International Dictionary of
OPERA

International Dictionary of

OPERA

EDITOR
C. STEVEN LARUE

PICTURE EDITOR
LEANDA SHRIMPTON

Volume 2: L-Z/Indexes

St J
St James Press

Detroit   London   Washington DC

STAFF

C. Steven LaRue, *Editor*
Leanda Shrimpton, *Picture Editor*
Emily J. McMurray, *Project Coordinator*
Paul E. Schellinger, *Associate Editor*
Robin Armstrong, David Ross Hurley, Robynn J. Stilwell, and Jeffrey Taylor, *Contributing Editors*

Cynthia Baldwin, *Art Director*
Mary Krzewinski, *Designer*
C. J. Jonik, *Keyliner*

Mary Beth Trimper, *Production Director*
Evi Seoud, *Assistant Production Manager*
Mary Kelley, *Production Assistant*

Cover photo: Luciano Pavarotti in *L'elisir d'amore*, 1990. Photo © Donald Cooper/Photostage, London.

Library of Congress Cataloging-in-Publication Data
International dictionary of opera / editor, C. Steven LaRue ; picture
editor, Leanda Shrimpton
    p.   cm.
    Includes bibliographical references and indexes.
    Contents: v. 1. A-K -- v. 2. L-Z/Indexes
    ISBN 1-55862-081-8 (set : alk. paper) : $250.00. -- ISBN
1-55862-112-1 (v.1 : alk. paper). -- ISBN 1-55862-113-X (v.2. :
alk. paper)
    1. Opera--Dictionaries. I. LaRue, C. Steven.
ML102.O6I6 1993
782.1'03--dc20
           92-44271
           CIP
           MN

British Library Cataloguing in Publication Data
International Dictionary of Opera
    I. Larue, C. Steven II. Shrimpton, Leanda
    782.103
    ISBN 1-55862-081-8

∞™ The paper used in this publication meets the minimum requirements
of American National Standard for Information Sciences—Permanence
Paper for Printed Library Materials, ANSI Z39.48-1984.

Printed in the United States of America.
Published simultaneously in the United Kingdom.

CONTENTS

INTRODUCTION

Scope

The *International Dictionary of Opera* provides students, teachers, researchers, and opera enthusiasts with a comprehensive source of biographical, bibliographical, and musicological information on people and works important to the history and development of opera. This two-volume set contains nearly 1100 entries on influential composers, librettists, performers, conductors, designers, directors, producers, and works representative of the genre from its beginnings to the present time.

Advisory Board

Entries were included in the *International Dictionary of Opera* based on the recommendations of advisers drawn from a number of fields associated with the study, performance, and recording of opera in both the United States and England. Advisers provided lists of suggested entries based on their individual expertise and their knowledge of the genre as a whole, from which the editor compiled the final selection of entries.

Entry Content

Each entry consists of a headnote containing biographical and bibliographical data followed by a signed critical essay. Headnotes were prepared by the editor and his staff from a number of different sources as well as from information supplied by individual contributors and advisers; thus the responsibility for the accuracy of the headnotes lies strictly with the editor and his staff, not with the contributors. Essays were provided by more than 200 music historians, theorists, teachers, critics, journalists, performers, recording executives, editors, publishers, and other individuals qualified to present interested readers with an informed critical opinion on the operatic work or person discussed. Viewpoints and interpretations found in the dictionary range from philosophical discussions of art and aesthetics to pragmatic considerations of performance and production.

Entries in the *International Dictionary of Opera* typically contain the following information:

- *BIOGRAPHICAL OUTLINE:* occupation; dates and places of birth and death; marriages and names of children; education and musical training, including institutions attended and names of teachers; career data, including musical posts held, milestones reached, and important performances, achievements, and awards; circle of important friends, associates, and students.

● *COMPOSITION AND PRODUCTION INFORMATION:* see the chart below for data unique to entry type:

Entry Type	Information Provided	Data Includes (where available)
Composer	List of Operas	Title (variant type; composer collaborators), librettist (source of libretto, including author and title of work), dates of composition, city, theater, and date of first performance, revisions under the composer's supervision, places and dates of performance.
Librettist	List of Librettos (selected)	Title, composer collaborator, date of first performance. (Note: further information can be found in the appropriate composer headnotes.)
Producer/ Director/ Designer	List of Productions (selected)	Title, city, theater, and date of performance.
Opera	Name of composer and librettist, and first performance information	List of roles and their general ranges. (Note: further information can be found in the appropriate composer headnote.)

● *SELECTED PRIMARY AND SECONDARY BIBLIOGRAPHIES:* title-by-title chronological lists of books and articles written and edited by the listee, including autobiographies and correspondence; and lists of books and articles written about the listee, including biographies, critical studies, chronologies, and dissertations. Readers seeking in-depth information about individual operas or librettists should also check appropriate composer bibliographies for additional sources to consult.

● *SIGNED CRITICAL ESSAY:* an evaluation or analysis of the contributions of the individual or importance of the work in question.

Illustrations

Individuals and operas in the *International Dictionary of Opera* come to life in 450 illustrations ranging from scenes from the contemporary opera stage to reproductions of period etchings, title pages of first-edition scores, portraits, and photographs.

Title and Nationality Indexes

Readers gain additional access to operas and individuals in the *International Dictionary of Opera* through the Title and Nationality indexes found in Volume 2. Titles in the "Operas" listing in each of the composer entries are indexed alphabetically, along with the composer's name and page number of the composer entry on which full composition information can be found. Operas for which full entries exist are further identified by boldface page numbers. In addition, users can explore national musical traditions by consulting the Nationality Index, in which individuals are arranged alphabetically by country of birth and/or citizenship and/or national affiliation.

Notes on Advisers and Contributors

Information about the areas of specialization of and additional music publications by the advisers and contributors to the *International Dictionary of Opera* can be found in the Notes on Advisers and Contributors section in Volume 2.

Acknowledgments

The editor wishes to recognize the pioneering efforts of Jim Vinson, founding editor of the *International Dictionary of Opera* and numerous other St James reference works, who died in 1991. Recognition is due as well to the late Greg Salmon, Russian music specialist and contributor of material for the essays on Glinka, Rimsky-Korsakov, Rubinstein, and Tchaikovsky. Special acknowledgment is also due to contributors Stephen Willier and Michael Sims, and advisers Bruce Burroughs, Andrew Farkas, and Thomas G. Kaufman for their editorial assistance in the late phases of this project; to the Gale Research Permissions Department for their help with photo sizing; and to Polly Vedder and Ken Shepherd for their technical assistance in the preparation of these volumes.

ADVISERS

Steven Barwick

Alan Blyth

Julian Budden

Bruce Burroughs

Norman Del Mar

Andrew Farkas

Paul Griffiths

Arthur Groos

Christopher Headington

John Higgins

Thomas G. Kaufman

Joseph Kerman

Herbert Lindenberger

George Martin

William R. Moran

Anthony Newcomb

Julian Rushton

John B. Steane

Denis Stevens

Michael Talbot

Alan Tyson

Arnold Whittall

LIST OF ENTRIES

COMPOSERS

Kagel, Mauricio
Keiser, Reinhard
Knussen, Oliver
Kodály, Zoltán
Korngold, Erich Wolfgang
Krenek, Ernst
Kurka, Robert
Lalo, Edouard
Leoncavallo, Ruggero
Ligeti, György
Lortzing, Albert
Lully, Jean-Baptiste
Magnard, Albéric
Malipiero, Gian Francesco
Marschner, Heinrich
Martín y Soler, Vicente
Martinů, Bohuslav
Mascagni, Pietro
Massenet, Jules
Mattheson, Johann
Maw, Nicolas
Mayr, Simon
Méhul, Étienne-Nicolas
Menotti, Gian Carlo
Mercadante, Saverio
Messiaen, Olivier
Meyerbeer, Giacomo
Milhaud, Darius
Moniuszko, Stanislaw
Montemezzi, Italo
Monteverdi, Claudio
Moore, Douglas
Mozart, Wolfgang Amadeus
Musorgsky, Modest
Nicolai, Otto
Nielsen, Carl
Nono, Luigi
Offenbach, Jacques
Orff, Carl
Pacini, Giovanni
Paer, Ferdinando
Paisiello, Giovanni
Penderecki, Krzysztof
Pepusch, Johann Christoph
Pergolesi, Giovanni Battista
Peri, Jacopo
Pfitzner, Hans Erich
Piccinni, Niccolò
Pizzetti, Ildebrando
Ponchielli, Amilcare
Porpora, Nicola Antonio
Poulenc, Francis

Pousseur, Henri
Prokofiev, Sergei
Puccini, Giacomo
Purcell, Henry
Rameau, Jean-Philippe
Ravel, Maurice
Reimann, Aribert
Rimsky-Korsakov, Nicolai
Rossini, Gioachino
Rousseau, Jean-Jacques
Rubinstein, Anton
Sacchini, Antonio
Saint-Saëns, Camille
Salieri, Antonio
Sallinen, Aulis
Scarlatti, Alessandro
Schmidt, Franz
Schoenberg, Arnold
Schreker, Franz
Schubert, Franz
Schumann, Robert
Sessions, Roger
Shostakovich, Dmitri
Smetana, Bedřich
Smyth, Ethel
Spohr, Ludewig
Spontini, Gaspare
Stockhausen, Karlheinz
Strauss, Richard
Stravinsky, Igor
Szymanowski, Karol
Tchaikovsky, Piotr Ilyich
Telemann, Georg Philipp
Thomas, Ambroise
Thomson, Virgil
Tippett, Michael
Vaughan Williams, Ralph
Verdi, Giuseppe
Villa-Lobos, Heitor
Vivaldi, Antonio
Wagner, Richard
Wallace, Vincent
Walton, William
Ward, Robert
Weber, Carl Maria von
Weill, Kurt
Weinberger, Jaromir
Wolf, Hugo
Wolf-Ferrari, Ermanno
Zandonai, Riccardo
Zemlinsky, Alexander von
Zimmermann, Bernd Alois

CONDUCTORS

Abbado, Claudio
Beecham, Thomas
Blech, Leo
Bodanzky, Artur

Böhm, Karl
Boulez, Pierre
Bülow, Hans von
Busch, Fritz

Caldwell, Sarah
Campanini, Cleofonte
Chailly, Riccardo
Cluytens, André
Coates, Albert
Damrosch, Leopold
Davis, Colin
De Sabata, Victor
Faccio, Franco
Furtwängler, Wilhelm
Giulini, Carlo Maria
Goodall, Reginald
Karajan, Herbert von
Keilberth, Joseph
Kempe, Rudolf
Kleiber, Carlos
Kleiber, Erich
Klemperer, Otto
Knappertsbusch, Hans
Krauss, Clemens
Krips, Josef
Kubelík, Rafael
Leinsdorf, Erich
Leppard, Raymond
Levi, Hermann
Levine, James
Maazel, Lorin
Mackerras, Charles

Mahler, Gustav
Mariani, Angelo
Monteux, Pierre
Mottl, Felix
Muck, Karl
Mugnone, Leopoldo
Muti, Riccardo
Nikisch, Arthur
Prêtre, Georges
Pritchard, John
Reiner, Fritz
Richter, Hans
Rosbaud, Hans
Rudel, Julius
Sanzogno, Nino
Sawallisch, Wolfgang
Schalk, Franz
Schippers, Thomas
Schuch, Ernst von
Seidl, Anton
Serafin, Tullio
Sinopoli, Giuseppe
Solti, Georg
Szell, George
Toscanini, Arturo
Walter, Bruno
Weingartner, Felix
Wolff, Albert

LIBRETTISTS

Auden, W. H.
Aureli, Aurelio
Boito, Arrigo
Brecht, Bertolt
Busenello, Giovanni Francesco
Calzabigi, Ranieri de
Cammarano, Salvadore
Cicognini, Giacinto Andrea
Da Ponte, Lorenzo
Forzano, Giovacchino
Gallet, Louis
Gay, John
Ghislanzoni, Antonio
Giacosa, Giuseppe
Goldoni, Carlo
Gregor, Joseph
Halévy, Jacques

Haym, Nicola Francesco
Hofmannsthal, Hugo von
Illica, Luigi
Meilhac, Henri
Metastasio, Pietro
Piave, Francesco Maria
Quinault, Philippe
Rinuccini, Ottavio
Rolli, Paolo Antonio
Romani, Felice
Rospigliosi, Giulio
Schikaneder, Emanuel
Scribe, Eugène
Solera, Temistocle
Striggio, Alessandro
Zeno, Apostolo

PERFORMERS

Albanese, Licia
Albani, Emma
Alboni, Marietta
Alda, Frances
Allen, Thomas

Alva, Luigi
Amato, Pasquale
Anders, Peter
Anderson, June
Anderson, Marian

Araiza, Francesco
Arnoldson, Sigrid
Arroyo, Martina
Baccaloni, Salvatore
Bacquier, Gabriel
Bahr-Mildenburg, Anna
Bailey, Norman
Baker, Janet
Bampton, Rose
Barbieri, Fedora
Barrientos, Maria
Battistini, Mattia
Battle, Kathleen
Behrens, Hildegard
Bellincioni, Gemma
Bene, Adriana Gabrieli del
Benucci, Francesco
Berganza, Teresa
Berger, Erna
Berglund, Joel
Bergonzi, Carlo
Bernacchi, Antonio Maria
Berry, Walter
Björling, Jussi
Blachut, Beno
Bockelmann, Rudolf
Bohnen, Michael
Bonci, Alessandro
Boninsegna, Celestina
Bordoni, Faustina
Borgatti, Giuseppe
Borgioli, Dino
Bori, Lucrezia
Borkh, Inge
Brouwenstijn, Gré
Bruscantini, Sesto
Bumbry, Grace
Burian, Karel
Burrows, Stuart
Caballé, Montserrat
Caffarelli
Callas, Maria
Calvé, Emma
Campanini, Italo
Caniglia, Maria
Cappuccilli, Piero
Carreras, José
Caruso, Enrico
Cavalieri, Catarina
Cavalieri, Lina
Cebotari, Maria
Chaliapin, Feodor
Christoff, Boris
Cigna, Gina
Corelli, Franco
Corena, Fernando
Cossutta, Carlo
Cotrubas, Ileana
Crespin, Régine
Cuénod, Hugues
Curtin, Phyllis
Cuzzoni, Francesca
Dal Monte, Toti

Danco, Suzanne
Del Bene, Adriana Gabrieli
  See Bene, Adriana Gabrieli del
Della Casa, Lisa
Del Monaco, Mario
De Los Angeles, Victoria
De Luca, Giuseppe
De Lucia, Fernando
De Reszke, Edouard
De Reszke, Jean
Dermota, Anton
Dernesch, Helga
Destinn, Emmy
Di Stefano, Giuseppe
Domingo, Plácido
Duprez, Gilbert-Louis
Eames, Emma
Elias, Rosalind
Evans, Geraint
Ewing, Maria
Falcon, Marie Cornélie
Farinelli
Farrar, Geraldine
Farrell, Eileen
Fassbaender, Brigitte
Faure, Jean-Baptiste
Ferrier, Kathleen
Figner, Medea
  See Mei-Figner, Medea
Figner, Nikolay
Fischer-Dieskau, Dietrich
Flagstad, Kirsten
Fleta, Miguel
Fremstad, Olive
Freni, Mirella
Frick, Gottlob
Gadski, Johanna
Galli-Curci, Amelita
Galli-Marié, Celestine
Garcia, Manuel
Garden, Mary
Gedda, Nicolai
Ghijaurov, Nicolai
Giannini, Dusolina
Gigli, Beniamino
Glossop, Peter
Gluck, Alma
Gobbi, Tito
Gorr, Rita
Grisi, Giuditta
Grisi, Giulia
Grist, Reri
Gruberova, Edita
Guadagni, Gaetano
Gueden, Hilde
Hammond, Joan
Heldy, Fanny
Hempel, Frieda
Hidalgo, Elvira de
Hines, Jerome
Homer, Louise
Horne, Marilyn
Hotter, Hans

Ivogün, Maria
Jadlowker, Hermann
Janowitz, Gundula
Janssen, Herbert
Jeritza, Maria
Jerusalem, Siegfried
Johnson, Edward
Jones, Gwyneth
Journet, Marcel
Jurinac, Sena
Kelly, Michael
Kiepura, Jan
King, James
Kipnis, Alexander
Kollo, René
Konetzni, Anny
Konetzni, Hilde
Köth, Erika
Kraus, Alfredo
Kunz, Erich
Kurz, Selma
Lablache, Luigi
Lauri-Volpi, Giacomo
Lawrence, Marjorie
Lear, Evelyn
Lehmann, Lilli
Lehmann, Lotte
Leider, Frida
Lemnitz, Tiana
Lewis, Richard
Lind, Jenny
Lipp, Wilma
London, George
Lorengar, Pilar
Lorenz, Max
Los Angeles, Victoria de
    See de Los Angeles, Victoria
Lubin, Germaine
Ludwig, Christa
MacNeil, Cornell
Malibran, Maria
Marcoux, Vanni
Mario, Giovanni
Martón, Eva
Mathis, Edith
Matzenauer, Margaret
Maurel, Victor
McCormack, John
McIntyre, Donald
Mei-Figner, Medea
Melba, Nellie
Melchior, Lauritz
Merrill, Robert
Merriman, Nan
Milanov, Zinka
Mildenburg, Anna von
    See Bahr-Mildenburg, Anna
Milnes, Sherrill
Minton, Yvonne
Mödl, Martha
Moffo, Anna
Moll, Kurt
Moore, Grace

Morris, James
Muzio, Claudia
Neidlinger, Gustav
Nesterenko, Evgeny
Nilsson, Birgit
Nilsson, Christine
Nordica, Lillian
Norman, Jessye
Nourrit, Adolphe
Novotná, Jarmila
Olivero, Magda
Onegin, Sigrid
Pagliughi, Lina
Pasero, Tancredi
Pasta, Giuditta
Patti, Adelina
Patzak, Julius
Pavarotti, Luciano
Pears, Peter
Peerce, Jan
Pertile, Aureliano
Peters, Roberta
Pilarczyk, Helga
Pinza, Ezio
Pons, Lily
Ponselle, Rosa
Popp, Lucia
Prey, Hermann
Price, Leontyne
Price, Margaret
Raaff, Anton
Raisa, Rosa
Ramey, Samuel
Raskin, Judith
Resnik, Regina
Rethberg, Elisabeth
Ricciarelli, Katia
Rossi-Lemeni, Nicola
Roswaenge, Helge
Rothenberger, Anneliese
Rubini, Giovanni-Battista
Ruffo, Titta
Rysanek, Leonie
Sammarco, Mario
Sanderson, Sybil
Sass, Sylvia
Sayão, Bidú
Schipa, Tito
Schlusnus, Heinrich
Schorr, Friedrich
Schreier, Peter
Schröder-Devrient, Wilhemine
Schumann, Elisabeth
Schumann-Heink, Ernestine
Schwarzkopf, Elisabeth
Scotti, Antonio
Scotto, Renata
Seefried, Irmgard
Sembrich, Marcella
Senesino
Shirley, George
Shirley-Quirk, John
Siems, Margarethe

Siepi, Cesare
Silja, Anja
Sills, Beverly
Simionato, Giulietta
Simoneau, Léopold
Singher, Martial
Slezak, Leo
Smirnov, Dmitri
Söderström, Elisabeth
Sontag, Henriette
Soyer, Roger
Stabile, Mariano
Stade, Frederica Von
  See Von Stade, Frederica
Steber, Eleanor
Stevens, Risë
Stich-Randall, Teresa
Stignani, Ebe
Stolz, Teresa
Storace, Nancy
Storchio, Rosina
Stracciari, Riccardo
Stratas, Teresa
Streich, Rita
Strepponi, Giuseppina
Supervia, Conchita
Sutherland, Joan
Svanholm, Set
Tagliavini, Ferruccio
Tajo, Italo
Talvela, Martti
Tamagno, Francesco
Tamberlick, Enrico
Tauber, Richard

Tebaldi, Renata
Te Kanawa, Kiri
Tetrazzini, Luisa
Teyte, Maggie
Thill, Georges
Thorborg, Kerstin
Tibbett, Lawrence
Tietjens, Therese
Tourel, Jennie
Tozzi, Giorgio
Traubel, Helen
Treigle, Norman
Troyanos, Tatiana
Tucker, Richard
Turner, Eva
Valletti, Cesare
Vallin, Ninon
Van Dam, José
Varady, Julia
Verrett, Shirley
Viardot, Pauline
Vickers, Jon
Vinay, Ramón
Vishnevskaya, Galina
Von Stade, Frederica
Wächter, Eberhard
Warren, Leonard
Weber, Ludwig
Weikl, Bernd
Welitsch, Ljuba
Windgassen, Wolfgang
Wunderlich, Fritz
Zenatello, Giovanni

PRODUCERS, DIRECTORS, and DESIGNERS

Appia, Adolphe
Arundell, Dennis
Benois, Alexandre
Benois, Nicola
Berghaus, Ruth
Bergman, Ingmar
Brook, Peter
Chéreau, Patrice
Ciceri, Pierre-Luc-Charles
Copley, John
Corsaro, Frank
Cox, John
Craig, Edward Gordon
Dexter, John
Ebert, Carl
Everding, August
Felsenstein, Walter
Freeman, David
Friedrich, Götz
Gentele, Göran
Graf, Herbert
Graham, Colin
Guthrie, Tyrone

Hartmann, Rudolf
Hall, Peter
Herz, Joachim
Hockney, David
Koltai, Ralph
Kupfer, Harry
Meyerhold, Vsevolod
Miller, Jonathan
Moshinsky, Elijah
Nemirovich-Danchenko,
  Vladimir
Pizzi, Pier Luigi
Ponnelle, Jean-Pierre
Pountney, David
Prince, Harold
Reinhardt, Max
Rennert, Günther
Roller, Alfred
Sanquirico, Alessandro
Schenk, Otto
Schneider-Siemssen, Günther
Sellars, Peter
Sendak, Maurice

Serban, Andrei
Shaw, Glen Byam
Stanislavsky, Konstantin
Strehler, Giorgio
Svoboda, Josef
Urban, Joseph
Visconti, Luchino

Wagner, Wieland
Wagner, Wolfgang
Wallerstein, Lothar
Wallmann, Margherita
Wilson, Robert
Zeffirelli, Franco

OPERAS

International Dictionary of
OPERA

L

LABLACHE, Luigi.

Bass. Born 6 December 1795, in Naples. Died 23 January 1858, in Naples. Married to singer Teresa Pinotti (13 children, many of them singers). Studied with Valesi at the Conservatorio della Pietà dei Turchini, Naples; debut in *L'erede senza eredita* at the Teatro San Carlino, Naples, 1812; sang in Messina as buffo and in 1815 in Palermo as basso cantante; Teatro alla Scala debut as Dandini in *La Cenerentola,* 1821, and appeared there until 1826; member of Domenico Barbaja's troupe in Vienna in the 1820s (sang at Beethoven's funeral, 1827); London debut at King's Theatre as Geronimo in *Il matrimonio segreto,* 1830, where he sang almost every year until 1852; appeared in Paris from 1830 until 1851; sang in St Petersburg and at Covent Garden in the mid 1850s.

Publications

By LABLACHE: books–

Méthode complète de chant. Paris, 1840.

About LABLACHE: books–

Castil-Blaze, F.H.J. *Biographie de Lablache.* Paris, 1850.
Widen, G. *Luigi Lablache.* Goteborg, 1897.

articles–

d'Ortigue, J. "Obituary." *Le journal des debats* [Paris] 24 February (1858).
Weinstock, H. "Luigi Lablache." *Opera* September (1966).

*　　*　　*

Luigi Lablache occupies an important place among opera singers from the first half of the nineteenth century. He started his public career at the age of seventeen as a "buffo napoletano" in Naples, where since the age of twelve he had studied with Valesi at the Conservatorio della Pietà dei Turchini. By the time he retired from the stage in 1857 he had appeared at most of the important operatic centers of Europe, scoring great successes in London and Paris and remaining a favorite among his countrymen Rossini, Bellini, and Donizetti, all of whom wrote roles especially for him.

Lablache gained considerable acclaim after his Teatro alla Scala debut as Dandini in Rossini's *La Cenerentola.* He continued to sing in Milan until 1826, as well as appearing in Rome, Turin, and Naples. Then in 1823 Lablache joined the Viennese troupe headed up by the famous impresario Barbaja, who hired him as the company's leading bass. After establishing a large repertoire, Lablache went to Paris, where he debuted as Geronimo at the Théâtre-Italien in 1830; he remained a favorite in that city until 1851.

Lablache matured through his performing of the fine buffo roles—some of them created for him—of Rossini, Donizetti, and Bellini. Historically, he brought to perfection the long-established buffo tradition. Closely associated with Rossini from early in his career, Lablache became known as that composer's definitive interpreter. (Rossini commented, "Many singers of my time were great artists, but there were only three true geniuses: Papa Lablache, Rubini, and that child so spoiled by nature, Maria Malibran.") With his rendering of Figaro in *Il barbiere de Siviglia,* he became known for his rapid articulation and distinction of diction; Lablache was associated with this role for the rest of his career. His other famous Rossini roles included Dandini, Assur, Don Bartolo, Don Magnifico, and Mustifa.

Lablache aroused great enthusiasm as well singing Mozart. In his younger years he sang Don Giovanni, but he became more widely renowned for his Leporello. A critic in London's *Musical World* wrote of him, "How he filled up the stage—not with size but with his intellect, every action had its propriety, every movement its meaning—every look its significance. No artist ever took greater liberties with his audience, but in all his freedom and 'gaggings' there was no extravagance or caricature. Few things are more amusing than to see this Rhodian Colossus caper and flit about the stage with the elasticity of a sylph."

Realizing that Paris and London offered more stable environments to singers of Italian opera, Lablache established himself in these two cities, sang annually in each of their seasons, and went on to triumph in new roles. From the 1830s to the 1850s, he had no rivals there. Famous for his role of Henry VIII in Donizetti's *Anna Bolena,* and for the title role of *Marin Falerio,* he was equally well known as Oroveso in Bellini's *Norma* and the title role of Rossini's *Guillaume Tell.* In 1835, Bellini composed *I Puritani* for the best voices of the day—Grisi, Rubini, Tamburini, and Lablache, known later as the "Puritani quartet." It was to prove one of the most successful operas of the era.

Lablache was able to leap naturally from serious to comic roles. Donizetti showcased Lablache's comic mastery when he wrote the charming romantic opera, *L'elisir d'amore,* as well as the "buffo classic," *Don Pasquale,* for him. His hilarious creation of this title role—Lablache's tenth Donizetti world premier—became legendary.

Dominating the opera stage for nearly half a century, Luigi Lablache was a thorough musician. He continued to sing his major roles while creating new ones in Paris, London, and St Petersburg. He also sang as a concert artist, appearing in England with the great prima donnas of his time, including Maria Malibran, Giulia Grisi, Jenny Lind, and Henriette Sontag.

—Clarissa Lablache Cheer

Luigi Lablache with Anna de Lagrange in Donizetti's *Don Pasquale,* Her Majesty's Theatre, London, 1852

THE LADY MACBETH OF MTSENSK DISTRICT [Ledi Makbet Mtsenskogo uezda].

Composer: Dmitri Shostakovich.

Librettist: A. Preis (after Leskov).

First Performance: Leningrad, 22 January 1934; revised as *Katerina Izmailova,* Moscow, 8 January 1963.

Roles: Katerina Izmailova (soprano); Sergei (tenor); Boris Timofeevich Izmailov (bass); Zinovi Borisovich Izmailov (tenor); Aksinya (soprano); Village Drunk (tenor); Sonetka (contralto); Police Inspector (bass); Priest (bass); several bit ports; chorus (SAATBB).

Publications

articles–

Brown, R.S. "The Three Faces of Lady Macbeth." In *Russian and Soviet Music: Essays for Boris Schwarz,* edited by Malcolm H. Brown, 245. Ann Arbor, 1984.
Emerson, Caryl. "Back to the future: Shostakovich's revision of Leskov's 'Lady Macbeth of Mtsensk District'." *Cambridge Opera Journal* 1 (1989): 59.

*   *   *

The finest and most significant Russian opera since Tchaikovsky's *Queen of Spades, The Lady Macbeth of Mtsensk District* (to give it its full translation) is also a link in the chain of victim-hero operas from Berg's *Wozzeck* to Britten's *Peter Grimes* and beyond (Britten heard a concert performance conducted by Albert Coates in 1936 and described it as "A most moving and exciting work of a real and inspired genius"). The target of an unsigned *Pravda* article, "Chaos instead of music" (28 January 1936), and attacked by influential Western critics for its passages of banality and emotional excess, *Lady Macbeth* languished until the early 1960s, when Shostakovich's revision, entitled *Katerina Izmailova,* sparked new interest. Rostropovich's 1979 recording of the original version was a landmark. In line with Shostakovich's increasingly high critical standing in the 1980s, *Lady Macbeth* has come to be recognized as one of the pinnacles of twentieth-century opera.

Katerina Lvovna Izmailova, wife of the merchant Zinovi Borisovich Izmailov, is childless, bored, and sexually frustrated. During her husband's absence on business she is seduced by Sergei, a recently hired worker on the estate. At the beginning of act II, Zinovi's father, Boris Timofeevich, catches Sergei emerging from Katerina's bedroom and brutally flogs him in front of her. Katerina laces Boris's supper with rat poison, and he dies in agony. For some days Katerina and Sergei continue their affair, she haunted by the ghost of Boris Timofeevich. Zinovi returns and confronts her with her infidelity; she calls Sergei from hiding, and they strangle Zinovi and hide his body in a cellar. In act III a peasant in

Lady Macbeth of the Mtsensk District, **with Josephine Barstow as Katerina, English National Opera, 1991**

search of vodka stumbles on the body and rushes off to the police station. The police are bored and angry with Katerina for failing to invite them to her wedding with Sergei; they taunt a local teacher suspected of "nihilism." Overjoyed at the peasant's news, they hurry to the wedding feast and arrest the newlyweds. Act IV sees the couple in a chain-gang marching through Siberia. Sergei has transfered his affections to a pretty convict-girl, Sonetka. He tricks Katerina into giving him her stockings, which he promptly passes to his new girl-friend. In utter despair Katerina throws herself and Sonetka into the lake. Both drown. The convicts sing a final lament for the cruelty of their captivity.

Just as Britten was to alter the original character of Peter Grimes, so Shostakovich and his co-librettist Alexander Preis set out to justify and excuse Katerina (the precise division of their labors on the text is not known). In Leskov's original short story, Katerina is a morally reprehensible character, who, in addition to the crimes seen in the opera, suffocates her young nephew, a co-heir to her late husband's estate. Shostakovich and Preis greatly increase the oppressiveness of her environment, in particular the domineering and lecherous character of her father-in-law. Thus the relevance of Shakespeare's Lady Macbeth is decreased, and the drama develops close parallels to Ostrovsky's *The Storm,* from which Janáček took the story of *Katia Kabanová* (there is no evidence to suggest that Shostakovich knew this opera, however). The scene in the police station—an addition to the original story—

is modeled on the writings of the nineteenth-century satirist Saltykov-Shchedrin.

It is impossible to separate out the three strands of Shostakovich's dramatic intentions. These are his own inner drives, reinforced by his stormy courtship with Nina Varzar whom he married in May 1932; his awareness of and commentary on social-political developments at a time of mass collectivization, show trials, and State terrorism; and his attempt to take official artistic doctrines into account (these were not properly formalized until 1934 and even then remained vaguely defined). At the present time, however, there is a strong tendency in Western productions and commentaries to emphasize the element of denunciation of the Stalin regime. In any case, the unusual vacillation of dramatic tone from introspection to brutality, burlesque comedy to hard-hitting tragedy, partly reflected in Shostakovich's own references to the genre of "tragedy-satire," has come to be regarded as a source of strength rather than an artistic miscalculation.

The musical language of *Lady Macbeth* reflects the full range of the young Shostakovich's eclectic enthusiasms— from the modal harmonic style of Musorgsky, through the lyricism of Mahler and the stylizations of Stravinsky, to the atonal-modernist trends of the 1920s as exemplified by Berg's *Wozzeck* and Krenek's *Der Sprung über den Schatten.* Katerina's boredom, Zinovi's ineffectuality, and the three scenes of obsessive brutality, are all memorably expressed in musical terms. In the interlude following the poisoning of Boris, Shostakovich rises to the dramatic challenge with the first of his great tragedy-absorbing passacaglias (again suggesting the influence of Berg).

In 1956, with the Khrushchev "Thaw" well under way, Shostakovich began revising the opera, which eventually appeared six years later as *Katerina Izmailova*. Here the excesses of the original are much toned down, vocal tessitura is less extreme, and there are newly composed, less "radical" entr'actes between scenes i and ii and scenes vii and viii. It should be noted, incidentally, that the version of *Lady Macbeth* to which the *Pravda* article took exception, and which was found shocking by many Western critics as well, had already had many of its most blatant excesses removed—notably the trombone glissandi at the height of the seduction scene. Again it is impossible to determine the role of self-criticism or imposed censorship in these changes. The composer's son, as well as many of his artistic associates now in the West and the majority of commentators outside the former Soviet Union, are united in preferring the original version and in considering the revisions to have been forced on the composer against his will.

—David Fanning

THE LADY OF THE LAKE
See LA DONNA DEL LAGO

Lily Pons as Lakmé, Metropolitan Opera, New York, 1928

LAKMÉ.

Composer: Léo Delibes.

Librettists: Edmond Gondinet and Philippe Gille (based on Gondinet's play *Le marriage de Loti*).

First Performance: Paris, Opéra-Comique, 14 April 1883.

Roles: Lakmé (soprano); Gérald (tenor); Nilakantha (bass); Frédéric (baritone); Hadji (tenor); Ellen (soprano); Rose (soprano); Mrs Benson (mezzo-soprano); Mallika (mezzo-soprano); chorus (SSTTBB).

Publications

book–

Loisel, Joseph. *"Lakmé" de Léo Delibes: étude historique et critique: analyse musicale.* Paris, 1924.

article–

Miller, Philip Lieson. "The Orientalism of Lakmé." *Opera News* 22 December (1941): 18.

*   *   *

To describe Léo Delibes as a one opera composer would be an oversimplification. His *Le roi l'a dit* (*The King Has Commanded it*) is a decent production and still is sporadically performed. Yet within the realm of opera (as contrasted with

ballet where he made a much greater impact), most people associate him only with the colorful oriental-motif masterpiece, *Lakmé*.

The tale takes place in mid-nineteenth century India. Two English officers with French names, Frédéric and Gérald, are intrigued by the attractive garden and mysterious temple of the foreigner-hating Brahmin priest, Nilakantha. They penetrate the fence surrounding the complex. Gérald is soon infatuated with the beauty and charm of Lakmé, Nilakantha's daughter, and the romantic interest is reciprocated. When Lakmé's father returns, Gérald leaves and almost manages to avoid detection by the fanatical Brahmin. But Nilakantha is aware that the sacred Hindu ground has been violated and vows vengeance as soon as he discovers the identity of the infidel. He cleverly arranges for Lakmé to sing in the town where the British soldiers are stationed, hoping that either Lakmé or the foreigner will in some way tip their hand. The ploy works, and angry Nilakantha stabs Gérald, but not seriously. Gérald awakes in Lakmé's hut in the forest, where Lakmé has had her lover transported. Gérald's fellow officer Frédéric finds Gérald, and Frédéric convinces his colleague to return to the garrison. When Lakmé realizes that Gérald is having trouble deciding between duty and his love for her, she makes the decision for him and poisons herself. After Lakmé has died, Nilakantha comes upon the scene, but his hatred is quickly dissipated when he finds that his daughter has gone to her celestial reward.

Delibes managed to capture the flavor of the Orient about as well as any western composer has. Ironically, this successful reflection of the culture of India was also a major factor in *Lakmé*'s substantial decline in public favor by the mid-twentieth century. Asian themes were in vogue at the time

Delibes wrote *Lakmé,* and when the vogue inevitably faded, the popularity of the opera correspondingly followed suit.

In spite of the limitations of the plot and the changing tastes of audiences, *Lakmé* continues to live on fairly strongly, and in recent years appears to be regaining a degree of the prominence it enjoyed in the late nineteenth and early twentieth century. Delibes' fine and at times quite brilliant score keeps *Lakmé* a persistent player in the repertory game. The legendary "Bell Song" ("Où va la jeune Hindoue?" or, "Where Does the Young Hindu Woman Go?") from act II is clearly the most famous portion of the music, but although sparkling and exciting it is not necessarily the best number. The Bell Song's renown owes as much to the demanding technical requirements of an agile, high soprano voice and to audience amazement at its execution as to its inherent beauty.

The Bell Song has tended to overwhelm other good sections, especially the excellent barcarolle "Dôme épais, le jasmin" ("Jasmine, the Dense Canopy") and the superlative aria "Fantaisie aux divins mensonges" ("Fantasy of the Divine Lies") in the first act. Furthermore, the act II ballet scene which precedes the Bell Song is colorful, vibrant, and quite well crafted, and there are additional high points throughout the production. *Lakmé* should be remembered and cherished for the innovative Bell Song, but the rest of the opera also deserves a comparable level of attention. *Lakmé* overall is a definite jewel of the lighter operatic muse, but it doesn't pretend to rival the more serious and substantial works of major masters like Wagner, Verdi, and Mozart.

—William E. Studwell

LALO, Edouard (-Victoire-Antoine).

Composer. Born 27 January 1823, in Lille, France. Died 22 April 1892, in Paris. Married: the contralto Mlle Bernier de Maligny, 1865. Studied with Baumann at the Lille branch of the Paris Conservatory; studied violin with Habeneck, and composition with Schulhoff and Crèvecoeur at the Paris Conservatory; violist of the Armingaud-Jacquard Quartet; published songs, 1848-49; gave up composition for a period of time; third place in an opera competition sponsored by the Théâtre-Lyrique for his *Fiesque,* 1867; success with his Violin Concerto, 1874, and his *Symphonie espagnole,* 1874; international success as an opera composer with *Le roi d'Ys,* 1888; officer of the Legion of Honor, 1888; Prix Monbinne, Académie des Beaux-Arts, 1888.

Operas

Fiesque, C. Beauquier (after Schiller, *Fiesko*), 1866-67.
Le roi d'Ys, Edouard Blau (after a Breton legend), 1875-1887, Paris, Opéra-Comique, 7 May 1888.
La jacquerie, Edouard Blau and Simone Arnaud, 1891-92 [unfinished; completed by Arthur Coquard and produced Monte Carlo, 9 March 1895].

Other works: ballets, choral works, songs, orchestral works, chamber music, piano pieces.

Publications

About LALO: books—

Dufour, Médéric. *Edouard Lalo.* Lille, 1908.
Séré, Octave. *Musiciens français d'aujourd'hui.* Paris, 1911; 8th ed., 1921.
Malherbe, H. *Edouard Lalo, conférence prononcée . . . 23 décembre, 1920.* Paris, 1921.
Sevières, Georges. *Edouard Lalo.* Paris, 1925.

articles—

Pougin, A. "Edouard Lalo." *Le ménestrel* 58 (1892): 139.
Dukas, P. "Edouard Lalo." *La revue musicale* 4/no. 5 (1923): 97.
Jullien, A. "Quelques lettres inédites de Lalo." *La revue musicale* 4/no. 5 (1923): 108.
Lalo, P. "La vie d'Edouard Lalo." *La revue musicale* 4/no. 5 (1923): 118.
Schultz, G. "A Northern Legend." *Opera News* 24 (1960): 12.
Brachtel, K.R. "Edouard Lalo zum 75. Todestag am 22 April." *Musica* 21 (1967): 130.
Fauquet, Joël-Marie. "Edouard Lalo de la Bretagne, les sources du *Roi d'Ys.*" In *Musique et société. La vie musicale en Provence aux XVIIIe, XIXe et XXe siècles.,* edited by Le Moigne-Mussat, Marie-Claire et al. Rennes, 1982.
Avant-scène opéra 65 (1984) [*Le roi d'Ys* issue].

*   *   *

Lalo is as an unusual figure in the history of opera in that he was not involved with the theater in any substantive way, and he focused his compositional and performance activities primarily on instrumental music until he was past forty. Eighteen sixty-six marks the year he tackled the opera world when he entered a competition sponsored by the Théâtre-Lyrique. *Fiesque,* an opera in three acts after Schiller's play, *Fiesko,* did not receive the prize, and although other theaters in Paris and Brussels showed interest, it was never performed. Lalo published the vocal score privately, and used much of the music in other compositions.

Despite this failure, Lalo continued to dream of success as an opera composer while continuing with his instrumental compositions. A series of solo violin and cello works and orchestra culminated in the next decade with the popular *Symphonie espagnole* (1874), and it was only in 1875 that he began work on what was to be his only performed opera, *Le roi d'Ys.* Extracts were performed in a concert version in 1881, but the opera was not immediately accepted by any Parisian theater. Lalo was considered a controversial figure in French music circles at this time, being regarded as too "germanic," even Wagnerian in style (the young Claude Debussy was an ardent admirer). However, on 7 May 1888, some thirteen years after its beginnings, *Le roi d'Ys* premiered at the *Opéra-Comique,* and was a success. It has never enjoyed overwhelming popularity at home or abroad, and yet over the next seventy-five years it received some 125 performances in Paris alone.

Lalo did not write another opera, and apart from *Fiesque* and *Le roi d'Ys,* his theatrical works include only one unperformed ballet, one pantomime, and one act of an opera left unfinished at his death. Although *Le roi d'Ys* continues to be mounted from time to time, only the overture is well known in modern musical life.

—Aubrey S. Garlington

LAURI-VOLPI, Giacomo.

Tenor. Born 11 December 1892, in Lanuvio, near Rome. Died 17 March 1979, in Valencia, Spain. Studied at Accademia di Santa Cecilia in Rome with Antonio Cotogni, and later with Enrico Rosati; debut as Arturo in *I Puritani,* Viterbo, 1919, using the name Giacomo Rubini; sang Massenet's Des Grieux under his own name, Rome, 1920; Teatro alla Scala debut as Duke of Mantua in Rigoletto, 1922, and sang regularly there in the 1930s and 1940s; at Metropolitan Opera, 1923-33; appeared at Covent Garden, 1925, 1936; also sang at Paris Opera and the Teatro Colon; continued to sing in public until 1959, and sang at the Teatro Liceo, Barcelona in 1972.

Publications

By LAURI-VOLPI: books–

L'equivoco (cosi e, e non vi pare). Milan, 1938.
Cristalli viventi. Rome, 1948.
A viso aperto. Milan, 1953.
Misteri della voce umana. Milan, 1957.
Parlando a Maria, Rome, 1972.

Giacomo Lauri-Volpi as the Duke in Verdi's *Rigoletto*

About LAURI-VOLPI: books–

Gustarelli, A. *Chi e Giacomo Lauri-Volpi?* Milan, 1932.
Bragaglia, L. *La voce solitaria: Cinquanta personaggi per Giacomo Lauri-Volpi.* Rome, 1982.

articles–

Williams, C. and T. Hutchinson. "Giacomo Lauri-Volpi." *Record Collector* 11 (1957): 245.
Celletti, R. " 'Il tenore eroico' del melodramma celeste." *Musica e dischi* 14 (1958).
Caputo, P., ed. "Tre generazioni di artisti festeggiano Lauri-Volpi." *Musica e dischi* 19 (1963).

After the death of Caruso in 1921, there were several exceptionally gifted tenors who might have assumed his mantle. Gigli was at the outset of a brilliant career and could rival Caruso for lyrical excellence but could not achieve the robust power of the great Neapolitan. Pertile could match Caruso's intensity and his excellent musicality but perhaps not his beauty of tone. Martinelli possessed nearly all of Caruso's qualities but his voice was of sterling silver rather than gold.

Not two years before Caruso's demise, the young Roman Giacomo Lauri-Volpi was beginning his career. In many respects Lauri-Volpi possessed much of the prodigious talent that made Caruso great; a voice of ravishing beauty, particularly in a honeyed mezza-voce (half-voice), Caruso's clarity of enunciation, nobility of manner, elegance of style and superb musicality. But, he was also gifted with a magnificent upper register for which Caruso was never renowned, particularly later in the latter's career. Lauri-Volpi shared with Caruso much of the standard tenor repertoire but was also able to sing the high tenor roles such as in *I Puritani* and *Guillome Tell* that were never Caruso's.

Lauri-Volpi's career was a major one: he sang in all the important theaters of the world and, owing to the excellence of his technique, sang well into his sixties. His early career was confined to the more lyric roles such as Rodolfo (*La bohème*), Des Grieux (*Manon*), Arturo (*I Puritani*) and roles which he soon dropped from his repertoire, such as Almaviva (*Il barbiere di Siviglia*). As his career progressed, he increasingly assumed more dramatic roles, which suited the more robust quality of the voice, such as Manrico (*Il trovatore*) and Radames (*Aida*). He continued to sing these roles until the end of his career, when he could still create a sensation with his top C, for which the public largely forgave the by now worn quality of the remainder of the voice.

Lauri-Volpi recorded extensively and, on records, his career can be nicely divided into early, middle and late periods. Few tenors have made both acoustic 78s and stereo LPs, though his late records can be difficult listening and are for his real admirers only. The early acoustic records for Fonotipia already show a surprising degree of artistry, considering they were made only shortly after his debut. The voice is somewhat dark, with a flickering vibrato as recorded (which may have been exaggerated by the close proximity of the recording horn), and is employed with skill and all the graces of the bel canto school. The thrilling quality of the high notes is already evident. Just occasionally, the relative immaturity of the artist is betrayed by exaggeration of the vocal line for effect.

Lauri-Volpi's voice was probably at its finest in the late twenties and thirties when he recorded, regrettably little, for Victor. Here, the voice is at its loveliest, the artistry at its most mature and his interpretations at their most satisfying. Later HMV recordings, from the forties, show somewhat of a loosening of the tonal quality, but this is compensated for by a more robust approach and a nobility of utterance in the heavier roles he had by then assumed, such as Otello. At the end of his career he participated in several complete operas, for Italian Radio and Cetra. Though the voice is undeniably worn, the artistry is that of the seasoned artist and the high notes still ring with a brilliance and quality worthy of a tenor half his age.

A deeply religious and cultured man, Lauri-Volpi wrote numerous articles for newspapers and magazines and several books. One, *Voci Parallele,* is a book of critical and comparative analyses of fellow singers, many of whom he had known personally. He was renowned as a singer but definitely not for his modesty, for, in this book, Lauri-Volpi suggests singers that he would consider *voci isolati* (unique voices), the first of them: Giacomo Lauri-Volpi.

—Larry Lustig

LAWRENCE, Marjorie (Florence).

Soprano. Born 17 February 1909, near Melbourne, Australia. Died 10 January 1979, in Little Rock, Arkansas. Studied in Paris with Cécile Gilly; debut as Elisabeth in *Tannhäuser,* Monte Carlo, 1932; sang at Paris Opéra, 1933-36; at Metropolitan Opera, 1935-41, first as Brünnhilde in *Die Walküre;* suffered paralysis from polio in 1941, but returned to sing Isolde at the Metropolitan Opera and Amneris in Paris; professor of voice at Tulane University, 1956-60; director of opera workshop at Southern Illinois University from 1960.

Publications

By LAWRENCE: books–

Interrupted Melody: the Story of my Life. New York, 1949.

*　　*　　*

Marjorie Lawrence's career was short by most standards, spanning the years 1931 through 1953. The first ten years encapsulated all the elements and the results of success: a fresh voice, acting ability, personal attractiveness, contracts with both the Paris Opéra and the Metropolitan Opera, a devoted international following, and "no end in sight" prospects. At thirty-one, her career was suddenly and jarringly over. In the spring of 1941, Miss Lawrence contracted polio which, if it did not altogether end her stage career, vastly curtailed its original promise. She spent the rest of her life confined to a wheelchair.

The irony of her particular disability is felt all the more when one remembers that Lawrence was one of the few Brünnhildes who was able to carry out the composer's instructions to leap upon her horse, Grane, and gallop into Siegfried's funeral pyre at the end of *Götterdämmerung.* One can imagine the New York audience's astonishment at this feat following her 1935 debut in *Die Walküre. New York Times* critic Olin Downes wrote, "The audience was taken by storm. . . ." Of her acting in this debut, *New York Post* critic Samuel Chotzinoff said "From a dramatic standpoint her Brünnhilde was

the most effective that the Metropolitan has seen in years." The *New York American* critic, Leonard Liebling, described her voice as "fresh, amply powered and richly timbered."

Another "physical" role with which Lawrence was associated was that of Salome in Strauss's opera. Here again, her mobility was the object of praise in Jerome Bohm's 1938 critique for the *New York Herald Tribune.* Speaking of her "Dance of the Seven Veils," he wrote, "It was a remarkable feat for a singing actress who has not been trained as a dancer to have surmounted an all but insurmountable problem so convincingly and to have sung the tremendous closing scene so magnificently."

Other critics wrote of her singing and characterizations with equal parts of enthusiasm and restraint, as though hesitant to bestow too much heady praise on a Wagnerian soprano under thirty who shared the stage with more prominent and experienced sopranos.

The second part of Lawrence's singing career can be said to have begun when she made a determined effort to regain her career after contracting polio. This she was able to do only with difficulty due to the reluctance of concert and opera managers who feared a decline in her vocal powers as well as the problems inherent in casting her in stage productions. Once offers began, however, she had to overcome the viewpoint that her infirmity had been exploited. It still remains open to debate whether it is the great singer who is remembered for her career or the handicapped singer who made a courageous comeback.

Of her comeback recital in Town Hall in 1943, critic Noel Straus wrote ". . . the long rest she has had did its share in giving freshness to the voice which was never before as absolutely firm in its tones, nor employed with such depth of feeling." Edward O'Gorman of the *New York Post* wrote ". . . I don't believe Miss Lawrence's voice has ever sounded as rich and as powerful . . . as it did last night." Other reviews could be interpreted more as tributes to her courage and determination than as evaluations of her singing. Few in number, but of special note, were the opera productions restaged to accommodate Lawrence's disability. Besides the war-time production of *Tannhäuser,* she sang the role of Isolde in a Montreal Opera production of *Tristan und Isolde* under the direction of Sir Thomas Beecham. She repeated this role at the Metropolitan in 1944, again under Beecham's direction. The *New York Times* critic wrote of it, "Hers was a brilliant artistic achievement. She infused her voice with an intensity hard to imagine being surpassed."

Marjorie Lawrence performed her last professional stage role as Amneris in Verdi's *Aïda* in 1947 at the Paris Opéra, where the *United Press* reported that she received "the greatest ovation ever heard in the Paris Opéra." Here again, one may read "sentiment and affection" in this generous statement, for she had many friends and admirers in Paris who had not seen her since her crippling disability.

While there are many recordings still available in reprints of Lawrence's contemporaries such as Flagstad, Traubel, and Farrell, one would have to search diligently for her 78's recorded during the 1930's. The only reprint of her work may be found on the German label *Preiser,* which contains excerpts from *Lohengrin, Götterdämmerung, Sigurd* (by Reyer) and Strauss's *Salome.* All are sung in French. As aesthetics change considerably over the decades, contemporary audiences might find her French tongue, French training and fast vibrato rather disconcerting in the works of Wagner and Strauss. In the final scene of *Salome,* she has a bright edge to her voice and brings a good deal of dramatic intensity to the characterization. However, one wishes for the more compelling sensuality that time and changing tastes allowed later sopranos such as Nilsson, Caballé and others to bring to the role.

After her retirement from the stage, Lawrence turned to teaching. During her thirteen-year tenure at Southern Illinois University, the *Marjorie Lawrence Opera Theater* was established in her honor.

—Helen Poulos

LEAR.

Composer: Aribert Reimann.

Librettist: Claus H. Henneberg (after Shakespeare).

First Performance: Munich, Nationaltheater, 9 July 1978.

Roles: King Lear (baritone); The King of France (bass-baritone); Duke of Albany (baritone); Duke of Cornwall (tenor); Kent (tenor); Gloucester (bass-baritone); Edgar (tenor or counter-tenor); Edmund (tenor); Goneril (soprano); Cordelia (soprano); Regan (soprano); Fool (speaking); A Servant (tenor); A Knight (speaking); chorus.

Publications

book–

Schulz, Klaus, ed. *Aribert Reimanns "Lear": Weg einer neuen Oper.* Munich, 1984.

Few operas premiered during the second half of the twentieth century have received such immediate acceptance by public and critics alike as *Lear.* Retained in the repertoire of the Bavarian State Opera until 3 August 1982, *Lear* was almost immediately recorded by Deutsche Grammaphon, a three-record LP album which sold over 9000 copies in three years, only 2000 of them in Germany.

The librettist of *Lear,* Claus H. Henneberg, quotes Sir Michael Tippett as saying, "Only foreigners could have the gall to lay a finger on *Lear!*" Dietrich Fischer-Dieskau had discussed the possibility of a *Lear* opera with Benjamin Britten long before the premiere of the *War Requiem* (1962), but the composer's preoccupation with his *Church Parables* and later illness made such a huge project impossible, although a German music dictionary at the time stated that Britten was working on *Lear.*

The action of Reimann/Henneberg's *Lear* is basically that of Shakespeare's tragedy, and it would serve little purpose to reproduce it except in essentials for readers in the English

Lear, **with Monte Jaffe in the title role, and Maria Moll as Regan, English National Opera, London, 1991**

language. In part I, King Lear disinherits and banishes his youngest daughter Cordelia because she cannot express her love for him to his satisfaction. Gloucester similarly banishes his true son Edgar, believing his bastard son Edmund's false accusation. Goneril and Regan shut out Lear and his followers, who take refuge on the stormy heath where they find Edgar pretending to be a madman. In part II, Goneril and Regan and their husbands, Cornwall and Albany, oppose the French forces and Cordelia who have come to rescue Lear. They blind Gloucester, an act that so horrifies the servant that he kills Cornwall. Edmund has won Goneril's favors; the latter plans to poison her sister Regan. Edgar (as Poor Tom) pretends to help Gloucester jump off the cliffs of Dover, then reverts to his real self, challenging and defeating Edmund, who has already ordered that the captured Cordelia be strangled. Regan is poisoned, Goneril stabs herself. Lear laments over Cordelia's corpse and dies.

The violent musical language of large portions of *Lear* drove some shocked listeners out of the opera houses in Munich, Düsseldorf, and San Francisco. For some, the bitingly aggressive clusters of sound, particularly in the storm and torture scenes, sound like uncontrolled noise, but a look at the huge and very complex score shows that Reimann's orchestral textures are precisely and carefully planned. Every dramatic phase of *Lear* was fixed by Reimann in verbal descriptions before he invented the musical materials that are specific to a particular stage character or scene. Some of this planning is evident at first hearing: the impersonal, wide vocal leaps accompanied by frozen chordal sound blocks for Goneril, the hysterical melismas and appoggiaturas of Regan's vocal line accompanied by tiny nervous figures in the high wind instruments, Cordelia's always calm, lyric vocal line created out of a twelve-tone row (Reimann uses this technique as a reservoir of motivic material although he rejected strict dodecaphony twenty-five years earlier), a row which, in reverse, supplies material for the similarly rejected Edgar. Obvious too is the uniquely effective beginning of the opera with Lear's unaccompanied chant "We have ordered your presence," the orchestra only entering with a stab of string tone at "Ah, ah, this longing for sleep." Not quite as obvious, though equally indicative of an instinctive genius for opera, is the first exchange between Goneril and Regan in scene ii. Their vocal line for "We swear to stand by each other," an expression of their joint determination to keep Lear and his soldiers out of their residences, shares the same notes but is staggered heterophonically to indicate that their different interests will eventually make bitter rivalries out of present harmony.

What Reimann has retained from his studies of the Second Viennese School is Anton Webern's strict reduction to essentials and Berg's *espressivo*, tempered by techniques deriving from Indian music, employing quarter-tones and building tremendous climactic scenes (such as the storm) out of minute cells that, taken together, form a double twenty-four-tone row and point toward a new principle of tension and relaxation to take the place of major/minor duality.

At first glance the line played by the bass strings looks like a conventionally notated twelve-tone melody with precisely fixed rhythms, until one notices that every instrument of the *divisi* section is playing a half or quarter tone apart so that a tone-cluster with precise metric definition results. Reimann feels his *Lear* score to be a commentary on "The isolation of a human being, completely alone, who is exposed to the whole brutality and uncertainty of life itself."

But *Lear* also has its ineffably tender pages, such as the moving reconciliations between Gloucester and Edgar, Lear and Cordelia, and the scene that closes the opera, Lear's

helpless monologue over his loving daughter's dead body, accompanied by a single sinuous string line which seems to symbolize the reduction of all life to nothingness. Such scenes show Reimann to be an opera composer capable of breathing life into his stage figures via the music. It is certainly this quality that has endeared *Lear* to those opera-goers capable of distinguishing between meretriciousness and dramatic veracity.

—James Helme Sutcliffe

LEAR, Evelyn (born Evelyn Shulman).

Soprano. Born 8 January 1926, in Brooklyn. Married: 1) Dr Walter Lear, 1943 (two daughters); 2) baritone Thomas Stewart, 1955. Studied piano and horn, then had vocal training with John Yard in Washington, D.C., with Sergius Kagen at Juilliard, and with Maria Ivogün in Berlin; debut as Composer in *Ariadne auf Naxos*, Berlin Städtische Oper, 1957; sang Cherubino in Salzburg, 1962-64; Covent Garden debut as Donna Elvira, 1965; Metropolitan Opera debut in premiere of *Mourning Becomes Electra*, 1967; farewell performance at Metropolitan Opera as Marschallin, 1985; created Jeanne in Egk's *Die Verlobung in San Domingo*, title role in Klebe's *Alkmene*, Irma Arkadina in Pasatieri's *The Seagull*, and Magda in Ward's *Minutes to Midnight*.

* * *

The key words for Evelyn Lear's extraordinary vocal career are versatility and flexibility. Her instinctive feeling for stage characterization made it possible for her to traverse the whole range of roles in the repertoire she loved most, Mozart and Richard Strauss, despite her dedication to 20th-century opera as Berg's Marie and Lulu and in seven other roles she created in operas by Kelterborn, Klebe, Egk, Levy, Pasatieri, Ward and others. Her vocal agility first made her right for Despina and Zerlina, the bright forward-placement of her tone creating an ideal Sophie. But after joining the West Berlin Opera ensemble her voice developed a rich breadth of tone enabling her to move at ease among *spinto*, heavier lyric and outright mezzo-soprano roles, even essaying several dramatic soprano roles on record, though never on stage.

Among Evelyn Lear's 33 recordings are excerpts from Nicolai's *Merry Wives of Windsor*, *Un ballo in maschera*, *Nabucco*, *Eugene Onegin*, *Der fliegende Holländer*, *Jonny spielt auf*, complete recordings of *Boris Godunov*, *Der Rosenkavalier*, *Le nozze di Figaro*, *Die Zauberflöte*, *Wozzeck*, *Lulu*, *Die Gezeichneten* (Schreker), The c minor Mass (Mozart), St. John Passion (J.S. Bach), Te Deum (Nicolai), Glagolithic Mass (Janáček), Klagende Lied (Mahler), Stabat Mater (Pergolesi), Songs by Richard Strauss, Hugo Wolf, Stravinsky, Schumann, Weill, Blitzstein, Bernstein and Sondheim together with five duet recordings with her husband. In 1974 Evelyn Lear starred together with Paul Newman, Joel Grey and Burt Lancaster in the Robert Altman film "Buffalo Bill and the Indians."

She is one of few sopranos to have sung Sophie, Octavian *and* the Marschallin in *Der Rosenkavalier*, Despina *and* Fiordiligi in *Così fan tutte*, Cherubino *and* the Countess in *Figaro*, Lulu *and* Geschwitz in *Lulu*, Zerbinetta *and* the Composer in *Ariadne auf Naxos*, the Countess *and* Clairon in

Capriccio, and Micaela *and* Carmen. An untiring seeker of perfection, her meticulous preparation of her roles and her Lieder programs meant that every aspect of interpretation—phrasing, language (for which she possessed instinctive feeling, making every word count), breath control, dynamics and the always tasteful use of expressive devices such as portamento and vocal coloration—underwent a conscious process of selection and control but without ever leading to interpretative coldness, as the grand cantilenas she could always call upon demonstrated. Perhaps because her innate musicianship first showed itself on the French horn (breath control) and the piano (in an emergency she taught herself the role of Micaela in two days) she became that rarity among singers, a vocalist who was first and foremost a musician.

—James Helme Sutcliffe

LEGEND OF THE INVISIBLE CITY OF KITEZH AND THE MAIDEN FEVRONIYA [Skazaniye o nevidimom grade Kitezhe i deve Fevronii].

Composer: Nicolai Rimsky-Korsakov.

Librettist: V.I. Bel'sky (after Pushkin).

First Performance: St Petersburg, 20 February 1907.

Roles: Fevroniya (soprano); Grischka Kuterma (tenor); Prince Juri (bass); Prince Vsevolod Jurivich (tenor); Fedor Poyarok (baritone); Otrok (mezzo-soprano); Guslee Player (bass); Bear Trainer (tenor); Two Men (tenor, bass); Bedyay (bass); Burunday (bass); Blind Huntsman (baritone); Sirin (soprano); Alkonost (contralto); Voices of Paradise Birds; chorus (SSAATTBB).

Publications

articles–

Kuharskij, Vasilij. "Postizenie Klassiki" [genesis of the libretto of *Legend of the Invisible City of Kitezh and the Maiden Fevroniya*]. *Sovetskaya muzyka* 10 (1984): 34.
Rahmanova, Marina. "K byloj polemike volsrug Kiteza" [*Legend of the Invisible City of Kitezh and the Maiden Fevroniya*]. *Sovetskaya muzyka* 10 (1984): 82.

*   *   *

Rimsky-Korsakov's *Legend of the Invisible City of Kitezh* is unique not only among his own compositions but in the history of Russian opera. Although its subject matter is based on folk legends, it is similar in many ways to Wagner's *Parsifal.* But it is so filled with Russian national elements and essentially Russian characters that in no way should it be regarded as a mere imitation of the Wagnerian masterpiece.

The opera opens with a prelude, "Hymn to the Wilderness," representing the Russian landscape, the vast forests stretching beyond the Volga, as well as the sounds of birds and the rustle of trees. Act I opens in the great Kerzhensky Forest beyond the Volga near Little Kitezh. Fevroniya is a lonely country girl, versed in the mysteries of nature, who lives with her brother in a poor hut. Her friends are the wild

Set design for *Kitezh* by Nicola Benois, Teatro alla Scala, Milan, 1930

beasts and birds, who come to her for healing and affection. The theme associated with her occurs all through the opera. She encounters Prince Vsevolod, who has lost his way while hunting in the forest. Fevroniya gives him traditional hospitality, and the prince is struck by her beauty and ingenuousness. In a long duet the pair express their mutual affection, and the prince places a ring on her finger. The sound of hunting horns is heard, the prince goes off to meet his men, and Fevroniya finds to her astonishment that she is betrothed to Vsevolod, son of Prince Yuri, ruler of Kitezh.

Act II takes place in the market-place of the town of Little Kitezh. A crowd awaits the wedding procession, which will pass through the town on the way to Great Kitezh. The wealthy citizens of the town, unhappy at the prince's choice of a bride, persuade Grishka Kuterma, a drunken simpleton, to make fun of Fevroniya. The sound of bells and *domras* announces the arrival of the wedding procession, which is greeted in traditional folk style, the wedding guests throwing honey cakes, ribbons and money to the people by way of "ransom" for the bride. The drunken Grishka Kuterma tries to interrupt proceedings but is chased away.

Suddenly the theme of the Tatar invasion is heard, and panic and terror fill the hearts of the people. The Tatars under their leaders Burunday and Bedyay enter and start a general massacre. Fevroniya is captured. The treacherous Grishka agrees to show the Tatars the way to Great Kitezh rather than be tortured. Fevroniya prays to the Lord to make the city invisible.

Act III opens in Great Kitezh where the princes, their retinue, and all the people are gathered. Prince Vsevolod leads his soldiers to fight the invaders. As they leave, a golden mist starts to rise above the lake and covers the town so thickly that it cannot be seen. Only the sound of bells can be heard. A symphonic picture ("The Battle of Kerzhenets"), marking the transition to the next scene, signifies the bitter fighting on the banks of the River Kerzhenets, with the predominance of the Tatar theme. When scene ii opens, Grishka Kuterma is seen leading the two Tatars, Bedyay and Burunday, to the lake, beyond which lies Great Kitezh. But because the town cannot be seen, the Tatars think he has tricked them; they bind him to a tree, promising to kill him in the morning.

The Tatar soldiers settle down by a fire and share the plunder before falling asleep. Burunday and Bedyay quarrel over Fevroniya, and Bedyay is killed. Fevroniya bewails the loss of her fiancé, who fell in battle with his men. Grishka begs Fevroniya to save him and, moved by compassion, she agrees. Tormented by the sound of bells and racked by guilt, he is about to throw himself into the lake when he is astonished by a vision of the City of Kitezh reflected in the water, illuminated by the rising sun. He runs away, screaming with terror, followed by Fevroniya. The Tatars are awakened by Grishka's cries and, seeing the reflection of the city, though not the city itself, take off in fright.

In act IV scene i, Fevroniya and Grishka are wandering through the forest exhausted. It is night. Grishka, raving, starts to dance and finally runs into the wood, not to be seen again. Fevroniya falls to the ground. Against a background of bird calls, rustling trees, strange lights, and beautiful flowers, the spirit of Vsevolod appears and, in an episode filled with religious mysticism, leads her to Kitezh. An orchestral interlude, filled with the sound of church chimes and voices of birds of paradise, leads into the final part, which takes place in Great Kitezh, wonderfully transformed. The transfigured Fevroniya appears with the prince and the people. Wedding songs are sung, Vsevolod and Fevroniya go to the altar, and the work ends in an atmosphere of incense, pealing chimes, and the words "eternal joy."

Musically the opera has some very fine moments: the long duet between Volodya and Fevroniya in act I, the Bard's song in act II and the vivid folk scene accompanying it, Fevroniya's moving lament in act III, and the great scene of Kuterma's madness in act IV. The final scene in *Kitezh,* often presented with wonderful vestments, opulence, and richness, is one of the great high points in Russian opera.

—Gerald Seaman

LEHMANN, Lilli.

Soprano. Born 24 November 1848, in Würzburg. Died 17 May 1929, in Berlin. Studied with mother Marie Loewe in Prague; debut as first boy and Pamina in *Die Zauberflöte* in Prague, 1865; sang in Danzig (1868), in Leipzig (1869), and the Berlin Court Opera (1869), in each case first appearing as Marguerite de Valois in *Les Huguenots;* principal singer in Berlin until 1885; appeared in the first Bayreuth *Ring* as Woglinde, Helmwige, and the Forest Bird, 1876; Vienna debut, 1882; moved into dramatic roles after 1884; London debut at Her Majesty's Theatre as Violetta, 1880; Metropolitan Opera debut as Carmen, 1885; returned to Berlin in 1891; pupils include Farrar, Fremstad, Kurt, and Lubin.

Publications

By LEHMANN: books—

Mein Gesangkunst. Berlin, 1902; English translation as *How to Sing,* New York, 1902; revised, 1924.
Mein Weg. Leipzig, 1913; published as *My Path Through Life,* New York and London, 1914.

About LEHMANN: books—

Ehrlich, A. *Berühmte Sängerinnen der Vergangenheit und Gegenwart.* Leipzig, 1895.
Newman, E. *The Life of Richard Wagner.* London 1933-47; reprinted 1977.
Kaap, J. *Geschichte der Staatsoper Berlin.* Berlin, 1937.
Henderson, W. *The Art of Singing.* New York, 1938.
Kolodin, I. *The Story of the Metropolitan Opera.* New York, 1951.
Fetting, H. *Die Geschichte der Deutschen Staatsoper.* Berlin, 1955.
Rosenthal, H. *Two Centuries of Opera at Covent Garden.* London, 1958.
Skelton, G. *Wagner at Bayreuth.* London, 1965.

*   *   *

No singer has been more respected and indeed more feared than Lilli Lehmann, whose technique, industry, musicianship, and executive authority made her one of the most daunting artists of her day. Her performances, and indeed her life,

Lilli Lehmann as Isolde

exemplified impassioned discipline, and her recordings, made as she approached sixty, reflect the praise of her colleagues precisely. She debuted at sixteen, and after almost a decade as Berlin's leading coloratura, went to Bayreuth in 1876, most importantly as Siegfried's charming Woodbird—and thereafter fought to remodel herself as a dramatic soprano. "One grows weary of singing nothing but princesses for fifteen years," she remarked, and gradually added Elsa, Elisabeth, Sieglinde, Isolde, Brünnhilde, Ortrud, Norma, Donna Anna, and Leonore (*Fidelio*) to her repertoire. After years of glory in these and similar roles at the Metropolitan and elsewhere, she returned in triumph to Bayreuth as Brünnhilde in 1896. Even after the turn of the century she continued to sing in opera and then in concert for two decades. Inevitably, she also taught, and was both demanding and caustic. "With her," said Geraldine Farrar, "Will was Power," and the nevertheless grateful Germaine Lubin called her Salzburg classes "veritable killers." Lehmann herself practised constantly, testing her voice sometimes for nearly an hour with a slow two-octave scale for faults of breath, attack, and dynamic control, and in rehearsals singing at full voice. Volume alone was not her goal: "One need not roar," she commented, finding that "one could sing well even with a little voice if the sound were noble."

Farrar thought that Lehmann combined the best of both the French and the Italian methods, and such a union of projection from the masque and diaphragmatic control is what emerges from Lehmann's records, made in 1906-07. It was a voice of modest size for Wagner, still absolutely steady, and glittering if occasionally pinched at the top, though by then a little pallid and worn in the middle. The legato technique of her coloratura days met with her dramatic thrust to produce a Norma of tragic command and a Lieder singer of lyric compulsion. With age and constricted recording to contend with, she relied on an iron control and support to send her triumphantly through the terrors of both Mozart ("Martern aller arten," for example) and Wagner ("Du bist der Lenz").

Of Lehmann's dramatic range it is more difficult to speak comprehensively. Critics (Hanslick, Krehbiel, Henderson), singers (Farrar, Calvé, Fremstad), and entrepreneurs and conductors (Mapleson, Walter Damrosch) all wrote of her noble and electrifying qualities as an actress, though others thought she lacked charm. Certainly Donna Anna's "Or sai, chi l'onore" and its recitativo, describing an attempted rape, have never been sung with such a sense of outrage; there is nothing of touching vulnerability in her delivery. Norma's "Casta diva" is splendidly articulated in her recording, but hardly visionary, although it certainly may have been so in the ambience of an opera house. One hears the same bright edge and foursquare approach in her excerpts from *La traviata,* doggedly accurate, and "Du bist der Lenz," fresh and intense but not really affectionate. This cannot be the whole story, however. In writing about performance, she often stresses the necessity of "life-giving style"—the real projection and not simply the indication of feeling, and the mingling of personal responses with those of the character in interpretation. To imagine her artistic aims in terms of recent singers, one might think of the technical mastery of the young Joan Sutherland wedded to the focused intensity of someone like Hildegard Behrens, in roles stretching from the Queen of the Night to Isolde.

Lehmann's extraordinary qualities become clearer in comparison with the work of other German sopranos of the time. Most of her exact contemporaries, in fact, had lost their voices and retired when she came to make records. What we can hear is largely the work of a somewhat younger generation

recording at the same period: Sophie Sedlmair, Thila Plaichinger, Anna Bahr-Mildenburg, Lucie Weidt and others. Bahr-Mildenburg (in her one extant record) has fine attack and reliable pitch, and Weidt some of Lehmann's sculptural sense, but none of them demonstrates her combination of sovereign authority in phrasing Mozart *and* Wagner, finish, lyricism, patrician utterance—and longevity. Perhaps her most moving and representative record is of Leonore's "Abscheulicher!" Its noble outrage and impassioned faith were touchstones of Lehmann's philosophy as well as her art. The voice, technique, and dramatic range, expanded throughout a lifetime of devoted study and performance, are here tested to the limit and emerge victorious. That was her way.

—London Green

LEHMANN, Lotte.

Soprano. Born 27 February 1888, in Perleberg, Germany. Died 26 August 1976, in Santa Barbara, California. Married Otto Krause in 1926 (died 1939). Studied at Berlin Hochschule für Musik in 1904 and under Mathilde Mallinger, 1908-9; debut as Second Boy in *Die Zauberflöte,* Hamburg, 1910; London Drury Lane debut as Sophie in *Der Rosenkavalier,* 1914; in Vienna 1916-37, where she created the Composer in the revised version of *Ariadne auf Naxos,* the Dyer's Wife in *Die Frau ohne Schatten,* and Christine in *Intermezzo;*

Lotte Lehmann as the Marschallin in Strauss's *Der Rosenkavalier*

Covent Garden debut as the Marschallin, 1924; appeared in Buenos Aires, 1922; in Paris, 1928-34; in Chicago, 1930-37; appeared at Salzburg 1926-37; Metropolitan Opera debut as Sieglinde, 1934, and sang there twelve seasons until 1946; gave recitals until 1951; taught in Santa Barbara.

Publications

By LEHMANN: books–

Anfang und Aufsteig: Lebenserinnerungen. Vienna, 1937; English translation as *Midway in My Song,* Indianapolis, 1938; as *Wings of Song,* London, 1934.
Orplid, mein Land. Vienna, 1937.
More Than Singing: The Interpretation of Songs. New York, 1945.
My Many Lives. New York, 1948.
Five Operas and Richard Strauss. New York, 1964; as *Singing with Richard Strauss.* London, 1964.
Gedichte. Salzburg, 1969.
Eighteen Song Cycles: Studies in Their Interpretation. London, 1971.

articles–

"The Singing Actor." In *Players at Work,* ed. M Eustis. New York, 1937.
"Twelve Singers and a Conductor" and "Goering, the Lioness, and I." *Opera '66,* edited by C. Osborne. London, 1966.

About LEHMANN: books–

Wessling, B. *Lotte Lehmann . . . mehr als eine Sängerin.* Salzburg, 1969.
Glass, B. *Lotte Lehmann: A Life in Opera and Song.* Santa Barbara, California, 1988.
Jefferson, A. *Lotte Lehmann: 1888-1976: A Centenary Biography.* London, 1988.

articles–

Miller, P. "Lotte Lehmann." *Record News* 4 (1960): 391, 440; 5 (1960): 20, 45.
Schauensee, M. de "The Maestro's Singers: Lotte Lehmann." *The Maestro* 3/nos. 1-2 (1971): 14.
Shawe-Taylor, D. "Lotte Lehmann and Elisabeth Schumann: A Centenary Tribute." *Musical Times* October (1988).

Lotte Lehmann was able to achieve astonishing vocal and physical effects on both the stage and the concert platform by relying on her personality and sweetness of delivery rather than on a naturally beautiful appearance, which she lacked. She came from a humdrum background in North Germany where her father, a civil servant, forbade his only daughter to become a professional singer. Her determination and sheer persuasiveness overcame this obstacle, though female professors insisted that she had no vocal talent. At last she managed to find her ideal teacher in Mathilde Mallinger (Wagner's first Eva), and was then "taken up" by a rich German family who helped smooth out some of her gauche manners and assisted her in obtaining her first contract with the Hamburg Opera in 1910.

Hard work, a cheerful spirit and constant pestering of the management gained her several small roles until, in 1912, a fortunate break gave her the opportunity to sing Elsa in *Lohengrin* under the savage tuition and the baton of Hamburg's young conductor, Otto Klemperer. From then on she rose in the ranks of the Hamburg company, eventually singing 56 different roles there before reluctantly leaving to join the Vienna Court Opera at the end of 1916.

At first Lehmann was a fish out of water in the elegant Habsburg capital and center of operatic Europe; although she had several interesting roles to sing with the most dazzling partners, nobody took much notice of her. Within a mere two months, partly due to the negligence at rehearsals of the great Marie Gutheil-Schoder, Lehmann was suddenly given the important new role of the Young Composer at the premiere of Richard Strauss's revised version of *Ariadne auf Naxos.* Her success was immediate, and she remained a member of the Vienna Opera until 1938, becoming Viennese herself in the process.

Her special relationship with Strauss gave her several more characters to create for him in his operas, but all the time she felt herself to be in the shadow of other sopranos more famous, certainly more beautiful and generally with more powerful political connections. As a result Lehmann assumed a sullen and defensive attitude, so that her relationships with some of her female colleagues deteriorated as she became acknowledged as the finest portrayer of certain roles, including the Marschallin in *Der Rosenkavalier,* Leonore in *Fidelio,* Sieglinde in *Die Walküre,* Eva in *Die Meistersinger* and as Massenet's Manon.

Although she completed her training with Mallinger, Lehmann had never perfected her technique due to her unhappiness with several previous teachers. Breath control was always difficult, although this mattered little when the performance was so thoroughly prepared and backed by a personality radiating charm, warmth and goodness through every note. The top of the voice was a little deficient in body, which makes it all the more amazing that Lehmann sang the first Vienna Turandot and eight more performances of it in the 1926-27 season. Although vocal deterioration is evident from her gramophone records of the following years, Lehmann was always game to take on a difficult role and conquer it, making it unmistakably her own creation.

Lehmann was a welcome visitor to many European cities, especially London and Paris, as well as South America and Chicago, though she did not arrive at the Metropolitan Opera until 1934, as a triumphant Sieglinde. There Lehmann was again confronted by competition from other sopranos and bore grudges against "unfair" casting. Initially in Hamburg her imagined antagonist had been Elisabeth Schumann, but that was soon put right; in Vienna her rival was Maria Jeritza, who really behaved obnoxiously towards her; upon Jeritza's departure, the bête-noire became Viorica Ursuleac. At the Met the enemy was Flagstad. Each of these voices offered such different timbres, coloring and dramatic qualities that they should have been considered alternatives rather than rivals, but Lehmann failed to understand this.

America was to become her home when she settled in California in 1939, away from both Nazi and professional enemies in Vienna. When engagements dwindled and then stopped altogether, she concentrated on her concert career, something which she had allowed to mature since the First World War and which had grown to a peak at Salzburg Festivals in the 1930s with Bruno Walter as her accompanist. Her concert repertoire was extensive and not exclusively German. She was always able to establish great *rapport* with her audiences in the concert hall, where she had learned to mould her projection and delivery to suit her varied and often humorous repertoire.

Despite vocal shortcomings from the beginning of her career, Lehmann's voice was long-lived. She was obliged to enter the last phase of her long and varied career as vocal teacher in Santa Barbara where she reveled in a life among dedicated young people, communicating to them the lessons which she had learned so painfully, urging them to grasp the wisdom of her experience.

Lehmann was greatly beloved by Arturo Toscanini, Bruno Walter, Otto Klemperer and Franz Schalk. She had a string of lovers and one husband (for a short time) but no children. She was an avid letter-writer, an author and novelist; she painted, potted and drew many penetrating sketches and caricatures.

Much of Lehmann's vocal output is preserved on records (455 sides of 78s) which are nearly all transfered to CD. They include much of the Marschallin's role in *Der Rosenkavalier* and Sieglinde in its entirety. In addition, many pictorial and vocal proofs of her art remain at a time when those who knew and heard her perform gradually disappear.

—Alan Jefferson

LEIDER, Frida.

Soprano. Born 4 April 1888, in Berlin. Died 4 June 1975, in Berlin. Married violinist Rudolf Deman. Studied with Otto Schwarz; debut as Venus in *Tannhäuser,* Halle, 1915; in Rostock, 1916-18; in Königsberg, 1918-19; at Hamburg State

Frida Leider as Isolde

Opera, 1919-23; at Berlin State Opera, 1923-40; appeared at Covent Garden, 1924-38; appeared at Bayreuth, 1928-38; Chicago debut as Brünnhilde in *Die Walküre,* 1928; Paris Opéra, 1930-32; Metropolitan Opera debut in *Tristan und Isolde,* 1933; after World War II she had a vocal studio at the Berlin State Opera until 1952; at Berlin Hochschule, 1948-58.

Publications

By LEIDER: books–

Das war mein Teil, Erinnerungen einer Opernsängerin. Berlin, 1959; English translation as *Playing My Part,* New York, 1966.

About LEIDER: articles–

Burros, H. "Frida Leider." *Record News* 2 (1958): 345.

* * *

Her obituary in a Berlin publication stated simply, "In the early morning hours of June 4, 1975, the Berlin Kammersängerin Professor Frida Leider, honorary member of the Deutsche Oper Berlin, died. She was one of the most important personalities in the music history of the first half of our century. Without her the Wagner repertoire during these years would not have been possible. Seldom has the fusion of text and music, seldom the art of phrasing and dramatic expression celebrated such triumphs as in the years that this great soprano was gracing our opera stages."

Frida Leider was born in Berlin on April 4, 1888. She studied voice with Otto Schwarz while supporting herself by working as a clerk in the Berliner Bank. In 1915 she made her debut in Halle as Venus in *Tannhäuser.* From 1916 to 1918 Leider was engaged by the City Opera in Rostock. In 1918-19 she sang in Königsberg and then joined the roster of singers at the Hamburg State Opera for the seasons 1919 through 1923. In 1924 Leider was engaged by the Berlin State Opera and soon celebrated the first of her many operatic triumphs.

Her guest appearances included performances in Milan's Teatro alla Scala, in Paris, Vienna, Munich, and Stuttgart, as well as in Stockholm, Amsterdam, and Brussels. Covent Garden invited her as a guest every year from 1924 through 1938. For ten years, between 1928-1938, Frida Leider was one of the greatest stars of the Bayreuth Festival. Her performances of the three Brünnhildes and Isolde led to her being considered the most important German Wagnerian soprano of her generation. She did not neglect other important roles for dramatic soprano. Frida Leider was also highly praised for her interpretations of Fidelio, the Marschallin in *Rosenkavalier,* Donna Anna, and Gluck's Armide.

Brünnhilde in *Walküre* was her debut role in Chicago during the 1928 season. Because the rivalry between the Metropolitan Opera and the Chicago Opera was so bitter, both companies had agreed not to raid one another's roster. This delayed Leider's Metropolitan career until January 16, 1933, when she appeared in a glorious performance of *Tristan und Isolde.* Her close friend Lauritz Melchior sang Tristan and contralto Maria Olczewska made her Metropolitan debut as Brangäne. All shared equally in the critical acclaim. Leider was praised for her "deep and enlarging tenderness, richness of feeling, poetry of imagination." Another critic described the performance as surpassing "any that memory can recall" since before the war and a third rejoiced with the words "At last a cast!"

The rise of the Nazi Party to power in Berlin made the last years of Leider's career very difficult. Her husband, Rudolf Deman, was Jewish. Deman, concertmaster of the Berlin State Opera, was forced to flee to Switzerland. Leider chose to remain with her husband and her career at the Berlin State Opera ended in 1940. It was through the financial generosity of Lauritz Melchior that the couple was able to exist in exile.

After World War II Leider sang only a few concerts. She became a stage director at the Berlin State Opera and began to teach. From 1945 to 1952 she directed the company's voice studio, and in 1948 Frida Leider accepted a professorship at the Berlin Hochschule für Musik, where she remained until her retirement in 1958.

On her eightieth birthday, Lauritz Melchior composed this tribute to his longtime colleague and friend: "I think there has never been a more sincere artist, and the greatness of her heart that you hear on the recordings is only a small percentage of what you heard when you saw her and heard her on the stage. As she filled her parts absolutely, she also made her partners do their very best, and through that made the performances something very special."

Frida Leider was the recipient of the German Service Cross, First Class. Her memoirs, *Das war mein Teil,* were published in Berlin in 1959.

—Suzanne Summerville

LEINSDORF, Erich.

Conductor. Born 4 February 1912, in Vienna. Studied piano with Paul Emerich, 1923-28; studied theory and composition with Paul Pisk; studied conducting briefly at the Mozarteum in Salzburg, and then at the University of Vienna; studied at the Vienna Academy of Music, 1931-33; conducting debut at the Musikvereinsaal, 1933; assistant conductor to the Worker's Chorus in Vienna, 1933; assistant to Walter and Toscanini at the Salzburg Festival, 1934; conductor of the Metropolitan Opera, New York, 1937; guest conductor at the Metropolitan Opera, 1938; succeeded Bodanzky as head of the German repertoire at the Metropolitan Opera, 1939; became a United States citizen, 1942; music director of the Cleveland Orchestra, 1943; served in the United States Army, 1943-44; conductor at the Metropolitan Opera, 1944-45; music director of the Rochester Philharmonic Orchestra, 1947-55; music director of the New York City Opera, 1956; conductor and music consultant at the Metropolitan Opera, 1957; guest conductor in the United States and Europe; music director of the Boston Symphony Orchestra, 1962-69; further guest conducting appearances; principal conductor of the West Berlin Radio Symphony Orchestra, 1978-80.

Publications

By LEINSDORF: books—

Cadenza: a Musical Career. Boston, 1976.
The Composer's Advocate: a Radical Orthodoxy for Musicians. New Haven, 1981.

*   *   *

Throughout Erich Leinsdorf's long and variegated career as a conductor, opera was the medium to which he ever returned, amidst tenures of varying duration as an orchestral conductor. At age eight he studied piano with Mrs Paul Pisk, at a local conservatory in Vienna, and three years later began lessons with the well-known piano teacher Paul Emerich. Angry that Leinsdorf had become involved in operatic and symphonic activities to the detriment of his pianism, Emerich ended their relationship in 1930.

At that point Leinsdorf began studying composition with Mr Paul Pisk, husband of his former piano teacher (and a student of Franz Schreker and Arnold Schoenberg). In this period Leinsdorf also became involved as a rehearsal pianist with Anton Webern's Sozialdemokratischen Musik Kunstelle, making his debut as an accompanist in a performance of Stravinsky's *Les noces.* He then became Bruno Walter's assistant at Salzburg, and later in that city accompanied Arturo Toscanini's performance of Zoltán Kodály's *Psalmus Hungaricus,* on very short notice. Successful in these difficult tasks, Leinsdorf became assistant to both Toscanini and Walter. These experiences, coupled with a timely recommendation from Lotte Lehmann, brought him an engagement as assistant to Artur Bodanzky, director of German repertoire at the Metropolitan Opera Company.

Leinsdorf made his New York debut in a performance of Wagner's *Die Walküre* in the Metropolitan subscription series. Successful in this endeavor, he then was asked to conduct Richard Strauss's *Elektra,* as well as Wagner's *Lohengrin* and *Tannhäuser* that same season, in which he was at last awarded a two-year contract as a regular conductor at the Met. After Bodanzky's death in 1939, Leinsdorf was put in charge of the German repertoire. In the meantime, he had also been engaged in 1938 by Gaetano Merola to participate in the fall season of the San Francisco Opera where he was engaged as assistant to Fritz Reiner, and given the assignment of conducting a performance of Debussy's *Pelléas et Mélisande.* This relationship with the San Francisco Opera continued successfully for the next four years.

In 1943 Leinsdorf left the Met, having been invited to replace Artur Rodzinsky as conductor of the Cleveland Symphony. Before he could assume duties there, however, he was drafted into the United States Army. Released a few months later, he found that the Cleveland position had been filled, and so returned to New York and the Metropolitan Opera Company. He continued to appear as an international guest conductor, particularly in London, where he recorded and concertized with most of the major orchestras, before traveling briefly on the continent. He returned to America to conduct the Rochester Philharmonic for five weeks as guest conductor, after which he was given a contract for several years as music director, to begin in 1947.

By 1953 greener pastures beckoned, and Leinsdorf accepted engagements in Philadelphia, in Israel, and sought to become permanent director of the New York City Opera. That appointment turned into a fiasco, a development which led him back to the Met once again. At Rudolph Bing's invitations, he undertook to replace Rudolf Kempe, conducting Wagner's *Die Walküre* and Richard Strauss's *Arabella.* During the same season he also accepted recording engagements with RCA and with Capitol Records, and, amidst the usual guest engagements, also undertook a new position as musical consultant to the Metropolitan Opera Company.

In 1962, upon the retirement of Charles Munch, Leinsdorf became music director of the Boston Symphony, a position he held with brilliant results for nearly seven years. His duties there included the Berkshire Music festival held annually each summer at Tanglewood, an activity which gave him great joy. After his tenure with the Boston Symphony, Leinsdorf became a world traveling conductor and a welcome guest for most world class orchestras and opera companies.

Leinsdorf's arrival in America before the outbreak of World War II was part of a general phenomenon which totally transformed American musical life. Quite suddenly American culture was enriched by an unexpected importation of the best conducting, performing and musicological talent in the world—all as a direct result of Hitler's policies. Men like Fritz Busch, Erich Kleiber, Erich Leinsdorf, Max Rudolf, William Steinberg, and George Szell might have visited America from time to time even without Hitler's actions. But it is unlikely that they would have invested their entire lives in America, as Erich Leinsdorf and many others did. Because of his investment, not only major institutions such as the Metropolitan Opera Company, or the Boston Symphony, but lesser communities, such as Rochester, New York, or Cleveland, Ohio, found their cultural lives incredibly enriched. Erich Leinsdorf, now in the sunset of a remarkable career, has given America much. His virtual retirement, which seems to coincide with the end of the Austro-German hegemony over our symphonic and operatic institutions, may well mark the beginning of an indigenous musical culture, led and nurtured by native talent.

—Franklin B. Zimmerman

LEMNITZ, Tiana (Luise).

Soprano. Born 26 October 1897, in Metz. Studied with Hoch in Metz and Anton Kohmann in Frankfurt; debut as Lortzing's Undine in Heilbronn, 1920; appeared at Aachen, 1922-28; Hannover, 1928-33; Dresden, 1933-34; at Berlin Staatsoper, 1934-57; at Covent Garden, 1936-38; appeared at the Teatro Colon in Buenos Aires, 1936, 1950.

Publications

About LEMNITZ: articles–

Seeliger, R. "Tiana Lemnitz." *Record Collector* 15 (1963): 29.

* * *

Tiana Lemnitz is the last of those statuesque and noble singers—both physically and vocally—from between the two wars, a soprano of superior merit. Lemnitz was born in Metz, German Alsace, in 1897, the tenth of eleven sisters, all daughters of an army bandmaster. Music flourished in the household. During the First World War, Lemnitz was a student at the Metz Conservatory of Music but later, when Alsace was returned to France, she lived with an elder sister in Frankfurt and attended the Conservatory there for two years. As a student in Frankfurt, she made her tentative debut as the heroine in Lortzing's *Undine*.

Her first proper engagement was in 1922 with the Aachen Opera. With patience and continuous instruction from the right teacher, she progressed to Hannover, went to Dresden with a guest contract, then to Berlin, where she was regarded as the successor of Maria Müller. She remained a member of the Berlin Staatsoper from 1934 to 1957 and was appointed

a *Kammersängerin* there in 1937. She frequently appeared abroad, but never in New York.

Several of her contemporaries had passed her and achieved fame sooner, but Lemnitz's slow progress paid off handsomely by preserving her voice. It was distinguished by a fully controlled pianissimo, used to special effect in Mozart; her nuances, expressiveness, and creamy voice made her an exceptional lyrical- and lyrico-spinto soprano. Her recording of Pamina in the Berlin *Zauberflöte* of 1938 (conducted by Beecham) illustrates her vocal quality, technical command and clear enunciation.

Between 1928 and 1934, when she was a guest artist at Dresden, Richard Strauss wanted her to sing Arabella in the premiere of his new opera. Because of Fritz Busch's departure (for political reasons) and his temporary replacement by Clemens Krauss, this did not come to pass until later; to Strauss's complete satisfaction, however, Lemnitz was the first and also the last Arabella in performances conducted by the composer himself in Berlin.

Lemnitz took part in the Covent Garden summer seasons of 1936 and 1938 as Eva in *Die Meistersinger* and as Octavian in *Der Rosenkavalier,* one of her most celebrated roles. Her boyish appearance, nobility of manner and her voice that alternated between warmth and coolness, combined with her exceptional acting ability, made her and Delia Reinhardt the two most sought-after Octavians in Europe. Later, she took over the role of the Marschallin in the same opera with great distinction, principally in Berlin.

Her repertoire was extensive. She was a key soprano in the German Verdi revival of the 1930s, sang Mozart, Wagner and Richard Strauss, as well as in less familiar Polish, Russian and Czech operas. She gave the South American premiere of Janáček's *Jenufa* at the Teatro Colón, Buenos Aires in 1951. Although she was then in her middle fifties, she looked considerably younger and retained her full vocal power and commanding presence.

Lemnitz remained with the Berlin Staatsoper throughout the war until July 1944, when all theaters in the Third Reich were closed. Afterwards, she was one of those who despite the dangers and hardships inflicted by invaders of the city, helped reopen the Opera at the Admiralspalast in East Berlin, Friedrichstrasse (an old music hall) when the Staatsoper Building no longer existed. She sang Eurydice at the opening performance in August 1945.

She appeared for only one season, 1939, at a Salzburg Festival as Agathe in *Der Freischütz,* another of her great roles. Surprisingly she never appeared at Bayreuth. After she retired from the stage in 1960, she became director of the Berlin State Opera Studio and took a small number of pupils.

—Alan Jefferson

LEONCAVALLO, Ruggero.

Composer. Born 23 April 1857, in Naples. Died 9 August 1919, in Montecatini. Studied piano with B. Cesi and composition with M. Ruta and L. Rossi at the Naples Conservatory;

read Italian at Bologna University. Pianist in Egypt, 1879; accompanist and song-writer in cafés in Paris, 1882-88; project to compose a trilogy on the Italian Renaissance entitled *Crepusculum* inspired by his study of Wagner, 1878-88; in Milan, *Pagliacci* composed and sold to the publisher Sonzogno, and achieved international success; first part of his trilogy *Crepusculum* entitled *I Medici,* unsuccessful; commissioned by Emperor Wilhelm II of Germany to compose *Der Roland von Berlin* for Berlin, 1904; United States and Canada tour, 1906; in London, 1912; conducting in San Francisco, 1913; continued composing opera and operetta in Italy until his death.

Operas

Publishers: Sonzogno, Choudens.

Tommaso Chatterton, Leoncavallo (after A. de Vigny), c. 1876, Rome, Nazionale, 10 March 1896; revised, Rome, Torre Argentina, 10 March 1896; revised Nice, 7 April 1905.
Pagliacci, Leoncavallo, Milan, Teatro dal Verme, 21 May 1892.
Crepusculum: I Medici, Leoncavallo, Milan, Teatro dal Verme, 9 November 1893.
La bohème, Leoncavallo (after Henri Murger), Venice, Teatro La Fenice, 6 May 1897; revised as *Mimi Pinson,* Palermo, Massimo, 14 April 1913.
Zazà, Leoncavallo (after P. Berton and C. Simon), Milan, Lirico, 10 November 1900.

Ruggero Leoncavallo, caricature by Romeo Marchetti, 1910

Der Roland von Berlin, Leoncavallo (after Willibald Alexis; German translation by G. Droescher), Berlin, Royal Opera, 13 December 1904.
La jeunesse de Figaro (operetta), after Sardou, *Les premières de Figaro,* United States, 1906.
Maia, A. Nessi (after Paul de Choudens), Rome, Costanzi, 15 January 1910.
Malbrouck (fantasia comica medioevale), A. Nessi, Rome, Nazionale, 19 January 1910.
Zingari, E. Cavacchioli and G. Emanuel (after Pushkin), London, Hippodrome, 16 September 1912.
La reginetta delle rose (operetta), G. Forzano, Rome, Costanzi, 24 June 1912.
Are you there? (farce), A. de Courville and E. Wallace, London, Prince of Wales, 1 November 1913.
Ave Maria, L. Illica and E. Cavacchioli, 1915 [unfinished].
La candidata (operetta), G. Forzano, Rome, Nazionale, 6 February 1915.
Goffredo Mameli (operetta), G. Belvederi, Genoa, Carlo Felice, 27 April 1916.
Prestami tua moglie (operetta), E. Corradi, Montecatini, Casino, 2 September 1916.
Edipo re, G. Forzano (after Sophocles) [unfinished; completed by G. Pennacchio, Chicago, Opera, 13 December 1920].
A chi la giarrettiera? (operetta), Rome, Adriano, 16 October 1919 [posthumous].
Il primo bacio (operetta), L. Bonelli, Montecatini, Salone di Cura, 29 April 1923 [posthumous].
La maschera nuda (operetta), L. Bonelli and F. Paolieri, Naples, Politeama, 26 June 1925 [unfinished; completed by S. Allegri].
Prometeo [unfinished].
Tormenta, G. Belvederi [unfinished].

Other works: songs, piano pieces, choruses, a symphonic poem, a ballet.

Publications/Writings

By LEONCAVALLO: librettos–

Mario Wetter (set by Augusto Machado), 1898.
Redenzione (set by G. Pennacchio), 1920.

About LEONCAVALLO: books–

Roux, O. *Memorie giovanili autobiografiche di Leoncavallo.* Florence, n.d.
Monaldi, G. *Ricordi viventi di artisti scomparsi.* Campobasso, 1927.
Adami, G. *G. Ricordi e i suoi musicisti.* Milan, 1933.
Rensis, R. de. *Per Umberto Giordano e Ruggiero Leoncavallo.* Siena, 1949.
Rubboli, Daniele. *Ridi pagliaccio.* Lucca, 1985.

articles–

Giani, R., and A. Engelfred. *"I Medici." Rivista musicale italiana* 1 (1894): 86.
Hanslick, E. *"Der Bajazzo* von Leoncavallo." In *Die moderne Oper,* vol. 7. *Fünf Jahre Musik (1891-1895): Kritiken,* 96. Berlin, 1896.
———. "Die Bohème von Leoncavallo." In *Die moderne Oper,* vol. 8. *Am Ende des Jahrhunderts (1895-1899); musikalische Kritiken und Schilderungen,* 123. Berlin, 1899.

Tabanelli, N. "La causa Ricordi-Leoncavallo." *Rivista musicale italiana* 6 (1899): 833.

Pastor, W. "Leoncavallos *Roland von Berlin.*" *Die Musik* 14/no. 7 (1904-05): 45.

Trevor, C. "Ruggiero Leoncavallo." *Monthly Musical Record* 49 (1919): 193.

Korngold, J. "Ruggiero Leoncavallo: *Zazà* (1909)." In *Die romantische Oper der Gegenwart,* 103. Vienna, 1922.

Angelis, A. de. "Il capolavoro inespresso di Leoncavallo? *Tormenta:* opera di soggetto sardo." *Rivista musicale italiana* 30 (1923): 563.

Fauré, G. "Leoncavallo." *Opinions musicales* (1930): 64.

Giachetti, G. "Leoncavallo a Milano prima dei *Pagliacci.*" *La sera* 20 March (1942).

Holde, A. "A Little-known Letter by Berlioz and Unpublished Letters by Cherubini, Leoncavallo, and Hugo Wolf." *Musical Quarterly* 37 (1951): 350.

Greenfield, E. "The Other Bohème." *Opera Annual* 5 (1958): 77.

Klein, John W. "Ruggero Leoncavallo (1858-1919)." *Opera* 9 (1958): 158, 232.

Morini, M. "Ruggero Leoncavallo: la sua opera." *La Scala* April (1959).

Giazotto, R. "Uno sconosciuto progetto teatrale di Ruggero Leoncavallo." *Nuova rivista musicale italiana* 2 (1968).

Lerario, T. "Ruggero Leoncavallo e il soggetto dei 'Pagliacci'." *Chigiana* 26-27 (1971): 115.

Marchetti, A. "Lo smisurato sogno dell' autore di 'Pagliacci'." *Rassegna musicale Curci* 25 (1972): 23.

Nicolodi, Fiamma. "Parigi e l'opera verista: dibattiti, riflessioni, polemiche." *Nuova rivista musicale italiana* 15 (1981): 577.

Hall, George. "Leoncavallo in London." *Opera* March (1984)[?]

———. "Leoncavallo in America." *Opera* February (1985).

Sansone, Matteo. "The 'Verismo' of Ruggero Leoncavallo: A Source Study of *Pagliacci.*" *Music and Letters* August (1989).

Maehder, Jürgen. "Immagini di Parigi. La trasformazione del romanzo 'Scènes de la vie de Bohème' di Henry Murger nelle opere di Puccini e Leoncavallo." *Nuova rivista musicale italiana* 3 (1990): 403.

*   *   *

Leoncavallo has been more easily vilified than praised, though it has often been stressed that he had a good literary education and a wide cultural background. He was the only composer of the young Italian school who could write his own librettos, but he was musically less gifted than his colleagues. Before 1892 (the year of *Pagliacci*), one opera could testify to Leoncavallo's cultural ambitions and genuine tastes, and that was *I Medici*, the first part of an "Epic Poem in the form of an Historical Trilogy" on the Italian Renaissance which the composer called *Crepusculum* (*Twilight*) in emulation of Wagner's *Götterdämmerung*. This large-scale project was conceived during Leoncavallo's stay in Bologna (the Wagnerian stronghold in Italy), and was to include *Gerolamo Savonarola* and *Cesare Borgia*, which were never written. The young composer put in a lot of work researching Lorenzo de' Medici, Poliziano, Savonarola and the Borgias, and the libretto of *I Medici* is meticulously annotated with literary and historical references. However, the opera failed hopelessly because of the pretentiousness of the text and the grandiloquence and lack of originality of the music. It could only be performed after the composer achieved sudden popularity

with *Pagliacci,* just as the youthful, romantic *Chatterton,* which did not reach the stage until 1896.

Three operas best exemplify Leoncavallo's skills as a librettist and musician: *Pagliacci* (*Clowns*), *La bohème* and *Zazà,* all of them composed in the heyday of *verismo*. His reputation, however, rests entirely on *Pagliacci,* the only opera in which his literary abilities were effectively matched by his musical talent.

Leoncavallo was a master in creating stylistic pastiche. The subject matter selected for his operas enabled him to contrive situations which justified the use of different linguistic registers and compositional styles. His creative limits made him turn to the relics of the dismantled romantic melodrama no less than to the fashionable light music of his time. With the sensibility of an operetta composer, Leoncavallo pieced together agitated duets, impassioned romanzas, drawing-room melodies, music-hall songs, waltzes and marches. Wagnerian reminiscences and borrowings from other major composers were interwoven with violet vocal outbursts in the new veristic fashion. The stylistic pastiche is a common feature of *Pagliacci, La bohème* and *Zazà*. In the most popular of the three operas it yields appreciable results.

It was the success of Mascagni's *Cavalleria rusticana* (*Rustic Chivalry*) that prompted Leoncavallo to turn to a naturalistic subject. As early as 1893, *Cavalleria* and *Pagliacci* were paired in a production at the Metropolitan Opera of New York and have since been identified by audiences and critics as the archetypes of *verismo*. In the case of *Pagliacci* the term covers two aspects that are only latent in Mascagni's opera: sensationalism and violence. The subtle use of the device of the play-within-the-play in Leoncavallo's libretto adds an intellectual, estranging dimension to the dramatization of a crime of passion. As for the music, the rococo style adopted for the *commedia dell'arte* farce in act II cleverly differentiates the stereotyped acting of the clowns from their violent exchanges in real life.

In *La bohème,* the larger, four-act structure of the "lyric comedy" shows up all the seams and threads of the pastiche and betrays the composer's lack of sustained inspiration and formal control. Clearly, Leoncavallo's clattering music does not stand comparison with Puccini's setting of the same subject. Yet it is only fair to acknowledge Leoncavallo's single-handed efforts in extracting a dramatic action from Murger's novel *Scenes of Bohemian Life*. His libretto makes a detailed and faithful use of the narrative material and respects Murger's own characterization of the bohemians. No fewer than six poems by Murger and Musset are used as texts for songs. Leoncavallo keeps the emphasis on the bohemians as a group and sets his first act *inside* the Café Momus on Christmas eve. All the characters of the source are included: Rodolfo, Marcello, Schaunard, Colline, Mimi, Musette, Eufemia (Schaunard's mistress) and the philosopher Barbemuche who volunteers to settle the huge bill of the bohemians' dinner party. The same group is featured in act II, set in a courtyard of Rue de la Bruyère on 15th April, when insolvent tenants are evicted. Musette's furniture has been moved out of her rented flat and assembled in the courtyard of the building. The bohemians organize a lively party during which Barbemuche's disciple, Viscount Paolo, succeeds in convincing Mimi to run away with him abandoning Rodolfo for a life of luxury and comfort. The separation between the two bohemians is thus more clearly motivated than in Puccini's opera (an early draft of the Illica-Giacosa libretto included a "Courtyard act" which was later deleted). The only weak part of Leoncavallo's version is act III, featuring Marcello's garret, almost a duplicate of Rodolfo's similar dwelling. The events of the act are inessential: a starving Musette decides to leave her penniless lover just when the elegant and healthy Mimi reappears to attempt a reconciliation with Rodolfo. In act IV, Mimi returns once more and dies in Rodolfo's cold garret on Christmas eve, remembering the happy time at the Café Momus the year before.

The problem with *La bohème* is that Leoncavallo cannot devise a suitable musical medium for the lively conversations of his characters, nor can he strike the right balance between humor and sentiment. The dialogues are often accompanied by perfunctory dance rhythms; Mimi's and Musette's songs are trivial operetta numbers while Marcello's and Rodolfo's romanzas (acts III and IV) exude pathos and emphasis. Sometimes the adoption of a different style has a clear parodic purpose, as in Schaunard's Rossinian cantata "The influence of blue on the arts" (act II) or in some Verdian choral passages, but the overall impression the opera makes is one of inadequacy and artistic insincerity.

No stylistic evolution is noticeable in *Zazà*, Leoncavallo's contribution to the gallery of *fin-de-siècle* great female roles (*Fedora, Tosca, Adriana Lecouvreur*). The choice of a contemporary French play centered on a music-hall singing actress evidences once more his adhesion to *verismo*. *Zazà* tries to mix opera with operetta. The device of the theater-within-the-theater, already used in *Pagliacci*, is now employed to present the backstage of a provincial music-hall. The cabaret numbers being performed on the front stage are part of the action (act I). That is the starting point of the love affair between Zazà, the local star, and a married man, Milio Dufresne. When Zazà finds out that he loves his wife and daughter more than her, she sends him away and weeps her heart out.

The cabaret songs seem to have a contagious effect on the music of the opera. Insincerity and vulgarity remain its dominant characteristics. Act III contains few enjoyable moments of subdued, expressive singing. The scene is set in Dufresne's bourgeois drawing-room in Paris. Zazà, disguising her identity, is there with her maid Natalia to find out about her lover's family. While Milio and his wife are away, she talks to their little daughter Totò, a spoken role. The girl plays Cherubini's *Ave Maria* on the piano and Zazà pours out her misery to Natalia. The idea of an emotional solo against the musical background of a piano piece was not new (Giordano had already used it in *Fedora*), but it retains its efficacy in *Zazà*.

In his later years, Leoncavallo drifted towards operetta or accepted texts prepared by third-rate dramatists like G. Forzano. In any case, these productions add nothing to the three operas of his best creative period.

—Matteo Sansone

LEONORA, ossia L'amore conjugale [Leonora, or Married Love].

Composer: Ferdinando Paer.

Librettist: F. Schmidt.

First Performance: Dresden, Court Theater, 3 October 1804.

Roles:

Publications

articles—

Schiedermair, L. "Über Beethovens 'Lenore'." *Zeitschrift der Internationalen Musik-Gesellschaft* 8 (1906-07): 115.
Engländer, Richard. "Paers *Leonora* und Beethovens *Fidelio.*" *Neues Beethoven Jahrbuch* 4 (1930): 118.

Paer's *Leonora* is known today (if at all) as a setting in typical Italo-international style of the same "rescue opera" libretto soon to be used by Beethoven (in a German translation) for *Fidelio*. The plot is therefore identical to the great masterpiece of a Singspiel, at least in Beethoven's first version of his work. As part of the Italian mode it uses recitativo rather than spoken dialogue, and there is no prisoners' chorus or final hymn of rejoicing from a massed populace, but otherwise all is recognizable: Leonora tries to free her husband Florestano by posing as a young man, Fedele, and hiring on at the political prison where her spouse is unjustly incarcerated. She foils the evil Pizzarro and at last gains her goal with the participation of the jailor Rocco, along with his daughter Marcellina and assistant Giachino.

Musically, Paer is quite graceful and able to turn a simple folk-like melody to charming account. However, the piece can make no claim to being a valid rival to its towering successor and has enjoyed its few performances in our century by virtue of its relationship to the well-known piece. A modern recording is, however, available as of this writing and may serve to elucidate the contemporary listener wishing to learn the standard operatic manner of circa 1800—those transitional years after Paisiello and Cimarosa (and, of course, Mozart) but before all the old ways paled before the brilliant *éclat* of Rossini, nationalism, and the victory of Romanticism.

—Dennis Wakeling

LEPPARD, Raymond (John).

Conductor/Composer. Born 11 August 1927, in London. Studied harpsichord and viola at Trinity College, Cambridge, receiving his M.A. in 1952; music director of the Cambridge Philharmonic Society; conducted his own ensemble, 1952; gave harpsichord recitals and lectures on early music, 1958-68; prepared a number of controversial editions of early operas, most notably those of Monteverdi; conducted his edition of Monteverdi's *L'incoronazione di Poppea* at the Glyndebourne Festival, 1964; guest conductor with a number of European opera houses and orchestras; United States debut conducting the Westminster Choir and the New York Philharmonic, 1969; principal conductor of the British Broadcasting Corporation Northern Symphony Orchestra in Manchester, 1973-80; conducted his edition of Cavalli's *L'Egisto* at the Santa Fe Opera, 1974; settled in the United States, 1976; conducted Britten's *Billy Budd* at the Metropolitan Opera in New York, 1978; principal guest conductor of the St Louis Symphony Orchestra, 1984-90; music director of the Indianapolis Symphony Orchestra, 1987; conducted his edition of

Purcell's *Dido and Aeneas* for the Prince of Wales at Buckingham Palace, 1988; conducted music for the ninetieth birthday of the Queen Mother, 1990; conducted a Public Broadcasting System performance of a concert of Mozart's music, 1983; Commander of the Order of the British Empire, 1983; composed many film scores, including *Lord of the Flies,* 1963, and *Hotel New Hampshire,* 1985.

Publications

By LEPPARD: books–

The Real Authenticity. London, 1988.

* * *

Raymond Leppard's interest in early opera led him to study and produce performing editions of Italian stage works of the baroque era. His first national success as a conductor of such music came at Aldeburgh in 1958, when he conducted Monteverdi's *Il ballo delle Ingrate.* This was followed by a stage version of Handel's *Samson* at the Royal Opera House, Covent Garden, in the following year.

Leppard has been criticized for taking liberties with the scores, making cuts, adding music from other sources and filling out the scoring, but his work, more than that of any other scholar or conductor, has made the operatic public at large aware of the stagecraft and musico-dramatic qualities of several fine scores that would otherwise have merely gathered dust on library shelves. He vigorously defends his approach, which is in any case always based on a thorough, scholarly and sympathetic study of the original sources.

Leppard has not confined his interest to baroque opera. In 1970, he was in charge of Nicholas Maw's *The Rising of the Moon* at Glyndebourne, a romantic comedy set in nineteenth-century Ireland and the first opera ever to be specially commissioned for the Glyndebourne house. He conducted Mozart's *Così fan tutte* and *Le nozze de Figaro* at the Royal Opera House, Covent Garden, in 1972 and has also been active in opera in France and the United States. In 1974, he conducted his edition of Cavalli's *L'Egisto* at Santa Fe, and in 1976, he conducted Virgil Thomson's *The Mother of Us All* at the Matthews Theater, Columbia University. At Glyndebourne, he has also conducted Janáček's *The Cunning Little Vixen* (1975) and Gluck's *Orfée* (1982), using an edition of his own with Italian text that drew music from both the original Italian and the later French versions of the piece.

Leppard's wide experience in the concert hall includes work with the English Chamber Orchestra (since 1960), the British Broadcasting Corporation Northern Symphony Orchestra (1973-80), the St Louis Symphony Orchestra (1984-90) and the Indianapolis Symphony Orchestra from 1986). He has also been very active in the recording studio; his recordings including Purcell's *Dido and Aeneas* and Rameau's *Dardanus* as well as a wide range of works from the baroque and classical repertoire. A versatile and scholarly musician whose prime concern is always to bring the music to vivid life for his audiences, his performances are notable for crisp rhythm, a sense of atmosphere and impeccable timing in older music and a meticulous regard for balance and textual accuracy in modern scores. Purists may question some of his

performing versions of baroque music, but no-one can doubt either his integrity or the verve and sparkle that he brings to its realization.

—James Day

LEVI, Hermann.

Conductor. Born 7 November 1839, in Giessen. Died 13 May 1900, in Munich. Studied with Vincenz Lachner in Mannheim, 1852-55; studied at the Leipzig Conservatory, 1855-58; conducted at Saarbrücken, 1859-61; conducted at the German Opera in Rotterdam, 1861-64; Hofkapellmeister at Karlsruhe, 1864; conductor, 1872, and Generalmusikdirektor, 1894-96, at the court theater in Munich; conducted the premiere of Wagner's *Parsifal* at Bayreuth, 26 July 1882; conducted the music at Wagner's funeral.

Publications

By LEVI: books–

Brahms Gesellschaft, ed. *Brahms Briefwechsel,* vol. 7 [correspondence with Brahms]. Berlin, 1912.

About LEVI: books–

Possart, E. von. *Erinnerungen an H. Levi.* Munich, 1900.

* * *

Hermann Levi first made his name in Karlsruhe where he conducted much of Brahms's music. He then became an ardent admirer of Wagner (but not at the cost of his allegiance to Brahms, although that composer certainly cooled toward him) and conducted the city's first staging of *Die Meistersinger* and *Rienzi* in 1869. In 1872 Levi moved to Munich, where he was to remain for the rest of his life, and once again won Wagner's recognition with a *Ring* cycle in 1878.

When Wagner reopened the Bayreuth Festival in 1882 with the premiere of *Parsifal,* he was obliged to contract the orchestra of the Munich Opera, and with it came its conductor Levi. Wagner tried to resist this contractual obligation but to no avail; if he wanted the orchestra, he also had to have its conductor. As it happened Levi proved himself worthy of the task and immediately took his place in the forefront of the first generation of Wagner conductors alongside Hans Richter, Felix Mottl and Anton Seidl. Apart from a futile attempt on Wagner's part to convert the Jewish Levi to christianity and an anonymous letter which falsely insinuated a liaison between Levi and Cosima Wagner (both of which nearly forced Levi to withdraw from the project), a warm relationship developed between the two men. It was during the last performance of *Parsifal,* on 29 August 1882, that Wagner made his only appearance as conductor in Bayreuth. Just before the orchestral interlude before the opera's final scene, the composer appeared in the pit and motioned Levi aside to take over the direction of the rest of the opera. Levi reported to his father that he "stood beside [Wagner] as I was worried he might lose his way, but my fears were unfounded—he conducted with a sureness as if he had been only a Kapellmeister for the whole of his life." After Wagner's death, Levi was entrusted with *Parsifal* by Wagner's widow Cosima. In 1888 she replaced him with Mottl, who was more pliant to her directorial ways, but the experiment proved a disaster—poor Mottl was left unsure of his tempi on account of her interference. From 1889 until his last appearance at Bayreuth in 1894, Levi conducted *Parsifal* once again. It was the only opera he ever conducted there.

Brahms and Wagner were not the only composers whose music Levi interpreted sympathetically. He made a strong case for Mozart and supplied German translations of *Le nozze di Figaro*, *Così fan tutte* and *Don Giovanni* which were in use in that country for half a century thereafter. For his performances of Mozart operas, he reverted to the use of a pianoforte to accompany the recitatives. Among the significant productions in Munich during Levi's twenty-five years there were his performances of operas by Chabrier, Ignaz Brüll, Hermann Goetz (*The Taming of the Shrew*), Goldmark, Humperdinck, Cornelius (*Barbier von Baghdad* and *Der Cid*) and Richard Strauss (*Guntram*), whose appointment as an assistant conductor in the city was secured by Levi.

Levi was an intuitive musician, above all else honest, sincere and of a serious-minded disposition. He was an able technician with a wide-ranging repertoire; Weingartner admired this "capacity which allowed him to master the style of [Auber's] *La muette de Portici* with the same elegance as the *Nibelungen Ring* or *Don Giovanni*.... He was a man directly inspired by his art, outwardly uniting in himself the advantages of his colleagues [Bülow, Richter and Mottl], inwardly penetrating far deeper than they did."

—Christopher Fifield

LEVINE, James (Lawrence).

Conductor. Born 23 June 1943, in Cincinnati. Soloist in Mendelssohn's Piano Concerto No. 2 at a youth concert of the Cincinnati Symphony Orchestra, 1953; studied music theory with Walter Levin, first violinist of the La Salle Quartet; piano lessons with Rudolph Serkin at the Marlboro School of Music, 1956; studied piano with Rosina Lhévinne at the Aspen Music School in Colorado, 1957; studied conducting with Jean Morel at the Juilliard School of Music, New York, 1961-64; joined the American Conductors Project associated with the Baltimore Symphony Orchestra, where he studied conducting with Alfred Wallenstein, Max Rudolf, and Fausto Cleva, 1964; apprentice to George Szell with the Cleveland Orchestra, 1964-65; assistant conductor to the Cleveland Orchestra, 1965-70; guest conductor with the Philadelphia Orchestra, summer 1970; conducted the Welsh National Opera and the San Francisco Opera, 1970; debuted *Tosca* at the Metropolitan Opera, New York, 1971; principal conductor, 1973, music director, 1975, and artistic director, 1986, of the Metropolitan Opera; music director of the Ravinia Festival of the Chicago Symphony Orchestra, 1973; music director of the Cincinnati May Festival, 1974-78; conductor at the Salzburg Festival, beginning 1975; conducted at Bayreuth, 1982; many performances as a pianist with various chamber music groups and ensembles.

James Levine

Publications

By LEVINE: interviews–

"James Levine on Verdi and Mozart." In *Conductors on Conducting*, edited by Bernard Jacobson. Frenchtown, New Jersey, 1979.
Matheopoulos, Helena. *Maestro: Encounters with Conductors of Today*. London, 1982.
Chesterman, Robert, ed. *Conductors in Conversation*. London, 1990.

*   *   *

Although his career is international, James Levine is the heartbeat of New York's Metropolitan Opera. His official title there is "Artistic Director" but seemingly everyone calls him "Jimmy." He is somewhat too young to be considered a patriarch of such a prestigious organization but among his "children" are some of the brightest talents of today. Kathleen Battle, Dawn Upshaw, Gary Lakes, Aprile Millo, Neil Shicoff, Maria Ewing, among others, owe a great deal to his inspiration and guidance as well as their own innate abilities. Perhaps because he was a "wunderkind" himself, he has an infinite amount of patience in working with young artists, helping shape their careers and instilling in them a sense of their own worth.

Levine's interest in singers refutes the accusations that he favors the orchestra. It cannot be denied that during his tenure, the Metropolitan Opera Orchestra has evolved into an ensemble second to none—praised by critics time and again. Levine is without a doubt an orchestra builder and with the invaluable assistance of the late David Stivender developed a chorus at the Metropolitan that is the orchestra's equal. When listening to operas in which the chorus is prominently featured, such as *Idomeneo, Fidelio, Aida* and *Peter Grimes,* it is easily recognizable what Levine and Stivender have accomplished.

Another area where Levine's artistic leadership has been felt is the introduction of new works into the repertory. Operas which had been bypassed by past Metropolitan Opera administrations, such as *Billy Budd, Mahagonny, Erwartung, Porgy and Bess, Lulu, La clemenza di Tito,* are now prominently featured.

Apart from being among the foremost conductors of the day, Levine is one of the most sought after accompanists as well. His is a true partnership with the recitalist, and nowhere is this more in evidence than in his work with Christa Ludwig and Jessye Norman. Whether playing a Brahms song or a Negro spiritual, he can capture the essence of each and adapt his style to both the singer and the song.

Levine started out as a pianist and his basic love for the instrument apparently has never diminished. Occasionally, he will participate in chamber music concerts with members of the Metropolitan Opera Orchestra—perhaps too rarely to satisfy the demand. These evenings are always met with high critical approval, and reviews never fail to mention what a fine pianist Maestro Levine really is.

Levine's energy seems limitless; his professional life is not only centered in the opera houses of the world but in the concert halls as well. He is a frequent guest conductor of the Berlin Philharmonic, the Vienna Philharmonic and, at Ravinia, the Chicago Symphony. His opera activities take him to Bayreuth and Salzburg regularly.

If one were asked to name a work which best shows what James Levine is all about, *Parsifal* would be the perfect choice. In his hands, the opera takes on a seamlessness which allows it to transcend time and space. Through his expert pacing of the score, the mystical element is made all the more pronounced and imparts to it a dimension that it does not attain in lesser hands.

—John Pennino

LEWIS, Richard [born Thomas Thomas].

Tenor. Born 10 May 1914, in Manchester. Died 13 November 1990, in Eastbourne. Studied at Royal Manchester College of Music and at Royal Academy of Music; debut with Carl Rosa Company, 1939; postwar debut as Male Chorus in *The Rape of Lucretia* at Glyndebourne, 1947, and sang there until 1979; Covent Garden debut as Peter Grimes, 1947; in San Francisco, 1955-68; created Troilus in Walton's *Troilus and Cressida,* Mark in Tippett's *Midsummer Marriage* and Achilles in Tippett's *King Priam;* named Commander of the Order of the British Empire, 1963.

Publications

About LEWIS: articles–

Rosenthal, H. "Richard Lewis." *Opera* March (1955).

*   *   *

The slow start of Richard Lewis's career was in part due to World War II, but it may also have had something to do with his unsophisticated Welsh background (his real name was Thomas Thomas); at any rate, it was not until he was in his early thirties that an agent recommended him to Glyndebourne as "a really excellent tenor who looks wonderful, has a very beautiful voice, is a superb musician and has absolute mastery of Mozart's style." Very soon after this he sang the lead in Britten's *Peter Grimes* at Covent Garden in 1947 and was preferred by some to Peter Pears, the creator of the role, although the composer remarked to me, "Peter does more with his voice." Britten's writing for the tenor voice, conceived for Pears, was considered difficult by many other singers, but Lewis was able to assimilate it easily and at Glyndebourne in 1947 he was an effective Male Chorus in *The Rape of Lucretia.*

Thus he began an association with Glyndebourne that was to last over thirty years, where he notably appeared as Mozart's Don Ottavio in *Don Giovanni* and Ferrando in *Così fan tutte;* he also sang the title role of the King in *Idomeneo* in Carl Ebert's first British production in 1951, so extending his range to more mature characters. He could convince, too, as the Emperor Nero in Raymond Leppard's famous revival of Monteverdi's *L'incoronazione di Poppea* and as Auden and Stravinsky's Tom Rakewell in *The Rake's Progress.* Indeed, the width of his musical and dramatic range was recognized to the extent that his roles covered nearly all the obvious tenor repertory from the young lovers Alfredo in Verdi's *La traviata* and Jenik in Smetana's *The Bartered Bride* to Beethoven's tormented prisoner Florestan in *Fidelio* and Offenbach's poet Hoffmann in *Les contes d'Hoffmann.* He could have been content with this, but in addition he was bold enough to work in much less familiar territory: he was a believable Troilus in the first production of Walton's *Troilus and Cressida* and created Mark in Tippett's *The Midsummer Marriage,* and beyond these new works he did not fear to take on, with success, such other roles as The Simpleton in Mussorgsky's *Boris Godunov,* the weak King Herod in Strauss's *Salome,* Aaron (the chief singing role) in Schoenberg's *Moses und Aron* and the young composer Alwa in Berg's *Lulu.*

Richard Lewis's versatility and intelligence were recognized by everyone, as was his ability to assimilate and memorize difficult new music. However, it is fair also to say that he lacked a really strong vocal personality of his own: his voice was mellow and flexible, but not especially large, and some roles that he sang at Glyndebourne (such as Florestan) might have been difficult for him in a larger theater. Like most British singers, he was also well known in oratorio and he was a memorably sincere Gerontius in Elgar's *The Dream of Gerontius,* which he recorded twice. In later life he was respected as a sympathetic teacher of musical and personal integrity.

—Christopher Headington

LIBUŠE.

Composer: Bedřich Smetana.

Librettist: J. Wenzig (Czech translation by E. Spindler).

First Performance: Prague, National Theater, 11 June 1881.

Roles: Libuše (soprano); Přemsyl of Stadice (baritone); Chrudoš (bass); St'ahlav (tenor); Lutobor (bass); Radovan (baritone); Krasava (soprano); Radmila (contralto); chorus (SSAT).

Publications

articles–

Jiránek, Jaroslav. "Problém hudebně dramatické reprezentace Krasavy ve Smetanové Libuši" [problem of musico-dramatic representation of Krasava in Smetana's *Libuše*]. *Hudebni veda* 11 (1974): 250; German summary, 274.
———. "Krystalizace významového pole Smetanovy Libuše" [the crystalization of the significant range of Smetana's *Libuše*]. *Hudebni veda* 13 (1976): 27; German summary, 55.
Ottlová, Marta, and Milan Pospíšil. "Český historismus a opera 19. století Smetanova *Libuše*." In *Historické vědomí v českém umění 19. století,* edited by Thomáš Vlček, 83. Praque, 1981.
———. "Smetanas *Libuše*. Der tschechische Historismus und die Oper des 19. Jahrhunderts." In *Festschrift Heinz Becker zum 60. Geburtstag am 26. Juni 1982,* edited by Jürgen Schläder and Reinhold Quandt, 237. Laaber, 1982.

*   *   *

"*Libuše* is not an opera of the old type, but a festive tableau— a form of musical and dramatic sustenance. I desire it to be used only for festivals which affect the whole Czech nation," Smetana wrote, explaining why the opera he regarded as his "most perfect work in the field of higher drama" had to wait nine years for its first performance. *Libuše* was conceived as a celebration of the Czech nation, and it was held back until 1881 in order to inaugurate the new National Theater.

The plot is built upon the legendary events around the founding of the first Bohemian dynasty. Two brothers of noble birth, Chrudoš and St'ahlav, are in dispute over their inheritance and decline to accept the judgment of the Queen of Bohemia, Libuše, on grounds of her feminine weakness. Chrudoš maintains that the German custom of the elder brother inheriting all should be followed, and Libuše decides that in the circumstances she must abdicate her power, suggesting that the people should choose her a husband with whom she can rule. Amid general rejoicing the choice is returned to her, and she names Přemsyl of Stadice, whom she has always loved. He gladly accepts the crown and effects a reconciliation of the two brothers, to the delight of the populace. In the final scene, Libuše prophesies the glory and eternal life of the Czech nation.

Much of *Libuše* is static, even monumental, in character. The basis for the drama is the opposition that exists between personal advantage and the well-being of the nation. For the simple reason that Přemsyl is portrayed as a countryman, Smetana suggests that the rural traditions, by which Czech culture has survived, should be seen as the highest expression of national identity. Yet though the subject matter is naturally grandiose, the musical characterization remains vivid and the individuals are keenly drawn.

The tendency toward profound declamation is an inevitable result of the chosen subject, but Smetana was at pains to point out that the new style remained his own: "I do not imitate any famous composer, I only wonder at their greatness and I take for myself what I consider good and beautiful in art, and above all truthful. In my case it is the libretto that decides the style of the music."

The linking of characters with their own identifying themes is more extensive in this opera than elsewhere in Smetana's work. For instance, the two brothers are each given a distinctive theme, heard in opposition or combination according to the dramatic circumstances. More telling still are the fine themes associated with Libuše and Přemsyl, which are first heard during the impressively grand overture, alongside festive fanfares. Only when the two principals make their formal entrance in the final act are the two themes fully unified, signifying how the new dynasty will lead the nation to a glorious future.

Přemsyl provides an example, found also in other operas, of how a central character's appearance can be delayed until the second act without diminishing his importance. This is partly because of the new focus he brings to the drama, but especially because of the portentous references to him made during act I. His arrival is prepared by a beautifully atmospheric evocation of the Czech countryside, complete with an off-stage chorus of harvesters. His aria "Jiz plane slunce" ("The sun is blazing") is a substantial achievement in its own right, revealing him as a figure of stature and principle. When he learns of his fate, his joy is reflected in a vigorous ensemble, in which the chorus represents the people. Then in the final act the ceremonial atmosphere shows Přemsyl in a new light, his nobility confirming his role as Libuše's husband and as king. And while a love duet would hardly be an appropriate element in this context, the two join together to ask for the blessing of God, preparing the way for the mood of general celebration and reconciliation.

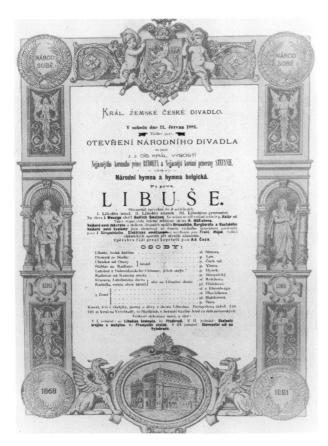

A poster for the first production of Smetana's *Libuše*, National Theater, Prague, 1881

Libuše's prophesy forms the final scene, in which she foretells the heroic destiny of the Czech people. The significant musical reference is the Hussite chorale, "Ye who are God's warriors," a theme Smetana used prominently in his cycle of symphonic poems, *Ma vlast* (*My Homeland*). Thus grandeur prevails over drama, in the spirit of Libuše's final proclamation: "My beloved Czech nation will not perish; gloriously she will vanquish the terrors of Hell!"

—Terry Barfoot

LICHT CYCLE (LIGHT CYCLE)
See LICHT: DIE SIEBEN TAGE DER WOCHE

LICHT: DIE SIEBEN TAGE DER WOCHE [Light: The Seven Days of the Week].

Composer: Karlheinz Stockhausen.

First Performance: *Der Jahreslauf* (scene from *Dienstag aus Licht*), 1977; *Donnerstag aus Licht*, Milan, 1981; *Samstag aus Licht*, Milan, 1984; *Montag aus Licht*, Milan, 1988.

Roles: Michael (tenor); Eve (soprano); Lucifer (bass); chorus.

Publications

interview–

Platz, Robert H.P. "Weder Anfang noch Ende. Zum Donnerstag aus Licht von Karlheinz Stockhausen. Ein Gesprach." Musiktexte 1 (1983): 26.

articles–

Frisius, Rudolf. "Komponieren heute: Auf der Suche nach der verlorenen Polyphonie. Tendenzen in Stockhausens *Licht*-Zyklus." *Neue Zeitschrift für Musik* 145/nos. 7-8 (1984): 24.
Oehlschlägel, Reinhard. "Wohlformulierte Teufelsmusik: zu Karlheinz Stockhausens *Samstag aus Licht*." *Musiktexte* 5 (1984): 50.
Kohl, Jerome. "Into the Middleground: Formula Syntax in Stockhausen's *Licht*." *Perspectives of New Music* 28/no. 2 (1990): 262.

*   *   *

Since 1977 Stockhausen has been wholly engaged on a cycle of seven operas, *Licht*, one for each day of the week, of which *Donnerstag, Samstag,* and *Montag aus Licht* have been completed, and the fourth, *Dienstag aus Licht,* is due for completion in 1991. Not only the week-long architecture of the entire cycle, but the essential lineaments of each opera, its dramatis personae, scenic divisions, temperament, actions, and musical textures are all derived from an initial three-line musical formula embodying in ornamental form the germ-cells of specific melodic, rhythmic, and harmonic functions.

These three strands of counterpoint are identified with mythic characters, a secular trinity, expressing three aspects of ideal humanity, approximately equivalent to the valiant knight (Michael), the eternal woman (Eve), and the wise man (or mad scientist) and anti-hero (Lucifer). Their roles and actions on stage are almost wholly symbolic, though alluding at times to events in the composer's life and his experiences with the public. This autobiographical dimension is most evident perhaps in the heroic imagery of *Donnerstag aus Licht,* in which Michael's getting of wisdom is clearly modelled on the turns and trials of the composer's life history. In *Samstag aus Licht* the character of Lucifer takes center stage, though the dramatic point has more to do with Lucifer as a representation of existential fear and how that fear is conquered: it leads the composer to some of his most brilliant scenic and musical inventions. *Montag aus Licht* is an opera in celebration of woman, motherhood, nature, and childhood; its imagery is fertile, green, and childlike, even hinting at the tonal kitsch of Disney or the Humperdinck *Hänsel und Gretel* Stockhausen directed for the Blecher town operetta society as a youth in the shell-shocked years after the end of World War II.

Stockhausen's approach to opera remains true to his abstract convictions while at the same time creating a compelling and often magical theatre. If his definition of opera seems to owe more perhaps to Berio and Kagel than Donizetti, his ideas for the stage are not lacking in references to more distant twentieth-century models, such as Kandinsky's dream for a series of operas based on colors, Piscator's theory of staging, and the concrete poetry of Hugo Ball. The imagery of *Licht* also reaches beyond European tradition to non-Western theatrical and musical rituals encountered by the composer in Japan, Bali, the African and Indian subcontinents, and Latin America. These older traditions provide a repertoire of dramatic or scenic templates for actions and processes essentially musical in inspiration. Rather than starting with an idea or libretto and finding the music to go with it, Stockhausen's visual and choreographic inventions, not to mention his libretti, are invented to fit the requirements of an existing musical formula, which is why so much of what happens seems mysterious at first encounter. The principle of the hidden agenda in music drama is ancient and honourable, and in Stockhausen's hands offers a rationale for wilfully unexpected results, intensities of experience and extraordinary audience reactions.

—Robin Maconie

A LIFE FOR THE TSAR [Zhizn' za tsarya].

Composer: Mikhail Glinka.

Librettist: G.F. Rosen.

First Performance: St Petersburg, Bol'shoy, 9 December 1836.

Publications

articles–

Abraham, Gerald. "A Life for the Tsar." In *On Russian Music,* 1. London, 1939.

Donnerstag aus Licht (from Stockhausen's *Licht* Cycle), Royal Opera, London, 1985

Homjakov, A. "Opera Glinki *Zhizn' za tsarya. Sovetskaya muzyka* 1 (1980): 91.

Bjørkvold, Jon-Roar. "*Ivan Susanni,* en russisk nasjonalopera under to despotier" [*Ivan Susanin (A Life for the Tsar): a Russian national opera under two rulers*]. *Studia musicologica Norvegica* 8 (1982): 9.

Mihajlov, Mihail. "Pol' skaja muzykal' naja citata v *Ivane Susanie* Glinka" [quotation of Polish music in *Ivan Susanin (A Life for the Tsar)*] In *Stilevye osobennosti russkoj muzyki XIX-XX vekov,* edited by Mihail Mihajlov. Leningrad, 1983.

Vasina-Grossman, Vera. "K istorii libretto *Ivana Susanina* Glinki" [history of the libretto of *Ivana Susanina (A Life for the Tsar)*]. In *Stilevye osobennosti russkoj muzyki XIX-XX vekov,* edited by Mihail Mihajlov. Leningrad, 1983.

*   *   *

The story of Ivan Susanin was well known by the time Glinka chose it as the subject for his first opera. The life of this seventeenth-century peasant hero and martyr who sacrificed himself to lead invading forces astray had already been treated by contemporary artists for its obvious parallels with the events of 1812. In fact, an Italian composer in Russia, Catterino Cavos, had already in 1815 composed an opera on the same subject. In Glinka's hands, however, *A Life for the Tsar* became one of the keystones of the great school of Russian opera that followed.

Tsar Nicholas I himself took an interest in the opera, attending one of the final rehearsals. Glinka got permission to dedicate the work to the tsar, and the title was changed from *Ivan Susanin* to *A Life for the Tsar.* Nicholas' approval is not difficult to understand. The opera's tsar Michael was the first of the Romanovs, Nicholas' own dynasty, and he could not help but be pleased at the depiction of such an extraordinarily loyal and self-sacrificing peasant as Susanin.

The action of the opera takes place toward the end of the "Time of Troubles," early in the seventeenth century. Act I opens in the village of Domnino, where a crowd of peasants waits to welcome back Sobinin from the wars. Ivan Susanin is there with his daughter Antonida, who is to marry Sobinin. Susanin gives his blessing to the wedding after learning that a new tsar has finally been selected. Act II switches to a ball at the fortress of the Polish commander. A messenger brings news that the Polish army has been defeated and that a new tsar has finally been elected. A plan is hatched to capture the new tsar in the monastery where he is staying, and the party resumes.

In act III, back in Domnino, wedding preparations are under way, despite the news of the Poles' hunt for the tsar. Suddenly Polish soldiers appear and try to force Susanin to reveal the location of the tsar. Susanin goes off with the Poles, planning to mislead them. Sobinin gathers a group to attempt to rescue Susanin. Act IV shows Sobinin searching for Susanin, then Vanya (Susanin's adopted son) warning the monastery of the tsar's danger. In the final scene, Susanin has led the Poles deep into the forest. He proudly tells them what he

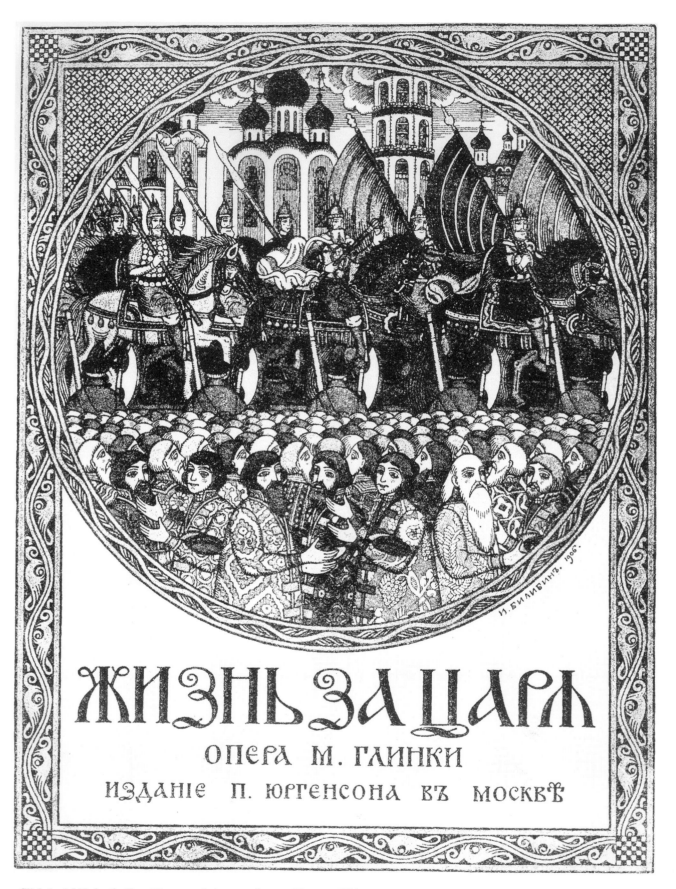

Glinka's *A Life for the Tsar,* **title page of piano-vocal score, Moscow, 1906**

has done and prepares to die at their hands. In the epilogue, Moscow prepares to greet the new tsar. Antonida, Sobinin, and Vanya tell what Susanin has done, and after an expression of grief, the crowd hails the tsar.

Tradition holds that it was homesickness which led to Glinka to write his first opera. He was attracted to remote places and traveled a good deal. He spent three years in Italy (1830-33) absorbing Italian music and briefly undertaking some studies in composition. Though he loved Italian music, he realized that he wanted to do something different: "I could not sincerely be an Italian. A longing for my own country led me gradually to the idea of writing in the Russian manner," he wrote in his memoirs.

When Glinka decided to write a large-scale national opera, he considered several different subjects before settling on the story of Ivan Susanin. Inspiration seized him; he wrote again in his memoirs, "I wrote the scene where Susanin is in the forest with the Poles in winter. . . . I often read it aloud, with feeling, and I put myself so vividly in the place of my hero that my hair would stand on end and I would be taken with cold shivers."

The main characters are peasants, and a crucial feature of their characterization in music is through the use of folk music. While previous composers had used Russian folk tunes in their operas, such elements were peripheral to the action and limited to comic operas. Glinka not only allowed the main characters to speak in folk inflections, he elevated this musical language to a high level of tragic heroism. Ironically, the use of folk music such as the quotation from a coachman's song was looked on disparagingly by some contemporaries; it was only later that such quotations were revered as evidence of Glinka's genius. Folk music only gradually became something for all levels of society to embrace as part of national identity, a transition helped along by Glinka.

Whether or not *A Life for the Tsar* is accepted as truly the first Russian opera, there is no doubting Glinka's status as the first composer to be internationally respected yet unmistakably Russian in identity, and his influence on subsequent generations of musicians was considerable. In common with many later Russian operas, *A Life for the Tsar* has the spectacular dance and choral crowd scenes typical of French opera, while at the same time Glinka attributed his handling of vocal writing to his knowledge of Italian opera. The dramaturgical construction in tableau-like scenes, as opposed to ongoing dramatic development, was also to prove a viable procedure for many subsequent Russian operas.

Renamed with the old title *Ivan Susanin,* the opera was resurrected (and partially rewritten) in the 1930s by the Stalinist regime as a model of socialist realism, the vague artistic guideline promulgated by the Soviet government for composers. But the composers to draw the greatest inspiration from Glinka's work were those working in the latter half of the nineteenth century, Tchaikovsky, Rimsky-Korsakov, and their contemporaries, who took Glinka as their starting point in the development of Russian opera.

—Elizabeth W. Patton

LIGETI, György (Sándor).

Composer. Born 28 May 1923, in Dicsöszentmartin, Transylvania. Studied composition with Sándor Veress and Ferenc Farkas at the Budapest Music Academy, 1945-49; instructor at the Budapest Music Academy, 1950-56; worked in the Studio for Electronic Music in Cologne, 1957-59; in Vienna, 1959-69; in Berlin, 1969-73; lectured at the International Courses for New Music in Darmstadt; guest professor of composition at the Musical High School in Stockholm, 1961; lectured in Spain, the Netherlands, Germany, Finland, and at Tanglewood; composer-in residence at Stanford University, 1972; professor of composition, Hochschule für Musik, Hamburg, 1973.

Operas

Publishers: Peters, Schott, Universal.

Aventures, Ligeti, 1962; arranged as a chamber opera, 1966.
Nouvelles aventures, Ligeti, 1962-65; arranged as a chamber opera, 1966.
Le grand macabre, M. Meschke (after Ghelderode), Stockholm, Royal Opera, 12 April 1978.
Rondeau, 1976, Stuttgart, 26 February 1977.

Publications

By LIGETI: articles–

Note: only post-1970 writings are listed here. For a complete bibliography of Ligeti's writings prior to 1970, see Nordwall, 1971.

"Apropos Musik und Politik." *Darmstädter Beiträge zur neuen Musik* no. 13 (1973): 42.

György Ligeti

"Musikalische Erinnerungen aus Kindheit und Jugend." In *Festschrift für einen Verlteger: Ludwig Strecker,* 54. Mainz, 1973.

"Mein Judentum." In *Mein Judentum.* Berlin and Stuttgart, 1978.

"Un foglio degli schizzi *San Francisco Polyphony."* In *Miscellanea del Cinquantenario; Die Stellung der italienischen Avantgarde in der Enwicklung der neuen Musik.* Milan, 1978.

"Zur Entstehung der Oper *Le Grand Macabre."* *Melos* (1978).

"Le grande macabre." *Österreichische Musikzeitschrift* 36 (1981): 569.

"Aspekte der Webernschen Kompositionstechnik." In "Zu Anton Weberns 100. Geburtstag." *Musik-Konzept* [Munich] (1983) [special issue].

"A zeneszerzés oktatásának új utjairól. I. II." *Virgilia* [Hungary] 3,4 (1984): 168, 298.

"Musik und Technik." In *Computer Musik,* edited by Batel et al. Laaber, 1987.

interviews–

Lichtenfeld, Monika. " 'Musik mit schlecht gebundener Kravatte.' György Ligeti in Gespräch mit Monika Lichtenfeld." *Neue Zeitschrift für Musik* 142 (1981): 471.

Wiesmann, Sigrid. " 'The Island is Full of Noise': György Ligeti in Gespräch mit Sigrid Wiesmann." *Österreichische Musikzeitschrift* 39 (1984): 510.

Lichtenfeld, Monika. "Gespräch mit György Ligeti." *Neue Zeitschrift für Musik* 145 (1984): 8.

About LIGETI: books–

Nordwall, Ove, ed. *Ligeti-Dokument.* Stockholm, 1968.
————. *György Ligeti: eine Monographie.* Mainz, 1971.
Klüppelholz, Werner. *Modelle zur Didaktik der Neuern Musik* [*Aventures*]. Wiesbaden, 1981.
Fischer, Erik. *Zur Problematik der Opernstruktur. Das künstlerische System und seine Krisis im 20. Jahrhunderts* [*Aventures*]. Wiesbaden, 1982.
Várnai, Péter. *Beszélgetések Ligeti Györggyel* [conversations with György Ligeti]. Budapest, 1979; English translation, London, 1983.
Griffiths, Paul. *György Ligeti.* London, 1983.
Kolleritsch, Otto. *György Ligeti: Personalstil—Avantgardismus—Popularität.* Vienna and Graz, 1987.

articles–

Stürzbecher, Ursula. "György Ligeti." In *Werkstattgespräche mit Komponisten,* Cologne, 1971.
Jungheinrich, Hans-Klaus. "György Ligetis *Le grand macabre.* Ein Avantgardist auf dem Seil und in der Manege." *Hi-Fi-Stereophonic* 17 (1978): 694.
Fabian, Imre. " 'Ein unendliches Erbarmen mit der Kreatur.' Zu György Ligetis *Le grande macabre."* *Österreichische Musikzeitschrift* 36 (1981): 570.
Wiesmann, Sigrid. "Bedingungen der Komponierbarkeit. Bernd Alois Zimmermanns *Die Soldaten,* György Ligetis *Le grande macabre."* In *Für und wider die Literaturoper. Zur Situation nach 1945,* edited by S. Wiesmann, 27. Laaber, 1982.
Fanselau, Rainer. "György Ligeti: *Le grand macabre.* Gesichtspunkte für eine Behandlung im Musikunterricht." *Musik und Bildung* 15 (1983): 17.

Hermann, Ingrid. "Ligeti-Bibliographie (und Schallplattenaufnahmen)." *Musik und Bildung* 15 (1983): 24.
Lichtenfeld, Monika. "Portret." *Ruch muzyczny* 18/no. 19 (1984): 3.

Ligeti is generally recognized as one of the most gifted composers to have emerged since the Second World War. While he is generally thought of as a radical member of the avant-garde, his compositions vary widely in style, from jokes to highly sophisticated pieces in the mainstream tradition.

The major change in Ligeti's compositional style can be directly related to his leaving his native Hungary in 1956. Up to that point the most important influence was Bartók, and Ligeti's education had included a period of research into Romanian folk music. Most of Ligeti's pre-1956 pieces continue Bartók's project of linking folk music with the concert hall, and show a thorough grasp of the traditional means of musical construction. However, any exploration of radically new compositional styles was strongly discouraged within Hungary at that time.

Ligeti's move to Austria in 1956 was into a new world, where the avant-garde was attempting to forge a new musical language. Ligeti was given the opportunity to work in the electronic studio of the West German Radio in Cologne, and he later described his study of the most fundamental elements of music as showing him the way to realize some of the sound worlds he had previously only been able to imagine.

Only two purely electronic pieces resulted from this work, *Glissandi* and *Articulation,* but this new way of hearing and analyzing sound led to the orchestral works *Apparitions* and *Atmospheres.* The principal characteristic of these pieces is the use of clusters of sound rather than individual pitches. The composer uses these to create shapes and lines by varying the dynamic levels, the size of the cluster, the registers, and the instrumentation. The effects which Ligeti achieves with this compositional technique range from a directionless soft fading in and out of colors to an aggressive play of contrasts. Further, Ligeti realized that one could make the surface texture of the music more lively by restricting the pitches used to the same narrow band, but giving each individual part many notes, played very fast. If each part has a different rhythm and pitch pattern, the ear can hear the music in two ways, following either the overall movement of the bands of sound or the texture in an attempt to follow the maze of lines that fill in the area. This technique of creating a broad, general effect by a proliferation of lines Ligeti termed "micropolyphony." The use of the technique is Ligeti's most individual characteristic, and it appears in many of his works, including works with voices, such as the *Requiem* and *Lux aeterna,* and sections of his opera *Le grand macabre.*

A different side of Ligeti is seen in the two works *Aventures* and *Nouvelle aventures,* written in the early sixties. Originally concert works, they were later transferred to the stage as chamber operas. They are scored for one male and two female singers, with a chamber orchestra of seven players, and together last a little over half an hour. The works pivot on the fact that the text is, in linguistic terms, completely meaningless, being a collection of vocal sounds and fragments of words. Ligeti shows us that this is no impediment to communication, as the combination of musical references and inflection— cries, laughter, sighs, and so on—make the thoughts and emotions of the singers perfectly transparent. Ligeti incorporates a huge number of sound effects in the instrumental parts, again exploring the boundary between conventional meaning and onomatopoeia. The pieces are truly grotesque, initially very funny, but by reducing emotion to its absurd appearance, somewhat sinister.

The most extreme example of Ligeti's humor is surely his *Poème symphonique,* scored for a hundred metronomes. Each of the metronomes is set to a different tempo, and they are released simultaneously. At the start of the piece there is a great cloud of ticking, which gradually thins out as the mechanisms run down, first forming a regular rhythmic pattern, and then reducing to a solitary pulse.

Alongside these exploratory works Ligeti has written a series of pieces appealing to more traditional aesthetic values. Each successive piece shows an increase in scope and assurance. One would expect that it is on these works that Ligeti's reputation will rest, provided they are not overshadowed by the sensationalism of his other styles. The piano concerto, first heard in its complete version in 1988, will surely take its place in the repertoire alongside the cello concerto of 1966, and the concerto for flute and oboe of 1972. Ligeti has also made a substantial contribution to the literature of chamber music with the trio for violin, horn and piano of 1982, and to that of the piano with the duets *Monument, Selbstporträt, Bewegung* of 1976, and the solo *Etudes* of 1985.

Given Ligeti's growing musical powers and his understanding of the voice which his choral music demonstrates, it is to be hoped that *Le grand macabre* will not be Ligeti's ultimate statement in the operatic medium. Much of Ligeti's music of the 1980s shows us that large scale forms constructed with a unified musical language are possible, and one cannot help hoping that this language, beyond irony, will be used to connect the abstract world of instrumental music with the social world of music theater.

—Robin Hartwell

LIGHT CYCLE
See LICHT: DIE SIEBEN TAGE DER WOCHE

THE LIGHTHOUSE.

Composer: Peter Maxwell Davies.

Librettist: Peter Maxwell Davies (after a story by Craig Mair).

First Performance: Edinburgh, 2 September 1980.

Roles: Sandy/Officer One (tenor); Blazes/Officer Two (baritone); Arthur/Voice of The Guards/Officer Three (bass).

*   *   *

By the time Davies came to write *The Lighthouse* in 1979 he had already written many works incorporating theatrical elements. *The Lighthouse* has more in common with the music he wrote for his chamber ensemble, "The Fires of London," than with his full-length opera, *Taverner. The Lighthouse* crosses the line into chamber opera, with an orchestra of twelve players, three singers doubling a total of six roles, and demanding some stage effects.

The libretto, written by Maxwell Davies himself, is one of the few texts by a composer which one can contemplate without embarrassment. The story is taken from a book by Craig Mair, who recounts how on Boxing Day, 1900, a supply boat visiting a lighthouse found that the keepers had disappeared. Their quarters were in good order, and there was no sign of a struggle. Mair dismisses the possibility that they were swept off the island by a storm, as the light was seen to be working after the storms had passed. It is this mystery that the opera explores.

The opera opens with the court of inquiry, where the officers of the supply ship give an account of the events of the night. We hear only their answers, as the questions are posed by a solo horn, which Davies suggests may be placed in the audience. The officers begin their answers in a stiff formal rhythmic unison, but as they begin to recount the story the emotions of the time return, and the music becomes increasingly flexible and expressive. They describe being lost in the fog and hearing a foghorn, though each hears it from a different direction. Once ashore by the lighthouse, the first officer sees three sellies (presumably seals), the second three scarfs (cormorants), and the third three gibbies (cats). It begins to emerge that the central theme of the opera is the different interpretations several individuals make of the same events.

The narrative then cuts back to the lighthouse men before their disappearance. Arthur is fervently religious, and his singing style resembles that of a priest's intonation. Blazes, on the other hand, has an unstable hysterical style, and mocks Arthur's religious beliefs as pretentious. Sandy, more placid, tries to calm the situation by suggesting a game of cards. In this scene the number symbolism found in Tarot cards, which Davies claims underlies the composition of the music, comes to the surface in both the music and the text. It also introduces a recurrent theme in Davies' works, the play of fortune. Naturalistic conventions are suspended as Arthur, off-stage, sings a part as the voice of the cards. An argument breaks out and Blazes suggests that each man sing a song.

Until this point the musical language has varied from the brittle Stravinskyan rhythms of the opening, through the mechanical processes of the card scene, to the apparently freely expressionistic music for Blazes. Each of the following songs, however, presents a parody of an external musical style. Blazes' song, with banjo and violin, is a cross between jolly hillbilly music and music-hall. But as the verses continue the level of violence rises, till Blazes, as if carried away by the rush of the song, confesses to battering an old woman to death for her money, allowing his father to be hanged for the crime and remaining silent while his mother died of grief. Sandy's song is a sentimental ballad. The originally innocent song becomes increasingly obscene when the others join in and the words are reordered across the voices. Arthur sings a hymn, but it becomes ever more bloodthirsty, setting brother against brother and father against son. The songs show the devilish underside to the family, love, and religion, and this conflict between appearance and reality is mirrored by the parodying of familiar and conventional musical styles.

The mists sweep in, and Arthur starts the foghorn, which he compares to the cry of the beast. Blazes begins to hallucinate, imagining the old woman he killed has come to haunt him. Sandy sees faces from the past, first his sister, then a boy, dead for twenty years. Arthur then sees the beast moving across the waters, with an army of ghosts. A light gradually grows brighter, shining fiercely into the audience, but at the climactic moment it is seen to be the lights of the boat of the officers arriving on the island.

The three officers are discussing what they will tell the inquiry, and we piece together that they found the lighthousemen berserk, and in self-defence killed them. They tidy the quarters and leave. The next watch of keepers move into the lighthouse, and begin to re-enact the opening of the scene. The image is obliterated by the orchestra taking up the rhythm of the automatic light (which in reality has replaced the men needed for the lighthouse), which gradually builds to a climax. The final suggestion is that we have witnessed a ghostly re-enactment of a drama repeated in perpetuity.

—Robin Hartwell

THE LILY OF KILLARNEY.

Composer: Julius Benedict.

Librettist: John Oxenford (after Dion Boucicault).

First Performance: London, Covent Garden, 8 February 1862.

Roles: Hardress Cregan; Eily O'Connor; Mr Corrigan; Ann Chute; Danny Mann.

* * *

Julius Benedict's *The Lily of Killarney* was one of the "big three" of mid-nineteenth century English opera. Along with Michael William Balfe's *The Bohemian Girl* (1843) and Vincent Wallace's *Maritana* (1845), *Lily* was the last of an extremely successful trio which dominated the British stage the generation before the incomparable duo of Gilbert and Sullivan overwhelmed all light operatic predecessors.

Ironically, the top operas by Irish born Balfe and Wallace were not based on Irish themes. Instead, it took the German-born Benedict to produce a masterpiece set in Ireland. Quite possibly, like Georges Bizet and *Carmen,* the novelty and intrigue of things foreign provided a special extra artistic and psychological stimulus.

Lily takes place in the early part of the nineteenth century. In a rural area, a wealthy landowner named Hardress Cregan is secretly married to the heroine Eily O'Connor. Beautiful Eily is also known as Colleen Bawn and the Lily of Killarney. The Cregan estate is mortgaged to the enterprising Mr Corrigan. In order to assure payment of the mortgage, Corrigan, ignorant of the vows between Eily and Hardress, encourages Hardress to woo wealthy heiress Ann Chute. Hardress reluctantly pretends to be romantically interested in Ann, but his heart is with Eily.

Danny Mann, a boatman who is a devoted supporter of Hardress, offers a shocking solution—he would be willing to kill Eily so that Hardress can marry the heiress. Hardress strongly rejects the idea, but Danny still embraces this drastic way out of the dilemma. Eily goes off with Danny, who pushes her out of the boat into life-threatening waters. Eily is saved by a hunter who is in love with her, and Danny accidentally dies.

Thinking that Eily is dead, Hardress is about to be married to Ann. Just before he died, Danny had made a confession about the murder attempt. Since Eily is missing, Corrigan and a group of soldiers arrest Hardress for his supposed role in the homicide. But then Eily appears, the clandestine marriage is revealed, and all more or less ends happily.

Secret weddings, abortive murders, missing persons—all are trite elements which make the story of *The Lily of Killarney* not the most original ever to be presented on the stage. The plot is not ridiculous, but it is far from superior. Add to this the saccharine, highly sentimental tone of the entire opera and it is easy to understand why *Lily* is only occasionally performed today. It seems that operas and musicals about Ireland and Irish people in other places tend to be charming enough to attract contemporary audiences and at the same time sufficiently maudlin to restrict long term interest. Such was the case for *Lily*—a smash in the nineteenth century and a relative obscurity in the twentieth.

Benedict's music, however, was bright, lively, fresh, lyrical, and melodic, and was the primary factor in *Lily*'s success. Each of the three acts has at least two notable numbers, all exhibiting elements of simple, ingenuous, folksy charm. A duet, "The Moon Has Raised Her Lamp Above," a love song, "It is a Charming Girl I Love," and Eily's aria, "The Cruickshank Lawn," grace act I. The popular air "Colleen Bawn" and Danny's "Yes, I'll Do My Duty" are features of act II. A serenade, "Your Slumbers," and Hardress' aria "Eily Mavourneen, I See Thee Before Me," highlight act III.

The Lily of Killarney is an effective blend of Benedict's original music intermixed with Irish folk melodies. Not only was the opera one of the very best of its time, it was one of the better productions for the musical theater which have dealt with the theme of Ireland and its almost inevitable dichotomy of pleasing warmth and oversentimentality.

—William E. Studwell

LIND, Jenny.

Soprano. Born 6 October 1820, in Stockholm. Died 2 November 1887, in Malvern Hills, Shropshire. Married: Otto Goldschmidt, 1852 (2 sons, 1 daughter). First stage appearance at age 10; formal opera debut as Agathe in *Der Freischütz,* Royal Opera, Stockholm, 1838; became regular member of Swedish Academy of Music, 1840; brief retirement, 1841-42, when she went to study with Manuel Garcia in Paris; returned to Stockholm and sang Norma, 1842; appeared at Leipzig Gewandhaus, 1845; Vienna debut as Norma at Theater an der Wien, 1846; gave her New York debut in 1850; settled in England in 1858; appeared in oratorio and concert performances until she retired in 1883.

Publications

By LIND: books–

The Lost Letters of Jenny Lind. London, 1926; New York, 1977.

About LIND: books–

Lyser, J. *G. Meyerbeer and Jenny Lind.* Vienna, 1847.
Rosenberg, J. *Lind in America.* New York, 1851.

Jenny Lind as Amina in *La sonnambula,* **embossed engraving published in London, 1848**

Wilkens, C. *Jenny Lind: Ein Cäcilienbild aus der evangelische Kirche.* Gutersloh, 1854.

Holland, H. and W. Rockstro. *Memoir of Mme. Jenny Lind-Goldschmidt.* London, 1891.

Rockstro, W. and O. Goldschmidt. *A Record and Analysis of the Method of the Late Jenny Lind-Goldschmidt.* London, 1894.

Maude, J. *The Life of Jenny Lind.* London, 1926.

Norlind, T. *Jenny Lind.* Philadelphia, 1928.

Wagenknecht, E. *Jenny Lind-Goldschmidt.* Boston, 1931.

Benet, L. *Enchanting Jenny Lind.* New York, 1939.

Headland, H. *The Swedish Nightingale: A Biography of Jenny Lind.* Rock Island, Illinois, 1940.

Pergament, M. *Jenny Lind.* Stockholm, 1945.

Bulman, J. *Jenny Lind: A Biography.* London, 1956.

Schultz, G. *Jenny Lind, the Swedish Nightingale.* Philadelphia, 1962.

Gattey, Charles Neilson. *Queens of Song.* London, 1979.

*　　*　　*

Jenny Lind studied first in Stockholm where she made her debut as Agathe in *Der Freischütz* in 1838. Puritanically, she refused to wear make-up when acting. Becoming unable to control sustained notes in the upper register without difficulty, she went to Paris to study with Manuel Garcia in 1841. He discovered that she had been taught an unsound way of breathing; to have continued singing in this way would have permanently destroyed her voice. She wrote to a friend: "I have had to begin again from the beginning." Garcia kept stressing his axiom that a singer should always keep something back. After a year she returned to Stockholm's Royal Opera to take the title role in Bellini's *Norma.* Critics were astonished by the improvement in her voice, which now ranged from B below the stave to C on the fourth line above it—two and three-quarter octaves. It had gained depth of tone and clarity and was capable of easily adapting itself to all shades of expression. In her shake, scales, *legato* and *staccato* passages, she employed such ornaments only when in harmony with the music's inner meaning.

In 1844, Lind made her Berlin Opera debut also as Norma. The first to play the Druid priestess, Pasta, had done so with fire and little tenderness. "Pasta presents a Norma *before* whom, our artist (Lind) a Norma *with* whom we tremble," wrote critic Ludwig Rellstab.

For her last role of the season, Jenny chose Amina in *La sonnambula,* for which her gentleness and crystal-pure voice were ideal. When she later sang the part in Vienna, the audience clamored for an encore of the rondo finale, so she went down to the footlights and pleaded: "May I first have five minutes to drink some lemonade?" This engaging lack of sophistication delighted the Viennese.

Jenny Lind made her London debut at Her Majesty's on 4 May 1847 as Alice in Meyerbeer's *Robert le diable* sung in Italian, chosen, as she confided to manager Lumley, because making her first appearance in a crowd would enable her to overcome any nervousness before she sang solo. He wrote of the first night that "the struggle for entrance was violent beyond precedent—so violent indeed, that the phrase 'a Jenny Lind crush' became a proverbial expression." *The Times* reported "torn dresses and evening coats reduced to rags; ladies fainting in the pressure and even gentlemen carried out senseless."

In the following year, the Swedish Nightingale made her London debut as Lucia. *The Times* wrote that in the second and third acts she brought out the distress and madness of the character with a force hitherto unknown. "The eye, glaring and vacant, appeared absorbed by fantasies, and blind to all external objects. The passions by which she is supposed to be influenced, while in this painful situation, are of the most varied kind; but she never for a moment lost sight of the insanity. At the conclusion, instead of running off the stage in the usual fashion, she fell senseless, which brought the situation to a more pointed conclusion."

On 29 July, Jenny's Elvira in Bellini's *I puritani* was the last new role in which she was seen on the operatic stage. The cadenza she composed for the opening movement of "Qui la voce" was one of the most brilliant and original of the passages of *fioritura* with which it was her practice to ornament the Italian arias she liked best. Arthur Coleridge in his *Musical Recollections* wrote: "She showered her trills and roulades like sparkling diamonds all over the place. It was the first time and the last, with the single exception of Rachel, that I have seen such unmistakable genius on the stage."

Brainwashed by associates who regarded the stage as a sort of ante-room to hell, Lind now announced that she would only sing in concerts in future. At Exeter Hall on 15 December, she sang with dramatic power the soprano part in Mendelssonn's last work, *Elijah,* which he had written with her in mind.

Probably it was as well that Jenny Lind retired from opera when she did. The critic H.F. Chorley thought that her repertory was so limited that it must have "exposed her on every side to comparisons should she have remained on the stage till enthusiasm cooled, as it must inevitably have done." She now played a new role, one of some importance in social history. Phineas T. Barnum was then the world's leading showman. While catering for the crude tastes of the masses had brought him immense wealth, his secret ambition was to make the American public acquire an appetite for culture and he regarded the "Swedish Nightingale" as the perfect vehicle for achieving this. In the negotiations that followed, Jenny Lind proved an astute businesswoman, conducting them entirely on her own.

Lind's farewell English concerts were a series of frenzied triumphs. At her final one in Liverpool, she gave *Messiah,* for the singing of which she was to rank supreme for the rest of her days. She held ninety-three concerts in America before falling out with Barnum and continuing to tour on her own with a new accompanist, Otto Goldschmidt, whom she married. But the public was tiring of programmes that were always the same and her husband proved a dull pianist. On 24 May 1852, nearly five months after arriving in New York, Lind gave her farewell concert at Castle Gardens; profits amounted to barely half of what they totalled at her debut. Barnum went to see her afterwards in her dressing-room. She told him she would never sing in public again. "Your voice is a God-given gift," he returned. "You must never cease using it." This appeal to her religious feelings succeeded and she relented, saying that she would continue so long as her voice lasted, but it would be mostly for charity as she now had all the money which she would ever need.

In 1862 Chorley wrote a perceptive estimation of Jenny Lind's talents: "It can now, without treason, be recorded that her voice was a soprano, two octaves in compass—from D to D—having a possible higher note or two available on rare occasions, and that the lower half and the upper one were of two distinct qualities. The former was not strong—veiled, if not husky, and apt to be out of tune. The latter was rich, brilliant and powerful—finest in its highest portions. . . . she could turn her 'very long breath' to account in every gradation of tone; and thus, by subduing her upper notes, and giving out her lower ones with great care, could conceal the disproportions of her organ."

—Charles Neilson Gattey

LIPP, Wilma.

Soprano. Born 26 April 1925, in Vienna. Studied in Vienna, and with Toti dal Monte in Milan; debut as Rosina in Rossini's *Il barbiere di Siviglia* in Vienna, 1943; joined the Vienna Staatsoper, 1945; Covent Garden debut as Queen of the Night in Mozart's *Die Zauberflöte,* 1950; Bayreuth Festival debut as the Woodbird in Wagner's *Siegfried* in 1951.

Publications

About LIPP: articles–

Bor, V. "Wilma Lipp a Tom Krause." *Hudebni Rozhledy* 24/7 (1971): 310.

*   *   *

Wilma Lipp joined the Vienna State Opera in 1945 (at the age of nineteen), where she specialized in (and established a substantial reputation for) coloratura roles, especially Konstanze and Blondchen (in Mozart's *Die Entführung aus dem Serail*) and the Queen of the Night (in *Die Zauberflöte*), which she first sang in 1948. Her debut role was Rosina in Rossini's *Il barbiere di Siviglia;* she also appeared as Zerbinetta in Richard Strauss's *Ariadne auf Naxos,* Sophie in *Der Rosenkavalier,* and sang Adele in Johann Strauss's *Die Fledermaus* at the Vienna Volksoper. As was characteristic of singers at the Vienna State Opera at that time, she sang a large number of performances each season: during the 1947-48 season, for instance, she gave fifty-eight performances. Lipp was made Kammersängerin—an honor bestowed by the Austrian and German governments—in 1955.

Lipp participated in the Salzburg Festival on several occasions, singing the Queen of the Night under Wilhelm Furtwängler's direction in 1949 and 1951. She recorded the Queen's two arias with Furtwängler and the Vienna Philharmonic in 1950 and shortly afterward recorded the entire role under Herbert von Karajan and the same orchestra. She appeared at the Bayreuth Festival in 1951, at performances marking the reopening of the festival after the war, singing the role of the Woodbird in Wagner's *Siegfried* under Herbert von Karajan's direction.

During the course of her career she moved from soubrette and coloratura roles to lyric ones and even some tending toward the dramatic end of the scale (Ilia in Mozart's *Idomeneo,* Pamina in *Die Zauberflöte,* Mimi in Puccini's *La bohème,* Marenka in Smetana's *The Bartered Bride,* Eva in Wagner's *Die Meistersinger,* Lady Harriet in Flotow's *Martha,* Wellgunde in Wagner's *Der Ring des Nibelungen,* Donna Elvira in Mozart's *Don Giovanni,* and Nedda in Leoncavallo's *Pagliacci*). In 1966 she sang Mistress Ford in Verdi's *Falstaff* in the performance that marked Leonard Bernstein's Vienna debut. In 1984, Lipp returned to the Salzburg Festival, where she performed the character role of Marianne Leitmetzerin in Strauss's *Der Rosenkavalier,* again with Karajan, with

whom she had recorded the role in 1982. She also sang the role in Turin in 1986.

Lipp's Teatro alla Scala and Covent Garden appearances also demonstrate her shift from coloratura to lyric roles. Her La Scala debut was as the Queen of the Night; she returned in 1960 to sing Marzelline in *Fidelio* under Karajan and in 1962 for Eva in *Die Meistersinger* under Karl Böhm and Euridice under Sanzogno. Covent Garden heard her Queen of the Night and Gilda (*Rigoletto*) in 1950 and her Violetta (*La traviata*) in 1955.

She also appeared at the Bregenz, Holland, Glyndebourne, and Wiesbaden festivals.

Her recordings do not quite substantiate her reputation. Her voice as recorded is pure, with accurate coloratura, but it sounds relatively small, without strong dramatic projection; the highest notes are pecked at and not sustained for as long as one would want. As the Queen of the Night she creates little character, partly because she sacrifices the words on higher vocal lines, but her staccato notes are impeccable.

—Michael Sims

THE LITHUANIANS
See I LITUANI

I LITUANI [The Lithuanians].

Composer: Amilcare Ponchielli.

Librettist: A. Ghislanzoni (after Mickiewicz, *Konrad Wallenrod*).

First Performance: Milan, Teatro all Scala, 6 March 1874; revised, Teatro alla Scala, 6 March 1875.

Roles: Arnoldo (baritone); Aldona (soprano); Walther/Corrado Wallenrod (tenor); Albano (bass); Vitoldo (bass);

Publications

article–

Attardi, Francesco. *"I Lituani."* In *Amilcare Ponchielli,* ed. by Giampiero Tintori. Milan, 1984.

*   *   *

I lituani was the first of Ponchielli's operas to be produced at the Teatro alla Scala, preceding the triumph of *La Gioconda* by two years and following a long and frustrating period of menial musical posts and insignificant theatrical opportunities. The text by Antonio Ghislanzoni, librettist of Verdi's *Aida,* was derived from the epic poem *Konrad Wallenrod* by the eminent Polish poet Adam Mickiewicz. The story involves a semi-legendary figure of Lithuanian origin who came to be appointed leader of the powerful Teutonic Order in the early Middle Ages and used this position to wreak vengeance upon this very group, as the oppressors of his Baltic homeland. Wallenrod's doom is proclaimed at the end by the fearsome Vehmic tribunal, the *francs juges* who also figure in Berlioz's fragmentary early opera of that title.

The prologue concerns the defeat of the Lithuanian armies at the hands of the Teutonic knights. The fires of distant combat are observed by Albano, an aged holy man who combines the roles of warrior, priest, and bard. After Albano leads his people in prayer, their prince, Arnoldo, returns from the battlefield. His companion Walther determines to undertake a last, apparently suicidal measure against the enemy. Walther consoles his wife, Aldona, with patriotic sentiments.

Act I takes place ten years later. By some unexplained means, Walther has been appointed supreme leader of the Teutonic Order, the erstwhile enemy. In the course of the festivities attending his accession to this high position, Walther (now "Corrado Wallenrod") grants clemency to the Lithuanian prisoners, Arnoldo among them. Arnoldo reflects on this unexpected turn of events (*Romanza,* "O rimembranze"), after which he encounters his sister, Aldona, who has come in search of her long absent husband, Walther. They determine to gain access to the Marienburg fortress where Walther, as Corrado, now holds court. In the midst of revelry and exotic dances (act II), the new leader demands some more edifying form of entertainment. Arnoldo steps forth with a strange and impassioned lament for his homeland ("Sui lituani fiumi"), to the consternation of all. Corrado is persuaded to save him from the general wrath by the intercession of Aldona, whom he quickly recognizes as his wife. The last act takes place against a frozen winter landscape, in the ruins of a cloister. Aldona is finally reunited with Walther/Corrado only to overhear his death sentence pronounced by the terrible Vehmic tribunal, the *franco giudici.* Back at the Marienburg fortress Walther takes poison, seeing no possibility of escape. At the last minute the victorious Lithuanian army arrives and drives away the remaining Germans, but it is too late. An off-stage chorus of nature-spirits (the "Willis") is heard calling for the soul of the deceased hero.

Ghislanzoni's libretto is beset by a number of those implausibilities endemic to the Italian *melodramma,* although what might seem the most glaring of these—Walther's unexplained transformation from Lithuanian warrior to Grand Master of the enemy Teutonic Order—is based on historical tradition, at least, if not documented fact. That all the characters should find themselves fortuitously reunited in the Marienburg fortress ten years after the first scene can by accepted as generic convention; but the patterns of recognition or non-recognition are too clearly dictated by dramatic contrivance. Why should Arnoldo and Aldona so readily identify Corrado as Walther when the pasteboard villain Vitoldo—a traitor to the Lithuanian cause, now in the service of the Teutonic knights—fails to do so until act III? The libretto contains various motifs reminiscent of *Aida,* such as the presence of a captive people amidst the grandiose celebrations of their oppressors (act I), or the manner in which Aldona overhears the sentence pronounced by the lugubrious tribunal against Walther, positioned analogously to the scene of Amneris and the Egyptian priests just prior to the tragic culmination of the drama.

Ponchielli's score may also owe something to the recent example of *Aida.* Like Verdi's work, it represents an Italianized response to French grand opera. The "exotic" dances of Andalusian, Moorish, and Greek women added to act II a year after the premiere lie somewhere between Verdi's "Egyptian" ballet music and that which he later provided for *Otello* in Paris. Elements of melodic style and orchestration can also be traced both back to *Aida* and forward to Verdi's late

operas. Ponchielli demonstrates a fondness here (as in *La Gioconda*) for high string textures with frequent solo or *divisi* writing and pizzicato accompaniments to delicately scored, sinuous woodwind melodies: examples can be found in the introduction to the opera's full-length *Sinfonia* and in Arnoldo's act-I *Romanza,* "O rimembranze." Another possible influence is Wagner's *Lohengrin,* which saw its much-publicized Italian premiere in the same year as Verdi's *Aida* (1871) and which would be a natural model for the northern-Gothic *tinta* Ponchielli sought to create. The use of stage trumpets in harmonic "counterpoint" with the orchestra and the melodic style of the act-I cathedral procession strongly suggest the impact of Wagner's opera. The shivering chromaticisms accompanying the opening scene (prologue), Arnoldo's lament ("Sui lituani fiumi") and various passages in act III may represent Ponchielli's own contribution to the characteristic *tinta* of the opera. Other features of the work anticipate the style of Puccini and the *verismo* generation (as does *Gioconda*), for instance the concentrated lyricism of "O rimembranze," its lush orchestration and the brief harmonic intensification of its central episode. The grandly conceived ensemble that follows (finale, act II), on the other hand, is cited by Francesco Attardi as "worthy of Verdi at his best, a masterpiece of its kind in later 19th-century Italian opera" with its counterpoise of dramatic solo lines over a majestically rising *fugato* subject.

—Thomas S. Grey

LIZZIE BORDEN.

Composer: Jack Beeson.

Librettist: K. Elmslie.

First Performance: New York, New York City Opera, 25 March 1965.

Roles: Lizzie (mezzo-soprano); Abbie (soprano); Margaret (soprano); Andrew Borden (bass-baritone); Captain Jason MacFarlane (baritone); Reverend Harrington (tenor); chorus (SA).

Publications

articles–

Eaton, Q. *"Hello Out There," "The Sweet Bye and Bye," "Lizzie Borden," "My Heart's in The Highlands."* In *Opera Production: A Handbook.* St Paul, 1961-74.
Beeson, Jack. "The Autobiography of Lizzie Borden." *Opera Quarterly* 4 (1986): 15.

*   *   *

Lizzie Borden went to trial for the ax murder of her wealthy parents in Fall River, Massachusetts, in 1892, but was acquitted and afterward lived a comfortable and social life. It is a famous case, but the opera changes all that. Lizzie becomes the older sister and the development of the opera places Lizzie squarely in a position, psychologically, to perform the murders. This story has been treated by Agnes deMille as a dance entitled *The Fall River Legend,* Lillian Gish played her in *Nine Pine Street,* she appeared as a character in Kaufman and Hart's comedy *The Man Who Came to Dinner,* and *New Faces of 1952* featured a humorous song and dance about her.

As Jack Beeson's opera tells it, the story is one of a repressed New Englander who finally explodes. Lizzie Borden, the daughter of wealthy Andrew Borden, is the victim of her father's discipline and derision. She must "make do" rather than buy a new dress for church. Later Lizzie's younger sister, Margaret, discusses with Lizzie Jason's arrival that evening and his possibly asking for Margaret's hand in marriage. After dinner, Abbie, Andrew's second wife, expresses her wish for a new organ, but Andrew isn't interested. She speaks accusingly of the two daughters' over-concern for their mother's possessions. Jason and Rev. Harrington enter: the Reverend to ask for money for the new church steeple and Jason for Margaret's hand. Andrew is offended on both counts and suggests Jason marry Lizzie instead. Even though Andrew forbids either daughter to see Jason, Margaret does leave with Jason when he comes the next day. Lizzie puts on Margaret's wedding dress, and Abbie taunts her by ripping it open to shame her. When Abbie leaves, Lizzie pounds on a mirror and breaks it.

Jason returns for Margaret's things, and Lizzie is barely aware of him. She asks him to write her as he wrote Margaret. Abbie returns to her room after speaking to Jason and Lizzie follows her. A scream is heard. When Andrew returns, Lizzie meets him on the stairs and follows him into the bedroom as the curtain falls. In the epilogue, Lizzie, several years later, is given back a church pledge by the minister, which the congregation voted not to accept following the murder of her parents. Lizzie is cold and distant. Children in the street sing a taunting song about her murdering her parents with an ax.

Lizzie Borden is generally considered to be stronger on story than on music. Kenward Elmslie was praised for his libretto, which creates the psychological climate for the murder by Lizzie. This emphasis on the interior life of the characters in the opera lifts the story from its penny dreadful reputation, as in the song: "Lizzie Borden took an ax/ Gave her mother forty whacks./ Lizzie stood behind the door/ and gave her father forty more," which the children sing at the end of the opera. It is unfortunate that this version sides with popular legend rather than lack of court evidence. Musically, the opera is lacking in a clear personality. There are Bergian elements, echos of Ives, hymn tunes, and bouncy New England hoedown rhythms. But Beeson has a good sense of English prosody and matches well the words with rhythms and music.

—Andrew H. Drummond

LOHENGRIN.

Composer: Richard Wagner.

Librettist: Richard Wagner.

First Performance: Weimar, Hoftheater, 28 August 1850.

Roles: Lohengrin (tenor); Henry I [Henry the Fowler] (bass); Frederick, Count Telramund (baritone); Elsa (soprano); Ortrud (soprano or mezzo-soprano); Royal Herald (baritone); Gottfried (mute); Four Nobles of Brabant (tenors, basses); Four Pages (sopranos, altos); Eight Ladies (sopranos, altos); chorus (SSAATTBB).

Publications

articles—

Kloss, E. "Richard Wagner über 'Lohengrin': Aussprüche des Meisters über sein Werk." *Richard Wagner-Jahrbuch* 3 (1908): 132.

Porges, H. "Über Richard Wagners 'Lohengrin'. *Bayreuther Blätter* 32 (1909): 173.

Kapp, J. "Die Urschrift von Richard Wagners 'Lohengrin'-Dichtung." *Die Musik* 11 (1911-12): 88.

Steinbeck, D. "Richard Wagners *Lohengrin*-Szenarium." In *Kleine Schriften der Gesellschaft für Theatergeschichte,* 25. Berlin, 1972.

Henry the Fowler, the tenth-century king of the Germans, comes to Brabant to gather forces for the defense of his states against the Hungarians and finds the northern duchy torn by dissent. Gottfried, the boy heir to the throne, has disappeared, and Count Telramund has accused the boy's older sister, Elsa, of murdering him. Elsa, called to court, says that she will be vindicated by a knight in shining armor, who has appeared to her in a dream. A summons is issued to the four winds, and the knight materializes, sailing up the Scheldt in a boat drawn by a swan. He will champion Elsa's cause if she will never ask his name. She consents, and the shining knight defeats Telramund in combat, but spares his life.

Telramund's pagan wife Ortrud plans revenge: as Elsa is about to marry her champion, she and Telramund interrupt the procession to tempt Elsa with doubts about the knight's origin. When the newlyweds are alone in their bedchamber, Elsa asks her husband the forbidden question, and at that moment Telramund enters with a drawn sword. The knight slays his assailant, and then says he must now leave Elsa forever; he will never, as the king had hoped, lead the combined German-Brabantian forces; his name is Lohengrin, and he must return to his father Parsifal, king of the Holy Grail. The swan boat reappears, and Ortrud in triumph recognizes, from the pendant around its neck, that the swan is the long-lost Gottfried, whom she had made disappear. Lohengrin kneels in prayer, and the swan sinks into the waves and rises again, now as Gottfried, ready to lead the pan-German crusade in Lohengrin's stead. Ortrud cries out in defeat, and Elsa, as she sees her husband fade from view, falls lifeless.

Lohengrin is the last opera Wagner wrote before the six-year silence from which the new musical world of the *Ring* emerged. It is also the last and greatest Romantic opera—if Romantic means visionary, lyrical, steeped in the folktales of the Middle Ages and, above all, German. Wagner was, at the time of the premiere, a political exile in Switzerland, and his still-active hopes for a united Germany are clearly part of the opera's texture. In many respects Lohengrin is, like Tannhäuser before him, a figure for the composer himself.

In *Lohengrin* Wagner's musical powers reach new heights, and he was never to surpass the orchestral coloring of the famous prelude, where soft divided strings in the traditionally "bright" key of A major suggest what Thomas Mann has

Lohengrin, **production by Herbert von Karajan for Salzburg Festival, 1976**

called "a silvery blue beauty." The score still features traditional arias, duets, choruses and ensembles, but each act builds with a new and impressive architectonic sense, and increasingly the orchestra comments on the action with leitmotifs in the manner that will eventually pervade the *Ring.*

The mythic aspects of *Lohengrin* have not always been properly appreciated, and Elsa in particular has been maligned as a weak character, though Wagner himself told us to think of her as "the unconscious, the intuitive . . . the feminine, hitherto not understood by me, now understood at last." (He was already moving on to Brünnhilde, the questioning, intuitive, saving woman of the *Ring.*) Elsa breaking an imposed taboo is not just an anticipation of Brünnhilde disobeying her father, but one of a whole pattern of mythic heroines who give way to curiosity and bring immediate tragedy but also hope for the future, even the promise of a world savior. Brünnhilde's disobedience brings, eventually, Siegfried, as in other mythologies Pandora's disobedience brings Elpis, Semele's Dionysus, Psyche's Eros, and Eve's (as the Church sings in her liturgy) the redeeming Jesus. These taboo-breaking myths describe a great evolutionary moment in prehistory, when the human race passed from unconsciousness to the much more problematic state of consciousness. ("You will be like gods," the tempter said to Eve.) Woman precipitates this, not because she is weaker, but because she is more intuitive. Elsa's questioning means the loss of Lohengrin, but restores Gottfried, the Grail-sent hope for the future, hidden for a time under a figure our mythologists would call a transcendence symbol—the swan.

Lohengrin is an astonishing work for anyone with ears for the pre-Raphaelite beauty and brassy glory of its music, and with the insight to see deeply into its text. Baudelaire, astonished, wrote that *Lohengrin* held him suspended "in an ecstasy compounded of joy and insight."

—M. Owen Lee

I LOMBARDI ALLA PRIMA CROCIATA [The Lombards at the First Crusade].

Composer: Giuseppe Verdi.

Librettist: Temistocle Solera (after Tommaso Grossi).

First Performance: Milan, Teatro alla Scala, 11 February 1843; revised as *Jérusalem,* libretto by Gustave Vaëz and Alphonse Royer, Paris, Opéra, 26 November 1847.

Roles: Arvino (tenor); Pagano (bass); Viclinda (soprano); Giselda (soprano); Oronte (tenor); Pirro (bass); Prior of Milan (tenor); Acciano (bass); Sofia (soprano); chorus (SATB).

A scene from Verdi's *I Lombardi,* Her Majesty's Theatre, London, 1846

Publications

article–

Kimbell, David R.B. "Verdi's First Rifacimento: *I Lombardi* and *Jérusalem.*" *Music and Letters* 40 (1969).

*   *   *

I Lombardi alla prima crociata, Giuseppe Verdi's fourth opera, was premiered at the Teatro alla Scala on 11 February 1843. The librettist Temistocle Solera based the work on Tommaso Grossi's novel-poem of the same name from 1826. The action takes place at the end of the eleventh century. Act I is subtitled "The Vendetta." Two brothers, Pagano and Arvino, both love Viclinda. She chooses Arvino; on their wedding day Pagano tries to kill his brother. Pagano is exiled but many years later returns to Milan dressed as a penitent; he is reconciled with his brother, with Viclinda, and with their daughter, Giselda. Pagano still seeks revenge, however. Thinking to attack his brother, he mistakenly kills his father; Pagano tries unsuccessfully to kill himself in remorse and is once again exiled. In act II, "The Man in the Cave," Oronte, the son of Acciano, the tyrant of Antioch, is in love with one of the Christian prisoners, Giselda. Pagano has become a hermit. His former follower, Pirro, comes to him offering to betray Antioch, which action allows the crusading Lombards, led by Arvino, to capture Antioch. Giselda, in the harem, learns that both Acciano and Oronte have been killed. When

the Lombards enter she curses the god who allowed this war; incensed at this, her father tries to kill her. Pagano, unrecognized, saves her, pleading that she is only "a poor mad girl." Act III, "The Conversion," takes place in the valley of Jehoshaphat outside Jerusalem. Oronte, in fact alive although critically wounded, disguised as a crusader, meets Giselda before he dies in her arms. In act IV, "The Holy Sepulchre," Giselda and her father are now reconciled. She has a vision of Oronte among the angels. In the battle for Jerusalem, Pagano is mortally wounded. He discloses his identity as he lies dying in Arvino's tent. He is forgiven; Arvino carries him to the entrance of the tent, where the two brothers regard the flags of the crusaders flying on the conquered city.

I Lombardi was Verdi's first opera after the extremely popular *Nabucco* of 1842. Because of the current political situation in Italy, *I Lombardi,* with its Lombards (seen allegorically as the Italians) pitted against the Saracens (the Austrian oppressors), caused even greater furor at its premiere than had *Nabucco.* One reads of stampedes in the theater and of frenzied applause and many demands for encores. Arvino's outcry in the final act calling the Lombards to battle, "La santa terra oggi nostra sarà" (The Holy Land will today be ours!) caused the audience to go wild; many shouted "Sì! guerra, guerra!" (Yes, war!) along with the chorus. The opera was performed a total of twenty-seven times before the end of the season. It was the right subject at the right time to stir such feelings, and some of the credit must also go to Verdi's rousing, full-blooded tunes. Yet *I Lombardi* is not on an artistic level with *Nabucco;* it is much more of a patchwork, and many of its effects are blatantly crude and banal. The critics recognized this immediately; some noted that Verdi's writing was unvocal and potentially damaging to good singing, and a correspondent of *France musicale* stated that "Nothing could be poorer than this work from the technical point of view. Counterpoint is inexcusably neglected and the deafening noise of the brass instruments and the big drum does not suffice to hide the emptiness of the orchestration."

Although *I Lombardi* does contain a great deal of town-band music (reflecting Verdi's earlier musical experiences), much of the music fits and even heightens the situation. The chorus "O Signore dal tetto natio" aroused great enthusiasm and for a time threatened to displace "Va, pensiero" from *Nabucco* in the public's affection as a sort of unofficial national hymn. Giselda's "Salve Maria," a lovely piece the elements of which are found almost half a century later in Desdemona's "Ave Maria," was much admired by Rossini. Of much poorer quality was Solera's libretto, muddled and perfunctory. Francis Toye went so far as to state that "It may be doubted whether the annals of opera contain a more uncouth libretto than this." In all fairness, it was an almost impossible task to fashion an intelligible libretto from Grossi's novel-epic because much of the complicated action, which takes place over a long span of time, is told out of sequence. In addition, there are too many secondary characters for the operatic stage. The resulting opera presents certain difficulties in staging: it requires eleven scenes, a number of them calling for a high degree of spectacle, two star tenors of quite different vocal weight, not to mention the ubiquitous town-band.

Even though *I Lombardi* was written against the backdrop of a volatile political situation, it was the Church rather than the political authorities that caused Verdi censorship problems. The Archbishop of Milan thought it sacrilegious in its onstage depiction of baptism, its biblical setting in the Holy Land, and in its incense and banners. This was Verdi's first major battle with censorship but it ended with him only being obliged to change Giselda's "Ave Maria" to "Salve Maria." In the manuscript one can see the addition of the "S" and the "l" in Verdi's own hand.

The success of *I Lombardi* was not repeated when it was staged in Venice later in 1843. Verdi, writing to the Countess Giuseppina Appioni, called the performance there "*un gran fiasco,* one of those fiascos that may truly be called classic." In 1847 the work was re-fashioned by Verdi as *Jérusalem* for Paris. It was his first attempt, carried through with *Les vêpres siciliennes,* the 1865 revision of *Macbeth,* and *Don Carlos,* to conquer the French capital. The librettists, Royer and Vaëz, abolished the crusades, transformed Milan into Toulouse, turning Italians into Frenchmen. Verdi added the obligatory ballet music, made many changes throughout, and even replaced some numbers with new ones. The effect of *Jérusalem* is not as immediate and vital as that of *I Lombardi.* Julian Budden sums up the Italian work thus: "If *I Lombardi* is a very imperfect work of art, it is nevertheless a rich compost-heap which fertilized the soil of many a later [Verdi] opera."

—Stephen Willier

THE LOMBARDS AT THE FIRST CRUSADE
See I LOMBARDI ALLA PRIMA CROCIATA

LONDON, George (born George Burnstein).

Bass-baritone. Born 5 May 1919, in Montreal. Died 23 March 1985, in Armonk, New York. Studied in Los Angeles with Richard Lert, voice with Hugo Strelitzer and Nathan Stewart; debut (as George Burnstein) as Dr Grenvil in *La traviata,* Hollywood Bowl; then studied in New York with Enrico Rosati and Paola Novikova; sang Monterone with San Francisco Opera, 1943; toured in 1947 with Frances Yeend and Paola Novikova; appeared as Amonasro at Vienna, 1949; in Edinburgh as Figaro, 1950; sang Amfortas at Bayreuth, 1951; Metropolitan opera debut as Amonasro, 1951, and sang with that company until 1966; appeared at Salzburg, 1952; at Teatro alla Scala as Don Pizarro in *Fidelio,* 1952; at Buenos Aires and Paris Opéra; suffered paralysis of vocal cords, 1967, but continued to work in arts management; artistic administrator of John F. Kennedy Center for the Performing Arts, Washington, D.C., 1968-71; executive director of National Opera Institute, 1971-77; staged *Ring* cycle in Seattle, 1975; directed Opera Society of Washington, 1975-77.

Publications

By LONDON: articles–

"Prima Donnas I Have Sung Against." *Opera Annual* 6 (1959).

George London as Amfortas in Wagner's *Parsifal,* Bayreuth, **1951**

About London: books–

London, N. *Aria for George.* New York, 1987.

articles–

Wechsberg, J. "The Vocal Mission." *New Yorker* 26 October and 2 November (1957).

*   *   *

Devotees of George London's vocal art value him not because his bass-baritone was a perfect voice used perfectly but because of the rare dramatic power and vocal conviction he conveyed at his best, especially onstage. Indeed J.B. Steane, remarking that London's singing is not flattered by recording, compares the interpretation of London and two other modern singers of Wotan's Farewell against the versions made by earlier singers Friedrich Schorr and Alexander Kipnis and finds all the moderns, including London, wanting. Smoothness of vocal emission and firmness of vocal control among Wagner baritones are something that, in Steane's view, had vanished at the time he was writing. Nevertheless, it is only fair to say, as indeed Steane himself does, that recording can only capture part of George London's dramatic excitement and not at all his dark, brooding theatrical presence.

Born in Canada, London's training and early career were in North America; his international career began with an Amonasro in Vienna in 1949. This was soon followed by Glyndebourne, Bayreuth, the Metropolitan Opera in 1951, and, among other notable milestones, the Bolshoi in 1960 as the first non-Russian to sing Boris Godunov there. Early in his career he began concentrating on the Wagner repertoire; an important phase in his development was his extensive collaboration with Wieland Wagner during the fifties and sixties which culminated in *Der Ring des Nibelungen* at Bayreuth and other centers, such as Cologne, in 1962. Perhaps his most memorable achievement with Wieland was his playing of Amfortas, an almost unbearably intense portrayal. He was also a notable Dutchman and Hans Sachs. His reputation as a leading Wagnerian made it natural that in the first complete recording of the *Der Ring des Nibelungen* in the late fifties and early sixties he was invited to assume the *Das Rheingold* Wotan under Solti and *Die Walküre* Wotan under Leinsdorf.

His achievements outside the Wagner repertoire were also distinguished. His Scarpia, the Count in *Le nozze di Figaro*, Don Giovanni, Mephistopheles (Gounod), Escamillo, and the villains in *Les Contes d'Hoffman* were among his successful stage assumptions and he has left recordings of these, in whole or in part. But one of his most exciting and moving recorded performances is to be found in the brief aria, "Standin' in the need of prayer" from Louis Gruenberg's *Emperor Jones,* a Lawrence Tibbett vehicle in the thirties at the Met. The fear, supplication, and above all the hallucinatory quality of the scene make it the most intense memorial he has left of his art. George London was forced into premature retirement while still in his prime (1967) for medical reasons. He pursued a career in arts administration until ill health gradually forced withdrawal from all activity; he died in 1985.

—Peter Dyson

———

LORENGAR, Pilar [born Pilar Lorenza Garcia].

Soprano. Born 16 January 1928, in Saragossa, Spain. Studied with Angeles Ottein in Madrid and later with Carl Ebert and Martha Klust in Berlin; debut in Zarzuelas, Madrid, 1949; concert debut, 1952; opera debut as Cherubino in Aix-en-Provence, 1955; New York concert debut as Rosario in *Goyescas,* 1955; Covent Garden debut as Violetta, 1955; appeared as Pamina at Buenos Aires, 1958; sang in Berlin from the late 1950s to the late 1980s; appeared at Glyndebourne, 1956-60; Salzburg, 1961-64; Metropolitan Opera debut as Donna Elvira, 1966, and sang there for twelve seasons; inagurated the Deutsche Oper, 1961, and named Kammersängerin, 1963.

Publications

About LORENGAR: books–

Elsner, W. and M. Busch. *Pilar Lorengar: ein Porträt.* Berlin, 1986.

*   *   *

During a career that stretched from the mid 1950s to the mid 1980s the Spanish soprano Pilar Lorengar sang a wide variety of roles in some of the world's leading opera houses. Her voice and stage *persona* evolved over the course of her career. A youthful Cherubino (Mozart's *Le nozze di Figaro*) grew gradually into a Countess. A specialist in Mozart expanded her repertory to Weber and Wagner, to Verdi and Puccini.

Lorengar's portrayal of Cherubino at the summer festival at Aix-en-Provence in the mid-1950s is among the many fine performances that established her international reputation. Her looks were not quite right; *Opera* called her "the most unboylike page imaginable, discarding the usual periwig in favor of a feminine hair-style which even the text of 'Non più andrai' could hardly justify." Recorded under Hans Rosbaud, Lorengar's Cherubino has a bright, pretty voice. In her aria "Non so più cosa son, cosa faccio" Lorengar projects a vivacious, fresh stage personality. Her clear enunciation of the words infuses the music with an infectious liveliness. Less successful, perhaps, is Lorengar's lyrical rendition of "Voi che sapete." The slower tempo and sustained notes here make Lorengar's wide vibrato more apparent than in "Non so più cosa son." The vibrato gives the voice a somewhat overripe quality that seems out of character. The clarity of enunciation that one can admire in "Non so più cosa son" is not so apparent here. Lorengar sacrifices words in the interests of smoothness of line; the result, however beautiful from a purely musical point of view, is a weakening of dramatic force and vividness of characterization.

A more mature Lorengar with a wider repertory won success later in her career. Her voice grew: a critic in *Opera* praised her performance in the title role of *Jenůfa* in Berlin (1976): "her once rather limited lyric soprano has grown surprisingly in volume and power while still retaining its perfection of tonal beauty and resonance in the upper register." Lorengar was loudly applauded for her subtle acting and pure voice when she portrayed Elisabetta (Verdi's *Don Carlos*) in Chicago in 1972. As Agathe in Weber's *Der Freischütz,* as Eva in Wagner's *Die Meistersinger,* and as the Countess in Mozart's *Figaro* at the Metropolitan Opera in New York, Lorengar was praised by listeners and critics alike.

Lorengar has sung successfully in light opera, including the zarzuelas of her native land. In Rafael Millan's *La dogaresa,* as recorded under Ataulfo Argento, one can hear Lorengar the zarzuela singer. Hers is a voice consistently pleasant to listen to. She delivers the aria "Ya muerto esta" with bright, clearly focused singing; but there is something impersonal, detached, about her performance. One misses in the aria "Las flores de mil colores," for example, a sense of the character's personality and emotional state. A listener with no knowledge of Spanish and no translation at hand might have difficulty in understanding what Lorengar's character is feeling.

—John A. Rice

LORENZ, Max.

Tenor. Born 17 May 1901, in Düsseldorf. Died 11 January 1975, in Salzburg. Studied in Berlin; debut as Walther von der Vogelweide in *Tannhäuser;* appeared at Berlin State Opera, 1931-44, where he was a member, 1933-37; at Vienna State Opera from 1937; appeared at Covent Garden, 1934, 1937; at Bayreuth, 1933, 1952; Metropolitan Opera debut as Walther von Stolzing in *Die Meistersinger,* and sang eleven roles there.

Publications

About LORENZ: books–

Schäfer, J. *Max Lorenz.* Hamburg, 1973.
Hermann, W. *Max Lorenz.* Vienna, 1976.

* * *

A supremely important and true heldentenor, Max Lorenz was perhaps the only artist in that category to rival the exploits of his Wagnerian colleague, Lauritz Melchior. While he also sang the same repertoire as Melchior, Lorenz' voice was naturally pitched a bit higher, allowing him to sing Walther in *Die Meistersinger,* a role which Melchior preferred not to attempt. Lorenz also sang Rienzi, Erik and Loge: the complete Wagnerian panoply.

Lorenz, too, ventured (or was given the opportunities to venture) into repertoires other than Wagner. He sang in the Strauss operas, *Salome* (Herod was his final performance, Vienna, 1962), *Elektra, Die ägyptische Helene, Die Frau ohne Schatten* and *Ariadne.* He even sang the Italian tenor in *Rosenkavalier.* He was a famous Otello (often compared favorably to Leo Slezak), and also sang Manrico, Alvaro, Riccardo, and Radames. He sang the Calif and Des Grieux in the Puccini operas, and a wide variety of other roles, from Offenbach to Irving Berlin (Buffalo Bill in *Annie Get Your Gun),* including Florestan, Don José, and Pfitzner's Palestrina. He sang the Idamantes of Mozart and Gluck's Achilles, Berg's

Drum Major and Pedro in *Tiefland,* Mussorgsky's False Dimitri and Weber's Max.

Max Lorenz appeared in several world premieres, among them Josef K. in von Einem's *Der Prozess,* and some of his last appearances were as Teresias in *Alcestiad* by the American composer Louise Talma in Frankfurt a. Main 1962. His repertoire included some 50 roles.

He was born in Düsseldorf in 1901 and made his stage debut in Dresden, 1927. He appeared in the major houses throughout Europe, was a regular at the Bayreuth and Salzburg Festivals, sang at Covent Garden, appeared at the Metropolitan Opera before the War (and returned after), and performed in South America. Berlin was his first artistic home, then Vienna. After his retirement from the stage, he taught at the Mozarteum in Salzburg and privately in Salzburg and Munich. He died in January 1975, in Salzburg. A memorial was held 10 days later at the Vienna State Opera before his interment in Vienna's Central Cemetery.

Max Lorenz is represented today by a myriad of recordings, many from live performances. There is an especially exciting *Tristan und Isolde* from Berlin, 1942, conducted by Robert Heger, among other *Tristan* live recordings; the *Götterdämmerung* Siegfried with Furtwängler from Milan; innumerable *Walküre* act I, scene III's; excerpts from *Tannhäuser,* led by Heger, 1943; a complete *Ariadne auf Naxos* conducted by Böhm; Bayreuth performance excerpts; a *Salome;* some singer portrait collections; and much else.

An always exciting singer, refined musically, and extremely versatile, Max Lorenz' 35-year professional career was a rewarding one for audiences everywhere.

—Bert Wechsler

LORTZING, Gustav Albert.

Composer. Born 23 October 1801, in Berlin. Died 21 January, 1851, in Berlin. Married: the actress Rosina Regina Ahles, Cologne, 30 January 1823 (11 children). Studied piano with Griebel and theory with Rungenhagen in Berlin; actor with the traveling troupe directed by Derossi, 1819; composed first opera, 1824; tenor with the Municipal Theater of Leipzig, 1833-44; conductor, Leipzig Opera, 1843-45; conductor at the Theater an der Wien, Vienna; music director of the Friedrich-Wilhelmstadt Theater in Berlin, 1850.

Operas

Ali Pascha von Janina, oder Die Franzosen in Albanien (Singspiel), Lortzing (after a "true incident"), 1824, Münster, 1 February 1828.
Der Pole und sein Kind, oder Der Feldwebel vom IV. Regiment (Liederspiel), Lortzing, Osnabrück, 11 October 1832.
Der Weihnachtsabend (Singspiel), Lortzing, Münster, 21 December 1832.
Andreas Hofer (Singspiel), Lortzing (after K. Immermann, *Trauerspiel in Tyrol),* 1832; arranged for performance by E.N. von Reznicek, Mainz, 14 April 1887.
Szenen aus Mozarts Leben (Singspiel), Lortzing, 1832.
Die beiden Schützen, Lortzing (after G. Cords), 1835, Leipzig, Municipal Theater, 20 February 1837.
Die Schatzkammer des Ynka, Robert Blum, 1836.

Gustav Albert Lortzing

Zar und Zimmermann, oder Die zwei Peter, Lortzing (after C. C. Römers), 1837, Leipzig, Municipal Theater, 22 December 1837.

Caramo, oder Das Fischerstechen, Lortzing (translated from A. Vilain de Saint-Hilaire and Paul Duport, *Cosimo, ou Le peintre badigeonneur,* after Eugène Prosper Prévost), 1839, Leipzig, Municipal Theater, 20 September 1839.

Hans Sachs, Lortzing (after J.L.F. Deinhardstein), Leipzig, Municipal Theater, 23 June 1840.

Casanova, Lortzing (after A. Lebrun), Leipzig, Municipal Theater, 31 December 1841.

Der Wildschütz, oder Die Stimme der Natur, Lortzing (after Kotzebue, *Der Rehbock*), Leipzig, Municipal Theater, 31 December 1842.

Undine, Lortzing (after Friedrich de la Motte-Fouqué), 1844-45, Magdeburg, 21 April 1845.

Der Waffenschmied, Lortzing (after Friedrich Wilhelm von Ziegler, *Liebhaber und Nebenbuhler in einer Person*), Vienna, Theater an der Wien, 30 May 1846.

Zum Grossadmiral, Lortzing (after A.W. Iffland, *Heinrich des Fünften Jugendjahre*), Leipzig, Municipal Theater, 13 December 1847.

Regina, Lortzing, 1848; arranged for performance by A. L'Arronge as *Regina, oder Die Marodeure,* Berlin, Royal Opera, 21 March 1899.

Rolands Knappen, oder Das ersehnte Glück, G.A. Musäus, Leipzig, Municipal Theater, 25 May 1849.

Die Opernprobe, oder Die vornehmen Dilettanten, Lortzing (after J.F. Jünger, *Die Komödie aus dem Stegreif*), 1851, Frankfurt am Main, 20 January 1851.

Other works: incidental music, choral works.

Publications/Writings

By LORTZING: books–

Kruse, G.R., ed. *A. Lortzing: Gesammelte Briefe.* Leipzig, 1901; 2nd ed., 1913; 3rd ed., 1947.

About LORTZING: books–

Düringer, P.J. *Albert Lortzing, sein Leben und Wirken.* Leipzig, 1851.

Kruse, G.R. *Albert Lortzing: Leben und Werk.* Berlin, 1899; 2nd ed., 1914; Wiesbaden, 1947.

Wittmann, H. *Lortzing.* Leipzig, 1890; 1902.

Schwermann, J. *Albert Lortzings Bühnentexte.* Wattenscheid, 1914.

Istel, Edgar. *Die Blütezeit der musikalischen Romantik in Deutschland.* Leipzig and Berlin, 1921.

Müller, Eugen. *Albert Lortzing.* Münster, 1921.

Laue, H. *Die Operndichtung Lortzings.* Würzburg, 1932.

Killer, Hermann. *Albert Lortzing.* Potsdam, 1938.

Schumann, O. *Albert Lortzing 1801-1851: sein Leben in Bildern.* Leipzig, 1941.

Dippel, Paul Gerhardt. *Albert Lortzing: ein Leben für das deutsche Musiktheater.* Berlin, 1951.

Freusberg, E. *Der reisende Student: aus Albert Lortzings Leben.* Cologne, 1951.

Petzoldt, R. *Albert Lortzing: Leben eines grossen Musikers.* Leipzig, 1951.

Burgmüller, Herbert. *Die Musen darben: ein Lebensbild Albert Lortzings.* Berlin, 1955.

Hoffmann, Max. *Gustav Albert Lortzing, der Meister der deutschen Volksoper.* Leipzig, 1956.

Schlöder, Jürgen. *Undine auf dem Musiktheater. Zur Entwicklungsgeschichte der deutschen Spieloper.* Bonn-Bad Godesberg, 1979.

Worbs, Hans Christoph. *Albert Lortzing in Selbstzeugnissen und Bilddokumenten.* Reinbek bei Hamburg, 1980.

articles–

Welti, H. "Lortzing und Wagner." *Richard Wagner-Jahrbuch* (1886): 229.

Komorzynski, E. von. "Lortzings 'Waffenschmied' und seine Tradition." *Euphorion* 8 (1901): 340.

Kruse, G.R. "Ein Mozart-Singspiel von Lortzing." *Mitteilungen für die Mozartgemeinde in Berlin* 12 (1901): 71.

———. "Albert Lortzing und seine 'Regina'." *Neue Zeitschrift für Musik* 79 (1912): 677.

Altmann, W. "Lortzing als dramaturgischer Lehrer." *Die Musik* 12 (1913-14).

Naylor, Bernard. "Albert Lortzing." *Proceedings of the Royal Musical Association* 58 (1931-32): 1.

Sanders, E. "*Oberon* and *Zar und Zimmerman*." *Musical Quarterly* 40 (1954): 521.

Hommel, Friedrich. "Lortzing and German Opera." *Opera* November (1963).

Bollert, W. "Romantischer Lortzing: Die Schallplatten-Première der Undine." *Fono forum* 12 (1967): 260.

Subotnik, Rose R. "Lortzing and the German Romantics: A Dialectical Assessment." *Musical Quarterly* (1976).

Hanemann, Dorothee. "Mozart in der Bearbeitung Lortzings. Untersuchungen zu *Szenen aus Mozarts Leben*." *Mozart-Jahrbuch* (1980-83): 355.

unpublished–

Butschek, R. "Die musikalischen Ausdrucksmittel in den Opern Lortzings." Ph. D. dissertation, University of Vienna, 1938.

Loy, M. "Lortzings 'Hans Sachs': ein Beitrag zur Geschichte und zum Stil der komischen Oper im 19. Jahrhundert." Ph. D. dissertation, University of Erlangen, 1940.

Lodemann, J. "Lortzing und seine Spielopern: deutsche Bürgerlichkeit." Ph. D. dissertation, University of Freiburg, 1962.

Wulf, E. " 'Die Opernprobe' von G.A. Lortzing. Untersuchungen zum Operneinakter in der Mitte des 19. Jahrhunderts." Ph. D. dissertation, University of Cologne, 1963.

Cowden, R.H. "A Translation and Production Notes for Albert Lortzing's Spieloper Der Wildschütz." A. Mus. D. Dissertation, University of Rochester, 1966.

Schirmag, H. "Das erste Auftreten des Proletariats als Klasse in der deutschen Opernliteratur des 19. Jahrhunderts: neue Aspekte für die Gewinnung eines realistischen Lortzingsbildes aus der Sicht der Lortzing-Oper 'Regina'." Dissertation, Pädagogische Hochschule, Potsdam, 1967.

————. "Das musik-theatralische Schaffen Albert Lortzings als progressives Erbe der deutschen Opernliteratur zur Zeit des Vormärz und der deutschen bürgerlich-demokratischen Revolution von 1848-49." Habilitationsschrift, Martin-Luther University, 1978.

*　　*　　*

As the creator and major composer of German *Spieloper* in the first half of the nineteenth century, Gustav Albert Lortzing holds a significant place in the history of opera. His best works, starting with *Zar und Zimmermann, oder Die zwei Peter* (Leipzig, 1837), all incorporate his professional experiences as an actor, singer, cellist, librettist, and composer, and they demonstrate his ability to entertain rather than enlighten his audience. Friedrich Hommel pointed out that "He is not immortal but he is Lortzing." His work is archetypical middle-class German theater.

In a very real sense a nationalist who annexed the Italian *buffo* tradition with characters who were equally funny but more profound, Lortzing represented the Mozart tradition with scenes such as the dramatic sextet in *Zar und Zimmermann,* and he extended the French vaudeville with tightly constructed, subtle, yet hilarious works such as *Der Wildschütz.* All of his thoughts and feelings were rooted in the vernacular idioms of Germany: immediate accessibility, everyday humor, an abundance of characters with whom one could identify, and spoken dialogue instead of recitative so that the pace of the drama approached that of the legitimate theater. All of these factors were dependent upon a reworking of well known material from contemporary plays, most of which he acted in himself.

Lortzing's mother Charlotte Sophie Seidel was a soubrette, and his father Johann, after his leather business failed, began a stage career as an actor in Breslau, Coburg, and Bamberg with marked success. Brought up in a theatrical family, Albert performed children's parts on the stage, played in the theater orchestra, and began to write incidental music for plays. An engagement in Freiburg i. Bresgau led to a meeting with the then famous theater director Derossi, whose acting troupe played engagements in the Rheinland. This was the so-called ABCD Theater, nicknamed because Derossi was director in Aachen, Bonn, Cologne, and Düsseldorf. Lortzing's parents were hired for the 1817 season, and Albert was given a job in the company in 1819. His first theater music dates from this period: music to Kotzebue's play, *Der Schutzgeist,* in which Lortzing was acting at the time. The pattern was set with Lortzing utilizing each facet of his career to complement and nourish the others.

The dramatic parameters of his works are limited in range, but they are effective in part because of this. Lortzing rarely attempted more than he could deliver; *Undine* in 1845 and *Regina* in 1848 are the exceptions. The audience came to be entertained in a comfortable way and they were. His special talent lay in the field of comedy, some would say typically Germanic rustic humor, but in his better works, such as *Der Wildschütz* (1842), the parallel with Mozart is unmistakable: wit, pace, charm and an unstoppable flow of action supported by a melodic and orchestral fabric of transparency and grace. Certainly one of the great comic ensembles in the literature is the incredible "Billiards Quintet" in act two, a minor masterpiece. In converting workable dramatic scenes from successful plays into musical ensembles, he sublimated the text to the music. Never one to spend a great deal of time with poetry, images, symbolism, or purity of rhyme, he allowed the music to dictate everything. Perhaps the very simplicity of his libretti encouraged a musical dominance.

In the middle of the nineteenth century, only Otto Nicolai's *Lustigen Weiber von Windsor* (1849) and Peter Cornelius's *Barbier von Bagdad* (1858) attained the excellence of *Der Wildschütz.* Of the remaining operas, *Undine* (1844-45) is a "Romantic Magic Opera" freely adapted from fairy tale by de la Motte-Fouqué. With its systematic use of leitmotifs, colorful orchestration, and symbolism, *Undine* is the closest thing to a German Romantic opera attempted by the composer. *Der Waffenschmied* (1846), although successful in Vienna, was notably less complicated musically than his previous efforts. His final effort, *Die Opernprobe* (1850) parodies the art form on which he had spent a lifetime, perhaps a fitting finale to the career of a composer who acted, composed, conducted, and sang his way into the history books.

Lortzing is a prime example of the perfect mating of native talent with the expectations of his audience. Relying upon Mozart as his prime influence, he managed to infuse the French legitimate stage and *opéra-comique* with the easy and comfortable German folk tradition so essential to his audiences. He had an unerring sense of the contemporary German theater, and he spent a lifetime catering to that public with humor, sentimentality (but not the religious sentimentality of the German Romantics), and well crafted folk-like melodies. Few of the leading roles are vocally demanding; what they do demand is verve and a sense of theatrical timing. His orchestrations were designed to exploit the small Mozartian pit orchestra then common in German theaters, and again the trademarks are conventionality and professional polish rather than experimentation and extension.

Totally immersed in both the practical and creative sides of the theater, it is amazing that Lortzing composed as much as he did. Although not well known outside of German speaking countries, four of his operas remain in the standard repertoire in Austria, Germany, and Switzerland: *Zar und Zimmermann, Der Wildschütz, Undine,* and *Der Waffenschmied.* All of these works (plus *Der Opernprobe* published by Universal Edition) are still in the catalogue of C.F. Peters Verlag.

If one pinpoints enlightenment and entertainment as the two major directions of opera in the mid-nineteenth century German theater, the latter was Lortzing's strength—immediacy and pleasure were his calling cards then as they are now.

His characters are all common stereotypes: his heros flirt and enjoy life, his young ladies manipulate and pretend, his comic bumpkins are obvious, and each character stays within his own special world, interacting most effectively in melody and song. One thinks of the undemanding period pieces of Jerome Kern or Sigmund Romberg that appealed to contemporary audiences and formed the basis of a country's musical heritage. Albert Lortzing gave a similar legacy to Germany, a legacy which is still fresh and appealing today.

—Robert H. Cowden

LOS ANGELES, VICTORIA DE
See DE LOS ANGELES, VICTORIA

LOUISE.

Composer: Gustave Charpentier.

Librettist: Gustave Charpentier [and Saint Pol-Roux].

First Performance: Paris, Opéra-Comique, 2 February 1900.

Roles: Louise (soprano); Julien (tenor); The Mother (mezzo-soprano); The Father (baritone); Irma (soprano); Camille (soprano); Gertrude (mezzo-soprano); Errand Girl (soprano); Elise (soprano); Blanche (soprano); Suzanne (mezzo-soprano); Streetwalker (mezzo-soprano); Young Ragpicker (mezzo-soprano); Forewoman (mezzo-soprano); Milk Woman (soprano); Newspaper Girl (soprano); Coal Gatherer (Mezzo-soprano); Marguerite (soprano); Madeleine (mezzo-soprano); Dancer (mute); Noctambulist (tenor); Ragman (bass); Old Bohemian (baritone); Song Writer (baritone); Junkman (bass); Painter (bass); Two Philosophers (tenor, bass); Young Poet (baritone); Student (tenor); Two Policemen (baritones); Street Arab (soprano); Sculptor (baritone); Old Clothes Man (tenor); Apprentice (baritone); King of Fools (tenor); chorus (SATB) [many of the bit parts may be doubled].

Publications

books–

Paoli, D. de. *Luisa.* Milan, 1922.
Himonet, A. *Louise de G. Charpentier.* Châteaurox, 1922.

article–

Rolland, Romain. "Louise." *Rivista musicale italiana* 7 (1900): 361.

*   *   *

One day at the Paris Conservatory Charpentier's teacher Jules Massenet is supposed to have said to him: "Don't try to surprise people with cleverness. Give your temperament a chance. Go to Montmartre, look at some pretty girl, and let

A poster for the first production of Charpentier's *Louise*, Paris, 1900

your heart say what it feels." Charpentier took his advice. There was, in fact, a real-life Louise, a working girl with shining eyes and black hair, who longed to be free. He never forgot her and always spoke of her in later years with respectful emotion. In the opera she is wooed by the poet Julien, who lives next door and who tries to persuade her to elope with him if her parents do not agree to their marriage. Her mother disapproves of a young man whom she, a respectable working-class woman, regards as a good-for-nothing Bohemian, although Louise's father, work-worn and weary, is more tolerant. A bitter quarrel between mother and daughter ends with the father trying to calm Louise and telling her that she must forget Julien. In act II Julien continues the siege by following her to her work as a seamstress. At last she agrees to go off with him, and by act III they are living in a hill-top Montmartre cottage overlooking the bright lights of Paris. Bohemian friends arrive and crown Louise "The Muse of Montmartre." The festivities are interrupted by the entry of Louise's mother, who reports that her father is desperately ill: will she try to save his life by giving him the joy of seeing her again? She does so, but the affectionate reunion ends in anger when she refuses his plea to give up Julien. She escapes, leaving him to curse the city of Paris for robbing him of his beloved daughter.

Although Charpentier is credited with the libretto of *Louise,* and certainly provided the words for the first act, his anonymous collaborator who pulled the whole thing into shape was a friend of his youth, the symbolist poet Saint-Pol-Roux. The original concept and the music, however, are entirely his own. The story line is clear and succinct, and the four main characters are vividly depicted. Charpentier follows Massenet in the cut and shape of his melodies and in his handling of the words. Note, for example, his unconventional prosody in Louise's famous aria "Depuis le jour," in which she recalls the first time she gave herself to Julien. He also draws, very successfully, on the *verismo* of Puccini to create a wholly realistic picture of Paris and its working people. Another device he adopts is the Wagnerian *leitmotif,* as in the leaping theme that introduces the opera and often recurs as a symbol of the passion between Julien and Louise. It is possible to argue that the main character of the opera is Paris itself. By weaving genuine street cries into his score and by his cunning depiction of the "petits gens" of the capital—especially in act II when he shows the city awakening at dawn and in the "Muse de Montmartre" episode of act III—Charpentier evokes an unforgettable impression of the greedy Paris which deprives Louise's father of his daughter. If *Louise* is an ardent plea for free love and for the right of every person to absolute liberty, it is also a wonderfully graphic re-creation of the atmosphere and personality of a great city.

—James Harding

THE LOVE FOR THREE ORANGES [Lyubov'k tryom apel'sinam].

Composer: Sergei Prokofiev.

Librettist: Sergei Prokofiev (after Gozzi).

First Performance: Chicago, Auditorium Theater, 30 December 1921.

Roles: The Prince (tenor); Fata Morgana (soprano); Truffaldino (tenor); Leandro (baritone); King of Clubs (bass); Princess Clarissa (contralto); Pantalon (baritone); Celio (bass); Ninetta (soprano); Smeraldina (mezzo-soprano); Cleonte (bass); Linetta (contralto); Nicoletta (mezzo-soprano); Farfarello (bass); Master of Ceremonies (tenor); Herald (bass); Ten Reasonable Spectators (five tenors, five basses); chorus (SSAATTTTTBBBBBBB).

Publications

articles–

Mitchell, Donald. "Prokofiev's *Three Oranges:* a Note on its Musical-Dramatic Organization." *Tempo* 41 (1956): 20.
Henderson, Robert. "Busoni, Gozzi, Prokofiev, and the *Three Oranges.*" *Opera* May (1982).

Prokofiev picked the subject for his second mature opera while still at work on *The Gambler.* In the artistic ferment of revolutionary Russia, the controversial theater director Vsevolod Meyerhold found a kindred spirit in the eighteenth-century Italian playwright Carlo Gozzi. Gozzi's concept of "abstract" theater owed a considerable debt to the improvisatory and stylized traditions of *commedia dell'arte.* Among advanced circles, Gozzi's *The Love for Three Oranges* was sufficiently well known to be adopted as the title of an avant-garde magazine: it would have been familiar to the composer

even before Meyerhold recommended it as ideal opera material.

The starting point of its central fairy-tale is the melancholia of a young prince, son of the King of Clubs. He will be cured, if only he can be made to laugh. Two wicked conspirators, the Prime Minister Leandro and the king's niece Clarissa, set out to ensure that he never recovers. The jester Truffaldino is summoned to organize festivities to amuse the prince, but all his efforts fail until Fata Morgana, Leandro's witch-protectress who is present in disguise, totters over in undignified fashion. Enraged by the prince's hysterical laughter, she curses him with a consuming love for three oranges which he must pursue to the ends of the earth. After various adventures, the oranges are successfully retrieved from under the nose of sorceress Creonta's enormous cook (amusingly cast as a *basso profondo*). One of the oranges contains the Princess Ninetta, with whom the Prince falls in love and eventually marries. There are hazards still to be overcome (Ninetta, for example, is promptly turned into a rat) but all complications are resolved in the end. In addition to the real personages of the story, we are privy to a world of magic: the ineffectual Celio (Tchelio), sorcerer to the king, set against a number of obstructive demons. A third ingredient, a sort of disparaging commentary, is provided by the chorus. Its various pressure-groups comment, criticize and disrupt—"a critical 'conscience' for composer and audience," suggests Donald Mitchell (*Tempo,* Autumn 1956).

The conceit of a play within a play whose spectators interfere with the inner action whenever so disposed had obvious appeal for Prokofiev. He could suggest serious morals without explicitly committing himself, and make fun of them (and anything else) at the same time. While the score abounds with his usual sly turns of wit and deceptive harmonic quirks, the scheme does have its disadvantages. The emphasis on dramatic *non sequitur* and the slender opportunities for characterization impose heavy demands on purely musical invention. With everyone singing in much the same idiom and differences between the fabulous and the earthy effectively ironed out, there can be little contrast of light and shade. At his best, notably in act III, where his heroine *and* his lyrical powers put in a belated appearance, Prokofiev manages to avoid the barren patches. The text maintains a farcical tone throughout, and the humor *is* sometimes a trifle unsubtle, as when the bass trombone produces a not unrealistic fart on behalf of the fanfaring stage trumpeter.

For Israel Nestyev, Prokofiev's Soviet biographer, *The Love for Three Oranges* is "a work of limited appeal" that offers further evidence of nihilism in its "rejection of the principles of classical operatic form." The opera may not be a flawless masterpiece; yet the structural problems which remain unsolved were created by the composer's scarcely unprecedented attempt to devise a dramatic form appropriate to the subject matter. He closely follows the text and spirit of Gozzi's play, and the result is a kaleidoscopic theatrical extravaganza rather than convincing drama or even conventional comedy. Some very familiar music accompanies the many dances, processions, and pantomimes: Prokofiev drew upon these sections for his orchestral suite of 1924, which includes the celebrated *March.* Most of what is sung, in his typical declamatory style, is too closely allied to the stage action (and to individual sight-gags) to survive outside the theater. As for hidden meanings, Prokofiev himself was insistent: "All I tried to do was write an amusing opera." It succeeds best if translated into the language of the audience and played very much for laughs.

Like most of Prokofiev's operas, *The Love for Three Oranges* had a lengthy gestation period, and it was not until

The Love for Three Oranges, English National Opera, London, 1990 (with, from left to right, Donald Maxwell as Leander, Fiona Kimm as Smeraldina and Anne Collins as Princess Clarissa)

after the success of his concerts in Chicago in December 1918 that Prokofiev returned to the project, prompted by an offer of production from Chicago Opera. Despite unseemly postponements and wrangles over financial compensation, the work finally reached the stage in December 1921. That initial Chicago production was followed by stagings worldwide: at New York (1922), Cologne (1925), Berlin (1926) and Leningrad (1927). And although the work was not introduced to British audiences until the Edinburgh Festival of 1962 (courtesy of Belgrade Opera), it has since been given at Sadler's Wells Theatre (1963), in a BBC television production, at Glyndebourne (1982), and (most sensationally) in the Richard Jones production, originally staged by Opera North in 1988, which grafted on a further level of audience participation through the use of "scratch-and-sniff" cards impregnated with "microfragrances"!

— David Gutman

THE LOVE OF THREE KINGS
See L'AMORE DEI TRE RE

THE LOWLANDS
See TIEFLAND

LUBIN, Germaine.

Soprano. Born 1 February 1890, in Paris. Died 27 October 1979, in Paris. Studied at the Paris Conservatory, 1909-12, and with F. Litvinne and Lilli Lehmann; debut as Antonia in *Les Contes d'Hoffmann,* Paris, Opéra-Comique, 1912; joined Paris Opéra, 1914, and remained on its roster until 1944; appeared at Covent Garden, 1937, 1939; appeared at Bayreuth in 1938, the first French singer to do so; became well known for her Wagnerian roles.

Publications

About LUBIN: books–

Casanov, N. *Isolde 39—Germaine Lubin* [with discography]. Paris, 1974.

articles–

Barnes, H. "Germaine Lubin Discography." *Recorded Sound* 19 (1965): 367.
Schauensee, M. de. "Lubin Revisited." *Opera News* 30/no. 12 (1966): 27.

*   *   *

Germaine Lubin is considered to be one of only a small handful of great twentieth-century French sopranos, preceded by Emma Calvé and followed only by Régine Crespin in terms of international reputation. Lubin was an exceptional stylist, a singer who was able to transcend the limits of French vocalism to excel in all repertoires. Her glory was the music of Wagner; although her recorded excerpts of his music are sung in French they are sung with beautiful, rounded, Italianate tone. Lubin possessed one of the greatest of all qualities for a singer, an immediately recognizable timbre. It is a sound of great clarity, power and warmth. Unlike some later Wagnerians, she does not chip away at the upward-sweeping phrases in "Dich, teure Halle" from *Tannhäuser,* for example, but always connects with a true legato. Indeed, she may actually be faulted for excessive use of portamento. Her "Ewig war ich" from *Siegfried* is marred by this tendency. Her Immolation Scene from *Götterdämmerung,* although impassioned and noble, also suffers from a surfeit of sliding from note to note.

Yet what a glorious sound it is. Lauritz Melchior sang *Parsifal* with her in Paris in 1937 and was then responsible for her appearances in Wagnerian roles in Berlin. There she relearned roles such as Sieglinde, Kundry, and Strauss' Ariadne in German. There followed several illustrious seasons at Bayreuth, where she became a favorite of various high-ranking Nazis, including Hitler. Like Flagstad, Lubin had begun in light roles, in her case at the Opéra-Comique with Antonia in *Les contes d'Hoffmann,* later moving to the Opéra with the role of Marguérite in *Faust.* When the Opéra began allowing performances of Wagner again in 1921 she undertook the "blond Wagnerian" roles of Elsa *(Lohengrin)* and Eva *(Die Meistersinger).* During these years she became associated with a number of illustrious names: she studied with Félia Litvinne to improve her acting ability; went for a number of summers to Salzburg to study roles with Lilli Lehmann, among them Donna Anna; sought out Marie Gutheil-Schoder, the first Oktavian in *Der Rosenkavalier,* to teach her the part; and began performing in Vienna where she became close to Strauss and von Hofmannsthal. She performed the title role in *Ariadne auf Naxos* under Strauss's baton, but she rejected Salome on religious grounds.

Although it is primarily as a Wagnerian that Lubin is remembered and prized today, she was extremely versatile and sang a vast number of roles, even creating a number of them. Some of the standard roles she sang include Juliette, Thaïs, Aida, Tosca, Isolde, Elektra, Leonore *(Fidelio),* Elisabeth, Kundry, and the Brünnhildes. Among the novelties were Fauré's Pénélope (as head of the Conservatoire when Lubin was a student there, he had personally taught her his songs), the role of Nicéa in d'Indy's *La légende de Saint Christophe,* Koethe in Ropartz's *Le pays;* Léonore in d'Indy's *Le chant de la cloche;* L'Impératrice Charlotte in Milhaud's *Maximilian;* Gina in *La chartreuse de Parma;* Salammbô in Reyer's opera; Monna Vanna in Février's setting; and Fausta in Massenet's *Roma.* Special mention should be made of the aria "Salut, splendeurs" from Reyer's *Sigurd;* this bit of "Wagnerisme" is arguably Lubin's best recording. In it she displays a richness of tone that reminds one of Rosa Ponselle. Certainly Lubin's singing in this aria may be characterized as effortless and supremely thrilling, as is the best of her Wagnerian singing.

Lubin was France's most significant operatic export of her time, but she was unfortunate in a number of respects. She made a career during the same period as Flagstad and Leider and to a certain extent was unfairly overshadowed by them. Hers was an overwhelming voice, what Rupert Christiansen has called "a lighthouse of a voice," if less engulfing than Flagstad's and more steely than Leider's. The closest comparison is to one of her contemporaries, Dame Eva Turner. Although not a Brünnhilde or Isolde, Dame Eva had a commanding, exhilarating voice and delivery. Hearing Lubin and Turner today on compact disc, one feels that both voices needed a lot of space to make the best effect and that perhaps recordings do neither of them full justice. Yet how fortunate we are to have evidence of Lubin's effortlessly supreme Wagnerian singing. Unappreciated and reviled in her own country for alleged collaboration for singing at the Paris Opéra during the German Occupation, condemned to "national degradation," allowed neither to sing nor leave the country for five years after the war, she is sorely needed today and would be welcomed as a vocal treasure.

—Stephen Willier

LUCIA DI LAMMERMOOR.

Composer: Gaetano Donizetti.

Librettist: S. Cammarano (after Sir Walter Scott, *The Bride of Lammermoor*).

First Performance: Naples, San Carlo, 26 September 1835; revised 1839.

Roles: Lucia (soprano); Edgardo (tenor); Enrico Ashton (baritone); Alisa (mezzo-soprano); Normanno (tenor); Arturo Bucklaw (tenor); Raimondo Bidebent (bass); chorus (SSTTBB).

Publications

books–

Baccaro, M. *"Lucia di Lammermoor" prima al S. Carlo di Napoli.* Naples, 1948.
Bleiler, H. *Lucia di Lammermoor by Gaetano Donizetti.* New York, 1972.

articles–

Barbiera, R. "Chi ispirò la 'Lucia'." In *Vite ardenti nel teatro (1700-1900).* Milan, 1930.
Gazzaniga, Arrigo. "Un intervallo nelle ultime scene di *Lucia.*" *Nuova rivista musicale italiana* 13 (1979): 620.
Black, John N. "Notes for the staging of *Lucia di Lammermoor.*" *Journal of the Donizetti Society* 4 (1980).
Avant-scène opéra September 1983 [*Lucia di Lammermoor* issue].

Ashbrook, William. "Popular Success, the Critics and Fame: the Early Careers of *Lucia di Lammermoor* and *Belisario*." *Cambridge Opera Journal* 2 (1990): 65.

*   *   *

Lucia di Lammermoor demonstrates how listening habits were changing in the Italy of the 1830s. Audiences who once only paid attention to choice plums in the score, who moved into their seats to hear a big aria by this or that *prima donna* and then went out again to chat or eat ices leaving the *hoi polloi* to the recitatives and the *comprimari,* now, it seems, could sit through a whole act with a musical logic intact from start to finish. In this unflinchingly romantic opera Donizetti held to a consistent orchestral coloring from the prologue onwards, with the sometimes athletic vocal line only underlining the mood, never fighting against it, as had been the norm.

Lucia di Lammermoor is set at Ravenswood Castle, whose true owners have been ousted by the Ashton family. The sole remaining heir of the former, Edgar (Edgardo), has, however, fallen in love with Lucy Ashton (Lucia) to the dismay of her brother Henry (Enrico), who wishes her to make a political marriage to boost his fortunes. He forges a letter from Edgardo, persuading the deceived Lucia into a reluctant marriage with Arthur Bucklaw (Arturo). At the marriage ceremony, Edgardo bursts into the castle, cursing Lucia for her faithlessness. During the celebrations which follow, however, Lucia emerges from the bridal chamber drenched in blood. She has stabbed Arturo and before the horrified guests enacts the wedding with Edgardo which should have taken place, singing crazily of love, ghosts, altars, and marital bliss, at the end of which she collapses. Edgardo, who has been bitterly watching the illuminated castle, is told of Lucia's death and falls on his sword in order to join her in heaven.

A few unconventional twists of plot notwithstanding, *Lucia di Lammermoor* cannot really be considered a radical score. It thrives on its stream of celestial melodies and on the passionate conviction which suffuses the tragic tale. At the first performance the great opera house in Naples resounded with sobs and tears; never before had Donizetti managed to encapsulate despair so fervently and with an ecstatic coloring surpassing mere charm. Various of the pieces were immediately enrolled in the musical pantheon, including the celebrated sextet "Chi mi frena in tal momento," Lucia's mad scene, and Edgardo's elegiac "Tu che a Dio spiegasti l'ali," its dying reprise given to the cello, which replaces the expiring hero's voice with an echo of his lament.

The score is a puzzle. The composer's autograph shows that he wrote it for singers very different from those who actually sang at the premiere. *Lucia* took quite a long time to come to the stage, and in the interim Donizetti got a different roster of artists. Even the instrumentation presents some problems unanswerable today. Did Donizetti really intend the heroine's mad scene to be accompanied by a glass harmonica? How could anyone have heard it beyond the first rows of stalls? No one really knows who wrote the celebrated cadenza for flute in the mad scene which urges her higher and higher, matching her note for note. It is not in the original score, though Donizetti would certainly have expected the soprano to interpolate a cadenza of her own. Even more astonishingly, the composer sanctioned alternatives in the choice of arias which, on the surface at least, diminish the effect of this fabled score. One of these arias he later incorporated in a French version of the opera (1839). To be precise,

he allowed Fanny Tacchinardi-Persiani, who was the first Lucia, to replace her magical "Regnava nel silenzio" with the all-purpose "Perchè non ho del vento," an *aria di sortita* she had sung in *Rosmonda d'Inghilterra* (1834).

—Alexander Weatherson

LUCIO SILLA.

Composer: Wolfgang Amadeus Mozart.

Librettist: Giovanni de Gamerra.

First Performance: Milan, Teatro Regio Ducal, 26 December 1772.

Roles: Lucio Silla (tenor); Giunia (soprano); Cecilio (soprano); Cinna (soprano); Celia (soprano); Aufidio (tenor); chorus (SATB).

*   *   *

The considerable success of Mozart's first *opera seria, Mitridate* (Köchel 87), written for Milan in 1770, led on the spot to a second commission for an opera to be presented two years later. The result was *Lucio Silla* (K. 135), an even greater success that ran, after a disastrous premiere, for twenty-six performances. A comparison between these two works shows how quick and dramatic was Mozart's musical growth through his teens.

As was his custom, Mozart tailor-made his music for the Milanese singers. Two of his favorites, Anna de Amicis and Venanzio Rauzzini, were cast in the principal roles, and they did have the best music in the opera. There were some problems with the cast, the most serious being the illness of the tenor who was to sing the title role. The last minute substitute was an inexperienced church singer, whose histrionic and singing abilities were clearly limited. The two of the four pieces for Bassano Morgnoni that Mozart did set show his skill in casting music appropriate to an artist of limited ability without loss in musical substance or any condescension to the singer. This skill is apparent in the trio that concludes act II. While the two leads sing parts that match their abilities, which included not only brilliance but, particularly in Rauzzini's case, a lovely line, the part for Morgnoni remains within a limited vocal range.

It is true that in *Lucio Silla,* as in *Mitridate,* characterization is limited, but it is by no means entirely lacking. Rauzzini's last act cavatina in A major shows identification with Mozart's famous pieces in that key. This is even more dramatically apparent in de Amicis' final scena in C minor (the only piece in this opera set in a minor key).

Even though *Lucio Silla* contains several modified da capo arias, the numbers in alternating slow-fast tempi are more subtly handled than in *Mitridate.* The accompanied recitatives are musically exciting and contain a wealth of telling instrumental effects.

The plot of *Lucio Silla* is simple, and Giovanni de Gamerra has been criticized for producing an inferior libretto. There is some evidence that Metastasio interpolated one scene. Silla, dictator of Rome, has spread the rumor that the banished senator, Cecilio, has died. By this ruse, he hopes to get Cecilio's wife, Giunia, to marry him. Cecilio, who returns to Rome and reveals to his surprised wife that he really is alive, resolves to kill Silla. He is, however, arrested and jailed. His friend Cinna persuades Celia, Silla's sister, to whom Cinna is betrothed, to intercede on Cecilio's behalf. Silla forgives all (rather surprisingly) and the lovers and spouses are reunited. The people praise Silla for his magnanimity.

The glory of this opera is its accompanied recitatives. In *Mitridate* Mozart had already shown delight in setting these portions of text, but in *Lucio Silla* we find more continuous and dramatic unity. Act I closes with a long episode set in the underground tomb of Roman heroes. A short instrumental prelude, which begins in B flat, plunges swiftly into A minor and is followed by an extended recitative in which Cecilio muses on the transitoriness of worldly glory. The music is marked by dark modulations. When Cecilio sees his wife, the quick current of emotion is revealed in musical sobs, resolved when Cecilio decides to hide. The music cannot make up its mind whether to stay in C major or move to C minor: it dissolves into E flat, which introduces a magnificent chorus in the Gluckian manner as the crowd calls on the spirits of the dead heroes. This moves without break (a technique brought to mastery in *Idomeneo*) into a short G-minor *molto adagio* for Giunia, who invokes the spirit of her father. The scene concludes with a chorus. This is but one example of Mozart's sense of drama throughout an entire episode. It is this scene which William Mann in his definitive book on Mozart's operas describes as "the finest music Mozart had yet composed," a verdict with which it is hard to argue.

No less astounding is Giunia's last scena. Believing her husband dead, she goes through the emotions of despair in the recitative. She thinks she hears her husband's spirit calling her. In thirds the flutes, with violas an octave lower, suggest his spirit while the violins accompany pizzicato. It is a breathless, beautiful moment, and it is followed shortly after by the finest aria in the opera, which is a large-scale but dramatically tight piece in C minor that jumps forward in time to the Mozart of the mature piano concertos, specifically the slow movement of K. 467 and the opening movement of K. 466. The opera ends much more satisfactorily than *Mitridate*, with a chorus in the home key of D major, with interpolations from the leading singers.

In *Lucio Silla* there are perhaps too many arias that march along in common time, and, for modern ears, there are too few ensembles. But this is a "Roman" opera, which calls for and gets splendid music (the strings are joined by a handsome band of flutes, oboes, bassoons, horns, trumpets, and drums). In *Lucio Silla* Mozart is growing more confident in his powers, and altogether more authoritative. Performances of the work may remain rare, for it requires at least three singers of great range, virtuosity, and character, which de Amicis and Rauzzini clearly possessed.

—Lawrence J. Dennis

THE LUCKY HAND
See DIE GLÜCKLICHE HAND

LUCREZIA BORGIA.

Composer: Gaetano Donizetti.

Librettist: Felice Romani (after Hugo).

First Performance: Milan, Teatro alla Scala, 26 December 1833.

Roles: Lucrezia Borgia (soprano); Alfonso d'Este (bass); Gennaro (tenor); Maffio Orsini (contralto); Jeppo Liverotto (tenor); Don Apostolo Gazella (bass); Ascanio Petrucci (bass); Oloferno Vitellozzo (tenor); Gubetta (bass); Rustighello (tenor); Astolfo (bass); chorus (SATB).

Publications

article—

Guaricci, J. "Lucrezia Borgia." *Journal of the Donizetti Society* 2 (1975): 161.

Even in Italy Lucrezia Borgia was a scandalous subject. In choosing it for an opera Donizetti was looking for change, even confrontation. From the start it was clear that the composer was planning a *coup,* dusting off the accepted routines of a score in numbers in favor of speed, a vast cast, a romantic gallimaufry of poisonings and *grand-guignol.* There was to be no love interest as such; Lucrezia was an anti-heroine, a thoroughly disreputable virago, the precursor of a whole succession of barnstorming Verdian sopranos whose violence and vehemence would be expressed with the same kind of energy, the same kind of leaping vocal lines.

The opera's layout was novel, a *prologo*—a flashback of sorts—followed by two acts set in Ferrara. There was to be only one concerted *finale,* and that was to the prologue. Both acts were to end with a vocal stint mostly on the part of the *prima donna.* It was to be a bold opera, fit to bring instant fame, had not all sorts of obstacles arisen (censorship, singers' protests, complaints from the Borgia descendents and a lawsuit from Victor Hugo amongst them). The *prologo* is set in Venice; a young soldier, Gennaro, sleeping peacefully in a doorway, awakes to find a splendidly-dressed woman bending over him. Astonished, he pours out his troubles, his unknown parentage, his unhappy upbringing, but when his friends return they begin insulting the lady. Gennaro is amazed: who is it, he asks? It's *La Borgia* they say, and snatch off her mask. Gennaro stares in fascinated bewilderment.

In Ferrara, the Duke (who has secretly witnessed his wife's encounter with the young man), determines to punish her "infidelity." When she comes to complain that her coat of arms has been desecrated (BORGIA has been altered to read ORGIA), he agrees that the culprit should be punished, but then triumphantly leads in Gennaro, who admits his guilt.

The Duchess is shaken. She pleads for Gennaro's release, but when this proves unsuccessful she threatens Alfonso, who remains unmoved and obliges her to administer a cup of poisoned wine to the witless youth. As soon as the Duke's back is turned, however, Lucrezia forces Gennaro to swallow an antidote and pushes him out through a secret panel. That evening there is a party at the Princess Negroni's palace. Gennaro's friends carouse joyfully, not much disturbed by the singing of a *miserere* in a nearby chapel. But when they try to leave they find the room locked, one door opening to

Lucrezia Borgia, with Joan Sutherland as Lucrezia, Stafford Dean as Alfonso d'Este and Alfredo Kraus as Gennaro, Royal Opera, London, 1980

admit the Duchess Lucrezia who has poisoned their wine in return for their insults in Venice. To her horror Gennaro is amongst them. This time he refuses to drink the antidote and attempts to stab her. In desperation she reveals that she is the mother he has so longed to find, and in agony Gennaro dies in her arms. At her cries Alfonso and all the courtiers rush in as Lucrezia, in a final elegy of despair and self-reproach, falls in extremis on the body of the son.

For this regrettable travesty of history (the real Lucrezia—whatever her despised dynasty—was noted for her piety), the composer supplied a stream of compelling music. Never before had he achieved quite such a momentum, nor such supreme flexibility. The superb trio which ends act I is a miracle of inventive variety, blending *cantilena* with *arioso,* declamation and vivid exchanges which look forward to Verdi and even beyond. It had everything that would focus Italian opera to come—a whispered colloquy *à la Macbeth,* innocence, insolence, insinuation, treachery, arrogance, heartbreak, and a devastating *stretta* which brought audiences to their feet. Perhaps most astonishingly, the opera preserved the expected contours perfectly intact. Certain of the *arie* became celebrated; Orsini's *brindisi* "Il segreto per esser felici" soon became staple diet for booming contraltos, with the ironical *miserere* that bisects it presaging *Il trovatore.*

As an operatic monster, this impure Lucrezia succeeded in capping the maternal anguish of Norma. Like Norma, she provided a vocal storehouse for several generations of great sopranos, most notably for Giulia Grisi and Thérèse Tietjens, both of whom made it the role for their final appearance on

the stage, the latter making her final collapse on the body of her son her own final collapse.

There have been disputes about the florid ending to this opera. Donizetti himself, true perhaps to the radical intentions behind the whole score, tried to dispense with the *cabaletta finale* and in 1840 supplied a new finale to replace it in which the curtain falls directly after Gennaro's death. But this, though theatrically viable, is an anti-climax, and *Lucrezia Borgia* has never thrived with this revised ending.

—Alexander Weatherson

LUDWIG, Christa.

Mezzo-soprano and soprano. Married: 1) baritone Walter Berry, 1957 (divorced 1970; one son); 2) actor and stage director Paul-Emile Deiber, 1972. Studied with her mother, Eugenia Besalla, and with Hüni-Mihaĉek in Frankfurt; debut as Orlovsky in *Die Fledermaus,* Frankfurt, 1946; in Salzburg from 1954; member of Vienna Staatsoper from 1955; Metropolitan Opera debut as Cherubino, 1959; at Metropolitan Opera for ten seasons; appeared at Bayreuth, 1966-67; Covent Garden debut as Amneris, 1969; created Claire Zachanassian in *Der Besuch der alten Dame,* 1971; received the Golden

Ring, 1980; became honorary member of Vienna Staatsoper, 1981.

Publications

About LUDWIG: books–

Lorenz, P. *Christa Ludwig, Walter Berry.* Vienna, 1968.

articles–

Osborne, C. "Christa Ludwig." *Opera* March (1973).

*   *   *

Christa Ludwig arguably possesses the most prodigious natural talent of our time. In years to come her powerful, radiant voice will be mentioned alongside those of Kirsten Flagstad and Rosa Ponselle. With such extraordinary resources her reputation would have been assured as a vocalist—but for Ludwig, the sound is never an end in itself. She brings to all of her roles potent insights and imagination. Ludwig is no mere virtuosa but one of the consistently thrilling artists of our time.

The sovereign technique which allows Ludwig such mastery is the happy alliance of a beautiful instrument with fastidious training. Ludwig's only teacher was her mother, and she has often described the detailed process by which the two of them quite literally "built" her voice, note by note, upon the solid foundation of proper breath support. This meticulous preparation has paid handsome dividends. Ludwig's lustrous mezzo-soprano—from the deep contralto of her lower notes to the gleaming soprano top tones—is a seamless whole, absolutely integrated in color. Her legato line is rock solid, yet she can cope with florid music with a nimbleness and ease that today we expect only from lighter voices. Her thorough schooling has also paid off with career longevity; at present she is well over sixty years old, and she continues to perform some of the most rigorous roles in opera with a freshness that would honor a singer half her age.

Her vocal command has allowed Ludwig to explore successfully an astonishingly broad repertoire. Although we do not associate her with the coloratura roles of Rossini, she made her debut as Angelina in *La cenerentola* and also sang in *Il barbiere di Siviglia:* a recording of Rosina's "Una voce poco fa," extensively decorated, is not entirely idiomatic but more than compensates through the skill of her fioratura and the palpable charm of her personality. She was a memorable Carmen and has sung Verdi's Amneris (*Aida*) and Eboli (*Don Carlos*) with distinction. For several years she focused on soprano roles, performing Verdi's Lady Macbeth and Strauss's Ariadne, the Marschallin (*Der Rovenkavalier*) and the Dyer's Wife. She even ventured—in concert—the Immolation Scene from *Götterdämmerung,* though Ludwig abandoned plans to sing Brünnhilde on the stage and decided to return to the mezzo-soprano repertoire. The choice was probably a wise one, but on records at least the higher roles appear completely comfortable for her—unlike so many mezzos who attempt this transition, Ludwig sounds like a real soprano. Also unlike many others, she managed the return to her original repertoire unscathed. Among Ludwig's excursions into the soprano repertoire there has been at least one major contribution: on records and in the theater she was the greatest Leonore in *Fidelio* of our time.

Ludwig's central recorded repertoire includes Octavian in *Der Rosenkavalier,* Dorabella in *Così fan tutte,* and in the mezzo soprano roles of Wagner, in which she has few if any equals. As Octavian, Ludwig is able to vividly characterize the boy's youthful brashness, yet at the same time her voice remains rich and vibrant, coping easily with the high tessitura and dense Strauss orchestration. She recorded Dorabella twice. In her early performance for Decca the singing is poised but a trifle anonymous, not yet the detailed reading it was to become. By her second recording for EMI, Ludwig is superbly humorous and feminine, marvelously knowing yet innocent. Her Fiordiligi here is the incomparable Schwarzkopf, and no two singers on records work together with more aplomb—the silvery sheen of Schwarzkopf's soprano is the perfect complement to Ludwig's warmer mezzo, and for once the two really do seem like sisters. It is no wonder that this pairing was, for several seasons, one of the glories of the Salzburg festival.

In the major Wagner roles—Kundry, Ortrud, Venus, Brangäne, and Fricka and Waltraute in *Der Ring des Nibelungen*—Ludwig was equally if differently impressive. Here the demands are less for personal charm than unflagging reserves of power, and the magisterial solidity of Ludwig's tone and the glow of her upper register are peerless. In this music we recognize that she is the fitting successor to the great Margaret Matzenauer. No doubt generations to come will wonder who is the fitting successor to the great Christa Ludwig.

—David Anthony Fox

LUISA MILLER.

Composer: Giuseppe Verdi.

Librettist: Salvadore Cammarano (after Schiller, *Kabale und Liebe*).

First Performance: Naples, San Carlo, 8 December 1849.

Roles: Luisa (soprano); Rodolfo (tenor); Miller (baritone); Count Walther (bass); Wurm (bass); Federica (contralto); Laura (mezzo-soprano); A Peasant (tenor); chorus (SSTTBB).

*   *   *

Luisa Miller has long been considered the all-important gateway to middle Verdi, especially in the intimacy of expression employed by the composer in the opera's third act. It represents the second time that Verdi conscientiously tried to come to grips with a drama by Schiller. The first, *I masnadieri* of 1847 (based on *Die Räuber*) was hampered by a text which, while relatively faithful to its parent play, was written by an intellectual friend who for all his scholarly accomplishments was a theatrical amateur. With his new work Verdi had learned better than to repeat that mistake, and instead collaborated with the most respected and established professional librettist in Italy, Salvatore Cammarano.

Kabale und Liebe (Intrigue and Love) is a play of social consciousness, pitting an innocent lower-middle-class girl against the evil machinations of a basically corrupt upper-crust society. While it is true that Cammarano was almost too slick for his own good when he ruthlessly cut out characters and scenes which either did not lend themselves to the

The title page of Verdi's *Luisa Miller,* piano-vocal score, c. 1849

standard dos and don'ts (the "Convenienze") of mid-century Italian opera or would have trouble getting past the censorship, still he presented Verdi with a text which elicited the most poetic and intimate music yet to issue from the composer's pen: a vital landmark on the road to the bourgeois apotheosis of *La traviata.* Indeed the correspondence between musician and poet as *Luisa Miller* was thrashed out of *Kabale und Liebe* makes fascinating reading for the insights it sheds on the artistic process.

In a Tyrolean village in the early seventeenth century lives a retired soldier named Miller and his only child, a daughter named Luisa. She has fallen in love, and her love is returned by a young man whom she knows as "Carlo" but who is actually Rodolfo, son of the local aristocrat Count Walther, who lives in the castle on the hill. Walther's steward, Wurm, also desires Luisa and threatens revenge when Miller refuses her hand to him. Meanwhile Count Walther, anxious to break up his son's romance with a lower-class girl, insists that he instead marry Federica, Duchess of Ostheim. Rodolfo refuses and has gone to Miller's cottage to claim Luisa when his father storms in with a group of soldiers. The count accuses Luisa of being a whore and is about to have both Millers thrown into prison when his son compels him to retreat by threatening to reveal to the world his father's guilty secret; namely, that he and Wurm had murdered the previous count in order to secure the succession.

In act II, however, Miller has been arrested after all and is threatened by torture and death. Wurm comes to Luisa, and as price for her father's life he forces her to write a letter of "confession," which he dictates. The letter states that she desires Wurm rather than Rodolfo, whom she pretended to love merely for the sake of his fortune. When the heartbroken

Rodolfo reads the false letter, he threatens Wurm with a duel, which the latter manages to evade. In the final act we return to the Miller cottage. Luisa is contemplating suicide, but her father's pleading causes her to relent, and the two of them decide to leave the village forever in the morning, even if they must become beggars. When Miller retires for the night, Rodolfo appears and secretly pours poison into a glass of wine which he forces Luisa to share with him. Told by Rodolfo that she soon will die, Luisa is freed from her unholy vow to Wurm and reveals the terms of his fatal bargain, to the despair of Rodolfo. The girl dies in her lover's arms as her hapless father looks on. Wurm, Count Walther and the villagers rush in to witness as Rodolfo, with his dying breath, stabs Wurm to the heart, leaving both fathers alone with their grief.

The loving father-daughter relationship and its centrality to Verdi's output (*Rigoletto, Simon Boccanegra, Aida,* etc.) has long been a topic of comment, as has, to a slightly lesser degree, that of father-son animosity (*Vêpres siciliennes, Don Carlos*). However, only in *Luisa Miller* do both themes appear in the same work, and indeed in many ways the polarity between the two fathers is one of the greatest strengths of this piece. It also has a well deserved reputation as a tenor's opera, inasmuch as Rodolfo's role takes extraordinary vocal stamina for its low-lying stentorian passages, yet must dominate equally in the many lyric moments, most particularly the famous aria "Quando le sere al placido" in act II. Luisa for her part must negotiate some awkward shifts from Bellini-esque ingenue in act I through typical early Verdian heroine with grandiose aria and cabaletta in act II on to the bona fide suffering and three-dimensionally characterized girl of the magnificent final act. Attention should also be drawn to the overture, arguably Verdi's finest structural achievement in that form. Amazingly, it is couched as a monothematic sonata movement, a format it shares with that which Mozart wrote for *Così fan tutte* but is otherwise quite rare in the operatic literature.

—Dennis Wakeling

LULLY, Jean-Baptiste (born Giovanni Battista Lulli).

Composer. Born 28 November 1632, in Florence. Died 22 March 1687, in Paris. Married: Madeleine Lambert, daughter of the musician Michael Lambert, 1662. Studied the elements of music with a Franciscan monk; taken by the Chevalier de Guise to Paris to become page to Mlle de Montpensier, 1646; position in the private band of Mlle de Montpensier; in the service of Louis XIV as a ballet dancer and composer, 1652; studied harpsichord and composition with Nicolas Métru, organist of St Nicholas-des-Champs, and François Roberday, organist at the Eglise des Petits-Pères; member of "les 24 violons du roi"; organized "les petits violons"; composer to the king, 1653; Surintendant de la Musique, 1661; composed music for comic ballets by Molière, 1663-71; acquired control of the Académie Royale de Musique, 1672; composed French operas from 1672, primarily with the librettist Quinault.

Operas

Editions:

Les chefs d'oeuvres classiques de l'opéra français. Edited by J.B. Weckerlin et al. Paris, 1878-83.

Jean-Baptiste Lully

J.B. Lully: Oeuvres complètes. Edited by H. Prunières. Paris, 1930-39; *Motets, iii,* edited by H. Prunières, revised by M. Sanvoisin, New York, 1972.

Les fêtes de l'Amour et de Bacchus (pastorale-pastiche), Philippe Quinault, Molière and Lully, Paris, Jeu de paume de Béquet, 15? November 1672.
Cadmus et Hermione, Philippe Quinault (after Ovid, *Metamorphoses*), Paris, Jeu de paume de Béquet, 27 April 1673.
Alceste, ou Le triomphe d'Alcide, Philippe Quinault (after Euripides, *Alcestis*), Paris, Opéra, 19 January 1674.
Thésée, Philippe Quinault (after Ovid, *Metamorphoses*), Saint-Germain, 11 January 1675.
Atys, Philippe Quinault (after Ovid, *Fasti*), Saint-Germain, 10 January 1676.
Isis, Philippe Quinault (after Ovid, *Metamorphoses*), Saint-Germain, 5 January 1677.
Psyché, Thomas Corneille (after Apuleius, *The Golden Ass*), Paris, Opéra, 19 April 1678.
Bellérophon, Thomas Corneille and Bernard le Bovier de Fontenelle (after Hesiod, *Theogeny*), Paris, Opéra, 31 January 1679.
Proserpine, Philippe Quinault (after Ovid, *Metamorphoses*), Saint-Germain, 3 February 1680.
Persée, Philippe Quinault (after Ovid, *Metamorphoses*), Paris, Opéra, 17 or 18 April 1682.
Phaëton, Philippe Quinault (after Ovid, *Metamorphoses*), Versailles, 6 January 1683.
Amadis, Philippe Quinault (after Montalvo, adapted by Herberay des Essarts, *Amadis de Gaule*), Paris, Opéra, 18 January 1684.
Roland, Philippe Quinault, Versailles, 18 January 1685.
Armide, Philippe Quinault (after Tasso, *Gerusalemme liberata*), Paris, Opéra, 15 February 1686.
Acis et Galatée (pastorale héroïque), Jean Galbert de Campistron (after Ovid, *Metamorphoses*), Anet, 6 September 1686; Paris.
Achille et Polyxène, Jean Galbert de Campistron (after Homer, *Iliad*), Paris, Opéra, 7 November 1687.

Other works: ballets, motets, instrumental works.

Publications/Writings

About LULLY: books–

Pure, M. de. *Idée des spectacles anciens et nouveaux.* Paris, 1668; 1972.
Guichard, H. *Requête servant de factums contre B. Lully.* Paris, 1673, 1675.
Perrault, C. *Critique de l'opéra, ou Examen de la tragédie intitulée "Alceste ou Le triomphe d'Alcide".* Paris, 1674.
Recueil général des opéras. Paris, 1703-46; 1971.
Le Cerf de la Viéville, J.L. *Comparaison de la musique italienne et de la musique françoise.* Brussels, 1704-06, 1972.
Titon du Tillet, E. *Le Parnasse françois.* Paris, 1732-43; 1971.
Durey de Noinville, J.-B. *Histoire du théâtre de l'Académie royale de musique en France.* Paris, 1757; 1969.
Le Prévost, d'Exmes. *Lulli musicien.* Paris, 1779.
Winterfeld, C. von. *"Alceste" von Lully, Händel, und Gluck.* Berlin, 1851.
Lajarte, T. *Lully.* Paris, 1878.
Pougin, A. *J.B. Lully.* Paris, 1883.
Nuitter, C. and E. Thoinan. *Les origines de l'opéra français.* Paris, 1886, 1977.
Radet, E. *Lully homme d'affaires, propriétaire et musicien.* Paris, 1891.

Prunières, Henri. *Lully.* Paris, 1909; 2nd ed., 1927.
La Laurencie, Lionel de. *Lully.* Paris, 1911; 2nd ed., 1919; 1977.
Gérold, T. *L'art du chant en France au XVIIe siècle.* Strasbourg, 1921; 1971.
La Laurencie, Lionel de. *Les créatures de l'opéra français.* Paris, 1921; 2nd ed., 1930.
Gros, E. *Philippe Quinault.* Paris, 1926.
Prunières, Henri. *La vie illustre et libertine de Jean Baptiste Lully.* Paris, 1929.
Campistron, Jean. *"Acis et Galatée": pastorale héroïque mise en musique par Lully, texte de livret de 1686.* Edited by Henri Prunières. Paris, 1933.
Mélèse, P. *Le théâtre et le public à Paris sous Louis XIV, 1659-1715.* Paris, 1934.
Borrel, Eugène. *Jean-Baptiste Lully: le cadre, la vie, la personnalité, le rayonnement, les oeuvres.* Paris, 1949.
Valensi, Théodore. *Louis XIV et Lully.* Nice, 1952.
Neumann, F.H. *Die Ästhetik des Rezitativs: zur Theorie des Rezitativs im 17. und 18. Jahrhundert.* Strasbourg, 1962.
Demuth, N. *French Opera: its Development to the Revolution.* Horsham, Sussex, 1963.
Anthony, James R. *French Baroque Music from Beaujoyeulx to Rameau.* London, 1973; 2nd ed., 1978.
Isherwood, R.M. *Music in the Service of the King: France in the Seventeenth Century.* Ithaca, New York, and London, 1973.
Newman, Joyce E. *Jean-Baptiste de Lully and his tragédies lyriques.* Ann Arbor, 1979.
Schneider, Herbert. *Die Rezeption der Oper Lullys im Frankreich des Ancien Régime.* Tutzing, 1982.
Heyer, John Hajdu, ed. *Jean-Baptiste Lully and the Music of the French Baroque: Essays in Honour of James R. Anthony.* Cambridge, 1989.
Fajon, R. *L'opéra à Paris du Roi-Soleil à Louis le Bien-aimé.* Geneva, 1984.
La Gorce, Jerome de, and Herbert Schneider. *Jean-Baptiste Lully, Actes du Colloque/Kongressbericht.* Laaber, 1990.

articles–

Lajarte, T. "Bellérophon de Lully." *Le ménestrel* 46 (1880): 153.
Pougin, A. "Les orgines de l'opéra français: Cambert et Lully." *Revue d'art dramatique* 21 (1891): 129.
Malherbe, C. "Un autographe de Lulli." *Le ménestrel* 1 (1898): 365.
Masson, P.-M. "Lullistes et Ramistes 1733-1752." *Année musicale* 1 (1911): 187.
Prunières, Henri. "Lettres et autographes de Lully." *Bulletin français de la Société Internationale de Musique* 8/no. 3(1912): 19.
Lote, G. "La déclamation du vers français à la fin du XVIIe siècle." *Revue de phonétique* 2 (1912): 313.
La Laurencie, Lionel de. "Une convention commerciale entre Lully, Quinault et Ballard en 1680." *Revue de musicologie* 2 (1920-21): 176.
Prunières, Henri. "Notes musicologiques sur un autographe musical de Lully." *La revue musicale* 10 (1928): 47.
Borrel, E. "L'interprétation de Lully d'après Rameau." *Revue de musicologie* 10 (1929): 17.
Torrefranca, F. "La prima opera francese in Italia?: L'Armida di Lulli, Roma 1690." In *Musikwissenschaftliche Beiträge: Festschrift für Johannes Wolf,* 191. Berlin, 1929.
Prunières, Henri. "La première tragédie en musique de Lully: Cadmus et Hermione." *La revue musicale* 11 (1930): 385.

Borrel, E. "L'interprétation de l'ancien récitatif français." *Revue de musicologie* 12 (1931): 13.

Grout, Donald J. "Seventeenth Century Parodies of French Opera." *Musical Quarterly* 27 (1941): 211, 514.

Mellers, Wilfrid. "Jean-Baptiste Lully." In *The Heritage of Music,* vol. 3, p. 32. Oxford, 1951.

Nagler, A.M. "Lully's Opernbühne." *Klein Schriften der Gesellschaft für Theatergeschichte* 17 (1960): 9.

Masson, C. "Journal du Marquis de Dangeau 1684-1720." *Recherches sur la musique française classique* 2 (1961-62): 193.

Maurice-Amour, L. "Comment Lully et ses poètes humanisent dieux et héros." *Cahiers de l'Association internationale des théâtres françaises* 17 (1965): 59.

Hibberd, L. "Mme de Sévigné and the Operas of Lully." In *Essays in Musicology: a Birthday Offering for Willi Apel,* 153. Bloomington, Indiana, 1968.

Isherwood, R.M. "The Centralization of Music in the Reign of Louis XIV." In *French Historical Studies* 6 (1969-70): 156.

Brossard, Y. de. "La vie musicale en France d'après Loret et ses continuateurs, 1650-1688." *Recherches sur la musique française classique* 10 (1970): 117.

Ducrot, A. "Lully créateur de troupe." *XVIIe siècle* 98-99 (1973): 91.

Dufourcq, A. "Les fêtes de Versailles: la musique." *XVIIe siècle* 98-99 (1973): 67.

———. "Lully: l'oeuvre, la diffusion, l'héritage." *XVIIe siècle* 98-99 (1973): 109.

Howard, Patricia. "Lully's Alceste." *Musical Times* 114 (1973): 21.

Mongrédien, G. "Molière et Lully." *XVIIe siècle* 98-99 (1973): 3.

Borowitz, A.I. "Lully and the Death of Cambert," *Music Review* 35 (1974): 231.

Seares, M. "Aspects of Performance Practice in the Recitatives of Jean-Baptiste Lully." *Studies in Music* [Australia] 8 (1974): 8.

Howard, Patricia. "The Académie Royale and the Performances of Lully's Operas." *The Consort* 31 (1975): 109.

Fajon, R. "Proposition pour une analyse rationalisée du récitatif de l'opéra lullyste." *Revue de musicologie* 64 (1978): 55.

Wolf, R.P. "Metrical Relationships in French Recitative of the Seventeenth and Eighteenth Centuries." *Recherches sur la musique française classique* 18 (1978): 29.

La Gorce, J. de. "L'opéra fraçaise à la cour de Louis XIV." Revue de la Société d'histoire du théâtre.

Muller, D. "Aspects de la déclamation dans le récitatif de Jean-Baptiste Lully." In *Basler Studien zur Interpretation der alten Musik,* edited by H. Oesch, vol. 2, p. 234. Winterhur, 1980.

Wood, C. "Orchestra and Spectacle in the *tragédie en musique,* 1673-1715: Oracle, *sommeil* and *tempête.*" *Proceedings of the Royal Musical Association* 108 (1981-82): 25.

Schneider, H. "Tragédie et tragédie en musique: querelles autour de l'autonomie d'un nouveau genre." *Komparatistische Hefte* nos. 5-6 (1982): 43.

Rosow, Lois. "French Baroque Recitative as an Expression of Tragic Declamation." *Early Music* 11 (1983): 468.

Turnbull, Michael. "The Metamorphosis of *Psyché.*" *Music and Letters* 64 (1983): 12.

Reckow, F. " 'Cacher l'Art par l'Art même': Jean-Baptiste Lullys 'Armide'—Monolog und die 'Kunst des Verbergens'." In *Analysen: Beiträge zu einer Problemgeschichte des komponierens: Festschrift für Hans Heinrich Eggebrecht zum 65. Geburtstag,* 128. Stuttgart, 1984.

Kintzler, C. "De la pastorale à la tragédie lyrique: quelques éléments d'un système poétique." *Revue de musicologie* 72 (1986): 67.

Palisca, C.V. "The Recitative of Lully's *Alceste:* French Declamation or Italian Melody?" *Actes de Baton Rouge, Biblio 17: Papers on Seventeenth-Century French Liturature* 25 (1986): 19.

Anthony, J.R. "Lully's Airs—French or Italian?" *Musical Times* 128 (1987): 126.

———. "The Musical Structure of Lully's Operatic Airs." In *Colloque Lully: Heidelberg and Saint-Germain-en-Laye 1987,* 65.

Avant-scène opéra January (1987) [*Atys* issue].

La revue musicale (1987) [*Lully Tricentenaire* (special volume)].

Schneider, H. "Strukturen der Szenen und Akte in Lullys Opern." In *Colloque Lully: Heidelberg and Saint-Germain-en-Laye 1987,* 77.

Rosow, Lois. "From Destouches to Berton: Editorial Responsibility at the Paris Opéra." *Journal of the American Musicological Society* 40 (1987): 285.

Brooks, W. "Lully and Quinault at Court and on the Public Stage, 1673-86." *Seventeenth-Century French Studies* no. 10 (1988): 101; supplementary note, no. 11 (1989): 147.

———. "Les monologues dans l'opéra de Lully." *XVIIe siècle* 40 (1988): 353.

Howard, Patricia. "Lully and the Ironic Convention." *Cambridge Opera Journal* 1 (1989): 139.

Massip, C. "Michel Lambert and Jean-Baptiste Lully: the Stakes of a Collaboration." In *Jean-Baptiste Lully and the Music of the French Baroque: Essays in Honor of James R. Anthony,* 25. Cambridge, 1989.

Rosow, Lois. "How Eighteenth-Century Parisians Heard Lully's Operas: the Case of *Armide's* Fourth Act." In *Jean-Baptiste Lully and the Music of the French Baroque: Essays in Honor of James R. Anthony,* 213. Cambridge, 1989.

———. "L'air dans la tragédie lyrique." *La tragédie lyrique,* edited by P. Van Dieren, 119. Paris, 1991.

Rosow, Lois. "Making Connections: Thoughts on Lully's Entr'actes." *Early Music* 21 (1993) [forthcoming].

unpublished–

Lang, Paul Henry. "The Literary Aspects of the History of Opera in France." Ph. D. dissertation, Cornell University, 1935.

Ducrot, A. "Recherches sur Jean-Baptist Lully (1632-1687) et sur les débuts de l'Académie royale de musique." Ph. D. dissertation, Ecole de Chartes, 1961.

Howard, Patricia. "The Operas of Lully." Ph. D. disertation, University of Surrey, 1974.

Schneider, H. "Der Rezeption der Lully-Oper im 17. und 18. Jahrhundert in Frankreich." Ph. D. dissertation, University of Mainz, 1976.

Brown, Leslie Ellen. "The *Tragédie lyrique* of André Campra and his contemporaries." Ph. D. dissertation, University of North Carolina, 1978.

Lang-Becker, Elke. "Szenentypus und Musik in Rameaus tragédie lyrique." Ph. D. dissertation, University of Heidelberg, 1977.

Rosow, Lois. "Lully's Armide at the Paris Opéra: a Performance History, 1686-1766." Ph.D. dissertation, Brandeis University, 1981.

Turnbull, T.M. "A Critical Edition of Psyché: an Opera with Words by Thomas Corneille and Philippe Quinault, and

Music by Jean-Baptiste Lully." Ph.D. dissertation, Oxford University, 1981.

Wood, C. "Jean-Baptiste Lully and his Successors: Music and Drama in the 'tragédie en musique,' 1673-1715." Ph.D. dissertation, University of Hull, 1981.

The leading figure in the musical court of Louis XIV, and the most influential musical figure in French culture in the seventeenth and eighteenth centuries, Giovanni Battista Lulli was born Italian, the son of a miller. He was thirteen years old when he arrived in France in March of 1646 to enter the service of Mlle de Montpensier, who had Lully brought to the household so that she would have someone with whom to practise her Italian. He worked as a musician/page (*garçon de chambre*) until he was 20, developing his musical skills as a guitarist, a violinist and a dancer all to a high level during this time.

His presence in Mlle de Montpensier's court at the Tuileries exposed Lully to the richness of the developing musical and cultural scene that surrounded the French court. Lully became a friend, and possibly a pupil, of the royal court composer, Italian violinist Lazzarini, and managed to attract the attention of the young Louis XIV through his exceptional skill as a dancer and mime. Managing to avoid any personal setback with the defeat of the Fronde, despite his employer's role in it, Lully secured his release from Mlle de Montpensier and returned to Paris in 1652.

When Mazarin died, in March of 1661, Italian music lost its most powerful advocate in France, but Lully's career continued to advance. Appointed director of music and composer for the royal household in May of that year, Lully then received his naturalization papers from Louis XIV the following December. In July of 1662 Lully married Madeleine, the daughter of Michel Lambert, chief musician for the royal family. The signatures of Louis XIV, the queen, and Colbert testify to Lully's expanding power in the musical scene at the French royal court. During these important times Lully not only changed the spelling of his name in the formal documents, he also erased his humble origins, declaring himself "Jean-Baptiste de Lully, esquire, son of 'Laurent de Lully,' Florentine gentleman."

After his admittance to the king's string orchestra, the *Vingt-quatre violons*, Lully secured Louis's permission to establish a new string ensemble, the *Petits violons*. Between 1656 and 1664 Lully developed this group to an exceptionally high level of performing precision, and thus attracted the musical attention of the royal court and of Europe. This achievement strengthened Lully's growing position in Louis XIV's centralized regime.

Lully's career as a composer proceeded in a rather orderly fashion from the preparation of court ballets (1655-1672) to *comédie-ballets* (1663-1671) and then to operas (1673-1687). Lully possessed a gift for comedy, which he utilized in his ballets and in the subsequent collaborations with Molière and Corneille. In these collaborations with the great playwrights, the composer skillfully exploited Louis XIV's great interest in dancing to further his own career—the *Gazette de France* in 1670 even described *Le bourgeois gentilhomme* as a "ballet accompanied by a comedy." In the later part of his career, however, Lully eschewed comedy in favor of epic drama in his operas.

The establishment of the French opera academies under a patent secured by Pierre Perrin in 1669 initially drew criticism from Lully, who then considered the French language inappropriate for large stage works. But the success of Perrin's *Pomone* in 1671 must have altered Lully's opinion, for when Perrin was incarcerated for debts, Lully quickly turned the situation to his own advantage, buying Perrin's privilege by offering him enough to pay off his creditors in addition to a pension for life. The royal privilege Lully obtained in 1672 gave him and his heirs the sole right to establish a royal academy of music. With that privilege, opera, defined as any work that was sung throughout, could only be performed with Lully's permission. So powerful did Lully become that subsequent legislation forbade more than two singers and six instrumentalists from appearing in productions independent of the newly established Royal Academy of Music.

Lully then secured a theater, the Jeu de paume de Béquet near the Luxembourg gardens, a stage machinist and architect, Carlo Vigarani, and a librettist, Philippe Quinault, with whom Lully had already worked in the ballets *La grotte de Versailles* (1668) and *Psyché* (1671). In this theater Lully's first operas were performed: *Les fêtes de l'Amour et de Bacchus,* a pastorale-pastiche, and *Cadmus et Hermione,* the first *tragédie-lyrique.* With this last work, what became known as French opera was born.

Lully and other composers preferred the term *tragédie en musique,* but the term *tragédie-lyrique* came into vogue and remained common until the time of the revolution. Lully's *tragédies-lyriques* were collaborations between the composer Lully, the librettist Quinault (who prepared 11 such works for Lully), and the French Academy, which held approval authority over the libretti. Lully's *Cadmus et Hermione* provided the model for the genre, which included a prologue followed by five acts, and the Lullian model became the standard for subsequent composers, including Campra, Rameau, and Gluck in his reform operas.

The subject matter of Lully's *tragédies-lyriques* came either from mythology (*Cadmus et Hermione, Alceste, Isis, Atys, Persée, Proserpine, Thésée* and *Phaëton*) or from tales of chivalry (*Amadis, Armide,* and *Roland*). Lully's prologues are usually separated distinctly from the subject material of the main action, and they generally pay homage to Louis XIV and his "heroic" achievements in war.

Lully's output of Latin sacred music is much smaller than that of his stage works, but because he composed sacred motets throughout his career, these works bear special significance to Lully's development as a composer. As early as 1664 he composed the *grand motet Miserere.* Other works followed for specific occasions: the *Plaude laetare Gallia* for the birth of the Dauphin in 1668, and the *Te Deum* of 1677 for the baptism of Lully's eldest son, for whom the king had agreed to serve as godfather. The last dated sacred work is the *Exaudiat te, Domine* of 1685, but two other motets, *Notus in Judaea* and *Quare fremuerunt gentes,* probably also came from Lully's last years. Fourteen *petits motets* are also credited to Lully.

On January 8, 1687, Lully struck his foot with a staff used to beat musical time while conducting 150 musicians in a performance of his *Te Deum.* The wound abscessed, but Lully refused to have a toe amputated, and he died of complications on the following March 22. He was interred according to his wishes in a private chapel at the church of the Petits-Pères, today Notre-Dame-des-Victoires, near the Bibliothèque Nationale.

Modern audiences tend to overlook Lully's importance in the history of western music. This remarkable figure stands alone in several respects: (1) he was the most influential individual composer of his era, for as the Italian and French styles came to dominate Europe from the late seventeenth through the eighteenth centuries, Lully alone personified a style that became the fashion in courts from England to Germany to Sweden and farther east; (2) he was an extraordinary administrator and businessman. Neal Zaslaw has pointed out that Lully was the only person who, during three centuries of the existence of the Paris Opéra, managed to make rather than to lose money. Lully built a personal fortune, at his death valued at more than P800,000 (at a time when the average court musician earned approximately P1500 annually). His wealth probably exceeded that of any musician of his time or before him. During his career he built several grand residences in Paris and in the surrounding communities in the direction of Versailles.

Lully jealously guarded the originals of his compositions, and the history of their existence after his death remains a subject of inquiry. None is known to have survived. Henri Prunières identified a fragment of manuscript from an unknown work and proposed it as a Lully autograph, but this identification has not been widely accepted by scholars. This absence of originals has made the preparation of a collected works difficult, and thus Lully remains one of the most important major figures in the history of western music for whom a collected edition has never been completed. The project, suspended with the outbreak of World War II, was recently resumed by an international team of scholars in a *New Collected Works* under the general editorship of Carl Schmidt.

The style that Lully developed in his decidedly French works separates itself sharply from Italian music in the mid to late seventeenth century. As a result, debate over the virtues of the two styles, French and Italian, developed and continued in various forms for more than a century. The crispness of rhythm appropriate to the French dance style, and the French classical requirement for clarity of declamation of text precluded the employment of the dense counterpoint found in Italian, and most particularly in German, Baroque music. The aesthetic values of proportion in time and balance in melodic contour came to the fore in French music, while the art of counterpoint was much less developed. As a result, canon and fugue are rare in Lully's music. Thus, Lully's music suffered in the assessment of later audiences who were captivated by eighteenth century counterpoint, the Italian Baroque style, and the German music it inspired. Only with the surge of interest in period instruments in the later twentieth century and with the renaissance of seventeenth- and eighteenth-century performance practices has Lully's music begun to find acceptance with modern audiences and critics. An important advancement occurred in 1987 with a critically acclaimed production of *Atys* at the Paris Opéra under the direction of William Christy and using period instruments, historically informed choreography, costumes and sets. The technology of film, video, and the faithfulness of digital sound reproduction lends promise to the hope that in the future Lully's achievements will be more widely understood and appreciated.

—John Hajdu Heyer

LULU.

Composer: Alban Berg.

Librettist: Alban Berg (after Frank Wedekind's *Erdgeist* and *Die Büchse der Pandora*).

First Performance: Zurich, Stadttheater, 2 June 1937; first complete performance, Paris, Opéra, 24 February 1979.

Roles: Lulu (soprano); Dr Schön (baritone); Countess Geschwitz (mezzo-soprano); Alwa (baritone); Painter (tenor); Schigolch (bass); Rodrigo (doubles with Animal Trainer, bass); Schoolboy (doubles with Wardrobe Mistress, contralto); Theater Manager (bass); Prince (tenor); Servant (tenor); Dr Goll (speaking part); Jack the Ripper (mute).

Publications

books–

Reiter, M. *Die Zwölftontechnik in Alban Bergs Oper Lulu.* Regensburg, 1973.

Cerha, F. *Arbeitsbericht zur Herstellung des 3. Akts der Oper Lulu von Alban Berg.* Vienna, 1979.

Lulu II. Musique et Musiciens [issued by the Opéra de Paris]. Paris, 1979.

Perle, George. *The Operas of Alban Berg II: Lulu.* Berkeley, 1985.

articles–

Offergeld, R. "Some Questions about *Lulu.*" *HiFi/Stereo Review* 13/4 (1964): 58.

Jarman, Douglas. "Dr. Schön's Five Strophe Aria: Some Notes on Tonality and Pitch Association in Berg's *Lulu.*" *Perspectives of New Music* 8 (1970): 23.

———. "Some Rhythmic and Metric Techniques in Alban Berg's *Lulu.*" *Musical Quarterly* 56 (1970): 349.

Herschkowitz, F. "Some Thoughts on *Lulu.*" *International Alban Berg Society Newsletter* 6 (1978): 11.

Jarman, Douglas. "*Lulu*: The Sketches." *International Alban Berg Society Newsletter* 6 (1978): 4.

Bachmann, Claus-Henning. "*Lulu* bisher: '. . . ein Anschlag auf den Dramatiker Berg.' Herstellung des dritten Aktes—Gespräch mit Friedrich Cerha." *Neue Zeitschrift für Musik* 140 (1979): 264.

Holloway, Robin. "The Complete *Lulu.*" *Tempo* 129 (1979): 36.

Perle, George. "The Cerha edition" [of *Lulu*, act III]. *Perspectives of New Music* 17 (1979): 251.

———. "The Complete *Lulu.*" *Musical Times* 120 (1979): 115.

Stephan, Rudolph. "Zur Sprachmelodie in Alban Bergs *Lulu*-Musik." In *Dichtung und Musik,* edited by Günter Schnitzler, 246. Stuttgart, 1979.

Jarman, Douglas. "Countess Geschwitz's series: a controversy resolved?" *Proceedings of the Royal Musical Association* 107 (1981): 111.

Perle, George. "Das Film-Zwischenspiel in Bergs Oper *Lulu.*" *Österreichische Musikzeitschrift* 36 (1981): 631.

———. "The tone-row as symbol in Berg's *Lulu.*" In *Essays on the Music of J.S. Bach and other Diverse Subjects: A Tribute to Gerhard Herz,* edited by Robert L. Weaver, 304. Louisville, Kentucky, 1981.

Carner, Mosco. "Alban Berg's *Lulu*—A Reconsideration." *Musical Times* 124 (1983): 477.

Pople, Anthony. "Serial and Tonal Aspects of Pitch Structure in Act III of Berg's *Lulu.*" *Soundings* 10 (1983): 36.

Carner, Mosco. "Berg e il riesame di *Lulu.*" *Nuova rivista musicale italiana* 18 (1984): 434.

Green, London. "Lulu Wakens." *Opera Quarterly* 3 (1985): 112.

Berg's autograph score for the prologue of *Lulu*, c. 1935

Perle, George. "Some Thoughts on an Ideal Production of *Lulu*." *Journal of Musicology* 7 (1989).

* * *

Wedekind's Lulu plays liberated Alban Berg from the rigid moral atmosphere of Vienna in the first decade of the twentieth century. On first reading them he proclaimed that "sensuality is not a weakness, does not mean a surrender to one's own will. Rather it is an immense strength that lies in us— the pivot of all being and thinking."

In the prologue to Berg's *Lulu,* an Animal Tamer presents the principal characters as animals. Lulu, the snake, embodies "the fundamental nature of womankind." She is desired by all the men in the first half of the opera (and truly loved only by the lesbian Countess Geschwitz, whose affection she does not reciprocate). She causes the death of two successive husbands when they discover her infidelity; and her marriage to the only man she ever loved, the wealthy newspaper editor Dr Schön, ends when he presses her to kill herself, and she shoots him instead.

In the second half of the opera Lulu escapes from prison through the Countess' self-sacrifice. She flees Germany with her new lover, Schön's son Alwa. Blackmailers force her to abandon a luxurious life in Parisian high society; she then becomes a London prostitute and dies at the hands of her third client, Jack the Ripper.

Wedekind's Lulu is the victim of men who cannot accept her sensuality and her honesty. They imprint upon her their own images of the ideal of feminine conduct (a point neatly symbolized by the new name which each of her lovers bestows upon her). By contrast, Lulu herself has an absolute integrity, a determination not to prostitute her sexuality or to compromise her love. This is why her descent into prostitution is so powerful an image; and her death at the hands of Jack the Ripper embodies the revenge of men on a female sensuality which is beyond male control.

The Lulu plays are a critique of contemporary German society, in particular of the tension between its monetary bases and the human feelings which mercantilism stifles. Berg responds to the strange mixture in Wedekind's texts of satire, farce, and tragedy with a music which can shift its perspective from moment to moment. In some parts of the opera, the music is of a Wagnerian or Mahlerian intensity; Berg demands a total involvement when he pours out his compassion for the tragedy of suffering humanity. Elsewhere, the composer offers a detached commentary, sardonic, ironic, and parodistic—a music which is essentially of its time, and frequently reflects the European mania for jazz in the twenties and thirties.

The most remarkable feature of *Lulu* is what Douglas Jarman has termed Berg's "extraordinary combination of technical calculation and emotional spontaneity." A score which unleashes some of the most tumultuous and passionate music of the twentieth century is also rigorously through-composed—clearly divided into formal numbers, and precisely controlled by Berg's intricate development of the twelve-tone technique.

Each act includes a form from instrumental music, which gives unity to the incidents which surround it. Act I is dominated by a sonata devoted to Dr Schön's unsuccessful struggle for freedom from Lulu, act II by a rondo which symbolizes Alwa's constant reversion to his passion for her, and act III by a theme and variations which evoke and chronicle the final descent of Lulu to her death.

Berg's compression of Wedekind's lengthy text is based on one basic structural principle. Lulu rises through the early scenes to the apex of her power and influence, when she has achieved her ambition and is married to Dr Schön. Then, after his death, she plunges inexorably towards her destruction. Berg sees her murder of Schön as the center point of his narrative, places it at the middle of the second of three acts, and enforces its centrality, firstly by constructing the film-interlude between the two scenes of act II as a palindrome, so that at the center point of the opera the music seems almost to be in equipoise; and secondly by the use of musical recapitulation, so that the second half of the opera seems almost to be a nightmarish reenactment of the events of the first.

Berg adapted the final scene of Wedekind's play, so that by extensive musical recapitulations, and by the doubling of parts on stage. Lulu's three clients reembody the three men whose deaths she caused in the first half of the opera. The third and last is Jack; there is hideous irony in the disjunction between text and music, as she haggles with him over the price for her favors to the most powerful presentation yet of the tragic music for her tortured affair with Dr Schön. Here, sexual need is seen simply as a lethal torment, for both men and women. But in his setting of the Countess' final, dying words Berg presents a counterbalancing image of the transcendent nobility and beauty of a love which can be fulfilled only in heaven.

Berg died before finishing the orchestration of act III. After initial enthusiasm, his widow banned completion of the opera, and *Lulu* had to be performed from 1937 to 1979 as a two-act torso. But Berg's publishers secretly commissioned from Friedrich Cerha an orchestration of the passages which Berg had left incomplete. Helene Berg died in 1976, and the opera was first performed in its entirety in Paris in February 1979. The completion allows us to appreciate, at last, Berg's symmetrical conception of the opera. And the London scene is an overwhelming finale, although the Paris scene is a disappointment. Berg's extraordinarily dense vocal ensembles in the Paris scene make comprehension difficult, even of crucial material; and the level of musical inspiration is lower than elsewhere. Despite this, *Lulu* is unquestionably one of the greatest operas of the twentieth century.

—Michael Evans

DIE LUSTIGEN WEIBER VON WINDSOR [The Merry Wives of Windsor].

Composer: Otto Nicolai.

Librettist: S.H. Mosenthal (after Shakespeare, *The Merry Wives of Windsor*).

First Performance: Berlin, Hofoper, 9 March 1849.

Roles: Sir John Falstaff (bass); Mr Ford/Herr Fluth (baritone); Mr Page/Herr Reich (bass); Fenton (tenor); Mistress Ford/Frau Fluth (soprano); Mistress Page/Frau Reich (mezzo-soprano); Anne Page (soprano); Slender Spärlich (tenor); Dr Caius (bass); chorus (SATB).

Publications

book–

Düre, Karl-Friedrich. *Opern nach literarischen Vorlagen. Shakespeares "The Merry Wives of Windsor" in den Vertonungen von Mosenthal-Nicolai "Die lustigen Weiber von Windsor" und Boito-Verdi "Falstaff." Ein Beitrag zum Thema Gattungstransformation.* Stuttgart, 1979.

article–

Kruse, George Richard. "Falstaff und die lustigen Weiber." *Die Musik* 6/no. 4 (1906-07): 63.

Nicolai's classic operatic treatment of Shakespeare's *Merry Wives of Windsor* was the culmination of a brief career theretofore devoted to Italian opera, in addition to smaller forms (*Lieder,* sacred music, part-songs, and miscellaneous instrumental music). Nicolai had aspired to the composition of a German opera ever since leaving Italy for Vienna in 1842. But difficulties in finding a suitable libretto, periods of bad health, and lack of co-operation from the Viennese Court Theater administration delayed the completion of the work by several years, by which time the composer had moved to Berlin.

The opera begins with Shakespeare's second act, as Mistresses Page (Reich) and Ford (Fluth) compare the identical letters they have received from the rotund and currently impecunious old knight, John Falstaff. To punish him for his presumption and Mr Ford for his habitual jealousy, the wives arrange an assignation between Sir John and Mistress Ford, intending that her husband should discover them. When Ford does arrive, posse in tow, Falstaff is quickly packed into a large laundry basket and unceremoniously deposited in the river while Ford and the others search the house in vain (finale, act I). Ford remains determined to catch the suspected intruder, and disguised as "Master Brook" ("Sir Bach") he enlists Falstaff as a surrogate lover to pry loose for him the rigid scruples of his beloved Mistress Ford, thus to verify her infidelity and the knight's guilt. In the meantime Squire Slender (Junker Spärlich) and the French physician Dr Caius are in competition with the impoverished young Fenton for the hand of Anne, daughter of the wealthy Mr Page (Herr "Reich," i.e. rich). Fenton serenades her ("Horch, die Lerche singt im Hain") while his rivals look on angrily, in hiding. In the finale to act II, Falstaff is again spirited out of the house, this time in the guise of the "fat old woman from Brainford," but not without receiving a beating from Mr Ford, who takes Falstaff for a fortune-teller and swindler. After Ford is let in on the merry wives' pranks, Mistress Page sings a ballad about Herne's Oak and together they plot their final act of revenge against Falstaff, to lure him into a mock fairy ritual in Windsor Forest. The elder Pages each set a plan to ensure the secret betrothal of Anne to their suitor of choice (Slender for Mr Page, Caius for his wife). But Anne determines to foil them by plighting her troth to Fenton first (the aria, "Wohl denn!, gefaßt ist der Entschluß"). As the moon rises on Windsor Forest in the final scene, Falstaff appears, adorned with stag horns, for his third attempted rendezvous. After a brief trio Mistresses Page and Ford suddenly flee, as the elfin pantomime begins. Falstaff is discovered, duly pinched and pummeled, and finally disabused of the masquerade. In the confusion of disguise, Slender and Caius find they have been wedded to one another, while Anne has been joined with Fenton.

The use of spoken dialogue, according to the convention of German comic opera, enables Nicolai and his librettist, S.H. Mosenthal, to preserve more details of Shakespeare's comedy than are found in the Verdi-Boito version (the role of Anne's third suitor, Slender, or Falstaff's second misadventure at Ford's house, for example). But conversely, Mosenthal's libretto cannot match the elegant economy of Boito's, and the act-II finale of Nicolai's opera (Falstaff's escape as the "fat woman of Brainford") seems redundant in terms of operatic dramaturgy, which cannot support the episodic density of incident characteristic of the spoken comedy. The frequency of dialogue scenes, on the other hand, is considerably curtailed in comparison with other German and French comic opera of the period, perhaps making its continued presence at all only more awkward. Act II, for instance, is only twice interrupted by dialogue. A rather long *secco* style recitative between Ford (as "Brook") and Falstaff introduces a continuous series of small, well-wrought musical numbers structured around Fenton's serenade to Anne in the garden. This well-known *Romanze,* "Horch, die Lerche singt im Hain," demonstrates Nicolai's experience as a composer of *Lieder* and his expertise as orchestrator.

Nicolai seized the lyric opportunities implicit in the originally rather subordinate love-intrigue of Anne and Fenton, as Verdi and Boito did in turn. Also like Verdi, he made the most of the romantic-fantastic atmosphere suggested by the nocturnal scene in Windsor Forest. This final scene, which provides much of the thematic material for the popular overture, is a good example of the blending of lyrical mood-painting (the "moonrise" with its shimmering sustained strings supporting a gradually rising line passed between woodwinds and brass) with the folk-like popular tunefulness of Lortzing or Flotow (the trio between Falstaff and the two wives). The essential quality of Nicolai's opera lies in this happy synthesis of brusque, earthy idiom of the German comic opera tradition with the more elevated manner of Mendelssohn's music to *A Midsummer Night's Dream* and with an easy control of the large-scale ensemble tableau of Italian opera (e.g., finale to act I, "Ich kam, ein Wild zu jagen, und finde keine Spur").

—Thomas S. Grey

M

MAAZEL, Lorin (Varencove).

Conductor. Born 6 March 1930, in Neuilly, France. Married:
1) Miriam Sandbank, pianist, 1952 (divorced); 2) Israela Margalit, pianist, 1969 (divorced); 3) Dietlinde Turban, 1986.
Studied violin with Karl Moldrem, piano with Fanchon Armitage, and conducting with Vladimir Bakaleinikov at an early
age; conducted a performance of Schubert's *Unfinished Symphony* with the University of Idaho Orchestra, 1938; conducted the National Music Camp Orchestra of Interlochen at
the World's Fair in New York, 1939; conducted the National
Broadcasting Company Symphony Orchestra, 1941; conducted an entire program with the New York Philharmonic,
1942; studied at the University of Pittsburgh; violinist and
apprentice conductor with the Pittsburgh Symphony Orchestra, 1948; Fulbright fellowship for travel to Italy, 1951; conducted in Catania, 1953; conducted at the Florence May
Festival, 1955; conducted at the Vienna Festival, 1957; conducted at the Edinburgh Festival, 1958; conducted *Lohengrin*
at the Bayreuth Festival, 1960; toured the United States with
the Orchestre National de France, 1962; conducted *Don Giovanni* at the Metropolitan Opera in New York, 1962; toured
Russia, 1963; honorary doctorate from the University of
Pittsburgh, 1965; artistic director of the Deutsche Oper in
West Berlin, 1965-71; principal conductor of the West Berlin
Radio Symphony Orchestra, 1965-75; associate principal
conductor, 1970-72, and principal guest conductor of the
New Philharmonia Orchestra of London, 1976-80; music director of the Cleveland Orchestra, 1972-82; principal conductor, 1977-82, principal guest conductor, 1982-88, and music
director, 1988-91, of the Orchestre National de France; artistic director of general manager of the Vienna State Opera,
1982-84; music consultant to the Pittsburgh Symphony Orchestra, 1984-86; music adviser, principal guest conductor,
and music director of the Pittsburgh Symphony Orchestra,
1986. Maazel has received the Sibelius Prize of Finland, the
Commander's Cross of the Order of Merit from West Germany, and the Grand Prix du Disque, Paris, among others.

Publications

About MAAZEL: books–

Geleng, I. *Die Direktion Lorin Maazel.* Vienna, 1984.

*   *   *

In 1960, Lorin Maazel became the first American, and, at
thirty, the youngest conductor, to conduct at the Bayreuth
Festival (his first performance was Wagner's *Lohengrin*). His
Salzburg Festival debut came in 1963 with performances of
Mozart's *Le nozze di Figaro*. His Metropolitan Opera debut
came in 1962, when he conducted Mozart's *Don Giovanni*
and, later in the same month, Richard Strauss's *Der Rosenkavalier*. In 1965 he conducted Tchaikovsky's *Eugene Onegin* at
the Rome Opera. He became artistic director of the Deutsche
Oper, Berlin, in 1965, where he had already conducted

Wagner's *Die fliegende Holländer* in 1964. He remained in
Berlin until 1971, conducting 300 performances of forty operas, including a double bill of Busoni's *Arlecchino* and
Turandot, the first German performance of Henze's *Die Bassaríden* and in 1968 the first performance of Dallapiccola's
Ulisse.

While at the Deutsche Oper, Maazel instituted several policy changes: he insisted that the same orchestral musicians
play at every performance of a production; he required at
least one full stage rehearsal of each opera; he double-cast all
operas, insisting on equal rehearsal time for both casts; and
he added baroque opera, Italian opera sung in Italian, and
the first *Ring* cycle to be heard in Berlin.

After leaving the Deutsche Oper, Maazel was guest conductor at several opera houses, conducting Verdi's *Luisa
Miller* at Covent Garden (1979), Mozart's *Die Entführung
aus dem Serail* at the Salzburg Festival (1980), and Verdi's
Falstaff, which opened the 1980-81 season at the Teatro alla
Scala. He returned to La Scala to open the 1983-84 season
with Puccini's *Turandot;* he opened the 1985-86 season with
Verdi's *Aida,* followed by Puccini's *Madama Butterfly* later
that season (a performance preserved on videotape), and *Fidelio* and Puccini's *La fanciulla del West* in 1990. In 1991
Maazel led a concert performance of Richard Strauss's *Elektra* at Carnegie Hall.

He returned to the Salzburg Festival in 1982 and 1983 with
Beethoven's *Fidelio*. In 1984 he led the world premiere of
Berio's *Un re in ascolta* at the festival, repeating it later
in Milan. In 1987 he conducted the festival production of
Falstaff.

Maazel became general director of the Vienna State Opera
in 1982. In his role as conductor, he has led performances of
Wagner's *Tannhäuser,* Verdi's *Falstaff,* Puccini's *Turandot,*
Berg's *Lulu,* Bizet's *Carmen,* and Verdi's *Aida*. As administrator, he instituted several policy changes, as he had done in
Berlin. One was to replace the repertory system, in which a
different opera is performed each night with varying casts,
with a "block" system of performing a series of up to six
operas for a short period with a single cast, followed by
another two-week series of five operas. This entailed the reduction of the number of operas performed each season from
nearly thirty to thirteen. He also expanded the repertoire to
include more French opera and more Slavic operas. Maazel
was a controversial figure to the Philharmonic musicians
because he asked them to rethink music on which they felt
they held proprietary rights. He resigned his position in 1984.

Maazel has a reputation for a certain coldness and emotional distance in his conducting. A highly sophisticated conductor with a profound and thorough knowledge of music,
he is sometimes leery of showing much involvement. His
performances demonstrate his precision, his drive and energy,
but also his tendency to overanalyze the score.

Maazel has made numerous recordings of complete operas.
These include Beethoven's *Fidelio* (1964), Bizet's *Carmen*
(1971), Gershwin's *Porgy and Bess* (1976) (the first recording
of the "complete" original score), Massenet's *Thaïs* (1976),
Puccini's *Tosca* (1966), *Il tabarro* (1976), *Suor Angelica*
(1976), *Gianni Schicchi* (1976), *Madama Butterfly* (1978), *Le*

villi (1979), *La rondine* (1983), and *Turandot* (a recording of a live performance from Vienna, 1983), Ravel's *L'enfant et les sortilèges* (1960 and, on videotape, 1986) and *L'heure espagnole* (1965), and Verdi's *La traviata* (1968) and *Luisa Miller* (1979).

Maazel has also recorded the soundtracks for a number of operatic films: Joseph Losey's *Don Giovanni* (1978), Franco Zeffirelli's *Otello* (1986), and Francesco Rosi's *Carmen*.

—Michael Sims

MACBETH.

Composer: Ernest Bloch.

Librettist: E. Fleg (after Shakespeare).

First Performance: Paris, Opéra-Comique, 30 November 1910.

Roles: Macbeth (baritone); Macduff (bass); Banquo (tenor); Duncan (tenor); Malcolm (tenor); Lennox (tenor); Porter (baritone); Old Man (bass); Server (tenor); Murderer (bass); Apparitions (bass, contralto); Lady Macbeth (soprano); Lady Macduff (soprano); Three Witches (soprano, mezzo-soprano, contralto); Macduff's Son (mezzo-soprano); Fleance (mute).

Publications

articles–

Hall, Raymond. "The *Macbeth* of Bloch." *Modern Music* 15 (1938): 209.
Cohen, Alex. "Ernest Bloch's *Macbeth.*" *Music and Letters* 19 (1938): 209.
Mariani, R. "Bloch e il suo *Macbeth.*" *La Scala* (1953): 29.
Kushner, David Z. "The Revivals of Bloch's *Macbeth.*" *Opera Journal* (1971): 9.
Kinkaid, Frank. "The Other *Macbeth.*" *Opera News* 37 (1973): 10.
Sills, David L. "Ruminations on *Macbeth.*" *Ernest Bloch Society Bulletin* (1986-87): 11.

*　　*　　*

Ernest Bloch's *Macbeth,* a lyric drama in seven scenes (a Prologue and three acts, each consisting of two scenes), is the composer's only complete opera. Sketches and drafts for the unfinished *Jezabel* (1911-18) are in the Library of Congress. Dedicated to the first woman to portray Lady Macbeth, Lucienne Bréval, *Macbeth* was composed in the woods and mountains of Geneva. The French libretto by Edmond Fleg was given to Bloch in 1904. Bloch stated, "My task was first of all to mirror Shakespeare." Italian and English versions of the libretto by, respectively, Mary Tibaldi Chiesa and Alex Cohen, have enabled productions to be mounted in Italy and in the United States.

The bulk of the action takes place amid the gloom of Macbeth's castle. Macbeth, Thane of Glamis, and Banquo, returning from quashing an armed revolt against King Duncan, are confronted by three witches who prophesy that Macbeth will be Thane of Cawdor, and then King of Scotland.

Banquo, it is foretold, will "get kings though he be none." The remainder of the opera closely follows the events of Shakespeare's drama, although with skillful compression. Unlike Giuseppe Verdi, Bloch is interested in dissecting his characters psychologically and in providing the appropriate musical and scenic atmosphere in which to do so. Macbeth, not Lady Macbeth, emerges as the central figure. It is his all-consuming guilt mixed with greed and lust for power that transfixes the audience.

The plasticity of the vocal lines, which are declamatory, suggests Debussy's model in *Pelléas et Mélisande*. Where Debussy's characters are ethereal and symbolic, however, Bloch's are human to a fault; i.e., they are so vividly realized that the audience is made to feel one with them. Words are not repeated; duets are eschewed, although dialogues between the principals do occur; ensembles are limited to the witches and the choruses (crowds) at climactic moments.

Like Modest Mussorgsky, Bloch places the drama first, with the result that the musical structure is determined by the necessities of the plot; consequently, there are assymetrical phrases, and there is a frequent state of flux among the meter, harmony, and texture. The metamorphoses of the several leitmotifs reveal the influence of the Liszt-Wagner school; however, Bloch's usage is limited to relatively few such examples. Understatement becomes a hallmark of Bloch's treatment of the characters. His music for Lady Macbeth's sleepwalking scene, to cite one example, is stark and dark. The pitches assigned to the Lady are closer to what we would expect from the normal speaking voice than from a full-blown aria. This treatment is in line with the composer's notion that Shakespeare's words should be the focus of attention, while the music provides atmosphere and enhances the perception that the Queen has separated herself from reality. In view of the tumultuous climax which follows, the sleepwalking scene is even more telling in its quietude (contrast this approach to the high drama given to this scene in Verdi's version).

Some of the orchestral writing, particularly in the interludes between scenes in acts I and III, is evocative and coloristic; it foreshadows the style which was to emerge in the "Jewish Cycle" works of 1912-16.

When *Macbeth* is viewed as a whole, it emerges as a musical drama of the first order. Critics such as Pierre Lalo, Henri Prunières, Romain Rolland, and Ildebrando Pizzetti were among the first to recognize the genius in this work, and yet, eighty years after its premiere, it remains largely unknown and neglected.

—David Z. Kushner

MACBETH.

Composer: Giuseppe Verdi.

Librettists: Francesco Maria Piave and Andrea Maffei (after Shakespeare).

First Performance: Florence, Teatro della Pergola, 14 March 1847; revised, Piave, French translation by Charles Nuitter and A. Beaumont, Paris, Théâtre-Lyrique, 21 April 1865.

Roles: Lady Macbeth (soprano); Macbeth (baritone); Macduff (tenor); Banquo (bass); Lady-in-Waiting (mezzo-soprano); Malcolm (tenor); Doctor (bass); Servant (bass);

Renato Bruson and Renata Scotto in Verdi's *Macbeth,* **Royal Opera, London, 1981**

Murderer (bass); Herald (bass); Apparitions (sopranos, bass); Hecate (dancer); Duncan (mute); Fleance (mute); chorus (SSAATTBB).

Publications

books–

Moscatelli, C. Il "Macbeth" di Giuseppe Verdi. L'uomo, il potere, il destino. Ravenna, 1978.
Degrada, Francesco. Il palazzo incantato. Fiesole, 1979.
Rosen, David, and Andrew Porter. Verdi's "Macbeth": a Sourcebook. New York and London, 1984.
John, Nicholas, ed. Giuseppe Verdi: Macbeth. London, 1990.

articles–

Hughes, Spike. "An Introduction to Verdi's Macbeth." Opera April (1960).
Osthoff, Wolfgang. "Die beiden Fassungen von Verdi's Macbeth." Archiv für Musikwissenschaft 29 (1972).
Noske, Frits. "Schiller e la genesi del Macbeth verdiano." Nuova rivista musicale italiana 10 (1976).
Degrada, Francesco. "Lettura del Macbeth di Verdi." Studi musicali 6 (1977).
Antokoletz, Elliot. "Verdi's Dramatic Use of Harmony and Tonality in Macbeth," In Theory Only 4/no. 6 (1978): 17.
Goldin, Daniela. "Il Macbeth verdiano: genesi e linguaggio di un libretto." Analecta musicologica 19 (1979): 336.
Noske, Frits. "Verdi's Macbeth: Romanticism or Realism?" In Ars musica, musica scientia. Festschrift Heinrich Hüschen zum fünfundsechzigsten Geburtstag am 2. März 1980, edited by Detlef Altenburg, 359. Cologne, 1980.
Avant-scène opéra March-April (1982) [Macbeth issue].
Rinaldi, M. "Il Macbeth di Verdi: un' opera 'più difficile delle altre'." Studi musicali 10 (1982).
Christen, Norbert. "Auf dem Weg zum szenischen Musikdrama: Verdis Macbeth in Vergleich der beiden Fassungen." Neue Zeitschrift für Musik 46/nos. 7-8 (1985): 9.

*   *   *

Macbeth is the first of three operas which Verdi drew from works by Shakespeare, the dramatist he most admired. There are two main versions of the work, one written for the 1847 carnival season in Florence, and a substantial revision for the 1865 season at the Théâtre-Lyrique in Paris. Although the earlier version was more successful with audiences than the revision, it is nonetheless the revised version that is heard today.

Verdi drew closely on the Shakespearean source for his plot, which he sketched in prose before turning the versification over to his librettist Piave, as was his usual practice. In act I, Macbeth and Banquo come across a band of witches, who prophesy that Macbeth will be Thane of Cawdor and King of Scotland, and that Banquo will be the father of future kings. The first prophecy is shortly thereafter proven, when messengers arrive to hail Macbeth as Thane of Cawdor, leaving him in turn to wonder about the truth of the other predictions. When Lady Macbeth hears of these events, and of King Duncan's intended visit to their castle, she decides Duncan must be murdered to fulfill the prophecy, and, convincing her more reluctant husband, they kill him in his sleep. In act II, King Macbeth broods over the predicted reign of Banquo's sons, and decides to hire an assassin to kill Banquo and his son Fleance, but Fleance escapes. At a banquet in the closing scene of the act, Macbeth learns of the escape, and is terrified by the ghost of Banquo, leading the guests to suspect his guilt—including Macduff, who decides to flee to England and gather support against Macbeth. In act III, Macbeth returns to the witches, and frightening apparitions appear from their cauldron to give him mysterious advice: to beware of Macduff, that "none of woman born" shall harm him, and that he need fear not until Birnam Wood advances. After the apparitions and witches vanish, he and Lady Macbeth decide that Banquo's son and Macduff's family must also die. Act IV begins as Macduff, along with the other Scottish refugees in England, mourns the death of his wife and children, and prepares for battle with the English army of Malcolm, now heir to the Scottish throne; they arm themselves with boughs of Birnam Wood for camouflage. Back in Scotland, Lady Macbeth is seen in her tormented nightly trance, trying to wash off the blood she imagines she sees on her hands. This is followed by a brooding scene in which Macbeth learns of his wife's death and of the advancing of Birnam Wood. In the final scene Macbeth is confronted and killed in battle by Macduff (who was not of woman born, but ripped from the womb), and Malcolm is joyously declared the new King of Scotland.

Notwithstanding his love for Shakespeare, Verdi's reason for choosing Macbeth as an operatic subject initially had little to do with the drama. The idea was proposed to him, along with two others, by the Florentine theater manager Lanari during contract negotiations; and it was the absence of a good romantic tenor on the one hand and the availability of a fine baritone on the other (more suited to the dark, non-romantic role of Macbeth), that determined Verdi's choice. However, after the initial, singer-related strategies, Verdi became deeply involved with the dramatic aspects of the project, so much so that Julian Budden, for instance, considers Macbeth to contain the composer's first "glimpses of a new freedom," as distinct from his earlier "years in the galley," in which Verdi primarily labored to please audiences, singers, and managers, rather than to fulfill his own dramatic conceptions. Although the many closed set-piece forms, especially the conventional cavatinas and cabalettas, seem to belie this new dramatic emphasis, Verdi's letters to his librettist Piave and to the lead singers tell a different story. For example, with Piave he insisted on a new approach of "FEW WORDS . . . FEW WORDS . . . CONCISE STYLE," and from the singers he demanded a departure from bel canto, suggesting to Varesi that he must sing the crucial murder duet with Lady Macbeth in act I "in a hollow voice such as will inspire terror," and to the soprano Barbieri-Nini that her singing in the sleepwalking scene must be "sotto voce and in such a way as to arouse terror and pity." Another forward-looking aspect of the 1847 version was Verdi's increasingly dramatic use of the orchestra, as seen for example in the evocative accompanimental pattern to the sleepwalking scene, made up of chromatically shuddering muted strings and sighing English horn.

Besides attempting (unsuccessfully) to answer the French tastes for ballet and general scenic grandeur, Verdi's revisions for the later Théâtre-Lyrique production reveal his stylistic evolution between 1847 and 1865, a period of striking experimentation in his operatic career. The result is a mixture of styles, with the early, crudely energetic music of the witches, the banquet scene, and the on-stage banda music for King Duncan's entry, for example, standing adjacent to scenes composed in the far more subtle, flexible style of melody and harmony which characterizes Verdi's late middle-period approach. The mixture is sometimes disconcerting and disturbing to the successful rhythm of dramatic flow present in the original version, but modern audiences would probably still be loathe to give up the special beauties of the revised score, such as Lady Macbeth's act II aria "La luce langue" ("The light fades," replacing the conventional cabaletta of the earlier version), the act IV Exiles' Chorus, and the revised act III apparition scene.

—Claire Detels

MACKERRAS, (Sir Alan) Charles (MacLaurin).

Conductor. Born 17 November 1925, in Schenectady, New York. Married: Judith Wilkins, clarinettist, 1947 (two daughters). In Australia, studied oboe, piano, and composition at the New South Wales Conservatorium; principal oboist of the Sydney Symphony Orchestra, 1943-46; joined the orchestra at Sadler's Wells in London, and studied conducting with Michael Mudie; studied conducting with Václav Talich at the Prague Academy of Music on a British Council Scholarship, 1947; conductor with Sadler's Wells Opera, 1948; principal conductor of the British Broadcasting Corporation Concert Orchestra, 1954-56; guest conductor with various British and European orchestras; principal conductor at the Hamburg State Opera, 1966-70; music director of the Sadler's Wells Opera (English National Opera, 1974), 1970-78; conducted Gluck's *Orfeo et Euridice* at the Metropolitan Opera, New York, 1972; Commander of the Order of the British Empire, 1974; knighted, 1979; chief conductor of the Sydney Symphony Orchestra, 1982-85; artistic director or the Welsh National Opera, Cardiff, 1987-92.

Publications

By MACKERRAS: articles—

"Sense About the Appoggiatura." *Opera* October (1963).
"Janáček's Makropulos." *Opera* February (1964).
"What Mozart Really Meant" [*Figaro*]. *Opera* April (1965).
"Is the Conductor the Boss?" *Opera* October (1967).
"Sir Charles Mackerras on Handel." In *Conductors on Conducting,* edited by Bernard Jacobson. Frenchtown, New Jersey, 1979.
"Handel in Performance." *Opera* February (1985).
"Where We Are Now." *Opera* February (1990).

interviews—

Matheopoulos, Helena. *Maestro: Encounters with Conductors of Today.* London, 1982.

About MACKERRAS: books—

Phelan, N. *Charles Mackerras: a Musicians' Musician.* London, 1987.

articles—

Rosenthal, Harold. "Charles Mackerras." *Opera* April (1970).
Milnes, Rodney. "The Mackerras Years" [with the Sadler's Wells/English National Opera] *Opera* January (1978).

* * *

Born in 1925 in the United States of Australian parents and educated at the New South Wales Conservatorium of Music in Sydney, where he studied oboe, piano, and composition, Charles Mackerras has become one of the most eminent opera conductors and scholars in Britain. To his conducting he brings his vast knowledge of editorial problems and performance practices but, as he says, he tries "to hit the happy medium between being a musician and a musicologist." Mackerras dislikes confining categories or being labeled a specialist: "Generally I prefer conducting works by unusual composers or unusual works by famous composers. I'm always interested in something new."

Despite the fact that Mackerras has conducted an astonishingly wide variety of operas, certain specializations do stand out, specifically music of the Baroque, the works of Mozart, and those of Janáček. In 1947 Mackerras received a British Council Scholarship to study conducting with Václav Talich at the Prague Academy of Music; there he first encountered Janáček's operas and has subsequently conducted them extensively in Brno, the composer's native city, and in London and elsewhere; Mackerras has also made authoritative recordings of most of them on Decca. His *Jenůfa* with Elisabeth Söderström restores many cuts and discards many of Kovařovic's "improvements." The recording also reinstates the overture, which Janáček had cut from the opera and had wanted played as an independent concert piece called "Jealousy." Also with Söderström are Mackerras's recorded versions of *Kát'a Kabanová,* clearly superior to any others, and *Věc Makropulos,* also featuring Peter Dvorský. Both are performed in editions prepared by Mackerras himself. Perhaps the most powerful account is of *From the House of the Dead,* on which Mackerras has done a great deal of editorial work to clean up a corrupt edition caused by the extreme difficulty in reading Janáček's notation. To many other composers' music Mackerras brings historical expertise. His Handel and Bach are "authentic," and there was the now legendary performance run of *Le nozze di Figaro* at Sadler's Wells in 1966 for which Mackerras ornamented the arias and added appoggiaturas liberally throughout the score. Of his *Figaro* Harold Rosenthal wrote that "There is no conductor whom I would rather hear conduct *Figaro* and that includes Karl Böhm." Mackerras has written a number of articles appearing in *Opera* about many of his editorial decisions.

In the mid-1950s Mackerras began free-lance work with the English Opera Group, where he conducted the world premieres of Lennox Berkeley's *Ruth* and Benjamin Britten's *Noye's Fludde.* His debut with Sadler's Wells as conductor was in 1948 with *Die Fledermaus* (he had previously played oboe in that orchestra); his second period of involvement conducting for that company began in the 1963-64 season when he gave the English version of Janáček's *Makropulos Case.* His debut at Covent Garden came in 1963 with Shostakovich's *Katerina Ismailova;* he has maintained an excellent reputation with that house. In 1966 Mackerras was invited to join the Hamburg State Opera, where he remained until 1970. There he extended his repertoire even further, conducting many works for the first time, some without rehearsal. Notable productions from Hamburg include Strauss's *Arabella,* *The Rake's Progress* by Stravinsky, *Boris Gudonov* of Mussorgsky, Cimarosa's *Matrimonio segreto,* Lortzing's *Zar und Zimmermann,* Glinka's *Russlan and Ludmilla,* and Wagner's *Der fliegende Holländer.*

After his stint with the Hamburg Opera, Mackerras served as music director of Sadler's Wells/English National Opera from 1970 to 1978; there he conducted 338 performances of 42 operas, built the orchestra into a fine ensemble, and tried to initiate a star system among the singers. In addition to

Janáček he conducted non-standard works such as Martinů's *Julietta,* Handel's *Semele,* Smetana's *Dalibor,* and Donizetti's *Maria Stuarda,* given in English as *Mary Stuart.* During these years Mackerras also emerged as a major conductor of both Verdi and Wagner. The production of *Mary Stuart* featured Janet Baker in the title role; she is lavish in her praise of Mackerras's talents: "And the rapport! Sometimes you stand up there and on a really good night, you feel as if the two of you are composing the music together there and then. Wonderful.... But I suppose that this can happen because he is not only a very brilliant man but also a *tremendous* worker . . . [and] allied together, brilliance and extreme industriousness are an incredible combination to find in a conductor. . . ."An HMV recording was made of this opera in 1982. On disc Mackerras is also the conductor for Beverly Sills's *Roberto Devereux* by Donizetti, made in 1969.

By this stage in his career Mackerras has conducted more operas than any other British conductor currently active. Of repertory not yet specifically mentioned, his Massenet is outstanding, he gave a highly praised *Aïda* in 1973, his Handel is vital but there has been all too little of it, his *Carmen* has had critics comparing him with Sir Thomas Beecham, and his Strauss is luminescent. Rodney Milnes notes in *Opera* that there have been "reservations" expressed by some about Mackerras's Wagner but that "In his most recent [*Ring*] cycle he made the music sound more beautiful simply as music than any other conductor I have heard in the theatre."

—Stephen A. Willier

MACNEIL, Cornell.

Baritone. Born 24 September 1922, in Minneapolis. Married: 1) Margaret Gavan, 1947 (two sons, three daughters, divorced 1972); 2) Tania Rudensky, 1972. Studied with Friedrich Schorr at the Hartt School of Music in Hartford, Connecticut; opera debut in Menotti's *The Consul,* on Broadway, 1950; New York City Opera debut as Germont in *La traviata,* 1953, and sang there until 1956; appeared at San Franc'co as Escamillo, 1955; appeared at Chicago as Puccini's Lescaut, 1957; Teatro alla Scala debut as Carlo in *Ernani,* 1959; Metropolitan Opera debut as Rigoletto, 1959; became president of American Guild of Musical Artists, 1971.

* * *

Cornell MacNeil was a natural singer from his earliest youth. He studied at the Hartt School of Music in Hartford, Connecticut with Friedrich Schorr. In 1945, he became a regular member of the glee club at Radio City Music Hall in New York City and joined the summer stock company at the Paper Mill Playhouse in Millburn, New Jersey. During this time he auditioned for Broadway parts. In 1947, he landed a small role in Victor Herbert's *Sweethearts* and understudied the juvenile lead in the long running musical *Where's Charley?,* which opened October 1948. MacNeil received his first major operatic opportunity when composer Menotti offered him the role of John Sorel in his musical drama *The Consul,* which opened in 1950 at the Ethel Barrymore Theatre on Broadway. It ran for 269 performances. The opera, which won the Pulitzer Prize for music and the Drama Critics Circle Award as Best Musical, also earned praise for MacNeil. Olin Downes

of the *New York Times* (17 March 1950) commended the young MacNeil for his "excellent" singing and the "appropriate pathos and simplicity" of his acting. MacNeil also impressed Menotti with his natural talent, and following Menotti's advice, MacNeil retired from the Broadway stage to prepare seriously for an operatic career. From 1953-56, after a successful debut, MacNeil sang a variety of roles while on the roster of the New York City Opera. After 1959 he traveled extensively, making guest appearances and debuts in San Francisco, Chicago, Caracas, Mexico City and Central City, Colorado.

MacNeil established himself internationally by singing two important debuts substituting for ailing singers. In March 1959, while performing in California, MacNeil received an urgent request from the Teatro alla Scala offering him a debut performance as Charles V in Verdi's *Ernani;* shortly after his warm reception in Italy, he received another urgent call from the Metropolitan Opera, to substitute for Robert Merrill in the title role of Verdi's *Rigoletto.* Both these substitutions served to establish MacNeil as a remarkably adaptable and versatile performer, with an almost instantaneous reputation nationally and internationally. He has also sung with great success in many houses throughout Europe including Covent Garden, the Vienna Staatsoper and the Paris Opéra. MacNeil would sing one more important premiere performance, *Nabucco,* again substituting for another singer, this time Leonard Warren. The Metropolitan Opera premiere in October 1960 was originally intended for Warren, but MacNeil was called on to fill the unexpected hole left by Warren's sudden death in March 1960.

MacNeil is a true Verdi baritone, who has been hailed throughout his career for his vocal consistency and his naturally produced sound. During his tenure at the Metropolitan Opera, MacNeil has shown himself to be well-rounded by presenting a truly broad spectrum of Verdi roles. His Verdi roles for the Metropolitan Opera have included Amonasro in *Aida,* Macbeth, the Count di Luna in *Il trovatore,* Simon Boccanegra, Iago in *Otello,* Guido di Monteforte in *I vespri siciliani* and Sir John Falstaff. He has presented himself equally well in non-Verdi literature and has offered such roles as the Baron Scarpia in Puccini's *Tosca* and Barnaba in Ponchielli's *La Gioconda.* He has also won recognition as a Wagnerian baritone with performances of the Dutchman in Wagner's *Der fliegende Holländer.*

His successes can be monitored by the many newspaper accounts which have recorded his premieres and performances. For the most part, he has always been received warmly and with high critical regard. Early in MacNeil's career, Paul Henry Lang of the *New York Herald Tribune* (25 October 1960) described his voice as "warm, with good color and carrying power" and although Lang mentioned some "slightly uncertain spots in the middle," he thought that MacNeil "sang well" and possessed the necessary "temperament." Winthrop Sargeant of the *New Yorker* (26 February 1966) assessed MacNeil as "one of the truly great Rigoletto's, with a voice of immense size and a fine grasp of character." Richard Freed of the *New York Times* (16 February 1966) proclaimed that MacNeil's Amonasro "reconfirmed" MacNeil as "the great Verdi baritone of this decade" and further that MacNeil's "characterizations seem to grow in subtlety and power from season to season."

No stranger to the American public, MacNeil has been seen many times on live telecasts from the Metropolitan Opera including: Verdi's *Rigoletto, Otello* and *La traviata;* Puccini's *Tosca* and *Il trittico,* and Kurt Weill's *Mahogonny.* He portrayed the elder Germont in Zeffirelli's film version of *La traviata* with Teresa Stratas and Placido Domingo, and can be seen in several "From the Met" video productions including a spectacular performance of the Baron Scarpia in Puccini's *Tosca* with Hildegard Behrens. His opera recording *La traviata* won him an American Grammy Award in 1984 for the Best Opera Recording.

Throughout his career, MacNeil has been committed to improving the life and working conditions of the artists and technicians connected with professional opera. This commitment culminated in his becoming the president of the American Guild of Musical Artists in 1971. In this capacity MacNeil was responsible for the contract negotiations between the on-stage performers and the management of the Metropolitan Opera. Robert Jones of the *New York Sunday News* (21 September 1975) suggests that MacNeil may well be best remembered for his "work as a musical political figure."

—Patricia Robertson

MADAMA BUTTERFLY.

Composer: Giacomo Puccini.

Librettists: Giuseppe Giacosa and Luigi Illica (after the drama by David Belasco based on the story by John Luther Long).

First Performance: Milan, Teatro alla Scala 17 February 1904; revised, Brescia, Grande, 28 May 1904; revised, London, Covent Garden, 10 July 1905; revised, Paris, Opéra-Comique, 28 December 1906.

Roles: Cio-Cio-San (soprano); Lt B.F. Pinkerton (tenor); Sharpless (baritone); Suzuki (mezzo-soprano); Kate Pinkerton (mezzo-soprano); Goro (tenor); Prince Yamadori (baritone); The Bonze (bass); The Imperial Commissioner (bass); The Official Registrar (baritone); Yakuside (baritone); Cio-Cio-San's Mother (mezzo-soprano); Aunt (mezzo-soprano); Cousin (soprano); Trouble (mute); chorus (SSATT).

Publications

books–

Carner, Mosco. *Madame Butterfly: a Guide to the Opera.* London, 1979.
John, Nicholas, ed. *Giacomo Puccini: Madama Butterfly.* London and New York, 1984.

articles–

Herz, Joachim. "Zur Urfassung von Puccinis *Madame Butterfly.*" In *Werk und Wiedergabe,* edited by Sigrid Wiesmann, 239. Bayreuth, 1980.
Smith, Julian. "A Metamorphosis Tragedy." *Proceedings of the Royal Musical Association* 106 (1980): 105.
Avant-scène opéra October (1983) [*Madama Butterfly* issue].
Groos, Arthur. "The Return of the Native: Japan in *Madama Butterfly/Madama Butterfly* in Japan." *Cambridge Opera Journal* 1 (1989): 167.

———. Madame Butterfly: The Story." *Cambridge Opera Journal* 3 (1991): 125.

*   *   *

Most likely due to the organized opposition of the dreaded Teatro alla Scala claque, Puccini's sixth opera, *Madama Butterfly,* was a fiasco in its 1904 Milan premiere, a failure so terrible that the composer withdrew the work and returned the royalties after the very first night. However, following some cuts in the originally lengthy act I, the addition of an intermission between what had been scenes i and ii of act II, and the removal three months later to the more intimate Teatro Grande at Brescia, the opera quickly became one of the most widely performed works in the repertory. Indeed, it is perhaps the most modern work in terms of harmonic style to achieve such popularity.

The dramatic source of *Madama Butterfly* was the American David Belasco's one-act play (itself adapted for the stage from an 1898 magazine story by John Luther Long) about a geisha girl (Butterfly) who marries and is abandoned by an American sailor. After admiring the play and securing the rights from Belasco during a trip to London in the summer of 1900, Puccini set quickly to work with his practiced team of librettists Luigi Illica and Giuseppe Giacosa (writers of *La bohème* and *Tosca*), focusing the story more directly on the title figure by enlarging on the tragic dimension of her character, in particular the dishonor and impoverishment of her family following her father's suicide (before the onset of the story), the passionate sincerity of her love for the American sailor and her desperate, doomed attempt to gain acceptance into his culture. Thus in act I, Madame Butterfly, or Cio-Cio-San, marries the American sailor, Lieutenant Benjamin Franklin Pinkerton; she for love (and to escape her life as a geisha girl) and he for amusement while he waits to find a "real" American wife. In doing so she renounces her religion and in turn brings the renunciation of her priestly uncle the Bonze and her family back on herself; but her love for Pinkerton and their rapturous wedding night overshadows the rest.

In act II, set three years later, Cio-Cio-San is patiently awaiting Pinkerton's return, despite everyone else's certainty that she has been abandoned. When the American ambassador Sharpless hints of Pinkerton's abandonment, she responds by showing him her son by Pinkerton, and he agrees to contact Pinkerton for her. When Pinkerton's ship suddenly appears in the harbor, the enraptured Cio-Cio-San and her maid Suzuki cover the house with flowers and hold a vigil for Pinkerton. In fact, Pinkerton has returned, but he has come with his American wife Kate, not to join Cio-Cio-San but to take the son away to America, as Kate explains in act III. Cio-Cio-San stoically agrees to the plan, but insists that Pinkerton come in person; then she prepares a ritualized death scene in imitation of her father's suicide, first saying good-bye to her son, blindfolding him, and stabbing herself with her father's hara-kiri knife, just as Pinkerton finally arrives.

Although initially criticized as derivative, *Madama Butterfly* stands apart from Puccini's earlier works in several respects. First there is the fully tragic dimension of the heroine. Cio-Cio-San is not just one of the passive "victim-women" that Puccini supposedly featured throughout his career (a clichéd supposition which does not account for the majority of his heroines); she is a brave woman who has made a fatal mistake, and whose discovery and accompanying reaction to

Madama Butterfly, **produced by English National Opera, London, 1986 (with Anne-Marie Owens as Suzuki, Magdalena Falewicz as Butterfly and Jungi Morikani as Sorrow)**

that mistake work well to evoke the definitively tragic mixture of fear and pity.

Second, Puccini's use of motivic and thematic recurrence to depict the main characters, ideas, and events in the drama is more psychologically acute and thorough-going than in any of his other works. That is to say, where Puccini had been content to repeat a good tune for its own sake in his earlier operas, all of the reprises in *Madama Butterfly* are psychologically revealing. For example, the main theme of Cio-Cio-San's late second-act aria—where she had explained to Sharpless that she would rather die than return to the geisha life—returns at the end of the opera as an orchestral accompaniment to her suicide, thus conveying a strong message to Pinkerton and the other persecutors that she will dance no more for their pleasure. Recurrences and transformations of other prominent themes and motives are also used to careful psychological effect, comparable to the leitmotivic usage of Wagner.

Other special features of *Madama Butterfly* include Puccini's use of authentic Japanese songs and other exotic details of style, such as whole tone and pentatonic harmonies, heterophonic textures and use of various gongs, bells, and other oriental-sounding percussion instruments. These exotic aspects of *Madama Butterfly* have sometimes been criticized as superficial, or merely indicative of the contemporary fad for the Orient, but they are actually very convincingly absorbed into Puccini's native Italian style, as demonstrated in the beauty and lyricism of the act-I love duet, among other scenes. Considered in their total effect, it is the above-mentioned unique features rather than the supposed sentimentality of the story which account for the longevity—following the initial fiasco—of this opera's extraordinary appeal.

—Claire Detels

THE MAGIC FLUTE
See DIE ZAUBERFLÖTE

THE MAGISTRATE
See DER CORREGIDOR

MAGNARD, (Lucien-Denis-Gabriel-) Albéric.

Composer. Born 9 June 1865, in Paris. Died 3 September 1914, in Baron, Oise. Magnard's father was editor of *Le Figaro;* studied with Dubois, Massenet, and d'Indy at the Paris Conservatory.

Operas

Yolande, Magnard, 1891. Brussels, Monnaie, 27 December 1892.

Guercoeur, Magnard, 1900, first complete performance [parts reconstructed by Ropartz, Paris, Opéra, 24 April 1931].
Bérénice, Magnard (after Racine), 1909, Paris, Opéra-Comique, 15 December 1911.

Publications

About MAGNARD: books–

Boucher, M. *Albéric Magnard.* Lyons, 1919.
Carraud, G. *La vie, l' oeuvre et la mort d'Albéric Magnard.* Paris, 1921.
Lalo, P. *De Rameau à Ravel: portraits et souvenirs.* Paris, 1947.
Cooper, M. *French Music from the Death of Berlioz to the Death of Fauré.* London, 1951.
Bardet, B. *Albéric Magnard, 1865-1914.* Paris, 1966.
Davies, L. *César Franck and his Circle.* London, 1970.

articles–

Laforêt, C. "L'esthétique d'Albéric Magnard." *La revue musicale* 1 (1920-21): 28.
Linden, A. van der. "Sur quelques lettres d'Albéric Magnard." *Revue belge de musicologie* 5 (1951).

Albéric Magnard was a strong-minded man who met a violent death in World War I, although he was a civilian, because he started a single-handed exchange of shots with a party of soldiers from the invading German army who had entered the garden of his country house. The story is relevant as well as colorful, because what it tells us about his character is also to be found in his music. He has been described by the critic Lionel Salter as "a withdrawn, austere misanthrope, pitilessly realistic about humanity," and though this paints a rather unfriendly picture it cannot be regarded as altogether unfair. Magnard was shamefully neglected in his lifetime in his native France, and the events of his death contributed to the long delay in the posthumous production of his opera *Guercoeur;* after the incident described above, the Germans set fire to his house and the orchestral score of acts I and III were destroyed. It was only later that his friend Guy Ropartz did a fresh instrumentation of the whole work from the vocal score, and the work finally reached the stage of the Paris Opéra in 1931, thirty years after its composition.

Magnard wrote his own libretto for *Guercoeur,* which tells the story of a noble hero and national liberator who has already died before the start of act I. In Heaven, he pleads with the supreme being, Truth, (a soprano role) to return to life, and is allowed to do so on the one condition that suffering, hitherto unknown to him, shall accompany him. In act II he discovers that his wife Giselle has betrayed him with his friend and disciple Heurtal, who in turn aims to seize political power and turn the free society Guercoeur has created into a new dictatorship. Even the people seem to want this, having tired of freedom, and when Guercoeur appeals to them they turn upon him and kill him. Penitent and chastened, he returns to Heaven in act III, declaring with some bitterness that all is vanity: to Truth, it seems that mankind can only look forward to a more enlightened future.

The powerful idiom of *Guercoeur* owes something to Magnard's principal teacher Vincent d'Indy and more than a little to Wagner, whose *Tristan und Isolde* had inspired him as a young man to become a composer. There is a full use of

Wagner's *leitmotiv* principles, but the technique is applied to a personal language, and though the opera is lengthy, the dramatic tension is maintained. The writing for the voices is skillful as is the instrumentation. It has been argued that the only weak music is in the crowd scenes, and that this reflects the composer's low opinion of his fellow men.

Magnard acknowledged his debt to Wagner in the preface to his third and last opera, *Bérénice,* writing with wry modesty, "My score is written in the Wagnerian style. Not having the genius needed to create a new lyric form, I chose from among existing styles that which suits my wholly classical tastes and completely traditional culture." It seems odd to call Wagner classical and traditional in 1911, but in the year that Stravinsky's *Petrushka* opened in Paris, that must have been how the great German master appeared to this very individual Frenchman.

—Christopher Headington

MAHAGONNY.

Composer: Kurt Weill.

Librettist: B. Brecht.

First Performance: Baden-Baden, 17 July 1927; revised as *Aufstieg und Fall der Stadt Mahagonny,* first performed Leipzig, Neues Theater, 9 March 1930.

Roles: Leocadia Begbick (contralto or mezzo-soprano); Fatty (tenor); Trinity Moses (baritone); Jenny (soprano); Jim Mahoney (tenor); Jack (tenor); Billy Bankbook (baritone); Alaska Wolf Joe (bass); Toby Higgins (tenor); chorus (SATB).

Publications

articles–

Blitzstein, M. "On Mahagonny." *Score* no. 23 (1958): 11.
Skulsky, A. "Rise and Fall of the City of Mahagonny." *American Record Guide* October (1958): 113.
Drew, D. "The History of Mahagonny." *Musical Times* 104 (1963): 18.
Kahnt, Harmut. "Die Opernversuche Weills und Brechts mit Mahagonny." In *Musiktheater heute,* edited by Hellmut Kühn, 63. Mainz, 1981.

*   *   *

In the summer of 1927 the Baden-Baden chamber music festival presented, together with premieres of serious works, a "Songspiel" as its authors Bertolt Brecht and Kurt Weill called it: in effect, a cross between a scenic cantata and cabaret-style skit. Entitled *Mahagonny,* the invented name for a symbolic American city that succumbs to corruption, the work used dance and popular music idioms of the day as the basis for a staged setting of satirical poems from Brecht's *Die Hauspostille* (*Domestic Breviary*). Brecht and Weill, encouraged by the rather scandalous success of their little piece, later that year agreed to incorporate it into what turned out to be their only joint full-blown opera, now entitled *Aufstieg*

und Fall der Stadt Mahagonny (*Rise and Fall of the City of Mahagonny*). Interrupted by other undertakings, most notably their *Die Dreigroschenoper* (*The Threepenny Opera*), the opera was finally given its premiere in Leipzig on March 9th, 1930, to a stormy reception whipped up by political demonstrations.

The subject of the opera is the history of the city of Mahagonny itself: from its founding and development to its disintegration, after several crises, and final downfall. The people of this city, common adventurers, criminals and prostitutes, are reduced to types representing modern, capitalist society, shown with all its insatiable greed, lust for pleasure, and supreme regard for money. Four men arrive in the city, flush with earnings from lumberjacking in Alaska, and determined to enjoy every penny's worth to the hilt. Soon, however, they become bored and disillusioned. A hurricane almost destroys the city, and Jim, their leader, is led to nihilism: absolute self-indulgence is now all that matters. Anarchy descends on Mahagonny. In the end Jim cannot pay for his pleasures and is condemned to death. After his execution, further catastrophes are followed by the city's destruction.

The opera is constructed according to Brecht's principles of epic theater, with which Weill at the time found himself in sympathy, seeing in them a means by which he could realize a neoclassical ambition to revive the old number opera while also injecting the genre with a modern approach and socially relevant content. Thus music, text, and staging do not fuse or reciprocally illustrate each other, but rather interact as independent forces to create a series of what Weill called "morality pictures of our time." The opera's twenty-one scenes, separated by spoken narrative and projected inscriptions, use music to comment on, and even take issue with, the text and stage action. Techniques of parody and caricature include musical quotation and allusions to already familiar idioms. Such popular styles of the day as tango, fox-trot, and shimmy, cast in dance-band instrumentation, appear in distorted form to point an accusing finger at the perversion of a world ruled by consumption. These mix with sections worked in "serious" operatic style, but made subject to a disjointedness which serves, similarly, a morally critical purpose. That is, Weill's constant interruption of expectations for formal continuity and closure, principally through a cleverly altered harmony but also through having a meter and rhythm that do not support the harmony as they should, has the effect of shocks that rupture any illusion of aesthetic unity. Through the gaps in the form we are shown reality, or, as Weill himself put it, "the state of things in their most crass form and without varnish." By detaching itself and refusing emotional support, the music does more, however, than merely report on what happens in the play; rather it is made to speak out, often with an expression of protest all of its own, against what are shown on stage as the evils inherent in the breakdown of humanity.

The *Mahagonny* opera must be viewed as a topical work in that it was concerned to illuminate, through an imaginative, perhaps even surrealistic treatment of character and situation, the social malaise which Brecht saw to be overtaking his own age. Weill may have lacked the political convictions of his collaborator, but he was possessed of a comparable social conscience and consciousness, such as would produce for this opera as well as other joint stage works of the period music of a peculiarly searching, critical, and perhaps even revolutionary quality. It is precisely this quality that explains the opera's troubled career in the few years before it fell victim to the Nazi regime. After the Leipzig premiere a series of revisions and cuts were forced on it by nervous producers; in particular the versions for Berlin and Vienna in 1931 and

1932 respectively, by reducing the work merely to its most striking numbers, robbed it of much of its operatic character. Revivals beginning in Germany (Darmstadt, 1957), followed by those in Britain, Canada, and America, while they have restored the authentic version, have struggled (not always successfully) to give a convincing interpretation of a score strung between the poles of the artful and the almost crudely subversive.

—Alan Lessem

MAHLER, Gustav.

Conductor/Composer. Born 7 July 1860, in Kalischt, Bohemia. Died 18 May 1911, in Vienna. Married: Alma Schindler, 1902 (two daughters). Studied piano with Julius Epstein, harmony with Robert Fuchs, and composition with Franz Krenn at the Vienna Conservatory, beginning 1875; studied history and philosophy at the University of Vienna, 1877-80; theater conductor at Ljubljana, 1881, Olmütz, 1882, Vienna, 1883, and Kassel, 1883-85; second Kapellmeister to Anton Seidl at the Prague Opera, 1885; assistant to Arthur Nikisch in Leipzig, 1886-88; music director of the Royal Opera in Budapest, 1888; conductor at the Hamburg Opera, 1891; music director of the Vienna Court Opera, 1897-1907; succeeded Hans Richter as conductor of the Vienna Philharmonic, 1898-1901; principal conductor of the Metropolitan Opera in New York, 1907-11; conductor of the New York Philharmonic, 1909-11. Mahler was also a composer of symphonies and vocal works.

Publications

By MAHLER: books–

Mahler, A., ed. *Briefe Gustav Mahlers.* Berlin, 1924; revised, H. Blaukopf, ed., Vienna, 1982; English translation, London, 1979.

————. *Gustav Mahler: Erinnerungen und Briefe.* Amsterdam, 1940; English translation, London, 1946.

Hansen, M., ed. *Gustav Mahler: Briefe.* Leipzig, 1981.

Blaukopf, H., ed., and E. Jephcott, trans. *Gustav Mahler— Richard Strauss: Correspondence 1888-1911.* London, 1984.

Blaukopf, H., ed. *Mahler's Unknown Letters.* Boston, 1987.

About MAHLER: books–

Lébl, V. "Gustav Mahler als Kappellmeister des deutschen Landestheaters in Prague." *Hudebni veda* 12 (1975).

Werba, R. "Il *Don Giovanni* nella interpretatione di Gustav Mahler." *Nuova rivista musicale italiana* 9 (1975).

Blaukopf, H., ed. *Mahler: a Documentary Study.* New York, 1976.

Willnauer, G.F. *Gustav Mahler und die Wiener Opera.* Vienna, 1979.

Filler, S. *Gustav and Alma Mahler: a Guide to Research.* New York, 1989.

Roman, Z. *Gustav Mahler's American Years: a Documentary History.* Stuyvesant, New York, 1989.

articles–

Stein, E. "Mahler and the Vienna Opera." *Opera* January, March, April, and May (1953).

Stomper, S. "Gustav Mahler als Dirigent und Regisseur: Ein Beitrag zur Geschichte der Operninterpretation." *Jahrbuch der Komischen Oper Berlin* 8 (1968).

* * *

One of music's greatest symphonists, Gustav Mahler embodies a supreme irony in that he spent the bulk of his working life in the opera pit. Opera touched his life early on when, as a teenage piano prodigy, he performed a program that included a Meyerbeer Fantasie, a medley from *Lucia di Lammermoor,* and Thalberg's Fantasia on themes from *Norma.* There are, in addition, four separate sets of fragments representing his unfinished operatic juvenilia. Most worthy of mention here are his *Herzog Ernst von Schwaben,* which pre-dates his departure for Vienna in 1875 to study at the Conservatory, and *Rübezahl,* an opera inspired by the myth of the Silesian mountain sprite, that intermittently occupied him for over ten years, from 1879 to 1890.

Mahler's career as opera conductor began in 1881 with his appointment to the provincial theater in Ljubjana (formerly Laibach), followed in short order by engagements in Olmütz, and Kassel. Among the first operas he conducted are: *Il trovatore, Die Zauberflöte, Der Freischütz, Il barbiere di Siviglia, Les Huguenots, Robert le Diable, Martha* (also Flotow's *Alessandro Stradella*), *Carmen,* as well as Maillard's *Les dragons de Villars,* Boieldieu's *La dame blanche,* and Marschner's *Hans Heiling.* In addition, he was responsible for operettas by Johann Strauss, Suppe, and Offenbach, to mention a few.

At the same time, Mahler was already developing a reputation for being a tyrannical perfectionist, obsessive about every detail of nuance, tempo, and balance. However, he was as restless as he was demanding. By 1885 he had arrived in Prague to assume the position of Kapellmeister at the Deutsches Landestheater, the very theater in which *Don Giovanni* had had its premiere a hundred years earlier. Indeed, it was in Prague that Mahler achieved his first major successes, particularly in the Mozart and Wagner repertory. It was on 1 August 1885 that he conducted his very first *Lohengrin.* The *Ring, Tristan und Isolde, Die Meistersinger,* and *Tannhäuser* followed during the same season. In early 1886, presumably to mark the 130th anniversary of Mozart's birth, Mahler conducted his first *Entführung aus dem Serail* and *Così fan tutte.* His performances of Mozart were praised for the diction of the recitatives, though there were understandable reservations about his use of strings in *secco* passages. But Mahler did not survive beyond one season because of differences with the ballet mistress and the theater director. Yet, during his final three months in Pague he was assigned new productions, of Marschner's *Hans Heiling,* Lortzing's *Undine,* and Meyerbeer's *Le prophète,* Gluck's *Iphigenie in Aulide* (Wagner's edition), and *Fidelio.* The *Fidelio* is interesting for the fact that Mahler adopted the practice of inserting the "Leonore" Overture no. 3 between the two acts. Mahler's tenure in Prague, though brief, did involve responsibilities that were worthy of his immense gifts. He was also able to begin conducting the major operas upon which his subsequent career in the theater was to be built.

Mahler's two years (1886-1888) in Leipzig were important for two main reasons: 1) as a subordinate to the first Kapellmeister, he was forced to compete with Arthur Nikisch, arguably Germany's foremost conductor; 2) there was some

Gustav Mahler, c. 1910

expansion of his repertoire to include Meyerbeer's *L'africaine* and works by Kreutzer and Weber (*Der Freischütz* and *Oberon*). The Weber connection was important for another reason; it was in Leipzig that Mahler completed the score of Weber's unfinished comic opera *Die Drei Pintos,* a task that, with generous publishing and performing rights, proved to be Mahler's greatest financial success to date. What is more, work on this project inspired his own creativity; several "Wunderhorn" songs and portions of the first and second symphonies were the result.

After two years in Leipzig, Mahler moved on to the Royal Budapest Opera, where matters were complicated by his impossible promise of creating a Hungarian National opera. There was a distrust of foreigners, especially Jews, and the inevitable quarrels ensued. In March 1891 he made his debut at the Hamburg opera conducting *Tannhäuser.* Critics were ecstatic and spoke of his "genius." It was during his tenure in Hamburg that Mahler made his only visit to England, conducting Wagner and Beethoven staples of the repertoire at Covent Garden in a series of eighteen performances during June and July of 1892. Most of the singers signed up by Sir Augustus Harris were from Hamburg as well.

Some five years later, on 11 May 1897, Mahler made his debut at the Vienna Hofoper with *Lohengrin.* The prodigal son had returned. It was a position that he had coveted for some time and one that Brahms had helped him obtain. Mahler's tempi in Wagner became a critical issue. He retorted with " . . . your tradition is really nothing but your comfort and your laziness." He did on occasion have to defer to director William Jahn's caprices (performing Leoncavallo's *La bohème* rather than Puccini's is a case in point). But Mahler was able to eventually assume full control of lighting, costumes, decor, and acting, sometimes engaging singers less for vocal prowess than for stage presence. His collaborations with stage designer Alfred Roller (friend of Gustav Klimt) were memorable in decisively shaping the productions of *Der Freischütz, Tristan,* and *Don Giovanni* with impressionist and Vienna Secession touches. However, much of this took a financial and emotional toll.

When, in 1907, Mahler left Vienna after "ten war years," he had only four more years to live. These were spent mainly in New York at the Metropolitan Opera in repertoire built on Mozart, Wagner, Smetana's *Bartered Bride* and Tchaikovsky's *Queen of Spades.* His Wagner was marveled at for the remarkable balance between voice and orchestra. Unfortunately matters deteriorated after his first season with changes in management. Giulio Gatti-Casazza, lured from the Teatro alla Scala, brought a shining new star in the person of Arturo Toscanini.

—Joshua Berrett

THE MAID OF ORLEANS [Orleanskaya deva].

Composer: Piotr Ilyich Tchaikovsky.

Librettist: Piotr Ilyich Tchaikovsky (after Zhukovsky's translation of Schiller, *Die Jungfrau von Orleans*).

First Performance: St Petersburg, Mariinsky, 25 February 1881; revised, 1882.

While browsing through his sister Alexandra's library one day, Tchaikovsky came across a copy of Schiller's drama, *Die Jungfrau von Orleans,* translated into Russian by Zhukovsky. In *Die Jungfrau,* Friedrich von Schiller, the leading German poet, playwright, and essayist of the latter eighteenth century, had reworked the facts about Joan of Arc into a heroic tale of good and evil. With the French arrayed against the English, Joan appears in the form of divine intervention as a savior for the French. No longer merely a stolid peasant girl, Schiller's Joan is an eloquent, elegant beauty who becomes involved in a fictional love affair with one of the enemy. Joan atones for this sin by her death on the battlefield rather than at the stake. Schiller's dramatization is thus a story of innocence, sin, guilt, and redemption.

Tchaikovsky, casting about for a new opera subject after *Eugene Onegin,* seized upon this famous historical tale. The subject itself, Tchaikovsky's treatment of it, and hints in his correspondence suggest that he was hoping to break into the world of international opera. It was Tchaikovsky's first opera from a non-Russian literary source, with a subject quite different from opera plots by Tchaikovsky's contemporaries. With its extensive use of a chorus, and the interpolation of a long ballet for the dwarves and pages, it exhibits the influence of the highly successful French grand opera style. "I do not think *The Maid of Orleans* the finest, or the most emotional, of my works, but it seems to me to be the one most likely to make my name popular," he wrote to his patron Madame von Meck. His hope, however, was not to be realized.

Fired by the subject, Tchaikovsky worked quickly. He planned a special trip to Paris to collect literary sources, but he was so eager to get started that he began to put together his own text from Zhukovsky's translation, and von Meck sent him a copy of Henri Wallon's *Jeanne d'Arc.* Even after the trip to Paris, he continued to work without a libretto or even a completely worked-out scenario. Each evening he would work on the text for the following day's music.

He followed up on plans to investigate other settings of the story of Joan of Arc, examining Auguste Mermet's opera *Jeanne d'Arc* and Verdi's *Giovanna d'Arco,* as well as a number of other literary sources. When he looked at Mermet's libretto, however, he was unimpressed. "In the end I have come to the conclusion that Schiller's tragedy, although it is not consistent with historical accuracy, still outstrips all other artistic presentations of *Joan* in its depth of psychological truth," he wrote to von Meck.

The opera opens with Joan at home on the farm with her father Thibault, when news arrives of the approach of the English army. Joan, overhearing this, suddenly speaks out and begins to prophesy. The time has come for action, and she bids farewell to her home. Act II finds Joan with king-to-be Charles VII in despair over the war situation approaching Orleans. Joan convinces everyone that she is sent from God by identifying the hidden Charles immediately and revealing his private prayers.

In act III Joan meets Lionel in battle, vanquishing him but hesitating to kill him when she catches sight of his face. In a peculiar emotional reversal, the two fall in love. Lionel refuses to flee, joining the French cause. But at the coronation, Thibault accuses his daughter of consorting with the devil rather than God. When challenged, she is overcome with guilt over her encounter with Lionel, and she cannot defend herself. In act IV, when Lionel pursues her to comfort her, she flees, but then yields to their mutual passion in a love scene. The English approach, but Joan refuses to escape. Lionel is killed trying to defend her. In the final scene, a chorus of angels sing support as Joan is led to her death at the stake.

When Tchaikovsky took up the strands of this drama, he was inspired by the image Schiller had woven of a noble girl trapped by fate, divinely inspired but susceptible to human love. Tchaikovsky's libretto was a Russified adaptation of Schiller's remaking of the historical Joan of Arc. The result is a hodgepodge of the Schiller version and Tchaikovsky's other sources, with a more historically accurate version of Joan's death at the stake tacked on at the end. However, Tchaikovsky's most notable embellishments involve the treatment of the love affair between Joan and Lionel. Schiller's Joan felt an involuntary attraction to the knight, though she fought against it and rejected his advances. Tchaikovsky, however, aggrandized the love affair, allowing Joan to wallow in and agonize over her feelings.

Much of the music in the opera is uninspiring, as if Tchaikovsky had watered down his style for an international audience. "I am glad to know that *The Maid of Orleans* is free from the faults of my earlier pseudo-opera style," he wrote to von Meck, "in which I wearied my listeners with a superfluity of details, and made my harmony too complicated, so that there was no moderation in my orchestral effects. . . . Opera style should be broad, simple, and decorative." But by and large, the music consists of discouragingly long stretches of eminently forgettable music and insipid dialogue, interspersed with stirring instrumental numbers and occasional moments of great beauty, such as Joan's farewell to the scenes of her childhood in act I.

Though the two works are not without interest, neither Schiller's play nor Tchaikovsky's opera are held in universally high esteem today. Ultimately *The Maid of Orleans* is most interesting for its revelations about Tchaikovsky's operatic technique, his interest in the successful tradition of French grand opera, and for his ongoing efforts to achieve a major operatic success.

—Elizabeth W. Patton

THE MAID TURNED MISTRESS
See LA SERVA PADRONA

THE MAKROPOULOS CASE [Věc Makropoulos].

Composer: Leoš Janáček.

Librettist: Leoš Janáček (after a play by Karel Čapek).

First Performance: Brno, National Theater, 18 December 1926.

Roles: Emilia Marty (soprano); Albert Gregor (tenor); Jaroslav Prus (baritone); Vitek (tenor); Kolenaty (baritone); Janek (tenor); Krista (mezzo-soprano); Hauk-Sendorf (tenor); Stagehand (bass); Servants (contraltos); chorus (TTBB).

Publications

articles–

Mackerras, Charles. "Janáček's *Makropoulos.*" *Opera* February (1964).

Pečman, Rudolf. "Janáčeks Oper vom ewigen Leben" [*Makropoulos Case*]. *Österreichische Musikzeitschrift* 34 (1979): 201.

✻   ✻   ✻

In act I we are in the law offices of Dr Kolenaty, whose assistant, Vitek, is working on a case of inheritance. This process has been, off and on, in the courts for about 100 years with no legal resolution, owing to the fact that a will said to have existed has never been found despite massive searches. The would-be inheritor is one Albert Gregor.

In the midst of the legal discussions between Vitek and Albert Gregor, Krista, Vitek's daughter, enters. She has just heard the great opera singer, Emilia Marty, the night before and is still in a trance. An opera student herself, she is inspired to work harder after hearing the great singer. They are interrupted by the entrance of Dr Kolenaty and the great Marty herself. Everyone is fascinated by her beauty and her cold

Anja Silja in *The Makropoulos Case,* Gunther Rennert's production for Stuttgart Opera, 1970

personality, while she, in turn, seems interested only in the Gregor case. She has come to Dr Kolenaty for a complete history of it. Kolenaty obliges with a didactic recital of the facts of the case. Emilia interrupts him with supposed facts about the people involved from generations ago. Dr Kolenaty and Albert Gregor are puzzled and irritated by her remarks, since they refer to things that she couldn't know, but still, they aren't quite sure what to make of her. She speaks as if she knew the founder of the family, Ferdinand Prus; in fact she uses his nickname, Pepi. She also knows that he had a son; she says that the mother was one Elliana MacGregor, a famous opera singer. Due to the son's illegitimacy, he was given the last name of MacGregor, or perhaps just Gregor.

Ferdinand Prus, it seems, left a will but nobody seems to know its whereabouts or whether, in fact, it really ever existed. But Marty knows, she says. It is to be found in a desk located in the Prus house. Marty urges Dr Kolenaty to break into that house to retrieve old "Pepi's" papers and the will; he flatly refuses. He thinks Marty is mad. But Albert, believing her, forces Dr Kolenaty to burglarize the house. While he is gone, Albert and Emilia talk. He becomes infatuated with the mysterious woman, but Emilia rejects his advances, treats him rudely, and angers him by her harsh rejection. Suddenly, Dr Kolenaty returns, and, stunningly, has the papers in his hand, including the will, which clinches the case for Albert Gregor.

The remainder of the plot is taken up with identifying the person of Emilia Marty. Pressed for an explanation, Emilia relates that when she was a young girl her father, Dr Makropoulos, was asked by Emperor Rudolf for a medication to postpone aging and death. When Makropoulos developed the drug, the emperor demanded that it be tested on someone, so Dr Makropoulos' own daughter, Elena, was chosen for the job. Elena suffered but recovered, and the drug was eventually proven successful, for Elena was to live much past the normal human life span. Through the years she moved around, with each move taking a new name, but always with the initials E.M. At various times she was known as Elliana MacGregor (from Ireland!), Elena Makropoulos, Eugenia Montez, and now Emilia Marty. Now 342 years old, she has experienced everything and has become embittered by the very process of life. To her there is no good, no evil, nothing moral or immoral any more. She has come to see all life as insubstantial, and has lost all capacity to feel anything. She rejects the chance to live longer by using the parchment with its drug prescription, which Prus has found among the papers of Ellian MacGregor. Emilia slowly falls into a stupor and then death. Before dying, she hands the parchment to Krista, who, after a moment's thought, burns it.

The Makropoulos Case, one of Janáček's most important operas, is also one of his most problematic. The first difficulty is the nature of the text. The libretto is taken directly from a play by Czechoslovakia's great playwright, Karel Čapek. Čapek's play was contemporary, with idiomatic language and very little of a poetic nature. Janáček remains faithful to Čapek's language. Thus, people order taxis, answer telephones, and speak the language of normal conversation.

Many years before, Janáček was engaged in researching the "music" of every day speech. He believed that speech was the major clue to a person's emotional life and identity, so he traveled over much of Eastern Europe transcribing into pitches what he heard people say in their normal conversations. How fast did they talk, how slow, how high, how low, when did they stutter, when did they hesitate? These and many other characteristics were of critical importance to the composer. He was particularly interested in the changes wrought in speech patterns under the pressure of emotional

stress. To Janáček, this was the "music" hidden in speech and it came to be more and more of a controlling factor in his compositions. It is the extreme of this method that one encounters in The Makropoulos Case, and it is perfectly suited to the language found there. It isn't valid to criticize Janáček for the absence of long line melodies as he was striving for the exact opposite, the melodic cell, always reflective of mind states, of the emotional temperature so to speak. It is an art of considerable subtlety, and its effect on the listener is likely to be variable. In a sense, it takes a gifted listener to make sense of Janáček's jagged, naturalistic rhythms, and his telegraphic melodic style.

Similarly, Janáček's orchestra lacks a conventionally beautiful sound. One's ears are constantly directed from one choir to another, as if one is hearing an extraordinary conversation about the stage action. As a fitfully convinced admirer of Wagner, Janáček assigns the orchestra a similar function assigned to it by the earlier master, but the leitmotif technique is not exactly what Janáček uses here. The orchestra acts as a commentary to the stage, but its musical material is often quite different from that of the voices. Despite its close mirroring of the stage events, it remains motivically separated from the action to a remarkable degree.

As for the harmonic language, Makropoulos is a thoroughly tonal score, but the tonal focus shifts very quickly, and the sense of incessant movement to new tonal centers can make one feel that it veers from conventional tonal thinking into pan-tonality.

Finally, one must ask whether Janáček's methods "work" for the listener. This is not difficult music to follow, but it requires an agile mind, and a developed ear to respond to its real nature. As of this writing (1990), the number of such listeners seems to be growing rapidly.

—Harris Crohn

MALIBRAN, Maria Felicità.

Mezzo-soprano. Born 24 March 1808, in Paris. Died 23 September 1836, in Manchester. Married: 1) merchant François Eugène Malibran, 1826 (divorced 1835); 2) violinist Charles de Bériot, 1836 (one son). Studied with her father, the tenor Manuel Garcia, and with Panseron and Herold in Naples; first appeared on stage at age six in Paer's Agnese, Naples, 1814; London debut as Rosina in Il barbiere di Siviglia, 1825; in New York with her father, 1825-26; returned to Europe in 1827; Paris debut in Semiramide, 1828; sang in Paris and London, 1829-32, then went to Italy; sang Bellini's Romeo in I Capuleti ed i Montecchi, Bologna, 1832; sang in La sonnambula, Naples, 1833; Teatro alla Scala debut as Norma, 1834.

Publications

About MALIBRAN: books–

Anon. Memoirs, Critical and Historical, of Madame Malibran de Beriot. London, 1836.
Barbieri, G. Notizie biografiche di M.F. Malibran. Milan, 1836.
Nathan, I. Memoirs of Madame Malibran de Beriot. London, 1836.

Maria Malibran as Leonora in *Fidelio*, 1836

Merlin, Countess de. *Memoirs of Madame Malibran.* London, 1840.

Chorley, H. *Thirty Years' Musical Recollections.* London, 1862.

Legouvé, E. *Maria Malibran.* Paris, 1880.

Heron-Allen, E. *Contributions towards an Accurate Biography of the Beriot and Malibran.* Paris, 1880.

Pougin, A. *Marie Malibran: histoire d'une cantatrice.* Paris, 1911.

Larionoff, P. and F. Pestellini. *Maria Malibran e i suoi tempi.* Florence, 1935.

Bielli, D. *Maria Malibran.* Castelbordino, 1936.

Desternes, S. and Henriette Chandet. *La Malibran et Pauline Viardot.* Paris, 1969.

Reparaz, C. *Maria Malibran: Estudio biográfico.* Madrid, 1976.

Gattey, C. *Queens of Song.* London, 1979.

Bushnell, H. *Maria Malibran: A Biography of the Singer.* University Park, 1979.

Giazotto, R. *Maria Malibran (1808-1836): Una vita nei nomi di Rossini e Bellini.* Turin, 1986.

Fitzlyon, A. *Maria Malibran, Diva of the Romantic Age.* London, 1987.

articles—

Teneo, M. "La Malibran d'apres des documents inedits." *Sammelbande der Internationalen Musik-Gesellschaft* 7 (1905-06): 437.

*   *   *

As the daughter of a great tenor, Maria Malibran (née Garcia) grew up in the theater and appeared onstage with her father whenever the plot called for a child. The earliest recorded mention of these instances was in Italy, during Garcia's engagements there 1811-16, when she appeared in Mayr's *Medea in Corinto* and Paer's *Agnese.* Legend says that in the latter, during a memory lapse by the soprano, little Maria delighted the audience by singing the melody herself. As she matured, her father devoted his considerable energies to training her voice, which at first seemed unpromising.

While in Italy, Garcia had refined his art under the great Italian masters, especially Giovanni Ansani, and was thus able to pass this knowledge to his daughter. In addition, he was very impressed with the art of Giuditta Pasta, his constant partner onstage in Paris and London. Pasta's ability to extend her upper and lower registers into the middle range enabled her to bring an unaccustomed drama to the music; she could sing a given note or passage in the lightness and sweetness of her head voice, or in the power and richness of her chest tones depending on the demands of the music or the dramatic situation. This was the ability that Garcia sought to give his daughter, and Maria's success in achieving it was one of the qualities that would establish her as the greatest singer of the age.

This period of Maria's life was not a happy one. Garcia was a brutal parent, merciless in his demands; in her later life Maria would remark that she learned how to sing through tears during her father's lessons.

In 1825, Garcia determined that his seventeen year old daughter, if not a finished artist, was at least marketable, and during a casting crisis at the King's Theatre in London he contracted her to that theater's desperate manager, John Ebers, at an absurdly high fee. Thus she made her formal operatic debut in June 1825 as Rosina, opposite her father's Almaviva in Rossini's *Il barbiere di Siviglia.* Despite the circumstances of this appearance, she succeeded in winning both public and critical approval and soon sang in the first London production of Meyerbeer's *Il Crociato in Egitto.* Subsequent performances in the English musical festivals that summer were less successful however, as both the inadequacies of her art and her status as a beginner became more apparent.

At this time, Manuel Garcia, now fifty years old and in vocal decline, accepted an engagement in the Americas. Assembling a troop largely consisting of his family, he arrived in New York in November 1825 and presented the first Italian Opera heard in the New World. In that less cultured land, before less demanding audiences, Maria Garcia spent two years perfecting her art and establishing herself as America's first prima donna. There too she escaped her father's unbearable cruelty by marrying Eugène Malibran, a French businessman three times her age. In the fall of 1826 the Garcia troop departed for Mexico and Maria Malibran retired from the stage, but within weeks her husband's business affairs suffered reversals that demanded her return to the theater at the highest fees possible, and by the autumn of 1827 his problems were such that the couple agreed that she should return to Paris where she could earn even more money.

Arriving in Paris in November 1827, Maria sought out family and friends, particularly the Countess Merlin and Rossini, who quickly presented her in the best salons before the musical *cognoscenti.* Then in January 1828 she appeared at the Académie Royale de Musique as Semiramide. Her success was immense. From this time until her death her career moved with a power hitherto unknown in the opera world. "She set the world on fire," wrote a contemporary, and such was the public hysteria in England, France, Italy, wherever she sang, that those words hardly seem overstated. Theaters in which she sang reported their highest gross receipts ever; drawings of her and incidents in her life were sold to an avid public; her arrival in Venice stopped the city for hours, and before she left a theater had been renamed for her. After her La Scala debut the audience unhitched her carriage and drew her home. Even governments in those revolutionary times trembled before her emotional control of crowds. At the premier of Persiani's *Ines de Castro,* which was written for her, the applause "rivalled Vesuvius's most violent eruptions" and people were carried fainting from the theater. All but deified, Maria Malibran redefined fame.

It would seem that everyone who attended a Malibran performance and who could hold a pen attempted to describe the indescribable. Her voice was "not exactly beautiful" (although many, including Chopin, disagreed), nor was it perfect, particularly in the middle register, which could be unfocused, even hollow, in sound. But its range was a remarkable three octaves, from low D to high D (sometimes E), and its quality, that of a rich contralto with a soprano register superadded, was distinguished by a strange and exciting timbre. The soprano register possessed a liquid sweetness; her contralto notes were richer, with a singular power and smoothness. The middle voice could be sung in either the brilliance of her soprano register or the rich power of her chest tones, which she used frequently and with more force than any singer before her. In addition, she executed the most difficult coloratura passages and embellishments as brilliantly as any singer before the public: her arpeggios and trills were astonishing, her ability to embellish and improvise apparently limitless. She was particularly adept at immense leaps of two and even three octaves, which she used to avoid the weakness between the mezzo and soprano registers. Her use of ornamentation for dramatic effect (as opposed to mere vocal display) was considered unique. That her voice was "unrivalled for compass, volume, and richness," might be ascertained from those legendary evenings when she sang both *Fidelio* and *Sonnambula* in sequence.

Malibran's vocal abilities were matched by a dramatic aptitude quite new to the operatic stage. Equally adept at both drama and comedy, she brought an unaccustomed naturalness, an emotional realism to her roles, eschewing the stock gestures then in currency. Giuditta Pasta, her only rival, was the perfection of the classic style, her "walk of terrible grandeur," the noble gestures, every movement accomplished with the full awareness that she was acting before an audience. In contrast, Malibran "forgot to find herself before a public," and varied her performances according to her mood, just as she could vary her musical embellishments according to her audience or inspiration. Furthermore, her very feminine appearance and appealing features immediately captured audience sympathy; visually she was always in character. Chorley tells us that although "not handsome, she was better than beautiful," that she possessed "great mobility of expression in her features," and that her style of dress indicated the character of a woman "thoroughly, fearlessly original." Acute swings of mood—her letters range from profound depression to the gayest hilarity—indicate both a manic-depressive temperament and an emotional range clearly mirrored in an art producing such a powerful impression that "few among her contemporaries could go home and sit in cool judgement upon one who, while she was before them, carried them as she pleased to the extremities of grave or gay."

Unfortunately, those same qualities would prove highly self-destructive. The impresario Alfred Bunn, who presented her in London, had long foreseen the inevitable outcome of such a life, the fate of one who would sing two operas on the same evening and rush off to the salons (where socialites would pay anything for a song from the throat of La Malibran), and even then dash off to town for further diversion. Bunn wrote, "The powerful and conflicting elements in her composition were gifts indeed, but of a very fatal nature—the mind was far too great for the body, and it did not require any wonderful gift of prophecy to foresee that, in their contention, the triumph would be but short, however brilliant and decisive."

In 1829, Maria fell in love with the Belgian violinist Charles de Bériot. As a citizen of Catholic France, she could not divorce Eugène, still an ocean away and with whom she had become thoroughly disgusted. In desperation, she wrote to General Lafayette, whom she had met only once but who was only too glad to help the famous and charming Maria Malibran. For years he tried, futilely, to push a divorce law through Parliament, but ultimately her lawyers had the marriage annulled under logic so flimsy that one suspects bribery or other political manipulation, and she married Charles. Meanwhile, she had given birth to their son, Charles Wilfred, who was, of course, illegitimate in a hypocritical age that did not accept such social transgressions gracefully and from which she suffered greatly.

In the spring of 1836 she was thrown from a horse and suffered cranial injuries (probably a severe concussion). Refusing to slow the pace of her career, she continued singing but died under the most dramatic of circumstances in Manchester during a music festival that September. She was twenty-eight years old. Her youthful demise sealed the immortality of her legend, and she remains one of the most famous and intriguing singers in musical history. After her final performances in Naples, 1835, a critic wrote: "And when we live in memories, recalling how nature and art lavished on you their utmost powers, we will have those memories with which to embitter the youth of our children." She must have been phenomenal.

—Howard Bushnell

MALIPIERO, Gian Francesco.

Composer. Born 18 March 1882, in Venice. Died 1 August 1973, in Treviso, near Venice. Grandfather, Francesco Malipiero, composed operas; father, Luigi, a musician; studied violin at the Vienna Conservatory, 1898; studied with Marco Bossi at the Liceo Musicale Benedetto Marcello; degree in composition from the Liceo Musicale G.B. Martini in Bologna, 1904; in Paris, 1913; returned to Italy, 1921, and taught composition at the University of Parma, 1921-23; director of the Liceo Musicale Benedetto Marcello in Venice, 1939; member of the National Institute of Arts and Letters, New York, 1949; member of the Royal Flemish Academy in Brussels, 1952; member of the Institut de France, 1954; member of the Akademie der Künste in West Berlin, 1967. Malipiero was also editor of collected editions of the works of Monteverdi and the instrumental music of Vivaldi.

Operas

Publishers: Birchard, Carisch, Chester, Eulenburg, Hansen, Ricordi, Senart, Suivini Zerboni, Universal.

Schiavona, early.

Elen e Fuldano, S. Benco, 1907-09.

Canossa, S. Benco, 1911-12, Rome, Costanzi, 24 January 1914.

Sogno d'un tramonto d'autunno, Gabriele D'Annunzio, 1913, Radio Audizioni Italiana, 4 October 1963.

Lancelotto del lago, A. De Stefani, 1914-15.

L'orfeide [triology: 1) *La morte delle maschere,* 1921-22; 2) *Sette canzoni,* 1918-19; 3) *Orfeo, ovvero l'ottava canzone,* 1919-20], Malipiero; *Sette canzoni* performed Paris, Opéra, 10 July 1920; complete performance, Düsseldorf, Stadtsoper, 5 November 1925.

San Francesco d'Assisi, Malipiero (after St. Francis), 1920-21; concert performance, New York, Carnegie Hall, 29 March 1922; staged performance, Perugia, 22 September 1949.

Tre commedie goldoniane [triology: 1) *La bottega del cafè;* 2) *Sior Todaro Brontolon;* 3) *Le baruffe chiozzotte*], Malpiero (after Carlo Goldoni), 1920, Darmstadt, Hessisches Landestheater, 24 March 1926.

Filomela e l'infatuato, Malipiero, 1925, Prague, Deutsches Theater, 31 March 1928.

Merlino maestro d'organi, Malipiero, 1926-27, Rome, Rome Radio, 1 August 1934; staged performance, Massimo, 28 March 1972.

Il mistero di Venezia [trilogy: 1) *Le aquile di Aquileia,* 1928; 2) *Il finto Arlecchino,* 1925; 3) *I corvi di Venezia,* 1928], Malipiero, 1925-28; *Il finto Arlecchino* performed Mainz, Stadttheater, 8 March 1928; complete performance, Coburg, Landestheater, 15 December 1932.

Torneo notturno, Malipiero, 1929, Munich, Nationaltheater, 15 May 1931.

I trionfi d'amore [trilogy: 1) *Castel smeraldo;* 2) *Mascherate* (after G.G. de Rossi); 3) *Giochi olimpichi*], Malipiero, 1930-31; *Mascherate* performed as *Il festino,* Turin Radio, 6 November 1937; staged performance, Bergamo, Donizetti, 2 October 1954 [numbers 1 and 3 never performed]

La bella e il mostro, Malipiero (after Perrault), 1930.

La favola del figlio cambiato, Luigi Pirandello, 1932-33, Brunswick, Landestheater, 13 January 1934.

Giulio Cesare, Malipiero (after Shakespeare), 1934-35, Genoa, Carlo Felice, 8 February 1936.

Antonio e Cleopatra, Malipiero (after Shakespeare), 1936-37, Florence, Comunale, 4 June 1938.

Ecuba, Malipiero (after Euripides), 1940, Rome, Opera, 11 January 1941.

La vita è sogno, Malipiero (after Calderón), 1940-41, Breslau, Opernhaus, 30 June 1943.

I capricci di Callot, Malipiero (after E.T.A. Hoffman), 1941-42, Rome, Opera, 24 October 1942.

L'allegra brigata, Malipiero (after Italian novels of the 14th-16th centuries), 1943, Milan, Teatro alla Scala, 4 May 1950.

Vergilii Aeneis, Malipiero (after Vergil, translated by A. Caro), 1943-44, Radio Audizioni Italiana, 21 June 1946; staged performance, Venice, La Fenice, 6 January 1958.

Mondi celesti e infernali, Malipiero, 1948-49, Radio Audizioni Italiana, 12 January 1950; staged performance, Venice, La Fenice, 2 February 1961.

Il figliuol prodigo, P. Castellano Castellani, 1952, Radio Audizioni Italiana, 25 January 1953; staged performance, Florence, Teatro della Pergola, 14 May 1957.

Donna Urraca, Malipiero (after Mérimée), 1953-54, Bergamo, Donizetti, 2 October 1954.

Il capitan Spavento, Malipiero (partly after N. de Fauteville), 1954-55, Naples, San Carlo, 16 March 1963.

Venere prigioniera, Malipiero (after E. Gonzales), 1955, Florence, Teatro della Pergola, 14 May 1957.

Rappresentazione e festa di Carnasciale e della Quaresima, Malipiero (after a Florentine text of 1558), 1961; concert performance, Venice, La Fenice, 20 January 1970.

Don Giovanni, Malipiero (after Pushkin), 1962, Naples, San Carlo, 22 October 1963.

Le metamorfosi di Bonaventura, Malipiero (after *Nachtwachen des Bonaventura*), 1963-65, Venice, La Fenice, 4 September 1966.

Don Tartufo Bacchettone, Malipiero (after Molière), 1966, Venice, La Fenice, 20 January 1970.

Il marescalco, Malipiero (after Aretino), 1960-68, Treviso, Comunale, 22 October 1969.

Gli eroi di Bonaventura, Malipiero, 1968, Milan, Teatro alla Piccola Scala, 7 February 1969 [exerpts from other works].

Uno dei dieci, Malipiero, 1970, Siena, Teatro Rinnuovati, 28 August 1971.

L'Iscariota, Malipiero, 1970, Siena, Teatro Rinnuovati, 28 August 1971.

Publications

By MALIPIERO: books–

L'orchestra. Bologna, 1920; English translation, 1920; Japanese translation, 1924.

Teatro. Preface by G.M. Gatti. Bologna, 1920; 2nd 3d., 1927.

Oreste e Pilade, ovvero "Le sorprese dell'amicizia". Parma, 1922.

I profeti di Babilonia. Milan, 1924.

Claudio Monteverdi. Milan, 1930.

La pietra del bando. Venice, 1945.

Strawinsky. Venice, 1945.

Anton Francesco Doni musico, ovvero L'armonioso labirinto. Venice, 1946.

Cossí va lo mondo (1922-45) [autobiography]. Milan, 1946.

L'armonioso labirinto (da Zarlino a Padre Martini, 1558-1774. Milan, 1946; reprinted in *Il filo d'Arianna* (1966): 3.

Antonio Vivaldi, il prete rosso. Milan, 1958.

Il filo d'Arianna (saggi e fantasie). Turin, 1966.

Ti co mi e mi co ti (soliloqui di un veneziano). Milan, 1966.

Cosí parlò Claudio Monteverdi. Milan, 1967.

Di palo in frasca. Milan, 1967.

Da Venezia lontan. Milan, 1968.

Maschere della commedia d' arte. Bologna, 1969.

Maria Teresa Muraro, ed. *Scrittura e critica.* Florence, 1984.

articles–

Numerous articles in *Rivista italiana musicale, Ars nova, The Chesterian, Il pianoforte, Musical Quarterly, La revue musicale, La rassegna musicale,* and many others; see G. Scarpa, ed., *L'opera di Gian Francesco Malipiero,* Treviso, 1952.

About MALIPIERO: books–

Prunières, Henri. *Le renouveau musical en Italie: G. Francesco Malipiero.* Bologna, 1919; reprinted from *Mercure de France* 16 May (1919); also in *La revue musicale* January (1927).

Alfano, F., A. Casella, M. Castelnuovo-Tedesco et al. *Malipiero e le sue "Sette canzoni".* Rome, 1929.

Fleischer, H. *La musica contemporanea.* 210ff. Milan, 1937.

Ballo, F. *"I 'Capricci' di Callot" di G. Francesco Malipiero.* Milan, 1942.

Bontempelli, Massimo, and R. Cumar. *Gian Francesco Malipiero.* Milan, 1942.

Scarpa, G., ed. *L' opera di Gian Francesco Malipiero* [catalogue of works, list of writings, bibliography]. Treviso, 1952.

Labroca, M. *Malipiero, Musicista veneziano.* Venice, 1957; 2nd ed., 1967.

Messinis, M., ed. *Omaggio a Malipiero.* Florence, 1977.

Muraro, M.T., ed. *Malipiero: scrittura e critica. Atti del Convegno 24-25 Settembre 1982, Venezia, Asolo.* Florence, 1984.

articles–

Luciani, S.A. "Una nuova forma di dramma musicale (le expressioni drammatiche di G.F. Malipiero)." *Ars nova* [Rome] 3 (1918): 4.

Gatti, G.M. "Le 'esspressioni drammatiche' di G.F. Malipiero (Sette canzoni)." *Rivista musicale italiana* 26 (1919): 690.

Laloy, L. "Les Sept chansons de Malipiero." *Comoedia* [Paris] 14/no. 2783 (1920): 1; reprinted in *Scarpa* (1952): 3.

Pratella, F.B. "*L'orfeide* di G. Francesco Malipiero." *Pensiero musicale* [Bologna] 3 (1923): 7, 28.

Gatti, G.M. "Gian Francesco Malipiero." *L' Esame* October (1923).

Rossi-Doria, G. "Il teatro musicale di G.F. Malipiero." *La rassegna musicale* 2 (1929): 354; French translation in *Musique* 3 (1929-30): 100, 168.

Redlich, H.F. "G.F. Malipiero und die neue Oper." *Musikblätter des Anbruch* 11 (1929): 325.

Goddard, S. "Malipiero's *L'orfeide.*" *The Chesterian* 12 (1930-31): 33.

Bruschettini, M. "Il *Torneo notturno* di G.F. Malipiero." *Italia musicale* 4/no. 8 (1931): 1.

Redlich, H.F. "Francesco Malipiero: dramaturge lyrique." *La revue musicale* no. 120 (1931): 300.

D'Amico, L.F. "Il *Torneo* di Malipiero a Roma." *Italia letteraria* 4/no. 50 (1932): 5.

_____. "Classicità di Malipiero." *Scenario* August (1932).

Paoli, D. de'. "Lettera da Coburgo" [*Il mistero di Venezia*] *La rassegna musicale* 6 (1933): 59.

Rossi-Doria, G. "Musica" [*Il finto Arlecchino*]. *Nuova antologia* 366 (1933): 312.

Gatti, G.M. "Malipiero and Pirandello at the Opera." *Modern Music* 11 (1934): 213.

Prunières, Henri. "Un opéra de Pirandello et Malipiero." *La revue musicale* no. 144 (1934): 207.

Rossi-Doria, G. "Lettera da Roma." [*La favola del figlio cambiato*]. *La rassegna musicale* 7 (1934): 228.

Stuckenschmidt, H.H. "Zu Malipieros Bühnenwerken." *Melos* 13 (1934): 47; Italian translation in Scarpa (1952): 71.

Gatti, G.M. "Malipiero: Romantic and Classic." *Monthly Musical Record* February (1935).

Malherbe, H. "Malipiero's *Pantéa.*" *The Chesterian* 17 (1935-36): 26.

Mantelli, A. "Lettera da Firenze: *Antonio e Cleopatra* di Malipiero." *La rassegna musicale* 11 (1938): 239.

Gasco, A. "Canzoni e burrasche al Teatro Reale (1929). In *Da Cimarosa a Strawinsky,* 422. Rome, 1939.

_____. "*La favola del figlio cambiato* al Teatro Reale (1934)." In *Da Cimarosa a Strawinsky,* 427. Rome, 1939.

Berger, Arthur V. "Gian Francesco Malipiero." In *The Book of Modern Composers.* New York, 1942.

La rassegna musicale March (1942) [Malipiero issue].

Gatti G.M. "Gian Francesco Malipiero." In *Musicisti moderni d'Italia e di fuori.* Bologna, 1945.

Fleischer, H. "Pour l'étranger: *L'allegra brigata* de G.F. Malipiero."*Il diapason* 1/nos. 6-7-(1950): 26.

D'Amico, F. "La farsa degli equivoci nella *Favola del figlio cambiato.*" *Vie Nuove* [Rome] 8/no. 33 (1952): 19.

Mila, M. "L'*Eneide* in bassorilievo." In *Cronache musicali 1955-1959,* 173. Turin, 1959.

D'Amico, F. "*Mondi celesti e infernali* di G.F. Malipiero." *Musica d' oggi* 4 (1961): 34.

Gavazzeni, G. "Le *Sette canzoni* di G. Francesco Malipiero." *La rassegna musicale* 32 (1962): 143.

D'Amico, F. "I vestiti che cantano" [*I capricci di Callot*]. *L' espresso* 14/no. 4 (Rome, 1968): 22.

_____. "Bonaventura vestito da Arlecchino" [*Gli eroi di Bonaventura*] *L'espresso* 15/no. 7 (1969): 22.

_____. "Un angelo nell' alcova" [*Il marescalco* and *Il capitan Spavento*]. *L'espresso* 15/no. 44 (1969): 30.

Pinzauti, L. "Malipiero and his *Sette canzoni.*" *Opera* 20 (1969): 670.

Waterhouse, J.C.G. "Malipiero's *Sette canzoni.*" *Musical Times* 110 (1969): 826.

Alberti, L. "Annotazioni drammaturgiche sul più recente Malipiero." *Chigiana* 28 (1971): 263.

D'Amico, F. "Giuda e i suoi ciceroni" [*Il figliuol prodigo, L' Iscariota,* and *Uno dei dieci*]. *L'espresso* 17/no. 37 (1971): 23.

_____. "Malipiero a Palermo: melodie prima del diluvio" [*Filomela, Merlino, Uno dei dieci*]. *L'espresso* 18/no. 15 (1972): 22.

Orselli, Cesare. "Oltre l'avanguardia: l'incontro fra Malipiero e Pirandello" [on *La favola del figlio cambiato*]. *Chigiana* 35 (1982): 67.

*　　*　　*

Malipiero, whose father and grandfather had been distinguished musicians, was the descendant of an aristocratic Venetian family. His nephew, Riccardo Malipiero, continued the family tradition. Gian Francesco had an eclectic training in music and was responsible for many experimental compositions throughout a long and fruitful career. He remained passionately interested in older music, especially Italian masters, throughout his life, and he was responsible for distinguished editions of the complete works of Monteverdi, which appeared from 1926-1942, and Antonio Vivaldi, 1947.

Malipiero was widely admired for inventive, original statements in his symbolic theatrical pieces, which include some 35 operas and six ballets of a decidedly personal nature. He wrote his own texts for subjects derived from a variety of sources. Such titles as *Giulio Cesare,* 1934-35, and *Antonio e Cleopatra,* 1936-37 (both after Shakespeare), *I capricci di Callot,* 1941-42 (based on E.T.A. Hoffmann), *Don Giovanni,* 1962 (after Pushkin), and *Rappresentazione e festa di Carnasciale e della Quaresima,* 1961 (an "opera with dancing" after a Florentine text of 1558), indicate a wide range of interests.

Malipiero's best known opera is the "triptych" *L'orfeide,* composed between 1918-1922 and first mounted *in toto* at Düsseldorf in 1925. Part I, *La morte delle maschere,* features the seven principal masks of the Italian commedia dell'arte being auditioned by an impressario. The action is interrupted by Pulcinella, who locks them in a wardrobe, reveals himself to be Orpheus, and announces that the masks will be put to death. They will be replaced by real life characters who will perform a new opera. One by one all the characters who are to appear in part II pass in review. After the stage empties,

Arlecchino breaks through the top of the wardrobe and escapes.

Seven different stories, *Sette canzoni,* with widely diverse subject matter are realized in dramatic form in part II. *I vagabondi, A Vespro, Il ritorno, L'ubriaco, La serenata, Il campanaro,* and *L'alba delle Ceneri* connect with the *commedia dell'arte* and Orpheus in a private, effective manner (in concert version the *Sette canzoni* remains Malipiero's most frequently performed vocal composition.) Part III, *Orfeo ovvero l'ottava canzone,* takes the form of a marionette show given for a king and queen. A figure disguised as Nero sings as his cruelty to his mother Agrippina and Rome is enacted. An argument breaks out among some of the spectators; Orpheus then appears dressed as a clown, i.e., Arlecchino from part I, and as he sings, the stage audience falls asleep. When Orpheus finishes, the queen kisses him, and the two leave together while the "audience" onstage remains asleep.

Each of the three parts can be mounted individually as an independent work or combined into a full, three act opera. The symbolism is as personal as it is complex, and whatever else may be said for such a conception, there is a remarkable wealth of lyrical beauty in part II balanced by demanding action in parts I and III. Malipiero was successful in breaking away from the traditional world of Italian opera in order to pursue his own ideals, and his works deserve to be better known.

—Aubrey S. Garlington

LES MAMELLES DE TIRÉSIAS [The Breasts of Tiresias].

Composer: Francis Poulenc.

Librettist: Francis Poulenc (after Guillaume Apollinaire).

First Performance: Paris, Opéra-Comique, 3 June 1947.

Roles: Thérèse/Card Reader (soprano); Husband (baritone); Gendarme (baritone); Manager (baritone); Newspaper Seller (mezzo-soprano); Elegant Woman (mezzo-soprano); Large Woman (mezzo-soprano); Presto (baritone); Lacouf (tenor); Newspaperman (tenor); Son (baritone); Bearded Man (bass); chorus (SSAATTBB).

Publications

articles–

Poulenc, Francis. "A propos des Mamelles de Tirésias." *Opera* 28 (1947).
Bellas, J. "Les mamelles de Tirésias en habit d'Arlequin." *Guillaume Apollinaire* 4 (1965): 30.

*   *   *

Poulenc did not begin work on his first opera until the years 1944-45, although he had been considering the project since before the Second World War. He finished orchestrating it in the summer of 1945. Based on Guillaume Apollinaire's

play, it is the high-point of Poulenc's settings of the poet's work, which also includes *Montparnasse* and the set of *Banalités.*

The story, inspired by the legend of Tiresias, concerns the barkeeper, called simply "The Husband," and his wife Thérèse. The setting is "Zanzibar," but its inhabitants resemble those of a typical Parisian *arrondissement.* Thérèse, during a marital squabble, declares herself a feminist; she discards her breasts, a pair of balloons that float away conveniently, and begins to grow a beard. The husband is forced to play the role of wife and mother, but in the end Thérèse returns and suggests that they "pluck the strawberry with the banana flower" and "hunt elephants the Zanzibar way." More importantly, the company turns to the audience and sings "Hear, o Frenchmen, the lessons of war's scares; make children, you who made scarce any." (This pun is untranslatable: 'Ecoutez, o Francais, les leçons de la guerre, et faites des enfants, vous qui n'en faisiez guère').

Poulenc had been present at the world premiere of Apollinaire's play in 1917; it has been claimed that it was for this event that the term surrealist was invented. The story, if such a word can really be used for the sequence of encounters and conversations which make up the action, nevertheless poses a number of ever-topical themes about conflicts of sexuality, children, and, even more in Poulenc's music, the longing of those who adore Paris and are away from it. This was exactly Poulenc's position when he wrote the opera, living in various places away from the occupied and still war-torn city. "In the text," wrote Poulenc, "the word Paris keeps cropping up; perhaps this, together with my nostalgia for its streets, enabled me to capture that moving tone in the midst of all the typically Apollinairian larks."

While working on the opera, Poulenc noted that he had studied Ravel's *L'heure Espagnole;* elsewhere he mentioned that people might be surprised that he had contented himself with "the orchestra of *Carmen.*" In other words, it was an opera tailor-made for the Paris Opéra-Comique, where it was eventually given its first performance. Poulenc had the action set, not in 1917, but in the earlier time of 1910-14; Thérèse's breasts fly away to the tune of "a 1912 Boston." The entr'acte contains a tango played with frenzy by a pianist, and throughout the opera nostalgic little waltzes and javas in the style of Parisian café-concerts ripple through the music. Poulenc's joyous tongue-in-cheek music seems to relate it far more to his earlier stage work, the carefree *Les biches.*

In addition to the main roles, *Les mamelles* has a splendid chorus contribution; the nostalgic ensemble "Comme il perdait au Zanzibar" (scene v) and the finale of act I, "Vous qui pleurez," both bear out Poulenc's contention, expressed during the opera's composition, that "It is madly scenic. . . . There is not one event on stage that is not directly connected to the music." When he read about it, Henri Sauget wrote to Poulenc, "The subject is precisely that which would have frightened me most in the world. But you are more daring, more modern than I am and above all you have mastered your art to such an extent that—through its intense musical colour and life—it transcends the subject and gives it quite a different dimension."

Despite this assertion, *Les Mamelles* has proved less easy to perform than Poulenc's other operas, although its music seems immediately more tuneful and accessible. The first production, which was designed by Erté, set the tone for its performance, and there have been other memorable stagings, especially that by John Dexter, designed by David Hockney, at the Metropolitan Opera in 1981.

—Patrick O'Connor

MANON.

Composer: Jules Massenet.

Librettists: Henri Meilhac and Philippe Gille (after Prévost).

First Performance: Paris, Opéra-Comique, 19 January 1884.

Roles: Manon (soprano); Des Grieux (tenor); Lescaut (baritone); Count des Grieux (bass); Guillot de Morfontaine (tenor); De Brétigny (baritone); Pousette (soprano); Javotte (soprano or mezzo-soprano); Rosette (soprano or mezzo-soprano); chorus (SATB).

Publications

books–

Hanslick, E. *Aus dem Tagebuch eines Musikers,* pp. 137 ff. Berlin, 1892.
Loisel, Joseph. *Manon de Massenet: étude historique et critique, analyse musicale.* Paris, 1922.
Colson, Percy. *Massenet: "Manon."* London, 1947.

Poëme de M. M.
MEILHAC et PH.GILLE

MANON

Musique de
J. MASSENET

A poster for the premiere of Massenet's *Manon,* Paris, 1884

John, Nicholas, ed. *Jules Massenet: "Manon". Opera Guide* 25. London, 1984.

articles–

Bellaigue, C. "À travers le répertoire lyrique (IX): 'Manon'." *Revue universelle* 1 October (1922): 59.
Cooke, J.F. "Massenet's Manon." *Étude* 40 (1922): 127.
Carner, Mosco. "The Two Manons." *Monthly Musical Record* 67 (1937); also in *Major and Minor,* London, 1944; 1980.
Jefferson, A. "Impressions of Manon." *Music and Musicians* 17/no. 4 (1968): 28.
Blyvh, Alan. "Manon." *Opera* February (1974).
Avant-scène opéra September (1989) [*Manon* issue].

unpublished–

Hiss, C.S. "Abbé Prévost's 'Manon Lescaut' as Novel, Libretto and Opera." Ph.D. dissertation, University of Illinois, 1967.

*   *   *

Like the Parisian gentlemen in Prévost's *Manon Lescaut,* Massenet found Manon irresistible. Most of his twenty-nine existing operas feature women characters, but Manon surpasses them all in unrestrained seductiveness. Aristocrats vie for her regard. At the sight of her, old men wish themselves young. All of sixteen, Manon lives only by the moment. Her appetite for pleasure is outrageous, her behavior scandalous; yet men indulge her excessive whims to the limit.

We first see her stepping from a couch outside an inn at Amiens where her cousin Lescaut, a soldier, inveterate gambler, and guardian of the family honor, awaits her. Guillot, a Minister of France, makes an unsuccessful pass at her, but confident in the power of his wealth and position, he hires a carriage for the two of them. Moments later the young Chevalier des Grieux sets his eyes on Manon and immediately falls in love with her. Forgetting both Lescaut and the convent she is bound for, she succumbs to Des Grieux's ardent advances, and departs with him to Paris in Guillot's carriage.

The lovers live together contentedly until Lescaut and De Brétigny, a nobleman infatuated with Manon, track them down. While Des Grieux tries to convince Lescaut that he truly loves Manon, De Brétigny secretly informs the covetous girl that Des Grieux's father, the Count des Grieux, will end his son's illicit affair by having the chevalier abducted that very day. De Brétigny promises to shower Manon with wealth if she will live with him instead and not reveal the count's plot to Des Grieux. The temptation of luxury proves too much for Manon, who bids a wistful farewell to their love nest. A knock from outside the apartment brings Des Grieux to the door. There are sounds of a struggle; Des Grieux does not return.

Manon appears lavishly dressed at a festival in the Cours la Reine. She overhears De Brétigny and the count discussing Des Grieux, who soon will be ordained an abbé of the Church, having "forgotten" his former love. This so distresses Manon that she hardly notices the ballet Guillot has engaged to impress her, and she hurries off to St Sulpice where Des Grieux has just delivered a sermon. After a few minutes alone with him, Manon wins him back.

Short of money, Des Grieux, accompanied by Manon, tries his luck at gambling in the Hotel Transylvania. Among the players is Guillot, who challenges Des Grieux to a game of chance and loses so badly that he accuses his young rival of cheating. Bent on vengeance, he has both Des Grieux and Manon arrested. The chevalier is soon released thanks to the count's influence, but Manon is imprisoned and later deported as a woman of ill repute. Lescaut and Des Grieux attempt to rescue her from a corps of prisoners taken under guard to Le Havre, but the plan fails. A bribe, however, procures the lovers brief privacy. Des Grieux talks of escape to a new life, but Manon is too ill to dream. Recalling their past happiness, she dies murmuring, "And so ends the story of Manon Lescaut."

Reconciling this melodramatic plot with the pleasantries of *opéra comique* required ingenuity. To accommodate the popular genre, Massenet strewed the score with affable tunes and diverting choruses; but he fused the patchwork of arias and ensembles with recitative and spoken dialogue by making every note of the accompaniment dramatically adroit and evocative, and by devising frequent orchestral allusions to representative themes. The abundance of blithesome music does not afford perfunctory entertainment, but evokes the gaity of Paris to offset Manon's amorous vicissitudes. Pleasures and agonies intensify against a background of frivolity. The score, in fact, enchants more advantageously than it emotes, for its most impassioned music is unabashedly sentimental. Massenet found passage from pathos to bathos the easiest of modulations. In *Manon,* there seems no clear boundary between them. Without large doses of *joie de vivre* to buoy it up, the work would sink into the maudlin ooze that imbues so many forgotten operas.

For more than a century *Manon* has held its place in the standard repertoire. During the composer's lifetime, the opera received over 700 performances at the Opéra-Comique alone. Massenet made musical portraiture in French opera a finer art by endowing Manon with inexhaustible fascination. Charpentier, Debussy, and Poulenc learned from him the subtle meanings couched in melodic inflection. With *Manon, opéra comique* became music theater *à la française,* but it preserved the best qualities of popular French opera in the 1880s. Audiences found it affecting and entertaining, and singers relished its fluent lyricism and virtuosic luster. Five of its arias remain perennial favorites from the French repertoire. Like *Carmen* and *Les contes d'Hoffmann, Manon* triumphs over banality. Massenet later courted many women characters, among them, Esclarmonde, Thaïs, Sapho, and Cléopâtre, and gave each something of Manon's illusive charm, but he reserved for her alone the blend of puissance and finesse that makes a cynosure of a brief flame.

—James Allen Feldman

MANON LESCAUT.

Composer: Giacomo Puccini.

Librettists: Ruggero Leoncavallo, Marco Praga, Domenico Olivia, Luigi Illica, and Giuseppe Giacosa (after Prévost).

First Performance: Turin, Regio, 1 February 1893.

Roles: Manon Lescaut (soprano); Lescaut (baritone); Chevalier des Grieux (tenor); Geronte di Ravoir (baritone); Edmondo (tenor); Singer (soprano or mezzo-soprano); Music Master (tenor); Naval Captain (bass); Sergeant (bass); Lamplighter (tenor); chorus (SATTBB).

Publications

article–

Carner, Mosco. "The Two Manons." In *Major and minor.* London, 1980.

*   *   *

Manon Lescaut was the first major success of Puccini's career, achieved after nine years of generous subsidy by publisher Giulio Ricordi, who had seen in the young composer of *Le villi* (1884) the most likely successor to the fame and riches of Giuseppe Verdi. Puccini had taken a dangerous chance by choosing for his subject the well-known story by Abbé Antoine Prévost (*L'histoire du Chevalier des Grieux et de Manon Lescaut,* 1731), given the successful Paris premiere of a setting, *Manon,* by Jules Massenet only nine years previously, not to mention other nineteenth-century musical settings by Balfe, Halévy, and Auber. However, Puccini's conception, maintained through six different librettists (including himself), was considerably different from that of Massenet and of Prévost, both in his more somber choice of scene and plot incident—excluding, for example, any scene of the blissful if poor lovers living together in Paris—and in his treatment of

Cesira Ferrani, the first Manon in Puccini's *Manon Lescaut,* 1893

the title character, by tradition a classic *femme fatale,* but in Puccini's eyes a helpless and mainly sympathetic figure who is herself the victim of greed, repression, and deceit.

In act I the young Chevalier des Grieux encounters Manon at an inn where she is staying *en route* to the nunnery her father is forcing her to enter; Des Grieux instantly falls in love and by the end of the act has convinced her to run away with him, a plan which in turn foils her brother's plan to sell her to the rich elderly Parisian, Geronte di Ravoir. In act II, Manon is nonetheless living a pampered, stilted existence with Geronte, having left Des Grieux at her brother's urging when the money ran short. When Des Grieux returns, she defies Geronte and leaves with her lover, but to the latter's despair she insists on returning to take the old man's jewels with her and is arrested in the process. In act III, Des Grieux and Lescaut follow Manon to Le Havre, the debarkation point to Louisiana for "fallen women," and attempt a rescue to no avail, but the captain does agree to allow the love-torn Des Grieux to accompany Manon to Louisiana. In act IV, Manon dies poverty-stricken, exhausted, and hopeless on a desolate wilderness plain, in the arms of Des Grieux.

In his sympathetic treatment of Manon as well as of later heroines, Puccini showed himself to be strikingly out of step with the disturbing, frequently demonic treatments of women by contemporary artists and writers such as Klimt, Wilde, d'Annunzio, Verga, and Louÿs, to mention a few. This is an important aspect of Puccini's success in his time as well as our own, and one that has often escaped notice, or if noticed, has evoked criticisms of excessive sentimentality or even sado-masochistic neurosis (as in Mosco Carner's *Puccini: A Critical Biography*). In addition, other aspects of Puccini's mature style, such as his colorful use of harmony and orchestration, his lyrical, languid vocal writing, his fluid, post-Wagnerian formal mixture of vocal set pieces and continuous orchestral melody, and his keen sense of theater are also fully in place in *Manon Lescaut,* with the possible exception of Manon's plodding, pathetic final scene and aria "Sola, perduta, abban-donata" ("Alone, lost, abandoned"), which Puccini consid-ered cutting as late as the 1922 Vienna production.

Fortunately for the young composer—whose career and future support from Ricordi were on the line—*Manon Les-caut* was a huge success in its premiere performance at the Teatro Regio in Turin (eight days before the Teatro alla Scala premiere of Verdi's *Falstaff*): Puccini was called for twenty-five bows between acts. Within the year, the opera had been performed all over Italy and in such far-away locales as Bue-nos Aires, Rio de Janeiro, St Petersburg, Madrid, and Ham-burg (in German translation), traveling faster and further than Massenet's *Manon* or any of Puccini's later operas. This popular success and the accompanying critical opinion served to establish Puccini's primacy within the world of Italian opera until his death in 1924 and even afterward. As George Bernard Shaw put it in his review of the Covent Garden premiere of *Manon Lescaut* on 14 May 1894, "Puccini looks to me more like the heir of Verdi than any other of his rivals." *Manon Lescaut* remains a solid part of the operatic repertory today, if less often performed than the perennial Puccini favorites *La bohème, Tosca* and *Madama Butterfly,* and, as it turns out, Massenet's *Manon.*

—Claire Detels

MARCOUX, Vanni (born Jean Emile Diogène).

Baritone and bass. Born 12 June 1877, in Turin. Died 22 October 1962, in Paris. Law student at University of Turin; studied at Paris Conservatory under Frederic Boyer; debut as Sparafucile in *Rigoletto,* Turin, 1894; Paris Opéra debut as Gounod's Mephistopheles, 1908; remained with Paris Opéra until 1947; at Covent Garden, 1905-12, where his debut was as Rossini's Don Basilio; Boston, 1912-14; in Chicago 1913 and 1926-32; Teatro alla Scala debut as Boris, 1922.

Publications

About MARCOUX: articles–

Shawe-Taylor, D. "Vanni Marcoux." *Opera* March (1963): 156.

*   *   *

The most celebrated French bass of his generation, Vanni-Marcoux's extraordinarily vivid accent and style seems to overcome a voice that often sounds dry and reedy in quality, though clearly of penetrating power and great endurance. His soft singing, his fine diction in the tradition of the great tragedians of the Comédie-Française, and his eclectic choice of repertory make his recordings among the most engaging of the 78 era. He shared with Chaliapin the distinction of giving the early performances of Massenet's *Don Quichotte;* Chaliapin gave the world premiere in Monte-Carlo, Vanni-Marcoux the first Paris performance. His performance as Boris Godunov in the first French-language performances of Mussorgsky's opera also suggests a direct comparison with Chaliapin, but the comparison reveals two great artists of such different impact that the contrast is less instructive than bewildering. Their voices and approach seem so completely different that it is hard to believe, as commentators have often noted, that Marcoux's voice is a bass at all. Indeed, he moved often from bass to baritone roles, and such is the delicacy of much of his singing that in the higher-lying passages he sounds like a tenor. Among his recordings from *Boris,* the "Clock scene," with its cries of "Là! Là-bas! Qui vas-là? Dans ce coin!" suggests a dramatic performance of enormous strength. Similarly the vivid, yet quiet, performance of the death of Don Quixote, has an immediacy that belies the accusations that have been made that Marcoux was a singer more in the tradition of popular song than opera. That he could produce a rich, romantically sensual sound is evidenced in, for instance, his 1931 recording of an aria from Massenet's *Cléôpatre,* "Solitaire sur ma terrasse," the fervour with which he sings the recitative and the clarity of his diction make even such a little-known passage seem at once important and dramatically apt. Another rare extract, from Massenet's *Panurge,* "Touraine est un pays au ciel bleu," sung with piano, is similarly so engaging that even with no other knowl-edge of the opera, the listener feels caught up in the action. Marcoux's many recordings of *mélodies* and *chansons,* includ-ing such items as Fragson's "Reviens!" and John Alden Car-penter's songs to texts by Langston Hughes, "Jazz Boys" and "Cryin' Blues," are all fascinating for his devotion to the text, and even within such minute items, he is able to conjure up a mood of sentimental nostalgia or suggest the unusual juxtaposition of styles without sacrificing his own manner. When the British critic Desmond Shawe-Taylor went to visit Marcoux in Paris a month or two before the singer's 80th birthday, he reported that "Genial, hale and hearty, he was the only man I have ever met who not only took a cold bath every morning of the year, but in summer put blocks of ice into it in order to correct the temperature." Shawe-Taylor summed up his singing by noting that "clear, luminous, perfectly poised tones trace the vocal line as though with a finely pointed pencil . . . here is a true basse chantante who can convey all the drama and pathos of the scene [Philip II in *Don Carlos*] without those sudden lapses which often deface the music's nobility."

—Patrick O'Connor

MARIA STUARDA [Mary Stuart].

Composer: Gaetano Donizetti.

Librettist: G. Bardari (after Schiller).

First Performance: Milan, Teatro alla Scala, 30 December 1835.

Roles: Maria (soprano); Elisabetta (mezzo-soprano or soprano); Leicester (tenor); Talbot (bass); Cecil (baritone); Anna (contralto); chorus (SATTB).

Publications

articles–

Schmid, Patric. "*Maria Stuarda* and Buondelmonte." *Opera* 24 (1973).
Ashbrook, William. "Maria Stuarda: The Vindication of a Queen." *About the House* (1977).
Commons, Jeremy. "*Maria Stuarda* and the Neapolitan Censorship." *Journal of the Donizetti Society* 3 (1977).
_____. "19th Century Performances of Maria Stuarda." *Journal of the Donizetti Society* 3 (1977).

*   *   *

Donizetti's *Maria Stuarda,* based on the final days of Mary Stuart and exhibiting the *primo ottocento* fascination for English historical subjects, was heard for the last time during the nineteenth century in 1865 in Naples; it was not revived until 1958, in Bergamo. The historically inaccurate libretto was fashioned by the obscure Giuseppe Bardari after Schiller, after Donizetti found the much sought-after librettist, Felice Romani, to be unavailable. At the opening of act I a tournament is being held for the French ambassador, who has come to England on behalf of the King of France to ask for Queen Elizabeth's hand in marriage. The queen, however, is in love with the Earl of Leicester. Talbot pleads with Elizabeth for mercy for Mary Stuart, while Cecil wants Mary to be executed. Elizabeth is inclined towards vengeance if Mary is indeed a rival for Leicester. When Leicester enters, Elizabeth gives him a ring, asking him to tell the French ambassador that she accepts the proposal tentatively. Leicester appears unmoved. Talbot gives Leicester a letter and a picture sent by Mary from Fotheringay Castle and Leicester rejoices, vowing either to free her or die with her. Leicester encounters Elizabeth and is obliged to give her the letter from Mary asking Elizabeth to meet her. Upon being questioned by the queen,

Leicester denies his love for Mary, although he describes her physical beauty in passionate terms. Elizabeth agrees to the meeting with Mary.

In act II Mary is enjoying the grounds at Fotheringay while lamenting her enforced exile from her beloved France. When Elizabeth arrives she is initially reluctant to speak to Mary. The latter kneels at Elizabeth's feet, begging her forgiveness, but Elizabeth's behavior repulses her. Mary, able to bear no more, insults the queen with the words "Vil bastarda." This meeting between the two queens never actually occurred in history. Mary is arrested and told by Elizabeth to prepare for death. In act III, scene i, Elizabeth signs Mary's death warrant and tells Leicester that he must witness the execution. In scene ii Mary's friends gather in a room next to the execution chamber, expressing repulsion at the sight of the instruments of execution. Mary enters and asks them to pray. As the cannon shots are fired she goes to her death.

Even though there are two queens and two soprano roles in Donizetti's opera, Mary Stuart is clearly the heroine and the character with whom one identifies emotionally. Schiller wrote that a tragic heroine is one who becomes transfigured through suffering; this is a drama that moves swiftly and inexorably to its fatal conclusion, Mary's death. Donizetti differentiates musically between the two queens, Elizabeth being given melodic lines of emphatic declamation in contrast to Mary's floating, limpid legato *cantilene*. A number of stylistic features heighten the tension and help achieve the ultimate catharsis. In the fictional confrontation scene, the "Dialogo delle due regine," the orchestration is telling, especially the use of the regal, foreboding trombone at certain points. This scene is a good illustration of the polarities on which the opera is built: with the difference in their musical material Mary is portrayed as a feminine figure and Elizabeth, with her great power and dominant personality, as masculine. There is also a suggestion of good pitted against evil and a display of chiaroscuro effects. In the corresponding scene of the play, Schiller specifies a moment of "general silence" as the two queens confront each other. This concept is especially apt for musical portrayal, and Donizetti provides a sparse accompaniment (mainly pizzicato strings) and extensive use of rests, as if time were suspended.

The prison motif is prominent in *Maria Stuarda*. At the beginning of act II Mary is incarcerated as she sings nostalgically of France. Following this *scena ed aria* is a duet with Leicester, in which much of Mary's character is revealed. Schiller had made Leicester Mary's lover, another detail contrary to history that became part of Bardari's libretto. In the opera, then, the love triangle propels the plot, and Mary is portrayed as a typical suffering Romantic heroine. Her roots are in the sentimental, pathetic figures found in gothic fiction and in *opera semiseria* earlier in the century.

After the fateful encounter with Elizabeth that seals Mary's fate, Mary is featured in a scene in which she confesses to Talbot; her suffering is reflected in the prominence of minor seconds in the orchestra, both in the prelude and in the accompaniment to her opening recitative. Mary then requests all her gathered friends to join her in a prayer forgiving all of those who have harmed her; it is a sublimely transcendent operatic scene. In the orchestral prelude to this prayer scene the character's emotions are most clearly portrayed: the key is E minor and the music is in the "horror" style of Weber's *Der Freischütz* and certain parts of *Fidelio* and *Don Giovanni,* full of ominous iterations and thudding figures. The chorus adds to the unsettled mood with a broadly elegiac melody ending in E major. The chorus then provides the musical underpinning for Mary's prayer, making it assume a broader meaning: Mary's personal plight stands for the plight of beleaguered Scotland. The mixture of personal and political sentiments becomes more explicit in Mary's final cavatina and cabaletta. The former begins in F minor, modulates to D-flat major, returns to F minor, and then goes to the parallel major in the Coda. The general effect is celestial and one of apotheosis in the F-major section of the Coda. Mary's solo vocal line ascends to high A and B-flat, pianissimo, hovering high above the chorus, often with long-held notes. The sentiment of the text is that Mary's blood will cancel all her sins.

The autograph manuscript of Donizetti's *Maria Stuarda* is lost. The opera was prohibited in Naples before it was ever performed; the music had to be adapted to a new subject, *Buondelmonte*. The score was first performed as *Maria Stuarda* in Milan with Maria Malibran in 1835. Although there is no original text there are several secondary ones, including at least four non-autograph manuscript scores and many vocal scores published around the time that Malibran assumed the role.

—Stephen Willier

MARIANI, Angelo.

Conductor. Born 11 October 1821, in Ravenna. Died 13 June 1873, in Genoa. Studied violin with P. Casalini and counterpoint with G. Roberti at the Ravenna Philharmonic Academy's music school; bandmaster of the city of Sant'Agata Feltria, 1842; violinist and violist in Rimini, 1843; attracted the attention of Rossini with three of Mariani's own compositions performed in Macerata, 1843, thus beginning a long-term relationship with Rossini; 1st violinist and maestro concertatore, Messina, 1844-45; Milan debut conducting Verdi's *I due Foscari,* Teatro Re, 1846; conducted at the Copenhagen Court Theater, 1847-48; went to Constantinople, where he conducted at the Pera theater until 1850; returned to Italy, 1851; appointed director and conductor of the Teatro Carlo Felice, Genoa; debut there conducting *Robert le diable,* 1852; assumed directorship of the Teatro Comunale, Bologna, 1860; conducted first Italian performances of *Lohengrin,* 1871, and *Tannhäuser,* 1872, in Bologna.

Publications

About MARIANI: books—

Busmanti, S. *Cenni su Angelo Mariani.* Ravenna, 1887.
Mantovani, T. *Angelo Mariani.* Rome, 1921.
Zoppi, U. *Angelo Mariani, Giuseppe Verdi e Teresa Stolz in un carteggio inedito.* Milan, 1947.

articles—

Ghislanzoni, A. "Angelo Mariani." *Gazzetta musicale di Milano* 23 (1868).
Fara, G. "Spigolature epistolari: Angelo Mariani." *Musica d'oggi* 8 (1926): 311.
Zoppi, U. "Documenti sulla giovinezza di Angelo Mariani." *La Scala* (1953): 40.
Baroni, M. "Note su Angelo Mariani, i: Le composizioni di Angelo Mariani." *Quadrivium* 14 (1973): 295.
Martinotti, S. "Angelo Mariani, direttore e musicista, nel suo tempo." *Studi musicali* 2 (1973): 315.
Vecchi, G. "II: Angelo Mariani, l'arte e gli artisti e gli amici accademici bolognesi." *Quadrivium* 14 (1973): 321.

Conductor Angelo Mariani played an important part in the development of Italian opera in the nineteenth century. In his day, Italian music was more of a vocal than an orchestral and instrumental medium, as opposed to German music, which was conceived from an instrumental perspective. Mariani's approach, or his propensity, increased the role of the orchestra in Italian opera. This complemented composers' increasing attention to the orchestra in their operatic writing.

A student of Rossini at the Liceo Filarmonico in Bologna, Mariani began his conducting career in 1844 in Messina, moving a short time later to two theaters in Milan, the Teatro Re and the Teatro Carcano. At both theaters he led performances of operas by Verdi: *I due Foscari* (an opera that exhibited greater attention to the orchestral writing), *I Lombardi* (in which he played the lengthy violin solo that precedes the trio "Qual voluttà trascorrere" that ends act III *Giovanna d'Arco,* and *Nabucco.* He left Italy to conduct at the Court Theater of Copenhagen until he returned to Italy to fight in the revolutions of 1848. As director of the Teatro Carlo Felice in Genoa from 1852 to 1873, Mariani earned the accolades of critic Henry Chorley, who said that the performance he heard in Italy was the "only good orchestral performance I have ever encountered in that country."

Mariani may be credited with raising the standard of the orchestra in Italy to match that already achieved in Austria, making the orchestra of the Teatro Carlo Felice in Genoa the best in Italy. He achieved this by enlarging the orchestra and by insisting on extensive rehearsals. A violinist and violist as well as a composer, Mariani was a persuasive figure who increased the influence of the conductor as authority figure in Italian orchestras.

Mariani saw opera as theater. His championing of contemporary works earned him the admiration of Meyerbeer, Mercadante, Hérold, Thomas, and Gounod, as well as Wagner. He introduced to Italy Meyerbeer's *Le prophète* and *L'Africaine.* He conducted the first Italian performances of Wagner's *Lohengrin* (1 November 1871) and *Tannhäuser* (1872), in response to which Wagner sent Mariani an autographed photograph inscribed "Evviva Mariani." It was appropriate that Mariani was the one to introduce Wagner to Italy, as his conductorial approach—his attention to the importance of the orchestra—emulated that of German conductors.

Mariani's personal association with Verdi began when he conducted the first performance of *Aroldo* (a revision of *Stiffelio,* Trieste, 1850), which opened the Teatro Nuovo, Rimini, on 16 August 1857. Verdi attended the orchestral rehearsals for *Aroldo;* when he noticed that the storm music made little effect despite Mariani's able conducting he withdrew the music and changed the scoring. By 1858 Verdi's friendship with Mariani had advanced to the point that they frequently went on hunting expeditions together. An interest in guns was a common bond; Verdi and Mariani arranged for the importation of rifles from England to the Duchy of Parma during the war of 1859. Mariani accompanied Verdi and Giuseppina Strepponi on many trips in the area. The closeness of their relationship by 1865 can be seen in their letters: Mariani wrote to Verdi that "My heart is completely devoted to you. My soul can nourish itself on your sublime musical creations. . . . You are everything to me." Verdi's respect for Mariani as a conductor is reflected in letters in which he suggested to the managers of the Théâtre Italien in Paris that the only way to improve the standards of their performances would be to hire Mariani. Mariani later arranged for Verdi and Giuseppina Strepponi to rent an apartment in his residence in Genoa.

The conductor led a successful revival of Verdi's *Un ballo in maschera* in Bologna and another of *Ernani* in 1864; this performance was significant in that it starred soprano Teresa Stolz, who became Mariani's mistress. In Genoa Mariani led performances of Faccio's *Amleto.*

Mariani introduced Verdi's *Don Carlos* to Italy (at the Teatro Communale in Bologna on 27 October 1867). He had attended the first performance of the opera at the Paris Opéra and was sufficiently dissatisfied with its execution that he became determined to produce the work at his own theater in Bologna. Verdi announced the success of Mariani's performance to publisher Léon Escudier and, through him, to the Opéra.

It was the knowledge of the capabilities of the orchestra under Mariani that freed Verdi to write more sophisticated music, leading him to greater virtuosity in his writing and to experimentation.

A rift with Mariani, however, began in 1869, when Verdi participated in the writing of a Mass to honor Rossini, who had died the previous year (each part of the Mass was to be written by a different composer). When the project foundered, Verdi held Mariani partly to blame; he felt that the conductor had failed to use his influence to encourage the project because he had been selected to conduct—but not compose—one of the parts of the Mass.

By 1870 Verdi had become critical of Mariani's imposition of his own interpretation on his music and his propensity for altering the score to suit his own interpretive ideas (Monaldi identified the insertion of a slur in the ballet music of *Don Carlos* as the alteration that first triggered Verdi's displeasure). Mariani's conducting of *La forza del destino,* his last collaboration with Verdi, was to Verdi a distortion of the character of the music. Verdi's feelings of affection toward Teresa Stolz, at that time Mariani's fiancée, also contributed to his annoyance with Mariani; Verdi reportedly disapproved of Mariani's treatment of Stolz. The final break between Verdi and Mariani may also have stemmed from Verdi's disapproval of Mariani for not returning to Stolz a sum of money she had asked him to hold for her—a matter that Stolz had asked Verdi to settle. There is also some implication that Strepponi drove Mariani from the Verdi's home at Sant'-Agata because she was jealous of Mariani's attentions toward Verdi.

Despite the termination of their friendship, Verdi still considered Mariani the best conductor in Italy and wanted him to conduct the premiere of *Aida* in Cairo in 1871. Mariani declined, and his subsequent embracing of the operas of Wagner, which he introduced to Italy, signaled the end of his association with Verdi's music.

Verdi heard Mariani conduct *Lohengrin* in Bologna on 19 November 1871 and was largely critical of the conducting and the cuts Mariani had made; he called the performance "mediocre." Apparently it was not as successful a performance as the premiere; Verdi had tried, unsuccessfully, to enter the theater incognito, and his presence in the audience, score in hand, seems to have disconcerted the cast. When someone in the audience shouted "Viva il Maestro Verdi" after the second act, a lengthy ovation ensued. Verdi refused to acknowledge the applause, and he left the theater immediately at the end of the opera. It was the last time he saw Mariani;

when Mariani died in Genoa in 1873 of intestinal cancer, Verdi did not attend the funeral.

—Michael Sims

MARIO, Giovanni Matteo.

Tenor. Born 17 October 1810, in Cagliari, Sardinia. Died 11 December 1883, in Rome. Lived with Giulia Grisi from about 1842 (six daughters). Officer in Sardinian army, but was exiled for his radical politics; studied in Paris with Louis Ponchard and Giulio Bordogni; coached by Meyerbeer for his debut at Paris Opéra as *Robert le diable,* 1838; London debut at Her Majesty's Theatre as Gennaro in *Lucrezia Borgia,* 1839; appeared in Paris, 1839-64; sang at Covent Garden, 1847-71; appeared in St Petersburg, 1849-53 and 1867-71, New York, 1854, and Madrid, 1864-65.

Publications

About MARIO: books–

Engel, L. *From Mozart to Mario.* London, 1886.
Pearse, Mrs. G. and F. Hird. *The Romance of a Great Singer: a Memoir of Mario.* London, 1910.
Forbes, E. *Mario and Grisi: A Biography.* London, 1985.

Giovanni Mario as Nemorino in *L'elisir d'amore,* 1839

articles–

Forbes, E. "The Purloined Cabaletta." *About the House* 4/ no. 3 (1973): 51.

Chancellor, V. "Rubini and Mario: An Historical Perspective." *Opera* January and February (1986).

*   *   *

Giovanni Matteo De Candia, generally known simply as Mario, was truly a prince of a tenor. Born to a noble Sardinian family, he started his public career relatively late in life, when he was already 28 years old. Because of his noble birth and his reluctance to embarrass his family, his entire singing career was pursued outside Italy. He started at the top of his profession, making his debut at the Paris Opéra, and maintained this high status throughout his entire professional career. He sang only in the world's most important houses (except during his countless tours of the British Isles), and in the company of the world's greatest stars.

Seven months after his Paris debut, he was engaged by the impresario of Her Majesty's Theatre in London to take over the roles of the Russian tenor, Nicolai Ivanoff, thus becoming to some extent Rubini's understudy, as Ivanoff had been. Mario was well received at his debut as Gennaro in *Lucrezia Borgia.* While he received fairly warm reviews, there is nothing in them to suggest that the critics were clairvoyant enough to realize that they had witnessed a historic event. The *Times,* for example, praised him for singing with considerable taste, but also stated that his voice was of good quality, as far as it went, but it was not very powerful.

During the next few seasons in London and Paris, Mario slowly began to replace Rubini in the "Puritani quartet," taking over more and more of the latter's roles. Yet, it must be pointed out that he only rarely sang in the company of Grisi, Tamburini and Lablache at the same time: in other words, what some historians call the "Great Quartet" seldom sang together, and certainly sang together much less frequently than the "Puritani quartet." By 1843 Rubini had stopped singing in London and Paris, and Mario had completely replaced him in the affections of the public. Yet Mario lacked Rubini's virtuosity, which was more than made up for by his much sweeter and much more beautiful voice. An assessment of Mario, written by an ordinary opera lover rather than a critic, was published shortly after his first New York appearance in 1854. It is of sufficient interest to justify repeating selected sections: "His voice combines the smooth, delicious beauty with the manly vigor and sonority of the two best tenors we have heard before. And his style is equally a fusion of the two; the chest notes are clear, ringing and powerful, taking the highest notes of the tenor register with entire absence of all effort or straining. He makes frequent use of the falsetto, and with most delicious effect, the two registers being so artistically fused together as to show no break or disunion of quality. His style seems to me the very perfection of the Italian school, declamatory, impassioned, graceful, vigorous and delicate, each in turn as the text required. His phrasing is superb, and his execution of fioriture clear, distinct, rapid and beautiful. You will perceive that my impression of him is fully to the mark of his great reputation."

Chorley also comments on his unparalleled abilities as an operatic lover in roles such as Raoul in *Les Huguenots:* "The passion duet, in the fourth act of M. Meyerbeer's greatest opera, as acted by Signor Mario, is a thing to be forgotten by no one that has ever seen it. The tenderness, the passion, the struggle, the fury,. . . ., under the eyes of the man faithless to his faith, and entrapped into a love alien from it—these things, helped by no ordinary youth and beauty of person, of voice, of pictorial and picturesque fancy, and of natural refinement in breeding, were represented by Signor Mario as we shall possibly never see them represented again."

These attributes made Mario much more suitable for the newly emerging repertory of the 1840s, 50s and 60s. He was probably at his best in operas like *Les Huguenots, La favorita, Lucrezia Borgia, Il trovatore,* and, towards the end of his career, *Faust* and *Romeo et Juliette.*

Mario dominated the lyric stage more than any other tenor except Caruso for close to a quarter century. During this period he completely changed the history of singing, becoming the first tenor to achieve his great popularity largely by dint of the natural beauty and sweetness of his voice. In a sense, he was the first of a new line of Italian tenors which eventually was to include names like Italo Campanini, Enrico Caruso, Beniamino Gigli, Giuseppe di Stefano and Luciano Pavarotti.

—Tom Kaufman

MARITANA.

Composer: Vincent Wallace.

Librettist: E. Fitzball.

First Performance: London, Drury Lane, 15 November 1845.

*   *   *

Vincent Wallace's masterpiece, *Maritana,* was written in 1845 to a libretto by Edward Fitzball, shortly after the composer's arrival in England, following his long sojourn overseas. Based on the play *Don Cesar de Bazan,* it was given at Drury Lane on 15 November 1845 and was so successful that it ran for more than fifty nights. It was performed subsequently in Dublin (1846), Vienna (1848), and Philadelphia (1848).

The action takes place in Spain, where, following the Overture, Maritana, a handsome *gitana,* is singing to a crowd of people in a square in Madrid. Her beauty has attracted the admiration of the king. Don José, an unscrupulous courtier, is in love with the queen, and determines to encourage the king in his passion and thus betray him. Don Caesar de Bazan, an impecunious knight, appears and, in order to protect a poor boy, Lazarillo, from arrest, challenges the Captain of the Guard to a duel, an action which the king has recently made punishable by hanging. In act II Don Caesar has been arrested and imprisoned. He does not mind dying but cannot bear the thought of his life being terminated by the hangman. Don José proposes that, if he marry a veiled lady, his sentence will be changed to that of being shot. This he consents to do, singing the aria "Yes, let me like a soldier fall." The marriage takes place and he is led away to face the firing-squad. However, Don Caesar is not killed, since Lazarello has succeeded in removing the bullets from the guns and after the blanks have been fired, he gets up from the ground, dresses himself as a monk, and sets off to try to find his wife. A pardon sent by the king to save Don Caesar is intercepted by Don José.

Maritana is now taken to the castle of the Marquis de Montefiore where she meets the king. Maritana has fallen in love with Don Caesar, however, and repudiates the king's advances. When Don Caesar arrives, the elderly Marchioness is persuaded by Don José to play the part of the veiled lady but, when he hears Maritana's voice, he is not deceived. Don José gives orders for him to be re-arrested. In the final act Maritana bewails her loss of liberty in the once well-known aria "Scenes that are brightest." She is joined by the king, who pretends to be her husband. When Don Caesar climbs in through the window and, not recognizing the king, asks who he is, the king replies that he is the Count de Bazan, to which Don Caesar retorts that he (Caesar) must be the king! The king departs, and Maritana and her husband are re-united. When the queen arrives, accompanied by Don José, a fight takes place in which José is killed. In the final scene the king, on hearing of Don Caesar's bravery, restores him to his bride and appoints him Governor of Valentia.

It is no accident that *Maritana* contains some of Wallace's best known tunes—the once immensely popular "Tis the Harp in the Air" in act I, Don Caesar's song "Yes! Let me like a Soldier Fall" with its accompaniment of trumpets and drums in act II, and Maritana's ballad "Scenes that are Brightest" in act III. But these are by no means the only good numbers in an opera that in general abounds in melody and vital rhythms. The finale to act II with the chorus singing "What mystery" *piano* in the background has a decidedly Verdian quality about it. The constant use of Bolero rhythms as in Maritana's Romance "It was a knight of princely mien" adds a distinct Spanish element to the work, while the presence of several sacred numbers such as the "Angelus" in act I and the Prayer Scene ("Sainted Mother") in act III all underline the composer's catholic background. *Maritana* is in many ways a predecessor of *Carmen*, which it anticipates in its strong rhythms, lively orchestration, and gypsy flavour.

—Gerald Seaman

THE MARRIAGE OF FIGARO
See LE NOZZE DI FIGARO

MARSCHNER, Heinrich (August).

Composer. Born 16 August 1795, in Zittau, Saxony. Died 14 December 1861, in Hannover. Studied music with Karl Hering and sang in the school choir in Zittau; studied law at the University of Leipzig, 1813; became a full-time musician at the recommendation of J.C. Schicht, cantor at the Thomasschule; music tutor to the family of Count Zichy in Pressburg, 1816; Kapellmeister to Prince Krasatkowitz, 1816; met Beethoven in Vienna, 1817; Marschner's *Heinrich IV und d'Aubigné* accepted by Weber for performance at the Dresden Opera, 1820; moved to Dresden, 1821; Kapellmeister of the Stadttheater, Leipzig, 1827; Kapellmeister of the Hanover Hoftheater, 1830.

Operas

Titus, Metastasio, 1816.

Der Kyffhäuserberg (Singspiel), Kotzebue, 1816, Zittau, 2 January 1822.

Heinrich IV und d'Aubigné, Hornbostel-Alberti, 1817-18, Dresden, 19 July 1820.

Saidar und Zulima, Hornbostel-Alberti, Bratislava, 26 November 1818.

Der Holzdieb, Friedrich Kind, 1823, Dresden, 22 February 1825.

Lukretia, August Eckschlager, 1820-26, Danzig, 17 January 1827.

Der Vampyr, Wilhelm August Wohlbrück (after the melodrama by Charles Nodier, François Adrien Carmouche, and Achille de Jouffroy), 1827, Leipzig, 29 March 1828.

Der Templer und die Jüdin, Wilhelm August Wohlbrück and Marschner (after Walter Scott, *Ivanhoe*), Leipzig, 22 December 1829.

Des Falkners Braut, Wilhelm August Wohlbrück (after Karl Spindler), 1830, Leipzig, 10 March 1832.

Hans Heiling, Eduard Devrient, 1831-32, Berlin, Court Opera, 24 May 1833.

Das Schloss am Ätna, E.A.F. Klingemann, 1830-35, Leipzig, 29 January 1836.

Der Bäbu, Wilhelm August Wohlbrück, 1836-37, Hanover, 19 February 1838.

Kaiser Adolf von Nassau, Heribert Rau, Dresden, 5 January 1845.

Austin, Marianne Marschner, 1850-51, Hanover, 25 January 1852.

Sangeskönig Hiarne, oder Das Tyringsschwert, Wilhelm Grothe, 1857-58, Frankfurt am Main, 13 September 1863 [posthumous].

Other works: orchestral works, chamber music, instrumental works, choruses, songs, piano pieces.

Publications/Writings

By MARSCHNER: letters–

Facsimile, letter to Meyerbeer, dated 27 March 1845. *Die Musik* 2 (1902).

[see "About MARSCHNER: articles" for additional letters]

About MARSCHNER: books–

Danzig, E. *Heinrich Marschner in seinen minderbekannten Opern und Liedern.* Leipzig, 1890.

Wagner, Richard. *Richard Wagner's Letters to his Dresden Friends.* Translated by J.S. Shedlock. London, 1980.

Wittmann, M.E. *Heinrich Marschner.* Leipzig, 1897.

Münzer, Georg. *H. Marschner.* Berlin, 1901.

Preiss, C. *Templer und Jüdin.* Graz, 1911.

Gaartz, Hans. *Die Opern Heinrich Marschners.* Leipzig, 1912.

Gnirs, Anton. *Hans Heiling.* Carlsbad, 1931.

Hausswald, Günter. *Heinrich Marschner, ein Meister der deutschen Oper.* Dresden, 1938.

Palmer, A. Dean. *Heinrich August Marschner 1795-1861: His Life and Stage Works.* Ann Arbor, 1980.

articles–

Borges, H. "Heinrich Marschners Oper 'Hiarne'." *Neue Zeitschrift für Musik* 79 (1883): 165, 173, 197.

Spitta, P. [article on *Austin*]. *Neue Musik-Zeitung* 19 (1898).

Istel, E. "Aus Heinrich Marschners productivster Zeit." *Süddeutsche Monatshefte* 7/no. 2 (1910).

———. "Heinrich Marschner beim Pariser Tannhäuser-Skandal." *Die Musik* 10 (1910-11): 42.

Batka, R. "Ein Brief Marschners an Herlossohn." *Der Merkur* 2 (1910-11): 192.

Istel, E. "Drei Breife Marschners an Wiedebein." *Die Musik* 11 (1911-12): 259.

———. "Ungedruckte Brief Marschners an seine Gattin Marianne." *Die Musik* 11 (1911-12): 285, 323.

———. "10 ungedruckte Briefe Marschners und Eduard Devrients." *Der Merkur* 5 (1914): 241, 325, 408.

Fischer, G. "Marschnererinnerungen." *Hannoversche Geschichtsblätter* 2 (1918); also published separately, Hannover, 1918.

Pfitzner, H. "Marschners Vampyr." *Neue Musik-Zeitung* 45 (1924): 134.

Schaum, W. "Beiträge zur Marschnerbiographie." *Neue Musik-Zeitung* 46 (1925): 279.

Rower, A. "Ein Brief Heinrich Marschners." *Neue Musik-Zeitung* 46 (1925): 16.

"Die Uraufführung des Hans Heiling." *Blätter der Staatsoper* 10/no. 7 (1929).

Tronnier, R. "Marschnernachlese." In *Von Musik und Musikern.* Münster, 1930.

Fiebiger, O. "Zwei unveröffentlichte Briefe Heinrich Marschners." In *Festschrift Martin Bollert.* Dresden, 1936.

Köhler, Volkmar. "Recitativ, Szene, und Melodram in Heinrich Marschners Opern." *Gesellschaft für Musikforschung Kongressbericht, Bonn 1970,* 461. Bonn, 1976.

Reising, Vera. "Zur Funktion des Phantastischen in den Opern von Ludwig Spohr und Heinrich Marschner." In *Romantikkonferenz 2. 1982,* edited by Günther Stephan and Hans John, 36. Dresden, 1983.

unpublished—

Bickel, A. "Heinrich Marschner in seinen Opern." Ph.D. dissertation, University of Erlangen, 1929.

Köhler, V. "Heinrich Marschners Bühnenwerke." Ph.D. dissertation, University of Göttingen, 1956.

*   *   *

In his own time Marschner's reputation rested on three operas written and premiered in close proximity: *Der Vampyr* (1828), *Der Templer und die Jüdin* (1829), and *Hans Heiling* (1833). These works fall precisely into the brief time span between the death of Weber (1826) and Richard Wagner's first completed opera, *Die Feen* (1834, unperformed). *Vampyr* and *Heiling,* with their folkloric and supernatural elements, carried on the consciously national strain of German Romantic opera inaugurated by Weber. Both operas, but especially *Der Vampyr,* continue to make an occasional appearance on smaller stages in Germany and elsewhere. *Templer und Jüdin,* one of several contemporary treatments of Scott's *Ivanhoe,* has not outlived its composer.

As a child Marschner acquired musical experience at home and as a chorister in the churches of Zittau and Bautzen. He received little formal training during his school years, but continued to study theory texts while a law student in Leipzig, as well as fashionable Italian operatic works (Righini) and the instrumental music of Beethoven, among others. While employed by the local aristocracy in Pressburg (Bratislava),

Marschner composed incidental music, *Singspiele* (*Der Kyffhäuserberg,* after Kotzebue), and several operas, of which *Heinrich IV* was produced by Weber in Dresden. Marschner soon moved to Dresden, where, like Weber, he championed the cause of national opera, serving as Weber's assistant at the court theater.

A brief turn as director of the Leipzig theater (1827-30) saw the creation of *Der Vampyr* and *Der Templer und die Jüdin,* which soon established his reputation throughout Germany. With these two works he appealed to two popular trends of contemporary culture: gothic *Schauerromantik* (i.e. supernatural, ghoulish, and macabre themes), and the historical Romanticism of Walter Scott. In 1830 the composer became musical director of the court theater in Hanover, where he remained to the end of his life, despite frequent disagreements with colleagues and authorities there. After *Hans Heiling* (1833), Marschner failed to achieve any further significant successes, although his many *Lieder,* partsongs, and choral works still sold well. In addition to five more operas (after *Heiling*), he produced occasional pieces ("allegorical pageants") for the Hanover court, incidental music, and a fair quantity of piano and chamber music.

Marschner was quickly recognized as Weber's heir in the realm of German Romantic opera to both the gothic-supernatural type, as in *Der Freischütz* (*Der Vampyr, Das Schloss am Ätna*), and the medieval-chivalric type, as in *Euryanthe* (*Templer und Jüdin*). For Marschner, as for Weber, the *Singspiel*—as a play provided with overture and a dozen or so small-scale lyric numbers—provided a starting point (*Der Kyffhäuserberg,* 1816, *Der Holzdieb,* 1823), and he continued to employ spoken dialogue until his last three operas, composed after 1845. The "Romantic" operas usually incorporate comic, rustic, and domestic elements as well, again like *Der Freischütz;* a similar mixture is to be found later in Wagner's *Fliegende Holländer.* Marschner's two attempts at comic opera, *Des Falkners Braut* and *Der Bäbu,* achieved little popular acclaim, however. The latter work, to a text by the composer's brother-in-law, W.A. Wohlbrück (who also provided the librettos of *Vampyr* and *Templer*), is unusual for its setting in contemporary India—involving a cast of British, Hindu, and Muslim characters in Calcutta—rather than an exotic-fantastic rendering of such a setting, as would have been more typical of the time.

In *Der Vampyr* Marschner tapped into the recent spate of vampire literature in the wake of Polidori's 1819 story. The score echoes many of the stylistic features of *Der Freischütz,* such as the folk-like background scenes (distinctly German-accented, despite the Scottish setting), the Wolf's Glen atmosphere of the opening scene (with its midnight colloquy between Ruthven and the "vampire master" with attendant spirits in a gloomy "accursed spot"), and the sentimental bourgeois lyricism of the protagonists Aubry and Malwina. Both here and in the similarly conceived *Hans Heiling* (to a text originally intended for Mendelssohn by the prominent singer, actor and critic, Eduard Devrient), Marschner attempts to expand on the Weberian model; greater emphasis is placed on ensemble and choral passages which (like Weber's Wolf's Glen scene) are able to encompass a variety of action and scenic effects. A good example of this new emphasis is the prologue to *Hans Heiling,* a continuous scene-complex placed before the overture depicting Heiling's departure from the subterranean gnome kingdom. This scene contrasts a characteristic chorus of "earth spirits," dramatic recitative and arioso, and a central lyrical duet for Heiling and his mother, the Queen of the underground realm. A similar expansion of conventional formal units may be found in the "grand scene and duet with chorus" in *Templer und Jüdin* (no. 6, Rebecca and Bois-Guilbert), which is directly tied to the Rebecca-Ivanhoe duet and, in turn, to the act I finale (nos. 7 and 8, respectively).

Wagner was familiar with Marschner's principal operas from the early stages of his career, and various dramatic and musical influences have been posited. It seems likely that the vampire Ruthven and especially the brooding and divided figure of Heiling were not without an impact on Wagner's Dutchman, although some apparently "proto-Wagnerian" symbolism in these works (a treasure-mining race of dwarves, Heiling's yearning for the human realm, his status as "outsider" and his need for self-sacrificing human love) are common Romantic themes. Wagner later dismissed Marschner's music as "Italian music rendered academic and impotent, resoled and re-leathered in the German style, nothing more." Yet there can be little doubt about its role in the formative stages of Wagner's musical development. Marschner himself attempted a kind of "Wagnerian" music drama in his last work, *Sangeskönig Hiarne* (1858), based on the early medieval *Fridthjof's Saga* and conceived along the structural lines of *Tannhäuser*. Ironically, the composer's efforts to achieve a Parisian production of *Hiarne* around 1860 were overshadowed and ultimately thwarted by the notorious French premiere of Wagner's opera.

—Thomas S. Grey

Playbill for the premiere of Flotow's *Martha*, Vienna, 1847

MARTHA, oder, Der Markt zu Richmond [Martha or, The Richmond Fair].

Composer: Friedrich von Flotow.

Librettist: F.W. Riese (after the ballet, *Lady Herriette*).

First Performance: Vienna, Kärntnertor, 25 November 1847.

Roles: Lady Harriet (soprano); Nancy (mezzo-soprano); Lionel (tenor); Plunkett (baritone or bass); Lord Tristan of Mickleford (bass); Sheriff (bass); chorus (SATB).

Publications

articles–

Hübner, W. "Martha, Martha, komm doch wieder." *Musik und Gesellschaft* 13 (1963): 618.
Kaiser, Fritz. "Flotow in Darmstadt. Zum 100. Todestag des Komponisten der *Martha*." In *Mitteilungen der Arbeitsgemeinschaft für mittelrheinische Musik-geschichte* 47 (1983): 278.

* * *

Martha, Flotow's most successful opera and virtually the only music of his which has survived into the late twentieth century, originated in a collaborative ballet, *Lady Harriet, or the Servant of Greenwich* (1844) for which Flotow wrote the music of the first act. Three years later, the Berlin journalist Friederich Wilhelm Riese, who had provided the libretto for Flotow's first international success, *Alessandro Stradella* (1844), supplied words to the music of act I of *Lady Harriet*

and added another three acts based on the ballet's story. The result, *Martha,* became one of the most popular operas of the nineteenth century, which survives through a few complete recordings and an ever-decreasing number of actual performances, even in the last stronghold of its success, provincial Germany.

The story Riese adapted is simple. Lady Harriet, on a whim, decides to disguise herself as a servant (calling herself Martha) to be auctioned for a year's employment at the Richmond Fair. Her services are won by a young farmer, Lionel, who immediately falls in love with her. She is likewise attracted, but realizing the impossible difference in their stations, she sneaks away before her caprice can cause further harm. Heartbroken at her disappearance, Lionel is driven into madness when he sees Martha among Queen Anne's retinue, dressed in finery. He gives his foster brother Plunkett a ring which reveals that Lionel is of noble birth, hidden among the peasantry as a baby because of political strife. Lady Harriet arranges a reprise of the Fair to restore him to sanity. Thus, all can end happily, with the lovers (including Plunkett and Lady Harriet's maid Nancy) reunited.

Ironically, neither of the two arias by which *Martha* is best remembered was composed for it. Lionel's lament, "Ach so fromm" (better known in its Italian translation "M'appari tutt'amor") originally appeared in Flotow's *L'ame en peine* (1846), while Lady Harriet's *"letzte Rose"* is none other than the traditional Irish melody of Thomas Moore's poem "The Last Rose of Summer," used as a leitmotif for Lionel's love of "Martha" both in the overture and throughout the opera. It is also noteworthy that these are the only numbers in the original score for one solo voice. Plunkett has the only other aria, a drinking song, but he shares it with the chorus (for later productions in Italian theaters Flotow added arias for Plunkett and Nancy).

Otherwise the opera is a succession of duets, trios, quartets, and concerted numbers, a fact that may explain why Flotow is at his most inventive in this score, reflecting the unsophisticated emotions of the characters with wit and a perfect sense of architecture. Act II provides the best example, opening with an animated quartet in which Lionel and Plunkett express their excitement at getting their new bondmaidens home, while the women grow more and more upset at the situation Lady Harriet's caprice has gotten them into. After an extremely brief recitative (in the 246 pages of the piano score, there are only about ten of recitative) in which Martha and Nancy refuse to do any menial work, Lionel begins another quartet at a reflective tempo, wondering at both the beauty and impertinence of his new acquisition. As Plunkett intrudes to instruct the women in sewing, the tempo reproduces that of the spinning wheel, then relaxes again in a duet for Lionel and Lady Harriet that culminates in her singing, at his request, "The Last Rose of Summer," in whose reprise he joins. Finally, in another quartet in which the four characters say good night, the music's accents follow those of a slowly-tolling clock. The terzettino/duet which actually concludes the act (and must, to get Lady Harriet and Nancy out of their rustic surroundings) is commendably brief, the "Gute Nacht" quartet being the true musico-dramatic conclusion of the act.

The high point, both musically and dramatically, is the ensemble "Mag der Himmel euch vergeben" which closes act III. To a sweeping melody first heard at the conclusion of the overture, Lionel berates Lady Harriet for her deception. While he recapitulates the main theme, first Nancy and Plunkett, then Lady Harriet react in sympathetic counterpoint, all to be swept up in the final statement of the theme in which the chorus joins, investing it with genuine pathos.

Though Flotow's career would not depend, while he lived, on *Martha*'s success, posterity has chosen it as his only work worthy of retention. Its wistful charm, sure-handed dramatic development, and lyric inventiveness, and the genius of the "Ach so fromm" melody, merit for its composer at least that small measure of remembrance.

—William J. Collins

MARTINŮ, Bohuslav.

Composer. Born 8 December 1890, in Polička. Died 28 August 1959, in Liestal, near Basel, Switzerland. Studied violin at home in his youth; enrolled in the Prague Conservatory, 1907-09; entered the Prague Organ School, but was dismissed, 1910; played second violin in the Czech Philharmonic in Prague, 1913-14; in Polička, 1914-18; reentered the Prague Conservatory, studied with Suk; private lessons with Albert Roussel in Paris, 1923; performances of his works at the festivals of the International Society for Contemporary Music; Elizabeth Sprague Coolidge Award for his String Sextet, 1932; in Portugal, 1940; in the United States, 1941; visiting professor at Princeton University, 1948-51; in Switzerland, 1957-59.

Operas

Publishers: Associated, Boosey and Hawkes, Cesky hubedny fond, Eschig, Heugel, Leduc, Schott, Universal.

The Soldier and the Dancer [*Voják a tanečnice*]. J.L. Budin (after Plautus, *Pseudolus*), 1926-27, Brno, 5 May 1928.
Les larmes du couteau, Ribemont-Dessaignes, 1928; Brno, 1968 [posthumous performance].
Les vicissitudes de la vie, Ribemont-Dessaignes, 1928 [unfinished].
Les trois souhaits. Martinů, Ilja Ehrenburg and Ribemont-Dessaignes, 1929.
The Miracle of Our Lady [*Hry o Marii*]. Martinů and Henri Ghéon, 1933, Brno, 1934.
The Voice of the Forest [*Hlas lesa*] (radio opera), 1935, Czech Radio, 6 October 1936.
The Suburban Theater [*Divadlo za bránov*], Martinů, 1935, Brno, 1936.
Comedy on the Bridge [*Veselohra na moste*] (radio opera), after Václav Klicpera, 1935, Czech Radio, 18 March 1937; revised c. 1950.
Alexandre bis, André Wormser, 1937, Mannheim, 18 February 1964 [posthumous production].
Julietta, or The Key to Dreams, Georges Neveux, 1936-37, Prague, 1938.
What Men Live By [*Cim clovek zije*] (television opera), Martinů (after Tolstoy), 1952, New York, 1953.
The Marriage [*Zenitba*] (television opera), Martinů (after Gogol), 1952, New York, 11 February 1953.
La plainte contre inconnu, 1953 [unfinished].
Mirandolina, 1954, Prague, 17 May 1959.
Ariadne, Georges Neveux, 1958, Gelsenkirchen, West Germany, 2 March 1961.
The Greek Passion [*Recké pasije*], after Nikos Kazantzakis, *Christ Recrucified,* 1955-59, Zurich, 9 June 1961.

Other works: orchestral works, chamber music, choral works, piano music, songs.

Publications

By MARTINŮ: articles–

"K voprosy o kritike sovremennoj muzyki" [on critiquing contemporary music]. In *O muzykal' noj kritike. Iz vyskazyvanij sovremennyh zurabeznyh muzykantov,* edited by Vera Bruanceva. Moscow, 1983.

About MARTINŮ: books–

Ferroud, P.O. *A Great Musician Today: Martinu.* London, 1937.
Copland, Aaron. *Our New Music.* New York, 1941.
Safránek, Milos. *Bohuslav Martinů: the Man and his Music.* London, 1946.
———. *Bohuslav Martinů: his Life and Works.* London, 1962; first published in Czech, Prague, 1961.
Pecman, R. *Stage Works of Martinů.* Prague, 1967.
Halbreich, H. *Martinů. Werkverzeichnis, Dokumentation und Biographie.* Zurich, 1968.
Mihule, J. *Martinů.* Prague, 1972; 2nd ed., 1978.
Large, B. *Martinů.* London, 1975.
Martinů, Charlotte. *My Life with Bohuslav Martinů.* Prague, 1978.

Polijaková, Ljudmila. *Ceskaja i sbvackaja opera XX veka, I* [Czech and Slovak opera of the twentieth century]. Moscow, 1978.

Pecman, R., ed. *Martinů v promenach casu* [Martinů symposium]. Praha-Brno, 1979.

Safránek, Milos. *Divadlo Bohuslava Martinů* [Martinů and the theater]. Praha, 1979.

Eyckeu, Karel van. *Bohuslav Martinů.* Steenokkerzeel, 1984.

articles—

Safránek, Milos. "Summing up Martinů's Output." *New York Times* 18 June (1939).

Nettl, Paul. [essay]. In *The Book of Modern Composers,* edited by David Ewen. New York, 1942.

Safránek, Milos. "Bohuslav Martinů." *Musical Quarterly* July (1943).

Hrabel, F. "Bohuslav Martinů." *Hudebni rozhledy* 10 (1957): 923, 960.

Safránek, Milos. "Martinů und das musikalische Theater." *Musica* no. 12 (1959).

Seaman, Gerald. "The Rise of Slavonic Opera." *New Zealand Slavonic Journal* 2 (1978): 1.

Barfoot, Terry. Chapter on Martinů. In *Opera: a History.* London, 1987.

* * *

Bohuslav Martinů's musical talents did not blossom in his conventional studies, for the Prague Conservatory found him incompetent in every subject except his ability to teach, and he was even expelled from the Organ School on grounds of "incorrigible negligence." Such was the unlikely background of one of the most prolific of composers; in fact, Martinů went on to write approximately four hundred compositions.

Although born in Bohemia, Martinů spent nearly all of his career in distant lands including Paris, the United States, Switzerland and Italy. He completed fourteen operas, all of them composed after he had left his homeland, and both musically and dramatically they represent a wide range of styles.

Martinů was much influenced by artistic developments in Paris during the 1920s. His first opera, *The Soldier and the Dancer,* was a comedy after Plautus's *Pseudolus* in which the composer attempted to emulate the wit of Offenbach by incorporating contemporary dances into the music. A jazz influence pervades *The Tears of the Knife,* a twenty-minute piece with surrealist imagery. More substantial altogether is his third opera, *Les trois souhaits.* This work reveals an interest in film, with the inner thoughts of the characters on stage portrayed on a screen behind them. The music reflects this complexity of thought, mixing elements of jazz with speech-song and advanced harmonies, and as in Stravinsky's *Oedipus Rex* a chorus comments on the action.

During the 1930s, Martinů's operas were more closely linked with his native Czechoslovakia. *The Miracle of Our Lady,* or *The Plays of Mary* is a cycle of four mystery plays based upon a tradition dating from twelfth century Prague. The chief consideration was not religious, however, since the composer chose them "because they are well suited to my music, that is treating them in folk style ... This work is a return to the old theatre, and that is the theatre I was looking for. It has been conceived, not in a religious sense, but in a folk or popular way." There are four sections, the shorter items preceding the longer ones. The longest and most complex story is that of Sister Pasqualina, which is set to music

of great expressiveness, and on a scale which brings the whole work to a powerful conclusion.

In 1935, Martinů composed two short operas for Radio Prague. The tuneful and lively *The Voice of the Forest* is based on the tale of a kidnapped hunter rescued by his wife, while in *The Comedy on the Bridge,* the basis of the story is an eighteenth-century play by Václav Klicpera. This brilliant comedy deals with the absurdities of war, its music characterizing the dramatic situation by means of elements such as fanfare figures and clashing harmonies. Another folk theme is treated in *The Suburban Theater,* namely, the entertainment given by traveling players at a fair. Accordingly, the scenes move along quickly and the musical language is simplified; the earlier part of the work is purely balletic. Here, the style is that of the commedia dell' arte, whereas in *Alexandra bis,* the single act adopts an *opera buffa* approach.

Both chronologically and musically, *Juliette* is the central composition in Martinů's output. Adapted from a play by Georges Neveux, *Juliette* deals with the relationship between reality, dreams and memory. Juliette is the idealized woman in the eyes of Michel, but he is the only character to possess a memory. He cannot therefore be sure if she is real, and the emotional intensity generated by the plot is enhanced by the arioso style and rich textures of the music, much of which achieves a truly haunting quality.

Martinů was blacklisted by the Nazis and in 1940 left Europe for the United States, where he turned to the one major genre he had not hitherto attempted, the symphony. After a gap of approximately fourteen years, the successful New York revival of *The Comedy on the Bridge* rekindled his enthusiasm for opera, and in 1953 he completed an adaptation of Tolstoy's *Tales for the People. What Men Live By* was intended to be a television opera, with chamber dimensions and a cast of seven. It was soon followed by *The Marriage,* in which Gogol's story is treated in a classical manner, using recitatives, arias, dances and ensembles.

The comedy *Mirandolina* is an altogether more striking achievement. Martinů described it as "a light, uncomplicated thing, with something of Goldoni," and its plot concerns the battle between the sexes, the hostess of the title reveling in the power she has over her guests. The leading soprano role has an exciting coloratura which skillfully enhances the characterization, while the interludes add considerable atmosphere.

In *Ariadne,* the inspiration was once again a play by Neveux, but Martinů had already made up his mind to write a chamber opera for Maria Callas, whose voice had so impressed him in broadcasts. She never sang the role, however, which seems a pity since its lyricism and wide vocal range would have been well suited to her artistry.

Martinů's final opera, *The Greek Passion,* is a tragedy based upon Nikos Kazantzakis's novel *Christ Recrucified.* The theme of the play within the play is used again, for in this story the actors of the village passion play take on the exact nature of their roles when they find that a group of refugees have arrived seeking help. At the end the refugees depart and continue their search for a new home. The music is atmospheric and dramatic, linking a series of short scenes and building a cumulative effect, and Martinů related its style to the hymns and chants of the Greek Orthodox Church.

The operas of Martinů cover many topics and styles, for like Stravinsky he had the ability to adopt different approaches and yet remain recognizably himself. His most significant operatic achievements are probably *The Miracle of*

Our Lady, Juliette and *The Greek Passion,* but all his music is thoroughly worthy of our attention.

—Terry Barfoot

MARTÍN Y SOLER, Vicente.

Composer. Born 18 June 1754, in Valencia, Spain. Died 30 January 1806, in St. Petersburg. Church organist at Alicante; first opera produced in Madrid, 1776; in Italy, composing operas for Naples, Turin, and Lucca, 1778-85; court composer to Catherine the Great, 1788; in London, 1795; returned to Russia, 1796. Lorenzo da Ponte was among the librettists who worked with Martín y Soler.

Operas

La Madrileña, o Tutor burlado (zarzuela), Madrid, 1776?.
Ifigenia in Aulide, L. Serio, Naples, San Carlo, 12 January 1779.
Ipermestra, Metastasio, Naples, San Carlo, 12 January 1780.
Andromaca, A. Salvi, Turin, Regio, 26 December 1780.
Astartea, Metastasio, Lucca, carnival 1781.
Partenope, Metastasio, Naples, Academy, 1782.
L' amor geloso, Naples, Regio, carnival 1782.
In amor ci vuol destrezza (*L'accorta cameriera*), C.G. Lanfranchi-Rossi, Venice, San Samuele, fall 1782.
Vologeso, after Zeno, *Lucio Vero,* Turin, Regio, carnival 1783.
Le burle per amore, M. Bernardini, Venice, San Samuele, carnival 1784.
La vedova spiritosa, Parma, Ducale, carnival 1785.
Il burbero di buon cuore, Da Ponte (after Goldoni), Vienna, Burgtheater, 4 January 1786.
Una cosa rara, o sia Belleza ed onestà, Da Ponte (after L. Vélez de Guevara), Vienna, Burgtheater, 17 November 1786.
L'arbore di Diana, Da Ponte, Vienna, Burgtheater, 1 October 1787.
The Unfortunate Hero Kosometovich [*Gore bogatyr Kosometovich*], Catherine II and A.V. Khrapovitsky, St. Petersburg, Hermitage, 9 February 1789.
Beloved Songs [*Pesnolyubie*], A.W. Khrapovitsky, St. Petersburg, Hermitage, 18 January 1790.
Il castello d'Atlante, A. Amelli, Desenzano, Communale, carnival, 1791.
La scuola dei maritati [*La capricciosa coretta, Gli sposi in contrasto*]. Da Ponte (after Shakespeare), London, King's Theatre in the Haymarket, 27 January 1795.
L' isola del piacere, Da Ponte, London, King's Theatre in the Haymarket, 26 May 1795.
Le nozze de' contadini spagnuoli (intermezzo), London, King's Theatre in the Haymarket, 28 May 1795.
La festa del villagio, F. Moretti?, St. Petersburg, Hermitage, 26 or 30 January 1798.

Other works: ballets, choral works, chamber cantatas, songs.

Publications/Writings

About MARTÍN Y SOLER: articles—

Fetis, F.-J. "Noticias biográficas de D. Vicente Martín." *Gaceta musical de Madrid* 1 (1855): 45.
Saldoni, B. "Apuntes biográficos del célebre maestro español Don Vicente Martín conocido . . . por Martini lo Spagnuolo." *Heraldo de las artes, de las letras y de los espectáculos* 14 December (1871).
Genée, R. " 'Una cosa rara' in Mozarts 'Don Juan'." *Mitteilungen für die Mozart-Gemeinde Berlin* 1 (1900): 63.
"Vinzenz Martin, der Komponist von 'Una cosa rara'." *Mitteilungen für die Mozart-Gemeinde Berlin* 2 (1906): 23.
Walter, E. "Mozarts Nebensonnen." *Mitteilungen der Salzburger Festspielhausgemeinde* 4/nos. 5-6 (1921): 5.
———. "Vicente Martin i Soler i la seva òpera 'Una cosa raro o sia bellezza ed onestà'." *Revista musical catalana* 33 (1936): 144.
Mooser, R.A. "Un musicien espagnol en Russie." *Rivista musicale italiana* 40 (1936): 432.
Prota-Giurleo, U. "Del compositore spagnuolo Vincente Martin y Soler." *Archivi* 27 (1960): 145.
Jesson, R. "Una cosa rara." *Musical Times* 109 (1968): 619.
———. "Martin y Soler's 'L'arbore di Diana'." *Musical Times* 113 (1972): 551.
Brophy, Brigid. "Da Ponte and Mozart." *Musical Times* 122 (1981): 454.
Sadie, Stanley. "Some Operas of 1787." *Musical Times* 122 (1981): 474.

unpublished—

Platoff, John. "Music and Drama in the *opera buffa* Finale: Mozart and his Contemporaries in Vienna, 1781-1791." Ph.D. dissertation, University of Pennsylvania, 1984.
Link, Dorothea. "The Da Ponte Operas of Vicente Martín y Soler." Ph.D. dissertation, University of Toronto, 1991.

* * *

Vicente Martín y Soler, a Spanish composer particularly successful in the composition of Italian comic operas, received musical training in his home town of Valencia. Around 1778 he traveled to Italy, and between 1779 and 1785 he enjoyed a successful career as a composer of operas for some of the principal theaters of Italy. In 1785 Martín settled in Vienna, where Joseph II had recently assembled a first-rate *opera buffa* troupe. Through the influence of the wife of the Spanish ambassador, Martín soon won the emperor's patronage. With *Il burbero di buon cuore* (1786) he began his successful collaboration with Da Ponte. *Una cosa rara,* first performed later the same year, won enthusiastic applause in Vienna and was soon being performed in theaters throughout Europe. Martín's third Viennese opera, *L'arbore di Diana* (1787) was also successful in Vienna and abroad.

Martín left Vienna shortly after the production of *L'arbore di Diana,* probably because of plans then being laid to disband the Viennese court opera troupe. He traveled to St Petersburg, where in December 1788 he was commissioned by Catherine II to write operas for the court theater. In the mid 1790s Martín moved to London, where he worked for two years as a composer at the King's Theater, reviving his collaboration with Da Ponte and composing at least three comic operas, the first of which, *La scuola dei maritati,* was greeted warmly by audiences and by the press. In 1796 Martín returned to St

Vicente Martín y Soler, engraving after Kreutzinger, 1787

Petersburg, where he stayed for the rest of his life composing, teaching, and managing the Italian court theater.

During his early years as an opera composer in Italy Martín wrote serious and comic operas in about equal numbers. But theatrical conditions in Vienna forced him to specialize in comic opera, a genre to which he was particularly suited; even after leaving Vienna, he continued to devote most of his attention to comic opera. Martín had full command of the wide variety of forms and styles expected in comic opera, and the ability to manipulate these to dramatic effect. He laid out ensembles and finales with a fine sensitivity to dramatic pacing. His ensembles often included canons or canonic passages; some of his canons enjoyed popularity as separate pieces ("Pietà, pietà di noi," in L'arbore di Diana, became an often-reprinted "favourite quartett"). Although he is not remembered as an innovator, Martín was capable of bold, dramatic strokes; for example, his idea of connecting the C-major overture of Una cosa rara, ending quietly on the dominant, directly with the following chorus in C minor.

Martín sometimes made recourse to a superficial prettiness that delighted audiences on first hearing, but had little staying power. A first-night critic writing enthusiastically of La scuola dei maritati (London, 1795) praised the music as "particularly adapted to the taste of an English audience," and expressed his conviction that the opera would enjoy a long and successful run, but in fact it was performed only a few times thereafter. But at its best, Martín's music could move audiences deeply; such was the case with the duet "Pace, caro mio sposo" in Una cosa rara, a copy of which decorates an engraved portrait of the composer. The Viennese theater-goer Zinzendorf found it "voluptuous," "tender," "expressive," and he feared for its effect on young people in the audience: "This duo . . . is truly dangerous for young spectators of both sexes: one needs to have some experience in order to keep one's head when seeing it performed."

—John A. Rice

MARTÓN, Eva (born Eva Heinrich).

Soprano. Born 18 June 1943, in Budapest. Studied with Endre Rosler and Jeno Sipos at the Franz Liszt Academy in Budapest; debut as Queen of Shemakhan in Le coq d'or, Budapest, 1968; member of Budapest State opera, 1968-72; sang in Frankfurt, 1972-77; Vienna debut, 1973; appeared in Munich as Donna Anna, 1974; in Hamburg as the Empress in Die Frau ohne Schatten, 1977; at Teatro alla Scala as Leonora in Il trovatore, 1978; Metropolitan Opera debut as Eva in Die Meistersinger von Nürnberg, 1976; appeared in Ring at San Francisco, 1985.

Publications

About MARTÓN: books–

Wilkens, C. Eva Martón. Hamburg, 1982.

articles–

Waleson, H. "Eva Martón." Ovation October (1987).
Blyth, A. "Eva Martón." Opera March (1990).

*   *   *

In the decade of the 1980s there were very few sopranos who could match the dramatic soprano from Hungary, Eva Martón, in power and attack, or who could expand the top notes so remarkably. These traits have served her well in such roles as Turandot, the Empress in Strauss's Die Frau ohne Schatten and Elektra, the last a role she has recently recorded under Sawallisch. She has performed this role onstage in very different productions under Abbado (in Vienna and Salzburg) and Navarro. Her assessment of Elektra is that "It's dangerous for the voice. I don't want to sing it too often, unlike Turandot, which suits me ideally. On record it's different." In Munich with Sawallisch, whom she greatly admires, Martón has sung Donna Anna (1974), the title role in Strauss' Die ägyptische Helena in 1981, and Ariadne, the last also at the Teatro alla Scala. She sang under Sawallisch in Ponnelle's production of Die Frau ohne Schatten, "one of the favorite stagings of my career." Not since Leonie Rysanek has there been a soprano equipped to project in such a dazzling manner the Empress's cruel tessitura. This role she has also performed in Hamburg with Dohnányi, at the Metropolitan Opera and the Teatro Colón in Buenos Aires with Birgit Nilsson as the Dyer's Wife, and at the Lyric Opera of Chicago. Although her repertoire is extensive and varied, she has made a specialty of Strauss roles. In addition to the above, there was a Salome with Janowski at the Metropolitan Opera that prompted Martin Mayer to declare that "If the title role is sung as splendidly as Martón sang it, you could set Salome as a tale of Martians on Mars and nobody would mind." A recording on CBS of the final scene from a live performance of Salome with the Toronto Symphony under Davis is less splendidly sung, catching most of Martón's more blatant faults, such as a tendency to wobble when attempting to sing softly and a certain fuzziness of timbre producing an unfocused pitch.

Martón has also appeared extensively in the operas of Wagner. Her early roles in Budapest included the Third Norn in Die Götterdämmerung and Elsa in Lohengrin. In 1977 she made her debut at Bayreuth, singing both Venus and Elisabeth in Tannhäuser. Her Elisabeth was subsequently brought to Geneva. Martón's first attempt at Brünnhilde was in San Francisco in 1984 in the Lehnhoff-Conklin Ring cycle; she had a notable success there in the Götterdämmerung Brünnhilde in 1985, of which Robert Jacobson noted that she "does not command the steely laser quality of a Nilsson . . . but suggests more the depth, roundness, and radiance of a Varnay or a Leider." He described her act I duet with René Kollo as Siegfried as "spectacular in its all-encompassing voluminousness, color and caloric content." She is currently recording the role in the complete Ring cycle under Bernard Haitink. Since her early years in Budapest she has made a great success in a number of houses with her Elsa and has even sung Ortrud at the Metropolitan to great acclaim. Her great ambition is to sing Isolde; she has recorded the Liebestod, sung a bit too grandly, negating the opening words of the text, "Mild und leise" (gently and softly).

Martón has by no means limited herself to German roles, although she is better suited to them than to most of the Italian roles she has undertaken. Her career began at the National Theater in Budapest with small parts such as the "Celestial Voice" in Verdi's Don Carlos and Kate Pinkerton in Madama Butterfly; her debut there, in 1968, was as a coloratura in the role of the Queen of Shemakha in Rimsky-Korsakov's Le coq d'or. She quickly progressed to the Countess Almaviva in Le nozze di Figaro and Manon Lescaut, among others.

Martón grew up singing the main roles in children's operas and in children's choirs. She loved to play the piano and still performs jazz when she has the spare time. At the Franz Liszt

Eva Martón as Elektra, Royal Opera, London, 1990

Academy she studied with Endre Rösler and left Hungary in 1972 to begin her career in the West in Frankfurt two years later, eventually settling in Hamburg where she makes her home today. In 1984 she was allowed back into Hungary because she held a German passport.

In the Italian repertoire Martón makes a fine Turandot, for her voice, when at its best (she is often uneven), is big, gleaming, and under firm control. She made her Covent Garden debut in this role in 1987 and can be heard performing it under Maazel in a live recording from Vienna with Carrerras as Calaf. Martón is very solid—she has power, attack, intensity and stamina—but she does not have a true Italianate sound. This is permissible and even desirable for Turandot but a serious fault when she undertakes a role such as Leonora in Verdi's *Il trovatore,* which she has sung in a telecast from the Metropolitan and at La Scala in 1978 under Mehta. Of her 1980 Aida at the Baths of Caracalla (her first Aida in Italy), Lanfranco Rasponi wrote that "Despite a lack of involvement and a rather routine stage presence, she possesses the vocal resources needed for the assignment. The instrument is strong, the pianissimos are well supported." Other Italian roles she has sung with varying degrees of success include Maddalena in *Andrea Chénier,* the title role in Ponchielli's *La Gioconda,* and Puccini's Tosca. Martón has recorded a recital disc of Puccini arias ranging from Musetta's Waltz to Turandot's "In questa reggia." In this album the tone is somewhat creamier than in many of her Italian endeavors. She claims a special affinity for the music of Puccini and has plans to add Minnie in *La fanciulla del West* at the Metropolitan with Domingo as Dick Johnson. Future plans also include a recording of Leonore in Beethoven's *Fidelio* under Colin Davis, but no plans to sing in a staged production of that opera. She has also recorded Bartók's *Bluebeard's Castle,* an opera learned in her early days, in Hungarian with Samuel Ramey, *Fedora* with Carrerras, *La Gioconda,* Catalani's *La Wally,* d'Albert's *Tiefland* with Kollo under Janowski, and act I of *Die Walküre* (from a live concert performance) with Peter Hofmann, Marti Talvela and the New York Philharmonic under Mehta.

—Stephen Willier

MARY STUART
See MARIA STUARDA

MASCAGNI, Pietro.

Composer. Born 7 December 1863, in Livorno. Died 2 August 1945, in Rome. Studied privately with Alfredo Soffredini in Livorno; studied with Ponchielli and Saladino at the Milan Conservatory, 1882, but dismissed from the conservatory in 1884; conductor of the municipal band of Cerignola, 1885; won first prize in the competition sponsored by the publisher Sonzogno for his one-act opera *Cavalleria rusticana,* 1890; knight of the Crown of Italy, 1890; director of the Rossini Conservatory in Pesaro, 1895-1902; conducted the premiere of his opera *Le maschere* in Rome, 1901, which was premiered simultaneously in Milan, Turin, Genoa, Venice, and Verona; United States tour, 1902; South American tour, 1911; member of the Italian Academy, 1929; supporter of the fascist regime in Italy during the Second World War.

Operas

Publisher: Sonzogno.

Pinotta, G. Targioni-Tozzetti, c. 1880, San Remo, Casino, 23 March 1932.
Il re a Napoli (operetta), Cremona, Municipale.
Guglielmo Ratcliff, A. Maffei (after Heine), c. 1885, Milan, Teatro alla Scala, 16 February 1895.
Cavalleria rusticana, G. Targioni-Tozzetti and G. Menasci (after Verga), Rome, Costanzi, 17 May 1890.
L'amico Fritz, P. Suardon [= N. Daspuro] (after Erckmann-Chatrian), Rome, Costanzi, 31 October 1891.
I Rantzau, G. Targioni-Tozzetti and G. Menasci (after Erckmann-Chatrian), Florence, Teatro della Pergola, Florence, 10 November 1892.
Silvano, G. Targioni-Tozzetti, Milan, Teatro alla Scala, 25 March 1895.
Zanetto, G. Targioni-Tozzetti and G. Menasci (after Coppée), Pesaro, Liceo Musicale, 2 March 1896.
Iris, L. Illica, Rome, Costanzi, 22 November 1898; revised, Milan, Teatro alla Scala, 19 January 1899.
Le maschere, L. Illica, simultaneous premiere in Rome, Costanzi; Milan, Teatro alla Scala; Turin, Regio; Genoa, Carlo Felice; Venice, La Fenice; Verona, Filarmonica; 17 January 1901.
Amica, P. Verel [= de Choudens], Monte Carlo, 16 March 1905.
Isabeau, L. Illica (after Lady Godiva legend), Buenos Aires, Coliseo, 2 June 1911.
Parisina, G. D'Annunzio, Milan, Teatro alla Scala, 15 December 1913.
Lodoletta, G. Forzano (after Ouida), Rome, Costanzi, 30 April 1917.
Sí (operetta), C. Lombardo and A. Franci, Rome, Quirino, 13 December 1919.
Il piccolo Marat, G. Forzano and G. Targioni-Tozzetti, Rome, Costanzi, 2 May 1921.
Nerone, Milan, G. Targioni-Tozzetti (after Cossa), Milan, Teatro alla Scala, 16 January 1935.

Other works: choral works, songs, orchestral works, chamber music, piano pieces.

Publications

By MASCAGNI: books–

Aus dunklen Tagen: Lebensabriss. Vienna, 1893.
Cinquantenario della "Cavalleria rusticana": le lettere ai librettisti. Milan, 1940.
Mascagni parla. Rome, 1945.
Stivender, David, ed. and trans. *The Autobiography of Pietro Mascagni.* New York, 1975, 1988.

About MASCAGNI: books–

Bastianelli, G. *Pietro Mascagni.* Naples, 1910.
Pompei, E. *Mascagni nella vita e nell'arte.* Rome, 1912.
Cogo, G. *Il nostro Mascagni: da Cavalleria a Parisina.* Milan, 1914.
Orisini, G. *Vangelo d'un Mascagnano.* Milan, 1926.
Mantovani, T. *Iris di Mascagni.* Rome, 1929.

Cogo, G. *Il nostro Mascagni.* Venice, 1931.
Donno, Alfredo de. *Modernità di Mascagni.* Rome, 1931.
———. *Mascagni nel 900 musicale.* Rome, 1935.
Cellamare, D. *Mascagni e la Cavalleria visti da Cerignola.* Rome, 1941.
Jeri, Alfredo. *Mascagni: quindici opere, mille episodi.* Rome, 1945.
Bonavia, F. *Pietro Mascagni.* London, 1952.
Anselmi, A. *Pietro Mascagni.* Milan, 1959.
Comitato nazionale delle onoranze a Pietro Mascagni nel primo centenario della nascità. Livorno, 1963.
Morini, M., ed. *Pietro Mascagni.* Rome, 1964.
Tedeschi, Rubens. *Addio, fiorito asil. Il melodramma italiano da Boito al Verismo.* Milan, 1978.
Casini, C., et al. *Mascagni.* Milan, 1984.
Studi su Pietro Mascagni (colloquium), Livorno 1985. 1987.
Iovino, R. *Mascagni: l'avventuroso dell' opera.* Milan, 1987.
Morini, M., and P. Ostali, eds. *Mascagni e l' "Iris" fra simbolismo e floreale. Atti del 2° Convegno di studi su Pietro Mascagni.* Milan, 1989.
Ostali, P., and N. Ostali, eds. *"Il piccolo Marat." Storia e rivoluzione nel melodramma verista. Atti del 3° Convegno di studi su Pietro Mascagni.* Milan, 1990.
———. *"Cavalleria rusticana" 1890-1990: cento anni di un capolavoro.* Milan, 1990.
Orselli, C. *Le occasioni di Mascagni.* Siena, 1990.

articles–

Torchi, L. " 'Guglielmo Ratcliff' di Mascagni." *Rivista musicale italiana* 2 (1895): 287.
———. " 'Iris' di Mascagni." *Rivista musicale italiana* 6 (1899): 71-118.
Klein, John W. "Mascagni and his Operas." *Opera* October (1955).
———. "Pietro Mascagni and Giovanni Verga." *Music and Letters* October (1963).
Goetz, H. "Die Beziehungen zwischen Pietro Mascagni und Benito Mussolini." *Analecta musicologica* no. 17 (1976): 212.
Nicolodi, Fiamma. "Parigi e l'opera verista: dibattiti, riflessioni, polemiche." *Nuova rivista musicale italiana* 15 (1981): 577.
Sansone, Matteo. "Verga and Mascagni: The Critics' Response to *Cavalleria rusticana.*" *Music and Letters* May (1990).

*   *   *

One hundred years since the sensational premiere of *Cavalleria rusticana,* Pietro Mascagni still owes his international reputation to that Sicilian story of love, jealousy and revenge, and any critical assessment of his work only credits him with being the initiator of operatic *verismo.* Yet Mascagni's sixteen operas covering a wide range of genres from romantic tragedy, veristic scenes, bourgeois idyll and symbolic music drama to Goldonian comedy and operetta and containing pages of inspired, imaginative music, should have elicited more critical attention or at least suggested caution before dismissing Mascagni as a negligible figure within the Young Italian School.

Cavalleria was undoubtedly the best libretto Mascagni ever set in his career. No innovative intentions were behind his choice of a veristic subject. The source was a play by the Sicilian writer Giovanni Verga, which had already enjoyed

Pietro Mascagni

the favor of the public and had a one-act format as required by the contest sponsored by the publisher Sonzogno for which the opera was intended. The operatic adaptation mostly preserved the vividness of dialogue and the quick pace of the action, but it distorted the social peculiarities of the story and capitalized on the "exotic" color of its setting.

With his coarse-grained, fresh, impassioned music Mascagni was able to delineate flesh-and-blood characters and give them a musical idiom consistent with their "rustic" nature. On the other hand, the inclusion of idyllic choruses, religious hymns, a serenade in Sicilian dialect, and a drinking song gave the opera a convenient balance between novelty and tradition that secured its initial and subsequently undiminished popularity.

The success of *Cavalleria* resulted in the adoption of the term *verismo* to define both the subject and the stylistic solutions devised by Mascagni to set Verga's story. The opera became the prototype of a new genre—operatic *verismo*—and, in the 1890s, a number of *Cavalleria* imitations flooded the opera houses to meet the demand for working-class tragedies: Giordano's *Mala vita,* Leoncavallo's *Pagliacci,* Massenet's *La navarraise,* and D'Albert's *Tiefland* are relevant examples to which Mascagni's own mediocre *Silvano* can be added.

When the whole of Mascagni's production is surveyed, however, it soon becomes clear how misrepresented he is under the label of *verismo.* The very next opera after *Cavalleria, L'amico Fritz,* baffled Mascagni's admirers for its definitely *un*veristic nature. The gentle idyll by Erckmann-Chatrian may have been a tenuous story to turn into a three-act "lyric comedy," but Mascagni took great care in shaping its pastoral setting and the three main characters, particularly the graceful Suzel, whose naive charm wins the bachelor Fritz over to marriage. Apart from some occasional lapses into his earlier *Cavalleria*-style, Mascagni's orchestra in *Fritz* sounds more refined, more elegant. The opera is full of tenderness, and the vocal part of Suzel contains exquisite melodies of Puccinian delicacy, such as the romanza "Son pochi fiori" (act I), the passionate lament "Non mi resta altro che il pianto" (act III). No less charming are the celebrated "Cherry Duet" (act II) between Suzel and Fritz, and the off-stage choruses for which Mascagni used two Alsatian folk-songs.

Even further away from *verismo* in terms of the subject and the musico-dramatic structures, is the four-act romantic tragedy *Guglielmo Ratcliff*, with its ghosts and bleak Scottish landscape. Although it was first performed in 1895, the opera had been a pet project of the composer since about 1885. Whereas the choice of *Cavalleria* was dictated by sheer expediency, the setting of the almost integral translation of Heine's gloomy tragedy was resumed with youthful zeal and earnest effort once Mascagni had achieved success. However, the unremarkable music and the length and frequency of the narrative monologues have doomed the opera to oblivion save for a Massenetian intermezzo (act III, 3) known as "Ratcliff's Dream."

The 1890s were the most prolific years in Mascagni's career. During this period, Mascagni composed no fewer than eight operas, each apparently marking the adherence to a different cultural trend, and demonstrating the composer's eclecticism. These works include one more Erckmann-Chatrian story (the unexciting and modest *I Rantzau*), *Silvano, Zanetto* (a one-act opera, set in Renaissance Florence and based on a play by the Parnassian poet François Coppée), the decadent *Iris,* and a revival of the commedia dell'arte masks with *Le maschere.*

One common feature is noticeable in these and in Mascagni's later operas; although they may well contain finer music than *Cavalleria,* their overall theatrical effectiveness is hindered by some intrinsic fault of the librettos. Mascagni lacks self-criticism and Puccini's unerring sense of the theater. It was not for him to pester his librettists and require extensive alterations and readjustments as his more perceptive colleague did. Mascagni may have occasionally complained, but the librettist had the last word. This was the case with the highly skilled and much sought-after librettist Luigi Illica, who wrote the librettos of *Iris, Le maschere* and *Isabeau.*

Iris exemplifies Mascagni's most advanced stage of artistic development. A Japanese legend is dramatized in the first two acts. Osaka, a lustful nobleman, sets his eyes on the ingenuous and beautiful Iris and engages Kyoto, the owner of a geisha house, to abduct the girl. Once in Kyoto's luxurious place, Iris does not respond to Osaka's passionate advances and is therefore put on public display. When her blind father curses her, flinging mud in her face, Iris, in despair, throws herself down a dark pit. The opera might come to an end on this gruesome event. Instead, act III shows the dying girl at dawn on the bank of an open sewer. Some ragpickers are attracted by her glittering attire. Iris dies as the sun rises and the horrid place is engulfed by flowers. After Baudelaire, Illica had read Maeterlinck, and a veil of symbolism is laid on people and events. The fashionable orientalism of the setting adds color to the decadent ingredients of the story, which include Osaka's eroticism, Kyoto's sadism, and Iris's passive, dreamy nature.

Stimulated by this material, Mascagni produces a sparkling score characterized by sophisticated harmonies and polychrome orchestration. A highly sensitive idiom is devised for Iris's nightmares and lyrical outbursts, such as in her dream monologue in act I, "Ho fatto un triste sogno," and the act II aria "Un dì (ero piccina)".

Despite Illica's pretentious text and its dramatic shortcomings, *Iris* has generally received a favorable critical response, to the point that some claim *Iris* to be an anticipation of Puccini's *Butterfly* and *Turandot.* The opera marks Mascagni's approach to *fin-de-siècle,* aestheticism, and, through the later *Isabeau* (Illica's adaptation of the Lady Godiva legend), leads to the "lyric tragedy" *Parisina* (1913), expressly written by Gabriele D'Annunzio for the composer.

Later, in *Il piccolo Marat,* Mascagni returned to his early *verismo* style with no appreciable results. Both this opera and his last, *Nerone* do not add much to the composer's artistic achievement.

—Matteo Sansone

THE MASK OF ORPHEUS.

Composer: Harrison Birtwistle.

Librettist: Peter Zinovieff.

First Performance: London, English National Opera, 21 May 1986.

Roles: Orpheus (tenor); Euridice (mezzo-soprano); Aristaeus (bass-baritone); Oracle of the Dead/Hecate (soprano); Troupe of Ceremony/Judges of the Dead (tenor, baritone, baritone); Three Women/Furies (soprano, mezzo-soprano, mezzo-soprano).

*   *   *

When, in 1970, Covent Garden and then London Weekend Television commissioned Harrison Birtwistle to write a second opera, he knew the story would have to reflect his musical preoccupations, which were primarily concerned with examining the same event from different angles, finding a balance between chance and necessity, and exploring new concepts of time. Birtwistle required a story which everybody knows, and for some time he wavered between Faust and Orpheus. He eventually selected Orpheus because Orpheus had been a musician and was possibly the more introspective of the two. The religion of Orphism, which Orpheus is said to have either founded or inspired, suggests he might have been a contemplative, as fascinated by the "divine dance of numbers" as Birtwistle himself. At first *The Mask of Orpheus* was intended to be an opera which could be put on in village halls, but in the event it turned out to be one of the most demanding ever composed. It demands elaborate stage mechanisms, very extensive electronic equipment, a dance troup capable of performing at breakneck speed, an orchestra containing large forces of percussion, wind instruments and plucked instruments (but no strings), and two conductors. Each of the three main characters, Orpheus, Euridice, and Aristaeus, must appear as singer, mime, and huge puppet. As human figures they are represented by masked singers, as heroic figures by masked mimes, as myths by very elaborate puppets with voices coming from amplified singers offstage.

Although Birtwistle presents different versions of the myth simultaneously or in close juxtaposition, he nevertheless follows the traditional story handed down to us mainly from Roman sources, notably Virgil and Ovid. Shortly after her

The Mask of Orpheus, **English National Opera, London, first production, 1986**

marriage to Orpheus, Euridice is walking by a river when Aristaeus, a beekeeper, tries to seduce her. In attempting to flee from him, a snake bites and kills her. Orpheus is so distraught that he determines to descend into Hades and win her back. There he charms Charon and the powers of darkness with his singing and crosses the river Styx. Pluto finds his song so moving that he takes pity on him and allows him to take Euridice back to earth. The condition is that Orpheus shall not turn back to look at her. In Birtwistle's version, the episode in Hades takes place in a dream, and Orpheus turns when blinded by the sun shining in his eyes on waking. Having lost his wife a second time, Orpheus renounces women and sings only to the animals, trees, and rocks. His rejection of women rouses the fury of the Maenads (the female followers of Dionysus) who tear him apart and cast his still murmuring head and lyre on the river Hebrus. From there they float to Lesbos where, on the intervention of Apollo, his ghost eventually passes into Hades and joins Euridice according to the usual ordinance.

Interspersed throughout the opera are two quite separate inserts. One involves the troupe of dancers who mime the stories which Orpheus tells to the animals, trees, and rocks, accompanied by electronic music on tape. As soon as they appear (and they do so at junctures which may take even the conductor by surprise) everything on stage freezes. Ideally their mime should be undertaken in accelerated motion to match the electric music, but this may prove impracticable. The other insert involves a troupe of singers who enact three Orphic ceremonies in such a way that the true content and meaning of them remain a mystery. Even today we have extremely limited knowledge of the religion know as Orphism. But what is revealed in these ceremonies is that they represent a backward evolution of man's development. According to Peter Zinovieff's libretto, "the Ceremonies are secret ritualistic dances which, by repetition and exposition of a gross and inner detailed structure, gradually become revealed as parts of a sacrificial murder."

To compose the electronic music for the mime inserts, Birtwistle had to go to IRCAM (L'Institut de Recherche et de Coordination Acoustique/Musique) in Paris for assistance. It was there that an engineer produced for him a sound suitable for the voice of Apollo, and from this came a late and unplanned perspective on the story. In the last act, Birtwistle causes Orpheus to be guilty of hubris by learning the language of the gods. With a sound for Apollo that has the quality of being incomprehensible and yet extremely authoritative, Birtwistle had at his disposal the means to contrast Orpheus's challenge to the gods with Apollo's commanding ability to repel it. The last act therefore plays out Birtwistle's central concern with the balance between caprice and order; for as well as being the god of music, Apollo is also the god of law, discipline, and necessity. In the end Orpheus also dies at the hand of his Olympian father. The return to a balanced state of affairs is suggested when Aristaeus's bees, which mysteriously disappeared when he seduced or attempted to seduce Euridice, return to him.

It took Birtwistle about fourteen years to complete *The Mask of Orpheus,* and the gap of six years between composing the first two acts and the last may have resulted in a slightly noticeable shift of style between acts II and III. But nevertheless his music is of the very highest quality. The opening of the opera with its evocation of the birth of music, the electronic inserts, and the extraordinary second act in which

Orpheus describes his journey through Hades in a huge aria which becomes more and more nightmarish, are outstanding.

—Michael Hall

MASKARADE [Masquerade].

Composer: Carl Nielsen.

Librettist: V. Andersen (after Holberg).

First Performance: Copenhagen, 11 November 1906.

Roles: Jeronimus (bass); Magdelone (mezzo-soprano); Leander (tenor); Henrik (bass-baritone); Arv (tenor); Leonard (tenor or baritone); Leonora (soprano); Pernille (soprano); Night Watchman (bass); Sergeant-Major of Cavalry (baritone); Mask Seller (baritone); Schoolmaster (baritone); Flower Seller (soprano); Steward (bass-baritone); Dance Master (mute); chorus (SSATTTB).

*   *   *

Having achieved a success with *Saul and David,* Nielsen turned his attention in 1905 to a comic subject, Holberg's *Maskarade.* Ludvig Holberg (1684-1754), Denmark's most famous comic playwright, modeled himself on Molière, but his work also invites comparison with that of Goldoni. *Maskarade* (1724) had become an established favorite with generations of Danish theater-goers, and by choosing it Nielsen ran a real risk of alienating his public. It is a story of how young love, hampered by mistaken identity and thwarted by hypocritical elders, wins acceptance through subterfuge and cunning and the exploitation of folly, the stock ingredients of comedy. It has been suggested that Nielsen looked upon the artifices of the masquerade as a child who sees in the magic of a toy theater the reflection of an idealized yet unattainable world. Nielsen's pragmatic attitude to life gives little support to this contention, and it is more likely that he saw these artifices as a comment on the mores of Danish society just as Holberg had.

Nielsen invited the historian Vilhelm Andersen to fashion the play into a suitable libretto. Andersen compressed Holberg's first two acts and added a street scene of his own invention. He also expanded Holberg's Intermezzo to meet the composer's demand for a full-length divertissement, rich in incident, from which could flow the actions leading to the dénouement. The relative importance of Holberg's characters was altered too; Leonora's was increased while Holberg's two respectable fathers, Jeronimus and Leonard, were reduced to comic stereotypes.

The plot is comparatively simple. Leander, son of Jeronimus, has been to the Masquerade with his servant Henrik. There he has fallen in love with a masked young lady. Unfortunately Jeronimus has betrothed him to Leonora, daughter of his friend Leonard. Leander has never seen Leonora and has no wish to marry her. Despite his father's disapproval of masquerading, he is determined to go back, and Henrik, who has his own amour afoot, plans to assist him. Jeronimus, determined to curb his son's addiction, orders him to be watched. Mr Leonard who is present confesses that his daughter is guilty of the same addiction. Henrik, in a spirited defense of the Masquerade as a democratic entertainment fit alike for servants and masters, almost wins Leonard over, but Jeronimus is adamant. Leander must pledge himself afresh to the unknown.

Act II begins in the street. Henrik, disguised as a ghost, terrifies the watching servant Arv, who confesses all his crimes believing he is about to die. Henrik declares himself and obliges the wretched Arv to let him and Leander escape to the masquerade. Realizing he has been outwitted, Jeronimus follows them disguised as Bacchus, with Arv disguised as Cupid. Meanwhile a secret dance addict, Jeronimus's wife Magdelone, suitably masked, joins the masquerade accompanied by the disguised Leonard.

The masquerade occupies most of act III. Leander is enjoying the company of his unknown lady-love. She, of course, is Leonora, Leonard's errant daughter. Henrik is pursuing Leonora's maid, and Leonard is trying to seduce the complaisant Mrs Jeronimus but is interrupted by an unsuspecting Jeronimus in search of his son. Henrik recognizes Jeronimus and alerts Leander; Arv recognizes Henrik but is sworn to silence. Jeronimus (alias Bacchus), now drunk, is making passes at the dancing master's fiancée. The time to unmask arrives. Magdelone and Leonard are dismayed to find who they have been dallying with; Leonora and Leander are delighted to discover each other at last, but Jeronimus is too befuddled to know that all has ended happily. Henrik approaches the audience and asks for their approval as the curtain falls.

While it is tempting to compare *Maskarade* with *Le nozze di Figaro,* there are some essential differences. Holberg's instinct was for broad comedy and Nielsen's for the exploitation of situations, whereas Beaumarchais's object was sharp social satire and Mozart's the development of character relationships. Nor should the coincidence that both plots revolve around wily servants be taken too seriously. Henrik, a wily bystander, merely profits from events as they occur while Figaro, the *deus ex machina,* creates the situations from which he ultimately profits.

Nielsen's music may sound Mozartian, and he employs devices familiar from *opera buffa,* but the differences are greater than the similarities. *Maskarade* is no pastiche; the music, unusually felicitous, is distinctive and follows closely the inflections of the Danish language. Where Nielsen does emulate Mozart is in the importance he accords the orchestra. A lively overture establishes the style, and the atmospheric prelude that opens act II indicates the breadth of Nielsen's orchestral imagination. There are few set pieces and none to compare with Mozart's act finales. There are no arias to hold up the action, and things are kept moving by a mixture of spoken dialogue, duets, recitative, and arioso. The composition went so well that Nielsen referred to himself as "a pipe through which flows a stream of music . . . in continual blissful vibrations." The core of the work is the masquerade itself. Like the Shrovetide Fair in Stravinsky's *Petrushka,* it is full of inventive if often irrelevant incident (the Dance of the Cocks is a triumph), and though it arguably upsets the balance of the opera its effervescent inventiveness offsets any dramatic shortcoming.

Maskarade gained immediate popularity in Denmark. First performed in 1906, it has remained an established part of the repertory ever since, passing its 100th performance in 1946. It has not established itself so easily elsewhere however, and only achieved its UK premiere in 1990.

—Kenneth Dommett

A MASKED BALL
See UN BALLO IN MASCHERA

I MASNADIERI [The Robbers].

Composer: Giuseppe Verdi.

Librettist: Andrea Maffei (after Schiller, *Die Räuber*).

First Performance: London, Her Majesty's, 22 July 1847.

Roles: Massimiliano (bass); Carlo (tenor); Francesco (baritone); Amalia (soprano); Arminio (tenor); Moser (bass); Rolla (baritone); chorus.

* * *

I masnadieri, for all its relative obscurity today, represents an important watershed in Verdi's career, his first commission for a premiere outside Italy. Her Majesty's Theatre in London was in 1844 under the direction of Benjamin Lumley, who needed a coup to offset the recently established rival opera company at Covent Garden. He was able to lure Verdi with a lucrative contract and a cast including famed basso Luigi Lablache and the London debut of Jenny Lind.

Verdi, for his part, was stretching his artistic wings both by choosing a play by Schiller as basis for the new work (*Die Räuber*) and taking as collaborator Andrea Maffei, a leading Milanese intellectual and translator of Schiller (among others) for Italian consumption. The resultant text was surprisingly faithful to the great German dramatist's play.

In early eighteenth-century Germany the elderly Count Massimiliano Moor has two sons. The elder, Carlo, is the embodiment of the wildly emotional and egocentric anti-hero of the period's literature. He has fled both family and sweetheart Amalia to lead a self-destructive life as head of a band of robber-brigands. Seizing the opportunity, his villainous younger brother Francesco concocts a false report of Carlo's death, which sends the old Count into a deep and nearly mortal faint. When, in his coffin, he revives, the enraged Francesco has him secretly imprisoned in a tower, then proceeds to force himself on the unwilling Amalia. Returning home, Carlo learns of all this and with his band swears a mighty oath of vengeance on his brother. Meanwhile Francesco, who has had a fiery dream full of images of judgment and damnation, summons Pastor Moser, who refuses to grant absolution to the tormented sinner. In the final scene Carlo's own life of crime is exposed, and in an excess of hysteria over a wasted life he tells his robber band "Hear me, you demons! You each have offered to me your own horrible head covered with shame, I offer to you an angel!" whereupon he stabs Amalia in the heart and rushes off to his own punishment and execution.

The play is very early Schiller and represents the worst excesses of the Sturm and Drang movement; indeed, Schiller repudiated it in later life. In turn, Maffei was too much of a scholar (and too much a theatrical amateur) to make those alterations which would have given Verdi the means to do what he did best, namely write scenes of violent confrontation between his principals. For example, not only do the two brothers never have a major scene together, they literally

THE THEATRES.

HER MAJESTY'S.

The great object of attraction is still Verdi's new opera, possessing, as it does, so much additional interest from the fact of its being one of the first operas ever written for our Anglo-Italian stage. We hope, however, it will not be the last, and that, the example once set, will be frequently followed. It redounds greatly to the credit of the management that this important step in art should have been taken in a season which all prophesied would be one of extraordinary difficulties for Her Majesty's Theatre, and which, on the contrary, will have been one of the most brilliant in its annals. Such performances as that of the "Masnadieri," a

MDLLE. JENNY LIND.   SIG. LABLACHE.

VERDI'S NEW OPERA "I MASNADIERI," AT HER MAJESTY'S THEATRE.—SCENE VI.

new opera by the first Italian composer, performed under his superintendence, by such artists as Lind, Gardoni, Coletti, and Lablache, followed by a ballet like the "Pas des Déesses," comprising three of the first dancers in the world—Taglioni, Cerito, and Rosati—such performances as these, we repeat, are indeed calculated to raise the character of the British nation for an enlightened and munificent patronage of the fine arts.

To proceed to Verdi's Opera. Let it be said, first, that nothing could be more perfect and admirable than the manner in which "I Masnadieri" is got up and performed. All the four artists, gifted with voices rarely equalled, with musical and dramatic skill of the first order, play with an ensemble, spirit, and genius, which brings every point of the libretto, every happy thought of the composer into prominence, while the orchestra and chorus seem as if inspired by one spirit, and work together in perfection. Nothing could be better done. The Opera itself is an essentially dramatic work. Of pieces which would make an effect in a drawing-room, there are few—fewer, perhaps, than in Verdi's other works, but in return, this professes more nicety of thought and conception, and the immense superiority of the libretto over that of any other opera Verdi has written, gives great advantage in its favour. Critics have already pronounced

SIG. GARDONI.   MDLLE. JENNY LIND.   SIG. LABLACHE.

VERDI'S "I MASNADIERI"—SCENE LAST.

Scenes from the premiere of Verdi's *I masnadieri*, Her Majesty's Theatre, London, 1847

never meet: a clash of wills between tenor and baritone would have to wait until the more mature Verdi of *Vêpres siciliennes.* Indeed since they (and Amalia) all live in separate emotional worlds, the majority of the first act is given over to ruminating expository arias for each, and it is very late in the game before the drama is finally allowed to get under way.

There are, as in all Verdi operas, some wonderful moments, particularly the finales of acts I, III, and IV and the savage Francesco/Moser duet. Amalia is given some very pretty and highly decorated music to sing, although it tends to be non-emphatic, naturally hand-tailored to the strengths (and weaknesses) of Jenny Lind. Francesco's dream narrative must be counted a noble failure, as Verdi had not yet acquired the musical language to bring to life a personalized *Dies irae* of this type. As a whole the opera can seem turgid and awkwardly paced, lacking the forward thrust and startling novelties of *Macbeth,* also of 1847: it is important to note in this context that while *I masnadieri* had its premiere after the composer's first Shakespearian opera, in its conception it in fact antedated that work and is a closer stylistic neighbor to the still earlier *Attila.*

—Dennis Wakeling

MASQUERADE
See MASKARADE

MASSENET, Jules (-Emile-Frédéric).

Composer. Born 12 May 1842, in Montaud, near St-Etienne, Loire. Died 13 August 1912, in Paris. Married: Constance de Sainte-Marie, 1866 (one daughter). Studied piano with Laurent, harmony with Reber, and composition with Savard and Ambroise Thomas at the Paris Conservatory, 1851; first prize for piano and fugue at the Paris Conservatory, 1859; Grand Prix de Rome for his cantata, *David Rizzio,* 1863; professor of composition at the Paris Conservatory, 1878; member of the Académie des Beaux-Arts, 1878. Massenet's students included Alfred Bruneau, Gabriel Pierné, Charles Koechlin, Reynaldo Hahn, Florent Schmitt, Henri Rabaud, and Gustave Charpentier.

Operas

Esmeralda, after Hugo, c. 1865.
La coupe du roi de Thulé, L. Gallet, c. 1866.
La grand'tante, Jules Adénis and Charles Grandvallet, Paris, Opéra-Comique, 3 April 1867.
Manfred, after Byron, c. 1869 [unfinished].
Méduse, M. Carré, 1870 [unfinished].
Don César de Bazan, Adolphe Philippe d'Ennery, P.E. Pinel Dumanoir and Jules Chantepie (after Hugo, *Ruy Blas*), Paris, Opéra-Comique, 30 November 1872.
L'adorable bel'-boul', Louis Gallet, Paris, Cercle des Mirlitons, 17 April 1874.
Les templiers [unfinished].
Bérengère et Anatole, Henri Meilhac and Paul Poirson, Paris, Cercle de l'Union Artistique, February 1876.

Le roi de Lahore, Louis Gallet, Paris, Opéra, 27 April 1877 [act III based on act II of *La coupe du roi de Thulé*].
Robert de France, c. 1880.
Les Girondins, 1881.
Hérodiade, Paul Milliet and Henri Grémont [=Georges Hartmann] and Zamadini (after Flaubert), Brussels, Théâtre de la Monnaie, 19 December 1881.
Manon, Henri Meilhac and Philippe Gille (after Prévost), Paris, Opéra-Comique, 19 January 1884.
Le Cid, Adolphe Philippe d'Ennery, Louis Gallet, and Edouard Blau (after Corneille), Paris, Opéra, 30 November 1885.
Esclarmonde, Alfred Blau and Louis de Gramont, Paris, Opéra-Comique, 14 May 1889.
Le mage, Jean Richepin, Paris, Opéra, 16 March 1891.
Werther, Edouard Blau, Paul Milliet, and Georges Hartmann (after Goethe) [libretto translated into German by Max Kalbeck], Vienna, Court Opera, 16 February 1892.
Thaïs, Louis Gallet (after Anatole France), Paris, Opéra, 16 March 1894.
Le portrait de Manon, Georges Boyer, Paris, Opéra-Comique, 8 May 1894.
La navarraise, Jules Claretie and Henri Cain, London, Covent Garden, 20 June 1894.
Sapho, Henri Cain and Arthur Bernède (after Daudet), Paris, Opéra-Comique, 27 November 1897.
Cendrillon, Henri Cain (after Perrault), Paris, Opéra-Comique, 24 May 1899.
Grisélidis, Paul Armand Silvestre and Eugène Morand, Paris, Opéra-Comique, 20 November 1901.
Amadis, Jules Claretie, c. 1902, Monte Carlo, Opéra, 1 April 1922 [posthumous].
Le jongleur de Notre Dame, Maurice Léna, Monte Carlo, 18 February 1902.
Chérubin, Francis de Croisset and Henri Cain, Monte Carlo, Opéra, 14 February 1905.
Ariane, Catulle Mendès, Paris, Opéra, 31 October 1906.
Thérèse, Jules Claretie, Monte Carlo, Opéra, 7 February 1907.
Bacchus, Catulle Mendès, Paris, Opéra, 5 May 1909.
Don Quichotte, Henri Cain (after Jacques Le Lorrain, *Le chevalier de la longue figure*), Monte Carlo, Opéra, 19 February 1910.
Roma, Henri Cain (after Dominique Alexandre Parodi, *Rome vaincue*), Monte Carlo, Opéra, 17 February 1912.
Panurge, Georges Spitzmüller and Maurice Boukay (after Rabelais), Paris, Théâtre de la Gaîté, 25 April 1913 [posthumous].
Cléopâtre, Louis Payen [=Albert Liénard], Monte Carlo, Opéra, 23 February 1914 [posthumous].

Other works: oratorios, incidental music, ballets, sacred and secular choral works, orchestral works, partsongs, piano pieces.

Publications/Writings

By MASSENET: books–

Discours prononcé à l'inauguration de la statue de Méhul à Givet, le 2 octobre, 1892. Paris, 1892.
Discours prononcé aux funérailles d'Ernest Guiraud. Paris, 1892.
Preface to Bonnal, G. *Dictionnaire des connaissances musicales.* Paris, 1898.

Mes souvenirs (1848-1912). Paris, 1912; English translation as *My Recollections,* Boston, 1919, 1970; German translation as *Mein Leben. Autobiographie,* Wilhelmshaven, 1982.

articles–

"Autobiographical Notes by the Composer Massenet." *Century Magazine* 45/November (1892): 122.
"Souvenirs d'une première." *Le Figaro* 29 August (1893).
"Discours prononcé aux obsèques d'Ambroise Thomas." *Le ménestrel* 63/23 February (1896).
"Discours à l'occasion du centenaire de Berlioz." *Revue illustrée* 1 April (1903).
Reply to "Confidences d'hommes arrivés." *La revue* 15 March (1904).
"La musique d'aujourd'hui et de demain." *Comoedia* 4 November (1909).
"19 lettres inédites de Massenet à Ernest Van Dyck." *Le ménestrel* 94 (1927): 45, 57, 69.

About MASSENET: books–

Hanslick, E. *Musikalische Stationen,* 86ff [*Le roi de Lahore*]. Berlin, 1885.
———. *Musikalisches und Litterarisches,* 79ff [*Le Cid*]. Berlin, 1889.
Malherbe, C. *Notice sur "Esclarmonde".* Paris, 1890.
Hanslick, E. *Aus dem Tagebuche eines Musikers,* 137ff [*Manon*]. Berlin, 1892.
———. *Fünf Jahre Musik,* 23ff [*Werther*]; 140ff [*La navarraise*]. Berlin, 1896.
Solenière, E. de *Massenet: étude critique et documentaire.* Paris, 1897.
Schneider, L. *Massenet: l'homme, le musicien.* Paris, 1908; 2nd ed., 1926.
Finck, Henry T. *Massenet and his Operas.* New York and London, 1910.
Séré, O. *Massenet.* Paris, 1911.
Soubies, A. *Massenet.* Paris, 1914.
Widor, C.M. *Notice sur la vie et les travaux de Massenet.* Paris, 1915.
Rigné, R. *Le disciple de Massenet.* 2 vols. Paris, 1920, 1923.
Loisel, Joseph. *Manon de Massenet: étude historique et critique, analyse musicale.* Paris, 1922.
Bouvet, C. *Massenet.* Paris, 1929.
Brancour, R. *Massenet.* Paris, 1930.
Delmas, M. *Massenet, sa vie, ses oeuvres.* Paris, 1932.
Bruneau, A. *Massenet.* Paris, 1935.
Augenot, R. *Esclarmonde ou Une forme divine de l'expression musicale au théâtre.* Brussels, 1939.
Morin, A. *Jules Massenet et ses opéras.* Montreal, 1944.
Colson, Percy. *Massenet: "Manon".* London, 1947.
Bruyr, José. *Massenet.* Geneva, 1948.
———. *Massenet: Musicien de la belle époque.* Lyons, 1964.
Coquis, André. *Jules Massenet: l'homme et son oeuvre.* Paris, 1965.
Bouilhol, Eliane. *Massenet: son rôle dans l'évolution du théâtre musical.* St Etienne, 1969.
Harding, James. *Massenet.* London, 1970.
Bessand-Massenet, Pierre. *Massenet.* Paris, 1979.
John, Nicholas, ed. *Jules Massenet: "Manon". Opera Guide 25.* London, 1984.
Salzer, Otto T. *The Massenet Compendium.* 2 vols. Fort Lee, New Jersey. 1984.

articles–

Bréville, W. "A propos de Sapho." *Revue blanche* 10 (1897): 457.
Debussy, Claude. "D'*Eve à Grisélidis*." *La revue blanche* 1 December (1901); reprinted in *Monsieur Croche et autres écrits,* edited by François Lesure, 58, Paris, 1980; English translation, London and Cambridge, Massachusetts, 1987.
Stojowski, S. "Grisélidis von Massenet." *Die Musik* 1 (1901-02): 513, 603, 696.
Debussy, Claude. "Reprise de *Werther* à l'Opéra-Comique." *Gil Blas* 27 April (1903); reprinted in *Monsieur Croche et autres écrits,* edited by François Lesure, 154, Paris, 1980; English translation, London and Cambridge, Massachusetts, 1987.
Pougin, A. "Le répertoire dramatique de Massenet." *Le ménestrel,* 79 (1912): 283.
Finck, H.T. "Massenet, Thaïs and Farrar." *The Nation* 104 (1917).
Parker, D.C. "Thérèse." *Musical Standard* 96 (1919).
Bellaigue, C. "A travers le répertoire lyrique (IX): 'Manon'." *Revue universelle* 1 October (1922): 59.
Cooke, J.F. "Massenet's Manon." *Etude* 40 (1922): 127.
Béraud, H. "Werther au phonographe." *Le ménestrel* 99 (1932): 9.
Carner, Mosco. "The Two Manons." *Monthly Musical Record* 67 (1937): 176; also in *Major and minor,* London, 1944; 1980.
Earl of Harwood. "Massenet's Opera *Werther*." *Opera* 3 (1952): 69.
Smith, Cecil, "The Operas of Massenet." *Opera* 6 (1955): 226.
Commons, J. "Genesis of *Werther*." in *Music and Musicians* 14/no. 10 (1966): 18.
Harding, J. "Massenet's *Werther*." *The Listener* 75 (1966): 958.
Jefferson, A. "Impressions of Manon." *Music and Musicians* 17/no. 4 (1968): 28.
Budden, J. "Massenet and the French Tradition." *The Listener* 72 (1969): 865.
Schlegel, Klaus. "Don Quichotte: die Fabellesart in der Inszenierung der Komischen Oper Berlin." In *Jahrbuch der Komischen Oper Berlin* 12 (1973).
Blyth, Alan. "Manon." *Opera* February (1974).
Becker, Heinz. "Massenets *Werther*: Oper oder vertonter Roman?" In *Ars musica, musica scientia. Festschrift Heinrich Hüschen zum fünfundsechzigsten Geburtstag am 2. März 1980,* edited by Detlef Altenburg, 30. Cologne, 1980.
Crichton, Ronald. "*Mireille* and *Esclarmonde*." *Opera* December (1983).
Avant-scène opéra March (1984) [*Werther* issue].
Avant-scène opéra December (1986) [*Don Quichotte* issue].
Avant-scène opéra May (1988) [*Thaïs* issue].
Avant-scène opéra September (1989) [*Manon* issue].

unpublished–

Hiss, C.S. "Abbé Prévost's 'Manon Lescaut' as Novel, Libretto and Opera." Ph.D. dissertation, University of Illinois, 1967.
Stocker, L.L. "The Treatment of the Romantic Literary Hero in Verdi's 'Ernani' and in Massenet's 'Werther'." Ph.D. dissertation, Florida State University, 1969.

*   *   *

In his time, Massenet was the most popular of all French composers for the stage. He owed his success to a brilliant sense of theater, a sharp awareness of prevailing fashions and an inexhaustible capacity for hard work.

Some of the qualities Massenet was to display in his triumphant career are clearly discernible in his first important opera, *Don César de Bazan* (1872). Although it bears traces of haste and clumsiness, it has a neat touch of Spanish local color, and the rhythms are handled to full theatrical effect. The stageworthy quality of the opera is what strikes one most, even in this early work. Here Massenet shows evidence of a remarkable gift for the theater despite the nature of the music, which today sounds conventional and often faded. Massenet knew instinctively how to create emotion by means of dramatic illusion; his natural talent, formed and instructed by years of humble work in the orchestra pit had begun to flower rewardingly.

Massenet's next important opera, *Le roi de Lahore* (1877), proved that he knew what the public of the Paris Opéra wanted: color, spectacle, exotic scenery, and all the grandiose delights which Meyerbeer had given them in profusion. Set in ancient India, *Le roi de Lahore* is modeled on Bizet's *Les pêcheurs de perles,* and makes clever use of pseudo-oriental harmonies. The third act is set in a Hindu paradise which, needless to say, gave excellent opportunities for the ballet without which no Parisian opera production would have been complete. The formula was impeccable.

Le roi de Lahore was a turning point in Massenet's career. It won rapturous acclaim and soon established itself in the repertory, not only at home but throughout the rest of Europe. The same exoticism marks *Hérodiade* (1881), which is inspired by one of Flaubert's *Trois contes.* In Salomé we see

Jules Massenet

the emergence of what was to become known as a typical Massenet heroine: the suave seductress, langorous and tempting. With her aria "Il est doux, il est bon," Massenet demonstrates his mature and most characteristic style. Rather like the Symbolist poets of the time, he breaks up the conventional rhythm of a line, shifts the accent and introduces enjambements (lines running over into the next one) which enable him to extend the melodic line in a novel way. There are links here with Debussy's *Enfant prodigue* and a forward glance at the unrealities of *Pelléas et Mélisande.*

If this style was not entirely suited to the torrid Eastern setting for which it was intended, it came fully into its own with *Manon* (1884). Prévost's short novel, a "passionate and beautiful romance" as Lytton Strachey called it, gave Massenet the chance of a lifetime. His mellifluous and caressing style fitted the eighteenth-century atmosphere of *Manon* to perfection. A setting of dainty boudoirs and rococo gambling rooms, an ambience of flowered waistcoats, silver shoe-buckles and swaying panniers, and above all a heroine of ravishing charm, were the elements that moved Massenet to write his masterpiece. Although there is a hint of Wagnerian techniques in his use of motifs associated with various characters, Massenet's handling of the material is wholly original. Manon herself is the best-known character in the gallery of operatic women that Massenet depicted. Like her creator, she has the art of wooing an audience, of captivating them with a seductive charm expressed in luscious melodies and ripe orchestration. While the opera belongs to Manon with her scintillating roulades and dizzying *ports de voix,* Massenet is careful nonetheless to give the men some fine opportunities. The score is unfailingly inventive and is embellished with many delicious pages of minuet, gavotte and ballet which add splendor to the production numbers.

The three operas which succeeded Massenet's greatest triumph are exercises on a more ambitious scale. *Le Cid* (1885), based on the Spanish epic, was hampered by a poor libretto and Massenet's inability to encompass the heroic gesture. *Esclarmonde* (1889) proved more congenial with its evocation of medieval sorcery, enchanted gardens, magic palaces and mystic chivalry. The style is bewilderingly eclectic and has decided echoes of Wagnerian pomp (the processional march in act 2, for example), not to mention hints of Gounod, Meyerbeer and Verdi. Massenet always maintained that *Esclarmonde* was his favorite opera—but that was only because he wrote it for his protégée, the American singer Sybil Sanderson, with whom he was infatuated at the time.

After *Le Mage* (1891), an overblown failure, Massenet returned to his best form with *Werther* (1892). In this version of Goethe's sentimental novel, the acts are conceived as unities rather than as a series of individual numbers, and the orchestral texture is rich in Wagnerian sonorities. Massenet knew which way the wind was blowing and shared with Puccini a flair for adapting whatever suited him best in the work of contemporaries and assimilating it into his own formulas. Yet he was very much more than just a snapper-up of other people's good ideas. *Werther* contains some of his most individual features: the naïf little melody of the short prelude which recurs from time to time, the innocent lyricism, and the exquisite simplicity of the famous moonlight scene where both Werther and Charlotte realize the impossibility of their love. As in *Manon,* the composer breaks up the line of verse and varies it with displaced accents to create a more fluid effect. Charlotte, another of his great heroines, is drawn in rather greater depth than he had attempted before, and she has a self-denial and a nobility that are foreign to his other women. Taken on its own terms, *Werther* is an artistic success. The sequences are shaped with perfect balance, climaxes are developed with sureness, and the variety of mood and action is wonderfully maintained. It is one of the most obvious examples of the freshness, the command of the stage, and the grateful writing for voice and orchestra that characterize Massenet at his best. It also shows how he could husband his gifts to the utmost and use them so as to achieve theatrical effect in every bar he wrote.

After *Werther*, Massenet composed a series of elegant variations on a theme he had made particularly his own. *Thaïs* (1894) offers yet another portrait of a temptress, in this case the beautiful Egyptian courtesan who brings about the downfall of a holy man and herself aspires to sainthood. The limpid irony of Anatole France's novel from which the opera is taken, whereby the saint becomes a sinner and the sinner turns into a saint, is blunted by adaptation for the stage, which calls for sharp dramatic contrast and the broad strokes which are necessary in the theater. Massenet's solution is to compress and simplify, as in the famous aria where Thaïs looks in the mirror and decides that, despite her luxurious life, she does not know the meaning of true happiness. Her only solace is her beauty, and that, too, she knows will fade. The melodic line rises, falls, then leaps again in a typically Massenetic way as she pleads with the goddess Venus to halt the passage of time. Another instance of compression is the interlude entitled *Méditation* for solo violin and orchestra, hackneyed now, but, if heard with fresh ears, an ingenious solution to the problem of showing the courtesan's dilemma as she wavers between thoughts of conversion and of carrying on her old sinful life. Within a very short space of time Massenet had to depict an event which France, in the leisurely pages of his novel, could describe with ample and convincing detail. From the point of view of characterization, Thaïs differs little, it must be admitted, from all the other heroines in Massenet's collection. Yet the music she has to sing is so ingratiating, the orchestration so inventive and flexible, that the charm of the opera still acts on a receptive audience. A few months after its premiere came the first performance of Debussy's *Prélude à l'après-midi d'un faune*, where the fluid line developed still further the direction Massenet had taken with his supple phrasing and broken rhythms. It is worth noting that Poulenc once remarked that he could never hear the second of Debussy's *Chansons de Bilitis* (1897) without thinking of the mirror aria in *Thaïs*.

La navarraise (1894), a piece of Spanish blood and thunder and doubtlessly the noisiest opera Massenet ever wrote, presents a heroine of Carmen-like intensity. It also shows the influence of the Italian *verismo* composers. Another passionate heroine is *Sapho* (1897), based on Alphonse Daudet's best-selling novel. This anguished account of how a vulnerable youth falls victim to his passion and is destroyed by it portrays the woman as the dominant partner and the man as the helpless object of her calculation. In some ways the opera is *Manon* brought up to date, and there are distinct parallels between each of the five acts of the two operas so far as action and plot are concerned. Like Manon, Sapho dominates the opera, although it is undeniably late nineteenth century with its Bohemian artists' studios and assignations in suburban taverns. Some of the music owes a debt to Tchaikovsky, whose influence was already apparent in *Werther*, and one of the big love arias carries an echo of *Eugène Onegin*.

By the nineteen hundreds, Massenet's star had begun to wane. Of the nine operas Massenet was to write in his last decade, only *Thérèse* (1907), a romance of the French Revolution, and *Don Quichotte* (1910), a moving portrayal of Cervantes's old hero, showed flashes of the old brilliance. Taken as a whole, however, the substantial body of work he left

proves that he is too complex a figure to be pigeon-holed merely as a writer of pretty tunes. Even in his minor operas there is usually some neat piece of invention or some clever technical device to be admired. He worked his talent with infinite care and made it yield up all that could be harvested.

The operas leading up to *Manon* show Massenet perfecting the unique style for which he became famous. *Werther* represents a new departure and demonstrates how he could adapt his gifts so that he moved with complete naturalness from the eighteenth century of Fragonard to early German romanticism.

—James Harding

MASTER PETER'S PUPPET SHOW
See EL RETABLO DE MAESE PEDRO

THE MASTERSINGERS OF NUREMBURG
See DIE MEISTERSINGER VON NÜRNBERG

MATHIAS THE PAINTER
See MATHIS DER MALER

MATHIS, Edith.

Soprano. Born 11 February 1938, in Lucerne, Switzerland. Studied at Lucerne Conservatory; debut as boy in *Die Zauberflöte*, Lucerne, 1956; engaged at Cologne Opera, 1959-62; member of Hamburg Staatsoper, 1960-75; has also appeared at Deutsche Oper, Berlin; Metropolitan Opera debut as Pamina, 1970; appearances at Salzburg and Glyndebourne.

* * *

Like her contemporary Mirella Freni, Edith Mathis has evolved over the course of a long and successful career from a light soprano (during the 1960s) to a more dramatic soprano. The maturing of Mathis's voice during the 1970s resulted in some miscasting and some flawed performances, but it also gave opera-goers a chance to hear Mathis give some memorable performances of works that she would not have been able to sing earlier.

During the first phase of her career, in the 1960s, Mathis won much applause for her Mozart singing: Cherubino, Susanna and Pamina were among her best roles. Outside of the Mozart operas she was successful also as Ännchen (Weber's *Der Freischütz*) and Sophie (Strauss's *Rosenkavalier*), roles in which Mathis could put to good use not only her light, pure soprano voice, but also her youthful wit and playfulness. Her portrayal of Marzelline (Beethoven's *Fidelio*) as recorded under Karl Böhm is a good example of her singing in the 1960s. In the opening duet with Jaquino we hear Marzelline as a young, innocent girl, cheerful and good-hearted. But Mathis's singing leaves some things to be desired. The way that Peter Schreier, as Jaquino, vividly enunciates his words makes one miss such enunciation when Mathis sings. And one can hear in Mathis's voice, even in this relatively early recording, a wide vibrato that sometimes obscures the pitch.

Some of her later performances were not so successful. In a recording of Mozart's *Zaide* under Bernhard Klee (1975) the big, full-bodied sound of the older Mathis seems out of place. Although she sings the beautiful aria "Ruhe sanft" with great feeling, one misses the purity that Stich-Randall or Margaret Price (or Mathis ten years earlier) could have brought to this music. When she sang Sophie at Covent Garden in 1975 she won praise for her acting; but one critic also noted that her voice "is now a trifle heavy for the part."

Trying to sound and act younger than she was, Mathis sometimes gave portrayals that sounded forced. She was criticized as "overly pert" in her portrayal of Susanna (Mozart's *Le nozze di Figaro*) in Paris in 1975. Her performance of Ännchen in a recording of Weber's *Der Freischütz* under Carlos Kleiber (1973), admirable in many ways, suffers from the same problem. Agathe's "young relative," with her heavy vibrato, sounds older than Agathe herself. Ännchen's light-hearted attempts to cheer up Agathe are pleasing to listen to, but dramatically unconvincing (and made more so by the unfortunate use, in this recording, of non-singing actors to perform the spoken dialogue).

Mathis's portrayals of another young woman, Pamina in *Die Zauberflöte*, have been consistently satisfying, even as the singer grew older. Her performance of the role as recorded under Karajan (c. 1980) has been hailed by Rodney Milnes as "a classic interpretation." Among other roles in which Mathis has won much applause are those of Mistress Ford in Nicolai's *Die lustigen Weiber von Windsor* (a role that she has recorded) and Mélisande in Debussy's *Pelléas and Mélisande*.

—John A. Rice

MATHIS DER MALER [Mathias the Painter].

Composer: Paul Hindemith.

Librettist: Paul Hindemith.

First Performance: Zurich, Stadttheater, 28 May 1938.

Roles: Mathis/St Anthony (baritone); Albrecht von Brandenburg/St Paul (tenor); Lorenz von Pommersfelden/Wealth (bass); Wolfgang Capito/Scholar (tenor); Ursula/Martyr (soprano); Regina (soprano); Riedinger (bass); Hans Schwalb/Knight (tenor); Countess von Helfenstein/Luxury (contralto); Truchsess von Waldburg (bass); Sylvester von Schaumberg (tenor); Piper (tenor); Count von Helfenstein (mute); chorus (SSAATTBB).

Publications

articles—

Paulding, James E. "*Mathis der Maler*—The Politics of Music." *Hindemith-Jahrbuch* 5 (1976): 102.
Schneider, Norbert J. "Prinzipien der rhythmische Gestaltung in Hindemiths Oper *Mathis der Maler.*" *Hindemith-Jahrbuch* 8 (1979): 7.
Rexroth, Dieter. "Hindemith and *Mathis der Maler.*" Booklet accompanying Angel recording SZCX-3869 (1979).
Hitchcock, H. Wiley. "Trinitarian Symbolism in the 'Engelkonzert' of Hindemith's *Mathis der Maler.*" In *A Festschrift for Albert Seay,* edited by M. Grace, 217. Colorado Springs, 1982.
Mainka, Jürgen. "Von innerer zu äusserer Emigration: Eine Szene in Paul Hindemiths Oper *Mathis der Maler.*" In *Musik und Musikpolitik im faschistischen Deutschland,* edited by Hanns-Werner Heister and Hans-Günter Klein, 265. Frankfurt am Main, 1984.

*   *   *

Mathis der Maler is a historical romance, a musically and dramatically vital stage piece which Hindemith himself came to regard as his masterpiece and which is generally taken to be the central work in his career.

The opera is unusual among Hindemith's compositions in that it has a strong autobiographical element. Having embraced a concept of music, loosely gathered under the term *Gebrauchsmusik,* which emphasized music's social functions rather than its aesthetic autonomy, Hindemith wrote the libretto as his first major literary effort and composed the music at a time when his personal circumstances were becoming unsettled and the political environment threatening. He was routinely denounced in the Nazi press as a "bolshevik atonalist" and had strong, longstanding personal and professional ties to Jewish musicians. Though suspect, his work was not officially banned until 1936. The premiere of the *Mathis* Symphony in 1934 met with great success, but the opera could not be produced, the particularly offending item being its book-burning scene.

Mathis describes a cycle of self-doubt, struggle, and final personal solution to the problem of the artist's role in society. The parallel between the opera's setting (Germany during the Peasants' Revolt, circa 1525) and the contemporary situation is hard to miss, as is the fact that the artistic personality ascribed to the principal character, the painter Mathias Grünewald, is Hindemith's own. Likewise, the central problem for both artists is the same: how can one justify creating art that is not politically engaged in a time of dangerous political uncertainty? Or, more basically, how can one continue to create art at all? In an apotheosis following a series of painful visions, Mathis's artistry is returned to him in the form of a "mission" to perfect an art that presents suffering but which is transformed by a moral power transcending its outward appearance.

Thus, the core of the plot is that the artist who cannot nurture his own creative abilities remains politically and socially impotent, no matter how much he uses activism in an attempt to quiet his conscience. This message, timely enough in 1935, was criticized after the end of World War II for an apparent capitulation to established power and lack of political forcefulness, but in more recent years its surprisingly complex parable of the artist in the world has received good productions and more positive press.

The music achieves a remarkable synthesis of stylistic and technical elements of Hindemith's stylistically varied music from the 1920s, as it shows the clearest evidence of his rediscovery of historical musics. The prevailing "modernist" style of the 1920s was characterized by great emphasis on melody and rhythm and, by extension, on counterpoint. Such music could also be indifferent (deliberately so) in motivic development and harmony, these being the two features of composition most deeply associated with the Romantic composers. In *Mathis,* however, Hindemith made his peace with the nineteenth century—he was once again willing to draw into his music motivic development and directed harmonic progression when they suited his purposes. This synthesis or, one might say, rounding out of his compositional tools and the careful planning exhibited on smaller and larger scales gave more substance to the modish "linear counterpoint" style, but simultaneously infused traditional romantic techniques with new vitality and movement. The manner achieved here remained characteristic of all his later work. In the course of achieving this personal solution to the Romantic-Modernist polarity, Hindemith exploited the most thorough-going historicism of any composer in this century. In the end, like *Mathis,* he came to see the need for this dialogue with history in moral terms.

As an example of this hard-won but fundamentally positive orientation toward both a contemporary musical aesthetic and the preservation of tradition, we may cite the opera's sixth tableau, which begins with an intense, dissonant orchestral recitative that has been (erroneously) described as twelve-tone. Both the second and third main divisions of the tableau are inspired by an altarpiece panel. At the climactic point of "The Temptation of Saint Anthony," also the high climax of the entire opera, a chorus of demons and a quintet of soloists pursue Mathis, who in his dream has been transmuted into St Anthony. To the text "Ubi eras bone Jesu . . .?" ["Where were you, good Jesus?"], which, incidentally, appears on a small piece of paper in a corner of the panel, Mathis sings a newly composed, typically Hindemithian melody—chromatic in its overall plan, but built out of diatonic cells of varying size and emphasizing the intervals of the major second and perfect fourth. At the same time, the upper winds accompany one of the quintet, Ursula, as she sings, to a new text, the melody of the sequence "Lauda Sion Salvatorem." Ursula (a character also based on a historical personage) had appeared earlier in the Temptation in three guises—beggar, seductress, and finally martyr. She appears here as the latter, and clearly the symbolism of the melody she sings is that of rising above chaos, holding out the hope of salvation or of healing, a process which takes place for Mathis/St Anthony in the third main section of the tableau, built around the scene depicted in the panel opposing the Temptation, The Visit of St Anthony to St Paul the Eremite. Their final "Alleluia" has become well-known as the dramatic ending of the *Mathis* Symphony.

Like Hindemith's other full-length operas, *Mathis* is an effective stage piece with several dramatic group scenes and ample opportunities for the singers to develop characterizations. It is, on the other hand, rather long and makes particularly heavy demands on the lead baritone part; a successful German production in 1979 changed some sections to dialogue.

—David Neumeyer

IL MATRIMONIO SEGRETO [The Secret Marriage].

Composer: Domenico Cimarosa.

Librettist: Giovanni Bertati (after Colman and Garrick, *The Clandestine Marriage*).

First Performance: Vienna, Burgtheater, 7 February 1792.

Roles: Geronimo (bass); Elisetta (mezzo-soprano or soprano); Carolina (soprano); Fidelma (contralto); Count Robinson (bass or baritone); Paolino (tenor).

Publications

book–

Chailly, Luciano. *Il matrimonio segreto.* Milan, 1949.

articles–

Engel, C. "A Note on Domenico Cimarosa's Il matrimonio segreto." *Musical Quarterly* 33 (1947): 201.
Dean, Winton. "The Libretto of 'The Secret Marriage'." *Music Survey* 3 (1950): 33.
Mondolfi-Bossarelli. "Due varianti dovute a Mozart nel testo del *Matrimonio segreto.*" *Analecta musicologica* no. 4 (1967): 124.
Dietz, Hanns-Bertold. "Die Varianten in Domenico Cimarosas Autograph zu *Il matrimonio segreto* und ihr Ursprung." *Die Musikforschung* 31 (1978): 273.
Degrada, Francesco. "Dal *Marriage à la mode* al *Matrimonio segreto:* genesi di un tema drammatico nel Settecento." In *Il palazzo incantato. Studi sulla tradizione del melodramma dal Barocco al Romanticismo.* Fiesole, 1979.

* * *

Cimarosa's opera buffa Il matrimonio segreto must be unique in having been encored in full on the evening of its premiere. So much did Emperor Leopold II enjoy the performance on 7 February 1792 at the Burgtheater in Vienna, that he provided supper for all the participants so that he could hear the opera through again.

Il matrimonio segreto has a libretto by Giovanni Bertati, who as Imperial Court Poet had all the right Viennese connections to aid the success of a composer who had only recently arrived in the city, having worked for several years in St Petersburg. And Bertati played his full part in the opera's success, for he was an experienced librettist who had already worked with Salieri and Paisiello. The tangled threads of the plot sustain the substance of the drama and its musical contrasts, and Bertati's mastery of pacing and clarity is never in doubt, for the whole concept relies upon the characters becoming aware of the truth as the action proceeds.

The basis of the action, as so often in opera buffa during this period, is how human relationships develop in the changing context of social circumstances. All six characters are important. They comprise the wealthy and socially ambitious Bolognese merchant Geronimo, who has two daughters, Elisetta and Carolina, and a sister, Fidelma. His patron is the English aristocrat Count Robinson, while the young Paolino is his lawyer and business associate. The story deals with events in Geronimo's house, where Fidelma is installed as mistress. Geronimo is anxious to marry off his elder daughter Elisetta to the count, whereby he will gain his family access to noble

Title page and frontispiece of Cimarosa's *Il matrimonio segreto*, libretto, 1793

blood, but he is unaware that his younger daughter Carolina has secretly married Paolino. Complications set in when the count decides he prefers Carolina, an option which appeals to Geronimo, since it involves only half the original dowry. Neither Carolina nor Paolino has the courage to admit the true situation, but in the course of a swift-moving final scene full of mistaken identities, the truth is eventually revealed. Now, to the delight of all concerned, the count agrees to marry Elisetta after all.

This plot provides excellent material for opera buffa, through the character studies of the arias to the developing relationships revealed in the ensembles. In the former case Geronimo's *"Udite, tutti udite"* is a masterpiece of characterization. Stylistically, this aria has a Mozartian sense of balance and of orchestral integration, as well as a tendency to develop the merchant's blustering self-importance in a direction which anticipates the wit of Rossini.

While Cimarosa does not plumb the depths of feeling as Mozart does in the countess' music in his *Le nozze di Figaro*, the roles of Carolina and Paolino do bring the contrast of sadness, expressed through their solo numbers as their plight worsens. For instance, when Paolino lays the plans for their elopement, the slow pulse of the strings, together with an obbligato clarinet, give the basis for the emotional release expressed in his vocal line.

Cimarosa was a master of pacing, his sense of drama enhanced by vivid characterization. Each number in the opera has its own musical identity, often building a pulse through repeated string figurations, and with a light and mobile bass line. The lively and bubbling overture immediately reveals a ready musical wit, and here, as in the opera itself, orchestral balance is of the highest order, tuttis balanced against lighter textures, staccato phrases against legato.

The buffo duet for the count and Geronimo, in which the former suggests he marry the younger daughter rather than the elder, to which arrangement the latter agrees, is a masterpiece of its kind. There is a ternary design, the outer sections brilliantly pointed through the close integration of both the voices and the orchestra, while at the center of the piece the plotting of the two men brings a more expressive characterization, including a sotto voce unison. Such subtleties abound in the finales to the two acts, as plot and music advance side by side, aided by Cimarosa's deft orchestration.

The famous critic Éduard Hanslick observed that "the marriage of *Il matrimonio segreto* with Mozart's *Figaro* resulted in the birth of Rossini's *Il barbiere di Siviglia*"; and there can be no doubts surrounding the historical significance of Cimarosa's opera, which within three years of its premiere had been staged in both London and Milan. But it would be a mistake to judge this sparkling and subtle work simply in these terms, for its achievement demands its own recognition. As Stendhal observed, Cimarosa's mastery lay in "his glittering array of comic verve, of passion, strength and gaiety."

—Terry Barfoot

MATTHESON, Johann.

Composer. Born 28 September 1681, in Hamburg. Died 17 April 1764, in Hamburg. Studied music with Joachim Gerstenbüttel at the Johanneum, Hamburg (graduated 1693); studied composition and keyboard with J.N. Hanff; performed as an organist in the churches of Hamburg, and sang in the chorus of the Hamburg Opera; studied law; became a page at the Hamburg court of Graf von Güldenlöw, Viceroy of Norway; solo debut with the Hamburg Opera at a performance in Kiel, 1696; singer (tenor), conductor, and composer for the Hamburg Opera, 1697-1705; tutor to Cyrill Wich, daughter of Sir John Wich, British envoy at Hamburg, 1704; secretary to Sir John Wich, 1706; music director of the Hamburg cathedral, 1715-28; Kapellmeister to the court of the Duke of Holstein, 1719; Legation Secretary to the Duke of Holstein, 1741; counselor for the Duke of Holstein, 1744.

Operas

Die Plejades oder Das Sieben-Gestirne, C.F. Bressand, Hamburg, 1699 [lost].
Der edelmüthige Porsenna, C.F. Bressand, Hamburg, 1702 [lost].
Victor, Hertzog der Normannen (pasticcio, with Schiefferdecker and Bronner), H. Hinsch, Hamburg, 1702 [lost].
Die unglückselige Cleopatra, F.C. Feustking, Hamburg, 1704.
Le retour du siècle d'or, Countess Löwenhaupt, Holstein, near Plön, 1705 [lost].
Boris Goudenow, Mattheson, Hamburg, 1710 [lost].
Die geheimen Begebenheiten Henrico IV, J.J. Hoe, Hamburg, 1711 [lost].
Nero (Orlandini, with added music by Mattheson), A. Piovene (translated by Mattheson), Hamburg, 1723 [lost].

Publications

By MATTHESON: books–

Das neu-eröffnete Orchestre. Hamburg, 1713.
Das beschützte Orchestre. Hamburg, 1717.
ed. *Niedtens Musicalischer Handleitung, dritter und letzter Theil.* Hamburg, 1717.
ed. Raupach, C. *Veritophili deutliche Beweis-Gründe.* Hamburg, 1717.
Exemplarische Organisten-Probe im Artikel vom General-Bass. Hamburg, 1719.
Réflexions sur l'eclaircissement d'un problème de musique pratique. Hamburg, 1720.
Das forschende Orchestre. Hamburg, 1721; 1976.
ed. *Niedtens Musicalischer Handleitung, andrer Theil.* Hamburg, 1721.
Melotheta, das ist der grundrichtige, nach jetziger neuesten Manier angeführte Componiste. Hamburg, 1721-22.
Critica musica. Hamburg, 1722-25; 1964.
Der neue göttingische, aber viel schlechter, als die alten lacedämonischen urtheilende Ephorus. Hamburg, 1727.
Der musicalische Patriot. Hamburg, 1728; 1975.
Grosse General-Bass-Schule, oder: der exemplarischen Organisten-Probe zweite, verbesserte und vermehrte Auflage. Hamburg, 1731; 1968.
De eruditione musica, ad virum plurimum reverendum, amplissimum atque doctissimum, Joannes Christophorum Krüsike. Hamburg, 1732.
Kleine General-Bass-Schule. Hamburg, 1735.
Kern melodischer Wissenschafft. Hamburg, 1737; 1976.

Gültige Zeugnisse über die jüngste Matthesonische-Musicalische Kern-Schrifft. Hamburg, 1738.
Der vollkommene Capellmeister. Hamburg, 1739; 1954.
Grundlage einer Ehren-Pforte. Hamburg, 1740; edited by M. Schneider, Berlin, 1910; 1969.
Die neueste Untersuchung der Singspiele, nebst beygefügter musicalischen Geschmacksprobe. Hamburg, 1744; 1975.
Das erläuterte Selah, nebst einigen andern nützlichen Anmerkungen und erbaulichen Gedanken über Lob und Liebe. Hamburg, 1745.
Behauptung der himmlischen Musik aus den Gründen der Vernunft, Kirchen-Lehre und heiligen Schrift. Hamburg, 1747.
Matthesons Mithridat wider den Gift einer welschen Satyre, genannt: La Musica [by Salvator Rosa]. Hamburg, 1749.
Matthesons bewährte Panacea, als eine Zugabe zu seinem musicalischen Mithridat, erste Dosis. Hamburg, 1750.
Wahrer Begriff des harmonischen Lebens. Der Panacea zwote Dosis. Hamburg, 1750.
Sieben Gespräche der Weisheit und Musik samt zwo Beylagen; als die dritte Dosis der Panacea. Hamburg, 1751.
Philologisches Tresespiel, als ein kleiner Beytrag zur kritischen Geschichte der deutschen Sprache. Hamburg, 1752; 1975.
Plus ultra, ein Stückwerk von neuer und mancherley Art. 4 vols. Hamburg, 1754-56.
Georg Friederich Händels Lebensbeschreibung [translation of J. Mainwaring, *Memoirs of the Life of the Late George Frederic Handel*]. Hamburg, 1761; 1976.

About MATTHESON: books–

Schmidt, H. *Johann Mattheson, ein Förderer der deutschen Tonkunst.* Leipzig, 1897; 1973.
Cannon, B.C. *Johann Mattheson, Spectator in Music.* New Haven, 1947; 1968.
Wolff, H.C. *Die Barockoper in Hamburg.* Wolfenbüttel, 1957.

articles–

Stege, F. "Johann Mattheson und die Musikkritik des 18. Jahrhunderts." *Zeitschrift für Musik* 106 (1939): 407.
Lenneberg, H. "Johann Mattheson on Affect and Rhetoric in Music." *Journal of Music Theory* 2 (1958): 47, 193.
Buelow, G.J. "Johann Mattheson, the Composer: an Evaluation of his Opera *Cleopatra* (Hamburg, 1704)." In *Studies in Eighteenth Century Music: a Tribute to Karl Geiringer.* London and New York, 1970.
Fenton, R.F.C. "Mattheson's 'Cleopatra' and Handel's 'Almira': the Transmission of a Tradition or a Case of Indebtedness?" *Göttinger Händel-Beiträge* 3 (1989): 50.

*   *   *

Details of Mattheson's life are found in an autobiography published in his *Grundlage einer Ehren-Pforte* (Hamburg, 1740). He was educated at Hamburg's famous school, the Johanneum, where he gained a strong background in the liberal arts, including musical instruction from Kantor Joachim Gerstenbüttel. By the age of six he had begun private lessons in keyboard playing and composition, as well as taking singing lessons and gamba, violin, flute, oboe, and lute instruction. As a child prodigy at nine, he performed on the organ and sang in churches. After being asked to join the Hamburg opera company, he decided since opera was a "musical university" he would not pursue a university education after completing the Johanneum curriculum in 1693. In 1696 he made his solo debut in opera singing female roles when the company visited Kiel. When his voice changed to tenor, he began a successful career in Hamburg, singing numerous roles until 1705. During these years as an opera singer he gained a rich musical experience singing and also conducting rehearsals under such important composers as Johann Georg Conradi, Johann Sigismund Kusser, and especially Reinhard Keiser.

While pursuing his professional career Mattheson sang in some sixty-five new operas, but he also wrote and had performed in Hamburg five of six operas of his own. His most famous opera is *Cleopatra,* largely because of the fact that George Frideric Handel was at that time a violinist in the Hamburg opera orchestra and served as harpsichordist while Mattheson sang the role of Mark Anthony. At one performance of *Cleopatra,* Mattheson returned to the orchestra after he had as Mark Anthony committed suicide on stage, and asked Handel to give up his place at the harpsichord. Handel refused, and this led to a famous duel with swords in which Handel's life was spared, according to Mattheson, only because the latter's sword struck a large button on Handel's coat. As far as can be determined the scores for all of the other operas of Mattheson were lost in the second world war.

In 1706 Mattheson became secretary to the English ambassador in Hamburg, a position of considerable social status and salary that he retained for most of his life. At the same time he became an outstanding figure in the musical life of Hamburg and one of the great names in German music history. In 1715 he was appointed music director of the Hamburg cathedral, a post for which he composed many sacred works, including more than two dozen oratorios. During a remarkably productive period between 1715 and 1740, he wrote not only numerous important scores and treatises, but also many translations from the English of books, pamphlets, and articles primarily connected with his secretarial duties. On 25 April 1764 he was buried in the crypt of Hamburg's St Michael's church, to which he had donated the bulk of his considerable fortune. At the burial service Telemann conducted a funeral ode composed by Mattheson for this occasion.

While Mattheson was active in opera only during the early part of his career, he became the most prolific and significant writer on music from the German Baroque. In his numerous treatises he presents in vivid details the musical world of the first half of the eighteenth century, years in which musical styles and critical values shifted in a transition from the Baroque to the Classic period. While most of his compositions are lost, it is fortunate that at least in his fine opera, *Cleopatra,* one finds supporting evidence for Mattheson's theoretical ideas, which he codified only subsequently. The theme of opera runs through many of his treatises, and his view is frequently stressed that opera was both an art form and a cultural necessity for the educated citizen (who he called the *galant homme*). Vocal music was for him the most significant form of composition. In one major passage in his *Der musicalische Patriot,* (Hamburg, 1728), he stresses that opera is essential to civic pride and metropolitan necessity: "Through celebrated performances [of opera] great princes and lords are often persuaded to stay and to bring their households to stay in a city, procuring for them frequent foodstuffs. Scholars, artists, artisans come along too, and the city takes on the kind of eminence with good opera as it has with good banks. For the latter are for service, the former give pleasure; the latter serve to give security, the former serve to instruct. It is

almost always true that where the best banks are found, so too are found the best opera houses."

—George J. Buelow

MATZENAUER, Margaret.

Mezzo-soprano/soprano. Born 1 June 1881, in Temeszvar, Hungary. Died 19 May 1963, in Van Nuys, California. Studied with Januschowsky in Graz, Mielke and Emerich in Berlin, and Ernst Preuses in Munich; debut as Puck in *Oberon,* Strasbourg, 1901; member of Munich Court Opera, 1904-11; Metropolitan Opera debut as Amneris, 1911, and stayed for nineteen seasons until 1930; in Boston, 1912-14; in Buenos Aires, 1912; Covent Garden debut as Ortrud, 1914; concertized extensively in the United States and Europe; after 1938 she taught in New York and California. Matzenauer's pupils include Blanche Thebom.

*   *   *

Margaret Matzenauer was neither the first nor the last mid-voiced soprano to decide that her extensive range entitled her to sing contralto to dramatic soprano. It is not that the contralto in her wished to forgo that rich lower range and recast her voice higher—for which there was ample precedent. It was that she would alternate within the same weeks

Margaret Matzenauer as Dalila, Metropolitan Opera, New York, early 1920s

Amneris and Erda with Isolde and Brünnhilde. Shirley Verrett and Grace Bumbry in our time share Matzenauer's philosophy with some of the same mixed results.

Possessor of a sumptuous contralto voice, Matzenauer sang that extensive repertoire as resident artist in her early Munich years preparing for her position as featured mezzo for two decades at the Metropolitan Opera in New York. American critics were unanimous in their praise of her opulent, well-focused mezzo. Were she content to dominate this natural range there would be no controversy as to her central position in the history of opera performance. It was her ambition, almost a vital internal need, to essay the dramatic soprano roles that made her controversial. She was not a failure in the dramatic soprano repertoire, for in fact she scored notable successes. But she compromised her voice in the process, and after the decade-long venture she had not achieved acceptance as a first-rate dramatic soprano and the lustre had rubbed off her remarkable lower range. By the time she was over forty years old the sheer glory of her lower voice would have been dulled from hard usage. At least she had the personal satisfaction of fulfilling her ambitions, even if the results were not all that she could have hoped.

Even though the New York critics had reservations about her Brünnhilde and Fidelio it was only when she assumed the Countess in Figaro that they were most unforgiving. There was ample precedent for a voice such as hers doing the Wagner "hochdramatic" roles, but not Mozart's Countess; transposing some of the music it was felt that she had neither the light touch, vocal ease or "physique du role." It is interesting that in her early Munich years the only non-Wagner role she essayed that did not fall in her "fach" was Donna Elvira in Don Giovanni, although there had been a Central European tradition of casting Elvira with other than a high soprano.

Her recordings are problematic but revelatory. The 1907-1910 Munich "takes" demonstrate a young, untarnished, wide-ranging voice, seemingly very large. The Walküre Shout and Ortrud's Curse indicate that she could encompass the high notes, but even this early in the career there is a stridency and effort that do not bode well. Both versions of Selika's Slumber song are remarkably successful. The early Victor records (1912) are more satisfying than the later ones made twelve years later. In all the recordings it is clear that the contralto foundation was the glory of her instrument. It is interesting that Victor recorded "D'amore sull ali" from Trovatore, "Patria Mia" from Aida, and "Casta Diva" from Norma, but none of these takes were ever published. Victor issued her successful if heavy "Ritorna Vincitor." Much has been made of the "Fort denn eile" from act III of Die Walküre where she sings the climactic exchange between Brünnhilde and Sieglinde. It is a curiosity record and shows that for three minutes she could pound out this high tessitura. One however senses that it would not be pleasant to hear such a voice going at full tilt a whole evening in the theatre. Contemporary reviews suggest that her act II "Todverkündung" was unmatched in actual performance; unfortunately no recording of this scene was made.

Matzenauer's musical culture was extensive. She was an accomplished pianist and learned new and difficult music very quickly. She had a solid grounding in the German Lied and sacred music tradition. She was a successful and prolific concert artist, and her regular appearances in the cantatas, Masses, and Passions of Bach, as well as the larger choral works of Beethoven and the Verdi Requiem were features of musical life in New York during her reign. A 1926 recording of arias from Messiah and Elijah show a majesterial command of this literature as well as the English language. Her Jocasta in the 1928 American premiere of Stravinsky's Oedipus Rex

with the Boston Symphony was considered historic. After leaving the Metropolitan in 1930 she continued with her interesting concerts and some guest appearances in opera. Teaching rounded out this remarkable artist's career.

—Charles B. Mintzer

MAUREL, Victor.

Baritone. Born 17 June 1848, in Marseilles. Died 22 October 1923, in New York. Studied in Marseilles, and with Duvernoy and Vauthrot at the Paris Conservatory; debut as Guillaume Tell, Marseilles, 1867; appeared at Paris Opéra as Di Luna, 1868; appeared in St Petersburg, Cairo, and Venice; Teatro alla Scala debut as Cacique in first performance of Gomes's Il Guarany, 1870; Covent Garden debut as Renato in Un ballo in maschera, 1873; Metropolitan Opera debut as Iago, 1894; created revised Simon Boccanegra, 1881, Iago in Otello, 1887, and Falstaff, 1893; taught in London, 1905-09.

Publications

By MAUREL: books–

A propos de la mise-en-scène du drame lyrique Otello. Rome, 1888.
Le chant rénové par la science. Paris, 1892.
Un problème d'art. Paris, 1893.

Victor Maurel as Don Giovanni

A propos de la mise-en-scène de Don Juan. Paris, 1896.
L'art du chant. Paris, 1897.
Dix ans de carrière. Paris, 1897.

About MAUREL: books–

Strakosch, M. *Souvenirs d'un imprésario.* Paris, 1887.
de Curzon, H. *Croquis d'artistes.* Paris, 1898.
Kellog, C. *Memoirs of an American Prima Donna.* New York, 1913.
Maurel, B. *Victor Maurel: Ses idées, son art.* Paris, n.d.

articles–

Rogers, F. "Victor Maurel: his Career and his Art." *Musical Quarterly* 12 (1926): 580.
Shawe-Taylor, D. "Victor Maurel." *Opera* 6 (1955): 293.

Described by critic W.J. Henderson as "the greatest of singing actors," Victor Maurel enjoyed a long and truly international career which culminated in his creation of two late Verdi roles—Iago and Falstaff.

When only twenty he sang Count Luna in *Trovatore* and Nevers in *Huguenots* at the Paris Opéra and within two years appeared at the Teatro alla Scala in the premiere of Gomes' *Il Guarany.* In 1872 he appeared at another of the great houses, the San Carlo in Naples in *Don Carlos* and *Favorita* and the following year he began a long association with Covent Garden with performances of *Un ballo in maschera, Le nozze di Figaro,* Meyerbeer's *Dinorah,* Donizetti's *Linda di Chamonix,* and Rossini's *Guillaume Tell.* Such a range suggests a rare versatility which was to be extended still further when he appeared in the belated London premieres of *Lohengrin* and *Tannhäuser,* which were both sung in Italian.

Perhaps there is a sense in which Maurel was beginning to don the mantle of leading Italian baritone on the world operatic stage. During the 1870s he sang extensively throughout Europe and also in New York, where he was the first Amonasro. It was not until 1879, after ten years' absence, that he returned to Paris to sing Hamlet, Don Giovanni, Méphistofélès, and Alfonso in *Favorita* at the Opéra. In 1881 he "re-created" the title role in Verdi's revised *Simon Boccanegra* at the Teatro alla Scala. It was to be the prelude to the later Verdi creations which would immortalize his name. In 1883 and 1884 he was artistic director for an attempt to revive the Théâtre Italien in Paris, beginning with the first French performance of *Simon Boccanegra.* At least one critic felt Maurel's performance to be perhaps too perfect—with exaggerated effects in the Italian manner! As an impresario Maurel was nothing if not ambitious—his production of Massenet's *Hérodiade* (in Italian) included the brothers de Reszke in the cast as well as himself. However, the time for a specifically Italian opera house in the French capital was over, and the venture was certainly not a financial success.

The climax of Maurel's career came with the creations of Iago in Verdi's *Otello* at the Teatro alla Scala in 1887 and Falstaff in 1893. He repeated both roles in Paris, London and New York. It is perhaps a mark of his continuing versatility that he also in 1892 created the role of Tonio in Leoncavallo's *I Pagliacci* and almost at the end of his operatic career a role in Erlanger's *Le Juif Polonais* at the Opéra-Comique in 1900.

Maurel's career continued into the age of recording, for his final performance was in 1905 at Naples as Rigoletto.

However, his few records could well give a misleading impression, important and exciting though it is to have creator discs of *Falstaff* and *Otello.* The voice is obviously old and worn and a little dry. There is though a great deal of the expressiveness which made such an impact on the stage. P.G. Hurst heard him towards the end of his career—"if the voice by then was useful rather than beautiful, the stupendous art and the gracious and noble manner, so free from platform trickery and calculated mannerism, was there in full measure; he was a really great actor."

For Bernard Shaw, Maurel "played like a man who had read Shakespeare." However, Shaw suggests that Maurel's status as a great actor was in considerable part conditioned by comparison with a generally low standard then prevalent at Covent Garden. As Don Giovanni he felt Maurel offered a description rather than an impersonation. Shaw discerned the influence of the earlier French baritone, Faure, and felt that Maurel "has a remarkable command of the sort of vocal effect he aims at."

There is a fine eye-witness account of Maurel's "sublime creation" of Iago in the fascinating book by Blanche Roosevelt, who was not a music critic—"his elegance, grace, subtlety and exquisite style in Iago find their most perfect expression." Perhaps, though, the finest tribute to Maurel's art was penned by that greatest of American critics W.J. Henderson who described the recitation of Cassio's dream as "one of the most consummate pieces of vocal finesse." Henderson felt sure that Maurel had never really had a great voice: "he sang chiefly from the mouth upwards. Perhaps there was never a time when he melted hearts. He was no handkerchief singer. He never came upon the stage silently invoking his audience: 'if ye have tears prepare to shed them now.' His art was intellectual, reflective, analytical, subtle, even hypnotically masterful at times. But it was the art of a mind ceaselessly active, enquiring, unsatisfied. . . . (he) enchanted auditors by the subtlety of his inflections, the shimmering variety of vocal colour and the far reaching eloquence of his interpretation."

—Stanley Henig

MAVRA.

Composer: Igor Stravinsky.

Librettist: B. Kochno (after Pushkin, *The Little House in Kolomna*).

First Performance: Paris, Opéra, 3 June 1922.

Roles: Parasha (soprano); The Neighbor (mezzo-soprano); The Mother (contralto); The Hussar (tenor).

Publications

articles–

Cambell, S. "The 'Mavras' of Pushkin, Kochno and Stravinsky." *Music and Letters* 58 (1977): 304.
Dan'ko L. "*Mavra* stravinskovo i *Nos* D. Shostakovicha." *Muzïkal'nïy sovremennik* [Moscow] 2 (1977): 73.

* * *

Set design for Stravinsky's *Mavra* by Roger Survage, Paris, 1922

When Stravinsky's new one-act opera *Mavra* opened at the Paris Opéra on 3 June 1922, the audience was more than a little puzzled. Not unnaturally, they were expecting something a good deal more exciting from the composer of *The Rite of Spring* than this odd little opera. To begin with, the plot is remarkably uncomplicated.

In the venerable tradition of borrowing inspiration from the great Russian poets, *Mavra* is based on Alexander Pushkin's poem, *The Little House in Kolomna*. Boris Kochno's libretto renders the simple story as follows: Parasha and a bold Hussar are in love. When her mother sends her out to look for a maidservant, Parasha returns with her Hussar in disguise as "Mavra." All goes well until the mother surprises the new cook shaving and chases him out of the house as a thief.

Completed in 1922, Stravinsky dedicated this short *opera buffa* to the memory of his forbears, Glinka, Tchaikovsky, and Pushkin. Stravinsky purposefully chose thus to associate himself with the cosmopolitan, all-embracing outlook of these Russian artists, rather than the anti-Western nationalists of the Balakirev kuchka. Like Tchaikovsky, Stravinsky worked with Western influences rather than rejecting them. Like Pushkin, he had a fruitful relationship with the Western spirit. Notably, the division of the opera into separate solos, ensembles, and duets (although not numbered) allies Stravinsky with the Italian and French style rather than the German; that is, he followed the Russian operatic tradition as developed by Glinka and Tchaikovsky.

The characters in *Mavra* are stock, stylized figures: the curmudgeonly old mother, the sweet young maiden, the nosey neighbor. The mother and the neighbor chatting about the weather and the price of cotton is a classic routine. The very existence of a handsome tenor and a love duet with his leading lady are clichés, and the disguise in the cause of love cannot fail to recall *opera buffa*. However, the presence of these elements in the drama sets up expectations which are not met. There is no resolution of the relationship between the two young people; the hapless Vasili simply vanishes out the window and the opera comes to an abrupt close.

Stravinsky's music too employs stock devices, only to rework them into a "burlesque" of comic opera. The melodies, while showing an affinity to Italian vocalism, could never be mistaken for true Italian coloratura. The material may be more sensual than usual for Stravinsky, but, infused with the inflections of the folk idiom, the melodic material has a harsh edge. This flowing vocal lyricism emerges over the tense, dry staccato chords and sounds of the wind instruments. The instrumentation is unusual and spare, dominated by a wind ensemble plus two violins, a viola, three cellos, and three basses.

The accompaniment often features mechanical oom-pah figures with "wrong notes," where the implied harmony contradicts the actual harmony. At one point, the harmonic progression implied by the bass, tonic to dominant seventh, is rhythmically offset from the chords above, which run dominant seventh to tonic, breaking the coordination among the parts. Such details are not always readily apparent, and the result can be thoroughly bemusing.

Though the audience may have been puzzled, the opera's total sound is entirely unique and characteristic of Stravinsky. The composer borrowed heavily from past operatic traditions for *Mavra,* but charges of pastiche are easily converted to a visionary eclecticism in the best sense of the word: borrowing freely from the best that the past has to offer.

—Elizabeth W. Patton

MAW, Nicholas.

Composer. Born 5 November 1935, in Grantham, Lincolnshire. Married: Karen Graham, 1960 (1 son, 1 daughter). Studied composition with Lennox Berkeley and Paul Steinitz at the Royal Academy of Music in London, 1955-58; studied with Nadia Boulanger and Max Deutsch in Paris, 1958-59; composer in residence, Trinity College, Cambridge, 1966-70; lecturer, University of Exeter, 1972-74; visiting professor, Yale, School of Music, 1984-85, 1989, Boston College, 1986; professor of music, Milton Avery Graduate School of the Arts, Bard College, 1989-.

Operas

Publishers: Boosey and Hawkes, Chester, Faber.

One Man Show, A. Jacobs, London, November 1964; revised, 1966.
The Rising of the Moon, B. Cross, 1967-70, Sussex, Glyndebourne, 19 July 1970.

Other works: orchestral works, chamber and instrumental music, choral and vocal works, incidental music.

Publications

About MAW: articles–

Bradshaw, S. "Nicholas Maw." *Musical Times* 103 (1962): 608.
Payne, A. "The Music of Nicholas Maw." *Tempo* no. 68 (1964): 2.
_____. "Nicholas Maw's 'One Man Show'." *Tempo* no. 71 (1964-65): 2.
Northcott, Bayan. "Nicholas Maw." In *Music and Musicians* 18/no. 9 (1970): 34, 82.
Walsh, S. "Nicholas Maw's New Opera." *Tempo* no. 92 (1970): 2.
Whittall, A. "Nicholas Maw." In *British Music Now,* edited by L. Foreman, 97. London, 1975.
_____. "Maw's Personae." *Tempo* no. 125 (1978): 2.
Hayes, Malcolm. "Nicholas Maw's 'Odyssey'." *Tempo* no. 163 (1987).

*   *   *

Nicholas Maw can be seen as something of a maverick among English composers of his generation. After a youthful period of exploration of the radical "European" techniques, his musical style crystallized into a "neo-romantic idiom" twenty five years before the term was coined. Maw has forged a musical language which is truly vibrant and sensuous, and which borrows both from the old and the new, not in any self-conscious, satirical, or dogmatic way but so that the expressive means may be as wide ranging as possible.

Scenes and Arias for soprano, mezzo, contralto and large orchestra (a BBC commission for the 1962 Promenade concerts) shows Maw's talent in its first maturity. Already he had developed a command of orchestral technique unusual among English composers, and this score, which is remarkable for its range of textures and colors amply demonstrates the acuity of his aural imagination. Despite its title, the work is in no way dramatic or operatic in the conventional sense, though Maw regarded it as a study for the maneuvres of opera. The text is taken from two fourteenth century macaronic poems, the first of which presents a girl's intimations of love, the second her beloved's response.

The characteristics of Maw's style manifested in *Scenes and Arias* include the dense yet mellow chromatic harmonic language (subtly evocative of diatonic relationships and often presenting static or slowly evolving chord structures reminiscent of Britten), an elegant, luxuriant, *bel canto* vocal style which articulates the harmonic units, a relatively conservative, pulse driven rhythmic idiom, and a mastery of pacing and musical architecture. Perhaps most alarmingly for the avant-garde status quo was Maw's acceptance of the importance of writing for a bourgeois audience in a way that was not antagonistic, either to their social position, or to their musical inclinations.

Maw would seem to have had the perfect kind of musical language for an opera composer, and yet his first opera, *One Man Show,* was not an unqualified success. The theme of Arthur Jacobs's Saki derived libretto was in essence that of *The Emperor's New Clothes,* for it concerns the impact on the capricious art world, with its endless craze for novelty, of a tattoo adorning the arm of Joe, the opera's hero, a choice of subject matter which could, perhaps, be seen as a side swipe at the avant-garde. While admitting that the work was flawed by inadequate character development and an overly complex use of leitmotifs, Maw has intimated that the experience of writing *One Man Show* provided a kind of operatic apprenticeship that allowed him to discover the techniques of characterization and dramatic timing.

Maw's operatic credentials are more amply testified to by his second opera, *The Rising of the Moon* (libretto by Beverley Cross), which was commissioned by the Glyndebourne Opera company. This three act romantic opera, described as a comedy of attitudes, would appear to locate Maw in the tradition of Britten; yet despite the work's fine craftsmanship, it seems to lack the humanity and moral commitment which mark Britten's most successful works.

For most of the 1970s and 1980s, Maw worked on the vast canvas of his orchestral work *Odyssey,* a single movement, ninety minute piece which has proved as large an enterprise as James Joyce's *Ulysses,* and it is, perhaps, in the musical and emotional autonomy of this work, and in *Life Studies,* Maw's other orchestral masterpiece, that his particular genius is most eloquently expressed.

—David Cooper

MAY NIGHT [Mayskaya noch'].

Composer: Nicolai Rimsky-Korsakov.

Librettist: Nicolai Rimsky-Korsakov (after Gogol).

First Performance: St Petersburg, Mariinsky, 21 January 1880.

Roles: Levko (tenor); Hanna (mezzo-soprano); Headman/ Mayor (bass); Sister-in Law (contralto); Village Clerk (bass); Distiller (tenor); Kalenik, the drunkard (baritone or bass); Nymphs, Hens, Ravens (sopranos); chorus (SATB).

*   *   *

Rimsky-Korsakov's opera *May Night* is based on a series of short stories by Gogol (*Evenings on a Farm near Dikanka*), a writer known for tales of Ukrainian peasant life as well as bizarre, macabre, and highly original stories. For Rimsky-Korsakov, *May Night* was the first of many operas to combine the comic and the fantastic in the unique style for which he was to become justly famous.

A political atmosphere of slavophilism in nineteenth-century Russia, and the concomitant interest in an idealized peasant way of life, meant that a fascination with paganism was current. Rimsky-Korsakov too developed an interest in pagan beliefs, especially sun worship. Ukrainian folklore, in the form of games, rituals, and stereotypical fears of ghosts and the devil, also figures prominently in *May Night*. There is a game of "raven," a *khorovod* (ring dance) of *rusalkas* (water sprites), and songs associated with the Christian church calendar. "All choral songs in my opera have a ceremonial coloring or a game-coloring," wrote Rimsky-Korsakov. "The very action of the opera I connected with the Trinity or Rusal'naya week, called Green Christmas."

May Night is like a staged folk tale, with the bizarre intermixture of the real and fantastic, ordinary and grotesque, historical and supernatural intermingled. With its standard peasant lads, lasses, and pompous officials, the story is fairly simple as comic operas go. Levko, son of the village Headman, is in love with Hanna and wants to marry her, but the Headman refuses his consent because he fancies Hanna himself. Meanwhile, after a love scene between Levko and Hanna, Levko tells the girl the legend of the old deserted manor house that stands beside the lake. Tormented by her stepmother's cruelty, a girl named Pannochka drowned herself and became a *rusalka*, a water-sprite. She haunted the lake at night, eventually luring her stepmother to her death in the depths. But the stepmother also became a *rusalka*, and Pannochka does not know which of them she is. Levko adds that the current owner of the house wants to set up a distillery there.

In revenge for the Headman's amorous advances toward Hanna, Levko and his unruly woodcutter friends arrive to make trouble while the Headman is busy with the distiller. There ensues a farcical sequence involving mistaken identities in which the wrong people are continually arrested. In act III Levko meets Pannochka at the house. When a game of "raven" reveals at last which *rusalka* is the wicked stepmother, the grateful Pannochka gives Levko an official-looking letter ordering the headman to permit Hanna and Levko's marriage. Fooled, the Headman is forced to consent, and the opera closes with a chorus of congratulations to the bride and groom.

This distinctly ridiculous and frequently hilarious sequence of events is burdened with several dramatically non-essential scenes, such as the one showing the village drunkard Kalenik trying to dance the Gopak while the village girls sing a mocking chorus. Again, while chatting with the Headman, the distiller relates a funny adventure involving his later mother-in-law, dumplings, and a greedy dinner guest who choked to death and then haunted the house. The plot is at times little more than a series of excuses for featuring the plentiful chorus and dance scenes. Levko's ghost story is followed by a chorus of girls singing a Pentecostal song, for example, and his meditative singing in the beginning of act III is followed by a chorus and a dance for the *rusalkas* who emerge from the lake.

There is a valid dramatic conflict between Levko and his father, but the resolution brought about by the brief intervention of a water-sprite is unconvincing at best (Pannochka herself, after all, has little to do with the action until her humorous *deus ex machina* rescue of the situation), and the human characters are more stereotypes than realistic human beings. Rimsky, however, did not worry too much about such things; he concerned himself more with the music than with the dramatic coherence of his operas, stating, "an operatic work is before everything a musical production." Indeed, while the plot development may be weak, the music is not.

Skill and imagination in the score lend a delightful touch to the musical characterizations. The music for the bombastic Headman is humorously breathless, suggesting corpulence, and the priceless scene with the village drunkard would be unthinkable without the lurching hopak music. Rimsky also developed unusual instrumental effects for the fantastical characters, such as the harp glissando accompanying Pannochka, or the progression of chromatically descending chords to suggest the magic of a moonlit night.

The orchestra is used masterfully throughout to create atmosphere—the distinct atmosphere of the Ukraine as it existed in the Russian's imagination. Combined with a generous sprinkling of folk melodies (borrowed from a collection of Ukrainian folk songs), the music is thoroughly evocative of the warm, sunny, picturesque and faintly mysterious southern province: a perfect setting for charming, innocent young lovers to frolic with mysterious *rusalkas* one magical May night.

—Elizabeth W. Patton

MAYR [MAYER], (Johannes) Simon (Giovanni Simone).

Composer. Born 14 June 1763, in Mendorf, Bavaria. Died 2 December 1845, in Bergamo. Studied music with his father, sang in a church choir, and played the organ; entered the Jesuit college in Ingolstadt, 1774; studied theology at the University of Ingolstadt, beginning 1781; taken to Italy by the Swiss baron Thomas von Bassus for further music education, 1787; studied with Carlo Lenzi in Bergamo, 1789; studied with Ferdinando Bertoni in Venice, and composed sacred music and oratorios; first opera, *Saffo*, performed in Venice, 1794; maestro di cappella at Santa Maria Maggiore in Bergamo, 1802; reorganized and directed the choir school of the Cathedral at Santa Maria, 1805; went completely blind in 1826; founded the Società Filarmonica of Bergamo. Noted as a teacher, Mayr included Donizetti among his pupils.

Operas

Saffo o sia I riti d'Apollo Leucadio. A. Sografi, Venice, La Fenice, 17 February 1794.

La Lodoïska, F. Gonella, Venice, La Fenice, 26 January 1796; revised, Milan, Teatro alla Scala, 26 December 1799.

Un pazzo ne fa cento (I rivali delusi; La contessa immaginaria), G. Foppa, Venice, San Samuele, 8 October 1796.

Telemaco nell' isola di Calipso, A. Sografi, Venice, La Fenice, 16 January 1797.

L'intrigo della lettera (In pittore astratto), G. Foppa, Venice, San Moisè, fall 1797.

Il segreto, G. Foppa, Venice, San Moisè, 24 September 1797.

Avviso ai mariati, F. Gonella, Venice, San Samuele, 15 January 1798.

Lauso e Lidia, G. Foppa, Venice, La Fenice, 14 February 1798.

Adriano in Siria, Metastasio, Venice, San Benedetto, 23 April 1798.

Che originali (Il trionfo della musica; Il fanatico per la musica; La musicomania), G. Rossi, Venice, San Benedetto, 18 October 1798.

Amor ingegnoso, C. Mazzonà, Venice, San Benedetto, 27 December 1798.

L'ubbidienza per astuzia, C. Mazzolà, Venice, San Benedetto, 27 December 1798.

Adelaide di Gueselino, G. Rossi, Venice, La Fenice, 1 May 1799.

Labino, e Carlotta, G. Rossi, Venice, San Benedetto, 9 October 1799.

L'avaro, G. Foppa, Venice, San Benedetto, November 1799.

L'accademia di musica, G. Rossi, Venice, San Samuele, fall 1799.

Gli sciti, G. Rossi, Venice, La Fenice, February 1800.

La locandiera, G. Rossi (after Goldoni), Vicenza, Berico, spring 1800.

Il caretto del venditor d'aceto, G. Foppa, Venice, Sant' Angelo, 28 June 1800.

L'imbroglione e il castiga-matti, G. Foppa, Venice, San Moisè, fall 1800.

L'equivoco, ovvero Le Bizzarie dell' amore, G. Foppa, Milan, Teatro alla Scala, 5 November 1800.

Ginevra di Scozia (Ariodante), G. Rossi, Trieste, Nuovo, 21 April, 1801 [for the inauguration of the theater].

Le due giornate (Il portatore d'acqua), G. Foppa (after Bouïlly, *Les deux journées*), Milan, Teatro alla Scala, 18 August 1801.

I virtuosi (I virtuosi a teatro), G. Rossi, Venice, San Lucca, 26 December 1801.

Argene, G. Rossi, Venice, La Fenice, 28 December 1801.

Elisa, ossia Il monte San Bernardo, G. Rossi, Malta, Manoel, 1801.

I misteri eleusini (Polibete), G. Bernardoni, Milan, Teatro alla Scala, 6 January 1802.

I castelli in aria, ossia Gli amanti per accidente, G. Foppa, Venice, San Benedetto, May 1802.

Ercole in Lidia, G. de Gamerra, Vienna, Burgtheater, 29 January 1803.

Gl'intrighi amorosi, G. Bertati, Parma, Ducale, carnival 1803.

Le finite rivali, L. Romanelli, 20 August 1803.

Alonso e Cora, G. Bernardoni (after Marmontel, *Les Incas*), Milan, Teatro alla Scala, 26 December 1803; revised as *Cora,* M. Salfa-Berico, Naples, San Carlo, 1815.

Amor non ha ritegno (La fedeltà della vedove), F. Marconi, Milan, Teatro alla Scala, 18 May 1804.

I due viaggiatori, G. Foppa, Florence, Risoluti, summer 1804.

Zanori, ossia L'eroe dell' Indie, L. Prividali, Piacenza, Nuovo Teatro Communale, 10 August 1804 [for the inauguration of the theater].

Eraldo ed Emma, G. Rossi, Milan, Teatro alla Scala, 8 January 1805.

Di locanda in locanda e sempre in sala, G. Buonavoglia, 5 June 1805.

L'amor conjugale (Il custode di buon cuore), G. Rossi (after Bouïlly, *Léonore, ou L'amour conjugal*), Padua, Nuovo, 26 July 1805.

La rocca di Frauenstein, G. Rossi (after Anelli, *I fuorusciti*), Venice, La Fenice, 26 October 1805.

Gli americani (Idalide), G. Rossi, Venice, La Fenice, carnival 1806.

Palmira, o sia Il trionfo della virtù e dell' amore, Florence, Teatro della Pergola, fall 1806.

Il piccolo compositore di musica, Venice, San Moisè, 1806.

Nè l'un, nè l'altro, A. Anelli, Milan, Teatro alla Scala, 17 August 1807.

Belle ciarle e tristi fatti (L'imbroglio contro l'imbroglio), A. Anelli, Venice, La Fenice, November 1807.

Adelasia e Aleramo, L. Romanelli, Milan, Teatro alla Scala, 25 December 1807.

I cherusci, G. Rossi, Rome, Torre Argentina, carnival 1808.

Il vero originale, Rome, Valle, carnival 1808.

La finta sposa, ossia Il barone burlato, M. Brunetti, Rome, Valle, spring 1808.

Il matrimonio per concorso, Bologna, Comunale, carnival 1809.

Il ritorno di Ulisse, Prividali, Venice, La Fenice, carnival 1809.

Amor non soffre opposizione, G. Foppa, Venice, San Moisè, carnival 1810.

Raùl di Créqui, L. Romanelli, Milan, Teatro alla Scala, 26 December 1810.

Il sacrifizio d'Ifigenia (Ifigenia in Aulide), G. Arici (after Du Roullet), Brescia, Grande, carnival 1811.

L'amor figliale (Il disertore), G. Rossi, Venice, San Moisè, carnival 1811.

La rosa bianca e la rosa rossa (Il trionfo dell' a amicizia), F. Romani, Genoa, Sant' Agostino, 21 February 1813.

Medea in Corinto, F. Romani, Naples, San Carlo, 28 November 1813.

Tamerlano, L. Romanelli, Milan, Teatro alla Scala, carnival 1813.

Elena (Elena e Costantino), A. Tottola, Naples, Teatro dei Fiorentini, carnival 1814.

Atar, o sia Il serraglio d'Ormus, F. Romani, Genoa, Sant Agostino, June 1814.

Le due duchesse, ossia La caccia dei lupi (Le due amiche), F. Romani, Milan, Teatro alla Scala, 7 November 1814.

La figlia dell' aria, ossia La vendetta di Giunone, G. Rossi, Naples, San Carlo, Lent 1817.

Mennone e Zemira, G. Rossi, Naples, San Carlo, 22 March 1817.

Amor avvocato, Naples, Teatro dei Fiorentini, spring 1817.

Lanassa, G. Rossi and B. Merelli (after Lemierre, *La veuve du Malabar*), Venice, La Fenice, carnival 1818.

Alfredo il grande, B. Merelli (after G. Rossi, *Eraldo ed Emma*), Rome, Torre Argentina, February 1818.

Le daniade, F. Romani, Rome, Torre Argentina, carnival 1819.

Fedra, L. Romanelli, Milan, Teatro alla Scala, 26 December 1820.

Demitrio, after Metastasio, Turin, Regio, carnival 1824.

Other works: oratorios, sacred dramas, cantatas, sacred and secular choral, orchestral works, chamber music, piano pieces.

Publications/Writings

By MAYR: books–

Breve notizie storiche della vita e della opere di G. Haydn. Bergamo, 1809
Begolamento delle Lezioni Caritatevoli di musica. Bergamo, 1822.
"Zibaldone," preceduto dalle "Pagine autobiografiche". Edited by Arrigo Gazzaniga. Bergamo, 1977.

articles–

"Cenni biografici di Antonio Capuzzi, primo violinista della chiesa di S Maria Maggiore di Bergamo." In *Poesie in morte di Ant. Capuzzi.* Bergamo, 1818.
"Considerazioni del vecchio suonnatore di viola dimorante in Bergamo, intorno ad un articolo di Seveilinges risguardante la vita e le opere di Luigi Palestrina." *Gazetta milanese* (1836).
Schiedermair, L., ed. "I sensali di teatro." *Sammelbände der Internationalen Musik-Gesellschaft* 6 (1904-05): 588.

unpublished–

Cenni autobiografici di G.S. Mayr.
Cenni istorici intorno all' oratorio musicale, ed ai misteri che lo precedetero.
Della musica e dei teatri presso le diverse nazioni antiche e moderne.
Di alcune invenzioni musicali, ed in specie della stampa ed incisione dei caratteri musicali, dell' arpa, del clarinetto, del serpento, del fagotto, e dell' organo.
Intorno alla storia del violino ed ai principali violinisti d'Italia.
Letturatura musicale, o Biografie di alcuni illusti compositori e artisti italiani: Arezzo, Pratok Lasso, Palestrina, Rinuccini, Doni, Astorga, Clementi, Martini, Corelli.
Memorie e studi sulla musica da chiesa.
Parere intorno ad un apposito maestro per la composizione teatrale, e particolarmente per L'istromentatione, scritto per direttore del Liceo musicale di Bologna.
Piano per una riforma del conservatorio di Napoli, particolarmente per i nuovi metodi dell' istruzione istromentale, stesso per quel ministro dell' interno.
Piano per l'istituzione d'una cattedra di musica nell' Università di Pavia, scritto per ordine del direttore generale della pubblica istruzione.
Piccola dizionnario di musica.
Saggio storico degli artisti e degli scrittori musicali di Bergamo.
La vita di Clementi.
La vita di S Cecilia.
Italian translation of Reicha, A., *Traité d'harmonie.*
Foppa-Mayr correspondence (manuscript in I-BGc).
Ricordi-Mayr correspondence (manuscript in I-Mr).

About MAYR: books–

Alborghetti, F., and M. Galli. *Gaetano Donizetti e G. Simone Mayr: notizie e documenti.* Bergamo, 1875.
Branca, F. *Felice Romani ed i più riputati maestri di musica del suo tempo.* Turin, Florence, and Rome, 1882.
Scotti, C. *Giovanni Simone Mayr: discorso.* Bergamo, 1903.

Schiedermair, L. *Beiträge zur Geschichte der Oper um die Wende des 18. und 19. Jahr.: Simon Mayr.* Leipzig, 1907-10; 1973.
Gazzaniga, Arrigo. *Il Fondo musicale Mayr della biblioteca civica di Bergamo.* Bergamo, 1963.

articles–

Kretzschmar, H. "Die musikgeschichtliche Bedeutung S. Mayrs." *Jahrbuch Musikbibliothek Peters* (1904): 27.
Schiedermair, L. "Briefe Teresa Bellocs, Giuseppe Foppas und Giuseppe Gazzanigas an Simon Mayr." *Sammelbände der Internationalen Musik-Gesellschaft* 8 (1906-07): 615.
Carner, Mosco. "Simone Mayr and his *L'amor conjugale.*" In *Major and minor.* London, 1980.
Gibelli, Vittorio. "Twórczósc operowa Simone Mayra i jego poglady na dramat muzuczny" [Mayr's concept of musical drama]. In *Pagine,* edited by Michal Bristiger, 93. Cracow, 1980.
Heartz, Daniel. "Mozarts *Titus* und die italienische Oper um 1800." *Hamburger Jahrbuch für Musikwissenschaft* 5 (1981): 225.

unpublished–

Sisk, Lawrence Theodore. "Giovane Simone Mayr (1763-1845); his Writings on Music." Ph.D. dissertation, Northwestern University, 1986.

* * *

Mayr began his musical studies with his father and was an accomplished musician by the age of eight. He entered the Jesuit College, Ingolstadt, in 1774 and later pursued theological studies at the local university. He was highly regarded locally as a gifted organist and wind instrument performer before he went to Bergamo in 1789 to study with Carlo Lenzi. Almost immediately he seized an opportunity to work with Ferdinando Bertoni in Venice. In 1790 Mayr demonstrated his abilities in vocal composition by composing an oratorio which was favorably received in Venice. He adopted the Italian form of his name at this time and remained in Italy for the rest of his life, returning only once to his native Bavaria.

Mayr's first opera, *Saffo,* was successfully produced in Venice, Teatro La Fenice, 1794, during carnivale, and the composer was to spend most of the next six years working in Venetian theaters. In all, a dozen operas appeared during these years to ever-increasing acclaim. His revised *opera seria, La Lodoïska,* was favorably received at Teatro alla Scala, Milan, and again at San Carlo, Naples, during 1799. *Ginevra di Scozia* (Venice, 1801) cemented his place in the Italian opera world, and for the next thirty years Mayr's works would figure prominently in Italian theaters. His operas were gradually replaced by those of Rossini, Mercadante, and Donizetti, his most famous pupil, as fashions and taste changed.

In 1802 Mayr returned to Bergamo to become *maestro di capella* at the cathedral; he remained in Bergamo for the rest of his life. Mayr composed his last opera in 1824, then turned his attention to critical and theoretical writings as well as church music after he became blind in 1826.

His masterpiece is generally considered to be *Medea in Corinto,* an *opera seria* with a distinguished libretto by the young Felice Romani (San Carlo, Naples, 1813). *Elisa, ossia il monte San Bernardo* and *L'amor conjugale,* a one act version of Bouïlly's important libretto for Gaveaux which became the foundation for Beethoven's *Fidelio,* along with *La rosa bianca e la rosa rossa,* also with a libretto by Romani, were among the works most widely admired and performed throughout Italy.

Mayr's operas reveal a solid harmonic foundation as befits his German heritage, and he was also justifiably regarded as a "natural" melodic composer. He has long been viewed as a major bridge between eighteenth- and nineteenth-century practices, and his place in the history of music is assured due to his combinations of the "science" of German practice with the elegant, cantabile vocal styles of late eighteenth-century Italian opera. His instrumentation is unusually sophisticated for Italian opera, and Mayr was especially effective with woodwind *concertato* writing.

While never overly elaborate, Mayr's sense of formal construction in arias and ensembles reveals a strong imagination, and his careful control of forces had its effect on Rossini. He was widely admired even to the extent of being praised by one Florentine critic as "the Petrarch of music" because of the elegance, grace, and charm of his compositions. His legacy consists of a large body of compositions largely unknown and unperformed today.

—Aubrey S. Garlington

MAZEPPA.

Composer: Piotr Ilyich Tchaikovsky.

Librettist: V. Burenin, revised by Tchaikovsky (after Pushkin, *Poltava*).

First Performance: Moscow, Bol'shoy, 15 February 1884.

Publications

article–

Warrack, John. "Tchaikovsky's *Mazeppa.*" *Opera* December (1984).

* * *

Tchaikovsky's *Mazeppa* is based on the historical character Ivan Mazepa, a prominent Ukrainian Cossack who in the early eighteenth century conspired with King Charles XII of Sweden against Tsar Peter the Great of Russia in hopes of attaining independence for the Ukraine. The story opens with Mazeppa, the military commander of the Ukraine, as a guest in the home of his colleague Kochubey. Maria, Kochubey's daughter, is in love with the much older yet in her eyes dashing hero Mazeppa. After Maria spurns the romantic advances of her longtime companion Andrei, Mazeppa asks Kochubey for Maria's hand in marriage. Kochubey refuses. A bitter quarrel follows, and ultimately Maria is forced to make a choice between her parents and Mazeppa. She decides on Mazeppa and the couple leaves amid a hostile atmosphere.

Driven by spite, Andrei, as a representative of Kochubey, reports to the Tsar that Mazeppa is plotting with the Tsar's archenemy King Charles. Peter refuses to believe Andrei, and

turns Kochubey over to Mazeppa. Kochubey is tortured and then sentenced to death. When Maria learns of her father's impending execution, she rushes to save him, but too late. Maria, consumed by grief, loses her mind and mentally reverts to her childhood. Soon Charles is defeated at the Battle of Poltava, and Mazeppa is similarly overwhelmed by the Tsar's troops who overrun and devastate the Ukraine. In flight, Mazeppa comes to get Maria at Kochubey's severely war-damaged villa. Andrei has also returned and Mazeppa mortally wounds the younger man. Seeing Maria's hopeless psychological state, Mazeppa departs. Andrei dies while Maria rocks him back and forth singing a lullaby.

The plot of *Mazeppa* has substance and irony, is believable, and is neither highly contrived nor completely predictable. The score is also above average, though not overall among the best of Tchaikovsky's compositions. Four sections of the music are particularly notable. If the entire opera were as attractive and well crafted as the overture, Tchaikovsky may have had a major hit. A beautiful, moderately slow melody and a taste of a rousing fast folk dance combine to make the overture memorable. In act I, the dance is reprieved more fully to produce an exciting ensemble. A fine love duet between Mazeppa and Maria, the best vocal scene in the opera, highlights act II. The symphonic section "The Battle of Poltava," at the beginning of act III, is another key point in the score that has from time to time been performed on the concert stage. Included in this description of the Russian victory is the famous Russian melody "Slava," which has also been used in a variety of other contexts. That three of these four notable sections of the opera are either orchestral or dance-oriented, rather than vocal, may help to explain why *Mazeppa* is not performed more often than it is.

—William E. Studwell

McCORMACK, John.

Tenor. Born 14 June 1884, in Athlone, Ireland. Died 16 September 1945, in Dublin. Married: Lily Folcy. Studicd with Vincent O'Brien in Dublin and with Vincenzo Sabatini in Milan; stage debut as Beppe in *L'amico Fritz,* Savona, 1906; Covent Garden debut as Turiddu, 1907, and sang there regularly until 1914; in Naples, 1909; Manhattan Opera debut as Alfredo, 1909; Metropolitan Opera debut in the same role, 1910; spent World War I in the United States and became a United States citizen in 1917, then returned to England; appeared in Monte Carlo, 1921 and 1923; gave recitals after retiring from stage.

Publications

By McCORMACK: books–

John McCormack: His Own Story. Boston, 1918.

About McCORMACK: books–

McCormack, L. *I Hear You Calling Me.* Milwaukee, Wisconsin, 1940.
Stragon, L. *John McCormack: The Story of a Singer.* New York, 1941.
Roe, L. *John McCormack, The Complete Discography.* London, 1956.

Foxall, R. *John McCormack*. London, 1963.
Ledbetter, G. *The Great Irish Tenor*. London, 1977.
Worth, P. and J. Cartwright. *John McCormack: A Comprehensive Discography*. New York, 1987.

*　　*　　*

John McCormack, an extremely popular and beloved recitalist, had a somewhat limited but very distinguished operatic career that began in Italy in 1906. He was barely past thirty years of age when his voice began to lose the fresh silvery quality of its youth and the high notes became problematic. Yet until the very end of his long life, and even in the last recordings where the tone is no longer rounded and the legato and portamento no longer melting, McCormack's impeccable diction and magical interpretations must be admired. It was principally in the realm of Irish ballads and songs, sung in English, that McCormack made his greatest impact.

In 1904 when McCormack was twenty years old, he heard Enrico Caruso sing at Covent Garden, which made an overwhelming impression on him. Even though McCormack wisely never attempted to imitate Caruso's vocal production, the experience left him with the resolve to become an Italian tenor. McCormack made some unsuccessful recordings in 1904 but then went to study with Vincenzo Sabatini in Italy, where he quickly mastered the Italian language and the core of his Italian operatic repertoire. In 1907 he debuted as Turiddu at Covent Garden, performing some fifteen roles there until World War I. In 1911 he toured Australia with Melba; their vocal timbres and even scales matched perfectly. He had already made his Metropolitan Opera debut in 1910 with Melba in *La traviata* and was especially popular with the large Irish population in New York City, but also with the public in general; in 1918 he sang in the Hippodrome for an audience of more than 7,000. McCormack's last opera performances were in Monte Carlo in the early 1920s; for the subsequent twenty years of his career he sang concerts, continued to make recordings, many of which sold at least 100,000 copies, and starred in a film, *Song of My Heart*, in 1929.

McCormack's voice was not large, but rather a nasal-sounding, lyrical, unforced, high tenor that, being well-placed, could fill vast spaces. He sang with a strong Irish brogue. Part of McCormack's magic was that he could make something spellbinding of the simplest material. Among his many charming recordings, the collector's items are pieces by Mozart and Handel. His "Il mio tesoro" from *Don Giovanni* set a standard that no subsequent tenor has been able to match on record. As with many other recorded selections (e.g., "Spirto gentil" from Donizetti's *La favorita*, in which he takes the first four phrases all in one breath), McCormack's breath control in "Il mio tesoro" is astonishing—a prime reason that his version stands above the rest. Also noteworthy is the seamless scale in which each note of the runs is quite distinct; and with all of the considerable demands of the aria, the lovely quality of sound of the voice never suffers. One of his best Handel recordings is "Come, my beloved" (original "Care selve") from *Atalanta*, for the above reasons; another is "Oh Sleep, Why Dost Thou Leave Me" from *Semele*, in which he sings a miraculous phrase on one breath on the rising line of the word "wandering."

Other noteworthy opera recordings by McCormack include "Una furtiva lagrima" from Donizetti's *L'elisir d'amore*, showing fine *bel canto* style and in general comparing favorably with Caruso's rendition. A typical McCormack feature is obvious here, however—the lack of dramatic tension on "m'ama," for example, and the stiffness of the cadenza. Similarly, the cadenza in Edgardo's final scene from *Lucia di Lammermoor*, "Fra poco a me ricovero," is too metrically strict in what is otherwise a stunning performance, complete with exemplary diction, sensitive phrasing, gorgeous, unrestrained outpouring of tone in the highest tessitura, and correct application of tempo rubato. The aria from act II of Donizetti's *La fille du régiment* is sung in Italian by McCormack as "Per viver vicino." Here he displays a model *messa di voce*, fine use of head voice and a well-controlled, beautiful tone throughout. As an interpreter of the music of Donizetti, McCormack is ideal among recorded tenors.

There exist a number of selections by McCormack from Verdi's *La traviata*, including a "De' miei bollenti spiriti" from 1910 with a long-held "Vivo" and an excellent cadenza; there is also a "Parigi, o cara" with Lucrezia Bori from 1914. The duet is very graceful, the voices blend together beautifully, yet McCormack cannot disguise his Irish accent and he does something no native Italian would do, dividing "Parigi" from "o cara."

For all his great storytelling ability, McCormack was no actor, and the operatic stage was not his natural milieu. As a recitalist he became, along with Ernestine Schumann-Heink, the first vocal "superstar"; with concerts and recordings he earned as much as a million dollars during certain years. There were a few faults. He never securely possessed the top notes above a B-flat and they soon disappeared; the Irish brogue, especially on the vowel "ee," could in later years be grating; and he was often harshly criticized for the popular quality of much of the material he presented in recital. Yet for vocal sweetness, prodigious breath control, crystal clear diction, exemplary legato and phrasing, and immediacy of communication to vast groups of people, McCormack had no peers. He is one of the most magical and enchanting singers on record.

—Stephen Willier

McINTYRE, (Sir) Donald (Conroy).

Bass-baritone. Born 22 October 1934, in Auckland, New Zealand. Studied at Guildhall School of Music, London; debut as Zaccaria in *Nabucco*, with Welsh National Opera, Cardiff, 1959; sang with Sadlers Wells Opera, 1960-67; Bayreuth debut as Telramund, 1967, and appeared there regularly until 1988; Metropolitan Opera debut as Wotan in *Das Rheingold*, 1975; became Officer of Order of British Empire, 1977; Commander of Order of British Empire, 1985, knighted, 1992.

Publications

About McINTYRE: articles—

Blyth, A. "Donald McIntyre." *Opera* 26/June (1975): 529.

*　　*　　*

At the outset of his career, Donald McIntyre scored important successes in two Wagnerian roles: the Dutchman in *Der fliegende Holländer* for Sadlers Wells in 1965, and Hunding in *Die Walküre* for Scottish Opera in 1966. These successes were prophetic. McIntyre's impressive physical presence, allied to a solid dark bass-baritone voice, firmly focussed and with unusual freedom in the upper register, proved ideally suited to Wagner. Invited to audition for Bayreuth in 1967, for the minor role of the Herald in *Lohengrin,* he gained instead the much larger part of the villainous Telramund. Critic Richard Law, hearing him repeat the role the following year, wrote in *Opera* (Autumn 1968), "He combines the weight of voice with total mastery of the innumerable cruelly high notes in the part, and he should be part of the Bayreuth scene for a long time to come." In fact, McIntyre was to appear regularly at the Bayreuth Festival until 1988, a record surpassed by few other singers and one which places him firmly as one of the leading Wagnerians of his generation.

The range of his Bayreuth repertoire is impressive: apart from Telramund, he has sung the Dutchman (1969-71, 1981), Klingsor in *Parsifal* (1968, 1970, 1972), Amfortas in *Parsifal* (1981, 1987-88), Kurwenal in *Tristan und Isolde* (1974), Wanderer in *Siegfried* (1973-80) and Wotan in *Der Ring des Nibelungen* (1975-80). It is for the dual role of Wanderer/Wotan in Patrice Chereau's controversial production of the *Ring* cycle that he will probably be most remembered.

Although McIntyre's voice has generally been described as a bass-baritone, he tends to reject categorization by vocal range, basing his approach to a role on what he can get out of it rather than on whether he exactly matches how it has been classified. This pragmatism has allowed him to encompass the extremes of Sarastro and Scarpia. He has recently expanded his repertoire by accepting the challenge of more contemporary roles—most notably Balstrode in *Peter Grimes,* the title role in Hindemith's *Cardillac,* the Doctor in *Wozzeck* and Prospero in Berio's *Un re in ascolto.*

McIntyre's concern has always been to keep his interpretations fresh and adventurous. He no longer sings Wotan because he feels he has exhausted the possibilities of the role. Instead, he has shifted his attention to perhaps the most complex of all Wagnerian creations, Hans Sachs in *Die Meistersinger von Nürnberg.* His Sachs is, characteristically, a powerful and charismatic figure in the vigorous prime of life. This reading gives a unique poignancy to his actions in the opera and is another example of the individuality with which McIntyre has always approached his art.

Considering his reputation, McIntyre has been poorly treated by recording companies. Relatively few of his major roles are represented on disc. However, his portrayals of the Wanderer and Wotan in the Chereau *Ring* cycle and of Hans Sachs in the 1988 Hampe production of *Die Meistersinger* for Australian Opera, have been preserved on video. They confirm the qualities on which his reputation is based: a dark, well-focussed voice with a dramatic edge to its timbre, an imaginative insight into character, and a commanding stage personality.

—Adrienne Simpson

MEDEA
See MÉDÉE

MÉDÉE [Medea].

Composer: Marc-Antoine Charpentier.

Librettist: Thomas Corneille.

First Performance: Paris, Opéra, 4 December 1693.

Roles: Créon (bass); Médée (soprano); Nérine (soprano); Créuses (soprano); Cléone (soprano); L'Amour (soprano); Italian Woman (soprano); two Specters (sopranos); Jason (tenor); Arcas (tenor); Oronte (baritone); two Corinthians (countertenor); La Jalousie (tenor); La Vengeance (bass); three Prisoners (soprano, contralto, countertenor); La Victoire (soprano); La Gloire (soprano); Bellone (contralto); chorus.

Publications

article–

Avant-scène opéra 68 (1984) [*Médée* issue].

*   *   *

Marc-Antoine Charpentier collaborated with dramatist Thomas Corneille in the composition of his opera *Médée* in 1693. Greek mythology had provided stories for the earliest operas in the seventeenth century and for many succeeding generations of opera libretti. The story of Medea has been one of particular interest for scholars, dramatists, and musicians. Euripides' play, *Medea,* dates from 431 BC; Medea also is a key figure in his *Peliades* (Daughters of Pelias) of 455 BC and *Aegeus* a few years later. He was fascinated with the idea of a figure who, initially sympathetic, became a criminally vindictive and vengeful woman, yet who somehow retained the sympathy of the gods. Over the centuries Euripides has been followed by many others in telling the story of Medea, including Ovid, Seneca, Franz Grillparzer, Jean Anouilh, and Pierre Corneille (in 1635) as well as his younger brother Thomas. Composers attracted to the story include Georg Benda (1775), Luigi Cherubini (1797), Simon Mayr (1813), Darius Milhaud (1938), and Samuel Barber (1946).

In the legend, Medea, the daughter of King Aetes of Colchis, had fallen in love with Jason during his quest for the Golden Fleece. She used her magic powers to help him get the fleece from her father and fled her home, killing her brother in the process. She helped Jason through various difficulties (she tricked the daughters of King Pelias of Iolcos into dismembering and boiling him so he supposedly could recover his youth) and went with Jason to Corinth, where they had two sons. At this point in the story the Charpentier/Corneille opera plot begins. Jason falls in love with Creusa, daughter of Corinthian King Creon. Gradually realizing her betrayal, Medea becomes vengeful and murders Creon, Creusa, and, as she sinks into madness, her two children as a final revenge against Jason.

Thomas Corneille had collaborated with Charpentier on previous projects as early as 1675 in the production of his play *Circé.* In adapting the Medea story for the opera stage he drew on his experience in tailoring speech for musical setting. He was also determined to present the story from a different perspective, emphasizing the misery and suffering of Médée from a human point of view. In the first act of the opera Médée is seen [in Hitchcock's description, in his biography of the composer, 1990] as "proud, jealous, and fierce," as Jason proves faithless and betrays her; in the second act Médée is shown as a "compassionate mother." In the third Médée sees the climax of the betrayal by Jason, and her anger grows, as she invokes "malignant sorcery" against those who have wronged her. The third act ends as she prepares a poisoned robe she will give to Créuses. The fourth act shows Médée's rage; there is a confrontation with Créon. In the fifth act Créon and Créuses die, and Médée kills her two sons, saying, "I could only see the sons of Jason in my sons."

When Jean-Baptiste Lully died in 1687 an official French musical monopoly ended. Charpentier's *Médée* was produced at the Royal Academy of Music in December of 1693—his first and only production there (the opera was published in 1694 by Christophe Ballard, a Parisian printer). Life in the court of the Sun King, Louis XIV, is extolled in an extensive prologue, for which Charpentier wrote a Lully-style French overture. Indeed, the orchestra calls for five string parts throughout the opera, according to the style set by Lully, perhaps as a bow to the Royal Academy of Music which was so dominated by the followers of that composer.

Charpentier's music is enormously sensitive to dramatic contrasts. The recitatives, airs, duets, choruses, and instrumental writing are characterized by unusual scoring to give a large palette of musical colors. The texture is generally homophonic, but there is interesting counterpoint (in the somewhat limited seventeenth century style), especially in the instrumental parts, which is dramatically effective. The melodic writing is typical of the composer, mixing Italian lyricism (there is even an Italian air in act II, scene vii, which must have given added fuel to Charpentier's anti-Italian detractors at the Royal Academy of Music) with French declamatory style. Charpentier's harmonies make great use of chromaticism and expressive dissonance. There is some variety of tonality, reflecting the composer's sensitivity to the character of different keys, as he had expressed earlier in a listing of keys and their moods *(énergies)* in his *Règles de composition* written for Phillippe d'Orléans, duke of Chartres.

Notable pictorial writing accompanies music sung by Médée, in which her anger is expressed in pulsating eighth-notes or rushing sixteenth-note passages in the strings. There are several *divertissements* in the opera which include dances typical of seventeenth-century France. The *divertissement* in act II concludes with a *passacaille en rondeau* for orchestra and chorus.

Médée was strongly praised by Charpentier's supporters; people in the camp of the Lully style were critical. Charpentier was very much in the middle of the debate over the relative worth of French and Italian styles. The significance of the opera is more readily seen in its 1984 revival on recording by William Christie and *Les Arts Florissants* and in the dedication of the complete issue of *Avant-scène opéra* (October 1984) to the opera.

—Donald Oglesby

MÉDÉE [Medea].

Composer: Luigi Cherubini.

Librettist: François Benôit Hoffman (after Euripides).

First performance: Paris, Théâtre Feydeau, 13 March 1797.

Roles: Jason (tenor); Médée (soprano); Néris (mezzo-soprano); Créon (bass); Dircé (soprano); First Maidservant (soprano); Second Maidservant (mezzo-soprano).

Publications

book–

Lega, Antonio. *Cherubini e l'opera "Medea": Cenno biografico con brani musicale.* Milan, 1909.

articles–

"Cherubini's Medea." *Dwights Journal of Music* 2 September (1865): 91.
Strobel, Heinrich. "Cherubinis *Medea.*" *Neue Musik-Zeitung* March (1925): 297.
Rinaldi, Mario. "*Medea* di Cherubini." *Nuova Antologia di Scienze, Lettere ed Arti* July (1953): 375.
Confalonieri, Giulio. "La rivoluzione de *Medea.*" *Teatro alla Scala* (1953-54): 27.
Damerini, Adelmo. "Rivive *Medea* di Cherubini." *Rivista musicale italiana* January-March (1954): 61.
Cooper, Martin. "Cherubini's *Medea.*" *Opera* June (1959): 349.
Wilks, John. "The Real 'Medea'." *Opera* May (1967): 372.
Ringer, Alexander L. "Cherubini's *Médée* and the Spirit of French Revolutionary Opera." In *Essays in Musicology in Honor of Dragan Plamenac on his 70th Birthday,* edited by Gustav Reese and Robert J. Snow. Pittsburg, 1969.
Rinaldi, Mario. "Due Medee." *Rassegna musicale Curci* September (1977): 57.
Jacobs, Arthur. "Authentic 'Médée'?" *Opera* [Festival Issue] (Autumn 1984): 40.
Stegemann, Michael. "Medea, oder: 'Störe unsere Kreise nicht!' Cherubinis Oper in Paris." *Neue Zeitschrift für Musik* May (1986): 37.
Deane, Basil. "Cherubini and opéra-comique." *Opera* November (1989): 1305.
Murray, David. "Médée." *Opera* January (1990): 103.

*   *   *

In act I of Cherubini's *Médée*, Dircé is fearful of marrying Jason but is convinced by her attendants that Médée is no longer a threat. Créon promises Jason protection for his sons, and Jason presents the Golden Fleece to Dircé during the March of the Argonauts. As the Corinthians are invoking Hymen to bless the marriage, Médée enters. Créon orders her to depart immediately, and the act ends with a prolonged duet between Médée and Jason during which both deplore the fatal influence of the Golden Fleece.

During act II, Médée convinces Créon to allow her to remain one day to have time to bid farewell to her children. She uses the time to have her children give a poisoned robe, crown, and jewels as presents to Dircé. The final act is preceded by an orchestral interlude depicting the storm raging both in nature and in Médée's heart. She curses her maternal weakness and, aided by cries from the palace, where Dircé is consumed by the flames of Médée's presents, drags the children into the temple to murder them. Jason rushes in with the people of Corinth, but too late. Médée, wielding her knife and surrounded by the three Eumenides, appears in the temple's doorway. She prophesies that Jason will wander homeless for the rest of his life and will meet her in Hades.

Frontispiece from the printed score of Cherubini's *Médée,* 1797

Médée rises into the air, the temple bursts into flames and the people flee terror-stricken as the curtain falls.

Although receiving critical approval, *Médée* enjoyed only a *succès d'estime,* disappearing after twenty performances. Paris did not see another production until the mid-twentieth century. However, the Germans were taken with the work, performing it on numerous occasions throughout the nineteenth century. Mme Margarite Luise Schick (1773-1809) was Médée in the first Berlin production on 17 April 1800, for which the *Allgemeine musikalische Zeitung* published an extensive analysis, and it was still performed there in 1880. Franz Lachner (1803-1890) set the spoken dialogue to a Wagnerian-style recitative for an 1855 Frankfurt production. This became the opera's standard form until the 1980s. Vienna was introduced to *Médée* in 1803 and it would appear that performances in 1809 were the occasion for Cherubini to make extensive cuts of about 500 bars which were supposedly incorporated into a Peters' published edition. It was revived again in 1812 for Mlle Pauline Anna Milder-Hauptmann (1785-1839) and was still in repertory in 1871.

The destiny of *Médée* in England and Italy was less fortunate. It was presented in London at Her Majesty's, Haymarket on 6 June 1865 with Mlle Thérèse Cathline Johanna Alexandra Tietjens (1831-1877) as Médée and recitatives by Luigi Arditi (1822-1903). It was repeated on 30 December 1870 at Covent Garden. In Italy, it was not staged until 30 December 1909 at the Teatro alla Scala, Milan in a translation by Carlo Zangarini, of which the edited version has been the standard Italian form of the score used until recently. The reception was mediocre, and it was not redone until the 16th Maggio musicale fiorentino in 1953, when Maria Callas (1923-1977) sang the title role and assured the opera's renewed success in the 20th century. The original French version, with reduced spoken dialogue, was mounted at Buxton Festival on 28 July 1984. Covent Garden presented the original version with nearly complete spoken dialogue on 6 November 1989.

Médée represents the culmination of Cherubini's work in the *opéra comique* genre. Although his *Les deux journées* of 1800 was more popular, *Médée* is far more innovative and extends the techniques of this genre to their limits. In many places, the music for an ensemble number or an aria continues into the dialogue and appears to stop only because some spoken words are required in order for the work to remain an *opéra comique*. In his use of form, Cherubini expresses himself as a classical musician; it is this quality which has been missed by audiences since the recitatives of Lachner were added in the mid-19th century. Only a revival of the complete opera without any musical excisions and with all the spoken dialogue will allow contemporary listeners to appreciate the symphonic proportions of the music and emotions of this work.

In its unmitigated horror, this opera has few equals. Its savage fury ties it closely to its Greek ancestry. Hoffman took one sentiment (revenge) and one action (murder) and expanded them into three hours of unrestrained emotion such as the French lyric stage had never seen. He provided excellent characterizations with which Cherubini could work, portraying the two main protagonists in depth. Because of the spoken dialogue, *Médée* is classed as an *opéra comique,* although the first edition labels it simply *opéra.* There are no comic interludes, and the majority of the musical numbers are ensembles (9 to 3 arias). In fact, the music of *Médée* foreshadows French or German Grand Opera of the mid-nineteenth century, and one has to wait until Bizet's *Carmen* to find a continuation of *Médée's* style and form. As Brahms

said: "This *Médée* is the work we musicians recognize among ourselves as the highest peak of dramatic music."

—Stephen C. Willis

THE MEDIUM.

Composer: Gian Carlo Menotti.

Librettist: Gian Carlo Menotti.

First Performance: New York, 8 May 1946.

Roles: Madame Flora, or Baba (contralto); Monica (soprano); Toby (mute); Mrs Gobineau (soprano); Mr Gobineau (baritone); Mrs Nolan (mezzo-soprano).

*   *   *

For a chamber opera lasting less than an hour, *The Medium* boasts an impressive list of credits. Composed for five singers, a tacit actor, and an orchestra of fourteen instruments, it is the first twentieth-century chamber opera to achieve international acclaim, advancing Menotti to the front rank of celebrity. It ran for two hundred and eleven performances on Broadway during the 1947-48 season at the Ethel Barrymore Theatre, and was filmed in 1950 under Menotti's direction by Scalera Studios in Rome. Artfully conceived both as music and theater, it has won the esteem of most critics and earned a secure place in the contemporary operatic repertoire.

Though manifestly a ghost story, *The Medium* harbors themes and poses questions worthy of ancient Greek drama. The action takes place in the contemporary parlor of Madame Flora (called Baba by her fanciful adolescent daughter Monica), a spiritualist who shams seances for her credulous clients. In the flat with Baba and her daughter lives Toby, a mute gypsy boy, whom the medium has taken in and incessantly abuses. Infatuated with Monica, he readily joins in her games of childish fantasy, sometimes arraying himself like an ancient king in Baba's finery.

As the opera begins, Baba interrupts one of the children's games and crossly tells them to get ready for a seance. The clients are Mr and Mrs Gobineau, whose infant son drowned in their garden fountain, and Mrs Nolan, who comes for the first time to communicate with her daughter, a girl about Monica's age. Monica impersonates the spirits while Toby manages the ghostly effects. They convince Mrs Nolan so completely that she becomes hysterical and must be calmed. As Monica imitates the laughing voice of the Gobineau's little boy, Baba suddenly wakes from her trance. She has felt a cold hand on her throat. "Who touched me?" she cries out, but the clients can tell her nothing and depart asking, "Why be afraid of the dead?" Terrified, Baba insists that Toby is at the bottom of this omen from the spirit world, and she wildly interrogates him. Monica intercedes, soothing Baba with the "Ballad of the Black Swan," but Baba hears the voice of Mrs Nolan's daughter and sends Toby on a fruitless search through the flat. As Monica resumes the song, Baba chants in a low voice over her rosary.

In act II, we see Toby performing a puppet show for Monica. The girl responds by singing him a gay waltz, then casts Toby and herself in a fairy tale about love, giving the mute boy her own voice. Baba comes in drunk and disheveled and accosts Toby. Certain of his duplicity, she tries to coax him, then to bribe him into telling what he knows, but the frightened boy reveals nothing. Finally Baba asks him if he would like to marry Monica, but even this desperate offer fails to penetrate Toby's enigmatic stare. Exasperated, Baba whips him until the doorbell distracts her. The Gobineaus and Mrs Nolan have arrived, expecting a seance. The guilt-ridden Baba admits to fraud and exposes all her tricks of ghostmanship, but the bereaved clients ignore her confession and implore her to conduct the seance. In despair, Baba orders them from the house; then, despite Monica's protests, she turns out Toby "before it is too late!" After locking Monica in her room, Baba ponders her unwonted fear, finally breaking into deranged laughter. Sick and exhausted, she falls into a drunken stupor. As she sleeps, Toby steals back into the flat to see Monica. While he rummages for his belongings, a trunk lid falls, waking Baba. Toby runs behind the white curtain of the puppet theater. Screaming, "Who's there?" Baba seizes a pistol from a drawer, sees the curtain move, and fires at it. Blood trickles down the white cloth, and the boy falls to the floor with the curtain wrapped about him. "I've killed the ghost!" Baba proclaims. She unlocks Monica's door. In a stifled voice, the horror-stricken girl calls for help, and rushes from the flat. Peering into Toby's vacant eyes, wide open in death, Baba whispers, "Was it you?"

Menotti himself interprets *The Medium* as "a play of ideas. . . . the tragedy of a woman caught between . . . a world of reality, which she cannot wholly comprehend, and a supernatural world, in which she cannot believe." Baba, he explains, represents Doubt, Monica Love, the three clients Faith, and Toby the Unknown. Like many artists discussing their work, Menotti has opened the door but not invited us in. The real and supernatural worlds compete within the medium herself. She is Madame Flora the spiritualist and Baba the mother. Youthful, compassionate, and innocent, Monica is everything her decrepit mother is not or no longer can be. Both contrive illusions, but Monica's are puerile while Baba's are devious. Toby serves as Baba's son, though the drama presents him as a foundling, making him a natural prey to Baba's assaults and preserving his romance with Monica from incest. He personifies the mystery of ripening sexuality. Forever mute, he keeps his secrets.

The score of *The Medium* is ingeniously eclectic, containing arias, ensembles, recitatives, a freely composed dramatic monologue, and orchestral music to support the wordless movement. The musical style shifts from one segment to the next. Gentle harmonies intersperse with peppery ones, homophonic texture with counterpoint, straightforward rhythms with complex syncopations, and diationic melodies with chromatically contorted ones of dubious tonality. Menotti liberally employs whatever suits the thought, the word, and the action.

—James Allen Feldman

MEFISTOFELE [Mephistopheles].

Composer: Arrigo Boito.

Librettist: Arrigo Boito (after Goethe, *Faust*).

First Performance: Milan, Teatro alla Scala, 5 March 1868.

Roles: Mefistofele (bass); Faust (tenor); Margherita (soprano); Marta (contralto); Wagner (tenor); Elena (soprano); Pantalis (contralto); Nereo (tenor); chorus (SATB).

Publications

books—

Risolo, M. *Il primo 'Mefistofele' di Arrigo Boito.* Naples, 1916.
Bonaventura, Arnaldo. *Mefistofele: Guido attraverso il poema e la musica.* Milan, 1924.
Vittadini, S. *Il primo libretto del "Mefistofele" di Arrigo Boito.* Milan, 1938.
Borriello, Antonio. *Mito poesia e musica nel Mefistofele di Arrigo Boito.* Naples, 1950.

articles—

Filippi, F. "Il 'Mefistofele' di Arrigo Boito." *La perseveranza* 9, 16 March (1868).
Ricordi, G. "Analisi musicale del 'Mefistofele' di Boito." *Gazzetta musicale di Milano* 23 (1868): 81.
Huneker, J. "Verdi and Boito"; "Boito's Mefistofele." In *Overtones: A Book of Temperaments,* 236, 272. New York, 1904.
Nicolaisen, Jay Reed. "The First *Mefistofele.*" *Nineteenth-Century Music* 1 (1978): 221.
Grim, William E. "Faust Manqué: Boito's *Mefistofele.*" In *The Faust Legend in Music and Literature,* 29. New York, 1988.
Taddie, Daniel. "The Devil You Say: Reflections on Verdi's and Boito's Iago." *Opera Quarterly* spring (1990).

*   *   *

Mefistofele is the best-known composition by Arrigo Boito, whose fame largely resides in the fact that he was the librettist for Verdi's *Otello* and *Falstaff.* Although it has now gained a foothold in the standard repertory, *Mefistofele*'s popular success has been achieved through a lengthy and incremental process. Boito had to revise (and greatly shorten) the opera several times before audiences discovered the intrinsic beauty and majesty of the opera's text and music.

The literary-minded Boito attempted to fashion a libretto that would remain true to Goethe's *Faust.* Of necessity, Boito had to condense and excise considerable portions of his model. The opera begins with the "Prologue in Heaven," in which Mefistofele and God (in the form of the Mystic Chorus and Celestial Host) make the wager concerning Faust's soul. Act I, scene i is set on Easter Sunday in the city of Frankfurt-am-Main (incidentally, Goethe's birthplace). Townspeople and students are celebrating the Paschal festivities. Faust comments on the change of seasons to his assistant, Wagner. They notice a grey friar approaching whom Faust views with apprehension. Scene ii is set at night in Faust's laboratory. The grey friar enters, reveals himself to be Mefistofele, and he and Faust sign a pact in which the latter agrees to a forfeiture of his soul if he ever says to the fleeting moment "Arrestati, sei bello!" ("Linger yet, thou art so fair!"). Act II, scene i is set in Marta's garden, in which the two couples (Faust-Margherita and Mefistofele-Marta) promenade. Faust and Margherita fall in love, and Faust gives Margherita a potion to make her mother fall asleep so that the two lovers may effect an illicit assignation. Scene ii is the "Witches' Sabbath," but even in this phantasmagorical setting Faust is unable to think of anyone or anything but Margherita. Act

Scenes from the first production of Boito's *Mephistofele,* **Milan, 1868**

III concerns itself with the imprisonment and death of Margherita, who has murdered her mother and the child that she bore to Faust. The delirious Margherita refuses the intercession offered by Faust, she prays to God for forgiveness, and ascends to Heaven at her death. Act IV is the "Classical Sabbath" in which Faust and Helen of Troy (the idealized counterpart to the quotidian Margherita) are introduced and fall in love. As is revealed later, the Helen episode is merely a dream. The epilogue is set once again in Faust's laboratory. Faust admits to world weariness, a dissatisfaction with both the real (Margherita) and the ideal (Helen). Mefistofele fails in his final attempt to entice Faust into sinful ways. Faust opens a Bible and prays to God for forgiveness, then asks for the fleeting moment to linger, falls dead, and ascends to Heaven much to the consternation of Mefistofele.

Although Boito's version is the most faithful of all Faust operas to Goethe's *Faust,* only a very few sections of Goethe's drama are actually utilized. These include from Part I: "Prologue in Heaven," "Outside the City Gate," "Study [from line 1322 ff.]," "Garden," "Walpurgis Night," and "Dungeon"; and from Part II: "Classical Walpurgis Night [of act III]," the Helen of Troy sections of act III, and a transformed version of act V. As the title of the opera indicates, Boito's main preoccupation is with the nature of evil rather than the potential of man to evolve and eventually possess a higher moral consciousness, as is the case with Goethe's *Faust.*

Some of Boito's alterations of Goethe's text may result from the necessities of adhering to the theatrical conventions of the day, catering to Italian taste, and avoiding problems with Italian censors. For example, in the "Prologue to Heaven," Mefistofele speaks to the Mystic Chorus rather than to God directly, as he does in Goethe's *Faust.* Additionally, Faust's salvation scene is significantly altered by Boito. Faust is saved not through the intercession of the "Eternal-Feminine" nor because of ceaseless striving after unobtainable goals, but because of his prayer for salvation.

In order to conform more closely with Christian theology, Boito has Faust's moment of supreme bliss come precisely at the point of spiritual reconciliation. Goethe's Faust, in contrast, never makes a sign of atonement. Boito's libretto minimizes the Goethean concept of *verweile doch, du bist so schön* (stay, thou art so fair) and, by extension, mitigates the necessity and logic of the wager between Mefistofele and God. In *Mefistofele* the wager is rendered moot by Faust's prayer for salvation.

The music of *Mefistofele* displays Boito's concern for harmonic structure and thematic organization. Even though Boito was forced to make severe cuts in the original version of the opera, its extant form reveals considerable musical unity. This is extremely important because the unifying structure of the music is essential to the realization of the tight organic structure with which Goethe held together the seemingly disparate and disjointed sections of his text. The unifying structure of *Mefistofele* is realized most effectively by Boito in his careful and consistent selection of tonalities. Flat keys are used for those sections of the opera dealing with movement, action, and reflection, whereas, sharp keys are reserved for moments of resolution and transcendence.

Boito emphasizes the paradoxical nature of Mefistofele in a number of ways. When Mefistofele first appears before the Celestial Host, his intoned style of declamation is a parody of the psalm tone-like recitation of the Celestial Host. Also, Mefistofele grotesquely parodies Faust's arias. The well-known aria "Dai campi" in F major sung by Faust reappears, transmogrified into F minor, when Mefistofele makes his first appearance before Faust ("Son lo spirito"). Boito's use of the same musical material for different sections of the text with

entirely contrasting literary connotations should not be considered infelicitous, but is rather the result of the composer's awareness of Goethe's preference for strophic over through-composed musical settings. Like Goethe, Boito employed a wide variety of technical devices and quotations to enhance his score. For instance, the beginning open 5th harmonies of the "Witches' Sabbath" are clearly and deliberately reminiscent of Franz Liszt's *Mephisto Waltz.*

In sum, *Mefistofele* is an opera of the highest literary and musical quality that is deserving of wider recognition and performance. Boito has successfully transfered Goethe's general conception of the Faust legend (if not in every detail) from spoken drama to the operatic stage, a feat seldom accomplished in the history of opera. Additionally, *Mefistofele* is one of those extremely rare operas in which the text of the libretto is both subtle and substantial, an equal partner to its accompanying music.

—William E. Grim

MÉHUL, Étienne-Nicolas [Nicholas].

Composer. Born 22 June 1763, in Givet, Ardennes. Died 18 October 1817, in Paris. Apprenticed to the organist at Couvent des Récollets in Givet; studied organ with Wilhelm Hansen, director of music at the monastery in Lavaldieu; studied with the composer Jean-Frédéric Edelmann in Paris, 1778; member of the Institut National de Musique, 1793; awarded an annual pension of 1,000 francs by the Comédie-Italienne, 1794; inspector of the new conservatory and elected to the Institut, 1795; numerous operas composed between 1795 and 1807; member of the Légion d'Honneur, 1804. The composer Hérold was one of Méhul's students.

Operas

Euphrosine, ou Le tyran corrigé, F.-B. Hoffman, Paris, Théâtre Favart, 4 September 1790; revised as *Euphrosine et Coradin.*

Cora (Alonso et Cora), Valadier, Paris, Opéra, 15 February 1791.

Stratonice, F.-B. Hoffman, Paris, Théâtre Favart, 3 May 1792.

Le jeune sage et le vieux fou, F.-B. Hoffman, Paris, Théâtre Favart, 28 March 1793.

Horatius Coclès, A.V. Arnault, Paris, Opéra, 18 February 1794.

Le congrès des rois (with H.-M. Berton, Blasius, Cherubini, Dalayrac, Devienne, Deshayes, Grétry, L. Jadin, R. Kreutzer, Solié, A.E. Trial), Desmaillot (=A.F. Eve), Paris, Théâtre Favart, 26 February 1794.

Mélidore et Phrosine, A.V. Arnault, Paris, Théâtre Favart, 6 May 1794.

Doria, ou La tyrannie détruite, G.M.J.B. Legouvé, C.J.L. d'Avrigny, Paris, Théâtre Favart, 12 March 1795.

La caverne, N.J. Forgeot, Paris, Théâtre Favart, 5 December 1795.

La taupe et les papillons, 1797?

Le jeune Henri (La jeunesse d'Henri IV), J.N. Bouilly, Paris, Théâtre Favart, 1 May 1797.

La prise du pont de Lodi, E.J.B. Delrieu, Paris, Feydeau, 15 December 1797.

Adrien (Adrien, empéreur de Rome), F.-B. Hoffman, Paris, Opéra, 4 June 1799.

Ariodant, F.-B. Hoffman, Paris, Téâtre Favart, 11 October 1799.

Epicure (with Cherubini), C.A. Demoustier, Paris, Téâtre Favart, 14 March 1800.

Bion, F.-B. Hoffman, Paris, Théâtre Favart, 27 December 1800.

L'irato, ou L'emporté, B.J. Marsollier, Paris, Opéra-Comique, 17 February 1801.

Une folie, J.N. Bouilly, Paris, Opéra-Comique, 5 April 1802.

Le trésor supposé, ou Le danger d'écouter aux portes, F.-B. Hoffman, Opéra-Comique, 29 July 1802.

Joanna, B.J. Marsollier, Paris, Opéra-Comique, 23 November 1802.

Héléna, J.N. Bouilly, Paris, Opéra-Comique, 1 March 1803.

Le baiser et la quittance, ou Une aventure de garnison (with Boieldieu, R. Kreutzer, Nicolo), L.B. Picard, C. de Longchamps and J.M.A.M. Dieulafoi, Paris, Opéra-Comique, 18 June 1803.

L'heureux malgré lui, C.G. d'A. de Saint-Just, Paris, Opéra-Comique, 29 December 1803.

Les deux aveugles de Tolède, B.J. Marsollier, Paris, Opéra-Comique, 28 January 1806.

Uthal, J.M.B.B. de Saint-Victor, Paris, Opéra-Comique, 17 May 1806.

Gabrielle d'Estrées, ou Les amours d'Henri IV, C.G. de Saint-Just, Paris, Opéra-Comique, 25 June 1806.

Joseph, A. Duval, Paris, Opéra-Comique, 17 February 1807.

Les amazones, ou La fondation de Thèbes (Amphion, ou Les amazones), V.J.E. de Jouy, Paris, Opéra, 17 December 1811.

Le prince troubadour, A. Duval, Paris, Opéra-Comique, 24 May 1813.

L'oriflamme (with H.-M. Berton, R. Kreutzer, Paër), C.G. Etienne and L.P. Baour-Lormain, Paris, Opéra, 1 February 1814.

La journée aux aventures, P.D.A. Chapelle, L. Mézières-Miot, Paris, Opéra-Comique, 16 November 1816.

Valentine de Milan, J.N. Bouilly, Paris, Opéra-Comic, 28 November 1822 [finished by Daussoigne-Méhul].

Psyché, C.H.F. de Voisenon [lost].

Anacréon, P.J.J. Bernard [lost].

Lausus ed Lydie, Valadier [lost].

Other works: ballets, incidental music, sacred and secular choral music, songs, orchestral an instrumental works, piano pieces.

Publications/Writings

About MÉHUL: books-

Vieillard, P.A. *Méhul, sa vie et ses oeuvres.* Paris, 1859.

Hanslick, E. *Die Moderne Oper, v: musikalisches und literarisches,* [241 ff]. Berlin, 1889.

Pougin, A. *Méhul: sa vie, son génie, son caractère.* Paris, 1889; 2nd ed., 1893.

Brancour, R. *Méhul.* Paris, 1912.

L'opéra aux XVIIIe siècle. Aix-en-Provence, 1982.

articles–

Hoffmann, E.T.A. Review of *La chasse du jeune Henri.* In *Allgemeine musikalische Zeitung* 14 (1812): column 743; reprinted in Hoffmann, *Schriften zur Musik,* edited by F. Schnapp, 115, Munich, 1963.

———. Review of *Ariodant.* In *Dramaturgisches Wochenblatt* 2/no. 25 (1816): 195; reprinted in Hoffmann, *Schriften zur Musik,* edited by F. Schnapp, 308, Munich, 1963.

Fétis, F.-J. "Biographie: Méhul (Etienne Henri)." *Revue musicale* 7 (1830): 193.

Weckerlin, J.-B. "Les quatre versions de la romance de Joseph, opéra de Méhul." *Revue et gazette musicale de Paris* 42 (1875): 252.

Quittard, H. "L'*Uthal* de Méhul." *La revue musicale* 8 (1908): 295.

Strobel, H. "Die Opern von E.N. Méhul." *Zeitschrift für Musikwissenschaft* 6 (1923-24): 362-402.

Barzel, C. "Notes et documents de musique: la jeunesse et le roman de Méhul." *Mercure de France* 15 September (1932): 730.

Masson, P.-M. "Les 'Chants anacréontiques' de Méhul." *Revue de musicologie* 15/no. 51 (1934): 129; 15/no. 52 (1934): 197.

———. "L'oeuvre dramatique de Méhul." *Annales de l'Université de Paris* 12 (1937): 523.

Longyear, R.M. "Notes on the Rescue Opera." *Musical Quarterly* 45 (1959): 49.

Dean, Winton. "Opera under the French Revolution." *Proceedings of the Royal Musical Association* 94 (1967-68): 77.

Charlton, D. "Motive and Motif: Méhul before 1791." *Music and Letters* 57 (1976): 362.

Galliver, David. "Jean-Nicolas Bouilly (1763-1842), successor of Sedraine." *Studies in Music* [Australia] 13 (1979): 16.

Grace, Michael D. "Méhul's *Ariodant* and the Early Leitmotif." In *A Festschrift for Albert Seay: Essays by his Friends and Colleagues,* edited by Michael D. Grace, 173. Colorado Springs, 1982.

Bartlet, M. Elizabeth C. "A Newly Discovered Opera for Napoleon." *Acta Musicologica* 56 (1984): 266.

unpublished–

De Cordes, Robert Clarence Christopher. "Etienne-Nicolas Méhul's *Euphrasine* and *Stratonice:* a Transition from *comédie mêlée d'ariettes* to *opéra-comique.*" Ph. D. dissertation, University of Southern California, 1979.

Bartlet, M. Elizabeth C. "Etienne Nicolas Méhul and Opera during the French Revolution, Consulate, and Empire: a Source, Archival, and Stylistic Study." Ph. D. dissertation, University of Chicago, 1982.

Étienne Méhul was a central figure in a largely forgotten era in French operatic history, the period following the French Revolution and the Napoleonic era. Méhul was one of the most original and influential composers of French opera between Gluck and Berlioz, and such diverse figures as Beethoven, Cherubini, Spontini, Weber, Berlioz, and Mendelssohn all felt his influence to varying degrees. Beethoven's style is largely distinguished from Haydn's and Mozart's by a strain of revolutionary ardor that owed a great deal to French opera of the revolutionary era, as the finale of his Fifth Symphony made abundantly clear. Beethoven envied Méhul's success with serious opera, and Méhul was a principal influence on Beethoven's own *Fidelio,* a "rescue opera" of the sort that was much in vogue in France in the decade following the French revolution. For Cherubini and Spontini, Méhul was a model worthy to stand beside Gluck for his seriousness of purpose and truth in expression. Berlioz's Romanticism and his sensitivity to the power of the orchestra were both anticipated by Méhul, and Berlioz included a warm appreciation of Méhul's operas in his *Soirées de l'orchestre* (Paris, 1852). Mendelssohn greatly admired the first of Méhul's two published symphonies, the Symphony in G minor of 1808, which he maintained in his active repertoire as a conductor. Weber was fanatically devoted to Méhul's operas, and they were an influence on Weber's own operatic output both for the variety of forms that Méhul succeeded in introducing into serious opera with spoken dialogue and for his brilliant orchestral invention. All of this should serve to suggest that the obscurity into which Méhul's operas have fallen has as much to do with changing tastes in operatic dramaturgy and with the peculiarly dated political dimensions of much of the operatic output of the period as it does with intrinsic artistic values, for Méhul's operas are the victims of an eclipse of the operatic output of an entire era. Méhul's operatic dramaturgy may never fully convince again, but he was capable of true brilliance as a composer of expressive dramatic music.

Méhul's earliest extant compositions were keyboard sonatas written under the tutelage of his teacher, Jean-Frédéric Edelmann. Edelmann himself was the author of keyboard sonatas that were dramatic in design (program music without a program, so to speak), and they were a principal influence on the young Méhul's own developing style. Equally important, Edelmann was the composer of a successful opera, *Ariane dans l'isle de Naxos* (1782), the success of which helped to fire Méhul's own operatic ambitions.

Under Edelmann's aegis, Méhul set about arranging popular airs from the operas of the day, and he thereby acquired a real familiarity with all of the trends in French opera of the period. When Méhul's setting of an ode by Jean-Jacques Rousseau was well received at one of the *Concerts Spirituels* of 1785, Méhul was offered the libretto of *Cora*, by the librettist Valadier, to set. Méhul wrote all of the music for *Cora* by 1789, the year of the French Revolution, but the work was not performed until two years later. Méhul began his career as an opera composer with this work, which was old-fashioned in its dramaturgy and remote in style from the genre in which Méhul would find his true path, the *opéra comique*.

Opéra comique refers not to comic opera, but to opera with spoken dialogue, and throughout the latter half of the eighteenth century and the better part of the nineteenth, *opéra comique* was a distinct genre in France with its own traditions and conventions. In the decade following the French Revolution, Méhul was the undisputed master of this genre as he developed the tradition that he had inherited from Grétry and Dalayrac. In Méhul's hands, *opéra comique* was transformed almost beyond recognition, transformed from something akin to musical comedy in form into a genre capable of great variety and dramatic power.

From a musical standpoint, Grétry's and Dalayrac's *opéras comiques* were modest in their ambitions at best. Their works were certainly tuneful, and Grétry in particular was capable of expressive dramatic music when the opportunity presented itself, but the harmonies in their works were restricted to the most simple tonal relationships. The forms of the *airs* in Grétry's and Dalayrac's operas were equally modest in scope, being limited to simple strophic songs, romances, and the like. Méhul far outstripped these predecessors in ambition.

Not only did Méhul's gifts and technique surpass those of his predecessors, he was well versed in the music of Rameau, Gluck, and Haydn, and he was well aware of the intellectual debates about opera current in the period as well. At the time of the French Revolution, Méhul was poised to transform *opéra comique* into a vehicle for lofty artistic ambitions, and

he largely succeeded in his goal, above all with the masterful *Ariodant*.

In transforming *opéra comique*, Méhul had the inestimable advantage of a worthy collaborator in the librettist François-Benoît Hoffman, who shared Méhul's views on operatic dramaturgy. Their first joint venture and the first of Méhul's operas to be performed was *Euphrosine*, which held the stage for over forty years in its modified three-act form. The duet from *Euphrosine*, "Gardez-vous de la jalousie," made Méhul famous overnight among amateurs of music for its revolutionary portrayal of extreme passion.

The most important of the Méhul-Hoffman collaborations were *Stratonice* and *Ariodant*. *Ariodant* remained Méhul's own favorite among his operas, and it represents Méhul at the pinnacle of his powers. The subject of *Ariodant* was taken from cantos V and VI of Ariosto's *Orlando furioso*, the Renaissance epic that had already furnished subjects for many an operatic composer of the eighteenth century, including Handel and Haydn. With his proto-Romantic style, a style more indebted to Gluck than he cared to admit, Méhul breathed new life into his *seria* characters and situations. In these operas Méhul made a characteristic use of "reminiscence" motives to recall specific characters or situations. He also introduced a great variety of forms into *opéra comique* and adapted aspects of Haydn's motivic development to operatic situations. At the same time, abandoning the perfunctory accompaniments of much *opéra comique*, he transformed orchestration into a vehicle for dramatic expression equal to the human voice. Each of Méhul's operas has its own distinctive sound, both by virtue of Méhul's handling of musical motives and because of his characteristically Gallic sensitivity to timbre and sonority. The overture to *Ariodant* opens with an effect both subtle and striking: the sound of three solo 'celli accompanied by the rest of the 'celli and double basses. In the Ossianic opera *Uthal*, the violinists are required to play violas, and the dark string sound of an orchestra without violins comes to seem a part of the "bardic" character that Méhul lent this opera.

In the early days of the Consulate, Méhul won the favor of Napoléon Bonaparte, the first Consul of the new French Republic, but French taste for operas exhibiting the high seriousness of Méhul's works was beginning to wane. In the early 1800s, there was a great vogue for light comic opera in France, and Méhul was forced to adapt to changing circumstances. Méhul's *Bion* was the first of a series of small-scale comic operas in which a new lightness of touch is manifest. Méhul also wrote his best known work, *Joseph*, during this period, an opera based on the well-known biblical story, but it is something of an exception among Méhul's works. None of the operas that Méhul wrote after 1800 ever quite attained the peak of *Ariodant*, as the composer himself admitted in maintaining his preference for that work.

Méhul also tried his hand at symphonic writing in 1808-09, completing three symphonies, only two of which were published. The style embodied in Méhul's symphonies was a curious amalgam. They represent a further development of the style already established in his own vivid and effective opera overtures, many of which had highly original forms of a programmatic nature, but he also gave free reign to a manner of symphonic development deriving from Haydn's style, which had a greater impact in France than either Mozart's or Beethoven's before the second quarter of the nineteenth century.

—David Gable

MEI-FIGNER, Medea (born Zoraide Amedea)

Soprano. Born in 1859, in Florence. Died 8 July 1952, in Paris. Married tenor Nikolay Figner, 1889 (divorced 1904). Trained as mezzo in Florence; debut as Azucena, Sinalunga, 1874 or 1875; sang in Italy, Spain and South America; by 1886 she was singing soprano roles; sang Valentine in *Les Huguenots* with Figner at Imperial Theater; at St Petersburg Opera, 1887-1912; Tchaikovsky chose her to create Liza in *The Queen of Spades*; created Iolanta in 1892; also in first performances of Nápravník's *Dubrovsky* (1895) and *Francesca da Rimini* (1902); remained in Russia, singing until 1923 and teaching.

Publications

By MEI-FIGNER: books–

Moi vaspominaniya [My memories]. St Petersburg, 1912.

About MEI-FIGNER: books–

Stark, E. *Peterburgskaya opera i eyo mastera* [The star singers of the St Petersburg Opera]. Leningrad, 1940.
Rosenthal, H. *Two Centuries of Opera at Covent Garden.* London, 1958.

articles–

Dennis, J. "Medea Mei-Figner." *Record Collector* 4 (1949).

*   *   *

Italian born and trained, Medea Mei-Figner spent the greater part of her career in Russia after establishing a reputation in Europe and South America. She accompanied tenor Nicolay Figner to Russia in the spring of 1887, and made a triumphant first appearance in St. Petersburg as Valentine to his Raoul in *Les huguenots.* Thereafter the two appeared as a team at the Imperial Opera in a varied, international repertory shrewdly chosen to accommodate their partnership. They were married in 1889.

Like her husband, Medea Mei-Figner remained most closely associated with the French and Italian repertory. But the size and flexibility of her voice were such that she was able to explore a wide range of roles without even cursory hesitation, and to expand her repertory in several directions at once. In addition to the dramatic and lyrical roles, she eventually cultivated a diverse, increasingly heavy repertory that came even to include the three Brünnhildes. While in residence at the Imperial Opera, she created four important Russian roles: Lisa in Tchaikowski's *The Queen of Spades,* and the title role in his *Iolanta,* and two of Napravnik's heroines—Mascha in *Dubrovsky* and Francesca in his *Francesca da Rimini.* Beyond the acclaim which initially greeted them, the importance of these interpretations—especially Lisa—can be weighed by the influence they exerted on her many successors.

Her versatility as an actress and imposing physical presence were as formidable as that of Figner's, and this does much to explain the couple's appeal at the box-office. Even after their divorce in 1904 they continued to appear together until his retirement from the Imperial Opera in 1907. Medea Mei-Figner remained there until 1912, retiring from the stage altogether in 1923. She lived and taught in Russia until 1930, and spent the remaining years of her life in Paris.

Medea Mei-Figner as Tosca

Mei-Figner's first recordings, six of them duets with her husband, were made in St. Petersburg in the Winter of 1901. She recorded again in 1903 for the Pathé Company, and made a handful of operatic titles for Columbia in 1904. Her recorded repertory included arias from *Tosca, Werther, Mefistofele,* Napravnik's *Harold,* and *Carmen,* as well as excerpts from a few of the roles she created: Mascha's Air and a duet (with Figner) from *Dubrovsky,* and Lisa's fourth-act aria from *The Queen of Spades* with an often-discussed low ending which, according to Mei-Figner, was her own contrivance sanctioned personally by the composer. The rest are songs, most of them Russian, but with a few charming Italian items performed in her native tongue. By a stroke of good fortune she was induced to record again in 1929 for the Soviet Mustrust, singing Billi's "Canta il grillo" and the lovely "Stornellatrice" from Respighi's *Re Enzo.* A recorded interview, made at her Paris home in 1949, has also survived, and in it the ninety-one-year-old singer discusses a number of important issues of interpretation, primarily with reference to her close association with Tchaikowski and her creation of Lisa in the 1890 premiere of *The Queen of Spades* under the supervision of the composer himself.

Even when singing in a language as uncompromising as Russian, which she did most often, Medea Mei-Figner remained unmistakably Italian in style and disposition. Her voice was large and resonant, and she used it to great dramatic advantage. Her scale was not entirely seamless, but neither was the breach between the registers excessive. Each region of her voice, moreover, exerted surprising authority: her chest tones were as warm and lucid as those at the top of her voice, and she was able to shade both with expert cunning—as we hear in her occasional flights to the extreme regions of the staff. In spite of her age at the time, the electrical recordings give us an even more vivid account of the dark, penetrating tone that was so often praised during her prime. Her singing is quite imaginative, and she uses her voice in a boldly expressive manner. Judging from the three recorded excerpts that have survived, her Carmen, one of her most celebrated roles, appears to have been most distinctive, possessing some of the inscrutability of Emma Calvé's, the suggestiveness of Zellie de Lussan's, and the uninhibited vulgarity of Maria Gay's, and yet, her interpretive liberties—the violent changes of mood and tempo, the seductive pauses, and the impetuous octave transpositions (which she takes so shamelessly throughout the "Seguidilla" and "Chanson Bohème") are altogether more eccentric.

—William Shaman

MEILHAC, Henri.

Librettist. Born 21 February 1831, in Paris. Died 6 July 1897, in Paris. Writer for the *Journal pour rire* and *Vie parisienne* (initially under the pseudonym Ivan Baskoff); began writing plays, 1856, and devoted himself to the theater, producing over 115 stage works (many in collaboration with other authors, most notably, Ludovic Halévy); elected a member of the Académie Française, 26 April 1888.

Librettos

[selected]

La belle Hélène (with L. Halévy) J. Offenbach, 1864.
Barbe Bleue (with L. Halévy), J. Offenbach, 1866.
La vie parisienne (with L. Halévy), J. Offenbach, 1866.
La Grande-Duchesse de Gérolstein (with L. Halévy), J. Offenbach, 1867.
Le château à Toto (with L. Halévy), J. Offenbach, 1868.
La Périchole (with L. Halévy), J. Offenbach, 1868.
Vert-Vert (with Nuitter), J. Offenbach, 1869.
Les brigands (with L. Halévy), J. Offenbach, 1869.
La diva (with L. Halévy), J. Offenbach, 1869.
Madame l'archiduc (with L. Halévy and Millaud), J. Offenbach, 1874.
La boulangère a des écus (with L. Halévy), J. Offenbach, 1875.
Carmen (with L. Halévy), G. Bizet, 1875.
La créole (with L. Halévy and Millaud), J. Offenbach, 1875.
Manon (with Gille), J. Massenet, 1884.
Kassya (with Gille), L. Délibes, 1893.

Publications

About MEILHAC: books–

Lacour, L. *Gaulois et parisiens*. Paris, 1883.
Brisson, A. *Portraits intimes*. Paris, 1884.

articles–

Flers, R. de. "Quelques souvenirs sur trois auteurs dramatiques: Labiche, Meilhac, Sardou." *Revue hebdomadaire* (1926).

The names of Meilhac and Halévy are as indissolubly linked in the history of nineteenth-century French theater as are those of Gilbert and Sullivan on the English stage. Henri Meilhac (1835-97) was a Parisian who, on leaving the Lycée Louis-le-Grand, one of the capital's most celebrated schools, became an assistant in a bookshop. His heart lay elsewhere, however, and soon he was contributing stories, articles and sketches to newspapers and magazines including *La vie parisienne*. Quite early on he turned to the stage, and comedies such as *Garde-toi, je me garde* (1855) and *L'autographe* (1858) showed his quick wit and deft grasp of stage technique. He became particularly adept at constructing opera libretti, one of his most famous being Massenet's *Manon*, which he wrote in collaboration with Philippe Gille.

Ludovic Halévy (1874-1908) came of a distinguished family: his uncles included the composer Fromenthal (*La Juive*) and the philosopher Léon, while his cousin Geneviève married Bizet and served as a model for the duchesse de Guermantes in Proust's *A la recherche du temps perdu*. He worked as a civil servant and eventually reached high rank in the Foreign Ministry. This did not prevent him from keeping up a prolific output of plays and books. One of his novels, still readable today, was *La famille cardinal* which the twentieth-century composers Honegger and Ibert later turned into an operetta. It has a scene where the father of a pretty ballerina interviews an elderly millionaire who has asked for her hand. With a fine show of indignation the father says that his daughter is not for sale, concluding his speech with the remark: "I leave, Monsieur, with the hope of saying to you, not *adieu*, but *au revoir!*" It was one of the best lines Halévy ever wrote.

One day Halévy was in a rush to complete an urgently needed play and happened to bump into Meilhac, with whom he had been at school. He asked him to help out. Meilhac did so to excellent effect, and so was born the famous partnership. One of their adaptations was from a German original which they called *Le réveillon*. By a curious turn of circumstances it later inspired Johann Strauss's *Die Fledermaus*. Together they wrote *Carmen* for Bizet and many libretti for Offenbach. From the very beginning they sensed a mutual affinity. Meilhac was the architect, the engineer who constructed the broad outline of the piece, while Halévy provided the verse for musical numbers. Together they blocked out the dialogue. Meilhac would have an idea and Halévy would bring it to life by transforming the inspiration into words. The two men had a perfect understanding. Their friendship, both personal and professional, was unclouded by argument. If a notion did not work they quietly dropped it and waited for another to turn up. The harmony between them was complete.

On his own or in collaboration with others Halévy wrote some twenty libretti for Offenbach, ranging from the early absurdity *Zing-zing, boum-boum aux Champs-Elysées* (later entitled *Entrez, Messieurs, Mesdames*) to the first great success *Orphée aux enfers*. Together with Meilhac, Halévy supplied *La belle Hélène* as their initial important libretto in the series they wrote for Offenbach. Offenbach, an incredibly quick worker, could write and score an operetta within a week (he did so once for a bet), and his demands for words to be set were imperious and urgent. He knew, however, that in Meilhac and Halévy he had found his ideal collaborators, and the impatient flood of suggestions and ideas he poured out on his "cher Ludo" was tempered with good humour. *La belle Hélène* set the tone of impudent satire and witty irreverence that became the hallmark of the Bouffes-Parisiens, Offenbach's own little theatre. The two librettists and their composer, together with their star Hortense Schneider, became the accredited entertainers of the Second Empire in its concluding phase. Even the Emperor Louis-Napoleon was amused by their pointed wit. Another of their hits was *La vie parisienne*, a celebration of Paris as the queen of pleasure and fashion and, at the same time, a wonderful gallery of characters who are depicted with typical boulevardier wit and resigned disenchantment. Another of their collaborations, *La Grande Duchesse de Gérolstein,* was launched with great trepidation. "How impatiently you wait for the first effect to come off!" Halévy wrote of its opening performance. "The great thing is to break the ice. Once the audience is in the mood everything's all right, but how difficult it is to tear out of them the first roar of laughter, the first murmur of approval, the first applause, and how delightful it is to hear it! . . . Our torture didn't last long." *La Grande Duchesse* went on to become another triumph with its satire on war and politics.

After the fall of the Second Empire and the inauguration of a more sober Third Republic, life was no longer so frivolous or so effervescent. Among the libretti which Meilhac and Halévy provided for Offenbach was *La Périchole,* in which the mood is less frenetic and the characterization, particularly of the heroine, is more thoughtful and penetrating. While, of course, "Meil" and "Hal," as Offenbach called his favourite collaborators, were superb men of the theatre, it must not be forgotten that the composer himself, with his constant revisions and new ideas, was as gifted for the stage as they were. That is why the triumvirate produced such brilliant results. Much later, when Meilhac and Offenbach were dead, Halévy turned up at a revival of *La belle Hélène.* Problems arose that called for rewrites. "No, no," cried Halévy, who was then an old man. "You're very kind, but I'm quite incapable of writing the lines you want from me. Naturally I'd enjoy it, but alas! I've lost the habit, the knack. And without Meilhac. . . ."

—James Harding

DIE MEISTERSINGER VON NÜRNBERG [The Mastersingers of Nuremburg].

Composer: Richard Wagner.

Librettist: Richard Wagner.

First Performance: Munich, Königliches Hof- und National-theater, 21 June 1868.

Roles: Eva (soprano); Walther (tenor); Hans Sachs (bass); Magdalena (soprano or mezzo-soprano); David (tenor); Beckmesser (bass); Pogner (bass); Kothner (bass); Vogelgesang (tenor); Nachtigall (bass); Zorn (tenor); Eisslinger (tenor); Moser (tenor); Ortel (bass); Schwarz (bass); Foltz (bass); A Nightwatchman (bass); chorus (SSSSAAATTTTTTBBBB).

Publications

books—

Bowen, A.M. *The Sources and Text of Wagner's 'Die Meistersinger von Nürnberg'.* Munich, 1899.

Tiersot, J. *Etude sur les Maîtres-chanteurs de Nuremberg de Richard Wagner.* Paris, 1899.

Kloss, E. *Richard Wagner über die 'Meistersinger von Nürnberg': Aussprüche des Meisters über sein Werk.* Leipzig, 1910.

Zademack, F. *Die Meistersinger von Nürnberg: Richard Wagners Dichtung und ihre Quellen.* Berlin. 1921.

Thompson, H. *Wagner and Wagenseil: a Source of Wagner's Opera "Die Meistersinger".* London, 1927.

Rayner, Robert M. *Wagner and "Die Meistersinger".* London, 1940.

Stoffels, Hermann. *Die Meistersinger von Nürnberg von Richard Wagner.* Berlin, 1965.

John, Nicholas, ed. *Richard Wagner: "Die Meistersinger von Nürnberg."* London, 1983.

Pahlen, Kurt, ed. *Richard Wagner: Die Meistersinger von Nürnberg.* Munich, 1986.

articles—

Abert, H. "Gedanken zu Richard Wagners 'Die Meistersinger von Nürnberg'." *Die Musik* 4 (1904-05): 254.

Altmann, W. "Zur Geschichte der Entstehung und Veröffentlichung von Richard Wagners 'Die Meistersinger von Nürnberg'." *Richard Wagner-Jahrbuch* 5 (1913): 87.

Grunsly, K. "Reim und musikalische Form in den Meistersingern." *Richard Wagner-Jahrbuch* 5 (1913): 138.

Mehler, E. "Die Textvarianten der Meistersinger-Dichtung: Beiträge zur Textkritik des Werkes" *Richard Wagner-Jahrbuch* 5 (1913): 187.

Roethe, G. "Zum dramatischen Aufbau der Wagnerschen Meistersinger." *Sitzungberichte der Preussischen Akademie* no. 37 (1919).

Hess, W. " 'Die Meistersinger von Nürnberg': ihre dichterische musikalische Gesamtform." *Zeitschrift für Musik* 113 (1952): 394.

McDonald, William E. "Words, Music, and Dramatic Development in *Die Meistersinger.*" *Nineteenth-Century Music* 1 (1978): 246.

Berkemeier, Georg. " 'Hin Ritter, wisst: Sixtus Beckmesser Merker ist!': 'Was nutzt mir meine Meisterpracht?' Noch eine anmerkung zum Merker in Wagners *Die Meistersinger von Nürnberg.*" In *Sequenzen. Maria Elizabeth Brockhoff zum 2.4.1982 gewidmet von Schülern, Freunden und Kollegen,* edited by Georg Berkemeier and Isolde Maria Weineck. Hagen, 1982.

Wildgruber, Jens. "Das Geheimnis der 'Barform' in R. Wagners *Die Meistersinger von Nürnberg.* Plädoyer für eine neue Art des Formbetrachtung." In *Festschrift Heinz Becker zum 60. Geburtstag am 26. Juni 1982,* edited by Jürgen Schläder and Reinhold Quandt, 205. Laaber, 1982.

Avant-scène opéra January-February (1989) [*Les maîtres chanteurs de Nuremburg* issue].

unpublished–

Stokes, Jeffrey Lewis. "Contour and Motive: a Study of 'Flight' and 'Love' in Wagner's *Ring, Tristan,* and *Meistersinger.*" Ph.D. dissertation, State University of New York, Buffalo, 1984.

Wagner wrote the libretto of *Die Meistersinger von Nürnberg* in 1845, but it was sixteen years before the work came to fruition. This, Wagner's only comic opera, dealt with an historical rather than a mythical subject. Wagner based his libretto on the life of Hans Sachs (1496-1576), cobbler, poet, composer, and a member of the Mastersingers' Guild. He also borrowed the names of various other sixteenth-century personages and added in an imaginary character, the knight Walther von Stolzing, who is portrayed as a musical innovator, like Wagner himself. Wagner did not scorn the guild's ideals and even quoted some of the original music, but he did convey his disapproval of the guild's inflexible nature. Sachs is portrayed more as a philosopher than as a writer, willing to incorporate Walther's new and disturbing artistic concepts within the traditional, "regulated" style. To emphasize the conflict between innovation and tradition, Wagner introduced Beckmesser, a master of the guild and die-hard representative of the Mastersingers' set manner of writing.

Act I opens in St Katherine's church, Nuremberg, with a chorale in which a full organ interrupts the overture. The

Die Meistersinger von Nürnberg, production by Wieland Wagner for Bayreuth Festspiele, 1956

chorale, apart from the orchestral interpolations between phrases, is written in pure Baroque style. Eva, her nurse Magdalena, Walther, and David (Sachs' apprentice) quickly establish themselves as real people, quite unlike the mythical personages of Wagner's other works. Walther, who is unfamiliar with the Mastersingers' craft, learns of a forthcoming song contest, and David explains to him some of the guild's regulations. The twelve masters enter. Pogner, the goldsmith, announces that his daughter Eva is to marry the winner of the contest. Walther, wishing to take part in the competition, asks to become a mastersinger. One of the mastersingers recites the guild's regulations, after which Walther sings a trial song for acceptance. This, however, is quickly rejected as breaking the masters' rules. All are outraged except Sachs, and Walther is disqualified.

The second act is set in a narrow street. It is late, and David closes Sachs' shop. Eva is alarmed to learn that if she were to reject the winner of the contest she would remain perpetually a spinster. Sachs, now alone, reflects on Walther's trial song. But when Eva arrives he warns her that Beckmesser intends to enter the contest. Eva secretly meets Walther outside Sachs' house, and the two plan to elope. Their expression of love is interrupted by the nightwatchman's horn, and they hide as Beckmesser appears and prepares to serenade Eva. Sachs, singing noisily over his work, interrupts Beckmesser's song. He agrees to be silent only if he is allowed to mark the serenade, using his shoemaker's hammer to record any errors, but the song is so clumsy and the hammering becomes so noisy that David is awakened. He notices that Beckmesser is serenading not Eva but Magdalena (to whom he is betrothed), and he attacks him. In the general brawl that follows, Walther and Eva try to escape, but Sachs hands Eva over to Pogner, mistaking her for Magdalena, and pulls Walther into his shop. Only when the nightwatchman's horn is heard does the tumult die away.

The long third act opens in Sachs' workshop as the cobbler reflects on attitudes towards tradition and innovation. When Walther appears and delivers a new song revealed to him in a dream, Sachs tries to adapt it slightly to a style more acceptable to the masters' requirements. After their departure, Beckmesser arrives. Finding the text of Walther's song in Sachs' handwriting, he pockets it, thinking he will be sure to win the contest. When Sachs realizes what Beckmesser has done, he allows him to keep the song and promises not to claim to be its author. In order to see Walther again, Eva uses the pretext of an ill-fitting shoe to enter Sachs' shop. Her words, as she explains the problem to Sachs, express her adoration for Walther, at which point Wagner introduces a musical quotation from *Tristan und Isolde*. In his happiness, Walther improvises the remaining stanza of his song and with David and Magdalena, they join together in a joyous quintet.

The scene moves to a meadow outside Nuremberg, where a large crowd has assembled. After the ceremonial entry of the masters, Sachs explains the terms of the contest. Beckmesser, with his lute, begins his song on the stolen sketch, but his memory fails: the words, becoming ludicrously garbled, provoke the onlookers first to astonishment and then ridicule. Beckmesser horrifies them by claiming that the text is by Sachs but Sachs disclaims responsibility and introduces the true composer. As Walther renders his Prize Song, all are amazed at its beauty. Despite his disqualification, Walther is declared the winner. He nevertheless impetuously refuses the golden chain of honor until Sachs, in a homily on German art, persuades him to accept it. As the opera ends, the people pay homage to Sachs.

The sheer size of *Die Meistersinger*, with its seventeen roles, a chorus of apprentices, three male choruses and the large full chorus, at once limits the possibilities of performance. Although, strangely enough, the orchestra is smaller than that of any of Wagner's other works, the instrumentation is weighty; the string players, for example, seldom stop playing throughout the entire opera.

Wagner uses pure melody to heighten the human dimensions of the story. Leitmotives draw the work together. The motives are associated more with emotions, places, and times (joy, Nuremberg, and midsummer day) than with people or objects, and are usually given to the orchestra rather than to the singers. Wagner's contrapuntal ingenuity in combining them first becomes evident in the overture, where three different motives appear at once.

The text of *Die Meistersinger,* unlike those of Wagner's other works, is written in rhyming verse. Its musical style is more diatonic than *Tristan und Isolde,* giving the work a certain solidity appropriate to its subject. Chromaticism is mostly associated with Walther's music—appropriately, perhaps, in view of the role's autobiographical associations.

Die Meistersinger appears as a hymn to German art, yet Wagner seems to have had some doubts over this in Sachs' final monologue, included only at his wife Cosima's insistence. Yet the opera's greatness, transcending national boundaries, comes from its richness in characterization and from the diversity, not only in the story and music, but in the essential relationship between characters.

—Alan Laing

MELBA, Nellie [born Helen Porter Mitchell].

Soprano. Born 19 May 1861, in Richmond, Victoria. Died 23 February 1931, in Sydney. Married: Charles Armstrong, 1882 (one son; divorced 1900). Studied with Mary Ellen Christian at Presbyterian Ladies College and Pietro Cecchi in Melbourne; gave concerts in Melbourne, from which her stage name derives; studied in Paris with Mathilde Marchesi, 1886-87; debut as Gilda in Brussels at Théâtre de la Monnaie, 1887; sang regularly at Covent Garden, where she first appeared as Lucia, from 1888 to 1926; Paris Opéra debut as Ophélie, 1889; appeared in Monte Carlo and St Petersburg, 1890-91; Teatro alla Scala debut as Lucia, 1893; Metropolitan Opera debut in same role, 1893; formal farewell concert at Covent Garden, 1926; teacher at Albert Street Conservatorium, Melbourne, from 1915.

Publications

By MELBA: books—

Melodies and Memories. London, 1925; New York, 1926.
The Melba Method. London, 1926.

About MELBA: books—

Murphy, A. *Melba: a Biography.* New York, 1909.
Colson, P. *Melba: an Unconventional Biography.* London, 1932.
Wechsberg, J. *Red Plush and Black Velvet: the Story of Dame Nellie Melba and her Times.* Boston, 1961.
Hutton, G. *Melba.* Melbourne, 1962.
Hetherington, J. *Melba: a Biography.* Melbourne, 1967.
Gattey, C. *Queens of Song.* London, 1979.

Moran, W., ed. *Nellie Melba: a Contemporary Review.* Westport, Connecticut, 1985.

Radic, T. *Melba: the Voice of Australia.* Melbourne and London, 1986.

articles–

Harvey, H. and G. Whelan. "Nellie Melba." *Record Collector* 4 (1949): 203.

Shawe-Taylor, D. "Nellie Melba." *Opera* February (1955).

* * *

"She [was] 32 when she came to the Metropolitan" wrote W.J. Henderson. "The voice was in the plenitude of its glory and it was quickly accepted as one of the great voices of operatic history. The quality of musical tone cannot be adequately described. No words can convey to a music lover who did not hear Melba any idea of the sounds with which she ravished all ears. . . . On the evening of her debut at the Metropolitan she sang in the cadenza of the mad scene a prodigiously long crescendo trill which was not merely astonishing, but also beautiful. Her stacatti were as firm, as well placed, and as musical as if they had been played on a piano. Her catilena was flawless in smoothness and purity. She phrased with elegance and sound musicianship as well as with consideration for the import of the text. In short, her technic was such as to bring out completely the whole beauty of her voice and to enhance her delivery with all the graces of vocal art."

Henderson was not by any means alone in his praise of the Melba technique. Writing in 1958, voice teacher J.H. Duval said: "Galli-Curci had some splendid vocal effects, as had Sembrich, but . . . whoever has heard [Melba's] marvelous crescendo on the trill in the Mad Scene in *Lucia* will remain unmoved by any vocal feat that has been performed since. It began pianissimo. It grew steadily stronger and stronger, more and more intense, and at last . . . that vast auditorium which is the Metropolitan Opera House of New York just vibrated with its wonderful fortissimo of crystalline purity. . . ."

Mary Garden's words about Melba's voice are famous but worth repeating: "I have no hesitation in declaring that Melba had the most phenomenal effect on me of any singer I have ever heard. I went once to Covent Garden to hear her do Mimi in *La boheme*. . . . Melba didn't impersonate the role at all—she never did that—but my God, how she sang it! You know, the last note for the first act of *La boheme* . . . is a high C, and Mimi sings it when she walks out the door with Rodolfo. She closes the door and then takes the note. The way Melba sang that high C was the strangest and weirdest thing I have ever experienced in my life. The note came floating over the auditorium of Covent Garden: it left Melba's throat, it left Melba's body, it left everything, and came over like a star and passed us in our box, and went out into the infinite. I have never heard anything like it in my life, not from any other singer, ever. It just rolled over the hall . . . My God, how beautiful it was! . . . That note of Melba's was just like a ball of light. It wasn't attached to anything at all— it was *out* of everything."

To those who know the Melba voice only from commercial phonograph records, it has always been difficult to understand how she could have had any success as Aïda. She first sang the part at Covent Garden 4 November 1892, "displaying greater energy as an actress than ever before, and displaying faultless vocalization." Hurst stated that as Aida

"her performance was so fine as to excite the highest admiration, for she threw aside her usual reserve to sing with passionate emotion, and easily dominated the great *ensemble* in the second act without apparent effort or loss of quality."

Of Melba's attempt to add the *Siegfried* Brünnhilde to her repertory in New York in 1896 much has been written. Most critics found her performance remarkable. In spite of the fact that, as one critic wrote, "her voice had the ring of true passion," all gave a word of warning that the attempt was "more potent than wise." Krehbiel wrote that "the music of the part does not lie well in her voice, and if she continues to sing it, it is much to be feared there will soon be an end to the charm which the voice discloses when employed in its legitimate sphere. The world can ill afford to loose a Melba, even if it should gain a Brünnhilde." But Nellie Melba needed no warning from others. In her typical frank style, she told her manager: "Tell the critics I am never going to do that again. It is beyond me. I have been a fool!" Melba knew her limitations. In 1914 she wrote, "I have never continued roles that proved unsuited to me," and in giving advice to young singers she maintained that she "always drew on the interest, never the principal." One experience taught her that Brünnhilde was "off limits," and as it became the fashion to sing Elsa and Elisabeth in German rather than French or Italian, she dropped those roles, as well as Aida.

Melba was unfortunate in that two operas written for her, Bemberg's *Elaine* and Saint-Saëns' *Hélène,* did not prove to be lasting works. She created Mascagni's *I Rantzau,* and while she created Nedda in Leoncavallo's *Pagliacci* in both London and New York at the composer's request, she did not attempt to maintain the role in her repertory. She can be credited, perhaps self-servingly, with recognizing Puccini's *La boheme* as a masterpiece, making it a point to study the opera with the composer. She virtually introduced the opera to the United States when touring with her own company, and she applied pressure to the managements of Covent Garden and the Metropolitan to include the work, promising to allow them to "give the public their money's worth" by supplementing each performance with a "free" mad scene from *Lucia* or *Hamlet* after Mimi expired, a practice which was actually carried on in both houses until the public indicated that the opera could stand on its own.

Melba's first commercial recordings were made in 1904, when she was forty-three years of age, and she continued to record into the beginning of the electrical recording era. Her farewell at Covent Garden in June 1926 was partially recorded, and her last records were made in December of that year. While there is no doubt that some of the bloom of youth had passed, some of her recordings are quite remarkable. Many of them are important documents, including material studied with Thomas, Gounod, Massenet, Verdi, and Puccini or songs written for her and often accompanied by composers such as Landon Ronald and Herman Bemberg. Recording technicians recognized the size and power of the Melba voice, and she was placed well back from the receiving horn, so that many of her recordings give the impression that she owned a small voice; as we have seen from quotations from critics who heard her, this was certainly not the case. We are fortunate that she left us some remarkable evidence of at least a part of one of the most remarkable careers which spanned the nineteenth and twentieth centuries.

—William R. Moran

Nellie Melba as Lakmé

MELCHIOR, Lauritz.

Tenor. Born 20 March 1890, in Copenhagen. Died 18 March 1973, in Santa Monica, California. Studied as a baritone with Paul Bang at Copenhagen Royal Opera School; debut as Silvio in *I pagliacci*, Copenhagen, 1913; sang as baritone for several seasons, then studied with Vilhelm Herold; second debut as tenor in *Tannhäuser*, Copenhagen, 1918; went to London in 1921 to study with Beigel; studied with Grenzebach in Berlin and Bahr-Mildenburg in Munich; appeared as Siegmund at Covent Garden, 1924, and returned regularly 1926-39; Bayreuth debut as Parsifal, 1924, and sang there until 1931; appeared in Hamburg (1928), Barcelona (1929), and Buenos Aires (1931-43); at Metropolitan Opera 1926-50, where he first appeared as Tannhäuser; after retiring in 1950 Melchior continued to work in film and operetta.

Publications

About MELCHIOR: books–

Hansen, H. *Lauritz Melchior: a Discography*. Copenhagen, 1965.
Nanlly, J. *Lauritz Melchior*. Copenhagen, 1969.
Emmons, S. *Tristanissimo: the Authorized Biography of Heroic Tenor Lauritz Melchior*. New York, 1990.

articles–

Mortersen, E. and J. Zachs. "A Lauritz Melchior Discography." *Record News* 3 (1959): 433; 4 (1959): 12, 49.
Blyth, A. "Gigli and Melchior—Blessed by the Gods." *Opera* April (1990).

*   *   *

It is the fate of all modern aspirants to the title of heldentenor to be compared to Danish tenor Lauritz Melchior. Melchior reigned as the king of Wagnerian tenors throughout his career, from the time he switched from singing baritone roles (which he sang from 1913 to 1918) until his farewell performance as Lohengrin at the Metropolitan Opera in 1950. After a hiatus of a decade, he made his final operatic appearance in 1960, when he was seventy, and his influence continues to the present thanks to his numerous recordings. Melchior's fame spread far beyond the opera house. He was the first male singer to be heard on radio, in an experimental broadcast from Chelmsford, England, in July 1920; his appearances in Hollywood films of the 1940s and 1950s, as both singer and comedian, helped popularize opera for the American public and reshape its image of opera singers.

Although Melchior's fame rests on his assumptions of the heavier roles in the tenor repertoire, he essayed several baritone roles (including di Luna in Verdi's *Il trovatore*, Giorgio Germont in Verdi's *La traviata*, and Silvio in Leoncavallo's *I pagliacci*, the role of his professional operatic debut in Copenhagen in 1913). After an audition before Wagner's son Siegfried, made possible by the Wagnerian soprano Anna Bahr-Mildenberg, Melchior first appeared at Bayreuth in 1924, where he was heard as Siegmund and Parsifal. His Metropolitan Opera debut came in 1926 as Tannhäuser; the performance was not completely successful, partly because the role lay too high for him at the time. By the 1930s he had become the company's leading Siegmund, Siegfried, and Tristan, and he remained at the Metropolitan Opera until 1950, singing only Wagnerian roles there.

Lauritz Melchior as Siegfried, Berlin, c. 1930

Physically imposing, Melchior possessed a voice that can be characterized as brilliant and enormously powerful, yet with the potential to be sweet and gentle. His singing had stamina, intensity, and enthusiasm; his sense of humor is apparent despite the heroic nature of the sound. Possibly because of his baritonal beginnings, his voice had a basic darkness; his secure technical foundation allowed him to master the difficult transitional vocal passage between E and F that are essential in the Wagnerian roles, and there is no discernible break between the registers.

What separates Melchior from virtually all other Wagnerian tenors is that he possessed a combination of full, firm, steady tone, brilliant high notes, the ability to maintain a lyrical quality even during the most strenuous passages sung over the heaviest orchestration, a liquid legato, excellent diction, and the skill to produce soft, caressing tones. His singing was remarkably consistent throughout his career, as attested to by his many recordings, including a recording of act I of *Die Walküre* made as late as 1960, and this consistency is a tribute to the soundness of his technique. The basic sound of the voice was maintained over the years, although it darkened somewhat as he got older, but without any loss of brilliance; his interpretive ability developed, gaining in subtlety as his career progressed.

In addition to his Wagnerian roles of Lohengrin, Parsifal, Siegfried, Siegmund, Tristan, and Tannhäuser, Melchior scored successes as Verdi's Otello, Canio in Leoncavallo's *I pagliacci*, Turiddu in Mascagni's *Cavalleria rusticana*, Florestan in Beethoven's *Fidelio*, Radamès in Verdi's *Aida*, John of Leyden in Meyerbeer's *Le Prophète*, and Samson in Saint-Saëns's *Samson et Dalila*, but he performed these roles relatively infrequently.

During his career, Melchior was criticized for several non-vocal failings: his appearance (early critics found the combination of unflattering costumes and Melchior's bulk laughable), his dramatic shortcomings, some rhythmic inaccuracy (especially a tendency to rush ahead of the beat and some sloppiness over note values), and a lack of discipline (he reportedly would leave the stage whenever his character had nothing to do but stand around, and he is said to have been liable to stay at card games in the wings until the last possible moment). His dismissal by Rudolf Bing from the Metropolitan Opera in 1950 apparently was precipitated by this kind of behavior; the intolerant Bing, in one of his first acts as general manager, thereby prevented Melchior from celebrating his twenty-fifth anniversary with the company.

His reputed rhythmic inaccuracy is little substantiated by his recordings, of which there is a vast number, beginning with several baritone arias in the period before he switched to tenor roles, and including most of his major roles. He was a prolific recording artist, making approximately 300 records between 1913 and 1954. His contribution as Siegmund in a recording of act I of *Die Walküre* made in 1935, with Bruno Walter conducting, Lotte Lehmann as Sieglinde, and Emanuel List as Hunding, helped make it one of the greatest of all opera recordings.

—Michael Sims

MENOTTI, Gian Carlo.

Composer. Born 7 July 1911, in Cadegliano, Italy. Basic music instruction from his mother: first opera attempt, *The Death of Pierrot*, composed at the age of ten; studied at the Milan Conservatory, 1923-27; in the United States, 1927; studied with Rosario Scalero at the Curtis Institute, 1927-33; taught composition at the Curtis Institute, 1941-58; Guggenheim fellowships, 1946-47; Pulitzer Prize and Drama Critics' Circle award for *The Consul*, 1950; Drama Critics' Circle Award and Music Critics' Circle Award for *The Saint of Bleecker Street*, 1954, and Pulitzer Prize, 1955; *The Unicorn, the Gorgon and the Manticore* commissioned by the Elizabeth Sprague Coolidge Foundation, 1956; *Maria Golovin* composed for the International Exposition at Brussels, 1958; organized the Festival of Two Worlds, Spoleto, Italy, 1958, and Charleston, South Carolina, 1977; settled in Scotland, 1974. Menotti was the librettist for Samuel Barber's *Vanessa* (1958), *A Hand of Bridge* (1959), and the libretto revisions of *Anthony and Cleopatra* (1975; original libretto by Zeffirelli, 1966).

Operas

Publishers: G. Schirmer, Ricordi.

Amelia al ballo, 1936, Philadelphia, 1 April 1937.
The Old Maid and the Thief (radio opera, 1939, National Broadcasting Company, 22 April 1939; stage premiere, Philadelphia, 11 February 1941.
The Island God, 1942, New York, Metropolitan Opera, 20 February 1942.
The Medium, 1945, New York, 8 May 1946.
The Telephone, 1946, New York, 18 February 1947.
The Consul, 1949, Philadelphia, 1 March 1950.

Amahl and the Night Visitors (television opera), 1951, National Broadcasting Company, 24 December 1951; stage premiere, Bloomington, Indiana, 21 February 1952.
The Saint of Bleecker Street, 1954, New York, 27 December 1954.
Maria Golovin, 1958, Brussels, 20 August 1958.
The Labyrinth (television opera), 1963, National Broadcasting Company, 3 March 1963.
Le dernier sauvage, 1963, Paris, Opéra-Comique, 21 October 1963.
Martin's Lie (children's church opera), 1964, Bristol, England, 3 June 1964.
Help, Help, the Globolinks!, 1968, Hamburg, Staatsoper, 21 December 1968.
The Most Important Man, 1971, New York, 12 March 1971.
Tamu-Tamu, 1973, Chicago, 5 September 1973.
The Egg (children's church opera), 1976, Washington, District of Columbia, 17 June 1976.
The Hero, 1976, Philadelphia, 1 June 1976.
The Trial of the Gypsy (children's opera), 1978, New York, 24 May 1978.
Chip and his Dog (children's opera), 1979, Guelph, Canada, 5 May 1979.
La loca, 1979, San Diego, 3 June 1979.
A Bride from Pluto, 1982, New York, 14 April 1982.
The Boy who Grew too Fast (children's opera), 1982, Wilmington, Delaware, 24 September 1982.
Goya, 1986, Washington, Kennedy Center for the Performing Arts, 15 November 1986.

Other works: orchestral and instrumental works, choruses, songs.

Publications/Writings

By MENOTTI: librettos–

A Hand of Bridge [libretto set by Samuel Barber, first performed 17 June 1959]. New York, 1960.
Introductions and Goodbyes [libretto set by Lukas Foss, first performed 5 May 1960]. New York, 1961.
Vanessa [libretto set by Samuel Barber, first performed 15 January 1958]. New York, 1964.

unpublished–

The Leper [stage play, first performed Tallahassee, Florida, 22 April 1970].

About MENOTTI: books–

Tricoire, R. *Gian Carlo Menotti: L'homme et son oeuvre.* Paris, 1966.
Grieb, L. *The Operas of Gian Carlo Menotti, 1937-1972: a Selective Bibliography.* Metuchen, New Jersey, 1974.
Gruen, John. *Menotti.* New York, 1978.
Ardoin, John. *The Stages of Menotti.* Garden City, New York, 1985.

articles–

Sargeant, W. "Orlando in Mount Kisco." *New Yorker* 39/4 May (1963): 49.

Ewen, D. "Gian Carlo Menotti." In *The World of Twentieth-Century Music*, 481ff. Englewood Cliffs, New Jersey, 1968.

Wolz, Larry. "Gian Carlo Menotti: Words Without Music." *Opera Journal* 10/no. 3 (1977): 8.

d'Amico, Fedele. "La musica e l' impegno" [on *The consul*]. *Nuovo rivista musicale italiana* 14 (1980): 321.

Ardoin, John. "A Welcome Gift." *Opera News* 45/no. 20 (1981): 9, 16.

*   *   *

Menotti is Italian by birth and also by citizenship, but, because from the age of sixteen he has studied, written, and premiered his music so extensively in the United States, even *The New Grove Dictionary of Music and Musicians* classifies him as an American composer. He is really an internationalist, "a man of two worlds," and the sad fact is that the two countries most integral to his life have been the most hostile to his talent, leading him to the refuge and solitude of a manor house in Scotland, which he acquired in 1974. "Italy created me; America nourished me; and Scotland will bury me," he has said; "I've chosen to live here, so that I could be completely cut off from my past . . . to take stock . . . [and] time for reflection."

When Gian Carlo Menotti accepted the scholarship at the Curtis Institute to study composition with Rosario Scalero, he could speak no English, but he tutored himself in this adopted language by going to the movies four times a week. Shortly after his graduation with honors from Curtis, he spent the winter in Vienna with his close friend, Samuel Barber, and while there began writing his first opera, *Amelia al ballo*. The Curtis years with Scalero had been steeped in contrapuntal studies, and although Menotti wrote two operas before the age of ten, he had come to regard opera as an inferior art form, not expecting the genre to dominate his life's work. He has dubbed *Amelia* "the beginning of my end!"

Amelia al ballo was an instant success; the premiere in Philadelphia was followed by a Metropolitan Opera performance the following March, and the opera was retained in the Met's repertoire for the next season. During the next decade, fame burst upon the young composer. The National Broadcasting Company commissioned an opera written especially for radio, and Menotti produced *The Old Maid and the Thief,* another one-act *opera buffa,* with high-spirited farce, lyric arias, and his first attempt at writing an English libretto.

After beginning his career with two works acclaimed by audiences and critics alike, Menotti's next opera, *The Island God,* commissioned by the Metropolitan Opera, was removed from the repertoire after only four performances and withdrawn from circulation by the composer, except for some concert editions of the orchestral episodes. Menotti quickly recognized that he was out of his element in attempting "a subject too heroic for my kind of music." It was a depressing setback, nonetheless, and he sought refuge in "Capricorn," the house in Mt. Kisco, New York that he and Barber had just acquired through their patron, Mary Louise Bok (now Mrs. Efrem Zimbalist). The house was a sprawling affair that provided separate work areas with ample seclusion and no interruptions. For the next four years, Menotti abandoned writing opera to concentrate on other musical forms, including a piano concerto, a commissioned ballet score, and an orchestral suite from the latter that became popular at concerts.

Meanwhile, Menotti was appointed in 1941 to the composition department at the Curtis Institute to teach a new course on "dramatic forms," and retained a teaching post there for the next seventeen years. Curtis awarded him an honorary bachelor of music degree in 1945, the same year that he won grants from the American Academy of Arts and Sciences and the National Institute of Arts. The following year, with a Guggenheim Fellowship and a grant from the Alice M. Ditson Fund of Columbia University, he began work on a new tragic opera more economic and modest in scope than *The Island God.* It was *The Medium,* a two-act chamber opera with its story "of a person caught between two worlds, the world of reality which she cannot wholly comprehend, and the supernatural world which she cannot believe," that set forth for the first time the fundamental elements that have become the mark of identity for Menotti as a composer. With its macabre text (written by the composer), the mixture of odd characters who evoke such strong feelings from the audience, and what Cocteau described as "a vocal style which elevates the ordinary and every-day into lyric drama," Menotti brought opera in America down from the heights to the level of the masses, and established it as a popular art form. *The Medium,* after its Columbia premiere, had a seven-month run the following year on Broadway, paired with *The Telephone,* an introductory one-act comedy for two actors.

The two works were lauded for their straightforward sincerity: the quality of *verismo* that led critics immediately to compare Menotti with Puccini, Rimsky-Korsakov, Ravel, and others. Critics and fellow composers stated then and have persisted in claiming that Menotti's work is all derivative; as one said, "Menotti has never written an original note in his life, and yet every note immediately has the signature of Menotti. . . . his music lasts." Menotti freely admits his debt to other composers, albeit a different list: Schubert ("I adore his simplicity, . . . the way he can communicate, can create something out of the most simple means . . ."); Monteverdi madrigals; Mussorgsky, Puccini, and Debussy ("Only in [their works] did I find admirable examples of what I myself was looking for"); and Stravinsky (". . . an indispensable item . . . He is like electricity: whether you approve of it or not, you can no longer do without it"). He is also grateful to Wolf-Ferrari, whose music he did not admire, for an early word of timely advice on writing opera: ". . . the orchestra and the voice must be knitted together like the cogs in tow wheels . . . the accents of either . . . must never meet, otherwise they will destroy each other."

Within the next few years, *The Medium* was given more than a thousand performances in Europe and America, was recorded, made into a motion picture, and taken to Europe on a State Department tour.

Broadway continued to produce popular operas by Menotti: his first full-length opera, *The Consul* (1949), premiered in 1950 and won the Pulitzer Prize, as well as the Drama Critics Award. As with *The Medium,* the dramatic tension and use of orchestral dissonance to heighten moments of emotional impact were well knit with contrasts of stark drama and tender lyricism, and *The Consul* was a sensation. The following year it was produced in London, Munich, Hamburg, Berlin, Zurich, Vienna, and even in Milan (the first American opera to be produced at the Teatro alla Scala). *The Consul* was acclaimed everywhere but in Italy, where left-wing demonstrations denounced it for its anti-communist stance, while others saw Menotti's American residency as an unpatriotic act.

The composer has cited *The Consul* as an example of his insistence on the unified whole of words, music and action: ". . . a good opera must be a happy marriage in which the music is the asserting husband, and the words the accepting wife." In his view, the music must shape the libretto: Menotti claims that some of the best literary phrases of his original text ended up on the cutting-floor to accommodate the music.

In Menotti's next opera, *Amahl and the Night Visitors,* verismo was replaced by the composer's love of folklore and his childhood absorption with puppet theater. There followed *The Saint of Bleecker Street,* set in New York City's Italian quarter, the composer's first opera with an American setting. When asked about his religious beliefs, Menotti said, "I definitely am not a religious man . . . [but it] is undeniable that the intense and incandescent faith which nourished my childhood and my adolescence has seared my soul forever. . . . [The loss of my faith] has left me uneasy . . . And it is this very duality in my character, this inner conflict, which I have tried to express in some of my operas. . . ." *The Saint of Bleecker Street* garnered for Menotti his second Pulitzer Prize, the Drama Critics and also the Music Critics Circle awards.

The lukewarm reception accorded *Maria Golovin,* commissioned as the American contribution to the 1958 Brussels Exposition, presaged a downward slant with his critical reviewers in Menotti's success as an opera composer. As Harold Schonberg pointed out, the 1930s and 40s hailed Menotti as a new hero of opera; his directness and romantic lyricism delighted the "aging lot" of critics "whose roots were in the nineteenth century. . . ." But after World War II, musical criticism was increasingly in the hands of a young generation weary of romanticism and eager for dissonance, serialism, and all other aspects of "the new speech," including the electronic medium. Menotti's works were still performed, but he was suddenly dismissed as old-fashioned, "hopelessly naïve," and not to be taken seriously. Many composers adapted their musical idioms to the new tastes, but Menotti refused: "Music history will place me somewhere," he said, "but that is no concern of mine." He would not forsake the cultivation of "the evocative power of melody," the fascinating problem of the *parlar cantando,* nor the gathering of melody "without harming or soiling its purity." He felt that many of the new breed of composers were confusing "the discoverer of a hidden natural force [with] the inventor of a fascinating and even at times useful gadget." He could not fathom why "modern" should be equated only with dissonance and nervousness, when consonance and serenity also had their place. Like Gottfried von Einem, he was dismayed at the idea of attempting to present the new and radical without a backdrop of the familiar, in the interest of form and coherence.

The 1960s were discouraging times for Menotti as a composer, compounded by the increasing demands of his role as founder of the Spoleto Festival of Two Worlds. *The Last Savage,* commissioned for Paris, was written with an Italian libretto (his first since *Amelia*), for translation into French and, later, English. It was dismissed by the critics, one of whom called it "a fiasco of American drivel." Americans objected to its French *opéra buffe* structure, with set numbers, arias, and duets. For the next seven years Menotti abandoned large forms and concentrated on chamber works. Vocal compositions in this period included a dramatic cantata and two one-act operas commissioned for television: *The Labyrinth,* which was so carefully designed for television's unique attributes that it is confined to that medium; and *Martin's Lie,* a medieval tale written for the Bath Festival in England.

The 1970s did not improve the critics' view of Menotti as a composer. *The Most Important Man,* his first full-length opera in almost a decade, was viciously denounced by the critics, who insisted that he was only repeating himself. *Amelia at the Ball* was called "maudlin," and a New York revival of *The Consul* brought cries of "overtheatrical," which Menotti retorted was rather like accusing music of being "too

musical." The composer was distressed by the vituperative quality of the criticism, which extended to any work that left his pen, including a magnificent cycle of songs commissioned by Elisabeth Schwarzkopf, called *Canti Della Lontananza.* The trouble lay not in the songs but in an unfortunate mismatch of music and musician; the critics were adamant in their conviction that only the composer was at fault. In a wonderful mix of drama and lyricism with touches of whimsy, Menotti's seven poems are a dramatic *scena* for soprano, and rank among the finest vocal writing of the century.

Menotti's one-act opera for children, *Help! Help! The Globolinks!,* was, in Harold Schonberg's opinion, the composer's polemic response to his critics. Written as a companion piece for a performance of *Amahl* in Hamburg, this fanciful tale of children threatened by extra-terrestrial creatures who "speak" in electronic sounds, was the first of several works for children, including *Chip and His Dog,* created for his adopted son, Francis Phelan, who now bears his name. The three mature "late" operas, all from the 1970s, were written for specific occasions and had the customarily uncertain response from the critics. *Tamu-Tamu, The Hero,* and *Juana La Loca* remain unpublished—principally because they were created for a specific audience, and would not have wide appeal. There are a host of Menotti works, including non-musical plays, which are not in print because they await revision and polishing, a task the composer confesses to avoiding.

The heavy commitment to the two Spoleto Festivals in Italy and the USA has taken its toll on Menotti's scores, but there is also his reluctance to "seal in" a work as a totally finished product: ". . . the agonizing process of freezing on the written page the fluctuations of my thoughts. . . ." He has a horror of the "frozen music" of recordings, which tend to be labelled definitive by the public regarding tempo and interpretation. Both, says Menotti, must be ". . . necessarily fluid according to temperament and mood and change as people change in an ever-changing world. . . . I don't think a definitive recording of my music exists."

Gian Carlo Menotti remains a figure of controversy, refusing to alter his basic philosophy regarding opera, wherein drama means strong texts allied closely to music and action in a "unified whole"; where there is little or no "gratuitous lyricism" and the vocal arias are actively essential to the drama; where a conscious attempt is made to keep the elements taut, the speech coherent and comprehensible, and the ingredients lean and spare. The critics still tend to dismiss him, but the number of performances, translated into more than 20 languages, increases annually. To Wiley Hitchcock's summation of Menotti's achievement in combining "the theatrical sense of a popular playwright and a Pucciniesque musical vocabulary with an Italianate love of liquid language and . . . characters as real human beings," Ned Rorem adds: "Whether you like his music or not, the fact exists that due to Menotti, and only Menotti, the whole point of view of contemporary opera in America, and perhaps in the world, is different from what it would have been had he not existed."

—Jean C. Sloop

MERCADANTE, (Giuseppe) Saverio (Raffaele).

Composer. Born 1795 (baptized 17 September), in Altamura, near Bari. Died 17 December 1870, in Naples. Married: Sofia

Gambaro, 1832 (1 daughter, 2 sons). Studied flute, violin, solfeggio, figured bass and harmony with Furno and counterpoint with Tritto at the Collegio di San Sebastiano, beginning 1808; studied composition with the director of the college, Zingarelli, 1816-20; first opera successfully performed in Naples, 1819; in Vienna, 1824; in Spain and Portugal, 1826-31; maestro di capella at the Cathedral of Novara, 1833-40; offered the directorship of the Liceo Musicale in Bologna by Rossini, 1839, but served only a short time; succeeded Zingarelli as director of the Naples Conservatory, 1840.

Operas

L'apoteosi d'Ercole, G. Schmidt, Naples, San Carlo, 19 August 1819.
Violenza e costanza, ossia i falsi monetari, A.L. Tottola, Naples, Nuovo, 19 January 1822.
Anacreonte in Samo, G. Schmidt (after J.-H. Guy, *Anacréon chez Polycrate*), Naples, San Carlo, 1 August 1820.
Il geloso ravveduto, B. Signorini, Rome, Valle, October 1820.
Scipione in Cartagine, J. Ferretti, Rome, Torre Argentina, 26 December 1820.
Maria Stuarda, regina di Scozia (Maria Stuart), G. Rossi, Bologna, Comunale, 29 May 1821.
Elisa e Claudio, ossia L'amore protetto dall' amicizia, L. Romanelli (after F. Casari, *Rosella*), Milan, Teatro alla Scala, 30 October 1821.
Andronico, Dalmiro Tindario P.A. [=G. Kreglianovich]. Venice, La Fenice, 26 December 1821.
Adele ed Emerico, ossia Il posto abbandonato, F. Romani, Milan, Teatro alla Scala, 21 September 1822.
Amleto, F. Romani (after Shakespeare), Milan, Teatro alla Scala, 26 December 1822.
Alfonso ed Elisa, after Alfieri, *Filippo,* Mantua. Sociale, 26 December 1822; performed as *Aminta ed Argira,* Reggio Emilia, Comunale, 1 May 1823.
Didone abbandonata, Metastasio, Turin, Regio, 18 January 1823.
Gli sciti, A.L. Tottola, Naples, San Carlo, 18 March 1823.
Costanzo ed Almeriska, A.L. Tottola, Naples, San Carlo, 22 November 1823.
Gli amici di Siracusa, J. Ferretti, Rome, Torre Argentina, 7 February 1824.
Doralice, Vienna, Kärntnertor, 18 September 1824.
Le nozze di Telemaco ed Antiope (pasticcio, mostly of music by other composers), C. Bassi, Vienna, Kärntnertor, 5 November 1824.
Il podestà di Burgos, Vienna, Kärntnertor, 20 November 1824.
Nitocri, Conte Piosasco (after Zeno), Turin, Regio, 26 December 1824.
Erode, ossia Marianna, L. Ricciuti, Venice, La Fenice, 26 December 1825.
Ipermestra, L. Ricciuti (after Metastasio), Naples, San Carlo, 29 December 1825.
Caritea, regina di Spagna, ossia La morte di Don Alfonso re di Portogallo, P. Pola, Venice, La Fenice, 21 February 1826.
Ezio, Metastasio, Turin, Regio, 2 February 1827.
Il montanaro, F. Romani, Milan, Teatro alla Scala, 16 April 1827.
La testa di bronzo, ossia La capanna solitaria, F. Romani (1816), Lisbon, private theater of Barone di Quintella at Larajeiras, 3 December 1827.
Adriano in Siria, A. Profumo (after Metastasio), Lisbon, San Carlos, 24 February 1828.

Gabriella di Vergy, A. Profumo (after Tottola), Lisbon, San Carlos, 8 August 1828; revised E. Bidera, Genoa, 16 June 1832.
La rappresaglia, F. Romani, Cádiz, Principal, March 1829.
Le nozze di Gamaccio, Cádiz, Principal, winter 1830.
Francesca da Rimini, F. Romani, 1830?.
Zaira, F. Romani, Naples, San Carlo, 31 August 1831.
I normanni a Parigi, F. Romani, Turin, Regio, 7 February 1832.
Ismalia, ossia Amore e morte, F. Romani, Milan, Teatro alla Scala, 27 October 1832.
Il conte di Essex F. Romani, Milan, Teatro alla Scala, 10 March 1833.
Emma d' Antiocchia, F. Romani, Venice, La Fenice, 8 March 1834.
Uggero il danese, F. Romani, Bergamo, Riccardi, 11 August 1834.
La gioventù di Enrico V, F. Romani (after Shakespeare), Milan Teatro alla Scala, 25 November 1834.
I due Figaro, F. Romani (after Martelly), c. 1827-29, Madrid, Principe, 26 January 1835.
Francesca Donato, ossia Corinto distrutta, F. Romani (after Byron), Turin, Regio, 14 February 1835; revised S. Cammarano, Naples, San Carlo, 5 January 1845.
I briganti, J. Crescini (after Schiller, *Die Räuber*), Paris, Théâtre-Italien, 22 March 1836.
Il giuramento, G. Rossi (after V. Hugo, *Angelo*), Milan, Teatro alla Scala, 11 March 1837.
Le due illustri rivali, G. Rossi, Venice, La Fenice, 10 March 1838.
Elena da Feltre, S. Cammarano, Naples, San Carlo, 26 December 1838.
Il bravo (La veneziana), G. Rossi and M. Marcello (after Cooper), Milan, Teatro alla Scala, 9 March 1839.
La vestale, S. Cammarano, Naples, San Carlo, 10 March 1840.
La solitaria delle Asturie, ossia La Spagna ricupertata, F. Romani, Venice, La Fenice, 12 March 1840.
Il proscritto, S. Cammarano (after F. Soulié), Naples, San Carlo, 4 January 1842.
Il reggente, S. Cammarano (after Eugène Scribe, *Gustav III*), Turin, Regio, 2 February 1843; revised Trieste, 11 November 1843.
Leonora, M. D'Arienzo, Naples, Nuovo, 5 December 1844.
Il Vascello de Gama, S. Cammarano, Naples, San Carlo, 6 March 1845.
Orazi e Curiazi, S. Cammarano, Naples, San Carlo, 10 November 1846.
La schiava saracena, ovvero il campo di Gerosolima (Il campo de' crociati), F.M. Piave, Milan, Teatro alla Scala, 26 December 1848; revised? Naples, San Carlo, 29 October 1850.
Medea, S. Cammarano (after F. Romani [1813]), Naples, San Carlo, 1 March 1851.
Statira, D. Bolognese (after Voltaire, *Olimpie*), Naples, San Carlo, 8 January 1853.
Violetta, M. D'Arienzo, Naples, Nuovo, 10 January 1853.
Pelagio, M. D'Arienzo, Naples, San Carlo, 12 February 1857.
Virginia, S. Cammarano (after Alfieri), early 1850s, Naples, San Carlo, 7 April 1866.
L'orfano di Brono, ossia Caterina dei Medici, S. Cammarano [unfinished].
Giovanna I [unfinished].

Other works: ballets, sacred choral works, cantatas with orchestra, orchestral works, chamber music, chamber vocal works.

Publications

About MERCADANTE: books—

Neumann, W. *Saverio Mercadante.* Kassel, 1855.

Colucci, R. *Biografia di Saverio Mercadante.* Venice, 1867.

Pomè, A. *Saggio critico sull' opera musicale di S. Mercadante.* Turin, 1925.

Pannain, G. "Saggio su la musica a Napoli nel sec. XIX da Mercadante a Martucci." *Rivista musicale italiana,* 35 (1928): 198, 331; revised and abridged as "Saverio Mercadante," in *Ottocento musicale italiano,* 114, Milan, 1952.

Napoli, G. de. *La triade melodrammatica altamurana: Giacomo Tritto. Vincenzo Lavigna. Saverio Mercadante* [67ff]. Milan, 1931.

Comitato "Pro Mercadante" di Altamura. *Saverio Mercadante, note e documenti.* Bari, 1945.

Schlitzer, F. *Mercadante e Cammarano.* Bari, 1945.

Notarnicola, Biagio. *Saverio Mercadante: biografia critica.* Rome, 1945; 2nd ed, 1948 as *Saverio Mercadante nella gloria e nella luce.*

Sardone, A.R. *Mercadante, le due patrie e "La gran madre Italia".* Naples, 1954.

Notarnicola, Biagio. *Verdi non ha vinto Mercadante.* Rome, 1955.

Kaufman, Tom. *Verdi and his Major Contemporaries. Annals of Opera,* vol. 1, New York, 1990.

articles—

Florimo, F. "Saverio Mercadante." In *Cenno storico sulla scuola musicale di Napoli.* Naples, 1869-71; 2nd ed. 1880-83; 1969.

Bustico, G. "Saverio Mercadante a Novara." *Revista musicale italiana* 28 (1921): 361.

Walker, Frank. "Mercadante and Verdi." *Music and Letters* 33 (1952): 311; 34 (1953): 33.

Roncaglia, G. "Il giuramento." *La Scala* 61 (1954).

d'Amico, F. "Il Ballo in Maschera prima di Verdi." *Verdi: bollettino dell' Istituto di studi verdiani* 1/no. 3 (1960): 1251.

Lippman,, F. "Vincenzo Bellini, und die italienische Opera Seria seiner Zeit." *Analecta musicologica* 6 (1969): 328.

Ballola, G. Carli. "Incontro con Mercadante." *Chigiana* 26-27 (1969-70): 465.

———. "Le due illustri rivali: un positivo ricupero di valori musicali." *Teatro la Fenice* December 3 (1970).

Rinaldi, M. "Significato di Mercadante." In *Ritratti e fantasie musicali.* Rome, 1970.

Ballola, G. Carli. "Mercadante e *Il bravo.*" In *Il melodramma italiano dell' ottocento; studi e ricerche per Massimo Mila.* Turin, 1977.

Jackson, Roland. "Mercadante Resumé of Opera Reform." In *"Ars musica, musica scientia." Festschrift Heinrich Hüschen zum fünfundsechzigsten Geburtstag am 2. März 1980,* edited by Detlef Altenburg, 271. Cologne, 1980.

Mioli, Piero. "Tradizione melodrammatica e crisi dei forma nelle *Due illustri rivali* di Saverio Mercadante." *Studi musicale* 9 (1980): 317.

Van, Gilles de. "Le travail du livret," "Les bals masqués." *Arc* 81 (1981).

*　　*　　*

Mercadante had a long career, which began while Rossini was already in his glory, and ended only shortly before Verdi's *Aida.* During this period, Mercadante had the poor fortune of almost always being in the shadow of his contemporaries, but for a brief period in the late 1830s and early 1840s when Donizetti was composing primarily for Paris and Vienna, and before Verdi came into prominence. Mercadante made his greatest contribution both to the musical splendors of Italian opera and to its development. While composing *Elena da Feltre,* and about a year after *Il giuramento,* Mercadante wrote an often quoted letter to Florimo in which he discusses his reforms. No evaluation of Mercadante would be complete without it, so it is provided here again: "I have continued the revolution begun with *Il giuramento*—varied the forms, abolished trivial cabalettas, exiled the crescendos; concision, less repetition; some novelty in the cadences; due regard paid to the dramatic side, the orchestration rich without swamping the voices; long solos in the concerted numbers avoided, as they obliged the dramatic parts to stand coldly by, to the harm of the dramatic action, not much big drum, and very little brass band."

Il giuramento is generally regarded as Mercadante's best and most successful opera. Its plot is derived from the same source as Ponchielli's *La gioconda.* Instead of ending with the usual solo scene for soprano, as is typical of bel canto operas, the finale and dramatic climax of *Il giuramento* is a violent confrontation between Elaisa (La gioconda) and Viscardo (Enzo) which ends with his killing her. The scene employs the greatest degree of dramatic intensity seen in Italian opera so far, and was undoubtedly strongly influenced by the composer's familiarity with Meyerbeer's *Les Huguenots,* gained while he was in Paris. Even more important, by depriving the prima donna, or some other star singer, of her until then inalienable right to have the stage to herself at the end, Mercadante sounded what was to be the death knell of the age of bel canto. Of course, many later works were still to display characteristics of bel canto and some highly successful operas such as Pacini's *Saffo* were, in some ways, a throwback to this earlier era, but the pendulum had begun to swing and with some exceptions the prima donna and her final rondo were to become less and less important.

The opening scene of *Il giuramento* is almost as interesting as its finale and can be cited as another example of the composer's experimentation with form. Manfredo is in love with Elaisa, who loves Viscardo. Viscardo, in turn, loves but has lost Bianca, little knowing that she is Manfredo's wife. Knights and ladies sing a chorus in praise of Elaisa. Viscardo sings a brief cavatina in which he pines for Bianca, which is then followed by a few bars for the chorus. Manfredo enters, singing another cavatina in which he expresses his fear that Elaisa may be betraying him. The scene is concluded by a repeat of a fragment of the opening chorus. This is a notable example of combining what would normally have been several separate numbers into a continuous whole, and was a device that Mercadante used again in *Il bravo* and several subsequent works.

The second of his reform operas, *Le due illustri rivali* (Venice, 1838) had a good initial run and was sufficiently liked to be repeated the following season. It was selected by the management of Teatro la Fenice to be revived to mark the 100th centenary of the composer's death: unfortunately, the poor cast did not do it justice and the revival failed. It is an unusually intimate work for the period, intimate and lyrical rather than dramatic. A tenor aria in act II, "Qual celeste tuo sembiante," was frequently sung by Mario in concert and even inserted by some singers in act II of *Lucrezia Borgia.* It is an unusually melancholy piece, similar in its general atmosphere to "Quando le sere al placido" in *Luisa Miller.*

Patric Schmid, writing in *Opera,* has this to say about the third of these works, *Elena da Feltre,* excerpts from which were broadcast by Italian radio in 1971.

A work of harmonic daring, subtly and originally orchestrated, it suddenly makes sense of oft quoted comparisons between Mercadante and Verdi. It has the overall coherence one looks for and finds in middle and late Verdi—a surprising anticipation, for *Elena da Feltre* dates from 1838, the year before Verdi's first opera.

The next opera, *Il bravo* (Milan, 1839), shows the French influence more than any other Italian work of the period. All that is lacking to have made it virtually the only French grand opera in Italian is a lengthy, formal ballet and two extra acts. Everything else is there: a grandiose procession and march, a huge party, an arson scene (foreshadowings of *Le prophète*), a benediction, a malediction, assassinations and a night watchman's chorus. The latter is particularly interesting since it so effectively depicts Venice as a police state. The chorus plays an unusually important role, and, as was customary in French grand opera, it takes part in the action rather than commenting on it. Another typically French touch is the insertion of an aria for Violetta as a bridge passage, not between Foscari's act I cavatina and cabaletta as in Donizetti, but between the first and second halves of the cabaletta.

Il bravo was the fourth of Mercadante's reform operas and the fourth work to have an atmosphere of its own: the underlying tension of *Il giuramento,* the intimacy of *Le due illustri rivali,* the gothic cruelty of *Elena da Feltre* and the Venetian grandeur of *Il bravo.*

By early 1840, Mercadante's career was thriving as it never had before. He was out of the shadow of his contemporaries, his works were being performed all over Italy and the world, and he had the most important musical position in his homeland. It is therefore not surprising that he experimented more than ever in *La vestale,* and wrote an opera with only three arias (none for the two principals) and one cabaletta. Considering the total absence of an aria for the prima donna, the most amazing thing about *La vestale* is its tremendous success, and the fact that it remained in the repertory for close to 25 years.

Other Mercadante works worth mentioning include *Il reg' gente* (Turin, 1843), which follows the same plot as Verdi's *Un ballo in maschera; Leonora* (Naples 1844), the most frequently performed of his later operas with close to 100 productions; *Orazi e Curiazi* (Naples 1846); and *Virginia* (Naples 1866, although composed around 1851). While Mercadante no longer adhered as strictly to his reforms in these operas as he had earlier, his emphasis on the dramatic seems even greater than before. *Orazi e Curiazi* has confrontations reaching feverish intensity between Curiazio and Orazio, and then between Orazio and his sister, while *Virginia* has one between the heroine and her father. The latter work also has a striking wedding procession, notable for its underlying, almost frightening feeling of tension.

If Mercadante was less successful than his contemporaries, the probable reason is that he was not quite their equal as a melodist, but there can be little doubt that Mercadante wrote the most dramatic music in Italian opera before Verdi's middle period.

—Tom Kaufman

THE MERCY OF TITUS
See LA CLEMENZA DI TITO

MERRILL, Robert.

Baritone. Born 4 June 1917, in Brooklyn. Married: Roberta Peters (divorced). Studied with his mother Lillian Miller Merril and with Samuel Margolis and Angelo Conarutto; debut as Amonasro, Trenton, 1944; Metropolitan Opera debut as Germont, 1945, and appeared there for thirty seasons; appeared in San Francisco, 1957; in Chicago, 1960; appeared in Venice as Germont, 1961; Covent Garden debut in same role, 1967.

Publications

By MERRILL: books–

Once More from the Beginning. New York, 1965.
Between the Acts: an Irreverant Look at Opera and Other Madness. New York, 1977.

*   *   *

Gifted with a powerful, resonant and biting voice, Robert Merrill frequently sang as if by rote, failing to communicate rhythmic pulse, much less musical ebb and flow, or feeling for drama in music. For him the basic unit of utterance was the note, not the phrase. The notes themselves stayed more or less at the same volume and thus lacked dynamic direction. As a result he couldn't prepare emphases with crescendos. This, combined with his tendency to treat legato passages as if they were declamation and to substitute bluster and cliched snarls for emotional substance, caused much of the music he sang to sound jagged. Nevertheless, his legato was excellent, for he was able to join notes together seamlessly (unlike many Americans who habitually disrupt legato passages with sudden, quick diminuendos before the consonants d and t).

On records from the forties and early fifties Merrill often sings marginally under pitch and, in Italian arias he is boring. In "Cortigiani," whenever he musters some feeling, as at the words "Marullo, signore," he fails to sustain it. Elsewhere, he has episodes where he interprets or is animated—but they usually don't last. A notable exception is Thaïs's death scene, with Dorothy Kirsten, recorded in 1947, where he sings with passion. Merrill's most successful early recordings are of light songs in English, in which he sounds fully at home with words and music. His best, "The Green Eyed Dragon," was made around 1949 (but it pales in comparison with John Charles Thomas's rendition). When Merrill does vary his sound here, as in another song, "Shadrack," it is with inflections seemingly borrowed from Lawrence Tibbett. Merrill recorded a number of duets with Jussi Björling—and it is to Björling that you end up paying attention.

By 1963, when Merrill recorded Ford's monolog from *Falstaff,* the voice had become bass tinged to the point that it was a dramatic baritone, suitable for heavy Verdi roles. By then, too, he had stopped sounding like an outsider to Italian opera and was not only vocally but also emotionally powerful throughout such selections as "Urna fatale."

As an actor on stage Merrill was wooden and lacked spontaneity. As the Toreador he had no pizzazz. As an actor with the voice, even at his best he didn't have Leonard Warren's or Giuseppe De Luca's ability to underscore the meaning of words, while as a vocal personality he lacked the latter's warmth and humanity. Merrill's diction was better than Warren's, who, however, had a beautiful pianissimo.

What enabled Merrill to become—and remain—a star? Particularly in the middle voice he had an imposing sound uncharacteristic of American baritones. Performing light music in concert and on radio, television and film made him famous throughout the U.S. (although he never achieved international stardom).

Merrill's opera career was based at the Met, where loudness counts for much. In the fifties he was in Warren's shadow. By the early seventies Sherrill Milnes got most of the great assignments. Merrill was, however, the leading American baritone of the sixties.

—Stefan Zucker

MERRIMAN, Nan [born Katherine-Ann Merriman].

Mezzo-soprano. Born 28 April 1920, in Pittsburgh. Studied with Alexia Bassian in Los Angeles; opera debut as La Cieca in *La Gioconda*, Cincinnati Summer Opera, 1942; sang often on Toscanini's National Broadcasting Company Symphony broadcasts; sang Dorabella in *Così fan tutte* at Aix-en-Provence, 1953; sang at Piccolo Scala, 1955-56; appeared at Glyndebourne, 1956; retired in 1965.

*   *   *

The inclusion of Nan Merriman in a dictionary of opera might at first seem difficult to justify. Her operatic career was confined to a small number of roles (many of them supporting parts) performed in a very few places. Although she appeared quite extensively as a concert and recital artist, Merriman is today much less well known than many of her contemporaries. In fact, we might reasonably if regrettably expect that many younger readers of this volume will not have heard of her.

Yet if excellence is its own justification for inclusion, Nan Merriman unquestionably belongs here. Her lush mezzo-soprano, instantly recognizable for its warm, characterful use of vibrato, was one of the finest of her generation. She brought to all of her operatic roles—small ones like Emilia in *Otello* or substantial ones like Meg Page—the same care and insight, the same unassuming sense of serving her art. In this she is very reminiscent of Kathleen Ferrier, and also of several other American singers—Eleanor Steber, Blanche Thebom, Risë Stevens—who made no pretentious distinctions between serious and popular music, interpreting all with equal aplomb. When we encounter Nan Merriman on records today it is always with real pleasure—and also with a constant sense of surprise that she is not more famous.

If she is not famous in the usual sense, however, Merriman is far from unknown, and is much appreciated by a small but knowledgeable circle of listeners; she is very much the connoisseur's singer. Two recitals of French and Spanish songs produced by Walter Legge were, for many years, among the most highly prized collectors' items in the EMI catalogue—and quite rightly too, for the singing is some of the loveliest and most stylish on records. Her recordings of the contralto solos in Mahler's *Das Lied von der Erde* may be played alongside the legendary ones by Ferrier with no apology. A few early 78 records of American show tunes by Vincent Youmans and excerpts from *Carousel* are marvelously idiomatic—and surely the songs have never been sung by a more gorgeous voice!

Although her operatic repertoire was small, we are fortunate that Merriman recorded most of her major roles. She was particularly well-known as Dorabella in *Così fan tutte*, which she recorded twice; in both performances there is a splendid richness of tone, a real flair for comedy, and the vibrato is used to bewitching effect in characterizing this chimerical, utterly feminine, creature. Merriman brings these same virtues to her delightful performances of Meg Page in *Falstaff.* As Gluck's Orfeo, the demands are very different, and she meets these also with assurance. In broadcast transcriptions of act II of *Orfeo ed Eurydice* under Arturo Toscanini, Merriman copes regally with the arching phrases and exhibits an admirable sense of restraint; the characteristic vibrato is lighter, no longer particularly feminine, and is now used as a coloristic device to create real pathos. It is a pity that she never recorded the complete role.

Merriman chose to leave the stage in 1965. Ever the modest artist, she closed the door far too early, for although at that time she had been performing publicly for a quarter of a century, she was just forty-five years old and still at the height of her powers. Her farewell performance with the Concertgebouw Orchestra included a fair sampling of some of the music with which she was closely associated—Mahler's "Lieder Eines Fahrenden Gesellen." It also included arias from Mozart's *La clemenza di Tito* and Tchaikovsky's *Jeanne d'Arc,* offering us a tantalizing glimpse of what might have been. Surely, had she so chosen, Merriman could have performed more opera. In particular, with her fluent, elegant French, what a Dalila she might have been, or Carmen or any number of other opera roles left untouched. Still there is much cause to rejoice, for in her unostentatious way, Nan Merriman remains one of the most completely satisfying singers of her time.

—David Anthony Fox

THE MERRY WIVES OF WINDSOR
See DIE LUSTIGEN WEIBER VON WINDSOR

MESSIAEN, Olivier.

Composer. Born 10 December 1908, in Avignon. Died 28 April 1992, in Paris. Married: 1) the violinist Claire Delbos (died 1959), 1936 (one son); 2) the pianist Yvonne Loriod, 1962. Studied organ, improvisation, and composition with Jean and Noël Gallon, Marcel Dupré, Maurice Emmanuel, and Paul Dukas at the Paris Conservatory, 1919-30; organist at Trinity church in Montmartre, Paris, 1930; teacher at the Ecole Normale de Musique and at the Schola Cantorum, 1930; also organized a group with André Jolivet, Ives Baudrier, and Daniel-Lesur called La Jeune France, 1936; in the French army, 1939; taken prisoner, and spent two years in a German prison camp in Görlitz, Silesia, where he composed his *Quatuor pour la fin du temps (Quartet for the End of Time);* returned to France, 1942, and reassumed his position as organist at Trinity; on the faculty of the Paris Conservatory; taught at the Berkshire Music Center in Tanglewood, 1948, and at Darmstadt, 1950-53. Messiaen is a Grand Officier de la Légion d'Honneur, a member of the Institut de France, the Bavarian Academy of the Fine Arts, the Santa Cecilia Academy in Rome, and the American Academy of Arts and Letters. Messiaen's pupils include Boulez, Martinet, Stockhausen, and Xenakis.

Operas

Publishers: Leduc, Durand.

St François d'Assise, Messiaen (after the anonymous 14th century *Fioreti* and *Contemplations of the Stigmata*), 1975-1983, Paris, Opéra, 28 November 1983.

Other works: orchestral works, choral and solo vocal works, piano pieces, organ works, works for instruments and tape.

Publications

By MESSIAEN· books–

Messiaen, et al. *Vingt leçons de solfège moderne.* Paris, 1933.
Vingt leçons d' harmonie. Paris, 1939.
Technique de mon langage musical. Paris, 1944; English translation, 1957.
Conference de Bruxelles. Paris, 1958.

articles–

"Ariane et Barbe-bleue de Paul Dukas." *La revue musicale* no. 166 (1936).
"Le rythme chez Strawinsky." *La revue musicale* no. 191 (1939): 331.
Preface to A. Jolivet. *Mana.* Paris, 1946.
"Maurice Emmanuel: ses 30 chansons bourguignonnes." *La revue musicale* no. 206 (1947).
Preface to Roustit, A. *La prophétie musicale dans l'histoire de l'humanité précédée d'une étude sur les nombres et les planètes dans leur rapports avec la musique.* Roanne, 1970.
Forword to Artaud, Pierre-Yves, and Gérard Geay. *Flûtes au présent.* Paris, 1980.
"Tribute" [to Iannis Xenakis]. In *Regards sur Iannis Xenakis,* edited by Hugues Gerhards. Paris, 1981.

About MESSIAEN: books–

Samuel, Claude. *Entretiens avec Olivier Messiaen.* Paris, 1967; English translation as *Conversations with Olivier Messiaen,* London, 1976.
Sherlaw-Johnson, Robert. *Messiaen.* London, 1974; 1989.
Nichols, Roger. *Messiaen.* Oxford, 1975; 1986.
Perier, A. *Messiaen.* Paris, 1979.
Halbreich, H. *Olivier Messiaen.* Paris, 1980.
Kaczynski, Tadeusz. *Messiaen.* Cracow, 1984.
Griffiths, Paul. *Olivier Messiaen and the Music of Time.* London, 1985.

articles–

Musik-Konzepte 28 (1982) [Messiaen issue].
Kaczynski, Tadeusz. "Messiaen o swojej operze" [on *St François*]. *Ruch Muzyczny* 3/no. 3 (1984): 13.

Messiaen was strongly influenced in his upbringing by the literary background of his parents. His mother was a poet (Messiaen was later to set some of her poetry to music) and his father translated the whole of Shakespeare into French. During his formative years, he obtained the scores of a variety of operas, including Debussy's *Pelléas et Mélisande.* Although, no doubt because of these early influences, there is a strong sense of theater running through much of his music, it was not until 1975 that he commenced work on his only stage work, the opera *St François d'Assise.* He entered the National Conservatoire de la Musique in Paris in 1919 to study a wide range of subjects: piano, organ, composition, harmony, history of music and percussion. Although he no doubt received some stimulus from the French organ school of composers, his own work for organ followed a very individual path and ultimately was to form only a small (and not the most important) part of his total output. He left the Conservatory in 1930, and was appointed organist at the church of the Sainte Trinité, Montmartre in 1931, a post which he still holds.

From the time of Messiaen's earliest compositions, one of the most important features of his music has been a highly developed sense of correlation between color and musical sound. Others have often claimed a rather simplistic relationship between color and specific keys, or even individual pitches, but with Messiaen, the phenomenon is much more complex. He rarely speaks of individual colors in connection with passages in his music; rather, whole combinations of colors set up by modal, harmonic, timbral and even rhythmic factors are present in his music. Connected with the sense of color in music is his predilection for his *Modes of Limited Transposition.* These are artificial modes of his own invention, from which he derives characteristic streams of harmonies or "color chords." A particular feature of his early work, Messiaen became less dependent on these modes as his musical language developed.

An equally important, but slightly less all-pervading influence on Messiaen's music is his own religious convictions. It might seem odd that, as a Catholic, he has published no works for liturgical use other than the short motet, *O Sacrum Convivium!.* He has preferred to write works of a meditative nature either for the organ, for use during services, or for the concert hall. It has been his aim in these works to express, as he puts it, theological truths, rather than to write mystical works (although he occasionally borders on mysticism in some movements). Because of their ritual nature, some works, such as *Trois petites liturgies de la présence divine,* approach a liturgical act within the context of the concert hall.

Also dating from his student days is his interest in exotic rhythm. His teachers at the Conservatory had stimulated his interest in Greek rhythms, an interest which he extended himself to Indian rhythms on his discovery of the table of deçi-tâlas published in Lavignac's *Encyclopédie de la Musique et Dictionnaire de la Conservatoire,* published in 1924 by Delagrave. Although he did not apply these rhythms to his own music until *La Nativité du Seigneur* for organ (written in 1935), the principles involved had a profound influence on the rhythmic shape of his music from that time onwards. Also dating from his student days was his interest in birdsong and his first attempts at notating it. In his early works there are occasional references to *style oiseaux,* but it was not until 1940 in *Quatuor pour la fin du temps* that he actually names birdsongs in the score. From that time on, birdsong plays an increasingly important role in his music, culminating in 1953 with *Réveil des oiseaux* for piano and orchestra, which is based entirely on birdsong. Birdsong subsequently remained a prominent feature of his music, and in 1958 he completed one of his most important piano works, *Catalogue d'oiseaux.* Prior to the composition of this work, he visited various parts of France, collecting birdsong. The work is in the nature of a documentary, painting a picture of specific regions and particular birds associated with those regions.

From his first published work in 1928 until 1956, Messiaen's musical language shows changes of emphasis from an early style, which is heavily based on the modes of limited transposition and Greek meters, through the incorporation of Indian rhythms into his music from 1935, to the crowning and most rhythmically complex work of this period, the *Turangalîla-symphonie* (1946-48). Following this, he experimented with serial methods involving the serialization of duration, intensity and timbre as well as pitch, but turned to works relying mainly on birdsong for their material from 1953. In *Catalogue d'oiseaux* and subsequent works, especially from the oratorio *La Transfiguration de Notre Seigneur Jésus-Christ* (1963-69), he returns, in part, to an earlier musical language involving the modes of limited transposition and Indian and Greek rhythms. This does not represent a return, however, to an earlier style, but a more integrated musical language, drawing from all periods of his working career.

A distinctly theatrical element is discernible in many of his larger works, such as the *Turangalîla-symphonie.* This is the central work in a trilogy in which he turns away from specifically Christian symbols to those of Hindu, Inca and Peruvian religions. He also draws on the Celtic myth of Tristan and Isolde, to exploit the same symbolism of the love-death which is the basis of Wagner's music-drama. In this work, the music is imbued with a sense of theatrical ritual which renders it complete in itself, without the need for a visual element. It is important to the surrealistic nature of the work and the experience which it arouses that the concepts behind such movements as the sixth, *Jardin du sommeil d'amour* and the seventh, *Turangalîla II,* should remain in the imagination of the listener. In the first of these we are asked to imagine the lovers sleeping in a garden full of exotic flowers, and the second is associated with pain and death as exemplified in Edgar Allan Poe's *The Pit and the Pendulum.* Even if it were feasible to represent these extra-musical elements theatrically, it would not add to, and might even detract from the music. As the imagination is often an important factor in listening to Messiaen's music, it is not surprising that it took him so long, and even then unwillingly, to embark on an actual opera, and that visually the result should consist of a series

of static tableaux rather than a dynamically developing drama which we would normally associate with the medium.

—Robert Sherlaw-Johnson

METASTASIO, Pietro (Antonio Domenico Bonaventura Trapassi)

Librettist/Poet. Born 3 January 1698, in Rome. Died 12 April 1782, in Vienna. Adopted by Gian Vincenzo Gravina; studied music with Porpora; wedding serenatas and other occasional pieces for the Neapolitan aristocracy; first opera libretto, 1723; lived in Rome and Venice, 1724-30; appointed court poet at Vienna (succeeding Zeno) by Emperor Charles VI, 1729.

Librettos

Note: only initial settings are listed.

Silface re di Numidia (after D. David, *La forza del virtù*), F. Feo, 1723.
Didone abbandonata, D. Sarro, 1724; revised, 1751.
Siroe re di Persia, L. Vinci, 1726.
Catone in Utica, L. Vinci, 1728; revised, 1729.
Ezio, N.A. Porpora, 1728.
Semiramide [Semiramide rinconosciuta]. L. Vinci, 1729; revised, 1752-53.
Alessandro nell' Indie L. Vinci, 1729; revised 1753-54.
Artaserse, L. Vinci, 1730, and J.A. Hasse, 1730.
Demetrio, A. Caldara, 1731.
Issipile, F. Conti, 1732.
Adriano in Siria, A. Caldara, 1732; revised, 1752-53.
Olimpiade, A. Caldara, 1733.
Demofoonte, A. Caldara, 1733.
La clemenza di Tito, A. Caldara, 1734.
Achille in Sciro, A. Caldara, 1736.
Ciro riconosciuto, A. Caldara, 1736.
Temistocle, A. Caldara, 1736.
Zenobia, L.A. Predieri, 1740.
Antigono, J.A. Hasse, 1743.
Ipermestra, J.A. Hasse, 1744.
Attilio Regolo (1740) J.A. Hasse, 1750.
Il re pastore, G. Bonno, 1751.
L'eroe cinese, G. Bonno, 1752.
La Nitteti, N. Conforto, 1756.
Il trionfo di Clelia, J.A. Hasse, 1762.
Romolo ed Ersilia, J.A. Hasse, 1765.
Ruggiero ovvero l'eroica gratitudine, J.A. Hasse, 1771.

Publications

By METASTASIO: books–

Brunelli, Bruno, ed. *Tutti le opere di Pietro Metastasio.* 5 vols. Milan, 1947-54.
Fubini, M., ed. *Pietro Metastasio: Opere.* Milan and Naples, 1968.
Gavazenni, F., ed. *Opere scelte di Pietro Metastasio.* Turin, 1978.

About METASTASIO: books–

Mattei, S. *Memorie per servire alla vita di Metastasio.* Colle, 1785.

Burney, C. *Memoires of the Life and Writings of the Abate Metastasio.* London, 1796; 1971.

Wotquenne, A. *Zeno, Metastasio et Goldoni. Table alphabétique des morceaux mesurés contenus dans leurs oeuvres dramatiques.* Leipzig, 1905.

Russo, L. *Pietro Metastasio.* Pisa, 1915; 2nd ed., 1921; 1945.

Della Corte, A. *L'estetica musicale di Pietro Metastasio.* Turin, 1922.

Giazotto, R. *Poesia melodrammatica e pensiero critico nel settecento.* Milan, 1952.

Binni, W. *L'Arcadia e Metastasio.* Florence, 1963.

Astaldi, M.L. *Metastasio.* Milano, 1979.

Metastasio e il mondo musicale. Atti del convegno. Venezio, 1982.

Metastasio e il melodramma. Atti del convegno. Cagliari, 1982.

Sala di Felice, E. *Metastasio: ideologia, drammaturgia, spettacolo.* Milan, 1983.

Teatro, pubblico e melodramma a Roma all' epoca di Metastasio [exhibition catalogue]. Rome, 1983.

Folena, G. *L'italiano in Europa. Esperienze linguistiche del Settecento.* Turin, 1983.

Lühning, H. *"Titus"-Vertonungen im 18. Jahrhundert. Analecta Musicologica,* vol. 20. Laaber, 1983.

Maragoni, G.P. *Metastasio e la tragedia.* Rome, 1984.

Gallarati, P. *Musica e maschera. Il libretto italiano del settecento.* Turin, 1984.

articles–

Calzabigi, R. de. "Dissertazione su le poesie drammatiche del Signor Abate Pietro Metastasio." In *Poesie del Signor Abate Pietro Metastasio,* vol. 1. Paris, 1755.

Cristini, C. "Vita dell'Abate Pietro Metastasio." In *Opere di Pietro Metastasio,* vol. 1. Nice, 1785.

Sanctis, F. de. "Pietro Metastasio." *Nuova antologia* 16 (1871): 807.

Baroni, J.M. "La lirica musicale di Pietro Metastasio." *Rivista musicale italiana* 12 (1905): 383.

Callegari, M. "Il melodramma e Pietro Metastasio." *Rivista musicale italiana* 26 (1919): 518; 27 (1920): 31, 458.

Corte, B.G. della. "Appunti sull'estetica musicale di Pietro Metastasio." *Rivista musicale italiana* 28 (1921).

Kunz, H. "Höfisches Theater in Wien zur Zeit der Maria Theresia." *Jahrbuch der Gesellschaft für Wiener Theaterforschung 1953-4* (1958): 3.

Binni, W. "Pietro Metastasio." In *Storia della letteratura italiana,* vol. 6, p. 461. Milan, 1968.

Gavazzeni, F. Introduction to *Opere scelte di Pietro Metastasio.* Turin, 1968.

Hortschansky, K. Introduction to *J.A. Hasse, "Ruggiero ovvero L'eroica gratitudine".* In *Concentus musicus,* vol. 1, p. ix. Cologne, 1973.

Paratore, E. "L' 'Andromaque' del Racine e la 'Didone abbandonata' del Metastasio." In *Scritti in onore di Luigi Ronga,* 515. Milan and Naples, 1973.

Heartz, D. "Hasse, Galuppi and Metastasio." In *Venezia e il melodramma nel settecento,* edited by M.T. Muraro, 309. Florence, 1978.

Monelle, R. "The Rehabilitation of Metastasio." *Music and Letters* 57 (1976): 268.

Lippmann, Friedrich. "Über Cimarosas *Opere serie.*" *Analecta Musicologica* 21 (1982): 21.

Neville, Don. "Moral Philosophy in the Metastasian Dramas." *Studies in Music* [Canada] 7 (1982): 28.

Pirrotta, N. "Metastasio and the Demands of his Literary Environment." *Studies in Music* [Canada] 7 (1982).

Robinson, Michael F. "The Ancient and the Modern: a Comparison of Metastasio and Calzabigi." *Studies in Music* [Canada] 7 (1982): 137.

Weiss, Piero. "Metastasio, Aristotle, and the *opera seria.*" *Journal of Musicology* 1 (1982): 385.

Cummings, Graham. "Reminiscence and Recall in Three Early Settings of Metastasio's *Alessandro nell' Indie* (1729)." *Proceedings of the Royal Musical Association* 109 (1982-83): 80.

Wiesend, R. "Metastasios Revisionen eigener Dramen und die Situation der Opernmusik in den 1750er Jahren." *Archiv für Musikwissenschaft* 40 (1983): 255.

Gronda, G. "Metastasiana." *Rivista italiana di musicologia* 19 (1984): 314.

Heartz, Daniel. "Farinelli and Metastasio: Rival Twins of Public Favour." *Early Music* 12 (1984): 358.

Pirrotta, N. "Metastasio e i teatri romani." In *Le Muse galanti. La musica a Roma nel settecento,* edited by B. Cagli. Rome, 1985.

Muraro, M.T., ed. *Metastasio e il mondo musicale.* Florence, 1986.

* * *

The rise of the Arcadian Academy in late seventeenth-century Italy was a direct answer to France's claim to inheritance of the poetic muse—passed to them, by their own report, as Italy

Pietro Metastasio, pastel portrait by Rosalba Carriera

wallowed in the sentimental age of Marinism. The Italian Arcadians sought to restore the luster of their poetry, and a profuse stream of didactic, polemical apologies flowed from such literati as Crescembeni, Muratori, and the most ascetic of all, Gian Vincenzo Gravina. To their view, the opera libretto *was* drama, but they criticized contemporary Italian efforts as decadent and capitulating to popular taste. This was the scene upon which the youth Antonio Trapassi entered. Gravina, having "discovered" the lad improvising poetry in Rome, adopted him, renamed him Pietro Metastasio, and saw him trained for law and classics, but upon Gravina's death in 1718 (and with the financial freedom this afforded his young ward), Metastasio returned to his best love, the poetry of the theater.

Metastasio's first tentative effort, a revision of D. David's *La forza del virtù,* was followed by a wholly original libretto, *Didone abbandonata* (an enormous success), for Rome in 1724 with music by Domenico Sarro. Over the next six years he provided Rome and Venice with a series of six more librettos, and his fame quickly surpassed even that of Zeno. For a time literary critics dared find no fault in him. In August of 1729 he accepted the position of court poet in Vienna and remained there for the rest of his life. Through the ensuing years, until the death of Charles VI in 1740, he provided operas and other theatrical poems for the court, most of which were first set to music by Antonio Caldara before the texts passed into the hands of virtually every important opera composer of the age. Upon Maria Theresia's rise to the throne, however, Metastasio saw his demand almost fully arrested; cost cutting and a low musical interest by the court were to blame.

Metastasio's twenty-seven three-act serious librettos *(opere serie)* and the other celebratory, occasional poems were set nearly 1,000 times before the century closed; but if revivals and pasticci are added, the figure is greatly magnified. His most popular librettos, such as *Artaserse,* were newly set over 100 times, and since many theaters pursued their libretto first and its music later, a single composer often set the same libretto several times for different theaters (though often maintaining some previous musical material). Metastasio is without peer in the history of Western opera in the sheer volume of operas set to his words.

While individual genre traditions of his librettos vary, the basic principles of his dramatic theory remain largely unchanged. In methodology he crystallized the Enlightenment philosophy of early eighteenth-century literature. The Metastasio libretto, particularly after his move to Vienna, is a type of laboratory, in which the virtues and vices of mankind are boiled up together. The characters of the drama do not represent individuals, in the way that was to fire the imagination of comic librettists of the later eighteenth century, but rather, as Calzabigi (Metastasio's contemporary) summarized, they represented either specific types of individuals or glorious examples of humanity. Into a single pot is thrown reason, virtue, and justice, along with such vices as unbridled passion, intemperance, and cruelty. These qualities are always presented in a lucid, unambiguous fashion. (Aminta, Licida's tutor in *L'Olimpiade,* for example, opens the opera by imploring Licida to "moderate this your violent, intolerant spirit"). Just as scientific observation leads to glorious discoveries, so the drama unveils the weaknesses and strengths of men and nature. In the end, of course, virtue inevitably triumphs; it is, after all, stronger. The popularly disparaged "lieto finale" is therefore a demonstration of dramatic logic, and not a mere capitulation to fashion. Metastasio viewed the *dramma per musica* (as his texts were called) as a school for the aristocracy, a model for the way in which monarchs ought to behave. In the same breath, as an employee for the court, he was responsible for its glorification and added *licenze* (epilogues) to tie noble attributes of the drama to the court.

Metastasio went to great lengths to defend his poetry against detractors and asserted that his dramas emulated Greek principles, as found in Aristotle and Homer. More pragmatically, however, many librettos were directly modeled on dramas of such French classicists as Moliere and Racine, whose ideas on Greek drama had been widely disseminated. Metastasio never apologized for allowing drama to fit the exigencies of a musical setting, alternating recitative and arias, etc., and actually found ways to defend that very structure: recitative represented dramatic speech, and the aria was like the Greek chorus. He followed contemporary notions and the demands of the public stage in providing "exit arias," alternation of aria types, two stanza arias (to accommodate the *da capo* format), etc., but despite these limitations he achieved a sympathetic and lyrical style that was itself frequently described as "musical" by his contemporaries. That Metastasio himself composed music surely contributed to this skill.

On the other hand Metastasio was not as dogmatic as some would suppose: his heroes and heroines did not always survive (see his early dramas *Didone abbandonata* and *Catone in Utica*), his oddly shaped arias were sometimes his most popular (e.g., "Se cerca, se dice," from *L'Olimpiade*), he sometimes experimented with new devices or genres (such as with the pastorale and the chorus), and his arias are at times actively dramatic. He was even willing to rewrite material to suit Farinelli's opera company in Madrid (whose voice and character he ardently admired).

Dozens of complete editions of Metastasio's poetry were published during his lifetime (the first authoritative edition by Bettinelli; the most widely quoted by Huirissant in Paris in 1780-82, which contained revisions of several dramas; the commonly accepted modern critical edition was edited by Brunelli), and he was everywhere praised. Still, aesthetics were changing, and the naturalism of Rousseau's France, along with the dramaturgy of the fluid and accessible *drammi giocosi* after 1750, led to constant emendations from without. His recitative was deemed too lengthy and was consistently cut (particularly in the third act); dramatic and emotive monologues, inserted as accompanied recitatives, increasingly appeared; new scenes were inserted; and by the 1790s often only the shell of Metastasio's poetry and plot remained—as Mazzola's Dresden-influenced reshaping of *Clemenza di Tito* for Mozart well demonstrates. Metastasio's verses continued to be set well into the nineteenth century.

—Dale E. Monson

MEYERBEER, Giacomo [born Jakob Liebmann Beer].

Composer. Born 5 September 1791, in Vogelsdorf, near Berlin. Died 2 May 1864, in Paris. Married: Minna Mosson, 25 May 1826 (two children who died in infancy). Studied piano with Lauska, and briefly with Clementi, who was a guest at his house in Berlin; studied theory with Zelter and Anselm Weber; studied with the Abbé Vogler (a fellow student was Carl Maria von Weber) at Darmstadt, 1810-12; opera productions in Munich, Stuttgart, and Vienna, 1812-14; opera productions in Venice, Padua, Turin, 1815-24; collaboration with

Eugène Scribe began, 1827; Chevalier of the Légion d'Honneur; member of the French Institut, 1834; Generalmusikdirektor to King Friedrich Wilhelm IV, Berlin, 1842; in England, 1862. Meyerbeer was friends with and was advised by Antonio Salieri, and assisted the young Wagner both artistically (he conducted the Berlin performances of *Rienzi*) and financially.

Operas

Jephtas Gelübde, Alois Schreiber, Munich, Court, 23 December 1812.

Wirth und Gast, oder Aus Scherz Ernst (Die beyden Kalifen, Alimelek), Johann Gottfried Wohlbrück, Stuttgart, 6 January 1813.

Das Brandenburger Tor, Emanuel Veith, written for Berlin, 1814 [not performed].

Romilda e Costanza, G. Rossi, Padua, Nuovo, 19 July 1817.

Semiramide riconosciuta, G. Rossi (after Metastasio), Turin, Regio, March 1819.

Emma di Resburgo (Emma di Leicester), G. Rossi, Venice, San Benedetto, 26 June 1819.

Margherita d'Anjou, Felice Romani (after René Charles Guilbert de Pixérécourt), Milan, Teatro alla Scala, 14 November 1820; revised Paris, 1826.

L'Almanzore, G. Rossi, intended for Rome, Torre Argentina, carnival 1821 [unfinished].

L'esule di Granata, Felice Romani, Milan, Teatro alla Scala, 12 March 1821.

Il crociato in Egitto, G. Rossi, Venice, La Fenice, 7 March 1824; revised Paris, 1826.

Robert le diable, Eugène Scribe and G. Delavigne, Paris, Opéra, 21 November 1831.

Les Huguenots, Eugène Scribe and Émile Deschamps, Paris, Opéra, 29 February 1836.

Ein Feldlager in Schlesien (Vielka), Eugène Scribe, Ludwig Rellstab, and C. Birch-Pfeiffer, Berlin, Court, 7 December 1844.

Le prophète, Eugène Scribe, Paris, Opéra, 16 April 1849.

L'étoile du nord, Eugène Scribe (partially after his ballet, *La cantinière*), Paris, Opéra-Comique, 16 February 1854; music based on *Ein Feldlager in Schlesien.*

Le pardon de Ploërmel (Le chercheur du trésor, Dinorah, oder Die Wallfahrt nach Ploërmel), Jules Barbier and Michel Carré, Paris, Opéra-Comique, 4 April 1859.

L'Africaine (Vasco de Gama), Eugène Scribe and F.J. Fétis, Paris, Opéra, 28 April 1865 [posthumous; final revisions by Fétis].

Other works: ballets, cantatas, incidental music, choral works, instrumental music, songs.

Publications/Writings

By MEYERBEER: books–

Becker, H., and G., eds. *Briefwechsel und Tagebücher.* 4 vols. Berlin, 1960-85.

———. *Giacomo Meyerbeer: Ein Leben in Briefen;* English translation as *Giacomo Meyerbeer: a Life in Letters,* London and Portland, Oregon, 1989.

About MEYERBEER: books–

Morel, A. *Le prophète: analyse critique de la nouvelle partition de Giacomo Meyerbeer.* Paris, 1849.

Lindner, E.O. *Meyerbeers "Prophet" als Kunstwerk beurtheilt.* Berlin, 1850.

Schladebach, J. *Meyerbeers Prophet (unter besonderer Berücksichtigung der Dresdener Aufführung.* Dresden, 1850.

Mirecourt, E. de. *Meyerbeer.* Paris, 1854.

Pougin, A. *Meyerbeer: notes biographiques.* Paris, 1864.

Blaze de Bury, H. *Meyerbeer et son temps.* Paris, 1865.

Mendel, H. *Giacomo Meyerbeer.* Berlin, 1868.

Schucht, J. *Meyerbeers Leben und Bildungsgang.* Leipzig, 1869.

Kohut, A. *Meyerbeer.* Leipzig, 1890.

Destranges, E. *L'oeuvre théâtral de Meyerbeer.* Paris, 1893.

Weber, J. *Meyerbeer.* Paris, 1898.

Curzon, H. de. *Meyerbeer.* Paris, 1910.

Eymieu, H. *L'oeuvre de Meyerbeer.* Paris, 1910.

Dauriac, L. *Meyerbeer.* Paris, 1913; 2nd ed., 1930.

Kapp, J. *Giacomo Meyerbeer.* Berlin, 8th ed., 1932.

Becker, H. *Der Fall Heine—Meyerbeer.* Berlin, 1958.

Frese, Christhard. *Dramaturgie der grossen Opern Giacomo Meyerbeers.* Berlin, 1970.

———. *Meyerbeer: Les Huguenots: Materialien zum Werk.* Leipzig, 1974.

Gossett, P. and C. Rosen, eds. *Early Romantic Opera,* vols. 18-25. New York, 1977.

Becker, H. *Giacomo Meyerbeer in Selbstzeugnissen und Bilddokumenten.* Reinbek, 1980.

Wessling, B.W. *Meyerbeer: Wagners Beute, Heines Geisel.* Dusseldorf, 1984.

Segalini, Sergio. *Diable ou prophète? Meyerbeer.* Paris, 1985.

Walter, Michael. *"Hugenotten"-Studien.* Frankfurt, 1987.

articles–

Tardel, H. "Die Sage von Robert dem Teufel in neueren deutschen Dichtungen und in Meyerbeers Oper." *Forschungen zur neueren Literaturgeschichte* 14 (1900).

Prod'homme, J.G. "Die Hugenotten-Premiere." *Die Musik* 3/no. 1 (1903-4): 187.

Bourgault-Ducoudray, L.A. "Meyerbeer: souvenirs d'autrefois." *Revue d'histoire et de critique musicales* 4 (1904): 452.

Brückner, F. "Meyerbeer en Allemagne." *Revue d'histoire et de critique musicales* 4 (1904): 455.

Combarieu, J. "Meyerbeer." *Revue d'histoire et de critique musicales* 4 (1904): 434.

Ettler, C. "Bibliographie des oeuvres de G. Meyerbeer." *Revue d'histoire et de critique musicales* 4 (1904): 436.

Kruse, G.R. "Meyerbeer's Jugendopern." *Zeitschrift für Musikwissenschaft* 1 (1918-19): 399.

Kapp, Julius. "Wagner-Meyerbeer: ein Stück Operngeschichte." *Die Musik* October (1923).

Brent Smith, A.E. "The Tragedy of Meyerbeer." *Music and Letters* 6 (1925): 248.

Istel, E. "Meyerbeer's Way to Mastership." *Musical Quarterly* 12 (1926): 72-109.

Servières, G. "Les transformations et tribulations de *L'africaine.*" *Rivista musicale italiana* 34 (1927): 80.

Abert, H. "Giacomo Meyerbeer." In *Gesammelte Schriften und Vorträge,* edited by F. Blume, 397. Halle, 1929.

Istel, E. "Act IV of *Les Huguenots.*" *Musical Quarterly* 22 (1936): 87.

Prod'homme, J.G. "Meyerbeer à Paris avant 'Robert le diable,' d'après son journal inédit." *Mercure de France* 14 April (1936): 275.

Becker, H. "Meyerbeers Ergänzungsarbeit an Webers nachgelassener Oper 'Die drei Pintos'." *Die Musikforschung* 7 (1954): 300.

Cooper, M. "Giacomo Meyerbeer." In *Fanfare for Ernest Newman,* 38. London, 1955.

Becker, H. "Meyerbeers Beziehungen zu Louis Spohr." *Die Musikforschung* 10 (1957): 479.

———. "Giacomo Meyerbeer." *Leo Baeck Institute: Yearbook* [London] 9 (1964): 178.

Brod, M. "Some Comments on the Relationship between Wagner and Meyerbeer." *Leo Baeck Institute: Yearbook* [London] 9 (1964).

Klein, J.W. "Giacomo Meyerbeer (1791-1864)." *Music Review* 25 (1964): 142.

Meyerowitz, J. "Giacomo Meyerbeer." *Musica* 19 (1965): 9.

Frederichs, H. "Das Rezitativ in den Hugenotten G. Meyerbeers." In *Beiträge zur Geschichte der Oper,* edited by H. Becker, 55. Regensburg, 1969.

Becker, H. "Giacomo Meyerbeers Mitarbeit an den Libretti seiner Opern." *Gesellschaft für Musikforschung Kongressbericht, Bonn 1970,* 155.

Kirchmeyer, H. "Ein Kapitel Meyerbeer." *Das zeitgenössische Wagner-Bild* 1 (1972): 51.

Döhring, S. "Les oeuvres tardives de Meyerbeer." *Studien zur Musikwissenschaft* 95 (1975): 57.

Loppert, M. "An Introduction to 'L'étoile du nord'." *Musical Times* 116 (1975): 130.

Thomson, J.L. "Giacomo Meyerbeer: the Jew and his Relationship with Richard Wagner." *Musica judaica* 1 (1975-76): 55.

Becker, H. "Die Couleur locale als Stilkategorie der Oper." In *Die Couleur locale in der Oper des 19. Jahrhunderts,* edited by H. Becker, 23. Regensburg, 1976.

Dahlhaus, Carl. "Motive der Meyerbeer-Kritik." *Jahrbuch des Staatlichen Institute für Musikforschung* (1979): 35.

Chabot, Carole. "Ballet in the Operas of Eugene Scribe: an Apology for the Presence of Dance in Opera." *Studies in Music* [Canada] 5 (1980): 7.

Dean, Winton. "Meyerbeer's Italian Operas." In *Music and Bibliography: Essays in Honour of Alec Hyatt King,* edited by Oliver Neighbor. London, 1980.

Join-Dieterle, C. "*Robert le diable:* Le premier opéra romantique." *Romantisme* (1980).

Becker, H. "'. . . Der Marcel von Meyerbeer.' Anmerkungen zur Entstehungsgeschichte der *Hugenotten.*" *Jahrbuch des Staatlichen Institut für Musikforschung* (1981): 79.

Fulcher, Jane. "Meyerbeer and the Music of Society." *Musical Quarterly* 67 (1981): 213.

Döhring, S. "Multimediale Tendenzen in der französischen Oper des 19. Jahrhunderts." In *International Musicological Society, Report of the Congress, Berkeley 1977,* edited by Daniel Heartz and Bonnie C. Wade, 497. Kassel, 1981.

———. "Die autographen der vier Hauptopern Meyerbeers. Ein erster Quellenbericht." *Archiv für Musikwissenschaft* 39 (1982): 32.

Walter, Michael. "'Man überlege sich nur alles, sehe, wo alles hinausläuft!' Zu Robert Schumanns *Hugenotten-Rezension.*" *Die Musikforschung* 36 (1983): 127.

Popíšil, Milan. "Der positive Beitrag der französischen *grand opéra* zur europäischen Opernentwicklung." In *Romantikkonferenz 2. 1982,* edited by Günther Stephan and Hans John, 78. Dresden, 1983.

Brzoska, Matthias. "*Majomet* et *Robert-le-diable:* L'esthétique musicale dans *Gambara.*" *Année balzacienne* (1983): 51.

Popíšil, Milan. "Dramatická úloha Meyerbeerovy harmonic." *Hudebni věda* 21 (1984): 323.

Döhring, S. "Giacomo Meyerbeer: Grand opéra jako drama ideji." *Hudebni věda* 21 (1984): 310.

Avant-scène opéra June (1985) [*Robert le diable* issue].

Dahlhaus, Carl. "Wagner, Meyerbeer, und der Fortschritt: Zur Opernästhetik des Vormärz." In *Festschrift für Rudolf Elvers zum 60. Geburtstag.* Tutzing, 1985.

Miller, Norbert. "Grosse Oper als Historiengemälde: Überlegungen zur Zusammenarbeit von Eugène Scribe und Giacomo Meyerbeer." In *Oper und Operntexte,* edited by Jens Malte Fischer. Heidelberg, 1985.

unpublished—

Haudek, R. "Scribes Operntexte für Meyerbeer: eine Quellenuntersuchung." Ph. D. dissertation, University of Vienna, 1928.

Roberts, John H. "The Genesis of Meyerbeer's *L'Africaine.*" Ph. D. dissertation, University of California, Berkeley, 1977.

Blessed with an independent income and a natural facility for both music and languages, Meyerbeer was, from the beginning, free to practice his art only when and wherever he chose. As a pupil of the Abbé Vogler in Darmstadt, and befriended by Vogler's most successful pupil, Carl Maria von Weber, Meyerbeer naturally gravitated to vocal music. Of his German student compositions, few have survived and none have been revived. Henri de Curzon describes them as overly complex, confused, and scholastic. Though the descriptions

Giacomo Meyerbeer

are abstract, they point to a natural tendency, even as a student, to impose on the vocal art a sophisticated orchestration, a trait which would distinguish his mature work.

A meeting with Antonio Salieri in Vienna led to Meyerbeer's departure for Italy, to study the methods of writing for the human voice. The immediate success of his operas written to Italian texts testifies to his ability to learn quickly, but the libretti to which he set his music did not overly please him. In an 1823 letter to the basso Prosper Levasseur, he expressed the wish to go to Paris; there alone did he feel he could find texts to satisfy his dramatic sensibilities.

In Italy, and later in Paris itself, he could not avoid comparison of his music with Rossini's. Certainly there is a formal similarity of approach, one he shares with his Italian contemporaries, but this is a matter of the style of the time, not of imitation. The Italian operas also reveal that Meyerbeer could write a fully-developed aria or ensemble, a fact that would always be evident in his French operas as well, despite criticism that he indulged in rhythmic complexity because he lacked the ability to develop a melody except at the most banal level.

His most popular Italian work, *Il crociato in Egitto,* has its Rossinian moments, notably the opening chorus and Armando's "Oh, come rapida," but also looks forward to the French operas, especially in his use of the brass band not only to accompany the crusaders into battle, but to replace the pit orchestra for a lyrical aria by Adriano.

In Paris a new spirit of historicism had begun to invade the dramatic arts. The success of Auber's *La muette de Portici* and Rossini's *Guillaume Tell* at the Opéra and the plays of Victor Hugo and Alexandre Dumas heralded a new approach to historical drama; romantic protagonists might remain in the persons of lovers, but the treatment of history as a complex web of sociopolitical forces rather than as a contrived excuse for a tragico-romantic denouement reflected a new, more realistic approach to drama, both legitimate and lyric.

Meyerbeer's arrival in Paris fortunately coincided with the ascendance of Eugene Scribe, librettist of *La muette de Portici,* as practitioner of the new romantic realism. Together they assembled what would become known as "grand opera." At its zenith, it consisted (almost always with variations, to be sure) of a love story set against a background of political and/or religious strife centered around a specific post-medieval historical event. The *mise-en-scène* sought to reflect the historical period and recognizable locales. At least one scene ought to provide a legitimate excuse for an extended ballet, usually but not exclusively in the third of five acts. The chorus played a prominent part in the drama, and original orchestral effects were looked forward to with as much anticipation as the contributions of the vocalists (this in spite of the myth that, like the Italian opera it replaced, grand opera displayed only spectacular vocalism and equally spectacular scenery). The ideal was that of a collaboration between composer, librettist, designer, conductor, chorus master and ballet master to produce a unified work, an ideal Richard Wagner would also embrace, with the one significant difference that he himself would be all the collaborators.

Meyerbeer and Scribe's first joint effort, *Robert le diable,* though it lacked historical specificity, combined the other elements of grand opera with an effectiveness and popularity which established its format as the measure for all subsequent works, a measure which stood for almost half a century in Paris. The excitement following *Robert*'s premiere has few parallels in music history; at the center lay Meyerbeer's score, whose originality and dramatic effectiveness Hector Berlioz both praised and emulated.

The most perfect (not necessarily the best) grand opera Meyerbeer composed was *Les Huguenots,* which portrayed the love of a Protestant nobleman for a Catholic lady-in-waiting on the eve of the infamous massacre of Huguenots by the Catholic nobility on St Bartholomew's Day, 1572. Meyerbeer displayed significant advances in his use of the chorus as protagonists representing the fanaticism of both religious camps, whereas in *Robert* the chorus had played a passive role as knights and ladies offering appropriate but anonymous commentary on the events of the plot. Also in *Les Huguenots,* the composer continues the move, begun in *Robert,* away from traditionally-constructed arias, replacing them with extended ariosos such as Raoul's "Plus blanche que la blanche herminée" and Nevers's "Noble dame." Meyerbeer includes a conventional aria/cabaletta (the queen's "O beau pays de la Touraine"), and a conventionally-constructed duet (such as that for the queen and Raoul), but prefers a more shifting structure, displaying a succession of themes. None of these themes is developed to the conventional extent; instead, they reflect subtle changes in the dynamics of the drama, as is the case in the long act III duet for Marcel and Valentine, and the justly-famous "Tu l'a dit" for Raoul and Valentine in act IV.

Following his return to Germany to compose the Singspiel *Ein Feldlager in Schlesien,* Meyerbeer returned to Paris to collaborate again with Scribe on *Le prophète.* In this opera, the obligatory love relationship (that of Jean for Berthe) is almost completely overshadowed by the love of mother for son (of the rejected Fidès for Jean the Prophet). Unfortunately, the plot also illustrates Scribe's increasing tendency to warp history in order to create a good story. The historical John of Leyden was a hypocritical voluptuary who used fundamentalist religion as a base for power and sexual license, and who was eventually captured and executed for his crimes. Scribe's protagonist is a dreamer prodded into action by the kidnapping of his fiancée.

Meyerbeer always tried to write for particular singers. The thirty years which elapsed between his first efforts to write *L'Africaine* and its final posthumous production resulted from the loss of his intended heroine, Cornélie Falcon, to irrevocable vocal decline, and the lack of a successor of her stature. Similarly, the availability of Pauline Viardot contributed much to Meyerbeer's treatment of the central character of *Le prophète:* Fidès three scenes overshadow even Jean's admittedly effective ariosos, the mad scene for Berthe, and the spectacular coronation scene at Münster Cathedral.

Having secured his place as the leading composer of grand opera, Meyerbeer turned to the quite different demands of the opéra-comique, where three acts rather than five, traditionally melodic arias and ensembles separated by spoken dialogue, and less complex plot and orchestral texture were the rule. Scribe adapted the libretto he had provided for translation as *Ein Feldlager in Schlesien* to a plot already set to music by Lortzing and Donizetti, that of Tsar Peter the Great's masquerading as a simple shipbuilder in Holland. The score seems to have been ignored by those who maintain that Meyerbeer could not write developed melodies; here they abound, especially in the music for the two soprano leads, with the orchestra reduced to accompaniment level.

For his second outing at the Opéra-Comique, Meyerbeer chose a Breton legend, *Le pardon de Plöermel* (better known under its Italian-language title, *Dinorah*), restricting much of his orchestral mastery to the overture, this one twenty minutes long and with an off-stage chorus. His arias, especially Dinorah's "Ombre légère," Höel's "Ah, mon remords," and the huntsman's aria beginning act III, show him still able to write effective traditional melody. No amount of sympathy with the different expectations and requirements of the mid-nineteenth century stage, however, can help to justify the opera's central drama, that of a peasant girl driven insane by the loss of her pet goat.

With the advent of the German soprano Marie Saxe, Meyerbeer turned again to the long-neglected *L'Africaine,* which owes its title to an earlier version of the libretto which had neither Vasco da Gama nor Hindu temples in its makeup. Meyerbeer's death before the opera went into rehearsal deprived the world of a definitive version, leaving its four and a half hours of music to be cut down by the Belgian musicologist Fétis. Even so, the score shows Meyerbeer at his most effective. The arias especially demonstrate a maturity of approach. Vasco's justly famous "O paradis" and Selika's "Sur mes genoux" strike a highly original balance between the traditional aria and the Meyerbeerian arioso. The argument between the liberal and conservative factions of the Grand Council, with the chorus of inquisitors injecting sinister asides, revives his mastery of the chorus-as-protagonist, and the opera's culmination, Selika's hallucinatory death scene, builds on the symphonic model of Fidès's "O prêtres de Baal" (and on the great "Adieu, fiere cité" from Berlioz' *Les Troyens,* which "O prêtres" influenced) to form a fitting finale to the career of the most influential musician of his time.

—William J. Collins

MEYERHOLD, Vsevolod Emilyevich.

Director. Born 9 February 1874, in Penza, Russia; died 2 February 1940, in Moscow. Married: Olga Munt, 1896 (divorced 1921); Zinaida Raikh, 1922 (died 1939). Studied law at Moscow University; studied acting at Moscow Philharmonic Society, 1896-98; became charter member of Moscow Art Theater in 1898; staged dramatic productions for Russian touring company, 1902-05; chosen by director Konstantin Stanislavsky to head the Theater-Studio in 1905, but studio closed the same year; in 1906-07 director of company of Vera Komissarzhevskaya, the leading Russian actress of her day; from 1908-18 director of the Imperial Theaters of St Petersburg, including the Alexandrinsky Theater, which produced straight plays, and the Mariinsky Theater, which produced opera; in 1919 took over municipal theater at Novorossiysk; in 1921 founded first Russian directing school, the Meyerhold Workshop; founded Meyerhold Theater in 1923 (after 1926 called the Meyerhold State Theater), and staged dramatic productions there until 1938; in 1935 staged production of Tchaikovsky's *The Queen of Spades* in Leningrad; in 1938 invited by Stanislavsky to work at his Opera Theater; after Stanislavsky's death later that year was appointed director, and completed Stanislavsky's production of *Rigoletto;* arrested in 1939; allegedly executed after brief trial in February of 1940.

Opera Productions (selected)

Tristan und Isolde, St Petersburg, Mariinsky Theater, 1909.
Boris Godunov, St Petersburg, Mariinsky Theater, 1911.
Orfeo ed Euridice, St Petersburg, Mariinsky Theater, 1911.
Elektra, St Petersburg, Mariinsky Theater, 1913.
The Stone Guest, St Petersburg, Mariinsky Theater, 1917.
The Snow Maiden, St Petersburg, Mariinsky Theater, 1917.
The Nightingale, St Petersburg, Mariinsky Theater, 1918.
The Queen of Spades, Leningrad, Maly Theater, 1935.

Publications

By MEYERHOLD: books–

Braun, Edward, ed. and trans. *Meyerhold on Theater.* New York, 1969.
Theaterarbeit: 1917-1930. Munich, 1974.

About MEYERHOLD: books–

Symons, James M. *Meyerhold's Theatre of the Grotesque: The Post-Revolutionary Productions, 1920-32.* Coral Gables, FL, 1971.
Hoover, Marjorie L. *Meyerhold: The Art of Conscious Theater.* Amherst, MA, 1974.
Braun, Edward. *The Theater of Meyerhold: Revolution on the Modern Stage.* London, 1979.
Schmidt, Paul, ed. *Meyerhold At Work.* Austin, TX, 1980.
Rudnitskii, Konstantin. *Meyerhold, the Director.* Ann Arbor, 1981.
Hoover, Marjorie L. *Meyerhold and His Set Designers.* New York, 1988.
Kiebuzinska, Christina Olga. *Revolutionaries in the Theater: Meyerhold, Brecht, and Witkiewicz.* Ann Arbor, 1988.
Leach, Robert. *Vsevolod Meyerhold.* Cambridge (England), 1989.
Leiter, Samuel L. *From Stanislavsky to Barrault: Representative Directors of the European Stage.* New York, 1991.

articles–

Houghton, Norris. "Theory into Practice: A Reappraisal of Meierhold." *Educational Theatre Journal* 20/3 (October 1968): 437.
Bristow, Eugene K. "The Making of a Regisseur: V.E. Meyerhold, The Early Years, 1874-1895." *The Theatre Annual* 25 (1969).
Barkhin, Mikhail, and Sergei Vakhtangov. "A Theatre for Meyerhold." *Theatre Quarterly* 2/7 (July-September 1972): 69.
Moore, Sonia. "Meyerhold: Innovator and Example." *Players* 48/1 (October-November 1972): 34.
Gladkov, Alexander. "Meyerhold Rehearses." Trans. Alma H. Law. *Performing Arts Journal* 3 (Winter 1979).

unpublished–

Beeson, Nora. "Vsevolod Meyerhold and the Experimental Pre-Revolutionary Theatre in Russia (1900-1917)." Ph.D. diss., Columbia University, 1961.
Schmidt, Paul. "The Theatre of V.E. Mejerxol'd" Ph.D. diss., Harvard University, 1974.

*   *   *

Meyerhold is remembered as an important Russian producer and actor. After first studying law at Moscow University, he entered the Moscow Philharmonic Dramatic School where, from 1896-98, he attended the classes of Nemirovich-Danchenko, who invited him to join the newly founded Moscow Art Theater in 1898. Over the following years he appeared in various productions of plays by Shakespeare, Hauptmann and Chekhov.

In 1902 Meyerhold left the Art Theater to found and head the Company of Russian Dramatic Artists, and, in 1903, the Comrades of the New Drama, in whose productions he started to formulate his aesthetic principles, based on symbolism, with an increasing emphasis on stage effects. From 1906-07 he was chief producer at the theater of actress V.F. Kommissarzhevskaya, where the extravagance of his productions of symbolist plays attracted widespread attention. On leaving Kommissarzhevskaya's theater, he became director of the Imperial Theaters, where he staged stylized productions of Molière's *Don Juan,* Lermontov's *Masquerade,* as well as Wagner's *Tristan und Isolde* (1909), Gluck's *Orpheus ed Euridice* (1911), Strauss's *Elektra* (1913) and Dargomïzhsky's *The Stone Guest* (1917).

Following the Revolution of 1917 Meyerhold joined the Communist Party and promoted the idea of "theatrical October," the purpose of which was to combine colorful spectacle with political propaganda. In endeavoring to reflect the spirit of the Revolution, Meyerhold found the work of Mayakovsky to be admirably suited to his ideas; and his productions of *Mystery-bouffe, The Bed-bug, The Bathhouse,* and other Soviet works, all given at the Meyerhold Theater, were of great significance.

Meyerhold did not hesitate to make changes in established classics such as Griboedov's *Woe from Wit* or Gogol's *The Inspector General* in order to exaggerate the social and political content; this extended to opera as well. His 1935 production of Tchaikovsky's *The Queen of Spades* not only used a new libretto by V.I. Stenich but transferred the action to the beginning of the nineteenth century, which, needless to say, intensified the polemics surrounding Meyerhold and his work. In 1938 the Meyerhold Theater was closed down by the State, and, though he was invited that year as a producer to Stanislavsky's Opera Studio and began work on Prokofiev's *Semën Kotko,* accusations that his theater had broken with Soviet reality increased and led to his arrest in 1939.

Meyerhold was one of the most colorful and original Russian producers of his era. Though often accused of taking away actors' initiative and using them as puppets, at the same time his productions were full of innovation and vitality, reflecting the influence of symbolism, constructivism, and what he termed "bio-mechanics"—a technique for developing actors' physical aesthetic sensibilities. His post-revolutionary productions, combining dramatic elements with circus and cinema were full of daring experiment, often with satirical or grotesque overtones. In the end, however, the Soviet Union was no longer sympathetic to anything suggestive of innovation or revolution, and Meyerhold died in humiliation in a concentration camp in 1940.

—Gerald Seaman

THE MIDSUMMER MARRIAGE.

Composer: Michael Tippett.

Librettist: Michael Tippett.

First Performance: London, Covent Garden, 27 January 1955.

Roles: Mark (tenor); Jenifer (soprano); King Fisher (baritone); Bella (soprano); Jack (tenor); Sosostris (contralto); Priest (bass); Priestess (mezzo-soprano); Dancing Man (tenor); Half-Tipsy Man (baritone from chorus); chorus (SSAATTBB).

Publications

articles—

Dickinson, A.E.F. "Round about The Midsummer Marriage." *Music and Letters* 37 (1956): 50.
Cairns, David. "The Midsummer Marriage." In *Responses.* London, 1973.

*　　*　　*

Tippett's first opera, *The Midsummer Marriage* is based on one of the most fundamental comic plots: overcoming the obstacles to a marriage. His initial vision was of a quarrel between an over-ardent boy and an icy, rebuffing girl—a couple kept apart by illusions about themselves and ignorance of each other, rather than the traditional interference from outsiders and relatives. The opera's subject is the quest for self-knowledge, and it takes its starting point from the words of the tenor in Tippett's oratorio *A Child of Our Time:* "I would know my shadow and my light, so shall I at last be whole."

The Midsummer Marriage was first produced in 1955 in a Cold War Britain which was wholly unprepared for its richness. The music was, and remains, remarkable for its nobility and lyrical warmth, and for a rhythmic drive and energy for which Tippett was indebted to his idol, Beethoven, but also, looking further back, to Handel. The opera wholly avoids the pomposity of some British neo-romantic music, and the gentle nostalgia of the English pastoral tradition is transcended in the fierce, evocative and justly famed "Ritual Dances."

The chromatic and contrapuntal complexity of some passages and the dense textures of the choruses and ensembles caused difficulties to the opera's first interpreters; but some of the early critics perceived the underlying clarity of Tippett's music, and Colin Davis' conducting of the 1968 new production (and the associated Philips recording) triumphantly vindicated the score.

The richness of the text caused many problems. Tippett wrote his own libretto, and it was at first generally regarded as obscure to the point of absurdity. In this opera, as in all of his subsequent stage works, two intersecting worlds are shown; the world of mysticism of magic, of the numinous and the prosaic world of everyday. Mark and Jenifer come for their marriage to a mysterious temple in a magic wood, and her hesitation and unwillingness plunge them into a visionary sequence of events, which unfold on a plane governed by dream-logic and by an inner, mystic necessity. The moment of their meeting is reenacted before the curtain falls; and now Jenifer, like Mark, is ready to be married, and all can depart for a new life.

Tippett evolved his text over a long period of gestation. He selected symbols and metaphors from traditional mythical material, from the images used by previous creative artists, and from his own imagination. They are designed to be more than a private, idiosyncratic language; with the support of the music, they unite the world of everyday with the deeper world beyond.

Though there are many influences upon the text—in particular Shaw and Eliot—Tippett based *The Midsummer Marriage* firmly on the story-pattern of its operatic precursor, *Die Zauberflöte.* As in Mozart's opera, there is a temple which symbolizes the power of traditional wisdom; there also is a parent opposing a daughter's need to break free from her family and find a mate. Furthermore, *The Midsummer Marriage, like Die Zauberflöte,* portrays two couples, not one. While Mark and Jenifer must take "the royal road," confronting the highest and most complex spiritual obstacles on their path to union, we are also shown the difficulties—and the joys of the mundane in the journey to marriage of their *alter egos,* the working-class couple Jack and Bella.

This is a *Zauberflöte* for our times, and the psychology of C.G. Jung underlies the opera. Mark and Jenifer have the potential to grow, and be adequate to marriage; but each must first develop his or her own self, and come to terms with their partner's. Tippett's metaphors for this are clear and appealing; a magic staircase to the light above, and below, a set of gates that lead to darkness. Above us, the refined purity at the heights of true femininity; below, the bestial violence which lurks beneath male sensuality. Neither Mark nor Jenifer can be complete until her over-precious spirituality and his Dionysiac power have been tempered by some degree of mutual exchange; and only after being reborn from the womb of the prophetess Sosostris, who represents infinite knowledge, can they relive the initial moment of confrontation and make themselves whole.

They must also overcome an external obstacle. Jenifer's father, King Fisher, dies at the climactic moment of the couple's rebirth. His name is derived from the wounded Fisher King in the Grail legend, whose sufferings symbolize the sterility of his society; Tippett's King Fisher, a businessman and a technocrat, embodies the features of modern society, which the composer regards as barren.

His death also evokes the ancient seasonal vegetation rites, in which the old king is ritually killed, and replaced by a new king, in the celebrations each midsummer for the birth and death of the crops. The opera's finale celebrates not just the psychological growth of Mark and Jenifer to maturity and wholeness, but also the triumph of emotion and intuition, and the renewal as a new generation takes over from the old.

Early critical responses separated the opera's text from the music; but this is increasingly seen as a grave injustice. The visionary lyricism and richness which were widely praised in Tippett's music are precisely matched to, and inspired by, exactly the same qualities in his libretto. Since 1968, new productions have been mounted both by the two main London houses and by Britain's major regional companies; and the belated Australian and American premieres (Adelaide 1978, San Francisco 1984) were both highly successful. *The Midsummer Marriage* is a landmark in English opera, a glorious affirmation of the magic and joy of human life and its perpetual self-renewal.

—Michael Ewans

A MIDSUMMER NIGHT'S DREAM.

Composer: Benjamin Britten.

Librettists: Benjamin Britten and Peter Pears (after Shakespeare).

First Performance: Aldeburgh, Jubilee Hall, 11 June 1960.

Roles: Oberon (counter tenor or contralto); Titania (soprano); Hippolita (contralto); Theseus (bass); Lysander (tenor); Demetrius (baritone); Hermia (mezzo-soprano); Helena (soprano); Bottom/Pyramus (bass-baritone); Puck (speaking part); Quince (bass); Flute (tenor); Snug (bass); Snout (tenor); Starveling (baritone); Peaseblossom, Cobweb, Mustardseed, Moth (treble).

Publications

articles–

Evans, Peter. "Britten's *A Midsummer Night's Dream.*" *Tempo* no. 53-54 (1960): 34.

Benjamin Britten, England's foremost opera composer, was blessed and cursed with an exceptionally keen ear for music. He could perceive and conceive sonic intricacies abstruse to general audiences and overweening critics. Always intending to communicate his art, he could not understand why his operas, esteemed by many, endeared so few. *A Midsummer Night's Dream* glimmers more than glitters with musical delights. To Shakespeare's natural and supernatural colorations, Britten adds one unnatural tone, the countertenor voice of Oberon. Children play the fairies attending Titania, a coloratura soprano. A boy-acrobat speaks Puck. The Rustics must modulate their voices to suit each line, especially Bottom when he wears the ass's head. A harpsichord, celesta, two harps, two recorders, and an array of percussion instruments augment the chamber orchestra. Indeed, the score is a veritable textbook on fanciful orchestration. Mutes, harmonics, glissandos, flutter-tonguing, and other effects embellish a profusion of textures, most of them lean. Like Debussy, Britten shifts the color scheme every few measures with inexhaustible invention, rarely reverting to the mixture as before. But the magic is subtle, elusive, ephemeral. There is no looking back, no dwelling place for thought, as if the listener were pursuing Puck himself.

To adapt the play as an opera of two and a quarter hours, Britten and Peter Pears omitted about half the lines and shuffled those retained, combining and redisposing entire scenes. Shakespeare's words, however, remain unchanged, with a single line invented to restore a link in the plot imparted in the deleted first scene. Although it transplants some events in the play, the opera tightens the action and faithfully presents the three entangled stories, while giving Theseus and Hippolita less to do.

Britten composed the work in only seven months to celebrate the 1960 reconstruction of Jubilee Hall, at the time the main concert facility of the Aldeburgh Festival. It was the eleventh of his sixteen operas, if we include his adaptation of *The Beggar's Opera.* Appropriately festive and jubilant, *A Midsummer Night's Dream* eschews psychological portrayal, evoking instead an ethereal enchantment quite unlike the stuff Britten's other operas are made of. He might have subtitled it

"Love the Magician," as Falla called his ballet, for Love is the guiding and confounding power behind the drama and its music. When passion subverts reason, volatility prevails. Recondite wishes emerge as in a dream, and in one night matches can be broken and remade by Puck's intrigues. Pyramus and Thisbe, farcically played by Bottom and Flute, die for Love's absurdity, mistaking it for Love's sorrow.

The characters, as Britten portrays them musically, are like enameled dolls, burnished but depthless, intoning measured lines with cold luster. We observe them from a distance by their own nocturnal light. Most substantial of the lovers is Helena, at first breathlessly pursuing Demetrius, later incredulous and indignant when her beloved and Lysander as well dote upon her. Among the Rustics, Bottom is easily the most ponderable and opaque. Too ebullient to know he plays the fool, he oversteps the boundaries of comedy as good clowns must. The rarefied and translucent realm of fairies cannot confine him. His angular declamations and immodest conduct immunizes him to the spell of the wood. Musically he is a lost character who seems to have stumbled into the wrong opera.

Like the play, Britten's music hinges on contrasts. Diatonic lines deflect to new modalities in mid-phrase. Modulatory legerdemain summarily shifts the tonal floor under our feet without a jog. Orthodox harmonies bear eccentric dissonances or fall together in solecistic clinches. Alien meters invade the iambic symmetry. Vocal and orchestral lines diverge and meet again in a network of interlacing streams. The score is a tour de force of circuitry behind an illusion.

—James Allen Feldman

MIGNON.

Composer: Ambroise Thomas.

Librettists: J. Barbier and M. Carré (after Goethe, *Wilhelm Meister*).

First Performance: Paris, Opéra-Comique, Salle Favart, 17 November 1866.

Roles: Mignon (soprano or mezzo-soprano); Philine (soprano); Wilhelm Meister (tenor); Lothario (bass); Frederick (tenor); Laerte (tenor); Giarno (bass); chorus (SATB).

Publications

article–

Klein, John W. "A Hundred Years of *Mignon.*" *Opera* November (1966).

* * *

Mignon, along with *Carmen* and *Faust,* has to be considered one of the most successful French operas ever composed. Premiered at the Opéra-Comique in 1866, it received its 1000th performance there in 1894 and eventually surpassed 2000. Translated into nearly twenty languages, *Mignon* did much to secure Thomas's reputation (along with *Hamlet,*

1868) as the leading composer of French opera and his appointment as Director of the Paris Conservatory five years later.

Based upon characters and selected situations from the first part of Goethe's *Wilhelm Meister,* the libretto by Carré and Barbier (who also provided for Gounod's *Faust*) was first offered to Meyerbeer and then to Gounod. Essentially a romantic triangle among Goethe's titular hero, the mysterious child/woman Mignon, and the extroverted actress Philine, the libretto bears little resemblance to the novel. In act I of the opera, a band of gypsies is entertaining the townspeople in the courtyard of an eighteenth-century German inn. When one of them, Mignon, refuses to dance as ordered, she is first shielded by Lothario, an old and partially-demented harper seeking his long-lost daughter, and then rescued by Wilhelm, a student. All this has been observed by Philine and Laerte, unemployed actors also staying at the inn. Wilhelm purchases Mignon's freedom from the gypsies. A letter borne by Frederick, Philine's Cherubino-like admirer, invites the acting troupe to perform at his uncle's castle. Wilhelm agrees to join the company, with Mignon in tow.

Act II contains two scenes, the first of which takes place at the castle in the bedroom assigned to Philine. Wilhelm, infatuated with the actress, seems not to notice that Mignon, serving as his page, is jealous. Philine prepares to perform as Titania in *A Midsummer Night's Dream.* Scene ii is set in a park outside the castle, where Mignon contemplates suicide because of Wilhelm's inattention. The heroine is consoled by Lothario, who hears her rhetorical wish that the theater in which Philine is performing be engulfed in flames. The play completed, Philine enters in triumph. She sends Mignon back into the theater on an errand, after which the building suddenly bursts into flames. Wilhelm dramatically rescues Mignon again.

In order to convalesce from the fire, Mignon is brought to an Italian palace for act III. Wilhelm finally assures her of his love. Now Lothario appears dressed as a nobleman, in possession of both his sanity and his ancestral home. Childhood mementos convince all that Mignon is really Lothario's lost daughter, Sperata, and rejoicing ensues.

Thus ends *Mignon* as it is ordinarily presented today, but this is not what the opening night audience witnessed. In fact, four different conclusions to the opera have been performed at one time or another. At the opera's premiere, the action continued with Philine's voice heard off-stage, causing Mignon to run out in fright. Act III had a second scene, set in the Italian countryside. After a brief ballet, Philine offers her hand in friendship to Mignon, claims Frederick as her husband, and even more rejoicing ensues. The next version of the ending, substituted soon after the premiere, omits act III's additional scene and the ballet but is essentially similar to the original. Version three, intended for German audiences, has Mignon die (as in Goethe's novel) in Wilhelm's arms after confronting Philine. The fourth version has the standard denouement, described in the synopsis above.

The opera contains some of Thomas's most memorable music, including a brilliantly scored overture and several highly effective arias. Among the best known are Mignon's gentle "Connais-tu le pays," a remarkably faithful adaptation of Goethe's "Kennst du das Land," and Philine's treacherous "Je suis Titania" from act II, surely one of the most demanding arias in the coloratura repertory. Frederick's "Me voici dans son boudoir," sometimes referred to as the gavotte from *Mignon,* is also notable.

Conceived originally as an opéra-comique, that is, with spoken dialogue, Thomas composed recitatives in 1868 for a production in Germany. It is in this latter form that the work is nearly always performed today.

—Morton Achter

Zinka Milanov as Leonora in *La forza del destino*

MILANOV, Zinka [born Mira Zinka Teresa Kunç].

Soprano. Born 17 May 1906, in Zagreb, Croatia. Died 30 May 1989, in New York. Married: 1) theater director Predrag Milanov, 1937 (divorced); 2) General Ljubomir Ilic, 1947. Studied at Zagreb Academy and with Milka Ternina, Maria Kostrenčić and Fernando Carpi (in Prague); debut at Ljubljana Opera as Leonora in *Il trovatore,* 1927; appeared at Zagreb Opera, 1928-35; began association with Toscanini in Verdi's Requiem at Salzburg, 1937; Metropolitan Opera debut as Leonora, 1937; Teatro alla Scala debut as Tosca, 1950; farewell performance at Metropolitan opera as Maddalena in *Andrea Chénier,* 1966.

Publications

About MILANOV: articles–

Einstein, E. "Zinka Milanov Discography." *Grand baton* 5/ no. 2 (1968): 7.
Opera News January (1958); May (1965); April (1977); December (1987).
Opera Quarterly 7, no. 1 (1990) ["Milanov Issue"].

* * *

Zinka Milanov towered over her generation of singers not as an innovator but as a standard-bearer. She stretched no boundaries; unlike so many artists of her time, she did not "reinterpret" a composer's intentions by filtering them through a raft of vocal shortcomings in the ostensible search for some elusive dramatic truth. She *did* become the very last singer of her type to realize every aspect of her potential and to maintain it in the heaviest Italian repertory throughout an unusually long career.

Milanov dedicated her life to what she considered the highest calling: serving an ideal of beauty that defined the reason for the very existence of the singer of opera. Her devotion to maintaining and perpetuating the vocal standards of her greatest predecessors (Rosa Ponselle, to whose place she succeeded at the Metropolitan Opera, was emphatically an admirer) produced "singing of a school already severely in decline, and it demanded attention," wrote Alan Blyth. Though she fell short of her self-set goal often enough, Milanov nonetheless fulfilled her destiny to a degree that made her, among her colleagues, the most esteemed of all singers.

Her majestic, larger-than-life stage persona seemed a throwback to an earlier era ("grand manner," it was called, and for no other singer was the designation invoked as often), but she had the goods to go with it: "To an age of somewhat dislocated musical values, Zinka Milanov stands as a kind of magnetic pole of old-fashioned musical virtue," was Irving Kolodin's 1953 assessment.

That "dislocation" had developed through the gradual abdication of critical responsibility to stress the importance of healthy vocalism vis-a-vis the presentation of dramatic values, until the two had become almost mutually exclusive. Milanov's priorities were clearly vocal, and hers was an instrument before which all other considerations paled. The sound was silver with a vein of amber, round and opulent, and all of a piece from top to bottom. Its hues ranged securely from brilliant to mellow, from honeyed and silky to dark and vibrant. Because of its prodigal size, Milanov could dominate any ensemble easily and impressively. But unlike other big voices, hers could be graded to the most refined and delicate of floated sounds, not just in midrange but to the very top of the compass. This extraordinary *pianissimo* seemed detached in space, not emanating from the stage at all but hovering directly at the listener's ear in any location inside the opera house. Milanov's finely spun legato, sense of phrasing, and feel for vocal color created a tone and line that conveyed all that was meaningful about her roles. Her emotional projection was "direct, deeply felt, infinitely touching," wrote John Ardoin. Olin Downes praised her "nobility of expression and complete mastery of every phase of the singer's art."

In the early years of her career, the going was indeed rough. Milanov sang constantly in Yugoslavia, in an extraordinary variety of roles, for very little money, and went as a guest artist to Germany, Bulgaria, and Czechoslovakia, often just for one-off performances with long train rides on the days she had to sing. Though she is remembered as a statuesque stand-pat diva who sang "old" music, she began as quite the vocal firebrand, and a good bit of her repertory was new by operatic standards. As one of her country's pioneer Turandots (1929), for instance, she introduced a role barely three years past its premiere; and she sang in several other operas written in her own lifetime.

An *Aïda* in Vienna in 1936 under Bruno Walter turned the tide; he loved her, and sent her to Toscanini, who engaged her at once for his 1937 performances of Verdi's Requiem at Salzburg. (Contrary to legend, she had already been invited to the Metropolitan *before* her spectacular success with Toscanini.) She was principal soprano in New York until the gala performance that closed the old Metropolitan Opera House, 16 April 1966, just prior to which she was granted a formal farewell. Though she made several historically important recordings, she did not commit a complete role to disc until her twenty-fifth year onstage. In any case, hers was a massive voice requiring the surrounding space of the theater to be heard to full advantage. Thus, generations that did not witness her in the house can never know the impact of her presence and her prime sound, the reasons for the tremendous extent of her influence.

As soon as Milanov retired, younger colleagues—Christa Ludwig, Régine Crespin, Grace Bumbry, Sandor Konya, Anna Moffo, Elinor Ross, Rosalind Elias, Walter Berry, and many others—flocked to her for lessons, all seeking the secrets that had made her singing so special, not to mention so healthy and durable. The root of their interest was summarized by Ludwig: "Zinka Milanov—this voice is really *the* voice of our century and not surpassed by other wonderful artists."

The international outpouring of analysis at the time of Milanov's death elucidated the source of her supereminent stature and made clear at just what point vocal history had taken the wrong turn: "It is a tragedy for operatic singing," wrote Hugh Canning, "that Callas rather than Milanov became the postwar icon," and Blyth recognized that American opera lovers, in particular, would rank Milanov as the "foremost of all *lirico-spinto* sopranos of the past fifty years." In so doing, a still grateful public simply seconds Rudolf Bing's valuation on the soprano's last night, when he acclaimed Milanov as "a supremely great singer."

—Bruce Burroughs

MILDENBURG, ANNA VON
See BAHR-MILDENBURG, ANNA

MILHAUD, Darius.

Composer. Born 4 September 1892, in Aix-en-Provence. Died 22 June 1974, in Geneva. Married: Madeleine Milhaud (his cousin), 1926 (one son). Studied violin with Berthelier and counterpoint with Gédalge at the Paris Conservatory, beginning 1909; secretary to the French Minister in Brazil, Paul Claudel, 1917-18; returned to Paris, 1918; active in French music circles until the outbreak of World War II; conducted and performed (as pianist) his own compositions and lectured at Harvard, Princeton, and Vassar during trips to the United States in 1922 and 1926; traveled and performed in Italy, Holland, Germany, Austria, Poland, and Russia, 1922-26; lived in the United States and taught at Mills College (Oakland, California), 1940-71; professor at the Paris Conservatory, 1947, and spent alternate years at the conservatory and

Mills; settled in Geneva, 1971. Milhaud was one of "Les Six" that included Auric, Durey, Honegger, Poulenc, and Tailleferre; his circle included Erik Satie and Jean Cocteau; his pupils include Gilbert Amy, Elinor Armer, Dave and Howard Brubeck, Richard Felciano, Betsy Jolas, Leland Smith, and Morton Subotnick.

Operas

Publishers: Eschig, Heugel, Israeli Music Publishers, Ricordi, Salabert, Universal.

La brebis égarée, Francis Jammes, 1910-14, Paris, Opéra-Comique, 10 December 1923.
Les euménides (last work in the three-part cycle, *L'Orestie*), Paul Claudel (after Aeschylus), 1917-22, Berlin, Berlin Opera, 18 November 1949.
Les malheurs d' Orphée, Armand Lunel, 1924, Brussels, Théâtre de la Monnaie, 7 May 1926.
Esther de Carpentras, Armand Lunel, 1925-26, Paris, Opéra-Comique, 3 February 1938.
Le pauvre matelot, Jean Cocteau, 1926, Paris, Opéra-Comique, 16 December 1927.
Trois opéras-minutes, Henri Hoppenot, 1927, 1) *L'enlèvement d'Europe,* Baden-Baden, 17 July 1927; 2) *L'abandon d' Ariane* and 3) *La délivrence de Thésée,* Wiesbaden, 20 April 1928.
Christophe Colomb, Paul Claudel, Berlin, State Opera, 5 May 1930.
Maximilien, R.S. Hoffman, translated by Armand Lunel (after Franz Werfel), 1930-31, Paris, Opéra, 5 January 1932.
Medée, Madeleine Milhaud (after Euripides), 1938, Antwerp, Flemish Opera, 7 October 1939.
Bolivar, Madeleine Milhaud (after Jules Supervielle), 1943, Paris, Opéra, 12 May 1950.
David, Armand Lunel, 1952-53, Jerusalem (King David Festival), 1 June 1954.
Fiesta, Boris Vian, 1958, Berlin, Städtische Opera, 3 October 1958.
La mère coupable, Madeleine Milhaud (after Beaumarchais), 1964-65, Geneva, Grand Théâtre, 13 June 1965.
Saint Louis, roi de France (opera-oratorio), Paul Claudel and Henri Doublier, 1970-71, Rome, Radio Audizioni Italiana, 18 March 1972.

Other works: incidental music, film music, orchestral works, instrumental and band music, vocal works, chamber music, ballets, piano pieces.

Publications

By MILHAUD: books—

Etudes. Paris, 1927.
Notes sans musique. Paris, 1949; revised, 1963; English translation by Donald Evans as *Notes Without Music,* edited by Rollo Meyers, London, 1952.
Ma vie heureuse. Paris, 1973.
Entretiens avec Claude Rostand. Paris, 1952.

articles, lectures, interviews—

Drake, Jeremy, ed. and comp. *Darius Milhaud: Notes sur la musique.* Paris, 1982.

About MILHAUD: books–

Collaer, Paul. *Darius Milhaud.* Paris, 1947; revised, 1982; translated and edited by Jane Hohfeld Galante, with a catalogue of works compiled from the composer's notebooks by Madeleine Milhaud, San Francisco, 1988; London, 1989.

Beck, Georges. *Darius Milhaud.* Paris, 1949.

Roy, Jean. *Darius Milhaud.* Paris, 1968.

Drake, Jeremy. *The Operas of Darius Milhaud.* New York, 1989.

articles–

Knapp, Bettina. "Paul Claudel's *The Diary of Christopher Columbus:* a Demiurge Journeys Forth." *Theatrical Journal* 33 (1981): 145.

Note: for additional articles on Milhaud, see Collaer, 1989.

*   *   *

Mention the name Darius Milhaud to most musicians and they will call to mind his huge output of scores (four hundred and forty-three opus numbers) but will probably not classify him as primarily an opera composer. Nevertheless, it is the contention of Milhaud's biographer, Paul Collaer, that the essence of this composer's style is dramatic and that the operas stand like pillars marking the path of his total musical journey. In fact, the first of his sixteen operas, *La brebis égarée* (*The lost lamb*), was begun when he was only eighteen

Darius Milhaud

years old, and the final one, an opera-oratorio commissioned by the French government to commemorate the seven-hundreth anniversary of King Louis IX's demise, was completed shortly before his own death.

Milhaud was catapulted into the conscience of the musical world in the 1920s when, as one of the group of "enfants terribles" of post-war Paris, his compositions elicited hoots and howls from the listening public and outraged invective from the press. Several composers, quite arbitrarily dubbed "Les Six" by a music critic, took up Erik Satie's battle cry, "Down with Wagner," and Milhaud, as the most prolific of the group, became a standard-bearer in the revolt against all that was pompous, obtuse and cloying in late nineteenth-century music. In Milhaud's operas, this revolt manifested itself in his insistence on meticulous matching of every element of the musical score to the expressive requirements of the text.

In his study of Milhaud's operas, Jeremy Drake divides the works into three periods. The first two operas, *La brebis égarée* and *Les euménides,* stand somewhat apart from this classification, and *Christophe Colomb* occupies a transitional position between the first and second periods. Drake includes *Les malheurs d'Orphée* (*The misfortunes of Orpheus*), *Esther de Carpentras, Le pauvre matelot,* and the three *Opéras-minutes* in the first period, and *Maximilien, Medée, Bolivar* and *David* in the second, which is characterized by thicker textures, minimal use of groups of solo instruments, less emphasis on counterpoint, and increased motivic development. *Fiesta, La mère coupable,* (*The guilty mother*), and *Saint Louis* make up the third period, which marks a return to the contrapuntal constructions that typified the first period. Whereas this classification is useful as a point of departure for examining the different works, close scrutiny will reveal that the stylistic elements that bind the operas together are far stronger than the chronology that separates them.

Melody is certainly the hallmark of Milhaud's operatic style, as it is of all his music. Sometimes the operas contain short, song-like sections, but more often the vocal lines are spun out either against an instrumental background or integrated polyphonically into the instrumental texture itself. The music responds to the nuances of each dramatic situation, and every melodic line has its own shape and symmetry which, far from "setting" the words of the libretto, expresses the mood of the text and, in fact, often subordinates the prosody to the metric pattern of the musical phrase.

Rhythmically, Milhaud uses mostly simple meters that contribute an element of cohesiveness to his flexible and often complex melodic structures. Harmonically, he is well known as the chief protagonist of polytonality and, as the word implies, his style is essentially tonal. His most typical compositional technique is counterpoint, which he applies in a variety of ways. The chamber orchestras of his early operas, such as *Les malheurs d'Orphée* and the *Opéras-minutes,* are perfectly adapted to his polytonal concept of using one instrument (or voice) to a part, each line standing out from the others by virtue of its special timbre. In later works involving full orchestra, his polyphonic structures are frequently festooned over great harmonic blocks, many times supported by powerful ostenati, while unequivocal cadences reaffirm the tonal centers of the music.

Three forces shaped Darius Milhaud as man and as musician, his Jewish faith, the heritage of his native Provence, and French rationality. As a result, his approach to art was both humanistic and fatalistic. Everything, he believed, including inanimate objects, plants, animals and people, is both spectator of and participant in the great eternal drama of mankind presided over by ineluctable fate. The protagonists of the individual operas may be simple people overcome by human passions, like Pierre and Françoise in *La brebis égarée* and the wife in *Le pauvre matelot;* they may be tragic characters, like Medea and Orestes, from Classical antiquity, or historical figures like Columbus and Bolivar. Some of the operas are short (each of the *Opéras-minutes* lasts eight to ten minutes), some provide an evening's entertainment, but every work is exactly as long as the particular dramatic situation demands. Nor does length necessarily equal importance. Writing to a friend about *Les malheurs d'Orphée,* Milhaud said: "It is such a magnificent subject, but I want to make it very human. . . ." The purity of the musical texture, the absolute economy of means should "project a total atmosphere of grandeur."

It is not surprising that Milhaud chose as collaborators people who shared his love of simplicity, his profound spirituality, and his affinity for his Provençal milieu. The poets Francis Jammes and Paul Claudel, his childhood friend Armand Lunel, and his wife Madeleine Milhaud provided most of the librettos. The recognition of Milhaud's world-wide prominence as an opera composer is borne-out by the wide range of cities in which first or second performances of his works have been given, such as Paris, Berlin, Brussels, Geneva, Graz, Rome, Milan, Rio de Janeiro, and Jerusalem. Whereas some of the larger works have received few performances because of the enormous resources required to stage them, the chamber operas are frequently presented, and interest in his entire operatic output never ceases to grow.

—Jane Hohfeld Galante

MILLER, Jonathan.

Producer/director. Born 21 July 1934, in London. Married: Helen Rachel Collet, 1956; three children. Educated at St Paul's School, London and St John's College, Cambridge; M.D., University College Medical School, London, 1959; first professional stage debut in *Beyond the Fringe,* which he also coauthored, Edinburough Festival, 1960; director, Nottingham Playhouse, 1963-69; associate director, National Theatre, 1973-75; member, Arts Council, 1975-76; visiting fellow in Drama, Westfield College, University of London, 1977-78; opera debut, Goehr's *Arden Must Die,* Sadler's Wells, 1974; associate director, English National Opera, 1978-81; since 1980, executive producer of BBC Shakespeare series; director, Old Vic, 1988-90; resident fellow in neuro-psychology, University of Sussex, 1985; also theater producer; has made numerous television appearances, including *The Body in Question,* 1978; Albert Medal, RSA, 1990.

Opera productions (selected)

Arden Must Die, Sadler's Wells, 1974.
Così fan tutte, Kent Opera, 1974.
Rigoletto, Kent Opera, 1975.
The Cunning Little Vixen, Glyndebourne, 1975, 1977.
Orfeo, Bath Festival, 1976.
Orfeo, Kent Opera, 1976.
Eugene Onegin, Kent Opera, 1977.
Le nozze di Figaro, English National Opera, 1978.
La traviata, Edinburgh Festival, 1979.
La traviata, Kent Opera, 1979.
Der fliegende Holländer, Frankfurt, 1979.
The Turn of the Screw, Kent Opera, 1979.

The Turn of the Screw, English National Opera, 1979, 1991.
Arabella, English National Opera, 1980.
Falstaff, English National Opera, 1980, 1981.
Così fan tutte, Opera Theatre of St Louis, 1982.
Otello, English National Opera, 1982.
Fidelio, English National Opera, 1982, 1983.
Rigoletto, English National Opera, 1982, 1984.
Die Zauberflöte, Scottish Opera, 1983.
Don Giovanni, English National Opera, 1985.
Die Zauberflöte, English National Opera, 1986.
Tosca, Maggio Musicale, Florence, 1986.
Tosca, English National Opera, 1986.
Il barbiere di Siviglia, English National Opera, 1987.
The Mikado, English National Opera, 1986, 1988.
La fanciulla del West, Teatro alla Scala, Milan, 1991.
Kat'a Kabanová, New York, 1991.
Le nozze di Figaro, Vienna, Theater an der Wien, 1991.

Opera Films

La traviata, BBC TV, 1979, 1987.
Così fan tutte, BBC TV, 1984.

Publications

By MILLER: books–

McLuhan. New York, 1971.
ed., *Freud: The Man, His World, His Influence.* 1972.
The Body in Question. New York, 1978.
Darwin for Beginners. With Borin Van Loon. New York, 1982.
The Human Body. New York, 1983.
States of Mind. New York, 1983.
Subsequent Performances. New York, 1986.
ed., *The Don Giovanni Book: Myths of Seduction and Betrayal.* London, 1990.

articles–

"Miller on Producing Opera." *Opera* 28 (October 1977): 932-38 and (November 1977): 1030-34.

About MILLER: books–

Romain, M. *A Profile of Jonathan Miller.* London, 1992.

About MILLER: articles–

Loppert, M. "Jonathon Miller (Interview)." *Music and Musicians* 22 (April 1974): 22-23.
Hartcup, A. "Miller on His *Vixen.*" *Opera* 26 (June 1975): 526-28.
Shames, L. "Is There Anything Jonathan Miller Can't Do?" *Saturday Review* 9 (June 1982): 32-34.
Sherlock, C. "An Enlightened View." *Opera News* 46 (June 1982): 10-12.

*   *   *

Qualified doctor, neurologist, coauthor of the fabulously successful show *Beyond the Fringe,* television pundit, theater and

Jonathan Miller's production of *Tosca* for English National Opera, London, 1990 (with Neil Howlett as Scarpia and David Redall as Cavaradossi)

opera director—Jonathan Miller can legitimately be described as a polymath. His first operatic staging of Alexander Goehr's historical thriller, *Arden Must Die,* for the New Opera Company in 1974, drew a criticism often leveled against him in later years: that his production appeared unfinished. The same year, Miller began an association with Kent Opera by directing *Così fan tutte;* this evoked a similar response from the critics. Only later did they realize that this state of incompletion was one of Miller's great strengths. His productions were able to flower, to adapt to new casts, and to grow in many ways because of it.

Miller held strongly to the theory that the date of an opera's composition was usually a good period in which to place it. His second production for Kent Opera, *Rigoletto,* set in the mid 1850s, was a great success. So were his third, a Poussin-inspired staging of Monteverdi's *Orfeo,* first seen in 1976 at the Bath Festival; his fourth, a delightful *Eugene Onegin* that stayed particularly close to Pushkin; and his fifth, an unconventional and unromantic reading of *La traviata* in which the medical details—and the behaviour of the Doctor—were, not surprisingly, authentic. This last production had its first performance in 1979 at the Edinburgh Festival.

Meanwhile Miller had scored another triumph, directing *The Cunning Little Vixen* at Glyndebourne. His approach was found original, as the animals were dressed and treated in almost the same way as the humans. This production of Janáček's opera was restaged in Frankfurt, for the Australian Opera in Sydney, and in 1988 for Glimmerglass Opera in Cooperstown, New York. Miller had returned to Frankfurt to direct *Der fliegende Holländer,* which for two acts succeeded superbly in evoking the Romanticism of the youthful Wagner's opera; the third act, unfortunately, was less of a success.

Miller's association with English National Opera began in 1978 with *Le nozze di Figaro.* Again the criticism of "not finished" was made and again the critics were confounded: this *Figaro* lasted for over 12 years. So did his second English National Opera staging of Britten's *The Turn of the Screw,* which was taken on tour to Kiev in 1990, and is still in the repertory in 1991. In the early 1980s Miller directed *Falstaff* and *Fidelio* for Kent Opera; Strauss's *Arabella* and Verdi's *Otello* for English National Opera and began a cycle of the Mozart/da Ponte operas at St Louis that did not progress beyond *Così fan tutte.* These productions, especially the latter, were well received, without attracting worldwide attention. Such recognition was to come with Miller's next staging.

In September 1982 Miller's "Mafia" *Rigoletto,* updated to the 1950s and set in New York's Little Italy, was unveiled at the London Coliseum by English National Opera. Its success was instantaneous and phenomenal; particularly relished was the moment in the last act when the "Duke," the Mafia boss, pressed the button of the juke box, which obliged with "La donna e mobile." Revived every season for five years, the production was taken on a tour in the United States which included New Orleans and the Metropolitan Opera House. Although it remained popular, Miller insisted on its withdrawal; it returned in 1992.

Miller next staged *Die Zauberflöte* for Scottish Opera. Set in an 18th-century Masonic library, it was presented as the dream of Tamino, who falls asleep in the library. This production was later taken over by English National Opera. Another production taken over by English National Opera was Miller's staging of *Tosca* for the 1986 Maggio musicale in Florence. This staging, which set the action in Nazi-occupied Rome during 1944, was second only to that of *Rigoletto* for the aptness and effectiveness of its period. A *Don Giovanni* in chiaroscuro for English National Opera proved very enduring, though *The Mikado,* set in a 1920s hotel (all-white decorations after Syrie Maugham), became even more popular, traveling to Houston and Los Angeles. Miller had made his Los Angeles debut with *Tristan und Isolde,* designed by David Hockney, a production subsequently seen in Florence. He also staged Weill's *Aufstieg und Fall der Stadt Mahagonny* in Los Angeles.

Despite repeated threats to abandon opera production, Miller continues to broaden his repertory and his sphere of activity. An exhilarating *Candide* for Scottish Opera (with comedian John Wells as codirector) later played at the Old Vic, London. He staged completely new productions of *Don Giovanni* and *Così fan tutte* in Florence. During 1991 he made his debut at the Teatro alla Scala, Milan, with a fairly traditional production of *La fanciulla del West* (his first attempt at a Puccini opera); he made a greatly acclaimed Metropolitan Opera debut directing *Kát'a Kabanová;* and, as part of the Mozart bicentennial celebrations in Vienna, he made his debut there, staging *Le nozze di Figaro* at the Theater an der Wien.

—Elizabeth Forbes

MILNES, Sherrill (Eustace).

Baritone. Born 10 January 1935, in Downers Grove, Illinois. Studied at Drake University with Andrew White, at Northwestern University with Hermanus Baer, and with Rosa Ponselle; at Santa Fe, 1960; toured with Boris Goldovsky's Opera Company, with whom he made his debut as Masetto, 1960; later sang Gérard in *Andrea Chénier* in Baltimore, 1961; New York City Opera debut as Valentin in *Faust,* 1964; Metropolitan Opera debut in same role, 1965; Covent Garden debut, 1971; created Adam in *Mourning Becomes Electra,* 1967.

Publications

By MILNES: articles–

"A Role in Hand." *Opera News* 36/no. 2 (1971): 12.

About MILNES: articles–

Sargaent, W. "Sherrill Milnes." *New Yorker* (1976): 36.
Lanier, T. "Sherrill Milnes." *Opera* June (1980).

*   *   *

Sherrill Milnes's art has improved as his voice has declined—the classic opera-singer syndrome. When he made his New York City Opera debut in 1964, he had the lean bright sound and easily accessible top notes characteristic of American baritones, exemplified by Lawrence Tibbett. But whereas from the start of his career Tibbett sang with imagination and pizzazz, Milnes was lacking in musical sensibility, detailed characterization and depth of feeling until the early eighties. He frequently didn't express words or music with enough intensity. He wasn't tender enough or distraught enough or sufficiently aflame. He did not have enough passion, urgency or emotional tension. He was boring in romantic or contemplative passages, rising to the occasion only when the music turned brilliant or vehement. His phrasing had little dynamic ebb and flow, for he seldom imparted forward motion to upbeats and he rarely tapered the ends of climactic downbeats with diminuendos. He routinely accentuated and held onto the last syllable of a phrase, even where that syllable was on a weak beat that resolved a dissonance. He thus dislocated the phrase's climax, inappropriately transfering it from a point of structural tension to one of structural repose. In addition to throwing music out of kilter, mislocating accents at phrase endings also caused him to stress Italian incorrectly: "amo*re*" instead of "a*mo*re." On a recording of *Don Carlo* from 1970, his singing is unresponsive to phrase shape and blighted by random and misplaced accentuations.

To negotiate the *passaggio*—the area of the voice where chest and head resonance abut—Milnes uses a technique called "covering." Older voice manuals make no mention of it. To judge from letters and reviews, covering gradually came into use in the nineteenth century. After World War I most singers—Italians in particular—covered the *passaggio* and sometimes other areas of the voice. Those who resort to covering often dispute when and where to use it. For many singers covering becomes a matter not of interpretive choice but of technical necessity. Milnes heavily covered notes in the area of his *passaggio*— around F. Although a chief benefit of covering is increased security, he often had intonation difficulties there.

On a 1974 aria album his voice rings forth, particularly on high notes—he sings a number of A-flats, A-naturals and even a B-flat, sounding more like a tenor than a baritone (he probably could have negotiated Siegmund with little difficulty). He trills agreeably and in Rodrigo's death scene encompasses in one breath phrases that many others take in two. His account of "Largo al factotum" surpasses most in variety of inflection. But his renditions of scenes from *I puritani, La favorite, Ernani, Don Carlos* and *La gioconda* suffer from predictability, sameness of expression and insufficient emotion. Although his high voice is not displayed to best advantage in the "Credo" from *Otello* or Rance's monologue from *La fanciulla del West,* he becomes more emotionally involved in them than in the generally more tender and introspective selections from the older operas, where among other things his music making lacks *Schwung,* with one downbeat thumped much like another.

In the early eighties Milnes dropped from sight, and rumors began to circulate that he was seriously ill. Returning, he started to sing with shading, nuance and structural awareness, contouring dynamics and lengthening dissonances so that the vocal line mirrored harmonic tension, moving phrases ahead by adding a touch of crescendo. He learned how to do appoggiaturas expressively, preparing them with crescendos and making diminuendos on resolutions, and came to phrase with regard to proportion and balance. Simon Boccanegra in the fall of 1984 was his zenith—memorable for depth of feeling—although by then the voice had begun to lose bloom and power and to sound constricted in the *passaggio.* Unfortunately, because of his vocal decline, many of New York's opera cognoscenti already had become hostile to him, to the point that they failed to recognize his artistic growth.

By the following season, when he reappeared in the role, his vocal problems had increased. By 1986 his sound was less true, thicker and more spread, also still more covered on top, while the *passaggio* was no better than before: most high Es were scooped (slid up to from below), if they ever reached pitch. In *I puritani* he sometimes failed to render dotted rhythms accurately, making short notes too long. His cavatina had little intense tenderness and his duet with the Arturo (Salvatore Fisichella) no ferocity. Yet he did have passion in some passages, for example, "E di morte lo stral." Recently, Milnes has sounded strangulated on such notes as the F-sharp of "delle lagrime *mie*" (*Un ballo in maschera*), the F of "grida*nò*", the F of "fan*ciul*li" and the F of "*era* voler" (all from *Aida*).

Cornell MacNeil's career paralleled Milnes's. Early on he too was lacking in feeling and characterization. He too developed them—even as his voice declined. The voice itself was bigger. Milnes's sound, particularly in recent years, hasn't seemed quite ample enough for the Met, except on high notes. Still, Milnes was the most prominent American baritone of the seventies and eighties.

—Stefan Zucker

MINTON, Yvonne (Fay).

Mezzo-soprano. Born 4 December 1938, in Sydney, New South Wales. Married: William Barclay, 1965; one son, one daughter. Studied with Marjorie Walker at Sydney Conservatory and with Henry Cummings and Joan Cross in London; won Kathleen Ferrier prize and Hertogenbosch Competition in 1961; debut as Britten's Lucretia, London, 1964; at Covent Garden since 1965, where she first appeared as Lola in *Cavalleria rusticana;* Cologne debut as Sesto in *La clemenza di Tito,* 1969; created Thea in Tippett's *The Knot Garden,* 1970; Chicago debut as Octavian, 1970; debut at Metropolitan Opera in 1973 and Paris Opéra in 1976 in same role; made a Commander of Order of the British Empire, 1980.

Publications

About MINTON: articles–

Rosenthal, H. "Yvonne Minton." *Opera* September (1977).

*   *   *

Few recent singers can compete with Yvonne Minton in versatility. She won applause for her performances of roles in operas by Mozart and Berg, Wagner and Bartók, Berlioz and Strauss. Her success as Dorabella (Mozart's *Così fan tutte*) hardly prepared opera-goers for her equally successful interpretations of Kundry (Wagner's *Parsifal*) and Waltraute (*Götterdämmerung*). Nor did her triumph as Charlotte (Massenet's *Werther*) prepare listeners for her fine portrayals of Countess Geschwitz (Berg's *Lulu*) and of Judith (Bartók's *Bluebeard's Castle*).

Minton's portrayal of Sesto in Mozart's *La clemenza di Tito* (as recorded under Colin Davis) reveals a big voice

marred sometimes, as in the opening duet "Come ti piace, imponi," by a wide vibrato that can obscure the pitch. Elsewhere her voice is less wobbly. In "Parto, ma tu, ben mio" Minton, perhaps inspired by the beautifully in-tune clarinet solo, sings admirably smooth, expressive melodic lines. She sings the great accompanied recitative "Oh dei, che smania è questa" with fire and passion; but to some of the more delicate and sentimental of Sesto's melodies, as in the trio "Se al volto mai ti senti," she brings too much heaviness and richness of voice.

That same richness and heaviness help make Minton a fine Wagner singer. She has won much praise for her many portrayals of Waltraute at Covent Garden, Bayreuth and elsewhere. "Urgent," "impassioned," and "most musical" are among the accolades that critics have awarded Minton for her Wagner singing, often concluding that Minton's Waltraute was the highlight of the entire performance of *Götterdämmerung.*

Minton shares some of her repertory with another leading mezzo-soprano, her younger contemporary Frederica von Stade. They are both first-rate Charlottes in Massenet's *Werther.* Like von Stade, Minton is effective in trouser roles. Early in her career she won praise for her portrayal of Ascanio in Berlioz's *Benvenuto Cellini;* the part was "exquisitely sung," according to one critic. She has sung a "youthful, eager" Octavian in a recording of Strauss's *Rosenkavalier;* she has also sung this latter role at Salzburg and the Metropolitan Opera with great success. And she has won applause for her portrayals of Cherubino (Mozart's *Figaro*), a role that von Stade too has sung to critical acclaim. Minton's voice is a good deal heavier than von Stade's, and this accounts for the difference in their repertories. Unlike von Stade, Minton has rarely ventured into opera of the baroque, classical (Mozart excepted), and early romantic periods. Minton has had little success in the bel canto operas of Rossini, while von Stade has won great applause in Rossini's operas, serious as well as comic. Von Stade, on the other hand, has not found the success achieved by Minton in Wagnerian and twentieth-century opera.

—John A. Rice

MIREILLE.

Composer: Charles Gounod.

Librettist: Michel Carré (after Frédéric Mistral, *Mirèio*).

First Performance: Paris, Théâtre-Lyrique, 19 March 1864; revised, performed 15 December 1864; restored, Henri Büsser, Paris, Opéra-Comique, 6 June 1939.

Roles: Mireille (soprano); Vincent (tenor); Ourrias (baritone); Ramon (bass); Taven (mezzo-soprano); Vincinette (soprano); Ambroise (bass); Andreloun (mezzo-soprano or tenor); Clémence (soprano); Boatman (bass); An Arlesien (baritone); Celestial Voice (soprano); chorus (SSTTBB).

Publications

articles–

Servières, G. "La version originale de *Mireille.*" *Quinzaine musicale* 1 April (1901).

Hahn, R. "La vraie *Mireille.*" In *Thèmes variés,* 101. Paris, 1946.

Crichton, Ronald. "*Mireille* and *Esclarmonde.*" *Opera* December (1983).

Huebner, Steven. "*Mireille* revisited." *Musical Times* 124 (1983): 737.

*   *   *

Charles Gounod is known world-wide as the composer of *Faust* and *Roméo et Juliette,* but his *Mireille* has undeservedly remained a seldom-performed novelty except in France. Based on the narrative poem *Miréio* by Frédéric Mistral, the simple tale of two Provençal lovers is, in Michel Carré's libretto, more faithful to the original than *Faust* was to Goethe or *Roméo* to Shakespeare.

Mistral tells of the love of Mireille, daughter of a wealthy farmer, and Vincent, a poor basket weaver; how it is thwarted by her proud father Ramon, who had chosen Ourrias, a rough "breaker and brander of wild cattle" from the Camargue, as her suitor; of an angry confrontation between the rivals, in which Vincent is believed killed, and the terrified Ourrias finds death awaiting in the Rhône. However, Vincent recovers, and hastens to the chapel of the Saintes-Maries, a seaside shrine, where he and Mireille had vowed to meet if trouble befell them. Aware of his plight, Mireille too makes the journey across the burning hot desert of the Crau, arriving exhausted and stricken by the sun at Saintes-Maries, only to die in Vincent's arms.

Melodramatic as it is, the plot of *Mireille* is no more extreme than those of many operas, and clothed as it is by Gounod in a never-ending wrap of Provençal-inspired melodies, the work would seem to have everything needed for success. Arias, duets, ensembles, choruses, and orchestral passages, all of great lyrical and pastoral beauty and force, follow one another to strong effect. The vigor of the overture (probably the best known excerpt), the ebullience of the lovers' duet "Song of Magali," a pulsating "farandole", a shepherd's plaintive air and Mireille's soul-stirring reply, and Vincent's pleading aria "Angels of paradise" are only some of the highlights of this opulent romantic score. A "Waltz of the Swallows," written as a show-piece by Gounod at the request of Mme Miolan-Carvallo, the first Mireille, was included in the original score, but since it was incidental to the action, it has seldom been repeated in subsequent productions. However, some divas still use it as a display number in concerts dedicated to coloratura acrobatics.

So the question arises, why is *Mireille* regarded as something less than a success? Was it because the public expected Gounod to compose another work comparable to the already

A scene from the first production of Gounod's *Mireille*, Paris, 1864

triumphant *Faust?* Did mid-nineteenth century audiences find its realistic country setting and characters too mundane for their tastes? (A later operagoer blamed its relapse on a lack of "des jolies costumes" for the prima donna). Were its Provençal melodies and traditions too unfamiliar to be accepted abroad? When *Roméo et Juliette* came along three years later to score a tremendous success, *Mireille* was naturally all but forgotten.

Nevertheless, Gounod continued to tinker with the opera, reducing its original five acts to three and making other changes, among them including a happy ending. Colonel Mapleson, the impresario who introduced *Mireille* to London (1864) and America (1884), devised revisions of his own. Sung in New York in Italian, it became *Mirella* with Emma Nevada in the title role singing the Waltz before collapsing in Vincent's arms at the finale, apparently having recovered from sun stroke. In 1901, a "new version by the Opéra-Comique" reverted to the original five acts and seven tableaux, which were retained in the Comique's 1939 presentation of yet another version credited to Reynaldo Hahn and Henri Büsser. After the liberation of Paris during World War II, opera goers could hear *Mireille* almost weekly with a variety of prima donnas. The Metropolitan Opera career of *Mireille* has been surprisingly brief—four performances in 1919 with Maria Barrientos in the title role, Pierre Monteux conducting, and designs by the long-retired baritone, Victor Maurel, a native of Provence.

With the resurgence of interest in French opera in the late 1980s and 1990s, which has led to the return from retirement of *Faust* and *Roméo et Juliette,* as well as the exploration of numerous works of Massenet, there remains the hope that *Mireille* will be rediscovered and appreciated for the unique creation that it is. Perhaps a revision to end all versions, including the best of each, will come from a serious musician enamoured of the melodic genius of Gounod and the Provence of Mistral.

—Louis Snyder

IL MITRIDATE EUPATORE.

Composer: Alessandro Scarlatti.

Librettist: G. Frigimelica Roberti.

First Performance: Venice, San Giovanni Grisostomo, carnival, 1707.

Roles: Laodicea (soprano); Stratonica (soprano); Issicratea (mezzo-soprano); Eupatore (castrato); Farnace (tenor); Pelopida (castrato); Nicomede (castrato); chorus.

Publications

article–

Westrup, Jack A. "Alessandro Scarlatti's *Il Mitridate Eupatore* (1707)." In *New Looks at Italian Opera: Essays in Honor of Donald J. Grout,* 133. Ithaca, New York, 1968.

* * *

Composed on a libretto by Girolamo Frigimelica Roberti for performance in Venice in 1707, *Il Mitridate Eupatore* stands alone among Scarlatti's extant operas in being a *tragedia per musica* (a tragedy with or by means of music). Operas do not, however, end unhappily in this period, even when the librettist's inspiration lies in ancient Greek tragedies; instead, the high purpose of *Il Mitridate Eupatore* is reflected in a straightforward setting of the story, unencumbered by the usual love sub-plots of the period and, unusual for the composer, devoid of comic scenes and characters.

In *Mitridate Eupatore,* as in Sophocles' *Electra,* the hero's mother (here named Stratonica) and her lover (Farnace) have murdered his father and usurped the throne, to the consternation of his sister (Laodicea). Scarlatti's music immediately establishes the dramatic substance of each of the principals in act I: an aria (marked *Rissoluto*) with strings in four parts for the resolute and faithful Laodicea (scene i), a moving invocation to the murdered king for Mitridate Eupatore (scene iv) in *recitativo accompagnato* (a style of declamatory recitative with string accompaniment that is reserved for moments of high drama), an aria in which two clashing obbligato violins contend with the tormented but still formidable Stratonica (scene vi), and yet another aria, now in minor mode, for Laodicea, this one emphatically threatening vengeance (scene vi).

By the end of act I, the typical aria structure of the period has been firmly established. Because each aria is marked *da capo* (repeat part A from the beginning) or *dal segno* (repeat A from the sign), every formal song in the opera will end with the same words with which it began. The result is a succession of static moods that has been described as a concert in costume; in *Mitridate Eupatore,* however, the effect is to reinforce compellingly the characters' obsessive broodings and the sense of inevitability that underlies the classical plot.

In acts II and III of the opera, Eupatore and his wife (disguised as Egyptians) offer to deliver the head of the missing heir to the uneasy royal couple, but they encounter the opposition of Laodicea (and her husband). Again there are strongly characterized arias by Eupatore (invoking the gods in the solemn repeated chords and dotted rhythms of "Patri numi") and Stratonica (her inner conflict between what she desires and the claims of maternal love once again reflected in the fiery obbligato violin parts of "Esci omai"). Also revealed is the cowardly nature of Farnace, not simply in the words and music of his aria ("Ottenga la paura") and his subsequent accompanied recitative (act III, scene i) but in his timbre; as a tenor among a clutch of castrati, his is the only natural—and therefore unheroic by Baroque standards—male voice in the opera.

As in Baroque society, the characters in the opera always remain conscious of their station. The themes and melodic inflections, the rhythms and the word accents, the treatment of dissonance and the varied instrumental accompaniments of the arias express not so much individual human beings as basic character-types in the throes of timeless human emotions. The drama thus takes on the character of a ritual—an effect supported by the highly stylized nature of the scenes, nearly all of which consist of a passage of recitative followed by a *da capo* aria. The measure of Scarlatti's success in *Mitridate* lies in the manner in which he uses the Baroque doctrine of affections to create contrast among the formal expressions of emotion.

After a stirring sinfonia (featuring a pair of trumpets and timpani aboard ship answered by muted trumpets in the orchestra), act IV moves swiftly to the musical climax of the opera. Laodicea watches Mitridate (still in disguise and unknown to her) disembark carrying an urn that supposedly contains his own head. Her ensuing expression of grief, beginning in simple recitative of surpassing intensity and concluding in one of the composer's finest laments ("Cara tomba"), is justly described by Edward Dent (*Alessandro Scarlatti, p.* 108) as reaching the "classic grandeur of Leonora [in *Fidelio*], Donna Anna [in *Don Giovanni*] and Iphigenie [in *Iphigenie en Tauride*]."

The remainder of act IV and a fifth act of equal proportion are required to complete the drama by re-establishing the rightful order of things. Following the expected recognition scene (featuring a *da capo* duet for brother and sister), Eupatore and Laodicea seize the upper hand from the tyrants, a shift of power expressed in a stirring call-to-arms aria with trumpet obbligato by Laodicea's husband. Stratonica is then presented with Farnace's severed head (in place of Eupatore's) and subsequently assassinated by Eupatore's wife. Finally, the opera concludes with the triumphal coronation of Mitridate Eupatore, an event celebrated by the quartet of principal characters that remain.

Il Mitridate Eupatore represents one of Scarlatti's finest operas, a determined but in the event unsuccessful attempt by a composer between secure court appointments to establish himself in the great operatic center of Venice. Not least among its virtues is the successful union of its Greek-derived subject matter with the conventions of Baroque operatic dramaturgy.

—David Poultney

MITRIDATE, RÈ DI PONTO.

Composer: Wolfgang Amadeus Mozart.

Librettist: Vittorio Amadeo Cigna-Santi (after Giuseppe Parini and Racine).

First Performance: Milan, Teatro Regio Ducal, 26 December 1770.

Roles: Mitridate (tenor); Aspasia (soprano); Sifare (soprano); Farnace (alto); Ismene (soprano); Marzio (tenor); Arbate (soprano); A Moor (mute); A Roman (mute).

*   *   *

Mitridate, rè di Ponto (Köchel 87) is the earliest of Mozart's four assays in the genre of *opera seria*. Many hold that the form is antithetical to modern tastes, but *Idomeneo*, arguably the greatest *opera seria* ever written, and *La clemenza di Tito*, a work which is now appreciated as the masterpiece it is, are almost repertory pieces. *Mitridate* is based in part on Racine's 1673 play of the same title, adapted in 1767 by Vittorio Amadeo Cigna-Santi. Mozart set the libretto three years later, when he was only fourteen. At that stage he was not able to breathe life into the characterizations, although there is plenty of emotion in the music. His chief concern, egged on by his father, was to make a splash in Italy, and he went to great lengths to please both singers and audience. While few of Mozart's works written before 1777 would have survived on their own merits had the wonder child not turned into a brilliant genius, intimations of the great Mozart do show up in *Mitridate*.

Mitridate is presumed to have been killed fighting the Romans. His two sons, Sifare and Farnace, are rivals, not so much for the throne as for the hand of Aspasia, who had been betrothed to Mitridate. Aspasia favors Sifare. Mitridate unexpectedly returns, accompanied by Ismene, who is engaged to Farnace. Mitridate is suspicious, believing Farnace to be traitorous and convinced that Aspasia returns Farnace's advances. He angrily offers Farnace to Aspasia, who says that she never loved him. Mitridate swears to kill them all, and Aspasia is offered poison. Just as she is about to take it, Mitridate is suddenly called to fight the Romans; he accepts the challenge even though he knows it will mean certain defeat. His two sons regret their treachery and swear to help their father. But it is too late; Mitridate is mortally wounded. He dies learning of his sons' loyalty and knowing that Sifare and Aspasia, Farnace and Ismene love each other.

The fact that the libretto had earlier been set by the Abbé Quirino Gasparino was to cause Mozart some trouble, as a cabal working against Mozart tried to get Antonia Bernasconi, who was singing the part of Aspasia (she had created the title role in Gluck's *Alceste* in 1767), to substitute Gasparini's arias for Mozart's. She refused, and was overjoyed with those he had written for her. In fact, they are among the best in the opera. Mozart received the libretto in July 1770, but delayed writing the arias until he met with the singers in Milan. He set all the recitatives before arriving in Milan in mid-October, and complained to his sister that his fingers were aching from the work. It seems to have been a stellar cast. Mozart had recently heard Giuseppe Cicognani (Farnace) sing in a performance of Hasse's *La clemenza di Tito,* and described him as having "a delightful voice and a beautiful cantabile." The *primo uomo* role (Sifare) was assigned to Pietro Benedetti, known as Sartorino. He did not arrive in Milan until December 1, two weeks before the first orchestral rehearsal. The part is extremely demanding; Sig. Sartorino must have been an exciting singer. The title role was sung by Guglielmo D'Ettore, who was in the employ of the Elector of Bavaria. His music is the least satisfactory, partly because he insisted on an over-abundance of high B flats and Cs that become tiresome. There is some justice here, as D'Ettore asked for constant revisions, and the Mozarts continued to regard him as the type of singer to avoid.

Mozart's eagerness to oblige the singers is demonstrated by the existence of alternative arias, many of them finished. It has been suggested that Mozart was inhibited by the demands of the singers, but most of the alternatives are not superior to the ones that replaced them, and, as we know, the peculiar talents of singers usually inspired rather than inhibited Mozart. One thinks immediately of such artists as Nancy Storace, Anton Raaff, Adriana Ferraresie del Bene, Josepha Dušek, not to mention Aloysia Weber.

Mitridate contains much music that is pleasing. The arias, taken separately, are generally well written, particularly with respect to the masterly and subtle handling of the orchestra, which at the opening performance numbered almost sixty players. The impact of the music is weakened by too many arias in modified da capo form or with alternating slow and fast sections. As the opera progresses there is considerable tightening of form with increased dramatic and musical effect (we do know the work was not composed in sequence). There is a notable solo for Mme Bernasconi (no. 4) in G minor that is a worthy predecessor of works in that key. There is a striking aria (no. 13) with horn obligato in the second act for Sartorino (in all probability the Milanese player could not cope with its technical demands since a version without horn exists). Apart from the final (and disappointing) *coro* at the end, the only concerted number is a duet for the *prima donna* and the *primo uomo* in A major (no. 18). Sartorino was so pleased with this number, written for him and Bernasconi, that he declared he would be willing to be castrated again if it were not a success. It is a fine piece, perhaps not quite as fine as the alternative version, but dramatically stronger. In the final act there is a remarkable scene for Aspasia (no. 21), which consists of an accompanied recitative, aria, and a concluding recitative with an alarming and effective passage for pizzicato bass. The musical highlight is Sifare's magnificent act III aria (no. 22). It is in C minor, and points the way even as far as the great D minor Piano Concerto.

Mitridate is now receiving some notice (it was performed at the Wexford Festival in 1989 and by the Opera Theatre of St. Louis in 1991). The fine, star-studded Deutsche Grammophon 1977 recording under Leopold Hager could hardly be bettered. It probably will not convince anyone that *Mitridate* is a great work, but it is certainly of more than passing interest, and substantial testimony to the remarkable musical fertility of the young Mozart.

—Lawrence J. Dennis

MÖDL, Martha.

Mezzo-soprano and soprano. Born 22 March 1912, in Nuremberg. Studied with Klinck-Schneider at Nuremberg Conservatory; debut as Hänsel in Nuremberg, 1942; sang mezzo roles in Düsseldorf, 1945-49; appeared at Hamburg

Martha Mödl as Isolde, Bayreuth Festspiele, 1952

Staatsoper, 1947-55; Covent Garden debut as Carmen, 1949; turned to soprano roles in early 1950s; at Bayreuth, 1951-67, where she first appeared as Kundry; Metropolitan Opera debut as Brünnhilde in *Götterdämmerung*, 1957; sang mezzo roles in 1960s; in first performances of Einem's *Kabale und Liebe*, Vienna, 1976, and Reimann's *Gespenstersonate*, Berlin, 1984.

Publications

About MÖDL: books–

Schafer, W. *Martha Mödl.* Hannover, 1967.

*   *   *

Martha Mödl had one of the longest and most interesting careers of any singer during the second half of the twentieth century. In a 1979 interview, she attributed the longevity of her working life to the fact that she did not begin to sing in public until her thirtieth year. The light mezzo-soprano repertory with which she began gave no hint of the dramatic heights she would later scale in the soprano and contralto roles. Cherubino, Dorabella and Hänsel were succeeded by Mignon and Octavian. Her performance as Azucena in Düsseldorf in the late 40s alerted casting directors to her dramatic strengths. She added the roles of Eboli, Lady Macbeth and Ulrica. A recording (in German) of *Un ballo in maschera* conducted by Fritz Busch preserves the impassioned quality she brought to these roles. Klytemnestra—a role she continued to sing for thirty years—and Carmen, which she even sang in English at Covent Garden, led the way to her debut at Bayreuth as Kundry in the famous Wieland Wagner *Parsifal* at the first postwar festival in 1951. This was succeeded by her Isolde and Brünnhilde. These performances have become the touchstone for all modern interpretations, and though later generations of sopranos have all elicited firmer control and more even pitch, no one seems to have equaled Mödl's grasp of the emotional possibilities in these roles.

She recorded the *Walküre* Brünnhilde with Furtwängler for EMI and later the whole *Ring* with the same conductor for Italian radio. In these recordings, as in her Kundry under Knappertsbusch and Isolde under Karajan, both from Bayreuth, one can hear the richness and power of the middle of her voice and the wholehearted commitment of her acting—as well as the strain apparent even then in the upper register. Inevitably her excursion into the soprano range took its toll on her voice; she also sang Marie in *Wozzeck* and Leonore in *Fidelio*, which she recorded with Furtwängler and also sang at the reopening of the Vienna Staatsoper in 1955.

By the 1960s she had forsaken these soprano parts and returned to her natural mezzo range. She then began what may be the most fascinating part of her career. In this later part of her career she was particularly admired in *Lulu*, as Geschwitz, and as the Countess in *Queen of Spades*. In addition to her vocal skill, Mödl was a dominating presence on the stage, able to establish a rapport with the audience, even (or perhaps especially) when they were unfamiliar with the work in performance. But it will always be Mödl's performances at Bayreuth in the early 1950s to which people will turn to know what it was that led Alan Blyth, for instance, to write that "*Wie wunder tönt, was wonnig du singst* might be a description of Mödl's performances—this kind of interpretive inspiration is something that simply cannot be caught in the studio."

—Patrick O'Connor

MOFFO, Anna.

Soprano. Born 27 June 1932, in Wayne, Pennsylvania. Studied with Giannini-Gregory at the Curtis Institute of Music and in Rome at the Accademia di Santa Cecilia with Luigi Ricci and Mercedes Llopart; debut as Norina in Spoleto, 1955; appeared as Butterfly for Milan television, 1956; Vienna Staatsoper debut, 1958; Salzburg, 1959; American debut as Mimì at Chicago Lyric Opera, 1957; Metropolitan Opera debut as Violetta, 1959; suffered a vocal breakdown in 1974, but resumed her career in 1976.

*   *   *

Anna Moffo was born in Wayne, Pennsylvania, on 27 June 1932, of Italian parentage. She studied at the University of Pennsylvania and the Curtis Institute of Music with Eufemia Giannini-Gregory. She received a Fulbright grant to study voice in Italy and attended Rome's Accademia di Santa Cecilia, where her teachers included Luigi Ricci and Mercedes Llopart. She has received honorary doctorates from Temple University and Ursinus College; and in 1985 she received a

Anna Moffo as Violetta in *La traviata*

Doctor of Humane Letters degree from Nazareth College of Rochester.

After several appearances over Italian radio, she sang the title role of Puccini's *Madama Butterfly* for a Milan television production. She also appeared as Norina in *Don Pasquale* at the Spoleto "Festival of Two Worlds." These two performances established her reputation as a singer in Europe. In 1956 she sang Zerlina at Aix-en-Provence. In 1958 she made her debut at the Vienna Staatsoper and in 1959 she sang at the Salzburg Festival, in Austria.

Meanwhile in 1957, she was engaged by the Chicago Lyric Opera, and sang her American opera debut there as Mimì in *La bohème.* She returned to the United States in 1959 for her Metropolitan debut as Violetta in Verdi's *La traviata.* Throughout the 1960s and early 1970s Moffo appeared in opera houses around the world including Milan, Vienna, Hamburg, Munich, London, Rome, Chicago, Buenos Aires, as well as performing eighteen major roles at the Metropolitan Opera in New York City. Her roles have included Norina in *Don Pasquale,* Pamina in *Die Zauberflöte,* Gilda in *Rigoletto,* Marguerite in *Faust,* Violetta in *La traviata,* as well as the heroines of *Les contes d'Hoffmann.*

Moffo's varied and successful career has helped to broaden the general appeal of opera. Her work in films and television, as well as her natural beauty, charming stage presence, and considerable dramatic talents have made her a role model for the modern opera singer.

Moffo has not confined herself to the operatic stage, but has made numerous television appearances, including her own Italian television series *The Anna Moffo Show.* She has also been a guest on special segments of *The Caterina Valente Show,* telecast live from Stuttgart, Germany, and on the American premiere of *Buonasera Raffaella* which was beamed live via satellite to forty-six countries on Radiotelevisione Italiana. She has also starred in film versions of *La traviata, Lucia di Lammermoor, La belle Hélène, Die Czardasfürstin* and *La serva padrona,* as well as in fourteen nonoperatic feature films.

In the fall of 1984, Video Arts International released a video cassette of *Lucia di Lammermoor* for home viewers. Her performance received glowing praise. *Video Now* (February 1985) called her "vocally radiant, dramatically convincing, and heartbreakingly beautiful as Lucia" and *Opera News* (March 30, 1985) called the video a "satisfying film" and lauded Moffo's "expressive" singing and acting ability.

Noteworthy among her recordings of complete operas, is Puccini's *La bohème* recorded with Maria Callas, recently released on compact disc by EMI. She has also made several recordings of operatic arias which have been well produced and well received. Her recording devoted to Verdi heroines was awarded the Orfée d'Or and her recording of coloratura arias, coached by Tullio Serafin, is probably her best work on record.

Moffo has a soprano quality which defies categorization; she has been critically assessed as a lyric, a coloratura and also a dramatic soprano. The broad range of her musical capabilities has enabled her to perform a broad range of roles rather than specialize in a certain "Fach" or "type." However, the exploitation of her musical and dramatic breadth by unsuitable choices in theater roles and in recordings led to vocal problems in the mid-1970s.

Her long list of honors include the Commendatore of the Order of Merit of the Republic of Italy and Rome's Masquera d'Argento, the prestigious Michelangelo Award and the Golden Rose of Montreux for the television production of *La sonnambula.* Recent additions include Liebe Augustin from the city of Vienna (1984), induction into the Academy of

Vocal Arts (Philadelphia) First Hall of Fame for Great American Opera Singers (1985) and the Citation of Merit from the New York Singing Teacher's Association (1986). In 1987 she was given the first annual Voice Award by the Academy of Arts and Culture under the auspices of the American Israel Opera Foundation. In 1990 Moffo received a special award from the Friends of the Staatsoper in Vienna and La Caveja d'Oro for "Artist of the Year" in Milan.

—Patricia Robertson

MOLL, Kurt.

Bass. Born 11 April 1938, in Buir, Germany. Studied at Cologne Hochschule für Musik and with Emmy Müller in Krefeld; small roles with Cologne Opera while a student, 1958-61; official debut as Lodovico in *Otello,* Cologne, 1961; in Aachen, 1961-63; Mainz, 1964-65; in Wuppertal, 1966-69; joined Hamburg Staatsoper in 1970; sang Fafner at Bayreuth, 1974; sang Marke at the Teatro alla Scala, 1974; appeared as Gurnemanz in *Parsifal* in San Francisco, 1974; Covent Garden debut as Caspar in *Der Freischütz,* 1975; Metropolitan Opera debut as Landgrave in *Tannhäuser,* 1978; Chicago Lyric Opera debut as Daland, 1983; created the King in Biala's *Der geistefelte Kater.*

* * *

Kurt Moll's voice encompasses the major bass roles of the German, Italian, Russian, and French repertoires, especially those of Wagner, Mozart, and Richard Strauss. His legato phrasing, which is to a large extent the key to the quality of his singing, may derive in part from his early training as a cellist. Moll's operatic career began in 1959 in small theaters of Germany—Aachen, Wuppertal, Mainz, Cologne—where he gained experience and slowly grew into his roles. He has been careful to remain within his *Fach* (vocal category)—true bass roles—performing roles that avoid the high Es, Fs, and F-sharps required for bass-baritone roles, which he feels would shorten his vocal life. His chief Wagner role is Gurnemanz in *Parsifal*—an extremely long role that the beauty of Moll's voice can make seem short—which he has sung at the Salzburg Easter Festival and at the Metropolitan Opera and which he has recorded under Herbert von Karajan; he has avoided the higher roles of Wotan and Hans Sachs. Musorgsky's *Boris Godunov* has also figured in Moll's career.

Since Moll's Metropolitan debut in 1978 he has sung there, in addition to Gurnemanz, Osmin in Mozart's *Die Entführung aus dem Serail,* Sparafucile in Verdi's *Rigoletto,* Rocco in Beethoven's *Fidelio,* Hermann in Wagner's *Tannhäuser,* Baron Ochs in Richard Strauss's *Der Rosenkavalier,* and Lodovico in Verdi's *Otello.*

A frequent performer at the major opera houses of Europe, Moll has appeared at many European opera festivals; he has portrayed King Marke in Wagner's *Tristan und Isolde* at the 1974 Bayreuth Festival; the King in Verdi's *Aida* and Baron Ochs at the Salzburg Festival; and Pogner in Wagner's *Die Meistersinger,* King Marke in Wagner's *Tristan und Isolde,* the Alcalde in Wolf's *Die Corregidor,* Sarastro in Mozart's *Die Zauberflöte,* and Abul Hassan in Cornelius's *Der Barbier von Bagdad* at the Munich Festival, among many other roles,

under the guidance of such directors as Peter Stein, August Everding, Otto Schenk, and Günther Rennert.

Moll's comic roles include a satisfyingly understated, almost noble Baron Ochs—in keeping with Strauss's description of Ochs as coarse and vulgar only on the inside, but outwardly presentable—and an Osmin who never needs to flirt with the flat side of the note for supposedly humorous effect.

Moll's voice has been described by critics as full, round-toned, resonant, richly sonorous, and plush, with a quality that has been called splendor. He conveys a vigorous, lively intelligence and an underlying sense of humor that preempt dullness, although he has been criticized for a certain interpretive blandness. His has been called the most beautiful German bass voice in the world today, and he is known for his human and characterful singing as well as his beautifully formed vocalism.

He has described himself as a "vocal painter, finding new colors in a role, bringing out the emotional chiaroscuro as well as stark blacks and whites" (in an interview in *Opera News,* 12 March 1983).

—Michael Sims

DER MOND [The Moon].

Composer: Carl Orff.

Librettist: Carl Orff (after the Brothers Grimm).

First Performance: Munich, 5 February 1939; revised, 1950.

Roles: The Narrator (tenor); Four Fellows Who Steal the Moon (tenor, bass, baritones); A Peasant (baritone); St Peter (bass); Village Mayor (speaking); Innkeeper (speaking); Child (speaking); chorus.

* * *

Carl Orff selected a fairy tale from the folk collection of the Brothers Grimm for this ninety-minute work, originally intended as a vehicle for musical puppet-theater. When Orff realized the complications that arose in staging, he abandoned the miniature idea and proceeded to develop a mature work for stage that of all his compositions most closely resembles an opera. Nine years before its creation, the composer had conducted the Bach Society of Munich in his stage adaptation of a St Luke's Passion, wrongly attributed to Bach, and from that performance Orff borrowed the concept of using a narrator for chronological cohesion, to be skillfully applied in *Der Mond.* Unlike the case with later works, there is here a close adherence to the original text; exact quotes from the Grimm version are given to the narrator, while most of the dialogue is original with Orff. Much of the remaining original material appears in stage directions, or is paraphrased in bits of dialogue.

Der Mond is the story of a moon-less country, from which four lads venture forth into another land, find the moon hanging on an oak tree, steal it, and carry it off to their hometown. They claim, of course, that they bought it as a gift for the town, and exact a weekly wage for its upkeep. The second part of the work begins with the deaths of the four lads, now quite elderly, who are each buried with their part of the moon as inheritance. In the town crypt, they emerge from their coffins, reassemble the moon, and hang it from a rafter. The dead stir uneasily, but gradually emerge and set up earthly revelries, which soon lead to quarrels, shouting, and general uproar. The noise is heard by Peter, the Wise Old Guardian of the Heavens, who comes down, restores order, takes the moon and hangs it once more in its rightful place in the sky. The proper balance of life to the living and rest to the dead is thus renewed.

Orff rejected the strong Christocentric emphasis in the Grimm version, deleting all references to the devil, canceling any identity of hell with the underworld, and stating emphatically that Peter is *not* Saint Peter but a Wise Old Guardian of the Heavens. Cited as Orff's last "romantic" work (mainly because of the orchestration), this delightful romp that the composer called "A Small World-Theater" is high-spirited and sketches broadly the foibles of mankind: "All of this is as in living,/No one wants to be forgiving,/Each one plays his crooked game,/No one ever gets his aim." The role of the chorus is major, and its vigorous rhythms bear the stamp of the earlier *Carmina burana.* Influences of early psalmody and plainsong are evident, amid snatches of *Sprechstimme* for soloists and chorus alike, and a percussion section that constitutes an orchestra within an orchestra.

Orff revised this work at least eight times, and the three published editions (1940, 1957, 1973) bear marked signs of this, chiefly in tempo changes. A major alteration, however, which most directly affects any planned production of this work concerns Peter's wonderful "aria," which was changed to a spoken version, but the 1957 score containing the musical setting, deserves serious consideration.

—Jean C. Sloop

IL MONDO DELLA LUNA [The World of the Moon].

Composer: Franz Joseph Haydn.

Librettist: C. Goldoni.

First Performance: Esterháza, 3 August 1777.

Roles: Ecclitico (contralto); Buonafede (bass); Lisetta (mezzo-soprano); Clarice (soprano); Flaminia (soprano); The Doctor (baritone); Cecco (tenor); Leandro (tenor); Ernesto (tenor); Four Zanies (two tenors, two baritones); Four Marionettes (two sopranos, two baritones); chorus (SATB).

Publications

articles–

Thomas, Günter. "Zu 'Il mondo della luna' und 'La fedeltà premiata': Fassungen und Pasticcios." *Haydn-Studien* 2 (1969): 113.
_____. "Observations on *Il Mondo della luna.*" In *Haydn Studies,* edited by Jens Peter Larsen, Howard Serwer, and James Webster, 144. New York and London, 1981.
Braga, Michael. "Haydn, Goldoni, and *Il mondo della luna.*" *Eighteenth-Century Studies* 17 (1983-84).

Thomas, Günter. "Zur Frage der Fassungen in Haydns *Il mondo della luna.*" *Analecta Musicologica* 22 (1984): 405.

*   *   *

Il mondo della luna is Haydn's first opera staged at Eszterháza following the institution of a regular opera season by his patron, Prince Nicholas, in 1776. It is also the last of three mid-century librettos by the Venetian comic poet Carlo Goldoni to be set by Haydn. (The other two are *Lo speziale* of 1768 and *Le pescatrici* of 1769-70.) Goldoni's fanciful story of life on the moon maintained its popularity well into the 1780s in revised texts set by Paisiello and Neri-Bondi. Haydn's libretto corresponds to Goldoni's original almost to the end of act II; beginning with the act II finale (scenes xv and xvi), Haydn's text follows that of Gennaro Astaritta's 1775 *Il mondo della luna* for Venice, with the exception of the act III closing chorus for which no concordant source is known.

Central to the opera is a plan devised by the false astrologer, Ecclitico, to trick Buonafede, a protective old father, into allowing his two daughters, Flaminia and Clarice, and his servant, Lisetta, on whom Buonafede has designs, to marry their lovers of choice, respectively Ernesto, Ecclitico, and Cecco (Ernesto's servant). After observing the delights of life on the moon through Ecclitico's telescope, Buonafede, literally "good faith," needs little persuasion to swallow an elixir, in reality a sleeping potion, by which he is to be transported to the lunar world. Upon awaking in Ecclitico's grandly decorated garden, Buonafede extols the moon's many beauties and watches as Cecco, disguised as the lunar emperor, crowns Lisetta empress.

This coronation scene is the sole event of Goldoni's act II finale, but the unknown author of Astaritta's revisions lengthens the finale. Included in this revised text are frequent comic interjections of nonsense language or "moonspeak" and several events from Goldoni's act III, including the betrothal of Buonafede's daughters and the old man's discovery of the hoax. By shoving these events into the second finale, act III is eviscerated dramatically—save for Clarice's and Ecclitico's beautifully evocative love duet "Un certo ruscelletto" and the closing reconciliation. With its enriched action, however, the second finale is better equipped to handle extended musical development. That the serious couple, Flaminia and Ernesto, are now permitted to participate in the finale's comic action further shows the tremendous changes in finale design since the form's mid-century inception. Although their characters are not as well-defined as the others, Flaminia and Ernesto are provided with exquisite music, of which her grand coloratura aria "Ragion nell' alma siede" and his austere yet beautiful "Qualche volta non fa male"—which Haydn later adapted as the Benedictus of his *Missa Cellensis* (the "Mariazell Mass," 1782)—are notable examples.

The moon held much fascination for eighteenth-century society, and to depict this exotic and distant land Haydn wrote several pastorale-style ballet and pantomime numbers. The three musical interludes accompanying Buonafede's observations of "life on the moon" (act I, scene iii) and the dances performed upon his arrival in "moonland" (opening of act II) lend themselves to imaginative stagings. Such extended use of instrumental music is found in no other Haydn opera.

Another interesting feature of this work is the use of harmony and tonality to link dramatic events across the opera. The overture, also known in an altered version as the opening movement of Symphony no. 63, "La Roxelane," opens in C major and closes in the dominant minor, G minor, leading to a choral introduction in E-flat major whose three flats symbolize the "triforme dea" ("threefold goddess") addressed by Ecclitico's students in "O luna lucente." A similar harmonic path is traced near the end of act I; as Buonafede contemplates swallowing the elixir, a passage of accompanied recitative beginning in C major and closing on a G minor chord precedes the act I finale's key of E-flat major. Here Buonafede's hallucinatory journey to the moon, depicted in the abundant assonance and alliteration of Goldoni's text ("Vado, vado, volo, volo") is mirrored by Haydn's delightful flight music. Attempts to trace associative tonalities across the opera, however, are hampered by the many revisions and transpositions the score underwent as a result of changes in cast and conceptions of vocal-type prior to the first production.

—Caryl Clark

MONIUSZKO, Stanisław.

Composer. Born 5 May 1819, in Ubiel, province of Minsk, Russia. Died 4 June 1872, in Warsaw. Studied with August Freyer in Warsaw, 1827-30; studied with Rungenhagen in Berlin, 1837-39; church organist in Vilnius, 1840-58; settled in Warsaw, 1858; professor at the Warsaw conservatory.

Operas

Edition: *S. Moniuszko: Dziela*. Edited by W. Rudziński. Cracow, 1965-

A Night's Lodging in the Apennines [*Nocleg w Apeninach*] (operetta), A. Fredo, Vilnius, 1839.
The Ideal or The New Preciosa [*Ideal czyli Nowa Precioza*] (operetta), O. Milewski, 1840, Vilnius, 1840.
Carmagnole or The French Like Joking [*Karmaniol czyli Francuzi lubia zartować*] (operetta), O. Milewski (after Théaulon de Forges and Jaime), 1841.
The Yellow Nightcap [*Zólta szlafmyca*] (operetta), F. Zablocki, 1841.
The New Don Quixote of One Hundred Follies [*Nowy Don Quichot Czyli Sto szaleństw*] (operetta), A. Fredo, 1841, Lwów, 1849.
The Lottery [*Loteria*] (operetta), O. Milewski, 1842 or 1843, Minsk, November 1843.
Halka, W. Wolski, 1846-47, concert performance, Vilnius, 1 January 1848; revised, 1857, staged performance, Warsaw, 1 January 1858.
Idyll [*Sielanka*], W. Marcinkiewicz, 1848? [lost].
Gypsies [*Cyganie*] (operetta), F.D. Kniaźnin, 1850, Vilnius, 20 May 1852; revised as *Jawnuta*, Warsaw, 5 June 1860.
Bettly, after Eugène Scribe and A.H.J. Mélesville, *Le chalet* (translated by F. Schober), 1852, Vilnius, 20 May 1852.
The Raftsman [*Flis*], W. Boguslawski, 1858, Warsaw, 24 September 1858.
Rokiczana, J. Korzeniowski, 1858-59 [unfinished].
The Countess [*Hrabina*], W. Wolski, 1859, Warsaw, 7 February 1860.
Verbum Nobile, J. Chęciński, 1860, Warsaw, 1 January 1860.
The Haunted Manor [*Straszny dwór*], J. Chęciński, 1861-64, Warsaw, 28 September 1865.

Paria, J. Chęciński (after C. Delavigne), 1859-69, Warsaw, 11 December 1869.
Beata (operetta), J. Chęciński, 1870 or 1871, Warsaw, 2 February 1872.
Trea, J.S. Jasiński, 1872 [unfinished].
The Bureaucrats [*Biuraliści*], F. Skarbek.
Water of Life [*Cudowna woda*] [lost].
The Seer's Dream [*Sen wieszcza*], after Rosier and de Leuven, *Le songe d'une nuit d'été* (translated W. Syrokomla) [lost].
The New Landlord [*Nowy dziedzic*] (operetta), M. Radziszewski.
The Musicians Struggle [*Walka muzyków*] (operetta), W. Marcinkiewicz [lost].
Conscription [*Pobór rekrutów*] (operetta), W. Marcinkiewicz [lost].

Other works: incidental music, ballets, sacred and secular vocal works, instrumental works.

Publications

By MONIUSZKO: books–

Pamiętnik do nauki harmonii [harmony textbook]. 1871.
Rudziński, W., and M. Stokowska, eds. *Stanisław Moniuszko: listy zebrane* [collected letters]. Cracow, 1969.

articles–

"Listy Stanisława Moniuszki do Leopolda Maruszyuskiego oraz do Pauliny i Augusta Wilkońskich" [letters to Matuszyński and Paulina and August Wilkoński; summary in English]. *Muzyka* 25/no. 1 (1980): 55.

About MONIUSZKO: books–

Walicki, A. *Stanisław Moniuszko*. Warsaw, 1873.
Poliński, A. *Moniuszko*. Kiev, 1914.
Jachimecki, Z. *Moniuszko*. Warsaw, 1924; 2nd ed., Cracow, 1983.
Opieński, H. *S. Moniuszko: życie i dziela* [life and early works]. Lwów, 1924.
Niewiadomski, S. *Stanisław Moniuszko*. Warsaw, 1928.
Rudziński, W., and J. Prosnak. *Almanach Moniuszkowski: 1872-1952*. Warsaw, 1952.
————. *Stanisław Moniuszko*. Cracow, 1954; 4th ed., 1972.
————. *Stanisław Moniuszko*. Cracow, 1955-61.
Prosnak, J. *Stanisław Moniuszko*. Cracow, 1964; 2nd ed., 1969.
Kaczyński, T. *Dzieje sceniczne "Halka" Stanisława Moniuszki* [performance history of *Halka*]. Cracow, 1969.
Maciejewski, Boguslaw M. *Moniuszko: Father of Polish Opera*. London, 1979.
Prosnak, J. *Moniuszko*. Cracow, 1980.

articles–

Karlowicz, J. "Rys ywota i twórczości Stanisława Moniuszki" [life and works]. *Echo muzycne teatralne i artystyczne* 2/nos. 66-68, 70, 72, 74, 76, 78 (1885).
Jachimecki, Z. "S. Moniuszko and Polish Music." *Slavonic Review* 2 (1924): 533.
————. "Stanislaus Moniuszko." *Musical Quarterly* 14 (1928): 54.
Belza, I. "Monyushko v Rossii." *Sovetskaya muzyka* no. 6 (1952): 73; Polish translation in *Muzyka* 3/nos. 9-10 (1952): 30.

Seaman, Gerald. "The Rise of Slavonic Opera, I." *New Zealand Slavonic Journal* 2 (1978): 1.

Bator, Zbigniew. "Halka-o czym to ject?" [dramaturgy of *Halka*]. *Ruch muzyczny* 15, 16 (1983): 3, 22.

Nowaczyk, Erwin. "Stanisława Moniuszki *Halka*." *Ruch muzyczny* 18/no. 21 (1984): 1, 24.

_____. "Niezwykle dzieje partytury *Strasznego dworu*" [history of the score of *The Haunted Manor*]. *Ruch muzyczny* 15/July (1984): 3.

Moniuszko was the leading Polish opera composer of the nineteenth century. Like Glinka in Russia, Erkel in Hungary and Smetana in the Czech lands, he has become associated above all with the concept of a national style in opera, and to some extent he himself fostered this idea.

Moniuszko was very much a product of his time and place. Apart from two years of study in Berlin (1837-39), he spent his active working career in Poland, where musical life—in the wake of the 1830 insurrection—was uneducated and conservative, with little in the way of sustained institutional development in any of the major cities. The music which responded most directly to the needs of the country during these years was not Chopin's, which so obviously transcended those needs, but Moniuszko's, in the twelve volumes of his *śpiewnik domowi* (home song-books) and in his operas. In the provincial setting of Vilnius and later in Warsaw he fathered a national operatic style of conservative bent, coloring the European styles of an earlier generation with the rhythms of Polish national dances in a manner which was to dictate the musical formulation of "Polishness" to later composers.

It was a during a visit to Warsaw in 1846 that Moniuszko met the poet and librettist Włodzimierz Wolski, with whom he collaborated in the first Polish "grand opera" *Halka*. The success of this work at its Warsaw premiere in 1858 (a shorter version was given in Vilnius 10 years earlier) belatedly launched Moniuszko's career, ensuring him a post as Director of Polish Productions at the Grand Theater and enabling him to produce there a succession of later operas, including *Flis* (*The Raftsman*), *Hrabina* (*The Countess*), *Verbum Nobile* and, above all, *Straszny dwór* (*The Haunted Manor*).

While working on *Straszny dwór*, Moniuszko was inevitably caught up in the growing political ferment which led to the insurrection of 1863. The work, regarded as excessively patriotic in tone, was withdrawn after three performances in 1865. From this point there was a decline in Moniuszko's creative powers and his last major works, the "Indian" opera *Paria* and the one-act operetta *Beata*, were failures with the Warsaw public at their first performances in 1869 and 1872 respectively.

Of his mature operas, only one (*Paria*) does not have a Polish setting. *Hrabina*, *Verbum Nobile* and *Straszny dwór* depict the world of the Polish gentry, *Flis* turns rather to the ordinary Polish people, while *Halka* concerns the relation between the two. In all there is a celebration of the social life and customs of Poland, past and present, and it was inevitable that the operas would become a focus for the nationalist sentiment of a people deprived of political status. The nationalist element would often be heightened in production, moreover, by idealizing the world of an earlier "Grand Poland" as a foil to contemporary discontents. In this context the national dances (polonaise, mazurka and krakowiak, which underpin so much of Moniuszko's music) carried powerfully symbolic values.

Halka set this national tone, with choral polonaises and polonaise arias depicting the nobility while mazurka and krakowiak arias represent the lower orders. In keeping with its setting, *Flis* employs only mazurka and krakowiak elements. *Hrabina*, *Verbum Nobile* and *Straszny dwór* again juxtapose polonaise- and mazurka-based movements with an additional krakowiak aria in act I of *Straszny dwór* and a sprinkling of polkas (a Czech "Polish dance") in *Hrabina*. Other national elements include the Highlander dances in act III of *Halka*, and the use of folksong for the Huntsmen's choruses in *Hrabina* and *Straszny dwór*. Most curious of all are the polonaise and mazurka elements which find their way into the thoroughly Indian setting of *Paria!*

National elements apart, Moniuszko's operas are indebted above all to early nineteenth century French models in their overall design. *Halka* and *Hrabina* are similar in general layout to French grand opera (Auber's *La muette di Portici* was a particular influence), especially in their extended scenic tableaux. The one-act *Flis* and *Verbum Nobile* resemble some of the one-act operas prepared by Scribe for the Opéra-Comique. It is mainly in solo vocal writing that Moniuszko comes closest stylistically to Italian composers, Rossini in particular. But in general solo arias are not extensive in the operas, and tend to be outweighed by duets, ensembles and choruses. In the choral writing and also in the orchestral style of *Halka* and parts of *Straszny dwór*, the primary influence was Weber; Moniuszko knew *Der Freischütz* well and regarded it as an important model for his own conception of national opera.

The particular "blend" of established European traditions and Polish national dances has ensured for Moniuszko's operas a special place in the Polish repertory, though there are as yet few signs that they can be exported with success.

—Jim Samson

MONTEMEZZI, Italo.

Composer. Born 4 August 1875, in Vigasio, near Verona. Died 15 May 1952, in Vigasio. Studied with Saladino and Ferroni at the Milan Conservatory, graduating 1900; in the United States, 1939, where he lived primarily in California; returned to Italy, 1949.

Operas

Publisher: Ricordi.

Bianca, Z. Strani.
Giovanni Gallurese, F. d'Angelantonio, Turin, 28 January 1905.
Hellera, Luigi Illica (after Benjamin Constant, *Adolphe*), Turin, 17 March 1909.
L'amore dei tre re, after S. Benelli, Milan, Teatro alla Scala, 10 April 1913.
La nave, G. d'Annunzio, Milan, Teatro alla Scala, 1 November 1918.
La notte di Zoraima, M. Ghisalberti, Milan, Teatro alla Scala, 31 January 1931.
L'incantesimo, S. Benelli, National Broadcasting Company, 1943; staged performance, Verona, 1952.

Other works: orchestral works, choral works, one chamber piece.

Publications

About MONTEMEZZI: books–

Navarra, U. *Noterelle critiche sulla tragedia . . . La nave. . . .* Milan, 1918.
Tretti, L., and L. Fiumi, eds. *Omaggio a Italo Montemezzi.* Verona, 1952.

articles–

Gilman, Lawrence. "A Note on Montemezzi." In *Nature in Music and Other Studies,* 155. New York, 1914.
Lualdi, A. "L'amore dei tre re di Montemezzi alla Scala." In *Serate musicali,* 237. Milan, 1928.
Tomelleri, L. "La nave (d'Annunzio e Montemezzi)." In L. Tomelleri, I. Pizzetti, et al., *Gabriele d'Annunzio e la musica,* 40. Milan, 1939; reprinted in *Rivista musicale italiana* 43 (1939): 200.
Serafin, T. "Italo Montemezzi." *Opera News* 17/no. 12 (1952-53): 10, 31.
Toni, A. "Italo Montemezzi." *Ricordiana* 2/new series (1956): 229.

*   *   *

Italo Montemezzi was born and died in Vigasio, near Verona, although from 1939 to 1949 he lived mainly in California. At the time of his death various world-class conductors paid him homage. Eugene Ormandy called him "one of the greatest Italian composers of our epoch"; Leopold Stokowski expressed "immense admiration for his creative powers"; and Bruno Walter noted that Montemezzi's place is "honorable and lasting in the great history of Italian opera." Much of Montemezzi's career was closely allied with that of another great conductor, Tullio Serafin. The two met as composition students at the Milan Conservatory, where Montemezzi took a diploma in 1900 and then taught harmony for a year. During that year he composed his first opera, a one-act work titled *Bianca,* for a prize competition.

Aside from his one year of teaching, Montemezzi was able to live entirely from composition for his entire career. His second opera, *Giovanni Gallurese,* was, like *Bianca,* originally written in one act for a competition; the work did not win Montemezzi the competition and was then recast in three acts to a libretto by d'Angelantonio. Serafin helped to get this work produced in Turin, where it premiered on 28 January 1905. Although Montemezzi and Serafin were apprehensive because they did not consider the chorus to be ready at the dress rehearsal, the opera was a great success and was given seventeen times in one month. In 1924 it was conducted at the Metropolitan Opera by Serafin with Giacomo Lauri-Volpi in the leading tenor role. With *Giovanni Gallurese* the principal features of Montemezzi's operatic style were already established: a dramatic instinct allied with solid craftsmanship; a score that included touches of local color; Wagnerian harmonies; and, in the Italian tradition, a texture that promotes predominance of the voice.

Montemezzi's second professional undertaking was the opera *Hellera,* composed to a three-act libretto by Puccini's librettist, Luigi Illica. Serafin likewise directed the premiere of this work, in addition to the revival at the Rome Opera in 1937. Montemezzi's reputation rests mainly on his next opera, *L'amore dei tre re,* the premiere of which was conducted by Serafin in 1913 and then given the following year at the Metropolitan with Toscanini in the pit. This opera has in fact proven far more popular in the United States than in Italy. It is characterized by a lack of vocal lyricism, even though the orchestral music is very stirring and closely depictive of emotions and events. The work is based on the play of the same name by Sem Benelli and Montemezzi's vocal writing has obviously been influenced by the sung-play declamation of Debussy's *Pelléas et Mélisande.* The two operas also have a number of elements of plot in common. Writing in *Opera* in June 1982, Patrick Smith deemed Montemezzi's *L'amore dei tre re* "weak-water stuff, expertly put together but sounding like this or that late nineteenth-century composition."

In an *Opera News* article just after Montemezzi's death, Serafin revealed that he considered *La nave,* premiered in 1918, to be the composer's best opera; it was a work that was well received by the critics at the time of its premiere. The libretto is by Gabriele D'Annunzio and the score shows decided Straussian influences. Serafin also notes that *La nave* is both difficult to sing and expensive to stage, for the ship of the title must sink in the last act. The work opened the 1919 Chicago season starring Rosa Raisa. After *La nave* Montemezzi's career entered a long silence, interrupted by a few stage works such as *La notte di Zoraima,* sung by Rosa Ponselle at the Metropolitan under Serafin's baton in 1931, and *L'incantesimo.* Neither of these works shows any advance in Montemezzi's musical language from his earliest works.

—Stephen Willier

MONTEUX, Pierre.

Conductor. Born 4 April 1875, in Paris. Died 1 July 1964, in Hancock, Maine. Married: Doris Hodgkins, singer, 1927. Studied violin with Berthelier, harmony with Lavignac, and composition with Lenepveu at the Paris Conservatory; first prize in violin, 1896; violinist and then chorus master of the Cologne Orchestra; violist with the orchestra of the Opéra-Comique, Paris; organized the Concerts Berlioz at the Casino de Paris, 1911; conductor for Diaghilev's Ballets Russes, 1911; conducted the premieres of Stravinsky's ballets *Petrouchka* and *Le sacre du printemps,* and his opera *Le rossignol,* Ravel's *Daphnis et Chloé,* and Debussy's *Jeux;* conducted at the Paris Opéra, 1913-14; founded the Société des Concerts Populaires in Paris, 1914; guest conductor throughout Europe; toured the United States with the Ballets Russes, 1916-17; conducted the Civic Orchestra Society of New York, 1917; conducted at the Metropolitan Opera, 1917-19; conductor of the Boston Symphony Orchestra, 1919-24; associate conductor of the Concertgebouw Orchestra of Amsterdam, 1924-34; principal conductor of the Orchestre Symphonique de Paris, 1929-38; conductor of the San Francisco Symphony Orchestra, 1936-52; naturalized United States citizen, 1942; guest conductor with the Boston Symphony Orchestra, beginning 1951; conducted at the Metropolitan Opera, 1953-56; principal conductor of the London Symphony Orchestra, 1961.

Publications

By MONTEUX: books–

with Doris G. Monteux. *Everyone is Someone.* New York, 1962.

About MONTEUX: books–

Monteux, Doris G. *It's All in the Music.* New York, 1965.
Schonberg, H. *The Great Conductors.* New York, 1967.

articles–

Canarina, J. "Pierre Monteux: a Conductor for All Repertoire." *April* (1986).

Pierre Monteux was a professional string player at the start of his career, and this gave him an inside knowledge of the orchestra that never left him. He led the Paris Opéra-Comique orchestra's violas for the premiere of Debussy's *Pelléas et Mélisande* in 1902 and never lost his admiration for "this inspired opera," while the other playing experience which he gained as a member of the Geloso String Quartet from 1894-1911 provided him with a wonderful ear for texture and ensemble. Similarly, his triumphant seasons with Diaghilev's Russian ballet before the First World War gave him a fine sense of theatrical timing as well as the ability to put over new scores by advanced contemporary composers, for he knew that winning his orchestra's understanding and trust was an essential preliminary to convincing an audience.

At the New York Metropolitan Opera from 1916, Monteux conducted French repertory above all: Bizet's *Carmen,* Gounod's *Faust* and *Mireille,* Saint-Saëns' *Samson et Dalila,* Massenet's *Thaïs* and (in 1917) the now somewhat forgotten *Mârouf, Cobbler of Cairo* by Rabaud which won brief fame for its blend of Wagnerian structure and Gallic orientalism. When the soprano Frances Alda demanded an extra aria in this last opera, Monteux was resourceful enough to suggest to the composer, who was at first reluctant to make any changes, how one might be added to it that would draw upon existing material. He always regretted that the New York public did not take to this "beautifully staged" opera, and that it was dropped from the repertory.

Monteux's time at New York seems to have been mainly a happy one, and for the most part he enjoyed working with singers. He was agreeably surprised by the modesty of the great tenor Enrico Caruso, who was then the highest paid singer in the operatic world, but who called him *Maître,* and at rehearsal deferred to his musical judgment; later Monteux said of Caruso, "we had an extremely happy, courteous relationship." Caruso was his Don José in several *Carmen* performances, opposite the American soprano Geraldine Farrar. Farrar could be charming, but in noticeable contrast to Caruso, liked people to remember her star status. Monteux had the tact to manage her, and indeed possessed a natural sympathy with singers. He once declared that an over-authoritative operatic conductor could stop them giving of their best: "a voice is such a personal thing, generated in a singer's body; it is not a mechanical instrument . . . I think a conductor should be aware of this and as helpful as it is within his powers to be with the singing artist."

Throughout his life, Monteux was much concerned with good casting, and his widow Doris Monteux has written that "this idea of the right personality for the role was carried into every work chosen by the Maestro." By the mid-1920s, when he reached fifty, he was well known also as a champion of new music and had conducted many premieres, although he remained loyal to the classical repertory with which he had fallen in love at the start of his career and to which he never ceased to give strong and sensitive performances (of such mainstream pieces as the Beethoven and Brahms symphonies and concertos). It seems a pity that much of his work during a very long career lay outside the opera house, to which his gifts were evidently well suited, although he did return to the Met for three seasons in the mid-1950s to give American audiences successful accounts of such works as *Faust, Samson et Dalila,* Massenet's *Manon* and Offenbach's *Les contes d'Hoffmann.* Late in his life he looked back with pleasure to a few other operatic performances of special quality such as Verdi's *Falstaff* (with Mariano Stabile in the title role), Debussy's *Pelléas et Mélisande,* Ravel's *L'heure espagnole* and Gluck's *Orfeo ed Euridice* (with Kathleen Ferrier as Orfeo), all of which took place in Amsterdam. Another memorable occasion for him was conducting Beethoven's *Fidelio* in San Francisco. Sadly, his operatic recordings are confined to *Orfeo ed Euridice* with the American mezzo Risë Stevens as Orfeo, Verdi's *La traviata* with Rosanna Carteri as Violetta, and *Manon* with Victoria de los Angeles in the name part.

—Christopher Headington

MONTEVERDI, Claudio (Giovanni Antoni).

Composer. Born 1567 (baptized 15 May), in Cremona. Died 29 November 1643, in Venice. Married: Claudia de Cattaneis (died 10 September 1607), a singer at the Mantuan court, 20 May 1599 (two sons, one daughter who died in infancy). Learned to play the organ, and studied singing and theory with Marc' Antonio Ingegneri, maestro di capella at the Cathedral of Cremona; visited Milan, 1589; viol and violin player at the court of Vincenzo I, Duke of Mantua, by 1592; met Giaches de Wert, maestro di capella at the Mantuan court; accompanied the Duke of Mantua on battles against the Turks in Austria and Hungary, and accompanied him to Flanders in 1599; appointed maestro di capella in Mantua, succeeding Pallavicino, 1601; *La favola d'Orfeo* performed for the Accademia degli Invaghiti in Mantua, 1607; membership in the Accademia degli Animori of Cremona, 1607; *L'Arianna* composed to celebrate the marriage of Francesco Gonzaga of Mantua to Margaret of Savoy, 1608; lost his post in Mantua after the death of Vincenzo I, 1612; maestro di capella at San Marco, Venice, 1613; cantata *Il combattimento di Tancredi e Clorinda* performed for the Venetian nobleman Girolamo Mocenigo, 1624; his late operas performed in the then recently opened public theaters of Venice, 1640-42. Monteverdi is buried in the church of the Fratri in Venice.

Operas

Editions:

C. Monteverdi: Tutte le opere. Edited by G.F. Malipiero. 16 vols. Asolo, 1926-42; 2nd revised edition, 1954; supplement, vol. 17, 1966.

C. Monteverdi: Composizioni vocali profane e sacre (inedite). Edited by W. Osthoff. Milan, 1958.

C. Monteverdi: Opera Omnia. Edited by Fondazione Claudio Monteverdi, Instituta e monumenta, *Monumenta,* vol. v. Cremona, 1970-.

La favola d'Orfeo, A. Striggio, Mantua, February 1607.
L'Arianna, O. Rinuccini, Mantua, 28 May 1608.
Le nozze di Tetide, 1616 [unfinished; lost].
Andromeda, E. Marigliani, 1618-20 [unfinished; lost].
La finta pazza Licori, G. Strozzi, composed for Mantua, 1927. [lost].
Gli amori di Diana e di Endimione, A. Pio, Parma, 1628 [lost].
Proserpina rapita, G. Strozzi, Venice, 1630 [music mostly lost].
Il ritorno d'Ulisse in patria, G. Badoaro, Venice, 1640.
Le nozze d'Enea con Lavinia, Venice, 1641 [lost].
L'incoronazione di Poppea, G.F. Busenello, Venice, 1642.

Other works: sacred and secular vocal works.

Publications

By MONTEVERDI: books–

Paoli, Domenico de', ed. *Lettere, dediche, e prefazioni.* Rome, 1973.
Stevens, Denis, trans. and ed. *The Letters of Claudio Monteverdi.* London, 1980.

About MONTEVERDI: books–

Canal, P. *Della musica in Mantova.* Venice, 1881.
Davari, S. *Notizie biografiche del distinto maestro di musica Claudio Monteverdi.* Mantua, 1884.
Bertolotti, A. *Musici alla corte dei Gonzaga in Mantova dal secolo XV al XVIII.* Milan, 1890; 1969.
Goldschmidt, H. *Studien zur Geschichte der italienischen Oper.* Leipzig, 1901-04; 1967.
Prunières, H. *La vie et l'oeuvre de C. Monteverdi.* Paris, 1926; 1931; English translation, 1926; 1972.
Malipiero, G.F. *Claudio Monteverdi.* Milan, 1929.
Tiby, O. *Claudio Monteverdi.* Turin, 1944.
Paoli, Domenico de'. *Claudio Monteverdi.* Milan, 1945.
Redlich, Hans F. *Claudio Monteverdi: Leben und Werk.* Olten, 1949; English translation, London, 1952; Westport, Connecticut, 1970.
Schrade, Leo. *Monteverdi, Creator of Modern Music.* New York, 1950; London, 1964; French translation, Paris, 1981.
Roux, M. le. *Claudio Monteverdi.* Paris, 1951.
Sartori, C. *Monteverdi.* Brescia, 1953.
Abert, Anna Amalie. *Claudio Monteverdi und das musikalische Drama.* Lippstadt, 1954.
Arnold, Dennis, and Nigel Fortune, eds. *The Monteverdi Companion.* London, 1968.
Osthoff, Wolfgang. *Das dramatische Spätwerk Claudio Monteverdis.* Tutzing, 1960.
Arnold, Dennis. *Monteverdi.* London, 1963, 1975.
Tellart, R. *Claudio Monteverdi: L'homme et son oeuvre.* Paris, 1964.
Barblan, Guglielmo, et al. *Claudio Monteverdi nel quarto centenario della nascita.* Turin, 1967.
Monterosso, Rafaello, ed. *Claudio Monteverdi e il suo tempo.* Verona, 1968.
Pirrotta, Nino, and Elena Povoledo. *LI due Orfei: da Poliziano a Monteverdi.* Turin, 1969; 2nd ed., 1975; English translation as *Music and Theatre from Poliziano to Monteverdi,* Cambridge, 1982.
Stevens, Denis. *Monteverdi: Sacred, Secular, and Occassional Music.* Rutherford, New Jersey, 1978.
Degrada, Francesco. *Il palazzo incantato. Studi sulla tradizione del melodramma dal Barocco al Romaticismo.* Fiesole, 1979.
Paoli, Domenico de'. *Claudio Monteverdi.* Milan, 1979.
Roche, Maurice. *Monteverdi.* Paris, 1979.
Hanning, Barbara R. *Of Poetry and Music's Power.* Ann Arbor, 1980.
Leopold, Silke. *Claudio Monteverdi und seine Zeit.* Regensburg, 1982.
Müller, Reinhard. *Der "stile recitativo" in Claudio Monteverdis "Orfeo": Dramatischer Gesang und Instrumentalsatz.* Tutzing, 1984.
Arnold, Dennis, and Nigel Fortune, eds. *The New Monteverdi Companion.* London, 1985.
Fabbri, Paolo. *Monteverdi.* Turin, 1985.
Whenham, John. *Claudio Monteverdi: Orfeo.* Cambridge, 1986.
Tomlinson, Gary. *Monteverdi and the End of the Renaissance.* Berkeley and Oxford, 1987.
Adams, Gary, and Dyke Kiel. *Claudio Monteverdi: a Guide to Research.* New York, 1989.
Chafe, Eric. *Monteverdi's Tonal Language.* New York, 1992.

articles–

Vogel, E. "Claudio Monteverdi." *Vierteljahrsschrift für Musikwissenschaft* 3 (1887): 315.
Sommi Picenardi, G. "D'alcuni documenti concernenti Claudio Monteverdi." *Archivio storico lombardo* 4/3rd series (1895).
Goldschmidt, H. "Monteverdis Ritorno d'Ulisse." *Sammelbände der Internationalen Musik-Gesellschaft* 4 (1902-03): 671.
———. "Claudio Monteverdis Oper: Il ritorno d'Ulisse in patria." *Sammelbände der Internationalen Musik-Gesellschaft* 9 (1907-08): 570.
Haas, R. "Zur Neuausgabe von Claudio Monteverdis 'Il ritorno d'Ulisse in patria'." *Studien zur Musikwissenschaft* 9 (1922): 3.
Prunières, H. "Monteverdi's Venetian Operas." *Musical Quarterly* 10 (1924): 178.
Borren, C. van den " 'Il ritorno d'Ulisse in patria' de Claudio Monteverdi." *Revue de l'Université de Bruxelles* 3 (1925).
Westrup, J.A. "Monteverdi's 'Il ritorno d'Ulisse in patria'." *Monthly Musical Record* 58 (1928): 106.
Benvenuti, G. "Il manuscritto veneziano della 'Incoronazione di Poppea'." *Rivista musicale italiana* 41 (1937): 176.
Redlich, H.F. "Notationsprobleme in Cl. Monteverdis 'Incoronazione di Poppea'." *Acta musicologica* 10 (1938): 129.
Ronga, L. "Tasso and Monteverdi." *Poesia* 1 (1945).
Osthoff, W. "Die venezianische und neapolitanische Fassung von Monteverdis 'Incoronazione di Poppea'." *Acta musicologica* 26 (1954): 88.
———. "Zu den Quellen von Monteverdis Ritorno d'Ulisse in Patria." *Studien zur Musikwissenschaft* 23 (1956): 67.
———. "Neue Beobachtungen zu Quellen und Geschichte von Monteverdis 'Incoronazione di Poppea'." *Die Musikforschung* 11 (1958): 129.
———. "Zur Bologneser Aufführung von Monteverdis 'Ritorno d'Ulisse' im Jahre 1640." *Anzeiger der phil.-hist.*

Klasse der Österreichischen Akademie der Wissenschaften 95 (1958): 155.

Westrup, J.A. "Two First Performances: Monteverdi's *Orfeo* and Mozart's *La clemenza di Tito*." *Music and Letters* 39 (1958): 327.

Gallico, C. "Newly Discovered Documents concerning Monteverdi." *Musical Quarterly* 48 (1962): 68.

Arnold, Dennis. " 'L'incoronazione di Poppea' and its Orchestral Requirements." *Musical Times* 104 (1963).

———. "*Il ritorno d'Ulisse* and the Chamber Duet." *Musical Times* 106 (1965): 183.

Rosenthal, A. "A Hitherto Unpublished Letter of Claudio Monteverdi." In *Essays Presented to Egon Wellesz*, 103. Oxford, 1966.

Rivista italiana di musicologia 2/no. 2 (1967) [special Monteverdi issue].

Pirrotta, Nino. "Early Opera and Aria." In *New Looks at Italian Opera: Essays in Honor of Donald J. Grout.* Ithaca, 1968.

———. "Early Venetian Libretti at Los Angeles." In *Essays in Musicology in Honor of Dragan Plamenac,* 233. Pittsburgh, 1969.

Fano, Fabio. "*Il combattimento di Tancredi e Clorinda* e *L'incoronazione di Poppea* di Claudio Monteverdi." In *Studi sul teatro veneto fra rinascimento ed età barocca.* Florence, 1971.

Frobenius, W. "Zur Notation eines Ritornells in Monteverdis 'L'Orfeo'." *Archiv für Musikwissenschaft* 28 (1971): 201.

Pirrotta, Nino. "Monteverdi e i problemi dell'opera." In *Studi sul teatro veneto fra rinascimento ed età barocca.* Florence, 1971.

Chiarelli, Alessandra. "*L'incoronazione di Poppea o Il Nerone:* Problemi di filologia testuale." *Rivista italiana di musicologia* 9 (1974): 117.

Hell, Helmut. "Zur Rhythmus und Notierung des 'Vi ricorda' in Claudio Monteverdi's *Orfeo.*" *Analecta Musicologica* no. 15 (1975): 87.

Avant-scène opéra September-October (1976) [*Orfeo* issue].

Hirsch, Hans-Ludwig. "Claudio Monteverdis 'Lamento d'Arianna': Genesis und Strukturanalyse." In *Oper heute: Ein Almanach der Musikbühne, I (1978),* edited by Horst Seeger, 9. Berlin, 1978.

Bragard, Anne-Marie. "Deux portraits de femmes dans l'oeuvre de Monteverdi: Ariane et Popée." *Bulletin de la Société Liégeoise de Musicologie* 24 (1979): 1.

Rosand, Ellen. "The Descending Tetrachord: an Emblem of Lament." *Musical Quarterly* 65 (1979): 346.

Godt, Irving. "A Monteverdi Source Reappears: The *Grilanda* of F.M. Fucci." *Music and Letters* 60 (1979): 428.

Tomlinson, Gary. "Madrigal, Monody, and Monteverdi's 'via naturale alla immitatione'." *Journal of the American Musicological Society* 34 (1981): 60.

Fischer, Kurt von. "Petit essay sur les opéras de Monteverdi." *Anuario musical* 37 (1982): 15.

McGee, Timothy J. "*Orfeo* and *Euridice,* the First Two Operas." In *Orpheus, the Metamorphosis of a Myth,* edited by John Warden, 163. Toronto, 1982.

Carter, Tim. "A Florentine Wedding of 1608." *Acta Musicologica* 55 (1938): 89.

Müller, Reinhard. "Basso ostinato und die 'imitatione del parlare' in Monteverdis *Incoronazione di Poppea.*" *Archiv für Musikwissenschaft* 40 (1983): 1.

Carroll, Charles Michael. "Eros on the Operatic Stage: Problems in Manners and Morals." *Opera Quarterly* 1 (1983): 37.

Tomlinson, Gary A. "Twice Bitten, Thrice Shy: Monteverdi's 'finta' *Finta pazza.*" *Journal of the American Musicological Society* 36 (1983): 303.

Michels, Ulrich. "Das *Lamento d'Arianna* von Claudio Monteverdi." In *Analysen: Beiträge zu einer Problemgeschichte des Komponierens. Festschrift für Hans Heinrich Eggebrecht zum 65. Geburtstag,* edited by Werner Berg et al., 91. Wiesbaden, 1984.

Fenlon, Iain. "Monteverdi's Mantuan *Orfeo:* Some New Documentation." *Early Music* 12 (1984): 163.

Osthoff, Wolfgang. "Contro le legge de' Fati: Polizianos und Monteverdis *Orfeo* als Sinnbild künstlerischen Wettkampfs mit der Natur." *Analecta Musicologica* 22 (1984): 11.

Rosenthal, Albi. "Monteverdi's Andromeda: a Lost Libretto Found." *Music and Letters* January, 1985.

Avant-scène opéra December (1988) [*L'incoronazione di Poppea* issue].

Rosand, Ellen. "Iro and the Interpretation of Il ritorno d'Ulisse in Patria." *Journal of Musicology* spring (1989).

———. "Monteverdi's Mimetic Art: *L'incoronazione di Poppea.*" *Cambridge Opera Journal* 1 (1989): 113.

McClary, Susan. "Constructions of gender in Monteverdi's dramatic music." *Cambridge Opera Journal* 1 (1989): 203.

*　　*　　*

Claudio Monteverdi is regarded not only as the first great opera composer, but one of the greatest of all time. That he has attained this stature is testimony to the extraordinary

Claudio Monteverdi, portrait from printed score of *Orfeo*, Venice, 1609

nature of his extant operas. Of his ten operas, the only to survive are his first opera *Orfeo* and a fragment from his second opera *Arianna*—both of which were written for the Mantua court during the early years of the genre—along with *Il ritorno d'Ulisse in patria* and *L'incoronazione di Poppea,* composed during his final years for the public opera theater in Venice. These four works, standing at the two opposite poles of Monteverdi's operatic career, thus necessarily provide only a glimpse into the development and full range of his operatic genius.

Monteverdi is the only seventeenth-century composer whose works have found a permanent position in today's operatic repertoire. This is not entirely surprising; he has received more scholarly attention than any other composer of his century. In addition, inquiry into seventeenth-century opera has tended to focus on the origins of the genre and the humanistic neo-classicizing impulses that inspired its birth. Thus, *Orfeo,* long regarded as the first great opera, has been the subject of intense scrutiny. At a time when much of the opera produced for the Venice stage languished in relative obscurity, Monteverdi's Venetian operas, and in particular *L'incoronazione di Poppea,* were acknowledged as masterworks.

Recent scholarship has long since increased the visibility of Monteverdi's Venetian contemporaries, yet this has only made more apparent the extent to which his latter two operas differ from those of his younger contemporaries writing for the Venetian theater. Monteverdi brought to opera composition his Renaissance heritage and a musical style shaped by decades of madrigal composition. The madrigal books, masterpieces in themselves, were also a sort of laboratory in which Monteverdi developed various rhythmic, tonal, and vocal styles that would accommodate the dramatic requirements of opera. As Eric Chafe has recently shown, Monteverdi also inherited a tonal language based on Renaissance modal-hexachordal thinking, which he transformed into a highly expressive device for the new genre. In a sense, the unique quality of Monteverdi's sound and style results from the application of the most fundamental precepts and principles of Renaissance style to opera—the genre that embodies the Baroque aesthetic.

Monteverdi's *La favola d'Orfeo* was performed in 1607 in Mantua under the auspices of the *Accademia degli Invaghiti.* For his librettist, Monteverdi chose Alessandro Striggio, a diplomat and lawyer in the service of the ruling Gonzaga family of Mantua who, as the son of a composer, also had considerable interest in music and poetry. Monteverdi's and Striggio's *Orfeo* was not the first work of its kind. As numerous scholars have pointed out, *Orfeo* was modeled after an earlier work, *Euridice,* by poet Ottavio Rinuccini and composer Jacopo Peri. Like Rinuccini, Striggio set his libretto within the pastorale tragicomedic world that was popular from other Mantuan and Florentine theatrical entertainments such as Guarini's play *Il pastor fido.* Striggio also followed a similar dramatic structure, organizing his libretto as a prologue followed by five acts or sections, with the first two acts of the two versions roughly analogous in terms of content. Specific resemblances between the two works occur particularly in recitative passages—as in the messenger's revelation of Euridice's death—and it is in those instance that Monteverdi's musical setting demonstrates its greatest debt to Peri's work. Monteverdi also drew upon the theatrical traditions of the Florentine and Mantuan court. Thus, rather than relying so heavily upon the *stile rappresentativo* favored by the Florentine opera pioneers, Monteverdi and Striggio designed *Orfeo* as a composite of various forms and styles for both voices

and instruments, enhanced by a wide spectrum of instrumental colors—indicated with great specificity by the composer— and with a greater variety of stage settings that undoubtedly contradicted classical demands for unity of place.

The appearance of the allegorical figure of Music in the prologue provides an important clue as to the actual purpose of this recounting of Orfeo's tale: a demonstration of music's power. In *Orfeo,* however, the ability to wield music's power does not necessarily rest in the hands of this gifted protagonist. Orfeo's songs are no doubt pleasing in times of joy, as in the delightfully simple strophic song "Vi ricorda" or as in the impetuous burst of emotional display of "Rosa del ciel," and his sorrow is movingly expressed in the sharply felt lament "Tu sei morta." Yet Orfeo's most virtuosic musical display and urgent evocation of music's power, "Possente spirto," only temporarily gains him his desired goal and ultimately cannot save him from his human failings. In *Orfeo,* it would seem that Monteverdi proves that the true power of music belongs to the composer. Indeed, the organization of *Orfeo* is by no means determined solely by the flow of the drama. Numerous scholars have noted the symmetrical design in the distribution of the closed forms, as in the patterns of choruses between the nymphs and shepherds in act I. More recently, Eric Chafe has shown the careful and logical way in which tonality is used both in terms of overall organization and in expressing the allegorical meaning of the drama. The dramatic tonal juxtapositions that occur in moments of rapidly shifting emotion—as in the messenger's announcement of Euridice's death—are not only localized effects, but rather can logically be accounted for within a rational tonal system that Monteverdi carefully employed in this work and explored in his contemporaneous madrigal composition.

In his musical characterization of the allegorical, somewhat two-dimensional Orfeo, Monteverdi provides only a glimpse of the psychological depth and human insight that was to mark the characters in his later operas. In the surviving fragment from the opera *Arianna,* written the following year, Monteverdi uses the monodic style to trace the various stages of Arianna's reaction to her abandonment by Theseus. Closely mirroring the intricacies of the text, Monteverdi sensitively evokes Arianna's despair, disbelief, hope, and anger. Yet the entire lament is musically unified by the repetitions of her obsessive cries for death, poignantly set with a striking chromaticism that has since become inseparable from the idea of lament.

In his latter two operas, Monteverdi also succeeds in creating characters with profoundly human depth; nevertheless, these works differ sharply from the earlier operas in musical and rhetorical style as well as in meaning. Undoubtedly, some of this is a result of the cultural and aesthetic climate in which they were produced. No longer employed by the Gonzaga family of Mantua, Monteverdi was now writing for the relatively new and successful public opera theater in Venice. Some of the striking peculiarities of these works thus reflect the intellectual leanings of those involved in Venetian opera production during its early decades. Both of the librettists for Monteverdi's late operas, Giacomo Badoaro and Gian Francesco Busenello, were members of the Accademia degli Incogniti, a group whose libertine and skeptical brand of philosophy was adopted by much of the noble intelligentsia of Venice. Opera librettos were but a small portion of their literary output, yet it is evident that these works reflect in some ways the numerous Incogniti discussions on love, women, virtue, death, and the survival of the flesh. As Ellen Rosand has pointed out, *Il ritorno d' Ulisse,* with its demonstration of the victory of virtuous love, and *L'incoronazione di Poppea,* with its celebration of illicit, passionate love, can be viewed as representing two sides of an Incogniti debate.

Neither the skepticism nor the intellectual leanings of these librettists interfered with Monteverdi's ability to infuse his characters with extraordinary humanity. Notably, among his contemporaries only Monteverdi chose to reshape portions of his librettos so as to alter their musical or dramatic implications. This is particularly evident in *Il ritorno d'Ulisse,* where the librettist Badoaro provided Monteverdi with mostly recitative poetry, with few stophic texts or other explicit indications for lyricism. In Penelope's opening lament, for example, Monteverdi rearranged the text in a manner that was not only more compelling dramatically—capturing Penelope's shifting moods as she longed for Ulisse's return—but also more musically coherent. Penelope's repeated lyrical plea for Ulisse's safe return, with its haunting melody and surprising tonal shifts, not only provides contrast from the recitative and bestows musical unity on the lengthy monologue, but also appropriately reflects Penelope's obsessive devotion to Ulisse, despite his continued absence. As Rosand has shown in her discussion of Iro, the *parte ridicolo* in *Il ritorno d'Ulisse*—whose expanded role in this libretto was librettist Badoaro's only significant departure from Homer—Monteverdi uses an extreme sort of musical imitation that captures and yet exaggerates the essence of each word, distorting the musical surface so as to realize Iro's amusing but highly disturbing craving for nourishment that precipitates his suicide.

It is precisely this kind of musical imitation, employed with such opposite results in Penelope's lament and Iro's suicide, that Monteverdi used to such advantage in his masterpiece, *L'incoronazione di Poppea.* These characters bear little resemblance to the allegorical Orfeo or the heroically lamentful Arianna. They are complex combinations of conflicting emotions and motivations, yet their depth is made explicit through Monteverdi's musical realizations. The listener may sympathize with the unfortunate predicament of Nero's abandoned wife Ottavia, but it is not solely on account of her murderous actions that she ultimately fails to inspire compassion. In Ottavia's act I monologue, Monteverdi uses a terse, somewhat angular recitative for her denouncement of women's fate and their victimization by men, moving easily into a strained lyricism as she visualizes Nero and Poppea's passion, then briefly employing the *guerriero* style in a futile gesture of anger as she decries Jove's impotence—and her own. The starkness of Ottavia's music is directly in contrast to the seductive, voluptuous nature of Poppea's music. In the first of Nero and Poppea's exquisite duets, for example, Monteverdi empowers Poppea with languid lyric gesture, seductive virtuosity, and tonal control that infuse the spent Nero with new passion and thus extract from him the first of several promises that ultimately lead to her coronation. Above all, it is Poppea's music that urges the listeners to abandon their moral reservations and rejoice with her in the triumph of love over virtue.

The complicated state of the surviving sources as well as some of their notational anomalies, noted most recently by Alan Curtis, have called into question the authorship of portions of *L'incoronazione di Poppea,* including the popular and highly sensuous final duet. Some commentators, however, have argued that the uniformity of features such as text setting, tonal style, melodic writing, and the application of musical devices from the madrigal tradition, still point to Monteverdi's authorship for much of the opera. While it is likely that these questions will never be definitively solved, the unique and subtle musical realizations of the characters throughout this opera would seem at the very least to argue

for Monteverdi's guiding spirit in the creation of this masterwork.

—Wendy Heller

MONTEZUMA.

Composer: Carl Heinrich Graun.

Librettist: Frederick II (translated by Tagliazucchi).

First Performance: Berlin, Opera, 6 January 1755.

Roles: Montezuma (soprano); Eupaforice (soprano); Tezeuco (tenor); Pilpatoè (soprano); Erissina (soprano); Hernán Cortés (tenor); Narvès (soprano); chorus.

Publications

book–

Helm, Ernest Eugene. *Music at the Court of Frederick the Great.* Norman, Oklahoma, 1960.

articles–

Quander, Georg. "Montezuma als Gegenbild des grossen Friedrich—oder: Die Empfindungen dreier Zeitgenossen beim Anblick der Oper *Montezuma* von Friedrich dem Grossen und Carl Heinrich Graun." In *Preussen—Dein Spree-Athen. Beiträge zu Literatur, Theater und Musik in Berlin,* edited by Hellmut Kühn. Reinbek bei Hamburg, 1981.

Klüppelholz, Heinz. "Die Eroberung Mexicos aus preussischer Sicht. Zum Libretto der Oper 'Montezuma' von Friedrich dem Grossen." In *Oper als Text. Romanistische Beiträge zur Libretto-Forschung,* edited by Albert Gier. Heidelberg, 1986.

Maehder, Jürgen. "Mythologizing the Encounter—Columbus, Motecuzoma, Cortés and Representation on the 'Discovery' on the Opera Stage." In *Musical Repercussions of 1492,* edited by Carol E. Robertson. Washington, D.C., 1992.

*   *   *

The discovery and conquest of the Americas resulted in a clash of cultures between the people of Europe and the indigenous people of America. Some of the first images of the "New World" seen by the people of Europe found expression in theater and opera. As Jürgen Maehder observes: "Nourished by the mythos through which Europe filtered its contact with the 'other,' these images and representations in turn gave form and substance to European views of the New World. The opera stage, in particular, offered an arena for the development of real and imagined characters that became the central protagonists in the process of mythologizing this pivotal encounter of culture" (Maehder, 427).

In the eighteenth century, the New World became an increasingly popular subject in Italian *opera seria.* The libretti of numerous operas were based on the discovery and conquest of Mexico, Peru, and the "native" peoples of America. One of the most popular plots portrayed the defeat of Montezuma by Spanish conquistador Hernán Cortés. Of the Montezuma settings, the opera composed by Carl Heinrich Graun is particularly interesting in that it reflects Frederick the Great's view of the conquest. As Eugene Helm states, "It is an important work in the history of eighteenth-century German opera because it represents the best artistic efforts of both Graun and Frederick, and because it contains some attempts at reform" (Helm, 67). This opera, in three acts, was first performed at the Royal Berlin Opera House on 6 January 1755. The libretto was written in French prose by Frederick in 1754, then translated into Italian verse by his court poet G.P. Tagliazucchi. Concerned less with the presentation of historical "facts," the libretto conforms to eighteenth-century operatic conventions; it focuses on intrigues of love and the duties of the ruling class, but concludes with an unexpected (and unconventional) tragic ending.

Set in the fifteenth century, the story is as follows: Montezuma, Emperor of Mexico, is happy because he is to marry his love Eupaforice, the Queen of Tlascala. His happiness is disturbed by Pilpatoè (General in the Imperial Army), who reports the arrival of Cortés (leader of the Spanish contingent) and warns Montezuma of the Spaniard's bad intentions. Ignoring Pilpatoè's warnings, Montezuma welcomes Cortés into his court. Montezuma's hospitality is abused and reciprocated with treachery. Cortés captures Montezuma. Eupaforice attempts to free Montezuma with the help of her confidant Erissina, Pilpatoè, and Tezeuco (Officer of the Imperial Crown). Her plans are divulged to Cortés, who in the name of Christianity kills Pilpatoè and Montezuma, and sets the city on fire. Reacting to these events, Eupaforice prophesies the fall of Spain and then kills herself.

Graun's Montezuma, only the third opera based on the conquest of the Americas, was considered innovative because it dealt with a comparatively modern historical subject. The text, which may have been influenced by Graun's recollections of Vivaldi's Motezuma opera (Venice, 1733), reflects Frederick's view, as librettist, of the conquest of the New World and shows strong influences of Voltaire's philosophy. Contrary to earlier beliefs, recent research tends to exclude any direct influence from Voltaire's drama Alzire (Maehder, 436). Frederick's strong prejudices against Spanish Catholicism and its missionary zeal—an attitude consistent with his seemingly anti-religious beliefs borrowed in part from Voltaire—were extended to his treatment of this libretto. In a letter written to Count Francesco Algarotti in October 1753, Frederick wrote: "You know, of course, that I shall be on the side of Montezuma, that Cortez will be the tyrant, and that as a result a few telling remarks can be made, even in music, against the barbarousness of the Christian religion." He continues by noting that "opera serves to reform customs and destroy superstitions" (Helm, 70).

As requested by Frederick, Montezuma begins with an Italian "Sinfonia" or the so-called "Italian Overture" in three movements. A notable musical feature of the opera is that most of its arias are in what was then called "cavatina" form, instead of the usual da capo form. Frederick, favoring the cavatina and taking credit for the innovation, wrote in a letter to his sister of 4 May 1754: "As for the cavatinas, I have seen some by Hasse which are infinitely more beautiful than [da capo] arias. . . . There is no need for repetition, except when the singers know how to make variations, but it seems to me, in any case, that it is an abuse to repeat the same thing four times." The cavatina contains no central contrasting section. The "B" section of the da capo aria and the usual repeats are omitted, limiting the amount of vocal display. The result is a simple binary form: A^1 - A^2 (exposition and recapitulation).

The first section (A^1), modulating from the tonic to the dominant, presents the primary theme(s). The second section (A^2) functions as a reprise, usually beginning in the dominant, sometimes incorporating a short harmonic development, and then returning to the tonic. Graun's incorporation of the cavatina—part of a reform movement preceding that of Gluck's—moves away from the rigid structures of Italian opera seria and the dramatically stagnant da capo aria, and allows for more dramatic fluidity.

Francesco Algarotti, in his Saggio sopra l'opera in musica (1755), wrote about Graun's Montezuma from a standpoint which differed from that of Frederick, and which may represent the way Europeans viewed the opera. He observed, "A display of the Mexican and Spanish customs, seen for the first time together, must form a most beautiful contrast; and the barbaric magnificence of America would receive heightenings by being opposed in different views to that of Europe" (Algarotti, 662).

—Anne Lineback Seshadri

MONTEZUMA.

Composer: Roger Sessions.

Librettist: A. Borgese (after Diaz del Castillo).

First Performance: West Berlin, 19 April 1964.

Roles: Bernal Diaz del Castillo the Elder (bass); Hernan Cortez (baritone); Pedro de Alvarado (tenor); Malinche (soprano); Montezuma (tenor); Bernal Diaz del Castillo the Younger (tenor); Cuauhtemoc (baritone); Father Olmedo de la Merced (bass); Cacamatzin (tenor); Netzahualcoyotl (bass); Teuhtlilli (tenor); several bit roles which may be doubled; chorus (SAATTBB).

Publications

articles–

Davies, P.M. "Montezuma." New York Times 21 April (1964).
Laufer, E.C. "Roger Sessions: Montezuma." Perspectives of New Music 4/no.1 (1965): 95.
Harbison, J. "Roger Sessions and Montezuma." New Boston Review 2/no. 1 (1976): 5; reprinted in Tempo no. 121 (1977): 2.
Porter, A. "The Matter of Mexico." New Yorker 102/19 April (1976): 115.
Stevenson, Robert. "American Awareness of the Other Americans to 1900." In Essays on Music for Charles Warren Fox, edited by Jerald C. Grave, 181. Rochester, 1979.
Porter, A. "The Magnificent Epic." New Yorker 108/8 March (1982): 128.
Olmstead, Andrea. "The Plum'd Serpent: Antonio Borgese's and Roger Sessions' Montezuma." Tempo no. 152 (1985).

unpublished–

Mason, Charles N. "A Comprehensive Analysis of Roger Sessions' Opera Montezuma." DMA dissertation, University of Illinois, Champaign-Urbana, 1982.

*   *   *

In act I of Roger Sessions' *Montezuma,* Cortez claims Mexico for Charles V, King of Spain. The soldiers choose Aztec girls and Cortez chooses Malinche, an enslaved princess. The Aztec ambassadors from Montezuma think that light-haired Cortez, or possibly his unfamiliar horse, is Quetzalcoatl, the Plum'd Serpent, prophesied to come from the East to save Mexico. Greeting Cortez as Quetzalcoatl, Malinche offers to lead him through the mountains to Montezuma. Cortez asks the priest to baptize Malinche and the other women. In a love duet Malinche asks Cortez directly whether he is the god Quetzalcoatl. He shrewdly allows the Aztecs to believe in his divinity.

In act II, the narrator Bernal the Elder describes the march up from Cholula to the city of Tenochtitlan and the battle of Cholula. Words desert him when he reaches the part of his tale where Cortez (and the audience) first meet Montezuma. A procession of eleven bound victims enters. When the mortal sacrifice is made atop the pyramid, the crowd rushes to eat their remains. Malinche bids Montezuma to accept the Spaniards' religious gospel. Montezuma is inclined to believe that Cortez is Quetzalcoatl. Cortez unveils a portrait of the Holy Roman Emperor and one of the Virgin Mary and Child. During a long discussion of religion, the two lieutenants, Alvarado and Cuauhtemoc, strain the delicate situation with their aggressiveness. The Indians present a ritual dance. Alvarado demands that Montezuma share his gold, but Cuauhtemoc's and Alvarado's argument prompts Cortez to apologize. When Cuauhtemoc challenges Malinche, she stands firm, precipitating a scuffle during which the Aztec Lord of Tacuba falls. Cortez sadly tells Montezuma that he must take him prisoner, and Montezuma is shackled by the ankles.

In act III, Montezuma watches an off-stage *auto-da-fé* and is clearly revolted by the execution. Cuauhtemoc conspires against the Spanish. Alvarado has ordered a massacre, an action that has rallied the Aztecs. He sings alone, quoting the Bible as justification for his plans to overthrow the king. Cortez returns and sharply rebukes Alvarado for having sought battle. Alvarado gives Cortez Machiavellian advice: since Cortez is not the son of a king, he must rule by example or by terror. Narvaez's men curse the war and grieve for their fallen comrades. Cortez pleads with Montezuma to speak to his people to end the strife. When Montezuma does so, some of the Aztecs retort that he is not their king. Montezuma praises the pregnant Malinche, beside him, as the builder of a new race. Cortez prompts Montezuma, saying the Spanish will leave the country, but the Indians call Montezuma a Christian and stone him to death. The opera ends with the chorus of clouds, "voices of eternity or fate" proclaiming, "We shall rain another time."

Sessions has said about the opera, "It's about the high-level relationships between human beings. And it has a sort of deeper implication, too. Because when it was written Borgese was a refugee from Mussolini. And I wasn't exactly a refugee from Hitler, but I'd been in Germany and seen Hitler come in and seen what he was doing to Germany and by implication the world. And we had those things on our minds very much as the text developed" (Interview with the author, 14 April 1976).

Both Borgese and Sessions separately visited Mexico in the late 1930s and had become enchanted with its history. They relied on Prescott's *History of the Conquest of Mexico* and Bernal Diaz's *The True History of the Conquest of New Spain* for historical information. Diaz appears in the opera both as an old narrator relating the adventures of his youth, and as the youth himself. The other main characters are paired as opposite numbers, Spanish on one side, Indian on the other.

For example, Cortez's opposite number is Montezuma, Alvarado's is Cuauhtemoc, and Father Olmedo is counterbalanced by Netzahualcoyotl. And the situations are also symmetrical: the Aztecs' human sacrifice is compared with the Spaniards' *auto-da-fé.* Such carefully planned symmetries give each side equal weight—humanity, sympathy, aggressiveness—and leaves the audience frustrated as to whom to blame for the death of Montezuma.

Musically the work is difficult to assimilate on one hearing. The vocal and orchestral writing is extremely (but typically for Sessions) dense; there are few formal demarcations and no literal musical repetitions; the most dramatic scenes are not sung, but mimed in tableaux; and the language of the libretto is highly poetical and includes Aztec, Spanish, and Latin. The fact that the work is written in a twelve-tone idiom is incidental to these other features, although in 1976 *Time* called it "indisputably twelve-tone music's finest hour on the operatic stage."

Montezuma represents Sessions' "magnum opus." His only other opera was written hastily in 1947 to a text by Bertolt Brecht, *The Trial of Lucullus.* Borgese never wrote another opera libretto (he was known for philosophical writing, poetry, and political work), and Sessions only once afterward approached opera: at the 1976 Boston production of *Montezuma,* he was encouraged by Sarah Caldwell to write another opera. Andrew Porter did not finish the libretto for the comic opera based on *The Emperor's New Clothes,* nor did Sessions finish the music.

The critical reaction to the only three productions of *Montezuma* has progressed from undisguised praise (Berlin), to mixed reactions (Boston), to outright negative opinions (New York). Only Porter and this writer defended the opera and the New York production, convinced that in the long run the high quality of the music will overshadow the obvious problems of the libretto.

—Andrea Olmstead

THE MOON
See DER MOND

MOORE, Douglas Stuart.

Composer. Born 10 August 1893, in Cutchogue, New York. Died 25 July 1969, in Greenport, Long Island, New York. Studied with D.S. Smith and Horatio Parker at Yale University; B.A., 1915, and Mus. Bac., 1917, from Yale; in the United States Navy, 1917-18; studied with Vincent d'Indy at the Schola Cantorum in Paris; studied organ with Tournemire and composition with Nadia Boulanger in Paris; studied with Ernest Bloch in Cleveland, upon his return to the United States; organist at the Cleveland Museum of Art, 1921-23, and at Adelbert College, Western Reserve University, 1923-25; in Europe on a Pulitzer traveling scholarship, 1925; on the faculty of Columbia University, 1926; succeeded Daniel

Gregory Mason as the head of the Columbia music department, 1940; honorable mention by the New York Music Critic's Circle for his Symphony in A, 1947; Pulitzer Prize for *Giants in the Earth,* 1951; retired, 1962.

Operas

Publishers: Boosey and Hawkes, C. Fischer, Galaxy, G. Schirmer.

Jesse James, J.M. Brown, 1928 [unfinished].
White Wings (chamber opera), Philip Barry, 1935, Hartford, Connecticut, 9 February 1949.
The Headless Horseman (high-school opera), S.V. Benét (after W. Irving, *A Legend of Sleepy Hollow*), 1936, Bronxville, New York, 4 March 1937.
The Devil and Daniel Webster, S.V. Benét, 1938, New York, 18 May 1939.
The Emperor's New Clothes (children's opera), R. Abrashkin (after Hans Christian Andersen, 1948, New York, 19 February 1949; revised 1956.
Giants in the Earth, Arnold Sundgaard (after O.E. Rølvaag), 1949, New York, 28 March 1951; revised, 1963.
Puss in Boots (children's operetta), R. Abrashkin (after C. Perrault), 1949, New York, 18 November 1950.
Ballad of Baby Doe (folk opera), J. Latouche, 1956, Central City, Colorado, 7 July 1958.
Gallantry ("soap opera"), A. Sundgaard, 1957, New York, 19 March 1958.
The Wings of the Dove, E. Ayer (after H. James), 1961, New York, 12 October 1961.
The Greenfield Christmas Tree, A. Sundgaard, 1962, Baltimore, 8 December 1962.
Carry Nation, W.N. Jayme, 1966, Lawrence, Kansas, 28 April 1966.

Other works: orchestral works, choral works, chamber music, songs.

Publications/Writings

By MOORE: books–

Listening to Music. New York, 1932; revised, 1963.
From Madrigal to Modern Music: a Guide to Musical Styles. New York, 1942; revised, 1962.

About MOORE: books–

Edmunds, J., and G. Boelzner. *Some Twentieth Century American Composers.* New York, 1959-60.

articles–

Rhodes, W. "Douglas Moore's Music." *Columbia University Quarterly* October (1940): 223.
Luening, O. "Douglas Moore." *Modern Music* 20 (1942): 248.
Beeson, J. "In Memoriam: Douglas Moore (1893-1969): an Appreciation." *Perspectives of New Music* 8 (1969): 158.
Gleason, H., and W. Becker. "Douglas Moore." In *20th-Century American Composers.* Music Literature Outlines, series 4, p. 129. Bloomington, Indiana, 2nd ed., 1981.

unpublished–

Weitzel, H. "A Melodic Analysis of Selected Vocal Solos in the Operas of Douglas Moore." Ph.D. dissertation, New York University, 1971.

*   *   *

Although Douglas Moore wrote a number of songs and purely instrumental pieces, opera was his primary concern. His creative impulses, like those of any successful opera composer, overflowed the confines of the strictly musical. A friend of Moore's, Jack Beeson, who is himself an opera composer, has succinctly described what his longtime colleague aimed for: "Moore's expressive intent was clear and unequivocal from early on: to write for the voice- and stage-dominated musical theater, using subject matter from his country's past."

Moore's sense of the American past might have reached back, through an awareness of his family history, to colonial settlements of the 1640s, but his operatic imagination was chiefly drawn to the time of his youth or, more expansively, to the nineteenth century. Within these limits his dramatic subjects have a considerable range. Sometimes his librettos have a factual basis for their stories (*The Ballad of Baby Doe, Carry Nation*); sometimes they are derived from substantial literary sources (Washington Irving, Henry James, O.E. Rølvaag, Stephen Vincent Benét). Their characters may face hardscrabble pioneer problems (*Giants in the Earth*) or, again, intrigues arising in the European world of deracinated Americans (*The Wings of the Dove*). Where the characters are unsophisticated, the homespun aspects of early American life are occasionally celebrated in an almost patronizing fashion. (Exceptionally, *Gallantry,* a short "soap opera," has not only a contemporary setting but also an openly parodistic tone.)

If Moore's librettos have plots and characters that are designed to be readily understood by audiences, even to be familiar to them, so too the musical layout of his operas builds upon the expectations of the seasoned operagoer. When John Houseman, the earliest director of *The Devil and Daniel Webster,* first heard Moore's score, he thought it "effective, melodious and conventional." This response could not have been unanticipated by so knowledgeable a composer as Moore. In fact, the music in his operas is effective in large part because it is melodious and relies firmly on operatic conventions. Love duets, ensembles of perplexity, mad songs, letter arias, the use of onstage music, and melodrama (as when the characters in *The Devil and Daniel Webster* speak over musical accompaniment)—such are the resources Moore tellingly exploits. By means of well-calculated arrangements of parlando passages, full-scale solo numbers and ensembles, and choruses, he and his librettists rework the standard opera components.

The style of Moore's music fits both his American themes and his traditional approach to operatic drama. One of its wellsprings is American popular and folk music in its broadest sense, including hymn tunes, dances, marches, and sentimental ballads. This gives his melodic writing a strong diatonic, at times even a pentatonic foundation. At the same time, the way in which a dramatic scene will emerge from preparatory parlando moments suggests especially nineteenth century Italian opera. *The Wings of the Dove* in particular seems to adapt Verdian techniques. But Moore seldom attempts elaborate or novel musical procedures, and he makes no extraordinary demands on the performers. Not the Metropolitan Opera House but opera workshops and regional opera companies are his most likely venues. Works with spoken dialogue (e.g., *The Headless Horseman*) are destined for this end.

Moore had been trained by gifted teachers—Horatio Parker, Nadia Boulanger, Vincent d'Indy, and Ernest Bloch—and the very breadth of his education may have helped him to stand apart from the various schools of modern music that flourished during his lifetime. He evidently reacted to modernism with a resistance such as was fairly common in American and English artistic circles of his day. For Moore the goal of being American transcended that of being modern. Yet he made his peace with twentieth-century trends; in 1926, years before his first opera, he wrote that he would "try to combine a reasonable modernity with attention to melody." Although this statement referred to a specific work he then had in mind, it evokes his musical style in general. Perhaps today, when twentieth-century modernism in all the arts is being re-evaluated, Moore's operas, well grounded in musical tradition and faithful to their national origin, deserve renewed respect.

—Christopher Hatch

MOORE, Grace.

Soprano. Born 5 December 1898, in Nough, Tennessee. Died 26 January 1947, in airplane crash near Copenhagen. Studied with Marafioti in New York; appeared in musical comedy and operetta in New York, 1921-26; worked with Richard Berthélemy in Antibes; Metropolitan Opera debut as Mimi, 1928, and sang there until 1946; Opéra-Comique debut, 1928; appeared at Covent Garden as Mimi, 1935; her many films include *One Night of Love,* 1934.

Publications

By MOORE: books–

You're Only Human Once. Garden City, New York, 1944.

About MOORE: books–

Thompson, O. *The American Singer.* New York, 1937.

articles–

Faria-Artsay, A. "Grace Moore." *Hobbies* 47 (1963): 31.

* * *

Although she appeared with other opera companies, New York's Metropolitan Opera was Grace Moore's home. During her career there, which began with a much publicized debut in 1928, until her tragic death in 1947, she had, at one time or another, soprano colleagues Lucrezia Bori, Amelita Galli-Curci, Rosa Ponselle, Elisabeth Rethberg, Claudia Muzio, Kirsten Flagstad, Lily Pons, Helen Traubel, Zinka Milanov, Bidu Sayao, Licia Albanese, Eleanor Steber and her protégé, Dorothy Kirsten, among others. Considering the vocal riches which surrounded her, the fact that an ex-Broadway review headliner such as Moore could not only reach the stage of one of the world's most important opera houses but

become one of its reigning stars is almost miraculous. In comparison with some others, her voice was not exceptional, but her charisma was. She could charm an audience into total and complete submission as easily as she could change outfits.

Grace Moore had an effervescence which was almost palpable. With her blond hair and her radiant smile she literally glowed. In addition, she had a voice of good size and texture. By the time she reached her third film and greatest success, *One Night of Love,* she was a very good actress. In Abel Gance's cinematic version of Charpentier's *Louise,* Moore had the good fortune to leave a lasting record of a role which is closely identified with her. Although she is not at her best vocally, she brings Louise to life in an appealing way and captures the essence of a young woman in love with love. Her acting abilities carried over into the opera house, but there she was called "stagey" more often than not—a complaint leveled a generation earlier against Geraldine Farrar. The "stigma" of Hollywood is hard to erase and Moore was thought by some to be too much the celebrity to be taken seriously as a classical artist. It is easy to fall into that trap when dealing with someone who carved out for herself a career which encompassed Broadway, opera, Hollywood, radio, recordings, recitals, concerts and war relief tours, the last of which took up as much of her time and energy as all of the rest combined. The fact that must not be overlooked is that she was a singer long before she was anything else. Her voice was a trained lyric soprano, at first, more suitable for musicals, but eventually through study and determination, an instrument quite capable of performing opera. Her recordings, while not vast, attest to this. Arias from *La bohème, Louise, Manon, Hérodiade* and *Tosca* are very expertly executed in a voice of agreeable timbre and sizeable range. The song literature is, as one would expect, where Moore shines best— not so much in the classic songs of Hahn or Duparc, which are rendered with great respect but little insight or attention to the fine points of French pronunciation, but in the semi-classical songs, especially "One Night of Love," "Ciribiribin," and, particularly "The Dubarry," from a show she starred in while on sabbatical from opera. There is enough evidence that her vocal production was erratic at times, most notably in intonation. In others this would have been a decided handicap, but in Moore it only seems to add to her glamour. "Glamour" is the key word here, for Moore personified it as much as her illustrious contemporaries Gertrude Lawrence and Carol Lombard. In the final analysis, it can be said that Grace Moore became an opera star not because of all she had going for her but in spite of it.

—John Pennino

MORRIS, James (Peppler).

Bass-baritone. Born 10 January 1947, in Baltimore. Studied with Frank Valentino at Peabody Conservatory, Nicola Moscona and Anton Guadagno; debut as Crespel in *Les contes d'Hoffman,* Baltimore Civic Opera, 1968; Metropolitan Opera debut as King in *Aida,* 1971, where he sang Don Giovanni in 1975; appeared widely in Europe; appeared as Wotan in *Die Walküre* in San Francisco, 1985.

Publications

About MORRIS: articles–

Current Biography (July) 1986.
Canning, H. "James Morris." *Opera* October (1988).

* * *

"A new super god . . . a Wotan of today and tomorrow," proclaimed the Vienna *Kronen Zeitung* upon the 1984 debut of James Morris at the Vienna State Opera in Wagner's *Die Walküre*—the American bass-baritone's first Wagnerian performance before a German-speaking audience. This and other laudatory reviews in Europe and the Americas have enabled Morris to take his place with such American-born predecessors as Clarence Whitehill, George London, and Jerome Hines among world-class Wagnerian interpreters.

Born in Baltimore, Maryland, on 10 January 1947, James Morris began his vocal studies as a teenager with a local teacher, Forrest Barrett. Upon graduating from high school Morris competed successfully for the first voice scholarship ever awarded by the University of Maryland; but, on the subsequent advice of soprano Rosa Ponselle, he completed his vocal studies at the Peabody Conservatory of Music under the tutelage of former Metropolitan Opera baritone Frank Valentino.

Although Rosa Ponselle is often cited as being Morris' first professional teacher (some sources, in fact, indicate that she came out of retirement in order to teach him), Ponselle in her memoirs (1982) wrote that although she "could hear the promise in [his] voice . . . I didn't feel I could take the responsibility for shaping his talents." After working with Morris in individual and group coaching sessions for a few months, Ponselle, with Valentino's concurrence, referred him to Metropolitan basso Nicola Moscona, with whom Morris studied for three years at Philadelphia's Academy of Vocal Arts. Still, the influence of Rosa Ponselle—to whom Morris was nominally related by marriage, from the maternal side of his family—did exert a lasting influence on his interpretive approach with new roles, instilling in him the necessity of "singing with your heart and emotion," as he expressed it.

Under Ponselle's artistic direction at the Baltimore Civic Opera Company, Morris sang comprimario roles in *La boheme, La forza del destino, Gianni Schicchi, La traviata* and other staples, in time advancing to Ramfis in *Aida,* the villains in *Les contes d'Hoffman,* and eventually to important roles in *Il barbiere di Siviglia, Rigoletto, Tosca,* and *Don Giovanni.* Morris' debut with the Baltimore Opera was as Crespel in *Hoffmann* (1968), which he sang opposite the Antonia of Beverly Sills, who also had coached under Ponselle.

In early November of 1970, at age twenty-three, Morris was given a Metropolitan Opera audition, which resulted in an invitation to join the company's Opera Studio. Morris declined the invitation, preferring instead to compete for a full-fledged contract at some later time. Through Moscona's influence, augmented by that of the Hurok agency (with whom Morris had recently signed as a client), a second Metropolitan audition was arranged; Rudolf Bing, then General Manager, was present. This second audition yielded an offer of a contract—which, when Morris accepted it, made him the youngest male singer ever engaged by the Metropolitan Opera.

After four seasons of singing smaller "character" parts (the Friar in *Don Carlos,* the Marquis in *Forza del destino,* Monterone in *Rigoletto*), Morris' self-described "longing for a real role" was partially satisfied when he was offered Timur in the Metropolitan production of *Turandot* (1974). Lacking many other opportunities for better roles at the Metropolitan, he accepted off-season engagements during the early 1970s with the Houston Grand Opera Company, the Philadelphia Lyric Opera, the Santa Fe Opera, and the Cincinnati Summer Opera. Other appearances in concertized operas produced by the Opera Orchestra of New York (including *Guillaume Tell,* 1972; Donizetti's *Parisina d'Este* and *Lucia,* 1974; and Gluck's *Semiramide,* 1976) enabled Morris to expand both his repertoire and his ensemble experience.

In 1976, under the aegis of Rosa Ponselle and Tito Capobianco, Morris returned to the Baltimore Opera to create the role of King Alfonso in the world premiere of Pasatieri's *Ines de Castro.* The following year, under the direction of Richard Bonynge, he created the role of Timur in the centenary revival of Massenet's *Le roi de Lahore.* But it was midway through the 1975-76 Metropolitan season that Morris achieved the greatest critical acclaim of his career up to that time: with only a few days' notice he replaced baritone Roger Soyer as Don Giovanni, also singing the role in that season's PBS "Live from the Met" telecast. It became one of the finest achievements of his career.

Having diversified his growing repertoire in challenging French and Italian roles, Morris prepared the role of Wotan in *Die Walküre* with Hans Hotter, generally considered the foremost Wotan of his time. Morris again returned to the Baltimore Opera for his first Wotan, and then followed it with a highly-praised Dutchman (also prepared under Hotter) at the Houston Grand Opera (1984). Morris' much-acclaimed Vienna State Opera debut as Wotan took place shortly afterward. The following year, when he appeared as Wotan in the San Francisco Opera Company's complete *Ring* cycle, he was judged "the greatest Wotan . . . since Hotter" (Arthur Bloomfield), and "a Wagnerian of the very first rank" (Paul Moor). Subsequent *Ring* performances at the Munich State Opera yielded the same enthusiastic responses from the critics.

Especially with Joan Sutherland, under the baton of Richard Bonynge, James Morris has made a number of well-received opera recordings, including *Maria Stuarda, Roi de Lahore,* Thomas' *Hamlet,* and Gay's *The Beggar's Opera,* all on the Decca/London label. He has also recorded *Così fan tutte* (under Riccardo Muti) and Haydn's *Die Schöpfung* (under Sir Georg Solti) in recent years. In all of his commercial recordings, Morris' pure *basso cantante* sound—dark in color, sonorous, impressively ductile, baritonal in range, and complemented by a profound musicality and artistic sensitivity—has been captured fully for contemporary audiences and, as his career continues at its zenith, for posterity as well.

—James A. Drake

MOSÈ IN EGITTO [Moses in Egypt].

Composer: Gioachino Rossini.

Librettist: A.L. Tottola (after F. Ringhierei, *L'Osiride*).

First Performance: Naples, San Carlo, 5 March 1818; revised as *Moïse et Pharaon,* Paris, 26 March 1827.

Roles: Pharaoh (bass); Amaltea (soprano); Osiris (tenor); Elcia (soprano); Mambre (tenor); Moses (bass); Aaron (tenor); Amenophis (mezzo-soprano).

Publications

articles–

Petrobelli, P. "Balzac, Stendhal e il *Mosè* di Rossini." *Conservatorio di musica 'G.B. Martini' di Bologna: Annuario 1965-1970* (1971): 205.

Isotta, P. "Da *Mosè* a *Moïse*." *Bollettino del Centro rossiniano di studi* (1971).

Conati, M. "Between Past and Future: the Dramatic World of Rossini in *Mosè in Egitto* and *Moïse et Pharaon*." *Nineteenth-Century Music* 4 (1980): 32

*   *   *

Mosè in Egitto is an opera designed to circumvent the ecclesiastical prohibition of opera performances during Lent; thus it has a biblical subject and proclaims itself an *"azione tragico-sacra"* (tragico-sacred action). In terms of plot it is very much a standard operatic love story, set in an exotic place and a remote time, with only the outlines of the Exodus account to get it past the censors.

In a stunning opening, Rossini reduces the overture to the briefest introduction in which the orchestra strikes the pitch "C" three times; on a dark stage the chorus laments in C minor until a change of key to C major signals the end of the plague and the return of light. Although Pharaoh has granted Moses permission to take the Israelites out of Egypt, the crown prince Osiris induces his father to change his mind, for Osiris is secretly married to Elcia, a Hebrew woman, whom he does not want to lose.

A plague of hailstones and fiery rain convinces Pharaoh to let the Israelites go, but again, influenced by his court, he revokes his permission and Moses threatens the death of Osiris and the other Egyptian first-born at God's hand. Although Osiris and Elcia attempted to hide, they have been discovered. Moses and Elcia are brought before Pharaoh and Osiris. Elcia reveals her marriage to Osiris and offers herself in return for her people's freedom. Osiris raises his sword to kill Moses but lightning from heaven strikes him down. In the final act, Moses and the Israelites, after praying for God's help, cross the Red Sea, but the pursuing Egyptian army drowns.

The music Rossini provided for the lovers is no different in style from that of his secular serious operas, but he treats the biblical elements of the story in a more majestic, oratorical way. Large ensembles and choral movements figure prominently, and the music for Moses himself is largely declamatory in nature. His well-known prayer, "Dal tuo stellato soglio" (From your starry throne), was not part of the original version: the staging of the crossing of the Red Sea so amused the audience that Rossini revised the third act the following year, adding this number.

In 1827 Rossini revised the entire opera for Paris, where it was presented on 26 March 1827 as *Moïse et Pharaon, ou Le Passage de la Mer Rouge* (*Moses and Pharaoh, or The Passage through the Red Sea*). The three-act libretto was expanded into the typical French four-act version by Luigi Balocchi and Etienne de Jouy. In addition to providing French texts for the Italian numbers, they created dramatic situations for additional pieces. An entirely new first scene was created in which the Israelites await the return of Moses' brother, who has gone to plead their cause with Pharaoh. Act II begins with the original opening of the plague of darkness. Aménophis (Osiris) is not yet married to Anaï (Elcia), and the queen persuades her son to agree to marry an Assyrian princess. The third act has an extended ballet performed in the Temple of Isis. When the Israelites refuse to worship the goddess, Pharaoh orders them expelled from Egypt. In the last act Aménophis, offering to give up the throne, asks Anaï to marry him, but she refuses to leave her people. Aménophis then joins his father in leading the doomed Egyptian army into the Red Sea.

The new music Rossini composed is admirable, although the added French spectacle weakens the drama. The best music from *Mosè in Egitto* was kept, while some which by then might have been considered old-fashioned was eliminated. Rossini's re-use of pieces from the first version in new dramatic contexts illustrates that his music is not intended to imitate specific emotions. For example, in an aria in *Mosè in Egitto* Elcia pleads with Osiris to marry a princess and allow her to leave with the Israelites; Osiris is killed, and Elcia expresses her grief in the cabaletta. In *Moïse et Pharaon* the aria is sung by Osiris' mother, the queen, who begs him to marry a princess and then in the cabaletta expresses her joy at his capitulation.

—Patricia Brauner

MOSES AND AARON
See MOSES UND ARON

MOSES IN EGYPT
See MOSÈ IN EGITTO

MOSES UND ARON [Moses and Aaron].

Composer: Arnold Schoenberg.

Librettist: Arnold Schoenberg (based on the Old Testament).

First Performance: partial performance [act III was never composed], Darmstadt, 2 July 1951; concert performance of acts I and II, Hamburg, 12 March 1954; staged performance of acts I and II, Zurich, Stadttheater, 6 June 1957.

Roles: Moses (bass-baritone); Aron (tenor); Young Maiden (soprano); Female Invalid (contralto); Young Man (tenor); Naked Youth (tenor); Man (baritone); Ephraimite (baritone); Priest (bass); Four Naked Virgins (sopranos, contraltos); Voice from Burning Bush (soprano, boy sopranos, contralto, tenor, baritone, bass); chorus (SSAATTBB).

Publications

books–

Wörner, K.H. *Gotteswort und Magie.* Heidelberg, 1959; English revision, *Schoenberg's 'Moses and Aaron',* 1963.

Boventer, H. ed. " 'Moses und Aron': zur Oper Arnold Schönbergs." Bensberg, 1979.

Krauss, Hans-Joachim, et al. *Moses und Aron: zur Oper Arnold Schönbergs.* Cologne, 1979.

Stec, Odil Hannes. *"Moses und Aron." Die Oper Arnold Schönbergs und ihr biblischer Stoff.* Munich, 1981.

White, Pamela C. *Schoenberg and the God-Idea: the Opera "Moses und Aron".* Ann Arbor, 1985.

articles–

Keller, H. "Schoenberg's 'Moses and Aron'." *The Score* no. 27 (1957): 30.

————. "Moses, Freud, and Schoenberg." *Monthly Musical Record* January-February and March-April (1958).

Serravezza, A. "Critica e ideologia nel 'Moses und Aron'." *Rivista italiana di musicologia* 15 (1980): 204.

Weaver, R. "The Conflict of Religion and Aesthetics in Schoenberg's 'Moses and Aaron'." In *Essays on the Music of J.S. Bach and Other Divers Subjects: a Tribute to Gerhard Herz,* edited by R. Weaver, 291. Louisville, 1981.

White, Pamela C. "The Genesis of Moses and Aron." *Journal of the Arnold Schoenberg Institute* 6 (1982): 8.

Yamaguchi, Koichi. "Der Gedanke Gottes und das Wort des Menschen: Zu Arnold Schönbergs *Moses und Aron." Neue Zeitschrift für Musik* 145 (1984): 8.

unpublished–

White, Pamela Cynthia. "Idea and Representation: Source-critical and Analytical Studies of Music, Text, and Religious Thought in Schoenberg's *Moses und Aron.*" Ph.D. dissertation, Harvard University, 1983.

*   *   *

Operas are usually concerned with love, in its comic or tragic aspects, or they are about intrigue or revenge; there are also political operas, satires, national epics, magical fantasies. Only Schoenberg could have conceived of writing an opera about the incommunicability of the nature of God. This is the philosophical core of *Moses und Aron;* but since it is a representation of the effect of that incommunicability on ordinary human beings—those wracked with the reality of it, and those unable to grasp it—the opera is also, paradoxically, the most dramatic work Schoenberg ever wrote, and one which has always "communicated" to its audiences with astonishing power.

Of the two acts for which Schoenberg actually composed the music, the first opens with Moses before the Burning Bush, receiving the Word of God. Subsequent scenes establish his relationship with his brother Aron, who eagerly accepts the role of priest and interpreter of Moses' vision in order to bring a finite political good—liberation from the power of Pharaoh—to the people of Israel, although to Moses this is a cheapening of the sacred Idea of God. They attempt to bring God's message to the fickle and sceptical people, who are only convinced when Aron performs three miracles: curing Moses' leprous hand, transforming the rod into a serpent,

and turning Nile water into blood (the last symbolizing liberation from Egypt)—all of which further distort the essence of Moses' insight. Encouraged by these signs of a God "more powerful than Pharaoh's gods," the Israelites prepare to follow the brothers on the quest for the Promised Land.

In act II the people are encamped in the desert, alarmed by Moses' long absence on the mountain of revelation. They demand of Aron a new and visible god like those of the surrounding tribes, and he eventually acquiesces in the creation of the Golden Calf. This leads to a huge communal orgy. Moses returns from the mountain bearing the Tables of the Law, and destroys the Calf in fury. But Aron defends himself, claiming the Tables are themselves a symbol, and yet another, the Pillar of Fire, appears to lead the Israelites onward. The music concludes with Moses' anguished monologue: "I too have fashioned an image, false, as an image must be . . . O word, thou word, that I lack!"

Moses und Aron can be seen to develop the dramatic themes of Schoenberg's (unperformed) stage-play *Der biblische Weg* (The Biblical Way) of 1927. Set in the contemporary world, this concerns an attempt to establish a Jewish homeland in Africa; the protagonist, Max Aruns, embodies within himself the conflicting forces of idealism and compromise that in the opera are separated out into the opposing characters of Moses and his brother. *Moses und Aron* was originally conceived as an oratorio, and goes back to the Book of Exodus and the original search for the Promised Land, which Schoenberg parallels with Moses' endeavour to forge the Israelites into a people dedicated to spiritual truth, to the "Only, infinite, omnipresent, unperceived and inconceivable God." In fact Moses also fails, for while his people are liberated from Egypt, they are not liberated from their craving for the symbols of nationhood. Despite—perhaps even because of—Schoenberg's inability to write the music for the brief, epilogue-like last act, which would have depicted Aron's death and Moses' triumph, the opera as it stands embodies a complete artistic design, which achieves its expressive purpose with unerring theatrical instinct. It is also the largest work Schoenberg ever composed according to the twelve-note method: its enormous variety of music derives from a single note-row (inhabiting the fabric of the opera like the "omnipresent and unperceived" God), and it exemplifies the entire range of his compositional mastery.

The core of the drama is implicit in the title: the contrasting mentalities of the two brothers, the prophet and the priest. All the other characters are merely representative figures from the Israelites, who are embodied *en masse* by the chorus. In a brilliantly effective stroke of operatic pathos, Schoenberg makes Moses—the only one who receives God's word, whose mind can encompass the spiritual reality—literally unable to sing. His part, notated throughout in a halting, uncouth *Sprechstimme* (Speech-song), cuts easily through the densest ensembles, yet it presents a man laboring under an immense interior burden. Moses therefore desperately *needs* Aron to get his message across, in words, which inevitably shackle and limit the force of the underlying idea; and for Aron, a golden-voiced lyric tenor, Schoenberg has composed some of the most seductive vocal lines in twelve-note music.

Indeed, for all the austerity of its philosophical message, *Moses und Aron* is probably the richest of all Schoenberg's works in sheer sonic invention, ranging from the mysterious disembodied glow of the Burning Bush (six solo voices doubled by six solo instruments), through the extreme complexity and layering of the massed choral sections, to the frenzied orgy-music of the Dances Round the Golden Calf—a kind of five-movement dance-symphony which ranks as one of his most staggering orchestral showpieces. Even this, however, is surpassed by the harrowing tragic grandeur of Moses' final monologue, accompanied only by a magnificently elegiac monody in the violins. Here, perhaps, Schoenberg gives us his self-portrait, as a prophet of musical truths which are always obscured through others' fascination with mere technical details: "how it is *done*," as he once wrote, "whereas I have always helped people to see: what it *is!*"

—Malcolm MacDonald

MOSHINSKY, Elijah.

Producer/Director. Born 8 January 1946, in Melbourne. Married: Ruth Dyttmann, 1970; two sons. Educated at Melbourne University, B.A.; St Antony's College, Oxford; producer at Covent Garden, 1973-; English National Opera, 1982-; and the Australian Opera; has also worked with the Royal Shakespeare Company and the National Theatre, as well as in the West End.

Opera Productions (selected)

Peter Grimes, London, Covent Garden, 1975.
Salome, Dallas, 1976.
Lohengrin, London, Covent Garden, 1978.
The Rake's Progress, London, Covent Garden, 1979.
Ernani, Cardiff, New Theatre, 1979.
Winter Cruise (Henkemans), Amsterdam, 1979.
Béatrice et Bénédict, Indianapolis, 1979.
Un ballo in maschera, New York, Metropolitan Opera, 1980.
Macbeth, London, Covent Garden, 1981.
Samson et Dalila, London, Covent Garden, 1981.
Le grande macabre (Ligeti), London Coliseum, 1982.
Death in Venice, Adelaide Festival, 1982.
Il trovatore, Adelaide Festival, 1983.
Les dialogues des Carmélites, Adelaide Festival, 1984.
Die Meistersinger von Nürnberg, London Coliseum, 1984.
Tannhäuser, London, Covent Garden, 1984.
I vespri siciliani, Geneva, 1985.
Samson, London, Covent Garden, 1985.
The Bartered Bride, English National Opera, 1985.
Macbeth, Canadian Opera, 1986.
Benvenuto Cellini, Florence, Teatro Communale, 1987.
Otello, London, Covent Garden, 1987.
Die Entführung aus dem Serail, London, Covent Garden, 1987.
La bohème, Glasgow, Theatre Royal, 1988.
Werther, Adelaide Festival, 1989.
La forza del destino, Glasgow, Theatre Royal, 1990.
Attila, London, Covent Garden, 1990.
Simon Boccanegra, London, Covent Garden, 1991.

Publications

By MOSHINSKY: articles–

"Verdi and *Macbeth*." *Opera* 32/April (1981): 340.
"*Tannhäuser* and the Unity of Opposites." *Opera* 35/September (1984): 963.

About MOSHINSKY: articles–

Sutcliffe, T. "A New *Lohengrin* (Producer, Elijah Moshinsky, Explains his New Approach)." *About the House* 5/3 (1977): 20.
Trilling, O. "Zweimal Britten." *Opernwelt* 20/6 (1979): 471.
Greenhalgh, J. "A New *Rake* for the Garden (interview)." *Music and Musicians* 27/June (1979): 24.
Wadsworth, S. "Making the Connection: Elijah Moshinsky." *Opera News* 44 (23 February 1980): 18.
Sutcliffe, T. "Elijah Moshinsky." In libretto, Hector Berlioz, *Benvenuto Cellini*. Florence, 1987.

* * *

The Australian producer/director Elijah Moshinsky has been one of the dominant figures in the British operatic scene during the past two decades. Although his career has been based mostly in Great Britain and Australia, some of his efforts have been seen in the United States, and he has created some productions in Italy and the Netherlands.

As assistant to John Tooley at Covent Garden he worked on productions of Wagner's *Ring* cycle with Götz Friedrich and *Tannhäuser* with Vaclav Kaslik. Also for the Royal Opera at Covent Garden he mounted Britten's *Peter Grimes* (1975); Wagner's *Lohengrin* (1978); Stravinsky's *The Rake's Progress* (1979); Wagner's *Tristan und Isolde* (a redirection of Peter Hall's production) (1980); Verdi's *Macbeth* (1981); Saint-Saëns's *Samson et Dalila* (1981); Richard Strauss's *Salome* (1982); Wagner's *Tannhäuser* (1984); Handel's *Samson* (1985, also seen at the Chicago Lyric Opera and the Metropolitan Opera); Verdi's *Otello* (1987); Mozart's *Die Entführung aus dem Serail* (1987); Verdi's *Attila* (1990); and Verdi's *Simon Boccanegra* (1991).

His American debut was a production of Richard Strauss's *Salome* for Dallas and Houston in 1976, and he also created a staging of Berlioz's *Béatrice et Bénédict* for Indianapolis (1979).

For the Scottish Opera he directed Puccini's *La bohème* (1988) and Verdi's *La forza del destino* (1990); for the Welsh National Opera, *Ernani* (1979); for the Metropolitan Opera, *Un ballo in maschera* (1980); for the English National Opera, Ligeti's *Le grand macabre* (1982), Wagner's *Die Meistersinger* (1984), Smetana's *The Bartered Bride;* for Geneva, Verdi's *I vespri siciliani* (1985); for Kent Opera, Mozart's *Die Entführung aus dem Serail;* and for the Australian Opera, *Boris Godunov* (using Musorgsky's original scoring). For the Adelaide Festival he staged Britten's *Death in Venice* (1982), Verdi's *Il trovatore* (1983), Poulenc's *Dialogues des Carmélites* (1984), and Massenet's *Werther* (1989, updated to the 1940s). In Amsterdam he mounted Hans Henkemans's *Winter Cruise* (1979); for the Canadian Opera, *Macbeth* (1986); and for the Maggio Musicale Fiorentino at the Teatro Communale, Florence, Berlioz's *Benvenuto Cellini* (1987). He has also directed a television production of *The Midsummer Marriage*.

Moshinsky's Covent Garden *Peter Grimes* was nonrepresentational—it took place in a large boxlike set with only minimal props. This was an effort to emphasize the mythic aspect of the work, in line with Moshinsky's belief that opera is "the last bastion of myth." He feels that each work has a particular point of connection, of identification: for example, in most Italian operas it is the singing, and the best performers of Italian opera are those who concentrate on the voice. In other works the point of identification may be betrayal, or

Elijah Moshinsky's production of Britten's *Peter Grimes*, Royal Opera, 1981

the political situation. What is important is that the interpretation of the work be derived from the meanings that exist within it and not from something imposed from without; nor should operas be staged as uni-dimensional works—political tracts, for example—when they actually contain a number of dimensions, such as the dynamic between the political context and the relationships between the characters. Creating a realistic environment allows the characters' motives to appear real as well. This is reflected in Moshinsky's admiration for works containing the most humane characters: Mozart's Da Ponte operas, Wagner's *Die Meistersinger,* Verdi's *Falstaff*— "humane comedies."

Moshinsky has been criticized for a tendency to overproduce, to encourage his singers to exaggerate action. He is considered by some critics, especially in Britain, however, to be one of the most intelligent and innovative directors active today.

—Michael Sims

THE MOTHER OF US ALL.

Composer: Virgil Thomson.

Librettist: Gertrude Stein.

First Performance: New York, 7 May 1947.

Roles: Susan B. Anthony (soprano); Anne (contralto); Daniel Webster (bass); Constance Fletcher (mezzo-soprano); John Adams (tenor); Jo the Loiterer (tenor); Gertrude S., the Narrator (soprano); Virgil T., the Master of Ceremonies (baritone); Indiana Elliot (contralto); Angel More (soprano); Chris the Citizen (baritone); Andrew Johnson (tenor); Thaddeus Stevens (tenor); Lillian Russell (soprano); Ulysses S. Grant (bass-baritone); Anthony Comstock (bass); Jenny Reefer (mezzo-soprano); Anna Hope (contralto); Herman Atlan (baritone); Donald Gallup (baritone); Gloster Heming (baritone); Isabella Wentworth (mezzo-soprano); Henrietta M. (soprano); Henry B. (bass-baritone); Indiana Elliot's Brother (bass-baritone); Negro Man (speaking); Negro Woman (speaking); chorus (TTAA); chorus (SATB).

Publications

article–

Smith, C. "Gertrude S., Virgil T., and Susan B." *Theatre Arts* 31/no. 7 (1947): 17.

*   *   *

After the scandalous success of their first opera, *Four Saints in Three Acts* in 1934, one might have expected that fellow expatriates in Paris Virgil Thomson and writer Gertrude

Stein would continue their fruitful association, bringing forth one unusual and evocative opera after another. However, the two suffered a falling out over financial matters. Thomson continued to compose and write prolifically, but no longer set Stein's off-beat melodious words. When World War II broke out, Stein remained in Europe, but Thomson returned to the U.S.A. in 1940, where he took up the post of music critic for the *New York Herald Tribune.* The two were not at work on an opera again until 1945, when Thomson returned to Paris for a time. He had a commission for an opera in hand and a deep interest in working on a subject from nineteenth-century American history. Stein leaped at the topic, chose Susan B. Anthony, leader of the women's suffrage movement, for her protagonist, and finished the libretto in March of 1946, just four months before her death.

The Mother of Us All is another Stein fantasy, this time centering on feminism and calling up such figures as John Adams, Daniel Webster, Ulysses S. Grant, and Lillian Russell. Even the characters Virgil Thomson and Gertrude Stein appear as narrators. Lacking a hard-and-fast plot per se, the work explores personalities and issues through boldly-drawn characters and their vivid words. Much of the time these figures do not seem to be speaking or listening to each other. With her usual liberating and liberated abandon, Stein ignores the conventions of chronology and conversation. These larger-than-life characters, even when they engage in sticho-mythia, often appear isolated and unable to connect emotionally. Speeches are made but communication is rare. Still there is a sense of progression through the scenes which include a political rally, a wedding, and several vignettes of Susan B. Anthony at home with her companion Anne. Quite moving is the final scene, the unveiling in the halls of Congress of a statue of Anthony some years after her death. An epilogue is delivered by the statue itself which sings of Anthony's "long life of effort and strife." The statue is at last left standing alone singing before a slow curtain fall.

Thomson's score is a brilliant nostalgic confusion of musical Americana. Echoing the flavor but never the exact melodies of popular parlor tunes, gospel and folk songs, maudlin ballads, and street bands, among others, Thomson deftly weaves the familiar, the trite, and the conventional in fresh, amusing, and evocative ways. In his autobiography Thomson himself described the harmonies as "plain-as-Dick's-hatband," but plain does not always mean simple or simplistic. Thomson's characteristic attention to instrumental texture and to the delicate interplay between voice and orchestra, and his marvelous ear for declamation and musical meaning shine through luminously here. The score of *The Mother of Us All* is by turns, amusing and poignant, but it is always well-wrought.

The premiere in 1947, with its student orchestra and blend of professional and amateur singers, was not a roaring success, but the work did receive acclaim. The Music Critics' Circle honored it with a special award. In 1949 Thomson arranged a suite for orchestra from *The Mother of Us All* which, brushing aside Stein's animating poetry, lacks the punch and appeal of the original work. This only serves as proof that the union of word and music in the work is miraculously robust, apt, and indissoluble. Thomson and Stein, both violent individualists, were a remarkable duo indeed.

—Michael Meckna

MOTTL, Felix (Josef).

Conductor. Born 24 August 1856, in Unter-Sankt Veit, near Vienna. Died 2 July 1911, in Munich. Married: 1) Henriette Standhartner, singer (divorced); 2) Zdenka Fassbender, singer, 1911. Studied piano with Door, theory with Bruckner, composition with Dessoff, and conducting with Hellmesberger at the Vienna Conservatory, graduating with high honors; assistant at the first Wagner festival at Bayreuth, 1876; succeeded Dessoff as court conductor at Karlsruhe, 1881; conducted *Tristan und Isolde* at the Bayreuth Festival, 1886; Generalmusikdirektor at Karlsruhe, 1893; conductor at Covent Garden, London, 1898-1900; conducted *Die Walküre* at the Metropolitan Opera in New York, 1903; Generalmusikdirektor of the Munich Court Opera, 1903; conductor of the Vienna Philharmonic, 1904-07. Mottl was also a composer whose works include four operas.

* * *

Austrian conductor and editor Felix Mottl, himself the composer of four operas (*Agnes Bernauer, Fürst und Sänger, Graf Eberstein,* and *Ramin*), held conducting posts at many of the major opera houses in Austria and Germany, as well as at the Metropolitan Opera in New York. After being appointed the conductor of the Academic Richard Wagner Society in Vienna, he became Wagner's assistant at Bayreuth in 1876. Four years later he was appointed Court Kapellmeister at the Karlsruhe Opera, during which tenure he led several Wagner operas and a cycle of the operas of Berlioz. Wagner considered his interpretation of *Tristan und Isolde* to be the best he had heard. In 1893, ten years after Wagner's death, Mottl became Karlsruhe's general music director, and during his time there he was responsible for making the standards of the company the highest in Germany. A skilled editor, he offered a reorchestrated version of Cornelius's *Der Barbier von Bagdad* in 1884 and temporarily rescued the work from obscurity. Also at Karlsruhe, he conducted all of the Wagner operas, as well as the first staging of the complete *Les Troyens* of Berlioz (1890, in German).

Mottl was the chief conductor at Bayreuth from 1886, first leading *Tristan und Isolde* and *Parsifal,* performances that established him as a leading exponent of Wagner's music. He was the conductor of *Tannhäuser* when it was first presented at Bayreuth in 1891.

At Covent Garden in 1898 Mottl led Wagner's complete *Ring* cycle. In 1903 he became the director of the Munich Opera, where he was again responsible for an improvement in standards. While there he led performances of his own editions of Bellini's *Norma* and Donizetti's *L'elisir d'amore.* While in Munich in 1910, Mottl conducted a performance of Wagner's early *Die Feen* at the Prinzregententheater (which had been built on the plan of the Bayreuth Festspielhaus expressly for the performance of Wagner in Munich). He also conducted Wagner's *Rienzi* there.

An early champion of the music of Richard Strauss (he had earlier orchestrated Strauss's lied "Ständchen"), Mottl had intended to conduct the world premiere of Strauss's first opera, *Guntram,* at Karlsruhe, but the plan was abandoned when the tenor withdrew because he believed that the title role was impossible to sing. Mottl did, however, give the first Munich performance of *Der Rosenkavalier* within a month of its Dresden premiere in 1911.

In 1903 Mottl was scheduled to conduct *Parsifal* at the Metropolitan Opera; the performance of 24 December was the first staging of the work outside Bayreuth and marked the first time an opera house abrogated Bayreuth's exclusive rights to its performance. He withdrew from the assignment because the Wagner family insisted that they still held the copyright and wanted no performances outside Bayreuth, but he did prepare the orchestra. He made his Metropolitan Opera debut later that season, leading *Die Walküre*. This was followed by *Lohengrin, Siegfried, Tannhäuser, Tristan und Isolde*, Mozart's *Le nozze di Figaro*, Gounod's *Roméo et Juliette*, Boieldieu's *La dame blanche*, Mozart's *Die Zauberflöte*, and Bizet's *Carmen*, all in the 1903-04 season. Dissatisfied because he was not granted sufficient authority by the Metropolitan's management, he resigned in 1904 and never returned to the company.

In addition to his conducting responsibilities, he edited several Berlioz and Wagner opera scores. For performances of *Tristan und Isolde* in Bayreuth shortly after Wagner's death, Mottl was asked to reduce the orchestration to improve the audience's ability to understand the text.

Mottl was criticized for being too easily influenced by others, especially by Cosima Wagner (with whom he maintained a correspondence for several years); it is rumored that Cosima instructed Mottl on how to conduct Wagner's scores, and he allowed her to dictate artistic policy at Bayreuth when he was chief conductor there.

As a conductor he is said to have favored slow tempos and, despite his reputation off the podium, to have led his orchestras with great authority. According to contemporary reviews, his performances were natural, tasteful, and free from mannerisms, and his technique perfect. In 1911, while conducting *Tristan und Isolde* in Munich, Mottl collapsed; he died a few weeks later.

—Michael Sims

MOZART, Wolfgang Amadeus (born Johannes Chrysostomus Wolfgangus Theophilus Mozart).

Composer. Born 27 January 1756, in Salzburg. Died 5 December 1791, in Vienna. Married: Constanze Weber, 4 August 1782. Studied with his father from a very early age; performed with his sister for the Elector of Bavaria, 17 January 1762, for Emperor Francis I at his palace in Vienna, September 1762, for Louis XV of France and Marie Antoinette, 1 January 1764, and for King George III of England, 1764; studied and performed with Johann Christian Bach in London; composed symphonies for performance in London; visited the Netherlands, Dijon, Lyons, Geneva, Bern, Zurich, Donaueschingen, and Munich on the way back to Salzburg, 1766; in Vienna, 1768, where he studied counterpoint with his father and worked on the opera *La finta semplice;* performance of his *Missa solemnis* in C minor for the royal family and court at the consecration of the Waisenhauskirche, 7 December 1768; Konzertmeister to Archbishop Sigismund von Schrattenbach in Salzburg, October, 1769; tour of Italy, 1770; elected to the Accademia Filarmonica in Bologna; made a Knight of the Golden Spur by the Pope, 1770; directed performances of his works in Milan, Salzburg, Vienna, and Paris, 1770-78; court organist in Salzburg, 1779; *Idomeneo* commissioned by the Elector of Bavaria, 1780; lost his position with the Archbishop in Salzburg, and moved to Vienna, 1781; joined the Masonic Order in Vienna, 1784; string quartets dedicated to Haydn, 1785; succeeded Gluck as Kammermusicus in Vienna, 1787; three last symphonies composed,

1788; performed as soloist in one of his piano concertos for the Elector of Saxony in Dresden, 1789; performed at the court of King Friedrich Wilhelm II, Berlin, 1789; in Frankfurt for the coronation of Emperor Leopold II, 1790; completed the score of *Die Zauberflöte,* 1791.

Operas

Editions:

W.A. Mozarts Werke. Edited by L. von Köchel et al. Leipzig, 1877-83; supplements, 1877-1910.
W.A. Mozart: Neue Ausgabe sämtlicher Werke. Edited E.F. Schmid, W. Plath, and W. Rehm, Internationale Stiftung Mozarteum Salzburg. Kassel, 1955-.

Apollo et Hyacinthus (intermezzo to *Clementia Croesi*), P.F. Widl? Salzburg, University, 13 May 1767.
La finta semplice, Marco Coltellini (after Goldoni), 1768, written for Vienna, performed Salzburg. Archbishop's palace, 1 May 1769.
Bastien und Bastienne (Singspiel), Friedrich Wilhelm Weiskern and J.A. Schachtner (after J.J. Rousseau, *Le devin du village,* and C.S. Favart, *Les amours de Bastien et Bastienne*), Dr F. Anton Mesmer's garden theater, September/October? 1768.
Mitridate, rè di Ponto, Vittorio Amadeo Cigna-Santi (after Giuseppe Parini and Racine), Milan, Teatro Regio Ducal, 26 December 1770.
Ascanio in Alba (festa teatrale), Giuseppe Parini, Milan, Teatro Regio Ducal, 17 October 1771.
Il sogno di Scipione (serenata), Metastasio, Salzburg, Archbishop's palace, c. May 1772.
Lucio Silla, Giovanni de Gamerra, Milan, Teatro Regio Ducal, 26 December 1772.
La finta giardiniera, Ranieri Calzabigi? (revised Coltellini), Munich, Assembly Rooms, 13 January 1775.
Il rè pastore, after Metastasio, Salzburg, Archbishop's palace, 23 April 1775.
Semiramide (melodrama), O. von Gemmingen [lost or projected].
Thamos, König von Ägypten (play with music), T.P. Gebler, Salzburg, 1776-79.
Zaide (Singspiel), Johann Andreas Schachtner (after F.J. Sebastiani, *Das Serail?*), 1779-80 [unfinished].
Idomeneo, Rè di Creta, Giambattista Varesco (after Danchet, *Idomenée*), Munich, Hoftheater, 29 January 1781.
Die Entführung aus dem Serail (Singspiel), J. Gottlieb Stephanie, Jr (after C.F. Bretzner, *Belmonte und Constanze*), Vienna, Burgtheater, 16 July 1782.
L' oca del Cairo, Giambattista Varesco, 1783 [unfinished].
Lo sposo deluso, Lorenzo Da Ponte?, 1783 [unfinished].
Der Schauspieldirektor, J. Gottlieb Stephanie, Jr, 1786, Vienna, Schönbrunn Palace, Orangery, 7 February 1786.
Le nozze di Figaro, Lorenzo Da Ponte (after Beaumarchais), Vienna, Burgtheater, 1 May 1786.
Il dissoluto punito, ossia Il Don Giovanni, Lorenzo Da Ponte, Prague, National Theater, 29 October 1787.
Così fan tutte, ossia La scuola degli amanti, Lorenzo Da Ponte, Vienna, Burgtheater, 26 January 1790.
La clemenza di Tito, Caterino Mazzolà (after Metastasio), Prague, National Theater, 6 September 1791.
Die Zauberflöte, Emanuel Schikaneder, Vienna, Theater auf der Wieden, 30 September 1791.

Other works: orchestral, including symphonies and concertos, chamber music, sacred and secular vocal music, songs, piano pieces.

Publications

By MOZART: books–

Anderson, Emily, trans. and ed. *The Letters of Mozart and his Family.* London and New York, 1938; 3rd ed., edited and revised by Alec Hyatt King and Stanley Sadie, London and New York, 1985.

Bauer, Wilhelm, and Otto Erich Deutsch, eds. *Mozart: Briefe und Aufzeichnungen. Gesamtausgabe.* 7 vols. Basel, 1962-75.

Curzon, Henry de, trans. *[Mozart] Lettres.* Paris, 1928; Ste Maxime, 1984.

About MOZART: books–

Niemetschek, Franz. *Leben des k. k. Kapellmeisters Wolfgang Gottlieb Mozart.* Prague, 1798; English translation by Helen Mautner as *Life of Mozart,* London, 1956.

Nissen, Georg Nikolaus von. *Biographie W. A. Mozarts.* Edited by Constanze von Nissen. Leipzig, 1828.

Gounod, C. *Le Don Juan de Mozart.* Paris, 1890; English translation, 1895; 1970.

Komorzynski, E. *Emanuel Schikaneder: ein Beitrag zur Geschichte des deutschen Theaters.* Vienna, 1901; 2nd ed., 1951; 3rd ed., 1955.

Dent, Edward J. *Mozart's Operas: a Critical Study.* London, 1913; 2nd ed., 1947; Italian translation by Luigi Ferrari as *Il teatro di Mozart,* Milan, 1979.

Lert, E. *Mozart auf dem Theater.* Berlin, 1918.

Dumesnil, R. *Le "Don Juan" de Mozart.* Paris, 1927.

Brukner, F. *Die Zauberflöte: unbekannte Handschriften und seltene Drucke aus der Frühzeit der Oper.* Vienna, 1934.

Blom, Eric. *Mozart.* London, 1935; 1974.

Stefan, P. *Die Zauberflöte: Herkunft, Bedeutung, Geheimnis.* Vienna, 1937.

Ben, C. *Mozart on the Stage.* London, 1946; 2nd 3d., 1947.

Jouve, P. J. *Le Don Juan de Mozart.* Freiburg, 1942, English translation, 1957.

Conrad, L. *Mozarts Dramaturgie der Oper.* Würzburg, 1943.

Einstein, Alfred. *Mozart: His Character, His Work.* Translated by Arthur Mendel and Nathan Broder. Oxford, 1945.

Levarie, S. *Mozart's "Le nozze di Figaro": a Critical Analysis.* Chicago, 1952; 1977.

Friedrich, Götz. *Die humanistische Idee der "Zauberflöte": Ein Beitrag zur Dramaturgie der Oper.* Dresden, 1954.

Greitler, A. *Die sieben grossen Opern Mozarts: Versuche über das Verhältnis der Texte zur Musik.* Heidelberg, 1956; 2nd ed. 1970.

Mitchell, Donald, and H.C. Robbins Landon. *The Mozart Companion.* London, 1956; 1965.

Wyzewa, T. de, and Georges de Saint-Foix. *Wolfgang Amédée Mozart: Sa vie musicale et son oeuvre.* 5 vols. Paris, 1912-46.

Deutsch, Otto Erich, ed. *Mozart: Die Dokumente seines Lebens.* Kassel, 1961; English translation by Eric Blom, Peter Branscombe, and Jeremy Noble as *Mozart: A Documentary Biography,* London, 1965.

Brophy, Brigid. *Mozart the Dramatist.* London, 1964; 2nd ed., 1988.

Rosenberg, A. *Die Zauberflöte: Geschichte und Deutung.* Munich, 1964.

Moberley, Robert B. *Three Mozart Operas: Figaro, Don Giovanni, The Magic Flute.* London, 1967.

Chailley, J. *La flûte enchantée: opéra maçonnique: essai d' explication du livret et de la musique.* Paris, 1968; English translation by Herbert Weinstock as *"The Magic Flute": Masonic Opera.* New York, 1972.

Batley, E.M. *A Preface to The Magic Flute.* London, 1969.

Abert, Anna Amalie. *Die Opern Mozarts.* Wolfenbüttel, 1970; English version in the *New Oxford History of Music,* vol. 7, Oxford, 1973.

King, Alec Hyatt. *Mozart: A Biography, with a Survey of Books, Editions, and Recordings.* London, 1970.

Massin, Jean, and Brigitte Massin. *Wolfgang Amadeus Mozart.* Paris, 1970.

Nettl, Paul. *Mozart and Masonry.* New York, 1970.

Levey, Michael. *The Life and Death of Mozart.* London, 1971.

Ascher, Gloria *"Die Zauberflöte" und "Die Frau ohne Schatten": Ein Vergleich zwischen zwei Operndichtungen der Humanität.* Berne, 1972.

Eggebrecht, Hans H. *Versuch über die Wiener Klassik: Die Tanzszene in Mozarts "Don Giovanni".* Wiesbaden, 1972.

Kunze, Stefan. *Don Giovanni vor Mozart: die Tradition der Don Giovanni-Opern im italienischen Buffo-Theater des 18. Jahrhunderts.* Munich, 1972.

Liebner, János. *Mozart on the Stage.* London, 1972.

Hutchings, Arthur. *Mozart: The Man, The Musician.* London, 1976.

Angermüller, Rudolf, and Otto Schneider. *Mozart-Bibliographie.* Kassel, 1976-85.

Gianturco, Carolyn. *Le opere del giovane Mozart.* Pisa, 1976; 2nd ed., 1978; English translation as *Mozart's Early Operas,* London, 1981.

Hildesheimer, Wolfgang. *Mozart.* Frankfurt, 1977; English translation by Marion Faber, London, 1982.

Mann, William. *The Operas of Mozart.* London, 1977.

Noske, F. *The Signifier and the Signified: Studies in the Operas of Mozart and Verdi.* The Hague, 1977.

Thomson, Katherine. *The Masonic Thread in Mozart.* London, 1977.

Amico, Fedele d'. *Attorno al "Don Giovanni" di Mozart.* Paris, 1978.

Deutsch, Otto Erich. *Mozart: Die Dokumente seines Lebens: Addenda und Corrigenda.* Kassel, 1978.

Hocquard, Jean-Victor. *Così fan tutte.* Paris, 1978.

———. *Le "Don Giovanni" de Mozart.* Paris, 1978.

Lippmann, Friedrich, ed. *Colloquium: Mozart und Italien.* Cologne, 1978.

Osborne, Charles. *The Complete Operas of Mozart.* London, 1978.

Pahlen, Kurt. *Wolfgang Amadeus Mozart—"Die Zauberflöte." Ein Opernführer.* Munich, 1978.

Raynor, Henry. *Mozart.* London, 1978.

Vill, S., ed. *Così fan tutte: Beiträge zur Wirkungsgeschichte von Mozarts Oper.* Bayreuth, 1978.

Degrada, Francesco. *Il palazzo incantato. Studi sulla tradizione del melodramma dal Barocco al Romaticismo.* Fiesole, 1979.

Gammond, Peter. *The Magic Flute: A Guide to the Opera.* London, 1979.

Hocquard, Jean-Victor. *La flûte enchantée.* Paris, 1979.

———. *Le nozze di Figaro.* Paris, 1979.

Massin, Jean, ed. *Don Juan, mythe littéraire et musical.* Paris, 1979.

Mila, Massimo. *Lettura della "Nozze di Figaro." Mozart e la ricerca di felicità.* Turin, 1979.

Ottaway, Hugh. *Mozart.* London, 1979.

Strohm, Reinhard. *Die italienische Oper im 18. Jahrhunderts.* Wilhelmshaven, 1979.

Hocquard, Jean-Victor. *"L' enlèvement au sérail," précédé de "Zaide."* Paris, 1980.

Keys, I. *Mozart: His Music in His Life.* London, 1980.

Pahlen, Kurt, ed. *Wolfgang Amadeus Mozart: Die Entführung aus dem Serail.* Munich, 1980.

Angermüller, Rudolf, and Robert Münster, eds. *Wolfgang Amadeus Mozart: "Idomeneo" 1781-1981.* Munich, 1981.

Csampi, Attila, and Dietmar Holland, eds. *Wolfgang Amadeus Mozart, "Don Giovanni." Texte, Materialien, Kommentare.* Reinbek bei Hamburg, 1981.

Rushton, Julian, ed. *W.A. Mozart: Don Giovanni. Cambridge Opera Guides.* Cambridge, 1981.

Angermüller, Rudolph, and Otto Schneider, comps. *Mozart, Bibliographie 1976-1980 mit Nachträgen zur Mozart-Bibliographie bis 1975.* Kassel, 1982.

Csampi, Attila, and Dietmar Holland, eds. *Wolfgang Amadeus Mozart: "Die Zauberflöte". Texte, Materialien, Kommentare.* Reinbek, 1982.

Hocquard, Jean-Victor. *Idoménée.* Paris, 1982.

Rickmann, Sonja P. *Mozart: Ein bürgerlicher Künstler: Studien zu den Libretti "Le Nozze di Figaro," "Don Giovanni," und "Così fan tutte".* Vienna, 1982.

Sadie, Stanley. *The New Grove Mozart.* London, 1982.

Allenbrook, Wye J. *Rhythmic Gesture in Mozart: "Le nozze di Figaro" and "Don Giovanni".* Chicago, 1983.

Csampi, Attila, and Dietmar Holland, eds. *Wolfgang Amadeus Mozart: Die Entführung aus dem Serail.* Reinbek, 1983.

John, Nicholas, ed. *Wolfgang Amadeus Mozart: Così fan tutte.* London and New York, 1983.

————. *Wolfgang Amadeus Mozart: Don Giovanni.* London and New York, 1983.

Lühning, Helga. *"Titus"—Vertonungen im 18. Jahrhundert: Untersuchungen zur Tradition der Opera Seria von Hasse bis Mozart.* Rome, 1983.

Peter, Christoph. *Die Sprache der Musik in Mozarts Zauberflöte.* Stuttgart, 1983.

Dieckmann, Friedrich, ed. *"Die Zauberflöte": Max Slevogts Randzeichnungen zu Mozarts Handschrift, mit dem Text von Emanuel Schikaneder.* Berlin, 1984.

Kaiser, Joachim. *"Mein Name ist Sarastro": Die Gestalten in Mozarts Meisteropern von Alfonso bis Zerlina.* Munich and Zurich, 1984.

Kunze, Stefan. *Mozarts Opern.* Stuttgart, 1984.

Henze-Döhring, Sabine. *Opera seria, Opera buffa und Mozarts "Don Giovanni": Zur Gattungskonvergenz in der italienischen Oper des 18. Jahrhunderts.* Laaber, 1986.

Kupferberg, Herbert. *Amadeus: A Mozart Mosaic.* New York, 1986.

Bauman, Thomas. *W.A. Mozart: Die Entführung aus dem Serail. Cambridge Opera Guides.* Cambridge, 1987.

Carter, Tim. *W.A. Mozart: Le nozze di Figaro. Cambridge Opera Guides.* Cambridge, 1987.

Hocquard, Jean-Victor. *"La clemenza di Tito" et les opéras de jeunesse.* Paris, 1987.

Tyson, Alan. *Mozart: Studies of the Autograph Scores.* Cambridge, Massachusetts, 1987.

Angermüller, Rudolph. *Mozart—Die Opern von der Uraufführung bis heute.* Freiburg, 1988; English translation as *Mozart's Operas,* New York, 1988.

Clément, Catherine. *Opera, or the Undoing of Women,* translated by Betsy Wing, with a forward by Susan McClary, Minneapolis, 1988.

Kivy, Peter. *Osmin's Rage: Philosophical Reflections on Opera, Drama, and Text.* Princeton.

Landon, H.C. Robbins. *1791: Mozart's Last Year.* New York, 1988.

Marty, Jean-Pierre. *The Tempo Indications of Mozart.* New Haven, 1988.

Nagel, Ivan. *Autonomie und Gnade: Über Mozarts Opern.* Munich, 1988; English translation by Marion Faber and Ivan Nagel, *Autonomy and Mercy: Reflections on Mozart's Operas,* Cambridge, Massachusetts, 1988.

Hastings, Baird. *Wolfgang Amadeus Mozart: A Guide to Research.* New York, 1989.

Landon, H.C. Robbins. *Mozart: The Golden Years, 1781-1791.* London, 1989.

Steptoe, Andrew. *The Mozart-Da Ponte operas: The Cultural and Musical Background to "Le Nozze di Figaro," "Don Giovanni," and "Così fan tutte".* Oxford, 1989.

Braunbehrens, Volkmar. *Mozart in Vienna.* London, 1990.

Heartz, Daniel. *Mozart's Operas.* Edited and with contributing essays by Thomas Bauman. Berkeley, 1990.

McLean, Ian. *Mozart.* London, 1990.

Miller, Jonathan, ed. *The Don Giovanni Book.* London, 1990.

articles—

Blümml, Emil Karl. "Ausdeutungen der 'Zauberflöte'." *Mozart-Jahrbuch 1* (1923): 109.

Lorenz, A. "Das Finale in Mozarts Meisteropern." *Musik 29* (1926-27): 621.

Blom, E. "The Literary Ancestry of Figaro." *Musical Quarterly 13* (1927): 528.

Einstein, Alfred. "Das erste Libretto des 'Don Giovanni'." *Acta musicologica 9* (1937): 149.

Komorzynski, E. "Die Zauberflöte: Entstehung und Bedeutung des Kunstwerks." *Neues Mozart-Jahrbuch 1* (1941): 147.

Redlich, H.F. "L'oca del Cairo." *Music Review 2* (1941): 122.

Wellesz, E. "Don Giovanni and the dramma giocoso." *Music Review 4* (1943): 121.

King, A.H. "The Melodic Sources and Affinities of *Die Zauberflöte*." *Musical Quarterly 36* (1950): 241.

Engel, H. "Die Finali der Mozartschen Opern." *Mozart-Jahrbuch* (1954): 113.

Raeburn, C. "An Evening at Schönbrunn." *Music Review 16* (1955): 96.

Keller, Hans. "The *Entführung's* Vaudeville." *Music Review 17* (1956): 304.

Tagliavini, L.F. "L'opéra italien du jeune Mozart." In *Les influences étrangères dans l' oeuvre de Mozart: Centre National de la Recherche Scientifique,* 125. Paris, 1956.

Raeburn, C. "Die textlichen Quellen des 'Schauspieldirektor'." *Österreichische Musikzeitschrift 13* (1958): 4.

Volek, T. "Über den Ursprung von Mozarts Oper 'La Clemenza di Tito'." *Mozart-Jahrbuch* (1959): 274.

Szabolcsi, B. "Mozart et la comédie populaire." *Studia musicologica Academiae scientiarum hungaricae 1* (1961): 65.

Friedrich, Götz. "Zur Inszenierungskonzeption *Così fan tutte:* Komische Oper Berlin 1962." *Jahrbuch der Komische Oper Berlin 3* (1962-63).

Gieglung, F. "Metastasios Oper *La clemenza di Tito* in der Bearbeitung durch Mazzola." *Mozart-Jahrbuch* (1962-63).

Kunze, Stefan. "Mozarts Schauspieldirektor." *Mozart-Jahrbuch* (1962-63): 156.

Köhler, K.-H. "Figaro-Miscellen: Einige dramaturgische Mitteilungen zur Quellensituation." *Mozart-Jahrbuch* (1962-63).

Neumann, F.-H. "Zur Vorgeschichte der Zaide." *Mozart-Jahrbuch* (1962-63): 216.

Livermore, A. "The Origins of Don Juan." *Music and Letters* 44 (1963): 257.

Floros, C. "Das 'Programm' in Mozarts Meisterouvertüren." *Schweizerische Musikzeitung/Revue musicale suisse* 26 (1964): 140.

Raeburn, C. "Die Entführungsszene aus 'Die Entführung aus dem Serail'." *Mozart-Jahrbuch* (1964): 130.

Moberly, Robert B. and C. Raeburn. "Mozart's 'Figaro': the Plan of Act III." *Music and Letters* 46 (1965): 134; reprinted in *Mozart-Jahrbuch* (1965-66): 161.

Münster, R. "Die verstellte Gärtnerin: neue Quellen zur authentischen Singspielfassung von W.A. Mozarts *La finta giardiniera*." *Die Musikforschung* 18 (1965): 138.

Branscombe, P. " 'Die Zauberflöte': some Textual and Interpretative Problems." *Proceedings of the Royal Musical Association* 92 (1965-66): 45.

Chusid, M. "The Significance of D minor in Mozart's Dramatic Music." *Mozart-Jahrbuch* (1965-66): 87.

Keahey, D.J. "*Così fan tutte*: Parody or Irony." In *Paul A. Pisk: Essays in his Honor*, 116. Austin, 1966.

Abert, A.A. "Beiträge zur Motivik von Mozarts Spätopern." *Mozart-Jahrbuch* (1967): 7.

Brophy, Brigid. "The Young Mozart." In *Opera 66*, edited by C. Osborne. London, 1967.

Giegling, F. "Zu den Rezitativen von Mozarts Oper 'Titus'." *Mozart-Jahrbuch* (1967): 121.

Köhler, K.-H. "Mozarts Kompositionsweise: Beobachtungen am Figaro-Autograph." *Mozart-Jahrbuch* (1967): 31.

Gruber, G. "Das Autograph der 'Zauberflöte'." *Mozart-Jahrbuch* (1967): 127; (1968-70): 99.

Abert, A.A. " 'La finta giardiniera;' und 'Zaide' als Quellen für spätere Opern Mozarts." In *Musik und Verlag: Karl Vötterle zum 65. Geburtstag*, 113. Kassel, 1968.

Noske, F.R. "Musical Quotations as a Dramatic Device: the Fourth Act of Le nozze di Figaro." *Musical Quarterly* 54 (1968): 185.

Tagliavini, L.F. "Quirino Gasparini and Mozart." In *New Looks at Italian Opera: Essays in Honor of Donald J. Grout*, 151. Ithaca, New York, 1968.

Döhring, S. "Die Arienformen in Mozarts Opern." *Mozart-Jahrbuch* (1968-70): 66.

Federhofer, H. "Die Harmonik als dramatischer Ausdrucksfaktor in Mozarts Meisteropern." *Mozart-Jahrbuch* (1968-70): 77.

Giegling, F. "Metastasios Oper 'La clemenza di Tito' in der Bearbeitung durch Mazzola." *Mozart-Jahrbuch* (1968-70): 88.

Köhler, K.-H. "Figaro-Miscellen: Einige dramaturgische Mitteilungen zur Quellensituation." *Mozart-Jahrbuch* (1968-70): 119.

Mahling, Christoph-Hellmut. "Typus und Modell in Opern Mozarts." *Mozart-Jahrbuch* (1968-70), 145.

Rech, G. "Bretzner contra Mozart." *Mozart-Jahrbuch* (1968-70): 186.

Henning, C. "Thematic Metamorphoses in Don Giovanni." *Music Review* 30 (1969): 22.

Noske, F. "Social Tensions in 'Le nozze di Figaro'." *Music and Letters* 1 (1969): 45.

Brophy, Brigid. " 'Figaro' and the Limitations of Music." *Music and Letters* 51 (1970): 26.

Noske, F.R. "Don Giovanni: Musical Affinities and Dramatic Structure." *Studia musicologica Academiae scientiarum hungaricae* 12 (1970): 167; reprinted in *Theatre Research/Recherches théâtrales* 13 (1973): 60.

Williamson, A. "Who was Sarastro?" *Opera* 21 (1970): 297.

Keller, Hans. "Mozart's Wrong Key Signature." *Tempo* no. 98 (1972): 21.

Goldschmidt, H. "Die Cavatina des Figaro." *Beiträge zur Musikwissenschaft* 15 (1973): 185.

Mahling, Christoph-Hellmut. "Die Gestalt des Osmin in Mozarts *Entführung*: Vom Typus zur Individualität." *Archiv für Musikwissenschaft* 30 (1973).

Moberly, Robert B. "Mozart and his Librettists." *Music and Letters* 54 (1973): 161.

Williams, B. "Passion and Cynicism: Remarks on 'Così fan tutte'." *Musical Times* 114 (1973): 361.

Lühning, H. "Zur Entstehungsgeschichte von Mozarts "Titus'." *Die Musikforschung* 27 (1974): 300; 28 (1975): 77, 312; 29 (1976): 127.

Moberly, R.B. "The Influence of French Classical Drama on Mozart's 'La clemenza di 'Tito'." *Music and Letters* 55 (1974): 286.

Gruber, G. "Bedeutung und Spontaneität in Mozarts "Zauberflöte'." In *Festschrift Walter Senn*, 118. Munich and Salzburg, 1975.

Koenigsberger, D. "A New Metaphor for Mozart's *Magic Flute*." *European Studies Review* 5 (1975): 229.

Scheel, H.L. "'Le mariage de Figaro' von Beaumarchais und das Libretto der 'Nozze di Figaro' von Lorenzo da Ponte." *Die Musikforschung* 28 (1975): 156.

Neville, Don J. "*La clemenza di Tito*: Metastasio, Mazzolà, and Mozart." *Studies in Music from the University of Western Ontario* 1 (1976).

————. "*Idomeneo* and *La clemenza di Tito*: Opera Seria and Vera Opera." *Studies in Music* [Canada] 5 (1978): 99.

Angermüller, Rudolf. "Mozart and Metastasio." *Mitteilungen der Internationalen Stiftung Mozarteum* 26/nos. 1-2 (1978): 12.

————. "Ein neuentdecktes Salzburger Libretto (1769) zu Mozarts *La finta semplice*." *Die Musikforschung* 31 (1978): 318.

————. "Wer war der Librettist von *La finta giardiniera?*" *Mozart-Jahrbuch* 1976-77 (1978): 1.

Carli Ballola, Giovanni. "Mozart e l'opera seria di Jommelli, De Majo e Traetta." *Analecta musicologica* 18 (1978): 138.

Gerstenberg, Walter. "Betrachtung über Mozarts Idomeneo." In *Festschrift Georg von Dadelsen zum 60. Geburtstag*, edited by Thomas Kohlhase and Volker Scherliess, 148. Stuttgart, 1978.

Goslich, Siegfried. "Über die Formentwicklung in Mozarts Opern." In *Mozart, Klassik für die Gegenwart*, 64. Oldenburg, 1978.

Heartz, Daniel. "Mozart, His Father, and *Idomeneo*." *Musical Times* 119 (1978).

Jaacks, Gisela. "Höllenfahrt und Sonnentempel. Das Bühnenbild der Mozart-Opern." In *Mozart, Klassik für die Gegenwart*, 98. Oldenburg, 1978.

Keys, Allwyn Charles. "Two Eighteenth-Century Racinian Operas." *Music and Letters* 59 (1978): 1.

Kunze, Stefan. "Mozarts *Don Giovanni* und die Tanzszene im ersten Finale." *Analecta musicologica*. 18 (1978).

Porena, Boris. "La parola intonata in *Così fan tutte*, ovvero l' esplorazione musicale di una lingua e del suo uso sociale." *Analecta musicologica* 18 (1978): 198.

Starobinsky, Jean. "Pouvoir et lumières dans la *Flûte enchantée*." *XVIIIe siècle* 10 (1978): 435.

Vill, Susanne, ed. "*Così fan tutte*": Beiträge zur Wirkungsgeschichte von Mozarts Oper. Bayreuth, 1978.

Agmon, Eytan. "The Descending Fourth and its Symbolic Significance in *Don Giovanni*." *Theory and Practice* 4 (1979): 3.

Angermüller, Rudolf. "*Les époux esclaves ou Bastien et Bastienne à Alger*. Zur Stoffgeschichte der Entführung aus dem Serail." In *Mozart und seine Umwelt*, edited by the

Internationale Stiftung Mozarteum Salzburg, 70. Kassel, 1979.

Dürr, Walther. "Zur Dramaturgie des *Titus*. Mozarts Libretto and Metastasio." In *Mozart und seine Umwelt*, edited by the Internationale Stiftung Mozarteum Salzburg, 55. Kassel, 1979.

Godwin, Jocelyn. "Layers of Meaning in *The Magic Flute*." *Musical Quarterly* 65 (1979): 471.

Heartz, Daniel. "Goldoni, *Don Giovanni* and the *dramma giocoso*." *Musical Times* 120 (1979): 993.

Valentin, Erich. " 'Don Ottavio balla Menuetto.' Anmerkungen zum *Don Giovanni*." *Acta mozartiana* 26 (1979): 66.

Croll, Gerhard. "Ein Janitscharen Marsch zur Entführung. Erster Bericht über einen Mozart-Fund." *Mitteilungen der Internationalen Stiftung Mozarteum* 28/no. 1-2 (1980): 2.

Kramer, Kurt. "Antike und christliches Mittelalter in Varescos *Idomeneo*, dem Libretto zu Mozarts gleichnamiger Oper." *Mitteilungen der Internationalen Stiftung Mozarteum* 28/no. 1-2 (1980): 6.

———. "Frauengestalten in Varescos *Idomeneo*. Ilia, die opferbereite Priamustochter und ihre dämonische Gegenspielerin Elektra." *Mitteilungen der Internationalen Stiftung Mozarteum* 28/no. 3-4 (1980): 16.

Wangermée, Robert. "Quelques mystères de *La flûte enchantée*." *Revue belge de musicologie* 34-35 (1980-81): 147.

Köhler, K.-H. "Zu den Methoden und einigen Ergebnissen der philologischen Analyse am Autograph der *Zauberflöte*." *Mozart-Jahrbuch* 1980-83): 282.

Ballantine, Christopher. "Social and Philosophical Outlook in Mozart's Operas." *Musical Quarterly* 67 (1981): 507.

Branscombe, Peter J. "*Così* in Context." *Musical Times* 122 (1981): 461.

Floros, Constantin. "Stileleben und Stilsynthese in den Opern Mozarts." In *Die frühdeutsche Oper und ihre Beziehungen zu Italien, England und Frankreich. Mozart und die Oper seiner Zeit*, edited by Martin Ruhnke, 155. Laaber, 1981.

Heartz, Daniel. " 'Che mi sembra morir': Donna Elvira and the Sextet." *Musical Times* 122 (1981): 448.

———. "Three Schools for Lovers: the Mozart—Da Ponte Trilogy." *About the House* spring (1981): 18.

Kramer, Kurt. "Zur Entstehung von Mozarts *Idomeneo*." *Mitteilungen der Internationalen Stiftung Mozarteum* 29 (1981): 23.

Mahling, Christopher-Hellmut. "Myslivecek (1737-1781) und Gretry (1741-1813). Vorbilder Mozarts?" In *Die frühdeutsche Oper und ihre Beziehungen zu Italien, England und Frankreich. Mozart und die Oper seiner Zeit*, edited by Martin Ruhnke, 203. Laaber, 1981.

Osthoff, Wolfgang. "Gli endecasillabi Villostistici in *Don Giovanni* e *Nozze di Figaro*." In *Venezia e il melodramma nel settecento*, edited by Maria Teresa Muraro, vol. 2, p. 293. Florence, 1981.

Pirrotta, Nino. "The Tradition of Don Juan Plays and Comic Operas." *Pamphlet of the Royal Musical Association* 107 (1981): 60.

Steptoe, Andrew. "The Sources of *Così fan tutte*: A Reappraisal." *Music and Letters* 62 (1981): 281.

Valentin, Erich. ". . . Punkte, die Opera betreffen." *Acta mozartiana* 28/no. 3 (1981): 49.

Williams, Bernard. "Mozart's Comedies and the Sense of an Ending." *Musical Times* 122 (1981): 451.

Allenbrook, Wye J. "Pro Marcellina: the Shape of 'Figaro' Act IV." *Music and Letters* 63 (1982): 69.

Angermüller, Rudolph. "*La finta semplice*. Goldoni/Coltellinis Libretto zu Mozarts erster Opera buffa (italienisch-deutsch)." *Mitteilungen der Internationalen Stiftung Mozarteum* 30 (1982): 15.

Autexier, Philippe A. "Rhapsodie philologique à propos du *Don Giovanni* de Mozart." *Studia musicologica* 24 (1982): 21.

Dabezies, André. "Le pardon dans les opéras de Mozart." In *L' opéra aux XVIIIe siècle*. Aix-en-Provence, 1982.

Dittrich, Michael. "Die Tanzmusik Joseph Haydns im Spiegel der Zeit." *Pannonia* 10/no. 1 (1982): 20.

Staehelin, Martin. "Ah fuggi il traditor . . . Bemerkungen zur zweiten Donna-Elvira-Arie in Mozarts *Don Giovanni*." In *Festschrift Heinz Becker zum 60. Geburtstag am 26. Juni 1982*, edited Jürgen Schläder and Reinhold Quandt, 67. Laaber, 1982.

Sulzer, Wolfgang. "Bretzner gegen Mozart? Ein Protest und seine Folgen." *Acta mozartiana* 29/no. 3 (1982): 53.

Wilkens, Lorenz. "Mozarts *Don Giovanni*." In *Notizbuch 5/6. Musik*, edited by Reinhard Kapp, 59. Berlin, 1982.

Analecta musicologica 20 (1983) ["*Titus*—Vertonungen in 18. Jahrhundert—Untersuchungen zur Tradition der Opera seria von Hasse bis Mozart"].

Bernich, Joan. "*The Marriage of Figaro*: Genesis of a Dramatic Masterpiece." *Opera Quarterly* 1 (1983): 79.

Carroll, Charles Michael. "Eros on the Operatic Stage: Problems in Manners and Morals." *Opera Quarterly* 1 (1983): 87.

Gurewitsch, Matthew. "In the Mazes of Light and Shadow: A Thematic Comparison of *The Magic Flute* and *Die Frau ohne Schatten*." *Opera Quarterly* 1/no. 2/(1983): 11.

Hirsbrunner, Theo. "Struktur und Dramaturgie in Mozarts *Don Giovanni*." *Universitas* 38 (1983): 985.

Nicolosi, Robert J. "The *tempo di minuetto* aria in Mozart's Operas." *College Music Symposium* 23 (1983): 97.

Parakilas, James. "Mozart's Mad Scene." *Soundings* 10 (1983): 3.

Stiefel, Richard. "Mozart's Seductions." *Current Musicology* 36 (1983): 151.

Avant-scène opéra 59 (1984) [*L' enlèvement au sérail* issue].

Cole, Malcolm S. "*The Magic Flute* and the Quatrain." *Journal of Musicology* 3 (1984): 157.

McClelland, John. "La function communicative des masques dans les comedies italiennes de Mozart." *Canadian University Music Review* 5 (1984): 179.

Plath, Wolfgang. "*Idomeneo*: Miszellen." *Acta mozartiana* 31 (1984): 5.

Wolff, Christoph. " 'O ew'ge Nacht! Wann wirst du schwinden?' Zum Verständnis der Sprecherszene im ersten Finale von Mozarts *Zauberflöte*." In *Analysen: . . . Festschrift für Hans Heinrich Eggebrecht zum 65. Geburtstag*, edited by Werner Breig et al., 234. Stuttgart, 1984.

Stone, John. "The Making of 'Don Giovanni' and Its Ethos." *Mozart-Jahrbuch* (1984-85): 130.

Freyhan, Michael. "Toward the Original Text of Mozart's *Die Zauberflöte*." *Journal of the American Musicological Society* 39 (1986): 355.

Steptoe, Andrew. "Mozart, Mesmer, and *Così fan tutte*." *Music and Letters* 67 (1986): 248.

Volek, Tomislav. "Prague Operatic Traditions and Mozart's *Don Giovanni*." In *Divadelni ústav* [Prague] no. 334 (1987): 23.

Platoff, John. "Writing about Influences: *Idomeneo*, a Case Study." In *Explorations in Music, the Arts, and Ideas: Essays in Honor of Leonard B. Meyer*, edited by Eugene Narmour and Ruth A. Solie, 43. New York, 1988.

Farnsworth, Rodney. "*Così fan tutte* as Parody and Burlesque." *Opera Quarterly* winter (1988-89).

Gallarati, Paolo. "Music and Masks in Lorenzo Da Ponte's Mozartian Librettos." *Cambridge Opera Journal* 1 (1989): 225.

Platoff, John. "Musical and Dramatic Structure in the Opera Buffa Finale." *Journal of Musicology* 7 (1989): 191.

Tyler, Linda. "Aria as Drama: A Sketch from Mozart's *Der Schauspieldirektor.*" *Cambridge Opera Journal* 2 (1990): 251.

————. "*Bastien und Bastienne:* The Libretto, Its Derivation, and Mozart's Text-Setting." *Journal of Musicology* 8 (1990): 520.

Webster, James. "Mozart's Operas and the Myth of Musical Unity." *Cambridge Opera Journal* 2 (1990): 197.

Platoff, John. "Tonal Organization in 'Buffo' Finales and the Act II Finale of 'Le nozze di Figaro'." *Music and Letters* 72 (1991): 387.

Rushton, Julian. "La vittima è Idamante': Did Mozart Have a Motive?" *Cambridge Opera Journal* 3 (1991): 1.

Tyler, Linda. " 'Zaide' in the Development of Mozart's Operatic Language." *Music and Letters* 72 (1991): 214.

Webster, James. "The Analysis of Mozart's Arias." In *Mozart Studies,* edited by Cliff Eisen, 101. Oxford, 1991.

unpublished–

Weichlein, William. "A Comprehensive Study of Five Musical Settings of *La clemenza di Tito.*" Ph.D. dissertation, University of Michigan, 1957.

Parakilas, James. "Mozart's *Tito* and the Music of Rhetorical Strategy." Ph.D. dissertation, Cornell University, 1979.

Henze, Sabine. "Das Problem der Gattungskonvergenz in der italienischen Oper des 18. Jahrhunderts, dargestellt an *opera buffa* und *opera seria* von der Jahrhundertmitte bis zu Mozarts *Don Giovanni.*" Ph.D. dissertation. University of Marburg, 1981.

Hasler, Renate. "Die Werke des Zauberflötentypus in Wien 1789-1810." M.A. dissertation, Hochschule für Musik und darstellende Kunst, 1982.

Platoff, John. "Music and Drama in the *opera buffa* Finale: Mozart and his Contemporaries in Vienna, 1781-1790." Ph.D. dissertation, University of Pennsylvania, 1984.

Tyler, Linda. "Mozart and Operatic Conventions in Austria and Southern Germany, 1760-1800." Ph.D. dissertation, Princeton University, 1988.

* * *

Mozart's career as an opera composer spanned over two decades, from *Apollo et Hyacinthus* in 1767 to *La clemenza di Tito* in 1791. He composed works in most of the major operatic genres of his day—including *opera seria, opera buffa,* and Singspiel—and received commissions from diverse institutions, including the Archbishop's court in Salzburg, the ducal court in Milan, the Electoral court in Munich, the imperial court in Vienna, the Prague National Theater, and the private theater of Emanuel Schikaneder. Throughout his career Mozart demonstrated remarkable mastery of the styles and conventions popular at the time, but he regularly pushed the conventions to fit with new ideas of his own. His later works reveal the confident hand of a master dramatist balancing aria and ensemble, voice and orchestra, sectional form and through-composed rhetoric, melodic inventiveness and motivic development. But his earlier works, too, often demonstrate adaptation rather than wholesale adoption of established styles.

Mozart's first experience in setting dramatic texts to music came in 1765-66 in London and The Hague, where he set some fifteen individual aria texts to music in a typical *opera seria* style. Work on a longer span of opera came in 1767 when Mozart composed *Apollo et Hyacinthus,* a Latin intermezzo performed between the acts of a Latin play. Drawing on a conservative Baroque style in keeping with the Salzburg practice of the period, Mozart demonstrated precocious inventiveness in both the vocal and accompanimental parts.

While spending almost a year in Vienna in 1768 at the age of twelve, Mozart composed his first full-length operas: *La finta semplice* and *Bastien und Bastienne. La finta semplice,* which eventually premiered in Salzburg rather than in Vienna, as first planned, demonstrates Mozart's astute grasp of the *opera buffa* ("comic opera") conventions of the 1760s. The opera is dominated by arias rather than ensemble numbers, and Mozart seized the chance to compose a wide range of different aria types, from short pattering comic pieces for the *buffo* characters to more extended lyrical soliloquies for the more serious characters. Though not especially daring in formal structure (most of the arias follow an ABA'B' or ABA' form), the pieces testify to Mozart's growing repertory of expressive techniques. The Singspiel *Bastien und Bastienne,* which probably premiered at the Viennese home of Dr Franz Anton Mesmer, shows Mozart grappling with a newer, less defined tradition: that of the Austro-German Singspiel. Mozart's music features simple, though not folk-like, melodies; some use of *buffo*-type patter and mock-*seria* elements, especially for the comic sorcerer, Colas; a direct, flexible, often elegant style of text-setting; and avoidance of strict sectional forms. In all, Mozart combined German, French, and Italian operatic conventions to achieve a musical effect highly suited to the one-act sentimental pastoral.

The operas Mozart composed during his teen years reflect his increasing experience with the broad range of operatic styles across late-eighteenth-century Europe. *Mitridate, rè di Ponto* (1770) and *Lucio Silla* (1772), both composed for the Milanese court, are full-scale *opere serie.* Dominated by extended multi-sectional arias in a typical Baroque *seria* vein, the two operas explore a wealth of highly-charged emotional states. Mozart manages his panoply of stylized expressions and virtuosic solo passages well and even at times adds compelling drama to the otherwise rigid, slow-moving stories.

Contrasting these two full-fledged operas are *Ascanio in Alba* (1771, Milan), *Il sogno di Scipione* (1772, Salzburg), and *Il rè pastore* (1775, Salzburg), all composed for important state occasions (the wedding of Archduke Ferdinand of Austria to Maria Ricciarda Berenice of Modena, the enthronement of Prince-Archbishop Colloredo, and the visit of the Archduke Maximilian Franz, respectively). All three generally adhere to the conventions of *opera seria,* but each exemplifies the adaptations necessary to serve the occasion. In *Ascanio in Alba* choruses and dances come to the fore, while most of the arias are shorter than in conventional *opere serie* and are for the most part built on the more modern ternary (ABA') structure. In *Sogno di Scipione,* dominated almost completely by arias, Mozart turns back to the more old-fashioned, drawn-out *dal segno* form, perhaps in reflection of the more conservative and solemn occasion for which the work was composed. *Il rè pastore,* revealing less pretentious musical expression, features shorter numbers and graceful expression that lend a dignified elegance to the pastoral work. *La finta giardiniera* (1775), which premiered at the

Wolfgang Amadeus Mozart, unfinished painting by Joseph Lange, c. 1790 (Mozarteum, Salzburg)

electoral court of Munich, was Mozart's only comic work of the 1770s. The libretto gave Mozart occasion to paint a variety of moods in his arias—passion, poignancy, anger, and humor—and to try his hand at two act-ending finales.

In the letters he wrote to his father during his long journey to Munich, Mannheim, and Paris in 1777-79, Mozart frequently voiced a desire to write more operas. He also indulged in increasingly opinionated assessments of works he heard. Some of his most notable comments were occasioned by performances in Mannheim and Munich of innovative German operas and melodramas, including those by Ignaz Holzbauer, Anton Schweitzer, and Georg Benda. So inspired was Mozart by Benda's melodramas that he even started, or at least planned to start, a melodrama of his own, entitled *Semiramide*. The Singspiel *Zaide* (1779-80) and new numbers added to his incidental music for the play *Thamos, König von Ägypten* (1773; revised in 1776-77 and 1779) were composed soon after Mozart returned from his highly stimulating trip and were, in a large part, the products of his grappling with ideas he had encountered. *Zaide* reveals a number of significant developments in his style, including the use of melodrama as a substitute for recitative, a bold mixture of comic and serious conventions, the streamlining and recasting of traditional aria structures, and more daring representation of texts.

Idomeneo, rè di Creta (1781), an *opera seria* commissioned by Munich's Electoral court, built on some of the experiments in *Zaide,* such as shorter and more fluid aria forms, flexible melodic phrasing, and colorful orchestral writing, but also reflected Mozart's maturing concern with the opera as a whole, not as a haphazard conglomerate of scenes and numbers. This concern was evident in the suggestions he made to his librettist, Gianbattista Varesco, about aria and recitative texts that were too long, unrealistic asides that needed elimination, and entire scenes that called for clearer direction. The overall result was an opera marked by careful dramatic pacing, effective juxtapositions of styles and expressions, compelling characterization, and brilliant orchestral and choral writing.

In the decade after *Idomeneo,* up until 1790, Mozart was commissioned to compose only comic operas, the genre of choice among residents of Mozart's new home city, Vienna. He wrote *Die Entführung aus dem Serail* (1782) for the Viennese National Singspiel, the theater for German opera that Emperor Joseph II had set up in 1778 in order to forward the cause of Austrian and German musical drama. Mozart, like many of the other composers writing for the National Singspiel, combined German elements with *opera buffa* gestures. For example, several of the servant characters rely on typical German strophic and rondo forms, while other characters depend on Italian-style lyrical, bravura, or pattering expression. In the same fashion, the second act ends with a long *buffo*-type finale, built of contrasting sections and rising dramatic intensity, but the third act concludes with a traditional German "Rundgesang," in which each character in turn sings one strophe in a verse-refrain number. A success among the Viennese and shortly thereafter in other Austrian and German cities, *Die Entführung* did much to boost Mozart's fame as an opera composer across Europe.

During 1783, rather than wait for further commissions, Mozart pursued two *opera buffa* projects on his own. For *L'oca del Cairo* Mozart solicited the help of the poet Varesco and, as in their previous collaboration, *Idomeneo,* made many suggestions as to the structure of the libretto and the number and types of characters. Mozart finished only a trio and sketched out six other numbers in the first act. Around that same time, he also began work on *Lo sposo deluso,* probably with librettist Lorenzo Da Ponte. Mozart finished only the overture, a trio, and a quartet and sketched out two other numbers before abandoning his work. His reasons for not completing the operas are not clear: perhaps he finally judged the librettos too weak or he was diverted by prospects of concertizing or composing other types of pieces. Whatever the reasons, Mozart never took up these operas again, nor did he express an interest in doing so in any of his surviving letters.

Mozart did not return to dramatic music until 1786, when he provided an overture and four numbers for the one-act "comedy with music" *Der Schauspieldirektor,* performed in the Orangery of the Schönbrunn palace for the visit of the Governor-General of the Austrian Netherlands. The story sets up a competition between two *prime donne,* and their arias, the first two numbers of the piece, reinforce the feud with a juxtaposition of the lyrical and bravura styles. In the trio the two sopranos indulge in fast-paced imitative bickering, while the final "Schlussgesang" allows each of the four main characters a strophe in a verse-refrain number. The satiric vein of the comedy and the small number of musical pieces limited Mozart's opportunity for elaborate musical-dramatic development, but the numbers show fine craftsmanship and a shrewd sense of characterization without caricature.

Mozart's next three operas, *Le nozze di Figaro* (1786, Vienna), *Il dissolute punito, ossia il Don Giovanni* (1787, Prague), and *Così fan tutte* (1790, Vienna), demonstrate his exceptional mastery of the *opera buffa* style and the full extent of his ability to shape the pacing, development, and tone of entire operas and their constituent parts. For all three operas Mozart collaborated with Lorenzo Da Ponte, Poet to the Imperial Theaters, who had a sharp eye for effective stagecraft and a versatile pen for appropriate texts.

Figaro gains much of its power from its characterizations: Da Ponte and Mozart did not rely on operatic stereotypes, but instead depicted characters with uncommon combinations of strengths, weaknesses, and idiosyncrasies. The characters are kept busy with a very intricate *buffo* plot, but the underlying themes of class struggle, social change, and gender ties are touched upon often and with dramatic and musical profundity. The three finales in the opera demonstrate the exceptional versatility and control of Mozart's compositional technique. The second-act finale, the longest, consists of careful alternation between playful action episodes that move the plot forward and more expansive, in places breathtaking, ensemble reflection on those events. In the third-act finale, Mozart relies on the wedding ceremony of Susanna and Figaro to define his musical sections. In the main sections of the finale, the processional march and the dance, he gives the orchestra the main melodic material while the characters interact in a simple melodic style above it. The fourth-act finale demonstrates how Mozart could shape a finale to climax not in loud, uproarious ensemble singing, but in the quiet sincerity of a contrite husband's apology.

The libretto to *Don Giovanni* derives much of its dramatic effect from the continuous battle between those who tolerate and those who condemn the Don's actions. Musically this translates into a struggle between the high moralism represented by the *seria* style (in the numbers for Donna Anna, Don Ottavio, Donna Elvira, and the Commendatore) and the earthy permissiveness embodied in the comic style. The continual juxtaposition of the disparate styles and sentiments is more glaring than in *Figaro,* where the stylistic polarities are not as extreme, and the tightly woven plot holds the numbers more closely together. In *Don Giovanni* Mozart succeeds at times in combining the divergent styles, as in the masterful first-act finale in which three stage orchestras simultaneously play an aristocratic minuet, a middle-class contredanse, and a peasant allemande. But the fundamental irreconcilability of clashing moralities and musical sentiments remains: neither Mozart nor Da Ponte simplistically reconciles them. The opera remains a dramatic testimony to powerful class and gender oppositions fuming in Enlightenment Europe.

Così fan tutte, based on a plot as clever and symmetrical as, if not more so than, *Figaro* or *Don Giovanni,* fails to tap the complex social issues of the period. Da Ponte's libretto contains even more ensemble numbers than the previous two librettos do, but this very emphasis on ensemble numbers leads in the end to characters that do not demonstrate the individuality of the main characters in *Figaro* or *Don Giovanni.* In addition, the characters are often called upon to feign emotions to deceive one another, again decreasing the opportunity for genuine characterization. Musically, *Così* demonstrates a distinctive turn in Mozart's operatic writing in that many of the ensemble numbers are slow and lyrical, not bouncy and comic. He relies on rich orchestral writing and the blending of long lyrical vocal lines in this departure from typical *buffo*-style ensemble writing. In all, the opera, though lacking somewhat in the directness and intensity of *Figaro* and *Don Giovanni,* is charming, elegant, and superbly crafted.

Mozart's final two operas, *La clemenza di Tito* and *Die Zauberflöte,* premiered within twenty-four days of one another in September 1791. *Tito,* commissioned for Prague on the occasion of Leopold II's coronation as King of Bohemia, is based on a Metastasian libretto, updated to include more ensemble numbers and fewer arias. Mozart, who composed most of the opera in eighteen days, reached back to the *opera seria* style he had practiced as a youth. But the frequency of ensemble numbers and Mozart's choice not to indulge in the long-windedness of typical *opere serie* lends a modern air to the work. His setting responds to the solemnity and profundity of the occasion and the libretto but reveals, too, an Enlightened elegance and restraint.

Die Zauberflöte, called a *grosse Oper* (grand opera) by Mozart and his librettist, Emanuel Schikaneder, combined elements of Viennese comedy, German fairy tales, Singspiel, *opera seria, opera buffa,* and the high Baroque polyphonic style. Mozart depicts the major conflict in the drama—that between Sarastro's realm of the Enlightened and the Queen's kingdom of the Night—with two distinctive musical styles: Sarastro and his followers sing in the German Baroque church style, while the Queen and her entourage use an Italianate operatic style, with the Queen relying on the consummate Italianate rhetoric, the coloratura virtuosic style. The two seekers, Tamino and Pamina, who must choose between the two kingdoms, sing in a more earnest lyrical style, while Tamino's comic sidekick, Papageno, offers up folk-like songs with occasional *buffo* flourishes. Though at times this hodgepodge of conventions results in a disparate, episodic drama, it nonetheless communicates a wide gamut and depth of emotion. As in so many of his other operas, in *Die Zauberflöte* Mozart adapted, recombined, and transformed the operatic conventions he inherited in the late eighteenth century to create a distinctive dramatic work. His unfailing instinct for the possibilities of compelling musical drama and his capacity for brilliant technical execution of his ideas distinguish his operas as tributes not only to the richness of operatic styles

in the Classical period, but also to Mozart's dramatic and musical genius.

—Linda Tyler

MUCK, Karl.

Conductor. Born 22 October 1859, in Darmstadt. Died 3 March 1940, in Stuttgart. Studied piano with Kissner in Würzburg; studied classical philology at the University of Heidelberg and the University of Leipzig, receiving Ph.D., 1880; studied at the Leipzig Conservatory; chorus master and then conductor at the municipal opera in Zurich; theater conductor in Salzburg, Brno, and Graz; conductor at the Landestheater in Prague, 1886; conductor for Angelo Neumann's traveling Wagner company (succeeding Seidl); conducted Wagner's *Ring* in St Petersburg and Moscow, 1889, 1891; first conductor of the Berlin Royal Opera, 1892; conducted the Silesian Music Festivals, 1894-1911; conducted Wagner operas at Covent Garden, London, 1899; conducted *Parsifal* at Bayreuth, 1901, and was a regular conductor there until 1930; conductor of the Vienna Philharmonic, 1904-06; conductor of the Boston Symphony Orchestra, 1906-08; returned to Berlin as Generalmusikdirektor, 1908; returned to conduct the Boston Symphony, 1912-17; arrested 25 March 1918 as an enemy alien, and was held until the end of World War I; returned to Germany, 1919; conducted the Hamburg Philharmonic, 1922-33.

Publications

About MUCK: books—

Schonberg, H. *The Great Conductors.* New York, 1967.

*　　*　　*

Karl Muck's name will inevitably be associated with Wagner's *Parsifal.* Performances of *Parsifal* were entrusted to him by Cosima Wagner, the composer's widow, from 1901-1930 at the annual Bayreuth Festival. He had inherited the opera from its first interpreter Hermann Levi, and only relinquished it on the deaths of Cosima and Siegfried Wagner in 1930, a year which saw the beginning of a new era with Winifred Wagner's administration of the Festival.

Some considered Muck's *Parsifal* to be the ultimate concept of the work, Herbert Peyser describing it as "neither of this age nor that age but of all time, the *Parsifal* in which every phrase was charged with infinities." Austere, dogmatic and passionately devoted to the memory of Wagner, the genuine Bayreuthian Muck became, when he retired in 1933, a remnant of the nineteenth century. Renowned for his exceptional ear, and capable of holding together an entire orchestra with an iron fist and uncompromising discipline, Muck developed a fearsome reputation in Germany and America (his principal spheres of operation) for obsession with rhythm. He had a metronomic sense of tempo which tolerated little plasticity for expression, although it gave him a unique sense of line and architecture for the large-scale Wagnerian music dramas. This approach placed him as the antithesis of such conductors as Mahler and Nikisch, whose romantic approach to melody and tempo Muck, together with Weingartner and

Strauss, studiously avoided. Muck was also a first-rate trainer of orchestras (even if feared as a daunting task-master), and had a considerable career as a concert conductor.

Given the background to Muck's musical apprenticeship, it is not surprising that he had little feel for the Italian *cantilena,* and that his operatic reputation was entirely based on the music of Wagner. His first meaningful appointment had been with Angelo Neumann in Prague, where he succeeded Anton Seidl as first Kapellmeister; his association with these two names alone confirmed him as a torch-bearer of the Wagnerian tradition. He conducted performances of the *Ring* with Neumann's touring Wagner company in St Petersburg and Moscow in 1889. Neumann was well satisfied with his protégé: "aside from Muck's understanding of his subject and his ability, he gave himself up to the work with such genuine eagerness and such unselfish devotion to his art that he deserved the highest possible praise, and called forth the admiration and the appreciation of all."

In spite of his single-minded devotion to Wagner, Muck nevertheless was an experienced Kapellmeister in the best sense of the word, and during his twenty-year tenure at the Berlin Opera he conducted 103 different operas of which thirty-five were new to the city. Muck's singers would fear his slow tempi only to find them revelatory, as Frida Leider did in his Berlin *Parsifal.* She remarked that "Muck's calmness and clarity enabled me to draw everything out of the role [Kundry], as I had always previously tried to do."

In 1928 Muck recorded several extracts from *Parsifal* with his Bayreuth forces for HMV and orchestral portions of other Wagner operas with the Berlin State Opera orchestra for CBS and HMV, all of which give a clear insight into his musicianship.

—Christopher Fifield

LA MUETTE DE PORTICI [The Mute Girl of Portici].

Composer: Daniel-François-Esprit Auber.

Librettists: Eugène Scribe and Casimir Delavigne.

First Performance: Paris, Opéra, 29 February 1828.

Roles: Fenella (dancer); Alfonso (tenor); Masaniello (tenor); Pietro (baritone); Elvira (soprano); Lorenzo (tenor); Selva (bass); Emma (mezzo-soprano); Borella (bass); Moreno (bass); chorus (SATTB).

Publications

articles—

Longyear, R. "La Muette de Portici." *Music Review* 19 (1958): 37.
Finscher, Ludwig. "Aubers *La muette de Portici* und die Anfänge der Grand-opéra." In *Festschrift Heinz Becker zum 60. Geburtstag am 26 Juni 1982,* edited by Jürgen Schlader and Reinhold Quandt, 87. Laaber, 1982.

* * *

The first performance of *La muette de Portici* began an epoch in operatic history with far-reaching effects. Auber turned from a long series of highly successful *opéras comiques* to compose this opera, which became the prototype of the genre ultimately known as *grand opéra.* Auber's masterpiece soon enjoyed performances all over the world, and by 1880 it had received 485 performances in Paris at the Opéra alone. Also known as *Masaniello,* after its central character (not to be confused with Carafa's 1827 work of the same name), it has gained notoriety as the opera which supposedly provided the spark for the revolution of 1830 in Belgium.

The plot is based upon familiar elements played out against the historical 1647 revolution of the Neapolitans against Spanish oppressors. Masaniello, leader of the tyrannized natives of Portici, calls his countrymen to arms to rid themselves of the Spanish, and not incidentally, to avenge the seduction of Fenella, a mute Neapolitan maid. Alfonso, son of the Spanish Viceroy of Naples, is guilty of the offense against Fenella, much to the chagrin of Elvira, a Spanish princess whom he loves. Alfonso apologizes for his indiscretions, but the revolt begins, nevertheless. Like so many revolutions, this one falls short of its ideals, so Masaniello, with mixed emotions, ultimately capitulates to Fenella's entreaties to shelter Alfonso and Elvira from the bloody mob. The latter is led by Masaniello's former confidant, Pietro, who poisons Masaniello. In his death throes, Masaniello madly goes off to rescue his former compatriots from the erupting Mt. Vesuvius, saves Elvira one more time from the mob, and is slain for his efforts by his fickle countrymen. Thereupon, Fenella commits suicide as Vesuvius begins to erupt.

Like most of the early grand operas, *La muette de Portici* is not often performed today, although its vibrant, almost Rossinian overture became a venerable chestnut of orchestral concerts. Grand opera has suffered more than its share of criticism for its excesses, but *La muette de Portici* was popular with the masses from the start. It succeeded as art because Auber based it upon a libretto by Eugène Scribe that was timely and well suited to the drama; included ballets that were integral to the action's development; and created a musical score that featured stirring tunes of revolution, effective use of the chorus, and a sparkling style of orchestration that carried it all. To this successful combination we must add the striking novelty of a principal ballerina in the non-singing role of the major female character and an emphasis upon Neapolitan local color that found its ultimate expression in the eruption of Mt Vesuvius that ends the opera. The major female character, mute Fenella, necessarily must communicate through pantomime, and this provides the impetus for superior orchestral passages of uncommon expressivity. Finally, the sumptuous staging accorded *La muette de Portici* at the Opéra cost some 150,000 francs, a huge sum, which allowed for unprecedented realism, including metal rather than cardboard stage properties. All of these factors played upon the public's taste in an impressive fashion.

The rousing success of *La muette de Portici* led straightway to the other early major examples of grand opera, Rossini's *Guillaume Tell* (William Tell, 1829); Meyerbeer's *Robert le diable* (Robert the Devil, 1831) and *Les Huguenots* (The Huguenots, 1836); and Halévy's *La Juive* (The Jewess, 1835). Wagner, an enthusiastic member of many an audience at the Opéra in Paris during the early years of his career, was effusive in his praise for *La muette de Portici* in an 1840 article that he published in the Parisian *Gazette musicale.* He lauded the work in later essays and observations, and evidently viewed it as having seminal importance. Various scholars, among them Redlich and Longyear, have directed attention

La muette de Portici, **Théâtre de la Monnaie, Brussels (the engraving shows the riot which followed the performance)**

to important connections between it and Wagner's *Tannhäuser* and *Lohengrin,* as well as later major Italian and Russian works.

Essential elements in *La muette de Portici* that played an important role in the development of French grand opera are: 1) a vivid plot based upon an incident from recent history; 2) its division into five tightly-constructed acts each of which builds in increasing tension; 3) adroit and evocative handling of the orchestra; 4) lavish, bold staging; 5) vivid local color; 6) important, relevant ballet divertissements; and 5) a role for the chorus that convincingly integrates it into the drama. The last major performance of the work took place long ago, and one should not look for a revival. Though its dated style would probably have little appeal today, in Wagner's words, it indeed is an opera of "true historical significance." Auber, building upon a highly successful career as a master of a lighter genre, drew upon a wealth of experience to produce an opera that was right for the times. His vigorous work united and articulated many of the essential dramatic and musical elements of early nineteenth-century romanticism. It laid the foundation for an operatic style that not only possessed great vitality, but which ultimately exercised a pervasive influence on much of the century's musical life.

—William E. Runyan

MUGNONE, Leopoldo.

Conductor. Born 29 September 1858, in Naples. Died 22 December 1941, in Naples. Studied with Cesi and Serrao at the Naples Conservatory. Conducted the premiere of Mascagni's *Cavalleria rusticana,* Rome, 17 May 1890; conducted the premiere of Puccini's *Tosca,* Rome, 14 January 1900. Mugnone was also an opera composer, and produced a number of relatively successful works in Naples and Venice.

*   *   *

Leopoldo Mugnone was a major Italian conductor of the late nineteenth and early twentieth century, especially associated with composers of the *verismo* school. He was a leading proponent of the operas of Mascagni, Puccini, and Leoncavallo, as well as Massenet and Richard Strauss.

Mugnone made his conducting debut at the Teatro La Fenice in Naples and later was a regular conductor at the Teatro Costanzi, Rome (now the Teatro dell'Opera). In 1888 he signed a contract giving him the right to conduct all non-Italian performances of operas published by the firm of Sonzogno. In 1889 he conducted at the Paris Opéra, and in 1890 he conducted the premiere of Mascagni's *Cavalleria rusticana,* one of the major events at the Costanzi. At the Liceo in Barcelona in 1893 an anarchist's bomb killed several people during a performance of Rossini's *Guglielmo Tell* that he was conducting.

Puccini requested that Mugnone conduct the premiere of *Manon Lescaut,* but this was vetoed by Puccini's publisher, Ricordi; Ricordi's choice was Arturo Toscanini. Mugnone was the conductor of the Palermo premiere of *La bohème* (at the Teatro Carolino), the performance that precipitated the fame of the work (despite Mugnone's superstitious reluctance to conduct the work on Friday the 13th). The success of the Palermo performance was such that Puccini insisted on

Mugnone as the conductor of the premiere at the Teatro alla Scala in Milan.

Mugnone had a long connection with La Scala, beginning with performances of Bellini's *I Puritani* and *La sonnambula,* Puccini's *La bohème,* and Franchetti's *Il signor di Pourceaugnac* in 1897. He returned in 1906 to lead Auber's *Fra Diavolo,* Tchaikovsky's *Queen of Spades,* Weber's *Der Freischütz,* Alfano's *Resurrezione,* Franchetti's *La figlia di Jorio* (which he introduced), Catalani's *Loreley,* Massenet's *Manon,* and Verdi's *La traviata* and *Falstaff;* in 1910 he led the premiere of Giordano's *Mese mariano* in Palermo. For the Verdi centennial celebration in 1913 he conducted *Nabucco.* In addition to his European engagements, Mugnone conducted Wagner's *Götterdämmerung* and Charpentier's *Louise* in South America.

Puccini had played the third act of *Tosca* for Mugnone and relayed the conductor's enthusiasm to Ricordi. *Tosca*'s first performance was at a packed Teatro Costanzi on 14 January 1900; this time, unlike the premiere of *Manon Lescaut,* Puccini was given the conductor he wanted. The tumultuous political climate of the time and the presence of Queen Margherita in the audience lent an air of tension to the proceedings. Shortly before the beginning of the performance, the police informed Mugnone of a bomb threat—by either some rival of Puccini or an anarchist; reminded of the explosion in Barcelona, the nervous conductor approached the orchestra pit with trepidation. Shortly after the opening bars were played a disturbance in the audience caused by latecomers and people telling them to be quiet sent him running terrified back to his dressing room. Only after the audience had settled down did the conductor return to the podium.

Mugnone conducted a revised version of Puccini's *Edgar* at the Teatro de la Opera in Buenos Aires on 8 July 1905. In the fall 1905 season, with the support of Sir Thomas Beecham, he conducted at Covent Garden, opening the season with *La bohème* and conducting every opera, which, with one exception (Gounod's *Faust*), were all Italian (Verdi's *Aida, Un ballo in maschera, Rigoletto, La traviata,* and *Il trovatore,* Mozart's *Don Giovanni,* Puccini's *Madama Butterfly, Manon Lescaut,* and *Tosca,* and Boito's *Mefistofele*). He gave the British premiere of Giordano's *Andrea Chénier;* his "noisy" approach, as well as the "blood-and-thunder" qualities of the music, were not popular with the British critics. The following year he introduced the British audience to Giordano's *Fedora* (the critics were slightly more positive) and added Cilèa's *Adriana Lecouvreur* and Bizet's *Carmen.* He returned when Covent Garden reopened after World War I to lead, among other works, Mascagni's *Iris* (not a popular or critical success). He was summoned back to Covent Garden in 1925 to take over the Italian repertoire after several less-than-successful performances by other conductors.

Puccini generally admired Mugnone's conducting of his operas, although the two men disagreed about some details during a revival of *Madama Butterfly* at the Costanzi in 1908. Later, Puccini wrote that Mugnone was "flabby and drags out the tempi to indecent lengths" when he led *La fanciulla del West* in Naples in 1911. Mugnone led several revivals of Puccini's *La rondine* shortly after its premiere in Monte Carlo in 1917, performances that were not well received and that apparently contributed to that opera's poor reputation. His pioneering—and largely successful—efforts in behalf of Puccini's operas, however, have caused Mugnone to be dubbed "the Puccini conductor."

—Michael Sims

MUSORGSKY, Modest Petrovich.

Composer. Born 21 March 1839, in Karevo, Pskov district, Russia. Died 28 March 1881, in St Petersburg. Studied piano with his mother, then with Anton Herke in St Petersburg; entered the cadet school of the Imperial Guard, 1852, and joined the Guard after graduation; met Dargomizhsky, Cui, and Balakirev, 1857; clerk at the Ministry of Communications, 1863-67; worked for the Forestry Department, 1869. Musorgsky was one of the "Mighty Handful" of Russian composers that included Dargomizhsky, Rimsky-Korsakov, Cui, and Balakirev; he frequently sought the advice and help of Rimsky-Korsakov and the music critic Stasov in musical matters.

Operas

Edition: *M.P. Musorgsky: Polnoye sobraniye sochineniy* [complete works]. Edited by P. Lamm, with B.V. Asaf'yev. Moscow, 1928-34; 1969; supplementary volume 8, 1939.

Salammbô, after Flaubert, 1863-66 [unfinished].
The Marriage [Zhenit'ba]. Musorgsky (after Gogol), 1868, [unfinished]: posthumous production of act I, St Petersburg, Suvorin Theater School, 1 April 1909.
Boris Godunov, Musorgsky (after Pushkin and Karamzin), 1868-69, Leningrad, 16 February 1928 [posthumous production]: revised 1871-72; further revised, 1873, St Petersburg, Maryinsky Theater, 8 February 1874.
Khovanshchina, Musorgsky, 1872-80 [unfinished]: completed and orchestrated by Rimsky-Korsakov, St Petersburg, February 21 1886.
Sorochintsy Fair [Sorochinskaya yarmarka]. Musorgsky (after Gogol), 1874-80 [unfinished]: completed by Lyadov, V.G. Karatïgin and others, Moscow, Free Theater, 21 October 1913.

Other works: orchestral works, choral works, piano pieces, songs.

Publications/Writings

By MUSORGSKY: books–

Rimsky-Korsakov, A.N., ed. *M.P. Musorgskiy: pis'ma i dokumentï* [letters and documents]. Moscow and Leningrad, 1932.
Keldïsh, U., ed. *M.P. Musorgskiy: pis'ma k A.A. Golenischchevu-Kutuzovu.* Moscow and Leningrad, 1939.
Pis'ma. Moscow, 1981.

About MUSORGSKY: books–

Stasov, V.V. *Modest Petrovich Musorgsky.* St Petersburg, 1881.
d'Alheim, P. *Moussorgski.* Paris, 1896.
Olenine-d'Alheim, M. *Le legs de Moussorgsky.* Paris, 1908.
Montagu-Nathan, M. *Musorgsky.* London, 1916.
Calvocoressi, M.D. *Moussorgsky.* Paris, 1908; 2nd ed., 1911; English translation, 1919.
Karatïgin, V. *Musorgskiy.* Petrograd, 1922.
Stasov, V.V. *Stat'i o Musorgskom.* Moscow, 1922.
Handschin, Jacques. *Mussorgski: Versuch einer Einführung.* Zurich, 1924.
Godet, Robert. *En marge de Boris Godounof.* 2 vols. Paris and London, 1926.

Riesemann, Oskar von. *Mussorgski.* Munich, 1926; English translation, London, 1935.
Wolfurt, Kurt von. *Mussorgskij.* Stuttgart, 1926.
Musorgsky i evo "Khovanshchina" [collection of essays]. Moscow, 1928.
Belyayev, Victor. *"Boris Godounov" in its Genuine Version.* London, 1928.
Glebov, Igor [=B.V. Asaf'yev]. *K vosstanovieniyu Borisa Godunova Musorgskovo* [restoration of *Boris Godunov*]. Moscow, 1928.
Lopashev, S., et al. *Musorgskiy i evo "Khovanshchina": sbornik statey* [collection of essays on *Khovanshchina*]. Moscow, 1928.
Belyayev, V., et al. *Boris Godunov: stat'i i issledovaniya* [collection of essays on *Boris Godunov*]. Moscow, 1930.
Keldïsh, Y. and V. Yakoviev, eds. *M.P. Musorgskiy k pyatid'esyatiletiyu co dnya smerti: stat'i i materialï* [essays, articles, annotated list of works, bibliography of writings in all languages from 1860-1928]. Moscow, 1932.
Keldïsh, Y. *Romansovaya lirika Musorgskovo.* Moscow, 1933.
Chiesa, Mary Tibaldi. *Musorgsky.* Milan, 1935.
Fédorov, V. *Moussorgsky.* Paris, 1935.
Golenishchev-Kutuzov, A.A. "Vospominaniya o M.P. Musorgskom" [memories of Musorgsky]. In *Muzikal'noe nasledstvo,* edited by M.V. Ivanov-Boretsky. Moscow, 1935.
Nilsson, Kurt. *Die Rimskij-Korsakoffsche Bearbeitung des "Boris Godunoff" von Mussorgskij als Objekt der vergleichenden Musikwissenschaft.* Münster, 1937.
Barzel, Charles. *Moussorgsky.* Paris, 1939.
Tumanina, N. *M.P. Musorgskiy: zhizn i tvorchestvo* [life and works]. Moscow and Leningrad, 1939.
Lukash, Ivan S. *Biednaya liubov Mussorgskago.* Paris, 1940.
Orlov, Georgy. *Letopis zhizni i tvorchestva M.P. Musorgskovo.* Moscow, 1940.
Calvocoressi, M.D. *Mussorgsky* [completed by Gerald Abraham]. London, 1946; 1974.
Leyda, Jay, and Sergei Bertensson, eds. *The Musorgsky Reader: a Life of M.P. Musorgsky in Letters and Documents.* New York, 1947; 1970.
Hofmann, Rotislav. *Moussorgski.* Paris, 1952.
Calvocoressi, M.D. *Modest Mussorgsky: his Life and Works.* London, 1956; 1967.
Orlova, Alexandra. *Trudï i dni M.P. Musorgskovo: letopis' zhizni i tvorchestva.* Moscow, 1963; English translation as *Musorgsky's Days and Works: A Biography in Documents,* edited and translated by Roy J. Guenther, Ann Arbor, 1983.
Ogolevets, A. *Vokal'naya dramaturgiya Musorgskovo.* Moscow, 1966.
Abraham, Gerald. *Slavonic and Romantic Music.* London, 1968.
Serov, V.I. *Modest Musorgsky.* New York, 1968.
Orlova, A.A., and M.S. Pekelis, eds. *M.P. Musorgskiy: literaturnoye nasledie.* Moscow, 1971.
Lloyd-Jones, David. *Boris Godunov: Critical Commentary.* London, 1975.
Shlifshteyn, S.I. *Musorgskiy: khudozhnik, vremya, sud'ba* [Musorgsky: artist, time, fate]. Moscow, 1975.
Hübsch, L. *Modest Musorgsky: Bilder einer Ausstellung.* Munich, 1978.
Schandert, M. *Das Problem der originalen Instrumentation des "Boris Godunov" von M.P. Mussorgski.* Hamburg, 1979.
Le Roux, Maurice. *Moussorgski: Boris Godounov.* Paris, 1980.
Reilly, E.R. *A Guide to Musorgsky: A Scorography.* New York, 1980.

Atti del Convegno Internazionale Musorgskij. Piccola Scala, 8-10 maggio 1981. Milan, 1981.

Sirinjan, Ruzanna. *Opernaja dramaturgija Musorgskogo* [Musorgsky's operatic dramaturgy]. Moscow, 1981.

Taruskin, Richard. *Opera and Drama in Russian as Practiced and Preached in the 1860s.* Ann Arbor, 1981.

Brown, Malcolm H. ed. *Musorgsky: In Memoriam 1881-1981.* Ann Arbor, 1982.

Csampai, Attila, and Dietmar Holland, eds. *Mussorgsky, Modest. Boris Godunow. Texte-Materialien-Kommentare.* Reinbek, 1982.

John, Nicholas, ed. *Modest Petrovich Mussorgsky: "Boris Godunov".* Libretto translation by David Lloyd-Jones. *English National Opera Guide* 11. London and New York, 1982.

Morazzoni, Anna Maria, ed. *Musorgskij: L'opera, il pensiero.* Milan, 1985.

Emerson, Caryl. *"Boris Godunov": Transpositions of a Russian Theme.* Bloomington, Indiana, 1986.

Orlova, Alexandra. *Musorgsky Remembered.* Bloomington, Indiana, 1991.

articles–

Stasov, V.V. "Modest Petrovich Musorgsky: biografichesky ocherk" [biography]. *Vestnik Evropï* no. 5 (1881): 285; no. 6 (1881): 506.

Muzikalny Sovremennik January-February (1917) [Musorgsky issue].

Glebov, I. "Die ästhetische Anschauungen Mussorgskij's." *Die Musik* 21 (1929): 561.

Abraham, Gerald. "Tolstoy and Musorgsky." In *Studies in Russian Music,* 87. London, 1936.

———. "*The Fair of Sorochintsy* and Cherepnin's Completion of it." In *On Russian Music,* 216. London, 1939.

Sovetskaya muzyka April (1939) [Musorgsky issue].

Abraham, Gerald. "Musorgsky's 'Boris' and Pushkin's." *Music and Letters* 26 (1945): 31.

Lloyd-Jones, David. "Musorgsky's *Khovanshchina.*" *Opera* December 1959.

Nagy, Ferenc. "És a Borisz kié?" *[Boris Godunuv]. Muzsika* 21 (1978): 29.

Seaman, Gerald. "The Rise of Slavonic Opera, I." *New Zealand Slavonic Journal* 2 (1978): 1.

Oldani, Robert W. "Boris Godunov and the Censor." *19th Century Music* 2 (1978-79): 245.

Avant-scène opéra May-August (1980) [*Boris Godunov* issue].

Andrew, Aleksej. "Zametki o soderzanii *Hovansciny.*" *Sovetskaja muzyka* 3 (1981): 95.

Vul'fson, Aleksej. "K problemann tekstologii." [on *Khovanshchina*]. *Sovetskaja muzyka* 3 (1981): 103.

Baroni, Mario. "La nozione de 'realismo' nella *Chovanscina* di Musorgskij." *Nuova rivista musicale italiana* 16 (1982): 313.

Avant-scène opéra November-December (1983) [*La Khovanshchina* issue].

Taruskin, Richard. "Handel, Shakespeare, and Musorgsky: the Sources and Limits of Russian Musical Realism." In *Music and Language,* edited Ellen S. Beebe et al., 247. New York, 1983.

———. " 'The Present in the Past': Russian Opera and Russian Historiography, ca. 1870." In *Russian and Soviet Music: Essays for Boris Schwartz,* edited by Malcolm H. Brown, 77. Ann Arbor, 1984.

———. "Musorgsky vs. Musorgsky: The Versions of *Boris Godunov.*" *19th Century Music* 8 (1984): 91.

Oldani, Robert W. "Musorgsky's Boris on the Stage of the Maryinski Theater: A Chronicle of the First Production." *Opera Quarterly* summer (1986).

unpublished–

Drukt, Aleksandr. "O prelomlenii narodnoj diatoniki v muzyke russkih kompozitor-kuckistov" [folk diatonicism in the operas of the Russian "Mighty Handful"]. Ph.D. dissertation, Leningradskij institut teatra, muzyki i kinematografii, 1978.

Bakaeva, Galina. "Istorija v narodnyh muzykalnyh dramah M.P. Musorgskogo" [history in Musorgsky's folk dramas]. Ph.D. dissertation, Inst. Iskusstvovedenija, Fol'klora i Etnografii HN, Kiev, 1982.

*   *   *

Modest Musorgsky is considered by most musicians and scholars to be the most innovative and imaginative of the group of Russian composers dubbed in its day as the "Moguchaia Kuchka," the "Mighty Handful." Musorgsky's freshness stems first from his intense spiritual kinship with the Russian people, identified by him most keenly in the peasantry—their lives, their feelings, their simplicity, and their language. From this, Musorgsky's fascination with Russian drama and poetry as well as his interest in the history of his native land follow logically, as does the further observation that his most important and most characteristic contributions to Russian music were his vocal works, especially his operas.

Modest Musorgsky, portrait by Ilja Repin, 1881

This image of Musorgsky's creative foundation pervades his total output, from his early songs (e.g., "Where Art Thou, Little Star") and the orchestral tone poem *Night on Bald Mountain* to his mature song cycles (*The Nursery* and *Sunless*), the piano masterpiece *Pictures at an Exhibition* and his three great operatic efforts (*Boris Godunov, Khovanshchina,* and *The Fair at Sorochintsy,* the latter two completed after his death by other composers). Throughout these works one observes not only an emphasis on things Russian—literary sources and scenes from life—but also Musorgsky's evolving and ever more free empirical approach to the craft of composition. While one might easily cite examples of his crudeness (by traditional standards) in harmony, structure, and the like, one cannot often justly criticize the composer for being unable to give clarity and succinctness to the musical imagery or expressive content he means to convey.

There are two principal characteristics of this clarity. One is melodic style, especially in Musorgsky's vocal music, where he shows the influences of both Glinka and Dargomizhsky as well as of Italian opera. Musorgsky's vocal lines have a rhythmic and intervallic freedom that allows them to follow the natural inflections of the Russian language without losing their inherent lyricism. The other is Musorgsky's realistic sense of visual and emotional drama which manifests itself musically in his unique harmonic style, his use of orchestral and vocal color, and in the intensely lyric and often folklike nature of his melodies. It is precisely this trait that gives such power to the psychological development of Czar Boris in *Boris Godunov* and to the pageantry of the coronation scene in the same work, to cite only the most familiar of several such examples.

On balance, Musorgsky's importance, perhaps, should be viewed less for his influence on other composers (although Debussy and Stravinsky must be mentioned in this regard) than for the skillful and determined manner in which he gave a musical voice to aspects of Russian culture and the segments of Russian society where that culture was seen in its purest state. In that sense, Musorgsky was part of an important trend in the arts of his day, following the examples of Pushkin in literature and Glinka in music.

—Roy J. Guenther

THE MUTE GIRL OF PORTICI
See LA MUETTE DE PORTICI

MUTI, Riccardo.

Conductor. Born 28 July 1941, in Naples. Married: Christina Mazzavillani, 1969 (two sons, one daughter). Studied violin and piano with his father, and then composition with Jacopo Napoli and Nino Rota at the Conservatorio di Musica San Pietro a Majella, Naples; studied conducting with Antonino Votto and composition with Bruno Bettinelli at the Verdi Conservatory, Milan; won the Guido Cantelli Competition in 1967; conducted with the Radio Audizioni Italiana, 1968; principal conductor of the Teatro Comunale, Florence, 1970; conductor at the Maggio Musicale Fiorentino, and artistic director, 1977; guest conductor at the Salzburg Festival, 1971, and the Berlin Philharmonic, 1972; conducted the Philadelphia Orchestra, 1972; conducted at the Vienna State Opera, 1973, and became principal conductor of the New Philharmonia Orchestra in London, 1974; conducted the Vienna Philharmonic, 1974; conducted at Covent Garden, London, 1977; principal guest conductor of the Philadelphia Orchestra, 1977; music director for the Philharmonia Orchestra (previously New Philharmonia Orchestra), 1979-82; music director of the Philadelphia Orchestra, succeeding Eugene Ormandy, 1980-92; music director of the Teatro alla Scala in Milan, 1986.

Publications

By MUTI: interviews–

Chesterman, R., ed. *Conversations with Conductors.* London, 1990.

About MUTI: articles–

Webster, D. "Riccardo Muti." *Ovation* February (1983).
Waleson, H. "Riccardo Muti: a Tale of Two Cities." *Ovation* December (1988).

*　　*　　*

For the last quarter of a century, Riccardo Muti has been active in both the concert hall and in the opera house. A leader of the "literalist" school of opera performance, in 1970 Muti quit the dress rehearsal of his intended Teatro alla Scala debut of Bellini's *I Puritani,* featuring Freni and Pavarotti, after a disagreement with the singers. He did not return to that house for a decade. He has stated that "In many opera houses all the bad things are called 'Italian tradition'," and that he wants to "avoid those cheap things that you hear in many opera houses, where operas are in the hands of singers or conductors who have no respect for the text." "The text" is an important consideration for Muti. He has been performing the operas of Verdi (*Nabucco, Ernani* and others), Puccini (*Tosca*) and other composers from "cleaned-up" modern editions that omit added high notes and ornamentation. His recording of Gluck's *Orfeo ed Euridice* on Angel with Agnes Baltsa is of the original 1762 Vienna version; the performance has been described as "reverential" and "sanctimonious." Marilyn Horne dropped out of an *Orfeo* with Muti at the Florence May Festival due to her insistence on singing Orpheus' interpolated bravura aria "Addio, o miei sospiri," a practice that the maestro would not allow. In Muti's recorded *Pagliacci* on Angel with Scotto and Carreras, he bans any high notes not indicated in the score, opens the cut in the love duet, and it is Tonio, not Canio, who delivers "La commedia è finita," all as written. For the recording of Bellini's *I Capuleti ed i Montecchi,* Muti allows the singers (Gruberova, Baltsa, and Dano Raffanti) to embellish only slightly on repeats of cabalettas, and in the recording of *I Puritani* with Caballé, the soprano is not allowed to decorate at all.

Along with his literal presentations of what he considers to be the composer's intentions, Muti is noted for conducting opera in a precise, orderly, at times authoritarian manner. Many times impressive results are achieved, but sometimes at a certain cost. Of Muti's 1985 *Macbeth* at the Bavarian State Opera, an *Opera* critic noted that "Not a single note or run was left to chance. For three hours, Muti pursued every nuance of tone coloring, responding with crystal clarity to the flickering shades of madness, the pretence of mourning, the sham festive splendor. Meaning rebounded from every note he conducted: didactic music *à la* Brecht." Muti himself has stated that ". . . music is not entertainment. It is a mutual exchange of culture and feelings between the orchestra and the public. It is a religious ceremony, a *communione*." Max Loppert, writing in *Opera* of a 1979 *Norma* with Scotto at the Teatro Comunale, Florence, called it a "fresh, dedicated, and deeply serious presentation" yet noted that "there were times when the unrelenting electricity of Muti's conducting began to nag at this listener's senses; . . . one longed for a tempering spaciousness, a hand that moulded and breathed the lines along with his singers." For this *Norma*, Muti typically went back to the original score, in an edition by Robbins Landon and Von Noë, one that restored traditional cuts yet truncated the act I trio and the "Guerra" chorus.

Maestro Muti is indisputably among the most respected and sought-after conductors in the world. He has received numerous accolades, as when a critic wrote of his conducting of *Aida* in Munich in 1979 that "frequently in the course of the evening we were reminded what feeling this conductor has for singers." Singers, too, have high regard for Muti's abilities, among them Carol Vaness, the Donna Elvira on Muti's Angel *Don Giovanni* and a singer who has given some of her best live performances under Muti's baton.

Many of Muti's opera recordings, such as *La forza del destino* with Freni and Domingo, *I vespri siciliani,* and Cherubini's *Lodoïska,* have been based on live performances. His range of recordings is wide and he is particularly proud of bringing some of the works of Cherubini to life again. As Muti explains, "He was one of the greatest composers of his time: not only Beethoven thought so but also Schumann, who . . . thought Cherubini was sublime; and the word 'sublime' from Schumann is quite a compliment." Certain recordings by Muti remain controversial. For his *Rigoletto* he wanted Gilda to be a genuine lyric soprano, not a *lirico-leggiero,* pointing out that "the tradition of coloratura is not what Verdi wanted: the traditional ornamentation does not exist in the score." The singer he chose, however, Daniela Dessi, has a tendency to sound like a mature spinto whose high notes are achieved only with effort. In *Gramophone* Alan Blyth noted of this recording that "As is his custom, Muti is more attentive to note values, dynamic advice and metronome markings than any other conductor. No license is allowed to singers or players. The singers sound overawed by the maestro. In the opening section of the first Gilda-Rigoletto duet they seem so concerned to keep up to Muti's rigorous tempo that no time is left for character or nuance in their phrasing and so . . . it continues throughout." However, Muti's first complete opera recording remains one of his very best and stands as one of the classics in the catalogue—*Aida* on Angel with Caballé, Domingo, and Cossotto all in top form.

—Stephen A. Willier

Riccardo Muti

MUZIO, Claudia [born Claudina Muzzio].

Soprano. Born 7 February 1889, in Pavia. Died 24 May 1936, in Rome. Studied with Annetta Casaloni in Turin and Viviani in Milan; debut as Massenet's *Manon,* Arezzo, 1910; Teatro alla Scala debut as Desdemona, 1913-14; appeared at Covent Garden, 1914; also appeared in South America; Metropolitan Opera debut as Tosca, 1916, and remained there until 1922; in Chicago 1922-32, where she first appeared as Aida; Teatro alla Scala, 1926-27.

Publications

About MUZIO: books–

Barnes, H. *Claudia Muzio: A Biographical Sketch and Discography.* Austin, Texas, 1947.
Arnosi, E. *Claudia Muzio: La unica.* Buenos Aires, 1987.

articles–

Richards, J. "Claudia Muzio." *Record Collector* 17 (1968): 197, 256.
Gualerzi, G. "The Divine Claudia." *Opera* June (1986).
Steane, J. "Claudia Muzio: A Centenary Tribute." *Musical Times* February (1989).

*   *   *

Fifty years after Claudia Muzio's death, her short career and her strikingly individual voice have given her legendary status. The enigma of Claudia Muzio (1889-1936) remains unsolved by any full-length biography in English. In *Prima Donna*, Rupert Christiansen writes that contemporaries remember her as a reclusive soprano "who never said anything." Writers praise her artistic achievements and portray her as a tragic figure whose recordings resonate with personal sadness. Most people know her voice only through opera and song recordings and her acting ability through dramatic poses in still photographs. Even so, the records and pictures make an impression of freshness, vitality and dramatic presence.

Opera figured strongly in Muzio's background: her father was a stage director at Covent Garden and the Metropolitan, her mother a chorus singer. Her teacher was Annetta Casaloni (the first Maddalena in *Rigoletto*). Through these influences and her natural abilities, Muzio perfected a style of *verismo* singing which never resorted to gasping, sobbing, or noise-making for effect, and which she could adapt to lyric roles. Admirers including Christiansen, Giorgio Gualerzi, and Rodolfo Celletti remark on the purity and subtle shading of her tone which avoided histrionics. Muzio's voice has an instantly recognizable timbre—a great melancholy with the capacity for lightness.

It is a voice of opposing forces, at times personal and small, yet large and flexible enough for her to have been the first Turandot of Buenos Aires. Her vocal negotiations between grand manner and endearing intimacy produced a sound which lent a human warmth to the most taxing of roles. She used opposing styles for dramatic effect, moving from sustained full voiced passages to pianissimi, from brightness of tone to darkness, with galvanizing ease. Some find this movement jarring, some find it a revelation. In either case, her records bear witness to the dramatic intensity of her voice.

Her recorded legacy spans the early acoustic age of 1911 to the later electrical EMI records of 1934-35. Some critics note in her last records a loss of the ease demonstrated in the diamond discs and attribute this to her bad health. However, for this listener, the ease and flexibility of voice are still there in her later efforts, and if I prefer the EMI sides to her Edison recordings it is because of technical sound quality. She was capable of great freshness during the EMI sessions, especially in "Per amor di Gesu," an aria she recorded in 1934 from Licino Refice's *Cecilia*, a mystical opera composed especially for her. The Angel of God beseeches listeners to hear the inspiring story of Cecilia (the patron saint of music). Muzio's voice has all the requisite brightness one might expect of an angel, but also a burnished melancholy which reads as impassioned concern that her listeners should take heed for their salvation. Her voice shimmers at the opening then deepens, and as the Angel describes Cecilia: "O chiara sposa, con socchiuso ciglio/a Dio cantasti: 'Deh! serbami pura!' " ["O

radiant bride, with veiled eyes to God you sang 'Ah, keep me pure!' "], Muzio descends to a chest note at "pura" with spine-tingling results—mystical indeed. Celletti describes her technique as the creation of sound which "lit certain words with a sudden flash." She achieved the flash with breath control and the contrast of light and dark sounds.

Just as freshness surfaces in her later records, the mature cast, the dark vocal inflection, of her voice appears in the early recordings, too. In "Ebben ne andro lontano" from Catalani's *La Wally,* recorded in 1920, she has the light timbre to be expected of youth, but also the gravity which portends things to come. From 1921, her recording from Leoncavallo's *Zaza* evinces depth of feeling set against youthful freshness of sound. Gualerzi suggests that Muzio used the contrast of light and dark vocal inflection to cope with divergent styles of opera, enabling her to sing Mascagni as well as Bellini. She judiciously contrasted volume and vocal coloring to bring to dramatic roles (such as Santuzza in *Cavalleria rusticana*) an effervescence which revealed character, and to lyric roles (such as Amina in *La sonnambula*) a dramatic pathos which added character. Her earliest recordings suggest Muzio was aware of the limitations and advantages of her voice and how to use them. Her distinction over typical *verismo* singers was the dimension which her pianissimi and restraint gave to melodramatic roles—without detracting from the drama.

Among her thirty or so EMIs, we find intense dramatic interpretations of arias from *Norma, Il trovatore, La traviata* (a legendary "Teneste la promessa" which many read biographically), and *Mefistofele,* each imprinted with Muzio's distinctive individuality. The palpable tension of "L'altra notte" provides as good an example of the singer's presence as we can get through recordings. Her visually suggestive voice inspires color associations (Christiansen cites brown and purple), but also suggests a persona. The strength of presence she had on stage comes through her voice "made of tears and sighs and restrained inner fire," as the tenor Giacomo Lauri-Volpi remarked. Photographs from roles such as Violetta, Tosca and the *Trovatore* Leonora show a remarkable combination of great dignity and inner fire.

We go to Muzio to hear reliably beautiful dramatic singing which achieves its effect through restraint. The effect of her singing is to endow characters with personality and dimension; she excels in the *verismo* style through a nearly impossible-to-describe form of breath control and vocal coloring, and in the lyric style through well-rounded tone and brightness tempered by melancholy. If her repertoire seems adventurous to modern ears, it is because she was a proponent of the *verismo* style and the music of her time.

—Timothy O. Gray

N

NABUCCO [Nabucodonosor].

Composer: Giuseppe Verdi.

Librettist: Temistocle Solera (after the ballet by A. Cortesi, 1838).

First Performance: Milan, Teatro alla Scala, 9 March 1842.

Roles: Nabucco (baritone); Ismaele (tenor); Zaccaria (bass); Abigaille (soprano); Fenena (soprano or mezzo-soprano); High Priest of Baal (bass); Anna (soprano); Abdallo (tenor); chorus (SSATTBB).

Publications

articles–

Avant-scène opéra April (1986) [*Nabucco* issue].

*   *   *

Nabucco occupies a unique place in the Verdi canon since Verdi himself dated the beginning of his artistic career from its composition, although it was his third opera. After the failure of *Un giorno di regno* and the deaths of his two children and then his wife, he was despondent and could do little musically. The story is well known how Merelli, the director of the Teatro alla Scala, forced the libretto of *Nabucco* onto the unwilling Verdi and how the words, *"Va, pensiero, sull' ali dorate"* ("Fly, O thought, on golden wings") caught his attention. These words, which became the choral lament of the Hebrew people exiled in Babylon, also became the cornerstone of the opera itself; raising the already excited opening night audience to unprecedented pitches of enthusiasm, the chorus went on to provide the dawning political movement toward a united Italy, the Risorgimento, with its battle hymn. The opera was played seventy-five times that year at La Scala alone and soon appeared all over Italy, Europe, and the Americas. Fifty-nine years later, the crowds lining the Milan streets for Verdi's funeral spontaneously broke out into the chorus that was still identified with him in a way none of his other compositions ever came to be. Revived in the 1930s, *Nabucco* has retained an important place in Verdi performances.

The introduction of the chorus to function as a protagonist came from the librettist, Temistocle Solera, who, basing his text on a French play and a ballet mounted at La Scala four years earlier (both called *Nabucodonosor*), emphasized the Old Testament element of Hebrew suffering implicit in the story. The action seems disjointed because it is divided, according to contemporary custom, into four parts each with a title taken from the Book of Jeremiah, four vast static tableaux culminating in bursts of activity. The action, set in 586 B.C. in Jerusalem and Babylon, is essentially a series of power struggles, first between Nabucco, King of Babylon, and the Hebrews; then between Nabucco and his supposed daughter,

Abigaille (revealed to be the offspring of slaves), who attempts to usurp the throne. Both of these are complicated by a love triangle of minor musical interest: Nabucco's real daughter, Fenena, at first a hostage of the Hebrews, converts to Judaism and loves Ismaele, nephew of the King of Jerusalem, who returns her love. He is also loved by the jealous Abigaille, who, seizing power in Nabucco's absence, almost succeeds in having the lovers executed. Nabucco himself is ultimately converted to Judaism, as is the defeated Abigaille, who, committing suicide, dies repentant.

Musically the work owes a debt to late Rossini, to *Guillaume Tell, Le siège de Corinth,* and structurally, to *Moïse,* but the musical language is unmistakably new, exhibiting the melodic breadth, vigor and dramatic drive we think of as characteristically Verdian. Structurally Verdi establishes several new directions in which he continued to move throughout his career: his use of the chorus both on its own and in relation to the principals; scoring for particular instruments or combinations to achieve special effects; creating duets and ensembles to express conflicting emotions in musical as well as dramatic terms, indeed, creating real music drama in the sense that the dialectic of the drama is developed in the music as well as in the stage action. Sensitive from the very beginning to the dramatic potential of different voice types, Verdi gives us in Nabucco himself the prototype of the Verdian baritone, the "high" deep masculine voice as the primary locus for expressing conflicting emotions.

Verdi's mastery is quickly demonstrated in the opening scene by the way in which the chorus, intervening in both the aria and cabaletta ("D'Egitto là sui lidi") of the solo bass, Zaccaria, establishes itself as a direct participant in the action. Abigaille's entry ("Prode guerrier"), a fiercely bitter declamation leaping from low B to high C, establishes her instantly both as a *persona* and the role as one of the most difficult soprano roles Verdi ever wrote. Her act II recitative (with a spectacular two-octave leap) and aria, ("Anch'io duschuiso un giorno") includes a decorated Bellinian *andante* followed, after the urging of the Babylonians to seize the throne, by a brilliantly exciting cabaletta ("Salgo già del trono aurato"). Act II, scene ii opens with another Verdian touch, an introduction to Zaccaria's prayer ("Tu che sul labbro") scored for six cellos, and moves toward an innovative finale. Beginning as a canonic quartet for Nabucco, Abigaille, Ismaele, and Fenena, gradually joined by the other minor characters and the chorus, it moves into a defiant recitative for Nabucco, who proclaims himself God. The resultant thunderclap leads not into the expected stretta but into a kind of mad scene for the king, a rapidly changing musical and emotional scenario (it points forward to Rigoletto's half-demented vilifications of the courtiers), which ends with Abigaille reasserting the glory of Baal.

The opening scene of act III contains one of the earliest of Verdi's wonderful father-daughter duets. Opening with an allegro dialogue, "Donna, chi sei?" it moves through a middle section full of powerful contrasts in which Nabucco grieves while Abigaille exults in dreams of glory, to the finale where Nabucco is led away as her prisoner. The "Va, pensiero," which now appears, is the emotional center of the opera.

A caricature of a performance of Verdi's *Nabucco,* at the Théâtre-Italien, Paris, 1844

Elegiac, melancholic, its leisurely yet grand, sweeping rhythm creates the effect of a thousand voices reaching out to a promised land; the shift from unison to harmony on the words, *"arpe dor,"* is a thrilling master stroke. Act IV is less gripping—the ending especially is a little routine—but the opening contains another fine scene as the distracted Nabucco moves into an oasis of orchestral tranquillity and prayer—a version of the tune we know as "Home Sweet Home"—to the God of the Hebrews (*"Dio di Giuda"*) to save his daughter Fenena.

—Peter Dyson

NEIDLINGER, Gustav.

Bass-baritone. Born 21 March 1910, in Mainz. Studied with Otto Rottsieper in Frankfurt; debut in Mainz, 1931, and sang there until 1934; appeared in Hamburg, 1936-50; in Stuttgart from 1950; debut at Teatro alla Scala, 1953; in Vienna from 1956; appeared at Bayreuth, 1952-75, where his roles included Kurwenal, Telramund, and Alberich; Covent Garden debut, 1963; appeared at Teatro Colón, Buenos Aires, 1968;

Metropolitan Opera debut as Alberich in *Siegfried,* 1972; retired 1975.

*   *   *

Gustav Neidlinger began in *buffo* roles and became one of the most admired *heldenbaritons* of the twentieth century. While in the early years of his career he was criticized as being too rough and coarse, his performances grew better and smoother through the years. He sang well into his sixties, and was praised for the wealth of experience he brought to his roles. He became famous as a Wagnerian singer, and his most famous role and crowning glory was Alberich in *Der Ring des Nibelungen.* Shortly before his retirement in the mid-1970s, he sang that role in his only Metropolitan Opera performance; the critics agreed that "his Alberich defies the years."

Neidlinger debuted in Mainz in 1931. He sang *buffo* roles in Mainz and Plauen until he joined the Hamburg opera company in 1936. He joined the Stuttgart State Opera in 1950, and began to enlarge his repertoire. He sang Pizarro in Beethoven's *Fidelio,* Iago in Verdi's *Otello,* Nick Shadow in Stravinsky's *The Rake's Progress,* Lysiart in Weber's *Euryanthe,* and had roles in Strauss's *Die Frau ohne Schatten* and Mozart's *Die Zauberflöte.* He began singing Wagnerian roles, too, including both Klingsor and Amfortas in *Parsifal,* Telramund in *Lohengrin,* Wotan in *Die Walküre,* and, of course, Alberich in the *Ring* cycle. In 1952, he joined the company of the Bayreuth festivals, and he originated several roles in the productions of Wieland Wagner. Wieland's production of the entire *Ring* cycle was repeated every year for over fifteen years by the Stuttgart company, and every year Neidlinger sang Alberich. He began appearing in opera houses all over Europe during the mid 1950s, making his London debut in 1955.

Niedlinger's early years were not auspicious. After abandoning both the violin and sports as professions, he settled into small roles in small German opera companies. When he started expanding his roles in the fifties, the critics suggested that he could use some refinement. In 1954, he sang both Amfortas and Klingsor in *Parsifal.* His Klingsor was "too coarse." *Opera* magazine reported that "Gustav Neidlinger's expostulations [as Amfortas] were on the rough side." Yet he improved, and critics were quick to notice. In 1957 he performed a "vocally and dramatically superb Pizarro." *Opera* reported in 1958 that "[his] Kurwenal . . . had improved immensely. It used to have over-rough edges, as if he had confused bluffness with coarseness. Now it was beautifully in focus. He no longer barked at Brangägne in Act 1. In Act 3 he knew—as few Kurwenals seem to know—how to be tender without falsifying the character by being sentimental. His voicing of the phrases was excellent, his shaping of some of them memorable." In the mid-1950s he also struck success with his Alberich. *Opera* again reported on his performance, saying it was "so musical as well as dramatically striking that [we] must question if it is to be bettered at the moment."

For over two decades Neidlinger sang with the Stuttgart State Opera and toured throughout Europe. He recorded some of the Wagner roles, and again, his Alberich received highest praises. He achieved fame and great respect in Europe, but was still little known in the United States. In 1972 he performed as Alberich in the Metropolitan Opera company's production of *Siegfried.* American critics agreed with their European counterparts that his interpretation was outstanding. Said critic George Movshon "Neidlinger's mastery in the part of Alberich is awesome: he is one of those artists who can change the entire atmosphere of the house with a few lines of song."

Neidlinger was sixty-two when he sang at the Met, but his age did not always seem to effect his performance. Said one critic "At sixty-two, [he] still sang Kurwenal with aplomb." Another critic, however, did suggest that age was taking its toll: "the veteran Gustav Neidlinger gave an impressive performance as Boris [Godunov], although his voice has no longer the power it used to have."

Neidlinger has made few recordings; again, his Alberich shines through. He has sung in three different recordings of the *Ring* cycle. *Opera* magazine's comparative review of different *Ring* recordings rates him above all others: "Three Neidlingers, each as wiley as the other, are pitted against two ineffectual Pernerstorfers and one too-melodramatic Kelewin." While critics of his early performances accused his singing of being too coarse and rough, his recordings prove him to be a rich and full-voiced singer. His musicianship is unassailable. J.B. Steane in his book *The Grand Tradition* says of his recordings "Gustav Neidlinger is superbly dark-toned and vibrant, entirely free of *sprechgesang,* and perhaps uniquely true to the letter of the score, without losing its spirit."

Because he performed little in the United States, Neidlinger remains relatively unknown here, despite his fame and success in Europe. Even after he retired, he was remembered in print as a model of perfection when a new recording of the *Ring* appeared. As his earlier German recordings are released in this country, his Alberich will keep his name alive for years to come.

—Robin Armstrong

NEMIROVICH-DANCHENKO, Vladimir.

Director/Producer. Born 11 December 1858, Ozurgety (now Makhardaze), Georgia; died 25 April 1943, Moscow. Married: Baroness Ekaterina Korf, August, 1886 (died 1938). Studied at Moscow University, 1876-1879; began career in 1877 as theater critic in Moscow; in 1881 also began work as playwright, eventually authoring eleven plays and contributing the libretto for Rachmaninov's *Aleko* (1893); taught drama at Moscow Philharmonic Society, 1891-1901; cofounded the Moscow Art Theater with Konstantin Stanislavsky in 1897, for which Nemirovich directed productions until the 1917 revolution; in 1919 founded Moscow Art Theater Musical Studio which in 1926 was renamed the Nemirovich-Dachenko Musical Theater: this studio later combined with Stanislavsky's Opera Theater and was renamed the Stanislavsky-Nemirovich-Danchenko Musical Theater (1941). Nemirovich-Danchenko was noteworthy for his creation of a stylized performance technique known as "Synthetic Theater" and his replacing of the conventional opera singer with what he called the "singing actor."

Opera Productions (selected)

La fille de Madame Angot (Lecocq), Moscow, Art Theater Musical Studio, 1920.
La périchole, Moscow, Art Theater Musical Studio, 1922.
Karmencita i soldat (based on Bizet's *Carmen*), Moscow, Art Theater Musical Studio, 1924.
Aleko (Rachmaninov), Moscow, Nemirovich-Danchenko Musical Theater, 1926.
Bakhchisarayskiy (Arensky), Moscow, Nemirovich-Danchenko Musical Theater, 1926.
Cleopatra (Glière), Moscow, Nemirovich-Danchenko Musical Theater, 1926.
Jonny spielt auf, Moscow, Nemirovich-Danchenko Musical Theater, 1929.
Dzhonny (Ksheneka), Moscow, Nemirovich-Danchenko Musical Theater, 1926.
The North Wind (Knipper), Moscow, Nemirovich-Danchenko Musical Theater, 1930.
Katerina Izmaylova (Shostakovich), Moscow, Nemirovich-Danchenko Musical Theater, 1934.
La traviata, Moscow, Nemirovich-Danchenko Musical Theater, 1934.
The Quiet Don (Dzerzhinsky), Moscow, Nemirovich-Danchenko Musical Theater, 1936.
V Buryu (Khrennikov), Moscow, Stanislavsky-Nemirovich-Danchenko Musical Theater, 1939.

Publications

By NEMIROVICH-DANCHENKO: books–

Gore ot uma v postanovke Moskovskogo Khudozhestvennogo teatra. Moscow, 1923.
Iz proshlogo. Moscow, 1936.

Cournos, John, trans. *My Life in the Russian Theatre*. New York, 1968.

P'esy. 1962.

Vl. I. Nemirovich-Danchenko o tvorchestve aktera; khrestomatiia. Moscow, 1973.

Izbrannye pisma: 1879-1943. Moscow, 1979.

Retsenzii; Ocherki; Stat'i; Interv'iu; Zametki, 1877-1942. Moscow, 1980.

Rozhdenie teatra: vospominaniia, stat'i, zametki, pis'ma. Moscow, 1989.

About NEMIROVICH-DANCHENKO: books–

Markov, Pavel Aleksandrovich. *V.I. Nemirovich-Danchenko i muzikal'niy teatr evo imeni*. Moscow, 1936.

Freidkina, Liubov' Markovna. *Vladimir Ivanovich Nemirovich-Danchenko*. Moscow, 1945.

Kryzhitskii, Georgii Konstantinovich. *Nemirovich-Danchenko o rabote nad spektaklem*. 1958.

Markov, Pavel Aleksandrovich. *Rezhissura Vl. I. Nemirovicha-Danchenko v muzikal'nom teatre*. Moscow, 1960.

Abalkin, Nikolai Aleksandrovich. *Khudozhnik i revoliutsiia*. Moscow, 1962.

Bertensson, Sergei. *V Khollivude s V.I. Nemirovichem-Danchenko, 1926-1927*. Monterey, 1964.

Knebel', M. *Shkola rezhissury Nemirovicha-Danchenko*. Moscow, 1966.

Korzov, Iurii Ivanovich. *Dramaturgiia V.I. Nemirovich-Danchenko*. Kiev, 1971.

Solov'eva, Inna Natanovna. *Nemirovich-Danchenko*. Moscow, 1979.

* * *

Nemirovich-Danchenko is renowned as a Russian playwright, director, and producer who, during the Soviet period, was a major force in creating the concept of Socialist Realism. On leaving Moscow University in 1879, he was active in the theater, being responsible among other things for the libretto of Rachmaninov's opera *Aleko* (1893), based on Pushkin's *The Gypsies*. Over the period 1891-1901 he was head of drama classes at the Moscow Philharmonic Society. In the course of time, however, he became increasingly concerned at the unimaginative and unenterprising nature of the productions of the state and provincial theaters, which he criticized in the press, stating that an opera-singer had to be not only a singer but an artist, and that operas required lively and intelligent librettos—just as much as drama. After meeting the young actor and director Konstantin Stanislavsky in 1897, Nemirovich-Danchenko joined forces with him to found, in 1898, the Moscow Art Theater (later known as the Moscow Art Academic Theater, under the abbreviation MKhAT). The Theater maintained the highest standards, with the role of the director being of great importance. It was Nemirovich-Danchenko who first discovered the plays of Chekhov and assisted other up-and-coming authors such as Maxim Gor'ky.

Following the October 1917 Revolution, Nemirovich-Danchenko and Stanislavsky were visited in 1918 by the Director of the Bol'shoy Theater, E.K. Malinovskaya, who (at Lunacharsky's suggestion) invited them to assist in the reform of the theater. The result was the creation in 1919 of a Musical Studio attached to the Bol'shoy Theater (renamed in 1926 the Nemirovich-Danchenko Musical Theater and in 1941 the Stanislavsky-Nemirovich-Danchenko Musical Theater), the purpose of which was to train "singing actors", to break away from stereotypes in traditional opera and to

search for new repertoire and means of expression. The performers were drawn from both the Art Theater and the Bol'shoy, great attention being paid to the role of the chorus and the mixing of music, singing, words and stage movement, in which could be observed the influence of the theories of Dalcroze. In particular Nemirovich-Danchenko was concerned with the devising of artistic ensembles, which were full of social consciousness, realism and were true to life.

The first performances of the Musical Studio were Lecocq's *La fille de Madame Angot* (1920), which was treated as a political comedy; Offenbach's *La périchole* (1922), which Nemirovich-Danchenko defined as a buffo-melodrama; Aristophanes's *Lysistrata* (1923) with music by Glière; and later such works as Krenek's *Jonny spielt auf* (1929), Knipper's *North Wind* (1930), Shostakovich's *Katerina Izmaylova* (1934), Dzerzhinsky's *Quiet Don* (1936) and Khrennikov's *V Buryu* (1939). Among his experimental works may be mentioned his *Karmencita i soldat* (1924), based on Bizet's *Carmen,* in which the libretto was rewritten and the character of Micaela omitted; and Verdi's *La traviata* (1934), which was given a new libretto stressing the social conflict between aristocratic society and the actress. Great imagination was shown in the staging of these works, which was influenced by Constructivist theories.

That Nemirovich-Danchenko was able to pilot his theater throughout turbulent periods over nearly four decades was due in no small measure to his personal tact. Though his innovations, especially in the matter of alterations to standard classical works, were by no means universally approved, the originality of Nemirovich-Danchenko's productions has been recognized far beyond the Soviet Union, and what has been described as his "masterly psychological analysis and the ability to convey the unique features of a social milieu" has undoubtedly left its mark on twentieth century theater.

—Gerald Seaman

NERO
See NERONE

NERONE [Nero].

Composer: Arrigo Boito.

Librettist: Arrigo Boito.

First Performance: Milan, Teatro alla Scala 1 May 1924 (version completed and performed by Arturo Toscanini, with the assistance of Vincenzo Tommasini; the opera was composed between 1862 and 1916).

Roles: Nero (tenor); Simon Magus (baritone); Phanuel (baritone); Asteria (soprano); Rubria (mezzo-soprano); Tigellino (bass); Gobrias (tenor); Dositeo (baritone); Perside (soprano); Cerinto (contralto).

Publications

articles–

Giani, R. Il *"Nerone" di Arrigo Boito*. Milan, 1901; reprinted in *Rivista musicale italiana* 31 (1924): 235.
Forzano, G. "La preparazione sceneca del 'Nerone'." *Lettura* March (1924).
Gui, V. "Arrigo Boito e il 'Nerone'." *Rivista musicale italiana* 31 (1924): 2.

As early as 1862, six years before the unsuccessful first version of *Mefistofele*, Boito had entertained the idea of an opera centered on the Emperor Nero, but throughout his life he seemed hesitant, first to complete it, then to offer it to the public. Following the success of the revised *Mefistofele* in 1875, the *Nerone* project gradually became common knowledge in Italian musical circles. Its postponement was seen as justified while Boito devoted himself to perfecting his consummate adaptations of Shakespeare, *Otello* and *Falstaff*, for Verdi to set to music. In 1891 Verdi himself read the libretto of *Nerone*, pronouncing it "splendid" and urging Boito, once *Falstaff* had been written, to go on to the music.

In 1901, the year of Verdi's death, Boito went so far as to publish the libretto, a character study not only of the emperor half-crazed by the memory of having murdered his mother, but also of the equally demented Asteria, whose unconsummated passion for Nero has led her not only to worship him as a god but to appear to him as a Fury. Engulfed in this madness are Phanuel, a Christian priest; Rubria, a convert who secretly maintains her position as a Vestal virgin; and the charlatan Simon Magus, who attempts unsuccessfully to use Asteria to control Nero. At the opera's end, Nero has gone totally mad, Rubria has been killed in the "Circus Maximus," and Simon Magus has been forced to his own suicide by Nero, leaving Phanuel and Asteria to escape from the flames of Rome, burned by Magus' followers. (The 1901 libretto also contains a fifth act, finally considered by Boito and his advisers to be unplayable, in which Asteria commits suicide in Nero's arms, leaving him to confront the phantasms of his multitude of victims, illuminated by the flames engulfing the city.)

By 1911 Boito seemed ready to submit the opera for performance, but the death of his publisher and friend Giulio Ricordi caused a delay. Again in 1913 Boito declared the score almost complete, and offered the title role to Enrico Caruso, but again withdrew it, ostensibly to rescore act I. At his death in 1918 the work was found to be nearly complete, with only some scoring and touching-up still needed. Arturo Toscanini and composer Vincenzo Tommasini undertook the editing (Paolo Rossini has written that examination of the autograph score shows the first three acts to have been completely scored, but significantly altered in matters of instrumentation and rhythmic indications by the editors). Toscanini finally saw the opera through its premiere at the Teatro alla Scala and took the production to other major northern Italian cities. With his semipermanent professional departure to the U.S., however, *Nerone* sank into obscurity.

Boito's six-decade hesitation can be traced to his own perfectionism as a dramatist, his knowledge of his limitations as a musician, the first of which had been confirmed by the immense success of his Shakespearean libretti for Verdi, the second probably affirmed by the painstaking revision he did on *Mefistofele*. In that work, he finally produced a lucky accident of a few extremely powerful scenes which have kept the opera on the fringes of the repertoire despite other scenes which verge on the banal. *Mefistofele* is an uneven opera, but its best music and its excellent libretto set up expectations on the part of the public that must have sorely tried Boito's self-confidence. As the years passed, and *Nerone* remained an unheard legend, the composer's sense of public anticipation must have become excruciating.

On the literary level, he need not have feared. Despite a donnish barrage of archaic Roman terms, both in sung passages and stage directions (Richard Arsenty has identified over 200 of them in the four acts set to music), *Nerone* emerges as a profoundly complex psychological study of Hegelian opposites, embodied not only in the obvious good-versus-evil of Phanuel and Simon Magus, but more rewardingly in the internal shifts of both Nero and Asteria, for which Boito had prepared, for his own use, a graph charting the shifting personas of each. Nero is both self-proclaimed god and cursed fugitive from the gods, both actor and emperor. Asteria worships the god-emperor but, touched by Rubria's recitation of the Lord's Prayer, betrays her god; to him she appears as both a snake-bedecked Fury demanding vengeance and as Astarte, the goddess of love. Though Phanuel and Rubria (despite her double identity as Christian and Vestal) are relatively one-dimensional, Simon Magus' love-hate relationship with what he perceives to be Phanuel's real divine power (as opposed to his own manufactured one) also contributes to a rare and welcome complexity.

Musically, Boito aims for a similar effect, and in some scenes he succeeds. The opening of act I, on the Appian Way at sunrise, with fragments of both urban and pastoral life (mostly taken from Roman poets) born briefly past the hearer on the shifting wind, evokes a spatial dimension seldom attempted on this scale. Similarly, the opening of act II, split both musically and in the *mise-en-scène* between Simon Magus' temple, with its suppliants worshipping the false deities, and the space behind the altar, where Simon's associates make ribald comments about the gullible devotees, effectively conveys the irony of the moment. Act III—in which Phanuel and Rubria lead a Christian service and are subsequently betrayed to the Praetorian Guard by Simon, who has been condemned by Nero to die and is determined that the Christians will join him in disgrace and death—finds Boito in total control of music which sustains a contemplative lyricism, turning appropriately magisterial in the confrontation between Phanuel and Simon.

Elsewhere, most notably in the extended solo passages for Nero, Asteria, and Simon Magus, declamation replaces a probably expected lyricism. The declamation is of a superior order, investing the text with a subtly heightened meaning and mood. In fact, *Nerone* here resembles the subsequent declamatory operas of Pizzetti and Respighi, though surpassing these in its greater warmth, majesty, and lyric approach to the text. The works of those composers, respected rather than loved by the Italian public and critics, are subject to occasional revival more as a civic duty to Italian art than from any genuine popular appeal. *Nerone*, which demands expensive, opulent, representational sets for a successful revival, thus remains absent from Italian stages while lesser, similar works are, infrequently, played. Despite its superior libretto and music which rewards the mind at all times but the heart only fitfully, *Nerone* remains silent, a victim less of its lavish physical demands than of its unrealized hopes.

—William J. Collins

NESTERENKO, Evgeny Evgenievich.

Bass. Born 8 January 1938, in Moscow. Studied at Leningrad Conservatory under V. Lukanin; debut as Prince Gremin in *Eugene Onegin,* Maly Theater in Leningrad, 1963; at Maly Opera 1963-67; at Kirov Opera, 1967-71; joined the Bolshoi Opera, Moscow, 1971; sang Boris on tour at the Teatro alla Scala (1973), the Vienna Staatsoper (1974), and the Metropolitan Opera (1975); Covent Garden debut as Don Basilio, 1978; sang Philippe II in *Don Carlos* at the Teatro alla Scala, 1978; taught at Leningrad Conservatory, 1967-71; chairman of voice department at Moscow Conservatory from 1975; first prize in Tchaikovsky Competition, Moscow, 1970; awarded Lenin Prize in 1982.

Publications

By NESTERENKO: books–

Thoughts on My Profession, 1985.

*   *   *

Since his debut as Prince Gremin in Tchaikovsky's *Eugene Onegin* at St Petersberg's Maly Theater in 1963, Russian bass Evgeny Nesterenko has sung at the Bolshoi, Covent Garden, San Francisco, La Scala, Rome, Verona, East Berlin, Savolinna, Nice, Munich, Wiesbaden, Vienna, Buenos Aires, Madrid, Barcelona, Budapest, and Bregenz, in roles including Bluebeard in Bartok's *Bluebeard's Castle,* Mussorgsky's Boris Godunov, Philip II in Verdi's *Don Carlos,* Mephistopheles in Gounod's *Faust,* Ruslan in Glinka's *Ruslan and Ludmila,* Prince Gremin in Tchaikovsky's *Eugene Onegin,* Don Basilio in Rossini's *Il barbiere di Siviglia,* Dosifei and Ivan Khovansky in Mussorgsky's *Khovanschina,* Rossini's Mosè, Colline in Puccini's *La bohème,* Tiresias in Stravinsky's *Oedipus Rex,* Sarastro in Mozart's *Die Zauberflöte,* Arkel in Debussy's *Pélleas et Mélisande,* Salieri in Rimsky-Korsakov's *Mozart and Salieri,* Zaccaria in Verdi's *Nabucco,* Verdi's Attila, Henry VIII in Donizetti's *Anna Bolena,* the Water Sprite in Dvořák's *Rusalka,* Boito's Mefistofele, Konchak in Borodin's *Prince Igor,* and Rachmaninoff's Aleko.

Nesterenko possesses a lyric bass voice that tends to be somewhat lighter than usual for some of the roles of his repertoire, yet can convey their grandeur. A versatile singer with a rich voice, he is an effective and interesting, even idiosyncratic, actor, with an especially expressive face, capable of bringing his characters to life. Possessing a monumental stage presence, he has been hailed for his powerful declamation and sense of character, a highly evocative style, majesty, and physical and vocal stature. While not massive, his voice in its prime was solid and imposing. Colorful, warm, and expressive, it was evenly distributed throughout its range.

Known especially for his work in the Russian repertoire, he has also had notable success in Italian roles, particularly those of Verdi; he was less adept at Rossini. Problems with his pronunciation of French limited his effectiveness in roles

in that language (and as seems to be true of many basses, the role of Mephistopheles brought out a tendency to overact). By the late 1980s signs of vocal strain, with concomitant lapses of intonation, an increasingly monochromatic sound, and a reduction in dynamic range began to reduce his vocal and dramatic capabilities. As his voice lost power, he tended toward a more baritonal sound and began to lack some of his former authority.

His appearances in recordings of complete operas include Sobakin in Rimsky-Korsakov's *The Tsar's Bride* under Mansurov (1972), Lanciotti in Rachmaninoff's *Francesca da Rimini* under Ermler (1979), Prince Gremin under Ermler (1980), Ruslan under Simonov (1982); Bluebeard under Ferencsik (1982), Zaccaria under Sinopoli (1983); Ferrando in Verdi's *Il trovatore* under Giulini (1984), and Mephistopheles under Colin Davis (1987).

—Michael Sims

NEUES VOM TAGE [News of the Day].

Composer: Paul Hindemith.

Librettist: Marcellus Schiffer.

First Performance: Berlin, Kroll, 8 June 1929; revised 1953.

Roles (in revised version): Laura (soprano); Eduard (baritone); Hermann (tenor); Frau Pick (mezzo-soprano); Baron D'Houdoux (bass); Elli (soprano); Olli (contralto); Ali (tenor); Ulli (bass); Museum Tour Leader (bass); Hotel Manager (bass); Wine Steward (baritone); Chambermaid (soprano); Bystander (bass); Six Managers (two tenors, two baritones, two basses); chorus (SSAATTBB).

*   *   *

Following his *Cardillac* (1926), which had enjoyed widespread critical acclaim as his first large-scale opera, *Neues vom Tage* represents Hindemith's contribution to the genre of *Zeitoper* first made famous by Ernst Krenek's *Jonny spielt auf* (1927). Before composing *Neues vom Tage,* however, Hindemith's *Hin und zurück,* a "Sketch mit Musik" on a libretto by Marcellus Schiffer, a writer of popular stage revues, appeared at the 1927 Baden-Baden Festival of chamber operas and amply demonstrated Hindemith's interest in representing and celebrating modern life, for which the *Zeitoper* was known. The reception of the "Sketch" was such that Hindemith decided to collaborate again with Schiffer.

In *Neues vom Tage,* Hindemith and Schiffer retained a number of the features of *Hin und zurück,* in particular the dramatic focus on domestic life and marriage. In *Hin und zurück,* marital squabbles lead to a murder-suicide that is then reversed in the manner of running a movie backwards, whereas in *Neues vom Tage,* the couple decide to divorce. Set in contemporary Paris, the opera, in three acts, opens with the couple, Laura and Eduard, arguing bitterly and deciding to divorce. Their friends, a newly-married couple known only as Herr and Frau M, enter, argue, and decide to divorce as well. Herr and Frau M successfully obtain their divorce and recommend to Eduard and Laura the services of handsome Herr Hermann, who, through his Office of Family Affairs, can supply them with the necessary grounds of infidelity. Herr Hermann arranges to meet Laura at the Louvre to stage their assignation, but Eduard takes it seriously and upon seeing the two together flies into a rage and destroys the Venus di Milo.

The second act opens with Laura in a hotel bathroom, which Herr Hermann enters professing his actual love for her. Frau M, who since her divorce has been Herr Hermann's lover, has followed him there and calls in the hotel personnel to reveal the scandal. Eduard learns of Laura's predicament, while she later learns that he is in jail for destroying the statue; both are confident they now have grounds for their divorce. Their divorce case causes such a sensation that Eduard is besieged by managers who wish to recount their story on stage. In the third act, Herr and Frau M remarry and meet Eduard and Laura in the foyer of a theater where, not yet divorced, they tell their story as part of a revue. In the last scene, they too reconcile, having earned enough money to cover Eduard's fines, and wish to retire as private citizens. However, their public will not allow it; they must continue to tell their story because they are the "news of the day."

As was the case with *Hin und zurück,* Hindemith formulated *Neues vom Tage* in the manner of an eighteenth-century number opera, thereby parodying the current interest in operatic revivals and neo-classical experiments. Each scene of the three acts is subdivided into two to five separate numbers, clearly marked in the score as recitatives, arias, choruses, duets, and the like, with a culminating finale. Hindemith burlesqued operatic conventions through his unconventional, even mundane approach. Thus, instead of the opening duet between Eduard and Laura being one in which they declare their love, as did Figaro and Susanna, the couple voice instead their mutual disgust for each other, ending in a unison, melismatic phrase on the line "we want a divorce." One of the most commented upon burlesques at the time, and for which Hindemith earned a reputation for immorality with the National Socialists, was Laura's arioso sung in praise of hot running water while in her hotel bathtub.

Overall the score is rhythmic and lively, and the orchestration favors brass and woodwinds. Of special interest is the use of pianos, two- and four-hands, which provide important harmonic and rhythmic support. In keeping with its *Zeitoper* distinction and Hindemith's own experiments with popular and concert music synthesis as in the Kammermusik no. 1, three sections borrow jazz dance idioms. Eduard and Laura argue to fox trot rhythms that reappear later in their theater act, and a triple-meter Boston waltz characterizes Frau and Herr M. Hindemith used the saxophone and banjo to recreate dance music timbres.

The work was premiered as part of the annual Berlin Festspiele, and though well-received by the audience, a number of critics judged the work flawed in its attempt to combine Schiffer's revue sketch and Hindemith's rigorous formal models. The opera's overture, however, was successful on its own. Hindemith revised the opera considerably in 1953, following the establishment of his new compositional principles. He restructured the work into two acts, changed the makeup of individual scenes, deleted Frau and Herr M, and added new characters. Like Krenek's *Jonny spielt auf,* Hindemith's original *Neues vom Tage* reflects the light-hearted satiric side of the Weimar culture before the political and cultural realities of National Socialism.

—Susan C. Cook

NEWS OF THE DAY
See NEUES VOM TAGE

NEW YEAR.

Composer: Michael Tippett.

Librettist: Michael Tippett.

First Performance: Houston, Grand Opera, October 1989.

Roles: Jo Ann (soprano); Donny (baritone); Nan (mezzo-soprano); Merlin (baritone); Pelegrin (tenor); Regan (soprano); Voice; chorus.

*   *   *

New Year is a fascinating work. Here again, as in Tippett's previous four operas, symbolism, ritual, and fantasy combine to create a modern myth. Libretto and musical dramatization—in which dance now becomes an integral part—are almost completely successful in delineating the fragments of space and time through which Tippett has us travel in search of the full potential of our humanity.

The plot is a modern fairy tale; Tippett's synopsis even begins: "Once upon a time there was a girl named Jo Ann." This young woman dreams of being able to help the people of her world. But she fears that world, a "Terror Town" in "Somewhere and Today," as Tippett calls it. She is frightened by the primitive, often outrageous behavior of her black, adopted step-brother Donny. As with all fairy tales, only the power of true love can redeem her from fear. This comes from Pelegrin, a handsome Space-Time Traveler from "Nowhere and Tomorrow." His platonic love nurtures Jo Ann through a ritualistic search for the courage to overcome her fear. In the end, far from living "happily ever after," Pelegrin leaves her, returning to "Tomorrow"; Jo Ann remains in the present, emboldened by love to face the world and work for "one humanity, one justice," as the last words of the opera declare.

What creates the fascination of this basically simple plot is the interaction between the present and future worlds as Tippett portrays them. He conjures a sterile nowhere and tomorrow of computer-filled rooms, robot-like machine operators, and, with the exception of Pelegrin, technology-and-future-fixated characters: Merlin, the computer wizard, and Regan, the icy commander of this tomorrow world. Tippett evokes an other-worldly atmosphere to depict space and time travel with specially taped electronic music for the take-off and landing of the space ship. The rich choral music (as luxuriant as in *The Midsummer Marriage*) and the driving energy of the crowd's dance music (here more exuberant than frightening, as in *The Ice Break*) create vivid street scenes in somewhere and today. Deliberately, then, today is a vital, immediate world; tomorrow, while numinous, is cerebral and remote.

Characterization is, perhaps, the opera's strongest feature. Tippett makes the main human characters especially vivid. Jo Ann's graceful melismatic vocal lines throughout, and her halting then strong dancing as she begins to experience new-found moral conviction, depict an appealing young woman. Pelegrin's melismatic tenor lines are the perfect match for Jo

Michael Tippett's *New Year*, Glyndebourne Festival, 1990

Ann's; their duet in act III, "Moments out of time and space," is the opera's most touching lyric moment and the only traditional love duet Tippett has written in any of his operas.

When Donny sings and dances his dream song of living with animals rather than humans, the ritual dances of *The Midsummer Marriage* come to mind. His sensual singing and dancing style depicts graphically a deep-seated frustration and longing for personal wholeness. On the strength of its individualized visceral impact, this ritual enactment evokes empathy and not just wonder.

One of *New Year*'s most delightful moments occurs when Regan, the dragon lady of the future, so to speak, is confronted by this primitive, Donny. Not understanding that the space ship has gone back to the past, Regan alights from it and asks who the people (of Terror Town) are. Donny boldly steps up, challenging her to talk to him. A rap-style speech duet with strut-like steps ensues, Regan entering into his style. She does not realize that the joke has been on her until Donny tells her "We are Earth." Tippett could not have pricked the balloon of her pompousness more aptly.

The exuberant interplay of traditional operatic techniques with elements of music theater throughout acts I, II and most of III makes for electrifying dramatic impact. But the closing *spoken* words of the opera's conclusion, "One humanity, one justice," leave the listener wondering if there is not more to come. Yet this anti-climactic ending is justified, perhaps, by weighing mythic message against musical expectations.

The fulfillment of *New Year*'s message occurs in social terms. If taken seriously, the challenge that Tippett has dramatized in act III is awe-inspiring. The rose of spiritual fortitude that Pelegrin gives Jo Ann in the ritual search for courage is not hers to keep. As she finally starts to enter the needy world around her, the rose returns to Pelegrin in tomorrow, the myth thus implying that the future is both our hope and our present strength; we must face the harsh realities of the present, the opera has said, and serve others in the light of hope that the future holds. Tippett clearly sees himself as an intermediary between one world and another, the Pelegrin who has led us to the brink of a new century. What artist would not stand in quiet awe before the mysteries of today and tomorrow?

—Margaret Scheppach

NICOLAI, (Carl) Otto (Ehrenfried).

Composer. Born 9 June 1810, in Königsberg. Died 11 May 1849, in Berlin. Studied piano with Zelter in Berlin, 1827; studied with Bernhard Klein at the Royal Institute for Church Music; concert debut in Berlin, 13 April 1833; organist to the embassy chapel in Rome by the German Ambassador, 1834; studied counterpoint with Giuseppe Baini; singing teacher and conductor at the Kärntnertor theater, Vienna, 1837; returned to Italy, 1838; first opera presented in Trieste, 1839; succeeded Kreutzer as court Kapellmeister in Vienna, 1841; conducted the inaugural concert of the Vienna Philharmonic Orchestra, 1842; Kapellmeister of the Royal Opera in Berlin, 1848. Hans Richter began an annual "Nicolai-Konzert" with the Vienna Philharmonic, which over the years has been conducted by such notable conductors as Gustav Mahler, Felix Weingartner, Wilhelm Furtwängler, Karl Böhm, and Claudio Abbado.

Operas

Enrico II (Rosmonda d'Inghilterra), Felice Romani, 1836, Trieste, 26 November 1839.
Il templario, Girolamo Maria Marini (after Scott, *Ivanhoe*), Turin, 11 February 1840; revised as *Der Tempelritter,* translated S. Kapper, Vienna, 20 December 1845.
Gildippe ed Odoardo, T. Solera, Genoa, 26 December 1840.
Il proscritto, G. Rossi, Milan, Teatro alla Scala, 13 March 1841; revised as *Die Heimkehr des Verbannten,* translated S. Kapper, 3 February 1846.
Die lustigen Weiber von Windsor, S.H. Mosenthal (after Shakespeare, *The Merry Wives of Windsor*), Berlin, Hofoper, 9 March 1849.

Other works: sacred and secular vocal works, orchestral works, chamber music.

Publications

By NICOLAI: books–

Schröder, B., ed. *Otto Nicolai: Tagebücher nebst biographischen Ergänzungen.* Leipzig, 1892.
Altmann, W., ed. *Otto Nicolai: Briefe an seinen Vater.* Regensburg, 1924.
Altmann, W., ed. *Otto Nicolais Tagebücher.* Regensburg, 1937.
Goslich, S. *Beiträge zur Geschichte der deutschen romantischen Oper.* Leipzig, 1937.
Jerger, W., ed. *Otto Nicolai: Briefe an die Wiener Philharmoniker,* 11ff. Vienna, 1942.

About NICOLAI: books–

Mendel, H. *Otto Nicolai.* Berlin, 1866; 1868.
Berlioz, Hector. *Mémoires.* Paris, 1870; English translation, 1969.
Hanslick, E. *Am Ende des Jahrhunderts. Die moderne Oper,* vol. 8, p. 100ff. Berlin, 1899.
Kolb, K.M. *Beiträge zur Geschichte der deutschen komischen Oper,* 87ff. Berlin, 1903.
Istel, E. *Die Blütezeit der musikalischen Romantik in Deutschland,* 157. Leipzig, 1909.
Kruse, Georg Richard. *Otto Nicolai; ein Künstlerleben.* Berlin, 1911.
Schünemann, G. *Geschichte des Dirigierens,* 269f. Leipzig, 1913.
Krebs, C. *Meister des Taktstocks,* 80ff. Berlin, 1919.
Schiedermaier, L. *Die deutsche Oper.* Leipzig, 1930.
Goslich, S. *Beiträge zur Geschichte der deutschen romantischen Oper.* Leipzig, 1937; revised as *Die Deutsche romantische Oper,* Tutzing, 1975.
Orel, A. *Musikstadt Wien,* 302f. Vienna and Stuttgart, 1953.

Düre, Karl-Friedrich. *Opern nach literarischen Vorlagen. Shakespeares "The Merry Wives of Windsor" in den Vertonungen von Mosenthal—Nicolai "Die lustigen Weiber von Windsor" und Boito—Verdi "Falstaff." Ein Beitrag zum Thema Gattungstransformation.* Stuttgart, 1979.
Konrad, Ulrich. *Otto Nicolai: Studien zu Leben und Werk.* Baden-Baden, 1986.

articles–

Kruse, George Richard. "Falstaff und die lustigen Weiber." *Die Musik* 6/no. 4 (1906-07): 63.
_____. "Otto Nicolai als Sinfoniker." *Allgemeine Musik-Zeitung* 35 (1908).
_____. "Goethe, Zelter und Otto Nicolai." *Goethe-Jahrbuch* 31 (1910): 163.
_____. "Otto Nicolais italienische Opern." *Sammelbände der Internationalen Musikgesellschaft* 12 (1910-11): 267.
Weissmann, A. *Berlin als Musikstadt: Geschichte der Oper und des Konzerts von 1740-1911,* 201, 203, 245. Berlin and Leipzig, 1911.
Kruse, George Richard. "Otto Nicolais 'Lustige Weiber' . . . mit unbekannt gebliebenen Nummern." *Die Musik* 28 (1936): 886.
Würz, A. "Otto Nicolai: eine Betrachtung zu seinem Gedenken." *Neue Musikzeitschrift* April (1949): 97.
Virneisel, W. "Otto Nicolai als Musiksammler." In *Festschrift Max Schneider,* 227. Leipzig, 1955.
Klein, J.W. "Verdi and Nicolai: a Strange Rivalry." *Music Review* 32 (1971): 63.

*   *   *

Like Georges Bizet, Nicolai lived just long enough to witness the production of the one opera on which his posthumous fame would entirely rest (*Die lustigen Weiber von Windsor,* 9 March 1849). If this premiere was on the whole better received than that of *Carmen,* neither composer survived to see the ultimate vindication of his final opera. Whatever Nicolai himself thought to be the merits of *Die lustigen Weiber* (his first comedy and first German opera, after 4 Italian works) its initial reception gave him no reason to believe that it would soon become a staple of the repertory.

As an adolescent Nicolai fled his East Prussian home to escape aggressive and exploitative treatment at the hands of his father, a minor musical figure in Königsberg. Later in Berlin he received instruction from Carl Friedrich Zelter, Goethe's friend and doyen of the musical scene in the Prussian capital. Other teachers included the pianist composer Ludwig Berger and a noted composer of liturgical music and oratorios, Bernhard Klein. Nicolai's training in Berlin was consequently geared toward sacred music, and when he went to Rome in 1834 as chapel organist to the German Embassy, his attention was at first directed to the musical institutions of the Catholic Church and the venerable tradition of Renaissance polyphony (especially as practiced by Palestrina) fostered by Giuseppe Baini and others.

The composition of a ten-voice setting of Psalm 54 in the "strict style" followed by a fantasy for piano and orchestra on themes from Bellini's *Norma* (Op. 25), both in the summer of 1835, is suggestive of the new orientation of the young composer's enthusiasm. This burgeoning interest in the world of Italian opera—despite complaints about poor standards and conditions for performance, so commonly voiced by foreign musicians in Italy—received still stronger symbolic manifestation in memorial compositions in honor of Bellini (a funeral march played as an entracte to *La sonnambula* in Rome, 14 October 1835) and Maria Malibran (Bologna, 1836). After a difficult year as Kapellmeister at the Vienna Court Opera (Kärntnertor theater) in 1837-38 Nicolai returned to Italy, determined to make a career in opera. A work begun for Vienna as *Rosmonda d'Inghilterra* (libretto by Felice Romani) was eventually staged in Trieste as *Enrico II* in 1839. Of three more operas produced in Italy, *Il templario* (Turin, 11 February 1840) and *Il proscritto* (Teatro alla Scala, Milan, 13 March 1841) achieved notable success and were subsequently performed in Vienna and in various German theaters as *Der Tempelritter* and *Die Heimkehr des Verbannten,* respectively. The libretto to *Il proscritto* was acquired in exchange for *Nabucodonosor* (later *Nabucco*), which was turned over to Verdi.

A longer period as Kapellmeister back at the Vienna Court Opera (1841-47) was distinguished by significant contributions to the musical life of the city, including a series of orchestral concerts which marked the establishment of the Vienna Philharmonic as an institution. However, Nicolai was continually frustrated by envy, intrigues, and general ill-will on the part of his colleagues, and the rejection of his nearly completed new opera *Die lustigen Weiber von Windsor* on the grounds of a contractual technicality led Nicolai to resign, assuming a similar post in Berlin. His meticulous musical standards and the expertise he had acquired as conductor were much appreciated during his two years in Berlin, where he also conducted the cathedral choir. *Die lustigen Weiber* finally reached the stage there two months before his early death at the age of 39.

Nicolai was perhaps the last German composer, following Meyerbeer, to undergo an active Italian apprenticeship. Like Meyerbeer, he appreciated the value of this induction into the traditions of the operatic stage and the techniques of vocal writing. Both composers ceased to write in the Italian style upon leaving the country, although both re-arranged their Italian operas for performance abroad, in translation.

Nicolai's Italian operas reflect something of his own mixed attitude toward the genre as he encountered it in the later 1830s. Like many Germans, he admired the quality of the vocal tradition in Italy, but lamented the tendency to sacrifice any serious concern for musical, dramatic, or even scenic matters to a narrow emphasis on the singer's art. He admired what he judged to be the most substantial products of the bel canto repertory, such as Bellini's, *La sonnambula* and *Norma*, Donizetti's *Anna Bolena,* and Rossini's *Guillaume Tell* (despite his distaste for the wider influence of Rossinian formulas). In *Il templario* (based on Scott's *Ivanhoe,* which had already served as the basis for operas by Giovanni Pacini and Heinrich Marschner, as well as a Rossini *pasticcio*) Nicolai displays a fluent command of the contemporary Italian idiom, occasionally betraying traces of a German accent. The symphonically conceived overture, for instance, suggests a grafting of the style of Weber and Marschner onto the conventional Italian *sinfonia*. Many of the solo numbers or passages are written in a typically bel canto style, as lyrical or virtuosic displays. But Rebecca's *preghiera* in act III (like Wagner's Elsa, she prays for a champion to come to her defense) is, despite her Jewish faith, clearly indebted to the Protestant chorale tradition, recalling the composer's original training in Berlin.

Given such a synthesis of Italian and German influences, it is no surprise that Nicolai held up Mozart as his musical idol. (Instrumental and vocal works of Mozart figured prominently on the programs of his "Philharmonic Academies" in Vienna.) Certainly the beloved image of Mozart informed Nicolai's ambitions to create a German opera for Vienna after returning there in 1841. Although these ambitions were to be frustrated for some time, they were fittingly realized at last in *Die lustigen Weiber von Windsor.* Perhaps the finest German comic opera since *Die Zauberflöte,* this score combines the spirit of Mozart's operas (especially *Figaro*) with the warm but light-footed "classical" romanticism of Mendelssohn at his best.

—Thomas S. Grey

NIELSEN, Carl (August).

Composer. Born 9 June 1865, in Nørre-Lyndelse, near Odense, on the island of Fyn. Died 3 October 1931, in Copenhagen. Studied violin with his father, and became second violin in the village orchestra; studied trumpet, and was a trumpeter in the Odense military band, 1879; studied composition with O. Rosenhoff, violin with V. Tofte, and music history with Gade at the Royal Conservatory in Copenhagen, 1884-86; violinist in the Royal Chapel Orchestra in Copenhagen, 1889-1905; conductor at the Royal Opera in Copenhagen, 1908-14; led the Musikföreningen in Copenhagen, 1915-27; conducted concerts in Germany, the Netherlands, Sweden, and Finland; appointed director of the Royal Conservatory in Copenhagen, 1931.

Operas

Publishers: Hansen, Samfundet til Udgivelse af Dansk Musik, Skandinavisk and Borups.

Snefrid (melodrama), Drachmann, 1893, Copenhagen, 10 April 1894; revised, 1899.
Saul og David [*Saul and David*], E. Christiansen, 1898-1901, Copenhagen, 28 November 1902.
Maskarade, V. Andersen (after Holberg), 1904-06, Copenhagen, 11 November 1906.

Other works: incidental music, orchestral works, accompanied and unaccompanied choral works, songs, chamber and instrumental music, piano and organ pieces.

Publications

By NIELSEN: books—

Levende musik. Copenhagen, 1925; English translation, 1953.
Min fynske barndom. Copenhagen, 1927; English translation, 1953.
Schousboe, Torben, ed. *Carl Nielsen: dagbøger og brevveksling med Anne Marie Carl-Nielsen* [critical edition of diaries and letters to his wife]. Copenhagen, 1983.

articles—

Jensen, Nick Martin, ed. " 'Den sindets stridighed.' Breve fra Carl Nielsen til Julius Lehmann" [letters to Julius Lehmann, the director of the opera *Saul and David* and *Maskarade*]. *Musik and Forskning* 6 (1980): 167.

About NIELSEN: books—

Meyer, Torben. *Carl Nielsen: Kunstneren of Mennesket: En Biografi.* 2 vols. Copenhagen, 1947-48.
Dolleris, Ludwig. *Carl Nielsen: En Musikografi.* Odense, 1949.
Fabricius, Johannes. *Carl Nielsen: a Pictoral Biography.* Copenhagen, 1965.
Miller, Mina F. *Carl Nielsen: a Guide to Research.* New York, 1987.

*   *   *

Nielsen's reputation, outside Denmark at least, rests mainly on his six symphonies. His two operas *Saul and David* and *Maskarade,* which belong to the early part of his career, have not so far gained wide circulation abroad, and it is a matter for regret that he never returned to opera in his later years. He held strong views about opera and placed great emphasis on the importance of plot as the "pole" or trunk from which all the strength of an opera is derived. Poetry, he averred, had no place in drama: "it melts." In common with many composers of his generation, he admired Wagner's aims but quite soon became critical of his methods, some of which he thought "unhealthy" (Nielsen was fond of words like "ruddy" and "healthy"). In particular, he disapproved of Wagner's reliance on leitmotif as a means of identifying his characters and their actions. He regarded this as "spoon feeding," and condemned it as being "naive" and insulting to the audience. He remained indifferent to Italian operatic tradition, although he must have been acquainted with it at first hand from his desk among the violins in the Copenhagen Opera. Verdi, its most potent representative, seems to have left him cold. He does, however, appear to have admired Puccini.

Always a perceptive critic, Nielsen attributed the divergent paths of operatic development during the nineteenth century to the opposing positions taken up in the eighteenth by Gluck in his "reform" of the *opera seria,* and by Mozart in his refinement of the Italian *buffo* tradition. This he interpreted as a conflict between the heroic and the humane, between music and movement. He saw Gluck's striving to elevate the literary quality of the libretto by the use of discursive recitatives, heavily orchestrated and impregnated with motifs, as the ancestor of Wagner's music drama. This tradition, he believed, made opera too symphonic and impeded plot development, and in *Saul and David,* which invited such treatment, he carefully steered around the recitative-aria formula in favor of a solution not dissimilar to that arrived at by Musorgsky in *Boris Godunov.* Mozart's awareness of the dramatic imperative (the need for pace, character development, clarity and relative simplicity of means) accorded more closely with his own ideas about the humanizing of character and the relationship of music to action, but being always more interested in action than character building, Nielsen never felt himself called on to imitate Mozart. *Maskarade* may sound Mozartian, but in reality it owes more to the buffo operas of Mozart's lesser Italian contemporaries, where movement takes precedence over motive.

Danish opera before Nielsen had no clear national identity. Kuhlau, Lange-Müller, Weyse, J.P.E. Hartmann and Heise followed in the wake of popular European models such as Rossini, Weber, Marschner and Wagner. Although vestiges of the romantic tradition exemplified by Heise's "Drot og Marsk" (King and Marshal) are to be found in *Saul and David,* that opera, and to an even greater extent *Maskarade,* demonstrate a determined and largely successful attempt to inject a specifically Danish spirit into Danish opera.

In 1922, Nielsen was invited to write another Holberg-based opera, *Kilderejsen,* but declined on the grounds that it was too much like *Maskarade,* and he had no wish to repeat himself. He did, however, seriously consider a project in connection with Hans Christian Andersen's 125th anniversary in 1930. The subject was Andersen's story *Den uartige Dreng,* which dealt with the author's love for Jenny Lind. The proposed opera never materialized, but became a play, *Amor og Digteren.* For this Nielsen wrote an overture (still performed), some songs and instrumental numbers. In all, he composed incidental music for fourteen plays, beginning in 1889 with Munch's *En aften paa Grike* and ending with Gruntvig's Easter play *Paaskeaftensspil,* completed some six months before his death in October 1931. Several songs from these now forgotten dramas achieved a separate life as recital pieces, but for the most part, the music written for them has likewise been forgotten.

Holberg apart, the most important playwright with whom Nielsen's name is associated is Adam Oehlenschläger (1779-1850). Nielsen wrote music for three of Oehlenschläger's plays, the most important, musically speaking, being *Aladdin* (1918). An orchestral suite drawn from this music has been successfully transfered to the concert hall. Unlike Grieg, Nielsen was never involved with a contemporary playwright, and it has been argued that his incidental music lacks the rapport with its subject that a contemporary theme might have given it. If one compares his work in this field with that of some of his predecessors, Kuhlau's *Elf-Hill* or Lange-Müller's *Once upon a time,* for instance, one can see that the argument has force. However, *Saul and David* and *Maskarade* suggest that given the right stimulus, contemporary or not, Nielsen was perfectly capable of creating a viable dramatic language.

—Kenneth Dommett

THE NIGHTENGALE
See LE ROSSIGNOL

NIKISCH, Arthur.

Conductor. Born 12 October 1855, in Szent-Miklós. Died 23 January 1922, in Leipzig. Studied composition with Dessoff and violin with Hellmesberger at the Vienna Conservatory, graduating 1874; played in the first violin section under Wagner's direction at the ceremonies surrounding the founding of Bayreuth, 1872; violinist in the Vienna Court Orchestra, 1874; second conductor at the Leipzig Theater, 1878; first conductor at the Leipzig Theater, 1882-89; conductor of the Boston Symphony Orchestra, 1889-93; music director of the Budapest Opera, 1893-95; many engagements as a visiting conductor; conductor of the Gewandhaus Concerts in Leipzig and of the Philharmonic Concerts, Berlin, 1895; toured with the Berlin Philharmonic; conducted Wagner and Richard Strauss at Covent Garden; director of studies at the Leipzig

Conservatory, 1902-07; general director of the Leipzig Stadt-theater, 1905-06; toured the United States with the London Symphony Orchestra, 1912.

Publications

About NIKISCH: books–

Pfohl, Ferdinand. *Arthur Nikisch als Mensch und Künstler.* Leipzig, 1900; revised as *Aurthur Nikisch: Sein Leben, seine Kunst, sein Werken.* Hamburg, 1925.
Dette, A. *Nikisch.* Leipzig, 1922.
Khevalley, H. ed. *Arthur Nikisch: Leben und Werken.* Berlin, 1922.

* * *

Arthur Nikisch, like his older compatriot Hans Richter before him, first learned his trade in the orchestra pit. For six years (1872-78) in the Vienna Court Opera, he was able to play for such composers as Wagner, Verdi, Brahms and Liszt as well as for Richter, who was appointed there in 1875. Nikisch sat amongst the first violins for the first two years as an extra player before his appointment was confirmed at the beginning of 1874. This was an invaluable training ground to learn repertoire and watch those conductors for whom he worked. This groundwork as a string player would become the core to his renowned production of a warm, rich and passionate sound from the strings of the orchestras he was later to conduct.

Nikisch's own tastes were molded and developed during his years as a player. Inevitably Wagner's influence predominated, particularly after the composer came to conduct *Lohengrin* in Vienna and the young Nikisch played for him in the orchestra at the 1872 foundation-laying ceremonial performance in Bayreuth of Beethoven's Ninth Symphony.

Nikisch's attitude to Italian opera was more equivocal. When Verdi came to conduct *Aida*, Nikisch was spellbound and, having absorbed every detail and nuance from the composer himself during the rehearsals, his own interpretation of the opera was, throughout his life, said to be as close as one could get to the composer himself. On the other hand, Nikisch would pay a deputy to take his place on evenings when Bellini's operas, such as *Norma,* were being played.

Called to Leipzig by Angelo Neumann to be chorus master, Nikisch soon progressed from his debut appearance conducting Lacome's operetta *Jeanne, Jeanette, Jeanetton* and Halévy's comic opera *L'eclair* to first conductor at only twenty-four years of age, and after only a year conducted performances of Wagner's *Tannhäuser* and *Die Walküre.* Nikisch immediately impressed his Leipzig orchestra with his infallible ear by spotting an error in the bassoon part of *Tannhäuser* which had gone unnoticed for many years. His manner with orchestral players (and here his early experience as one of them proved invaluable) became legendary. He rarely raised his voice and would disarm his players with personal touches, for example by publicly greeting as an old and cherished friend anyone he recognized in an orchestra with which he was guest-conducting.

Nikisch not only devoted himself to the established repertoire during his ten Leipzig years, he also conducted new works such as Rubinstein's *The Demon* and *Die Makkabäer,* Ignaz Brüll's *Königin Mariette,* Nessler's *Der Trompeter von Säkkingen* and Goldschmidt's *Helinthus.* Tchaikovsky heard Nikisch conduct *Das Rheingold* and *Die Meistersinger* during his period in Leipzig. He described him as "elegantly calm,

sparing of superfluous movements, yet at the same time wonderfully strong and self-possessed." The Russian composer became aware of what so many others were to sense, the hypnotic spell which Nikisch could cast upon players and audience alike when he conducted and the way in which he came to play the orchestra as if it were a huge instrument. Boult described Nikisch's performance of *Tristan* as "transcendent, electric and memorable."

After Leipzig Nikisch rarely worked in the field of opera (Budapest, where as director of the Budapest Opera he spent a miserable four years, being the only other city to win him), although occasionally, as with a production of the *Ring* in London in 1913, he would guest-conduct. At the time of his death in 1922 he was negotiating a first-appearance at Bayreuth two years later. That his name had been missing from the ranks of the conductors who worked there was probably attributable to Cosima Wagner's reluctance to invite those whose principal work and reputation was in the concert hall. It could only have been to her and the Festspielhaus's loss that Nikisch's mercurial *Tristan* was never heard there.

—Christopher Fifield

NILSSON, Birgit.

Soprano. Born 17 May 1918, in Vastra Karups, Sweden. Studied with Joseph Hislop in Stockholm; debut as substitute for role of Agathe in *Der Freischütz,* 1946; formal debut as Lady Macbeth at Stockholm; with Stockholm Opera, 1947-51; appeared as Elektra in *Idomeneo* at Glyndebourne, 1951; Bayreuth debut as Elsa, 1954, and sang there regularly until 1970; appeared at Covent Garden from 1957; appeared at Teatro alla Scala from 1958, first as Turandot; Metropolitan Opera debut as Isolde, 1959, and sang there until 1982.

Publications

By NILSSON: books–

Mina minnesbilder. Stockholm, 1977; English translation as *My Memoirs in Pictures,* New York, 1981.

About NILSSON: articles–

Jeffries, W. "Birgit Nilsson." *Opera* September (1960).

* * *

The Swedish soprano Birgit Nilsson dominated the soprano Wagnerian roles after World War II and was considered the Wagnerian soprano of her generation and the heir to Kirsten Flagstad. She made her debut in Stockholm as Agathe in *Der*

Freischütz in 1946 and gained international attention as a result of her stellar Elektra in Mozart's *Idomeneo* at Glyndebourne in 1951. In 1954 and 1955 she sang Brünnhilde (in Wagner's *Ring* cycle) and the title role of *Salome* in Munich; thereafter, she was a real superstar.

Nilsson became famous for the power and force of her voice, in addition to her ability to sing wonderfully with portamento; her interpretations also impressed with their insight and drama. She was best known for the main Wagnerian soprano roles: all three Brünnhildes in the Ring cycle, Isolde in *Tristan und Isolde,* Elsa in *Lohengrin,* and both Elisabeth and Venus in *Tannhauser.* She also sang Mozart with success, Donna Anna in *Don Giovanni* and Elektra being her best Mozart roles. In the Italian repertory, she was best in the title roles of *Turandot, Tosca, Aïda,* and Minnie in *La Fanciulla del West.* By the early 1960s Nilsson had created sensations in Milan, Chicago, London, Munich, and New York. She also collaborated in the 60s with Wieland Wagner at Bayreuth for wonderful productions of the *Ring* cycle and *Tristan und Isolde.*

Toward the end of her career, Nilsson sang two Strauss roles with great acclaim: the Dyer's Wife in *Die Frau ohne Schatten* and the title role in *Elektra.* She appeared at all the great opera houses, but was especially familiar at New York's Metropolitan Opera, Milan's Teatro alla Scala, Munich's Bavarian State Opera, and London's Covent Garden.

Nilsson has left a fine recorded legacy, particularly in her fruitful collaboration with the conductor Sir Georg Solti. They recorded a wonderful *Ring* cycle with her as all three

Brünnhildes, plus Strauss' *Salome* and *Elektra.* With the conductor Karl Böhm she also recorded an exciting *Ring* cycle plus *Tristan und Isolde* with the tenor Wolfgang Windgassen.

—John Louis DiGaetani

NILSSON, Christine (Kristina).

Soprano. Born 20 August 1843, in Sjöabol, Sweden. Died 22 November 1921, in Stockholm. Studied with Franz Berwald in Stockholm, and in Paris with Wartel, Massé and Delle Sedie; debut as Violetta in *La traviata* at Théâtre-Lyrique, Paris, 1864; London debut in same role, 1864; created Ophélie in *Hamlet,* Paris, Opéra, 1868; Covent Garden debut in *Lucia di Lammermoor,* 1869, and appeared there and at Drury Lane regularly until 1881; U.S. debut as Mignon, Academy of Music, New York, 1871; sang Marguerite in *Faust* for opening of new Metropolitan Opera House, 1883.

Publications

About Nilsson: books–

Charnacée, Guy de. *Christina Nilsson.* Paris, 1869.
Mapleson, J. *The Mapleson Memoirs.* London, 1888.
Norlind, T. *Kristina Nilsson.* Stockholm, 1923.
Headland, T. *Christine Nilsson: the Songbird of the North.* Rock Island, Illinois, 1943.
Leche-Lofgren, M. *Kristina Nilsson.* Stockholm, 1944.
Franzén, Nils Olof. *Christina Nilsson: en svensk saga.* Stockholm, 1976.

*　　*　　*

Recordings have a considerable effect on our perception of a singer. Christine Nilsson was an exact contemporary of Adelina Patti, but because she retired twenty years earlier while still in her forties and made no gramophone records, she seems a very much more distant figure from an earlier period of operatic history.

Nilsson's debut was at the Théâtre-Lyrique in Paris as Violetta. One can surmise that musical Paris knew something was afoot, for the audience is said to have included both Madame Miolan-Carvalho, reigning prima donna of the house, and Patti herself. Nor it seems did the newcomer disappoint despite her evident nervousness—"a voice eminently pure, flexible and true in the upper range, though decidedly weak and defficient in the lower register [and she imparted] a great charm to her rendering of the part."

Nilsson remained with the Théâtre-Lyrique until 1867 when another astute impresario, Mapleson, engaged her for Her Majesty's in London as a rival to Patti, then supreme at Covent Garden. Nilsson was to remain one of Mapleson's trump cards in his many operatic campaigns. She still returned frequently to Paris, although now to sing at the Opéra where she created Ophélia in Thomas' *Hamlet* with Faure in the title role in 1868. She also sang in Bruxelles, Munich, Moscow, St Petersburg and Vienna. However, London was her home base. In her first season she followed *Traviata* with *Faust, Martha* and *Don Giovanni.* In the latter she appeared as Donna Elvira with Tietjens, Mapleson's other great prima donna, as Donna Anna.

Birgit Nilsson as Isolde, Bayreuth

According to the *Musical World,* no Elvira had ever "endowed the part with an individuality at once so marked and prepossessing. . . . The voice of Mdlle Nilsson, were she far less accomplished a singer than she is, would alone exercise an irresistible fascination. There is a liquid quality, a youthful freshness of tone in every note of its range from the lowest to the highest." Tietjens and Nilsson next collaborated in *Die Zauberflöte* with the latter as Queen of the Night. This may seem surprising given the later predominance of lyrical roles in her repertoire—Mignon, Marguerite in both *Faust* and *Mefistofele,* Elsa in *Lohengrin,* Alice in *Robert le diable.* Interestingly, Herman Klein recounts that when Rossini heard her Queen of the Night he advised her not to sing above high D, Klein felt that she had taken his advice; even in the mad scenes of Lucia and Hamlet she did no more than touch higher notes. Later as the high notes were lost, her voice "acquired in its 'dramatic' range a degree of opulence and power." Klein praised her brilliance, ease and precision as Donna Elvira and Lucia as well as "the rare elegance of her execution in the more showy passages of Verdi."

From a very different musical perspective Bernard Shaw appraised Christine Nilsson as "the most gifted of our leading soprani. That position she has made good . . . by the force of her inborn dramatic instinct and the charm of a voice whose beauty asserts herself in spite of a most destructive method of production." Shaw goes on to laud Nilsson's dramatic genius, particularly as Marguerite in *Faust:* "we are carried away in defiance of bad phrasing, breathing in awkward places, wilful trifling with the tempo to the destruction of all rhythm, and any other liberty which the impulsive audacity of the singer may suggest. Her acting at the death of Valentine, once witnessed, cannot easily be forgotten; and in the church scene she attains the highest tragic expression." Yet by the last act Shaw felt that the real Madame Nilsson had again replaced the ideal Marguerite.

Shaw's assessment seems very different from that of Klein, but it does offer a perspective both on Nilsson's popularity and perhaps on the relative brevity of her career. She had sung at New York's Academy of Music from 1870. In 1883 she was engaged for the first Metropolitan season; in six months she gave fifty-nine performances. Krehbiel points out that "she was no longer in her prime, neither her voice nor her art having stood the wear of time as well as those of Mme Patti." That the magic was still there is testified by a review of her Gioconda, ostensibly a somewhat improbable role but evidently "a part that enables her to display her strong tragic powers—[she] kept the audience in a state of almost painful excitement by the vivid manner in which she depicted the sufferings of the street singer."

This first Metropolitan season was the final high point of Nilsson's career. She retired after her second marriage in 1887. She may seem an ideal prima donna type, more calculating than truly temperamental. George Upton thought she was "a singular bundle of moods, contrarities and little superstitions, and yet she was a sunshiny, optimistic creature. She would have made an accomplished diplomat." Henry Lahee found "her singing cold, clever and shrewd and she calculated her effects so well that her audience was impressed by the semblance of her being deeply moved." But he also felt her to have been "a dramatic artist of the finest intuitions . . . a refinement, a completeness and an imaginative quality in her acting which was altogether unique."

—Stanley Henig

NINA, ossia La pazza per amore [Nina, or Mad for Love].

Composer: Giovanni Paisiello.

Librettist: G. Carpani (after B.J. Marsollier de Vivetière, with additions by G.B. Lorenzi).

First Performance: Caserta, Royal Palace, 25 June 1789; revised, Naples, Teatro dei Fiorentini, 1790.

Roles: Nina (soprano); Lindoro (tenor); The Count (bass); Susanna (soprano); Giorgio (bass); Shepherd (tenor); chorus (SATB).

Nina, Giovanni Paisiello's *opera semiseria* in two acts, was premiered on 25 June 1789. The libretto was a translation into Italian by Giuseppe Carpani of Benoît Joseph Marsollier de Vivetières's French sentimental domestic comedy, *Nina; ou, La folle par amour,* which had been set by Eugène Dalayrac in 1786. The plot and musical settings of the Nina story are important models for full-fledged "mad scene" operas (e.g., Donizetti's *Lucia di Lammermoor* of 1835) of the early romantic era in which a girl under the domination of powerful male family figures is prohibited from being with her beloved and thus loses her reason. In act I of Paisiello's *Nina,* the title character's nurse, Susanna, tells an assembled group of country folk about Nina's predicament. Nina's father, the count, promised her to Lindoro but then changed his mind in favor of a wealthy nobleman. It is generally believed that Lindoro has been mortally wounded in a duel fought between him and his rival. Nina has gone mad over her love for Lindoro; she raves every time she hears her father's name. Her father regrets his actions and fervently desires Nina's recovery. Whenever he attempts to approach his daughter, she fails to recognize him; much of her time is spent in looking for Lindoro. Susanna advises her to go down to the village, which she does, following a shepherd playing the bagpipes.

With the opening of act II, the count receives the news that Lindoro is not dead, but has recovered from his wounds. The gamekeepers have arrested him for trying to climb the wall into the estate gardens. Lindoro is astonished to be welcomed and embraced as a son by the count, but chagrined to hear of Nina's affliction. She has amnesia and spends much time wandering the countryside dressed in white, fantasizing about the return of Lindoro. When she is brought in to see him, she does not at first recognize him, but as they begin talking and recalling past events she starts to recover her sanity. Eventually Nina realizes that she is with her beloved Lindoro and that her father approves the match. The country folk, who have been following the situation with much interest, rejoice with her.

The Nina story is a prime example of the *larmoyante* aspect of *opéra-comique* of the late eighteenth century. Due to dramatic conventions of the period and because the work is in the comic genre, the opera has a happy ending, but not without some true suffering by the heroine. Paisiello's setting was a huge success and remained popular into the early nineteenth century, showing the public's taste for the sentimental. Especially affecting was Nina's mad scene lament, "Il mio ben quando verrà." Here, and throughout the opera, Paisiello displayed his ability to heighten the drama and psychological situation through musical means. This lament, during which Nina imagines that Lindoro has been restored to her, is a cavatina in free rondo form with agitated syncopated accompaniment, chromatic inner parts, and broken phrases that capture her troubled nature and unfocused thinking. The sound of the shepherd's piping in the background distracts her as if she is hearing voices in her own mind, in addition to providing a bit of local color. The recurring musical themes in Nina's lament and throughout the work are indicative of her own fixation and impaired reason.

—Stephen Willier

NIXON IN CHINA.

Composer: John Adams.

Librettist: Alice Goodman.

First Performance: Houston, Houston Grand Opera, 22 October 1987.

Roles: Chou En-lai (baritone); Richard Nixon (baritone); Henry Kissinger (baritone); Nancy T'ang (mezzo-soprano); Second Secretary to Mao (mezzo-soprano); Third Secretary to Mao (mezzo-soprano); Mao Tse-Tung (tenor); Pat Nixon (soprano); Chiang Ch'ing (soprano); chorus (SATB).

Publications

articles–

"Nixon in China" [Interview with John Adams by Andrew Porter]. *Tempo* December (1988).

*   *   *

Nixon in China begins with the arrival of the presidential plane at the Beijing airport. A chorus of troops sings a revolutionary hymn to the sky as the American jet lands. Premier Chou En-lai greets the Nixons and Henry Kissinger. The action continues with the historic meeting and discussions between Richard Nixon and Chairman Mao. The first act closes with a state banquet in the Great Hall of the People.

In the second act, Patricia Nixon visits various Communist showplaces—a medical clinic, a model pig farm, and finally the Ming Tombs. She sings a long, melancholic aria about life in middle class America. Later, Madame Mao (Chiang Ch'ing) entertains the dignitaries with a performance of her revolutionary ballet entitled "The Red Detachment of Women." The three Americans become mesmerized and are drawn into the atrocities portrayed in the ballet. In the midst of the chaos Madame Mao sings her spectacular aria which displays all the revolutionary charismatic fervor of China's first lady.

Made up of only one scene, act III is the shortest act in the opera. Played out in the individual bedrooms, it is a weary sequence of soliloquies interwoven with a double duet. The couples dance a slow fox-trot. They each reminisce about the past—Nixon about his tour of duty in World War II and Madame Mao about the days spent with the young chairman in the caves at Yenan. At the end of the opera, Chou En-lai, who has seemed a peripheral figure up to now, emerges as

the opera's philosophical hero. Taking up the thread of the soliloquy, he sings the aria which ends the opera.

The opera is uniquely constructed, in that its structural units decrease proportionally throughout the opera. There are three scenes in the first act (sixty minutes), two scenes in the second act (forty-five minutes) and one scene in the third act (thirty minutes). The dramatic plot parallels the diminishing construction. The first act presents a flurry of events depicting the ceremonial and public nature of the celebrated visit; in the second act the women are seen in closer focus; and in the third act, we see the main characters stripped of their public faces. We peer into their private memories, their lack of comprehension and their fatigue. In an interview with Andrew Porter, reported in *Tempo* (December 1988), Adams stated that one of the things which drew him to this vehicle was the "opportunity" to explore the "uncertain, vulnerable human beings" who stand behind the public figures. He described the diminishing structure as a narrowing of focus, until finally, in the third act, we see the characters in their "psychological and emotional undress."

To premiere of *Nixon in China* on 22 October 1987, by the Houston Grand Opera, took place amid a storm of publicity, which is understandable because the subject matter alone is newsworthy, and must be weighed carefully. Critical response was strongly divided. David Patrick Sterns reported for *Gramophone* (October 1988) that "the music was either considered so insubstantial as to be boring or so entrancing as to be unforgettable." Among the opera's strong supporters, John Rockwell, critic for the *New York Times* (6 December 1987), held that the opera was "full of charm and wit, and in the end, beauty." Other voices in favor of the Houston production included Michael Walsh of *Time Magazine* (9 November 1987), who praised the "dramatic qualities" and its "theatricality," and John Ardoin, critic for the *Dallas Morning News* (24 October 1987) who hailed the appropriateness of Peter Sellar's staging and praised its suitability as "that sort of simplicity that brings dramatic necessities down to musical essentials." Two months after its Houston premiere, the production traveled to the Brooklyn Academy of Music's *Next Wave Festival* and shortly afterwards to the Kennedy Center in Washington D.C. The production was also mounted with positive response at the Netherlands Opera in Amsterdam (June 1988) and at the Edinburgh Festival (August 1988).

Despite its foundations in minimalism, *Nixon in China* is dramatically moving rather than simply repetitive. Adams has not abandoned the repetition and arpeggiation of minimalism; he simply relegates them to the orchestral accompaniment, and by doing so makes the vocal lines stand out in dramatic relief. This preservation of minimalistic elements in the orchestral scoring allows a freedom of vocal writing previously unseen in minimalistic opera. Furthermore, Adams has a gift for melody and is able to strike an amiable compromise between soaring melody and the rhythmic demands of inflected speech. This melodic sense, along with Alice Goodman's eloquent libretto, allows Adams to mold his characters into melodic types, as demonstrated by a comparison of the melodic writing for the three main Communist characters: Madame Mao sings in a compositional voice that is fiery, the Chairman requires a more sustained vocal style, while Premier Chou En-lai sings always with a seemingly fluid and chant-like line. Many great moments stand out in the score, among them Nixon's breathless act 1 aria, Chou En-lai's noble lyricism during the State banquet as well as his stunning final aria. The arias of the women also deserve mention. One recording of *Nixon in China* has been made, on the Nonesuch Label, recorded between performances at the Brooklyn Academy of Music in New York City. It features the original cast members and can therefore be considered a good, if not exact, representation of the original performance.

—Patricia Robertson

NONO, Luigi.

Composer. Born 29 January 1924, in Venice. Died 8 May 1990, in Venice. Married: Nuria Schoenberg, daughter of the composer, 1955 (two daughters; divorced). Studied law at the University of Padua, graduated 1946; studied composition with Malipiero at the Benedetto Marcello Conservatory in Venice; studied advanced harmony and counterpoint with Bruno Maderna and Hermann Scherchen; involved in the Italian resistance movement against the Nazis at the end of World War II; electronic music research at the Studio di Fonologia Musicale, 1954-60; teacher, Ferienkurse für Neue Musik, Darmstadt, 1957-; elected to the Central Committee of the Italian Communist Party, 1975; three visits to the Soviet Union, 1963, 1973, and 1976.

Operas

Publishers: Ars Viva, Ricordi, Schott.

Intolleranza 1960 (scenic action), after an idea by A.M. Ripellino (based on texts by Brecht, Eluard, Sartre, and Mayakovsky), Venice, 13 April 1961; revised as *Intolleranza 1970*, new scene after J. Karsunke, Florence, 1974.
Il gran sole carico d'amore (*Au grand soleil d'amour chargé*) (scenic action), Nono, 1972-75, Milan, 4 April 1975; revised, 1977, Milan, 11 February 1978.
Prometeo: Tragedia dell' ascolto, Cacciari, 1981-85, Venice, 25 September 1984.

Other works: works for both acoustic and electronic instruments, tape.

Publications

By NONO: books–

Stenzl, J., ed. *Texte: Studien zu seiner Musik.* Zurich, 1975.

articles–

"Zur Entwicklung der Serientechnik." *Gravesaner Blätter* no. 4 (1956): 14 [includes English translation].
"Die neue Kompositionstechnik." *Gravesaner Blätter* no. 6 (1956): 19 [includes English translation].
"Die Entwicklung der Reihentechnik." *Darmstädter Beiträge zur neuen Musik* no. 1 (1958): 25.
"Diario polacco '58: Bemerkungen eines Komponisten." *Blätter und Bildung* no. 8 (1960): 55.
"Presenza storica nella musica d'oggi." *La rassegna musicale* 30 (1960): 1; reprinted in Degrada, F. ed., *Al gran sole carico d'amore,* 7, Milan, 1975; German translation in *Melos* 27 (1960): 69, and in *Darmstädter Beiträge zur neuen Musik* no. 3 (1960): 41; English translation in *Score* no. 27 (1960), 41; Slovak translation in *Slovenska hubda* 12 (1968): 174.

"Vorwort zum Kranichsteiner Kompositions-Studio." *Darmstädter Beiträge zur neuen Musik* no. 2 (1960): 67.
"Appunti per un teatro musicale attuale." *La rassegna musicale* 31 (1961): 418.
"Alcune precisazioni su 'Intolleranza 1960'." *La rassegna musicale* 32 (1962): 277.
"Possibilità e necessità di un nuovo teatro musicale," *Il verri* no. 9 (1963): 59; reprinted in Degrada, F. ed., *Al gran sole carico d'amore,* 11, Milan, 1975.
"Su 'Fase seconda' di Mario Bortolotto." *Nuova rivista musicale italiana* 3 (1969): 847.
"Ricordo di due musicisti." *Cronache musicali Ricordi* no. 3 (1973): 1.

Note: other writings by Nono can be found in Stenzl, 1975.

About NONO: books–

Degrada, F. *Al gran sole carico d'amore.* Milan, 1975.
Stenzl, J., ed. *Luigi Nono: Texte: Studien zu seiner Musik.* Zurich, 1975.

articles–

Stockhausen, K. "Sprache und Musik." *Dartmstädter Beiträge zur neuen Musik* no. 1 (1958): 65; English translation, *Die Reihe* no. 6 (1964): 40.
Unger, U. "Luigi Nono." *Die Reihe* no. 4 (1958): 9; English translation in *Die Reihe* no. 4 (1960):5.
Pestalozza, L. "Luigi Nono e 'Intolleranza 1960'." *Biennale di Venezia* 11/no. 43 (1961): 18; German translation in Stenzl, 1975, 348.
Smith Brindle, R. "Current Chronicle: Italy" [*Il canto sospeso*]. *Musical Quarterly* 47 (1961): 247.
Weissmann, J.S. "Luigi Nono und sein Werk" *Schweizerische Musikzeitung/Revue musicale suisse* 101 (1961): 358.
D'Amico, F. "La polemica su Luigi Nono." *Paragone* [Milan] 13/no. 156 (1962): 13.
Bartolotto, M. "La mission teatrale di Luigi Nono." *Paragone* [Milan] 13/no. 146 (1962): 25.
Vedova, E. "Interventi" [*Intolleranza 1960*]. *Collage* [Palermo] no. 6 (1966): 93.
Poné, G. "Webern and Luigi Nono: the Genesis of a New Compositional Morphology and Syntax." *Perspectives in New Music* 10 (1972): 111.
Pestalozza, L. "Luigi Nono—Musik, Text, Bedeutung." *Melos* 41 (1974): 265.
Feuer, Mária. "Konvenciók nélkül. Holland Fesztwál '79." *Muzsika* 22/no. 10 (1979): 10.
Stenzl, Jürg. "*Azione Scenica* und Literaturoper. Zu Luigi Nonos Musikdramaturgie." *Musik-Konzepte* 20 (1981): 45.

* * *

Luigi Nono achieved fame and notoriety as much for his compositional techniques as for his political propensities. Like many composers before him, he studied law, the culmination of which was, in his case, a doctoral degree (Padua). Concurrent with his legal preparation, Nono studied musical composition. From 1941-1945, he worked with Gian Francesco Malipiero at the Venice Conservatory; his other principal teachers were Bruno Maderna and Hermann Scherchen. From the latter two in particular, Nono learned the intricacies of twelve-tone and electronic composition, and, indeed, it was this orientation which charted his entire creative career.

Set design by Josef Svoboda for Nono's *Intolleranza*, Teatro la Fenice, Venice, 1961

Nono's first flush of fame emerged with the *Variazioni Canoniche,* a dodecaphonic work based on a tone row employed in Schoenberg's *Ode to Napoleon.* It was premiered August 27, 1950 under Scherchen's direction at the Darmstadt summer music school. Of the chamber and symphonic works which followed, *Polifonica, Monodia, Ritmica* for flute, clarinet, bass clarinet, saxophone, horn, piano, and percussion (1951) and *Due Espressioni* (1953) are representative. The former was introduced by Scherchen, again at Darmstadt, while the latter was presented first by Hans Rosbaud and the Donaueschingen Festival Orchestra for which it was commissioned. William Steinberg and the Pittsburgh Symphony brought *Due Espressioni* to the United States in 1958. The work established Nono as a colorist and sonorist within the serial sphere.

The twelve-tone approach was extended to the ballet in *Der rote Mantel* (1954), based on the poetry of Garcia Lorca, whose work had a lasting effect on the composer. The melodic contours are, as might be expected, free and seemingly unpredictable; they are, however, systematically determined by means of serial techniques. The *Epitaph for Federico Garcia Lorca,* a homage to the poet, is a three-part composition featuring solo voices, chorus, and orchestra. Bruno Maderna conducted part one at Darmstadt (July 21, 1952) and part three via the Northwest German Radio in Hamburg on February 16, 1953; Hans Rosbaud presented part two at Baden-Baden on December 12, 1952. In the first and third parts, the vocal soloists and chorus have speaking parts (in Spanish) and sometimes utter words penned by Lorca and by Pablo

Neruda. The middle part, a concertante for flute and orchestra, reveals an intense emotionality not often encountered in serial works of this type.

Nono's leftist political attitude manifested itself unmistakably in the opera *Intolleranza 1960,* which, when premiered in Venice on April 13, 1961 at the Festival of Contemporary Music, resulted in a riot. Using the opera as a scaffold upon which to build a text which attacked intolerance in general, Nono mounted a musical pulpit to lash out against segregation and Fascism, as well as the atomic bomb. Electronic sounds are introduced within the framework of strict serialism. The composer's membership in the Communist Party in Italy helped to polarize the audience as well as the various pro-Nazi and Fascist demonstrators inside and outside the theater. Interestingly, the American premiere in Boston (1965) resulted in only mild protestation. A State Department reversal of an earlier denial of a visa for the composer resulted in "free" publicity. By now the serial techniques employed (including pointilism) and sequences on magnetic tape no longer had the shock value of earlier forays along these lines.

Nono found himself at the center of another controversy at the first performance of his oratorio *The Representative* (text by Peter Weiss), based on portions of Dante's *Divine Comedy.* The inflammatory text, much more than the Webernian serialism, provoked the audience. The subject matter deals with the trial of Auschwitz guards in Franfurt in 1965. In this sense, the subject, as well as the music, was both topical and contemporary.

Intolleranza 1960 and *The Representative* firmly clarified Nono's chosen mode of expression. In the opera especially it becomes apparent that the vocal/choral component is the conveyor of the central ideas and thus needs to be understood both figuratively and literally. The orchestral writing moves away from the translucence and subtle expressivity associated with Webern's serialism and toward a massed polychromatic and sometimes static series of layers of sound. Expressionism is therefore linked with agitation-propaganda themes as in the musical theater of the 1920s.

Collectivism emerges in the 1975 opus, *Al gran sole carico d'amore* (a celebration of the Paris commune of 1871). Here, Nono collaborated with the scenographer Borovsky and the director Lyubimov (of Moscow's Taganka Theater), and, ultimately, with the choreographer Jakobson and the conductor Abbado (the work was dedicated to Abbado and Pollini). The libretto contains a curious mix of Marxist quotations and words by forgotten workers punctuated by both instrumental and electronic interjections. Unlike *Intolleranza,* this work possesses self-contained scenes. Of particular interest, because of its break with Nono's past utterances, is the inclusion of a classical ballet which symbolizes the domination of the bourgeoisie.

Luigi Nono, along with Maderna, Dallapiccola, and Berio, is a luminous figure in late twentieth-century Italian art music. He has found a language which, while complex and modeled on the formulations of the Second Viennese School, is nevertheless one well-suited to the polemical messages its creator wished to enunciate.

—David Z. Kushner

NORDICA, Lillian [born Lillian Norton].

Soprano. Born 12 December 1857, in Farmington, Maine. Died 10 May 1914, in Batavia, Java. Married: 1) Frederick Gower, 1883 (died); 2) singer Zoltan Dome, 1896 (divorced 1904); 3) George Young, 1909 (divorced). Studied with John O'Neill at New England Conservatory, Boston, and with Sangiovanni in Milan; debut as Donna Elvira at Teatro Manzoni, Milan, 1879; after appearing in St Petersburg she studied in Paris with Giovanni Sbriglia, 1881-82; Paris Opéra debut as Marguerite, 1882; New York debut in same role at Academy of Music, 1883; Covent Garden debut as Violetta, 1887, and appeared there regularly until 1902; Metropolitan Opera debut as Valentine in *Les Huguenots,* 1891, and appeared there until 1902; first American to sing at Bayreuth; last opera appearance as Isolde, Boston, 1913.

Publications

By NORDICA: books–

Armstrong, W, ed. *Lillian Nordica's Hints to Singers.* New York, 1923.

About NORDICA: books–

Glackens, I. *Yankee Diva: Lillian Nordica and the Golden Days of Opera.* New York, 1963.

*　　*　　*

Seldom were our most respected musical critics at the turn of the century so unanimous in their opinions, both at the time of reviewing performances or in later years while reminiscing about the glories of the past: the most revered, almost mythical Lilli Lehmann (1848-1929) had but one possible rival and certainly only one possible successor, Lillian Nordica. W.J. Henderson, writing about the 27 November 1895 Metropolitan performance of *Tristan und Isolde* (the first for Jean de Reske as well as Nordica) said: "Mme. Nordica, by her performance of Isolde, simply amazed those who thought they had measured the full limit of her powers. She has placed herself beside the first dramatic sopranos of her time. Her declamation was broad and forcible. . . . Nothing more beautiful than the close of the 'Sink hernieder' passage in the duo between her and Mr. de Reszke has been heard here, and certainly it has never been better sung anywhere."

After several appearances in Italy and an engagement for the 1880 season to sing in St Petersburg, Nordica went to Paris, where she developed close friendships with both Gounod and Thomas. She made her debut there as Marguerite at the Opéra 22 April 1882 after working on the role with the composer. This was followed by her first Ophélie in Thomas's *Hamlet,* on 25 December, with Jean Lassalle in the title role, and again after study of the work with the composer. She sang for eighteen months at the Opéra, working on her Italian, French and German. She learned one role after another, even if there was no hope of ever singing them, and she was always ready to step in for a fellow artist in case of an emergency. She later learned the part of Valentine in *Les Huguenots* in six days, in order to sing the role in London with the De Reszke brothers (their first time in that city) in a cast that also included Engle, Fabbri, Foli and Maurel. She

Lillian Nordica as Cherubino in *Le nozze di Figaro*

was also heard as Donna Elvira (in *Don Giovanni*) and in *Aida,* in which she stepped on the stage with no rehearsals. While in England she took part in a number of oratorio performances, including a last minute substitution for Albani in Sullivan's *Golden Legend.*

In 1892, Nordica studied the role of Venus in *Tannhäuser* at Bayreuth with Cosima Wagner, who engaged her to sing Elsa in *Lohengrin* at the next festival, an unprecedented honor for an American. Rehearsals took three months, and Lillian devoted her extra time to the perfection of her German, and study of Sieglinde with Cosima "just in case she might need it sometime" (she never did). She became completely absorbed in the Bayreuth tradition, and when she returned to New York was able to persuade Jean de Reszke to learn *Lohengrin* in German. In New York she had the great fortune to work with Anton Seidl, who had been Wagner's assistant for five years, and it was Seidl who suggested that Lillian and Jean undertake *Tristan und Isolde.* Nordica went back to Bayreuth to study Isolde with Cosima. Gustav Kobbe tells us that ". . . from ten in the morning until one in the afternoon, and again from three until five the prima donna studied with Mme. Wagner in a little room, where she was drilled just as if it were a stage."

After her London Isolde, Sebastian Schlesinger wrote: "How Nordica has mastered the German language, of which she knew nothing a little while ago, is wonderful; her enunciation is perfect and she knows 'how to sing' . . . her fatigue of voice is very little. . . . While we have many singers whose high registers call forth our warmest admiration, we have few, and with the exception of Lilli Lehmann I know none, whose mezza voce is as fine as Mme. Nordicas's. . . . [She has had] that vocal instruction which makes the voice *biegsam,* or *bel canto,* and this is required for the ideal Isolde."

In spite of her very successful adoption of the heavier roles in grand opera, Nordica did not forget her early training or lose her ability to revert to some of her old triumphs. On 17 February 1900 she was asked to replace Sembrich in *La traviata* that night. She had sung Brünnhilde in *Götterdämmerung* only two nights before, and had not appeared as Violetta for six years, but she "consented to sing to oblige the management." She spent the entire day at the piano, brushing up her old role, while costumes were hastily arranged. Wrote David Bispham, "the night was a triumph for one of the most beautiful and obliging prima donnas America ever produced." Two days later she sang Valentine in *Les Huguenots.* W.J. Henderson wrote "Lillian Nordica began [with Violetta] and never abandoned it even after she became a Brünnhilde and Isolde. . . ."

As the years progressed, Nordica turned more and more to the concert stage, where her work received the same painstaking preparation she had always shown in her operatic roles. Her German, French and Italian were by this time impeccable, and she was highly praised especially for her Lieder. Her last performance in opera was in Boston as Isolde, on 16 March 1913.

One of the most regrettable failures of the phonograph in the pre-electric days was its inability to capture in a satisfactory manner the voice of Lillian Nordica. Some distant echos can be heard in brief snippets from *Götterdämmerung, Huguenots* (Valentine), *Siegfried, Tristan* and *Walküre* (Brünnhilde) in the transcriptions from the amateur wax cylinders made by Lionel Mapleson during Metropolitan performances in 1902-03. Her only commercial recordings were made by American Columbia in 1906, 1907, 1910, and 1911. Of some 38 recordings known (from sketchy documentation) to have been made, only nine received regular publication; four more have been issued from fortuitously discovered test pressings.

None can be described as really successful: apparently Nordica's voice was just too large or presented other problems for the primitive Columbia recording apparatus. Some idea of the voice can be obtained from the recording of the recitative and aria from the Hungarian opera *Hunyadi Laszlo* by Ferenc Erkel, perhaps because the technicians placed the soprano so far from the recording machine that she sounds as though she were in the next room. Of interest are two test pressings of "Tacea la notte" from *Trovatore* which contain variations and ornamentation said to have been sung by Therese Tietjens (1831-1877), and given to Nordica by Herman Klein who had arranged the experimental recording sessions at which they were made. It seems rather improbable that Nordica ever used these variations in her own performances of Leonora. In another recording made at the same experimental session, the Miserere from *Trovatore,* Nordica has interpolated a long-held high C. which may or may not reflect performance practice.

—William R. Moran

NORMA.

Composer: Vincenzo Bellini.

Librettist: Felice Romani (after Louis Alexandre Soumet).

First Performance: Milan, Teatro alla Scala, 26 December 1831.

Roles: Norma (soprano); Adalgisa (mezzo-soprano or soprano); Pollione (tenor); Oroveso (bass); Flavio (tenor); Clotilde (mezzo-soprano); chorus (SSTTBB).

Publications

books–

Damerini, A. *Vincenzo Bellini, 'Norma': guida attraverso il dramma e la musica.* Milan, 1923.
Andolfi, O. *Norma di Vincenzo Bellini.* Rome, 1928.
Atti del simposio Belliniano celebrato in occasione del 150 anniversario de l'esecuzione di "Norma." Catania, 1981.

articles–

Pannain, G. " 'Norma': Cento anni." In *Ottocento musicale italiano,* 49. Milan, 1936.
Galatopoulos, Stelios. "The Romani-Bellini Partnership." *Opera* November (1972).
Monterosso, R. "Per un' edizione di *Norma.*" In *Scritti in onore di Luigi Ronga,* 415, Milan and Naples, 1973.
Brauner, Charles S. "Textual Problems in Bellini's *Norma* and *Beatrice di Tenda.*" *Journal of the American Musicological Society* 29 (1976): 99.
Avant-scène opéra September-October (1980) [*Norma* issue].

*   *   *

Vincenzo Bellini's *Norma* transcended the Italian operatic tradition of vocal elegance to reaffirm with Monteverdi,

Gluck, and Mozart the supremacy of dramatic representation. By purging bel canto of its affectations while retaining its functional qualities, Bellini imbued *Norma* with trenchant character portrayals and a prodigious emotional intensity without sacrificing melodic beauty or harmonic cordiality. Felice Romani's exceptionally adroit adaptation of Soumet's play (produced in Paris only eight months before the opera's premiere) may well have inspired Bellini to abandon the facile rubric of his early operas. Never before had he confronted so volatile and paradoxical a heroine as Norma. She is the axis and prime agent of a plot incited by human viscousness. Providing her with musical mind and marrow demanded supreme ingenuity of a bel canto composer, but Bellini, like Mozart, both permeated and absorbed his characters. To make Norma musically authentic, he had to transform Italian opera, surpassing even the stylistic advances of Donizetti. Soon French composers followed suit, and Wagner, despite his contempt for Italian opera, praised the intimacy of music and drama achieved by Bellini and savored his vinaceous melodies.

Norma is deeply troubled as the story begins. As high priestess of the Druid temple in Gaul during the Roman occupation (ca. 50 B.C.), she avows chastity, but has born two children by Pollione, the Roman preconsul who has vanquished her people. Assisted by her confidante Clotilde, Norma has managed to conceal her children from all Gaul, even from her father Oroveso, the Archdruid. Pollione, however, has redirected his passions to Adalgisa, a young virgin of the temple for whom Norma shows maternal fondness. The Druids, eager to revolt against the Roman conquerors, consult Norma, who prophesies disaster should they take up

Domenico Donzelli, Giulia Grisi and Giuditta Pasta in Bellini's *Norma*, **1833**

arms. She prays to the goddess Irminsul for peace, a devotion even more personal than collective.

Meeting Pollione secretly in act II, the vulnerable Adalgisa succumbs to his ardor and promises to depart with him for Rome. Without naming her lover, she confides her plans to Norma, who sympathizes knowingly and frees Adalgisa from her vows. A moment later, Pollione enters; Adalgisa addresses him as her lover, Norma addresses him as the father of her children. The mutually astounded women berate Pollione until the temple gong summons Norma to the altar.

In act III, overwrought with shame and obsessed with vengeance, Norma stands over her sleeping children, dagger in hand, but, after some eloquent soul searching, proves herself a kinder mother than Medea. She charges Adalgisa to take the children to their father, who will raise them as Romans. After much remonstration, Adalgisa agrees, hoping that the sight of the children will move Pollione to return to Norma. Softened by the girl's altruism, Norma embraces her rival and the two vow eternal friendship. But Pollione insists on leaving for Rome with Adalgisa. The despairing girl returns in act IV to the temple, and Norma at last calls for war. Pursuing Adalgisa, Pollione is captured and brought before Norma. With magisterial aplomb, the priestess offers to spare his life if he will abandon Adalgisa. When Pollione refuses, Norma threatens to immolate his preferred mistress; she enjoys Pollione's tormented attempts to die in her stead. Then, to Pollione's amazement, Norma turns her moment of retribution into a confession of impiety. Persuading her father to look after the children, she commits herself to death by fire. Loving her in sacrifice more than in sacrilege, Pollione joins her in the flames.

The Romantic excesses of *Norma* accentuate its psychological validity. The agonized priestess compresses and intensifies the pivotal struggles of womanhood. Her lover literally subverts her father and usurps her allegiance. She is biological mother to Pollione's children, vicarious mother to Adalgisa, and spiritual mother to the Druids, but the momentum of vindictiveness makes her maternal burdens almost unbearable, and she nearly adds murder and treason to her offenses before regaining her higher nature. She is both sanctified and profane, conspicuous and clandestine, formidable and benign. She drives those she loves to utmost distress while placating her war-minded people. Her music, best suited for a dramatic soprano, is by turns resounding and mellifluous. It requires unfaltering agility, sustaining power, minute control of dynamics, and a wide spectrum of vocal colors. Remarkably few sopranos have attempted the role, and fewer still have proved equal to its technical and interpretive demands.

Although *Norma* hardly typifies its genre, Bellini preserved the formalities of *opera seria*. For the most part, he clearly distinguishes arias and ensemble from recitatives, cavatinas from cabalettas, and ariosos from all else. The opera begins with a formal overture, and punctuates the end of each number with conclusive harmonies. Arpeggiated and repeated chords abound in the accompaniment, except during recitatives where Bellini braces the vocal lines with discrete chords, or vivifies them with a vocabulary of rhetorical figures that the young Verdi learned well. The chorus has much to sing, and the orchestra much to play on its own with all its thematic introductions and postludes. Nor does Bellini renounce melodic appeal for dramatic expression; Norma's prayer in act I sets linear beauty and poignant emotion in perfect balance.

In style and substance, *Norma* pointed the way for Verdi. Romani's libretto integrates lyricism and plot, making the visually static arias and ensembles essential to the drama. Everywhere Bellini's music reinforces the thrust of Romani's verse, charting the interplay of characters and confiding their secret musings and inducements. Even the recitatives impart poetic nuances and implicit meanings, as Norma's filicidal monologue affectingly demonstrates. The harmonic current, spurred by accented dissonances, diverted by altered chords, and delayed by circuits and reversals, frequently brings the emotional intensity to a fervid glow. More prospector than reformer, Bellini amplified the language of bel canto to sound the churning of affinities and disengagements. He heard the inner music of opera's most forbearing woman, and enriched the singer's art with her prophetic voice.

—James Allen Feldman

NORMAN, Jessye.

Soprano. Born 15 September 1945, in Augusta, Georgia. Studied with Carolyn Grant at Howard University, Washington, DC, with Alice Duschak at Peabody Conservatory and with Pierre Bernac and Elizabeth Mannion at the University of Michigan; debut as Elisabeth in *Tannhäuser,* Deutsche Oper, Berlin, 1969; appeared in Florence as Selika in *L'africaine,* Maggio Musicale, 1971; Teatro alla Scala debut as Aida, 1972; Covent Garden debut as Cassandre in *Les Troyens,* 1972; U.S. stage debut with Opera Company of Philadelphia as Jocasta in *Oedipus Rex* and Purcell's Dido; Metropolitan Opera debut as Cassandre, 1983.

*   *   *

Born into a musical family in Augusta, Georgia, Jessye Norman learned the piano at an early age and first remembers singing in public at age six when she performed "Jesus is Calling" in the key of C. In 1961 she went to study singing with Carolyn Grant at Howard University in Washington, DC. Grant did not attempt to put her voice into a specific category but let her explore a wide range of music. Study with Alice Duschak at Peabody and Pierre Bernac at the University of Michigan followed. As might be expected, Norman has an affinity for songs of all kinds, from the German Lieder of Schubert, Brahms, Mahler, and Schoenberg, to French *mélodies,* Russian songs, spirituals, and the songs of Jerome Kern. Miss Norman performs spirituals, usually at the close of a recital, to "bring music to people who have no interest in classical music on a grand scale but who can approach folk music." With spirituals and the music of composers such as Kern she feels a "Lied-like unity of poem and melody." Norman has recorded copious examples of this wide range of song literature, reflecting her extensive activity in the recital hall.

As an opera singer Norman has had to find her way gradually. Her sumptuous voice, one of the richest and most expressive of recent decades, is in range and timbre a cross between a soprano and a mezzo-soprano and is shown to advantage only in certain repertory. Her operatic debut was as Elisabeth in *Tannhäuser* at the Deutsche Oper, Berlin, in 1969. The three years Norman spent at that house, singing Aida, the Countess, Elsa, and many other roles, brought her only partial success for she did not want to sing standard soprano repertory and was still finding her way. Of the major Verdi soprano roles, for example, Aïda is the only one she cares for:

"I've turned down all the Leonoras." She has since sung, at least on disc, a few of the early Verdi heroines, appearing as Medora on the Philips *Il corsaro* set with Caballé and Carreras and on Philips's *Un giorno di regno.* From 1975 to 1980 Norman turned down all opera engagements and gave only Lieder recitals and orchestra concerts. Her statuesque appearance has also been a factor in selecting appropriate roles and it is perhaps significant that her first appearance after her operatic hiatus was in that most static of roles, Strauss's Ariadne. Harold Rosenthal, writing in *Opera* of Norman's Ariadne, which she has subsequently recorded, called her "a prima donna to her fingertips. 'Es gibt ein Reich' was gloriously projected. . . ."

Two standard roles that Norman performed in her Berlin years have been recorded commercially. Her Elsa in *Lohengrin* may be heard on Decca with Domingo in the title role, conducted by Solti. In the recording of her Countess in Mozart's *Le nozze di Figaro,* Norman's spacious voice (she says her voice "can only go *so* quickly" and "needs space in which to resound") conveys dignity, yet Norman's characterization displays the Countess's sense of humor, never letting the listener forget that she is Rosina who was not born with a title. Much more recently Norman has recorded roles in Offenbach's *Les contes d'Hoffmann, Fidelio,* and *Carmen,* operas that she has not performed on stage. She has always kept a long list of roles to be considered, rejecting many but working gradually up to others. One direction she moved towards was to sing more Wagner and Strauss, with Isolde as her ultimate goal. To that end she has sung the three acts of *Tristan und Isolde* on separate nights in concert. Isolde is a part that she is afraid of "using up every ounce of [my] energy in the first act alone." Sieglinde is a character she has been identified with, in a recording of *Die Walküre* from Dresden under Janowski and in the Metropolitan Opera telecast in the summer of 1990. Her Sieglinde has much of the femininity and passion of Lotte Lehmann with more sumptuousness of voice.

In the 1972-73 season at Covent Garden, Norman performed in Berlioz' *Les Troyens* and made her Metropolitan Opera debut as Cassandre in 1983. At the Met she has also sung, in addition to Sieglinde, Didon in *Les Troyens,* Jocasta, Ariadne, Elisabeth, and Mme. Lidoine in Poulenc's *Les dialogues des Carmélites.* Poulenc seems to be a favorite; in addition to his songs Miss Norman has also appeared in *La voix humaine.* In addition to early Verdi works, rarities or unusual repertoire that Norman has sung or recorded include Selika in Meyerbeer's *L'africaine* conducted by Muti at the 1971 Florence May festival, of which a pirate recording exists; a recording of Mozart's *La finta giardiniera;* Faure's *Pénélope* on disc; and, from the late 1970s recordings of seldom-performed operas by Haydn. These include *La vera costanza* (1977) under Dorati with Norman as a dashing Rosina and *Armida* (1979) with Norman in the title role in magnificent voice, ranging in mood from terrifying vengeance to heartfelt pleas. In the French repertoire there is a stunning recorded account of Gluck's French *Alceste* with Gedda in which Norman sings poignantly and, from the Baroque, she has sung Rameau's *Hippolyte et Aricie* at Aix-en-Provence. As a result of her upbringing Norman has an affinity with music of a spiritual nature: she has sung *Messiah,* some Haydn oratorios, and Mahler's Second and Eighth symphonies. She has recorded an affecting *Gurrelieder* of Schoenberg and has performed Shostakovich's Symphony No. 14 with Giulini and the Los Angeles Philharmonic.

Jessye Norman will no doubt continue to explore the possibilities of her unique voice, discarding or rejecting certain roles while at the same time rising to new challenges.

—Stephen A. Willier

THE NOSE [Nos].

Composer: Dmitri Shostakovich.

Librettists: E. Zamyatin, G. Yonin, and A. Preis (after Gogol).

First Performance: Leningrad, 18 January 1930.

Roles: Platon Kusmich Kovalev (baritone); Ivan Yakovlevich (bass-baritone); Police Commissioner (tenor); Ivan (tenor); Nose as Councilor of State (tenor); Praskovia Ossipovna (soprano); Alexandra Grigorievna Podtotchina (mezzo-soprano); Her Daughter (soprano); Advertising Editor (bass-baritone); Doctor (bass-baritone); Yarizhkin (tenor); several bit roles and speaking parts; chorus (SATB).

Publications

articles–

Norris, Geoffrey. "Shostakovich's *The Nose*." *Musical Times* 120 (1979): 393.
Fay, L.E. "The Punch in Shostakovich's *Nose*." In *Russian and Soviet Music: Essays for Boris Schwarz*, edited by Malcolm H. Brown, 229. Ann Arbor, 1984.

* * *

Taken at face value, *The Nose* is pure grotesque fantasy, a play of masks in comparison with the human engagement of Shostakovich's later opera, *The Lady Macbeth of Mtsensk District*. For while the latter presents a credible human being caught up in the tragic consequences of a fatal passion, *The Nose* is a surrealist satire presenting a petty official in the time of Nicolas I, whose sole concern is with rank and success with the ladies. While Katerina stands out as a flawed but fully human figure amongst a gallery of ordinary, more or less evil and ignoble characters in *Lady Macbeth*, *The Nose* presents a tragi-comic episode in the life of one of many ordinary little people who throng the stage. (In this sense, perhaps, *The Nose* is a more sharply social and politicized opera than *Lady Macbeth*.)

There is no equivalent in *The Nose* of the "direct" use of a lyrical idiom that is in harmony with human feelings with which the audience can identify. Where a contemplative lyrical idiom *does* exist—and there are plenty of passages in *The Nose* in which the music is beautiful, serious, or lyrically grave in expression (for example the scene in Kazan Cathedral)—it contradicts a situation that is to be perceived as farcical or grotesquely improbable. How can we possibly identify with a person who has lost his nose, thereby taking on a superior social identity? This is the same technique as the indirect use of falsely gay music in *Lady Macbeth*, and it is what Shostakovich meant when he wrote that the music of *The Nose* does not wisecrack, but takes the story perfectly seriously, as Gogol did.

Reinforcing this "clash of the planes of perception" (Meyerhold) is a contrapuntal sub-text using the machine rhythms and figurational clichés of baroque counterpoint in a "busy" style that is rendered abnormal by such things as angular leaps, fragmentation, extreme registral displacement, and multi-voiced textures which lie beyond the aural perception of linearity. Fugue and canon (or at other times the interplay of independent lines) establish a kind of lunatic logic of continuity, counterpointing the fantastic events on stage with a poker-faced commentary of its own, hurrying the movement on at a hectic pace. (Such a style spilled over into Shostakovich's symphonies of the period: both the Second and Fourth Symphonies contain parallel passages.) As in *Wozzeck* (which was much admired by the Leningrad avant-garde after its premiere there in 1927), contrapuntal forms in the orchestra provide their own objective structural support to the nightmare events on stage and, in the interludes, develop their own rhetorical style of address—whether extravagant, farcical, or totally indifferent.

Like much of *Lady Macbeth*, *The Nose* is a speech intonation opera which sets the text in an exact reproduction of speech rhythms and inflections. The music could not exist without the text, and the contemplative vocal aria is rigorously excluded. What songs there are (for example, the policemen's long note unison ditty to keep up their courage in act III, scene vii or Ivan's balalaika aria at the beginning of act II) are intentionally comic in effect, creating an out-of-context tonal lyricism that clashes with the serious business of Kovalev's pursuit of his nose. Again (as in *Lady Macbeth*) there is no system of *leitmotifs*, only a number of small motivic ideas that recur in a local (as distinct from global) context. Such is the tiny drooping fourth motif of the nose which Kovalev vainly tries to stick on before the mirror. It becomes obsessive, raising the trivial to a level of musical importance that is ludicrously farcical as Kovalev continues to seek a remedy for the restoration of his symbolic organ. (This use of a microscopic *idée fixe*, totally at variance with the grand gestures of Romanticism, is characteristic both of the Ten Aphorisms for Piano Op. 13 [1927] and of the motivic technique of *Lady Macbeth*, where the smallest gestural ideas take on musical significance.)

The theoretical ideas that inform this new conception of opera—its total lack of romantic subjectivity, its organic dependence on a text, the "truthfulness" of its exact reproduction of human speech—recall the ideas that had informed Dargomyzhsky's unfinished opera *The Stone Guest* (1866-1869), which for Stasov and the "Kuchka" became the epitomy of truth to life and the human spirit. (Stasov had actually hailed *The Stone Guest* as the "music of the future" in contradiction to Wagner's "accepted conventions, sham and clap-trap of the theatre.") This is a reminder of the traditional Russianness of Shostakovich's artistic conscience, seemingly paradoxical in an avant-garde Soviet opera. The brilliant Marxist-Leninist critic I.I. Sollertinsky hailed *The Nose* as "orudie dal'noboynoe" ("a long range gun") in the development of Soviet opera, but the advent of Stalin and the doctrine of Socialist Realism brought about its disappearance (together with the later ill-fated *Lady Macbeth*) until it was successfully rehabilitated in a Moscow revival (1974) at the end of the composer's life.

—Eric Roseberry

NOURRIT, Adolphe.

Tenor. Born 3 March 1802, in Montpellier, France. Died 8 March 1839, in Naples. Despite discouragement from father, tenor Louis Nourrit, he studied with the elder Manuel Garcia; debut as Pylade in *Iphigénie en Tauride,* Paris Opéra, 1821; principal tenor at Paris Opéra, 1826-37; appointed professeur de déclamation lyrique at Paris Conservatoire, 1827; traveled to Italy when Duprez came to Paris in 1837; Naples debut in Mercadante's *Il giuramento,* 1838; created Neocle in *Siège de Corinthe* (1826), Arnold in *Guillaume Tell* (1829); title role in *Robert le Diable* (1831); Raoul in *Les Huguenots* (1836), among others.

Publications

About NOURRIT: books–

Quicherat, M. *Adolphe Nourrit: Sa vie.* Paris, 1867.
Boutet de Morvel, E. *Un Artiste d'autrefois, Adolphe Nourrit.* Paris, 1903.

articles–

Rogers, F. "Adolphe Nourrit." *Musical Quarterly* January (1939).

*　　*　　*

It was Adolphe Nourrit's good fortune to succeed his father as leading tenor at the Paris Opéra during an era that featured Rossini and Meyerbeer as principal composers; it was his contribution to inspire these composers and others to treat the operatic tenor as a viable tragic hero, fully equal for the first time to his colleagues in both dramatic and vocal stature. Nourrit's convincing dramatic manner and exemplary declamation of recitative was inspired by the great stage tragedian François Talma. Not especially favored by nature to cut a fine figure on the stage, being short and inclined to stoutness, Nourrit seems to have taken much more care than was customary at the time with his costumes and with thorough research and preparation of each role so that every gesture, like every note, would contribute to his characterization. He had a gift for stage movement and, in tragedy, a commanding dramatic presence. The extraordinary succession of roles that he created reveals a great deal about his dramatic art as well as his vocal attributes: Neocles—*Le siège du Corinth,* Rossini (October, 1826); Amenophis—*Moïse,* Rossini (March, 1827); Masaniello—*La muette de Portici,* Auber (Feb., 1828); Count Ory—*Le Comte Ory,* Rossini (August, 1828); Arnold—*Guillaume Tell,* Rossini (August, 1829); Robert—*Robert le Diable,* Meyerbeer (November, 1831); Eléazar—*La juive,* Halévy (February, 1835); Raoul—*Les Huguenots,* Meyerbeer (February, 1836).

Despite his vocal training in the Italian method with the renowned tenor Manuel Garcia, Nourrit's vocal strengths were not those of Italian singers—virtuoso agility, mastery of embellishment, and purity of line. Rather, he employed sung words as he did gestures—to plumb the depths of character. His true art lay in the subtle vocal nuances of color, dynamics, and inflection. Not for Nourrit were the stunning high notes taken in chest voice that so distinguished his rival Duprez. Indeed, his roles would not be so difficult that the operas are seldom given if modern tenors had the training and temperament to use as he did the voix-mixte (a blending of chest and head registers) and the voix de tête (the head

Adolphe Nourrit

register). Perhaps the most revealing critical opinion (by Edouard Thierry) refers to Nourrit's ability to phrase like a violoncello and to sound like the viola or the oboe and English horn—precisely the effect heard (in a lower register) in recordings by such later French singers as Pol Plançon.

Nourrit was an unusually well-educated and cultured man. In 1828, despite his youth, he was appointed professor of lyric declamation at the Paris Conservatory. Among his friends were Mendelssohn, Liszt, and Chopin (the last of whom played the organ at his funeral service in Marseilles); among his musical interests were the songs of Schubert, some of which he introduced in France by singing them in his own French versifications. Also noteworthy are the several scenarios he wrote for ballets danced by Taglioni and Fanny Elssler. The singer's social conscience is evidenced by his whole-hearted support of the revolution of 1830, when he went about to the various theaters singing patriotic songs. His professional advice was solicited and respected by composers: the words for Halévy's great aria "Rachel, quand du Seigneur" (*La juive*) are his, as was the suggestion for a grand love duet as the climax of act IV of Meyerbeer's *Les Huguenots.* Nevertheless, despite enthusiastic audiences, critical acclaim, and supportive friends, Nourrit fell victim at the very zenith of his career to his own sensitive temperament and what must have been an unusual degree of insecurity.

In 1838, following a highly successful singing tour of Belgium and France, Nourrit set off on a self-imposed odyssey to Italy and an ill-fated attempt to Italianize his singing. The event was precipitated by the hiring in 1837 of tenor Gilbert-Louis Duprez, ostensibly to lighten the burden on Nourrit, who had reigned without a rival (and without missing a scheduled performance) for fifteen years. Although Nourrit agreed with the decision in principle, the director's insistence upon assigning lead tenor roles by lot forced the singer's resignation. Not even the offer to draw up his own contract at the Opéra Comique in Paris could dissuade him from what had now become his quest. In Italy he was coached by Donizetti, but their hopes for a triumph in *Poliuto* were dashed by the Neapolitan censor. Under the stress of learning a new repertory, of harsh treatment by the impresario Barbaia, and of increasing vocal troubles, Nourrit's mental state deteriorated rapidly. In his own words (as expressed in a letter translated in a *Musical Quarterly* article of Jan., 1939 by Francis Rogers), Nourrit realized that "in gaining certain qualities—or, at least, in developing them somewhat—I had lost other essential ones. I continued to hope that with time I could regain the subtleties that characterized my talent and the variety of inflections that I had to give up in conforming to Italian standards. . . . My former voice was no longer there; both my mixed voice and my head voice had disappeared." Although well-received in Italy, Nourrit had lost his unique command of vocal nuance. On March 8, 1839, after singing at a benefit concert in Naples, he took his life by jumping from his apartment window.

—David Poultney

NOVOTNÁ, Jarmila.

Soprano. Born 23 September 1907, in Prague. Married: Baron George Daubek, 1929. Studied with Emma Destinn, Hilbert Vávra. Major debut as Mařenka in *The Bartered Bride,* Prague, 1925; at National Theater in Prague 1925-26; Italian debut in *Rigoletto* at the Arena di Verona, 1927; at the Berlin State Opera, 1928; Vienna State Opera 1933-38; created title role of Lehár's *Giuditta,* Vienna, 1934; American debut in *Madama Butterfly,* San Francisco, 1939; Metropolitan Opera debut as Mimì in *La bohème,* 1940; with Metropolitan Opera, 1940-56, roles including Orlofsky, Cherubino, Elvira, Pamina, Octavian, Violetta, Freia, and Mélisande; performed frequently at the Salzburg Festival. Also a film actress; appeared on Broadway in Korngold's adaptation of *La belle Hélène.*

Publications

About NOVOTNÁ: articles–

"Reflected Glory." *Opera News* 48/October (1983): 72.
Freeman, John W. "The Good Life." *Opera News* 54/ December (1989): 8.

*   *   *

Born in Prague on 23 September 1907, Jarmila Novotná took an early interest in music. When the conservatory turned her away as too young, she took some lessons from Emma Destinn, whom her parents knew, and then studied with the baritone Hilbert Vávra, whom Destinn recommended. As a member of the gymnastic organization Sokol, she received a background in lifelong physical fitness and a chance to do some choral singing. At seventeen, after about two years' study with Vávra, she joined her teacher in stage performances of *Il barbiere di Siviglia* and *La traviata* in a provincial theater at Louny, northwest of Prague. Vávra then arranged

an audition with Otakar Ostrčil, chief conductor at the National Theater in Prague, where she was engaged for a *Bartered Bride* and a *Traviata* at the end of the 1924-25 season. She sang as guest with the company until January 1926, when she was taken on the roster, but a year later, feeling the need for further study, she left for Milan, where she found not only a teacher but an engagement for *Rigoletto* at the Arena di Verona for the summer of 1927.

Throughout her career, Novotná enjoyed good connections and an active social life, but while these helped her advancement (as did her phenomenal physical beauty), they did nothing to lessen her seriousness as an artist. Thomas Masaryk, the Czechoslovak president, took an interest in her singing, as did his son Jan, who often accompanied her at the piano. (Together they recorded a set of folk songs). She was engaged for a number of films but refused to consider giving up the opera stage for a career as film actress. Instead she worked at the Vienna State Opera (1928), Otto Klemperer's Kroll Oper and in several operettas staged by Max Reinhardt in Berlin. After her marriage in 1929 and the birth of her children, she looked for a more settled life, joining the Vienna State Opera's permanent roster in 1933. There she appeared often in numerous roles for five years, under such eminent conductors as Weingartner and Krips, and in 1934 she created the title role of Lehár's *Giuditta* there. For a more international audience she sang at the Salzburg Festival in Mozart roles—in *Così fan tutte* and *Le nozze di Figaro* with Weingartner and Bruno Walter, *Die Zauberflöte* with Toscanini.

Not wishing to sing in Nazi Germany or "annexed" Austria, Novotná welcomed an invitation from Toscanini to come to the New York World's Fair for *La traviata* and *Falstaff,* but those productions were called off after her arrival in March 1939. Toscanini helped her get an engagement with the Metropolitan Opera for the following season, but first she had to return to Europe to retrieve her family, who left with her hurriedly, bringing little with them. There followed a series of opera performances on short notice in San Francisco and St Louis before her Metropolitan Opera debut in *La bohème* on 5 January 1940, with Jussi Björling. With the exception of the 1951-52 season, she remained with the company for a fifteen-year period, making her final appearance as Orlofsky in *Die Fledermaus* on 15 January 1956. This was her most frequent role with the company, closely followed by Cherubino and Octavian; her other roles were Elvira, Pamina, Violetta, Antonia, Mařenka, Euridice, Freia, Massenet's Manon and Giulietta, altogether 193 performances—142 in the house, 51 on tour. She resumed appearances in Europe from 1949 through 1957 and settled in Vienna until the death of her husband, Baron George Daubek, in 1981, after which she moved back to New York. She never took up teaching.

Novotná's films give the best impression of her personal charm, in which she is comparable to such colleagues as Lucrezia Bori and Bidù Sayão, but her records, while not numerous, capture the warmth, flexibility and considerable strength of her voice, which combined the sweetness and smoothness of a lyric coloratura with the expressive range of a spinto soprano. There is a quality of soul in the pliancy and occasional urgency of her singing. In the Salzburg *Zauberflöte,* for example, which survives from a 1937 Selenophon recording, Toscanini coaxed from her a sense of the anxiety and despair of Pamina's plight, and her *Traviata* at the Met (unfortunately not recorded) carried rare elegance together with a gently tragic accent suggestive of Greta Garbo's *Camille.* It was her ladylike quality, as well as her secure musicianship and captivating stage appearance, that ranked Novotná alongside such artists as Tiana Lemnitz, Maria

Cebotari and Sena Jurinac as models of the Middle European lyric/dramatic soprano.

—John W. Freeman

LE NOZZE DI FIGARO [The Marriage of Figaro].

Composer: Wolfgang Amadeus Mozart.

Librettist: Lorenzo Da Ponte (after Beaumarchais).

First Performance: Vienna, Burgtheater, 1 May 1786.

Roles: Figaro (baritone); Count Almaviva (baritone); Countess (soprano); Susanna (soprano); Cherubino (soprano or mezzo-soprano); Marcellina (soprano or mezzo-soprano); Dr Bartolo (bass); Don Basilio (tenor); Don Curzio (tenor); Antonio (bass); Barbarina (soprano); chorus (SATB).

Publications

books–

Levarie, S. Mozart's "Le nozze di Figaro": a Critical Analysis. Chicago, 1952; 1977.
Hocquard, Jean-Victor. Le nozze di Figaro. Paris, 1979.
Mila, Massimo. Lettura della "Nozze di Figaro." Mozart e la ricerca di felicità. Turin, 1979.
Rickmann, Sonja P. Mozart: Ein bürgerlicher Künstler: Studien zu den Libretti "Le Nozze di Figaro," "Don Giovanni," und "Così fan tutte". Vienna, 1982.
Allenbrook, Wye J. Rhythmic Gesture in Mozart: "Le nozze di Figaro" and "Don Giovanni". Chicago, 1983.
Carter, Tim. W.A. Mozart: Le nozze di Figaro. Cambridge Opera Guides. Cambridge, 1987.
Steptoe, Andrew. The Mozart-Da Ponte Operas: The Cultural and Musical Background to "Le Nozze di Figaro," "Don Giovanni," and "Così fan tutte". Oxford, 1989.

articles–

Blom, E. "The Literary Ancestry of Figaro." Musical Quarterly 13 (1927): 528.
Köhler, K.-H. "Figaro-Miscellen: Einige dramaturgische Mitteilungen zur Quellensituation." Mozart-Jahrbuch (1961-63).
Moberly, Robert B. and C. Raeburn. "Mozart's 'Figaro': the Plan of Act III." Music and Letters 46 (1965): 134; reprinted in Mozart-Jahrbuch (1965-66): 161.
Köhler, K.-H. "Mozarts Kompositionsweise: Beobachtungen am Figaro-Autograph." Mozart-Jahrbuch (1967): 31.
Noske, F.R. "Musical Quotations as a Dramatic Device: the Fourth Act of Le nozze di Figaro." Musical Quarterly 54 (1968): 185.
————. "Social Tensions in 'Le nozze di Figaro'." Music and Letters 1 (1969): 45.
Brophy, Brigid. " 'Figaro' and the Limitations of Music." Music and Letters 51 (1970): 26.
Scheel, H.L. " 'Le mariage de Figaro' von Beaumarchais und das Libretto der 'Nozze di Figaro' von Lorenzo da Ponte." Die Musikforschung 28 (1975): 156.
Osthoff, Wolfgang. "Gli endecasillabi Villostistici in Don Giovanni e Nozze di Figaro." In Venezia e il melodramma nel settecento, edited by Maria Teresa Muraro, vol. 2, p. 293. Florence, 1981.
Allenbrook, Wye J. "Pro Marcellina: The Shape of 'Figaro' Act IV." Music and Letters 63 (1982): 69.
Bernich, Joan. "The marriage of Figaro: Genesis of a Dramatic Masterpiece." Opera Quarterly 1 (1983): 87.

* * *

Le nozze di Figaro was Mozart's second opera for Vienna, and his first major collaboration with the librettist Lorenzo Da Ponte (1749-1838). The composer had found it hard to establish himself in the imperial city since his arrival in 1781; not surprisingly, he took some time to settle on the subject for his first Italian opera buffa for the sophisticated Viennese. After two false starts, he chose a controversial French play by Pierre-Augustin Caron de Beaumarchais (1732-99), La folle journée ou Le mariage de Figaro (1784). This, the second of a trilogy about the Spanish barber Figaro, had recently created a scandal across Europe for its political content: the notion of a count getting his come-uppance for his wicked designs on Susanna, the fiancée of his servant, Figaro, at the hands of his wife, the countess, and of his social inferiors was clearly inflammatory. Louis XIV called the play "detestable," while Napoleon claimed it "the revolution in action."

But social satire apart, the play is also a sparkling comedy of manners: the harridan Marcellina and the pedantic lawyer Dr Bartolo—who are both enlisted to help the count, but who turn against him on the discovery that they are Figaro's parents— plus the fawning music-master, Don Basilio, and the love-sick adolescent, Cherubino, are splendid characters. All this, and its succès de scandale, surely made the play attractive for Mozart. It also enabled him to rival Paisiello, whose Il barbiere di Siviglia (St Petersburg, 1782), based on Beaumarchais' first Figaro play, had been an outstanding success when performed in Vienna in 1783.

Lorenzo Da Ponte was a good librettist who knew what worked on a stage. He could also write polished verse well suited to music. The account in his Memoirs of working with Mozart on Le nozze di Figaro, hoodwinking Emperor Joseph II into accepting the project, and engineering that the act III finale should not be cut despite a recent ban on dances within operas, should be read with caution. But Da Ponte and Mozart were certainly at work by mid 1785, and on 11 November Leopold Mozart reported that his son was up to his eyes in the score: "I know the piece: it is a very tiresome play and the translation from the French will certainly have to be altered very freely if it is to be effective as an opera. God grant that the text may be a success. I have no doubt about the music. But there will be a lot of running about and discussions before he gets the libretto so adjusted as to suit his purposes exactly."

Da Ponte had to tone down the more obviously seditious passages of the play, and also focus and simplify the dialogue to accommodate the slower speed of sung rather than spoken delivery. But he did not alter the play as much as one might expect (or as much as the emperor was led to believe); it was too tautly structured to be cut extensively, and much of the libretto simply translates Beaumarchais word for word. Indeed, most of the comic masterstrokes in the opera are thanks to the playwright. And even though the play was reduced from five acts to four, Da Ponte still had to apologize for its length in his preface to the libretto.

In deciding which sections of the play would be treated as arias and ensembles, the librettist and composer sometimes

Le nozze di Figaro: **extract from Mozart's autograph score, showing beginning of Cherubino's aria in act II, "Voi che sapete"**

took their cue from musical references in the play: for example, Chérubin's *romance* "Mon coursier hors d'haleine" sung to the countess in act II of Beaumarchais' play was transformed into Cherubino's "Voi che sapete." Elsewhere Beaumarchais' episodic organization allowed the choice of sections suitable for extended musical treatment by virtue of their pace, their importance to the overall intrigue, and their possibilities for comic characterization: good examples are provided by the act I trio "Cosa sento! tosto andate" (from act I, scene ix in the play) and by the act II finale. Finally, arias had to be provided for the main members of the cast, if only to meet the demands of the singers, each of whom required at least one show-piece.

These arias also raise further issues. Although some (e.g., Cherubino's "Non so più cosa son, cosa faccio" and Figaro's "Non più andrai farfallone amoroso") translate parallel speeches in the play, elsewhere Da Ponte was forced to halt the action to provide an aria and thus to develop his characters more extensively. Beaumarchais generally maintains a fast pace in the play, reveling more in comic action and witty repartee than in emotional introspection. But Figaro's "Se vuol ballare," the count's "Vedrò mentre io sospiro," Susanna's "Deh vieni, non tardar, o gioia bella," and the countess' "Porgi amor, qualche ristoro" and "Dove sono i bei momenti," take the opera into a different world: the carefully calculated transformation of the countess, whose renewed self-understanding becomes the focal point of the action, is particularly striking. And if the libretto had to delve more deeply into the characters than Beaumarchais might have

wished, Mozart's music delves deeper still. For everyone in the opera, what starts out as a rather innocent game becomes (by the middle of act II) an intense, almost frightening, and ultimately revelatory experience.

Mozart renders his characters far more human than their derivation from *commedia dell'arte* stereotypes would suggest. He also found ways of restoring the political elements cut from the libretto: the music for Figaro and Susanna goes beyond what *opera buffa* conventions decreed suitable for the lower classes, and dance patterns, in particular the courtly minuet, allow the servants to challenge their masters in subtle ways. Finally, Mozart develops a musical style that fully meets the demands of comedy. This is especially apparent in the glorious ensembles. Two structural procedures that Mozart was currently developing in his instrumental works come to fruition here: contrapuntal techniques that enable characters to present different points of view simultaneously, and sonata-form organization exploiting the ability of tonality to establish and resolve musical conflicts that mirror the conflicts and resolutions of the action. The best example is the act III sextet, "Riconosci in questo amplesso"—reportedly Mozart's favorite piece in the opera—where the drama of Figaro recovering his long-lost parents is matched perfectly by Mozart's music. Similarly, the magnificent act II finale elaborates a well-founded musical structure of unprecedented length to support the ebb and flow of the action. Perhaps for the first time, Mozart has fully realized the potential of the Classical style. The result is a comic masterpiece.

Although the premiere of *Figaro* was planned for early 1786, it was delayed until 1 May. The performance was not outstanding: it is a difficult score, and anti-Mozart factions in the audience sought to sabotage the event. But it was by no means a disaster: according to Michael Kelly, "At the end of the opera, I thought the audience would never have done applauding and calling for Mozart: almost every piece was encored, which prolonged it nearly to the length of two operas. . . . Never was any thing more complete, than the triumph of Mozart, and his 'Nozze di Figaro,' to which numerous overflowing audiences bore witness." The opera was even more successful in Prague, from where Mozart wrote excitedly on 15 January 1787, "here they talk about nothing but 'Figaro.' Nothing is played, sung or whistled but 'Figaro.' No opera is drawing like 'Figaro.' Nothing, nothing but 'Figaro'." It was revived for Vienna in 1789, when Mozart wrote two substitute arias for Susanna (K 577, 579) and made other adjustments to suit his new cast.

—Tim Carter

O

OBERON.

Composer: Carl Maria von Weber.

Librettist: J.R. Planché (after C.M. Wieland).

First Performance: London, Covent Garden, 12 April 1826.

Roles: Oberon (tenor); Puck (contralto); Reiza (soprano); Fatima (mezzo-soprano); Huon of Bordeaux (tenor); Sherasmin (baritone); Droll (contralto); First and Second Mermaids (sopranos); Speaking Roles: Titania; Haroun al Rashid; Babekan; Mesru; Almansor; Roschana; Nadine; Abdulla; First and Second Gardeners; Charlemagne; chorus (SATB).

Publications

"Oberon, or The Elf King's Oath." *Quarterly Musical Magazine and Review* 8 (1826): 84.
Warrack, John. "*Oberon* und der englische Geschmack." In *Musikbühne 76,* edited by H. Seeger. Berlin, 1976.
Avant-scène opéra April (1985) [*Oberon* issue].

* * *

Set in the thirteenth century and in places as different as Shakespeare's fairyland and Baghdad, *Oberon,* Weber's last opera, was designed for a London production with a libretto in English. But the story is taken mostly from an old French *chanson de geste* called *Huon of Bordeaux.* Unlike that of *Euryanthe,* the music for *Oberon* is interrupted by scenes of spoken dialogue and stage action without music.

Although Oberon, Titania, and Puck all play their part in the opera, Shakespeare and his "wood near Athens" are soon left far behind in act I, as the story takes a variety of new turns. But it resembles *A Midsummer Night's Dream* in that it begins with the King of Fairyland and his Queen at odds. Oberon has vowed not to be reconciled with her until he finds two lovers who shall remain faithful through all temptations and dangers. Soon he regrets his vow, despairing of success, but he then hears of the knight Huon of Bordeaux, who has killed Charlemagne's son in a duel and is to be sent as a punishment to Baghdad to claim the Caliph's daughter as a bride after killing the man who sits on the Caliph's right hand. In a vision, Oberon shows Huon the beautiful Reiza whom he must claim and with whom he at once falls in love. Then he gives the young knight a magic horn and transports him to the Middle East along with his squire Sherasmin. In their first adventure they rescue Prince Babekan from a lion, but it turns out that he is evil and about to be married to Reiza—against her will, as we learn in the final scene of the act, which shows her in Haroun el Rashid's palace with her attendant Fatima. But Reiza too has seen a vision, sent by Oberon, of the knight who will save her from the hated Babekan, and Fatima tells her mistress that she foresees her deliverance. Huon, too, has reaffirmed his chivalrous mission in a big aria earlier in the act.

Act II begins still in the palace, where attendants praise the Caliph, who sits with Babekan beside him. Dancing girls precede Reiza's entrance, but Huon is on hand with his sword, and, after overcoming Babekan and blowing his magic horn to subdue the court he and Sherasmin, take Reiza and Fatima away. A number of adventures and hardships ensue, which place all four characters in danger, these being Oberon's test of their strength, but the love which binds them (for Sherasmin and Fatima now also love each other) carries them through: among these adventures is the storm at sea and shipwreck, after which Reiza sings her florid and dramatic aria "Ocean, thou mighty monster." Pirates separate the lovers, too, when Reiza is taken into slavery in Tunis, as are Fatima and Sherasmin. But in act III her master, the Emir Almanzor, respects her chastity, and when Huon is guided by Puck to Tunis he is able to rescue her despite being courted by the Emir's wife. This rescue can occur only after greater dangers (Huon is arrested and condemned to be burned alive) and the intervention of Sherasmin armed with the horn of Oberon. To its magical music, all must dance and be reconciled, and Oberon himself appears and tells the lovers that all their prayers are answered, after which he transports them back to Charlemagne's Frankish court. There Huon claims his pardon, and the opera ends with a chorus of thanksgiving.

The music of *Oberon* makes us regret the composer's untimely death in London less than two months after the premiere. The work is remarkable perhaps above all for the orchestral writing, and indeed the magic horn of Oberon, heard in the orchestra in the very first notes of the famous overture, returns as a kind of motto throughout. The music of fairyland, too, occurs not only in act I but also in other places such as the end of act II, where Oberon and Puck and their attendants once again appear. Oberon and Huon are both tenor roles, and each singer has interesting music although that of the heroic young knight is more varied and challenging, while Reiza too has fine solos to sing besides her famous address to the ocean after the shipwreck. Even Sherasmin and Fatima are well characterized vocally, not least in their charming exchanges at the start of act III. Dramatically, we can see parallels in act III not only with Mozart's *Die Entführung aus dem Serail* but also with the same composer's *Die Zauberflöte* in both of which pairs of lovers are held captive and in some way spiritually tested. Because of its spoken scenes and sheer length, the opera is difficult to stage, but as always with the mature Weber we are clearly in the presence of a highly imaginative and often masterly musical mind. After the London production the composer planned to reshape *Oberon* and use more recitative instead of the speech, but unfortunately he did not live to carry out this plan. However, Gustav Mahler later made a carefully arranged performing version.

—Christopher Headington

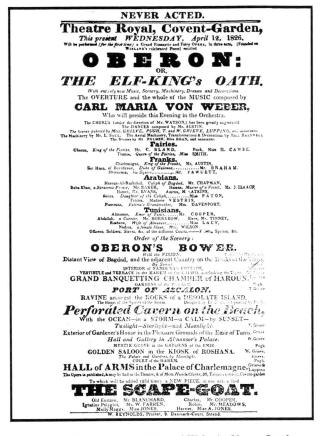

A playbill for the first performance of Weber's *Oberon*, London, 1826

OEDIPE À COLONE [Oedipus at Colonus].

Composer: Antonio Sacchini.

Librettist: N.-F. Guillard.

First Performance: Versailles, Court, 4 January 1786.

Roles: Antigone (soprano); Erifile (soprano); Thésée (tenor); Polinice (tenor); Oedipe (bass); High Priest (bass); An Athenian Lady (soprano from the chorus); A Voice (tenor from the chorus); chorus (SATB).

Publications

article–

Villars, F. de. "Oedipe à Colone et Sacchini." *Art musicale* 3 (1863): 345, 361.

*   *   *

The story of *Oedipe à Colone* follows loosely that of Sophocles' *Oedipus at Colonus,* the third and last Sophoclean treatment of the Theban Oedipus cycle. Oedipe's exiled and beleaguered son, Polinice, seeks assistance from Thésée, King of Athens, for his attempt to be restored to the throne of Thebes. The noble Athenian consents to lend aid and to join Polinice in marriage with his daughter Erifile, an act highlighted by a melodically rich trio. But the gods will not bestow their

blessing on the union, for Polinice had offered little resistance to the expulsion of Oedipe from Thebes. In act II Oedipe appears with his faithful daughter Antigone. After they encounter the hostile crowd on Mt Cithaeron, a danger which the noble Athenian Thésée once again averts, Antigone pleads with her father, also an exile, to forgive the exiled Polinice. The once angry Oedipe relents, and by the end of the third act Polinice's marriage with Erifile merits both the blessing of the gods and the joy of the chorus.

After a long, periodically successful international career which brought him from his native Florence to Naples, Padua, Rome, Venice, Munich, Stuttgart, and London, Sacchini at age fifty-two left the financial difficulties which he helped create for himself in London and prospered again under Marie Antoinette's patronage (at the encouragement of her brother, Joseph II of Austria). It was at Versailles that Sacchini saw his *Oedipe à Colone,* by all accounts his masterpiece, performed early in 1786. Still admired today are the first-act hymn sung before the Temple of the Eumenides and, above all, the second-act duet for Oedipe and Antigone ("Filles du Styx, terribles Euménides").

Nonetheless, ever since his arrival in France five years earlier, his operas *Renaud (Armida), Chimène,* and *Dardanus* had provided the artistic battleground, as it were, for the struggle between the French followers of Piccinni and those of Gluck. In addition, continual resentment against the queen's preference for foreigners accounted for even more resistance to Sacchini's continued success. These cultural and political factions in Paris and at the court interfered specifically with Sacchini's plans to produce *Oedipe à Colone* in Paris. Greatly disappointed because of all the intrigue, Sacchini died that October. Ironically, once *Oedipe à Colone* was posthumously performed in Paris the next year, it became a huge success. Remaining one of the Paris Opéra's most popular works for almost sixty years, it was performed nearly 600 times.

Unlike two of Sacchini's early Paris operas, *Oedipe à Colone* consisted of original musical material. The libretto, by Nicolas-François Guillard, was only the first since that by P. Torri (1729), to be based on Sophocles' Colonus drama, a great irony since Sophocles' *Oedipus at Colonus,* like Sacchini's, was the artist's last complete work, the success of which came only posthumously. The unique choice of subject can probably be attributed to that aspect of Gluckian reform, also encouraged by Diderot and the Encyclopedists, which called for simplified subject matter. For this aim Greek tragedy provided the ideal sources, and Sacchini had as immediate models Gluck's most recent versions of Euripides' *Alceste* (1776), *Iphigénie en Aulide* (via Racine, 1774), and *Iphigénie en Tauride* (1779), the latter with the libretto by Guillard. Despite (and, in part, as a result of) the cultural, political tug of war which preceded and undermined the composition and production of *Oedipe à Colone* and led ultimately to his death, Sacchini, musically speaking, created a satisfactory compromise in which the drama of this French *tragédie lyrique* based on a Greek original was beautifully colored by his Italian melodies and tempered with Gluckian economy.

—Jon Solomon

OEDIPUS AT COLONUS
See OEDIPE À COLONE

OEDIPUS REX.

Composer: Igor Stravinsky.

Librettist: J. Cocteau (translated into Latin by J. Danielou).

First Performance: concert performance, Paris, Sarah Bernhardt, 30 May 1927; staged performance, Vienna, 23 February 1928; revised, 1948.

Roles: Oedipus (tenor); Jocasta (mezzo-soprano); Creon (bass-baritone); Tiresias (bass); Shepherd (tenor); Messenger (bass-baritone); chorus (TTBB).

Publications

articles–

Cocteau, J. "La Collaboration Oedipus rex." *La revue musicale* no. 212 (1952): 51.

Mellers, W. "Stravinsky's Oedipus as 20th-century Hero." *Musical Quarterly* 48 (1962): 300; reprinted in *Stravinsky: a New Appraisal of His Work*, edited by Paul Henry Lang, 34, New York, 1963.

Sorokina, T. [article on neoclassical aspects of *Oedipus Rex*]. *Nauchno-metodicheskiye zapiski* [Novosibirsk] (1970).

Hirsbrunner, T. "Ritual und Spiel in Igor Strawinskys *Oedipus Rex*." *Schweizerische Musikzeitung/Revue musicale suisse* 117 (1974): 1.

Alfeyevskaya, G. " 'Tsar' Edip Stravinskovo: k probleme neoklassitsisma." *Teoriticheskiye problemï muzïki XX veka* [Moscow] 2 (1978): 126.

Hansen, M. "Igor Strawinskys 'Oedipus Rex': Anmerkungen zum Wort-Tonverhältnis." *Musik und Gesellschaft* 28 (1978): 329.

Vinay, G. "Da *Oidipous* a *Oedipus rex* e ritorno: un itinerario mertico." *Rivista italiana di musicologia* 18 (1982): 333.

Schubert, Werner. "Prima le parole, dopo la musica? Igor Strawinsky, Sophokles und die lateinische Sprache im *Oedipus Rex*." *Ntike und Abendland* 29 (1983): 1.

*   *   *

In the mid-1920s, Stravinsky, whose career to that point had been devoted primarily to works for the ballet and for the theater, turned to composing the kind of instrumental works that suited his new neo-classical style: the Octet for Winds, the Piano Sonata and Serenade, and the Concerto for Piano and Winds. He returned to the theater with the opera-oratorio *Oedipus Rex* (1927), written partly as a surprise gift to Diaghilev on his twentieth anniversary as ballet and opera impresario. Indeed, since the existence of the work was kept secret from Diaghilev until virtually the last minute, it was initially produced by Diaghilev's Ballets Russes in concert form. In the opinion of many, *Oedipus Rex* has never fully recovered from this inauspicious launching; when plunked in the midst of a program that included a full mounting of *Firebird*, the work seemed especially impenetrable to audience and critics alike. Diaghilev himself regarded the work, according to Stravinsky, as "un cadeau très macabre."

Subsequent stagings have done little to improve upon that first impression, for in composing his opera-oratorio, Stravinsky was experimenting with a theatrical style in which the work would be seen as a "still-life," with stationary characters in masks placed at various heights on an immobile set. By adapting a story the plot of which was well-known, Stravinsky would be free to concentrate on musical dramatization; by having the work sung in Latin, he would be able to distance the emotions from the directness of word-to-word comprehensibility and thus be able to use the text more for its purely phonetic qualities than for the exigencies of exposition and elucidation.

Stravinsky enlisted the aid of librettist Jean Cocteau, whom he had known for over fifteen years and who certainly was no stranger to Diaghilev projects. When Stravinsky informed Cocteau that his verses were to be recast in Latin, the latter must have surely felt the same artistic side-stepping as had occurred ten years earlier, when, as scenarist and putative librettist for *Parade*, his text was jettisoned in favor of a purely balletic approach. Nevertheless, the two authors came up with a compromise scheme in which a narrator, in evening dress and speaking French, would introduce the drama's various scenes, with the bulk of the work sung, by the soloists and male chorus, in Latin. In Cocteau's eyes, the sternness of the musical presentation would be relieved by the Parisian chic of the narration.

The story is taken directly from Sophocles. The people of Thebes implore Oedipus, their king, to save them from the plague. Creon, who has been sent to consult the oracle, returns with the information that for the plague to cease, the murder of King Laius must be avenged, and that the murderer is amongst them. Tiresias, the blind seer, is consulted, but he knows the truth and will not speak. Only when Oedipus impetuously accuses him of the murder does Tiresias reply that the murderer of the king is himself a king.

In the opera's second act, the facts fall into place. Oedipus' wife Jocasta mentions that Laius was killed at a crossroads; the chorus reminds Oedipus that he killed a man at a crossroads; the death of the elderly King Polybus is announced, and it is revealed that he was not the true father of Oedipus, as the latter had thought; Oedipus' lineage is revealed, whereupon he realizes that he has actually killed his father and married his mother (fulfilling an earlier oracle). Jocasta commits suicide, Oedipus gouges out his eyes, and the chorus mourns their fallen leader.

The implacable ostinatos (predominantly of minor thirds) of the chorus' initial appeal to Oedipus set the severe tone of the work's emotional atmosphere, and most of the music of the first act, though superficially forbidding, is nevertheless wonderfully expressive even in the sense of "expressive" to which Stravinsky himself might admit. From Oedipus' proud fioritura, to the blaring C-major of Creon's revelations, to the heart-piercing wind chords of Tiresias' refusal to speak (the 1920s was Stravinsky's "wind decade"), to the brilliant chorus hailing Jocasta at the end of the act, the first half of the drama surges forward with a determination and logic that are always compelling.

The second act is more diffuse and less successful, starting with Jocasta's strangely vampy aria, with its teasing alterations of raised and lowered sevenths. The choral contributions, except for the magnificent conclusion (essentially a tonally altered recapitulation of the work's opening) are far less focused, and in two instances are rather silly: the "Mulier in vestibulo" episodes in the rondo announcing Jocasta's death, and the "Aspikite" fugue ending that section (having the chorus sing a pompous academic fugue at this point is mannerist excess).

Like the contemporaneous German playwright Bertolt Brecht, whose name will be forever linked to his theory of "Verfremdung" ("alienation," as it is often translated; keeping the audience at an emotional distance), Stravinsky so often spoke polemically of music being "powerless to express

Stravinsky's *Oedipus Rex,* **English National Opera, London, 1991 (Philip Langridge in the title role)**

anything but itself" that audiences and commentators often prejudge his works as cold and uninvolving. There can be little doubt that *Oedipus Rex,* given its elaborate strategems of remoteness, figures among the most austere of Stravinsky's many theater works. But there is as little doubt that Stravinsky's incomparable techniques of word-setting, of orchestrational mastery and refinement, of character portrayal by means of harmonic and tonal delineation are all but lost on this uninvolved public.

—Gerald Moshell

OFFENBACH, Jacques.

Composer. Born 20 June 1819, in Cologne. Died 5 October 1880, in Paris. Studied cello with Vaslin at the Paris Conservatory, 1833-34; cellist in the orchestra of the Opéra-Comique; conductor at the Théâtre Français, 1850; opened the Théâtre des Bouffes-Parisiens, 1855, and managed it until 1866; operas produced in Ems, Germany, and Vienna; management of the Théâtre de la Gaîté; toured the United States, 1877.

Operas

L'alcôve, P.P. de Forges and A. de Leuven, Paris, Tour d'Auvergne, 24 April 1847.

Le trésor à Mathurin, L. Battu, Paris, Salle Herz, May 1853; revised as *Le mariage aux lanternes,* J. Dubois [=M. Carré] and L. Battu, Paris, Bouffes-Parisiens, 10 October 1857.

Pépito, J. Moinaux, L. Battu, Paris, Variétés, 28 October 1853.

Luc et Lucette, P.P. de Forges, E.-G. Roche, Paris, Salle Herz, 2 May 1854.

Oyayaie, ou La reine des îles, J. Moinaux, Paris, Folies-Nouvelles, 26 June 1855.

Entrez, messieurs, mesdames, F.-J. Méry and J. Servières [=L. Halévy], Paris, Bouffes-Parisiens (at Salle Marigny), 5 July 1855.

Les deux aveugles, J. Moinaux, Paris, Bouffes-Parisiens (at Salle Marigny), 5 July 1855.

Une nuit blanche, E. Plouvier, Paris, Bouffes-Parisiens (at Salle Marigny), 5 July 1855.

Le rêve d'une nuit d'été, E. Tréfeu, Paris, Bouffes-Parisiens (at Salle Marigny), 30 July 1855.

Le violoneux, E. Mestépès and E. Chevalet, Paris, Bouffes-Parisiens (at Salle Marigny), 31 August 1855.

Madame Papillon, J. Servières [=L. Halévy], Paris, Bouffes-Parisiens (at Salle Marigny), 3 October 1855.

Paimpol et Périnette, P.P. de Forges, Paris, Bouffes-Parisiens (at Salle Marigny), 29 October 1855.

Ba-ta-clan, L. Halévy, Paris, Bouffes-Parisiens, 29 December 1855.

Elodie, ou Le forfait nocturne, L. Battu and H. Crémieux, Paris, Bouffes-Parisiens, 19 January 1856.

Le postillon en gage, E. Plouvier and J. Adenis, Paris, Bouffes-Parisiens, 9 February 1856.

Trombalcazar, ou Les criminels dramatiques, C.D. Dupeuty and E. Bourget, Paris, Bouffes-Parisiens, 3 April 1856.

La rose de Saint-Flour, M. Carré, Paris, Bouffes-Parisiens (at Salle Marigny), 12 June 1856.

Les dragées du baptême, C.D. Dupeuty and E. Bourget, Paris, Bouffes-Parisiens (at Salle Marigny), 18 June 1856.

Le "66", P.P. de Forges and M. Laurencin [=P.A. Chapelle], Paris, Bouffes-Parisiens (at Salle Marigny), 31 July 1856.

Le savetier et le financier, Choiseul, Paris, Bouffes-Parisiens, 23 September 1856.

La bonne d'enfants, E. Bercioux, Paris, Bouffes-Parisiens, 14 October 1856.

Les trois baisers du diable, E. Mestépès, Paris, Bouffes-Parisiens, 15 January 1857.

Croquefer, ou Le dernier des paladins, A. Jaime, E. Tréfeu, Paris, 12 February 1857.

Dragonette, E. Mestépès and A. Jaime, Paris, Bouffes-Parisiens, 30 April 1857.

Vent du soir, ou L'horrible festin, P. Gille, Paris, Bouffes-Parisiens, 16 May 1857.

Une demoiselle en lôterie, A. Jaime and H. Crémieux, Paris, Bouffes-Parisiens, 27 July 1857.

Les deux pêcheurs, C.D. Dupeuty and E. Bourget, Paris, Bouffes-Parisiens, 13 November 1857.

Mesdames de la Halle, A. Lapointe, Paris, Bouffes-Parisiens, 3 March 1858.

La chatte metamorphosée en femme, Eugène Scribe and Mélesville, Paris, Bouffes-Parisiens, 19 April 1858.

Orphée aux enfers, H. Crémieux and L. Halévy, Paris, Bouffes-Parisiens, 21 October 1858; revised, Paris, Théâtre de la Gaîté, 7 February 1874.

Un mari à la porte, A. Delacour and L. Morand, Paris, Bouffes-Parisiens, 22 June 1859.

Les vivandières de la grande armée, A. Jaime and P.P. de Forges, Paris, Bouffes-Parisiens, 6 July 1859.

Geneviève de Brabant, A. Jaime and E. Tréfeu, Paris, Bouffes-Parisiens, 19 November 1859; revised, H. Crémieux, Paris, Menus Plaisirs, 26 December 1867; revised, H. Crémieux, Paris, Théâtre de la Gaîté, 25 February 1875.

Le carnaval des revues, E. Grangé, P. Gille, L. Halévy, Paris, Bouffes-Parisiens, 10 February 1860.

Daphnis et Chloé, Clairville [=L.F. Nicolaie], J. Cordier [=E.T. de Vaulabelle], Paris, Bouffes-Parisiens, 27 March 1860.

Barkouf, Eugène Scribe and H. Boisseaux, Paris, Opéra-Comique, 24 December 1860; revised as *Boule de neige,* Nuitter and E. Tréfeu, Paris, Bouffes-Parisiens, 14 December 1871.

La chanson de Fortunio, H. Crémieux and L. Halévy, Paris, Bouffes-Parisiens, 5 January 1861.

Le pont des soupirs, H. Crémieux and L. Halévy, Paris, Bouffes-Parisiens, 23 March 1861; revised, Paris, Variétés, 8 May 1868.

M. Choufleuri restera chez lui le . . ., Saint-Rémy [=Duc de Morny], E. L'Epine, H. Crémieux, L. Halévy, Présidence du Corps Législatif, 31 May 1861.

Apothicaire et perruquier, E. Frébault, Paris, Bouffes-Parisiens, 17 October 1861.

Le roman comique, H. Crémieux and L. Halévy, Paris, Bouffes-Parisiens, 10 December 1861.

Monsieur et Madame Denis, M. Laurencin [=Chapelle] and M. Delaporte, Paris, Bouffes-Parisiens, 11 January 1862.

Le voyage de MM. Dunanan père et fils, P. Siraudin and J. Moinaux, Paris, Bouffes-Parisiens, 23 March 1862.

Les bavards (Bavard et bavarde), Nuitter (after Cervantes, *Los habladores*), Bad Ems, 11 June 1862.

Jacqueline, P. d'Arcy [=H. Crémieux and L. Halévy], Paris, Bouffes-Parisiens, 14 October 1862.

Il Signor Fagotto, Nuitter and E. Tréfeu, Bad Ems, 11 July 1863.

Lischen et Fritzchen, P. Dubois [=P. Boisselot], Bad Ems, 21 July 1863.

L'amour chanteur, Nuitter and E. L'Epine, Paris, Bouffes-Parisiens, 5 January 1864.

Die Rheinnixen, A. von Wolzogen (after Nuitter and E. Tréfeu), Vienna, Hofoper, 4 February 1864.

Les géorgiennes, J. Moinaux, Paris, Palais-Royal, 16 March 1864.

Jeanne qui pleure et Jean qui rit, Nuitter and E. Tréfeu, Bad Ems, July 1864.

Le fifre enchanté, ou Le soldat magicien, Nuitter and E. Tréfeu, Bad Ems, 9 July 1864.

La belle Hélène, H. Meilhac and L. Halévy, Paris, Variétés, 17 December 1864.

Coscoletto, ou Le lazzarone, Nuitter and E. Tréfeu, Bad Ems, 24 July 1865.

Les refrains des bouffes, Paris, Bouffes-Parisiens, 21 September 1865.

Les bergers, H. Crémieux and P. Gille, Paris, Bouffes-Parisiens, 11 December 1865.

Barbe-bleue, H. Meilhac and L. Halévy, Paris, Variétés, 5 February 1866.

La vie parisienne, H. Meilhac and L. Halévy, Paris, Palais-Royal, 31 October 1866.

La Grande-Duchesse de Gérolstein, H. Meilhac and L. Halévy, Paris, Variétés, 12 April 1867.

La permission de dix heures, Mélesville [=A.H.I. Duveyrier] and P.F.A. Carmouche, Bad Ems, 9 July 1867.

La leçon de chant, E. Bourget, Bad Ems, August 1867, Folies-Marigny, 17 June 1873.

Robinson Crusoé, E. Cormon and H. Crémieux (after Defoe), Paris, Opéra-Comique, 23 November 1867.

Le château à Toto, H. Meilhac and L. Halévy, Paris, Palais-Royale, 6 May 1868.

L'île de Tulipatan, H. Chivot and A. Duru, Paris, Bouffes-Parisiens, 30 September 1868.

La périchole, H. Meilhac and L. Halévy, Paris, Variétés, 6 October 1868; revised, 25 April 1874.

Vert-vert, H. Meilhac and Nuitter, Paris, Opéra-Comique, 10 March 1869.

La diva, H. Meilhac and L. Halévy, Paris, Bouffes-Parisiens, 22 March 1869.

La princesse de Trébizonde, Nuitter and E. Tréfeu, Baden-Baden, 31 July 1869; revised, Paris, Bouffes-Parisiens, 7 December 1869.

Les brigands, H. Meilhac and L. Halévy, Paris, Variétés, 10 December 1869.

La romance de la rose, E. Tréfeu and J. Prével, Paris, Bouffes-Parisiens, 11 December 1869.

Mam'zelle Moucheron, E. Leterrier and A. Vanloo, c. 1870, Paris, Renaissance, 10 May 1881.

Le roi Carotte, Sardou (after Hoffmann), Paris, Théâtre de la Gaîté, 15 January 1872.

Fantasio, P. de Musset, Paris, Opéra-Comique, 18 January 1872.

Fleurette, oder Näherin und Trompeter, J. Hopp and F. Zell [=C. Walzel] (after Pittaud de Forges, M. Laurencin [=P.-A. Chapelle]), Vienna, Carl-Theater, 8 March 1872.

Der schwarze Korsar, J. Offenbach and R. Genée, Vienna, Theater an der Wien, 21 September 1872.

Les braconniers, H. Chivot and A. Duru, Paris, Variétés, 29 January 1873.

Pomme d'api, L. Halévy and W. Busnach, Paris, Renaissance, 4 September 1873.

La jolie parfumeuse, H. Crémieux and E. Blum, Paris, Renaissance, 29 November 1873.

Bagatelle, H. Crémieux and E. Blum, Paris, Bouffes-Parisiens, 21 May 1874.

Madame l'archiduc, H. Meilhac, L. Halévy and A. Millaud, Paris, Bouffes-Parisiens, 31 October 1874.

Whittington, Nuitter, E. Tréfeu, H.B. Farnie, London, Alhambra, 26 December 1874.

Les hannetons, E. Grangé and A. Millaud, Paris, Bouffes-Parisiens, 22 April 1875.

La boulangère a des écus, H. Meilhac and L. Halévy, Paris, Variétés, 19 October 1875.

La créole, A. Millaud and H. Meilhac, Paris, Bouffes-Parisiens, 3 November 1875.

Le voyage dans la lune, E. Leterrier, A. Vanloo, and A. Mortier, Paris, Théâtre de la Gaîté, 26 November 1875.

Tarte à la crème, A. Millaud, Paris, Bouffes-Parisiens, 14 December 1875.

Pierrette et Jacquot, J. Noriac and P. Gille, Paris, Bouffes-Parisiens, 13 October 1876.

La boîte au lait, A. Grangé and J. Noriac, Paris, Bouffes-Parisiens, 3 November 1876.

Le docteur Ox, A. Mortier and P. Gille (after J. Verne), Paris, Variétés, 26 January 1877.

La Foire Saint-Laurent, H. Crémieux and A. de Saint-Albin, Paris, Folies-Dramatiques, 10 February 1877.

Maître Péronilla, Nuitter and Ferrier, Paris, Bouffes-Parisiens, 13 March 1878.

Madame Favart, H. Chivot and A. Duru, Paris, Folies-Dramatiques, 28 December 1878.

La marocaine, Ferrier and L. Halévy, Paris, Bouffes-Parisiens, 13 January 1879.

La fille du tambour-major, H. Chivot and A. Duru, Paris, Folies-Dramatiques, 13 December 1879.

Belle Lurette, E. Blum, E. Blau, R. Toché, Paris, Renaissance, 30 October 1880 [unfinished; completed by Delibes].

Les contes d'Hoffmann, J. Barbier, Paris, Opéra-Comique, 10 February 1881 [unfinished; completed by Guiraud].

Other works: vocal works, ballets, dance music, various works for violon cello.

Publications

By OFFENBACH: books—

Notes d'un musicien en voyage. Paris, 1877; 1979; English translation as *Offenbach in America,* New York, 1877; as *America and the Americans,* London, 1877; as *Orpheus in America,* Bloomington, Indiana, 1957; London, 1958.

Jacob, Walter K., ed. *Jacques Offenbach in Selbstzeugnissen und Bilddokumenten.* Hamburg, 1969.

About OFFENBACH: books—

Mirecourt, E. de. *Les contemporains: Auber, Offenbach.* Paris, 1869.

Argus. *Célébrités dramatiques: Jacques Offenbach.* Paris, 1872.

Martinet, A. *Offenbach: sa vie et son oeuvre.* Paris, 1887.

Bekker, P. *Jacques Offenbach.* Berlin, 1909.

Northcott, R. *Jacques Offenbach: a Sketch of his Life and a Record of his Operas.* London, 1917.

Rieger, E. *Offenbach und seine Wiener Schule.* Vienna, 1920.

Schneider, L. *Offenbach.* Paris, 1923.

Brancour, R. *Offenbach.* Paris, 1929.

Henseler, A. *Jakob Offenbach.* Berlin, 1930.

Kristeller, H. *Der Aufstieg des Kölners Jacques Offenbach: ein Musikerleben in Bildern.* Berlin, 1931.

Kracauer, Siegfried. *Jacques Offenbach und das Paris seiner Zeit.* Amsterdam, 1937; English translation as *Orpheus in Paris: Offenbach and the Paris of his Time.* London, 1937; New York, 1938.

Brindejont-Offenbach, J. *Offenbach, mon grand-père.* Paris, 1940.

Lyon, Raymond, and Louis Saguer. *Les Contes d'Hoffmann: Etude et analyse.* Paris, 1947.

Decaux, A. *Offenbach, roi du Second Empire.* Paris, 1958; 3rd ed., 1975; German translation, Bergisch Gladbach, 1978.

Silbermann, A. *Das imaginäre Tagebuch des Herrn Jacques Offenbach.* Berlin, 1960.

Hughes, G. *Composers of Operetta.* London, 1962.

Sollertinsky, I.I. *Offenbach.* Moscow, 1962.

Schneidereit, Otto. *Jacques Offenbach.* Leipzig, 1966.

Jacob, P.W. *Jacques Offenbach in Selbstzeugnissen und Bilddokumenten.* Hamburg, 1969.

Faris, Alexander. *Jacques Offenbach.* New York, 1981.

Gammond, Peter. *Offenbach: his Life and Times.* Tunbridge Wells, 1980.

Harding, James. *Jacques Offenbach: a Biography.* London and New York, 1980.

Heinz-Klaus Metzger and Rainer Riehn, eds. *Offenbach.* Munich, 1980.

Pourvoyeur, R. *Offenbach idillio e parodia.* Turin, 1980.

Rissin, David. *Offenbach ou le rire en musique.* Paris, 1980.

articles—

Wolff, A. "Jacques Offenbach." In *La gloire à paris.* Paris, 1886.

Grau, R. "When Offenbach Came to Town." *Musical America* (1913).

Lamb, A. "How Offenbach Conquered London." *Opera* 20 (1969): 932.

Folstein, Robert L. "A Bibliography on Jacques Offenbach." *Current Musicology* 12 (1971): 116.

Pourvoyeur, R. "Verne et Offenbach." *Bulletin de la Société Jules Verne* 20 (1971): 87; 21 (1972): 112.

Mailer, F. "Jacques Offenbach—ein Parisier in Wien." *Österreichische Musikzeitschrift* 27 (1972): 246.

Reininghaus, Frieder. "'Sinnenrausch'—Jules Verne und Jacques Offenbach." *Stadtrevue—Vier Wochen Köln* 3/no. 12 (1978): 15.

———. "Wieder in die Oper gehen? Zwei neue Offenbach—Inszenierungen." *Spuren Zeitschrift für Kunst und Gesellschaft* 1/no. 5 (1978): 59.

Avant-scène opéra January-February (1980) [*Les Contes d'Hoffmann* issue].

Irmer, Hans-Jochen. "Offenbach und das Musiktheater." *Bulletin* [Berlin] 17/no. 2 (1980): 12.

Lamb, Andrew. "Offenbach in One Act." *Musical Times* 121 (1988): 615.

Loewen, Jan van. "*La Périchole*. Zum Schicksal einer *opéra bouffe*." *Neue Zürcher Zeitung* 231 (1980): 69.

Rosset, Clément. "Le rire en musique." *Critique* 407 (1981): 390.

Avant-scène opéra 66 (1984) [*La périchole* issue].

Peschel, Enid Rhodes, and Richard E. "Medicine, Music, and Literature: The Figure of Dr. Miracle in Offenbach's *Les Contes d'Hoffmann*." *Opera Quarterly* summer (1985).

* * *

"There is in Paris a very young celebrity whose existence is, alas, not suspected by the musical world," remarked the Paris paper *Le ménestrel*, shortly after the appearance of a waltz called "Fleurs d'hiver" (Flowers of winter) in 1836. "M. Offenbach regularly composes three waltzes before luncheon, a mazurka after dinner, and four gallops between the two meals." At the age of seventeen, Offenbach had begun to make his name as a composer. Though he went on to write for the theater, he retained both his affinity for dance music and his prolific speed of composition.

Jacques (born Jakob) Offenbach, king of French comic operetta, began his musical career as a cellist. He was determined to pursue his ambition to write for theater, although his antagonistic relationship with the operatic establishment, especially the prestigious Opéra-Comique, meant that the only sources of commissions were closed to him. He finally joined the orchestra of the Opéra-Comique as a cellist, though he soon grew bored with this activity, and escaped to his first theatrical appointment: conductor for the Théâtre-Français. But he wanted to write his own music. Still unable to obtain commissions to write his music for the established theaters, Offenbach in 1855 applied for the necessary government permission to start his own theater, *Les Bouffes-Parisiens*. Success came immediately on opening night with *Les deux aveugles* (The Blind Beggars), among others. With this new-found popularity, Offenbach's career as a professional composer for the theater was launched.

Popular approval did not automatically bring critical acclaim, and critics were often hostile toward the immoral content of the librettos. But Offenbach slowly won more widespread approval. By 1857, the company was ready to tour London, with nineteen operettas by Offenbach in their repertoire. Offenbach had already been to London in 1844 as a cello virtuoso, but now he took London by storm with a season of operettas, an example on which Gilbert and Sullivan were to build—and from which they sometimes borrowed heavily. Offenbach's hold on London taste lasted more than twenty years.

Eager to write larger-scale works, Offenbach acquired a new license and used a large cast for the first time with *Mesdames de la Halle* (The Ladies of the Marketplace) in 1858. But the first truly large-scale production was *Orphée aux enfers* (Orpheus in the Underworld). Thereafter there was no turning back, and Offenbach continued to turn out music at an extraordinary pace. Though he wrote other music—songs and miscellaneous instrumental music—Offenbach is remembered for his great bulk of operettas, about 100 works. Many are short one-act pieces, but he worked quickly and constantly. Once, on a bet, he set a libretto in eight days.

Offenbach's fame rests on a mere handful of his works: *Les contes d'Hoffmann* (Tales of Hoffmann), his one relatively serious major opera, plus six comic operettas: *Orphée aux enfers, La belle Hélène* (Fair Helen), *La vie parisienne* (Life in Paris), *Barbe-bleu* (Bluebeard), *La Grande-Duchesse de Gerolstein* (The Grand Duchesse of Gerolstein), and *La Périchole* (The Périchole).

During his lifetime, Offenbach's stature was considerable. He often profited from good relations and good standing at court and in government circles, using his connections to acquire licenses and gain French citizenship, among other things. In 1861, Louis Napoleon awarded him the title "Chevalier de la Légion d'honneur." But Napoleon's empire collapsed after the Franco-Prussian war, and for the rest of his life Offenbach suffered suspicion from both the French and the Germans as a man with potentially divided loyalties. He fell on harder times, and faced continuing hostility from the Republicans seeking scapegoats from the second empire. Late in life, suffering from poor health, he continued to write, producing a few successes, though his masterpiece, *Les contes d'Hoffmann*, was left incomplete upon his death on 5 October 1880.

Offenbach's mature musical style owes much to the tradition of comic opera, with spoken dialogue rather than recitative separating the musical numbers. And Offenbach's love of Mozart shows unmistakably in the skillful part-writing for the larger vocal ensembles, influenced by *Die Zauberflöte* and *Così fan tutte*. Offenbach made effective use of the *opera buffa* patter song, with its breathless one syllable per note, popularized earlier by Rossini ("Largo al Factotum") and later by Gilbert and Sullivan. But perhaps the most striking aspect of Offenbach's musicality is his lyrical flair. Brilliant, memorable melodies scintillate throughout his scores, especially in the solos and duets. Many of the melodies are based on dances; the cancan immortalized by Offenbach is a breathlessly exciting 2/4 dance with the nonstop beat. But the most important characteristic of his music is parody.

Offenbach loved parody and satire. Meyerbeer and serious grand opera were frequent victims of his attentions, with a notable instance in the finale of *Ba-ta-clan*, when the oriental ruler Fé-ni-han decides to die in the noble manner of *Les Huguenots*. He calls on his comrades to join him in the German chorale "Ein' feste Burg," with voices preposterously imitating trumpet fanfares. Meyerbeer maintained a reasonably good humor over the situation, attending the Bouffes regularly, though he always waited until the second night rather than attend the opening.

Offenbach's irreverent imitations brought him popularity with the public, but not all his victims were so forgiving. Richard Wagner, who had come to Paris in 1859, avowed a high-minded pretentiousness that made him an obvious target. Following Wagner's book *Das Kunstwerk der Zukunft* (The Work of Art of the Future), Offenbach lampooned his style with *La symphonie de l'avenir* (The symphony of the future), and again in *Le carnaval des revues* (The Carnival of Revues, 1864). The result was an exchange of invective and a lifelong feud. Wagner retaliated with *Eine Kapitulation* (Capitulation), in which he mercilessly mocked the hapless Parisians suffering during the disastrous Franco-Prussian War, 1870-71.

For a long time Offenbach's work was largely ignored, due partly to a belief that the satire was too topical to be of interest today. But interest has grown since the centenary of his death in 1980. Attempts have been made to write entirely new scripts to accompany Offenbach's music, and recent efforts have also been made to update librettos with modern references. Further, in recent scholarship, an attempt has been made to analyze the social, cultural, and political basis of Offenbach's parody within the context of France's second empire, potentially lending serious theoretical weight to Offenbach's frivolity. The composer did indeed poke fun at

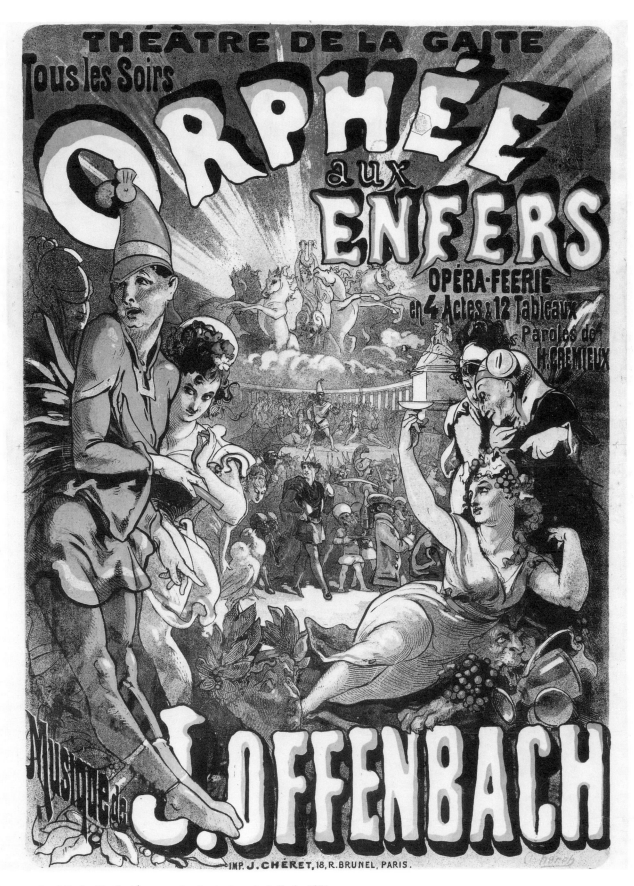

A poster for Offenbach's *Orphée aux enfers* (revised version), Paris, 1874

contemporary political situations, as in *The Grand Duchesse of Gerolstein*'s mockery of petty duchies, or the question of legitimate rule in *The Brigands,* or the critique of the Paris Commune in *King Carrot.* But Offenbach did not parody war and the military, or satirize court life, with any revolutionary intent.

Offenbach's popularity was undoubtedly connected with the rise of the middle class and the concomitant need for music somewhere between highbrow and vulgar. His work may be thoroughly entrenched in its time, but it can still be enjoyed today in the spirit in which it was intended: delicious entertainment.

—Elizabeth W. Patton

OLIVERO, Magda.

Soprano. Born 14 March 1914, in Saluzzo. Studied with Luigi Gerussi, Simonetto and Ghedini in Turin; debut as Lauretta in *Gianni Schicchi,* Turin, 1933; sang Adriana Lecouvreur in Rome, Naples, Venice and Florence, 1939-40; married and retired, 1941, but upon Cilèa's urging reappeared at Teatro Grande, Brescia after ten years; London debut as Mimì, Stoll Theatre, 1952; U.S. debut as Medea in Dallas, 1967; Metropolitan Opera debut as Tosca, 1975.

Publications

By OLIVERO: articles–

"Cilèa and 'Adriana Lecouvreur.' " *Opera* 14 (1963): 523.

About OLIVERO: articles–

Celletti, R. "Magda Olivero, ieri, oggi, domani." *Discoteca* nos. 1-2 (1969): 21.
Morini, M. "Magda Olivero: l'artista, le scelte, il personaggio." *Discoteca* nos. 1-2 (1969): 16.
Connolly, R. "The Rediscovery of Magda Olivero." *Stereo Review* 23 (1960): 70.

* * *

When Magda Olivero made her Metropolitan Opera debut in 1975, as Tosca, she was more than sixty. Though she had behind her an international career spanning forty years and including a few blazingly successful Dallas appearances, her only recording widely circulated in America was of Liu in the first complete *Turandot,* done in 1938. Nevertheless, her reputation as a singing actress was legendary. Her appearance at the Metropolitan, however, was not, as it turned out, merely a nostalgic evocation of former grandeur in present ruins, but an artistic event, similar to the display of an hypnotic painting from a passing age. Her voice, even in pianissimo, cut through the orchestra; it was steady, with a full complement of colors, a vehicle for yearning. Above all, she gave us Tosca: imperious, mercurial, passionate, lost, distraught—a performance in the great tradition of committed *theatrical* realism (verismo) that had all but left the operatic stage a decade before. "One must have such a technique that the voice can be put at the service of the character being portrayed," she once told Jerome Hines. "Go onstage and think of performing, not singing!"

Olivero's voice was not beautiful in the Milanov or Caballé sense, but it was an *unavoidable* voice, with acid and fibre and even some seeds in it: a pomegranate voice. In any other singer that might be interesting but eventually tiresome, but Olivero had dramatic imagination, complete control of vocal dynamics, and a range of hues developed by stringent technique and coordinated by art. One can hear this alike in her recorded Liu of 1938 and her Fedora of 1969. As a student she was intrepid. She went through three terrible teachers before she found a knowledgeable mentor who told her, "This is the last time you are going to say *I can't.* If necessary I'll see you dead to get what I want! Die, afterward, if you wish, but first you must do what I want!" She later heard a Ponselle record and determined that she would learn to swell and diminish on high C. "It was always my dream to do pianissimi," she told Hines. "And I achieved them by studying. . . . I do it all with breath, breath, breath. When you do pianissimi you must support twice as much as when you sing forte." As an artist she remained constantly analytical: "I am like two persons: one lives in the character, and the other vigilantly watches, saying, 'Why did you do this? Why did you do that?' "

In another sense also she was two people: Olivero the singer and Olivero the icon. She began in 1933 when the verismo style of singing was at its height. Muzio, Pampanini, and Scacciati were in full career, and Favero, Tassinari, and Caniglia had recently started. By the seventies, they and most of their successors were gone, but Olivero was still singing splendidly, the potent advocate of a style all but vanished. Articulation, tone color, and sensitive phrasing were her weaponry. Her contemporaries vouched for her authenticity: Maria Laurenti, Gilda dall Rizza, and Germana di Giulio, prominent sopranos all, have spoken in retirement of her spellbinding qualities. "God has helped Magda to keep going," said Dalla Rizza to Lanfranco Rasponi, "so people can still know what it was like when singing was art."

Olivero's records attest to the subtlety and variety of her approach. Her Puccini is often sung with extraordinary intimacy; the exhaustion and despair of her Mimì, Manon Lescaut, and Suor Angelica suggest a dazed madness. Her early Liu has a simplicity (despite a burst of tears) that seems Oriental. The climax of "Vissi d'arte" is a great arch of deep feeling: she is *compelling* God to listen. About the arias from *Adriana Lecouvreur* and *Louise* there is a hushed lyricism, a private ecstasy which is Olivero's trademark. Sometimes, in our day and at such close range, one almost seems to be hearing a brilliant analysis of the music and the style in which it was written rather than the music itself. No matter. The art is there in the records even if the tradition seems to have gone from the stage.

—London Green

ONEGIN, Sigrid [born Sigrid Elisabeth Elfriede Emilie Hoffman].

Contralto. Born 1 June 1889, in Stockholm. Died 16 June 1943, in Magliaso, Switzerland. Married: 1) pianist and composer Eugene Onegin, 1913 (died 1919); 2) Fritz Penzoldt, 1920. Studied with Resz in Frankfurt, with E.R. Weiss in Munich and with di Ranieri in Milan, as well as with Lilli

Lehmann and Margarethe Siems; debut as Carmen, Stuttgart, 1912; sang at Bavarian State Opera in Munich, 1919-22; Metropolitan Opera debut as Amneris, 1922, and remained there until 1924; sang Orfeo at Salzburg, 1931-32; appeared at Bayreuth, 1933-34; last appearance in United States in recital, 1938; created Dryade in *Ariadne auf Naxos.*

Publications

About ONEGIN: books–

Penzoldt, F. *Sigrid Onegin.* Magdeburg, 1939; as *Alt-Rhapsodie: Sigrid Onegin: Leben und Werk.* Neustadt an der Aisch, 1953.

Sigrid Onegin, Rudolf Bing wrote in his memoirs, was "a very difficult woman.... temperamentally the character of Lady Macbeth came naturally to her." Bing's evaluation was the consequence of his association with the Swedish contralto at the Städtische Oper Berlin, in the early 1930s, where she sang Verdi's Lady Macbeth under the baton of Fritz Stiedry. But it is the codicil to the future Metropolitan Opera general manager's comment on her personality that illuminates the undimmed high regard in which Onegin is held by connoisseurs: "Hers was one of the most individual and beautiful voices I have ever heard." Onegin's unlikable disposition may well account for the slight aloofness evident in her singing, but it may also have made possible her dedicated search for perfection of tone production and evenness of scale, a quest that resulted in as near-flawless a vocal method as has existed in the twentieth century.

Although every description of Onegin onstage in any of her great roles—Orfeo, Fidès, Amneris, Lady Macbeth, Brangäne, and Carmen—indicates that her physical presence, emotive powers, and dramatic projection were in no respect wanting, it was the voice that primarily occupied commentators; it remains the voice that defines her importance today. Listening to Onegin amounts to an extraordinary lesson in vocal genealogy, for hers is a prodigious aural demonstration of what it means to have been a truly great singer of a voice type that is no longer practiced. She is an artist who causes us to grapple with our labels and categories, indeed, with our very concepts.

Late twentieth-century vocal pedagogy and the taste that fueled its evolution have pretty much eradicated the true low female voice. In its place has been cultivated the "mezzo-soprano," a hybrid instrument designed to produce, through a certain amount of force and pressure, a uniformly exciting sound that is very much overbalanced toward the top, is somewhat driven and hard in timbre and lacking in real repose and refinement. To "sound" in the lower part of the range, where much important music lies, the modern mezzo all too often has recourse only to an angry snarl.

Onegin proves herself a true contralto in the characteristic low passages of Dalila and Fidès, for example, which are dark and weighty but never heavy, raw, or pushed, and yet she can float and sustain a pianissimo high B-flat worthy of envy by any lyric soprano. Moreover, her chest voice blends without a break into her middle register. Like the young Marian Anderson, nowhere is Onegin's voice thick or artificially darkened, and it is paradoxically both lighter and more flexible than the supposedly higher and brighter *genus* mezzo-soprano.

Other virtues that come through consistently in all of her recordings are exact and unwavering intonation; clear and identifiable vowel formation (albeit usually limited to *ah* and *oh* above the stave, to facilitate the production of firm, round sound without attenuation); the impression of natural motion in the sound, ensuing from an emission that is perfectly on the breath and a vibrato that is free and never widens; the capacity to swell the voice without forcing and to withdraw it without squeezing; and the ability to maintain the integrity of the musical line at all times because that line is invariably traced in a true legato.

This mechanical facility and technical polish—the "voice as instrument"—are in Onegin mated to an artistic sensibility of the highest order, so that the singer is able to accomplish virtually any vocal *and* expressive intention with ease. If her effects are occasionally a bit less than spontaneous-sounding, if there is a particle of calculation in the exploitation of so wide a range, so complete a command of dynamics, so long a breath line, and such a varied palette of vocal colors, the virtuosity is nonetheless downright nonchalant.

Onegin's calm, majestic legato gives way in a flash to the fastest, most fluid runs, scales, and trills, with no yodeling over register breaks; nothing is held onto and there is no constriction. Her musical manners are fastidious, but very much a product of her time. We would not now countenance so many tempo fluctuations, so much rhythmic taffy-pulling in a piece like the "Alleluia" from Mozart's "Exsultate, jubilate" motet. We require our bravura, when we can get it, to be metronomical and lacking eccentric individuality.

Her many recordings, made for Polydor, HMV, Brunswick, and Victor, traverse all the important operatic repertory in her voice range, a considerable amount of Lieder, a breathtaking vocalise on Chopin's A-flat Impromptu (op. 29), and Brahms' "Alto Rhapsody." In all things, as Richard Aldrich wrote, Onegin's voice is "one of great power controlled with smoothness and beauty, its emotional color prevailing[ly] of the 'darker' sort, but stirred with the true gleam of temperamental fire."

The historic synergy of that fire and that technique make Sigrid Onegin, along with fellow Swede Karin Branzell, one of the two last great exemplars of the genuine, now extinct, grand opera contralto.

—Bruce Burroughs

OPERA.

Composer: Luciano Berio.

Librettists: Luciano Berio, U. Eco, and F. Colombo.

First Performance: Santa Fe, New Mexico, 12 August 1970; revised, 1977.

Publications

book–

Berio, Luciano. *Two Interviews with Rossana Dalmonte and Bálint András Varga,* translated by David Osmond-Smith. New York, 1985.

* * *

Berio intended the title *Opera* to convey the plural of the Latin word *opus* for work rather than *opera* in the traditional sense. Indeed, Berio includes elements of at least three works, or *opera,* within *Opera:* 1) quotations from Striggio's libretto for Monteverdi's *Orfeo;* 2) scenes from *Terminal,* a dramatic work about terminally ill persons in a hospital ward, and also about travelers arriving at a terminal; and 3) the sinking of the Titanic, an event which took place in 1912 and which in 1957 became the basis for Berio's collaboration with Umberto Eco and Furio Colombo in the writing of a *Rappresentazione.* (This latter project was never completed.) In Berio's words, "all three [works within *Opera*] have one subject in common: death. *Opera* is a celebration of ending."

Berio has punctuated *Opera* with three different performances of an Aria, designated as Air I, Air II, and Air III, performed by a Soprano and accompanied on the piano by her vocal coach. The text is sung in English, and based in part on Striggio's libretto for *Orfeo.*

> Now, as the tunes change, now gay, now sad,
> Behold the trav'ler
> For whom, only a short time ago
> Sighs were food and tears were drink.

The opening line is similar to that sung in Italian by La musica (the Spirit of Music) at the end of the Prologue of Monteverdi's *Orfeo,* while the sources for lines three and four are the words sung by the Chorus of Nymphs and Shepherds which comes at the end of act I of *Orfeo.* By adding the line "Behold the trav'ler," Berio included all of the travelers in *Opera:* those on the Titanic, those in *Terminal,* as well as Orfeo himself. Each time the Aria is repeated in *Opera,* the quality of performance improves—as if the Soprano is making progress in her voice lessons. This is in keeping with Berio's idea that various episodes in *Opera* are developmental. Berio comments that: "The structure of the music, the expressive nature of certain elements continue to grow while everything on stage is dying. This contrary motion is one of the basic elements of *Opera....*"

The musical and dramatic elements of Air III provide a smooth transition to Memoria in act III. This is the third of three Memoria in *Opera.* For these episodes, Berio extracted part of the text sung by the Messenger in act II of *Orfeo.* All three episodes (Memoria) are similar to each other in musical and dramatic content. A tritone prevails throughout the melodic setting of this text, which creates a haunting sound in keeping with the devastating news delivered by the messenger.

In act I, the Memoria episode serves as a transition to scene one. This is also the case in act II where Memoria moves directly to scene ii, in which the texture becomes more complicated since all three works of *Opera* are intertwined. Shortly after Berio's musical reference to Stravinsky's *Fireworks,* the choir sustains the diminished triad of scene i (F#, A, C) as a continuous sound block, as some of the instruments alternate pitches of an ascending chromatic scale fragment. This leads the choir to utterances of "addio," which spins off into some vocal alliteration, almost as a warning of a later episode which is entitled "Addio." The reference is to Orfeo's lament at the end of act II.

The tritone which was so evident in scenes i and ii in the Chorus of Spirits, and in Memoria where the Messenger announced death, is also used to characterize the reference to the Westwind in Melodrama. This thread of melodic dissonance is also carried through to Documentario I and II. In Documentario I (act II), a feeling of stasis is created by the repetition of the ascending melodic pattern of the tritone and perfect fourth on the piano which creates a feeling that the dramatic motion as well as the Titanic are standing still. At this point, the actors are mimicing the sounds of the ship's engine. In the second Documentario, the feeling of stasis is even more extreme than that of Documentario I, because of the repeated notes and blocks of sound created by instrumentalists and members of the chorus. In the introductory bars, the marimba and vibraphone share the same tritone E—B flat as if *Opera* is moving to a climax. In fact, this is the point at which Berio frees *Opera* from the influences of the Titanic, *Terminal,* and *Orfeo* and focuses the dramatic and musical action on dead children.

Immediately before the second Documentario, Berio has placed Concerto II (based on his earlier work, *Tempi Concertati* [1958]), which helps to complete Concerto I (act I). In *Opera,* Berio used these episodes as the backdrop for the surviving passengers of the Titanic to introduce themselves to each other. He says that "The episode [Concerto II] continues at the end of the piece, before the scene of the children: we can hear a development of the concerto and of the characters." The musical texture of both of these concertos is characterized by long sustained notes. There are also layers of melodic activity which result in jagged lines. The overall effect is only mildly dissonant because of the blocks of sound. Contrast is achieved by tempo changes.

For the musical labyrinth surrounding the "Non-Story" of *Opera,* Berio succeeded in weaving numerous fragments together in support of the episodic nature of the work. Certain motives appear in the Aria which are transformed in the haunting references to the Westwind in Melodrama, having to do with the Titanic, or to the musical background of the Chorus of Spirits in scene i, and so on. Berio's quotation and elaboration of the most futuristic segment of Stravinsky's *Fireworks* is also revealing, since Berio's compositional style in *Opera* often resembles that of the youthful, forward-looking Stravinsky. The technique is freely atonal, with emphasis on motivic development in the sections that are melodically and contrapuntally oriented. In *Opera,* Berio was always able to support the drama with his musical instincts. By controlling the libretto and the music, he had a clear idea of how to use expressive means to the advantage of *Opera.* Because of the overall sequence of episodes within each act, a certain symmetry is evident in the revised version (1977) of *Opera,* which might not have been apparent in the original version (1970).

It should come as no surprise that Berio himself has suggested that "... a discussion of *Opera* would need a book by itself..." At the very least, a documentary film ought to be considered as a means of preserving some of the scenes from *Opera* for further study by scholars.

—Maureen A. Carr

ORFEO [Haydn]
  See L'ANIMA DEL FILOSOFO

ORFEO [Monteverdi]
   See LA FAVOLA D'ORFEO

ORFEO [Gluck]
   See ORFEO ED EURIDICE

ORFEO ED EURIDICE [Orpheus and Eurydice].

Composer: Christoph Willibald von Gluck.

Librettist: Ranieri de Calzabigi.

First Performance: Vienna, Burgtheater, 5 October 1762; revised as *Orphée et Euridice,* Moline (translated and adapted from Calzabigi), Paris, Académie Royale, 2 August 1774.

Roles: Orfeo (mezzo-soprano); Euridice (soprano); Amor (soprano); Ombra Felice [Happy Spirit] (soprano); chorus (SATB).

Publications

books–

La Laurencie, L. de *Orphée de Gluck: étude et analyse.* Paris, 1932.
Howard, Patricia. *C.W. von Gluck: "Orfeo".* Cambridge, 1981.
Pozzoli, Barbara Eleonora. *Dell' alma amato oggetto: gli affetti nel "Orfeo ed Euridice" di Gluck a Calzabigi.* Milan, 1989.

articles–

Furstenau, M. "Über die Schluss-Arie des ersten Aktes aus Glucks französischem Orpheus." *Berliner Musikzeitung Echo* 19 (1869): 261, 269.
_____. "Glucks Orpheus in München 1773." *Monatshefte für Musikgeschichte* 4 (1872): 218.
Tiersot, J. "Etude sur Orphée de Gluck." *Le ménestrel* 62 (1896): 273.
Kurth, E. "Die Jugendopern Glucks bis 'Orfeo'." *Studien zur Musikwissenschaft* 1 (1913): 193.
Abert, H. "Glucks italienische Opern bis zum 'Orfeo'." *Gluck-Jahrbuch* 2 (1915): 1; reprinted in *Gesammelte Schriften,* edited by F. Blume, 287, Halle, 1929.
Engländer, R. "Zu den Münchener Orfeo-Aufführungen 1773 und 1775." *Gluck-Jahrbuch* 2 (1915): 26.
Vetter, Walther. "Stilkritische Bemerkungen zur Arienmelodik in Glucks 'Orfeo'." *Zeitschrift für Musikwissenschaft* 4 (1921): 27.
Brück. "Glucks Orpheus." *Archiv für Musikwissenschaft* 7 (1925): 436.
Loewenberg, Alfred. "Gluck's *Orfeo* on the Stage with some Notes on Other Orpheus Operas." *Musical Quarterly* 26 (1940): 311.

Finscher, L. "Der verstümmelte Orpheus: über die Urgestalt und die Bearbeitung von Glucks 'Orfeo'." *Neue Zeitschrift für Musik* 124 (1963): 7.
_____. "Che farò senza Euridice? ein Beitrag zur Gluck Interpretation." In *Festschrift Hans Engel,* 96. Kassel, 1964.
Sternfeld, F.W. "Expression and Revision in Gluck's *Orfeo* and *Alceste.*" In *Essays Presented to Egon Wellesz,* edited by Jack Westrup, 114. London, 1966.
Allroggen, G. "La scene degli Elisi nell' 'Orfeo'." *Chigiana* 29-30 (1975): 369.
Heartz, Daniel. " 'Orfeo ed Euridice': some Criticisms, Revisions, and Stage-realizations during Gluck's Lifetime." *Chigiana* 29-30 (1975): 383.
Paduano, Guido. "La 'costanza' di Orfeo. Sul lieto fine dell' *Orfeo* di Gluck." *Rivista italiana di musicologia* 14 (1979): 349.

Gluck's *Orfeo* is in fact two operas. The first version, *Orfeo ed Euridice,* was presented in Vienna on 5 October 1762. The principal part was sung by the celebrated Gaetano Guadagni (1725-1792), who was much admired by Handel, having sung the part of Didimus in the premiere of *Theodora.* He was trained by David Garrick. Burney notes that Guadagni as an actor "seems to have had no equal on any stage in Europe; his figure was uncommonly elegant and noble; his countenance replete with beauty, intelligence, and dignity." These characteristics must have made him the ideal Orfeo, for, although with *Orfeo* Gluck consciously set out to reform opera, he did not for this opera abandon the prevailing custom of assigning the leading male role to a castrato.

The opera opens with Orfeo standing by Euridice's tomb, mourning her death. Gluck instructed a later singer to deliver the heart-rending cries for Euridice during the opening chorus "as if he were having his leg sawn off." Amor, the god of love, is moved to tell Orfeo that he may go to Hades to fetch Euridice on condition that he does not look at her until they are back on earth. In act II, Orfeo is repelled by the furies who guard the underworld but he soothes the savage beasts while accompanying himself on the lyre. They let him enter. Orfeo gazes in wonder at the beauty of the Elysian fields. Euridice is restored to him, but she cannot understand his indifference. She pleads with him to look at her, and he eventually does so. She dies once again, at which point Orfeo sings the most famous aria in the piece, "Che farò senza Euridice." Amor again takes pity on Orfeo, and Euridice is restored to him amid general rejoicing.

With *Orfeo,* the forty-eight year old composer of almost three dozen operas set out, aided by his excellent librettist Ranieri de Calzabigi (1714-90), to change the course of opera and to break with the conventions of opera seria. This is best expressed in Gluck's own introduction to *Alceste:* "I resolved to divest it [opera] entirely of all those abuses, introduced into it either by the mistaken vanity of singers or by the too great complaisance of composers, which have so long disfigured Italian opera and made of the most splendid and most beautiful of spectacles the most ridiculous and wearisome." Gluck goes on to mention specifically ornamentation, extended ritornelli, cadenzas, da capo arias. He also notes that the overture should anticipate the nature of the action. Most significantly he adds, "I believed that my greatest labour should be devoted to seeking a beautiful simplicity." Burney attested to the success of Gluck's goals when he wrote

C. Monnet inv. del. 1764.

N. le Mire Sculp.

Euridice amor ti rende.

atto II. Sce. II....

Gluck's *Orfeo ed Euridice,* **engraved title page from printed score, Paris, 1764**

that most of the arias in *Orfeo* "are as plain and simple as English ballads."

Calzabigi wrote the libretto of *Orfeo* expressly for Gluck. The convention of six characters (occasionally a few more) was broken by having only three, and two of them fairly small at that. The chorus, traditionally relegated to a minor role and sometimes eliminated altogether, plays a major part, and the opera omits any aria in full da capo form. Secco recitatives are completely abandoned.

The Viennese version is short, direct, and quite stunning. Twelve years later Gluck revised the work for Paris under the title, *Orphée et Euridice.* The title role was rewritten for a high tenor, Joseph Legros (1739-93), who became director of the Concerts Spirituels in Paris, and not only befriended Mozart but commissioned works from him for these concerts. He performed parts in several of Gluck's Paris operas. His was a high tenor voice, which has perhaps militated against the greater use of the Paris version. It is longer and less dramatically concise than its predecessor, but enormously rich in detail. There are noticeable differences in the orchestration between the two versions. The Paris version is more colored than its predecessor. It is worthwhile to compare the two settings of scene ii of act II. It is preceded in the Paris version by the "Air de Furies," which is omitted in the Viennese version, not surprisingly as it is lifted from the final movement of Gluck's 1761 ballet *Don Juan.* Then follows the famous "Dance of the Blessed Spirits" in both scores, but extended in the Paris version by the well-loved middle section in D minor for the solo flute. Euridice's first aria follows. It is a tender piece in F major, hard to give up but missing in the Vienna score. Next is Orfeo's wonderful "Che puro ciel," which is more subtly scored in the earlier version, with the solo flute much more in evidence than in the 1774 version. The remainder of the act is similar in both scores, but subtle differences abound. As might be expected, the Paris version contains considerably more ballet music throughout the opera.

Which version is to be preferred is perhaps a matter of taste, but what is not to be preferred is the uncomfortable mixture of the two, with which innocent audiences have frequently been presented. The origins of the mixture go back to Berlioz's famed version of the opera prepared specially in 1859 for Pauline Viardot-Garcia, and which she sang with outstanding success for almost 150 performances. That text is a retranslation from the French. Since that time the opera in hybrid form has been much favored by contraltos.

In 1936 Alfred Einstein, one of the important Gluck scholars, wrote, "Anyone who wishes to stage *Orfeo ed Euridice* nowadays should not keep wholly to the Vienna or to the Paris version, but will have to attempt to fashion the ideal form of the work out of both." And as recently as 1972 the writer in Kobbe's *Complete Opera Book* stated, "Some reconciliation between the Vienna and the Paris versions has, to this day, to be made for each and every production." With the importance attached nowadays to "authentic" performances, those views are no longer acceptable. Directors and singers must make a choice, for this is not one but two operas, in much the same way as are Strauss's *Ariadne auf Naxos* and Verdi's *Macbeth.* They both have their strengths—the Vienna score, tightness, directness, simplicity; the Paris score, a greater richness, more brilliant (though not necessarily more effective) orchestration, and some additional music.

Handel said that his cook knew more about counterpoint than Gluck! *Orfeo,* in both versions, is sustained by the composer's inventive imagination, subtle scoring, and structural daring, but there is little of that rich musical texture one finds, even as early as 1770, in Mozart's operatic writing.

Handel was correct. That is doubtless why Gluck's works, with the exception only of a few of the reform operas, have never held the stage. But *Orfeo* is appropriately accorded an important place in opera for it is not merely a museum piece, but one charged with great beauty, dramatic intensity, and genuine feeling.

—Lawrence J. Dennis

ORFF, Carl.

Composer. Born 10 July 1895, in Munich. Died 29 March 1982, in Munich. Studied with Heinrich Kaminski and at the Academy of Music in Munich; founded the Günther School (with Dorothee Günther) for gymnastics, dance, and music, in Munich, 1924; professor at the Hochschule für Musik in Munich, 1950-60. Orff invented a system of music education that has been adopted by schools internationally.

Operas

Publisher: Schott.

Klage der Ariadne, after Monteverdi, Karlsruhe, 1925; revised, Gera, 1940.
Orpheus, after Monteverdi, Mannheim, 1925; revised, Munich, 1931; revised, Dresden, 1940.
Tanz der Spröden, after Monteverdi, Karlsruhe, 1925; revised, Gera, 1940.
Der Mond, Orff (after the Brothers Grimm), Munich, 5 February 1939; revised, 1950.
Catulli carmina, Leipzig, 1943.
Die Kluge, Orff (after the Brothers Grimm, *Die kluge Bauerntochter*), Frankfurt, 20 February 1943.
Die Bernauerin, Orff, Stuttgart, 15 June 1947.
Antigonae, after Sophocles (translated by Friedrich Hölderlin), Salzburg, 9 August 1949.
Astutuli, Orff, Munich, 1953.
Trionfo di Afrodite, Milan, Teatro alla Scala, 13 February 1953.
Oedipus der Tyrann, Orff (after Sophocles, translated by Friedrich Hölderlin), Stuttgart, 1960.
Ein Sommernachtstraum, after Shakespeare, 1939-62; revised, Stuttgart, 1964.
Prometheus, after Aeschylus, Stuttgart, 24 March 1966.

Other works: choral works, orchestral works.

Publications/Writings

By ORFF: books–

Schulwerk. 1930-35; revised, 1950-54.
Schmidt, H.W., ed. *Carl Orff: sein Leben und sein Werk in Wort, Bild and Noten.* Cologne, 1971.
Bairisches Welttheater. Munich, 1972.
Gersdorf, Lilo, ed. *Carl Orff in Selbstzeugnissen und Bilddokumenten.* Reinbek bei Hamburg, 1981.

articles–

"Lehrjahre bei den alten Meistern." In *Carl Orff und sein Werk.* Tutzing, 1975-.

"*Antigonae.* Ein Trauerspiel des Sophokles von Friedrich Hölderlin." *Neue Zeitschrift für Musik* 143 (1982): 19.

About ORFF: books–

Sachs, C., and O. Lang. *Einführung in der Neugestaltung von Orfeo.* Mainz, 1925.
Keller, W. *Carl Orffs Antigonae.* Mainz, 1950.
Liess, A. *Carl Orff: Idee und Werk.* Zurich, 1955; 2nd ed., 1977; English translation, 1966; 2nd ed., 1971; 1980.
Ruppel, K.H., G.R. Sellner, and W. Thomas. *Carl Orff, ein Bericht in Wort und Bild.* Mainz, 1955; 2nd ed., 1960; English translation, 1960.
Wagner, W., and W.E. Schäfer. *Carl Orff.* Bayreuth, 1955.
Etienne, F., and P. Vanderschaeghe. *Carl Orff.* 1957.
Klement, U. *Vom Wesen der Alten in den Bühnenwerken Carl Orffs.* Leipzig, 1958.
Schadewaldt, W. *Carl Orff.* Zurich, 1960.
Willnauer, F., ed. *Prometheus: Mythos, Drama, Musik: Beiträge zu Carl Orffs Musikdrama nach Aischylos.* Tübingen, 1968.
Münster, R., ed. *Carl Orff: das Bühnenwerk.* Munich, 1970.
Carl Orff und sein Werk. Tutzing, 1975-.
Leont'eva, Oksana. *Karl Orff.* Moscow, 1984.

articles–

Häusler, Joseph. "Carl Orff und sein Werk für das Musiktheater der Gegenwart." *Universitas* 34 (1979): 343.
Thomas, Werner. "Carl Orffs *Antigonae.* Wieder-Gabe einer antiken Tragödie." In *Werk und Wiedergabe,* edited by Sigrid Wiesmann, 349. Bayreuth, 1980.

unpublished–

Klement, U. "Das Musiktheater Carl Orffs: Untersuchungen zu einem bürgerlichen Kunstwerk." Ph. D. dissertation, University of Leipzig, 1969.

*   *   *

Carl Orff is a controversial but highly influential composer whose contribution to musical theater has yet to be sufficiently explored and appreciated. What sets him apart from all other twentieth century opera composers is that his stage works owe far more allegiance to traditional theater than to the opera genre. Indeed, Orff insisted that his compositions were not opera, but music for the stage. Only two works, *Der Mond* and *Die Kluge,* can be identified with traditional operatic forms; the rest lie somewhere between scenic cantata and a variant of "straight theater."

Orff's musical efforts have been devoted almost exclusively to the stage; this is not surprising, in view of his many years employment with the Munich Kammerspiele and theaters in Mannheim and Darmstadt. As part of the post-Wagnerian "alienation theory" era, whose chief exponent was Bertolt Brecht, Carl Orff and others (Stravinsky, the early Hindemith, Krenek, Weill) were influenced by Brecht's idea of reform, resulting in essentially epic and static drama based on themes of simple but universal human significance, presenting the dramatis personae not as individual characters but as types.

Largely self-taught, Orff immersed himself in a study of the old masters, chiefly from the Italian Renaissance, as well as later composers. Although his professional work brought him in close contact with works by Richard Strauss, he reacted against the late-Romantic ideal, and was more drawn to Schoenberg and Stravinsky, the latter of whom he called "a synopsis of music history and—perhaps its last possibility," adding that "Every new score from him is for me an event." Like Stravinsky, Orff used folk elements, motor-rhythms, and short motives based on a configuration of notes within a small interval, often as an ostinato. His refinement of these elements, however, contained no "development" in the classical sense, severing the planes of "melody" and "accompaniment" to elevate the musical elements within the language as an integral factor. The formal structure of Carl Orff's works is block-like, with the instrumentation providing color and rhythmic pulse, using *Sprechstimme* and passages of speech as a contrasting extension of musical flow. There is little counter-rhythm or -melody; the vocal line is uppermost, and frequently reflects the influence of early psalmody. The chorus is always an important part of the drama, serving in the old Greek role as commentator and agitator within the play. And throughout all these elements is the ever-present dominance of rhythm: the percussion section is an orchestra within an orchestra, which binds the whole. Orff weaves within the spare and economic means of "bare" sets and static movement a unified texture of sight and sound which sublimates everything to the text.

Accused of being thoroughly derivative in his writing, Orff generously acknowledged his debt to the following: to Monteverdi, for magnificent choral textures and paired-voice writing in the Italian madrigal tradition; to Debussy, for his respect for language and explorations with color; to Shakespeare, without whom the use of the composite stage, and the following are "unthinkable": the witches' scene in *Die Bernauerin,* and characters such as the four lads in *Der Mond,* the three hoodlums in *Die Kluge,* the shepherds and soldiers in the Christmas and Easter plays, and the tricksters in *Astutuli;* to Otto Falkenberg, director of the Munich Kammerspiele, from whom he learned the secrets of staging and dramatic tension; and to his close friend, Kurt Huber, the German folklore authority, who collaborated with him in choosing subjects for his early works and stimulated his interest in using the literature of bygone eras to illuminate the core of the present, "the self-contained sphere that represents the mirror of the world." Finally, Orff's fascination with dance accompaniment by African rattles confirmed for him the importance of rhythm and percussion instruments: "the music of an African tribal dance is more genuine and has more to say in our time than a cleverly crafted neo-classical symphony."

Because the historical origins of theater were so much a part of Carl Orff, his musical theater places great responsibility on the player, who is once more required to be singer/dancer/actor, the *homo ludens* of antiquity. Gustav Sellner states that what is unique to Orff's stage is "theater lifted out of its framework, on which the symbolic precedents are allowed to appear among minimum decor and display." Orff asserted that his "entire interest is in the expression of spiritual realities," which has given rise to much misinterpretation in performing his work. The realm of the spirit is seen to encompass more than any theological tenet, but as Udo Klement has stated, the composer must resign himself to "religious punctuation" from those who would confine his artistic statements to their own particular ethic. Thus, although Orff specifically cites Peter in *Der Mond* as *not* a Christocentric saint but rather the Wise Old Keeper of the Heavens, the 1974 edition by Schott marks every entrance for that character as "St Peter"! Similarly, just as Orff has refused to "operaticize" a text for the sake of the music, so will the best productions of his works refrain from adding undue overlay to force hidden meanings and connotations that were meant to be left free for the finding.

It is futile to judge Carl Orff's works by criteria appropriate to opera or music drama. The inherent concept of *Urgrundmusik* espoused by him produced a unique hybrid form that continues to engender heated argument. As post-Romantic experimentation continues, with continued developments in works for musical theater that move beyond the traditional opera genre (such as minimalism), scholarly research will turn to the eight-volume commentary on his professional work, in which Orff discusses his experimental views and the many influential forces that aided him, and at last discern the impact this man has made on twentieth-century musical theater. Meanwhile, in the words of Henry Pleasants, "One can at least understand why those who [espouse] . . . musical means and conventions in vogue since the 17th century should exclude from their reckoning one who has seen fit to throw the entire apparatus overboard."

—Jean C. Sloop

ORLANDO.

Composer: George Frideric Handel.

Librettist: after C.S. Capeci (based on Ariosto, *Orlando furioso*).

First Performance: London, King's Theatre in the Haymarket, 27 January 1733.

Roles: Orlando (contralto); Angelica (soprano); Medoro (contralto); Dorinda (soprano); Zoroastro (bass).

Publications

Flesch, S. "Händels 'Orlando'." In *Festschrift der Händelfestspiele*, 42. Halle, 1961.
Jorgens, Elise B. "*Orlando* metamorphosed: Handel's Operas after Ariosto." *Parnassus* 10/no. 2 (1982): 45.

*   *   *

Orlando tells the story of Orlando (Roland), the warrior knight, whose love for the Princess Angelica is thwarted by her preference for the Moorish youth Medoro. Although it lacks the memorable arias that make other Handel operas so well-known, the opera is remarkable for its spectacle and for its characterization of Orlando's madness. The libretto is based on Ariosto's epic poem *Orlando furioso* of 1516, as are Handel's operas *Ariodante* (1734) and *Alcina* (1735). In the poem, Orlando's love-sickness causes him to rage uncontrollably; Ariosto writes that he pulls up tall pines at a single pull. Orlando is cured when the knight Astolpho, with St John as his guide, takes the chariot of Elijah to the moon and recovers Orlando's lost senses in a vessel labeled "Orlando's wit."

Handel's libretto, which is based on a libretto from Rome, 1711, by C.S. Capeci, elaborates upon this skeletal story. Capeci's libretto of *La resurrezione* (*The Resurrection*) had been written directly for Handel in 1708, and his *Tolomeo,*

also of 1711, formed the basis of Handel's opera of the same name (1728). In 1728, Handel's adaptor had been his regular librettist, Nicola Haym. The adaptor of *Orlando* is not known, but it may be that Haym prepared this libretto before his death in 1729 or that Handel revised it himself. Capeci's libretto adds to Ariosto's story the shepherdess Dorinda, who is in love with Medoro. It also includes a second pair of lovers, Isabella and Zerbino from Ariosto's epic, but these characters are omitted in Handel's version. Handel's version adds the sorcerer Zoroastro, who in the opening scenes urges Orlando to forsake love for duty (which advice Orlando chooses to ignore), and who in the closing scenes restores Orlando to his senses, the "golden vessel" containing his wits arriving in the beak of an eagle.

Orlando marks the first time since the early London operas (1711-1715) that Handel worked with a libretto containing magic, sorcery, and transformations. In fact, comparison with *Rinaldo* (1711), *Teseo* (1713), and *Amadigi* (1715) reveals many similarities to the extent that one might easily conclude the moments of spectacle were devised with the old stage machinery and equipment in mind. To pick but one example, Angelica's magical rescue from Orlando in act II, scene x ("Angelica flies, and Orlando pursues her, on which a large Cloud descending, covers Angelica, and bears her away into the Air, accompanied by four Genij that surround her") closely parallels Almirena's abduction in *Rinaldo,* act I, scene vii ("a black Cloud descends, all fill'd with dreadful Monsters. . . . The Cloud covers Almirena and Armida, and carries 'em up swiftly into the Air, leaving in their place, two frightful Furies . . ."). In Capeci's source libretto, as in Ariosto's poem, Angelica escapes from Orlando simply by putting in her mouth the magic ring that makes her invisible. The visual display in Handel's libretto that is lacking in the source libretto is frequently summoned directly by Zoroastro, a new character in Handel's version. His addition may thus have been less an aid to the story line than an aid to the desired spectacle.

Orlando's madness is depicted musically by playing on the convention of the *da capo* (from the beginning) aria, in which two distinct sections of text and music were invariably followed by a repetition of the first, during which the singer was expected to add ornamentation. An average Handel opera contained thirty such arias separated by simple recitative (sung speech) accompanied only by harpsichord and cello. *Orlando* offers a very different picture.

After the opening scenes with Orlando and Zoroastro, which show Orlando in a magical realm wrestling with his destiny, the scene changes to "A little Wood, interspers'd with the Cots of Shepherds." Almost immediately the music falls into normative patterns. Beginning with Dorinda's aria "Ho un certo rossore" ("I feel a strange confusion"), there follow seven *da capo* arias, including the act-ending trio for Medoro, Angelica and Dorinda, "Consolati, Oh bella" ("Lovely one, be comforted"), one of the rare ensembles in Handel's operas. During this series, only the duet for Angelica and Medoro, "Ritornava al suo bel viso" ("Restored to that fair face") fails to fall into the *da capo* pattern; all the recitatives are simple.

The same regularity of structure obtains throughout most of the second act. Beginning with Dorinda's "Se mi rivolgo al prato" ("If I wander to the meadow"), there are six *da capo* arias separated by simple recitative. At this point, Angelica is borne into the heavens on a cloud, and Orlando goes mad. He begins in recitative, "Ah, stigie larve" ("Ah, Stygian monsters"), accompanied by full orchestra (accompanied recitative) and moves freely through sections more song-like. A very unusual passage of music in 5/8 time (five eighth notes to a bar) marks his belief that he is crossing the River Styx into the underworld. The scene culminates with a rondo (refrains separated by contrasting interludes) in which the last refrain sets a changed text. For Orlando at this point nothing is stable, not even the rondo form, and his loss of mind is equated with the musical loss of the *da capo*. This continues in the third act, where the only non-*da capo* pieces are sung by the demented hero.

The dramatically intense scenes written for Orlando without recourse to the conventional *da capo* form, and the extraordinary visual effects, have made *Orlando* one of Handel's most frequently performed operas in this century. Although it was also admired when it was written—one contemporary writer deemed it "extraordinary fine & magnificent"—it did not prevent the temporary collapse of Handel's operatic venture. *Orlando* was the last opera of Handel's Second Academy.

—Ellen T. Harris

ORLANDO [originally called Orlando finto pazzo].

Composer: Antonio Vivaldi.

Librettist: G.B. Braccioli (after Ariosto, *Orlando furioso*).

First Performance: Venice, Sant' Angelo, fall 1714; revised as *Orlando,* first performed Venice, Sant' Angelo, fall 1727.

Roles: Orlando (mezzo-soprano); Angelica (soprano); Alcina (mezzo-soprano); Bradamante (contralto); Medoro (tenor); Ruggiero (baritone); Astolfo (bass).

Publications

book–

Collins, M., and E.K. Kirk, eds. *Opera and Vivaldi.* Austin, Texas, 1984.

article–

Tammaro, F. "Contaminazione e polivalenze nell' *Orlando finto pazzo.*" *Rivista italiana di musicologia* 17 (1982).

Perhaps the first thing to be said of the 1978 Verona and 1980 Dallas productions of "Vivaldi's" three-act opera *Orlando* (subsequently given in San Francisco in 1989) is that neither one was entirely the handiwork of the celebrated "Red Priest." Then again, the same also could be said of Vivaldi's staging of the work in 1727. There, in addition to composing music especially for the occasion, Vivaldi borrowed from his own 1714 *Orlando finto pazzo,* in turn a reworking of the 1713 *Orlando,* libretto by Grazio Braccioli, music by Giovanni Alberto Ristori, from which he retained a fair portion of Ristori's music (John Walter Hill has argued that almost all the music used by Vivaldi in act II of the 1727 score is Ristori's). In addition, he also may have used numbers from his 1727 *Siroe re di Persia* (Siroes, King of Persia). The 1714 opera bore the title *Orlando finto pazzo;* the 1727 work was

called simply *Orlando.* The use of the title *Orlando furioso* for the modern revival of the 1727 opera, an unnecessary change that succeeded only in complicating an already confusing state of affairs, evidently was the inspiration of the editor of the Verona/Dallas score, Claudio Scimone. Nor was this the only change Scimone wrought. The role of Ruggiero, for example, in Vivaldi's day sung by a castrato, was transposed down an octave for the performances in Verona (in Dallas it was taken by a countertenor); the score, particularly act I, was heavily cut, and at least one aria was imported from another Vivaldi work.

Vivaldi based his 1727 opera on Ludovico Ariosto's immensely popular epic poem *Orlando furioso,* an exhilarating mélange treating "Of Dames, of Knights, of armes, of love's delight" (to quote from the opening of John Harington's 1591 English verse translation), but mainly given over to the adventures of the Christian knight Roland (Orlando), nephew of Charlemagne. Begun in 1502 or 1503, Ariosto completed the poem some forty-six cantos later in 1532 when the work was brought out in its third edition. Vivaldi's operatic accounts of the saga necessarily were considerably condensed. Although Braccioli says in the preface to his 1713 libretto that the numerous exploits of the epic roam half the world, he limits his setting to the sorceress Alcina's enchanted island and takes as his main action the love, madness, and recovery of Orlando. But "the loves of Bradamante and Ruggiero, Angelica and Medoro, the various inclinations of Alcina, and diverse passions of Astolfo serve to accompany this action and lead to its end." Amorous machinations therefore abound in the 1727 opera. Orlando loves Angelica, the proud princess of Cathay, who has turned the heads of half of Europe's heroes and whose inconstancy in love has angered the God of Love; as punishment he wills that she fall in love with a completely unsuited person—in the event the lowborn but handsome Saracen warrior Medoro. Angelica first encounters Medoro mortally wounded; she cures him with Oriental potions and the pair retire to a shepherd's hut, are married, and afterwards carve their names in the bark of nearby trees. The two depart, whereupon Orlando comes upon the carved trees, learns of their marriage, and consequently loses his reason. Meanwhile, Alcina, King Arthur's sister, an old woman still craving sensual pleasures, maintains her seductive beauty by her sorcery; the latter she presently works on Ruggiero, another Christian knight. Bradamante, niece of Charlemagne, seeing her beloved Ruggiero under Alcina's spell, seeks help from the enchantress Melissa. Legions of plot twists later, the opera ends with Orlando's recovery of his senses thanks to the intervention of his cousin Astolfo; Alcina's vow of vengeance and loss of magical powers; and the reunion of Bradamante and Ruggiero. Orlando calmly pardons Angelica and Medoro and blesses their marriage.

Before the Verona and Dallas revivals of *Orlando*—the latter evidently the first Vivaldi opera staged in America—the received wisdom was pretty much dependent on the appraisals of mid eighteenth-century critics who cited them as evidence of Vivaldi's supposed inability to keep pace with changing styles. Thus Tartini declared in 1740: "a gullet is not the neck of a violin. Vivaldi, who wanted to practice both genres [i.e., operatic and instrumental writing], always failed to go over in the one, whereas in the other he succeeded very well." And Quantz, in his 1752 treatise *On Playing the Flute,* was of the opinion that after Vivaldi began to write "theatrical vocal pieces [the first in 1713 at age thirty-five], he sank into frivolity and eccentricity both in composition and performance."

While it would be a mistake to hazard an evaluation of all ninety-four operas Vivaldi claimed late in life to have written based on only a single composition, his 1727 *Orlando* nevertheless forcefully disproves Tartini's and Quantz's pronouncements. *Orlando* also explodes one of the "rules" set forth in 1720 by Benetto Marcello in his satirical *Teatro alla moda* when he says that a composer should see to it "that the arias, to the very end of the opera, are alternately lively and pathetic, without regard to the words [of the libretto]." Vivaldi broke with convention and grouped within each of the opera's nine stage settings arias of the same type, the result being an infinitely more trenchant and dramatic whole than that derided by Marcello. Similar emotions—tenderness, vengeance, etc.—thus catch different characters differently. Other dramatic surprises at variance with the "rules" include launching an aria without recitative, halting a number at an unexpected moment, and keeping a character onstage after an apparent "exit aria." (Such innovations are just one reason why the changes introduced by Scimone are to be regretted.) Borrowings from his own work and from the work of others notwithstanding, Vivaldi crafted the 1727 *Orlando* with unusual care, creating a work abounding with energy and beautiful, stirring music. If *Orlando* is in any way representative of Vivaldi's achievement as an operatic composer, it can only be hoped that it will not be long before more of his operas are revived as well.

—James Parsons

L'ORMINDO.

Composer: Francesco Cavalli.

Librettist: Giovanni Faustini.

First Performance: Venice, San Cassiano, carnival 1644.

Roles: Ormindo (tenor); Amida (baritone); Sicle (mezzo-soprano); Erisbe (soprano); Ariadeno (bass); Nerillo (mezzo-soprano); Melide (mezzo-soprano); Erice (tenor); Mirindi (mezzo-soprano); Osmano (baritone).

Publications

books–

Rosand, Ellen. *Opera in Seventeenth-Century Venice.* Berkeley, 1991.

articles–

Rosand, Ellen. " 'Ormindo travestito' in *Erismena.*" *Journal of the American Musicological Society* 28 (1975): 268.

* * *

Ormindo, Prince of Tunis, and Amida, Prince of Tremisene, have succeeded in stopping the Spanish assault on King Ariadeno's territories of Morocco and Fez. Both princes have fallen victim to the charms of Erisbe, Ariadeno's young queen, who adores them both and cannot choose between them. Amida's former lover, Princess Sicle, arrives in Fez with her old nurse, Erice. Disguised as Egyptians, the newcomers are not recognized by Amida and soon learn that he is courting Erisbe. Seizing an opportunity to expose Amida's deception and faithlessness, Sicle tells his fortune and reveals his desertion of a certain princess in Torodenta. He is furious and Erisbe stunned by the revelation. Consequently, she pledges her true love to Ormindo. He and his army are on the point of departure from Fez, and Erisbe impulsively decides to sail with them.

Meanwhile, Erice has arranged to meet Amida on the old city ramparts where she promises to restore Erisbe to his arms. Erice brings Sicle to keep the appointment but hides her. When Amida enters, Erice casts a magic spell designed to obtain the release of Sicle's soul from Hades. The presumed spirit of Sicle appears. Amida, seeing Sicle once more, confesses a resurgence of the old fire. Overjoyed, she exclaims that she is really alive, and the couple sing a rapturous duet of restored love.

Ariadeno learns from his captain Osmano that Ormindo and Erisbe have both been captured while trying to escape from Fez. The old king orders their deaths by poisoning, but Osmano administers a sleeping potion instead of poison. Both lovers expire, expecting to be united forever in the happy gardens of eternity. As a repentant Ariadeno expresses deep regret at his rash execution order, Ormindo and Erisbe awaken. Ariadeno, touched at their devotion and, realizing his own age and fragility, offers his throne, country, and wife to Ormindo. All ends happily as the company sing the praises of love in the obligatory closing ensemble.

L'Ormindo is one of Cavalli's earliest operas and the third of the group set to libretti by Giovanni Faustini. It contains many of the familiar comic elements that characterize the seventeenth-century Venetian opera: a wise and scheming nurse, waiting women more sophisticated than their mistresses, a naive page, and two pairs of lovers. Erice felicitously and magically resolves one of the love stories. Sicle's Melide and Erisbe's Mirinda present the views of canny young female servants who are aware of men's escapades but who are determined to avoid their traps. Nerillo, Amida's page, is at least as foolish as his master; however, his youth and experience demand that he be forgiven his biting comments on men's foibles. Each of these minor characters is elevated by important solo monologues in which he assumes the role of critical commentator on the actions and emotions of his social superiors.

The development of the *personae* of the highly ranked characters is an especially fascinating component of the plot. Their love stories present librettist and composer with fruitful opportunities to explore the emotional ambiguities of the mind. The foolish behavior of a well-born lover may obviously be cause for derision and ridicule but can subtly suggest the emergence of wisdom. Erisbe's frivolous unfaithfulness certainly evokes amusement. However, one cannot help being moved by her eventual unselfish devotion to Ormindo, or by her determination to accompany him in death. One can also appreciate Ariadeno's abdication as the noble sacrifice that can be inspired by intense devotion of the old for the young.

—Martha Novak Clinkscale

ORPHEUS AND EURYDICE [Haydn]
See L'ANIMA DEL FILOSOFO

ORPHEUS AND EURYDICE [Monteverdi]
See LA FAVOLA D'ORFEO

ORPHEUS AND EURYDICE [Gluck]
See ORFEO ED EURIDICE

OTELLO, ossia il moro de Venezia [Othello, or The Moor of Venice].

Composer: Gioachino Rossini.

Librettist: F. Berio di Salsa (after Shakespeare).

First Performance: Naples, Teatro del Fondo, 4 December 1816.

Roles: Otello (tenor); Desdemona (soprano); Rodrigo (tenor); Iago (tenor); Elmiro (bass); Emilia (mezzo-soprano); The Doge (tenor); Gondolier (tenor); chorus (SATB).

Publications

articles–

Klein, J.W. "Verdi's "Otello' and Rossini's." *Music and Letters* 45 (1964): 130.

Tammaro, F. "Ambivalenza dell' *Otello* rossiniano." In *Il melodramma italiano dell' ottocento: studi e ricerche per Massimo Mila.* Turin, 1977.

Dahlhaus, Carl. "Zur Methode der Opern-Analyse" [*Otello* finale]. *Musik und Bildung* 12 (1980): 518.

Rozett, Martha Tuck. "*Othello, Otello* and the Comic Tradition." *Bulletin of Research in the Humanities* 85 (1982): 386.

Although the opera is based on Shakespeare's play, it treats its source more freely than Verdi's *Otello.* Rossini's opera plays down the love between Otello and Desdemona, who have no love duet (their only duet is the frantic one leading up to the murder of Desdemona). Desdemona is given a father, Elmiro, who despises Otello and curses his daughter when she tells him of her love for the Moor. The intricate

Set design by Karl Friedrich Schinkel for Rossini's *Otello,* Berlin, 1821

process by which Shakespeare (and Verdi) have Iago gradually enflame Otello's jealousy is much abridged and simplified; Rossini's opera leaves out Cassio (a character crucial to Shakespeare and Verdi) altogether.

But comparisons with Shakespeare and Verdi do little to reveal the real worth of Rossini's *Otello,* a fine example of early nineteenth-century *opera seria,* and a work that can stand securely on its own. Rossini composed the opera for the San Carlo theater in Naples, whose company included three tenors capable of taking leading roles; this led to the casting of not only Otello but also Rodrigo and Iago as tenors (Desdemona's father is the only bass among the principals). Rossini used his plethora of tenors to dramatic purpose. He composed the confrontation between Rodrigo and Otello (in the second-act trio "Ah vieni, nel tuo sangue") as a kind of singing contest between the two rivals: the ensemble begins with Rodrigo and Otello singing, in turn, almost exactly the same music, culminating in a high C and a run of coloratura.

This was not the only place where Rossini left the singers themselves to differentiate their characters. He also did so in the first-act duet for Emilia and Desdemona, "Vorrei che il tuo pensier," where Emilia tries to cheer up Desdemona. The duet lacks the kind of musical characterization with which Weber, in an analogous scene in *Der Freischütz* (composed five years later), distinguished Agathe and Aennchen. But Weber did not surpass the beauty of Rossini's duet, with its delicate intertwining of soprano voices.

Among the many remarkable features of Rossini's drama is its orchestral writing. The plot unfolds at a leisurely pace, interspersed with orchestral passages of considerable length and complexity. Otello's triumphant aria "Ah! sì per voi sento," in act I, is followed by an orchestral postlude that recapitulates the march that accompanied Otello's arrival in Venice; later in act I a long orchestral introduction with beautiful woodwind writing and an elaborate horn solo sets a mood of gentle melancholy for the scene in which Emilia tries to comfort Desdemona. The intensely lyrical clarinet solo in Rodrigo's aria "Che ascolto?" (act II) and the harp solo in Desdemona's Willow Song (act III) are among the instrumental passages that embellish *Otello* and evoke its shifting moods.

Rossini's manipulation of harmonic resources is no less effective. The simple shift from minor to major near the end of each strophe of the Willow Song is rich in pathos. In the trio "Ah vieni, nel tuo sangue," a quiet yet daring modulation after a long, harmonically static passage shows Rossini, with a perfect sense of timing, preparing the audience for an explosion of emotion as the trio ends.

—John A. Rice

OTELLO.

Composer: Giuseppe Verdi.

Librettist: Arrigo Boito (after Shakespeare).

First Performance: Milan, Teatro alla Scala, 5 February 1887.

Roles: Otello (tenor); Iago (baritone); Desdemona (soprano); Cassio (tenor); Emilia (mezzo-soprano); Roderigo (tenor); Lodovico (bass); Montano (bass); A Herald (bass); chorus (SSATB).

Publications

books–

Degrada, Francesco. *Il palazzo incantato.* Fiesole, 1979.

Csampai, Attila, and Dietmar Holland, eds. *Giuseppe Verdi: Otello: Text, Materialien, Kommentare.* Reinbek, 1981.

Hepokoski, James A. *Giuseppe Verdi: Otello.* Cambridge, 1987.

Bush, Hans, ed. *Verdi's Otello and Simon Boccanegra (Revised Version) in Letters and Documents.* 2 vols. Oxford, 1988.

articles–

Schueller, H. "*Othello* Transformed: Verdi's Interpretation of Shakespeare." In *Studies in Honor of John Wilcox.* Detroit, 1958.

Klein, John W. "Verdi's *Otello* and Rossini's." *Music and Letters* April (1964).

Dean, Winton. "Verdi's *Otello:* A Shakespearean Masterpiece." *Shakespeare Survey* 21 (1968).

Hauger, George. *Othello* and *Otello." Music and Letters* January (1969).

Aycock, Roy Edwin. "Shakespeare, Boito, and Verdi." *Musical Quarterly* October (1972).

Avant-scène opéra May-June (1976) [*Otello* issue].

Lawton, David. "On the 'bacio' Theme in *Otello.*" *Nineteenth-Century Music* 1 (1977-78): 211.

Coe, Doug. "The Original Production Book for *Otello:* an Introduction." *Nineteenth-Century Music* 2 (1978): 148.

Noske, Frits. "*Otello:* Drama through Structure." In *Essays on Music for Charles Warren Fox,* edited by Jerald C. Grave, 14. Rochester, New York, 1979.

Budden, Julian. "Time Stands Still in *Otello.*" *Opera* 32 (1981).

Cone, E.T. "On the Road to *Otello:* Tonality and Structure in *Simon Boccanegra.*" *Studi verdiani* 1 (1982): 72.

Rozett, Martha Tuch. "*Othello, Otello* and the Comic Tradition." *Bulletin of Research in the Humanities* 85 (1982): 386.

Parker, Roger, and Matthew Brown. "*Ancora un bacio:* Three Scenes from Verdi's *Otello.*" *Nineteenth-Century Music* 9 (1985): 50.

Gualerzik, Giorgio. "Otello: the Legacy of Tamagno." *Opera* February (1987).

Taddie, Daniel. "The Devil, You Say: Reflections on Verdi's and Boito's Iago." *Opera Quarterly* spring (1990).

* * *

It was publisher Giulio Ricordi's fondest wish in the late 1870s to bring Giuseppe Verdi out of his post-*Aida* retirement and back to the business of writing new operas. He ultimately accomplished this feat by arranging a collaboration between the composer and the brilliant librettist Arrigo Boito, whose flamboyant, youthful views in the 1860s on the need for operatic reform had once alienated Verdi. They worked together first on a revision of Verdi's much lamented mid-career fiasco, *Simon Boccanegra* (1857), and, beginning almost simultaneously, on a work that fired Verdi's imagination from the beginning: *Otello,* based on the play *Othello* by his most beloved playwright, Shakespeare. The project was secret at first, and Verdi refused to make any promises that the opera would ever be finished or performed; indeed his eventual contract for the 1887 Teatro alla Scala season included

A scene from the first production of Verdi's *Otello*, Milan, 1887

stipulations that he could withdraw the work at any time for any reason. The control Verdi thus exercised over the compositional process of *Otello* contrasts strikingly with that of the operas of his early-period "years in the galley" (as he called them); and the results of this control, along with Boito's poetic and scenic input, are intensely dramatic, very much in keeping with Verdi's stated aims for opera throughout his career.

The plot involved some significant changes from the Shakespearean source, including the removal of the play's act I in Venice, and the telescoping of Iago's tempting of Otello to jealousy and destruction into fewer, more melodramatic scenes. To review the main action: act I begins on a stormy night in Cyprus, as the jealous Iago sets up Otello's favored lieutenant Cassio into drinking too much, losing his temper, and wounding a fellow soldier, Montano, in a fight. Iago has his henchman Roderigo sound the alarm, and when Otello, the Moorish commander of the Venetian forces and Governor of Cyprus, arrives, Iago allows him to believe that Cassio is completely at fault. Otello dismisses Cassio from his service, and the act closes with a love scene between Otello and his beautiful wife Desdemona, reminiscing on their early courtship. In act II, Iago advises Cassio to beg Otello's forgiveness through his wife Desdemona, and then encourages Otello to be suspicious of the intimate scene he sees between Desdemona and Cassio (as the latter follows Iago's advice), and of her ensuing intercession on Cassio's behalf. In act III Otello becomes increasingly filled with the jealousy Iago sows in him; he believes that a special handkerchief of Desdemona's which Iago steals and plants on Cassio furnishes the proof of Desdemona's unfaithfulness. In front of the Venetian ambassador—who has come to deliver the orders of Otello's recall to Venice and his replacement by Cassio—Otello strikes and curses Desdemona, and yields to Iago's insistence that Desdemona and Cassio be punished immediately, before the change in command takes effect. Dismissing the crowd, who are then heard in the distance shouting praise to Otello, "Leon di Venezia" ("Lion of Venice"), he collapses in a psychotic rage, leaving Iago to snarl with triumph his ironic line "Ecco il Leone"—"Here's the Lion!" Act IV begins with the frightened Desdemona's Willow Song and prayer, followed quickly by Otello's entrance and the murder. But Otello realizes his mistake when Emilia arrives with the news that Roderigo, dead at Cassio's hand, has revealed Iago's treachery. The opera ends as Otello takes a final kiss from the dead Desdemona and kills himself with his dagger.

Verdi's musical language in *Otello* illustrates his successful late-period merging of the vocally-oriented set piece traditions of Italian opera, with a thematically and harmonically unified approach, more characteristic of the French and German traditions. Thus Iago, for instance, communicates his evil act II "Credo" in a traditional aria form, and elsewhere employs the traditional drinking song (act I) and cabaletta form (the closing duet of act II, with Otello); but on the other hand his appearances are just as powerfully characterized by recurring orchestral ideas, such as the ragged brass fanfare and the long, eery woodwind trills of the Credo, and the winding unison melody of "É un idra fosca, livida" ("It's a dark, malign monster," referring to jealousy), which appears again as the prelude to act III to symbolize the working of Iago's poison on Otello's mind. Otello and Desdemona too have powerful solo moments, she in the haunting Willow Song and "Ave Maria" of act IV, and he in the passionate act III arioso "Dio! mi potevi scagliar" ("Heaven! Had it pleased thee to try me") and his death scene in act IV. At the same time, the large-scale tonal and thematic design, as well as deceptive cadences and connecting orchestral interludes, serve to override the separations of these vocally-oriented segments and give coherence, at least subliminally, to the drama.

Probably the most brilliant sections of the opera are the duets and ensembles, for which Verdi combines his new-found skills with large-scale tonal and thematic unity, with the dissimilar ensemble technique he had developed in the middle period, where dissimilarity in the vocal lines of each of the characters reveals the separate qualities of their personalities and/or situations. Thus for example in the act III ensemble "A terra! si . . . nel livido fango" ("Yea, prostrate I lie in the dust"), Desdemona's high leaps and soothing stepwise descents express her pleas for restored peace and love, and contrast against the more hymn-like sympathies of the crowd, and the speech-like dialogue of Otello and Iago, as they plan to expedite the punishments of Cassio and Desdemona. Meanwhile, symmetries of theme and key provide unity to the scene and link it with the drama of the rest of the act.

Out of his first complete collaboration with the gifted Boito, Verdi received the benefits of some excellent dramatic advice, leading for example to the powerful ironic ending of act III, and a poetic style featuring the very concision and scenic focus that he had long hoped and asked for from other librettists. The powerful concision of such lines as "Ecco il Leone!" and "Ancora un bacio" ("One more kiss") when accompanied with such deft musical imagery as the swelling "Bacio" theme, create the most memorable moments in *Otello*. In addition, Verdi's orchestration of the score is masterfully colorful and dramatic, especially in his unique solo melodic use of muted double basses at Otello's act IV entrance to Desdemona's bedchamber.

The opera was an immense success in its La Scala premiere, and within two years had reached most of the operatic theaters in the world. Verdi received all the adulation that one might expect for a long-missed national hero and theatrical genius; he was carried through the streets and applauded through the night, according to the account in the *Musical Times*. Today *Otello* remains among the most admired works of the operatic literature.

—Claire Detels

OTHELLO
See OTELLO

OWEN WINGRAVE.

Composer: Benjamin Britten.

Librettist: M. Piper (after Henry James).

First Performance: broadcast premiere: British Broadcasting Corporation, 16 May 1971; stage premiere, London, Covent Garden, 10 May 1973.

Roles: Owen Wingrave (baritone); Spencer Coyle (bass-baritone); Lechmere (tenor); Miss Wingrave (soprano); Mrs

Coyle (soprano); Mrs Julian (soprano); General Sir Philip Wingrave (tenor); Narrator (tenor); chorus.

Publications

article–

Corse, Sandra. "Owen Wingrave." In *Opera and the Uses of Language: Mozart, Verdi, and Britten.* New Jersey, 1987.

Owen Wingrave was not the first opera for which Britten (through his librettist Myfanwy Piper) had turned to Henry James for a congenial subject. Some sixteen years earlier *The Turn of the Screw* had provided him with an eerie and ambiguous tale of a haunted country house: two innocent children secretly possessed by evil spirits are yet in the end perhaps "saved" by the "good" governess whose struggle with the ghosts of a former manservant and his mistress leads to the confession and death of Miles, one of her two charges. *Wingrave,* set in an English country mansion belonging to a family with a proud military tradition, is also a tale of the supernatural. Here the ghosts are ancestral: a cruel Colonel and his son—the son accidentally killed by a blow from his father for refusing to fight in some childhood quarrel, the father subsequently found dead in his room. Young Owen Wingrave, studying strategy with Spencer Coyle, head of a military establishment in London, has turned against his family's proud tradition of dying in battle for King and Country and has become a pacifist. For this he has to face the fury of "the living and the dead" at Paramore, the Wingraves' country seat. Disinherited in an interview with his senile old grandfather (his father had died in battle too), proudly free (as he now thinks) of his family's outraged sense of honor and bullying, Owen is taunted by his fiancee Kate to sleep in the haunted room to prove that he is not a coward. Accepting the challenge, he allows himself to be locked in the room overnight and, after an uneasy passage of time in which the house guests are unable to sleep, is discovered there lifeless by a remorseful Kate. The Wingraves have claimed their own after all, yet in a sense Owen has won.

In *Owen Wingrave* Britten speaks out against war through the mouth of his chief protagonist. It is thus a "morality" no less than previous operas such as the *Church Parables* or *Noyes Fludde* or *Paul Bunyan,* a protest as vehement and intense as the *War Requiem.* Its lyrical high point is a radiant monologue in the (much shorter) act II when, against a succession of sustained common chords setting out in B flat major and surrounded by bells, Owen sings of peace as a positive force in the world. (This passage has been compared with the awesome chordal interlude after the trial and Vere's aria ["I accept their verdict"] before the final scene of *Billy Budd.*) The release brought about here is memorable in the context of large-scale musico-dramatic tensions that are spelt out with concentrated precision in the prelude to the opera. The passion and imagery of *Wingrave* are fired by two characteristic and inter-related elements in Britten's technique that had already come to the fore in previous works. These are (1) "heterophony" (or the overlapping of the notes of a melody to form—as in a peal of bells—harmonic "clusters" or "aggregates" of sound) which was the leading principle of *Curlew River* and the *Church Parables;* (2) what Schoenberg referred to as "the unity of musical space"—the ordering of all twelve notes of the chromatic scale into characteristic "rows" which are manipulated to form a kind of magnetic field of horizontal (i.e. melodic) and vertical (i.e. harmonic) forces. It is Britten's masterly deployment of these techniques, both vocally and instrumentally, together with his (to use another definition from Schoenberg) "emancipation of the dissonance" within an expanded sense of traditional tonality, that gives this opera its unique resonances—resonances that continue to vibrate in his next and final opera, *Death in Venice.*

It should not be forgotten that *Wingrave* was composed in the first place for television—a medium Britten had already thought about deeply in connection with the mounting of *Peter Grimes* for a British Broadcasting Corporation television production in February 1969 (see his conversation with Donald Mitchell in *The Britten Companion,* London, 1984, pp. 88-92). The surrealistic potential and fluidity of the film medium (for which Britten had shown an early flair in his work for the GPO Film Unit in the 1930s) is here deliberately exploited in direct opposition to that popular brand of photographic realism which, in Britten's view, was not to be countenanced in the televised presentation of opera. Cross-cutting, "dissolves," fading out, collage, music as an expression of unspoken thought on the part of the assembled characters, swift transitions—all these devices applied to the musical conception make of *Wingrave* an opera which, as it is sometimes said of certain works by Berlioz (e.g. *Romeo and Juliet, Faust* or *Les Troyens*) is perhaps heard to advantage in the theater of the imagination. In this respect, Britten's fine recording with the original cast for whom the opera was written and the English Chamber Orchestra in 1970 is indispensable.

—Eric Roseberry

P

PACINI, Giovanni.

Composer. Born 17 February 1796, in Catania. Died 6 December 1867, in Pescia. Studied with Marchesi and Padre Mattei in Bologna, and with Furlanetto in Venice; composed forty-six operas up to the failure of *Carlo di Borgogna,* 1835, when he stopped composing operas for a period; established a music school at Viareggio, near Lucca, later moving it to Lucca; *Saffo* a great success, 1840; thirty-one more operas up to 1867. Pacini was a contributor to several musical journals; his brother Emilio Pacini (1810-98) was a well-known librettist.

Operas

Don Pomponio, G. Paganini, 1813 [not performed].
Annetta e Lucindo, F. Marconi, Milan, S. Radegonda, 17 October 1813.
La ballerina raggiratrice, G. Palomba, Florence, Teatro della Pergola, spring 1814.
L'ambizione delusa, G. Palomba, Florence, Teatro della Pergola, spring 1814.
L'escavazione del tesoro, F. Marconi, Pisa, Ravvivati, 18 December 1814.
Gli sponsali de' silfe, F. Marconi, Milan, Filodrammatici, carnival 1814-15.
Bettina vedova (Il seguito di Ser Mercantonio), A. Anelli, Venice, San Moisè, spring 1815.
La Rosina, G. Palomba, Florence, Teatro della Pergola, summer 1815.
La Chiarina (?), A. Anelli, Venice, San Benedetto, carnival 1815-16.
L'ingenua, Marconi, Venice, San Benedetto, 4 May 1816.
Il matromonio per procura, A. Anelli, Milan, Re, 2 January 1817.
Dalla beffa il disinganno, ossia La poetessa, A. Anelli, Milan, Re, carnival 1816-17; revised with a new text as *Il carnevale di Milano,* P. Latanza, Milan, Re, 23 February 1817.
Piglia il mondo come viene, Anelli, Milan, Re, 28 May 1817.
I virtuosi del Teatro (?), G. Rossi, Milan, Re, 1817.
La bottega di Cafè (?), G. Foppa, Milan, Re, 1817.
Adelaide e Comingio, Rossi, Milan, Re, 30 December 1817.
Atala, A. Peracchi, Padua, Nuovo, June 1818.
Gl' illinesi, F. Romani, 1818 [not performed].
Il barone di Dolsheim (Federico II re di Prussia, Il barone di Felcheim, La colpa emendata dal valore), F. Romani, Milan, Teatro alla Scala, 23 September 1818.
La sposa fedele, Rossi, Venice, San Benedetto, 14 January 1819; revised, Milan, Teatro alla Scala, 1 August 1819.
Il falegname di Livonia, F. Romani, Milan, Teatro alla Scala, 12 April 1819; revised, Florence, Teatro della Pergola, 28 February 1823.
Vallace, o L'eroe scozzese, F. Romani, Milan, Teatro alla Scala, 14 February 1820.
La sacerdotessa d'Irminsul, F. Romani, Trieste, Grande, 11 May 1820.
La schiava in Bagdad, ossia il papucciajo, Turin, Carignano, 20 October 1820.

La gioventù di Enrico V (La bella tavernara, ossia L'avventure d'une notte), G. Tarducci or J. Ferretti (in part after Shakespeare), Rome, Valle, 26 December 1820.
Cesare in Egitto, J. Feretti, Rome, Torre Argentina, 26 December 1821.
La vestale, L. Romanelli, Milan, Teatro alla Scala, 6 February 1823.
Temistocle, P. Anguillesi (after Metastasio), Lucca, Giglio, 23 August 1823.
Isabella ed Enrico, L. Romanelli, Milan, Teatro alla Scala, 12 June 1824.
Alessandro nell' Indie, A.L. Tottola (after Metastasio), Naples, San Carlo, 29 September 1824.
Amazilia, G. Schmidt, Naples, San Carlo, 6 July 1825; revised, Vienna, 20 February 1827.
L'ultimo giorno di Pompei, A.L. Tottola, Naples, San Carlo, 19 November 1825.
La gelosia corretta, L. Romanelli, Milan, Teatro alla Scala, 27 March 1826.
Niobe, A.L. Tottola, Naples, San Carlo, 19 November 1826.
Gli arabi nelle Gallie, ossia Il trionfo della fede, L. Romanelli (after d' Arlincourt, *Le renégat*), Milan, Teatro alla Scala, 8 March 1827; revised, Paris, Théâtre-Italien, 30 January 1855.
Margherita, regina d'Inghilterra, A.L. Tottola, Naples, San Carlo, 19 November 1827.
I cavalieri di Valenza, Rossi, Milan, Teatro alla Scala, 11 June 1828.
I crociati in Tolemaide, ossia Malek-Adel (La morte di Malek-Adel), C. Bassi, Trieste, Grande, 13 November 1828.
Il talismano, ovvero La terza crociata in Palestina, G. Barbieri (after Scott), Milan, Teatro alla Scala, 10 June 1829.
I fidanzati, ossia Il contestabile di Chester, D. Gilardoni (after Scott), Naples, San Carlo, 19 November 1829.
Giovanna d' Arco, G. Barbieri, Milan, Teatro alla Scala, 14 March 1830.
Il corsaro, J. Ferretti (after Byron), Rome, Apollo, 15 January 1831.
Il rinnegato portoghese (Gusmano d' Almeida), L. Romanelli, written for Venice, La Fenice, 1831 [not performed].
Ivanhoe, Rossi (after Scott), Venice, La Fenice, 19 March 1832.
Don Giovanni Tenorio, o Il convitato di pietra, G. Bertati, Viareggio, Casa Belluomini, spring 1832.
Gli elvezi, ovvero Corrado di Tochemburgo, Rossi, Naples, San Carlo, 12 January 1833.
Fernando duca di Valenza, P. Pola, Naples, San Carlo, 30 May 1833.
Irene, o L' assedio di Messina, Rossi?, Naples, San Carlo, 30 November 1833.
Carlo di Borgogna, Rossi, Venice, La Fenice, 21 February 1835.
La foresta d' Hermanstadt, Viareggio, 1839 [not performed].
Furio Camillo, J. Ferretti, Rome, Apollo, 26 December 1839.
Saffo, S. Cammarano, Naples, San Carlo, 29 November 1840.
L'uomo del mistero, D. Andreotti (after Scott), Naples, Nuovo, 9 November 1841.

Il duca d'Alba (Adolpho di Warbel), G. Peruzzini and F.M. Piave, Venice, La Fenice, 26 February 1842.

La fidanzata corsa, S. Cammarano (after Mérimée, *Colomba*), Naples, San Carlo, 10 December 1842.

Maria, regina d' Inghilterra, L. Tarantini, Palermo, Carolino, 11 February 1843.

Medea, B. Castiglia, Palermo, Carolino, 28 November 1843.

Luisella, ossia La cantatrice del molo [di Napoli], L. Tarantini, Naples, Nuovo, 13 December 1843.

L' ebrea, G. Sacchèro, Milan, Teatro alla Scala, 27 February 1844.

Lorenzino de' Medici, F.M. Piave, Venice, La Fenice, 4 March 1845; revised as *Elisa Velasco,* Rome, Apollo, 3 January 1854; revised as *Rolandino di Torresmondo,* D. Bolognese, Naples, San Carlo, 20 March 1858.

Bondelmonte, S. Cammarano, Florence, Teatro della Pergola, 18 June 1845.

Stella di Napoli, S. Cammarano, Naples, San Carlo, 11 December 1845.

La regina di Cipro, F. Guidi, Turin, Regio, 7 February 1846.

Merope, S. Cammarano, Naples, San Carlo, 25 November 1847.

Ester d'Engaddi, F. Guidi, Turin, Regio, 1 February 1848.

Allan Cameron, F.M. Piave, Venice, La Fenice, 28 March 1848.

Alfrida, Bertolozzi [not performed].

Zaffira, o La riconciliazione, A. de Lauzières, Naples, Nuovo, 15 November 1851.

Malvina di Scozia, S. Cammarano, Naples, San Carlo, 27 December 1851.

L' assedio di Leida (Elnaya), F.M. Piave, 1852? [not performed].

Rodrigo di Valenza, written for Palermo, Carolino, carnival 1852-53 [not performed].

Il Cid, A. de Lauzières, Milan, Teatro all Scala, 12 March 1853.

Lidia di Brabante, Gaetano, 1853 [not performed].

Romilda di Provenza, G. Miccio, Naples, San Carlo, 8 December 1853.

La donna delle isole, F.M. Piave, written for Venice, La Fenice, carnival 1853-54 [not performed].

La punizione, C. Perini, Venice, La Fenice, 8 March 1854, [revision of *Lidia di Brabante*].

Margherita Pusterla, D. Bolognese, Naples, San Carlo, 25 February 1856.

Il saltimbanco, G. Checchetelli, Rome, Torre Argentina, 24 May 1858.

Lidia di Bruxelles, G. Cencetti, Bologna, Comunale, 21 October 1858 [revision of *Lidia di Brabante,* 1853].

Gianni di Nisida, G. Checchetelli, Rome, Torre Argentina, 29 October 1860.

Il mulattiere di Toledo, G. Cencetti, Rome, Apollo, 25 May 1861.

Belfagor, A. Lanari (after Machiavelli), Florence, Teatro della Pergola, 1 December 1861 [composed 1851?].

Carmelita, F.M. Piave (after Dumas, *Don Juan de Marana*), written for Milan, Teatro alla Scala, 1863 [not performed].

Don Diego di Mendoza, F.M. Piave, Venice, La Fenice, 12 January 1867.

Berta di Varnol, F.M. Piave, Naples, San Carlo, 6 April 1867.

Nicola de Lapi, C. Perini, 1855, Florence, Pagliano, 1873 [revision of *Lidia di Brabante*].

Publications/Writings

By PACINI: books–

Sulla originalità della musica melodrammatica italiana del sec. XVIII: ragionamento. Lucca, 1841.

Corso teorico-pratico di lezioni di armonia. Milan, c. 1844.

Principi elementari col metodo del Meloplasto. Lucca, 1849.

Memoria sul migliore indirizzo degli studii musicali. Florence, 1863.

Cenni storici sulla musica e trattato di contrappunto. Lucca, 1864.

Le mie memorie artistiche. Florence, 1865; edited by F. Magnani, Florence, 1875; edited by Luciano Nicolosi and Piannavaria Salvatore, Lucca, 1982.

unpublished–

Lettera ai municipi italiani per una scuola musicale (1863).
Progetto dei giovani compositori (1863).
Vita di Guido d'Arezzo (1865?).

About PACINI: books–

Carlez, J. *Pacini et l'opéra italien.* Caen, 1888.

Giovanni Pacini. Pescia, 1896.

Davini, M. *Il maestro Giovanni Pacini.* Palermo, 1927.

Lippman, F. *Vincenzo Bellini und die italienische Opera Seria seiner Zeit.* Cologne, 1969.

Kaufman, Tom. *Verdi and his Major Contemporaries. Annals of Italian Opera,* vol. 1. New York, 1990.

articles–

Clément, F. "Giovanni Pacini." In *Les musiciens célèbres.* Paris, 1868.

Lianovsani, L. [=G. Salvioli]. "Serie cronologica delle opere teatrali cantate ed oratio del maestro Giovanni Comm. Pacini." *Gazzetta musicale di Milano* 31 (1876): 215.

Ghislanzoni, A. "Giovanni Pacini." *Libro serio* [Milan] (1879): 49.

Chilesotti, O. "Giovanni Pacini." In *Nostri maestri del passato.* Milan, 1882.

Barbiera, R. "Pacini e un suo carteggio." In *Immortali dimenticati.* Milan, 1901.

———. "Paolina Bonaparte e la sua passione per il Maestro Pacini." In *Vite ardenti nel teatro.* Milan, 1931.

Cametti, A. "La musica teatrale, a Roma cento anni fa: 'Il corsaro' di Pacini." In *Annuario della R. accademia di Santa Cecilia.* Rome, 1931.

Lippmann, F. "Giovanni Pacini: Bemerkungen zum Stil seiner Opern." *Chigiana* 24 (1967): 111.

Profeta, R. "Giovanni Pacini e la *Saffo.*" *L'opera* [Milan] no. 6 (1967): 31.

Ugolini, G. "Pacini alle origini del melodramma ottocentesco." *L'opera* [Milan] no. 6 (1967): 22.

Commons, Jeremy. "Pacini and Maria R. Tudor." *Donizetti Society Journal* no. 6 (1988).

*   *   *

With the possible exception of Saverio Mercadante, no nineteenth-century Italian opera composer was as successful in his day, or as forgotten in ours as Giovanni Pacini. Even Mercadante does not really qualify, in that some eight Mercadante operas have had recent revivals; while there have been only two recent revivals of works by Pacini.

During his lifetime, Pacini composed some 73 operas (the exact number is difficult, if not impossible, to establish, because some of the titles listed may have been revisions of earlier works). His first 30 or so operas, composed during the time when Rossini was still in Italy were, not surprisingly, in the Rossini style, but so were everybody else's. Pacini and his contemporaries (Meyerbeer, Bellini, Donizetti and Mercadante) started to modify the nature of Italian opera around 1824. Collectively, they started to create a new style for bel canto opera.

It would be inaccurate to say that each of these composers evolved a style of his own, and followed it throughout his career. Instead, they were strongly influenced by one another; with the exception of Meyerbeer's French works, the differences in style between these composers are much less apparent than the similarities. Similarly, the differences in style between operas by different composers dating from the same period (e.g. the early 1840s or the late 1810s) are less significant than the differences between one composer's early and late operas. These composers did, however develop their own trademarks; thus, just as Bellini was best known for his long melodic line, Pacini earned considerable fame by the vigor and variety of his cabalettas.

Early in his career, Pacini became one of the most prominent composers in Italy. His position was greatly enhanced by the success of *Gli arabi nelle Gallie* (Milan, 1827), which eventually reached many of the world's most important stages, and was the first of Pacini's operas to be given in the United States. It was mounted quite frequently in Italy, and in fact it was not until 1830 that Bellini's first success, *Il pirata* (also Milan, 1827) passed *Gli arabi nelle Gallie* in performances at the Teatro alla Scala.

While almost each of Bellini's subsequent works was moderately to highly successful, and Donizetti also had more than his share of triumphs, Pacini was unable to keep up, most of his ensuing operas being failures. He was the first to recognize his defeat and made the following entry in his memoirs: "I began to realize that I must withdraw from the field—Bellini, the divine Bellini has surpassed me." Some years later, he decided to reenter the field, and, after one more setback, enjoyed his greatest success, *Saffo* (Naples, 1840).

After *Saffo*, Pacini entered into another period of great prominence in the early and mid 1840s. Bellini had passed away years ago, Donizetti had left for Paris, and only Mercadante and the young Verdi were important enough to be serious rivals. Mercadante's major successes were already behind him, thus Verdi offered the only important competition, and it was not until 1844 that Verdi eclipsed Pacini with the unparalleled triumph of *Ernani*. (Successful as *Nabucco* was, it was less so than *Saffo*.) It was in these 1840s that Pacini enjoyed his most glorious years, with one hit after another. These included *La fidanzata corsa* (Naples, 1842), *Medea* (Palermo, 1843), *Lorenzino de'Medici* (Venice, 1845) and *Bondelmonte* (Florence, 1845). This was followed by another, and much longer, period of gradual decline, marked only by *Il saltimbanco* (Rome, 1858).

The bel canto revival of recent years has not been particularly kind to Pacini. All of Verdi's output, almost all of Bellini's, most of Rossini's, much of Donizetti's and even eight Mercadante operas have already been revived, but only two of Pacini's: *Saffo* and *Maria, regina d'Inghilterra*. Judging from the revivals and recordings of these works, Pacini's abilities as a melodist do not seem to be far behind those of Donizetti and Bellini, and they clearly surpass those of Mercadante.

Like *Saffo*, *Maria, regina d'Inghilterra* contains many individual pieces of great beauty, especially the closing arias for the two protagonists, Mary Tudor and Riccardo Fenimoore. The latter's prison scene is particularly effective in all of its movements: a melancholy prelude, an elegiac first part sung with great feeling and a striking cabaletta. It is superior to many prison scenes by better known composers. The final scene for the Queen is just as beautiful, in which Pacini first sets the mood and builds tension with a heart-rending funeral march.

While only *Saffo* ever attained the favor achieved by the best of Verdi's early works, several of Pacini's middle period operas eclipsed a number of Verdi scores. Due to the recent publication of complete nineteenth century chronologies of many of the works of the period (Kaufman, *Annals of Italian Opera*), it is now possible to establish the relative popularity of selected Verdi and Pacini titles in terms of the number of their nineteenth-century revivals:

Pacini		Verdi	
Bondelmonte	92	Aroldo	88
Medea	44	Giovanna d'arco	88
Lorenzino de'Medici	37	Simon Boccanegra (1857)	31
La fidanzata corsa	36	La battaglia di Legnano	25
Il saltimbanco	22	Il corsaro	16
La regina di Cipro	19	Stiffelio	14
Stella di Napoli	13	Alzira	13
Maria, regina d'Inghilterra	8	Oberto	7
Merope	6	Un giorno di regno	3

It can be seen that four Pacini rarities actually were more popular in the nineteenth century than the original version of *Simon Boccanegra*, and six were performed more often than *Stiffelio*.

It seems reasonable to suggest that had any of the first four to six works in the above list been by a better known composer, it would already have had numerous recent revivals. It would appear that all of these titles (as well as the much earlier *Gli arabi nelle Gallie*) might present a gold mine to musical archeologists looking for potential treasures to explore. The hoped for performances of more of Pacini's works would also facilitate a more accurate and realistic evaluation both of him as a composer and of the degree of his influence on the development of Italian opera.

If Pacini was less successful than some of his contemporaries, it may be because he was less of an innovator. Just as his early operas were modeled on Rossini, some of his middle period works show the heavy influence of his idol, Vincenzo Bellini, as well as some of Donizetti. His still later operas, none of which has yet been revived, show many influences of Mercadante and even Verdi. Yet there can be little doubt that Pacini contributed to the changes in style away from Rossini, or that he, like Mercadante, exerted an influence on the far greater changes to be eventually made by Verdi.

—Tom Kaufman

PAER, Ferdinando.

Composer. Born 1 June 1771, in Parma. Died 3 May 1839, in Paris. Studied with Fortunati and Ghiretti; honorary maestro di cappella to the court of Parma, 1792; in Vienna, 1797-1802; succeeded Naumann as court Kapellmeister at Dresden, 1802; in Paris, maître de chapelle to Napoleon and conductor of the Opéra-Comique, 1807; succeeded Spontini as director of the Italian Opera in Paris, 1812, but forced to resign due to financial problems, 1827; cross of the Legion of Honor, 1828; member of the Institut, 1831; conductor of the royal chamber music, 1832.

Operas

Orphée et Euridice, Duplessis, Parma, Court, 1791.
Circe (Calypso), D. Perelli, Venice, San Samuele, carnival 1792.
Le astuzie amorose, o Il tempo fa giustizia a tutti [*La locanda dei vagaboni*]. Parma, Ducale, fall 1792.
I portenti del magnetismo Vienna, Kärntnertor, carnival 1793.
Icilio e Virginia, G. Foppa, Padua, Nuovo, June 1793.
Laodicea (Tegene e Laodicea), G. Foppa, Padua, Nuovo, June 1793.
I pretendenti burlati, G.C. Grossardi, Medesano, Teatrino privato Grossardi, summer 1793.
L'oro fa tutto (Geld ist die Lösung) A. Anelli, Milan, Teatro alla Scala, August 1793.
L'inganno in trionfo, Florence, Palla a Corda, 1794.
Il nuovo Figaro, Lorenzo da Ponte (libretto written for Mozart after Beaumarchais), Parma, Ducale, January 1794.
Il matrimonio improvviso (I due sordi), G. Foppa, Venice, San Moisè, 22 February 1794.
I molinari, G. Foppa, Venice, San Moisè, 22 February 1794.
Il fornaro, Venice, San Moisè, 1794.
L'Idomeneo, G. Sertor, Florence, Palla a Corda, spring 1794.
Ero e Leandro, Naples, San Carlo, 13 August 1794.
Una in bene e una in male (Le astuzie di Patacca), G. Foppa, Rome, Teatro alla Valle, 1794.
La Rossana, A. Aureli, Milan, Teatro alla Scala, carnival 1795.
Il Cinna, A. Anelli, Padua, Nuovo, 13 June 1795.
Anna, Padua, Nuovo, June 1795.
L'intrigo amoroso (Saidi ossia Gl'intrighi del serraglio; Il male vien dal buco), G. Bertati, Venice, San Moisè, 4 December 1795.
L'orfana riconosciuta, Florence, Teatro della Pergola, 2 April 1796.
L'amante servitore, A. Sografi, Venice, San Moisè, 26 December 1796.
Il principe di Taranto, F. Livigni, Parma, Ducale, 11 February 1797; revised as *La contadina fortunata,* A.L. Tottola.
Il fanatico in Berlina, Vienna, Kärntnertor, 1797.
Griselda, ossia La virtù al cimento, A. Anelli, Parma, Ducale, January 1798.
Camilla, ossia Il sotterraneo, G. Carpani, Vienna, Kärntnertor, 28 February 1799.
Il morto vivo, P. Franceschi, Vienna, Kärntnertor, 12 July 1799.
La testa riscaldata, G. Foppa, Venice, San Benedetto, 20 January 1800.
La sonnambula, G. Foppa, Venice, San Benedetto, 15 February 1800.
Poche, ma buone, ossia Le donne cambiate (Der lustige Schuster), G. Foppa, Vienna, Kärntnertor, 18 December 1800.
Achille, G. De Gamerra, Vienna, Kärntnertor, 6 June 1801.
Ginevra degli Almieri, Dresden, Court Theater, 1802.
I fuorusciti di Firenze, A. Anelli, Dresden, Court Theater, 27 November 1802.
Sargino, ossia L'allievo dell'amore, G. Foppa, Dresden, Court Theater, 26 May 1803.
Lodoiska, F. Gonella, Bologna, Comunale, summer 1804.

Leonora, ossia L'amore conjugale, G. Schmidt, Dresden, Court Theater, 3 October 1804.
Sofonisba, D. Rossetti, Bologna, Corso, 19 May 1805.
Il maniscalco, Florence, Palla a Corda, summer 1805.
Numa Pompilio, M. Noris, Paris, Théâtre des Tuileries, carnival 1808.
Diana e Endimione, ossia Il ritardo, S. Vestris, Paris, Théâtre des Tuileries, fall 1809.
Agnese, L. Buonavoglia, Parma, Villa Scotti, Teatro Ponte d'Altaro, October 1809.
La Didone, Metastasio, Paris, Théâtre des Tuileries, 1810.
Un pazzo ne fa cento, Florence, Teatro della Pergola, fall 1812.
I Baccanti, G. Rossi, Paris, Théâtre des Tuileries, 7 January 1813.
Poche ma buone, ossia La moglie ravveduta, De Gamerra, Rome, Valle, summer 1813.
L'oriflamme [with Méhul, Berton, and Kreutzer]. C.G. Etienne and L.P.M.F. Baour-Lormian, Paris, Opéra, 31 January 1814.
Oro non compra amore, Pavia, Quattro Signori, 1814.
L'eroismo in amore, L. Romanelli, Milan, Teatro alla Scala, 26 December 1815.
La primavera felice, L. Balocchi, Paris, Italien, 5 July 1816.
Lo sprezzatore schernito, Florence, Teatro della Pergola, 22 November 1816 [pasticcio of works by Pacini, Paganini, Guglielmi, Sampieri, Generali, Portogallo, and Farinelli].
Le maître de chapelle, ou Le souper imprévu, S. Gay, Paris, Feydeau, 29 March 1821.
Blanche de Provence, ou La cour des fées [with Berton, Boieldieu, Cherubini, and Kreutzer], M.E.G.M. Théaulon and de Rancé, Paris, Opéra, 3 May 1821.
La marquise de Brinvilliers [with Auber, Batton, Berton, Blangini, Boieldieu, Carafa, Cherubini, and Hérold], Paris, Opéra-Comique, 31 October 1831.
Un caprice de femme, J.P.F. Lesguillon, Paris, Opéra-Comique, 23 July 1834.
Olinde et Sophronie, after Tasso, intended for Paris, Opéra [unfinished].

Other works: cantatas, oratorios, sacred and secular vocal works, orchestral works, chamber music.

Publications

About PAER: books—

Massé, T. and A. Deschamps. *De MM. Paer et Rossini.* Paris, 1820.
Schiedermair, L. *Beiträge zur Geschichte der Oper um die Wende des 18. und 19. Jahrhunderts.* Leipzig, 1907-10.
Della Corte, A. *L'opera comica italiana nel '700.* Bari, 1923.
Radiciotti, G. *Rossini.* Tivoli, 1927-29.
Engländer, Richard. *Ferdinando Paer als Hofkapellmeister in Dresden.* Dresden, 1929.

articles—

Schiedermair, L. "Über Beethovens 'Lenore'." *Zeitschrift der Internationalen Musik-Gesellschaft* 8 (1906-07): 115.
Tiersot, J. "Lettres de musiciens écrits en français du XVe au XXe siécle." *Rivista musicale italiana* 21 (1914): 479; published separately, Turin, 1924.
Engländer, R. "Zur Musikgeschichte Dresdens gegen 1800." *Zeitschrift für Musikwissenschaft* 4 (1921-22): 199.
Engländer, Richard. "Paers *Leonora* und Beethovens *Fidelio.*" *Neues Beethoven Jahrbuch* 4 (1930): 118.

Pelicelli, N. "Musicisti in Parma nel sec. XVIII." *Note d'archivio per la storia musicale* 12 (1935): 27.

Tebaldini, G. "Ferdinando Paer." *Aurea Parma* 2 (1939).

Uhrig, Dieter. "Die Staatskapelle Dresden und ihr Beitrag zur Pflege der Werke Mozarts in Historie und Gegenwart." *Wiener Figaro* 46/no. 1 (1979): 55.

Lippmann, Friedrich. "Mozart und die italienischen Komponisten des 19. Jahrhunderts." *Mozart-Jahrbuch* (1980-83): 104.

Cagli, Bruno. "Rossini a Londra e al Théâtre Italien di Parigi. Con documenti inediti dell' impresario G.B. Benelli" [letters by Paer]. *Bolletino del Centro Rossiniano di Studi* 1-3 (1981): 5.

Heartz, Daniel. "Mozart *Titus* und die italienische Oper im 1800." In *Mozart und die Oper seiner Zeit,* edited by Martin Ruhnke. Laaber, 1981.

Ruhnke, Martin. "*Opera semiseria* und *dramma eroicomico.*" *Analecta musicologica* 21 (1982): 263.

*   *   *

Paer is one of those composers who enjoyed some success during his lifetime only to be almost completely forgotten before the end of his century. Especially prolific in opera, he left behind over fifty titles in that genre, written during a career of considerable international acclaim.

Paer began his career in Venice, where as a young man he was thoroughly grounded in the traditions and musical language of Paisiello and Cimarosa. Called to Vienna, he managed to assimilate some of the orchestral techniques associated with the scores of Mozart and Haydn, and enjoyed his first great success with *Camilla* in 1799.

A stylistic weathervane minutely and nimbly attuned to audience tastes and whims, Paer's path next led him to Dresden, and then in 1807 to Paris, having fortuitously found himself in the entourage of Napoleon at Warsaw the previous year. Having attracted the emperor's ear with his graceful and none too demanding music, he remained in the French capital for the remainder of his life, being the last in that string of transplanted Italians (Lully, Cherubini, Spontini, et al.) to find a niche there as musical arbiter and savant before the onslaught of nineteenth century nationalism.

By all accounts a personally unpleasant and conniving man, Paer had the politician's uncanny ability to land on his feet when regimes changed, and he died with many honors, although he was often despised and distrusted by his musical colleagues. Stendhal is particularly cutting in his descriptions of Paer, yet this author (who in his championship of Rossini had an axe to grind) also admired the man's music.

During Paer's life, his most important successes included such works as *Achille* and *Sargino,* while a later comedy, *Le maître de chapelle,* proved to be the most durable of all, and continued to be performed throughout much of the nineteenth century.

Ironically, Paer is remember today chiefly for a work which was not one of his most brilliant successes. In 1804, while in Dresden, he set an Italian translation of the French libretto by Bouilly which would soon serve Beethoven (in a German version) as the text of *Fidelio*. Paer's *Leonora* has in fact been recorded, and while primarily of historical importance, it claims a good deal of grace and charm. Indeed, the composer seems to have had a penchant for being second best in his choice of subject matter, having set at one time or another an *Orfeo ed Euridice, Griselda, Idomeneo, La sonnambula* and under the title *Il nuovo Figaro* da Ponte's very libretto for Mozart's *Le nozze di Figaro.*

A solid craftsman, Paer is a typical example of a lesser talent who manages to straddle a period of transition without ever making an important statement of his own in any style. With no depth of passion to command he was nonetheless well equipped to entertain, which he did with aplomb (if not always honor) over the course of many productive years.

—Dennis Wakeling

———

I PAGLIACCI [The Clowns].

Composer: Ruggero Leoncavallo.

Librettist: Ruggero Leoncavallo.

First Performance: Milan, Teatro dal Verme, 21 May 1892.

Roles: Canio (tenor); Nedda (soprano); Tonio (baritone); Silvio (baritone); Beppe (tenor); chorus (SSTTBB).

Publications

book–

Rubboli, Daniele. *Ridi pagliaccio.* Lucca, 1985.

articles–

Giachetti, G. "Leoncavallo a Milano prima dei *Pagliacci.*" *La sera* 20 March (1942).

Lerario, T. "Ruggero Leoncavallo e il sogetto dei 'Pagliacci'." *Chigiana* 26-27 (1971): 115.

Marchetti, A. "Lo smisurato sogno dell' autore di 'Pagliacci'." *Rassegna musicale Curci* 25 (1972): 23.

Sansone, Matteo. "The 'Verismo' of Ruggero Leoncavallo: a Source Study of Pagliacci." *Music and Letters* August (1989).

*   *   *

I Pagliacci was composed in the wake of the sensational success of Mascagni's *Cavalleria rusticana,* which started a fashion for veristic subjects in the Italian music theater. Leoncavallo wrote both the libretto and the music. By his own admission, he took the subject from an incident that occurred in a Calabrian village where he lived for a few years while his father was posted there as a judge. As a *verismo* opera, *Pagliacci* should, therefore, have the best possible claim to authenticity, since it is based on a true story. However, an examination of the court records of that incident (the murder of a young man by two brothers due to the jealousy over a local woman) shows that most of the opera's plot is pure fiction, to be attributed to Leoncavallo's own imagination or traced back to other sources.

A troupe of strolling players arrives in a village to put on a *commedia dell'arte* show. One of the clowns, Tonio, makes advances to Nedda, the leader's wife, but she is in love with a villager, Silvio. The two lovers agree to run away together after the performance. Their conversation is overheard by Tonio who alerts Canio, Nedda's husband. Canio tries in vain to make her reveal the man's name. The clowns' farce seems to reproduce their real-life situation since Columbine (Nedda) is secretly in love with Harlequin, and Pagliaccio (Canio) demands the name of her lover, which she refuses to give. The enraged clown can no longer keep up the pretence. Mad with jealousy, he stabs Nedda and then Silvio who had rushed to her help.

The village murder on which Leoncavallo claimed to have based his opera is hardly more than a pretext for the Calabrian setting of the plot. The brutal violence of the double

Nellie Melba and Fernando de Lucia as Nedda and Canio in *Pagliacci,* **London, 1893**

murder committed by the white-faced clown in front of his audience is at the same time more sensational and more sophisticated than the rustic challenge and the off-stage fight of *Cavalleria rusticana.* The *verismo* of *Pagliacci* is, in fact, of a different nature from that of Mascagni's archetypal opera.

The characterization of Canio/Pagliaccio is focused on the antitheses of appearance/reality, clown/man. The device of the play-within-a-play with *commedia dell'arte* masks and the Pierrot-like personality of Pagliaccio point to broader cultural influences that should be dated back to the 1880s, the years Leoncavallo spent in Paris trying to make a living as a songwriter. In that period two works were produced which contain similarities with *Pagliacci: Tabarin* (1885), an opera in two acts by Émile Pessard based on a comedy by Paul Ferrier, and *La Femme de Tabarin* (1887), a one-act play by the Parnassian poet Catulle Mendès. Both feature the seventeenth-century *commedia dell'arte* clown Tabarin, and both deal with the unfaithfulness of his wife Francisquine. A substantial part of the action in the two pieces consists in the sudden shift from the performance of a light farce to real-life tragedy on the small stage of Tabarin's open-air theater, in front of an audience responding with loud comments to the unusually impressive acting. Pessard's opera, in particular, seems close to the plot of *Pagliacci,* even though it ends with the reconciliation of the clown and his wife.

The 1880s also witnessed a revival of interest in pantomimes centered on the sad and violent Pierrot, a *commedia dell'arte* mask similar to Pagliaccio both in character and costume. In 1883, even the great Sarah Bernhardt donned the white costume of the male mask to perform *Pierrot assassin,* a pantomime by Jean Richepin.

Leoncavallo was well aware of the latest fashions in the French theater while he worked and made friends in Paris. A few years later, when he chose to follow Mascagni's example and wrote a veristic opera, his Parisian recollections were probably more influential than his childhood memories. So the libretto of *Pagliacci* resulted from the skilful blending of a veristic crime of passion with the well-tried device of the play-within-a-play, which allowed the composer a clever differentiation in the musical treatment of the main story and the inset "comedy." This is the opera's best asset besides the strongly emotional numbers such as Canio's "Vesti la giubba" ("Put on the costume").

On the whole, the music of *Pagliacci* exhibits the typical characteristics of the new veristic genre inaugurated by *Cavalleria:* loud and coarse orchestration, sensational effects, hybrid style. Reviewing a Viennese production of the opera in 1893, Eduard Hanslick compared *Pagliacci* with *Cavalleria* and noted that Leoncavallo's music is "less fragmented and disjointed" than Mascagni's, though "his melodic invention can scarcely be praised for its richness and originality."

A distinctive feature of *Pagliacci* is the unnecessary and pretentious prologue where Tonio informs us that the author has tried to portray a "squarcio di vita," a slice of life, that is the naturalistic *tranche de vie:* though we will be seeing "le antiche maschere," the old masks, we are invited to consider that comedians are flesh and blood creatures. A "nest of memories" moved the author to write "with real tears," and "his sobs beat the tempo for him." We shall hear "shouts of rage" and "cynic laughter" from his true-to-life characters. Was this meant to be an aesthetic manifesto of operatic *verismo?* Or was it, rather, a cunning device to reconcile the clown's story with the sordid incident dug out from the composer's childhood memories? Possibly both, but, in the first place, the prologue was to be a reward for the baritone Victor Maurel (the first Tonio) who used his influence on the impresario of the Teatro dal Verme in Milan to have *Pagliacci* premiered there. With this addition, Leoncavallo gave Maurel the opportunity to introduce the opera and conclude it with the spoken line "The comedy is ended" which was eventually appropriated by the tenor.

—Matteo Sansone

PAGLIUGHI, Lina.

Soprano. Born 27 May 1907, in New York. Died 2 October 1980, in Rubicone, Italy. Married: tenor Primo Montanari. Studied with Manlio Bavagnoli, Milan; debut as Gilda at Teatro Nazionale, Milan, 1927; sang at Teatro alla Scala, 1930-47; at Monte Carlo, 1931; appeared as Lucia at San Carlo, Naples, 1936; Covent Garden debut as Gilda, 1938; appeared at Maggio Musicale, Florence, as Queen of the Night, 1940; sang Elvira at Rome opera, 1949; sang with Italian Radio until her retirement in 1956.

Publications

About PAGLIUGHI: books–

Cernaz, B. *Lina Pagliughi.* Savignano, 1982.

articles–

Cave, L. di. "Lina Pagliughi." *Record Collector* 21 (1973): 101.

*   *   *

Born in Brooklyn of Italian parents, Lina Pagliughi began giving public recitals at the age of eight, displaying remarkable voice control and impressive capabilities in lyric, dramatic, and coloratura styles. It soon became clear that not only the beauty and flexibility of her voice but also her innate musicianship and her sensitive emotional reaction to what she sang would carry her far in an operatic career. When Luisa Tetrazzini heard her sing in San Francisco she immediately named the girl as her ultimate successor. In order not to endanger her gifts by forcing her voice, she stopped singing in public. After studying with Brescia she was taken to Milan for further tuition with Bavagnoli. Her impressive debut as Gilda in *Rigoletto* at the Teatro Nazionale there in 1927 was followed by an equally successful one as Lucia at the Teatro Vittorio Emanuele in Turin. Carlo Sabagno, who was getting ready to produce for Italian H M V the first electric recording of *Rigoletto,* chose her for Gilda. Her voice on this recording is creamy and attractive in its freshness, despite the inadequacies of the recording.

Having married the tenor Primo Montanari, Lina then sang at the other major opera houses in Italy, including the Teatro alla Scala (1930-31, 1937-38, 1940, 1947). The highlight of her career came in 1937 when she triumphed as Sinaide in Rossini's *Mosè in Egitto* at the Teatro alla Scala. She was acclaimed the following year as Lucia with Gigli as Edgardo, and also in 1940 at the Maggio Musicale in Florence in the challenging role of the Queen of the Night in *Die Zauberflöte.*

Unfortunately Pagliughi's appearance by now was making it difficult for her to portray convincingly certain characters.

Even in 1938 when Walter Legge engaged her to sing Gilda at Covent Garden, one finds him writing: "She was almost as broad as she was short, but musically and vocally the best interpreter of the part at that time. At his first glimpse of her on the stage, Beecham said, 'My dear boy, we can't let her be seen. She looks like a tea cosy.' " After appearing as Elvira in 1948 at the Teatro dell' Opera in Rome and as Lucia at the San Carlo, she gave up the stage and began singing on Italian radio instead. That year listeners heard her in *L'elisir d'amore* with Schipa and in *Rigoletto* with Lauri-Volpi and Gobbi. She retired in 1956 and taught singing in Milan.

Pagliughi recorded for H M V, Parlophone, and Oetra. The latter's discs are usually regarded as the best. Apart from four Victor recordings, few do full justice to the mellowness of her voice. Noel Strauss, musical critic of the *New York Times,* wrote after her Carnegie Hall concert in 1940: "The voice, pure, even in scale throughout its wide range and extraordinarily flexible, had much of the body and weightiness formerly demanded of coloratura singers, and above all it possessed real brilliancy." Such scintillating vocal virtuosity had not been heard in New York since Tetrazzini's times. It closely resembled hers in timbre, accuracy and assurance.

—Charles Neilson Gattey

PAISIELLO, Giovanni.

Composer. Born 9 May 1740, in Taranto. Died 5 June 1816, in Naples. Studied with Durante, Cotumacci, and Abos at the Conservatorio di Sant'Onofrio in Naples, 1754-59; taught at the Conservatorio, 1759-63; commissioned to write an opera for the Marsigli-Rossi theater in Bologna as a result of the success of one of his comic intermezzos, 1763; invited to St Petersburg by Empress Catherine II, 1776; maestro di cappella to Ferdinand IV of Naples, 1784-99; maître de chapelle to Napoleon in Paris, 1802-03; various posts of importance under Napoleon's government, but lost them with the restoration of the Bourbons in 1815.

Operas

Il ciarlone, A. Palomba, Bologna, Marsigli-Rossi, 12 May 1764.
I francesi brillanti, P. Mililotti, Bologna, Marsigli-Rossi, 24 June 1764.
Madama l'umorista, o Gli stravaganti, A. Palomba, Modena, Rangoni, 26 January 1765.
I bagni d'Abano, C. Goldoni, Parma, Ducale, spring 1765.
Demetrio, Metastasio, Modena, Rangoni, Lent 1765; revised, Tsarskoye Selo, 1779.
Il negligente, C. Goldoni, Parma, Ducale, 1765.
Le virtuose ridicole, C. Goldoni, Parma, Ducale, 1765.
Le nozze disturbate, G. Martinelli, Venice, San Moisè, carnival 1766.
Le finte contesse, after P. Chiari, *Marchese Villano,* Rome, Valle, February 1766.
La vedova di bel genio, P. Mililotti, Naples, Nuovo, spring 1766.
L'idolo cinese, G.B. Lorenzi, Naples, Nuovo, spring 1767.
Lucio Papirio dittatore, Zeno, Naples, San Carlo, summer 1767.
Il furbo malaccorto, G.B. Lorenzi, Naples, Nuovo, winter 1767.

Le 'mbroglie de la Bajasse, P. Mililotti, Naples, Teatro dei Fiorentini, summer 1767; revised as *La serva fatta padrona,* Naples, Teatro dei Fiorentini, summer 1769.

Alceste in Ebuda, ovvero Olimpia, A. Trabucco, Naples, San Carlo, 20 January 1768.

Festa teatrale in musica (Le nozze di Peleo e Tetide), G.B. Basso-Bassi, Naples, Royal Palace, 31 May 1768.

La luna abitata, G.B. Lorenzi, Naples, Nuovo, summer 1768.

La finta maga per vendetta, G.B. Lorenzi, Naples, Teatro dei Fiorentini, fall? 1768.

L'osteria di Marecchiaro, F. Cerlone, Naples, Teatro dei Fiorentini, winter 1768; performed with a separate third act, *La Claudia vendicata.*

Don Chisciotte della Mancia, G.B. Lorenzi, Naples, Teatro dei Fiorentini, summer 1769.

L'arabo cortese, P. Mililotti, Naples, Nuovo, winter, 1769.

La Zelmira, o sia La marina del Granatello, F. Cerlone, Naples, Nuovo, summer 1770.

Le traume per amore, F. Cerlone, Naples, Nuovo, 7 October 1770.

Annibale in Torino, J. Durand, Turin, Regio, 16 January 1771.

La somiglianza de'nomi, P. Mililotti, Naples, Nuovo, spring 1771.

I scherzi d'amore e di fortuna, F. Cerlone, Naples, Nuovo, summer 1771.

Artaserse, Metastasio, Modena, Court, 26 December 1771.

Semiramide in villa (intermezzo), G. Martinelli?, Rome, Capranica, carnival 1772.

Motezuma, V.A. Cigna-Santi, Rome, Teatro delle Dame, January 1772.

La Dardanè, F. Cerlone, Naples, Nuovo, spring 1772.

Gli amanti comici, G.B. Lorenzi (after his *Don Anchise*), Naples, Nuovo, fall 1772; revised as *Don Anchise Campanone,* Venice, 1773.

L'innocente fortunata, F. Livigni, Venice, San Moisè, carnival 1773; revised as *La semplice fortunata,* Naples, Nuovo, summer 1773.

Sismano nel Mogol, G. de Gamerra, Milan, Regio Ducale, carnival 1773.

Il tamburo, G.B. Lorenzi (after Addison, *The Drummer*), Naples, Nuovo, spring 1773.

Alessandro nel' Indie, Metastasio, Modena, Court, 26 December 1773.

Andromeda, V.A. Cigni-Santi, Milan, Regio Ducale, carnival 1774.

Il duello, G.B. Lorenzi, Naples, Nuovo, spring 1774; revised as *Il duello comico,* Tsarskoye Selo, 1782.

Il credulo deluso, after C. Goldoni, *Il mondo della luna,* Naples, Nuovo, fall 1774.

La frascatana, F. Livigni, Venice, San Samuele, fall 1774.

Il divertimento dei numi (scherzo rappresentativo per musica), G.B. Lorenzi, Naples, Royal Palace, 4 December 1774; performed as *Lo scherzo degli dei Caserta,* 1771, with Gluck, *Orfeo.*

Demofoonte, Metastasio, Venice, San Benedetto, carnival 1775.

La discordia fortunata, Abate F.B.A.F., Venice, San Samuele, carnival 1775.

L'amore ingegnoso, o sia La giovane scaltra, Padua, Obizzi, carnival 1775.

Le astuzie amorose, F. Cerlone, Naples, Nuovo, spring 1775.

Socrate immaginario, G.B. Lorenzi, Naples, Nuovo, fall 1775.

Il gran Cid, R. Pizzi, Florence, Teatro della Pergola, 3 November 1775.

Le due contesse (intermezzo), G. Petrosellini, Rome, Valle, 3 January 1776.

La disfatta di Dario, N. Morbilli, Rome, Torre Argentina, carnival 1776.

Dal finto il vero, S. Zini, Naples, Nuovo, spring 1776.

Nitteti, Metastasio, St Petersburg, Court, 28 January 1777.

Lucinda ed Armidoro, M. Coltellini, St Petersburg, fall 1777.

Achille in Sciro, Metastasio, St Petersburg, Court, 6 February 1778.

Lo sposo burlato, G. Casti, St Petersburg, Court, 24 July 1778.

Gli astrologi immaginari, G. Bertati, St Petersburg, Hermitage, 14 February 1779.

Il matrimonio inaspettato (La contadina di spirito), Kammeniÿ Ostrov, 1779.

La finta amante, G. Casti?, Mogilev, Poland, 5 June 1780.

Alcide al bivio, Metastasio, St Petersburg, Hermitage, 6 December 1780.

La serva padrona (intermezzo), G.A. Federico, Tsarskoye Selo, 10 September? 1781.

Il barbiere di Siviglia, ovvero la precauzione inutile, G. Petrosellini (after Beaumarchais), St Petersburg, Court, 26 September 1782.

Il mondo della luna, Kammeniÿ Ostrov, 1782.

Il re Teodoro in Venezia, G. Casti, Vienna, Burgtheater, 23 August 1784.

Antigono, Metastasio, Naples, San Carlo, 12 January 1785.

La grotta di Trofonio, G. Palomba, Naples, Teatro dei Fiorentini, December 1785.

Olimpiade, Metastasio, Naples, San Carlo, 20 January 1786.

Le gare generose, G. Palomba, Naples, Teatro dei Fiorentini, spring 1786 [seperate, untitled third act].

Pirro, G. de Gamerra, Naples, San Carlo, 12 January 1787.

La modista raggiratrice, G.B. Lorenzi, Naples, Teatro dei Fiorentini, fall 1787.

Giunone e Lucina, C. Sernicola, Naples, San Carlo, 8 September 1787.

Fedra, L.B. Salvioni, Naples, San Carlo, 1 January 1788.

L'amor contrastato [La molinara], G. Palomba, Naples, Teatro dei Fiorentini, carnival 1789.

Catone in Utica, Metastasio, Naples, San Carlo, 5 February 1789.

Nina, o sia La pazza per amore, G. Carpani (after B.J. Mersollier, with additions by G.B. Lorenzi), Caserta, Royal Palace, 25 June 1789; revised, Naples, Teatro dei Fiorentini, 1790.

I zingari in fiera, G. Palomba, Naples, Fondo, 21 November 1789.

Le vane gelosie (with Silvestro Palma), G.B. Lorenzi, Naples, Teatro dei Fiorentini, spring 1790.

Zenobia in Palmira, G. Sertor, Naples, San Carlo, 30 May 1790.

Ipermestra, Metastasio, Padua, Nuovo, June 1791.

La locanda, G. Toniolo (after Bertati), London, Pantheon, 16 June 1791.

I giuochi d'Agrigento, A. Pepoli, Venice, La Fenice, 16 May 1792.

Il ritorno d'Idomeno in Creta, S. Salsi, Perugia, Teatro del Verzaro, fall 1792.

Elfrida, R. Calzabigi, Naples, San Carlo, 4 November 1792.

Elvira, R. Calzabigi, Naples, San Carlo, 12 January 1794.

Didone abbandonata, Metastasio, Naples, San Carlo, 4 November 1794.

Chi la dura la vince, S. Zini, Milan, Teatro alla Scala, 9 June 1797.

La Daunia felice (festa teatrale), Foggia, 26 June 1797.

Andromaca, G.B. Lorenzi (after A. Salvi), Naples, San Carlo, 4 November 1797.

L'inganno felice, G. Palomba, Naples, Fondo, 1798.

Proserpine, M. Guillard (after Quinault), Paris, Opéra, 28 March 1803.
I pittagorici, V. Monti, Naples, San Carlo, 19 March 1808.
Epilogue for Mayr's Elise, 1807.

Other works: sacred and secular cantatas and oratorios, masses and other liturgical works, orchestral works, piano pieces.

Publications

About PAISIELLO: books–

Dominicis, G. de. *Saggio su la vita del Cavalier Don Giovanni Paisiello.* Moscow, 1818.

Ferrari, G.G. *Aneddoti piacevoli e interessanti.* London, 1830; edited by S. Di Giacomo, Milan, 1929.

Schizzi F. *Della vita e degli studi di Giovanni Paisiello.* Milan, 1833.

Rosa, C.A. de [Marchese di Villarosa]. *Memorie dei compositori di musica del regno di Napoli.* Naples, 1840.

Panarco, S. *Paisiello in Russia.* Trani, 1910.

Corte, A. della. *Settecento italiano: Paisiello.* Turin, 1922.

_____. *L'opera comica italiana nel '700.* Bari, 1923.

Prota-Giurleo, U. *Paisiello ed i suoi primi trionfi a Napoli.* Naples, 1925.

Faustini-Fasini, E. *L'ultima opera di Paisiello, I pittagorici.* Taranto, 1937.

_____. *Opere teatrali, oratori e cantate di Giovanni Paisiello.* Bari, 1940.

Mooser, R.-A. *Annales de la musique et des musiciens en Russie au XVIIIe siècle.* Geneva, 1948-51.

Ghislanzoni, A. *Giovanni Paisiello: valutazioni critiche rettificate.* Rome, 1969.

Michtner, O. *Das alte Burgtheater als Opernbühne von der Einführung des deutschen Singspiels (1778) bis zum Tod Kaiser Leopolds II (1792).* Vienna, 1970.

Robinson, Michael F. *Naples and Neapolitan Opera.* Oxford, 1972.

Hunt, J.L. *Giovanni Paisiello: his Life as an Opera Composer.* New York, 1975.

Kruntjaeva, Tat'jana. *Ital'janskaja komiceskaja opera XVIII veka.* Leningrad, 1981.

Muraro, Maria Teresa, ed. *Venezia e il melodramma nel Settecento.* Florence, 1981.

articles–

Cassitto, L. "Elogio storico." In *Onori funebre renduti alla memoria di Giovanni Paisiello,* edited by Gagliardo. Naples, 1816.

Mazzarella da Cerreto, A. "Giovanni Paisiello." In *Biografia degli uomini illustri del regno di Napoli,* edited by D. Martuscelli, vol. 3. Naples, 1816.

Nicolini, F. "Dal carteggio dell'Ab. Galiani." *La critica* 2 (1904): 503.

Giacomo, S. di. "Paisiello e i suoi contemporanei." *Musica e musicisti* 60 (1905): 762; reprinted in *Napoli: figute e paesi,* Naples, 1969.

Barbiero, F. "Giovanni Paisiello tra le ire di un copista e di un innovatore." *Rivista musicale italiana* 22 (1915): 301.

_____. "Disavventure di Paisiello." *Rivista musicale italiana* 23 (1916): 534.

_____. "Lettere inedite di Paisiello." *Rivista musicale italiana* 24 (1917): 73.

Abert, Hermann. "Paisiellos Buffokunst und ihre Beziehung zu Mozart." *Archiv für Musikwissenschaft* 1 (1918-19): 402.

Barverio, Francesco. "I primi dieci anni di vita artistica di Paisiello." *Rivista musicale italiana* II (1922): 264.

Cortese, N. "Una autobiografia inedita di Giovanni Paisiello." *La rassegna musicale* 3 (1930): 123.

Speziale, G.C. "Ancora per Paisiello." *La rassegna musicale* 4 (1931): 1.

Faustini-Fasini, E. "Documenti paisielliani inediti." *Note d'archivio per la storia musicale* 13 (1936): 105.

Somerset, H.V.E. "Giovanni Paisiello: 1740-1816." *Music and Letters* 18 (1937): 20.

Loewenberg, Alfred. "Paisiello's and Rossini's 'Barbiere di Siviglia'." *Music and Letters* 20 (1939): 157.

Rolandi, U. "Contributi alla bibliografia di Giovanni Paisiello." In *Rinascenza salentina.* Lecce, 1940.

Pannain, G. " 'Don Chisciotte della Mancia' di G.B. Lorenzi e Giovanni Paisiello." *Rivista musicale italiana* 56 (1954): 342.

Einstein, A. "A 'King Theodore' Opera." In *Essays on Music,* edited by Paul Henry Lang. New York, 1956; 2nd ed., 1958.

Samson, I. "Paisiello—'La bella Molinara'." *Neue Zeitschrift für Musik* 120 (1959): 368.

Corte, A. della. "Un'opera di Paisiello per Caterina II di Pietroburgo: Gli astrologi immaginari (1779)." *Chigiana* 23 (1966): 135.

Tartak, Marvin. "The Two *Barbieri.*" *Music and Letters* October (1969).

Dietz, Hanns-Bertold. "Die Varianten in Domenico Cimarosas Autograph zu *Il matrimonio segreto* und ihr Ursprung." *Die Musikforschung* 31 (1978): 273.

Heartz, Daniel. "Mozart and his Italian Contemporaries: *La clemenza di Tito.*" In *Mozart und seine Umwelt,* edited by the Internationale Stiftung Mozarteum Salzburg, 275. Kassel, 1979.

Scherliess, Volker. "*Il barbiere di Siviglia:* Paisiello und Rossini." *Analecta musicologica* 21 (1982): 100.

Lippmann, Friedrich. "Haydn e l'opera buffa: tre confronti con opere italiane coeve sullo stesso testo." *Nuovo rivista musicale italiana* 17 (1983): 223.

Bimberg, Guido. "Die italienische Opera seria im russischen Musiktheater des 18. Jahrhunderts. II." *Händel Jahrbuch* 30 (1984): 121.

Blanchetti, Francesco. "Tipologia musicale dei concertati nell'opera buffa di Giovanni Paisiello." *Rivista italiana di musicologia* 19 (1984): 234.

Lang, Paul Henry. "The Original *Barber:* Paisiello's Great Model for Mozart and Rossini." *Opus* 3/no. 1 (1986): 20.

Lippmann, Friedrich. "Il mio ben quando verra: Paisiello creatore di una nuova semplicità." *Studi musicali* 19 (1990): 385.

unpublished–

Candiani, Rosy. "L'attività di Ranieri de'Calzabigi nel periodo napoletano (1780-1795)." Ph.D. dissertation, Università degli Studi, Milan, 1981-82.

Wilson, J. Kenneth. "*L'Olimpiade:* Selected Eighteenth Century Settings of Metastatio's Libretto." Ph.D. dissertation, Harvard University, 1982.

Platoff, John. "Music and Drama in the *opera buffa* Finale: Mozart and his Contemporaries in Vienna, 1781-1790." Ph.D., University of Pennsylvania, 1984.

*   *   *

Paisiello was perhaps the most prominent of the Italian composers whose works formed the basis for Mozart's operatic achievement. In fact, the talent, facility, and operatic successes of such wily Italians as Piccinni, Paisiello, Cimarosa, and Salieri made it difficult for Mozart to find the court position that could have made his career secure. No composer in that era of courtly patronage was to please more royal masters longer and more felicitously than Giovanni Paisiello.

Trained under Durante in Naples, Paisiello began his career in Bologna and Modena before returning to Naples and establishing his reputation with such operas as *L'idolo cinese* (1757) and *Socrate immaginario* (1775). Awkwardness in the control of rhythm, a limited harmonic vocabulary, and characters that seldom rise above stereotypes suggest that the young composer's success in *L'idolo cinese* rested heavily on pleasing melodies and a strong libretto by the estimable Giambattista Lorenzi. Musically, the opera displays a curious mixture of styles, ranging from highly ornamented serious arias in the fashionable manner of Hasse to simple comic songs that frequently rely too much upon literal repetition of short contrasting motives. Although present at the ends of acts, ensembles do little more than offer the characters singing in turn or in simple homophony. *Socrate immaginario,* composed on another unusual libretto by Lorenzi, reveals substantial progress in the technique of dramatic composition.

Giovanni Paisiello

Even so, the moments that linger in memory are those in act II when, none too subtly, Paisiello parodies the scene in Gluck's *Orfeo* in which Orpheus entreats the Furies.

From 1776 to 1784, Paisiello served as court composer to Catherine II in St Petersburg, his major achievement being *Il barbiere di Siviglia* (1782). This opera reveals not only a mastery of aria, ensemble, finale, and orchestration, but also full possession of a gift for musical characterization that was to influence contemporaneous composers. Despite regular reappointment, Paisiello became displeased with his duties at the Russian court. Without revealing his intention not to return, he took a leave of absence (with pay), and made his way to Vienna, where a significant success with *Il re Teodoro in Venezia* (1784) consolidated his favor with Emperor Joseph II. In addition, Alfred Einstein suggests that *Il re Teodoro a Venezia* had considerable bearing on Mozart's *Le nozze di Figaro* (1786) *(Essays on Music).*

During the last period of his life, with the exception of several years (1801-1804) spent in Paris as court composer and great favorite of Napoleon, Paisiello repeatedly refused invitations to compose abroad, preferring to remain in Naples in the service of King Ferdinand IV. Partly by inclination and certainly in deference to courtly taste, the composer turned increasingly to the composition of serious opera and sacred music. A successful setting of Metastasio's *Antigono* in 1785 led to a significant number of *opere serie,* among them *Pirro* (1787), which Paisiello claims was the first opera of its kind to use introductions and ensemble finales. Two collaborations with Gluck's influential librettist Raniero di Calzabigi followed (*Elfrida* and *Elvira*), both of them apparently distinguished by such elements of Gluckian reform as simpler arias and more expressive recitatives.

Despite the success in Naples of the composer's serious operas, Paisiello's international reputation rested then, as now, on his comedies. Two of the most played works from his later years are *L'amor contrastato* (better known as *La molinara*) and *Nina. La molinara* remains noteworthy for its parody of serious opera in the music of Calloandro and for the generally popular qualities of its melody and sentiment, which may be heard at their best in the aria "Nel cor piu non mi sento" (made famous through Beethoven's set of variations) and in the memorable quartet (praised by Stendhal in his *Vie de Rossini*). *Nina* is distinguished by a pervading lachrymose sentimentality that at times (as in Nina's "Il mio ben") foreshadows the melancholy vein of Donizetti's *L'elisir d'amore.* It has been called "one of the best examples of sentimental comedy in the whole period" (Donald J. Grout, *A Short History of Opera*). It seems significant that Paisiello, once an influence on Mozart, appears in both *La molinara* and *Nina* to have been influenced by Mozart. For example, it does not seem possible to hear Lindoro's "Questo e dunque" *(Nina)* without being reminded of Mozart's music for Don Ottavio (*Don Giovanni,* 1787).

After a long and noteworthy career that produced more than eighty operas and an old age replete with honors, the elderly Paisiello finally fell victim to the patronage system that had served him so well. Not once, but twice he chose to remain in Naples when Ferdinand IV was forced to abandon the city in the rapidly changing world of Napoleonic politics. The second time he even composed an opera, his last (*I pittagorici,* 1808), which alluded to the revolution of 1799 and was in fact commissioned by the reigning monarch, Joseph Buonaparte. When his Bourbon master returned, Paisiello had to live out the remainder of his days in disgrace.

—David Poultney

PALESTRINA.

Composer: Hans Erich Pfitzner.

Librettist: Hans Erich Pfitzner.

First Performance: Munich, Prinzregententheater, 12 June 1917.

Roles: Palestrina (tenor); Pope Pius IV (bass); Giovanni (baritone); Bernardo (tenor); Cardinal Madruscht (bass); Carlo (baritone); Cardinal from Lorraine (bass); Abdisu (tenor); Anton (bass); Luna (baritone); Bishop of Budoja (tenor); Theophilus (tenor); Avosmediano (bass-baritone); Ighino (soprano); Silla (mezzo-soprano); Bishop Ercobe Severolus (bass-baritone); chorus.

Publications

articles–

Osthoff, Wolfgang. "Pfitzner—Goethe—Italien: die Wurzeln des Silla-Liedchens im *Palestrina.*" *Analecta musicologica* no. 17 (1976): 194.

See, Max. "Berühung der Sphären. Gedanken zu einer musikalischen Reminiszenz." *Melos/Neue Zeitschrift für Musik* 4 (1978): 312.

Osthoff, Wolfgang. "Eine neue Quelle zu Palestrinazitat und Palestrinasatz in Pfitzners musikalischer Legende." In *Renaissance Studien. Helmuth Osthoff zum 80. Geburtstag,* edited by Ludwig Finscher, 185. Tutzing, 1979.

Gersdorff, Dagmar von. "Der Komponist Palestrina in Bewusstsein E.T.A. Hoffmanns, Thomas Manns, und Pfitzners." *Mitteilungen der Hans Pfitzner-Gesellschaft* 42 (1981): 50.

Adamy, Bernhard. "Schopenhauer in Pfitzners *Palestrina.*" *Schopenhauer Jahrbuch* 63 (1982): 67.

———. "Das *Palestrina*-Textbuch als Dichtung." In *Symposium Hans Pfitzner,* edited by Wolfgang Osthoff, 21. Tutzing, 1984.

Ermen, Reinhard. "Der 'Erotiker' und der 'Asket': Befragung zweier Klischees am Beispiel der *Gezeichneten* und des *Palestrina.*" In *Franz Schreker (1878-1984) zum 50. Todestag,* edited by Reinhard Ermen, 47. Aachen, 1984.

Kurze, Stefan. "Zeitschichten in Pfitzners *Palestrina.*" In *Symposium Hans Pfitzner,* edited by Wolfgang Osthoff, 69. Tutzing, 1984.

Lee, M. Owen. "Pfitzner's *Palestrina:* A Musical Legend." *Opera Quarterly* spring (1986).

*   *   *

Palestrina, Pfitzner's three-act "musical legend," was published with an epigraph from the nineteenth-century German philosopher Schopenhauer, asserting the independence of intellectual and artistic life from the "bloodstained" history of man's political and social development. This viewpoint is elaborated in an interesting, if ultimately compromising manner in Pfitzner's distinguished libretto, whose treatment of the fabled rescue of polyphonic choral music from an ecclesiastical ban by Palestrina's *Missa Papae Marcelli* was elaborated from careful reading in the history of the period. *Palestrina* is less a historical grand opera, however, than a post-Wagnerian drama of ideas about creativity and inspiration in the context of the pressure exerted upon artists by political controversy and social fashion.

In keeping with its setting at the time of the concluding sessions of the Council of Trent in 1563, the opera's broadly Wagnerian musical language is tempered by stylized effects of spare sixteenth-century harmony and contrapuntal figures. The long first act focuses upon Palestrina and his refusal to compose an exemplary mass for Cardinal Borromeo, with which the latter might persuade the council against an interdiction on polyphonic music. A ghostly visitation by ancient German masters, who press Palestrina to fulfil his artistic mission, is succeeded by a miraculous revelation of the angelic host, ecstatically singing music based on leading motifs from the historical *Missa Papae Marcelli.* In accordance with the legend, Palestrina writes the mass down in a sustained flow of divinely-dictated inspiration (we subsequently learn that it is taken to the authorities by his son Ighino—a travesty role for soprano—only after the composer has been imprisoned for his disobedience to Cardinal Borromeo). Act II presents, with great brilliance and some intentional humor, the relevant session of the Council of Trent, whose pedantic arguments conclude in chaos and brutal physical violence (a satire on democratic debate was apparently intended). The shorter concluding act finds Palestrina returned to his home, wearily awaiting the council's decision on the mass, which is being performed before Pope Pius IV. The work is received favorably, and the Pope himself arrives to thank Palestrina. Neither papal commendation nor the adulation of the crowd in the street below greatly interest the weary composer, however. He is finally left alone on stage, improvising on a chamber organ as he devoutly consigns his remaining days to God.

The work's musical construction depends upon an elaborate repertoire of leitmotifs and a deliberate contrast between the introspective, "spiritual" music of the outer, Roman acts and the more dynamic style of the grandly ceremonial and "worldly" second act. Palestrina's pupil Silla (a friend of Ighino and similarly a travesty role) is also given music affecting the new style of secular song-composition which he intends to go to Florence to study, forsaking his current master. The opera rapidly established itself in Germany and Austria as a worthy successor to *Parsifal,* but Pfitzner himself, in conversation with the novelist Thomas Mann, referred to it as an autumnal version of *Die Meistersinger.* Mann had been strongly impressed by the first performances of *Palestrina* in Munich under Bruno Walter, finding much to sympathize with in its nobly pessimistic reflection of the current state of the German spirit in the midst of the First World War. Mann was later, however, to distance himself from Pfitzner's chauvinistic conservatism, which Mann regarded as readier to engage with "bloodstained" political debates than *Palestrina*'s idealism appeared to warrant.

Mann thus began to appreciate the historical role of *Palestrina* as a work which revealed the mysterious nexus between artistic ideals and cultural ills that would occupy him in his 1947 novel, *Dr Faustus.* Guided by his interest in the work, we may regard it as historically important not for its immediate attractiveness or theatricality, nor for its place in any mythically "progressive" development of Western musical style, but for its movingly self-reflexive dramatization of some of the conservative sentiments which would fuel the dark chapters of Germany's cultural history in the 1930s and 40s. The post-Romantic notion of transcendent art is here presented revealingly (if unintentionally) as a precisely contextualized and historically-oriented *musical,* as well as intellectual, construction.

—Peter Franklin

PARSIFAL (originally Parzival).

Composer: Richard Wagner.

Librettist: Richard Wagner.

First Performance: Bayreuth Festspielhaus, 26 July 1882.

Roles: Kundry (soprano); Parsifal (tenor); Amfortas (baritone); Gurnemanz (bass); Klingsor (bass); Titurel (bass); First and Second Knights of the Grail (tenor and bass); Four Esquires (soprano, contralto, tenors); Flower Maidens (six sopranos); chorus (SSSAAATTTTBBBB).

Publications

books–

Kufferath, M. *Parsifal de Richard Wagner: légende, drame, partition.* Paris, 1890; English translation, 1904.

Wechsler, E. *Die Sage vom heiligen Gral in ihrer Entwicklung bis auf Richard Wagners "Parsifal".* Halle, 1898.

Golther, W. *Parsifal und der Gral in deutscher Sage des Mittelalters und der Neuzeit.* Leipzig, c.1911.

d'Indy, Vincent. *Introduction à l'étude de Parsifal.* Paris, 1937.

Geck, M., and E. Voss, eds. *Dokumente zur Entstehung und ersten Aufführung des Bühnenweihfestspiels Parsifal. R. Wagner: Sämtliche Werke* 30. Mainz, 1970.

Bauer, H.-J. *Wagners Parsifal: Kriterien der Kompositionstechnik.* Munich, 1977.

Chailley, Jacques. *"Parsifal" de Richard Wagner, opéra initiatique.* Paris, 1979.

Reinhardt, Heinrich. *Parsifal. Studien zur Erfassung des Problemhorizonts von Richard Wagners letztem Drama.* Straubing, 1979.

Beckett, Lucy. *Richard Wagner: Parsifal.* Cambridge, 1981.

Csampai, Attila, and Dietmar Holland. *Richard Wagner, "Parsifal": Texte, Materialen, Kommentare.* Reinbek bei Hamburg, 1984.

articles–

Drews, A., "Mozarts 'Zauberflöte' und Wagners 'Parsifal': eine Parallele." *Richard Wagner-Jahrbuch* 1 (1906): 326.

Sakolowski, P. "Wagners erste Parsifal-Entwürfe." *Richard Wagner-Jahrbuch* 1 (1906): 317.

Grunsky, K. "Die Rhythmik im Parsifal." *Richard Wagner-Jahrbuch* 3 (1908): 276.

Altmann, W. "Zur Entstehungsgeschichte des 'Parsifal'." *Richard Wagner-Jahrbuch* 4 (1912): 162.

Koch, M. "Die Quellen der 'Hochzeit'." *Richard Wagner-Jahrbuch* 4 (1912): 105.

Petsch, R. "Zur Quellenkunde des 'Parsifal'." *Richard Wagner-Jahrbuch* 4 (1912): 138.

Wolzogen, H. von. "Parsifal-Varianten: eine Übersicht." *Richard Wagner-Jahrbuch* 4 (1912): 168.

Heuss, A. "Die Grundlagen der Parsifal-Dichtung." *Die Musik* 12 (1912-13): 214.

Unger, M. "The Cradle of the Parsifal Legend." *Musical Quarterly* 18 (1932): 428.

Adorno, T.W. "Zur Partitur des 'Parsifal'." In *Moments musicaux,* 52. Frankfurt am Main, 1964.

Blissett, William. "The Liturgy of *Parsifal.*" *University of Toronto Quarterly* 49 (1979): 117.

Avant-scène opéra January-February (1982) [*Parsifal* issue].

Musik-Konzepte 25 (1982) [special *Parsifal* issue].

Sutcliffe, James Helme. "*Parsifal:* Summation of a Musical Lifetime." *Opera* July-August (1982).

White, David A. "Who is Parsifal's 'pure fool'? Nietzsche on Wagner." *Music Review* 44 (1983): 203.

Lewin, David. "Amfortas's Prayer to Titurel and the Role of D in *Parsifal:* the Tonal Spaces of the Drama and the Enharmonic C-flat/B." In *Essays for Joseph Kerman,* edited by D. Kern Holoman. *Nineteenth-Century Music* 7 (1984).

Kinderman, William. "Wagner's *Parsifal:* Musical Form and the Drama of Redemption." *Journal of Musicology* 4 (1986): 431; 5 (1987): 315.

*   *   *

Parsifal is Wagner's final work, and the culmination of his long and turbulent career; the composer himself once described it as his "last card," in recognition of both his failing health and of the fact that *Die Sieger* (*The Victors*), the work that was to have followed *Parsifal,* would never be composed. Wagner's preoccupation with *Parsifal* stretched over almost four decades, from his first inspiration for the subject at Marienbad in 1845, and his later notion, soon rejected, of introducing the character of Parsifal into the third act of *Tristan,* to the writing of the first prose draft in 1865 and eventual completion of the poem in April 1877. The composition of the music was begun tentatively in 1876 and sustained over the period from August 1877 to April 1879, with the writing of the full score and revision or insertion of certain passages occupying Wagner until January of 1882. Recent research on Wagner's manuscripts has shown that the last extended musical passage he conceived was actually the second half of the transformation music in act I, which was added to his drafts in March 1881. *Parsifal* was painstakingly rehearsed and given a series of exemplary performances to reopen the Bayreuth Festival in July and August 1882, six months before Wagner's death. Wagner called it a *Bühnenweihfestspiel* ("stage consecration festival play") and meant to confine performances of the work to Bayreuth.

The text is based mainly on the medieval epic poem *Parzival* by Wolfram von Eschenbach, but Wagner characteristically departed from his sources to create a highly concentrated drama heavily laden with symbolic import. He viewed the wounded Grail king in *Parsifal,* Amfortas, as analogous to the wounded Tristan in act III of *Tristan und Isolde* but with an enormous dramatic intensification. Amfortas' wound will not heal because it is the outward symbol of his inward state of moral impurity, and whenever he serves his duty of revealing the Holy Grail the wound opens afresh. This dilemma of Amfortas threatens to cause the downfall of the Order of Knights and bring the Grail into the hands of the diabolical Klingsor, who has already seized the Holy Spear and covets the Grail as well. Amfortas' inability to perform his office after the communion scene in the second half of act I eventually causes the death of his father Titurel, founder of the Grail Temple, whose funeral procession forms the transformation music at the change of scene in act III. Only the intervention of Parsifal as redeemer reverses this dissipation of the Order of the Grail in the final moments of the drama, as Parsifal returns the Spear, heals Amfortas' wound and assumes the role of leader of the Order.

The drama of *Parsifal* thus turns on the conflict between two opposing and incompatible realms. The crucial encounter that decides the outcome of this struggle is Kundry's attempt to seduce Parsifal in Klingsor's magic garden in act II. Only in this great duet scene, moreover, are the deeper layers of

The final scene from *Parsifal,* **wood engraving after Theodor Pixis, 1882**

symbolic meaning unveiled. Kundry, the sole female figure in *Parsifal* and perhaps the most fascinating and complex of all Wagner's characters, was developed as an amalgam of characters in Wolfram von Eschenbach's poem: in act I she is a wild heathen, distrusted by the knights but nonetheless bound to serve Amfortas for some undisclosed reason; in act II, she is an irresistible temptress and unwilling agent of the evil Klingsor in his magic castle; and in act III, she is a penitent who attains release through death in the opera's closing moments. As Kundry eventually reveals, she is under a curse and has experienced untold reincarnations through history, as Herodias and others. The cause of her curse and domination by Klingsor, was her spiteful laughter at the redeemer on the cross. Paradoxically, she can only be set free of her curse if her seductive charms are resisted, but no such "redeemer," with an insight transcending the sway of the senses, ever emerges until Parsifal. The seduction attempt, centered on the delivery of Kundry's poisoned kiss to Parsifal, acts like a replay of her earlier seduction of Amfortas, which led to his loss of the Spear and his wounding by Klingsor. Unlike Amfortas, Parsifal resists the temptation of her seduction because his capacity for compassion, as predicted in the prophecy of act I ("Knowing through Compassion, the Pure Fool"), enables him to identify with the agony of Amfortas, and gradually to grasp the significance of his calling to the Grail. Since the seduction has failed, and the protective shield of Parsifal's purity remains intact, the Spear when thrown by Klingsor cannot harm him. As Parsifal makes the sign of the cross with the Spear, Klingsor's realm is destroyed. Parsifal's return journey to the Grail is tortuous, since his path has been cursed by Kundry. His eventual return to the Grail, on Good Friday, coincides with Kundry's final reincarnation, and his first duty as redeemer is to baptise her. Act III concludes, as had act I, with the Communion service and revelation of the Grail, now no longer under threat from Klingsor.

The music of *Parsifal* assumes great dramatic weight and importance, especially in view of the ritualistic nature of the Grail scenes, the sparsity of text in portions of act III, which approach pantomime, and the inward, psychological nature of the Parsifal-Kundry encounter in act II. The largest single vocal part, on the other hand, is given to the narrator, Gurnemanz. At a formative stage in composition, Wagner described the "core of the drama" as the first Grail scene, and it is indeed the music for this section that is anticipated in the prelude to act I and eventually reinterpreted and resolved in the concluding Grail scene of act III. Noteworthy in this respect is Wagner's control of tonal relations on different levels of the musical structure. The opening Communion or Last Supper theme thus begins and ends in A-flat major, but turns prominently to C minor in its third bar, in a motivic gesture later associated with Amfortas' wound and hence with the threat to the Grail. Wagner also employs this A-flat/C axis to generate the ensuing tonal sequence of the entire theme beginning in C minor, with its internal dissonances intensified; and on the most gigantic level he plans the entire first act to modulate to the major mode of C at the entrance into the Grail Temple, where this tonality is affirmed by the fixed pitches of the temple bells. A grim reinterpretation of the fixed pitches of the bells occurs during the funeral procession in act III, in the key of E minor.

The music associated with Kundry and Klingsor, with Amfortas' agony, and with Parsifal's tortuous journey back to the Grail in the third-act prelude, displays a chromaticism sometimes even more advanced than in *Tristan* but which nevertheless retains contact with the music of the Grail. The

so-called Magic motive, heard when Kundry delivers her kiss to Parsifal, outlines the dissonant interval of the tritone, instead of rising through the perfect fifth to the major sixth, as does the Communion theme; its intervallic configuration is constructed as a chromatic distortion of the latter. At Parsifal's response to Kundry's kiss, furthermore, this chromatic material is juxtaposed with the familiar dissonant inflection within the Communion theme itself, which enables the listener to hear that material with new insight as a "chromatic contamination"—stemming from Kundry's earlier seduction of Amfortas—of the otherwise diatonically pure music of the Grail. This "chromatic contamination" is purged from the music of the Grail in act III, after Parsifal's return of the Spear, as the head of the Communion theme receives a new ascending resolution. The enormous time-scale of Wagner's drama requires an appropriately massive musical resolution of tensions, which is supplied in part in the "Good Friday" music and capped by the closing music to act III, with its choral text "Erlösung dem Erlöser!" ("Redeemed the Redeemer!"). Here the various themes and motives heard successively in the first-act prelude are combined in a larger formal synthesis symbolizing the wholeness of the redemption.

The controversy that has always surrounded *Parsifal* is connected in part to its close relationship to Christianity. "Christus" is never mentioned by name, however, and there is no need to interpret *Parsifal* within a Christian framework. (To be sure, the analogy between "Adam and Eve: Christ" and "Amfortas and Kundry: Parsifal" lies close at hand, and was drawn by Wagner himself.) *Parsifal* is a major monument to the aesthetic of the sublime and to Wagner's conviction that art could "salvage the kernel of religion" through its "ideal representation" of mythical religious images. The theme of redemption, which obsessed Wagner throughout his career, is developed and radicalized here to concern not just individuals but a collective society. The resulting political and ideological overtones have seemed sinister to some commentators, especially in view of subsequent German history. Nevertheless, Parsifal's qualities of pity and renunciation are incompatible with fascism, and performances of the work at Bayreuth were discontinued during the Second World War.

Yet another critical problem is the imbalance between *Agapē* and *Eros;* the brotherhood of knights leaves no place for sexuality, and the "redemption" of Kundry renders her dumb before eliminating her. As Josef Chytry has pointed out, *Die Sieger* would have confirmed the compatibility of *Agapē* and *Eros,* but it remained unrealized.

It is above all the music of *Parsifal* that represents a summation of Wagner's achievement, in its exquisite textures and orchestration, richness of allusion, in the gigantic simplicity of its large-scale formal relations, and as an unconsummated symbol for those aspects of the drama that transcend action and concepts to embrace the ineffable and the numinous.

—William Kinderman

PASERO, Tancredi.

Bass. Born 11 January 1893, in Turin. Died 17 February 1983, in Milan. Studied with Arturo Pessina in Turin; debut as Rodolfo in *La sonnambula,* Vicenza, 1917; appeared at Teatro Colon, Buenos Aires, 1924-30; on roster of Teatro alla Scala, 1926-52, where he first appeared as Philippe II in *Don*

Carlo; Metropolitan Opera debut as Alvise in *La Gioconda,* 1929; at Covent Garden, 1931; appeared in Florence and Verona, 1933; at the Teatro alla Scala he created Miller in Giordano's *Re* and Babilio in Mascagni's *Nerone* (1935).

Publications

About PASERO: articles–

Winstanley, S. "Tancredi Pasero." *Record Advertiser* 3/no. 4 (1974): 2.
Clerico, C. *Tancredi Pasero: Voce verdiana.* Scomegna, 1985.

* * *

Pasero was in the grand line of Italian basses whose most acclaimed representative this century was probably Ezio Pinza. This is not the only type of Italian bass, but the particular line has a very distinctive national character about it. Without the depth of the Russians, the lightness of the French, the "blackness" of the Germans or the "straight," oratorio-orientated tone of the English, the Italians have valued and cultivated richness: a vibrant quality, authoritative and dignified certainly, but passionate rather than heavy, luscious rather than dry.

In the earlier part of Pasero's career the vibrancy on records may be too much, especially to Anglo-Saxon ears. In 1927 and the years immediately following, he recorded a large selection of arias with a voice of magnificent freshness, but the quick, reiterative vibrato is a very insistent presence. Sometimes it is assimilated more readily into the main body of the tone, which raises the question of the extent to which the recordings of those times pick it out and present it as a separate, inescapable feature. Comparison with other singers also suggests that it is characteristic of a young voice and that it diminishes with age. By the late 1930s it is less prominent in Pasero's recordings, though it never disappears entirely. At no time does it seem to have been a feature which American or British critics pounced on when he sang at the Metropolitan Opera or Covent Garden.

In both of these houses he was regarded as an asset, though not one of long duration. At the Teatro alla Scala he was an institution, the indispensable bass of all seasons from 1926 till near the end of the war. He was versatile and reliable, and in certain operas rose to meet the greatness of the role. This was particularly so in *Don Carlos,* where his portrayal of King Philip had pathos and dignity in just proportions. His recordings of the solo ("Ella giammai m'amò") are touchingly colored with sorrow, and there are moments when the agony is almost disconcertingly vivid. It was no doubt something of the same sympathy that he brought to his Boris Godunov and which helped to make his Fiesco in *Simon Boccanegra* so moving in the restrained expression of suffering in this dignified patrician.

Less congenial to him was the lowlife character of Leporello, though for Don Basilio's Slander Song in *Il barbiere di Siviglia* he is able to draw resourcefully on a capacious bag of tricks. His devils (in Gounod and Boito) do not sound particularly satanic—though an exception has to be made for Mefistofele's "Son lo spirito," which he recorded in 1944 with a dark menace and a chillingly devilish chuckle. While he is generally a fine master of the legato style, he sometimes indulges in the vice of aspirating, but then that never seems to have worried the Italians much, and Pasero was essentially an Italian singer. At one time it seemed that he was among

the best of a type that could be relied on to continue indefinitely into the future. It is none too easy to recognize his successor today.

—J.B. Steane

PASTA, Giuditta (born Giuditta Maria Costanza Negri).

Soprano. Born 26 October 1797, in Saronno, near Milan. Died 1 April 1865, in Blevio, Lake Como. Studied with Bartolomeo Lotti and Giuseppe Scappa; made debut in 1815; appeared in Scappa's *Le tre Eleonore* at the Teatro dei Filodrammatici di Milano, 1816; Paris debut in Paer's *Il principe di Taranto,* Théâtre-Italien, 1816; London debut as Telemachus in Cimarosa's *Penelope,* King's Theatre, 1817; appeared in Venice, Padua, Rome, Brescia, Trieste and Turin; appeared as Rossini's Desdemona at the Théâtre-Italien, Paris, 1821; appeared in Vienna, 1829; in St Petersburg, 1840; created title roles in Pacini's *Niobe* (Teatro San Carlo, Naples, 1826), Donizetti's *Anna Bolena* (Milan, 1830), Bellini's *Norma* (Teatro alla Scala, 1831) and Amina in Bellini's *La sonnambula* (Milan, 1831).

Publications

About PASTA: books–

Ferranti-Giulini, M. *Giuditta Pasta e i suoi tempi.* Milan, 1935.
Cambi, L., ed. Bellini, V. *Epistolario.* Milan, 1943.
Pastura, F. *Bellini secondo la storia.* Modena, 1959.
Pini, V., ed. *Giuditta Pasta: i suoi tempi e Saronno.* Saronno, 1977.

articles–

Stendhal. "Madame Pasta." In *Vie de Rossini,* Paris, 1824; English translation as *Life of Rossini,* London, 1824.

* * *

Giuditta Pasta was one of three great sopranos who helped mould the first years of the romantic period of opera. At a time when London opera house managers could afford to pay the highest fees, Pasta, Sontag and Malibran were the superstars, to be followed by Grisi and Lind. Arguably, in comparison with her rivals Pasta had much the least "romantic" life and career, but for many contemporaries she remained on a pedestal. She also has unique historic importance as one of the first great interpreters of the three greatest Italian romantic composers—Rossini, Bellini, Donizetti— creating various of their works, including two which remain central to the repertoire—Norma and Amina in *La Sonnambula.*

After a debut in Brescia, Pasta made a false start to her international career at the Théâtre des Italiens in Paris in 1816 and the King's Theatre in London in 1817. She made little impact and returned to Italy for further study with Scappa and appearances all over Italy, often in minor houses and mostly in long since forgotten works of minor composers.

During these years and subsequently Pasta slowly moulded her voice, which she both lengthened and strengthened. Ebers, impressario of the King's commented on her appetite for hard work—"she leaves nothing to chance." He labeled

Giuditta Pasta in the title role of Bellini's *Beatrice di Tenda*

her voice a mezzo soprano: "its present excellence is in great measure due to cultivation, its natural tone being far from perfect." Stendhal describes a register extending from low A to high C or even D, but draws attention to the different registers of voice. Indeed many contemporaries refer to the veiled quality of the middle register. Given the range and scope of Pasta's repertoire—Amina and Semiramide which we associate with lyric coloratura; Norma and Anna Bolena, true dramatic soprano territory; and Tancredi, bravura mezzo—the critics could easily have been describing Maria Callas! Indeed there are striking similarities in their careers, separated by nearly a century and a half.

From her reappearance in Paris in 1821 Pasta attained the status of international stardom and from 1824, when she again sang in London, she was for some years unrivaled. During this period she also appeared in Vienna, Naples, Milan and other centres, culminating in her 'creations'—Rossini's *Viaggio a Reims* in 1825, Anna Bolena in 1830, Norma and Amina in 1831 and the leading roles in Donizetti's *Ugo, conte di Parigi* in 1832 and Bellini's *Beatrice di Tenda* in 1836. Ultimately her repertoire extended to over 50 roles, including at least eleven by Rossini.

That Pasta's success was as much due to her acting as to her singing is another point of similarity with Callas. Chorley points to the way in which Pasta would first create and then maintain her interpretation, but though he knew what was coming both in terms of ornamentation and histrionically, Pasta's genius was such that he always felt as if he were seeing something quite new. From her first entry she was riveting. As late as 1837, when her voice had markedly deteriorated, he wondered "where has ever been seen any greater exhibition of art" than in her performance of Medea in Mayr's opera.

Ebers felt "there is no perceptible effort to resemble the character she plays . . . . she comes upon the stage the character itself transformed into the situation."

The creation of Norma was the climax of Pasta's career. In June 1833 she sang the role in London and if the critics were initially lukewarm about the opera, there was no doubt about the heroine. "She (Pasta) was in grand voice and sang with a purity of intonation, with a truth of expression, with an intensity of feeling perfectly unrivalled." Pasta had carried the opera: "no other artiste now in existence could have produced a similar result."

Pasta's career began to dwindle by the late 1830s, although in 1840 and 1841 when she was only forty-four she appeared extensively in Eastern Europe—Berlin, Moscow, St. Petersburg, Vienna and Warsaw. Once again there is a premonition of the Callas career, for nine years later Pasta reappeared in London in an ambitious program of arias and scenes from operas including the taxing finale of *Anna Bolena*. Chorley gives an evocative account of the heart-rending spectacle of a great voice in ruin, its owner unable to recapture past glory, and he ends with an unforgettable quotation from another witness—Pauline Viardot, sister of Malibran and then at the peak of her own career: "You are right! It is like the Cenacolo of da Vinci at Milan—a wreck of a picture, but the picture is the greatest picture in the world." The single epithet "greatest" given by the younger artist at such a moment is the final acknowledgement of Pasta's status.

—Stanley Henig

PATTI, Adelina [Adela] Juana Maria.

Soprano. Born 19 February 1843, in Madrid. Died 27 September 1919, in Craig-y-Nos Castle, near Brecon, Wales. Married: 1) Marquis de Caux, 1868 (divorced); 2) tenor Ernesto Nicolini, 1886 (died 1898); 3) Baron Rolf Cederström, 1899. Studied in New York with her half-brother Ettore Barilli, then toured as a prodigy; opera debut as Lucia di Lammermoor, 1859; Covent Garden debut as Amina in *La sonnambula*, 1861; in Berlin, 1861; Brussels, 1862; Paris, 1862; Vienna 1863; in Italy, 1865-66, then in Russia; appeared at the Teatro alla Scala, 1877-78, first as Violetta; appeared at Paris Opéra, 1874, 1888; presented at Metropolitan Opera, 1887; Covent Garden farewell season, 1903-04; appeared in recital until 1914.

Publications

About PATTI: books—

de Grave, T. *La Biographie d'Adelina Patti.* Paris, 1865.

de Charnacé, G. *Adelina Patti.* Paris, 1868.

Dalmazzo, G. *Adelina Patti's Life.* London, 1877.

Lauw, L. *Fourteen Years with Adelina Patti.* New York and London, 1884.

Klein, H. *The Reign of Patti.* New York and London, 1920.

Castán Palomar, F. *Adelina Patti: Su vida.* Madrid, 1947.

Cabezas, J. *Adelina Patti: La cantante de la voz de oro.* Madrid, 1956.

Rosenthal, H. *Twelve Centuries of Opera at Covent Garden.* London, 1958.

Hernandez Girbal, F. *Adelina Patti: La reina del canto.* Madrid, 1979.

Gattey, Charles Neilson. *Queens of Song*. London, 1979.
Cone, J. *Adelina Patti: Regina*. Portland, 1993.

*   *   *

Born in Madrid of Italian parentage, Adelina Patti was taken
to the United States where, aged seven, she began her career,
then after giving some 300 concerts retired at ten to allow
her voice to develop without risk of becoming strained. Six
years later, Patti made an impressive debut as Lucia in New
York. She had from the start the facility of learning a new
part completely by singing it two or three times *sotto voce*,
and once sung in public never forgot it, proving her best in
roles with opportunities for the display of exuberance and her
natural gift for comedy. The longevity of her voice was due
to her avoiding overexertion, helped perhaps, when once established, by her refusal to attend rehearsals. Making an
immediate impact at her Covent Garden debut as Amina in
1861, she was hailed as Grisi's successor. Enthusiasm even
surpassing that roused by Jenny Lind in 1848 followed the
final cadenza in the Mad Scene when Adelina sang Lucia.
She next became the youngest Violetta London had ever seen
in *Traviata;* James H. Davison, critic of *The Times*, judged
her acting "more elaborately finished than any previous impersonation of the character we remember." By the close of
the season she had sung twenty-five times in six operas within
eleven weeks, ending with Rosina in *Il barbiere di Siviglia*,
which was destined to be the role in which she excelled.

Patti went on to establish herself in all the capitals of
Europe. Wilhelm von Lenz, the Russian music critic, called
her "the Paganini of voice virtuosity." When he originally

Adelina Patti as Rosina in *Il barbiere di Siviglia*

heard her, he was struck at once with the fact that she
launched a tone in a manner characteristic only of great
instrumentalists. "She attacks the first note with a security
and an exactness of intonation which the majority of singers
achieve only in the course of a cantilena."

In Vienna, the distinguished critic Eduard Hanslick attended all Patti's major performances. He thought that as she
grew older her understanding of her roles deepened, and he
noticed in particular the greater fullness of her lower notes
which resembled "the dark tones of a Cremonese violin."
Her singing as Violetta was admirable, but the performance
suffered from an inability to convince one that this was a
courtesan. Patti made her first entrance like a high-spirited
child, for whom lilies would have been more appropriate than
camellias to wear in her corsage. All the same, in the last
scene, she was most moving. Such exquisite transition from
piano to expiring *pianissimo*, as when Violetta lay dying, and
from *mezza voce* to *fortissimo*, as in her duet with Alfredo,
he had never before witnessed. Verdi had no reservations;
Patti always was to him the ideal singer of his great role.

Hanslick thought Adelina failed to portray convincingly
Marguerite's tranquil unworldliness in *Faust*. She was too
lively, with her features continually in motion, but her singing
of the "King of Thule" and of the "Jewel Song" were flawless.
He was present once when the latter aria was followed by
demands for an encore. Suddenly, without signalling the orchestra, Patti took up again the trill on B—they joined her
in the next bar, and there was not the slightest difference in
the pitch.

Patti's friendship with the Empress Eugénie led to her
marriage in 1868 to the Marquis de Caux, equerry to Napoleon III, and eighteen years her senior. It soon proved a
mistake, and pursued by a Don Juan of a tenor, Ernesto
Nicolini, whom she first detested, Adelina eventually yielded
and eloped with him. When in 1876 *Aïda* had its Covent
Garden premiere with her in the title role and Nicolini as
Radamès, Hermann Klein, the critic, who was present, called
the first night the most exciting in her whole career. "There
was a new note of tragic feeling in the voice; there were shades
of poignant expression in the 'Ritorna vincitor' and the three
superb duets . . . that seemed to embrace the whole gamut of
human misery and passion."

The critic of the *Daily Telegraph* wrote in a similar vein.
On no other occasion had he witnessed at Covent Garden
anything "more impassioned than her acting, declamation
and singing." The truth undoubtedly was that she had experienced a grand passion for the first time in her life and it was
for the tenor originally so hated. Eventually they married and
it was because he longed to lead the life of an English country
squire that she bought her mock Gothic castle, Craig-y-Nos
in South Wales.

It was there in 1905 when Patti was sixty-two and gramo-
phones were in their infancy that the Gaisbergs recorded her
singing for posterity. An excellent assessment of these historic
discs is given by J.B. Steane in *The Grand Tradition—Seventy
Years of Singing on Record*. His overall impression is of "an
imaginative interpreter, an accomplished technician with a
warm middle voice and a remarkable, sometimes disconcerting fund of energy." He compares her recording of "Ah,
non credea mirarti" ("Scarcely could I believe it") from *La
sonnambula* with those of other prima donnas and finds hers
the most richly varied. "She colours with more emphasis than
Callas. . . . The elderly lady singing into the old horn gives
one some uneasy moments: a sudden forte in one phrase, a
loose bit of timing in another . . . But Callas in her prime and
with all EMI at her service gives more." On the whole, Steane
prefers Patti who in addition to an intimate feeling for the

music has retained some accomplishments—"swift turns, the trill with its fantastically fine texture and lightness—that few of the others have ever really acquired."

When Bernard Shaw, in his guise as the music critic, "Corno di Bassetto," heard Patti sing at the Albert Hall at the age of forty-seven, he disapproved of the program. There were few things more terrible to a seasoned musician than to have "Within a Mile" tacked on to "Ombra leggiera" or "Home, Sweet Home" introduced by "Il bacio." But he could not help wanting to hear those florid arias of the old school "on that wonderful vocal instrument, with its great range, its bird-like agility and charm of execution, and its unique combination of the magic of a child's voice with the completeness of a woman's."

—Charles Neilson Gattey

PATZAK, Julius.

Tenor. Born 9 April 1898, in Vienna. Died 26 January 1974, in Rottach-Egern, Bavaria. Studied conducting in Vienna with Guido Adler and Franz Schmidt; self-taught as a singer; debut as Radames, Reichenberg, 1926; member of Munich State Opera, 1928-45; member of Vienna State Opera, 1945-59; at Salzburg, 1948-50; also sang Herod and Palestrina; teacher at Vienna Academy of Music and at Salzburg Mozarteum; retired from stage in 1966.

Publications

About PATZAK: articles–

Branscombe, P. "Julius Patzak." *Opera* 5 July (1954): 403.
Dennis, J. "Julius Patzak." *Record Collector* 19 (1971): 197.

*　　*　　*

Celebrated Austrian tenor of the pre-and post-war years, Julius Patzak was born in Vienna where he went to University then to the Music Academy, studying composition, and conducting with Franz Schmidt. Having graduated, he conducted a dance orchestra and began to sing in a modest fashion, realising that this was his true métier. With constant practice in cafés, he began to teach himself and with such success that he was engaged by the Opera House at Reichenberg, Bohemia in 1926 and made his début as Radames in *Aida*. He was then called by Brno to sing the same role and this resulted in a year's contract from 1927-8.

Patzak was invited by the prestigious Bavarian State Opera in Munich for the 1928-9 season and remained with them until 1945, becoming internationally famous for his Mozart interpretations at the annual Munich festivals in the 1930s. He sang in three world premieres there: Pfitzner's *Das Herz* in 1931; Richard Strauss' *Friedenstag* in 1938 and Carl Orff's *Der Mond* in 1939. He also made many guest performances in Europe, including Tamino at Covent Garden in 1938 under Beecham, and was sought by Clemens Krauss at the Berlin State Opera, having already sung for him in Vienna. Patzak left Munich for the Vienna State Opera in 1945, and remained there as principal tenor until 1959.

He did not appear in as many operatic performances at Salzburg as might be thought, considering his prowess as a Mozartean. Although he had sung there in sacred music concerts since 1938, his first stage appearance was in 1943 as Tamino in Krauss's "Alt Wiener" *Zauberflöte,* a Krauss-produced-and-conducted affair which was never repeated. However, in 1945 Patzak sang Belmonte in *Die Entführung* and two years later in von Einem's *Dantons Tod,* and in *Arabella* (as Count Elemer).

His chief success in Salzburg came relatively late: in 1948 as Florestan in *Fidelio,* when his voice had grown stronger; then again in the next two seasons with Kirsten Flagstad as Leonore and under Furtwängler's direction. Patzak also sang Titus in the first Salzburg production of Mozart's opera, in 1949; but Florestan, which he again sang with Flagstad at Covent Garden in 1951, was one of his two greatest creations, the other being Palestrina in Pfitzner's Musical Legend. All Patzak's clarity of diction, insight into the characters and a complete range of even vocal tone marked him as a great singer.

To some ears, though, his voice sounded nasal, a shade dry, or even acid in tone from time to time; but there was never any doubting his exceptional and scrupulous musicianship based on a fine intelligence: he knew his strengths and his limitations precisely.

Patzak sang in four languages, and his Verdi and Puccini in German, some of which has been preserved on record, may strike a little hard, verbally, on Anglo-Saxon and Latin ears, though there can be absolutely no doubt about the tender phrasing and vocal precision. He was equally at home in operetta as in opera, his Eisenstein in *Fledermaus* was unsurpassed; and the purity and authenticity, devoid of mannerisms in his Viennese *Schrammel* indicated a broad and unaffected outlook, a great sense of humor and a delight in everything Viennese.

His stage presence was always effective in spite of a withered arm which, with great skill, he always contrived to make inconspicuous in keeping with full characterization of the role he was playing. Before and after his retirement from the opera stage in 1959, Julius Patzak became a professor at the Vienna Music Academy as well as a member of the staff of the Salzburg Mozarteum.

—Alan Jefferson

PAUL BUNYAN.

Composer: Benjamin Britten.

Librettist: W.H. Auden.

First Performance: New York, Columbia University, Brander Matthews Hall, 5 May 1941.

Roles: Narrator (baritone or tenor); Voice of Paul Bunyan (speaking); Johnny Inkslinger (tenor); Tiny (soprano); Hot Biscuit Slim (tenor); Sam Sharkey (tenor); Ben Benny (bass); Hel Helson (baritone); Four Swedes (tenors, basses); John Shears (baritone); Western Union Boy (tenor); Fido (soprano); Moppet (mezzo-soprano); Poppet (mezzo-soprano); chorus.

Publications

article–

Mitchell, D. "The Origin, Evolution and Metamorphoses of Paul Bunyan, Auden's and Britten's 'American Opera'." In *W.H. Auden: Paul Bunyan.* London, 1988.

Despite negative criticism when it was first produced, and the fact that it is not well known even today, *Paul Bunyan* maintains a significant place among Britten's numerous works for the stage. *Paul Bunyan* was Britten's first attempt at writing opera, and as such it foreshadows many of the compositional traits, techniques, and textual themes that characterize the composer's important future contributions to the operatic repertoire of the twentieth century.

Paul Bunyan, set to a libretto by the poet W.H. Auden (his most extended collaboration with Britten), is an operetta for young voices based on the exploits of the American folk hero Paul Bunyan. At first glance, the story appears merely to chronicle certain events from Paul's life having to do with the physical mastery of man over the American wilderness. However, Auden skillfully directs the focus to the complex question of how, having accomplished this, man will choose to live in the "civilization" he has created.

After a prologue in which the coming of Paul Bunyan is prophesied, act I opens in an unspoiled, innocent America which is about to be set upon by Paul and his team of lumberjacks, assembled from immigrants of many nationalities. Eventually a leader (Hel Helson) is identified, as well as those to cook (Sam Sharkey and Ben Benny), and someone to keep the books (Johnny Inkslinger). As months pass, the enthusiasm felt in any new, exciting venture begins to give way to boredom and discontentment as the lumberjacks grow weary of their lot, particularly the changeless diet of soup and beans. The men appeal to Johnny Inkslinger to intercede. Fortunately, a new arrival to the camp, Hot Biscuit Slim, is an excellent cook, and he is assigned to that chore (over the protestations of two very hurt colleagues, Sam and Ben). Meanwhile, Paul has been away to get his daughter Tiny and bring her to live with him, now that her mother has passed away. Tiny immediately becomes the center of everyone's attention, and much to the regret and envy of all the men, especially Inkslinger, she is assigned to help Hot Biscuit Slim in the kitchen. (By the close of act I the common cause of man's struggle for survival, which has united the camp thus far, begins to disintegrate as the challenges of the life of choice begin to emerge.)

Act II opens some time later, and Paul realizes that it is now time to cultivate the land that has been cleared. Farmers (among them John Shears) are sought to follow Paul to an ideal spot he has selected, some 1,000 miles away, while the lumberjacks, who remain behind, are to be dispatched to a new and difficult site to clear. Hel Helson, feeling underappreciated and exploited, is urged by his cronies to confront and, if necessary, fight Paul upon his return. Though he is no match for Paul, Helson does fight him but in defeat realizes what a fool he has been. Slim and Tiny, in the meantime, have proclaimed their love for each other. In the final scene, "The Christmas Party," Paul acknowledges that his work is done and that he must now move on to conquer other wildernesses. Those who remain begin the life of choice, wherever it may lead, knowing that America's future rests in the choices they and succeeding generations make.

From the outset, Britten and Auden faced enormous obstacles. The subject matter, if approached at all realistically, would require dimensions of impossible proportions, especially those of the main character and his exploits. Hence, the part of Paul is assigned to an unseen speaker. Also, an opera with potentially only one female voice created a different type of challenge. Auden's solution is to invent singing trees and animals to accommodate the needed diversity in sound. (Britten was later to address quite successfully the all-male issue in *Billy Budd* and the three *Church Parables.*) And of course the sheer audacity of two expatriate Englishmen creating on American soil a work based on an American myth in a structure and style reflective of American musical idioms undoubtedly contributed to the unfavorable press which greeted the premiere. Shortly thereafter the piece was exiled to the composer's file, not to be revisited again for over thirty years.

That *Paul Bunyan* was the first operatic venture for both artists may explain, if not excuse, its lack of musical and dramatic focus. Auden was clearly influenced by a type of socially conscious musical theater practiced by Kurt Weill, and in *Bunyan* he raises many issues for the audience to contemplate: world hunger, ecology, the generation gap, brain versus brawn, order versus disorder, etc. What he failed to provide was a specific enough dramatic argument on which the opera could develop. And while Britten's score shows amazing compositional skill for one relatively inexperienced, the result lacks continuity. There is a juxtaposition (rather than an assimilation) of styles and idioms (including musical theater, jazz, opera parody, choral music, etc.) which might explain the audience's initial confusion. Yet there is much to admire in Britten's ability to combine words, music, instrumentation, and textures in uniquely expressive and dramatic ways.

—Michael Sells

LE PAUVRE MATELOT [The Poor Sailor].

Composer: Darius Milhaud.

Librettist: Jean Cocteau.

First Performance: Paris, Opéra-Comique, 16 December 1927.

Roles: Sailor (tenor); His Wife (soprano); His Father-in-Law (bass); His Friend (baritone).

Le pauvre matelot tells the story of a sailor's wife who has been waiting faithfully for fifteen years for her husband's return. Her father-in-law urges her to marry again because they are poor, but she declares that her husband will return rich from his travels. The sailor husband does indeed return a wealthy man. First he goes to his friend's house and determines to visit his wife without revealing his identity, in order to view her constancy for himself. He finds his wife hungry for news of her husband, and he tells her that her man is alive but very poor. At first she is worried because she herself is penniless, but then expresses her joy that her husband is alive.

Throughout this scene the disguised sailor boasts to her about his own wealth and about the gold and pearls he carries with him, but she replies to him "And what about my husband?" When she asks to stay the night, she consents. During the night she kills him with a hammer, because the wealth of this stranger will help to pay the debts of her loved one.

Jean Cocteau's libretto was inspired by a newspaper article with a similar plot. Other writers, such as Camus in *Le malentendu* and Cervantes in *Don Quixote,* have been interested in variants of this gruesome tale with its roots in folklore. Cocteau added the seafaring setting. As a result *Le pauvre matelot* is really a dramatization of a sea ballad or sailor's lament. While writing the opera Milhaud made frequent visits to the harbor at Marseilles to absorb the music and atmosphere of the bars and streets; the results of his visits are evident in the opera. Much of the music is imbued with the simplicity and repetitiveness of folksong. The opera opens with a jaunty tune in the style of a "java." The melodic outline is strikingly modal with the fourth degree of the scale raised and the leading note flattened. The music depicts the shabby bar where the sailor's wife works, and the repetitiveness and incessant character of the tune evoke the player piano Milhaud had encountered in similar bars. Just as the bar is the setting for the plot and the place where such a tale would be told, the music that characterizes the bar is the focus of the opera: it is heard repeatedly at the opening, referred to throughout, and concludes the opera.

Act III is dominated by another tune, this time not of Milhaud's creation, but the well known folk song "Blow the man down." On its first appearance on the horn it assumes tragic weight to the point of exaggeration. It is possible that Milhaud chose this tune partly because of the appropriate title: the wife has indeed blown her man down. The folksong forms only part of the musical substance in the last act. Suspense is created by a jazz-inspired rhythmic figure uttered by the bassoon, double-bass, and percussion in combination, and repeated after short but irregular intervals. Its unpredictability and rhythmic drive add to the suspense. Musical depiction affects not only the setting and the events, but also the characters themselves. This is most striking in the case of the wife and the sailor. The wife's music is simple and tuneful, suggesting that she is a simple, even a stupid woman with but one obsession: her husband. Once she has killed him, she sings a triumphant song, which, because of its inappropriateness to the tragic events, distances her from the audience and makes her appear ridiculous. Milhaud emphasizes this ridiculousness by setting this song in a particularly high register: her obsession has gone too far.

The music associated with the husband is of a different ilk. It is a characterization Milhaud used in other operas, such as with the creditors in *Christophe Colomb* (1928). The sailor is a tenor, and his part is also continually placed high in that range. His excessive pride and confidence are matched with a fast-paced vocal line. Both the pitch and the speed of his part make it difficult for the listener to take him seriously.

Le pauvre matelot is a chamber opera, requiring only four singers and thirteen solo instruments and lasting only forty-five minutes. It was Milhaud's second of several chamber operas, the shortest of which, *L'enlèvement d'Europa* (*The Abduction of Europa*) of 1927, lasts only nine minutes. This brevity of expression shows but one side of Milhaud's diverse musical interests. *Le pauvre matelot* can be contrasted with such large-scale works as *L'Orestie* (1913-22, adapted from Aeschylus's *Oresteia*), *Christophe Colomb* and *Maximilien* (1930) which require large forces and deal with mythological and historical subjects. Yet *Le pauvre matelot* by no means fades under their shadow, and it remains Milhaud's most frequently performed opera. This slight but cruel subject is handled by both poet and musician with utter precision, and there is no room for elaboration. The brutal tale is unraveled with an unrelenting and emotionless drive in one of Milhaud's most dramatically compelling works.

—Barbara L. Kelly

PAVAROTTI, Luciano.

Tenor. Born 12 October 1935, in Modena. Studied with Arrigo Pola in Modena and Ettore Campogalliani in Mantua; debut as Rodolfo in *La bohème,* Reggio Emilia, 1961; same role for debuts in Vienna (1963), Covent Garden (1963), Naples (1964) and the Teatro alla Scala (1965); appeared as Idamante in *Idomeneo* in Glyndebourne, 1964; toured Australia with Sutherland, 1965; Metropolitan Opera debut as Rodolfo, 1968; Chicago debut in same role, 1973.

Publications

By PAVAROTTI: books–

My Own Story. New York and London, 1981.

About PAVAROTTI: books–

Gatti, G. and G. Cherepelli, eds. *Luciano Pavarotti: Vent'anni di teatro.* Modena, 1981.
Mayer, M. *Grandissimo Pavarotti.* Garden City, New York, 1986.

articles–

Rubin, S. "Luciano Pavarotti." In *The Tenors,* edited by H. Breslin. New York, 1974.
Gualerzi, G. "Luciano Pavarotti." *Opera* February (1981).

*   *   *

Luciano Pavarotti has in the last few decades been billed variously as "the greatest singer in the world," "the world's greatest tenor," and "the greatest tenor since Caruso." He has taken to singing in stadiums, large parks, and other vast arenas such as the Baths of Caracalla in Rome with fellow tenors José Carreras and Placido Domingo during the 1990 World Soccer Cup match; this concert of "The Three Tenors" subsequently became a best-selling video. He has appeared in a movie ("Si, Giorgio," which was quickly dubbed "No, Luciano" by several critics) and frequently on talk shows. He has sponsored a singing competition based in Philadelphia and made a number of popular albums that have become best-sellers by any standard, not just those by which recordings by classical artists are judged.

None of these activities—many of which were practiced by his illustrious tenor predecessors Enrico Caruso and John McCormack in the early part of this century—should divert attention from the seriousness with which Pavarotti has studied and practiced his art. His vocal qualities come across strongly in his many gramophone recordings: his is a silvery, Italianate tenor voice with a ringing top, a fine *pianissimo,* smooth legato, a beguiling *mezza voce,* and liquid Italian

Luciano Pavarotti as Nemorino in *L'elisir d'amore,* Royal Opera, London, 1990

diction. Like his tenor idol, Giuseppe di Stefano, Pavarotti has the passion of Italy in his voice, yet his is a sound unlike the dark tone of di Stefano. As Pavarotti notes, "Occasionally I worry that my voice is not 'brown' and rich enough . . . [but] I really want to have a clear voice, with a strong metallic sound." Thus, in terms of vocal timbre, Pavarotti is not in the line of Caruso, di Stefano, or his own contemporary, Placido Domingo, but has more in common with Beniamino Gigli, Giacomo Lauri-Volpi, and Jussi Bjoerling.

Allied with stunning natural vocal equipment—which Pavarotti comes by naturally from his baker father who sang tenor and owned a good collection of tenor recordings—is the indefinable factor of Pavarotti's great charm, his obvious enjoyment of life, and his ability to communicate human emotions to vast numbers of people through his singing. John Steane notes a "kind of tension in his singing which, for one thing, focuses interest . . . and more important, enforces the urgency of the music and the conviction that this is . . . *the* performance." But there has also been a great deal of hard work, beginning with seven years of study in his native Modena and in nearby Mantua, first with Arrigo Pola, who refused to let him indulge in excessive *portamenti,* and then with Ettore Campogalliani, who also trained Pavarotti's childhood friend from Modena, Mirella Freni. From the first, Pavarotti was fascinated by every technical detail of *bel canto* singing and was determined to learn it correctly and thoroughly. "Many singers find studying voice—the *solfeggio,* the endless vocalizing, the exercises—very boring . . . [but] I became intrigued with the process." Pavarotti describes *bel*

canto mastery as "agility, elasticity, a smooth, even flow of liquid, well-focused sound, uniform of color, the ability to spin long, expressive legato lines without recourse to *portamenti* and, most important, without ever overdoing anything or giving the impression that you are over-exerting yourself, something you can do in *verismo.*"

Many fellow musicians and critics realized that the young tenor had indeed mastered the art of singing when Pavarotti began his career as Rodolfo in Puccini's *La bohème* at Reggio Emilia in 1961. This remains, along with Nemorino in Donizetti's *L'elisir d'amore,* one of Pavarotti's two favorite roles. As Rodolfo he eventually made debuts at La Scala, San Francisco, the Metropolitan, the Paris Opéra, and at Covent Garden, where he replaced di Stefano in 1963 after having been heard and "discovered" by Joan Ingpen in Dublin. After this break, two important engagements occurred: the first was his involvement in the tenor version of Idamante in Mozart's *Idomeneo* at Glyndebourne; second was the 1965 tour of Australia with Joan Sutherland and Richard Bonynge. The noted accompanist Geoffrey Parsons heard Pavarotti at Glyndebourne: ". . . there was this glorious voice! I'd never heard anything like it before in my life. A really astonishing, silvery, yet full-bodied sound that possessed a wonderful, sweet quality." Pavarotti considers learning Idamante an invaluable experience: "I learned to sing in the Mozart style—piano and legato. Also, the Glyndebourne people have a very pure, almost cold approach to opera; this was a good counterbalance to some of my Italian excesses." It was, however, his connection with the illustrious Sutherland that brought

Pavarotti's name before the opera world at large. Since that 1965 tour, the soprano and tenor have sung and recorded together extensively, matching each other in vocal brilliance and physical size. Ever serious about the study of singing, Pavarotti was astonished by Dame Joan's consistently high quality of performance night after night; from her he learned better breath support by, as Bonynge explains, putting "his hands on my wife's tummy trying to figure out . . . how she breathed." Good breathing, Pavarotti believes, "amounts to eight per cent of the art of singing because leaning on the diaphragm, . . . a strong and highly elastic muscle, removes the strain from the vocal cords and ensures the sound will come out as it should."

The role that Pavarotti sang with Dame Joan that catapulted him into the realm of the legendary was Tonio in Donizetti's *La fille du régiment,* where in numerous live performances and on their Decca recording he poured out without obvious strain the nine high C's in Tonio's air, "Pour mon âme." Pavarotti has in fact been dubbed "King of the High C's," yet there are qualities he considers much more important for a tenor. "To make so much of the high C is silly. Caruso didn't have it. Neither did Tito Schipa . . . [who] was a great singer. He had a great line. For producing music, that is ten times more important."

In the 1960s Pavarotti was the perfect example of the *tenore di grazia,* turning down any large roles that might harm his voice, such as Cavaradossi, Arnold in Rossini's *Guillaume Tell,* Manrico, Radamès, Rodolfo in *Luisa Miller,* Ernani, and especially Verdi's *Otello,* instead concentrating on Tonio, Pinkerton, Arturo in *I Puritani,* Nemorino, Elvino in *La sonnambula,* and the Duke of Mantua. He has since sung most of these heavier roles, finally adding Otello to his repertoire in 1990 in concert performances with Sir George Solti and recorded on Decca. With the addition of the bigger parts there has been somewhat of a decline in Pavarotti's pure *bel canto* style, but at the same time his interpretive powers have increased. While his Radamès and Otello were only partially successful, by far his best *spinto* role has been Riccardo in Verdi's *Un ballo in maschera.* He has recorded it twice on Decca, the first time with Renata Tebaldi and again with Margaret Price.

Pavarotti considers Elvino the most difficult *bel canto* role, one that "requires great phrasing in the *mezza voce* as well as an easy top." The real measure of a tenor according to Pavarotti, however, is the Duke in Verdi's *Rigoletto.* He has made stylish and exciting recordings of most of his roles. The following complete recordings with Dame Joan Sutherland may be especially recommended: *La fille du régiment* (1967); *I Puritani* (1973) with its falsetto high f; *Rigoletto* (1972); *L'elisir d'amore* (1970); *Lucia di Lammermoor* (1971); and *Turandot* (1972). With Mirella Freni he has made affecting recordings of Puccini's *La bohème* and *Madama Butterfly,* Mascagni's *L'amico Fritz,* and Boito's *Mefistofele.* Pavarotti and Montserrat Caballé have appeared together in recordings of Verdi's *Luisa Miller,* Ponchielli's *La Gioconda,* and Giordano's *Andrea Chénier.* Of the many recital albums, his debut album of Verdi and Donizetti arias (Pavarotti considers Verdi the greatest dramatic composer but "my voice likes Donizetti"), *Primo Tenore,* and *O Sole Mio* give special pleasure.

—Stephen A. Willier

THE PEARL FISHERS
See LES PÊCHEURS DE PERLES

PEARS, Peter.

Tenor. Born 22 June 1910, in Farnham, England. Died 3 April 1986, in Aldeburgh, England. Studied with Elena Gerhardt and Dawson Freer, 1934-38; studied with Thérèse Behr and Clytie Hine-Mundy, 1938-40; sang with the BBC Singers, 1934-38; sang with the New English Singers, 1936-38; first joint recital with Benjamin Britten in 1937; first tour in the United States in 1939; opera debut as Hoffmann in Offenbach's *Les contes d'Hoffmann* at the Strand Theatre in London, 1942; premiered Britten's *Peter Grimes,* 1945; premiered the role of the Male Chorus in Britten's *The Rape of Lucretia,* 1946; premiered Britten's *Albert Herring,* 1947; co-founded the Aldeburgh Festival, 1948; other Britten premiers include: *Billy Budd,* 1951, *Gloriana,* 1953, *The Turn of the Screw,* 1954, *A Midsummer Night's Dream,* 1960, *Curlew River,* 1964, *The Burning Fiery Furnace,* 1966, *The Prodigal Son,* 1968, *Death in Venice,* 1973; made a Commander of the Order of the British Empire, 1957; knighted, 1978.

Publications

About PEARS: books–

Steane, J.B. *The Grand Tradition.* London, 1974.
Thorpe, M., ed., *Peter Pears: a tribute on his 75th Birthday.* Aldeburgh, England, 1985.

articles–

Keller, H. "Peter Pears." *Opera* 2 (1950-51): 287.
Blyth, A. "Peter Pears Talks." *Gramophone* 46 (1968-69): 331.
Heinitz, T. "The Art of Peter Pears." *Records and Recording* 16/9 (1973): 6.
Richards, D. "Peter Pears at 70." *Music and Musicians* 28 (980): 20.
Norris, G. "Pears at 70." *Musical Times* 121 (1980): 509.
"Sir Peter Pears, an appreciation." *Opera Quarterly* 4/13 (1986): 1.
Davis, P.G. "Sir Peter Pears." *Opera News* 51 (1986): 32.

* * *

Peter Pears was an influential figure in British opera from 1945 until his death in 1986, not only as a performer but as an inspiration to composers and other singers. In *The Grand Tradition* John B. Steane suggests that Pears may be the best representative of the "educated modern singer," whose musicality and intelligence must embrace the music of all periods. Certainly, Pears's wide-ranging activities would support such a claim. He was particularly associated with Benjamin Britten, who wrote a dozen operatic roles for him—fourteen, if one adds the realizations of *The Beggar's Opera* and *Dido and Aeneas.* Pears also sang *Oedipus Rex* under Stravinsky, created Pandarus in Walton's *Troilus and Cressida* (1954) and Boaz in Berkeley's *Ruth* (1956), and appeared in important productions of Holst's *Savitri* (1956) and

Peter Pears as Aschenbach in Britten's *Death in Venice,* **English Opera Group, Aldeburgh Festival, 1973**

Poulenc's *Les mamelles de Tirésias* (1957). His activities were not restricted to contemporary music. As a young singer he sang the standard lyric tenor repertoire, appearing in leading roles with the Sadler's Wells Opera (1943-45) in *Il barbiere di Siviglia, Rigoletto, Die Zauberflöte, Così fan tutte, The Bartered Bride, La traviata,* and *La bohème;* he appeared at Covent Garden as Tamino and as David in *Die Meistersinger von Nürnberg* in the 1950s and added Idomeneo to his repertoire at Aldeburgh as late as 1969. To this marked versatility in opera should be added an even more striking range of music in concert work: he was a distinguished interpreter of the works of the English lutenists, Purcell, Schütz, Bach, and the great nineteenth-century Lieder composers. In addition, the archives at the Britten-Pears Library indicate that he sang the first performances of more than ninety non-operatic works, many of them written specifically for him.

The voice itself was not conventionally beautiful. It could sound unsteady at times (although this trait seems to have been more pronounced in recordings than in the concert hall), and it lacked richness. This rather vulnerable-sounding timbre, together with an unusually high register break and a well-developed capacity for pianissimo singing, was often exploited in the music written for him, particularly moments that present the character as a victim or a visionary. Among the most famous instances that call upon this unique sound are "Now the Great Bear" and "What harbour shelters peace" in *Peter Grimes.*

Pears's many recordings demonstrate the sensitivity to words and music that made him such a sought-after interpreter. His last operatic recording (*Death in Venice*) provides many illustrations. For example, his handling of the rising interval at the end of the phrase "Should I go too beyond the mountains?" is a lesson in avoiding false accentuation (moun*tains*) while maintaining the musical line. Everywhere the text is evocatively colored: the caressing tone at "low-lying clouds, unending grey," the delivery of "Ah, here comes Eros" (scene v, besotted already), the physical decay of "O Aschenbach . . . Famous as a master," the numbed clarity of the Phaedrus passage. Pears's interpretation, however, is never fussy, and the performance never lapses into a demonstration of the role.

In addition, Pears was a gifted comic actor as well. His flair for sung comedy is evident on records in his operatic performances as Albert Herring and (even more subtly) Nebuchadnezzar in *The Burning Fiery Furnace.* That his abilities extended to the legitimate stage can be heard in his recorded portrayal of Feste in Shakespeare's *Twelfth Night* and, during his last years, in his readings at the Aldeburgh Festival.

Pears's contributions to musical life were not limited to his career as a performer. One of the founders (with Britten and Eric Crozier) of the Aldeburgh Festival, he contributed many witty and informative notes to its program books, and, with Britten, adapted Shakespeare's text for *A Midsummer Night's Dream.* In 1972 he and Britten established the Britten-Pears School for Advanced Musical Studies, where he was director of singing studies, a duty he shared with Nancy Evans after 1976. There he worked with promising young singers from all over the world, helping them establish careers.

—Joe K. Law

LES PÊCHEURS DE PERLES [The Pearl Fishers].

Composer: Georges Bizet.

Librettists: Michel Carré and Eugène Cormon.

First Performance: Paris, Théâtre-Lyrique, 30 September 1863.

Roles: Léïla (soprano); Nadir (tenor); Zurga (baritone); Nourabad (bass); chorus (SATTBB).

Publications

articles—

Klein, J.W. "The Centenary of Bizet's *The Pearl Fishers.*" *Music Review* 25 (1964): 302.
Poupet, Michael. "Les infidélités posthumes de partitions lyriques de Georges Bizet: *Les Pêcheurs de perles.*" *Revue de musicologie* 51 (1965): 170.
————. "Le Rétablissement de la partition originale des *Pêcheurs de perles* de Georges Bizet." Choudens, 1976; in *Revue de musicologie* 62 (1976): 343.
Wright, Lesley A. "*Les Pêcheurs de perles:* Before the Premiere." *Studies in Music* 20 (1986): 27.
Avant-scène opéra October (1989) [*Les pêcheurs de perles* issue].

* * *

Bizet was only twenty-four in late March or April 1863 when Léon Carvalho, then director of the Théâtre-Lyrique in Paris, commissioned him to write a three-act score on a libretto by Eugène Cormon and Michel Carré. Rehearsals were to begin in August for an anticipated premiere in mid-September. To meet the tight schedule, the young composer borrowed from the earlier, incomplete *Ivan IV* and may well have cannibalized much of his now lost one-act *opéra comique, La guzla de l'Émir.* During rehearsals, he made numerous revisions and composed recitatives for acts I and II so that *Les pêcheurs de perles,* at that time entitled *Léïla,* no longer contained spoken dialogue. The premiere was postponed until 30 September due to the soprano's illness.

Most reviewers in 1863 pointed to passages they felt were derived from the work of established composers (notably Gounod, David, Verdi, and Wagner). And since Bizet was already identified as a leader of the younger generation, the critics also mounted their standard attack against "noisy" orchestration and unnatural harmonies; however, in the *Journal des débats* Berlioz testified to finding a "considerable number of beautiful pieces full of fire and rich coloring." The libretto was universally condemned. Though the work had a *succès d'estime* in certain circles, the public failed to embrace it, and *Les pêcheurs de perles* disappeared from the stage after eighteen performances that autumn. It was not performed again until the 1880s, when *Carmen*'s popularity induced directors to look at other works by Bizet.

The plot, centered on the traditional operatic love triangle and set in exotic Ceylon, is driven and resolved by coincidence. Léïla and Nadir are lovers pitted against the jealous and powerful Zurga; the dynamics of the triangle are complicated by a long-term friendship between the two men and by Léïla's oath before the pearlfishers to forswear all men. Nadir comes to the isolated camp where he is welcomed as a long-lost friend by Zurga, who has just been chosen leader of the

A poster for the first production of Bizet's *Les pêcheurs de perles*, Paris, 1863

pearlfishers. The two reminisce about the evening when both saw and fell in love with a beautiful "goddess" at the temple in Kandi; both had then pledged to avoid her rather than jeopardize their friendship. In the next scene the same woman (Léïla) appears, veiled, and is sworn in as the chaste, solitary Hindu priestess who will pray for the safety and good fortune of the pearlfishers. Before the end of act I Léïla and Nadir have recognized one another, for Nadir had broken his oath to Zurga and returned to hear her songs in Kandi. The lovers meet that night (act II), but are discovered by the high priest Nourabad and are then condemned to death at sunrise by the furious Zurga. At the opening of act III, Zurga is tormented by guilt about sentencing his dear friend to death and thinks, too, of Léïla's great beauty; but when Léïla enters to plead for Nadir's life and confesses her love for him, she ignites Zurga's jealousy once more. Before leaving she asks him to give her necklace to her mother. He discovers that it is the very necklace he had given to a brave girl who had saved his life many years earlier. Zurga's jealousy evaporates, and he starts a fire in the camp, to distract the bloodthirsty pearlfishers and permit the lovers to escape.

In an effort to improve the dramatic impact of the score, posthumous editors (c. 1885, 1893) felt free to tinker with both music and plot in the final scene and elsewhere. The original form of these sections was not widely available until 1975 when Choudens issued a corrected score. Since the autograph manuscript has been lost, Arthur Hammond used the first-edition piano-vocal score and orchestrated sections missing since the 1880s. The strongest of the ensembles, the tenor/baritone duet from act I ("Au fond du temple saint"), has ironically become widely popular in a non-authentic posthumous version that discards the original triple meter closing allegro in praise of "sacred friendship" for a dramatically nonsensical return to the goddess theme ("Oui, c'est elle, c'est la déesse"). This wonderfully memorable goddess theme is first introduced in an effective flute and harp scoring and recurs, perhaps too often, whenever Bizet wishes to call attention to Léïla's effect on the men's friendship; it is effectively used, however, in the original version of the final scene after Zurga has saved the lovers from imminent death.

Very little of the score predicts that Bizet would write *Carmen* a little more than a decade later, but there is a good deal of lovely music for the soloists. Each has at least one strong aria, but the finest of them are Zurga's dramatically expressive recitative and aria in act III ("L'orage s'est calmé"/ "O Nadir, tendre ami de mon jeune âge"); Nadir's exotic act II Chanson ("De mon amie"); and Nadir's often excerpted Romance in act I ("Je crois entendre encore"). Bizet supports the haunting Romance melody with an equally memorable scoring: the plangent English horn, muted violins, and two solo cellos that provide a rocking figure for the lullaby.

Choral music occupies a fairly substantial portion of the opera. It succeeds nicely in some places and sounds banal or dated in others. At their best the choruses help create the exotic setting, as in the opening choral dance for act I ("Sur la grève en feu"), where energetic rhythms are combined with interesting modulations; or in the offstage chorus opening act II, where simple choral parts and an ostinato rhythm in the male voices contrast with striking harmonies interjected by shrill piccolos. One of the weakest choral passages, judged embarrassingly old-fashioned even in 1863, accompanies Léïla's coloratura at the end of act I.

Only a few operas from Second Empire France are now more widely performed than *Les pêcheurs de perles*, and even fewer works by twenty-four-year-old composers have earned a place in the repertory. Though Bizet's distinctive musical personality emerges only occasionally and the more dramatic situations fall short of truth and power, this more than creditable score often transcends its weak libretto, largely due to Bizet's gift for melody and his colorful and effective orchestration.

—Lesley A. Wright

PEER GYNT.

Composer: Werner Egk.

Librettist: Werner Egk (after Ibsen).

First Performance: Berlin, 24 November 1938.

Roles: Peer Gynt (baritone); Solveig (soprano); Aase (contralto); Ingrid (soprano); Mads (tenor); Old Man (tenor); The Red-headed Dancer (soprano); Three Merchants (tenor, baritone, bass); The President (bass); Three Black Birds (soprano); The Unknown One (bass); Blacksmith (baritone); Bailiff (tenor), Bailiff's Wife (mezzo-soprano); Chief Troll (soprano); Six Trolls (basses); Little Troll (boy soprano); Waiter (tenor); chorus.

*　　*　　*

It is with his third opera, *Peer Gynt* (1938), above all that Egk has made an enduring contribution to European culture, thanks to revivals within Germany and a recent recording now available world-wide on compact disc. Egk's not inconsiderable literary abilities enabled him to fashion (as with all of his operas) his own libretto from Ibsen's long verse drama, described as "freely adapted," "took considerable liberties with" would be nearer the mark. While on one level his compression of the plot works remarkably effectively, it does so at the expense of the wider moral issues of the original. It is possible that Egk had other motives: the opera was banned by the Nazis, who apparently recognized themselves in the acid treatment of the trolls. If they really were Egk's target, it can only have been by way of a side-swipe, since there is never any doubt of the main concern of the opera.

Although retaining the general topography of Ibsen's story, Egk obviously felt that the relationship between Peer and the various women in his life was the most important aspect and the most ripe for operatic setting. Yet this is by no means a conventional romantic opera—the music is too caustic in tone—and true romance only appears in the very last scene. In concentrating on the love interest, he relinquished some of Ibsen's more fantastical elements, such as Peer's encounters with the Boyg and the Button-moulder (a folk variant on the Grim Reaper, equating to the Unknown One in the opera's last act), while the rejection of Ingrid, the courting of the Old Man's daughter and the relationship with Solveig all gain in intensity since they loom larger in the overall scheme. But the most radical difference between opera and source is the plot's elapsed time: Egk compressed it to barely more than ten years against Ibsen's half-century. The ramifications of this change are immense: when Peer returns home he is barely into middle-age, with Solveig a presumably still nubile woman in her mid-thirties, not blind or ancient, as in Ibsen. The primary significance of Peer's journey home as an all-but-forgotten liar called to account for his actions at the end of his days would therefore have made no sense in the opera. He is still redeemed by the impossibly patient Solveig, but Egk has her save him from the trolls (from whom he had fled ten years before) and not the divine judgement of Ibsen's Button-moulder. Effective enough both musically and dramatically in balancing the scene with the trolls in act I, philosophically it deprived the story of one of its main ironic points: that in refusing to become a troll by proving false to the Old Man's daughter, as well as abandoning Solveig for a career around the world, Peer acted exactly like a troll ("to thyself be—*enough*") and not as a man ("to thyself be true"). That is precisely what had caused the Old Man such ire in Ibsen's final act (if the Nazis were the trolls, this outcome would have been unthinkable). In Egk's final act it is only through the intercession of his mother's shade, Aase (in Ibsen, Peer is present when she dies, not so in Egk), that he has the chance of salvation, just as the implicit prayer to his mother in act I had saved him when the ringing of church bells caused the trolls to flee.

The Old Man's red-headed daughter assumed a more central role in Egk by replacing the sultry Arabic dancer Anitra, though with much the same result. For whatever reasons, Egk eschewed the North African setting of Ibsen's fourth act, and the compositional opportunities for exoticism as in Grieg's (and eroticism in Saeverud's) incidental music for the stage play, by switching the location to Central America. The resulting burlesque (not particularly Latin in tone, however) of the scene with the three merchants and the ponderous President (an invention of Egk's) is delightful and one of the most enjoyable scenes in the opera, showing that Egk had heard and learned from the music of Kurt Weill. But when

Peer's ship is destroyed, he fetches up not in the Sahara but in a desert of an altogether different kind, a local bar, so that instead of his adventures in Egypt with Memnon and Anitra, he now courts the unnamed redheaded dancer, directed to be sung by the same performer as the Old Man's daughter.

The intercontinental presence of the trolls, and the fact that they claim Peer on his return, increases their position in the overall scheme to one of much greater importance. The local, albeit thoroughly nasty, imps of Ibsen acquire almost diabolic power in the opera. The first appearance of the Old Man reinforces this new, sinister image through the doubling of his folk-like air by the trumpet, giving the music a cutting edge that makes him a much more formidable and menacing character, whatever he may seem on the surface. While the music that portrays the trolls en masse is more akin to the circus, there is little really clown-like in their behavior, and their evil accordingly acquires greater depth. The orchestral accompaniment to the Dancer's pantomime at the close of act II has all the power and bite of the interludes from Shostakovich's *Lady Macbeth of Mtsensk,* and there is a real sense in the second half of the opera of fate catching up with Peer to drag him down into tragedy.

It has been claimed that *Peer Gynt* ends not so much with a full stop as with a semi-colon; in this it is close in spirit to the original, but a more satisfying close than Solveig's incandescent final aria, with its magnificent accompaniment from the horns, I cannot imagine. It is the high point of the opera, on which the whole emotional weight is thrown. The quiet and subdued close reflects Peer's exhaustion and relief and seems complete enough. If *Peer Gynt* fails, in the end, to attain quite the heights of the greatest of twentieth century German opera, it is only because Egk's theme does not match that of *Doktor Faust* or *Mathis der Maler* in its breadth or scale. If it does not always do justice to the full range of Ibsen's at times unwieldy drama, it must be said that no opera could do so, and Egk's reduction to more manageable proportions is entirely successful in its own terms. It is the final integrity of both text and music that makes *Peer Gynt* so enduring.

—Guy Rickards

PEERCE, Jan [born Jacob Pincus Perelmuth].

Tenor. Born 3 June 1904, in New York. Died 15 December 1984, in New York. Married: Sara Tucker. Sang at Radio City Music Hall, 1932; then studied with Giuseppe Boghetti; debut in Baltimore, 1938; became regular tenor soloist for Toscanini's broadcasts; Metropolitan Opera debut as Alfredo, 1941; on staff at Metropolitan Opera until 1966 and appeared there 1967-68; retired 1982.

Publications

By PEERCE: books–

with A. Levy. *The Bluebird of Happiness: The Memoirs of Jan Peerce.* New York, 1976.

*   *   *

"Between the high notes," said Jan Peerce, "there's something to be said in the middle of the aria." The middle of the aria often means the middle of the voice, and one of Peerce's most celebrated characteristics was his tonal consistency, a virtue he shared with some great cantors, with Giovanni Martinelli, and also with Aureliano Pertile, Toscanini's earlier "favorite tenor" at the Teatro alla Scala. For Peerce, to sing well was to breathe well; one senses immediately in his work not only responsible musicianship but total physical support. It was a luscious, forward sound, lyric in size but dramatic in quality, and crammed with texture. He gave to his Puccini roles and Don Ottavio a Verdian rectitude—quite the opposite of (for example) Beniamino Gigli, who often sentimentalized Verdi and Mozart as if they were Puccini. Peerce's forthright manner lent substance to all his Bach Aria Group performances and to his *Rigoletto* Duke in the opera house, and his earnest concern and full lyric voice made him a distinguished Alfredo and a vibrant Rodolfo, if not flirtatious in the manner of Ferruccio Tagliavini or Giuseppe di Stefano. Though his voice became drier, it remained steady and full until a stroke felled him in his seventies: he maintained strong vocal health as long as any other tenor of the century. His stage acting was dutiful, but his singing tone sounded even more persuasive in the opera house than on most of his records, which in RCA Victor's Studio 8H emphasized blatancy and harshness. In the house these were softened by distance, and his exceptional evenness of emission, now and then monotonous on record, meant in a live event that one heard *all* of his role very richly sung—an effect he shared with Jussi Bjoerling, who had a very different sort of voice.

Peerce knew his limits of volume and style, and refused to sing Wagner, even for his beloved Toscanini, who originally engaged him (after hearing Peerce's first and only concert performance of the first act of *Die Walküre!*) two years before the tenor's contract with the Metropolitan Opera. One understands the conductor's enthusiasm for the full, rattling voice, the dramatic commitment, and the rhythmic alacrity and clean musicianship of this dedicated tenor. Such qualities must have recalled his days in the twenties reshaping the Teatro alla Scala company with Pertile and others. Peerce and Toscanini performed together for fifteen years.

Aside from his Toscanini performances, Peerce made many records throughout his long career. Among them are some splendid moments of *La forza del destino*'s Alvaro, whose manly lyricism suits him very well, and his 1941 final scene from *Lucia di Lammermoor*, a performance of great richness and dramatic drive (hear his articulation of "No! No! No!" as he stabs himself) under complete artistic control. Perhaps his most representative work is in the Toscanini *La bohème*, ringing in tone, not subtly poetic but musically scrupulous and driven by passion, and wholly persuasive in its own special terms. Here, in short, was an artist whose musical style and vocal means were uniquely complementary and who fought for a repertoire which gave scope to his prodigious gifts without destroying them.

—London Green

PELLÉAS ET MÉLISANDE.

Composer: Claude Debussy.

Librettist: Claude Debussy (after Maeterlinck).

First Performance: Paris, Opéra-Comique, 30 April 1902.

Roles: Mélisande (soprano); Pelléas (tenor or high baritone); Golaud (baritone); Arkel (bass); Geneviève (mezzo-soprano); Yniold (soprano); Physician (bass); Shepherd's Voice (baritone); Serving Women (mute); chorus (AATBB).

Publications

books—

Gilman, Lawrence. *Debussy's "Pelléas et Mélisande": A Guide to the Opera*. New York, 1907.
Emmanuel, Maurice. *Pelléas et Mélisande*. Paris, 1926.
Jardillier, R. *Pelléas*. Paris, 1927.
Inghelbrecht, D.-E. *Comment on ne doit pas interpréter Carmen, Faust, Pelléas*. Paris, 1933.
Ackere, Jules van. *Pelléas et Mélisande*. Brussels, 1952.
Goléa, Antoine. *Pelléas et Mélisande: analyse poétique et musicale*. Paris, 1952.
Büsser, H. *De Pelléas aux Indes galantes*. Paris, 1955.
Kerman, Joseph. *Opera as Drama*. New York, 1956; 2nd ed., 1988.
Lerberghe, C. van. *Pelléas et Mélisande: notes critiques*. Liege, 1962.
Lesure, François. *Esquisses de Pelléas et Mélisande*. Paris, 1977.
John, Nicholas, ed. *Claude Debussy: Pelléas et Mélisande. English National Opera Guides,* vol. 9. London and New York, 1982.
Orledge, Robert. *Debussy and the Theatre*. Cambridge, 1982.
Terrasson, René. *Pelléas et Mélisande; ou, L'initiation*. Paris, 1982.
Grayson, David A. *The Genesis of Debussy's "Pelléas et Mélisande"*. Ann Arbor, 1986.
Nichols, Roger, and Richard Langham Smith. *Claude Debussy: Pelléas et Mélisande*. Cambridge, 1989.

articles—

D'Indy, Vincent. "À propos de Pelléas et Mélisande: essai de psychologie du critique d'art." *L'occident* June (1902).
Evans, E. "Pelléas et Mélisande." *Musical Standard* 29 May (1909).
Peter R. "Ce que fut la 'générale' de Pelléas et Mélisande." In *Inédits sur Claude Debussy,* Collection Comoedia Charpentier, 3. Paris, 1942.
Dukas, Paul. "Pelléas et Mélisande." In *Les écrits de Paul Dukas sur la musique*. Paris, 1948.
Abraham, M. "Sous le signe de Pelléas." *Annales du Centre Universitaire Mediterranéen* 7 (1953-54).
D'Estrade-Guerra, O. "Les manuscrits de Pelléas et Mélisande." *Revue musicale* no. 235 (1957): 5.
Leibowitz, R. "Pelléas et Mélisande; ou, le 'No-Man's Land' de l'art lyrique." *Critique* 13 (1957).
Stewart, Madear. "The First Mélisande: Mary Garden on Debussy, Debussy on Mary Garden." *Opera* May (1962).
Williams, B. "L'envers des destinées: Remarks on Debussy's *Pelléas et Mélisande*." *Cambridge University Quarterly*. (1975).

Avant-scène opéra, March-April (1977) [*Pelléas et Mélisande* issue].

Stirnemann, Kurt. "Zur Frage des Leitmotivs in Debussys *Pelléas et Mélisande.*" In *Schweizer Beiträge zur Musikwissenschaft, IV: Studien zur Musik des 19. und 20. Jahrhunderts,* edited by Jürg Stenzel. Bern and Stuttgart, 1980.

White, David A. "Echoes of Silence: The Structure of Destiny in Debussy's *Pelléas et Mélisande.*" *Music Review* 41 (1980): 266.

Abbate, Carolyn. "*Tristan* in the Composition of *Pelléas.*" *Nineteenth-Century Music* 5 (1981): 117.

Tammaro, Ferruccio. "Mélisande dai quattro volti." *Nuovo rivista musicale italiana* 15 (1981): 95.

Spieth-Weissenbacher, Christine. "Prosodes et symboles mélodiques dans le récitatif de Pelléas et Mélisande ou place du figuralisme dans l'écriture vocale de Debussy." *International Review of the Aesthetics and Sociology of Music* 13 (1982): 82.

Kunz, Stefan. "Der Sprechgesang und das Unsagbare: Bemerkungen zu *Pelléas et Mélisande.*" In *Analysen: Beiträge zu einer Problemgeschichte des Komponierens. Festschrift für Hans Heinrich Eggebrecht zum 65. Geburtstag,* edited by Werner Breig, et al., 338. Wiesbaden, 1984.

Grayson, David A. "The Libretto of Debussy's *Pelléas et Mélisande.*" *Music and Letters* (1985).

Boulez, Pierre. "Reflections on *Pelléas et Mélisande.*" In *Orientations.* London, 1986.

unpublished–

Grayson, David Alan. "The Genesis of Debussy's *Pelléas et Mélisande:* a Documentary History of the Opera, a Study of its Sources, and 'Wagnerian' Aspects of its Thematic Revisions." Ph.D. dissertation, Harvard University, 1983.

*   *   *

Pelléas et Mélisande is Debussy's only completed opera score. It is a slightly adapted version of Maeterlinck's play by the same title. Debussy began working on *Pelléas* in 1892, and the work was completed a decade later.

The opera takes place in an imaginary period, in the imaginary kingdom of Allemonde. While hunting, Golaud, a member of the royal family, finds a mysterious and lovely woman, Mélisande, weeping beside a well. The two of them become enamored of each other, and Mélisande agrees to go back to the kingdom and marry Golaud, who is a widower with a small son. Golaud announces that he must go get his son, Yniold, and asks Pelléas, his brother, to accompany Mélisande while he is away. While out walking with Pelléas, Mélisande drops her wedding ring in a fountain whose waters are said to cure the blind. Golaud returns home to find that Mélisande is not wearing the ring. She explains that she lost it in a cave on the seashore, and he insists that she go look for it at once, taking Pelléas for protection. A romance grows between Pelléas and Mélisande which devastates Golaud. Pelléas decides he must leave the kingdom and asks Mélisande for one last meeting, at which they confess their love and embrace for the first and last time. Golaud has been spying on them from the shadows and now leaps forward, running a sword through his brother. The final act of the opera takes place in the castle shortly after Mélisande has given birth to a daughter. Mélisande is dying, and the grieving, jealous Golaud asks whether she betrayed him with Pelléas. She never seems to understand him and dies without replying.

When Debussy had finished the opera, Albert Carré, the director of the Opéra-Comique, was alarmed at the language and the dramatic structure of the work. The premiere was a tense occasion: Maeterlinck had quarreled with both Debussy and the theater management because his wife was not chosen to play the heroine. The Scottish singer Mary Garden had been chosen instead. Maeterlinck publicly wished failure on the opera, and indeed its novel style of music outraged the public initially. Despite the public's first reaction, the opera played for fourteen nights, and gradually the hostility died down.

The style of *Pelléas et Mélisande* is unique. Debussy took the scenes just as he found them, making few cuts from Maeterlinck's play, which he set in reticent declamation over a subtle, shadowy layer of music. Musically, Debussy utilized modal, whole-tone, or pentatonic melodies and harmonies. He also used seventh and ninth chords, often in organum-like parallel movement.

The vocal line is murmuring, with much monotone recitation, and few sudden rhythms. By means of the slightest deviations of pitch and rhythm, Debussy was able to capture natural speech patterns.

Debussy linked the scenes all together within the acts through the use of musical interludes, a technique that deepens the mood and intensifies the concentration needed on the part of the audience. In addition, each scene has its own theme which is a subtle variant of the overall mood. *Pelléas* contains leitmotives in the Wagnerian tradition: short, flexible recurring fragments, associated with a person, or an idea.

Pelléas is considered one of the great works in opera literature and truly holds a significant place in opera development. It was this work that made Debussy a leader of a school, and brought about his revered position in music history. On the other hand, some say that this opera suffers because the drama is constructed out of ideas instead of persons and action. Nonetheless, the work has been closely examined and frequently performed, and will continue to be for quite some time.

—Kathleen A. Abromeit

—————

PENDERECKI, Krzysztof.

Composer. Born 23 November 1933, in Debica, Poland. Married: Elzbieta Solecka, 1965 (one son, one daughter). Studied privately with F. Skoyszewski; studied theory with Artur Maawski and Stanisaw Wiechowicz at the Superior School of Music in Cracow, 1955-58; taught at the Superior School of Music, 1958-66; UNESCO award for *Threnos,* 1961; taught at the Folkwang Hochschule für Musik in Essen, West Germany, 1966-68; faculty member at Yale University, 1973-78; honorary member of the Royal Academy of Music in London, 1974, of the Arts Academy of West Berlin, 1975, of the Arts Academy of the German Democratic Republic, 1975, and of the Royal Academy of Music in Stockholm, 1975; honorary member, Accademia di Santa Cecilia, 1976; member of the Academia Nacional de Bellas Artes, Buenos Aires, 1982. Penderecki has been the recipient of numerous international composition awards and prizes.

Pelléas et Mélisande, **stage design for act IV by Jusseaume, Paris, 1902**

Operas

Publishers: Moeck, Polskie Wydawnictwo Muzyczne, Schott.

The Devils of Loudon [*Diably z Loudon*]. Penderecki (after Huxley/Whiting), 1969, Hamburg, Staatsoper, 20 June 1969.
Paradise Lost [*Raj utracony*] C. Fry (after Milton), 1975-78, Chicago, Lyric Opera, 29 November 1978.
Die schwarze Maske, after G. Hauptmann, 1984-86, Salzburg, 15 August 1986.

Other works: incidental music, film scores, various vocal and orchestral works, instrumental works and works for tape.

Publications

By PENDERECKI: interviews–

Robinson, Ray. "Krzysztof Penderecki: An Interview and an Analysis of *Stabat Mater.*" *Choral Journal* 24 (1983): 7.

About PENDERECKI: books–

Lisicki, K. *Szkice o Krzysztofa Pendereckim.* Warsaw, 1973.
Schwinger, Wolfram. *Penderecki. Begegnungen, Lebensdaten, Werkkommentare.* Stuttgart, 1979.
Fischer, Erik. *Zur Problematik der Opernstruktur. Das künstlerische System und seine Krisis im 20. Jahrhundert. Bei-*

hefte zum Archiv für Musikwissenschaft 20. Wiesbaden, 1982.
Schwinger, Wolfram. *Krzysztof Penderecki: his Life and Works.* London, 1990.

articles–

Zielinski, T.A. "Der einsame Weg des Krzysztof Penderecki." *Melos* 29 (1962): 318.
Pociej, B. "Krzysztof Penderecki: en traditionell kompositör." *Nutida musik* 8/nos. 1-2 (1965-66).
Erhardt, Ludwik. *Spotkania z Krzysztofem Pendereckim* [a meeting with Penderecki]. Cracow, 1975.
————. "Chicago: 29 listopada 1978. Bóg, Szatan i Czlowiek" [on *Paradise Lost*]. *Ruch muzyczny* 1, 2, 3 (1979): 3, 14, 12.
Komorowska, Malgorzata. "Penderecki w teatrze." *Dialog* 26 (1979): 131.
Niemöller, Klaus Wolfgang. "Zur musikalischen Ausdruckwelt der religiösen Oper im 20. Jahrhundert." In *Das Religiöse in Opern des 20. Jahrhunderts zum Domfest 1980. Bonn (1981).* Bonn, 1981.
Rasmussen, Bo. "Djaevlene fra Loudon." *Musik og teater* 3/nos. 10, 11 (1982): 16, 18.
Ivaškin, Aleksandr. *Kšištof Pendereckij. Monografičeskij očerk.* Moscow, 1983.

*   *   *

Krzysztof Penderecki, a Polish composer who shot to international attention after the "thaw" of Stalinist repression in Poland in the early 1960s, has to date written three operas.

Only the first, *The devils of Loudon,* first performed in 1969, represents the aggressive avant-garde style (featuring dense tone-clusters, wide-ranging *glissandi* and garish tone-colors) with which his name is still most closely associated. By the mid 1970s, Penderecki had abandoned his *enfant terrible* attitude and with it his trademark orchestral effects. Like so many of his contemporaries, he attempted a rapprochement with such traditional musical devices as singable melody, periodic rhythm and clear-cut tonal centers. Whereas *The devils of Loudon* is a deliberately harsh and pungent treatment of Aldous Huxley's novel about alleged witchcraft and demonic possession in central Europe in the seventeenth century, the 1978 *Paradise Lost* is a lushly orchestrated, unabashedly tonal treatment (rich in references to hymnody and E major brilliance) of the biblical story of creation as told in verse by the seventeenth century English poet John Milton.

If Penderecki can be said to have become a neo-Romantic with *Paradise Lost* and such other works as the 1972 Violin Concerto, the 1979 Te Deum and the 1980 Symphony No. 2, he can be said to have turned into something of a neo-Expressionist with his 1986 *The Black Mask.*

Based on the 1929 play of the same title by the German dramatist Gerhart Hauptmann, *The Black Mask,* like Penderecki's first two operas, has a religious subject with ties to the seventeenth century. Its setting is the well-stocked but seriously troubled home of the Dutch-born mayor of a small town in the state of Silesia on the German-Polish border; the action takes place in the winter of 1662, shortly after the Thirty Years' War and on the eve of an epidemic of bubonic plague. The cast of characters (including the Calvinist mayor, his Catholic wife, their Huguenot and Jansenist servants, a Jewish merchant, a Lutheran clergyman) is a metaphor for the region's troubled political situation. The gathering only appears to be friendly and civil; beneath the surface of pleasant chit-chat runs a deep stream of ugly hatreds. The stream floods over in the last act when a mysterious villain, to whom the mayor's wife once bore an illegitimate child, visits the house; he is a black man, dressed as a black masquer, and he presents the household not only with guilt but also with death.

The music of *The Black Mask* is turbulent, with dissonant harmonies and angular melodic lines. The score is freely atonal; in its extreme moments, it calls to mind both the dynamic intensity and the actual sounds of Schoenberg's *Erwartung.*

—James Wierzbicki

Krzysztof Penderecki

PÉNÉLOPE.

Composer: Gabriel Fauré.

Librettist: René Fauchois.

First Performance: Monte Carlo, 4 March 1913.

Roles: Ulysses (tenor); Eumée (baritone); Pénélope (soprano); Antinous (tenor); Eurymaque (baritone); Euryclée (mezzo-soprano); Cléone (mezzo-soprano); Mélantho (soprano); Alkandre (mezzo-soprano); Phylo (soprano); Lydie (soprano); Eurynome (soprano or mezzo-soprano); Léodes (tenor); Ctésippe (baritone); Pisandre (tenor or baritone); Herdsman (tenor); chorus (SATB).

Publications

articles–

Jankelevitch, V. "Pélléas et Pénélope." *Revue du Languedoc* 6 (1945): 123.
Loppert, Max. "Faure's *Pénélope.*" *Opera* March (1982).

*　　*　　*

The action of Pénélope takes place on the island of Ithaca, ten years after the Trojan War, from the evening of one day to the next morning. It corresponds very closely to Books XVII-XXII of Homer's *Odyssey,* but the character of Telemachus, Odysseus' son, is omitted and the role of Athena and the other Olympians is reduced almost to invisibility. Ulysses (Odysseus), King of Ithaca, has now been absent twenty years, ten years at the war and ten delayed on the homeward voyage. His wife Pénélope is besieged within her own palace by arrogant suitors who, believing her husband dead, have taken over his property and are living off the fat of his land. Her delaying stratagems have finally failed, and the suitors will force her to choose one of them as a new husband the next day. During a banquet celebrating this fact Ulysses returns, disguised as an aged beggar, and weathers their insults until Pénélope grants him hospitality. Act II is largely a dialogue between Pénélope and Ulysses on a cliff overlooking the sea; still in disguise, he urges her to have courage and to suggest that only he who can draw Ulysses' great bow can have her in marriage. When she departs he reveals himself to the herdsmen and people of Ithaca as their rightful king, and calls on them for aid. In act III the trial of the bow takes place; only the beggar can draw it, and finally appearing in his true identity the hero slays his importunate rivals and is reunited with his faithful wife.

Fauré had been eager to begin an opera, preferably on a classical subject, since the considerable success of his music for *Prométhée* as produced at Béziers in 1900 and 1901. But he did not find a suitable libretto until, in early 1907, the Wagnerian soprano Lucienne Bréval put him in touch with the young dramatist René Fauchois, who had already written a drama on the subject of Pénélope with Bréval in mind. From that year until the premiere at Monte Carlo in 1913, Fauré devoted his principal creative efforts to *Pénélope,* and they are chronicled in a fascinating series of letters to his wife, who tended to stay in Paris while he spent the summer months composing at various retreats.

Fauchois was an inexperienced librettist and only an average poet; Fauré, ever mindful of dramatic pacing, drastically cut much of his original text and demanded various revisions, always in the service of greater simplicity. But Fauchois' unbounded admiration for the Homeric original was a sentiment Fauré fully shared, and it is evident that the clumping couplets of the libretto (which, when all is said and done, is no worse than that of many operatic masterpieces) were often

Lucienne Bréval and Maurice Raveau in the first Paris production of Fauré's *Pénélope,* Théâtre des Champs-Élysées, 1913

merely a springboard for imaginative identification with the great myth that stands behind them.

Fauré's operatic technique is a very personal adaptation and refinement of Wagner's. The principal characters are identified by strongly contrasted leitmotifs ("It is Wagner's system, but there is none better," Fauré wrote to his wife), arrived at by a long process of testing for potential development and combination. These define the opera's most memorable images—the grave, sighing chordal motif of Pénélope, the vaunting, wide-spanned trumpet call of Ulysses, the suitors' shifting (and shifty) chromatics, the mystically unfolding chord of the shroud that Pénélope daily weaves and nightly undoes. There are also other themes used in a more or less symphonic manner, notably a sequentially aspiring love-theme that appears first in Pénélope's act I apostrophe to the absent Ulysses, and is used to close act I and (in generous apotheosis) the entire opera.

Essentially the work is through-composed, though dividing loosely into scenes with some set-pieces (the somewhat conventially "oriental" ballets in the outer acts) and vocal solos which (like Pénélope's song already referred to) carry the imprint of Fauré the great lyric song-writer. It was long rumored that the orchestration was not Fauré's own, but it is known now that the whole of act I and the bulk of act II were indeed orchestrated by him, and that he merely consigned portions of the remainder to his young pupil Fernand Pécoud as it became evident he would not be able to complete the job himself in time for the premiere.

In fact, Fauré regretted that in many post-Wagnerian operas the interest was overwhelmingly centered on the orchestra, and he sought in *Pénélope* to give the voice greater primacy. Nevertheless some of the work's greatest moments are in the orchestra: the dark and fateful opening of act III, the virile ending of act II, achieved by strict canonic stretto of Ulysses' theme, while the statuesque act I prelude has some claim to be regarded as Fauré's greatest purely orchestral work. The characters are simply and efficiently drawn, and include the attractive baritone role of Eurymaque, the faithful retainer. Ulysses himself does not entirely shake off the image of a conventional *Heldentenor,* but that is his essential function. It is Pénélope who is treated with greatest depth and who provides the opera's (literal) center of gravity: a mature and mindful heroine, both passionate and patient.

What no mere description of this opera can convey is its almost continual sense of contemplative ecstasy, its vision of an epic age viewed with a calm clarity that in itself has the force of piercing emotion. Identifying so strongly with characters and story, Fauré's music at the same time removes them further from us, turns them into an ideal myth taking place upon a *horizon chimérique* (to quote the title of one of Fauré's last song-cycles) towards which we all yearn. By the same token the opera seems to stand curiously outside time, a representative of an eternal "classicism" that has much to do with Greece and nothing to do with the "classical" period in late eighteenth-century Vienna. Premiered in the same year as Stravinsky's *Le Sacre du Printemps, Pénélope* was truly born out of its time, and it has never found great favor. Maybe it is caviar to the general, but Fauré's work (whose select progeny certainly includes George Enescu's *Oedipe*) retains its fascination as a vision of one possible kind of twentieth-century opera. Perhaps it is indeed too idealized for the operatic stage, but it is a peerless work of the imagination.

—Malcolm MacDonald

PEPUSCH, Johann Christoph [John Christopher].

Composer. Born 1667, in Berlin. Died 20 July 1752, in London. Married: the singer Marguerite de l'Epine, 1730. Studied theory with Klingenberg and organ with Grosse; position at the Prussian court, 1681-97; in the Netherlands, and then London, 1700; violinist in the Drury Lane orchestra, then became harpsichordist and composer for the theater; founded with Needer, Gates, Galliard, and others the Academy of Ancient Music, 1710; preceded Handel as organist and composer to the Duke of Chandos, 1712; Mus. Doc. from Oxford University, 1713; director of Lincoln's Inn Fields Theatre, 1715-30; arranged the music for the enormously successful *Beggar's Opera,* 1728; organist of the Charterhouse from 1737 until his death.

Operas and Masques

Thomyris, Queen of Scythia (pasticcio), P.A. Motteux, London, Drury Lane, 1 April 1707.
Venus and Adonis (masque), C. Cibber, London, Drury Lane, 12 March 1715.
Myrtillo (masque), C. Cibber, London, Drury Lane, 5 November 1715.
Apollo and Daphne (masque), J. Hughes, London, Drury Lane, 12 January 1716.
The Death of Dido (masque), B. Booth, London, Drury Lane, 17 April 1716.
The Prophetess, or The History of Dioclesian, T. Betterton and J. Dryden (after Fletcher and Massinger), London, Lincoln's Inn Fields, 28 November 1724 [lost].
The Beggar's Opera (ballad opera), J. Gay, London, Lincoln's Inn Fields, 28 January 1728.
The Wedding (ballad opera), E. Hawks, Lincoln's Inn Fields, 6 May 1729.
Polly (ballad opera), J. Gay, London, Little Theatre in the Haymarket, 19 June 1777.

Other works: songs, odes, secular cantatas, sacred vocal works, instrumental music.

Publications/Writings

By PEPUSCH: books–

Rules, or A Short and Compleat Method for attaining to Play a Thorough Bass upon the Harpsichord or Organ, by an Eminent Master. London, c. 1730.
A Treatise on Harmony: containing the Chief Rules for Composing in Two, Three and Four Parts. London, 1730; 2nd ed., 1731; 1966; 1976.

articles–

"Of the Various Genera and Species of Music among the Ancients." *Philosophical Transactions of the Royal Society* 44 (1746).

unpublished–

A Short Account of the Twelve Modes of Composition and their Progression in Every Octave. Manuscript, 1751 [lost].

About PEPUSCH: books–

Downes, J. *Roscius anglicanus.* London, 1708; 1927.

Baker, C.H.C. and M.I. *The Life and Circumstances of James Brydges, First Duke of Chandos.* Oxford, 1949.
Deutsch, O.E. *Handel: a Documentary Biography.* London, 1955.
Wilson, J., ed. *Roger North on Music.* London, 1959.
Fiske, R. *English Theatre Music in the Eighteenth Century.* London, 1973.

articles–

Hughes, Charles W. "Johann Christoph Pepusch." *Musical Quarterly* 31 (1945): 54.
Moor, E.L. "Some Notes on the Life of Françoise Marguerite de l'Epine." *Music and Letters* 28 (1947): 341.
Lello, A.J.E. "Dr Pepusch." *Musical Times* 93 (1952): 209.
Tilmouth, M. "A Calendar of References to Music in Newspapers published in London and the Provinces (1660-1719)." *Royal Musical Association Research Chronicle* 1 (1961): 1.
Beeks, Gradon. " 'A Club of Composers': Handel, Pepusch and Arbuthnot at Cannons." In *Handel Tercentenary Collection,* edited by Stanley Sadie and Anthony Hicks, 209. New York and London, 1987.

unpublished–

Williams, J.G. "The Life, Work and Influence of J.C. Pepusch." Ph. D. dissertation, University of York, 1976.
Cook, D.F. "John Christopher Pepusch in London: his Vocal Music for the Theatre." Ph. D. dissertation, University of London.

*   *   *

The son of a clergyman, Johann Christoph Pepusch is best known as the arranger of the sixty-nine popular songs in the ballad opera known as *The Beggar's Opera.* This immensely and timelessly popular English work has had performances and revivals well into the present day, and has spawned many imitations and versions, the best known being Kurt Weill's *Dreigroschen Oper* (*Threepenny Opera*).

Pepusch received most of his musical training in Prussia before moving to England. His first employment in England came as a violist, and later as a harpsichordist at Drury Lane Theatre, where he collaborated on several masques, his most successful being *Venus and Adonis.* Pepusch's greatest success came as a result of his work on *The Beggar's Opera,* although the extent of Pepusch's contributions to this work is not entirely known. The first edition (1728) makes no mention of Pepusch and contains only the melodies of the airs; it is not until the second edition (in the same year) that overtures and harmonies appear and Pepusch is cited. It is believed that John Gay (1685-1732), author of the libretto for *The Beggar's Opera,* was responsible for the selection of the tunes and the lyrics (with the exception of five songs with lyrics composed by Lord Chesterfield and others), while Pepusch arranged the songs, set bass lines for them, and composed a few "overtures" for individual sections.

Some of Pepusch's dramatic works are lost, including his opera directly preceding *The Beggar's Opera,* entitled *The Prophetess, or The History of Dioclesian.* Pepusch also composed another ballad opera with E. Hawkes entitled *The Wedding* (performed at Lincoln's Inn Fields in 1729), and a sequel to *The Beggar's Opera* entitled *Polly,* which was not performed until after Pepusch's death (the first production was in 1777), due to censorship problems. Ballad operas were

Johann Christoph Pepusch

full of parody and satire which incensed critics; *The Beggar's Opera* alone satirized the political situation, several professions, and the upstanding public, drawing broad analogies between the thieves and prostitutes portrayed in the opera and public figures of high position in England at that time.

The overwhelming popularity of *The Beggar's Opera* has overshadowed Pepusch's other musical contributions, both dramatic and non-dramatic. He is to be remembered for a myriad accomplishments: his work as co-founder and organizer of the Academy of Ancient Music in London, his theoretical writings, his work as a historian and music librarian whose personal collection of music included the harpsichord pieces which were later to be gathered and published as the *Fitzwilliam Virginal Collection,* his chamber music, secular and sacred compositions and odes, and his dramatic music. For many years Pepusch has been regarded as a mere German academic whose career in England was motivated by a vicious rivalry with Handel. There is, however, little evidence to support the theory that Pepusch and Handel were bitter rivals; in fact, Pepusch aided Handel in arranging for performances for his operas through the Academy of Ancient Music. Handel turned successfully to oratorio writing, but Pepusch never had another success that equaled that of *The Beggar's Opera.*

—Meredith Wynne

PERGOLESI, Giovanni Battista.

Composer. Born 4 January 1710, in Iesi, near Ancona, Italy. Died 16 March 1736, in Pozzuoli. Studied with Francesco Santi, choir director at Iesi Cathedral; entered the Conservatorio dei Poveri in Naples as the result of a stipend given to him by the Marchese Cardolo Pianetti; studied violin with Domenico de Matteis, theory with Gaetano Greco, and later studied with Durante, Vinci, and Feo at the Conservatorio; first performed work the oratorio *La conversione di San Guglielmo d'Aquitania* at the monastery of Sant' Angelo Maggiore, summer 1731; commissioned by the municipal authorities of Naples to write a Mass (after a series of violent earthquakes), December, 1732; in Rome, May 1734; in Pozzuoli, where he died of consumption, 1736.

Operas

Editions:

Opera omnia di Giovanni Battista Pergolesi. Rome, 1939-42.
Pergolesi Complete Works Edition. New York and Milan, 1986-.

Salustia, Sebastiano Morelli? (after Zeno, *Alessandro Severo*), Naples, San Bartolomeo, January 1732.
[untitled intermezzo], Domenico Caracajus [performed with *Salustia;* lost].
Lo frate 'nnamorato, Gennarantonio Federico, Naples, Teatro dei Fiorentini, 27 September 1732; revised, Naples, carnival 1734.
[untitled work performed with *Lo frate 'nnamorato;* lost]
Il prigionier superbo, Naples, San Bartolomeo, 5 September 1733.
La serva padrona (intermezzo), Gennarantonio Federico [performed with *Il prigionier superbo*].
Adriano in Siria, Metastasio, Naples, San Bartolomeo, 25 October 1734.
La contadina astuta (intermezzo), Tommaso Mariani [performed with *Adriano in Siria*].
L'Olimpiade, Metastasio, Rome, Tordinona, 8 or 9 January 1735.
Il Flaminio, Gennarantonio Federico, Naples, Nuovo, fall 1735.

Other works: sacred dramas, oratorios, masses and other sacred vocal music, chamber vocal works.

Publications

By PERGOLESI: articles–

Luciani, S.A., ed. "G.B. Pergolesi (1710-1736): note e documenti." *Chigiana* 4 (1928).

About PERGOLESI: books–

Rousseau, J.-J. *Lettre de MM. du coin du roi à MM. du coin de la reine sur la nouvelle pièce intitulée La servante maîtresse.* Paris, 1754.
Rosa, C. de, Marquis of Villarosa. *Lettera biografica intorno alla patria ed alla vita di Gio: Battista Pergolese celebre compositore di musica.* Naples, 1831; 2nd ed., 1843.
Brosses, C. de. *L'Italie il y a cent ans, ou Lettres écrites d'Italie à quelques amis en 1739 et 1740.* Paris, 2nd ed., 1836.
Florimo, F. *La scuola musicale di Napoli e i suoi conservatorii.* Naples, 1880-83, 1969.

Annibaldi, G. *Alcune delle notizie più importanti intorno al Pergolesi recentemente scoperte: il Pergolesi in Pozzuoli: vita intima.* Iesi, 1890.

Radiciotti, G. *G.B. Pergolesi: vita, opere ed influenza su l'arte.* Rome, 1910; 2nd ed., 1935.

Giacomo, S. di. *I quattro antichi conservatorii musicali di Napoli.* Vol. 2. Palermo, 1928.

Corte, A. della. *G.B. Pergolesi.* Turin, 1936.

Schlitzer, F. *G.B. Pergolesi.* Turin, c. 1940.

Strohm, Reinhard. *Die italienische Oper im 18. Jahrhundert.* Wilhelmshaven, 1979.

Troy, Charles. *The Comic Intermezzo: a Study in the History of Eighteenth-Century Opera.* Ann Arbor, 1979.

Muraro, Maria Teresa, ed. *Venezia e il melodramma nel settecento.* Florence, 1981.

Degrada, Francesco, ed. *Studi pergolesiani.* 2 vols. Scandici, 1986-88.

articles–

Boyer, C. "Notices sur la vie et les ouvrages de Pergolèse." *Mercure de France* July (1772).

Schletterer, H.M. "Giovanni Battista Pergolesi." *Sammlung musikalischer Vorträge* 3 (1898): 127.

Dent, E.J. "Ensembles and Finales in 18th-century Italian Opera." *Sammelbände der Internationalen Musik-Gesellschaft* 11 (1909-10): 543; 12 (1910-11): 112.

————. "Italian Opera in the Eighteenth Century and its Influence on the Music of the Classical Period." *Sammelbände der Internationalen Musik-Gesellschaft* 14 (1912-13): 500.

Walker, F. "Two Centuries of Pergolesi Forgeries and Misattributions." *Music and Letters* 30 (1949): 297.

————. "Goldoni and Pergolesi." *Monthly Musical Record* 80 (1950): 200.

————. "Pergolesiana." *Music and Letters* 32 (1951): 295.

Prota-Giurleo, U. "Breve storia del teatro di corte e della musica a Naploi nei secoli XVII-XVIII." in *Il teatro di corte del Palazzo reale di Napoli.* Naples, 1952.

Walker, F. "Orazio: the History of a Pasticcio." *Musical Quarterly* 38 (1952): 369.

————. "Pergolesi Legends." *Monthly Musical Record* 82 (1952): 144, 180.

Degrada, Francesco. "Falsi pergolesiani: dagli apocrifi ai ritratti." *Convegno musicale* 1 (1964): 133.

————. "Linee d'una storia della critica pergolesiana." *Convegno musicale* 2 (1965): 13.

————. "Alcuni falsi autografi pergolesiani." *Rivista italiana di musicologia* 1 (1966): 32.

————. "Uno sconosciuto intermezzo di Giovanni Battista Pergolesi." *Collectanea historiae musicae* 4 (1966): 79.

Hucke, Helmut. "Die musikalischen Vorlagen zu Igor Strawinskys Pulcinella." In *Helmuth Osthoff zu seinem siebzigsten Geburtstag,* 241. Tutzing, 1969.

————. "Pergolesi: Probleme eines Werkverzeichnisses." *Acta musicologica* 52 (1980): 195.

unpublished–

Wilson, J. Kenneth. "*L'Olimpiade:* Selected Eighteenth Century Settings of Metastasio's Libretto." Ph.D. dissertation, Harvard University, 1982.

Monson, Dale Eugene. "*Recitativo semplice* in the *opere serie* of G.B. Pergolesi and his Contemporaries." Ph.D. dissertation, Columbia University, 1983.

*　　*　　*

Few composers in the history of western art music have been more misunderstood than Giovanni Battista Pergolesi, whose short productive career was followed by a posthumous rise in fame and mystique that culminated in his canonization as an early master of expressive affect (De Brosses) and of divine inspiration (Rousseau). He was championed as embodying the perfection of the Italian style during the so-called *Querelle des Bouffons,* in which the perennial Parisian battle of French versus Italian music and language was once again fought through a barrage of pamphlets and articles. Hundreds of misattributed compositions appeared under Pergolesi's name, often with music completely incongruous with his style and time; works such as the twelve concertini (by von Wassanauer) and *Il maestro della musica* (Auletta) still sometimes appear under Pergolesi's name. The proper estimation of Pergolesi places him with Vinci, Leo, and others, as a composer instrumental in transforming the contemporary musical language of the early eighteenth century through opera, a transformation that led to many of the characteristic features of the Classic style, such as a slow harmonic rhythm and melodies built of motivic repetition. At his best, he achieved high drama, generally through either the most expressive pathos or an inspired comic characterization.

Pergolesi's first public operatic work, a *dramma sacro* for the monastery of Sant' Angelo Maggiore on the conversion

Giovanni Battista Pergolesi

of William of Acquitaine, came at the end of his study in one of the famous Neapolitan music conservatories of the eighteenth century, the Conservatorio dei Poveri di Gesù Cristo, where he had studied for at least six years (and perhaps as many as ten) under the supervision of Gaetano Greco, Leonardo Vinci, and Francesco Durante. *San Guglielmo* is a limited work, but flashes of Pergolesi's soon-to-blossom genius are evident, particularly in the *buffo* scenes. The opera, overall, was tentative and less developed than those that would soon appear. Pergolesi's schooling must have gone well, for he was not required to pay tuition (as he led one of the conservatory's orchestras for hire), and the commission for *San Guglielmo* was arranged and performed by the conservatory, an honor reserved for only the best students. The boy was apparently a versatile and refined violinist, whose improvisations amazed even his fellow musicians (as reported by Villarosa), but he also may have studied voice—at least a set of solfeggi attributed to Pergolesi is found in the Naples Conservatory library.

From 1732 through 1735 a series of Pergolesi's operas appeared in Naples and Rome. Of his four serious operas, *Adriano in Siria* and *L'Olimpiade* (which borrowed heavily from *Adriano* and which was likely prepared in a rush) are the most developed. *Adriano* is one of his greatest works, at least in part inspired by his cast, which included the great Caffarelli in its ranks; Caffarelli's arias (such as the gorgeously lyric "Lieto così tal volta," with obbligato oboe, and the tumultuous "Torbido in volto e nero," with double orchestra) received his most careful and expressive treatment. Extensive alterations in the Metastasio libretto are everywhere to be found. *L'Olimpiade* was particularly singled out in contemporary accounts for its lyric beauty and passionate expression. Megacle's (the *primo uomo*) parlante aria, "Se cerca, se dice," which forms the centerpiece of the tragedy, was singled out as an "aria classicus" by later writers. Its poignant, sighing melodic line, reinforced by an orchestral "agitato" accompaniment, was in fact widely imitated in other settings of the same text in years to follow. *Salustia*, an adaptation of Zeno's *Alessandro Severo*, was plagued by sudden, last-minute cast changes (the *primo uomo*, Nicolini, died only days before the scheduled premiere), and the surviving scores suggest at least two possible performance formats. His second serious opera, *Il prigionier superbo*, was written for a rather undistinguished cast, although the orchestral writing is more secure. Both of these earlier operas seem tentative compared to the last two works.

The comic intermezzo written to separate the acts of *Salustia* is lost, but the two written for *Prigionier* and *Olimpiade*, *La serva padrona* and *La contadina astuta* (*Livietta e Tracollo*), are masterworks of comic writing. *La serva padrona*, whose renewed revival in Paris in 1752 precipitated, or at least encouraged, the *Querelle*, stands as a nearly unique example of an intermezzo largely unaltered in its transference and revival across European stages in the eighteenth century. *Livietta* brings to life its commedia dell'arte origins in a lively way, while the sometimes poignant arias of *La serva padrona* encourage a marvelously expressive dramatic flow.

Of his full-length operas, his most famous and successful works were his two *commedie musicali*, *Lo frate 'nnamorato* and *Flaminio*. Both works were revived on numerous occasions. The famous duet, "Per te ho io nel core," from the finale of *Flaminio* was later inserted into *La serva padrona* (one of its few alterations). *Flaminio* is closely modeled on the opera seria tradition, both in its dramaturgical design and its choice of cast. When *Lo frate* was revived in the Teatro Nuovo in Naples in 1748, it was reported that the opera had been sung in the streets for the previous twenty years (sic).

It is a wonderful amalgam of music, from serious arias in a high style to lower, apparently popular tunes and allusions—references (both in music and text) that, though obvious in intent, are sometimes unidentifiable today. It is one of the earliest complete Neapolitan dialect comedies and represents an important transition in the history of Italian comic opera. It was such works as this, traveling through Rome to Venice, that inspired the development of other full-length comic works there in the 1740s and eventually led to the birth of the *dramma giocoso*.

—Dale E. Monson

PERI, Jacopo.

Composer. Born 20 August 1561, in Rome. Died 12 August 1633, in Florence. Studied with Cristoforo Malvezzi in Lucca; maestro at the court of Fernando I and Cosimo II de' Medici, Florence; maestro at the court of Ferrara, 1601; member of the Florentine Camarata, formed by the counts Bardi and Corsi. Peri's setting of Rinuccini's *Euridice* composed for the marriage of Maria de' Medici and Henry IV of France, 6 October 1600.

Operas

La favola di Dafne (with J. Corsi), O. Rinuccini, Florence, carnival 1598; revised, 1598-1600.
L'Euridice O. Rinuccini, Florence, Palazzo Pitti, 6 October 1600.
Tetide, F. Cini, for Mantua, 1608 [not performed].
Lo sposalizio di Medoro e Angelica (with M. da Gagliano), A. Salvadori, Florence, Palazzo Pitti, 25 September 1619; revised, c. 1622.
Adone, J. Cicognini, 1611, for Mantua, May 1620 [not performed].
La Flora, overo Il natal di Fiori (with M. da Gagliano), A. Salvadori, Florence, Palazzo Pitti, 14 October 1628.
Iole ed Ercole, A. Salvadori, for Florence, 1628 [not performed].

Other works: intermezzi, ballets, oratorios, songs, instrumental works.

Publications/Writings

About PERI: books—

Davari, S. *Notizie biografiche del destinto maestro di musica Claudio Monteverdi.* Mantua, 1884.
Ademollo, A. *La bell' Adriana ed altre virtuose del suo tempo alla corte di Mantova.* Città di Castello, 1888.
Corazzini, G.O. *Jacopo Peri e la sua famiglia.* Florence, 1895.
Goldschmidt, H. *Studien zur Geschichte der italienischen Oper im 17. Jahrhundert.* Leipzig, 1901.
Solerti, A. *Le origini del melodramma.* Turin, 1903; 1969.
———. *Gli albori del melodramma.* Milan, 1904; 1969.
———. *Musica, ballo e drammatica alla corte medicea dal 1600 al 1637.* Florence, 1905; 1968; 1969.
Haas, R. *Die Musik des Barocks.* Potsdam, 1928.
Ghisi, F. *Feste musicali della Firenze medicea.* Florence, 1939; 1969.

Ghisi, F. *Alle fonti della monodia: due nuove brani della 'Dafne'.* Milan, 1940.

Nagler, A.M. *Theater Festivals of the Medici, 1539-1637.* New Haven, Connecticut, 1964.

Pirrotta, N., and Elena Povoledo. *Li due Orfei: da Poliziano a Monteverdi.* Turin, 1969; 2nd ed., 1975; English translation as *Music and Theatre from Poliziano to Monteverdi,* Cambridge, 1982.

Hanning, Barbara R. *Of Poetry and Music's Power.* Ann Arbor, 1980.

articles–

Vogel, E. "Marco da Gagliano: zur Geschichte des Florentiner Musiklebens von 1570-1650." *Vierteljahrsschrift für Musikwissenschaft* 5 (1889): 396, 509.

Sonneck, O.G. " 'Dafne,' the First Opera: a Chronological Study." *Sammelbände der Internationalen Musik-Gesellschaft* 15 (1913-14): 102.

Mila, M. "Jacopo Peri." *La rassegna musicale* 6 (1933): 219.

Boyer, F. "Les Orsini et les musiciens d'Italie au début du XVIIe siècle." In *Mélanges de philologie, d'histoire et de littérature offerts à Henri Hauvette,* 301. Paris, 1934.

Pirrotta, H. "Tempermenti e tendenze nella Camerata florentina." In *Le manifestazioni culturali dell' Accademia nazionale di Santa Cecilia.* Rome, 1953; English translation as "Temperaments and Tendencies in the Florentine Camarata." *Musical Quarterly* 40 (1954): 169.

Mila, M. "La nascita del melodramma." *Rivista musicale italiana* 56 (1954): 307.

Palisca, C.V. "The First Performance of 'Euridice'." *Queens College Twenty-fifth Anniversary Festschrift,* 1. New York, 1964.

Porter, William V. "Peri and Corsi's *Dafne:* Some New Discoveries and Observations." *Journal of the American Musicological Society* 18 (1965): 170.

Pirrotta, N. "Early Opera and Aria." In *New Looks at Italian Opera: Essays in Honor of Donald J. Grout,* 39. Ithaca, 1968.

Monterosso Vacchelli, A.M. "Elementi stilistici nell' 'Euridice' di J. Peri in rapporto al 'Orfeo' di Monteverdi." In *Congresso internazionale sul tema Claudio Monteverdi e il suo tempo: Venezia, Mantova e Cremona 1968,* 117.

Brown, Howard M. "How Opera Began: An Introduction to Jacopo Peri's *Euridice.*" In *The Late Italian Renaissance 1525-1630,* edited by Eric Cochrane, 401. London, 1970.

Sternfeld, F.W. "The First Printed Opera Libretto." *Music and Letters* 59 (1978): 121.

Carter, Tim. "Jacopo Peri (1561-1633): Aspects of his Life and Works." *Proceedings of the Royal Musical Association* 55 (1978-79): 50.

Carter, Tim. "Jacopo Peri." *Music and Letters* 61 (1980): 121.

Palisca, Claude V. "Peri and the Theory of Recitative." *Studies in Music* [Australia] 15 (1981): 51.

Tomlinson, Gary. "Madrigal, Monody, and Monteverdi's 'via naturale alla immitatione'." *Journal of the American Musicological Society* 34 (1981): 60.

Brown, Howard M., ed. Preface to *Jacopo Peri: Euridice.* Madison, Wisconsin, 1981.

Carter, Tim. "Jacopo Peri's *Euridice* (1600): A Contextual Study." *Music Review* 43 (1982): 83.

McGee, Timothy. "*Orfeo* and *Euridice,* the First Two Operas." In *Orpheus, the Metamorphosis of a Myth,* edited by John Warden, 163. Toronto, 1982.

Savage, Roger. "Prologue: Daphne Transformed." *Early Music* November (1989).

unpublished–

Tomlinson, Gary. "Rinuccini, Peri, Monteverdi, and the Humanist Heritage of Opera." Ph. D. dissertation, University of California, Berkeley, 1979.

Carter, Tim "Jacopo Peri (1561-1633): his Life and Works." Ph. D. dissertation, University of Birmingham, 1980.

*   *   *

Despite the fact that historians practically from the very start have dubbed Peri the "inventor" of opera, the composer himself seems to have viewed his ground-breaking efforts in an altogether more modest light. Indeed, he later categorized his earliest work in the genre, *Dafne* (first performed during carnival 1598; all music lost save six numbers), as nothing more than a "simple trial." But however fortuitous his role may have been in setting in motion the new art form, there is no mistaking the fact that he envisioned his labor as a joining of the old and new: on the one hand a backward glance at the courtly entertainments and philosophical speculations of the Renaissance, on the other, an experimental first step toward the emergence, in music, of the Baroque. Ottavio Rinuccini, librettist of *Dafne,* in fact touched on both points when he wrote in the preface to *Euridice* (1600), his next collaboration with Peri: "It has been the opinion of many . . . that the ancient Greeks and Romans, in representing their tragedies on stage, sang them throughout. But until now this noble manner of recitation has been neither revived nor (to my knowledge) even attempted by anyone, and I used to believe this was due to the imperfections of modern music, by far inferior to the ancient. But the opinion thus formed was wholly driven from my mind by Jacopo Peri, who . . . set to music with so much grace the fable of *Dafne* ([the words of] which I had written solely to make a simple test of what the music of our age could do), that it gave pleasure beyond belief to the few who heard it."

Rinuccini was not alone in praising Peri's achievement. Marco da Gagliano, a colleague of Rinuccini's and Peri's who in 1608 composed his own setting of the poet's *Dafne* text, enthusiastically recalled "the pleasure and astonishment" afforded by the "novel spectacle" of *Euridice* and how it "aroused admiration and delight" in those who heard it. Arguably an even greater tribute had already taken place in 1607 when Claudio Monteverdi, in creating his first opera, *Orfeo,* modeled much of the style of his dialogues and monologues on those of *Euridice* (to judge by the evidence of his reliance on them, the passages of Peri's score that most captivated Monteverdi are those that first strike listeners today: Daphne's narration in which she recounts Euridice's death; Orpheus's response; Orpheus's plea in the underworld). Nevertheless, at least one contemporary listener found Peri's most novel accomplishment, that is, his "noble manner of recitation," rather tedious—"like the chanting of the passion."

Curiously, given both his contemporaneous fame and the prominence accorded him by posterity, most twentieth century historians have shown a greater interest in the theories that gave rise to Peri's work than in the music he actually composed. Along with *Dafne* and *Euridice,* Peri composed five other operas between 1608-28 although three of them seem never to have been performed; the two others were written in collaboration with Gagliano. While with the lost *Dafne* this is unavoidable, with *Euridice* it can only be regretted.

Who was this shadow figure whose name is mentioned in all opera histories worthy of the name but whose music is so little known? As the musical scholar Tim Carter has written, in two important articles impressive for the way they build on original archival research and a review of existing information, Peri was "a singer and composer in rather routine, and for his part diffident, service at the Medici court. Some of his music is of the first order; but it needs to be seen in the context of his life and times." Part of that context is provided by the only other work of Peri's besides *Euridice* to have been published during his lifetime, the 1609 *Le varie musiche* (*The True Music;* 2nd ed., 1619), a volume of eighteen chamber songs containing fourteen for solo voice and two each for two and three voices with poetic forms running from the sonnet, madrigal, aria and a single example of strophic variation. From the literary point of view, the collection is especially telling in that it reveals the composer's tastes to have tended toward the conservative, with texts not only by Rinuccini but four by Petrarch, the latter inspiring songs of intense emotionalism that show Peri to have been the master of a compositional control matched by few of his contemporaries.

All told, Peri was at his most successful with highly-charged, dramatic texts. Although obviously drawn to the plaintive, the charge of "lugubrious" brought against him during his day has been shown to have been the vituperative handiwork of the pupils of Giulio Caccini, a fellow Florentine singer and composer who on more than one occasion seems to have delighted in impeding Peri's creative undertakings. While it is true that the lament on the death of Euridice along with Orpheus's first invocation in the underworld are among the most impressive moments of *Euridice,* these are not the only things treated in the opera, a point borne out variously by the vitality of the pastoral dances or the aristocratic mien given to the character of Pluto. Throughout the whole of the work one is aware of an unerring sense of proportion and drive. Howard Mayer Brown, describing *Euridice* in 1970, has elegantly and lovingly written that the work is one that "deserves repeated hearings and study, not merely for its historical significance as the first extant opera, but because it is capable of moving listeners even today." Brown himself has responded to the work with what one reviewer has termed "a landmark edition of early Baroque music" (Recent Researches in the Music of the Baroque, vol. 36, Madison, Wisconsin, 1982). Brown's words, but even more his edition of Peri and Rinuccini's unfaded allegory of music's power to influence and alter our lives, remain challenges not often enough taken up. Nowhere is that more apparent than in the continued need for a recording that does the work justice.

—James Parsons

PERTILE, Aureliano.

Tenor. Born 9 November 1885, in Montagnana. Died 11 January 1952, in Milan. Studied with Orefice and Fugazzola; debut as Lionel in *Martha,* Vicenza, 1911; then worked in Italy and South America; Teatro alla Scala debut as Paolo, 1916; Metropolitan opera debut as Cavaradossi, 1921; sang at Teatro alla Scala, 1922-37; appeared in Buenos Aires, 1923-29; sang at Covent Garden, 1927-31; taught at Milan Conservatory from 1945 and after his retirement in 1946.

Publications

About PERTILE: books–

Silvestrini, D. *Aureliano Pertile e il suo metodo di canto.* Bologna, 1932.
Tosi, B. *Pertile, una voce, un mito.* Venice, 1985.

articles–

Morley, P. "Aureliano Pertile." *Record Collector* 7 (1952): 245, 267.

"Sing! Sing it the way Pertile does!" Toscanini is said to have exclaimed when frustrated by rehearsals in which his singers and orchestra could not achieve the effect he was seeking. This single phrase, above all, sums up the influence of Aureliano Pertile during his great career.

"Il tenore di Toscanini" was the title accorded the tenor, the doyen of the Teatro alla Scala company for twenty years. His was an exceptional career, for in Pertile was embodied every requirement of the supreme opera singer: a fine instrument, musicality of a high order, intelligence and an innate histrionic ability.

Two factors in particular endeared him to Toscanini: an outstanding command of the musical idiom and an interpretive ability that was quite special. With a magnetic personality, Pertile would bring his characters to life. No longer were the characters merely a peg on which to hang the musical performance, but living, plausible human beings with whom the audience could identify. The quintessential singing actor, Pertile sought interpretive truth and restored to opera the proper amalgam of words, music and drama.

"Singing actor" is a term often reserved for an artist with an inferior voice, whose histrionic ability somehow compensates for a less than first-class instrument. In Pertile's case the voice was a fine one: a ringing *lirico-spinto* (lyric-dramatic) tenor, with an exceptionally vibrant tone quality which added an intensity to his portrayals. What distinguished Pertile from other fine contemporary tenors was his musicianship, brought about by a technique which permitted him the scrupulous observation of the directions of the composer's score, enhancing the authenticity of his portrayal. Although he was called upon mainly to sing dramatic roles such as Manrico (*Il trovatore*), Lohengrin, Canio (*Pagliacci*) and Radamès (*Aida*), he could sing with ease the more lyric roles such as Riccardo (*Un ballo in maschera*), Pinkerton (*Madama Butterfly*) and Edgardo (*Lucia di Lammermoor*), lightening the tonal color of the voice for the lyric and darkening and intensifying the sound for the dramatic repertoire.

With his magnetic personality and his sincerity of creation, little surprise that Pertile has passed into operatic history not just as another singer but as a legend. He is still thought of with reverence among some opera singers of later generations. Tenors like Pavarotti, Bergonzi and Corelli, who were influenced by Pertile in their earlier years, have all praised his technique and style.

Fortunately Pertile recorded extensively, both acoustically and by the electric process, for Pathé, Columbia and Fonotipia. His best period was probably between the years 1923 and 1929. Then his art was at its most mature, the voice thrilling in its intensity yet capable of every dynamic from a delicate *piano* to a ringing *fortissimo.* The control of the instrument is admirable. Add to this a scrupulous musicianship, a wide variety of tone color and a keen interpretive ability and it is not difficult to see why he became Toscanini's favorite tenor.

Pertile also recorded, a little later in his career, for HMV. By then, however, his style had become a little too intense, the tone a little too vibrant. Unfortunately, these also suffer from a technically over-amplified quality which clashes with the already vibrant sound of the singer. They are generally best avoided.

At a time when many singers were still content just to stand and sing, Pertile sought a greater truth in the portrayal of real characters, capable of the vast spectrum of human emotion. With his vocal and interpretive power, he would rivet the attention of his audience with the sincerity of his creation and the magnetism of his stage persona.

—Larry Lustig

PETER GRIMES.

Composer: Benjamin Britten.

Librettist: M. Slater (after the poem "The Borough," by George Crabbe).

First Performance: London, Sadler's Wells, 7 June 1945.

Roles: Peter Grimes (tenor); Ellen Orford (soprano); Captain Balstrode (baritone); Auntie (contralto); Niece (I and II, both soprano); Bob Boles (tenor); Swallow (bass); Mrs Nabob Sedley (mezzo-soprano); Rev. Horace Adams (tenor); Ned Keene (baritone); Hobson (bass); Dr Thorp (mute); Boy (mute); chorus (SSAATTBB).

Publications

books–

Crozier, Eric. *Peter Grimes.* London, 1945.
Stuart, C. *Peter Grimes.* London, 1947.
Abbiati, F. *Peter Grimes.* Milan, 1949.
Brett, Philip. *Britten: Peter Grimes. Cambridge Opera Guides.* Cambridge, 1983.
John, Nicholas, ed. *Benjamin Britten: Peter Grimes and Gloriana. Opera Guide 24.* London and New York, 1983.

articles–

Stein, Erwin. "Opera and *Peter Grimes.*" *Tempo* no. 12 (1945): 2.
Brett, Philip. "Britten and Grimes." *Musical Times* 118 (1977): 995.
Avant-scène opéra. January/February (1981) [*Peter Grimes* issue].
Brett, Philip. "Grimes and Lucretia." In *Music and Theatre: Essays in Honour of Winton Dean.* Cambridge, 1987.

*   *   *

Benjamin Britten's *Peter Grimes* occupies a unique place in the history of British music. A Koussevitsky Foundation commission had enabled Britten to devote himself to its composition. The Sadler's Wells Opera Company boldly decided to re-open its theater after World War II with a new work by a British composer. The resulting production drew together the composer's return from America to his English roots, the postwar sense of national rejuvenation, and the hope of a new era for English opera. Generally applauded, *Peter Grimes* rapidly established itself in the international repertoire.

The fisherman, Peter Grimes, appears in "The Borough," a poem describing English small-town life by George Crabbe, a native of Aldeburgh not far from Britten's own birthplace of Lowestoft. Montagu Slater's libretto, however, depicts a radically different Grimes from Crabbe's villainous monster. The protagonists in the opera are Peter Grimes himself, and (individually and collectively) the Borough as a whole. In the Prologue, an inquest pronounces the death of Grimes's apprentice to have been accidental, but Borough gossip continues to implicate him. In act I the townsfolk for the most part shun Grimes, but Ellen Orford (the schoolmistress) braves opposition to help him acquire a new apprentice and clear his name. With a storm raging outside, the Borough's superficial social life is depicted in The Boar pub, as Grimes, in a great lyrical aria, reveals his more profound sensitivity. But the following Sunday (act II), evidence of Grimes's harshness towards John, the new apprentice, in pursuit of his ambition, alienates Ellen (whom he had hoped to marry). As she deserts him, he defiantly resolves to go his own way, provoking a chorus of suspicion from the Borough, who angrily march to his hut. In the hut Peter and the apprentice are preparing to go to sea, but at the approach of the Borough Peter hurries the boy through the cliffside door. We hear his cry as he falls, but the crowd finds nothing. The final act begins with the conviviality of a town ball, but evidence of the boy's death emerges, causing suspicion against Grimes to intensify. A venomous manhunt ensues. Grimes re-appears, distraught to madness by his sufferings, and on the advice of the sea captain Balstrode he commits suicide.

Britten set out to compose a "numbers" opera of the traditional kind, with set-pieces defining key moments in the action, linked by continuous music. Six orchestral interludes depict both the natural elements, sunshine and storm, against which the community labors for its existence and the psychological tensions of the plot. Notable among those interludes is the passacaglia on Grimes's theme in act II, delineating Grimes's mental turmoil. The oscillation in the presentation of the minor characters, between individual expressions of musical personality and their merging in the collectivity of the crowd, reflects the fearful hold of mass psychology, while the extended choruses of mob fury are developed with great power. They contrast with the calm beauty of the reflections given to those (Ellen, the women, Balstrode) who stand aside from the hounding of a scapegoat, and the combination of strength, sensitivity, and destructive self-pity in the music of Peter himself.

Britten said that the opera concerned "a subject very close to my heart—the struggle of the individual against the masses. The more vicious the society, the more vicious the individual." Within that framework, Grimes has been interpreted as "an ordinary weak person, at odds with society, who offends against the conventional code"; "a maladjusted aggressive psychopath"; "a spiritual visionary"; "a misunderstood aesthete"; or "a rejected homosexual." As Philip Brett has shown, preliminary libretto drafts suggest that the last-mentioned view was in mind as the opera took shape. But overt suggestions of homoeroticism were steadily expunged as work progressed. Grimes is a harsh taskmaster, but hardly

Peter Pears and Joan Cross in Britten's *Peter Grimes*, London, 1947

merits death on that account, and since the opera intends, I think, to absolve him of responsibility for the deaths of his apprentices, his enforced suicide requires explanation. British society may have ignored or even denigrated the unconventional, the visionary or the aesthete, but it has not pressurized them into suicide. For the homosexual, the sense of guilt arising from society's rejection has all too often had just that outcome. The dynamics of Grimes's relationship with the Borough reflect this experience.

The vignettes of the townsfolk reveal their various infringements of "morality" so that, confronted by Ellen Orford, none "dare throw the first stone." Like Grimes, "each one's at his exercise." Judged by this parallel, a homicidal tendency is too extreme to constitute Peter Grimes' "exercise"; but homosexuality would readily fill the bill. Moreover, the proposal for rehabilitation through financial success and a marriage of convenience is (in the 1940s) understandable in regard to a despised homosexual. When, at the mid-point of the opera, Grimes makes his defiant affirmation of his right to go his own way: "So be it! . . . ," the townsfolk, in the ensuing chorus, take up the *same* musical theme. This parallelism makes a profound dramatic point. If Grimes is asserting his self-identity, the Borough likewise asserts (however hypocritically) *its* right "to keep its standards up." Britten's answer to this unresolvable conflict of values is the plea for understanding expressed by the women (act II:1). Incapable of such understanding, the men of the Borough sink their individual judgment in a hysterical chorus, powerfully expressive of homophobia. Astoundingly, even Balstrode (earlier, Peter's friend) comes to endorse the mob's rejection. Grimes, on the other hand (in Brett's illuminating analysis) internalizes in self-hatred his rejection by society, and buckles under the strain to the point of self-destruction.

Writing his first opera in the 1940s, when homosexual acts were still criminal, Britten could hardly be explicit. Yet the unmentioned theme of homosexuality aptly fits the psychological dynamics of the work, and supplies the missing key to a full interpretation. For those who find such psychologizing not to their taste, the opera still works as a moving statement of the universal theme of the individual against society.

—Clifford Hindley

PETERS, Roberta [born Roberta Peterman].

Soprano. Born 4 May 1930, in New York. Married: Robert Merrill (divorced). Studied with William Pierce Hermann; debut as replacement in role of Zerlina in *Don Giovanni* at the Metropolitan Opera, 1950, where she remained for thirty-five seasons; sang Arline in *The Bohemian Girl* at Covent Garden, 1951; appeared at Salzburg, 1963; appeared as Violetta in *La traviata* at the Bolshoi Opera, 1972; has appeared in recital, musical comedy, and film.

Publications

By PETERS: books—

with L. Biancolli. *A Debut at the Met.* New York, 1967.

* * *

There are relatively few persons in opera whose fate in singing seems to have been established during their teenage years. Roberta Peters, however, was one who appeared to control the direction of her career at a very early age. Her desire to sing gained support from her parents, both of Austrian descent, although neither parent was musically inclined. Her father was a shoe salesman and her mother a milliner. As Roberta Peterman, she came into serious vocal study as a result of a contact made by her grandfather. He had a prestigious position in a hotel located in the Catskill Mountains that was often frequented by the tenor Jan Peerce. When Peters was yet very young, Peerce was asked by her grandfather to listen, assess, and make a recommendation about Peters' musical training. Peerce, though impressed, was hesitant to endorse any talent, let alone one so young and inexperienced; however, he did help the family arrange for voice lessons with William Pierce Hermann, teacher of Patrice Munsel.

Because Peters was a native of New York City, all her training began and revolved around tutors in this metropolitan area. Hermann almost immediately recognized the potential in his young, energetic singer. After Peters completed junior high school, he was able to persuade her parents and school officials that she should withdraw from the public schools and continue her formal musical education with him. From the age of thirteen until her audition with the Metropolitan Opera at the age of nineteen, she learned a total of twenty operatic roles under his guidance. The first she learned was Lucia in Donizetti's *Lucia di Lammermoor.* Hermann arranged additional lessons in other areas essential in her preparation for a career in opera. These included ballet, acting, French, German, and Italian.

Even though she was given an opportunity to appear on Broadway at the age of sixteen, she declined because she was interested only in opera. Three years later Jan Peerce, who had checked on her progress throughout the years, took her to Sol Hurok, who, in turn, signed her to a contract and arranged auditions for her. In January of 1950, Max Rudolf heard her sing, and a week later Rudolf Bing engaged her to sing the Queen of the Night (*Die Zauberflöte*) and Rosina (*Il barbiere di Siviglia*) in performances scheduled nearly a year later. Her debut at the Metropolitan Opera did not wait until then, however. Because of her command of numerous roles and her participation in the Kathryn Turney Long program at the Metropolitan, she was able to replace an indisposed Nadine Conner as Zerlina in Mozart's *Don Giovanni* on six hours notice in November of 1950 without ever having performed an opera role on any stage.

As a result, she endeared herself to the critics, and the media immediately helped her to become an overnight sensation and a name known by virtually everyone in American operatic circles. Other demanding roles she has successfully assumed on short notice at the Metropolitan Opera include Gilda (*Rigoletto*), Sophie (*Der Rosenkavalier*), Susanna (*Le nozze di Figaro*), and Adele (*Die Fledermaus*). She created the role of Kitty in the American premiere of Menotti's *The Last Savage.* Her frequent appearances on television, on film, and in musical comedy have kept her name constantly before the American public.

The longevity of her career substantiates the artistic qualities present in her singing as a result of her meticulous preparation. Those persons who theorize that the singing of demanding operatic literature at an early age damages the human vocal instrument must ignore the ingredients of Peters' successes. In her youth she tackled a difficult coloratura repertory, beginning at the age of thirteen, and she maintained a rigorous and strenuous schedule thereafter in developing all facets of a singing career. She never pampered herself, but she was never without the help of a constant, trained technician. She studied with Hermann five and six days every week. She was proud of her command of exacting coloratura cadenzas, but she was also able to perfect the demanding Klosé clarinet studies for additional agility.

There are those who criticize her failure to create both warmth and excitement in her tone. At the height of her career, Peters was rather unfavorably compared, at first, to the fiery and passionate Maria Callas and later on to the dramatic and spectacular Joan Sutherland. In spite of the success of these two singers, Peters maintained an approach to coloratura singing which was more popular in the earlier part of this century and which was used by such singers as Galli-Curci and Pons. The demand for Callas and Sutherland in European venues possibly precluded any lasting acclaim for Peters on the international scene. Her appearances in 1951 in a gala performance at Covent Garden (*La bohème* under Beecham), in 1963 at Salzburg (*Die Zauberflöte*), in 1963 at Vienna (*Rigoletto*), and in 1972 in Russia at the Bolshoi Opera (*La traviata*) are highlights of her European performances.

Peters steadfastness as a performer is evidenced by the fact that by the end of her thirty-fifth anniversary with the Metropolitan Opera (1985), she had sung over three hundred sixty performances of twenty-three roles. Setting house records for her roles of Zerlina, the Queen of the Night, Oscar, and Gilda, she has experienced a career characterized by dependability, charm, and a perennial Cinderella quality which resulted from her fairy-tale debut at the Metropolitan Opera at the age of twenty.

—Rose Mary Owens

PFITZNER, Hans Erich.

Composer. Born 5 May 1869, in Moscow. Died 22 May 1949, in Salzburg. Married: daughter of James Kwast, in England, 1899. Studied piano with James Kwast and composition with Iwan Knorr at the conservatory in Frankfurt; taught piano and theory at the Conservatory of Coblenz, 1892-93; assistant conductor of the Municipal Theater in Mainz, 1894-96; on the faculty of the Stern Conservatory in Berlin, 1897-1907; conductor at the Theater des Westens, 1903-06; conducted the Kaim concerts in Munich, 1907-08; municipal music director of Strasbourg and dean of the Strasbourg Conservatory, 1908-18; conductor at the Strasbourg Opera, 1910-16; conducted at the Munich Konzertverein, 1919-20; master class at the Berlin Academy of Arts, 1920-29; taught composition at the Akademie der Tonkunst in Munich, 1929-34. Pfitzner stood trial for his supposed involvement with the Nazis in 1948, but was exonerated.

Operas

Der arme Heinrich, James Grun (after a medieval epic poem by Hartman von Aue), 1891-93, Mainz, Municipal Theater, 2 April 1895.
Die Rose vom Liebesgarten (prologue), James Grun, 1897-1900, Elberfeld, Munich, Municipal Theater, 9 November 1901.

Das Christ-Elflein, Ilse von Stach and Pfitzner, [incidental music, Munich, 1906, recast as a "Spieloper," Dresden 1917].
Palestrina, Pfitzner, 1912-15, Munich, Prinzregententheater, 12 June 1917.
Das Herz, Hans Mahner-Mons, 1930-31, Munich and Berlin, State Opera, 12 November 1931.

Other works: incidental music, choral works, orchestral works, concertos, chamber music, songs, piano pieces.

Publications

By PFITZNER: books–

Gesammelte Schriften. Augsburg, 1926-29.
Über musikalische Inspiration. Berlin, 1940.
Abendroth, W., ed. *Reden-Schriften-Briefe.* Berlin, 1955.

articles–

Adamy, Bernhard. "Zwei wiederaufgefundene Pfitzner Beiträge: *Das Herz* und *Die "Symbolik" in der Rose vom Liebesgarten.* " *Mitteilungen der Hans Pfitzner Gesellschaft* 40 (1979): 3.

About PFITZNER: books–

Cossmann, P.N. *Hans Pfitzner.* Munich, 1904.
Louis, R. *Hans Pfitzners 'Rose vom Liebesgarten'.* Munich, 1904.
Halusa, K. *Hans Pfitzner.* Leipzig, 1907.
Riezler, W. *Hans Pfitzner und die deutsche Bühne.* Munich, 1917.
Wandrey, C. *Hans Pfitzner.* Leipzig, 1922.
Kroll, E. *Hans Pfitzner.* Munich, 1924.
Lütge, W. *Hans Pfitzner.* Leipzig, 1924.
Abendroth, W. *Hans Pfitzner.* Munich, 1935.
Valentin, E. *Hans Pfitzner: Werk und Gestalt eines Deutschen.* Regensburg, 1939.
Müller-Blattau, Josef. *Hans Pfitzner.* Potsdam, 1940.
———. *Hans Pfitzner: sein Leben in Bildern.* Leipzig, 1941.
Unger, H. *Von Wagner bis Pfitzner und Weismann.* Cologne, 1942.
Abendroth, W., ed. *Hans Pfitzner: ein Bild in Widmungen anlässich seines 75. Geburtstages.* Leipzig, 1944.
Rutz, H. *Hans Pfitzner: Musik zwischen den Zeiten.* Vienna, 1949.
Müller, K.F. *In memoriam Hans Pfitzner.* Vienna, 1950.
Rüdiger, C. *Hans Pfitzner: eine Zusammenstellung über ihn und sein Werk.* Cologne, 1959.
Schrott, L. *Die Persönlichkeit Hans Pfitzner.* Freiburg and Zurich, 1959.
Rectanus, H. *Leitmotivik und Form in den musikdramatischen Werken Hans Pfitzners.* Würzburg, 1967.
Abendroth, W., and K.-R. Danler, eds. *Festschrift aus Anlass des 100. Geburtstags und des 20. Todestags Hans Pfitzner.* Munich, 1969.
Müller-Blattau, J. *Hans Pfitzner.* Frankfurt am Main, 1969.
Osthoff, Wolfgang, ed. *Symposium Hans Pfitzner Berlin 1981.* Tutzing, 1984.
Vogel, Johann Peter. *Hans Pfitzner.* Reinbek, 1989.

articles–

Mann, T. "Hans Pfitzner." In *Betrachtungen eines Unpolitischen.* Berlin, 1919; English translation by Walter D.

Morris as *Reflections of a Nonpolitical Man,* Ungar, New York, 1983.

Dent, Edward J. "Hans Pfitzner." *Music and Letters* 4 (1923): 119.

Abendroth, W. "Hans Pfitzner." In *Vier Meister der Musik.* Munich, 1952.

Schwarz, W. "Die Bedeutung des Religiösen im musikdramatischen Schaffen Hans Pfitzner." In *Festgabe für Joseph Müller-Blattau,* 95. Saarbrücken, 1960.

Kindermann, J.E. "Zur Kontroverse Busoni-Pfitzner: Futuristengefahr-Missverständnis einer Kritik?" In *Festschrift für Walter Wiora,* 471. Kassel, 1967.

Rectanus, H. "Pfitzner als Dramatiker." In *Beiträge der Geschichte der Oper,* edited by H. Becker, 139. Regensburg, 1969.

Osthoff, W. "Pfitzner—Goethe—Italien: die Wurzeln des Silla-Liedchens im *Palestrina.*" *Analectica Musicologica* no. 17 (1976): 194.

Carner, M. "Pfitzner v. Berg, or Inspiration v. Analysis." *Musical Times* 117 (1977): 379.

See, Max. "Berührung der Sphären. Gedanken zu einer musikalischen Reminiszenz" [on *Palestrina*]. *Melos/Neue Zeitschrift für Musik* 4 (1978): 312.

Osthoff, Wolfgang. "Eine neue Quelle zu Palestrinazitat und Palestrinasatz in Pfitzners musikalischer Legende." In *Renaissance Studien. Helmuth Osthoff zum 80. Geburtstag,* edited Ludwig Finscher, 185. Tutzing, 1979.

Rectanus, Hans. " 'Ich kenne Dich, Josquin, du Herrlicher . . .'. Bermerkungen zu thematischen Verwandtschaften zwischen Josquin, Palestrina und Pfitzner." In *Renaissance Studien. Helmuth Osthoff zum 80. Geburtstag,* edited Ludwig Finscher, 211. Tutzing, 1979.

Gersdorff, Dagmar von. "Der Komponist Palestrina in Bewusstsein E.T.A. Hoffmanns, Thomas Manns und Pfitzners." *Mitteilungen der Hans Pfitzner-Gesellschaft* 42 (1981): 50.

Niemöller, Klaus Wolfgang. "Zur musikalischen Ausdruckwelt der religiösen Oper im 20. Jahrhundert." In *Das Religiöse in Opern des 20. Jahrhunderts zum Domfest 1980. Bonn (1981).* Bonn, 1981.

Adamy, Bernhard. "Schopenhauer in Pfitzners *Palestrina.*" *Schoenhauer Jahrbuch* 63 (1982): 67.

———. "Das *Palestrina* - Textbuch als Dichtung." In *Symposium Hans Pfitzner,* edited by Wolfgang Osthoff, 21. Tutzing, 1984.

Ermen, Reinhard. "Der 'Erotiker' und der 'Asket': Befragung zweier Klischees am Beispiel der *Gezeichneten* und des *Palestrina.*" In *Franz Schreker (1878-1984). zum 50. Todestag,* edited by Reinhard Ermen, 47. Aachen, 1984.

Kurze, Stefan. "Zeitschichten in Pfitzners *Palestrina.*" In *Symposium Hans Pfitzner,* edited by Wolfgang Osthoff, 69. Tutzing, 1984.

Lee, M. Owen. "Pfitzner's *Palestrina:* A Musical Legend." *Opera Quarterly* spring (1986).

Williamson, John. "Pfitzner and Ibsen." *Music and Letters* April (1986).

unpublished–

Halusa, K. *Pfitzners musikdramatisches Schaffen.* Ph.D. dissertation, University of Vienna, 1929.

Hirtler, F. *Hans Pfitzners 'Armer Heinrich'.* Ph.D. dissertation, University of Freiburg, 1939.

*   *   *

Although associated with the "modernists" of the pre-World War I era, Pfitzner was steeped in the traditions of both Viennese classicism and German romanticism, and his idealism expressed itself in a deliberately retrospective way. Whether as a composer, a conductor, a teacher or a polemical pamphleteer, he held himself aloof from what he regarded as wrong-headed "futuristic" experimentation, as well as from any inclination to seek easy, popular success in the theater.

Pfitzner's first opera, *Der arme Heinrich,* is a somewhat gloomy but finely wrought essay in Romantic medievalism in which a command of post-Wagnerian chromatic harmony and orchestral color is controlled by a dramatic ethos related more closely to *Tannhäuser* and *Lohengrin* than to the Wagner of *Tristan* or the *Ring* operas. The central character of this "music drama" after Hartman von Aue is an early twelfth-century German knight who suffers from a mysteriously debilitating malady that can supposedly be cured only by the sacrifice of a pure young girl. Agnes, the fourteen-year-old daughter of Heinrich's servant, devotedly offers herself, but Heinrich's cure is effected by his remorse as the sacrifice is about to be carried out under religious supervision in the monastery of Salerno. He intervenes and saves Agnes, who becomes the focus of the final tableau of transfigured renewal in the light of the rising sun.

The formal declamatory style of *Der arme Heinrich* and its use of clearly characterized leitmotivic material established the fundamental Wagnerian mode of Pfitzner's later dramatic development, which made its boldest inroad into his *fin de siècle* style and preoccupations in his second "Romantic opera", *Die Rose vom Liebesgarten.* Here the legacy of *Parsifal* is more strongly felt in the composer's treatment of a perhaps over-complex and turgid libretto by his friend James Grun. Rosicrucian symbolism and Romantic nature mysticism give birth to the idealized Germanic nobles of the Garden of Love and Siegnot, Guardian of the Gate of Spring, who is enticed into the subterranean realm of the mysterious Night-Sorcerer. There he meets his death, only to be restored to life in the Garden of Love through the quasi-divine intervention of the Star-Maiden, to whom Siegnot returns the mystic rose with which she had entrusted him. First performed in 1901, the opera was given an influential production, designed by Roller, in Vienna in 1905 under Gustav Mahler (who regarded it as having emotional appeal but too stuffy and "stagnant" a mystical atmosphere).

In the following year (1906) Pfitzner wrote incidental music for a children's Christmas play by Ilse von Stach. This infused pagan fairy tale material (anthropomorphic fir trees and elves) with sentimental bourgeois Christianity. In 1917 Pfitzner recast the work as the "Spieloper" (though still with spoken dialogue) *Das Christelflein.* The manner is that of Hans Andersen after Engelbert Humperdinck (*Hänsel und Gretel*), but von Stach's German nationalism combines with the deliberately simplified melodic style of Pfitzner's music to produce a work which, in retrospect, confirms the darker conservative implications detectable in his major opera, *Palestrina.*

Palestrina was to become Pfitzner's best known stage work, and was first performed in the same year as the revised *Das Christelflein* (1917); it had been composed between 1912 and 1915, to the composer's own libretto. In his depiction of the aging sixteenth century composer, feeling himself to have become an irrelevant historical figure in his own lifetime, Pfitzner created an idealized operatic self-portrait that was as sympathetic as it was vulnerable. Palestrina's resignation and self-doubt are nobly expressed in the first act, but the transcendent idealism of his artistic philosophy is somewhat compromised by a haughtily anti-democratic chauvinism that reflected the cultural temper of the period in Germany. Pfitzner's subsequent polemical debates with Busoni and Paul Bekker revealed trenchantly nationalistic and even anti-semitic attitudes that led, with or without his consent, to official acclaim during the Nazi period.

For a variety of reasons—and a measure of critical self-awareness must have played its part—Pfitzner withdrew from the world in which he found himself caught between hostile modernist detractors and compromising Nazi admirers. As an opera director in Strasbourg before World War I, he had already begun to revive the works of earlier German Romantic opera composers—particularly Marschner—and his own final stage work of 1931, *Das Herz,* was appropriately in a Gothic-Romantic vein and set once more in a far away time (around 1700). Its black-magician hero, Daniel Athanasius, unintentionally sacrifices the heart of his own wife in order to restore the life of his master's son. Condemned and contrite, he is finally conducted into an elysian after-world by the astral figure of his wife, her glowing heart restored, even as the executioners arrive to lead him to the scaffold.

Although uneven in its quality and effectiveness, Pfitzner's operatic music, like that of his many concert and chamber works, was of wide imaginative and expressive range, for all the outward conservatism of its tonal language (acerbically contrapuntal, if at times given to Romantic lushness). Few composers have so argumentatively preached transcendent aesthetic values while so eloquently portraying their contingent and worldly self in their works. As a result, Pfitzner remains a composer of more than passing historical interest, for all that his ponderous and theatrically uncertain operas seem likely to remain unattractive to commercially-minded producers.

—Peter Franklin

PIAVE, Francesco Maria.

Librettist. Born 18 May 1810, in Murano. Died 5 March 1876, in Milan. Studied for the priesthood; published translations, articles, and short stories, 1830s; proofreader, 1838; introduced to Verdi through the directors of the Teatro La Fenice, Venice.

Librettos (selected)

Ernani, G. Verdi, 1844.
Il duca d'Alba (with Giovanni Peruzzini), G. Pacini, 1842.
Cromvello, for G. Verdi, 1843 [never set].
I due Foscari, G. Verdi, 1844.
Pittore e Duca, M.W. Balfe, 1844.
Lorenzino de' Medici, G. Pacini, 1845.
Macbeth, G. Verdi, 1847; revised, 1865.
Allan Cameron, G. Pacini, 1848.
Il Corsaro, G. Verdi, 1848.
La schiava saracena, ovvero Il campo de' crociati, S. Mercadante, 1848.
Stiffelio, G. Verdi, 1850.
Rigoletto, G. Verdi, 1851.
La traviata, G. Verdi, 1853.
Simon Boccanegra, G. Verdi, 1857.
Don Diego di Mendoza, G. Pacini, 1867.
Berta di Varnol, G. Pacini, 1867.

La forza del destino, G. Verdi, 1862; revised, A. Ghislanzoni, 1869.
La donna delle isole, G. Pacini [not performed?].
Vico Bentivoglio, for A. Ponchielli [not set].

Many other librettos for T. Benvenutti, C. Boniforti, C.E. Bosoni, G. Braga, A. Buzzolla, A. Cagnoni, Casalini, S. Levi, De Liguoro, C. Pedrotti, A. Peri, Petroncini, B. Pisani, F. and L. Ricci, C. Romani, P. Serrau, Clary, Chiaramonte, Forati, Noseda, the count Litta, Perelli, Ritter, Rota, and Stanzieri, as well as eleven incomplete librettos.

Publications

About PIAVE: books—

Miragoli, L. *Il melodramma italiano nell' ottocento.* Rome, 1924.
Quarti, G.A. *F.M. Piave, poeta melodrammatico.* Rome, 1939.
Rolandi, U. *Libretti e librettisti verdiani.* Rome, 1941.
Portinari, F. *Pari siamo: io la lingua, egli ha il pugnale. Storia del melodramma ottocentesco attraverso i suoi libretti.* Turin, 1981.
Conati, M. *La bottega della musica. Verdi e la Fenice.* Milan, 1983.

articles—

Checchi, E. "Librettisti e libretti di Giuseppe Verdi." *Nuova antologia di lettere, scienze ed arti* 167 (1913): 529.
Mantovani, T. "Librettisti verdiani: Francesco Maria Piave." *Musica d'oggi* 6 (1924): 258.
Adami, G. "Librettisti e poeti verdiani." In *Verdi. Studi e memorie.* Rome, 1941.
Aycock, R.E. "Shakespeare, Boito and Verdi." *Musical Quarterly* (1972).
Biddlescombre, George. "The Revision of 'No, mon morrai, che' i perfidi.' Verdi's Compositional Process in *I due Foscari.*" *Studi verdiani* 2 (1983): 59.
Schrader, Steven W. "Verdi, *Aroldo,* and Music Drama." *Verdi Newsletter* 12 (1984): 8.

*   *   *

From the beginning of his career, Verdi had strong views about the layout of a libretto. He usually chose the subject and often sketched a synopsis; as a result, he needed compliant librettists. Francesco Maria Piave was the most compliant of all, and was selected by Verdi for more operas than any other writer; he was responsible for one of the first great successes, *Ernani,* for the "watershed opera" *Macbeth,* the composer's most popular operas *Rigoletto* and *La traviata,* and the complex, epic *Forza del destino.*

Piave has been ridiculed by Italian critics for the poverty of his verses, and praised for his effective construction. In fact, it is hard to know how far he is responsible for either; the only libretto he wrote for Verdi which was not planned and radically adapted by the composer was *Cromvello* (1843) which Verdi never set. The same year, Piave was commissioned to adapt Victor Hugo's play *Hernani,* but Verdi fussed over details of the adaptation, excusing his interference by saying, "Sig. Piave has never written for the theatre, and is naturally deficient in these things." The poet consented to all the proposed alterations, of course, but he may still be given

Francesco Maria Piave

some credit for the masterly compression of the play and the simple and direct language.

In the case of *Macbeth,* his contribution was more limited. "I wrote the scenario myself," Verdi tells us, "and, indeed, more than the scenario; I wrote out the whole drama in prose, with divisions into acts, scenes, numbers, etc., etc., . . . then I gave it to Piave to put into verse. Since I found things to criticize in the versification, I asked [Andrea] Maffei, with the consent of Piave himself, to go over those lines, and rewrite entirely the witches' chorus from Act III, as well as the sleepwalking scene."

The *Rigoletto* text was prepared in the usual way, with Piave following Verdi's instructions. While the opera was being composed, Verdi constantly badgered his librettist; he wanted, for example, a passage "in *decasillabi,*" or a passage which "expresses the joy of revenge," and the unfortunate poet replied pathetically, "I have written some lines, but none that would satisfy you, so I don't think there's any point in my sending them to you."

The success of *La traviata* may perhaps be credited to Piave in some degree. Verdi forced the librettist to change the words and meters a good deal, but the layout may have been Piave's, with its rapid changes of focus and stunning climaxes. The writing, however, is conservative and "operatic," "as though translated into a dead language" (Luigi Baldacci). *Simon Boccanegra* was sketched first by Verdi, as usual, and when several of Piave's verses did not please the composer, he had them rewritten by Giuseppe Montanelli.

The composer's letters to Piave often show such irritable contempt that it is hard to imagine that the two men were close friends. Nevertheless, Piave nursed Verdi through his serious illness in 1846, and the musician continued to help

his friend even after the stroke which took away his speech (1867). Piave was also the faithful fixer who put things right with the censors, getting politically risky subjects accepted by the Venice authorities. He was a profoundly limited man who knew how to make himself useful to a great composer, and so passed into history.

—Raymond Monelle

PICCINNI, Niccolò.

Composer. Born 16 January 1728, in Bari, Italy. Died 7 May 1800, in Paris. Piccinni's father was a violinist at the Basilica di San Nicola in Bari, and his uncle Gaetano Latilla was an opera composer; the Archbishop of Bari, Muzio Gaeta, arranged for Piccinni to enroll at the Conservatorio di Sant' Onofrio in Naples, where he studied with Leo and Durante; instructor at the Conservatorio di Sant' Onofrio, 1755; produced operas in Rome and Naples; in Paris, December 1776; director of the Italian opera troupe in Paris, 1778; appointed maître de chant at the Ecole Royale de Chant et de Déclamation Lyrique in Paris, 1784; lost his position at the Ecole Royal de Chant after the Revolution, and returned to Naples; given a small pension by the King of Naples; returned to Paris, where he received honors and 5,000 francs, 1798; honorary position of sixth inspector, Paris Conservatory (Ecole Royal de Chant prior to the revolution); in Passy for the last months of his life.

Operas

Le donne dispettose, A. Palomba, Naples, Teatro dei Fiorentini, fall 1754.
Il curioso del suo proprio danno, A. Palomba, Naples, Nuovo, carnival 1755-56?; revised, with A. Sacchini, as *Il curioso imprudente,* Naples, Teatro dei Fiorentini, fall 1761.
Le gelosie. G.B. Lorenzi, Naples, Teatro dei Fiorentini, spring 1755.
Zenobia, Metastasio, Naples, San Carlo, 18 December 1756.
L'amante ridicolo, A. Pioli, Naples, Nuovo, 1757.
La schiava seria (intermezzo) Naples, 1757.
Caio Mario, G. Roccaforte, Naples, San Carlo, 1757?.
Farnace (with D. Perez), M.A. Lucchini, Naples, San Carlo, 8 May 1757, or Messina?, 1753.
Nitteti (G. Cocchi), Metastasio, Naples, San Carlo, 4 November 1757.
Gli uccellatori, after C. Goldoni?, Naples/Venice, 1758.
Alessandro nelle Indie, Metastasio, Rome, Torre Argentina, 21 January 1758.
Madama Arrighetta. A. Palomba (after C. Goldoni, *Monsieur Petitone*), Naples, Nuovo, fall/winter 1758.
La scaltra letterata, A. Palomba, Naples, Nuovo, winter 1758.
Siroe rè di Persia, Metastasio, Naples, 1759.
Ciro riconosciuto, Metastasio, Naples, San Carlo, November-December 1759.
La buona figliuola, ossia La Cecchina, C. Goldoni, Rome, Teatro delle Dame, 6 February 1760.
L'Origille, A. Palomba, Naples, Teatro dei Fiorentini, spring 1760.
Il rè pastore, Metastasio, Florence, Teatro della Pergola, fall 1760.

La furba burlata, P. di Napoli? (after A. Palomba), Naples, Teatro dei Fiorentini, fall 1760, or Naples, Nuovo, summer 1762.

Le beffe giovevoli, after C. Goldoni, Naples, Teatro dei Fiorentini, winter 1760.

Le vicende della sorte (intermezzo and comedy), G. Petrosellini (after C. Goldoni, *I portentosi effetti della madre natura),* Rome, Valle, 3 January 1761.

La schiavitù per amore (intermezzo), Rome, Capranica, carnival 1761.

Olimpiade, Metastasio, Rome, Teatro delle Dame, carnival 1761.

Tigrane, V.A. Cigna-Santi (after C. Goldoni's revision of F. Silvani?), Turin, Regio, carnival 1761.

Demofoonte, Metastasio, Reggio, Pubblico, May fair 1761.

La buona figliuola maritata, C. Goldoni, Bologna, Formagliari, May 1761.

Lo stravagante, A. Villani, Naples, Teatro dei Fiorentini, fall 1761.

L'astuto balordo, G.B. Fagiuoli, Naples, Teatro dei Fiorentini, winter 1761.

L'astrologa, P. Chiari, Venice, San Moisè, carnival 1761-62.

Amor senza malizia, Nuremburg, Thurn und Taxis, 1762.

Artaserse, Metastasio, Rome, Torre Argentina, 3 February 1762; revised, Naples, 1772.

Le avventure di Ridolfo (intermezzo), Bologna, Marsigli-Rossi, carnival 1762.

La bella verità, C. Goldoni, Bologna, Marsigli-Rossi, 12 June 1762.

Antigono, Metastasio, Naples, San Carlo, 4 November 1762.

Il cavalier parigino? (with Sacchini), Naples, Nuovo, winter 1762.

Il cavaliere per amore, G. Petrosellini, Naples, Nuovo, winter 1762, or Rome, Valle, carnival, 1763.

Le donne vendicate (intermezzo), after C. Goldoni, Rome, Valle, carnival 1763.

Le contadine bizzarre, G. Petrosellini, Rome, Capranica, February 1763, or Venice, San Samuele, autumn 1763; revised as *La contadina bizzarra,* Naples, 1774.

Gli stravaganti, ossia La schiava riconosciuta (intermezzo), Rome, Valle, 1 January 1764.

La villeggiatura, after C. Goldoni?, Bologna, Formagliari, carnival 1764 [possible revision of *Le donne vendicate*].

Il parrucchiere (intermezzo), Rome, Valle, carnival 1764.

L'incognita perseguitata, G. Petrosellini, Venice, San Samuele, carnival 1764.

L'equivoco, L. Lantino [=A. Villani], Naples, Teatro dei Fiorentini, summer 1764.

La donna vana, A. Palomba, Naples, Teatro dei Fiorentini, November 1764.

Il nuovo Orlando, Modena, Rangoni, 26 December 1764.

Berenice?, B. Pasqualigo, Naples, c. 1764.

Il barone di Torreforte (intermezzo), Rome, Capranica, 10 January 1765.

Il finto astrologo (intermezzo), after C. Goldoni?, Rome, Valle, winter 1765.

L'orfana insidiata (with G. Astarita), Naples, Teatro dei Fiorentini, summer 1765.

La pescatrice, ovvero L'erede riconosciuta (intermezzo), after C. Goldoni?, Rome, Capranica, 9 January 1766.

La baronessa di Montecupo (intermezzo), Rome, Capranica, 27 January 1766.

L'incostante (intermezzo), G. Palomba, Rome, Capranica, February 1776.

La molinarella, Naples, Nuovo, fall 1766.

Il gran Cid, G. Pizzi, Naples, San Carlo, 4 November 1766.

La francese maligna, Naples, 1766-67, or Rome, 1769.

La fiammetta generosa (with P. Anfossi?), Naples, Teatro dei Fiorentini, 1766.

La notte critica, C. Goldoni, Lisbon, Salvaterra, carnival 1767.

La finta baronessa, F. Livingni, Naples, Teatro dei Fiorentini, summer 1767.

La direttrice prudente, Naples, Teatro dei Fiorentini, fall 1767.

Mazzina, Acetone e Dindimento, Naples?, c. 1767?.

Olimpiade [second setting], Metastasio, Rome, 1768.

Li napoletani in America, F. Cerlone, Naples, Teatro dei Fiorentini, 10 June 1768.

La locandiera di spirito, Naples, Nuovo, fall 1768.

Lo sposo burlato (intermezzo), G.B. Casti, Rome, Valle, 3 January 1769.

L'innocenza riconosciuta, Senigallia, 11 January, 1769.

La finta ciarlatana, ossia Il vecchio credulo, Naples, Nuovo, carnival, 1769.

Demetrio. Metastasio, Naples, San Carlo, 30 May 1769.

Gli sposi perseguitati, P. Mililotti, Naples, Nuovo, 1769.

Cesare in Egitto, G.F. Bussani, Milan, Ducale, January 1770.

Didone abbandonata, Metastasio, Rome, Torre Argentina, 8 January 1770.

La donna di spirito, Rome, Capranica, 13 February 1770.

Il regno della luna, Milan, Ducale, spring 1770.

Gelosia per gelosia, G.B. Lorenzi, Naples, Teatro dei Fiorentini, summer 1770.

L'olandese in Italia, N. Tassi, Milan, Ducale, fall 1770.

Don Chisciotte, G.B. Lorenzi, Naples?, 1770.

Il finto pazzo per amore, Naples?, 1770.

Catone in Utica, Metastasio, Naples, San Carlo, 1770, or Mannheim, 4 November 1770.

Antigono, Metastasio, Rome, Torre Argentina, carnival 1771.

Le finte gemelle (intermezzo), G. Petrosellini, Rome, Valle, 2 January 1771.

La donna di bell' umore, Naples, Teatro dei Fiorentini, 15 May 1771.

La Corsala, G.B. Lorenzi, Naples, Teatro dei Fiorentini, fall 1771.

L'americano (intermezzo), Rome, Capranica, 22 February 1772.

L'astratto, ovvero Il giocator fortunato, G. Petrosellini, Venice, San Samuele, carnival 1772.

Le trame zingaresche, G.B. Lorenzi, Naples, Teatro dei Fiorentini, summer 1772.

Ipermestra, Metastasio, Naples, San Carlo, 4 November 1772.

Scipione in Cartagena, A. Giusti, Modena, Corte, 26 December? 1772.

Le quattro nazioni o La vedova scaltra, after C. Goldoni's play, Rome?, 1773.

La sposa collerica (intermezzo), Rome, Valle, 9 January 1773.

Il vagabondo fortunato, P. Mililotti, Naples, Teatro dei Fiorentini, fall 1773.

Gli amanti mascherati, Naples, Teatro dei Fiorentini, 1774.

Alessandro nelle Indie, Metastasio, Naples, San Carlo, 12 January 1774.

Il sordo (intermezzo), Naples, 1775.

L'ignorante astuto, P. Mililotti, Naples, Teatro dei Fiorentini, carnival 1775.

I viaggiatori, P. Mililotti (after C. Goldoni?), Naples, Teatro dei Fiorentini, fall 1775.

Enea in Cuma, P. Mililotti, Naples, Teatro dei Fiorentini, spring? 1775.

La contessina, Coltellini (after C. Goldoni?), Verona, Filarmonico, fall 1775.

Radamisto, A. Marchi, Naples?, 1776.

Vittorina, C. Goldoni, London, King's Theater in the Hay Market, 16 December 1777.

Roland, J.-F. Marmontel (after Quinault), Paris, Académie Royale de Musique, 27 January 1778.

Phaon, C.H. Watelet, Choisy, Court, September 1778.

Il vago disprezzato, Paris, Académie Royale de Musique, 16 May 1779.

Atys, J.-F. Marmontel (after Quinault), Paris, Académie Royale de Musique, 22 February 1780.

Iphigénie en Tauride, A. de C. Dubreuil, Paris, Académie Royale de Musique, 23 January 1781.

Adèle de Ponthieu, J.-P.-A. de R. de Saint-Marc, Paris, Académie Royale de Musique, 27 October 1781; revised (reset?), Paris, 1785 [not performed].

Didon, J.-F. Marmontel, Fontainebleau, 16 October 1783.

Le faux lord, G.M. Piccinni, Fontainebleau, 6 December 1783.

Le dormeur éveillé, J.-F. Marmontel, Paris, Comédie-Italienne, 14 November 1783.

Diane et Endymion (with J.F. Espic Chevalier de Lirou), Espic, Paris, Académie Royale de Musique, 7 September 1784.

Lucette, G.M. Piccinni, Paris, Comédie-Italienne, 30 December 1784.

Pénélope, J.-F. Marmontel, Fontainebleau, 2 November 1785.

L'enlèvement des Sabines?, Paris, 1787.

Clytemnestre, L.G. Pitra, Paris, 1787 [not performed].

La serva onorata, Lorenzi?, Naples, Teatro dei Fiorentini, carnival? 1792.

Der Schlosser?, 1793.

Le trame in maschera, Naples, Teatro dei Fiorentini, carnival 1793.

Ercole al Termedonte, Naples, San Carlo, 12 June 1793.

La Griselda, after A. Anelli?, Venice, San Samuele, 8 October 1793.

Il servo padrone ossia l'amor perfetto, C. Mazzolà, Venice, San Samuele, 17 January 1794.

I Decemviri.

Il finto turco.

Sermiculo?

La pie voleuse, ou La servante de Valaiseau?

Other works: oratorios, sacred and secular vocal works, instrumental pieces.

Publications/Writings

About PICCINNI: books–

Marmontel, J.-F. *Essai sur les révolutions de la musique en France.* Paris, 1777.

La Borde, J.-B. de. *Essai sur la musique ancienne et moderne.* Paris, 1780; 1972.

Leblond, G.M. *Mémoires pour servir à l'histoire de la révolution opérée dans la musique par M. le Chevalier Gluck.* Naples and Paris, 1781.

Ginguené, P.L. *Notice sur la vie et les ouvrages de Nicolas Piccinni.* Paris, 1801.

Desnoiresterres, Gustave le Brisoys. *La musique française aux XVIIIe siècle: Gluck et Piccinni 1774-1800.* Paris, 1872.

Jullien, A. *La cour et l'opéra sous Louis XVI.* Paris, 1878.

Thoinan, E. *Notes bibliographiques sur la guerre musicale des Gluckistes et Piccinnistes.* Paris, 1878.

Jullien, A. *L'opéra secret au XVIIIe siècle.* Paris, 1880.

Curzon, Henri de. *Les dernières années de Piccinni à Paris.* Paris, 1890.

Abert, H. *Piccinni als Buffokomponist.* Leipzig, 1913.

Popovici, Josefine Dagmar. *La buona figliuola von Nicolo Piccinni.* Vienna, 1920.

Della Corte, A. *Piccinni: settecento italiano.* Bari, 1928.

La Rotella, P. *N. Piccinni: commemorato nel II centenario della nascità.* Bari, 1928.

Pascazio, N. *L'uomo Picini e la querelle célèbre.* Bari, 1951.

Robinson, M.F. *Naples and Neapolitan Opera.* London, 1972.

Degrada, Francesco. *Il palazzo incantato. Studi sulla tradizione del melodramma dal Barocco al Romaticismo.* Fiesole, 1979.

Strohm, Reinhard. *Die italienische Oper im 18. Jahrhundert.* Wilhelmshaven, 1979.

articles–

Cametti, Alberto. "Saggio cronologico delle opere teatrali (1754-1794) de Niccolò Piccinni." *Rivista musicale italiana* 8 (1901): 75.

Blom, E. "A Misjudged Composer." In *Stepchildren of Music.* London, 1925.

Parisi, A. "Intorno al soggiorno di N. Piccinni in Francia." *Rivista musicale italiana* 30 (1928): 219.

Abert, H. "Piccinni als Buffokomponist." *Jahrbuch der Musikbibliothek Peters* (1913): 29; reprinted in *Gesammelte Schriften und Vorträge,* Halle, 1929.

Bellucci La Salandra, Maro. "Opere teatrali serie e buffe di Niccolò Piccinni dal 1754 al 1794." *Note d'archivio* 12 (1935): 43, 114, 235.

Gastoué, A. "Nicolò Piccinni et ses opéras à Paris." *Note d'archivio* 13 (1936): 52.

Bollert, W. "L'opera *Griselda* de Piccinni." *Musica d'oggi* 19 (1937): 43.

Holmes, William C. "Pamela Transformed." *Musical Quarterly* 38 (1952): 581.

Prota-Giurleo, U. "La biografia di Nicola Piccinni alla luce di nuovi documenti." *Il fuidoro* 1 (1954): 27.

————. "Sacchini fra Piccinnisti e Gluckisti." *Gazzetta musicale di Napoli* 3 (1957): 57, 76.

Rushton, J.G. "The Theory and Practice of Piccinnisme." *Proceedings of the Royal Musical Association* 98 (1971-72): 31.

————. " 'Iphigénie en Tauride': the Operas of Gluck and Piccinni." *Music and Letters* 53 (1972): 411.

Allroggen, G. "Piccinnis *Origille.*" *Analecta Musicologica* no. 15 (1975): 258.

Lippmann, Friedrich. *Nuova rivista musicale italiana* (1983).

Torrefranca, T. "Strumentalità della commedia musicale: *Buona figliuola, Barbiere,* e *Falstaff.*" *Nuova rivista musicale italiana* 18 (1984): 1.

Hunter, Mary. "The Fusion and Juxtaposition of Genres in Opera buffa 1770-1800: Anelli and Piccinni's *Griselda.*" *Music and Letters* October (1986).

unpublished–

Rushton, J.G. "Music and Drama at the Académie Royale de Musique, Paris, 1774-1789." Ph. D. dissertation, Oxford University, 1970.

Liggett, Margaret McGinness. "A Biography of Niccolò Piccinni and a Critical Study of his *La Didone* and *Didon.*" Ph. D. dissertation, Washington University, St Louis, 1977.

Wilson, J. Kenneth. "*L'Olimpiade:* Selected Eighteenth Century Settings of Metastasio's Libretto." Ph. D. dissertation, Harvard University, 1982.

*   *   *

One of the most inventive and popular composers of the mid-eighteenth century, Piccinni played a pivotal role in the development of both Italian and French opera. In his day he was almost universally in high regard; Burney placed Piccinni "among the most fertile, spirited and original," and La Borde found in his music "a vigour, a variety, and especially a new grace, a brilliant and animated style." He is frequently discussed today as a master of pathetic, sentimental affects, particularly in his Italian comedies. At his best he was brilliantly lyrical and emotive, yet Piccinni's music shows him to be much more than a writer of pretty melodies; he strove for a flexible approach to musical form and mood, and was unusually skilled in joining music and drama.

After Piccinni's education at the Sant' Onofrio Conservatory of Naples (where he studied under both Leo and Durante), his operas first began to appear in that city in 1754. His fame soon spread to other Italian houses, and within ten years he had written for Venice, Bologna, Reggio, Turin, and elsewhere. The vast majority of his works before 1776, however, were performed on the stages of Naples and Rome, including a large number of both comic and serious works. Among his youthful successes in comedy was his extremely popular *La Cecchina, ossia La buona figliuola,* produced in Rome on 6 February 1760 to a Goldoni libretto (first set in Parma with music by Dunì). From this moment his fame

Niccolò Piccinni

was assured. The often fickle Roman public finally deserted Piccinni for Anfossi in carnival 1776, however, during which Piccinni's *La capricciosa* was hissed from the stage—with no apparent musical motivation. Piccinni fell ill and returned to Naples.

With the promise of a royal pension in Paris from Marie Antoinette (the same enticement that had lured Gluck), Piccinni settled there on 31 December 1776, but found himself in another awkward, contrived rivalry, now with Gluck. The verbal battle between the "Gluckists" and the "Piccinnists" was only superficially over the merits of French and Italian music, however; in reality both Gluck and Piccinni represented a similar desire to join the two national styles. Gluck remained the more grand and was the master of high drama, and Piccinni excelled in versatility, adaptability, and melody. The debate first arose late in 1777; the poet Marmontel, in plot with the empress, sought to have Piccinni and Gluck simultaneously write for the same libretto, *Roland*. Gluck caught wind of the idea and destroyed his incomplete score. His *Armide* was produced instead, and was then held up by his admirers as a model that others were not likely to match; yet Piccinni's *Roland* early the next year was uncommonly successful. In February of 1778 Mozart summarized the French reaction: "My favourite type of composition, the chorus, can be well performed there [in Paris]. I am indeed glad that the French prize it highly. Their only objection to Piccinni's new opera *Roland* is that the choruses are too weak and thin, and that the music on the whole is a little monotonous; otherwise the work has been a success. To be sure they are used to Gluck's choruses in Paris."

Piccinni's French operas over the next ten years show remarkable inventiveness, but were not universally well received. An untimely staging of his *Iphigénie en Tauride* encouraged its poor reception (it followed by two years Gluck's version of the same story and is overall a less polished work). Still it abounds in expressive and coloristic effects, such as in Iphigénie's first act scene, "A la triste clarté de flambeaux palissants," in which swift changes of mode and key contribute greatly to the drama. He continued to experiment with a wide variety of musical styles and forms, with the rich orchestral palette of the French orchestra at his disposal (which Mozart also praised). Among his most successful, innovative, and influential works were *Atys* (a *tragédie lyrique* whose integration of French and Italian traits was perhaps his most successful), *Didon,* and *Pénélope.* In these operas, the advice and inspiration of his librettist, Marmontel (one of the loudest voices in the cries against French excesses in the Gluck/Piccinni controversy) was likely crucial.

Piccinni's popularity faded in the mid 1780s, and with the outbreak of the French revolution and the loss of his pension he left Paris and returned to Naples, where he settled in 1791. Falsely accused of political intrigue, he was placed under house arrest in 1794 for the next four years; upon his release he went again to Paris, but found little favor.

—Dale E. Monson

PILARCZYK, Helga (Käthe).

Mezzo-soprano and soprano. Born 12 March 1925, in Schönigen, near Brunswick. Studied with Dziobek in Hamburg beginning in 1948; mezzo debut as Irmentraude in Lortzing's *Der Waffenschmied,* Brunswick, 1951; sang as soprano from

1953 in Hamburg Staatsoper; at Covent Garden, 1958; Glyndebourne, 1958; Teatro alla Scala, 1963; has also appeared in Paris and Vienna; Metropolitan opera debut as Marie in *Wozzeck,* 1965.

Publications

By PILARCZYK: articles–

"On Singing Modern Opera." *Opera* September (1962).

* * *

Dramatic soprano Helga Pilarczyk was just about unexcelled in her limited but extremely difficult repertoire. She enjoyed a distinguished career, if not an especially long one.

A long twisting road led to her eventual expertise and international recognition. She was first a pianist. Then, discovering her vocal abilities, she sang mezzo in operetta. She began her stage career as a member of the Braunschweig Theater (near her birthplace). Afterwards, from 1954 to 1968, she was based at the Hamburg opera, a major company. She was a guest on many of the leading operatic and concert stages.

Pilarczyk sang primarily the music of Schoenberg, Berg, Dallapiccola and the like. She was a noted Marie in *Wozzeck,* in which she made her only appearances at the Metropolitan Opera, not then a bastion of contemporary opera, and was an arresting Lulu. Other roles which fit her unique talents were Renata in Prokofiev's *The Flaming Angel* and the Mother in *The Prisoner* by Dallapiccola, as well as in operas by Henze and Liebermann. She also sang Jocasta in Stravinsky's *Oedipus Rex* and, at Glyndebourne, was heard in *Arlecchino* by Busoni.

Perhaps surprisingly, Pilarczyk was also an exciting Salome in the Strauss opera, which she sang at Covent Garden, 1958, and the same year in a pan-European Radio broadcast from Copenhagen with Set Svanholm as Herod, conducted by Robert Heger. She also concertized extensively.

Pilarczyk was an exemplary musician. Her voice was not lush, in the usual sense, but was more wiry, and could be almost unbearably intense. It was also unusually expressive, and she was able to color it and project characterization throughout its considerable range. She was a strong actress, which showed, too, in her vocal interpretations, as well as in her riveting stage presence.

There are not many recordings extant by Helga Pilarczyk. The best known is that of Schoenberg's *Erwartung* with the Northwest German Philharmonic conducted by Hermann Scherchen. This is marked by a glowing warmth and romanticism, not always associated with the work. There is another recording of *Erwartung,* conducted by Robert Craft which grew out of the Washington performances (Igor Stravinsky was associated with these) and a *Pierrot Lunaire.* Denmark's Radio has, in the past, rebroadcast the *Salome,* but it is not known if professional copies exist at the present time.

—Bert Wechsler

THE PILGRIM'S PROGRESS.

Composer: Ralph Vaughan Williams.

Librettist: Ralph Vaughan Williams (after Bunyan).

First Performance: London, Covent Garden, 26 April 1951; revised, 1951-52.

Roles: The Pilgrim (baritone); John Bunyan (baritone); Evangelist (baritone); many lesser roles.

Publications

articles–

Mullinar, M. "The Pilgrim's Progress." *Royal College of Music Magazine* 47 (1951): 46.
Murrill, H. "Vaughan Williams's Pilgrim." *Music and Letters* 32 (1951): 324.
Smith, C. "The Pilgrim's Progress." *Opera* 2 (1951): 373.
Foss, H.J. "*The Pilgrim's Progress* by Vaughan Williams." In *Music 1952,* edited by A. Robertson, 32. Harmondsworth, 1952.

* * *

Vaughan Williams completed his operatic "morality" based on John Bunyan's *The Pilgrim's Progress* in 1949. It represents the culmination of a fascination with this subject that occupied the composer intermittently for over forty years. A series of works composed over this time-span anticipate the finished score: incidental music provided for a dramatization of *The Pilgrim's Progress* produced in 1906 at the Reigate Priory uses the hymn tune "York" which opens the opera; virtually the complete score of *The Shepherds of the Delectable Mountains* of 1922, a "pastoral episode" in one act, is incorporated into the fourth act; the incidental music of 1942 for a BBC radio adaptation of Bunyan's book employs music used in the opera; and the Fifth Symphony of 1943 is largely based on thematic material from the first act. Vaughan Williams adapted the libretto himself, skillfully interpolating passages of the Bible among scenes drawn from Bunyan, while paring down the elaborate Christian allegory to the essential framework of a spiritual quest. Further additions were made by the poet Ursula Wood (later Ursula Vaughan Williams). These are found primarily in the passages where Vaughan Williams revised and expanded the score in 1951-52.

The plot is developed in four concise acts with a prologue and epilogue, presented in a series of tableaux of gradually increasing intensity. After a prologue showing Bunyan in prison writing his book, the first act opens with the Pilgrim's cry "What shall I do to be saved?" An Evangelist appears and, despite the protests of conventional neighbors, encourages the Pilgrim to begin his quest. The Pilgrim journeys to the House Beautiful, where he receives absolution and inspiration. The second act consists of the Pilgrim's battle with the monstrous giant Apollyon, the hero's revival after defeating the giant, and the dark warnings of the Evangelist. In the next act, the Pilgrim encounters and rejects the worldly allurements of Vanity Fair, is tried and sentenced to death, but is miraculously freed from prison. The last act finds the Pilgrim among the shepherds of the Delectable Mountains. A Celestial Messenger arrives and summons him to the river of death; he crosses the river and enters into the Celestial City. As the radiant vision fades, Bunyan reappears in his cell and offers his book to the audience.

The Pilgrim's Progress does not conform to traditional expectations suggested by the term "opera"; Vaughan Williams recognized the unique quality of his score by titling it a "Morality." While acknowledging the origin of his material in seventeenth-century Puritanism, Vaughan Williams stressed its universality, and distanced his work from any specific set of beliefs: he pointedly changed his protagonist's name from Bunyan's "Christian" to the more general "Pilgrim." Thus *The Pilgrim's Progress* is neither an oratorio disguised as an opera nor an opera in the nineteenth-century tradition, but rather a music drama designed to appeal to the catholic beliefs of a wide audience. The premiere of *The Pilgrim's Progress,* given at Covent Garden on 26 April 1951 as part of the Festival of Britain, was marred by a hurried production, uninspired stage design, and an inexperienced conductor. Subsequent productions, such as those by Dennis Arundell at Cambridge and Geoffrey Ford at Charterhouse, and also the recording made by Sir Adrian Boult, have begun to tap the dramatic power and musical richness of this noble score.

—Byron Adams

PIMPINONE.

Composer: Georg Philipp Telemann.

Librettist: after Pietro Pariati, partially translated into German by Philipp Praetorius.

First Performance: Hamburg, Gänsemarkt, 27 September 1725.

Roles: Vespetta (soprano); Pimpinone (bass).

Publications

article–

Wolff, H.C. "*Pimpinone* von Albinoni und Telemann: ein Vergleich." *Hamburger Jahrbuch für Musikwissenschaft* 5 (1981).

*   *   *

One consequence of the reform of Italian "heroic" opera (*opera seria*) at the beginning of the eighteenth century was that scenes for comic characters were removed from the fabric of the opera proper, reemerging as comic intermezzi—in effect, miniature comic operas whose component scenes (each of which was termed an "intermezzo") were interspersed within the host work, generally between acts. This segregation enabled the two or three comic characters to participate—for the first time in operatic history—in a work with a contemporary setting and satirical flavor far removed from the historical, exotic, or legendary world of *opera seria.* In formal terms the comic intermezzo is not the direct ancestor of *opera buffa,* which is related in length and structure to *opera seria,* but there is no doubt that its musical and literary style and slapstick elements left their mark on the *buffo* genre.

The first generation of comic intermezzi appeared in Venice after 1705. A prominent surviving early example (1708) was Tomaso Albinoni's setting of a group of three intermezzi for the characters Vespetta and Pimpinone. The author of the text was Pietro Pariati, a master of dramatic dialogue on whom the famous librettist Apostolo Zeno came to rely for the versification of his operatic scenarios. Albinoni's setting proved very popular and during the next few decades was taken all round Italy and as far afield as Moscow, Ljubljana, and Brussels by pairs of comic singers. In 1717 Francesco Conti provided a new setting for Vienna, Vespetta being renamed Grilletta. Then in 1725 Johann Philipp Praetorius provided Telemann with a revised version of the libretto in which the recitatives were translated into German but the arias and duets (except for Praetorius's own additions) remained in Italian. The modern edition of Telemann's setting by Theodor W. Werner (1936) supplies German versions of all the Italian texts; nowadays the work is most often given in German throughout. Telemann's new setting was first performed together with Handel's *Tamerlano* at Hamburg's Gänsemarkt (Goosemarket) theater on 27 September 1725. It was revived there at least once, in 1730; on that occasion Johann Gottfried Riemenschneider took the role of Pimpinone and Margaretha Susanna Kayser that of Vespetta.

Pimpinone, a rich but gullible bourgeois, and Vespetta, a cunning and ambitious maidservant, are merely updated versions of the *vecchio* (old man) and *servetta* (female servant), stock characters of the comic scenes in seventeenth-century Venetian opera. They are also forerunners of the protagonists in Pergolesi's *La serva padrona.* In the first scene (Intermezzo I) Vespetta talks Pimpinone into employing her with extravagant promises of good housekeeping and exemplary conduct. In Intermezzo II, having made herself indispensable, she inveigles him into marrying her by threatening to leave. In Intermezzo III she breaks her promises of good wifely behavior and announces her intention to go out to enjoy herself: Pimpinone is furious, but ultimately powerless to stop her.

In his superbly witty libretto, Pariati exploits the traditional antitheses of male and female, age and youth, innocence and guile. But he also satirizes Venetian society on its most sensitive point: the growing espousal of a "noble" life-style by members of the citizenry or—even more threateningly—the lower class. The text is shot through with ambivalence: Pimpinone is more risible than Vespetta but also more reassuring, since he does not aspire above his proper station in life; Vespetta commands admiration for her resourcefulness but nonetheless constitutes a social danger.

Using no more than orchestral strings, continuo, and two singing parts (soprano and bass), Telemann produces a sparkling and varied work that completely outclasses its Albinonian predecessor and fully attains the level of *La serva padrona.* His expression of the comic reaches glorious heights in an aria for Pimpinone (Intermezzo III) where the frustrated husband mimics the malicious gossip of two women—in the soprano and alto registers respectively. With great irony he casts the final duet (where Vespetta is breezily exultant, Pimpinone morosely subdued) in the Polish style, creating a music that is at once courtly and folklike, sweet and bitter.

That *Pimpinone* is the one stage work by Telemann to achieve popularity in modern times is partly due to the vagaries of preservation, partly to the ready intelligibility of its simple comic plot and partly to its sheer practicality, which has turned it into a true "chamber opera" of the late Baroque.

No better illustration of its composer's musical and dramatic gifts can be found.

—Michael Talbot

————————

PINZA, Ezio.

Bass. Born 18 May 1892, in Rome. Died 9 May 1957, in Stamford, Connecticut. Studied voice with Ruzza and Vizzani at the Bologna Conservatory; debut as Oroveso in *Norma* at Soncino, 1914; military service in World War I; appeared as Comte Des Grieux in Rome, 1920; Teatro alla Scala debut as Pimen in *Boris,* 1922; selected by Toscanini to sing Tigellino in the premiere of Boito's *Nerone* at La Scala, 1924; Metropolitan Opera debut as Pontifex Maximus in Spontini's *La Vestale,* 1926; remained on the staff of the Metropolitan until 1947; also appeared in films.

Publications

By PINZA: books—

Ezio Pinza: An Autobiography, edited by R. Magidoff. New York, 1958.

About PINZA: books—

Verducci, P. *The First Pinza Discography.* New York, 1957.

articles—

Tuggle, R. "Ezio Pinza." In *The Golden Age of Opera,* New York, 1983.

*   *   *

Pinza did much to restore the authority and importance of the operatic bass, especially at the Metropolitan Opera, in works such as *Don Carlos, Simon Boccanegra, Norma, Mefistofele* and *Boris Godunov.*

He was born in Rome, seventh among nine children of a poor family, but lived in Ravenna during his childhood years when he hoped to become a civil engineer. Having given up that idea, Pinza's father dissuaded him from being a racing cyclist and persuaded him to train for music. He underwent two years of vocal study in Bologna and made his debut in Soncino as Oroveso in *Norma.* He then took leading bass roles in smaller Italian opera companies until he was called up into the Italian artillery during the First World War. In 1920 he resumed his singing career at the Teatro Reale, Rome and two years later was called to the Teatro alla Scala.

His Milan debut was as Pogner in an Italian *Meistersinger,* and after that he was cast in the première of Pizzetti's *Deborah e Jaele.* Toscanini was so impressed with Pinza's voice and personality that he cast him as Nerone in Boito's opera of that name, which received its premiere in 1924.

This was the making of Pinza, who was immediately snatched by Giulio Gatti-Casazza for the Metropolitan Opera, where his debut performance was in Spontini's *La vestale*

with Rosa Ponselle. Pinza's success that night assured his acceptance for the next twenty-two seasons.

He could sing Osmin in *Il seraglio* and had always wanted to be a *basso profundo,* but that was not to be. He was, instead, a *basso cantante* of sumptuous quality with an even tone over two octaves, a smooth legato with edge and carrying power, combined with a magnetic stage presence: handsome appearance and carriage, a good intelligence and the understanding to mould phrases with innuendo, humor, or malice.

Hence Don Giovanni, usually a baritone role, was not only possible for him vocally, but eminently suitable when related to his noble, dashing appearance that turned many a woman's head on and off stage. He sang it about two hundred times, although it took him a while to perfect the role. In 1929 at the Met (where Scotti had last sung it in 1908) Pinza was criticized for "lack of elegance, grace, adroitness and charm," which sounds biased; but he quickly amended these "faults," although it was not until he met Bruno Walter in Salzburg and sang it under him there, that Pinza admitted he was accomplishing all he could with the Don.

Toscanini was his other mentor, especially for general style, enabling Pinza to be considered the finest acting bass since Chaliapin, whose Italian repertoire he inherited. Pinza's favorite roles were Figaro and Boris Godunov. He first sang Pimen in the Mussorgsky opera at the Teatro alla Scala (with Vanni-Marcoux as the Czar), but then he made the title role his own, always singing it in Italian. They couldn't persuade him to do otherwise, even at the Met, where the rest of the cast sang in English.

He sang Figaro frequently at Salzburg—for the last time three days before the outbreak of war in 1939—as well as Don Giovanni, of course, and Basilio in *Il barbiere.* Salzburg welcomed him every season but one between 1934 and 1939.

After Pinza had mastered and sung almost one hundred major bass operatic roles (fifty-one of them at the Met) and could find no appropriate new ones, he became restless and left the Met for Broadway, appearing in the musicals *South Pacific* and *Fanny.* He also made a few films. Although he lived on until 1957 and the voice was still in reasonable trim, he lacked the impetus and glamour and companionship of the opera stage to which he truly belonged.

—Alan Jefferson

————————

IL PIRATA [The Pirate].

Composer: Vincenzo Bellini.

Librettist: Felice Romani (after M. Raimond, *Bertram ou le pirate*).

First Performance: Milan, Teatro alla Scala, 27 October 1827.

Roles: Imogene (soprano); Ernesto (baritone); Gualtiero (tenor); Goffredo (bass); Itulbo (tenor); Adele (soprano); boy (mute); chorus (SSAATTBB).

Publications

articles—

Willier, Stephen A. "Madness, the Gothic, and Bellini's *Il pirata*." *Opera Quarterly* summer (1989).

* * *

Bellini's *Il pirata, opera seria* in two acts with libretto by Felice Romani, was based on the three-act *mélodrame* by Raimond (Isidore J.S. Taylor) which was in turn based on Charles Robert Maturin's five-act gothic verse-play, *Bertram*. The title of the opera was undoubtedly taken from Walter Scott's *The Pirate* (1821). The story is set in the thirteenth century in and around the castle of Caldora in Sicily. With the Angevin victory, Imogene, although she loves Gualtiero, a fellow Swabian, has been forced to marry Ernesto, Duke of Caldora, to save her aged father's life. Gualtiero, forced by circumstances to become an outlaw and a leader of a band of pirates, has been defeated in a battle at sea by Ernesto. This is the background to the action. In act I, scene i, Gualtiero and his men are swept ashore near the castle during a raging storm. Imogene offers them aid, relates a strange prophetic dream that makes her ladies-in-waiting concerned for her slipping sanity, and fails to recognize Gualtiero. In scene ii, Gualtiero reveals his identity to Imogene. He is extremely distraught to find her married, for he had turned to piracy and battling the Angevins out of his love for her. Imogene explains the situation, whereupon Gualtiero decides to challenge the Duke to a duel. Ernesto returns triumphant to the castle after his victory over the pirates and reproves his wife for not sharing his joy. In act II Ernesto discovers that his old enemy Gualtiero is on the island. Discovering him in his wife's chambers, he draws a sword on him; in the ensuing duel Ernesto is killed. The knights of Caldora condemn Gualtiero to death. As the scaffold is erected for his execution, Imogene's latent madness blossoms fully: in an extended mad scene she runs a wide gamut of emotions, one moment singing tenderly to her son, the next calling on the sun to veil the sight of the fatal scaffold.

Although Romani acknowledged neither Raimond nor Maturin as a source for his libretto, the plot does not deviate far from its antecedents, even though for operatic purposes much of the length and complexity of the original had to be excised. In the opera, as might be expected, much is made of the opening storm at sea. It is impossible to discount the impression Bellini's music in this scene must have made on Verdi when he composed the opening storm scene of *Otello*, some sixty years later.

Imogene is the most fully-drawn character in both Maturin's play and in the opera. Between her opening dream sequence ("Sorgete; è in me dover"; "Lo sognai ferito") and her concluding mad scene one can trace the collapse of an already frail sensibility. The chorus is usually prominent in Bellini's operas, even in ostensibly solo scenes, where it provides affective commentary. Significantly, Imogene's dream narrative is interrupted several times by choral interjections, the chorus supplying the information, in the manner of Greek tragedy, that she has for some time exhibited a melancholy disposition. The fantastic nature of this dream aria allowed Bellini greater compositional freedom than arias dealing with more mundane matters. The form is nearly through-composed, and the melody is not as continuous or lyrical as in the preponderance of slow arias from the period. There is more musical continuity between recitative and aria style than was usual; the unsettled, rich harmonies help to underline the lamentations of the text, as do the orchestral coloring and the use of appoggiaturas on words such as "dolor" (sorrow).

In the final scene of the opera, Imogene's *gran scena di pazzia*, the dark timbre of the orchestra is paramount in painting the physical and psychological situations. To a harp accompaniment (the harp in this period suggests the unreal or fantastic, as in the fountain scene of Donizetti's *Lucia di Lammermoor*) of triplets and sustained viola chords, a long English horn solo (really a small orchestral tone poem) mirrors Imogene's bodily contortions and her mental fragmentation after she learns of Gualtiero's condemnation. Especially telling is the use of rhythm: on one level, tension is created by the contrast between the repeated triplets in the accompaniment and the simple duple meter of the solo line; the English horn melody itself is full of jarring rhythmic movement—dotted notes with or without preceding short appoggiaturas, double-dotted rhythms, gruppetti after longer-held notes, and smooth rhythms followed by jerky ones. Much of the sense of physical contortion comes from the use of repeated pitches that "twitch" back and forth; the dynamics also keep shifting. In the concluding fast aria, "Oh, Sole! ti vela di tenebre oscure," in which Imogene invokes the sun to blot out the scaffold, the ferocious rhythmic drive, jagged melodic contours, and projections of naked emotion become the prototype for subsequent scenes of madness and extreme anger, as in Anna's final cabaletta, "Coppia iniqua," from Donizetti's *Anna Bolena*, Lady Macbeth's part in Verdi's 1847 setting of *Macbeth*, and Abigaille's vocal lines in Verdi's *Nabucco*. This is one of the relatively few points in the opera that Bellini has invested with a great deal of embellishment (most of the vocal delivery in *Il pirata* is in unadorned, *declamato* style) and a wide melodic range in order to portray Imogene's state of delirium. Words such as "affanno" (anguish) and "angoscia" (distress) are repeated several times to long, semichromatic scalar runs.

Romani's libretto for *Il pirata* ends with an insurrection in which Gualtiero's band of pirates tries to save its leader. Gualtiero, however, rejects their assistance and throws himself from a bridge into an abyss. The opera as intended for performance, however, concludes with Imogene's mad scene. Although Bertram's onstage demise was suppressed in the case of *Il pirata*, Donizetti's *Lucia di Lammermoor*, composed a few years later, included both the heroine's mad scene and the hero's suicide in the church graveyard as Lucia's funeral cortege passes by. There are numerous ways in which the mad scene in *Lucia*—the *locus classicus* of the Romantic mad scene for a century and a half—is indebted to that of the extremely influential but relatively little known one in *Il pirata*. As the nineteenth-century composer Ferdinand Hiller noted, "*Lucia di Lammermoor* scarcely would have existed had there not been *Il pirata*."

—Stephen Willier

THE PIRATE
See IL PIRATA

PIZZETTI, Ildebrando.

Composer. Born 20 September 1880, in Parma. Died 13 February 1968, in Rome. Studied piano with his father, Odvardo Pizzetti, in Parma, and composition with Tebaldini at the Conservatory of Parma, graduating 1901; on the faculty of the Conservatory of Parma, 1907-08; on the faculty of the Conservatory of Florence, 1908-24; founded with G. Bastianelli the new music journal *Dissonanza,* 1914; director of the Conservatory of Florence, 1917; director of the Milan Conservatory, 1924-36; taught at the Santa Cecilia Academy in Rome, 1936-58; president of the Santa Cecilia Academy, 1947-52; in New York, 1935, and Buenos Aires, 1931, for performances of his operas.

Operas

Publishers: Chester, Curci, Forlivesi, Pizzi, Ricordi, Sonzogno, Suivini Zerboni.

Several unperformed operas, 1899-1907, several unfinished.
Fedra, Gabriele d'Annunzio (after his tragedy), 1909-12, Milan, Teatro alla Scala, 20 March 1915.
Gigliola, Gabriele d'Annunzio, 1914-15 [unfinished].
La sacra rappresentazione di Abram e d'Isaac (incidental music expanded into a one-act opera), F. Belcare, 1925, Turin, Nuovo, 11 March 1926.
Debora e Jaele, Pizzetti, 1915-21, Milan, Teatro alla Scala, 16 December 1922.
Lo straniero, Pizzetti, 1922-25, Rome, Teatro Reale dell' Opera, 29 April 1930.
Fra Gherardo, Pizzetti, 1925-27, Milan, Teatro alla Scala, 16 May 1928.
Orséolo, Pizzetti, 1931-35, Florence, Comunale, 4 May 1935.
L'oro, Pizzetti, 1938-42, Milan, Teatro alla Scala, 2 January 1947.
Vanna Lupa, Pizzetti, 1947-49, Florence, Comunale, 5 May 1949.
Ifigenia (radio opera), Pizzetti, 1950, Radio Audizioni Italiana, 3 October 1950; stage premiere, Florence, Comunale, 19 May 1951.
Cagliostro (radio opera), Pizzetti, Radio Audizioni Italiana, 5 November 1952; stage premiere, Milan, Teatro alla Scala, 24 January 1953.
La figlia di Iorio, d'Annunzio (abridged by Pizzetti), 1953-54, Naples, San Carlo, 4 December 1954.
Assassinio nella cattedrale, Eliot (translated by A. Castaldi), abridged by Pizzetti, 1957, Milan, Teatro alla Scala, 1 March 1958.
Il calzare d'argento, R. Bacchelli, Milan, Teatro alla Scala, 23 March 1961.
Clitennestra, Pizzetti, 1961-64, Milan, Teatro alla Scala, 1 March 1965.

Other works: incidental music, film scores, orchestral works, vocal works, chamber and instrumental music, piano pieces.

Publications

By PIZZETTI: books—

La musica dei greci. Rome, 1914.
Musicisti contemporanei. Milan, 1914.
Intermezzi critici. Florence, 1921.
Paganini. Turin, 1940.
Musica e dramma. Rome, 1945.
La musica italiana dell' 800. Turin, 1947.

articles—

"La musica per 'La nave' di Gabriele d'Annunzio." *Rivista musicale italiana* 14 (1907): 855.
"Ariane et Barbebleue." *Rivista musicale italiana* 15 (1908): 73.
"Questa nostra musica." *Pan* [Milan, Florence, and Rome] 1 (1933-34): 321.

About PIZZETTI: books—

Fondi, R. *Ildebrando Pizzetti e il dramma musicale italiano di oggi.* Rome, 1919.
Gatti, G.M. *"Debora e Jaele" di Ildebrando Pizzetti: guida attraverso il poema e la musica.* Milan, 1922.
Pilati, M. *Fra Gherardo di Ildebrando Pizzetti.* Milan, 1928.
Rinaldi, M. *L'arte di Ildebrando Pizzetti e "Lo straniero".* Rome, 1930.
Tebaldini, G. *Ildebrando Pizzetti nelle memorie.* Parma, 1931.
Damerini, A., et al. *Parma a Ildebrando Pizzetti.* Parma, 1932.
Gatti, Guido M. *Ildebrando Pizzetti.* Turin, 1934; 2nd ed., 1955; English translation, 1951.
Pilati, M. *"L'orseolo" di Ildebrando Pizzetti.* Milan, 1935.
Gavazzeni, G. *Tre studi su Pizzetti.*
Rinaldi, M. *"Lo straniero" di Ildebrando Pizzetti.* Florence, 1943.
Gavazzeni, G. *"L'oro" di Pizzetti: guida musicale.* Milan, 1946.
Bucchi, V., L. Dallapiccola et al. *Firenze a Ildebrando Pizzetti.* Florence, 1947.
Gavazzeni, G. *Altri studi pizzettiani.* Bergamo, 1956.
La Morgia, Manilio, ed. *La città dannunziana a Ildebrando Pizzetti: saggi e note.* Pescara, 1958.
Pizzetti, Bruno, ed. *Ildebrando Pizzetti: cronologia e bibliografia.* Parma, 1980.

articles—

Corte, A. della. "Ildebrando Pizzetti e la *Fedra." Rivista d' Italia* [Rome] 18 (1915): 558.
Barini, G. *"Fedra* di Gabriele d'Annunzio e Ildebrando Pizzetti." *Nuova antologia* 260 (1915): 652, 664.
Sincero, D. "La première di Fedra alla Scala." *Rivista musicale italiana* 22 (1915): 319.
Pratella, F.B. "Due avvenimenti musicali: *Fedra* di Ildebrando Pizzetti." In *L'evoluzione della musica dal 1910 al 1917,* vol. 2, p. 60. Milan, 1919.
Prunières, H. "Ildebrando Pizzetti." *Nouvelle Revue d' Italie* July (1920).
Bastianelli, G. "Ildebrando Pizzetti." *Il convegno* March-April (1921).
Barini, G. "Debora e Jaele: dramma di Ildebrando Pizzetti." *Nuova antologia* 306 (1923): 80.
Pagano, L. " 'Debora e Jaele' di Ildebrando Pizzetti." *Rivista musicale italiana* 30 (1923): 47; reprinted in *La fionda di Davide.* Turin, 1928.
Gatti, G.M. "L'opera drammatica di Pizzetti." *Il pianoforte* 8. Turin, 1926.
Musella, S. "Fra Gherardo (riflessioni)." *Bollettino bibliografico musicale* 3/no. 5 (1928): 21.
Brusa, F. *"Fra Gherardo* di Ildebrando Pizzetti." *Rivista musicale italiana* 35 (1928): 386.
Lualdi, A. *"Debora e Jaele* di I. Pizzetti alla Scala," "*Abramo e Isacco* di Feo Belcari musiche di I. Pizzetti al teatro di Torino." *Serate musicali* [Milan] (1928): 3, 222.

Bonaccorsi, A. "*Lo straniero* di Ildebrando Pizzetti." *Rivista musicale italiana* 38 (1931): 429.

Baronti, A. "La *Debora e Jaele* di Ildebrando Pizzetti al Carlo Felice." *Italia musicale* [Genoa] 5/no. 3 (1932): 3.

Rinaldi, M. "Il valore della *Fedra* di d'Annunzio nel dramma di Pizzetti." *Rassegna dorica* 8 (1936-37): 2.

Gasco A. "La *Fedra* di Ildebrando Pizzetti alla Scala di Milano (1915)," "*Fra Gherardo* al Teatro reale (1929)." In *Da Cimarosa a Strawinsky*, 364, 378. Rome, 1939.

Ponz de Leon, G. "Il dramma lirico nell'arte di Ildebrando Pizzetti." *Rivista musicale italiana* 43 (1939): 539.

Pugliatti, S. "Il dramma musicale nella poetica di Ildebrando Pizzetti." *La rassegna musicale* 14 (1941): 277.

Gaizo, V. del. "Considerazioni sull' *Orséolo* di Ildebrando Pizzetti." *Musica d'oggi* 24 (1942): 115.

Gavazzeni, G. "Brano di un commento all' *Orséolo* di Pizzetti." *La rassegna musicale* 16 (1943): 105.

Confalonieri, G. "*Orséolo* di Ildebrando Pizzetti." In *Bruciar le ali alla musica*, 153. Milan, 1945.

Barblan, G. "*L'oro*, ultima opera di Pizzetti alla Scala." *Rivista musicale italiana* 48 (1947): 57.

Gavazzeni, G. "Commenti alla *Debora e Jaele* di Pizzetti." In *La musica e il teatro*, 83. Pisa, 1954.

Mila, M. "Ascoltando *La figlia di Iorio* di Pizzetti." *La rassegna musicale* 25 (1955): 103; reprint in *La rassegna musicale* 32 (1962): 264.

Pannain, G. "*La figlia di Iorio* di d'Annunzio e Pizzetti." *Rivista musicale italiana* 57 (1955): 51.

Mila, M. "L'assassinio nella cattedrale." In *Cronache musicali 1955-1959*, 163. Turin, 1959.

———. "L'*Ifigenia* di Pizzetti." *Cronache musicali 1955-1959*, 167. Turin, 1959.

Aprahamian, F. "Pizzetti in Coventry." *Ricordiana* [London] 7/no. 3 (1962): 1.

Porter, A. "Coventry and London: Murder in the Cathedral." *Musical Times* 103 (1962): 544.

Santi, P. "Il mondo della *Debora*." *La rassegna musicale* 32 (1962): 151.

Paratore, E. "Introduzione a *La figlia di Iorio* di Pizzetti." *Studi dannunziani* [Naples] (1966): 331.

* * *

Ildebrando Pizzetti (1880-1968), Italian composer, conductor, and music journalist, was the son of a piano teacher. In addition to music, Pizzetti displayed an interest in the theater early in life. In 1895 he entered the Parma Conservatory and received his diploma in 1901. Giovanni Tebaldini, an important figure among Italian musicologists, became the director of the conservatory in 1897 and took a personal interest in Pizzetti, introducing him to music of various styles and eras, in particular plainsong and Italian church music of the Renaissance. Pizzetti's great ambition, though, was to succeed as an opera composer. From the beginning he always viewed opera not primarily as a musical form, but more as a unified work of art in which "words, music, and action must coexist harmoniously." These are the words of G.M. Gatti, a long-time advocate of and commentator on Pizzetti's works.

Pizzetti began to explore operatic composition as a student, leaving several youthful efforts unfinished, among them a *Sardanopolo* based on Byron and a *Mazeppa* after Pushkin. An early work, *Il Cid*, written for the Concorso Sonzogno, was, in the composer's own words, "made up of melodic *fioriture* from start to finish, the scenic action concentrated into a series of lyric effusions [patterned after] Rossini, Bellini, Verdi...." In his mature operas, Pizzetti turned away from this lyric style, coming to believe that "if one expends such effort to embark on the vertiginous current of lyric effusion, he is carried so far away from the path of drama that he may well be unable to find the way back."

In 1905 Pizzetti read parts of Gabriele d'Annunzio's play *La nave*, then in progress. It made a profound impact on him; the two artists became friends and Pizzetti was asked to furnish incidental music for the premiere of *La nave*. During the years 1909-12 the playwright and composer collaborated on a production of *Fedra*, premiered 20 March 1915 at the Teatro alla Scala. Meanwhile, Pizzetti had become professor of composition at the Parma Conservatory (1907) and subsequently professor of harmony and counterpoint in Florence (1908). He resided in Florence from 1908-24, succeeding to the directorship of the conservatory there in 1917. During his Florentine years Pizzetti associated with many of the prominent philosophers, writers, and artists connected with the avant-garde periodical *La voce*, published from 1908 to 1916. From 1917-19 Pizzetti was a part of Casella's Società Italiana di Musica Moderna, although his links were at times tenuous. Pizzetti, in fact, began to display decidedly conservative traits, as attested to, for example, by his shock upon attending the premiere of Stravinsky's *Sacre du Printemps* in Paris in 1913. Conservative traits became overt when on 17 December 1932 Pizzetti joined Respighi, Zandonai, and others in signing a manifesto, published in several Italian newspapers, attacking progressive music and calling for a return to tradition.

After his time in Florence, Pizzetti became director of the Milan Conservatory in 1924 and in 1936 went to Rome to teach at the Accademia di Santa Cecilia. Throughout his life he continued to write music criticism, for such journals as *La rassegna musicale* and the *Corriere della sera*. Many of his articles were subsequently collected and published in book form. His most ambitious and significant contribution to music lies, however, in the realm of opera. A notable feature of his stage works is their avoidance of the sweeping melodies of his predecessors Mascagni and Puccini. Pizzetti instead tends to write in a flexible arioso style that captures both the rhythms of the Italian language and the nuances of the text. Sources of this style are to some extent Wagnerian, but Debussy's techniques in *Pelléas et Mélisande* play an even larger role, as do the examples of the seventeenth century Florentine monodists and Monteverdian recitative. The "Pizzettian declamation" has been the subject of much heated debate; on the negative side, it can sometimes lead to monotony, for Pizzetti tends to include a great deal of philosophical discussion in his operas. Yet there are also some of the most lyrical, moving moments in all of twentieth century Italian opera, for example the "Trenodia per Ippolito Morto" from *Fedra* or Mara's song at the end of act I of *Debora e Jaele*.

These two operas—*Fedra* and *Debora*—are are considered Pizzetti's best works. *Debora* was heavily influenced by Musorgsky's *Boris Godunov*, particularly in its choral writing, which is superbly dramatic. Pizzetti, Gatti notes, was drawn to choral composition by an innate religious feeling. Pizzetti's *Assassinio nella cattedrale*, while not on the level of *Fedra* or *Debora*, also contains striking choral writing. As with most of Pizzetti's operas, *Assassinio* is best appreciated by audiences able to understand every nuance and inflection of the Italian language.

—Stephen Willier

PIZZI, Pier Luigi.

Designer and producer. Born 15 June 1930. Studied at Polytechnic School of Architecture, Milan; lighting designer, also scenic and costume designer for theater (especially with di Lullo), film, and television, as well as opera; theater debut, Piccolo Teatro dell Città, Genoa, 1951; first opera design was *Don Giovanni,* Teatro Comunale, Genoa, 1952; began producing operas in 1977; has designed for most of the major opera houses. Awards include San Genesio Prize, 1965, and Golden Neptune.

Opera Productions and Designs (selected)

Design only

Maria Stuarda, Florence, 1957.
Eugene Onegin, Glyndebourne, 1968.
Les vêpres siciliennes, Teatro alla Scala, 1970.
The Queen of Spades, Glyndebourne, 1971.
Nabucco, Verona, 1971.
Boris Godunov, Venice Fest, 1973.
La forza del destino, Vienna, 1974.
La bohème, Metropolitan Opera, 1977.

Direction and design

Don Giovanni, Turin, 1977.
Orlando Furioso, 1978.
Semiramide, Aix-en-Provence, 1980.
Les vêpres siciliennes, Teatro alla Scala, 1989.

Publications

About PIZZI: articles–

Kaplan, A. "Pier Luigi Pizzi on *Semiramide* (Interview)." *San Francisco Opera Magazine* no. 1 (Fall 1981): 56-58.
Labie, J.F. "Pier Luigi Pizzi: 'Comment j'ai travaillé Rinaldo.' " *Diapason-Harmonie* no. 306 (June 1985): 10.
Bauzano, G. "Pier Luigi Pizzi, un regista diferente." *Monsalvat* no. 56 (January 1988): 14-15.

*   *   *

The influence of Pier Luigi Pizzi's training as an architect can be seen in much of his work for the theater. His fine draftsmanship is reflected in his sense of volume and perspective, which is complemented by a judicious use of a deliberately restrained range of colors. Always elegant, often postmodern (before the word was invented), his sets and costumes have been featured in over 300 productions, mostly of opera.

Don Giovanni was the first opera that Pizzi designed (Genoa, 1952), and over the next twenty-five years he was to work with many of Italy's most noted producers (Strehler, Di Lullo, Ronconi) before becoming a producer himself. Some of his most memorable works include *Eugene Onegin* for Glyndebourne (1968); and, in the seventies, *Orfeo ed Euridice* and *Nabucco* (conducted by Riccardo Muti) in Florence and the *Ring* at the Teatro alla Scala.

In 1977, Pizzi designed and produced *Don Giovanni* in Turin and, since then, he has always been responsible for both the production and design of the operas he has staged. Two distinct styles emerged from Pizzi's approach to solving the problems of staging opera. "Darker" scores (e.g., *Macbeth, Khovanshchina,* etc.) showed an almost Brechtian starkness and simplicity which displayed Pizzi's effective handling of the chorus and his fondness for somber sets with splashes of bright color. His style for baroque operas evolved from his *Orlando Furioso* (1978), in which lavish use was made of columns, mirrors and ornate costumes. This was followed by a series of eighteenth-century works (Rameau and Handel) for which he became widely known. Pizzi's reactualization of neo-classical taste led to his all-white *Semiramide* at Aix-en-Provence (1980), a production which was seen in several other opera houses.

In the 1980s, Pizzi was much in demand, especially for works which have rarely been revived; *I due Foscari, Guillaume Tell* and several rediscovered Rossini operas in Pesaro. He has been taxed with undertaking too much in too short a time. Certainly, there have been Pizzi productions which have verged on self-parody or which show signs of over hasty preparation. Both of these tendencies were well in evidence at the opening of the Opéra de la Bastille for which Pizzi mounted yet another all-white staging (*Les troyens*), not long after a not entirely successful *Vêpres siciliennes* for the opening of the Teatro alla Scala season. Future generations may see in Pizzi's work the operatic equivalent of the designer-label mentality which so marked the two decades up to 1990. As with many a "grand couturier," finding new ideas for each new season has often proved the hardest task of all.

—Oliver Smith

———————

**THE POACHER
See DER WILDSCHÜTZ**

———————

IL POMO D'ORO [The Golden Apple].

Composer: Antonio Cesti.

Librettist: Franco Sbarra.

First Performance: Vienna, 13-14 July 1668.

Roles: Proserpina (soprano); Pluto (bass); Discordia (soprano); Bacchus (bass); Mars (tenor); Venus (soprano); Jupiter (bass); Juno (soprano); Pallas Athene (soprano); Apollo (contralto); Neptune (bass); Mercury (contralto); Jupiter's Cupbearer (soprano); Ganymede (contralto); Momo Buffone (bass); Ennone (soprano); Aurindo (contralto); Filaura (tenor); Caronte (bass); Aletto (soprano); Tesifore (soprano); Megera (contralto); Cecrope (bass); Alceste (contralto); Adrasto (contralto); various personified figures; chorus.

Publications

articles–

Shock, D.H. "Costuming for 'Il pomo d'oro'." *Gazette des beaux-arts* 69 (1967): 251.

Antonicek. "Antonio Cesti alla Corte di Vienna." *Nuova rivista musicale italiana* 4 (1970): 93.

Schmidt, Carl B. "Antonio Cesti's *Il pomo d'oro:* a Reexamination of a Famous Hapsburg Court Spectacle." *Journal of the American Musicological Society* 13 (1978): 442.

* * *

Il pomo d'oro is an important example of the large-scale Baroque court opera. Composed for the marriage festivities of the Austrian Emperor Leopold I and the Infanta Margherita of Spain, it was first performed in Vienna in 1668. Its historical importance stems from the qualities of Cesti's music, especially the forward-looking relationship between music and text, and from the sumptuousness of the production, particularly of Burnacini's original sets and stage machinery. The music from the prologue, acts I, II, and IV is extant as well as some individual arias from acts III and V.

In a laudatory prologue Cupid, Hymen, and the allegorical personifications of numerous kingdoms appear. Then follows a plot based on the Greek myth of the golden apple, which is to be the prize given to the most beautiful of the three goddesses Juno, Pallas Athene, and Venus. After plotting with Pluto and Proserpina, Discord appears with the golden apple at a banquet of the gods in Jupiter's palace. Venus, Juno, and Pallas Athene agree to let Paris decide who is to win the golden apple. Ennone, who loves Paris, and Aurindo, who loves Ennone, are both worried. When Venus is awarded the apple, Juno and Pallas devise various intrigues to hinder Paris in carrying out his choice. Before all has finished Pallas and the Athenian army have even attacked the fortress of Mars. Difficulties are resolved with the required happy ending, in which Jupiter sends his eagle to carry the apple to the most worthy of all, the empress Margherita.

Il pomo d'oro is the crowning work of Cesti's career, during which he composed more than a dozen operas, beginning in Venice with *Orontea* (1649) and concluding in Vienna with *Il pomo d'oro*. Cesti, participating in the exportation of Venetian opera to the Viennese court, adhered to the general mid-seventeenth century Italian style. In *Il pomo d'oro* the separate roles of recitative and aria are clearly defined, the former carrying the burden of the plot and the latter serving as commentary. In the recitatives Cesti does not often cultivate that particularly expressive (affective) quality frequently found in the work of the older composers Monteverdi and Cavalli, although occasional lyrical outbursts within the recitative can still be found. For special effect, recitative is occasionally accompanied by an orchestral texture fuller than the continuo alone. It is the arias and occasional ensembles, however, which are the chief points of musical attraction, a trait by which Cesti looks forward to the operas of the later Baroque. The arias may be strophic or through-composed, and they are accompanied by continuo or by the orchestra in a five-part texture. Arias may include an instrumental ritornello to be played at the beginning and/or the end. Arias are sometimes shared by more than one character, so that the characters sing successively without joining together in duet

Il pomo d'oro, engraving by Matthaeus Küsel after Burnacini's design for act II, scene 6 (the entrance to Hell)

fashion. The chorus, used occasionally and to spectacular musical effect, also appears onstage in a supernumerary capacity. The smaller ensembles, duets and trios for protagonists in the drama provide much scope for melodic imitation and rhythmic vigor.

Since *Il pomo d'oro* appeared under the patronage of the imperial court, there were vast resources available for the production of the work. The orchestra, unusually large for its time, includes brass and woodwinds as well as strings. The five acts provide ample opportunity for changes of scene, the province of the set-designer and court architect, Burnacini. Extant engravings from Burnacini's two dozen sets for *Il pomo d'oro* show a monumental, spectacular style requiring sophisticated machinery for the ascents and descents of deities. Because of the splendor of its production *Il pomo d'oro* had sensational success and was long remembered in the seventeenth century.

—Edward Rutschman

PONCHIELLI, Amilcare.

Composer. Born 31 August 1834, in Paderno Fasolaro, Cremona. Died 16 January 1886, in Milan. Married: the soprano Theresa Brambilla. Studied at the Milan Conservatory, 1843-54; organist at Sant' Ilario in Cremona, later a bandmaster; professor at the Milan Conservatory, 1880; maestro di capella at the Cathedral of Bergamo, 1881-86. Puccini and Mascagni were among Ponchielli's students.

Operas

Il sindaco babbeo (farsa) (with C. Marcòra, D. Cagnoni, A. Cunio), G. Giacchetti, Milan, Conservatory, March 1851.
I promessi sposi, after Manzoni, Cremona, Concordia, 30 August 1856; revised, E. Praga, Milan, Teatro dal Verme, 4 December 1872.
Bertrando dal Bormio, 1858 [not performed].
La Savoiarda, F. Guidi, Cremona, Concordia, 19 January 1861; revised 1870; revised as *Lina,* C. D'Ormeville, Milan, Teatro dal Verme, 17 November 1877.
Roderico re dei goti, F. Guidi (after R. Southey, *Roderick*), Piacenza, 26 December 1863.
La vergine di Kermo (with ten others), F. Guidi, 1860, Cremona, Concordia, 22 February 1870.
Il parlatore eterno, A. Ghislanzoni, Lecco, Sociale, 18 October 1873.
I Lituani, A. Ghislanzoni (after Mickiewicz, *Konrad Wallenrod*), Milan, Teatro alla Scala, 6 March 1874; revised, Teatro alla Scala, 6 March 1875.
I Mori di Valenza, A. Ghislanzoni (after Scribe, *Piquillo Alliaga*), 1874 [unfinished; act 4 completed by Annibale Ponchielli and A. Cadore], Monte Carlo, Opéra, 17 March 1914.
La Gioconda, Tobia Gorrio [=Arrigo Boito] (after Hugo, *Angelo, tyran de Padoue*), Milan, Teatro alla Scala, 8 April 1876; revised, Venice, Rossini, 18 October 1876.
Il figliuol prodigo, A. Zanardini, Milan, Teatro alla Scala, 26 December 1880.
Marion Delorme, E. Golisciani (after Hugo, *Marion de Lorme*), Milan, Teatro alla Scala, 17 March 1885.

Other works: ballets, cantatas, vocal chamber music, orchestral works, instrumental works, piano pieces.

Publications

About PONCHIELLI: books–

Adami, G. *Giulio Ricordi e i suoi musicisti.* Milan, 1933.
Cesari, G. *Amilcare Ponchielli nell' arte del suo tempo: ricordi e carteggi.* Cremona, 1934.
Rolandi, Ulderico. *Nel centenario ponchielliano: Amilcare Ponchielli librettista.* Como, 1935.
De Napoli, Giuseppe. *Amilcare Ponchielli (1834-1886): la vita, le opere, l'epistolario, le onoranze.* Cremona, 1936.
Damerini, A. *A. Ponchielli.* Turin, 1940.
Tedeschi, Rubens. *Addio, fiorito asil. Il melodramma italiano da Boito al Verismo.* Milan, 1978.
Nicolaisen, Jay. *Italian Opera in Transition 1871-1893.* Ann Arbor, 1980.
Albarosa, Nino, et al. *Amilcare Ponchielli* [colloquium]. Casalmorano, 1984.

articles–

Hanslick, E. "Gioconda." In *Die moderne Oper,* vol. 4. *Musikalisches Skizzenbuch.* Berlin, 1888; 3rd ed., 1911; 1971.
Farina, S. "Amilcare Ponchielli." *Gazzetta musicale di Milano* 55 (1900): 523, 535, 547.
Wolf, H. "Gioconda." In *Musikalische Kritiken.* Leipzig, 1911.
Shaw, George Bernard. *Music in London 1890-94,* vol. 1. London, 1932.
Mila, M. "Caratteri della musica di Ponchielli." *Pan* 2 (1934): 481.
Tebaldini, G. "Amilcare Ponchielli." *Musica d'oggi* 16 (1934): 239.
Damerini, A. "Una lettera inedita di A. Ponchielli." *Musica d'oggi* 17 (1935): 141.
Sartori, C. "Il primo rimaneggiamento dei *Promessi sposi.*" *Rassegna dorica* 20 May (1938).
Tebaldini, G. "Il mio maestro." *La Scala* March (1952).
Morini, M. "Destino postumo dei *Mori di Valenza.*" *La Scala* March (1957).
Gavazzeni, G. "Considerazioni su di un centenario: A Ponchielli." In *Trent' anni di musica,* 57. Milan, 1958.
Klein, J.W. "Ponchielli: a Forlorn Figure." *The Chesterian* 34 (1959-60): 116.

*   *   *

After taking his diploma with highest honors from the Milan Conservatory in 1854, Ponchielli began working in Cremona as organist and piano teacher. His goal was to conquer the Italian opera stage, which at that time meant challenging Giuseppe Verdi. To this end Ponchielli began working on a setting of Manzoni's *I promessi sposi,* to a libretto that he and several friends had devised. It was premiered in Cremona in 1856 at the Teatro Concordia; although the work was given fifteen times in Cremona, its success was purely local. Ponchielli's second opera, *Bertrando dal Bormio,* was slated for a premiere in Turin in 1858, but for unexplained reasons was not performed. His next effort, *La Savoiarda* (*The Girl from Savoy*), was given at Cremona; the revision, a return to the *opera semiseria* of the early nineteenth century renamed *Lina,* was heard in Milan in 1877.

In 1861 Ponchielli was appointed town band-master in Piacenza for three years, and his next opera, *Roderico re dei goti* (*Roderick, King of the Goths*), was given in 1863 at the Teatro Comunale. After his three-year stint in Piacenza, Ponchielli returned to Cremona as conductor of the town band. He also conducted operas there and was able to have one of his own ballets performed. It was a frustrating time for Ponchielli: he had not achieved his goal of becoming a recognized composer of opera; among other disappointments, Piave (the librettist of Verdi's *Rigoletto*) had agreed to write a libretto for him in 1867, but then had fallen ill.

Ponchielli's operatic success did not begin until his much revised *I promessi sposi,* now with libretto by Emilio Praga, was produced in December 1872 at the Teatro dal Verme in Milan. Soon after (in February of 1873), the Teatro alla Scala gave his ballet *Le due gemelle.* Success was now Ponchielli's: Ricordi began to publish his music and to get it performed, and commissioned an opera from him for La Scala. This turned out to be *I Lituani,* to a libretto by Ghislanzoni,

premiered at La Scala on 6 March 1874 and rearranged as *Aldona* for St Petersburg a decade later. This work is particularly notable for Ponchielli's attempts at Slavic coloring; it may profitably be compared with Musorgsky's *Boris Godunov* of the same year, an opera unknown to Ponchielli.

Ponchielli's greatest operatic triumph came in 1876 with *La Gioconda,* a melodrama set to a text by Boito (writing under the pseudonym Tobia Gorrio) based on Victor Hugo's *Angelo, tyran de Padoue.* However, *La Gioconda* was the apex of Ponchielli's operatic career. Subsequent works—such as *Il figliuol prodigo,* with its oriental coloring, and *Marion Delorme,* in the *opéra comique* tradition with bows to Verdi's *Traviata*—did not come close to the popularity of *La Gioconda,* which is the only opera by Ponchielli to have survived until the present.

Even *La Gioconda* is often maligned, although it has many strong points: vivid characters portrayed indelibly by musical means, sure and exact musical heightening of Venetian local color, seemingly inexhaustible melodic invention, and imaginative treatment of the orchestra. Many of Ponchielli's scores, even though each contains inspired pages and at the very least highly competent workmanship and a natural flair for drama, lack a strong musical personality, a facet of Ponchielli's own nature. As a man he was reticent, kindly, and passive to a fault.

—Stephen Willier

PONNELLE, Jean–Pierre.

Director/Scenic Designer. Born 19 February 1932, in Paris. Married: Margit Saad (one child). Studied philosophy at the Sorbonne, and music with Hans Rosbaud; began career as a scenic designer, later made the transition to director/designer; design debut, *Boulevard Solitude,* Hannover, 1953; directing debut, *Tristan und Isolde,* Düsseldorf, 1963; especially noted for his Mozart and Monteverdi cycles, his work on Rossini, and his opera films.

Opera Productions (selected)

Tristan und Isolde, Düsseldorf, 1963.
Le nozze di Figaro, Freiburg, 1967.
Il barbiere di Siviglia, Salzburg, 1968.
Così fan tutte, Salzburg, 1969.
La clemenza di Tito, Cologne, 1969.
La Cenerentola, San Francisco, 1969.
Così fan tutte, San Francisco, 1970.
Don Giovanni, Cologne, 1971.
Manon, Vienna, 1971.
Così fan tutte, Cologne, 1972.
Le nozze di Figaro, Salzburg, 1972.
Die Zauberflöte, Cologne, 1972.
Tosca, San Francisco, 1972.
La Cenerentola, Milan, 1973.
L'italiana in Algeri, New York, 1973.
Ariadne auf Naxos, Cologne, 1973.
Die Entführung aus dem Serail, Cologne, 1974.
Idomeneo, Cologne, 1974.
Der fliegende Holländer, San Francisco, 1975.
Le nozze di Figaro, Chicago, 1975.
L'Orfeo, Zurich, 1975.
Rigoletto, Düsseldorf, 1976.

Amilcare Ponchielli, portrait by E. Pagliano, 1887

Salome, Cologne, 1976.
L'incoronazione di Poppea, Zurich, 1977.
Pelléas et Mélisande, Milan, 1977.
Turandot, San Francisco, 1977.
Il ritorno d'Ulisse in patria, Zurich, 1977.
La traviata, Houston, 1979.
Les contes d'Hoffmann, Salzburg, 1980.
Lucio Silla, Zurich, 1981.
Parsifal, Cologne, 1983.
Fidelio, Berlin, 1984.
Cavalleria rusticana/Pagliacci, Vienna, 1985.
Falstaff, San Francisco, 1985.
Manon, New York, 1987.
Moses und Aron, Salzburg, 1987.
Peter Grimes, Florence, 1988.

Opera Films

Il barbiere di Siviglia, 1972.
Madama Butterfly, 1974.
Carmina Burana, 1975.
Le nozze di Figaro, 1976.
Monteverdi cycle: *L'Orfeo, L'incoronazione di Poppea, Il ritorno d'Ulisse in patria,* 1978-79.
La clemenza di Tito, 1980.
La Cenerentola, 1981.
Rigoletto, 1982.
Die Zauberflöte, 1982.
Idomeneo, 1982.
Tristan und Isolde, 1983.
Manon, 1983.
Mitridate, re di Ponto, 1986.
Cardillac, 1986.
Così fan tutte, 1988.

Publications

By PONNELLE: articles–

Jean-Pierre Ponnelle: Arbeiten für Salzburg [includes several articles by Ponnelle]. Salzburg, 1989

About PONNELLE: books–

Jacobsen, Robert. *Magnificence: Onstage at the Met.* New York, 1985.
Keck, Sabine. *Die Regie hat das Wort.* Westermann, 1988.
Jean-Pierre Ponnelle: Arbeiten für Salzburg. Salzburg, 1989.

articles–

Marker, Frederick J. and Lise-Lone. "Retheatricalizing Opera: A Conversation with Jean-Pierre Ponnelle." *Opera Quarterly* summer (1985).

*   *   *

Of the many contemporary designer/directors whose staging of opera has evoked controversy, Jean-Pierre Ponnelle is probably the most interesting, because his concepts, unlike those of so many of his fellow craftspersons, came not from ignorance (wilful or accidental) of operatic tradition, but from a conscious decision to traduce the existing libretto and the composer's expressed or implied wishes.

At his worst, Ponnelle blatantly disregards both the specific words and the sense of the situation in his desire to produce a visually striking image. His act III of Verdi's *Rigoletto* exemplifies this approach. After the Duke's poignant aria "Parmi veder le lagrime," the courtiers (most of whose wives and daughters the Duke has seduced) enter his private chambers through a dozen or more secret doors. If all these people he has wronged know a secret way to his living quarters, it is difficult to believe he could have survived this long. Further, instead of rushing into his bedroom to deflower the kidnapped Gilda (as the libretto indicates), he accomplishes the seduction/rape (with curtains drawn, to be sure) in a center-stage ebony bed whose columns resemble those of the high altar at St Peter's. It is a breathtaking picture, but makes nonsense of the text when Rigoletto seeks to get beyond "la porta," ("the door"—to the Duke's bedroom) to save his daughter—she's just behind the drapes.

In *Cavalleria rusticana,* the opportunity to present a parade of self-flagellating penitents proved so strong a lure that Ponnelle changed the day on which the work takes place from Easter Sunday to Good Friday, which justifies the sadomasochism, but not the church chorus singing "He is risen," a hymn reserved for Easter Sunday. Santuzza is followed around by a group of pregnant furies, and the simple carter Alfio is transformed into a mafia *capo* with sunglasses and a slavish male chorus to whom he has obviously made an offer they can't refuse.

Perhaps Ponnelle's most determinedly wrongheaded production is his infamous San Francisco staging of Wagner's *Der fliegende Holländer* (later seen in New York), in which the composer's expressed intention of exalting woman's sacrifice as redemptive of the protagonist's suffering is reduced to a sex dream by a minor character, the Steersman. His fantasy of the whole encounter with his captain's daughter, the otherworldly suitor, and his own rejection by her, in the more romantic guise of the hunter Erik, is that of a self-pitying (albeit imaginative) loser. Though the production abounds in eye-catching detail—the Russian dolls who accompany Senta's domestic duties, the rolling sea, the appearance of the Dutchman's ghostly crew as rotting corpses—the overall feeling is of having participated in the trivialization of the message Wagner sought to convey.

When not self-driven to excesses, Ponnelle's vision of familiar operas could revivify them for the viewer. In his film of Puccini's *Madama Butterfly,* he not only used a gumchewing Lt Pinkerton and a straw-hat and blazer clad Goro to typify the United States Navy's cultural imperialism in its Asiatic ports of call, but commendably avoided the overly-obvious irony of abusing the Nagasaki location, with its atomic fate, to engage in trivial but trendy imperialist-bashing.

Perhaps Ponnelle's most successful staging of a mainstream opera was his *Pagliacci,* in which his updating of the story to the mid-1920s did no violence to Leoncavallo's text, but allowed the strolling comedians to enter the small Calabrian town in a vintage Oldsmobile truck, use its cab for Silvio's seduction of Nedda and its battery to light the stage for the play-within-a-play.

Ponnelle was most generally successful in staging comic opera of almost any era, in interpreting Monteverdi's and Mozart's serious operas, and, though not always, in directing

Jean-Pierre Ponnelle's production of *Idomeneo,* **Salzburg Festival, 1983**

works with a strong mythic content. Though Andrew Porter once damned his production of Verdi's *Falstaff* as having "all the proliferation of vulgar detail that marks much of his work," others have noted that the comic details he adds never deviate from either Shakespeare's spirit or Boito's libretto; he provided sight-gags the libretto did not contain, but also did not bar. His productions of Rossini operas, particularly *La Cenerentola,* are justly famous for enhancing the possibilities for physical comedy to match the music's humor, as is also evident in his loving approach to Mozart's *Così fan tutte.*

Ponnelle's Monteverdi cycle for Zurich and his much-traveled staging of Mozart's *Idomeneo* demonstrated the fact that he was not afraid to take another's successful idea and give it his own stamp. He was by no means the first to decide that baroque *opera seria* might best be staged using costumes, sets and stage machinery redolent of Mozart's or Monteverdi's time, rather than that of the libretto's classical Greece or Rome. However, through his use of dominant colors, a mixture of classical and baroque costumes, Palladianesque architecture and restrained allusion to the stagecraft of the composer's period, he managed to integrate the formalism of the genre with a more contemporary view of the human problems exhibited in the text, so often overlooked or submerged in more academically correct stagings.

Aside from a penchant for priest-bashing, understandable in the context of the Catholic anticlericalism of his native France, Ponnelle grinds no political or social axes in his productions. Whatever his politics, he does not impose them overtly on music that cannot support them. He obviously knew and (almost always) loved the works he designed and staged. To disagree with his concepts, one has to rethink one's own ideas, to confront the possibility of atrophied or unexamined acceptance of traditionalism for its own sake. In a climate of polemics and deconstruction, he provides both visual pleasure and the pleasure of informed debate.

—William J. Collins

PONS, Lily.

Soprano. Born 16 April 1898, in Draguignan (near Cannes); died 13 January 1976, in Dallas, Texas. Married: André Kostelanetz in 1938. Studied with Alberti de Gorostiaga at the Paris Conservatoire; debut as Lakmé at Mulhouse, 1928; Metropolitan Opera debut as Lucia in Donizetti's *Lucia di Lammermoor,* 1931; sang with the Metropolitan Opera, 1931-60; Covent Garden debut as Rosina in Rossini's *Il barbiere di Siviglia,* 1935; made several films, including *I Dream Too Much,* and *That Girl from Paris.*

Publications:

About PONS: books–

Rasponi, L. *The Last Prima Donnas.* New York, 1982.

articles–

Park, B. "Lily Pons." *Record Collector* 14 (1961): 245.
Schaumkell, C.D. "In memoriam Lily Pons." *Opernwelt* 4 (1976): 53.
Robinson, F. "Lily Pons." *Opera News* 40 (1976): 38.
Miller, P.L. "Lily Pons in retrospect." *American Record Guide* 40 (1977): 49.
Jellinek, G. "Lily Pons coloratura assoluta." *Stereo Review* 38 (1977): 114.

* * *

Lily Pons was "Mr. Gatti's little Christmas gift from a kind providence." Thus wrote W.J. Henderson in the *New York Herald Tribune* of the petite French coloratura whom Metropolitan Opera general manager Giulio Gatti-Casazza put on, with no advance publicity, for an American debut as Lucia di Lammermoor on 3 January 1931. The success she scored then, which was nothing short of sensational, endured long after Pons had already become, in her unique way, a legend in her own lifetime.

Lily Pons as Cherubino in *Le nozze di Figaro*

In the eyes of both the operatic public and society at large, she was the very last of her voice type to be a full-fledged *prima donna.* Following the mid-twentieth-century advent of big-voiced Lucias such as Callas and Sutherland, it was no longer possible for a genuine *haute-colorature* to find consideration as an operatic "first lady." Voices of the size of Pons' became soubrettes for life, only rarely performing the "mad scene" heroines. And when they did, it was all too often not with the voices nature gave them but rather with instruments made wiry and intractable in the vain attempt to achieve feats that came naturally to their larger-voiced colleagues.

But Pons, following in the Galli-Curci tradition, knew better. She possessed style and sense and savvy and complete awareness of what she could and could not do. She stayed securely within the bounds of appropriate repertory. (She attempted Violetta only once, in her fifties, and did not return to it.) Moreover, she had a chic and bewitching kind of glamour that captivated the public at once.

During the 1930s Pons was the Metropolitan's principal box-office attraction, rivaled only by Kirsten Flagstad in the second half of the decade. And her influence upon her generation went beyond the excitement aroused in the public. Risë Stevens recalled that Pons singlehandedly made that era "a glamour time, when everyone dressed and was bejewelled. You were expected to be very glamorous. And we were."

Pons' voice, though small, was of utmost purity and carrying power. Beyond that, its quality was warm and appealing, not blanched and piercing like so many voices of the type, despite the brilliance that characterized it. The top range was so fluent that she always performed the *Lucia* mad scene transposed up a whole tone, in F, including the very last time she sang it (Fort Worth Opera, 30 November 1962, with Placido Domingo in his first Edgardo).

Although on the operatic stage she was never less than a serious and dedicated artist, her manipulation of the uses and possibilities of publicity was second to none. She made her first motion picture shortly after her American debut. At one point she acquired a pet ocelot, later donating it to the Bronx Zoo when it grew too large (both events were well covered in the press), and another time she was photographed eating a meal with some of the zoo's resident monkeys.

Like many other artists who left Europe before achieving real fame, Pons remained intensely loyal to the American public, which had regarded her as a star immediately. She sang rarely in her native land after her Metropolitan debut and not at all in opera after 1935. She visited Covent Garden for Rosina in the latter year and had made two brief stops at the Colón in Buenos Aires earlier (1932 and 1934).

Pons' profoundest effect was not as Lucia or Lakmé in the comfort and security of an opera house, however. She took her American citizenship in 1940 and during World War II spent a great deal of time traveling to entertain troops, enduring tremendous hardship and putting her own life in jeopardy continually. She performed in evening gowns in freezing cold at the Belgian front, in blistering heat in the Persian Gulf, and all temperatures between in China, Burma, India, Russia, Germany, Italy, and Africa. After the liberation of Paris she stood on the balcony of the Opéra, having been a full participant in the horror of the war, and before 250,000 of her compatriots sang the "Marseillaise." To the end of her days thousands of Allied servicemen who never went near an opera remembered with deep affection the tiny, plucky French nightingale who came to dangerous places to raise their spirits, often alone with only the pilot and her gown in the plane that transported her.

At her final appearance (in 1972, on a New York Philharmonic Promenade concert conducted by her former husband André Kostelanetz), Pons at seventy-four contrived not only to look as she had years before but to produce a sound almost palpably that of a much earlier day. Irving Kolodin's words then are a summation of the impact and appeal of Lily Pons, who "made an entrance that could only have been the product of nearly fifty years' practice in perfecting the unreality that is every *prima donna*. The exquisite way in which she was turned out assured her a triumph by sight alone." As a singer, "she had, literally decades ago, done herself less justice than she did this May 31. It was a kind of afterglow, a final flaring up of the barely smoldering vocal flame, a stirring about of the all but exhausted embers." It was equally the afterglow of a long bygone era, of which Pons herself was the symbol.

—Bruce Burroughs

PONSELLE, Rosa [Rose Ponzillo].

Soprano. Born 22 January 1897, in Meriden, Connecticut. Died 25 May 1981, in Baltimore. Married: Carle A. Jackson, 1936. Sang in cinema and vaudeville theaters with her sister Carmela; studied with William Thorner, Romano Romani; debut as Leonora in *La forza del destino*, Metropolitan Opera, 1918, with Enrico Caruso; twenty-two roles at the Metropolitan Opera, including Norma, Aida, Violetta in *La traviata,* Donna Anna in *Don Giovanni;* created the role of Carmelita in Breil's *Legend,* 1919; Covent Garden debut as Norma, 1929; sang Zoraima in American premier of *La notte di Zoraima* by Montemezzi, 1931; retired from opera stage, 1937. Served as artistic director of the Baltimore Civic Opera and taught; students include William Warfield, Sherrill Milnes, James Morris.

Publications

By PONSELLE: books–

with James A. Drake. *Ponselle: A Singer's Life.* New York, 1982.

About PONSELLE: books–

Armstrong, William Dawson. *The Romantic World of Music.* New York, c.1922.
Thompson, O. *The American Singer.* New York, 1937.
Steane, J.B. *The Grand Tradition.* London, 1974.

articles–

Cook, Ida. "Rosa Ponselle." *Opera* 3/February (1952): 75.
Favia-Artsay, Aida. "Rosa Ponselle." *Hobbies,* October 1952.
Riemens, L. and Rodolfo Celletti. "Ponselle, Rosa." *Le grandi voci.* Rome, 1964.
Villella, T. and B. Park. "Rosa Ponselle Discography." *Grand Baton* 8/1-2 (1970): 5.
Ardoin, John. "A Footnote to Ponselle's Norma." *Opera* 27/ March (1976): 225
"Ponselle at 80." *Opera* January (1977).
Opera News, 12 March (1977).
Legge, Walter. "La Divina." *Opera News* 42/5 (1977): 9.
Forbes, M. "A Diva's Legacy." *Opera News* 48/July (1983): 32.

Emmons, S. "Voices from the Past." *The NATS Bulletin* 41/ 2 (1984): 41.
Sills, B. "Studying with Garden and Ponselle." *Opera* 39/ March (1988): 270.
Freeman, John W. "The Good Life." *Opera News* 54 (1989): 8.

*   *   *

Second only to that of Caruso, the voice of Rosa Ponselle has come to be regarded, simply, as the most beautiful in the history of recorded sound. Brash as such a valuation seems, more than half a century after the soprano's retirement, dissenters remain virtually unheard-of. The number of those living who actually saw her in performance has naturally dwindled, but, as with Caruso, the legion of her admirers only grows with time. The activating force behind this ongoing phenomenon is the same in both cases: the powerful legacy of a great singer's recordings.

Ponselle's career itself was hardly remarkable for length (two decades), nor was it really an international one. Except for three summer seasons at Covent Garden, a 1924 visit to Havana, and several performances at the 1933 Florence May Music Festival, it transpired entirely in the United States. Nonetheless, she is universally revered. For Tullio Serafin, she was one of only three "vocal miracles" in his lifetime (Caruso and Ruffo were the others). When Maria Callas made her Covent Garden debut (as Norma, 1952), Ernest Newman's astute summation was, "She's wonderful, but she is not a Ponselle."

The remarkable quality of her instrument allowed Ponselle to break every rule that existed for making an operatic career when she began. "Nobody taught me to sing," she said. "I was one of those fortunate few just 'born to sing'." American by birth (to Neapolitan immigrant parents), she was nonetheless an Italian singer in every respect. After a not exceptional amount of private study and coaching and a moderate accumulation of experience on the vaudeville stage, partnered by her older sister Carmela (also possessor of an exceptional voice), Ponselle sang in opera for the first time anywhere at the Metropolitan Opera. She was only twenty-one and made immediate history not only for the glory of her vocalism but for coming in as Leonora in the company premiere of Verdi's *La forza del destino* opposite Caruso (15 November 1918) without previous experience in anything approaching the demands of such an undertaking, let alone the then prerequisite apprenticeship in European opera houses. "Her voice disclosed a tonal beauty such as has not been surpassed by another soprano within memory. It is a big, luscious voice with a texture like a piece of velvet." Pierre Key's words presaged what would become the standard reaction to a voice darker, warmer, rounder, and richer than that of any recorded soprano predecessor, contemporary, or successor, whatever such other artists' manifest virtues.

With that voice, Ponselle was much more an instinctive than a calculated technician, and had from the beginning an inordinate fear where the top range was concerned. Moreover, as a performer she was beset by an excessive anxiety about getting on the stage at all, and this never abated. Set against these inseparable insecurities, which contributed not only to a vibrant dramatic temperament but also to a tendency toward emotional unreliability, was her devotion to work and study, her fanatical insistence on absolutely complete musical preparation. She demonstrated steady and admirable growth, maturing from the callow debutante with the golden voice into an artist for whom the Metropolitan Opera exhumed

Rosa Ponselle as Leonora in *La forza del destino*

works long "dead." Most notable of these were *La vestale* and *Norma,* the revivals of which (in 1925 and 1927, respectively) have entered the realm of operatic legend.

The preservation on discs of the soprano's characteristic sound in such music, allied with her noble delivery, reposed legato, neatly articulated fioritura, and a trill quite exceptional for so large an instrument, has created not only a personal monument but a touchstone for the measurement of sheer beauty of voice. Commentary by those professional listeners who were of long experience when Ponselle was a beginner and who found her wanting, vocally and musically, must be taken somewhat on faith. If anyone before her possessed anything close to a timbre of such nurturing immediacy, the extant recording equipment was too primitive to do it justice, though one *can* discern more rarefied stylistic accomplishment, purer vowels, and more highly placed, radiant tone quality in certain older sopranos. No matter. Ponselle, just by having the voice she had and using it as eloquently as she did, superseded all previous models and became herself the one that female singers, from coloraturas to contraltos, want to sound like. Ponselle is the archetypal "modern" soprano, whose sound is a universal ideal, whose style and manner are broad and general enough (but not in any sense careless or unconscientious) not to reflect in some limiting or archaic way the era in which she herself performed. She is uniquely the Soprano for all Seasons.

She retired early, or so it seemed at least from the standpoint of chronological age. But by the mid-1930s, high notes that had felt precarious to her all along for the first time began to sound that way to the astute listener as well. For both that reason and what she felt to be a real temperamental affinity, Ponselle took on the title role of *Carmen.* There are no two opinions alike about this assumption (some said presumption) on her part; it was controversial from the start and remained so. When, in 1937, general manager Edward Johnson wanted her to return to Norma—in what turned out to be her last two seasons at the Metropolitan Opera she had sung only Carmen and Santuzza—Ponselle balked. She asked for a revival of *Adriana Lecouvreur* instead, and Johnson refused. Negotiations stalled and, over time, separation undramatically became divorce. Ponselle never appeared again at the Metropolitan Opera or anywhere else in an operatic role.

The quality of her sound was unaltered and retained its power to enthrall for two decades after her final appearance in opera, as visitors to her Baltimore home and an album recorded in her living room by RCA Victor in 1954 attested. (Numerous private recordings, several from as late as 1977, also exist.) In Aida Favia-Artsay's words, Rosa Ponselle's was "a perfectly phonogenic voice." Because of this fact, virtually everyone who comes to love opera eventually acquires also a special affection and admiration for that voice and for the particularly communicative artistry of its owner.

—Bruce Burroughs

THE POOR SAILOR
   See LE PAUVRE MATELOT

POPP, Lucia.

Soprano. Born 12 November 1939, in Uhorská Veš, Czechoslovakia. Studied at the Bratislava Academy, 1959-63; also studied in Prague, principally with Anna Hrušovska-Prosenková; debut at the Bratislava Opera, 1963; Vienna debut as Barbarina, Theater an der Wien, 1963; joined the Vienna State Opera, 1963, became principal member; appeared frequently at the Salzburg Festivals; Covent Garden debut as Oscar, 1966; Metropolitan Opera debut as the Queen of the Night, 1967; made an Austrian Kammersängerin, 1979.

Publications

About POPP: articles–

Blyth, Alan. "Lucia Popp." *Opera* February (1982).

*   *   *

To properly do justice to Lucia Popp we must really examine three careers, or at least three aspects of one remarkable career. In the beginning she was particularly celebrated for the clarity and freedom of her highest notes, and Popp followed an auspicious debut as the Queen of the Night by singing many of the German roles for coloratura soprano with great success. As her voice developed more bloom and richness, Popp went on to perform most of the soubrette parts in Mozart as well as much of the traditional lyric soprano repertoire. In the last decades, Popp's voice has continued to grow in size and depth, allowing her to take on challenges reserved for more powerful spinto voices. On records she has recently essayed with great success the essentially dramatic soprano part of Elisabeth in Wagner's *Tannhäuser,* and it seems reasonable to expect her stage repertoire to expand along similar lines.

So Popp has come full circle, now singing with equal success the heavier roles in operas whereas she once portrayed lighter heroines. There is a certain sense of balance in this; the great Queen of the Night in *Die Zauberflöte* of the 1960s has become one of the finest Paminas of the next decades, or in *Fledermaus,* as the sparkling Adele has been transformed into a suave, insinuating Rosalinde. Popp has more than mastered the hurdles posed in *Der Rosenkavalier:* an incomparable Sophie has become an equally distinguished Marschallin.

Popp is not the first singer to have made this transition successfully, but she is one of a very small number who have also matured as interpreters, so that the dramatic roles suit her today as well as the lyric repertoire did in years past. For the growth of Popp as a singer isn't merely vocal; as her instrument has developed in size and fullness she has also deepened as an artist. Lucia Popp today is not merely an accomplished virtuoso but one of today's important singing-actresses, and at this time—and her career is by no means over—there is every indication that she may join that select company of the century's greatest singers.

If it is Popp's interpretive intelligence that has been the great glory of her mature career, it must be said that she was able to build on a truly extraordinary natural gift, for there have been few if any voices in our time of more flawless quality and greater natural beauty. Popp's instantly recognizable soprano blends the natural creaminess found in the finest German singers with a distinctive Slavic edge, which lends a thrilling glamour to the tone color. From the start she has had the musical skills to deploy the voice like a virtuoso instrumentalist, and in fact her singing—perfect in intonation and sense of attack—often resembles great violin playing. And perhaps this is a bit of a drawback too, for in producing her voice like a string player Popp will sometimes "squeeze" the tone, draining it of all vibrato. Over the years this tendency has become more pronounced: often it is used effectively as a coloristic device, but sometimes Popp's singing can sound mannered and artificial, and very occasionally the sound is uncomfortably constricted and will not ring out freely. It should also be noted that although the basic timbre of Popp's voice has remained largely and amazingly unchanged over the nearly twenty-five years of her career, the highest notes have not come easily for several years now. But these small issues are comparatively insignificant in the face of such glorious singing and superb artistry.

We are fortunate that Popp has been and continues to be a prolific recording artist, and her discography abundantly supports her exalted reputation. Like Elisabeth Schwarzkopf, in whose distinguished steps she seems to follow, Popp is at her best in the operas of Mozart. She has preserved for posterity her Susanna, Despina, Zerlina, and Blondchen, and to each of these soubrette roles she brings not only the requisite bell-like tone but a sense of humor and humanity as well. As the Countess and Pamina, Popp invests her perfectly poised classical line with an almost unbearable poignancy and tonal beauty. And, in one of her first recorded performances, she remains an unbettered Queen of the Night: the staccati gleam with astonishing accuracy, the highest notes are not merely present but are integrated into the body of the voice, and in the role's two short arias Popp paints an unusually detailed and sympathetic character: a wondrous and promising debut for this young singer, and the career that has followed has amply fulfilled the promise.

—David Anthony Fox

PORGY AND BESS.

Composer: George Gershwin.

Librettist: DuBose Heyward (after DuBose and Dorothy Heyward, *Porgy,* with lyrics by Ira Gershwin).

First Performance: New York, Alvin Theater, 10 October 1935.

Roles: Porgy (bass-baritone); Bess (soprano); Sportin' Life (tenor); Crown (baritone); Clara (soprano); Serena (soprano); Maria (contralto); Jake (baritone); Mingo (tenor); Robbins (tenor); Peter (tenor); Frazier (baritone); Annie (mezzo-soprano); Lily (mezzo-soprano); Strawberry Woman (mezzo-soprano); Jim (baritone); Undertaker (baritone); Nelson (tenor); Crab Man (tenor); chorus (SSAATBB).

Publications

articles–

Kolodin, I. "Porgy and Bess: American Opera in the Theatre." *Theatre Arts Monthly* 19 (1935): 853.

Crawford, R. "It ain't necessarily Soul: Gershwin's *Porgy and Bess* as Symbol." *Yearbook for Inter-American Musical Research* 8 (1972): 17.

———. "Gershwin's Reputation: a Note on Porgy and Bess." *Musical Quarterly* 65 (1979): 257.

Shirley, W.D. "Reconciliation on Catfish Row: Bess, Serena, and the Short Score of Porgy and Bess." *Library of Congress Quarterly Journal* 38 (1981).

Starr, L. "Toward a Reevaluation of Gershwin's Porgy and Bess." *American Music* 2 (1984): 25.

Gershwin's enduring fame is based almost entirely on music he wrote for theatrical situations, yet the 1935 *Porgy and Bess* is his only contribution to the operatic literature.

Some would say that *Porgy and Bess* is not an opera, that it is, like Leonard Bernstein's *West Side Story* and recent efforts by Andrew Lloyd Webber, merely a "musical" that aspires to operatic status. That it was first produced not in an opera house but in a Broadway theater is less relevant to this argument than the song-like nature of its segments. *Porgy and Bess* indeed contains a bounty of solid numbers; most of them are easily extractable from the score, and many of them—"Summertime," "It ain't necessarily so," "There's a boat that's leavin' for New York"—have enjoyed dazzling success in the repertoire of pop and jazz performers. It remains, though, that *Porgy and Bess* is a through-composed work whose spotlit songs are connected more or less deftly with recitative and dialogue set over orchestral backdrops, as rich in atmosphere as it is in detail of plot and characterization, a tight-knit music-drama whose momentum flows consistently over its entire three-act course.

The lyrics for the song-like numbers are by Gershwin's brother Ira, but the libretto as a whole is by DuBose Heyward, based on his 1926 play *Porgy* and modeled loosely after real life characters in Heyward's native Charleston, South Carolina.

It is set in the city's Afro-American ghetto neighborhood near the harbor, once called "Cabbage Row" but renamed "Catfish Row" by the playwright. Porgy is a crippled beggar, in love with Bess, but troubled by Bess's involvements with various other members of the community. One of them is a thug named Crown, who loses his hold on Bess only when he is killed by Porgy during a quarrel at the opening of act III. Another, a gambler named Sportin' Life, eventually convinces Bess to accompany him to New York. The opera ends with Porgy, undaunted, hitching up his goat-cart and setting off in pathetic pursuit.

—James Wierzbicki

PORPORA, Nicola Antonio.

Composer. Born 17 August 1686, in Naples. Died 3 March 1768, in Naples. Studied with Gaetano Greco, Matteo Giordano, and Ottavio Campanile at the Conservatorio dei Poveri, beginning 1696; maestro di capella to Philip, Landgrave of Hesse-Darmstadt, 1711-25; taught singing at the conservatories of Sant' Onofrio, 1715-22, 1760-61, Santa Maria di Loreto, 1739-41, 1760-61, in Naples, the Ospedali degli Incurabili, 1726-33, 1737-38, the Ospedali della Pietà, 1742-46, and the

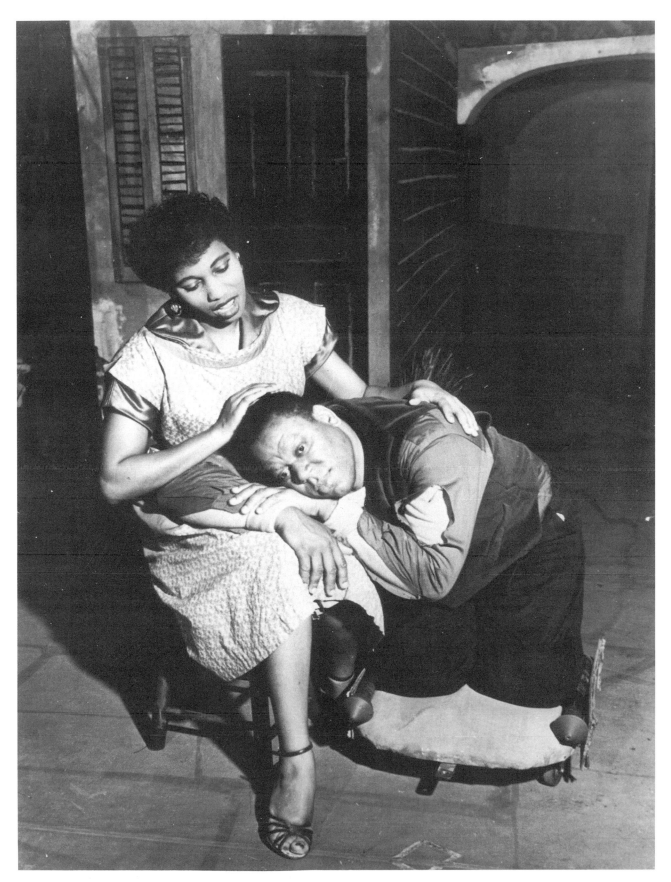

William Warfield and Leontyne Price in a Berlin production of Gershwin's *Porgy and Bess*, 1952

Ospedaletto, 1746-47, in Venice; settled in Venice, 1726; applied for the post of maestro di capella at San Marco in Venice, but did not get it, 1733; composed operas for the Opera of the Nobility in London, 1733-36; in Dresden as a singing teacher to the Electoral Princess, 1747-51; in Vienna, 1751, where Porpora taught composition to Joseph Haydn; returned to Naples, 1758. As a singing teacher, Porpora taught the famous castrati Carlo Broschi (known as Farinelli), Gaetano Majorano (known as Caffarelli), Antonio Uberti, and Salimbeni. He also taught music to the librettist Pietro Metastasio.

Operas

Agrippina, N. Giuvo, Naples, Palazzo Teale, 4 November 1708.
Flavio Ancio Olibrio, Zeno and P. Pariati, Naples, San Bartolomeo, carnival 1711.
Basilio re d'oriente, G.B. Neri?, Naples, Teatro dei Fiorentini, 24 June 1713.
Arianna e Teseo, P. Pariati, Vienna, Hoftheater, 1 October 1714; revised.
Berenice regina d'Egitto (with D. Scarlatti), A. Salvi, Rome, Capranica, carnival 1718.
Temistocle, Zeno, Vienna, Hoftheater, 1 October 1718.
Faramondo, Naples, San Bartolomeo, 19 November 1719.
Eumene, Zeno, Rome, Alibert, carnival 1721.
Adelaide, A. Salvi, Rome, Alibert, carnival 1723.
Amare per regnare, F. Silvani, Naples, San Bartolomeo, 12 December 1723.
Damiro e Pitia, D. Lalli, Munich, 1724.
Semiramide regina dell'Assiria, F. Silvani?, Naples, San Bartolomeo, spring 1724.
Griselda, Zeno?, 1724?.
Didone abbandonata, Metastasio, Reggio Emilia, Pubblico, Ascension 1725.
Silface, Metastasio, Milan, Ducale, 26 December 1725; revised.
La verità nell'inganno, F. Silvani?, Milan, Ducale, carnival 1726.
Meride e Selinute, Zeno, Venice, San Giovanni Grisostomo, carnival 1726.
Imeneo in Atene, S. Stampiglia, Venice, San Samuel, 1726.
Siroe re di Persia, Metastasio, Rome, Teatro delle Dame, carnival 1727.
Ezio, Metastasio, Venice, San Giovanni Grisostomo, fall 1728.
Ermenegildo, Naples, 1729.
Semiramide riconosciuta, Metastasio, Venice, San Giovanni Grisostomo, carnival 1729.
Mitridate, F. Vanstryp, Rome, Capranica, carnival 1730.
Tamerlano, A. Piovene, Turin, Regio, carnival 1730.
Poro, after Metastasio, *Alessandro nell'Indie,* Turin, Regio, carnival 1731.
Annibale, F. Vanstryp, Venice, San Angelo, fall 1731.
Germanico in Germania, N. Coluzzi, Rome, Capranica, carnival 1732.
Issipile, Metastasio, Rome, carnival 1733.
Arianna in Nasso, P. Rolli, London, Lincoln's Inn Fields, 29 December 1733.
Enea nel Lazio, P. Rolli, London, Lincoln's Inn Fields, 11 May 1734.
Polifemo, P. Rolli, London, King's Theatre in the Haymarket, 1 February 1735.
Ifigenia in Aulide, P. Rolli, London, King's Theatre in the Haymarket, 3 May 1735.

Mitridate, Gavardo da Gavardo [=C. Cibber], London, King's Theatre in the Haymarket, 24 January 1736.
Lucio Papirio, G. Boldoni (after A. Salvi), Venice, San Cassiano, carnival 1737.
Rosbale, after C.N. Stampa, *Eumene,* Vencie, San Giovanni Grisostomo, fall 1737.
Carlo il calvo, Rome, Teatro delle Dame, fall 1738.
Il barone di Zampano, P. Trinchera, Naples, Nuovo, spring 1739.
L'amico fedele, G. di Pietro, Naples, Teatro dei Fiorentini, fall 1739.
Il trionfo di Camilla, S. Stampiglia, Naples, San Carlo, 20 January 1740.
Tiridate, after Metastasio, *Zenobia,* Naples, San Carlo, 19 December 1740.
Partenope, Naples, 1742.
La Rosmene, Vienna, 1742.
Statira, F. Silvani, Venice, San Giovanni Grisostomo, carnival 1742.
Temistocle, Metastasio, London, King's Theatre in the Haymarket, 22 February 1743.
Filandro, V. Cassani, *L'incostanza schernita,* Dresden, Hoftheater, 18 July 1747.
Il trionfo di Camilla, G. Lorenzi (after S. Stampiglia), Naples, San Carlo, 30 May 1760.
Giasone (serenata?), Naples, 1742.
Tolomeo re d'Egitto.

Other works: secular cantatas, serenatas, oratorios, sacred operas, motets, instrumental works.

Publications

About PORPORA: books–

Carpani, G. *Le Haydine, ossia lettere sulla vita e sulle opere di G. Haydn.* Milan, 1812.
Fürstenau, M. *Zur Geschichte der Musik und des Theaters am Hofe zu Dresden.* Dresden, 1861-62; 1971.
Fassini, S. *Il melodramma italiano a Londra nella prima metà del settecento.* Turin, 1914.

articles–

Walker, Frank. "A Chronology of the Life and Works of Nicola Porpora." *Italian Studies* 6 (1951): 29.
Prota-Giurleo, U. "Per una esatta giografia di Nicolò Porpora." *La Scala* January 21 (1957).
Robinson, Michael, F. "Porpora's Operas for London, 1733-1736." *Sounding* 2 (1971-72): 57.
Corti, Gino. "Il Teatro della Pergola di Firenze e la stagione d' opera per il Carnevale 1726-1727: lettere di Luca Casimiro degli Albizzi a Vivaldi, Porpora, e altri." *Rivista italiana musicologia* 15 (1980): 182.
———. "How to Demonstrate Virtue: The Case of Porpora's Two Settings of *Mitridate.*" *Studies in Music* [Canada] 7 (1982): 47.

*   *   *

Nicola Antonio Porpora in many ways personified mainstream Italian *opera seria* in the first half of the eighteenth century. His own incessant travels and popularity accompanied the spread of Italian opera throughout Europe—he rarely remained in a city more than three or four years at a time. Both in his operas and in his instruction, a clear focus on vocal virtuosity paralleled a similar rise of embellished castrato singing that surpassed in sheer technique and brilliance anything previously heard. Finally, his musical style mirrored more general changes of the day: slow harmonic rhythmic, static bass lines, melodic generation by motivic repetition, and heavy reliance on formal traditions and performance improvisation. His music is above all else melodic, with expression generally limited to nuances within a clear homophonic texture in sometimes conventional formulas.

Porpora was enrolled at the age of ten in the Conservatorio dei Poveri di Gesù Cristo in Naples, but by the time he was thirteen he no longer had to pay tuition (as one of the school's best students). Before his early thirties he wrote few operas, although his appointments in the courts of the Prince of Hessen-Darmstadt and with the Portuguese ambassador (by 1713) gave him increasing access to other international venues. His reputation in Naples propelled him through several posts, both pedagogical and professional; among his singing pupils was Farinelli, perhaps the greatest of all castrato singers in the eighteenth century, and Caffarelli. The vocal exercises and *solfeggi* he created for his singers show his emphasis on fundamentals (long tones, scales, *mezze di voce,* etc.) and improvisational patterns (interval sequences, trills, etc.). By his late twenties Porpora had established a link with the imperial court in Vienna, which he favored throughout his life; he had several early operas and serenatas performed there.

In the 1720s his fame had spread throughout Italy, and by 1726 he moved his principal residence from Naples to Venice. He stayed there until 1733, enjoying a variety of posts, until he was hired by the Opera of the Nobility in London to compete directly with Handel. His operas there were the most adventuresome of his career, with great attention to inner-voice writing, dramatic effect, counterpoint, and harmonic complexity. *Arianna in Nasso* (1733), the first of his London operas, already displays many of those new traits, as Porpora apparently imitated the style of his famous German rival; typical is the opening of the opera, an aria for Arianna, in which the "B" section of the aria gradually breaks down through dramatic pauses, and finally abandons lyric singing altogether, lapsing into recitative before returning "da capo" to the initial opening. Brief accompanied recitatives occur throughout the score. Some of these traits remained after his return to continental Europe, including the occasional use of French overtures. The close competition of the two rival companies in London eventually proved the undoing of both, and by 1737 Porpora was back in Venice, teaching and composing opera.

Over the next several years he travelled freely between Venice and his former home, Naples, and held various positions in both locations. For four years after 1747 Porpora was in Dresden, where he composed opera at the same court as Hasse, and served as the singing instructor to the Princess Maria Antonia. Through most of the 1750s Porpora again lived in Vienna; among his many pupils there was the young Haydn, who later reported that he learned "the true foundations of composition" from the opera composer. Financial burdens, primarily brought on by the spreading wars in Europe, forced him to return to Naples in 1759, where he remained until his death. His past glory had now faded, and although he was given positions at two conservatories, he was apparently unable to fulfill his duties and retreated into retirement.

—Dale E. Monson

POSTCARD FROM MOROCCO.

Composer: Dominick Argento.

Librettist: J. Donahue.

First Performance: Minneapolis, Center Opera Company, 14 October 1971.

Roles: Lady with Hand-mirror/Operatic Singer (soprano); Lady with Cake Box (soprano); Lady with Hat Box/Foreign Singer (mezzo-soprano); Man with Old Luggage/First Puppet/Operatic Singer (tenor); Man with Paint Box (tenor); Man with Shoe Sample Kit/Second Puppet (baritone); Man with Cornet Case/Puppet Maker (bass).

Postcard from Morocco is Dominick Argento's most frequently performed opera. Accompanying the seven singers is a small ensemble consisting of clarinet (and bass clarinet), saxophone, trombone, violin, viola, bass, guitar piano and violin. The ninety-minute surrealistic fantasy is based on a book by John Donahue, who uses the metaphor of an isolated band of travelers waiting in a train station in Morocco in the year 1914. According to Donahue, "The scene is like a memory, like an old postcard from a foreign land showing the railway station of Morocco or some place, hot and strange, like the interior of a glass-covered pavilion or spa." During their wait, the fears, dreams, and desires of seven people are revealed. According to Raymond Ericson of the *New York Times,* "Their earthly travels are like their lives, and this symbolism is compounded by sideshows put on for their benefit, with puppets, magicians, and singers of romantic songs, who reflect their condition . . . Onstage there are puppets who resemble real people, and sometimes the people behave like puppets." The climax of the opera occurs when each of the individuals refuses the ultimate symbolic self-revelation—the opening of their respective suitcases.

As the opera progresses we hear an on-stage dance band which entertains the waiting travelers with a medley of themes taken from various operas by Wagner, including the "Spinning Song" from the *Flying Dutchman.* Argento's use of this reference is intended as more than just a bit of musical color. It is meant to suggest contemplation of Wagner's hero, who is doomed by supernatural forces to sail forever across the oceans until, by an act of compassion and love from a stranger, the curse is broken and the journey ended. In *Postcard from Morocco,* the journey is not launched by supernatural forces, but by humans who fail to demonstrate charity, pity, love, or compassion for their fellow creatures. According to Argento, "Perhaps this unkindness is self protective or thoughtless and not malicious; perhaps it is the result of curiosity, suspicion, selfishness; or a form of grieving. Whatever the reason, when it does occur, another Dutchman is born and—if only in a swan-drawn boat or in a ship of one's own making—a new voyage begins."

In composing *Postcard from Morocco,* Argento was very much influenced by Mozart's *The Magic Flute.* While Mozart assimilated much of the music of his day from *opera seria, opera buffa,* folk songs, fugues, and other sources, Argento realized a similar effect in his opera by juxtaposing diverse twentieth-century styles such as blues, twelve-tone rows, ragtime, and atonality. As the composer writes, "this emulation of Mozart's opera doesn't *sound* like Mozart but the *procedure* and the *attitude* are certainly borrowed from him and the reason must be abundantly evident: despite the exotic trappings of *Postcard,* it too belongs to no specific time, people or place."

—Roger E. Foltz

LE POSTILLON DE LONGJUMEAU [The Coachman of Longjumeau].

Composer: Adolphe Adam.

Librettists: Adolphe de Leuven and L.L. Thérie Brunswick.

First Performance: Paris, Opéra-Comique, 13 October 1836.

Cast: Chappelou/St Phar (tenor); Bijou/Alcindor (bass); Marquis de Corcy (tenor); Madeleine/Madame de Latour (soprano); Rose (soprano); Bourdon (chorus member); chorus (SATTB).

*   *   *

Le postillon de Longjumeau, a light opera whose novelties include the cracking of a coachman's whip and the vocal imitation of a coachman's horn during the key song of the opera, features the coachman Chappelou as the principal character. On top of his transportation profession, Chappelou is also a fine but undiscovered singer. On his wedding night, Chappelou sings to his guests, and one of the listeners, the Marquis de Corcy, Director of the Paris Opéra, offers Chappelou a singing job in Paris. Unfortunately, there is a catch: Chappelou has to depart immediately, leaving behind his new bride Madeleine. Chappelou chooses career over spouse and in time becomes the principal tenor at the Opéra, under the stage name of St Phar. Later on, his jilted wife, the heiress to a fortune, also goes to the big city under a pseudonym, Madame de Latour. Ten years have passed and Chappelou/St Phar does not recognize Madeleine/Madame de Latour who, posing as a rich noble lady, flirts with

Le postillon de Longjumeau, **wood engraving, 1837**

Chappelou. While Madeleine's original motive for coming to Paris was spite and revenge, she realizes that her love for her husband is still strong. Chappelou in turn falls in love with his wife for a second time. Since he is already married, Chappelou asks his friend Bijou to disguise himself as a priest and "marry" the couple. Madeleine finds out about the mock ceremony and substitutes a real priest. The Marquis de Corcy, who also is infatuated with Madeleine, charges Chappelou with bigamy, but in the end Madeleine discloses her true identity and all turns out well.

Le Postillon de Longjumeau is the best known of Adam's numerous operas, and probably the most competently composed. *Si j'étais roi,* another better-than-average work, to an extent rivals the fame of *Postillon.* But *Postillon* must be regarded as Adam's top operatic production, although by no means a real masterpiece. It is lively, light-hearted, and entertaining, with a fun plot and reasonably good music. In addition, *Postillon* is an important milestone in the development of comic opera and its later derivative, twentieth-century musical comedy. In the total context of opera, it is a relatively minor work. However, in the historical context of light opera and operetta, *Postillon* and Adam are major phenomena.

—William E. Studwell

POULENC, Francis.

Composer. Born 7 January 1899, in Paris. Died 30 January 1963, in Paris. Piano lessons with Ricardo Viñes; served in the French Army, 1918-21; studied composition with Koechlin, 1921-24; accompanist to the baritone Pierre Bernac, 1935; commissioned by Diaghilev to write for the Ballets Russes. Poulenc was one of "Les Six" that included Auric, Durey, Honegger, Milhaud, and Tailleferre.

Operas

Les mamelles de Tirésias, Poulenc (after Guillaume Apollinaire), 1944, Paris, Opéra-Comique, 3 June 1947.
Dialogues des Carmélites, Poulenc (after Georges Bernanos), 1953-56, Milan, Teatro alla Scala, 26 January 1957.
La voix humaine, Poulenc (after Jean Cocteau), 1958, Paris, Opéra-Comique, 6 February 1959.

Other works: ballets, orchestral works, chamber music, sacred and secular vocal works, piano pieces.

Publications

By POULENC: books–

Francis Poulenc: entretiens avec Claude Rostand. Paris, 1954.
Emmanuel Chabrier. Paris, 1961; English translation by Cynthia Jolly, London, 1981.
Audel, S., ed. *Moi et mes amis.* Paris, 1963; English translation by James Harding as *My Friends and Myself,* London, 1978.

Journal de mes mélodies. Paris, 1964; English translation as
    Diary of My Songs, London, 1985.
Wendel, Hélène de, ed. *Correspondance 1915-1963.* Paris,
    1967.
Journal de vacances. Boulogne, 1979.

articles–

"A propos de Mavre." *Feuilles libres* June-July (1932).
"Eloge de la banalité." *Presence* no. 3 (1935): 24.
"Mes maîtres et mes amis." *Conferencia* no. 21 (1935): 521.
"Igor Stravinsky." *Information musicale* 3 January
    (1941): 195.
"Le coeur de Maurice Ravel." *Nouvelle revue française* no.
    323 (1941): 237.
"Centenaire de Chabrier." *Nouvelle revue française* no. 329
    (1941): 110.
"A propos d' un ballet." *Comoedia* 29 August (1942).
"La leçon de Claude Debussy." In *Catalogue de l' exposition
    Claude Debussy,* edited by A. Martin, p. xii. Paris, 1942.
"Sur deux premières auditions." *Comoedia* 19 June (1943): 1,
    5.
"Le Musicien et le Sorcier." *Lettres françaises* 5 May (1945).
"Francis Poulenc on His Ballets." *Ballet* 2 no. 4 (1946): 57.
"Un nouveau musicien: Anton Heiller." *Contrepoints* no. 4
    (1946): 60.
"Oeuvres récentes de Darius Milhaud." *Contrepoints* no. 1
    (1946): 59.
"A propos des Mamelles de Tirésias." *Opera* 28 (1947).
"Mes mélodies et leurs poètes." *Les annales* (1947): 507.
"Rêverie monégasque." *Opéra/Revue* 22 January (1947).
"Tribute to Christian Berard." *Ballet* April (1949): 30.
Article in "Opera Forum." *Music Today* (1949): 137.
"Extrait d' un journal de voyage aux USA." *Table ronde* no.
    30 (1950): 66.
"La musique de piano d' Erik Satie." *La revue musicale* no.
    214 (1952): 23.
"La musique de piano de Prokofieff." *Musique russe* 2
    (1953): 269.
"Souvenirs à propos de la musique de scène d' Intermezzo de
    Jean Giraudoux." In *Jean Giraudoux et 'Pour Lucrèce'.*
    Paris, 1953.
"Souvenirs sur Jean Giraudoux." *Samedi soir* 5 November
    (1953).
"Hommage à Béla Bartók." *La revue musicale* no. 224
    (1955): 18.
"Lorsque je suis mélancolique." *Mercure de France* 1 January
    (1956): 72.
"Inventur der modernen französischen Musik." *Melos* 23
    (1956): 35.
Preface to Laplane, G. *Albéniz: sa vie, son oeuvre.* Paris, 1956.
"Comment j'ai composé les *Dialogues des Carmélites.*" In
    Opéra de Paris no. 14 (1957): 15.
"La musique et les Ballets Russes de Serge Diaghilev." In
    Histoire de la musique, edited by Rolland Manuel, 985.
    Paris, 1960.
"Opera in the Cinema Era." *Opera* 12 (1961): 11.
"A propos d'une lettre d'Arthur Honegger." *Schweizerische
    Musikzeitung/Revue musicale suisse* 102 (1962): 160.
"Hommage à Benjamin Britten." In *Tribute to Benjamin
    Britten on his Fiftieth Birthday,* 13. London, 1963.

interviews–

"Entretien avec Francis Poulenc." *Guide du concert* April-
    May (1929).

"Francis Poulenc on his Ballets." *Ballet* September
    (1946): 57.

About POULENC: books–

Rostand, C. *La musique française contemporaine.* Paris, 1952.
Hell, Henri. *Francis Poulenc, musicien français.* Paris, 1958;
    1978; English translation as *Francis Poulenc,* London,
    1959.
Roy, Jean. *Francis Poulenc: L'homme et son oeuvre.* Paris,
    1964.
*Catalogue de l' exposition à Tours: Georges Bernanos, Francis
    Poulenc et les "Dialogues des Carmélites".* Paris, 1970.
Bernanos, Georges. *Francis Poulenc et les "Dialogues des
    Carmélites".* Paris, 1970.
Medvedeva, I. *Francis Pulank.* Moscow, 1970.
Bernac, Pierre. *Francis Poulenc.* Paris, 1977; English transla-
    tion, 1977.
Guarracino, Georges. *Jean Cocteau, magicien du spectacle.*
    Marseille, 1983.
Daniel, Keith W. *Francis Poulenc: his Artistic Development
    and Musical Style.* Ann Arbor, 1989.

articles–

Lockspeiser, E. "Francis Poulenc and Modern French Po-
    ets." *Monthly Musical Record* 70 (1940): 29.
La Maestre, André Espiau de. "Francis Poulenc und seine
    Bernanos-Oper." *Österreichische Musikzeitschrift* 14
    (1959).
Lockspeiser, Edward. "An Introduction to Poulenc's *La voix
    humaine.*" *Opera* August (1960).
Bellas, J. "Les mamelles de Tirésias en habit d' Arlequin."
    Guillaume Apollinaire 4 (1965): 30.
Kestner, Joseph. "The Scaffold of Honor: the Strength to
    Conquer Fear Figures as a Central Theme in the Carmelite
    Dialogues of Bernanos and Poulenc." *Opera News* 45
    (1981): 12.
Avant-scène opéra 52 (1983) [*Dialogues des Carmélites* and
    La voix humaine issue].

*   *   *

The music of Francis Poulenc presents few challenges, either
to the critic or to the casual listener, for, though he continued
writing well into the avant-garde period, his style remained
resolutely tonal and accessible throughout his career. Despite
an active interest in serialism and electronic music, he eschewed both, preferring to remain in the neo-classic and neo-
romantic realms that had served him during his formative
years (1916-1936). Poulenc reveled in eclecticism, borrowing
unashamedly from Stravinsky, Debussy, Verdi, and Parisian
music hall composers, and seeking stimulation from the parallel worlds of painting and poetry.

Poulenc launched his career with a *succès de scandale* of
the kind dreamed about by every young composer, when his
Rapsodie nègre outraged wartime audiences in December of
1917. He was soon grouped with five other young, audacious
composers—Darius Milhaud, Arthur Honegger, Georges
Auric, Germaine Tailleferre, and Louis Durey—under the
collective name "The Six," a title bestowed upon them by an
obscure critic who compared them to "The Russian Five."
The rhetoric surrounding each of their concerts, and their
association with Erik Satie and Jean Cocteau, did much to
launch successful careers for four of the six.

In 1958, Poulenc wrote to his friend and collaborator of more than twenty years, singer Pierre Bernac, saying: "I am decidedly a man of the theater." Though he was often guilty of hyperbole when speaking of his loves and pursuits, he was not exaggerating in this statement. His enthusiasm undoubtedly sprang from the fact that he was in the midst of composing his third, and final, opera, *La voix humaine,* which also turned out to be his last stage work. By that time, in addition to three operas, he also had to his credit three ballets, nine of the ten sets of incidental music he was to compose, music for five films, and minor contributions to three other stage works.

Though Poulenc had the intention of writing an opera early in his career (he toyed with setting Raymond Radiguet's *Paul et Virginie* in the early 1920s), he, like many other composers, was unable to find the "right" libretto. His first opera, *Les mamelles de Tirésias,* was thus not written until the summer of 1944, prompted by a new encounter with the play, which Guillaume Apollinaire had written in 1917. The two-act *opéra-bouffe* enjoyed a lengthy run at the Opéra-Comique and has been performed frequently in the ensuing years; it remains one of Poulenc's most popular works. His two other operas, *Dialogues des Carmélites* and *La voix humaine,* were both written in the 1950s, his last full decade of composition.

If *Mamelles* and *Dialogues* represent throwbacks to the comic and serious operatic traditions of the nineteenth century, the former suggesting Offenbach or Chabrier and the latter deriving from Verdi, Moussorgsky and Debussy (to whom it was dedicated), then *La voix* falls into the twentieth-century tradition of shorter, more intense operatic monodramas, which began with *Erwartung.* All three are essentially seamless operas, with the predominant vocal style occupying a middle ground between accompanied recitative and lyric aria, though there are obvious "tunes" or "numbers" in *Mamelles,* and much of the vocal line in *La voix* is subdued, narrow, almost chant-like, with repeated notes abounding. In general, Poulenc treated the texts carefully in his operas, but allowed himself some freedom and lighthearted fun with prosody in *Mamelles.* A further characteristic which sets *Mamelles* apart from the others is in the use of the orchestra, for it is strictly accompanimental, with an occasional coloristic effect, in the *opéra-bouffe,* whereas it is called upon to enhance the drama, by setting or deepening a mood, or by providing unifying musical motives (often leading motives in *Dialogues*), in the two dramas.

Poulenc's skill as a prosodist (few twentieth-century composers have set the poetry of their time more successfully) and composer of solo songs served him well in his operas. *La voix* is little more than an extended art song, while the bulk of the vocal writing in the other two operas is for solo voice, or an occasional duet. There are few ensembles and no attempt to construct a scene with them. Choral writing plays a large part in *Mamelles* and *Dialogues:* in the former, the style of writing ranges from mock-serious (a comment on rapid repopulation, thanks to men giving birth, wrapped in Poulenc's sensuous sacred choral style) to boisterous finales for both acts; in the latter, the sensuous sacred style, which had been perfected in such works as the *Mass,* the *Lenten Motets,* and *Figure humaine,* is kept subdued until the exultant, dramatic "Salve Regina" of the final scene.

Poulenc chose his opera texts carefully, selecting three contemporary writers who meant a great deal to him. Guillaume Apollinaire and Jean Cocteau were poets to whom he turned often throughout his career. Though his choice of Apollinaire poems that he set as *mélodies* (art songs) ran the spectrum from whimsical, to obscure, to quite serious, he turned to Apollinaire's World War I farce about repopulation during the darkest days of another war, when the French were facing a similar concern and were once again in need of a lighthearted laugh. Poulenc's choice of *La voix humaine,* of all of Cocteau's plays, suggests that the composer, as he approached the age of sixty, was concerned with more serious matters, such as the anguish of being alone (Poulenc had lived that way his entire life). On the other hand, Georges Bernanos, author of *Dialogues,* spoke to Poulenc's devout, personal view of Roman Catholicism. In each case, he prepared his own libretto, deleting and altering where he felt it was necessary.

Though he was not an innovator—and it increasingly seems that radical innovation is slower to gain acceptance in opera than in other genres—Poulenc will certainly be recognized as an important opera composer for, apart from those like Britten, whose output has been largely in the operatic field, few composers of this century have produced three popular operas that have entered the repertory and that continue to hold musical and dramatic sway on stage.

—Keith W. Daniel

POUNTNEY, David.

Director. Born 10 September 1947, in Oxford. Married: Jane Henderson, 1980; one son, one daughter. Educated at St. John's College Choir School, Cambridge, and St. John's College, M.A.; at Scottish Opera, 1971-, director of productions 1976-80; director of productions, English National Opera, 1982-93; directed world premiere of Glass's *Satyagraha.*

Opera Productions (selected)

Trionfo dell' onore, Cambridge, 1967.
The Kiss, Cambridge, 1969.
The Seven Deadly Sins, Cambridge, 1969.
Die Verurteilung des Lukullus (Dessau), Cambridge, 1970.
The Rake's Progress, Glasgow, Theatre Royal, 1971.
Katya Kabanová, Glasgow, Theatre Royal, 1972.
Jenůfa, Cardiff, New Theatre, 1975.
Macbeth, Edinburgh, 1976.
Toussaint (Blake), London Coliseum, 1977.
The Bartered Bride, Glasgow, Theatre Royal, 1978.
Die Entführung aus dem Serail, Glasgow, Theatre Royal, 1978.
Don Giovanni, Glasgow, Theatre Royal, 1980.
Werther, Amsterdam, 1982.
Queen of Spades, London Coliseum, 1983.
From the House of the Dead (Z mrtvého domu), Cardiff, New Theatre, 1983.
Rusalka, London Coliseum, 1983.
The Midsummer Marriage, London Coliseum, 1985.
Orphée aux enfers, London Coliseum, 1985.
Osud, Bremer, 1986.
Satyagraha, Holland.

Carmen, London Coliseum, 1987.
Lady Macbeth of Mtsensk, London Coliseum, 1987.
The Cunning Little Vixen, London Coliseum, 1988.
Hänsel und Gretel, London Coliseum, 1988.
Falstaff, London Coliseum, 1989.
Christmas Eve, London Coliseum, 1989.
Der fliegende Holländer, Bregenz Festival, 1989.
Doktor Faust, London Coliseum, 1990.
Clarissa, London Coliseum, 1990.
Pelléas et Mélisande, London Coliseum, 1991.
Wozzeck, 1991.
Elektra, Los Angeles Music Center Opera, 1991.

Publications

By POUNTNEY: articles–

Translated libretto *Der fliegende Holländer,* Opera Guide no. 12. New York, 1982.
"Words, Music and Tradition." *Opera* 38/December (1987): 1375.
"The Joy of Rimsky." *Opera* 39/December (1988): 1405.

About POUNTNEY: article–

Rosenthal, Harold. "David Pountney." *Opera* 34/October (1983): 1072.

*   *   *

David Pountney is one of London's most innovative and controversial opera producers. He is also author of numerous translations used in the English-language productions of the English National Opera and other British companies.

Pountney's first operatic production was Scarlatti's *Trionfo dell' onore* for the Cambridge University Opera Society in 1967. While at Cambridge he began his association with Czech opera with Smetana's *The Kiss* (1969), and later produced Weill's *The Seven Deadly Sins* (1969), Dessau's *Die Verurteilung des Lukullus* (1970), and Stravinsky's *The Rake's Progress* (1971).

A controversial staging of *The Rake's Progress* at the Scottish Opera in 1971 (later seen in Holland) marked Pountney's first independent work with that company. He became the Scottish Opera's director of productions in 1976 and held the post until 1980. A specialist in Janáček, Pountney has staged *Katya Kabanová, Jenůfa, The Makropoulos Case, From the House of the Dead, The Cunning Little Vixen,* and *Osud* for the Scottish Opera (shared with the Welsh National Opera); and he has produced *Katya Kabanová* for the Wexford Festival. Also for Scottish Opera he has mounted Wagner's *Die Meistersinger von Nürnberg,* Mozart's *Don Giovanni* and *Die Entführung aus dem Serail,* Smetana's *Bartered Bride,* and Weill's *Street Scene.* For the Edinburgh Festival he has produced Henze's *Elegy for Young Lovers,* Verdi's *Macbeth,* Tchaikovsky's *Eugene Onegin* (which was also seen in Rome), and Rimsky-Korsakov's *The Golden Cockerel.* The Wexford and Perth Festivals saw his production of Smetana's *The Two Widows.*

Pountney has directed productions in several companies throughout Britain, including Holst's *Savitri* and *The Wandering Scholar* at Aldeburgh, and Puccini's *La Rondine* for the Sadler's Wells company. His American debut was at the Houston Opera with a production of Verdi's *Macbeth.* Richard Strauss's *Elektra* is planned there for 1993.

Pountney has also worked in Australia (*Katya Kabanová* in Sydney; Prokofiev's *The Fiery Angel* at the Adelaide Festival), Holland (the world premier of Glass's *Satyagraha,* Puccini's *La fanciulla del West,* Tchaikovsky's *The Queen of Spades,* Prokofiev's *The Gambler*), East Berlin (Gilbert and Sullivan's *Iolanthe*), and at the Bregenz Festival (Wagner's *Der fliegende Holländer*).

Pountney is most closely associated with the English National Opera (ENO), where he has been director of productions since 1982. His first ENO production was David Blake's *Toussaint* in 1977. He has also directed Wagner's *Der fliegende Holländer,* Tchaikovsky's *The Queen of Spades,* Dvořák's *Rusalka,* Wagner's *Die Walküre,* Tippett's *The Midsummer Marriage,* Offenbach's *Orphée aux enfers, Katya Kabanová,* Busoni's *Doktor Faust,* Bizet's *Carmen,* Shostakovich's *Lady Macbeth of Mtsensk,* Humperdinck's *Hänsel und Gretel,* Verdi's *La traviata,* Rimsky-Korsakov's *Christmas Eve,* Verdi's *Falstaff,* Verdi's *Macbeth,* Holloway's *Clarissa,* and Berg's *Wozzeck,* several in his own English translations. In 1991 he announced his resignation, effective in 1993.

In an effort to express the meaning of operas in visual terms, Pountney has increasingly set his productions in times and places at variance with, or unidentifiable as, the composer's original, specified locations. His 1981 production of *La fanciulla del West,* for example, takes place in a Hollywood film studio of 1910 rather than in the California of the Gold Rush, with opening and closing credits, film clips for chase scenes, and stagehands on stage manipulating lights and props. The 1983 *Rusalka* is an adolescent girl's dream in a Victorian nursery, with the Water Sprite a wheelchair-bound grandfather and the Witch a governess; the production reflects the fact that Dvořák composed the opera the year Freud's *Interpretation of Dreams* was published. His 1987 production of Bizet's *Carmen* is updated to the recent past and places the action in an automobile graveyard, with machine-gun-toting urchins, a pink Cadillac for Escamillo, and a giant billboard. *Hänsel and Gretel* live in a housing project in post-World War II London.

One of Pountney's intentions is to remove the elitist character of operatic productions. He stresses the importance of good acting and attempts to clarify the relationships between characters. He relies heavily on visual symbols and seeks visual images that can compete with those of television and cinema in an effort to attract younger audiences. He frequently makes use of flashbacks and dream sequences in his productions—also cinematic techniques.

Pountney's productions with the English National Opera have altered the expectations of the public and the critics of what characterizes an ENO staging. They have contributed to the ENO's reputation as a company that presents an alternative to the traditional stagings of Covent Garden. But whether these productions are stimulating or self-indulgent and distracting is a matter for debate. Audiences expect that a new Pountney staging, especially of a traditional opera, will be greeted with a mixture of cheers and boos, and wildly divergent responses from the critics. Whether or not they are successful at conveying the composers' intentions, Pountney's productions often succeed as brilliant, indelible theatrical experiences.

—Michael Sims

David Pountney's production of *Carmen* for English National Opera, London, 1986 (Sally Burgess as Carmen and John Treleaven as Don José)

POUSSEUR, Henri.

Composer. Born 23 June 1929, in Malmédy, Belgium. Studied at the Liège Conservatory, 1947-52; studied at the Brussels Conservatory, 1952-53; studied composition with Pierre Boulez and André Souris; worked in electronic music studios in Cologne and Milan, where he met Stockhausen and Berio; member of the avant-garde group "Variation" in Liège; taught in Belgian schools, 1950-59; founder and director of Studio de Musique Electronique APELAC in Brussels (now with Centre de Recherches Musicales in Liège); lectured and taught at Darmstadt, 1957-67, Cologne, 1962-68, Basel, 1963-64, and State University of New York at Buffalo, 1966-68; professor, 1970-75, and director, since 1975, of the Liège Conservatory.

Operas

Publishers: Universal, Suvini Zerboni.

Votre Faust (fantaisie variable genre opéra), M. Butor, 1960-67, Milan, Piccola Scala, 15 January 1969.

Other works: orchestral works, chamber and instrumental music, vocal works.

Publications/Writings

By POUSSEUR: books–

Ecrits d'Alban Berg. Monaco, 1956.
Quel enseignement musical pour demain? I: Approches fondamentales. Paris, 1957.
Fragments théoriques I sur la musique expérimentale. Brussels, 1970.
Musique sémantique et société. Paris, 1972.
La musica elettronica. Milan, 1976.

articles–

"A l'écoute d'un dialogue." *Musique en jeu* [Paris] (1971).
"La musique aujourd'hui." *Socialisme* nos. 139, 140, 142 (1977).
"Webern, de la lettre à l'esprit, une autre mutation." *Musica/Realtá* 1 (1980).
"Le sacré et la musique aujourd'hui." In *Les sacrés et les formes.* Paris, 1982.
"L'héritage dans la musique actuelle." *Traces et dires* (1983).

"La Vision de la Rose fait éclorer les Voix de Namur." In *La Vision de Namur à l'intention de la Rose des Voix,* edited by Michel Butor and Pousseur. Yverdon les Bains, 1983.
"Une expérience de musique microtonale." *Interface* 14/nos. 1-2 (1985).
"Musique et identité culturelle." *Harmonique* 2 (1987).

interview–

"Notre Faust is 'Votre Faust.' Conversations with Michel Butor and Henri Pousseur." *The Opera Journal* 1/no. 2 (1968): 13.

unpublished–

Musique sérielle, musique actuelle (fragments théoriques II). 1954-78.

About POUSSEUR: articles–

Wolf, Muriel Hebert. "Votre Faust: Take Your Chance!" *The Opera Journal* 1/no. 2 (1968): 5.
Revue Belge de musicologie (1990) [Pousseur issue].
Musikkonzepte (1990) [Pousseur issue].

*   *   *

Henri Pousseur, in his essay *Musique, sémantique et société,* compares similarities between musical and social structures, and philosophically makes special note of man's search in contemporary works for models to control the growing complexities of life, ultimately anticipating a utopian social organization for mankind. This phenomenological interpretation appears to be a strong motivational factor in his writing throughout his career. Viewed from his compositional development, it may be the basis of a great deal of his aleatoric experimentation, which led to the composition of his first opera, "Fantaisie variable genre opéra," *Votre Faust* ("a variable operatic fantasy," *Your Faust*), 1960-7. One of his most important works, it is a retrospective synthesis of his musical experience and productivity.

The impact of Webern on Pousseur is reflected in his earliest works, and his encounter with Stockhausen resulted in complex experimentation with "total serialism" (*Symphonies,* for 15 instruments, 1954-55). However, after Darmstadt, the focus of his interest has been aleatory procedures and he has played a prominent role in the development of these techniques, as well as in the uses of extra-musical materials and mixed media.

As Pousseur has explained in his lectures, there were three important pieces which led up to his writing *Votre Faust: Rimes,* for different sound sources, 3 orchestral groups, 2-track tape (Studio de Musique, Brussels), 1958-9, premiered at Donaueschingen, 1959; *Répons,* for flute, harp, 2 pianos, violin, cello, 1960, including a new version with actor (Butor), 1965, and a new version as *Répons avec son paysage* (Butor); and *Electre* (after Sophocles), a commissioned television ballet for 2-track tape (Studio de Musique, Brussels), 1960, which Pousseur wrote simultaneously with *Répons.* In relating the history of his opera, the composer speaks of these diverse pieces as solving different problems, which at the same time could be considered convergent. In *Rimes* he considered the question of relating electronic music to instrumental sounds, thus relating all possible sounds—musical and noise elements—to one another. He had already worked out the question in much larger pieces, including better spatial

and formal concepts and a stronger sense of unity than in previous serial music. On the other hand, in *Répons* the seven instrumentalists play in a very mobile form, not at all with a fixed unity. Although this problem had been previously considered with one or two musicians, such a piece involving seven musicians, in which each would have responsibilities in the composing, presented a strong creative challenge. The psycho-game element in the work proved to be very exciting for the musicians, but in its first version it was confusing for the audience to understand what was occurring on stage. In a new version with the addition of an actor, using poetic metaphors to explain to the audience the happenings, the communication exchange was improved. In addition to this effort to include the audience, Pousseur also tried to make the original material more significant and expressive, which consequently made the work less indeterminant and more fixed.

At the same time he was composing the ballet *Electre,* in which the music alone exists and nothing can be changed. The music here is very aggressive and expressive as determined by the text and action of the ballet. When the director of the theater where *Electre* was performed let it be known indirectly that he would like Pousseur to compose an entire evening of music, the timing was auspicious. Pousseur not only had been thinking of writing a large mobile piece for theater involving audience participation, but he had worked through a group of complementary works which anticipated a number of the problems he expected to encounter in his new project. With *Votre Faust* (1960-7) he achieved for the mobile form a higher level of synthesis than previously attempted. The several choices of direction for the work are supposedly determined by audience vote, although in practice are generally predetermined by the performers. As Luciano Berio views it, "In reality, the main personage in *Votre Faust* is the history of music, not out of the old Faustian urge to use the past but out of the desire and need to deal with the realities wherever they may be" (*Dictionary of Contemporary Music,* 1972 ed.). There have been those who have asked Henri Pousseur in the course of a lecture if he is indeed Henri, the protagonist of his opera, to which he has replied, "I am Henri in life! I am a composer but it is not exactly the same situation. *Votre Faust* would be quite a simplification!"

The use of literary quotations by Butor and musical quotations by Pousseur introduced vast and subtle possibilities for several "satellite" pieces: *Miroir de Votre Faust* (1964-65); *Portail de Votre Faust* (1960-66); *Jeu de miroirs de Votre Faust* (1967); *Echos de Votre Faust* (1967); *Ombres de Votre Faust;* and *Fresques de Votre Faust* (collaboration with J.-Y. Bosseur). Most important, the musical quotations projected a new approach to harmonic organization and stimulated Pousseur's further exploitation of harmonic energy previously abandoned by serialism.

Pousseur has published several essays discussing the development of his work towards a "more complex musical expression," as well as problems—artistic and philosophical—of serious concern to him, particularly the role of harmony in the maturation of relationships among men and between nature and man.

—Muriel Hebert Wolf

PRÊTRE, Georges.

Conductor. Born 14 August 1924, in Waziers. Studied at the Douai Conservatory, then at the Paris Conservatory; studied conducting with Cluytens; conducting debut at the Marseilles Opera, 1946; guest conducting engagements; music director of the Opéra-Comique, Paris, 1955-59; conducted at the Lyric Opera of Chicago, 1959-71; conductor, 1959, and music director, 1970-71, at the Paris Opéra; conducted *Samson et Dalila* at the Metropolitan Opera in New York, 1964; principal guest conductor of the Vienna Symphony Orchestra, beginning 1986.

*　　*　　*

Georges Prêtre has been extremely active in international opera life for over three decades. While he has had a certain success in the symphonic repertoire, he is generally considered to be better suited to opera. Although he is French and thus a natural advocate of French opera, he is by no means limited to works in that language; he has done much in the German and Italian repertoires. Two superb recordings that display his gifts in the latter are both on the RCA label: the *Traviata* starring Montserrat Caballé, a vivid and dramatic reading, and the affecting *Lucia di Lammermoor* with Anna Moffo. Prêtre has also led Régine Crespin in an EMI recital of somewhat unidiomatic Verdi arias, among them a very stately "Ritorna vincitor." In the French repertoire he has conducted much-lauded recital discs of Maria Callas performing a wide selection of French arias—Callas's Carmen is rather light and very Gallic—and Victoria de los Angeles and Nicolai Gedda in a beautiful but overly sentimental interpretation of Massenet's *Werther*. He is a dedicated promoter of the works of Francis Poulenc, having given the premieres of both *La voix humaine* and the *Gloria*. In addition, there are a number of French operas that Prêtre has considered unjustly neglected, among them Rabaud's *Marouf,* Berlioz' *Benvenuto Cellini,* several by Massenet, and Gounod's *Mireille*.

Certain features stand out in many of Prêtre's performances. He has been criticized for letting the grand sweep of the music prevail over a concern for precision. In 1978 a correspondent writing in *Opera* was prompted to ponder in frustration why the Teatro alla Scala in Milan seemed to give every Puccini opera to Prêtre, who, in the reviewer's opinion, did not do the composer justice. Cited was the uneven flow of the music, "with its enthusiasms and sudden pauses," where an "argument between orchestra and stage is always at risk: everybody tends to go his own way." Earlier, in 1975, in writing of a *Don Carlos* led by Prêtre at the Paris Opéra, a critic in *Opera* stated that "if this revival was less successful than it might have been, then the fault lay with Prêtre who actually managed to get the superb chorus to sing off the beat and the orchestra, which the evening before had been in fine form for Jésus Lopez-Cobos in *Trovatore,* to sound hopelessly lackadaisical. Never have so many fingers been waggled in so many directions to so little effort!"

Prêtre, however, has been just as often praised for his emotional manner of music-making, even when it has led to ensemble difficulties. The following was written about his *Samson et Dalila* at La Scala in 1971: "[Prêtre's] . . . personal and passionate conducting brought out every nuance of the score, ranging from barely audible pianissimo to the bacchanalian frenzy of the last-act ballet. Exciting throughout, his approach had the defect of occasionally neglecting the singers—rushing them in some moments and overpowering them

in others." In a difficult French score, Debussy's *Pelléas et Mélisande,* conducted by Prêtre at La Scala in 1973, he "inspired some splendid playing from the Scala orchestra and guided his cast through moments of magic singing," as reported in *Opera.*

—Stephen Willier

PREY, Hermann.

Baritone. Born 11 July 1929, in Berlin. Married: Barbara Pniok, two daughters, one son. Sang with Berlin Mozart Choir as a child; studied with Günter Baum at Berlin Academy for Music 1948-51; also studied with Harry Gottschalk; debut as Moruccio in *Tiefland* at the Hessische Oper, Wiesbaden, 1952; at Hamburg Opera 1953-60 in a number of contemporary operas; debuts at the Vienna State Opera, 1957, the Bavarian State Opera, Munich, 1957, and the Salzburg Festival, 1959; Metropolitan Opera debut as Wolfram von Eschenbach in *Tannhäuser,* 1960; Bayreuth debut in same role, 1965; Covent Garden debut as Figaro in *Il barbiere di Siviglia,* 1973; directorial debut *Le nozze di Figaro,* Salzburg, 1988. Prominent Lieder singer.

Publications

By PREY: book–

with Robert D. Abraham. *Premierenfieber.* London, 1986. Translated into English by Andrew Shackleton as *First Night Fever: The Memoirs of Hermann Prey,* New York, 1986.

About PREY: articles–

Fabian, Imre. "Zeitlos—im barocken Rahmen." *Opernwelt* 20/5 (1979): 16.
von Lewinski, W.E. "Das Interview" *Opernwelt* 20/6 (1979): 24.
Honolka, K. "Krise in Hohenems: macht Herman Prey weiter?" *Opernwelt* 20/8 (1979): 26.
Profile. *San Francisco Opera Magazine* 4/Fall (1982): 1959.
Meider, H. "Gespräch mit Kammersänger Hermann Prey." *Oper und Konzert* 31/June (1988): 32.
Van Tassell, E. "An Interview with Hermann Prey." *Fanfare* 13/1 (1989): 502.

*　　*　　*

Although most noted as a distinctive interpreter of German Lieder, the baritone Hermann Prey has also had an extensive and illustrious operatic career. In his native Germany he is also known as a comedian, an operetta singer, and a popular television personality. In opera he has sung an astonishingly wide repertoire ranging from Monteverdi and his contemporaries, Telemann, Bach, Mozart, Rossini, to Wagner and Alban Berg. Even though most of his extensive recording career has been devoted to Lieder (most of these recordings are unfortunately currently unavailable) rather than major operatic roles, Prey has made quite a few opera and oratorio recordings, a number of them of rather unusual works. These include Cavalieri's *La rappresentazione di anima e di corpo* with Troyanos, Zylis-Gara, and Adam; C.P.E. Bach's *Israel in Egypt* with Geszty and Häfliger; Schubert's *Alfonso und Estrella*, an EMI recording with Mathis, Schreier, and Fischer-Dieskau, which sounds like a *Liederabend;* Weber's *Die drei Pintos* (completed by Gustav Mahler) with Popp and Hollweg; a true classic of the gramophone, EMI's monaural version of Cornelius' *Der Barbier von Bagdad* with Schwarzkopf and Gedda, conducted by Leinsdorf; Weinberger's *Schwanda the Bagpiper* from 1981 in German translation with Popp and Jerusalem, conducted by Heinz Wallberg; Humperdinck's *Königskinder,* an opera even more Wagnerian than his *Hänsel und Gretel,* with Donath, Dallapozza, and Ridderbusch and Korngold's *Die tote Stadt* on RCA Victor with Neblett and Kollo, conducted by Leinsdorf.

In the more standard repertoire he has recorded most of the major Mozart baritone roles: Figaro in *Le nozze di Figaro* with Böhm in 1967 (although Prey normally performed Count Almaviva on the stage); Guglielmo in Böhm's third recording of *Così fan tutte* from 1984, and a fine Papageno in *Die Zauberflöte* with Solti conducting. Prey has also recorded the role of Figaro in Rossini's *Il barbiere di Siviglia* conducted by Abbado, but in this role his coloratura is somewhat inelegant.

Prey was born in Berlin in 1929 and sang in the Berlin Mozart Choir as a boy. In 1951 he won a singing competition sponsored by the Hesse State Radio and made his stage debut at the Wiesbaden State Theater in 1952. The next year he began working with Günther Rennert at the Hamburg State Opera. Various debuts followed: in 1957 at both the Bavarian State Opera in Munich and at the Vienna State Opera; in 1960 at the Metropolitan Opera as Wolfram von Eschenbach in Wagner's *Tannhäuser;* in the same role (one of his best) in 1965 at Bayreuth. Since 1959 Prey has been a regular at the Salzburg Festival, singing Rossini's Figaro and Mozart's Guglielmo and Papageno. His Covent Garden debut came in 1973 as Figaro in *Il barbiere.* As a young singer Prey sang several Italian roles in German, such as the Count di Luna in Verdi's *Il trovatore,* Don Carlo in *La forza del destino,* and the Marquis of Posa in Verdi's *Don Carlos.* His later concentration on the German roles include five parts in three Strauss operas: Arlecchino and the Musikmeister in *Ariadne auf Naxos,* Storch in *Intermezzo,* and Olivier and the count from *Capriccio.* Of the Wagnerian roles, in addition to Wolfram he has also made a great success of performing Beckmesser. In this role his interpretation runs counter to the traditional one. Prey considers Beckmesser a gentleman, an intellectual, a respectable town clerk whose tragedy comes from falling in love with Eva. Moreover, he really sings the role, paying special care to the coloratura demands. Prey refers to Beckmesser as "one of two peak achievements of my career," the other being his portrayal of Papageno. Other endeavors undertaken by Prey include Eisenstein in *Die Fledermaus* and works by Henze and other modern composers. He also recorded early on the role of Escamillo in German with Christa Ludwig as Carmen. According to Rodney Milnes, Prey's Escamillo has "charm in abundance and more edge to the voice than we hear from him nowadays."

As his career progressed Prey has been criticized for a tendency to droop with the voice, presumably in an effort to sound expressive. His instrument is naturally a beautiful one, more satisfying in its purely tonal resources and command of legato than his older contemporary, Dietrich Fischer-Dieskau. Like Fischer-Dieskau, Prey has a tendency to perform, in Lieder as well as opera, in a somewhat affected manner, overloading the music with a too emphatic expression. He will not often enough sing a simple line as do the baritones Willi Domgraf-Fassbänder or Gerhard Hüsch, and

from this point of view his singing can sometimes fail to satisfy a basic requirement. On the positive side, much of Prey's artistry is based on spontaneity and immediacy. Unlike Fischer-Dieskau, who has a much more "set" interpretation of a song cycle such as Schubert's *Die schöne Müllerin,* Prey's performance will often depend on his own particular mood and the response from the audience.

—Stephen A. Willier

PRICE, Leontyne.

Soprano. Born 10 February 1927, in Laurel, Mississippi. Married: William Warfield in 1952; divorced in 1973. Studied at Juilliard School of Music with Florence Page Kimball and Frederic Cohen; sang in Virgil Thomson's *Four Saints in Three Acts,* 1952; sang in Gershwin's *Porgy and Bess* in the United States and in Europe, 1952-54; premiered Barber's *Prayers of Kierkegaard* in Boston, 1954; television debut as Tosca, 1955; Vienna debut as Aida, 1958; London debut as Aida, 1958; Teatro alla Scala debut as Aida, 1959; Metropolitan Opera debut as Leonora in *Il trovatore,* 1961; premiered Barber's *Anthony and Cleopatra,* 1966. Received Lifetime Achievement award from the National Academy of Recorded Arts and Sciences, 1989.

Publications

About PRICE: articles–

Blyth, A. "Leontyne Price Talks." *Gramophone* 49 (1971): 303.
Cliburn, V. and R. Mohr, "In praise of Leontyne." *Opera News* 46 (1982): 8.
Corelli, F. "In praise of Leontyne." *Opera News* 46 (1982): 10.
Koelker, J. "Rintornao vincitrice." *San Francisco Opera Magazine* 2 (1984): 8.
"Spotlight: Leontyne Price a farewell to greatness." *Opera Digest* 5/2 (1985): 1.
Jacobson, R. "Collard Greens and Caviar." *Opera News* 50 (1985): 18.

* * *

Leontyne Price is the first American-born black prima donna in opera history. Although she is at times hesitant to accept accolades related to her race, her accomplishments helped to eliminate much of the prejudice prominent in opera at the beginning of the twentieth century. It is not surprising that one of her first significant musical impressions came to Leontyne (her name then spelled Leontine) when, at the age of nine, she heard Marian Anderson sing a concert in Jackson, Mississippi. Price, born in Laurel, Mississippi, was encouraged in music by her parents, both singers in the Methodist

Church choir. Her father, a carpenter, and her mother, a midwife, influenced her musical training by providing piano lessons for Leontyne and encouraging her to sing in public school and at church. This family support was essential to Price as she pursued a performing career, her mother serving as a constant inspiration until her death.

Price's parents financed her attendance at the College of Education and Industrial Arts (now Central State College) in Wilberforce, Ohio, where she received a Bachelor of Arts with preparation to teach public school music. In these surroundings she made her solo singing a vital ingredient to her education by performing in the school glee club, participating in as many musical functions as possible, and singing solo performances on the radio, for civic clubs, and in churches.

A teaching vocation slipped into the background for Price, however, when she was offered a full scholarship to the Juilliard School of Music. A long-time family friend from Laurel, Mrs. Elizabeth Chisholm, provided financial aid to meet her additional living expenses. Four years of study with Florence Page Kimball established for Price a secure vocal technique. She was almost magnetically drawn to opera by seeing productions of *Turandot* at New York City Center and *Salome* at the Metropolitan Opera. Her personal introduction to singing opera came first as Nella in *Gianni Schicchi* and then as Mistress Ford in *Falstaff* in productions at Juilliard. Composer-critic Virgil Thomson, hearing her in *Falstaff,* engaged her to appear as Saint Cecilia in a revival on Broadway of his opera *Four Saints in Three Acts.* It was the role of Bess in Breen's production of *Porgy and Bess,* however, that launched first her national and then her international career. After the opera had played in several American metropolitan areas, it settled in the Ziegfeld Theatre in New York for a rather

Leontyne Price as Leonora in *Il trovatore,* **Salzburg Festival, 1977**

lengthy run before being taken throughout Europe under the auspices of the Department of State. William Warfield, who sang the role of Porgy in these performances, became her husband, their marriage lasting legally until 1973, even though the couple separated much earlier.

The enjoyment of singing Bess apparently evoked in Price a desire to continue pleasing listeners with her appealing, quality-filled tone, which critics often describe as *dunkel* (dark). Price seemed unrestricted by registers in her voice, the vocal range forming a unit rather than being segmented.

Premier performances of works by Igor Stravinsky, Lou Harrison, Henri Sauguet, William Killmayer, and John LaMontaine helped to establish her as a singer of contemporary music, but meeting Samuel Barber had a more direct impact on her American career. Barber had begun his *Hermit Songs* in 1953 before he heard Price sing. Those he completed after meeting her were composed for her. In later years, at the pinnacle of her success, Price was chosen to sing the role of Cleopatra in Barber's new opera *Antony and Cleopatra* for the opening of the Metropolitan Opera House at Lincoln Center in 1966.

Beginning in 1955 she accomplished something significant to her career almost annually. That year the National Broadcasting Company Opera, under Peter Herman Adler, cast her in *Tosca,* making her the first black singer to appear in a major operatic role on television. In 1957 she sang her first staged opera in a major house. After debuting as Madame Lidoine in the America premiere of Poulenc's *Dialogues des Carmélites* with the San Francisco Opera, she went on to sing Leonora (*Il trovatore*), Aïda, and both Donna Elvira and Donna Anna (*Don Giovanni*) with that company.

While Samuel Barber assisted her to fame in America, Price had the aid of another musical giant in establishing her career abroad. André Mertens, her personal manager, arranged a brief but significant meeting with Herbert von Karajan during his first tour to the States with the Berlin Philharmonic. Immediately charmed by her voice, Karajan became a springboard for her further success, especially in Europe.

In 1958 Price made her European debut as Aïda at the Vienna State Opera under Karajan. Triumphant performances followed at Covent Garden in London, Verona Arena, Brussels, and Yugoslavia. With her debut at the Teatro alla Scala in Milan, Price became the first black singer to perform a major role in an Italian opera in that house. Performances of Liù (*Turandot*) and Thaïs at Chicago in 1959 gave her further preparation for her debut at the Metropolitan Opera in 1961. Her premiere performance there came as Leonora (*Il trovatore*) in January, quickly followed by performances of Aïda, Donna Anna, Liù and Cio-Cio-San. Even though she was the fifth black singer to sing on the stage in this famous house, she was the first to attain stardom. Her performances, both live and recorded, have not, however, escaped criticism. There are those who fault the quickness of her vibrato, often more noticeable in recordings than in live performances, even though it displays a uniqueness that has been a trademark of her singing. Her failure to execute all the Mozart roles she attempted, especially Fiordiligi (*Così fan tutte*), in the style expected has gathered some disapproval for her interpretations. It has been her Verdi performances, however, that have reached the hallmark of her profession. Reviewers and audiences were eager to praise her singing of these parts, many calling her the greatest Verdi soprano of the century. Her ability to execute the soaring phrases while capturing astonishing, sudden pianissimo throughout the vocal range without losing her delectable tone is a feat not often attained even over the span of an entire career. Luckily, recordings have captured her development as a singer and serve as a chronicle of her vocal artistry.

One of her most significant achievements was that she sang in virtually every major opera house in the world. Except for brief explorations of unsuitable roles, she remained selective in those parts she undertook. This selectivity was a true strength of her entire tenure in opera. Although her performances at the Metropolitan and in opera were somewhat sporadic, she continued her reign as one of America's greatest divas during this century until her retirement from the stage in 1985. Her receipt of numerous national and international awards attests to her preeminence as a singer.

—Rose Mary Owens

PRICE, Margaret.

Soprano. Born 13 April 1941, in Tredegar, Wales. Studied with Charles Kennedy Scott, 1956-60; sang with the Ambrosian Singers, 1960-62; debut as Cherubino in *Le nozze di Figaro,* Welsh National Opera, 1962; Covent Garden debut as Cherubino, 1963; U.S. debut as Pamina in *Die Zauberflöte,* San Francisco Opera, 1969; Metropolitan Opera debut as Desdemona in Verdi's *Otello,* 1985. She was made a Commander of the Order of the British Empire in 1982.

Publications

About PRICE: articles–

"Das Buehne Profil." *Die Buehne* 248 (1979): 13.
Matheopoulos, H. "Here and there: Margaret Price." *Gramophone* 60 (1983): 811.
Blyth, A. "People: Margaret Price." *Opera* 36 (1985): 607.

*   *   *

Margaret Price is one of the finest sopranos of the second half of the twentieth century. She made her professional debut as Cherubino (Mozart's *Le nozze di Figaro*) in 1962, and for the first decade of her career her repertory focused on Mozart; in the 1970s, as her voice matured in richness and size, she expanded her repertory to include nineteenth-century opera, especially Verdi. Price is not slim: her weight has made her reluctant to take on some roles. She could sing Violetta (in Verdi's *La traviata*) and Mimi (in Puccini's *La bohème*) beautifully, from a musical point of view, "but whoever heard of a consumptive my size?" she asked an interviewer in 1985.

As a student Price hoped to become a concert and recital singer; the operatic stage had little attraction for her. She has always moved audiences more with her voice than with her acting or appearance. Price is not an especially lively actress: she lacks the high-energy passion of Callas; nor does comedy come naturally to her. Her stage persona is noble, dignified; as a portrayer of tragic heroines she is unsurpassed.

Among Price's Mozart roles are the Countess (*Le nozze di Figaro*), Constanze (*Die Entführung aus dem Serail*), Pamina (*Die Zauberflöte*) and Fiordiligi (*Così fan tutte*). She has also made a recording of some of Mozart's greatest concert arias, conducted by James Lockhart, in which it is possible to hear some of her most attractive qualities. Hers is a warm, rich voice, yet without the excessive vibrato that mars the singing

of so many twentieth-century operatic voices. In Price's performance of such arias as "Vorrei spiegarvi, oh Dio!" we can admire her extraordinary accuracy of pitch, her lovely legato and the ethereal splendor of her high coloratura.

Some of Price's Mozart performances have left critics searching desperately for ways to describe her adequately; thus Brian Magee (in *Opera*), trying to put into words his reaction to Price's portrayal of Fiordiligi in *Così fan tutte* (Vienna, 1977), described her as "looking and sounding like pears and cream—each of her arias stopped the show." This was not the first time that the image of cream had come up in connection with Price's voice. A critic praised her "full, creamy tone," when she performed Donna Anna (*Don Giovanni*) in Paris in 1974. When she sang the title role of Bellini's *Norma* at Covent Garden in 1987, a critic described her voice as "rich, creamy, even from top to bottom." There is a combination of richness, smoothness and purity in Price's voice that makes critics think of cream when they hear her sing.

Price has won much applause as a singer of Verdi's heroines, most notably Desdemona (a role that she first sang in 1976) and Aida (which she first sang in 1979). In a recording of *Otello* made under Solti in 1977 we can hear the qualities that make her such a successful Desdemona. Her light, perfectly pure high notes sometimes remind us of Teresa Stich-Randall at her best. Her rendition of the Willow Song is memorable: when she sings the word "cantiamo" for the last time her vibratoless tone is of truly angelic beauty.

—John A. Rice

IL PRIGIONIERO [The Prisoner].

Composer: Luigi Dallapiccola.

Librettist: Luigi Dallapiccola (after Villiers de l'Isle Adam and Charles de Coster).

First Performance: Radio Audizioni Italiana, 1 December 1949; stage premiere, Florence, Comunale, 20 May 1950.

Roles: The Mother (soprano); The Prisoner (baritone); The Jailer (tenor); The Grand Inquisitor (tenor); A "Fra Redemptor" (tenor); Two Priests (mute); chorus.

Publications

articles–

Mila, M. "Il prigioniero di Luigi Dallapiccola." *La rassegna musicale* 20 (1950): 303; French translation in *Musique contemporaine* no. 1 (1951): 53.
Pestalozza, L. "Pour l'étranger: Il prigioniero de Dallapiccola au XIII Maggio Musicale Fiorentino." *Il diapason* [Milan] 1 (1950): 22.
Goldman, R.F. "Current Chronicle: New York" [*Il prigioniero*]. *Musical Quarterly* 37 (1951): 405.
Dallapiccola, L. "The Genesis of the Canti di prigionia and Il prigioniero." *Musical Quarterly* 39 (1953): 355.
Rufer, J. "Luigi Dallapiccola: 'Il prigioniero'." In *Oper im XX Jahrhundert,* edited by H. Lindlar, *Musik der Zeit* 6, 56. Bonn, 1954.

D'Amico, F. "Liberazione e prigionia." In *I casi della musica,* 139. Milan, 1962.

Ugolini, G. "Il prigioniero di Luigi Dallapiccola." *La rassegna musicale* 32 (1962): 233.

Dallapiccola, L. "What is the Answer to 'The Prisoner'?" *San Francisco Sunday Chronicle* 2 December (1962): 27, 36.

Kaufmann, H. *Spurlinien* [p. 67ff on *Il prigioniero*]. Vienna, 1969.

Kämper, Dietrich. "Uno sguardo nell' officina: gli schizzi e gli abbozzi del *Prigioniero* di Luigi Dallapiccola." *Nuova rivista musicale italiana* 14 (1980): 227.

*   *   *

Probably the single most formative experience in Dallapiccola's early life was the period of twenty months of internment at Graz between 27 March 1917 and 18 November 1918. The impact, psychologically, aesthetically, politically, of this period sent shock waves reverberating throughout his life and erected a philosophical frame upon which most of his mature music would later hang. *Il prigioniero,* conceived in the darkest days of the Second World War before Mussolini's overthrow, was composed between 1944 and 1948. It is unquestionably the most gripping of all Dallapiccola's operas, due mainly to the complete marriage of music and subject through every bar of the score. Primarily adapted from Villiers de L'Isle-Adam's short story *La torture par l'espérance,* the opera is set in sixteenth-century Spain and tells simply of the final torment of a condemned prisoner tricked into an escape by the jailer who will ultimately lead him to the stake. Dallapiccola equated the Inquisition's terror in Philip II's reign with Hitler's and Mussolini's totalitarian states; in the depiction of the Spanish king as a death's head (as seen in a vision related by the prisoner's mother in the prologue) the contempt for and dread of the latter-day dictators is clearly audible. This makes the hostile reception accorded *Il prigioniero* after its premiere in 1950 all the more ironic: the Catholic Church regarded it as an attack upon itself by virtue of the role of the Inquisition, while the communists assumed that Philip II stood for Stalin. Dallapiccola's choice of Job as his next subject may not, therefore, have been entirely fortuitous.

Musically and dramatically, *Il prigioniero* is exceptional among Dallapiccola's stage works. It is by far the best known and most often performed; it is the only one to have been commercially recorded; it is also the shortest. *Ulisse,* undoubtedly the composer's magnum opus, is the work the majority of his post-War music led towards, while in *Job* his use of dodecaphony became more thorough-going and consistent, but *Il prigioniero* has a compositional integrity and simple theatricality that the others lack. Allied to its brevity (under fifty minutes in performance) these elements were forged into one of the finest and most powerful of twentieth-century operas.

Dallapiccola's searing orchestration is one of the most remarkable aspects of the score, not least in the restraint and delicacy of much of the writing, as can be heard right from the start. Gone are the chamber textures and counterpoint that gently opened *Volo di notte;* instead a dissonant three-chord motif (recurring later on at crucial moments) is unleashed without warning, creating a scarcely bearable tension for the mother's long declamation and vision of Philip II in the prologue. When the prisoner later attempts his escape through the labyrinthine corridors of his prison, the suspense is underlined by the spare instrumentation, one prominent feature of which is the use of the vibraphone. The chorus forms an additional range of colors to the orchestra; there is no direct role for them (unlike in *Volo di notte* and *Ulisse*), but their two intermezzi form important lynchpins in the musical development, coming between the prologue and first scene, and immediately prior to the prisoner's Alleluias of relief at his apparent escape. The deployment of first a chamber chorus and later the full group through the opera's final pages provides a chilling backdrop to the dénouement: the fuller, glowing textures of voices intoning a Latin hymn is in almost horrific contrast to the victim's sudden awareness of his torment and imminent execution.

Il prigioniero closes with a question: "La libertà?" uttered in disbelief by the prisoner as he is led away. No hope remains for him: the uneasy acceptance of Rivière is impossible here in the implacability of the prisoner's fate. No succor would be found, despite an artificial glimmer at the end of *Job,* until the final bars of *Ulisse,* where the wanderer snatches a revelation of peace quite unlooked for. In 1948, however, the memory of recent pain and horror was too fresh for such redemption.

—Guy Rickards

PRINCE, Harold.

Director and producer. Born 30 January 1928, in New York City. Married: Judith Chaplin, 26 October 1962. Two children, Charles and Daisy. Earned A.B. at University of Pennsylvania, 1948; began career as stage manager with Robert E. Griffith, then worked with and studied under George Abbott; co-produced (with Griffith) his first musical comedy, *The Pajama Game,* in 1954; in 1959 co-produced *Fiorello!,* which won a Pulitzer Prize in 1961; directed his first opera, Josef Tal's *Ashmedai,* in 1976; continued to produce and direct both musicals and operas, as well as several pieces (such as Bernstein's *Candide* and Sondheim's *Sweeney Todd*) that fuse the two genres; president, League of New York Theaters, 1964-65; in 1983 became president of the National Institute for Music Theatre; winner of sixteen Tony Awards and five New York Drama Critics' Circle Awards.

Opera Productions (selected)

Ashmedai, New York City Opera, 1976.
La fanciulla del West, Chicago Lyric Opera, 1979.
Der Silbersee, New York City Opera, 1980.
Willie Stark, Houston Grand Opera, 1981.
Madama Butterfly, Chicago Lyric Opera, 1982.
Turandot, Vienna Staatsoper, 1983.
Don Giovanni, New York City Opera, 1989.
Faust, New York, Metropolitan Opera, 1990.

Publications

By PRINCE: book–

Contradictions: Notes on Twenty-Six Years in the Theatre. New York, 1974.

About PRINCE: books—

Morrden, Ethan. *Better Foot Forward: The History of the American Musical Theater.* New York, 1976.
_____. *Broadway Babies: The People Who Made the American Musical.* New York, 1983.
Aronson, Arnold. *American Set Design.* New York, 1985.
Mast, Gerald. *Can't Help Singin': The American Musical on Stage and Screen.* Woodstock, 1987.
Hirsch, Foster. *Harold Prince and the American Musical Theatre.* Cambridge, 1989.
Ilson, Carol. *Harold Prince: from Pajama Game to Phantom of the Opera.* Ann Arbor, 1989.

articles—

"The New York Harold" (interview). In *Theatre One.* New York, 1969.
Saal, Hubert. "How to Play at Hal Prince." *Newsweek* (26 July 1971): 68.
Waterhouse, Robert. "Hal Prince and Boris Aronson Talk to Robert Waterhouse." *Plays and Players* 19/6 (1972): 16.
"On Collaboration between Authors and Directors." *Dramatists Guild Quarterly* 16 (1979): 14.
Corry, John. "Harold Prince: Craft is the Key." *New York Times* (20 January 1980): 1.
Flatow, Sheryl. "Working with Hal." *Opera News* 54/12 (1990): 14.

unpublished—

Huber, Eugene Robert. "Stephen Sondheim and Harold Prince: Collaborative Contributions to the Development of the Modern Concept Musical, 1970-81." Ph.D. dissertation, New York University, 1990.

*   *   *

Director Harold ("Hal") Prince, known primarily for his work on the Broadway stage, has long championed the American musical as a serious art form parallel to the Viennese operetta and the German Singspiel. Although he does not feel that all musicals are appropriate for such treatment, he believes that many of the finest musicals should be performed by both American and international opera companies.

Prince's fame rests primarily on his stagings of such serious Broadway musicals as Leonard Bernstein's *West Side Story,* Andrew Lloyd Webber's *Evita,* and Stephen Sondheim's *A Little Night Music, Pacific Overtures, Company,* and *Sweeney Todd.* In venturing across the murky region that separates these works from certified operas, he has highlighted questions of definition—and has perhaps added even more confusion to the issue (and one may regret that so many true operas remain neglected by the major opera companies).

When Prince was asked by Carol Fox of the Chicago Lyric Opera to stage Puccini's *La fanciulla del West* in 1979, he had directed only one other opera, Josef Tal's *Ashmedai* for the New York City Opera in 1976. Having staged numerous Broadway musicals, Prince did not find the transition to opera difficult, as he sees opera primarily as a theatrical medium. The musicals he had staged, including several of Sondheim's, were already approaching opera; Prince's life-long love of opera may have drawn him to these works. His approach to staging musicals has been to take them seriously, as if they actually were operas.

Prince's *Fanciulla* was marked by careful attention to detail to create the appropriate atmosphere; an example is his placement of foraging bears in the background of one scene. The staging is full of revealing character touches, establishing the identity of each character clearly. His next operatic production—this time a work that straddles the line separating opera and Broadway musical—was the New York City Opera's staging of Kurt Weill's *Der Silbersee,* a 1980 production that interpolated music from other Weill works to provide a continuous score and further blur the distinction between the genres. This was followed by a Houston staging of Carlisle Floyd's *Willie Stark,* another borderline opera, in its world premiere (1981). Prince emphasized the contrast between the problems of the individual characters and those of American society in this production. Bernstein's *Candide*—yet another Broadway orphan—followed at the New York City Opera in 1982. The same year Prince mounted a production of Puccini's *Madama Butterfly* (done in two acts rather than the three of Puccini's revised version) for the Chicago Lyric Opera, a production that drew on the traditions of Japanese Noh theater, with black-clad supernumeraries moving the sets, carrying the flower petals for the Flower Duet, and pulling a long red ribbon from Cio-Cio-San's heart at the moment of her suicide. A production of Puccini's *Turandot* at the Vienna Staatsoper in 1983 followed. In 1989 Prince staged Mozart's *Don Giovanni* for the New York City Opera, a production that was criticized for being ordinary, the implication being that it had too much stale operatic routine and not enough Broadway. His Metropolitan Opera directorial debut came in 1990 with a production of Gounod's *Faust;* he had previously been asked to stage Mascagni's *Il piccolo Marat* for the Met, but the production, originally set for 1979, was canceled. The *Faust* production was not well received by the majority of critics, partly because of their displeasure with the sets and choreography, and partly because they felt that Prince concentrated only on those who were in the spotlight and paid insufficient attention to the actions of whoever was not singing at any given moment.

Prince is primarily interested in the theatrical—rather than the realistic—aspects of opera. He is more concerned with the acting of the principals than with the singing. This emphasis has been made possible by what he sees as an improvement in operatic acting in recent years; yet some singers with wonderful voices are still too static on stage, he believes, and their voices do not sufficiently compensate for their lack of acting ability.

Prince has said that he does not want to stage operas to which he feels he can bring nothing. He will not do something different for its own sake. He is disinclined to make use of updatings, transfers to different locations, and the imposition of directorial "concepts" in his stagings; he feels he occupies a middle ground between tradition and innovation.

—Michael Sims

PRINCE IGOR [Kniaz' Igor'].

Composer: Alexander Borodin (completed by Rimsky-Korsakov, Liadov and Glazunov).

Librettist: Alexander Borodin (after a scenario by V.V. Stasov based on the medieval chronicle *Tale of Igor's Campaign*).

First Performance: St Petersburg, Marinsky, 16 November 1890.

Roles: Yaroslavna (soprano); Konchakovna (contralto); Vladimir (tenor); Prince Igor (baritone); Khan Konchak (bass); Galitsky (bass); Khan Gzak (bass); Ovlour (tenor); Sulka (bass); Eroshka (tenor); Nurse (soprano); Maiden (soprano); chorus (SSAATTTTBBBB).

Publications

book–

Bobeth, Marek. *Borodin und seine Oper "Furst Igor": Geschichte—Analyse—Konsequenzen.* Munich, 1982.

articles–

Abraham, Gerald. "Prince Igor." In *Studies in Russian Music,* 119. London, n.d.
Glazunov, A.K. "Kapiski o redaktsii Knzazya Igorya Borodina" [notes on the editing of *Prince Igor*]. *Russkaya muzikal' nayva gaseta* 3 (1896): 155.
———. "The History of 'Prince Igor'." In *On Russian Music,* 147. London, 1939.
Dmitriyev, A. "K istorii sozdaniya operi A.P. Borodina Knayaz' Igor" [history of the composition of *Prince Igor*]. *Sovetskaya muzyka* no. 11 (1950): 82.
Listova, N.A. "Iz istorii sozdaniya operi *Knyaz' Igor'* A.P. Borodina" [history of the composition of *Prince Igor*]. *Soobsh cheniya Instituta istorii iskusstv* 15 (1959): 36.
Kiselyov, V.A. "Stsenicheskaya istoriya pervoy postanovki Knyazya Igorya" [history of the first performance of *Prince Igor*]. In *Muzikal' noye nasledstvo* 3, edited by M.P. Alexeyev and others, 284. Moscow, 1970.
Vyzgo-Ivanova, Irina and Ivanov-Ehvet, A. "Ešče Raz ob istokah *Knazja Igoria*" [More of the sources of *Prince Igor*]. *Sovetskaya muzyka* 4 (1982): 89.
Lamm, Pavel. "K podlinnomu tekstu *Knjazja Igoria*" [toward an authentic text of *Prince Igor*]. *Sovetskaya muzyka* 12 (1983): 104.
Temirbekova, Alma. "Iz istorii russko—kazahskih muzykal' nyh svjazej" [historical connections between *Prince Igor* and Kayah music]. *Prostor* 1 (1983): 194.

*   *   *

Based primarily on the "Slovo o polku Igoreve," a mysterious and famous (at least to Slavicists) medieval Russian poem, *Kniaz' Igor' (Prince Igor),* Alexander Borodin's only opera, tells the oddly inconclusive tale of the defeat of Prince Igor Sviatoslavich (1151-1202) of Novgorod-Seversk at the hands of the nomadic Polovtsy tribe in 1185. Borodin began *Igor* at the urging of nationalist critic Vladimir Stasov, who prepared the original libretto from the "Slovo" ("The Tale of Igor's Campaign") and early Russian chronicles. Though fragmentary, unwieldy, and dramatically unfocused, the subject offered the composer rich opportunities to draw on his country's history, folk songs, and folk music, and to stress the glories of the Russian past. Stasov believed it "met all the demands of Borodin's talent and artistic nature: broad epic motives, nationalism, variety of characters, passion, drama, the oriental." The subject also conformed with the aesthetic

of the *moguchaia kuchka* ("mighty handful"), whose five members—including Borodin—came together in the 1860s largely in an attempt to build a native Russian operatic repertoire.

If Borodin had followed Stasov's original outline, the opera would surely have benefited. But the part-time composer (and full-time chemist) never even bothered to write an actual libretto. Instead, he produced *Igor* in fits and starts over a period of 18 years, drawing rather haphazardly on Stasov's scenario and on his own research, jumping between acts and scenes as his whims dictated, proceeding on impulse, responding to the spirit, not the details of the Igor story. As a result, when Borodin died in 1887 while attending a costume ball in Russian national dress, the opera remained far from finished. According to Alexander Glazunov, Borodin had completed in piano-vocal score only the Prologue; act I, scene i; and the whole of act IV. He had managed to orchestrate even less: only ten numbers. It fell, therefore, to Glazunov and Nicolai Rimsky-Korsakov (a fellow member of the *kuchka*) to flesh out the remaining sections, relying on the piles of fragments and sketches their colleague left behind. Glazunov restored act III and the Overture, and Rimsky-Korsakov the rest.

The opera opens on the main square of the southern Russian city of Putivl. In the Prologue, Igor and his Christian army prepare to march against the pagan Polovtsy, despite the omen of an eclipse. Yaroslavna, Igor's wife, bids a tearful farewell to her noble husband. In the first scene of act I, Yaroslavna's lascivious brother, Prince Galitsky, egged on by the comic characters Skula and Eroshka (invented by Borodin), stirs up trouble in Igor's absence, threatening to take over the kingdom. In the second, Yaroslavna struggles to defend her husband's throne and the honor of her violated female subjects.

Acts II and III unfold in the exotic Polovtsian encampment, where Igor and his son Vladimir are being held captive after the rout of their Russian forces. Against a background of much "Oriental" choral singing and dancing, the Polovtsian ruler, kindly Khan Konchak, befriends Igor. As act III ends, Igor escapes, but Vladimir stays behind, enchanted by Konchak's daughter Konchakovna, with whom he has fallen in love. (Act III has frequently been cut in performances and recordings, even though its omission robs the narrative of what little sense it makes.) Back in Putivl, act IV opens with one of the opera's most successful and famous arias, Yaroslavna's lament, inspired by the Russian folk tradition of the *plach.* At last, Igor returns to her waiting arms, amidst general rejoicing. The city's fate remains unclear, however, for as the curtain falls, the Polovtsy are approaching. Supported by his valiant and virtuous countrymen, Igor vows to defeat them.

More a collection of colorful scenes than a coherent dramatic whole, the scenario leaves many basic conflicts unresolved. Prince Galitsky plays a central role in act I but disappears thereafter; Vladimir and Konchakovna suddenly vanish after act III. Igor is also absent from the stage for long periods, and emerges as a considerably less dominant and psychologically less compelling character than Tsar Boris in Musorgsky's *Boris Godunov.*

Where Borodin excels, however, is in his use of the chorus, which assumes a dramatic and musical role so important as to become the work's real protagonist. The lengthy patriotic choruses ("*Slava*"—"Glory") of the people *(narod)* of Putivl in the Prologue and act IV; the plaintive songs of the maidens in act I; and the languid celebrations of the Polovtsy in acts

Prince Igor, title page of first edition of full score, Leipzig, 1888

II and III are the heart and soul of *Prince Igor.* The prominence of the choral episodes, which fill the stage with hundreds of colorfully costumed singers and dancers, also contributes to the opera's "Russianness," and sets it apart from those composed by Borodin's European contemporaries.

At the same time, Borodin's writing for the solo voice, unlike Musorgsky's, draws heavily on Italian *bel canto* models. In this and other features, he was following in the footsteps of his Russian predecessor Mikhail Glinka, whose operas *A Life for the Tsar* and *Ruslan and Lyudmila* had combined Russian subject matter and folk tunes with an Italianate style. From Glinka, too, Borodin inherited a fascination with the exotic East. In *Igor,* the scenes set in the Polovtsian encampment grabbed most of the composer's attention and inspiration. Himself the illegitimate son of an elderly Caucasian prince, Borodin had already given evidence of his special affinity for "Oriental" material in "The Steppes of Central Asia" (1880). Significantly, about one-half of the sections of *Igor* which Borodin managed to orchestrate belong to the Polovtsian scenes, including the opera's most celebrated pages: the wild and often-recorded "Polovtsian Dances" which end act II.

Similarly, the characters of the noble Konchak and the seductive, spontaneous Konchakovna receive such vivid musical and dramatic embodiment that Igor and Vladimir—and even the Russian people back in Putivl—almost pale by comparison. Whereas Borodin allows the Polovtsy to be decisive, romantically appealing figures, he portrays the Russians as a fractious, debauched, and querulous bunch of crybabies. Only Yaroslavna, in her act I arioso and her haunting act IV lament, achieves genuine heroic stature. For a supposedly patriotic Russian opera, *Prince Igor* is surprisingly defeatist.

—Harlow Robinson

THE PRISONER
  See IL PRIGIONIERO

PRITCHARD, (Sir) John (Michael).

Conductor. Born 5 February 1921, in London. Died 5 December 1989, in Daly City, California. Studied violin with his father; studied music in Italy; served in the British army during World War II; vocal coach at Glyndebourne, 1947; chorus master and assistant to Fritz Busch at Glyndebourne, 1948; conductor, 1951-63, and music director, 1969-77, at Glyndebourne; principal conductor of the Royal Liverpool Philharmonic, 1957-63; Commander of the Order of the British Empire, 1962; principal conductor of the London Philharmonic, 1962-66; guest conductor with the Pittsburgh Symphony Orchestra, 1963; conducted at the Chicago Lyric Opera, 1969; conducted at the San Francisco Opera, 1970; conducted *Così fan tutte* at the Metropolitan Opera, New York, 25 October 1971; principal conductor of the Cologne Opera, 1978-89; principal guest conductor, 1979, and principal conductor, 1982, of the British Broadcasting Corporation Symphony Orchestra, London; joint music director of the

Opéra National, Brussels, 1981-89; knighted, 1983; first music director of the San Francisco Opera, 1986-89.

The son of a professional violinist, John Pritchard made his name in the operatic world in performances at Glyndebourne, at John Christie's private opera house in Sussex. When he joined the staff there as a vocal coach in 1947, it was in some ways a conservative place, and although it had given the premieres of Britten's *The Rape of Lucretia* and *Albert Herring,* Christie thought the second of these operas "common" because it was in English and set in a shop. Pritchard fitted in better to this scene and style, for he was sophisticated and had studied in Italy, and he showed a quiet competence in his work coaching solo singers and, from 1948, as chorus master. When Fritz Busch's indisposition during a Glyndebourne Festival performance of Mozart's *Don Giovanni* in 1949 presented him with the chance to conduct, he took it firmly; in the 1951 season, Busch again gave him *Don Giovanni* and two other operas by Mozart, and Pritchard's ability attracted wider attention.

Later in his career, Pritchard's cool competence became something of a legend. "Unflappability" was a word sometimes used of him and was meant as a compliment, for he seemed to be able to turn in good, well-prepared opera performances whatever last-minute hitches might occur in a production. On the other hand, he could also seem too "laid back," so that, while things ran smoothly, there could also be a shortage of sheer electricity in his performances. However, in the two seasons following his Covent Garden debut in 1952 in Verdi's *Un ballo in maschera,* he conducted more than eighty performance of eleven operas, and it would be unfair to blame him for the notorious failure of Britten's Coronation opera *Gloriana* in 1953, although we may still wonder whether another conductor might have communicated its qualities more successfully to the gala audience of mostly unmusical dignitaries.

From 1953 Pritchard's skills were rightly in demand on both sides of the Atlantic, but he also kept his loyalty to Glyndebourne, conducting there in every season from 1951 to 1963, when he was appointed "principal conductor and artistic counsellor"; later he was made music director. Apart from this, he worked mostly as a freelance conductor and not always in opera, and he may have felt that concert work (for example with the Liverpool Philharmonic Orchestra, where he gave pioneering concerts of new music) and as a chief conductor of the British Broadcasting Corporation Symphony Orchestra gave him more musical freedom. His commitment to contemporary music made him a natural choice as the first conductor of Tippett's *The Midsummer Marriage* and *King Priam,* and the Glyndebourne production of Henze's *Elegy for Young Lovers.*

Though Britain was Pritchard's early professional base and largely remained so, he had few personal ties to his native land, and later made his home in Monte Carlo. He was never quite a national figure or a star performer in the eyes of the British press and public, though he conducted the last night of the Proms in 1989, and this is perhaps because he did not project a strong individual personality, at least when compared to a Bernstein or Boulez. Another factor may have been his never very robust health. Nevertheless, during three and a half decades he contributed much to the raising of standards in opera house orchestras, and he aided many of the singers with whom he worked. It was generally felt in musical circles that the knighthood which he received toward the end of his life had been well earned, and after his death, following performances of *Idomeneo* in San Francisco, his body was brought to Britain to be buried near Glyndebourne.

—Christopher Headington

PRODIGAL SON
See CHURCH PARABLES

PROKOFIEV, Sergei.

Composer. Born 27 April 1891, in Sontzovka, near Ekaterinoslav, Russia. Died 5 March 1953, in Moscow. Married: the soprano Lina Llubera [=Carolina Codina], 1923 (two sons). Studied with Glière in Moscow; studied composition with Rimsky-Korsakov, Wihtol, and Liadov, piano with Mme Essipova, and conducting with Nicolas Tcherepnin at the St Petersburg Conservatory, graduating 1914; Anton Rubinstein Prize for his First Piano Concerto; first performance of his *Classical Symphony*, 1918; traveled to Siberia, Japan, and then the United States; performed concerts of his music in New York, Chicago, and other American cities; in Paris, 1920, where he composed for Diaghilev's Ballets Russes; Koussevitzky commissioned several works from Prokofiev; in Chicago for the production of his opera, *Love for Three Oranges*, 1921; concertized in Russia, 1927, 1929, 1932; last United States visit, 1938.

Operas

Publishers: Boosey and Hawkes, Editions Russes de Musique, Gutheil, Jürgenson, Muzgiz.

The Giant [*Velikan*]. 1900 [unorchestrated].
On Desert Islands [*Na pustïnnïkh ostrovakh*], 1900-02 [unfinished].
A Feast in the Time of Plague [*Pir vo vremya chumï*], after Pushkin, 1903 [unorchestrated]; revised, 1908-09.
Undina, M. Kilstett (after de la Motte Fouqué), 1904-07.
Maddalena, after M. Lieven, 1911-13 [unfinished]: orchestrated by E. Downes and performed for the British Broadcasting Company, London, 25 March 1979.
The Gambler [*Igrok*], Prokofiev (after Dostoevsky), 1915-17, revised 1927-28, Brussels, Théâtre de la Monnaie, 29 April 1929.
The Love for Three Oranges [*Lyubov'k tryom apel'sinam*], after Gozzi, 1919, Chicago, Auditorium Theater, 30 December 1921.
The Fiery Angel [*Ognennïy angel*], after V. Bryusov, 1919-23, revised, 1926-27, act II concert performance, Paris, 14 June 1928; concert performance, Paris, Champs Elysées, 25 November 1954; staged performance, Venice, La Fenice, 14 September 1955.
Semyon Kotko, V. Katayev, Prokofiev (after Katayev), 1939, Moscow, Stanislavsky, 23 June 1940.
Betrothal in a Monastery [*Obrucheniye v monastïre*], Prokofiev and Myra Mendel'son (after Sheridan), 1940-41, Leningrad, Kirov, 3 November 1946.

Khan Buzay, 1942-[unfinished].
War and Peace [*Voyna i mir*], Prokofiev (after Tolstoy), 1941-43, concert performance Moscow, 16 October 1944; revised, 1946-52; complete performance Moscow, Stanislavsky, 8 November 1957.
The Story of a Real Man [*Povest'o nastoyashchem cheloveke*], Prokofiev and Myra Mendel'son (after B. Polevoy), 1947-48, private concert performance, Leningrad, Kirov, 3 December 1948; staged performance, Moscow, Bol'shoy, 8 October 1960.
Distant Seas [*Dalyokiye morya*], Prokofiev (after V.A. Dïkhovichnïy), 1948- [unfinished].

Other works: incidental music, film scores (including *Alexander Nevsky* for Eisenstein), ballets, orchestral works, chamber music, piano pieces.

Publications/Writings

By PROKOFIEV: books–

Kozlova, M.G., ed. *Avtobiografiya*. Moscow, 1973; 2nd ed., 1982; edited and translated by Francis King as *Prokofiev by Prokofiev: a Composer's Memoir*, London, 1979.
Blok, Vladimir, ed. *Materials, Articles, Interviews* [in English]. Moscow, 1978.
Barenbojm, Lev, and Natum Fišman, compilers. *L.V. Nikolaev. Stat'i i vospominanija sovremennikov. Pis'ma*. Leningrad, 1979.
Detstvo [childhood]. 5th ed., Moscow, 1983.

About PROKOFIEV: books–

Nestyev, Israel V. *Prokofiev: his Musical Life*. New York, 1946; revised edition as *Prokofiev*, Stanford, California, 1960.
Shlifshteyn, S.I., ed. *S.S. Prokof'yev: materialï, dokumentï, vospominaniya* [documents and materials]. Moscow, 1956; 1961; English translation, 1960; 1968; German translation 1965.
Samuel, Claude. *Prokofiev*. Paris, 1960. English translation, London, 1971.
Klimovitsky, A. *Opera Prokof'yeva "Semyon Kotko"*. Moscow, 1961.
Danko, L. *Operï S. Prokof'yeva*. Moscow, 1963.
Hofmann, M.R. *Serge Prokofiev*. Paris, 1963.
Brockhaus, H.A. *Sergej Prokofjew*. Leipzig, 1964.
Hanson, Lawrence and Elizabeth. *Prokofiev: the Prodigal Son*. London, 1964.
Rayment, M. *Prokofiev*. London, 1965.
Seroff, V. *Sergei Prokofiev: a Soviet Tragedy*. New York, 1968.
Moisson-Frank Franckhauser, S. *Serge Prokofiev et les courants esthétiques de son temps*. Paris, 1974.
Robinson, Harlow. *Sergei Prokofiev: a Biography*. London and New York, 1987.
Gutman, David. *Prokofiev*. London, 1990.

articles–

Sabinina, M. " 'Voyna i mir'." *Sovetskaya muzyka* no. 12 (1953).
Bruch, C. " 'Ognennïy angel'v Parizhe." *Sovetskaya muzyka* no. 7 (1955).
Keldïsh, Ya. "Eshcho ob opere 'Voyna i mir' " [*War and Peace*]. *Sovetskaya muzyka* no. 7 (1955).
Mitchell, Donald. "Prokofiev's *Three Oranges*: a Note on its Musical-Dramatic Organization." *Tempo* 41 (1956): 20.

Swarenki, H. "Prokofieff's *The Flaming Angel*." *Tempo* 39 (1956): 16.

Zolotov, A. "Ode to Heroism: 'The Story of a Real Man' at the Bolshoy Theatre." *Current Digest of the Soviet Press* no. 48 (1960).

Renate, J. "Von 'Spieler' zur 'Erzählung von wahren Menschen'." *Musik und Gesellschaft* 11 (1961).

Lloyd-Jones, David. "Prokofiev and the Opera." *Opera* 13 (1962): 513.

Porter, Andrew. "Prokofiev's Early Operas." *Musical Times* 103 (1962): 528.

Sabinina, M. "Ob opere kotoraya ne bïla napisana" [*Khan Buzay*]. *Sovetskaya muzyka* no. 8 (1962).

Polyakova, L. "O poslednem opernom zamïsle S. Prokof'yeva 'Dalekie morya' " [*Distant Seas*]. *Sovetskaya muzyka* no. 3 (1963).

Jefferson, A. "The Angel of Fire." *Music and Musicians* 13 (1965): 32.

Mnatsakanova, E. "Neskol'ko zametok ob opere 'Igrok'." *Muzyka i sovremennost* 3 (1965): 122.

_____. "Prokof'yev i Tolstoy." *Muzyka i sovremennost* 4 (1966).

Pugliese, G. "The Unknown World of Prokofiev's Operas." *High Fidelity* 16 (1966): 44.

Porter, Andrew. "Prokofiev's Late Operas." *Musical Times* 108 (1967): 312.

McAllister, R. "Prokofiev's Early Opera *Maddalena*." *Proceedings of the Royal Musical Association* 96 (1969-70): 137.

_____. "Natural and Supernatural in *The Fiery Angel*." *Musical Times* iii (1970): 785.

_____. "Prokofiev's Tolstoy Epic." *Musical Times* 113 (1972): 851.

Brown, M.H. "Prokofiev's *War and Peace:* a Chronicle." *Musical Quarterly* 63 (1977): 297.

Potapova, Natal'ja. "Contribution to the History of the Second Version of the Opera *Igrok* by Sergej Prokof'ev." In *Vosprosy muzhkal'nogo stilja,* edited by Mark Aranovskij. Leningrad, 1978.

Fedorov, Georgij. "Trinadcat'ih" [sketches and stage directions by Sergej Eisenstein for *War and Peace*]. *Sovetskaya muzyka* 9 (1979): 83.

Halif, Viktorija. *Perepiska S.S. Prokof'eva s L.M. Glagolevoj.* [letters between Prokofiev and Glagolevoj]. In *Pamjatniki kul'tury: novye otkrytija pis'menost', iskusstvo, arheologija. Ezegodnik, 1979,* 227. Leningrad, 1979.

McAllister, R. "Prokofiev's *Maddalena:* A Première." *Musical Times* 120 (1979): 205.

Grzegorzek, Aleksandra. "Recytatyw jako podstawowy element dramaturgii muzycznej w operze Prokofiewa *Wojna i pokój*." *Muzyka* 25 (1980): 75.

Birjukov, Jurij. "Tvorec sovremennoj opery: k 90-letiju so dnja roždenija S.S. Prokof'eva." *Teatral' naja žizn* 8 (1981): 15.

Downes, Edward. "Prokofjews Oper *Maddalena*." *Österreichische Musikzeitschrift* 36 (1981): 577.

Henderson, Robert. "Busoni, Gozzi, Prokofiev, and *The Oranges*." *Opera* May (1982).

Konieczna, Aleksandra. "Postać przestrzeń i czas w finałowym akcie *Gracza* Sergiusza Prokofiewa" [last act of *The Gambler*]. *Muzyka* 28 (1983): 31.

Wierzbicki, James. "*Maddalena,* Prokofiev's Adolescent Opera." *Opera Quarterly* 1 (1983): 17.

Abraham, Gerald. "Dostoevsky in Music." In *Russian and Soviet Music: Essays for Boris Schwarz,* edited by M.H. Brown. Ann Arbor, 1984.

Robinson, Harlow. "Dostoevsky and Opera: Prokofiev's *The Gambler*." *Musical Quarterly* 70 (1984): 96.

unpublished–

McAllister, R. "The Operas of Sergei Prokofiev." Ph. D. dissertation, Cambridge University, 1970.

Robinson, Harlow. "The Operas of Sergei Prokofiev and their Russian Literary Sources." Ph. D. dissertation [Slavic Literature], University of California, Berkeley, 1980.

* * *

French critic Rostislav Hofman may have been guilty of overstatement when he wrote that "musically speaking, Prokofiev's operas have nothing in common." But no one could argue that it is easy to reconcile the vast aesthetic differences between the early *The Gambler,* a radical application of Musorgskian principles to an intensely psychological subject, and the late *War and Peace,* a loose collection of patriotic military-domestic tableaux heavily indebted to Borodin and Tchaikovsky. Much of the explanation for the erratic course of Prokofiev's operatic career lies in the peculiar circumstances of his life: born and trained in Tsarist Russia, he lived in the West from 1918 to 1936, then returned to Stalin's Russia where he died in 1953. As a result, he composed for several different operatic markets and audiences, achieving at best limited public success. Ignoring the warnings of countless critics, including his countrymen Sergei Diaghilev and Igor Stravinsky, that full-length opera was *passé,* Prokofiev devoted great time and effort to this genre. Sadly, his work in

Sergei Prokofiev

the field has never achieved the popularity or recognition of his ballet, symphonic, film or piano music, and even today his operas, full of his trademark ironic humor, strong illustrative sense and quirky originality, all too rarely take the stage.

Obstacles and disappointment dogged Prokofiev throughout his operatic career. While still a student at St Petersburg Conservatory, he finished a charming (and uncharacteristically romantic) one-act opera, *Maddalena*, in piano score, but orchestrated only the first of its four scenes and failed to find a producer. His first completed mature opera, *The Gambler*, was written for the Mariinsky Theater in St Petersburg on the eve of the 1917 Bolshevik Revolution, but received its belated premiere in Brussels more than ten years later. His second, and by far most successful, *Love for Three Oranges* was commissioned and produced (in 1921) by the Chicago Opera and soon went on to international fame. His third, *The Fiery Angel,* was intended for a 1927 Berlin Staatsoper production, but reached the stage (in Florence) only in 1955, two years after Prokofiev's death.

One of the factors that led Prokofiev to return to the Soviet Union was his belief that it would be easier for him to get his operas produced there. Language had always been a problem in Europe and America. Moreover, because of the more conservative and closely controlled cultural climate, opera in the Soviet Union had remained a prestigious and viable form that attracted talented performers, directors and designers. Operating with huge state subsidies, the Kirov in Leningrad and the Bolshoi in Moscow seemed to represent great opportunities. And yet the harsh and ever-changing realities of Soviet history and cultural policy created a new set of problems no less vexing. Not a single one of Prokofiev's four "Soviet" operas traveled a smooth road to the stage.

Semyon Kotko fell out of the repertoire very soon after its 1940 Moscow premiere, tainted by its controversial portrayal of German participation in the 1918 Civil War in the Ukraine. The happily escapist *Betrothal in a Monastery* was produced in 1946, six years after it was completed. Prokofiev spent nearly 13 years working on his epic *War and Peace*, the opera he hoped would bring him official recognition, but this, too, proved problematic to the enforcers of Socialist Realism, and the composer died without seeing it staged in full. Nor did the composer live to see *Story of a Real Man* produced, for it, too, fell afoul of Stalin's censors in 1948 and reached the stage only in 1960. Of Prokofiev's four "Soviet" operas, only *War and Peace* and *Betrothal in a Monastery* (which deserves to be better known) have achieved any measure of international success.

Prokofiev also left two of his last operas unfinished. The most nearly completed, *Khan Buzay,* begun in the early 1940s, was a "lyric-comic opera" based on folk legends and folk songs of Kazakhstan. In 1948, Prokofiev began an "opera-vaudeville," *Distant Seas,* inspired by a comedy by the Soviet playwright Dïkhovichnïy, but abandoned the project in the preliminary stages.

Of Prokofiev's seven mature operas, only *Love for Three Oranges* has managed to establish itself—and even then just barely—in the standard international repertoire. Like all of them, it is far from a singers' opera, and demands strong acting, tight ensemble work and a physical, highly imaginative production to succeed (The one directed by Frank Corsaro and designed by Maurice Sendak for Glyndebourne in 1982 is a good example). Intended at least in part as a parody of outmoded operatic conventions, *Oranges* also exemplifies the fierce and unresolved conflict between tradition and innovation that drives all of Prokofiev's best music, including his operas. Here and elsewhere, the composer attacks the very values he cherishes, alternating between nasty sarcasm and

boyish lyricism. This uncertainty of tone (should we laugh or sympathize?) can also undermine the emotional impact of Prokofiev's operas; *The Fiery Angel* provides a good example, veering between vicious caricature of Catholic prelates and Renata's self-inflicted psychological torment.

One thing all of Prokofiev's operas share is an unusual respect for and fidelity to their literary sources. Only one, *Betrothal in a Monastery* (also known as *Duenna*), uses a non-Russian source. To some extent this marks the continuation of a tradition among nineteenth century Russian operatic composers of turning to the masterpieces of the national literature for libretti. What sets Prokofiev apart from them, however, is a preference for large works of narrative prose. Five of his operas (all except *Betrothal* and *Oranges*) use hefty pieces of fiction. Two come from the Russian nineteenth century literary mainstream: Dostoevsky's short novel *The Gambler* and Tolstoy's mammoth *War and Peace. The Fiery Angel* uses a Decadent novel of the same title by the twentieth century Russian Symbolist Valery Bryusov. The remaining two are from bland "official" works of Soviet Socialist Realism, by authors contemporary with Prokofiev. *Semyon Kotko* is based on Valentin Katayev's *I Am a Son of the Working People,* and *Story of a Real Man* on a novel of the same title about a brave Soviet fighter pilot by the hack journalist Boris Polevoy.

Unlike Stravinsky or Shostakovich, both of whom—for different reasons—paid considerably less attention to opera, Prokofiev authored or coauthored all his mature libretti. (Three were his own, four were collaborations.) Initially, he detested "libretto verse," insisting as much as possible upon prose, which guaranteed greater dramatic truth and power. He was encouraged in this belief by his friend and collaborator the avant-garde Russian stage director Vsevolod Meyerhold (1874-1940), a sworn enemy both of Wagnerism and of *verismo* melodrama who saw in Prokofiev the new hope of twentieth century operatic theater. Meyerhold also suggested the subject of *Oranges* and was collaborating with Prokofiev on a production of *Semyon Kotko* when he was arrested on Stalin's orders in 1939.

In *The Gambler,* Prokofiev followed the example set by Musorgsky in his experimental opera *The Marriage.* He transfered unedited chunks of Dostoevsky's text into the libretto, setting them to an uncompromisingly declamatory vocal line surrounded by a dense, dissonant and dynamic orchestral texture. Forward movement and dramatic truth were his early goals, which he hoped to achieve by virtually eliminating pauses in the action for arias, ensembles and choruses. Unfortunately, Prokofiev's "Scythian" orchestration (heavy, brassy and full of brilliant pictorial effects, like the spinning of the roulette wheel created by the woodwinds and xylophone) frequently upstaged the text and plot, and made the going rough for singers.

As was the case with Musorgsky himself, Prokofiev's early radical championship of the word in the word-music relationship modified as time went on. While still highly "literary," and placing great emphasis on dramatic values, *Oranges* and *The Fiery Angel* make greater concessions to the singers and to the audience's need for the emotional breathing space provided by arias, ensembles and choruses. When Prokofiev came back to revise *The Gambler* in 1927-28, he similarly incorporated some of the lessons he had learned in the meantime as an operatic composer.

Although Musorgsky's music exerted the central influence on Prokofiev during the time he was working on *The Gambler,* other Russian composers also played a role in the development of this highly impressionable composer's operatic style. One was Rimsky-Korsakov, the author of ten operas, and Prokofiev's teacher at the St Petersburg Conservatory. In his diary, Prokofiev remarked that he especially loved *The Legend of the Invisible City of Kitezh and the Maiden Fevronia, Sadko,* and *Snegurochka,* which he saw as a student. This interest in the devils and spirits of Rimsky's fairy-tale operas later turned up, with a strongly satirical twist, in *Oranges* and *The Fiery Angel,* as well as in the ballets *Chout, Cinderella* and *The Stone Flower.*

The operas of Borodin and Tchaikovsky also influenced Prokofiev. Certain features (a sense of color and visuality, a strong melodic gift, Orientalism) had always linked Prokofiev and Borodin, but these became more prominent in the operas he wrote after returning to the USSR in the late 1930s, at a time when Borodin was being held up to Soviet composers as a model to be followed. *Semyon Kotko, War and Peace,* and, to a certain extent, *Story of a Real Man,* share with *Prince Igor* a strongly patriotic message; a dramatic structure loosely constructed around a series of historical "tableaux"; imitation of folk music as an integral part of the style; and many important scenes for the chorus. *War and Peace,* of course, owes the most to *Prince Igor,* concerned as it is with huge military/historical issues stretching across an entire country.

Prokofiev came later to Tchaikovsky. Although he knew both *Eugene Onegin* and *The Queen of Spades* as a young man, his own early operas, especially *Oranges* and *The Fiery Angel,* represent a firm rejection of the "pretty," highly sentimental style Tchaikovsky brought to Russian opera (Prokofiev once remarked that he considered *The Queen of Spades* to be "in very bad taste.") After his return to the Soviet Union in the late 1930s, however, Prokofiev's attitude towards Tchaikovsky became more positive. *War and Peace* even includes scenes directly modeled on scenes in Tchaikovsky's operas: scene i, the duet between Natasha and Sonya, refers to the Polina-Lisa duet in act I, scene ii of *The Queen of Spades,* and scene ii, Natasha's first ball, refers to act II of *Eugene Onegin.* As was the case with Prokofiev's renewed interest in Borodin, his apparent reappraisal of Tchaikovsky stemmed in part from the demands of Soviet cultural policy, which looked increasingly to the nineteenth-century classics as the appropriate models for Soviet composers.

Oddly enough, then, Prokofiev, who lived abroad for almost twenty years, long enough to become a suspicious "cosmopolitan" in the eyes of Stalin's cultural officials, remained strongly Russian in his operatic aesthetic. Showing little use for or interest in twentieth-century European opera, he claimed to particularly dislike Richard Strauss (although *Maddalena,* his 1913 student one-act opera, shows a definite Straussian influence in its decadent theme and lush harmonic language). In his voluminous writings, Prokofiev showed no knowledge of Janáček, blamed Wagner for killing the vitality of opera, and displayed little enthusiasm for or curiosity about the music (operatic or otherwise) of Schoenberg, Berg and Webern.

In the final analysis Prokofiev's love for opera remained unrequited and his legacy uncertain. Every one of his operas boasts marvelous moments, from the fetching lament of the princesses in *Oranges* to Andrei's harrowing death-bed scene in *War and Peace,* from the wild convent orgy that concludes *The Fiery Angel* to the ironic music-making scene in *Betrothal in a Monastery.* For the most part, however, they remain isolated moments. Strangely, Prokofiev never achieved once in opera the complete artistic synthesis of the ballet *Romeo and Juliet,* remarkable precisely for its infallible dramatic sense, compassion and psychological insight. One of the most

instinctive and "natural" of composers, Prokofiev had to work too hard at opera.

—Harlow Robinson

THE PROPHET
See LE PROPHÈTE

LE PROPHÈTE [The Prophet].

Composer: Giacomo Meyerbeer.

Librettist: Eugène Scribe.

First Performance: Paris, Opéra, 16 April 1849.

Roles: Berthe (soprano); Fidès (mezzo-soprano); Jean de Leyden (tenor); Count Oberthal (bass or bass-baritone); Jonas (tenor); Mathisen (bass); Zacharias (bass); Two Children (soprano, mezzo-soprano); Two Peasants (tenor, bass); Soldier (tenor); Two Bourgeois (tenors); Two Officers (tenor, bass); chorus (SSAATTBB).

Publications

books–

Morel, A. *Le prophète: analyse critique de la nouvelle partition de Giacomo Meyerbeer.* Paris, 1849.
Lindner, E.O. *Meyerbeers "Prophet" als Kunstwerk beurtheilt.* Berlin, 1850.
Schladebach, J. *Meyerbeers Prophet (unter besonderer Berücksichtigung der Dresdener Aufführung.* Dresden, 1850.

article–

Fulcher, J. "Radicalization, Repression, and Opera: Meyerbeer's *Le Prophète.* In *The Nation's Image: French Grand Opera as Politics and Politicized Art.* Cambridge, 1987.

When *Le prophète* was finally produced in 1849, thirteen years had elapsed since Meyerbeer's last great success at the Paris Opéra, *Les Huguenots.* Plans for the new opera had begun in 1837, again with the accomplished playwright-librettist Eugène Scribe, and the score was largely completed by 1841, but a number of factors conspired to cause long delays: casting problems, administrative difficulties at the Opéra, the composer's tenure as Generalmusikdirektor in Berlin from 1842-46, and the political turmoil of 1848, to name a few. Such a long period of anticipation may actually have contributed to the eventual triumph of the opera, as did the performance of the famed Pauline Viardot-Garcia in the maternal role of Fidès (she was only twenty-eight at the time). Scribe's libretto, based on events surrounding the early sixteenth-century Anabaptist leader John (here named Jean) of Leyden, afforded a variety of picturesque scenes, splendid

The coronation scene from Meyerbeer's *Le prophète*, London, 1849

tableaux, and dramatic *coups de théâtre* such as Parisian audiences had come to expect. The underlying theme of popular rebellion, furthermore, had a timely appeal for European audiences in the wake of the revolutions of 1848-49.

The motivating force behind the action is the group of three Anabaptist preachers—Zacharie, Jonas, and Mathisen—who prey on the discontents of the peasant class to garner support for the political ambitions of their sect (act I). When the impending marriage of the innkeeper Jean to the orphan girl Berthe is thwarted by the tyrannical and rapacious Count Oberthal (who invokes his feudal *droits du seigneur*), Jean is convinced to act as leader of the Anabaptists, who notice his resemblance to a holy image in the Münster cathedral. He is forced to yield his fiancée to Oberthal in order to save his mother, Fidès (act II). In act III the Anabaptist faction succeeds in capturing Oberthal, but Jean is encouraged to pursue his chosen path still further and help them take the city of Münster. Act IV finds Jean on the point of being crowned Prophet-King of the victorious Anabaptists. Berthe and Fidès fortuitously encounter one another in Münster and resolve to avenge themselves against the false "prophet" whom they believe to be responsible for Jean's death. Amidst a grand coronation ceremony, Fidès recognizes the prophet as her son, but Jean is forced to deny his mother in his role as the new Messiah. In the final act Berthe is attempting to infiltrate the palace at Münster in order to set fire to a munitions storeroom and destroy the Anabaptist leader. On discovering his identity, she kills herself. When he learns that he has been betrayed and the emperor's troops are approaching to

suppress the heretical rebellion, Jean himself determines to have Berthe's plan carried out. While the prophet and his court indulge in a riotous bacchanale, the enemy troops arrive, as does Fidès, to pardon her son. But all perish together as the hall collapses in the sudden conflagration.

Le prophète was the principal target of Wagner's famous diatribe against its composer in *Opera and Drama*, written soon after the opera's triumphant premiere and during a time when it was conquering nearly all the stages of Europe—unlike Wagner's own scores. Meyerbeer himself made no apologies about tailoring his music to the strengths of his cast, nor about taking full advantage of the resources offered by the Opéra. It may be an inevitable consequence of the long gestation period of Meyerbeer's later operas and the endless tinkerings to which this perfectionist craftsman subjected these scores that they appear more heterogeneous than organic. Yet despite the unconcealed artifice of the work, and Meyerbeer's obvious delight in experimenting with novel, often isolated instrumental effects, *Le prophète* is unified, in a sense, by several distinctive styles. The first two acts, for instance, set in a bucolic Dutch landscape near the river Meuse (Maas), are characterized by a pastoral idiom: the echoing of solo clarinets in the introduction (suggesting a rustic *chalumeau* sound), the "Valse villageoise" beginning act II, and an array of double-drone effects ("Choeur pastoral," entrance of Fidès, duo-romance for Berthe and Fidès in act I; the "Valse villageoise" and Jean's "Pastorale" in act II). The opening pastoral chorus includes a kind of ritornello scored for high pizzicato strings and arpeggiated parallel woodwind triads (with triangle), which produces a striking "polytonal" effect. On the other hand, the soprano cavatina ("Mon coeur s'élance et palpite") inserted after this chorus at the request of the first Berthe, Jeanne Castellan, is a blatant vocal display piece, demonstrating Meyerbeer's willingness to sacrifice stylistic continuity to singers' demands.

Meyerbeer himself cited a "somber and fanatic" tone as characteristic of Le prophète. This is achieved in part by the recurring Anabaptist chant, "Ad nos, ad salutarem undam," with its mock-antique modal idiom. The use of four bassoons (in another parody of the sacred style) to accompany the entrance of the Anabaptist trio is another example of this "somber" tone. The "fanatic" element—related to the "Benediction of the Daggers" scene in Les Huguenots—is well represented by the Anabaptist chorus opening act III, combining a trumpet-like call-to-arms, a fragment of choral prayer and an orgiastic, bloodthirsty rhythmic refrain ("Dansons sur leur tombe—du sang!"). The antiphonal off-stage trumpet calls introducing this number define yet another tone, dominant in the later acts. This character, appropriate to the military camp setting of act III, is manifested in numerous march rhythms so favored by the genre of grand opera and in opulent brass scoring in the larger choral scenes.

Aside from the use of roller skates for the ice-skating chorus and divertissement in act III and the innovative application of electric light to effect the sunrise at the end of this act ("Hymne triomphal"), the fame of this opera is concentrated on the great coronation scene of act IV. Many ingredients of the scene—grand march, Latin hymns with organ, the solo prayer—were already hallmarks of the genre. New elements here include the addition of children's chorus and the mezzo/contralto role (Fidès) as focal point. The powerful moment of Jean's enforced denial of his mother is possibly undermined by the somewhat trivial tune that dominates the closing ensemble (introduced by Fidès: "L'ingrat, il ne me reconnait pas"). Nevertheless, Scribe's compelling dramaturgical conception and Meyerbeer's exploitation of Viardot-Garcia's impressive range and theatrical presence contribute to one of nineteenth-century opera's most effective scenes, deeply admired by Verdi, among many others.

—Thomas S. Grey

PUCCINI, Giacomo.

Composer. Born 22 December 1858, in Lucca. Died 29 November 1924, in Brussels. Married: Elvira Gemignani, 1904 (one son). Puccini came from a long line of musicians; studied with Carlo Angeloni at the Istituto Musicale of Lucca; church organist in Mutigliano, 1875; organist at San Pietro in Somaldi; submitted his cantata Juno to a contest in Lucca, but did not win, 1877; studied with Antonio Bazzini and Amilcare Ponchielli at the Milan Conservatory, 1880-83; Edgar commissioned by the publisher Ricordi, 1884; lived in Torre del Lago from 1891; in New York for the American premiere of Madama Butterfly, 1907; La fanciulla del West commissioned by the Metropolitan Opera of New York.

Operas

Le villi, Ferdinando Fontana, Milan, Teatro dal Verme, 31 May 1884; revised, Turin, Regio, 26 December 1884.

Edgar, Ferdinando Fontana (after de Musset, La coupe et les lèvres), Milan, Teatro alla Scala, 21 April 1889; revised, Ferrara, 28 February 1892; further revised, Buenos Aires, 8 July 1905.

Manon Lescaut, Leoncavallo, Marco Praga, Domenico Olivia, Luigi Illica, and Giuseppe Giacosa (after Prévost), Turin, Regio, 1 February 1893.

La bohème, Giuseppe Giacosa and Luigi Illica (after Murger), Turin, Regio, 1 February 1896.

Tosca, Giuseppe Giacosa and Luigi Illica (after Sardou), Rome, Costanzi, 14 January 1900.

Madama Butterfly, Giuseppe Giacosa and Luigi Illica (after the drama by David Belasco based on the story by John Luther Long), Milan, Teatro alla Scala, 17 February 1904; revised, Brescia, Grande, 28 May 1904; revised, London, Covent Garden, 10 July 1905; revised, Paris, Opéra Comique, 28 December 1906.

La fanciulla del West, Guelfo Civinini and Carlo Zangarini (after David Belasco, The Girl of the Golden West), New York, Metropolitan Opera, 10 December 1910.

La rondine, Giuseppe Adami (translated from a German libretto by Alfred Maria Willner and Heinrich Reichert), Monte Carlo, 27 March 1917.

Il trittico: 1) Il tabarro, Giuseppe Adami (after Didier Gold, La houppelande), 2) Suor Angelica, Giovacchino Forzano, 3) Gianni Schicchi, Giovacchino Forzano (scenario based on lines from Dante, Inferno), New York, Metropolitan Opera, 14 December 1918.

Turandot, Giuseppe Adami and Renato Simoni (after Gozzi), Milan, Teatro alla Scala, 25 April 1926 [unfinished; completed by Franco Alfano].

Other works: sacred and secular vocal music, orchestral works, chamber music, keyboard pieces.

Publications/Writings

By PUCCINI: books—

Adami, Giuseppe, ed. Giacomo Puccini: epistolario. Milan, 1928; English translation by Ena Makin, London, 1931; revised ed., edited by Mosco Carner, 1974.

Gatti, G.M. Puccini in un gruppo di lettere inedite a un amico. Milan, 1944.

Gara, Eugenio. Carteggi pucciniani. Milan, 1958.

Marchetti, Arnaldo, ed. Puccini com'era. Milan, 1973.

Pintorno, Giuseppe, ed. Puccini: 276 lettere inedite. Milan, 1974.

Puccini, Simonetta, ed. Lettere a Riccardo Schnabl. Milan, 1981.

About PUCCINI: books—

Dry, Wakeling. Giacomo Puccini. London, 1906.

Torrefranca, Fausto. Puccini e l'opera internazionale. Turin, 1912.

Coppotelli, A. Per la musica d'Italia: Puccini nella critica del Torrefranca. Orvieto, 1919.

Weissmann, Adolf. Giacomo Puccini. Munich, 1922.

Coeuroy, André. La Tosca de Puccini: étude historique et critique. Paris, 1923.

Chop, M. Die Tosca. Leipzig, 1924.

Monaldi, G. Giacomo Puccini e la sua opera. Rome, 1924.

Fraccaroli, A. La vita di Giacomo Puccini. Milan, 1925.

Neisser, Arthur. Giacomo Puccini: sein Leben und sein Werk. Leipzig, 1928.

Billeci, A. *La Bohème di Giacomo Puccini: studio critico.* Palermo, 1931.

Specht, Richard. *Giacomo Puccini: das Leben - der Mensch - das Werk.* Berlin, 1931; English translation by Catherine Alison Phillips, London, 1933.

Maisch, W. *Puccinis musikalische Formgebung, untersucht an der Oper "La Bohème".* Neustadt an der Aisch, 1934.

Adami, Giuseppe *Puccini.* Milan, 1935.

Fellerer, Karl Gustav. *Giacomo Puccini.* Potsdam, 1937.

Gerigk, H. *Puccini.* Potsdam, 1937.

Knosp, Gaston. *G. Puccini.* Brussels, 1937.

Seligman, Vincent. *Puccini among Friends.* London, 1938.

Marini, R.B. *La "Turandot" di Giacomo Puccini.* Florence, 1942.

Adami, Giuseppe. *Il romanzo della vita di Giacomo Puccini.* Milan, 1944.

Carner, Mosco. *Of Men and Music: Collected Essays and Articles* [numerous essays on Puccini and his operas]. London, 1944; 3rd ed., 1945.

Thiess, Frank. *Puccini: Versuch einer Psychologie seiner Musik.* Vienna, 1947.

Marchetti, Leopoldo. *Puccini nelle immagini.* Milan, 1949.

Marotti, Guido. *Giacomo Puccini.* Florence, 1949.

Bonaccorsi, Alfredo. *Giacomo Puccini e i suoi antenati musicali.* Milan, 1950.

Marek, George R. *Puccini: a Biography.* New York, 1951.

Del Fiorentino, Dante. *Immortal Bohemian: an Intimate Memoir of Giacomo Puccini.* London, 1952.

Ricci, L. *Puccini interprete di se stesso.* Milan, 1954.

Carner, Mosco. *Puccini: a Critical Biography.* London, 1958; New York, 1959; revised ed., London, 1974; New York, 1977; French translation, 1983.

Sartori, C. *Puccini.* Milan, 1958.

Hughes, Spike. *Famous Puccini Operas.* London, 1959; New York, 1972.

Sartori, C., ed. *Puccini* [essays by numerous authors]. Milan, 1959.

Ashbrook, William. *The Operas of Puccini.* New York and London, 1968.

Hopkinson, Cecil A. *A Bibliography of the Works of Giacomo Puccini 1858-1924.* New York, 1968.

Titone, Antonio. *Vissi d'arte: Puccini e il disfacimento del melodramma.* Milan, 1972.

MacDonald, Ray S. *Puccini, King of Verismo.* New York, 1973.

Winterhoff, H.J. *Analytische Untersuchungen zu Puccinis "Tosca".* Regensburg, 1973.

Galli, N.A. *Puccini e la sua terra.* Lucca, 1974.

Jackson, Stanley. *Monsieur Butterfly: the Story of Puccini.* London, 1974.

Magri, G. *Puccini e le sue rime.* Milan, 1974.

Pinzauti, L. *Puccini: una vita.* Florence, 1974.

Christen, Norbert. *Giacomo Puccini: Analytische Untersuchungen der Melodik, Harmonik, und Instrumentation.* Hamburg, 1975.

Siciliano, E. *Puccini.* Milan, 1976.

Casini, Claudio. *Giacomo Puccini.* Turin, 1978.

Knaust, Rebecca. *The Complete Guide to "La bohème".* New York, 1978.

Tedeschi, Rubens. *Addio, fiorito asil. Il melodramma italiano da Boito al Verismo.* Milan, 1978.

Weaver, William. *Puccini: the Man and his Music.* New York, 1977; London, 1978.

Carner, Mosco. *Madame Butterfly: a Guide to the Opera.* London, 1979.

Csampi, Attila, and Dietmar Holland, ed. *la Bohème: Texte, Materialien, Kommentare.* Reinbek, 1981.

Greenfield, Howard. *Puccini.* New York, 1980; German translation, 1982.

Osborne, Charles. *The Complete Operas of Puccini.* London, 1981.

Weaver, William, ed. and trans. *Seven Puccini Librettos.* New York, 1981.

Ceresa, Angelo. *Puccini. Schauplätze seines Lebens.* Vienna and Munich, 1982.

John, Nicholas, ed. *Giacomo Puccini: "La bohème".* London and New York, 1982.

———. *Giacomo Puccini: "Tosca".* London and New York, 1982.

Courtin, Michèle. *Tosca de Giacomo Puccini.* Paris, 1983.

Gossett, Philip, et al. *Masters of Italian Opera: Rossini, Donizetti, Bellini, Verdi, Puccini. The New Grove Composer Biography Series.* London, 1983.

Leukel, Jürgen J. *Studien zu Puccinis "Il trittico".* Munich, 1983.

Stewart, Robert S., ed. *Giacomo Puccini: La bohème.* London, 1983.

Baldacci, Luigi, ed. *Tutti i libretti di Puccini.* Milan, 1984.

Höslinger, Clemens. *Giacomo Puccini.* Reinbek bei Hamburg, 1984.

Krause, Ernst. *Puccini. Beschreibung eines Welterfolges.* Berlin, 1984.

John, Nicholas, ed. *Giacomo Puccini: "Madama Butterfly".* London and New York, 1984.

———. *Giacomo Puccini: "Turandot".* London and New York, 1984.

Carner, Mosco. *Giacomo Puccini: Tosca.* Cambridge, 1985.

Martino, Daniele A. *Metamorfosi: del femminino nei libretti per Puccini.* Turin, 1985.

Groos, Arthur, and Roger Parker. *Giacomo Puccini: La bohème.* Cambridge, 1986.

DiGaetani, John Lewis. *Puccini the Thinker.* New York, 1987.

Musco, Gianfranco. *Musica e teatro in Giacomo Puccini.* Vol. 1. Cortona, 1989.

Schickling, Dieter. *Giacomo Puccini: Biographie.* Stuttgart, 1989.

Ashbrook, William, and Harold Powers. *Puccini's "Turandot": the End of the Great Tradition.* Princeton, 1991.

articles–

Fontana, F. "Giacomo Puccini." *Gazzetta musicale di Milano* 39 (1884): 381; reprinted as 'Puccini visto dal suo primo librettista." *Musica d'oggi* 15 (1933): 148.

Pizzetti, I. "Giacomo Puccini." In *Musicisti comtemporanei: saggi critici.* Milan, 1914.

Dean, Winton. "Giacomo Puccini." In *The Heritage of Music,* vol. 3, edited by H. Foss, 153. London, 1951.

La Scala December (1958) [Puccini issue].

D'Amico, Fedele. "Una ignorata pagina 'maliperiana' di *Suor Angelica.*" *Rassegna Musicale Curci* March (1966).

Smith, Gordon. "Alfano and *Turandot.*" *Opera* March (1973).

Meyerowitz, J. "Puccini: musica a doppio fordo." *Nuova rivista musicale italiana* 10 (1976): 3.

Avant-scène opéra September-October (1977) [*Tosca* issue].

Casini, C. "Introduzione a Puccini." In *Il melodramma italiano dell' ottocento; studi e ricerche per Massimo Mila.* Turin, 1977.

Gherardi, L. "Appunti per una lettura delle varianti nelle opere di Giacomo Puccini." *Studi musicale* 6 (1977): 269.

Martinotti, S. "I travagliati Avant-Propos di Puccini." In *Il melodramma italiano dell' ottocento; studi e ricerche per Massimo Mila.* Turin, 1977.

Sartori, C. "I sospetti di Puccini." *Nuova rivista musicale italiana* 11 (1977): 233.

Avant-scène opéra March-April (1979) [*La bohème* issue].

Revers, Peter. "Analytische Betrachtungen zu Puccinis *Turandot.*" *Österreichische Musikzeitung* 34 (1979): 342.

Ross, P., and D. Schwendimann Berra. "Setta lettere di Puccini a Giulio Ricordi." *Nuova rivista musicale italiana* 13 (1979): 851.

Carner, Mosco. "The Two Manons." In *Major and Minor.* London, 1980.

Herz, Joachim. "Zur Urfassung von Puccinis *Madame Butterfly.*" In *Werk und Wiedergabe,* edited by Sigrid Wiesmann, 239. Bayreuth, 1980.

Smith, Julian. "A Metamorphosis Tragedy" [*Madama Butterfly*] *Proceedings of the Royal Musical Association* 106 (1980): 105.

Avant-scène opéra May-June (1981) [*Turandot* issue].

Perusse, Lyle F. "Tosca and Piranesi." *Musical Times* 121 (1981): 743.

Nicolodi, Fiamma. "Parigi e l'opera verista: dibattiti, riflessioni, polemiche." *Nuova rivista musicale italiana* 15 (1981): 577.

Lederer, Josef-Horst. "Mahler und die beiden Bohèmes." In *Festschrift Othmar Wessely zum 60. Geburtstag,* edited by Manfred Angerer et al., 399. Tutzing, 1982.

Leukel, Jürgen. "Puccinis kinematographische Technik." *Neue Zeitschrift für Musik* 143/nos. 6-7 (1982): 24.

———. "Puccini et Bizet." *Revue musicale de Suisse romande* 35/no. 2 (1982): 61.

Avant-scène opéra October (1983) [*Madame Butterfly* issue].

Corse, Sandra. " 'Mi chiamo Mimi': The Role of Women in Puccini's Operas." *Opera Quarterly* 1 (1983): 93.

Ashbrook, William. "*Turandot* and its Posthumous *prima.*" *Opera Quarterly* 2 (1984): 126.

DiGaetani, John Lewis. "Comedy and redemption in *La fanciulla del West.*" *Opera Quarterly* 2 (1984): 88.

———. "Puccini's *Tosca* and the Necessity of Antagonism." *Opera Quarterly* 2 (1984): 76.

Döhring, Sieghart. "Musikalischer Realismus in Puccini's *Tosca.*" *Analecta Musicologica* 22 (1984): 249.

Green, Susan. "Comedy and Puccini's Operas." *Opera Quarterly* 2 (1984): 102.

Maehder, Jürgen. "Studien zum Fragmentcharakter von Giacomo Puccinis *Turandot.*" *Analecta Musicologica* 22 (1984): 279.

Avant-scène opéra December (1985) [*Gianni Schicchi* issue].

Budden, Julian. "The Genesis and Literary Source of Giacomo Puccini's First Opera." *Cambridge Opera Journal* 1 (1989): 79.

Groos, Arthur. "The Return of the Native: Japan in *Madama Butterfly/Madama Butterfly* in Japan." *Cambridge Opera Journal* 1 (1989): 167.

Atlas, Allan W. "Newly discovered sketches for Puccini's *Turandot* at the Pierpont Morgan Library." *Cambridge Opera Journal* 3 (1991): 173.

———. "Madame Butterfly: The story." *Cambridge Opera Journal* 3 (1991): 125.

*   *   *

The phenomenon of Puccini's success from the period of *Manon Lescaut* (1893) until his death in 1924, a popularity that has if anything increased since then, sets him off from his chief contemporaries, the other members of what used to be called La Giovane Scuola or The Generation of the '90s. These composers, men like Mascagni, remembered primarily for *Cavalleria rusticana,* or Leoncavallo, regarded as another one-opera figure with *I pagliacci,* or Francesco Cilea with *Adriana Lecouvreur,* made their mark with a single major success that they could never, try as they might, quite equal. Why should one man have an almost unbroken string of triumphs and leave his rivals far behind? To provide some answers to this question, to try to isolate some of the strengths of Puccini's talent that were less prominent in the others provides one way to take some measure of this phenomenon.

Puccini had, usually, a powerful sense of theater, of dramatic timing, and he would hone his works, even after they had been first introduced, modifying them as he experienced them in the opera house until they satisfied his discriminating taste. For instance, after the opening run of *Manon Lescaut* he rewrote the ending of act I. He expanded the Café Momus scene in *La bohème.* He tightened up the second act of *Tosca.* Over a period of three years (1904-07), he pared away at *Madama Butterfly,* modifying it and focusing more fully on his heroine. Up until the final *Turandot,* which was left incomplete at his death, there is not one of his operas that did not undergo some later revision. This acute sensibility for dramatic effect, kept alive through his personal supervision of a number of local premieres of his works, shows up in other ways as well.

Puccini was notorious for giving his librettists a hard time. His first two operas, *Le villi* and *Edgar* (although he revised them both, and the second on several occasions) suffered from weak texts. When he worked on *Manon Lescaut,* it took six people's efforts to come up with the scenes and diction adjusted as he wanted them. He participated actively in the preparation of the librettos he set, asking for revisions and then revisions of revisions, because he knew how much the viability of an opera depended upon its emphasis and timing. There is little evidence that any of his contemporaries were nearly as demanding or as discriminating about the fine tuning of the plots they had chosen or as fussy about the words they set to music.

Mascagni's *Cavalleria rusticana* (1890) is famous for introducing *verismo,* the operatic equivalent of naturalism in literature, to the musical theater. In contrast to the romantic *melodrama* that had dominated the Italian opera stage for most of the nineteenth century, the veristic approach involved a lessening of the aesthetic distance between the action on the stage and the audience. Part of the appeal of *La bohème* is that it is about ordinary people, although removed in time, being set in Paris of the 1830s, the period of Louis-Philippe. The neatly adjusted mixture of light-heartedness and pathos in this work helped to assure its popularity. Leoncavallo composed a setting of *La bohème* to his own libretto that appeared one year after Puccini's opera; he derived his text from the same source Puccini had turned to, but Leoncavallo's work is heavy-handed and lacks the clarity of dramatic focus of Puccini's setting. Not surprisingly, Puccini's opera is performed with great frequency, while Leoncavallo's is revived only very occasionally as a curiosity.

In *Madama Butterfly* Puccini sought to make an exotic setting vivid by employing some Japanese music as well as composing his own Japanese-style music, a course he would later follow with Chinese music in *Turandot:* borrowing some and inventing some, even imitating the sounds of Oriental instruments on occasion. Orientalizing, however, was not Puccini's only move in this direction; settings closer to home were important to him as well. The locations of the three acts of *Tosca,* for example, each involve historic landmarks of

Giacomo Puccini (left) with Giuseppe Giacosa and Luigi Illica, c. 1905

Rome, and Puccini was concerned enough with detail that he found out the note sounded by the great bell of St Peter's (low E) so that he might introduce it into the prelude of act III of *Tosca.*

The only simon-pure example of *verismo* among Puccini's output is the one-act *Il tabarro,* with its action involving working-class characters taking place upon a barge on the river Seine. Puccini understood the poignancy of the aspirations of poor or defenseless people and could give such feelings memorable musical expression in such arias as "Mi chiamono Mimì" from *La bohème* and "Un bel dì" from *Butterfly.* Puccini would occasionally exploit the sordid or violent aspects of *verismo* (a movement that spent its momentum fairly rapidly), but he understood how to counter-balance them with genuine sentiment and moments of pathos.

The creation of atmosphere, an effort to make as palpable as possible the physical and emotional climate in which the action takes place, was always a matter of close concern to Puccini. The dancing lesson in act II of *Manon Lescaut,* with its aura of minuets and other court dances, establishes a sense of eighteenth-century Parisian luxury. The snowy scene at the opening of act III of *La bohème* provides a background for a scene in which love has grown cold. Verdi had provided an example for his followers of how effective a strikingly evocative setting could be in the storm scene in the last act of *Rigoletto* and the raging tempest depicted at the opening of *Otello,* or the moonlight on the rippling Nile at the beginning of act III of *Aida.* None of Puccini's contemporaries, however, could equal him in the sheer variety and poetic appropriateness of the scenic atmosphere he developed. A wonderful example of this is the opening of *Il tabarro* that summons up a sense of Seine-side sound and movement as vivid as any Utrillo cityscape of Montmartre.

There is a lighter side to Puccini's art as well, a range that eluded most of his contemporaries. Only Wolf-Ferrari among them could match his deftness. *La rondine* is a work that started out to be a Viennese-style operetta and ended up as a sentimental comedy with a slightly acerbic outcome; in it Puccini's flair for humor and charm shows up not only in the wonderful act II quartet but in the many examples of dance music in this score. His greatest comic achievement, thanks in no small measure to Forzano's pungent text, is the one-act *Gianni Schicchi,* with its sharply etched characters and its comic afflatus humanized by brief flights of lyric expansiveness. Among his other major works, there is not one that does not have some humorous or light-hearted moment to contrast with its more serious conflicts. A brilliant example of this is the trio of Ministers, Ping, Pang and Pong, in *Turandot.* One problem with *verismo* operas is that violent plots too easily tend to find expression in strident and over-vehement music, a defect that afflicted Puccini's contemporaries with embarrassing frequency, but his keen sense of proportion and his ability to make a deft transition from one mood to another, as at the end of "Nessun dorma" (Let no one sleep) in act III of *Turandot,* saves him from the worst of the excesses of the Generation of the '90s. Puccini understood the utility of occasional understatement as well as the precise position for a climax. His mental theatrical clock was more finely adjusted than the sense of stage time demonstrated by his rivals.

It is only comparatively recently that Puccini has become critically respectable. Not so long ago he was regarded with suspicion and jealousy just because of his great popularity, and the fact that he did not aim at grandly tragic or epic material was held against him. His music was faulted for appealing too directly to carnal emotions and less to spiritual values. It has taken time, however, to realize that Puccini had a profound instinctive feeling for the epoch in which he lived and possessed a combination of artistry and sensitivity to give it lasting expression to a degree that none of his contemporaries could match.

—William Ashbrook

PUNCH AND JUDY.

Composer: Harrison Birtwistle.

Librettist: Stephen Pruslin.

First Performance: Aldeburgh Festival, Jubilee Hall, 8 June 1968; revised London, 3 March 1970.

Roles: Pretty Poll/Witch (soprano); Judy/Fortuneteller (mezzo-soprano); Punch (baritone); Lawyer (tenor); Doctor (bass); Choregos/Jack Ketch (baritone).

Publications

articles–

Crosse, G. "Birtwistle's *Punch and Judy.*" *Tempo* no. 85 (1968): 24.

*   *   *

Punch and Judy is based on the traditional children's puppet show which was established when Italian actors and puppeteers flocked to Britain with the opening of theaters at the time of the Restoration. As well as having its roots in the Italian *commedia dell' arte,* the original show also drew on memories of the medieval morality play. Punch clearly takes over the role of Old Vice, the outrageous buffoon who encapsulated all the vices of the other characters in the old allegory. What attracted Birtwistle to the show was its stylization and the way it goes through the same event from different perspectives. The standard routine has become a series of ritual murders. Punch throws baby out of the window, beats and kills Judy, a doctor, and various other characters, and cheats the hangman. As in the old morality play, the show usually ends with the defeat of the devil.

To give his opera greater depth and significance, Birtwistle adds two more strands to this series of melodramas. The first turns the events into a genuine comedy and relates the work to the medieval Romance. It concerns Punch's quest for Pretty Poll, his ideal woman, and the obstacles he needs to overcome before he can win and marry her. Pretty Poll was one of the characters who appeared for a time when the show was reshaped at the beginning of the nineteenth century. Unlike the other characters, which are hand puppets, she was a doll on a stick, and this distinction is preserved in the opera. Every time he commits a murder, Punch, like some knight-errant, sets out on his hobby-horse to win her. But the obstacles to his success are his own misdeeds. She accepts him only when he has purged himself by defeating the devil. In the final apotheosis, the whole company sing and dance round a maypole with one of the dancers dressed as the traditional Green Man, symbol of rebirth and regeneration: "Man and wife, wife and man together complete the celestial plan."

The other additional strand to the plot turns the proceedings into a potential tragedy. It involves the showman whom Birtwistle calls Choregos, the name originally given to the person who sponsored the chorus in the ancient Greek theater, but used here to suggest the chorus itself. The relationship between Punch and Choregos, protagonist and chorus, is perhaps the most important in the opera, for it represents the relationship between chance and necessity, or caprice and order, factors which, in Birtwistle's music, as well as in life itself, must always be held in balance. Without chance nothing new could emerge, there would be no growth or development; without necessity there would be no continuity or stability. Needless to say, Punch represents caprice (has there ever been a character as capricious or wilful?) and Choregos order. The opera's peripeteia comes when Punch murders Choregos by placing him in a huge bass viol case and sawing him in half! Suddenly the tables are turned, and Punch is plunged into a nightmare. The quest takes him northward "to the land of infinite night." Judy has become a fortune-teller with a wicked pack of tarot cards; Pretty Poll has become a witch. When he awakens in terror to continue his journey, Pretty Poll's pedestal is deserted.

Everything about the opera—set—lighting, acting, singing—is intended to be as stylized as possible. Birtwistle has no time for naturalism in the theater. The murders being ritual, those killed appear again, take on other roles and join in the singing chorus. Since the traditional show is now played almost exclusively to young children, the opera abounds in childish puns and riddle games. And in a way, the music can also be considered childlike, at least as far as its structure is concerned, for *Punch and Judy* is the number opera par excellence. There are well over a hundred numbers. One, Judy's Passion Aria "Be silent, strings of my heart," which she sings after Choregos has been ushered into the bass viol case, is a fullblown baroque aria with an obbligato for oboe d'amore. Others, like the toccatas which frame the Passion chorales, sung by four singers acting as a chorus whenever a murder has been committed, last only a few seconds. They are meant to sound "like some mechanical process switched on and off."

Judy's Passion Aria provides the clue to the unchildlike aspect of the score. Birtwistle makes reference to Bach's *St Matthew Passion* throughout the opera. Choregos, in the way he comments on and links the various episodes, is both chorus and evangelist, a role emphasized by the expressive, *parlando* style of his delivery. One of the most poignant moments in *Punch and Judy*—"Weep my Punch. Weep out your unfathomable, inexpressible sorrow"—is not unlike the music given to Evangelist reporting Peter's denial.

Birtwistle believes that to make a worthwhile statement, a composer has to go to extremes. But if the character of Punch necessitates music of extreme violence (so violent that Benjamin Britten and other members of the audience at the first performance felt obliged to walk out), there are also moments of extreme lyricism and tenderness.

—Michael Hall

PURCELL, Henry.

Composer. Born c. 1659, in London. Died 21 November 1695, in Dean's Yard, Westminster. Married: Frances Peters, c. 1681 (six children). In the choir of the Chapel Royal under the direction of Cooke and Humfrey, 1669; studied with John Blow; appointed Assistant Keeper of the Instruments for the Chapel Royal, 1673; composer to the King's Band, 1677; succeeded Blow as the organist of Westminster Abbey, 1679; activity as a composer of dramatic music beginning 1680; organist of the Chapel Royal, 1682; Keeper of the King's Wind Instruments, 1683. Purcell is buried in the north aisle of Westminster Abbey.

Operas

Edition: *The Works of Henry Purcell.* The Purcell Society. London, 1878-1965; revised 2nd ed., 1961-.

Dido and Aeneas, Nahum Tate, London, Josias Priest's Boarding School for Young Ladies, Chelsea, December 1689.
The Prophetess, or The History of Dioclesian (semi-opera), Thomas Betterton (after J. Fletcher and P. Massinger), London, Dorset Gardens Theatre, spring 1690.
King Arthur, or The British Worthy (semi-opera), John Dryden, London, Dorset Gardens Theatre, spring 1691.
The Fairy Queen (semi-opera), Elkanah Settle? (after Shakespeare, *A Midsummer Night's Dream*), London, Dorset Gardens Theatre, April 1692.
The Indian Queen (semi-opera) (with Daniel Purcell), John Dryden and R. Howard, London, Drury Lane Theatre, 1695.
The Tempest or The Enchanted Island (semi-opera), T. Shadwell (after Shakespeare), c. 1695.

Other works: incidental music, sacred and secular vocal music, instrumental music, organ pieces.

Publications

About PURCELL: books—

Oettel, J. *Purcells Opern.* Leipzig, n.d.
Cummings, William H. *Purcell.* London, 1881.
Nicoll, A. *A History of Restoration Drama, 1660-1700.* Cambridge, 1923; 4th ed., 1952.
Svanepol, P.F. *Das dramatische Schaffen Purcells.* Vienna, 1926.
Arundell, Dennis. *Henry Purcell.* Oxford, 1927; 1971.
Dupré, Henri. *Purcell.* Paris, 1927; English translation by Catherine Alison Phillips and Agnes Bedford, New York, 1928.
Dent, Edward J. *Foundations of English Opera.* Cambridge, 1928; 1965.
Meyer, Ernst Hermann. *Die mehrstimmige Spielmusik des 17. Jahrhunderts in Nord-und Mittel-europa.* Kassel, 1934.
Westrup, J.A. *Purcell.* London, 1937; 4th ed., 1980; Russian translation, 1980.
Demarquez, S. *Purcell: la vie, l'oeuvre.* Paris, 1951.
Ravenzaaij, G. van. *Purcell.* Haarlem and Antwerp, 1954.
Sietz, R. *Henry Purcell: Zeit, Leben, Werk.* Leipzig, 1956.
Holst, Imogen, ed. *Henry Purcell (1659-1695): Essays on his Music.* London, 1959.
Wilson, J., ed. *Roger North on Music.* London, 1959.
Moore, R.E. *Henry Purcell and the Restoration Theatre.* London, 1961.
Schjelderup-Ebbe, Dag. *Purcell's Cadences.* Oslo, 1962.
Zimmerman, Franklin B. *Purcell, 1659-1695: his Life and Times.* New York and London, 1967; 2nd ed., Philadelphia, 1983.

Price, Curtis A. *Henry Purcell and the London Stage.* Cambridge and New York, 1984.

————, ed. *Purcell: Dido and Aeneas: an Opera.* New York, 1986.

Harris, Ellen T. *Henry Purcell's Dido and Aeneas.* Oxford, 1987.

Zimmerman, Franklin B. *Purcell: a Guide to Research.* New York, 1989.

articles–

Gray, Alan. "Purcell's Dramatic Music." *Proceedings of the Royal Musical Association* 43 (1917).

Squire, William Barclay. "Purcell's 'Dido and Aeneas'." *Musical Times* June (1918).

————. "Purcell's 'Fairy Queen'." *Musical Times* January (1920).

Rendall, E.D. "Purcell's Dramatic Music." *Music and Letters* 1 (1920): 135.

Espinós, Victor. "Las realizaciones musicales del Quijote: Enrique Purcell y su 'Comical History of Don Quixote'." *Revista de la Biblioteca* [Madrid] (1933) [on Purcell's music for Durfey, *The Comical History of Don Quixote*].

Miller, Hugh M. "Henry Purcell and the Ground Bass." *Music and Letters* 29 (1948): 340.

Laurie, M. "Did Purcell Set *The Tempest?*" *Proceedings of the Royal Musical Association* 90 (1963-64): 43.

Buttrey, John. "Dating Purcell's *Dido and Aeneas.*" *Proceedings of the Royal Musical Association* 94 (1967-68): 51.

Covell, R. "Seventeenth-century Music for the Tempest." *Studies in Music* [Australia] 2 (1968): 43.

Savage, Roger. "The Shakespeare-Purcell *Fairy Queen:* a Defence and Recommendation." *Early Music* 1 (1973): 200.

————. "Producing Dido and Aeneas: an Investigation into Sixteen Problems." *Early Music* 4 (1976): 393.

Alssid, Michael. "The Impossible Form of Art: Dryden, Purcell, and King Arthur." *Studies in the Literary Imagination* spring (1977).

Avant-scène opéra November-December (1978) [*Didon et Enée* issue].

Craven, Robert R. "Nahum Tate's Third *Dido and Aeneas:* the Sources of the Libretto to Purcell's Opera." In *The World of Opera.* 1979.

Baldwin, Olive, and Thelma Wilson. "Purcell's Sopranos." *Musical Times* 123 (1982).

Charlton, David. "King Arthur: Dramatick Opera." *Music and Letters* July-October (1983).

Young, Percy M. "John Dryden: Klassische Literatur und neue Musik." In *Thematik und Ideenwelt der Antike bei Georg Friedrich Händel,* edited by Walther Siegmund-Schultze, 51. Halle, 1983.

Harris, Ellen T. "Recitative and Aria in *Dido and Aeneas.*" *Studies in the History of Music* 2 (1987).

unpublished–

Laurie, M. "Purcell's Stage Works." Ph. D. dissertation, Cambridge University, 1962.

Buttrey, J. "The Evolution of English Opera between 1656 and 1695: a Reinvestigation." Ph. D. dissertation, Cambridge University, 1967.

Rinkel, Lawrence S. "The Forms of English Opera: Literary and Musical Responses to a Continental Genre." Ph. D. dissertation, Rutgers University, 1977.

*   *   *

Henry Purcell II, alias 'Orpheus Britannicus, was born between 22 November 1658 and 10 June 1659, probably in Westminster. His father, Henry Purcell I, who served as a singing man and Master of the Choristers at Westminster Abbey, died on 11 August 1664. Soon thereafter, young Henry was adopted by his paternal uncle, Thomas Purcell, Gentleman of the Chapel Royal, Musician for Lute, Viol and Voice, Composer for the Violins, leader of the band of violins, and Groom of the Robes to Charles II.

Within a few years of his father's death, Henry Purcell joined the Children of the Chapel Royal, serving steadily until age fourteen, when his voice broke, and he was discharged, in 1673. Of his education otherwise, we know only that he held a "Bishop's Boy" scholarship at St Peter's, Westminster from 1678 to 1680, and that he complained publicly, in the preface to his *Sonatas of 1683,* that his education was inadequate.

Purcell did receive excellent musical training under Captain Henry Cooke and Pelham Humfrey, however, both of whom studied music abroad. He also was taught by Matthew Locke, John Blow, and Christopher Gibbons, organist. Further, he served for fourteen years as apprentice to John Hingeston, Keeper and Repairer of His Majesty's Instruments. Hingeston was also his godfather, as we know from his will, which, incidentally, identifies Henry Purcell as son of Elizabeth Purcell, who was wife to the elder Henry Purcell.

In 1677, upon the death of his mentor, Matthew Locke, Purcell was appointed Composer in Ordinary for the Violins at the Chapel Royal. Two years later, in 1679, he assumed duties as Organist at Westminster Abbey. Thus, even before finishing his twentieth year, Purcell held three important posts, and a scholarship as well.

Henry Purcell, portrait by J. Closterman, 1695

About 1681, Purcell entered into matrimony, marrying one Frances Peters, daughter of Captain John Baptist Peters, wealthy citizen of Westminster. Altogether, six children were to be born of the marriage; but only Frances, Edward and Mary Peters survived their father, the latter by a scant few weeks.

Already by 1680, Purcell's reputation as a rising musical genius had begun to spread. In 1677 he had made his debut as a composer of instrumental music for theater, with *The Stairre-Case Overture,* and also attracted favorable attention with his wonderfully affective "Elegy on the Death of his worthy Master, Matthew Locke" (*What shall we do, now he is gone?*) During this period, Purcell's songs began to appear in all the major published collections. Many of these were theater songs, which together with his instrumental pieces reflected Purcell's rapid rise to popularity with London's theater public. Some Purcell songs, like "Now the fight's done," and "Britons, strike home," reached a much broader popular audience once they were established as the tunes to which various nationalistic, political, or downright scurrilous texts were circulated daily throughout England.

Further clear evidence of Purcell's mastery of the art of composition appeared in the summer of 1680, when he composed most of his ingeneous fantasias and *In nomines* for consorts of from three to seven instruments. In these elegant, deeply conceived creations, Purcell not only revived England's oldest and most important instrumental tradition. He climaxed that tradition with works of such expressive power and beauty as former generations had never known. Purcell's fantasias and *In nomines* closed a century and a half's tradition of England's finest instrumental polyphony, as developed by such famous masters as Tye, Tallis, Taverner, Byrd and Gibbons. Though still a youth, Purcell appears here as a master among masters.

From the same period, Purcell's anthems, royal welcome songs and odes for various occasions continue the British tradition, despite their more modern Italianate and "Frenchyfied" trappings, which had been the vogue in England from the time or Charles I onward. By 1660, when Charles II renewed the Stewart monarchy, the music of Bassani, Carissimi, Gratiani, Lully and Lelio Colista had become part of British musical culture. Performers, such as Niccolo Matteis, virtuoso violinist, and Giovanni Battista Draghi, harpsichordist, soon popularized this new repertoire, which thereafter profoundly influenced England's musical life. From Purcell's use of forms and techniques characteristic of the works of these composers, as well as from elements of stylistic influence apparent in his own works, it is clear that the new Italian style had caught his fancy. But there is even more persuasive direct evidence, in the meticulous study scores of various Italian masters which Purcell copied during these years, most particularly in his close study of some of the revolutionary madrigals of Claudio Monteverdi, principal pioneer of this new, affective Italian style of the Baroque.

Purcell's most overtly Italianate works were his twenty-two trio sonatas. In a century in which Italianate trio-sonata publications proliferated in every quarter of the musical world, these trio sonatas are unique creations, the foremost of their kind. Paradoxically these twenty-two compositions, even while bringing the latest Italianate styles, forms and techniques to the English public, still retained the essence of the old English praxis.

Meanwhile, various problems had complicated Purcell's life, both at court and at home. His uncle, Thomas, who had fulfilled the role of father to him for nearly two decades, died suddenly, on 31 July 1682. Just a week after the burial of his uncle, Purcell then attended the birth of a new son, John

Baptist, who survived only two months of infancy. As if all this were not enough, on 4 February 1683, Purcell was required to take the Sacrament according to the Church of England, before witnesses. It is not known whether Purcell was suspected of being a Papist, or merely was undergoing a formality contingent upon his new appointment as organist to the Chapel Royal, as of 14 July 1682.

Nevertheless, Purcell continued to compose industriously. After seeing the first set of trio sonatas through the press in June of 1683, he composed eight songs for Playford's *Fourth Book of Choice Ayres and Songs,* seven more for the fifth book in the same series, and a royal ode of thanksgiving for the King's providential delivery from the assassins of the Rye House Plot. The ode, "Fly bold rebellion" shows considerable advances in Purcell's skill of fusing the new Italianate instrumental style with a more traditional English vocal style, as do the three St Cecilian odes composed at this time—"Welcome to all the pleasures," "Raise, raise the voice" and "Laudate Ceciliam" and the ode celebrating the marriage of Princess Ann and Prince George of Denmark, "From hardy climes."

The year 1684 found Purcell involved in a widely discussed organ competition between Bernard Smith, Purcell's candidate, and Renatus Harris, in which, after much heat and a certain amount of skulduggery, Smith was awarded the palm. That year, too, his long and patient service under John Hingeston was rewarded, upon the latter's death, with the award of a livery and annual salary to Purcell as Keeper of His Majesty's Instruments. Throughout the year, he continued to produce odes, anthems, chamber music and theatrical music apace.

Then quite suddenly, on 3 February 1685, King Charles II died of an apoplectic stroke. As the nation mourned, Purcell wrote another touching funeral lament, "If prayers and tears," a warmly personal setting of an evocative text, published with an affective sub-title, "Sighs for our late sovereign, King Charles the second." The accession of James II brought no change in Purcell's official position. Musically, however, Purcell's compositions began to show new strength of inspiration and grander style and design. "My heart is inditing," the anthem he composed for James II's coronation on 23 April, breathes a new air of courtly grandeur, in the Lullian manner. The same sort of style animates his birthday ode for James II, "Sound the trumpet, beat the drum," and the anthem "Blessed are they that fear the Lord," which, according to a rubric in the John Gostling part-books at York Minster, was "Composed for the Thanksgiving appoint'd to be observed in London and 12 miles around and upon the 29th following over England for the Queen's being with child."

Purcell's stylistic development was not restricted to these forms, however, as may be seen in the twenty-nine songs published just then in the four books of *The Theatre of Music,* printed by John Playford and published by his son, Henry, during the years 1685 and 1686, or in the catches and duets that appeared in the same period. One of Purcell's most impressive small masterpieces was the pastoral threnody, "Gentle shepherds, you that know" set to verses penned by Nahum Tate (according to William Cummings, the piece was occasioned by the sudden, tragic death not of "Honest John Playford," but rather of his son, John Jr). It is a fine composition, in the newly developed style, as are Purcell's anthems and sacred songs appearing at that time in Henry Playford's *Harmonia Sacra,* along with several masterful anthems such as "O, sing unto the Lord" and "The Lord is King, the earth may be glad." All reveal him in full mastery of the late, expanded style mentioned above.

For Purcell himself the signal event of the year was the birth of his daughter Frances, one of three children who were to survive him. But he was also surely pleased that, with the fall of James II at the end of 1688 and the establishment of William and Mary as monarchs of Great Britain, he received a new appointment at court as Gentleman of the Private Music. Seemingly, this was a sinecure, adding to his fees without heavily increasing his responsibilities. From a charming anecdote first reported by Hawkins, we learn that his new duties involved performing chamber works for Queen Mary. Apparently the Queen, growing tired of Purcell's songs as sung by John Gostling and accompanied by Arabella Hunt on the lute, asked Hunt to sing the old Scots ballad "Cold and raw." Purcell, biding his time, set the tune as bass to a movement of his next birthday ode for the Queen, to the suggestive couplet: "May her blest example chase/Vice in troops out of the land."

These events coincided with Purcell's rise to preeminence as the foremost composer for the stage in London. His popularity in this realm was soon to be greatly expanded by the entirely new activity he entered into as an opera composer. His first operatic venture was to set Nahum Tate's libretto, *Dido and Aeneas* as an opera, with a great deal of dance intermixed, to satisfy the needs of the Royal choreographer Josias Priest, who had an active dance program at a boarding school for young ladies in Chelsea. These elements were not uncommon in seventeenth-century opera, particularly in France, so it seems clear that Purcell and Tate had studied the field carefully. What was unusual about Purcell's approach to *Dido and Aeneas* was that he should have attempted to perform such a work with amateurs, an attempt that is all the more astonishing in view of the superb quality of the music and the drama itself.

Although quite short, the opera has more dramatic power than any yet heard on the English stage and measures up in this regard to anything performed on any stage in Europe up to that time. Its four principal characters—Dido, Aeneas, Belinda and the Sorceress—are clearly drawn and dramatically convincing. The dramatic pace, greatly abetted by the seventeen intercalated dances, moves quickly and forcefully to the denouement, and the melodic beauty and general musical inspiration are profoundly moving.

Each year after the premiere of *Dido and Aeneas* (1689) until his death, Purcell mounted one major operatic event for the London season (these actually were called "semi-operas," since dialogue, dance and pantomime were included in their performances). First, in 1690, came *The Prophetess, or The History of Dioclesian,* with a plot paralleling the fall of James II. Musically, *Dioclesian* was a resounding success, being the first example of Purcell's new resplendant orchestral style, replete with trumpets and drums, which characterized all his productions during the reign of William and Mary.

King Arthur (1691) was less successful, perhaps due to an incomprehensible story line. But Purcell's music for *King Arthur* is all clarity and delight, expressed again in his resplendant, late style. This fact, added to its excellent adornment "with scenes and machines . . . and dances made by Mr. Jo: Priest" brought great success to the company. Unfortunately, Purcell's autograph score was lost, so that no further performances were possible until the work was reconstructed for presentation at Drury Lane Theatre in 1770.

Purcell's opera for the next season, the longest of his works in this genre, was reported as follows by Peter Motteux in *Gentleman's Journal* for May, 1692: "The opera of which I have spoken to you in former hath at last appeared, and continues to be represented daily; it is called *The Fairy Queen.* The drama is originally [that of] Shakespeare, the music and

decorations are extraordinary. I have heard the dances commended, and without doubt the whole is very entertaining." Aesthetically, the production was a great success, but financially, it did not do well, as Downes observes: ". . . in ornaments [it] was superior to the other two; especially in clothes for all the singers, and dancers, scenes, machines and decoration, all most profusely set-off; and excellently performed, chiefly the instrumental and vocal part composed by the said Mr. Purcell and dances by Mr. Priest. The Court and the town were wonderfully satisfied with it; but the expenses in setting it out being so great, the company got very little by it."

Purcell's last semi-opera, *The Indian Queen,* is filled with irrational, even paradoxical qualities. Musically it is one of the most imaginative, and expressive of all of Purcell's stage works. His penchant for the occult and the mystical, demonstrated from the very beginning of his career, here found profoundly effective expression. In terms of musical composition and style, it is modern beyond belief. However its libretto is the most old-fashioned of all his major works, harking back to the early Restoration period when the London stage was showing the first feeble signs of revival. The plot is bizarre, and filled with historical inaccuracies: Howard set the play against a background of wars between Mexico and Peru as if these were neighboring principalities. Such total disregard of history and geography would have been totally uncharacteristic of Dryden. Nor would Dryden have created such an improbable cardboard villainess as Queen Zempoalla, as depicted in the original play, nor been responsible for the vast amounts of bombast with which the original was stuffed.

However, as Curtis Price suggests, his might well have been the skilful hand that revised the play as an opera for the production of 1695, for which Henry Purcell provided music. He set all but the additional act, which death prevented him from completing, and which consequently was passed on to his brother, Daniel. Whatever the truth here, Purcell rose magnificently to the challenge. Indeed he somehow managed to turn the weaknesses of the original play into sources of remarkable musical power, with new musical characterizations, awesome scenarios, and orchestral music that marks the pinnacle of his career as a dramatic composer.

During the last five or six years of his life, Purcell's creative development manifested itself not only in the sudden appearance of the English semi-opera, but in many other forms as well. Of the forty-three plays for which Purcell provided incidental music, all but half a dozen were written during this final period. These, too, reflect the rapid maturation and fulfillment of style which are so impressive in the semi-operas, as do several anthems, his numerous songs and dialogues, and his odes and welcome songs. Of the latter variety, his five birthday odes for Queen Mary and his last great St Cecilia Ode, "Hail, bright Cecilia." In the latter, a tour-de-force of instrumental and vocal virtuosity, Purcell is said to have sung the counter-tenor solo, " 'Tis Nature's voice," with the "incredible graces" he himself had written.

Amidst all this creative flow, Purcell died on the eve of another annual St Cecilia's Day celebration, which he had done so much to maintain and enrich during the whole tradition of the London society that he had helped to found. The exact cause of death is not known. Hawkins reports that he died because his wife locked him out to punish him for late-night carousing, but this may be dismissed as mere gossip. Several modern physicians to whom I have shown late portraits of Purcell suggest that he may have suffered from a thyroid ailment. However, Westrup's conjecture that he may have died of consumption is perhaps as plausible as any.

From the rudely scrawled signature to his will, and from the obvious haste in which this document was drawn up it is clear that death came unexpectedly. And yet from the annotations to two songs, Altisidora's "From rosy bowers," *Don Quixote* III and "Lovely Albina's come ashore," it seems that Purcell had been ill for quite some time when he died.

Buried in Westminster Abbey near the organ he once played and took care of, Purcell still lives in the memory of his countrymen and of some few beyond the seas, as "the British Orpheus." His reputation on the continent had impressed no less a musician than Archangelo Corelli who, according to Cummings, was actually on his way to England to visit Purcell personally when news of his death turned him back. Elsewhere on the continent, Purcell was equally popular; witness the following statement from *Mackays's Journey Through England* of 1722: "The English affect more the Italian than the French music, and their own compositions are between the gravity of the first and the levity of the other. They have had several great masters of their own. *Henry Purcell's* works in that kind are esteemed beyond Lully's everywhere."

—Franklin B. Zimmerman

PURGATORY.

Composer: Gordon Crosse.

Librettist: Gordon Crosse (after Yeats).

First Performance: Cheltenham, Everyman, 7 July 1966.

Roles: Old Man (baritone); Boy (tenor); chorus (nine to twelve women).

Publications

articles–

Crosse, Gordon. "A Setting of W.B. Yeats." *Opera* 17 (1966): 534.
Walsh, Stephen. "First Performances: Crosse's *Purgatory.*" *Tempo* 77 (1966): 23.

*   *   *

Gordon Crosse's *Purgatory* is an opera in one act based on the play by William Butler Yeats. Crosse's libretto is for the most part faithful to Yeats's text. To the Old Man and the Boy, the only two characters who participate in the dialogue, Crosse has added the ghosts of the Old Man's mother and father as mysterious presences in the music and drama. He has also added two sopranos and an alto who sing off stage (in ensemble) and without words in order to intensify the dramatic action. The number of singers can be increased to as many as twelve. The instrumental ensemble, which includes the standard orchestral instruments, emphasizes per-

cussion and wind instruments for special effects which heighten the doomsday atmosphere of *Purgatory*.

The plot involves the struggle between father (the Old Man) and son (the Boy), and the father's attempt to end the cycle of his mother's misery in purgatory. The Old Man attempts to accomplish this through a series of horrible deeds, which include the murder of his father and son with the same knife. Yet the Old Man does not succeed in releasing his mother from her recurring dream which brings her back to her family's house on her wedding night. Not only does the Old Man continue to be haunted by his mother's wretched situation, but his mother is unable to reverse the unhappiness initiated by her unfortunate marriage to his father. Stephen Walsh, reviewing the first performance of the opera, noted that "Yeats was dealing with questions, both general and particular, . . . the general one the problem of inherited guilt, the particular one the social and political predicament of the young Irish republic, of which perhaps *Purgatory* is conceivably an allegory."

Crosse's motivic style of writing lends itself well to the fragmentary nature of the dialogue between the Old Man and the Boy. In addition to repeating motives at different pitch levels, Crosse also transformed his melodic ideas by modifying rhythmic patterns and by changing the order in which melodic intervals occurred. By rearranging the intervals within a motive, he was able to reshape melodic fragments to serve the expressive needs of the text.

Two of the most significant melodic motives of *Purgatory* are closely related to each other both musically and dramatically. They evolve from places in the opera where the Old Man instructs the Boy to "Study that house," and to "Study that tree." A third motive, which is whole tone in nature and represents the Old Man as the murderer of his father and son, shares three pitches with the "tree motive." In addition to appearing in the vocal line, the motives signifying the house, the tree, and the murder appear in the instrumental parts as well. The melodic and harmonic connections among these motives become unifying factors among sonorities which are seemingly disparate.

By building a network among melodic and harmonic atonal patterns which are linked by the dramatic action, Crosse succeeded in developing a musical network that is audible to the listener. The melodic fragments are not extensive enough to evolve into lyrical melodies, nor are they likely to be recalled by members of the audience as they walk away from a performance of *Purgatory*. Nevertheless, Crosse's careful attention to musical detail brings about a subtle unity and variety which strengthens the listener's understanding of the drama. Crosse himself has said that "one of the reasons the subject [*Purgatory*] appealed to me is that it suited the sort of musical language that I was using at the time . . . a language very much concerned with unity of idea."

In speaking of the musical quality of the play Crosse said, "Its very structure is a musical one; words and images recur in the manner of musical motives, every line reverberates beyond its immediate sense." One can only assume that had Yeats been present at the first performance of the opera he would have approved of Crosse's sensitivity to the musical nuances of *Purgatory*.

—Maureen A. Carr

I PURITANI [The Puritans].

Composer: Vincenzo Bellini.

Librettist: Carlo Pepoli (after Jacques-Arsène Ancelot and Joseph Xavier Boniface, *Têtes rondes et cavaliers*).

First Performance: Paris, Théâtre-Italien, 24 January 1835.

Roles: Elvira (soprano); Arturo (tenor); Riccardo (baritone); Giorgio (bass); Lord Walton (bass); Enrichetta (soprano or mezzo-soprano); Sir Bruno Robertson (tenor); chorus (SSATTBB).

Publications

articles–

Porter, Andrew. "Bellini's Last Opera." *Opera* May (1960): 315.
Petrobelli, P. "Nota sulla poetica di Bellini: a proposito di *I puritani.*" *Muzikoloski zbornik* 8 (1972): 70.
_____. "Bellini e Paisello: altri documenti sulla nascita dei *Puritani.*" In *Il melodramma italiano dell'ottocento: studi e ricerche per Massimo Mila.* Turin, 1977.
Avant-scène opéra March (1987) [*Les Puritains* issue].

*   *   *

The action of *I Puritani* takes place in a fortress near Plymouth during the English civil war. The residents of the

Giulia Grisi and Luigi Lablanche as Elvira and Giorgio in *I Puritani*, London, 1835

fortress prepare to celebrate the forthcoming wedding of Elvira, the daughter of the governor of the fortress, Lord Gualtiero Walton, a supporter of Cromwell. Riccardo, a rejected suitor, laments that he has lost Elvira. Elvira's uncle Giorgio tells her that her father has given permission for her to marry the man she loves, Arturo Talbo, although he is a supporter of the Stuarts. Arturo enters the fort and discovers that Enrichetta, the widow of Charles I, is being held prisoner there. He disguises her in Elvira's wedding veil and the two of them flee, urged on by Riccardo. When Elvira discovers her bridegroom has run off she lapses into madness.

In act II, Giorgio describes Elvira's aberrant behavior to the residents of the fortress. Riccardo announces that Arturo has been proscribed by the Parliament; if he is caught he will be executed. Elvira wanders in, at first melancholic over Arturo's disappearance but then manic as she enacts the start of the wedding ceremony. Giorgio tells Riccardo he must find a way to save Arturo or there will be two victims— Arturo and Elvira. They unite in a paean to their country, to victory, and to honor.

Act III takes place three months later. Arturo returns to the fortress, in the midst of a storm, pursued by soldiers. Hearing Elvira singing his love song, he goes to her and explains why he had abandoned her. The search party draws closer and Arturo tries to hide, but the possibility of Arturo running off again unhinges Elvira's mind. Arturo stays with her, is caught, and condemned to death. Just then it is announced that the war has ended and there is a general amnesty.

I Puritani, Bellini's last opera, contains many ravishing melodies, supported by lush chromatic harmonies; it is the most carefully orchestrated of all his works. Recitative is reduced, replaced by arioso and parlante—still flexible but musically more substantial means of setting the text. Free-standing solo pieces are minimized—neither Elvira nor Arturo has a traditional aria. Instead there are a number of ensembles which show imaginative experimentation with form, allowing both greater fluidity and greater control over larger units of time. Thus it is unfortunate that *I Puritani* makes use of the weakest libretto Bellini ever set. For all of his other mature operas Bellini set libretti written for him by Felice Romani. For *I Puritani* Bellini recruited Count Carlo Pepoli who, according to Bellini, possessed "a talent for good verse and the facility to use it." However, Pepoli had no experience writing for the stage, and Bellini undertook to be his guide. The libretto they created together was full of touching situations and opportunities for expressive music. Unfortunately, it is peopled with stock characters and lacks dramatic consistency.

I Puritani shows Bellini at his most expansive, both in his abilities as a composer and in his willingness to let the music, rather than dramatic necessities, determine the course of the opera. For example, the second act contains four musical numbers—each one a gem. A chorus laments ("Ahi! dolor"), Giorgio describes Elvira's unhappy state ("Cinta di fiori"), Elvira appears for a mad scene ("Qui la voce"), and Giorgio and Riccardo assert their patriotism ("Il rival salvar tu dei"). A study of any one of these numbers reveals Bellini's richer and surer handling of form, melody, harmony, and orchestration. But it must be noted that at the end of the second act the dramatic action has not advanced at all. A plot summary which omitted the second act would be no less coherent than one which included it.

Before *I Puritani* received its premiere in Paris, Bellini agreed to revise and adapt it for a performance at the Teatro San Carlo in Naples. Thus Bellini was in the unusual position of working on two different versions of the opera at the same time. The Paris version was composed for Grisi, Rubini, Tamburini, and Lablache; the Naples version was to star Malibran, Duprez, Pedrazzi, and Porto. That is, instead of soprano, high tenor, baritone, bass, the Naples version is written for mezzo soprano, tenor, tenor, baritone. As things turned out, the Naples version was never performed in the nineteenth century. In the past decade there has been a certain amount of critical debate about the relative merits of these two versions. The changes made for Naples—some music added, some taken out, transpositions and adjustments made to accommodate different singers—are musical ones; dramatic issues are not addressed. Since it can certainly be argued that dramatic issues are the most problematic ones in the opera, it can also be argued that these musical changes do not make an essential difference in the value of the work.

—Charlotte Greenspan

THE PURITANS
See I PURITANI

Q

THE QUEEN OF SHEBA
See DIE KÖNIGIN VON SABA

THE QUEEN OF SPADES [Pikovaya dama].

Composer: Piotr Ilyich Tchaikovsky.

Librettists: M. and P. Tchaikovsky (after Pushkin).

First Performance: St Petersburg, Mariinsky, 19 December 1890.

Roles: Lisa (soprano); Countess (mezzo-soprano); Herman (tenor); Count Tomsky (baritone); Prince Eletsky (bass); Pauline (mezzo-soprano); Governess (mezzo-soprano); Mascha (soprano); Chekalinsky (tenor); Surin (bass); Chaplitsky (tenor); Narumov (bass); Master of Ceremonies (tenor); Characters in interlude at the masked ball: Chloe (soprano); Daphnis (Pauline); Plutus (Tomsky); chorus (SSSAATTBB).

Publications

articles–

Vasil'ev, Jurij. "K rukopisjam *Pikovoj damy.*" *Sovetskaya muzyka* 7 (1980): 99.

Bjalik, Mihail. "Das Romantische in Tschaikowskis *Pique Dame.*" In *Romantikkonferenz (2.) 1982,* edited by Günther Stephan and Hans John, 106. Dresden, 1983.

Schläder, Jürgen. "Operndramaturgie und musikalische Konzeption zu Tschaikowskijs Opern *Eugen Onegin* und *Pique Dame* und ihren literarischen Vorlagen." *Deutsche Vierteljahrsschrift für Literaturwissenschaft und Geistesgeschichte* 57 (1983): 525 [summary in English].

Avant-scène opéra April-May (1989) [*La dame de pique* issue].

* * *

The tense overture to *The Queen of Spades,* full of foreboding, introduces several themes to be heard later on in the work; it leads directly into act I, which takes place in the Summer Garden, St Petersburg, where children are playing, accompanied by their nurses and governesses. Two soldiers, Surin and Chekalinsky, discuss their melancholy friend, Herman, who is obsessed by gambling, yet never makes a bet. Tomsky cannot understand Herman's incessant gloom, and Herman explains that he has fallen in love with a girl whose name he does not know. Tomsky tells him that he must make every effort to learn this, but Herman is afraid that a difference in social rank will make any relationship impossible.

Herman states that if his pursuit of the unknown woman fails, he will commit suicide. Prince Eletsky, Chekalinsky, and Surin appear. The prince is elated over his recent engagement; his mood contrasts with Herman's wretchedness, and their conflicting emotions are expressed in a duet. The prince greets his fiancée, Lisa, who is accompanied by her grandmother, the countess. To his horror, Herman recognizes that Lisa is the girl with whom he has become infatuated. Lisa and the countess note Herman's strange looks as they, along with Herman, Tomsky, and the prince, sing an ensemble.

Tomsky then tells the story of the countess, who was once a celebrated beauty, though passionately addicted to cards. In a ballad he describes how, after she had lost everything at the tables, the Count St Germain gave her the secret of three cards, which would enable her to regain her fortune. She was successful and passed the secret on to two others. She was warned in a dream that if she ever conveyed the secret to a third party, however, she would die. Surin and Chekalinsky jokingly suggest that Herman should try to secure the countess's secret himself. A storm breaks and Herman, left alone on the stage, muses over what has been said and resolves to win Lisa from the prince.

Act II opens in a luxurious home where a ball is in progress. The master of ceremonies invites the guests into the garden to see the fireworks, and Chekalinsky and Surin decide to play a trick upon Herman. The prince is upset by Lisa's depression and, in a well-known aria, expresses his love and respect. Herman appears with a letter from Lisa requesting a meeting. As he thinks of the three cards, Chekalinsky and Surin whisper to him in such a way that he thinks he has heard a ghost. Lisa slips Herman a key which will give him access to her room via that of the countess. Herman insists on coming to see her that night. The scene ends with a triumphal chorus to mark the arrival of Empress Catherine.

The next scene takes place in the countess's bedroom at midnight. Herman hides himself while the countess is escorted to her boudoir by her maids and Lisa. When all is quiet and the servants have departed, Herman enters and looks at the countess, who stares back terrified. Herman beseeches her to tell him the secret of the cards, but she remains silent. To try to persuade her he draws out a pistol, and she falls back dead. Lisa enters and is convinced that Herman did not love her but was using her for his own ends. The scene now changes to the barracks, where Herman is reading a letter from Lisa forgiving him and requesting a midnight rendezvous. As the wind howls and a funereal chorus is heard, the countess's ghost appears and tells him that he must marry Lisa and that the cards he seeks are the Three, The Seven, and the Ace.

The next scene takes place at the canal near the Winter Palace where Lisa waits anxiously for Herman and expresses her feelings in a powerful aria. As the clock strikes midnight, Herman arrives and they express their love in an impassioned duet. But the illusion is shattered when he announces that they are going to the gaming table. Herman's wild obsession is too much for Lisa, and she drowns herself in the canal. The final scene takes place in the gambling house, where men are having supper. All are surprised to see the prince, whose engagement with Lisa has been broken off. Herman enters and, playing against Chekalinsky, wins twice with the Three and the Seven. He sings an aria about fate. Recklessly he calls for another opponent. The prince volunteers, but when Herman turns up a card saying that it is the Ace, it proves to be the Queen of Spades. The ghost of the countess appears, Herman stabs himself and, as he dies, begs the prince's forgiveness. The chorus sings a prayer for Herman's soul.

Obsessed with the element of fate, Tchaikovsky could not help but be fascinated by Pushkin's story. The opera is a masterpiece of the highest order in which, from the very beginning, a feeling of apprehension and foreboding is never far from the surface. The audience's attention is sustained by a series of contrasting scenes in which normalcy vies with abnormality, such elements sometimes occurring simultaneously as in the duet of Herman and the prince in act I. The opera abounds in fine numbers, which provide an almost inexhaustible repertoire for opera singers. The system of fate motives, especially those associated with the three cards, runs like a thread throughout the whole work, binding and fusing it together in a most effective manner. *The Queen of Spades* must be considered one of Tchaikovsky's outstanding achievements.

—Gerald Seaman

A QUIET PLACE
See TROUBLE IN TAHITI [AND] A QUIET PLACE

QUINAULT, Philippe.

Librettist. Born 5 June 1635, in Paris. Died 26 November 1688, in Paris. Married: Louise Goujon [born Bouvet], a wealthy widow, 29 April 1660. Received his literary education from the poet Tristan l'Hermite, for whom he was a valet; his comedy *Les rivales* performed in Paris, 1653; became a jurist; secretary to the Duc de Guise, 1655; wrote verses for the court divertissement *La grotte de Versailles* for the court of Louis XIV, 1668; member of the Académie Française, 1670; collaborated with Molière and Corneille on the tragédie-ballet *Psyché*, set by Lully for the court of Louis XIV, 1671; member of the Académie des Inscriptions et Belles Lettres, 1674.

Librettos

Les fêtes de l'Amour et de Bacchus (pastoral), J.B. Lully, 1672.
Cadmus et Hermione, J.B. Lully, 1673.
Alceste, J.B. Lully, 1674; G.C. Schurmann, 1719; F.-A.-D. Philidor, 1776.
Thésée, J.B. Lully, 1675; J.J. de Mondonville, 1765; F.J. Gossec, 1782; Grenier, 1782.
Atys, J.B. Lully, 1676; N. Piccinni, 1780.
Isis, J.B. Lully, 1677.
Proserpine, J.B. Lully, 1680; G. Paisiello, 1803.
Persée, J.B. Lully, 1682; F.-A.-D. Philidor, 1780.
Phaëton, J.B. Lully, 1683.
Amadis, J.B. Lully, 1684; De La Borde and H.M. Berton, 1771; J.C. Bach, 1779.

Roland, J.B. Lully, 1685; N. Piccinni, 1778.
Armide, J.B. Lully, 1686; T. Traetta, 1761; C.W. Gluck, 1777; J. Mysliveček, 1779.

Publications/Writings

By QUINAULT:books–

Recueil des plus beaux vers qui ont eté mis en chant. Paris, 1668.
Nouveau recueil de vers mis en chant. Paris, 1670.
Recueil de tous les plus beaux airs bachiques. Paris, 1671.
Théâtre. 5 vols. Paris, 1739.

About QUINAULT:books–

Crapelet, G.A. *Notice sur la vie et les ouvrages de Quinault.* Paris, 1824.
Lindemann, F. *Die Operntexte Ph. Quinaults vom literarischen Standpunkte aus betrachtet.* Leipzig, 1904.
Richter, E. *Philippe Quinault.* Leipzig, 1911.
Gros, E. *Philippe Quinault: sa vie et son oeuvre.* Paris, 1926.
Buijtendorp, J.B.A. *Philippe Quinault, sa vie, ses tragédies et ses tragicomédies.* Amsterdam, 1928.
Lancaster, H.C. *A History of French Dramatic Literature in the 17th Century,* vol. 3, no. 2. Baltimore, 1936.
Girdlestone, C.M. *La tragédie en musique considerée comme genre littéraire.* Geneva, 1972.
Anthony, J. *French Baroque Music from Beaujoyeulx to Rameau.* London, 1973; 2nd ed., 1978.

articles–

Courville, X. de. "Quinault, poète d'opéra." *La revue musicale* 6/no. 3 (1925): 74.
Eerde, J. van. "Quinault, the Court and Kingship." *Romantic Review* (1962): 174.
Maurice-Amour, L. "Comment Lully et ses poètes humanisent dieux et héros." In *Opéra et littérature français* (1965): 59.
Giraud, Y. "Quinault et Lully ou l'accord de deux styles." *Marseille* 95 (1973): 195.
Howard, Patricia. "Lully and the Ironic Convention." *Cambridge Opera Journal* 1 (1989): 139.
_____. "The Positioning of Women in Quinault's World Picture." In *Actes du Colloque Lully,* 193. 1990.
_____. "The Influence of the Précieuses on Content and Structure in Quinault's and Lully's *tragédies-lyriques.*" *Acta musicologica* 63/no. 1 (1991): 57.

*　　*　　*

Philippe Quinault has won an enduring place in music history as co-founder of French opera. Together with the composer Jean-Baptiste Lully, he devised a literary and musical structure which satisfied the national taste for over a hundred years, making earlier experiments seem insignificant forerunners, and later departures decadent distortions. His influence even extended into the nineteenth century, and many of the structures found in the grand operas of Meyerbeer, Auber and Berlioz originated in the integrated tableaux of solos, choruses and ballets devised by Quinault.

Both Lully and Quinault had established reputations before coming together, but the fourteen stage works they completed collaboratively far outshone their previous independent achievements. Their working relationship was complex: while

Lully had to please no-one but himself, Quinault wrote for three masters: the king, the punctilious Académie Française, and the autocratic composer. Each libretto, often upon a subject suggested by Louis XIV, was submitted to be judged by the Académie for literary merit and by Lully for dramatic truth. Although the artistic priorities of the day gave a higher status to the poet than to the musician, Quinault seems to have been wholly pliable to Lully's demands, allegedly rewriting one libretto (*Phaëton*) some twenty times at the composer's insistence.

Quinault's operas (properly, *tragédies lyriques*) are devised in five acts, preceded by a prologue eulogizing the king. Most of the subjects are mythological; the last three operas set stories from the age of chivalry. Some of Quinault's innovations mark a conscious departure from contemporary Italian opera: he aimed at creating a continuous dramatic flow across each act, reducing scene-changes to a minimum, and linking scenes with plausible entrances and exits. He ended most acts with a set-piece finale, incorporating chorus and dance, providing Lully with the opportunity to create large-scale musical structures from a minimum of text. After the first two librettos, he dropped the comic scenes popular in Venetian opera, but even so, the operas are rarely genuinely tragic; love-intrigues, often involving gods and goddesses, make up the majority of his plots, and most contrive happy endings.

Quinault's ability to write witty exchanges in what a contemporary called his "dialectic of love" resulted in a wealth of sparkling (sadly untranslatable) two-liners. His characters reproduce the elegant logic and verbal play of the best court conversation and so delighted the courtiers who made up a large proportion of his public. The court connection, however, was to prove dangerous for him: in 1677 Quinault was banished from court and forbidden to work with Lully, after writing scenes in *Isis* in which he was thought to have used scenes between Jupiter, Juno and the persecuted nymph, Io, to caricature the notorious domestic rivalries between Louis, his principal mistress, Madame de Montespan and his new entanglement, Madame du Ludres. Two years later he was reinstated, having been deemed indispensable.

Deeply influenced by his contemporaries Corneille and Racine, Quinault could also write in the noble manner. Cornellian conflicts between love and duty surface in the last three operas. Parallels with Racine are apparent in a handful of all too brief monologues given to embittered or rejected women (Medea in *Thésée,* Merope in *Persée*); these show Quinault as a remarkable if biased psychologist who perceived the issue of women in love to be fit subject matter for tragedy.

Quinault's success gave rise to many jealous attacks in his lifetime, but in the eighteenth century his standing was higher than Lully's, with praise from Pierre-Charles Roy, Marmontel, D'Alembert and Voltaire. Remarkable testimony to his reputation lies in the many resettings of his librettos by such forward-looking composers as Traetta, Paisiello, Piccinni and Gluck: at a time when Lully was thought to be replaceable, Quinault's work was regarded as enshrining the secret of the perfect libretto.

—Patricia Howard

R

RAAFF, Anton.

Tenor. Baptized 6 May 1714, in Gelsdorf, near Bonn. Died 28 May 1797, in Munich. Studied with Ferrandini in Munich, 1736, and with Bernacchi in Bologna, 1737; entered the service of Clement Augustus, the Elector of Cologne, 1736; sang at the betrothal of Maria Theresa in Florence, 1738; sang in Venice, 1739; sang in Bonn, 1741-42; sang in Vienna, 1749; sang in Italy, 1751-52; principal tenor in Naples and Florence, 1760-70; sang throughout Germany and Austria, 1770-80.

Publications

About RAAFF: books–

Schubart, C.F.D. *Ideen zu einer Ästhetik der Tonkunst.* Vienna, 1806.
Kelly, M. *Reminiscences.* London, 1826.
Freiberger, H. *Anton Raaff (1714-1797): sein Leben und Wirken.* Cologne, 1929.
Anderson, E. ed. *The Letters of Mozart and his Family.* London, 1938.

articles–

Prota-Giurleo, U. "Notizie biografiche intorno ad alcuni musicisti d'oltralpe a Napoli nel settecento." *Analecta musicologica* 2 (1965): 136.
Petrobelli, P. "The Italian years of Anton Raaff." *Mozart-Jahrbuch 1973-74.* (1975): 233.
Heartz, D. "Raaff's last Aria: a Mozartian Idyll in the Spirit of Hasse." *Musical Quarterly* 40 (1974): 517.

* * *

Anton Raaff was one of the most famous tenors of the 18th century. He studied first with Ferrandini in Munich, then with Bernacchi in Bologna, where he met Padre Martini. Active principally in Italy, Raaff sang throughout Europe, specializing in *opera seria.* Many of the major composers of the day, including Jommelli, J.C. Bach, Sacchini, Piccinni, Hasse, Holzbauer, and Mozart wrote music for him. His correspondence with Martini survives (see Petrobelli) and is an important source of information about musical life in the 18th century. Raaff's present day notoriety rests to a large extent on his creating the title role in Mozart's *Idomeneo.* Mozart's own letters reveal much about Raaff's aging voice and the problems Mozart went through to please the singer (see Heartz article).

Raaff's vocal style centered on a beautiful legato technique, portamento, exacting intonation, and proper declamation of the text. He is said to have relied on falsetto as well. The effect of his singing was considerable though perhaps somewhat old-fashioned, as the following 1751 account from Tartini to Martini suggests: "I sincerely confess that I have never yet heard such extraordinary singing . . . I continue to thank God that I find myself alive and as a result that I am able to reassure myself that the true style of singing has not been lost in the present (in general very unhappy) time: on the contrary, it has been perfectly restored in this most worthy man, in whom one does not know how to divide musical virtues from moral ones, for in him these qualities are present in the highest degree" (trans. Petrobelli).

Schubart's report in his *Ideen zu einer Ästhetik der Tonkunst* is more specific, noting a wide range ("from the alto to bass"), and full and pure tone quality. Schubart also mentions Raaff's inimitable agility, beautiful skill at tasteful ornamention and cadenzas, and depth of expression.

Metastasio, however, wrote that Raaff lacked the vocal power to be effective in large settings, as "all the finesse and delicacy, and in sum all that is most admirable in his singing will be lost," and further complained of Raaff's poor acting skills. Ironically, Raaff's love of Metastasian text was absolute, and he even subscribed to the complete edition of his libretti.

In later years, Raaff's range appears to have narrowed considerably. Although Michael Kelly found Raaff (then in his seventies) to still possess a "fine voce de petto and pure style of singing," Mozart was not so kind upon hearing Raaff in Holzbauer's *Günther von Schwarzburg* in 1777. As he wrote to his father: "Raaff sang four arias in such a fashion as to call forth the remark that his voice was the strongest reason why he sang so badly. Anyone who hears him begin an aria without at once reminding himself that it is Raaff, the once famous tenor, who is singing, is bound to burst out laughing." Mozart further confirmed Raaff's lack of stage presence, which became quite noticeable during the rehearsals for *Idomeneo.* Again in a letter to his father, Mozart is quite to the point: "Raaff is like a statue."

Despite Mozart's harsh criticism of Raaff and the difficulties he encountered in composing for him, the two seem to have gotten along quite well. Raaff was instrumental as well in helping Mozart obtain the commission for *Idomeneo* and was an important contact for Mozart during his 1777 trip to Mannheim.

—David Pacun

RADAMISTO.

Composer: George Frideric Handel.

Librettist: Nicola F. Haym (after D. Lalli, *L'amor tirannico, o Zenobia,* Florence, 1712).

First Performance: London, King's Theatre in the Haymarket, 27 April 1720; revised 28 December 1720, January-February 1728.

Anton Raaff

Roles: Farasmane (bass); Radamisto (soprano); Zenobia (contralto); Tigrane (soprano); Polissena (soprano); Fraarte (soprano); Tiridate (tenor).

Publications

articles–

Edlemann, Bernd. "Die zweite Fassung von Händels Oper 'Radamisto' (HWV 12b)." *Göttinger Händel-Beiträge* 2 (1986): 99.
Milhous, Judith, and Robert D. Hume. "A Prompt Copy of Handel's *Radamisto*." *Musical Times* June (1986).

Radamisto is George Frideric Handel's first opera for the Royal Academy of Music. It differs from his previous London operas by eschewing mythological, magical, and pastoral texts; its plot is derived from Book xii of the *Annals* of Tacitus. Nicola Haym adapted the libretto for Handel from an earlier libretto, *L'amor tirannico (Tyrannical Love)* by Domenico Lalli. The extended family relationships and the entangled love interests make this story as modern as any television serial.

The opera tells the saga of Farasmane, king of Thracia, and his two children: Radamisto, who is married to Zenobia, and Polissena, who is married to Tiridate, king of Armenia. Tiridate falls in love with Zenobia and "to satisfy his unjust Amours" makes war on Farasmane, whom he takes prisoner. Tiridate threatens Radamisto with his father's death unless he surrenders the city. Farasmane orders his son not to accede to these demands. Radamisto and Zenobia flee from Tiridate's approaching soldiers, and Zenobia, fearing captivity more than death, urges Radamisto to kill her. Radamisto half-heartedly tries, and she throws herself into the river. Radamisto surrenders to Tigrane, Tiridate's ally. Meanwhile, Fraarte, Tiridate's brother, rescues Zenobia from the river. Complicating the story further, Fraarte is also in love with Zenobia, and Tigrane is in love with Polissena.

Tigrane, rejecting the tyranny of Tiridate, helps Radamisto disguise himself as Ismeno, one of Radamisto's servants. Radamisto fails, however, to convince his sister Polissena to turn against her husband Tiridate, even to save her father and brother. Rather, she, faithful to her marriage vows, protects her husband's life and then begs his forgiveness for Farasmane and Radamisto. Tiridate does not concede, but Radamisto and Zenobia are later saved when Polissena brings the news that his army, led by Tigrane and Fraarte, are in revolt against him. Ultimately, Farasmane regains his throne, Polissena forgives her husband his mistreatment of her, and Radamisto reinstates Tiridate as king of Armenia.

Radamisto exists in two versions written only a few months apart for different casts. Farasmane was the only role to keep the same singer and voice range. The changes assist the modern casting director, showing, as they do, that Handel did not follow a regular pattern in assigning treble male roles to male or female singers. At first Radamisto and Tigrane were sung by women, then by men. On the other hand, Fraarte was at first sung by a man, then by a woman. Further, Handel did not identify individual female singers exclusively with roles of one sex. Thus Margherita Durastanti first played the role of Radamisto, then the role of Zenobia.

One of the most striking dramatic differences between these two versions concerns the role of Fraarte. Before the April 1720 performance, the castrato Baldassari had complained to the directors of the Royal Academy about his part "that he had never acted any thing, in any other Opera, below the Character of a Sovereign; or, at least, a Prince of the Blood; and that now he was appointed to be a Captain of the Guard, and a Pimp." The Directors consented "that he should make love to ZENOBIA, with proper limitations. The Chairman signified to him, that the Board had made him a Lover, but he must be contented to be an unfortunate one, and be rejected by his mistress. He expressed himself very easy under this." This contretemps is clearly the origin for Fraarte becoming the brother of Tiridate in Handel's original version, and a competitor for the hand of Zenobia. In the December 1720 version, after Baldassari's departure, Fraarte is demoted to minister, the love interest excised, and the entire role contracted.

In addition to this dramatic change, the December 1720 version included a number of musical additions and alterations to reflect the changes in range for a number of the parts and the general superiority of the cast. In particular, the roles of Radamisto and Tigrane were expanded. All in all, Handel composed ten new arias, one duet, and one quartet as additions to or substitutions for the December version. Of these the most remarkable is the quartet. Ensembles in Handel's operas are rare. Most operas can claim at least one duet, but trios occur in only four operas: *Tamerlano, Orlando, Alcina,* and *Imeneo.* The quartet in the December 1720 version of *Radamisto* is unique in Handel's operas. Polissena, Zenobia, and Radamisto tell Tiridate "Surrender or die" ("O cedere o perir"). Tiridate remains obdurate. Handel sets this by pairing the two women, often giving them sustained, lyrical lines in imitation as they plead with Tiridate to concede. Radamisto's part is sometimes joined to theirs, but is frequently given musical prominence by sixteenth note runs in the top half of the singer Senesino's range as he insists on surrender. Tiridate's part is distinguished by a repetitive syllabic setting in sixteenth notes, depicting his dogged refusal to listen to any of them.

Even without the quartet, however, the first version is filled with musical riches. The opera opens with Polissena's cry from the heart, "Sommi Dei" ("Great Gods!"), in which she asks the gods to take pity on her heartache. Her angular opening line is completely unaccompanied. Thereafter the orchestra alternates between the barest support and angry descending unison scales. In this briefest of arias, Polissena is shown to be totally alone and emotionally assaulted.

When Radamisto thinks he has lost Zenobia, his aria "Ombra cara" ("Dear shade") depicts his anguish in long, sustained lines set against an intricate, contrapuntal and sometimes chromatic string accompaniment. The complexity of the accompaniment explores the depth of emotion Radamisto feels but cannot express. The simplicity of his vocal line is therefore all the more heartbreaking.

Radamisto was one of Handel's most popular operas. The composer's first biographer, John Mainwaring, writing in 1760, states that the "assembly of ladies . . . , who had forc'd their way into the house with an impetuosity but ill suited to their rank and sex, actually fainted through the excessive heat and closeness of it."

—Ellen T. Harris

RAISA, Rosa [Rose Burchstein].

Soprano. Born 30 May 1893, in Bialystok, Poland. Died 28 September 1963, in Los Angeles. Married: singer Giacomo Rimini. Studied with Eva Tetrazzini, and at San Pietro a Majella, Naples, with Barbara Marchisio; debut as Leonora in *Oberto,* Parma, 1913; debuts at Chicago Opera, 1913, and Covent Garden, 1914, both as Aida; debut at Teatro alla Scala as Lida in 1916; created the roles of Asteria in Boito's *Nerone,* 1924, Turandot, 1926, both at the Teatro alla Scala, and Leah in Rocca's *The Dybbuk,* 1936; primarily associated with the Chicago Opera 1913-37, with roles including Aida, Maddalena, Tosca, Valentine, Norma, and Donna Anna.

* * *

Rosa Raisa is an outstanding example of an artist who is so identified with one opera company and city that her achievements elsewhere are overlooked. She was so greatly admired in her home theater that she did not need to travel the world in search of fame. The historian must realize, however, that an understandable sense of proprietorship is at issue when such an icon is critiqued by local reviewers.

Because Raisa's non-Chicago career is substantial, ample perspectives exist to help gauge her place in history. The Chicago Opera in Raisa's time toured North America every season for almost three months; Raisa was therefore regularly scrutinized by the critics of Boston, New York, Cleveland,

Dallas, San Francisco and other important musical centers. Her seven South American and Mexican seasons as well as the European career capped with her three Toscanini-Teatro alla Scala seasons (world premieres of Turandot and Nerone) add an additional body of mainstream criticism. This balance is important as those writers, critics, and historians who best knew her work in Chicago maintain that she had no equal. As Chicago was a world-class music center, which heard her illustrious predecessors and contemporaries, these assertions lend credibility to her fame.

The much loved Claudia Muzio shared nine Chicago seasons with Raisa. The two sopranos were constantly in each other's shadows throughout their best years not only in Chicago but also in South America and Italy. Though they shared some of the same repertoire (*Aida, Trovatore,* and *Cavalleria rusticana*), they represented totally different vocal and dramatic values. Raisa gloried in her voluminous and brilliant voice capable of bravura feats delivered with intense emotionalism. Muzio seduced with her soft-grained voice with its delicate chiaroscuro and her intensity and emotion wedded to poetic suggestion. It was possible for the same public to adore both divas for their unique qualities. When Muzio first unveiled her Aida at the Chicago Opera the critics, unstinting in their praise of her presentation, called her the best "Italian born" Aida on the current stage.

Raisa was one of the twentieth century's true dramatic sopranos with a dark-hued and brilliant voice and sweeping emotional delivery. Wherever she appeared critics invariably

Rosa Raisa as Aida, London, 1914

singled out the physically powerful sensation her voice produced. Her voice had its strengths and weaknesses. The clarion upper register balanced the sepulchral chest register at the loss of a consistently rich and even mid range. Recordings confirm that in so wide ranging a voice the inevitable weakness was the middle. Depending on the requirements of the music she could adjust her placement to make beautiful and powerful sounds in the middle, but one is conscious of adjustment of technique to suit the situation. Trained in the florid skills of nineteenth-century singing Raisa possessed a genuine trill and she could sing coloratura passages accurately. Her musical taste was not aristocratic; her impulse was to be dramatically vivid and realistic, thrilling in vocal display, even reckless in her need to make vocal effects. An unconventional beauty, her superior stage presence and regal bearing wedded to her imposing voice created a unique dramatic artist.

As to Raisa's work as a recording artist, much has to be taken on faith. She made five groups of recordings from 1917 to 1933 for four labels (Pathé, Vocalion, Brunswick, and Voce del Padrone). We have always been told that very large and brilliant voices were almost impossible to capture acoustically and even difficult electrically. Raisa herself passionately disliked her recordings, maintaining that none adequately revealed the power of her voice. Many of her recordings are mere blueprints of what she could do. Most are not distinguished, but there are a handful that are remarkable: *Mefistofele, Vespri siciliani, Aida,* and *Il trovatore* among the acoustics, and *Gioconda* and *Andrea Chénier* among the electricals. Duets with baritone husband Giacomo Rimini from their concert repertoire such as Don Pasquale and Luisa Miller are sad omissions.

Although very different in vocal and artistic values Raisa was most often compared to Ponselle and Muzio. Unlike Muzio, Ponselle was a close personal friend who admired Raisa and saw her as having a secure high register, with its potential for trills, which was denied her. Ponselle has written that she proposed to Raisa that they perform Aida together with Ponselle as Amneris, thinking their voices heard together on the same stage would produce proper colors and contrasts. Muzio lifted her art to yet another level of expressiveness and ultimately became a figure of tragedy and legend. Raisa's gifts were more obvious, and her artistic bent did not rise to levels of mystery. She viewed her gifts as an opportunity to thrill audiences with the power, range, drama and beauty of her voice.

—Charles B. Mintzer

THE RAKE'S PROGRESS.

Composer: Igor Stravinsky.

Librettists: W.H. Auden and C. Kallman (after Hogarth's series of engravings).

First Performance: Venice, La Fenice, 11 September 1951.

Roles: Anne (soprano); Tom Rakewell (tenor); Nick Shadow (baritone); Baba the Turk (mezzo-soprano); Trulove (bass); Mother Goose (mezzo-soprano); Sellem (tenor); Keeper of the Madhouse (bass); chorus (SATB).

Publications

book–

Griffiths, P. *Igor Stravinsky: The Rake's Progress.* Cambridge, 1982.

articles–

Craft, R. "Reflections on *The Rake's Progress.*" *The Score* no. 9 (1954): 24.
Cooke, D. "*The Rake* and the 18th Century." *Musical Times* 103 (1962): 20.
Abert, A.A. "Strawinskys *The Rake's Progress:* strukturell betrachtet." *Musica* 25 (1971): 243.
Josipovici, G. "*The Rake's Progress:* Some Thoughts on the Libretto." *Tempo* no. 113 (1975): 2.
Ordzhonikidze, G. "Nravstvennye uroki nasmeshlivoy pritchi." *Sovetskaya muzyka* no. 1 (1979): 56.
Schneider, Frank. "*The Rake's Progress* oder Die Oper der verspielten Konventionen. Eine dramaturgische Studie." *Jahrbuch Peters 1980* 3 (1981): 135.
Spiegelman, Willard. "The *Rake,* the *Don,* the *Flute:* W.H. Auden as Librettist." *Parnassus* 10 (1982): 171.

*   *   *

Stravinsky first saw prints of William Hogarth's engravings depicting the life of an eighteenth-century libertine at the Chicago Art Institute in 1947. He had long wanted to write an opera with an original text in English, and Hogarth's pictures immediately suggested to him a succession of operatic scenes. His friend Aldous Huxley suggested W.H. Auden as a librettist, and the two worked together instinctively from the start. Hogarth's scenes are not followed closely in the opera, which adds to the simple story depicted in the engravings a mythic dimension ranging from the Greek myths of Venus and Adonis to the Faust legend with the introduction of Nick Shadow, who is none other than the devil himself. The libretto is a masterpiece of balance and symmetry, with moralizing counterbalanced by the element of chance, Hogarth's pregnant servant girl replaced by the chaste Anne, the ne'er-do-well rake by the innocent but fatally weak Tom (more reminiscent of Faust than Don Juan) and the element of evil personified by Nick Shadow.

The opera is cast in the mold of an eighteenth-century "number opera," with a succession of separate arias, recitatives, duets, trios, choruses, and instrumental interludes. Although in the earlier scenes the action is carried forward by the *secco* recitatives, as the opera progresses, the story unfolds almost entirely in song. While Stravinsky limited his outside listening during the work's composing almost exclusively to Mozart's *Così fan tutte,* there is little direct resemblance between the two works. Accused of avoiding the complex issues facing the twentieth-century composer by escaping into neoclassicism, Stravinsky always maintained that it was possible for a composer to re-use the past and still move forward, and he asked listeners to focus instead on discovering the real qualities of the opera.

Throughout his life, Stravinsky was known to have an extraordinarily sensitive ear, and his preoccupation with harmony and color are ever-present in *The Rake.* The degree of control over the tonal organization is almost without precedent. The opera rises tonally to the dominant E, the dramatic turning point, with each episode in Tom's progress centered on an ever higher key area. As the action unfolds, Tom has

The Rake's Progress, **Glyndebourne Festival, 1989**

moments of insight and doubt indicative of a psychologically complex character, and these points are distinguished musically by the use of keys outside the main tonal framework. The use of key circles within each act is close to Mozart's in *Così fan tutte,* the source of the more easily attributable derivations. Tom's cavatina "Love, too frequently betrayed" uses an opening motive from "Un aura amorosa," the arioso and terzettino are modeled on "Vorrei dir," and the whores' chorus seems inspired by the quintet "Di scrivermi ogni giorno." The harpsichord figurations for the card-playing scene, on the other hand, come from Tchaikovsky's *The Queen of Spades,* an opera Stravinsky must have known from his youth in Russia, rather than from any baroque model. The entire Bedlam scene was likely suggested to Hogarth by the popular ballads on the "Mad Tom of Bedlam" theme, so ubiquitous that one was included in a collection of Purcell songs.

Whatever the final verdict, Stravinsky's opera is no mere exercise in musical antiquarianism. Its music is vital and compelling, and it supports the drama in terms of both comedy and tragedy—the same elements Mozart fused so powerfully in *Don Giovanni.* As to why *The Rake* has been somewhat neglected since its initial flurry of performances, one may ask whether our craving for originality and hunger for the new has blinded us to this and other neoclassic works. It is true that Stravinsky declined a second Auden libretto, thinking that it would have meant composing a sequel to *The Rake.* After the premiere, Stravinsky began to turn toward

serial composition, which was rapidly gaining the attention of the avant garde among the musical establishment.

—Robert H. Danes

RAMEAU, Jean-Philippe.

Composer. Born 25 September 1683, in Dijon. Died 12 September 1764, in Paris. Attended the Jesuit College of Dijon, 1693-97; in Italy, 1701; with a traveling French opera troupe as a violinist; assistant organist at Notre Dame in Avignon, and organist at Clermont-Ferrand, 1702; succeeded his father as church organist at the cathedral in Dijon, 1709; organist in Lyons, 1713; organist at the cathedral in Clermont-Ferrand, 1715-23; *Traité de l'harmonie* published in Paris, 1722; organist at Sainte-Croix-de-la-Bretonnerie, 1732; *Nouveau système de musique théorique,* 1726; music master to the wife of La Pouplinière, through whom he obtained the libretto for *Samson* from Voltaire; composer of the King's chamber music; granted a patent of nobility. Rameau was the subject of numerous vigorous debates comparing his music and his theories to those of previous generations of musicians, most notably those of Lully.

Operas

Edition:

J.-P. Rameau: Oeuvres complètes. Edited by C. Saint-Saëns, C. Malherbe, M. Emmanuel, and M. Teneo. Paris, 1895-1924; 1968.
_____. Edited by N. Zaslaw and F. Lesure. Paris and New York, 1983-.

Samson, Voltaire, 1733.
Hippolyte et Aricie, S.-J. Pellegrin, Paris, Opéra, 1 October 1733; revised, 11 September 1742.
Les Indes galantes (opéra-ballet), L. Fuzelier, Paris, Opéra, 23 August 1735; revised 10 March 1736, 28 May 1743, 8 June 1751, and 14 July 1761.
Castor et Pollux, P.-J. Bernard, Paris, Opéra, 24 October 1737; revised, 8 June 1754.
Les fêtes d'Hébé (opéra-ballet), A.G. de Montdorge, Paris, Opéra, 21 May 1739.
Dardanus, C.-A. Le Clerc de la Bruyère, Paris, Opéra, 19 November 1739; revised, 23 April 1744.
La princesse de Navarrre (comédie-ballet), Voltaire, Versailles, 23 February 1745; revised as *Les fêtes de Ramire,* Versailles, 22 December 1745.
Platée, J. Autreau and A.-J. Le Valois d'Orville, Versailles, 31 March 1745; libretto revisions, 9 February 1749.
Les fêtes de Polymnie (opéra-ballet), L. de Cahusac, Paris, Opéra, 12 October 1745.
Le temple de la gloire (opéra-ballet), Voltaire, Versailles, 27 November 1745.
Les fêtes de l'Hymen et de l'Amour, ou Les Dieux d'Egypte (ballet-héroïque), L. de Cahusac, Versailles, 15 March 1747.
Zaïs (ballet-héroïque), L. de Cahusac, Paris, Opéra, 29 February 1748.
Pygmalion (acte de ballet), Ballot de Savot (after A.H. de La Motte, *Le triomphe des arts*), Paris, Opéra, 27 August 1748.
Les suprises de l'Amour, J.-P. Bernard, Versailles, 27 November 1748.
Naïs, L. de Cahusac, Paris, Opéra, 22 April 1749.
Zoroastre, L. de Cahusac, Paris, Opéra, 5 December 1749; revised, 19 January 1756.
Linus, Le Clerc de la Bruyère, c. 1752.
La guirlande, ou Les fleurs enchantées (acte de ballet), J.-F. Marmontel, Paris, Opéra, 21 September 1751.
Acante et Céphise, ou La symphathie, J.-F. Marmontel, Paris, Opéra, 19 November 1751.
Daphnis et Eglé, C. Collé, Fontainebleau, 30 October 1753.
Lysis et Délie (pastorale), J.-F. Marmontel, October 1753 [not performed; lost].
Les Sybarites (acte de ballet), J.-F. Marmontel, Fontainebleau, 13 November 1753.
La naissance d'Osiris, ou La fête Pamilie (acte de ballet), L. de Cahusac, Fontainebleau, 12 October 1754.
Anacréon [i] (acte de ballet), L. de Cahusac, Fontainebleau, 23 October 1754.
Anacréon [ii] (acte de ballet), P.-J. Bernard, Paris, Opéra, 31 May 1757.
Le procureur dupé sans le savoir, 1758-59 [private performance].
Les Paladins (comédie-ballet), D. de Monticourt, Paris, Opéra, 12 February 1760.
Abaris, ou Les Boréades, L. de Cahusac, intended for fall 1763.
Nélée et Myrthis (acte de ballet) [not performed].
Zéphyre [*Les nymphes de Diane*] (acte de ballet) [not performed].
Io (acte de ballet) [not performed].

Other works: incidental music, sacred and secular vocal works, instrumental works, keyboard pieces.

Publications

By RAMEAU: books–

Jacobi, E.R., ed. *Jean Philippe Rameau: Complete Theoretical Writings.* Rome, 1967-72.
Traité de l'harmonie réduite à ses principes naturels. Paris, 1722; English translation, 1737; edited and English translation by Philip Gossett, New York, 1971.

About RAMEAU: books–

Raguenet, F. *Paralèle des italiens et des françois, en ce qui regarde la musique et les opéra.* Paris, 1702; English edition, London, 1709; 1968; reprinted in *Musical Quarterly* 32 (1946): 411.
Le Cerf de la Viéville, J.-L. *Comparaison de la musique italienne et de la musique française.* Brussels, 1704-06; 1972.
Rousseau, J.J. *Lettre sur la musique française.* Paris, 1753.
Bourges, E. *Quelques notes sur le théâtre de la cour à Fontainebleau (1747-1787).* Paris, 1892.
Pougin, A. *Un ténor de l'opéra au XVIIIe siècle: Pierre Jélyotte et les chanteurs de son temps.* Paris, 1905.
La Laurencie, L. de. *Rameau.* Paris, 1908.
Laloy, L. *Rameau.* Paris, 1908.
Graf, G. *Jean-Philippe Rameau in seiner Oper Hippolyte et Aricie: eine musikkritische Würdigung.* Wädenswil, 1927.
Masson, P.-M. *L'opéra de Rameau.* Paris, 1930; 1972.
Vallos, L. *Un siècle de musique et de théâtre à Lyons, 1688-1789.* Lyons, 1932; 1971.
Gardien, J. *Jean-Philippe Rameau.* Paris, 1949.
Tiénot, Y. *J.-Ph. Rameau: esquisse biographique, suivi d'un tableau chronologique comprenant une liste complète des oeuvres de Rameau.* Paris, 1954.
Berthier, P. *Réflexions sur l'art et la vie de Jean-Philippe Rameau (1683-1764).* Paris, 1957.
Girdlestone, C. *Jean-Philippe Rameau: his Life and Work.* London, 1957; 2nd ed., 1969; French translation, 1963; 2nd ed., 1983.
Malignon, J. *Rameau.* Paris, 1960; in Russian, 1983.
Demuth, N. *French Opera: its Development to the Revolution.* Horsham, Sussex, 1963.
Seefrid, G. *Die Airs de danse in den Bühnenwerke von Jean-Philippe Rameau.* Wiesbaden, 1969.
Girdlestone, C. *La tragédie en musique (1673-1750) considérée comme genre littéraire.* Geneva, 1972.
Bertrando-Patier, Marie-Claire. *L'exoticisme dans la musique françoise du XVIIIe siècle: "Les Indes galantes" du Jean-Philippe Rameau.* Strasbourg, 1974.
Launay, D., ed. *La querelle des bouffons.* Geneva, 1974.
Lang-Becker, Elke. *Szenentypus und Musik in Rameaus tragédie lyrique.* Munich and Salzburg, 1978.
Malignon, Jean. *Rameau.* Paris, 1978.
Beaussant, Philippe. *"Dardanus" de Rameau.* Paris, 1980.
Brjanceva, Vera. *Zan Filipp Ramo. Francuzskij muzykal'nyj teatr.* Moscow, 1981.
Kintzler, Catherine. *Jean-Philippe Rameau.* Paris, 1983.
De la Gorce, Jérôme, ed. *Jean-Philippe Rameau: colloque international organisé par la Société Rameau. Dijon, 21-24 septembre 1983; actes.* Paris, 1987.

Foster, Donald H. *Jean-Philippe Rameau: A Guide to Research.* New York, 1989.

articles–

Dacier, E. "L'opera au XVIIIe siécle: les premières représentations de Dardanus." *La revue musicale* 3 (1903): 163.
Masson, P.-M. "Lullistes et Ramistes." *Année musicale* i (1911): 187.
Tiersot, J. "Rameau." *Musical Quarterly* 14 (1928): 77
Kisch, E. "Rameau and Rousseau." *Music and Letters* 22 (1941): 97.
Mellers, W. "Rameau and the Opera." *The Score* 4 (1951): 26.
Masson, P.-M. "Les deux versions du 'Dardanus' de Rameau." *Anuario musical* 26 (1954): 36.
Anthony, J.R. "The French Opéra-ballet in the Early Eighteenth Century: Problems of Definition and Classification." *Journal of the American Musicological Society* 18 (1965): 197.
Gervaise, F. "La musique pure au service du drame lyrique chez Rameau." *La rassegna musicale* no. 260 (1965): 21.
Girdlestone, C. "Voltaire, Rameau, et 'Samson'." *Recherches sur la musique française classique* 6 (1966): 133.
Anthony, J.R. "Some Uses of the Dance in the French Opéra-ballet." *Recherches sur la musique française classique* 9 (1969): 75.
Sadler, G. "Rameau's Last Opera: Abaris, ou Les Boréades." *Musical Times* 116 (1975): 327.
Anderson, Nicholas. "Performing Early Music on Record 4: the Operas of Rameau," and "Complete Discography of Music from Rameau's Stage Works." *Early Music* 4 (1976): 284, 499.
Sadler, G. "Rameau's Harpsichord Transcriptions from *Les Indes galantes*." *Early Music* 7 (1979): 18.
———. "Rameau's *Zoroastre:* the 1756 Reworking." *Musical Times* 120 (1979): 301.
Cyr, Mary. "Eighteenth-Century French and Italian Singing: Rameau's Writing for the Voice." *Music and Letters* 61 (1980): 318.
Sadler, G. "*Naïs,* Rameau's Opéra pour la Paix'." *Musical Times* 121 (1980): 431.
Kintzler, Catherine. "Rameau et Voltaire: les enjeux théoretiques d'une collaboration orageuse." *Revue de musicologie* 67 (1981): 139.
Avant-scène opéra December (1982) [*Les Indes galantes* issue].
Sadler, G. "Rameau and the Orchestra." *Proceedings of the Royal Musical Association* 108 (1981-82): 47.
Boucher, Thierry, G. "Promenade dans les théâtres de Rameau." *Diapason* 285 (1983): 21.
Libin, Laurence. "A Rediscovered Portrayal of Rameau and *Castor and Pollux*." *Early Music* 11 (1983): 510.
Rice, Paul Francis. "Mid-Eighteenth Century Changes in French Opera: the Two Versions of Rameau's *Zoroastre*." *Recherches* 21 (1983): 128.
Rosow, Lois. "French Baroque Recitative as an Expression of Tragic Declamation." *Early Music* 11 (1983): 468.
Sadler, Graham. "Rameau, Pellegrin and the Opéra: the Revisions of *Hippolyte et Aricie* During its First Season." *Musical Times* 124 (1983): 533.
Savage, Roger. "Rameau's American Dancers." *Early Music* 11 (1983): 441.
Paquette, Daniele. *Jean-Philippe Rameau, musicien bourguignon.* St-Seine-l'Abbage, 1984.
Recow, Fritz. " 'Cacher l'Art par l'Art même': Lullys *Armide* -Monolog und die Kunst des Vergebens." In *Festschrift für Hans Heinrich Eggebrecht zum 65. Geburtstag,* edited by Werner Breig et al., 128. Wiesbaden, 1984.

Zimmermann, Michael. " '. . . laissons à l'Italie. De tous ces faux brillans l'éclatante folie' - Rameau und die 'närrische' Musik Italiens." In *Gesellschaft für Musikforschung, Report, Bayreuth 1981,* edited by Christoph Hellmut Mahling and Sigrid Wiesmann, 532. Kassel, 1984.
Sadler, G. "A Re-Examination of Rameau's Self-Borrowings." In *Jean-Baptiste Lully and the Music of the French Baroque: Essays in Honor of James R. Anthony,* edited by John Hajdu Heyer. Cambridge, 1989.

unpublished–

Ahnell, E.G. "The Concept of Tonality in the Operas of Jean-Philippe Rameau." Ph.D. Dissertation, University of Illinois, 1958.
Smith, Mary-Térey. "Jean-Philippe Rameau: Abaris ou les Boréades, a Critical Edition." Ph.D. dissertation, University of Rochester, 1971.
Cyr, M. "Rameau's 'Les fêtes d'Hébé'." Ph.D. dissertation, University of California, Berkeley, 1975.
Wolf, R. Peter. "Jean-Philippe Rameau's comédie-lyrique, *Les Paladins (1760):* a Critical Edition and Study." Ph.D. dissertation, Yale University, 1977.
Brown, Leslie Ellen. "The *tragédie lyrique* of André Campra and his Contemporaries." Ph.D. dissertation, University of North Carolina, 1978.
Verba, E. Cynthia. "A Hierarchical Interpretation of the Theories and Music of Jean-Philippe Rameau." Ph.D. dissertation, University of Chicago, 1979.
Rice, Paul F. "The Fontainebleau Operas of Jean-Philippe Rameau: a Critical Study." Ph.D. dissertation, University of Victoria, 1981.

*   *   *

Jean-Philippe Rameau is regarded, along with Lully and Gluck, as one of the finest composers of pre-revolutionary opera in France. He is equally renowned for his theoretical works, especially the monumental *Traité de l'harmonie.* Though he made important contributions to other genres, including harpsichord solos, motets, cantatas, and instrumental music, his thirty operas bear the most vivid stamp of his musical personality.

Rameau fostered an early interest in the stage, but it was not until his fiftieth year that his first *tragédie, Hippolyte et Aricie,* was produced at the *Académie Royale de Musique* (later the Paris Opèra) in Paris. Despite the novelty of his music to eighteenth-century listeners, his operas are closely bound to the traditions of French opera found in works by Lully, Collasse, Campra and others. The *tragédies* include a mythological prologue, five acts, declamatory recitative, vocal airs, and prominent use of chorus and dancing in each act. Rather than transform these traditional elements, Rameau invigorated them with orchestral writing of an astonishing variety and often used instruments in new ways, either by giving them prominent solos or using them in pairs (such as flute and bassoon). Other tragedies, including *Dardanus* and *Zoroastre* contain some of Rameau's finest music, but they suffer from poor librettos, and their success in both cases rested upon significant revisions undertaken by both librettist and composer for later revivals. Rameau's last tragedy, *Les Boréades,* was rehearsed in 1763 but was not performed.

Of the other operatic genres in which Rameau wrote, the most important is the *opéra-ballet,* usually containing a prologue and three separate acts or *entrées.* In these works dance, costumes, and exotic locales are featured, and the music has

Jean-Philippe Rameau

a freshness and expressiveness completely removed from tragedy. Among the finest works in this genre are *Les Indes galantes* and *Les fêtes d'Hébé*. Rameau's only *comédie lyrique, Platée,* is a burlesque with a lovesick nymph (sung by a man), a bravura air for Folly in imitation of an Italian aria (act II, scene 4), and other comic music such as animal sounds in the overture and prologue. An occasional work written for the marriage of the Dauphin in 1745, it was greeted with praise by virtue of its novelty, but twentieth century writers have viewed its libretto more critically as a grotesque satire.

Among the most memorable music in Rameau's oeuvre are the extended vocal solos (*ariettes*) and duets, most of which were written for Marie Fel (soprano) and Pierre Jélyotte (*haute-contre* = high tenor). His instrumental dances are often marked by irregular phrase lengths and unusual instrumental timbres (such as musettes or clarinets), while the chaconnes, usually found at the end of an opera, are grand and extended pieces of unusual diversity. Some of the overtures, such as those in *Hippolyte et Aricie* and *Castor et Pollux* retain the traditional two-part Lullian form, to which Rameau added piquant harmonies and solo instrumental textures; the overtures to *La princesse de Navarre* and several later works are Italianate (fast-slow-fast), and still others are programmatic, including those in *Acante et Céphise* and *Zoroastre*. A particularly unusual one is the overture to *Zaïs,* which depicts the "unravelling of chaos." Its irregular phrasing and jarring harmonies were judged by some to be "shocking and disagreeable" when first performed, but despite the initial reservations Rameau's works sometimes encountered,

they usually achieved successful first runs, and many remained in the repertoire long after his death.

—Mary Cyr

RAMEY, Samuel E.

Bass. Born 28 March 1942, in Colby, Kansas. Married: Carric Ramey. Studied with Arthur B. Newman at Wichita State University, then with Armen Boyajian in New York City while working as an advertising copywriter; debut as Zuniga in *Carmen,* New York City Opera, 1973; various debuts as Figaro in *Le nozze di Figaro*: Glyndebourne (1976), Teatro alla Scala (1981), Covent Garden (1982); Metropolitan Opera debut as Argante in *Rinaldo,* 1984.

Publications

About RAMEY: articles–

Paolucci, Bridget. "The New Young Lions." *Hi Fidelity/ Musical America* 31/January (1981): 56.
Seabury, D. "A Boy from Kansas." *Opera News* 46/July (1981): 8.
Mai, C. "Das Interview." *Opernwelt* 23/3 (1982): 24.
Soria, D.J. "Samuel Ramey." *Hi Fidelity/Musical America* 34/July (1984): MA6.
Profile. *San Francisco Opera Magazine* 3/Fall (1984): 52.
Zakariasen, B. "Samuel Ramey." *Ovation* 5/November (1984): 14.
Mayer, Martin. "Samuel Ramey." *Opera* 37/April (1986): 399.
Matheopoulos, Helena. *Bravo,* London 1986.
Gurewitsch, Matthew. "Primo basso." *Connoisseur* 216/August (1986): 18.
Profile. *San Francisco Opera Magazine* 2/Fall (1986): 36.
Greenfield, E. "Samuel Ramey." *Gramophone* 64/October (1986): 533.
Gurewitsch, Matthew. "Sam Shadow." *Opus* 3/5 (1987): 30.
Loebl, H. "Samuel Ramey." *Bühne* 346-347/July-August (1987): 13.
Koltai, Tamas. "Aki eb enekelt, mit latott operat: beszelgetes Samuel Ramey." *Muzsika* 31/March (1988): 26.
Wirthmann, J. "Samuel Ramey." *Muzsika* 31/March (1988): 25.
Profile. *San Francisco Opera Magazine* [*Mefistofele* issue] 1989: 36.
Hart, C. "Entrevista Samuel Ramey." *Monsalvat* 179/July-August (1989): 8.
Profile. *San Francisco Opera Magazine* 68/7 (1990): 7.
von Rhein, John. "A Rake's Progress." *Opera News* 54 (14 April 1990): 11.

* * *

American bass Samuel Ramey's operatic career began when, after being a finalist in the Metropolitan Opera auditions in 1972, he made his operatic debut at the New York City Opera in the small role of Zuniga in Bizet's *Carmen,* followed at the end of the season by the substantially larger role of Don Basilio in Rossini's *Il barbiere di Siviglia*. At the time, the reigning bass at the company was Norman Treigle; upon

Treigle's death in 1975, Ramey stepped into several of his roles, most notably Mefistofele in Boito's opera. But it was in the bel canto repertoire that Ramey made his mark, in roles such as Lord Walton in Bellini's *I puritani,* and especially in the florid roles of Rossini (of which he has now sung a large number, including Mustafa in *L'italiana in Algeri,* Selim in *Il turco in Italia,* Lord Sidney in *Il viaggio a Reims,* Moïse, Maometto II, and Assur in *Semiramide*) and early Verdi—*Attila* especially stands out. It was as Argante in Handel's *Rinaldo* that Ramey first appeared—belatedly, to many—at the Metropolitan Opera. Largely restricting himself to the Italian and French repertoire, Ramey has increased his range of roles to encompass Massenet's *Don Quichotte,* Nick Shadow in Stravinsky's *The Rake's Progress,* both Leporello and Don Giovanni in Mozart's opera, Figaro in Mozart's *Le nozze di Figaro,* Philip II in Verdi's *Don Carlos,* Méphistophélès in Gounod's *Faust,* and Bluebeard in Bartók's *Bluebeard's Castle,* and he has now appeared at Covent Garden, Salzburg, Aix-en-Provence, Pesaro, the Deutsche Oper in Berlin, the Théâtre de la Monnaie in Brussels, the Chicago Lyric Opera, the Vienna Staatsoper, the Hamburg Opera, the Netherlands Opera, Glyndebourne, and the Teatro alla Scala.

Ramey, a *basso cantante,* possesses a formidable technique for the coloratura bass roles—the requisite agility as well as the ability to spin out a long line. With a voice clearly focused throughout its wide range (from D below the stave to G above, although the tone loses color, but not volume, at the very bottom), a vibrant, sensual sound, substantial stage presence, and both good diction and skill with languages, Ramey lacks little to command the roles of his repertoire.

Ramey tries to maintain a balance between acting and singing. He prefers dramatic characters to comic ones—his skills are greater in conveying drama than comedy—and, in his more florid roles, he feels it is essential to understand the reasons behind the ornamentation in order to keep it from being empty vocal display.

Ramey's voice is notable for its authority, virility, and sturdiness. He is especially successful in conveying the combination of power and resignation that characterizes many of the kingly roles in his repertoire. What he somewhat lacks is introspection, charm, gentleness, sentiment, and humor when these characteristics are called for. He can sometimes seem rather detached, his characters appearing deficient in spiritual depth.

Ramey possesses one of the necessary, if not sufficient, elements of a great singer: a distinctive, recognizable timbre. What he does not possess, at least not in abundance, is the ability to differentiate his various characters; he fits his characters to his voice rather than fitting his voice to the characters. Nor does one look to him to find revelations of character; one finds instead incidental interpretive touches, sudden vivid illuminations created through a variation of vocal color or accent. These may seem relatively superficial rather than growing out of a holistic conception of the character, but as Ramey employs them they are nonetheless effective in projecting and underscoring the meaning of the text.

Ramey's contributions to recordings of complete operas (other than those taken from staged performances) include Angelotti in Puccini's *Tosca* (1976, under Colin Davis), Jacopo Loredano in Verdi's *I due Foscari* (1976, under Gardelli), Mustafà (1980, under Scimone), Figaro (1982, under Solti), Douglas d'Angus in Rossini's *La donna del lago* (1983, under Pollini), Nick Shadow (1984, under Chailly), Don Giovanni (1985, under Karajan), Banquo in Verdi's *Macbeth* (1988, under Chailly), Bluebeard (1988, under Fischer), Oroveso in Bellini's *Norma* (1988, under Bonynge),

and Sarastro in Mozart's *Die Zauberflöte* (1989, under Marriner).

—Michael Sims

THE RAPE OF LUCRETIA.

Composer: Benjamin Britten.

Librettist: Ronald Duncan (after A. Obey).

First Performance: Glyndebourne, 12 July 1946; revised, 1947.

Roles: Lucretia (contralto); Collatinus (bass); Junius (baritone); Prince Tarquinius (baritone); Bianca (mezzo-soprano); Lucia (soprano); Male Chorus (tenor); Female Chorus (soprano); chorus (SATB).

Publications

books–

Keller, H. *The Rape of Lucretia; Albert Herring.* London, 1947.
Crozier, Eric, ed. *The Rape of Lucretia: A Symposium.* London, 1948.

articles–

Brett, Philip. "Grimes and Lucretia." In *Music and Theatre: Essays in Honour of Winton Dean.* Cambridge, 1987.

*   *   *

The Rape of Lucretia remains one of Benjamin Britten's most controversial operas. Ronald Duncan's libretto does not merely retell the old legend as it is found in Livy, Ovid, and indeed in Shakespeare, as an incident illustrative of unchanging human nature, but adds a Christian interpretation, reviewing the story in terms of sin and forgiveness. The opera tells of the Etruscan tyrant, Tarquinius, who is goaded by a drunken bet to "prove" the chastity of an honorable Roman matron, Lucretia. Tarquinius hurries to Rome, imposes himself on the quiet house, and that night forces Lucretia at swordpoint. The next morning, overcome with grief and guilt, Lucretia stabs herself. These events, however, are framed by two singers, a Male and Female chorus, who sit on either side of the stage, narrate and comment on the action, personifying the male and female principles which are opposed in this violent legend. The libretto has been criticized both for the deliberately anachronistic intrusion of the choruses and for its intricate poetic language, not easily projected to an audience. The opera offers a confusingly rich experience which both celebrates the power of human sexuality and endorses a doctrine which condemns its consequences.

This is a continuously lyrical opera—which raises another problem: vice and virtue are made equally attractive in the soaring lines of, for example, the thrilling narration of Tarquinius's ride to Rome, or the long lament (for cor anglais) during which Lucretia prepares to take her own life. Consequently the theme of the opera turns out to be not rape but rather seduction. The audience is continually seduced by the memorable melodies; through melody, the characters charm us and each other; Lucretia's capitulation is ambivalent, and the concluding redemption is offered as much for her fall from innocence as for her ravisher's act of violation. Despite the lyricism, however, the score is tightly organized. It is based on two leitmotives—Britten's first thorough-going excursion into this technique. A nest of interlocking thirds represents Lucretia (or the female principle) and a descending tetrachord indicates Tarquinius (or the male). The motifs appear on every page of the score, easily—some would say too easily—detectable by the audience in all their ingenious transformations. This musical coherence goes a long way to resolve problems set by the dramatic inconsistencies.

The Rape of Lucretia was the first of Britten's chamber operas, and the genre was to prove an important stimulus for him. It is a demanding medium. The orchestra are soloists, virtuoso exponents of just twelve instruments and piano. The singers have to take their place within textures which rarely accompany, but which interweave and engage in dialogue with them. The audience has to remain alert to every line in the score, which, by means of a word or a motif, may reveal a crucial moment in the drama. Some of the timbres are stunningly original: the lullaby for the sleeping Lucretia is a trio for bass flute, muted horn and bass clarinet, which is interrupted by the pointillist percussion representation of the approaching Tarquinius. Many later operas deal with the confrontation between good and evil, but no other opera makes evil so dangerously attractive. Brilliant but problematic, *The Rape of Lucretia* is an opera to delight the ear while it puzzles the mind.

—Patricia Howard

A RARE OCCURENCE.
See UNA COSA RARA

RASKIN, Judith.

Soprano. Born 21 June 1928 in New York. Died 21 December 1984, in New York. Married: Raymond Raskin in 1948; two children. Studied at Smith College, and then with Anna Hamlin in New York; debuted in the title role of Douglas Moore's *The Ballad of Baby Doe* in Central City, Colorado, 1956; television debut as Susanna in Mozart's *Le nozze di Figaro* with the NBC Opera, 1957; New York City Opera debut as Despina, 1959; Metropolitan Opera debut as Susanna, 1962; sang at the Metropolitan Opera, 1962-72; European debut, Glyndebourne, 1963; taught at the Manhattan School of Music from 1975; taught at Mannes College of Music from 1976.

Publications

By RASKIN: articles–

"American Bel Canto." *Opera News* 30/2 (1966): 6.

About RASKIN: articles–

Soria, D.J. "Judith Raskin: 'ina' to 'ona'." *High Fidelity/ Musical America* 17 (1967): MA4.
Movshon, G. "The Metropolitan Opera." *High Fidelity/Musical America* 19 (1969): MA12.
"How does a singer do it?" *Opera News* 33 (1969): 28.
"Reflected Glory (recollections of life at the Met)." *Opera News* 48 (1984): 34.

*   *   *

Few singers arriving on the American operatic scene successfully in the 1950s did so without first establishing a career in Europe. Judith Raskin, however, a native of New York City, was able to circumvent the need for overseas performances. In addition to this unusual aspect of her career, Raskin's development as a singer began later than usual. Both of her parents were educators. Her father was the chairman of the music department of a high school in the Bronx, and her mother was an elementary teacher. Because of his knowledge of music, her father did not want her to overtax what he felt was a fine young singing voice. As a result Raskin studied only violin and piano as a child. Raskin's studies at Smith College in Northampton, Massachusetts, continued with the same emphasis until her piano teacher heard her sing and realized she was concentrating on the wrong musical instrument. She immediately began studying voice with Anna Hamlin, herself once a student of Marcella Sembrich. The close alliance Raskin felt with her teacher did not end with her college days; her serious vocal study continued for several years after her graduation in 1949. During her senior year in college, Raskin married Dr Raymond A. Raskin, a physician. Although she devoted most of her time to her husband and two young children for nearly ten years, she never relinquished her goal of becoming a singer.

Solo singing in synagogues and other sporadic musical engagements comprised her vocal development until 1957, when she successfully auditioned for George Schick, music coordinator of National Broadcasting Company Opera. Her debut on the stage came that same year with her portrayal of Susanna (*Le nozze di Figaro*) in Ann Arbor, Michigan, in a live performance with the NBC Opera. It was evident in her initial tour with this company that her interpretation of Mozart was excellent because of the thought and preparation she brought to her performances. As a result of her successes on the tour, Raskin was cast in Poulenc's *Dialogues des Carmélites* in an NBC telecast at the end of 1957. Performances with companies in Santa Fe, Dallas, Washington, D.C., Central City, Colorado, and in New York with the American Opera Society and Juilliard School of Music followed in the next two years.

Her debut at New York City Opera in 1959 and the Metropolitan Opera in 1962 were both in Mozart roles. Her European debut came in the 1963 summer season of the Glyndebourne Festival. The role she sang then and the following summer was Pamina (*Die Zauberflöte*). A repeat of this performance on British Broadcasting Corporation TV gave her talent greater exposure to the public.

Raskin's performances were not limited to Mozart. Notable roles she portrayed included Ann Brice in the world premier of Leonard Kastle's *Deseret,* the Wife in Menotti's *The Labyrinth* for television, the title role in *The Ballad of Baby Doe,* Nannetta in Verdi's *Falstaff* (produced by Franco Zeffirelli and conducted by Leonard Bernstein), Sophie in *Der Rosenkavalier* and Micaëla in *Carmen.* One of her most prestigious recordings is Anne Truelove in Stravinsky's *The Rake's Progress* under the baton of the composer.

Raskin was a very popular singer with colleagues, audiences, and critics. Her vocal purity and agility resulted in her being compared to the singer Elisabeth Schumann. Her interpretations were readily understood because of her absolute command of any language she was singing. The clarity of her English dispelled for many the rationale that only tone is important in opera. Although it is often difficult to understand words sung in the higher range of a soprano, this was not true with Raskin. In addition, her precise use of the language allowed her to effectively manipulate the shaping of the musical phrases. These two emphases—her ability to communicate well and her shaping of phrases—along with her vocal and physical attractiveness, worked hand in hand to reveal her as a consummate artist. Ill health necessitated Raskin's early departure from the operatic stage, but her loss of physical energy did not prevent her from giving occasional recitals and teaching at varying music schools in New York City until shortly before her death in 1984.

—Rose Mary Owens

RAVEL, (Joseph) Maurice.

Composer. Born 7 March 1875, in Cibourne, Basses-Pyrénées. Died 28 December 1937, in Paris. Studied piano with Henri Ghis and harmony with Charles René; studied piano with Anthiome and Charles de Bériot (won first prize, 1891), and harmony with Emile Pessard at the Paris Conservatory, beginning 1889; studied composition with Fauré and counterpoint and fugue with Gédalge, 1897; debut as a conductor leading a performance of his *Shéhérazade* with the Société Nationale, Paris, 27 May 1899; second place Prix de Rome for his cantata *Myrrha,* 1901; served in the ambulance corps, 1914; visited Amsterdam and Venice, 1922; in London, 1923; in Sweden, England, Scotland, 1926; American tour as conductor and pianist, 1928; honorary D. Mus *honoris causa,* Oxford University, 1928.

Operas

Publishers: Durand, Schig.

L'heure espagnole, Franc-Nohain, 1907-09, Paris, Opéra-Comique, 19 May 1911.
L'enfant et les sortilèges, Colette, 1920-25, Monte Carlo, 21 March 1925.
Other works: ballets, orchestral works, vocal works, instrumental and chamber music, piano pieces.

Publications

By RAVEL: books—

Chalupt, R., and M. Gerar, eds. *Ravel au miroir de ses lettres.* Paris, 1956.
Orenstein, A., ed. *Lettres, écrits, entretiens.* Paris, 1989; English translation, 1990.

About RAVEL: books—

Roland-Manuel. *Maurice Ravel et son oeuvre dramatique.* Paris, 1928.
Landowsky, W.A.L. *Maurice Ravel, sa vie, son oeuvre.* Paris, 1938; 2nd ed., 1950.
Roland-Manuel. *A la gloire de Ravel.* Paris, 1938; 2nd ed., 1948; English translation as *Maurice Ravel,* London, 1947; New York, 1972.
Vuillermoz, E., et al. *Maurice Ravel par quelques-uns de ses familiers.* Paris, 1939.
Jankélévitch, V. *Ravel.* Paris, 1939; 2nd ed., 1956; English translation, 2nd ed., 1959.
Goss, M. *Bolero: the Life of Maurice Ravel.* New York, 1940.
Aubin, T., et al. *Maurice Ravel.* Paris, 1945.
Jourdan-Morhange, H. *Ravel et nous.* Geneva, 1945.
Demuth, N. *Ravel.* London, 1947.
Machabey, A. *Maurice Ravel.* Paris, 1947.
Onnen, F. *Maurice Ravel.* Stockholm, 1947.
Malipiero, R. *Maurice Ravel.* Milan, 1948.
Fargue, L.-P. *Maurice Ravel.* Paris, 1949.
Bruyr, J. *Maurice Ravel ou Le lyrisme et les sortilèges.* Paris, 1950.
Tappolet, W. *Maurice Ravel: Leben und Werk.* Olten, 1950.
Seroff, V. *Maurice Ravel.* New York, 1953.
Ackere, J. van. *Maurice Ravel.* Brussels, 1957.
Fragny, R. de. *Maurice Ravel.* Lyons, 1960.
Myers, R.H. *Ravel: Life and Works.* London, 1960.
Léon, G. *Maurice Ravel.* Paris, 1964.
Stuckenschmidt, H.H. *Maurice Ravel: Variationen über Person und Werk.* Frankfurt, 1966; English translation, 1968.
Petit, P. *Ravel.* Paris, 1970.
Orenstein, A. *Ravel, Man and Musician.* New York, 1975.
Nichols, R. *Ravel.* London, 1977.
James, B. *Ravel: his Life and Times.* New York and Tunbridge Wells, 1983.
Marnat, M. *Maurice Ravel.* Paris, 1986.
Nichols, R. *Ravel Remembered.* London, 1987; New York, 1988.

articles—

Lalo, P. "Encore le Debussysme: une lettre de M. Ravel." *Le temps* 9 April (1907).
Roland-Manuel. "Maurice Ravel." *La revue musicale* 2/no. 6 (1921): 1.
La revue musicale 6/no. 8 (1925) [Ravel issue].
La revue musicale no. 187 (1938) [Ravel issue].
Melos 14/no. 12 (1947) [Ravel issue].
Lesure, F. " 'L'affaire' Debussy-Ravel: lettres inédites." In *Festschrift Friedrich Blume,* 231. Kassel, 1963.
Orenstein, A. "*L'enfant et les sortilèges:* correspondence inédite de Ravel et Colette." *Revue de musicologie* 52 (1966): 215.
———. "Maurice Ravel's Creative Process." *Musical Quarterly* 53 (1967): 467.
———. "Some Unpublished Music and Letters by Maurice Ravel." *Music Forum* 3 (1973): 291.

Crosland, M. "Colette and Ravel: the Enchantress and the Illusionist." In *Colette: the Woman, the Writer*, 116. University Park, 1981.

Green, M.S. "Ravel and Krenek: Cosmic Music Makers" [*L'enfant et les sortilèges*]. *College Music Symposium* 24 (1984): 96.

* * *

Maurice Ravel has been hailed as the leading French composer of his generation, but during his lifetime he was a subject of controversy, and with good reason· he had a flair for upsetting French complacencies. Nothing that this great provocateur wrote was as strange and shocking as his two tiny operas, *L'heure espagnole* and *L'enfant et les sortilèges.*

Before *L'heure espagnole*, Ravel's first opera, there was a play of the same name, which in itself was scandalous stuff. The author was Franc-Nohain, pen name for Maurice-Etienne Legrand (1873-1934), who wrote several one-act comedies. This one-act *comédie bouffe* takes place in a Spanish clockmaker's shop and is about the amorous affairs of the clockmaker's wife, aptly named Concepcion. Every Thursday, while her husband Torquemada is away from the shop for an hour, Concepcion receives her lovers on the sly. On this particular Thursday there is young Gonzalve, who gushes poetical nonsense, and then Don Inigo Gomez, a fat, middle-aged banker who struts about like a peacock. Neither lover can satisfy Concepcion upstairs in her bedroom, so she ultimately sets her cap on a bumbling but sturdy mule driver named Ramiro, who does. The play concludes with a moral from Boccaccio: "There comes a moment in the pursuit of love when the muleteer has his turn."

Franc-Nohain wrote not only a sex comedy, but also a paradoxical tale in which the characters are so shrewd and calculating that they resemble clockwork, rather than people with any real feelings. The craftiest of the lot may well be Torquemada: upon returning toward the end of the play and catching two of his wife's lovers hiding inside his grandfather clocks, he is hardly upset but seizes the moment to sell the clocks. On account of the play's comic vision, however, the many intrigues never have tragic results.

In his adaptation of the play, Ravel left the story basically intact, since it was already tailor-made to his personal musical style and to aspects of his autobiography. Surely, Torquemada's occupation and the Spanish setting reminded him of his own heritage. His father was a Swiss civil engineer who, like his son, had an interest in all things mechanical. His mother was a Basque, and it was from her that Ravel inherited a lifelong attachment to Spanish folk music. In this opera he made use of several quintessential Spanish rhythms, like those of the jota, malagueña, and habanera.

The paradoxical aspect of the story, of humans behaving like machines, also must have appealed to him since he himself was an expert at drawing paradoxes. In the extraordinary orchestral introduction he inserted ticking clocks and whirring automatons that practically vibrate with a life force. Conversely, the characters sound wooden and unmusical since Ravel instructed the singers to give the impression of speaking, rather than of singing, their parts (the one exception is the role of Gonzalve, which is "affectedly lyrical"). There are all too few solo arias and ensembles, the customary places where singers vent their feelings. The characters simply chatter incessantly throughout the twenty-one little scenes, like puppets in a puppet play.

Ravel's primary aim in writing *L'heure espagnole* was to resurrect eighteenth-century Italian *opera buffa*, and in so doing, he created a suitable musical counterpart to Franc-Nohain's *comédie bouffe*. The dry "quasi parlando" vocal style relates to *buffo* recitative, and the concluding habanera, in which all five members of the cast take part, resembles *buffo* ensemble finales. There is even a *basso buffo*, the portly Don Inigo Gomez, who chirps falsetto "cuckoos" when stuffed inside the grandfather clock.

Ravel also captured the comic spirit of the *buffo* tradition, and made it his own, by writing funny music that enhanced the wittiness of the text. Often, his sense of humor is quite subtle and satirical. A case in point is his punctuation of Gonzalve's dramatic question, "Isn't [love] stronger than death?" with a plain C major chord, a chord that sounds so banal here that it instantly deflates the earnestness of the remark.

Predictably, the 1911 premiere of the opera drew a fair amount of controversy, and several critics faulted the work. A "miniature pornographic vaudeville" was how one writer described the libretto. Other critics liked the opera and praised Ravel's daring and original orchestration, especially that of the "symphony of clocks" in the introduction. *L'heure espagnole* went on to become a resounding success and remains to this day a delightful and entertaining comedy, as long as the shady side of the characters—their heartlessness and cunning—are not taken too seriously.

As for *L'enfant et les sortilèges,* it dates from 1916 when the famous author Colette (1873-1954) sent Ravel a copy of her eighteen-page libretto in the hope that he would set it to music. At this time of course the world was at war, and Ravel, a fervent patriot, had enlisted in the French army and was driving an army truck, sometimes near the front at Verdun. Apparently, the libretto was lost, for he never received it. Colette had to wait another three years before he agreed to collaborate, and another six years before the opera had its premiere. It was worth the long wait, however, for their joint efforts resulted in one of the most imaginative and enchanting operas of the twentieth century.

In brief, Colette's libretto, which is in two scenes, is a magical fairy tale about a naughty little boy who learns the meaning of compassion the hard way. When we first see him, he is ensconced in a cozy room; it is late afternoon and he is in a perverse mood. Not only does he refuse to do his homework, but the little brat also sticks his tongue out at his mother. For punishment he is confined to the room, whereupon he has a temper tantrum and wreaks havoc on nearly everything in it. But then the room comes under a spell of sorcery, and all the objects of his fury magically take on life to seek retribution.

The nightmare gets worse in the second scene, which is set in a moonlit garden outside his house. There the boy discovers that the trees, insects and animals are angry with him as well, and they take him to task for a whole host of other crimes, from pinning a dragonfly to the wall, to bashing a bat to death with a stick. The tension quickly escalates to the point where the garden becomes a battleground. All the animals encircle the terror-stricken child, jostle him back and forth, and then claw at each other in a terrible brawl. At the height of the frenzy, a squirrel is injured and the boy, filled with a new compassion, attempts to heal its wounded paw. Because of this one small act of kindness, the animals stop fighting and forgive him. The story comes to an end as he calls out softly for his mother. He has learned his lesson, the wicked spell is broken, and the natural order restored.

Magical as it is, Colette's story is more than just a fable for children. To be sure, behind the fairy-tale façade is a wartime story, and the implied message it carries is that war is triggered by hostile behavior while peace is ensured by love and

Maurice Ravel, 1937

compassion. Still deeper, and running through all aspects of the story, is a motif of progression and expansion that testifies to Colette's penetrating and coherent mind: the setting shifts from a small room to an outside garden, from afternoon to night; an act of aggression leads to chaos; a child develops; the pageant of bewitched characters begins with inanimate objects (from chairs to arithmatic homework), moves to plant life (trees), and then to more complex life forms (dragonflies, bats, frogs, squirrels). The exceptions to the overall progression are the two cats that appear in both scenes and merely ignore the child.

In short, Colette's libretto is multivalent, and Ravel understood this. To depict the fantastic side of the story, he broke it up into individual episodes—each distinguished by its own musical style and unrelated to the surrounding ones—and strung them all along in one continuous flow. He constructed, in effect, a musical dreamscape which, like our own dreams and fantasies, has a bizarre and haphazard sequence of events. In one memorable episode, a black Wedgwood teapot, representing an African-American boxer, and a Chinese teacup dance to a ragtime/foxtrot tempo and are accompanied by a contemporary jazz band. By contrast, in the following episode a tempestuous soprano, personifying "Fire," sings a coloratura aria that brings to mind eighteenth- and nineteenth-century opera arias.

To translate conflict and disorder in musical terms, Ravel relied on a wide variety of musical procedures. A standout is the temper tantrum episode where he inserted clashing bitonal passages to convey the boy's oppositional and perverse nature. There are plenty of examples of growth and expansion in the score; witness the orchestration of the openings of the two scenes. The first, which takes place in the child's room, suggests a sense of compression because the orchestra hovers over the boy's part, thereby blanketing him and emphasizing his smallness. The beginning of the second scene, which takes place in the moonlit garden, gives the opposite impression, that of depth and of the vast expanse between the ground and stars. Here, the muted strings, altogether sweeping an airy five-octave range, sound in the background, while the slide flute and piccolo (birds and crickets) are heard in the foreground.

Clearly, each opera in its own way is unique. *L'heure espagnole* is a dry and earthy comedy without an ounce of sentimentality. *L'enfant et les sortilèges* is a lyric fantasy that has traces of tenderness and real feeling. At the same time, the two operas may be viewed as opposite sides of the same coin. Both operas have similar formal designs that consist of a succession of brief scenes or episodes, and each lasts only an hour. Both give evidence that Ravel was drawn to stories with multiple layers of meaning, with the superficial layer on top and the darker or more serious layers underneath. His music as a whole is well-constructed, and he would spend years planning a new piece in his mind before writing a single note (the composition of *L'heure espagnole* is an exception to the rule as it was completed in about six months). In this light, it is hardly surprising that this finicky perfectionist only finished two operas and that his total output is rather limited.

Finally, both operas highlight Ravel's penchant for inconsistencies and paradoxes: pulsing clocks and heartless people, beastly child and humane animals. For him, the remarkable balance of contradiction, surprise, and technical perfection was the goal to which he always aspired. For us, that balance is a key to the understanding of his music.

—Teresa Davidian

UN RÈ IN ASCOLTO [A King Listens].

Composer: Luciano Berio.

Librettist: Italo Calvino.

First Performance: Salzburg, 7 August 1984.

Roles: Prospero (bass-baritone); Director (tenor); Friday (speaking part); Female Protagonist (soprano); Soprano I; Soprano II; Mezzo-soprano; Three Singers (tenor, bass, baritone); Sick Sister (soprano); Wife (mezzo-soprano); Doctor (tenor); Lawyer (bass); various musicians, mimes, dancers; chorus.

Publications

article–

Vogt, Matthias Theodor, "Listening as a Letter of Uriah: A Note on Berio's *Un rè in ascolto* (1984)." *Cambridge Opera Journal* 2 (1990): 173.

*   *   *

Un rè in Ascolto by Luciano Berio received its world premiere at the somewhat unlikely venue of the 1984 Salzburg Festival, where innovation is or was rarely the order of the day. The opera was conducted by Lorin Maazel and produced by Götz Friedrich. This production was seen later in Vienna, and in 1986 at the Teatro alla Scala, Milan. A new production was mounted in 1986 by the Deutsche Oper am Rhein in Düsseldorf. It received a British premiere at the Royal Opera House in February 1989 in a new production by Graham Vick, making a highly successful debut at Covent Garden. This version was a critical and public triumph, and Berio himself was delighted. He conducted the first three performances and was followed by Berio specialist Stephen Harrap.

By the time *Un rè* got to London, the composer stated that it was not in fact an opera, but an "azione musicale," a musical action. The libretto was written by Italo Calvino (who died in 1985) in collaboration with Berio himself and is very loosely based on Shakespeare's *The Tempest* and various adaptations from W.H. Auden and other writers. Opera or not, *Un rè* contains no shortage of "azione." The highly elaborate staging surrounds the character of an impresario, Prospero, who is rehearsing a musical version of *The Tempest.* The device of a play within a play about a play is thus used. As the piece develops members of the audience are left to come to their own conclusions.

—Sally Whyte

IL RÈ PASTORE [The Shepherd King].

Composer: Wolfgang Amadeus Mozart.

Librettist: after Metastasio.

First Performance: Salzburg, Archbishop's palace, 23 April 1775.

Roles: Allesandro (tenor); Aminta (soprano); Elisa (soprano); Tamiri (soprano); Aegenore (tenor).

* * *

Il rè pastore, a pastoral drama written by Pietro Metastasio and first set to music by Giuseppe Bonno for the Viennese court on 27 October 1751 (the Empress's birthday), over the next twenty-five years found new settings by Hasse, Lampugnani, Galuppi, Piccinni, Gluck, and Jommelli (and at least six others), and had spread as far as Lisbon, Stockholm, Copenhagen, Naples, and London by Mozart's day. The occasion for Mozart's setting was the celebration of a visit to Salzburg by Maria Theresa's youngest son, the Archduke Maximillian, later Archbishop of Cologne, on his way to Italy from Vienna. The Archduke referred to the work in his travel journal on 23 April 1775: "The evening concluded again with a music concert and supper in the palace; . . . whereas for the previous day the well-known Kapellmeister Fischietti had written the music, for the sung cantata of this evening the music was by the not less renowned Mozart." The reference to the work as a "cantata" is indicative of its scaled-down mode of performance as a *serenata* rather than as an *opera seria:* it was cut to two acts and was almost surely given without costumes or scenery. Varesco, a Salzburg cleric at the court (and later the librettist for *Idomeneo*), collapsed acts II and III into a single act, eliminated a number of arias and much recitative, and added a single new aria and an accompanied recitative for Aminta.

In Mozart's opera the basic outline of Metastasio's plot is retained. Aminta lives as a shepherd and plans a simple life with his beloved Elisa (of royal, but foreign, lineage), unaware that he is heir to the kingdom of Sidon. His father's servant Aegenore had him hidden and raised by a shepherd, as the king feared for his son's life when Stratone (mentioned in the opera only by name) stole the throne. Now Alessandro (Alexander the Great) has defeated Stratone and wishes to restore Aminta to his kingdom. The plot is complicated when Alessandro thinks to show clemency to Aminta and the deposed Stratone by arranging the marriage of Aminta to Stratone's daughter, Tamiri, who loves Aegenore. In the end Elisa pleads with Alessandro for Aminta, who joins that complaint and reasons that although Tamiri's royal station merits her ruling the kingdom, he cannot abandon Elisa. Aminta proposes to Alessandro that he be allowed to forfeit his throne and give up the kingdom, and thus marry Elisa. Aminta and Elisa are in the end united by Alexander and are given the kingdom of Sidon, and Tamiri is joined with Aegenore; they will be given some as yet unnamed, unconquered kingdom.

This little known, rarely performed Mozart opera contains some of his most beautiful early compositions. In the main, the work reflects the altered face of *opera seria* in the late eighteenth century, in which a flexible, dynamic approach was increasingly common. Arias are mostly in a rounded binary, lightly ornamented style, the latter probably a reflection on the anonymous, likely non-operatic cast. The most famous aria, Aminta's "L'amerò, sarò costante," is a rondo with an obligato solo violin, flutes, English horns, bassoons, horns, and strings. Its gentle lyricism is broken into short phrases (probably for the singer's sake), and the counterpoint with the solo violin is particularly lovely. It was for this aria, in a later performance of the early 1780s, that Mozart composed a set of popular cadenzas. The pastoral character of the drama is echoed in several arias, such as the two opening ones for Aminta and Elisa; Mozart's sense and loyalty to appropriate musical style seeks here the same ends he

continued through his later operas. Elisa's rage aria, "Barbaro, o Dio! mi vedi divisa dal mio ben," contains some of the most ornate writing in the opera. The closing finale alternates a rondo homophonic choral section in praise of Alessandro with short small ensembles; such mixed elements were increasingly common in revisions of Metastasio's librettos at that time, as sometimes seen in Jommelli and others.

Despite modern criticism of this and other of Mozart's serious operas as artificial and unconvincing, in the context of its day *Il rè pastore* was neither of these, but rather a demonstration of Mozart's growing ability to adapt a variety of musical forms and devices in compelling, dramatic roles. Three years later, in 1778, he was to give four of the *Pastore* arias to the object of his affection in Paris, Aloysia Weber, whose career he hoped to further and whose sister, Constanze, he eventually married.

—Dale E. Monson

THE RED LINE [Punainen viiva].

Composer: Aulis Sallinen.

Librettist: Aulis Sallinen (after the novel by I. Kianto).

First Performance: Helsinki, 30 November 1978.

Roles: Topi (baritone); Riika (soprano); Puntarpaa (baritone); Simana Arhippaini (bass); A Young Priest (baritone); The Vicar (tenor); Kisa (soprano); Jussi (tenor); Tiina, Raapana, Kunilla, Epra (all non-singing); Pirhonen (baritone).

* * *

In his second opera, Sallinen moved away from the obtrusive and often obscure symbolism of *Ratsumies* (The Horseman, 1974) towards a clearer expression of less equivocal themes. Symbolism still plays a part in *The Red Line* but is a less potent element of the plot. Sallinen constructed the libretto from a popular and influential novel of the same name (*Punainen viiva* in Finnish) by Ilmani Kianto (born Calamnius), written in 1909 and published two years later. Kianto (1874-1970) was born and lived most of his life in the northern province of Kainuu, a land of harsh contrasts which imposes great hardships on those who live there. This is the landscape of *The Red Line,* and the pitiless struggle of its characters against the predators, beast and men, who exploit their poverty and misery is the story of the opera. At the time, Finland was still a Russian province, albeit a semi-autonomous one, and the political events hinted at in the story can be linked to the reform of representation in the Finnish Diet and the elections of 1907, which led Finland to become the first country in the world to adopt universal suffrage and give votes to women.

The opera is in two acts, of four and three scenes respectively, with an epilogue. There is no overture or other orchestral introduction. A poor farmer, Topi, ekes out a living with his wife Riika and their children, but their existence is threatened by a bear (symbol perhaps of the alien environment or of revolutionary Russia just over the border). Topi seeks help from the neighbors but is refused because the parson considers he has failed in his religious duties. An agitator arrives to whip up local support for an election that is soon to take place. He promises democracy and freedom from oppression if only the people put a red line on the ballot paper. Topi, who has never held a pencil in his hand, wonders how such an action can change his world. He makes his mark, but his world does not change, and his children die of malnutrition. The bear strikes again and Topi sets out to hunt it. The bear kills him instead, leaving a wound in the shape of a red line across his throat. Now quite alone, Riika stands facing the bleak future, but behind her is a green birch tree, symbol of new hope.

By the time he wrote *The Red Line,* Sallinen's writing for voices had matured, and he had largely abandoned his earlier involvement with atonalism in favor of a freely lyrical style based on a loosely structured tonality. The scoring reveals a strong feeling for orchestral color, especially in the use of brass and percussion (bells and gongs), and in fastidiously atmospheric string writing. Both have become a feature of Sallinen's music. The grim struggle which is at the core of *The Red Line* would seem to demand the cold relentlessness of Sibelius's *Tapiola* perhaps, but Sallinen's opera is a hopeful as well as a tragic work, and though there is little humor in it there is warmth and a sense of the enduring heroism of the human spirit in the face of adversity that saves the work from any charge of nihilism.

—Kenneth Dommett

REGINA.

Composer: Marc Blitzstein.

Librettist: Marc Blitzstein (after Lillian Hellman, *The Little Foxes*).

First Performance: New York, 46th Street Theater, 31 October 1949.

Roles: Regina Giddens (soprano); Alexandra Giddens (soprano); Birdie Hubbard (soprano); Addie (contralto); Horace Giddens (bass); Benjamin Hubbard (baritone); Oscar Hubbard (baritone); Leo Hubbard (tenor); Cal (baritone); William Marshall (tenor); Jabez (baritone); John Bagtry (mute); Belle (mute).

Publications

article–

Gordon, Eric. "The Roots of 'Regina'." *Performing Arts* 3 (1980): 6.

* * *

The 1940s and 1950s were not distinguished by the premieres of outstanding new American operas. Marc Blitzstein's *Regina*, first performed on Broadway in 1949, is a symptom of this slump if considered by its performance history. Even today it is unappreciated by many in the press and opera administrations. But those who know the score find it an exciting, vividly dramatic work, easily Blitzstein's best work for the stage. Its solid dramatic core comes from its source,

Lillian Hellman's play *The Little Foxes,* which had opened on Broadway only ten years before.

The story concerns the Hubbard family: Regina Giddens and her brothers Ben and Oscar Hubbard; Oscar's wife Birdie, daughter of an old and distinguished Southern family, and their scapegrace son Leo; and Regina's husband Horace, a local banker, and their daughter Alexandra. The time is spring, 1900; the place, Bowden, Tennessee. The Hubbard siblings plan to build a cotton mill with the financial support of a Chicago banker, William Marshall. A short prologue on the veranda of the Giddens home sets the scene: Alexandra and the servants, singing spirituals, are silenced irritably by Regina. The first act begins with the after-dinner drinks as Marshall flatters Regina. When he leaves, she and her brothers start to argue over the terms of the deal. Regina sends Alexandra off to get Horace, who is in a hospital in Baltimore with a bad heart, for his financial support. Oscar's wife Birdie warns Alexandra of a plan to marry her to Leo; at the curtain, Oscar, who has overheard her, slaps her across the face.

Act II opens on the night of a party Regina gives for Marshall, at which they are to close the deal. Leo and Oscar discuss stealing a box of Horace's bonds to ensure it. Horace arrives, tired and ill. He and Regina have a brief reconciliation, but when she tells him why she summoned him home, he refuses to participate. During the party Leo is sent by his father and uncle to steal the bonds. Oscar insults Birdie, who is comforted by the servant Addie in a blues number. During a wild gallop for the guests, Ben tells Marshall that the deal can be considered settled. Regina is astonished, not knowing what has happened. She blames Horace and declares that she hopes he dies.

The third act opens the next day, with Horace, Alexandra, Birdie, and Addie commenting on the falling rain. Birdie, who has drunk a bit much, reflects in an aria on the miserable life she has had with the Hubbards. Horace tells Regina that the bonds have been stolen and that he will say they are a loan from her to her brothers. Regina goads him into having a heart attack by saying she has always detested him and refuses to get his medicine. He collapses and dies trying to go upstairs for it. Regina announces to her brothers that unless she gets seventy-five percent of the interest in the mill, she will report them and Leo to the police. They give in. Alexandra, recognizing the evil of her family and strengthened by her father's, Birdie's, and Addie's examples, decides to leave her mother. At the curtain Regina is alone.

There are three versions of the opera: the first version written for the Broadway premiere in 1949; the version for the New York City Opera in 1953; and that for the second New York City Opera production in 1958. The original Broadway version came closest to being a "musical," with spoken dialogue separated by musical numbers. For the first City Opera production Blitzstein cut some of the plotting, set most of the dialogue to music, and divided the two acts into three. In the second City Opera version, that which is performed today, Blitzstein cut the music for the black Angel Band; most of these cuts come during the prologue and the party scene.

The music, lying between opera and Broadway, is as successful as the drama. It ranges from the sublime—the "Rain Quartet" that opens the last act—to the anguished—Birdie's aria—to the almost demonic—the gallop during the party and Regina's "The Best Thing of All." The score is diatonic with use of blues and jazz rhythms and harmonies. Blitzstein shows his gift for melody, and his ability to mold it to fit the individual characters, throughout. Regina's raging outbursts are as finely crafted as Addie's gentle blues number to comfort

Birdie. Leo's number before the party sounds as inane as the character.

Blitzstein's attempt to contrast the servants and field hands as good characters with the evil Hubbards is ineffective although characteristic of the composer's interest in social causes, as demonstrated in almost all of his other works. His use of spirituals to open and close the opera is a clever musical/dramatic device; the cuts of the Angel Band music were probably well-considered as they reduce the racial subplotting.

The few failings include some of Blitzstein's cadences (a problem found in other works), which sound like a return to Broadway formulas after the operatic music that has come before. The ending of Ben's last number, for example, sounds like a contrivance rather than a naturally evolved climax. Some of the accompanied dialogue composed for the second production is interesting but not notable—but, then, the same can be said about recitatives by Verdi or Rossini. The Brechtian device of the characters commenting on the action in the first scene would have been brilliant if used throughout the opera, but occurring as it does in only one scene, it now seems only an odd interpolation.

Regina is an opera that deserves to become a repertory piece, with its memorable score and strong drama. The roles are difficult ones; it would be sad to see the work consigned to mediocre college productions. Perhaps if performed in summer opera festivals or in theaters away from critics who have not reconsidered their opinions of it recently, it will reveal to audiences its stature as a major twentieth-century opera.

—David E. Anderson

REIMANN, Aribert.

Composer. Born 4 March 1936, in Berlin. Studied with Blacher and Pepping; studied at the German Academy in Rome; became an accompanist as well as a composer, most notably to Dietrich Fischer-Dieskau; professor for twentieth-century solo vocal music, Hamburg, 1974-1983; professor, Berlin Hochschule der Künste, 1983-. Reimann's opera *Lear,* 1978, has been produced in Munich, Düsseldorf, Mannheim, San Francisco, Nuremberg, Paris, Berlin, Brunswick, Zurich, and London.

Operas

Publisher: Bote and Bock, Schott.

Ein Traumspiel, after Strindberg, translated by Peter Weiss, 1965, Kiel, 20 June 1965.
Melusine, Claus H. Henneberg (after Y. Goll), 1970, Schwetzingen Festival, 29 April 1971.
Lear, Claus H. Henneberg (after Shakespeare), Munich, Nationaltheater, 9 July 1978.
Die Gespenstersonate (chamber opera), Reimann and Uwe Schwendel (after Strindberg), 1983, Berlin, Hebbel-Theater, 25 September 1984.
Troades, Reimann and Gerd Albrecht (after Euripides, translated by Franz Werfel), Munich, Nationaltheater, 1985, 7 July 1986.
Das Schloss, Reimann (after Max Brod's dramatization of Kafka's novel), Berlin, Deutsche Oper, 2 September 1992.

Other works: vocal works, two piano concertos, a cello concerto, orchestral works, chamber music, piano pieces.

Publications

By REIMANN: articles–

"Salut für die junge Avantgarde." *Neue Zeitschrift für Musik* 140 (1979): 25.
"Krise des Liedes? Zum Lied im 20. Jahrhundert." *Musica* 35 (1981): 235.

interviews–

Burde, Wolfgang. "Aribert Reimann als Komponist und Interpret. Interview mit Aribert Reimann." *Neue Zeitschrift für Musik* 141 (1980): 535.

About REIMANN: books–

Zimmermann, Michael. "Aribert Reimann. Komponistenporträt." *Neue Zeitschrift für Musik* 142 (1981): 29.
———. "*Padrona la serva?* Text und Musik im 19. und im 20. Jahrhundert." In *Für und Wider die Literaturoper,* edited by Sigrid Wiesmann, 13. Laaber, 1982.
Schulz, Klaus, ed. *Aribert Reimanns "Lear": Weg einer neuen Oper.* Munich, 1984.

* * *

As the son of a pair of respected practicing musicians—his mother was a concert singer, his father a leading church musician in the Leipzig circle surrounding Max Reger—Aribert Reimann's path to music and particularly vocal music was a natural one. With six operas, five choral works and twenty-nine compositions for voice with piano or instruments among his published works (as of 1992) compared to seventeen compositions for solo instruments, chamber or orchestral ensembles, the bias is evident. This does not even take into account his juvenile and youthful unpublished output. His first composition was a song—*Morgentau* for soprano with piano accompaniment (1946), and he was to compose some twenty-nine vocal pieces, one a seven-number cycle for this same combination, together with piano pieces (Divertimenti, Fantasie, Melodie, Ballade and three Impressions) by 1955 when he graduated from high school and entered the Berlin High School of the Arts to major in piano with Otto Rausch and study counterpoint with the important German church composer, Ernst Pepping.

The first of his song cycles to be performed in public (1956) was *Five Songs from the Chinese,* one of eight works (for solo instruments, chorus or string quartet) written before *Elegie for Orchestra* (1957), the first of his works to be published by his teacher Boris Blacher's publishing house, Bote & Bock of Berlin, midway in his musical studies. From this year also dates Reimann's active participation in Berlin's concert life as a sought-after and extraordinarily sensitive piano accompanist to such singers as Barbara Scherler, Ernst Haefliger, Elisabeth Steiner, Elisabeth Grümmer, Rita Streich, Catherine Gayer, Barry McDaniel and Joan Carroll, many of whom were soloists with the Städtische Oper in West Berlin where Reimann had worked as a coach since graduating from high school. His collaboration with Dietrich Fischer-Dieskau dated from 1962 when the baritone sang the world premiere of "Five Poems by Paul Celan" at the Berlin Festival. It was

Fischer-Dieskau's performance in the title role of Reimann's *Lear* (1978) which, together with a hand-picked supporting cast and Ponnelle's brilliant staging, made the work that rarity among contemporary opera, an unqualified public success. Fischer-Dieskau, besides being a moving force in the creation of *Lear*, also sang the world premieres of Reimann's *Zyklus* (1971), *Wolkenloses Christfest* (1974), *Nunc dimittis* (1984), the Michelangelo poems (1986) and the James Joyce cycle *Shine and Dark* (1991). Only the Americans Barry McDaniel and Catherine Gayer have inspired Reimann to as many vocal works. The lead roles in *Melusine* (1971) were tailored expressly to their voices.

As a teacher, Boris Blacher—himself the composer of ten operas—was able to put his finger on the stylistic elements in Reimann's music that were characteristic of the composer and to encourage Reimann's development along those lines. Strict twelve-tone composition, Blacher's own technique of variable meters, Webernesque "Punktmusik," strict serialism (á la Boulez, soon discarded as a straitjacket) and aleatoric effects were all tested for their usefulness and absorbed. Now no longer accepted as part of the canon, a Piano Sonata (1957), a Ballet *Stoffreste* (scenario by Günter Grass, 1958) and a Cello Concerto (1959) were all created during his conservatory years. But it is the "Celan"-Songs and the first Piano Concerto (26 October 1962) which mark the beginning of Reimann's authentic compositional voice.

Reimann has consciously avoided association with any of the "schools" of avant-garde music (Darmstadt, Cologne, Donaueschingen), preferring to develop a musical vocabulary of his own independent of dodecaphonic trends in Germany which, until the 80s, made many composers sound like Webern clones. Reimann employs rows and their permutations undogmatically but achieves his own, highly individual and unmistakable sound-textures in orchestral works by presenting the note-series and its transpositions simultaneously (e.g., divided basses at the beginning of *Lear*, violas divisi ten ways, basses six, moving in and out of *sul tasto* or *ponticello*, at the beginning of *Wolkenloses Christfest*), by staggering the presentation of the row at different pitches, or by undulating a three- or four-segment section of the row among banks of solo wind instruments (Double Concerto).

Reimann's solo writing, whether for voice or instruments, is extremely demanding, extending the technical command required of the performer to but never beyond its limits. The solo cello voice in *Wolkenloses Christfest*, for example, is even more difficult than the cello part of the Double Concerto and shares with the baritone soloist Reimann's love of rapid *appoggiature* of a second, third or fourth on the main beat of the melody, *glissandi* between neighboring notes, and quarter tones, the latter used consistently in chamber works like *Invenzioni* and *The Ghost Sonata*. But often textures are cleared in order to present long, melodic *cantilene* above pedal-tone clusters, as with the violas at the end of the *Requiem* section of *Wolkenloses Christfest* (II), throughout the string section in the final moving pages of *Lear*, and as plaintive wind unison commentary in *Troades*. In all of his operas, Reimann clearly characterizes his stage figures by the kind of vocal line they have to sing, but nowhere is this more necessary than in *Troades*, where most of the soloists are women. Without even seeing the stage, the difference between the high coloratura flightiness of the self-justifying seductress Helen, the hysterical rapid arpeggios of the mezzo prophetess Cassandra, the long-drawn lament of the dramatic alto Hecuba, the expressive declamation of the still queenly soprano Andromache, even the hidden compassion of the Greek officer

Talthybios (baritone) whose orders are to throw her son Astynax from the ramparts, put Troy to the torch and disperse its widowed women, is audible.

Some of Reimann's scores present difficulties on first encounter, but all reveal beauties of form, texture, melody and dramatic truth with repeated hearing.

—James Helme Sutcliffe

REINER, Fritz.

Conductor. Born 19 December 1888, in Budapest. Died 15 November 1963, in New York. Studied piano with Thomán and Bartók and composition with Koessler at the Royal Academy of Music, Budapest; conductor of the Volksoper, Budapest, 1911-14; conductor of the Hofoper (later Staatsoper), Dresden, 1914-21; various conducting engagements in Europe; music director of the Cincinnati Symphony Orchestra, 1922; became a United States Citizen, 1928; professor of conducting at the Curtis Institute of Music, Philadelphia, 1931-34; guest conductor at Covent Garden, 1936-37; guest conductor at the San Francisco Opera, 1935-38; music director of the Pittsburgh Symphony Orchestra, 1938-48; conductor at the Metropolitan Opera, 1948-53; music director of the Chicago Symphony Orchestra, 1953-62. Among Reiner's conducting students were Leonard Bernstein and Lukas Foss.

Publications

About REINER: articles–

Harrison, Jay S. "Return of Reiner" (Interview). *Musical America* October (1963).

unpublished–

Potter, R. "Fritz Reiner, Conductor, Teacher, Musical Innovator." Ph.D. dissertation, Northwestern University, 1980.

*   *   *

In an interview in *Musical America* conducted shortly before his death, Fritz Reiner, when asked about his early career, stated that "We can't get away from opera because that's how my career began." At the time of his death in November 1963 Reiner was in New York preparing for his return to the Metropolitan Opera, where he had not appeared for a decade, to conduct Wagner's *Götterdämmerung*. From 1953, the year he left the Metropolitan and became music director of the Chicago Symphony, until the end of his life, the only opera Reiner conducted was *Die Meistersinger* in 1955 during the opening postwar season of the Vienna Staatsoper. In this same interview Reiner noted that the opera house is the right training ground for conductors: "There you learn about repertory, about ensembles, about singers, about how to cope with emergencies."

After studying piano with Thomán and Bartók, the latter of whom signed his diploma in 1909, and composition with Koessler at the Royal Academy of Music, Budapest, Reiner made his conducting debut as Chorus Master for *Carmen* in Budapest. His first post was at Laibach (now Ljubljana), "in a typical Austrian-style opera house where we played everything in the world," in Reiner's words. Repertory there included *Tannhäuser,* Lehár's *Die lustige Witwe, La bohème,* and Smetana's *Dalibor.* Reiner then returned to his native city, where he conducted at the Volksoper from 1911-14. The very moment it became possible to produce Wagner's *Parsifal* outside Bayreuth, Reiner staged it in Budapest, sounding the first note at one minute after the stroke of midnight of 31 December 1913 (when copyright restrictions were lifted). The performance lasted until 5:00 a.m. Also in Budapest Reiner gave the local premiere of Wolf-Ferrari's *The Jewels of the Madonna.*

Reiner spent the years 1914-22 at the Court Opera in Dresden, one of the most important operatic posts in Europe. There he came into contact with Richard Strauss, whose music he came to conduct with special insight and flair. During his Dresden years Reiner guest conducted orchestras in Berlin, Hamburg, and Vienna. He would travel to Berlin and Leipzig to watch Artur Nikisch, whose protégé Reiner became: from both Nikisch and Strauss Reiner learned how to achieve clarity of line and transparency of sound. During this time Reiner's characteristic conducting features were developed: the constant right-hand beat, the extreme economy of motion, and the ability to direct with his eyes, eyebrows, tilt of head, and line of shoulders. Of Nikisch, Reiner later said that "It was he who told me that I should never wave my arms in conducting and that I should use my eyes to give cues." Although Reiner had tenure at Dresden, he gave up his post there in 1921 to be free to conduct in Rome and Barcelona and wherever else he chose.

In 1922 Reiner took on the first of several missions as orchestra builder when he became music director of the Cincinnati Symphony Orchestra. There, as when he took over the Pittsburgh Symphony Orchestra in 1938 and the Chicago Symphony Orchestra in 1953, he was faced with disspirited personnel and low performance standards. Reiner remained in Pittsburgh for nine years, becoming an American citizen in 1928. From 1926-30 he made various appearances at Teatro alla Scala. In 1931 he became a professor of conducting at the Curtis Institute of Music in Philadelphia, with perhaps an eye to succeeding Stokowski as leader of the Philadelphia Orchestra. At Curtis his pupils included Leonard Bernstein, Lukas Foss, and Walter Hendl. Reiner stressed discipline and scrupulous preparation, insisting that his pupils be ready to conduct a performance at a moment's notice by virtue of knowing the score thoroughly and being able to convey one's wishes to the players with the greatest economy of motion. In his Dresden days Reiner had, for example, conducted the entire *Ring* cycle without rehearsal. In addition to teaching at Curtis, Reiner conducted opera in Philadelphia in the early 1930s, including a performance of Strauss' *Elektra* in the 1934-35 season.

Reiner returned to regular opera activity as guest conductor at San Francisco and Covent Garden in the late 1930s, specializing in Wagner. A number of these performances were with Flagstad and Melchior, and some are now available on compact disc, including a *Tristan und Isolde* from San Francisco and act II of *Die Walküre* from Covent Garden. In 1938 Reiner went to Pittsburgh, where many of his best players from Cincinnati joined him. During his Pittsburgh years he was a regular guest conductor of major American and European orchestras; beginning in 1941 he conducted the NBC Symphony annually at Toscanini's invitation.

From 1948 to 1953 Reiner was a shining light at the Metropolitan Opera. He conducted 143 performances of, among others, *Carmen, Falstaff, Salome, Elektra, Le nozze di Figaro,*

Don Giovanni, Der Rosenkavalier, and the United States premiere of *The Rake's Progress.* His prowess as a Strauss conductor was displayed in the now legendary performances of *Salome* from 1949 with Ljuba Welitsch in the title role. A tape of the broadcast exists and there is also a commercial recording of the final scene. Reiner may also be heard on a live recording of 30 December 1950 of Wagner's *Fliegende Höllander* with Hans Hotter. Another famous collaboration from these Metropolitan years was with Risë Stevens as Carmen. A commercial recording exists of this interpretation. Reiner also recorded excerpts from *Elektra* and *Salome* with the soprano Inge Borkh.

From 1953 to 1962 Reiner was music director of the Chicago Symphony, which he built into one of the premiere orchestras in the world. Among the factors that enabled Reiner to be such an effective orchestra builder was his role as a rigid disciplinarian, one who refused to socialize with his players. If he was not beloved as a conductor, he was greatly respected for his precision (he had the smallest beat since Richard Strauss) and almost inhuman demand for perfection, for his profound musical scholarship, his strong sense of line and proportion, his ability to build climaxes over long time spans, and his mastery of orchestral balance and color. Like Toscanini, Reiner believed in the authority of the score. His conducting, anything but sentimental, conveyed force and grandeur. He was especially ingenious at clarifying the complex scores of composers such as Strauss and Bartók.

—Stephen A. Willier

REINHARDT, Max (Goldman).

Director, also actor, manager, producer. Born 9 September 1873, in Baden, Austria. Died 30 October 1943, in New York City. Founded Kleines Theater, 1902; initially an actor, by 1903 devoted exclusively to production; collaborated with Alfred Roller in premiere of *Der Rosenkavalier,* 1911; noted for spectacles such as *The Miracle,* 1911, and Hofmannsthal's *Jedermann,* 1920; cocreator of the Salzburg Festival, 1920; forced to leave Germany, 1937; produced Shakespeare's *Midsummer Night's Dream* in the Hollywood Bowl, then on film, 1935.

Opera Productions (selected)

Orphée aux enfers, Neues Theater, Berlin, 1906.
Oedipus Rex, Vienna, 1910.
Le belle Hélène, Venice, 1911.
The Miracle, Olympia, London, 1911.
Der Rosenkavalier, Dresden, 1911.
Ariadne auf Naxos, Stuttgart, 1912.
Die Fledermaus, Paris, 1929.
Die Fledermaus, Berlin, 1930.
Les contes d'Hoffmann, Grosses Schauspielhaus, Berlin, 1931.

Publications

By REINHARDT: books–

Ausgewählte Briefe, Reden, Schriften und Szenen aus Regiebüchern. Edited by F. Hadamowsky. Vienna, 1963.

Briefe, Reden, Aufsätze, Interviews, Gespräche, Auszüge aus Regiebüchern. Edited by H. Fetting. Berlin, 1974.

articles—

"Weingartner suscite l'enthousiasme de Romain Rolland pour Beethoven." *Revue Musicale de Suisse Romande* 41, no. 4 (1988): 196.

About REINHARDT: books—

Herald, H., and E. Stern. *Reinhardt und seine Bühne.* Berlin, 1918.
Sayler, Oliver Martin, ed. *Max Reinhardt and His Theatre.* New York, 1924.
Horch, F., ed. *Die Spielpläne Max Reinhardts 1905-1930.* Munich, 1930.
Stern, E. *My Life, My Stage.* London, 1951.
Strauss, Richard. *Recollections and Reflections.* Edited by Willi Schuh. Translated by L.J. Lawrence. New York, 1953.
Strauss, Richard, and Hugo von Hofmannsthal. *The Correspondence between Richard Strauss and Hugo von Hofmannsthal.* Translated by Hanns Hammelmann and Ewald Osers. London, 1961.
Carter, Huntly. *The Theatre of Max Reinhardt.* New York, 1964.
Hadamowsky, F. *Reinhardt und Salzburg.* Salzburg, 1964.
Braulich, H. *Max Reinhardt.* Berlin, 1969.
Eisner, Lotte H. *The Haunted Screen: Expressionism in the German Cinema and the Influence of Max Reinhardt.* Translated by Roger Greaves. Berkeley, 1969.
Reinhardt, G. *Der Liebhaber.* Munich, 1973.
Fuehrich-Leisler, E., and G. Prossnitz, eds. *Max Reinhardt in Amerika.* Salzburg, 1976.
Reinhardt, Gottfried. *The Genius: A Memoir of Max Reinhardt.* New York, 1979.
Hartmann, Rudolf. *Richard Strauss, The Staging of His Operas and Ballets.* New York, 1981.
Styan, J.L. *Max Reinhardt.* New York, 1982.
Fuehrich-Leisler, E., and G. Prossnitz, eds. *Max Reinhardt-ein Theater, das den Menschen weider Freude gibt.* Munich, 1987.
Leiter, Samuel L. *From Stanislavsky to Barrault: Popular Directors of the European Stage.* Westport, Connecticut, 1991.

articles—

Cuno, Franz. "Reinhardts Inszenierung von 'Hoffmanns Erzählungen.'" *Maske und Kothurn* 3, Heft 3 (1957).
Prossnitz, G. "Max Reinhardt und das Musiktheater." *Oesterreichische Musikzeitschrift* 24 (August 1969): 454-56.
Marek, G.R. "The Lord of Leopoldskron." *Opera News* 36 (1 April 1972): 26-29; (15 April 1972): 26-30.
Heinsheimer, H. "Es gibt, ob Tanzen und Singen tauge—zum hundertsten Geburtstag von Max Reinhardt." *Neue Zeitschrift für Musik* 134, no. 9 (1973): 570-72; *Das Orchester* 21 (October 1973): 599-600.

*   *   *

For the first third of the twentieth century, Max Reinhardt was the most famous stage director in the western world. Based in Berlin, with two (and later three) theaters housing his large and versatile acting company, Reinhardt produced a wide repertoire of classic and modern plays. From his first season as director at the Kleines Theater in 1902, Reinhardt fused a stolid German theatrical tradition with new energy. His genius lay in his ability to find a style suited to each individual dramatic work he tackled. Inspired by Wagner's concept of the *Gesamtkunstwerk,* he employed all the arts to achieve this end: visual and musical elements were integrated with the spoken word; the right theater or theatrical venue was found for the work. In addition, the director made use of new technical devices being developed at the time.

At a distance of half a century, Reinhardt's name now conjures up such magnificent spectacles as Vollmoeller's *The Miracle,* for which venues like the London Olympia or the Century Theatre in New York were turned into cathedrals, and the awesome pageantry of the performance exalted its spectators into a quasi-religious state. This in fact would be an erroneous impression. The director was at home in many varying styles: his Ibsen naturalistic and intimate, his Shakespeare fluid and clearly-spoken. Büchner's *Danton's Death* conveyed the terrifying sense of being in the grip of a revolutionary Parisian mob, while Goldoni's *Servant of Two Masters* embodied the *commedia dell'arte* spirit. Berlin soon became a focus of international attention with season after season of Reinhardt's outstanding theatrical productions. He toured them on the continent, reproduced them in London and New York City with English-speaking casts. His name was synonymous with theatrical excitement and excellence, and his work stood as a landmark in its time.

Max Reinhardt began his theatrical career as an actor in his native Austria. He moved to Berlin in 1894 to join the company of Otto Brahm, whose naturalistic approach to acting was in stark contrast to the then-prevailing declamatory style of the late nineteenth century. The young actor began to chafe at the constraints of this wholly-naturalistic style. In the artistic ferment of *fin de siècle* Berlin, Reinhardt and friends founded a satirical cabaret in order to experiment and stretch themselves. Within a year it had become the theatrical company of the Kleines Theater, with Reinhardt as director. The repertoire of its first season (1902) included Strindberg and Oscar Wilde, the latter's *Importance of Being Earnest* as well as the German premiere of his *Salome.* By 1905, three theaters were under Reinhardt's aegis, and his groundbreaking production of *A Midsummer Night's Dream* had made him world famous.

Although the bulk of Reinhardt's productions were spoken drama, he did occasionally include an operetta in the season's roster. The first such was Offenbach's *Orphée aux enfers,* produced in 1906, followed by the same composer's *La belle Hélène* in 1911. Both productions were revived, *Orphée aux enfers* in 1921, *La belle Hélène* in 1931, which was later reincarnated on Broadway in 1944 as *Helen Goes to Troy.*

Revivals were facilitated by the existence of the *Regiebuch,* a Reinhardt innovation. To the customary theatrical prompt-book was added each nuance of movement and gesture evolved during rehearsals, the scenic plans, set and costume sketches, lighting plot and musical score, as well as all of Reinhardt's textural and historical research, and his interpretive ideas. A production could therefore be remounted, merely by following these detailed instructions. This did not prevent the director from adding new touches to his revivals, and he was always willing to accommodate his conception to circumstances at hand.

That Reinhardt brought the same fastidious attention to his productions of operetta as spoken drama is attested to by Otto Klemperer who, at the age of 21, served in 1906 as chorus master during rehearsals of *Orphée aux enfers,* and subsequently conducted some fifty performances of the work during the season. He recalled the production as having been "musically and scenically prepared down to the smallest detail" and described it to Reinhardt's son Gottfried thus: "An indescribable freedom on the stage was bridled by an indefinable authority."

Perhaps the most magical of Reinhardt's operetta productions was his mounting of Johann Strauss's *Die Fledermaus* in 1929. "What he had done," says Gottfried Reinhardt, "was to remove the arbitrariness from the old shotgun marriage of sublime music and ridiculous plot, strip that plot of its triteness and the music of its anti-theatre hegemony, take the relic out of operetta's home for the aged and make a happy home for it in the living theatre.... Reinhardt's unorthodox concept ... with its emphasis on acting, necessitated modification of the score (melodies composed for voices had to be transferred to instruments, story changes called for musical additions from other Strauss works)."

Gottfried Reinhardt has noted that one of his father's hallmarks was the invention of "a single, symbolic scene [which would] reveal a play in its entirety and quintessence." The opening pantomime, with the overture as its accompaniment, was a case in point. It set the scene for a *Die Fledermaus* that contained the essence of Biedermeier Vienna, minus the "coy and sentimental kitsch" and "characters without character" that Reinhardt deplored. The director had gone instead to the heart of Strauss's work.

The addition of new music or the elimination of songs from the roles of non-singing actors, while anathema perhaps to the musical purist, was a conscious choice on Reinhardt's part: thus could he give new life to works that had become ossified. None of his musical productions were immune from this process, but it was always done with the intention of presenting what Reinhardt felt to be true to the author's vision.

His last musical presentation in Berlin, Offenbach's *Les contes d'Hoffmann,* produced at the Grosses Schauspielhaus in 1931, continued this process. With Leo Blech as conductor and musical adaptor, and Friedell and Sassman as literary adaptors, Reinhardt felt himself at liberty to rework an opera which the composer himself had never finished.

In order to strengthen the Hoffmann-Stella relationship— the framework against which the stories of the poet's three loves are contrasted—two short dialogue scenes between Hoffmann and Stella were inserted at the beginning of the opera; in addition Stella made two other appearances in the tavern as Hoffmann told his stories. Her serious presence thereby gave force to Reinhardt's *coup de théâtre* at the end: Reinhardt's audience was presented with the backs of the singers and beyond them their auditorium. As Stella sings into the "stage opera house," Hoffmann storms on and takes her in his arms, trying forcibly to remove her from her Art. But Stella resists, and Hoffmann is left to his Muse. The critics did not take kindly to this interpretation, nor did they like Offenbach's original spoken dialogue, familiar as they were to the sung recitatives completed after the composer's death and by then the normally accepted version. But "Berlin," Gottfried Reinhardt tells us, "took *Les contes d'Hoffmann* to its heart." Even the president of Germany, Hindenburg, wished to see it, but was too old to climb the stairs to the official box.

Reinhardt's other association with the operatic world is far better known and documented: his staging of the premieres of two Richard Strauss/Hugo von Hofmannsthal works, *Der Rosenkavalier* (1911) and the original version of *Ariadne auf Naxos* (1912). Strauss had long been familiar with Reinhardt's stage productions. In *Recollections and Reflections* he records his visits to Wilde's *Salome* in 1902 and Hofmannsthal's German-language version of *Elektra* in 1903. Both productions were catalysts in the composition of the Strauss operas based on those dramatic works.

It was probably inevitable that the composer and librettist should turn to Reinhardt for assistance with *Der Rosenkavalier* when it became apparent that the regisseur at Dresden, where the opera was to receive its world premiere, was inadequate to the task of realizing the style and scope of their vision. Thus Max Reinhardt, as his son puts it, "pioneered yet another development that has since become the order of the day: the preeminence of the stage director in opera." With his ability to mold singers into singing actors, Reinhardt prefigured developments in late twentieth-century performance style.

Hofmannsthal, who had had several dramatic works produced in the Reinhardt theaters, and who was as pleased as Strauss with the miracles wrought on the *Rosenkavalier* cast, proceeded to work on his next libretto for Strauss with Reinhardt in mind as producer. The combination of Molière's *Bourgeois gentilhomme* with a one-act opera (*Ariadne*) was conceived specifically as something that would appeal to the talents of Reinhardt and his company. In the end, however, the Reinhardt company could not provide Strauss with the singers and orchestra he needed for the one-act opera, and Strauss settled on Stuttgart for the premiere. Reinhardt agreed to work in Stuttgart, and the premiere went ahead. The evening was, however, only modestly successful, despite the "splendid" performance and "gorgeously brilliant ... scenery effects by Reinhardt." The work could not please the public, as the composer himself acknowledged. But the debt to Reinhardt was generously acknowledged with the publication of the score.

There was to be one last Strauss-Hofmannsthal-Reinhardt collaboration: the founding of the Salzburg Festival in 1920. The idea for the Festival had been Reinhardt's, born of his desire to present "a fusion of all the arts" and inspired by the idea of presenting Hofmannsthal's version of *Everyman*— originally produced by Reinhardt in Berlin in 1911—in the square before the Salzburg cathedral. Local opposition to the idea of a festival was overcome by enlisting the support of Hofmannsthal and Strauss, but it was Reinhardt's commitment that kept the impetus from faltering, and he was the festival's principal animator until his American exile in 1937.

Today Reinhardt's achievements have been largely forgotten, *The Miracle* or his Hollywood film of *A Midsummer Night's Dream* appearing as footnotes in theatrical histories. In fact, he was the pioneer who cleared the ground for much that constitutes current production style, whether in the spoken theatre or on the opera stage. His belief that every art should be brought into play to serve the work in hand, then a revolutionary concept, now is accepted without question. The intensity of his efforts to fulfill each writer's intentions, with the resulting wealth of production styles, and the concommitant fostering of acting, design and musical talent around him, was unique in his time.

—Louise Stein

RENNERT, Günther.

Producer. Born 1 April 1911, in Essen, Germany. Died 31 July 1978, in Salzburg. Married: Elisabeth de Freitas; four children. Educated in Essen, Buenos Aires, and Cologne; attended the Universities of Munich, Berlin, and Halle, 1930-33; began directing short comedy films, 1933; first opera production was *Parsifal,* Frankfurt, 1935; appointments in Wuppertal, Frankfurt, and Mainz, 1935-39; chief producer, Königsberg, 1939-42; chief producer, Berlin Städtische Oper, 1942-44; chief producer, Bayerische Staatsoper, 1945; general administrator and chief producer, Hamburg Staatsoper, 1946-56; theater debut, Kammerspiele, Hamburg, 1947; head of production and joint artistic counsellor, Glyndebourne, 1960-67; Staatsintendant, Bayerische Staatsoper, 1967-76. Awards include Grosses Bundesverdienstkreuz, FR Germany; Austrian Bundesverdienstkreuz für Kunst und Wissenschaft; Bayerischer Verdienstorden; and Brahms Medal, City of Hamburg.

Opera Productions (selected)

Parsifal, Opera House, Frankfurt, 1935.
Dama Boba, Mainz, 1938.
Fidelio, Bayerische Staatsoper, 1945.
Heimkehr, Hamburg, 1947.
Totz wider Trotz, Hamburg, 1948.
Un ballo in maschera, Covent Garden, 1952.
Les contes d'Hoffmann, Covent Garden, 1954.
Pallas Athene weint, Hamburg, 1955.
Fidelio, Glyndebourne, 1959.
Oedipus der Tyrann, Stuttgart, 1959.
Nabucco, Metropolitan Opera, 1960.
Volpone, Stuttgart, 1960.
Un ballo in maschera, Metropolitan Opera, 1962.
Manon, Metropolitan Opera, 1963.
Flood, Hamburg, 1963.
Salome, Metropolitan Opera, 1965.
Die Zauberflöte, Metropolitan Opera, 1967.
Jenůfa, Metropolitan Opera, 1974.
Gestiefelte Kater, Schwetzingen/Hamburg, 1975.
Le nozze di Figaro, Metropolitan Opera, 1975.

Publications

By RENNERT: books–

Opernarbeit: Inszenierungen 1963-1973 (Munich, 1974).

articles–

"Glyndebourne and Its Future," with V. Gui. Translated by G. Morris. *Opera* 11 (Autumn 1960): 7.
"My Aims in Munich." *Opera* 18 (October 1967): 831-33.
"Gedenkrede." *Pfitzner* no. 23 (September 1968): 2-4.
"Three Strauss Operas for London." *Opera* 23 (March 1972): 200-02.
"Zur Inszenierung der *Frau ohne Schatten,*" with G. Schneider-Siemssen. *Opernwelt* no. 8 (August 1974): 24-25.
"The Function of the Intendant." *Opera* 26 (February 1975): 139-42.
"Mehr als realistisches Musiktheater." *Opernwelt News* 12 (December 1975): 25.
"Meine Begegnung mit dem Werk Carl Orffs." *Opernwelt News* no. 7 (July 1975): 15-16.

About RENNERT: books–

Schäfer, W.E. *Günther Rennert—Regisseur in dieser Zeit.* Bremen, 1962.

articles–

Hartog, H. "Günther Rennert." *Opera* 3 (September 1952): 542-546.
Fuchs, P.P. "Opera in West Germany; Post-War Conditions Have Produced New Visual Approaches and Techniques." *Musical America* 76 (15 February 1956): 16-17.
Besch, A. "A Triptych of Producers." *Opera* 9 (April 1958): 227-29.
Honolka, K. "Rennert und das Musiktheater." *Musica* 13 (March 1959): 180-81.
"Staging Pure and Simple." *Opera News* 25 (3 December 1960): 14-15.
Joachim, H. "Günther Rennert, Oskar Fritz Schuh, Wieland Wagner—Three Eminent Opera Producers." *Canon: Australian Music Journal* 16 (December-January 1962-1963): 16-19.
Schäfer, W.E. "Der Opernregisseur Günther Rennert." *Melos: Zeitschrift für neue Musik* 30 (July-August 1963): 224-28.
Koegler, H. "German Producers on 'Musical Theatre'." *Opera* 15 (June 1964): 378-81.
Golea, A. "Vu et entendu." *Musica* no. 126 (September 1964): 17-22.
"Portrait." *Neue Zeitschrift für Musik* 127 (February 1966): 79.
Honolka, K. "Offenbarung des Mitleidens." *Opernwelt* no. 5 (May 1967): 38-39.
"Günther Rennerts Münchner Pläne." *Opernwelt* 6 (June 1967): 24-25.
Krause, E. and K. Schumann. "Einstand und Abschied." *Opernwelt* no. 9 (September 1967): 10-13.
"Günther Rennert: Unklare Alternativen (Interview)." *Opernwelt* no. 12 (December 1967): 19-21.
Harewood, Lord. "Operatic Bounty in Germany." *Opera* 19 (January 1968): 21-22.
Ruppel, K.H. "Rennert and Rennert." *Opernwelt* no. 1 (January 1968): 36-38.
Loney, G. "Günther Rennert, Opera Doctor (Interview)." *Music Journal* 27 (January 1969): 28-31.
K.R. Danler. "Gespräch mit dem Intendaten der Bayerischen Staatsoper München, Dr. Günther Rennert." *Das Orchester* 18 (April 1970): 166-67.
Ludwig, H. "Das Interview: Günther Rennert." *Opernwelt* no. 4 (April 1973): 26-27.
"Gedanken zum Nachfolge-Rennert-Quiz." *Oper und Konzert* 12, no. 3 (1974): 20-22.
Lesch, H. "Wie Münchens Opernzukunft aussehen könnte: ein Kommentar zum Ende der Ära Rennert." *Opernwelt* no. 3 (March 1974): 16.
Breuer, R. "Great Directors: Günther Rennert." *Opera News* 40 (21 February 1976): 8-12.
Schwinger, W. "Oper von A bis Z—Günther Rennert zum Füenfundsechzigsten." *Musica* 30, no. 3 (1976): 238-39.
Christie, George. "Günther Rennert." *Opera* 29 (October 1978): 956-58.
Fabian, I. "Günther Rennerts letzte Inszenierung." *Opernwelt* Yearbook (1978): 76-78.

* * *

When the Hamburg Staatsoper was rebuilt after its destruction by Allied bombs in World War II, Günther Rennert was its general administrator, and he remained with the company for the first ten years of its new existence. It was he who built the company's reputation. This came about through

Günther Rennert's production of *The Makropoulos Case*, Stuttgart Opera, 1970

an expansion of repertoire back to Handel and Purcell and forward to such twentieth-century composers as Britten, Schoenberg, Berg, and Hindemith. He also introduced a new manner of staging opera based on his experience in the legitimate theater, replacing the traditional, often stilted and clichéd operatic approach with a more modern, theatrical, integrated one. This approach was carried on by Rennert's successors, Rolf Liebermann and August Everding.

Rennert served as an apprentice to Walter Felsenstein before beginning his own career, and it was Felsenstein who steered him toward opera. He began producing operas in Frankfurt in 1935 with a production of Wagner's *Parsifal.* From 1939 to 1942 he was chief producer at Königsberg. Rennert became principal producer at the Städtische Oper, Berlin, in 1942 and remained there for two seasons. In 1945 he served as principal producer at the Bavarian State Opera; he was its intendant from 1967 to 1976. He served as intendant of the Hamburg State Opera from 1946 to 1956, where his productions included Britten's *Peter Grimes,* Stravinsky's *The Rake's Progress,* Hindemith's *Mathis der Maler,* and the operas of Alban Berg. In 1952 he mounted a production of Verdi's *Un ballo in maschera* at Covent Garden, which was followed by a staging of Offenbach's *Les contes d'Hoffmann* there in 1954. In 1960 Rennert was named head of production at Glyndebourne, where he had produced Beethoven's *Fidelio* the previous year; he remained at Glyndebourne until 1967. Rennert died in 1978.

Rennert produced six operas for the Metropolitan Opera: Verdi's *Nabucco* (1960), Massenet's *Manon* (1963), Richard Strauss's *Salome* (1965, with Birgit Nilsson), Mozart's *Die Zauberflöte* (1967), Janáček's *Jenůfa* (1974), and Mozart's *Le nozze di Figaro* (1975).

Rennert was especially adept in directing crowd scenes and in staging comedies, perhaps because of his early experience in directing comedy films. A specialist in twentieth-century opera, Rennert was also known for his productions of Rossini, for which he prepared his own versions that are considered unscholarly by today's standards.

Rennert believed that the source of opera's impact is "deliberate unreality." He saw music as a medium of communication, the carrier of the work's ideas, and an enhancement to the words that compensates for the loss of realism inherent in opera.

—Michael Sims

RESNIK, Regina.

Soprano and mezzo-soprano. Born 30 August 1922, in New York. Studied with Rosalie Miller and Giuseppe Danise; concert debut at the Brooklyn Academy of Music, 1942; sang opera in Mexico, 1943; Metropolitan Opera debut as Leonore in *Il Trovatore,* 1944; sang regularly with the Metropolitan, turning to mezzo-soprano roles in 1955; appeared as Sieglinde at Bayreuth, 1953; Covent Garden debut as Carmen, 1957; sang there until 1972; active as an opera producer from 1971.

Publications

About RESNIK: articles–

Cook, I. "Regina Resnik." *Opera* 1 (1963): 13.
Rosenthal, H. "Regina Resnik." In *Great Singers of Today*, London, 1966.

We so strongly think of Regina Resnik as a mezzo that it comes as a surprise to realize that this was really a second career, for she began as a soprano. Yet a soprano she was, and not as a brief, incidental foray into a repertoire which was abandoned early on; after her debut (as Lady Macbeth, no less) Resnik sang for a number of years such major and unequivocally soprano roles as Tosca, Aida, Butterfly, both Donna Anna and Donna Elvira in *Don Giovanni,* and—most interestingly—Chrysothemis in *Elektra,* the opera in which she would later score such a great success in the contralto part of Klytemnestra.

Indeed, that we tend to forget about these early years is not at all a negative comment on Resnik's achievements as a soprano; radio broadcasts preserve her in several of these roles and reveal a bright, shining instrument secure throughout the range and coping easily with top notes. It is instead that her achievements as a character mezzo are considerable, and the voice is the real thing—no topless soprano trying to maintain a career in a new repertoire, but a genuine mezzo of a particularly ripe and fruity color. This "second voice" is, in fact, so dark and formidable—and Resnik's sense of identification in mezzo roles is so complete and commanding—that it seems inconceivable that she was once an altogether different kind of singer.

Take, for example, the aforementioned role of Klytemnestra, in which she had few if any equals. Whether on records (the Decca performance under Georg Solti) or on the stage, Resnik's characterization is absolutely vivid, portraying the arrogance, rage, and ultimately terror and pathos of this character with unrivaled intensity and authority. She meets every arduous demand that Strauss makes with an instrument that is absolutely steady, although it should be said also that—here as elsewhere—Resnik is willing to use the voice for maximum dramatic impact. This means she will frequently bear down and force the tone, so that the dark color becomes almost suffocating, and the timbre will curdle a bit; at its most extreme, the sound can be really rather ugly and she can seem quite the harridan. This is always used in an appropriate and artistic way, but though it is eminently suitable for some roles—Ulrica in *Ballo in maschera,* for example, or the Principessa in *Suor Angelica*—it is rather less desirable in *Carmen* or as Eboli in *Don Carlo,* where a handsomer and more sensuous voice better suit these characters.

That Resnik has impersonated Carmen and Eboli with considerable success is yet another testimonial to her fine artistry. Records preserve her Carmen under less than ideal circumstances—del Monaco and Sutherland are in poor form and Resnik herself was past her best years for this role—but her distinction is still in evidence. Although without her handsome stage presence this Carmen sounds rather matronly, Resnik's word-painting is exceptionally fiery and full of innuendo—for once, she really sounds as though she might

have worked in a cigarette factory. Later, when Carmen achieves a certain nobility, Resnik's conception of the part pays off especially well with a maturity and richness that are strikingly in contrast with her hoydenish early scenes. And turning from this to her wonderfully comical Mistress Quickly in Bernstein's superb recording of *Falstaff* is to see yet another remarkable facet of the art of this singing actress.

Resnik continues to make use of her dramatic skills. At the time of this writing a number of years have passed since she retired from singing opera and concerts, but she has performed to excellent reviews and predictably positive audience response in musicals, including a Broadway revival of *Cabaret.* Resnik has also achieved considerable success as a director of opera, and it is encouraging to realize that the stage instincts which made her such a memorable singer are still serving the opera world.

—David Anthony Fox

EL RETABLO DE MAESE PEDRO [Master Peter's Puppet Show].

Composer: Manuel de Falla.

Librettist: Manuel de Falla (based on Cervantes, *Don Quixote*).

First Performance: concert performance, Seville, San Fernando, 23 March 1923; staged performance, Paris, home of Edmond de Polignac, 25 June 1923.

Roles: Don Quixote (bass or baritone); Master Peter (tenor); Boy-Narrator (boy soprano); Sancho Panza, Innkeeper, Page, Scholar (all mute); various puppets.

Though the Princess Edmond de Polignac commissioned works for her private puppet-theater from Igor Stravinsky and Erik Satie as well as from Manuel de Falla, only de Falla's *El retablo de Maese Pedro* came to be presented, in 1923, under her auspices. It is fitting that de Falla, fascinated by puppetry since childhood, would be the one to fulfill the commission, and *El retablo de Maese Pedro* holds an honored place among that difficult-to-categorize species of mixed-genre works that flourished in the first few decades of the twentieth century—works that combine aspects of opera, ballet, pantomime and recitation.

De Falla fashioned his own libretto from an episode in Part II of Cervantes' *Don Quixote*. Don Quixote and his squire Sancho Panza have arrived at an inn where the traveling showman Master Peter presents a puppet play in which Don Gayferos, knight at the court of Charlemagne, rescues his wife Melisendra (who is also the daughter of Charlemagne) from Moorish captivity in Spain. At the point in the interior play in which Melisendra and Gayferos, on horseback, are being pursued by the Moors, Quixote agitatedly jumps up, takes his sword, and confusing the drama with reality, slashes the pursuers to wooden bits (much to the anguish of Master Peter, who sees this "madman" slice his livelihood to nothingness). The work ends with Quixote proudly singing a peroration to knight errantry and to his beloved Dulcinea.

Though the story is simple, and though the work takes slightly less than half an hour to perform, there are artistic and intellectual rewards in abundance. For in de Falla's conception, not only is the play-within-the-play performed with puppets, but those watching that play (Quixote, Panza, the Innkeeper) and those putting on the play (Master Peter and his assistant, the Boy-Narrator) are portrayed by larger, life-size puppets. Quixote's quandary with illusion is thus mirrored by de Falla's structural scheme in which puppets watch other puppets manipulate yet other puppets. The prismatic effect is heightened when, from time to time, Master Peter and Quixote chide the Boy-Narrator for unduly embellishing or editorializing the story as well as for being mistaken on points of historical accuracy.

Only three of the characters sing (Quixote—baritone, Master Peter—tenor, and Boy—soprano), the voices emanating from the orchestra pit in which their human counterparts are stationed (an effect developed by Stravinsky in *Le rossignol, Pulcinella, Renard,* and *Les noces*). The orchestra itself comprises fewer than twenty-five players, with special anti-romantic prominence accorded the oboes, the muted trumpet and horns, and, most significantly, the harpsichord, performed in the original production by the already-then-celebrated Wanda Landowska. (De Falla was to write his *Harpsichord Concerto* for Landowska just a few years later.)

It is perhaps not coincidental that de Falla's *Puppet Show* is influenced, in style and substance, by works from the pens of de Polignac's two other commissionees. From Satie's *Parade* (1917), the ballet in which circus performers present a come-on performance that the public mistakes for the real show, is derived the phenomenon of confusing the artifice of show business with the cool logic of reality (and then questioning the legitimacy of that reality). From Stravinsky's *Histoire du soldat* (1918) comes the device of the narrator, the fanciful fairy-tale atmosphere, and the artistic aesthetic of emotional distancing. And as in *Histoire,* in which Stravinsky trades the exuberance of his earlier Russian style for the asceticism of a neo-classicized and internationalist stance, so de Falla turns from the luxuriant Hispanicisms of *La vida breve, El amor brujo,* and *El sombrero de tres picos* to the more neutral truthfulness of his *Puppet Show.* Time and time again, we hear Stravinskyan harmonic effects in the *Puppet Show:* in Master Peter's Symphony, which spikes the 16th-note bustle of its C-major good-naturedness with polytonal clashes (though equally good-natured ones); in Melisendra's forlorn chords as she languishes in the Moorish tower; in the violent music (so similar to *Histoire*'s "Devil's Dance") that accompanies the king's punishment of the Moor who steals a kiss from Melisendra.

But there is much that is independently and gloriously Fallaesque: the stately music of the court of Charlemagne, with its mock-ancient modality; the picturesque klip-klopping of the ride across the Pyrenees; and Quixote's noble self-vision ending the opera. The Boy-Narrator and Master Peter sing primarily in a manner of recitation combining plainsong with Spanish street-cries, and invention that surely owes nothing to Stravinsky.

El retablo de Maese Pedro is rarely performed, primarily because of the difficulty of fitting it into (or adapting it to) the repertoire of an opera and ballet company. (And how many puppet theaters with singers and orchestras are there in continuous operation?) Nevertheless, it remains, after almost seventy years, a work of exquisite sensibilities and proportions (and still-potent modernisms). It is surely one of the most neglected of twentieth-century masterpieces.

—Gerald Moshell

RETHBERG, Elisabeth (Lisbeth Sättler).

Soprano. Born 22 September 1894, in Schwarzenberg, Germany. Died 6 June 1976, in Yorktown Heights, New York. Married: baritone George Cehanovsky, 1957. Naturalized as an American citizen, 1939. Studied piano, then voice at the Dresden Conservatory with Otto Watrin, 1912; debut at Dresden Hofoper, 1915; at Dresden 1915-22; Salzburg debut, 1922; Metropolitan Opera debut as Aida, 1922; at the Metropolitan Opera 1922-42, 30 roles including Sieglinde, Eva, Elsa, Madama Butterfly, Elisabeth, Aida, Desdemona; Covent Garden debut as Aida, 1925; also sang in Rome, Milan, Paris, Florence, San Francisco, Chicago; created the title role of *Die ägyptische Helena,* Dresden, 1928.

Publications

About RETHBERG: book—

Henschel, Horst, and Erhard Friedrich. *Elisabeth Rethberg: Ihr Leben und Künstlertum.* Schwarzenberg, 1928. Reprinted 1977.

articles—

Richards, J.B. "Elisabeth Rethberg: The Discography." *Record Collector* 3 (1948): 51.
_____. "Elisabeth Rethberg's Recordings." *Record Collector* 8 (1953): 5.
_____. "Rethberg, Elisabeth." In *Le grandi voci,* ed. by R. Celetti, Rome, 1964.

*   *   *

Few singers of the inter-war years were celebrated in such grand terms, and with such abandon, as Elisabeth Rethberg. Testimonials to the beauty of her voice and the breadth of her technique abound in her legend. Toscanini is said to have compared her voice to a Stradivarius, insisting that she was the world's greatest soprano. She was made an honorary member of the State Theaters of Saxony in a 1930 tribute at the Dresden Opera. She was even subjected to the kind of beauty-contest pageantry typical of the times—in 1928, the New York Guild of Vocal Teachers bestowed upon her a gold medal for "Perfection in Singing," and a year later the New York Society of Singers proclaimed her's the world's "most perfect voice." Is it any wonder that when her singing teacher, Otto Watrin, assumed a modest teaching post at a small midwestern college in 1929, his arrival in America was reported in the *New York Times?*

The surviving recorded evidence, which is fairly plentiful, does little to contradict the extravagance of these claims. In its prime, roughly between 1924 and 1935, Rethberg's voice was indeed of surpassing beauty. Its large compass, even scale, absolute consistency of tone, and melting legato were further complemented by an effortless production rare even among great singers. Her legendary precision, the product of musical instincts as acute as her training was thorough, made all the standard deceptions unnecessary, for she had few inadequacies to hide and still fewer to overcome. What she seems to have lacked in spontaneous passion and depth of character penetration—charges frequently leveled against her—she made up for in the intelligence and tastefulness with which her voice was used, and in her consuming obligation to the composer's written intentions. Rethberg's was a simple and direct style of singing in the best sense, unburdened by contrivance, and guided by what seems to have been a faultless intuition. The absolute control she exerted over her instrument made her as adept an interpreter of Handel as of Richard Strauss, and allowed her voice to meet the boisterous demands of *verismo* as easily, if not as convincingly, as it dealt with the subtleties of Mozart.

Rethberg's repertory was primarily Italian and German, but her functional command of languages, aided by a prodigious memory, enabled her to maintain a familiarity with more than 100 of the most demanding lyric and dramatic soprano roles. It was boasted that she had committed 1000 songs to memory in their original languages, and had more than a passing acquaintance with the large-scale sacred works of Bach, Handel, Haydn, Mozart, and Brahms, many of which she performed throughout her career.

Born into a musical family, Rethberg showed great promise at an early age, singing and playing the piano with some proficiency by the time she was four—indeed, she was said to have performed the entire *Winterreise* cycle of Schubert by the age of seven. Her first formal musical instruction began at the Dresden Conservatory in 1912, where she studied voice with Otto Watrin. Watrin was himself a pupil of August Iffert (1859-1930), whose vocal method stressed breath control above all else. This was a revelation to Rethberg, and having mastered it to her own satisfaction, she undertook no further study. In the spring of 1915, and at the urging of then assistant conductor Fritz Reiner, she successfully auditioned for a contract at the Dresden Opera, and remained there for seven formative seasons. She quickly assumed many of the leading roles that would remain prominent in her repertory: Michaela in *Carmen*, Mimi in *La bohème*, Butterfly, Octavian and Sophie in *Der Rosenkavalier*, and Tosca. Guest performances in Vienna, Berlin, and Milan followed, and included notable appearances with the Berlin Philharmonic and Leipzig Gewandhaus Orchestras under Artur Nikisch's direction.

From 1922 until her retirement in 1942, Rethberg was an outstanding fixture at the Metropolitan Opera in New York, singing some thirty roles over twenty consecutive seasons. Her debut as Aida on 22 November 1922 received sturdy if not unrestrained notices. Richard Aldrich's review in the *New York Times* noted that, despite her obvious nervousness, her "crude costuming" and the stentorian vocal demands placed upon her in the noisier segments of the score, Rethberg was, in all "essentials," a success. She became possibly the leading Aida of her generation, performing the role fifty-one times at the Metropolitan Opera alone. The role also served as her debut vehicle at Covent Garden, a last-minute engagement during the 1925 Grand Opera Season. There, she was hailed as the freshest interpreter of the role that house had seen in years. Her subsequent appearances at Covent Garden were surprisingly few, amounting to less than ten roles during the 1934-1936 and 1939 Royal Opera Seasons. Upon the invitation of Lilli Lehmann, she first appeared at the Salzburg Festival in 1922, and even after her American debut, continued to appear regularly in Europe—at the Salzburg Festivals of 1933 and 1939, in Italy, and in her native Dresden, where she created the title role in Strauss' *Die Ägyptische Helena* on 6 June 1928. She performed frequently with the San Francisco

and Chicago Opera companies as well. In her prime, Rethberg's fame in Mozart was unmatched, but her stage repertory came also to stress Verdi and the lighter Wagnerian heroines—an exception being what Irving Kolodin considered a disastrous Brünnhilde (Siegfried), foolishly undertaken during her final season. Her retirement from the Metropolitan Opera, which brought her stage career to an end, was ostensibly the result of a contract dispute, but almost undoubtedly this was the culmination of her numerous quarrels with the management over repertory. An Aida on 6 March 1942, served as a quiet, surprisingly uneventful farewell. There followed only a few more years of concert and radio activity. By then, her powers had declined dramatically: her tone had become forced, its previous warmth sacrificed for volume; even her intonation was at times unpredictable.

Rethberg recorded somewhat discontinuously between 1920 and 1939, but her prime is well documented. Her earliest recordings were made in Berlin for Odeon when she was still singing at the Dresden Opera, and included duets with tenor Richard Tauber. Later sessions for that company in 1928 and 1933 yielded more pleasing results, though the operatic repertory she recorded, much of it Italian, was burdened by the German translations. Her first American recordings, made for Brunswick in Chicago between 1923 and 1925 are perhaps her best, for they preserve the voice as it was at the dawn of her prime—still fresh and miraculously responsive. Thereafter, her studio output, at least the operatic portion of it, tended to be repetitious, confining her to only a small portion of her vast repertory. Certain of her most prominent roles are scarcely represented at all. There is a fairly substantial amount of Baroque music by which to judge her activities in oratorio, but on the whole, the recordings are dominated by Mozart and Verdi, especially Aida (in addition to several versions of the two major arias, she recorded the entire third-act Nile Scene with Giacomo Lauri-Volpi and Giuseppe De Luca in 1929 and 1930). She often appeared on the radio throughout the 1930s and early 1940s, and a good many of her recitals and opera broadcasts have survived in transcription, including a matinee of *Otello* from 12 February 1938 with Giovanni Martinelli and Lawrence Tibbett, the original principals from the Metropolitan Opera's heralded 1937 revival of the work. Much of this off-the-air material, especially the performances dating from the final years of her career, has done her reputation a tragic disservice, documenting her decline with cruel efficiency.

—William Shaman

THE RETURN OF ULYSSES TO THE HOMELAND
See IL RITORNO D'ULISSE IN PATRIA

DAS RHEINGOLD
See DER RING DES NIBELUNGEN

RICCIARELLI, Katia.

Soprano. Born 18 January 1946, in Rovigo, Italy. Studied with Iris Adami-Corradetti at the Venice Conservatory; debut as Mimì in Mantua, 1969; U.S. debut as Lucrezia in *I due Foscari,* Chicago, 1972; Covent Garden debut as Mimì, 1974; Metropolitan Opera debut as Mimì, 1975; appeared as Desdemona in Zeffirelli's film version of *Otello.*

*   *   *

Of a clutch of Italian sopranos to emerge in the post Callas/Tebaldi era, Katia Ricciarelli is perhaps the most important. A pupil of Iris Adami-Corradetti, herself an outstanding lyric soprano of the thirties, Ricciarelli emerged onto the world operatic stage through winning no less than three major vocal competitions—at Milan, Parma and one organized by Italian radio and television to mark the seventieth anniversary of the death of Verdi. Within months she made her debut in *La bohème* at Mantua with the equally youthful and unknown José Carreras.

Within two years Ricciarelli was singing all over Italy and further afield—Verdi's *Il corsaro* in Venice and his *Giovanni d'Arco* in Rome, Puccini's *Suor Angelica* at Teatro alla Scala and Verdi's *I due Foscari* in Chicago. In 1974 she made her first appearances at both Covent Garden and the Metropolitan Opera.

In the high pressure world of international opera, Ricciarelli's career suggests the superstar. For twenty years she has sung all over the world; she has regularly partnered the tenor trio of Carreras, Domingo and Pavarotti and she has made a formidable number of recordings, particularly of complete operas. Nonetheless as was pointed out in a major profile in *Opera* her performances have been controversial throughout her career. Of her first Leonora in *Trovatore,* Giorgio Gualerzi spoke of "the smoothness of her warm and luminous timbre, the firmness of her high register." However, within months another critic spoke of "lack of real musical preparation. . . . phrasing is unvaried and monotonous" in a performance of Violetta in *La traviata.* Later in the 1970s Andrew Porter offered a balanced assessment of her Desdemona: "serious in intention, subtle and musical, not always limpid in timbre yet more satisfying than those who are sweeter in voice but not alert to the shades of Verdi's music."

Ricciarelli's very first LP disc was an ambitious Verdi recital, mostly little-known arias. Apart from some slightly tentative high notes, it is stunning—perhaps one of the finest first recordings. Her voice is expressive and much of the singing is of the greatest beauty. This pure beauty is still very much in evidence in a complete recording of *Luisa Miller* and in some fine duets with Carreras, where there is an almost magical quality to items from Verdi's *Lombardi* and Donizetti's *Poliuto.* On the other hand, she seems quite simply wrongly if not over-parted in her recordings of *Aida, Tosca* and *Turandot.* One criticism of the latter considers it more "sensuously feminine than usual" and goes on to argue that "Ricciarelli is a far more vulnerable figure than one expects of the icy princess, and the very fact that the part strains her

Katia Ricciarelli in the title role of Verdi's *Luisa Miller,* **Royal Opera, London, 1981**

beyond reasonable vocal limits adds to the dramatic point, even if it subtracts from the musical joys." As a recorded performance this is frankly best forgotten, but the conductor was Karajan. Ricciarelli in the same *Opera* interview admitted that she did not think such roles suitable for her voice, "but when Abbado or Karajan asks you to sing them, what do you do?" We can only speculate what equivalent stars of an earlier generation might have done or said! Ricciarelli's next comment goes some way perhaps to explaining her relationship to the world of musical criticism: "I don't regret anything. I relied on my instinct, and I really don't mind what anybody says."

Although Ricciarelli has more than sixty roles in her repertoire, her instinct now seems to be telling her to concentrate on the early Italian romantic repertoire—Rossini, Donizetti, Bellini and early and middle Verdi, plus Desdemona in Verdi's *Otello.* Indeed it is in this last role that she will be remembered best by the general public. Opposite Domingo in the filmed version of *Otello,* Ricciarelli is an expressive, vulnerable and beautiful Desdemona.

Afficionados may prefer to turn to her stunning 1986 Anna Bolena at the Bregenz festival—"she works miracles with her piano phrases which here assumed a Tebaldi-ish glow and shimmer. . . . the most complete performance of a role I have ever experienced from this variable singer. . . . if the real Anna Bolena had pleaded only half so eloquently . . . no male jury in all the world would judge her guilty." Significantly, the conductor was not Abbado or Karajan, but the under-rated Giuseppe Patanè who was one of the most sensitive and idiomatic of Italian maestri. Later that same year there was a superb performance at Pesaro of Rossini's *Bianca e Falliero* in which Ricciarelli's voice blended in perfect harmony with that of Marilyn Horne in one of the truly great operatic performances.

—Stanley Henig

RICHARD COEUR-DE-LION [Richard the Lionhearted].

Composer: André Grétry.

Librettist: Michel-Jean Sedaine (after *La Curne de Sainte-Palaye*).

First Performance: Paris, Comédie-Italienne, 21 October 1784; revised 1785.

Roles: Marguerite (soprano); Laurette (soprano); Richard (tenor); Blondel (baritone); Antonio (mezzo-soprano); Sir William (bass); Florestan (bass); several bit parts, mostly speaking; chorus (SSTTBB).

* * *

Grétry's opera *Richard Coeur-de-Lion* opens at the Castle of Linz in the twelfth century. Workers are returning at sundown from the fields, ready to celebrate a fiftieth wedding anniversary scheduled for the next day. Blondel de Nesle, valet and court troubadour, arrives looking for his master, King Richard I, who has been unjustly imprisoned. Disguised as a blind minstrel, he hires the young shepherd Antonio as

guide. Later he overhears conversation about a note surreptitiously sent from the prison governor Florestan to Laurette, but intercepted by her father, William. After meeting Laurette, Blondel decides he can turn her predicament to her advantage as well as to Richard's. Marguerite, Countess of Flanders and of Artois, arrives with her entourage searching for her beloved Richard.

In act II, outside the castle, Blondel, hidden from the castle guards, determines his king's presence in the fortress by singing the royal troubadour song within earshot of Richard, who is taking the morning air on the fortress terrace. Richard answers with the second couplet and the two conclude in duet. Blondel is seized by the guards and taken inside the fortress. He asks to see Florestan with news of Laurette. In act III Blondel pays a visit to Marguerite, informing her of Richard's presence. As he removes his disguise, Marguerite's attendants recognize him. Plans are made for the rescue. The next day peasants arrive singing and dancing as Mathurin and his wife renew their wedding vows. This is followed immediately by the ball. When Florestan arrives to meet Laurette, he is forced to allow the siege of the fortress and the rescue of Richard, who can now return to England with Marguerite. The piece concludes with celebration and rejoicing.

In the opening of the overture, G minor string tremoli cast a gloomy mood over the fortress. A pastoral G major with bagpipe drone dispells the tragic overtones, as peasants return from the fields singing in an ancient folk style. Orchestral and choral forces are dovetailed to produce dramatic flow.

It is Blondel de Nesle, not King Richard I of England, who sings the lion's share of the opera. The ensembles offer a wide variety of forms and styles. There is motivic unity in Blondel's grand C-major air (act I, scene ii), which motives are reflected by those of Richard's grand air in act II, scene ii. Blondel's C major key denotes goodness, purity, and constancy. He introduces on his violin a medieval romance, the pivotal piece of the opera, which recurs nine times and further unifies the opera. Blondel in his role of blind minstrel has occasion to play Cupid as well in the *chanson à deux* ("A Blindfold Covers the Eyes"). The milieu of the twelfth century troubadour is suggested by means of a simple popular melodic style, intended for dance or mime. Pizzicati and hocket imitate a lute accompaniment. In act I, scene viii, Blondel sings and dances a convivial drinking song with a choral refrain. When he confronts soldiers of the fortress in act II, scene v, horns—symbolic of former victories— bassoons, and lower strings march in whole notes, since the soldiers have just returned from the Holy Land. The chorus sings in a mock contrapuntal style.

Richard's justly famous grand air ("If the whole universe forgets me") is a picture-gazing aria which captures both his former glory and his broken spirit in the E-flat heroic key. Dotted rhythms assert Richard's royalty while Lombardic figures and audible chains express both his sorrow and incarceration. Lyrical passages recall his longing for Marguerite. The air is written for the *haute contre* voice, a close relative of the countertenor, and spans a range of nearly two octaves. Strains in apparent anticipation of the "Marseillaise" go back to Gluck's *Paris and Helen,* 1770. Outside of this air, Richard has only the romance duo (act II, scene ii) and the final ensemble to sing, yet Grétry has characterized him finely in but a few brush strokes.

Richard Coeur-de-Lion is significant in the history of opera for the following reasons: the nine-fold appearance of the romance foreshadows the reminiscence motive of the nineteenth century; the orchestra and the real-life ensembles have expanded in size and importance; stock characters have all but disappeared; and subtle expressions of inner thoughts and desires are coupled with more boisterous modes of expression. The opera is a prototype of the rescue opera, serving as a model for Cherubini, Méhul, and Beethoven as well as for Meyerbeer, Halévy, and Auber.

—Linda M. Stones

RICHARD THE LIONHEARTED
See RICHARD COEUR-DE-LION

RICHTER, Hans.

Conductor. Born 4 April 1843, in Raab, Hungary. Died 5 December 1916, in Bayreuth. Studied theory with Sechter, violin with Heissler, and french horn with Kleinecke at the Vienna Conservatory, 1860-65; horn player in the Kärntnertor theater orchestra, Vienna, 1862-66; met Wagner in 1866, and became a copyist of the score and performing parts for the premiere of *Die Meistersinger;* chorus master of the Munich Court Opera, 1867; assistant to von Bülow as conductor, Court Orchestra in Munich, 1868-69; conducted many Wagner revivals; principal conductor of the Pest National Theater, 1871-75; first principal conductor of the Vienna Court Opera, 1875-99; conducted the Vienna Philharmonic, 1875-82, 1883-97; conductor at the Gesellschaft der Musikfreunde, 1880-90; chosen by Wagner to conduct the *Ring* at Bayreuth, 1876; went to London with Wagner to conduct his music at the Wagner Festival in Royal Albert Hall, 1877; conductor of the Hallé Orchestra in Manchester; conducted at Covent Garden, London, 1882, 1886, and of Wagner operas produced there, 1903-10; conductor of the Birmingham Festivals, 1885-1909; conductor of the London Symphony Orchestra, 1904-11.

Publications

About RICHTER: books–

Kufferath, M. *L'art de diriger.* Paris, [3rd ed] 1909.
Karpath, L. *Wagners Briefe an Hans Richter.* Vienna, 1924.
Schonberg, H. *The Great Conductors.* New York, 1967.

articles–

Klickmann, F. "Dr. Hans Richter." *Windsor Magazine* September (1896).

*   *   *

Hans Richter's mother was an opera singer and, on the death of his father in 1853, the young boy became a chorister at the Hofkapelle. At the Vienna Conservatory he mastered all instruments save the oboe and harp, and, while a student, earned his living as a horn player (after just nineteen months study) in the Kärntnertor Theater. This mastery of orchestral instruments was to become part of the Richter legend, but no less important was his background and training in vocal technique and operatic music. In October 1866 he was sent to Wagner at Tribschen as copyist of *Die Meistersinger* and assisted as vocal coach and chorus master for the opera's premiere in Munich (1868) under von Bülow, whom Richter succeeded at the Hoftheater in 1869. He resigned in protest when the staging of the first performance of *Das Rheingold* did not meet with Wagner's approval, and he went to Brussels in 1870 to conduct the premiere there of *Lohengrin.* He then returned to Tribschen to copy the third act of *Siegfried* for Wagner, who, together with Liszt, secured him a post as Kapellmeister (and later musical director) at the Opera in Budapest (1871-75). After a guest appearance in Vienna in 1875 he virtually took over conducting all the major musical organizations of that city, including the Hofoper where he remained until 1899. Mahler had been appointed music director the previous year and the two men had difficulty in reconciling their musical differences. Richter, after a short spell as music director in Budapest (only a year or two of the four he spent there), had vowed never to accept the post anywhere again, for he loathed the administrative responsibility and political intrigues which inevitably accompanied such a position.

Hans Richter (left) with Felix Mottl, Bayreuth, 1888

In 1876 Richter conducted the premiere of Wagner's *Ring* cycle at the first Bayreuth Festival. Following their differences ten years earlier he had gained Wagner's musical trust and, in the years leading up to the first festival, would travel many miles and spend many hours hearing singers and orchestral players on Wagner's behalf. The summer of 1875 was devoted to a whole series of vocal and orchestral rehearsals in Bayreuth in preparation for the performances a year later.

In 1877 Richter joined Wagner in London to share the conducting of the Wagner Festival, mounted to try to recoup financial losses incurred at Bayreuth in 1876. The concerts at the Royal Albert Hall were devoted to orchestral and vocal extracts from all the Wagner operas from *Rienzi* to *Götterdämmerung*. Wagner proved incapable of conducting (he became so involved when conducting his own music that his orchestral players had difficulty in following him), and so he devolved most of the work on to his young assistant, who scored a personal triumph with players and public alike. Richter soon came to dominate London's musical life in the way he was doing in Vienna.

Though his operatic work was largely confined to Vienna together with regular appearances in Bayreuth, Richter conducted the German opera seasons in London of 1882 (when he gave the British premieres of *Tristan* and *Die Meistersinger*), 1884 and, in 1908, the first *Ring* cycle in English. Richter passionately believed in opera sung in the vernacular, but it was to be a further sixty years before his dream of a permanent English National Opera was to be realized. His final performance was at Bayreuth in 1912, where he conducted the work he had made his own, *Die Meistersinger* (the opera with which he had also made his 1875 debut in Vienna).

Though Richter's operatic repertoire was dominated by Wagner (he conducted all the operas after *Rienzi* except *Parsifal*), Mozart, Beethoven, Bizet, Auber, Meyerbeer and Gounod were also favorites. His interest in Italian opera was limited to a handful of operas by Cherubini, Bellini, Donizetti, Ponchielli and Verdi (*La traviata, Il trovatore* and *Aida*).

Hans Richter was one of the most prominent musical personalities of his day, and for nearly forty years his influence upon the opera houses and concert halls of Vienna and London was second to none. His interpretations were marked by their simplicity and breadth. The sheer magnitude of a Wagner score presented no problem for Richter, who, though no intellectual, was prodigious of memory, assured in technique and intuitive in musicianship.

—Christopher Fifield

RIDERS TO THE SEA.

Composer: Ralph Vaughan Williams.

Librettist: Ralph Vaughan Williams (after J.M. Synge).

First Performance: London, Royal College of Music, 1 December 1937.

Roles: Maurya (contralto); Bartley (baritone); Cathleen (soprano); Nora (soprano); A Woman (mezzo-soprano); chorus (SSAA).

Publications

articles—

Ottaway, H. "Riders to the Sea." *Musical Times* 93 (1952): 358.
Forbes, Anne-Marie H. "Motivic Unity in Ralph Vaughan Williams's *Riders to the Sea.*" *Music Review* 44 (1983): 234.

As a composer, Ralph Vaughan Williams was an outdoorsman. His musical wanderings through the English countryside led him twice to the sea. First came the vast Sea Symphony for chorus and orchestra (1903-09) based on poems of Whitman. Sixteen years after its completion, Vaughan Williams began to sketch *Riders to the Sea,* a thirty-five minute opera based on Synge's seminal one-act play. Despite its modest forces (five singing roles, a small women's chorus, and an orchestra with mostly single winds), the work took him seven years to compose. He even asked his composer friend Gustav Holst for technical advice, knowing that this compact opera transcended his three full-length operas in theme and substance. Its chief player is the sea itself, never visible but ubiquitous and everlasting. We sense its cadence, its moods, and its boundless eminence.

The opera is set in a cottage on an island off the west coast of Ireland. It is the weathered home of a dwindling family. The sea has claimed father, grandfather, and five of the six sons. Remaining with Maurya, the mother, are two daughters, Cathleen and Nora, and their brother Bartley. As the curtain rises, the sisters are about to open a bundle containing a shirt and stocking taken from a drowned man whose body was washed ashore far to the north. The garments may belong to Michael, a brother lost only nine days before. But Maurya wakes from her nap, and the sisters hide the bundle, afraid of distressing their mother.

The wind is strong and the sea rising. Bartley prepares to transport a red mare and a grey pony by boat to Galway Fair. Fearing that he too will not return, Maurya tries to dissuade him from going, asking "What is the price of a thousand horses against a son where there is one son only?" But the determined young man goes forth, without his mother's blessing and his bit of bread forgotten. Apprehensive on both counts, the sisters send Maurya after Bartley with the bread. Left to themselves, they open the bundle, recognize Michael's clothes, and quickly hide them.

Maurya returns, lamenting distractedly. She has given Bartley neither bread nor blessing, for she saw Michael, wearing fine clothes, astride the pony Bartley was leading as he passed her. This portends disaster. The deaths of all but one of her men haunt Maurya's thoughts as women's voices mourn offstage. A procession of old women enters the cottage. They carry in Bartley's drowned body and lay it on the table. One of the women tells the tale: "The grey pony knocked him into the sea, and he was washed out where there is a great surf on the white rocks." Now Maurya finds peace. There is no man left for the sea to take from her. She asks God's blessing on the souls of the dead and the living. The last of her sons soon will rest in a fine white coffin. "No man at all can be living for ever, and we must be satisfied." The curtain falls on the fading music of the sea.

Critics have received *Riders to the Sea* more warmly than most prestigious opera companies have. Some attribute its exclusion from the basic repertoire to the scarcity of short operas suitable for performance on the same bill. It has, however, been paired with Pasatieri's *Signor Delusa,* and placed between Debussy's *The Prodigal Son* and Ibert's *Angélique.* Vaughan Williams' somber work thrived in both productions, evidence that contrast outweighs affinity when programming a monolithic opera.

Vaughan Williams has left the text of Synge's play almost unaltered. The music's blending modes and sloping melodic contours derive from British folk music, the composer's perpetual inspiration. The vocal lines commingle arioso style with recitative, supported by sustained orchestral counterpoint rather than disjointed rhetorical figures. This textural relation of voices and orchestra owes much to Debussy, although the musical locution is steadfastly British. The slow-paced tertial harmonies are often double-layered, their components diverging and converging to form polychordal dissonances. Parallel triads abound, giving the orchestral current a ponderous mobility reminiscent of the sea. Although Vaughan Williams threads a few motives through the score, his concentrated style provides a single-minded intensity that congeals the music as a single thought. No opera is more homogeneous or less diverting.

Maurya is the only character given lyric music or cause for lyricism. She has lived so long bound with the sea that it has crept into her soul. Those nurtured by the sea love the sea as a mother. It draws them back time and again and cradles them in eternal sleep. It is the matriarch of earthly life. In time its will prevails, for it outlasts the headstrong resolutions of men. It rolls with a majestic and unyielding pulse, but its melody is doleful and ancient as music. And Maurya, ageless in maternal grief and impassive to the untamed brunts of nature, keens like the sea.

—James Allen Feldman

RIENZI, der Letzte der Tribunen [Rienzi, the Last of the Tribunes].

Composer: Richard Wagner.

Librettist: Richard Wagner (after E. Bulwer-Lytton and M.R. Mitford).

First Performance: Dresden, Königliches Hoftheater, 20 October 1842; revised, 1843.

Roles: Cola Rienzi (tenor); Irene (soprano); Steffano Colonna (bass); Adriano (mezzo-soprano); Paolo Orsini (bass); Raimondo (bass); Baroncelli (tenor); Cecco (bass); Messenger of Peace (soprano); Herald (tenor); chorus (SSSATTBB).

Publications

book–

Deathridge, John. *Wagner's Rienzi: a Reappraisal based on a Study of the Sketches and Drafts.* Oxford, 1977.

articles–

Dinger, H. "Zu Richard Wagners 'Rienzi'." *Richard Wagner-Jahrbuch* 3 (1908): 88.

Mehler, E. "Beiträge zur Wagner-Forschung: unveröffentlichte Stücke aus 'Rienzi', 'Holländer' und 'Tannhäuser'." *Die Musik* 12 (1912-13): 195.
Geck, M. "Rienzi-Philologie." In *Das Drama Richard Wagners als musikalisches Kunstwerk,* edited by Carl Dahlhaus, 183. Regensburg, 1970.
Strohm, Reinhard. "*Rienzi* and Authenticity." *Musical Times* (1976).
Deathridge, John. "*Rienzi* . . . a Few of the Facts." *Musical Times* 124 (1983): 546.

* * *

Rienzi, der Letzte der Tribunens, first performed at the Dresden Court Opera on 20 October 1842, made Richard Wagner famous. Intended for the Paris Opéra, *Rienzi* augmented the grand operatic tradition of Meyerbeer and Spontini. The young Wagner, his ego aflame, hoped to overwhelm even the most seasoned operagoers with a prodigious extravaganza. Aggrandized by luxuriant choruses, processions, and an imposing ballet, *Rienzi* did just that. Dresden audiences loved the work despite its excessive length. (The premiere lasted five and a quarter hours.) Wagner himself suggested cuts which the management declined, and for a while *Rienzi* was given split performances on two successive nights. The first published score, however, trimmed the mammoth opus to Wagner's specifications, but the version most used in twentieth-century productions is based on a redaction by Wagner's wife Cosima and the conductor Julius Kneise. Unhappily, the original manuscript, a prized item among Hitler's personal possessions, has disappeared, preventing reconstruction of the opera as Wagner initially conceived it.

In various abridgments, productions of Rienzi abounded throughout Europe during the last half of the nineteenth century, with almost two hundred performances given in Dresden alone. Most opera companies, however, have long since dismissed it as a long-winded blaze of youthful immodesty. Yet *Rienzi* is far more, for Wagner's musical prowess matures from act to act, laying the seeds for his music dramas and consummating his transition from journeyman to master. He was already an accomplished orchestrator and found in the Germanic style of Weber the sinewy vitality he needed. The orchestra for *Rienzi* is exceptionally large, including a serpent, four horns (two with valves), four trumpets (two with valves), three trombones, an ophicleide, and enough percussion to busy four players. Although the music in acts I and II is derivative and often tedious, the remainder of the score sounds distinctively Wagnerian. We hear proliferating chromatic harmonies, remote key relations, subordinate counterpoint in the orchestra, and melodic adumbrations of works to come. Arias, ensembles, and choruses expand climactically in an upsweeping curve, while recitatives shed their formality and become melodically compelling.

Wagner based *Rienzi* on Bulwer-Lytton's novel of the same name (1835) about the fourteenth-century Roman notary who successfully led the plebeian citizens in an insurrection against the dissolute patricians, and briefly ruled the city, hoping to restore the freedom and glory of the ancient republic. Though he first tried to interest Eugène Scribe in providing a libretto, Wagner wrote the dramatic verse himself (as he always did), constructing it in five acts and sixteen scenes with rhymed quatrains for the traditional vocal pieces.

The curtain rises on a street in Rome. It is night. The patrician Paolo Orsini and friends are abducting Rienzi's sister, Irene; but Steffano Colonna, a rival patrician, and a

The final scene of act IV of *Rienzi*, Dresden, 1843

party of men including his son Adriano, Irene's suitor, intercept the marauders. (Following eighteenth-century practice, Wagner composed Adriano's music for a mezzo-soprano.) A fight breaks out with both factions wielding their weapons until Rienzi appears and lays down the law to the nobles. He invokes the civic pride and allegiance of the citizens and wins their support, as well as sanction from a papal legate who has witnessed and tried to stop the skirmish. The patricians plan to resume combat at dawn outside the city. Their departure prompts Rienzi to lock the gates and rally the people against the miscreant nobles until they agree to abide by Roman law.

Word of the incident spreads quickly, and soon all the Roman commoners champion Rienzi. They offer him the crown, but he prefers the republican title of Tribune. Appointing Adriano as Irene's protector, Rienzi urges the young man to join the plebeian cause, but Adriano's loyalty to his family prevents him from endorsing Rienzi's ideals.

Disdaining their gratuitous subservience, the patricians plot Rienzi's assassination despite Adriano's attempts to dissuade them. At a festival procession in front of the Capitol, Orsini attacks Rienzi with a dagger, but the wary tribune has girded himself in chain-mail and the weapon pierces only his robe. The outraged citizens demand death for the conspirators. Rienzi orders their executions but changes his mind when Adriano and Irene plead for leniency to save Colonna's life. Forced to accept Rienzi's terms, the patricians speciously swear fealty to the new government.

The deposed patricians raise an army in the provinces and march on Rome, determined to regain their former power.

Adriano appeals for conciliation, but Rienzi, exasperated by the patricians' disloyalty, will not hear of it. He rouses his Romans to a bellicose frenzy, leads them in battle, and returns triumphant with the bodies of many slain patricians, including Orsini and Colonna.

The patricians now resort to political intrigue, convincing the Pope and the German emperor that Rienzi's rebellion is heretical and dangerous to the sovereignty of Rome. The emperor recalls his ambassadors, and the Vatican censures Rienzi by issuing a papal ban against him. The tribune suddenly finds himself friendless and defenseless. Adriano, who in vengeance set out to murder Rienzi but lost his nerve, urges Irene to desert her brother before it is too late. Irene, however, will not leave Rienzi to face peril alone and sends Adriano away. He returns to entreat her more affectingly, only to receive the same reply.

Rienzi's faith in God and in Rome remains unshattered, but Rome has lost faith in him. He appears with Irene on a balcony of the Capitol to address the unruly Romans who stone them both and set fire to the building. As Adriano tries to rescue Irene, the balcony tower crashes down, burying him with the woman he loves and the man he has come to despise.

The story of Rienzi contains several themes and character types found in Wagner's subsequent stage works: the visionary hero, the self-sacrificing woman, the discomfited and ineffectual patriarchs, the betrayal of greatness, the volatility of judgment, the supersedure of the old order by the new, the sublimity of freedom and democracy, the fragility of transcendent morality, the tenacity of convention, and the inclination of the people to destroy its saviors. Rienzi, composed between 1838 and 1840, was the third and most egocentric of Wagner's early operas. It is a vast parable, a critical prospectus on politics, society, and the arts. A bold leader must arise to marshal the people or they will not venture forth, but his supremacy will make him a tragic figure, persecuted and ultimately brought down by his inferiors.

Wagner's score exalts its hero, probably the first operatic role requiring a *Heldentenor,* unless we so consider Florestan in Beethoven's *Fidelio.* Rienzi's music is titanic and wholly explicit. The thoughts behind his words, like the musings of Heracles or Theseus, remain unknown. Of the opera's nine characters, only Adriano shares with us something of his inner life. The others declaim but rarely intimate, leaving the music nothing to express beyond the categorical meaning of the text. The libretto exhibits the kind of histrionic dialogue that typified early Romantic drama. Learning to channel the indirect currents of metaphor and irony that charge the later music dramas took the composer another ten years. *Rienzi* brought to a close Wagner's artistic adolescence and compelled the prevailing motif of his music dramas: redemption through suffering, love, and spiritual enlightenment.

—James Allen Feldman

RIGOLETTO.

Composer: Giuseppe Verdi.

Librettist: Francesco Maria Piave (after Hugo, *Le roi s'amuse*).

First Performance: Venice, La Fenice, 11 March 1851.

Roles: Duke of Mantua (tenor); Gilda (soprano); Rigoletto (baritone); Sparafucile (bass); Maddelena (mezzo-soprano or contralto); Count Monterone (bass); Giovanna (mezzo-soprano); Count Ceprano (baritone); Borsa (tenor); Marullo (baritone); Countess Ceprano (mezzo-soprano or soprano); A Page (mezzo-soprano); chorus (SATB); chorus (TTBB).

Publications

books–

Lavagetto, Mario. *Un caso di censura: il "Rigoletto".* Milan, 1979.
Osborne, Charles. *Rigoletto: a Guide to the Opera.* London, 1979.
John, Nicholas, ed. *Giuseppe Verdi: Rigoletto.* London, 1982.

articles–

Roncaglia, G. "L'abbozzo del *Rigoletto* di Verdi." *Rivista musicale italiana* 48 (1946).
Verdi Bollettino 7, 8, 9 (1969-82). [*Rigoletto* issue].
Chusid, Martin. "Rigoletto and Monterone: a Study in Musical Dramaturgy." In *International Musicological Society Congress Report 11, Copenhagen 1972.*
Della Corte, Andrea, and Marcello Conati. "Saggio di bibliografia delle critiche al *Rigoletto." Verdi Bollettino* 9 (1982).
Lawton, David. "Tonal Structure and Dramatic Action in *Rigoletto." Verdi Bollettino* 9 (1982).
Marchesi, Gustavo. "Gli anni del *Rigoletto." Verdi Bollettino* 9 (1982).
Mauceri, John. "Rigoletto for the 21st Century." *Opera* October (1985).
Avant-scène opéra September-October (1988) [*Rigoletto* issue].

* * *

Rigoletto, a hunchbacked jester, encourages his young master, the libertine Duke of Mantua, to debauch the wives and daughters of his courtiers, all the while hiding his own innocent young daughter, Gilda. The courtiers, in turn, plot revenge after discovering the hiding place of Gilda, whom they take to be Rigoletto's mistress. The venerable Count Monterone publicly protests the dishonoring of his own daughter by the duke. Rigoletto mocks him, and the old nobleman curses both duke and jester. Tricking Rigoletto into helping them, the courtiers seize Gilda for the duke, who has already pledged his love to her and she to him. Rigoletto mistakenly believes the curse to have been fulfilled.

His daughter dishonored, Rigoletto swears vengeance. Gilda, still in love with the duke, tries to dissuade her father. A month later, Rigoletto arranges for the duke to visit a dilapidated tavern occupied by an assassin, Sparafucile; the nobleman is now in pursuit of the assassin's attractive sister, Maddelena. The jester brings Gilda to watch; she does and is griefstricken. Rigoletto then sends her away and pays the assassin to murder the duke; but Gilda returns and dies in his place. Rigoletto finds that the true curse, far more terrible than dishonor, is the death of his daughter.

For Verdi, Triboulet (Rigoletto) in Victor Hugo's drama *Le roi s'amuse* was a character worthy of Shakespeare, the composer's favorite dramatist; and the play inspired him to write an opera, his seventeenth, which he considered to be the finest of his early and middle period operas.

Avoiding a number of the conventions of Italian operas in his day (for example, in *Rigoletto* there is no large ensemble finale), Verdi used the orchestra and wind band brilliantly. There are no female or mixed choruses in the opera, but a male chorus is used to astonishing effect. It serves in the first and second acts to represent the courtiers of the Duke of Mantua who, as a group, rival the principals in dramatic importance. In act III the same chorus hums offstage to help create the effect of wind during a storm. The storm and the drama build simultaneously in the music. Their gradual development is brilliantly portrayed by the composer: lightning by rapid arpeggios played on the piccolo and flute; additional wind sounds produced by the cellos and double basses. At the climax of the storm comes the climax of the drama: the stabbing of Gilda.

Verdi once said that the second act of an opera should be better than the first and the third should be the best of all. In none of his operas is this crescendo of excellence more visible than in *Rigoletto.* The third act is incomparably masterful. It opens with a brief, soft prelude, followed by the duke's song "La donna é mobile," one of the most famous arias in all opera. Next comes the equally famous quartet, a tour-de-force of individual characterization, together with the extended storm scene described above. Finally, there is Rigoletto's exultant monologue, and the closing duet during which the buffoon discovers his dying daughter in a sack supposed to contain the body of the duke. Not a moment of the act is extraneous, and the tension never relaxes.

Leo Nucci and Mariella Devia in the final scene of *Rigoletto,* **Royal Opera, London, 1991**

Highly successful from its premiere, *Rigoletto* is the first of Verdi's stage works to establish itself permanently in the operatic repertory; and, as one of the most popular operas in history, it has been translated and performed in almost every European language.

The composer first asked Salvadore Cammarano to prepare the libretto, but the Neapolitan poet refused, fearing the censors. Subsequently Francesco Maria Piave undertook the by no means simple task of converting Hugo's five-act play into a three-act opera libretto; and he did so with relative fidelity to the original. The opera is sometimes performed in four acts, with an intermission between the Introduction and remainder of the act. However, this weakens considerably the psychological and tonal connections between the two parts so vital to the drama and the music.

As Cammarano had foreseen, there were serious problems with *la censura* both while Verdi was writing the music and after the premiere. The composer was compelled to sacrifice the title he wanted, *La maledizione* (The Curse), to change the names of the characters, and to alter the venue from Paris at the time of Francis I to Mantua during the reign of the Gonzagas. He also had to forego Hugo's scene for Blanche and Francis in the latter's bedroom. This created a problem for the beginning of the second act of the opera that was never really solved. The duke's lament on the disappearance of Gilda strikes a false note dramatically. Some of the changes by the censor were not replaced by the text Verdi originally intended until the 1983 critical edition by Martin Chusid.

For a decade after the first performance, until the unification of Italy, censors in many Italian cities regularly altered the libretto of *Rigoletto,* in some cases deleting segments of the music as well. The changed texts were usually accompanied by new titles of which *Viscardello* was the most common. *Lionello* was performed in Naples and surrounding areas, and *Clara di Perth* in Naples alone. It was less the political aspect—the attempt to assassinate a ruler—that disturbed the censors than their perception that both play and opera shared a low moral tone. They objected to the failure of either the libertine duke or the assassin to be punished, and they were especially bothered by the fate of the innocent Gilda. In some versions the kidnapping of the heroine could not be shown on stage, and the first act ended with the chorus "Zitti, zitti." At times, Giovanna accompanied the girl into the duke's bedroom; and in several versions Gilda does not die of her wounds. Rigoletto then sings of Heaven's clemency with exactly the same music to which he had sung "la maledizione" in the version set by Verdi.

—Martin Chusid

RIMSKY-KORSAKOV, Nicolai.

Composer. Born 18 March 1844, in Tikhvin, near Novgorod, Russia. Died 21 June 1908, in Liubensk, near St Petersburg. Studied at the Naval School in St Petersburg, 1856-1862; studied piano with Théodore Canillé, who introduced him to Balakirev; served on the clipper *Almaz,* 1862-65; first symphony premiered at the Free Music School in St Petersburg with Balakirev conducting, 31 December 1865; professor of orchestration and composition at the St Petersburg Conservatory, 1871; inspector of the military orchestras of the Russian Navy, 1873-1884; assistant director of the court chapel, and conductor of the chorus and orchestra, 1883-94; conducted the annual Russian Symphony concerts sponsored by the publisher Belaieff, 1886-1900; elected a corresponding member of the French Academy, succeeding Grieg, 1907. Rimsky-Korsakov's students included Glazunov, Liadov, Arensky, Ippolitov-Ivanov, Gretchaninov, Nicolas Tcherepnin, Maximilian Steinberg, Gnessin, Miaskovsky, and Stravinsky.

Operas

Edition: *N. Rimsky-Korsakov: Polnoye sobraniye sochineniy: Literaturniye proizvedeniya i perepiska* [Complete edition of musical and literary works and correspondence]. Edited by A. Rimsky-Korsakov et al. 50 vols. Moscow, 1946-70.

The Maid of Pskov [*Pskovityanka*], Rimsky-Korsakov (after L.A. Mey), 1868-72, St Petersburg, Mariinsky, 13 January 1873; revised 1876-77, 1891-92 (St Petersburg, Panayevsky, 18 April 1895), and 1898 [one new aria].

Mlada (with Borodin, Cui, Musorgsky, and Minkus) (opera-ballet), V.A. Krïlov, 1872 [unfinished].

May Night [*Mayskaya noch'*], Rimsky-Korsakov (after Gogol), 1878-79, St Petersburg, Mariinsky, 21 January 1880.

The Snow Maiden [*Snegurochka*], Rimsky-Korsakov (after A.N. Ostrovsky), 1880-81, St Petersburg, Mariinsky, 10 February 1882; revised, c 1895, St Petersburg, 1898.

Mlada (opera-ballet), Rimsky-Korsakov (after Krïlov), 1889-90, St Petersburg, Mariinsky, 1 November 1892.

Christmas Eve [*Noch' pered Rozhdestvom*], Rimsky-Korsakov (after Gogol), 1894-95, St Petersburg, Mariinsky, 10 December 1895.

Sadko, Rimsky-Korsakov and V.I. Bel'sky, 1894-96, Moscow, Solodovnikov, 7 January 1898.

The Barber of Baghdad [*Bagdadskiy borodobrey*], Rimsky-Korsakov, 1895 [sketches].

Mozart and Salieri [*Motsart i Sal'yeri*], after Pushkin, 1897, Moscow, Solodovnikov, 7 December 1898.

Boyarïnya Vera Sheloga, Rimsky-Korsakov (after L.A. Mey), 1898, Moscow, Solodovnikov, 27 December 1898.

The Tsar's Bride [*Tsarskaya nevesta*], after L.A. Mey (one scene by I.F. Tyumenev), 1898, Moscow, Solodovnikov, 3 November 1899; revised 1899 [one new aria].

The Tale of Tsar Saltan [*Skazka o Tsare Saltane*], V.I. Bel'sky (after Pushkin), 1899-1900, Moscow, Solodovnikov, 3 November 1900.

Serviliya, Rimsky-Korsakov (after L.A. Mey), 1900-01, St Petersburg, Mariinsky, 14 October 1902.

Kashchey the Immortal [*Kashchey bessmertnïy*], Rimsky-Korsakov (after E.M. Petrovsky), 1901-02, Moscow, Solodovnikov, 25 December 1902; conclusion revised, 1906.

Pan Voyevoda, Tyumenev, 1902-03, St Petersburg, Conservatory, 16 October 1904.

Legend of the Invisible City of Kitezh and the Maiden Fevroniya [*Skazaniye o nevidimom grade Kitezhe i deve Fevronii*], V.I. Bel'sky, 1903-05, St Petersburg, 20 February 1907.

The Golden Cockerel [*Zolotoy petushok*], V.I. Bel'sky (after Pushkin), 1906-07, Moscow, Solodovnikov, 7 October 1909.

Sten'ka Razin, V.I. Bel'sky, 1906 [sketches].

Heaven and Earth [*Zemlya i nebo*], after Byron, 1906 [sketches].

Other works: incidental music, choral works, orchestral works, instrumental and chamber music, piano pieces.

Publications

By RIMSKY-KORSAKOV: books–

My Musical Life. Translated by Judah A. Joffe. New York, 1923; London, 1924.
Polnoye sobraniye sochiniy: lituraturnïye proizvedeniya i perepiska [complete written works] Moscow, 1955-.

About RIMSKY-KORSAKOV: books–

Gike van der Pals, N. van. *N.A. Rimsky-Korsukov: Opernschaffen nebst Skizzen über Leben und Wirken.* Paris and Leipzig, 1929.
Abraham, Gerald. *Studies in Russian Music* [142-310]. London, 1935.
———. *Rimsky-Korsakov: a Short Biography.* London, 1945.
Assafiev, Boris. *Nikolay Andreyevich Rimsky-Korsakov.* Moscow and Leningrad, 1945.
Belza, I.F. *Motsart i Sal'yeri, tragediya Pushkina: dramaticheskiye stsenï Rimskovo-Korsakova.* Moscow, 1953.
Gozenpud, A.A.*N.A. Rimsky-Korsakov: temï i idei evo opernovo tvorchestva* [themes and ideas in Rimsky-Korsakov's operas]. Moscow, 1957.
Danilevich, L. *Posledniye operï N.A. Rimskovo-Korsakova* [last operas]. Moscow, 1961.
Kunin, I.F. *Nikolay Andreyevich Rimsky-Korsakov.* Moscow, 1979.
Ozercovskaja, Irina. *Shazka o core Saltane Rimskogo-Korsakova: Putevoditch'po opere* [guide to *Tzar Sultan*]. 4th ed., Moscow, 1984.
Yastrebtser, V.V. *Reminiscences of Rimsky-Korsakov.* Edited by Florence Jonas. New York, 1985.
Seaman, Gerald S. *Nikolay Andreyevich Rimsky-Korsakov: a Guide to Research.* New York, 1988.

articles–

Calvocoressi, M.D. and Gerald Abraham. "Rimsky-Korsakov." In *Masters of Russian Music,* 335. London, 1936.
Abraham, Gerald. "Rimsky-Korsakov's *Mlada.*" In *On Russian Music,* 113. London, 1939.
———. "*Tsar Saltan.*" In *On Russian Music,* 122. London, 1939.
———. "*Pskovityanka:* the Original Version of Rimsky-Korsakov's First Opera." *Musical Quarterly* 54 (1968): 58.
———. "Satire and Symbolism in *The Golden Cockerel.*" *Music and Letters* 52 (1971): 46.
Seaman, Gerald. "The Rise of Slavonic Opera, I." *New Zealand Slavonic Journal* 2 (1978): 1.
Lischké, André. "Les leitmotive de *Snegourotchka* analysés par Rimsky-Korsakov." *Revenue de musicologie* 65 (1979): 51.
Aleksandrov, Dmitrij. "*Mlada* Rimskogo-Korsakova i e problemy." *Sovetskaya Muzyka* 3 (1982): 73.
Kuharskij, Vasilij. "Postiženie klassiki" [genesis of the libretto of *Legend of the Invisible City of Kitezh and the Maiden Fevronia*]. *Sovetskaya Muzyka* 10 (1984): 34.
Pashalov, V. "Pojuščaja živopis Kiteža." *Teat'r* 47/no. 11 (1984): 111.
Rahmanova, Marina. "K byloj polemike volsrug Kiteža" [*Legend of the Invisible City of Kitezh and the Maiden Fevronia*]. *Sovetskaya Muzyka* 10 (1984): 82.
Taylor, Philip. "Gogolian Interludes: Gogol's Story 'Christmas Eve' as the Subject of Operas by Tchaikovsky and Rimsky-Korsakov." In *Essays on Russian and East European Music.* London, 1984.
Taruskin, Richard. "'The Present in the Past': Russian Opera and Russian Historiography, ca. 1870." In *Russian and Soviet Music: Essays for Boris Schwartz,* edited by Malcolm H. Brown, 77. Ann Arbor, 1984.
Poultney, David. "The Joy of Rimsky." *Opera* December (1988).

*　　*　　*

Rimsky-Korsakov's interest in the fantastic and exotic elements of Russian folklore is evident in his choice of opera subjects and in his musical treatment of those subjects. As one of "The Five" Russian composers responsible for the movement toward the development of national Russian music during the second half of the nineteenth century, his operas cover a wide range of folk topics as well as a number of historic episodes, reflecting his preoccupations with pre-Christian societies as well as with particular historical figures (most notably Ivan the Terrible). At the same time, Rimsky-Korsakov was also influenced by the works of western European composers, so that his operas contain nationalist Russian elements in both music and text as well as western operatic elements.

Rimsky-Korsakov's stylistic development as an opera composer is clearly visible in his scores. The first few operas are not as lyrical as his later works, although none come close to *The Maid of Pskov* in terms of monotonal recitative. With the opera-ballet *Mlada* (composed in collaboration with Borodin, Cui, Musorgsky, and Minkus), Rimsky-Korsakov's numbers become more lyrical, as in the big set pieces found in the dance music, the divertissements, etc. A gradual change of style can be discerned, however, in *May Night* and *The Snow Maiden,* in which Rimsky-Korsakov blurs the distinction between recitative and aria, and does not include the large set pieces as found in his earlier operas. From this point on in Rimsky-Korsakov's opera composition, number opera is abandoned in favor of a continuous, through-composed approach.

The influence of Glinka, who in turn had been influenced by French grand opera, is evident in Rimsky-Korsakov's use of thematic recurrence functioning as identification motives in many of his works. These motives or themes rarely are used as a means of symphonic development, since most of them are never altered. The theme associated with the *The Snow Maiden,* for example, is constant, except for its transformations in act IV to show Leshii fooling Mizgir. Even in this instance, however, the thematic transformations are more closely related to those found in the works of Liszt and Berlioz than they are to the leitmotive technique developed by Wagner.

Wagner's influence on Rimsky-Korsakov is evident, however, in his orchestration and in some of the motives he employs. This is particularly noticeable in the opera-ballet *Mlada,* in which both orchestral techniques and motives can be linked to Wagner. In addition, Rimsky-Korsakov seems to have been particularly attracted to Wagner's nature music; there is Rhine-like music in *Sadko* (which uses an octatonic rather than a diatonic scale as its basis), as well as forest murmurs in *The Tale of Tsar Saltan.*

With the composition of the first of his last two operas, *Legend of the Invisible City of Kitezh,* Rimsky-Korsakov drew most successfully on Wagnerian theories. He interwove two legends to produce a tone poem based setting for a medieval

Rimsky-Korsakov's *The Golden Cockerel,* **title page of score designed by Ivan Bilibin, 1908**

miracle play (called "a Russian *Parsifal*"). Here, Rimsky-Korsakov delineated his characters, particularly the maiden Fevronia of Murom, with evocative expression, unlike his previous dramatizations.

Alexander Pushkin's works had influenced Rimsky-Korsakov's earlier experimental short opera *Mozart and Salieri.* In his final opera, Rimsky-Korsakov derived *The Golden Cockerel* from Pushkin's verse *Fairy Tales,* using poetic ridicule of aristocrats for a thinly-veiled satire of current officials. Rimsky-Korsakov deftly blended myth, Orientalism, fantasy, Wagnerism and originality. His melodic themes at last created both scenes and characters worthy of his technical scholarship, and it is fitting that *The Golden Cockerel* marked the end of both Rimsky-Korsakov's work and the fifty-year era of "The Five."

—Gregory Salmon

RINALDO.

Composer: George Frideric Handel.

Librettist: Giacomo Rossi (after a scenario by A. Hill based on Tasso, *La Gerusalemme liberata*).

First Performance: London, Queen's Theatre in the Haymarket, 24 February 1711; revised 1717, 1731.

Roles: Goffredo (contralto); Almirena (soprano); Rinaldo (contralto); Argante (bass); Armida (soprano); Eustazio (contralto); Christian Magician (contralto); Herald (tenor); Two Mermaids.

Publications

book–

Kubik, Reinhold. *Handels "Rinaldo". Geschichte—Werk—Wirkung.* Neuhausen, 1981.

articles–

Avant-scène opéra February (1985) [*Rinaldo* issue].
Price, Curtis. "English Traditions in Handel's *Rinaldo*." In *Handel Tercentenary Collection,* edited by Stanley Sadie and Anthony Hicks. Ann Arbor and London, 1987.

*   *   *

Rinaldo introduced both George Frideric Handel and newly composed Italian opera to London. Its libretto resulted from a collaboration of English and Italian hands. Aaron Hill, as he writes in the preface, was given the responsibility "to frame some Dramma," after which Giacomo Rossi proceeded "to fill up the Model I had drawn" into Italian verse.

Hill based his story on Torquato Tasso's *Gerusalemme liberata* (*Jerusalem delivered*) of 1581. His intent, as explained in his preface, was to address two issues: the desirability, first, of having a resident composer write specifically for a group of resident singers and, second, of imbuing Italian opera with the conventions of English musical theater. The presence of Handel and the resident singers answered the first need; the second was addressed by adding the spectacle that Italian opera, at that time mostly heroic and historical, lacked. As a result, *Rinaldo* is based not simply on Tasso's epic poem, but on recent English dramatic operas (operas in English with spoken text, elaborate spectacle, and extensive musical interludes) with the same or similar story line including both heroism and sorcery, such as *King Arthur* (1691) with music by Henry Purcell, *Rinaldo and Armida* (1699) with music by John Eccles, and *The British Enchanters* (1706) with music by Eccles and others.

The Hill-Rossi-Handel *Rinaldo* follows Tasso loosely. Goffredo, chief of the Christian armies, is engaged in a crusade to liberate Jerusalem from pagan forces, led by the warrior Argante. Rinaldo, one of Goffredo's most heroic knights, is enchanted by the sorceress Armida. Only by securing his release and return to battle is Jerusalem delivered.

In Tasso, Rinaldo, enchanted, dallies with Armida. Argante is killed, and Armida, repentent, continues to love Rinaldo. He returns her love, and they are reconciled. In Hill's version, on the other hand, Argante is King of Jerusalem, who is in love and in league with Armida. Goffredo has a daughter Almirena who is promised to Rinaldo on the condition that Jerusalem is delivered to the Christians. Almirena is abducted by Armida, and Rinaldo, while seeking to recover her, is captured himself through the siren call of singing mermaids. Rinaldo successfully repulses Armida's advances and with the help of Goffredo and his brother, who arrive in the nick of time, overpowers Armida. The Christians ultimately win Jerusalem, and the captured Argante and Armida convert to Christianity. Almirena and Rinaldo are united.

Two-thirds of Handel's music for this opera derives from his earlier works, mostly from Italy. There are two obvious reasons for this. First, Rossi states in his introduction that the opera was composed in fourteen days, so that the pressures of time may have encouraged Handel to borrow. Secondly, however, Handel may have wanted his first major work for London to offer an anthology of his best music. Thus, although the music is not always dramatically apt, it is generally of the highest quality.

Certain arias stand out as extraordinary, even within their new dramatic context. "Lascia ch'io pianga" ("Leave me to weep") is one of Handel's most beautiful melodies. The saraband dance rhythm (in slow triple time with a secondary accent on the second beat) lends a nobility and grace to the lament of Almirena in captivity. This air comes to *Rinaldo* from *Almira* (1705) through *Il trionfo del tempo* (1707; *The Triumph of Time*); nevertheless, it fits its new dramatic position perfectly. The same may be said of Rinaldo's lament at the moment of Almirena's abduction, "Cara sposa" ("Dear betrothed"). Its long vocal lines set against an intertwining string accompaniment capture the sense of tragedy. In the second section, Rinaldo breaks out of his shock just long enough to rail angrily at the gods, before falling back into despair and a repetition of the first section. Based on the aria in *La resurrezione* (1708; *The Resurrection*), "Caro figlio" ("Dear son"), in which S. Giovanni (St. John) describes

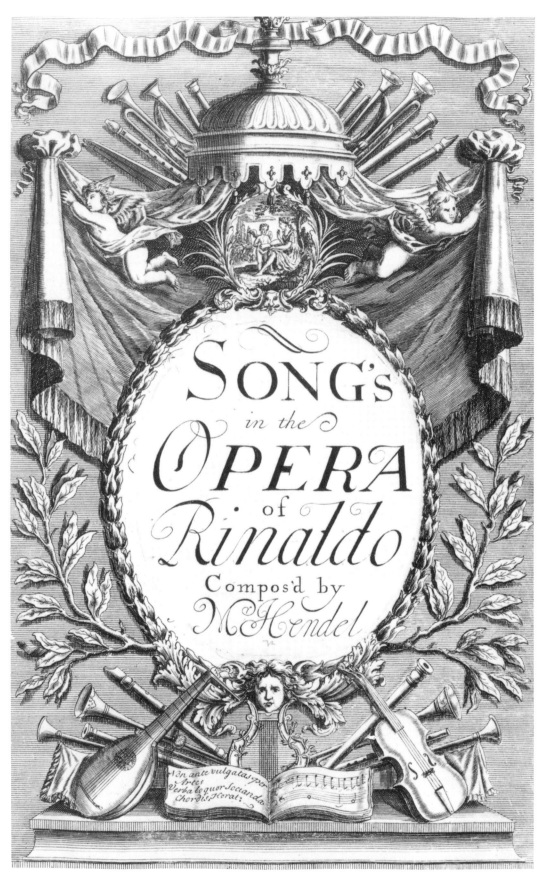

Rinaldo, **title page from first edition of score, London, 1711**

Mary's reaction to seeing the resurrected Christ, "Cara sposa" has many of the same serious and intense qualities, but its angry middle section and string accompaniment are entirely new. Charles Burney, the late eighteenth-century music historian, proclaimed this aria "by many degrees the most pathetic song, and with the richest accompaniment, which had been then heard in England."

In addition to its music, *Rinaldo* succeeded because of its spectacle. Act I opens with the city of Jerusalem under full siege. Soon after, Armida arrives "in the Air, in a Chariot drawn by two huge Dragons, out of whose Mouths issue Fire and Smoke." When the scene then changes to "A delightful Grove," live sparrows were released into the theater. Shortly thereafter Almirena is abducted in a black cloud "all fill'd with dreadful Monsters spitting Fire and Smoke on every side." Acts II and III demand similar displays. In act III, for example, a full war is waged between the Christians and the supernatural spirits: "Godfrey, Eustatio [his brother] and the Soldiers, having climb'd half way up the Mountain, are stopp'd by a Row of ugly Spirits, who start up before 'em; The Soldiers, frighted, endeavour to run back, but are cut off in their Way by another Troop, who start up below 'em. In the midst of their Confusion, the mountain opens and swallows 'em up, with Thunder, Lightning, and amazing Noises."

The triumph of *Rinaldo* led detractors of Italian opera to ridicule the extravagant spectacle. Sir Richard Steele wrote in March of 1711 that the performance he attended had "but a very short Allowance of Thunder and Lightning, . . . [that] the Sparrows and Chaffinches at the Hay-Market fly as yet very irregularly over the Stage; and instead of perching on the Trees and performing their Parts, these young Actors either get into the Galleries or put out the Candles, . . . [and that] the Undertakers forgetting to change their Side-Scenes, we were presented with a Prospect of the Ocean in the midst of a delightful Grove." Nevertheless, *Rinaldo* was performed more in Handel's lifetime than any other of his operas.

—Ellen T. Harris

RING CYCLE
See DER RING DES NIBELUNGEN

DER RING DES NIBELUNGEN [The Ring of the Nibelung].

Das Rheingold [The Rhinegold].
Die Walküre [The Valkyrie].
Siegfried [originally, *Der junge Siegfried;* The young Siegfried].
Götterdämmerung [Twilight of the Gods].

Composer: Richard Wagner.

Librettist: Richard Wagner.

First Performances: *Das Rheingold:* Munich, Königliches Hof- und Nationaltheater, 22 September 1869; *Die Walküre:* Munich, Hof- und Nationaltheater, 26 June 1870; *Siegfried:*

Bayreuth Festspielhaus, 16 August 1876; *Götterdämmerung:* Bayreuth Festspielhaus, 17 August 1876; performance of the entire cycle, Bayreuth Festspielhaus, 13, 14, 16, 17 August 1876.

Roles: *Das Rheingold:* Fricka (mezzo-soprano); Loge (tenor); Wotan (baritone); Alberich (baritone); Freia (soprano); Erda (mezzo-soprano); The Rhinemaidens (sopranos or mezzo-sopranos); Froh (tenor); Donner (baritone); Mime (tenor); Fasolt (baritone); Fafner (bass); Nibelungs (shout, groan, etc., but do not sing).

Die Walküre: Sieglinde (soprano); Brünnhilde (soprano); Siegmund (tenor); Wotan (baritone or bass-baritone); Fricka (soprano or mezzo-soprano); Hunding (bass); Helmwige (soprano); Ortlinde (soprano); Gerhilde (soprano); Waltraute (mezzo-soprano); Siegrune (mezzo-soprano); Rossweise (mezzo-soprano); Grimgerde (mezzo-soprano); Schwertleite (mezzo-soprano).

Siegfried: Brünnhilde (soprano); Siegfried (tenor); Mime (tenor); Der Wanderer (bass or bass-baritone); Alberich (bass); Fafner (bass); Voice of the Forest Bird (soprano); Erda (contralto).

Götterdämmerung: Brünnhilde (soprano); Siegfried (tenor); Hagen (bass); Gutrune (soprano); Gunther (bass or bass-baritone); Alberich (bass); Waltraute (mezzo-soprano); Three Norns (contralto, mezzo-soprano, soprano); The Rhinemaidens (soprano, mezzo-soprano, contralto); chorus (STTBB).

Publications

books—

Shaw, George Bernard. *The Perfect Wagnerite: a Commentary on the Niblung's Ring.* London, 1898; 4th ed., 1923; 1972.

Smolian, A. *Richard Wagners Bühnenfestspiel Der Ring des Nibelungen: ein Vademecum.* Berlin, 1901.

Golther, W. *Die sagengeschichtlichen Grundlagen der Ringdichtung Richard Wagners.* Berlin, 1902.

Kloss, E. and H. Weber. *Richard Wagner über den Ring des Nibelungen: Aussprüche des Meisters über sein Werk in Schriften und Briefen.* Leipzig, 1913.

Wiessner, H. *Der Stabreimvers in Richard Wagners "Ring des Nibelungen."* Berlin, 1924; 1967.

Leroy, L.A. *Wagner's Music Drama of the Ring.* London, 1925.

Hapke, W. *Die musikalische Darstellung der Gebärde in Richard Wagners Ring des Nibelungen.* Leipzig, 1927.

Strobel, O. *Richard Wagner: Skizzen und Entwürfe zur Ring-Dichtung, mit der Dichtung 'Der junge Siegfried'.* Munich, 1930.

Buesst, A. *Richard Wagner: The Nibelung's Ring.* London, 1932; 2nd ed., 1952.

Hutcheson, E. *A Musical Guide to the Richard Wagner Ring of the Nibelung.* New York, 1940; 1972.

Donington, Robert. *Wagner's "Ring" and its Symbols: the Music and the Myth.* London, 1963; 3rd ed., 1974.

Westerhagen, Curt von. *Die Entstehung des 'Ring', dartgestellt an den Kompositionsskizzen Richard Wagners.* Zurich, 1973; English translation, 1976.

Grieg, W., and H. Faldt, eds. *Dokumente zur Entstehungsgeschichte des Bühnenfestspiels Der Ring des Nibelungen. R. Wagner, Sämtliche Werke 29/1.* Mainz, 1976.

Culshaw, John. *Reflections on Wagner's Ring.* New York, 1976.

Westerhagen, Curt von. *Die Entstehung des "Ring".* Zurich, 1973; English translation as *The Forging of the "Ring".* Cambridge, 1976.

DiGaetani, John Louis, ed. *Penetrating Wagner's Ring: an Anthology.* Rutherford, New Jersey, 1978; New York, 1983.

Cooke, Deryck. *I Saw the World End: a Study of Wagner's Ring.* London, 1979.

Barth, Herbert, ed. *Bayreuther Dramaturgie. "Der Ring des Nibelungen."* Stuttgart and Zurich, 1980.

Blyth, Alan. *Wagner's "Ring": an Introduction.* London, 1980.

Ewans, Michael. *Wagner and Aeschylus: the "Ring" and the "Orestia".* London, 1982.

McCreless, Patrick. *Wagner's "Siegfried": its Drama, History, and Music.* Ann Arbor, 1982.

Benvenga, Nancy. *Kingdom on the Rhine: History, Myth and Legend in Wagner's "Ring".* Harwick, Essex, 1983.

Cord, William O. *An Introduction to Richard Wagner's Der Ring des Nibelungen: a Handbook.* Athens, Ohio, 1983.

John, Nicholas, ed. *Richard Wagner: "Die Walküre".* London, 1983.

Fay, Stephen. *The Ring: Anatomy of an Opera.* London, 1984.

John, Nicholas, ed. *Richard Wagner: "Siegfried".* London, 1984.

Fitzgerald, Gerald and Patrick O'Connor, eds. *The Ring: Metropolitan Opera.* New York, 1988.

White, David A. *The Turning Wheel: a Study of Contracts and Oaths in Wagner's Ring.* Selinsgrove, Pennsylvania, 1988.

articles–

Ellis, W.A. "Die verschiedenen Fassungen von "Siegfrieds Tod." *Die Musik* 3 (1903-04): 239, 315.

Petsch, R. "Der 'Ring des Nibelungen' in seinen Beziehungen zur griechischen Tragödie und zur zeitgenössischen Philosophie." *Richard Wagner-Jahrbuch* 2 (1907): 284.

Istel, E. "Wie Wagner am 'Ring' arbeitete: Mitteilungen über die Instrumentationsskizze des 'Rheingold' und andere Manuskripte." *Die Musik* 10 (1910-11): 67; abridged English translation in *Musical Quarterly* 19 (1933): 33.

Altmann, W. "Zur Geschichte der Entstehung und Veröffentlichung von Wagners 'Der Ring des Nibelungen'." *Allgemeine Musik-Zeitung* 38 (1911): 69, 101, 129, 157, 185, 217, 245.

Strobel, O. " 'Winterstürme wichen dem Wonnemond': zur Genesis von Siegmunds Lenzgesang." *Bayreuther Blätter* 53 (1930): 123.

————. "Zur Enstehungsgeschichte der *Götterdämmerung:* unbekannte Dokumente." *Die Musik* 25 (1932-33): 336.

Engel, H. "Versuch einer Sinndeutung vom Richard Wagners *Ring des Nibelungen.*" *Die Musikforschung* 10 (1957): 225.

Serauky, W. "Die Todesverkündigungsszene in Richard Wagners *Walküre* als musikalisch-geistige Achse des Werkes." *Die Musikforschung* 12 (1959): 143.

Westernhagen, Curt von. "Die Kompositionsskizze zu 'Siegfrieds Tod' aus dem Jahre 1850." *Neue Zeitschrift für Musik* 124 (1968): 178.

Bailey, Robert. "Wagner's Musical Sketches for *Siegfrieds Tod.*" In *Studies in Music History: Essays for Oliver Strunk,* edited by Harold Powers, 459. Princeton, 1968.

Dahlhaus, Carl. "Formprinzipien in Wagners 'Ring des Nibelungen'." In *Beiträge zur Geschichte der Oper,* edited by H. Becker, 95. Regensburg, 1969.

Brinkmann, R. " 'Drei der Fragen stell'ich mir frei': zur Wanderer-Szene im I. Akt von Wagners 'Siegfried'." *Jahrbuch des Staatlichen Institut für Musikforschung Preussischer Kulturbesitz 1972:* 120.

Nitsche, P. "Klangfarbe und Form: das Walhallthema in Rheingold und Walküre." *Melos/Neue Zeitschrift für Musik* 1 (1975): 83.

Avant-scène opéra November-December (1976) [*L'or du Rhine* issue].

Avant-scène opéra January-February (1977) [*La Walkyrie* issue].

Avant-scène opéra November-December (1977) [*Siegfried* issue].

Deathridge, John. "Wagner's Sketches for the *Ring.*" *Musical Times* 118 (1977).

Bailey, Robert. "The Structure of the *Ring* and its Evolution." *Nineteenth-Century Music* 1 (1977-78).

Avant-scène opéra nos. 13-14 (1978) [*Le crépuscule des Dieux* issue].

Breig, Werner. "Der 'Rheintöchtergesang' in Wagners *Rheingold.*" *Archiv für Musikwissenschaft* 38 (1980): 241.

Coren, David. "Inspiration and Calculation in the Genesis of Wagner's *Siegfried.*" In *Studies in Musicology in Honor of Otto E. Albrecht,* edited by John Walter Hill, 266. Kassel, 1980.

Kinderman, W. "Dramatic Recapitulation in Wagner's Götterdämmerung." *Nineteenth-Century Music* 4 (1980): 101.

Lek, Robbert van der. "Zum Begriff Übergang und zu seiner Anwendung durch Alfred Lorenz auf die Musik von Wagners *Ring.*" *Die Musikforschung* 35 (1982): 129.

Schäfer, Wolf Dieter. "Syntaktische und semantische Bedingungen der Motivinstrumentation in Wagners *Ring.*" In *Festschrift Heinz Becker zum 60. Geburtstag am 26. Juni 1982,* edited by Jürgen Schläder and Reinhold Quandt, 191. Laaber, 1982.

Coren, David. "The Texts of Wagner's *Der junge Siegfried* and *Siegfried.*" *Nineteenth-Century Music* 6 (1982-83).

Cumbow, Robert C. "The Ring is a Fraud: Self, Totem, and Myth in *Der Ring des Nibelungen.*" *Opera Quarterly* 1 (1983): 107.

Dahlhaus, Carl. "Tonalität und Form in Wagners *Ring des Nibelungen.*" *Archiv für Musikwissenschaft* 40 (1983): 165.

Floros, Constantin. "Der 'Beziehungszauber' der Musik im *Ring des Nibelungen* von Richard Wagner." *Neue Zeitschrift für Musik* 144 (1983): 8.

Gloede, Wilhelm. "Dichterisch-musikalische Periode und Form in Brünnhildes Schlussgesang." *Österreichische Musikzeitung* 38 (1983): 84.

Hirsbrunner, Theo. "Wagners *Götterdämmerung.* Motivgeschichte in Tradition und Gegenwart." *Universitas* 38 (1983): 43.

Lee, M. Owen. "Wagner's *Ring:* Turning the Sky Round." *Opera Quarterly* 1 (1983): 28.

Nitsche, Peter. "Operntraditionen im Musikdrama Richard Wagners. Zu Formkonzeption des ersten Aufzugs der *Walküre.*" *Musica* 37 (1983): 29.

Potter, John. "Brünnhilde's Choice." *Opera News* 47 (1983): 8.

Dahlhaus, Carl. "Entfremdung und Erinnerung: zu Wagners *Götterdämmerung.*" In *Bericht über den Internationalen Musikwissenschaftlichen Kongress Bayreuth, 1981,* edited by Christoph Hellmut Mahling and Sigrid Wiesmann, 416. Kassel, 1984.

Hirsbrunner, Theo. "Musik über Musik: zu Wagners *Götter-dämmerung*." In *Analysen: Beiträge zu einer Problem-geschichte des Komponierens. Festschrift für Hans Hein-rich Eggebrecht zum 65. Geburtstag,* edited by Werner Breig et al., 292. Wiesbaden, 1984.

Dyson, J. Peter. "Ironic Dualities in *Das Rheingold.*" *Current Musicology* 43 (1987).

Darcy, Warren. " 'Everything that is, ends!': the Genesis and Meaning of the Erda Episode in *Das Rheingold.*" *Musical Times* September (1988).

unpublished—

Coren, D. "A Study of Richard Wagner's 'Siegfried'." Ph.D. dissertation, University of California, Berkeley, 1971.

Breig, W. "Studien zur Entstehungsgeschichte von Wagners 'Ring des Nibelungen'." Ph.D. dissertation, University of Freiburg, 1973.

Heidgen, Norbert. "Textvarianten in Richard Wagners *Rheingold* und *Walküre.*" Ph.D. dissertation, Technische Universität, Berlin, 1981.

Stokes, Jeffrey Lewis. "Contour and Motive: a Study of 'Flight' and 'Love' in Wagner's *Ring, Tristan,* and *Meister-singer.*" Ph.D. dissertation, State University of New York, Buffalo, 1984.

*   *   *

Perhaps the greatest operatic work ever composed, the tetralogy *Der Ring des Nibelungen* creates a mythic world encompassing both tragedy and comedy. A universe in itself, the Ring cycle deserves study for its richness of characters, situations, themes, and leitmotifs, and for the development of its ideas.

Das Rheingold opens in the river Rhine as the Rhinemaidens celebrate (and guard) the Rhinegold. Into this world comes the dwarf Alberich, who tries to seduce the lovely Rhinemaidens. They laugh and tease him, and finally reject him. He then notices the Rhinegold and asks about it; they explain that whoever renounces love, steals the gold, and forms the gold into a ring will have power over the whole world. Rejected repeatedly in his quest for love, Alberich now curses it and steals the gold.

In the second scene of *Das Rheingold* the gods find themselves in a quandary. They have given their sister, the goddess of love Freia, to the giants Fasolt and Fafner in return for building them their fortress Valhalla. The god of fire, Loge, suggests that the newly stolen ring, made from the Rhinegold, would be a suitable substitute for Freia to pay the giants.

In the third scene of *Das Rheingold* Alberich has enslaved his brother Mime and the other Nibelung dwarves and forced them to make golden trinkets only for him. But Wotan and Loge enter Nibelheim and capture Alberich along with his magical ring. In the final scene of the opera, Wotan steals the ring from Alberich, who then puts a curse of death on whoever owns it. Wotan is very tempted to keep the ring because of its ultimate power, but finally—at the urgings of Erda, the Earth Mother—gives the ring to the giants and leads the gods into Valhalla.

Die Walküre presents the story of the Wälsungs (children of Wotan), specifically of Sieglinde, married to Hunding, but

The Rheinmaidens from a production of *Das Rheingold* at Bayreuth, 1905

Set design by Joseph Hoffmann for *Die Walküre,* **1876**

in love with a stranger—who turns out to be her brother Siegmund. Their love horrifies Fricka, the goddess of marriage, who successfully urges Wotan to kill Siegmund as an incestuous adulterer. Wotan unhappily orders his daughter, the Valkyrie Brünnhilde, to let Siegmund die in battle against Hunding. When she goes to Siegmund to announce his fate, he threatens to commit suicide rather than abandon his sister. Brünnhilde then promises to help him in his battle against Hunding. She tries to do this but Wotan intervenes, and in the end first Siegmund and then Hunding are killed.

In the last act of *Die Walküre,* Brünnhilde leads Sieglinde to her sister Valkyries for protection against the angry Wotan. They fear him but try to protect their sister and Sieglinde (who is now pregnant with Siegfried). However, Wotan furiously enters and orders them off. His final confrontation with his disobedient daughter Brünnhilde results in a compromise: Wotan will take away her godhead because of her disobedience and then put her in a magic sleep, but he will protect her from cowards by a circle of fire. Whoever kisses her will awaken her and can have her as a wife.

Siegfried involves the young manhood of Siegfried, the son of Siegmund and Sieglinde. Because of his mother's death, he has been raised by a Nibelung dwarf named Mime (brother of Alberich) and raised for the purpose of getting the ring from the dragon Fafner who is guarding it. Through a series of adventures, Siegfried kills the dragon, gets the powerful ring, but outsmarts Mime and keeps the ring himself. The opera's final act involves his climbing through the fire, finding

Brünnhilde, and kissing her into consciousness and love. The opera ends with their wonderful duet.

The tetralogy ends with *Götterdämmerung,* which opens with the three Norns predicting the action of the opera: the death of all the characters and the final end of this greedy struggle for the all-powerful ring. The next scene presents Siegfried and Brünnhilde, joyfully in love. Siegfried then goes off on heroic adventures, leaving Brünnhilde on her mountain. Siegfried next comes to the land of the Gibichungs, ruled by Gunther, his sister Gutrune, and their half-brother Hagen (who is the son of Alberich, the original thief of the ring). The Gibichungs give Siegfried a sleeping potion which makes him forget Brünnhilde and fall in love with Gutrune. Gunther then proposes a marriage—Gutrune will marry Siegfried if he can find a suitable wife for Gunther. Gunther then proposes Brünnhilde, whom Siegfried seizes while disguised as Gunther.

The second act of *Götterdämmerung* begins with Hagen plotting with his father Alberich for their possession of the ring. The next scene involves a wedding celebration which becomes a public humiliation. Gunther marches in with the captive Brünnhilde, and Siegfried happily enters with Gutrune. Brünnhilde immediately accuses Siegfried of betrayal and demands revenge. By the end of the act Hagen, Gunther, and Brünnhilde have vowed to revenge themselves with Siegfried's death.

The final act of *Götterdämmerung,* perhaps the most glorious in the whole cycle, begins with comedy as the Rhinemaidens enter and try to tease Siegfried into returning their

Siegfried, from Patrice Chéreau's Ring cycle at Bayreuth, 1976

ring. When this fails, they leave, saying they will get their ring back by the end of the day in any case. In the next scene, Hagen, Gunther, and the Gibichungs enter, and Hagen kills Siegfried. His body is taken back to the hall of the Gibichungs, with the famous Funeral Music playing. Gutrune tries to claim his body, but Brünnhilde claims to be his real wife. In the fight over the ring, which is still on Siegfried's hand, Gunther is killed. Ultimately, Brünnhilde takes the ring from Siegfried's finger, sings her famous Immolation scene, and starts a fire which burns up first the hall of the Gibichungs and then Valhalla. The Rhine then overflows, bringing with it the Rhinemaidens who get their ring back at last. The evil of the ring has been purged through fire and water, and the gold is finally back where it belongs, in the waters of the river.

In the fairy-tale world of the Ring cycle exist first of all the gods—Wotan, Fricka, Freia, Donner, and Froh; there are also creatures who serve the world of the gods—the Valkyries, especially Brünnhilde and Waltraute, their mother Erda, and the Rhinemaidens. While the gods are creatures of the air and the Rhinemaidens live in water, underground are the Nibelung dwarves, including Alberich and his brother Mime. The creatures who live on the earth are the human beings, the Wälsungs, primarily the brother and sister Siegmund and Sieglinde and their son Siegfried, but also the giants Fasolt and Fafner, and the Gibichungs. Into this complex world enters the Rhinegold, lying at the bottom of the Rhine adding beauty to the river while the Rhinemaidens swim around it, both praising and guarding it. But the person who makes the

gold into a ring and renounces love will have power over the entire complex world of gods, dwarves, giants, and people. The cycle involves the power struggles through these various segments of the population to take possession of the ring and its awesome power, but with it the curse of a loveless life.

In the process we see the corruption of various characters and their altering situations as the moral and political issues connected with the powerful ring affect their lives and those around them. Wotan, the god who originally coveted the gold and stole it from Alberich, appears in three of the four operas and changes from an arrogant young god into an elder, wiser god who desires the end of the conflict and his own death. His daughter Brünnhilde begins as a warrior-maiden, a Valkyrie, who sees the grief of her father Wotan and the despair of Siegmund when told that he will have to leave his sister and lover Sieglinde when ordered to Valhalla. Brünnhilde ultimately becomes the humanized, all-wise woman at the end of this vast tetralogy who sings the famous Immolation scene, hoping that by her death and the sacrifice of her husband Siegfried, the world will finally be rid of the evil ring so love and happiness can return.

Siegfried begins as an innocent though sometimes cruel adolescent, yet becomes a helpless and naive victim of the ring's power. He is accused of treacheries that he is unaware of having committed, thereby constituting the suffering innocent who will become the scapegoat for all the evil plotters around him. His murder will ultimately cause the return of the ring to the Rhine and its rightful owners, the Rhine-

A scene from *Götterdämmerung*, showing the death of Siegfried (woodcut, c. 1890, after a painting by Theodor Pixis)

maidens. Only when in the Rhine, giving off beautiful reflected light to the river's flowing waters, does the Rhinegold provide any goodness for the universe. Human beings and the other creatures of this world can now begin again with hope.

This magnificent work lends itself to many moral, political, religious, philosophical, psychological, and ecological interpretations. The conflict of love and power, one of the recurrent themes in Western literature, finds operatic embodiment in the Ring cycle. To enter the world of Wagner's Ring is to enter a uniquely fascinating place, a place of both magical fairy-tale and profound philosophy, and that fascination will repay study with musical and dramatic enjoyment.

—John Louis DiGaetani

THE RING OF THE NIBELUNG
See DER RING DES NIBELUNGEN

RINUCCINI, Ottavio.

Librettist/Dramatist. Born 20 January 1562, in Florence. Died 28 March 1621, in Florence. Began to write for the court entertainments in Florence, c. 1579; member of the Accademia Fiorentina; member of the Accademia degli Alterati (also in Florence), 1586; collaborated with Peri on *Dafne*, composed in the new recitative style, 1598; wrote librettos for Monteverdi in Mantua; member of the Accademia degli Elevati in Mantua.

Librettos

La favola di Dafne, J. Peri and J. Corsi, 1598; revised for M. da Gagliano, 1608; H. Schütz (translation by Martin Opitz), 1627.
L'Euridice, J. Peri, 1600; G. Caccini, 1600 (first performed 1602).
L'Arianna, C. Monteverdi, 1608.
Narciso, 1616 [not set].

Publications/Writings

By RINUCCINI: books–

Poesie. Florence, 1622.

articles–

Preface to *Euridice*. Florence, 1600; English translation in *Source Readings in Music History*, edited by O. Strunk, New York, 1950; 1965.

unpublished–

L'Annunziazione. 1619.
Versi sacri cantati nella Capella della serenissima Archiduchessa d'Austria. 1619.

About RINUCCINI: books–

Raccamadoro-Ramelli, F. *Ottavio Rinuccini*. Fabriano, 1900.
Solerti, A. *Le origini del melodramma*. Turin, 1903; 1969.
_____. *Gli albori del melodramma*. Milan, 1904-05; 1969.
_____. *Musica, ballo e drammatica alla corte medicea dal 1600 al 1637*. Florence, 1905; 1969.
Schild, M. *Die Musikdramen O. Rinuccinis*. Würzburg, 1933.
Calcaterra, C. *Poesie e canto: studi sulla poesia melica italiana e sulla favola per musica*. Bologna, 1951.
Abert, A.A. *Claudio Monteverdi und das musikalische Drama*. Lippstadt, 1954.
Hanning, B. *Of Poetry and Music's Power*. Ann Arbor, 1980.
Rosand, Ellen. *Opera in Seventeenth-Century Venice*. Berkeley, 1991.

articles–

Mazzoni, G. "Cenni sul Ottavio Rinnuccini, poeta." *Atti dall' accademia del Rinuccini. Istituto musicale di Firenze* 33 (1895).
Sonneck, O.G. "*Dafne*, the First Opera: a Chronological Study." *Sammelbände der Internationalen Musik-Gesellschaft* 15 (1913-14): 102.
Porter, W.V. "Peri and Corsi's *Dafne*: Some New Discoveries and Observations." *Journal of the American Musicological Society* 18 (1965): 170.
Palisca, C.V. "The Alterati of Florence, Pioneers in the Theory of Dramatic Music." In *New Looks at Italian Opera: Essays in Honor of Donald J. Grout*, 9. Ithaca, New York, 1968.

Pirotta, N. "Early Opera and Aria." In *New Looks at Italian Opera: Essays in Honor of Donald J. Grout,* 39. Ithaca, New York, 1968.

———. "Scelte poetiche di Monteverdi." *Nuova rivista musicale italiana* 2 (1968): 10.

———. "Teatro, scene e musica nelle opere di Monteverdi." In *Congresso internazionale sul tema Claudio Monteverdi e il suo tempo: Venezia, Mantova e Cremona, 1968.*

Hanning, B. "Apologia pro Ottavio Rinuccini." *Journal of the American Musicological Society* 26 (1973): 240.

Tomlinson, G.A. "Ancora su Ottavio Rinuccini." *Journal of the American Musicological Society* 28 (1975): 351.

Strainchamps, E. "New Light on the Accadamia degli Elevati of Florence." *Musical Quarterly* 62 (1976): 507.

Sternfeld, F.W. "The First Printed Opera Libretto." *Music and Letters* 59 (1978): 121.

Hill, J.W. "Oratory Music in Florence, I: *Recitar Cantando,* 1583-1655." *Acta musicologica* 51 (1979): 108.

Brown, Howard. Introduction to Peri, Jacopo, *Euridice: an Opera in One Act, Five Scenes. Recent Researches in the Music of the Baroque Era,* vols. 36, 37. Madison, Wisconsin, 1981.

Carter, Tim. "Jacopo Peri's *Euridice* (1600): a Contextual Study." *Music Review* 43/no. 2 (1982): 83.

Tomlinson, Gary. "Music and the Claims of Text: Monteverdi, Rinuccini, and Marino." *Critical Inquiry* 8/no. 3 (1982): 565.

*　　*　　*

Title page to the score of Jacopo Peri's *L'Euridice,* to a libretto by Ottavio Rinuccini, Venice, 1608

As the creator of the first opera librettos, Ottavio Rinuccini played a fundamental role in the early development of the genre of opera. His works are a link between the first operas and the Florentine *intermedii*-the drama with musical interludes performed for sixteenth-century Florentine court celebrations. In addition, his poetry was infused with a kind of rhetorical expression that was particularly well-suited to the heightened declamation and emphasis on text expression that was so critical to the first opera composers. Indeed, the settings of his poetry by Claudio Monteverdi, both in numerous madrigals and in the surviving fragment of the opera *Arianna* (1608) are among that composer's greatest works.

Rinuccini was stimulated by his youthful contact with the Florentine academies—including Count Giovanni Bardi's famous Camerata—and what was likely a classical education. His desire to explore the power of music and poetry led to what he would later call the "first test of music," the creation of *La favola di Dafne* with the singer-composer Jacopo Peri, which was first performed in the home of Jacopo Corsi, one of Florence's leading intellectuals. With *La favola di Dafne,* Rinuccini established a model that he would follow in his subsequent librettos. Set in the pastorale, mythological realm of its primary source, Ovid's *Metamorphoses,* this first opera libretto is more typical of the genre of tragicomedy as exemplified by Guarini's popular *Il pastor fido* (1589) than any genuine emulation of classical tragedy that so preoccupied the Florentine intellectuals. In a mere 445 lines of verse, Rinuccini provided Peri with a prologue and series of six scenes or tableaux that were particularly apt for musical representation. The success of the work was apparently unexpected and unprecedented, after its first performance in 1598 at the house of Jacopo Corsi, it was performed numerous times and Rinuccini himself revised the libretto for a setting by Marco da Gagliano for the Mantuan carnival in 1608.

Rinuccini explored the dramatic potential of the new genre in his second collaboration with Jacopo Peri, *Euridice* (1600).

(*Euridice* was also set by Caccini and published in 1600, but not performed until 1602.) Like *Dafne, Euridice* is a mythological pastoral based on Ovid, but also somewhat dependent upon Virgil. Rinuccini may also have known Poliziano's 1480 play *La favola d'Orfeo* which likewise relies heavily on Ovid and Virgil. Yet Rinuccini differed from Poliziano by altering the myth's tragic ending so that Euridice and Orfeo both survive happily, thus creating one of opera's earliest happy endings. The historical significance accorded this work, however, is a result of its use as a model for the more famous Orfeo setting of the early seventeenth century, Monteverdi and Striggio's *La favola d'Orfeo* (1607). It is evident that Monteverdi and Striggio's *Orfeo* resembles the earlier work not only in terms of dramatic organization and sources, but also in its direct correspondence between specific speeches and the musical settings of those speeches.

Rinuccini's indirect relationship with Monteverdi through *Euridice* came to fruition in their successful collaboration on the opera *Arianna.* As Monteverdi expressed in one of his letters, *Arianna* provided him with something he apparently had not found in *Orfeo:* a poetry that would allow his music to imitate the text more perfectly. In *Arianna,* Rinuccini transcended the emotional restraint of the pastoral world and provided Monteverdi with characters of greater depth and humanity, and in particular, with a heroine whose tragic abandonment inspired some of Monteverdi's greatest music. In the only surviving fragment of the opera, Arianna's famous lament, Rinuccini and Monteverdi eloquently express all of the various phases of Arianna's reaction to her abandonment by Theseus: her outrage and disbelief, despair, and pleading, her highly volatile outbursts juxtaposed with her obsessive thoughts of death. Arianna's lament, published both as a monody and a set of madrigals, was one of the most popular and widely-circulated operatic excerpts of the century, and as a result, the lament became an almost mandatory feature of subsequent operas. In this single surviving excerpt from what was undoubtedly a masterpiece, Rinuccini and Monteverdi provided future generations of opera composers and librettists with a specific vocabulary of musical and poetic gestures that would be forever identified with the idea of the lament.

—Wendy Heller

THE RISE AND FALL OF THE CITY OF MAHA-
GONNY
See MAHAGONNY

THE RISING OF THE MOON.

Composer: Nicholas Maw.

Librettist: Beverley Cross.

First Performance: Sussex, Glyndebourne, 19 July 1970.

Roles: Brother Timothy (tenor); Donal O'Dowd (baritone); Cathleen Sweeney (mezzo-soprano); Col. Lord Francis Jowler (bass-baritone); Major Max von Zastrow (baritone); Captain Lillywhite (tenor); Lady Eugenie Jowler (soprano); Frau Elizabeth von Zastrow (mezzo-soprano); Miss Atalanta Lillywhite (soprano); Corp. of Horse Haywood (bass-baritone); Cornet John Stephen Beaumont (tenor); The Widow Sweeney (contralto); Young Gaveston (tenor); Willoughby (baritone); chorus (TTTBBBBBB).

Publications

article–

Walsh, S. "Nicholas Maw's New Opera." *Tempo* no. 92 (1970): 2.

*   *   *

Nicholas Maw's second opera, a romantic comedy, was written in the years between 1966 and 1970 while he was employed as composer in residence at Trinity College, Cambridge. The title, though not the subject matter (at least not directly), derives from an Irish folk-song whose lyrics express the patriotic fervor of the Fenian revolutionaries as they prepare to mount a nighttime attack on the British forces. The theme of Beverley Cross's libretto, which avoids direct discussion of politics or religion, is that of people's attitudes to honor, whether in the relationships between men and women, in patriotism, or directed towards their vocations.

The opera is set in the year 1875 in County Mayo, Ireland. The 31st Royal Lancers, an English regiment, occupies the village of Ballinvourney to the consternation of the few remaining inhabitants. Cornet Beaumont, a young aristocratic recruit, arrives, and it soon becomes clear that as an artist and aesthete, he is not best suited to the life of the regiment. Major Max von Zastrow, a Prussian professional soldier who has been seconded to the regiment, challenges him to a test of his virility in the form of a libertine triathlon, the initiate being required to smoke three cigars, drink three bottles of champagne, and sleep with three women in the same night. At this point the Irish cunningly take the initiative, and lead Beaumont to a local inn, where, unknown to himself, Eugenie and Elizabeth, the wives of Jowler (the English colonel) and von Zastrow, and Atalanta, the virgin daughter of the adjutant, are staying. Unaware of their real identities, Beaumont successfully tackles the first two ladies, but Cathleen, a local Irish girl who has fallen for the recruit, substitutes herself for Atalanta, who is visited instead by von Zastrow. The following morning brings turmoil as the truth is revealed, though once Beaumont has resigned his commission and the troops have retreated in disarray, peace is restored to the village. Aware of the hopelessness of a relationship with Cathleen, Cornet Beaumont departs.

On the surface, the opera might seem to fall into the tradition of Berg's *Wozzeck,* and indeed a number of superficial stylistic similarities can be detected, especially Cathleen's second act lullaby, which bears more than a passing resemblance to *Wozzeck's* Marie's similarly phrased aria. Maw's concerns are not, however, for the miseries of the proletariat, or for the arbitrariness of existence, and he has no intention to preach to or cajole his audience. His stated intention was to entertain the well-heeled Glyndebourne audience, aware that non-subsidized theater could not afford the luxury of antagonizing its public, an attitude which seems unusual for late 1960s Britain (most of Maw's contemporaries were oblivious of, or antipathetic to, market forces). The work's title takes on an ironic significance when related to the sentiment of the folk-song source, for the events which take place at the rising of the moon involve sexual athleticism as Beaumont attempts to uphold his honor, and that of the regiment (while of course dishonoring his paramours), rather than the patriotic vigor of the Fenians gathering with their pikes by moonlight in preparation for an attack on the British.

Maw had developed a sensuous chromatic musical idiom which was as much influenced by Richard Strauss and Benjamin Britten as by the second Viennese school, a harmonic idiom that could accommodate the diatonicism of military marches and Irish folk melody without stylistic rift. He had served his operatic apprenticeship in *One Man Show* (1964), developing a technical mastery of the genre in terms of pacing and characterization. *Scenes and Arias* (1961-62) had indicated Maw's ability to write powerful erotic music lacking self-consciousness or anxiety, and this skill is especially apparent in Elizabeth and Beaumont's ecstatic act II duet at the very core of the opera.

The music, which is tightly organized, finely scored, and contains beautifully shaped vocal melodies, is almost entirely successful within its own terms. If the opera has a weakness, it lies not in the music but in the relative superficiality of the plot and the lack of any really finely drawn moral conclusions. Presenting itself as a quasi-Straussian opera, but in an incongruent social and temporal frame, it appears, perhaps, rather naive, even anachronistic, in a way that the operas of Britten, an analogous musical figure, rarely do.

—David Cooper

IL RITORNO D'ULISSE IN PATRIA [The Return of Ulysses to the Homeland].

Composer: Claudio Monteverdi.

Librettist: G. Badoaro.

First Performance: Venice, 1640.

Roles: Human Frailty (soprano); Time (bass); Fortune (soprano); Love (soprano); Jove (tenor); Neptune (bass); Minerva (soprano); Juno (soprano); Ulysses (tenor); Penelope (soprano); Telemachus (tenor); Antinous (bass); Peisander (tenor); Amphinomus (contralto); Eurymachus (tenor); Melantus (soprano); Eumete (soprano); Irus (tenor); Eurykleia (soprano); chorus.

Publications

articles—

Goldschmidt, H. "Monteverdis Ritorno d'Ulisse." *Sammelbände der Internationalen Musik-Gesellschaft* 4 (1902-03): 671.
———. "Claudio Monteverdis Oper: Il ritorno d'Ulisse in patria.: *Sammelbände der Internationalen Musik-Gesellschaft* 9 (1907-08): 570.
Hass, R. "Zur Neuausgabe von Claudio Monteverdis 'Il ritorno d'Ulisse in patria'." *Studien zur Musikwissenschaft* 9 (1922): 3.
Borren, C. van den. "Il ritorno d'Ulisse in patria' de Claudio Monteverdi." *Revue de L'Université de Bruxelles* 3 (1925).
Westrup, J.A. "Monteverdi's 'Il ritorno d'Ulisse in Patria'." *Monthly Musical Record* 58 (1928): 106.
Osthoff, W. "Zu den Quellen von Monteverdis Ritorno d'Ulissc in Patria." *Studien zur Musikwissenschaft* 23 (1956): 67.
———. "Zur Bologneser Aufführung von Monteverdis 'Ritorno d'Ulisse' im Jahre 1640." *Anzeiger der phil.-hist. Klasse der Österreichischen Akademie der Wissenschaften* 95 (1958): 155.
Arnold, Denis. "*Il ritorno d'Ulisse* and the Chamber Duet." *Musical Times* 106 (1965): 183.
Rosand, Ellen. "Iro and the Interpretation of Il ritorno d'Ulisse in Patria." *Journal of Musicology* Spring (1989).

*   *   *

Unfortunately, nothing is known of the public's reception of *Il ritorno d'Ulisse in patria.* Nor, if truth be told, is it certain that all of the work was composed by Monteverdi. The story, as worked into a libretto from the last twelve books of Homer's *Odyssey* by the amateur Venetian author, Giacomo Badoaro, is quite simple and straightforward: Act I opens at the Royal Palace in Ithaca, where Penelope mourns the absence of her husband, Ulysses, who even then is nearing home, though she is unaware of the fact. Her immediate concern is that in his absence, numerous suitors for her hand—she calls them hostile rivals—have gathered at the palace, and she fears for her safety. In the next scene Ulysses, born homeward by Phaeacian sailors, awakens on an unknown shore to discover that his mentors, terrified by Neptune's anger, have abandoned him. However, he learns from Minerva, who appears disguised as a shepherd, that he has been cast ashore near Ithaca. She transforms him into an old, bald beggar, and guides him towards his old residence. On the path he meets

Eumete, an old, faithful servant who encourages him to the palace even though he does not recognize him as Ulysses. The bald beggar prophesies that Ulysses will return.

Act II begins as Ulysses' son, Telemachus, who is returning to Ithaca to assist his mother, encounters Eumete and the beggar. Soon Ulysses reveals to Telemachus that he is his father, and they proceed happily to the palace. There they find Penelope, surrounded by suitors, Antinous, Peisander and Amphinomus, who, upon learning of Telemachus' presence, and the impending return of Ulysses, redouble their efforts to seduce the queen. Actually, Ulysses is there already, disguised as the bald beggar, and immediately challenges Irus, another suitor, to a fight, in which Ulysses is the victor. Penelope, inspired by Minerva, then produces Ulysses' bow, suggesting that the rival suitors engage in an archery contest. All fail in their attempts to string the bow except the bald beggar, who with deadly aim promptly dispatches all the suitors. In act III, Ulysses at last convinces Penelope that he truly is her husband, by describing an embroidered sheet that earlier had graced their connubial bed, and they are blissfully reunited.

Monteverdi's handiwork is readily identifiable throughout most of the opera. No longer are the scenes so short-coupled as in *Orfeo,* but the stamp of his genius is clearly apparent. Formally and technically, the composition is more highly developed, the phrases longer, the sequences more intricate, and the musical characterization elaborated in greater detail throughout. The arias, the duets, and the ensembles reflect not only the old principles of *seconda prattica,* but also the innovations of *bel canto,* showing that Monteverdi had grown with the times and was ably competing with his brilliant students, such as Cavalli, Fedeli, Manelli, and Sacrati. It has been suggested that one or more of these may have collaborated with Monteverdi in the composition of *Il ritorno d'Ulisse.* Given that only one complete manuscript is now extant, further sources will have to be discovered before this interesting suggestion may be fully investigated.

—Franklin B. Zimmerman

———

THE ROBBERS
See I MASNADIERI

———

ROBERT LE DIABLE [Robert the Devil].

Composer: Giacomo Meyerbeer.

Librettists: Eugène Scribe and G. Delavigne.

First Performance: Paris, Opéra, 21 November 1831.

Roles: Robert le Diable (tenor); Albert (baritone); Raimbaut (tenor); Bertram (bass-baritone); Alice (soprano); Isabella (soprano); Herald (tenor); Provost (tenor); Priest (baritone); Lady of Honor (mezzo-soprano); Helen (mute); Cavaliers (two tenors, baritone, bass); chorus (SSATTBB).

The prologue from Monteverdi's *Il ritorno d'Ulisse,* **production by David Freeman for English National Opera, London, 1989**

Publications

articles–

Tardel, H. "Die Sage von Robert dem Teufel in neueren deutschen Dichtungen und in Meyerbeers Oper." *Forschungen zur neueren Literaturgeschichte* 14 (1900).

Prod'Homme, J.G. "Meyerbeer à Paris avant 'Robert le diable,' d'après son journal inédit." *Mercure de France* 14 April (1936): 275.

Join-Dieterle, C. "*Robert le diable:* Le premier opéra romantique." *Romantisme* (1980).

Brzoska, Matthias. "*Majomet* et *Robert-le-diable:* L'esthétique musicale dans *Gambara.*" *Année balzacienne* (1983): 51.

Avant-scène opéra June (1985) [*Robert le diable* issue].

*   *   *

Meyerbeer, whose Italian operas *Margherita d'Anjou* and *Il crociato in Egitto* had made the composer's name known in Paris, came to the French capital from Italy in 1826, having learned much about writing for the voice, but yearning for libretti that would allow him to extend the drama into the orchestra as well. His meeting with Eugène Scribe, soon to be the librettist of the first "grand opera," Auber's *La muette de Portici,* resulted in an agreement to collaborate on a three-act opéra comique based on the legend of Robert, Duke of Normandy, spawn of the devil and a mortal woman, saved from hell by his foster-sister.

The story itself was well known; it had played on the Paris stage as early as 1815. Had Meyerbeer gone ahead with staging the original version, it might, thanks to his gifts as a melodist, have become a period piece such as Boieldieu's *La dame blanche,* and the history of opera would have been far different. Instead, thanks in part to extrinsic circumstances, he urged Scribe to turn the story into a full-fledged five-act work which could be through-composed, like *La muette de Portici.* Armed with his understanding of how Mozart and Weber had treated drama in music, and with his understanding from his Italian operas of the capacities of the voice, Meyerbeer produced a work which changed the face of opera and influenced even those who would later become the composer's musical adversaries.

With *Robert,* Meyerbeer and Scribe indicated the direction that opera would take for the next forty years. Perhaps Meyerbeer's most lasting contribution (though he himself had borrowed the idea from both Weber and Gluck) was the use of the orchestra as dramatic protagonist. His latter-day detractors sneer at his "effects for their own sake," but his method of enhancing and underscoring dramatic situations through the use of unusual instruments and instrumental combinations in *Robert* has been exhaustively analyzed by Hector Berlioz, whose reputation as a musician, unlike Meyerbeer's, has survived the same kind of criticism.

Meyerbeer diminished the importance of the solo aria in his French operas, beginning with *Robert.* The tenor of the title has no aria at all, the occasionally recorded "Sicilienne" being a short solo passage in an ensemble. The second tenor, Raimbaut, a folksinger who sets the stage for the opera's events, has a strophic tune for the legend of Robert the Devil, but even here Meyerbeer uses the simplicity of the first two verses as a foil for the inventive orchestration of the third. Isabelle, the princess Robert loves, and Bertram, his fiend-father, both have two "arias" apiece, but they reflect the beginning of a particularly Meyerbeerian treatment of solo melody, neither in classical ABA form nor in the development of a single tune, but rather a succession of undeveloped tune-forms which change at the bidding of the text's changing emotions, instead of forcing themselves on a text compelled by a single melodic development. Fitfully, especially in the injection of the demonic chorus beneath the stage, Meyerbeer also began to develop his idea of the chorus as a protagonist on its own, one he was later to perfect in *Les Huguenots* and *L'Africaine.*

In sum, *Robert le diable* is a laboratory from which Wagner took the idea of the orchestra as a coequal participant in the drama (and Tannhäuser as a character is obviously patterned on Robert); Berlioz the impact of unexpected, original orchestral effects; Gounod the structure for the final trio in *Faust;* Verdi the concept of human drama played out against historical perspective. Perhaps only a time-traveler from whose memory all subsequent musico-dramatic developments had been erased could appreciate the impact of *Robert le diable* as it was first played. Like Beethoven's *Eroica* Symphony and Stravinsky's *Le sacre du printemps,* it changed the course of its own musical form irrevocably.

—William J. Collins

ROBERT THE DEVIL
See ROBERT LE DIABLE

ROBERTO DEVEREUX, ossia Il conte di Essex.

Composer: Gaetano Donizetti.

Librettist: S. Cammarano (after F. Ancelot, *Elisabeth d'Angleterre*).

First Performance: Naples, San Carlo, 29 October 1837.

Roles: Elisabetta (soprano); Roberto (tenor); Sara (mezzo-soprano); Nottingham (baritone); Lord Cecil (tenor); Sir Walter Raleigh (bass); Page (bass); Servant (bass); chorus (SATTB).

*   *   *

More than any other opera of Donizetti's prime, *Roberto Devereux* was born under a tragic star. It followed the deaths of both his parents, and in between the receipt of Cammarano's libretto and the opera's successful first performance at the Teatro San Carlo in Naples on 29 October 1837, Donizetti

lost both his wife and his still-born son. In an abyss of despair he wrote to a friend: "Without a father, without a mother, without a wife, without children. . . . Why then do I labour on? Why?"

The opera was composed in the middle of a cholera epidemic, in an apartment where his wife's room was kept locked. Such bitter tragedy provoked a prolonged cry of anguish fully appropriate to Cammarano's remorseless plot; the fury, the regret, the almost embarrassingly intrusive cries of despair in this opera, are unhappily Donizetti's own. The opera is set in London, where an aging Elisabetta (Queen Elizabeth I) refuses to believe in the treachery of Roberto Devereux (Earl of Essex). But he has indeed betrayed her, with Sara, her lady-in-waiting. These guilty lovers agree to part, exchanging momentos; he gives her a safe-conduct ring (a present from the Queen), she gives him a scarf she has embroidered. Despite the pleas of innocence made on his behalf by Sara's husband, Roberto is found guilty of treason. But the scarf is then produced; recognizing it, Sara's husband swears revenge on his erstwhile friend, and Elisabetta condemns him to the block.

Sara's attempts to take the ring to the Queen are frustrated by her husband, who locks her in her room. Meanwhile Elisabetta waits in vain for the token which will give her the excuse to save his life. Just as the execution is announced, Sara bursts in with the ring; Elisabetta goes almost mad with grief, and in a swan-song of terrible anguish she abdicates before the terrified courtiers.

Roberto Devereux was the last of Donizetti's "Tudor" operas, all but one of them making an operatic star out of Queen Elizabeth I (the others were *Il castello di Kenilworth* of 1829, *Anna Bolena* of 1830, and *Maria Stuarda* of 1834-5). As with those other operas, *Roberto Devereux* is not really about its title character, but about Elizabeth. Elisabetta has all the power of a reigning queen, but none at all where love is concerned and is destroyed as a consequence. Opera, like love, is a great leveler. It is Elisabetta, not Roberto, who has the lion's share of the music: Donizetti gives her three of his most extended arias, including the astonishing *gran' scena finale* to the opera with its spun-out cabaletta in which the distraught sovereign sees the angel of death hovering over her, a tour-de-force with a huge arch of melody worthy of Bellini's inordinate tunes and with a cumulative anguish only Donizetti knew how to achieve.

These Tudor operas, while often melodramatic, were mostly derived from picturesque French plays which often contained at least a grain of truth. Essex's ring for example really did exist; it was presented to Westminster Abbey in 1927 and is today fixed below the effigy of Elizabeth on the great Queen's tomb. Indeed, *Roberto Devereux* is more faithful to the facts than most operas of its day. Its libretto shows a greater concentration on detail as well as a concern for vivid portraiture—exaggerated to be sure—but convincing, even overwhelming.

Roberto Devereux did not really hold the stage until its twentieth-century revivals. A Parisian revision in 1838 was not well received, possibly because Donizetti had the grotesque idea of including "God Save the Queen" in a specially-composed overture, but more probably because the French capital was already seething with the scenic-marvels of Meyerbeerian *grand opéra.* Elisabetta harkens back to Dido, Medea, Iphigenia, and other distraught heroines who perhaps embarrassed the Victorians with their naked emotion. In today's revivals Elisabetta's struggle between duty, pleasure, and passion finds an echo in our lives, and its exalted *finale* seems far more appropriate to our everyday existence, combining lyricism with despair, as well as excercising the talents of two or three of our genuinely sovereign sopranos.

—Alexander Weatherson

RODELINDA, Regina de' Longobardi.

Composer: George Frideric Handel.

Librettist: Nicola F. Haym (after A. Salvi, based on P. Corneille, *Pertharite*).

First Performance: London, King's Theatre in the Haymarket, 13 February 1725; revised 18 December 1725, 4 May 1731.

Roles: Rodelinda (soprano); Bertarido (contralto); Grimoaldo (tenor); Edwig (contralto); Garibaldo (bass); Unulfo (contralto); Flavio (mute).

*   *   *

Rodelinda is set in Lombardy in the seventh century. Upon the death of King Ariberto, the kingdom was divided between his two sons: Bertarido, who took Milan, and Gundeberto, who took Pavia. Gundeberto, with the help of Grimoaldo, Duke of Benevento, has conquered Milan, and Bertarido is presumed dead. Before his own death, Gundeberto has offered the hand of his sister Eduige to Grimoaldo, now the ruler of Lombardy. Grimoaldo, however, is enamored of Rodelinda, the supposed widow of Bertarido. She remains at court with their son Flavio.

These are the background events to the opera, whose pre-echoes of French rescue opera, in particular Beethoven's *Fidelio,* have often been noted: Rodelinda, for example, seeks her husband in a dungeon and her cry of "Perfido!" matches Leonore's passionate "Abscheulicher!" In act I, scene ii, Bertarido returns in disguise from exile and watches secretly as his wife and his son mourn at his tomb. Grimoaldo snatches Flavio from Rodelinda, threatening to kill him if Rodelinda will not marry him. Rodelinda consents but privately determines that Grimoaldo will die. In act II, when Rodelinda tells Grimoaldo that she will marry him, she stipulates that there is one condition: he must kill Flavio. Rodelinda never believes for a moment that Grimoaldo would do such a thing. In torment, Grimoaldo leaves. Later in the act, as Bertarido and Rodelinda are reunited, Grimoaldo, not recognizing Bertarido, orders him imprisoned. In the third act Eduige helps to rescue her brother from prison. In the escape Bertarido has wounded Unulfo with a sword, even though Unulfo has come to rescue him through a secret passage. When Eduige leads Rodelinda and Flavio into the cell they find only Bertarido's cloak and drops of blood. For the second time, Rodelinda believes her husband dead. In the final scene Bertarido thwarts an attempt on Grimoaldo's life. In gratitude Grimoaldo, whose conscience has been torturing him, returns the throne to Bertarido, who is joined by his wife and son.

The libretto of *Rodelinda* is one of the best Handel ever set, and the opera, one of three masterpieces composed by

Handel in less than a year's time (the other two being *Tamerlano* and *Giulio Cesare*), is considered to be one of the composer's most inspired scores. According to Charles Burney, it "contains such a number of capital and pleasing airs as entitles it to one of the first places among Handel's dramatic productions," and Chrysander deemed it "one of his most complete and satisfying operas." One strength is the relative clarity of the plot and credibility of the characters. As with any *opera seria* there are certain unmotivated dramatic situations and plot complexities, but these are both fewer and less strained in *Rodelinda* than in the bulk of Baroque opera. Even though the work was held in such high esteem in Handel's day and later, it was nevertheless unheard and unseen for the better part of two centuries. It was with *Rodelinda* that the twentieth-century Handel revival began: a production was given in Göttingen in 1920, but based on a corrupt text; the true revival began with the foundation in 1955 of the Handel Opera Society in England. Four years later, on the bicentenary of the composer's death, three of his operas were given, *Rodelinda* among them, with Joan Sutherland in the cast.

The first act of *Rodelinda* is notable for a string of allegro arias, each one distinct from the others only when one learns to distinguish various types of Handelian allegros. After this series of fast arias, the character of Bertarido makes his entrance with the most famous air in the opera, the poignant "Dove sei?" It is pure melody projecting personal and tender emotions. After the first four measures of the melody there is a brief silence during which his plea to his absent wife is unanswered. Rodelinda's own *largo* aria, "Ombre piante," an aria that Handel rewrote more than once, follows Bertarido's in order to display the closeness of the married couple even though physically separated, and to serve as an illustration of Handel's willingness to abandon the convention of contrasting slow-quick-slow aria patterns for dramatic and psychological purposes. Several allegro arias then follow, but the act ends in B minor as Bertarido voices his belief that Rodelinda is in love with another.

The character of Rodelinda is among the most grandly dignified of opera heroines. Her strength and command of her destiny are displayed in the wide range of music Handel wrote for her, music that variously exhibits fury, grief, tenderness and passion, and exultation. She is given eight arias, consisting of three laments, three denunciations, and two love songs, one of desperate longing and one of joyous fulfillment as she and her beloved are united. As Winton Dean noted in the program for the 1959 Handel Opera Society production: "Handel expresses every facet of conjugal emotion—separation, longing, despair, hope, relief—in music of marvelous eloquence."

—Stephen Willier

LE ROI ARTHUS. [King Arthur].

Composer: Ernest Chausson.

Librettist: Ernest Chausson.

First Performance: Brussels, Théâtre de la Monnaie, 30 November 1903 [posthumous production].

Roles: Guinevere (mezzo-soprano); King Arthur (baritone); Lancelot (tenor); Mordred (baritone); Lionel (tenor); Allan (bass); Merlin (baritone); A Farmhand (tenor); A Knight (bass); A Horseman (bass); Four Soldiers (two tenors, two basses); chorus.

Publications

Hallays, A. "Le Roi Arthus." *Revue de Paris* 10 (1903): 846.

*   *   *

Chausson's only opera, *Le Roi Arthus,* begun in 1886, six years after its composer's first exposure to Wagner's *Tristan und Isolde* in Munich, was well received at its Brussels premiere and for some time thereafter. Yet it is an opera one is not ever likely to see; and no complete recording of it exists. Thus a working knowledge of its music depends entirely on a careful study of its score, preferably at the piano. One writer and commentator dismissed the opera for being "impeccably Wagnerian from beginning to end," but had he examined Chausson's libretto and score in greater detail, he could hardly have failed to see how exaggerated and unfair his pronouncement was. It is true that the principal elements of the story are those of *Tristan,* yet Chausson who, like Wagner, was his own librettist, interpreted his libretto very differently from Wagner. And parts of some scenes are musically Wagnerian (meaning Tristanesque). Both points will be treated more fully following the plot exposition.

Le Roi Arthus consists of three acts, each divided into two tableaux. As the opera opens King Arthur is at his court, surrounded by his knights of the Round Table with whom he is celebrating his recent victory over the Saxons. He and his queen, Guinevere, especially congratulate Lancelot for his exploits, thereby inflaming the jealous Mordred, ringleader of a small group of malcontents. Mordred's mood turns to fury when he overhears Guinevere quietly reminding Lancelot of their coming nocturnal tryst. In the second tableau Lancelot's squire, Lionel, keeps watch on the castle terrace and duly warns the lovers of the swiftly approaching day, but they pay no heed. Mordred bursts in, is pierced by Lancelot's sword and left for dead, although Guinevere sees him rise, helped by his henchmen. The third tableau (act II) finds the guilty couple later on at the edge of a forest, and in disagreement as to what course to pursue. Lancelot is consumed by guilt and remorse while the unrepentant Guinevere loudly demands that Lancelot save her honor. This difference is temporarily overcome, and the two sing an impassioned duet. The fourth tableau is set in Arthur's court where the king, beset by doubts as to the loyalty not only of Lancelot and Guinevere but also of the dissident knights, consults Merlin, his old magician. Merlin's prophecy is filled with gloom: Arthur will soon die and the Order of the Round Table will be destroyed. As the act closes Arthur prepares for war with his rebellious knights. Act III opens with Guinevere and an attendant watching the distant battle between Arthur's loyal knights and those who support Mordred. The king is now fully aware of Guinevere's and Lancelot's unfaithfulness. The wounded Lancelot approaches the queen to tell her of his decision to die with honor. After his departure the deserted queen strangles herself with her long hair. In the final tableau, following a battlefield reconciliation with the dying Lancelot, Arthur, his earthly tasks completed, is ferried away in a barge by invisible forces to a hereafter where he is promised rest from his labors and rewards for his idealism in establishing the Order of the Round Table, now unfortunately in ruins.

The illicit love which is the generating force in both *Le Roi Arthus* and *Tristan und Isolde* leads to circumstances and conclusions that are radically different in each opera. The key to these differences lies in the titles chosen by Chausson and Wagner, the former electing to emphasize Arthur as the noble, betrayed king, while the latter gives first place to the guilty lovers. Chausson's decision to make Arthur the central figure in *Arthus* meant that he was virtually obligated to develop the king's character to the extent of portraying him as the personification of all that is noble and good; and that, of course, depended on Arthur's reaction to the love that had developed between the two most important persons in his life. As time was an essential factor in the gradual delineation of Arthur's character, Chausson placed the lovers' nocturnal tryst in the first act, thereby allowing two whole acts for the king's disillusionment, not only with Lancelot and Guinevere but also with the dissident knights, to be transmuted into noble resignation and ultimate forgiveness. In the course of this successful character study, Chausson unwittingly revealed his own character, for his idealism and high moral standards made a deep impression upon all who were fortunate enough to know him.

One of the musically Tristanesque scenes in *Le Roi Arthus* is that containing the first-act love duet between Lancelot and Guinevere. The musical texture in Chausson's scene is largely composed of the emotionally charged chromaticism whose irresistible power made *Tristan* one of the great watersheds in western music. Such an influence is almost inevitable in a scene whose participants and events exactly parallel those in *Tristan*'s love duet. Yet other Wagnerian components such as a highly developed leitmotive system are totally absent in *Arthus.*

While it is neither possible nor appropriate to ignore the Wagnerian influences on *Arthus,* it would be a serious mistake to assume that the opera is *Tristan*-dominated. The style most consistently present interweaves the ordinary diatonicism of nineteenth-century opera—at times in a formula-ridden way—with the more complex language of Chausson's mature works. Thus the music of *Arthus* is made up of disparate elements, although considering the numerous interruptions over the nine years spent on the project the stylistic mixture is not surprising.

—Ralph S. Grover

LE ROI DE LAHORE [The King of Lahore].

Composer: Jules Massenet.

Librettist: Louis Gallet.

First Performance: Paris, Opera, 27 April 1877.

Roles: King Alim (tenor); Sitâ (soprano); Seindia (baritone); Timour (bass); Indra (bass); Kaled (mezzo-soprano); a Commander (baritone); a Soldier (baritone); chorus.

*   *   *

The action of *Le roi de Lahore* takes place in India in the eleventh century. Scindia, King Alim's First Minister, is in love with Sitâ, a priestess. Timour, the high priest, refuses to release her from her sacred vows. Sitâ confesses to Timour her nocturnal trysts with a mysterious lover. She is publicly denounced by Scindia for her refusal to love him. Her lover turns out to be King Alim himself, who, to atone for his crime, must fight the invading Muslims. In act II Scindia announces that the army has been defeated and Alim mortally wounded. Scindia, believing this to be a judgment on Alim's devious actions, usurps the throne. Alim is imprisoned and dies as Sitâ swears to love him forever. Act III takes place in the Garden of the Blessed in the god Indra's Paradise. Alim appears; Indra is so moved by his story that he allows him to return to life, not as king, but as an ordinary man who will die at the same instant as Sitâ. In act IV Alim awakens on the steps of the palace in Lahore as an ordinary man. It is the day of Scindia's coronation. As the grand procession moves toward the palace, Alim tries to kill Scindia. Act V takes place in Indra's sanctuary. Alim finds Sitâ, who is in hiding from Scindia. Scindia discovers the two lovers together, Sitâ stabs herself, and Alim, as divinely ordained, dies along with her.

Le roi de Lahore is in the French grand opera tradition, with five acts, much spectacle, and a ballet. The production, extremely popular with the public, was designed to exploit the vast resources of the Paris Opéra. The work was given almost sixty times in its first three years, and already in 1878 it had become extremely popular throughout Italy. This is especially noteworthy for, as Massenet notes in *Mes Souvenirs,* "at that time the only works translated into Italian and given in that country were those of the great masters." Within five years Dresden, Budapest, Munich, London, Buenos Aires, Rio de Janeiro, Prague, Madrid, and St Petersburg had

seen it. It was Massenet's first great success and only the third opera of his to be staged. Typically for French grand opera, grand, spectacular scenes—in this case temple scenes, royal processions, grand ensembles, off-stage but audible battles—alternate with intimate moments of lyrical beauty, projected in solos and duets.

An important component of the opera is the local color used for the Eastern exoticism and theme of mysticism. Massenet's obvious model in this regard was Georges Bizet's *Les pêcheurs de perles,* especially in act IV where Massenet's "C'est un Dieu qui l'inspire!" is clearly indebted to Bizet's duet "Au fond du temple saint." Massenet calls for a standard orchestra, but adds, for the first time, the saxophone. Exotic effects are also achieved through pseudo-Oriental harmonies and by use of the triangle. Previous to this opera Massenet had already made a name for himself as an orchestral composer with programmatic works such as "Scènes hongroises." The initial reviews for *Le roi de Lahore* praised his use of orchestra, especially in the overture and in the ballet music in act III, a melodic pastiche including a slow waltz for saxophone and a "Hindu" melody for flute with five variations. In this same act the influence of Charles Gounod is apparent, although not by way of mere imitation.

It is known that Massenet spent a number of years drafting *Le roi de Lahore,* its inception possibly going as far back as 1869. Large portions of the final work are probably drawn from earlier unfinished or unperformed pieces, such as an abandoned opera of his called *Les templiers.* The scene in Indra's Paradise is drawn from act II of Massenet's *La coupe du roi de Thulé,* a score he wrote for a competition in 1867 that won second place but was never performed. Massenet was an inveterate reviser and changer of his scores. During the initial Parisian run of the opera he added a "Romance-Sérénade" to the French original and subsequently made further changes for Italy, including a new scene at the beginning of act IV, a duet for Nair (Sitâ's name in the Italian version) and Timour; this duet was then replaced by an aria, "Ma non tremar d'orror," composed especially for Maddalena Marianna-Masi.

In April of 1879 the Opéra revived the work to great success. Tchaikovsky heard it, bought the score, and wrote the following to his patroness, Mme von Meck: *Le roi de Lahore* "has captivated me by its rare beauty of form, its simplicity and freshness of ideas and style, as well as by its wealth of melody and distinction of harmony."

—Stephen Willier

A poster for Massenet's *Le roi de Lahore*, Paris, 1877

LE ROI D'YS [The King of Ys].

Composer: Edouard Lalo.

Librettist: Edouard Blau (after a Breton legend).

First Performance: Paris, Opéra-Comique, 7 May 1888.

Roles: Mylio (tenor); Karnac (baritone); Saint Corentin (bass or baritone); Jahel (baritone or tenor); Margared (mezzo-soprano); Rozenn (soprano); chorus.

Publications

articles–

Fauquet, Joël-Marie. "Edouard Lalo et la Bretagne, les sources du *Roi d'Ys.*" In *Musique et société. La vie musicale en provence aux XVIIe, XIXe, et XXe siècles,* edited by Marie-Claire, Le Moigne-Mussat et al. Rennes, 1982. *Avant-scène opéra* 65 (1984) [*Le roi d'Ys* issue].

* * *

Lalo is an unusual figure in the history of French opera. From 1839 when he first came to Paris from Lille until 1885 when *Le roi d'Ys* premiered, his major interests and musical activities lay not in theater but in instrumental music. He is that rare composer who wrote a single important opera without any significant hands-on experience in the theater. When his first opera, *Fiesque,* after Schiller's play, *Fiesko,* did not win the competition sponsored by the Théâtre Lyrique in 1866, the composer had the vocal score published at his own expense and used the music in several different compositions.

In 1875 he began work on *Le roi d'Ys.* Extracts were performed in a concert version in 1881, but no theater in Paris would produce the work. Finally, in 1888 it was mounted at the Opéra-Comique to general approval. Whereas this opera was never overwhelmingly popular, it continues to enjoy critical esteem and over the years has been mounted in Paris alone over 125 times. The overture remains the best known portion of the opera.

The story is taken from an ancient Breton legend hammered into shape by Edouard Blau. In its legendary and mythic foundations it is curiously Wagnerian in its treatment of nationalistic mythic subjects which certain French critics and musicians of the time believed would be the means by which Wagnerian ideals could be translated into French music. Chabrier's *Gwendoline,* Reyer's *Sigurd,* even Debussy's *Pélleas et Mélisande,* come to mind in this context.

The complicated and twisted action takes place in the ancient Breton kingdom of Ys where two sisters, Margared and Rozenn, are secretly attracted to the same man, Mylio, who had mysteriously disappeared when a young boy. He reappears just as mysteriously when Rozenn mentions his name. Margared has been promised in marriage to Karnac, whom King Jahel has named as his successor. When Margared confesses her love for Mylio, who loves Rozenn, Karnac denounces Margared and threatens to destroy the city.

Mylio, Rozenn, and King Jahel believe Saint Corentin will deliver them. When Karnac challenges the Saint and seems to emerge the winner, the desperate Margared joins forces with him and reveals that Ys is protected from the sea by a chain of dikes. As the waters rise, Margared is seized with remorse and throws herself into the sea. St Corentin appears, and as Mylio and Rozenn fall on their knees and the people pray, the waters recede. Ys has been delivered.

The orchestral music is more successfully realized than are the vocal parts. One semi-effective scene follows another, and whereas there is obvious evidence of a talented composer at work, the opera in its entirety lacks overwhelming conviction. Yet, there is sufficient power within the music to warrant the occasional revival, particularly those scenes which use the organ, and one in which an offstage ghost and heavenly choir interact. The young Debussy was known to be an admirer of Lalo, and some find a reminiscence of this opera in *La cathédral engloutie* from the First Book of Preludes.

—Aubrey S. Garlington

LE ROI MALGRÉ LUI [The King in Spite of Himself].

Composer: Emmanuel Chabrier.

Librettists: Emile de Najac, Paul Burani, and J. Richepin (after a comedy by A. and M. Ancelot).

First Performance: Paris, Opéra-Comique, 18 May 1887.

Roles: Henri de Valois (baritone); Count of Nangis (tenor); Duke of Fritelli (baritone); Count Laski (bass); Basile (tenor); Villequier (bass); Liancourt (tenor); Elbeuf (tenor); Maugiron (baritone); Quelus (baritone); Soldier (bass); Minka (soprano); Alexina (soprano); chorus.

* * *

As usual, the composer of *Le roi malgré lui* was ill served by his librettists, and despite a number of improvements suggested by Chabrier himself, the libretto remains generally feeble, with little of the sparkling repartee one expects in light opera, of the sort provided for Offenbach by his librettist, Ludovic Halévy. Perhaps sixteenth-century history and farce do not make good bedfellows. The action is as follows. In a castle near Cracow, the Frenchman Henri de Valois is about to be crowned King of Poland: it was custom of the time for a foreigner to assume the Polish crown. Henri is homesick and wishes he were back in his native France. He discovers from Minka, his beloved, that a group of Polish noblemen, headed by Count Laski, has formed a conspiracy to dethrone and murder him. Henri disguises himself as his friend, the Count of Nangis, and joins the group of would-be murderers, offering to perform the fatal deed himself. When the real Nangis approaches the conspirators' hideout, his life is clearly at risk. After the usual confusion consequent upon such operatic disguises, both Henri and Nangis emerge unscathed, and Henri reluctantly agrees to be crowned King of France and Poland.

As in several of his stage works, Chabrier suffered the misfortune of seeing *Le roi malgré lui* taken off prematurely—in this case after only three performances—due to fire damage at the Opéra-Comique. Although the work was revived six months later, for some reason it failed to establish itself in Paris. Despite these setbacks, *Le roi malgré lui* set the seal on Chabrier's reputation, and the opera is regarded today as his masterpiece. It proves, beyond any doubt, that Chabrier's gifts lay in the field of comic rather than serious opera. *Le roi* is perhaps one of the clearest examples of an opera that triumphs over the absurd complications of its libretto by its wealth of musical resource. Unlike the earlier stage works, here the spoken dialogue complements rather than holds up the musical argument, a desirable feature that is usually striven for in opera with spoken dialogue. Ten years previously, *L'étoile* (The Star), musically the precursor of *Le roi,* had consisted of a string of delightful numbers often too condensed for what one feels the musical argument might have been capable of sustaining. However, in *Le roi* the phraseology is greatly expanded. The formal structures, though still basically simple in design, cover a broader canvas; the orchestration, more sumptuous and varied than it was in *L'etoile,* seems to enhance these extended musical parameters. Both the masterly "Fête polonaise" at the start of the second act, and the ensemble which brings the whole opera to a close, furnish indisputable proof of this breadth of utterance. The "Danse slave" (Slavonic Dance) embodies all the bounce and verve associated with Chabrier at his most inventive. Despite the conventionality of many of the lightweight characters in the work, Chabrier manages to infuse these prototypes with something approaching genuine emotional feelings.

Harmonically, the opera is an advance even on *Gwendoline,* particularly in its free employment of unprepared and unresolved seventh and ninth chords, which are heard to particularly good effect in the brief overture. Many of these harmonic originalities pass almost unnoticed due to the lightness of hand and coruscating wit with which Chabrier invests them. The work is a landmark in French opera because it demonstrated that it was possible to ally wit and sparkle with an advanced harmonic idiom. *Le roi* thus left its mark on a whole generation of French composers, notably Satie and Ravel. Owing to the enthusiastic propagation of Felix Mottl, the work had a great success in Germany, despite the censorious disapproval of Cosima Wagner, who heard the opera (with great distaste) at Karlsruhe in 1890. In the twentieth century, however, the opera has all but disappeared from the boards even in France. If Ravel's famous comment "I would rather have written *Le roi malgré lui* than *The Ring of the Nibelungs!*" betrays an excusable if exaggerated chauvinism, it does at least put into context the completeness of Chabrier's achievement. The fact that *Le roi* is heard of but never heard does nothing to diminish this achievement.

—J. Barrie Jones

ROLAND.

Composer: Jean-Baptiste Lully.

Librettist: Philippe Quinault.

First Performance: Versailles, 18 January 1685.

*   *   *

Roland, Lully's thirteenth opera, his twelfth *tragédie lyrique*—or, to use his own term, *"tragédie mise en musique"*—

takes as its dramatic point of departure "the delusions in which love can entangle a heart that disregards *la gloire.*" A standard of society reflected in almost all of Lully's imposing operatic entertainments, *la gloire* is in many ways an attribute not easily defined in terms of late twentieth-century sensibilities. Indeed, egalitarian-minded individuals likely will find it a difficult concept to come to terms with altogether. One definition might be the willingness to abide by an exalted code of conduct. In pre-1789 France, the characteristic evidently was the exclusive domain of the first estate, assuming of course the aristocratic person in question was disposed to performing some all-encompassing, magnanimous deed. As the idea was taken up by Lully and his librettist, Philippe Quinault, the deed itself was generally less important than the motivation of the protagonist. In other words, virtue is its own reward. Maidens are rescued from some calamitous fate, whole nations are freed from some menacing monster.

More specifically, Lully based his opera on Ludovico Ariosto's immensely popular epic poem *Orlando furioso* (completed in 1532), an action-packed mélange treating "Of Dames, of Knights, of armes, of love's delight" (to quote from the opening of John Harington's 1591 English verse translation), but given over in the main to the adventures of the Christian knight Roland (Orlando), nephew of Charlemagne, and the love triangle that develops between him, his beloved Angélique, and her subsequent infatuation with and marriage to the lowborn but handsome Saracen warrior Médor. The essential thread running throughout the opera is that badly-conceived love will bring ruin even to a noble soul.

French opera of the seventeenth century has aptly been described as "a product directed toward a specific audience of one, the king"—Louis XIV, the Sun King, who in his own estimation was a near relative of God. Not surprisingly, the Prologue that introduces the five-act *Roland* is a celebration in praise of Louis, who, personified by the mythological king Démogorgon, sings to his subjects that "Ruthless war will never ravage your happy hearts." The parallel undoubtedly was intended to favorably spotlight the recently signed Truce of Regensburg, a treaty concluded with the Habsburg Empire in August 1684 from which France otherwise peacefully annexed a number of territories in Lorraine and Alsace. Other current events were incorporated into the main body of the five-act opera. The first was the arrival of ambassadors from Siam in October of 1684. Knowing the Sun King's love of the unusual, Quinault and Lully obliged by creating scenes for "oriental natives" whenever dramatically appropriate in order to underscore the exotic origins of Angélique, Queen of Cathay. Similarly, Médor is billed as a "follower of one of the African Kings," a not-so-veiled reference to the fact that the French navy under Admiral Abraham Duquesne had conducted a campaign against Barbary pirates off the coast of Tripoli and had bombarded Algiers during the autumn of 1684. Whereas in Lully's previous *tragédies lyriques* both love and *la gloire* had been inseparable, in *Roland* love is judged less important. For while most of the opera revolves around Roland's indecision between his desire for love and his sense of duty to defend his country, he eventually is convinced by the allegorical embodiments of Fame and Glory that he has a more important mission than love: to deliver his country from its enemies and in turn safeguard his *gloire.*

It is perhaps difficult to understand how conventions as seemingly stifling as these could have blended with music to result in what Jacques Bonnet spoke of in his 1715 *Histoire de la musique* (speaking of the *tragédies lyriques* as a whole) as a force "moving enough to melt hearts and to make the very rocks to groan." And one must recall as well that unlike

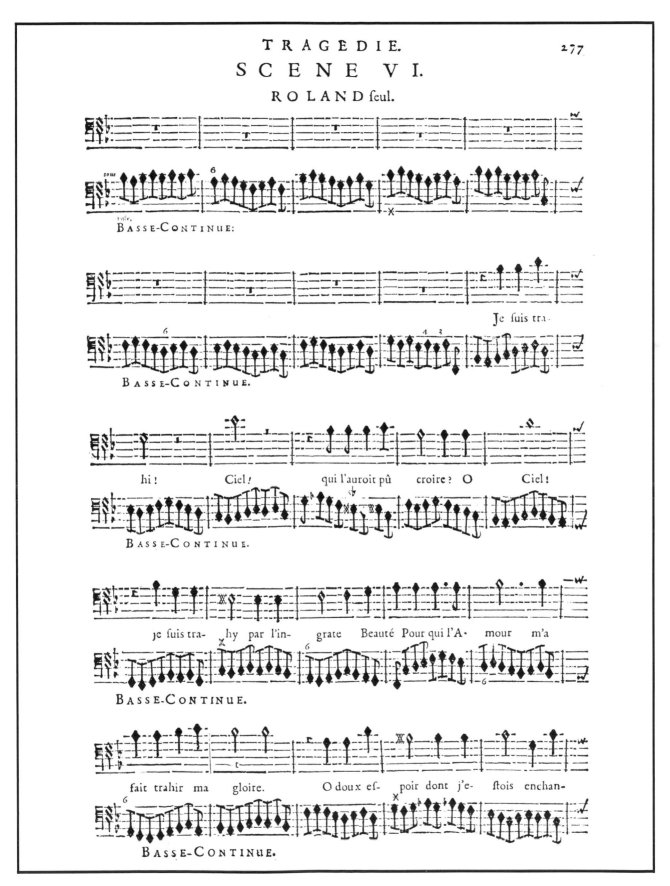

A page from Lully's *Roland,* first edition of full score, Paris, 1685

Lully's younger contemporary Marc-Antoine Charpentier, whose fortunes are running very high these days thanks to the efforts of H. Wiley Hitchcock (author of the impressive Charpentier thematic catalogue and lately of a study of the composer's life and music), only three of Lully's operas have appeared in modern performing editions (all in a series undertaken by Henry Prunières before his death in 1942). *Roland*, alas, is not one of them. Critical assessments therefore are obviously provisional. Nevertheless, reading through the sumptuous score of 1685, published by Christophe Ballard, one is struck by a number of deft touches. One example will have to suffice here.

Contrary to the famous 1683 assessment of the *tragédie lyrique* by Saint-Denys de Saint-Évremond, in which he described the genre as "something magnificently foolish laden with music, dances, machines, and scenery," one notes the remarkable way in which Lully integrates the divergent elements of dance, chorus, and song to heighten by contrast Roland's solitary tragedy in act IV. In scenes iii through v Roland has witnessed the village wedding of Angélique and Médor, an occasion that affords Lully the use of an elaborate succession of choruses and dances of joyful shepherds and shepherdesses. Disrupting the festivities at the end of scene v, Roland moves forward to address the faithless Angélique, saying that she has pierced his heart with "the most terrible blow." The chorus, already dramatically established, here interjects: "Ah! fuyons, fuyons tous" ("Ah! let us flee, let us all flee"), after which follows Roland's air of vengeance "Je suis trahi!" ("I am betrayed!"). The air, accompanied by only basso continuo (harpsichord and a bass string or woodwind instrument), a model of musical economy, stands in vivid contrast to the forces employed in the preceding three scenes. Delivering his invective with an almost motionless and understated intensity (the voice part is entirely syllabic and confined to the range of a single octave), Roland laments the folly upon which he had embarked, thereby emphasizing the didactic thrust of the entire opera: "I am betrayed! Heaven!" he intones, "I am betrayed by ungrateful Beauty, for whom Love has caused me to betray my *gloire!*"

—James Parsons

ROLLER, Alfred.

Designer. Born 2 October 1864, in Vienna. Died 12 June 1935, in Vienna. Studied painting with Griepenkerl and Lichtenfels, Vienna Academy; founding member of Vienna Sezession, 1890s; professor at the Vienna Kunstegewerbeschule, 1909, and director, 1909-34; designer, Hofoper, 1902; chief designer, 1903-09, 1918-34; chief designer, Burgtheater, 1918-34; also worked at major theaters in Berlin, Dresden, Salzburg, New York City, Philadelphia, and Bayreuth.

Opera Productions (selected)

Tristan und Isolde, Vienna, Hofoper, 1903.
Fidelio, Vienna, Hofoper, 1904.
Don Giovanni, Vienna, Hofoper, 1906.
Fidelio, Metropolitan Opera, 1907.
Elektra, Vienna, Hofoper, 1909.
Der Rosenkavalier, Dresden, 1911.
Die Frau ohne Schatten, Dresden, 1919.
Ring Cycle, Dresden.

Publications

By ROLLER: books and writings–

Regieskizze "Der Rosenkavalier." Berlin, 1910.
Skizzen zu Kostümen und Dekorationen von R. Strauss' "Die Frau ohne Schatten." Berlin, 1919.
Gedächtnisausstellung: Alfred Roller. Reichenberg, 1939. [catalogue of designs].

articles–

"Bühnenreform?" *Der Merker* 1 (1909): 193.
"Das Theater ist zweiern." *Die Szene* 18 (1928): 12.
"Bühne und Bühnenhandwerk." In *Thespis.* Edited by R. Roessler. Berlin, 1930.

About ROLLER: books–

Hevesi, L. *Altkunst-Neukunst: Wien 1894-1908.* Vienna, 1909.
Mell, M. *Alfred Roller.* Vienna, 1922.
Schuh, W., ed. *Der Rosenkavalier: Fassungen, Filmszenarium, Briefe.* Frankfurt, 1971.

articles–

Strauss, Richard. "Gedankworte für Alfred Roller." *Schweizerische Musikzeitung* 104, no. 4 (1964): 216-17.
Hadamowsky, F. "Regisseure und Bühnenbildner um Richard Strauss in Salzburg." *Österreichische Musikzeitschrift* 19 (August 1964): 366-68.
de la Grange, H.L. "Uproar in Vienna—When Gustav Mahler and Alfred Roller Staged 'Don Giovanni' in 1906, Tradition Was Thrown to the Winds." *Opera News* 38 (13 April 1974): 8-12.
Greisenegger, W. "Alfred Roller: Neubedeutung des szenischen Raumes." *Studia Musica* 31, nos. 1-4 (1989): 271.
Pausch, O. "Mahlerisches in den Rollerbeständen der Wiener Theatersammlung." *Studia Musica* 31, nos. 1-4 (1989): 343.

unpublished–

Kitzwegerer, L. *Alfred Roller als Bühnenbildner.* Ph.D. dissertation, University of Vienna, 1960.

*   *   *

Austrian designer Alfred Roller is an important figure in the history of opera for his trailblazing productions with Gustav Mahler at the Vienna Hofoper that prepared the way for designers and producers such as Wieland Wagner decades later. If Roller was not known for any other production, his elegant designs for Richard Strauss's *Der Rosenkavalier* would ensure him a place in operatic history. His career at the Hofoper reflected the ebb and flow of its production values: he was brought in under Mahler, left under Felix Weingartner, returned during Franz Schalk's directorship, and made his final innovations under Clemens Krauss.

Roller's background prepared him well for his role as an operatic iconoclast. He had been a founding member of the Vienna Sezession and was both teacher at and later director of the Kunstgewerbschule (School of Arts and Crafts). His first production with Mahler, who acted as both conductor and producer in Vienna in 1903, was Wagner's *Tristan und*

Isolde. This caused a furor among audiences and the press because of Roller's minimalist use of props and scenery, and more importantly, the striking lighting: blazing reddish-orange in act I, deep purple signifying night in act II; and gray in act III. Roller was often criticized in later years for his dim lighting, again anticipating post-World War II Bayreuth; "a night at the opera" became a running joke. In his experiments with lighting and color, he began to use velvet for sets, as it absorbed light and thus tended to intensify the colors on stage.

After the success of *Tristan,* the Hofoper offered Roller a contract. A production of *Don Giovanni* for the Mozart 150th anniversary year saw the introduction of what came to be known as "Roller Towers": massive and angular covered scaffolding at either side of the stage that could be moved to change the width of the stage, or turned to represent other buildings or structures. Roller could use this "permanent scenery"—now a standard concept in opera design—to change the scene with the use of only a few other props and backdrops.

Some of Roller's most important designs were for the premieres of operas by Strauss, designs which left their mark on later productions: the massive, towering castle with the narrow doorway through which all the characters had to pass in *Elektra;* the stunning rococo costume designs for *Rosenkavalier* and the silver hall of Faninal's palace for act II; the earth-tone sets of the human world contrasted with the Eastern-inspired elements for the spirit world in *Die Frau ohne Schatten;* and the elegant Grecian—by way of Paris—gowns for Maria Jeritza playing the most beautiful woman of all time in *Die ägyptische Helena.*

Roller's designs did not always aim toward simplicity; his set for *Siegfried* was so complicated that it took a day to set up and another day to strike. He continued to experiment with minimalist techniques and new ideas from the avant-garde in art. In his later years, a production of *Die Walküre* was strongly criticized because he omitted the tree under which Wotan puts Brünnhilde to sleep. Roller's son Ulrich also established himself as a talented designer before he was killed on the Russian front.

—David Anderson

ROLLI, Paolo Antonio.

Librettist/Poet. Born 13 June 1687, in Rome. Died 20 March 1765, in Todi. Studied with Gian Vincenzo Gravina; invited to England by the Earl of Pembroke and/or the Earl of Stair, 1715, where he taught Italian language and literature to noble families; Italian secretary to the Royal Academy of Music, 1719-22; secretary to the Opera of the Nobility, 1733-37; Fellow of the Royal Society, 1729; first to translate Milton's *Paradise Lost* into Italian, 1729-35; patent of nobility from Todi, 1735; applied unsuccessfully for Zeno's post as court poet in Vienna, 1736.

Librettos

Numitore, G. Porta, 1720.
Muzio Scevola (after S. Stampiglia), F. Amadei, G. Bononcini, G.F. Handel, 1721.
Floridante, (after Silvani, *La costanza in trionfo*), G.F. Handel, 1721.

L'Astarto, G. Bononcini, 1720.
L'odio e l'amore, A. Ariosti, 1721.
Crispo, G. Bononcini, 1722.
Griselda, G. Bononcini, 1722.
Erminia, G. Bononcini, 1723.
Scipione (after A. Salvi), G.F. Handel, 1726.
Alessandro (after O. Mauro, *La superbia d'Alessandro*), G.F. Handel, 1726.
Riccardo Primo (after F. Briani, *Isacio tiranno*), G.F. Handel, 1727.
Arianna, N. Porpora, 1734.
Fernando, Cerrigoni, 1734.
Enea nel Lazio, N. Porpora, 1734.
Polifemo, N. Porpora, 1735.
Ifigenia in Aulide, N. Porpora, 1735.
Sabrina (pasticcio), 1737.
Partenio, F.M. Veracini, 1738.
Busiri, ovvero il Trionfo d'Amore, G.B. Pescetti, 1740.
Deidamia, G.F. Handel, 1741.
Penelope, B. Galuppi, 1741.
Rosane, G.B. Lampugnani, 1743.
Alfonso, G.B. Lampugnani, 1744.
Alceste, G.B. Lampugnani, 1744.
Roselinda (after Shakespeare, *As You Like It*), F.M. Veracini, 1744.

Also many librettos for *pasticcios.*

Publications

By ROLLI: books–

Tondini, G.B., ed. *Marziale in Albion . . . premesse le memorie della vita dell' autore* [memoires]. Florence, 1776.

About ROLLI: books–

Fassini, S. *Il melodramma italiano a Londra nella prima metà del settecento.* Turin, 1914.
Vallese, T. *Paolo Rolli in Inghilterra.* Milan, 1938.
Deutsch, O.E. *Handel: a Documentary Biography.* London, 1955; New York, 1974.
Dorris, G.E. *Paolo Rolli and the Italian Circle in London.* The Hague, 1967.
Lindgren, Lowell. *A Bibliographic Scrutiny of Dramatic Works set by Giovanni and his Brother Antonio Maria Bononcini.* Ann Arbor, Michigan, 1974.
Dean, Winton, and John Merrill Knapp. *Handel's Operas: 1704-1726.* Oxford, 1987.
Gibson, Elizabeth. *The Royal Academy of Music 1719-1728: the Insitution and its Directors.* New York, 1989.
Harris, Ellen T. *The Librettos of Handel's Operas.* 13 vols. New York, 1989.

articles–

Fassini, S. "Il melodramma italiano a Londra ai tempi del Rolli." *Rivista musicale italiana* 19(1912): 35, 575.
Cellesi, L. "Un poeta romano e un sopranista senese." *Bullettino senese di storia patria* 37 (1930): 320.

*　　*　　*

Paolo Rolli, like his more famous contemporary Pietro Metastasio, was a pupil of Gian Vincenzo Gravina, a founding member of the Roman Arcadian Academy. In 1715 he came to London, staying for almost thirty years as poet, librettist, translator, editor, and teacher. As a librettist, Rolli was always connected to George Frideric Handel, either as collaborator or antagonist. Handel's settings of Rolli's texts include three cantatas written between 1718 and 1720, at least five operas for the Royal Academy of Music (1719-1729), and a handful of later operas, including Handel's last, *Deidamia* (1741).

At the opening of the Royal Academy, Rolli was appointed Secretary and principal librettist. Of the first ten Academy operas, only one opera did not have a libretto by him: *Radamisto* (1720), Handel's first opera for the Academy, was probably prepared by Nicola Haym. In 1722, Haym replaced Rolli as Secretary, undoubtedly with Handel's approval. From this point on, if not before, Rolli's relationship to Handel was strained. As early as 1720, he wrote to a friend, "I submit myself to all shows of humility towards [Handel] within the limits of decorum, and we shall see whether that bristly nature of his will soften."

As was generally the case with London opera, many of Rolli's operatic texts are adaptations of previous librettos. True to the goals of the Arcadian Academy (which favored operatic reform), his sources tend to be more recent than those of his competitor Haym. Giuseppe Riva, the Modenese envoy in London and Rolli's friend, points to this difference in a letter of 1725: he writes that Haym, "a complete idiot," has "been adapting—or rather making worse—the old librettos which are already bad enough in their original form." On the other hand, also true to the Arcadians, Rolli esteemed classical and neo-classical authors. He translated Virgil, Boccaccio, and Ariosto, among others, and made the first complete Italian translation of John Milton's *Paradise Lost*. His libretto for *Sabrina* (1737) is based on Milton's *Comus*.

Despite Rolli's long association with opera in London, his talent was not predominantly dramatic in character, and his librettos are most interesting in their lyrical moments. One characteristic that marks his work and indicates his tendency toward balance and symmetry rather than dramatic flexibility is the use of refrain structures in both recitative and aria. The first scene of *Floridante* (Handel, 1721) opens with an aria-like refrain enclosing dialogue in recitative. Act II, scene vii of the same opera is entirely composed of an accompanied recitative surrounded by refrains. The first scene of *Scipione* (Handel, 1726) breaks up a *da capo* so as to create a refrain structure: the first part of the aria is followed by extensive dialogue, after which the second part of the aria and the repetition of the first completes the scene. In act II, scene ii of this opera, Rolli again provides a refrain beginning for the scene (refrain-recitative-refrain), but in setting the text Handel chose to eliminate the opening refrain and recitative and thereby moved more quickly to the dramatic content of the scene.

Rolli's librettos are also typified by their lack of scenic descriptions and actions. Because this lack of visual imagination so contradicted Handel's style, it is sometimes possible to discover what is missing by comparing the printed libretto to Handel's score. In *Riccardo primo* (Handel, 1727), the libretto completely lacks a setting in two scenes, and in others the description is strikingly reduced: where the libretto's description reads "A royal pavilion. Richard and afterwards Pulcheria," the equivalent scene in Handel's score is headed by the composer: "The shore of Lamissus, with a royal pavilion, and a chair of gold on the side. Richard comes accompanied by his army, and afterwards Corrado and Pulcheria with her attending Ladies."

Rolli's style is also typified by long aria texts. The *da capo* aria calls for a text in two parts, which are set musically by repeating the first section after the second to create a large ABA form. Whereas Haym favored texts with three lines in each section, Rolli's texts frequently use more than four. For example, *Muzio Scevola* contains frequent five and six line strophes with rhymes that are tagged both within sections and across sections, such as abbcd/aeecd (I, iv) and aabbac/ddeedc (II, iii).

The stylistic features of librettos attributed to Rolli help to identify those that are unattributed. *Admeto* (Handel, 1727) has been assigned variously to Rolli and Haym, but its style argues strongly for Rolli's authorship. The aria texts are predominantly in four line strophes, with seven arias even longer. Act I, iv begins with recitative bounded by refrain, and act II, iv-v uses refrain structure in a more dramatic way, similar to the opening scene in *Scipione*. As in *Riccardo,* set descriptions are lacking and scenic layout is sloppy.

The increasing number of librettos by Rolli for Handel in the last four years of the Academy (four out of six Handel librettos from 1725 to 1728) coupled with Haym's death in 1728 might have led Rolli to believe that with the establishment of a second Academy in 1729 he would once again be appointed Secretary. In the event, this position went to another. Nevertheless, Rolli may have adapted Handel's *Sosarme* (1732). Shortly thereafter, however, he took the opportunity to become Secretary and principal librettist for the rival Opera of the Nobility (1733-37). In this capacity, he prepared *Arianna in Nasso* (Porpora, 1734) in direct competition with Handel's *Arianna in Creta* (1734); after Handel's revival of *Acis and Galatea* in 1734, he wrote an opera based in part on the same story, *Polifemo* (Porpora, 1735); and his *Sabrina* (1737), telling of an enchanter who turns his victims into animals and stone, surely was written in competition with Handel's *Alcina* (1735). He also adapted Handel and Haym's *Ottone* (with additional music by Porpora (1734), which competed with Handel's own revival of the same opera (1733).

After the collapse of the Opera of the Nobility in 1737, Rolli and Handel again collaborated, but *Deidamia* (1741) was Handel's last opera. In his last years in London, Rolli worked for an opera company formed by Lord Middlesex. Even so he was unable to escape Handel. In 1743 he adapted his and Handel's *Alessandro* under the new title of *Rossane* (with additional music by Lampugnani). Rolli's last libretto for London was *Rosalinda* (Veracini, 1744), an adaptation of Shakespeare's *As You Like It*.

—Ellen T. Harris

ROMANI, Felice.

Librettist. Born 31 January 1788, in Genoa. Died 28 January 1865, in Moneglia. Married: Emilia Branca, 1844. Studied at the University of Pisa; taught in Genoa; traveled extensively; settled in Milan, where he produced his first librettos for Mayr, beginning 1813; literary critic for the *Gazette ufficiale piemontesse,* and moved to Turin to become editor, 1834; career as a librettist until 1855; retired to Moneglia.

Librettos (selected)

Aureliano in Palmira, G. Rossini, 1813.
La rosa bianca e la rosa rossa, S. Mayr, 1813; P. Generali, 1819.

Medea in Corinto, S. Mayr, 1813; P. Selli, 1839; revised as *Medea,* S. Mercadante, 1851.

Atar ossia Il serraglio d'Ormus, S. Mayr, 1814; C. Coccia, carnival 1820-21; A.L. Mirò, 1836.

Il Turco in Italia (after Caterina Mazzola), G. Rossini, 1814.

Le due duchesse, ossia La caccia dei lupi, S. Mayr, 1814; F. Celli, 1824.

La testa di bronzo ossia La capanna solitaria, C.E. Soliva, 1816; S. Mercadante, 1827; D. Fontemaggi, 1835; V. Mela, 1855.

La sacerdotessa d'Irminsul, G. Pacini, 1817 (performed 1820).

Gianni di Parigi, F. Morlacchi, 1818; A. Speranza, 1836; G. Donizetti (set 1831), 1839.

Il finto Stanislao, A. Gyrowetz, 1818; as *Un giorno di regno,* G. Verdi, 1840.

La gioventù di Enrico V, G. Mosca, 1818; F. Morlacchi, 1823; S. Mercadante, 1834.

Il barone di Dolsheim, G. Pacini, 1818; F. Schoberlechner, 1827.

Le danaidi, S. Mayr, 1819; as *Danao re d'Argo,* G. Persiani, 1827.

Il contraccambio, G. Cordella, carnival 1819; as *La rappresaglia,* H. Stuntz, 1819.

Il falegname di Livonia, G. Pacini, 1819.

Il califfo e la schiava, F. Basili, 1819; G. Guaquerini, 1842; as *Adina* (revised by G. Bevilacque), Rossini, 1826.

Bianca e Falliero, o sia Il consiglio dei tre (after A. Arnhault, *Blanche et Montcassin*), Rossini, 1819.

Vallace, o L'eroe scozzese, G. Pacini, 1820.

I due Figaro, M. Carafa, 1820; G. Panizza, carnival 1823-24; Brogialdi, 1827; S. Mercadante, 1835; revised A. Speranza, 1839.

Margherita d'Anjou, G. Meyerbeer, 1820.

L'esule di Granata, G. Meyerbeer, 1821; revised as *Almanzor,* G. Tadolini, 1827.

Adele ed Emerico, ossia Il posto abbandonato, S. Mercadante, 1822.

Chiara e Serafina (after R.C.G. de Pixérécourt, *La cisterne*), G. Donizetti, 1822; as *I corsari,* A. Mazzucato, 1840.

Amleto, S. Mercadante, 1822.

Francesca da Rimini, F. Strepponi, 1823; S. Mercadante [not performed]: Carlini, 1825; M. Quilici, 1829; G. Staffa, 1831; G. Tamburini, 1835; E. Borgatta, 1836; E. Canneti, 1843; Franchini, 1857.

Giulietta e Romeo, L. Vaccaj, 1825; E. Torriani, 1828; revised as *I Capuleti e i Montecchi,* V. Bellini, 1830.

Il montanaro, S. Mercadante, 1827; as *L'incognito,* P. Campiuti, 1832; revised as *Il podestà di Gorgonzola,* G. Cagnola, 1854.

Il pirata (after M. Raimond), V. Bellini, 1827.

Bianca e Fernando (after Gilardoni), V. Bellini, 1828.

Alina, regina di Golconda (after S.J. de Boufflers), G. Donizetti, 1828.

La straniera (after Victor Charles Prévost), V. Bellini, 1829.

Rosmonda d'Inghilterra, C. Coccia, 1829; G. Donizetti, 1834; as *Rosmonda,* A. Belisario, 1835; revised, *Il castello di Woodstock,* P. Tonassi and P. Collavo, 1839; as *Enrico II,* O. Nicolai, 1839.

Zaira (after Voltaire), V. Bellini, 1829; A. Gandini, 1829; S. Mercadante, 1831; Mami, 1845.

Ernani, late 1830 [unfinished].

Anna Bolena (after Pindemonte and Pepoli), G. Donizetti, 1830.

La sonnambula (after a ballet-pantomime by Eugène Scribe and Jean-Pierre Aumer), V. Bellini, 1831.

Norma (after Louis Alexandre Soumet), V. Bellini, 1831.

I Normanni a Parigi, S. Mercadante, 1832.

Ugo, conte di Parigi (after Bis, *Blanche d'Acquitaine*), G. Donizetti, 1832.

L'elisir d'amore (after Scribe), G. Donizetti, 1832.

Ismalia, ossia Amore e morte, S. Mercadante, 1832; Carnicer, 1838; revised as *La fattucchiera,* V. Cuyás, 1838.

Beatrice di Tenda (after a novel by Carlo Tebaldi Fores and a ballet by Antonio Monticini), V. Bellini, 1833; R. Ticci, 1837; F. Guimaraes, 1882.

Parisina (after Byron), G. Donizetti, 1833; Giribaldi, 1878.

Lucrezia Borgia (after Hugo), G. Donizetti, 1833; revised by A. Pendola and P. Coppola as *Giovanna I Regina di Napoli,* 1840.

La figlia dell'arciere (with G.M. Mariani), C. Coccia, 1834; as *Adelia,* G. Donizetti, 1841.

Emma d'Antiocchia, S. Mercadante, 1834; revised as *Emma e Ruggero,* G. Bracciolini, 1838; Pontani, 1852; E. Cavazza, 1877.

Uggero il danese, S. Mercadante, 1834.

Francesca Donato ossia Corinto distrutta, S. Merdacante, 1835.

La solitaria delle Asturie, ossia La Spagna ricuperata, C. Coccia, 1838; S. Mercadante, 1840; L. Ricci, 1845; G. Sordelli, 1846; as *Matilde di Scozia,* G. Winter, 1852.

Publications

About ROMANI: books–

Regli, F. *Elogio a Felice Romani.* Turin, 1865.

Lianovosani, L. [G. Salvioli]. *Saggio bibliografico relativo ai melodrammi di F. Romani.* Milan, 1878.

Branca, E. *F. Romani ed i più reputati maestri di musica del suo tempo.* Turin, 1882.

Paschetto, C. *Felice Romani.* Turin, 1907.

Miragoli, L *Il melodramma italiano nell'ottocento.* Rome, 1924.

Schlitzer, F. *Mondo teatrale dell' 800.* Naples, 1954.

Rinaldi, M. *Felice Romani dal melodramma classico al melodramma romantico.* Rome, 1965.

Smith, P. *The Tenth Muse.* New York, 1970.

Portinari, F. *Pari siamo: io la lingua egli ha il pugnale. Storia del melodramma ottocentesco attraverso i suoi libretti.* Turin, 1981.

Dapino, C., and F. Portinari, eds. *Il libretto del melodramma dell'ottocento. Il Teatro Italiano,* 5/1. Turin, 1983.

articles–

Bustico, G. "Saggio di una bibliographia di libretti musicali di Felice Romani." *Rivista musicale italiana* (1906).

Tamassia Mazzarotto, B. "La riforma del Romani e i primi librettisti di Verdi." *Ateneo veneto* 118 (1935).

Tintori, G. "La Grisi, Bellini e Felice Romani." *L'Opera* (1966).

Fischer-Williams, B. "Prince of Sluggards." *Opera News* 37/ no. 15 (1973): 24.

Galatopoulos, Stelios. "The Romani-Bellini Partnership." *Opera* November (1977).

Collins, Michael. "The Literary Background of Bellini's *I Capuletti ed i Montecchi.*" *Journal of the American Musicological Society* 35 (1982): 532.

Parker, Roger. "*Un giorno di regno.* From Romani's Libretto to Verdi's Opera." *Studi verdiani* 2 (1983): 38.

Henze-Döhring, Sabine. " 'Combinammo l'ossatura . . .' Voltaire und die Librettistik des frühen Ottocento." *Die Musikforschung* 36/no. 3 (1983): 113.

Joly, Jacques. "Felice Romani; ou, Le Classicisme romantique." *Avant-scène opéra* July (1989).

*　　*　　*

Felice Romani was the most important Italian librettist of the first half of the nineteenth century. His librettos provided texts for more than one hundred composers including Mayr, Meyerbeer, Mercadante, Vaccai, Pacini, Rossini, Donizetti, Verdi, and probably most importantly, Bellini. Romani's career as a librettist spanned more than forty years—from 1813 to 1855. His librettos record the gradual disappearance from the Italian operatic world of the virtuous, noble, and rational characters of *opera seria* and also of the light-hearted, comic figures of *opera buffa*. Most of his librettos belong in the categories of *opera semiseria* and *melodramma*. The protagonists of his *melodrammas,* both male and female, frequently follow hopeless causes—most often desired union with an unattainable figure—to their deaths at the end of the opera. Preferred settings were the middle ages or renaissance—but the renaissance of Lucrezia Borgia rather than some more rational spirit.

Despite the romantic trappings and romantic patterns of behavior to be seen in his libretti, Romani was not a romantic. Patrick Smith noted that "trained as a classical poet, he never ventured far beyond classicism, and although he dutifully used the work of such poets as Victor Hugo or Byron, he never concealed his dislike for all the tenets of Romanticism they stood for (*Tenth Muse,* 201). In his stance as a critic he launched a polemic objecting to the romanticism of Manzoni's *I promessi sposi*. It is no coincidence that although Romani's life overlapped with Verdi's career for several decades, Verdi's single setting of a libretto by Romani—*Un giorno di regno,* previously set in 1818 as *Il finto stanislao* by Gyrowetz—resulted in one of his least characteristic and least successful operas. The disaffection was mutual: Romani was not an admirer of Verdi's works.

Romani's first librettos, *La rosa bianca e la rosa rossa* and *Medea in Corinto* were written for Simon Mayr, an important composer of the generation before Rossini, and the teacher of Donizetti. Romani provided three librettos for Rossini, ten for Donizetti, and sixteen for Mercadante. Although several of the librettos which Romani had written before meeting Bellini were successful in their own time, it was only during and after his collaboration with Bellini that he wrote librettos for operas which are still performed today. *La sonnambula* and *Norma, Anna Bolena, L'elisir d'amore* and *Lucrezia Borgia,* to name only the most famous, were all written between 1830 and 1833, the final years when Romani and Bellini worked together. Bellini and Romani sensed, and later commentators have agreed, that each found his truest voice through the other. Bellini, although no contemporary accounts describe him as a dominating or forceful personality, somehow persuaded Romani to work carefully and meticulously, to shape and reshape his texts, so that they were not merely satisfactory vehicles for music but rather a true partner in the expression of a sentiment.

Romani was the foremost practitioner of a profession whose status had declined considerably since its heyday in the time of Metastasio. One example of this is that at the end of a long and successful career, Romani was unable to arrange a publication of his collected librettos (indeed, there is still no such publication). Moreover, librettist was only one of the strings on Romani's literary bow; he was also a poet, essayist, journalist, critic, and editor.

Romani's librettos were based on pre-existing texts—usually French plays, but sometimes ballet scenarios or novels. Originality was not highly valued in librettists at that time. What was valued was fluency and fecundity, and those talents Romani had in abundance. In his most prolific year, Romani churned out eight librettos. Even his most routine texts show polished and refined verses arranged with good dramatic sense. His best works—*L'elisir d'amore, Anna Bolena,* and *Lucrezia Borgia* for Donizetti, *Il pirata, La straniera, La sonnambula,* and *Norma* for Bellini—provided the foundations for masterpieces.

—Charlotte Greenspan

Poster for Bellini's *Norma*, to a libretto by Felice Romani, Teatro alla Scala, 1834

ROMEO AND JULIET
　See ROMÉO ET JULIETTE

ROMÉO ET JULIETTE [Romeo and Juliet].

Composer: Charles Gounod.

Librettists: Jules Barbier and Michel Carré (after Shakespeare).

First Performance: Paris, Théâtre-Lyrique, 27 April 1867; revised to include ballet, Paris, Opéra, 28 November 1888.

Roles: Juliette (soprano); Roméo (tenor); Mercutio (baritone); Friar Laurence (bass); Stephano (soprano or mezzo-soprano); Gertrude (mezzo-soprano); Tybalt (tenor); Count Capulet (bass); Gregory (baritone); Benvolio (tenor); Duke of Verona (bass); Count Paris (baritone); chorus (SATB).

Publications

articles–

Avant-scène opéra 41 May-June (1982) [*Roméo et Juliette* issue].

There are more than eighty operas based on Shakespeare's *Romeo and Juliet,* including Bellini's version in which the part of Romeo is sung by a woman. It is, of course, impossible to equal Shakespeare's beauty of language or to preserve the complicated sub-plots and large number of characters. Gounod's librettists adopted a bold approach and reduced the play to the barest and most important elements. The narrative becomes a straightforward tale of tragic love between two young and attractive people, while the remaining characters—Friar Laurence, Gertrude, Capulet, and so on— are kept firmly in their places as minor cogs in the machinery of the plot.

Roméo et Juliette is, in effect, a series of four love duets. The madrigal sung by the lovers at their first meeting, "Ange adorable" ("Adorable angel"), is a stylized piece with an attractive archaic flavor, the mannered style justified by the preciosity of Shakespeare's language at this point. The balcony scene of act II opens with Roméo's "Ah! lève-toi soleil!" ("Ah! rise o sun!"), a cavatina that reproduces the spirit of the soliloquy "Arise, fair sun, and kill the envious moon." The second love duet, "O nuit divine," mingles recitative and aria and changes of mood and rhythm with a suppleness of style that mirrors every fluctuating emotion. Fully half of act IV is taken up with the duet portraying the fearful joy of the two lovers when Roméo visits Juliette by night. Their mellifluous "Nuit d'hyménée!" is suddenly shot through with anguish when Roméo hears "the lark, the herald of the morn." The final duet that leads to double suicide is underlined by solemn music that changes with the speed of April weather into a triumphant affirmation of love.

But the love duets, although they provide the basic structure of the opera, are by no means the whole of the story. A happy stroke gives us a prologue sung by unaccompanied voices with occasional interjections from the harp. The harmonies, strangely novel for the time and austere only in their prophecy of later developments in French music, wander tragically through unusual modulations. More traditional is Friar Laurence's "Dieu qui fit l'homme à ton image" ("God who made man in thy image"), an aria which recalls Sarastro

Jean De Reszke and Adelina Patti in Gounod's *Roméo et Juliette,* **Paris, 1888**

in *Die Zauberflöte*. Mercutio is also given a fine opportunity with the Queen Mab song, all quicksilver and urgent rhythms. So is Stephano, a character not found in Shakespeare, who, as a soprano *en travesti*, sings an Italianate *chanson*.

Apart from such minor blemishes as the waltz song and the pompous Second Empire mazurka that booms unrepentantly throughout the ball at the Capulets' in act I, *Roméo et Juliette* is notable for the consistency of its inspiration. The orchestral writing is fluently responsive to the demands that are made on it. Moods and atmosphere are quickly established with economy. While composing the opera Gounod lived like a man possessed, sorrowing with his characters and rejoicing in their pleasure. He believed passionately in what he was creating, and he felt, he said, like a young man of twenty again. This fresh quality, this keenness of feeling unblunted by the cynicism of middle age or the disillusionment of the years, are what give *Roméo et Juliette* a vitality and a spontaneity which keep it alive in performance today.

—James Harding

LA RONDINE [The Swallow].

Composer: Giacomo Puccini.

Librettist: Giuseppe Adami (translated from a German libretto by Alfred Maria Willner and Heinz Reichert).

First Performance: Monte Carlo, 27 March 1917.

Roles: Magda de Civry (soprano); Lisette (soprano); Ruggero Lastouc (tenor); Prunier (tenor); Rambaldo Fernandez (baritone); Périchaud (bass or baritone); Gobin (tenor); Crébillon (bass or baritone); Yvette (soprano); Bianca (soprano); Suzy (mezzo-soprano); Rabonnier (bass); a Butler (bass); a Singer (soprano); a Grisette (soprano); a Student (tenor); chorus (SSTTBB).

*   *   *

By 1913, Puccini was firmly established as the leading figure in Italian opera. His latest work, *La fanciulla del West,* which was premiered at the Metropolitan Opera in 1910, had scored remarkable successes around the world. In October of 1913, it was given in Vienna, and Puccini attended the production. It was during this stay in Vienna that he was approached by Harry Berté and Otto Eisenschütz, the directors of the *Karltheater,* at that time the foremost operetta theater in Vienna. Out of this encounter grew a commission for a new operetta, which is to say a piece consisting of separate numbers interspersed with spoken dialogue. This would have been a new and unaccustomed genre for Puccini; indeed, after some objections on his part, it was decided that the new piece would be a full-scale opera, with music throughout. The result was *La rondine*.

The genesis of the libretto is remarkable. The operetta text was to be provided for Puccini in German, and Puccini was to arrange for a translation into Italian. He would then set the music, and the finished result would be re-translated into German. Eventually, when the decision was made that spoken dialogue would be altogether omitted, Giuseppe Adami became in essence the sole librettist, and the two Viennese

writers, Willner and Reichert, who had supplied the original German text, were to translate the finished result into German.

The story of *La rondine* is set in Paris and on the French Riviera during the Second Empire. Magda, concubine of the wealthy Parisian banker Rambaldo, is hosting a party with Rambaldo at her salon in Paris. Ruggero, the son of an old school friend of Rambaldo, appears at the party. As it is the first time Ruggero is in Paris, the guests suggest several dance halls to him as suitable places for a first night's entertainment. Lisette, Magda's maid, suggests that he visit *Chez Bullier.* When Ruggero and the guests have left, Magda, who had barely noticed Ruggero, decides to spend the evening at *Bullier*'s as well.

Magda, wearing her maid's dress so as to remain incognito, chances upon Ruggero, who does not recognize her. She introduces herself as Paulette, and in the course of the evening they fall in love. Magda decides to break up with Rambaldo and leaves with Ruggero to live on the Riviera. One day, Ruggero tells Magda that he has asked his mother's permission to marry Magda. His mother has sent a letter in which she approves of the marriage, provided that Magda is a pure and virtuous woman. When Magda reads this letter, she is deeply moved and decides to reveal her past to Ruggero. Against his protests, she tells him that she cannot marry him; she can be his mistress, but not his wife. She leaves him to return to Rambaldo.

As is all too clear, the story shows remarkable parallels to *La traviata,* except that Magda, unlike Violetta, does not die in the end. Upon closer examination, however, it is difficult to regard *La rondine* as having the same seriousness of intent as *La traviata.* Clearly, the work was never intended as a tragedy, given its original conception as an operetta. At the same time, it is not light-hearted enough to pass as a comedy, and therein lies its greatest flaw. It is difficult to feel empathy for any of the characters because the emotional appeal is not strong enough; on the other hand, not enough room is given for any comic development. The lack of commitment to either dramatic option in *La rondine* ultimately fails to involve the listener in the story.

Overall, *La rondine* is one of Puccini's most disappointing operas. Its greatest weakness lies in the libretto, and it is hard to avoid the conclusion that Puccini was uninspired by it himself. But the score is certainly not without merit. In a letter to Sybil Seligman from September 1914, Puccini writes regarding *La rondine:* "it's a light sentimental opera with touches of comedy—but it's agreeable, limpid, easy to sing, with little waltz music and lively and fetching tunes . . . it's a sort of reaction against the repulsive music of today— which, as you put it so well, is very much like the war!"

The characterization is fitting. The score contains some exquisite melodies in the typical Puccinian mold, the most famous example being Prunier's/Magda's aria "Chi il bel sogno di Doretta." While the harmonic style is mostly straightforward, there are some conspicuous passages of bolder invention, with expanded harmonies, unresolved dissonances, instances of bitonality, and unmitigated harmonic shifts. The orchestration is skillfully handled and delicately scored. Despite the opera's dramatic shortcomings, Puccini's attention to musical detail is noticeable throughout the score.

—Jürgen Selk

ROSBAUD, Hans.

Conductor. Born 22 July 1895, in Graz. Died 29 December 1962, in Lugano. Studied at the conservatory in Frankfurt; director of the Hochschule für Musik in Mainz, 1921-30, and conducted the city orchestra there; first Kapellmeister of the Frankfurt Radio and of the Museumgesellschaft concerts, 1928-37; Generalmusikdirektor in Münster, 1937-41; Generalmusikdirektor in Strasbourg, 1941-44; Generalmusikdirektor of the Munich Philharmonic, 1945; principal conductor of the Southwest Radio, Baden-Baden, 1948; music director of the Tonhalle Orchestra, Zurich, 1957; conducted the premiere of Schoenberg's *Moses und Aron* (radio performance), Hamburg, 1954.

Publications

About ROSBAUD: articles–

Evans, J. "The Hans Rosbaud Library at Washington State University, Pullman, Washington, U.S.A." *Notes* September (1984).

* * *

Conductor Hans Rosbaud is remembered as a champion of contemporary music. He was a close associate of several twentieth-century composers, including Hindemith, Schoenberg, Berg, Webern, Stockhausen, Stravinsky, Bartók, and Boulez, and was known for the clarity and classical balance of his performances of the modern repertoire as well as music of the classical and late romantic periods.

Highly regarded by Stravinsky, who called him "the most scrupulous of musicians and one of the few non-delinquent conductors," Rosbaud conducted Stravinsky's *Mavra* in a double-bill with *Oedipus Rex* in a radio concert in Frankfurt in 1932. With the composer in the audience, he led *Oedipus Rex* again in 1952 at the Théâtre des Champs-Elysées. In a letter of recommendation, Stravinsky wrote in 1936: "I know Hans Rosbaud, a pure-blooded musician, an aristocrat among conductors. I know his fine talent, his exemplary humility, his perserverence, his tenacity, the exactitude of his baton, his artistic conscience and integrity."

On 11 June 1934 Rosbaud conducted a concert performance (although with substantial cuts) of Richard Strauss's rarely performed first opera, *Guntram,* on the occasion of the composer's seventieth birthday, a concert that was broadcast by Berlin Radio.

Rosbaud has been connected with the Aix-en-Provence Festival from its inception in 1948. He was the conductor of its initial production, Mozart's *Così fan tutte* (which he repeated in 1957), and later led Mozart's *Le nozze di Figaro* (1955) and *Don Giovanni* (1956). He remained with the festival until 1959.

Rosbaud has been closely associated with the operas of Schoenberg. Having worked extensively with Schoenberg on many of his nonoperatic works, he was selected to conduct the first performance of *Moses und Aron* on a few days notice when the scheduled conductor, Hans Schmidt-Isserstedt, became ill. A radio performance from the Hamburg Musikhalle, this formed the basis for the first recording of the work. In 1957 Rosbaud led the first stage production, at the Zurich Stadttheater, for which he reportedly had held 350 choral and fifty orchestral rehearsals. At the Holland Festival, in 1958, he led a double bill of the same composer's *Erwartung* and *Von heute auf morgen.*

Despite his renown for leading twentieth-century music, Rosbaud's relatively few recordings were predominantly of the eighteenth-century repertoire. These include Mozart's *Don Giovanni* (1956), based on the Aix-en-Provence festival performance of that year, and a highly regarded recording of Gluck's *Orfeo ed Euridice* (1956); of this recording, Max Loppert wrote "If I wished to explain what I meant by a spacious, serene moulding of the music, in which steadiness of tempo is the dominant feature and in which emotional weight is never lacking nor allowed to become mere heaviness of statement, I would base my demonstration on long stretches of his Philips recording. . . . Number after number, whether it be the cumulative dark energy of the Dance of the Furies or the luminous poignancy of 'Objet de mon amour,' is unfolded with an unwavering, never rigid hand. There is air and light in the orchestral playing, and breath for the length of the singers' phrases."

—Michael Sims

DER ROSENKAVALIER [The Knight of the Rose].

Composer: Richard Strauss.

Librettist: Hugo von Hofmannsthal.

First Performance: Dresden, Court Opera, 26 January 1911.

Roles: Princess von Werdenberg, The Marschallin (soprano); Octavian (mezzo-soprano or soprano); Sophie (soprano); Baron Ochs von Lerchenau (bass); Herr von Faninal (baritone); Singer (tenor); Marianne (soprano); Valzacchi (tenor); Annina (contralto); Police Commissioner (bass); Marschallin's Majordomo (tenor); Faninal's Majordomo (tenor); Attorney (bass); Innkeeper (tenor); Three Noble Orphans (soprano, mezzo-soprano, contralto); Milliner (soprano); Animal Vendor (tenor); Four Footmen (two tenors, two basses); Four Waiters (tenor, three basses); Scholar, Fluteplayer, Hairdresser, His Assistant, a Widow, Mahomet (all mute); chorus (SAATTBB).

Publications

books–

Pryce-Jones, A. *Richard Strauss: Der Rosenkavalier.* London, 1947.
Pörnbacher, K. *Hugo von Hofmannsthal/Richard Strauss: Der Rosenkavalier.* Munich, 1964.
Schnoor, H. *Die Stunde des Rosenkavalier: 300 Jahre Dresdener Oper.* Munich, 1968.
Schuh, W. *Der Rosenkavalier: 4 Studien.* Olten, 1968.
———, ed. *Hugo von Hofmannsthal, Richard Strauss: Der Rosenkavalier: Fassungen, Filmszenarium, Briefe.* Frankfurt am Main, 1971.
Erté's Costumes and Sets for "Der Rosenkavalier". Introduction by John Cox. New York, 1980.
Stewart, Robert Sussman, ed. *Richard Strauss: Der Rosenkavalier.* New York, 1982.
Jefferson, Alan. *Richard Strauss: Der Rosenkavalier.* Cambridge, 1985.
Schlötterer, Reinhold, ed. *Musik und Theater im "Rosenkavalier" von Richard Strauss.* Vienna, 1985.

articles–

Wasdruszka, A. "Das *Rosenkavalier* Libretto." *Öster-reichische Musikzeitschrift* 24 (1969).

Gerlach, R. "Die ästhetische Sprach als Problem im *Rosenka-valier.*" *Neue Zeitschrift für Musik* 1 (1975).

Perusse, Lyle F. "*Der Rosenkavalier* and Watteau." *Musical Times* 119 (1978): 1042.

Zimmerschmied, D. "Integration in Liebe oder brutale Ver-treibung? Versuche zur Deutung der Sängerepisode im *Rosenkavalier.*" *Die Musikforschung* 32 (1979).

Heldt, Gerald. ". . . aus der Tradition gestaltet: Der Rosenka-valier und seine Quellen." in *Ars musica, musica scientia. Festschrift Heinrich Hüschen,* 233. Cologne, 1980.

Partsch, Erich Wolfgang. "Die 'missglückte' Operette. Zur stilistischen Position des *Rosenkavaliers.*" *Österreichische Musikzeitschrift* 38 (1983): 159.

Avant-scène opéra November-December (1984) [*Le chevalier à la rose* issue].

Springer, Morris. "The Marschallin: a Study in Isolation." *Opera Quarterly* 2 (1984): 56.

*   *   *

"That summer, the summer of 1914, it seemed as if the whole of London was a ballroom. . . . The dance tunes continued until the end to sound through the windows: fox-trots, tangos, and waltzes. And though that summer the waltzes were fewer in number when compared with other rhythms, nevertheless one of them reigned supreme in every ballroom, the waltz from *Rosenkavalier,* that mocking parody of the old order, that triumph of Ritz-Eighteenth Century. With its seductive rhythms, its carefully hidden cleverness, it was the last song of an era. . . ." Thus Osbert Sitwell wrote in his novel *Those Were the Days,* a chronicle of British high society life. In the summer of 1914, *Der Rosenkavalier* was only three years old, yet it already symbolized a pleasant past in which slightly scandalous intrigue flourishes but young love conquers all.

Strauss' favorite librettist, the poet Hugo von Hofmanns-thal, set his plot in the Vienna of Maria Theresa (i.e., mid-eighteenth century). A field marshal's wife (the Marschallin), still beautiful but beginning to age, is having a dalliance with the 17-year-old Octavian. The Marschallin's country-bred cousin, the boorish Baron Ochs, is about to marry the lovely Sophie, daughter of a wealthy bourgeois, von Faninal. According to local custom, Ochs requires a young cavalier to present a silver rose to his intended, and the Marschallin recommends Octavian for the task. When the actual presenta-tion takes place, in act II, Octavian and Sophie fall forthwith in love. In act III, Octavian, dressed as a girl, entices the philandering baron to an inn to expose his true character. All ends happily, with the two young lovers singing an ecstatic duet (to which the sound of the celesta lends an ethereal quality) while Ochs decamps and the Marschallin is left to face the realization that the ravages of time are coming ever closer.

For all the skill and variety of Hofmannsthal's libretto, it is Strauss' richly lyrical and psychologically apt score that

Act II of *Der Rosenkavalier,* **production by Herbert von Karajan, Salzburg Festival, 1983**

has elevated *Der Rosenkavalier* to its generally accepted rank as an operatic comedy that can bear comparison to such masterpieces as Mozart's *Le nozze di Figaro,* Wagner's *Die Meistersinger* and Verdi's *Falstaff.* As in all of Strauss' works, the orchestra is not least among his protagonists. The work opens with a near-symphonic episode designed to depict, before the curtain rises, the passionate nature of the affair between Octavian and the Marschallin. Similarly, act III is preceded by a brilliant instrumental *fugato* suggesting the conspiratorial activities of Valzacchi and Annina, two intriguers hired by Ochs to aid his amatory pursuit of the disguised Octavian. The orchestra is even accorded the final music of the opera, which ends with a black pageboy scampering across an otherwise empty stage to pick up a handkerchief dropped by Sophie.

It also is Strauss' delectable music rather than the sometimes convoluted stage action that saves the day in several drawn-out episodes during which a listener might be tempted to remark, with Christopher Sly: "'Tis a very excellent piece of work. . . . Would 'twere done!" A case in point is a good portion of act III, in which the farcical antics of Valzacchi and Annina grow wearisome, perhaps because one is impatiently awaiting the incadescently beautiful trio in which Octavian, with Sophie at his side, takes final leave of the Marschallin, who quietly and resignedly calls for God's blessing on the young couple.

Despite the sexual innuendo of its opening scene (in which Octavian and the Marschallin are practically discovered in bed), *Der Rosenkavalier* breathes a more wholesome air than either of Strauss' previous operatic successes, *Salome* and *Elektra.* It also is far longer (well over three hours) and musically expansive, with a huge cast and an orchestra of over one hundred. Ironically, Hofmannsthal had originally proposed it as a short comic opera, even including a ballet. The character of the Marschallin was not in the original *dramatis personae,* but once she entered she took over as the dominant personality. As the work expanded in size, it developed a radiant and robust quality of its own. The ballet episode never came to pass, but in its place there is a good deal of lusty stage business, most notably the Marschallin's act I *levée,* a madcap reception in her salon in which she receives a motley crowd of petitioners, suppliants, entertainers (including an Italian tenor who sings a fine aria), salespersons, attendants, and household staff—an enchanting and vivid portrayal of eighteenth-century Viennese society as it may or may not have existed.

In addition to its period flavor and scenic variety, *Der Rosenkavalier* flourishes in opera houses throughout the world because of its rich musical characterizations. The Marschallin, Ochs, and Octavian are all unmistakably identifiable by the music they sing. Strauss wanted the Marschallin not to be depicted as decrepit, superannuated or even past her prime. "Octavian is neither her first lover nor her last," he wrote, suggesting that she display sorrow in one eye and gaiety in the other as their affair comes to an end. He also wanted her to exhibit "Viennese grace and lightness" and expressed the hope that conductors wouldn't give her draggy tempos. She is a woman afraid not of life, but of time. Her most moving words of all (are there any simpler in all opera?) are the cryptic "Ja, ja!" with which, at the close, she replies to Faninal's hearty but not very original observations that young people will be young people. Finding just the right way to sing these words is a constant challenge for Marschallins.

Ochs, too, is a more complicated character than he seems. It is a mistake for singers to present him as an out-and-out buffoon; he is, after all, an aristocrat, even if rough around the edges, and he is hopelessly out of his depth among a courtly coterie of sophisticated intriguers and voluptuaries whose moral level really isn't much higher than his. Strauss' music for Ochs, with its bluff heartiness, broad melodic appeal and artful touches of vulgarity, limns his character perfectly.

Octavian is frequently compared to Cherubino in *Le nozze di Figaro,* and indeed Strauss, after completing *Elektra,* had announced his intention of composing a Mozartean opera. No doubt there are certain resemblances: the mezzo voices, the fact that both are trouser-roles, the ease with which many singers slip from one part to the other. Yet the differences are significant: Cherubino has a quality of innocence lacking in the worldly Octavian, and he certainly is less discursive. Still, who is to say that the two "boys" might not enjoy comparing notes—and not necessarily musical ones?

—Herbert Kupferberg

ROSPIGLIOSI, Giulio.

Librettist/Statesman/Leader of the Catholic Church. Born 28 January 1600, in Pistoia. Died 9 December 1669, in Rome. Studied philosophy, theology, and law at Pisa; in the service of the Barberini family, Rome; papal nuncio in Spain, 1644-55; apostolic secretary of state under Alexander VII and became a cardinal, 1657; elected to the papacy (Pope Clement IX), 1667.

Librettos

Sant' Alessio, S. Landi, 1631.
Erminia sul Giordano (after Tasso, *La gerusalemme liberata*), M. Rossi, 1633.
Santa Theodora ovvero Didimo e Teodora, 1635.
Il Falcone (Che soffre speri) (after Boccacio, *Decameron*), V. Mazzocchi, 1637; revised as *L'Egisto,* or *Che soffre speri,* V. Mazzocchi and M. Marazzoli, 1639.
San Bonifatio, V. Mazzocchi, 1638.
L'innocenza difesa, V. Mazzocchi, 1641.
Il palazzo incantato d'Atlante ovvero La guerria amante (after Ariosto, *Orlando furioso*), L. Rossi, 1642.
Il Sant' Eustachio, M. Marazzoli and V. Mazzocchi, 1643.
La comica del cielo, ossia La Baltasara, A.M. Abbatini, c. 1653.
Dal male in bene, A.M. Abbatini and M. Marazzoli, 1654.
Le armi e gli amori, M. Marazzoli, 1656.
La vita humana ovvero Il trionfo della pietà, M. Marazzoli, 1656.
La Datira.
L'Adrasto.
La Sofronia.

Publications

About ROSPIGLIOSI: books–

Sanesi, J. *Poesie musicale di Giulio Rospigliosi.* Pistoia, 1894.
Canevazzi, G. *Papa Clemente IX poeta.* Modena, 1900.
Murata, M.K. *Operas for the Papal Court, 1631-1668.* Ann Arbor, 1981.

articles–

Ademollo, G. "Il melodramma italiano e Clemente IX (Rospigliosi)." *Opinioni* (1879).

Salsa, A. "Drammi inediti di Giulio Rospigliosi, poi Clemente IX." *Rivista musicale italiana* 14 (1907): 473.

Rolandi, U. "La prima commedia musicale rappresentata a Roma nel 1639." *Nuova Antologia* (1927).

Reiner S. "Collaboration in *Che soffre speri.*" *Music Review* (1961).

Murata, M.K. "Rospigliosiana, ovvero Gli equivoci innocenti." *Studi musicali* (1975).

Witzenmann, W. "Die römische Barock Oper *La vita umana ovvero Il trionfo della pietà.*" *Analecta Musicologica* 15 (1975).

Murata, M.K. "Il carnevale a Roma sotto Clemente IX Rospigliosi." *Rivista italiana di musicologia* 12 (1977): 83.

The development of a distinctly Roman style of opera in the seventeenth century is due largely to the efforts of Giulio Rospigliosi, who was a student of philosophy and theology, diplomat and administrator, patron of arts under two Popes, and himself elected Pope under the title of Clement IX. In this highly successful career, Rospigliosi achieved an extraordinary balance between artistic and political accomplishments. Rospigliosi was a gifted librettist with a highly acute sense of theater. He was able to both incorporate and modify elements from such disparate sources as early Florentine opera and mid-seventeenth century Spanish theater, yet all the while working within the political and moral constraints of the papal administration in which he was so deeply involved. The operas set to Rospigliosi's librettos were by no means ephemeral productions. Rather, they were among the most important full-length theatrical works of their time. Frequently repeated in subsequent years, they featured the best Roman and foreign singers and highly elaborate and intricate stage effects, all to project the glory of Rome and the papacy to visiting heads of state, ambassadors, and the like.

Despite his likely exposure to Florentine opera, Rospigliosi was apparently not preoccupied with the neo-classic urges that inspired the first generations of librettists and opera composers. As compared with Rinuccini's *Euridice* or *Arianna*, for example, Rospigliosi's librettos are longer and more substantial. Rather than writing tragicomedies set exclusively in the mythological or pastoral realm—an example followed by some of his Roman colleagues—Rospigliosi's librettos represent a broad range of genre types: romantic secular comedy, *rappresentazioni spirituali,* and tragic secular drama. This assortment of genres resulted in operas with varied musical realizations, differing in such features as recitative style or number and distribution of arias and other closed musical forms. Nevertheless, Rospigliosi's works are surprisingly consistent in their preoccupation with certain themes, in particular with man's personal dilemma and responsibility in the eternal struggle between evil and good.

Rospigliosi's career as a librettist can be divided into two distinct periods: those works written during the reign of Pope Urban VIII (1623-44) and those completed under the reign of Pope Alexander VII (1655-67). In Rospigliosi's first major libretto, *Sant' Alessio* (1631) a *dramma spirituale* set to music by Stefano Landi, the central character is torn between the temptations of a pagan world, the evils of humanity, and the desire to lead a Christian life. The long lost Alessio tries to adhere to an ascetic Christian life while living among his family disguised as a hermit. He resists the efforts of the devil to seduce him into the world of paganism and luxury, and he dies and ascends to heaven (not without stage machinery and special effects depicting the glories of heaven and the horrors of hell). Rospigliosi explores the conflicts of the Christian saints again in *Santa Theodora* (1635), which also places the pagan and Christian worlds in opposition, culminating in the martyrdom of saints Didimo and Theodora. A similar tragic fate awaits the title characters of *San Bonifatio* (1638), and *Sant' Eustachio* (1643). In *Genoinda*, also known as *L'innocenza difesa* (1641), a *dramma tragico per musica,* considered by Margaret Murata as one of Rospigliosi's most serious and tightly constructed dramatic works, the evil of mankind is personified in a genuine human villain. *Chi soffre speri* (1637), a *commedia in musica* based on a tale of Boccaccio, is a secular but largely serious work, often cited in discussions of early comic opera for its use of *commedia dell'arte*-type characters. Rospigliosi briefly visits the pastorale world in his two works based on popular sixteenth-century crusade epics: *Erminia sul Giordano* (1633), based on Tasso's *La gerusalemme liberata;* and *Il palazzo incanto* (1642), based on Ariosto's *Orlando Furioso*. Both of these works are distinctive in their increased use of subplots, their mixture of the comic and serious, resulting in a less tightly constructed dramatic narrative and more elaborate musical display.

The second period in Rospigliosi's literary career is marked by his first-hand exposure to the Spanish theater during his ambassadorship in Spain. As the often-noted relationship between Italian seventeenth-century opera and the contemporary Spanish theater is not entirely understood, Rospigliosi's direct adaptation of three of his later operas from known Spanish dramatic sources is particularly notable. *Dal male in bene* (1654), based on a play by Antonio Sigler de Huerta, is a romantic comedy in which the union of two pairs of lovers is frustrated by such conventional devices as mistaken identity and misconstrued intentions, assisted by well-meaning and irreverent servants. Similar themes predominate in *Le armi e gli amori* (1656) based on Pedro Calderón de la Barca's *Los empeños de un acaso*. *La comica del cielo* (not performed until 1668; likely written in Spain before 1653), based on the Spanish play *Baltasara,* is somewhat reminiscent of Rospigliosi's earlier works, as it deals with Baltasara's conversion to Christianity and temptations by the devil. *La vita humana* (1656) is in many ways a culmination of themes with which he was preoccupied for much of his life. In this opera, the central character is the allegorical representation of Human Life, who, assisted by Innocence and Human Understanding, faces the ultimate battle with Pleasure and Guilt.

Poised at the end of the Renaissance and the beginning of the early modern age, Rospigliosi's focus is on man's internal battle in both the sacred and secular realms. As Margaret Murata points out, for Rospigliosi, "the significant battle takes place in individual souls; the personal struggle defines and strengthens their worthiness for salvation. . . . He makes it clear that the burden of responsibility lies within man himself."

—Wendy Heller

LE ROSSIGNOL [Solovey; The Nightingale].

Composer: Igor Stravinsky.

Librettists: Igor Stravinsky and S. Mitussov (after Andersen).

First Performance: Paris, Opéra, 26 May 1914.

Roles: Fisherman (tenor); Nightingale (soprano); Cook (soprano); Emperor of China (baritone); Chamberlain (bass); Bonze (bass); Three Japanese Envoys (tenors, bass); chorus.

Publications

book–

Albright, Daniel. *Stravinsky: The Music Box and the Nightingale.* New York and London, Gordon and Breach, 1989.

articles–

Stravinsky, Igor, and Fëdor Saljapin. "Pis'ma I.F. Stravinskogo i F.I. Saljapin k A.A. Saninu" [letters to opera producer A. Sanin concerning *Le rossignal*]. *Sovetskaya muzyka* 6 (1978): 92.

Sorokina, Tat'jana. "The Evolution of Igor Strawinsky's Harmonic Thinking as Seen in the Opera *Solovey.*" In *Theoreticeskie voprosy vokal'noj muzyki,* compiled by Nikolaj Tiftikidi. Moscow, 1979.

Craft, Robert. "Stravinsky at his 'bird-best'." *Opera News* 46/no. 8 (1982): 14.

* * *

Stravinsky worked on his first opera, *The Nightingale* between the years 1908 and 1914. He received tremendous encouragement for this project from his teacher, Rimsky-Korsakov, who saw the initial sketches of the first act in 1908. The first act was completed in the summer of 1909, just before Stravinsky began work on his first ballet, the *Firebird,* which was premiered at the Paris Opéra on 25 June 1910. After that his attention focused on two other ballets—*Petrushka* (first performance, Paris, Théâtre du Chatelet, 13 June 1911) and *The Rite of Spring* (first performance, Paris, Théâtre des Champs-Elysees, 29 May 1913).

In spite of these interruptions, Stravinsky had hopes of completing the *Nightingale* in 1913, to fulfill a commission which had originally come from the Moscow Free Theater. But, because of financial difficulties, the Theater was forced to abandon *Nightingale.* As a result, Diaghilev took over the production of the opera. Stravinsky eventually completed his work on 28 March 1914, and *The Nightingale* received its first performance on 26 May 1914, at the Paris Opéra with Ansermet as conductor. Benois designed the costumes and sets. Romanov was responsible for the dances. The singing parts, which were in Russian for this performance, were designed to be "mimed" by the actors on stage, with the singers placed in the orchestra—a format which exemplifies Stravinsky's philosophy that "the music is more important than the action, as the words were more important than the action in Shakespeare."

The libretto for *The Nightingale* was the result of a collaboration between Stravinsky and his friend Mitussov, and is based on a fairy-tale by Hans Christian Andersen. The first act begins with an introduction modeled after *Nuages*—one of the Orchestral Nocturnes written by Debussy between 1897-99. The Fisherman prays to the heavenly spirit and asks to hear the Nightingale sing. The Nightingale responds with a beautifully embellished vocal line, addressed to the roses in the palace garden. Eventually, the Chamberlain, Bonze, Courtiers, and Cook enter and patiently wait to tell the Nightingale of the Emperor's wish to hear her sing.

The second act begins with an interlude entitled Entr'Acte "Breezes." Curtains made of gauze envelop the stage as if to conceal the activities in preparation for the appearance of the Emperor. Two choruses sing of lanterns, torches, light, and the music of silver bells, made by the flowers in the wind. As the Emperor approaches to hear the Nightingale, the gauze curtains are lifted. The famous Chinese March forms the second scene of the second act. In the third scene, the song of the Nightingale is now even more highly embellished than in the first act. When asked by the Emperor how he should reward her for singing so beautifully, the Nightingale responds that she is rewarded by the tear drops shining in his eyes. This sentiment is expressed in the third act as well. The last scene of the second act involves the performance of the mechanical Nightingale, which the Japanese envoys have brought for the Chinese Emperor. Suddenly, someone notices that the real Nightingale has disappeared. The scene ends with the Fisherman exclaiming that the music of the real Nightingale has the power to conquer death.

The third act opens in the Emperor's chamber, where he lies ill. He is surrounded by ghosts and by Death. Suddenly, the real Nightingale reappears to tell the Emperor of the beauty of his garden, which is reflected in the beauty of her song. The most powerful dramatic action in the entire opera occurs with the Nightingale singing, "and over there beyond the white wall there is another garden," to which Death responds "I like to hear you singing. Why have you fallen silent? Sing on!" The dialogue continues between the Nightingale and Death, and ultimately the music of the Nightingale triumphs over Death. The Emperor recovers from his illness. The Nightingale reminds the Emperor that she is rewarded by the tears that fill his eyes.

The opera closes with a solemn procession. The members of the Emperor's court, who have assumed that he has died, are surprised to hear him say, "Be welcome here!" The Fisherman urges us to "Listen to them, with them rejoice, they are the spirits' heavenly voice."

In *Memories and Commentaries,* Stravinsky stated that "The premiere [of *The Nightingale*] was unsuccessful only in the sense that it failed to create a scandal. Musically and visually, the performance was excellent." What Stravinsky is referring to here is that the members of the Paris audience received the first performance of *Nightingale* calmly, in contrast to the their riotous reaction just one year earlier to *The Rite of Spring.*

From all reports, Ravel was pleased with *The Nightingale,* but strangely enough, Stravinsky is convinced that Debussy did not like it. In Stravinsky's own words: ". . . I heard nothing whatever from him about it. I remember this well, for I expected him to question me about the great difference between the music of Act I and the later acts, and though I knew he would have liked the Mussorgsky-Debussy beginning, he probably would have said about that, too, 'Young man, I do it better.'"

Stravinsky was too hard on himself in his *Apologia* for the dichotomy of style within *The Nightingale.* What his first opera provides for the listener is a fascinating study of the evolution of Stravinsky's style between the years 1908 and 1914. Regardless of the stylistic contrasts within this work, however, the diverse elements fit together in a remarkable way. Various unifying elements appear throughout, such as the Fisherman's chant at the end of the opera which is quite similar to those which occur after the introduction in act I, and at the end of act I. The vocalises sung by the real Nightingale herself provide another means of consistency. The diversity of style, especially apparent when comparing the musical context for the real Nightingale with that of the mechanical one, is supported by the opera's plot. The chromaticism of the real Nightingale's vocalise-style contrasts markedly with the pentatonic melody of the mechanical Nightingale. The one is expressive and the other hypnotic.

—Maureen A. Carr

ROSSI-LEMENI, Nicola.

Bass. Born 6 November 1920, in Istanbul. Died 12 March 1991, in Bloomington, Indiana. Married: 1) Vittoria Serafin; 2) soprano Virginia Zeani. Studied with his mother, Xenia Macadon; debut as Varlaam in *Boris Godunov*, Venice, 1946; at Teatro alla Scala, 1947-61, debuting as Verlaam; San Francisco debut as Boris Godunov, 1951; Covent Garden debut, 1952; Metropolitan Opera debut as Mefistofele in Gounod's *Faust*, 1953; created the role of Tommasso in Pizzetti's *L'assassinio nella cattedrale*, Teatro alla Scala, 1958. Taught at the University of Indiana, 1980-1991.

Publications

By ROSSI-LEMENI: books–

Oltrè l'angoscia. Bologna, 1972.

About ROSSI-LEMENI: articles–

Celletti, Rodolfo. "Rossi-Lemeni, Nicola." *Le grandi voci.* Rome, 1964.
"Ils se souviennent." *Diapason-Harmonie* 329/July-August (1987): 36.
Battaglia, C. "Keepers of the Flame." *Opera News* 52/November (1987): 28.

*   *   *

There are some artists whose vision magnetizes zeal no matter how contentious their actual achievements may be. Callas, Vickers, and Rysanek have been among them—and so was Nicola Rossi-Lemeni. When in 1951 he made his American stage debut (as Boris) in San Francisco, it was immediately sensed that he had brought an obsessive intensity back to the operatic theatre—and this in a city devoted to such galvanic singers as Lotte Lehmann, Vinay, Albanese, Gobbi, Pinza, and Baccaloni. His granitic features, disciplined physique, and, above all, his extraordinarily moving vocal approach evoked a theater beyond the merely human. Rossi-Lemeni seemed to bear another world with him: an emotional energy and a lightning response, a divine disillusion and encompassing humanity that distinguish tragedy from lesser drama. In retrospect, one is reminded of Edmund Kean, the great

nineteenth-century tragedian: "His eyes are marvelous," said Mrs. Siddons, "having a sort of fascination, like that attributed to the snake." Rossi-Lemeni's Boris (and his Boito Mefistofele) was that sort of hypnotizing performance, even for an audience used to Pinza in the role.

In the theatre of forty years ago Rossi-Lemeni's voice was cavernous, fibrous, and shadowed, with little of the focused sheen of (for example) Boris Christoff's, but deeply expressive of both frenzy and intimate melancholy. He was, of course, accused of copying Feodor Chaliapin, but even that influence seems to have been molded by his own brilliant theatricality. In *Mefistofele* the voice became an ironic snarl, and later we learned that he could sing Rossini with witty accuracy (*Il Turco in Italia*) and inventiveness (*Il barbiere di Siviglia*). It was claimed that he had never had formal training. That is believable: at times the voice could tire and there were occasional pitch problems. He could over-inflect. On records alone, a role like Rossini's Mosè, which demands invincible technique and a continual burnished grandeur of tone, defeats him. But he has left behind a series of live and studio performances which, even with their vocal compromises, show him to have been a visionary singing actor: one of the few on a level with Maria Callas, with whom he often sang. In Verdi's *Don Carlo*, for example, he gets the saddened, exhausted tone of King Philip's dawn meditation to the life, despite uncertainties of pitch and line. With Callas in *Il Turco in Italia*, he enacts consummate gallantry against her feline modesty, matching her vocal precision surprisingly well. In Bellini's *I puritani* he sings with tender dignity, his phrasing and dynamics shaped compellingly by the words, again despite some technical difficulties. As Oroveso in *Norma* he creates a mystic high priest driven by vengeance, anger, and then sorrow: a monumental characterization. One of his most gripping live recordings is as the Pontifex Maximus in Spontini's *La vestale*, at the Teatro alla Scala in 1954. In regard to this very role, critic Lawrence Gilman long ago wrote, "High Priests are usually the dullest animals in the operatic herd," but Rossi-Lemeni, firm in voice in pitch, creates a horrifying zealot, inplacable and yet fascinating in his confrontations with the brilliant Callas. Here is blazing animation of the recitativo by each of the two great singing actors. In sum, like Callas, he was so weighted with gifts and with flaws, too, that, even with documentation, we must at times thrust almost painfully with our imaginations to recall or envision how powerful he really was in the theater.

—London Green

ROSSINI, Gioachino (Antonio).

Composer. Born 29 February 1792, in Pesaro, Italy. Died 13 November 1868, in Paris. Married: 1) Isabella Colbran, soprano, 16 March 1822 (divorced 1837); 2) Olympe Pélissier, 16 August 1846. Studied French horn with his father and singing with the local canon in Lugo; studied singing, harpsichord, and music theory with Padre Tesei in Bologna; served as maestro al cembalo in local churches and opera houses; studied voice with the tenor Matteo Babbini; studied singing and solfeggio with Gibelli, cello with Cavedagna, piano with Zanotti, and counterpoint with Padre Mattei at the Liceo Musicale in Bologna, beginning 1806; received a prize from the Liceo Musicale for his cantata *Il pianto d'Armonia sulla morte d'Orfeo*, performed 11 August 1808; his successful early opera compositions led to a commission from the Teatro alla Scala, 1812; commissioned by the impresario Barbaia, 1814; numerous operas, 1814-1822, including *Il barbiere di Siviglia* (1816); met Beethoven in Vienna, 1822; received in London by King George IV of England, 1823; director of the Théâtre-Italien in Paris, 1824; *Il viaggio a Reims* composed for the coronation of King Charles X, 1825; met Meyerbeer in Paris; Premier Compositeur du Roi and Inspecteur Général du Chant; contract with the government of Charles X to compose operas for the Paris Opéra, 1829 (invalidated with the outbreak of the revolution of 1830); consultant to the Liceo Musicale in Bologna, 1836-1848; in Florence, 1848; in Paris, 1855.

Operas

Editions:

Quaderni rossiniani, a cura della Fondazione Rossini. Pesaro, 1954-.
Edizione critica delle opere Gioachino Rossini. Edited by the Fondazione Rossini. Pesaro, 1979-.

Demitrio e Polibio, V. Viganò-Mombelli, c. 1809, Rome, Valle, 18 May 1812.
La cambiale di matrimonio, G. Rossi (after Camillo Federici), Venice, San Moisè, 3 November 1810.
L'equivoco stravagante, G. Gasparri, Bologna, Teatro del Corso, 26 October 1811.
L'inganno felice, G. Foppa (after G. Palomba), Venice, San Moisè, 8 January 1812.
Ciro in Babilonia, ossia La caduta di Baldassare, F. Aventi, Ferrara, Comunale, 14? March 1812.
La scala di seta, G. Foppa (after Planard, *L'echelle de soie*), Venice, San Moisè, 9 May 1812.
La pietra del paragone, L. Romanelli, Milan, Teatro alla Scala, 26 September 1812.
L'occasione fa il ladro, L. Prividali, Venice, San Moisè, 24 November 1812.
Il Signor Bruschino, ossia Il figlio per azzardo, G. Foppa (after A. de Chazet and E.-T. Maurice Ourry, *Le fils par hazard*), Venice, San Moisè, January 1813.
Tancredi, G. Rossi and L. Lechi (after Voltaire), Venice, La Fenice, 6 February 1813.
L'italiana in Algeri, A. Anelli (for L. Mosca), Venice, San Benedetto, 22 May 1813.
Aureliano in Palmira G.-F. Romani, Milan, Teatro alla Scala, 26 December 1813.
Il turco in Italia, F. Romani (after Caterino Mazzdà), Milan, Teatro alla Scala, 14 August 1814.
Sigismondo, G. Foppa, Venice, La Fenice, 26 December 1814.
Elisabetta, regina d'Inghilterra, G. Schmidt (after Carlo Federici), Naples, San Carlo, 4 October 1815.
Torvaldo e Dorliska, C. Sterbini (after J.-B. de Coudry, *Vie et amours du chevalier de Faubles*), Rome, Valle, 26 December 1815.
Almaviva, ossia L'inutile precauzione (Il barbiere di Siviglia), C. Sterbini (after Beaumarchais and G. Petrosellini), Rome, Torre Argentina, 20 February 1816.
La gazzetta, G. Palomba (after C. Goldoni, *Il matrimonio per concorso*), Naples, Teatro dei Fiorentini, 26 September 1816.
Otello, ossia Il moro di Venezia, F. Berio di Salsa (after Shakespeare), Naples, Teatro del Fondo, 4 December 1816.
La Cenerentola, ossia La bontà in trionfo, G. Ferretti (after Perrault, *Cendrillon,* C.-G. Etienne, and F. Fiorini), Rome, Valle, 25 January 1817.

La gazza ladra, G. Gherardini (after d'Aubigny and Caigniez, *La pie voleuse*), Milan, Teatro alla Scala, 31 May 1817.
Armida, G. Schmidt (after Tasso, *La Gerusalemme liberata*), Naples, San Carlo, 11 November 1817.
Adelaide di Borgogna, G. Schmidt, Rome, Torre Argentina, 27 December 1817.
Mosè in Egitto, A.L. Tottola (after F. Ringhieri, *L'Osiride*), Naples, San Carlo, 5 March 1818; revised as *Moïse et Pharaon, ou Le passage de la Mer Rouge,* L. Balocchi and E. de Jouy, Paris, Opèra, 26 March 1827.
Adina, G. Bevilacqua-Aldobrandini, 1818, Lisbon, Saõ Carlo, 22 June 1826.
Ricciardo e Zoraide, F. Berio di Salsa (after Niccolò Forteguerri, *Ricciardetto*), Naples, San Carlo, 3 December 1818.
Ermione, A.L. Tottola (after Racine, *Andromaque*), Naples, San Carlo, 27 March 1819.
Eduardo e Cristina, G. Schmidt (revised by Bevilacqua-Aldobrandini and A.L. Tottola), Venice, San Benedetto, 24 April 1819.
La donna del lago, A.L. Tottola (after Scott, *The Lady of the Lake*), Naples, San Carlo, 24 September 1819.
Bianca e Falliero, ossia Il consiglio dei tre, F. Romani (after A. van Arnhault, *Blanche et Montcassin*), Milan, Teatro alla Scala, 26 December 1819.
Maometto II, C. della Valle (after his *Anna Erizo*), Naples, San Carlo, 3 December 1820; revised as *Le siège de Corinthe,* L. Balocchi and A. Soumet, Paris, Opéra, 9 October 1826.
Matilde di Shabran, ossia Bellezza, e cuor di ferro, G. Ferretti (after F.-B. Hoffmann, *Euphrosine,* and J.M. Boutet de Monvel, *Mathilde*), Rome, Apollo, 24 February 1821.
Zelmira, A.L. Tottola (after Dormont de Belloy), Naples, San Carlo, 16 February 1822.
Semiramide, G. Rossi (after Voltaire), Venice, La Fenice, 3 February 1823.
Il viaggio a Reims, ossia L'albergo del giglio d'oro, L. Balocchi (after Staël, *Corinne*), Paris, Théâtre-Italien, 19 June 1825; partial revision as *Le Comte Ory* E. Scribe and C.G. Delestre-Poirson (after their play), Paris, Opéra, 20 August 1828.
Guillaume Tell, E. de Jouy, H.-L.-F. Bis et al. (after Schiller), Paris, Opéra, 3 August 1829.

Other works: sacred works, cantatas, incidental music, hymns, choruses, solo vocal works, instrumental and chamber music, piano pieces.

Publications/Writings

By ROSSINI: books–

Mazzatinti, G., ed. *Lettere inedite di Gioacchino Rossini.* Imola, 1890; 2nd ed. as *Lettere inedite e rare di G. Rossini,* 1892; 3rd ed. as *Lettere di G. Rossini,* 1902.
Allmayer, A., ed. *Undici lettere di Gioachino Rossini pubblicate per la prima volta.* Siena, 1892.
Cagli, Bruno, and Sergio Ragni, eds. *Lettere e Documenti,* vol. 1. Pesaro, 1992.

About ROSSINI: books–

Stendhal. *Vie de Rossini.* Paris, 1824; 2nd ed. by Henri Prunières, 1922; English translation, 1956; 2nd ed., 1970.
Stendhal. *Rome, Naples, et Florence en 1817.* Paris, 1817; English translation, 1959.

Zanolini, A. *Biografia di Gioachino Rossini.* Paris, 1836; 2nd ed., Bologna, 1875.

Escudier, M. and L. *Rossini: sa vie et ses oeuvres.* Paris, 1854.

Montazio, E. *Gioacchino Rossini.* Turin, 1862.

Aulagnier, A. *G. Rossini: sa vie et ses oeuvres.* Paris, 1864.

Azevedo, A. *G. Rossini: sa vie et ses oeuvres.* Paris, 1864.

Pacini, G. *Le mie memoire artistiche.* Florence, 1865; 2nd ed., 1872.

Edwards, H.S. *The Life of Rossini.* London, 1869; 2nd ed. as *Rossini and his School,* 1881.

Pougin, A. *Rossini: notes, impressions, souvenirs, commentaires.* Paris, 1871.

Silvestri, L.S. *Della vita e delle opere di Gioachino Rossini: notizie biografico-artistico-aneddotico-critiche.* Milan, 1874.

Staeten, E. vander. *La mélodie populaire dans l'opéra "Guillaume Tell" de Rossini.* Paris, 1879.

Dauriac, L. *Rossini: biographie critique.* Paris, 1906.

Fara, G. *Genio e ingegno musicale: Gioachino Rossini.* Turin, 1915.

Vatielli, F. *Rossini a Bologna.* Bologna, 1918.

Curzon, H. de. *Rossini.* Paris, 1920.

Gatti, G.M. "Le 'Barbier de Séville' de Rossini." Paris, 1925.

Radiciotti, G. *Gioachino Rossini: vita documentata, opere ed influenza sull' arte.* Tivoli, 1927-29.

———. *Aneddoti rossiniani autentici.* Rome, 1929.

Derwent, G.H.J. *Rossini and some Forgotten Nightingales.* London, 1934.

Toye, F. *Rossini: a Study in Tragi-comedy.* London, 1934; 2nd ed., 1954; 1963.

Faller, H. *Die Gesangkoloratur in Rossinis Opern und ihre Ausführung.* Berlin, 1935.

Roncaglia, G. *Rossini l'olimpico.* Milan, 1946; 2nd ed., 1953.

Rognoni, L. *Rossini.* Parma, 1956; 2nd ed., 1968; 3rd ed., 1977.

Schlitzer, F. *Un piccolo carteggio inedito di Rossini con un impresario italiano Vienna.* Florence, 1959.

Viviani, V., ed. *I libretti di Rossini.* Milan, 1965.

d'Amico, F. *L'opera teatrale di Gioacchino Rossini.* Rome, 1968.

Bonaccorsi, A., ed. *Gioacchino Rossini.* Florence, 1968.

Weinstock, H. *Rossini: a Biography.* New York, 1968.

Cagli, Bruno *"Guglielmo Tell": La guida all' opera.* Milan, 1971.

Harding, James. *Rossini.* London, 1971.

Cagli, Bruno, ed. *Bollettino del centro rossiniano de studi, anno 1976.* Pesaro, 1976.

Gossett, Philip. *The Tragic Finale of "Tancredi."* Pesaro, 1977.

Questa, C. *Il ratto del serraglio: Euripide, Plauto, Mozart, Rossini.* Bologna, 1979.

John, Nicholas, ed. *Gioachino Rossini: "La Cenerentola."* London and New York, 1980.

Weaver, William. *The Golden Century of Italian Opera from Rossini to Pacini.* New York, 1980.

Atti del convego di studi: Rossini, edizioni critiche e prassi esecutiva—Siena, 30 agosto-1 settembre 1977. Florence, 1981.

Till, Nicholas. *Rossini: his Life and Times.* New York and Tunbridge Wells, 1983.

John, Nicholas, ed. *Il barbiere di Siviglia and Moïse et Pharaon.* London and New York, 1985.

Osborne, Richard. *Rossini.* London, 1986.

Beghelli, M., and N. Gallino, eds. *Tutti i libretti di Rossini.* Milan, 1991.

articles—

Berlioz, H. "Guillaume Tell." *Gazette musicale* 1/October-November (1834): 326, 336, 341, 349; English translation in *Source Readings in Music History,* edited by Oliver Strunk, New York, 1950.

Wagner, R. "Eine Erinnerung an Rossini." *Allgemeine Zeitung* 17 December (1868); reprinted in *Gesammelte Schriften und Dichtungen* vol. 8, Leipzig, 1883; 2nd ed., 1888; English translation, 1895; 1966.

Romagnoli, G. "Gioacchino Rossini, Giulio Perticari e la 'Gazza ladra'." *Vita italiana* 3 (1897): 106.

Cametti, A. "Il 'Guglielmo Tell' e le sue prime rappresentazioni in Italia." *Rivista musicale italiana* 6 (1899): 580.

Radiciotti, G. "Il *Signor Bruschino* e il *Tancredi* di Rossini." *Rivista musicale italiana* (1920).

De Rensis, R. "Rossini intimo: lettere all' amico Santocanale." *Musica d'oggi* 13 (1931): 343.

Prod'homme, P.-G. "Rossini and his Works in France." *Musical Quarterly* 17 (1931): 119.

Della Corte, A. "La drammaturgica della *Semiramide* di Rossini." *La rassegna musicale* (1938).

Capri, A. "Rossini e l'estetica teatrale della vocalità." *Rivista musicale italiana* (1942): 353.

Della Corte, A. "Fra gorgheggi e melodie di Rossini." *Musica* 1 (1942): 23.

Rolandi, U. "Librettistica rossiniana." *Musica* 1 (1942): 40.

Hughes, Spike. "An Introduction to *La Cenerentola.*" *Opera* June (1952).

Kirby, P.R. "Rossini's Overture to 'William Tell'." *Music and Letters* 33 (1952): 132.

La rassegna musicale 24/no. 3 (1954) [Rossini issue].

Porter, A. *"Le Comte Ory."* *Opera* 5 (1954).

Melica, A. "Due operine di Rossini" [*L'inganno felice, L'occasione fa il ladro*]. *Chigiana* 13 (1956): 59.

Schlitzer, F. "Rossiniana: contributo all' epistolario di G. Rossini." *Chigiana* 35 (1956).

Bonaccorsi, A. *"La donna del lago."* *La rassegna musicale* (1958).

Melica, A. "L'aria in rondò de *La donna del lago.*" *Bollettino del Centro rossiniano di studi* (1958).

Porter, A. "William Tell." *Opera* 9 (1958).

Gavazzeni, G. *"Il turco in Italia."* *La rassegna musicale* 1 (1959).

Confalonieri, G. "Avventure di une partitura rossiniana: l'Adina ovvero Il califfo di Bagdad'." *Chigiana* 20 (1963): 206.

Klein, J.W. "Verdi's 'Otello' and Rossini's." *Music and Letters* 45 (1964): 130.

Porter, A. "A Lost Opera by Rossini" [*Ugo, re d'Italia*]. *Music and Letters* 45 (1964): 39.

Damerini, A. "La prima ripresa moderna di un' opera giovanile di Rossini: 'L'equivoco stravagante' (1811)." *Chigiana* 22 (1965): 229.

Celletti, R. "Vocalità rossiniana." *L'opera* 2 (1966): 3.

Zedda, A. "Appunti per una lettura filologica del 'Barbiere'." *L'opera* 2 (1966): 13.

Gossett, Philip. "Le fonti autografe delle opere teatrali di Rossini." *Nuova rivista musicale italiana* 2 (1968): 936.

Celletti, R. "Origini e sviluppi della coloratura rossiniana." *Nuova rivista musicale italiana* 2 (1968): 872.

———. "Il vocalismo italiano da Rossini a Donizetti: Parte I: Rossini." *Analecta musicologica* no. 5 (1968): 267.

Gossett, P. "Rossini and Authenticity." *Musical Times* 109 (1968): 1006.

———. "Rossini in Naples: some Major Works Recovered." *Musical Quarterly* 54 (1968): 316.

Lippmann, F. "Rossinis Gedanken über die Musik." *Die Musikforschung* 22 (1969): 285.

Tartak, M. "The Two 'Barbieri'." *Music and Letters* 1 (1969): 453.

Gossett, Philip. "Gioachino Rossini and the Conventions of Composition." *Acta musicologica* 42 (1970): 48.

Isotta, P. "*La donna del lago* e la drammaturgica di Rossini." *Bollettino del Centro rossiniano di studi* (1970).

Carli Balola, G. "Una *pièce à sauvetage* da Salvare" [*Torvaldo e Dorliska*]. *Bollettino del Centro rossiniano di studi* (1971): 11.

Gossett, Philip. "The *candeur virginale* of *Tancredi.*" *Musical Times* 112 (1971).

Petrobelli, P. "Balzac, Stendhal e il *Mosè* di Rossini." *Conservatorio di musica 'G.B. Martini' di Bologna: Annuario 1965-1970* (1971): 205.

Zedda, A. "Problemi testuali della *Cenerentola.*" *Bollettino del Centro rossiniano di studi* (1971).

Carli Ballola, G. "Lettura dell' *Ermione.*" *Bollettino del Centro rossiniano di studi* no. 3 (1972): 13.

Gossett, Philip. "*La gazza ladra:* Notes Towards a Critical Edition." *Bollettino del Centro rossiniano di studi* (1972).

Cagli, B. "Le fonti letterarie dei libretti di Rossini." *Bollettino del Centro rossiniano di studi* no. 2 (1972): 10 [*Maometto II*]; no. 1 (1973): 8 [*Bianca e Falliero*].

Tartak, M. "Matilde and her Cousins." *Bollettino del Centro rossiniano di studi* no. 3 (1973): 13.

Isotta, P. "I diamanti della corona: grammatica del Rossini napoletano." In *Mosè in Egitto, Opera: collana di guide musicali,* 4. Turin, 1974.

Cacaci, F. "*La cambiale di matrimonio* da Federico a Rossi." *Bollettino del Centro rossiniano di studi* 1-2 (1975).

Caswell, A. "Vocal Embellishment in Rossini's Paris Operas: French Style or Italian?" *Bollettino del Centro rossiniano di studi* 1-2 (1975).

Scott, Michael. "Rossini in England." *Opera* March-May (1976).

Chigiana 34 (1977).

Gallarati, P. "Dramma e ludus dall' *Italiana* al *Barbiere.*" In *Il melodramma italiano dell' ottocento: studi e ricerche per Massimo Mila.* Turin, 1977.

Tammaro, F. "Ambivalenza dell' *Otello* rossiniano." In *Il melodramma italiano dell' ottocento: studi e ricerche per Massimo Mila.* Turin, 1977.

Bisogni, Fabio. "Il melodramma rossiniano e le ideologie correnti." *Chigiana* 33 (1979): 211.

Lippmann, F. "Autographe Briefe Rossinis und Donizettis in der Bibliothek Massimo, Rom." *Analecta musicologica* no. 19 (1979): 330.

Tozzi, Lorenzo. "*Edipo a Colono* di Rossini." *Chigiana* 33 (1979): 361.

Viale Ferrero, M. "*Guglielmo Tell* a Torino (1839-1840) ovvero una *Procella* scenografica." *Rivista italiana di musicologia* 14 (1979): 378.

Gossett, Philip. "The Overtures of Rossini." *Nineteenth-Century Music* 3 (1979): 3.

Dahlhaus, Carl. "Zur Methode der Opern-Analyse" [*Otello* finale]. *Musik und Bildung* 12 (1980): 518.

Kallberg, Jeffrey. "Marketing Rossini: sei lettere di Troupenas ad Artaria." *Bollettino del Centro rossiniano di studi* 1-3 (1980): 41.

Mauceri, Marco. "F.F. Padre ignoto dell' *Agatina* di Pavesi." *Bollettino del Centro rossiniani de studi* 1-3 (1980): 65.

Conati, M. "Between Past and Future: the Dramatic World of Rossini in *Mosè in Egitto* and *Moïse et Pharaon.*" *Nineteenth-Century Music* 4 (1980): 32.

Avant-scène opéra November-December (1981) [*Le barbier de Seville* issue].

Lanfranchi, A. "Alcune note su *Zelmira.*" *Bollettino del Centro rossiniano di studi* (1981).

Lippmann, Friedrich. "Rossini—und kein Ende." *Studi musicali* 10 (1981): 279.

d'Amico F. "A proposito d'un *Tancredi:* Dioniso in Apollo." In *Die stylistische Entwicklung der italienischen Musik zwischen 1770 und 1830 und ihre Beziehungen zum Norden,* edited F. Lippmann, 61. Laaber, 1982.

Kunze, Stefan. "Ironie des Klassizismus: Aspekte des Umbruchs in der musikalischen Komödie um 1800." In *Die stylistische Entwicklung der italienischen Musik zwischen 1770 und 1830 und ihre Beziehungen zum Norden,* edited F. Lippmann, 72. Laaber, 1982.

Rozett, Martha Tuck. "*Othello, Otello* and the Comic Tradition." *Bulletin of Research in the Humanities* 85 (1982): 386.

Scherliess, Volker. "*Il barbiere di Siviglia:* Paisiello und Rossini." *Analecta musicologica* 21 (1982): 100.

Gerhard, Anselm. "L'eroe titubante e il finale aperto: un dilemma insolubile nel *Guillaume Tell* di Rossini." *Rivista italiana di musicologia* 19 (1984): 113.

Avant-scène opéra November (1985) [*Le siège de Corinthe* issue].

Avant-scène opéra March (1986) [*La Cenerentola* issue].

Avant-scène opéra June (1988) [*La pie voleuse* issue].

Avant-scène opéra March (1989) [*Guillaume Tell* issue].

Crichton, Ronald. "An Overture to *Guillaume Tell.*" *Opera* June (1990).

unpublished–

Gossett, Philip. "The Operas of Rossini: Problems of Textual Criticism in Nineteenth-Century Opera." Ph. D. dissertation, Princeton University, 1970.

Balthazar, Scott Leslie. "Evolving Conventions in Italian Serious Opera: Scene Structure in the Works of Rossini, Bellini, Donizetti, and Verdi 1810-1850." Ph.D. dissertation, University of Pennsylvania, 1985.

* * *

Rossini's operatic career was short but intensely busy and productive. Only 19 years separated the composition of his first complete opera (*La cambiale di matrimonio,* 1810) from his last (*Guillaume Tell,* 1829); those nineteen years saw the composition of thirty-eight operas (not including the very early *Demetrio e Polibio,* the extent of Rossini's contribution to which is not clear). Rossini's career took him from Bologna, where he studied, first to the major theaters of northern Italy, then to Naples, and finally to Paris. This geographical progress coincided with three phrases of Rossini's career and of the development of his operatic art. During the first and most prolific phase, 1810-1815, he wrote thirteen operas, most for the theaters of Venice and Milan. Many of these were one-act comic operas; the full-length operas, like those of Rossini's great eighteenth-century predecessors Cimarosa and Paisiello, were about evenly divided between *opera buffa* and *opera seria.* Naples witnessed the second phase of Rossini's career (1815-1822), devoted almost exclusively to serious opera, but with trips to Rome for the composition of two of his greatest comic operas, *Il barbiere di Siviglia* (1816) and *La Cenerentola* (1817). The third and final phase (1823-29) brought Rossini to Paris, saw a brief return to

Gioachino Rossini as a young man, painting by Vincenzo Camuccini, c. 1816

comic opera (*Le Comte Ory*, 1828), and culminated in his last opera, *Guillaume Tell.*

Rossini wrote many of his earliest works for the Teatro San Moisè in Venice. This theater specialized in one-act *farse,* comic operas that required simple staging, a small orchestra, no chorus and few rehearsals: perfect conditions for a young and inexperienced composer to try out new works. Rossini's early comic *farse* are infused with the spirit of late eighteenth-century *opera buffa. La cambiale di matrimonio* is a conventional story along the lines of Cimarosa's *Il matrimonio segreto.* One can sense in Rossini's music his eagerness to challenge what was regarded at the time as a twenty-year-old classic. The entrance aria of Slook, a rich man engaged in absentia to the young heroine Fanny, was an open invitation for Rossini to match Cimarosa's "Senza tante cerimonie." "Dite presto dove stà," the duet for the two comic basses Slook and Sir Tobia (Fanny's father), rivals Cimarosa's duet "Se fiato in corpo avete." To these and other conventional dramatic situations Rossini responded with his own effortless inventiveness. Sometimes a single delightful idea brings an entire number to life: this happens near the end of the duet "Dite presto dove stà," when, at the words "grazie tante," a pretty sequential passage suffuses everything with unexpected charm.

From the beginning of his career Rossini revealed himself to be a skillful and original composer of overtures. Using the same sonata form that the Viennese masters used for the first movements of their symphonies, Rossini created overtures that were totally different from anything written in Vienna—or in Italy, for that matter—and were instantly recognizable as products of his particular mind. Rossini's crescendos

earned the disdain of Berlioz and Wagner, but others have felt and appreciated the excitement and originality of Rossini's overtures. When Bernard Shaw attended a concert in celebration of the centenary of Rossini's birth in 1892, he reported of the performance of several of Rossini's overtures: "Nobody was disgusted, *à la Berlioz,* by 'the brutal crescendo and big drum.' On the contrary, we were exhilerated and amused; and I, for one, was astonished to find it all still so fresh, so imposing, so clever, and even, in a few serious passages, so really fine."

With *Tancredi* and *L'italiana in Algeri* (both first performed in Venice in 1813) Rossini began to establish an international reputation as a brilliant composer of both *opera seria* and *opera buffa.* Everywhere in these operas one finds evidence of Rossini's extraordinary melodic and harmonic gifts. Working comfortably within the musical conventions of his time, Rossini managed to bring subtle originality to his melodic lines and their harmonic underpinnings. Also admirable is Rossini's endless supply of imaginative orchestral figuration with which he accompanied both long, lyrical lines and parlando passages.

In 1815 Domenico Barbaia, the impresario of the Teatro San Carlo in Naples, persuaded the 23-year-old Rossini to settle in Naples as the music director of San Carlo. During the next seven years Rossini devoted most of his compositional efforts to the genre which predominated at San Carlo, *opera seria.* Rossini's Neapolitan operas show him taking inspiration from the operatic conditions that confronted him, and not only in terms of operatic genre. The ample and well-trained chorus of San Carlo encouraged Rossini to give the chorus an increasingly important role in his music dramas. The large and fine orchestra of the Teatro San Carlo caused him to use orchestral color to great dramatic effect. Rossini's first opera for Naples, *Elisabetta, regina d'Inghilterra* (1815) was also his first opera to abandon simple recitative in favor of orchestrally accompanied recitative throughout.

Rossini's flair for orchestral music, already evident in the overtures for many of the earlier operas, takes on new vigor and grandeur in the Neapolitan operas. Not only overtures, but marches, orchestral interludes, and long introductions (often with beautiful and elaborate solos), enrich *Otello* (1816), *La donna del lago* (1819) and *Maometto II* (1820); even as early as *Elisabetta,* Rossini made effective use of San Carlo's orchestral resources, coloring Leicester's prison scene with two English horns and strengthening the orchestration of the overture that he had composed for *Aureliano in Palmira* (1813) and now reused for *Elisabetta.* The fine canonic quintet near the beginning of *Mosè in Egitto* (1818), with harp, low strings (no violins), horns, and delicate touches of woodwind color may serve as one example of Rossini's orchestrational genius as it was inspired by the orchestra of San Carlo.

The availability of certain singers also shaped Rossini's art, as, for example, when the presence of several talented tenors in Naples caused Rossini to write three major tenor parts in *Otello* and to represent the conflicts between Otello and Rodrigo on the one hand and between Otello and Iago on the other as contests between tenors. In other Neapolitan operas too much of the drama is a product of the way in which Rossini engineered the relationship between the great virtuosos for whom he wrote and the audience that heard them sing. Rossini's genius was theatrical as well as musical. Arsace's entrance in *Semiramide* (Venice, 1823), preceded by a long orchestral introduction, is a great *coup de théâtre* in which the composer presented the singer to the audience at La Fenice, "Eccomi alfine in Babilonia" ("Here I am finally in Babilonia"). An innocuous platitude becomes, in Rossini's hands, one of the most memorable and dramatic moments in all of opera.

In 1821, the impresario Barbaia left Naples and took over the direction of the Court Opera in Vienna. Rossini accepted Barbaia's invitation to come to Vienna to present his operas there; this trip was followed by another to Paris and London (1823). The successes that Rossini achieved abroad encouraged him to take up the position of music director at the Théâtre Italien in Paris the following year, but not before composing one more opera for the city that saw most of his earliest successes. *Semiramide,* Rossini's last opera for Italy, was first performed at La Fenice, Venice, in February 1823, ten years almost to the day after *Tancredi* was first performed in the same theater.

Rossini arrived in Paris a celebrity whose musical supremacy was acknowledged by most of Europe; yet, as often in the past, he felt a need to rework older material. Rossini based most of his Parisian operas on Italian works: his Neapolitan opera *Maometto II* served as the basis for *Le siège de Corinthe* and *Mosè in Egitto* as the basis for *Moïse.* But to *Guillaume Tell* he devoted all his creativity and originality, recasting his musical style in the service of grand opera at its finest.

Everything in *Guillaume Tell* is on a grand scale. The splendid overture, so overplayed that it has, for modern audiences, lost much of the effect with which it must have stunned and delighted early audiences, shows Rossini to have been fully in command of the resources of the Opéra's large and disciplined orchestra. In the first-act duet "Où vas-tu? Quel transport l'agile" for Arnold and Guillaume we can see how Rossini could use the extraordinary flexibility of structure that he learned, above all, in the composition of ensembles for *opera buffa,* to construct a serious, dramatic confrontation between a young lover and a mature patriot. The duet for the lovers Arnold and Mathilde "Oui, vous l'arrachez à mon ame" (act II) is on a similarly enormous scale, but lacks some of the inventiveness and pure theatrical excitement that animates some of the ensembles in Rossini's earlier operas. Arnold's aria "Asile hérétidaire" (act IV) is a grandiose display of tenor heroics, a rousing call to arms that makes some of Rossini's earlier tenors (Edward in *La cambiale di matrimonio,* Lindoro in *L'italiana in Algeri,* even Otello) sound a little boyish in comparison. As one listens to *Guillaume Tell,* with its astonishing richness of invention, one is tempted to believe that Rossini thought it likely, as he wrote this opera, that he would compose no more operas after it. He lavished all his craft, all his dramatic power, on a last, triumphant spectacle.

—John A. Rice

ROSWAENGE [Rosvaenge], Helge Anton Hansen.

Tenor. Born 29 August 1897, in Copenhagen. Died 19 June 1971, in Munich. Self-taught. Operatic debut as Don José in Neustrelitz, 1921; in Cologne, 1927-1930; leading "Italian" tenor, Berlin State Opera, 1930-44; Salzburg debut as Tamino, 1933; Bayreuth debut as Parsifal, 1934; created roles in Künnecke's *Die grosse Sünderin,* Berlin, 1935, and Wille's *Königsballade,* Berlin, 1939; Vienna State Opera, 1936-58; Covent Garden debut as Florestan, 1938; American debut as a recitalist, 1962.

Publications

By ROSWAENGE: books–

Skratta Pajazzo, Copenhagen, 1945. Translated into German as *Lache Bajazzo: Ernstes und Heiteres aus meinem Leben.* Munich, 1953.
Mach es besser, mein Sohn: Ein Tenor erzählt aus seinem Leben. Leipzig, 1962.
Leitfaden für Gesangsbeflissene: Eine heitere Plauderei über ernste Dinge. Munich, 1964. Translated into English as *Guidelines for Aspiring Singers,* Ipswich, n.d.

About ROSWAENGE: book–

Tassie, Franz. *Helge Roswaenge.* 1975.

articles–

Natan, A. "Roswaenge, Helge." *Primo uomo.* Basel, 1963.
Gualerzi, G. "Roswaenge, Helge." In *Le grandi voci,* ed. by R. Celetti, Rome, 1964.
Dennis, J. "Helge Rosvaenge." *Record Collector* 23 (1976): 101.
Sahlin. "Danska vaerldstenor." *Musikrevy* 33/6 (1978): 271.
Krauese, E. "Schöne Stimmen von damals: Helge Rosvaenge." *Opernwelt* 21/1 (1980): 15.

*   *   *

There are a number of normally accepted rules or guidelines that an aspiring singer who hopes to achieve a long and

Helge Roswaenge as Tamino in *Die Zauberflöte*

distinguished career in opera is encouraged to follow, but Helge Roswaenge is an exception to them all. First, the singer is expected to undertake a long period of study with an established voice teacher in order to develop the necessary mastery of vocal technique. Roswaenge was principally self-taught. He studied by listening to the recordings of Enrico Caruso. Second, a singer would normally be encouraged to limit his repertoire to those roles suitable for his voice type. Roswaenge's repertoire consisted of over one hundred different roles, ranging from operetta through the operatic repertoire from Mozart to Wagner. Third, in particular, a lyric tenor with an extended top range up to high Cs and Ds would be advised not to undertake heavier lyrico-spinto or dramatic roles, the usual consequences being the loss of the high notes. Roswaenge, like his idol Caruso, began his career in lyric roles then evolved into the lyrico-spinto and dramatic repertoire, yet at the age of sixty-eight, in his first concerts in America (as documented on a "private" recording) still produced ringing high Cs. Finally, a singer would normally be advised not to sing too often because overworking the voice normally results in loss of vocal quality and a shortened career. Roswaenge's capacity for work is legendary. In one year he sang over two hundred times in twenty-five different cities. It was not unusual for him to sing three or four performances of opera during the week and on weekends to sing in operetta. Despite this amazing quantity of performances, he preserved his voice throughout his long career.

Not only did this unique artist break all of the accepted rules of singing, but his career itself was unusual. Roswaenge never achieved the kind of international recognition that his talents deserved, because his performances were principally confined to Germany and Austria during the Second World War. He rarely traveled outside of the continent, although he did appear in Cairo (*Aida*) in 1933 and at Covent Garden (*Die Zauberflöte*) in 1938. His international reputation, particularly in America, was established by his recordings.

Roswaenge's earliest recordings were made in 1927, and throughout the 78 era he recorded over two hundred seventy-one sides. After the war English Decca issued a highlights from Verdi's *Un ballo in maschera* and highlights from Lehar's *Der Zarewitsch*, as well as a recital of operetta arias on long playing discs. Like Caruso's, Roswaenge's recordings have been continually available. Preiser has issued an almost complete collection of his 78s on eleven long playing discs. In addition, early recordings of Danish popular songs made in 1928 are also available as well as selections from several wartime opera broadcasts.

Roswaenge recorded a complete *Die Zauberflöte* under Sir Thomas Beecham in 1938 for HMV. Deutsche Grammophon issued three complete operas featuring Roswaenge: Leoncavallo's *Pagliacci* (1943), Verdi's *Rigoletto* (1944) and *I vespri siciliani* (1951), all sung in German. In the 1930s he participated in a series of opera highlights recordings of Bizet's *Carmen*, Puccini's *La bohème* and Gounod's *Faust* (again all sung in German) as well as highlights of Kalman's operetta *Die Czardasfüerstin*.

Roswaenge's vocal transition from lyric to lyrico-spinto is documented by his recordings, and in particular by his rendition of the coachman's aria from Adam's *Le postillion de Lonjumeau*. In 1928 he made two versions of this aria for Parlophone-Odeon. The style is lyrical and the climactic high D is sung softly in the head voice. In 1936 he made another version of the aria for HMV, which was instrumental in advancing his international reputation, principally because of the incredible full chest voice high D, which never fails to astonish a first time listener.

Roswaenge's preference for the non-German repertoire is confirmed by the fact that in performance he most often sang *Carmen* (twenty-seven times); *Il trovatore* (twenty-six); *Aida* (twenty-three); and *Un ballo in maschera* (twenty-one). He always sang these operas in German. In operas written to a German text his most frequent roles were Tamino (*Die Zauberflöte*, twenty-one performances); Florestan (*Fidelio*, fifteen), and Belmonte (*Die Entführung aus dem Serail*, fifteen). He frequently sang the major Puccini operas and was a famous exponent of the role of Canio (Leoncavallo's *Pagliacci*).

His recordings also confirm this preference. He recorded arias and duets from sixteen different operas in the Italian repertoire, eight from the French, nine from the German, and four from the Russian. He made no commercial recordings from Italian or French operas in the original text. There are, however, three exceptions: a 1941 radio air-check of "Nessun dorma" (*Turandot*), sung in Italian and available on volume seven of the aforementioned Preiser collection; an "Una furtiva lagrima" (*L'elisir d'amore*) and a "Salut! demeure" (*Faust*) issued on an unfortunately undocumented Preiser LP, probably from a radio concert. Outside of the tenor serenade from *Der Rosenkavalier*, which, of course, was written to an Italian text, the only other recording he sang in Italian was an early (1932) rendition of the song *Santa Lucia*.

The fact that Roswaenge's recordings are almost exclusively sung in German strongly affects any critical evaluation of Roswaenge's recorded legacy in the Italian and French repertoire. Not even an artist as gifted as Roswaenge can overcome the handicap of the more guttural, consonant rich German language in music set to the vowel-rich Italian or French. His attack is sometimes criticized as being too vehement, and the German text often emphasizes this quality—at times he seems to hammer out notes. In particular, the lyric cantilena (smoothness) is lost, and the recordings are never ideally idiomatic. To many, this flaw is compensated by his vocal virtuosity, musicianship and interpretative authority.

Roswaenge was possibly the only tenor of his generation to sing in performance and record Alfredo's cabaletta "O mio rimorso" in *La traviata*. He is also one of the very few tenors with the technique to sing the final high B flat in "Celeste Aida," softly, pianissimo, as Verdi intended. In his only performance of Verdi's *Otello*, which he sang for the Berlin radio and which has been excerpted on disc, he sings the final high note in the first act love duet softly in accordance with Verdi's score marking. It is more difficult to sing tenor high notes softly than to bang them out full voice because the ability to do so requires extraordinary breath control.

It is to Roswaenge's recordings from German opera that one must turn to gain a full appreciation of his talents. The voice in his peak years was a lyrico-spinto tenor of amazing power and brilliance. In fact, to some ears too bright and ringing. His technique encompassed all of the attributes of bel canto. He possessed a smooth legato, a command of vocal nuance from pianissimo through mezza voce (half voice) to a ringing forte of astounding power. He was especially admired for his high notes. He was an authentic "King of the high C's" throughout his long career.

Roswaenge's Tamino in the complete recording of *Die Zauberflöte* has inspired mixed critical evaluation. Detractors maintain that the voice is too heavy for the role, admirers point out that Tamino is a strong character who must undergo severe trials and defend his interpretation. He was the only tenor in the 78 era to record the technically demanding "Von Jugend auf in dem Kampfgefild" from Weber's *Oberon*, which requires not only fortissimo high notes but lyrical soft singing. His recording of Ivan Sussanin's aria from Glinka's *Life for the Czar* is another tour-de-force, notable for several brilliant high Cs as well as a soft, beautiful reflective passage. His recording of Florestan's aria "Gott! welch' Dunkel hier" is possibly the definitive version.

Most of Roswaenge's recordings have marks of distinction. Despite the language obstacle, his singing in the Italian and French repertoire always reveals a sound musical interpretation combined with an excellent vocal technique. He claimed that only one of his recordings completely satisfied him, that of Hugo Wolf's song "Die Feuerreiter." He was a fine singer of German Lieder, which he often sang in concert but rarely recorded.

His impact on the live theater audience, which was tremendous throughout his career is documented in various critical reviews. Indeed as late as 1956, in his "second career," Christopher Raeburn reported in the December issue of *Opera* magazine that in a performance of *Aida* at the Vienna Staatsoper, Roswaenge's "Sacerdote, io resto a te" (at the end of the third act) "was absolutely astonishing. For the record, the applause continued right through the interval and delayed the beginning of the fourth act."

—Bob Rose

ROTHENBERGER, Anneliese.

Soprano. Born 19 June 1924, in Mannheim. Married: journalist Gerd W. Diebenitz. Studied with Erika Müller at the Mannheim Conservatory; debut in Koblenz, 1943; Hamburg debut as Oscar in *Un ballo in maschera,* 1949; Hamburg State Opera, 1946-56, 1958-73; Salzburg debut creating Telemachus in Liebermann's *Penelope,* 1954; created Agnes in Liebermann's *Die Schule der Frauen,* Salzburg, 1957; Metropolitan Opera debut as Zdenka in *Arabella,* 1960; created the title role in Sutermeister's *Madame Bovary,* Zurich, 1967; specialized in Mozart and Strauss, although she also sang Violetta in *La traviata,* and the title role in *Lulu.*

Publications

By ROTHENBERGER: book–

Melodie meines Lebens: Selbsterlebtes, Selbsterzähltes. Munich, 1972.

About ROTHENBERGER: book–

von Lewinski, Wolf-Eberhard. *Anneliese Rothenberger.* Velber, 1968.

articles–

Bor, V. "Sest pevcu ve ctyrech vecerech." *Hudebni Rozhledy* 35/8 (1982): 361.
"Reflected Glory." *Opera News* 48/October (1983): 74.

*   *   *

A prominent soprano who specialized in the roles of Mozart and Richard Strauss, as well as those of Viennese operetta, Anneliese Rothenberger began her career in Koblenz in 1943.

She sang numerous Mozart roles (including Cherubino and Susanna in *Le nozze di Figaro,* Blondchen in *Die Entführung aus dem Serail,* Ilia in *Idomeneo,* and Pamina in *Die Zauberflöte*), as well as coloratura roles such as Olympia in Offenbach's *Les contes d'Hoffmann* and lyric roles such as Sophie in Richard Strauss's *Der Rosenkavalier,* Zdenka in the same composer's *Arabella,* with Violetta in Verdi's *La traviata* representing the heavier end of Rothenberger's repertoire. The extent of her range is shown in her assumption of the killing title role in Berg's atonal *Lulu.* She also created several modern roles, notably Madame Bovary in Sutermeister's opera and Telemachus in Liebermann's *Penelope,* and she also appeared in Hindemith's *Mathis der Maler* and Liebermann's *Die Schule der Frauen.*

Rothenberger appeared at the Hamburg Staatsoper from 1946 to 1956, and later at the Vienna Staatsoper, in Salzburg, at Glyndebourne, at the Edinburgh Festival, in Munich, and at the Metropolitan Opera (between 1960 and 1966, as Zdenka, Oscar in Verdi's *Un ballo in maschera,* Adele in Johann Strauss's *Die Fledermaus,* Susanna, Amor in Gluck's *Orfeo ed Euridice,* and Sophie). A skilled actress, Rothenberger could encompass this exceptionally wide range of roles; but vocally as well as dramatically her true métier would appear to have been the lighter parts. It was a fluent, nimble, graceful voice that matched in flavor her lively characterizations— not a voice weighed down by tragedy or marked by an inherent pathos. Her voice tended to sound a bit cold despite a rather pronounced, but not obtrusive, vibrato. She was proficient at coloratura; it tended to be accurate but not brilliant. Although her very highest notes took on a pinched quality, even in her prime, her timbre remained relatively even throughout the greater part of her range.

Rothenberger's recordings of complete operas and operettas include Arsena in Johann Strauss's *Der Zigeunerbaron* (1960, under Hollreiser); Susanna (1964, under Suitner); Adele (1964, under Danon); Gretel (1964, under Cluytens); Euridice in Gluck's *Orfeo ed Euridice* (1966, under Neumann); Konstanze (1965, under Krips); Harriet in Flotow's *Martha* (1988, under Heger), Rosalinde (1972, under Boskovsky); Pamina (1972, under Sawallisch); Ilia (1973, under Schmidt-Isserstedt); and Fatima in Gluck's *Le Cadi dupé* (1974, under Suitner).

Other Rothenberger appearances in complete operetta recordings include Josepha Vogelhuber in Benatzky's *Im weissen Rössl* (under Mattes), Johann Strauss's *Ein Nacht in Venedig* (under Allers), Gabriele in Johann Strauss's *Wiener Blut* (under Boskovsky), Sylvia Varescu in Kálmán's *Csárdásfürstin* (under Mattes), the countess in Kálmán's *Gräfin Mariza* (under Mattes), Eurydice in Offenbach's *Orfee aux enfers* (under Mattes), Kurfürstin Marie in Zeller's *Der Vogelhändler* (under Boskovsky). More recently (1982) she has appeared as Carlotta in a recording of Millocker's *Gasparone* (under Wallberg).

—Michael Sims

ROUSSEAU, Jean-Jacques.

Composer. Born 28 June 1712, in Geneva. Died 2 July 1778, in Ermenonville, near Paris. Self-taught in music; delivered a paper to the Académie in Paris, 1724, later published as *Dissertation sur la musique moderne,* 1743; opera composition between 1745-70. Rousseau sided with the partisans of Italian opera in the famous "guerre des bouffons," 1952.

Operas

Iphis et Anaxorète, Chambéry, c. 1740 [lost].
La découverte du nouveau monde, Lyons, 1741 [lost].
Les muses galantes (opéra-ballet), Paris, residence of La Pouplinière, 1745? [lost].
Les fêtes de Ramire, Versailles, late 1745 (revision of Rameau's *La princesse de Navarre*) [lost].
Le devin du village, Fontainebleau, 18 October 1752; six new airs posthumously published 1778.
Pygmalion (with H. Coignet) (scène lyrique), Lyons, Hôtel de Ville, 1770.
Daphnis et Cloé, P. Laujon [not performed].

Other works: vocal works, instrumental pieces.

Publications

By ROUSSEAU: books–

Écrits sur la musique. Paris, 1838; 1979.
Oeuvres complètes. Paris, 1782-83.

About ROUSSEAU: books–

Istel, E. *J.-J. Rousseau als Komponist seiner lyrischen Szene Pygmalion.* Leipzig, 1901.
Mooser, A. *Pygmalion et Le devin du village en Russie au XVIIIe siècle.* Geneva, 1946.
Oliver, A.R. *The Encyclopaedists as Critics of Music.* New York, 1947.
Sénelier, J. *Bibliographie générale des oeuvres de Jean-Jacques Rousseau.* Paris, 1949.
Veen, J. van der. *Le mélodrame musical de Rousseau au Romantisme.* The Hague, 1955.
Ebisawa, Bin. *Rousseau to ongaku.* [Japan], 1981.
L'opéra aux XVIIIe siècle. Aix-en-Provence, 1982.

articles–

Arnheim, A. "Le devin du village von J.J. Rousseau and die Parodie 'Les amours de Bastien et Bastienne.' " *Sammelbände der Internationalen Musik-Gesellschaft* 4 (1902-03): 686.
Plan, P.P. "Jean-Jacques Rousseau et Malesherbes: documents inédits." *Mercure de France* 92 (1912): 5.
Bruyère, A. "Les muses galantes, musique de Jean-Jacques Rousseau." *La revue musicale* no. 218 (1952): 5.
Whittall, Arnold. "Rousseau and the Scope of Opera." *Music and Letters* 45 (1964): 369.
Morelli, G. " 'Eloges rendus à un singulier mélange de philosophie, d'orgueil, de chimie, d'opéra, etc.': sulle ascendenze melodrammatiche della antropologia di Jean-Jacques Rousseau." *Rivista italiana di musicologia* 9 (1974): 175.
Lichtenhahn, Ernst. "Jean Jacques Rousseau: *Le devin du village.*" *Schweizerische Musikzeitung/Revue musicale suisse* 119 (1979): 299.
Heartz, Daniel. "The Beginnings of the Operatic Romance: Rousseau, Sedaine, and Monsigny." *Eighteenth-Century Studies* 15 (1981): 149.
Kintzler, Catherine. "Rameau et Voltaire: les enjeux théoriques d'une collaboration orageuse." *Revue de musicologie* 67 (1981): 139.

Morelli, Giovanni, and Elvidio Surian. "*Pigmalione* a Venezia." In *Venezia e il melodramma nel settecento, II,* edited by Maria T. Muraro. Florence, 1981.
Thacher, Christopher. "Rousseau's *Devin du village.*" In *Das deutsche Singspiel im 18. Jahrhundert,* edited by Renate Schusky, 119. Heidelberg, 1981.
Rex, Walter E. "Sobering Reflections on a Forgotten French Opera Libretto" [includes discussion of *Pygmalion*]. *Eighteenth–Century Studies* 16 (1983): 389.

Rousseau's reputation as a composer rests on only two pieces, the little opera, *Le devin du village* of 1752, and the melodrama, *Pygmalion* of 1770. In fact this amounts to a large slice of the music Rousseau composed, and of the remainder much has been lost. These are sufficient to vindicate the worth of Rousseau's theories, however, and to assess his place in music history. In the later work, *Pygmalion,* Rousseau attempted to combine the spoken word with instrumental accompaniment, and while the medium was taken up by many German composers, the form was not destined to survive. The opera *Le devin du village,* on the other hand, was an astounding success, not just in Paris where it was performed for over seventy-five years, but across Europe, where many imitations were spawned, the most illustrious example of which is Mozart's *Bastien und Bastienne* of 1768. It embodies Rousseau's belief in the value of melody and simplicity, and in its artlessness still has great charm.

Rousseau was one of the great polymaths of the eighteenth century, for as well as composing music he was a music theorist, novelist, and engaged in political speculation. It is for his non-musical interests that he is usually studied today, resulting in a vast, and still expanding, body of secondary works. The interest in his ideas is due to their articulating, or indeed forming, a new consciousness which led to Romanticism. In particular one notes an emphasis on individual sensibility, and on the artificiality of social institutions. Lying behind this is the belief that man is by nature good and sympathetic to the emotions of others, but that he is corrupted by society which creates unnecessary and harmful barriers between individuals.

The most famous of his writings is the *Discourse on the Origins and Foundations of Inequality among Men,* which in its emphasis on the natural equality between individuals helped formulate ideas which led to the struggle for democracy. *Emile,* a sort of didactic novel, still appears in the reading lists of those studying education, for its exposition of a method which utilizes the innate curiosity of the child to learn, rather than imposing a system of learning from the outside. Rousseau also wrote an autobiography, *The Confessions,* which as well as being an invaluable historical record of his life and times can be read with great pleasure, purely as literature.

Despite his central position in the history of European ideas, for much of his life he moved on the margins of society, usually reliant on the protection of patrons. He earned his daily bread mostly through music copying, which though doubtless tiresome, he took a characteristic pride in doing to a high professional standard.

Rousseau wrote the entries on music in Diderot's *Encyclopédie,* which later formed the basis of his own *Dictionary of Music.* Typically, Rousseau used these as opportunities to present his own opinions, with little pretence at impersonal objectivity.

Other writings include the *Essay on the Origin of Language,* which connects Rousseau's thoughts on music, language and society. The most notorious text is his *Letter on French Music* which discusses, if that is the right word, the relative virtues of French and Italian music. The clarity of the argument is confused by his personal dislike of the greatest French composer then living, Rameau. Rousseau puts forward rather more philosophical arguments for preferring the Italian style to the French, by starting with the belief that the natural is to be preferred to the artificial. As feeling precedes reason, so melody, as emphasized in Italian opera, is superior to harmony, as emphasized in French opera. However, it would appear that the cool logic of his argument was swept away by the pleasure of making sweeping attacks, as Rousseau eventually claims that it is impossible to connect music with the French language. One target was certainly Rameau, and another the Paris Opéra. Presumably excluded from the criticism is his own work, *Le devin du village,* composed the previous year to a French text.

The reasons for Rousseau's dislike of Rameau one finds in the *Confessions.* One of the most wounding occasions arose when Rousseau had sections of his opera, *Les muses galantes,* performed for Rameau, who voiced the thought that the best parts could not be by the same person as the worst, leaving Rousseau, and others present, to draw the conclusion that Rameau regarded him as a talentless plagiarist.

By an odd twist Rousseau was soon involved in re-writing Rameau's opera *La princesse de Navarre,* with a text by Voltaire. Rousseau claims that he managed the task well, writing several introductory pieces, an overture, and a great number of recitatives, but was subjected to a great deal of petty criticism. The last insult came when Rameau's name was removed from the concert program, seemingly because he did not want to be publicly associated with Rousseau. As the music is lost, unfortunately we are unable to judge for ourselves.

The *Letter on French Music* sparked off a heated public debate, known as the war of the bouffons. On one side were the pro-French and Rameau faction known as the King's Corner, and on the other the supporters of Rousseau and the Italian style known as the Queen's Corner. Despite the fact that Rousseau's group was initially the smaller, the controversy appears in retrospect to mark the death of the Baroque style of Lully and Rameau, and the rise of the taste for a simpler pre-classical style.

—Robin Hartwell

RUBINI, Giovanni Battista.

Tenor. Born 7 April 1794, in Romano, Italy. Died 3 March 1854, in Romano. Studied with Rosio di Bergamo; debut in Generali's *Le lugrime di una vedova,* Pavia, 1814; sang in Naples, 1815-25; Paris debut, 1825; premiered many works in Italy and Paris by Bellini and Donizetti between 1825 and 1835, including *Anna Bolena,* 1830, *La sonnambula,* 1831, and *I puritani,* 1835; London debut, 1831; sang in London and Paris, 1831-43; retired in 1844.

Publications

About RUBINI: books–

Locatelli, A. *Cenni biografici sulla stoardinaria carriera teatrale percossa da Giovanni Battista Rubini.* Milan, 1844.
Gara, E. *Giovanni Battista Rubini nel centenario delle morte.* Bergamo, 1954.
Traini, C. *Il cigno di Romano: Giovanni Battista Rubini.* Bergamo, 1954.

articles–

Zucker, S. "Last of a breed." *Opera News* 46 (1982): 24.
Chancellor, V. "Rubini and Mario: an historical perspective." *Opera* 37 (1968): 8.

* * *

Although famous for his remarkable ability to extend his normal tenor compass upwards to f (or even g) in alt, and for his having supposedly introduced vibrato as an expressive contribution to singing technique, Rubini was more than just another vocal virtuoso. Rejected by his first teacher as being unfit for music, he persevered under his father's guidance and served an honorable apprenticeship as violinist and member of the chorus in a traveling opera company. His lessons with Andrea Nozzari, like himself a native of the country around Bergamo, first gave him the idea of refining and shaping his voice in such a way that he became a natural partner for such composers as Bellini and Donizetti.

Giovanni Rubini in *Il pirata* with his wife Adèle Comelli, 1828

His first successes, however, were scored in Rossini operas, notably *Cenerentola* in which he sang at his debut in Paris (6 Oct. 1825), and in *Otello* and *La donna del lago*. But many of the Parisian singers tended to shout in what was called "une déclamation criarde," which Rubini contrasted with his own special combination of alternating soft and loud passages. As a beginner in Naples he had come under the influence of Giuditta Pasta, who wished to protest against the shouters and screamers and thus save Italian singing from the twin depradations of volume and vulgarity. Together with Brambilla and Galli, they persuaded Bellini and Donizetti to write operas in a more subtle vein, where the voice could be light, intimate, mellow and yet audacious.

Rubini, who at one time lodged with Bellini, helped him considerably in perfecting the arias in *Il pirata,* and he also encouraged Donizetti to reach new heights in *Anna Bolena,* whose principal tenor part was written for him. The exploitation of the upper part of his tessitura—where he changed to his falsetto register—was largely due to certain passages in act II of *I puritani.* Bellini simply fell in with the prevailing custom of the Pasta followers (who opted for lighter and more flexible singing), and with the established habit of Rubini himself, who maintained to the French tenor Gilbert-Louis Duprez that, while Duprez sang on his capital, Rubini survived quite nicely on the interest.

In fact Duprez over-strained his voice and had to retire early, while Rubini from his misuse of the falsetto ruined his throat and stopped singing at fifty. Wagner heard Rubini in Paris, and was much put off by a performance of *Don Giovanni* in which the famous tenor sang arias softly throughout, only to break forth into a loud interlarded cadenza ending with an explosive fermata.

He was in fact a master of florid execution, but could not always be trusted to sing these passages with taste. His vibrato, although by no means the first in vocal history, lent expression and pathos to certain arias, which were also occasionally vehicles for the "sob" effect which has since been much abused. Rubini is supposed to have broken his collarbone in an attempt to reach a high note, but considering his reliance on the gentler sounds of the falsetto this legend may not be reliable. He was not a great actor, but his presence was such that the English critic Chorley had no hesitation in hailing him as a genius. Rubini, who died a very rich man, had sung throughout his native land, and in Paris, Berlin, London, St Petersburg and many other operatic cities, always to the amazement and enthusiasm of his audiences. His art, if a very unusual one, apparently enjoyed an almost universal appeal, and his technique served him well in the roles especially written for him.

—Denis Stevens

RUBINSTEIN, Anton.

Composer. Born 28 November 1829, in Vykhvatinetz, Podolia, Russia. Died 20 November 1894, in Peterhof, near St Petersburg. Studied piano with Alexandre Villoing in Moscow; taken to Paris by Villoing in 1839, where he played for Chopin and Liszt; concert tour of the Netherlands, Germany, Austria, England, Norway, and Sweden, 1841-43; studied composition with S.W. Dehn in Berlin, 1844; toured Hungary with the flutist Heindl; in St Petersburg, 1848; opera composition under the patronage of the Grand Duchess Helena Pavlovna; tour of western Europe, 1854-58; court pianist and conductor of the court concerts in St Petersburg, 1858; director of the Russian Musical Society, 1859; founded the Imperial Conservatory in St Petersburg, 1862, and was its director until 1867; concerts in Europe, 1867-70; American tour, 1872-73; directorship of the St Petersburg Conservatory, 1887-1891; established the Rubinstein prize, 1890; in Dresden, 1891-94; returned to Russia before his death.

Operas

Dmitry Donskoy, V.A. Sollogub, V.R. Zotov (after Ozerov), 1849-50, St Petersburg, 1852.

The Siberian Huntsmen [*Sibirskiye okhotniki*], A. Zherebtsov, 1852, Weimar, 1854.

Stenka Razin, M. Voskresensky, 1852 [unfinished].

Hadji-Abrek (performed as *Mest'* [*Revenge*]), A. Zhemchuzhnikov (after Lermontov), 1852-53, St Petersburg, 1858.

Tom the Fool [*Fomka-durachok*], M.L. Mikhaylov, 1853, St Petersburg, 1853.

Das verlorene Paradies (sacred opera), A. Schlönbach (after Milton), 1856, Düsseldorf, 1875.

Die Kinder der Heide, S.H. Mosenthal (after Beck), 1860, Vienna, 1861.

Feramors, J. Rodenberg (after T. Moore), 1862, Dresden, 1863.

Der Thurm zu Babel (sacred opera), J. Rodenberg, 1869, Königsberg, 1870.

Demon, P.A. Viskovatov (after Lermontov), 1871, St Petersburg, 1875.

Die Makkabäer, S.H. Mosenthal (after O. Ludwig), 1874, Berlin, 1875.

Nero, J. Barbier, 1875-76, Hamburg, 1879.

Kalashnikov the Merchant [*Kupets Kalashnikov*], N. Kulikov (after Lermontov), 1877-79, St Petersburg, 1880.

Sulamith (opera/oratorio), J. Rodenberg (after the *Song of Songs*), 1882-83, Hamburg, 1883.

Unter Räubern, E. Wichert, 1883, Hamburg, 1883.

Der Papagei, H. Wittmann (after a Persian story), 1884, Hamburg, 1884.

The Careworn One [*Goryusha*], D. Averkiyev, 1888, St Petersburg, 1889.

Moses (sacred opera), S.H. Mosenthal, 1885-91, Prague, 1892.

Christus (sacred opera), H. Bulthaupt, 1887-93, Bremen, 1895.

Other works: sacred and secular vocal music, orchestral works, chamber music, piano pieces.

Publications

By RUBINSTEIN: books–

Avtobiograficheskiye vospominaniya (*1829-1889*). St Petersburg, 1889; English translation as *Autobiography of Anton Rubinstein, 1829-1889,* 1890; 1969.

Muzïka i eyo predstaviteli. Moscow, 1891; English translation as *Music and its Masters: a Conversation on Music,* 1891.

Barenboym, Lev, ed. *Izbrannïye pis'ma* [selected letters]. Leningrad, 1954.

Literaturnoye nasledie. V trek tomak I. Stat'i. Knigi. Dokladnye zapiski. Reči. Moscow, 1983.

articles–

"Istoriya literaturï fortepiannoy muzïki." In *Muzïkal' noye
obozreniye.* Petersburg, 1888; German translation as *Die
Meister des Klaviers,* 1899.

About RUBINSTEIN: books–

Droucker, S. *Erinnerungen an Anton Rubinstein.* Leipzig,
1904.
Findeyzen, N.T. *A.G. Rubinshteyn: ocherk evo zhiznii muzïkal'noy deyatel'nosti* [life and musical activities]. Moscow,
1907.
Hervey, A. *Rubinstein.* London, 1913; 2nd ed., 1922.
Glebov, I [B. Asef'yev]. *Anton Grigor'yevich Rubinshteyn v
evo muzïkal'noy deyatel'nosti i otzïvakh sovremennikov*
[musical activities and contemporary opinions]. Moscow,
1929.
Drinker Bowen, C. *Free Artist: the Story of Anton and Nicholas Rubinstein.* New York, 1939.
Alexeyev, A. *Anton Rubinshteyn.* Moscow and Leningrad,
1945.
Barenboym, L. *Anton Grigor'yevich Rubinshteyn.* Leningrad,
1957-62.

articles–

Bennigsen, O. "The Brothers Rubinstein and their Circle."
Musical Quarterly 25 (1939): 407.
Abraham, G. "Anton Rubinstein: Russian Composer." *Musi-
cal Times* 86 (1945): 361.
Stolte, Heinz. *"Ein Steinwurf oder Opfer um Oper.* Zur Inter-
pretation von Friedrich Hebbels Operntext." *Hebbel-
Jahrbuch* (1979): 12.
Jazvinskaja, Elena. "K sceničeskoj istorii opery A.G. Rubin-
štejna *Kupec Kalašnikov*" [Theatrical history of *Kupec
Kalašnikov*]. In *Pamjatniki kul'tury: novye otkrytija pis'-
mennost', iskusstvo, arheologija. Ezegodnik, 1979,* 152. Le-
ningrad, 1980.

*   *   *

Anton Rubinstein, 1879

Of Anton Rubinstein's enormous output as a composer, almost nothing is performed today outside of Russia, and only
a small percentage within. Although he wrote twenty stage
works (few of which had any great success in his lifetime),
only *Demon* is performed today. Nonetheless, these works
are the output of an important pedagogue and an influential
(if controversial) figure on the Russian scene.

Rubinstein belongs to the post-Glinka generation of Russian composers to whom fell the burden of keeping alive the
newly founded national school. After early efforts at writing
operas based on nationalist subjects failed with the public,
Rubinstein denounced "The Five" (Balakirev, Borodin, Cui,
Musorgsky, and Rimsky-Korsakov), and what he saw as their
amateurish approach to the compositional problems of creating a genuinely Russian music. Rubinstein's reaction may in
part be explained by his extensive western European training
as a musician and his international reputation as pianist
(whose only rival was Liszt).

Rubinstein was an incredibly prolific composer, perhaps
too prolific. No composer has ever had quite his work ethic,
nor was any more eager to compose. Indicative of this aspect
of Rubinstein's compositional process is the story that at
one time he arrived at the apartment of his librettist, Jules
Rodenburg, and sang through thirty pages of opera to the

words "rats, mice, rats, mice," saying that he had to write
his own words if the libretto was too slow in coming. Appropriately, this music became part of *Der Thurm zu Babel* (*The
Tower of Babel*).

Probably due to his traditional training at various western
European musical centers and his conservative views, Rubinstein's greatest stylistic and aesthetic influence was Mendelssohn. Unlike Mendelssohn, however, Rubinstein used little
of the neo-Baroque and *stile antico* found in *Elijah* or *Paulus*
(excepting the occasional fugue). Instead, Rubinstein wrote
in the common, international style of the mid-nineteenth century, so that the colorlessness of what we might term his
personal style is all too evident. He is most effective when he
writes in an exotic vein (*Feramors,* for example), but he is
less sure of himself in more conventional, straightforward
passages. As a result, almost every act of his stage works has
at least one effective number, but there is much padding and
passagework.

In his recitatives, Rubinstein is frequently quite dull, making surprising overuse of the completely unaccompanied recitative: for four or five measures at a time, the texture is given
over to the solo voice. The employment of this technique was
perhaps influenced by Glinka's masterful use of the device in
Ivan Susanin's great monologue in act IV of *A Life for the
Tsar,* but, unlike Glinka, Rubinstein does not reserve the
technique for moments of high drama or psychological revelation; instead, Rubinstein frequently uses it for the most pedestrian of purposes, such as in passages of plot exposition (it is
tempting to view some of these passages as the result of words
being grafted to existing music). In his ensemble writing,
there is usually one clear principal voice, the others frequently

singing in a monotone, which gives the ensembles a feeling of being vocal arrangements of piano accompaniments.

Perhaps as a result of Mendelssohn's influence, Rubinstein wrote a number of Biblical operas, a kind of hybrid of opera and oratorio, with the large choral role characteristic of the latter, but the staging and attempted dramatic design of the former. In actuality, these works read more like oratorios; the plots are episodic, as in *Christus,* whose prologue, seven scenes, and epilogue condense the life of Christ into a series of events, including the temptation in the wilderness, the Sermon on the Mount, and the betrayal in the garden. *Moses* is similarly constructed in eight scenes. *Christus* is more effective in part, however, because of the important role accorded to Satan—not only in the temptation episode, but also in the final scene of death on the cross, where the devil's triumph is interrupted by a chorus of heavenly spirits in a manner quite similar to the final scene in the better planned and executed *Demon.*

In his dramatic works, Rubinstein is clearly at his best in both the most impersonal passages and the most personal, that is, the exotic scene-setting passages and the more intimate demon-type conflicts (Rubinstein was fascinated with the conflict of spiritual good and evil). His importance to opera, however, was more as a pedagogue: in particular, Rubinstein influenced his student Tchaikovsky's opera composition considerably. He did not, however, keep up with contemporary opera, due in part to his feud with the Balakirev circle, and was not familiar with such works as Musorgsky's *Boris Godunov.* As a result, much of Rubinstein's operatic music is more pan-European than it is specifically Russian.

—Gregory Salmon

RUDEL, Julius.

Conductor. Born 6 March 1921, in Vienna. Studied at the Vienna Academy of Music; emigrated to the United States, 1938, and became a naturalized citizen, 1944; studied at the Mannes School of Music, New York; United States conducting debut as conductor at the New York City Opera, 1944; music director of the New York City Opera, 1957-79; honorary insignia for arts and sciences from the Austrian government, 1961; music director of the Buffalo Philharmonic Orchestra, 1979-85.

*   *   *

Julius Rudel is one of the rare breed of musicians who excel equally as performers and administrators. Although since 1980 he has been active principally on the podium, his most significant contribution to American musical life undoubtedly came during the nearly twenty-five years in which he was the general director, as well as the principal conductor, of the New York City Opera.

With Rudel, versatility and virtuosity go hand in hand. Although he resists identification as a specialist in any one epoch or style of music, Rudel is regarded as a conductor who has an affinity for Mozart, a feeling for nineteenth-century Romantics, a flair for French music, and a keen insight into such moderns as Kurt Weill, Benjamin Britten and Alberto Ginastera—many of whose works he has introduced to this country. He has been a strong exponent of American composers from George Gershwin to the present, and he has an innate sympathy for the lilting music of his native Vienna.

Rudel learned to conduct in the United States, but he received his earliest musical training in Vienna. Following the Nazi Anschluss in 1938, he emigrated with his mother and younger brother to New York. Armed with a conducting diploma from the Mannes School of Music, he got a non-paying job as a rehearsal pianist with the New York City Opera, then in the process of formation. The next year he received his first conducting assignment there, Johann Strauss's *Der Zigeunerbaron.* In succeeding seasons he undertook more frequent conductorial duties until he became one of the company's mainstays on the podium. His lucid style, musical command and no-nonsense approach won him the respect of performers and the approval of critics and audiences.

In the mid-1950s the New York City Opera was afflicted by managerial and financial crises and, largely as a result of a petition by company members to the board of directors, Rudel was put in charge. He forthwith began a series of brilliant productions, many of which he conducted himself. With the aid of the Ford Foundation he staged such American works as Douglas Moore's *The Ballad of Baby Doe,* Carlisle Floyd's *Susannah,* Robert Ward's *The Crucible* and Kurt Weill's *Street Scene.* Equally enterprising were his productions of contemporary works from abroad including Britten's *A Midsummer Night's Dream,* Poulenc's *Dialogues des Carmélites,* Prokofiev's *Flaming Angel* and von Einem's *Dantons Tod.* Standard repertory works were given innovative stagings, and the company's emphasis on stylish singing and tightly-knit ensemble work enabled it to triumph even in such large-scale operas as *Die Meistersinger, Der Rosenkavalier, Mefistofele* and *Les contes d'Hoffmann.*

In 1966 the company moved from its somewhat tacky quarters at the City Center—a converted Masonic hall—to a new home at Lincoln Center for the Performing Arts, literally side-by-side with the Metropolitan Opera House. Typically, Rudel chose for his inaugural work there Ginastera's *Don Rodrigo,* never before given in North America, and introduced to New York audiences a young tenor named Placido Domingo. It was at Lincoln Center that the soprano Beverly Sills, long a company mainstay, burst into international stardom with unforgettable performances in Massenet's *Manon* and Handel's *Giulio Cesare.* In the latter she was joined by the fine bass Norman Treigle, also one of the company's bulwarks, who unfortunately died at the peak of his career.

Involved as he was at the New York City Opera, Rudel—who was fond of quoting the saying "If you want something done, ask a busy man"—found time to serve stints as head of the Caramoor Festival in Katonah, New York, and as music adviser to the Kennedy Center for the Performing Arts in Washington, D.C. He also pursued his own conductorial career, both operatic and symphonic, in the United States and abroad.

In 1979 Rudel resigned as director of the New York City Opera, being succeeded by Beverly Sills. He forthwith expanded his conducting activities, becoming music director of the Buffalo Philharmonic (until 1985) and also working extensively in opera. Among the companies with which he appears regularly is the Metropolitan Opera, where audiences always greet him with particular warmth. He has not conducted at the New York City Opera since his departure.

—Herbert Kupferberg

RUFFO, Titta [Ruffo Cafiero Titta].

Baritone. Born 9 June 1877, in Pisa. Died 6 July 1953, in Florence. Studied with Senatore Sparapani, Venceslao Persichini, and Lelio Casini. Debut as the Herald in *Lohengrin,* at the Teatro Costanzi in Rome, 9 April 1898; appeared in Chile, 1900; appeared at Teatro Massimo in Egypt, 1901, Buenos Aires in 1902, Covent Garden in 1903, and as Rigoletto at Teatro alla Scala in 1904; United States debut as Rigoletto in Philadelphia, 1912; served in Italian army 1917-18; debut at Metropolitan Opera as Rossini's Figaro, 1922, and remained at Met until 1929.

Publications

By RUFFO: books–

La mia parabola. Milan, 1937; edited by T. Ruffo, Jr, and C. Marinelli Roscioni, Rome, 1977.

About RUFFO: books–

Monaldi, G. *Cantanti celebri.* Rome, 1929.
Gaisberg, F. *The Music Goes Round.* New York, 1943; reprinted as *Music on Record,* 1946.
Lauri-Volpi, G. *Voci parallele.* Milan, 1955.
Farkas, A., ed. *Titta Ruffo: An Anthology.* New York, 1984.

articles–

Wolf, A. "Titta Ruffo." *Record Collector* 2/no. 5 (1947): 11.

*   *   *

Titta Ruffo (Ruffo Cafiero Titta) was born in Pisa, on 9 June 1877. His father, Oreste, was an iron worker and young Ruffo, never allowed to attend school, started to work in his father's shop when he was ten years old. As he was growing up, his older brother Ettore, a music student at the time, took young Ruffo to a performance of *Cavalleria rusticana.* He was so impressed by the performance that upon returning home from the theater, he begged Ettore to play the "Siciliana" on his flute. As Ruffo later recalled, almost unaware of what he was doing, he began to sing "in a tenor voice of such beauty and spontaneity that when the music ended we looked at each other with astonishment. [Ettore] could not explain where my voice came from, and clasping his flute with trembling hands exclaimed: 'This is a miracle!'"

Years later, fellow baritone and colleague Giuseppe de Luca expressed the same sentiment. Asked to comment on Titta Ruffo's voice, he said: "That was no voice—it was a miracle!" This assessment is borne out by all contemporary reviews and the recordings. Ruffo's voice had a natural placement, and it only needed schooling and refinement. Senatore Sparapani taught him the rudiments of singing and breath control; he then attended the classes of Venceslao Persichini at the Accademia di Santa Cecilia of Rome for about six months. After quitting the Academy, he received sporadic private instruction from the baritone Lelio Casini. With his funds depleted, he could wait no longer: he either had to obtain an engagement or give up the dream of a singing career. After a series of auditions he was engaged to sing the Herald in *Lohengrin* at the Teatro Costanzi in Rome. He made his debut on 9 April 1898, under the name of Titta Ruffo, reversing his given and family name upon the suggestion of an impresario who found it more euphonious.

Titta Ruffo in the title role of Franchetti's *Cristoforo Colombo*

Ruffo's first engagements were in the Italian provinces, and he advanced slowly to larger and more important theaters. His first South American engagement took him to Chile, from July through October 1900. On the long sea voyage he met mezzo-soprano Adelina Fanton Fontana (1867-1907), a member of the company, who had a lasting influence on his life and career. She helped him artistically and became his companion until her premature death.

A series of important milestones followed. Ruffo appeared at the Teatro Massimo of Palermo and in Egypt in 1901, Buenos Aires and Montevideo in 1902, Covent Garden and La Fenice in Venice in 1903, the Teatro alla Scala in 1904, Russia and Paris in 1905, Vienna in 1906, and the San Carlo of Naples in 1908. During his Russian tours (1905-07) he sang in Moscow, St Petersburg, Kiev, Odessa, and Khar'kov. In 1908 he took part in the inaugural season of the Teatro Colón in Buenos Aires, and he returned to that city for the next three summers (and five more seasons between 1915 and 1931). He made his North American debut as Rigoletto in Philadelphia, on 4 November 1912, and his success prompted the company to rent the Metropolitan Opera House for a single performance of Ambroise Thomas' *Hamlet,* a great personal triumph for Ruffo. He then moved on to Chicago where he first appeared on 29 November 1912, again in *Rigoletto.* He soon became a local favorite and returned there for several seasons before and after the war.

Ruffo served two years in the Italian army (1917-18) and after resuming his career he rejoined the Chicago company in 1920. He became a member of the Metropolitan Opera Company in the season following Caruso's death, and made his debut as Rossini's Figaro on 19 January 1922. He remained a member of the company until 1929, singing seven roles in 55 performances, 47 of those in the house. After leaving the Met he returned to North America once more, to participate in the festive opening program of Radio City Music Hall (27 December 1932).

Between his extended engagements, Ruffo toured extensively. He sang in most major cities, opera houses, and auditoriums of Europe, and North and South America. He sang most often in Argentina, where he was lionized by his devoted public. During his best years his fees were the highest among baritones, ranking with those of Caruso and Chaliapin. He took part in five world premieres; on 13 December 1920 he created the title role of Leoncavallo's *Edipo re* in Chicago, a role that was expressly composed for him.

Lacking any formal education, Ruffo was an autodidact. He had a great interest in the arts, and he read extensively, particularly about the historical characters he was to impersonate and the period in which they lived. Purely fictional characters he would occasionally model on real persons. One of his most successful creations, Tonio in *Pagliacci,* was based on a poor retarded man he met several times in a forest near the place where he was vacationing. His other widely acclaimed roles were Rigoletto, the title role of *Hamlet,* and Figaro. His large repertoire included 56 roles, among them the major Verdi, Puccini, Leoncavallo, and Giordano roles; from the French repertory Hamlet, Escamillo, Nelusko, Athanael, Valentin and Méphistophélès *(Faust);* from the Russian repertory Boris Godunov, Eugene Onegin, and the title role of Rubinstein's *Demon.* His only Mozart role was Don Giovanni. Ruffo's versatility extended to the legitimate theater as well: in 1915 he participated in a stage performance of *Amphion* at the side of actor Gustavo Salvini. Ruffo spoke pure Italian with exemplary diction, which can be heard in his two recorded monologues from Shakespeare's *Hamlet.*

Because of overuse, the prodigal voice began to fail by the time Ruffo reached fifty, and he was obliged to retire in his mid-fifties. Some maintain that he was forced into early retirement because he never learned to sing properly, but logic suggests otherwise. His steady engagements lasted from 1898 until the end of 1932, and a thirty-four year time-span is anything but a short career. Furthermore, a faultily produced voice could not have withstood the relentless demands imposed upon it for over three decades.

Ruffo's voice was unique in every respect. It had extraordinary power without parallel in his lifetime, a highly individual and appealing timbre with a brilliant sheen and an incisive vibrato. He produced the voluminous sound with a free, unobstructed throat, and the voice, like Caruso's, seemed to open up and gain in brilliance with every note moving up on the scale. In his best years Ruffo had an easy top to a recorded high A and a privately witnessed high C. The forward placement of the voice, "in the mask," gave it unique resonance, supported by a spectacular breath control that made his cadenza of the *Hamlet* "Drinking Song" a perennial showstopper. Although the voice was perfectly equalized, the recordings show that the lowest notes of his range were less secure, and they noticeably weakened toward the end of his career.

Titta Ruffo was an honest, ethical man, a staunch anti-fascist who suffered great indignities at the hands of the fascist regime. Plaques commemorating his appearances in Pisa and Terni were vandalized by the blackshirts; before an appearance in Marseille he was attacked by fascist thugs; his passport was revoked and he was even briefly incarcerated on the orders of Mussolini. The socialist leader Giacomo Matteotti, kidnapped and assassinated by the fascists in 1924, was the husband of his sister Velia. Restricted in his movements, Ruffo spent most of his retirement years in his native Pisa,

where he died on 5 July 1953. He left a recorded legacy against which all other baritones are measured. The recordings have a lasting appeal and have been frequently reissued, most recently in a two-album set containing all of his records, including unpublished takes. He made fifteen sides for Pathé in 1904, and thereafter recorded only for the Gramophone Company ("His Master's Voice") in Milan and London, and the Victor Talking Machine Co. in Camden, N.J. and New York. His records show the maturing of his interpretations and the development, zenith, and eventual decline of his immense voice that Andrès de Segurola likened to the "imposing mass of the Niagara Falls—no end in sight."

—Andrew Farkas

RUSALKA.

Composer: Antonin Dvořák.

Librettist: J. Kvapil.

First Performance: Prague, National Theater, 31 March 1901.

Roles: Rusalka (soprano); Prince (tenor); Watersprite (bass); Ježibaba (contralto); Foreign Princess (soprano); Hunter (baritone); Gamekeeper (tenor); Kitchenboy (soprano); Three Dryads; chorus (SATB) (SSAA).

Publications

article–

Schläder, Jürgen. "Märchenoper oder symbolistisches Musikdrama? Zum Interpretationsrahm der Titelrolle in Dvořáks *Rusalka.*" *Die Musikforschung* 34 (1981): 25.

unpublished–

Bykovskih, Majja. "Principy dramaturgii pozdnih oper Antonína Dvorzaka *Čert i Káča* i *Rusalka*" [principles of dramaturgy in Antonín Dvořák's later operas *Kate and the Devil* and *Rusalka*]. Ph.D. dissertation, Gosudarstvennaja Konservatorija, Moscow, 1984.

*   *   *

The ninth of Dvořák's ten operas, *Rusalka* was composed in 1900, the same year in which Puccini's *Tosca* and Gustave Charpentier's *Louise* were first performed. And yet in contrast to the verismo, or realistic, treatment of everyday life in *Tosca* and *Louise* (in the case of the former some have said overly realistic, most notably Joseph Kerman when he penned his oft-quoted assessment of the opera as "that shabby little shocker" dressed up in "café-music banality"), *Rusalka*, like Humperdinck's *Hänsel und Gretel* which reached Prague five years earlier in 1895, is a reaction against the blood-and-guts violence of verismo. Dvořák in fact called *Rusalka* a "lyric fairy-tale in three acts." His librettist, Jaroslav Kvapil (not to be confused with the composer of the same name, a pupil of Janáček's), in fashioning the opera's sequence of dreamlike scenes, noted that he was inspired to take up the subject "in the land of [Hans Christian] Andersen, on the island of Bornholm, where I was spending my summer holidays. The fairy-tales of Karel Jaromír Erben and Božena Němcová accompanied me to the seashore, and there merged into a single tale in the manner of Andersen." As it happens, the sea had a profound effect on Kvapil, for what he produced was another version of the ancient French story of Mélusine, the Lorelei, Friedrich de La Motte-Fouqué's *Undine*, Andersen's *The Little Mermaid*, and the Ruthie in Gerhardt Hauptman's *Sunken Bell*, all of which tell of the doomed love of a water nymph and a mortal man.

Kvapil's account, praised by no less a master librettist than Hugo von Hofmannsthal (librettist of six of Richard Strauss's operas) for its "pleasing musical verse, full of tender, shimmering and shadowy moods, the work of an artist who was also a fine connoisseur of the stage and its requirements,"

The first production of *Rusalka*, with Ruzena Maturova in the title role, National Theater, Prague, 1901

opens not by the shore of some large sea, but rather at the edge of a forest lake. There the water nymph Rusalka sings of her love for a handsome prince. She describes her love to the old Water Sprite, whom she calls father, in unequivocally sensual terms: "He comes here often, reposes in my embrace, he leaves his clothes on the shore and plunges into my arms. Yet I am just a wave, he cannot sense my being." And so Rusalka yearns to be made human, to "live in the sunshine," so that she might love. Her wish is granted by the witch Ježibaba, but for a price: in human form she must remain mute, and should she be rejected in love both she and her lover will be cast into the lake in "eternal damnation." Although Rusalka has been taken by the prince to his castle by act II, we soon discover that her embrace "is always cold," that she does not "burn with passion." Thus the prince turns his attention to a lovely foreign princess. At the start of act III, rejected by the prince, Rusalka sits again at the edge of the forest lake, her youth vanished, her hair turned white. Ježibaba emerges from her cottage and sings, "Short has been your honeymooning, long will be your lamenting." Rusalka again asks the witch to grant her a wish: return her to her life as a water nymph. Once more there is a price. She must slay her seducer. Her refusal prompts Ježibaba to deliver a jeering rebuke: "Into silly human form you have been lured—and now you lack the strength to spill human blood. Man attains manhood only when he has dipped his hand in blood, when moved by passion he becomes drunk with his neighbor's blood." Rusalka seeks refuge in the lake but is rebuffed by her former sisters, the three Dryads. "Do not descend to us," they ominously intone, lest "with the will-o'-the-wisps you play, to entice people to their graves!" At the opera's end it is the prince who now approaches the lake's edge, the place where he first met Rusalka. She suddenly appears, lighted by the glow of the moon. The prince ardently begs her for a kiss. She warns him, "If I kiss you now, you are lost for all time." Staggering toward her he repeats the request. At last she yields. To his now mute and lifeless body she sings: "Because you loved, because you were humanly fickle, because of all that makes up my fate—God have mercy on your human soul!" The curtain falls as Rusalka returns at last to the depths of the forest lake.

Lovingly and intelligently produced, the "sweet sadness"—as one critic has aptly put it—at the heart of *Rusalka* can make for an intensely moving theatrical experience. (Despite its success and undeniable merit, one must wonder if the English National production, available on videotape, set as it is by David Poultney in an Edwardian nursery replete with incestuous undertones, is really in touch with the story envisioned by its creators.) The score, rich and ample in its orchestration, contains some of the most beautiful melodies Dvořák would ever compose. His use of recurring motives for the principal characters, a system he appears to have conceived independently of Wagner or of Smetana, is as ingenious as it is subtle. His bewitching tone-painting of the moonlight forest is capable of holding a modern, cough-prone audience in rapt silence. Evocations of nature clearly brought out the very best in Dvořák. The only one of his operas to win a place in the international repertory, *Rusalka* nevertheless deserves to be known by a far greater number of listeners than the record collector who occasionally puts on Rusalka's lovely aria "O silver moon" or those lucky enough to live near operatic companies dedicated to adventurous fare. Opera houses—and their audiences—in need of a rest from the same handful of war-horses could do well by *Rusalka*. Dvořák at his very best can be glorious indeed.

—James Parsons

RUSLAN AND LYUDMILA [Ruslan i Lyudmila].

Composer: Mikhail Glinka.

Librettists: V.F. Shirkov, N.V. Kukol'nik, M.A. Gedeonov, N.A. Markevich (after Pushkin).

First Performance: St Petersburg, Bol'shoy, 9 December 1842.

Roles: Svietozar (bass); Lyudmila (soprano); Ruslan (baritone); Ratmir (contralto); Farlaf (bass); Finn (tenor); Naina (mezzo-soprano); Gorislava (soprano); Bayan (tenor); Chernomor (tenor); Aedo (tenor); chorus (SSATB).

Publications

article–

Abraham, Gerald. *"Ruslan and Lyudmila."* In *On Russian Music*, 20. London, 1939.

*   *   *

Ruslan and Lyudmila, Glinka's second and last opera, was to have a profound and lasting effect on Russian music. In spite of its flaws, it was hailed at once as a masterpiece equal to Mozart's greatest operas by those interested in promoting nationalist music, and it remained influential for generations of composers after Glinka.

The opera is based on a poem of the same name by the young Alexander Pushkin, the poet whose work so often provided inspiration for Russian composers. Pushkin's poem is a romantic fairy tale of abduction, seduction, and enchantment. By turns erotic, violent, frightening, humorous, and satirical, it has been called a "mock-romantic fairy tale ballad parody of pseudo-Kievan sham-chivalry."

Glinka had indeed wanted the poet himself to prepare the libretto, but Pushkin's death early in 1837 scotched that plan. Valerian Shirkov was the main librettist, though several others, including the composer, helped write various scenes—contributing further to the confusing nature of the libretto. Little remains of Pushkin's original.

The opera opens in Kiev, with a feast celebrating the incipient wedding of Lyudmila and Ruslan. Suddenly darkness falls, and Lyudmila is kidnapped, whereupon her father the Grand Prince Svietozar promises her hand and half his kingdom to the man who rescues her. Ruslan eagerly sets out in pursuit, accompanied by Ratmir and Farlaf, two previously unsuccessful suitors.

Ruslan meets an old magician, the Finn, who tells him that the dwarf Chernomor has abducted Lyudmila and warns him against Naina, a wicked enchantress. After a series of adventures, Ruslan and Ratmir both find themselves in Naina's palace under the spell of her seductive maidens. The Finn finally arrives to break the spell, bring Ratmir together

with his slave Gorislava, and set the three of them on their way to rescue Lyudmila.

At Chernomor's palace, the captive Lyudmila vents her despair and defiance. When Ruslan is seen approaching, Chernomor casts a spell on Lyudmila, plunging her into a deep sleep, and departs to fight Ruslan. Ruslan enters victorious, having cut off the dwarf's long beard—the source of his evil power. Lyudmila, however, cannot be wakened. En route back to Kiev, Lyudmila is stolen away by Farlaf, who also is unable to waken Lyudmila. When Ruslan arrives with Ratmir, he breaks the spell with the aid of a magic ring from the Finn, and the opera ends in general rejoicing.

The unreality of the subject affords little opportunity for deep human emotion, and, lacking dramatic emotional crises to spur the action, this tale is ill-suited to the stage. The opera focuses instead on such dramatic irrelevancies as narrations of past events of marginal importance to the plot. Furthermore, it is frequently difficult to make out the connection between scenes, particularly when information from the story has been omitted. During Ruslan's encounter with the head, for example, it is not explained why the knight is in need of a sword (he broke it in his encounter with Rogdai, the third rival suitor from Pushkin's poem, who is eliminated entirely from the opera).

Puzzling omissions are matched by equally puzzling additions, especially with respect to the character of Ratmir. Gorislava, a slave girl conveniently in love with Ratmir, is invented for him to have in place of Lyudmila; this is made clear in act III, where the only goal aside from the creation of atmosphere is the elimination of Ratmir as a rival. Pushkin made him out to be a frighteningly serious rival for Ruslan, and his easy transference of affection from Lyudmila to Gorislava is unconvincing. There is no emotional crisis; the Finn simply appears and reminds them that Ruslan is destined to have Lyudmila and Ratmir to have Gorislava.

Though there is little to bind everything together into a coherent dramatic whole, many of these set pieces contain very fine music. Some is inevitably derivative; the bravura arias of both Lyudmila and Farlaf, her comically cowardly suitor, are meritorious examples of the Italian style. But Chernomor's famous march, so suggestive of jerky, lurching movements, has served as a model for "musical grotesques" in the music of Musorgsky, Prokofiev, Stravinsky, and Shostakovich. Here too is the source of orientalism and the magic idiom so pervasive in later Russian operas. Many of Glinka's innovative practices became standard, such as the use of a combination of piano and harp to mimic the sound of a *gusli*, a plucked string folk instrument.

Glinka is often credited with the earliest use of the wholetone scale in *Ruslan and Lyudmila*. The harmonic destabilization of this scale can represent the effect of Chernomor's magical machinations. In act IV, where Ruslan opposes the dwarf's whole-tone assault with a firm E major, the conflict between the two is even more clearly represented in the music.

Perhaps the most important of musical techniques in Glinka's legacy is his use of folk music. Turkish, Tatar, Caucasian, Persian, Finnish, and Russian melodies appear in the opera, albeit not in the dramatic scenes holding the opera together; rather, they are used in the set pieces which are, dramatically speaking, merely decorative. Their chief interest lies in what Glinka does with them. His "changing-background" technique for incorporating folk melodies into larger musical structures was to prove especially valuable for a broad range of composition, operatic and instrumental alike.

The differences between Glinka's first opera (*A Life for the Tsar*) and *Ruslan and Lyudmila* engendered a great deal of controversy regarding the relative merits of the two operas.

But Tchaikovsky, reviewing a performance of *Ruslan* in 1872, wrote, "*Ruslan* cannot be included among the model operas; it is simply a magical spectacle accompanied by outstandingly fine music."

—Elizabeth W. Patton

RUSTIC CHIVALRY
See CAVALLERIA RUSTICANA

RYSANEK, Leonie.

Soprano. Born 12 November 1926, in Vienna. Married: musicologist E.L. Gausmann. Studied at Vienna Conservatory, with Alfred Jerger, Rudolf Grossman, and Clothilde Radony von Ottean; debut as Agathe in *Der Freischütz,* Innsbruck, 1949; sang Sieglinde in first postwar Bayreuth Festival, 1951; Bavarian State Opera, Munich, 1952-54; Covent Garden debut as Danae, 1953; Vienna State Opera debut, 1954; American debut as Senta in *Der fliegende Holländer,* San Francisco, 1956; Metropolitan Opera debut as Lady Macbeth, 1959; Metropolitan Opera Gala celebrated her 25th anniversary with the company, 1984; her twenty roles there include Elisabeth, the Marschallin, Tosca, Salome, Aida, Elsa, and Desdemona.

Publications:

By RYSANEK: articles–

"Née pour chanter Strauss (conversation with Monique Barichella)." *Avant-scène opéra,* November 1986.
"De Kostelnicka à Kabanikha." *Avant-scène opéra,* November 1988.

About RYSANEK: articles–

Gualerzi, G. "Rysanek, Leonie." In *Le grandi voci,* ed. by R. Celetti, Rome, 1964.
Rosenthal, Harold. "Leonie Rysanek." *Great Singers of Today.* London, 1966.
Profile. *Opera News* 43 (20 January 1979): 26.
Ecker, T. "Leonie Rysanek Keeps Earning Ovations." *The Christian Science Monitor* 71 (8 February 1979): 19.
[Leonie Rysanek]. *Oper und Konzert* 17/11 (1979): 25.
Baxter, R. "Leonie Rysanek." *Fugue* 4/November (1979): 28.
von Buchau, S. "Silver Anniversary for Rysanek." *San Francisco Opera Magazine* 3/Fall (1980): 34.
Asche, G. "Leonie Rysanek: Wieland hatte Mühe, mich zu zähmen." *Opernwelt* Yearbook 1981: 23.
Kaplan, A. "Rysanek on Ortrud." *San Francisco Opera Magazine* 10/Fall (1982): 58.
Mahlke, S. "Traumbild Elektra; der Opernfilm von Karl Böhm und Götz Friedrich und eine Dokumentation seiner Enstehung." *Opernwelt* 23/11 (1982): 31.
Profile. *San Francisco Opera Magazine* 2/Summer (1983): 39.
O'Connor, T. "The Singers View their Characters (Sieglinde in *Die Walküre*)." *San Francisco Opera Magazine* 2/Summer (1983): 55.
Ulrich, A. "Leonie Rysanek meets Elektra." *San Francisco Opera Magazine* 1/Fall (1983): 45.
"Reflected Glory." *Opera News* 48/October (1983): 3.
Kerner, L. "Music: The Celebrated (Tribute upon 25th Anniversary of Met Debut)." *Village Voice* 29 (20 March 1984): 69.
Sandow, G. "Music: The Possessed (Performance at 25th Anniversary of Met Debut)." *Village Voice* 29 (20 March 1984): 69.
"Leonie Rysanek 25 Jahre an der Met." *Opernwelt* 25/5 (1984): 2.
"Rysanek Returns." *San Francisco Opera Magazine* 1/Summer (1984): 49.
Lanier, Thomas P. "Total Woman." *Opera News* 49 (13 April 1985): 30.
Jacobson, Robert. "I'm Still Here!" *Opera News* 50 (15 March 1986): 11.
Profile. *San Francisco Opera Magazine* 3/Fall (1986): 35.
Loebl, H. "Vom Herrgott noch ein Zuckerl." *Bühne* 338/November (1986): 10.
Flinois, P. "Leonie Rysanek." *Diapason-Harmonie* 322/December (1986): 21.
"Leonie Rysanek 60." *Oper und Konzert* 24/12 (1986): 20.
Flinois, P. "Interview." *Diapason-Harmonie* 335/February (1988): 46.
Conrad, Peter. "A Night at the Opera." *Opera News* 52/June (1988): 38.
Fabian, Imre. "Gespräche mit Leonie Rysanek." *Opernwelt* Yearbook 1989: 5.
Conrad, Peter. "Vanishing Act." *Opera Now,* May 1990.
"Leonie Rysanek: 40 Jahre Staatsoper." *Bühne* 381/June (1990): 93.
Kennicott, Philip. "Song of the Wild." *Opera News* 56 (11 April 1992): 34.

*   *   *

Throughout her forty-year career, Leonie Rysanek has garnered some of the warmest accolades imaginable from critics, the public, and from her fellow singers. Not only has she been acclaimed as one of the most exciting actresses to mount the opera stage; not only has her voice not deteriorated over the decades but actually grown stronger in terms of the middle voice; not only has she never lost the soaring, gleaming top that allows her to excel in a number of Strauss roles; but she has constantly expanded her repertoire until it encompasses an astonishing diversity of parts. With the heights have, admittedly, come also the depths. In addition to the early problems with the insecurity of the middle voice, there was initially no low register to speak of. In her own words, however, she had "two things by nature: an extremely good top and extremely easy pianissimo, . . . and fortissimo up there, from the G up." It was not until her early forties (around 1970) that the middle voice was suddenly there.

Inevitably Rysanek is compared to her Germanic predecessors. It has been pointed out that with her glorious top register, she was able to assume the Strauss roles associated with the glamorous Maria Jeritza, and John Steane hears in her something of the creamy quality of Tiana Lemnitz. Rysanek's is a voice to experience above all in the theater. On recordings the unsteady middle voice, the lack of bite sometimes apparent, and the overt histrionics do not always make for a satisfying listening experience. Fortunately a number of her recordings are products of the theater rather than the studio. In her 1967 Sieglinde for Karl Böhm at Bayreuth she is, as in a number of recordings, not in the best vocal estate but, as always, expressive, and her high notes are exhilarating. One can hear the "coital scream" she unleashes in act I as Siegmund wrenches the sword from the tree. Her Kundry from Bayreuth, where she sang frequently, exists in a nearly complete version with Siegfried Jerusalem under Janowski. Although she made a studio recording of *Die Frau ohne Schatten* under Böhm in conjunction with the 1955 Vienna staging, a more vital one exists, also under Böhm (whom she has termed her "musical father"), live from the Staatsoper in 1977. Rysanek in this performance typically takes a portion of the evening to warm up but is very impressive in the power and radiance she brings to the high-lying role, especially when one considers that she had been singing this difficult music for nearly twenty-five years and only doing it better with the passage of time.

Other Rysanek recordings were made in the studio, yet were, as with the early *Frau,* associated with concurrent stagings. Such was the 1959 Lady Macbeth under Leinsdorf, made when she substituted for Callas in the Metropolitan Opera production. Rysanek's Lady is beautifully sung and typically thrilling dramatically. In addition to Sieglinde, the Empress in *Die Frau ohne Schatten* (a role in which no one could challenge her), and Kundry, Rysanek's other greatest roles were Senta and Elisabeth. It should be noted that she declined certain parts, e.g., Isolde, Turandot, Elektra, and Brünnhilde, because she considered that Birgit Nilsson did them to perfection. Yet she and the Swedish soprano were good colleagues, appearing together not only in *Die Frau* but also in *Elektra,* in which Rysanek took on the soaring soprano

role of Chrysothemis. She was slated to do this part for Solti's recording of *Elektra* with Nilsson, but had to cancel.

Recorded documents exist of Rysanek's greatest roles. In addition to the 1967 Bayreuth Sieglinde, she made one in the studio in 1954 with Furtwängler in which she begins act I poorly but ends triumphantly, giving a tantalizing glimpse of how inspired she was on the stage; there is also an act III from 1951 with Karajan that includes a thrilling "O hehrstes Wunder." In 1961 she recorded Senta with George London as the Dutchman; here she displays her gorgeous pianissimo singing, although she is not overall in best voice. Her arias from *Tannhäuser* probably most readily display the quality of Lemnitz that can be heard in the voice.

Additional Germanic roles include the Marschallin, captured on a 1955 highlights disc with the Berlin Philharmonic under Schuchter, a famous revival of *Die ägyptische Helena* in Munich under Keilberth (which was for Harold Rosenthal the finest soprano singing he heard that year, 1956), Salome, Leonore, and Ortrud. Her rapturously confident top register can be heard to good advantage in a 1958 recording of Leonore in *Fidelio* under Fricsay. Of the Italian repertoire, in addition to Lady Macbeth there is an early Abigaille at the Metropolitan Opera, as well as Tosca, Aida, Gioconda, Elisabetta in *Don Carlos, Un ballo in maschera,* and *La forza del destino.* There is a sumptuous recording of Verdi's *Otello* with Jon Vickers and Tito Gobbi, conducted with great love and mastery by the veteran Tullio Serafin. Other notable roles undertaken by Rysanek included Medea, and Kostelnicka in Janáček's *Jenůfa.*

There is no doubt that in everything she performed, Rysanek gave the utmost of herself. She was a singing-actress who gambled mightily and when that gamble paid off, as it often did, she was supreme.

—Stephen Willier

S

SACCHINI, Antonio (Maria Gasparo Gioacchino).

Composer. Born 14 June 1730, in Florence. Died 6 October 1786, in Paris. Studied composition with Francesco Durante, violin with Nicola Fiorenza, and singing with Gennaro Manna at the Conservatory of Santa Maria di Loreto, Naples; performances of his operas in Naples, 1756-62; succeeded Traetta as director of the Conservatorio dell' Ospedaletto in Venice, 1768; in Munich, 1769; in London, 1772; invited by Marie Antoinette to go to Paris, and commissioned to compose three operas for Paris, 1781; remained in Paris, composing two more operas.

Operas

Fra Donato (intermezzo), P. Trinchera?, Naples, Conservatorio Santa Maria di Loreto, 1756.
Il giocatore (intermezzo), Naples, Conservatorio Santa Maria di Loreto, 1757.
Olimpia tradita, Naples, Teatro dei Fiorentini, 1758.
Il copista burlato, G.A. Federico, Naples, Nuovo, fall 1759.
Il testaccio, Rome, Capranica, 1760.
La vendemmia (intermezzo), C. Goldoni, Rome, Capranica, carnival 1760.
I due fratelli beffati, Naples, Nuovo, fall 1760.
Andromaca, A. Salvi, Naples, San Carlo, 30 May 1761.
La finta contessa, Rome, Capranica, 1761.
Li due bari, Naples, Teatro dei Fiorentini, 1762.
L'amore in campo, Rome, Valle, 1762.
Alessandro Severo, Zeno, Venice, San Benedetto, carnival 1763.
Alessandro nell' Indie, Metastasio, Venice, San Salvatore, Ascension 1763; revised, Naples, 1768.
Olimpiade, Metastasio, Padua, Nuovo, 9 July 1763; revised, Paris, 2 October 1777.
Semiramide riconosciuta, Metastasio, Rome, Torre Argentina, carnival 1764.
Eumene, Zeno, Florence, Teatro della Pergola, carnival, 1764.
Il gran Cidde, G. Pizzi, Rome, Torre Argentina, 1764; revised as *Il Cid,* G. Bottarelli, London, King's Theatre in the Haymarket, 19 January 1773; revised as *Chimène,* N.P. Guillard, Fontainebleau, 18 November 1783.
Lucio Vero, Zeno, Naples, San Carlo, 4 November 1764.
Il finto pazzo per amore (intermezzo), T. Mariani, Rome, Valle, spring 1765.
Il Creso, G. Pizzi, Naples, San Carlo, 4 November 1765; revised, London, King's Theatre in the Haymarket, 1774.
La contadina in corte (intermezzo), Rome, Valle, carnival 1766.
L'isola d'amore, A. Gori, Rome, Valle, carnival 1766; revised, London, King's Theatre in the Haymarket, 1776.
Le contadine bizzarre, G. Petrosellini, Milan, Regio Ducale, 1766.
Artaserse, Metastasio, Rome, Torre Argentina, carnival 1768.
Nicoraste, B. Vitturi, Venice, San Benedetto, Ascension 1769.
Scipione in Cartagena, E. Giunti, Munich, Court, 8 January 1770.
Calliroe, M. Verazi, Stuttgart, Residenz, 11 February 1770.
L'eroe cinese, Metastasio, Munich, Court, 27 April 1770.
Adriano in Siria, Metastasio, Venice, San Benedetto, Ascension 1771.
Ezio, Metastasio, Naples, San Carlo, 4 November 1771.
Armida, G. de Gamerra, Milan, Regio Ducale, carnival 1772; revised as *Rinaldo,* London, King's Theatre in the Haymarket, 22 April 1780; revised as *Renaud,* J. Leboeuf and S. Pellegrin, Paris, Opéra, 28 February 1738.
Vologeso, Zeno, Parma, Ducale, 1772.
Tamerlano, A. Piovene, London, King's Theatre in the Haymarket, 6 May 1773.
Perseo, A. Aureli, London, King's Theatre in the Haymarket, 29 January 1774.
Nitteti, Metastasio, London, King's Theatre in the Haymarket, 19 April 1774.
Motezuma, Botarelli, London, King's Theater in the Haymarket, 7 February 1775.
Didone abbandonata, Metastasio, London, King's Theatre in the Haymarket, 11 November 1775.
Erifile, De Gamerra, London, King's Theatre in the Haymarket, 7 February 1778.
L'amore soldato, N. Tassi, London, King's Theatre in the Haymarket, 4 May 1778.
L'avaro deluso, o Don Calandrino, G. Bertati, London, King's Theatre in the Haymarket, 24 November 1778.
Enea e Lavinia, Botarelli, London, King's Theatre in the Haymarket, 25 March 1779.
Mitridate, Zeno, London, King's Theatre in the Haymarket, 23 January 1781.
Dardanus, N.P. Guillard, Versailles, Trianon, 18 September 1784.
Oedipe à Colone, N.P. Guillard, Versailles, Court, 4 January 1786.
Arvire et Evelina, N.P. Guillard, Paris, Opéra, 29 April 1788 [unfinished; completed by J.-B. Rey].

Other works: oratorios, sacred and secular vocal music, orchestral works, instrumental and chamber works, keyboard pieces.

Publications/Writings

About SACCHINI: books–

Nohl, A.L. *Lettres de Gluck et de Weber.* Paris, 1870.
Jullien, A. *La cour et l'opéra sous Louis XVI.* Paris, 1878.
Onoranze a G.B. Pergolesi e Antonio Sacchini. Lesi, 1890.
Prod'homme, J.G. *Ecrits de musiciens.* Paris, 1912.
Schlitzer, F. *Antonio Sacchini: schede e appunti per una sua storia teatrale.* Siena, 1955.
Prota-Giurleo, U. *Sacchini a Napoli.* Naples, 1956.
———. *Sacchini fra Piccinisti e Gluckisti.* Naples, 1957.

articles–

Villars, F. de. "Oedipe à Colone et Sacchini." *Art musicale* 3 (1863): 345, 361.

Florimo, F. "Antonio Sacchini." In *La scuola musicale di Napoli e i suoi conservatorii,* vol. 2, p. 358. Naples, 1882.

Prod'homme, J.G. "L'héritage di Sacchini." *Rivista musicale italiana* 15 (1908): 23.

———. "Un musicien napolitain à la cour de Louis XVI: les dernières années de Gasparo Sacchini." *Le ménestrel* 87 (1925): 505.

Morelli, V. "Antonio Sacchini fra i Gluckisti e i briganti di Londra." *Vita musicale italiana* 7-8 (1926).

unpublished–

Thierstein, E.A. "Five French Operas of Sacchini." Ph. D. dissertation, University of Cincinnati, 1974.

Wilson, J. Kenneth. "*L'Olimpiade:* Selected Eighteenth-Century Settings of Metastasio's Libretto." Ph. D. dissertation, Harvard University, 1982.

*   *   *

One of the leading opera composers of the second half of the eighteenth century, Antonio Sacchini had an adventurous career that can be divided into three periods. From 1756 to 1772 he worked mostly in Italy, first as a composer and music director in Naples, where he had received his musical education, then later in Rome and Venice. From 1772 to 1781 he lived and worked in London, writing Italian operas both comic and serious. From 1782 to his death in 1786 he lived in Paris, devoting himself to the *tragédie lyrique.* The success that he achieved in all three phases of his career attests to the cosmopolitan nature of his talent.

Antonio Sacchini

Sacchini's early works reveal him to be a composer equally gifted in comic and serious opera. The fine craftsmanship and lyric beauty in such operas as *Olimpiade* (Padua, 1763) made his name known throughout Italy. The success of his comic works (among them *La contadina in corte,* first performed in Rome in 1766) brought international recognition; it was not long before invitations from Germany and London tempted him to leave Italy.

Sacchini's *Perseo,* first performed in London in January 1774, is a good example of the serious operas with which he won the favor of English opera-lovers. The drama begins powerfully and immediately with the overture, a stormy C minor movement that ends with a menacing *pianissimo.* Large choruses like "Qual fiero caso" add to the opera's substance and richness. Several long accompanied recitatives anticipate, in some respects, the sound of Sacchini's Parisian *tragédies lyriques* ("Qual improvviso, oh numi, tremor m'assale" is 85 measures in length). Sacchini contributed to the development of the two-tempo aria known as the rondò; an incipient form of the rondò, although not labelled as such by Sacchini, is represented by Perseo's aria "Il caro ben perdei," in which the opening slow melody returns twice after contrasting episodes, and a final allegro brings the aria to a conclusion. Also rondò-like (but lacking a final fast part) is Andromeda's "Son felice," a ravishing triple-meter andante. Not surprisingly, *Perseo* was a great success in London, according to the *Public Advertiser* (31 January 1774): "The music is worthy of Sacchini; [it] has all the fire, all the elegance, all the pathos of that celebrated composer. The airs are excellent. . . . The chorusses are pleasing, and that of unrevenged Shades of Youths and Virgins ["Fra queste tenebre"], beautifully pathetic."

Sacchini's French operas bring together some of the finest characteristics of Italian opera seria and Gluckian music drama. The most celebrated among them is *Oedipe à Colone,* first performed in 1786, shortly before the composer's death. This is a somber work, neo-classical in its seriousness and nobility. Polinice's recitative and aria at the beginning of act II will serve here as an example of the musical and dramatic strength of *Oedipe.* Polinice, alone in a desolate spot, expresses his sadness and desperation in a recitative in which the orchestra vividly reflects his emotional state with syncopations, tremolos, and a predominance of the minor mode. A melodic idea introduced in the recitative later serves to accompany the beginning of Polinice's aria, "Hélas! d'une si pure flamme." The aria is full of rich melodic ideas. Sacchini achieves dramatic effects by the simplest of means: his modulation from minor mode to major at the words "Cet amour vertueux eût épuré mon âme" is as effective dramatically as it is simple musically; the same can be said for the sudden return to the minor mode at the word "pleurs." Sacchini's fine sense of drama is united with impeccable craftsmanship here and elsewhere in *Oedipe,* resulting in an opera that richly deserves study and revival.

—John A. Rice

SADKO.

Composer: Nicolai Rimsky-Korsakov.

Librettists: Nicolai Rimsky-Korsakov and V.I. Bel'sky.

First Performance: Moscow, Solodovnikov, 7 January 1898.

Roles: Sadko (tenor); Liubava Bousslayevna (mezzo-soprano); Nejata (contralto); Volkova (soprano); King of the Sea (bass); Duda (bass); Sopiel (tenor); Viking Merchant (bass); Hindu Merchant (tenor); Venetian Merchant (baritone); Foma Nasaritch (tenor); Luka Senovitch (bass); Two Mountebanks (mezzo-sopranos); Two Soothsayers (tenors); Apparition (bass); Pilgrim (baritone); chorus (SSAATTBB).

* * *

The notion of using the legendary hero Sadko as the inspiration for a musical composition originated with Stasov, who mentioned the idea in a letter to Balakirev. In turn, Balakirev suggested the topic to Musorgsky. Finally, Musorgsky gave the idea to Rimsky-Korsakov. At first, Rimsky-Korsakov used Sadko as the basis for a symphonic poem which he completed in 1867, entitled "Episode from the Legend of Sadko." The second and third versions appeared in 1869 and 1892 as "Musical Picture—Sadko."

In the years 1894-96 Rimsky-Korsakov worked on the so-called "opera bylina" *Sadko,* in seven tableaux. With the help of friends, Rimsky-Korsakov wrote the libretto, drawing upon a wide range of Russian folklore and literature. Originally, Rimsky-Korsakov had not included Sadko's wife Liubava Bousslayevna (tableau III) in the opera, nor was she included in tableaux IV or VII. However, Vladimir Ivanovich Bel'sky encouraged his friend Rimsky-Korsakov to make these changes as well as others having to do with the incorporation of certain folk elements into the opera.

The first tableau depicts a festive gathering of the wealthy merchants of Novgorod. Sadko sings of his wish to take a

Sadko **by Rimsky-Korsakov, first edition of score, 1896**

fleet of thirty-one ships on an ocean voyage, in spite of the fact that there is no direct outlet to the ocean from Novgorod. The elders openly criticize Sadko's blind ambition. Twelve years later, their criticism turns to praise (tableau VII) when, upon Sadko's return, the river Volkov miraculously appears in Novgorod providing access to the ocean. Herein lies the legend of Sadko.

The second tableau finds Sadko on the shore of Lake Ilmen, when Volkova, the Princess of the Sea, and her sisters appear at first in the form of swans and sea gulls. They are daughters of the King of the Sea. The princess promises to marry Sadko (the wedding ceremony takes place twelve years later, in tableau VI). As dawn approaches, the king arrives and summons his daughters to return home. The princess and her sisters are transformed into swans as they descend into the depths of the sea. Before they leave, the princess gives Sadko three golden fish to bring him power and wealth.

Tableau III opens with Liubava Bousslayevna, Sadko's wife, lamenting the disappearance of her husband, and wondering if he still loves her. Sadko returns, drifting in and out of a dream-state. He decides to return to the sea, even though Liubava is sad about his leaving.

The action of tableau IV takes place in Novgorod, in an atmosphere similar to that of the first tableau. At first, the activities revolve around the visit of the pilgrims and the foreign merchants, with special attention given to the Viking, the Hindu and the Venetian. As Sadko sings of the golden fish that can be found in Lake Ilmen, the Elders mock him. To prove his point about the golden fish, Sadko challenges his people and offers his head if he is wrong, in return for their wealth if he is correct. A fishing boat is prepared for Sadko, the Elders and others. Sadko draws in a fishing net with three golden fish—reminiscent of the gift given to Sadko by Princess Volkova in the second tableau. Sadko emerges victorious and, feeling sorry for having depleted the resources of his people, suggests that they check the fishing nets to see if any fish were left there. Suddenly the contents of the net are transformed into gold. The people of Novgorod rejoice. Sadko encourages his friends to buy whatever they want and to sail with him. Before departing, however, Sadko expresses sorrow for the poverty of those he is leaving behind. He returns whatever possessions he had taken from his people as the spoils of his victory. Each of the three special guests (the Viking, the Hindu, and the Venetian) sings of his homeland. (They will appear in the seventh tableau to sing praise to Sadko when he returns.) The tableau ends with Liubava Bousslayevna lamenting again Sadko's departure. Sadko tells his wife not to weep. The thirty crimson ships depart together with Sadko's ship, *The Falcon.*

In the fifth tableau, *The Falcon* is stalled in calm waters. Treasures are thrown overboard to lighten the load. Nothing seems to help. Sadko encourages his crew to join him in paying tribute to the King of the Sea by writing their names on parchment. Strips of the parchment are then cast into the sea. Sadko writes his name on a branch which is also thrown into the sea. He then climbs out of the boat and floats on a plank. *The Falcon* sails away and eventually Sadko drowns. As he descends to the depths of the sea, Sadko is consoled by the sounds of the swans and the voice of the princess.

In tableau VI, Sadko arrives at the palace of the King of the Sea, where the princess is spinning seaweed. The King of the Sea, having waited twelve years for Sadko, says that he wants his head. But after hearing Sadko sing a song of praise, the King of the Sea changes his mind and offers him his daughter's hand in marriage. The king calls everyone home for the wedding feast—his daughters (rivers), nieces (streams), and so on. The sturgeon serves as the minister and the dolphins are the attendants for the bride. There follows a procession of the Marvels of the Sea.

After the ceremony and towards the end of the dance, an apparition comes through an elderly pilgrim who proclaims that the turbulence of the dancing has created problems with ships. He orders the princess to go to Novgorod in order to be changed into a river. The power over the sea is then taken away from the king.

In the final tableau, Sadko and the princess take a wedding voyage to Novgorod. The Princess Volkova is miraculously transformed into the River Volkov. Sadko returns to his wife, Liubava Bousslayevna. *The Falcon* sails on the river Volkov leading the other ships of Sadko's fleet home to Novgorod. There is much rejoicing in honor of Novgorod and Sadko. He has returned victorious after twelve years. The visiting merchants (the Viking, the Hindu, and the Venetian) join in the celebration.

Rimsky-Korsakov provided motivic linkages among the tableaux. These unifying elements enabled him to juxtapose many diverse events within the opera plot. Thus, the dramatic action is supported by the composer's meticulous work in establishing a musical network among the motives signifying Sadko, Sadko's wife, the Princess Volkova, the king and other marvels of the sea, the Elders, the Viking, the Hindu, and the Venetian.

Sadko is outstanding for its experimentation with melodic and harmonic patterns that expanded the traditional tonal system. These innovations would have an important effect on the composers of the next generation. For example, Stravinsky benefited from compositional techniques utilized by Rimsky-Korsakov, such as the melodic and harmonic fragments derived from the octatonic scale and the layering of different textures simultaneously. Furthermore, Rimsky-Korsakov's careful attention to detail allowed him to show his students just how a motivic network could be implemented.

—Maureen A. Carr

SAFFO.

Composer: Giovanni Pacini.

Librettist: S. Cammarano.

First Performance: Naples, San Carlo, 29 November 1840.

Roles: Alcandro; Climene; Saffo; Faone; Dirce; Ippia; Lisimaco; chorus.

Publications

article–

Profeta, R. "Giovanni Pacini e la *Saffo.*" *L'opera* [Milan] no. 6 (1967): 31.

*   *   *

While it is badly neglected today, *Saffo* was one of the most successful operas of the mid nineteenth century, actually rivalling works such as *Lucrezia Borgia* and *Il Giuramento* in popularity, and easily exceeding contemporary operas like *Nabucco* and *I Lombardi.* Yet it was hardly ever given in Northern Europe, especially in the British Isles. It had only one production in London (in English!), Amsterdam, and Berlin, none in the British provinces, two each in Paris and Vienna, four in St Petersburg, and was apparently never given in Belgium or Sweden. It was much more popular in the United States, having some six revivals in New York alone, and also heard in Boston, Chicago, Cincinnati, Louisville, Philadelphia and St Louis. It was a repertory opera in Italy, Spain, Portugal, and South America.

Alcandro, Priest of Apollo, is furious at Saffo because she had given an impassioned speech denouncing him, and tells her lover, Faone, that Saffo is betraying him with another man. To revenge himself, Faone decides to marry a former flame, Climene, Alcandro's daughter. When Saffo discovers this she is so filled with despair that she destroys the altar of Apollo. To repent, she offers to throw herself from the sacred rock. It is soon discovered that she is Alcandro's long lost daughter. Alcandro pleads in vain to save Saffo's life and bitterly repents having initiated the chain of events that will result in her death. Faone, too, realizes how much he has loved Saffo and has to be restrained from following her to the grave.

The plot has some superficial similarities with that of Bellini's *Norma,* although many of the specific details differ. Not surprisingly, it was frequently sung by the same sister teams that specialized in the Bellini opera. It remained in the repertory in Italy until the early years of the twentieth century, thus outlasting much better known works such as *Anna Bolena, Maria Stuarda* and *Roberto Devereux,* and has had occasional revivals ever since.

Its great erstwhile popularity was due as much to its audience appeal as to its status as a favorite vehicle for many of the great dramatic sopranos of the nineteenth century. Some famous Saffos include Carlotta Marchisio, Alice Urban, Carolina Ferni, Hericlea Darclée and Eva Tetrazzini. Climene was a favorite role of Barbara Marchisio and Adelaide Borghi-Mamo, while the likes of Enrico Tamberlick, Augusto Scampini, Domenico Donzelli and Francesco Tamagno all sang Faone. Finally, famous Alcandros include Leone Giraldoni, Felice Varesi, and Giuseppe Bellantoni. The latter even recorded the baritone aria from *Saffo.* In recent times, the title role has been considered by Maria Callas, and sung by Leyla Gencer, Adelaide Negri, and Montserrat Caballé.

Each of the four protagonists has a striking two part aria. Alcandro's "Di sua voce il suon giungea" with its superb cabaletta "Un Erinnni atroce, orrenda" comes first, soon followed by Climene's "Ah! con lui mi fui rapita". But Pacini, as usual, saves the best for last: Faone's repentant "Ah! giusta pena!" and the highlight of the score: Saffo's finale "Teco dall' are pronube." The elegiac quality of the tenor aria and the chorus before the final scene for Saffo tends to look back to the bel canto years, and especially to Bellini, more than to the forthcoming music of Verdi. There is also a wonderful duet for Climene and Saffo, sung before they realize that they are sisters. This duet is generally considered to be on a par with the Norma-Adalgisa duets. On the other hand, the ensembles are highly dramatic, much more so than Bellini's music, and are definitely pre-Verdian in character. The best of these is the trio between Alcandro, Climene and Saffo, in which Alcandro realizes that Saffo is his daughter and expresses his guilt at being her murderer.

—Tom Kaufman

ST FRANCIS OF ASSISI
See ST FRANÇOIS D'ASSISE

ST FRANÇOIS D'ASSISE [St Francis of Assisi].

Composer: Olivier Messiaen.

Librettist: Olivier Messiaen (after the anonymous 14th-century *Fioretti* and *Contemplations of the Stigmata*).

First Performance: Paris, Opéra, 28 November 1983.

Roles: The Angel (soprano); St Francis (baritone); The Leper (tenor); Brother Leon (baritone); Brother Massée (tenor); Brother Elie (tenor); Brother Bernard (bass); Brother Sylvester (bass); Brother Rufin (bass); chorus.

Publications

article–

Kaczynski, Tadeusz. "Messiaen o swojej operze." *Ruch Muzyczny* 3/no. 3 (1984): 13.

*   *   *

It is perhaps surprising that for a composer who in his early days took an intense interest in opera and the plays of Shakespeare should not have embarked on writing an opera himself until the age of sixty-six. By his own admission, he would not have started such a project even then had it not been for the insistence of Rolf Liebermann of the Paris Opéra, who commissioned the work. Messiaen himself felt that he had no gift for the theater, in spite of his early interest in works written for it. The choice of subject was the composer's own, and it was natural, in the light of his own religious convictions, that he should choose St Francis of Assisi as his subject. In addition, the legend of St Francis preaching to the birds gave Messiaen the opportunity to indulge his own love of birdsong as part of the musical material of the opera. The libretto is by the composer himself, who began work on the poem in the summer of 1975. The music was composed between 1975 and 1979 and orchestrated from 1979 to 1983.

The opera does not attempt to present the complete story of St Francis' life, but consists rather of a series of tableaux representing events or episodes which were crucial in St Francis' spiritual development as based on *Fioretti* and *Contemplations on the Stigmata* by anonymous Franciscan friars of the fourteenth century. The work contains three acts, the first two divided into three tableaux each and the third into two tableaux. In the first tableau, *La croix* (The Cross), Francis explains to a fellow-friar, Brother Leon, that it is essential to endure all sufferings with patience for the love of Christ. In the second tableau, *Les laudes* (Lauds), after the morning office, Francis asks God to let him meet a leper and make him capable of loving him. The third tableau, *Le baiser au lépreux* (The Kissing of the Leper) fulfils Francis' prayer. He visits a leper hospital and meets a leper. Francis eventually overcomes his revulsion and embraces the man, thus curing him of his leprosy. Simultaneously with the cure of the leper, Francis experiences grace; this is the point, says Messiaen, at which Francis achieves sanctity and becomes Saint Francis.

The fourth tableau, *L'ange voyageur* (The traveling angel), at the beginning of the second act, is the only one in which St Francis does not appear. An angel, who is taken for a traveler by the characters in the opera, appears outside the friary. He knocks at the door with a loud noise (symbolizing the inrush of grace) and asks a question about predestination. In the fifth tableau, *L'ange musicien* (The Angel as Musician), the angel appears to St Francis and plays to him on the viol (represented by three ondes martenot in the orchestra) in order to give him a foretaste of heavenly bliss. The sixth tableau, *Le prêche aux oiseaux* (The Sermon to the Birds), takes place at Carceri in Assisi. The birds reply to St Francis' sermon with a grand chorus. In this section Messiaen exploits a new technique in his treatment of birdsong. Although the rhythms are notated exactly, some songs commence at a signal from the conductor and are played at their own tempo, independent of the rest of the orchestra.

Act III begins with the tableau in which St Francis receives the stigmata (*Les stigmates*). Five luminous rays shine out from the cross and pierce both hands and feet and the right side of St Francis, accompanied by the same hammer-blows from the orchestra which were used for the angel's knock on the door of the friary. The five wounds are the divine seal of the sanctity of St Francis. The last tableau, *La mort et la nouvelle vie* (Death and New Life), portrays Francis' death as he sings the last verse of his *Canticle of Creatures*. Surrounded by his brethren, the angel and the leper, he dies. Bells toll, everyone disappears, and while the chorus sings of the Resurrection, a spot of light, which increases to blinding intensity, shines on the place where the body of St Francis lay.

Theatrically, the work is very static, but it nevertheless makes a powerful impact, and the music contains some of Messiaen's most imaginative and inventive. While there is no use of *leitmotiv* in the Wagnerian sense, the main characters are symbolized by themes associated with them, varying according to the theatrical context. St Francis has five themes: a violin melody (the principle one), a harmonic theme consisting of a cluster followed by a trombone chord which accompanies his solemn pronouncements, a Decision theme, a theme of Joy, and in particular the song of the blackcap (*fauvette à tête noire*). Messiaen made a special journey to Carceri (the scene of the sermon to the birds) in order to note the song of the local blackcap which would have been familiar to St Francis.

In addition to birdsong, color (as in other works of Messiaen) plays an important role. The composer prescribes the color of the angel's wings, in particular, with great precision, and all the costumes are described in detail. Much of the inspiration comes from the frescoes and altar-pieces of Fra Angelico in Florence; the angel is modeled on one of the Annunciations of Fra Angelico in the San Marco Museum.

—Robert Sherlaw-Johnson

ST JOHN'S EVE
See FEUERSNOT

THE SAINT OF BLEECKER STREET.

Composer: Gian Carlo Menotti.

Librettist: Gian Carlo Menotti.

First Performance: New York, 27 December 1954.

Roles: Annina (soprano); Desideria (mezzo-soprano); Michele (tenor); Don Marco (bass); Assunta (mezzo-soprano); Carmela (soprano); Maria Corona (mezzo-soprano); Salvatore (baritone); chorus (SSAATTBB).

*　　*　　*

The Saint of Bleecker Street was written four years after *The Consul,* in the same period as *Amahl* and Menotti's first major works for the concert hall. It won a Drama Critics Award and the Pulitzer Prize (his second for both awards) and is the one composition of Menotti's that can possibly be classified as "verismo." The human emotions characterized here are devoid of supernatural imagery and dream sequences, and the people are real. To quote John Ardoin, ". . . religion and faith are no longer side issues or subplots but the main event—the opera's heart and soul." The chorus is not just a vehicle for commentary, but a protagonist in its own right.

Michele and Annina, brother and sister, live in a cold-water flat on Bleecker Street, in the Little Italy section of New York's Greenwich Village. Annina, a young woman of extremely fragile health, has religious visions accompanied by bleeding stigmata in her hands, and is considered by the neighborhood to be a saint with miraculous powers, occasionally effecting miracle-healings. Her brother is a sceptic; to him the hysterically adoring mob and the Church's clerics have only exacerbated his sister's poor health, and were she (and they) rich, there would be no visions. His all-consuming love for and protective stance toward his sister border on incest, a situation he has never admitted to himself until confronted with it by Desideria, his girlfriend and lover. Evicted by her mother because of her liason with Michele, Desideria longs for marriage or at least a live-in arrangement, and in her fury at Michele's refusal, she accuses him of incestuous love for Annina. In a blind rage, he stabs Desideria in the back, an act that is witnessed by the celebrants leaving Carmela's and Salvatore's wedding reception. Michele flees for his life as his lover dies.

In a clandestine meeting, Annina begs Michele to turn himself in and accept his punishment, and reveals that she is determined to take holy orders and become a nun. Michele is desperate; he tells his sister that she is all he has to live for, and his need is greater than God's. Failing to win his argument, he curses her, shoves her away, and disappears into the subway, while Annina collapses in tears.

The final scene is back in Annina's tenement flat; pale and extremely ill, she is wrapped in a shawl and is resting in an armchair, surrounded by a nun and several women friends, including Carmela. To the latter Annina confides that her voices have told her she will take the veil today, and she asks Death to postpone his coming until permission arrives from Rome for her investiture. When Annina worries about having the required white dress and veil, Carmela produces her own wedding gown which she has brought for that purpose. Don Marco receives the letter from Rome, and relays the joyful news that Annina's wish has been granted, so the nun and Carmela help her to the bedroom to dress. Just then word comes that the ceremony might be interrupted by Michele, who is still determined to prevent her from becoming a nun. He does indeed arrive but is too late to prevent the investiture. Annina, in a holy trance, does not hear his outcry, and Michele can only stand staring as the initiate's hair is cut off and the ceremony draws toward an end. As Don Marco extends the gold wedding ring by which Annina becomes the Bride of Christ, she falls to the floor and dies as the priest kneels to place the ring on her finger.

The Saint marked the last of Menotti's works with which he tried to present opera as a self-sustaining financial endeavor. Although it ran for three months to packed houses, this theater piece never made money. Its autobiographical elements portray the ongoing conflict within Menotti between his Catholic upbringing and subsequent lack of faith. Menotti considers Michele and Annina as opposing parts of himself.

—Jean C. Sloop

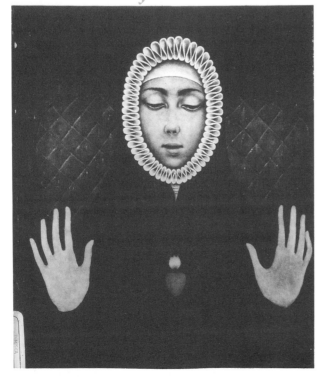

The Saint of Bleecker Street by Menotti, cover of score

SAINT-SAËNS, (Charles-) Camille.

Composer. Born 9 October 1835, in Paris. Died 16 December 1921, in Algiers. Married: Marie Truffot, 1875 (separated 1881; two sons who died in infancy). Studied piano with his great-aunt, Charlotte Masson; studied with Stamaty, beginning 1842; debut as a pianist at the Salle Pleyel, 6 May 1846; studied harmony with Pierre Maleden; studied organ with Benoist and composition with Halévy at the Paris Conservatory; two unsuccessful attempts to win the Prix de Rome,

1852 and 1864; first prize of the Société Sainte-Cécile for his *Ode à Sainte-Cécile,* 1852; first symphony performed, 11 December 1853; organist at the church of Saint-Merry, Paris, 1853-57; succeeded Lefébure-Wély as organist at the Madeleine, 1857-76; taught piano at the Ecole Niedermeyer, 1861-65; Chevalier of the Legion of Honor, 1868; one of the founders of the Société Nationale de Musique, 1871; elected to the Institut de France, 1881; Officer of the Legion of Honor, 1884, Grand-Officier, 1900; in the United States, 1906; Grand-Croix of the Legion of Honor, 1913; tour of South America, 1916; honorary Mus. D. from Cambridge University; gave many of his manuscripts and belongings to the municipal museum in Dieppe, where they are preserved in a special section. Pupils included André Messager and Gabriel Fauré.

Operas

Publisher: Durand.

La princesse jaune, L. Gallet, Paris, Opéra-Comique, 12 June 1872.
Le timbre d'argent, J. Barbier and M. Carré, Paris, National-Lyrique, 23 February 1877.
Samson et Dalila, F. Lemaire, Weimar, Hoftheater, 2 December 1877.
Etienne Marcel, Lyons, Grand Théâtre, 8 February 1879.
Henry VIII, Détroyat and A. Silvestre, Paris, Opéra, 5 March 1883.
Proserpine, L. Gallet (after V. Vacquerie), Paris, Opéra-Comique, 14 March 1887.
Ascanio, L. Gallet (after P. Meurice), Paris, Opéra, 21 March 1890.
Phryné, L. Augé de Lassus, Paris, Opéra-Comique, 24 May 1893.
Frédégonde (with E. Guiraud), L. Gallet, Paris, Opéra, 18 December 1895.
Les barbares, V. Sardou and P.B. Gheusi, Paris, Opéra, 23 October 1901.
Hélène, C. Saint-Saëns, Monte Carlo, 18 February 1904.
L'ancêtre, L. Augé de Lassus, Monte Carlo, 24 February 1906.
Déjanire, Saint-Saëns (after L. Gallet), Monte Carlo, 14 March 1911.

Other works: ballets, incidental music, sacred and secular vocal music, orchestral works, chamber music, piano pieces.

Publications

By SAINT-SAËNS: books–

Notice sur Henri Reber. Paris, 1881.
Harmonie et Mélodie. Paris, 1885; 9th ed., 1923; German translation by Eva Zimmermann, Leipzig, 1978.
Charles Gounod et le 'Don Juan' de Mozart. Paris, 1893.
Problèmes et mystères. Paris, 1894; revised as *Divagations sérieuses,* 1922.
Portraits et souvenirs. Paris, 1899; 3rd ed., 1909.
Essai sur les lyres et cithares antiques. Paris, 1902.
Quelques mots sur 'Proserpine'. Alexandria, 1902.
Ecole buissonnière: notes et souvenirs. Paris, 1913; English translation, abridged, 1919; 1969.
Notice sur Le timbre d'argent. Brussels, 1914.
Germanophilie. Paris, 1915.
Bowie, H.P., ed. *On the Execution of Music, and Principally of Ancient Music.* San Francisco, 1915.

Au courant de la vie. Paris, 1916.
Les idées de M. Vincent d'Indy. Paris, 1919.
Outspoken Essays on Music [selected essays]. Translated by F. Rothwell. New York and London, 1922; 1970.
Nectoux, J.-M., ed. *Camille Saint-Saëns et Gabriel Fauré: correspondance: soixante ans d' amitié.* Paris, 1973.

articles–

"Lyres et cithares." In *Encyclopédie de la musique et dictionnaire du Conservatoire* 1/no. 1 (1921): 538.
Nectoux, J.-M., ed. "Correspondance Saint-Saëns Fauré." *Revue de musicologie* 58 (1972): 65, 190; 59 (1973): 60.
"Correspondance inédite." *Revue musicale* 358-60 (1983) [special issue].

About SAINT-SAËNS: books–

Bellaigue, C. *M. Camille Saint-Saëns.* Paris, 1889.
Neitzel, O. *Camille Saint-Saëns.* Berlin, 1899.
Augé de Lassus, L. *Saint-Saëns.* Paris, 1914.
Bonnerot, J. *C. Saint-Saëns: sa vie et son oeuvre.* Paris, 1914; 2nd ed., 1922.
Montargis, J. *Camille Saint-Saëns: l'oeuvre, l'artiste.* Paris, 1919.
Chantavoine, Jean. *L'oeuvre dramatique de Camille Saint-Saëns.* Paris, 1921.
Hervey, A. *Saint-Saëns.* London, 1921.
Collet, H. *Samson et Dalila de C. Saint-Saëns.* Paris, 1922.
Lyle, W. *Camille Saint-Saëns: His Life and Art.* London, 1923; Westport, Connecticut, 1970.
Servières, G. *Saint-Saëns.* Paris, 1923; 2nd ed., 1930.
Handschin, J. *Camille Saint-Saëns.* Zurich, 1930.
Aguétant, P. *Saint-Saëns par lui-même d'après des lettres reçues.* Paris, 1938.
Chantavoine, J. *Camille Saint-Saëns.* Paris, 1947.
Harding, James. *Saint-Saëns and his Circle.* London, 1965.
———. *Massenet.* London, 1970.

articles–

Rolland, R. "Camille Saint-Saëns." In *Musiciens d'aujourd'-hui.* Paris, 1908; 1946; English translation 1915; 1969.
Séré, O. "Camille Saint-Saëns." In *Musiciens français d'aujourd'hui.* Paris, 1911; 2nd ed., 1921.
Boschot, A. "Saint-Saëns." In *Portraits de musiciens* vol. 2. Paris, 1947.
Lalo, P. "Camille Saint-Saëns." In *De Rameau à Ravel.* Paris, 1947.
Avant-scène opéra 15 (1978) [*Samson et Dalila* issue].
Ratner, Sabina. "Richard Wagner and Camille Saint-Saëns." *Opera Quarterly* 1 (1983): 101.

*   *   *

Saint-Saëns was an unusually prolific musician who wrote in every medium, so it is not surprising that he should have been attracted to opera, which, in his day, was the surest way to fame and riches for the composer lucky enough to succeed. He wrote, in all, thirteen operas on a wide variety of subjects. They range from the charming little one-act *La princesse jaune* to the blood-boltered melodrama of *L'ancêtre,* from the pageantry of *Henry VIII* to the musical comedy frivolity of *Phryné.* His best-known opera is, of course, *Samson et Dalila,* although it took nearly twenty years to establish itself. When it did, however, it became one of the most popular items in

the repertory—much to Saint-Saëns's annoyance when he
reflected on how much it overshadowed his eleven other
operas, none of which achieved real success.

The reason why Saint-Saëns never won fame as a major
opera composer was that he had little sense of theater. Prodigiously gifted in every branch of music and endowed with a
Mozartian facility, he lacked that precious instinct which his
detested rival Massenet possessed in abundance. When he
embarked on *Etienne Marcel,* an ambitious historical opera
based on the leading figure in the struggles between the medieval guilds of Paris and the king, he tackled a subject to which
only the grandiose and flashy technique of Meyerbeer could
have done full justice. The music, as always, is elegant and
skillfully shaped, but it fails to make its point on the stage.
As in *Henry VIII,* for which he studied sixteenth-century
manuscripts in the then music library at Buckingham Palace,
the most telling passages are the more intimate moments: the
love duets, the occasional meditative aria, the limpid ballet
music. The attempt at Wagnerian grandeur does not come
off.

The same verdict applies to *Les barbares,* in which, despite
the collaboration with Victorien Sardou, the day's most successful playwright, Saint-Saëns failed to create an epic drawn
from French history in the way Wagner had utilized the
heroic legends of his own country. The story of a vestal virgin
of ancient Gaul who breaks her vow to save a town from
pillaging barbarians remains lifeless and unmoving. *Ascanio*
will never rival Berlioz's opera *Benvenuto Cellini* which has
the same hero, and it now belongs to the obscurity that
shrouds *Déjanire* and *Proserpine.* The most successful, and
the most deserving of revival, are the smaller works that do
not call for extended inspiration or for accomplished stage
technique. The best of them is *La princesse jaune,* an attractive example of *Japonaiserie* spiced with an amusingly Parisian brand of exoticism, deftly orchestrated and wittily
written.

There remains the paradox of *Samson et Delila.* It has
survived because, here, for once, the quality of inspiration
rarely fails Saint-Saëns, and, more important still, the opera
could almost as well be performed as an oratorio without
harming any of the effect. It also has at least three big arias
which are a gift for star singers, besides a colorful ballet
familiar as an independent suite in the concert hall. Given
these advantages, the only survivor of Saint-Saëns's operas
shows no signs of losing its popularity.

—James Harding

SALIERI, Antonio.

Composer. Born 18 August 1750, in Legnago, near Verona.
Died 7 May 1825, in Vienna. Studied with his brother Francesco, a violinist, and with the organist Simoni; taken to
Venice by a patron upon the death of his father, 1765; studied
singing with Pacini and harmony with Pescetti; taken to Vi-
enna by the composer Gassmann, 1766; conducted at the
Burgtheater, 1770; succeeded Gassmann as court composer
(Vienna), 1774; studied with Gluck, who recommended Sa-
lieri to the Académie de Musique in Paris; succeeded Bonno
as court Kapellmeister (Vienna), 1788; conductor of the
Tonkünstler-Sozietät until 1818. Salieri's students included
Beethoven, Schubert, and Liszt.

Operas

La vestale, Vienna, 1768 [lost].

Le donne letterate, G. Boccherini, Vienna, Burgtheater, January 1770.

L'amore innocente, G. Boccherini, Vienna, Burgtheater,
1770.

Don Chisciotte alle nozze di Gamace (divertimento teatrale),
G. Boccherini, Vienna, Burgtheater, 1770.

La moda, ossia I scompigli domestici, P. Cipretti, Vienna,
1771.

Armida, M. Coltellini, Vienna, Burgtheater, 2 June 1771.

La fiera di Venezia, G. Boccherini, Vienna, Burgtheater, 29
January 1772.

Il barone di Rocca antica, G. Petrosellini, Vienna, Burgtheater, 12 May 1772.

La secchia rapita, G. Boccherini, Vienna, Burgtheater, 21
October 1772.

La locandiera, D. Poggi (after C. Goldoni), Vienna, Burgtheater, 8 June 1773.

La calamità de' cuori, G. Gamerra, Vienna, Burgtheater, 11
October 1774.

La finta scema, G. Gamerra, Vienna, Burgtheater, 9 September 1775.

Daliso e Delmita, G. Gamerra, Vienna, Burgtheater, 29 July
1776.

L'Europa riconosciuta, M. Verazi, Milan, Teatro alla Scala,
3 August 1778.

La scuola de' gelosi, C. Mazzolà, Venice, San Moisè, 27 December 1778.

Il talismano (with G. Rust), C. Goldoni, Milan, Cannobiana,
21 August 1779.

La partenza inaspettata, G. Petrosellini, Rome, Valle, 22 December 1779.

La dama pastorella, G. Petrosellini, Rome, Valle, 1780.

*Der Rauchfangkehrer, oder Die unentbehrlichen Verräther
ihrer Herrschaften aus Eigennutz* (Lustspiel), T. Auen-
brugger, Vienna, Burgtheater, 30 April 1781.

Semiramide, Metastasio, Munich, court, 1782.

Les Danaides, Du Roullet and Tschudi, Paris, Opéra, 26
April 1784.

Il ricco d'un giorno, Da Ponte, Vienna, Burgtheater, 6 December 1784.

La grotta di Trofonio, G.B. Casti, Vienna, Burgtheater, 12
October 1785.

Prima la musica e poi le parole (operetta), G.B. Casti, Schönbrunn Orangerie, 7 February 1786.

Les Horaces, N.F. Guillard, Paris, Opéra, 7 December 1786.

Tarare, Beaumarchais, Paris, Opéra, 8 June 1787; revised
as *Axur, Re d'Ormus,* Da Ponte, Vienna, Burgtheater, 8
January 1788.

Cublai, gran kan de Tartari, G.B. Casti, 1788 [not per-
formed].

Il talismano, Da Ponte, Vienna, Burgtheater, 10 September
1788.

Il pastor fido, Da Ponte, Vienna, Burgtheater, 11 February
1789.

La cifra, Da Ponte, Vienna, Burgtheater, 11 December 1789.

Catilina, G.B. Casti, Vienna, 1792 [not performed].

Il mondo alla rovescia, C. Mazzolà, Vienna, Burgtheater, 13
January 1795.

Eraclito e Democrito, G. Gamerra, Vienna, Burgtheater, 13
August 1795.

Palmira, Regina di Persia, G. Gamerra, Vienna, Kärntnertor,
14 October 1795.

Il moro, G. Gamerra, Vienna, Burgtheater, 7 August 1796.

I tre filosofo, 1797 [unfinished].

Falstaff ossia Le tre burle, C.P. Defranceschi, Vienna, Kärntnertor, 3 January 1799.
Cesare in Farmacusa, C.P. Defranceschi, Vienna, Kärntnertor, 2 June 1800.
L'Angiolina, ossia Il matrimonio per sussurro, C.P. Defranceschi, Vienna, Kärntnertor, 22 October 1800.
Annibale in Capua, A.S. Sografi, Trieste, Nuovo, April 1801.
La bella selvaggia, G. Bertati, Vienna, 1802 [not performed].
Die Hussiten vor Naumberg (Schauspiel), Kotzebue, Vienna, court, 1803.
Die Neger, Treitschke, Vienna, Theater an der Wien, 10 November 1804.
Die Generalprobe [unfinished; lost].
Das Posthaus [unfinished; lost].

Other works: cantatas, sacred vocal music, orchestral works, instrumental and chamber works.

Publications/Writings

By SALIERI: unpublished–

Libro di partimenti di varia specie per profitto della gioventù [lost].
Scuola di canto, in versi, e i versi in musica. 4 vols.

About SALIERI: books–

Mosel, I.F.E. von. *Über das Leben und die Werke des A. Salieri.* Vienna, 1827.
Neumann, W. *A. Salieri.* Kassel, 1855.
Hermann, A. von. *A. Salieri: eine Studie zur Geschichte seines künstlerischen Wirkens.* Vienna, 1897.
Magnani, G. *Antonio Salieri: musicista legnaghese.* Legnago, 1934.
Delle Corte, A. *Un italiano all' estero: Antonio Salieri.* Turin and Milan, 1937.
Thayer, Alexander Wheelock. *Salieri, Rival of Mozart.* Edited by Theodore Albrecht. Kansas City, Missouri, 1989.

articles–

Rochlitz, F. "Antonio Salieri." *Nekrolog: allgemeine Theaterzeitung und Unterhaltungsblatt für Freunde der Kunst, Literatur und des geselligen Lebens* 18/no. 99 (1825): 405.
Jullien, A. "Salieri: sa carrière en France (1782-1787)." *Revue et gazette musicale de Paris* 42 (1875): 58.
Serini, C. "Antonio Salieri." *Rivista musicale italiana* 32 (1925): 412.
Bollert, W. "Antonio Salieri und die italienische Oper." In *Aufsätze zur Musikgeschichte,* 43. Bottrop, 1938.
———. "Antonio Salieri e l'opera tedesca." *Musica d'oggi* 20 (1938): 122.
Pisarowitz, K.M. "Salieriana: eine streiflichtende Dokumentarstudie." *Mitteilungen der Internationalen Stiftung Mozarteum* 9/nos.3-4 (1960): 11.
Damerini, A., and G. Roncaglia. "Volti musicale di Falstaff." *Chigiana* 18 (1961): 23.
Angermüller, R. "Beaumarchais und Salieri." In *Gesellschaft für Musikforschung Kongressbericht, Bonn 1970,* 325.
Swenson, E.E. " 'Prima la musica e poi le parole': an Eighteenth-Century Satire." *Analecta musicologica* no. 9 (1970): 112.
Heinzelmann, J. " 'Prima la musica, poi le parole': zu Salieris Wiener Opernparodie." *Österreichische Musikzeitschrift* 28 (1973): 19.
Rushton, J. "Salieri's *Les Horaces:* a Study of an Operatic Failure." *Music Review* 37 (1976): 266.
Angermüller, R. "Salieris Vorbemerkungen zu seinen Opern." *Mitteilungen der Internationalen Stiftung Mozarteum* 25/nos. 3-4 (1977): 15.
———. "Die entpolitisierte Oper am Wiener und am Fürstlich Esterházyschen Hof." *Haydn Yearbook* 10 (1978): 5.
———. "Salieri's *Tarare* (1787) und *Axur, Re d'Ormus* (1788). Vertonung eines Sujets für Paris und Wien." In *Mozart und die Oper seiner Zeit,* edited by Martin Ruhnke, 211. Laaber, 1981.
Sadie, Stanley. "Some Operas of 1787." *Musical Times* 122 (1981): 474.

unpublished–

Angermüller, R. "Antonio Salieri: sein Leben und seine weltlichen Werke unter besonderer Berücksichtigung seiner 'grossen' Opern." Ph.D. dissertation, University of Salzburg, 1970.
Platoff, John. "Music and Drama in the *opera buffa* finale: Mozart and his Contemporaries in Venice, 1781-1790." Ph.D. dissertation, University of Pennsylvania, 1984.

*　　　*　　　*

A native Italian, Antonio Salieri spent the majority of his life in Vienna except for four years between 1784-1788 when he was active in Paris. He was already musically proficient at the age of sixteen when the composer Florian Gassmann took him to Vienna where he was to meet Gluck and Metastasio and seize every opportunity to advance his career.

In 1770, when Salieri was 20, his first opera, *Le donne letterate,* was performed at the Burgtheater. In 1774 Salieri became *Kapellmeister* to the Habsburg court where he was responsible for producing Italian operas. He was a recognized figure in Viennese musical life long before Mozart settled in the city. The two knew each other well, Salieri being only six years Mozart's senior, and on one occasion in 1786 they shared a double bill when Mozart's *Der Schauspieldirektor* and Salieri's *Prima la musica e poi le parole* premiered at Joseph II's command.

Salieri was honored in 1778 when his opera, *L'Europa riconosciuta,* opened the new Teatro alla Scala in Milan: his operas were produced in Rome and Naples during the next several years. His career was enhanced when at Gluck's request he came to Paris in 1784 and produced his first French opera, *Les Danaïdes,* to critical acclaim. His second French opera, *Les Horaces,* composed 1784, was a failure at its premiere in 1786. The highlight of his French work was his collaboration with the controversial Pierre-Augustine Caron de Beaumarchais, who had decided ideas concerning opera as stated in his preface to *Tarare* composed by Salieri in 1787. This work was the composer's greatest Parisian success, and while regarded as his masterpiece, its fame survives primarily because of Beaumarchais's controversial libretto, particularly the preface which sets forth a new theory of opera. *Tarare* was fitted with a new libretto by Lorenzo Da Ponte as *Axur, Re d'Ormus,* under which title it was performed in Prague, Vienna, Germany, and England.

Salieri remained a vital component of Viennese musical life for over fifty years, thirty-six of which were spent as court composer, where he gained a reputation as an exemplary administrator. He wrote some 44 operas, including revised

A scene from Salieri's opera *Falstaff,* illustration from piano score, 1799

versions, and whereas a limited number of instrumental compositions survive, his compositions were overwhelmingly vocal in nature. His theatrical career ended with the death of Joseph II in 1790, and his music, always solidly constructed but never daring, became increasingly out-of-step as taste for the traditional Italian cantabile style found less and less favor during the next three decades. To examine a Salieri score is to find competent workmanship, an understanding of staging, and evidence of elegant melodic construction. The harmonic scheme is never advanced, and in general, the net-effect is one of stability and competency.

Even more than with his operas, Salieri left his mark on the future by giving composition lessons to Beethoven, Schubert, Czerny, and the young Liszt, among others. He went insane in 1823, and his reputation was subsequently defamed by insidious rumors, the most outrageous of which was that he had poisoned Mozart. It is unfortunate that such a falsehood still clouds his accomplishments.

—Aubrey S. Garlington

SALLINEN, Aulis.

Composer. Born 9 April 1935, in Salmi, Finland. Studied with Aarre Merikanto and Joonas Kokkonen at the Sibelius Academy, 1955-60; managing director of the Finnish Radio Symphony, 1960-70; taught at the Sibelius Academy, 1963-76; named Arts Professor by the Finnish State, 1976-81; life appointment as Arts Professor, 1981-.

Operas

Publishers: Fazer, Novello.

The Horseman [*Ratsumies*], P. Haavikko, 1973-74, Savonlinna Opera Festival, 17 July 1975.
The Red Line [*Punainen viiva*], after I. Kianto, 1977-78, Helsinki, 30 November 1978; English version, London, 14 July 1979.
The King Goes Forth to France [*Kuningas lahtee ranskaan*], Haavikko, 1983, Savonlinna Opera Festival, 7 July 1984; English version, Santa Fe, New Mexico, 26 July 1986.
Kullervo op 61, Kalevala, 1988, Los Angeles, February 1992.

Other works: orchestral works, chamber and instrumental music, vocal works.

Publications

By SALLINEN: books–

Salmenhaara, E., ed. *Miten sävellykseni ovat syntyneet* [*Origin of my works*]. Helsinki, 1970 [contains worklist and discography].

About SALLINEN: articles–

Parsons, Jeremy. "Aulis Sallinen." *Musical Times* 122 (1980): 693.

*　　*　　*

Aulis Sallinen is by nature a symphonist who tends to think instinctively in instrumental rather than vocal terms. Since the mid 1950s, when his first serious work began to appear, the tally of his compositions shows that orchestral and instrumental music heavily outweighs that for the voice and have been a more reliable indicator of his development over the years. This development shows clear signs of having been influenced by Aarre Merikanto (1893-1958) and Joonas Kokkonen (born 1921), his principal teachers at the Sibelius Academy in Helsinki.

Merikanto's only opera *Juha* (composed 1922, first performed 1957) is now acknowledged to have been a milestone in the history of opera in Finland. It has played a part in Sallinen's own evolution as an opera composer and its influence is especially noticeable in *The Red Line* (1977-78), not merely because both operas deal with remote communities in the grip of elemental forces, but because of the way in which the two composers have managed to combine the starkness of nature with the warmth of human emotions. A work of considerable intrinsic merit, *Juha* was for years thought too avant-garde in his native land, but since its first performance, Merikanto's sensitive characterization and his dramatic handling of a theme not unlike that of Janáček's *Kat'a Kabanová* have served as a model for other Finnish composers, among them Kokkonen, whose only opera, *The Last Temptations,* is one of the most successful of all modern Finnish operas.

Kokkonen, also by instinct a symphonist, was at first strongly influenced by Sibelius, but that influence has since been diluted by exposure to western, mainly French, models. The resulting amalgam has contributed to the formulation of Sallinen's own musical language, which also owes something to Berg and Bartók. Kokkonen's chief influence on Sallinen, however, has been in exploring the potential of instruments, particularly strings, and in the use of orchestral color and the development of unusual sonorities.

Sallinen's own music reveals an acute ear for unconventional harmony and subtle color; his highly individual use of the combination of tuned percussion and low brass has become something of a feature of his orchestral palette. With the passage of time, he has refined his style, discarding an early flirtation with serialism in favor of a freely developing tonality, uncluttered melodic lines, open harmonies and suspended chords, a technique employed to great effect in the short orchestral work *Shadows* and in the Symphony "Washington Mosaics" (no. 5).

Sallinen's three operas are all basically tragic and in varying degrees symbolic. In his first, *Ratsumies* (*The Horseman*) (1974), an opera imbued with a haunting sense of unreality, the symbolism is of a teasingly obscure kind that leaves the listener suspended and unsure. In *The Red Line,* the equivocations have been largely rationalized, but in *The King Goes Forth to France,* a surreal fantasy about war, intrigue and death set in an ice age during an unhistorical Hundred Years War, we are again in a world of shadows and hauntingly elliptical meanings never quite made clear. An orchestral interlude, "The King passes by," has been heard in the concert hall and gives a strong flavor of the opera in general; its subdued color and steady muffled rhythm powerfully evoke the impression of a doom-laden excursion under the deadening hand of winter. Like Sibelius, Sallinen has an unerring talent for evoking the feeling of timelessness, numbing cold, and the silent, limitless space of the bleak northern latitudes with music of muted but exciting intensity. It would be wrong, though, to imply that his music is consistently cold or doom-laden. His themes are tragic, but he himself is an optimist who always leaves us on a rising note; however wretched the prospect, there is always light somewhere at the end of the tunnel.

Sallinen may not aspire to the epic quality that makes Sibelius's finest work monumental and compelling, but he does have a regard for humanity, a quality absent from Sibelius's music, which gives his own work genuine stature and a unique quality. As a composer he is in the forefront of what for want of a better description may be termed the lyric-contemporary school of Finnish music, a group which includes among others Rautavaara and Kokkonen, and whose work contrasts with the determinedly experimental music of the followers of Erik Bergmann. In Sallinen's case these trends are well defined in his operas but are perhaps to be found more consistently expressed in his five symphonies, his string quartets, and in the short chamber-orchestral pieces that are signposts of his development.

—Kenneth Dommett

SALOME.

Composer: Richard Strauss.

Librettist: Richard Strauss (based on H. Lachmann's translation of Oscar Wilde's play).

First Performance: Dresden, Court Opera, 9 December 1905.

Roles: Salome (soprano); Herod (tenor); Herodias (mezzo-soprano); Jokanaan (baritone); Narraboth (tenor); Page of Herodias (contralto); Five Jews (four tenors, bass); Two Nazarenes (tenor, bass); Two Soldiers (two basses); Cappadocian (bass); Slave (soprano).

Publications

books–

Gilman, L. *Strauss' Salome: a Guide to the Opera.* New York, 1906.
John, Nicholas, ed. *Richard Strauss: Salome, Elektra.* London and New York, 1988.
Puffett, Derrick, ed. *Richard Strauss: Salome.* Cambridge, 1989.

articles–

Marsop, P. "Italien und der 'Fall Salome,' nebst Glossen zur Kritik und Ästhetik." *Die Musik* 6 (1906-07): 139.
Hoslinger, C. "Salome und ihr österreichisches Schicksal 1905-19." *Österreichische Musikzeitschrift* 22 (1977).
Avant-scène opéra January-February (1983) [*Salome* issue].

Kramer, Lawrence. "Culture and musical hermeneutics: The Salome complex." *Cambridge Opera Journal* 2 (1990): 269.

*　　*　　*

Strauss was not the first to use the story of the death of John the Baptist as the basis of a dramatic work, nor was Oscar Wilde, the author of Salome's literary source. Indeed, images of the beheading of John the Baptist are scattered throughout the visual as well as literary art of the latter nineteenth century. Wilde was drawn to the story by the paintings of Gustave Moreau, and the cruel, sultry illustrations produced by Aubrey Beardsley for Wilde's play are famous. Violent biblical women were a current source of subject material, Klimt having already painted Judith (from the Apocrypha) more than once. The art of Gustav Klimt, leader of the Viennese Secession, shows an obsession with beautiful, sensuous, and frighteningly cruel women, thoroughly congruent with the aesthetic of *Salome.*

The character of the daughter of Herodias in these artistic imaginations evolved considerably beyond the mindless girl of the brief biblical tale. The new Salome—determined, mature, beautiful, chaste, perverse—acts quite independently of any vengeful designs on the part of her mother. Yet in all its gory psychotic perversion, *Salome* is a brilliant reflection of the artistic tenor of Austria and Germany at the turn of the century, and deeply rooted in the currents of nineteenth-century literary Decadence, with its contorted language and macabre imagery, and its interest in death, the occult, and the erotic.

The story of the opera runs as follows: Herod the tetrarch holds John the Baptist imprisoned. Salome, daughter of Herod's wife Herodias, is obsessed with the captive, admiring his voice, his body, hair, and above all his mouth. When John sternly rebuffs her, she becomes obsessed. Herod in his turn is obsessed with Salome, insisting that she dance for him the dance of the seven veils. After Herod swears to give her whatever she asks, Salome agrees, afterwards demanding the head of John. In a lurid apostrophe to the head, Salome exults in her triumph, ecstatically kissing the severed head. The horrified king orders his soldiers to kill Salome.

With the very opening line "How beautiful Princess Salome is tonight!" the opera dives into the realm of sexual obsession, and the tension only builds from that moment until the end. The obsessive and neurotic atmosphere is underscored by the weird repetitive nature of the text. John drones on with his imprecations, the Jews bicker over the nature of John, and Herod in his overpowering anxiety repeatedly worries that "something terrible" will happen. The recurrence of textual themes, together with the visual motif of the moon and the constantly recurring musical motifs, is not only suggestive of obsession, but eerily reminiscent of biblical language.

Strauss' score forms a brilliant exegesis of the neurotic, sensual obsessions of the characters on the stage. Opening

The first production of *Salome,* **with Marie Wittich as Salome, Karl Burian as Herodes, and Irene von Chavanne as Herodias, Dresden Hofoper, 1905**

directly, without a prelude, the music is a dense network of tense *Leitmotifs* which appear over and over, altered in rhythm, harmony, and color as they recur in a changing web of meaning and association. The crisp and memorable motives developed in Strauss' tone poems are here employed to devastating effect, moving far beyond such musical depictions as Don Quixote's harmless obsession or Till Eulenspiegel's death knell. *Salome*'s motifs are nagging, uneasy, piercing, vicious. By the end, the *idée fixe* of Salome's obsession, piercing through a veil of harsh trills, is scarcely endurable.

Despite the execution of Salome at the end, there is no moral judgment passed on her behavior. A desperate and amoral hunt for pure sensation and novelty, characteristic of Decadence, leads inevitably away from moral strictures. When sensation is all that matters, rules do not apply: not to the linguistics of poetry, the harmony of music, or the morals of social behavior. An oblique theological justification is advanced by one of the bickering Jews, who says, "God is in what is evil even as He is in what is good." But Wilde himself wrote, "I myself would sacrifice everything for a new experience, and I know there is no such thing as a new experience at all . . . I would go to the stake for a sensation and be a sceptic to the last!"

Certainly not everyone was sympathetic to the sentiments, aesthetic or otherwise, expressed in *Salome*. The 1905 premiere in Dresden caused a terrific scandal. In London and in Berlin, where Strauss was conductor of the Royal Court Opera, premieres were delayed and the opera censored. When *Salome* was given at the Metropolitan Opera House in New York, in 1907, it was withdrawn after one performance. "Bestial!" "corrupt!" "blasphemous!" cried viewers. But the opera did not die. Perhaps it was irresistible precisely because it was such an accurate reflection of its time; indeed, *Salome* is remarkable for expressing so clearly so many contemporary cultural currents. Herodias' crazed daughter is a vision at once compelling and troubling of Old Testament society, reinterpreted for the modern age and given vivid expression by musicians, artists, and writers alike, united in the multimedia genre of opera.

Salome triumphed in spite of, or perhaps because of, the scandal and shock it caused, to become Strauss' first operatic triumph and one of the most influential works of the time. As Strauss later commented wryly, "Wilhelm II once said, 'I am sorry Strauss composed this *Salome*. I really like the fellow, but this will do him a lot of damage.' The damage enabled me to build my villa in Garmisch."

—Elizabeth W. Patton

SAMMARCO, Mario.

Baritone. Born 13 December 1867, in Palermo. Died 24 January 1930, in Milan. Studied with Antonio Cantelli; debut as Valentine in *Faust*, Palermo, 1888; appeared as Scarpia at Covent Garden, 1904; sang at Covent Garden until 1914; American debut as Tonio, Manhattan Opera House, 1908; sang with the Chicago Grand Opera, 1910-13; created Gerard in *Andrea Chénier* and Cascart in *Zazà*.

Publications

About SAMMARCO: articles–

Freestone, J. "Giuseppe Mario Sammarco." *Gramophone* 24 (1951): 96.
Celletti, R. "Sammarco, Mario." In *Le grandi voci,* Rome, 1964.

*   *   *

Within scarcely more than a decade Italy produced a rich array of baritones, including Scotti, De Luca, Stracciari, Viglione-Borghese, Giraldoni, Ruffo, Amato, and Sammarco. Of these, Scotti and Sammarco are the two least convincingly "explained" by their recordings. Both, we know, were good actors, and Sammarco's was certainly the richer and more resonant voice, though as recorded it is not of such a distinctive or memorable character as to make it instantly identifiable. His high notes have plenty of body, and he copes easily with a high tessitura (the Italians describe him as "tenoreggiante"). Stylistically, he is hardly a suave exponent of *bel canto,* and yet he can turn his hand to a Donizetti aria and sing it with genuine accomplishment, as he does in "A tanto amor" from *La favorita.* While these recordings may not always show him as a great singer in an age of great singers, the facts of his career suggest that that is exactly what he was.

Sammarco's stage performances presented a particularly satisfying mixture of elements. He sang well and acted well,

Mario Sammarco as Sharpless, with Giovanni Zenatello as Pinkerton, in *Madama Butterfly*

and in combination these two factors amounted to excellence. There was a great vitality about his performances: the recurrent description is "vigorous." He had considerable versatility, so that in addition to the standard Italian and French operas his repertoire included Wagnerian roles, such as Wolfram in *Tannhäuser* and Sachs in *Die Meistersinger;* and in 1919 Sommarco sang the title-role in Monteverdi's *Orfeo,* a rarity at that time, at the Milan Conservatory. He was also extremely hard working: the opera critic of *Musical Opinion* recalled that in the 1910 season at Covent Garden he appeared in 35 out of 83 performances. On his return as Rigoletto in 1919 the same critic wrote of him: "We heard him in a part that he always made great, and great his representation of it still is, but Time is relentless and unsparing in its toll. . . . There were glad moments enough that had the real old Sammarco hallmark, especially in 'Pari siamo,' and his acting was more polished than ever." Herman Klein, looking back to Sammarco's best days, said he "had a voice of singular purity, breadth and vibrant power, always in tune, well controlled, and capable of deep as well as varied expression." If there is something a little formal about such critical appreciation, it might also be recalled that at the Manhattan Opera House in New York, where Sammarco was one of the mainstays, "enthusiasm ran riot, the audience rising to its feet, applauding and waving programmes and handkerchieves" when he had finished the Prologue to *Pagliacci:* "a Caruso among baritones," proclaimed the *New York Press.*

—J.B. Steane

SAMSON AND DALILAH
See SAMSON ET DALILA

SAMSON ET DALILA [Samson and Delilah].

Composer: Camille Saint-Saëns.

Librettist: F. Lemaire.

First Performance: Weimar, Hoftheater, 2 December 1877.

Roles: Samson (tenor); Dalila (mezzo-soprano or contralto); High Priest to Dagon (baritone); Abimelech (bass); An Old Hebrew (bass); chorus (SSAATTBB).

Publications

book–

Collet, H. *Samson et Dalila de C. Saint-Saëns.* Paris, 1922.

articles–

Avant-scène opéra 15 (1978) [*Samson et Dalila* issue].

*　　　*　　　*

The plot of *Samson et Dalila* closely follows the story of Samson as told in Chapter XVI of the Book of Judges. The only main change is that Dalila hands Samson over to the Philistines for patriotic reasons and not, as in the Bible, for eleven hundred pieces of silver—an alteration probably introduced to avoid offending the susceptibilities of opera audiences at the time. The work had originally been intended as an oratorio, but the librettist, a Creole poet named Ferdinand Lemaire who was distantly related to Saint-Saëns by marriage, insisted that it should be an opera. Portions of the second act were quickly written in 1867, but, when tried out privately, they met with little enthusiasm. Then, on a visit to Liszt in Weimar, Saint-Saëns was encouraged by the remark: "Finish your opera. I will have it performed in Weimar." Liszt was as good as his word: in 1877 he sponsored the world premiere in that town. But French impresarios remained uninterested since they traditionally regarded biblical subjects as box-office poison, and *Samson et Dalila* had to wait a long time before reaching the Paris Opéra in 1892.

It is Saint-Saëns' only successful opera, largely because its oratorio-like form and uncomplicated story line enabled him to concentrate on the purely musical aspects instead of seeking after theatrical effect. The many gifts Saint-Saëns possessed did not include a highly developed sense of theater, which is why none of his other stage-works survives today. In *Samson et Dalila* this lack of feeling for the stage did not matter greatly, and Saint-Saëns could give full rein to his musical genius. He was an eclectic composer able to assimilate a wide variety of different styles, absorb them, and turn them deftly to his own use. As an early enthusiast of Handel, whose music was then little known in France, he brought a sombre Handelian power to the choral writing, notably in the laments of the oppressed Hebrews, and his contrapuntal style is, as always, impeccable. Samson's impassioned arias—"Arrêtez, ô mes frères," for example, and "Israël romps ta chaîne,"—are an inspired continuation of Meyerbeer at his most stirring. *Samson et Dalila* is historically important too in that it brings exoticism into French music. However facile the oriental languors of the ballet music may seem today, it should be remembered that prior to Saint-Saëns none of his insular compatriots, with the possible exception of that minor figure Félicien David, had sought inspiration very far beyond the frontiers of their own country.

Most important of all, Saint-Saëns rose to the occasion by giving Dalila melodies of a delectable but subtle sensuality. Passion is not normally a strong point of his music, yet in depicting the great temptress he drew on reserves of unexpected voluptuousness. "Printemps qui commence" is full of an amorous yearning which flames into raging desire with "Amour viens aider ma faiblesse," where Dalila's sexual longing mingles ardently with feelings of patriotism. "Mon coeur s'ouvre à ta voix" is one of the most famous arias ever written, a love song in which the effect is skillfully ensured by chromatic variation of the melodic line. Dalila's music alone, together with the sensational climax when Samson brings the pillars of the temple crashing down, is enough to guarantee the continued success of the work.

—James Harding

SANDERSON, Sybil.

Soprano. Born 7 December 1865, in Sacramento, California. Died 15 May 1903, in Paris. Studied music in San Francisco

An engraving showing act III of *Samson et Dalila*, Paris Opéra, 1890

before going to Paris to study with Massenet, Giovanni, Sbriglia, and Mathilde Marchesi; debut as Manon, The Hague, 1888; created role of Esclarmonde at Opéra-Comique, 1889; created role of Thaïs, Opéra, 1894; Metropolitan Opera debut as Manon, 1895.

*　　*　　*

A good deal of mystery surrounds the true status of Sybil Sanderson in the operatic world. A pupil of both Mathilde Marchesi and Giovanni Sbriglia, her name is indissolubly linked with the operas of Massenet. Her debut at the Hague was in *Manon* and the composer considered her the ideal interpreter. Massenet thereafter wrote both Esclarmonde and Thaïs specifically for Sanderson and she created the title roles respectively at the Opéra–Comique in 1889 and the Paris Opéra in 1894. Although the middle-aged composer was undoubtedly affected, if not obsessed with Sanderson's incredible beauty, this was clearly not the sole reason for her success in the two roles.

In their annals of the Paris stage Noel and Stoullig refer to Sanderson's ravishing voice and theatrical instinct in *Esclarmonde* and wax lyrical over her performance as Thaïs— "absolutely ideal with a voice like crystal." Her success in Paris was enormous and she was a huge favorite at both the Opéra and the Opéra–Comique. She also sang in the premieres of Massenet's *Le mage* and Saint-Saëns' *Phryne.*

Having conquered Paris, Sanderson as an American citizen was in due course lured to the Metropolitan Opera in New York to make her debut as Manon in 1895 opposite Jean de Reszke. According to Krehbiel it was a "radiant vision," but

unfortunately by the beginning of act II "it became noticeable that she was wanting in passionate expression as well as in voice and that her histrionic limitations went hand in hand with her vocal." Her voice was "pure and true in intonation (but) lacking in volume and in penetrative quality." The critic could not accept that her voice was "of a kind to be associated with serious opera." Lahee was kinder in describing Sanderson's voice as "light, pure and flexible" and he praised her upper register, which Krehbiel felt was composed of "mere trickles of sound."

Earlier in 1891 she had a similar lack of success at Covent Garden, where she was the first to sing Manon in the original language opposite Van Dyck whose voice simply overwhelmed hers. It is reasonable to conclude that this was not a voice for the larger houses. On the other hand Noel and Stoullig felt that when singing Thaïs her voice had filled the Opéra despite what might have been expected and this was three years after her appearances at Covent Garden.

Sanderson's career simply withered at the turn of the century. Re-engaged by the Metropolitan to sing on tour over the winter of 1901-2 she appeared infrequently and was unable to continue a performance of *Manon* in Memphis. She returned to Paris, died aged only 37 and left behind no records. Certainly Sanderson was a glory of the operatic stage, but almost exclusively in one city singing largely the works of one composer.

—Stanley Henig

Sybil Sanderson, c. 1890

SANQUIRICO, Alessandro.

Designer. Born 27 July 1777, in Milan. Died 12 March 1849, in Milan. Worked in collaboration with Landriani, Pedroni, Perego, and Fuentes; first major solo design, *La festa della rosa,* 1811; sole designer and chief scene painter for Teatro alla Scala, 1817-32; designed hundreds of operas and ballets at Teatro alla Scala, including works of Mercadante, Bellini, Rossini, Donizetti, Pacini, and Meyerbeer; redecorated the interior of Teatro alla Scala, 1829.

Opera Productions (selected)

La festa della rosa, Teatro alla Scala, 1811.
La gazza ladra, Teatro alla Scala, 1817.
Il pirata, Teatro alla Scala, 1827.
Norma, Teatro alla Scala, 1831.
Lucrezia Borgia, Teatro alla Scala, 1834.

Publications

By SANQUIRICO: books and writings–

Raccolta di scene teatrali eseguite o disegnate dai più celebri pittori scenici di Milano, 1819-24.
Raccolta di varie decorazioni sceniche inventate ed eseguite per il R. Teatro alla Scala di Milano da Alessandro Sanquirico, c1827.

About SANQUIRICO: articles–

Rigotti, D. "Sanquirico Scenografo Principe." *Rassegna Musicale Curci* 30, no. 1 (1977): 53-55.

* * *

Alessandro Sanquirico was one of the more remarkably talented and prolific scenographers in the history of the Italian music theater. He trained in the lively, bustling atmosphere of the theatrical workshops in Milan where he quickly became adept at every feature of theatrical design and production. As was customary, he collaborated on many different projects throughout his career, but especially during his youth. His first major solo design was made for Stefano Pavesi's opera *La festa della rosa,* produced at Teatro alla Scala, 1811. This work marked the beginning of a series of over 200 different scenographic designs for the opera theater in Milan and environs for the next three decades. Between 1817-1832, Sanquirico was the dominant scenographer at Teatro alla Scala, and his designs were crucial for the premieres of many major operas including *Norma, La gazza ladra, Otello,* and *Il pirata,* among others.

Sanquirico was highly respected for his abilities to organize elaborate architectural perspectives in terms of massive backgrounds which served as elegant frameworks for foreground acting space. While the result was almost always one of epic grandeur, his designs were primarily intended to function as frameworks for the work at hand. Thus, as visually extravagant as were the realizations of his projects, Sanquirico seems never to have lost sight of the fact that stage designs were not spectacles for their own sake but were to connect with the musical action.

The Milanese master was responsive to new technical innovations, and towards the end of his career he took advantage of new effects offered when gas lighting was introduced to Teatro alla Scala. Although Sanquirico never traveled extensively outside Milan and Lombardy, his fame and influence were not limited to Italy. Two collections of his drawings and designs were published during his lifetime, one between 1819 and 1824, the other in 1827. These publications allowed him to become as highly regarded as more internationally based compatriots such as Ciceri in Paris.

Sanquirico was a master of the Pompeiian style which swept Europe in the late eighteenth century. In turn, this style went hand in glove with prevailing neoclassical theories and practices which dominated European artistic activity. Although Sanquirico was justifiably esteemed as a leading master of neoclassical techniques—his structural sense determined by such organizational modes—he was neither rigid nor pedantic. His understanding of geometric design permitted him almost total control, freeing him from restrictive rigidities.

Concern with design proprieties did not blind Sanquirico to the efficacy of local color. Sanquirico's fascination with subtle variants of shading—both color and traditional chiaroscuro—reveals him sensitive to certain aspects of Romanticism which came to the fore in Italian stage design during the last two decades of his career. There is a grace and power in Sanquirico's work which more than justifies one Milanese critic's audacity in comparing him to Michelangelo.

—Aubrey S. Garlington

SANZOGNO, Nino.

Conductor/Composer. Born 13 April 1911, in Venice. Died 4 May 1983, in Milan. Studied composition with Malipiero in Venice; studied conducting with Scherchen in Brussels, 1935; conductor at the Teatro La Fenice, Venice, 1937, and principal conductor, 1938-40; conducted at the Teatro alla Scala, Milan, 1939, and principal conductor, 1962-65; conducted in South America; gave conducting courses at Darmstadt. Sanzogno composed a number of orchestral and chamber works.

* * *

Chief conductor at the Teatro La Fenice, Venice, from 1938 to 1940, Nino Sanzogno was one of the regular conductors at the Teatro alla Scala in Milan, where he appeared during most seasons between 1941 and 1972 and was principal conductor from 1962 to 1965. He also made guest appearances in Vienna, Moscow, Buenos Aires, and at the Edinburgh Festival. He was especially associated with twentieth-century music, to which he dedicated himself, leading numerous world and Italian premieres, and he was known for his proficiency in reading complex modern scores. From 1956, beginning with a production of Cimarosa's *Il matrimonio segreto,* he was closely tied to the 500-seat Piccola Scala, where he conducted such twentieth-century works as Luciano Chailly's *Una domanda di matrimonio* (in its world premiere performance on 22 May 1957), Rota's *Il cappello di paglia di Firenze* and *La notte di un nevrastenico* (world premiere, 8 February 1960), Malipiero's *Sette canzoni* (1960) and *Torneo notturno* (1961), Berio's *Passaggio* (1963), Manzoni's *Atomtod* (1964), and Weill's *Aufstieg und Fall der Stadt Mahagonny* (1964), in addition to eighteenth- and nineteenth-century operas including Piccinni's *La Cecchina* (1958), Rossini's *La pietra del Paragone* (1959), Cimarosa's *Le astuzie femminili* (1960), and Paisiello's *Nina ossia La pazza per amore* (1961).

Sanzogno's assignments at La Scala reveal the number of world or Italian premieres he led and his wide-ranging experience with operas little known outside Italy as well as the standard repertoire: 1941—Richard Strauss's *Salome;* 1942—Mascagni's *Lodoletta,* Humperdinck's *Hänsel und Gretel,* Puccini's *Madama Butterfly;* 1943—Verdi's *La forza del destino* and *La traviata;* 1944—Busoni's *Arlecchino ovvero Le fenestre;* 1948—Stravinsky's *Oedipus Rex;* 1949—Pizzetti's *La sacra rappresentazione di Abraham e d'Isaac,* Humperdinck's *Hänsel und Gretel,* Offenbach's *Les contes d'Hoffmann,* Milhaud's *Le pauvre matelot,* Petrassi's *Il cordovano* (world premiere, 12 May); 1950—Ferrari-Trecate's *L'orso re,* Wolf-Ferrari's *Il campanello,* Malipiero's *L'allegra brigata* (world premiere, 4 May); 1951—Menotti's *Il console,* Monteverdi's *Il combattimento di Tancredi e Clorinda,* Peragallo's *La collona,* Paisiello's *La serva padrona,* Cherubini's *L'osteria portughese,* Cimarosa's *Il credulo;* 1952—Donizetti's *Don Pasquale;* 1953—Napoli's *Mas'aniello,* Verdi's *Rigoletto;* 1954—Mortari's *La figlia del diavolo,* Peragallo's *La gita in campagna,* Menotti's *Amelia al ballo;* 1955—Milhaud's *David* (world stage premiere, 2 January), Tosatti's *Il giudizio,* Stravinsky's *Mavra;* 1956—Walton's *Troilus and Cressida* (the first Italian performance), Leoncavallo's *Pagliacci,* Donizetti's *L'elisir d'amore, Il matrimonio segreto,* Prokofiev's *The Fiery Angel* (the first Italian performance), Lattuada's *Caino;* 1957—Piccinni's *La cecchina ossia La buona figliuola,* Hindemith's *Mathis der Maler,* Gluck's *Iphigenie en Tauride* (with Maria Callas), Poulenc's *Les dialogues des Carmelites* (world premiere, 26 January); 1958—Ravel's *L'heure espagnole* and *L'enfant et les sortilèges*, Donizetti's *L'elisir d'amore*, Janáček's *The Cunning Little Vixen*, Cimarosa's *Il matrimonio segreto*, Menotti's *Maria Golovin*; 1959—Bizet's *Carmen*; 1960—Verdi's *Macbeth, Aida,* and *Carmen*; 1961—Tchaikovsky's *The Queen of Spades*, Britten's *A Midsummer Night's Dream*, Offenbach's *Les contes d'Hoffmann*; 1962—Dallapiccola's *Il prigioniero*, Busoni's *Turandot*, Kurka's *Good Soldier Schweik*, Gluck's *Orfeo ed Euridice*; 1963—Berg's *Lulu* (the first Italian performance), Bizet's *Carmen*, Verdi's *Falstaff*, Cherubini's *Ali Baba*; 1969—Donizetti's *La figlia del reggimento* with Mirella Freni and Luciano Pavarotti.

At La Fenice in 1948 he conducted a performance of Puccini's *Turandot* that was one of Maria Callas's first professional appearances and marked her first assumption of the role. Also at La Fenice he conducted the world premiere of Tosatti's *Partita a pugni* (8 September 1953), and the world stage premiere of Prokofiev's *The Fiery Angel* (14 September 1955). He also led the first Italian performance of Shostakovitch's *Lady Macbeth of Mtsensk.*

The Teatro Massimo in Palermo heard Verdi's *Otello* under his baton in 1962 and Bellini's *La straniera* in 1968. At the 1957 Edinburgh Festival he led Cimarosa's *Il matrimonio segreto* and Donizetti's *L'elisir d'amore.* He also conducted at the 1966 Maggio Musicale Fiorentino (Verdi's *Luisa Miller*). Not a prolific recording artist, Sanzogno was the conductor of Joan Sutherland's first recording of Verdi's *Rigoletto* (1961).

Sanzogno's reputation lies more on the world premieres he led, his championing of contemporary opera, and the length of his career than on the quality of his performances. Not a strong taskmaster or the possessor of a charismatic authority, he is not known for raising the level of achievement of the orchestras he conducted despite his long tenure with them. Italian critics have remarked on his quiet, subtle control, his precision, and his deep musical knowledge, as well as an elegance and charm that mask his firm discipline, but his ranking has not been high in the eyes of American critics, who may be unaware of his importance in introducing modern operatic works to Italy and the world.

—Michael Sims

* * *

SASS, Sylvia.

Soprano. Born 12 July 1951, in Budapest. Married: György Hajdu. Studied with her mother, and with Olga Revhegyi at the Liszt Academy; debut as Violetta in *La traviata,* Sofia, 1971; British debut as Desdemona, Scottish Opera, 1975; Covent Garden debut as Giselda in *I lombardi,* 1976; Metropolitan Opera debut as Tosca, 1977. Teaches voice in Europe.

Publications

About SASS: article–

Muñoz, J.A. "Entrevista." *Monsalvat* 151/July-August (1987): 20.

* * *

Sylvia Sass, who began her international career in the mid-1970s, was then hailed as "the new Callas," a prophecy the Hungarian singer has not fulfilled. Such a prediction is a curse, setting a standard which is unfair, not to mention undesirable (Elena Suliotis was once the "new Callas" and her career went into a downward spiral after she assumed roles too taxing for her voice). Despite vocal qualities which invite comparisons to Callas, such as a covered, hooded tone, and an upper range which tends to be wiry, she has developed vocal colorings and strengths of her own. Sass can bring off the lightest of pianissimi and the most unearthly of chest notes; in between, she has strength and clarity. She possesses a large voice and is able to draw on great reserves of breath support for the steadiest of sound. Indeed, she sounds very robust, especially on the records she made for Decca in 1977 and 1978.

Sass appeared at a time when audiences were looking for successors to Callas, Sutherland and Caballé. This state of affairs was a disadvantage, because those sopranos cast three of the longest shadows of recent operatic history, and the search for their successor predisposes listeners to look for duplicates rather than artists with new styles of singing. Sass has acquitted herself nicely and is no longer the "next" so-and-so, although her career does not have the international dimension her early work promised. Despite what some consider a premature Metropolitan Opera debut as Tosca in 1977 (she was twenty-six), she has maintained a steady reputation recording, performing and teaching voice regularly in Hungary and much of Europe. While she has wisely avoided trying to please those looking for the next Callas, she has developed as a reliable and imaginative interpreter of Puccini, Mozart and Verdi roles as well as Strauss songs.

She came from a musical family. Sylvia was trained early by her mother, a coloratura, and then studied with Olga Revhegyi at the Academy in Budapest. Her father was a pianist who taught at high school and encouraged the development of her voice by staging an opera for her. After winning several European competitions, she earned fame as a prodigy. Now almost twenty years after her meteoric rise, her voice remains full and her technique sound. Like Suliotis, she performed roles before she was ready, singing "Medea" before she was thirty. She differs, though, from "too much too soon" sopranos by taking great care in accepting roles and in preserving her voice.

However, Sass does have a vocal flaw, but not as a result of early abuse. The problem is that her voice fits neither the lyric nor the dramatic repertoire precisely. To accommodate her ventures into either repertory, she combines lyric and dramatic qualities, sometimes producing a highly mannered sound. On a recording such as the letter scene from Tchaikovsky's *Eugene Onegin,* her vocal point of view is not clearly lyric or dramatic and the mannered sound predominates, although she produces some exquisitely beautiful notes.

She can separate her lyric and dramatic propensities according to the demands of a given role. Her recording of "Un bel di" from *Madama Butterfly* shows a light plaintive quality with plenty of warmth. On the contrary, her "In questa Reggia" from *Turandot,* in which the imperious princess scares potential suitors with the story of her violated ancestor, shows off a glacial "dove si spensa la sua fresca voce" ["when they stilled her young voice"] which could stop admirers in their tracks. Though it is not as cold or authoritative a reading as Birgit Nilsson's, it is nonetheless impressive in its surety.

Her range is much greater than either of these two examples would indicate; despite problems, her middle range combines suppleness and dramatic heft to produce an odd sound which is somehow thick, but at the same time brilliant. The combination provides an incandescent glow which informs arias as diverse as "Io son l'umile ancella" from Cilèa's *Adriana Lecouvreur* and "Dei tuoi figli la madre" from Cherubini's *Medea*. Her incandescence results in part from the noticeable interplay between unforced legato and the effort she makes to push her voice. For some listeners, this "pushing" suggests the human struggle which many arias dramatize and results in intense communication. For others, it is a severe irritation.

Sass's soprano sometimes "works" when she shows effort, but it is often seamless at places and "works" in them, too. Some listeners find seamless, flawless voices dull. Rupert Christiansen quotes Victor Gollancz's appraisal of Joan Sutherland: "God, she's as dull as Melba" (*Prima Donna*, New York, 1985: 317). It is important to note that a seamless voice does not automatically produce dull sound, and a large steely voice does not automatically produce vocal drama. While Sass is certainly not dull, neither does her voice always "work" in a role. For example, her recording of the mad scene from *Lucia di Lammermoor* offers some beautiful plaintive singing, but when a flexible upper range is called for, Sass glides over the notes which are too fast to negotiate. Her strong point in this recording is the lustre she offers. To her credit, Sass's pianissimi are supple and seamless, and while her fully projected voice sounds forced at the top, she has great presence and dramatic quality in her interpretations.

Despite vocal problems, Sylvia Sass's performances always have something to recommend them. Recently she has undertaken a series of early Verdi roles for Hungaroton Records, and provides committed, intelligent readings of them. She excels in roles which call for pianissimo and in roles which call for the lower registers. She is interesting but not always satisfying when she reaches for high notes in full voice. Her voice has a distinctive timbre, and, taken together, her strengths and weaknesses often add up to compelling performances.

—Timothy O. Gray

SATYAGRAHA
See TRIPTYCH

SAUL AND DAVID
See SAUL OG DAVID

SAUL OG DAVID [Saul and David].

Composer: Carl Nielsen.

Librettist: E. Christiansen.

First Performance: Copenhagen, 28 November 1902.

Roles: Saul (bass-baritone); Jonathan (tenor); Mikal (soprano); David (tenor); Samuel (bass); Abner (bass); Abisay (soprano); The Witch of Endor (contralto); chorus.

* * *

The story of the friendship and subsequent rivalry between the old king Saul and the young shepherd David is to be found in the First Book of Samuel. It is a story full of incident; of battles fought between the Israelites and their foes, centering on the momentous encounter between David and Goliath; of aspects of love, the love of Saul and of his son Jonathan for David, and of David's love for Saul's daughter Mikal; of jealousy, anger and revenge; of arrogance and overthrow. By abrogating to himself the sacred authority vested in the prophet Samuel, Saul invokes divine anger. Ever jealous of His authority and displeased that the Israelites should have chosen any king but Him, Jehovah revenges himself on the sacrilegious Saul, by first making him mad, then having Samuel anoint the submissive hero David as his successor. Jonathan is allowed to die and the defeated Saul is consigned to his fate, defiant still and cursing God.

Apart from Handel, whose *Saul* is an opera in all but name, no composer has had much success in reducing this epic to tractable dramatic form. Nielsen was first drawn to the story in 1896, the year of his lyric cantata *Hymnus amoris*. He was thirty, but despite having already written his first Symphony he did not feel psychologically ready to meet the challenge of so dramatic a subject. A story as rich in conflicts and subplots as this whose outcome is familiar demands skill and imagination to turn it to account: it must either be refashioned so as to give the plot novelty or throw new light on the characters. Nielsen chose to treat the characters.

The dominant theme, the "pole" as Nielsen called it, from which *Saul and David* springs, is the role of kingship. Are kings who are appointed by God empowered to rule independently of Him? Saul's fate provides the answer. He, the vain, troubled and misguided king, not the virtuous, insipid David, is the real hero of the opera, and it is his descent from grace that preoccupies us. His arrogance, cunning and tragic destiny call to mind another tortured hero, Boris Godunov, though his refusal to repent in the face of destruction confers on him an uneasy comradeship with the unregenerate Don Giovanni.

The task of constructing the libretto was given to the dramatist Einar Christiansen, who stuck closely to the story as set out in I Samuel, skilfully reducing it to a coherent narrative. He divided his text into four acts which contain clearly defined scenes, though they are not described as such. Acts I and II take place in Saul's house in Gilgal, the scene of Saul's blasphemous sacrifice, of his meeting with David, his love for and later jealousy of his favorite, of Mikal's love for David and David's flight from Saul's rages. Act III, in Saul's camp in the Wilderness of Ziph, marks the temporary reconciliation of Saul with David. Act IV is divided between the house of the Witch of Endor, where Saul receives from the ghost of Samuel the final prophecy of his death, and Mount Gilboa, where Saul makes his last defiant stand, and where David receives the plaudits of the people.

Although by temperament a symphonist, Nielsen avoided the trap from which Beethoven struggled to extricate himself in *Fidelio* of turning *Saul and David* into an operatic symphony. He repudiated Verdi's singer-dominated lyricism and Wagner's reliance on leitmotifs to identify his characters and their motives. Instead he adopted a continuously evolving mixture of accompanied recitative and arioso to advance the all-important action. Only rarely, as in Mikal's expression of her love for David, and David's musing over the sleeping Saul in act III does he come close to full-blown aria.

By the time he finished the score in 1902, Nielsen had written his Second Symphony, "The Four Temperaments." In this he expresses varying and often contradictory aspects of character as bands of color refracted through the prism of a basic temperament. Robbed of dramatic surprise (we are told almost at the outset and on two further occasions what the outcome is to be) Nielsen relied on this new-found ability, further refined by action and text, to build up rounded and credible portraits of each of the main participants—Saul as friend and foe, spiritually anguished or defiant; Samuel as sage and disillusioned friend, a man of stature and dignity even in death; David as humble musician, noble hero, and tender lover. Jonathan, fated warrior, and Mikal, promised bride, are subsidiary characters and, inevitably perhaps, largely one-dimensional.

The opera begins without an overture. Only rarely does Nielsen resort to the orchestra to create atmosphere or advance the action, but when he does, in the interlude in which David slays Goliath (off stage) and in the Israelites' defeat by the Philistines (between the two parts of act IV) he does so most effectively. The use of a hidden chorus to comment on this battle was a miscalculation, but considering Nielsen's lack of operatic experience, mistakes are rare. The writing for the voices is always sensitive and that for the choruses remarkably assured.

It remains to ask though whether Nielsen might have turned a good opera into a great one if he had deferred work on *Saul and David* for perhaps a decade. As it is it has become the most firmly established dramatic opera in the Danish repertory, and wider exposure could well ensure it greater universal esteem than it currently enjoys.

—Kenneth Dommett

SAVITRI.

Composer: Gustav Holst.

Librettist: Gustav Holst (after an episode in the Mahabharata).

First Performance: London, Wellington Hall, 5 December 1916.

Roles: Satyavan (tenor); Savitri (soprano); Death (bass); chorus (SSAA).

*   *   *

Savitri is one of the most successful of Holst's works taken from the Sanskrit scriptures. Composed to his own libretto, it was written in 1908 and first performed at the London School of Opera on 5 December 1916; its first professional performance was at the Lyric Theatre, Hammersmith, on 23 June 1921, with Dorothy Silk in the title role. Other notable interpreters of the part have been Arda Mandikian and Dame Janet Baker.

The opera is on a small and intimate scale, with only three characters, a wordless offstage female chorus and an

orchestra of twelve players: two flutes, cor anglais, double string quartet and double bass. It takes just over half an hour to perform. A prefatory note by the composer says that it is expressly designed for staging either out of doors or in a small building.

Savitri contains little action. Savitri, wife of the woodman Satyavan, is waiting for her husband to come home from his day's work. Instead, she hears the distant voice of Death summoning her husband. Satyavan enters: he has seen a stranger moving amid the trees. He falls to the ground: the stranger is Death. When Death enters, Savitri welcomes him as the "Just One," and he is so moved that he promises her anything but her husband's life. She asks for her own life "in its fulness"; and when Death agrees, she points out that without Satyavan, her life is not full. Defeated, Death walks off; Satyavan wakes and finds himself in his wife's arms.

Holst's subdued and austere vocal writing, a fluent arioso-type line that suits the subtle ebb and flow of the exchange of argument between Savitri and Death, underlines the dream-like other-worldliness of the action. Though he makes no attempt to reproduce an oriental style, Holst's spare and skillfully balanced vocal and orchestral texture (the whole of the opening dialogue between Savitri and Death is unaccompanied), gives the work a half-light, "un-Western" intensity that makes it very effective theater. The work can justly be claimed as the first and one of the finest of modern chamber operas, a genre for which British composers seem to have a particular flair.

—James Day

SAWALLISCH, Wolfgang.

Conductor. Born 26 August 1923, in Munich. Studied with Ruoff, Haas, and Sachse in Munich; in the German army during World War II, 1942; studied music at the Hochschule für Musik in Munich; vocal coach, 1947, then conductor, 1950, for the Augsburg Opera; Generalmusikdirektor of the opera house at Aachen, 1953-57; Generalmusikdirektor at the opera house in Wiesbaden, 1957-59; Generalmusikdirektor of the opera house at Cologne, 1959-63; conducted at the Bayreuth Festival, 1957-61; principal conductor of the Vienna Symphony Orchestra, 1960-70; Generalmusikdirektor of the Hamburg State Philharmonic, 1961-73; principal conductor of the Orchestre de la Suisse Romande, Geneva, 1970-80; Generalmusikdirektor of the Bavarian State Opera, Munich, beginning 1971; Staatsoperndirektor, Munich, 1982; named music director of the Philadelphia Orchestra, effective 1993.

Publications

By SAWALLISCH: books–

Im Interesse an Deutlichkeit: Mein Leben mit der Musik. Hamburg, 1988.

About SAWALLISCH: books–

Krellmann, H., ed. *Stationen eines Dirigenten: Wolfgang Sawallisch.* Munich, 1983.

articles–

Loney, G. "Wolfgang Sawallisch." *Musical America* May (1989).

*   *   *

Conductor Wolfgang Sawallisch represents the central Austro-German operatic tradition. A specialist in the operas of Mozart, Wagner, and Strauss who has devoted the greater part of his career to these composers, he has also championed such modern operatic scores as Hindemith's *Mathis der Maler* and has had a successful career as an accompanist in Lieder recitals.

Although during the early years of his conducting career Sawallisch led performances of operas by Spontini, Bellini, Donizetti, and Verdi, he decided early on that he wanted to devote himself to the German repertoire, feeling that there are others more appropriate to lead works of the French, Italian, and Eastern European schools. He is known as a conservative conductor interested in the composers of the classical and romantic periods rather than those of the Second Viennese School and their followers. He chooses to specialize in a relatively limited range of works in order to perfect his approach over long periods. Thus, the complete Wagner canon was performed under Sawallisch's baton in Munich in 1983, including the rarely performed *Die Feen* and *Das Liebesverbot,* and in the summer of 1988 he led performances of every Richard Strauss opera—*Guntram* to *Capriccio*—as part of the Munich festival, fulfilling a lifelong ambition.

Sawallisch prefers small European theaters with relatively permanent ensembles to major houses with casts of international stars, and for this reason he has refused offers to become music director of the larger theaters. He also has limited his guest appearances to the Teatro alla Scala in Milan in order to remain close to his home theater in Munich, having turned down offers from the Metropolitan Opera in New York and the Berlin Opera.

Sawallisch has expressed a reluctance to be placed in the limelight, as he feels that performers should avoid placing themselves above the music. His performances are straightforward and unidiosyncratic, closely following the composer's markings; he rarely imposes his own personality on the music. His interpretations derive from his attention to the structure of the works and his long-standing familiarity with every opera he leads, a benefit of his specialization in a relatively limited repertoire. His close attention to the score has led some critics to accuse Sawallisch of choosing a dry-eyed, intellectual approach at the expense of emotion and sensuality, preferring the intimate to the grand.

In addition to recordings of Orff's *Die Kluge* (1956) and *Der Mond* (1958), Mozart's *Die Zauberflöte* (1972), Bartók's *Duke Bluebeard's Castle* (1979), Weber's *Abu Hassan,* and *Die Feen* (1983), Sawallisch has led a distinguished series of recordings of the operas of Richard Strauss, beginning with the pioneering set of *Capriccio* in 1957. More recent recordings of Strauss operas include *Arabella* (1981), *Die Frau ohne Schatten* (1987, the first recording of the complete score), and *Elektra* (1990).

—Michael Sims

SAYÃO, Bidú (Balduina de Oliveira Sayão).

Soprano. Born 11 May 1902, in Niteroi, near Rio de Janeiro. Married: 1) impresario Walter Mocchi, 1927 (divorced); 2) baritone Giuseppe Danise, 1947 (died 1963). Studied in Rio de Janeiro and in Bucharest with Elena Theodorini, and later with Jean de Reszke, Lucien Muratore, Reynaldo Hahn, and Luigi Ricci; operatic debut as Rosina in *Il barbiere di Siviglia,* Rome, 1926; Opéra-Comique debut, Paris, 1926; Teatro alla Scala debut as Rosina, 1930; created the role of Rosalina in Giordano's *Il rè,* Rome, 1930; Metropolitan Opera debut as Manon, 1937; seventeen roles at the Metropolitan opera, including Mimi, Gilda, Violetta, Zerlina, Mélisande, Susanna; Chicago Opera, 1941-45; San Francisco, 1946-52; retired 1957.

Publications

About SAYÃO: books–

Rasponi, Lanfranco. *The Last Prima Donnas.* New York, 1982.

articles–

Léon, J.A. and A. Ribeiro Guimaries. "Bidú Sayão." *Record Collector* 13 (1960): 125.
Celletti, Rodolfo. "Sayão, Bidú." In *Le grandi voci,* Rome, 1964.

*   *   *

As a child, Bidú Sayão had set her mind on a career as an actress, but because of family objections and her early love of music, she settled on a career as a recitalist. Fortunately, the great Rumanian opera singer Elena Theodorini had retired and opened a singing school in Rio, and she was persuaded to accept Bidú as a pupil at the age of fourteen. Initially the voice was of very limited range, but Theodorini began to build it. By the end of World War I, when the teacher decided to move back to her native Rumania, Sayão had made such spectacular progress that she felt she could not possibly change teachers, so she (accompanied by her mother) followed, and resumed lessons in Bucharest.

Sayão later studied with Jean de Reszke, and after the latter's death in 1925 Sayão's mother agreed that the young soprano should consult the famous Emma Carelli (1877-1928) who, along with teaching singing, was co-manager, with her husband Walter Mocchi (1870-1955), of the Teatro Costanzi in Rome. From 1910, when they took over the operation of the Teatro Costanzi until the theater was nationalized in 1926, Carelli and Mocchi were powerful figures on the Italian operatic scene.

In 1925, Carelli placed Bidú Sayão under the tutelage of Maestro Luigi Ricci to learn repertoire. "The voice is limited," she commented, "but sometimes it is the tiny birds who fly the greatest distances and for the longest times!" Sayão's operatic debut took place as Rosina in *Il barbiere di Siviglia* at the Costanzi on 25 March 1926; this was followed by Gilda in *Rigoletto* and Carolina in *Il matrimonio segreto.* This was the final season at the Costanzi under the Carelli-Mocchi ageis. Walter Mocchi had long been associated with opera management in South America; in 1926 he accepted the post of director of the Teatro Municipal in São Paulo which also included an opera season each year in Rio. He drew many of his artists from the Costanzi, among them Bidú Sayão.

Sayão's debut in her native Rio was as Rosina on 15 July 1926. She was also heard in two Brazilian operas, as Mario Maria in Carlos de Campo's *Un caso singular* and as Margarida in her uncle Alberto Costa's *Soror Madalena.* The Rio season was interwoven with the season at the Teatro Municipal in São Paulo, where Sayão was heard in the same roles.

In 1927 Bidú Sayão became Mrs. Walter Mocchi, a marriage which the singer said later in an interview "lasted . . . until 1934, with the divorce coming later." The singer made Rome her base, making many extended concert tours throughout Europe, with occasional opera appearances. In 1928 and 1929 she was heard at the Teatro Colón in Buenos Aires in *Il barbiere di Siviglia, Rigoletto, Il rè,* and *Lucia di Lammermoor.* On 24 January 1930 she was chosen by Giordano to create Rosalina in his new opera *Il rè* for its first performance in Rome. She then made extensive engagements in Europe and South America.

Bidú Sayão had sung frequently with the veteran baritone Giuseppe Danise (1882-1963), especially in South America. In an interview with Lanfranco Rasponi in 1979, Sayão said that Danise "took me in hand to steer me gradually into some of the lyric roles. He was fantastic as a teacher, and tremendously strict. . . . Watching me like a hawk, he ignored my pleas to take on Desdemona, Fiora, and Butterfly. He allowed me to try Violetta . . . and then Mimi, Mélisande, and Manon. I had sung Marguerite in *Faust* at the Opéra in Paris, but Danise did not approve, for he considered the Church Scene too heavy, so I dropped it. At the end of my career, I appeared in San Francisco as Margherita in *Mefistofele,* and as Nedda [in *Pagliacci*], but by then I was willing to take risks. . . . It was Danise who was totally responsible for my American career [for] in 1936 he persuaded me to accompany him to New York."

In New York Sayão was introduced to Toscanini, who at the time was looking for a soloist for Debussy's *La damoiselle élue;* she was given the part, and made her debut with sensational critical acclaim at Carnegie Hall in April 1936. The Sayão-Danise timing for a New York debut could not have been more perfect: Lucrezia Bori had left the Metropolitan on 29 March, and the question as to who could possibly replace her seemed to be automatically answered. Sayão returned to the local seasons at Rio and São Paulo with a Metropolitan contract for the 1936-37 season in her pocket. If there were any doubts about Sayão's ability to replace Bori, they were quickly dispelled at her Metropolitan debut as Manon on 13 February 1937.

Sayão remained with the Metropolitan Opera for sixteen seasons, during which she sang twelve roles, including Violetta, Mimi, Juliet, Susanna (in *Le nozze di Figaro*), Norina, Zerlina, Adina, Mélisande and Serpina (in *La serva padrona*). Of her 226 performances in New York and on tour with the company, a total of thirty-six were broadcast, and recordings thus exist of all of her Metropolitan roles except Serpina. During 1939, 1940, and 1946, she also took part in seasons in Rio, São Paulo and Buenos Aires, and she was a great favorite on the Pacific Coast where she sang with the San Francisco Opera Company, both at its home base and on tour, during 1939-42, 1946-48, and 1950-52.

With the advent of Rudolph Bing at the Metropolitan Opera (1950), Sayão's performances were drastically reduced, and she was only offered a few performances of *La bohème.* When a new production of *Pelléas et Mélisande* was mounted in November 1953, the role with which Sayão had been so closely identified was given to Nadine Conner. It did not take Danise (whom she had married in 1947) to tell her that it was time to leave the Metropolitan and concentrate on concerts, for which her services were in great demand throughout

the United States and Canada. Her final performance at the Metropolitan Opera was as Mimi on 26 February; her last with the company was on tour in Boston, as Manon, on 23 April 1952.

Sayão's voice was that of a true lyric coloratura. It was even throughout its extensive range, and had a peculiar sweetness. Perhaps most distinctive was the singer's ability to change the color of the tone. This feature of the Sayão voice was especially effective during a song recital and was a technique she had learned from Jean de Reszke. Another feature of her voice was its projection: although small, it could always be heard in solo or ensemble from the back of a large hall, perhaps again because it could be colored in a distinctive way and thus the ear could separate it from other sounds and voices. But Sayão did not live by voice alone. She was a fine actress: as Mélisande she seemed an ethereal thing that could glide rather than walk; as Zerlina she was a country girl who could give as well as take; as Manon her mood changed as the story developed: the audience would be laughing with her at one minute and crying with her the next.

Bidú Sayão's first commercial recordings were made by RCA Victor in Brazil in 1933. Only two selections from *Il Guarany* received world circulation. After Sayão's arrival in New York, she continued to record for Victor, at sessions late in 1938, 1939 and 1940. In 1941 she went with Columbia, with whom she recorded a complete *La bohème* in 1947 (with Tucker). She stayed with Columbia until 1950. Her only other commercial recording was made after her retirement, when she was persuaded by Villa-Lobos to record his last composition, released on the United Artists label in 1959. Of her Metropolitan Opera roles which were broadcast, one, a performance of *Romeo et Juliette* on 1 February 1947 with Jussi Bjoerling, has been officially released by the Metropolitan; many others have found their way into circulation.

—William R. Moran

SCARLATTI, Alessandro.

Composer. Born 2 May 1660, in Palermo. Died 22 October 1725, in Naples. Married: Antonia Anzalone, 1678 (10 children, including the musicians Pietro Filippo and the famous composer Domenico). Studied with Carissimi in Rome, 1672; referred to as maestro di cappella to Queen Christina of Sweden on a manuscript copy of his opera *Il Pompeo,* 25 January 1683; taught at the Conservatorio di Santa Maria di Loreto in Naples, 1689; maestro to the Viceroy at Naples, 1694; assistant maestro to Foggia at Santa Maria Maggiore in Rome; succeeded Foggia as first maestro at Santa Maria Maggiore, 1707; resigned in 1709 and returned to Naples; maestro of the Royal Chapel, Naples. Among Scarlatti's private pupils was J.A. Hasse, 1724.

Operas

Edition: *The Operas of Alessandro Scarlatti.* Edited by D.J. Grout. Cambridge, Massachusetts, 1974-.

Gli equivoci nel sembiante, D.F. Contini, Rome, Capranica, 5 February 1679.
L'honestà negli amori, F. Parnasso, Rome, Palazzo Bernini, 6 February 1680.

Tutto il mal non vien per nuocere, G.D. de Totis, Rome, Palazzo Rospigliosi, 1681.

Il Pompeo, N. Minato, Rome, Colonna, 25 January 1683.

La guerriera costante, F. Orsini, Rome, palace of Duchess of Bracciano, carnival 1683.

L'Aldimiro o vero Favor per favore, G.D. de Totis, Naples, Palazzo Reale, 6 November 1683.

La Psiche o vero Amore innamorato, G.D. de Totis, Naples, Palazzo Reale, 21 December 1683.

Olimpia vendicata, A. Aureli, Naples, Palazzo Reale, 23 December 1685.

La Rosmene o vero L'infedeltà fedele, G.D. de Totis, Rome, Palazzo Doria Pamphili, carnival 1686.

Clearco in Negroponte, A. Arcoleo, Naples, Palazzo Reale, 21 December 1686.

La santa Dinna (with Alessandro Melani and B. Pasquini), B. Pamphili, Rome, Palazzo Doria Pamphili, carnival 1687 [lost].

Il Flavio, M. Noris, Naples, Palazzo Reale, 14? November 1688.

L'anacreonte tiranno, G.F. Bussani, Naples, San Bartolomeo, 9 February 1689.

L'Amazzone corsara [guerriera] o vero L'Alvilda, G.C. Corradi, Naples, Palazzo Reale, 6 November 1689.

La Statira, P. Ottoboni, Rome, Tordinona, 5 January 1690.

Gli equivoci in amore o vero La Rosaura, G.B. Lucini, Rome, Palazzo della Cancelleria, December 1690.

L'humanità nelle fiere o vero Il Lucallo, Naples, San Bartolomeo, 25 February 1691 [lost].

La Teodora augusta, A. Morselli, Naples, Palazzo Reale, 6 November 1692.

Gerone tiranno di Siracusa, A. Aureli, Naples, Palazzo Reale, 22 December 1692.

L'amante doppio o vero Il Ceccobimbi, Naples, Palazzo Reale, April 1693 [lost].

Il Pirro e Demetrio, A. Morselli, Naples, San Bartolomeo, 28 January 1694.

Il Bassiano o vero Il maggior impossibile, M. Noris, Naples, San Bartolomeo, spring 1694 [lost].

La santa Genuinda, o vero L'innocenza difesa dall'inganno (with G.L. Lulier and C.F. Cesarini), B. Pamphili, Rome, Palazzo Doria Pamphili, 1694.

Le nozze con l'inimico o vero L'Analinda, Naples, San Bartolomeo, 1695.

Nerone fatto Cesare, M. Noris, Naples, Palazzo Reale, 6 November 1695.

Massimo Puppieno, A. Aureli, Naples, San Bartolomeo, 26 December 1695.

Penelope la casta, M. Noris, Naples, San Bartolomeo, 23? February 1696.

La Didone delirante, F.M. Paglia (after A. Franceschi), Naples, San Bartolomeo, 28 May 1696.

Comodo Antonino, F.M. Paglia (after F. Busani), Naples, San Bartolomeo, 18 November 1696.

L'Emireno o vero Il consiglio, F.M. Paglia, Naples, San Bartolomeo, 2 February 1697.

La caduta de' Decemviri, S. Stampiglia, Naples, San Bartolomeo, 15 December 1697.

La donna ancora è fedele, D.F. Contini (revised), Naples, San Bartolomeo, 1698.

Il prigioniero fortunato, F.M. Paglia, Naples, San Bartolomeo, 14 December 1698.

Gl' inganni felici, A. Zeno, Naples, Palazzo Reale, 6 November 1699.

L'Eraclea, S. Stampiglia, Naples, San Bartolomeo, 30 January 1700.

Odoardo (with the intermezzo *Adolfo e Lesbiana*), A. Zeno, Naples, San Bartolomeo, 5 May 1700.

Dafni, F.M. Paglia (after E. Manfredi), Naples, Casino del Vicerè a Posillipo, 5 August 1700.

Laodice e Berenice, after M. Noris, Naples, San Bartolomeo, April, 1701.

Il pastor di Corinto, F.M. Paglia, Naples, Casino del Vicerè a Posillipo, 5 August 1701.

Tito Sempronio Gracco (with the intermezzo *Bireno e Dorilla*), S. Stampiglia, Naples, San Benedetto, carnival? 1702.

Tiberio imperatore d'Oriente, G.D. Pallavicino, Naples, Palazzo Reale, 8 May 1702.

Il Flavio Cuniberto, M. Noris, Pratolino, Villa Medicea, September 1702?

Arminio, A. Salvi, Pratolino, Villa Medicea, September 1703.

Turno Aricino, S. Stampiglia Pratolino, Villa Medicea, September 1704 [lost].

Lucio Manlio l' imperioso, S. Stampiglia, Pratolino, Villa Medicea, September 1705 [lost].

Il gran Tamerlano, A. Salvi (after Pradon), Pratolino, Villa Medicea, September 1706 [lost].

Il Mitridate Eupatore, G. Frigimelica Roberti, Venice, San Giovanni Grisostomo, carnival, 1707.

Il trionfo della libertà, G. Frigimelica Roberti, Venice, San Giovanni Grisostomo, carnival 1707.

Il Teodosio, V. Grimani?, Naples, San Bartolomeo, 27 January 1709 [lost].

L'amor volubile e tiranno, G.D. Pioli and G. Papis, Naples, San Bartolomeo, 25 May 1709.

La principessa fedele, D.A. Parrino? (after A. Piovene), Naples, San Bartolomeo, 8 February 1710.

La fede riconosciuta, B. Marcello?, Naples, San Bartolomeo, 14 October 1710.

Giunio Bruto o vero La caduta dei Tarquini (with C.F. Cesarini and A. Caldara), G. Sinibaldi, intended for Vienna [unperformed].

Il Ciro, P. Ottoboni, Rome, Palazzo della Cancelleria, carnival 1712.

Il Tigrane o vero L'egual impegno d'amore di fede, D. Lalli, Naples, San Bartolomeo, 16 February 1713.

Scipione nelle Spagne (with the intermezzo *Pericca e Varrone*), A. Zeno and N. Serino (intermezzo by Salvi?), Naples, San Bartolomeo, 21 January 1714.

L'amor generoso (with the intermezzo *Despina e Niso*), G. Papis and S. Stampiglia, Naples, Palazzo Reale, 1 October 1714.

Carlo re d'Allemagna (with the intermezzo *Palandrana e Zamberlucco*), F. Salvani, Naples, San Bartolomeo, 30 January 1716.

La virtù trionfante dell' odio e dell' amore, F. Silvani, Naples, San Bartolomeo, 3 May 1716 [lost].

Telemaco, C.S. Capece, Rome, Capranica, carnival 1718.

Il trionfo dell'onore, F.A. Tullio, Naples, Teatro dei Fiorentini, 26 November 1718.

Il Cambise, D. Lalli, Naples, San Bartolomeo, 4 February 1719.

Marco Attilio Regolo (with the intermezzo *Leonzio e Eurilla*), Rome, Capranica, carnival 1719.

La Griselda, after A. Zeno, 1720; revised, Rome, Capranica, January 1721.

Other works: sacred and secular vocal music (including madrigals), instrumental works, keyboard pieces.

Publications

About SCARLATTI: books–

Crescimbeni. *L'arcadia*. Rome, 1711.

Dent, Edward J. "The Operas of Alessandro Scarlatti." *Sammelbände der Internationalen Musik-Gesellschaft* 4 (1902-03): 143.

———. "Alessandro Scarlatti." *Proceedings of the Royal Musical Association* 30 (1903-04): 77.

———. *Alessandro Scarlatti: his Life and Works*. London, 1905; 2nd ed., with additions by F. Walker, 1960.

Borren, C. van der. *Alessandro Scarlatti et l'esthétique de l'opéra napolitain*. Brussels and Paris, 1921.

Prota-Giurleo, U. *Alessandro Scarlatti 'il Palermitano'*. Naples, 1926.

Lorenz, A. *Alessandro Scarlattis Jugendoper*. Augsburg, 1927.

Fabbri, Mario. *Alessandro Scarlatti e il Principe Fernando de' Medici*. Florence, 1961.

Pagano, Roberto, Lino Bianchi and Giancarlo Rostirolla. *Alessandro Scarlatti*. Turin, 1972.

Colloquium Alessandro Scarlatti. Wurzburg, 1975.

Strohm, Reinhard. *Italienische Opernarien des frühen Settecento (1720-1730)*. Cologne, 1976.

Grout, Donald J. *Alessandro Scarlatti: an Introduction to his Operas*. Berkeley, 1979.

Strohm, Reinhard. *Die italienische Oper im 18. Jahrhundert*. Wilhelmshaven, 1979.

Holmes, William C. *"La Statira" by Pietro Ottoboni and Alessandro Scarlatti: The Textual Sources with a Documentary Postscript*. New York, 1983.

D'Accone, Frank A. *The History of a Baroque Opera: Alessandro Scarlatti's "Gli equivoci nel sembiante"*. New York, 1985.

Pagano, Roberto. *Scarlatti: Alessandro e Domenico*. Milan, 1985.

articles–

Junker, H. "Zwei *Griselda* Opern." In *Festschrift zum 50. Adolf Sandberger*, 51. Munich, 1918.

Lorenz, A. "Alessandro Scarlattis Opern und Wien." *Zeitschrift für Musikwissenschaft* 9 (1926-27): 86.

Cametti, A. "Carlo Sigismondo Capeci (1652-1728), Alessandro e Domenico Scarlatti e la Regina di Polonia a Roma." *Musica d'oggi* 13 (1931): 55.

Paoli, D. de'. "*Diana ed Endimione* di Alessandro Scarlatti." *La rassegna musicale* 13 (1940): 139.

Sartori, C. "Il *Dafni* di Alessandro Scarlatti." *Rivista musicale italiana* 45 (1941): 176.

———. "*Dori e Arione* due opere ignorate di Alesandro Scarlatti." *Note d'archivio per la storia musicale* 18 (1941): 35.

Dent, Edward J. "A Pastoral Opera by Alessandro Scarlatti." *Music Review* 12 (1951): 7.

Pauly, R.G. "Alessandro's *Tigrane*." *Music and Letters* 35 (1954).

Sartori, C. "Una Arianna misconosciuta: La Laodice di A. Scarlatti." *La Scala* no. 79 (1956): 4.

Grout, Donald J. "*La Griselda* di Zeno e il libretto dell' opera di Alessandro Scarlatti." *Nuova rivista musicale italiana* 2 (1968): 207.

Trowell, B. "Scarlatti and Griselda." *Musical Times* 109 (1968): 527.

Westrup, Jack A. "Alessandro Scarlatti's *Il Mitridate Eupatore* (1707)." In *New Looks at Italian Opera: Essays in Honor of Donald J. Grout*, 133. Ithaca, New York, 1968.

Boyd, Malcolm. "Scarlatti's *La Statira*." *Musical Times* 111 (1970): 495.

Rose, G. "Two Operas by Scarlatti Recovered." *Musical Quarterly* 58 (1972): 420.

Grout, Donald J. "The Original Version of Alessandro Scarlatti's *Griselda*." In *Essays on Opera and English Music in Honour of Sir Jack Westrup*, 103. Oxford, 1975.

Strohm, Reinhard. "Hasse, Scarlatti, Rolle." *Analecta Musicologica* 15 (1975): 221.

Jones, G. "Alessandro Scarlatti's *Il Ciro*." *Hamburger Jahrbuch für Musikwissenschaft* 3 (1978): 225.

Collins, Michael. "An Introduction to Alessandro Scarlatti's *Tigrane*." In *Essays on Music for Charles Warren Fox*, edited Jerald C. Grave, 82. Rochester, 1979.

Grout, Donald J. "*Opera seria* at the Crossroads: Scarlatti's *Eraclea*." In *Studia Musicologica, Aesthetica, Theoretica, Historia*, edited by Elzbieta Dziebowska, 223. Cracow, 1979.

Hucke, Helmut. "Alessandro Scarlatti und die Musikkomödie." In *Studia Musicologica, Aesthetica, Theoretica, Historia*, edited by Elzbieta Dziebowska, 177. Cracow, 1979.

Wolff, H.C. "Die Buffoszenen in den Opern Alessandro Scarlattis." In *Colloquium Alessandro Scarlatti Würzburg 1975*, edited by Wolfgang Osthoff and Jutta Ruiledronke, 191. Tutzing, 1979.

Lionnet, J. "A Newly Found Opera by Alessandro Scarlatti." *Musical Times* 128 (1987): 80.

unpublished–

Morey, C.R. "The Late Operas of Alessandro Scarlatti." Ph.D. dissertation, Indiana University, 1965.

The aristocratic tradition of Italian opera that was established about 1600 in Florence and Mantua reached its culmination after 1700 in the works composed for Rome and Naples by Alessandro Scarlatti. His operas continue to touch the heart today even while expressing the stylized words and doctrinal affections of his Baroque poets and their ever more schematicized libretti. To appreciate the masterpieces of Scarlatti's maturity, one must accept their unlikely circumstances of plot (as in modern adventure films) as situations contrived to test the mettle of the principal characters. Unlike films, however, the *dramma per musica* centered not on exciting actions but largely on the characters' emotional states, creating an internal drama in the heart and mind such as must often have engaged those occupying the higher rungs of the era's tightly structured social order.

Audiences readily accepted the use of the greatest singers of the time—the castrati—to express their own idealized responses to the situations presented in the *dramma per musica*. The largest obstacle to the acceptance of modern performances of these works is not the improbable plots (often based on events from Roman history very freely embellished) or the unbelievable disguises, but the well-intended modern attempts at realism, whether in the replacement of the male sopranos with natural male voices (generally employed at the time only in minor or comic roles) or in realistic stage action not in keeping with a character's station.

Scarlatti established his reputation in Rome, where he forged relationships with aristocratic patrons that endured throughout his subsequent court appointments in Naples and brought him commissions for many of his approximately 800 cantatas, 40 oratorios, and 30 serenatas. His first opera, *Gli*

Alessandro Scarlatti

equivoci nel sembiante (Rome, 1679), proved to be one of the most successful works of his career. An unpretentious pastoral drama, it perfectly suited the varied small-scale forms of Scarlatti's early period and his inclination to draw his music from the rhythms and inflections of the words. Unlike the later libretti, scenes unfold freely and the verse forms allow the composer to write expanded binary and ground-bass arias as well as small-scale ternary forms. Arias can even change meter and tempo for contrasting sections (act II, scene 6: "V intendo, si"), and the music can rise to considerable eloquence at moments of climax, as in the duet "Ecco l'alma ti dono" (act III, scene 8). It is also true, however, that in Scarlatti's early operas the singers seem to bear the burden of varying an undue amount of literal repetition, as in the habitually repeated phrases and sections of an aria written in ternary form that is also given an identical second strophe. Of the early operas, Donald Grout (*Alessandro Scarlatti*, Berkeley, 1979) named *Rosmene* (Rome, 1686) "certainly one of the best, if not the very best."

Most of Scarlatti's eighty-five or so operas (of which about thirty are extant) were written for Naples, where the composer served the court three times (1684-1702, 1708-18, and 1722-25). It was in Naples that the composer's operatic language underwent transformation, the bass line gradually changing from a contrapuntal role to a mainly harmonic one and the melody being differentiated from the chamber style of the cantata by its greater breadth and virtuosity. Instead of expressing faithfully every nuance of the words, Scarlatti comes to stress the primary affection of the aria, allowing the melody to unfold freely and breaking up the poetic lines and fitting words to the motives when necessary.

In *Tigrane* (Naples, 1713), for example, far from being daunted by a libretto that provides almost exclusively *da capo* arias and scenes that seldom consist of more than a recitative and an aria, the composer seizes the opportunity of working within a fixed form to expand his range of aria types and styles and to extend his musical language with wider-ranging modulations, more varied rhythms, and a new attitude towards tone-painting that raises it to an integral facet of his art. In addition, he makes greater use of accompanied recitatives and independent instrumental pieces, including the three-movement Italian overture (which he had established in 1697); he even differentiates the thematic material of the instruments from that of the voice, as in the act I *aria concertata* entitled "All acquisto di gloria" (the first known use of horns in opera). Other significant operas of Scarlatti's mature years include *Mitridate Eupatore* (Venice, 1707), the subject of a separate essay, and *La principessa fedele* (Venice, 1710).

The composer's last years found his music falling out of fashion in the public theaters of Naples but still in demand by his Roman patrons and, more significantly, growing ever more expressive within his established parameters. Grout found *Telemaco* (Naples 1718) "one of Scarlatti's most interesting operas." *Griselda,* composed in 1720 on a story from Boccaccio's *Decameron* and revised in 1721 for performance in Rome, also offers great depth of musical richness, including more independent instrumental writing (as in the act III simile aria "Come va l'ape"). Perhaps its most striking moment occurs when the ever faithful Griselda reacts to a threat on her son's life with a dramatic aria (act II, scene 4: "Figlio! Tiranno!") whose agitated style *(stile concitato)* and declamatory power place Scarlatti firmly within the distinguished tradition established by Monteverdi.

The operas of Alessandro Scarlatti represent a variety of musical styles and dramatic types, ranging from the *dramma per musica* (which required comic scenes in Naples) to the *commedia (Tutto il mal)* and including as well the pastoral *(Gli equivoci nel sembiante)* and even the *tragedia in musica (Mitridate Eupatore)*. They deserve revival, if only in concert performances (which would eliminate many of the obstacles to successful performance), because they reveal as does no other medium the spirit and character of their age.

—David Poultney

SCHALK, Franz.

Conductor. Born 27 May 1863, in Vienna. Died 2 September 1931, in Edlach. Studied with Bruckner at the Vienna Conservatory; conducted in Liberec, 1886, Reichenbach, 1888-89, Graz, 1889-95, Prague, 1895-98, and the Berlin Royal Opera, 1899-1900; conducted at the Vienna Hofoper, 1900; co-director of the Vienna Staatsoper (previously Hofoper) with Richard Strauss, 1919-24, and then sole director, 1924-29; regular conductor with the Vienna Philharmonic, 1901-31; conductor of the Gesellschaft der Musikfreunde, 1904-21; conducted *Die Walküre* at the Metropolitan Opera, New York, 1898; conducted Wagner's *Ring* at Covent Garden, London, 1898, 1907, 1911; conducted at the Salzburg Festival; taught conducting in Vienna.

Publications

By SCHALK: books–

Schalk, L. ed. *Franz Schalk: Briefe und Betrachtungen.* Vienna, 1935.

*   *   *

Franz Schalk's initial experience was gained in Graz, where it was mainly limited to conducting operetta. His first move to Prague, where his eminent predecessors had included Anton Seidl, Karl Muck and Gustav Mahler, ended in 1898 after three years, and coincided with invitations to replace Weingartner in Berlin and to guest-conduct a single performance of Wagner's *Lohengrin* in London. The success he encountered in London led in turn to an invitation to conduct at the Metropolitan Opera in New York, due to the untimely death of Seidl. Schalk triumphed in New York with an excellent *Tristan* sung by Lehmann, Böhmer, van Rooy and the De Reszke brothers. Schalk was offered inducements to stay in America and had a secure appointment in Berlin (where he was not happy), but when Mahler wrote from Vienna with an offer of Hans Richter's post of first Kapellmeister he gratefully accepted. Schalk opened his account in the great opera house with *Lohengrin* on 8 February 1900, and for the next thirty years played an increasingly vital and important role in the running of the organization. Taking *Die Meistersinger* as an example, Richter conducted sixty-three performances between 1875-99, Mahler ten between 1898-1900, Weingartner eleven between 1909-27, but Schalk outstripped

Franz Schalk, silhouette by Hans Schliessmann, 1900

them all with 149 performances of the opera between 1901-28. Mahler saw in Schalk a musician who could perpetuate the Bayreuth tradition hitherto practised by Richter.

At the Vienna Opera, Schalk was to be overshadowed by musicians such as Mahler and Weingartner. After the First World War, nothing changed when both he and Richard Strauss held the joint directorship, though this dual operation became untenable and Strauss left in 1924. Only for the final four years of his work in Vienna was Schalk solely in control, but once given free rein, he both instigated an era of inventive and original program planning at home and increased the reputation of the Vienna Opera abroad with highly successful tours. Works introduced under Schalk's personal direction included Pfitzner's *Palestrina,* Strauss's *Salome, Die Frau ohne Schatten, Intermezzo* and *Die ägyptische Helena* (in spite of personal differences with Strauss the man there were none with Strauss the composer), Schreker's *Die Gezeichneten* and *Der Schatzgräber,* Musorgsky's *Boris Godunov,* Giordano's *Andrea Chénier,* Puccini's *Trittico* and *Turandot.* Contemporary Austrian composers such as Korngold (*Die tote Stadt* and *Heliane*) and Schmidt (*Fredigundis*) featured among lesser figures, while new productions of such works as Gluck's *Alceste,* Weber's *Euryanthe,* Smetana's *Dalibor,* Wolf's *Der Corregidor* and Verdi's *La forza del destino* sustained Schalk's growing reputation as musical director.

Schalk extended his activities within the city by directing the opera class at the Hochschule für Musik and by presenting small-scale operas such as Weber's *Abu Hassan,* Mozart's *Bastien und Bastienne,* Pergolesi's *La serva padrona* and Donizetti's *Don Pasquale* at the reopened Redoutensaal. In 1923 he took the Vienna Opera to Ghent (Mozart's *Don Giovanni* and *Marriage of Figaro*) and to Paris in the following year with a smaller group forming a Mozart ensemble. Its success led to a return visit in 1927 with *Fidelio* as part of the Beethoven centenary celebrations, and in 1928 with the full company to perform *Tristan* and *Fidelio,* to Cologne later in the year and to Stockholm in 1929. The Cologne visit included taking the opera house's ballet company, which Schalk had also improved considerably.

Schalk left Vienna in 1929, and his last years were spent as a free-lance conductor working throughout Europe. His last appearances were in Vienna in 1931 with *Götterdämmerung* and *Tristan.*

Franz Schalk was a renowned and respected conductor of keen ear and trusty eye. His interpretations were widely regarded as convincing, his reputation as an orchestral and choral conductor was equally high, and his opera singers could always depend upon him for sympathetic support from the orchestra pit.

—Christopher Fifield

DER SCHAUSPIELDIREKTOR [The Impresario].

Composer: Wolfgang Amadeus Mozart.

Librettist: J. Gottlieb Stephanie, Jr.

First Performance: Vienna, Schönbrunn, Palace, Orangerie, 7 February 1786.

Roles: Madame Herz (soprano); Mlle Silberklang (soprano); Monsieur Vogelsang (tenor); Buff (bass).

Publications

articles–

Raeburn, C. "Die textlichen Quellen des 'Schauspieldirektor'." *Österreichische Musikzeitschrift* 13 (1958): 4.

Kunze, Stefan. "Mozarts Schauspieldirektor." *Mozart-Jahrbuch* (1962-63): 156.

Tyler, Linda. "Aria as Drama: A Sketch from Mozart's *Der Schauspieldirektor.*" *Cambridge Opera Journal* 2 (1990): 251.

*   *   *

Der Schauspieldirektor, a one-act "comedy with music" or "occasional piece," was commissioned for a grandiose social gathering sponsored by Emperor Joseph II in the Orangerie garden of the Schönbrunn Palace. The work, which contains only four vocal numbers in addition to the overture, pokes fun at theatrical companies—at the arrogance, pettiness, and greed that were regularly displayed by actors, singers, and troupe directors in the late eighteenth century. The story revolves around the impresario Frank, who is hiring performers to take with him to an engagement in Salzburg. In the opening scenes, three actresses approach the director: each recites a scene from a well-known play and—after haggling over the contract—is hired. Two singers, Madame Herz, and Mademoiselle Silberklang, then audition with arias and are also offered positions in the company. In a third musical number, a trio, the two sopranos argue over who will be the prima donna of the troupe, while the tenor, Monsieur Vogelsang, attempts to keep the peace. The antagonists declare a truce in the last scene, which concludes with a vaudeville.

The focus of the four vocal numbers in the work is the conflict between the two sopranos. Much of Mozart's musical characterization of these two roles seems to have been based on the careers and reputations of the singers who sang the roles at the premiere: Catarina Cavalieri and Aloysia Weber. Cavalieri enjoyed her greatest Viennese successes in Italian opera, and the very name of her character, Mademoiselle Silberklang, alludes to her operatic specialty—brilliant, "silvery" passagework. Aloysia Weber, by contrast, was more closely linked with German opera in Vienna. Her strong suit—as the name of her character, Madame Herz, suggests—was the lyrical, "heart"-felt sentimental style. Mozart clearly seized on the trademark roles and fortes of these two singers in composing their arias in *Der Schauspieldirektor.* Mademoiselle Silberklang's aria is typically Italian: a two-tempo, duple-meter rondo form set with gavotte rhythmic patterns and dazzling vocal embellishments in the second section. Madame Herz's two-section aria differs from her counterpart's in a number of ways: it is through-composed rather than set in a conventional aria form; it features slower tempos; its conjunct

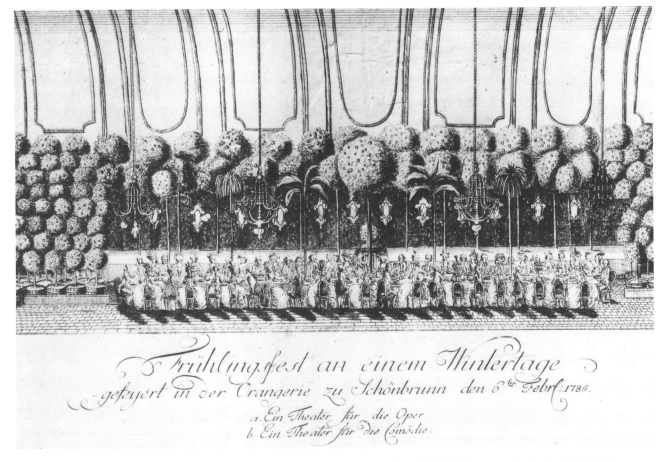

The Orangery at Schönbrunn where Mozart's *Der Schauspieldirektor* was first performed in 1786 (the engraving by Loschenkohl shows a banquet held by Joseph II for the occasion)

melodic movement contrasts with the buoyant, triad-based motion of Mademoiselle Silberklang's vocal line; and the rhythmic character, based on 3/4 meter and the rhythmic gestures of a sarabande, sets the solo apart from the gavotte motion and distinctly accented style of the rival diva's number.

The characterizations established in the two arias recur in the trio and the vaudeville. In the trio, the two ladies argue with each other over the hierarchy of singers in the troupe through a series of imitative duets. When Mademoiselle Silberklang leads the argument, the tempo is "allegro assai," and the meter duple. When Madame Herz takes the lead, the meter changes to 3/4 and the tempo to "andante." Thus the lead singer in each section brings the meter and tempo of her aria to the ensemble. In the final vaudeville, all the characters except Madame Herz sing their solo stanzas in gavotte rhythms in "allegro" tempo with a 2/2 time signature. Madame Herz, however, follows another rhythmic pattern: one featuring many dotted notes and an uneven distribution of syllables—a clear allusion to the rhythmic patterns of her arietta. Mozart, deprived of opportunities for subtle musical characterization otherwise available in a more expansive Singspiel or *opera buffa* format, depicts the two sopranos from the start with starkly distinguishable musical characteristics and maintains these throughout the work.

—Linda Tyler

SCHENK, Otto.

Director. Born 12 June 1930, in Vienna. Married: Ruth Michaelis; three children. Studied acting at the Reinhardt Seminar and production at the University of Vienna, beginning his career at the Josefstadt Theater as an actor; later a producer of plays; debut as operatic director, *Die Zauberflöte,* Salzburg Landestheater, 1957; Oberspielleiter, Vienna Staatsoper, since 1965; a regular director in Munich, also guest director in European and American theaters; has worked in films and television.

Opera Productions (selected)

Die Zauberflöte, Salzburg Landestheater, 1957.
Don Pasquale, Vienna Volksoper, 1961.
Lulu, Vienna Festival, 1963.
Dantons Tod, Vienna Festival, 1963.
Die Zauberflöte, Salzburg Festival, 1963.
Der Rosenkavalier, Frankfurt, 1963.
Otello, Stuttgart, 1963.
L'heure espagnole, Vienna Volksoper, 1964.
Jenůfa, Vienna Stattsoper, 1964.
Macbeth, Munich, 1967.
Tosca, Metropolitan Opera, 1968.
Fidelio, Metropolitan Opera, 1970.
Der Rosenkavalier, Munich, 1972.
Der Freischütz, Vienna Staatsoper, 1972.
Manon, Vienna Staatsoper, 1972.
La traviata, Vienna Staatsoper, 1972.
Le nozze di Figaro, Teatro alla Scala, 1974.
Der Rosenkavalier, Munich, 1975.
Un ballo in maschera, Covent Garden, 1975.
Tannhäuser, Metropolitan Opera, 1977.
Les contes d'Hoffmann, Metropolitan Opera, 1982.

Arabella, Metropolitan Opera, 1983.
Die Walküre, Metropolitan Opera, 1986.
Die Fledermaus, Metropolitan Opera, 1986.
Der Ring des Nibelungen, Metropolitan Opera, 1986-89.
Rigoletto, Metropolitan Opera, 1989.
Parsifal, Metropolitan Opera, 1991.
Elektra, Metropolitan Opera, 1992.
Fidelio, Metropolitan Opera, 1992.

Publications

About SCHENK: articles–

Knessl, L. "Poppeltes 'giocoso.' " *Opernwelt* no. 8 (August 1967): 11-12.
Rizzo, F. "Why the Director?" *Opera News* 33 (15 February 1969): 26-30.
Brunner, G. "Ballade von blutiger Machtgier." *Opernwelt* no. 6 (June 1970): 30-31.
Brunner, G. "Die radikalsten Talente des Theaters muessen von der Ideologie abweichen (Interview with Otto Schenk)." *Opernwelt* 12 (December 1975): 17-18.
"Das *Buehne*-Profil: Otto Schenk." *Die Buehne* no. 215 (August 1976): 13-15.
Loney, G. "Otto Schenk: The Actor/Regisseur." *Opera News* 43 (September 1978): 14-21.
von Lewinski, W.E. "Das Interview." *Opernwelt* 22, no. 5 (1981): 15.
Soria, D.J. "Otto Schenk." *High Fidelity/Musical America* 32 (October 1982): MA10-11.
Loebl, H. "Ich geh' gerne fremd." *Die Buehne* no. 321 (June 1985): 13-15.
Loebl, H. "Titel (Interview)." *Die Buehne* no. 352 (January 1988): 6-8.
"Zeitgenossen." *Die Buehne* no. 381 (June 1990): 92.
Kathrein, K. " 'Ich bin ein auslaufendes Modell' (Interview)." *Die Buehne* (Summer 1991): 14-18.

*   *   *

A former actor, producer Otto Schenk directed his first operatic production at the Salzburg Landestheater, a staging of Mozart's *Die Zauberflöte* in 1957. This was followed by a production of Donizetti's *Don Pasquale* for the Vienna Volksoper in 1961. Stagings of von Einem's *Dantons Tod* and Berg's *Lulu* at the Vienna Festival were his first major successes and led to productions at other important German and Austrian theaters, most notably in Frankfurt and Stuttgart. He has been the chief stage director of the Vienna Staatsoper since 1965 and has directed productions at many of the major opera houses of Europe and America. He first came to the Metropolitan Opera at the recommendation of Birgit Nilsson, where he staged Puccini's *Tosca* (1968). This was followed by Beethoven's *Fidelio* (1970, commemorating the 200th anniversary of Beethoven's birth), Wagner's *Tannhäuser* (1977), Offenbach's *Les contes d'Hoffmann* (1982), Richard Strauss's *Arabella* (1983), Johann Strauss's *Die Fledermaus* (1986), and Wagner's *Der Ring des Nibelungen* (1986-1989). Other productions have included Mozart's *Le nozze di Figaro* at Teatro alla Scala (1974) and Verdi's *Un ballo in maschera* at Covent Garden (1975).

Schenk often bases his productions on the particular characteristics and abilities of the singers originally cast in the roles; he is dissatisfied with the practice of most opera companies of remounting productions in later seasons with different casts.

Schenk works closely with his designers and has maintained a working relationship with a relatively small number of them, most notably Jürgen Rose and Günther Schneider-Siemssen. His productions generally are realistic and representational, based on attention to the composer's stage directions and the use of available technology to realize the composer's intentions. With his close attention to detail, Schenk attempts to create productions in styles appropriate to the context of the work, often turning to the music rather than the libretto for inspiration, as in his Italianate production of Verdi's *Macbeth*. He feels that the music often contains more clues to the characters than does the libretto, even in such an area as movement, and he is especially concerned with the acting ability of his singers in communicating character to the audience. Although his productions are realistic, Schenk makes use of stylized elements where necessary to create a feeling of fantasy or transcendence of reality. He tries to make his characters real, intelligent creatures, relying to an extent on the instincts of his actors. His productions have been devoid of idiosyncrasy and the imposition of directorial "concepts;" he does not feel the need to make a statement with his stagings. He avoids the introduction of modern elements into historical works, preferring to highlight what these works still have to say to audiences today.

Schenk feels that music adds a tremendous force to the plays on which operas are based—a power not present in the words alone—and that because of this, even a badly staged opera can succeed as a play could not. The physical appearance and acting talent of a singer are not as important as his or her ability to convey the character through the voice.

—Michael Sims

SCHIKANEDER, Emanuel [born Johann Joseph Schikeneder].

Librettist/Composer/Actor/Singer/Impresario/Dramatist. Born 1 September 1751, in Straubing. Died 21 September 1812, in Vienna. Married: actress Maria Magdalena (known as Eleonore) Arth, in Augsburg 1777. Studied at the Jesuit Gymnasium at Regensburg; actor with F.J. Moser's troupe, 1773/74; his (Singspiel) *Die Lyranten* performed at the court in Innsbruck, 1775/76; moved to Augsburg with the Innsbruck company, 1776; in Nuremberg with F.J. Moser's troupe, 1777-78; guest appearance at the Munich court theater as Hamlet, 1777; director of Moser's troupe, 1778; leased the Kärntnertor theater, 1783-84; member of the National Theater, 1785-86; his troupe moved to the Freihaus-Theater auf der Wieden, Vienna, 1788-1801; formed a Singspiel Company, 1788; opened the new Theater an der Wien, 1801; left Vienna after the sale of the Theater an der Wien, and took over the Brno Theater, 1806; back in Vienna, 1809.

Librettos

Die Lyranten (Das lustige Elend, oder Die drei Bettelstudenten) (Singspiel), Schikaneder, 1775/76.
Der Müllertomerl, oder Das Bergmädchen (Kaspar der Müller Tomerl), J. Haibel, 1785.
Der Luftballon (operetta), B. Schack, 1786.
Das Urianische Schloss (Singspiel), Schikaneder, 1786.
Die drei Ringe oder [Kaspar] Der lächerliche Mundkoch (Singspiel), B. Schack and F.X. Gerl, 1787.

Lorenz und Suschen (Singspiel), B. Schack, 1787.
Der Krautschneider (Singspiel), B. Schack, 1788.
Jacob und Nannerl, oder Der angenehme Traum, B. Schack, 1789.
Der dumme Gärtner aus dem Gebirge, oder Die zween Anton, B. Schack and F.X. Gerl, 1789.
Die verdeckten Sachen, B. Schack and F.X. Gerl, 1789.
Was macht der Anton im Winter?, B. Schack and F.X. Gerl, 1790.
Der Fall ist noch weit seltner, oder Die geplagten Ehemänner, B. Schack, 1790.
Der Frühling, oder Der Anton ist noch nicht tot, 1790.
Der Stein der Weisen, oder Die Zauberinsel, B. Schack, F.X. Gerl, and others, 1790.
Anton bei Hofe, oder Das Namensfest, B. Schack, 1791.
Die Zauberflöte, W.A. Mozart, 1791.
Der Renegat, oder Anton in der Türkei, 1792.
Der Zauberpfeil, oder Das Kabinett der Wahrheit, J.G. Lickl, 1793.
Die Waldmänner, J.B. Henneberg, 1793.
Die Hirten am Rhein, 1794.
Der Spiegel von Arkadien, F.X. Süssmayr, 1794.
Das Häuschen im Walde, oder Antons Reise nach seinem Geburtsort, B. Schack, 1795.
Der Scherenschleifer, J.B. Henneberg, 1795.
Der Königsohn aus Ithaka, F.A. Hoffmeister, 1795.
Der Höllenberg, oder Prüfung und Lohn, J. Wölfl, 1795.
Der Tyroler Wastel, J. Haibel, 1796.
Östreichs treue Brüder, oder Die Scharfschützen in Tirol (Singspiel), J. Haibel, 1796.
Das medizinische Konsilium, J. Haibel, 1797.
Der Löwenbrunn, I.X.R. von Seyfried, 1797.
Babylons Pyramiden, J. Gallus-Mederitsch and P. Winter, 1797.
Das Labyrinth, oder Der Kampf mit den Elementen, P. Winter, 1798.
Die Ostindier vom Spittelberg (Die Rückkehr aus Ostindien) (Singspiel), I.X.R. von Seyfried, M. Stegmayer, and others, 1799.
Mina und Peru, oder Die Königspflicht (Singspiel), J.B. Henneberg and I.X.R. von Seyfried, 1799.
Der Wundermann am Rheinfall, I.X.R. von Seyfried, 1799.
Amors Schiffchen in der Brigittenaue, I.X.R. von Seyfried and others, 1800.
Proteus und Arabiens Söhne (Singspiel), I.X.R. von Seyfried, M. Stegmayer, 1801.
Alexander, F. Teyber, 1801.
Tsching! Tsching! Tsching!, J. Haibel, 1802.
Die Entlarvten (Singspiel), A. Fischer, 1803.
Pfändung und Personal-Arrest (Singspiel), F. Teyber, 1803.
Swetards Zaubertal, A. Fischer, 1805.
Vestas Feuer, J. Weigl, 1805; fragmentary setting by Beethoven.
Die Kurgäste am Sauerbrunn (Singspiel), A. Diabelli, 1806.
Das Zaubermädchen im Schreywald, not set: passed by Brno censor, 1809.
Das Fest der Götter, not set: passed by Brno censor, 1809.

Publications

About SCHIKANEDER: books—

Komorzynski, Egon. *Emanuel Schikaneder: Ein Beitrag zur Geschichte des deutschen Theaters*. Berlin, 1901; 2nd ed., 1951.
Blümml, E.K. *Aus Mozarts Freundes- und Familienkreis*. Vienna, 1923.

Hadamowsky, F. *Das Theater in der Wiener Leopoldstadt.*
Vienna, 1934.

Deutsch, O.E. *Das Freihaus-Theater auf der Wieden 1787-1801.* Vienna, 1937.

Anderson, Emily. ed. *The Letters of Mozart and his Family.*
London, 1938; 3rd ed., 1985.

Komorzynski, E. *Der Vater der Zauberflöte: Emanuel Schikaneders Leben.* Vienna, 1948.

Bauer, A. *150 Jahre Theater an der Wien.* Vienna, 1952.

Bauer, W.A., O.E. Deutsch and J.H. Eibl, eds. *Mozart: Briefe und Aufzeichnungen.* Kassel, 1962-75.

Brophy, Brigid. *Mozart the Dramatist.* London, 1964; 2nd ed., 1988.

Rosenberg, A. *Die Zauberflöte.* Munich, 1964; 2nd ed., 1972.

Batley, E.M. *A Preface to The Magic Flute.* London, 1969.

Honokla, Kurt. *Papageno: Emanuel Schikaneder: Der grosse Theatermann der Mozart-Zeit.* Salzburg, 1984.

articles–

Schikaneder, J.K. "Emanuel Schikaneder." *Der Gesellschafte*
[Berlin] 18/nos. 71-74 (1834).

Endrös, H. "E. Schikaneder und das Augsburger Theater."
Zeitschrift des Historischen Vereins für Schwaben [Augsburg] 55-56 (1942-43): 203.

Dent, E.J. "Emanuel Schikaneder." *Music and Letters* (1956).

Friedrich, Götz. "Der Theaterman Schikaneder als Dramatiker und als Direktor." *Theater der Zeit* 11 (1956).

Hess, W. "Vestas Feuer." *Beethoven-Jahrbuch* (1957-58): 63.

Senn, W. "Schikaneders Weg zum Theater." *Acta mozartiana*
9 (1962): 39.

Deutsch, O.E. "Schikaneders Testament." *Österreichische Musikzeitschrift* 18 (1963): 421.

Schuh, W. *"Il Flauto Magico."* In *Festschrift F. Blume.* Kassel, 1963.

Batley, Edward Malcolm. "Emanuel Schikaneder, the Librettist of *Die Zauberflöte.*" *Music and Letters* July (1965).

Branscombe, P. *"Die Zauberflöte:* some Textual and Interpretive Problems." *Proceedings of the Royal Musical Association* 92 (1965-66): 45.

Fischer, F.J. "Emanuel Schikaneder und Salzburg." *Jahrbuch der Gesellschaft für Wiener Theaterforschung* 15-16 (1966): 179.

Koch, H.-A. "Das Textbuch der *Zauberflöte.* Zu Entstehung, Form und Gehalt der Dichtung Emanuel Schikaneders."
Jahrbuch der Freien deutschen Hochstifts (1969): 76.

Gurewitsch, Matthew. "In the Mazes of Light and Shadow: a Thematic Comparison of *The Magic Flute* and *Die Frau ohne Schatten.*" *Opera Quarterly* 1/no. 2 (1983): 11.

Henderson, Donald G. "The 'Magic Flute' of Peter Winter."
Music and Letters 64 (1983): 193.

*   *   *

The second half of the eighteenth century was a time of
dramatic change for German theater in general and opera in
particular. As one of the outstanding theater figures of the
period, Emanuel Schikaneder (born Johann Joseph Schikeneder) contributed significantly to this change. Convivial, talented, and endowed with abundant energy, he developed rapidly as composer, singer, actor, theater director, and
dramatist.

His immersion in theater profoundly influenced Schikaneder the librettist. As an actor excelling in serious roles,
he was acclaimed one of the finest Shakespearean interpreters
of his time and place. As a singer, he performed chiefly bass

Emanuel Schikaneder as Papageno in the first production of *Die Zauberflöte,* engraving by Ignaz Albert from original libretto, 1791

buffo roles, the most memorable being that of Papageno in
Die Zauberflöte. As a director committed to effective theater,
Schikaneder enthusiastically indulged his penchant for spectacle and the grand scene. In 1789, his twelve-year reign
as director of Vienna's Theater auf der Wieden (Freihaus
Theater) began. He assembled a company that included excellent singers, backed them with a capable orchestra, and undertook to fulfill his dream, the cultivation of German opera.
Armed with a privilege granted in 1786 by Emperor Joseph
II, Schikaneder ultimately built the Theater an der Wien
(1801), a temple to German opera.

As a dramatist, Schikaneder wrote plays and operas. With
Die Lyranten, oder das lustige Elend (1775/76), he produced
a thoroughly German *Singspiel* libretto, drawing from his
own life experience to create three memorable characters:
Leichtsinn, the youthful lover (sung by Schikaneder to his
own music); Stock, the elderly tippler; and Vogel, the youth
of noble birth who has fled his gilded cage. The comic
vein continued with *Der dumme Gärtner aus dem Gebirge, oder
Die zween Anton* (Vienna, 1789; music by B. Schack and
F.X. Gerl). In Anton, Schikaneder not only perpetuated the
hallowed Viennese low-comedy figures of Hanswurst and
Kasperl; he also generated a model for Papageno. Having
become a Viennese by adoption, Schikaneder, with his enormously successful *Der Tyroler Wastel* (1796, music by J.J.
Haibel), pioneered the so-called *Lokalstück,* a piece specifically Austrian in setting, sentiment and dialect, and with a
strong social-critical vein.

Schikaneder had long imagined another kind of German
opera, a generally lofty, serious opera that included comic

episodes, magic, and machines. With its exotic setting and its trial by fire and water for the hero, *Der Stein der Weisen, oder Die Zauberinsel* (1790, music by Schack and Gerl) established the tone. Of Schikaneder's numerous achievements, it is *Die Zauberflöte* (1791, music by W.A. Mozart) that assures his immortality. Here, against a heady mixture of Egyptian exoticism, Enlightenment ideals, and precepts of Freemasonry, a quest for inner harmony and wisdom unfolds. Books, contemporary operas, Masonic ritual, prior Mozart compositions, and Schikaneder's own earlier works and his Shakespearean experience supplied ideas, scenes, characters, and plot details. From these disparate elements, the collaborators forged a unified whole, various surface inconsistencies notwithstanding. The spoken portions of the libretto are set in prose; portions to be sung are rendered in verse. Admittedly, Schikaneder's writing pales in comparison to that of Goethe, Schiller, or Lessing. Still, simple in diction, intelligible, pictorial, and often inspiring, it stands well above the average German opera libretto of its time. Schikaneder's stage directions are often more poetic than his poetry per se. Those for describing the trials scene, for example, suggest a cinematic fantasy.

Generally discredited now is the long-held theory that Schikaneder reversed the original plot, transforming the apparently evil Sarastro into an enlightened ruler and the ostensibly good Queen of the Night into a destructive force. Similarly, the question of who actually authored the libretto is argued less vehemently. As in the art studios of the Renaissance, others such as Karl Ludwig Giesecke may well have provided details under the guiding hand of Schikaneder, the master responsible for the overall conception. A far more intriguing question concerns Mozart's share in the shaping of the libretto. In the absence of concrete evidence, one can only observe that this libretto, with its action, suspense, spectacle, low comedy, and lofty idealism, surpasses those of Schikaneder's other magic operas.

Schikaneder's later magic operas, all of them variations on the basic theme of trial and purification, failed to attain the level of *Die Zauberflöte*. While they might well match or even surpass it in spectacle, their texts lack symbolic depth, and their music cannot rival Mozart's. To be mentioned in particular are *Der Spiegel von Arkadien* (1794, F.X. Süssmayr); *Babylons Pyramiden* (1797, J. Gallus-Mederitsch and P. Winter), the piano-vocal score of which contains elegant illustrations of the sets; and *Das Labyrinth, oder Der Kampf mit den Elementen* (1798, Winter), part II of *Die Zauberflöte*.

In retrospect, Schikaneder's decision to publish several of his dramas in 1792 proved ill advised. Because he wrote not for readers but for the stage, his verse invited merciless lambasting when divorced from the scenic effects and character portrayals he envisioned. One critic bluntly labeled him a "completely miserable dramatic bungler." Schikaneder engaged in a bitter war of words with Goethe's protegé, the Weimar Court Theater poet Christian August Vulpius, who published "improved" versions of Schikaneder's librettos. In response, Schikaneder rightly complained that Vulpius had "worsened" *(verbösert)* the operas, not "improved" them *(verbessert)*. At issue in this feud were the distinct literary sensibilities that still separated north and south German opera traditions.

Schikaneder candidly confessed his approach to writing: "I write to amuse the public and do not wish to appear learned. I am an actor—a director—and work for the box office" (1794). Consequently, he created the principal roles for himself, the others for players whose strengths and limitations he knew. To offset his literary shortcomings, he devised

ever more magnificent theatrical exhibitions. No less an authority than Goethe admitted that Schikaneder understood extraordinarily the art of producing great theatrical effects.

With his lifelong veneration of German art, Schikaneder the theater person provided Mozart the opportunity to think as a German, to act as a German, to speak German, and, "Heaven help us, to sing in German!!" (Mozart letter of 21 March 1785, to Anton Klein). Ten years before *Die Zauberflöte*, Mozart confided to his father: "The best thing of all is when a good composer, who understands the stage and is talented enough to make sound suggestions, meets an able poet, that true phoenix" (letter of 13 October 1781). For Mozart, Schikaneder the librettist proved to be that phoenix.

—Malcolm S. Cole

SCHIPA, Tito [baptized Raffaele Attilio Amadeo].

Tenor. Born 2 January 1888, in Lecce, Italy. Died 16 December 1965, in New York. Studied with A. Gerunda in Lecce and E. Piccoli in Milan; debut in Verdi's *La traviata* in Vercelli, 1910; Teatro alla Scala debut, 1915; premiered Ruggero in Puccini's *La rondine*, Monte Carlo, 1917; joined the Chicago Opera, 1919-32; Metropolitan Opera debut as Nemorino in *L'elisir d'amore*, 1932; toured extensively until he retired from opera in 1954; farewell concert in New York in 1961; he was the teacher of Cesare Valletti.

Publications

By SCHIPA: books–

Si confessi. Genoa, 1961.

About SCHIPA: articles–

Hutchinson, T. and S. Winstanley, "Tito Schipa." *Record Collector* 14 (1960): 77.
Reid, C. "Tenore di grazia." *Music and Musicians* 14 (1966): 27.
Mason, E. "Tito Schipa," *Music and Musicians* 14 (1966): 35.

* * *

During the last half of the nineteenth century the repertoire of the major opera houses of the world underwent a substantial change. In Italy during the first half of the century the dominant composers were Rossini, Bellini, Donizetti and Verdi, all of whom followed the principles of *bel canto* (beautiful singing—a style characterized by brilliant vocal display and purity of tone). By the 1870s the concepts of music drama, exemplified by Wagner, had become the new critical standard of opera composition. These changes produced the *verismo* school of Italian composers and resulted in the last great period of Italian opera composition. The vocal category most affected by this change was that of the tenor, and the singer who popularized the new style of singing was Enrico Caruso. The emphasis was now on dramatic declamation and sheer power. The tenor who was accepted as the foremost exponent of the older *bel canto* tradition during his career (1911-1950) was Tito Schipa.

The light, lyric tenor, in the older tradition, was termed a *tenore leggiero* (light, agile, nimble). All voice ranges from bass to soprano were required to develop the technique of what is called coloratura—the ability to sing runs and trills, and to ornament and decorate the music with aspects of vocal virtuosity. By Schipa's time coloratura had become almost the exclusive property of the high soprano. In the operas that remained in the repertoire—principally Rossini's *Il barbiere di Siviglia,* Bellini's *La sonnambula,* Doni-^tti's *L'elisir d'amore, Lucia di Lammermoor* and *Don Pasquale,* along with Verdi's *La traviata* and *Rigoletto,* which constituted the basic Italian repertoire that Schipa sang during his career—tenor *cabalettas,* which were written to display vocal virtuosity, were traditionally cut out and not performed. Schipa's operatic repertoire was extended into the French lyric school,

Tito Schipa as Des Grieuz in *Manon*

Delibes' *Lakmé,* Thomas' *Mignon,* Massenet's *Manon* and *Werther.* The Mozart revival of the late 1920s provided him with the role of Don Ottavio in *Don Giovanni.* These thirteen operas constituted the basic repertoire that he sang during his long career. At the outset of Schipa's career, however, he did sing in operas of the newer *verismo* school: Mascagni's *Cavalleria rusticana,* Leoncavallo's *Zaza,* Cilèa's *Adriana Lecouvreur* and Puccini's *Tosca,* and even recorded arias from *Cavalleria* and *Tosca* in his earliest series of recordings (1913/14). By about 1920 he had wisely abandoned that repertoire.

Michael Scott in *The Record of Singing, Volume Two 1914-1925* states that "Schipa was never, not even at the beginning of his career, a *bel canto* singer." By the traditional definition of the term, Scott is probably correct; however, Schipa's reputation as a master of *bel canto* can be defended by noting the change in the critical attitude toward the term. No longer was the *leggiero* aspect of the method considered important. Indeed the light, lyric tenor was by then defined as a *tenore di grazia,* gracefulness replaced agility as the touchstone of the *bel canto* method.

Schipa's own recordings give evidence to the fact that he was primarily a *tenore di grazia.* In 1916 he recorded the original version of "Ecco ridente in cielo" on two sides of a ten inch disc for Pathé. The tempo is slow and the runs are breathy and labored. In 1926 when he again recorded the aria for Victor, he was content with the then current simplified version. In both his commercial (c1927) and later air check (1941) of "Il mio tesoro" from *Don Giovanni,* he again chooses an inordinately slow tempo and comes to grief on the long run.

Schipa's reputation as a *bel canto* artist is justified by the fact that he was, first, a highly trained musician; second, because he had an instinctive, intuitive sense of rhythm—a sense of knowing just how a phrase should go; and finally because he had adopted and mastered the art of equalization of tone quality throughout the range. This aspect of singing became the most important touchstone of the newer definition of *bel canto.* In Schipa it produced a seamless *legato* and a command of breath control, gracefully and tastefully used.

Schipa's voice, while not remarkable in either range or power, was unique and totally distinctive. He was what is termed a "short" tenor. Although early recordings show that he had a high C, his top notes disappeared about 1920. In fact, he was famous for transposing arias down to accommodate his limited range. But within that limited range his command of nuance and purity of tone enabled him to encompass all aspects of the music he sang. He was a prime example of the fact that pure, resonant projection of the voice, rather than simply volume, is the touchstone of audibility—that a relatively small voice, purely produced will carry, even in a large opera house, better than a louder, larger, unfocused voice.

John Freestone testifies to the special qualities of Schipa in a record note: "He possessed, like McCormack, the truly miraculous ability of making a perfect crescendo and dimuendo on one note. He possessed a whole armory of superbly subtle effects and though the voice seemed small in scale and a little lacking in range, he seemed incapable of uttering an ill-balanced note." Furthermore, one is always impressed by Schipa's ease of production; the voice floats in an effortless stream of sound, and the purity of tone enabled him to modulate from the pure soft head voice to a ringing, passionate fortissimo. Rodolfo Celletti notes that Schipa's voice "had also just a trace of that guttural quality which somehow recalls Spanish tenors, and gives a rare and exotic sound to the voice."

Schipa's recorded output in the operatic repertoire began in 1913 and concluded in 1942. Unfortunately he only recorded one complete role, that of Ernesto in *Don Pasquale* (1933). Air checks issued on private recordings exist of excerpts from *Manon, Werther,* and *Don Giovanni* and Cimarosa's *Il matrimonio segreto* from the Teatro alla Scala in 1949. He was equally famous as a singer of Neapolitan and Spanish songs of the more popular vein and recorded extensively in this area as well as classical *arie antiche.* In the popular songs his intuitive sense of rhythm and delicacy of phrasing convinces the listener that even the most simple song sounds like a work of artistic merit.

After his retirement from the opera stage he continued to concertize and also devoted himself to teaching voice. His pupil, Cesare Valletti, was his successor in the basic repertoire of the *tenore di grazia.*

The fact that Schipa preserved his voice over a span of more than fifty years is attributable to his perfect technique, and that, once having found his *Fach,* he never ventured into the heavier tenor repertoire. At the age of 73 in 1962 he gave a farewell concert tour. The recording issued of his New York concert gives proof of the fact that the unique timbre, the nuance and phrasing remained intact. Even at that age the distinctive voice could have issued from no other throat.

—Bob Rose

SCHIPPERS, Thomas.

Conductor. Born 9 March 1930, in Kalamazoo, Michigan. Died 16 December 1977, in New York. Studied piano at the Curtis Institute of Music, Philadelphia, 1944-45, and with Olga Samaroff, 1946-47; studied composition with Paul Hindemith at Yale University; won second place in a contest for young conductors sponsored by the Philadelphia Orchestra, 1948; organist at the Greenwich Village Presbyterian Church, New York; involved in founding and conducting the Lemonade Opera Company; conducted the New York premiere of Menotti's *The Consul,* 15 March 1950; conducted the television premiere of Menotti's *Amahl and the Night Visitors,* 24 December 1951; conducted Menotti's *The Old Maid and the Thief* at the New York City Opera, 9 April 1952; guest conductor with the New York Philharmonic, 1955; conducted Donizetti's *Don Pasquale* with the Metropolitan Opera, New York, 1955; worked with Menotti on the Spoleto Festival of Two Worlds, 1958-76; alternate conductor for the Soviet Union tour of the New York Philharmonic, 1959; conducted the premiere of de Falla's cantata *Atlantida* at the Teatro alla Scala, Milan, 1962; conducted at the Bayreuth Festival, 1964; conducted the premiere of Menotti's opera *The Last Savage,* 1966; conducted the opening of the new Metropolitan Opera House with Barber's *Antony and Cleopatra,* 16 September 1966; music director of the Cincinnati Symphony Orchestra, 1970-77; professor at the University of Cincinnati, 1972-77; conducted the Metropolitan debut of the original version of Musorgsky's *Boris Godunov,* 1974; named conductor laureate of the Cincinnati Symphony, 1977.

* * *

Thomas Schippers was regarded during his lifetime (which was cut short at the age of forty-seven due to cancer) as one of the leading young conductors of opera.

Starting out as an organist, Schippers entered the Curtis Institute of Music in Philadelphia at the age of fifteen and later studied composition with Paul Hindemith at Yale University. Schippers became the organist at Greenwich Village Presbyterian Church in New York City, and it was here that his career as an opera conductor developed when he took over the directorship of the Lemonade Opera Company, which performed in the basement of the church.

Schippers' career was closely identified with the music of the composers Samuel Barber and Gian Carlo Menotti. He premiered the former's *Antony and Cleopatra* (1966) and was one of the first interpreters of the latter's *The Consul* (1950). One of Schippers' triumphs was as conductor of the premiere in 1951 on NBC television of Menotti's *Amahl and the Night Visitors.* Along with Menotti, Schippers co-founded the Spoleto Music Festival in Italy in 1958 and was its music director. Schippers also conducted frequently at Bayreuth, Teatro alla Scala, New York City Opera, and the Metropolitan Opera, where he debuted in 1955 at the age of twenty-five. Before his death, he conducted 287 performances of twenty-eight different operas at the Met.

Schippers taught at the College-Conservatory of Music of the University of Cincinnati from 1972 to 1977 and was music director of the Cincinnati Symphony Orchestra from 1970 to 1977. At the time of his death, Schippers had been engaged as the music director of the Santa Cecilia Orchestra in Rome.

Although he conducted operas from the German, French, and Russian repertoires, the clarity and understatement of Schippers' conducting technique was best suited for American and Italian operas, especially those of Barber, Menotti, Verdi, and Rossini. In his short lifetime Thomas Schippers managed to create a very large body of live and recorded performances, and his interpretations of a number of operas are considered by many to be, if not definitive, at least as yet unsurpassed.

—William E. Grim

SCHLUSNUS, Heinrich.

Baritone. Born 6 August 1888, in Braubach am Rhein. Died 18 June 1952, in Frankfurt am Main. Studied voice in Frankfurt and Berlin; debut in *Lohengrin* at the Hamburg Opera, 1915; sang in Nuremberg, 1915-17; leading member of the Berlin Royal (later State) Opera, 1917-45; also appeared in Chicago, 1927, Bayreuth, 1933, and Paris, 1937.

Publications

About SCHLUSNUS: books–

Naso, E. von and A. Schlusnus. *Heinrich Schlusnus, Mensch und Sänger.* Hamburg, 1957.
Steane, J.B. *The Grand Tradition.* London, 1974.

articles–

Csan, E. and A.G. Ross. "A Schlusnus Discography." *Record News* 3 (1959): 164, 196, 319, 402.

Smolian, S. "Heinrich Schlusnus: a Discography." *BIRS Bulletin* no. 14 (1959): 5; no. 15-16 (1960): 16.

*　　*　　*

He was the leading Verdi baritone for nearly thirty years at the Berlin State Opera, but Heinrich Schlusnus was equally comfortable with the music of Wagner, and played a wide range of operatic roles. American audiences loved his recordings and his few appearances in the United States as much as Europeans enjoyed his many performances all over the continent. He sang lieder as well as opera for almost forty years, and his voice remained smooth and pure into his sixties. His records have been re-released since his death, keeping his name and voice alive.

Heinrich Schlusnus debuted in *Lohengrin* in 1915 with the Hamburg Opera. Two years later, he joined the Berlin State Opera and stayed with them until 1945 as their finest Verdi singer. His operatic roles were varied; he took part in the Verdi revival in Berlin in the 1920s and 1930s, singing in *I vespri Siciliani, La forza del destino, Don Carlos, Rigoletto, Otello, La traviata,* and *Il trovatore.* He also sang in the operas of Wagner as well as in Borodin's *Prince Igor,* Bizet's *Carmen,* Donizetti's *Don Pasquale,* Offenbach's *Les contes d'Hoffmann,* and Tchaikovsky's *Eugene Onegin.* When not singing in Berlin, he sang with other opera companies all over Europe, and he toured as a recitalist in Europe, the United States, and South Africa. World War II interrupted his career. He lost his son, who fought against Russia; his home was bombed, and he lost all of his personal records. He resumed singing and touring after the war. Age did not seem to touch his voice. Shortly before his death at the age of 64, the *New York Times* commented that "[His] voice, still a high baritone, is fresh and beautiful, its employment a model of fine vocalism."

Schlusnus was an immensely popular performer during his day. Critics admired the pure, natural beauty of his voice and the smoothness and strength of his upper register. A.J. Coetsee, writing about a concert in South Africa, described how Schlusnus "scored [a] phenomenal success with *Verschwiegene Liebe* by Wolf, sustaining the high B with ease in perfect *mezza voce.*" Another critic, Erich Hermann, wrote "Schlusnus, at the age of sixty, once again proved that he is unique in his sincerity and the unspoilt beauty of his voice." While Schlusnus was not known as an extremely dramatic singer, critics hailed his sensitive interpretations in live performance. A.J. Coetsee wrote "with incomparable beauty of tone, diction, phrasing and genuine artistry, he created an atmosphere of close intimacy right from the opening group of songs. . . ." He was a close friend of Richard Strauss and frequently worked with him; he was considered an "ideal interpreter of Strauss' lieder." Age seemed only to deepen the sensitivity of his expression.

Throughout his life Schlusnus made many recordings of Italian opera, German opera, and Lieder. His eighty recordings include duets with Selma Kurz, Frida Leider, and Lotte Lehmann. While the vocal quality comes through on record, his interpretive ability is less audible on recordings than it apparently was in life. His smooth texture and lyrical lines, his perfect legato, and even, sweet tone strike the listener at once. Recordings made shortly before his death attest to the soundness of his vocal production; his voice was always velvet-like and unpressured. His singing is economical, unforced, and unmannered. His musicianship, his pitch and rhythmic accuracy, and his diction, are impeccable. He recorded six Strauss songs with the composer as his accompanist. On these records, his interpretations shine through; yet on many others, his expressiveness is less than exciting. As he grew older, he lost spontaneity, and he frequently seemed to strive for general, rather than specific, meaning, as can be heard in his Mahler Lieder recordings. He used dynamics expressively, but he seemed to sacrifice drama for an undisturbed beauty of tone and smooth delivery. He was at his best with purely lyrical pieces.

Schlusnus' simple and undramatic approach to his singing fit his personality, for he was a simple, humble man. He reportedly hated flattery and preferred evenings spent with his friends to large parties after recitals. If someone would comment on his performance, he would respond with praise of the composition. He concentrated his efforts on the beauty of the music he sang, producing the most beautiful tones he could. We are fortunate he left such a prodigious recorded legacy for a singer of his generation, for as J.B. Steane says in his book *The Grand Tradition,* "I think that if I was a singing teacher, I would send my baritones to records of Schlusnus more often than the records of any other singer."

—Robin Armstrong

SCHMIDT, Franz.

Composer. Born 22 December 1874, in Pressburg. Died 11 February 1939, in Perchtoldsdorf, near Vienna. Studied with Mader in Pressburg, and then with Leschetizky in Vienna, 1888; studied composition with Bruckner, theory with Fuchs, and cello with Hellmesberger at the Vienna Conservatory, beginning 1890; cellist in the orchestra of the Vienna Hofoper, 1896-1911; taught cello at the conservatory of the Gesellschaft der Musikfreunde, 1901-08; professor of piano, 1914-22, and of counterpoint and composition, beginning 1922, at the Vienna Staatsakademie; director of the Vienna Staatsakademie, 1925-7; director of the Vienna Hochschule für Musik, 1927-31; honorary doctorate from the University of Vienna, 1934; Beethoven Prize of the Prussian Academy in Berlin shortly before his death.

Operas

Notre Dame, Schmidt and L. Wilk (after Hugo), 1902-04, 1 April 1914.
Fredigundis, Schmidt (after F. Dahn), 1916-21, Berlin, 1922.

Other works: orchestral works (including four symphonies), chamber music, piano pieces.

Publications

About SCHMIDT: books–

Korngold, J. *Deutsches Opernschaffen der Gegenwart.* Vienna and Leipzig, 1922.
Liess, A. *Franz Schmidt: Sein Leben und Schaffen.* Graz, 1951.
Nemeth, C. *Franz Schmidt: Ein Meister nach Brahms und Bruckner.* Vienna, 1957.
Tschulik, N. *Franz Schmidt.* Vienna, 1972; English translation, 1980.
Leibnitz, T. *Österreichische Spätromantiker: Studien zu Emil Nikolaus von Reznicek, Joseph Marx, Franz Schmidt, und Egon Kornauth.* Tutzing, 1986.

articles–

Franklin, P. "The Case of Franz Schmidt." *Musical Times* February (1989).

*   *   *

Franz Schmidt is known today for his four symphonies composed in a post–romantic style and his huge oratorio *Das Buch mit sieben Siegeln* based on the book of Revelation. Schmidt was for the most part self-taught. He had the ability of almost total musical recall, and he was an accomplished pianist and cellist. Schmidt played in the Vienna Opera orchestra for many years and occupied many important teaching positions. Arnold Schoenberg remarked that his friend and advocate had too much talent. Like many composers of the period, Schmidt decided to try his hand at opera, first with *Notre Dame* (1914), based on Victor Hugo's novel, and then with *Fredigundis* (1922), based on a novel by Felix Dahn.

For *Notre Dame,* Schmidt adapted Hugo's novel with Leopold Wilk. The intermezzo and carnival music were performed in 1903 before the opera's completion as *Zwischenspiel aus einer unvollständigen romantischen Oper* (intermezzo from an incomplete romantic opera) by the Vienna Philharmonic under Dresden court conductor Ernst von Schuch. In 1904 Schmidt submitted the score to Gustav Mahler for production at the Vienna Opera. Schmidt had already had conflicts with Mahler, caused in part by intrigues among other members of the orchestra. After Schmidt had played through the score, Mahler complimented his piano playing, but turned down the opera, saying that it lacked "great ideas." The score waited a decade until 1914 when it was accepted by Mahler's successors. The administration of the Opera seemed surprised by the work's success, and in response to queries from other houses surmised that it was due in large part to Schmidt's local standing. Because of the war, *Notre Dame* was only slowly taken up elsewhere (at Budapest in 1916 and in Berlin not until 1918). It has enjoyed occasional revivals in Vienna.

Notre Dame is a summation of Schmidt's early style, but even here one sees his exploitation of chromatic harmony leading toward the freer use of dissonance that was to mark his later works. Schmidt was almost exclusively a composer of symphonies and chamber music (he wrote no published songs and only a handful of piano pieces), and for the most part he eschewed programmatic devices. Even in this opera the dramatic tension is based more in his musical forms—for example, the first scene is a sonata movement—than in the text, and his lyricism is more instrumentally than vocally inspired. The score is like a symphony with vocal parts, and in fact the sketches reportedly show that Schmidt often fitted the vocal lines over the orchestra. The solo parts are lyrical but undramatic, and the chorus often sounds like a choral society. Scoring is full throughout, but without the contrasts between instrumental groups and the intermittent lightened textures that would make it more effective. Frequently one finds passages that a more experienced composer for the stage would have expanded to build the dramatic effect; the ending sounds particularly abrupt and unprepared. Yet the music is lush and not without merit: concert performances doubtless prove more effective than staged ones. The gipsy music for Esmeralda is often noted (Schmidt was three-fourths Hungarian). Hungarian composer Karl Goldmark said it was the most beautiful gipsy music he had ever heard.

Schmidt devoted almost six years exclusively to work on his second opera, *Fredigundis,* which is about a murderous sixth-century Frankish queen. As with *Notre Dame,* part of it was first performed separately, the *Variations on the King's Fanfares* for organ. This opera was also initially rejected by the Vienna Opera. After many problems, it premiered in Berlin in 1922. As is the case with many operas, it was popular with audiences but not with the critics. It received only a few other productions, including one in Vienna.

Many claim that *Fredigundis* contains some of Schmidt's finest music. By the time he wrote his second opera, his harmonic language had advanced significantly over that found in *Notre Dame;* the new ideas Schmidt had acquired through his advocacy of Schoenberg and other young composers have found their way into his own music here. Movement by semitone in contrary motion often leads almost to bitonality, and dissonances resolve less frequently and less regularly than in most of Schmidt's other works. Schmidt rarely wrote music as thick and contrapuntal as he did here, although the linear emphasis is characteristic of his late style. He compensated for the awkward libretto, condemned even by his admirers, by an outflowing of symphonic music that is even less dramatic than that in *Notre Dame.*

Schmidt remarked that there were three symphonies in the music for *Fredigundis.* Richard Strauss told him that the music covered everything like a lava flow and that he (Strauss) could have made four operas out of the thematic material. Of Schmidt's three large-scale vocal works, *Das Buch mit sieben Siegeln* has proved most enduring, although the intermezzo and carnival music from *Notre Dame* are still occasionally heard.

—David E. Anderson

SCHNEIDER-SIEMSSEN, Günther.

Designer. Born 7 June 1926, in Augsburg. Married: Eva Mazar; four children. Studied in Munich with Emil Preetorius at the Akademie der bildenden Kunst, with Ludwig Sievert at the Akademie für angewandte Kunst, Professor Kutscher at the University, and Rudolf Hartmann; began professional opera career at Bremen Stadttheater, 1945; film designer, 1946-51; joined the staff at the Bavarian State Opera, 1948-52; debut as set designer in *The Consul,* Salzburg, 1951; debut as costume designer in *Ariodante,* Staatstheater, Bremen, 1956; designed productions at the Salzburg Marionette Theater, where he created several Mozart operas, 1952-72; resident designer, Bremen State Theater, 1954-59; also active in theater and film in Munich, Berlin, and Salzburg; chief designer, Vienna Staatsoper, Burgtheater, and Volksoper, since 1962; staff of Salzburg Festival, from 1965; designer, Easter Festival, 1967-89; exhibitions of his designs in Vienna in 1969, New York City in 1970, Berlin in 1971, Reinhard Museum in Salzburg in 1972; faculty member of the International Summer Academy for the Visual Arts in Salzburg. Honors include fellow at M.I.T., U.S.A., 1980-85 and President, Society of the Stage of the Future.

Opera Productions (selected)

The Consul, Salzburg, 1951.
Ariodante, Staatstheater, Bremen, 1956.
Pelléas et Mélisande, Vienna Staatsoper, 1960.
Siegfried, Covent Garden, 1962.
Die Erwartung, Covent Garden, 1962.

Der Ring des Nibelungen, Covent Garden, 1962-64.
Dame Kobold, Städt Bühnen, Frankfurt, 1964.
Boris Godunov, Salzburg, 1965.
Don Giovanni, Salzburg, 1967.
Der Ring des Nibelungen, Salzburg, 1967-70.
Der Ring des Nibelungen, Metropolitan Opera, 1967-72.
Aucassin und Nicolette, Munich Staatsoper, 1969-70.
Otello, Salzburg, 1969.
Tristan und Isolde, Metropolitan Opera, 1971.
Fidelio, Salzburg, 1971.
Besuch der alte Dame, Vienna Staatsoper, 1972.
De Temporum fine comoedia, Salzburg Festival 1973.
Le nozze di Figaro, Teatro alla Scala, 1973.
Jenůfa, Metropolitan Opera, 1974.
Tannhäuser, Metropolitan Opera, 1977.
Les contes d'Hoffmann, Greater Opera of Miami, 1979-80 season.
Les contes d'Hoffmann, Metropolitan Opera, 1981.
Arabella, Metropolitan Opera, 1983.
Die Fledermaus, Metropolitan Opera, 1986.
Der Ring des Nibelungen, Metropolitan Opera, 1986-89.
Der Ring des Nibelungen, Warsaw, 1988.
Parsifal, Metropolitan Opera, 1989.
Samson und Dalila, Berlin, 1990.
Arabella, Berlin, 1990.
Katya Kabanova, Metropolitan Opera, 1991.
Rusalka, Seattle, 1991.

Publications

About SCHNEIDER-SIEMSSEN: articles–

Jenkins, S. "*The Ring*—East and West." *Opera News* 32 (25 November 1967): 15-17.
Eaton, Q. "Guenther and Eva." *Opera News* 36 (18 December 1971): 26-27.
"Gespraech mit Guenther Schneider-Siemssen." *Oper und Konzert* 11, no. 5 (1973): 18-19.
Adam, K. "Holographie: Der dreidimensionale Lichtraum erstmals im Buehnenbereich." *Oper und Konzert* 23, no. 10 (1985): 23-25.
"Operascope." *Opera News* 51 (28 February 1987): 6.
Fabian, I. "Ein romantischer *Ring* mit den heutigen Mitteln des Theaters: Gespraech mit dem Buehnenbildner Guenther Schneider-Siemssen." *Opernwelt* 28, no. 11 (1987): 18-20.
Persche, G. "Den Menschen nicht erschlagen . . . (Interview)." *Opernwelt* 31 (April 1990): 15-16.

* * *

As an apprentice scenery painter at the Bavarian Staatsoper in the 1930s, and later in his studies with Emil Preetorius and Rudolf Hartmann in Munich, German designer Günther Schneider-Siemssen absorbed the 1930s Bayreuth style. He began his professional career in opera at the Bremen Stadttheater in 1945. From 1952 to 1972 he designed productions for the Salzburg Marionette Theater. An invitation from Herbert von Karajan brought him to the Vienna Staatsoper, where he has been the chief designer since 1962. His designs for the Metropolitan Opera have included several Wagnerian operas: the *Der Ring des Nibelungen* (two productions, 1967-72 and 1986-89), *Tristan und Isolde* (1971), *Tannhäuser* (1977), and *Parsifal* (1989); other operas include Janáček's *Jenůfa* (1974), Offenbach's *Les contes d'Hoffmann* (1982,

based on his designs for the Greater Opera of Miami), Richard Strauss's *Arabella* (1983), and Johann Strauss's *Die Fledermaus* (1986). He has also created sets for Covent Garden (Schoenberg's *Erwartung* [1962] and *Der Ring des Nibelungen* [1962-64]) and the Teatro San Carlo in Naples (including *Der Ring des Nibelungen*). He has worked with such directors as Otto Schenk and August Everding.

The abstract and heavily symbolic sets Schneider-Siemssen created for Herbert von Karajan's neo-Bayreuth *Der Ring des Nibelungen* in Salzburg (and on which the first of his two Metropolitan Opera *Ring* cycles was based) employed constantly moving, fluid projections to create an unworldly atmosphere. For his subsequent Wagner productions, the designer has attempted to realize many of Wagner's stated intentions—a combination of the spirit of nineteenth-century theater with the expectations of twentieth-century audiences. Schneider-Siemssen feels that the standards for "realistic" productions are now higher because of modern audiences' exposure to film and television. This has dictated his approach to the sets and props of his current Metropolitan Opera *Ring* cycle—an attempt to achieve accuracy of detail in geological formations, plant life, utensils, and architecture.

This aspect of Schneider-Siemssen's style is marked by a realism imbued with a poetic, delicate feeling. His sets are highly detailed—designed with an understanding of the opera's historical context—with elements of fantasy, as in his sets for the Metropolitan Opera's *Les contes d'Hoffmann.* This is especially evident in the menacingly dark Venetian courtyard and in Spalanzani's laboratory, festooned with his mad inventions, the entire room rolling forward to fill the stage as the equally atmospheric set for the prologue of act I descends, courtesy of the stage elevator. In Crespel's home, Dr Miracle can walk through walls, while projections of the tiers of an opera house reveal Antonia's dreams.

Schneider-Siemssen's sets for the Metropolitan Opera's 1977 *Tannhäuser* also make use of realistic projections and scrims to create a fairy-tale atmosphere surrounding Otto Schenk's realistic direction. In this production's major *coup de théâtre,* the steamy Venusburg grotto—scene of the orgiastic bacchanal, with its waterfalls and lakes, stalagmites and stalagtites—dissolves in an instant into the pristine, springlike atmosphere of the Wartburg. For the Hall of Song in act II, Schneider-Siemssen recreated in historic detail the architecture of the actual castle in Thuringia, conveying a sense of tradition and stability.

For Wagner's *Tristan und Isolde,* as presented at the Metropolitan Opera in 1971, Schneider-Siemssen has taken his cue from the work's central theme of the contrast between day and night. Employing his technique of "painting with light," he created spare sets and depended on projections to produce an almost cinematic realization of the opera. In act I, the huge billowing sails of the ship provide a screen onto which the looming silhouette of Tristan is cast. The heightened reality of the sets is paralleled by a stage effect in which the singers are transported into the heavens, via the stage elevator. The castle gardens of act II change from lushness to bleakness as the story progresses. The far more abstract set for act III reflects Tristan's hopelessness and delirium.

This "romantic realism," combining the romanticism of fantasy with reality as seen through dreams, tempered by the accuracy of detail expected by modern audiences, defines Schneider-Siemssen's achievement.

—Michael Sims

SCHOENBERG [SCHÖNBERG], Arnold (Franz Walter).

Composer. Born 13 September 1874, in Vienna. Died 13 July 1951, in Los Angeles. Married: 1) Mathilde von Zemlinsky (1877-1923), 1901 (two children); 2) Gertrud Kolisch, 1924 (three children). Studied at the Realschule in Vienna; learned the cello and the violin; first work, three piano pieces, 1894; studied counterpoint with Alexander Zemlinsky, and played in his instrumental group Polyhymnia; public performance of his first String Quartet in D major, Vienna, 17 March 1898; in Berlin, 1901, where he and E. von Wolzgen, F. Wedekind, and O. Bierbaum started a cabaret called Überbrettl; string sextet *Verklärte Nacht* performed, Vienna, 18 March 1902; met Richard Strauss, who recommended him for a Liszt stipend and a teaching position at the Stern Conservatory; met Mahler in Vienna, 1903, who helped Schoenberg establish his career; Vereinigung Schaffender Tonkünstler organized for the performance of new music; symphonic poem *Pelleas und Melisande* performed 26 January 1905; *Kammersymphonie* performed 8 February 1907, but not well received; began painting seriously, 1907; took on Alban Berg, Anton von Webern, and Egon Wellesz as private students; appointed to the faculty of the Vienna Academy of Music, 1910; instructor at the Stern Conservatory, Berlin, 1911; his *Fünf Orchesterstücke* premiered in London, under the direction of Sir Henry Wood, 3 September 1912; *Pierrot Lunaire* premiered in Berlin, 16 October 1912, and condemned by critics; Verein für Musikalische Privataufführungen formed by Schoenberg for the performance of new music at the exclusion of critics, 1918-22; taught a master class at the Prussian Academy of Arts in Berlin, 1925; taught at the Malkin Conservatory of Boston, 1933; professor of music at the University of Southern California, 1935; professor of music at the University of California at Los Angeles, 1936-44; turned down for a Guggenheim fellowship; United States citizenship, 11 April 1941; Award of Merit for Distinguished Achievements from the National Institute of Arts and Letters, 1947.

Operas

Publishers: Belmont, Dreililien, Hansen, G. Schirmer, Schott, Universal.

Edition: *A. Schoenberg, Sämtliche Werke.* Mainz, 1966-.

Erwartung (monodrama), M. Pappenheim, 1909, Prague, Neues Deutsche Theater, 6 June 1924.
Die glückliche Hand, Schoenberg, 1910-13, Vienna, Volksoper, 14 October 1924.
Von Heute auf Morgen, M. Blonda [=G. Schoenberg], 1928-29, Frankfurt, Opernhaus, 1 February 1930.
Moses und Aron, Schoenberg, 1930-32 [unfinished: act III never composed], partial performance, Darmstadt, 2 July 1951; concert performance of acts I and II, Hamburg, 12 March 1954; staged performance of acts I and II, Zurich, Stadttheater, 6 June 1957.

Publications/Writings

By SCHOENBERG: books—

Harmonielehre. Vienna, 1911; 3rd ed., 1922; abridged English translation, 1948; complete English translation, 1978.
Models for Beginners in Composition. Los Angeles, 1942; 2nd ed., 1943; revised by L. Stein, 1972.
Style and Idea. New York, 1950; expanded 2nd ed., London, 1975; 1984.

Searle, H. ed. *Structural Functions of Harmony.* London, 1954; revised by L. Stein, 1969; 1983.
Stein, E., ed. *Arnold Schoenberg: Briefe.* Mainz, 1958; enlarged and in English translation, 1964; French translation, 1983.
Stein, L. ed. *Preliminary Exercises in Counterpoint.* London, 1963.
Reich, W. ed. *Schöpferische Konfessionen.* Zurich, 1964.
Stein, L., ed. *Fundamentals of Musical Composition.* London, 1967; German translation, Vienna, 1979.
Rognoni, L., ed. *Testi poetici e drammatici.* Milan, 1967.
Heller, F.C. ed. *Arnold Schönberg-Franz Schreker: Briefwechsel.* Tutzing, 1974.
Rufer, J., ed. *Berliner Tagebuch.* Frankfurt, 1974.
Busoni, F. *Entwurf einer neuen Ästhetik der Tonkunst, mit handschriftlichen Anmerkungen von A. Schönberg.* Frankfurt, 1974.
Vojtech, I., ed. *Gesammelte Schriften.* Frankfurt, 1976.
Kimmey, J., ed. *The Arnold Schoenberg—Hans Nachod Collection.* Detroit, 1979.
Hahl-Koch, J., ed. *Arnold Schönberg, Wassily Kandinsky: Briefe, Bilder und Dokumente.* Salzburg, 1980; English translation, 1984.

articles—

"A Four-Point Program for Jewry." *Journal of the Arnold Schoenberg Institute* 3 (1979): 49.
"About Rudolf Kolisch." *Journal of the Schoenberg Institute* 4 (1980): 21.
Schönberg Nono, Nuria, translator. "Napoleon Patience" [short story]. *Journal of the Arnold Schoenberg Institute* 5 (1981): 54.
" 'Jede blinde Henne . . .'. Aphorismen nach einem Manuskript von 1929, mit einem Nachwort von Ivan Vojtech." *Österreichische Musikzeitung* 39 (1984): 286.

texts for music—

Totentanz der Prinzipien. Published in *A. Schoenberg: Texte,* Vienna, 1926.
Wendepunkt. Published in Maegaard, J., *Studien zur Entwicklung des dodekaphonen Satzes bei Arnold Schönberg,* Copenhagen, 1972.
Requiem. Published in *A. Schoenberg: Texte.* Vienna, 1926.
Psalmen, Gebete und Andere Gespräche mit und über Gott. Mainz, 1956.

unpublished—

Das Komponieren mit selbständigen Stimmen. June, 1911.
Der musikalische Gedanke und seine Darstellung. 1925-36.
Die Lehre von Kontrapunkt. October 1926.
Der biblische Weg [drama]. 1926-27.
Aberglaube [fragmentary opera libretto].
Odoaker [fragmentary opera libretto].
Die Schildbürger [fragmentary opera libretto].

Note: for additional unpublished writings, see Rufer, 1959.

About SCHOENBERG: books—

Wellesz, E. *Arnold Schönberg.* Vienna, 1921; revised English translation, 1925; 1971.
Rufer, Josef. *Das Werk Arnold Schönbergs.* Kassel, 1959; English translation as *The Works of Arnold Schoenberg: a*

Catalogue of Compositions, Writings, and Paintings. London, 1962.

Wörner, K.H. *Gotteswort und Magie.* Heidelberg, 1959; English revision as *Schoenberg's 'Moses and Aron',* 1963.

Payne, Anthony. *Schoenberg.* London, 1968.

Reich, Willi. *Schoenberg.* Vienna, 1968; English translation as *Schoenberg: a Critical Biography,* London, 1971.

Stuckenschmidt, H. *Schönberg: Leben, Umwelt, Werk.* Zurich, 1974; English translation as *Schoenberg: his Life, World, and Work,* London and New York, 1977.

Rosen, C. *Arnold Schoenberg.* New York, 1975.

MacDonald, M. *Schoenberg.* London, 1976.

Satoh, T., compiler. *A Bibliographic Catalogue with Discography and a Comprehensive Bibliography of Arnold Schoenburg.* Tokyo, 1978.

Boventer, H. ed. *'Moses und Aron': zur Oper Arnold Schönbergs.* Bensberg, 1979.

Krauss, Hans-Joachim, et al. *Moses und Aron: zur Oper Arnold Schönbergs.* Cologne, 1979.

Lessem, A. *Music and Text in the Works of Arnold Schoenberg.* Ann Arbor, 1979.

Newlin, D. *Schoenberg Remembered: Diaries and Recollections (1938-76).* New York, 1980.

Garcia-Laborda, José Maria. *Studien zu Schönbergs Monodram "Erwartung" op. 17.* 2 vols. Laaber, 1981.

Stec, Odil Hannes. *"Moses und Aron." Die Oper Arnold Schönbergs und ihr biblischer Stoff.* Munich, 1981.

White, Pamela C. *Schoenberg and the God-Idea: the Opera "Moses und Aron".* Ann Arbor, 1985.

Smith, Joan Allen. *Schoenberg and his Circle: a Viennese Portrait.* New York, 1986.

Haimo, Ethan. *Schoenberg's Serial Odyssey.* Oxford, 1990.

articles–

Keller, H. "Unpublished Schoenberg Letters: Early, Middle and Late." *Music Survey* 4 (1952): 499.

———. "Schoenberg's 'Moses and Aron'." *The Score* no. 27 (1957): 30.

Birke, J. "Richard Dehmel und Arnold Schönberg, ein Briefwechsel." *Die Musikforschung* 11 (1958): 279; 17 (1964): 60.

Keller, H. "Moses, Freud, and Schoenberg." *Monthly Musical Record* January-February and March-April (1958).

———. "Schoenberg's Comic Opera." *The Score* no. 23 (1958): 27.

"Letters of Webern and Schoenberg to Roberto Gerhard." *The Score* no. 24 (1958): 36.

Reich, W. "Ein unbekannter Brief von Arnold Schönberg an Alban Berg." *Österreichische Musikzeitschrift* 14 (1959): 10.

Glück, F. "Briefe von Arnold Schönberg an Adolf Loos." *Österreichische Musikzeitschrift* 6 (1961): 8.

Adorno, T.W. "Sakrales Fragment." In *Quasi una fantasia,* 306. Frankfurt, 1963.

Wörner, K.H. "Die glückliche Hand, Arnold Schönbergs Drama mit Musik." *Schweizerische Musikzeitung/Revue musicale suisse* 204 (1964): 274.

Vojtech, I. "Arnold Schönberg, Anton Webern, Alban Berg: unbekannte Brief an Erwin Schulhoff." *Miscellanea musicologica* 18 (1965): 31.

Buchanan, H. "A Key to Schoenberg's 'Erwartung'." *Journal of American Musicological Society* 20 (1967): 434.

Klemm, E. "Der Briefwechsel zwischen Arnold Schönberg und dem Verlag C.F. Peters." *Deutsches Jahrbuch der Musikwissenschaft* 15 (1970): 5.

Wörner, K.H. "Schönberg's 'Erwartung' und das Ariadne-Thema." In *Die Musik in der Geistesgeschichte,* 91. Bonn, 1970.

Vlad, R. "Arnold Schönberg schreibt an Gian Francesco Malipiero." *Melos* 38 (1971): 461.

Lampert, V. "Schoenbergs, Bergs und Adornos Briefe an Sándor (Alexander) Jemnitz." *Studia musicologica Academiae scientiarum hungaricae* 15 (1973): 355.

Crawford, J. "Die glückliche Hand: Schoenberg's Gesamtkuntwerk." *Musical Quarterly* 60 (1974): 583.

Glück, F. "Briefe von Arnold Schönberg an Claire Loos." *Österreichische Musikzeitschrift* 29 (1974): 203.

Hilmar, E. "Arnold Schönbergs Briefe an den Akademischen Verband für Literatur und Musik in Wien." *Österreichische Musikzeitschrift* 31 (1976): 273.

Berman, Marsha, compiler. "Current Bibliography: Articles in Periodicals and Collections of Essays." *Journal of the Arnold Schoenberg Institute* 1 (1977): 78.

———. "Bibliography: Books and Dissertations." *Journal of the Arnold Schoenberg Institute* 1 (1977): 11.

Theurich, J. "Briefwechsel zwischen Arnold Schönberg und Ferruccio Busoni 1903-1915 (1927)." *Beiträge zur Musikwissenschaft* 19 (1977): 163.

Budde, E. "Arnold Schönbergs Monodrama 'Erwartung': Versuch einer Analyse der ersten Szene." *Archiv für Musikwissenschaft* 36 (1979): 1.

Beck, Richard Thomas. "The Sources and Significance of *Die glückliche Hand.*" In *Bericht über den Internationalen Musikwissenschaftlichen Kongress Berlin 1974,* edited by Helmut Kühn and Peter Nitsche, 427. Kassel, 1980.

Crawford, J. "*Die glückliche Hand:* Further Notes." *Journal of the Arnold Schoenberg Institute* 4 (1980): 68.

Kirsch, Winfried. "Die 'Opera domestica'. Zur Dramaturgie des bürgerlichen Alltags im aktuellen Musiktheater der 20er Jahre" [*Von heute auf morgen*]. *Hindemith-Jahrbuch* 9 (1980): 179.

Mauser, S. "Forschungsbericht zu Schönbergs 'Erwartung'." *Österreichische Musikzeitschrift* 35 (1980): 215.

Ringer, Alexander L. "Schoenberg, Weill, and Epic Theater." *Journal of the Arnold Schoenberg Institute* 4 (1980): 77; in German as "Weill, Schönberg und die 'Zeitoper'," *Die Musikforschung* 33 (1980): 465.

Serravezza, A. "Critica e ideologia nel 'Moses und Aron'." *Rivista italiana di musicologia* 15 (1980): 204.

Steiner, E. "The 'Happy' Hand: Genesis and Interpretation of Schoenberg's Monumentalkunstwerk." *Music Review* 41 (1980): 207.

Mauser, Siegfried. "Die musikdramatische Konzeption in *Herzog Blaubarts Burg*" [compares Bartók's *Bluebeard's Castle* to Schoenberg's *Die glückliche Hand*]. *Musik-Konzepte* 22 (1981): 169.

Penney, Diane, compiler. "Current Bibliography (1978-June 1981)." *Journal of the Arnold Schoenberg Institute* 5 (1981): 213.

Weaver, R. "The Conflict of Religion and Aesthetics in Schoenberg's 'Moses and Aaron'." In *Essays on the Music of J.S. Bach and Other Divers Subjects: a Tribute to Gerhard Herz,* edited by R. Weaver, 291. Louisville, 1981.

Hahl-Koch, J., with Rudolf Mengelberg. "The Schoenberg-Mengelberg Correspondence I." *Journal of the Arnold Schoenberg Institute* 6 (1982): 181.

White, Pamela C. "The Genesis of Moses und Aron." *Journal of the Arnold Schoenberg Institute* 6 (1982): 8.

Neighbour, Oliver. "*Veraltete Sentimentalität:* Arnold Schoenberg in Defence of Richard Strauss." In *Festschrift Albi Rosenthal,* edited by Rudolf Elvers, 253. Tutzing, 1984.

Weissweiler, Eva. " 'Schreiben Sie mir doch einen Operntext, Fräulein!' Marie Pappenheims Text zur Arnold Schönbergs *Erwartung*." *Neue Zeitschrift für Musik* 145 (1984): 4.

Yamaguchi, Koichi. "Der Gedanke Gottes und das Wort des Menschen: Zu Arnold Schönbergs *Moses und Aron*." *Neue Zeitschrift für Musik* 145 (1984): 8.

unpublished–

Mauser, Siegfried. "Das expressionistische Musiktheater der Wiener Schule. Stilistische und entwicklungsgeschichtliche Untersuchungen zu Arnold Schönbergs *Erwartung* op. 17, *Die glückliche Hand* op. 18 und Alban Bergs *Wozzeck* op. 7." Ph. D. dissertation, University of Salzburg, 1981.

White, Pamela C. "Idea and Representation: Source-critical and Analytical Studies of Music, Text, and Religious Thought in Schoenberg's *Moses und Aron*." Ph.D. dissertation, Harvard University, 1983.

Auner, Joseph. "Schoenberg's Compositional and Aesthetic Transformations 1910-1913: the Genesis of *Die Glückliche Hand*." Ph. D. dissertation, University of Chicago, 1991.

*　　*　　*

During army service in World War I, Arnold Schoenberg was asked by an officer if he was that controversial composer of the same name, to which he replied: "Somebody had to be, and nobody else wanted the job, so I took it on myself." That answer neatly encapsulates his sense of the inevitability of his creative mission, and the belief that personal wishes

Arnold Schoenberg, c. 1930

had little to do with it. He was in many ways an unwilling revolutionary, driven by the need for continual clarification of his emotional and artistic concerns. Pursuing his ideals, he effected the most profound transformation of the terms of musical discourse; a revolution that forced a revaluation of all aspects of musical creativity.

Schoenberg was virtually self-taught, apart from some tuition from Alexander von Zemlinsky (himself a prolific composer of operas), who became his brother-in-law and lifelong friend. Both of them, in the early 1900s, were befriended and supported by Mahler, who as conductor of the Vienna Hofoper was enormously influential, and whose opera performances were of great significance to younger Viennese musicians. As early as 1897 Schoenberg collaborated with Zemlinsky on the libretto of the latter's first opera, *Sarema,* and prepared the vocal score.

Schoenberg's own music, which soon began to outpace Zemlinsky's in the swiftness of its stylistic development, first acquired a personal profile by an exceptionally thoroughgoing synthesis of Brahmsian contrapuntal texture and motivic development with Wagnerian chromaticism, harmonic ambiguity and large compositional spans. This idiom attained its magnificent early flowering in the *Gurrelieder,* a cantata for five singers, reciter, large chorus and enormous orchestra, composed to texts by Jens Peter Jacobsen in 1900-1, but not fully scored until 1911. Although designed for concert performance, its equally intense dramatic and lyrical features refer back constantly to the world of Wagnerian music-drama, especially *Tristan* and *Götterdämmerung.*

It is notable that the work owes almost nothing to Richard Strauss, whose style is only very occasionally hinted at in subsequent pieces, such as the symphonic poem *Pelleas und Melisande* (written at Strauss's suggestion, and in ignorance of Debussy's opera). This was the first of several scores in which Schoenberg began to compress four movement symphonic schemes into a single unbroken span, while radically increasing the degree of contrapuntal and motivic development of every thematic element—a kind of rage for maximum communication that was already, as far as his contemporaries were concerned, causing serious difficulties for comprehension of his purpose.

The emotionally and intellectually supercharged style of these works of the early 1900s exploded, after 1908, into the music of Schoenberg's "Expressionist" phase, where he strove to represent extreme states of mind and feeling more or less directly, without any intervening decorum of form. His ideal, he once said, was a music "without architecture, without structure. Only an ever-changing, unbroken succession of colors, rhythms and moods." His works of this period are accordingly characterized by an unprecedented degree of harmonic ambiguity, asymmetry of melody and phrase-lengths, wide and dissonant melodic intervals, abrupt contrasts in register, texture, stasis and dynamism. All twelve notes of the chromatic scale occur with extreme frequency; consequently the harmonic language shifts away from any kind of diatonic hierarchy towards a state of total chromaticism—an "emancipation of dissonance" which does not, however, prevent the covert and allusive operation of tonal functions, and so belies the popular misnomer of "atonality" which is so often applied to this idiom.

The apotheosis of musical Expressionism was attained in two extraordinary short operas, the monodrama *Erwartung* and the "Drama with Music" *Die glückliche Hand* (the virtually untranslatable title ironically combines the concepts of "A happy knack" with "The hand of fate"). Both works have more often been presented in the concert-hall than on stage—not inappropriately, as both inhabit what are essentially regions of the unconscious mind.

Schoenberg once described *Erwartung*—composed and scored at fantastic speed in a creative brainstorm of uncompromising intensity and freedom—as an *Angsttraum* (anxiety dream), a slow-motion representation of a single second of maximum spiritual stress. Its action is purely psychological, and the moonlit forest through which the female protagonist moves is the stage embodiment of her unconscious fears. Apprehensive, somnambulistic, she wanders in search of her lover, giving voice in broken, discontinuous sentences analogous to a stream of consciousness. Eventually she discovers his corpse, but it remains unclear whether she herself may have done the deed, or whether the entire episode is taking place in her fevered imagination. Despite the chaos of the protagonist's mind, however, the score of *Erwartung* is not in any sense chaotic. There is a willed unity of atmosphere, created through a myriad of intensely imagined details, which could only have been achieved under iron control. Yet the daring juxtapositions of lyricism, violence, anguish and *Angst*-ridden terror attain the effect of high-pressure improvisation, and the solo part demands a tremendous variety of expression, from near-*Sprechstimme* to big moments of Valkyrie-like power and stamina.

Schoenberg, himself an "amateur" painter of near-genius within severe technical limitations, discerned a kinship between what he was doing in works like *Erwartung* and the art of the contemporary Expressionist painters, above all Kandinsky, whom he came to know personally. The parallels are perhaps even clearer in *Die glückliche Hand,* a new kind of *Gesamtkunstwerk* in which music, staging, movement and especially color (achieved by "orchestration" and "color modulation" of the lighting) are expected to play equal parts in a symbolic drama. There are striking similarities to Kandinsky's own contemporary stage-work *Der gelbe Klang,* though it is now known that the two works were conceived entirely independently. "I called it, in my own private language, *making music with the media of the stage,"* Schoenberg commented in a lecture preceding a production in Breslau in 1928: "This kind of art, I don't know why, has been called Expressionist: it has never expressed more than was *in it!* I also gave it a name, which did not become popular . . . I said that it is the *art of the representation of INNER processes."*

Die glückliche Hand is a symbolic representation of the eternal struggles of any creative artist, and as such probably contains a strong autobiographical element. The action again centers on a single unnamed protagonist, male in this case, who is the only vocal soloist. Other characters—his unattainable *innamorata,* a wealthy gentleman, metalworkers, and a monstrous "mythical beast," presumably an exteriorization of the protagonist's self-lacerating consciousness, which has him pinioned to the ground at the beginning and end of the drama—are mimed. A small choir of twelve voices performs the role of a Greek chorus, commenting on the action in a complex vocal texture combining song and *Sprechstimme.* Even more than in *Erwartung,* the sung text is dreamlike, fragmentary, a short verbal index of the inner emotional drama expressed through the medium of the orchestra. On the other hand the structure is, after *Erwartung,* comparatively easy to grasp, and the orchestration has a wonderful iridescence. However, since the solo baritone part of the Man offers far fewer attractions than *Erwartung*'s great soprano role, and the other technical difficulties are no less fearsome, *Die glückliche Hand* has been far less often performed.

No sooner had the Expressionist style attained its climacteric than Schoenberg was concerned to reintroduce "architectural" principals into his music, aware that the supremely intuitive, quasi-improvisational achievement of *Erwartung* was by definition unrepeatable, and that his linguistic revolution had for the moment put traditional means of large-scale organization beyond his grasp. The problems are already reflected in the three years it took to compose *Die glückliche Hand* (as against *Erwartung*'s three weeks) and its more consciously patterned and symmetrical structure. Most of his works of the next decade were vocal, the text helping to determine the progress of the form. At the same time he began to concentrate on intensive development of the constituent tones of principal thematic ideas, and cultivated a wide range of canonic and other "ancient" structural devices to provide structural backbone.

All these tendencies appear in *Pierrot Lunaire* (1912) for instrumental ensemble and *Sprechstimme* ("Speech-song," i.e. half-sung recitation), an ironic cycle of rondel-settings with elements of an Expressionist cabaret. However, they reached a new density, and an impasse, in the unfinished oratorio *Die Jakobsleiter* (1917-22), which grew out of a project for a gigantic choral symphony dealing with modern man's spiritual problems, but which began to assume operatic proportions with a large number of clearly-characterized soloists taking the parts of souls undergoing judgment in purgatory, justice being dispensed by the Angel Gabriel. Though it remains a 40-minute torso (completed for performance after Schoenberg's death by his pupil Winfried Zillig), *Jakobsleiter* brings his musical, philosophical, and religious dilemmas into sharp focus with extraordinary power, and contains the seeds of the idea that would resolve his creative difficulties.

Schoenberg's central problem was how to accept and assimilate the "traumatic" forces of Expressionism as a natural extension and enrichment of the existing scheme of musical discourse: to "objectify" the intense subjectivity of the new idiom within an enlarged musical language which he could apply consciously—not merely intuitively—in further works. We should observe that his pupil Alban Berg found a personal solution to this conundrum, somewhat ahead of Schoenberg, in *Wozzeck* (1917-22), where total chromaticism is balanced by passages with fairly strong tonal orientation, and the large-scale form is articulated by building each scene upon an "abstract" or traditional classical form—passacaglia, sonata, invention on one note, and so on. Berg, however, was always a slow and painstaking worker: Schoenberg's problem was different in kind as well as degree, for he desired a solution that would give him the means to recapture his spontaneity of inspiration.

Schoenberg's approach to this problem, characteristically, was far more radical than Berg's: he developed the "method of composition with twelve tones related only to each other"; the "twelve-note method", or "twelve-note serialism" for short. A fixed series of all the notes of the chromatic scale, derived from the initial melodic and harmonic ideas for a particular work, becomes the kernel, the essence, the germinating cell of that work's unique tonal properties. The series is developed continually through transposition, inversion, retrograde motion, in whole or in part, in melodic lines and in chords, in "punning" similarities between different segments (which, at different transpositions, may employ identical pitches), to provide an inexhaustible and self-consistent source of invention.

Schoenberg developed the techniques of twelve-note serialism progressively through the 1920s in the revivification of classical forms, beginning with dance-movements (in the op. 23 Piano Pieces and op. 25 Suite for Piano), and working up through large-scale chamber scores (Wind Quintet, String Quartet no. 3) and orchestral compositions (Variations for Orchestra). His logical goal was opera, and the one-act comic opera *Von heute auf morgen* (1928-9, to a libretto by his second wife Gertrud, writing under the pseudonym of 'Max Blonda') and the three-act biblical parable *Moses und Aron* (1930-2, to his own libretto) remained his largest twelve-note scores, even though the latter was nominally unfinished.

The oddity of Schoenberg writing a comic opera is lessened when one recalls his Viennese background and his unashamed enthusiasm for the operettas of Franz Lehar. *Von heute auf morgen* is a domestic comedy, reputedly inspired by the home-life of Schoenberg's Berlin colleague Franz Schreker, and a satire on fashionable modernity in social life. A bourgeois couple, dissatisfied with their ordinary lives, become involved with a sophisticated woman-friend and a famous tenor, a sort of Richard Tauber figure, whose smartness and "up-to-dateness" they envy. A night's flirtation with the idea of adopting the latter pair's standards gives way by morning to a reaffirmation of the virtues of a stable marriage. The score is musically almost over-rich, the tone benevolently satirical, with some sharp parodic touches that range from Wagner through Puccini to jazz. Seldom staged, it needs careful handling to bring it alive in the theater—yet it is one of Schoenberg's most humane and positive works, and was clearly invaluable preparation for his operatic masterpiece, *Moses und Aron*. It is that work above all (discussed separately in this dictionary) which sums up a lifetime's musical development and applies it to dramatic ideas of the epic, religious and philosophical scope towards whose expression Schoenberg's genius had always struggled.

—Malcolm MacDonald

SCHORR, Friedrich.

Bass-Baritone. Born 2 September 1888, in Nagyvárad, Hungary. Died 14 August 1953, in Farmington, Connecticut. Studied law at the University in Vienna, and music with Adolf Robinson; minor roles with the Chicago Opera, 1911-12; major debut as Wotan in *Die Walküre*, Graz, 1912; in Graz, 1912-16; in Prague, 1916-18; in Cologne, 1918-23; Berlin State Opera, 1923-32; Metropolitan Opera debut as Wolfram in *Tannhäuser*, 1924; at Metropolitan Opera, 1924-43, singing eighteen roles, primarily Wagner; Covent Garden debut in *Das Rheingold*, 1924; Bayreuth debut as Wotan, 1925; at Bayreuth, 1925-31; sang Daniello in American premiere of *Jonny spielt auf*, 1929; at San Francisco, 1931-38; sang in American premiere of Weinberger's *Schwanda*, 1931; appointed vocal advisor to Wagner department at the Metropolitan Opera, 1938; taught at The Manhattan School of Music and Hartt School of Music, 1943-53; advisor on German opera, New York City Opera, 1950. Became United States citizen.

Publications

About SCHORR: articles–

"Torch Bearers of Opera." *Opera News* 13 November 1950: 13.

"Recreating Hans Sachs." *Music Clubs Magazine* February 1951: 9.

"Schorr's Shoemaker." *Music and Musicians* 12/November (1963): 53.

"Friedrich Schorr's Hans Sachs." *American Record Guide* 30/June (1964): 976.

"Hans Sachs." *HiFidelity* 14/June (1964): 63.

Shawe-Taylor, Desmond. "Friedrich Schorr." *Opera* May, 1965.

Frankenstein, A. "Friedrich Schorr." *Record Collector* 19 (1971): 245.

Fischer, J.M. "Sprachgesang oder Belcanto—zur Geschichte des Wagner-Gesangs." *Opernwelt* 27/5 (1986): 57.

Friedrich Schorr's career spanned over forty years and two continents. He sang Lieder and sacred music as well as opera, but he was above all a Wagnerian. Schorr gave his first performance singing Wotan, and in his final performance he sang the Wanderer in *Siegfried*. At the end of his career, he coached and taught Wagnerian singers at the Metropolitan Opera and elsewhere. As J.B. Steane said in his book *The Grand Tradition*, "It is in Wagner, particularly as Sachs and Wotan, that Schorr is most himself and irreplaceable." He was a true *Heldenbariton*, and it was said that his impressively noble Wotan spoiled his audiences for any other performer.

Schorr began his long career in 1912 in Graz, Austria, debuting as Wotan; that same year he also sang several small roles with the Chicago Opera company in the United States. He sang in Europe—mostly Graz, Prague, and Berlin—for a decade before his Metropolitan Opera debut, again as Wotan, in 1924. Although he concentrated on Wagnerian roles, he sang in other operas as well, including Beethoven's *Fidelio*, Strauss's *Rosenkavalier*, Puccini's *Tosca*, and lesser know works like Weinberger's *Schwanda* and Krenek's *Jonny spielt auf*. In 1938, he was made vocal advisor to the Metropolitan Opera's Wagnerian singers. After he retired from the company in 1943 and until his death in 1953, he taught singing at The Manhattan School of Music in New York City, and at Hartt School of Music, in Hartford, Connecticut.

Audiences loved Schorr. Arthur Notcutt, who saw his debut at Covent Gardens in 1924, wrote later: "His singing in *Rheingold* on the opening night at once stamped him as an artist of outstanding gifts. The commencing phrase when Wotan is asleep and dreaming, 'Der Wonne seligen Saal' was sung in the softest of tones—followed later by the full opulence of his voice in his address to the castle, 'Vollendet das ewige Werk.' One could sense the reaction of the audience immediately. *Die Walküre* on the following evening confirmed one's initial impression." Both his vocal quality and his acting were lavishly praised. Notcutt mentioned the "ravishing beauty of his mezza-voce" and described his "nobility of . . . expression, his intensity and dramatic fire, and [his] melting tenderness and pathos." His first New York season was equally well-received, and he continued to reap such praise. In 1934, New York critic W.J. Henderson wrote of him: "He sang all the music like a great artist and some of it as it had never been sung."

Schorr left a large recorded legacy. He did, of course, record a substantial amount of Wagner, but he recorded other literature as well. His recordings of the difficult excerpts from Beethoven's *Fidelio* are masterful, while his recording from Weber's *Der Freischütz* is not his most successful. He recorded passages from Bach's *Mass in B Minor*, Mendelssohn's *Elijah*, and Hayden's *The Seasons*, as well as some Lieder.

While many of Schorr's Wagnerian predecessors had sung in a generally dry and declamatory style, Schorr's voice was pure velvet. His fortes were powerful, steady, and smooth, not shouted. He never obscured the pitch with excess vibrato. His quiet singing was beautifully controlled and always focused; the effect was rich and dignified. The recordings made towards the end of his life do show some signs of age—he sings the higher notes with more care, but the voice is still free of excess wobble, and retains its warmth and color. An even legato and a command of the messa di voce always underlay his singing; while he always sang expressively, he never sacrificed the musical line for the drama.

Schorr's recordings show the same interpretive care and dramatic ability ascribed by critics to his live performances. His Wagnerian recordings demonstrate a constant sensitivity to the smallest nuances, handling the changes of mood and tempo with great expressive effect. In all of his opera recordings, from his evil and energetic Pizarro in *Fidelio* to his warm-hearted Sachs in *Die Meistersinger von Nürnberg,* he portrays a variety of moods. Boris Semeonoff, in his commentary on Schorr's discography, described Schorr as "a noble and impressive Wotan," yet he showed the proper resignation when required. Schorr's recordings of sacred music are simple and reverent. His Lieder recordings are slightly less successful, but while some of them may fail to come to life, he does great justice to the dramatic *Prometheus* of Wolf.

As a teacher, Schorr had very strong ideas about singing and teaching. "Personally, I think non-professional singers are not capable of teaching voice. They aren't able to *show* their students the pros and cons of singing," he said in an interview with *Opera News.* "People who have never done strenuous parts like Otello or Isolde or Wotan aren't able to instruct their students as to vocal economies so that they will be fresh to the very end—no matter how hard the role." He taught careful Wagnerian singing: "Some say that singing Wagner spoils the voice. That is not true. If a voice is fundamentally of the right volume and trained properly, the voice will not be hurt at all by singing Wagner . . . A singer with a sound voice and correct vocal production shouldn't be afraid to sing anything." The secret, he continued, was to learn how "to conserve and preserve the voice." He was a nurturing teacher, attentive to all aspects of a student's development. "The teacher has to develop not only voice but personality of each student."

Although Schorr died several decades ago, his name and reputation live on. He holds a notable place in the history of Wagnerian singing, and his Wotan and Sachs are still held up as examples. His recordings are regularly re-issued and re-released in the newest formats, standing up solidly to more recent recordings of higher electronic fidelity made by younger singers. He still holds interest for music critics, and his performances, both live and recorded, are still discussed in print. He will not soon be forgotten, for, as J.B. Steane says, "no one who carries in his head Schorr's singing . . . in [for example] *Das Rheingold,* is likely to hear another performer without some yearning to get back to the gramophone and listen again to Friedrich Schorr."

—Robin Armstrong

SCHREIER, Peter Max.

Tenor. Born 29 July 1935, in Meissen, Germany. Sang in the Dresden Kreuzchor; studied with Polster in Leipzig from 1954-56, and with Winkler at the Dresden Musikhochschule, 1956-59; as a child, he sang as one of the three boys in Mozart's *Die Zauberflöte* at Dresden's Semper Opera House, 1944; debut as the First Prisoner in Beethoven's *Fidelio,* Dresden State Opera, 1959; joined the Dresden State Opera, 1961; joined the Berlin State Opera, 1963; Metropolitan Opera debut as Tamino in *Die Zauberflöte,* 1967; began conducting in 1970.

Publications

By SCHREIER: books–

Aus meiner Sicht: Gedanken und Erinnerungen. Vienna, 1983.

About SCHREIER: books–

Schmiedel, G. *Peter Schreier: Für Sie porträtiert.* Leipzig, 1976.
Schmiedel, G. *Peter Schreier: eine Bildbiographie.* Berlin, 1979.

articles–

Blyth, A. "A singing maestro." *Gramophone* 65 (1987): 65.
Kutschera, E. "Musik ist nicht alles!" *Die Buehne* 342 (1987): 16.

* * *

During a long and busy singing career that has spanned the 1960s, 70s and 80s, Peter Schreier has won recognition as one of the world's leading lyric tenors. He has been particularly successful as an interpreter of Mozart's tenor roles, but he has also won applause for his performances in nineteenth-century German opera.

Schreier's portrayals of Mozart's Belmonte, Ottavio, Ferrando and Tamino are among the best in recent times; and his Mozart interpretations have not been limited to young lovers. He has sung the title role of *La clemenza di Tito* (Berlin, 1978); his recording of arias from that opera shows him to be an exciting and sympathetic emperor and makes one wish that he had performed the role more often. In 1987 he took on the role of Idomeneo for the first time. (He had previously sung Arbace and Idamante). In singing this role only late in his career Schreier followed in the footsteps of the first Idomeneo, the tenor Anton Raaff, who created the role at the end of his career, when he was sixty-six years old.

Schreier's voice is distinctive, lyrical yet virile, with a touch of baritone quality to it. His enunciation is admirably clear and vivid. He is at his best in gentle, lyrical passages. High notes and loud passages sometimes strain his voice. For example, in his recorded portrayal of Tamino (under Sawallisch), the "Portrait aria" is on the whole elegant and expressive, but at the word "Götterbild" Schreier shouts out the A flat harshly. Much the same criticism can be leveled at his portrayal of the hero Gomatz in Mozart's rarely performed Singspiel *Zaide* (recorded under Bernhard Klee). When Schreier relaxes and sings lyrically his voice is remarkably beautiful, but when he sings loudly an unpleasant, harsh tone enters his voice (as, for example, in the aria "Rase, Schicksal").

Schreier is a master of recitative, especially in German. One can hear this in the long orchestrally accompanied recitative in act I of *Die Zauberflöte* (again as recorded under Sawallisch), where he brings the text to life with his vivid and emphatic delivery. Characteristically for Schreier, this vividness comes, to some extent, at the expense of pure beauty of tone. But how sweetly and movingly he projects the line "Man opferte vielleicht sie schon?" as he expresses his fear for Pamina's life.

Schreier has shown little interest in nineteenth-century Italian opera, preferring opera in German. His recorded performance of Max (*Der Freischütz*) shows that his voice is not entirely suitable to the interpretation of Romantic heroes; the strain that is heard only rarely in his portrayals of Mozart's heroes is much more obvious here. But his performances of lesser and lighter roles in German Romantic opera, like David (*Die Meistersinger*), have been praised for their strong acting as well as their fine singing. (Schreier's David can be heard in a recording of *Die Meistersinger* under Karajan). In a rare revival of Strauss's *Die ägyptische Helena* (Vienna 1971), Schreier won applause for his portrayal of Da-ud. Among his other nineteenth-century roles are Baroncelli in *Rienzi* (a fine portrayal recorded under Hollreiser), Fenton in Nicolai's *Die lustigen Weiber von Windsor* and Lensky in *Eugene Onegin* (a German version presented in Vienna in 1974).

As Schreier's vocal power declined in recent years, he has directed much of his musical energy to operatic conducting; in this new phase of his career he seems to have made an auspicious start.

—John A. Rice

SCHREKER, Franz.

Composer. Born 23 March 1878, in Monaco. Died Berlin, 21 March 1934. Studied violin with Rosé and theory with Robert Fuchs in Vienna; organized and conducted the Vienna Philharmonic Chorus, 1908; professor of composition at the Akademie für Musik; director of the Hochschule für Musik in Berlin, 1920-32; professor for an advanced class at the Prussian Academy of Arts, 1932; lost his post with the Prussian Academy due to the rise of the Nazis, 1933. Schreker's pupils included Ernst Krenek, Karol Rathaus, and Alois Hába.

Operas

Publisher: Universal.

Flammen, D. Leen, c. 1900, concert performance Vienna, Bösendorfersaal, 24 April 1902.
Der ferne Klang, Schreker, c. 1901-10, Frankfurt am Main, 18 August 1912.
Das Spielwerk und die Prinzessin, Schreker, 1909-12, Frankfurt am Main and Vienna, Hofoper, 15 March 1913; revised as *Das Spielwerk*, 1916, Munich, National, 30 October 1920.
Die Gezeichneten, Schreker, 1913-15, Frankfurt am Main, 25 April 1918.
Der Schatzgräber, Schreker, 1915-18, Frankfurt am Main, 21 January 1920.
Irrelohe, Schreker, 1919-23, Cologne, 27 March 1924.
Der singende Teufel, Schreker, 1924-28, Berlin, Staatsoper, 10 December 1928.
Christophorus, oder Die Vision einer Oper, Schreker, 1924-27, intended for Freiburg, 1933 [cancelled by the Nazis]: first performance Freiburg, 1 October 1978.

Der Schmied von Gent, Schreker (after Charles de Coster), 1929-32, Berlin, Deutsches Opernhaus, 29 October 1932.

Other works: orchestral works, vocal works, songs, instrumental music, piano pieces.

Publications

About SCHREKER: books–

Bekker, P. *Franz Schreker: Studie zur Kritik der modernen Oper*. Berlin, 1919; 1983.
Musikblätter des Anbruch 2/no. 1-2 (1920) [special Schreker issue].
Hoffmann, R.S. *Franz Schreker*. Leipzig and Vienna, 1921.
Kapp, J. *Franz Schreker: der Mann und sein Werk*. Munich, 1921.
Musikblätter des Anbruch 6/no. 2 (1924) [special Schreker issue].
Musikblätter des Anbruch 10 (1928): 81.
Schreker-Heft. Berlin, 1959.
Neuwirth, G. *Franz Schreker*. Vienna, 1959.
Bures-Schreker, H. *El caso Schreker*. Buenos Aires, 1969; revised and in German translation with contributions by H.H. Stuckenschmidt and W. Oehlmann as *Franz Schreker*, 1970.
Neuwirth, G. *Die Harmonik in der Oper 'Der ferne Klang' von Franz Schreker*. Regensburg, 1972.
Heller, F.C. ed. *Arnold Schönberg-Franz Schreker: Briefwechsel*. Tutzing, 1974.
Kolleritsch, O. ed. *Franz Schreker am Beginn der neuen Musik*. Graz, 1978.
Budde, Elmar, and Rudolf Stephan, eds. *Franz Schreker Symposium*. Berlin, 1980.
Brzoska, Matthias. *Franz Schrekers Oper "Der Schatzgräber."* Stuttgart, 1988.

articles–

Chadwick, N. "Franz Schreker's Orchestral Style and its Influence on Alban Berg." *Music Review* 35 (1974): 29.
Döhring, S. "Franz Schreker und die grosse musiktheatralische Szene." *Die Musikforschung* 27 (1974): 175.
Blackburn, Robert. "Franz Schreker, 1878-1934." *Musical Times* (1978): 224.
Molkow, Wolfgang. "Untergang der Transzendenz. Franz Schrekers Oper *Die Gezeichneten*." *Melos/Neue Zeitschrift für Musik* 4 (1978): 304.
Franklin, Peter R. "Style, Structure and Taste: Three Aspects of the Problem of Franz Schreker." *Proceedings of the Royal Musical Association* 109 (1982-83): 134.
Roberge, Marc-André. "Franz Schreker (1878-1934): de la gloire à la renaissance en passant par l'oubli." *Sonances* 2 (1983): 2.
Wickes, Lewis. "A Jugendstil Consideration of the Opening and Closing Sections of the Vorspiel to Franz Schreker's Opera *Die Gezeichneten*." *Miscellanea musicologica* [Australia] 13 (1984): 203.
Dahlhaus, Carl. "Schreker and Modernism: On the Dramaturgy of *Der ferne Klang*." In *Schoenberg and the New Music*. Cambridge, 1987; original German, 1978, as "Schreker un die Moderne: zur Dramaturgie des *Fernen Klangs*," in *Franz Schreker am Beginn der neuen Musik*, O. Kolleritsch, ed., 9. Graz, 1978.

Franklin, Peter R. "Distant sounds—Fallen music: *Der ferne Klang* as 'woman's opera'?" *Cambridge Opera Journal* 3 (1991): 159.

* * *

By the early 1920s, Franz Schreker had become one of the most popular of the "modern" operatic composers active in Germany, his style rooted in the elaborate and luxuriant manner of pre-1914 late romanticism. His efforts to come to terms with new artistic manners, while adhering to subject matter compiled from symbolist, expressionist and veristic sources, nevertheless failed to convince either the radical entrepreneurs of "new music" or the fascist opponents of so-called "decadent" modernism (particularly as practised by part-Jewish composers). Schreker's reputation, career and personal health suffered rapidly and irrevocably. His fate was in many ways comparable to that of his Viennese compatriot Alexander Zemlinsky, but Schreker failed to arrange emigration to the United States after 1933. He died in Berlin, following a stroke, not long after completing an ambitious orchestral overture to a projected opera (*Memnon*) which, like all his operas after the youthful *Flammen,* would have been to his own libretto.

Schreker's control over all aspects of his stage works fueled the adverse criticism of those who admired his exotically-colored musical language but remained scornful of his supposedly "penny-dreadful" libretti. His most enthusiastic support came from the critic Paul Bekker, who hailed Schreker,

Franz Schreker, c. 1920

in a short 1919 study, as a stage-composer who, like Wagner, wrote precisely the libretti that his essentially *musical* inspiration required. This resulted, Bekker felt, in operas of greater imaginative freedom and depth than those of many of his contemporaries.

Schreker's first staged opera, *Der ferne Klang,* achieved a celebrated success in 1912 and remains by any standards a remarkable work. The influence of *Der ferne Klang* on his contemporaries was considerable (they included Berg, deviser of its first piano-score). Combining elements of the romantic *Künstlerroman* with those of expressionistic realism, its underlying orchestral discourse was innovative in the complexity of its expressive modeling of its protagonists' emotional experience. Schreker's next opera, *Das Spielwerk und die Prinzessin* (revised as the one-act "Mysterium," *Das Spielwerk*) went on to problematize its own lush, post-Wagnerian language, which it symbolized in the mysterious music-machine of Meister Florian, capable equally of elevating listeners or exciting them to Dionysian excess. This latter ability, ensured by malicious sabotage in the machine's construction, is employed by the sexually voracious Princess. She is escorted safely back into her fairy tale castle only by a simple lad whose innocent flute playing triggers the Spielwerk, in the opera's closing scene, just as an angry mob prepares to set fire to it. The finale is an extraordinary choral and orchestral study in magical enchantment mixed with death-obsessed fatality. It inspired composers amongst Schreker's contemporaries, like Karol Szymanowski, but otherwise confused both audience and critics.

The two large-scale operas that followed, *Die Gezeichneten* and *Der Schatzgräber,* nevertheless achieved wide critical and public success around the time of Schreker's 1920 removal from Vienna, where he had occupied the post at the Academy originally held by Fuchs (offered to both Richard Strauss and Sibelius before Schreker accepted it). The remarkable overture to *Die Gezeichneten,* with its iridescent textures and polytonal harmonic effects, rapidly establishes the atmosphere of its decadent Renaissance subject matter, the text having been inspired initially by a libretto request from Zemlinsky. Art once more features symbolically as the socially dangerous sublimation of the passions of its central character, the crippled young nobleman Alviano Salvago. As in *Der Schatzgräber,* which returns to a mediaeval fairy-tale setting, Schreker's individual treatment of such standard dramatic *topoi* as the hunch-backed hero and the decadent *femme fatale* is matched by a powerful control of choral crowd-scenes and an ultimately dominant orchestral underlay of great coloristic brilliance and leitmotivic richness.

The squandering of such technical and coloristic resources on the apparently overwrought romantic transformation drama *Irrelohe* led to comprehensive critical denunciation in 1924 (although the work has great musical beauty). The posthumous *Christophorus,* dedicated to Schoenberg (with whom Schreker discussed it at length), *Der singende Teufel* and *Der Schmied von Gent* all bear the marks of a thoroughgoing rethinking by Schreker of his earlier style. *Christophorus* is part spoken opera-within-an-opera about the nature of the medium. *Der singende Teufel* dramatizes a music-centered power struggle between pagan and Christian world views in a newly chastened musical language (indicating awareness of Hindemith and others). *Der Schmied von Gent* is a comic pantomime opera after Charles de Coster on the subject of heaven, hell and individual freedom of conscience.

European revivals of Schreker's works, particularly *Der ferne Klang,* have slowly begun to re-establish his place as one of the most richly problematic and attractive Austro-German opera composers of the first half of the twentieth century. His works open up to the fullest extent the late-romantic expressive and imaginative world, often associated with Viennese "Jugendstil" and the *fin de siècle*, which Zemlinsky and the younger Strauss and Schoenberg had begun to explore before the First World War.

—Peter Franklin

SCHRÖDER-DEVRIENT, Wilhelmine.

Soprano. Born 6 December 1804, in Hamburg. Died 26 January 1860, in Coburg. Married: 1) Karl Devrient, four children (divorced, 1828); 2) Van Döring (divorced before 1850); 3) Baron von Bock in 1850. Studied with her father Friedrich Schröder and her mother Antoinette Sophie Bürger in Hamburg; studied with Mozatti in Vienna; debut as Pamina in Mozart's *Die Zauberflöte*, Vienna, 1821; sang in the Dresden Court Opera, 1823-47; toured Europe in concert and opera until 1856.

Publications

About SCHRÖDER-DEVRIENT: books–

Chorley, H. *Thirty Years' Musical Recollections.* London, 1862.
Glümer, C. von. *Erinnerungen an Wilhelmine Schröder-Devrient.* Leipzig, 1862.
Wolzogen, W. von. *Wilhelmine Schröder-Devrient.* Leipzig, 1863.
Hagemann, C. *Wilhelmine Schröder-Devrient Berlin.* 1904.
Bab, J. *Die Devrients.* Berlin, 1932.

articles–

Rellstab, L. "Wilhelmine Schröder-Devrient." *Gesammelte Schriften* (1844): 9.
Wagner, R. "Über Schauspieler und Sänger." *Gesammelte Schriften* (1873): 9.
Bonacci, G. "Guglielmina Schröder-Devrient e Gasparo Spontini." *Nuova antologia* 106 (1903): 306.

*   *   *

Although generally known as a dramatic soprano, Wilhelmine Schröder-Devrient was trained by her mother as an actress until her seventeenth year, which may account for her remarkable and instantaneous success as Leonore in Beethoven's *Fidelio*. Beethoven, who was deaf by 1822, took such note of her acting that he realized her power as an interpreter of such roles, and promised to write an opera for her. Wagner maintained that her mastery of mime taught him all he ever knew about this aspect of the singer's art, and, although Clara Novello, on hearing her in Weigl's *Schweizerfamilie*, found her "distressingly German" (Dresden, 1838), it is undoubtedly true that dramatic roles remained her strong point. This, however, was by no means to the exclusion of her work in comic opera, widely admired and commented upon, for she enjoyed in her younger days an enviable breadth of expression and sympathy. Her main problem was that, although a professional singer, she was not instinctively musical, with the result that she often found it difficult to learn new roles.

In 1822 Schröder-Devrient sang Agathe in *Der Freischütz* under Weber's direction, receiving his whole-hearted approval. Goethe also sang her praises and she was widely admired as an exponent of Italian as well as German opera, notably in Mozart, Bellini, Donizetti and Rossini. Her early successes took place in Vienna, Berlin, Dresden and Paris, while later on she sang frequently in London. Her performances at Drury Lane, however, proved financially fruitless due to the bankrupt director and poetaster Alfred Bunn.

A clue to the strength of her portrayals seems to lie in her private life, which was stressful and unsettled. She was thrice married and subsequently became involved in various love affairs. The publisher Prinz even went so far as to have a quasi-pornographic book of purported memoirs issued (Altona, 1861) but this contains wild exaggerations. There is no doubt, however, about her passionate feelings, which she used creatively in her interpretation of major roles.

The actress Karoline Bauer tells of an appearance of Schröder-Devrient as Leonore in Budapest, when she rushed off the stage and collapsed in her dressing-room. While her admirers praised her performance, she seized upon one of

Wilhelmine Schröder-Devrient as Leonore in *Fidelio*

them and upbraided him with an accusation concerning his criticism of her private life. She invited him to send out onto the stage one of the soberly sedate wives whose moral example he had exalted, and have her project the role as she did. "When I have to represent a passion I must possess one, for I can only be carried away by what I feel with great intensity."

Towards the close of her life those very qualities that had made her famous became tedious and over-emphasized—her acting and her declamation were both adversely criticized by Berlioz. She also developed the habit of dragging out the tempo, which eventually contributed to the breakdown of her vocal powers.

Her first marriage (to Karl Devrient) lasted five years, during which time they had four children. Her second, to a Saxon officer, van Döring, was of brief duration and disastrous consequences, for he robbed her of her earnings. Her third husband, Baron von Bock, succeeded in getting her out of political trouble with the Saxon authorities, but she ceased to sing in 1856 and died four years later.

Her main contribution to operatic singing was a powerful, accurate and incisive voice, a readiness to feel and express passion, an ability to reflect comedy through character, and slowly digest great roles which she flung with abandon into the midst of the operatic public of her day.

—Denis Stevens

SCHUBERT, Franz (Peter).

Composer. Born 31 January 1797, in Himmelpfortgrund, Vienna. Died 19 November 1828, in Vienna. Studied violin with his father, piano with his brother, and piano, organ, singing, and theory with Holzer, the choirmaster at Himmelpfortgrund; sang in the Vienna Imperial Court chapel choir, 1808; studied music with the Imperial Court organist Wenzel Ruzicka and opera with the court composer Antonio Salieri at the Stadtkonvikt, a school for singers; attended a training college for teachers in Vienna, and taught in his father's school, 1814-17; lodged with the poet Schober, 1817; music tutor to the family of Count Esterházy, Zélesz, Hungary, 1818 and 1824; Schubert's circle included the famous baritone Johann Michael Vogl, the poets Johann Mayrhofer and Franz von Schober, and the painter Moritz von Schwind.

Operas

Editions:

F. Schuberts Werke: kritisch durchgesehene Gesamtausgabe. Edited by E. Mandyczewski, J. Brahms et al. Leipzig, 1884-97; 1964-69.
F. Schubert: Neue Ausgabe sämtlicher Werke. Edited by W. Dürr, A. Feil, C. Landon et al. Kassel, 1964-.

Der Spiegelritter (Singspiel), A. von Kotzebue, 1811-12 [unfinished], Swiss Radio, 11 December 1949.
Des Teufels Lustschloss, A. von Kotzubue, 1813-15, Vienna, Musikvereinsaal, 12 December 1879.

Adrast, J. Mayrhofer, 1817?-19 [unfinished], Vienna, Redoutensaal, 13 December 1868.
Der vierjährige Posten (Singspiel), T. Körner, 1815, Dresden, 23 September 1896.
Fernando (Singspiel), A. Stadler, 1815, Vienna, 13 April 1907.
Claudine von Villa Bella (Singspiel), Goethe, 1815 [unfinished], Vienna, Gemeindehaus Wieden, 26 April 1913.
Die Freunde von Salamanka (Singspiel), J. Mayrhofer, 1815, Halle, 6 May 1928.
Die Bürgschaft, 1816 [unfinished], Vienna, 7 March 1908.
Die Zauberharfe (melodrama), G. von Hofmann, 1820, Vienna, Theater an der Wien, 19 August 1820.
Die Zwillingsbrüder (Singspiel), G. von Hofmann, 1819, Vienna, Kärntnertor, 14 June 1820.
Sakuntala, J.P. Neumann (after Kalidasa), 1820, Vienna, 12 June 1971.
Alfonso und Estrella, F. von Schober, 1821-22, Weimar, 24 June 1854.
Die Verschworenen (Der häusliche Krieg) [Singspiel], F. Castelli (after Aristophanies, *Lysistrata*), 1823, Vienna, Musikvereinsaal, 1 March 1861.
Rüdiger, I. von Mosel?, 1823 [unfinished], Vienna, Redoutensaal, 5 January 1868.
Fierabras, J. Kupelwieser, 1823, Karlsruhe, 9 February 1897.
Der Graf von Gleichen, E. von Bauernfeld, 1827 [unfinished].
Der Minnesänger (Singspiel) [unfinished; lost].

Other works: orchestral works, sacred and secular vocal works, Lieder (over 600), chamber music, piano pieces.

Publications/Writings

About SCHUBERT: books–

Deutsch, Otto Erich. *Franz Schubert: die Dokumente seines Lebens und Schaffens.* 2 vols. Munich, 1913-14; English translation by Eric Blom as *Schubert: a Documentary Biography,* London, 1946.
Gador, Agnes, ed. and trans. *Franz Schubert levelei.* Budapest, 1978.

articles–

Liszt, F. "Alfonso und Estrella." In *Gesammelte Schriften,* v. 3/1, translated by L. Ramann, 68. Leipzig, 1881.
Brown, M.J.E. "Schubert's Two Major Operas." *Music Review* 20 (1959): 104.
Racek, F. "Franz Schuberts Singspiel 'Der häusliche Krieg' und seine jetzt aufgerfundene Ouvertüre." *Biblos* 12 (1963): 136.
Brown, M.J.E. "Schubert's *Fierabras.*" *Musical Times* 112 (1971): 338.
Szmolyan, W. "Schubert als Opernkomponist." *Österreichische Musikzeitung* 26 (1971): 282.
Hoorickx, R. van. "Les opéras de Schubert." *Revue belge de musicologie* 28-30 (1974-76): 238.
Arnold, Hans Dieter. "Zur Geschicte von Schuberts Oper *Des Teufels Lustschloss.*" *Musik und Gesellschaft* 28 (1978): 662.
Branscombe, P. "Schubert and his Librettists—1." *Musical Times* 119 (1978): 943.
Dalmonte, R. "Die Bedeutung der Skizzen des *Zauberharfe* D 644 zur Erkenntnis der Schubertschen Schaffensweise." In *Schubert-Kongress Wien 1978. Bericht.,* edited by O. Brusatti, 141. Cracow, 1979.

Kritsch, Cornelia. "Die Texte zu Schuberts theatralischen Auftragswerken." In *Schubert-Kongress Wien 1978. Bericht.*, edited by O. Brusatti, 269. Cracow, 1979.

Ortner, Gerhard E. and Erwin G. "Schuberts Opern: verlegt und weggelegt. Anmerkungen zu *Alfonso und Estrella.*" *Morgen* 12 (1980): 129.

Hoorickx, Reinhard van. "An Unknown Schubert Letter" [*Alfonso und Estrella*]. *Musical Times* 122 (1981): 291.

Norman-McKay, E. "Schubert as a Composer of Operas." In *Schubert Studies: Problems of Style and Chronology*, edited by Eva Badura-Skoda and Peter Branscombe, 85. Cambridge, 1982.

Dalmonte, R. "*Die Zauberharfe* in der Zauberwelt." In *Franz Schubert: Jahre der Krise, 1818-1823. Arnold Feil zum 60. Geburtstag*, edited by W. Aderhold et al., 72. Kassel, 1985.

Dieckmann, Friedrich. "*Fidelios* Erben: *Fierabras* und das biedermeierliche Bewusstein." *Oper heute* 8 (1985): 77.

Thomas, Werner. "Bild und Aktion in *Fierabras*: ein Beitrag zu Schuberts musikalischer Dramaturgie." In *Franz Schubert: Jahre der Krise, 1818-1823. Arnold Feil zum 60. Geburtstag*, edited by W. Aderhold et al., 85. Kassel, 1985.

unpublished–

Krott, R. "Die Singspiele Schuberts." Ph.D. dissertation, University of Vienna, 1921.

Norman-McKay, E. "The Stage-Works of Schubert, Considered in the Framework of Austrian Biedermeier Society." Ph.D. dissertation, Oxford University, 1962-63.

Citron, M.J. "Schubert's Seven Complete Operas: a Musico-Dramatic Study." Ph.D. dissertation, University of North Carolina, 1971.

Cunningham, G.R. "Franz Schubert als Theaterkomponist." Ph.D. dissertation, University of Freiburg, 1974.

Wischusen, Mary Ann. "The Stage Works of Franz Schubert: Background and Stylistic Influences." Ph.D. dissertation, Rutgers University, 1983.

*   *   *

From 1812, when he composed the Singspiel *Der Spiegelritter* at the age of fifteen, until the crushing disappointment of the cancellation of *Fierabras* in 1823 after he had rushed to complete it, Schubert devoted much of his time to the musical stage, and was rewarded with practically no success or recognition at all. His teacher Salieri had advised him that a composer was most likely to make his name with a successful stage work; and his friends included many who hoped to establish a German operatic style to match the French and Italian ones. Unfortunately, there was so little to build on, so little tradition either to use or to resist, that most of these efforts failed due to their creators' lack of experience. Even Weber failed with *Euryanthe*, his most ambitious opera, which eschewed spoken dialogue. Not until Wagner would there be any successes outside of Singspiel; and even his success was rarely emulated. Schubert's Vienna was not receptive to innovation and experiment; in 1819, for instance, there were about forty performances each, all in German, of works by Mozart, Boieldieu, and Rossini. Lesser imitators of Rossini were also very popular in the years that followed; and there was little public sympathy for the artists' yearning for a national style of musical theatre.

Schubert's first completed stage work, *Des Teufels Lustschloss* (1813-15), was based on a popular libretto from which several versions had been performed in Vienna. Schubert had no concrete hopes for performance; after submitting it to Salieri (who had encouraged Schubert to write operas to advance his career), he revised it thoroughly. In 1815, Schubert set three more pre-existing Singspiel libretti and part of a fourth; none was considered for performance. Of these, *Die Freunde von Salamanka* has attracted the most attention; it contains some of Schubert's best dramatic music, including some examples of his attention to lyrical detail. After abandoning *Die Bürgschaft* (1816) with two of its three acts complete, he wrote no more for the stage for almost three years. (The substantial fragment of *Adrast* may date from this interval.)

In 1819, his career as a composer of Lieder well-established, Schubert set a one-act Singspiel, *Die Zwillingsbrüder*. Written to accommodate Johann Michael Vogl, Schubert's great partner in Lied performance, in a double lead role, the work was not a success. Soon thereafter, he composed choruses and melodramas for a three-act play, *Die Zauberharfe*. (Like most other composers for the German stage in his time, Schubert used the melodrama for dramatic effect: free-form music, often very chromatic, underlining highly dramatic spoken passages in a play or Singspiel.) Schubert later salvaged some of the material from this piece (which was performed shortly after *Die Zwillingsbrüder*) for the overture and incidental music to another play, *Rosamunde*, in 1823. These were the only three stage works of Schubert performed in his lifetime.

Determined to compose a successful grand opera that would gain him renown and provide a model for German musical theater to come, Schubert and his friend Franz von Schober retired to the country in the autumn of 1821 to collaborate on what became *Alfonso und Estrella*. This was Schubert's favorite among his stage works, no doubt because of its attractive music and innovative style. It is through-composed, with sung recitative instead of dialogue, several years before Weber's similar attempt in *Euryanthe*. But Schober's drama is hopelessly inept, and Schubert neither saw the deficiencies nor wrote music that might have minimized them; indeed, many of the set pieces, however beautiful, actually dissipate any dramatic tension.

First performed in 1861, *Die Verschworenen* (1823) entered the repertory of the German theatre—the only Schubert opera to do so—and remained there until the 1930s. In this one-act version of the Lysistrata story, Schubert endowed a well-crafted libretto with appropriate, witty music of considerable charm. Immediately thereafter, he began work on what was to be his final opera, *Fierabras* (q.v.). After hopes for its performance were suddenly dashed in the autumn of 1823, Schubert, having rushed the completion of the work, withdrew from the musical stage and took up the series of instrumental works that stand beside the Lieder as his monument. In 1827 he sketched two numbers for *Der Graf von Gleichen*, but soon gave up on that as well.

One is easily overwhelmed by reasons for the failure of Schubert's operas, both in his time and after. The sad state of German opera and Viennese theater have already been described. The young inexperienced Schubert had no connections or influence with the theaters of Vienna, nor do we have evidence that Schubert concerned himself greatly with the workings of the theatre, or with issues of drama and stagecraft, or that he attended rehearsals.

Schubert's music for the stage rarely heightened the drama, even when the generally weak libretti he had to work with were not hindering him; although he (like all the progressive critics of his time) was dissatisfied with number opera, he composed set-pieces perfectly rounded in form and unable to advance whatever tension was in the situation. Nor was Schubert a good judge of dramatic suitability or practicality: despite the closest possible collaboration with the librettist, *Alfonso und Estrella* is a monstrosity. Even *Fierabras,* the one major work that might have had a career in the repertory once Schubert's works were revived, is spoiled by its perfunctory ending and suffers from one-sided characters and too much theatrically static music.

Many have noted the irony: the inventor of the Romantic art song not only failed at dramatic music, but rarely produced lyrical moments in his stage works to rival those of his hundreds of exemplary songs. But the best-known songs are usually static, self-contained character studies, moments or moods (*Gretchen am Spinnrade, Mignon*), or lyrical meditations (*An die Musik*), or narrations, complete dramas told in hindsight (*Erlkönig, Die Forelle*). Even *Die Winterreise,* whose cumulative characterization of its narrator produces a unique dramatic effect, presents the changing personality one phase at a time; each song ends firmly, making a poetic point with its close. Staged drama could not sustain such emphasis and dependency on closure, and Schubert was either unwilling or did not recognize the need to develop forms that could withstand interruption for the sake of drama, prepare and build to climactic events, and support the action on the stage with first-rate music. That he did not, however, in no way diminishes his greatness, especially since no German composer between Mozart and Wagner created a satisfactory musical-dramatic style in more than a few works; and the best moments in Schubert's operas, from the earliest ones to *Fierabras,* leave us to speculate that, given a normal lifespan, he would have succeeded.

—Roger L. Lustig

SCHUCH, Ernst von.

Conductor. Born 23 November 1846, in Graz. Died 10 May 1914, in Kötzschenbroda, near Dresden. Married: Clementine Procházka, soprano, 1875 (one daughter, the soprano Liesel von Schuch). Studied law, and music with Eduard Stolz in Graz; director of the Musikverein in Graz; completed his law degree in Vienna, and studied music with Otto Dessoff; played professionally as a violinist; music director of Lobe's theater in Breslau, 1867-68; conducted in Würzburg, 1868-70, in Graz, 1870-71, and Basel, 1871; conductor of Pollini's Italian Opera in Dresden, 1872; Royal Music Director at the Court Opera, 1872; Royal Kapellmeister at Dresden with Julius Rietz, 1873-79, with Franz Wüllner, 1879-82, and then sole Kapellmeister, 1882; conductor of the concerts of the Königliche Kapelle, 1877; Generalmusikdirektor of Dresden, 1889; made a nobleman by Emperor Franz Joseph of Austria-Hungary, 1897; toured the United States in 1900. Schuch conducted the premieres of Richard Strauss's *Feuersnot,* 1901, *Salome,* 1905, *Elektra,* 1909, and *Der Rosenkavalier,* 1911.

Publications

About SCHUCH: books–

Brescius, H. von. *Die königliche musikalische Kapelle von Reissiger bis Schuch (1826-1898): Festschrift zu Feier des 350-jährigen Kapelljubiläums.* Dresden, 1898.
Sakolowski, P. *Ernst von Schuch.* Leipzig, 1901.
Schuch, F. von. *Richard Strauss, Ernst von Schuch und Dresdens Oper.* Dresden, 1952; 2nd ed., 1953.

articles–

Schmiedel, G. "Ernst von Schuch and the Dresden Opera." *Opera* January (1960).

Ernst von Schuch, like Franz Schalk in Vienna a little later, suffered somewhat by being exclusively associated with one city throughout his entire career. Though Richter spent years in Vienna and Nikisch held appointments in Leipzig and Berlin, both men ensured their wider reputations by traveling and guest-conducting in other parts of Europe.

Schuch made his home in Dresden, yet managed to secure for himself a lasting memory as a gifted conductor, brilliant administrator and the man who gave the premieres of several operas by Richard Strauss, (*Feuersnot, Salome, Elektra* and *Der Rosenkavalier*). Of the first performance of *Elektra,* Strauss himself wrote in his *Recollections and Reminiscences:* "Once again he [Schuch] knew the score as well as if it were the twentieth performance. Schuch was famous for his elegant performances of Italian and French operas and as a discreet accompanist. He had perfected this praiseworthy art to such a pitch that under him even Wagner's scores sounded a little undistinguished. One hardly ever heard a real fortissimo from the brass of this exemplary Dresden orchestra. . . . I was stupid enough to find fault during rehearsals with Schuch . . . I insisted on hearing secondary thematic parts so much that he played with such fury during the dress rehearsal that I was forced to confess 'the orchestra was really a little strong today.' 'You see,' said Schuch triumphantly, and the first performance had perfect balance." Strauss went on to find fault with Schuch's speciality of making cuts in operas; "He never, I believe, conducted an opera without cuts and was particularly proud when he could leave out a whole act of a modern opera." In 1948 Strauss referred to "the ingenious Schuch's tireless magic wand" when congratulating the Dresden orchestra on its 400th anniversary.

Schuch was not only a devotee of Strauss. He introduced the *Ring* and *Tristan* to Dresden after Wagner had regained his respectability in the post-1848 revolutionary years in the city, and on Palm Sunday 1884 he introduced fragments of *Parsifal,* a full performance of which had to wait until 1913, when Wagner's ban on performances outside Bayreuth expired. Schuch was equally at home interpreting the Italian repertoire, giving the German premiere of *Cavalleria rusticana* in 1891, and introducing the works of Puccini (*Tosca, La bohème* and *Madama Butterfly*), who described him as "maître incomparable," and Verdi, whose *Falstaff* received a hearing only a year after its first performance in Milan.

For more than four decades (1872-1914) Schuch built up the opera ensemble and orchestra (the Dresdener Staatskapelle) to an international reputation which persists to this day, and during his tenure gave fifty-one premieres and 117 first performances in the city. His personality was a combination of temperament and elegance which produced detailed and refined performances motivated by an inspired musical mind. He was a tireless rehearser intent on painstakingly detailed accuracy, but his performances were relaxed affairs founded on this secure preparation. His singers (he was married to one, Clementine Schuch-Procházka) always felt able to improvise in the knowledge that he would be able to follow them. His outward style belied his inner feel for the music he performed; sparing of movement and shunning extrovert exhibitionism, he appeared to give only the beat, the left hand used only intermittently and primarily to subdue loud dynamics, but his eyes and ears were everywhere.

—Christopher Fifield

SCHUMANN, Elisabeth.

Soprano. Born 13 June 1885, in Merseburg, Germany. Died 23 April 1952, in New York. Studied with Natalie Hänisch in Dresden, Marie Dietrich in Berlin, and Alma Schadow in Hamburg; debut as the Shepherd in *Tannhäuser,* Hamburg Opera, 1909; remained on roster there until 1919; Metropolitan Opera debut as Sophie in *Der Rosenkavalier,* 1914; principal member of the Vienna State Opera, 1919-38; concert tour of the U.S. with Richard Strauss, 1921; lived in the U.S. after 1938; taught at the Curtis Institute of Music in Philadelphia; became naturalized citizen, 1944.

Publications

By SCHUMANN: books–

German Song. London, 1948.

About SCHUMANN: books–

Puritz, E. *The Teaching of Elisabeth Schumann.* London, 1956.

articles–

Owen, H.G. and J. Cone. "Elisabeth Schumann." *Record Collector* 7 (1952): 221.
Mathis, A. "Elisabeth Schumann." *Opera* 24 (1973): 672, 783, 968.
Shawe-Taylor, D. "Lotte Lehmann and Elisabeth Schumann: A Centenary Tribute." *Musical Times* October (1988).

*   *   *

Elisabeth Schumann was born in Merseburg, Thuringia in 1885 (not 1888 as she claimed) and was descended from the German soprano Henriette Sontag, who had created Euryanthe for Weber in 1823 and had also been the first solo soprano in Beethoven's Mass in D and in his Ninth Symphony. Sontag's voice was described as being "clear, bright, and used with exquisite taste"—these words describe Schumann's voice equally well. Her personality was full of fun and mischief, but she was astute enough to preserve the voice's youthful qualities until the late 1940s.

Schumann's parents always intended that she should become a singer and provided her with sound training in Dresden, whence she went to Marie Dietrich (a Pauline Viardot pupil) in Berlin. As soon as she finished her studies, she was given a contract by the Hamburg State Theater where she made her debut as the Shepherd Boy in *Tannhäuser.* The audience was entranced by the sweetness and brilliance of her tone and by the purity of sound.

In the following season, Schumann was the Sophie in Hamburg's first production of *Der Rosenkavalier,* a role with which later gramophone records have always associated her. No other Sophie has produced such crystal notes, especially in the act II Presentation Scene. This is the character of Sophie personified, all sweetness and virginity. In Hamburg she also sang a number of the same roles as Lotte Lehmann: Eva in *Die Meistersinger,* Mimi and one performance of Octavian as the result of a romantic scandal in which she was involved with the conductor, Otto Klemperer.

Schumann sang for one season at the Metropolitan Opera in 1914-15 and her debut there was as Sophie. "A clear and high soprano of pure quality and agreeable timbre, a voice possessing the bloom of youth," said a critic that night. She

Elisabeth Schumann as Sophie in *Der Rosenkavalier*

also sang Musetta, Gretel and Papagena in New York. Her London debut was again as Sophie, ten years later when, it was said, "for sheer beauty of tone and perfection of technique she towered above the rest of the cast," which included Lotte Lehmann and Richard Mayr.

Despite these positive assessments of Schumann's voice, it has been stated (by Michael Scott) that she suffered from "technical inadequacy," that "the voice was not fully developed and lacked support." Considering her training and immense success in all major opera houses, this view seems difficult to uphold. Of course it was not a large voice and could even be called soubrettish without any intended slur. Her Adele in *Fledermaus* when heard in Paris and admitted reluctantly to Covent Garden by Bruno Walter—both in 1930—was certainly a soubrette role, but how magically she did it!

In 1919 Richard Strauss, who was very partial to Schumann's voice and personality, engaged her for the Vienna Opera, especially to sing Mozart. He also took her to Salzburg for four of the Festivals between 1922-36 where she gave memorable characterizations of Despina, Susanna, Zerlina and Blondchen, and one performance of Marzelline in *Fidelio*. In Vienna, where she remained until 1937, she sang Micaela, Nedda and Norina, together with her usual Mozart roles and Ilia in Strauss's adaptation of *Idomeneo*—and of course Sophie.

When the Anschluss came, Elisabeth Schumann went to the USA, a refugee on account of her Jewish husband, the conductor Karl Alwin. She gave up the stage and devoted the rest of her life to *Lieder* and to teaching. But within this teaching were many operatic roles and she often demonstrated how to sing them, the voice still capable, pure and fresh as ever.

—Alan Jefferson

SCHUMANN, Robert Alexander.

Composer. Born 8 June 1810, in Zwickau. Died 29 July 1856, in Endenich, near Bonn. Married: the reknowned pianist Clara Wieck, 12 September 1840; eight children. Studied piano with J.G. Kuntzsch, organist of the Zwickau Marienkirche; entered Leipzig University as a law student, 1828; studied piano with Friedrich Wieck in Leipzig; in Heidelberg, 1829; in Leipzig, 1830, where he studied composition with Heinrich Dorn; founded the *Neue Zeitschrift für Musik* with J. Knorr, L. Schunke, and Friedrich Wieck, 1834; wrote extensively for that journal during its first decade, under the names Florestan, Eusebius, and Meister Raro; asked by Mendelssohn to join the faculty of the newly founded Conservatory in Leipzig as a teacher of piano, composition, and score reading, 1843; concert tour of Russia with Clara, 1844; lived in Dresden, 1844-1850; conductor of the Liedertafel, 1847; organized the Chorgesang-Verein in Dresden, 1848; town music director in Düsseldorf, 1850; attempted suicide, 27 February 1854; placed in a sanatorium at Endenich at his own request, 4 March 1854, where he spent the rest of his life.

Operas

Edition: *R. Schumann: Werke.* Edited by C. Schumann, J. Brahms et al. Leipzig, 1881-93.

Der Corsar, O. Marbach (after Byron), 1844 [fragment].
Genoveva, R. Reinick (after L. Tieck and C.F. Hebbel, as altered by Schumann), 1847-48, Leipzig, 25 June 1850.

Other works: orchestral works, vocal works, Lieder, chamber music, piano pieces.

Publications

By SCHUMANN: books—

Gesammelte Schriften über Musik und Musiker. Leipzig, 1854; 4th ed., 1891; 1968; 5th ed., 1914; English translation, 1877; new partial English translation, 1947; 1983.
Schumann, Clara, ed. *Jugendbriefe von Robert Schumann.* Leipzig, 1885; 4th ed., 1910; English translation, 1888.
Jansen, F., ed. *Robert Schumanns Briefe: neue Folge.* Leipzig, 1886; 2nd ed., 1904; English translation, 1890.
Tagebücher, vol. 1, (*1827-38*). Leipzig, 1971.
Pis'ma. 2 vols. Compiled, edited, and translated by Daniel Zitomirskij et al. Moscow, 1982.
With Clara Schumann. *Briefe einer Liebe. Robert und Clara Schumann.* Edited by Hanns-Josef Ortheil. Königstein, 1982.
with Clara Schumann. *Briefe und Notizien Robert und Clara Schumanns.* Edited by Siegfried Ross. Bonn, 1978; 2nd ed., 1982.
Häusler, Josef, ed. *Schriften über Musik und Musiker.* Stuttgart, 1982.

articles—

"Aufzeichnung über Mendelssohn." In *Felix Mendelssohn-Bartholdy,* edited by Heinz-Klaus Metzger, 97. Munich, 1980.

About SCHUMANN: books—

Erler, H. *Robert Schumanns Leben: aus seinen Briefen geschildert.* Berlin, 1886-87; 3rd ed., 1927.
Boetticher, Wolfgang, ed. *Briefe und Gedichte aus dem Album Robert und Clara Schumanns.* Leipzig, 1979.
Oliver, Willie-Earl. *Robert Schumanns vergessene Oper "Genoveva".* Freiburg im Breisgau, 1978.

articles—

Hanslick, E. "R. Schumann als Opernkomponist." In *Die moderne Oper,* 256. Berlin, 1875; 1971; 3rd ed., 1911.
Gensel, J. "Robert Schumanns Briefwechsel mit Henriette Voigt." *Die Grenzboten* 51 (1892): 269, 324, 368; enlarged and printed separately, Leipzig, 1892.
Jansen, F. "Briefwechsel zwischen Robert Franz und Robert Schumann." *Die Musik* 8 (1908-09): 280-346.
Abert, H. "R. Schumann's Genoveva." *Zeitschrift der Internationalen Musik-Gesellschaft* 11 (1910): 227.
Shaw, George Bernard. *Music in London 1890-94* Vol. 3, p. 107. London, 1932.
Abraham, G. "The Dramatic Music." In *Schumann: a Symposium,* edited by Gerald Abraham, 260. London, 1952.
Wolff, H. "Schumanns 'Genoveva' und der Manierismus des 19. Jahrhunderts." In *Beiträge zur Geschichte der Oper,* 89. Regensburg, 1969.
Cooper, F. "Operatic and Dramatic Music." In *Robert Schumann: the Man and his Music,* edited by A. Walker, 324. London 1972; 2nd ed., 1976.

Siegel, L. "A Second Look at Schumann's *Genoveva.*" *Music Review* 36 (1975): 17.

Avant-scène opéra January (1985) [*Genoveva* issue].

*   *   *

Robert Schumann composed only one opera, but he contemplated operatic projects at several stages of his career. As early as 1830, he thought of a *Hamlet* opera, but soon realized that he was not ready for such a project. For most of the 1830s, he was not especially sympathetic toward vocal music in general; but by 1838 he was considering E.T.A. Hoffmann's *Doge and Dogeressa* as a subject. After he had established himself around 1840 as a composer of song cycles, his plans became more serious and connected to his nationalistic intentions for German music as a whole; as he wrote to his friend Kossmaly: "Do you know my artist's morning and evening prayer? It is: German opera. There is work to be done there."

At the same time, however, he began to seek alternatives to staged dramas. His writings, and to some extent his activity as performer and conductor, had done much to advance the new institution of the symphonic concert as central to musical life. From 1841, when he began work on the mythological oratorio *Paradise and the Peri,* to 1853, when *Scenes from Goethe's Faust* was completed, Schumann attempted to fuse scenic and narrative ideas with the symphonic ideal, following the lead of Mendelssohn's *The First Walpurgis Night.* None of these works, which use soloists, chorus, and orchestra, is very popular today, though *Paradise and the Peri* and the short *Requiem for Mignon* (based on an episode in Goethe's *Wilhelm Meister*) attract some attention. *Manfred* is a melodrama—that is, it calls for spoken declamation over an instrumental accompaniment.

In 1847-48 Schumann wrote his only opera, *Genoveva.* Like so much German opera of the time, it had its source in a fairy tale; in this case, Ludwig Tieck's 1779 play about a countess who preserves her virtue in the face of treachery, but dies in the end. When Schumann's friend Robert Reinick was already more than half done with an adaptation, the composer encountered a recent play on the same subject by the Romantic realist Friedrich Hebbel, and asked Reinick to include elements of the newer work in the libretto. After Reinick failed at this task, and a meeting between Schumann and Hebbel produced nothing, Schumann wrote his own libretto, based on Hebbel but including some of Tieck's ideas. Unfortunately, his version magnified some of the crudities of Hebbel's drama; at the same time, he removed both Tieck's tragic ending in favor of reunion and rejoicing, and let the villain escape instead of having him killed. The opera was performed in 1850, and was not a success. There have been few revivals or recordings.

Schumann shared Wagner's distaste for number operas punctuated by applause. Like Wagner, he avoided simple recitative; in *Genoveva* this led to a heavy through-composed texture that lacked Wagner's genius for punctuating action with narrative monologues and otherwise varying the pace of the drama. Worst of all, though, he showed little flair for musical characterization; much of the music in the opera could belong to any role.

Schumann not only used motivic reminiscence as Weber, Lortzing, Marschner, and others had done before him, but also employed leitmotives not unlike Wagner's, sometimes using a motive to inform the listener of a dramatic point not explicit in the words or action. Moreover, the integration of the recurring motives into the musical texture was more advanced than anything Wagner had achieved up to that time. Unfortunately, Schumann's motives were not always as characteristic and memorable as Wagner's vivid, painstakingly crafted ones. Some of them appear too often, or in inappropriate locations; this compromises their effectiveness in furthering the drama. (In fact, they went almost entirely unnoticed by critics in Schumann's time.)

In his writings, Schumann revealed himself as less than fully sympathetic to the ways of opera itself. He took an absolutist view toward music; that is, proper compositional technique took precedence over dramatic effectiveness. Writing to Mendelssohn in 1845, Schumann criticized the score of *Tannhäuser* on grounds of technical ineptitude and "pallid, forced" writing, though he recognized Wagner's brilliance, originality, and daring. After seeing the opera, he wrote to Mendelssohn again, amending his view in light of the work's dramatic effect. In later years, Schumann retained this ambivalence: "Many passages of his operas, once heard from the stage, cannot but prove exciting. And if you do not find clear sunlight in them, such as that which radiates from the works of genius, they distill a strange magic which captivates the senses. But, as I said, the music itself (that is, disregarding its stage effect) is poor and frequently amateurish, empty, and distasteful" (letter to van Bruyck, 8 May 1853). On the other hand, he was entirely enthusiastic about Wagner's 1851 essay, *Opera and Drama,* which presented an ideal of music that flowed directly out of its poetry.

Schumann criticized Rossini on different grounds. His music was competent, to be sure—but too easy. Instead of rising to the artistic challenges of composition, Rossini offered little of musical substance, and merely contributed to a culture in which singers, not musical substance, were the focus of the audience's attention.

But the most notorious outburst, in 1837, was reserved for Meyerbeer. Not only were that composer's mixed style and deficient compositional skills at odds with the ideal of German music that Schumann was campaigning for; but the shock, gory spectacle, and approbation for religious war in *Les Huguenots* raised his moral hackles as well.

In all, Schumann did not focus on opera in his published critiques (which he stopped writing in 1844) any more than in his own compositional endeavors. *Genoveva,* with its Germanic theme and symphonic orientation at the expense of dramatic effect, is perhaps best seen as a polemic in musical terms, Schumann's crusade against musical mediocrities, quacks, and infidels, and his attempt to unite opera with his vision of what was best about German music.

—Roger L. Lustig

SCHUMANN-HEINK, Ernestine (Rössler).

Contralto. Born 15 June 1861, in Lieben, near Prague. Died 17 November 1936, in Hollywood. Married: 1) Ernst Heink, 1882 (divorced, 1893), three sons, one daughter; 2) Paul Schumann, 1893 (died), two sons, one daughter; 3) William Rapp, Jr., 1905 (divorced, 1914). Studied with Marietta von Leclair in Graz, then with Karl Krebs, Franz Wüllner and G.B. Lamperti; debut as Azucena in *Il trovatore,* Dresden, 1878; in Dresden 1878-82; in Hamburg 1882-97; performed in a London production of *Der Ring des Nibelungen* under Gustav Mahler, 1892; Bayreuth debut in *Der Ring des Nibelungen,* 1896; Berlin Opera, 1898; at Covent Garden 1897-1900;

American debut as Ortrud in *Lohengrin,* Chicago, 1898; Metropolitan Opera debut as Ortrud, 1899; created the role of Klytemnestra in *Elektra,* Dresden, 1909; also a performer in musical comedy, radio, and films. Naturalized as an American citizen 1908.

Publications

About SCHUMANN-HEINK: books–

Armstrong, William Dawson. *The Romantic World of Music.* New York, c.1922.
Mayfield, John S. *Conversation in 1026.* Austin, 1925.
Lawton, Mary. *Schumann-Heink, the Last of the Titans.* New York, 1928; reprinted with discography, New York, 1977.

articles–

McPherson, James B. "Schumann-Heink." *Record Collector* 17/5-6 (June/August 1967): 99, 154.
Brandt, L.J. "Rubini Records: Voices from the Past." *Fanfare* 4/3 (1981): 46.
Emmons, S. "Voices from the Past." *The NATS Bulletin* 40/4 (1984): 33; 40/5 (1984): 25.

Ernestine Rössler, later known to the world as Ernestine Schumann-Heink, was born in Lieben, on the outskirts of Prague, in what was then Austria. While her mother had been well educated in Italy, her father had to support his family on a soldier's pay. Ernestine was raised around the army barracks wherever her father happened to be stationed, eventually in Graz where she was heard by an ex-singer who offered to give her lessons. At the age of fifteen she made her first public appearance, singing the alto part in the Beethoven Ninth from memory as she could not read music. The soprano, Marie Wilt of the Vienna opera, was so impressed with her little colleague that she arranged an audition in Vienna. Funds had to be borrowed for the trip, but the thin, scrawny girl in a made-over dress and army boots failed to impress. She was advised to go home and become a dressmaker. Ernestine was broken-hearted; fortunately her case was taken up by Amalie Materna who arranged an audition in Dresden, and this time she was successful. Her debut, on 15 October 1878, was as Azucena in *Il trovatore.* She was seventeen. She continued to sing a variety of small parts, from Puck in *Oberon* to Martha in *Faust;* from Merceedes in *Carmen* to the Shepherd in *Tannhäuser.* She also sang in the services at the Dresden Cathedral and had the opportunity to study seriously with Franz Wüllner and other musicians who lived in the city.

In 1882, Ernestine married Ernst Heink, a secretary at the opera. Their marriage was without the consent of the management, which was required by contract, and they were dismissed from the Dresden opera. After several months of bleak despair, Tini Rössler, now Frau Heink, obtained an engagement at the Hamburg Opera. As her biographer James McPherson put it, "during her first four years at Hamburg, Ernestine had nothing but bit parts and babies. To the latter category belonged August, Charlotte and Henry. When a fourth child grew imminent, Ernst Heink fled back to Saxony." In spite of her pleas with the management at Hamburg for larger and more substantial roles (and higher fees) Frau Heink continued to sing small roles, night after night, often giving as many as twenty-two performances in one month. At last, in 1889, the break finally came: Marie Goetze, the principal contralto of the opera, had a fit of temperament and refused at the last minute to go on as Carmen. In desperation, the management turned to Heink. Could she sing the opera? "I'll sing it if I die on the stage" was her answer, and sing it she did, in spite of no rehearsal and an improvised costume. She was a sensation, and Goetze was so put out that she cancelled her next appearance, Fidès in *Prophet.* Frau Heink came through again. The drudgery experienced on the lower rungs of the ladder had paid off. Then followed appearances at the Hofoper in Berlin, a tour of Scandinavia, and Paris. In 1892 she appeared in London, opening with Heink as Erda and Max Alvary as Siegfried. There the company performed two *Ring* cycles, two *Tristan und Isolde,* and England's first performances of *Der Trompeter von Sackingen,* in which the critics found special praise for Frau Heink.

In 1896 Schumann-Heink (she had in the meantime married Paul Schumann) was coached by Cosima Wagner at Bayreuth in the roles of Erda, Waltraute and the First Norn. She participated in five complete *Ring* cycles in July and August, and then back to Hamburg where she took part in 128 performances between September and May. Now most of the parts were major ones, and her repertory was enlarged by roles in several new operas, including *Rienzi, Andrea Chénier,* Meyerbeer's *Star of the North, The Bartered Bride, Hänsel und Gretel,* Kreutzer's *Verschwender,* Kienzl's *Evangelimann,* and even Gilbert & Sullivan's *Mikado.* In 1897, she returned to Covent Garden, Bayreuth, and without a break, back to Hamburg with still new operas like *Bohème, Cavalleria, Gioconda, Aida, Odysseus, Undine,* and *Fra Diavolo.*

With the death of the intendant of the Hamburg Opera in November 1897, the contract which had regulated Schumann-Heink's life for the past fourteen years was broken. She began accepting engagements in Berlin and elsewhere, and wrote "Ende—Finis" to Hamburg in her performance log on 31 May 1898. She was in London in June and July, and in August signed a new contract with the Berlin Hoftheater. Next it was the Metropolitan: the company was on tour, and Schumann-Heink made her debut in Chicago as Ortrud, with Eames, Dippel, Bispham and Edouard de Reszke, and received twenty curtain calls. There was a second triumphant Ortrud on the 10th, followed by Fricka in *Walküre* on the 18th and 23. Her New York debut was again in *Lohengrin,* this time with Nordica, Bispham, Jean and Edouard de Reszke.

For the next four years, she spent winters in New York and the balance of the year in Berlin and elsewhere. In the spring of 1903, Maurice Grau retired from the Metropolitan, and Schumann-Heink decided it was time for a change. A comic opera called *Love's Lottery* with book by Stanislau Stange and music by Julian Edwards, cast the singer as a Hausfrau laundress and ran for fifty performances on Broadway after its opening on 3 October 1903. After the Broadway closing, the show went on tour: the opening night in Boston brought the news of Paul Schumann's death in Dresden. Leaving the children in the care of their grandmother, Ernestine finished the tour, which was a great financial success. Events moved rapidly. The singer took out American citizenship, married her business manager, William Rapp Jr., brought the children to the United States, purchased a new home at Singac, New Jersey, and began a 40,000-mile concert tour in the United States. The great love affair between Ernestine Schumann-Heink and the American people had begun. During the next few years there were many such tours, both in the United States and in Europe, with an occasional appearance at an opera house squeezed in. The Metropolitan saw her again in 1907 when she sang ten performances, including the Witch in *Hänsel und Gretel;* there was an *Il trovatore* for Hammerstein in 1908; and she created Klytemnestra in Strauss' *Elektra* in Dresden, 25 January 1909. Now and again there were Bayreuth performances until the war, with occasional visits to the operatic stage in Boston and Chicago. In February and March 1926, to celebrate her "Golden Jubilee" as a singer, she sang Erda in *Das Rhinegold* and *Siegfried* at the Metropolitan; another *Rhinegold* followed in February 1929; and in 1932, she sang Erda in *Das Rhinegold* and *Siegfried* in her 71st year.

When World War I broke out, Schumann-Heink's eldest son August joined the German navy; shortly after, her son Hans contracted typhoid and died. When America entered the war, her youngest three boys enlisted in the American forces, and Schumann-Heink plunged into war work. Paying concerts were cancelled. She turned her home, then in Chicago, into a servicemen's canteen. She began an endless procession of appearances in hospitals and military camps; between these visits, she sang for Liberty Loan drives. She became known as "Mother Schumann-Heink" to countless service men. Actually, the work for "her boys" went on until her death, as she made it known that she was always available at no fee to any group of disabled veterans or the American Legion, no matter how inconvenient the engagement to the aging singer.

In 1926 Schumann-Heink made her first venture into radio; in the following year she made three Vitaphone shorts, and there was talk of "retirement" which was ended abruptly by the stock market crash of 1929. She was supporting a small army of relatives and hangers-on, and she desperately needed funds. The only way seemed to be vaudeville engagements in a nation-wide tour of motion picture houses, and radio appearances, including her weekly "show" for a maker of canned baby food, during which she told yarns about her career and sang a few songs. In 1935 she was signed to play herself in a "musical" film featuring Nino Martini called *Here's to Romance.* She turned out to be the hit of the show, and suddenly she was assailed by offers to make her own feature film. Unfortunately, it was not to be: she was taken ill in November 1936, returning from a Disabled Veterans convention in Milwaukee. She died of leukemia in Hollywood on 17 November. Two days later, the American Legion held a funeral service at their Hollywood post.

Schumann-Heink has left us some remarkable recordings, even though her voice had had some twenty-five years' hard usage before she made her first commercial discs for Columbia, early in 1903. In 1906, she began her long association with Victor, which ended in 1931, some forty-three years after her debut. Regretfully, her great Wagnerian roles are poorly represented, but the 1908 recording of "Gretcher Gott" from *Rienzi* must stand as a model of declamation and style. Her Erda's warning from *Das Rhinegold* can be compared in her acoustical version of 1907 and the electrical recording made in 1929 which, in spite of her age, commands tremendous respect. There are excellent examples of her coloratura in the Arditi "Bolero" (1907), in the aria from Mozart's *La clemenza de Tito* (1909), the two-part prison scene from *Le prophète,* and there are the famous renditions of the *Lucrezia Borgia* "Brindisi" with extended trills and two-octave leaps. She has left us "Ah mon fils" in both German and French, several versions of the *Samson* arias, and some Schumann, Schubert, Strauss and Brahms Lieder, the latter being especially important as she was given (she said) these songs by the composer. While some of her concert songs are of little lasting value, others are miniature works of art. Most will agree that her recordings of "Stille Nacht" have never been surpassed, and playing one of these recordings on Christmas Eve is still an important ritual in many American homes. A good deal of her fabulous personality comes through in the four sound films of 1927 and 1935, brief as her appearances in them are.

—William R. Moran

SCHWARZKOPF, Elisabeth.

Soprano. Born 9 December 1915, in Jarotschin, near Poznan. Married: record producer Walter Legge, 1953 (died 1979). Studied with Lula Mysz-Gmeiner at the Berlin Hochschule für Musik, and later with Maria Ivogün and her husband, accompanist Michael Raucheisen; joined Berlin Städtische Oper in 1938, making debut as a Flowermaiden in *Parsifal;* gave successful recital at Beethoven Saal in Berlin, 1942, and was subsequently asked by Karl Böhm to join the Vienna Staatsoper; Covent Garden debut as Donna Elvira during Staatsoper's visit there in 1947, and remained with the Covent Garden company five seasons; at Salzburg Festival, 1947-64, and Teatro alla Scala, 1948-63; created role of Anne Trulove in Stravinsky's *The Rake's Progress,* Venice, 1951; also in 1951 sang Eva and Woglinde at Bayreuth; San Francisco debut as Marschallin in *Der Rosenkavalier,* 1955; debut at Paris Opéra (1962) and Metropolitan Opera (1964) in same role; from the 1950s recorded extensively, usually in collaboration with husband; retired from opera in 1972 and from concerts in 1975; holds honorary Doctorate from Cambridge University and the Grosses Verdienst-Kreuz der Bundesrepublik Deutschland.

Publications

By SCHWARZKOPF: books–

Ed., *On and Off the Record* [memoirs of Walter Legge]. New York, 1982; second ed., New York, 1988.

About SCHWARZKOPF: books–

Tubeuf, André. *Le chant retrouvé. Sept divas: renaissance de l'opéra.* Paris, 1979.
Segalini, Sergio. *Elisabeth Schwarzkopf.* Paris, 1983.

articles–

Mann, W. "Elisabeth Schwarzkopf." *Gramophone Record Review* 56 (1958): 659.
Interview, *Collegium musicum* new ser., no. 8 (1971): 7.
Legge, Walter. "Her Master's Voice." *Opera News* 39/22 (1975): 9.
Greenfield, E. "Elisabeth Schwarzkopf" (interview). *Gramophone* 54 (1976): 555.
Jolly, J. "Elisabeth Schwarzkopf" (interview). *Gramophone* 68 (December 1990): 1173.

*   *   *

In Mozart and as Richard Strauss's Marschallin and Countess Madeleine (*Capriccio*), Elisabeth Schwarzkopf may lay claim as the most significant interpreter in our time. Yet she antagonizes as many listeners as she pleases, so that the distinguished critic John Steane will write of a Schwarzkopf performance that "what one hears is the most beautiful legato, the finest of lightenings, the least fussy and most sensitive of interpretations," while the equally respected Robin Holloway describes "narcissism to the point of incest . . . this isn't renunciation; it's a pettish *grande dame* with migraine."

What is the reason for such contradictory opinions? Certainly not in dispute is the quality of Schwarzkopf's natural talents: Holloway himself rather grudgingly admits to her "singing of extraordinary technical accomplishment; it is perfect, even great, in its way." Indeed, few singers in our time have been so prodigiously gifted. A great physical beauty, Schwarzkopf also possessed a superb lyric soprano voice—instantly recognizable and managed with the precision of an instrumentalist. Although over time the top of the voice hardened somewhat, Schwarzkopf's technical mastery and canny artistic intelligence allowed her to mask this weakness and even turn it to her advantage; the lighter, slightly crooning quality employed in some of her later recordings has the suggestion of elegant and sophisticated artistic choice. If this fact reveals a degree of calculation, perhaps we have arrived at the source of the controversy. Much has been written about Schwarzkopf's marriage to record producer and EMI executive Walter Legge, a union of two perfectionists with seemingly insatiable appetites for refinement. Their collaboration meant that music, text and interpretation were prepared with the meticulous care of a diamond-cutter. The resulting performances had a specificity and richness of detail which are quite unique, but a certain lack of naturalness and spontaneity could also characterize the finished product.

Ultimately one's reaction to Schwarzkopf is very much a matter of personal taste. Like Maria Callas in a rather different repertoire, Schwarzkopf is an artist of bold choices, and audiences tend to be deeply factionalized about her work. Some cannot tolerate her often fussy diction and find her insufferably arch and mannered in almost every role. Others think Schwarzkopf incomparable in achieving a unification of dramatic insight and superb vocalism. For the latter group of listeners, Schwarzkopf ranks with Callas as one of the complete operatic artists of our time—as much actress as singer.

Certain operas suited Schwarzkopf's aristocratic approach better than others, and in her mature career she cagily restricted her stage portrayals to a limited number of roles which she performed internationally. The music of Mozart figured prominently. She brought a towering, tragic stature to Donna Elvira, a part which in lesser hands can seem merely hectoring and pathetic, and her singing of the difficult music—demanding a perfectly controlled legato line as well as a formidable florid technique—was superb in every way. Schwarzkopf's touching Countess in *Figaro* was equally distinguished. As Fiordiligi, she revealed a delicious flair for comedy and sang the fiendishly difficult music as well as it has been sung in recent memory: year after year, her portrayal was one of the highlights of the Salzburg Festival.

Even Schwarzkopf's most virulent detractors allow that she has few peers as the Marschallin, a role which needs a singer who can provide a steady outpouring of beautiful tone as well as illuminate the profound, often difficult and abstract poetry of Hofmannsthal's masterly libretto. Since the premiere performance of *Der Rosenkavalier* in 1911, only a few sopranos have really made the part their own. The great Lotte Lehmann was indelibly identified with the opera in the 1930s and 1940s, and, since the 1950s, it is Schwarzkopf's portrayal which has become legendary. Many first-class singers have performed the Marschallin with distinction since Schwarzkopf's retirement—the list includes Elisabeth Söderström, Kiri Te Kanawa, Lucia Popp and others—but none has displaced her memory in the part.

Although Elisabeth Schwarzkopf retired from singing in the late 1970's, she continues to play a significant role in the musical world. In 1976, she and Walter Legge offered a highly successful series of Master Classes at the Julliard School in New York City. Since Legge's death in 1979, Schwarzkopf has continued her career as a master teacher in venues around the world. Among her students have been the American baritone Thomas Hampson; soprano Margaret Marshall, whose cultivated assumptions of the Mozart heroines are very much in the tradition of her mentor; and Mitsuko Shirai, the noted Japanese concert singer. As a teacher Schwarzkopf continues to promote the exacting standards which made her one of the century's greatest singers.

—David Anthony Fox

Elisabeth Schwarzkopf as Rosalinda in *Die Fledermaus*

DIE SCHWEIGSAME FRAU [The Silent Woman].

Composer: Richard Strauss.

Librettist: Stefan Zweig (after Ben Jonson, *Epicoene*).

First Performance: Dresden, Staatsoper, 24 June 1935.

Roles: Aminta (soprano); Henry Morosus (tenor); Cutbeard (baritone); Sir Blunt Morosus (bass); Housekeeper (contralto); Isotta (soprano); Carlotta (mezzo-soprano); Morbio (baritone); Vanuzzi (bass); Farfallo (bass); chorus (SATTBB).

Publications

article–

Partsch, Erich Wolfgang. "Utopie und Wirklichkeit: Anmerkungen zu Konzeption und Stil der *Schweigsamen Frau* von Richard Strauss." In *Bericht über den Internationalen Musikwissenschaftlichen Kongress Bayreuth, 1981,* edited by C.-H. Mahling and S. Wiesman, 528. Kassel, 1984.

unpublished–

Partsch, Erich Wolfgang. "Artifizialität und Manipulation. Studien zur Genese und Konstitution der 'Spieloper' bei Richard Strauss unter besonderer Berücksichtigung des *Schweigsamen Frau.*" Ph.D. dissertation, University of Vienna, 1983.

* * *

The plot of *Die schweigsame Frau* is derived from the play *Epicoene* by Ben Jonson. Morosus, who wants a silent wife, is duped by Henry, Aminta, the buffa troupe, and the barber, into a fake marriage with Henry's wife, Aminta, who turns out to be anything but silent. When, in act II, she turns his world upside down, Morosus despairs of life. In act III, these conflicts are resolved, and Morosus comes to the conclusion that a wife who stays with someone else is the best wife.

The vocal distributions give Strauss ample opportunities for exploring the contrasts and the blendings possible between the ten characters in this opera. From the standpoint of vocal requirements and the possibilities of those voices set free by a master like Strauss, this opera should be a successful masterpiece. But singers who concertize and make recordings want memorable arias (duets, even) for such programs. Strauss provides such arias and duets in other operas, but not in *Die schweigsame Frau.* Only Morosus, Henry, and Aminta have aria sections which could be extracted (along with some Henry-Aminta duets) for such solo performances. But even these sections which could be extracted are not memorable in the ways in which excerpts for similar voices from other works by Strauss are memorable. While this opera contains many delightful touches and shows Strauss' mastery of the orchestra, it is very seldom performed.

—Samuel B. Schulken

SCOTTI, Antonio.

Baritone. Born 25 January 1866, in Naples. Died 26 February 1936, in Naples. Studied with Ester Triffani-Paganini and Vincenzo Lombardi; debut as Amonasro in *Aida,* Malta, 1889; major debut as Cinna in *La vestale,* Naples, 1889; Teatro alla Scala debut as Hans Sachs, 1899; Covent Garden debut as Don Giovanni, 1899; Metropolitan Opera debut as Don Giovanni, 1899; at Metropolitan Opera, 1899-1933, roles including Scarpia, Falstaff, Rigoletto, Iago, Tonio; created the role of Chim-Fen in Leoni's *L'oracolo,* Covent Garden, 1905; his Scotti Opera Company toured the United States for four years; retired in 1933.

Publications

About SCOTTI: books–

Gatti-Casazza, G. *Memories of Opera.* New York, 1941.
Lauri-Volpi, G. *Voci parallele.* Milan, 1955.

articles–

Celletti, Rodolfo. "Scotti, Antonio." *Le grandi voci.* Rome, 1964.
Reutlinger, D. "Antonio Scotti." *The Maestro* 1/1-2, 3-4 (1969): 35, 31.
Bott, M.F. "On Tour with Scotti—1921." *Opera* 27 (1976): 1101.
"Chaliapin, Scotti and Lytton." *Gramophone* 60/July (1982): 174.
Albright, William. *Opera Quarterly* 7/3 (Autumn 1990): 166.

* * *

On 20 January 1933, five days before his sixty-seventh birthday, Antonio Scotti, seeming even older than his years, stood alone in front of the great gold curtain at the Metropolitan

Antonio Scotti as Scarpia in *Tosca*

Opera and said to the assemblage, "I do not want to leave you, but I must." The role he had just performed at this official farewell was that of Chim-Fen in Leoni's *L'oracolo,* one which he had created at Covent Garden (1905) and of which he had been sole interpreter at the Metropolitan (in a total of fifty-five performances between 1915 and 1933).

Scotti's honest remark to his final audience acknowledged that his voice, never his most important asset and eventually his greatest liability, would simply no longer bear the strain of performance. Perhaps the body, too, was at last in rebellion against the histrionic requirements of his signature roles—Scarpia, Marcello, Sharpless—parts that he "owned" in New York from the first moment he brought them to life there. Scotti's 217 Scarpias with the Metropolitan constitute an unbreakable record: the most performances of a leading role by any artist in the company's history.

What kept Scotti onstage for so many years beyond his time of prime vocal accomplishment was his almost unparalleled sense of the theater, impossible to part with until there was absolutely no choice but to do so. He had debuted in Naples as Cinna in *La vestale* in 1889, and followed this with a decade of hard singing throughout Italy, as well as in Spain, Portugal, Poland, Russia, and South America. He came both to London and New York in 1899 (in each case as a dapper Don Giovanni), singing in a smoothly produced, well-schooled *bel canto* style, supported by a high level of musical understanding that gave him rank even though his voice was quite the least of those baritone instruments that emerged from Italy at the end of the nineteenth century. Battistini, De Luca, Ancona, Ruffo, and Amato, all of whom were prominent at various points during Scotti's lengthy time before the public (the first two enjoyed similarly long careers), all possessed voices either larger or of much greater natural beauty, and all were much more suited to the high-lying *cantilena* of early and middle-period Verdi, for instance.

But Scotti was completely aware of his strengths and limitations and began to specialize in verismo roles, along with occasional others (Iago, Falstaff) wherein his command of characterization and dramatic nuance went largely unchallenged. In 1924, W.J. Henderson wrote of Scotti that "now when his voice has passed its meridian his skill in impersonation, which years ago became the chief part of his stock, still chains the interest of operagoers." Despite the considerable, nearly Verdian, vocal hurdle posed for him by the "Prologue" (from which he omitted the two stand-out high notes), Scotti retained the otherwise verismo part of Tonio in *I pagliacci* in his repertory all the way up until 1930, simply because it appealed to him so much from the dramatic standpoint.

Even though the evidence of Scotti's recordings, being strictly aural, belies for some commentators his high historical standing (William Albright has written that Scotti "is a singer whose legendary status tends to elude me. I find his tone dry, hooded, and stiff, his legato gluey"), the impression he made in person was overpowering. Max Smith described his Chim-Fen as "a gruesomely realistic characterization of the villainous Chinaman, every detail of his portrayal, even to the forward inclination of his head, the indrawing of his shoulders and elbows and the ghastly limpness of his pendulous fingers, showing careful study and elaboration. Few persons are likely to forget the uncanny sight Scotti presented as he sank, loose and spineless, under the onslaught of his murderer, and later as he flopped forward in a heap and rolled over on the stage."

Offstage, Scotti possessed a sophistication and innate elegance that his fellow Neapolitan and frequent colleague Enrico Caruso lacked, particularly in matters of dress. But Caruso, "natural man" that he was, endured unfavorable

comparisons with good humor, perhaps privately noting that he had considerably more success in matters of the heart than Scotti: urged on by William J. Guard, the Metropolitan's publicist, the New York papers in 1911 carried a statement containing "the annual announcement of [Geraldine] Farrar's rejection of Scotti's proposal of marriage." Whatever their differences in character, Caruso and Scotti were lifelong friends, and left to posterity recordings of duets from *Don Carlo, La forza del destino, La bohème,* and *Madama Butterfly* that stand among the most important documents in operatic history.

Scotti could not live without the stage, and he had an ego, too. One of the most celebrated incidents in Metropolitan annals occurred at the 1925 revival of *Falstaff.* When the audience clamored for the young American baritone Lawrence Tibbett, who was singing Ford, following the act II inn scene, Scotti mistook the applause as being for himself and insisted on bowing again and again with Tibbett ("the modest Mr Tibbett evidently did not want to get between the limelight and Mr Scotti," wrote Lawrence Gilman). But the opera was not allowed to proceed until Tibbett finally showed himself alone before the curtain. His compatriots "split the roof" and created a new star simultaneously.

Scotti retired, poverty-stricken (a fact known only to a faithful servant), to his native Naples. Death came within three years to the man we still honor as the greatest Italian operatic actor of his day.

—Bruce Burroughs

SCOTTO, Renata.

Soprano. Born 24 February 1934, in Savona. Started to study music in Savona at age fourteen; studied in Milan with Emilio Ghirardini, Merlini, and Mercedes Llopart; debut as Violetta, Savona, 1952; formal debut in same role, Milan, Teatro Nuovo, 1953; sang at Teatro alla Scala; U.S. debut as Mimi, Chicago Lyric Opera, 1960; Metropolitan Opera debut as Madama Butterfly, 1965; won wide recognition as Mimi in the "Live from Lincoln Center" telecast of *La bohème,* 1977.

Publications

By SCOTTO: books–

Scotto: More than a Diva, with O. Roca. New York, 1984.

About SCOTTO: books–

Tosi, B. *Renata Scotto. Voce di due mondi.* Venice, 1990.

*   *   *

In the opera house a diva creates her own world. Whatever the means, she obliterates for the moment any other realization of the role she is playing: she fills you with herself. The effect is quite unlike the reasoned appreciation roused by an accomplished professional performance. Renata Scotto was, by common consent, a diva. She brought to the operatic stage at first a truly beautiful lyric voice, full of unexpected light and shadow. She had curiosity, intelligence, and the gift of

Renata Scotto with Renato Bruson in *Macbeth,* **Royal Opera, London, 1981**

perception; her *Trittico* heroines, for example, were works of great skill as well as great art.

Scotto also had a dangerous audacity. Against strong advice she went on in the second half of her career to sing dramatic soprano roles such as Gioconda, Norma, and Lady Macbeth. Her dramatic gifts illuminated some of them—one thinks particularly of Gioconda—but she destroyed her voice and sometimes seriously compromised the music in the process, a fate predicted for her by a number of major Italian sopranos of the previous generation, from Pagliughi to Caniglia to Tebaldi.

Scotto's voice had everything: a forward lyric quality, a silvery edge that did not belie warmth, the brilliant high range and mobility to conquer Lucia, and, when she wished it, a fascinating darkness that qualified her for a lovely Violetta, the role in which she made her debut at age eighteen. She also had discipline. Seeing herself in the Met's televised *Bohème* of 1977, she decided to lose thirty pounds, did so, and never regained it. She was a graceful, if slight, stage figure. She was the subtlest vocal actress of the post-Callas period in not one but three repertories (bel canto, Verdi, and verismo), and the only one to provide a conviction and a complexity of dramatic effect sufficient to recall the occasional glories of the previous two generations. Typically, Mafalda Favero, one of the great La Scala lyric sopranos of the thirties and forties, called Scotto the finest of the later Italians.

Early recordings of *La serva padrona* and *Lucia* show her in splendid voice, with lovely phrasing and an exquisite projection of both vitality and warmth in characterization. As

Lucia, even in 1959, before she had sung the role onstage, she had a technique and beauty of tone to match any of her later rivals except possibly the young Sutherland, and a concept excelled in subtlety and romantic fervor only by Callas. The very way she sings the word "Ascolta!" ("Listen!") before her first aria draws us in to hang upon her mysterious tale. From the beginning, her Lucia's love is unconditional, and expressed with a noble economy of means which is in itself a comment on Lucia's character: color, phrasing, and just a hint of hysteria in the tone. The mad scene is deliciously warm, though it settles for pathos and misses the tragic: that was to come later. Of her mature recordings the 1966 *Butterfly* is typically memorable: beautifully voiced save for a few top notes, grave and yet youthful, shy but sensual, full of humor but never coy, intimate and yet somehow far more tragic in its effect than the creations of darker voices, and rich with a thousand fine-grained vocal effects.

Unlike many singers, Scotto was even more touching when seen. Her three roles in Puccini's *Trittico*—rather dull when done by three other sopranos in the same production previously in New York, were gripping in her live performance. The restless despair of Georgetta, the ecstatic purity of Suor Angelica, and the charm of young Lauretta were separately winning and together overwhelming. Only Scotto among modern sopranos could build the second half of *Suor Angelica* in such a way as not to lose dramatic tension in sentimentality. On television she made of the melodrama *Gioconda* a genuine tragedy. One of the few great operatic videotapes is of her *Manon Lescaut,* conducted by Levine, directed by Menotti, beautifully set and costumed, and also featuring Placido Domingo in one of his most fervent performances. Scotto herself is in fine voice. Her skill and spontaneity, and the mystery, frivolity, and passion of her performance are in heartbreaking balance. It is, in short, the diva experience.

—London Green

SCRIBE, (Augustin) Eugène.

Librettist/Dramatist. Born 24 December 1791, in Paris. Died 20 February 1861, in Paris. Studied at the Collège Ste-Barbe in Paris; elected to Académie Française, 1835. Scribe was one of the most prolific dramatists of the nineteenth century.

Librettos (selected)

La petit lampe merveilleuse (with Mélesville), L.A. Piccinni, 1822.
Leicester (with Mélesville), D.F.E. Auber, 1823.
La neige (with Delavigne), D.F.E. Auber, 1823.
Le concert à la cour (with Mélesville), D.F.E. Auber, 1824.
Léocadie (with Mélesville), D.F.E. Auber, 1824.
Robin des Bois (with Castil-Blaze), music arranged from Weber's *Der Freischütz*, 1824.
Le maçon (with Delavigne), D.F.E. Auber, 1825.
La dame blanche, F.A. Boieldieu, 1825.
La vieille (wtih Delavigne), F.J. Fétis, 1826.
Le timide (with Saintine), D.F.E. Auber, 1826.
Fiorella, D.F.E. Auber, 1826.
Le mal du pays (with Mélesville), A. Adam, 1827.
La muette de Portici (with Delavigne), D.F.E. Auber, 1828.
Le Comte Ory (with Delestre-Poirson), G. Rossini, 1828.
La fiancée, D.F.E. Auber, 1829.
Les deux nuits (with Bouilly), F.A. Boieldieu, 1829.
Fra Diavolo, D.F.E. Auber, 1830.
Le dieu et la bayadère (opéra-ballet), D.F.E. Auber, 1830.
La sonnambula, V. Bellini, 1831.
Le philtre, D.F.E. Auber, 1831.
L'elisir d'amore, G. Donizetti, 1832; also set by Macfarren.
La Marquise de Brinvilliers (with Castil-Blaze), D.F.E. Auber and F.H.J. Castil-Blaze, 1831.
Robert le diable (with Delavigne), G. Meyerbeer, 1831.
Le serment (with Mazères), D.F.E. Auber, 1832.
Gustave III, D.F.E. Auber, 1833; set as *Un ballo in maschera*, G. Verdi, 1859.
Ali Baba (with Mélesville), L. Cherubini, 1833.
Lestocq, D.F.E. Auber, 1834.
Le châlet (with Mélesville), A. Adam, 1834; also set by Vilnius, and as *Betly* by G. Donizetti and S. Moniuszko.
La juive, J.F.E. Halévy, 1835.
Le cheval de bronze, D.F.E. Auber, 1835.
Actéon, D.F.E. Auber, 1836.
Les Huguenots (with Deschamps), G. Meyerbeer, 1836.
Les chaperons blancs, D.F.E. Auber, 1836.
L'ambassadrice (with Saint-Georges), D.F.E. Auber, 1836.
Le domino noir, D.F.E. Auber, 1837; also set by L. Rossi.
Le fidèle berger (with Saint-Georges), A. Adam, 1838.
Guido e Ginevra, J.F.E. Halévy, 1838.
Marguerite (de Planard), F.A. Boieldieu [unfinished].
L'africaine, 1838; G. Meyerbeer, 1865.
Régine, A. Adam, 1839.
Le lac des fées (with Mélesville), D.F.E. Auber, 1839.

Les treize (with Duport), J.F.E. Halévy, 1839.
Le shérif, J.F.E. Halévy, 1839.
La reine d'un jour (with Saint-Georges), A. Adam, 1839.
Le Duc d'Albe, 1840, G. Donizetti [unfinished]: also set by G. Pacini?, and by G. Verdi [*Les vêpres siciliennes*] (as revised by Duveyrier].
Le drapier, J.F.E. Halévy, 1840.
Les martyrs (after Corneille, *Polyeucte*), G. Donizetti, 1840.
Zanetta (with Saint-Georges), D.F.E. Auber, 1840.
L'opéra à la cour (with Saint-Georges), arranged A. Grisar and L. Boieldieu, 1840.
La favorite (with Royer and Vaez), G. Donizetti, 1840.
Le guitarrero, J.F.E. Halévy, 1841.
Les diamants de la couronne (with Saint-Georges), D.F.E. Auber, 1841.
Carmagnola, A. Thomas, 1841.
Le main de fer (with de Leuven), A. Adam, 1841.
Le Duc d'Olonne (with Saintine), D.F.E. Auber, 1842.
La part du diable, D.F.E. Auber, 1843.
Le puits d'amour (with de Leuven), M.W. Balfe, 1843.
Lambert Sinnel (with Mélesville), H. Monpou [finished by Adam], 1843.
Dom Sébastien, G. Donizetti, 1843.
Cagliostro (with Saint-Georges), A. Adam, 1844.
La sirène, D.F.E. Auber, 1844.
La barcarolle, D.F.E. Auber, 1845.
Haydée, D.F.E. Auber, 1847.
Adrienne Lecouvreur (with Legouvé), 1849; adapted by A. Colautti for F. Cilèa as *Adriana Lecouvreur*, 1902; also set by G. Setaccioli [unfinished] and by Alexandrov.
Le prophète, G. Meyerbeer, 1849.
La fée aux roses (with Saint-Georges), J.F.E. Halévy, 1849.
La tempesta (after Shakespeare, translated by Giannone), J.F.E. Halévy, 1850.
Giralda, A. Adam, 1850.
L'enfant prodigue, D.F.E. Auber, 1850.
La dame de pique, J.F.E. Halévy, 1850.
Zerline, D.F.E. Auber, 1851.
Le juif errant (with Saint-Georges), J.F.E. Halévy, 1852.
Marco Spada (with Mazillier), D.F.E. Auber, 1852.
Le nabab (Saint-Georges), J.F.E. Halévy, 1853.
L'étoile du nord, G. Meyerbeer, 1854.
La nonne sanglante (with Delavigne), C.F. Gounod, 1854.
Jenny Bell, D.F.E. Auber, 1855.
Manon Lescaut (with Aumer), D.F.E. Auber, 1856.
La chatte métamorphosée en femme (with Mélesville), J. Offenbach, 1858.
Barkouf (with Boisseaux), J. Offenbach, 1860.
La circassienne, D.F.E. Auber, 1861; also set by F. von Suppé, as *Fatinitza*.
La fiancée du Roi de Garbe (with Saint-Georges), D.F.E. Auber, 1864.
L'africaine (with F.J. Fétis), Meyerbeer, 1865.

Publications

By SCRIBE: books–

E. Scribe: *Oeuvres complètes*. Paris, 1874-85.

About SCRIBE: books–

Arvin, N.C. *Eugène Scribe and the French Theater*. New York, 1924; 1967.
Crosten, W.L. *French Grand Opera*. New York, 1948.
Smith, P. *The Tenth Muse*. New York, 1970.

Pendle, Karin. *Eugène Scribe and French Opera of the Nineteenth Century.* Ann Arbor, 1979.

articles—

Scherle, A. "Eugène Scribe und die Oper des 19. Jahrhunderts." *Maske und Kothurne* 3 (1957): 141.
Wallis, Cedric. "Eugène Scribe." *Opera* March (1959).
Forbes, Elizabeth. "The Age of Scribe at the Paris Opéra." *Opera* January (1968).
Chabot, C. "Ballet in the Operas of Eugène Scribe: an Apology for the Presence of Dance in Opera." *Studies in Music from the University of Western Ontario* 5 (1980).
Switzer, Richard. "Dawn of *The vespers.*" *Opera News* 46/no. 14 (1982): 26.
Miller, Norbert. "Grosse Oper als Historiengemälde: Uberlegungen zur Zusammenarbeit von Eugene Scribe und Giacomo Meyerbeer." In *Oper und Operntexte,* edited by Jens Malte Fischer. Heidelberg, 1985.

*   *   *

Born the son of a Parisian draper, Augustin Eugène Scribe studied to become a lawyer. He soon deserted his studies, however, and wrote his first play at the age of nineteen. Its failure did not deter him, and he went on to turn out some four hundred plays and libretti, often in collaboration with a small army of hacks whom he drilled to produce the necessary raw material which his theatrical flair would then transform.

The stage technique Scribe evolved was glossily efficient. He worked like a skillful watchmaker, contriving ingenious situations and bringing off *coups de théâtre* with cynical ease. His plays were often written in reverse, starting with the climax and working backwards so that every twist in the plot would lead with smooth and irresistible logic to the *dénouement,* or "untying" of the various threads cunningly woven together by a master hand. So clever was his stage sense that he could make a telling point merely by the placing of a chair.

To read Scribe's theatrical pieces nowadays is a daunting task: his characters are pasteboard, his dialogue is trite, and he subordinates everything to dramatic effect. This resulted from catering slavishly to the audience of the day and following, and even flattering, conventional opinion. When that audience passed away, so, inevitably, did the plays intended for it. *Le verre d'eau* (1840), a comedy about politics, survives fitfully, and so does *Adrienne Lecouvreur* (1849), a play about the eighteenth-century actress which was once in the repertory of the Comédie Française. They are in the collected edition of his works (running to no less than seventy-five volumes), 1874-1885, of which six contain his opera libretti and twenty the libretti he wrote for opéras-comiques.

With Meyerbeer, Scribe was largely responsible for perfecting the nineteenth-century formula for French grand opera. Meyerbeer was as theatrically gifted as Scribe, and together this formidable team created those "grandes machines" *Le prophète* (1849), *L'étoile du nord* (1854) and *L'africaine* (1865). They knew exactly what audiences at the Paris Opéra wanted: glamour, showmanship, romance, and excitement; and they gave it to them in full measure. With his talent for the spectacular and his dexterity at manipulating plot and sub-plot, Scribe would probably, in a later age, have been a very successful Hollywood film maker. Among the other composers for whom he wrote effective libretti were Auber, Boieldieu, Rossini *(Le Comte Ory),* Cherubini, Halévy, Gounod, Offenbach and even Verdi *(Les vêpres siciliennes).*

Scribe lacked culture and was notorious for the gaffes he made. Working always at high speed, he littered his dramas with such absurdities as: "D'avoir pu le tuer vivant/Je me glorifierai sans cesse!" ("I shall always glory in having been able to kill him alive!"), and "Quoiqu'il advienne ou qu'il arrive" ("Although it happens or whatever happens"). Such was the penalty of creating in haste over half a dozen plays and libretti a year for half a century. What cannot be denied, however, is his unfailing ability to engineer situations and to hold an audience's interest until the fall of the curtain. Without Scribe, the history of nineteenth-century French opera would have been very different, and he must be allowed a very important part in its evolution.

—James Harding

Eugène Scribe, c. 1840

THE SECRET MARRIAGE
See IL MATRIMONIO SEGRETO

THE SECRET OF SUSANNA
See IL SEGRETO DI SUSANNA

SEEFRIED, Irmgard.

Soprano. Born 9 October 1919, in Köngetried, Germany. Died 24 November 1988, in Vienna. Married: violinist Wolfgang Schneiderhan, 1948; two daughters. Studied with her father, with Albert Meyer at the Augsburg Conservatory, and with Paola Novikova; debut as Gretel at age 11; adult debut as Priestess in *Aida,* Aachen, 1940; at Aachen 1940-43; Vienna State Opera debut as Eva in *Die Meistersinger von Nürnberg,* 1943; at Vienna State Opera 1943-76; Covent Garden debut as Fiordiligi in *Così fan tutte,* 1947; Teatro alla Scala debut as Susanna in *Le nozze di Figaro,* 1949; Metropolitan Opera debut as Susanna, 1953; after 1976, performed some character parts at the Deutsche Volksoper and taught.

Publications

About SEEFRIED: books–

Fassbind, Franz. *Wolfgang Schneiderhan, Irmgard Seefried: Eine Künstler-und Lebensgemeinschaft.* Berne, 1960.
Rasponi, Lanfranco. *The Last Prima Donnas.* New York, 1982.

articles–

Werba, Erik. "Irmgard Seefried." *Opera* 28/August (1966): 611.
Schumann, J. "Irmgard Seefried Discography." *Fono-forum* 9 (1974): 812, 1226.
"Geburtskalendarium." *Österreichische Musikzeitschrift* 34/ October (1979): 512.
Seward, William. "Golden Days." *Opera News* 51 (28 February 1987): 20.
Blyth, A. "Irmgard Seefried: An Appreciation." *Opera* 40/ January (1989): 35.
Mayer, G. "Musik ist eine heilige Kunst: zum Tode von Irmgard Seefried." *Bühne* 364/January (1989): 4.

*   *   *

Seldom is a world-famous soprano as much liked by her colleagues as she is by her public, but Irmgard Seefried never acted the prima donna. She was born in Bavaria in 1919 of Austrian parents, both musical, and her father became her first teacher, training her thoroughly in piano and violin. She became a vocal student in Augsburg and later at the Munich Music Academy with such success that she was engaged for the 1940-41 season at Aachen Opera by its director, Herbert von Karajan. While there, she also sang in the Cathedral Choir and learned a great deal from its director, Dr Theodor Rehmann. It was indirectly through him that Seefried was invited by Karl Böhm as a guest artist to Dresden. When Böhm moved to Vienna in 1943, Seefried went as a contract member of Vienna's famous opera company. Her debut was as Eva in *Die Meistersinger,* though her career was to become centered on Mozart.

In 1944, Richard Strauss asked that Seefried be cast as the Young Composer in his 80th Birthday Festival performance of *Ariadne auf Naxos;* she subsequently sang Octavian in *Der Rosenkavalier,* and in both of these trouser roles she displayed great gusto, even though she was innately feminine and graceful.

Seefried appeared with the Vienna Staatsoper at Covent Garden in 1947 as Fiordiligi in *Così fan tutte* (its first appearance at that house) and also as Susanna in *Figaro* which, together with Pamina in *Die Zauberflöte* and Zerlina in *Don Giovanni,* were to be her staple roles at Salzburg and elsewhere for the next twenty years.

Irmgard Seefried was a very intelligent musician and has left several perceptive indications of the way in which she approached Mozart. She particularly liked singing Pamina: "there is no greater test for the production of smooth legato. Some of my colleagues found her dull; I never did." And "Zerlina suited my voice and sense of comedy. She is really the audience's key to understanding what the Don is like." About Fiordiligi: "She is hard to sing, but in my estimation one must think of her as a violin. Although many people think the role is ideal for an Italian soprano, that is not true."

Later in her career, Seefried filled out her repertoire with contrasting roles: Blanche in *Les dialogues des Carmélites,* Cleopatra in Handel's *Giulio Cesare* and Marie in *Wozzeck*— probably the most appealing Marie on any stage, sung from a firm Mozartian technique and not screamed.

She was always full of admiration for other great singers, which indicates total self-confidence in her own artistry. The voice was, as the roles she sang indicate, full of expression, warm and sunny like her nature, and thoroughly trained always to produce the very best. The frequency with which she sang her Mozart roles added to, rather than detracted from, their impression on audiences; she was not only seeking fresh insights into her characters and new, convincing ways round vocal difficulties (with which they abound) but was always prepared to adapt to other singers' needs when in ensemble.

Seefried had a successful marriage with Wolfgang Schneiderhan, leader of the Vienna Philharmonic Orchestra throughout the war and afterwards, and was vocally, as well as personally, a happy, relaxed and grateful singer whose gifts were given generously.

—Alan Jefferson

IL SEGRETO DI SUSANNA [The Secret of Susanna].

Composer: Ermanno Wolf-Ferrari.

Librettist: E. Golisciani.

First Performance: Munich, Hoftheater, 4 December 1909.

Roles: Susanna (soprano); Count Gil (baritone); Sante (mute).

Publications

article–

Bontempelli, E. "Il segreto di Susanna." *Rivista musicale italiana* 18 (1911): 839.

*   *   *

Il segreto di Susanna, with libretto by Enrico Golisciani, is one of the most successful operas composed by Wolf-Ferrari. The work was conceived as an intermezzo in the Italian comic tradition of the eighteenth century. The plot is reminiscent of Goldoni's comedies, which are mostly based on a series of misunderstandings, resolved eventually in the reestablishment of the truth. The action and the situations described in both the libretto and the music are always concise, prolixity being the last resort of Wolf-Ferrari's compositional method.

Count Gil questions the fidelity of Susanna when he comes home and smells tobacco. On another occasion, when embracing her, he smells tobacco again. His suspicion and jealousy grow, so that Susanna's strange behavior seems to suggest that she has a lover and that she wants to get rid of her husband. Having searched the house unsuccessfully, the count disappears. Susanna then lights a cigarette, but when the count appears at the window, she hides the cigarette behind her back. In a burst of rage, Count Gil seizes her hand and burns himself, realizing that Susanna is a smoker. He apologizes and falls at her knees. Susanna gives him a cigarette, and they both retire in the bedroom in a cloud of smoke, while Sante, the servant, blows out the candle leaving the scene in total darkness.

The music, brilliantly orchestrated, follows and underlines the vocal parts (two singers only) in the spirit of a comic opera worthy of comparison with Cimarosa, Paisiello and Pergolesi, without being a mere imitation of the respective styles of those composers. The overture is a model of wittiness and freshness of pure instrumental music.

As with *Quattro rusteghi* and *Gioielli della Madonna,* which enjoyed great popularity when they were produced in Germany before the First World War, *Il segreto di Susanna* is still considered an Italian opera par excellence by those students who feel that the composer was more inclined to stress his Italian descent.

—Edward Neill

SEIDL, Anton.

Conductor. Born 7 May 1850, in Pest. Died 28 March 1898, in New York. Married: Auguste Kraus, soprano, 1882. Studied at the University and at the Conservatory in Leipzig; chorus master at the Vienna Hofoper; assisted in preparing the *Ring* score and parts for the Bayreuth Festival, 1876; first conductor of the Leipzig Opera, 1879-82; engaged by the impresario Angelo Neumann for a grand tour of Wagner's operas, 1882; conductor of the Bremen Opera, 1883; engaged to conduct German operas at the Metropolitan Opera, New York, 1885; conducted the New York Philharmonic, 1891-98; Seidl conducted the premiere of Dvořák's *New World Symphony,* 15 December 1893.

Publications

By SEIDL: books–

The Music of the Modern World. 2 vols. New York, 1895.

About SEIDL: books–

Krehbiel, H. *Anton Seidl.* New York, 1898.
Finck, H.T., ed. *Anton Seidl: a Memorial by his Friends.* New York, 1899.

*   *   *

Throughout his career, Hungarian-born conductor Anton Seidl was closely associated with the operas of Richard Wagner. Wagner's personal secretary, friend (he lived in Wagner's house for six years), and assistant at the first Bayreuth Festival in 1876, Seidl was helped by Wagner's recommendation in being selected conductor of the Leipzig Opera House in 1879; he remained there until 1882. That year he became conductor of Angelo Neumann's "Nibelungen" opera troupe, and with this company he toured Europe. The following year he became conductor of the Bremen Stadttheater.

In 1885, seeking a replacement for the late Leopold Damrosch, Metropolitan Opera board secretary Edmund C. Stanton traveled to Germany to offer Seidl the position of music director and chief conductor—such was Seidl's reputation as Wagner's protégé. Seidl retained this position throughout the Metropolitan's "German" seasons (during which all operas were sung in German, regardless of their original language). His first conducting assignment was leading *Lohengrin,* and during his tenure at the Metropolitan Opera he led the American premieres of *Die Meistersinger von Nürnberg* (1886), *Tristan und Isolde* (1886), *Siegfried* (1887), *Götterdämmerung* (1888), and *Das Rheingold* (1889). He also led the first complete *Ring* cycle to be given in America, in 1889.

In 1891, the new management changed the house from its German-only policy to one favoring Italian singers. Relegated, as a result, to Sunday-night concerts, Seidl was reinstated as a regular conductor in the 1892-93 season, partly at the insistence of leading tenor Jean de Reszke. At the Metropolitan Opera until 1897, he led a wide range of operas in the French, German, and Italian repertoires, including Meyerbeer's *L'Africaine,* Verdi's *Aïda,* Cornelius's *Der Barbier von Bagdad,* Bizet's *Carmen,* Berlioz's *La damnation de Faust,* and Mozart's *Don Giovanni,* in addition to Wagner and several lesser known works.

Seidl quickly established his reputation as a master conductor. The critic W.J. Henderson reported that his *Lohengrin* was "finely managed, the fortissimos being wrought up by well-nigh imperceptible gradations." He did not allow himself to be unduly influenced by his singers, seeing them as servants to the music, and he once stopped a performance while waiting for the wealthy box-holders to quiet down—an attempt to teach them proper discipline in the opera house, which he equated with a house of worship. He immediately won the respect of the orchestra by identifying and correcting 180 errors in the instrumental parts of *Lohengrin.* Modeling his productions of Wagner's operas on those he had observed under the composer's supervision in Bayreuth, he insisted on extensive rehearsals to ensure a high standard of performance.

Despite his reverence for Wagner's scores, he made significant cuts in them, a practice for which he has been criticized by subsequent conductors.

Seidl was married to soprano Auguste Seidl-Kraus, who sang *Aïda* and Eva in *Die Meistersinger* under his baton. He died suddenly at age forty-seven in 1898. His funeral was conducted on the Metropolitan Opera's stage; he was the first person to be so honored.

—Michael Sims

SELLARS, Peter.

Producer. Born 27 September 1957, in Pittsburgh. Attended Harvard University, where he directed operas and plays and studied music, film, and art history; staged *Don Giovanni* for New Hampshire Symphony, 1980; staged *The Inspector General,* American Repertory Theater, Cambridge, Massachusetts, 1980; director of the Boston Shakespeare Company, 1983-84; director of the American National Theater at the Kennedy Center, Washington, D.C., 1984-86; oversaw the Los Angeles Festival in 1990.

Opera and Musical Theater Productions (selected)

Don Giovanni, New Hampshire Symphony, 1980.
Orlando, Cambridge, Massachusetts, 1981.
Saul, Cambridge, Massachusetts, 1981.
Mikado, Chicago Lyric Opera, 1983.
My One and Only, New York, 1983.
The Lighthouse, Boston Shakespeare Company, 1983; Purchase, New York, 1985.
Così fan tutte, Ipswich, Massachusetts, 1984.
Hang on to Me, New York, 1984.
Giulio Cesare, Purchase, New York, 1985.
Così fan tutte, Purchase, New York, 1986.
Giulio Cesare, Boston, 1987.
The Electrification of the Soviet Union, Glyndebourne, 1987.
Nixon in China, Houston Grand Opera, 1987; Edinburgh Festival, 1988.
Giulio Cesare, Brussels, 1988.
Le nozze di Figaro, Purchase, New York, 1988.
Tannhäuser, Chicago Lyric Opera, 1988.
Le nozze di Figaro, Purchase, New York, 1989.
Don Giovanni, Purchase, New York, 1989.
Così fan tutte, Purchase, New York, 1989.
Die Zauberflöte, Glyndebourne, 1990.
The Death of Klinghoffer, Brussels, 1990/91 season.

Publications

About SELLARS: articles–

Malitz, N. "John Adams' Revolutionary New Opera: *Nixon in China." Ovation* 8 (October 1987): 16-18.
van der Klis, J. "Satire en actualiteit in Haendelopera van Peter Sellars." *Tijdschrift voor Oude Muziek* 3, no. 3 (1988): 75-76.
"Uj szelek—uj rendezok az amerikai operahazakban." *Muzsika* 31 (May 1988): 20-21.

Crutchfield, Will. "The Triumphs and Defeats in Sellars's Mozart." *The New York Times* 138 (25 July 1988): B1 or C13.
Gray, M. "Peter Sellars: Opera's Enfant Terrible Reaches Mark Two." *Ovation* 9 (September 1988): 18.
Mayer, M. "Purchase, N.Y.: Social Distances (Summer Festival)." *Opera* 39 (Autumn 1988): 120-21.
Milnes, R. "Glyndebourne: Changing Partners." *Opera* 39 (Autumn 1988): 20-21.
Dyer, Richard. "Mozart American Style." *Connoisseur* 219 (April 1989): 144.
Parouty, M. "Peter Sellars." *Diapason-Harmonie* no. 354 (November 1989): 26.
Littlejohn, David. "Reflections on Peter Sellars's Mozart." *Opera Quarterly* 7, no. 2 (1990): 6-36.
Jacobson, M. "Peter Sellars." *Musical America* 110, no. 3 (1990): 48-49.
Reiter, S. "Sellars Meets Mozart." *Classical* 3 (February 1991): 38-44.

* * *

Since 1980, Peter Sellars has become the most written-about director in the American theater. Unique among the more creative and venturesome American stage directors, he has recently focused most of his attention on opera.

Sellars's best-known and most controversial productions are those of the three Mozart-Da Ponte operas, *Don Giovanni, Così fan tutte,* and *Le nozze di Figaro.* The operas attracted international attention when they were presented together at Purchase, New York in 1989, and later televised and released in videocassette versions in 1991, the Mozart bicentennial year. Almost as well-publicized have been *Nixon in China* and *The Death of Klinghoffer,* two "current events" musical docudramas in semioratorio form that Sellars is usually credited as having thought up, and then persuaded composer John Adams and librettist Alice Goodman to write. Each of the Sellars/Adams/Goodman operas was cosponsored, and offered sequentially by six major American and European institutions.

But Sellars has also produced at least a dozen other works of traditional and modern musical theater, including radically innovative stagings of Mozart's *Die Zauberflöte,* and dramatic scores by Bach, Handel, Haydn, Wagner, Gilbert and Sullivan, Stravinsky, Brecht and Weill, Peter Maxwell Davies, and Nigel Osborne. His new production of Olivier Messiaen's *St. François d'Assise* is scheduled for the Salzburg Festival in 1993.

Sellars appears to have made the shift from spoken theater to opera because of the greater expressive range of the latter, and the greater opportunity it offers (by way of radical productions in a tradition-bound form) to disconcert, shock, and outrage—whether in defiantly "contemporary" productions of works from the standard repertory, or in new works of an aggressively political cast. In his notorious and inimitable program notes, Sellars defensively asserts the pertinence of his late 20th-century readings, which he regards as urgent "statements" about industrial capitalism, modern geopolitics, and contemporary struggles over sex, class, and race. His own stance is inevitably against the existing order, although his nontheatrical ideas are not always clear.

Extravagant theatrical conceits, in fact, usually seem to precede intellectual rationales in Sellars's opera productions. There is, admittedly, something unique and ingenious in setting *The Mikado* among the business tycoons and flamboyant new youth of contemporary Tokyo; in seeing *Tannhäuser* as

Peter Sellars's production of *The Magic Flute*, Glyndebourne Festival, 1991

the drama of a modern American TV evangelist of the Jimmy Swaggart sort; or in trying to make the three Mozart-Da Ponte operas work when interpreted by jaded, tormented, or drug-addled New Yorkers in a burnt-out, post-Vietnam War world. But as there is no way to force the original librettos to fit these novel conceptions, a great deal of the text must remain nonsensical in such productions (which is easier to get by with when it is sung instead of spoken, usually in a foreign language); or be jettisoned altogether, as Sellars did with the spoken dialogue of his "Los Angeles freeway" version of *Die Zauberflöte* for the Glyndebourne Festival in 1990, a production that was almost universally disliked.

If his productions of the two operas by John Adams have sometimes been more hospitably received, it is probably because there is no performance tradition for them to defy, no pre-modern text or score for the director to pervert, or reinterpret. In these cases, some of Sellars's *coups de théâtre*—the great onstage airplane, Mao poster, and "Red Detachment" ballet of *Nixon in China;* the giant video screens, dancer-doubles, and abstract metal-frame set for *Klinghoffer*—can be admired for their own sake. Fundamental objection to these works (apart from one's assessment of text and score) tends to be directed more at their simplistic, reductionist readings of important recent events, by which contemporary history is disfigured in the interests of theatricalist effects and muddled moral messages—a problem with "docudramas" in other media as well.

Sellars's greatest strengths as an opera producer are precisely his creative instinct and attraction for the stunning theatrical effect (his Mozart-Da Ponte operas, his *Tannhäuser,* his *Giulio Cesare,* and his *Nixon in China* are full of unforgettable scenes, which on occasion seem pertinent to the music and drama); and his ability—sometimes in concert with a choreographer—to shape the physical motions of well-disciplined performers in complex and compelling ways. (He tends to work with the same people, through long rehearsal periods, in one production after another.) Sellars weaves many different theatrical genres, Eastern as well as Western, traditional and "avant-garde," highbrow and lowbrow—into antinaturalist and musically expressive forms of stage movement, "deeds of music made visible" (in Wagner's phrase), for his troupe of singing actors to use during their arias and (especially) ensembles. In his inventiveness, attention to detail and rigor as an operatic stage director, Sellars has been compared with distinguished European predecessors such as Giorgio Strehler, Walter Felsenstein, and Peter Brook. This characteristic, although present to some degree in all his opera productions, is especially notable (and successful) in his *Orlando,* his *Così fan tutte,* and in some scenes of his *Le nozze di Figaro.* Long stretches of other productions, by contrast, can be static or embarrassingly crude.

Sellars's greatest deficiencies seem to be a profound lack of historical imagination—the willingness or ability to comprehend the times and cultures of the composers whose work he reinterprets—and an unashamed deafness to deeper musical meanings and the potential power of the singing voice. The scores of Handel, Mozart, Wagner, and Stravinsky are of course *ours* now, and no longer theirs. Expressed verbal "intentions" of such composers may legitimately be ignored, if a contemporary producer can find in their music coherent and defensible new meanings.

Sellars seems unwilling or unable to do this. Instead, he has an array of defiant and "outraged" cultural/political statements (more often, gestures) he wishes to make, and an apparently limitless trove of novel theatrical effects he wishes to display. To attract the greatest possible attention to these effects, he imposes them on (rather than extracting them from) complex opera scores, even where only minimal justification can be discovered in the original text and score.

—David Littlejohn

SEMBRICH, Marcella [real name Praxede Marceline Kochanska].

Soprano. Born 15 February 1858, in Wisniewczyk, Galicia. Died 11 January 1935, in New York. Married Wilhelm Stengel in 1877. Studied at the Lemberg Conservatory with Wilhelm Stengel; studied with Viktor Rokitansky in Vienna and with G.B. Lamperti in Milan; debut as Elvira in Bellini's *I puritani,* Athens, 1877; sang Lucia in Donizetti's *Lucia di Lammermoor* at the Dresden Court Opera, 1878; Covent Garden debut as Lucia, 1880; Metropolitan Opera debut as Lucia, 1883; sang with the Metropolitan Opera Company, 1898-1900 and 1901-09; retired in 1917; served as department head at the Curtis Institute of Music in Philadelphia, and at the Institute of Musical Art in New York.

Publications

About SEMBRICH: books–

Arnim, G. *Marcella Sembrich und Herr Prof. Julius Hey.* Leipzig, 1898.
Owen, H.G. *A Recollection of Marcella Sembrich.* New York, 1950.

articles–

Haughton, J.A. "Opera Singers from the golden age." *Musical America* 69 (1949): 18.
Charbonnel, A.B. "Touring with Sembrich." *Musical Courier* 140 (1949): 6.
Owen, H.G. "A Recollection of Marcella Sembrich." *Record Collector* 19/5-6 (1969): 101.

*   *   *

The life of Marcella Sembrich, the famous Polish coloratura, is the story of a rise from obscurity to celebrity, a rags to riches tale, accomplished, not with the support of wealthy patrons or happy coincidences of fate, but by her own hard work and the successful channeling of extraordinary innate talents to achieve their maximum effect. Born Praxede Marcelline Kochanska in 1858 in rural Galicia, she was the daughter of an itinerant musician who taught her at an early age to play both piano and violin. With the modest help of a local music lover, she was enrolled in nearby Lemberg Conservatory for further study of piano and violin, where for four years her piano teacher was Wilhelm Stengel, a pupil of

Moscheles. Professor Stengel, who became her mentor (and in 1877 her husband), arranged for her to study in Vienna in 1873 with three renowned pedagogues, Julius Epstein (piano), Joseph Helmesberger (violin), and as her first teacher of voice, Viktor Rokitansky.

Here legend enters the picture. For years, the story was told that Marcella was brought before the venerable Franz Liszt to perform first on the piano, then the violin, both of which aroused his enthusiasm, but when she sang he was overwhelmed, and reportedly said: "My little angel, God has given you three pairs of wings with which to fly through the country of music; they are all equal: give up none of them, but sing, sing for the world, for you have the voice of an angel."

Sembrich herself never told this story, nor denied it. However, she made it clear that it was Epstein, not Liszt, who discovered her voice. "Things get told this way and that" was her comment.

At full maturity, the range of Sembrich's voice was from C below the treble clef to the F above it, with no breaks or inequalities between registers. Flexibility and lyric warmth were among its qualities, and her early designation as a dramatic coloratura explained the impact of her performances of such roles as the Queen of the Night, Gilda, Violetta, and Mimi—Puccini called her "*the* Mimi." Coupled with her natural beauty of timbre and technical skill was an empathic feeling for interpretation and characterization which never failed to impress her hearers in opera and concert. Wisely, she undertook only two Wagnerian roles, Eva and Elsa, particularly suited to her voice and temperament, at a time when some critics were becoming impatient with the bel canto repertoire. Cognizant of her own abilities, she never made the mistakes of Patti in attempting Aïda and Carmen, or of Melba's one try at the *Siegfried* Brünnhilde. Despite the inroads of Wagnerian and verismo works, audiences never failed to welcome Sembrich's Susanna and Zerlina, Lucia and Rosina, Martha, Marie in *La fille du régiment,* and Adina in *l'elisir d'amore* throughout her career.

From her operatic debut as Elvira in *I Puritani* in 1877 at Athens to her tumultuous farewell gala at the Metropolitan Opera on 6 February 1909, she had been heard with amazement and pleasure in most of the great opera houses of the world. Her consistent display of artistry and the personal warmth and conviction that she always communicated made her a favorite ranking with such illustrious colleagues as Adelina Patti, Emma Albani, Etelka Gerster, Christine Nilsson, Nellie Melba and Emma Calvé. Her devoted friends on stage and in private life included all the great names in music, theater, the visual arts and public life. Kings, queens, czars, presidents, composers and everyday citizens, including critics, acknowledged being proud to know her.

When the Columbia company made its Grand Opera Series in 1903, "the First Recordings of Opera in America," Sembrich joined six other prominent singers (Suzanne Adams, Giuseppe Campanari, Edouard De Reszke, Charles Gilibert, Ernestine Schumann-Heink, and Antonio Scotti) in this historic enterprise. Her selections were arias from *Ernani* and *La traviata* and the Strauss waltz *Voices of Spring,* for which she is said to have received $3000. She was then forty-five, and admittedly the new experience of standing before the recording horn was unsettling. Later she recorded extensively for Victor Talking Machine under improved technical conditions, and although these Red Seal discs were popular and profitable, Sembrich never felt they truly represented her voice at its best.

Following her retirement from opera, Sembrich confined her public appearances to the concert stage where her programs of Lieder in as many as six languages broke with the tradition of diva "aria recitals," and revealed a new world of song to concert goers. The death of Wilhelm Stengel in 1917 brought an end to her singing career, and from then until her death in 1935, Sembrich devoted herself to teaching— privately and as head of the vocal departments at the Juilliard School in New York and the Curtis Institute in Philadelphia.

—Louis Snyder

SEMIRAMIDE.

Composer: Gioachino Rossini.

Librettist: G. Rossi (after Voltaire).

First Performance: Venice, La Fenice, 3 February 1823.

Roles: Semiramide (soprano); Arsace (contralto); Assur (baritone); Idreno (tenor); Oroe (bass); Azema (soprano); Mitrane (tenor); chorus (SSATB).

Publications

article–

Della Corte, A. "La drammaturgica della *Semiramide* di Rossini." *La rassegna musicale* (1938).

* * *

Although the plot of *Semiramide* seems and in fact is overwhelmingly complex, it is nonetheless comprehensible. The story takes place in ancient Babylon. Queen Semiramide has years earlier plotted but failed to kill Ninias, the son she bore King Nino. Nino, however, has himself been assassinated by the wicked Semiramide and her lover Prince Assur. Now that the oracle has declared that a new king will be designated, Arsace, the commander of the army, has returned to Babylon. In love with Princess Azema, Arsace angers Assur because Assur also loves Azema and plans to make her his queen once he has taken over the throne. The Indian King Idrino also loves Azema.

Misinterpreting a divine oracle, Semiramide has now fallen in love with Arsace. She arranges for Idreno to marry Azema and for herself to marry Arsace, who would thereby become king. The ghost of Nino declares that Arsace will indeed become king once certain ancient crimes have been atoned.

Set design for the sanctuary scene in Rossini's *Semiramide* by Alessandro Sanquirico, 1824

(At its premiere in 1823, this much of the opera—act I—reportedly lasted two and one-half hours.)

In act II Arsace is told by the High Priest (Oroe) that it was Semiramide and Assur who had murdered Nino and that he, Arsace, is in fact Ninias, the long-lost son of Nino and rightful heir to the throne. When Arsace confronts Semiramide with her crime, she confesses, but he is unable to avenge his father's death on his own mother. In the dark of Nino's tomb, however, Arsace mistakes his mother for Assur and kills her instead. Arsace nobly contemplates suicide, but when all is revealed, Assur is arrested, and the people declare as their new king Arsace, who finally makes Azema his queen.

The legend of Semiramis can be traced back to an historical Assyrian queen, Sammuramat, wife of Shamshi-Adad V, who lived during the late ninth century B.C. On the other hand, the popularized legend of Semiramis was promulgated in Italy by Muzio Manfredi as early as 1593, set as an opera in 1648, and was reworked by Metastasio in the eighteenth century. Rossini's libretto, based on Voltaire's treatment of the legend in 1748, was written again by Gaetano Rossi, the same librettist who had rendered Rossini a libretto for Voltaire's *La cambiale di matrimonio* in Venice some years before at the outset of his career. Remarkably (but characteristically), Rossini claims and seems to have completed the opera in less than forty days.

The premiere at La Fenice on 3 February 1823, was well received, although the extraordinary length of the first act had the audience at first somewhat perplexed. Nonetheless, the finale of the first act was captivating, and Rossini's reputation did not suffer. The opera was repeated almost nightly for an entire month and played well subsequently in France, Germany, and England. Chronologically, however, *Semiramide* was the last opera Rossini wrote in Italy. After returning to Bologna that spring, Rossini and Mme Colbran-Rossini signed a contract to work in London, an arrangement which ultimately brought them to Paris. For the new Parisian production of *Semiramide* in 1825, Rossini stretched out the quickly unfolding events at the end of act II by extending Semiramide's death scene.

The splendidly atmospheric music Rossini composed for Arsace's visions in Nino's tomb, for the finale of act I, and even for the substantial overture typify his particular ability at composing a convincing *opera seria* in the mystical world of (what was then called) the Orient with an obviously Italian idiom. Previous examples include *Ciro in Babilonia, Aureliano in Palmira, Otello, Mosè in Egitto,* and *Maometto II.*

—Jon Solomon

SENDAK, Maurice.

Designer. Born 10 June 1928, in Brooklyn. Educated at Lafayette High School, Brooklyn, Art Students' League, New York; employed at All American Comics; window display work, Timely Service, 1946-48; F.A.O. Schwartz, 1948-50; illustrations for *The Wonderful Farm,* 1951; illustrated over 60 books by others; first book as author and illustrator, *Kenny's Window,* 1956; international fame from *Where the Wild Things Are,* 1963, which won the Caldecott Medal; retrospective one-man exhibitions 1964-; first theatrical endeavor, wrote and directed the film *Really Rosie, Starring the Nutshell Kids,* 1975 which ran as an Off-Broadway play with music, 1980; story, costumes, and sets for *Nutcracker and the Mouse King,* Pacific Northwest Ballet, 1983 and later remade into a movie, 1986; artistic director, Sundance Children's Theatre, 1988; artistic director, The Night Kitchen, national children's theater; has taught at Yale University and Parsons School of Design. Awards include first American recipient Hans Christian Andersen Illustrator's Award, 1970; a *New York Times* award for best illustrated children's book with *Fly by Night,* 1976; Laura Ingalls Wilder Award for contributions to children's literature, 1983; President's Fellow Award, Rhode Island School of Design, 1985.

Opera Productions (selected)

Die Zauberflöte, Houston Grand Opera, 1980.
Where the Wild Things Are, La Monnaie, Brussels, 1980; National Theatre, London, 1983; Glyndebourne, 1984.
The Cunning Little Vixen, New York City Opera, 1981.
The Love for Three Oranges, Glyndebourne, 1982.
Higglety, Pigglety, Pop!, Glyndebourne, 1984.
L'oca del Cairo, Lyric Opera, Kansas City, 1986.
L'enfant et les sortilèges, Glyndebourne, 1986.
Idomeneo, Los Angeles Opera, 1989.
L'heure espagnole, Glyndebourne, 1986/87 season; New York, 1991.

Publications

By SENDAK: selected books and illustrations–

Ritchie, Jean. *Singing Family of the Cumberlands.* Illustrated by Maurice Sendak. New York, 1955.
Minarik, Else Holmelund. *Father Bear Comes Home.* Illustrated by Maurice Sendak. New York, 1959.
Where the Wild Things Are. Illustrated by Maurice Sendak. New York, 1963.
Alderson, Brian. *Catalogue for an Exhibition of Pictures by Maurice Sendak at the Ashmolean Museum, Oxford.* London, 1975.
Corsaro, Frank, and Maurice Sendak. *The Love of Three Oranges: The Glyndebourne Version.* London, 1984.
Hoffmann, E.T.A. *Nutcracker.* Pictures by Maurice Sendak. New York, 1984.
Tesnohlídek, Rudolf. *The Cunning Little Vixen.* Illustrated by Maurice Sendak. Translated by Tatiana Firkusny, Maritza Morgan, and Robert T. Jones. New York, 1985.
Posters by Maurice Sendak. New York, 1986.
Caldecott & Co.: Notes on Books and Pictures. New York, 1988.

About SENDAK: books–

Lanes, Selma G. *The Art of Maurice Sendak.* New York, 1984.

articles–

Mendl-Schrama, H. "Een kinderopera van Sendak en Knussen op komst." *Mens en Melodie* 41 (January 1986): 44-45.
Heymont, G. "Hunting the Wild Things (Stage Design)." *Opera News* 51 (September 1986): 24-26.

*   *   *

After achieving fame as a children's book author and illustrator, Maurice Sendak has embarked on a career as stage designer for opera productions. He has designed operas that are most appropriate to his experience, those occupying a fantasy world close to that of his books. His sets and costumes have graced productions of Mozart's *Die Zauberflöte,* Janáček's *The Cunning Little Vixen,* Prokofiev's *The Love for Three Oranges,* Knussen's *Where the Wild Things Are,* Mozart's *L'oca del Cairo,* and Ravel's *L'heure espagnole* and *L'enfant et les sortilèges.* Sendak has also written the librettos for two one-act operas, each based on one of his books: *Where the Wild Things Are* and *Higglety Pigglety Pop!*

Sendak's designs for *Die Zauberflöte*—his first operatic venture—were created for the Houston Grand Opera in conjunction with Frank Corsaro for the 1980 season and were later seen in several other cities. As is typical of Sendak's designs, this production emphasized the fantasy elements of the story, the human emotions and dilemmas rendered secondary to the fanciful plants and animals. The designs for every scene feature a menagerie of grotesque yet unthreatening creatures. The sets encompass the dark, sinister aspects of the work without shortchanging its childlike character, combining Egyptian and Masonic motifs with those of the eighteenth century. Some critics objected to the incongruity of the cute animals (including the *Schlange*—here a steam-breathing dragon—chasing Tamino in the opening scene) and the serious elements of the plot.

Where the Wild Things Are, which originated at La Monnaie in Brussels in 1980 in a production by Frank Corsaro, was later seen at Glyndebourne in the same production.

Mozart's uncompleted opera *L'oca del Cairo* gave Sendak the opportunity to design a giant goose that serves as an oracle. The sets for *L'heure espagnole,* first seen at Glyndebourne in 1987 in Frank Corsaro's production, featured elaborate clockwork. *L'enfant et les sortilèges,* also seen in a Corsaro production at Glyndebourne, took advantage of Sendak's brand of whimsy in its costumes for the Squirrel, the Frog, the Tea Pot, and the other characters who wreak vengeance on the wicked child. Projected cartoons complemented (or intruded upon, depending on one's viewpoint) the live action.

Prokofiev's *The Love for Three Oranges* originated in a production for Glyndebourne by Corsaro in 1982 and later was produced at the New York City Opera. Based on the concept of the toy theater and employing theatrical devices of the baroque, such as rapidly moving flats and flying machines. The production was criticized for Sendak's misunderstanding of the character of the Cook, intended to be a woman with a bass voice, which he portrayed and costumed as a man.

Critical reaction to Sendak's designs has followed individual critics' feelings about storybook approaches to operas. Some find his work disarming, delightful, and imaginative, avoiding sentimentality; others see it as flimsy, trivial, and overly cute, with the banality of comic books.

—Michael Sims

SENESINO [real name Francesco Bernardi].

Contralto castrato. Born in Siena, Italy, died 27 January 1759, probably in Siena; sang in Venice 1707-08 and 1714-15; Bologna, 1709, Genoa, 1712; sang at the Dresden Court,

1717-20; sang in London, 1720-28 and 1730-36; returned to Italy and retired in 1740.

Publications

About SENESINO: books–

Haböck, F. *Die Kastraten und ihre Gesangskunst.* Stuttgart, 1927.
Heriot, A. *The Castrati in Opera.* London, 1956.

Senesino (a nickname derived from his birthplace) was one of the most important castrato singers of the early 18th century. While in high demand in Italy, he spent the majority of his time abroad in England, where he was always enthusiastically received. Quantz summarized: "He had a powerful, clear, equal and sweet contralto voice, with a perfect intonation and an excellent shake. His manner of singing was masterly and his elocution unrivaled. Though he never loaded Adagios with too many ornaments, yet he delivered the original and essential notes with the utmost refinement. He sang Allegros with great fire, and marked rapid divisions, from the chest, in an articulate and pleasing manner. His countenance was well adapted to the stage, and his action was natural and noble. To these qualities he joined a majestic figure."

Over his career Senesino appeared widely. His public debut was in Venice in 1707, which was followed by numerous engagements in Italy and abroad, including performances in Bologna, Genoa, Venice, Reggio Emilia, and a two year stay in Naples from 1715 through early 1717 (appearing in two Scarlatti operas). From Naples he was hired on a three-year appointment at the Dresden court from 1717. He returned briefly to Italy, but from September 1720 he was found in Handel's company in London, where he remained until 1728. He moved to Siena the following year, gloating over his bounty and his fat purse, the "folly of the English," but was soon re-engaged for London. From October 1730 through 1736 he again sang for Handel, as well as for the rival Opera of the Nobility (which he helped found). He returned to Italy and appeared only a few more seasons, in Turin, Florence, and Naples, before giving up the stage in 1740 and returning to Siena.

His artistry as a singer is probably best attested by the many operas he sang during his London years, including seventeen original Handel operas and several oratorios. His voice was continually praised by the London public, which found in Senesino's clear sound, precise technique, and moving expression a standard often used to judge others in the theater. He was a superb actor as well, with an imposing and commanding stage presence. His voice gradually fell over his career, as was typical of most castrati; the f″ reported by Quantz had fallen to a d″ by his late career. His voice was capable of much diversity, excelling both in the rich, long, lyric phrases often praised in castrati, as well as in passages of extended coloratura. Among his many talents was his delivery of recitative, which both Hawkins and Burney regarded highly.

Despite his many virtues as a singer, Senesino's personality frequently caused him difficulties. His behavior was heavily salted with intolerance and professional jealousy; he had a sharp tongue and a virulent ego, and apparently never got

Engraved songsheet by George Bickham on the departure of Senesino from London for Italy, satirizing the British enthusiasm for Italian singers, c. 1736

along well with Handel, who called Senesino a "damned fool" soon after Senesino's arrival in London.

—Dale E. Monson

SERAFIN, Tullio.

Conductor. Born 1 September 1878, in Rottanova de Cavarzere, Venice. Died 2 February 1968, in Rome. Studied at the Milan Conservatory; conducting debut in Ferrara, 1898; assistant conductor to Toscanini at the Teatro alla Scala, Milan, 1901; principal conductor at La Scala, 1909-14, 1917-18; conductor at the Metropolitan Opera, New York, 1924-34; principal conductor and artistic director of the Rome Opera, 1934-43; artistic director at La Scala, 1946-47; conductor of the Lyric Opera of Chicago, 1956-58; artistic adviser to the Rome Opera, 1962.

Publications

By SERAFIN: books–

with A. Toni. *Stile, tradizioni e convenzioni del melodramma italiano del Settecento e dell' Ottocento.* Milan, 1958-64.

About SERAFIN: books–

Rubboli, D. *Tullio Serafin: vita, carriera, scriti inediti.* Cavarzere, 1979.
Celli, T., and G. Pugliese. *Tullio Serafin: il patriarca del melodramma.* Venice, 1985.

*   *   *

In his obituary of Tullio Serafin (*Opera,* 1968), William Weaver wrote that "Like Callas, Wieland Wagner, and Felsenstein, Serafin made an all-important, unique contribution to opera in the past twenty years. The *bel canto* revival . . . would have been impossible without him." Actually, Serafin's involvement with the *bel canto* repertoire (used in this sense to mean the masterworks of Rossini, Donizetti, Bellini, and the early Verdi) goes much further back than 1948, the year in which Maria Callas sang her first Norma with him. Callas is not the prime object in the resuscitation of many of these roles; Serafin is. It was because of him, first of all, that Callas undertook parts such as Norma and Elvira in *I Puritani;* furthermore, the revival had begun long before this, for in the 1920s and 1930s a number of dramatic sopranos in Italy sang Norma and also some of the more obscure Donizetti and Rossini operas. Even though Serafin's name became closely linked with that of Callas for about a decade beginning in 1948, it should not be forgotten that Serafin's conducting career had begun around 1900 and that he was associated with numerous other singers, his "three miracles" being Rosa Ponselle, Enrico Caruso, and Titta Ruffo. Serafin worked closely with Ponselle on Norma and *La vestale* by Spontini, and even attempted to persuade Renata Tebaldi to tackle the role of Norma. Yet even Serafin, whom Ethan Mordden labels the "wizard of *Fach,*" could not induce her.

That Serafin was conducting *bel canto* operas all along, before they became "fashionable" (a fashion he unwittingly helped to create), is symptomatic of his career and artistic credo: if he admired a work, he conducted it. Throughout his career he was a champion of the obscure and the "difficult": he conducted the first Italian *Wozzeck,* with Tito Gobbi, in Rome in 1942 and, amid jeers from the audience, the Teatro alla Scala premiere of *Der Rosenkavalier* in 1911. His La Scala career had begun in 1909; he came to the Metropolitan Opera in 1924. It is no surprise that he introduced Puccini's *Turandot* to the United States, but it is remarkable that, as an Italian conductor whose specialty was Rossini-Bellini-Donizetti-Verdi, Serafin was to conduct the premieres at the Metropolitan of *Emperor Jones, Merry Mount, The King's Henchman,* and *Peter Ibbetson.* But then, perhaps Serafin did not believe in "specialties" or attempt to limit himself.

Serafin helped launch the Florence May Festival in the 1930s and appeared often at the Rome Opera in 1930s and 1940s, because of him a great period for that house. Tito Gobbi, who worked with him for nearly thirty years, called him a "complete 'man of the theatre' " and "an infallible judge of voice and character"; Gobbi maintained that Serafin's performances were "like an arch, beautifully shaped in a curve from the first bar to the last." After Serafin's death in 1968 Callas revealed some of his secrets: "He opened a world to me, showed me there was a reason for everything, that even fioriture and trills . . . have a reason in the composer's mind, that they are the expression of the *stato d'animo* [state of mind] of the character. . . . He would coach us for every little detail, every movement, every word, every breath. . . . But in performance he left you on your own. . . . He was helping you all the way. He would mouth all the words. If you were not well, he would speed up the tempo, and if you were in top form he would slow it down to let you breathe, to give you room. He was breathing with you, living the music with you, loving it with you. It was elastic, growing, living."

After World War II Serafin experienced serious disagreements with the management of La Scala; thus, although he was closely associated with Callas during her great decade of the 1950s, it was through recording; he never conducted Callas in a staged performance at La Scala. Thanks to the record producer Walter Legge, however, Serafin conducted a number of "La Scala" recordings with Callas and other illustrious singers, all on the EMI/Angel label. Among them are two complete recordings of Bellini's *Norma,* the monophonic version in 1954 and the stereo one in 1960. Like his contemporary, Vittorio Gui, Serafin places *Norma* in its rightful time period as before, rather than after, the masterpieces of Verdi and Wagner. Serafin also conducted both of Callas' commercial recordings of *Lucia di Lammermoor,* the *Rigoletto* with Callas, Di Stefano, and Gobbi (in which Rigoletto's and Gilda's scenes are incomparable), and an elegant reading of the veristic *Cavalleria rusticana* with Callas and Di Stefano. There is also a dramatic *Aida* and an insightful *La forza del destino,* both with Callas and with Richard Tucker as the tenor.

With other singers and on other labels, there are passionate Puccini performances of *La bohème* and *Madama Butterfly* on the Decca-London label, both sung gloriously by Renata Tebaldi and Carlo Bergonzi, and an *Un ballo in maschera* from 1943, with Beniamino Gigli and Maria Caniglia in which the principal focus is on the singers. Of special interest because of what Serafin makes of the orchestral writing is his recording of Verdi's *Otello* with Rysanek and Vickers and the Iago of Tito Gobbi. Even though they made no recordings together, it was Serafin who coached and conducted Joan Sutherland in her landmark performances as Lucia at Covent Garden in 1959. Serafin subsequently conducted Sutherland

INTERNATIONAL DICTIONARY OF OPERA

in *La sonnambula* at that same house, which led David Cairns to write of the conductor's "grasp of style and spacing and his wonderfully tactful accompanying of the singers."

—Stephen Willier

SERBAN, Andrei.

Producer. Born 21 June 1943, Bucharest, Rumania. Educated at the Institute of Theatrical and Cinematographic Arts, Bucharest, where he was active in student theater, and the University of Bucharest; came to the United States to direct at La Mama Experimental Theatre Club in New York, producing *Arden of Faversham,* 1970; assisted Peter Brook in Paris; assistant director, Yale Repertory Theatre, 1977; visiting professor, Yale, 1977-78; has also taught at University of California, Carnegie-Mellon, Sarah Lawrence College, the Paris Conservatoire d'Art Dramatique, and the A.R.T. Institute; operatic debut, *Die Zauberflöte,* Nancy, 1979; permanent position with Boston Repertory Theatre; director, National Theatre, Romania, 1990. Awards include Ford, Guggenheim, and Rockefeller Foundation grants.

Opera Productions (selected)

Die Zauberflöte, Nancy, 1979.
Eugene Onegin, Welsh National Opera, 1980.
La traviata, Julliard Opera Center, New York, 1981.
I puritani, Welsh National Opera, 1981.
Norma, Welsh National Opera, 1981; New York City Opera, 1985; Opera North, 1987.
Alcina, New York City Opera, 1983.
Turandot, Olympic Arts Festival, Los Angeles, 1984; Covent Garden, 1983/84 season.
Il trovatore, Opera North, 1984.
The Juniper Tree, American Repertory Company, Cambridge, Massachusetts; Baltimore Opera, 1985.
Fidelio, Covent Garden, 1986/87 season.
Les huguenots, Covent Garden.
Fiery Angel, Los Angeles Music Drama, 1989 and Geneva.
Don Carlos, Geneva and Bologna.
Prince Igor, Covent Garden, 1990.
Lucia di Lammermoor, Lyric Opera, Chicago, 1990.
Elektra, San Francisco, 1991/92 season.

Publications

About SERBAN: articles–

"Serban, Andrei." In *Current Biography* (1978): 376-80.
Mann, W. "Sense (Colin Davis' Jahre am Royal Opera House)." *Opernwelt* 27, no. 10 (1986): 48-50.
"Uj szelek—uj rendezok az amerikai operahazakban." *Muzsika* 31 (May 1988): 19-20.

* * *

Serban was brought to the United States in 1969 by avant-garde leader Ellen Stewart, who had discovered Serban while he was still a student at The Central Drama School in Bucharest. Following his directorial debut at Stewart's La Mama Club, Serban was invited to Peter Brook's International Center of Theatre Research in 1970.

Serban has received critical acclaim for his versions of Aeschylus, Sophocles, Shakespeare, and Chekhov. Perhaps most influenced by the 18th-century Italian playwright Carlo Gozzi, Serban has directed the operas *Turandot* and *The Love for Three Oranges,* both based on works by Gozzi, as well as the plays *The Serpent Woman* and *The King Stag. The King Stag,* first produced in 1984, toured throughout the United States in 1986 to extremely favorable reviews. Serban worked with composer Elliott Goldenthal on the production, which incorporated masks and life-size puppets.

In his trilogy of Greek tragedies, Serban and composer Elizabeth Swados attempted to reinvent opera; one play, *The Trojan Women,* was even subtitled "An Epic Opera." The text was spoken, chanted, shrieked, whispered, and sung mainly in ancient Greek, to focus attention on the emotive possibilities of sound, not on the meanings of words. When the Welsh National Opera invited him to direct *La traviata,* he thought it was a joke, but when the offer was repeated with Tchaikovsky's *Eugene Onegin,* Serban accepted because of his familiarity with the poem by Pushkin. Thus his career as an opera director was begun in 1980.

Serban is described as "an auteur who feels the modern theater has become increasingly bogged down in sociology." Despite his production of *Il trovatore* in modern dress, set surrealistically in an abandoned train station, he described modern German productions as follows: "You watch something that is so crazy, so off-the-wall, that your mind is puzzled and intellectually you are challenged and, at the same time, your heart is totally left hungry. . . . I don't really see Norma with a machine gun in her hand singing 'Casta diva.' It's been done."

Serban also feels that current opera singers "have the tendency to exaggerate too much. For them to act interiorly means to be boring, to be unseen, unnoticed." *The Wall Street Journal* says of him, "Mr. Serban has a reputation for creating lyrically visual and playfully imagistic productions that have only a nodding relationship with the neo-Stanislavskian realism practiced in his native Romania."

For a New York City Opera production of *Norma* in 1985, Serban emphasized the contrast between Norma the priestess and Norma the private woman through masks, headdresses, and robes for the public scenes. Also in 1985, Serban directed the American Repertory Company premiere of *The Juniper Tree,* an opera by Philip Glass and Robert Moran, with a libretto by Arthur Yorinks, based on a Grimm fairy tale. The fantasy element that Serban had responded to in Gozzi was evident here in the cutout sets, the tableaux, and the slow stylized movements that matched the minimalist music. As he had done in some of his plays, Serban had the actors singing from the audience. Julius Novick likened *The Juniper Tree* to "a Robert Wilson piece in which something actually happens." Serban has said of it, "It's a mistake to try to be intellectual about material from fairy tales. They exist in our experience, in our bodies. We will lose many aspects of them if we try to analyze them. The visual images are very important. Something happens almost every second. Each minute has a symbol and an enigma. The piece really has the echoes of Greek tragedy; it is a barbaric, primitive myth."

A calibration of the artistic success of *The Juniper Tree* can be determined from the vastly different reviews of the production; the less uniform the reaction, the better from an

Andrei Serban's production of *Turandot* for the Royal Opera, London, 1984

artistic standpoint. *The Philadelphia Inquirer* pronounced, "Throughout, the staging by Andrei Serban, the Romanian visionary, proceeded from surprise to surprise, from one inspired detail to another. . . . The magic was sustained for ninety minutes, carrying through the intermission." A *Boston Globe* critic labeled it "just awful;" a critic from the *Phoenix,* "pretentious." *The Herald* echoed: "The staging is *The Juniper Tree's* undoing. Nowhere is Serban extreme enough. His stylistic approach with its impressive display of visual gimmicks never shocks, never approaches the grotesque." Others found it "stunning" and "spellbinding." The work was frequently compared with Humperdinck's *Hänsel und Gretel* and Ravel's *L'enfant et les sortilèges* and the staging with that of Glass's collaborator Robert Wilson. Serban's intent—did he mean to portray fantasy, realism, or a cartoon?—was unclear to some, although this author felt the staging was the most successful element in the production.

Whenever an *auteur* director approaches opera, one of two things can happen. A war-horse can be seen in a new and different light with allusions to contemporary life which enhance its meaning. Conversely, a new opera can be distorted from the composer's intentions without the audience knowing exactly where or how because of an unfamiliarity with the libretto and music. Despite almost no middle ground, a composer would be lucky to have Serban direct his operas. Serban is one of the most distinguished *auteur* opera directors today.

—Andrea Olmstead

SERSE [Xerxes].

Composer: George Frideric Handel.

Librettist: unknown (after S. Stampiglia, Rome, 1694, based on N. Minato).

First Performance: London, King's Theatre in the Haymarket, 15 April 1738.

Roles: Serse (soprano); Arsamene (soprano); Amastre (contralto); Ariodate (bass); Romilda (soprano); Atalanta (soprano); Elviro (bass).

Publications

article–

Powers, Harold S. "*Il Serse* trasformato." *Musical Quarterly* 47 (1961): 481; 48 (1962): 73.

Serse is one of Handel's last operas. It is based on an earlier libretto by Silvio Stampiglia entitled *Il Xerse,* which was performed in Rome in 1694 with music by Giovanni Bononcini. Handel's text may have been adapted by Paolo Rolli, who prepared *Deidamia* for Handel in 1741. In the story, Serse, King of Persia, is betrothed to Amastre. He, however,

Handel's *Xerxes*, English National Opera, London, 1985

prefers Romilda, who loves and is loved by Arsamene, Serse's brother. Serse, impatient that Arsamene will not help him win Romilda's hand, exiles him from court. Amastre, Serse's fiancée, enters the court disguised as a man. Atalanta, Romilda's sister, further complicates matters by playing the coquette, and Elviro, Serse's servant, creates endless confusion by his mistakes. When Ariodate, father of Romilda and Atalanta, returns successful from battle, Serse obliquely makes his wishes known by promising him that Romilda "shall have a royal bridegroom of Serse's line, equal to Serse." Ariodate interprets this to mean that he has Serse's permission to give Romilda in marriage to Arsamene, Serse's brother, and he oversees their union. Amastre then reveals her true identity; she forgives Serse, and they are united. Atalanta cheerily says she will look for another lover elsewhere. All rejoice.

In Handel's operatic career, *Serse* is followed chronologically only by *Imeneo* (1740) and *Deidamia* (1741). These three operas have much in common. Unlike many of Handel's operas, none is heroic in the sense that none contains a political conflict between two rulers that needs to be resolved. Furthermore, none is dependent on magical or mythological elements. Rather, the plot of each opera tells of love relationships and complications without a strong secondary focus. All three operas contain choral movements (which is somewhat unusual), and all three are freer in structure than the typical Handel opera. Finally, both *Serse* and *Deidamia* have decidedly comic elements, which is very rare in Handel's oeuvre. The argument of *Serse* specifically mentions "that basis of the story" that resides partially in "some imbicilities," and

the cast list describes Serse's servant, Elviro, as "a facetious Fellow."

The three late operas are also similar in their flexible scenic construction, which deviated from normal patterns. The accepted conventions of Baroque *opera seria* (serious opera) included the pervasive use of a single aria form (the *da capo*, meaning "from the beginning" or having a three-part structure: ABA), the placement of these arias with very few exceptions at the end of scenes (so that the end of a scene could normally be defined by the occurance of an aria), and the immediate exit of the character who has sung the aria (thus the term "exit aria"). Handel's last three operas, however, are very fluid in their formal layout, as the first three scenes of *Serse* can demonstrate. The first scene is for Serse alone. It ends with a through-composed aria (an aria without formal repetition), after which Serse remains on stage. In the second scene, Arsamene arrives with Elviro. They overhear a woman in the summer house begin an aria, and as she sings, they recognize the singer as Romilda and comment upon this. Serse, hearing Romilda mention his name, joins Arsamene and Elviro. This marks the beginning of scene iii. Romilda finishes her song (which, like Serse's in scene i, is through-composed) and remains in the summer house. Serse and Arsamene then have a brief conversation, after which Romilda sings another song, which Handel sets in ternary form (in three parts with the last a variation of the first). She then exits. Serse and Arsamene continue their conversation. Scene iii ends with a *da capo* aria that is first sung by Serse with one text, after which he exits, and then by Arsamene with another text, after which he remains on stage. Thus, in *Serse* the typical scenic construction of recitative leading to an aria does not apply. Arias can come anywhere in the scene (and even across scenic boundaries) and be in various formal designs; exits are not tied to *da capo* arias or to the ends of scenes. Although this increased flexibility contributed enormously to the structural variety of Handel's opera, it was not the panacea some modern authors have described it to be. Without a rigid convention to control expectation, Handel lost the element of surprise, one of his most important dramatic tools.

Handel's music for *Serse* is lighter in style than that of his earlier operas. It is often charming, and sometimes stunning. Serse's opening aria, "Ombra mai fu" ("Never was there shade more soothing"), is one of Handel's most beautiful and popular melodies; like other movements in this opera, it is based on Bononcini's setting of the same text. When Elviro disguises himself as a flower-seller, he sings "Ah! chi voler fiora" ("Ah! who will buy my flowers?"), which is apparently based on the street cry of a London match-boy, thus antedating Haydn's use of London street cries in his "London" Symphony (no. 104) by more than fifty years. Handel's copy of the cry still exists. Perhaps referring in part to this song, Lady Luxborough reports in a 1748 letter that "The great Handel has told me that the hints of his very best songs have several of them been owing to the sounds in his ears of cries in the street."

Although *Serse* was not successful in Handel's lifetime, closing after only five performances, its performances coincided with the placement of a white marble statue of the composer by the sculptor Louis François Roubiliac in Vauxhall Gardens in London. In this century, because of its melodiousness, comic elements, and structural freedom, *Serse* has become one of Handel's most frequently performed operas.

—Ellen T. Harris

LA SERVA PADRONA [The Maid Turned Mistress].

Composer: Giovanni Battista Pergolesi.

Librettist: Gennarantonio Federico.

First Performance: Naples, San Bartolomeo, 5 September 1733.

Roles: Serpina (soprano); Uberto (bass); Vespone (mute).

Publications

books–

Rousseau, J.-J. *Lettre de MM. du coin du roi a MM. du coin de la reine sur la nouvelle pièce intitulée La servante maîtresse.* Paris, 1754.
Troy, Charles. *The Comic Intermezzo: a Study in the History of Eighteenth-Century Opera.* Ann Arbor, 1979.

*   *   *

La serva padrona, Pergolesi's most famous stage work, comprises two comic intermezzi, or brief scenes, originally interposed between the acts of his serious opera *Il prigioniero superbo* (Naples, San Bartolomeo, 28 August 1733). The libretto, by Gennarantonio Federico (one of the finest comic librettists of the early eighteenth century), tells the simple story of a scheming yet enchanting servant girl, Serpina, who teases and torments her master, Uberto, and who ultimately tricks the temperamental miser to consent to marriage. As her pleading goes unheeded (he swears he would marry anyone but her), she dresses up another servant (Vespone, a mute role) as a Bulgarian captain and presents him to Uberto as her fiancé. When she informs Uberto that he must choose among giving her a dowry for her wedding, facing death at the hands of the soldier, or marrying her himself, he chooses what he thinks is the least objectionable and consents to the marriage. Though he soon sees he has been swindled, they still admit their mutual love.

The plot and characters are not wholly original; numerous plays and libretti of the day portrayed a similar action. Jacopo Angelo Nelli's comic play of the same title, written for Naples probably in the first decade of the century and then revised for Rome shortly thereafter, includes several episodes perpetuated by Federico, including a scene of the master complaining about his missing chocolate. Pietro Pariati's libretto, *Pimpinone, ossia Vespetta e Pimpinone,* was extremely popular, set by Telemann (1725) and others, and is perhaps Federico's closest model. The characters, drawn from standard *commedia dell' arte* stock, act in a predictable way. Serpina ("little serpent"—compare Pariatti's "Vespetta," or "little wasp") deftly manipulates Uberto to her own ends. The use of disguise is particularly clever, but again common.

La serva padrona was continually revived through the eighteenth century, and in a singularly astonishing manner. It is practically unique in the extent to which it was preserved, largely without changes, over the many revivals staged both by traveling companies and resident theaters throughout Europe. That singers left it relatively undisturbed attests to its tight dramatic impact, the convincing logic of its musical setting, and its universal musical appeal. The only change consistently made (and still practiced) was the deletion of the original final duet of the second intermezzo, "Contento tu sarai," and the substitution of a duet taken from Pergolesi's last full-length comic opera, *Flaminio:* "Per te ho io nel core."

The work was revived in most of the operatic centers of Europe. In London, for example, the work was often restaged, primarily in the Marybone Gardens (four times in the original language, seven times in English translation). Its most famous revival, however, occurred in Paris. The work had been mounted there already in 1746, to little public response, but when an Italian opera company began to stage full-length comic works and shorter intermezzi for the Parisian public in 1752, the work immediately became the rallying cry for the opponents of French music, led by Rousseau (who even wrote his own opera in direct imitation of *La serva padrona*'s style). A vitriolic pamphlet war ensued, the so-called *querelle des bouffons,* another reincarnation of the perennial battle over the merits of Italian and French music.

Pergolesi's music in *La serva padrona* is representative of the new musical language arising in the 1730s in Italy. Phrases are built by simple repetition of short motives (sometimes in melodic sequence, but usually repeated at pitch). The harmonic rhythm has slowed enormously, necessitating an alteration of the bass line into such patterns as the "drum bass" or "Alberti bass." Phrases are irregular in the main; it is only in the obvious imitation of popular musical styles that the music squares up into the four-measure patterns sometimes thought to be typical. The buffo arias are marvelous caricatures (such as Uberto's opening "Aspetare" aria), with imitations of every comic effect, from long patter passages and wildly disjunct melodies, to text-painting devices (such as his wailing at "morire"). Serpina can be plaintive and emotive, or cocky and impertinent (both are juxtaposed in "A Serpina penserete," for example). Overall, the work is one of the finest masterpieces of characterization and comedy of its age.

—Dale E. Monson

SESSIONS, Roger.

Composer. Born 28 December 1896, in Brooklyn. Died 16 March 1985, in Princeton, New Jersey. Married: 1) Barbara (Sessions), 1920 (divorced 1936); 2) Elizabeth Franck. B.A. Harvard University, 1915; studied with Horatio Parker at Yale University, B.M., 1917; studied privately with Ernest Bloch in Cleveland and New York; taught music theory at Smith College, 1917-21; on the faculty of the Cleveland Institute of Music as assistant to Ernest Bloch, and then as department head, 1921-25; Guggenheim fellowships, 1926-27; American Academy in Rome fellowship, 1928-31; Carnegie fellowship, 1931-32; on the faculty at the Boston Conservatory of Music, 1933-36, New Jersey College for Women, 1935-37, Princeton University, 1935-45, and the University of California, Berkeley, 1945-53; returned to Princeton, 1953-65, Berkeley, 1966-67, Harvard, 1968-69, and Juilliard, 1965-83; citation by the Pulitzer Award Committee for his distinguished career as an American composer, 1974; Pulizer prize for his *Concerto for Orchestra* (1981), 1982. Sessions students included Milton Babbitt, Peter Maxwell Davies, David Diamond, Andrew Imbrie, Leon Kirchner, Frederic Rzewski, and Hugo Weisgall.

Operas

Publishers:

The Trial of Lucullus, after Brecht, Berkeley, 18 April 1947.
Montezuma, after A. Borghese, 1962-63, West Berlin, 19 April 1964.

Other works: orchestral works, vocal works, chamber music, piano pieces, organ music.

Publications

By SESSIONS: books–

The Musical Experience of Composer, Performer, Listener. Princeton, 1950.
Harmonic Practice. New York, 1951.
Reflections on the Music Life in the United States. New York, 1956.
Questions About Music. Cambridge, Massachusetts, 1970.
Cone, E.T., ed. *Roger Sessions on Music: Collected Essays.* Princeton, 1979.

About SESSIONS: books–

Olmstead, Andrea. *Roger Sessions and his Music.* Ann Arbor, 1985.
_____. *Conversations with Roger Sessions.* Boston, 1987.
_____. *The Correspondence of Roger Sessions.* Boston, 1992.

articles–

Davies, P.M. "Montezuma." *New York Times* 21 April (1964).
Laufer, E.C. "Roger Sessions: *Montezuma.*" *Perspectives of New Music* 4/no. 1 (1965): 95.
Harbison J. "Roger Sessions and Montezuma." *New Boston Review* 2/no. 1 (1976): 5; reprinted in *Tempo* no. 121 (1977): 2.
Porter, A. "The Matter of Mexico." *New Yorker* 102/19 April (1976): 115.
Stevenson, Robert. "American Awareness of the Other Americas to 1900" *[Montezuma].* In *Essays on Music for Charles Warren Fox,* edited by Jerald C. Grave, 181. Rochester, 1979.
Porter, A. "The Magnificent Epic." *New Yorker* 108/8 March (1982): 128.
Olmstead, Andrea. "The Plum'd Serpent: Antonio Borghese's and Roger Sessions's *Montezuma.*" *Tempo* no. 152 (1985).

unpublished–

Mason, Charles N. "A Comprehensive Analysis of Roger Sessions' Opera *Montezuma.*" DMA dissertation, University of Illinois, Champaign-Urbana, 1982.

Sessions's first work, created when he was thirteen years old, was an opera on Tennyson's *Idylls of the King* called *Lancelot and Elaine* (1910). His first operatic influences were Wagner and Strauss, about whose music he published articles while still a teenager. However, he recoiled from Strauss in 1915 and outgrew his "Wagner phase." Although he wrote incidental music for Andreyev's play *The Black Maskers* in 1923, Sessions did not return to the operatic—or even vocal—medium until the mid-1930s, when, prodded by his Sicilian friend Antonio Borgese, he began work on an opera about Cortez's conquest of Mexico.

The completion of this opera, eventually titled *Montezuma,* was so long delayed, due to Sessions's slow pace of composition and to the interruption of other orchestral commissions, that the librettist did not live to see the work produced. In the meantime, at the urging of Heinrich Schnitzler to write a work for an upcoming performance at the University of California, Sessions composed a one-act opera on a radio play by Bertolt Brecht, *The Trial of Lucullus.* Uncharacteristically, he finished the work within a few months during the spring of 1947, and he conducted the student production. By the time Sessions completed *Montezuma* in 1963, he had adopted the twelve-tone technique of his friend Arnold Schoenberg. After the Boston production in 1976, *Time* magazine pronounced *Montezuma* "indisputably twelve-tone music's finest hour on the operatic stage."

The composer saw a connection between his two only operas: "Fundamentally *The Trial of Lucullus* and *Montezuma* are about the same thing: the futility of conquest." The two also share the oratorio-like device of a narrator and they both deal with historical and fictional events as vehicles to display universal human emotions. *The Trial of Lucullus* is more successful as opera not because it is tonal and *Montezuma* is twelve-tone, but because the libretto, a translation from Brecht's German, is succinct and powerful. Borgese's libretto, which consists of lengthy fancy poetry incorporating Spanish, Aztec, and Latin, has been widely criticized, although Andrew Porter defended it by writing, "It [the libretto's diction] seems to me now an awkwardness that, since Sessions accepted it, we, too, must accept—as an integral part of his opera." The fundamental difference between the two works lies in the fact that Brecht was one of the greatest dramatists of the twentieth century, while Borgese was known as a newspaper columnist and poet (he wrote in Italian, German, and English), who had never before written an opera libretto. Without Borgese, however, the opera would certainly never have been written.

Sessions is seen as an instrumental composer first and foremost. His nine symphonies, four concertos, and numerous other orchestral and chamber works attest to this view of him. However, his two operas and six other vocal works, including a forty-two minute monodrama for soprano and orchestra *(Idyll of Theocritus)*, the Three Choruses on Biblical Texts, and his monumental cantata, *When Lilacs Last in the Dooryard Bloom'd,* demonstrate his overarching concern with the voice and the vocal line. In all, Sessions wrote almost as many notes for works for voice as for purely instrumental combinations, and at the end of his life was working on another opera, *The Emperor's New Clothes,* to a libretto by Porter. Perhaps when his two operas are recorded and performed more frequently in public, a full recognition of Sessions the vocal composer will enlarge our appreciation of Sessions the composer.

Always revered in the musical community, Sessions has taken a long time to achieve public success. This wider appreciation has not yet fully been realized, but is inevitable when recordings of all of his works and frequent performances acquaint a larger audience with his music. Music critics have not always been supportive; frequently denounced as too "cerebral," "academic," or "knotty" by the press (particularly the *New York Times*), Sessions's music is widely known and loved among musicians and particularly among the several generations of composers he taught. His obituary quoted the *bon mot:* "Everybody loves Roger Sessions except the public."

—Andrea Olmstead

SHAW, Glen Byam.

Producer. Born Glencairn Alexander Byam Shaw, 13 December 1904, in London. Died 29 April 1986, in London. Married: Angela Baddeley; two children. Educated at Westminster School, London, 1918-22; received stage training as a member of James Bernard Fagan's Oxford Players Company; stage debut in *At Mrs. Beam's,* Torquay, England, 1923; Oxford University Dramatic Society, 1936; Member of the Directorate, Old Vic Theatre, 1946-51; first production as director, *The Winslow Boy,* Lyric Theatre, London, 1946; director of Old Vic Theatre School, 1951; codirector of Shakespeare

Memorial Theatre, Stratford-upon-Avon, 1952-56; director of Shakespeare Memorial Theatre, Stratford-upon-Avon, 1956-59 and Governor, 1960-75; operatic debut as producer in *Rake's Progress,* Sadler's Wells, 1962; director of productions, Sadler's Wells Opera company, 1962-68; director, English National Opera, 1968-81; made Commander of the British Empire, 1953.

Opera Productions (selected)

The Rake's Progress, Sadler's Wells, 1962.
Idomeneo, Sadler's Wells, 1962.
Orfeo ed Euridice, Sadler's Wells, 1963.
Così fan tutte, Sadler's Wells, 1963.
Der Freischütz, Sadler's Wells, 1963.
Hänsel und Gretel, Sadler's Wells, 1963.
Faust, Sadler's Wells, 1964.
Un ballo in maschera, Sadler's Wells, 1965.
Die Fledermaus, Sadler's Wells, 1966.
Orfeo ed Euridice, Sadler's Wells, 1967.
Die Meistersinger von Nürnberg, Sadler's Wells, 1968 (with John Blatchley).
Die Walküre, London Coliseum, 1970 (with Blatchley).
Götterdämmerung, London Coliseum, 1971 (with Blatchley).
Das Rheingold, London Coliseum, 1972 (with Blatchley).
Duke Bluebeard's Castle, London Coliseum, 1972.
Siegfried, London Coliseum, 1973 (with Blatchley).
Tristan und Isolde, English National Opera, 1981.

Publications

About SHAW: articles—

"New Appointment at Sadler's Wells (Production Director)." *Musical Events* 17 (April 1962): 26-27.
"Glen Byam Shaw." *Music and Musicians* 11 (October 1962): 5.

*   *   *

Glen Byam Shaw began his career in 1923 as an actor; after World War II he became first codirector and then director of the Shakespeare Memorial Theatre (now the Royal Shakespeare Company) at Stratford-upon-Avon. In 1962, he was appointed the director of productions for Sadler's Wells Opera. During the years that he worked with the company, he staged a number of interesting productions, frequently designed by Motley, that were admired by the critics and public alike. These included two very successful stagings of Mozart's *Così fan tutte* (1963) and *Idomeneo* (1962), as well as Igor Stravinsky's *The Rake's Progress* (1962), which was taken to Stuttgart, Frankfurt, Munich, Berlin, Cassel, and other cities in Germany, where it was very well received.

Der Freischütz (1963) and an extremely popular staging of *Hänsel und Gretel* (1963) were followed by Gounod's *Faust* (1964) and Verdi's *Un ballo in maschera* (1965), both designed by Motley, whose plain but highly imaginative sets suited Byam Shaw's own style particularly well. *Die Fledermaus* (1966) was another popular success, but Gluck's *Orfeo ed Euridice* (1967) was marginally less successful. In 1968 *Die Meistersinger von Nürnberg,* coproduced by Shaw and John Blatchley, scored a veritable triumph, despite the enormous difficulty of fitting Richard Wagner's opera onto the small stage of Sadler's Wells Theatre. When in 1968 the company moved to the much larger London Coliseum, the production was expanded to its full artistic stature.

As the climax to his years with Sadler's Wells (in 1974 to be renamed English National Opera), Shaw, with coproducer Blatchley and designer Ralph Koltai, planned and executed a long-cherished project: a complete cycle in English of *Der Ring des Nibelungen.* Starting in 1970 and progressing at the rate of one opera a year, in the order of *Die Walküre, Götterdämmerung, Das Rheingold* and *Siegfried,* the complete *Ring* cycle was performed in the 1973-74 season and repeated many times, both in London and on tour. The exceptional ability of the production to explain all the ramifications of Wagner's text and plot, the meticulous care taken over character detail and motivation, and the open, lunar-landscape sets which utilized the whole of the vast London Coliseum stage illustrated those qualities of simplicity, clarity and dramatic credibility for which Shaw had striven throughout his career. The production marked the apotheosis of his life's work.

—Elizabeth Forbes

THE SHEPHERD KING
See IL RÈ PASTORE

SHIRLEY, George.

Tenor. Born 18 April 1934, in Indianapolis. Married: artist and educator Gladys Lee Ishop, 1956; one daughter, one son. Studied with Amos Ebersole, Edward Boatner at Wayne State University; also with Themy S. Georgi, Cornelius Reid; debut as Eisenstein in *Die Fledermaus,* Woodstock, New York, 1959; Italian debut as Rodolfo at Teatro Nuovo, Milan, 1960; New York City Opera debut as Rodolfo, 1961; Metropolitan Opera debut as Ferrando in *Così fan tutte,* 1961; at Metropolitan Opera, 1961-73, singing twenty-seven roles including Ottavio, Alfredo, Pinkerton, Tamino, Romeo, Almaviva; Glyndebourne debut as Tamino, 1966; Covent Garden debut as Don Ottavio, 1967; Alwa in *Lulu,* Santa Fe, 1973. On the faculty of Staten Island Community College; Artist-in-Residence, Morgan State College, Baltimore.

Publications

By SHIRLEY: articles–

"The Black Performer." *Opera News,* 30 January 1971.
Preface to Patterson, Willis, compiler. *Anthology of Art Songs by Black American Composers.* New York, c.1972.

About SHIRLEY: articles–

Turner, P. "Afro-American Singers: An Index and Discography of Opera, Choral Music and Song." *Black Perspectives in Music* 9/1 (1981): 75.
Cheatham, William M. "Black Male Singers at the Metropolitan Opera." *Black Perspectives in Music* 16/1 (1988): 6.

———. "Conversation with George Shirley." *Black Perspectives in Music* 18/1-2 (1990): 141.

* * *

The American tenor George Shirley sang in a wide variety of operas during a relatively short career that unfolded primarily during the 1960s and 1970s. His repertory was remarkable for the extent to which it went beyond the standard repertory of late eighteenth- and nineteenth-century classics. Shirley was as successful with Haydn and Britten as he was with Mozart, Wagner and Debussy.

One of Shirley's best Mozart roles was the title role of *Idomeneo,* which he performed under Colin Davis at Covent Garden. He was less successful in some of his performances of Mozart tenor roles that require a gentler touch. His portrayals of Ferrando (in *Così fan tutte*) earned mixed reviews. Shirley was praised for the passion and nobility he brought to the role, but was criticized for the tightness of voice that one could hear in his rendition of "Un' aura amorosa", an aria that demands more delicacy and tenderness than Shirley could convey.

Wagner's operas offered Shirley roles well suited to his voice. His portrayals of Loge in the *Ring* were much applauded at Covent Garden during the 1970s. One critic praised his performance as "subtle and musical"; another praised his "dazzling portrayal of Loge"; others called him "eloquent," even "superb."

Writing of Shirley's Loge, a critic noticed in his voice "a baritonal sound." He was referring no doubt to a dark quality that was characteristic of Shirley's voice and to his tessitura, which was lower than those of some other tenors. Shirley was a tenor, not a baritone, but he was never completely comfortable with high notes. One could hear this in one of his best roles, that of Pélleas in Debussy's *Pelléas et Mélisande.* When he performed the role with the Scottish Opera in 1975 he was praised for his portrayal, but also criticized for the strain perceptible in his voice.

Pelléas was not Shirley's only successful role with the Scottish Opera. He won much applause for his portrayal of Quint in Britten's *Turn of the Screw* when the Scottish Opera presented the opera at the King's Theatre in 1979. *Opera* praised his performance as "insinuating, physically threatening and mesmerizingly sung."

Shirley's portrayal of the title character in Haydn's *Orlando paladino,* recorded under Dorati, gives listeners some idea of the singer's weaknesses and strengths. This is a very strong, vivid depiction of the violent, love-crazed Orlando. But Shirley sometimes goes too far, seemingly forcing his character on the audience. In such arias as "D'Angelica il nome" we can admire the beauty of Shirley's voice in lyrical passages, but in louder passages he sometimes shouts rather than sings. He seems to be able to express his character's rage only with a harsh fortissimo. Shirley's voice sounds like a high baritone rather than a tenor; high notes sometimes sound forced. A tremulous vibrato often mars the gentler, more lyrical passages. And yet we remember this character. Shirley's passion, energy and enthusiasm stay with us, as the rest of the performances in this recording fade from memory.

—John A. Rice

SHIRLEY-QUIRK, John Stanton.

Bass-Baritone. Born 28 August 1931, in Liverpool. Married: physician Patricia Hastie, 1955 (died 1981), one daughter, one son; 2) Sara V. Watkins, 1981, one daughter, one son. Educated at Liverpool University, in chemistry 1948-53; Education Branch of the Royal Air Force, 1953-57; taught chemistry at Acton Technical College, 1957-61; studied voice with Roy Henderson, sang in St Paul's Cathedral Choir; debut as Docteur in *Pelléas et Mélisande* at Glyndebourne, 1961; joined English Opera Group, 1964, creating a number of Britten roles, including the Traveler in *Death in Venice,* the Ferryman in *Curlew River,* Ananias in *The Burning Fiery Furnace,* the Father in *The Prodigal Son,* and Coyle in *Owen Wingrave;* Metropolitan Opera debut as the Traveler (and associate roles) in *Death in Venice,* 1974; created roles in *Confessions of a Justified Sinner,* 1976, and Tippett's *The Ice Break,* Covent Garden, 1977.

*   *   *

The voice of this gifted British singer has been variously described as a baritone and as a bass-baritone, and this no doubt reflects not only his vocal range but also his flexibility of vocal color and character, which can vary from brighter to darker according to the demands of the music. Britten took full advantage of this when he wrote for Shirley-Quirk the multiple roles in *Death in Venice,* which required him to play no less than seven characters who are externally different although all of them symbolize the same unsettling force of the psyche (or the Greek god Dionysus) that drives the lonely writer Aschenbach towards his destiny. Britten had first heard him in oratorio early in the 1960s and at once recognized his high musical intelligence and his potential as a singing actor—so much so that he wrote a role for him in each of his operas thereafter. But initially, the singer was quite taken aback that the composer saw him as capable of the dour unfriendliness of the Ferryman in *Curlew River,* and—though he played more sympathetic roles as Ananias in *The Burning Fiery Furnace,* the Father in *The Prodigal Son* and the tutor Coyle in *Owen Wingrave*—in *Death in Venice* he was once again somewhat sinister in his seven guises, despite having some moments of irony and comedy.

This side of Shirley-Quirk's vocal personality has always been exploited fully by composers and producers alike. Four years after *Death in Venice,* in Tippett's *The Ice Break* he created another character with a dark past though not a dark soul; at the start of the opera, Lev has just emerged from twenty years in Russian prison camps as a fifty-year-old "drab figure" of a dissident teacher bearing the burden of the world's wrongs—and Tippett actually designates this role as for a bass. He has played the egoistic poet Mittenhofer in Henze's *Elegy for Young Lovers,* and in Debussy's *Pelléas et Mélisande,* another opera of this century (just), he was the broodingly jealous husband Golaud. He has sung the aged King Arkel, Golaud's grandfather in the same opera, as well as Death in Holst's *Savitri,* again bass roles.

If this were the whole story, Shirley-Quirk would appear to be an artist entirely limited to somewhat sombre characters. But he has also had the charm to play the Count in Mozart's *Le nozze di Figaro* and the Don in *Don Giovanni,* the latter being a young nobleman with the power to win women's hearts even though his own is uneasy and unsatisfied. The same may perhaps be said of his title role in Tchaikovsky's *Eugene Onegin,* a character who realizes too late that he loves Tatyana and is finally dismissed by her to a life of loneliness. All three of these are baritone roles, for a voice usually associated less with romance than with maturity, and although Shirley-Quirk's personality is easy and convivial off stage, his theatrical appearance and presence are somewhat saturnine, and this has perhaps always militated against his being given romantic parts to play. It seems that he was never considered for the baritone role of the handsome sailor Billy Budd in Britten's opera of that name. In the recording of *Billy Budd* the composer chose him to play the ship's First Lieutenant Redburn, a role which he also sang in a production for BBC Television. Shirley-Quirk has made many recordings, though not so many of them are of opera and those operas are mainly by Britten. Like so many British opera singers, he is equally known in oratorio and in concert work, where his sensitivity, dignity and intelligence find full expression.

—Christopher Headington

THE SHORT LIFE
See LA VIDA BREVE

SHOSTAKOVICH, Dmitri.

Composer. Born 25 September 1906, in St Petersburg. Died 9 August 1975, in Moscow. Early musical training from his mother, a professional pianist; studied piano with Nikolayev and composition with Maksimilian Shteinberg at the Petrograd Conservatory, 1919-25 (piano degree, 1923; composition degree, 1925); his first symphony performed by the Leningrad Philharmonic, 12 May 1926.

Operas

Publishers: State Music Printing House [Moscow], Boosey and Hawkes, Sikorski.

Edition: *D. Shostakovich: Collected Works.* 42 vols. Moscow, 1980-84.

The Gypsies, after Pushkin, before 1918 [destroyed by the composer].
The Nose [Nos]. E. Zamyatin, G. Yonin, and A. Preis (after Gogol), 1927-28, Leningrad, 18 January 1930.
The Lady Macbeth of Mtsensk District [Ledi Makbet Mtsenskogo uezda]. A. Preis (after Leskov), 1930-32, Leningrad, 22 January 1934; revised as *Katerina Izmailova,* 1956-63, Moscow, 8 January 1963.
The Gamblers [Igroki] after Gogol, 1941 [unfinished].
Moscow, Cheremushki [Moskva Cheremushki] (operetta), V. Mass and M. Chervinsky, 1958, Moscow, 24 January 1959.

Other works: ballets, incidental music, film scores, orchestral works, vocal works, chamber music, piano pieces.

Publications

By SHOSTAKOVICH: books–

The Power of Music. New York, 1968.
Volkov, Solomon, ed. *Testimony: the Memoirs of Dmitri Shostakovich.* London and New York, 1979.
Pribegina, G., ed. *D. Shostakovich o vremeni i o sebe: 1926-1975.* Moscow, 1980; English translation, 1981.

articles–

"Nos." *Krasnaya gazeta* 24 June (1928).
"Ekaterina Izmailova." *Sovetskoye iskusstvo* 57/14 December (1933): 4.
"My Opera 'Lady Macbeth of Mtsensk'." *Modern Music* 12 (1934-35): 23.
Gojowy, Detlef, trans. "Briefe an einen Studenten (Edison Denissow)." *Neue Zeitschrift für Musik* 142 (1981): 152.

interviews–

Brown, R.S. "An Interview with Shostakovich." *High Fidelity* 18 (1973): 86.

Note: for a selected list of Shostakovich's writings, see *The New Grove Russian Masters 2.* New York, 1986.

About SHOSTAKOVICH: books–

Seroff, V. *Dmitri Shostakovich.* New York, 1943; 1970.
Martynov, I. *D.D. Shostakovich.* Moscow, 1946; 2nd ed., 1956; English translation, 1947; 1969; 1974; Hungarian translation, 1965.
Rabinovich, D. *Dmitri Shostakovich—Composer.* Moscow and London, 1959.
Brockhaus, H.A. *Dmitri Schostakowitsch.* Leipzig, 1962; abridged 2nd ed., 1963 [includes German translations of some articles by Shostakovich].
Hofmann, R.-M. *Dmitri Chostakovitch: l'homme et son oeuvre.* Paris, 1963.
Danilevich, L. *Nash sovremennik: tvorchestvo Shostakovicha.* Moscow, 1965.
Orlov, G. *Dmitri Shostakovich.* Leningrad, 1966.
Danilevich, L. ed. *Dmitri Shostakovich.* Moscow, 1967.
Lazarov, S. *Dmitri Shostakovich.* Sofia, 1967.
Kay, N. *Shostakovich.* London, 1971.
Meyer, K. *Szostakowicz.* Cracow, 1973; German translation, 1980.
Shneerson, G., ed. *D. Shostakovich: stat'i i materialy.* Moscow, 1976.
Bogdanova, Alla. *Opery i balety Shostakovicha.* Moscow, 1979.
Danilevich, L. *Dmitri Shostakovich: zhizn' i tvorchestvo.* Moscow, 1980.
Sollertinski, Dmitry and Ludmilla. *Pages from the Life of Dmitri Shostakovich.* London, 1980.
Norris, Christopher, ed. *Shostakovich: the Man and his Music.* London, 1982.
Roseberry, Eric. *Shostakovich: his Life and Times.* New York and Tunbridge Wells, 1982.
Gojowy, D. *Dmitri Schostakowitsch mit Selbstzeugnissen und Bilddokumenten.* Reinbek, 1983.
Schwartz, Boris. *Music and Musical Life in Soviet Russia, 1917-81.* Bloomington, 1983.
Sofiya, Ziv, compiler. *Muzykal'nyi sovremennik. V.* [includes an essay on *The Gamblers*]. Moscow, 1984.

Kröplin, Eckart. *Frühe sowjetische Oper: Schostakowitsch, Prokofjew.* Berlin, 1985.
Khentova, S. *Shostakovich: zhizn'i tvorchestvo.* 2 vols. Moscow, 1985-86.
The New Grove Russian Masters 2. New York, 1986.
MacDonald, Ian. *The New Shostakovich.* London, 1990.
Hulme, D.C. *Dmitri Shostakovich: a Catalogue, Bibliography and Discography.* Oxford, 1991.

articles–

Thomson, V. "Socialism at the Metropolitan." *Modern Music* 13 (1935).
Sakva, K. "Novaya vstrecha s. Katerinoi Izmailovoi." *Sovetskaya muzyka* no. 3 (1963): 57; German translation in *Musik und Gesellschaft* 13 (1963): 428.
Sovetskaya muzyka no. 9 (1976) [special issue].
Seaman, Gerald. "The Rise of Slavonic Opera, I." *New Zealand Slavonic Journal* 2 (1978): 1.
Norris, Geoffrey. "Shostakovich's *The Nose.*" *Musical Times* 120 (1979): 393.
Fay, L.E. "Musorgsky and Shostakovich." In *Musorgsky: In Memoriam 1881-1981,* edited by M.H. Brown, 215. Ann Arbor, 1982.
Yudin, Gavriil. "... Vasva rabota dlha menya sobytie na vsyu zyiznh" [Letters between Smolic and Shostakovich about the production of Shostakovich's operas]. *Sovetskaya muzyka* 6 (1983): 84.
Bogdanova, Alla. "Einige stilistische Besonderheiten der Oper *Der Spieler* von Dmitri Schostakowitsch." In *Sowjetische Musik: Betrachtungen und Analysen,* edited by H. Gerlach, 162. Berlin, 1984.
Brown, R.S. "The Three Faces of Lady Macbeth." In *Russian and Soviet Music: Essays for Boris Schwarz,* edited by Malcolm H. Brown, 245. Ann Arbor, 1984.
Fay, L.E. "The Punch in Shostakovich's *Nose.*" In *Russian and Soviet Music: Essays for Boris Schwarz,* edited by Malcolm H. Brown, 229. Ann Arbor, 1984.
Emerson, Caryl. "Back to the future: Shostakovich's revision of Leskov's 'Lady Macbeth of Mtsensk District'." *Cambridge Opera Journal* 1 (1989): 59.
Taruskin, Richard. "The Opera and the Dictator." *New Republic* 20 March (1989): 34.

* * *

A single newspaper article blighted one of the most promising operatic careers of the twentieth century and diverted the entire operatic tradition of a nation. On 28 January 1936, *Pravda* denounced Dmitri Shostakovich's *The Lady Macbeth of Mtsensk District* as "Chaos instead of Music." The article was unsigned, and there have been disputes as to its authorship, but it clearly carried the authority of Stalin, who had seen a production of the opera the previous month. As the Soviet intellectual community had already discovered, the price of such disapproval could be loss of livelihood, victimization of relatives, internal exile, imprisonment, or even death.

Shostakovich abandoned his planned operatic trilogy (later announced as a tetralogy) about heroic Russian and Soviet women, and he never completed another serious opera; instead his dramatic instincts were redirected and he became one of the great twentieth century symphonists. Meanwhile Soviet composers, if they ventured into musical drama at all, took refuge in nationalistic song operas of the kind known to

Dmitri Shostakovich

appeal to Stalin. Here the approved model was Ivan Dzerzhinsky's *The Quiet Don* (after Sholokhov's novel), which ironically enough had been completed under Shostakovich's artistic supervision.

Lady Macbeth was a huge popular and critical success in Leningrad and Moscow, notching up nearly 200 performances in 1934 and 1935. It was also performed all over Europe and in both American continents, where its reception was more mixed. Russian and Western commentators alike saw its emotional excesses as a product of Soviet society, although their reasons for drawing this conclusion were very different. It would almost certainly be wrong to see *Lady Macbeth* as dissident or even consciously non-conformist, even if later events made it seem so. By the time of the opera's completion in 1932 the Party's policy directives for the arts had only just been formulated, and their relevance to music was far from clear. *Lady Macbeth* was almost certainly an attempt to influence the direction of that policy rather than a gesture of either compliance or defiance. Its subject matter (an indictment of the merchant class in nineteenth-century Russia) and its dramatic tone (summed up by the composer as "tragedy-satire") represented considerable modifications of Leskov's original story, in line with what might have been understood as Socialist/Realist principles at the time.

Shostakovich's early musical development was remarkable. His First Symphony, finished at the age of 18, was an international sensation, and on the strength of it he was acclaimed as the first significant composer to have spent his formative years under the Bolsheviks. Among the juvenilia he burned after his graduation in 1925 was an opera *The Gypsies,* after Pushkin, probably composed before 1918—three vocal numbers survive, but are unpublished.

In the ideological battlefield of Soviet music in the 1920s, Shostakovich sided with those who favored increased contact with new Western music. His satirical opera *The Nose* (1927-28) has many features in common with the burlesque tone of Prokofiev's *The Love for Three Oranges,* the atonal caricatures in Berg's *Wozzeck,* and the music hall elements of Krenek's *Der Sprung über den Schatten,* all produced in Leningrad in 1926 and 1927. Shostakovich always played down their influence, however, and it is probable that his imagination was fired more intensely by the work of the famous actor-director Vsevolod Meierkhold, with whom he lodged during the composition of *The Nose.* The eighty-odd solo roles in this work are something of an obstacle to staged performance, and the first Soviet production had great difficulties coping with Shostakovich's musical demands. Nevertheless the score, which includes parts for domra and balalaika and an interlude for percussion alone, is brilliantly inventive and succeeds in matching Gogol's text in its refusal to allow any single interpretation of its meaning.

Much of Shostakovich's work between *The Nose* and *Lady Macbeth* consisted of ballet and film scores and incidental music for the theater. The thirty-five numbers for the music hall review *Conditionally Killed* (1931) make this virtually a full blown operetta; in 1929 he supplied two additional movements for the opera *Columbus* by the young German composer Erwin Dressel; and in 1932 he began work on a comic opera to Nikolai Aseev's *The Great Lightning,* whose nine published numbers (rediscovered in 1980) suggest the influence of Weill's *Die Dreigroschenoper.* All of these activities left their mark on the music of *Lady Macbeth*—less avant-garde than that of *The Nose,* but still immensely vivid. Subsequently there are two film scores—for the cartoons *The Tale of the Priest and his Servant Balda* (1933-34) and *The Silly Little Mouse* (1939)—which Shostakovich regarded as "little operas," since the films were put to the music rather than vice versa.

Shostakovich's rehabilitation after *Lady Macbeth* came with the Fifth Symphony in 1937 and was consolidated with the Seventh (the "Leningrad") in 1941. His interest in the stage was kept alive, however, by his edition and orchestration of Musorgsky's *Boris Godunov* in 1939-40, and in 1942 he started work on the Gogol play *The Gamblers.* His word-for-word setting of the latter was abandoned at the end of act I, ostensibly because it was becoming unmanageable, but more importantly because there were no realistic prospects of performance, still less of approval (a posthumous three-act completion has been made by his Polish pupil, Krzysztof Meyer).

In 1944, Shostakovich completed the orchestration of the 40-minute one-act opera *Rothschild's Violin* (a Chekhov short story) by his pupil Veniamin Fleishman who had died at the battlefront. This encounter with Jewish folk idioms was to bear fruit in many of Shostakovich's later instrumental works, as well as in the general enrichment of his modal harmonic style; there are direct echoes of Fleishman's music in the Twenty-four Preludes and Fugues (1950-51) and the Tenth Symphony (1953).

Shostakovich's operetta (or musical comedy) *Moscow, Cheremushki* (1958) deals with the lives of workers in a Moscow suburb and incorporates at least half a dozen folk and popular songs of the 1920s, as well as references to his own songs of that period. In an explanatory article he professed admiration for the work of Offenbach, Lecocq, Johann Strauss, Kálmán and Lehár (the notorious invasion music of the "Leningrad" Symphony is based partly on a snatch of melody from Lehár's *The Merry Widow*). In the same year he prepared an edition and orchestration of Musorgsky's *Khovanshchina,* originally undertaken for a film version of the opera. Between 1956 and 1963 he worked on a revision of *Lady Macbeth,* toning down its most lurid extremes. His closest musical associates consider the revisions politically rather than artistically motivated. The new version was entitled *Katerina Izmailova.*

Throughout his career, Shostakovich was offered various operatic projects and in some cases made sketches. These include Ilf and Petrov's *The Twelve Chairs* (1937-38), *Quiet Flows the Don* (mentioned in the Soviet press between 1965 and 1970) and, perhaps most tantalizing of all, Chekhov's story *The Black Monk,* which he was considering in his last years and which he claimed was a sub-text to the Fifteenth Symphony of 1971.

—David Fanning

THE SICILIAN VESPERS
See LES VÊPRES SICILIENNES

LE SIÈGE DE CORINTHE [The Siege of Corinth].

Composer: Gioachino Rossini.

Librettists: L. Balocchi and A. Soumet (after della Valle's libretto for Rossini's *Maometto II,* 1820).

First Performance: Paris, Opéra, 9 October 1826.

Roles: Mahomet II (bass); Pamira (soprano); Néoclès (tenor); Hiéros (bass); Adraste (tenor); Omar (tenor); Ismène (soprano); Cléomène (tenor); chorus.

Publications

article–

Avant-scène opéra November (1985) [*Le siège de Corinthe* issue].

* * *

Le siège de Corinthe is a reworking of Rossini's Neapolitan opera *Maometto II.* It was his debut at the Paris Opéra, for which Rossini was apparently as yet reluctant to write a completely new work in French (his first opera for Paris, the Italian *Il viaggio a Reims,* was performed at the Théâtre-Italien in June of 1825).

The plot of the opera basically follows that of *Maometto II,* but the place, time, and names of characters as well as some details are changed. It is based on the historical Turkish victory at Corinth in 1459 (in *Maometto II* the Turks conquer the Venetians at Negroponte in 1476). Cléomène (Paolo Erisso in *Maometto II*), the Greek governor of Corinth, has called his council to determine whether to fight the Byzantines who have besieged the city for two months or to surrender. The young officer Néoclès (Calbo), to whom Cléomène has promised the hand of his daughter Pamira (Anna), encourages the Greeks to resist. However, Pamira is in love with a man named Almanzor (Uberto), whom she met in Athens, and refuses to wed Néoclès. Cléomène gives her a dagger with which to kill herself if the city is captured. The Turks breach the wall of the city, and Mahomet confides to his friend Omar (Selimo) that while traveling under the name of Almanzor he met a Greek girl whose memory makes him feel clemency toward her compatriots. Cléomène is brought before him and Mahomet and Pamira recognize each other. Still rejecting Néoclès, Pamira brings her father's wrath upon herself.

The second act opens in Mahomet's tent as the Turkish maidens exhort Pamira to enjoy the delights of love. Torn between love for Mahomet and loyalty to her country, she prays to her dead mother to watch over her destiny. Mahomet, trying to lessen her sorrow, offers her his crown and says they will appease her father's anger. Pamira's confidante, Ismène, and the chorus joyfully anticipate the wedding, dancing and singing a marriage hymn. Néoclès tries to prevent the wedding, and to save him Pamira tells Mahomet that he is her brother; Omar interrupts them to say the Greek women and soldiers are defending the citadel. Pamira says she loved Almanzor but will die for her country.

In the final act, Néoclès brings Pamira to her father in the catacombs, where the Greeks have prepared their last defense, and convinces him to forgive her; Cléomène then unites them in marriage. Cléomène and Néoclès go to join the Greeks in battle as Pamira and the Greek women pray. When Mahomet and the victorious Turks burst in, Pamira stabs herself. Flames engulf the stage, for the Greeks have set fire to their city, leaving only ruins to the conquerors.

Rossini's approach to the revision ranges from minor changes of the Italian originals to composition of entirely new pieces. *Maometto II* was a work in which he had pushed his musical techniques to new limits, using richly elaborated vocal lines and forms that expand into long continuous musical and dramatic units. He himself coined the term "Terzettone" (big trio) for its astounding trio. *Le siège de Corinthe* is reworked to moderate both the vocal floridity and the formal innovations. The "Terzettone" is reduced to a more conventional form, and the solo arias for Mahomet, Pamira, and Néoclès are adapted to what Rossini perceived to be French dramaturgy. The new music for the French stage includes an overture, which the Italian original had lacked (the thematic material, to be sure, is derived from earlier works). There are grand numbers in which the chorus joins the soloists as a dramatic character, as in the second finale. True to French taste, dance and patriotic spectacle are provided. The score, more uniform in style than that of *Maometto II,* lacks the boldness which characterized the earlier version.

—Patricia Brauner

THE SIEGE OF CORINTH
See LE SIÈGE DE CORINTHE

SIEGFRIED
See DER RING DES NIBELUNGEN

SIEMS, Margarethe.

Soprano. Born 30 December 1879, in Breslau. Died 13 April 1952, in Dresden. Studied with Orgéni; debut at the Prague May Festival, 1902; joined the Prague Opera that same year; joined the Dresden Court (later State) Opera, 1908; leading dramatic coloratura soprano there until 1920; created role of Chrysothemis in *Elektra,* 1909, and of the Marschallin in *Der Rosenkavalier,* 1911, both in Dresden; created role of Zerbinetta in *Ariadne auf Naxos,* Stuttgart, 1912; Covent Garden debut, 1913; taught at the Berlin Conservatory, 1920-26, then in Dresden and Breslau.

Publications

About SIEMS: articles–

Wilhelm, P. "Margarethe Siems." *Record News* 2 (Toronto, 1958): 421.

Initially a violin and piano student, Margarethe Siems turned to voice study in Dresden with Aglaja von Orgéni, then with Pauline Viardot-Garcia (Orgéni's own teacher). Siems' debut was in 1902 at the German Theater, Prague in the leading soprano role of Marguerite de Valois in Meyerbeer's *Les Huguenots.* She was twenty-three, and remained in Prague until 1908, when she was called to the Royal Dresden Opera as successor to the brilliant soprano, Irene Abendroth, who had retired prematurely—a fortunate event for Siems, who was able to take over most of her roles.

During her eleven years there, Siems sang with much ease and success Aida, Amelia in *Un ballo in maschera,* Mimi and Madame Butterfly (always in German); Venus in *Tannhäuser,* and Isolde as well as the florid coloratura sopranos such as Lucia, Gilda and the Queen of Night. In 1908, Richard Strauss cast her as Chrysothemis in his new opera *Elektra,* and in 1911 she became the first Marschallin in *Der Rosenkavalier,* also premiered in Dresden. She fulfilled all his vocal requirements and responded to Max Reinhardt's stage direction.

When Strauss and Hofmannsthal staged their next opera in Stuttgart, Siems was invited as a guest to sing the extremely taxing coloratura soprano role of Zerbinetta (afterwards greatly simplified). Siems's voice was probably centered round the dramatic soprano register but with an amazing extension to well above the staff which almost made it seem like two voices. Siems wore a tragic expression, suitable for the Marschallin. In the few surviving pictures of her as Zerbinetta in *Ariadne auf Naxos,* however she looks curiously unrelated to the character. It is likely that her successes resulted from her voice more than her appearance and acting.

In London in 1913 and 1914 Siems sang seven performances of the Marschallin, and it was in this role that she gave her farewell appearance in 1925 at Breslau. It was her most famous role and some recordings were made soon after the premiere. They give a certain insight into her style of singing,

but it sounds more tentative than it must have been in the opera house.

Between 1926-37, Siems lived in Dresden and again from 1946 until her death in 1952. She taught in Berlin, Breslau and Dresden between 1920 and 1940. Siems was a grande-dame with a voice whose equal has never since been heard.

—Alan Jefferson

SIEPI, Cesare.

Bass. Born 10 February 1923, in Milan. Studied at the Milan Conservatory; debut as Sparafucile in Verdi's *Rigoletto,* Schio, near Vicenzo, 1941; Teatro alla Scala debut as Zaccaria in Verdi's *Nabucco,* 1946; sang at La Scala, 1946-58; Metropolitan Opera debut as Philip II in *Don Carlo,* 1950; sang at the Met, 1950-73; sang at Covent Garden 1962-73.

Publications

About SIEPI: articles–

Gualerzi, G. "Siepi, Cesare." *Le grandi voci.* Rome, 1964.
Pluta, E. "Das Porträt: Cesare Siepi." *Opernwelt* 8 (1975): 22.
Kaplan, A. "Cesare Siepi: reflections on a 40-year career." *San Francisco Opera Magazine* 2 (1988): 58.
Pluta, E. "Das Porträt." *Opernwelt* 24/2 (1983): 10.
"Cesare Siepi." *Die Bühne* 353 (1988): 47.

The first season of Rudolf Bing's regime at the Metropolitan Opera, which commenced on November 6, 1950 with an innovative production of Giuseppe Verdi's *Don Carlo,* served to introduce to the New York scene the bass, Cesare Siepi. Originally, Siepi was not to have been cast as King Philip and was engaged when Boris Christoff could not acquire the proper visa to enter the country. The premiere was to be televised and along with Siepi, the powerhouse Italian mezzo-soprano Fedora Barbieri, the Argentinian soprano Delia Rigal and the young American soprano Lucine Amara were all scheduled to make their debuts in company with the "veterans," Jussi Björling, Robert Merrill and Jerome Hines. It was a triumph for everyone concerned and especially for Siepi whose delivery of King Philip's, "Ella giammai m'amò," brought the entire proceedings to a halt with a thunderous ovation. It did not take long for the newspapers to want to know more about this new bass, and soon it was discovered that under the grey exterior of the aging monarch was a young man of twenty-seven years who could rival any of Hollywood's matinee idols in appearance. The reign of Siepi began at the Metropolitan where he was thought of as the natural heir to Ezio Pinza, who concluded his twenty-two year association with that house in 1948.

The similarities between Pinza and Siepi are striking; physically both were tall, athletically built men who could dominate a stage by their presence alone. However, it is in their voices where they were most similar, but certainly not because they could ever be mistaken for one another. Each had a unique sound which is immediately identifiable by hearing just one note. Their voices had a lushness and a warmth which imparted an aura of palpable sensuality. Siepi's voice was the more evenly produced of the two, giving him the edge over Pinza in legato singing. Both excelled as Mozart's Don Giovanni and Figaro. Siepi's "Là ci darem la mano" was a veritable textbook of *bel canto* singing, his "Se vuol ballare" a showcase for the many faceted shadings and colors in his voice.

There was another side to Siepi, the romantic lead, and that was the consummate comedian. His Don Basilio in *Il barbiere di Siviglia* was a comic masterpiece of subtle timing and innuendo. For those not old enough to have seen Pinza and the great *buffo* Salvatore Baccaloni as Don Basilio and Don Bartolo, the pairing of Siepi with Baccaloni's successor, Fernando Corena, as the two Dons left nothing to be desired. The master artist Eugene Berman who created designs for the Metropolitan's *Il barbiere di Siviglia* in the 1953-1954 season gave each a chair in the second act which conformed to the figures of the characters they played. The expansive, rotund one for Bartolo and the spindly ladder-back for Basilio could certainly have been abstractions of the singers themselves, and each made the most of the prop he was given.

Cameo roles such as Colline, Sparafucile, and Ramfis were etched as carefully as was the tortured Boris Godunov (performed in English, which he took great pains to enunciate clearly). Siepi's death of Boris was not only heart-rending but also hair-raising when he toppled head first down a staircase at its conclusion. When playing opposite Maria Callas in *Norma*, his granite exterior as the implacable Oroviso visually crumbled under her pleadings for forgiveness for her children and gave the audience the soul-stirring experience of two great singing-actors playing off one another. No less effective was his Méphistophélès in Gounod's *Faust* with its proper blend of elegance and evil so often overlooked by others.

Siepi was no stranger to the recording studios and the old Cetra-Soria label championed his cause early on when they issued two albums devoted to him, one of arias and another of Italian songs. The collection of songs in particular remains a treasured part of any collector's holdings as does his anthology of Cole Porter which is rendered in delightfully (and ever so lightly) accented English. Fortunately, he recorded a number of operatic roles and his Don Giovanni, Figaro, Mefistofele, Alvise, Padre Guardiano, among others, have been preserved.

Siepi came upon the operatic scene when good, even great, voices were plentiful. That he dominated his surroundings speaks volumes for the singular abilities which made him an international star of the first magnitude. When Pinza chose to leave the Metropolitan, Siepi followed two years later, and he remains irreplaceable.

—John Pennino

THE SILENT WOMAN
See DIE SCHWEIGSAME FRAU

SILJA, Anja.

Soprano. Born 17 April 1940, in Berlin. Married conductor Christoph von Dohnányi, 1979; one son, one daughter. Studied with her grandfather, Egon van Rijn; debut as Rosina in *Il barbiere di Siviglia*, Berlin, 1956; at Brunswick, 1956-58; American (Chicago) and Bayreuth debuts as Senta in *Der fliegende Holländer*, 1960; London debut as Leonore in *Fidelio*, 1963; Metropolitan Opera debut as Leonore in *Fidelio*, 1972; directed *Lohengrin*, Brussels, 1990.

Publications

About SILJA: book–

Heinzelmann, Josef. *Anja Silja*. Berlin, 1965.

articles–

Schwinger, Wolfram. "Anja Silja." *Opera* 20/March (1969): 193.
Profile. *San Francisco Opera Magazine* 3/Fall (1981): 43; 3/Fall (1983): 47; 2/Fall (1985): 34; 67/12 (1989): 35.
von Buchau, S. "All About Anja." *San Francisco Opera Magazine* 3/Fall (1983): 45.
Zondergeld, R.A. "Endlich kein ferner Klang mehr . . ." *Neue Zeitschrift für Musik* 149/September (1988): 47.

*　　*　　*

Silja's early career is inextricably bound up with that of her mentor, Wieland Wagner. In his productions she became the most famous Lulu and Salome of her time, and, transcending modern ideas about what one singer's repertoire might be, seemed to sing everything from The Queen of the Night and Zerbinetta to Brünnhilde and Isolde.

Silja's ambition was from the beginning directed towards the Wagner roles, something that seemed unlikely considering that she made her debut, still in her teens, as Rosina in Rossini's *Il barbiere di Siviglia* in Brunswick. Only four years later Wieland Wagner brought her to Bayreuth to sing Senta. Silja's voice as a young singer was very high—she claims to have been able to sing a whole octave above top C ("like Yma Sumac"). Many eyebrows were raised at the casting for the 1960 Bayreuth Festival, but after her debut, William Mann wrote in the London *Times* that if Silja were to attempt more Wagner she would "light those roles with a glorious new flame." That was precisely what happened. Returning every summer to Bayreuth until Wieland Wagner died in 1966, she sang Elisabeth and Venus in *Tannhäuser*, Elsa in *Lohengrin* and Eva in *Die Meistersinger*. Elsewhere she also sang Isolde and the three Brünnhildes (notably in Cologne with George London as Wotan). But after Wieland's death, she at first said she wanted to abandon her career: "I didn't want to sing any more and I couldn't think of anything that was not connected with him. Even the operas I'd sung that he hadn't staged, still there was a connection in my eyes."

Under the influence first of Otto Klemperer, however, who chose her to be his Senta and Leonore in *Fidelio* for London, and later Christoph von Dohnányi (whom she married) she expanded her repertory, first turning to French roles. She sang all three soprano parts in Offenbach's *Les contes d' Hoffmann*, the title role in *Carmen* and Cassandre in *Les troyens*. Later she concentrated on Russian and Czech roles—*Katya Kabanová*, Emilia Marty in *The Makropoulos Case* and Shostakovich's *Lady Macbeth of Mtsensk*.

Just as Callas had seemed for many a throw-back to the times of Pasta and Grisi, so Silja seemed to be the successor to Wilhelmine Schroeder-Devrient, Wagner's adored "Queen of Tears." In conventional terms, Silja's voice had not equipped her to be a recording or concert artist, it being essential to see and hear her. (From this point of view it is sad that almost nothing of her work with Wieland was video-taped, except one performance of *Lulu,* although she did film both Jenny in *Mahagonny* and the title role in *Fidelio.*) A totally committed stage actress, no one who saw her as Fidelio at Covent Garden in 1969, with Klemperer conducting, is likely to have forgotten the moment when, at "Tot erst sein Weib!" she tore off the grey prison-cap (designed by Wieland), and her red-gold tresses tumbled to her shoulders. Her command of the stage, her ability to carry off supremely melodramatic gestures within the confines of the drama continued to be hers for three decades. When she took on the role of Kostelnicka in Lehnhoff's memorable production of *Jenůfa* at Glyndebourne in 1989, she revealed a voice that had gained in power and strength in the lower register. She claimed to have added an octave at the bottom, having discarded the notes *in alt,* and became for a new generation one of the most powerful singing actresses. The dangerous quality in her tone, a whining sound and apparent insecurity on the high notes, makes hers an art that will always provoke extreme controversy, but as Harold Rosenthal wrote of her Salome in the 1960s, "her voice is not beautiful by any stretch of the imagination, but it is clearly projected, and every phrase carries its overtones—psychological not musical—which suggests the child-like degenerate, over-sexed princess in all too clear a manner. Her nervous, almost thin body is never still; she rolls on her stomach and her back; she crawls, she slithers, she leaps, she kneels . . . There is no denying that this is one of the great performances of our time."

—Patrick O'Connor

SILLS, Beverly [Belle Miriam Silverman].

Soprano. Born 25 May 1929, in Brooklyn. Married: Peter B. Greenough, 1956; one son, one daughter. Child prodigy, sang on radio; studied with Estelle Liebling from age 11; debut as Frasquita in *Carmen,* Philadelphia, 1947; toured with the Charles Wagner Company; San Francisco debut as Elena in *Mefistofele,* 1953; at New York City Opera, 1955-79, debuting as Rosalinde; Vienna debut as the Queen of the Night in *Die Zauberflöte,* 1967; Teatro alla Scala debut as Pamira in *Le siège de Corinthe,* 1969; Covent Garden debut as Lucia di Lammermoor, 1970; Metropolitan Opera debut as Pamira, 1975; sang in premier of Menotti's *La Loca,* San Diego, 1979; celebrated as Violetta; retired from stage, 1979; director of New York City Opera 1979-89.

Publications

By SILLS: books–

Bubbles: A Self-Portrait. Indianapolis, 1976; 1981.
with Lawrence Linderman. *Beverly: An Autobiography.* New York, 1987.

articles–

"Beverly Sills: A Portrait of the Artist as a Young Singer." *The NATS Bulletin* 38/4 (1982): 26.
"Studying with Garden and Ponselle." *Opera* 39/March (1988): 270.

About SILLS: books–

Sargeant, Winthrop. *Divas.* New York, 1973.
Steane, J.B. *The Grand Tradition.* London, 1974.

articles–

Weinstock, Herbert. "Beverly Sills." *Opera,* December 1970.
Livingstone, W. "Beverly Sills." *Stereo Review* 42/February (1979): 80.
Eaton, Quaintance. "Madness Is as Madness Sings." *Music Clubs Magazine* 49/2 (1979): 10.
Terry, K. "Beverly Sills: Opera's Superstar Takes on New Role." *Opera Canada* 20/2 (1979): 14.
Oppens, K. "Beverly Sills nahm Abschied von der Bühne." *Opernwelt* 20/3 (1979): 37.
Heinsheimer, H. "USA: Drei Opern-Amazonen." *Neue Zeitschrift für Musik* 4/July-August (1979): 382.
"Beverly! Her Farewell Performance." *Music Clubs Magazine* 60/2 (1980): 14.
Jacobson, R. "Miss American Superstar." *Opera News* 45/October (1980): 8.
Soria, D.J. "For Beverly, Farewell and Welcome." *High Fidelity/Musical America* 31/February (1981): MA6.
Andrews, P. "Beverly Sills as Impresario." *Saturday Review* 8/May (1981): 12.
Sandler, K. "Zero Hour for the New York City Opera." *Opera News* 47/July (1982): 28.
Hiller, C.H. "Ein Musiktheater der amerikanischer Künstler; Gespräch mit Beverly Sills, der Leiterin der New York City Opera." *Opernwelt* 23/8-9 (1982): 87.
Paolucci, Bridget. "Remembrance of Recordings Past with Beverly Sills." *Ovation* 6/April (1985): 14.
Wakeling, Dennis W. "A Sills Cornucopia." *Opera Quarterly* 3/4 (1985-86): 1058.
Passy, C. "Evening Treasures: A Serenade to Sills." *Ovation* 10/August (1989): 40.

*   *   *

To many of those who saw Beverly Sills in performance or who listen to her records, she was unquestionably one of the greatest—some would claim *the* greatest—bel canto sopranos of the nineteen-sixties and seventies. While audiences everywhere adored her, there were ongoing reservations from some critics. Peter Davis in the Sills entry in the *New Grove Dictionary of Music and Musicians* can be taken as representative of this reserve when he describes her mainly in terms of drawbacks, as lacking the dramatic weight of Callas or the sheer tonal beauty of Sutherland or Caballé, as not dramatically commanding and with a stage personality that is merely in-gratiating. While no one is likely to question Callas's supremacy, J.B. Steane is nearer the mark when he describes Sills as achieving "profundity perhaps more genuinely" than her rivals, and remarks about her, "The interesting thing, finally, is that Sills is so satisfying, not as a sweet-sounding, highly-trained nightingale, but as a singer of remarkable intellectual and emotional strength."

Sills's career as a radio child-prodigy is as well-known as the fact that she began her serious vocal training at age 11 with Estelle Liebling who had been a pupil of Mathilde Marchesi and who remained Sills's only teacher. A debut in Philadelphia as Frasquita (1947) was followed two years later by a tour as Violetta during which she sang the role fifty-four times in nine weeks; it was to become one of her most celebrated roles, one which she was to sing more than three hundred times in the course of her career. A contract with the New York City Opera singing a variety of roles eventually led to her appearance in 1958 as the heroine of Douglas Moore's *The Ballad of Baby Doe,* a high-soprano role which brought considerable recognition and which became identified with her. But it was eight more years and many more roles—her repertoire eventually totalled more than seventy—before her appearance as Cleopatra in Handel's *Giulio Cesare* (1966) brought her international acclaim.

Sills then entered on a period of intense activity both abroad—debuts in Vienna, the Teatro alla Scala, Covent Garden, Teatro Colón quickly followed—and at home in America. Her debut at the Metropolitan Opera in Rossini's *Le siège de Corinthe* (1975) was delayed by Rudolph Bing until after his departure from the house. The New York City Opera remained her home base, at which she appeared as the three heroines in *Les contes d'Hoffmann,* the Queen in Rimsky-Korsakov's *Le coq d'or,* Manon, Elvira in *I puritani,* Lucia, *La Fille du Régiment, Lucrezia Borgia,* and, in some ways her most important achievements, the so-called Donizetti three queens trilogy—*Roberto Devereux, Maria Stuarda,* and *Anna Bolena.*

Onstage, Sills enjoyed a considerable dramatic advantage over her rivals; Sutherland, never at ease with her own physicality, overcame her awkwardness to achieve a measure of sincerity onstage, while Caballé belonged to the philosophy of stage deportment associated with Zinka Milanov whose baroque acting style was once described by Irving Kolodin in the *Saturday Review* as a cross between Eleanora Duse and Mack Sennett. Sills, like Sutherland, is a tall woman but one who is at home with the fact; allying her natural acting ability to a shrewd practical training resulted in a series of highly skilled and moving stage impersonations.

Sills sang many of the Italian roles associated with the bel canto revival of the fifties and sixties, as well as remaining a Mozart singer—Donna Anna, Donna Elvira, Constanze—and also specializing in the French repertoire—she sang Marguerite, Manon, Thaïs, Louise, the three heroines in *Les contes d'Hoffmann,* Philine in *Mignon,* among others. She was always willing to push herself vocally and histrionically, and this led to her assuming roles which in some ways were, as she herself acknowledged, unwise for her. Her middle voice, though evocative in timbre, could betray signs of stress under pressure; but it was her high voice that was her claim to glory. Although some perceived it as shallow in tone, her high singing in the theatre was extraordinarily telling; it had carrying power, flexibility, brilliance, and, thanks to excellent pitch, accuracy. Again J.B. Steane goes to the heart of the matter when he remarks that there is "something exalted, non-pedestrian, even crazy, about the high notes of the soprano voice (so far above the pitch of the woman's normal speaking voice), especially when taken in context with fast passage-work. No 'coloratura' seems quite to have sensed this as Sills has done." He proceeds on this basis to analyze her recording of Lucia's first aria in terms of the eerie supernatural chill she evokes, and provides a number of other examples from her *Roberto Devereux.* Her recording of Olympia's aria from *Les contes d'Hoffmann* can be seen to provide a zany version of the same phenomenon, including a perfectly tuned running-down as the doll unwinds.

At the same time, one cannot overlook the sheer beauty of sound evidenced in many of Sills's recording. In the St Sulpice scene from Manon she spins a gossamer web of erotic magnetism; in "O luce di quest'anima" (*Linda di Chamonix*) the staccatos are feathery light; in Mozart's lullaby, "Ruhe sanft, mein holdes Leben" (*Zaïde*) her tone is preternaturally beautiful, in Strauss's "Breit über mein Haupt" full of unbearable pathos. It is not an exaggeration to say that she scarcely ever made a recording which does not provide exquisite moments.

It is typical that Sills chose to end her career with a challenge—the premiere of Menotti's *La Loca* (1979); indeed in later interviews she attributed her decision to retire comparatively early to two factors, the first an operation for cancer in 1972 which robbed her of perfect security in her breath control, and second, the decision to take on roles like *Norma* which she knew perfectly well were too heavy for her voice, consequently shortening her vocal life, but which she felt were worth doing. It was, indeed, that very desire to rise to the great artistic challenges available to her and if possible to go beyond them that made her one of the formidable figures of the lyric stage of her day.

—Peter Dyson

SIMIONATO, Giulietta.

Mezzo-soprano. Born 12 May 1910, in Forli. Studied with Locatello and Palumbo; won first place in a bel canto competition in Florence, 1933; sang in premiere of Pizzetti's *Orsèolo* at Florence Festival, 1935; Teatro alla Scala debut in Puccini's *Suor Angelica,* 1936; appeared regularly at La Scala until 1966; British debut as Cherubino at 1947 Edinburgh Festival; appeared as Adalgisa, Amneris, and Azucena at Covent Garden in 1953; in 1954 a revival of Bellini's *I Capuleti ed i Montecchi* was staged for her in Palermo; made United States debut in Chicago in same year, and sang for the Metropolitan Opera, 1959-65; made farewell appearance (as Servilia in *La clemenza di Tito*) at the Piccola Scala, 1966.

Publications

About SIMIONATO: books–

Hanine–Vallaut, J.J. *Giulietta Simionato—Come Cenerentola divenne regina.* Parma, 1987.

About SIMIONATO: articles–

Kolodin, I. "Great Artists of Our Time: Giulietta Simionato." *High Fidelity* 11 (1959): 37.
Natan, A. "Giulietta Simionato." In *Prima donna,* 30. Basle, 1962.

Guarlezi, G. "Giulietta Simionato." *Opera* 2 (1964): 87.
"Giulietta Simionato." *Bühne* no. 380 (1990): 62.

*   *   *

For many opera-goers of the 1950s one of the greatest voices and most beloved personalities of that decade was the mezzo-soprano Giulietta Simionato. She seemed to combine the coloratura agility of Conchita Supervia with the lush authority of manner of Ebe Stignani into the ideal versatile mezzo-soprano. Her voice exhibited the richness of a contralto's with the upward extension of a soprano's—indeed she sang some soprano roles (Donna Elvira, Ännchen, Fedora, and Santuzza) early on, but on a number of occasions wisely resisted taking on others. She turned down offers of Norma, Lady Macbeth, and Minnie; she agreed to learn Leonora in *Il trovatore,* but Antonino Votto eventually dissuaded her from performing it.

Simionato's range of roles was nevertheless astonishing. She undertook the coloratura repertoire, represented by the operas of Handel, Rossini, Bellini, Donizetti, and Verdi; lyric mezzo roles such as Mignon, Octavian, Dorabella, and Cherubino; and the heavy, dramatic characters such as Dalila, Azucena, Amneris, Eboli, Leonora in *La favorita,* the Aunt in Puccini's *Suor Angelica,* and the Princess in *Adriana Lecouvreur.* Some of her roles were curiosities from the past, as when she appeared in Alessandro Scarlatti's *Mitridate Eupatore* at Piccolo Scala with Victoria de los Angeles in 1956. At La Scala, where she debuted in 1936, she also sang, in addition to many of the roles mentioned above, Dido in Berlioz's *Les Troyens,* Gluck's *Iphigénie en Aulide,* and undertook the soprano role of Valentine in a renowned 1962 production of *Les Huguenots* with Sutherland and Corelli. A well-circulated pirate recording exists of this production in which Simionato sings in a grand veristic style that is not true to Meyerbeer or the period but is nevertheless exciting. The enjoyment of the La Scala audience is palpable. Also from La Scala with Sutherland during the same period is a live performance of Rossini's *Semiramide.* Yet another famous La Scala production in which Simionato took a prominent part, and for which recorded documentation exists, was the 1957 revival of Donizetti's *Anna Bolena* for Maria Callas, a soprano with whom Simionato often appeared. Simionato is in splendid form in the role of Jane Seymour; she is perhaps all the more forthright and unsubtle in contrast to Callas's vulnerability.

Much of the admiration and respect accorded Simionato comes from those who heard her often and regularly on the stage; her regal timbre, great versatility, and endearing physical presence made her a beloved operatic personality. Yet the recordings reveal problems, some of them basic. It must also be admitted that some of the flaws—such as the sharp register breaks and unequalized tone—are intentional products of her training, and owe something to the fact that she was an Italian singer performing during a certain era. Blatant aspirates and lack of a seamless scale clearly are more acceptable at certain times and in certain places than others. If one compares Simionato to Marilyn Horne in such parts as Arsace (*Semiramide*), Rosina in *Il barbiere di Siviglia,* and Isabella in *L'Italiana in Algeri,* Simionato emerges a distinct second-best in technical accuracy. Horne is near perfect in this regard, with Simionato displaying all of the problems mentioned above to a blatant degree. Then there is the matter of charm. Horne's fioriture sparkle and delight; even for all

Simionato's agility, which is quite considerable, Simionato rarely charms or delights in a Rossini comic role. We hear her instead as an Azucena or a commanding Amneris who is, astonishingly, able to toss off roulades with an amazing degree of accuracy. Many of these recordings were admittedly made when Simionato was rather mature, such as the *La Cenerentola* from 1964 when she was fifty-four years old. Even in Simionato's Verdi recordings there are shortcomings: she rarely follows Verdi's copious and explicit expressive markings, although in the several recordings that display her Amneris, Ulrica (when this recording was made in 1961 she could no longer adequately sustain the low notes necessary for the role), Preziosilla, and Dame Quickly, she is almost always in sumptuous, authoritative-sounding voice. This assessment holds true of her Laura, sung to Anita Cerqueti's Gioconda, and her Aunt to Renata Tebaldi's Suor Angelica.

Simionato retired without fanfare in the mid-1960s without any discernible deterioration in vocal quality. She left the opera stage a greatly beloved singer; when she retired she perhaps left an older era behind her.

—Stephen Willier

SIMON BOCCANEGRA.

Composer: Giuseppe Verdi.

Librettists: Francesco Maria Piave and G. Montanelli (after Antonio García Gutiérrez).

First Performance: Venice, La Fenice, 12 March 1857; revised, Arrigo Boito, Milan, Teatro alla Scala, 24 March 1881.

Roles: Amelia Grimaldi (soprano); Gabriele Adorno (tenor); Simon Boccanegra (baritone); Fiesco (bass); Paolo Albiani (baritone); Pietro (baritone); Maid (soprano or mezzo-soprano); A Captain (tenor); chorus (SSAATTTBB).

Publications

books—

Bush, Hans, ed. *Verdi's Otello and Simon Boccanegra (Revised Version) in Letters and Documents.* 2 vols. Oxford, 1988.
Sopart, Andreas. *Verdis Simon Boccanegra (1857 und 1881): Eine musikalisch-dramaturgische Analyse.* Laaber, 1988.

articles—

Walker, Frank. "Verdi, Giuseppe Montanelli, and the Libretto of *Simon Boccanegra.*" In *Verdi: bollettino dell' Institute di Studi Verdiani* 1 (1960).
Klein, John W. "Some Reflections on Verdi's *Simon Boccanegra.*" *Music and Letters* April (1962).
Osthoff, Wolfgang. "Die beiden *Boccanegra*-Fassungen und der Beginn von Verdis Spätwerk." *Analecta Musicologica* 1 (1963).
Avant-scène opéra January-February (1979) [*Simon Boccanegra* issue].
Kerman, Joseph. "Lyric Form and Flexibility in *Simon Boccanegra.*" *Studi verdiani* 1 (1982): 47.

Várnai, Péter Pál. "Paolo Albiani. Il cammino di un perso-
    naggio." *Studi verdiani* 1 (1982): 63.
Puccini, Dario. "Il *Simon Boccanegra* di Antonio García
    Gutiérrez e l'opera di Giuseppe Verdi." *Studi verdiani* 3
    (1985): 120.

unpublished–

Detels, Claire Janice. "Giuseppe Verdi's *Simon Boccanegra:*
    a Comparison of the 1857 and 1881 Versions." Ph.D.
    dissertation, University of Washington, 1982.

*   *   *

Although this vast, complicated, and much-revised melodrama has never been very successful, *Simon Boccanegra* has
great historical importance in Verdi's career in that it helped
to bring the composer out of his post-*Aida* retirement to
compose his great Shakespearean operas, *Otello* and *Falstaff.*
There are two main versions of *Simon Boccanegra:* one which
premiered as a fiasco at the 1857 Venice carnival season (and
received minor revisions over the next several years), and a
substantially revised version which premiered in the 1881
Teatro alla Scala season, which Verdi prepared with the assistance for the first time of the most gifted librettist of the
day, Arrigo Boito, and which is the version heard in theaters
today.

Based on a complex political melodrama by the Spanish
playwright García Gutiérrez (also the source of Verdi's *Il
trovatore*), *Simon Boccanegra* deals with the conflict between
the patrician and plebeian parties in the fourteenth-century
sea-going republic of Genoa. In brief, the prologue presents
us with the famous pirate Simon Boccanegra, as he returns
from hiding to accept election as Doge of Genoa in a vote
controlled by Paolo, an organizer of the plebeians. Simon
accepts the position in the hope that it will allow him to
reunite with his beloved Maria, daughter of the patrician
Fiesco, as well as unwed mother of their lost child, also named
Maria. Twenty-five years later in act I, the mysteriously
adopted Amelia Grimaldi (actually the young Maria) loves
the young patrician Gabriele Adorno; they receive permission
to marry from her guardian Andrea, who is actually Fiesco in
disguise. But meanwhile, Paolo has asked Simon the political
favor of interceding on his behalf and courting Amelia. During their encounter Simon and Amelia realize they are father
and daughter, and Simon desists from pleading Paolo's case,
after which the angry Paolo avenges himself by having Amelia abducted. In act I, scene ii (completely revised from the
original plot), Simon is meeting with his council when Gabriele breaks onto the scene, followed by a plebeian mob,
which is enraged that he has murdered one of their members,
Lorenzin. Admitting to the murder, Gabriele reveals that
Lorenzin conspired in the abduction of Amelia (but he suspects that Simon was behind the abduction). Amelia, having
secured her own release, calls for peace among the warring
factions. Suspecting Paolo as the perpetrator of the abduction,
Simon calls on him to curse the abductor (himself), and the
act closes on the crowd's repetition of the curse.

Simon Boccanegra, **Royal Opera, London, 1991**

In act II the vengeful Paolo secretly poisons Simon's cup and tries to persuade Fiesco/Andrea and Gabriele to kill him as well. Gabriele agrees, responding mainly to Paolo's hints of a romantic relationship between Simon and Amelia, who have been together frequently. He hides in Simon's private chamber, preparing to strike. Amelia finds him, and pleads with him to accept peace with Simon, but refuses to explain her own relationship with the doge. Next, Amelia begs for Simon's consent to her marriage with Gabriele, and he reluctantly agrees, provided that Gabriele repents his opposition. Alone, Simon unknowingly drinks Paolo's poison, and falls asleep. Gabriele rises from hiding to strike him, but Amelia appears again and stops him just as Simon awakens and reveals that Amelia is his daughter. As the act closes, Simon gives his blessing for the marriage of Gabriele and Amelia, and Gabriele decides to join Simon's side in the upcoming battle he has helped to brew with the patricians. In act III, Simon has won the battle, but Fiesco/Andrea learns from the condemned Paolo that Simon will nonetheless die from poisoning, Paolo's revenge. Fiesco/Andrea then confronts Simon for a last accusatory scene, but instead learns from a gratified Simon of his granddaughter Amelia/Maria. Simon dies as the opera ends, and Gabriele is proclaimed Doge.

In letters to his librettist for the first version of *Simon Boccanegra*, Francesco Maria Piave, Verdi had insisted that "the layout of the libretto, of the numbers, etc. etc. must be as original as possible," in keeping with the unusual features of the drama. But the fact that Piave's work, never superior, was especially convoluted cannot be blamed on the librettist alone, since he closely followed the prose sketch which Verdi himself had prepared from the Gutiérrez drama, and since the worst problems in the opera were inherent in the political complexity of the subject—a complexity little suited to the lyrical language of Italian opera. Besides, the aspect of *Simon Boccanegra* that most troubled audiences in 1857 was not the text but rather the music, which was considered overly somber and lacking in lyrical vocal melody. In fact, Verdi had taken special pains to avoid conventional set pieces in the scenes he considered particularly dramatic, including the prologue and act III scenes between Simon and Fiesco. Moreover there is no real aria for the central figure of Simon (one of the main reasons he fails to achieve the necessary weight in the 1857 version of the opera), and there is very little in words or music to convey Paolo's crucial role in the drama. On the other hand, there are many conventional set pieces for the less central characters and situations, including three cavatina-cabaletta pairs in act I, scene i for Amelia, Amelia and Gabriele, and Amelia and Simon respectively.

The 1881 revisions reveal Boito's skill at refocusing the weight of the dramatic action onto the central characters of Simon and Paolo, and they also show the remarkable evolution in Verdi's compositional style between 1857 and 1881, a twenty-four-year gap in which the composer had blended the vocal traditions of Italian opera with the French emphasis on scenography and orchestral accompaniment, as well as with his own unique brand of melodic vigor and characterization. Grafting this blend onto a twenty-four-year-old dramatic failure was no easy matter, and many of Verdi's solutions were weak compromises. For instance, he made very few changes in acts II and III, and, although he cut a cabaletta for Amelia in act I, he only lightly revised the remaining two, at a time when the cabaletta was considered terribly outdated and dramatically stifling. However, there are two sections of the opera, the beginning of the prologue and the Council Chamber scene (act I, scene ii) which are largely new. In these sections, the orchestra unifies the drama with large-scale tonal symmetries and thematic recurrences, similar to those found in the later operas *Otello* and *Falstaff.* Vocal melody is perhaps less prominent than usual here, but that is owing to the dark, political nature of these scenes. Still, when Simon has a heroic moment in his efforts to unite the Genoan people in the Council Chamber after Amelia's abduction, Verdi gives him full lyrical opportunity with the dramatic "Plebe! Patrizi! Popolo!" ("Plebeians! Patricians! People!"). Some parts of the score foreshadow the style of *Otello,* particularly in the Council Chamber scene, where Amelia's melodic plea for peace resembles that of Desdemona in act III of *Otello,* and the brass fanfare and trill accompanying Paolo's self-cursing is a harbinger of Iago's act II "Credo."

The revised *Simon Boccanegra* of 1881 brought mixed reviews, ranging from Filippo Filippi's claim of "A Triumph" following the La Scala premiere, to Eduard Hanslick's assessment at the 1882 Vienna debut that "The old Verdi is distracted, tired, and in a bad mood." Still, the revision succeeded in gaining a place for *Simon Boccanegra* in the modern repertory; the somber, heavily masculine tone of the opera is so unique and so uniquely Verdian that it has developed a following among the composer's most avid fans.

—Claire Detels

SIMONEAU, Léopold.

Tenor. Born 3 May 1918, in St Flavien, Canada. Married: Pierrette Alarie in 1946. Studied with Émile Larochelle and with Salvator Issaurel; debut as Hadji in *Lakmé,* Variétés Lyriques, Montreal, 1941; studied in New York with Paul Althouse, 1945-47; European debut as Mireille, Paris, Opéra-Comique, 1948; Metropolitan Opera debut as Ottavio in Mozart's *Don Giovanni,* 1963; founding member of L'Opéra du Québec, 1971; joined the faculty of the San Francisco Conservatory in 1972. He was made an Officer of the Order of Canada in 1971.

Publications

By SIMONEAU: articles–

"Style and Mozart." *Opera Canada* 27/2 (1986): 14.

About SIMONEAU: books–

Maheu, R. *Pierrette Alarie, Leopold Simoneau; deux voix, un art.* Montreal, 1988.

articles–

Schneider, R. "Schöne Stimmen von damals: Leopold Simoneau." *Opernwelt* 27/10 (1986): 59.
McLean, E. "A grand tradition: Leopold Simoneau." *Opera Canada* 32 (1991): 11.
Pluta, E. "Schöne Stimmen von damals." *Opernwelt* 32/5 (1991): 64.

*　　*　　*

Léopold Simoneau was the Mozart tenor of his generation. For the bicentennial of the composer's birth in 1956, he recorded the roles of Belmonte with Sir Thomas Beecham,

Idamante with Sir John Pritchard, Ottavio with Rudolf Moralt, Ferrando with Herbert von Karajan, Tamino with Karl Böhm, some of Titus with Bernard Paumgartner, and the tenor part of the Requiem with Bruno Walter. In the same period he also sang Mozart in public performances worldwide with such conductors as Busch, Kempe, Klemperer, Krips, Mitropoulos, Reiner, and Solti. The greatest maestros valued him for his consummate musicianship, silvery tone, faultless technique, and heartfelt projection of the inner drama of the Mozart roles. The best critics said that he sang "Il mio tesoro" more beautifully than any tenor since McCormack, and with an intelligence that was all his own.

But Simoneau, born in Quebec and married to the Montreal-born soprano Pierrette Alarie, was equally accomplished in and dedicated to the French repertory. The language and its classics were like the air he breathed, and he made indelible impressions as (on record and broadcast only) Faust, Don José, Hoffmann, des Grieux, and Pelléas and (in performance) Orphée, Pylade, Nadir, Gérald in *Lakmé,* and Wilhelm Meister in *Mignon.* He and his wife often sang together in both concert and opera, notably as Roméo and Juliette, Vincent and Mireille, Tonio and Marie, Damon and Fatime in *Les Indes galantes,* as well as such standard duos as Almaviva and Rosina, Alfredo and Violetta and, most often, Belmonte and Blondchen. Pierrette won the Metropolitan Opera Auditions of the Air when she was only twenty-four, and sang at the Metropolitan Opera (as Oscar, Olympia, Blondchen, and Xenia) at the time of her marriage to Léopold in 1946. Simoneau, who triumphed in Chicago with Callas, Schwarzkopf, Gobbi, and other great singers, sang only Ottavio at the Metropolitan, triumphantly but in a single season at the end of his career, in 1963. Together the Simoneaus made many recordings, including a performance of the first Canadian opera, *Colas and Colinette* by Joseph Quesnel, and in 1961 they won the Grand Prix du Disque for their *Concert Arias and Duets of Mozart.*

Simoneau retired from the operatic stage in 1964, again as Ottavio, a role he sang 185 times. When he left the concert stage, in 1970, his voice was still in its prime, but he said, speaking as always for his wife as well as himself, "We didn't want to appear before the public with anything less than the very best to give." Since then the Simoneaus have been indefatigable teachers, in Montreal (where the Opéra du Québec did not meet their exacting standards), in San Francisco, and in Victoria, B.C. (where they founded Canada Opera Piccola).

Simoneau's voice recorded with astonishing fidelity, and his art is perhaps best sampled, apart from Mozart, in his "Una furtiva lagrima," which Steane has called "surely the most even and finely poised modern recording." Connoisseurs will also want to hear Simoneau sing on records the work of such widely divergent composers as Vivaldi, Couperin, Bach, Handel, Haydn, Berlioz, Schubert, Schumann, Honneger, Duparc, and Werner Egk. The high value that people of genius placed on his musicianship is perhaps best illustrated by the fact that he was accompanied in concert at the Stratford (Ontario) Festival by Glenn Gould, attracted Nadia Boulanger to every performance of the first run of *The Rake's Progress* in Paris, and dared to perform *Oedipus Rex* with its creators, Igor Stravinsky and Jean Cocteau.

—M. Owen Lee

SINGHER, Martial Jean-Paul.

Baritone. Born 14 August 1904, in Oloron-Sainte-Marie, France. Died 9 March 1990, in Santa Barbara, California. Married Eta Busch, 1940; three sons. Studied at Paris Conservatory with André Gresse; debut as Orestes in *Iphigénie en Tauride,* 1930; Paris Opéra debut as Athanael in *Thaïs,* 1930; at Paris Opéra 1930-43; Covent Garden debut as High Priest in *Alceste,* 1937; Metropolitan Opera debut as Dapertutto in *Les contes d'Hoffmann,* 1943; Metropolitan Opera, 1943-59; sang both Pelléas (1944) and Golaud (1953); created the roles of Bassanio in Hahn's *Le marchand de Venise,* Bazaine in Milhaud's *Maximilien,* and Ascanio in Le Roucher's *La duchesse de Padoue;* taught at Mannes College; head of the vocal department, Curtis Institute; head of the vocal department, Music Academy of the West, Santa Barbara, 1962-81; pupils include James King, Louis Quilico, Donald Gramm, John Reardon, Jeannine Altmeyer.

Publications

By SINGHER: book–

An Interpretive Guide to Operatic Arias: A Handbook for Singers, Coaches, Teachers, and Students. University Park, Pennsylvania, c.1983.

article–

"La musique française." *Esquisse de la France.* Montreal, 1946.

About SINGHER: articles–

Riemens, L. "Singher, Martial." In *Le grandi voci.* ed. by R. Celletti, Rome, 1964.
Eaton, Quaintance. "Beau Idéal." *Opera News* 51 (11 April 1987): 10.

* * *

On 27 January 1956, the two-hundredth anniversary of the birth of Mozart, Martial Singher performed the title role in a celebratory *Le nozze di Figaro* at the Metropolitan Opera. Two months later, on 28 March, the not-quite fifty-two year-old baritone was onstage again in the same work in the same theater, but this time as Figaro's employer, the Count Almaviva. During that particular New York season Singher was also much occupied singing Hoffmann's four nemeses in a new production of *Les contes d'Hoffmann,* the High Priest of Dagon in *Samson et Dalila,* and Amfortas in *Parsifal.* Such a demonstration of versatility was for him no extraordinary feat, but merely standard routine in a thirty-year-long manifestation of the art of the operatic singing actor at its highest level.

Martial Singher was the prime mid-twentieth-century example of that uniquely French phenomenon, the *baryton martin.* That is to say, he possessed a voice of such properties (though it was neither large nor of outstanding beauty) that he could encompass a repertory ranging from Boris Godunov, the dominion of operatic basses, to the much higher, lighter Pelléas, many of whose most famous interpreters have been tenors.

Singher's was not an instrument that was stentorian or ringing in the Titta Ruffo or John Charles Thomas manner, nor one that evidenced real comfort in high tessitura passages as did those of Igor Gorin or the young Theodor Uppman (singers Singher much admired); it was, in fact, a voice with a tendency toward dryness and lack of sheen, especially as it aged, and one that was at no time in the artist's career invariably steady or pitch-true. What set Singher apart from his contemporaries almost from the beginning, later made him a revered model to younger colleagues while he was still performing, and finally resulted in his becoming one of the most influential teachers of his time, was an acutely developed musico-dramatic sensibility far surpassing that available to the majority of those who *did* have effulgent, impressive Italianate voices. Because of this, he was able to impart complete verisimilitude to characters as diverse and with vocal requirements as dissimilar as Musorgsky's haunted tsar and Debussy's prince of Allemonde—even if he did, in truth, always have to strain a bit for the lowest notes of the one and the highest notes of the other. As an actor, he was compelling, charismatic, and lithe. "Together we became ballet dancers," he said of himself and Bidú Sayão as Figaro and Susanna.

For a certain period of time, Singher was in constant demand in the United States for the great roles of the French repertory. "His singing of that language," wrote Virgil Thomson after a 1944 *Pelléas et Mélisande* in New York, "is as different from the way anybody else here sings it as a real French dress or pastry is from what is currently available to us." Indeed, for some years Singher and Lily Pons constituted the entire contingent of French singers on the Metropolitan Opera roster.

When Singher was only twenty-eight, Maurice Ravel dedicated one of the three songs ("Chanson épique") of his 1932 cycle "Don Quichotte à Dulcinée" to the young singer. (In later years, Singher was wont to insist that he was actually offered all three but had been too modest to accept, which may or may not have amused the other dedicatees, Robert Couzinou and Roger Bourdin.) Modesty notwithstanding, it was Singher who sang the world premiere of the whole cycle (in Paris, 1 December 1934) and subsequently recorded it in Ravel's presence. Not only the vocal span itself, but the very specific palette of dynamic demands and the wide emotional range required in this music give to us now a real indication of the depth and extent of Singher's artistic capacity.

A prominent teacher for three decades, among other places at the Curtis Institute in Philadelphia and later in succession to Lotte Lehmann at the Music Academy in Santa Barbara, California, Singher passed on to his students more than just his knowledge of the vanishing French tradition, of which he was guardian and principal exponent outside of France in his time. He gave them as well the guiding principles by which he lived: that music, words, and drama are of absolutely equal significance and that one never subsumes the position of another; that the designation "singing actor" does not imply permission to shirk the responsibilities of virtuoso vocalism; and that even though drama and words are on a plane with the music, it must be understood that they have their origin *in* the music, and never vice versa. Singher's paramount achievement may well be the conspicuous degree of success with which he inculcated these tenets in a large number of pupils who subsequently became prominent performers themselves.

—Bruce Burroughs

SINOPOLI, Giuseppe.

Conductor/Composer. Born 2 November 1946, in Venice. Studied organ and harmony in Messina; studied harmony and counterpoint at the Venice Conservatory; studied medicine at the University of Padua (psychiatry degree, 1971); studied composition with Donatoni in Paris; studied composition with Swarowsky at the Vienna Academy of Music; organized the Bruno Maderna Ensemble, 1975; guest conductor at the Teatro La Fenice, Venice, 1976; guest conductor at the Deutsche Oper, Berlin, 1980, the Hamburg State Opera, 1980, and the Vienna State Opera, 1982; conducted at Covent Garden, London, 1983; conducted at the Metropolitan Opera, New York, 1985; principal conductor of the Orchestra dell' Accademia Nazionale di Santa Cecilia, Rome, 1983-87; principal conductor of the Philharmonia Orchestra, London, beginning 1984; Generalmusikdirektor of the Deutsche Oper, Berlin, 1990; principal conductor of the Dresden Staatskapelle. Sinopoli has composed an opera and a number of orchestral and chamber works.

Publications

About SINOPOLI: articles–

Stearns, D. "The Psychodynamics of Sinopoli." *Ovation* March (1989).

Having been born in Italy but educated in Vienna under conductor Hans Swarowsky, Giuseppe Sinopoli brings to his performances a combination of Germanic weightiness and an Italianate sense of bel canto. He also holds a doctorate of medicine in psychiatry, and is known for his keen powers of musical and dramatic analysis. As a result, he is known for innovative readings of well-known works and gives unusual dramatic credibility to works that were previously not considered to be especially stageworthy. Sinopoli is clearly a revisionist, and has even admitted in interviews that he becomes somewhat uncomfortable when his notices from critics are unanimously favorable.

To be sure, Sinopoli's notices weren't always that way. When he first arrived on the international opera circuit, he was sometimes a shocking presence in the orchestra pit. Though his bearded, bespectacled appearance suggested someone professorial, there was nothing academic about his contorted conducting motions, which seemed to typify what at first seemed a somewhat perverse approach to music. He often found fresh insights into well-worn works by underscoring inner voices and with rhetorical effects achieved with a flexibility of tempo. This sometimes resulted in performances with an emphasis on the grotesque, such as in Verdi's *Macbeth,* which can seem lurid even in the most conservative interpretations.

Sinopoli's iconoclasm, combined with unusual casting (Hildegard Behrens as Tosca and Mara Zampieri as Lady Macbeth, for example), suggested he is a deconstructionist, a musical counterpart to some of the more radical, post-modern stage directors. But as Sinopoli has matured, eccentricities have become less pronounced, and his performances have become more deeply considered.

While his casting instincts have become more sound and traditional, he still excites considerable controversy with unusual interpretive choices. Sinopoli's treatment of Elisabeth's aria, "Dich, teure Halle," from *Tannhäuser* is unusually sub-dued and rounded, which some might say goes against the grain of the essentially ecstatic music. However, it could also be said that such an extroverted outburst is not in keeping with the rest of the character, and that Sinopoli's emphasis on the warm, nurturing side of her personality might be more appropriate for her pious nature.

Such highly debatable details in Sinopoli's interpretations are typical of his probing mind and the thoughtfulness with which he approaches even the most over-exposed operas. He makes *Madama Butterfly* into musical drama of feverish intensity, though not always with success. Sinopoli telegraphs to the audience exactly what is going to happen in the story by self-consciously italicizing the musical references to the United States national anthem in Pinkerton's act I duet with Sharpless. Most listeners know the plot anyway, but Sino-poli's emphasis on this key moment does not allow the listener to re-discover the plot as the opera progresses.

In that sense, Sinopoli is a post-modernist: he seems to assume that all of his listeners know the work at hand inti-mately and his job is to shake them out of their torpor at the expense of the music's flow and naturalness of the texture. However, Sinopoli often justifies his idiosyncracies with a sense of fresh discovery that would seem almost impossible with many overexposed masterpieces in the late twentieth century.

In this sense, Sinopoli's art is often most distinguished in its use of timbre. He frequently searches for the right sound for a particular dramatic situation, often favoring muted, darker colors to impart a sense of mystery. In *Madama Butterfly*, Sinopoli gives the title character a radiant halo of sound in her entrance, and the so-called "Humming Chorus" that ends act II is treated as a luminous, homogeneous texture. Often, Sinopoli will find a certain sound vocabulary for an entire piece, stating and developing timbres much the way themes are argued symphonically. In doing this, he is occa-sionally guilty of emphasizing one aspect of the score at the expense of another.

Because these rather special ideas—not to mention the slow tempos that frequently go with them—can only be fully realized by the finest instrumentalists and singers, Sinopoli's influence to other orchestras and conductors is perhaps des-tined to be limited. Moreover, Sinopoli's ideas—even at their most resonant—are no doubt ineffective without his special sort of Dionysian passion.

Sinopoli's repertoire is a source of some disappointment. Despite being a composer and having championed contempo-rary composers at the beginning of his career, his repertoire has become remarkably conservative, favoring the works of Verdi, Puccini, Mahler, Schumann and other romantics. Usu-ally, Sinopoli begins with a composer's early and middle-period works, implying he is saving their late works for when he is older. He occasionally champions a lesser-known work such as Verdi's *Nabucco*, but the most remote item in his discography is some excerpts from his own, alban berg-influenced opera, *Lou Salome.*

—David Patrick Stearns

THE SLEEPWALKER
See LA SONNAMBULA

SLEZAK, Leo.

Tenor. Born 18 August 1873, in Mährisch-Schönberg (now Sumperk), Moravia. Died 1 June 1946, in Egern am Teg-ernsee, Germany. Married: Elsa Wertheim. Studied with Ad-olf Robinson, Jean De Reszke; debut as Lohengrin in Brno, 1896; in Berlin, 1898-99; Breslau, 1899; Vienna State Opera as Guillaume Tell, 1901, remained until 1933; Covent Garden debut as Lohengrin, 1900; Teatro alla Scala debut, 1902; Metropolitan Opera debut as Otello, 1909; Boston Opera, 1911-13; retired from opera, 1933; continued to act in film; his son was actor Walter Slezak.

Publications

By SLEZAK: books–

Meine sämtlichen Werke. Stuttgart, 1922.
Der Wortbruch. Berlin, 1927.
Song of Motley: Being the Reminiscences of a Hungry Tenor, London and New York, 1938. (Abridged translation of *Meine sämtlichen Werke, Der Wortbruch*)
Rückfall. Hamburg, 1940.
Mein Lebensmärchen. Stuttgart and Berlin, 1948.
Slezak, Walter, editor. *Mein lieber Bub: Briefe eines besorgten Vaters.* Munich, 1966.

About SLEZAK: books–

Kleinenberger, L. *Leo Slezak.* Munich, 1910.
Leitenberger, Friedrich Alfons. *Der göttliche Leo: Ein Volks-buch über Leo Slezak.* Vienna, 1948.
Slezak, M. *Der Apfel fällt nicht weit vom Stamm.* Munich, 1958.
Slezak, Walter. *What Time's the Next Swan?* New York, 1962.

articles–

Kaufman, Thomas G. and J. Dennis. "Leo Slezak." *Record Collector* 15 (1964): 197.
"Next Time Call a Cab." *The Instrumentalist* 45/September (1990): 4.

*   *   *

Having studied initially with baritone Adolf Robinson, Leo Slezak's rise to prominence was fairly rapid, with few signifi-cant setbacks. His earliest professional activity at Brno and Berlin was not especially distinguished, but neither was the repertory that was entrusted to him. At Breslau he was given more demanding roles, but still seemed to show more promise than accomplishment. A British tour of the Breslau company afforded him the opportunity of making his Covent Garden debut during the 1900 Royal Opera Season as Lohengrin to Milka Ternina's Elsa. Bitter political developments managed to distract his audience, considerably diminishing his impact, but an invitation to sing before Queen Victoria at Bucking-ham Palace during his stay provided some consolation. Guest appearances in Vienna followed in 1901, when he attracted the attention of Gustav Mahler, and the twenty-eight-year-old tenor was offered a contract to sing in the conductor's extraordinary ensemble of principals at the Vienna State Opera.

If his manner was in many ways rather typical of the German vocal style, Slezak's repertory was international, made up primarily of the brash, pre-*verismo* Italian and French dramatic heroes: Raoul (*Les Huguenots*), Jean (*Le prophète*), Arnold (*Guillaume Tell*), Gounod's Faust, Des Grieux (*Manon*), Gerald (*Lakmé*), Eléazar (*La juive*), and Julien (*Louise*); Canio (*I pagliacci*) and Rodolfo (*La bohème*); Flotow's Alessandro Stradella and Goldmark's Assad (*Die Königin von Saba*); Hermann (*The Queen of Spades*); Radames (*Aida*), Manrico (*Il trovatore*), the Duke (*Rigoletto*), and Otello. His reputation as a Wagnerian is surprising, for he generally confined himself to that composer's less taxing vehicles, those which his voice could accommodate. An early, unhappy flirtation with the young Siegfried, a role he first sang at Brno, ended abruptly with a poorly-received 1900 Covent Garden performance. Thereafter he wisely limited himself to Walther (*Die Meistersinger*), Lohengrin, and Tannhäuser.

Unable to negotiate a suitable contract with Mahler's successor, Felix Weingartner, Slezak left the Vienna Opera temporarily after Mahler's departure in 1907, and spent the next six years abroad. Though already well established, he clearly had his sights set upon an international career, which led him to study the non-German repertory that same year with Jean De Reszke in Paris and Lieder interpretation with Reynaldo Hahn. Sporting a new-found refinement that did not go unnoticed, he made an auspicious second debut at Covent Garden on 2 June 1909 as Otello, though his Radames that season was not similarly well received. Under Toscanini's direction, he made his Metropolitan Opera debut, also as Otello, on 17 November 1909, and this was an unqualified success. His portrayal of the Moor received excellent notices, and despite "a certain huskiness at times in his voice" attributed to nervousness, Henry Krehbiel was impressed with the "fine power" of his voice, and the "more than ordinary discretion" with which it was used.

Slezak's success in America was altogether remarkable, owing as much to his overwhelming physical stature as to his singing. Certainly, at over six feet, Slezak cast an enormous, almost menacing presence, but his bearing was anything but clumsy, prompting Krehbiel to remark that he presented "such a figure as would have delighted the audience that once applauded the heroics of Tommaso Salvini"—high praise indeed, bestowed at a time when the haunting memory of the great Italian tragedian still lingered. Unlike many European artists, whose soft tones and subtle manner were more or less wasted on a public accustomed to the more robust Italian wing already so well-established in America, Slezak had no difficulty making a profound and lasting impression. Both his voice and his physical stature were of the same vast proportions as his repertory, and he enjoyed immediate favor. At the Metropolitan Opera he sang Radames, Manrico, Stradella, Hermann, Gounod's Faust, Walther, and Lohengrin, and added Tamino (*Die Zauberflöte*) during his last season. He was given relatively little to do during his two seasons with the Boston Company, and was obliged to share his major roles—Otello, Manrico, and Radames—and even some peripheral ones—Julien, Faust, and the Duke—with Boston's own leading tenors. In the 1912-1913 Boston season he was called upon only once for a single Otello, substituting for Giovanni Zenatello.

Slezak returned to Europe in 1913, and remained there for the rest of his career, undertaking successful tours of Sweden, Russia, Holland, and the Scandinavian countries. His final appearance at the Vienna State Opera, his artistic home until 1928, was made as Canio on 26 September 1933, by which time he had already established himself with equal success as a singer of operetta and as a character actor in films.

In addition to his records, there are four delightful volumes of memoirs that have long served as testimonials to his wit; indeed, mention of him in the literature has seldom resisted the temptation of recalling some clever remark or further embellishing one of the particularly mischievous backstage pranks for which he was famous.

At his best, Slezak was a singer of the first rank. His voice could be as attractive as it was robust, and richly expressive. He could shade his voice as sensitively as the most renowned Italian and French stylists, aided by what must have been among the most beautifully-contrived head voices in the tenor business—a *voix mixte* as rich in tone as it was well-controlled. Examples of it abound in his records, exerting an almost magic presence—the ending high Cs of his 1905 *Lakmé* "Fantaisie," the 1905 "Magische Töne" from *Der Königin von Saba,* and the celebrated 1905 "Viens, gentille dame" from Boieldieu's *La dame blanche.* Accounts vary, but it would appear that Slezak was not so great an *actor* as he was an effectively dramatic *singer*—something he had in common perhaps with Caruso and Martinelli, both of whom shared his repertory and experienced a similar histrionic growth over the course of their respective careers.

Between about 1901 and 1931 Slezak left nearly 400 souvenirs of his voice, among them operatic excerpts drawn from the four corners of the international tenor repertory, and an imposing number of superbly-executed Lieder. Generally, they maintain a consistency of quality comparable to that of other prolific recorders. His huge voice recorded exceptionally well from the very beginning, as many big voices did, and it remained more or less unchanged over a period of some forty years, enabling him to record electrically with great effectiveness. His many recordings for the Gramophone Company, made between 1901-1912, are among his best, and give a thorough accounting of his behavior in the repertory in which he clearly excelled. This notwithstanding the often brutal German translations. Only rarely did he record the non-German repertory in its original language, which makes the few items he recorded for American Columbia during his seasons with the Boston Opera especially precious. Perhaps the most extraordinary of all his records are the Lieder, the best of which were made when he was already past his sixtieth year. These are as expressively sung as any on disc, and help us to understand Richard Aldrich's observation after a 1912 Carnegie Hall recital that "Mr. Slezak has an unusual power of giving apt and significant expression to a variety of moods, expression that is gained by subtle means in the molding of a phrase, the color of the voice, the suggestion of dramatic or emotional motive." Herman Klein, reviewing a batch of Slezak's recorded Lieder in the April 1927 issue of *The Gramophone,* wrote that "For my part I do not want to hear a more perfect or more poetic diction, better phrasing, an apter sense of colourful contrast, clearer rhythm, or greater depth and purity of expression."

As a whole, Slezak's records impress us with a voice of distinctive timbre and clarion strength. He was not above forcing his voice, however, with the kind of senseless abandon characteristic of the worst exponents of the German school, hence the slow wobble, and coarseness of tone so frequently encountered among his records. His interpretations, especially those of his Verdi specialties, can be overwhelmingly dramatic, yet at the same time keenly perceptive. His many recordings from *Otello* suggest that, with Zenatello, he was clearly one of that generation's most striking exponents of the role, certainly ranking high among its definitive interpreters. It is perhaps significant that Slezak was the last to sing Otello at the Metropolitan (on 31 January 1913) until the opera was revived for Martinelli in December 1937, a suitable replacement having taken nearly a quarter of a century to appear.

—William Shaman

SMETANA, Bedřich (Friedrich).

Composer. Born 2 March 1824, in Leitomischl. Died 12 May 1884, in Prague. Married: Katharina Kolař (died 1859), pianist, 1849. Studied piano with Proksch in Prague; music teacher to the family of Count Thun; financially disastrous piano tour 1848; aided by Liszt in opening a piano school, 1848; conductor of the Philharmonic Society of Göteborg, Sweden, 1856; returned to Prague to support the nationalist artistic movement, 1861; composition of nationalist operas, 1863-74; conductor of the Provisional Theater, 1866; symphonic poems collectively entitled *Má vlast* composed 1874-79; further opera composition from 1876-82.

Operas

Editions:

Souborná díla Bedřicha Smetany. 4 vols. Edited by Z. Nejedlý and O. Ostrčil. Prague, 1924, 1932-36.
Studijní vydání děl Bedřicha Smetany. Edited by F. Bartoš, J. Plavec, et al. Prague, 1940-.
Klavírní dílo Bedřicha Smetany. Edited by M. Očadlík et al. Prague, 1944-73.
B. Smetana: Písne. Edited by J. Plavec. Prague, 1962.
Operni librety Bedřicha Smetany: kritické vydání [critical edition of Smetana's opera librettos]. Various editors. Prague, 1918-62.

The Brandenburgers in Bohemia [Braniboři v Čechách], K. Sabina, 1862-63, Prague, Provisional Theater, 5 January 1866; various revisions up to 1870.
The Bartered Bride [Prodana nevěsta], K. Sabina, 1863-66, Prague, Provisional Theater, 30 May 1866; revised, 1869, Prague, Provisional Theater, 29 January 1869; revised, 1869, Prague, Provisional Theater, 1 June 1869; revised, 1869-70, Prague, Provisional Theater, 25 September 1870.
Dalibor, J. Wenzig (Czech translation by E. Špindler), 1865-67, Prague, New Town Theater, 16 May 1868; revised, 1870.
Libuše, J. Wenzig (Czech translation by E. Špindler), 1869-72, Prague, National Theater, 11 June 1881.
The Two Widows [Dvě vdovy], E. Züngel (after P.J.F. Mallefille), 1873-74, Prague, Provisional Theater, 27 March 1874; revised, 1877, Prague, Provisional Theater, 15 March 1878.
The Kiss [Hubička], E. Krásnohorská (after K. Světlá), 1875-76, Prague, Provisional Theater, 7 November 1876.
The Secret [Tajemství], E. Krásnohorská, 1877-78, Prague, New Czech Theater, 18 September 1878.
The Devil's Wall [Čertova stěna], E. Krásnohorská, 1879-82, Prague, New Czech Theater, 29 October 1882.
Viola, E. Krásnohorská (after Shakespeare, *Twelfth Night*), 1874, 1883-84 [unfinished].

Other works: orchestral works, chamber music, vocal works, piano pieces.

Publications

By SMETANA: books–

Teige, K., ed. *Příspěvky k životopisu a umělecké činnosti mistra Bedřicha Smetany.* Vol. 2, *Dopisy Smetanovy* [letters]. Prague, 1896.
Srb-Debrnov, J., ed. *Z deníků Bedřicha Smetany (1856-1861)* [from Smetana's diaries]. Prague 1902.
Zelenka-Lerando L., ed. *B. Smetana a E. Züngel* [correspondence]. Nymburk, 1903.
Löwenbach, J., ed. *Bedřich Smetana a dr Ludevít Procházka: vzájemná korespondence.* Prague, 1914.
Reisser, J., ed. *Bedřich Smetana: články a referáty 1862-1865.* [articles and reviews]. Prague, 1920.
Očadlík, M., ed. *Bedřich Smetana: To, co my komponisté jako v mlhách tušime* [facsimile edition of Smetana's statements on creating a national style]. Prague, 1940.
———. *Bedřich Smetana: Zápisník motivů* [facsimile edition of Smetana's notebook of themes]. Prague, 1942.
———. *Prodaná nevěsta: první náčrtek Bedřicha Smetany* [facsimile edition of *The Bartered Bride* sketches]. Prague, 1944.

articles–

Hostinský, O., ed. "Smetanovy dopisy" [letters]. *Dalibor* 7 (1885); 8 (1886); 9 (1887).

Note: for additional letters, see below and *The New Grove Dictionary of Music and Musicians,* 1980 ed.

About SMETANA: books–

Nejedlý, Z. *Zpěvohry Smetanovy* [Smetana's operas]. Prague, 1908; 3rd ed., 1954.
Balthasar, V. *Bedřich Smetana* [includes letters to Srb-Debrnov]. Prague, 1924.
Bartoš, J. *Prozatimní divadlo a jeho opera* [The Provisional Theater and its Opera]. Prague, 1938.
Očadlík, M. *Libuše: vznik Smetanovy zpěpohry* [the origin of *Libuše*]. Prague, 1939.
———. *Eliska Krásnohorská-Bedřich Smetana* [includes correspondence]. Prague, 1940.
Rutte, M. and O. Šourek, eds. *Smetanův operní epilog* [Smetana's operatic epilogue]. Prague, 1942.
Pražák, P. *Smetanovy zpěvohry* [Smetana's operas]. Prague, 1948.
———. *Smetanova Prodaná nevěsta: vznik a osudy díla* [the origins of *The bartered bride*]. Prague, 1962.
Large, Brian. *Smetana.* London, 1970.
Clapham, John. *Smetana.* London and New York, 1972.
Honolka, Kurt. *Bedřich Smetana in Selbstzeugnissen und Bilddokumenten* [includes analysis of *Dalibor*]. Reinbek bei Hamburg, 1978.
Tyrrell, John. *Czech Opera.* Cambridge, 1988.

articles–

Dolanský, L. "Bedřich Smetana v letech studentských" [includes diary extracts]. *Naše doba* 10 (1903): 241, 360.
Nejedlý, Z. "Opera Tajemství ve Smetanových denících" [*The Secret* in Smetana's diaries]. *Hubedni revue* 1/no. 8 (1908).
Abraham, Gerald. "The Genesis of The Bartered Bride." *Music and Letters* 28 (1947): 36.

Belza, I. "Pisma Smetany i St. Moniuszko k E.P. Nápravník" [letters to Nápravník from Smetana and Moniuszko]. *Akad. nauk SSSR Inst. slavyanovedeniya: Kratkiye soobschcheniya* [Moscow] 14 (1955): 72.

Pospíšil, V. "Talichova Prodaná nevěsta" [Talich's *Bartered Bride*]. *Hudebni revue* 10 (1957): 741.

Jiránek, Jaroslav. "Das Problem der Beziehung von Musik und Wort im Schaffen Bedřich Smetanas." In *Colloquium: Music and Word: Brno IV*, 107. Brno, 1969.

Vokurka, Z. "Ještě k vavřínům Smetanovy Hubičky" [On *The Kiss*] *Opus musicum* 2 (1970): 198.

Jiránek, Jaroslav. "Vstah hudby a slova ve Smetanově Prodané nevěstě" [word-music relations in *The Bartered Bride*]. *Hudebni veda* 8 (1971): 19; German summary, 123.

———. "Statistika jako pomocný nástroj intonační analýzy" [Statistics and analysis; analysis of *Libuše*]. *Hudebni veda* 8 (1971): 165; English summary, 252.

Jareš, S. "Obrazová dokumentace nejstarších inscenací Prodané nevěsty" [Pictoral documentation of the first production of *The Bartered Bride*]. *Hudebni veda* 11 (1974): 195; German summary, 198.

Jehne, L. "K prolematice Smetanovských hlasových oburů pěveckých typů" [voice types and singers in Smetana's works]. *Hudebni veda* 11 (1974): 125; German summary, 135.

Jiránek, Jaroslav. "Problém hudebně dramatické reprezentace Krasavy ve Smetanové Libuši" [problem of musico-dramatic representation of Krasava in Smetana's *Libuše*]. *Hudebni veda* 11 (1974): 250; German summary, 274.

Clapham, John. " 'Dalibor': an Introduction." *Opera* 27 (1976): 890.

Jiránek, Jaroslav. "Krystalizace významového pole Smetanovy Libuše" [the crystalization of the significant range of Smetana's *Libuše*]. *Hudebni veda* 13 (1976): 27; German summary, 55.

Large, B. "Smetana's Brandenburgers." *Musical Times* 119 (1978): 329.

Seaman, Gerald. "The Rise of Slavonic Opera, I." *New Zealand Slavonic Journal* 2 (1978): 1.

Goebel, Albrecht. "Zur rechten Zeit in den Ehestand. *Die verkaufte Braute* und ihre Epoche." *Musik und Medizin* 3 (1979): 37.

Jiránek, Jaroslav. "Sabinovo libreto ke Smetanově proní opeře" [libretto for *Brandenburgers*] *Česká literatura* 27 (1979): 206.

Clapham, John. "Smetana's Sketches for *Dalibor* and *The Secret*." *Music and Letters* 61 (1980): 136.

Jiránek, Jaroslav. "K problému operníko libreta a jeho analýzy" [analysis of *The Bartered Bride* libretto]. *Hudebni veda* 17 (1980): 221.

Ottlová, Marta, and Milan Pospíšil. "Český historismus a opera 19. století Smetanova *Libuše*." In *Historické vědomí v českém umění 19. století*, edited by Thomáš Vlček, 83. Praha, 1981.

———. "K problematice české historické opery 19. století" [libretto of *The Brandenburgers in Bohemia*]. *Hudebni rozhledy* 34 (1981): 169.

———. "Smetanas *Libuše*. Der tschechische Historismus und die Oper des 19. Jahrhunderts." In *Festschrift Heinz Becker zum 60. Geburtstag am 26. Juni 1982*, edited by Jürgen Schläder and Reinhold Quandt, 237. Laaber, 1982.

Vít, Petr. "Libuše-proměny mýtu ve společnosti a v umění." *Hudebni veda* 19 (1982): 269.

Beechey, Gwilym. "The First Czech National Opera." *Musical Opinion* 107 (1984): 318, 323, 332.

Jiránek, Jaroslav. "Smetanova operní tvorba. 1: Od *Braniborů v Čechách* k *Libuši.*" *Dílo a život Bedřicha Smetany* [Praha] 3 (1984): 437.

Střítecký, Jaroslav. "Tradice a obrozeni—Bedřich Smetana." *Opus musicum* 16 (1984): 194.

* * *

Until the end of the World War I, the Czech regions—Bohemia, Slovakia and Moravia—remained provinces of the Austro-Hungarian Empire. In common with all members of the Czech middle classes during the earlier nineteenth century, Bedřich Smetana was educated and brought up speaking the "official" language, which was German. His musical training was classical, in the German and Italian traditions. The emergence of Czech nationalism caught Smetana's imagination, and he determined to help create a distinctively national musical style, using opera as its central focus. Among the challenges that this commitment brought was that of learning his native language; for instance, it was not until the age of thirty-two that Smetana could summon the confidence to write a letter in Czech. A little later, in 1860, he wrote: "I am not ashamed to write in my mother tongue, however imperfectly, and am glad to be able to show that my fatherland means more to me than anything else."

Smetana did not gain early recognition in his homeland, however, and he worked in Gothenburg in Sweden for the six years from 1856. The opportunity he needed to achieve a breakthrough came from a competition set up by Count Jan Harrach to encourage the creation of new Czech operas. Two types of opera were suggested: one to be based upon the

Bedřich Smetana

history of the Czech people, the other to be "of lighter content and taken from the national life of the people in Bohemia and Moravia." This development made Smetana aware of the new potential for the arts in his homeland, especially when in 1862 the Provisional Theater was opened in Prague, for opera as well as drama, in order to stage performances in Czech.

The two types of work stipulated in the competition regulations reflect the two basic approaches Smetana was to follow in his eight completed operas. Czech history was a natural subject for nationalist opera, as was the life of the people, which reflected the rural communities and their peasant customs as well as the preservation of the Czech language. In order to become a significant and lasting phenomenon, however, any emergent national trend had to gain a composer of genius, as had previously been the case with Glinka in Russia. Smetana's Czech predecessors were worthy but mediocre, and his duty became the creation of the repertory of opera which his homeland lacked.

In 1863, Smetana submitted the score of *The Brandenburgers in Bohemia* to the competition judges. It won the first prize and in due course received a triumphant premiere in the Provisional Theater. The opera is set at a time when Bohemia was overrun with foreign troops, its dramatic potential captured and enriched by Smetana's music. The experience already gained in his symphonic poems on literary subjects enabled him to create vivid scenes and rounded characters, which he combined with writing for the chorus that is both subtle and assured.

The premiere of a second opera, *The Bartered Bride* (which has proved to be Smetana's most popular work for the stage) fulfilled the second of the competition's options, being in a lighter style. The composer claimed he wrote it "not out of vanity but for spite, because I was accused after *The Brandenburgers* of being a Wagnerian who was incapable of writing anything in a lighter vein." At first, *The Bartered Bride* was not well received, but various revisions up to 1870 transformed it, particularly by means of the addition of distinctive material such as the dances and "beer chorus," in which the national element really came to the fore. However, the characterization is strong and so too are the dramatic pacing and the melodic invention. The piece was performed more than one hundred times during Smetana's lifetime, although its style was not always understood; when he was accused of modeling it on the operettas of Offenbach, his indignant response was: "Did none of those gentlemen realise that my model was Mozart's comic opera?" Smetana much admired *The Marriage of Figaro,* and in its general features his opera has similarities to it: its bubbling presto overture, as well as its plot, structure and basic themes. There are two pairs of lovers in each case, as well as an identical resolution of the drama, brought about by the discovery of a long-lost son.

Yet Smetana believed that more important tasks awaited him, for his next two operas, *Dalibor* and *Libuše,* are concerned with heroic and epic themes. *Dalibor* presents the story of the hero of the title, who stood bravely and selflessly for the cause of right and for the most noble aspirations. Having avenged the murder of his beloved friend Zdeněk, Dalibor is imprisoned, but despite the efforts of his enemy's sister Milada to rescue him, the opera ends tragically. Thus the moral stance taken by Beethoven in *Fidelio* is adapted by Smetana for his own ends, one of which was surely the nationalist vision of freedom from oppression.

The composer was bitterly disappointed by the adverse critical response to *Dalibor*, caused largely by the misconception that it was deliberately Wagnerian. In fact, if an influence is at work it is that of Liszt's "transformation of themes," a procedure already evident in Smetana's symphonic poems.

The chorus, representing the Czech people, has some stirring music, and the range of emotion and balance of dramatic urgency and release of tension show *Dalibor* to be a masterpiece of the first order.

Libuše, designed as a national epic, was composed by 1872 but held back for a further nine years in order to coincide with the opening of the new National Theater. The music has a special festive quality, in keeping with Smetana's intention that it should celebrate the Czech nation itself. Its plot treats the legendary creation of the Přemyslid dynasty, an historical episode of great symbolic significance. Libuše herself is the Queen of Bohemia, and her abdication by marriage allows the firm rule of Přemysl to unite the conflicting elements within the nation. Smetana described this opera as "a glorious tableau animated by musical drama," and decreed that its performance should be reserved for ceremonial occasions. This patriotic scheme immediately preceded the completion of his cycle of six symphonic poems, *Ma Vlast* (*My Homeland*), and the two works are intimately linked in their imagery.

Throughout his career as an opera composer, Smetana continued to diversify his approach to the medium. *The Two Widows* is a lively comedy in which subtleties of characterization are enhanced both by the vocal writing and the role of the orchestra. Stylistically this work is very advanced for its time, with an intimate story in which one widow pretends to be in love with the landowner Ladislav in order to encourage the other to commit herself to him. It is set as a number opera with linking recitatives, the latter replacing the original spoken dialogue in a subsequent revision, and among its strongest admirers was Richard Strauss, who may even have used it as the model for his own opera *Intermezzo*.

By 1875-76, when Smetana composed his sixth opera, *The Kiss,* he had become completely deaf. This was his first collaboration with the excellent librettist Eliska Krásnohorská, and though the plot, based upon a lovers' quarrel, may seem slight, the humanity with which it is treated transcends the surface level by virtue of wide-ranging characterization and the atmospheric creation of mood in the contrasting scenes.

Smetana could by now work only slowly, and for no longer than an hour at a time, since the concentration required when composing had the effect of intensifying the buzzing sensation in his ears. Despite the distress these circumstances caused him, his will remained strong, as he explained in a letter to Krásnohorská written during October 1877, while he was working on *The Secret,* their second collaboration: "I am afraid my music is not cheerful enough for a comedy. But how could I be cheerful? Where could happiness come from when my heart is heavy with trouble and sorrow? I should like to be able to work without having to worry. When I plunge into musical ecstasy, then for a while I forget everything that persecutes me so cruelly in my old age." Yet this new three act opera was completed within nine months, and warmly received. Set in the Bohemian countryside in the eighteenth century, its dramatic situation, characterization and musical structure are more sophisticated than in *The kiss.* The vocal writing, particularly for the principal soprano, Kalina, is wide-ranging and often declamatory, and the musical flow is continuous rather than in separate numbers. Accordingly, the orchestral writing is distinguished, and dramatically the tensions build until they release large scale ensembles with splendid choral contributions.

Smetana described *The Devil's Wall* as a "comic-romantic opera," a strange terminology stemming from the fact that it is a parody set in the age of chivalry, when men of the church plotted in order to acquire power and wealth. In this, his last completed opera, there are few indications of musical weakness, though the complex plot does not avoid confusions. One fundamental and forward-looking aspect of this work is that one of the leading characters appears simultaneously as two different personalities, with two different singers onstage, one representing the hermit Beneš and the other his alter-ego, the devilish Rarach, though the other characters see them as one and the same person. Rather more than elsewhere, Smetana used recurring themes, perhaps to unify the potential confusions inherent in the drama.

At the time of his death Smetana was working on *Viola,* an adaptation by Krásnahorská of Shakespeare's *Twelfth Night,* but he only reached the stage of preliminary sketches, since his condition deteriorated rapidly during his final months. He complained frequently of "a pounding and intense hissing in the head, day and night without ceasing, as if I were standing underneath a huge waterfall." His mind gave way, and he was eventually taken to the Prague lunatic asylum on 23 April 1884, where he died nearly three weeks later.

Apart from *The Two Widows,* based on a French comedy but reset in Bohemia, all Smetana's completed operas are thoroughly Czech in subject matter. He succeeded in establishing a national operatic tradition, and his firm commitment to opera ensured the achievement of this goal. Yet each of his operas brings its own approach and its own identity within his style. Perhaps the most clearly Czech elements in these works are the folklike peasant choruses and the vigorous dances, but these features are less significant than his extraordinary and often intensely personal expressive range, from historical epic grandeur to light lyric comedy. In retrospect, Smetana must be viewed as one of the giants of nineteenth century opera.

—Terry Barfoot

SMIRNOV, Dmitri.

Tenor. Born 19 November 1882, in Moscow. Died 27 April 1944, in Riga. Married: soprano Lydia Smirnova-Maltseva. Student of Emiliya Pavlovskaya; also studied in Milan; debut as Gigi in the premiere of Esposito's *Camorra* at the Hermitage Theater in Moscow, 1903; after Bol'shoy Opera debut in 1904 (as Sinodal in *The Demon*), sang with the company until 1910; member, Imperial Opera, St Petersburg, 1910-17; debut at Paris Opéra, as Gregori in *Boris Godunov,* 1908; debut at Metropolitan Opera in 1910 as Duke in *Rigoletto;* sang there until 1912; sang *Lakmé* with Boston opera in 1911; in summer of 1914 sang Levko in Rimsky-Korsakov's *May Night* under Beecham at Drury Lane; was regular guest in Paris at Théâtre du Châtelet and Théâtre Sarah Bernhardt, singing in *Prince Igor, Russalka, Russlan and Lyudmila,* and Serov's *Judith;* during 1920s sang mainly in Europe; made concert tours in the USSR, 1926-30; sang Gregori in new production of *Boris Godunov* at Théâtre des Champs Elysées in Monte Carlo, 1931; in later life was active as teacher.

Publications

About SMIRNOV: articles–

Stratton, J. "Dmitri Smirnov." *Record Collector* 14 (1962): 245.

Kesting, Jürgen. "Der Manierist: Dimitri Smirnow." In *Die Grossen Sänger,* Vol. 2, 734. Düsseldorf, 1986.

*   *   *

In the early years of the twentieth century, pre-Revolution Russia boasted a formidable array of tenor talent: Ershov, Klementiev, Davidov, Labinsky and Figner, to name but a few. Of the lyric tenors, two stood out from the rest: Leonid Sobinov and Dmitri Smirnov. Among record collectors they are usually considered together, though their careers were quite different. While Sobinov largely confined his career to his homeland, Dmitri Smirnov also sang extensively in the West and thus achieved greater popularity, particularly in Europe.

Smirnov, like his exact Italian contemporary Giuseppe Anselmi, who also sang with great acclaim in Russia, was a supreme exponent of the art of bel canto, in particular of the high pianissimo and the morendo (where the voice is slowly filtered away to the merest thread of tone). Smirnov's voice was, according to contemporary reports, not of outstanding beauty nor especially large, but of a fascinating timbre, wedded to a fine stage appearance and a musicality of a high order. His musicianship was at times a cause for some qualification by the critics, however, for he was inclined to gratuitous distortions of the music for effect, a practice in which he was hardly alone among the singers of his day.

In Russia, Smirnov vied successfully for public favor with all the great singers of his day. Abroad, however, his fortunes were somewhat mixed. He was a great favorite in France,

Dmitri Smirnov as Lenski in *Eugene Onegin*

Belgium and Monte Carlo and was well-enough liked when he sang in London. In America, however, he made a less favorable impression. He sang during two seasons at the Metropolitan Opera in Italian and French roles, at a time when the tenor competition was fierce. His delicate, lyrical style did not impress a public accustomed to the more robust and thrilling tones of Caruso. The critic W.J. Henderson, for example, found his Roméo "dead flat and colourless." Perhaps he would have done better in his native repertoire, but Russian opera was not part of either of the seasons in which he participated.

On records, Smirnov is a collectors' favorite, particularly for those fascinated by the art of singing. The tone has a vibrancy and a timbre which is most appealing, and his singing shows a fascinating variety of nuance. His pianissimi are exquisite, often plucked at will as if from the air. His exemplary breath control enables the shaping of long, legato phrasing that is a pleasure to listen to. The high notes are of generally good quality and are produced with panache and without cost to the singer.

His recorded repertoire is wide-ranging, encompassing Russian, Italian and French opera and the song repertoire. Exquisite singing can, however, alternate with his taking liberties with the music that would raise the eyebrows of even the most tolerant listeners. In his recording of "Donna non vidi mai" (*Manon Lescaut*), for example, he alters the finale of the aria so as to end a whole octave higher than Puccini's score. For an artist whose musicality could be praiseworthy, these gratuitous interpolations are lapses of taste which are all the more regrettable.

Despite these caveats, Smirnov had an individuality that is typical of the greatest artists. On records, his finest work more than compensates for his occasional shortcomings and fully rewards the patient attention of the listener.

—Larry Lustig

SMYTH, (Dame) Ethel (Mary).

Composer. Born 22 April 1858, in Marylebone. Died 9 May 1944, in Woking, Surrey. Studied at the Leipzig conservatory; studied with Heinrich von Herzogenberg in Leipzig and Berlin; string quartet performed in Leipzig, 1884; returned to London, 1888, where numerous works of hers were performed; Dame of the British Empire, 1922.

Operas

Publishers: Universal, Novello, Curwen/Faber

Fantasio, Smyth (after Alfred de Musset), 1892-94, Weimar, 1898.
Der Wald, Smyth, 1899-1901, Berlin, 1902.
The Wreckers, Smyth, 1903-04, Leipzig, 1906.
The Boatswain's Mate, Smyth (after W.W. Jacobs), 1913-14, London, 1916.
Fête galante, Smyth (after Maurice Baring), 1923, Birmingham, 1923.
Entente cordiale, Smyth, 1925, London, 1925.

Other works: sacred and secular vocal music, orchestral works, chamber music, songs.

Publications

By SMYTH: books–

Impressions that Remained. London, 1919; 1981; abridged version edited by Ronald Crichton, 1987.
Streaks of Life. London, 1921.
A Three-legged Tour in Greece. London, 1927.
A Final Burning of Boats. London, 1928.
Female Pipings in Eden. London, 1933.
Beecham and Pharaoh. London, 1935.
As Time Went On. London, 1935.
Inordinate (?) Affection. London, 1936.
What Happened Next. London, 1940.

About SMYTH: books–

White, E.W. *The Rise of English Opera* [129 ff]. London, 1951.
St John, C. *Ethel Smyth.* London, 1959.
Howes, F. *The English Musical Renaissance* [65 ff]. London, 1966.
Collis, Louise. *Impetuous Heart: The Story of Ethel Smyth.* London, 1984.

articles–

McNaught, W. "Dame Ethel Smyth." *Musical Times* 85 (1944): 207.
Dale, K. "Dame Ethel Smyth." *Music and Letters* 25 (1944): 191.
————. Ethel Smyth's Prentice Work." *Music and Letters* 30 (1949): 329.
Beecham, T. "Dame Ethel Smyth (1858-1944). *Musical Times* 99 (1958): 363.
Wood, Elizabeth. "Women, Music, and Ethel Smyth: a Pathway in the Politics of Music." *Massachusetts Review* 24 (1983): 125.
Crichton, Ronald. "Ethel Smyth at the Opera." *Opera* October (1986).
Abromeit, Kathleen A. "Ethel Smyth, *The Wreckers,* and Sir Thomas Beecham." *Musical Quarterly* 73 (1989).

* * *

Ethel Smyth was a leader in the suffrage movement as well as an author of considerable distinction, but her most considerable success was in the field of opera. She wrote six operas between 1892 and 1925.

Ethel Smyth's first opera, *Fantasio,* was premiered at Weimar in 1898. The work is based on Alfred de Musset's comedy and is two acts in length. The Weimar premiere received bad press, with critics praising only the orchestration. Smyth destroyed most of the printed scores in 1916.

Completed in 1901, *Der Wald* is a one-act work which was heavily influenced by German symbolist art. With its forest setting and theme of salvation through death, the work shows Wagnerian influence. The main protagonist is the chorus of forest spirits. *Der Wald* was produced in Berlin and Covent Garden in 1902, followed by a New York performance in 1903. This performance made history as it was the first opera by a woman to be performed at the Metropolitan Opera House.

The Wreckers, probably the major musical achievement of Smyth's career, was written in 1903-04. The libretto was originally in French and titled *Les Naufrageurs* (The Wreckers). Rumor had it that French conductor André Messager would be the new artistic director of the English opera company, Covent Garden. Because of this, Smyth and Brewster felt that a French libretto would give *The Wreckers* its best chance for a performance in England. However, the work was never performed in its original French version (usually, the work is performed in English, although there is a German version as well). The large orchestra, the use of leitmotifs, and the dense contrapuntal writing all demonstrate again a Wagnerian influence.

In 1916, Smyth wrote her fourth opera, *The Boatswain's Mate.* This two-act comedy was written in the traditional English ballad opera style with spoken dialogue and folk song quotations. Smyth based the libretto on a short story by W.W. Jacobs. The plot centers around an ex-boatswain, Harry Benn, who tries to attract Mrs Waters, a widowed innkeeper. Benn's plan involves staging a robbery; he hopes that Mrs Waters will get scared and call him for help. Benn thinks that he will then rush in and supposedly "save" Mrs Waters. Rather, she becomes aware of Benn's false interest and turns the joke on him. The strength of the main female character parallels Smyth's personal strength.

In 1913, Smyth began noticing that her hearing was gradually failing. Despite the hardship, Smyth wrote two more operas. *Fête galante* is a "dance-dream" based on a short story by Maurice Baring. Many of the opera's features capture the new musical idiom of neoclassicism, such as the use of baroque dances and an *a cappella* madrigal. Unlike Stravinsky's, Smyth's interest in neoclassicism was shortlived, and she never used it again in any of her later works.

Smyth's final opera, *Entente cordiale,* concerns itself with British soldiers and their difficulties in a northern French town. World War I put an end to performances of Smyth's works on the continent, so she began writing. Her books remain a valuable source of information on her as well as other musical figures of the time. Smyth stands out as one of the most important figures in British music and was made a Dame by King George V. She staked the claim and proved that a woman could be a successful professional opera composer. In this way, she paved the path for generations to come.

—Kathleen A. Abromeit

THE SNOW MAIDEN [Snegurochka].

Composer: Nicolai Rimsky-Korsakov.

Librettist: Nicolai Rimsky-Korsakov (after A.N. Ostrovsky).

First Performance: St Petersburg, Mariinsky, 10 February 1882; revised version, St Petersburg, 1898.

Roles: The Snow Maiden, Snegurochka (soprano); King Winter (bass); Fairy Spring (mezzo-soprano); Lel (tenor or contralto); Kupava (mezzo-soprano); Mizgir (baritone or tenor); The Tsar (tenor); Villager (tenor); His Wife (mezzo-soprano); Wood Ghost (tenor); Carnival King (bass); Bermyata (bass); Two Heralds (tenor, baritone); Page (mezzo-soprano); chorus (SATB).

*   *   *

For the summer of 1880, Rimsky-Korsakov retired to the countryside, surrounded by an enchanting pastoral scene of fields, forests, rivers, lakes, and little villages with ancient names. "For the first time in my life I spent the summer in the heart of the Russian countryside. Everything delighted me," he recalled. The setting was just right for working on his new opera, *The Snow Maiden,* with its focus on fantasy and pagan pantheism. Counted among Rimsky-Korsakov's best operas, it is based on a play by Ostrovsky (*Snegurochka*) about a well-known folk tale.

In late nineteenth-century Russia, interest in pantheism and pagan rituals and beliefs was not uncommon. In Rimsky's operas this fascination with paganism shows up in either direct borrowing of subject-matter from the ancient pagan world (as in *The Snow Maiden* and *Mlada*) or indirect reference to related subjects from later Christian times (as in *May Night* or *Christmas Eve*). Wrote the composer, "though sun-worship had entirely faded before the light of Christianity, yet the whole cycle of ceremonial songs and games to this very day rests on the ancient pagan sun-worship which lives unconsciously in the people." When Rimsky re-read Ostrovsky's play, he wrote, "My mild interest in the ancient Russian customs and heathen pantheism flamed up. There seemed no better subject in the whole world than this ... no better religion and philosophy of life than the worship of the sun god, Yarilo."

The Snow Maiden is the unplanned daughter of an affair that the Fairy Spring had with King Winter. It is rumored that the angry sun waits to destroy the girl by warming her heart with love, so her father keeps her hidden deep in the snowy forests of Berendey. But the Snow Maiden is attracted by the songs of the shepherd Lel, and she begs her parents to let her live like a mortal. Lel does not return her interest, and she is passionately wooed instead by Mizgir, a young Tartar merchant.

When Mizgir's erstwhile bride-to-be Kupava demands justice from the Tsar, Mizgir can only show the beautiful Snow Maiden to the court to explain his behavior. Already hoping to appease the sun god with mass marriages, the sympathetic Tsar promises to marry her off to the one who can win her love before the next sunrise. In the forest, Lel and the jilted Kupava join together while wood-sprites help the Snow Maiden to escape Mizgir's aggressive pursuit. The unhappy girl calls upon her mother to grant her the power to love like a mortal. Upon seeing Mizgir again, she falls in love with him; but with the warmth of her new human love, a ray of sunlight pierces the clouds to melt her away. Yarilo is appeased, and the people sing a hymn in praise of the sun.

In its unusual half-human, half-mythological anthropomorphisms, *The Snow Maiden* was something new in the arena of lyric drama. The Tsar Berendey is human, yet sitting on his golden throne surrounded by blind *gusli* players, he is straight out of legend. His role as adjudicator for love affairs is also part of the benevolent "father-tsar" figure found in so many Russian folk tales. More than a two-dimensional caricature, he personifies a deeply-rooted type out of the folk mythology.

Except for a couple of mere mortals (Kupava and Mizgir), the characters in the opera are mythical. In addition to wood-sprites and the Snow Maiden herself, Spring and Winter are presented as people; birds, flowers, and a scarecrow are also living parts of the tale. Even the shepherd Lel can be interpreted as the personification of music, drawing on the sun as the source of its miraculous power. The Snow Maiden, when asked by her father what the attraction of the mortals is for her, replies simply: the music.

Rimsky developed a delightful musical language for his characterization. There is for example a short-breathed, rhythmically precise music suggesting the music of puppets, which is associated with the Tsar. For the bird characters, Rimsky used real bird-calls in the music, recording that "One of the motives of Spring is the accurately reproduced song of a bullfinch which had lived rather long in our cage; only that dear little bullfinch sang it in F-sharp major, while I took it a tone lower for the convenience of the violin harmonics. Thus, in obedience to my pantheistic frame of mind, I had hearkened to the voices of folk creation and of nature, and what they had sung and suggested."

The Snow Maiden is an odd combination of the fantastic, sensuous, humorous, and grotesque—perhaps mostly grotesque. The story is complete with all-too-authentic folk tale crudities like Mizgir's passionate demands or Lel's blunt cruelty, but the crude is joined with the sublime through Rimsky's enchanting music. Furthermore, apart from the music itself, *The Snow Maiden* is a stylistically unified, cohesive drama with the decorative element of spectacle well integrated. The big dance and chorus of the birds in the Prologue, for instance, is introduced as an activity for the shivering birds to get warm. Other choruses fade off gently, through a bit of dialogue, rather than end abruptly. After completing *The Snow Maiden*, Rimsky correctly realized he had written a masterpiece, stating that he felt he was a "mature musician, standing firmly on my feet as an opera composer."

—Elizabeth W. Patton

SÖDERSTRÖM, Elisabeth.

Soprano. Born 7 May 1927, in Stockholm. Married: Sverker Olow, 1950; three sons. Studied with Andrejeva von Skilondz and at Royal Academy of Music and Opera School in Stockholm; debut as Mozart's Bastienne at Drottningholm Court Theater, 1947; joined Swedish Royal Opera, 1949; Glyndebourne debut as the Composer in *Ariadne auf Naxos*, 1957; debut at Metropolitan Opera as Susanna, 1959; debut at Covent Garden, with Royal Swedish Opera (as Daisy Doody in Blomdahl's *Aniara*), 1960; sang Ellen Orford in *Peter Grimes* at Metropolitan, 1983; sang in premiere of Argento's *The Aspern Papers*, Dallas, 1988; appointed artistic director, Drottningholm Court Theater, 1990.

Publications

By SÖDERSTRÖM: books–

I min tonart. Stockholm, 1978. English translation by Joan Tate (as *In My Own Key*), London, 1979.

About SÖDERSTRÖM: articles–

Amis, John. "People 17: Elisabeth Söderström" (interview). *Opera* 20/1 (1969): 16.

Salter, S. "Söderström and Friends" (interview). *San Francisco Opera Magazine* 68/5 (1990): 60.

Söderström, like her near contemporaries Kerstin Meyer, Nicolai Gedda and Birgit Nilsson, had the benefit of belonging to the company at the Royal Opera in Stockholm and being part of a tightly-knit ensemble, before launching out on an international career. Like Nilsson, Söderström first came to Great Britain to sing at Glyndebourne, where she made a specialty of Strauss roles, the Composer in *Ariadne*, the title-role in *Der Rosenkavalier*, the Countess in *Capriccio* and Christine in *Intermezzo*.

The mantle of Schwarzkopf descended upon Söderström to an extent once, after 1965, Schwarzkopf began to withdraw from the opera stage. Whereas Schwarzkopf's interpretations depended upon her analytic approach to the text and music, something which she continued to develop in her Lieder recitals, Söderström's great theatricality and obvious spontaneity—by her own admission she found it difficult to hold back tears on stage—and her intense desire to include the audience in her confidence made her one of the most fascinating singing actresses of the day. Consequently, her recording career was slow to take off, and despite the allure of her recordings of the three great Janáček parts, Jenůfa, Kat'a and Emilia Marty, they might have benefited from being caught a little earlier.

Söderström's voice was essentially a lyric soprano; when she undertook heavier roles such as Leonore in *Fidelio*, Emilia Marty and the Marschallin, in the theatre one became conscious of her need always to negotiate the music fairly cautiously. But as Tatyana, the *Capriccio* Countess and Jenůfa she was unsurpassed in her time. She brought to these roles the same qualities which distinguish her singing in the enormous repertory of Lieder, Mélodies and folk-songs that she included in her recitals. A quiet intensity, the ability to make the audience feel that she was abandoning herself completely to each moment in the music and drama, was added to a voice which although neither large nor conventionally beautiful had an individual quality, a quick vibrato in the middle range and a silver purity on the highest notes, plus exemplary diction in German, English, Italian, French and Swedish.

Söderström was an accomplished comedienne and mimic, as can be heard in her performance as Octavian—unfortunately not recorded complete, but a souvenir of each act is to be heard on the disc of highlights conducted by Varviso, with Crespin as the Marschallin. Like the singers of the nineteenth century, Söderström was always willing to learn and sing the music of living composers. In 1969 she claimed that her favorite role was that of the Governess in *The Turn of the Screw*. Equally memorable was her Jenny in Richard Rodney Bennett's *The Mines of Sulphur*, Daisie Doody in Blomdahl's *Aniara*, Elisabeth Zimmer in Henze's *Elegy for Young Lovers*, and her final role, as the aged primadonna in Argento's *The Aspern Papers*. To all of these she brought that same responsive, alert enthusiasm mixed with a wry femininity that made her more a Countess in *Figaro* than a Fiordiligi. It was this very warmth that told against the total success of her Mélisande; Mélisande has seldom seemed so vibrant, and it is not really conceivable that such a vivid presence can succumb to the gloomy inevitability of the plot.

Because her career was so diversified, Söderström never had the international fame or notoriety that lesser singers have achieved. She was one of the last of the true ensemble singers and a great star in her own right.

—Patrick O'Connor

DIE SOLDATEN [The Soldiers].

Composer: Bernd Alois Zimmermann.

Librettist: Bernd Alois Zimmermann (after Lenz).

First Performance: Cologne, 15 February 1965.

Roles: Wesener (bass); Marie (soprano); Charlotte (mezzo-soprano); Wesener's Old Mother (contralto); Stolzius (baritone); Stolzius' Mother (contralto); Obrist (bass); Desportes (tenor); Pirzel (tenor); Eisenhardt (baritone); Lt Mary (baritone); Major Haudy (baritone); Countess de la Roche (mezzo-soprano); Count de la Roche (tenor); Three Young Officers (tenors); several lesser roles; chorus.

Publications

book–

Zimmermann, Bernd Alois. *Die Soldaten* [Livret, correspondance, textes, études]. Strasbourg, 1988.

articles–

Seipt, A. "Die Soldaten." In *Neue Musik seit 1945,* 360. Stuttgart, 1972.

Becker, Peter. "Aspekte der Lenz-Rezeption in Bernd Alois Zimmermanns Oper *Die Soldaten.*" In *Musiktheater heute,* edited by Hellmut Kühn, 94. Mainz, 1981.

Fischer, Erik. "Bernd Alois Zimmermanns Oper *Die Soldaten.* Zum Deutung der musikalisch-dramatischen Struktur." In *Festschrift Heinz Becker zum 60. Geburtstag am 26. Juni 1982,* edited by Jürgen Schläder and Reinhold Quandt, 268. Laaber, 1982.

Wiesmann, Sigrid. "Bedingungen der Komponierbarkeit. Berndt Alois Zimmermanns *Die Soldaten,* György Ligetis *Le grand macabre.*" In *Für und Wider die Literaturoper. Zur Situation nach 1945,* edited by Sigrid Wiesmann, 27. Laaber, 1982.

*   *   *

Bernd Alois Zimmermann's *Die Soldaten* (1958-60; revised 1963-64) stands at a particularly important juncture in the history of opera. It represents the first major effort in the genre by a composer of the post-World War II *avant-garde,* and it is considered to be the most significant opera by a German composer since those of Alban Berg. Zimmermann's debt to Berg is as often cited as it is over-rated. The similarities between *Die Soldaten* and Berg's *Wozzeck* (1921) are due as much to Georg Büchner (the author of *Woyzeck* [1836], Berg's source for *Wozzeck*) as to Zimmermann. Büchner based characters and themes in *Woyzeck* on the play *Die Soldaten* (1775) by J.M.R. Lenz, the same play which forms the basis for Zimmermann's opera. The similarity between Marie of *Die Soldaten* and the title character of Berg's other

opera, *Lulu* (1935), is perhaps coincidental, since the character in Zimmermann's opera is no different from that in Lenz's play.

Zimmermann's real contribution is that he successfully integrates several of the innovative techniques pioneered by European composers at mid-century—including integral serialism, textural "sound-mass" effects, and *musique concrète* (the technique of manipulating tape-recorded sounds through cutting, splicing, and other methods)—into a newly conceived operatic framework. By re-working the narrative of J.M.R. Lenz into an increasingly fragmentary and mercurial braid of fifteen scenes, some of which overlap in simultaneous montages of visual and aural images, Zimmermann was able to effect a formal revolution in the drama analogous to, and in concordance with, that which originates in the music.

The libretto deals with the immoral behavior of soldiers in relation to the society that they are supposed to protect. During the course of the opera, Marie—the beautiful but flighty daughter of a merchant, M. Wesener—becomes the object of several knavish soldiers' amorous intents. Her downfall, and that of her spurned suitor Stolzius, is linked to the failure of society to protect itself adequately from its own protectors: the soldiers. Marie is, in a sense, sacrificed by a society which depends on an unnatural separation between several classes. The soldiers and their immoral behavior are creations of society; as a result of her social ambitions, Marie becomes entangled in an uncontrollable sequence of events.

The innovative features for which the opera is famous—the quotation of pre-existing music (Bach chorales, Gregorian chant, Jazz), the simultaneous presentation of disparate "scenes" in separate stage locations, the use of multi-media through projection of film and recorded sound playback—are all representative of the composer's pluralistic attitude toward time which he summed up in the novel concept "Kugelgestalt der Zeit" (sphere-form of time). This may briefly be described as an opening up of the present to include the past and the future. Zimmermann's quotation of older music, combined always with his "own" music, is the result of this opening up. It presents another layer of significance to the drama, which is itself opened up through the gradual breakdown of the barriers between temporally and spatially separate localities, as well as the erosion of any causality implied by traditional narrative structure.

The first scene of act IV is perhaps the single most representative realization of these innovations. Zimmermann's depiction of the action takes on completely the characteristically fragmentary and overlapping presentation in which the classical unities of time and place are discarded in favor of the more contemporary view that reality is closer to the confused, the contingent, and the fortuitous than to any clearly delineated straight-line narrative. While Zimmermann's techniques in this scene are thoroughly innovative in terms of operatic treatment, the composer couches the action in the age-old dramatic scenario of the dream. Marie has a dream in which various scenes from her past, present, and future are simultaneously entangled. The persons who have been a part of this dream finally come together in a tribunal to pass judgment on her behavior.

In the final scene of the opera, Zimmermann makes a significant alteration over Lenz's original. In Lenz's play, the penultimate scene shows Wesener accosted by his daughter Marie, who has become unrecognizable to him as a destitute beggar. Wesener finally recognizes Marie and they are reunited. Zimmermann opts for the completely desolate alternative in which Wesener pushes Marie away without recognition. This underscores Zimmermann's apocalyptic and thoroughly twentieth-century ending in which images projected on screens depict soldiers marching in endless columns, shouting orders in several languages, only to be stopped when an atomic explosion ends the opera.

—Richard Blocker

THE SOLDIERS
See DIE SOLDATEN

SOLERA, Temistocle.

Librettist/Composer/Impresario. Born 25 December 1815, in Ferrara. Died 21 April 1878, in Milan. Married: the singer Teresa Rosmini. Published poems and a novel early in his career; wrote librettos and set a number of them himself; impressario in Spain, 1846-59; secret courier between Napoleon III and the Khedive of Egypt, 1859; superintendent of police, region of Basilicata, 1860, and police chief in several cities; reorganized the police force for the Khedive of Egypt; antique dealer in Paris. Solera set many of his librettos himself.

Librettos

Oberto, Conte di San Bonifacio (Solera?)(after A. Piazza), G. Verdi, 1839.
Ildegonda, Solera, 1840.
Il contadino d'Agleiate, Solera, 1841; revised as *La fanciulla di Castelguelfo,* 1842.
Galeotto Manfredi, Hermann, 1842.
Nabucodonosor (Nabucco), G. Verdi, 1842.
I lombardi alla prima crociata, G. Verdi, 1843.
Genio e sventura, Solera, 1843.
La hermana de Palayo, Solera, 1845.
Giovanna d'Arco, G. Verdi, 1845.
Attila (with Piave), G. Verdi, 1846.
La conquista di Granata, J. Arrieta, 1850.
La fanciulla delle Asturie, B. Secchi, 1856.
Sordello, A. Buzzi, 1856.
Pergolesi, A. Ronchetti-Monteviti, 1857.
Vasconcello, A. Villanis, 1858.
Una notte di festa, A. Villanis, 1859.
L'espiazione, A. Peri, 1861.
Zilla, G. Villate, 1877.

Publications

About SOLERA: books–

Barbiera, A. *Figure e figurine del secolo che muore.* Milan, 1899.
Ramelli, A. Cassi. *Cinquanta librettisti dell' ottocento.* Milan, 1971.

articles–

Checchi, E. "Librettisti e libretti di Giuseppe Verdi." *Nuova antologia* 167 (1913): 528.
Mantovani, T. "Librettisti verdiani: Temistocle Solera." *Musica d'oggi* 5 (1923): 286.
Pugliese, G. "Dai Lombardi alla Gerusalemme." *Quaderni dell' Istituto di Studi Verdiani* no. 2 (1963).
Cavicchi, A. "Verdi e Solera, considerazioni sulla collaborazione per *Nabucco.*" In *Atti del congresso "Studi Verdiani".* Venice, 1966.
Giovanelli, P.D. "La storia e la favola dell' *Oberto.*" *Studi Verdiani* 2 (1983): 29.

*   *   *

Temistocle Solera lived an adventurous life in the Casanova tradition. As a youth he ran away from boarding school in Vienna to join a traveling circus; he was reputed to be Queen Isabella's lover; he worked as a theater manager in Madrid; he made his living as an editor of a religious magazine in Milan; he sold antiques in Paris and elsewhere; and he became a secret courier between Napoleon III and the Khedive of Egypt, for whom he organized a police force.

As a poet and novelist, Solera came to be admired by the impresario of the Teatro alla Scala, Bartolomeo Merelli, who gave him Antonio Piazza's libretto of *Oberto* to refashion. This was Verdi's first opera (premiered in 1839) and for the next several years Solera and Verdi worked very closely together. In 1846, however, with the libretto of *Attila* not yet completed, Solera abandoned Verdi to follow his wife, the prima donna Teresa Rosmina, to Spain, where he began his career as an impresario. Fifteen years later Solera approached Verdi with a libretto, but Verdi showed no desire to renew their collaboration. Personal feelings aside, Verdi's concepts of musical theater had changed radically by the beginning of the 1860s. In 1878 Solera died in poverty and neglect in Milan.

Solera also served as librettist to a number of composers besides Verdi, among them Arrieta, Secchi, Ronchetti-Monteviti, Villanis, and Villate. Solera's operas to his own libretti include *Ildegonda* (1840); *Il contadino D'Agleiate* (1841), revised in 1842 as *La fanciulla di Castelguelfo; Genio e sventura* (1843); and *La hermana de Palayo* (1845). His libreti for Verdi coincided with that composer's early *Risorgimento* works, to which spirit Solera contributed greatly. His verse was vigorous and crude and his plots contained grand theatrical effects. The plot of *I Lombardi* is especially sprawling and confusing, although the poetic language is direct and simple in order to speak directly to the emotions of the public in general. For the libretto of *Nabucco* (1842), Solera adapted the poetry to the reverent tone appropriate to a Biblical drama, which was not a feature of the play *Nabucodonosor* by Anicet-Bourgeois and Francis Cornue. Solera's libretto for *Attila,* based on Zacharias Werner's play, *Attila, König der Hunnen,* purposely used barbaric and violent language to capture the spirit of the title character. Solera used Werner's play very freely for his own purpose, which was to appeal to Italian, specifically Venetian, patriotic sentiments. Thus he added a scene showing the foundation of Venice, changed Hildegonde to Odabella, an Aquileian warrior maiden who fights for the Italians, and omitted many characters extraneous to his aims.

Although Solera tended to treat his sources very freely, he was accused of outright plagiarism a number of times, especially with *Nabucco.* This was despite the fact that he made several distinct departures from the original French play, for example in portraying Abigail's love for Ishmael, a necessary element for Italian romantic opera. With the libretto of *Giovanna d'Arco,* Solera claimed originality but at various points resorted to language from Schiller's *Die Jungfrau von Orleans.* Julian Budden notes that "For poetry and humanity [in Schiller] we are given theatrical sensationalism," and detects the shadow of Scribe's libretto for Meyerbeer's *Robert le diable* behind *Giovanna d'Arco,* "with its invisible demons and angels, its storms and its instrumental trickery."

Solera's dramatic-poetic style was very much attuned to the passions and interests of Italians in the 1840s—indeed, he helped to ignite those very passions. Yet his style was hopelessly out-dated by the beginning of the 1860s when, with the end of the *Risorgimento,* composers such as Verdi were looking for new ideas.

—Stephen Willier

SOLTI, (Sir) Georg [Györgyi].

Conductor. Born 21 October 1912, in Budapest. Studied piano with Dohnányi and Bartók at the Franz Liszt Academy of Music, Budapest, 1925; took composition courses with Kodály; vocal coach with the Budapest Opera, 1930; assistant to Bruno Walter, 1935, and Toscanini, 1936-37, at the Salzburg Festival; conducting debut with *Le nozze di Figaro* at the Budapest Opera, 1938; left Hungary as a result of antisemitic hostilities; concert pianist in Switzerland, 1939; winner of the Concours International de Piano, Geneva, 1942; conductor with the orchestra of the Swiss Radio, 1944; American occupation authorities asked him to conduct *Fidelio* at the Bavarian State Opera, Munich, 1946; Generalmusikdirektor of the Bavarian State Opera, 1946-52; Generalmusikdirektor in Frankfurt, 1952; conducted *Elektra* at the San Francisco Opera, 1953; various guest conducting engagements; named music director of the Los Angeles Philharmonic, but never got started as a result of administrative conflicts; music director of the Dallas Symphony Orchestra, 1960-61; music director of the Royal Opera House, 1961-71; honorary Commander of the Order of the British Empire, 1968; music director of the Chicago Symphony Orchestra, 1969-91; toured Europe with the Chicago Symphony, 1971-91; became a British subject and was knighted, 1972; music adviser to the Paris Opéra, 1971-73; music director of the Orchestre de Paris, 1972-75; toured China with the Orchestre de Paris, 1974; principal conductor and artistic director of the London Philharmonic, 1979-83; conducted the *Ring* at the Bayreuth Festival; Laureate Conductor of the Chicago Symphony, 1991-; engaged as artistic director of the Salzburg Festival, 1992.

Publications

About SOLTI: books–

Culshaw, John. *Ring Resounding.* New York, 1967.
Furlong, W. *Season with Solti: a Year in the Life of the Chicago Symphony.* New York and London, 1974.
Robinson, P. *Solti.* London, 1979.

articles–

Thomas, E. "Georg Solti." *Opera* August (1961).
Mann, W. "Solti, Champion of Strauss." *Opera* December (1984).
Rhein, J. von. "Solti at Seventy-five." *Ovation* November (1987).

During the late 1950s and the 1960s Georg Solti held a dominating position on the international operatic scene, and his decade of tenure at the Royal Opera House, Covent Garden from 1961 came when he had reached the heights of an already long and varied career. When he declared his intention of making Britain's national opera house "quite simply, the best" in the world, some people thought him boastful or at least unrealistically ambitious, but by the end of his time there, there were as many who argued that he had succeeded in his aim, or at least made it the equal of other great houses.

Solti's training and first experience were as a pianist and a vocal coach, and at the Salzburg Festivals of 1936 and 1937 he had the valuable experience of working under Toscanini in a varied repertory. Though anti-Semitism restricted his early career in his native Hungary, he did make his conducting debut there in Mozart's *Le nozze di Figaro,* but it was not until after the Second World War that he could resume his operatic career with a performance in Munich of Beethoven's *Fidelio,* an opera which Toscanini had conducted memorably at Salzburg and which carried a message of hope to a newly liberated Europe.

Although Solti once confessed his youthful disillusion and disappointment that the German-speaking world could produce a man such as Hitler as well as Mozart and Beethoven, his Jewishness never stopped him from appreciating all that was best in German and Austrian music, and in fact it was in this part of Europe and its musical repertory that he made his name, first at the Bavarian State Opera in Munich and then with the Frankfurt Opera. The power and urgency of his work was soon recognized, as was the fact that it went hand in hand with thorough preparation and a generally good rapport with singers. His performances of the two very different Strauss operas *Salome* and *Der Rosenkavalier* were among his early successes, and his Covent Garden years also saw daring innovations with the same composer's metaphysical piece *Die Frau ohne Schatten* as well as Schoenberg's *Moses und Aron* with its famous orgy scene—which, however, proved a little tame when actually staged. This was also the time of his celebrated performances of Wagner's *Ring* cycle, and he said at the time of these four operas that he chose to forget their perhaps dubious *Weltanschauung* or moral-philosophical outlook in favor of concentrating on their wonderful music. This was the time too of his colossally successful Decca recording of the same tetralogy, made with mainly German singers and the Vienna Philharmonic Orchestra but using the notably gifted British producer John Culshaw; it was the first complete recording of the work to be issued and it made pioneering and skilful use of stereo techniques to give listeners the illusion of theatrical space and movement.

At this stage of his career, Solti's style was decisive and authoritative, and although it would be unfair to call it authoritarian, those who had reservations about it sometimes considered it too driving and bold to capture all the nuances of an operatic score or allow singers quite the degree of freedom that might allow them to give of their very best; certainly his way with Wagner was very different from the

Sir Georg Solti

more spacious delivery of Reginald Goodall, an older man who languished in a small Covent Garden post during his rule and only emerged later as a major Wagner conductor. Subsequently, Solti's style has broadened and somewhat softened without any loss of strength; he has become an expert conductor in nearly all parts of the repertory, with Verdi being another area in which he excels. He has also been successful with modern opera scores such as those of Britten and Henze, though he has avoided the avant-garde. His recordings over some three decades are as numerous as those of any other conductor of his generation.

—Christopher Headington

LA SONNAMBULA [The Sleepwalker].

Composer: Vincenzo Bellini.

Librettist: Felice Romani (after a ballet-pantomime by Eugène Scribe and Jean-Pierre Aumer).

First Performance: Milan, Teatro Carcano, 6 March 1831.

Roles: Amina (soprano); Lisa (soprano); Elvino (tenor); Rodolfo (bass); Teresa (mezzo-soprano); Alessio (bass); Notary (tenor); chorus (SSATTBB).

Publications

books—

Andolfi, O. *La sonnambula di V. Bellini*. Rome, 1930.

articles—

Porter, Andrew. "An Introduction to *La sonnambula*." *Opera* October (1960): 665.
Degrada, Francesco. "Prolegomeni a una lettera della *Sonnambula*." In *Il melodramma italiano dell'ottocento: studi e ricerche per Massimo Mila*. Turin, 1977.

*   *   *

La sonnambula is set in a Swiss village at some unspecified time. The villagers are preparing to celebrate the betrothal of Amina, an orphan, to Elvino, a prosperous farmer. The only unhappy person at the gathering is Elvino's former flame, Lisa, the innkeeper. The notary and Elvino arrive and the betrothal ceremony takes place. A stranger arrives, on his way to the castle. As evening approaches, the villagers warn the stranger of their local phantom. He decides to spend the

Set design by Alessandro Sanquirico for the final scene of Bellini's *La sonnambula*, first production, Teatro alla Scala, Milan, 1831

evening at the inn and offers a few courteous compliments to the bride-to-be, provoking a jealous response from Elvino.

The scene changes to the stranger's room in the inn. Lisa tells him that the villagers have learned he is the new Count; they will soon be coming to offer their respects. Amina wanders in through the window; she is sleepwalking. Dreaming, she converses with Elvino and enacts the wedding ceremony. The Count, not wanting to compromise Amina, leaves. The villagers appear and find Amina, in her nightgown, in the Count's room. Amina's foster mother Teresa wraps Amina in the shawl Lisa had left in the room. Elvino denounces Amina and calls off the wedding.

In the second act the villagers decide to go to the castle to ask the Count directly if Amina is innocent, as she protests she is. Elvino angrily rejects Amina and declares he will marry Lisa instead. Teresa accuses Lisa of having been in the Count's room and produces Lisa's shawl as evidence. When the Count arrives and explains that Amina is an innocent sleepwalker Elvino refuses to believe him. Amina appears, perilously sleepwalking across the roof of the mill, sorrowing over Elvino who has so unjustly rejected her. Amina wanders onto safe ground, Elvino awakens her by slipping a ring on her finger, and the villagers once again prepare to celebrate a wedding.

La sonnambula is not a typical Bellini opera. An *opera semiseria,* it dispenses with heroic gestures and historic trappings. Instead the work celebrates romanticized pastoral virtues—rustic innocence, naivete, simplicity. References to the supernatural are tongue-in-cheek. What we are meant to take completely seriously, however, are the sentiments of the protagonists—Amina's pure love for Elvino, Elvino's passionate love for Amina and his equally passionate sense of betrayal, the Count's affection for his homeland and his general good will. There are no villains in *La sonnambula,* only misunderstandings which are relatively easily set right.

La sonnambula shows almost no conflict between dramatic ends and musical means. Bellini composed it quickly (in approximately two months) after he discontinued work on a projected *Ernani.* Unlike most of his operas, Bellini produced *La sonnambula* seemingly effortlessly. The work has an abundance of set numbers that do not strain against the received Rossinian formulas. All of the characters are well served with arias: Amina has two full-scale double arias, Elvino and the Count one double aria each; even Lisa has two arias, though of more modest size and shape. Elvino is not given an entrance cavatina but he dominates both of the act I duets he sings with Amina. The first duet begins with his action of giving Amina a ring ("Prendi l'anel ti dono") and the second duet begins by discussing his feelings of jealousy ("Son geloso del zeffiro errante"). He also leads off the second-act quartet. In all of the set numbers, the sentiments stated, their musical expression, and their appropriateness to the characters and action are in perfect balance.

In *La sonnambula* the characters seem to be notably at ease with their status as musical beings. In her first duet Amina complains, with no irony intended, that she cannot find words to express her feelings—but of course, expressing feelings through words is not what this preeminently lyrical opera is about. Indeed, the opening chorus hardly bothers with a text at all; an occasional "Viva Amina" punctuates the pervasive "la, la, la." The chorus is on stage for more than half of the opera. It functions as a kind of collective comic character, a useful balance for the sentimentalized principal characters.

The abundance of numbers in compound time or with accompaniments with triplet subdivision helps establish and maintain the pastoral atmosphere. Indeed, only Lisa's and Elvino's arias in the second act—sung when pastoral contentment is at the point of greatest disruption—are entirely free from triplet rhythms.

Critical opinion on *La sonnambula* is divided. For some, this is a very silly work. For others it is Bellini's finest opera— "Bellini's genius at its purest." In order to enjoy it, one needs to suspend not only disbelief but sophistication. But if one can enter its idyllic, pastoral world, one is rewarded by gifts of beauty and kindliness.

—Charlotte Greenspan

SONTAG, Henriette.

Soprano. Born 3 January 1806, in Koblenz. Died 17 June 1854, in Mexico City. Married: Count Carlo Rossi, 1828. Studied with her mother Franziska Martloff Sonntag, and Anna Czegka at the Prague Conservatory, 1815; as a child sang Salome in Kauer's *Das Donauweibchen,* 1811; debut as the princess in Boieldieu's *Jean de Paris,* 1821; sang in Vienna, 1822; premiered Weber's *Euryanthe,* 1823; premiered Beethoven's Ninth Symphony and *Missa Solemnis,* 1824; sang in opera houses all over Europe, 1826-30; gave up the stage, 1830-49; then sang in London, Paris, the United States, and Mexico until her death of Cholera in 1854.

Publications

About SONTAG: books–

Gautier, T. *L'ambassadrice: Biographie de la Comtesse Rossi.* Paris, 1850.
Stümcke, H. *Henriette Sontag.* Berlin, 1913.
Pirchan, E. *Henriette Sontag: die Sängerin des Biedermeier.* Vienna, 1946.

articles–

Kaufman, T. "The Arditi tour: The Midwest gets its first real taste of Italian Opera (1852-1854)." *Opera Quarterly* 4/4 (1986-87): 43.

Henriette Sontag was one of the most popular sopranos of the first half of the nineteenth century, one of the few German singers to challenge the great Italian singers in their native repertoire. Her success came at a very early age. Making her formal operatic debut at fifteen in Boieldieu's *Jean de Paris* in Prague, she was chosen two years later by Weber to create the title role of *Euryanthe* in Vienna. She was acclaimed there, as she was at the first performances of Beethoven's Ninth

Symphony and *Missa solemnis* the following year (1824). Debuts followed in Berlin as Isabella in Rossini's *L'italiana in Algeri* (1825) and as Rosina in *Il barbiere di Siviglia* at Paris's Théâtre-Italien (1826), both inspiring great enthusiasm. It reached epidemic proportions in Berlin, where it was described as a fever (Sontagsfieber). Her London debut in 1828, once more as Rosina, was also a great success.

While much of the interest in Sontag was doubtless generated by her prowess as a singer (and she was said to be on a level with Angelica Catalani), much of that interest also originated in her life, which followed the archetypal pattern of certain familiar fairy tales, romantic novels—and operas. A strikingly beautiful woman of humble origins, she achieved almost unheard of adulation. In Germany, young men drank champagne from her slipper stolen especially for that purpose, Ludwig Rellstab was jailed for writing critically of the enthusiasm about her, and even Goethe wrote poetry in her honor. In England, she was soon welcomed into the highest circles of society and was reportedly proposed to by the Duke of Devonshire. In 1827 she contracted a secret marriage with Count Carlo Rossi, a Sardinian diplomat, whose career was seriously jeopardized when the court refused to approve the marriage. After the King of Prussia conferred a title upon her, the court agreed to sanction the marriage if she would retire from the stage. This she did in 1830, at the height of her fame, singing only privately thereafter and at a few charity concerts. The political turmoil of 1848, however, put an end to Rossi's career as a diplomat, and financial difficulties forced Sontag to return to the stage. After nearly twenty years' retirement, she appeared in London in July 1849, singing once more to great acclaim. Her voice, by Henry Chorley's account, showed only the slightest decline. This return was followed by a grueling schedule of performances, including not only roles she had sung earlier but a number of operas written in the intervening years, including the first performances of Jacques Fromenthal Halévy's *La tempestà* (London 1850) and Giulio Alary's *The Three Marriages* (Paris 1851). Her career ended only with her death of cholera in Mexico in 1854 during an extended American tour. (A brief but moving glimpse of Sontag on this tour is provided in Eyre Crowe's *With Thackeray in America*).

Although she was the daughter of an actor and actress and had much stage experience as a child, contemporary accounts suggest that Sontag won acclaim less by her dramatic abilities than by her attractive presence and beautiful voice. William Makepeace Thackeray's nostalgic essay "De juventute" mentions her 1828 London appearances, stressing her physical beauty, while J.E. Cox's account of those same performances emphasizes the great flexibility of her voice and the coolness of her interpretations. She was, according to Chorley, "essentially a singer, not a declamatory artist." He also commented, however, that "emotion and warmth increasingly animated her performances" as the years went on. Certainly she eventually won the admiration of Hector Berlioz, whose obituary tribute credited her with "all the gifts of art and nature: voice, musical feeling, dramatic instinct, style, the most exquisite taste, passion, reflection, grace, everything, and something more than everything." Merely mentioning her technical brilliance in trifling music, Berlioz dwelt on her abilities as an interpreter of great music, providing a poetic account of an 1851 performance of *Le nozze di Figaro* in London. There, in her singing of Susanna's final aria, were faithfully rendered "the song of solitude, the song of voluptuous revery, the song of mystery and of night."

While these and other contemporary accounts of her singing leave no doubt as to the reasons for Sontag's immediate popularity, her lasting contributions to opera are more difficult to assess. Of the operatic roles written especially for her, only Euryanthe retains even the slightest currency, while Beethoven can hardly be said to have written with her voice in mind. Although it cannot be demonstrated conclusively, it does seem possible that Sontag contributed in some part to the modern practice of categorizing soprano voices. Unlike her contemporaries Maria Malibran and Giuditta Pasta, heavy-voiced singers who sang florid music in both comic and tragic roles, Sontag, a light soprano, achieved her greatest successes in comic and serious rather than tragic parts (e.g., the heroines of *Linda di Chamounix* or *La sonnambula*). Her great popularity may have been one of the factors helping associate that voice type with those roles in preference to heavier voices. Certainly, the aviary terminology used to praise Sontag has also been applied to her "coloratura" successors, suggesting a clear line of descent.

—Joe K. Law

THE SOUL OF THE PHILOSOPHER
See L'ANIMA DEL FILOSOFO

SOYER, Roger.

Bass. Born 1 September 1939, in Paris. Studied with Georges Daum and Georges Jouatte at the Paris Conservatory, sang with the Paris Opéra in small roles, 1962-63; sang Pluto in Monteverdi's *Orfeo* at the Aix-en-Provence Festival, 1965; British debut in Bizet's *La jolie fille de Perth*, 1968; Metropolitan Opera debut as Mozart's Don Giovanni, 1972; premiered Mr. Broderick in Stanton Coe's *Sud* at the Paris Opéra, 1972.

Publications

About SOYER: articles–

Fogel, S. "Roger Soyer: his own master." *Opera News* 39 (1975): 15.

*   *   *

Roger Soyer is perhaps best-known for his portrayal of Don Giovanni, and also for his work in the French romantic repertoire.

According to an interview by Susan Lee Fogel (*Opera News* February 1975), Soyer "generally prefers roles that require acting as well as singing" (e.g., Giovanni, Basilio, Mephistopheles) but stage work has not always suited him. "I used to be terribly *renfermé,* closed inside myself. I was forced to come out of my shell in the theatre," states Soyer himself.

Margaret E. Davies (*Opera News* September 1969) found his early Don Giovanni in the Aix-en-Provence Festival "vocally rich and exciting . . . His cold, supercilious manner," however, "made it hard to believe in Leporello's catalogue of his conquests." At Soyer's Metropolitan Opera debut in November 1972, Gerald Fitzgerald (*Opera News* January

1973) reported that the bass "sang a low-key Don Giovanni of baritonal timbre"; he was "stylish, trim and elegant, but as the evening wore on he ran short of the swashbuckling sensuousness of the classic Don" and "did not seem quite at home in the large dramatic framework of the Met production, though [he] sang well enough."

Soyer returned for the Metropolitan Opera's January 1975 presentation of *Don Giovanni.* Lackluster musical direction and staging disappointed Robert Lawrence (*Musical America* April 1975): "Soyer, the Don Giovanni, had played the part once before at the Metropolitan . . . to wide approval. I heard him . . . at the Munich Festival, singing what then seemed the finest Don in my experience. This time he was sadly out of form, dispirited perhaps by the pedestrian pace . . . or the general aura of non-staging. Also his ingratiating voice . . . sounded just too small for the large spaces of the Metropolitan. Lower tones were sometimes weak, the breath short in arched phrases."

On the other hand, Alfred Frankenstein (*Musical America* March 1975) was impressed by the San Francisco Opera production in the same season. "Roger Soyer was a Don Giovanni of black moods and furies, rather different from the usual cynic, and all the more effective for that."

Soyer's recording of Giovanni, with the English Chamber Orchestra conducted by Daniel Barenboim, received favorable reviews. "Roger Soyer's Don is smoothly sung," wrote Dale S. Harris (*High Fidelity 21st Annual,* 1976); "The Serenade is handsomely done, the second verse is a very seductive *mezza voce.* Soyer, no doubt about it, is a very good singer, though I find him too phlegmatic to be entirely satisfactory in this role."

Soyer's definite strengths seem to lie in French opera recording. His work on Berlioz discs has elicited praise for noble French diction, "a fine, sensitive Joseph" (*L'Enfance du Christ,* 1968), and "a Pope of imposingly rich profundity" (*Benvenuto Cellini*). In Delibes' *Lakmé,* "Roger Soyer is a splendid Nilakantha. He sings his high-lying aria with a full and expressive line that is very satisfying, especially as his scale is so even" (D. Harris, *High Fidelity Annual,* 1974).

—Kiko Nobusawa

THE SPANISH HOUR
See L'HEURE ESPAGNOLE

SPOHR, Ludewig (Louis).

Composer. Born 5 April 1784, in Braunschweig. Died 22 October 1859, in Kassel. Married: 1) the harp player Dorette Scheidler, 1805 (died 1834); 2) the pianist Marianne Pfeiffer, 1836. Studied violin with Rector Riemenschneider and Dufour in Seesen, 1789; studied with the organist Hartung and the violinist Maucourt in Braunschweig; the Duke of Brunswick appointed him to the ducal orchestra and arranged for his study with Franz Eck; toured Russia with Eck, 1802-03, where he met Clementi and John Field; tour of Berlin, Leipzig, and Dresden as a violinist, 1804; concertmaster of the ducal orchestra at Gotha, 1805; concert tour of Germany with his first wife, 1807; concertmaster of the orchestra of the Theater an der Wien, 1812-15; grand tour of Germany and Italy, 1815; appointed opera conductor in Frankfurt, 1817; concert tour of England with his first wife, 1820; court Kapellmeister in Kassel, 1822; conductor and composer at musical festivals in Düsseldorf, 1826, Nordhausen, 1829, Norwich, 1839, Bonn, 1845, and others; toured England, 1847, and Frankfurt, 1848; last tour of England, 1853; retired from his position in Kassel, 1857; last public appearance conducting *Jessonda* in Prague (with a broken arm), 1858. Spohr's students included Ferdinand David and Moritz Hauptmann.

Operas

Die Prüfung (operetta), E. Henke, Gotha, 1806.
Alruna, die Eulenkönig, 1808 [unperformed].
Der Zweikampf mit der Geliebten (Singspiel), J.F. Schink, 1810-11, Hamburg, 15 November 1811.
Faust, J.K. Bernhard, 1813, Prague, 1 September 1816; revised, London, 4 April 1852.
Zemire und Azor, J.J. Ihlee (after Marmontel), 118-19, Frankfurt am Main, 4 April 1819.
Jessonda, E. Gehe (after A.M. Lemièrre, *La veuve de Malabar*), Kassel, 28 July 1823.
Der Berggeist, G. Döring, 1824, Kassel, 24 March 1825.
Pietro von Abano, K. Pfeiffer (after L. Tieck), Kassel, 13 October 1827.
Der Alchymist, F.G. Schmidt [=K. Pfeiffer] (after W. Irving), 1829-30, Kassel, 28 July 1830.
Die Kreuzfahrer, L. and M. Spohr (after Kotzebue), 1843-44, Kassel, 1 January 1845.

Other works: orchestral works, solo instrumental works and concertos, chamber music, sacred and secular vocal music, songs.

Publications/Writings

By SPOHR: books—

Selbstbiographie. 2 vols. Kassel and Göttingen, 1860-61; English translation, 1865; 1969.

articles—

"Briefe L. Spohr's an das Haus Peters in Leipzig." *Allgemeine musikalische Zeitung* new series/vol. 2 (1867): 290.
Göthel, F. ed. *Louis Spohr: Briefwechsel mit seiner Frau Dorette.* Kassel, 1957.
———. *Spohr: Lebenserinnerungen.* Tutzing, 1968.

About SPOHR: books—

Ebers, I.J. *Spohr und Halévy.* Breslau, 1837.
Neumann, W. *Louis Spohr.* Kassel, 1854.
Giehne, H. *Zur Erinnerung an Louis Spohr.* Karlsruhe, 1860.
Malibran, A. *Louis Spohr.* Frankfurt am Main, 1860.
Schletterer, H.M. *L. Spohr.* Leipzig, 1881.
Mayer, Dorothy Moulton. *The Forgotten Master: the Life and Times of Louis Spohr.* London, 1959; 1981.
Homburg, H., ed. *Louis Spohr: Bilder und Dokumente seiner Zeit.* Kassel, 1968.
Marschner, Wolfgang. *Louis Spohr. Avantgardist des Musiklebens seiner Zeit.* Stuttgart, 1979.
Göthel, Folker. *Thematisch-bibliographisches Verzeichnis der Werke von Louis Spohr.* Tutzing, 1981.

Katow, Paul. *Louis Spohr: Persönlichkeit und Werk.* Luxembourg, 1983.
Becker, H., and R. Krempien, eds. *Louis Spohr: Festschrift und Ausstellungskatalog zum 200. Geburtstag.* Kassel, 1984.
Brown, Clive. *Louis Spohr: a Critical Biography.* Cambridge, 1984.
Ederer, Walter. *Louis Spohr—heute.* Helmstedt, 1984.

articles—

Spitta, P. "Jessonda." *Zur Musik* [Berlin] (1892); reprinted 1975.
Istel, E. "Fünf Briefe Spohrs an Marschner." In *Restschrift Rochus Freiherrn von Liliencron*, 110. Leipzig, 1910.
Schmitz, E. "Louis Spohrs Jugendoper Alruna." *Zeitschrift der Internationalen Musik-Gesellschaft* 13 (1911-12): 293.
———. "Louis Spohrs erster Opernversuch." *Archiv für Musikforschung* 7 (1942): 84.
———. "Zu Louis Spohrs Selbstbiographie." *Deutsche Musikkultur* 9 (1944): 45.
Becker, H.J. "Meyerbeer in seinen Beziehungen zu Louis Spohr." *Die Musikforschung* 10 (1957): 479.
Uhlendorff, E. "Chronik des Kasseler Musiktheaters 1814-1944." In *Theater in Kassel* (Kassel, 1959).
Abert, A.A. "Webers 'Euryanthe' und Spohrs 'Jessonda' als grosse Opern." In *Festschrift für Walter Wiora*, 35. Kassel, 1967.
Brown, Clive. "Spohr's *Jessonda.*" *Musical Times* 121 (1980): 94.
Reising, Vera. "Zur Funktion des Phantastischen in den Opern von Ludwig Spohr und Heinrich Marschner." In *Romantikkonferenz (2.) 1982*, edited by Günther Stephan and Hans John, 56. Dresden, 1983.

unpublished—

Wasserman, R. "Louis Spohr als Opernkomponist." Ph.D. dissertation, University of Rostock, 1909.
Greiner, D. "Louis Spohrs Beiträge zur deutschen romantischen Oper." Ph.D. dissertation, University of Kiel, 1960.
Berrett, J. "Characteristic Conventions of Style in Selected Instrumental Works of Louis Spohr." Ph.D. dissertation, University of Michigan, 1974.

*   *   *

Louis Spohr's ten operas and two scores of incidental stage music (*Macbeth* and *Der Matrose*) were written during the period from 1806 to 1844. Spohr's earliest efforts for the stage date from his tenure at the Gotha court, where he wrote the one-act opera *Die Prüfung*, a gentle evocation of Mozart's *Così fan tutte* in that its female protagonist (Natalie) puts her lover's fidelity to the test. In addition there are affecting chromatic touches and details of woodwind orchestration that are reminiscent of Mozart, particularly in the overture. Influences of Benda, Cherubini, and Dalayrac are present in the vocal numbers.

Spohr's next opera, *Alruna, die Eulenkönig* marks a significant departure in its use of supernatural elements. These focus on the realm of the Owl Queen herself into which the knight Hermann and his squire Franz wander. The character of the Owl Queen, not to mention her coloratura, invite comparison with Mozart's Queen of the Night. Another Mozartean touch of the supernatural involves the ghost of Hermann's ancestor

Poster for a farewell performance of *Jessonda*, conducted by Spohr himself, Kassel Hoftheater, 1857

speaking from the grave. Also worthy of comment are Spohr's growing skill in handling an extended scene-complex, most notably in act III, and reminiscence motifs, particularly where Alruna reflects on her past. The fugal Allegro of the overture offers a characteristic chromatic reworking of Mozart's overture to *Die Zauberflöte*. Following this, Spohr's *Die Zweikampf mit der Geliebten* represents a stylistic retreat in hewing closer to *opera seria* or *semi-seria* traditions. In does, however, include some effective writing, ranging from a bantering duet for servants to a sensitively drawn treatment of both the public and private sides of one of the central cnaracters, Princess Matilde.

Faust represents a major achievement in German romantic opera, anticipating later achievements by Weber, Halévy, Meyerbeer, and Wagner, only to be overshadowed by them. Most significant is Spohr's use of the leitmotif, particularly those associated with hell and love, applied with a subtlety that was not to be surpassed until Wagner. Notable too is the Blocksberg scene, particularly the invocation by Mephistopheles to the witch Sycorax. The Walpurgisnacht music later written by Loewe, Lortzing, and Mendelssohn owes a debt to Spohr. There is also a rich variety of recitatives, arias, duets, and trios combined with such elements as a drinking song with chorus and a chorale sung within a cathedral. Spohr's *Faust* was a staple of the repertoire for well over fifty years, appearing in German, Italian, French, English, and Czech versions.

Zemire and Azor, a retelling of the Beauty and the Beast story, dates from Spohr's Frankfurt period. Written in a lighter vein than *Faust*, it has its share of stock characters, including the servant Ali, whose affinity with Papageno is

unmistakable. In general there is a fresh charm to the score with individual items attaining great popularity in the concert hall. The romanza "Rose softly blooming" is a case in point.

Jessonda, completed in 1822 shortly after Spohr's arrival in Kassel, is recognized as his masterpiece. Inspired by Lemièrre's drama *La veuve de Malabar* (1770), its eponymous heroine is the young widow of the Rajah of Goa who has been condemned to the funeral pyre. She is, however, eventually reunited with her true love Tristan d'Achuna, thanks to the intervention of the young priest Nadori. Spohr's great achievement involves creating large scene-complexes as well as integrating chorus and ballet and dramatic recitative into the structure. Tonality, timbre, and rhythm serve to differentiate between Portuguese and Indians. Conducted by Wagner, Mahler, and Richard Strauss, *Jessonda* remained a staple until the early twentieth century.

Spohr's *Der Berggeist* is a tale of earth gnomes digging for treasure beneath a mountain; their ruler, the Berggeist, determined to learn the nature of love, kidnaps a mortal woman. The work is in effect a proto-music drama being essentially through-composed and open-ended, with long stretches of continuous action. By the same token it dramatized Spohr's own aesthetic, whereby German opera was adjudged as superior to Italian.

Pietro von Abano after a novel by Ludwig Tieck, is set in medieval Padua. Pietro, a Faustian mix of teacher and sorcerer-necrophiliac, re-animates the corpse of Cacilie, the intended of a Florentine nobleman, so as to satisfy his lust. The orchestral writing is especially strong in its depiction of invisible spirits, treatments of incantation and resurrection, but shop-worn mannerisms are present in too many of the arias and ensembles. Again, the subject matter of the plot proved too offensive to Kassel, Berlin, and Frankfurt.

Der Alchymist is a study in Spanish exoticism, particularly in its use of orchestral color and ethnic dance rhythms. While there is an underlying scene-complex structure, individual components show a wide variety, including the ariette and romanza.

Spohr's final opera, *Die Kreuzfahrer*, is an attempt to emulate the grand opera of Spontini and Meyerbeer. Crusaders, Saracens, and the Holy Land provide the broad context within which the heroine is condemned to being entombed for a carnal sin only to be saved, *deus ex machina*, by the last-minute attack of the Saracens. A fluid intermixture of secco recitative and arioso sustains much of the dramatic action. Although there is some deft orchestral writing, the work as a whole lacks the spontaneity of Spohr's best earlier efforts; Spohr reached his zenith as an opera composer with his *Faust* and *Jessonda*, coinciding with a time when post-Napoleonic Germany was hungry for art works to claim as its own.

—Joshua Berrett

SPONTINI, Gaspare (Luigi Pacifico).

Composer. Born 14 November 1774, in Majolati, Ancona. Died 24 January 1851, in Majolati, Ancona. Married: the daughter of Jean-Baptiste Erard, 1810. Studied singing with Tritto and composition with Sala at the Conservatorio della Pietà de' Turchini in Naples, 1793; commissioned by the Teatro della Pallacorda in Rome, 1796; aided by Piccinni in the composition of his second opera, *L' eroismo ridicolo;*

composed three operas for the Neapolitan court, 1800; in Rome, 1081, Venice, 1802, and Naples and Paris, 1803; appointed "compositeur particulier" by the Empress Josephine of France; with *La vestale,* won the prize offered by Napoleon (and judged by Méhul, Gossec, and Grétry) for best dramatic work, 1807; director of the Italian Opera in Paris, 1810-12, where he staged the Paris premiere of Mozart's *Don Giovanni;* appointed court composer to Louis XVIII, 1814; court composer and general music director to King Friedrich Wilhelm III, Berlin, 1820-41; knight of the Prussian Ordre pour le Mérite; member of the Berlin Akademie, 1833; member of the French Institut, 1839; returned to Paris, 1842, and then retired to his birthplace; given the rank and title of Conte de Sant' Andrea by the Pope, 1844; Ph.D. from Halle University.

Operas

Li puntigli delle donne, Rome, Teatro della Pallecorda di Firenze, carnival 1796.

Il finto pittore, Rome, 1797-98 [lost].

Adelina Senese, o sia L'amore secreto, after G. Bertati, *La principessa d' Amalfi,* Venice, San Samuele, 10 October 1797.

L'eroismo ridicolo, D. Piccinni, Naples, Nuovo, carnival 1798.

Il Teseo riconosciuto, C. Giotti, Florence, Intrepidi, spring 1798.

La finta filosofa, D. Piccini?. Naples, Nuovo, summer 1799; revised, Paris, Théâtre-Italien (Salle-Favart), 11 February 1804.

La fuga in maschera, G. Palomba, Naples, Nuovo, carnival 1800.

I quandri parlante, Palermo, Santa Cecilia, 1800 [lost].

Gli Elisi delusi, M. Monti, Palermo, Santa Cecilia, 26 August 1800 [only act I survives].

Gli amanti in cimento, o sia Il geloso audace, Rome, Valle, 3 November 1801 [lost].

Le metamorfosi di Pasquale, o sia Tutto è illusione nel mondo, G. Foppa, Venice, San Samuele, carnival 1802 [lost].

[*Che più guarda meno vede,* Florence, 1798?]

La petit maison, A.M. Dieulafoy and N. Gersaint, Paris, Opéra-Comique (Feydeau), 12 May 1804.

Milton, E. de Jouy and Dieulafoy, Paris, Opéra-Comique (Feydeau), 27 November 1804.

Julie, ou Le pot de fleurs, A.G. Jars, Paris, Opéra-Comique (Feydeau), 12 March 1805.

La vestale, E. de Jouy, Paris, Opéra, 15 December 1807.

Fernand Cortez, ou La conquète du Mexique, E. de Jouy, J.A. d'Esmenard, Paris, Opéra, 28 November 1809; revised, Paris, Opéra, 8 May 1817.

Pélage, ou Le roi et la paix, E. de Jouy, Paris, Opéra, 23 August 1814.

Les dieux rivaux ou Les fêtes de Cythère (opéra-ballet, with Kreutzer, Persuis, and Berton), A.M. Dieulafoy and C. Briffaut, Paris, Opéra, 21 June 1816.

Olimpie, A.M. Dielafoy and C. Briffaut (after Voltaire), Paris, Opéra, 22 December 1819; revised as *Olympia,* revised and translated by E.T.A. Hoffman, Berlin, Opéra, 14 May 1821.

Nurmahal, oder Das Rosenfest von Caschmir, C.A. Herkotz (after T. Moore. *Lalla Rookh*), Berlin, Opéra, 27 May 1822.

Alcidor, G.M. Théaulon de Lambert (after Rochon de Chabannes, translated into German by C.A. Herklotz), Berlin, Opéra, 23 May 1825.

Agnes von Hohenstaufen, S.B.E. Paupach, performance of act I, Berlin, Opéra, 28 May 1827; revised, Berlin, Opéra, 12 June 1829; revised, Lichtenstein, Berlin, Opera, 6 December 1837.

Other works: songs, duets, choral music, instrumental works, piano pieces.

Publications/Writings

By SPONTINI: books–

with Berton, H. and M. Carafa. *Reconstruction de la Salle Favart: observations à MM les membres de la Chambre des députés.* Paris, 1839?

Opinion de M. Spontini sur les changements à introduire dans le règlement du concours de grand prix de composition musicale tels qu'ils avaient été proposés par le même académicien et adoptés par la commission spéciale designée par l'académie. Paris, n.d.

Mes propositions pour la réorganisation des musiques militaires de France. Paris, 1850.

articles–

"Rapport à l'Académie royale des beaux arts de l'Institut de France." In J.G. Prod'homme and A. Dandelot, *Gounod (1818-1893): sa vie et ses oeuvres,* vol. 1, 253 ff. Paris, 1911.

unpublished–

Rapporto intorno alla riforma della musica sacra. 1838.

About SPONTINI: books–

St Victor. *Réflexions d'un amateur sur l'opéra La Vestale.* Rouen, 1809.

Oettinger, E.M. *Spontini.* Leipzig, 1843.

Raoul-Rochette, D. *Notice historique sur la vie et les oeuvres de M. Spontini.* Paris, 1852.

Berlioz, H. *Les soirées de l'orchestre.* Paris, 1852; English translation, 1965.

Robert, C. *Spontini: eine biographische Skizze.* Berlin, 1883.

Bouvet, C. *Spontini.* Paris, 1930.

1° congresso internazionale di studi spontiniani: Iesi, Maiolati, Fabriano, Ancona 1951.

Ghislanzoni, A. *Gaspare Spontini.* Rome, 1951.

Fragapane, P. *Spontini.* Bologna, 1954.

Schlitzer, F. *La finta filosofa di Gaspare Spontini.* Naples, 1957.

Becker, H. *Der Fall Heine-Meyerbeer: neue Dokumente revidieren ein Geschichtsurteil* [81ff, 118ff]. Berlin, 1958.

articles–

Hoffmann, E.T.A. "Nachträgeliche Bemerkungen über Spontinis Oper Olympia." *Zeitung für Theater und Musik* 1 (1821); reprinted in *Schriften zur Musik: Nachlese,* 354, Munich, 1963.

Rellstab, L. "Spontinis Oper *Agnes von Hohenstaufen.*" *Berliner allgemeine musikalische Zeitung* 4 (1828).

Marx, A.B. "Eine Betrachtung über den Heutigen Zustand der deutschen Oper, angeknüpft an Nurmahal von Spontini und Oberon von Weber." *Caecilia* 7 (1828): 135-82.

Loménie, L.L. de. "Spontini." *Galerie des contemporains illustres par un homme de rien* [Paris] 10 (1847?).

Gathy, A. "Berlioz über Spontini." *Neue Berliner Musikzeitung* 5 (1851): 88, 97.

Krigar, H. "Spontini." *Almanach für Freunde der Schauspielkunst* 16 (1852): 136.

Wagner, R. "Erinnerungen an Spontini." In *Gesammelte Schriften,* vol. 3, p. 86. Leipzig, 1972; English translation, 1894.

Spitta, P. "Spontini in Berlin." In *Zur Musik,* 291. Berlin, 1892.

Maecklenburg, A. "Der Fall Spontini-Weber: ein Beitrag zur Vorgeschichte der Berliner Erstaufführung der *Euryanthe.*" *Zeitschrift für Musikwissenschaft* 6 (1924-5): 449.

Abraham, G. "The Best of Spontini." *Music and Letters* 23 (1942): 163.

Engel, H. "Wagner und Spontini." *Archiv für Musikwissenschaft* 12 (1955): 167.

Mueller von Asow, H. "Gasparo Spontinis Briefwechsel mit Wolfgang von Goethe." *Chronik des Wiener Goethe-Vereins* 61 (1957): 42.

Ghislanzoni, A. "Un opera di Spontini rintracciata: *Gli Elisi delusi.*" *Musica d'oggi* [new series] 2 (1959): 10.

Schnapp, F. "E.T.A. Hoffmanns Textbearbeitung der Oper 'Olimpia' von Spontini." *Jahrbuch des Wiener Goethe-Vereins* 66 (1962): 126.

Vander Linden, A. "Notes de Madame Gaspare Spontini sur la vie et l'oeuvre de son mari." *Revue belge de musicologie* 28-30 (1974-76): 222.

Loschelder, J. "Spontini und Rossini." In *Bollettino del Centro Rossiniano di Studi.* Pesaro, 1975.

Döhring, Sieghart. "Spontinis Berliner Opern." In *Studien zur Musikgeschichte Berlins im frühen 19. Jahrhundert,* edited by Carl Dahlhaus, 469. Regensburg, 1980.

Miller, Norbert. "Hoffmann und Spontini. Vorüberlegungen zu Einer Ästhetik der Romantischen *opera seria.*" In *Studien zur Musikgeschichte Berlins im frühen 19. Jahrhundert,* edited by Carl Dahlhaus, 451. Regensburg, 1980.

* * *

The Italian composer Gaspare Spontini was a major international figure during the first part of the nineteenth century. He worked in Naples and other Italian centers until around 1800, gaining considerable operatic experience. Throughout his life, opera dominated his creative work. Most of his early operas have been lost; however, the most successful of them, *Li puntigli delle donne,* gave him a reputation in comic opera.

It was his move to Paris after 1802 which proved the decisive factor in Spontini's career, since it enabled him to fulfill his potential in new directions. His first Parisian works were in fact *opéras comiques;* they were, however, badly received, to some extent because of anti-Italian resentment in the city's musical fraternity. In 1804 his *opéra comique Milton* revealed a tendency towards the French preference for a noble style and serious subjects, and the following year Spontini confirmed this trend by composing *La vestale* to a libretto by Etienne de Jouy, a text already rejected by Boieldieu, Cherubini and Méhul, three leading contemporaries.

La vestale was a *tragédie lyrique* written for the Paris Opéra, and its triumph there in 1807 revived the flagging fortunes of that institution and established Spontini as a major figure in the operatic world. Its style is founded on Gluck, but updated to suit the tastes of Napoleonic audiences through its melodrama and spectacle. It remains an impressive achievement, with a brilliantly paced drama built around the perennial operatic issue, the conflict between love and duty.

Although Spontini wrote some two dozen operas, only three—*La vestale, Fernand Cortez* and *Olimpie*—have become established enough to form the basis for his reputation.

Fernand Cortez was another collaboration with Jouy, and it has been suggested that Napoleon himself put forward the subject, hoping that an opera dealing with the conquest of Mexico might reflect favorably upon his Spanish campaign. However, the work only became popular several years later, following substantial revisions. This version, first staged in 1817, received hundreds of performances during Spontini's lifetime.

In *Fernand Cortez* the hero is a complex character who falls in love with his enemy's daughter. Therefore it is mistaken to view this opera merely as a grand historical epic, even though its staging was particularly spectacular. There is a cavalry charge stipulating seventeen horses, the burning of the Spanish fleet, and the destruction of the Aztec temple in the final scene. The chorus understandably plays a central role, the two sides characterized by march-like music and exotic percussion effects.

Spontini had a typically Italian gift for vocal melody and a sure command of the orchestra. He used the full modern orchestra of his day, preferring to separate the roles of cellos and basses, and to divide the violas as Mozart had done. His woodwind writing was distinctive, especially as an aid to developing character, and he was fond of the spatial potential of the on-stage band and the exotic sounds of tam-tam, bells and other percussion. The next generation recognized his special talent, as the words of Berlioz confirm: "Spontini's orchestration has no antecedents. Its special colour is achieved by a use of wind instruments which contrasts skillfully with that of the strings. The frequent stressing of weak beats, dissonances whose resolution is transplanted into a different part, bass figures rising and falling majestically beneath the bulk of the orchestra, the sparing but ingenious use of trombones, trumpets, horns and timpani, the almost total exclusion of the very top register of piccolos, oboes and clarinets—all this gives Spontini's great works a grandiose character, an incomparable power and energy, and often a poetic melancholy."

Spontini's last *tragédie lyrique, Olimpie,* was begun in 1815 but only performed four years later. Despite being his most grand conception, it remained in the repertory for only a few performances (Spontini's ability to make enemies contributed to his downfall). This disappointment led to his accepting an offer from the King of Prussia to direct the Berlin Opera, and one of his first decisions was to stage *Olimpie* using E.T.A. Hoffmann as an adviser. This 1821 production was a success, but it was soon overshadowed by Weber's *Der Freischütz,* which was premiered only a month later.

The formal pageantry of Spontini is at its height in *Olimpie.* For instance, it ends with a lengthy divertissement, a spectacle which comes after the resolution of the plot; and the hero is directed to make his entry riding on an elephant, as indeed he did in the Berlin production.

Spontini responded to his new circumstances by incorporating fairy-tale supernaturalism, so effective in Weber's *Freischütz,* into his own opera *Nurmahal.* But he could hardly have expected to create a real German romantic opera, especially since his music drew heavily on earlier works, even from his Italian period. Then, in *Agnes von Hohenstaufen,* he adapted a medieval German subject in his efforts to respond to the taste of his Berlin audience. This opera has massive ensemble scenes of great formal complexity, as in *Olimpie,* but his position in Berlin was declining by this stage, and in 1842 he returned to Paris, where he tried unsuccessfully to rekindle past glories. In 1850, just a year before his death, he returned to Italy.

Spontini had much in common with Meyerbeer, whose rise to prominence he resented, but who continued the tradition of grand opera which he had largely established. Despite his reputation as a creator of spectacle, it is for his music that Spontini should be remembered. He was an important influence on Weber and Wagner as well as on Berlioz, who believed him to be the greatest composer he ever met, the "genius of the century." Most of all, Spontini followed Gluck's precedent as a composer of powerful operas, whose chief concern was the expression of human passions.

—Terry Barfoot

STAATSTHEATER [State Theater].

Composer: Mauricio Kagel.

First Performance: Hamburg, Staatsoper, 25 April 1971.

*　　*　　*

Much of Kagel's output since the early 1960s has included theatrical elements, and in many ways *Staatstheater,* composed between 1967-70, offers a synthesis of his main musical preoccupations during that decade. The work, typically iconoclastic, is described by the composer as "not just the negation of opera, but of the whole tradition of music theatre." *Staatstheater* comprises nine scenes or tableaux, as follows with the composer's sub-titles:

> Repertoire (scenic concert piece)
> Einspielungen (music for loudspeaker[s])
> Ensemble for 16 voices
> Debüt for 60 voices
> Saison (a singspiel in 65 tableaux)
> Spielplan (instrumental music in action)
> Kontra-Danse (dance for non-dancers)
> Freifahrt ("gliding chamber music")
> Parkett (concertante mass-scenes)

In the score, the composer offers the option of the performance of extracts with the proviso that "Repertoire," if performed, should always be placed first. Described as a scenic concert piece, "Repertoire" specifies a hundred instruments or props (the distinction is often blurred), each of which features in one of the short scenes; the way in which these are to be played/used is carefully drawn and notated on each page of the score, though the order of the component sections may be varied.

Normally only one performer is visible at a time, although it is possible to have unseen (i.e., off-stage) sound-events happening simultaneously. Visually, "Repertoire," like much of what follows it, inhabits the world of the theatre of the absurd. "Einspielungen" (Recordings) for Choir and Orchestra may only be heard on tape when performed alongside other sections of *Staatstheater;* the piece is based around the performance of particular musical intervals, with instrumentation and order of the sections left to the performers. Nevertheless, it is typical of the composer that the sequence of events within each section, rhythm and dynamics should be precisely marked and specified. "Ensemble," for sixteen voices, similarly offers a series of precisely notated sections which the performers may arrange in whichever order they wish. Here, however, the composer hopes that the voices performing will correspond to those of typical operatic roles, and the scenic

action may be borrowed from "Saison" (Season), which may also in turn use vocal sections from "Debüt."

Reference to the world of opera is overt, with the performers being required to wear a mélange of costumes from the opera wardrobe and employing vocal lines that range from distortions of simple recitative to bizarre caricatures of full-blown aria. With so many performance options, and indeed with the simultaneous performance of "Ensemble" and "Debüt," "Einspielungen," "Spielplan," "Kontra-Danse," "Freifahrt" and "Parkett" a possibility, a performance of *Staatstheater* will be very different in each production. At its heart, however, remains a strong sense of parody; Kagel focusses upon opera's performance mannerisms, its traditions, its characters and even some of its more unfortunate accidents. "Kontra-Danse," for example, stipulates that the performers should have "no training in dance whatsoever"; the harder they work to perfect their performance "the clearer it becomes that the task is hopeless." A performance of "Kontra-Danse" may well revive memories of ill-starred balletic interludes at some of opera's more lowly outposts. As may be apparent, humour plays an important part in Kagel's work; he has recently commented that it is the only thing he is very serious about.

—Stephen Pratt

STABILE, Mariano.

Baritone. Born 12 May 1888, in Palermo. Died 11 January 1968, in Milan. Studied with Antonio Cotogni at the S. Cecilia Conservatory in Rome; debut at Teatro Biondo, Palermo, as Marcello in *La bohème,* 1909; chosen by Toscanini to sing title role in *Falstaff* for opening of the Teatro alla Scala 1921-22 season; while at La Scala also sang Gerard, Scarpia, Beckmesser, and created title role in Respighi's *Belfagor* (1923); sang Falstaff at Covent Garden, 1926; sang frequently at Covent Garden during next five years; at Salzburg, 1931-39; at Glyndebourne, 1936-39, appearing in *Le nozze di Figaro* and as Dr Malatesta in *Don Pasquale;* sang Don Alfonso in *Così fan tutte* at Edinburgh Festival, 1948; appeared frequently at Cambridge and Stoll Theaters, 1946-49; officially retired in 1961, but continued to sing occasionally until 1963.

Publications

About STABILE: articles–

Earl of Harewood. "People 31: Mariano Stabile." *Opera* 7/5 (1956): 271.
Gualerzi, Giorgio. "Stabile—A Centenary Tribute." *Opera* 39/10 (1988): 1190.

*　　*　　*

The great Sicilian baritone Mariano Stabile will probably go down in history as the finest Falstaff in living memory. He is believed to have sung it over one thousand times, although his sixty other major roles must not be overlooked.

Stabile came from a distinguished Palermo family, and in spite of their reservations and distaste he began to study singing in 1906 with the celebrated baritone, Antonio Cotogni (Jean de Reszke's and Gigli's master). Stabile was an excellent actor and a thorough musician, qualities which helped compensate for his moderate size of voice, which he used carefully and with great discretion from his debut as Amonasro (*Aida*), 1909, until his last Falstaff at Siena in 1961. Although he sang Iago and Belfagor (in Respighi's opera of that name, a role he created) and fairly "beefy" baritone roles for some years, it was in the subtle and gracious parts of Scarpia, Figaro (both Mozart and Rossini) and as Don Giovanni where he excelled both vocally and histrionically.

Stabile was always ruled on stage by his particular feelings (and possibly metabolism) of the occasion; and while he did not deviate from the planned interrelationships with other singers, his own, smaller personal movements might change. As his wife, Gemma Bosini, has described while she was singing "Vissi d'arte" in act II of *Tosca* opposite him, Stabile as Scarpia sometimes "went to the window and stood there, or he went back to his desk signing papers, or he came and stood quite near me." All the time his very acting, in its uncertainty, added to her own performance by chilling her (his real wife!) and again reacting with a magnetism upon the audience. He was not trying to steal the show, for he was always considerate to other artists, refusing to take solo calls when others of equal fame were performing with him.

Scarpia was one of Stabile's most thrilling serious roles. He did not play him as a crude bully, nor as a tyrant (like Tito Gobbi was to do later with such success). All Stabile's characterizations were stamped with nobility: he might be playing a cruel man, but nevertheless he was polite and civilized about it.

The voice was likewise elegant and well produced with a smooth and pleasant tone; but it was the subtle, always natural changes of mood and of inference in Stabile's vocal performances which raised them from the merely good to the superb. His Figaro (Mozart) in the 1936 Glyndebourne production was a revelation because he dominated the whole opera in a manner previously unheard in England, with every nuance in place and the role teasingly sung. His Don Giovanni was magnificent: a nobleman to the core.

Stabile's career first blossomed when Toscanini engaged him to sing Falstaff for the opening performance of the 1921 Teatro alla Scala season, when Toscanini returned there for the third and last time. This led to engagements at the Salzburg Festivals where, especially under Toscanini's direction between 1931-39, Stabile's appearances became highlights in a glowing career.

At one time he sang such lighter Wagnerian baritone roles as Beckmesser in *Die Meistersinger,* whom he played with sympathy. Two generations of singers came together at Teatro alla Scala in 1955 when Stabile sang the (Don Alfonsolike) Poet to Maria Callas's Fiorilla in Rossini's *Il Turco in Italia.* Stabile could sing Mozart, Rossini, Verdi and Puccini with equal facility but probably got and gave most from Dr Malatesta, Don Giovanni, Scarpia and Falstaff.

—Alan Jefferson

STADE, FREDERICA VON
See VON STADE, FREDERICA

STANISLAVSKY, Konstantin.

Producer. Born Konstantin Sergeyevich Alekseyev, 5 January 1863, in Moscow. Died 7 August 1938, in Moscow. Also theater director, actor, and theorist; gained practical experience performing and directing operettas in the private family theater; studied voice with Fyodor Komisarzhevsky; studied at Lazarev Institute of Oriental Languages, Moscow, 1878-81; from 1885, one of the directors of the Russian Musical Society, with Tchaikovsky, Taneyev, Jürgenson, and Tretyakov; co-founded the Society of Art and Literature, 1888; first notable production was Tolstoi's *Fruits of Enlightenment,* 1891; co-founded the Moscow Art Theatre, 1898, where he later developed the Stanislavsky method for training actors; last twenty years of his life he focused on opera more than theater; established the Bolshoi Theatre Opera Studio, 1918, which began an independent studio in 1920; later renamed the Stanislavsky Opera Theatre, 1926; organized a new Operatic-Dramatic Studio, 1938; among his greatest achievements were productions of Chekhov's plays as lyric dramas. Awards include Order of Lenin; Order of the Red Banner of Labor.

Opera Productions (selected)

Eugene Onegin, Act I, Bolshoi Theatre Opera Studio, 1919.
Werther, Bolshoi Theatre Opera Studio, 1921.
Eugene Onegin, Bolshoi Theatre Opera Studio, 1922.
Il matrimonio segreto, Bolshoi Theatre Opera Studio, 1925.
The Tsar's Bride, Bolshoi Theatre Opera Studio, 1926.
La bohème, Stanislavsky Opera Theatre, 1927.
May Night, Stanislavsky Opera Theatre, 1928.
Boris Godunov, Stanislavsky Opera Theatre, 1929.
The Queen of Spades, Stanislavsky Opera Theatre, 1930.
The Golden Cockerel, Stanislavsky Opera Theatre, 1932.
Il barbiere di Siviglia, Stanislavsky Opera Theatre, 1933.
Carmen, Stanislavsky Opera Theatre, 1935.
Don Pasquale, Stanislavsky Opera Theatre, 1936.
Madama Butterfly, Stanislavsky Opera Theatre, 1938.
Rigoletto, Stanislavsky Opera Theatre, 1939.

Publications

By STANISLAVSKY: books–

Moya zhizn' v iskusstve [*My Life in Art*]. London, 1923.
Rabota aktyora nad soboy [*An Actor Prepares*]. Translated by Elizabeth Reynolds Hapgood. London, 1936.
Stanislavsky Produces Othello. London, 1948.
Rabota aktyora nad soboy [*Building a Character*]. 2nd ed. Translated by Elizabeth Reynolds Hapgood. New York, 1949.
Rabota aktyora nad rol'yu [*Creating a Role*]. London, 1949.
Stanislavsky on the Art of the Stage. Translated with an introduction by David Magarshak. London, 1950.
ed. M.N. Kedrov. *K.S. Stanislavsky: sobraniye sochineniy* [Collected Works]. Moscow, 1954-61.
An Actor's Handbook: An Alphabetical Arrangement of Concise Statements on Aspects of Acting. Edited and translated by Elizabeth Reynolds Hapgood. New York, 1963.

About STANISLAVSKY: books–

Antarova, K.E., ed. *Besedï K.S. Stanislavskovo v Studii Bol'shovo v 1918-22 gg.* [Conversations with Stanislavsky at the Bol'shoy Studio during the Years 1918-22]. Moscow, 1939, rev. 3/1952.
Magarshack, David. *Stanislavksy: A Life.* London, 1950.

Kristi, G.V. *Rabota Stanislavskovo v opernom teatre* [Stanislavsky's Work in the Opera Theater]. Moscow, 1952.

Rumyantsev, P.I. *Rabota Stanislavskovo nad opernoy Rigoletto* [Stanislavsky's Work on *Rigoletto*]. Moscow, 1955.

Lewis, Robert. *Method—or Madness?* New York, 1958.

Hapgood, E.R., ed. *Stanislavsky's Legacy.* 1959.

Moore, Sonia. *The Stanislavski Method: The Professional Training of an Actor.* New York, 1960.

Edwards, Christine. *Stanislavsky Heritage.* New York, 1965.

Cole, Toby. *Acting: A Handbook of the Stanislavski Method.* New York, 1971.

Kelly, Elizabeth Y. *The Magic If; Stanislavski for Children.* Baltimore, 1973.

Vinogradskaya, I.N., ed. *Zhizn' i tvorchestvo K.S. Stanislavskovo: letopis'* [The Life and Work of Stanislavsky: A Chronicle]. 3rd ed. Moscow, 1973.

Rumiantsev, Pavel Ivanovich. *Stanislavski on Opera.* Translated by Elizabeth Reynolds Hapgood. New York, 1975.

Moore, Sonia. *Training an Actor: The Stanislavski System in Class.* Harmondsworth, N.Y., 1979.

Toporkov Vasilii Osipovich. *Stanislavki in Rehearsal: The Final Years.* New York, 1979.

Benedetti, Jean. *Stanislavski, an Introduction.* New York, 1982.

Hirsch, Foster. *A Method to Their Madness: The History of the Actors Studio.* New York, 1984.

Driver, John. *Chekhov in Yalta: Featuring a Rare and Delightful Visit by the Moscow Art Theatre.* New York, 1986.

Jones, David Richard. *Great Directors at Work: Stanislavsky, Brecht, Kazan, Brook.* Berkeley, California, 1986.

Strasberg, Lee. *A Dream of Passion: The Development of the Method.* Edited by Evangeline Morphos. Boston, 1987.

Benedetti, Jean. *Stanislavski.* New York, 1988.

Vineberg, Steve. *Method Actors: Three Generations of an American Acting Style.* New York, 1991.

articles–

Kamernitsky, D. "Thirty-Five Years of the Stanislavsky and Nemirovich-Danchenko Music Theatre." *Opera* 6 (January 1955): 25-28.

Roslavleva, N. "Stanislavski and the Ballet." *Dance Perspectives* no. 23 (1965).

Adler, K. "Stanislavsky and Opera." *Opera News* 29 (6 February 1965): 6-7.

Lemeshev, S. "Iz avtobiograffi; v studii K.S. Stanislavskogo." *Sovetskaya Muzyka* 29 (February 1965): 42-51.

Khaykin, B. "Vstrechi i razmyshleniya." *Sovetskaya Muzyka* 29 (April 1965): 54-58.

Sobolevskaya, O. "Kak stavilas' 'Tsarskaya Nevesta.' " *Sovetskaya Muzyka* 32 (August 1968): 80-86.

Stanislavsky, K. "Idet rabota nad *Karmen.*" *Sovetskaya Muzyka* 32 (August 1968): 87-92.

Grosheva, E. "Rozhdennyy revolyutsiey." *Sovetskaya Muzyka* 33 (December 1969): 28-37.

Pokrovsky, B. "Vospitanie artista-pevtsa i printsipy K.S. Stanislavskogo." *Sovetskaya Muzyka* 36 (January 1972): 59-64.

Osborne, C.L. "The Mouth-Honored Prophets: Stanislavski and Felsenstein." *Musical Newsletter* 5, no. 4 (1975): 3-13.

Cannon, R. "Stanislavski—and the Opera." *Opera* 33 (November 1982): 1112-17.

Cannon, R. "Stanislavski and the Opera—in Production." *Opera* 34 (July 1983): 714-20.

* * *

Konstantin Stanislavsky is celebrated as an outstanding Russian theater and opera director, actor, teacher and theorist, and a founder of the scientific theory of realistic stage art. Born into an art-loving family (his father was a wealthy Moscow merchant), he received an excellent private education, which apart from the usual school subjects included foreign languages, music, dancing, sport, and various crafts. After high school, he studied at the Lazarev Institute of Oriental Languages. His interest in the theater manifested itself at an early age, as he participated in the operettas and vaudevilles given by the "Alekseev Circle" in his own home. (Stanislavsky was the nephew of the celebrated theatrical maecenas Savva Mamontov.) A frequent visitor to the Bol'shoy Theatre (which presented more than fifty works a season), he took opera singing lessons with the tenor Felix Kommissarzhevsky, studied the techniques of leading artists at the Imperial Theatres, and was struck by the performance of Chaliapin, the music of Rachmaninov, and the conducting of Koussevitsky. In 1888, together with F.P. Kommissarzhevsky and A.F. Fedotov, he founded the Society of Art and Literature, where he performed numerous roles in plays by Russian and European playwrights and later became a producer.

A turning point came in Stanislavsky's life when he was invited by V.I. Nemirovich-Danchenko to co-found the Moscow Art Theatre in 1898. The Moscow Art Theatre included students from the Society of Art and Literature as well as members of Nemirovich-Danchenko's School of Music and Drama, associated with the Moscow Philharmonic Society. The ensuing productions of Chekhov's *The Sea-gull* (1898), *Uncle Vanya* (1899), *The Three Sisters* (1901), and *The Cherry Orchard* (1904), in which acting, scenery, lighting, sound effects and music were all interlinked to form a homogeneous, aesthetic whole, were startling in their originality and psychological insight; a strong contrast to the stereotyped uniformity of preceding Russian theatrical performances.

In 1918 Stanislavsky and Nemirovich-Danchenko, at the encouragement of Lunacharsky, the first Commissar of the Arts, established an Opera Studio, which was attached to the Bol'shoy Theatre. In 1920 the Studio achieved independent existence, being renamed the Stanislavsky Studio Theatre and, in 1926, the Stanislavsky Opera Theatre. Commencing with productions such as Rimsky-Korsakov's *Vera Sheloga* (1921), Massenet's *Werther* (1921), and Tchaikovsky's *Eugene Onegin* (1922), the following years saw a host of memorable performances, which have gone down in the annals of Russian operatic history: Cimarosa's *Il matrimonio segreto* (1925), Rimsky-Korsakov's *The Tsar's Bride* (1926), Puccini's *La bohème* (1927), Rimsky-Korsakov's *May Night* (1928), Mussorgsky's *Boris Godunov* in its original version (1929), Tchaikovsky's *The Queen of Spades* (1930), Rimsky-Korsakov's *The Golden Cockerel* (1932), and many others.

In the course of Stanislavsky's work from about 1907 onwards he employed what has become known as the "Stanislavsky Method." Basing his theories on outstanding European and Russian theatrical theorists and performers such as Diderot, Riccoboni, Goethe, and Shchepkin, he sought in a performance sincerity and truth. Since acting had a psychological basis and rested on the ability to recall particular emotions at specific times, the performer had to be intellectually aware of the chief motivating force in a role, without which a performance could not be completely convincing. Attention also had to be paid to physical action and gesture.

In the last twenty years of his life Stanislavsky was particularly interested in opera production. He saw the musical score itself as the prime source for any interpretation, not the libretto. Stanislavsky's theories had influence not only on the development of the contemporary Soviet theater but on productions outside the U.S.S.R. His ideas were set out in literary form in 1938 in his book entitled *An Actor Prepares.*

—Gerald Seaman

STATE THEATER
See STAATSTHEATER

STEBER, Eleanor.

Soprano. Born 17 July 1916, in Wheeling, West Virginia. Died 3 October 1990, in Langhorne, Pennsylvania. Attended New England Conservatory in Boston, and studied privately with Paul Althouse and William Whitney; debut as Senta, Boston, 1936; in 1940 won Metropolitan Opera radio auditions, which led to Metropolitan debut (as Sophie) in same year; remained at Metropolitan until 1962, singing Violetta, 1943, Konstanze in Metropolitan premiere of *Die Entführung aus dem Serail,* 1946, the Marschallin, 1949, title role in American premiere of *Arabella,* 1955, title role in world premiere of Barber's *Vanessa,* 1958, and Marie in Metropolitan's first *Wozzeck,* 1959; appeared at Edinburgh Festival, 1947, as Elsa at Bayreuth, 1953, in Vienna, 1953, and in Florence, as Minnie, 1954; sang in first performance of Barber's *Knoxville: Summer of 1915,* 1948; sang Miss Wingrave in American premiere of Britten's *Owen Wingrave,* Santa Fe, 1973; in later years appeared frequently in musical comedies and as concert artist, and was active as teacher at Cleveland Institute and Juilliard School, among other schools.

Publications

By STEBER: books–

Mozart Operatic Arias, with R. Beatie. New York, 1988.

About STEBER: articles–

Moore, D. "Eleanor Steber—A Tribute." *The NATS Journal* 47/2 (1990): 4.
Rubinstein, L. "Improper Diva" (interview). *Opera News* 55 (1990): 10.

*　　*　　*

One of the most renowned operatic sopranos of the twentieth century, Eleanor Steber was born on 17 July 1916 in Wheeling, West Virginia. She studied at the New England Conservatory and won the 1940 Metropolitan Opera auditions. Steber's lengthy career at the Met (1940-1962) and other operatic venues established her as a singer of astonishing breadth and depth. Steber's popularity may be gauged by the fact that she had a very active fan club with numerous chapters throughout the United States which even published a regular newsletter entitled "The Silvertone." A noted performer of Richard Strauss (especially the roles of Sophie, the Marschallin, and Arabella) and Mozart (including but not limited to the roles of Donna Anna, Donna Elvira, Pamina, and Fiordiligi), Steber also successfully tackled more modern roles such as Marie of Berg's *Wozzeck* and Miss Wingrave of Britten's *Owen Wingrave.*

Steber's flexibility as a singer and her stage presence contributed greatly to the development of an uniquely American approach to opera singing, with a much greater emphasis placed on the singer as actor. Convincing characterization was an essential element of this approach and led Steber as her career matured to take successively older roles in operas in which she had already starred in younger roles.

Steber's singing was particularly associated with the music of the American composer Samuel Barber. She premiered the title role of Barber's *Vanessa* (1958) and also commissioned and premiered the composer's well-known *Knoxville: Summer of 1915* (1948) based on a text by the American writer James Agee. Steber's championing of American music was paralleled in her great concern for correct instruction in English diction, which the singer believed was not being properly taught in European conservatories.

Eleanor Steber as Elsa in *Lohengrin,* Bayreuth Festival, 1953

After her retirement from the Met in 1962, Steber continued to perform in operas and solo recitals. One of the most notable performances of her post-Met career was as old Miss Wingrave in the Santa Fe (New Mexico) Opera's production of *Owen Wingrave*

Steber dedicated her later years to teaching (at the Juilliard School of Music in New York City, Temple University in Philadelphia, the New England Conservatory in Boston, and the Cleveland Institute of Music, among other institutions) and providing financial support to aspiring singers through the agency of the Eleanor Steber Music Foundation, which is dedicated to financing, in Steber's words, "the no man's land that lies between school training and big-time debut."

—William E. Grim

STEVENS, Risë.

Mezzo-soprano. Born 11 June 1913, in New York. Married: Walter Surovy, 1939. Studied at the Juilliard School of Music with Anna Schoen-René; studied in Salzburg with Marie Gutheil-Schoder and Herbert Graf; debut in Thomas's *Mignon,* Prague, 1936; sang Octavian in Strauss's *Der Rosenkavalier,* 1938; Metropolitan Opera debut as Octavian, 1938; sang at the Glyndebourne Festival, 1939; films include *The Chocolate Soldier,* 1941, and *Going My Way,* 1944; sang at the Met, 1938-61; Teatro alla Scala debut, 1954; retired from the stage in 1964; co-director of Metropolitan Opera National Company, 1965-67; president, Mannes College of Music, 1975-78; managing director, Metropolitan Opera Board, 1988—.

Publications

About STEVENS: books–

Chrichton, K. *Subway to the Met: Risë Stevens' Story.* New York, 1959.

articles–

Soria, D.J. "Artist Life" *High Fidelity/ Musical America* 27 (1977): MA6.
Waleson, H. "Off and Running." *Opera News* 46 (1981): 16.
"Reflected Glory (Personal recollections of life at the Met)." *Opera News* 48 (1983): 78.
Price, W. "Irreplaceable: Risë Stevens remains the Carmen of all time." *Opera News* 51 (1987): 8.
Mayer, M. "Risë." *Opera News* 53 (1988): 12.

*   *   *

Possessor of one of the most sensuous mezzo-soprano voices of her generation, Risë Stevens virtually owned the roles of Carmen and Dalila at the Metropolitan Opera during the 1940s and 1950s. Her vocal texture was pure velvet, not meant for the heavy dramatic mezzo heroines of Verdi and Wagner. She had the good sense to drop Amneris, as well as her weighty Wagnerian sisters, Fricka and Erda, early in her career. From the start Stevens was more suited to the classic line of Gluck's Orfeo than the heroic outpourings of Beethoven's Leonore—a role she was offered by Bruno Walter and wisely declined.

Like several of her opera colleagues—Gladys Swarthout, Lawrence Tibbett, Grace Moore and Lily Pons—Stevens built a career notable for its diversity. She was a popular star of radio and television, an appealing recitalist, an opera singer of the first rank, a much sought after concert performer, a film actress (who had the good fortune to be in *Going My Way*), and a recording artist whose extensive output included classical, semi-classical, Broadway and popular songs. Her rendition of Cole Porter's "Ev'rything I love" ranks with the best, and the excitement generated in her final scene from *Carmen* with Raoul Jobin leaves all others far behind (even her own later version with Jan Peerce). Her occasional pairing with the dynamic Italian tenor and congenial colleague, Mario Del Monaco at the Metropolitan, produced superlative performances of *Carmen* and *Samson et Dalila* which set standards unchallenged to this day. Recorded highlights of *Samson et Dalila* with these two artists preserve the chemistry which existed between them.

Carmen was Stevens's most famous role because she willed it to be. She molded herself to a part which actually was wrong for her. The Nordic-American beauty which was hers is light years away from that of a Spanish Gypsy's. At first, her interpretation followed conventional lines, but after her encounter with Tyrone Guthrie, who directed a production of *Carmen* at the Metropolitan Opera done especially for her, she completely changed her conception of the central character. Stevens's Carmen was not pretty, but rather hard, calculating, tough and one step away from a prostitute. This approach was a gamble, for she walked a fine line between characterization and caricature. To her credit, she completely avoided the obvious and probed deeper and deeper into the role. The death of Carmen, set in the grimy dressing room of Escamillo, with her defiant rejection of Don José constitutes one of the greatest moments of theater.

As with anyone who is so closely identified with a part, we tend to forget that Stevens was also brilliant as Octavian. Her early collaboration with Lotte Lehmann in *Der Rosenkavalier* is what operatic legends are made of. She was one of the very few who could bring Dalila to vivid realization, present an Orfeo of compelling beauty and pathos, a Prince Orlofsky of endearingly wacky charm, a beguiling Cherubino and a bewitching Mignon. That she also received critical acclaim as Laura in *La gioconda,* Marfa in *Khovanshchina* and Marina in *Boris Godunov* further defines the versatility she possessed.

When speaking of Stevens, one can not avoid the word "multi-faceted." She excelled in a wide variety of forms of entertainment; today's "superstars" would be hard pressed to duplicate her achievements. Her greatest asset was her uncanny ability to communicate. No matter if it was in the large expanse of an opera house or the intimacy of the television screen, Stevens could give the impression that she was singing to you alone.

—John Pennino

STICH-RANDALL, Teresa.

Soprano. Born 24 December 1927, in West Hartford, Connecticut. Studied voice at the Hartford School of Music and at Columbia University; created role of Gertrude Stein in Thomson's *The Mother of Us All,* 1947; sang under Toscanini and NBC Symphony Orchestra as the Priestess in *Aïda,* 1949, and Nannetta, 1950; European debut as Mermaid in *Oberon,* Florence, 1952; Vienna State Opera debut, 1952; Metropolitan Opera debut as Fiordiligi in *Così fan tutte,* 1961; first U.S. singer to be named Austrian Kammersängerin, 1962.

Publications

About STICH-RANDALL: articles–

Gualerzi, G. "Stich-Randall, Teresa." In *Le grandi voci,* Rome, 1964.

*   *   *

The American-born soprano Teresa Stich-Randall made an early and auspicious debut: in 1947, while still a student at Columbia University she created the role of Gertrude Stein in Virgil Thomson's opera *The Mother of Us All.* By 1950 she had been recruited by Arturo Toscanini, who, no doubt impressed by her pure tone and secure intonation, cast her as the Priestess in *Aida* and Nanetta in *Falstaff* in his NBC broadcasts of these operas. These performances, still available on records, testify to Stich-Randall's excellence even then—particularly in *Falstaff* where, surrounded by a formidable cast, she shines by virtue of the flute-like purity of her tone.

Stich-Randall's voice, basically a lyric soprano with some bloom, was notable for a concentrated silvery sharpness which could penetrate large orchestrations with ease, creating the illusion of a dramatic size which was perhaps not hers by nature. Also striking was a remarkable sense of attack: the voice moved in even the fastest and most complex passagework with the uncanny accuracy of an instrument, always—or nearly always—landing in the dead center of a note. If the instrumental analogy suggests efficiency more than poetry, that is probably just: Stich-Randall's singing is often distinguished more by its brilliance and gleam than by its humanity. In addition, particularly in the latter part of her career, the virtuosic florid singing could sound mannered and mechanical. A recorded recital includes performances of arias from *I Puritani* and *La traviata.* Here the tempi are almost freakishly fast, and the manic precision of the scale work becomes comically inappropriate. In fact, none of the arias as recorded (all from the French and Italian repertoires) really satisfies. The glinting tone seems much better suited to German music, and although Stich-Randall's stage repertoire encompassed Gilda and even Norma it is unsurprising that she is best known for her significant contributions to the music of Strauss and Mozart. The EMI recording of *Der Rosenkavalier* (conducted by Herbert von Karajan) in which Stich-Randall sings Sophie introduced her to many listeners, and the performance remains justly celebrated; there have been more human, vulnerable Sophies but none who negotiates the rise to the soft B flat in the Presentation of the Rose with such superb ease.

As an interpreter of the music of Mozart, Stich-Randall left many significant recorded souvenirs of her artistry. Among the operatic roles she was perhaps best known as Donna Anna (*Don Giovanni*), and her performance recorded live at Aix-en-Provence captures the fleet, shining voice at its best—as well as a memorable impersonation, alive to every nuance of the chimerical, neurotic character. This vividness of interpretation is the exception rather than the rule among Stich-Randall's recorded performances, and although critics and audiences who saw her in the theater invariably comment on her fine acting, her records tell a somewhat different story. Her Fiordiligi in *Così fan tutte,* for example, barely hints at the critical change of heart which is foreshadowed in "Per pietà," although the arching legato line is masterly. In "Come scoglio," the fearsome leaps are negotiated with almost impudent ease—but the critical sense of fun is absent. Similarly, Stich-Randall's recording of the Countess in *Le nozze di Figaro* is a first-rate piece of singing but a leaden and unmemorable interpretation placed against those of Elisabeth Schwarzkopf, Lisa Della Casa, Sena Jurinac and other contemporaries. Several recital records of Mozart opera arias include, in addition to the roles noted above, characters as diverse as Pamina (*Die Zauberflöte,* Ilia (*Idomeneo*) and Constanze (*Die Entführung aus dem Serail*)—all are sung with care and artistry, shining tone, musicianly attention to detail, and all are indistinguishable from one another as personalities.

The concert arias of Mozart require less specific insights, and Stich-Randall's recordings of these show her at her marvelous best. The extended motet *Exsultate, Jubilate* with its celebrated "Alleluja" (taken here at an especially brisk pace) is sung with gorgeous tone and invigorating accuracy, the extreme difficulties of "Ah, se in ciel benigne stelle" are tossed off with seeming ease, and in the long legato lines of "Bella mia fiamma" the instrumental purity is a joy to hear. All of these preserve the remarkable artistry at its finest, and all go far to justify the inclusion of Stich-Randall in the pantheon of great Mozart singers of the middle of our century.

—David Anthony Fox

———————

STIFFELIO.

Composer: Giuseppe Verdi.

Librettist: Francesco Maria Piave (after E. Souvestre and E. Bourgeois).

First Performance: Trieste, 16 November 1850; revised as *Aroldo,* Rimini, Nuovo, 16 August 1857.

Roles: Stiffelio (tenor); Lina (soprano); Stankar (baritone); Jorg (bass); Raffaele (tenor); Dorotea (mezzo-soprano); Federico (tenor); chorus.

Publications

articles–

Quaderni dell' Istituto di Studi Verdiani 3 (1968).

*   *   *

In the few years since Julian Budden's description of *Stiffelio* as Verdi's most unjustly neglected opera—he was writing after the 1968 Parma performances of the opera, the first in more than a hundred years—little has happened to alter its status except perhaps a remarkable 1985-86 staging (in tandem with *Aroldo,* Verdi's 1857 reworking of *Stiffelio*) by Pier Luigi Pizzi at La Fenice. The neglect up until 1968 is understandable given that Verdi used the autograph score of

Stiffelio, as the manuscript for the *Aroldo* revisions and ordered other copies destroyed; consequently no autograph exists for *Stiffelio,* and it was only with the discovery of two copyists' full scores in the 1960s that performance became possible once again. Considering that it was composed between *Luisa Miller* and *Rigoletto,* the comparative lack of interest still shown for *Stiffelio* is extraordinary.

The frustration which led Verdi to abandon *Stiffelio* as unperformable in his day stemmed primarily from censorship difficulties. The subject was the most contemporary Verdi had tackled; the play on which it was based, *Le pasteur, ou L'évangile et le foyer* by Emile Silvestre and Eugène Bourgeois, had premiered in Paris only the year before. The adultery of a Protestant clergyman's wife was bewildering to the Italian public, who were unused to clergymen having wives, let alone adulterous ones, while the Church censors found it presumptuous and offensive on numerous grounds. Verdi had to agree unwillingly to changes—indeed some of them made nonsense of the drama—to get it onstage at all. The alterations to the climax in act III, scene i, for example, when Lina, the erring wife, having failed to move Stiffelio to listen to her as a husband, suddenly asks him to hear her confession as a minister, rendered it pointless. A bowdlerized version, *Guglielmo Wellingrode,* made the rounds for a few years, but Verdi's detestation of it brought about the decision to revise it into *Aroldo.*

Act I begins with Stiffelio's return from his travels to be greeted by his wife, Lina, her father, Stankar, and his elderly colleague, Jorg. Magnanimously refusing to investigate a possible adulterous liaison brought to his attention, Stiffelio soon has reason to suspect that the liaison is in fact his wife's. Her father discovers the truth and challenges Raffaele, the lover, to a duel in the graveyard of the castle that night, where act II takes place. Lina, waiting to warn Raffaele, prays at the grave of her mother. He enters, followed by Stankar; they fight, bringing Stiffelio out of the church onto the scene. Stankar informs him that Raffaele is Lina's lover; enraged, Stiffelio moves to revenge himself on Raffaele. Suddenly the congregation in the church is heard singing "Non punirmi, Signor, nel tuo furore" ("Do not punish me, O Lord, in thine anger"); Jorg, appearing at the church door, persuades Stiffelio to renounce his anger and reenter the church. Act III, scene i brings the confrontation between Stiffelio and Lina; he offers her a divorce freeing her to marry Raffaele but refuses to listen to her. She eventually signs the document but swears she loves him and that she was Raffaele's victim. Stiffelio, again enraged, is about to take vengeance on Raffaele but is forestalled by Stankar, who enters announcing that *he* has killed Rafaele. The concluding scene is set in the church, where the congregation, singing the same psalm begging for mercy, waits for Stiffelio to preach. He enters and, not perceiving Lina, mounts the pulpit praying for guidance; at Jorg's urging he opens the Bible for inspiration and, finding himself at the story of the woman taken in adultery, reads the passage aloud, forgiving his wife before the congregation.

There are problems in the libretto, chiefly the necessity of compressing the very complicated action of the play; in effect, Piave dramatized only the last two acts of the four-act drama. The chief loss is a clear sense of the context of Lina's adultery, of her motivation apart from a sense of guilt so that her music alone has to establish her as a figure with whom the audience can identify unquestioningly. Today's audiences may also have difficulty accepting that the modern society depicted could hold to a moral code in which the "wronged" husband and father assume the right to murder the seducer while remaining reluctant to forgive the "fallen" woman.

Much of the music, as one would expect at this point in Verdi's career, is extraordinarily mature. Opening the opera with Jorg's sombre meditation on the holy book ("O santo libro") rather than with the more usual chorus, establishes the elder preacher as the drama's voice of moral aspiration. The septet following Stiffelio's entrance is unable to distinguish the characters and their relative positions very satisfactorily, but Stiffelio's aria, "Vidi dovunque gemere," establishes him as a kind of tenor character different from any Verdi had yet tackled: a balanced man of mature years, a kind of early Otello-figure, whose struggle will be between his magnanimity and his impulses. Lina's aria after Stiffelio's suspicions are awakened, "A te ascenda," leads to a splendidly varied duet with her father, "Dite che il fallo a tergere," in which the true Verdian baritone vents its fury while the soprano's fragmented laments anticipate Gilda's vocal line in the soon-to-be-completed *Rigoletto* quartet. Act II works well both dramatically and musically, moving from Lina's opening aria, "Ah daglie scanni eternei" (whose luminous accompaniment looks forward to Amelia's first-act act aria in *Simon Boccanegra*) into a powerful quartet, "Ah, era vero." However, it is the act-III duet between husband and wife ("Opposto è il calle") that realizes their full stature and marks the greatness of the work. The musical austerity of the final scene, from the simple organ opening through the choral psalm punctuated by Stankar's prayer for mercy and Lina's hopeful cries, gradually builds up a tremendous tension which is released only by the ensemble's repeated cry of "Perdonata."

—Peter Dyson

STIGNANI, Ebe.

Mezzo-soprano. Born 11 July 1903, in Naples. Died 5 October 1975, in Imola. Studied piano and singing with Agostino Roche, San Pietro di Maiella Conservatory, Naples; debut as Amneris in *Aïda,* Naples, 1925; Teatro alla Scala debut, 1926; leading mezzo there until 1953; created the Voice in Respighi's *Lucrezia;* created Cathos in Lattuada's *Le preziose ridicole,* Teatro alla Scala, 1929; retired, 1958.

Publications

About STIGNANI: books—

de Franceschi, Bruno, and Pier Fernando Mondini. *Ebe Stignani: Una voce a il suo mondo.* Imola, 1980.
Rasponi, Lanfranco. *The Last Prima Donnas.* New York, 1982.

articles—

Rosenthal, Harold. "Ebe Stignani." *Opera* 6/June (1952): 334.
Celletti, Rodolfo. "Stignani, Ebe." *Le grandi voci.* Rome, 1964.
Davidson, E. "All About Ebe." *Opera News* 35/21 (1971): 28.

*   *   *

By almost any standard, Ebe Stignani was regarded as the greatest Italian mezzo-soprano of her time. Gianna Pederzini was a better actress, Elena Nicolai was more overtly histrionic, and Irene Minghini-Cattaneo, Cloe Elmo and others had their triumphs, but in the long period between Gabriella Besanzoni and, say, Fedora Barbieri and Giulietta Simionato, no one had the grandeur of tone, technique, and phrasing of this great mezzo. "I was given a magnificent gift," she once told Lanfranco Rasponi, "and in a way I am like a priestess, for I feel that it is my responsibility to keep this flame lit in the best possible manner.... I am Stignani because of my voice." This extraordinary dedication is part of what one experienced of her in the opera house and of what one hears even now on her many recordings. She sang all the great Verdi roles, the popular Bellini and Donizetti works, some Rossini, and such characters as Dalila, Laura, Santuzza, Waltraute, Ortrud, and Brangaene. The voice was enormous, evenly balanced, and steady throughout its range, with a flexibility exciting in Rossini and a piercing richness at the top. It was unexpectedly lyric—at times even shallow—in the middle, which was also powerful, and the chest voice was thrilling in its edge.

Stignani was, she freely admitted, not a great stage figure, but in virtually all of her roles her technical command allowed her to work through the music to find characterization: a classicist in the age of verismo. She said her favorite role was Gluck's Orfeo, but one need only hear her Judgment Scene (in *Aïda*) to sense the classical orientation; each phrase is sculpted for proportionate expressiveness, the whole a structure of profound power, next to which Gigli and Del Monaco, her tenors in different recordings, sound respectively sentimental and self-righteous. Her Dalila recordings (in Italian) are similarly impressive. In the tone quality itself is a measure of sexual allure, but beyond this, Stignani's flexibility and often sumptuous phrasing allow her to project what many other mezzos can only reach for: psychological power. She is what she wishes you to think she is: a force. For her audiences, her voice alone projected something inimitably compelling.

Stignani's distinguishing qualities can be heard clearly in two other recordings: the young hero Arsace's entrance aria, "Ah! quel giorno", from Rossini's *Semiramide,* and a live performance of *Il trovatore* at the Teatro alla Scala in 1953, her final year there, twenty-six seasons after her debut. In the Rossini, the tone quality is both rich and focused and the technique dazzling. Her Azucena differs from others not only in its power and control but in its musical dignity and profound motherly concern. Here Azucena's madness is not a theatrical affectation nor a gypsy exoticism but the tragic result of a tangle of betrayals: a completely believable portrayal and the more deeply moving because of it. For Stignani, realizing a role in musical terms demanded, as she said, the intensity and commitment associated with religious belief. For us there is a depth of pleasure to be gained from her art that transcends the event and borders on the philosophical.

—London Green

STOCKHAUSEN, Karlheinz.

Composer. Born 22 August 1928, in Mödrath, near Cologne. Studied piano and music education at the Hochschule für Musik in Cologne, 1947-51; studied composition with Frank Martin at the Hochschule, 1950-51; studied with Olivier Messiaen at the Paris Conservatory, musique concrète at Pierre Schaeffer's Club d'Essai, and privately with Darius Milhaud in Paris, 1951-53; production assistant, Studio for Electronic Music, WDR Cologne, 1953-63; summer seminars for the Ferienkurse für Musik in Darmstadt, 1953-74; lecture tour of Canadian and American Universities, 1958; founder and artistic director of the "Cologne Courses for New Music," 1963-68; artistic director, Studio for Electronic Music, WDR Cologne, 1963-75; visiting professor at the University of California, Davis, 1966-67; public lectures in England, 1969-71; performances at the World's Fair in Osaka, Japan, 1970; professor of composition at the Hochschule für Musik, Cologne, 1971-77; Ernst von Siemens Music Prize, 1986; honorary membership, the Royal Academy of Music, London, 1987; honorary membership, the American Academy of Arts and Sciences, 1989.

Operas

Publishers: Universal, Stockhausen-Verlag.

'Atmen gibt das Leben...' (choral opera), 1974-77, Cologne, Cologne Radio, 10 February 1979.
Licht: die sieben Tage der Woche, 1977-: 1) *Der Jahreslauf* (scene from *Dienstag aus Licht*), 1977; 2) *Donnerstag aus Licht,* 1978-80, Milan, 1981; 3) *Samstag aus Licht,* 1981-84, Milan, 1984; *Montag aus Licht,* 1984-88, Milan, 1988.

Other works: various works for conventional and unconventional instruments, electronics, etc.

Publications

By STOCKHAUSEN: books–

Texte zur Musik. 6 vols. Cologne, 1963-89.
with others. *Stockhausen in Calcutta.* Translated by Sharmila Bose. Calcutta, 1984.
Karlheinz Stockhausen in Musikwissenschaftlichen Seminar der Universität Freiburg i. Br. 3 bis 5 Juni 1985. Murrhardt, 1986.
with others. *Karlheinz Stockhausen.* Paris, 1988.
with Robin Maconie. *Stockhausen on Music.* London, 1988.
Towards a Cosmic Music: Texts by Karlheinz Stockhausen. Selected and translated by Tim Nevill. Shaftesbury, 1989.

articles–

"Actualia." *Die Reihe* 1 (1958).
"Structure and Experimental Time." *Die Reihe* 2 (1958).
"... how time passes ...." *"Die Reihe* 3 (1959).
"Electronic and Instrumental Music." *Die Reihe* 5 (1961).
"Music in Space." *Die Reihe* 5 (1961).
"The Concept of Unity in Electronic Music." *Perspectives of New Music* 1/no. 1 (1962).
Bennett, Sheila, and Richard Toop, trans. "Stockhausen Miscellany." *Music and Musicians* 21/no. 2 (1972).
"Die Zukunft der elektroakustischen Apparaturen in der Musik." *Musik und Bildung* 7-8 (1974).
"World Music." *World Music* 21 (1979): 3.

interviews–

"Notes and Commentaries." *New Yorker* 18 January (1964).
Heyworth, Peter. "Spiritual Dimensions." *Music and Musicians* 19/no. 9 (1971).

Oesch, Hans. "Interview mit Karlheinz Stockhausen." *Melos/Neue Zeitschrift für Musik* 1/no. 6 (1975).

Frankfurter Allgemeine Zeitung 18 July (1980).

Platz, Robert H.P. "Weder Anfang noch Ende. Zum *Donnerstag aus Licht* von Karlheinz Stockhausen. Ein Gespräch." *Musiktexte* 1 (1983): 26.

About STOCKHAUSEN: books–

Wörner, Karl H. *Karlheinz Stockhausen: Werk und Wollen 1950-1962.* Rodenkirchen, 1963; revised as *Stockhausen: Life and Works,* edited and translated by Bill Hopkins. London, 1973.

Cott, Jonathan. *Stockhausen: Conversations with the Composer.* New York, 1973.

Harvey, Jonathan. *The Music of Stockhausen.* London, 1975.

Maconie, Robin. *The Works of Karlheinz Stockhausen.* Oxford, 1976; 2nd ed., 1990.

Sabbe, Hermann. *Karlheinz Stockhausen: '. . . wie die Zeit verging . . .'.* Munich, 1981.

Manion, Michael, Barry Sullivan, and Frits Weiland. *Stockhausen in Den Haag.* The Hague, 1982.

Tannenbaum, Mya. *Intervista sul genio musicale.* Milan, 1985; English translation as *Conversations with Stockhausen.* Oxford, 1987.

Kurtz, Michael. *Stockhausen: eine Biographie.* Kassel, 1988; English translation by Richard Toop, London, 1992.

Conen, Hermann. *Formal-Komposition: zu Karlheinz Stockhausens Musik der siebziger Jahre.* Mainz, 1991.

articles–

Schnebel, Dieter. "Karlheinz Stockhausen." *Die Reihe* 4 (1958); English translation, *Die Reihe* (1960).

Toop, Richard. "Stockhausen's *Konkrete Etüde.*" *Music Review* 37/no. 4 (1976).

———. "Stockhausen's Other Piano Pieces." *Musical Times* April (1983).

Blumröder, Christoph von. "Stockhausen-Bibliographie 1952-1982." *Neuland* 3 (1983): 178.

Frisius, Rudolf. "Komponieren heute: Auf der Suche nach der verlorenen Polyphonie. Tendenzen in Stockhausens *Licht*—Zyklus." *Neue Zeitschrift für Musik* 145/nos. 7-8 (1984): 24.

Oehlschlägel, Reinhard. "Wohlformulierte Teufelsmusik: zu Karlheinz Stockhausens *Samstag aus Licht.*" *Musiktexte* 5 (1984): 50.

Britton, Peter. "Stockhausen's Path to Opera." *Musical Times* September (1985).

Kohl, Jerome. "Into the Middleground: Formula Syntax in Stockhausen's *Licht.*" *Perspectives of New Music* 28/no. 2 (1990): 262.

Maconie, Robin. "Great Vintages." *Classic CD* 5 (1990): 52.

*   *   *

The cultural environment in which Stockhausen grew up was hardly the comfortable life of regular opera-going, but a real world of Germany in the 1930s, in which material deprivation, spiritual anguish, state persecution, the threat and reality of war, the solace of music and the saving grace of religion all played a part. As a youthful conscript he played the piano to the wounded and dying in a camp hospital, then when the war was over worked for two years as operetta *repetiteur* in Blecher, a country town, which led to his directing Humperdinck's *Hansel and Gretel.* His philosophy and music studies in Cologne were paid for by working as a nightclub pianist and accompanist to a touring magician, capitalizing on his skills at jazz improvisation. In 1950, he co-authored and composed *Burleska,* a pantomime extravaganza for speaker, solo singers, choir and chamber ensemble. It was his nearest venture into opera for twenty-seven years.

The avant-garde composing milieu in which Stockhausen rapidly assumed a leading role had little sympathy for either the social or the narrative conventions of traditional operatic entertainment, thriving instead on the ritual of the concert platform and a music of deliberately cryptic codes and utterances as well as dazzling instrumental effects. The taboo against representational elements, forbidding the use of a conventional tonal language, continuous narrative or recognizable characters, arose from a desire to reinvent music from ground zero, and it led to a style of spiritual abstraction strangely similar in inspiration to the mathematical patterning of traditional Islamic art. Nevertheless, the ecstatic verbal confusion of *Gesang der Jünglinge* (1955-56) for five-channel electronic sound incorporating a boy soprano's voice, had undeniable dramatic impact as an image of the biblical fiery furnace and its divinely-protected survivors, and the cantata *Momente* (1961-64; revised 1971-74), an accompanied stream-of-consciousness monologue for soprano solo, though static and essentially radiophonic in conception, betrayed a well-developed sense of comedy and impressive emotional and dramatic range.

After 1970, elements of visible ritual, often parodying the stiffness of concert-hall behavior, but always in strict obedience to the underlying musical agenda, gradually infiltrated Stockhausen's instrumental and orchestral compositions. Anecdotal events from everyday musical life provide comic relief in *Trans* (1971), in *Tierkreis* (1975) and the choir opera '*Atmen gibt das Leben . . .*' (1974-77) the musical form is translated into through-composed and choreographed stage actions. The underlying motive of his visionary cantata *Sirius* (1975-77) for soprano, bass, trumpet and bass clarinet is self-evidently the same kind of visitation celebrated by Steven Spielberg in the movie *Close Encounters of the Third Kind.* The increasingly visual choreography of all of Stockhausen's music during this time (and retrospectively in his revivals of earlier compositions) can be regarded in part as a gradual progress toward finding a gestural and scenic vocabulary; but it can equally be seen as a shrewd pre-emptive tactic to ensure control of the visual presentation of his works in a new age of video and interpretative license in opera generally.

—Robin Maconie

STOLZ, Teresa (Teresina [Terezie] Stolzová).

Soprano. Born 5 June 1834, in Elbekosteletz (now Kostelec nad Labem), Bohemia. Died 23 August 1902, in Milan. Studied at Prague Conservatory, with Luigi Ricci in Trieste, and with Lamperti in Milan. Operatic debut in Tbilisi, 1857; Spoleto debut as Leonora in *Il trovatore,* 1864; Teatro alla Scala debut as Giovanna d'Arco, 1865; sang Leonora in the revision of *La forza del destino,* 1869; the first Italian Aïda, 1872; created soprano role in Verdi's Requiem, Milan, 1874; in St Petersburg, 1876-77; retired, 1879.

Publications

By STOLZ: correspondence–

Luzio, A., editor. "Il carteggio di Verdi con la Stolz e la Waldmann." *Carteggi verdiani* 2 (Rome, 1935): 222; 4 (Rome, 1947): 189.
Zoppi, Umberto, editor. *Angelo Mariani, Giuseppe Verdi e Teresa Stolz in un carteggio inedito.* Milan, 1947.

About STOLZ: books–

Šolin, J. *T. Stolzová: první a nejslavější Aida* [*Stolz: The First and Most Celebrated Aïda*]. Melnik, 1944; second edition, 1946.

articles–

Cenzato, G. "Verdi e la Stolz." *Corriere della sera* 30 October 1932; reprinted in *Itinerari verdiana.* Parma, 1949: 148; Milan 2/1955: 127.
Walker, Frank. *The Man Verdi.* London, 1962: 283.
Jares, S. "Pevkyne Tereza Stolzová (1834-1902)." *Hudebni Veda* 22/3 (1985): 268.

* * *

Dramatic soprano Teresa, or Teresina, Stolz is most closely associated with the works, and life, of Giuseppe Verdi. Having made her debut in Tbilisi in 1857, she subsequently sang in Odessa and Constantinople and scored significant successes in Nice and Granada, singing Leonora in Verdi's *Il trovatore* and Bellini's Norma (both in 1863), followed by Anaide in Rossini's *Mosè* and Elvira in Verdi's *Ernani* (in 1864). Her first appearance in Italy was in Spoleto as Leonora, also in 1864. Between 1864 and 1872 she appeared throughout Italy, singing in the opera houses of Palermo, Florence, Cesena, Reggio Emilia, Treviso, Parma, Rome, Genoa, Vicenza, Padua, Trieste, Turin, Sinigaglia, Venice, and Brescia, in such roles as Gilda in Verdi's *Rigoletto,* Verdi's Lady Macbeth, Giselda in Verdi's *I lombardi,* Elena in Verdi's *I vespri siciliani,* Amelia in Verdi's *Un ballo in maschera,* and Malipiero's Linda d'Ispahan—a list that shows Stolz's range, from lyric coloratura roles to heavy dramatic ones. At the Teatro alla Scala she sang Verdi's Giovanna d'Arco, Pisani's Rebecca, and Donizetti's Lucrezia Borgia in 1865, and Leonora in Giannini's *Fieschi* in 1869. Her performances in *Ernani* and Rossini's *Guillaume Tell* in Bologna in 1864 were conducted by Angelo Mariani, a conductor with close ties to Verdi who later became Stolz's lover. When Verdi's *Don Carlo* was first given in its Italian version at La Scala in 1868 (its premiere had been held in Paris, in French), Stolz was chosen to sing Elisabetta. The first Italian performances of *La forza del destino* (the premiere had been in St Petersburg), a production supervised by Verdi at La Scala in 1869, had Stolz as Leonora, and she was also the first Italian Aïda (Cairo had seen the work's premiere) in 1872. After 1872 she sang only Verdi roles, with the exception of Alice in *Robert le diable* and Rachel in Halévy's *La juive.* Her last creation of a Verdi part (although not an operatic role) was in the Requiem in 1874, which she sang at La Scala and on a European tour. She continued to appear on the operatic stage until 1877, and she sang a final Requiem in 1879 at the Teatro alla Scala.

Stolz's voice has been described as a powerful instrument, both passionate and disciplined; she exhibited a substantial upper extension above high C and possessed the prodigious breath control required for the long arching lines of Verdi's music. Blanche Roosevelt's 1875 review of Stolz's performance in the Requiem, published in the *Chicago Times,* communicates her achievement: "Mme Stoltz's [*sic*] voice is a pure soprano, with immense compass and of the most perfectly beautiful quality one ever listened to, from the lowest note to the highest. Her phrasing is the most superb I ever heard and her intonation something faultless. She takes a tone and sustains it until it seems that her respiration is quite exhausted, and then she has only commenced to hold it. The tones are as fine and clearly cut as diamond, and sweet as a silver bell; but the power she gives a high C is something amazing. She is said to be the greatest singer in the world. . . ."

Stolz had a significant influence on Verdi, both professionally and personally. He apparently had her voice in mind when he created the role of Aïda, and she therefore had a major part in creating the voice type we now refer to as a "Verdi soprano." Verdi's close professional connection with Stolz put a strain on his relationship with Mariani, leading to a complete break by 1870; Mariani then shifted his allegiance to Wagner and led the first performance of his music in Italy, making Stolz, in a sense, a catalyst in the introduction of Wagner's music to the Italian public. In addition, Verdi's attentions to Stolz were the source of a great deal of tension in Verdi's marriage to Giuseppina Strepponi. The nature and extent of Verdi's nonprofessional relationship with Stolz remain unclear, although most writers feel there was at least strong affection between them.

After her separation from Mariani, Stolz remained a frequent guest at the Verdis' home at Sant' Agata, and she remained close to the family until Verdi's death in 1901. She died the following year in Milan.

—Michael Sims

————————

THE STONE GUEST [Kamenniy gost].

Composer: Alexander Dargomïzhsky [completed by C.A. Cui and scored by Rimsky-Korsakov].

Librettist: set to the poem by Alexander Pushkin.

First Performance: St Petersburg, Mariinsky, 28 February 1872.

Roles: Don Juan (tenor); Leporello (bass); Donna Anna (soprano); Don Carlos (baritone); Laura (mezzo-soprano); A Monk (bass); First and Second Guests (tenor, bass); Statue of the Commandant (bass).

Publications

book–

Levik, B. *'Kammeniy gost' Dargomïzhskovo—'Mozart i Salieri' N. Rimskovo-Korsakovo—'Skupoy rïstar S. Rakhmaninova* [Dargomïzhsky's *Stone Guest*—Rimsky-Korsakov's *Mozart and Salieri*—Rachmaninov's *The Miserly Knight*]. Moscow and Leningrad, 1949.
Cui, C.A. *Izbranniye stat'i* [selected articles, some of which are on *Rusalka* and *The Stone Guest*]. Leningrad, 1952.

articles–

Abraham, Gerald. "*The Stone Guest.*" In *Studies in Russian Music,* 68. London, 1936.

Rabinovich, D. "K. vozobnovlenniyu *Kammenovo gostya* [the revival of *The Stone Guest*]. *Sovetskaya muzyka* no. 1 (1960): 62.

Blagovidova, N. "Kammaniÿ gost" [*The Stone Guest*]. *Sovetskaya muzyka* no. 7 (1963): 87.

Bremini, I. "Trieste." *Opera* 20 (1969): 535. [*The Stone Guest*].

Baker, Jennifer. "Dargomizhsky, Realism, and *The Stone Guest.*" *Music Review* 37 (1976): 193.

Cuker, Anatolij. "*Kamennyi gost*' kak muzykal'naja koncepcija" [*The Stone Guest* as a musical work]. *Sovetskaya muzyka* 5 (1980): 108.

Mikseeva, Galina. "O dramaturgiceskoj roli garmonii v *Kamennom goste* Dargomyzskogo" [dramaturgical function of harmony in *The Stone Guest*]. In *Problemy stilevogo obnovlenija v russkoj klassiceskoj i sovetskoj muzyke. Sbornik naucnyh trudov Moskovskoi konservatorii,* edited by Irina Stepanova and Irina Brezneva. Moscow, 1983.

*　　*　　*

The Stone Guest is an anomaly—an opera much talked and written about, but one which is seldom performed. As a result of this paradox, much that is reported about the work is based on hearsay or upon early commentary rather than upon first-hand knowledge or experience.

This three-act work was left unfinished by Dargomïzhsky; Cesar Cui, as per Dargomïzhsky's expressed wishes, wrote the prelude and the end of the first scene, and Nicolai Rimsky-Korsakov orchestrated the piano score. The story line which Pushkin developed is essentially the same Don Juan legend that served Mozart so admirably in his *Don Giovanni:* after being exiled for killing the Commandant in a duel precipitated by his untoward attention to Donna Anna, the older gentleman's wife, Don Juan maintains his reputation as a skilled rake and swordsman by killing Don Carlos in a duel over the latter's betrothed, Laura. The Don resumes his love-making with the Commandant's wife in the shadow of her deceased husband's stone statue. Donna Anna, by no means the grieving widow, makes a tryst with her lover as the Don taunts the statue to appear at the designated rendezvous. In the midst of a sumptuous dinner of which Don Juan and his latest "victim" are partaking, the statue, a.k.a the stone guest, does indeed appear and, in one of opera's major examples of retribution, carries the unwilling lothario off to hell.

Although *The Stone Guest* cannot be called a masterpiece, it is, nevertheless, of historic importance because of the influence it exerted on the course of Russian opera. For one thing, Dargomïzhsky broke with the conventional operatic practices of the Italians and the French and, in league with the Russian Realist philosophers, such as Chernyshevsky, proclaimed "truth in art" as his primary goal. The meaning of the words was to be the focal point around which the opera revolved; consequently, coloratura arias and, indeed, melodic ornamentation of any kind, were to be eschewed in favor of what is essentially a continuous recitative or arioso. The vocal lines in *The Stone Guest* are determined by the inflections, stresses, and emotive suggestions of the words. The orchestral background consists mainly of chords, a good number of which were regarded by critics of the day as "strange" owing to the fact that they were often derived from the whole-tone scales which characterize the vocal declamation. Dargomïzhsky

himself referred to his opera as a "strange work." To varying degrees, Cui, Rimsky-Korsakov, and Mussorgsky were influenced by their colleague's theories of naturalness, although none of them applied them with rigor (cf. Rimsky-Korsakov's *Mozart and Salieri*). The rejection of arias and other set pieces bears a superficial resemblance to the approach taken by Richard Wagner, but Dargomïzhsky had a strong aversion to Wagner's "music of the future"; the Realist thinkers were undoubtedly the spark for his radical departure from the Glinka tradition. Rubinstein and Tchaikovsky disavowed the declamatory style, the latter pointing out that opera, by its very nature, was based on *pseudo,* and that it was an art form in which truth, in its common definition, was not at all necessary.

The Stone Guest will continue to intrigue, to tantalize, and to invite commentary. Its ultimate merits as a stage work will not be determined until there are more frequent performances which do full justice to the composer's intentions.

—David Z. Kushner

STORACE, Nancy [Ann Selina].

Soprano. Born 27 October 1765, in London. Died 24 August 1817, in London. Married: John Abraham Fisher, 1783. Studied in London with Sacchini and Rauzzini; Italian opera debut, 1780; sang prima donna roles in Vienna, 1783-87; premiered the role of Susanna in Mozart's *Le nozze di Figaro,* 1786; sang in London, performing in many of the operas by her brother Stephan, 1787-1808; retired in 1808.

Publications

About STORACE: articles–

Sands, Mollie. "Mozart's First Susanna." *Monthly Musical Record* (1944): 178.

Matthews, B. "The Childhood of Nancy Storace." *Musical Times* 40 (1969): 733.

Flothuis, M. "Mozart and Anna Selina Storace." *Notes on Notes.* Buren, 1974.

Geiringer, K. and I. Geiringer, "Stephen and Nancy Storace in Vienna." *Essays on Bach and Other Matters: a Tribute to Gerhard Herz.* Louisville, Kentucky, 1981.

Hodges, S. "One of the Most Accomplished Women of Her Age." *Music Review* 50 (1989): 93.

*　　*　　*

Ann Selina Storace is remembered today because she was the original Susanna in Mozart's *Le nozze di Figaro.* Since at that time opera composers tailored their music to suit the singers who were to perform it, and since Mozart was particularly compliant in this respect, as well as being a close friend of Nancy (as she was generally called), it seems likely that the role of Susanna mirrors some of her own characteristics—the charm which captivated audiences wherever she sang (even in middle age, when she had little voice left), her gaiety, generosity, quick wit, strong personality, acting ability, and especially the humor which rarely failed her.

On the stage, Nancy sang only in comic opera. Neither her voice nor her temperament was suited to *opera seria,* which she never attempted. Some critics, such as Burney and Earl Mount Edgcumbe, thought her voice harsh, but no one disputed her profound knowledge or her musicianship.

When she first went to Vienna to sing at the Burgtheater, her acting was criticized as being greatly exaggerated. With the ready intelligence which characterized the whole of her career she quickly modified it, and for the four years during which she sang *prima donna* roles at the Burgtheater she was the undisputed favorite of the Viennese public. She threw herself with total commitment into every role she played, so that the spectators were bewitched and the other actors were put entirely in the shade. "She united in her person," the *Allgemeine musikalische Zeitung* wrote, "all the gifts of nature, education and technique which one may hope for in performances of Italian comic opera." The tenor Michael Kelly, who often sang with her both in Vienna and in London, believed that in her line she was the finest singer in Europe.

Le nozze di Figaro was the only one of Mozart's operas in which she sang, but her friendship with Mozart is documented through the scena and rondo "Ch'io mi scordi di te . . ." (K 505), which he wrote for her farewell concert before she left Vienna, himself accompanying her on the piano. The autograph score, which is lost, bore the inscription *Composta per la Signora Storace, dal suo servo e amico W.A. Mozart.* Michael Kelly, too, records a chamber music concert at the Storaces' house in Vienna (her mother and composer brother were there with her) at which Mozart played the viola, Haydn and Dittersdorf the first and second violins and Vanhal the cello.

Nancy was probably the first person to introduce Mozart's opera music to English audiences, when on 9 May 1789 she and the bass baritone Francesco Benucci introduced the duet "Crudel! perche finora" into Gazzaniga's opera *La vendemmia.* The next year, in a *pasticcio,* she sang one air each from *Don Giovanni* and *Figaro.*

Vienna marked the apex of her career, for though she sang for another twenty years she appeared mainly in indifferent English comic operas written by indifferent composers to bad libretti. Her voice deteriorated quickly, presumably because she had been singing in public since the age of seven, but her craftsmanship and acting ability stayed with her always. She sang not only in opera but also in oratorio in London and the provinces, especially at the annual concerts in Westminster Abbey that began in 1784. Mount Edgcumbe thought that this was where she was heard to the greatest effect, "for in that space the harsh part of her voice was lost, while its power and clearness filled the whole of it."

Storace was a professional through and through. Fair weather or foul, she turned up at the opera house to sing her role; and when, as often happened, the theaters were in difficulty because a singer had proved inadequate, she was brought in to fill the gap. Together with Michael Kelly she raised the standard of performance in the London opera houses to a level hitherto unknown; and with him, too, she introduced a new style of acting whereby the performers, who had previously stood in a straight line facing the audience, moved about the stage in a more natural way. Once, during a performance of her brother's opera *The Haunted Tower,* the kettle drummer was suddenly found to be missing just when he was needed. Nancy seized the sticks and drummed away as if to the manner born. On another occasion, when she was singing in *Il re Teodoro in Venezia* and the orchestra was proving itself totally incompetent, she baffled the efforts of the musicians to make her sing out of tune, quick or slow— as they fiddled, she modulated.

Sweetness her voice may have lacked, but of her charm, musicality and ability to hold an audience spellbound there is overwhelming evidence.

—Sheila Hodges

Nancy Storace, engraving, 1788

STORCHIO, Rosina.

Soprano. Born 19 May 1876, in Venice. Died 24 July 1945, in Milan. Studied under A. Giovannini and G. Fatuo at the Milan Conservatory; debut as Micaela in *Carmen,* Teatro dal Verme, Milan; Teatro alla Scala debut in *Werther,* 1895; created the role of Mimì in Leoncavallo's *La bohème,* Venice, 1897; created several other roles, including the title role of *Madama Butterfly,* Teatro alla Scala, 1904; continued to appear at La Scala until 1918; toured South America and Europe; engaged at Manhattan Opera House, New York, and appeared at the Chicago Grand Opera, 1920-21.

Publications

About STORCHIO: articles–

Celletti, R. "Rosina Storchio." *Musica e dischi* no. 91 (1954): 4.
Hutchinson, T. "Rosina Storchio." *Record Collector* 7 (1958): 53.

Celletti, R. "Rosina Storchio" [with discography]. *Record News* 4 (1960): 429.

* * *

It is Storchio's misfortune that her name is indissolubly linked with one of the greatest of operatic fiascos—the premiere of *Madama Butterfly* at the Teatro alla Scala on 17th February 1904. Puccini had not only been confident of success, but certain that in Storchio he had an ideal interpreter for perhaps the most taxing role he had ever written and his favorite heroine. The performance was to turn into an anti-Puccini demonstration by the audience—hisses, cat-calls, laughter. Storchio herself was subjected to ribald remarks.

Traditional history has it that the opera was then withdrawn, revised and presented for a new premiere three months later at Brescia with Salomea Kruszelnicka in the title role. In fact the modifications were not substantial; it is by no means clear that they were included in the performance in Buenos Aires five weeks after the Brescia premiere when Storchio again undertook the role with Toscanini conducting. Nonetheless she declined to sing the role in Italy again, only finally relenting near the end of her career in 1920.

Storchio was only seventeen when she made her debut in Milan as Michaela in *Carmen*. After singing successfully around Italy she made her first appearance at the Teatro alla Scala in 1895 as Sophie in *Werther*. She was to remain a favorite at Italy's leading opera house for more than twenty years. At the same time a major international career took her to Germany, Portugal, Russia and Spain, Argentina, Cuba and Mexico. Curiously she did not sing in the USA until she appeared with the Chicago company in 1920-21 when she was well past her best: Toscanini, a life-long friend, advised her not to appear in New York at this stage in her career.

Apart from Madama Butterfly Storchio appeared in four other premieres—Leoncavallo's *Bohème* at Venice in 1897 and *Zazà* at La Scala in 1900; Giordano's *Siberia* again at La Scala in 1903, and finally Mascagni's *Lodoletta* in Rome in 1917.

Storchio's voice is an attractive light lyrical soprano. She was clearly an affecting actress and there is certainly a great deal of expressiveness in her singing on her few records. Filippo Sacchi wrote, "There will never be another Violetta to sing with such unutterable perfection, moving, laughing, loving, suffering as the slight and gentle Rosina Storchio (with) her enormous seductive eyes, her delightful coquetry, her gay tenderness, her fresh spontaneity."

Such qualities are apparent on her discs, even if some have argued that they do not do full justice to her voice. Her recorded repertoire extends from Bellini and Donizetti to Giordano's *Siberia*. There is some beautiful singing in the arias from *Don Pasquale* and *Linda di Chamonix* and a sparkling vivacity to Musetta's aria from Leoncavallo's *Bohème*, although she actually sang the role of Mimi on stage! In view of Sacchi's comment we can only regret the non-publication of the long duet from the second act of *La traviata* which she recorded with Stracciari.

—Stanley Henig

STRACCIARI, Riccardo.

Baritone. Born 26 June 1875, in Casalecchio di Reno, Italy. Died 10 October 1955, in Rome; studied with Ulisse Masetti in Bologna; opera debut as Marcello in Bologna, 1898; sang at Teatro alla Scala 1904-24; sang at Covent Garden, 1905; sang at the Metropolitan Opera, 1906-08; sang throughout Europe, 1909-17; sang with Chicago Opera, 1917-19; sang in Europe, 1920-46; taught in Naples and Rome; teacher of Boris Christoff and Alexander Svéd.

Publications

About STRACCIARI: articles–

Schauensee, M. de, "A Visit with Riccardo Stracciari." *Opera News* 9 (1954): 8.
di Cave, Luciano et. al. "Riccardo Stracciari." *Record Collector* 30 no. 1-2 (1985): 3.
Celleti, R. "Riccardo Stracciari." *Record News* 3 (1958): 75.
"Opera has lost." *Opera News* 20 (1955): 28.

* * *

Riccardo Stracciari was, in many respects, the odd man out in an epoch of unparalleled baritone splendor. With Battistini still active, and contemporaries such as Scotti, Sammarco, Amato, Ruffo, and De Luca in their prime, he enjoyed the stature of a major artist, but was never able to secure real international preeminence. It would be hazardous to single him out above these many gifted contemporaries for sheer beauty of voice, dramatic insight, breadth of expression, or even technical virtuosity, but few singers can be said to have merged so many of these attributes as naturally or as thoroughly as did Stracciari. Lacking the eloquence of Battistini, the power of Ruffo, and perhaps the finish of Amato, he nonetheless had an imposing technique and an equally robust, colorful tone—and the good sense not to overextend himself, which allowed him to keep his voice decades after the careers of Amato and Ruffo were prematurely spent. His instrument was certainly superior to Scotti's, and by all accounts, including the recorded evidence, he was a considerably more refined interpreter than Sammarco. But as glorious as he sounds on the recordings made in this first decade of his career, he was received on the stage less enthusiastically than either. He was overshadowed by these better-established rivals during some of his most important international engagements—by Battistini and Sammarco at Covent Garden, Scotti at the Metropolitan Opera, and Ruffo at the Teatro Real in Madrid—and was rarely judged comparable to any of them by either the critics or the public.

Stracciari is perhaps best compared to De Luca, an artist whom he thought vocally his inferior, but whose singing and acting he greatly admired. Both were most comfortable in the pre-*verismo* repertory, and they shared a similar stable of roles more or less dominated by Figaro (*Il barbiere di Siviglia*) and Rigoletto. Both were acknowledged as true exponents of the *bel canto* style, and were formidable technicians, renowned as masters of legato and detailed phrase construction. Stracciari's voice was larger than De Luca's, and darker, but to its discredit, lacked much of the warmth and smoothness of tone that was the latter's great natural gift.

Europe remained the scene of Stracciari's greatest success. He was scarcely noticed at Covent Garden during Rendle's 1905 Autumn Season, where he sang four Amonasro (*Aïda*), a single Germont (*La traviata*), shared Rigoletto with Battistini and the Count Di Luna (*Il trovatore*) with Franz Costa, but where his voice was dismissed as muffled and not especially attractive. His two seasons at the Met (1906-1908) were eventful, but for him, undistinguished. Indeed, he appears to have aroused only the critics, who thought him well below the average of the artists then in residence. W.J. Henderson, reviewing his debut as Germont, described his voice as "throaty," which it often was, but also as "pallid," a charge that is difficult to reconcile with even the weakest of the contemporary recorded evidence. In all, he performed ten leading roles at the Met in 52 appearances. Thereafter his career was largely confined to Italy, notably at the Teatro alla Scala, where he remained for twenty years, and South America, though there were two seasons with the Chicago Opera in 1917-1919, guest appearances and tours in Spain, Russia, Mexico, Cuba, Canada, and Switzerland, and sporadic visits to Paris, Berlin, and Vienna. He did not appear in England after 1905.

Stracciari's stage repertory, which continued to expand as late as the 1930s, consisted of some sixty roles, most of them from earlier nineteenth-century Italian works. He sang fewer than a dozen French roles, but did manage to admit a number of interesting curiosities into the fold—Alfano's *La Risurrezione* and *L'ultimo Lord,* Strauss' *Feuersnot,* and revivals of Spontini's *La vestale* in Paris, and Ricci's *Crispino e la Comare* at the Chicago Opera. Contemporary accounts describe his acting as intelligent, uninhibited but rarely prone to excess, and calculated without being at all tentative.

He recorded prolifically between late 1904 and the summer of 1930, leaving well over 150 recordings. The overwhelming majority of them, down to the most ephemeral popular songs and folk tunes, are splendid. As a Verdi specialist he left fragmentary accounts of a dozen roles, along with a large sampling of titles drawn from the French and earlier Italian repertory, and a few arias from the dozen *verismo* roles with which he was more tentatively associated—works of Leoncavallo, Giordano, and Franchetti. Wolfrom (*Tannhäuser*), which he retained in his repertory as late as 1916, and for which he was highly acclaimed, is the only Wagnerian role from which he recorded, though he also appeared as Kurvenal (*Tristan und Isolde*) and Telramund (*Lohengrin*) on the stage. Like De Luca's, Stracciari's career lasted nearly a half century, during which his voice remained more or less unimpaired. He was still singing on Italian radio as late as the autumn of 1934 and concertizing in 1946, forty-eight years after his stage debut. His last studio sessions, made in Milan for Columbia, included complete recordings of *Il barbiere di Siviglia* (1929) and *Rigoletto* (1930), both stunning documents—as much for the singer's unexpected state of vocal preservation as for his fine dramatic disposition and the vitality of his interpretations. The voice we hear is large and responsive, with a prevailingly dark, often gloomy timbre that he was able to use to great expressive advantage. For all its distinctiveness, it was certainly flexible enough to accommodate with ease and equal conviction whatever was demanded of his most characteristic roles, whether it be foolishness, treachery, or pathos. The penetrating throatiness of the voice, its least attractive feature, grew more pronounced with age, but was tempered by an extraordinary working range of more than two octaves, which on top had a tenor-like clarity and forcefulness. This is especially evident in his early Fonotipia recordings which abound with taxing high notes and engaging

vocal characterizations all managed with little effort and great effect.

—William Shaman

LA STRANIERA [The Foreign Lady].

Composer: Vincenzo Bellini.

Librettist: Felice Romani (after Victor-Charles Prévost, Vicomte d'Arlincourt, *L'etrangère).*

First Performance: Milan, Teatro alla Scala, 14 February 1829.

Roles: Alaide (soprano); Lord of Montolino (bass); Isoletta (mezzo-soprano); Arturo (tenor); Baron Valdeburgo (baritone); Prior (bass); Osburg (tenor); chorus.

Publications

articles–

Lippmann, Friedrich. "Su *La Straniera* di Bellini." *Nuova rivista musicale italiana* 5 (1971): 565.

La straniera is a romantic story of doomed love, set in fourteenth-century Brittany. Arturo, count of Ravenstel, is engaged to Isoletta, daughter of the Lord of Montolino. But he is passionately attracted to a mysterious stranger, Alaide, a femme fatale despite herself. She is shunned by all the inhabitants of the castle, who have never seen her face (she goes about veiled). Her secluded existence suggests to them some unknown crime in her past. They believe she may be a witch. Arturo is warned by Alaide herself and by his friend the Baron Valdeburgo, that his love for her is absolutely hopeless. In a jealous rage Arturo stabs Valdeburgo, whom he believes to be his rival, and Alaide reveals that Arturo has stabbed her brother. Arturo plunges into the lake after Valdeburgo. When Alaide is found, more or less delirious, holding a bloody sword, she is arrested.

In the second act Alaide and Arturo are tried for Valdeburgo's slaying, but the wounded Valdeburgo appears at the trial and takes Alaide away. Arturo is coerced into marrying Isoletta. After the marriage ceremony a messenger announces that the queen has died and the king is now free to legitimize his bigamous union with Alaide, whom he had been forced to banish from his court. Arturo stabs himself, and the stranger, blaming a cruel fate, collapses before the horrified people.

La straniera, Bellini's fourth opera, led both the composer and the contemporary critics to assert that his was a significant, individual, and independent talent. Bellini was no simple, servile imitator of Rossini's style. His experiments in *La straniera* involved both the quality of the vocal declamation and the structure of the set numbers. A contemporary reviewer remarked on Bellini's melodic style in *La straniera* that "we hardly know whether to describe [it] as declaimed song or sung declamation." Actually, *La straniera* is not denuded of florid, coloratura lines. But at moments when characters are expressing their sentiments most urgently and sincerely—such as in the first act when Arturo first declares his love to Alaide ("Ah se tu vuoi fuggir") or when Valdeburgo first appears before the judges in act II ("Si, li sciogliete, o Giudici")—Bellini chooses to set their texts syllabically.

A shift in vocal style goes hand in hand with experimentation with set numbers in this opera. There are relatively few arias in *La straniera*—fewer than ensembles or even choruses. The impulsive and impetuous Arturo is given no aria. All his set numbers are ensembles; his vocal utterances are all results of interactions with other people, not reflection. Alaide receives her due as the prima donna—each act ends with a showy aria-finale for her. Her entrance number, however, is more imaginatively handled. When Alaide is first seen she is veiled; when she is first heard she is offstage, singing a romanza which she breaks off, mid-phrase, when she sees Arturo. Thus, her mysterious character is revealed not only by the words or melody she sings, but by the fragmented shape and obscured presentation of her entrance number.

The chorus is used for two different functions. It establishes ambience and local color, as with the opening barcarolle ("Voga, voga, il vento tace") or the hunting chorus ("Campo ai vetri") later in act I. Bellini was very pleased with the stereophonic effects he had composed into these choruses, having the voices sound from different parts of the stage. The chorus is also used, less successfully, as a kind of collective villain. In "La Straniera a cui fe" the chorus is meant to act as a malevolent force, stimulating Arturo's worst fears and suspicions, but Bellini seems not to have had the musical means for such a task, and the effect is more comic than ominous.

Perhaps one of Bellini's most successful creations in *La straniera* was the role of Valdeburgo, one of the earliest in a line of sympathetic, well-rounded baritone roles that Verdi would later develop more fully. Bellini was convinced that "a baritone can not play a lover." But the types of roles he created for baritones—father or uncle, jealous husband, friend—show far more variety than do his tenor roles.

—Charlotte Greenspan

STRATAS, Teresa [real name, Anastasia Strataki].

Soprano. Born 26 May 1938, in Toronto. Studied with Irene Jessner at Toronto Conservatory; from age twelve sang at nightclubs and at father's restaurant in Toronto; debut as Mimi with Canadian Opera, Toronto, 1958; won 1959 Metropolitan Opera Auditions of the Air and made Metropolitan debut that year as Poussette in *Manon*; created title role in Glanville-Hicks's *Nausicaa*, Athens Festival, 1960; Covent Garden debut as Mimi, 1961; sang Queen Isabella in Falla's *Atlántida*, Teatro alla Scala, 1962; sang Susanna in *Figaro* in Salzburg, 1972-73; sang *Salome* for German television, 1974; has made regular appearances in Munich, Hamburg, Paris, and at the Bol'shoy Theater; performed title role in first three-act production of Berg's *Lulu*, Paris, 1979; was Violetta in Zeffirelli's film version of *La traviata* (1983); was subject of film portrait by Harry Rasky, *StrataSphere;* Broadway debut in musical *Rags,* 1986; made an Officer of the Order of Canada, 1972.

Publications

About STRATAS: books–

Rasky, Harry. *Stratas: An Affectionate Tribute.* New York, 1988.

articles–

Morey, C. "Canadian Singers and the International Stage." *Opera Canada* 31/1 (1990): 32.

When Stratas auditioned for the Opera School at the Royal Conservatory of Music, University of Toronto in 1954, she was completely untrained, her only singing experience having been in the clubs and cafes of the local Greek community. She was nevertheless accepted, so striking was her natural ability, and she studied there for four years with Irene Jessner, her only teacher. Her progress was remarkably swift and unfolded with the intensity that has characterized everything she has done. In 1958 she made an impressive professional debut in Toronto as Mimi in *La bohème,* joined the Metropolitan Opera in October 1959, sang Cio-Cio-San at Vancouver in 1960, and in 1961 made her Covent Garden debut as Mimi. Through the 1960s she appeared at most of the principal opera houses in Europe and America in roles as varied as Yniold in *Pelléas et Mélisande,* Tatyana in *Eugene Onegin,* the Composer in *Ariadne auf Naxos,* and Despina in *Così fan tutte.* During this period she maintained about fifteen roles in her active repertoire, roles that covered a great vocal and dramatic range.

The alluring timbre of her voice has been described as "smoky" but that alone does not convey the tension in the sound. It is by no means a big voice, but it is especially well-focussed and projected with great power. In the Puccini roles in which she first established her reputation it is foregone that one of the requirements is beautiful, even voluptuous singing, but mere beauty of voice is only the starting point for a Stratas portrayal. More important are the shadings of the voice, the textual inflections, the exclamations that give varied insights into the character of the role. Although diminutive in stature (something that allowed her to play soubrettes and youths so convincingly) she has great presence on stage, and has developed an acting ability of extraordinary subtlety and detail to make her one of the greatest and most affecting actress/singers on the operatic stage.

In 1974 she sang the title role in *Salome* for German television in a performance that records everything that makes Stratas so remarkable. Vocally she is able to rattle off the chatter of the girlish Salome, to express the bewilderment and growing sensuality when she first encounters Jochanaan, and finally to give free rein to Salome's depraved rapture in the final scene. Visually Stratas depicts with flashing detail the broad development of Salome from a naive, puzzled and spoiled child to a woman overwhelmed by sensual desire. At the climactic moments she does not hesitate to push her voice to the emotional edge to project the intensity of the action.

In the 1970s Stratas sharply curtailed her appearances and became more and more selective about what and when she would sing. She did allow herself one of her greatest triumphs in the title role in the full three-act premiere of Berg's *Lulu* at Paris in 1979, and later that same year she appeared at the Metropolitan as Jenny in Weill's *Aufstieg und Fall der Stadt Mahagonny.* Through the latter work she came to know

Weill's music and when, in the 1980s she had virtually stopped singing in public, she devoted herself to the recording of his songs. She did appear in Zeferelli's 1983 film of *La traviata* where the exaggerated production could not diminish the riveting tension, the vulnerability and desperation that she brought to the role of Violetta.

Her interest in exploring new avenues brought her to the Broadway show *Rags,* which had a disastrously short run but which brought Stratas a Tony Award for the best actress in a musical, and to the recording of Julie in Jerome Kern's *Showboat.* Stratas was always unpredictable and with the passing of time she had more and more the need to live her own life privately. The self-evaluation and the exhaustive scrutiny with which she considered any role have had the result of fewer Stratas performances, but she has maintained the finesse, the shading, and the conviction of her performances.

—Carl Morey

STRAUSS, Richard.

Composer. Born 11 June 1864, in Munich. Died 8 September 1949, in Garmisch-Partenkirchen. Married: the singer Pauline de Ahna, 10 September 1894. Studied piano with A. Tombo, harpist of the court orchestra, 1868; studied the violin with Benno Walter, concertmaster of the court orchestra, 1872; studied music theory and instrumentation with F.W. Meyer, court conductor, 1875-1880; graduated from the Gymnasium, 1882; went to lectures on philosophy at the University of Munich, 1882-83; Symphony in D minor performed in Munich, conducted by Hermann Levi, 30 March 1881; violin concerto performed in Munich by Benno Walter, 5 December 1882; American premiere, Symphony in F minor, conducted by Theodore Thomas and performed by the New York Philharmonic, 13 December 1884; in Berlin, 1883-84; assistant conductor to Bülow's orchestra in Meiningen, then principal conductor, 1885; in Italy, spring 1886; a conductor of the court opera in Munich, 1886-89; conductor of the Weimar court orchestra, 1889-94; tone-poem *Don Juan* premiered 11 November 1889; in Greece, Egypt, and Sicily, 1892-93; conductor of the Berlin Philharmonic, 1894-95; conducted his own works in Brussels, Liège, various German cities, and Moscow, 1896; visited Amsterdam, Paris, London, and Barcelona, 1897; worked for the Berlin Opera, 1898-1918; honorary Ph.D., University of Heidelberg, 1903; premiere of *Symphonia domestica* in the United States, 1904; co-director (with Franz Schalk) of the Vienna State Opera, 1919-24; concert tour in America, 1921; V.P.O. concert tour of South America, 1923; president of the Reichsmusikkammer under the Nazi regime, 15 November 1933 (resigned 1935); concert tour in London, 1936; Gold Medal of the London Philharmonic Society; English concert tour, 1947; faced the post-war court in Munich for collaborating with the Nazis, but was not found guilty.

Operas

Guntram, Strauss, 1892-93, Weimar, Court Theater, 10 May 1894; revised, Weimar, Deutsches Nationaltheater, 29 October 1940.

Feuersnot, E. von Wolzogen, 1900-01, Dresden, Court Opera, 21 November 1901.

Salome, O. Wilde (translated H. Lachmann), 1904-05, Dresden Court Opera, 9 December 1905.

Elektra, H. von Hofmannsthal, 1906-08, Dresden, Court Opera, 25 January 1909.

Der Rosenkavalier, H. von Hofmannsthal, 1909-10, Dresden, Court Opera, 26 January 1911.

Ariadne auf Naxos, H. von Hofmannsthal, 1911-12, Stuttgart, Court Theater, 25 October 1912; revised, 1916, Vienna, Court Opera, 4 October 1916.

Die Frau ohne Schatten, H. von Hofmannsthal, 1914-18, Vienna, Staatsoper, 10 October 1919.

Intermezzo, Strauss, 1918-23, Dresden, Staatsoper, 4 November 1924.

Die ägyptische Helena, H. von Hofmannsthal, 1923-27, Dresden, Staatsoper, 6 June 1928; revised (act II), L. Wallerstein, 1932-33, Salzburg, Festspielhaus, 14 August 1933.

Arabella, H. von Hofmannsthal, 1929-32, Dresden, Staatsoper, 1 July 1933.

Die schweigsame Frau, S. Zweig (after Jonson), 1933-34, Dresden, Staatsoper, 24 June 1935.

Friedenstag, J. Gregor, 1935-36, Munich, Staatsoper, 24 July 1938.

Daphne, J. Gregor, 1936-37; Dresden, Staatsoper, 15 October 1938.

Die Liebe der Danaë, J. Gregor (after H. Hofmannsthal), 1938-40, Salzburg, Festspielhaus, dress rehearsal for canceled premiere, 16 August 1944; first performance, Salzburg, Festspielhaus, 14 August 1952 [posthumous].

Capriccio, Krauss and Strauss, 1940-41, Munich, Staatsoper, 28 October 1942.

Other works: incidental music, orchestral works (including tone poems), instrumental and chamber music, vocal music, songs, piano pieces.

Publications/Writings

By STRAUSS: books–

Strauss, F., ed. *Richard Strauss: Briefwechsel mit Hugo von Hofmannsthal.* Berlin, 1925; English translation, 1928.

Schuh, W., ed. *Betrachtungen und Erinnerungen.* Zurich, 1949; 2nd ed., 1952; 3rd ed., 1981; English translation as *Recollections and Reflections,* London, 1953; 1974.

Richard Strauss et Romain Rolland: correspondance, fragments de journal. Paris, 1951; English translation, edited by Rollo Meyers, London, 1968.

Schuh, W. ed. *Richard Strauss und Hugo von Hofmannsthal: Briefwechsel: Gesamtausgabe.* Zurich, 1952; 2nd ed., 1955; English translation, 1961; 1980.

———. *Richard Strauss: Briefe an die Eltern 1882-1906.* Zurich, 1954.

Trenner, Franz, ed. *Richard Strauss: Dokumente seines Lebens und Schaffens.* Munich, 1954.

Tenschert, R., ed. *Richard Strauss und Joseph Gregor: Briefwechsel 1934-1949.* Salzburg, 1955.

Schuh, W., ed. *Richard Strauss, Stefan Zweig: Briefwechsel.* Frankfurt am Main, 1957; English translation as *A Confidential Matter: the Letters of Richard Strauss and Stefan Zweig, 1931-1935,* Berkeley, 1977.

Kämper, D., ed. *Richard Strauss und Franz Wüllner im Briefwechsel.* Cologne, 1963.

Kende, G.K., and W. Schuh, eds. *Richard Strauss, Clemens Krauss: Briefwechsel.* Munich, 1963; 2nd ed., 1964.

Grasberger, F., ed. *Der Strom der Töne trug mich fort: die Welt um Richard Strauss in Briefen.* Tutzing, 1967.

Ott, A. *Richard Strauss und Ludwig Thuille: Briefe der Freundschaft 1877-1907.* Munich, 1969.

Schuh, W., ed. *Richard Strauss: Briefwechsel mit Willi Schuh.* Zurich, 1969.

Trenner, Franz, ed. *Cosima Wagner—Richard Strauss. Ein Briefwechsel.* Tutzing, 1978.

with Hans Guido von Bülow. *Correspondence.* Edited by Willi Schuh and Franz Trenner, translated by A. Gishford. Westport, Connecticut, 1979.

Blaukopf, Herta, ed. *Gustav Mahler/Richard Strauss: Briefwechsel 1888-1911.* Munich, 1980; English translation, Chicago, 1984.

Krause, E., ed. *Richard Strauss Dokumente: Aufsätze, Aufzeichnungen, Vorworte, Reden, Briefe.* Leipzig, 1980.

Trenner, Franz, ed. *Briefwechsel* [with Ludwig Thuille]. Tutzing, 1980.

Brosche, G., ed. *Ein Briefwechsel* [with Franz Schalk]. Tutzing, 1983.

Schlötterer, Roswitha, ed. *Ein Briefwechsel: Richard Strauss—Rudolf Hartmann.* Tutzing, 1984.

articles–

Gregor, Joseph. "Strauss—Bahr Briefwechsel." In *Meister und Meisterbriefe um Hermann Bahr,* p. 49. Vienna, 1947.

Schuh, W., and Franz Trenner, eds. "Hans von Bülow/Richard Strauss: Briefwechsel." *Richard Strauss Jahrbuch* (1954): 7; English translation as *Correspondence,* London, 1955.

Krause, E., ed. "Richard Strauss: ein Brief an Dora Wihan-Weis." *Richard Strauss Jahrbuch* (1959-60): 55.

Schuh, W., ed. "Richard Strauss und Anton Kippenberg: Briefwechsel." *Richard Strauss Jahrbuch* (1959-60): 114.

"Erlebnis und Bekenntnis des jungen Richard Strauss" [letter to Cosima Wagner]. *Internationale Mitteilungen: Richard-Strauss-Gesellschaft* no. 30 (1961): 1.

Schmieder, W. "57 unveröffentlichte Briefe und Karten von Richard Strauss in der Stadt-und Universitätsbibliothek Frankfurt/Main." In *Festschrift Helmuth Osthoff,* 163. Tutzing, 1961.

Kende, G.K. "Aus dem Briefwechsel Richard Strauss/Clemens Krauss: 12 unveröffentlichte Briefe." *Schweizerische Musikzeitung/Revue musicale suisse* 106 (1966): 2.

"Richard Strauss-Ernest Roth: Correspondence." *Tempo* 98 (1972): 9.

Birkin, K.W. "Strauss, Zweig and Gregor: Unpublished Letters." *Music and Letters* 56 (1975): 180.

"Richard Strauss—Ludwig Karpath: Briefwechsel." *Richard Strass-Blätter* new series 6 (1975): 2; 7 (1976): 1.

"Richard Strauss—Roland Tenschert: Briefwechsel." *Richard Strauss-Blätter* (1977): 1.

"Zeitgemässe Glossen für Erziehung zur Musik." *Zeitschrift für Musikpädagogik* 3/no. 6 (1978): 74.

with Hans Adler. "Richard Strauss und Hans Adler im Briefwechsel." Edited by G. Klaus Kende. *Richard Strauss-Blätter* new series 4 (1980): 18.

Wünsche, D., ed. "Richard Strauss—Heinz Tiessen: Briefwechsel." *Richard Strauss-Blätter* no. 6 (1981): 23.

———. "Richard Strauss—Gerhart Hauptmann: Briefwechsel." *Richard Strauss-Blätter* (1983).

———. "Richard Strauss—Heinz Tietjen: Briefe der Freundschaft." *Richard Strauss-Blätter* (1988).

About STRAUSS: books–

Gilman, L. *Strauss' Salome: a Guide to the Opera.* New York, 1906.

Schmitz, E. *Richard Strauss als Musikdramatiker: eine aesthetisch-kritische Studie.* Munich, 1907.

Newman, E. *Richard Strauss.* London, 1908.

Bekker, P. *Das Musikdrama der Gegenwart.* Stuttgart, 1909.

Fischer-Plasser, E. *Einführung in die Musik von Richard Strauss und Elektra.* Leipzig, 1909.

Gräner, G. *Richard Strauss: Musikdramen.* Berlin, 1909.

Hübner, O.R. *Richard Strauss und das Musikdrama: Betrachtungen über den Wert oder Unwert gewisser Opernmusiken.* Leipzig, 1910.

Hutcheson, E. *Elektra by Richard Strauss: a Guide to the Opera with Musical Examples from the Score.* New York, 1910.

Steinitzer, Max. *Richard Strauss.* Berlin, 1911; 4th ed., 1927.

Specht, Richard. *Richard Strauss und sein Werk.* Leipzig, 1921.

Kapp, J. *Richard Strauss und die Berliner Oper.* Berlin, 1934-39.

Krüger, K.-J. *Hugo von Hofmannsthal und Richard Strauss: Versuch einer Deutung des künstlerischen Weges Hugo von Hofmannsthals, mit einem Anhang: erstmalige Veröffentlichung der bisher ungedruckten einstigen Vertonung eines Hofmannsthalschen Gedichtes durch Richard Strauss.* Berlin, 1935.

Röttger, H. *Das Formproblem bei Richard Strauss gezeigt an der "Die Frau ohne Schatten".* Berlin, 1937.

Gregor, J. *Richard Strauss: der Meister der Oper.* Munich, 1939; 2nd ed., 1942.

Hartmann, R. *Capriccio: ein Konversationsstück für Musik in l Aufzug von Clemens Krauss und Richard Strauss, op. 85: Regieangaben nach Erfahrungen der Uraufführung, Staatsoper München, 28. Oktober 1942.* Berlin, 1943.

Pryce-Jones, A. *Richard Strauss: Der Rosenkavalier.* London, 1947.

Schuh, W. *Uber Opern von Richard Strauss.* Zurich, 1947.

Busch, Fritz. *Aus dem Leben: eines Musikers.* Zurich, 1949; English translation by M. Straghey, London, 1953.

Pfistner, Kurt. *Richard Strauss, Weg—Gestalt—Denkmal.* Vienna, 1949.

Lindner, D. *Richard Strauss/Joseph Gregor: Die Liebe der Danae: Herkunft, Inhalt und Gestaltung eines Opernwerkes.* Vienna, 1952.

Schuch, F. von. *Richard Strauss, Ernst von Schuch und Dresdens Oper.* Leipzig, 1952; 2nd ed., 1953.

Schuh, W., ed. *Hugo von Hofmannsthal: Danae oder die Vernunftheirat: Szenarium und Notizen.* Frankfurt, 1952.

Hausswald, G. *Richard Strauss: ein Beitrag zur Dresdener Operngeschichte seit 1945.* Dresden, 1953.

Roth, E. ed. *Richard Strauss: Bühnenwerke.* London, 1954.

Schuh, W. *Das Bühnenwerk von Richard Strauss in den unter Mitwirkung des Komponisten geschaffenen letzten Münchner Inszenierungen.* Zurich, 1954.

Krause, E. *Richard Strauss: Gestalt und Werke.* Leipzig, 1955; English translation as *Richard Strauss: The Man and his Work,* London, 1964.

Kende, G.K. *Richard Strauss and Clemens Krauss: eine Künstlerfreundschaft und ihr Zusammenarbeit an "Capriccio".* Munich, 1960.

Scanzoni, Signe. *Richard Strauss and his Singers.* Munich, 1961.

Baum, G. *"Hab' mir's gelobt, ihn lieb zu haben . . .": Richard Strauss und Hugo von Hofmannsthal nach ihrem Briefwechsel dargestellt.* Berlin, 1962.

Del Mar, N. *Richard Strauss: a Critical Commentary on his Life and Works.* London, 1962-72; with corrections, 1978.

Petzoldt, R. *Richard Strauss: sein Leben in Bildern.* Leipzig, 1962.

Jefferson, A. *The Operas of Richard Strauss in Britain 1910-1963*. London, 1963; revised up to 1986, *Richard Strauss-Blätter* no. 15 (1986): 104.

Kralik, Heinz. *Richard Strauss Weltburger der Musik*. Vienna, 1963.

Natan, A. *Richard Strauss: die Opern*. Basle, 1963.

Baum, G. *Richard Strauss und Hugo von Hofmannsthal*. Berlin, 1964.

Böhm, Karl. *Begegnung mit Richard Strauss*. Vienna, 1964.

Lehmann, L. *Five Operas and Richard Strauss*. New York, 1964; as *Singing with Richard Strauss*, London, 1964.

Mann, W. *Richard Strauss: a Critical Study of the Operas*. London, 1964.

Ortner, O. ed. *Richard-Strauss-Bibliographie, Teil 1: 1882-1944*. Vienna, 1964.

Pörnbacher, K. *Hugo von Hofmannstal/Richard Strauss: Der Rosenkavalier*. Munich, 1964.

Schuh, W. *Hugo von Hofmannsthal und Richard Strauss: Legende und Wircklichkeit*. Munich, 1964.

Marek, George R. *Richard Strauss: the Life of a Non-Hero*. New York and London, 1967.

Schäfer, R.H. *Hugo von Hofmannsthals "Arabella"*. Berne, 1967.

Deppisch, Walter, ed. *Richard Strauss in Selbstzeugnissen und Bilddokumenten*. Reinbek, 1968.

Schnoor, H. *Die Stunde des Rosenkavalier: 300 Jahre Dresdener Oper*. Munich, 1968.

Schuh, W. *Der Rosenkavalier: 4 Studien*. Olten, 1968.

Grasberger, F. *Richard Strauss und die Wiener Oper*. Tutzing, 1969.

Knaus, J. *Hugo von Hofmannsthal und sein Weg zur Oper Die Frau ohne Schatten*. Berlin, 1971.

Schuh, W. ed. *Hugo von Hofmannsthal, Richard Strauss: Der Rosenkavalier: Fassungen, Filmszenarium, Briefe*. Frankfurt am Main, 1971.

Abert, A.A. *Richard Strauss: Die Opern: Einführung und Analyse*. Hanover, 1972.

Ascher, G.I. *Die Zauberflöte und die Frau ohne Schatten: ein Vergleich zwischen zwei Operndichtungen der Humanität*. Berne, 1972.

Lenz, Eva-Maria. *Hugo von Hofmannsthals mythologische Oper "Die ägyptische Helene"*. Tübingen, 1972.

Brosche, G., ed. *Richard-Strauss-Bibliographie, Teil 2: 1944-1964*. Vienna, 1973.

Daviau, D.G., and George J. Buelow. *The "Ariadne auf Naxos" of Hugo von Hoffmannsthal and Richard Strauss*. Chapel Hill, 1975.

Jefferson, A. *Richard Strauss*. London, 1975.

Kennedy, M. *Richard Strauss*. London, 1976; 1988.

Schuh, W. *Richard Strauss: Jugend und frühe Meisterjahre: Lebenschronik 1864-98*. Zurich, 1976; as *Richard Strauss: a Chronicle of the Early Years 1864-1898*. Cambridge, 1982.

Trenner, Franz. *Die Skizzenbücher von Richard Strauss aus dem Richard-Strauss-Archiv in Garmisch*. Tutzing, 1977.

Overhoff, K. *Die "Elektra"—Partitur von Richard Strauss*. Salzburg, 1978.

Pantle, Sherrill Hahn. *"Die Frau ohne Schatten" by Hugo von Hofmannsthal and Richard Strauss: an Analysis of Text, Music, and their Relationship*. Bern, 1978.

Erté's Costumes and Sets for "Der Rosenkavalier". Introduction by John Cox. New York, 1980.

Hartmann, Rudolf. *Richard Strauss: Die Bühnenwerke von der Uraufführung bis heute*. Freiburg, 1980; English translation as *Richard Strauss: The Staging of his Operas and Ballets*, Oxford, 1982.

Heldt, Gerhard. ". . . aus der Tradition gestaltet: Der Rosenkavalier und seine Quellen." In *Ars Musica, Musica Scientia. Festschrift Heinrich Hüschen*, 233. Cologne, 1980.

Schultz, K. and S. Kohler, eds. *Richard Strauss: "Feuersnot"*. Munich, 1980.

John, Nicholas, ed. *Richard Strauss: Der Rosenkavalier*. London, 1981.

Mayer, Hans. *Versuche über die Oper*. Frankfurt am Main, 1981.

Schuh, W. *Straussiana aus vier Jahrzehnten*. Munich, 1981.

Forsyth, Karen. *Ariadne auf Naxos by Hugo von Hoffmansthal and Richard Strauss: its Genesis and Meaning*. Oxford, 1982.

Stewart, Robert Sussman, ed. *Richard Strauss: Der Rosenkavalier*. New York, 1982.

Wilhelm, Kurt. *Richard Strauss: persönlich*. Munich, 1984; English translation, London, 1989.

———. *Fürs Wort brauche ich Hilfe—Die Geburt der Oper "Capriccio" von Richard Strauss*. Munich, 1984.

Winterhager, Wolfgang. *Zur Struktur des Operndialogs: Komparative Analysen des musikdramatischen Werks von Richard Strauss. Europäische Hochschulschriften 36/9*. Frankfurt am Main, 1984.

Jefferson, Alan. *Richard Strauss: Der Rosenkavalier*. Cambridge, 1985.

John, Nicholas, ed. *Arabella*. London, 1985.

Schlötterer, Reinhold, ed. *Musik und Theater im "Rosenkavalier" von Richard Strauss*. Vienna, 1985.

Schlötterer, Roswitha, and Victoria Ursuleac. *Singen für Richard Strauss*. Vienna, 1986.

John, Nicholas, ed. *Richard Strauss: Salome, Elektra*. London and New York, 1988.

Konrad, Claudia. *Studien zu "Die Frau ohne Schatten" von Hugo von Hofmannstal und Richard Strauss*. Hamburg, 1988.

Osborne, Charles. *The Complete Operas of Richard Strauss*. London, 1988.

Birkin, Kenneth W. *"Friedenstag" and "Daphne": an Interpretive Study of the Literary and Dramatic Sources of the Two Operas by Richard Strauss*. New York, 1989.

———. *Richard Strauss: Arabella*. Cambridge, 1989.

Puffett, Derrick, ed. *Richard Strauss: Salome*. Cambridge, 1989.

———. *Richard Strauss: Elektra*. Cambridge, 1989.

Nice, David. *Richard Strauss*. London, 1990.

Birkin, Kenneth. *Stefan Zweig—Joseph Gregor: Correspondence 1921-1938*. Otago, New Zealand, 1991.

articles—

Marsop, P. "Italien und der 'Fall Salome,' nebst Glossen zur Kritik und Ästhetik." *Die Musik* 6 (1906-07): 139.

Bekker, P. "*Elektra:* Studie," *Neue Musik-Zeitung* 30 (1909): 293, 330, 387.

Mennicke, C. "Richard Strauss: *Elektra.*" In *Riemann-Festschrift*, 503. Leipzig, 1909.

Klein, W. "Die Harmonisation in *Elektra* von Richard Strauss: ein Beitrag zur modernen Harmonisationslehre." *Der Merker* 2 (1911): 512, 540, 590.

Diebold, B. "Die ironische *Ariadne* und der *Bürger als Edelmann.*" *Deutsche Bühne* 1 (1918): 219.

Specht, R. "Vom *Guntram* zur *Frau ohne Schatten.*" In *Almanach der Deutschen Musikbücherei auf das Jahr 1923*, 150. Regensburg, 1923.

Rosenzweig, Alfred. "Les adaptations de Lulli et de Couperin par Richard Strauss." *Revue Musicale* 7 (1926).

Westphal, K. "Das musikdramatische Prinzip bei Richard Strauss." *Die Musik* 19 (1926-27): 859.

Reich, W. "Bemerkungen zum Strauss'schen Opernschaffen, anlässlich des 70. Geburtstages." *Der Auftakt* 14 (1934): 101.

Ruppel, K.H. "Richard Strauss und das Theater." *Melos* 13 (1934): 175.

Gregor, J. "Zur Entstehung von Richard Strauss' *Daphne.*" In *Almanach zum 35. Jahr des Verlags R. Piper and Co., München,* 104. Munich, 1939.

Tenschert, R. "Hosenrollen in den Bühnenwerken von Richard Strauss." *Zeitschrift für Musikwissenschaft* 106 (1939): 586.

Mathis, A. "Stefan Zweig as Librettist and Richard Strauss." *Music and Letters* 25 (1944): 163, 226.

Schuh, W. "Eine nicht komponierte Szene zur *Arabella.*" *Schweizerische Musikzeitung/Revue musicale suisse* 84 (1944): 231.

Erhart, O. "The Later Operatic Works of Richard Strauss." *Tempo* 12 (1949).

————. "Richard Strauss's *Die Frau ohne Schatten.*" *Tempo* 17 (1950).

Beinl, S. "A Producer's Viewpoint: Notes on Die Frau ohne Schatten." *Tempo* 24 (1952).

Tenschert, R. "A 'Gay Myth': The Story of *Die Liebe der Danae.*" *Tempo* 24 (1952).

Friess, H. "Richard Strauss and the Bavarian State Opera." *Tempo* 43 (1957).

Tenschert, R. "*Arabella:* die letzte Gemeinschaft von Hugo von Hofmannsthal und Richard Strauss." *Österreichische Musikzeitschrift* 13 (1958).

————. "The Sonnet in Richard Strauss's Opera *Capriccio.*" *Tempo* 47 (1958).

Graf, E. "Die Bedeutung von Richard Strauss's *Intermezzo.*" *Österreichische Musikzeitschrift* 18 (1963).

Wurmser, Leo. "Richard Strauss as an Opera Conductor." *Music and Letters* January (1964).

Ott, A. "Richard Strauss und sein Verlegerfreund Eugen Spitzweg." In *Musik und Verlag: Karl Vötterle zum 65. Geburtstag,* 466. Kassel, 1968.

Wasdruszka, A. "Das *Rosenkavalier* Libretto." *Österreichische Musikzeitschrift.* 24 (1969).

Schuh, W. "Richard Strauss und seine Libretti." In *Gesellschaft für Musikforschung Kongressbericht* (1970): 169.

Mühler, Robert. "Hugo von Hofmannsthals Oper *Ariadne auf Naxos.*" *Interpretationen zur Österreichischen Literatur* 6 (1971).

Könneker, Barbara. "Die Funktion des Vorspiels in Hofmannsthals *Ariadne auf Naxos.*" *Germanisch-Romanische Monatsschrift* 12 (1972).

Abert, A.A. "Richard Strauss' Anteil an seinen Operntexten." In *Musicae scientiae collectanea: Festschrift Karl Gustav Fellerer,* 1. Cologne, 1973.

Keller, W. "*Die Liebe der Danae:* ein Wagner-Oper von Richard Strauss." *Neue Zeitschrift für Musik* 134 (1973).

Gerlach, R. "Die ästhetische Sprache als Problem im *Rosenkavalier.*" *Neue Zeitschrift für Musik* 1 (1975).

Ott, A. "Die Briefe von Richard Strauss in der Stadtbibliothek München." In *Beiträge zur Musikdokumentation: Franz Grasberger zum 60. Geburtstag,* 341. Tutzing, 1975.

Schuh, W. "Hofmannsthals Randnotizen für Richard Strauss im *Ariadne* Libretto." In *Für Rudolf Hirsch zum siebzigsten Geburtstag.* Frankfurt, 1975.

Hoslinger, C. "Salome und ihr österreichisches Schicksal 1905-1919." *Österreichische Musikzeitschrift* 22 (1977).

Perusse, Lyle F. "*Der Rosenkavalier* and Watteau." *Musical Times* 119 (1978): 1042.

Brosche, Günter. "Der Schluss der Oper *Ariadne auf Naxos.* Neue Aspekte zur Enstehung des Werkes." *Österreichische Musikzeitschrift* 34 (1979): 329.

Enix, M. "A Reassessment of *Elektra* by Strauss." *Indiana Theory Review* 2 (1979).

Schnitzler, Günter. "Kongenialität und Divergenz. Zum Eingang der Oper *Elektra* von Hugo von Hofmannsthal und Richard Strauss." In *Dichtung und Musik,* edited by Günter Schnitzler, 175. Moscow, 1979.

Zimmerschmied, D. "Intergration in Liebe oder brutale Vertreibung? Versuche zur Deutung der Sängerepisode im *Rosenkavalier.*" *Die Musikforschung* 32 (1979).

Kohler, Stephan. "Machen wir mythologische Opern. . . . Zur *Ägyptischen Helena* von Hugo von Hofmannsthal und Richard Strauss." In *Richard Strauss-Blätter* new series 4 (1980): 43.

Brosche, Günther. "Beiträge zur Richard-Strauss-Bibliographie 1882 bis 1964. Ergänzungen zu den erschienenen Verzeichnis." In *Festschrift Hans Schneider zum 60. Geburtstag,* edited by R. Elbers and E. Vögel. Munich, 1981.

Erwin, C. "Richard Strauss's Presketch Planning for *Ariadne auf Naxos.*" *Musical Quarterly* 67 (1981): 348.

Carsity, Turner. "The Egyptian Pauline." *Parnassus* 10/no. 2 (1982): 115.

Avant-scène opéra January-February (1983) [*Salome* issue].

Birkin, Kenneth W. "Collaboration Out of Crisis (Strauss—Zweig—Gregor)." *Richard Strauss–Blätter* 9 (1983): 50.

————. "Stefan Zweig—Richard Strauss—Joseph Gregor. An Evaluatory Assessment of Zweig's Influence upon the Strauss/Gregor Operas. Part 1. *Friedenstag* and *Danaë.*" *Richard Strauss-Blätter* new series/no. 10 (1983).

Gurewitsch, Matthew. "In the Mazes of Light and Shadow: a Thematic Comparison of *The Magic Flute* and *Die Frau ohne Schatten.*" *Opera Quarterly* 1/no. 2 (1983): 11.

Hoppe, Manfred. "Das 'Musikalische Gespräch' in *Der Bürger als Edelmann:* Ein 'richtiges Gedicht' Hofmannsthals?" *Modern Philology* 81 (1983): 159.

Partsch, Erich Wolfgang. "Die 'missglückte' Operette. Zur stilistischen Position des *Rosenkavaliers.*" *Österreichische Musikzeitschrift* 38 (1983): 389.

Petersen, Peter. "Programmusik in den Opern von Richard Strauss." *Hamburg Jahrbuch für Musik wissenschaft* 6 (1983): 598.

Potter, Pamela M. "Strauss's *Friedenstag:* a Pacifist Attempt at Political Resistance." *Musical Quarterly* 69 (1983): 408.

Avant-scène opéra November-December (1984) [*Le chevalier à la rose* issue].

Birkin, Kenneth. "Zweig—Strauss—Gregor Part 2. *Daphne.*" *Richard Strauss-Blätter* new series/no. 12 (1984).

Neighbour, Oliver. "Veraltete Sentimentalität: Arnold Schoenberg in Defense of Richard Strauss." In *Festschrift Albi Rosenthal,* edited by Rudolf Elvers, 253. Tutzing, 1984.

Partsch, Erich Wolfgang. "Utopie und Wirklichkeit: Anmerkungen zu Konzeption und Stil der *Schweigsamen Frau* von Richard Strauss." In *Bericht über den Internationalen Musikwissenschaftlichen Kongress Bayreuth, 1981,* edited by C.-H. Mahling and S. Wiesmann, 528. Kassel, 1984.

Springer, Morris. "The Marschallin: a Study in Isolation." *Opera Quarterly* 2 (1984): 56.

Avant-scène opéra July (1985) [*Ariadne à Naxos* issue].

Birkin, Kenneth W. "The Last Meeting: *Die Liebe der Danae* Reconsidered." *Tempo* 153 (1985): 13.

Avant-scène opéra November (1986) [*Elektra* issue].

Birkin, Kenneth. "Über den Wagner Gipfel hinaus." *Richard Strauss-Blätter* new series/no. 23 (1990): 4.

Kramer, Lawrence. "Culture and musical hermeneutics: The Salome complex." *Cambridge Opera Journal* 2 (1990): 269.

unpublished–

Pfister, Werner. "Hofmannsthal und die Oper." Ph.D. dissertation, University of Zurich, 1979.
Partsch, Erich Wolfgang. "Artifizialität und Manipulation. Studien zur Genese und Konstitution der 'Spieloper' bei Richard Strauss unter besonderer Berücksichtigung der *Schweigsamen Frau.*" Ph.D. dissertation, University of Vienna, 1983.
Kaplan, Richard Andrew. "The Musical Language of *Elektra:* a Study in Chromatic Harmony." Ph.D. dissertation, University of Michigan, 1985.

* * *

In terms of continuity and output, Richard Strauss, whose work dominates the first four decades of this century, must be considered one of the most successful—and by implication one of the most important—of twentieth century opera composers. His first music drama, *Guntram,* was completed in 1893, his last opera, *Capriccio,* in 1941, while *Die Liebe der Danaë* (1940) despite the Salzburg General probe of 1944, was not officially premiered until 1952, four years after his death. Strauss came to opera relatively late (he was 29 when he wrote *Guntram*), but the Munich environment, the growing influence upon him of Wagner's music and the spirit of

Richard Strauss, 1933

times heady with post *Tristan*-esque romanticism and Nietzschean polemic inevitably drew him to opera.

The goal of opera was approached by Strauss, perhaps subconsciously, through the medium of the tone poem where, continuing the Berlioz/Liszt tradition, he demonstrated a mastery of large-scale formal procedures and orchestration as well as, prophetically enough, an astounding dramatic flair. The overcomplexity of which he was accused was a symptom of an exuberance which swept him into a position, alongside Gustav Mahler, as one of Europe's most avant-garde composers. His palette of unconventional sounds, together with the opulent forces involved in works such as *Also Sprach Zarathustra* (1896) and *Ein Heldenleben* (1898), raised establishment eyebrows and stamped him as something of an *enfant terrible* in late nineteenth century music.

Encouraged by his mentor, the Wagnerian Alexander Ritter, and having conducted *Tristan* for the first time (Weimar, 1892), he was, when he set out upon *Guntram* in 1892, both orchestrally and formally "armed at all points," even, in true Wagnerian tradition, writing his own text for the work. In itself *Guntram* is, perhaps, relatively unimportant. It does, however, identify Strauss's Wagnerian starting point and (despite miscalculations from which he was quick to learn), together with *Feuersnot* (1901), acts as a palpable link with a tradition upon which he was to build and to which in the fullness of time he was to return.

The climax of the first phase of Strauss's operatic career arrived with *Salome* and *Elektra* (1905 and 1908 respectively), single act works which, eclectic in nature, project the salient features of the symphonic tone poem into the field of music drama. Strauss's absolute confidence and consequent success in this one-act format stems from a clear-headed objectivity which subsequently never left him: an ability to learn from past errors, and to exploit—in this case by transference of technique from one medium to another—universally acknowledged strengths. *Salome,* highly illustrative in musical effect, employs an orchestrally motivated symphonic design as well as firmly establishing what was to become an almost legendary predilection for the soprano voice.

Strauss saw *Elektra,* his first collaboration with Hugo von Hofmannsthal, as a logical extension of the *Salome* line. The notorious success of *Salome,* which utilized flagrantly expressionist devices to interpret the psychological conflict of the drama, confirmed his avant-garde position in the eyes of his contemporaries. Once committed to Hofmannsthal, however, Strauss's horizons manifestly broadened as the poet, assuming the role of "cultural arbiter," guided him in an up to then unforeseen direction. He encouraged Strauss to adopt his own, admittedly somewhat rarified, aestheticism and to renounce a Wagnerian heritage which was, nonetheless, to retain a powerful hold upon the composer's imagination.

The path, from *Elektra* to *Arabella* (the last Hofmannsthal/Strauss collaboration), was unpredictable to Strauss's peers. The perceived stylistic U-turn which fueled the romantic "classicism" of *Rosenkavalier* (1910) was labeled retrogressive, by implication an opting out, a symptom of artistic complacency. Nevertheless, posterity has uniquely benefited from the Strauss/Hofmannsthal theatrical experiments of the 1920s and 30s which in the search for a new rationality of form, means, and expression attempted to establish a working balance between the musical, literary, visual and psychological elements of the drama. The ultimate achievement, which transcended Hofmannsthal's tragic death in 1929, was substantial.

Hofmannsthal's first "purpose built" Strauss libretto, *Der Rosenkavalier* (*Elektra* was adapted from the already existing stage play), deliberately sought to win the composer away from the "through-composed" Wagnerian style to a more "classical" format which would provide for set pieces in the traditional manner. The lyrical moments of the score emerge naturally from a recitative-like, conversational medium, a technique enabled by the rhythmic fluidity of Hofmannsthal's text. It was this flexibility, centered as it was upon a conceptual equality of "word" and "music" that was new. From it developed the parlando manner whose pace and expressivity contributed greatly to *Rosenkavalier's* success and which was to be further refined in *Ariadne* (1912), *Intermezzo* (1923) and *Arabella* (1932).

It was the *direction* in which Hofmannsthal pointed Strauss that had such important implications. *Ariadne*—written for Max Reinhardt—looked forward, in its later "prologue" version, towards the developed "conversational" style of *Intermezzo* (for which, once again, Strauss provided his own text). The pace and modernity of this work, with its cinematographically inspired scenic "takes," is remarkable. Even Hofmannsthal, who deplored its bourgeois domesticity, recognized that it took the "new style" of *Rosenkavalier* and the *Ariadne* Vorspiel one step further. Their last opera, *Arabella*, sought to reconcile the parlando "extreme" of *Intermezzo* with the more popular lyricism of *Rosenkavalier*. Here, the marriage, on equal terms, of text and music operates with even greater flexibility than heretofore. Its "fined-down" romanticism, orchestral restraint, lyrical charm, and artistry create a stylistic synthesis that is the ultimate achievement of the collaboration, establishing a new genre of music theater—the "conversation" opera.

It is surely here, in the obsession with "conversation opera" that Strauss's longterm significance lies. That is not, however, to discount works of a more eclectic nature such as *Salome, Elektra* or *Die Frau ohne Schatten;* they also played an important part in the development of his *oeuvre*. Masterpieces in their own right, they bear out, viewed in context, Strauss's own admission that the specific nature and form of each work is dictated by the resolution of technical problems propounded by text, ethos, environment and musical-theatrical resource. Bound together by a common cultural ideal and heritage, Strauss and Hofmannsthal realized a unique (great poet/great composer) collaboration. Working out of a clearly defined tradition, the starting point for *Rosenkavalier* was Mozart's *Marriage of Figaro. Ariadne* (based on Molière's *Le bourgeois gentilhomme*) has pronounced neo-classical overtones derived from Baroque opera, while *Die Frau ohne Schatten* (1918), links the world of Wagner to that of *The Magic Flute*. It is, perhaps, significant that *Die ägyptische Helena* (1927), which has no obvious antecedents, has proved—despite its music and craftsmanship—their least successful work.

Hofmannsthal's death was a bitter blow to Strauss. A new unexpectedly fortuitous liaison with the gifted Austro/Jewish writer Stefan Zweig seemed to hold out new collaborative hopes, but these were soon dashed by the political turmoil of the 1930s. The fruit of this brief but happy partnership, Strauss's only truly Italian-inspired opera, *Die schweigsame Frau* (1934) (based on Ben Jonson's play *The Silent Woman*) was banned in Germany on anti-semitic grounds after only four performances. Condemned to self-exile but still anxious to serve, Zweig provided a successor, his friend Joseph Gregor, who texted three operas for Strauss, the first of which was the Zweig-inspired *Friedenstag* (closely modeled on Beethoven's *Fidelio*). Here, the woman, Maria, is the catalyst; as a "peace" advocate she transcends religious enmity and engineers universal reconciliation. *Friedenstag* (1936) was, for the reclusive Strauss of the late 1930s, a rare "political"

document—a plea, albeit fruitless, for peace and brotherhood at a crucial time in European history.

Of the two remaining Gregor works, *Daphne* (1937) is a psychological version of the Greek myth worked on post-Nietzschean lines, and *Die Liebe der Danaë*, (1940) another mythological subject, summarizes the cultural influences which had guided the composer throughout his life. Deeply read, historically aware and culturally literate, Strauss retreated into his shell in these late years, disassociating himself from the insanity of the contemporary world. His works of the period demonstrate a reassessment of longheld cultural beliefs, a reaffirmation of aesthetic values, and an attempt to renew his identification with, and to salvage something from, a tradition which he saw endangered in the bigoted, war-torn world of the 1940s. It was upon this tradition, he believed, that the future depended. Evidence suggests that he regarded *Die Liebe der Danaë*, which in its final act integrates Classical (Mozartian) and Romantic (Wagnerian) impulses, as something of an artistic testament, while *Capriccio* occupies itself exclusively with the central problem of his career, that of the relationship between words and music. As a philosophical treatise upon relativity in theater-related arts, *Capriccio*, designated by its authors Strauss and Clemens Krauss as a "Konversationsstück" (conversation piece), confirms, reinforces and justifies the stylistic thrust discernible from *Rosenkavalier* onwards.

It is all too easy to theorize about Strauss's operas. His work is, indeed, characterized by superb craftsmanship and by a consummate and practical instinct for theater. His level of musical intelligence is phenomenal—every effect is calculated and where effect failed, he was himself the first to recognize the fact. In his treatment of the soprano voice, he reaches his greatest inspirational heights. His range of operatic heroines from Salome to Madelaine still challenge, and are as roles still coveted by, the greatest singing artists of today. New productions of his operas are significant and prestigious events calling for the most advanced production techniques and demanding the ultimate in vocal and instrumental virtuosity. He ranks high among musical lyricists and it is, indeed, melody that dominates the last period works (which include his final incomplete "school" opera *Des Esels Schatten*). Strauss's own hope that he might merit "an honourable place at the end of the rainbow" of tradition has been amply realized—from a total of fifteen operas at least ten are regularly performed while seven (a conservative estimate), undisputed mainstays of the repertoire, are universally regarded as classics of the genre.

—Kenneth Birkin

STRAVINSKY, Igor.

Composer. Born 18 June 1882, in Oranienbaum, near St Petersburg. Died 6 April 1971, in New York. Married: 1) Catherine Nossenko (died 1939), 24 January 1906 (four children); 2) Vera de Bosset (died 1982), 9 March 1940. Stravinsky's father was Feodor Stravinsky, a famous bass at the Russian Imperial Opera. Studied piano with Alexandra Snetkova and then with Leokadia Kashperova; studied music theory with

Akimenko and then Kalafati, 1900-03; studied law at St Petersburg University, 1901; traveled to Germany, 1902; composition of a piano sonata for Nicolai Richter, 1903-04; lessons in orchestration from Rimsky-Korsakov, 1905; commission from the impressario Diaghilev to compose a work for the Ballets Russes, which resulted in *The Firebird*, performed in Paris, 25 June 1910; became a resident of Paris, 1911, and composed numerous works for the Ballets Russes, including *Pétrouchka*, 1911, and *Le sacre du printemps*, 1913; work on *Les noces*, 1914-18; piano concerto commissioned by Koussevitzky and performed by Stravinsky, 22 May 1924; commissioned by the Elizabeth Sprague Coolidge foundation, which resulted in *Apollon Musagète*, performed at the Library of Congress, 27 April 1928; *Symphony of Psalms* composed for the fiftieth anniversary of the Boston Symphony Orchestra, 1930, but premiered in Brussels; the Violin Concerto commissioned by the violinist Samuel Dushkin, 1931; the melodrama *Perséphone* commissioned by the ballerina Ida Rubenstein; became a French citizen, 1934; *Dumbarton Oaks* concerto commissioned by Mr and Mrs Robert Woods Bliss, 1938; Charles Eliot Norton lecturer at Harvard University, 1939-40; became an American citizen, 1945; composed *Circus Polka* on a commission from Ringling Brothers; worked with George Balanchine, who choreographed a number of his ballets; the choral work *Canticum Sacrum* his first attempt at serial composition for the theater; visited Russia, 1962, where some of his works were finally accepted.

Operas

Publishers: Associated, Belyayev, Bessell, Boosey and Hawkes, Breitkopf und Härtel, Chappell, Charling, Chester, Faber, Hansen, Henn, Jurgenson, Leeds, Mercury, Edition Russe de Musique, Schott, Sirène.

Le rossignol [*Solovey*], Stravinsky and S. Mitusov (after Anderson), 1908-09, 1913-14, Paris, Opéra, 26 May 1914.
Mavra, B. Kochno (after Pushkin, *The little house in Kolomna*, 1921-22), Paris, Opéra, 3 June 1922.
Oedipus Rex (opera-oratorio), J. Cocteau (translated into Latin by J. Danielou), 1927, concert performance, Paris, Sarah Bernhardt, 30 May 1927; staged performance, Vienna, 23 February 1928; revised 1948.
The Rake's Progress, W.H. Auden and C. Kallman (after Hogarth's series of engravings), 1947-51, Venice, La Fenice, 11 September 1951.

Other works: ballets, orchestral works, choral works, chamber music, piano pieces.

Publications

By STRAVINSKY: books—

with W. Nouvel. *Chroniques de ma vie*. Paris, 1935-36; 2nd ed., 1962; English translation, 1936; as *An Autobiography*, 1936; 1975; Spanish translation, 1936-37; German translation, 1937; Russian translation, 1964; Bulgarian translation, 1966; Hungarian translation, 1969.
Poétique musicale. Cambridge, Massachusetts, 1942; English translation, 1947; German translation, 1949; 3rd ed., 1966; Italian translation, 1954; English-French edition, 1970.
Leben und Werk. Zurich and Mainz, 1957.
with Robert Craft. *Conversations with Igor Stravinsky*. London and New York, 1959; Berkeley, 1980; Russian translation, 1971.

———. *Memories and Commentaries*. London and New York, 1960; London and Berkeley, 1981; Russian translation, 1971.
———. *Dialogues and a Diary*. New York, 1961; 2nd ed., London, 1968; as *Dialogues*, Berkeley, 1982; Russian translation, 1971.
———. *Expositions and Developments*. London and New York, 1962; 1981; Russian translation, 1971.
———. *Themes and Episodes*. New York, 1966; 2nd ed., 1967.
———. *Reptrospectives and Conclusions*. New York, 1969.
Kutateladse, L., ed. *Statï, pisma, vospominaniya*. Leningrad, 1972.
D'yachkova, L.S., and B.M. Yarustovsky, eds. *Statï i materiali*. Moscow, 1973.
Lindlar, Heinrich, ed. *Aufsätze, Kritiken, Erinnerungen*. Frankfurt am Main, 1982.
Craft, Robert, ed. *Stravinsky, Selected Correspondence, I*. New York, 1982.
Schriften und Gespräche. Introduced by Wolfgang Burde. Mainz, 1983.
Craft, Robert, ed. *Stravinsky, Selected Correspondence, II*. New York, 1984.

articles—

and Šaljapin, Fëdor. "Pis'ma I.F. Stravinskogo i F.I. Šaljapin k A.A. Saninu" [letters to opera producer A. Sanin concerning *Le rossignol*]. *Sovetskaya muzyka* 6 (1978): 92.
" 'Dear Bob[sky]' (Stravinsky's Letters to Robert Craft, 1944-1949)." *Musical Quarterly* 65 (1979): 392.
Ricci, Carlo Franco. "Lettere inedite di Strawinsky a Vittorio Rieti." *Note d'archivio per la storia musicale* 1 (1983): 228.

About STRAVINSKY: books—

Lederman, M., ed. *Stravinsky in the Theatre*. London and New York, 1949; 1975.
Stravinsky and the Theatre: a Catalogue of Decor and Costume Designs for Stage Productions of his Works. New York, 1963.
Routh, Francis. *Stravinsky*. London, 1975.
Stravinsky, Vera, and Robert Craft. *Stravinsky in Pictures and Documents*. New York and London, 1978.
Möller, D. *Jean Cocteau und Igor Strawinsky: Untersuchungen zur Ästhetik und zu Oedipus Rex*. Hamburg, 1981.
Griffiths, P. *Igor Stravinsky: The Rake's Progress*. Cambridge, 1982.
Schouvaloff, A., and V. Borovsky. *Stravinsky on Stage*. London, 1982.
Van der Toorn, Pieter C. *The Music of Igor Stravinsky*. New Haven, 1983.
Pasler, Jann, ed. *Confronting Stravinsky: Man, Musician, Modernist*. Berkeley, 1986.
Walsh, Stephen. *The Music of Stravinsky*. London and New York, 1988.
Albright, Daniel. *Stravinsky: the Music Box and the Nightingale*. Rochester, New York, 1989.

articles—

Milhaud, D. "Strawinskys neue Bühnenwerke." *Musikblätter des Anbruch* 4 (1922): 260.
Cocteau, J. "Critics and the Comic Spirit." (1922); reprinted in *Igor Stravinsky*, edited by E. Corle, 21, New York, 1949.

Cocteau, J. "La collaboration Oedipus rex." *La revue musicale* no. 212 (1952): 51.

Mason, C. "Stravinsky's Opera." *Music and Letters* 33 (1952): 1.

Kerman, J. "Opera à la mode." *Hudson Review* 6 (1953-54): 560.

Craft, R. "Reflections on *The Rake's Progress.*" *The Score* no. 9 (1954): 24.

Cooke, D. "*The Rake* and the 18th century." *Musical Times* 103 (1962): 20.

Mellers, W. "Stravinsky's Oedipus as 20th-century Hero." *Musical Quarterly* 48 (1962): 300; reprinted in *Stravinsky: a New Appraisal of his Work,* edited by Paul Henry Lang, 34, New York, 1963.

Whittall, Arnold. "Stravinsky and Music Drama." *Music and Letters* 1 (1969).

Sorokina, Tat'jana. [article on neoclassical aspects of *Oedipus Rex*]. *Nauchno-metodicheskiye zapiski* [Novosibirsk] (1970).

Abert, A.A. "Stravinsky's *The Rake's Progress:* strukturell betrachtet." *Musica* 25 (1971): 243.

Kraus, R. "Bibliographie, Igor Strawinsky." *Musik und Bildung* 3 (1971): 304.

Klein, L. "Stravinsky and Opera: Parable as Ethic." In *Cahiers Canadiens de Musique* 4 (1972).

Hirsbrunner, T. "Ritual und Spiel in Igor Strawinskys *Oedipus rex.*" *Schweizerische Musikzeitung/Revue musicale suisse* 117 (1974): 1.

Thompson, Virgil. "Stravinsky's Operas." *Musical Newsletter* 4 (1974).

Josipovici, G. "*The Rake's Progress:* Some Thoughts on the Libretto." *Tempo* no. 113 (1975): 2.

Cambell, S. "The 'Mavras' of Pushkin, Kochno and Stravinsky." *Music and Letters* 58 (1977): 304.

Dan'ko, L. "*Mavra* Stravinskovo i *Nos* D. Shostakovicha." *Muzikal'niy sovremennik* [Moscow] 2 (1977): 73.

Alfeyevskaya, G. " '*Tsar' Edip* Stravinskovo: k probleme neoklassitsisma" [*Oedipus rex*]. *Teoriticheskiye problemï muzïki XX veka* [Moscow] 2 (1978): 126.

Hansen, M. "Igor Strawinskys 'Oedipus Rex': Anmerkungen zum Wort-Tonverhältnis." *Musik und Gesellschaft* 28 (1978): 329.

Ordzhonikidze, G. "Nravstvennye uroki nasmeshlivoy pritchi" [*The Rake's Progress*]. *Sovetskaya muzyka* no. 1 (1979): 56.

Sorokina, Tat'jana. "The Evolution of Igor Strawinsky's Harmonic Thinking As Seen in the Opera *Solovey.*" In *Theoretičeskie voprosy vokal'noj muzyki,* compiled by Nikolaj Tiftikidi. Moscow, 1979.

Dahlhaus, Carl. "Strawinskijs episches Theater." *Beiträge zur Musikwissenschaft* 23 (1981): 163.

Schneider, Frank. "*The Rake's Progress* oder Die Oper der verspielten Konventionen. Eine dramaturgische Studie." *Jahrbuch Peters 1980* 3 (1981): 135.

Threlfall, Robert. "The Stravinsky Version of *Khovanshchina.*" *Studies in Music* [Australia] 15 (1981): 106.

Craft, Robert. "Stravinsky at his 'bird-best'." *Opera News* 46/no. 8 (1982): 14.

Dömling, Wolfgang. "Über Strawinskys Bühnenwerke." *Die Musikforschung* 35 (1982): 345.

Hirsbrunner, Theo. "Igor Strawinskij. Verwerfung und Wiederherstellung von Opernklischees." In *Für und Wider die Literaturoper. Zur Situation nach 1945,* edited by Sigrid Wiesmann, 39. Laaber, 1982.

————. "Strawinsky und die Antike." *Österreichische Musikzeitschrift* 37 (1982): 320.

Kindlar, Heinrich. "Geist vom Geist Mozarts. Klassizität in Strawinskys Bühnenwerken." *Acta Mozartiana* 29/no. 4 (1982): 82.

Spiegelman, Willard. "The *Rake,* the *Don,* the *Flute:* W.H. Auden as Librettist." *Parnassus* 10 (1982): 171.

Vinay, G. "Da *Oidipous* a *Oedipus rex* e ritorno: un itinerario metrico." *Rivista italiana di musicologia* 18 (1982): 333.

Karlinsky, Simon. "Stravinsky and Russian Pre-literate Theater." *Nineteenth–Century Music* 6 (1983): 232.

Schubert, Werner. "Prima le parole, dopo la musica? Igor Strawinsky, Sophokles und die lateinische Sprache im *Oedipus Rex.*" *Antike und Abendland* 29 (1983): 1.

unpublished–

Zinar, R. "Greek Tragedy in Theater Pieces of Stravinsky and Milhaud." Ph.D. dissertation, University of New York, 1968.

Stravinsky's life-work falls, both stylistically and historically, into three periods: Russian, neoclassical and serial. His four operas belong to the first two periods, *Le rossignol* and *Mavra* being Russian works, *Oedipus Rex* and *The Rake's Progress* neoclassical. He did not write a serial opera, being primarily concerned in the later stage of his life with religious choral music and the style and structure appropriate for that. But it is through the theater (using the term in its widest sense) that Stravinsky has most profoundly affected the twentieth century. He belonged to the theater by birth, by tradition, and by inclination. Never was there a composer less willing to repeat himself, and each of his eighteen major theater works represents a different solution to a different problem. With each, he altered the face of his music.

Stravinsky disliked many aspects of opera. He was disenchanted with the aesthetic basis on which, since Wagner, it rested. "Music-drama" was an idea to which he was antipathetic, while the conception of "endless melody" was for him a contradiction in terms. The composition of opera, therefore, presented aesthetic problems to him which did not exist in the case of ballet. The path to the discovery of a new classicism appropriate to ballet was unimpeded, but classicism in opera had been practically obliterated by the "inflated arrogance" of the Wagnerian conception of "music-drama," which represented no tradition and fulfilled no musical necessity. The operas of Stravinsky's maturity, particularly *Mavra* and *The Rake's Progress,* may be seen as his solutions to this problem.

His first opera, *Le rossignol,* which he calls "a lyric tale," stands midway between opera and ballet, with a marked leaning to the latter. It seeks a solution to the opera problem along Debussy's path of lyric drama; it is the only one of his operas capable of being adapted into a symphonic poem for concert use with a minimum of alteration. It was concerned not with action or character but with a story, and a disembodied, tongue-in-cheek fairy story at that. It was also a spectacle, sumptuous and impressive, the last to be staged by Diaghilev before Europe was plunged, two months later, into war.

The opera is short (only forty-five minutes), and the story, which hardly qualifies as a plot, concerns the miraculous power of the Nightingale's song, which in the end restores the dying Emperor to health and vigor. The chief moment of this stage-spectacular is the Emperor of China's march, which so affected the designer Alexandre Benois that for the first time in his life he felt genuinely moved by one of his own creations. Stravinsky had the model before him of the coronation scene in Musorgsky's *Boris Godunov*; as for the love of things oriental, this was something that was equally strongly felt in Paris and St Petersburg at this time.

Mavra is more of an opera than *Le rossignol,* and has clean, formal divisions into solos, duets, and ensembles. It is in one act, lasting less than thirty minutes, and marks the end of Stravinsky's Russian period. It is an *opera buffa,* a charming take-off of the *romances sentimentales* of nineteenth century Russian composers, built around a Russo-Italian melodic line. The music stays within the hundred-years-old tradition of Glinka and Dargomizhsky, not in an attempt to reestablish that tradition, but to realize the form of *opera buffa,* which was so well suited to the subject. The plot tells of a hussar who dresses up as a cook (Mavra) to obtain admission into the household of his betrothed (Parasha), only to be discovered shaving by Parasha's mother and a neighbor. The joke contained in Kochno's libretto, based on the Pushkin story *The little house in Kolomna,* is well matched by the wit contained in Stravinsky's music: on to the long melodic lines of bel canto with frequent repetition of words and phrases, the composer has grafted his recently minted metrical discoveries. The score thus has a freshness, a subtlety, which the nineteenth century period and the Italian influence cannot conceal, only offset. In this respect, although the joke fell distinctly flat at the first performance, the opera marks a turning point in Stravinsky's creative thought. Its stylistic successor, though not for thirty years, was *The Rake's Progress.*

Although *Oedipus Rex* was completed in 1927, only some five years after the completion of *Mavra,* the contrast between these two operas could hardly be greater. Stravinsky had felt the desire to write a large-scale dramatic work for some time; one might almost speculate that this desire was itself a reaction to the smallness of *Mavra.* The story of *Oedipus Rex* is the universal, timeless Greek myth of Oedipus. The composer's choice of the Latin language and his use of the oratorio procedure whereby the characters address not each other but the audience combine to give the work its uniqueness. The events themselves are concentrated in the music, and the only stage movements are entrances and exits; moreover the moving characters (Speaker, Tiresias, Messenger, Shepherd) are secondary figures; the agents of Destiny, not its victims. Nothing could afford a greater contrast to the lightweight, charming, satirical *Mavra.*

Oedipus Rex is static, monumental, archetypal drama. Just as Greek tragedy was itself a compound of drama, history and myth, with the action taking place off-stage, so Stravinsky's work is part profane (opera), part sacred (oratorio). With the chorus stretched across the stage, the singers appear like statues, at different heights, in masks which restrict their movements. With the use of stage lighting, they can be made to appear disembodied; *Oedipus Rex* invites multi-media production. Conceptions such as these, combined with the narrator in contemporary dress and the use of a dead language combine to hold the audience at a distance, and to portray nervous energy and mystery; indeed the themes of detachment and alienation are Brechtian concepts.

The music too has a monumental quality, and is tonally and harmonically simple. The rhythms are four-square, unlike earlier works, and are more static and regular as they follow the rhythms of Sophocles's choruses (an idea which Stravinsky was to pursue further in his next stage work *Apollo*). Moreover, unlike Stravinsky's earlier vocal style, accentuation is decided by musical, not linguistic, considerations. The second syllable of "Oedipus" is a case in point. The word "oracula" also gives rise to an insistent rhythmic pattern. As for the *melos,* a minor tonality predominates,

gradually dropping, but is offset by the occasional section in the major, such as the music for Creon's first appearance, and the sudden outburst of C major on the word "gloria" at the end of the first act. The harmony and the orchestral sonority are built up from the bass line, as Handel would have done. For this reason, the texture has a firmness and a classical solidity. There is also a strong Verdi influence, particularly in the use of the chorus.

Twenty years after *Oedipus Rex, The Rake's Progress* (1947-51) marks the end of Stravinsky's neoclassical period. Not only is it the longest and most substantial of the four operas, lasting 150 minutes, it also uses a libretto which is a work of art in its own right (by a leading poet, W.H. Auden). Its first production in Venice was a spectacular success; its subsequent popularity has been unbroken. With this opera, Stravinsky resumed consideration of the operatic problem where he had left it with *Mavra.* In the meantime, Berg's *Wozzeck,* whose premiere took place in December 1925, had moved twentieth century European opera even further away from pre-Wagnerian clichés. Stravinsky did not set out to outflank Berg as a "reformer"; instead he returned to the very clichés of the Italian-Mozartian Classical style that the contemporary German composers had sought to supersede.

Stravinsky maintained a lifelong acquaintance with opera; such works as *Un ballo in maschera* and *Rigoletto* were familiar to him beyond the point where criticism of their obvious absurdities made any difference. While he was working on *The Rake's Progress,* Mozart's *Così fan tutte* was his musical diet. He deliberately sought to revitalize the conventions of a period that many might have imagined were long since dead. The structure is built round arias, recitatives, choruses, and ensembles, with a definite scheme of tonality. Generally speaking, prose is used for the recitatives, while the arias and ensembles are in verse. The orchestra is correspondingly small. As so often before, Stravinsky strove for a period piece; in this case the conventions of ostinato accompaniment were more appropriate for the eighteenth century than polyphony, whose effect could be timeless or hieratic, as in *The Symphony of Psalms.*

The presence of Mozart is pervasive throughout *The Rake's Progress.* Not only is the orchestra one of classical proportions, including a harpsichord for the recitatives, but the demonic atmosphere of the churchyard scene, as Rakewell and Shadow play cards, and the moralizing epilogue with which the opera ends, all point unmistakably to one model— *Don Giovanni.*

The Rake's Progress marked both the end and the culmination of that "incubation" period of Stravinsky's work known as neoclassicism. This was a universal musical phenomenon, to which diverse composers subscribed, particularly (but not exclusively) those of the Franco-Russian tradition. In the case of this opera, the origins both of the score and the libretto are well documented in primary sources, chiefly the correspondence between Auden and Stravinsky. Comparing it with the earlier operas, the composer said: "*The Nightingale* seems more remote to me now than the English operas of three centuries ago, or than the Italian-Mozartian opera which has been so neglected and misunderstood by the world of the musical dramatists. In so far as *Mavra* suggests any comparison to my present work, it is in my conception of opera. I believe 'music drama' and 'opera' to be two very, very different things. My life work is a devotion to the latter."

—Francis Routh

THE STRAYED WOMAN
See LA TRAVIATA

STREET SCENE.

Composer: Kurt Weill.

Librettists: E. Rice and L. Hughes.

First Performance: New York, Adelphi, 9 January 1947.

Roles: Anna (soprano); Steve (baritone); Frank (bass-baritone); Sam (tenor); Rose (soprano); Abraham (tenor); Greta (soprano); Carl (bass); Emma (mezzo-soprano); Olga (contralto); Shirley (contralto); Henry (baritone); Willie (child); Daniel (tenor); George (baritone); Lippo (tenor); Jennie (mezzo-soprano); Second Graduate (soprano); Third Graduate (mezzo-soprano); Mrs Hildebrand (mezzo-soprano); Mary (child); Grace (child); Harry (baritone); other lesser roles, dancers, etc.; chorus.

*   *   *

The action of *Street Scene* unfolds in a working-class neighborhood of New York City during one eventful hot day in June. On one level, *Street Scene* attempts to portray the personal concerns and convictions of the people who live there. They include a number of characters of various nationalities, religious beliefs, political opinions, occupations, and educational backgrounds. However, at its more immediate and most dramatic level, *Street Scene* concentrates on two ill-fated love affairs involving members of the neighborhood: Anna Maurrant's affair with Steve Sankey and the consequences of her infidelity to her husband Frank; and the thwarted romance between Anna's daughter Rose and the overly-sensitive law student Sam Kaplan.

Early in the first act we learn in the "Gossip Trio" that Anna has tried to escape her unhappy marriage by taking a lover. In the second act, when a suspicious and heavily drinking Frank returns unexpectedly from a dress rehearsal in New Haven, he discovers the liaison of the two lovers. He races up to the apartment, draws his gun and murders them. Meanwhile, the bookish Sam is in love with Rose, both of whom want desperately to leave the dreadful circumstances in which they live. But the murder of Rose's mother and the capture of her father have caused drastic changes in her life. Rose leaves Sam behind as she heads out with her brother Willie to begin a new life of her own.

One of Weill's primary goals in the United States was to write a definitive American opera, using indigenous American materials and sources. He believed this could be achieved only in the "living American theater," that is, on the Broadway stage. According to his own liner notes to the original cast recording of *Street Scene,* he believed that in *Street Scene*

Street Scene, Scottish Opera, 1989

he had synthesized all those elements necessary for a truly American operatic style.

Set against the norms of the 1940s Broadway musical (for example, the work of Richard Rodgers, whom Weill came to regard as his chief rival), *Street Scene* represents a significant change in direction regarding subject matter and musical technique. Weill believed that each of his earlier works was a "stepping stone" toward the fully-integrated musical structure in *Street Scene*. Apparently he also believed that *Street Scene*'s success would inaugurate a new era in the American musical theater.

Weill tried to unify the work in several ways. By far the most important and dramatically effective of these is his attempt to extend the techniques of film music to the stage medium. In *Street Scene* he utilizes the film technique of underscoring (spoken scenes in which music accompanies speech) as a formal and dramatic device to enormous advantage. Film composers such as Max Steiner had used a relatively sophisticated leitmotive technique to provide structure and dramatic continuity for films of the 1930s. By utilizing a similar technique in *Street Scene,* the music connecting the individual numbers serves not merely as incidental music, but illuminates and shapes the dramatic action just as effective film music cues could create continuity in a film. Some features of this underscoring technique can be found in Kern's *Showboat* (1927), Gershwin's *Porgy and Bess* (1935), and Rodgers' *Carousel* (1945), for example, but the means utilized are for the most part quite different from those in *Street Scene,* both musically and dramatically.

The complete aria Weill wrote for Anna Maurrant in act I illustrates in microcosm the compositional technique he employed throughout the work. Weill exploits several different recurring motives and themes during the course of the aria. These motives and themes connect the aria to events both prior and subsequent to it. In effect, the aria occupies a position central to the entire work through its foreshadowing and motivic connections to widely scattered events. Thus, Weill constructed the aria so that it would serve two specific purposes: first, it reveals Anna's life and character through reference to her past; and second, it presents those musical motives associated with her and her fate throughout the course of the opera.

Within the context of the work as a whole, the aria functions as a springboard for much of the motivically unifying material. Certainly, this complex construction gives to the aria a musical sophistication well beyond the normal requirements of Broadway, and yet the aria apparently succeeds on both counts of quality and popular accessibility. From the very first, critics extolled the dramatic impact and craftsmanship of the aria.

Weill's apparent enthusiasm for *Street Scene* can be justified to some extent. While in his other American works he attempted various means of integrating text and music with varying degrees of success, certainly no other American work consistently displays the formal continuity and interdependence both of the underscoring and of this aria in *Street Scene.*

When viewed in its proper social and temporal context, *Street Scene* should dispel any doubts as to its central position in the American musical theater of the 1940s, and of its continuing relevance. If *Street Scene* does hold a special place in Weill's oeuvre, as the abundance of recent revivals seems to suggest, then perhaps Weill predicted accurately to Arnold Sundgaard (his librettist for *Down in the Valley*) when he

stated, "Seventy-five years from now *Street Scene* will be remembered as my major work."

—William Thornhill

STREHLER, Giorgio.

Producer. Born 14 August 1921, in Barcola, Trieste. Studied at Accademia dei Filodrammatici, Milan; began career as an actor in 1940 and as a producer of plays in 1941; operatic debut, *La traviata,* Teatro alla Scala, 1947; co-founded the Piccolo Teatro di Milano, 1947; famous for his productions of plays by Brecht, Shakespeare, and Goldoni; helped found the Piccolo Scala, an experimental opera studio, 1955; supervisor and resident stage director, Salzburg Festival, since 1973; art consultant to Karajan; first Italian stagings of *Lulu, Judith,* and *Fiery Angel.*

Opera Productions (selected)

La traviata, Teatro alla Scala, 1947.
The Love for Three Oranges, Teatro alla Scala, 1947.
Die Dreigroschenoper, Piccolo Teatro, Milan, 1956 and 1973.
Die Entführung aus dem Serail, Salzburg, 1965; Teatro alla Scala, 1978.
Verurteilung des Lukullus, Teatro alla Scala, 1973.
Die Zauberflöte, Salzburg Festival, 1974.
Macbeth, Teatro alla Scala, 1975/76 season.
Simon Boccanegra, Teatro alla Scala; Covent Garden, 1976; Washington, D.C., 1976.
Le nozze di Figaro, New York?, 1976.
Falstaff, Teatro alla Scala, 1980.
Lohengrin, Teatro alla Scala, 1981/82 season.
Salome, Munich, 1987.
Falstaff, Munich, 1987.

Publications

By STREHLER: books–

Piccolo Teatro, 1947-58. Milan, 1958.
Piccolo Teatro di Milano, 1947-67. Milan, 1967.
Fuerein menschlicheres Theater. Edited and translated by S. Kessler. Frankfurt am Main, 1975.

About STREHLER: books–

Gaipa, E. *Giorgio Strehler.* Bologna, 1959.
Guazzotti, G. "*L'Opera da tre soldi di Bertolt Brecht e Kurt Weill.*" Bologna, 1961.
Fechner, E. *Giorgio Strehler inszeniert.* Velbert, 1963.
Gaipa, E. *Giorgio Strehler.* Berlin, 1963.

articles–

Besch, A. "A Triptych of Producers." *Opera* 9 (April 1958): 229-31.
Kesslet, G. "Zauberer Strehler." *Opernwelt* no. 8 (August 1969): 15.
Weaver, W., and L. Alberti. "Florence in Transition." *Opera* 205 (Autumn 1969): 109-11.
Kessler, G. " 'Schluss mit den Tenoeren im Lightkegel!' " *Opernwelt* no. 1 (January 1972): 23-25.

Breger, P. "Versailles (Strehler's 'Total Theatre')." *Opera* 24 (May 1973): 423-24.

Rasponi, L. "Giorgio Strehler, the Poet Musician." *Opera News* 41 (September 1976): 16-23.

Ashman, M. "Into Europe?" *Opera* 30 (November 1979): 1036-42.

Segalini, Sergio. "Giorgio Strehler: Une Pratique du théâtre." *Avant-scène opéra* (November-December 1980).

Dziewulska, M. "Kim jest Giorgio Strehler?" *Ruch Muzyczny* 27, no. 14 (1983): 21-23.

"Giorgio Strehler." *Die Buehne* no. 335 (August 1986): 58.

* * *

Throughout his long career as a producer, Strehler has been equally successful in staging both plays and operas. A number of his productions have been seen outside his native Italy, and nearly all of them have been acclaimed for their clarity, depth, and powerful theatricality. His stagings of opera, in particular, often seem to have illustrated the music itself, not just the libretto. With his Central European background and his penetrating musicianship, Strehler has proved himself to be the master craftsman of "beautiful" stage pictures which allow the eyes and ears of the audience to respond to an opera as a whole.

Early in life, Strehler discovered his passion for the theater through the works of Shakespeare and Goldoni. His feeling for music probably came from his family—his mother was a gifted violinist and his grandfather had been director of the opera in Trieste, Strehler's birthplace. On returning from prison camp in 1945 (his communist sympathies are well known), Strehler co-founded the Piccolo Scala in Milan, putting into practice his ideas for "popular" culture, some of which he owed to Louis Jouvet and Jacques Copeau and their work in Paris.

La traviata was the first opera to be staged by Strehler (1947), and he went on to mount many opera productions in Milan, Venice, Genoa, and later, outside of Italy. His understanding of music was such that Victor de Sabata once thought of offering Strehler a codirectorship at Teatro alla Scala. Many of Strehler's productions were *opera buffa*—consistent with the commedia dell'arte style he was developing at the Piccolo Scala. (His constantly revised production of *Harlequin, Servant of Two Masters* has held a permanent place in the repertory there since 1952.) Strehler also worked on operas in other genres, just as he worked on plays by many dramatists other than Goldoni; Brecht and Shakespeare in particular.

International recognition of Strehler's skill in making opera accessible came with his production of *Die Entführung aus dem Serail* at the 1965 Salzburg Festival. Together with the designers with whom he had most often worked (Damiani for sets, Frigerio for costumes), Strehler created a series of shadow pictures by backlighting singers onto a decor of sliding panels which allowed for swift scene changes and effects matching the playful nature of the *singspiel*. After this, he was invited by Karajan to become artistic director of the Salzburg Festival, although he did not produce another opera there until his *Die Zauberflöte* in 1974. In the meantime, Strehler mounted a stark *Cavalleria rusticana* and *Pagliacci* at the Teatro alla Scala and a truly "Sturm und Drang" *Fidelio* in Florence.

With *Simon Boccanegra*, which had often been considered a problematic (and rarely revived) work, Strehler put opera-lovers in his debt by bringing the piece back into the main-stream repertory. By using simple, well-delineated but imposing sets designed by Ezio Frigerio and lighting them to achieve a chiaroscuro effect, Strehler created a taut, fast-moving production. A huge sail was deployed, not only to divide the stage space, but to remind the audience that this is an opera which constantly evokes the sea. The complexities of the plot which intertwines private and political feelings were so clearly unraveled that a new Verdi opera seemed to have been discovered. Conducted by Abbado and sung by the finest available cast, the production was recorded and toured all over the world by the Teatro alla Scala. This production, seen by more people than any other by Strehler, is probably the one for which he will be best remembered.

In 1973, Rolf Liebermann, to whom fell the unenviable task of restoring the Paris Opéra to its former glory, engaged Strehler to stage *Le nozze di Figaro* in the opera house at Versailles. Those who saw the production there say it never reached the same level of sublimity when it was transferred to the Palais Garnier. Without resorting to pastiche or *espagnolade*, Strehler and Frigerio seemed to capture the very essence of Mozart's score, and at the same time gave the audience the impression they were watching the Beaumarchais play. Here again, diffused lighting and a small number of scenic elements were enough to make stage pictures which suggested a mixture of Fragonard and Longhi. This production has been revived frequently with excellent casts and will be the only Liebermann-era staging to be taken to the Opéra de la Bastille.

These two productions (*Simon Boccanegra* and *Le nozze di Figaro*) showed that Strehler had reached the full maturity of his style. His work in the opera house from then on was usually in the same vein, although absolute perfection seemed more elusive. Damiani returned to design the Salzburg *Die Zauberflöte* in 1974 and the Teatro alla Scala *Macbeth* in 1975. In the 1980s, Strehler again worked with Frigerio on *Falstaff*, *Lohengrin* and *Don Giovanni* in Milan, as well as on a none-too-happy *Die Dreigroschenoper* at the Châtelet in Paris, where he later mounted his last opera production, *Fidelio*, in 1989. After rehearsals fraught with difficulties, Strehler virtually disowned the production by refusing to take a curtain call on the first night. Afterwards he declared that he had abandoned all hope of being able to find the ideal conditions needed for the successful staging of an opera, due to the chaotic state of affairs which reigns in so much of the operatic world.

—Oliver Smith

STREICH, Rita.

Soprano. Born 18 December 1920, in Barnaul, Russia. Died 20 March 1987, in Vienna. Studied with Willi Domgraf-Fassbänder, Maria Ivogün and Erna Berger; debut as Zerbinetta in Strauss's *Ariadne auf Naxos,* Aussig, 1943; sang with the Berlin Staatsoper, 1946-51; sang with the Berlin Städtische Oper, 1951-53; London debut as Zerlina in Mozart's *Don Giovanni,* 1954; American debut in San Francisco in 1957; joined the faculty at the Folkwang-Hochschule in Essen, 1974.

Publications:

By STREICH: articles–

"Titelpartie und Welturaufführung." *Österreichische Musikzeitschrift* 14 (1959): 335.

About STREICH: articles–

"Three singers and a dancer join Colbert-LaBerge Management." *Musical Courier* 154 (1956): 6.
"Rita Streich." *Musical America* 79 (1959): 32.
"Rita Streich." *Musical Courier* 159 (1959): 38.

Rita Streich enjoyed a prominent place on the European operatic stage during the 1950s and 1960s. A charming and vivacious actress, Streich used her small but pretty voice to memorable effect in a wide variety of operas, most of them by German and Austrian composers. She specialized in comic opera, and in the portrayals of lively young women. Her performances of Mozart's lighter female leads delighted audiences at Aix and Salzburg; she was a fine Adele in *Die Fledermaus;* she won applause in her performances of Strauss's coloratura roles.

A recording of her Susanna at Aix, made under Rosbaud during the 1950s, shows Streich the Mozart singer at her prime. She had a lovely voice, free of the strain with which many opera singers attempt to fill large halls. In "Venite, inginocchiatevi" there is an admirable freshness and clarity to her singing that beautifully expresses Susanna's character. Streich was capable of elaborate coloratura; but she could also sing "Deh vieni, non tardar" with moving simplicity, embellishing her performance with delicate *portamento* and gentle, caressing *pianissimo* passages.

The qualities that made Streich a memorable Susanna also brought her success in her portrayals of some of Mozart's other young women: Blondchen, Zerlina and Despina were among her best roles. But she was less successful in serious roles. A recording of her performance of the Mad Scene in Donizetti's *Lucia di Lammermoor* (part of a six-record retrospective issued by Deutsche Grammophon in the mid 1980s) lacks drama. Streich seems to have had difficulty conveying the personality and the feelings of serious characters.

Streich devoted much of her career to opera in German. Her performance at Salzburg of Aennchen (*Der Freischütz*) won praises for the naturalness with which she expressed her character's affection for Agathe, but listeners also noticed that her voice was too small for the cavernous Festspielhaus. At Bayreuth she sang one of the few Wagner roles suitable to her voice, that of the Forest Bird in *Siegfried*.

Streich was especially admired for her portrayals of two of Richard Strauss's most attractive young women: Sophie in *Der Rosenkavalier* and Zerbinetta in *Ariadne auf Naxos*. In her performance of Zerbinetta's great recitative and aria "Grossmächtige Prinzessin," recorded under Karajan in the mid-1950s, we can hear what made Streich so successful an interpreter of Strauss's operas. She sings with delicacy and sweetness. She enunciates words clearly, so that Hofmannsthal's text is almost always easily understood by the listener. The lightness and wit of Streich's singing corresponds perfectly to the text. Her coloratura is effortless, with high notes always light and beautiful to the ear, never shrill. One gets a chance in this aria to hear the lower part of Streich's vocal range, which has its own color and charm, quite different from the more familiar upper register.

—John A. Rice

STREPPONI, Giuseppina.

Soprano. Born 8 September 1815, in Lodi. Died 14 November 1897, in Sant'Agata, near Busseto. Married: Giuseppe Verdi, 1859. Studied piano and voice at Milan Conservatory, where she won the first prize for bel canto; may have had debut at Adria in 1834; first major appearance in Rossini's *Matilda di Shabran,* Trieste, 1835; also in 1835 appeared in Vienna as Adalgisa in *Norma* and Amina in *La sonnambula;* debut at Teatro alla Scala, 1839; created title roles in Donizetti's *Adelia,* Rome, and Abigaille in Verdi's *Nabucco,* Milan, 1841; retired from stage in 1846.

Publications

About STREPPONI: books–

Mundula, M. *La moglie di Verdi: Giuseppina Strepponi.* Milan, 1938.
Walker, F. *The Man Verdi.* London, 1962.
Cazzulani, Elena. *Giuseppina Strepponi.* Lodi, 1984.

articles–

Luzio, A. "La 'Traviata' e il dramma intimo di Verdi." *Nuova antologia* no. 390 (1937): 270. Reprinted in *Carteggi verdiani* 4 (1947): 250.
Gara, E. "La misteriosa giovinezza di Giuseppina Strepponi." *Corriere della sera* (27 January 1951).
de Amicis, E. "Giuseppina Verdi-Strepponi." In *Nuovi ritratti letterari ed artistici,* Milan, 1902; reprinted in *Verdi: bolletino quadrimestrale dell'Istituto di studi verdiani* 1/2 (1960): 779.
"Ebbe una figlia a Trieste la moglie di Giuseppe Verdi." *Corriere della sera* (6 March 1965).
Medici, M. " 'Quel prete' che sposò Verdi." *Verdi: bolletino quadrimestrale dell'Istituto di studi verdiani* 1/2 (1970): 657.
Sartori, C. "La Strepponi e Verdi a Parigi nella morsa quarantottesca." *Nuova rivista musicale italiana* 8 (1974): 239.
Phillips-Matz, M.J. "A Time of Stress." *Opera News* 55 (5 January 1991): 10.

Giuseppina Strepponi's name came to be inextricably connected with that of Giuseppe Verdi, first as an interpreter of his music, then as his musical adviser, his paramour, and eventually his wife and trusted companion. The relationship between the two lasted nearly sixty years, from Strepponi's creation of the role of Abigaille in Verdi's *Nabucco* in 1842 until her death in 1897. Yet before she encountered Verdi, Strepponi was an established prima donna known for her roles in the operas of Rossini, Bellini, Donizetti, and their contemporaries. She was from a well-connected musical family. Her father, Feliciano Strepponi (1797-1832), was organist at the Cathedral at Monza and composer of several operas, of which *Ulla di Bassora* had a certain success at the Teatro alla Scala in 1831. Giuseppina was admitted as a paying pupil at age fifteen to the Milan Conservatory, where she studied piano and voice. In 1834 Strepponi won first prize for *bel canto* and left the conservatory. Her first success came in Rossini's *Matilda di Shabran* in Trieste in the spring of 1835; in that same year she appeared in Vienna as Adalgisa in Bellini's *Norma* (a role created for a soprano even though it is sung by rich-voiced mezzos today) and as Amina in Bellini's *La sonnambula,* one of her most celebrated roles.

The latter part of the 1830s was Strepponi's heyday. Her Teatro alla Scala debut was in 1839. Verdi's first opera, *Oberto,* was given there primarily as a result of her and Ronconi's recommendation. Strepponi's approval of Verdi's *Nabucco* in 1842 was also decisive in allowing that opera to be premiered at the Teatro alla Scala, the occasion when she and Verdi met. Strepponi had overused her voice during the previous few years and her creation of Abigaille—an extremely demanding role that sopranos today undertake only with the greatest trepidation—was only a partial success. Donizetti, although a friend of hers, was critical of Strepponi at this time. He wrote to his brother-in-law on 4 March 1842 that "There remains la Strepponi. Tell him [an impresario in Rome] that this singer, in *Belisario* [by Donizetti] here, made such a furore that she was the only one who never received any applause, that Verdi did not want her in his opera and the management has forced her on him...." Not only had Strepponi sung too frequently over a period of many years but she had been involved in a liaison with the tenor Napoleone Moriani and had borne him two illegitimate children and undergone an abortion. In an 1840 account, Temistocle Solera (the future librettist of *Nabucco*) wrote that "In the mere five years that she has been exercising her art, with rapid and happy acclaim, and at the fresh age of twenty-four years, she has gloriously covered all of twenty-seven theaters—Vienna, Florence, Venice, Bologna, Rome, Turin, and, last spring, the cultivated Milan, have admired in this young woman the finest gifts of nature, improved by constant study...."

In addition to Verdi's Abigaille, Strepponi had created the title role in Donizetti's *Adelia* in Rome in 1841. She suffered a disastrous season in Palermo in 1845 and sang only intermittently for the next year, mainly in works by Verdi. Her retirement from singing came in 1846 at the age of thirty-one. In October of that year she arrived in Paris with a letter from Verdi to his French publishers, the Escudiers. After giving some concerts, she set herself up as a singing teacher. In July of 1847 she was joined in Paris by Verdi as he was returning from the premiere of *I masnadieri* in London. The two were together from that point on: in 1849 she was installed at Verdi's estate Sant' Agata, which engendered a great deal of gossip among the villagers. Only in 1859, for reasons still unknown, were the couple finally married. A number of Verdi scholars see Strepponi, with her morally checkered past and rejection by society, as the impetus for Verdi's setting of *La traviata* in the early 1850s. Verdi naturally left no clues on this count, but in a letter of 21 January 1852 to his father-in-law, Antonio Barezzi, Verdi made clear his feelings about moral hypocrisy: "In my house there lives a Lady, free, independent, who, like me, is fond of solitary life.... Neither she nor I owes anyone an account of our actions.... Who knows whether or not she is my wife?... Who has the right to cry scandal?... in my house she is owed the same, indeed greater respect than is owed to me, and no one is allowed to fail in his duty towards her in any way; and finally she is fully entitled to it, both by her demeanor and her spirit, and by the special regard she never fails to show others." Although there were troubled times in the late 1870s, when Verdi's

feelings towards the soprano Teresa Stolz caused Strepponi a great deal of anguish, she and Verdi were closely attuned to one another for decades. With Strepponi's intelligence, tactfulness, generosity, sense of humor, and gifts as a linguist, she was able to take on much of Verdi's most important correspondence. A number of revealing letters also exist between the two written during periods when they were apart.

If Abigaille, with its treacherous tessitura and acrobatic leaps, was not suited to Strepponi's vocal talents, then most of the tragic heroines of Bellini and Donizetti (e.g., *Lucia di Lammermoor*) were. She also successfully performed the role of Elaisa in Mercadante's *Il giuramento.* Strepponi was equally adept at comedy, starring as Adina in Donizetti's *L'elisir d'amore* and as Sandrina in Luigi Ricci's *Un'avventura di Scaramuccia.* A contemporary reviewer described Strepponi as possessing a "limpid, penetrating, smooth voice, seemly action, a lovely figure; and to Nature's liberal elements she adds an excellent technique."

—Stephen Willier

STRIGGIO, Alessandro.

Librettist/Statesman/Musician. Born 1573?, in Mantua. Died 15? June 1630, in Venice. Viol player for the festivities surrounding the wedding of Grand Duke Ferdinando I in Florence, 1589; studied law in Mantua; secretary to Duke Vincenzo (Gonzaga) I, 1611, and ambassador to Milan; made a count, a marquis, and then a chancellor in 1628; member of the Accademia degli Invaghiti; died of the plague in Venice, where he was attempting to obtain military aid for Mantua in the war over the succession to Vincenzo II.

Librettos (selected)

La favola d'Orfeo, C. Monteverdi, 1607.

Publications

About STRIGGIO: books–

Volta, L.C. *Compendio chronologico-critico,* vol. 4. Mantua, 1833.

Abert, A.A. *Claudio Monteverdi und das musikalische Drama.* Lippstadt, 1954.

Mazzoldi, L., R. Giusti and R. Salvadori. *Mantova: la storia,* vol. 3. Mantua, 1963.

Hanning, B.R. *Of Poetry and Music's Power.* Ann Arbor, 1980.

Rosand, Ellen. *Opera in Seventeenth-Century Venice.* Berkeley, 1991.

articles–

d'Arco, C. "Due cronache di Mantova dal 1628 al 1631." In G. Muller, *Raccolta di cronisti e documenti storici lombardi inediti,* vol. 2. Milan, 1857.

Pirotta, N. "Teatro, scene, e musica nelle opere di Monteverdi." In *Claudio Monteverdi e il suo tempo,* edited by R. Monterosso, 45. Venice, 1968.

———. "Scelte poetiche di Monteverdi." *Nuova rivisti musicale italiana* 2 (1968): 10.

_____. "Monteverdi e i problemi dell' opera." In *Studi sul teatro veneto fra rinascimento ed età barocca*, edited by M.T. Muraro, 321. Florence, 1971.

Osthoff, W. "Contro le legge de' Fati: Polizianos und Monteverdis *Orfeo* als Sinnbild künstlerischen Wettkampf mit der Natur." *Analecta Musicologica* 22 (1984): 11.

* * *

Alessandro Striggio (the Younger) played an important role in the development of opera as the librettist for Monteverdi's *La favola d'Orfeo*, regarded by many as the first masterpiece of the new genre. Striggio was a diplomat and lawyer in the service of the ruling Gonzaga family of Mantua. He was also the son of a composer with interests in music and poetry, and as such was a likely choice as collaborator for Monteverdi's first operatic venture. As attested to in Monteverdi's surviving letters—many of which are addressed to Striggio—Monteverdi regarded Striggio not only as a patron but as a friend, and they frequently conferred on both musical and practical matters. Their collaboration apparently continued long after Monteverdi's departure for Venice in 1613; in this letter of 9 January 1629, Monteverdi describes his thoughts on the musical setting of one of Striggio's texts that was subsequently lost: "I am sending your Lordship the lament of Apollo. By the next post I shall send you the beginning, up to this point, since it is already almost finished; a little revision in passing still remains to be done. At the place where Amore begins to sing, I would think it a good idea if your Lordship were to add three more short verses of like meter and similar sentiment, so that the same tune could be repeated (hoping that this touch of gladness will not produce a bad effect when it follows—by way of contrast—Apollo's previous doleful mood) and then go on as it stands, changing the manner of expression in the music, just as the text does" (translation by Denis Stevens, *The New Monteverdi Companion*, p. 37).

La favola d'Orfeo was written under the auspices of the Accademia degli Invaghiti to be performed at the court in Mantua in 1607 during carnival season. Striggio himself was a member of the Accademia degli Invaghiti, whose interests included poetry and oration. Undoubtedly, both Striggio and Monteverdi used as a model the opera *Euridice* (1600) by Florentine poet Ottavio Rinuccini and composer-singer Jacopo Peri. As numerous scholars have noted, the resemblance between these two works consists of more than their mutual reliance upon Ovid and Virgil or Poliziano's *La favola d'Orfeo* of 1480. Like Rinuccini, Striggio set his libretto within the pastoral tragicomedic world that was popular from other Mantuan and Florentine theatrical entertainments, such as Guarini's play *Il pastor fido*. Striggio also followed a similar dramatic structure, organizing his libretto as a prologue followed by five acts or sections with the first two acts of the two versions roughly analogous in terms of content. Moreover, speeches at important dramatic junctures contain obvious correspondences both in terms of content and poetic style, and in several of those instances Monteverdi's musical setting also demonstrates its debt to the earlier work.

There are also important differences between Striggio's *Orfeo* and Rinuccini's *Euridice*, which may reflect the contrasting circumstances in which these works were performed as well as the differing goals of their creators. With its comfortable fitting of the happy ending onto the popular tragic myth, Rinuccini's *Euridice* is a more straightforward work, and as such was highly appropriate for the celebration of the Medici wedding. Orfeo loses Euridice yet wins her back unambiguously from the underworld by means of his musical skill. In the prologue, Rinuccini makes his dramatic intentions clear; the personification of tragedy uncharacteristically describes her intention to banish sorrow and tears and bring pleasure to her listeners.

La favola d'Orfeo, however, was not part of a court celebration but rather was performed for the private enjoyment of the Accademia degli Invaghiti during carnival. Striggio and Monteverdi may thus have had more freedom in their treatment of this well-known subject. The protagonist of their prologue is not La Tragedia but rather La Musica herself, who proclaims her intention to demonstrate the power—and perhaps the limitations—of music. It is also no coincidence that Striggio and Monteverdi chose to name their work after Orfeo rather than Euridice. In Striggio's libretto, Orfeo has a more prominent role, yet he is also more problematic. Striggio and Monteverdi give their Orfeo ample opportunity to demonstrate his considerable lyric prowess in the opening acts (Rinuccini's Orfeo does not even appear until the second scene, and his Euridice is given a larger role); yet this musical proficiency proves ineffective at the most critical moment. Orfeo's most potent demonstration of his musical skill—his "Possente spirto"—is in Monteverdi's hands a veritable catalogue of all of the available vocal styles, yet it only lulls Charon to sleep. Although Orfeo subsequently succeeds in slipping by the sleeping Charon in order to gain Pluto's conditional permission to lead Euridice out of the underworld, his triumph is only temporary. Orfeo's musical prowess can in no way compensate for his human failings.

While most critics have maintained that Monteverdi's operatic setting of the Orfeo myth surpasses its model both in terms of its music and its dramatic effect, they have been more ambivalent about the virtues of Striggio's poetry. Monteverdi's decision to use Rinuccini as the poet for his next opera *Arianna*, and his famous claim to have found a superior kind of musical imitation in the setting of that poet's work, has prompted some commentators to turn a more critical eye to Striggio's libretto. Gary Tomlinson, for example, who compares Monteverdi's style of recitative in *Orfeo* to that of the surviving lament from *Arianna*, attributes what he feels to be weaknesses in the recitative for *Orfeo* as in part due to "musical reflections of rhetorical deficiencies in Striggio's text." The existence of two different endings for the opera—the one from the printed libretto in which Orfeo is killed by the Bacchantes and the happier but somewhat dissatisfying version contained in Monteverdi's score in which Orfeo is rescued by Apollo—has further complicated the critical issues surrounding Striggio's libretto.

Numerous hypotheses have been put forth to account for the chronology and circumstances surrounding the differing endings of the work as found in the 1607 libretto and the 1609 score. Monteverdi may have preferred to employ the *lieto fine* for this opera as he would for all of his subsequent operas. It is also possible, as Iain Fenlon suggests, that the more violent ending may have been deemed inappropriate for a given occasion. Others have suggested that the hall in Mantua may have been too small to accommodate the descent of Apollo and that the ending with the Bacchantes was added later as it would have been easier to stage. Gary Tomlinson proposes that the more awkward *lieto fine* may actually have been written by somebody other than Striggio, such as Francesco Gonzago. Nevertheless, whether Orfeo's eventual denunciation of women—another conspicuous feature of the myth omitted from the earlier libretto—precipitates the furious attack of the Bacchantes or Apollo's benevolent rescue, Striggio—and Monteverdi—present a darker, more enigmatic, and perhaps more human Orfeo, whose arguably greater musical proficiency ultimately fails to achieve for him his desired goals.

—Wendy Heller

SUOR ANGELICA
See TRITTICO

SUPERVIA, Conchita.

Mezzo-soprano. Born 9 December 1895, in Barcelona. Died 30 March 1936, in London. Married: Sir Ben Rubenstein, 1931. Studied at the Colegio de las Damas Negras in Barcelona; debut in Stiattesi's opera *Blanca de Beaulieu,* Buenos Aires, 1910; European debut in Bari as Casilda in Marchetti's *Ruy Blas,* 1911; sang with the Chicago Opera, 1915-16; London debut, 1934.

Publications

About SUPERVIA: articles–

Barnes, H.M. and V. Girard. "Conchita Supervia." *Record Collector* 6 (1951): 54.
Shawe-Taylor, D. "Conchita Supervia (1895-1936)." *Opera* 6 (1960): 16.
Barnes, H.M. "Conchita Supervia." *Recorded Sound* 52 (1973): 212.
Newton, I. "Conchita Supervia." *Recorded Sound* 52 (1973): 205.

*   *   *

Born into an old Andalusian family in Barcelona, Conchita Supervia studied voice there from the age of ten. At the young age of fifteen she made her operatic debut with a traveling Spanish company led by Francesco Vignas, at the Colón, Buenos Aires, singing the part of an old woman.

In the following year, 1911, Supervia sang Octavian in the Rome premiere of Richard Strauss's new opera *Il cavalliere della rosa (Der Rosenkavalier)*—still today the youngest singer to have done so professionally. She then began to take on the heavier roles of Carmen, Delila, Mignon and Charlotte in *Werther.* She had a great success in the latter during her season with the Chicago Opera in 1915-16. From about 1920, Supervia was in much demand throughout Italy and made her Teatro alla Scala debut in 1924 as Hänsel. She never appeared at the Metropolitan Opera.

Her coloratura ability, which had been so well trained by Professor Alfredo Martino in Rome, gave her the opportunity to assist the conductor, Vittorio Gui, in reviving Rossini's bel canto operas. She again enlarged her repertoire with *Italiana in Algeri, Cenerentola* and especially as Rosina in *Il barbiere di Siviglia,* which she sang in the original key for coloratura contralto.

She also made as keen an impression on audiences in song as on the opera stage. In songs by Falla, Granados and other Spanish composers, she achieved a new order of interpretation, which was sometimes used effectively in her operatic characterizations. In 1926 at La Scala she gave a concert version of Falla's *El amor brujo* in Italian, when her almost savage rendering and her luscious chest voice surprised and delighted that Milanese audience.

Supervia was a volatile personality. In 1934 she sued the management of Covent Garden (Sir Thomas Beecham and Geoffrey Toye) for omitting one of her performances from the schedule, and won (out of court). Her excessive demands included a strong voice in the casting of "her" operas in the following season! She was a determined young *prima donna:* in fact she was the first contralto, as opposed to a soprano, to be regarded as *prima donna,* for it is almost a contradiction in terms.

Supervia was not only an exceptional singer but also an excellent actress. She made a wonderful Carmen, but because she was so very Spanish herself, there were moments when Bizet's frenchified version of her own country and people seemed a trifle pallid. Rossini's charming and playful women suited her far better, and with the theater in her bones, she was able to extract every histrionic and vocal nuance from her roles.

Those who remember hearing her sing say that the vibrato that many feel is part and parcel of Supervia was not always evident from the stage. Although it is such a characteristic of her recordings, she apparently was able to produce it or restrain it at will on the stage or platform. Only the merciless "ear" of the recording microphones have picked it up throughout, with one exception—the song *Hay en mi jardin* which is said to express the purity of her live singing. With a voice that had two octaves of beautifully moulded notes, an enchanting personality to deliver them and a passion that sometimes went beyond the bounds of mid-1930s "decency," Supervia possessed the kind of magnetism which was not to be found again until the arrival of Maria Callas.

Supervia married a Jewish-English industrialist and became Lady Rubinstein after meeting him while she was on a UK tour in 1931. They had a son, George. But in 1936 she died while giving birth to a second child in London, at the early age of forty, a quarter of a century to the day after her first operatic success as Octavian in Rome.

—Alan Jefferson

SUSANNAH.

Composer: Carlisle Floyd.

Librettist: Carlisle Floyd.

First Performance: Florida State University, Tallahassee, 24 February 1955.

Roles: Susannah Polk (soprano); Sam (tenor); Olin Blitch (bass-baritone); Lil Bat McLean (tenor or speaking); Elder McLean (bass); Elder Gleaton (tenor); Elder Hayes (tenor); Elder Ott (bass); Mrs McLean (mezzo-soprano); Mrs Gleaton (soprano); Mrs Hayes (soprano); Mrs Ott (contralto); chorus.

*   *   *

When Carlisle Floyd's *Susannah* premiered, the critical reaction was overwhelmingly favorable. Here is an opera in which the subject matter is thoroughly American in flavor although the story is based on the Biblical tale of "Susannah and the Elders" from the *Apocrypha*. Stories of Bible Belt preachers and their shenanigans have precedence in Mark Twain, Sinclair Lewis, and more recently television evangelism. Even though it is an old subject, the treatment in this case—operatic, or as "musical theater" as Floyd prefers to name it—is fresh and vital mainly because the story yields two flesh and blood characters in Susannah, a vivacious, pretty girl, and Olin Blitch, a traveling preacher. Using hymn tunes, modality, and folk song sources, the musical structure is straightforward. With non-polyphonic textures, it communicates easily and is not difficult to execute.

Susannah gains the attention of Rev. Olin Blitch, who is to preach at the local church. When she returns home, she sings "Ain't it a Pretty Night" and is answered by her brother, Sam, who lives with her. Later he sings "Jaybird sittin' on a hick'ry limb." The next day the four elders discover Susannah bathing nude in the creek where they propose to hold a baptism. Scandalized, they vow punishment of Susannah. Li'l Bat, a feeble minded friend, tells Susannah of the elders' plan. However, she attends the revival service where Blitch preaches a hell-fire sermon, a musically powerful scene, which moves from spoken dialogue to singing. Susannah refuses to be "saved," and Blitch comes to her house later. He tells her of his loneliness and succeeds in seducing her. The next day as the baptism proceeds, Sam returns to hear the whole story from Susannah. Infuriated and somewhat drunk, he takes a gun and goes to the baptism. Susannah hears shots; Blitch is killed. The townspeople want to hang Sam and run Susannah out of the Valley. She stands them off with a gun, laughing defiantly, as the curtain falls.

Floyd has fashioned a piece that is dramatically and musically viable. The libretto is a mixture of words spoken, spoken on pitch and in rhythm, and full singing voice—all of this with a fluidity that respects natural speech rhythms and dramatic intensity. Floyd is striving to create a more viable musical theater, and in some respects he has. *Susannah* moves with a logical development and feeling for the situation of the characters, who are allowed space in which to move emotionally as they build the story. However, Floyd, a Methodist minister's son with a background of church music, employs orchestration and musical development that is thin and lacking in resourcefulness. But this opera is good theater and connects with the audience, an ideal Floyd respects. It has been produced repeatedly at the New York City Opera as well as in many professional and university opera companies.

—Andrew H. Drummond

SUTHERLAND, Joan.

Soprano. Born 7 November 1926, in Sydney. Married: pianist/conductor Richard Bonynge, 1954; one son. Studied piano and voice with her mother; later studied with Joan and Aida Dickens in Sydney and, in London, with Clive Carey at the Royal College of Music and at the Opera School; won first of many singing competitions at age 19; sang first operatic role, Dido in *Dido and Aeneas,* in concert performance at Lyceum Club in Sydney, 1947; operatic debut at Sydney Conservatorium, in title role of Goosens's *Judith,* 1951; Covent Garden debut as First Lady in *Die Zauberflöte,* 1952; while with the company sang *Aida* (1954), Jennifer in Tippett's *The Midsummer Marriage* (1955), Gilda in *Rigoletto* and the title role in *Alcina* (both 1957); greatest triumph of the period came with Zeffirelli's production of *Lucia di Lammermoor* (1959); Teatro alla Scala and Metropolitan Opera debuts, both as Lucia, 1961; returned to Australia for 1965-66 season; later made many appearances there while husband was director of Australian Opera in Sydney, 1976-86; farewell appearance at Sydney in *Les Huguenots,* 1990; made Dame Commander of the Order of the British Empire, 1979.

Publications

By SUTHERLAND: books–

The Joan Sutherland Album, with Richard Bonynge. London, 1986.

About SUTHERLAND: books–

Braddon, Russell. *Joan Sutherland.* London, 1962.
Greenfield, Edward. *Joan Sutherland.* London, 1972.
Tubeuf, André. *Le chant retrouvé. Sept divas: renaissance de l'opéra.* Paris, 1979.
Adams, Brian. *La Stupenda: A Biography of Joan Sutherland.* London, 1980.
Major, Norma. *Joan Sutherland.* London, 1987.
Quaintance, Eaton. *Sutherland and Bonynge: An Intimate Biography.* New York, 1987.

articles–

Dunlop, Lionel. "People 42: Joan Sutherland." *Opera* 11/10 (1960): 675.
Jacobson, Robert. "Conversation Piece: A Free-Wheeling Visit with the Bonynges." *Opera News* 47/6 (1982): 8.

*   *   *

Joan Sutherland's early career as a member of the company at the Royal Opera House, Covent Garden, during the 1950s is particularly interesting and relevant when one considers her later position as the most celebrated and popular coloratura soprano in the world. She achieved a three-decade-long succession of triumphs with the public, a great deal of it in the face of quite hostile criticism from the music critics of the English-speaking world.

During the decade that led to her most famous performance, her debut in the title role of Donizetti's *Lucia di Lammermoor* on 17 February 1959, she had built up a repertory that included not only roles by Handel, Mozart, Donizetti and Verdi—parts that she continued to sing for the rest of her career—but also Weber, Wagner, Britten, Tippett, Poulenc, Bizet and heavier Verdi roles (such as Amelia in *Ballo in maschera* and Aida). This career as member of a company, something which few of her successors have had the chance to develop to such an extent, laid the foundations for her formidable technique and assurance, which meant that even past the age of sixty she still took on new roles, maintaining to an impressive degree the flexibility and security for which she was most prized. Of her early roles, one which she allegedly disliked was that of Jennifer in the world premiere of

Michael Tippett's *The Midsummer Marriage.* In her recording of this work, one can hear that as early as January 1955 all of Sutherland's characteristics were already there: the agility and brilliant attack on staccato notes *in alt,* especially in the passage beginning "Then the congregation of the stars began to dance" and the legato that made the longest arching phrases seem easy. Her English diction was then at its best. The low-lying passages obviously pose a problem, as they were always to do. It is hard to imagine now that there were people who considered that Sutherland should have taken on the heaviest Strauss and Wagner parts; her future obviously lay in the lyric-coloratura range.

Sutherland's career will always be inseparable from that of her husband, Richard Bonynge, who is usually credited with encouraging her to study the early nineteenth-century Italian repertory, especially the operas of Bellini and Donizetti. Once her position as leading soprano of the Covent Garden company had been established, with her singing of Pamina, Desdemona, Gilda and the three soprano roles in *Les Contes d'Hoffmann,* her assumption of Lucia seemed inevitable. Here Sutherland owed a great deal to the example of Callas, approaching the role as one of dark drama instead of the prettiness that sopranos of the previous generation, Pons and Robin among them, had been said to bring to it. The 1959 performances of *Lucia* at Covent Garden, repeated shortly afterwards in Paris, Milan and other Italian cities, and her assumption of the role of Elvira in *I Puritani* at Glyndebourne in 1960 marked the very peak of the early Sutherland style. One hears in it the complete freedom and purity of her voice, unimpaired by the swooping portamenti and the veiled diction that later marred it for so many. This sound differs from that which she developed in the early 1960s, in which in the middle and lower registers her enunciation had a "thick" quality in contrast to the mercurial quality which she always found for the upper registers.

It is idle to speculate where Sutherland's career would have gone without Bonynge. His coaching, their exploration together of the nineteenth-century opera and song repertory and the many recordings that resulted gained for them a huge and loyal following. If critics in the late 60s were inclined to carp, referring to their set-up as "a circus," and to criticize her poor diction, which in fact was no worse than most other coloraturas, they seemed always to ignore the very things which made her performances such a pleasure: the total security, accuracy of pitch, retention of the natural quality of her voice right up to the highest regions, and her always generous stage presence.

If Sutherland's acting never had the spontaneous or psychological insight that, say, Silja or Callas seemed to bring to their roles, she was always engaged in the role, was a commanding figure on stage, and moved with grace and often surprising swiftness. After her success as Norma at the New York Metropolitan Opera in 1970, Sutherland began to move into somewhat heavier, more dramatic-soprano roles. Donizetti's Maria Stuarda, Lucrezia Borgia and eventually Anna Bolena, Massenet's Esclarmonde and Leonora in *Il trovatore,* all challenged her voice. Of these parts the Lucrezia seemed to suit her the best, although her Maria Stuarda had some impressive moments dramatically, her vehement "Vil bastarda!" quite the equal of Gencer, Caballé or Sills, all of whom were performing the role at the same time.

Always noticeable, even as late as her 1988 Anna Bolena at Covent Garden, was the rhythmic pulse and energy that she could put into ensemble passages. However, she never achieved to the same degree as her contemporaries Caballé and Leontyne Price the melting smoothness when holding on to the long, sad lines of a Verdi aria such as "Tacea la notte."

Sutherland was an accomplished comedienne, and in Donizetti's *La fille du Régiment,* Strauss's *Fledermaus* and Lehàr's *Merry Widow,* she demonstrated her good-natured personality (as she did in the television series "Who's Afraid of Opera?," in which she added the roles of Rosina in *Il barbiere di Siviglia* and Offenbach's *La Périchole,* neither of which she sang on the stage).

If one wished to analyze Sutherland's particular greatness, the best role to examine is not Lucia, the most famous, but her own favourite, that of Violetta in *La traviata.* Her last London performances of this, in 1975, found her in the best possible voice, her diction better than ever, and her ability to bring off the staccato high Cs in the Tetrazzini variations which she interpolated into the second verse of "Sempre libera," a pulse-racing crescendo on the final E flat, all superb. If the drooping, mooning quality was still there in the second-act duet with Germont père, her total commitment to the death scene, in which she seemed to have found a perspective on the slowness of the dying woman's movements, as well as a stream of solid, golden tone that had not only pathos but variation in color within individual notes, made even her harshest critics sit up in surprise.

Sutherland has left a formidable recorded legacy. All her records made up to and including *Lucrezia Borgia,* issued in 1980, have fascination and provide great pleasure; the later ones are inclined to accentuate the greater beat in the voice, the absence of the remembered radiance in her tone, and a sameness of characterization. This did not seem so apparent when one heard her in the opera house. Of those roles she sang only for the gramophone, supreme is the title-role in *Turandot,* conducted by Mehta, and a very enjoyable Adina in *L'elisir d'amore.*

—Patrick O'Connor

SVANHOLM, Set.

Tenor. Born 2 September 1904, in Västerås, Sweden. Died 4 October 1964, in Saltsjö-Duvnäs, near Stockholm. Studied as baritone with John Forsell at the Opera School of the Stockholm Conservatory; debut, as baritone, as Silvio in *I Pagliacci,* Stockholm, 1930; tenor debut as Radames, Stockholm, 1936; appeared at the Salzburg Festival and the Vienna State Opera, 1938, the Berlin State Opera, Teatro alla Scala, 1941-42, and Bayreuth Festival, 1942; appeared as Tristan in Rio de Janeiro, 1946, and as Lohengrin in San Francisco, 1946; Metropolitan Opera debut as Siegfried, 1946; remained on roster of the Metropolitan until 1956; also sang at Covent Garden, 1948-56; director of the Royal Theater in Stockholm, 1956-63.

Publications

About SVANHOLM: articles—

Rosenthal, H. "Set Svanholm." *Opera* 6 (1955): 357.
_____. "Set Svanholm." In *Great Singers of Today,* London, 1966.

*   *   *

Like a number of distinguished dramatic tenors before him—Jean De Reszke, Giovanni Zenatello, Lauritz Melchior, Eric Schmedes, and Renato Zanelli among them—Set Svanholm came to opera as a baritone. Having studied with the eminent Swedish baritone John Forsell at the Stockholm Conservatory (Björling was a fellow Forsell pupil), he made his debut in 1930 at the Royal Opera of Stockholm in the same role in which Melchior had made his—Sylvio in *I Pagliacci*. Six years later he successfully re-emerged a tenor, singing Radames in a well-received *Aïda*. He remained a principal at the Royal Opera until 1956, and by the late 1930s had already assumed a busy schedule of guest appearances that would continue throughout his career. He was offered a Metropolitan Opera contract as early as 1940, but the volatile political climate of the times prevented him from accepting it. He remained in Europe during the war, and appeared with some success at the Teatro alla Scala and Bayreuth. The post-war restoration of the Wagnerian repertory finally brought him to Britain and the United States. His Metropolitan Opera debut on 15 November 1946 received impressive if not spectacular notices, but he came eventually to sing seventeen roles there in 105 performances between 1946 and 1956, the majority of them Wagnerian. In similar roles, he was also a regular guest at Covent Garden between 1948 and 1956, and finished his career as an innovative director of the Royal Opera of Stockholm, with a strong commitment to a wide and varied repertory.

Svanholm was appreciated most for his energy, his youthful appearance, and his good looks. Clearly, the physical illusion he created was far more considerable than any lasting vocal or dramatic impression he may have made. Ernest Newman for example, was genuinely taken with his young Siegfried, which "really looked and behaved like the young boy Wagner had in mind," but had misgivings about his Tristan, one of the singer's most important and popular roles, which Newman dismissed as "musical but unpoetical."

Svanholm's musicianship was reputed to be as impeccable as his faithfulness to the composer's written intentions, but his singing seems always to have lacked the drama and individuality of those heldentenors to whom he was hastily proclaimed a natural successor, notably Melchior. His reviews, like his performances, were remarkably consistent throughout his career, both cast from a palette of few colors, which says something about his limitations and his inability to transcend them. Olin Downes' account of Svanholm's 1946 Met debut, which noted that he was obviously "a sound musician who sings his part accurately as written," that he was "youthful in action as well as in song," and that dramatically, "his conception was fully rounded and always significant" was, in retrospect, a virtual prototype for the majority of reviews that would follow.

Svanholm was a diligent craftsman, always intelligent and determined even at his least inspired. His voice was outstanding for its vitality and for a clean, open tone uncommon to even the best singers normally associated with his repertory, but in the more intimate resources of warmth, vibrance and sweetness, it was somehow deficient. His repertory, developed prior to his post-war triumphs, was large and international in scope, and included many of the heaviest Italian and French dramatic roles along with a complement of German specialties—Florestan (*Fidelio*), Herod (*Salome*), Eisenstein (*Die Fledermaus*), and Aegisth (*Elektra*). But it was as a Wagnerian that he is best remembered. Given such a diverse repertory, he suffered remarkably few setbacks, Lohengrin being perhaps the most perplexing.

His most successful roles, Siegfried, Siegmund, Tristan, Florestan, and Aegisth, certainly stand alongside the better post-war intrepretations, as he does generally among the better post-war interpretors, and these have all survived in extensive recorded segments and even complete performances, some of them commercial studio recordings, others live broadcasts taken off the air. His celebrated partnership with Kirsten Flagstad was as persistent in the studio as it was on the stage, and is exceedingly well documented. It is most unfortunate that no recordings of him as a baritone seem to have been made: considering that his timbre lacked virtually any trace of latent baritone weight and resonance, it would be especially interesting to compare the before with the after. That he had the physical resources to meet the demands of such taxing heldentenor roles is unquestionable, and this is borne out not only by the length of his career, but by the fact that his voice underwent little significant change between 1946 and the assumption of his administrative duties in Stockholm a decade later. The same youthful but manly sound, albeit a bit dryer, is as evident in his last studio recordings of the late 1950s as it is in his earliest ones for Victor just after the war.

—William Shaman

SVOBODA, Josef.

Set designer. Born 10 May 1920, in Caslav, Czechoslovakia. Married: Libuše Svobodova. Trained as an architect at the Academy of Applied Arts, Prague, where he is now a professor; chief designer, National Theater, Prague 1947-. Svoboda invented the Polyecran system of simultaneous projection, and is especially well known for his work with Lanterna Magika, 1973, and for his production of *Der Ring des Nibelungen*, Covent Garden, 1974-76.

Opera Productions (selected)

Dalibor, National Theater, Prague, 1961.
Intoleranza, The Opera Group of Boston, 1965.
Tristan und Isolde, State Theater, Wiesbaden, 1967.
Die Zauberflöte, Munich State Opera, 1970.
From the House of the Dead, Hamburg, 1972.
Carmen, Metropolitan Opera, 1972.
Tannhäuser, Royal Opera, London, 1973.
I vespri siciliani, Metropolitan Opera, 1974.
Der Ring des Nibelungen, Royal Opera, 1974-76.
Der Ring des Nibelungen, Grand Theater, Geneva, 1975-77.
Fidelio, Zurich, 1975.
Tristan und Isolde, Bayreuth, 1976.
Turandot, Reggio, Turin, 1976.
The Queen of Spades, National Arts Centre, Ottawa 1976.
Otello, Paris Opéra, 1976.
Ein Engel kommt nach Babylon, Zurich, 1977.
The Bartered Bride, Metropolitan Opera, 1978.
Rusalka, Stuttgart, 1980.
Idomeneo, National Arts Centre, Ottawa, 1981.
The Queen of Spades, Houston, 1982.
Salome, 1985.

Publications

About SVOBODA: books–

Skelton, Geoffrey. *Wagner at Bayreuth*. New York, 1965.

Gollancz, Victor. *The "Ring" at Bayreuth*. London, 1966.

Bablet, Denis. *Josef Svoboda*. Lausanne, 1970.

Burian, Jarka. *The Scenography of Josef Svoboda*. Middletown, Connecticut, 1971.

Berezkin, Viktor. *Teatr Jozefa Svobody*.

Mack, Dietrich, ed. *Theaterarbeit an Wagners "Ring"*. Munich, 1978.

Burian, Jarka. *Svoboda: Wagner*. Middletown, Connecticut, 1983.

articles–

Nagler, Alois. "Wagnerian Productions in Postwar Bayreuth." In *The German Theater Today*, edited by Leroy R. Shaw. Austin, Texas, 1963.

Burian, Jarka. "Czechoslovakian Stage Design and Scenography, 1914-1938." *Theater Design and Technology* summer (1975): 14, 35; fall (1975): 23.

————. "A Scenographer's Work: Josef Svoboda's Designs, 1971-1975." *Theater Design and Technology* summer (1976): 10.

*   *   *

As he enters his sixth decade of professional stage designing, or scenography (a term he prefers), Josef Svoboda can look back on a career that has included exhibitions, international awards and honorary degrees, and some six hundred productions, of which about half have been operas. Perhaps half of those operas have been in his native Czechoslovakia, the rest in other parts of Europe and in North America. Although he is probably best known as an exemplar of the employment of technology in the service of theater, Svoboda's significance extends beyond that particular association. It is rather his way of thinking and his approach to his craft and art that more truly defines his lasting contribution to twentieth century scenography.

Educated as an architect, Svoboda has consistently applied an architect's sense of order and discipline in the organization of space to his work in theater. Although Svoboda also studied painting and brings a painter's eye to his work, it is his demarcation and shaping of space by tangible and intangible means that is most characteristic of his work.

Underlying Svoboda's great range and versatility are a few fundamental principles. He views scenography not as a way of providing realistic background settings for drama or opera, but as a vital expressive force to be integrated with the flow of action and, in the case of opera, with the shadings and dynamics of music. Primarily, scenography should function as poetic imagery or as a metaphor of some essential aspect of the action and music. Sometimes the scenography may retreat or virtually disappear, but at other times it should be ready to provide an effective complement or supplement to that music. Moreover, in order to be adequately expressive, the scenography must be capable of transformation during the course of the action; it must be as capable as a performer of responding to certain cues. Such transformation or response may be overt and physical, but just as often subtle and intangible, above all by means of lighting, by itself or in conjunction with other techniques. Furthermore, Svoboda

has consistently urged a contemporary approach to scenography: not only should contemporary materials and technologies be adapted to theater use, but even the most simple and realistic treatment ought to have about it some clear indication that it is being presented now, at the end of the twentieth century, rather than existing as an archival echo of earlier styles and techniques.

Two final characteristics of Svoboda's orientation: scenography is not to be regarded as an end in itself, but as an instrument to be placed at the service of a director; and whatever its unique features may be, opera is essentially theater. From a scenographer's point of view, opera generally gives freer play to the imagination (one designs more for the music than the plot), and opera budgets are generally larger than those of drama (a scenographer is more likely to be able to afford special instruments and materials).

A brief consideration of specific examples will suggest Svoboda's inventiveness and variety. His use of lighting has been especially important. Light as light, creating an almost tangible atmosphere, was strikingly evident in *Carmen* (1972) as high intensity beams captured the sensuality and passions of the first and last scenes. Light in conjunction with aerosol particles created a virtually tangible column of light for *Tristan and Isolde* (1967), and light in conjunction with abstract projections on literally miles of vertical thin cords gave the impression of mysterious, unending space in another *Tristan*, at Bayreuth (1976). Light in the form of projected laser images contributed to the impact of two different productions of Wagner's *Ring* (1974-76 and 1975-77), as well as Mozart's *The Magic Flute* (1970). More complex projections were the basis of the scenography in such milestone productions as *Tannhäuser* (1973), which created the Venus grotto by means of projections on pneumatic, vaguely erotic forms. Projections onto a special construction of scrim surfaces established the break of past and present and the expressionistic disturbances of mind in the protagonist in *The Queen of Spades* (1976). Still more sophisticated use of projections was evident in Orff's *Prometheus* (1968) and Nono's *Intoleranza* (1965), as Svoboda employed closed circuit television to project live images of the characters and the action onto various surfaces on the stage as a reinforcement of or ironic counterpart to the live action.

An emphasis on architectural, frequently kinetic elements was evident in Smetana's *Dalibor* in 1961 (two huge towers, each placed eccentrically on a separate turntable), Verdi's *Sicilian Vespers* in 1969 (several massive sections of stairs and two towers that moved into varying configurations), Verdi's *Otello* in 1976 (curved concentric walls, each rotating on its own rails), and Mozart's *Idomeneo* in 1981 (a twenty-foot high sculpted head of Poseidon that was sliced into vertical sections, each of which was mobile and placed in various positions for different scenes). These very limited examples, of course, also involved expressive lighting and sometimes projections.

Mirrors, in conjunction with other elements, have also figured prominently in a number of Svoboda's opera productions. An earlier *Magic Flute* (1961) and an earlier *Idomeneo* (1971), as well as Strauss's *Salome* (1985) incorporated mirror effects not only to reinforce the mood of certain scenes but also to extend the sense of stage space in striking ways.

Svoboda's version of Wagner's Ring cycle at Covent Garden (1974-76), with director Götz Friedrich, combined a number of characteristic elements. Central to the scenography was a large platform on hydraulic lifts that could rise and descend, rotate and tilt. Its underside was mirrored to convey the effect of the swimming Rhinemaidens as well as the foundry of the Nibelungs (located below stage) in *Das*

Rheingold. Its top surface was varied for each opera, as were the various elements placed on it or suspended above it: stairs in *Das Rheingold,* abstract cliffs in *Die Walküre,* a forest of suspended pliant plastic strips for *Siegfried,* and a system of rigid glass-like plastic panels with distorting lenses in *Götterdämmerung.* Projections and other special lighting effects, including laser images, enhanced all of these settings.

One other production merits attention in this brief survey. Mozart's *Don Giovanni* had its premiere in Prague under Mozart's direction in what is now called the Tyl theater. To exploit these unique Prague roots of the opera for a 1969 revival in that same theater, Svoboda created a copy of the rococo interior of the auditorium itself—on the stage itself— as a background to the action of the opera and a place to situate the chorus, thus metaphorically reinforcing the "Pragueness" of this particular work.

—Jarka M. Borian

THE SWALLOW
See LA RONDINE

SZELL, George [György].

Conductor. Born 7 June 1897, in Budapest. Died 30 July 1970, in Cleveland. Studied piano with Richard Robert and composition with Mandyczewski in Vienna and J.B. Foerster in Prague; studied with Max Reger in Leipzig; child prodigy as a pianist, performing a Mozart piano concerto with the Vienna Symphony Orchestra, 1907; conducted the Berlin Philharmonic, 1914; assistant conductor at the Royal Opera, Berlin, 1915; conducted opera in Strasbourg, 1917-18, Prague, 1919-21, Darmstadt, 1921-22, and Düsseldorf, 1922-24; principal conductor of the Berlin State Opera, 1924-29; conducted in Prague, 1929-37; guest conductor of the St Louis Symphony Orchestra, 1930; conductor of the Scottish Orchestra, Glasgow, 1937; conductor with the Residentie Orkest, The Hague, 1937-39; conducted in Australia; conductor at the Metropolitan Opera, New York, 1942-46; naturalized United States citizen, 1946; conductor of the Cleveland Orchestra, 1946-70; music adviser and senior guest conductor of the New York Philharmonic, 1969-1970.

Publications

About SZELL: books–

Marsh, R. *The Cleveland Orchestra.* Cleveland and New York, 1967.
Schonberg, H. *The Great Conductors.* New York, 1967.

articles–

Landon, H.C. Robbins. "In Memoriam: George Szell, 1897-1970." *Ovation* July (1985).

*   *   *

Widely considered to be one of the greatest conductors of the century, George Szell was born in Budapest in 1897, grew up largely in Vienna, and developed a great emotional and artistic affinity with Czech culture and music. A child piano prodigy, Szell made his debut as composer-pianist at age eleven with the Vienna Symphony Orchestra, playing works by Mozart, Mendelssohn, and his own Rondo for Piano and Orchestra. He studied composition in Vienna with the eminent music historian and friend of Brahms, Eusebius Mandyczewski and with the Czech Johann Bohuslav Foerster, a close friend of Mahler. Szell also studied with Max Reger in Leipzig. In Berlin, where Szell conducted the Philharmonic in 1914 and became assistant conductor at the Royal Opera in 1915, Richard Strauss took him under his wing. In addition to providing Szell with opportunities to conduct opera, Strauss gave the premiere of Szell's *Variations for Orchestra,* which subsequently had eighty performances worldwide. Szell came to model his conducting technique after that of Strauss, Arturo Toscanini, and Artur Nikisch.

Szell's greatest loves were the classics, especially Haydn and Mozart, but he also championed a number of early twentieth-century composers such as Sibelius, Prokofiev, Bartók, Janáček, and Walton. Elegant phrasing and shortened note values gave Szell's Haydn, Mozart, and Beethoven an incomparable clarity. Like Fritz Reiner, Szell was anti-sentimental, precise, a conductor who maintained great fidelity to the score, yet his interpretations had grace, impeccable taste, and a broad sweep. He was the last of a generation of great conductor-composers whose roots lay in the nineteenth century; aside from his connections with Strauss, Szell grew up under the influence of Mahler and was able to hear the first performances of Schoenberg's music as a student in Vienna.

Strauss helped Szell to obtain a post in Strasbourg, where he conducted opera in the 1917-18 season. From there he moved through a succession of opera positions from Darmstadt, Düsseldorf, Berlin, and Prague, where he remained from 1929 to 1937, meanwhile guest conducting widely. The outbreak of World War II found Szell in America, where he decided to remain. From 1942-46 and briefly in the 1953-54 season he was active at the Metropolitan Opera in New York, conducting 76 performances in all. These included his debut with *Salome,* and also *Der Rosenkavalier, Boris Gudonov, Don Giovanni, Tannhäuser, Die Meistersinger, Der Ring des Nibelungen,* and Verdi's *Otello.* Szell's recorded legacy of opera is unfortunately small. For a number of years he had close ties with the Salzburg Festival; from the 1949 Festival there is a live recording of Strauss's *Der Rosenkavalier* with Maria Reining as the Marschallin, Jarmila Novotná as Octavian, and Hilde Gueden as Sophie, in which the elegance of Szell's style is evident. Although a classicist, at Salzburg Szell gave the world premiere of Rolf Liebermann's *Penelope* in 1953 and of Werner Egk's *The Irish Legend* in 1956. At Salzburg he also led a new production of Mozart's *Die Entführung aus dem Serail.*

Szell's greatness as an orchestra builder became evident when he took over the Cleveland Orchestra in 1946, an ensemble that he left at his death in 1970 as one of the greatest orchestras in the world. Under Szell the Cleveland Orchestra became the quintessential Classical ensemble, giving performances that were astonishing for their clarity and precise execution. Fortunately, many recordings attest to this. Szell was a great technician in the manner of Nikisch and Strauss, with a firm belief that the music should be allowed to speak for itself without histrionics from the conductor. A meticulous disciplinarian, respected but feared, Szell was adamant about ensemble playing, demanding a chamber-like balance based on the players listening carefully to one another. Szell was known to boast that "In Cleveland we begin to rehearse when most orchestras leave off." He noted that "In Cleveland I wanted to combine the American purity and beauty of sound and their virtuosity of execution with the European sense of tradition, warmth of expression and sense of style." With the Cleveland Orchestra he left exciting recordings of orchestral excerpts from Wagner's *Der Ring des Nibelungen.*

—Stephen A. Willier

SZYMANOWSKI, Karol.

Composer. Born 6 October 1882, in Timoshovka, Ukraine. Died 28 March 1937, in Lausanne. Studied with Gustav Neuhaus in Elizavetgrad; studied with Noskowski in Warsaw, 1901; in Berlin composing symphonic music, 1906-08; returned to Warsaw, where his first symphony was performed, 26 March 1909; second symphony completed 1911; in Vienna, 1912-14; in Timoshovka, 1914-17, where he composed his third symphony; performed his violin works with the violinist Paul Kochanski in Moscow and St Petersburg; in Elizavetgrad, 1917-19; settled in Warsaw, 1920; visited Paris, London, and New York, 1921; director of the Warsaw Conservatory, 1927-29; rector of the Warsaw Conservatory, 1930-32.

Operas

Edition: *K. Szymanowski: Dziela.* Edited by T. Chylińska. Cracow, Paris, and Vienna, 1973-.

Lottery for a husband [Loteria na mężów] (operetta), J. Krewiński-Haszyński, 1908-1909.
Hagith, after F. Dörmann, 1912-13, Warsaw, 13 May 1922.
Król Roger, Szymanowski and J. Iwaszkiewicz, 1918-24, Warsaw, 19 June 1926.

Other works: ballets, incidental music, orchestral works (including four symphonies), vocal works, chamber music, piano pieces.

Publications

By SZYMANOWSKI: books–

Wychowawcza rola kultury muzycznej. [educational role of music culture in society]. Warsaw, 1930; 1984.
Bronowicz-Chylińska, ed. *Szymanowski Karol: z listów* [selected letters]. Cracow, 1957.
Chylińska, T., ed. *Dzieje przyjazni: korespondencja Karola Szymanowskiego z Pawłem i Zofia Kochańskimi* [correspondence between Szymanowski and Paweł and Zofia Kochański]. Cracow, 1971.
Smoter, J.M., ed. *Wspomnienia o Karolu Szymanowskim.* Cracow, 1974.
Chylińska, T. ed. *Zakopianskie dni Karola Szymanowskiego.* Cracow, 1976.
———. *Między kompozytorem i wydawca. Korespondencja Karola Szymanowskiego z Universal Edition.* Cracow, 1978.
———. *Karol Szymanowski. Korespondencja. Pelna edycja zachowanych listów od i do kompozytora* [complete edition of letters, 1902-19]. Cracow, 1982.

Nikol'skaja, Irina, and Julia Krejnina, eds. *Vorponicnanija, stat'i publikacii.* Moscow, 1984.
Michatowski, K. and T. Chylińska, eds. *Karol Szymanowski: Pisma.* 2 vols. Cracow, 1984-89.

articles–

"Uwagi w sprawie wspólczesnej opinii muzyczncj w Polsce" [observations on contemporary musical opinion in Poland]. *Nowy przegląd literatury i sztuki* July (1920).
"Fryderyk Chopin." *Skamander* no. 28 (1923).
"Drogi i bezdroza muzyki wspólczesnej" [on contemporary music] *Muzyka* no. 5 (1926).
"O romantyzmie w muzyce." *Droga* no. 1 (1929).
"Frédéric Chopin et la musique polonaise moderne." *La revue musicale* no. 2 (1931): 30.
"Wstęp do pamiętnika" [introduction to Szymanowski's memoires]. *Wiadomości literackie* no. 1 (1938).
Bronowicz-Chylińska, T., ed. *Z pism* [selected essays]. Cracow, 1958.
"Iz Ametok o souvremennom sostojanii muzykal'noj kritiki v Pol'se." In *O muzykal'noj. kritike,* edited by Vera Brjanceva. Moscow, 1983.

About SZYMANOWSKI: books–

Chylińska, T. *Szymanowski.* Cracow, 1962, 3rd ed., 1973; English translation, 1973.
Rubinstein, A. *My Young Years* [116ff, 371ff]. London, 1973.
Jachimecki, Z. *Karol Szymanowski.* London, 1938.
Golachowski, S. *Karol Szymanowski.* Warsaw, 1948; 2nd ed., 1956.
Lobaczewska, S. *Karol Szymanowski: życie i twórczość (1882-1937)* [life and works]. Cracow, 1950.
Chomiński, J.M., ed. *Z życia i twórczości Karola Szymanowskiego.* Cracow, 1960.
Maciejewski, B.M. *Karol Szymanowski: his Life and Music.* London, 1967.
Waldorf, Jerzy. *Serce w plomieniach: opowieść o Karolu Szymanowskim.* Warsaw, 1980.
Sierpiński, Zdzislau, compiler. *O Karolu Szymanowskim Antologia.* Warsaw, 1983.
Bristiger, Michał, et al., eds. *Karol Szymanowski in seiner Zeit.* Munich, 1984.

articles–

Seaman, Gerald. "The Rise of Slavonic Opera, I." *New Zealand Slavonic Journal* 2 (1978): 1.
Samson, Jim. "Szymanowski. An Interior Landscape." *Proceedings of the Royal Musical Society* 106 (1980): 69.
Konold, Wulf. "Karol Szymanowski." *Musica* 36 (1982): 419.
Kresánek, Josef. "K storocnici Karola Szymanovského." *Hudobny zivot* 19 (1982).

*   *   *

Apart from childhood pieces—*Roland, Złocisty szczyt* ("The Golden Summit")—which have been lost without trace, Szymanowski's first stage work was the operetta *Loteria na mężów* ("Lottery for a husband"), composed to a libretto by Juliusz Krewiński-Haszyński in 1908-09, shortly after the composer's student days in Warsaw. Undoubtedly his least happy artistic venture ("I decided to finish it with clenched teeth"), the work remains unpublished and unperformed.

Szymanowski's first major opera, the one-act *Hagith,* was composed to a German libretto by Felix Dörmann (Polish translation by Stanisaw Baracz) in 1912-13. Based on oriental legends of King David as well as on the bible, its central theme is the demand for the sacrifice of Hagith's young body to restore youth and strength to the old king. Her refusal to make the sacrifice (because of her love for the young prince) results in Hagith being stoned to death. The libretto was modeled on Hofmannsthal and the music—by the composer's own admission—on the Strauss of *Salomé* and *Elektra.* "I often fall into the Straussian manner," he conceded in a letter to his friend Stefan Spiess. At times the music veers alarmingly from Straussian frenzy to banal echoes of Puccini, as in the love-duet between Hagith and the young prince. Wagner is also echoed here, and again in Hagith's final love-death. Yet at the dramatic climax of the work—the final duet between Hagith and the Old King—there is music of genuine power, already foreshadowing the world of *Król Roger* (King Roger).

Hagith was followed by a year of extensive travel (including Sicily and North Africa) in the course of which Szymanowski steeped himself fully in the worlds of classical and oriental mythology, as well as in the history and culture of the Arab lands. On his return to Poland in 1915, he found himself as a composer, achieving (belatedly) full creative maturity and branching out in quite new aesthetic directions, inspired both by his travels and by his extensive reading. His most prolific period followed, coinciding almost exactly with the war years and culminating in his masterpiece *Król Roger,* begun in 1918. In some ways, *Król Roger* may be regarded as an autobiographical statement, exorcising the creative crisis which Szymanowski experienced in 1917, when his private world of composition was brutally shattered by the Russian Revolution, which totally destroyed the Szymanowski estate in the Ukraine.

Already before the completion of *Król Roger* in 1924 Szymanowski's music began to take a new turn, evidenced in the simpler idiom of the ballet-pantomime *Mandragora* (1920) and the folk-influenced ballet *Harnasie* (1923). Apart from some incidental music to Tadeusz Miciński's drama *Kniaź Patiomkin* ("Prince Potemkin") (1925), these were his only other stage works. His later music was broadly nationalist in tone, responding to the new-found political independence of Poland with music much indebted to the folk music of the southern Tatra highlands. In addition to *Harnasie* there is a cycle of mazurkas, the song-cycle *Słopiewnie* ("Word-songs"), a *Stabat Mater* and several extended instrumental compositions.

In later life Szymanowski was dogged by ill health and straitened circumstances. Following an unhappy period as director of the Warsaw Conservatory (1927-29), during which he wrote extensively about music, he was appointed Rector of the State Academy of Music in Warsaw, a post which did even more to fray his nerves. He was dismissed, along with others, in a controversy of monumental proportions in 1932 and spent his remaining years trying to make a living through concert performances. He died of tuberculosis in a Lausanne sanatorium at the age of fifty four.

—Jim Samson

T

IL TABARRO
See TRITTICO

TAGLIAVINI, Ferruccio.

Tenor. Born 14 August 1913, in Barco, Reggio Emilia. Married: soprano Pia Tassinari (divorced). Studied with Brancucci in Parma and Amadeo Bassi in Florence; debut as Rodolfo in *La bohème*, Florence 1938; at Teatro alla Scala, 1942-53; U.S. debut in Chicago, 1946; at Metropolitan Opera, 1947-54 and 1961-62; sang Nemorino in *L'elisir d'amore* during La Scala's 1950 visit to Covent Garden; also appeared in London as Cavaradossi in *Tosca* and Nadir in *Les pêcheurs de perles*; retired from opera in 1965.

Publications

About TAGLIAVINI: books–

Tedeschi, C. *Ferruccio Tagliavini*. Rome, 1942.
Gualerzi, G. *Ferruccio Tagliavini: un Reggiano che voleva vivere cosi.* Reggio Emilia, 1988.

articles–

Sanguinetti, H. and C. Williams. "Ferruccio Tagliavini." *Record Collector* 29 (1984): 197.

*   *   *

While Italy's reputation as "The Land of Song" is not as indisputable as it once was, we still look to Italy for one type of voice in particular: the tenor. At its best the warmth of the Italian sun pervades its timbre and, when combined with the forward placement and rounded vowel sounds of the language, results in a tonal quality that is unique in its beauty. Ferruccio Tagliavini, whose voice was typical of the genre, achieved glory over a long and brilliant career.

When Tagliavini made his debut, there was no shortage of great Italian tenors: Martinelli was at his zenith; Lauri-Volpi and Pertile had seen their greatest triumphs but were by no means at the end of their careers; Gigli, who had already won every accolade in his outstanding career, would still sing with honor for almost two more decades. To triumph in the face of such formidable competition may have seemed an awesome task, yet Tagliavini achieved the status of his older colleagues.

It was Gigli whom Tagliavini most resembled in quality and weight of voice. Tagliavini began as a lyric tenor; the voice not overly large but well-produced and even throughout its range. Its greatest asset was its sweetness of timbre and a lovely mezza-voce (half-voice) of ravishing quality.

In the early years of his career he wisely did not stray from roles suitable for the light lyric tenor: Rodolfo (*La bohème*), The Duke (*Rigoletto*), Fritz (*L'amico Fritz*), Elvino (*La sonnambula*) and Almaviva (*Il barbiere di Siviglia*). Tagliavini scored over his contemporaries because of an innate sense of style which he brought to his interpretations, at once placing him on a plane above most Italian tenors.

Tagliavini conquered all the important operatic stages of the world, none more so than the Metropolitan Opera, and at a time when several fine tenors such as Jussi Björling, Richard Tucker and Jan Peerce were already firmly established there. Of his debut role, Rodolfo, Virgil Thompson (*New York Herald Tribune*) wrote "Not in a very long time have we heard tenor singing at once so easy and so adequate." Irving Kolodin (*New York Sun*) waxed even more poetic: "(He) was the best the old house has had in a decade at least. A quantity of listeners limited only by the fire laws took Tagliavini to their hearts almost immediately, and he responded by charming their hearts away by the beauty of his voice and the artistry of his singing. The suggestions in his record were supported by the airy brightness of his vocal quality, the style and verve which he used it to make Rodolfo a tangible figure on the stage. Not by any means the largest tenor voice the work has had (even this season) it floats superbly, and reaches the ear with ring and vibrance at all levels of force. As if being an Italian tenor who is also a musician is not enough, Tagliavini added a lively sense of stage action. . . ." His singing elicited similar reactions wherever he appeared.

Fortunately for collectors, Tagliavini recorded extensively, both solo items and several complete recordings. His earliest Cetra recordings from the 1940s are treasures indeed, the voice ravishing in its lyricism, stylish and of beautiful quality. As a general rule, the earliest recordings are the ones to seek out. Of the complete recordings, most have much to commend them; only the very late Supraphon *L'elisir d'amore* is to be avoided: recorded at the very end of his career, the voice is coarse and unattractive. His complete recording of *L'amico Fritz* is particularly worth searching for: for not only was Tagliavini a famous interpreter of Fritz, but the performance is conducted by the composer. It is a document of true historic value and a worthy testimony to a glorious career.

—Larry Lustig

TAJO, Italo.

Bass. Born 25 April 1915, in Pinerolo, Italy. Studied with Nilde Stinchi Bertozzi in Turin, 1932-34; debut as Fafner in Wagner's *Das Rheingold,* 1935; sang with the Rome opera,

1939-44; sang intermittently at Teatro alla Scala, 1946-56; sang at the Metropolitan Opera, 1948-50; sang with the San Francisco Opera, 1948-56; sang on Broadway in *Fanny,* 1956; joined the faculty at the Cincinnati Conservatory of Music in 1966; sang at the Metropolitan Opera, 1980-91; farewell performance in Puccini's *Tosca,* 1991.

Publications

About TAJO: books—

Clerico, C. *Italo Tajo—La parte del basso.* Turin, 1985.

About TAJO: articles—

Hastings, R. "Italo Tajo." *Opera Annual* 7 (1960): 1.
Giannini, V. "Italo Tajo: a great basso looks at his repertoire." *Opera Quarterly* 5 no. 4 (1987-88): 58.

*　　*　　*

Few artists, in any discipline, have enjoyed the length of a career such as the one enjoyed by basso Italo Tajo. Born in 1915, he made his debut in 1935 in Turin, as Fafner in *Das Rheingold,* and continued to sing at the Metropolitan and with American regional opera companies into the 1990s.

He was interrupted early by army service but returned to the stage in 1939 in Rome, where he sang until 1948. His longstanding association with the Teatro alla Scala began in 1940, and he appeared on the other Italian stages. The 1947 film of Rossini's *Il barbiere di Siviglia* with Tajo, Ferruccio Tagliavini and Tito Gobbi made the three of them internationally famous, and Tajo was then in demand everywhere. He sang in London first in 1947, and appeared in Edinburgh and Glyndebourne as Mozart's Figaro and as Banquo in *Macbeth.* He was heard in Paris, Germany and Buenos Aires.

He first sang in San Francisco in 1948, after which the Metropolitan Opera engaged him to help fill the void created when Ezio Pinza left that house for Broadway. Tajo's Metropolitan Opera debut role was as Don Basilo *Il barbiere di Siviglia.* His singing of Basilo in the film plus his San Francisco reviews made his first Metropolitan appearance so eagerly anticipated that Lily Pons canceled her Rosina that evening, or so it was said.

Tajo sang only five roles at the Metropolitan before the new regime of Rudolf Bing failed to rehire him. He continued to sing in other houses and to concertize. He made films, one being an ambitious setting of the Faust legend with music from the operas of Gounod, Berlioz and Boito. He then went into stage direction and in 1966, joined the Cincinnati Music Conservatory in Ohio.

Upon the ascension of James Levine as Music Director of the Metropolitan Opera, Tajo returned there, singing smaller parts such as the Sacristan (*Tosca*), the Bailiff (*Werther*), and the *La bohème* Benoit and Alcindoro. He also sang two performances as Don Pasquale which were superb, in spite of his age.

Italo Tajo had a large, varied repertoire ranging from the classic buffo roles to the Doctor in *Wozzeck* (in the Italian premiere of the opera in Rome), to tragic figures, to modern roles in works by Milhaud and Nono. He sang Mozart magnificently. The voice was immense, easily projected, and could adopt a comic, cavernous quality. His acting was always highly imaginative and unique to him. He played Colline in *La bohème* as a blond young man, not a gray-haired ancient as had been usual before, and now Colline is universally

interpreted as the same age as the other Bohemians. His Dulcamara in *L'elisir d'amore* will never be forgotten and his *Faust* Mephisto could be quite bawdy. He has sung over 80 roles on the stage.

Cetra recorded an album of Mozart concert arias with Tajo, the Mozart Requiem, with Pia Tassinari and Tagliavini and conducted by Victor de Sabata, and *Le nozze di Figaro.* RCA put out 78rpm's of arias, not re-released; and Tajo also figures in their *Rigoletto* recording with Erna Berger, Jan Peerce, and Leonard Warren. There is a *Tannhäuser* from Florence, 1951, on Melodram; a *Macbeth* with Callas, Teatro alla Scala, 1952; an *Il trovatore,* Naples, 1951; an *Attila,* Venice, 1951; and some Metropolitan Opera air checks of his original engagement there including *Faust, Gianni Schicchi,* and *L'elisir d'amore.* Italian Radio broadcast several operas with Tajo over the years and they should be made available. Italo Tajo's first recording was as Roucher in *Andrea Chénier,* with Gigli, Caniglia and Bechi in 1942.

—Bert Wechsler

THE TALES OF HOFFMANN
See LES CONTES D'HOFFMANN

TALVELA, Martti (Olavi).

Bass. Born 4 February 1935, in Hittola, Finland. Died 22 July 1989, in Juva, Finland. Studied at the Lahti Academy of Music, 1958-60, and then with Carl Martin Oehmann in Stockholm; debut as Sparafucile in Verdi's *Rigoletto,* Stockholm, 1961; joined Berlin's Deutsche Opera, 1962; Metropolitan Opera debut as the Grand Inquisitor in *Don Carlos,* 1968; sang many Verdi and Wagner roles; artistic director of the Savonlinna Festival, 1972-80.

Publications:

About TALVELA: articles–

Fabian, I. "Das Interview." *Opernwelt* 24/10 (1983): 10.
Robinson, H. "Believer: Finnish bass Martti Talvela." *Opera News* 50 (1986): 30.

*　　*　　*

Although few artists ever achieve the status of national hero in their homeland, basso Martti Talvela was so venerated in Finland. His untimely death at the age of 53 while dancing at his daughter's wedding was considered a national calamity. Having been the director of the Savonlinna Opera Festival for many years, and after instigating the Finnish National Opera's 1983 triumphant appearance at the Metropolitan Opera House in New York, he had been appointed to lead the National Opera into their newly built home in Helsinki when death intervened.

A former heavyweight boxing champion, he was an immensely imposing man, six feet eight inches tall and weighing almost 300 pounds, and had a large beard. He loved his farm.

He was working as a schoolteacher when his voice developed: he then studied with Carl Martin Ohman in Stockholm. His debut was as Sparafucile in Helsinki, 1960, but he then sang regularly with the Royal Opera in Stockholm. The Berlin Opera called, and so did Bayreuth, where Talvela sang many roles. He also sang at the Salzburg Festival and performed many times at Covent Garden. He came to the Metropolitan Opera in 1968 and immediately became a favorite there. The Teatro alla Scala, Paris, Moscow, Leningrad and further music centers experienced his opera roles and concerts.

Talvela possessed a large, commanding voice, as was his stage presence. His acting was intelligent and always in character. The Finnish opera *The Last Temptations* by Joonas Kokkonen allowed the opportunity for one of Talvela's greatest roles, the itinerant preacher Paavo Ruotsalainen, a Finnish historical figure. Other roles in which he excelled were Hunding, Pimen, the *Don Carlo* Inquisitor, Rocco, Daland, and King Marke. He also widely sang Boris Godunov, King Philipp, Sarastro, and other leading roles, but did not reach the supreme excellence in those that he did in the others. He was also a dedicated concert singer, offering extremely serious programs.

Talvela's many recordings range from Finnish folk songs to the role of Boris Godunov in Musorgsky's original orchestration. He has also recorded Musorgsky's cycle *Songs and Dances of Death* in an orchestration he commissioned from Kalevi Aho, Schubert's *Winterreise,* the Wagner roles, and a Sarastro from Salzburg.

—Bert Wechsler

TAMAGNO, Francesco.

Tenor. Born 28 December 1850, near Turin. Died 31 August 1905, in Varese. Studied at the Turin Conservatory with Carlo Pedrotti; debut as Gasparo in Cortesi's *La colpa del cuore,* Turin, 1872; major debut as Riccardo in *Un ballo in maschera,* Palermo, 1874; Teatro alla Scala debut as Vasco da Gama in *L'Africaine,* 1877; created Fabiano in Gomes's *Maria Tudor* (1879), Azaele in Ponchielli's *Il figliuol prodigo,* (1880), Adorno in the revised *Simon Boccanegra* (1881), Didier in Ponchielli's *Marion Delorme* (1885), the title role in *Otello* (1887—a role on which much of his reputation was made and rests), and Helion in de Lara's *Messaline* (1899); Metropolitan Opera debut as Otello, 1890; singer at the Metropolitan Opera, 1894-95; sang in first performance of Leoncavallo's *I medici,* Milan, 1893; Covent Garden debut as Otello, 1895; last complete operatic performance, 1903, in Rome.

Publications

About TAMAGNO: book–

Ruberi, Mario. *Francesco Tamagno (Otello fu. . .) La vita del grande tenore.* Turin, 1990.

article–

Gualerzi, Giorgio. "*Otello:* The Legacy of Tamagno." *Opera* 38/February (1987): 122; postscript in June 1987 issue.

* * *

By midday on 31 August 1905, news of the death of Francesco Tamagno had spread by telegraph and courier from the tenor's palatial villa at Varese to the opera capitals of his native Italy. In Milan, critic Ettore Moschino wrote simply, "Otello fu." No other headline would have been more appropriate: throughout Europe and the Americas, Francesco Tamagno was not only the greatest dramatic tenor Italy had yet produced; he was Otello.

One of five surviving children, Francesco Tamagno was born near Turin on 28 December 1850. His father, an amateur baritone, sang popular songs and attempted an occasional aria for the diners at his small *trattoria;* as youths, Francesco and his brother, Domenico, each of whom had penetrating alto voices, followed their father's example. Both boys were good enough to merit a place in the local diocesan choir, where they learned nominal solfeggio. What rudimentary voice lessons they had were obtained from a local teacher who held group sessions in the resonant archway of a local bridge.

When Francesco was eighteen, in 1868, he and his brother sought an audition at the local conservatory, then headed by Carlo Pedrotti, conductor at the Teatro Regio and the leading musical force in Turin. Pedrotti could only commend the

Francesco Tamagno as Otello

brothers' "excellent lungs"; otherwise, he rated their musicianship and artistic promise in one word: "zero." Francesco, heartbroken yet unwilling to give up completely, sought the help of influential patrons who, in time, prevailed upon Pedrotti to admit the young man to the Teatro Regio chorus.

Although Francesco Tamagno's debut is usually cited as having occurred at the Teatro Regio in 1873 in the second-tenor role of Nearco in Donizetti's *Poliuto,* recent research (T.G. Kaufman, 1990) has established that Tamagno's first appearance on the Teatro Regio stage took place on 27 February 1872 in a performance of Cortesi's *La colpa del cuore,* in which Tamagno sang the comprimario role of Gasparo. It was not in Turin but in Palermo—at the Teatro Bellini in the 1873-74 season, where he sang the role of Riccardo in Verdi's *Un ballo in maschera*—that Tamagno first earned genuine critical acclaim. From there his reputation grew rapidly, undergirded by his virile stage presence and clarion voice.

By the time he made his debut at the Teatro alla Scala (1877), where he was heralded in Verdi's *Don Carlos,* Massenet's *Le roi de Lahore,* and in Gomes' revised version of *Fosca* (1878), Tamagno was already being spoken of as "the preeminent interpreter" in most of the dramatic roles he had undertaken. At La Scala he would also create the tenor roles in Gomes' *Maria Tudor* (1879), as well as Ponchielli's *Il figliuol prodigo* (1880) and *Marion Delorme* (1885).

Late in 1880 in Milan, reports began to circulate that Giuseppe Verdi had secretly begun work on a new opera based upon Shakespeare's *Othello.* Verdi's public silence subtracted from the story's credibility; but it did not dissuade two singers from making known their interest to the composer—Victor Maurel and Francesco Tamagno, who would soon sing together in Verdi's 1881 revision of *Simon Boccanegra.* Six years would pass, however, before Tamagno would be chosen by Verdi for the title role in *Otello.*

The premiere of *Otello,* at the Teatro alla Scala on 5 February 1887, was a triumph for the composer and the principal singers alike. Victor Maurel's Iago, especially his rendering of the "Credo," was heralded as a dramatic tour de force. But for all of Maurel's triumph, it was Tamagno's elemental human touches—"his passion, tenderness and love, contrasted with his explosive violence," in the words of *Il Monaldi*—that put his Otello on a level with the brilliant acting of Italy's great tragedian, Tommaso Salvini.

Rapidly and enduringly, Otello became Tamagno's signature role. In Europe and the Americas he performed the role in both large and comparatively small cities; in the United States, for example, he bestowed his Otello not only upon New York, Boston, Philadelphia, Washington, and Chicago audiences, but also ventured to San Francisco, Denver, Louisville, and eventually St Louis to create the role in each locale. At each touring stop, one critic noted, audiences sat on the edges of their seats, awestruck by the power of "notes hurled from his deep, prodigious chest like missiles from a catapult."

In scope, the active career of Francesco Tamagno spanned nearly three decades, and encompassed approximately 365 productions staged in different cities during a thirty-year period. Although it is not feasible to specify an exact number of Tamagno's operatic and concert performances, it seems safe to estimate that he sang at least one thousand operatic performances; the figure may be increased slightly if his concert appearances were to be included in the sum. He performed frequently, and with no appreciable loss of vocal splendor, from his first triumph in *Un ballo* in 1874 past the turn of the century.

Slowed by congestive heart problems which increased in severity by 1902, Tamagno was forced thereafter to put reasonable limits on his performing. His last complete performance as Otello took place in Rome in 1903, and his final operatic performances—of the second and third acts of *Poliuto,* perhaps his favorite role—occurred successively in Rome, Naples, Turin, and Milan in the spring of 1904. By the following spring, at age 54, he had become convinced that the end of his life was near. As spring turned to summer he had a premonition of his death. On 30 August 1905, a massive cerebral hemorrhage befell him; he died at 7:30 that morning, in the presence of his family.

The international obituaries of Francesco Tamagno paid tribute not only to his heroic voice and enduring operatic accomplishments, especially as the creator of Otello, but also noted the qualities of personality which defined him both as a man and an artist. Physically, he had been well suited for Otello: he was above average in height, powerfully built, with refined facial features and dark auburn hair. Especially considering his celebrity, Tamagno was approachable and was unfailingly considerate of the public. His personality, as Quaintance Eaton summarized it from the words of many of his colleagues, was that of an "extremely pleasant and cheerful man . . . [who] turned a good-natured face to the world."

The voice and artistry of Francesco Tamagno—at the end of his life, at least—are accessible to contemporary listeners by way of the thirteen arias he recorded from his repertoire for the infant Gramophone and Typewriter Company. As these valuable early discs have been reissued (though not always reliably as regards playback speed) in a variety of formats in the intervening decades, they warrant consideration here. Details of the making of most of the Tamagno G & T discs have come to us from the memoirs of F.W. Gaisberg, the company's senior recording technician at the time. "To carry out this recording my brother, as Tamagno's guest, spent a week in his mountain home at Sousa in the Mont Cenis pass," Gaisberg notes in his *The Music Goes 'Round* (1942). A second, brief session appears to have been held in Rome in April of 1904, coincident with the tenor's abridged *Poliuto* performance there.

Had Tamagno recorded only the brief "Esultate!" he would have left evidence for succeeding generations of the accuracy of the descriptions of the timbre, or sound quality, of his voice as it was characterized by contemporaries: a voice of "enduring brass" (David Bispham), a "trumpet from Jericho" (Carlo Nasi). These qualities are also apparent in his "Ora a per sempre addio!" which he recorded, however, at an unusually broad tempo.

Of Tamagno's "Niun mi tema" recording, the judgment of Henry Pleasants (1966, 1981) is worth noting: "The production is primitive, and the piano accompaniment ludicrous. But the searing despair of his 'E tu, come sei pallida, e stanca, e muta, e bella!—And you, how pale you are, and spent, and silent, and beautiful!', uttered after Othello has strangled Desdemona, is possibly unmatched by anything else on wax."

In the remaining discs, as in the three *Otello* recordings, both the volume, range, and unique timbre of the Tamagno voice are fully in evidence. His fabled high tones, the ease of which enabled him to add five successive high Cs to the final act stratta in *Guillaume Tell,* are heard in sustained clarion form in his recordings of "Di quella pira" from *Il trovatore,* "Corriam! voliam!" and "O muto asil" from *Tell,* "Re del ciel" from *Il profeta,* and "Quand nos jours" from *Hérodiade.* Yet in the second of his *Profeta* recordings, of the aria "Sopra Berta, l'amor mio," Tamagno tempered his stentorian approach and incorporated nominal *mezza voce* in the shaping of some of the aria's long, sustained phrases. In the end, however, one must bear in mind the verdict of F.W. Gaisberg when assessing the Tamagno recordings: "I regret to say, [they] can only be considered a faint reflection of that extraordinary voice."

Of all of his recordings, the very last one he made at his summer home at Sousa—a record not released until five years after his death—perhaps reveals more of Francesco Tamagno's basic personality than any of the others. As Will Gaisberg lowered the cutting stylus of the recording device onto the last of the wax plates which would preserve his voice, Tamagno paused before his accompanist began the opening measures of the *Trovatore* aria "Deserto sulla terra"—"Alone in the world." Then he spoke the words "Dedico alla memoria di mio padre" into the apparatus—"This I dedicate to the memory of my father."

The speaking voices of other singers had been heard before on recordings, usually announcing the selections they were about to sing. But no artist had ever spoken words as personal as these were. The man who spoke them was an international celebrity. His father, by contrast, was known only to the patrons of his little *trattoria* near Turin.

—James A. Drake

TAMBERLICK, Enrico.

Tenor. Born 16 March 1820, in Rome. Died 13 March 1889, in Paris. Studied with Zirilli in Rome and Guglielmi in Naples; debut as Tebaldo in Bellini's *I Capuleti ed i Montecchi*, Naples, 1841; London debut as Masaniello in Auber's *La muette de Portici*, 1850; sang in London, 1850-77; premiered Verdi's *La forza del destino*, 1862; toured the United States in 1873.

*   *   *

Enrico Tamberlick is the forerunner of the dramatic tenor as we know it today. It is true that he is not really the first such tenor to specialize in heavier roles. Andrea Nozzari, Domenico Donzelli and Adolphe Nourrit all had the same specialty. But Tamberlick was the first dramatic tenor with an international career to possess the chest high C, and also to sing the new dramatic repertory, which included operas by Meyerbeer, Halévy, Verdi and even Donizetti.

The chest high C was first introduced by Gilbert-Louis Duprez in 1837, and has since become a favorite weapon of those tenors who could reach it. Duprez, of course, sang it in French opera, more specifically in Rossini's *Guillaume Tell*. Tamberlick has frequently been credited with bringing this high note into Italian opera by interpolating it in the third act of *Il trovatore*. Even though Verdi was reportedly very dismayed by this unauthorized change to his score, the practice eventually became a tradition far beyond the composer's control. This was not Tamberlick's innovation, however, for Carlo Baucardé had already sung it in Florence in the autumn of 1853. However, Carlo Baucardé's career was too short and too limited to Southern Europe for him to have made a significant impact on the history of singing. Considering the length and scope of Tamberlick's career (from the early 1840s to the early 1880s and in most of the major capitals of Northern Europe, with seasons in the United States, Cuba and

Mexico) he left a great impact and had many would-be imitators.

Like many dramatic tenors after him, Tamberlick started his career in lighter roles. Although he had made his debut in Rome as Arnoldo in a concert version of *Guillaume Tell*, he made his "stage" debut in Naples as Tebaldo in *I Capuleti ed i Montecchi*, and frequently sang Rodrigo in Rossini's *Otello* and Idreno in the same composer's *Semiramide*. He sang three seasons in Naples, and six more in the Iberian peninsula (Lisbon, Madrid, and Barcelona) before achieving true international prominence when he became a regular in London, Paris, Madrid and St Petersburg. His voice probably did not start to darken until the early 1850s when he began to specialize in a heavier repertory than he had sung in Southern Europe.

Unlike many of the more prominent singers of the mid-nineteenth century, Tamberlick did not achieve much of his fame by dint of the roles he created. While he did take part in a number of operatic premieres, most of the works involved are now completely forgotten. The most notable exception is Alvaro in Verdi's *La forza del destino*, a role he created in St Petersburg in 1862 and repeated there for two more seasons. But Alvaro never became a part of his regular repertory; in fact, there is no record of his ever impersonating him outside Russia. Another exception is the role of Jorge in Arrietta's *Marina*, which he created when it was first given as an opera in Madrid in 1871.

Tamberlick had an unusually long career. He had made a concert debut in 1837, and a stage debut in 1841, after which he sang almost non-stop until 1883. His last confirmed appearance was as Poliuto in the Spanish city of La Coruña in September of 1883, but the company proceeded to the nearby town of El Ferrol, and Tamberlick may well have sung there as well. His favorite roles were Poliuto, Manrico, Arnoldo, Vasco de Gama and Rossini's Otello. Had he kept his voice for a few years more there is little doubt that he would have sung both Otellos.

Tamberlick was compared to the great Mario by a correspondent of the Musical World during his first London season (in 1850). Portions of this comparison may be of interest: "Tamberlick, the new tenor of the Covent Garden Opera, whose art and voice are of totally different character, appears to be the only contemporary tenor who has in any way rivalled the incomparable Mario. Their styles are, however, so different that, whilst they may be equals, they are both masters of their own model and originality . . . I should describe Tamberlick's singing as mystic, subtle and insinuating. His voice, contrary to Mario's, appears to have its great distinguishing features towards the treble, where, in astonishing force, it was never exceeded, if equalled. It is of a metallic, and, at the same time of a silvery tone. His shrill cry outvies and overcomes the mighty mass of concerted music, and is heard above the thundering tones of the great basses and baritones, above the lark-like notes of the sopranos, then he strikes lightning into your very soul."

The writer goes on to say that the breadth, volume and distinctness in the lower part of Mario's voice are absent in Tamberlick's. Therefore, he regards Mario as the more perfect of the two singers. Yet, if Tamberlick was less perfect than Mario, he still ranked second on the world's operatic stages for a period of twenty years when great tenors were much more abundant than they are today.

—Tom Kaufman

TAMERLANO.

Composer: George Frideric Handel.

Librettist: Nicola F. Haym (after A. Piovene, Il *Bajazet*; and as revised for 1719, based on J. Pradon, *Tamerlan, ou La mort de Bajazet*).

First Performance: London, King's Theatre in the Haymarket, 31 October 1724; revised 13 November 1731.

Roles: Bajazet (tenor); Asteria (soprano); Andronico (contralto); Tamerlano (contralto); Irene (contralto); Leone (bass).

Publications

article–

Knapp, J. Merrill. "Handel's *Tamerlano:* the Creation of an Opera." *Musical Quarterly* 56 (1970): 405.

*   *   *

The story of Tamerlano as set by Handel originally comes from the tragedy *La mort de Bajazet* (1675) by the French playwright Jacques Pradon. It was not directly from Pradon's play that Handel and his librettist Nicola Haym took their subject, however, and before the first performance of the work Handel's original version of the opera underwent a number of drastic alterations as the result of the introduction of a new singer and a new version of the story. For the sake of clarity, the plot of Handel's ultimate first performance version will be summarized here.

The Turkish Emperor Bajazet, who has lost his empire in battle to the Tartar Emperor Tamerlano, has been imprisoned with his daughter Asteria. The first act concerns itself with Bajazet's loathing of Tamerlano, with the love between Asteria (originally played by the internationally famous soprano Francesca Cuzzoni) and the Greek prince Andronico (played by the renowned alto castrato Francesco Bernardi, known as Senesino), and Tamerlano's lust for Asteria, as well as his desire to marry her. Act II shows Asteria's feigned interest in Tamerlano in order to get close enough to him to murder him, but by the end of act II, Asteria has failed in her task, and has reunited with Andronico and her father, both of whom had doubted her faithfulness. In the final act, Bajazet gives his daughter a vial of poison, saying that he will soon take the same, and advises her to drink it before Tamerlano forces himself upon her. He promises her that they will meet each other in the afterlife, free of the tyrant who imprisons them. The dramatic finale involves Bajazet's on-stage death as he succumbs to the poison he has taken while fiercely denouncing Bajazet and tenderly bidding his daughter farewell. In the last scene, Tamerlano, deeply moved by Bajazet's words and action, gives Andronico the rule of Greece and Asteria's hand in marriage, saying "Now Hatred's banish'd, and we're Friends again;/From this Day's Joy, we'll date our happy Reign" (translation from the original London libretto).

The ultimate first performance version of Handel's *Tamerlano* was based on a mixture of Agostino Piovene's 1710 libretto of the same title, as adapted by Nicola Haym, and on the revision of Piovene's text for Reggio in 1719, prepared by a group of anonymous librettists. The Reggio version of the opera, set by F. Gasparini, probably came into Handel's

hands by way of the tenor Francesco Borosini, who created the role of Bajazet at the premiere of Handel's opera. Borosini was clearly not the tenor Handel originally wrote the part for, however, and a virtually complete first version of the work based exclusively on Haym's adaptation of Piovene's 1710 libretto survives in Handel's autograph manuscript of *Tamerlano,* in which the part of Bajazet was quite possibly intended for the Scottish tenor Alexander Gordon, who had appeared in previous Royal Academy productions.

In Handel's original version of *Tamerlano,* Bajazet remains static throughout the opera in terms of his fierce determination to die rather than be imprisoned by Tamerlano. Piovene's version of the story, upon which Haym's initial libretto was based, places dramatic emphasis on Asteria and her reaction to her father's tragic death. By contrast, the revision of Piovene set by Gasparini in 1719 shifts the emphasis to Bajazet's character by showing him both as the proud, defeated ruler of the original version, and as a compassionate father, concerned about his daughter's welfare. In the original Piovene version, Bajazet cannot conceive how he or Asteria can continue to live in the shame of defeat, whereas in the revised 1719 version, Bajazet is torn between his own desire to die and his concern for his daughter's future in his absence.

Clearly, the Italian tenor Francesco Borosini influenced the decision of the anonymous 1719 librettists to alter the 1710 version of the story to accommodate the tenor's interpretation of the character of Bajazet. Like Handel's ultimate 1724 score, Gasparini's contains the on-stage death of Bajazet, an extremely unusual event in *opera seria*. It also seems likely that it was Borosini's musico-dramatic abilities that led Handel to alter the existing version of his opera to include his own setting (in part based on Gasparini's) of the death scene, as well as a number of other revisions necessary as a result of this monumental change.

While the intense drama of the on-stage death of Bajazet cannot be denied, Handel's pre-first-performance revisions of his original version of *Tamerlano* compromised the integrity of the work in a number of ways. Perhaps the most striking of these is the shifting of the act II ending aria "Cor di Padre, e cor d'Amante," which was originally addressed to Bajazet ("Padre") and Andronico ("Amante"), to the first scene of act III, where Asteria addresses her father in private. While many practical reasons for this can be proposed (such as the need to create equal numbers of arias for the leads), the excision of the original act III, scene i aria is in itself tragic. The original aria here, "Su la sponda del pigro Lete," was completely revised by Handel prior to its ejection as a result of the Borosini-invoked changes, in order to render this scene a high point of the drama. In this scene, Bajazet and Asteria make a pledge to one another that they will poison themselves and meet each other in the afterlife on the banks of the river Lethe. Needless to say, such a dramatic situation evoked a powerful musical response from Handel; composing in the unusual (for him) key of B-flat minor, Handel's interweaving of voice and accompaniment creates an atmosphere in which the transition from this world to the next can be imagined, and suggests the powerful bond between father and daughter as well as the desperation of their plight.

While it is to be regretted that Handel's initial conception of the drama was altered, the resultant first performance version of *Tamerlano* is considered by most to be superior, depicting as it does Bajazet's death in a highly dramatic manner. Perhaps more than any other of Handel's operas, however, *Tamerlano* reveals the extent to which *opera seria*

Title page from the score of Handel's 1724 opera

was created based upon the musico-dramatic abilities of the cast for whom it was initially written; revisions were necessarily compromises of the original product. In the case of *Tamerlano,* the advantages gained by the introduction of a superlative singing-actor and the changes suggested by him have to be weighed against the compromises to the original musico-dramatic structure of the opera his introduction entailed.

In any of its versions, *Tamerlano* remains a stunningly dramatic work from an age in which opera was accused of pandering to the audience's desire to hear singers at their virtuosic best, regardless of the drama at hand. While in part this characteristic of the work can be attributed to the excellent plot and inherent dramatic situations, Handel's and his librettist Haym's treatment of the story of Bajazet's imprisonment resulted in an *opera seria* masterpiece, and indeed in one of the great masterpieces of the eighteenth century.

—C. Steven LaRue

TANCREDI.

Composer: Gioachino Rossini.

Librettists: G. Rossi and L. Lechi (after Voltaire).

First Performance: Venice, La Fenice, 6 February 1813.

Roles: King Argirio (tenor); Orbazzano (bass); Amenaide (soprano); Tancredi (mezzo-soprano); Isaura (mezzo-soprano); Roggiero (tenor); chorus.

Publications

book–

Gossett, Philip. *The Tragic Finale of "Tancredi".* Pesaro, 1977.

articles–

Radiciotti, G. "Il *Signor Bruschino* e il *Tancredi* di Rossini." *Rivista musicale italiana* (1920).
Gossett, Philip. "The *candeur virginale* of *Tancredi.*" *Musical Times* 112 (1971).
Amico Fedele d'. "A proposito d'un *Tancredi:* Dioniso in Apollo." In *Die stylistische Entwicklung der italienischen Musik zwischen 1770 und 1830 und ihre Beziehungen zum Norden,* edited by F. Lippmann, 61. Laaber, 1982.

*　　*　　*

Tancredi was the first opera composed by Rossini for La Fenice, Venice's leading theater. Its success confirmed Rossini's newly-won reputation as one of Italy's leading operatic composers. He was then twenty-one years old.

The action, loosely based on Voltaire's tragedy *Tancrède,* takes place in Syracuse, on Sicily, during the middle ages. After an unsuccessful rebellion against King Argirio, Orbazzano swears allegiance to Argirio; the king, to celebrate their reconciliation, promises his daughter Amenaide to Orbazzano in marriage. But Amenaide loves Tancredi, an exiled

hero. Tancredi, returning to Syracuse in secret, presents himself to the audience in a memorable *scena* that anticipates in some respects the appearance of Arsace in act 1 of *Semiramide* (1823). He reveals his identity only to Amenaide, with whom he sings a passionate love duet ("L'aura che intorno spiri"). As Amenaide is led toward the nuptial alter, Orbazzano enters with a love letter by Amenaide and addressed, he believes, to Solamir, ruler of the Saracens who threaten Syracuse; the first act ends with all expressing their astonishment, confusion, anger, and fear.

In the second act Argirio condemns his daughter to death for treason. Even Tancredi believes her to be unfaithful and, in despair, he goes off to court death in battle with the Saracens. The drama comes to a climax in the final scenes, set in a Romantically conceived forest with gullies, caves, and waterfalls (cf. Weber's Wolf Glen). Tancredi leads his troops against the enemy; victorious, he hears from the dying Solamir that Amenaide is innocent. Argirio happily blesses the marriage of Tancredi and Amenaide as the opera ends.

With *Tancredi* Rossini came of age as a composer of *opera seria.* Craftsmanship and inspiration are at a consistently high level throughout. The music breathes freshness and vitality. Tancredi's arrival in act I, with its celebrated cabaletta "Di tanti palpiti," has tended to overshadow the opera's many other beauties. Argirio's accompanied recitative "Dall patria ogni nemico" (also in act 1) is full of the excitement of battle. The aria that follows, "Pensa che sei mia figlia," conveys a sense of energy, even violence, with music that is splendidly heroic and dramatic. The king's confusion and indecision, as he condemns his daughter to death in the great recitative and aria (with chorus) "Oh Dio crudel!" (act II) is vividly expressed by rests between syllables and sudden modulations, by coloratura and extremes of vocal range. In the quiet passage at the words "Ma, la figlia," we can feel Argirio's remorse.

No less successful is Amenaide's prison scene, which begins with a long, atmospheric oboe solo over throbbing strings. The beautiful orchestration of Amenaide's aria, with English horn, clarinet and flute, anticipates the wonderful orchestral experiments of Rossini's Neapolitan operas. Rossini's ability to differentiate characters is apparent in the first-act duet for Amenaide and Tancredi. Amenaide's disjunct line reveals her distracted state of mind; Tancredi's smoother line helps Amenaide (and us) believe him when he says confidently "Contra il destin crudele / Trionferà amor" ("Against cruel destiny love will triumph").

—John A. Rice

TANNHÄUSERund der Sängerkrieg auf Wartburg [Tannhäuser and the Song Contest at the Wartburg].

Composer: Richard Wagner.

Librettist: Richard Wagner.

First Performance: Dresden, Königliches Hoftheater, 19 October 1845; revised, text alterations with C. Nuitter, Paris, Opéra, 13 March 1861; revised, Munich, Königliches Hof- und Nationaltheater, 5 March 1865; revised, Vienna, Hofoper, 22 November 1875.

Roles: Elisabeth (soprano); Venus (soprano or mezzo-soprano); Tannhäuser (tenor); Wolfram von Eschenbach (baritone); Hermann (bass); Walther von der Vogelweide (tenor); Biterolf (bass); Heinrich der Schreiber (tenor); Reinmar von Zweter (bass); Young Shepherd (soprano); Four Noble Pages (sopranos, altos); chorus (SSAATTBB).

Publications

books–

Smolian, A. *The Themes of 'Tannhäuser'.* London, 1891.
Lindner, E. *Richard Wagner über 'Tannhäuser': Aussprüche des Meisters über sein Werk.* Leipzig, 1914.
Steinbeck, D. *Interszenierungsformen des Tannhäuser (1845-1904): Untersuchungen zur Systematik der Opernregie.* Regensburg, 1964.
———, ed. *Richard Wagners Tannhäuser-Szenarium: das Vorbild der Erstaufführung mit der Kostümbeschreibung und den Dekorations-plänen.* Berlin, 1968.
Hopkinson, C. *Tannhäuser: an Examination of 36 Editions.* Tutzing, 1973.
Mack, Dietrich, ed. *Richard Wagner, "Tannhäuser".* Frankfurt am Main, 1979.
John, Nicholas, ed. *Wagner: Tannhäuser.* London, 1988.

articles–

Altmann, W. "Richard Wagner und die Berliner General-Intendantur: Verhandlungen über den 'Fliegenden Holländer' und 'Tannhäuser'." *Die Musik* 2/no. 11 (1902-03): 331; no. 14 (1902-03): 92; no. 16 (1902-03): 304.
Golther, W. "Die französische und die deutsche Tannhäuser-Dichtung." *Die Musik* 2 (1902-03): 271.
Panzer, F. "Richard Wagners Tannhäuser: sein Aufbau und seine Quellen." *Die Musik* 7 (1907-08): 11.
Mehler, E. "Beiträge zur Wagner-Forschung: unveröffentlichte Stücke aus 'Rienzi,' 'Holländer' und 'Tannhäuser'." *Die Musik* 12 (1912-13): 195.
Robertson, J.G. "The Genesis of Wagner's Drama 'Tannhäuser'." *Modern Language Review* 18 (1923): 458.
Steinbeck, D. "Zur Textkritik der Venus-Szenen im 'Tannhäuser'." *Die Musikforschung* 19 (1966): 412.
Strohm, Reinhard. "Dramatic Time and Operatic Form in Wagner's *Tannhäuser*." *Proceedings of the Royal Musical Association* 104 (1977-78).
Abbate, C. "The Parisian 'Venus' and the 'Paris' Tannhäuser." *Journal of the American Musicological Society* 36 (1983).
Kestner, Joseph. "Romantic Rebel: Wagner's Hero Tannhäuser, Forged from a Wealth of Literary Sources, Straddles Worlds Sacred and Profane—Much Like its Creator." *Opera News* 47 (1983): 16.
Avant-scène opéra April-May (1984) [*Tannhäuser* issue].
Daverio, John. "Narration as Drama: Wagner's Early Revisions of *Tannhäuser* and their Relation to the Rome Narrative." *College Music Symposium* 24 (1984): 55.
Wolf, Hugo, et al. "*Tannhäuser und der Sängerkrieg auf Wartburg* von Richard Wagner." *About the House* 6/no. 12 (1984): 33.

unpublished–

Abbate, Carolyn. "The 'Parisian' *Tannhäuser*." Ph.D. dissertation, Princeton University, 1984.

*   *   *

Tannhäuser, a medieval minstrel, has deserted his beloved Elisabeth and the cliffed castle of the Wartburg and fled to the pagan goddess of love and her underground Venusberg. But when he hears a distant churchbell, he tells Venus that he is weary of a life of the senses and longs to return to a life of striving, piety, and pain. The goddess' spell over him is broken when he invokes the Virgin Mary. He wakes in the green valley of the Wartburg and is found there by the minstrels he had deserted.

In the Wartburg's hall of song, Landgrave Hermann holds a contest for the hand of Elisabeth. The pious minstrel Wolfram sings the praises of courtly love, and Tannhäuser answers him with a song about his erotic encounter with Venus. The court is shocked, and the men draw their swords. Elisabeth intervenes, and the landgrave orders the repentent Tannhäuser to make a pilgrimage to Rome and ask pardon from the Pope.

Later in the year, the pilgrims return without Tannhäuser, and Elisabeth, after a prayer to the Virgin, dies of grief. As the evening star appears in the sky, the faithful Wolfram meets Tannhäuser in the Wartburg valley and hears that the Pope has denied him absolution: sooner will the papal sceptre put forth green leaves than such a sinner will find redemption.

A scene from *Tannhäuser,* showing Elisabeth in prayer, drawing by Theodor Pixis, 1894

The disillusioned Tannhäuser is about to return to Venus when Wolfram tells him that Elisabeth has died and is interceding for him in heaven. Tannhäuser, shattered by the revelation, dies in Wolfram's arms as messengers arrive from Rome carrying the Pope's staff which, in a miracle of grace, has blossomed in green leaves.

The complete title, *Tannhäuser und der Sängerkrieg auf der Wartburg,* underlines the fact that Wagner blended two figures to make his hero—the legendary Tannhäuser who sinned with Venus, and the quasi-historical Heinrich von Ofterdingen who competed in song with Wolfram von Eschenbach and other Minnesingers in the Wartburg. The opera itself exists in two main versions, the earlier written for Dresden in 1845, the latter a revision, especially of the Venusberg scene, for the Paris Opéra in 1861. Its stormy reception there was perhaps the greatest musical scandal of the nineteenth century. The Paris version has passages of post-*Tristan* complexity, but in either version *Tannhäuser* is a more or less traditional blend of arias, duets, ensembles, choruses, and even a ballet. One remarkably prophetic moment is the hero's "Rome Narrative," which anticipates the powerful narratives of the music dramas to follow.

Tannhäuser has lost some of its popularity as Wagner's later scores have come to be better known, and is now often regarded as a melodious but simplistic conflict between good and evil. This verdict does the work a grave disservice. *Tannhäuser* is set in a historical era of some complexity, a time when a stable Christian society, confident of its political and spiritual values, was challenged by a renascent paganism. The opera's hero is a man torn not between good and evil so much as between two opposing sets of values, each important and essential to him, and he rises above his two experiences to achieve a new synthesis of them. His redemption (to use Wagner's word) is won through what Goethe had called *das Ewig-Weibliche,* the ability of a woman intuitively to understand a man and lead him upwards (like the famous "evening star" of Wolfram's song). Tannhäuser's victory is sounded on the score's last page when, to quote the composer, "The music of the Venusberg sounds amid the hymn of God." The greening of the papal sceptre is a sign of the integration of medieval and Renaissance sensibilities promised in the fifteenth century, and a sign too of what twentieth-century Jungians would call the healing of the psyche.

The opera may thus be seen as a kind of psycho-biographical statement by a young Romantic composer defying the society he knows and seeking to change it, a neo-pagan unable to win a hearing for his music because of his unorthodoxy, an idealist soon to be driven into exile and forced to act out the scenario he has written. But ultimately the opera's hero is anyone who has had to relate a new world of intellectual or spiritual or sensual awareness to the traditional values of the world in which he is placed. *Tannhäuser* represents that human struggle in mythic symbols and in music that, to listeners as varied as Hanslick and Baudelaire, came as a kind of self-revelation. "It seemed to me," the latter said, "that I already knew this music. It seemed to me it was my *own* music."

—M. Owen Lee

TARARE.

Composer: Antonio Salieri.

Librettist: Beaumarchais.

First Performance: Paris, Opéra, 8 June 1787; revised as *Axur, Re d'Ormus* (libretto by Da Ponte), Vienna, Burgtheater, 8 January 1788.

Roles: The Spirit of Nature (soprano); Spirit of Fire (bass); Atar (bass); Tarare (tenor); Astasie (soprano); Arthénée (bass); Altamort (bass); Urson (bass); Calpigi (tenor); Spinette (soprano); Élamir (soprano); chorus.

Publications

articles—

Angermüller, R. "Beaumarchais und Salieri." In *Gesellschaft für Musikforschung Kongressbericht, Bonn 1970,* 325.
———. Salieri's *Tarare* (1787) und *Axur, Re d'Ormus* (1788). Vertonung eines Sujets für Paris und Wien." In *Mozart und die Oper seiner Zeit,* edited by Martin Ruhnke, 211. Laaber, 1981.

*   *   *

Antonio Salieri came to Paris in 1784 at Gluck's behest to produce his opera *Les Danaïdes.* Following the failure of his second French opera *Les Horaces* in 1786 he was persuaded to compose yet a third French opera, this time on a text by the controversial Pierre-Augustine Caron de Beaumarchais, whose *Barber of Seville* and *The Marriage of Figaro* had scandalized Paris. Beaumarchais conceived *Tarare* as an exercise in operatic reform, and his preface, "Aux abonnés de l'Opéra qui voudraient aimer l'Opéra," proved more significant than the body of the text.

In keeping with French practices, Beaumarchais claimed that opera was to be neither serious nor comic but a unique genre combining the two. Subject matter could be drawn from history or be a product of the imagination. Allegory and realism could be mingled; it was important only that the subject treat great philosophical ideas. Subplots, however, were permitted to share the scene with the main action. Since the story might combine history with fantasy, the action should be in an exotic location, preferably the Orient. Magic was permitted, but if present it should be relegated to a secondary position. Language need not be restricted to that of Classical French theatre but could employ everyday, familiar expressions and even bizarre phraseology. Language could even be offensive if the subject demanded such treatment. Finally, the plot could be as complex and arcane as suited the author's taste and purpose. While Beaumarchais makes a strong case for music to be secondary to the text, he calls for close collaboration between composer and librettist. Such a stricture is in keeping with Gluckian principles.

Beaumarchais' proposals seem unnecessarily provocative if not inappropriate to the French opera theater, but *Tarare* is organized traditionally, containing a Prologue and five acts with a ballet in its time-honored place in the third act. As complicated as the plot is, verbal precision clarifies the focus. In the Prologue the spirits of Nature and Fire summon unborn souls of characters from the opera proper to be examined before they are sent to earth. The opera's action concerns a noble Christian warrior, Tarare, whose principles are at odds with the Moslem tyrant Atar and his henchman. Atar has taken Tarare's wife Astasie into his harem in Ormuz on the Persian Gulf, and much of the opera centers on the hero's efforts to achieve Astasie's freedom while remaining the tyrant's obedient subject. All is to no avail: Tarare is condemned to death, and Atar agrees to allow Astasie to die with him. Although the soldiers turn against Atar, Tarare refuses to accept their loyalty, his freedom and that of Astasie, because they are disobedient to their lawful monarch, hence unworthy of respect. In a fury Atar commits suicide because his countrymen prefer Tarare's rule to his own. Tarare is eventually forced to accept the crown as the Spirits of Nature and Fire appear and deliver a final moral to the effect that man's station in life is not important; nobility of character is the crucial element.

Salieri's musical realization, sufficiently competent but not outstanding, is not the opera's center. The major interest in the French version lies in the richly convoluted action and scenic richness offered by the text and staging. Yet Salieri's style permits the action to be clearly grasped in terms of honor and nobility, and the composer is at his best in the Prologue, where a mysterious atmosphere is musically created to match the fantasy. In common with other Italian opera composers of his generation, Salieri was not particularly gifted in creating descriptive music, and his storm music for the Prologue shows no signs of an incipient Romanticism (unlike Beaumarchais's ideas, which proved fruitful for the development of Romantic opera). *Tarare* remains a work more honored for idea and text than for musical realization.

—Aubrey S. Garlington

TAUBER, Richard.

Tenor. Born 16 May 1891, in Linz. Died 8 January 1948, in London. Married: 1) soprano Carlotta Vanconti; 2) actress Diana Napier, 1936. Studied conducting and composition at Frankfurt Conservatory, and voice with Carl Beines at Frieburg; debut as Tamino in *Die Zauberflöte,* at the Chemnitz Neues Stadt-Theater, where his father was director, 1913; his success prompted a five-year contract with the Dresden Opera; debut at German Opera House in Berlin as Bacchus in *Ariadne auf Naxos,* 1915; member Vienna Staatsoper, 1922-28 and 1932-38, and Berlin State Opera, 1923-33; sang to great acclaim at Mozart Festivals in Munich and Salzburg, appearing as Tamino, Belmonte and Don Ottavio; after 1925 began appearing frequently in light opera, singing in Lehár's *Das Land des Lächelns* at Drury Lane in 1931; Covent Garden debut as Tamino, 1938; in 1947 made final operatic appearance (as Don Ottavio) during a visit of the Vienna Staatsoper to Covent Garden; became a naturalized British citizen in 1940.

Publications

About TAUBER: books—

Ludwig, Heinz. *Richard Tauber.* Berlin, 1928.
Tauber, Diana Napier. *Richard Tauber.* London, 1949.
Tauber, Diana Napier. *My Heart and I.* London, 1959.
Korb, Willi. *Richard Tauber.* Vienna, 1966.
Castle, Charles, and Diana Napier Tauber. *This was Richard Tauber.* London, 1971.

articles—

Dennis, J., et al. "Richard Tauber." *Record Collector* 18 (1969): 171.
Scott, M. "Tamino and Beyond." *Opera News* 56 (August 1991): 17.

* * *

The development of the phonograph in the first half of the twentieth century made it possible for the first time for singers to achieve popularity with a large section of the public. The phonograph record can be used as a valid yardstick to measure the popularity of singers, and during this period three tenors stand out above all others. First, the immortal Enrico Caruso, whose records outsold all others; second, the peerless John McCormack, the most prolific recording artist of all time with over 800 recorded titles to his credit; and third, the Austrian, Richard Tauber, second only to McCormack in the quantity of records produced—over 700 titles. All three singers were idolized by the public and were held in high esteem by critics—the only negative critical opinion that was voiced in regard to them was their common fondness for popular, less serious, music.

Of the three, Tauber was undoubtedly the most versatile. Caruso was primarily an opera singer, while McCormack was principally a concert artist, although he appeared in opera. Tauber, whose formal musical education was more thorough, achieved recognition not merely as a singer but also as a composer and conductor. From 1913, when he contracted to appear with the Dresden Opera, until 1922, Tauber devoted himself to opera, not only at Dresden, but at principal opera houses in Berlin and Vienna. From 1923 up to the time he fled to England in the mid-1930s to escape Nazi persecution, Tauber divided his time between opera and operetta. In the final years of his career he sang principally in concerts and appeared in films.

Tauber possessed a unique, utterly distinctive voice that was instantly recognizable. During his career several colleagues achieved a degree of celebrity because they supposedly "sounded like Tauber," but none succeeded in approximating Tauber's vocal personality. Apart from its individualistic *timbre,* Tauber's voice was not remarkable either in power or in range. It was a lyric tenor, modeled on the old *bel canto* tradition, aided and abetted by consumate musicianship, technical proficiency marked by impeccable intonation, outstanding breath control, and a seamless *legato.* In order to produce the distinctive resonant quality that characterizes his voice, Tauber sacrificed the highest notes of the tenor range, and is generally considered a "short" tenor because he had no high C from the chest register. Thus he reverted to the older tradition of singing high notes in either the pure head voice, or the mixture of head and chest resonance, a technique that came from the French lyric tradition and known as the *voix-mixte.* Nor did he eschew the use of the vocal technique known as *falsetto.*

Henry Pleasants defines *falsetto* as "a kind of vocal production, now normally applied only to males, by which the upper range is extended and takes on the character of the female (or boy) alto or soprano." Pleasants adds "Nor does everyone agree on just where a 'legitimate' head voice ends and *falsetto* begins." One of the earliest works on the technique of singing is Piero Francesco Tosi's *Opinion d' cantori antiche e moderni o siano osservazioni sopra il canto figurato* published in 1723. Tosi considered the use of *falsetto* necessary for successful singing. Throughout the early period of opera up to the early nineteenth century, tenors traditionally sang high notes in either the head voice or *falsetto*. It was Gilbert-Louis Duprez who first sang the high C from the chest in a performance of Rossini's *Guillaume Tell* in 1837. Rossini detested the sound and preferred the traditional use of the head voice. But gradually other tenors began to emulate Duprez and by the end of the nineteenth century the ringing chest voice tenor high notes were critically and publicly acclaimed. Conversely the use of the *falsetto* fell into critical disapproval. Thus critics applying modern standards have criticized Tauber for his use of the technique, which he employed more often in operetta and popular songs than he did in opera. However, the quality and resonance of the tone which Tauber produced by the use of this technique, even in the softest *pianissimo,* overcomes all objections.

From 1920-25, during the acoustical era, Tauber recorded twenty-six operatic arias for Odeon. With the advent of electrical recordings, he made another forty-two operatic recordings from 1925 to 1947. Of these only eight were repeats of arias which he had previously recorded. Thus out of his recorded legacy of 725 records only 86 were of operatic music. He followed the contemporary custom of singing almost exclusively in German, notable exceptions being two arias from *Don Giovanni* in Italian, the flower song from *Carmen* and an aria from Lalo's *Le Roi d'Ys* in French. His operatic recorded repertoire ranged from Rossini to Wagner, but he achieved his greatest acclaim as a Mozart specialist. Critics noted that his personal magnetism and vocal brilliance transformed Don Ottavio in *Don Giovanni* into a major role, and his success as Tamino in *Die Zauberflöte* was so brilliant that both critics and colleagues referred to the opera as "*Tauberflöte.*"

Tauber's early acoustical recordings consist of arias and duets from twenty-one operas, ten of which are from Italian opera, with the emphasis on Verdi and Puccini. Because of his command of *legato* and *bel canto* style, his singing of Italian opera is not severely compromised by the constant use of a German text. A notable example is his recording of the drinking song from *La traviata,* which he sings as a solo. Despite the language, Tauber's instinctive rhythmic sense captures the essence of the music. During this period he ventured into the dramatic tenor repertoire, recording duets from *Aida* and arias and duets from *Il trovatore.* Unfortunately his lack of a chest voice high C necessitated his lowering the pitch in the aria "Di quella pira" a full tone. However, his recordings of Puccini arias are justly admired. Six operas are represented from German opera, only one from Mozart, a recording of "Dalla sua pace" from *Don Giovanni,* also sung in German. Two recordings are of Wagner operas which he never sang on stage. The list is completed by three arias from French opera, one each from Russian and Czech.

In his later electrical recordings the emphasis shifts to German opera. Only the *Tosca* arias are repeated from the Puccini canon, and he forsakes Verdi, except for a duet from *La forza del destino* with Benno Zeigler. His most critically acclaimed recordings are his Mozart arias from *Die Entführung aus dem Serail, Die Zauberflöte* and *Don Giovanni.* From the latter opera he sings the correct Italian text. All of his electric operatic recordings are noteworthy, the most outstanding being his two arias from Offenbach's *Les contes d'Hoffmann,* which are examples of his most ravishing style despite the use of a German text. His recording of "Durch die Wälder, durch die Auen" from Weber's *Der Freischütz* is justly considered to be the classic version.

During his early career, Tauber's impact was so exceptional that he reinstituted an older tradition in a new genre. Nineteenth-century composers invariably wrote operas for specific singers to create the roles. By the twentieth century this practice had become obsolete, but Tauber's relationship with composers of operetta, notably Franz Lehár and Emmerich Kálmán, was such that both composers wrote operetta specifically for him. Every operetta had to have a "Tauberlied," the most famous of which is "Dein ist mein ganzes herz" (Yours is my heart alone) from Lehár's *Das Land des Lachlens* (The Land of Smiles).

Tauber was undoubtedly the most versatile tenor of all time. He sang and recorded nearly everything: "pop" tunes of Irving Berlin and Jerome Kern, Strauss waltzes, Irish songs, Neapolitan songs, operetta, oratorio arias, German lieder, and grand opera. Whatever the music, he brought to it his inimitable musical style. He was gifted with an instinctive, intuitive feeling for rhythm, perfect pitch, exemplary breath control, and a unique sound.

In addition to his voluminous output of commercial recordings, air checks have been published of various radio broadcasts. Also published is a private recording of Tauber's own operetta *Old Chelsea* as well as a record of the soundtrack from his film of *Pagliacci.* Twenty-seven commercial recordings have been issued with Tauber as the conductor of various orchestras.

His legacy of recordings prove that his voice did not deteriorate with age. On 27 September 1947, already stricken with lung cancer, he sang his final operatic performance of *Don Giovanni* at Covent Garden as a guest artist with the visiting Vienna State Opera Company. Air checks of a duet and his two principal arias reveal that, in spite of his illness, singing on virtually one lung, he still produced the resonance and vocal quality that made him unique.

—Bob Rose

TAVERNER.

Composer: Peter Maxwell Davies.

Librettist: Peter Maxwell Davies.

First Performance: London, Covent Garden, 12 July 1972.

Roles: John Taverner (tenor); Richard Taverner (later St John, baritone); Cardinal (later Archbishop, tenor); King Henry VIII (bass); Jester (later Death and Joking Jesus, baritone); White Abbot (baritone); Priest Confessor (later God the Father, counter-tenor); Rose Parrowe (later Virgin Mary, mezzo-soprano); Boy (treble); Captain (bass); Antichrist (soprano); Archangel Gabriel (tenor); Archangel Michael (bass); First Monk (tenor); Second Monk (tenor); chorus (TTBB) (SATB).

Publications

articles—

Arnold, S. "The Music of *Taverner.*" *Tempo* no. 101 (1972): 20.
Josipovici, G. "*Taverner:* Thoughts on the Libretto." *Tempo* no. 101 (1972): 12.

Sutcliffe, T. "A Question of Identity: *Blind Man's Buff* and *Taverner." Music and Musicians* 20 no. 10 (1972): 26.

* * *

Peter Maxwell Davies's opera *Taverner* was long in gestation. Davies first became familiar with the music of John Taverner (ca 1490-1545) in 1956, while studying at Manchester University. He was very much affected by the story of Taverner's life (as found in the introduction to volume I of Edmund Fellows' *Tudor Church Music*) as well as by his music, and he conceived the idea for an opera at that time. In 1962, he wrote his *First Fantasia on an 'In Nomine' by John Taverner;* the themes from this composition of Taverner's would continue to influence his own compositions, including the opera on which he was working. He completed act I of *Taverner* in 1964 while at graduate school in music at Princeton, and during the same year wrote his second *Fantasia* on Taverner's *In Nomine.* Act II of *Taverner* was completed in 1968; however, the score was mostly destroyed in a fire at Davies's cottage, and the composer was forced to rewrite practically the entire work. *Taverner* was premiered in London, Covent Garden, 12 July 1972.

The libretto which Davies wrote for *Taverner* is based on Fellows' biography, according to which the crucial events in Taverner's life were these: having attained a post as an ecclesiastical musician, Taverner was imprisoned for (Lutheran) heresy in 1528 but pardoned by Cardinal Wolsey in recognition of his musical abilities; subsequently, he quit his musical career and, following Henry VIII's schism, became a persecutor of Catholics and an informer in the service of Thomas Cromwell. Of his earlier career as musician, he said that he "repented him very much that he had made songs to popish ditties in the time of his blindness." Although this biography is now generally discredited, Davies himself has said that the action of the opera really takes place more in the mind of the character John Taverner rather than being an accurate picture of historical events: he was concerned with "the nature of betrayal at the deepest levels." It is one man's struggle with the turmoil of religion and truth. (Davies has also remarked that one of the things he had in mind while composing *Taverner* was the situation of Soviet composer Dmitri Shostakovich.)

The opera is in two acts of four scenes each. As the first act begins, Taverner is on trial for heresy. The White Abbot sits in judgment. After lengthy testimony by various characters, Taverner is sentenced to death. The Cardinal then appears and reverses the sentence in view of Taverner's value as a composer, saying "He is but a poor musician." In the second scene, as the monks in his chapel sing his music, he expresses doubts about his profession. The third scene portrays the Reformation: King and Cardinal discuss what is to come (the Royal Divorce). A new character appears, the Jester; gradually, it appears that the Jester controls the progress of the Reformation. During the fourth scene, the Jester leads Taverner through a terrifying "conversion," conjuring up a Pope-Antichrist, Taverner's mistress Rose Parrow, and a passion play. At the end, Taverner signs his confession: "I repent me very much that I have made songs to popish ditties in the time of my blindness."

The four scenes of act II are all, in various ways, inversions of the corresponding scenes in act I. In the first scene, John Taverner sits in judgment of the White Abbot. The second scene, which takes place in the Throne Room, represents the establishment of the Church of England over the Church of Rome: the Jester controls the scene and changes the Cardinal

into an Anglican Archbishop. The dissolution of the monasteries is announced. In scene III, the White Abbot is celebrating Mass, in the presence of Taverner and his monks. Soldiers enter, interrupting the ceremony, and carry out the dispossession of the monastery; the monks sing Taverner's original setting of the *Benedictus.* In the fourth scene, Taverner carries out the execution of the White Abbot—as Davies says, Taverner's final act of destruction, destroying his own spiritual nature.

Taverner is a complex yet compelling work. More than one critic has seen it as a theater piece in the tradition of Wagner's *Gesamtkunstwerk.* Martin Cooper, however, though taking note of this, points out that unlike Wagner's ideal, *Taverner* is "primarily visual image seen through a musical atmosphere." True to its complex musical structure, the drama as it unfolds is open to many levels of interpretation, a complex intellectual exercise demanding on the audience as well as on the performers.

Musically, Davies employs themes and motives derived from John Taverner's *In Nomine* and his plainsong Mass *Gloria Tibi Trinitas.* Each of these works, in turn, was based on an antiphon *Gloria Tibi Trinitas* sung at Lauds and Second Vespers on Trinity Sunday. This theme serves as a *cantus firmus* for the opera, both in its pure form and in many permutations. Davies' use of the compositional techniques of early music is very evident. He quotes directly from Taverner's Mass. The opera is a melding of styles: precomposed music, musical quotations, and new music deliberately intertwined. Complex contrapuntal writing serves as contrast to open, stark sections. The juxtaposition of early styles and techniques with highly contemporary material, often in a way reminiscent of Stravinsky, serves the composer well.

—Carolyn J. Smith

TCHAIKOVSKY, Piotr Ilyich.

Composer. Born 7 May 1840, in Votkinsk, Viatka district. Died 6 November 1893, in St Petersburg. Married: Antonina Milyukova, 18 July 1877. Became a government clerk, 1859; studied music with Lomakin; studied harmony and counterpoint with Zaremba and composition with A. Rubinstein at the music school established by Rubinstein (ultimately the St Petersburg Conservatory), 1861-65; silver medal for his cantata on Schiller's *Hymn to Joy;* professor of harmony at the Moscow Conservatory, 1866-78; composition of orchestral works, 1866-1870; music criticism for Moscow newspapers, 1868-74; world premiere of his Piano Concerto by Hans von Bülow in Boston, 25 October 1875; numerous trips to Paris, Berlin, Vienna; covered the first Bayreuth Festival for the Moscow newspaper *Russkyie Vedomosti,* 1876; in Italy, Switzerland, Paris, and Vienna, 1877-78; in America, 1891; concert tour of Russia, Poland, and Germany, 1892. Tchaikovsky was financially supported throughout much of his life by the patronage of Nadezhda von Meck.

Operas

Edition: *P.I. Tchaikovsky: Polnoye sobraniye sochineniy.* Moscow and Leningrad, 1940-71.

Voyevoda, Ostrovsky and Tchaikovsky (after Ostrovsky, *Son po Volge*), 1867-68, Moscow, Bol'shoy, 11 February 1869 [destroyed by the composer; reconstructed by Pavel Lamm].

Undina, V. Sollogub (after Zhukovsky's translation of F. de la Motte Fouqué), 1869, excerpts performed Moscow, 28 March 1870 [destroyed by the composer].

Mandragora, S. Rachinsky, 1870, Moscow, 30 December 1870 [unfinished; one chorus only].

Oprichnik, Tchaikovsky (after I. Lazhechnikov), 1870-72, St Petersburg, Mariinsky, 24 April 1874.

Vakula the Smith [*Kuznets Vakula*]. Ya. Polonsky (after Gogol, *Noch' pered rozhdestvom*), 1874, St Petersburg, Mariinsky, 6 December 1876; revised as *The Slippers [Cherevichki]* (comic-fantastic opera), 1885, Moscow, Bol'shoy, 31 January 1887.

Eugene Onegin [*Evgeny Onegin*], K. Shilovsky and Tchaikovsky (after Pushkin), 1877-78, Moscow, Maliy, 29 March 1879.

The Maid of Orleans [*Orleanskaya deva*]. Tchaikovsky (after Zhukovsky's translation of Schiller, *Die Jungfrau von Orleans*), 1878-79, St Petersburg, Mariinsky, 25 February 1881; revised, 1882.

Mazeppa, V. Burenin, revised by Tchaikovsky (after Pushkin, *Poltava*), 1881-83, Moscow, Bol'shoy, 15 February 1884.

The Sorceress [*Charodeyka*], I. Shpazhinsky, 1885-87, St Petersburg, Mariinsky, 1 November 1887.

The Queen of Spades [*Pikovaya dama*]. M. and P. Tchaikovsky (after Pushkin), 1890, St Petersburg, Mariinsky, 19 December 1890.

Iolanta, M. Tchaikovsky (after V. Zotov's translation of H. Hertz's *King René's Daughter*) 1891, St Petersburg, Mariinsky, 18 December 1892.

Other works: symphonies, ballets, other orchestral works, chamber music, vocal works, piano pieces.

Publications/Writings

By TCHAIKOVSKY: books–

Rukovodstvo k prakticheskomu izucheniyu garmoniy. Moscow, 1872; English translation as *Guide to the Practical Study of Harmony*, Leipzig, 1900.

Kratkiy uchebnik garmoniy, prisposoblenniy k chteniyu dukhovnomuzïkal'nïkh sochineniy v Rossiy [study of harmony adapted to the study of religious music in Russia]. Moscow, 1875.

One of the editors of *Slovar' russkovo yazïka* [Russian language dictionary]. Moscow, 1892, 1895.

Newmarch, Rosa, ed. Tchaikovsky, Modest. *The Life and Letters of Peter Ilyich Tchaikovsky*. London, 1906.

Tchaikovsky, I.I. ed. *P. Chaykovsky: dnevniki (1873-1891)*. [Diaries]. Moscow and Petrograd, 1923; English translation and edited by Lakond, Vladimir as *Diaries*, New York, 1945.

––––––. *P. Chaykovsky: perepiskas P.I. Yurgensonom* [correspondence with Jürgenson]. Moscow, 1938-52.

P. Chaykovsky: literaturnïye proizvedeniya i perepiska [literary works and correspondence]. Moscow, 1953-81.

Zhdanov, V.A., ed. *P. Chaykovsky: pis'ma k blizkim* [letters to his family]. Moscow, 1955.

Young, Percy M., ed. *Letters to his Family: an Autobiography*. New York, 1982.

articles–

Avtobiograficheskoye opisaniye puteshestviya za granitsu v 1888 godu. [autobiography of travel abroad, 1888]. *Russkiy vestnik* no. 2 (1894): 165.

"Vagner i evo muzïka" [Wagner's music]. *Morning Journal* [New York] 3 May (1891).

"Beseda s Chaykovskim v noyabre 1892 g. v Peterburge" [conversation with Tchaikovsky in St Petersburg, November 1892]. *Peterburgskaya zhizn'* 24 November (1892).

Note: see also *P. Chaykovsky: Literaturniye proizvedenya i perepiska* [literary works and correspondence]. Moscow, 1953-81.

unpublished–

Diaries, 1858-59 [destroyed 1866], 1873, 1882 [lost], 1884-91 [1885 lost; 1888 published (see above)].
Autobiography. 1889 [lost].

About TCHAIKOVSKY: books–

Laroche, H.A. *Chaykovsky kak dramaticheskiy kompozitor* [Tchaikovsky as dramatic composer]. St Petersburg, 1895.

Newmarch, R. *Tchaikovsky: his Life and Works*. London, 1900.

Tchaikovsky, M.I. *Zhizn' P.I. Chaykovskovo* [biography]. Moscow, 1900-02; abridged English translation, 1906.

Lyapunov, S.M. ed. *Perepiska M.A. Balakireva s P.I. Chaykovskim* [Balakirev's correspondence with Tchaikovsky]. St Petersburg, 1913; reprinted in *M.A. Balakirev: vospominaniyai pis'ma*, edited by A. Orlova, 115, Leningrad, 1962.

Bogdanov-Berezovsky, V.M. *Opernoye i baletnoye tvorchestvo Chaykovskovo* [operas and ballets]. Moscow, 1940.

Shaverdyan, A.I., ed. *Chaykovsky i teatr*. Moscow, 1940.

Yakovlev, V.V. *Chaykovsky na moskovskoy stsene: perviye postanovki v godï evo zhizni* [Tchaikovsky on the Moscow stage: premieres]. Moscow and Leningrad, 1940.

Asaf'yev, B.V. *"Evgeny Onegin": opït intonatsionnovo analiza stilya i muzïkal'noy dramaturgii* [intonation analysis of style and musical dramaturgy]. Moscow and Leningrad, 1944.

Abraham, Gerald, ed. *Tchaikovsky: a Symposium*. London, 1945.

Weinstock, Herbert. *Tchaikovsky*. London, 1946.

Yarustovsky, B. *Opernaya dramaturgiya Chaykovskovo* [Tchaikovsky's operatic dramaturgy]. Moscow and Leningrad, 1947.

Sokolova, T, ed. *P. Chaykovsky: muzïkal'no-kriticheskiye stat'i*. Moscow, 1953.

Protopopov, V.V., and N.V. Tumanina. *Opernoye tvorchestvo Chaykovskovo* [operas]. Moscow, 1957.

Al'shvang, A.A. *P.I. Chaykovsky*. Moscow, 1959; 1967.

Tumanina, N. *Chaykovsky*. Moscow, 1962-68.

Koniskaya, L. *Chaykovsky v Peterburge*. Leningrad, 1969.

Chaykovsky i zarubyozhniye muzïkanti: izbranniye pis'ma inostrannïkh korrespondentov [selected letters from foreign musicians]. Leningrad, 1970.

Garden, Edward. *Tchaikovsky*. London, 1973; 1984.

Warrack, John. *Tchaikovsky*. London, 1973.

Volkoff, V. *Tchaikovsky: a Self-Portrait*. Boston and London, 1974.

Yoffe, Elkhonon. *Tchaikovsky in America: the Composer's Visit in 1891*. New York, 1986.

Brown, David. *Tchaikovsky: a Biographical and Critical Study*. 4 vols. London, 1978-.

Strutte, Wilson. *Tchaikovsky: his Life and Times.* Tunbridge Wells, 1979.

Šol'p, Aleksandra. *"Evgenij Onegin" Čajkovskogo. Očerki.* Leningrad, 1982.

Taylor, Philip. *Gogolian Interludes: Gogol's Story "Christmas Eve" as the Subject of Operas by Tchaikovsky and Rimsky-Korsakov.* London, 1984.

Zajaczkowski, Henry. *Tchaikovsky's Musical Style.* Ann Arbor, 1987.

Kendall, Alan. *Tchaikovsky: a Biography.* London, 1988.

Mountfield, David. *Tchaikovsky.* London, 1990.

articles–

Newmarch, R. "Tchaikovsky." In *The Russian Opera,* 334. London, 1914.

Shemanin, M. "Literatura o P.I. Chaykovskom za 17 let (1917-34)" [bibliography]. In *Muzïkal'noye nasledstvo.* Moscow, 1935.

Abraham, Gerald. *"Eugene Onegin* and Tchaikovsky's Marriage." In *On Russian Music,* 225. London, 1939.

Ferman, V. *"Cherevichki (Kuznets Vakula).* Chaykovskovo i *Noch' pered rozhdestvom* Rimskovo-Korsakova: opït sravneniya" [comparison of Tchaikovsky's *The slippers* and Rimsky-Korsakov's *Christmas Eve*]. *Voprosï muzïkoznaniya* 1 (1953-54): 205.

Abraham, G. "Tchaikovsky's First Opera." In *Festschrift Karl Gustav Fellerer,* 12. Regensburg, 1962.

———. "Tchaikovsky's Operas." In *Slavonic and Romantic Music.* London, 1968.

Lloyd-Jones, D. "A Background to Iolanta." *Musical Times* 109 (1968): 225.

Berlin, I. "Tchaikovsky, Pushkin, and Onegin." *Musical Times* 60 (1979).

Vasil'ev, Jurij. "K rukopisjam *Pikovoj damy."* *Sovetskaya muzyka* 7 (1980): 99.

Avant-scène opéra September (1982) [*Eugène Onéguine* issue].

Bjalik, Mihail. "Das Romantische in Tschaikowskis *Pique Dame."* In *Romantikkonferenz (2.) 1982,* edited by Günther Stephan and Hans John, 106. Dresden, 1983.

Gliede, Edmund. *"Eugen Onegin*—Metamorphosen eines Stoffes." *Musik und Bildung* 15 (1983):18.

Schläder, Jürgen. "Operndramaturgie und musikalische Konzeption zu Tschaikowskijs Opern *Eugen Onegin* und *Pique Dame* und ihren literarischen Vorlagen." *Deutsche Vierteljahrsschrift für Literaturwissenschaft und Geistesgeschichte* 57 (1983): 525 [summary in English].

Warrack, John. "Tchaikovsky's *Mazeppa."* *Opera* December (1984).

Avant-scène opéra April-May (1989) [*La dame de pique* issue].

unpublished–

Macokina, Elena. "Polifonija v operah P.I. Čajkovskogo." Ph.D. Leningrad Conservatory, 1979.

*   *   *

Although *Eugene Onegin* and *The Queen of Spades* are the only operas by Piotr Ilyich Tchaikovsky that are regularly performed in the West today, he composed ten operas, and no genre spans his career quite so neatly. Tchaikovsky's opera composition demonstrates a wide range of aesthetic and compositional approaches, from works based on the French grand opera tradition as represented by Meyerbeer (usually with a nationalist bent) to attempts at realism (inspired by Balakirev and his circle). His influences were both from traditional western European opera and from the attempts of "The Five" (Balakirev, Borodin, Cui, Musorgsky, Rimsky-Korsakov) to create a genuinely nationalist Russian opera. Like Rubinstein, however, Tchaikovsky's works remain on the more traditional, conservative, and heavily western-based side of the equation.

All of Tchaikovsky's operas are number operas, but in spite of this conservative approach, there is at times considerable originality to its use in relation to dramatic structure, such as in *Eugene Onegin,* for example. Tchaikovsky was a great admirer of Gounod's (he said that he valued Gounod's *Faust* above any other opera) and was influenced by his lyricism, although, unlike Gounod, Tchaikovsky frequently allows his lyricism to dominate dramatic considerations. In keeping with his primarily musical rather than dramatic aesthetic, Tchaikovsky was frequently accused of being a symphonist in his operas rather than a true dramatic composer (especially by Cesar Cui, an experienced if not successful opera composer who could hardly let a critique pass without summoning the epithet). This symphonism is evident in numerous facets of his operas, from some of the most effective passages (such as the near leitmotivic manipulation of the love theme in *Eugene Onegin*) to the weakest moments (such as the excessive filigree in some of the choruses in *The Maid of Orleans*).

None of Tchaikovsky's operas are without fine musical moments; unfortunately, however, these moments do not always coincide with the drama. In *The Sorceress,* for example, the opening genre numbers, which are musically some of the best in the opera, have nothing to do with the drama, and the real dramatic events fall so weakly in the midst of it all that act II is barely explainable. Similarly, Tchaikovsky's orchestration is at his best in the dances, where he is able to free himself from the constraints of accompanying and supporting the voice. He also excelled at divertissements, the style of which provide much of the best music in *The Queen of Spades,* and at melodrama, which in *Oprichnik* is surprisingly well paced and well-balanced musically.

Tchaikovsky was very fond of connecting numbers within an opera by quoting a previous tune as a transition to the next piece, perhaps as an attempt at continuity within the segmented number opera format. This tendency toward melodic self-quotation is also evident in the echo voice over a measure of rest in both accompanied recitatives and arias. His operas also frequently contain mad scenes, such as in *Mazepa* and *The Sorceress,* the latter of which was probably influenced by the Mad Miller in Dargomyzhsky's *Rusalka.* His dramatic music was also influenced by Ostrovsky; his first opera, *Voyevoda* was based on Ostrovsky's *A Dream on the Volga,* and he composed an overture for Ostrovsky's play *The Storm,* as well as incidental music for *The Snow Maiden* and other Ostrovsky plays. Perhaps the most puzzling omission in Tchaikovsky's works, however, particularly in the context of post-*Ruslan* Russian opera, is the almost total absence of Orientalism. The part of the Moorish doctor in *Iolanta,* added to the *Nutcracker,* and a slight touch of Orientalism in the *Mazepa* overture is the extent of its use in Tchaikovsky's works.

Piotr Ilyich Tchaikovsky, c. 1890

Tchaikovsky's choice of librettos was not always fortunate; he was given some weak librettos and prepared a few himself. The success of *The Queen of Spades,* for example, is largely in spite of its libretto rather than because of it. Tchaikovsky's librettos do span a wide range of subjects, however, from Pushkin to historical and political topics to melodrama and fantasy.

In general, Tchaikovsky excelled in the musical parts of his operas (song, ballet), but not in the dramatic aspects. He is at his best in the purely domestic scenes (as in much of *Eugene Onegin*) and genre numbers, but he does not always succeed in building musico-dramatic tension. He had a real lyric gift rather than a genuine dramatic sense, and as a result, individual numbers work very well and could easily be lifted from one work and placed in another without any real loss of effect (as Tchaikovsky did in *Oprichnik,* using several numbers from *Voyevoda*). Tchaikovsky's operatic strength was therefore rooted in his abilities as a lyricist, which is not surprising in light of the fact that his international reputation and fame rested primarily on his symphonic and instrumental compositions.

—Gregory Salmon

TEBALDI, Renata.

Soprano. Born 1 February 1922, in Pesaro. Studied with Brancucci and Campogalliani at the Parma Conservatory, 1937-40; studied with Carmen Melis and Giuseppe Pais at the Pesaro Conservatory, 1940-43; debut as Elena in *Mefistofele,* Rovigo, 1944; among the artists chosen by Toscanini to re-open the Teatro alla Scala in 1946; sang at La Scala until 1954; British debut as Desdemona with the visiting La Scala company, Covent Garden, 1950; U.S. debut as Aïda, San Francisco, 1950; Metropolitan Opera debut as Desdemona, 1955; sang at Metropolitan until 1973.

Publications

About TEBALDI: books–

Panofsky, W. *Renata Tebaldi.* Berlin, 1961.
Seroff, V. *Renata Tebaldi: The Woman and the Diva.* New York, 1961.
Harris, K. *Renata Tebaldi: An Authorized Biography.* New York, 1975.
Casanova, C. *Renata Tebaldi: La voce d'angelo.* Milan, 1981.
Segond, André. *Renata Tebaldi.* Lyons, 1981.

articles–

Rosenthal, H. "Renata Tebaldi." *Opera* July (1955).
———. "Renata Tebaldi." In *Great Singers of Today,* London, 1966.
Rasponi, Lanfranco. "Renata Tebaldi." In *The Last Prima Donnas,* New York, 1982.

*　　　*　　　*

Assessment of Tebaldi's career will always be influenced by two extramusical factors: the misinterpretation of a remark by Arturo Toscanini and the fact that her twenty-nine years on stage spanned the shorter, more intense career of Maria Callas. Toscanini, having accepted Tebaldi as the only young singer to participate with pre-war veterans in the 1946 re-opening of the Teatro alla Scala, had, for his performance of Verdi's *Four Sacred Pieces,* positioned her in the organ loft for her brief contribution. At rehearsal, partly in tribute to her beauty of voice but mainly making a pun on her location high above the orchestra, he exclaimed "Ah! La voce d'angelo!" (Ah, the voice of an angel). The offhand play on words soon transformed via the operatic grapevine into a benediction of her artistry by the world's leading conductor, but to hear the voice in the Trio from Rossini's *Mosé,* recorded at that reopening concert, one can believe Toscanini had meant it more seriously. Tebaldi's sound, full, clear, and seamless, agile and fresh, does sound "angelic," a sound she would retain well into the late years of her career.

Her role vis-à-vis Callas did not have such positive results. It originated in Rio de Janeiro in 1951, when Callas had the role of Tosca taken from her after a sub-par performance and given to Tebaldi, who had been 400 miles away in Sao Paulo and thought she was replacing a different singer entirely (Elisabetta Barbato) when she returned to Rio. Callas saw a conspiracy where none had existed. Back in Italy, fueled by hysterical fans of both singers (called by the Italian press "tifosi," a word otherwise used only to describe rabid football fans and typhoid fever sufferers), Tebaldi became identified with the traditional, antidramatic, voice-for-its-own-sake school of singing, while Callas was seen as the wind of change, the exponent of opera as theater, of voice in the service of

Renata Tebaldi as Tosca, Vienna, 1959

art. According to the myth, Callas revived forgotten operas and revealed their hidden greatness, while Tebaldi regurgitated the mainstream repertoire in admittedly golden but psychologically empty tones.

In fact, in the early years of their coincident careers, Tebaldi had been as active in reviving long-buried operas as Callas: Rossini's *Le siège de Corinthe*, Spontini's *Fernando Cortez* and *Olympie*, Handel's *Giulio Cesare*. They had both made excursions into Wagner and Tebaldi had even created a contemporary work, Casavola's *Salammbô*. But to some extent the myth created by Callas and by the tifosi, and fanned by the Italian newspapers, whose critics almost to a man were in the Callas camp, became a reality. Tebaldi retreated to a small group of traditionally popular operas in the mid-1950s. At the same time Callas gave up a number of soprano parts in which sheer beauty of voice and effortless emission were worth more than psychological nuance or subtle coloration. Only with the virtual withdrawal of Callas from the stage in the early 1960s did Tebaldi once again venture into more dramatic parts: Minnie in *La fanciulla del West*, Gioconda, and Adriana Lecouvreur (a meaty dramatic role Callas strangely never sang).

Tebaldi's recordings span almost her entire career. Her earliest 78s reveal a youthful freshness well suited to lyric roles such as Mimi. The most thoroughly satisfying discs from this period are those of her complete *Giovanna d'Arco*. "O fatidica foresta" demonstrates a perfect command of legato, as do her duets with Carlo Bergonzi, in which she rises to the climaxes without apparent effort, the purity of tone at the core of the sensuous overall sound reflecting the conflicting emotions of a saint in love. Tebaldi's Verdi heroines (leaving aside Elisabeth in *Don Carlos* and Amelia in *Un ballo in maschera* which she never sang on stage and recorded late in her career) are her most satisfying. She recorded *Aida* twice; the second recording, under Karajan, shows off her aristocratic style and ability to convey emotion in purely vocal terms, though her voice is much more voluptuous in a third act duet with Mario Filippeschi from a 1954 Rio de Janeiro broadcast which has not yet been put on disc.

From that same year come several recordings of complete performances of *La forza del destino*, of which the best is the commercial Decca/London release. In the duet with the Father Guardian she demonstrates that the agility of the 1940s has not left her, especially in the "Plaudite, o cori angelici" passage. At "Voi mi scacciate? Voi?" she displays her opulent chest voice and an aristocratic projection which illuminates the character's nobility and desperation. Her "Pace, pace, mio Dio" must rank with Ponselle's for pure beauty of sound and the phenomenal breath control which supports long phrases without apparent effort. One's choice will probably depend on whether one prefers the duskiness of Ponselle or the brighter Tebaldi sound.

She was equally at home in the spinto-dramatic roles of Puccini, though most of her studio recordings of that repertoire date from the period in which she sacrificed, to some extent, characterization to sound. On stage at this time she could be unusually variable. Under a conductor such as Karajan, her Tosca could thrill an audience not only vocally, but with an underplayed intensity and economy of gesture which conveyed a character as well-conceived as the more celebrated Callas interpretation, though less vulnerable as a human being. Given a more indulgent conductor and costars, her *Tosca* could turn into a concert in costume, its arias and duets directed at the audience.

Tebaldi had little empathy for 18th-century music, though she obstinately included it in recital throughout her career. Despite reports that her Countess in *Le nozze di Figaro* was

excellent, most of her pre-Rossini repertoire has a sameness which, despite the beautiful sounds, is empty of commitment. At the other chronological extreme of her repertoire, she sang *canzone* of the post-verismo composers with an understanding of style that makes it all the more tragic that, despite its being announced for both Florence and San Francisco, she never sang in her one-time teacher Zandonai's *Francesca da Rimini*, only recording the love duet long after her smoothness of emission had become a mechanical chore rather than a natural attribute.

Representing, as she did for a generation of operagoers, one pole of a controversy as to the nature of operatic singing, Tebaldi's contributions to that art have been both praised and castigated for the wrong reasons. At her best, she demonstrated how the possessor of a magnificent sound could serve the text without sacrificing the sheerly sensual appeal of that sound. Even at less than her best, she exemplified how much pleasure could be gained from hearing an Italian dramatic-lyric role sung by the finest pure voice of its generation—or, so far, since.

—William J. Collins

TE KANAWA, (Dame) Kiri Janette.

Soprano. Born 6 March 1944, in Gisborne, Auckland. Married: company director Desmond Stephen Park, 1967; one daughter, one son. Studied with Sister Mary Leo, Auckland; at London Opera Centre; and with Vera Rosza; debut as Carmen, Northern Opera, 1968; London debut as Idamante in *Idomeneo*, Chelsea Opera Group, 1968; Covent Garden debut as Blumenmädchen in *Parsifal*, 1971; major debut as Countess Almaviva in *Le nozze di Figaro*, Covent Garden, 1971; Glyndebourne debut, 1973; Metropolitan Opera debut as Desdemona, 1974; Paris debut as Elvira, 1974; Dame of the British Empire, 1982.

Publications

About TE KANAWA: book–

Fingleton, David. *Kiri Te Kanawa: A Biography*. London, 1982.

articles–

Harris, Norman. "Kiri: Music and a Maori Girl." Sydney, 1966.
Barichella, M. "Kiri Te Kanawa." *Opera* 106 (1975): 64.
"Kiri Te Kanawa, Soprano." *Hi Fidelity/Musical America* 29/July (1979): MA35.
Soames, N. "Catching Up with Kiri Te Kanawa." *Fugue* 4/October (1979): 26.
Profile. *San Francisco Opera Magazine* 58/8 (Fall 1980): 63; 10/Fall (1985): 34; 2/Fall (1986): 35.
"Das *Bühne* Profil." *Bühne* 266/November (1980): 13.
Percy, G. "Kiri Te Kanawa—aennu en australisk storstjaerna." *Musikrevy* 36/6 (1981): 308.
Forbes, Elizabeth. "Kiri Te Kanawa." *Opera* 32/July (1981): 679.
Jacobson, R. "Dame Kiri." *Opera News* 47 (26 February 1983): 8.
Portrait. *Vanity Fair* 46/May (1983): 58.

Soria, D.J. "Kiri Te Kanawa." *Hi Fidelity/Musical America* 33/June (1983): MA6.

Blyth, A. "Kiri Te Kanawa Interviewed." *Gramophone* 61/ November (1983): 603.

Renk, H.E. "Porträt." *Opernwelt* 25/1 (1984): 44.

Lanier, T.P. "Hearts and Flowers." *Opera News* 48 (4 February 1984): 27.

"Divas." *Ovation* 6/August (1985): 20.

Malitz, N. "Kiri Te Kanawa: Up Close and Personal." *Ovation* 6/September (1985): 10.

Fraser, Antonia. "My Heroine." *Opera News* 51 (20 December 1986): 21.

Wollen, Peter. "On Kiri Te Kanawa, Judy Garland, and the Culture Industry." In *Modernity and Mass Culture*, edited by James Naremore and Patrick Brantlinger. Bloomington, 1991.

*   *   *

New Zealand-born soprano Kiri Te Kanawa received her early vocal training (as a mezzo-soprano) in New Zealand, but her first performances in staged opera took place in England: Idamante in Mozart's *Idomeneo* for the Chelsea Opera Group in 1968, Ellen in Rossini's *La donna del lago* at the Camden Festival in 1969, and a Bridesmaid in Mozart's *Le nozze di Figaro* at the Royal Festival Hall in 1970 under the baton of Otto Klemperer. Small roles followed at Covent Garden: a Flowermaiden in Wagner's *Parsifal,* the High Priestess (an offstage role) in Verdi's *Aida.* Her breakthrough came in December 1971 with a performance of the Countess Almaviva in *Le nozze di Figaro.* Desdemona in Verdi's *Otello* and Micaela in Bizet's *Carmen* followed, and to these roles were soon to be added Amelia in Verdi's *Simon Boccanegra* and Donna Elvira in Mozart's *Don Giovanni.* Signed to make her Metropolitan Opera debut as Desdemona in 1974, she made an unscheduled early debut when the announced Desdemona, Teresa Stratas, canceled. The performance was well received and launched her American career.

Te Kanawa has had particular success in the Mozart and Strauss repertoire, most notably as the countess in *Le nozze di Figaro* and Fiordiligi in *Così fan tutte,* and in the title role of *Arabella,* which she first sang in 1977, the Marschallin in *Der Rosenkavalier,* which she added in 1981, and the countess in *Capriccio.* She brings to the Strauss roles the soaring top notes, if not quite the careful attention to the text, that these roles ideally require.

Te Kanawa is less suited to the Verdi and Puccini roles, although she has sung Puccini's Mimi, Tosca, and Manon Lescaut, and Verdi's Desdemona, Amelia, and Violetta in *La traviata;* she lacks sufficient expansiveness, heft, and dramatic thrust, as well as the combination of *spinto* strength and agility needed to negotiate the difficulties of many of these parts, nor does she have the strong chest register needed for verismo roles. She has had greater success in the French and German repertoires; among her French roles are Marguerite in Gounod's *Faust,* while her German roles include Rosalinde in Johann Strauss's *Die Fledermaus.*

Kiri Te Kanawa as Amelia in *Simon Boccanegra,* with Michael Sylvester as Gabriele Adorno, Royal Opera, London, 1991

Primarily a lyric soprano, Te Kanawa possesses a creamy, silky sound, a clear, plangent vocal tone with a shimmery brightness allied to physical beauty and poise, a combination that, for many, more than compensates for some failings in intonation and dramatic projection. Her voice is free from an obtrusive vibrato, and she avoids the common fault of scooping into notes. She has the ability to sing softly and is at least proficient in floating her piano high notes, notes that have extended to the high E-flat.

Te Kanawa's detractors find her an unimaginative singer, prone to swallowing her words and creating generalized portrayals. They complain about her lethargic delivery of the vocal line and the text, a droopy quality to her phrasing, an imperturbability that persists even in the most dramatic situations. Her projection of the words is not strong; her enunciation tends to be cloudy and her pronunciation of German and French is not ideally idiomatic, resulting in the production of sounds that, while lovely in an abstract sort of way, do not incisively project the music, the text, or the emotions of the character she is portraying. Her Italian roles are compromised by a lack of fire. Nor is she particularly able to differentiate one of her characters from another—they all appear to be cast in the same, rather passive, unemotional mold, if an exceptionally beautiful one. It is this characteristic combination of vocal beauty and emotional remoteness that makes Te Kanawa a frustrating singer for some.

Early in her career, Te Kanawa performed tiny roles in some recordings of complete operas. She was heard, if briefly, as the groom Dmitri in Gardelli's recording of Giordano's *Fedora* in 1969, was the Countess Ceprano in Bonynge's recording of Verdi's *Rigoletto* in 1972, and was a Flowermaiden in Wagner's *Parsifal* (also in 1972, under Solti's baton). Once her international career had been launched, she was assigned to major roles in numerous recordings, especially in her specialty roles of Mozart and Strauss. Her complete operatic recordings include her portrayals of the Countess Almaviva (1973, under Colin Davis; 1978, under Solti; and 1991, under Levine); Donna Elvira (1973, under Colin Davis, and 1978, under Maazel); Micaela in Bizet's *Carmen* (1975, under Solti); Fiordiligi (1977, under Lombard, and 1989, under Levine); the Sandman in Humperdinck's *Hänsel und Gretel* (1978, under Pritchard), Pamina in *Die Zauberflöte* (1978, under Lombard, and 1989, under Marriner); Magda in Puccini's *La rondine* (1983, under Maazel), Tosca (1986, under Solti); Manon Lescaut (1988, under Chailly); Amelia (1989, under Solti), Arabella (1987, under Tate); Mademoiselle Silberklang in Mozart's *Der Schauspieldirektor* (1990, under Pritchard), Rosalinde (1991, under Previn); the Marschallin (1991, under Haitink); and the Woodbird in Haitink's recording of Wagner's *Ring* cycle.

—Michael Sims

TELEMANN, Georg Philipp.

Composer. Born 14 March 1681, in Magdeburg. Died 25 June 1767, in Hamburg. Married: 1) Louise Eberlin, 1709 (died 1711); 2) Maria Katharina Textor, 1714 (eight sons, two daughters). Studied theory with the cantor Benedikt Christiani; studied law at the University of Leipzig, beginning 1701; organized a collegium musicum at the University of Leipzig, 1702; music director of the Leipzig Opera; in Sorau as Kapellmeister to Count Erdmann II of Promnitz, 1705; Konzertmeister to the court orchestra and later Kapellmeister in Eisenach, 1708; music director of the city of Frankfurt, 1712; director of the Frauenstein Society; music director of five churches in Hamburg, 1721; music director of the Hamburg Opera, 1722-38; visited France, 1737-38.

Operas

Editions:

G.P. Telemann: Musikalische Werke. Kassel and Basel, 1950-.

G.P. Telemann: Orgelwerke. Edited by T. Fedtke. Kassel, 1964.

Sigismundus, 1693.
Adonis, 1708 [fragmentary].
Narcissus, 1709 [fragmentary].
Mario, 1709 [fragmentary].
Die Satyren in Arcadien, Leipzig, 1719 revised, 1724, as *Der neu-modische Liebhaber Damon.*
Der geduldige Sokrates, J.U. von König (after Minato), Hamburg, 1721.
Sieg der Schönheit, Hamburg, 1722; revised, 1725, and 1732 as *Genserich.*
Belsazar, 1723 [fragmentary].
Pimpinone (comic intermezzi), Hamburg, 1725; 1728.
La capricciosa e il credulo (comic intermezzi), 1725 [fragmentary].
Sancio, 1727 [fragmentary].
Calypso, 1727 [fragmentary].
Miriways, 1728.
Die Last-tragende Liebe, oder Emma und Eginhard, 1728 [destroyed?].
Die verkehrte Welt, 1728 [fragmentary].
Flavius Bertaridus, 1729.
Aesopus, 1729 [fragmentary].
Don Quichotte der Löwenritter, 1761.
Adam und Eva, [fragmentary].
Hercules und Alceste, [fragmentary].
Herodes und Mariamne, [fragmentary].
[texts to 7 operas and 2 sets of intermezzi].

Other works: sacred and secular vocal music, concertos, chamber music, keyboard works, lute pieces.

Publications/Writings

By TELEMANN: books–

Singe-Spiel- und Generalbass-Übungen. Hamburg, 1733-34; Leipzig, 1983.
Beschreibung der Augen-Orgel. Hamburg, 1739.
Grosse, H., and H.R. Jung, eds. *Georg Philipp Telemann, Briefwechsel.* Leipzig, 1972.
Fleischhauer, G., W. Siegmund-Schultze, and E. Thom, eds. *Autobiographien, 1718, 1729, 1739.* Blankenburg, 1977; English translation, 1982.
Rackwitz, Werner, ed. *Singen ist das Fundament zur Musik in allen Dingen: Eine Dokumentensammlung.* Leipzig, 1981.

articles–

"Neues musicalisches System." In L.C. Mizler, *Musikalische Bibliothek,* vol. 3/no. 4 (Leipzig): 713; revised as *Letzte Beschäftigung G. Ph. Telemanns im 86. Lebensjahre, be-*

stehend in einer musikalischen Klang- und Intervallentafel, in *Unterhaltungen,* 3, Hamburg, 1767.

About TELEMANN: books–

Valentin, E. *Georg Philipp Telemann.* Burg, 1931; 3rd. edition, 1952.

Kahl, W. *Selbstbiographien deutscher Musiker des 18. Jahrhunderts.* Cologne and Krefeld, 1948; 1970.

Wolff, H.C. *Die Barockoper in Hamburg 1678-1738.* 2 vols. Wolfenbüttel, 1957.

Magdeburger-Telemann Festtage 1-6. Magdeburg, 1963-78.

Petzoldt, R. *Telemann und seine Zeitgenossen.* Magdeburg, 1966.

————. *Georg Philipp Telemann: Leben und Werk.* Leipzig, 1967; English translation, 1974.

Georg Philipp Telemann: Leben und Werk: Beiträge zur gleichnamigen Ausstellung. Magdeburg, 1967.

Grebe, K. *Georg Philipp Telemann in Selbstzeugnissen und Bilddokumenten.* Reinbek, 1970.

Allihn, I. *Georg Philipp Telemann und J.J. Quantz.* Magdeburg, 1971.

Füredi, L. and D. Vulpe. *Telemann.* Bucharest, 1971.

Telemann-Renaissance: Werk und Wiedergabe. Magdeburg, 1973.

Siegmund-Schultze, Walther, and Günther Fleischhauer, eds. *Telemann und seine Dichter.* Magdeburg, 1978.

Georg Philipp Telemann: Leben—Werk—Wirkung. Berlin, 1980.

Klessmann, E. *Telemann in Hamburg 1721-67.* Hamburg, 1980.

Siegmund-Schultze, W. *Georg Philipp Telemann.* Leipzig, 1980.

Wettstein, H. *Georg Philipp Telemann: Bibliographischer Versuch zu seinem Leben und Werk,* 1681-1767. Hamburg, 1981.

Muller, Jean-Pierre. *Georg Philipp Telemann.* Brussels, 1981.

Fleischhauer, Günther, et al., eds. *Die Bedeutung Georg Philipp Telemanns für die Entwicklung der europäischen Musikkultur im 18. Jahrhundert.* Magdeburg, 1983.

articles–

Baselt, Bernd. "Georg Philipp Telemanns Serenade *Don Quichotte auf der Hochzeit des Comancho.* Beiträge zur Entstehungsgeschichte von Telemanns letztem Hamburger Bühnenwerk." *Hamburger Jahrbuch für Musikwissenschaft* 3 (1978): 85.

Buelow, George J. "Opera in Hamburg 300 Years Ago." *Musical Times* 119 (1978): 26.

Baselt, Bernd. "Bemerkungen zum Opernschaffen Georg Philipp Telemanns." *Musica* 35/no. 1 (1981): 19.

————. "Telemann und die deutsche Oper." *Musik und Gesellschaft* 31 (1981): 140.

Ruhnke, M. "Komische Elemente in Telemanns Opern und Intermezzi." *Bericht über den Int. Musikwissenschaftlichen Kongress. Bayreuth, 1981,* edited by Christoph-Hellmut Mahling and Sigrid Wiesmann, 94. Kassel, 1981.

————. "Telemanns Hamburger Opern und ihre italienischen und französischen Vorbilder." *Hamburger Jahrbuch für Musikwissenschaft* 5 (1981): 9.

Wolff, H.C. "*Pimpinone* von Albinoni und Telemann: Ein Vergleich." *Hamburger Jahrbuch für Musikwissenschaft* 5 (1981).

unpublished–

Peckham, M.A. "The Operas of Georg Philipp Telemann." Ph.D. dissertation, Columbia University, 1969.

* * *

Most versatile and industrious of all baroque composers, Telemann was bound to turn his hand to opera. In fact, opera remained a major interest of his from the time when, as a twelve-year-old in his birthplace Magdeburg, he penned *Sigismundus* to 1761, when as an octogenarian he composed *Don Quichotte der Löwenritter (Don Quixote the Lion-hearted Knight).* His most successful works were those written for the Gänsemarkt (Goosemarket) theater in Hamburg, of which he held the musical direction between 1722 and 1738 (this despite his responsibility, as cantor, for the city's church music and the consequent opposition of some city councilors to his dual activity). Prior to his arrival in Hamburg in 1721 he wrote numerous operas for Leipzig, Weissenfels, Bayreuth and Eisenach, although only isolated fragments of these works remain. Some of the librettos for these operas were his own handiwork, and he enjoyed occasional opportunities in Hamburg to put this gift to use.

Of the eight stage works by Telemann surviving in performable state four can be classified as "serious" operas (though with an admixture of comic elements), three as "comic" operas and one as a set of three comic intermezzi. The serious works are *Miriways* (1728), *Emma und Eginhard* (1728), *Flavius Bertaridus* (1729) and *Genserich* (1722, revived 1732);

Georg Philipp Telemann

the comic works are *Der geduldige Sokrates* (1721), *Der neumodische Liebhaber Damon* (1724) and *Don Quichotte der Löwenritter* (1761); the set of intermezzi is *Pimpinone*.

Telemann had neither the wish nor, one suspects, the talent to construct movements on the monumental scale found in J.S. Bach and Handel. His gift was to invent "cameo" movements of short to moderate length with an original melodic or harmonic cast and often interesting instrumentation. He liked to wear his counterpoint lightly and did not cultivate either vocal or instrumental virtuosity for its own sake, although in the interests of expression he could certainly write technically challenging parts. These gifts found a perfect vehicle in opera as practised in Hamburg: stylistically (sometimes also linguistically) eclectic, willing to juxtapose the comic and the serious and favoring a kaleidoscopic succession of short numbers (at a time when in Italy, under the influence of reforming librettists such as Metastasio, the trend was toward fewer but longer numbers). To illustrate the last point: *Der geduldige Sokrates,* which in a recent recording lasts just over four hours, contains nearly 120 separate numbers.

Telemann's feeling for musical characterization, particularly in a comic or simple lyrical vein, is outstanding. Here is one baroque composer whose recitatives, smoothly flowing and sensitively shaped, strongly resist cutting. He was also a master of ensemble writing. *Sokrates,* a study of the problems of polygamy in ancient Athens, is full of attractive duets for the female roles—the philosopher's quarrelsome wives Xantippe and Amitta and the rival princesses Rodisette and Andronica—and ensembles for his pupils. The arias that perhaps stick longest in the mind are those in a wistful vein, whose intimacy is sometimes heightened by having no other accompaniment than continuo.

Telemann's experience of dance music (he wrote hundreds of *ouvertures,* or orchestral suites in the French style) is very evident in his operas, where the minuet, the passepied and other dance measures inform the rhythmic movement of many numbers.

Telemann is a complex musical personality to whom facile labels such as "galan" or "pre-classical" do scant justice. He may probe less deeply into the soul than Handel but he gratifies on other counts. The success in modern times of *Pimpinone,* which through its brevity and humor leaps over the usual barriers to the revival of baroque operas, points the way forward to the more substantial works.

—Michael Talbot

THE TENDER LAND.

Composer: Aaron Copland.

Librettist: H. Everett (after E. Johns).

First Performance: New York, New York City Opera, 1 April 1954; revised 1955, Oberlin, Ohio, 20 May 1955.

Roles: Laurie (soprano); Ma Moss (contralto); Martin (tenor); Top (baritone); Grandpa Moss (bass); Beth Moss (child, mostly speaking); Mr Splinters (tenor); Mrs Splinters (mezzo-soprano); Mr Jenks (baritone); Mrs Jenks (soprano); Three Guests (soprano, tenor, bass); chorus (SATB).

*　　*　　*

The Tender Land, the only full-length opera by Aaron Copland, is about a farm family in the American midwest in the mid-1930s. Laurie Moss is about to graduate from high school. Her mother, grandfather, and younger sister, Beth, are planning a celebration. Two migrant workers, Martin and Top, appear to help with the harvest. The first act ends with a quintet, "The Promise of Living." During the graduation party at the farm that opens the second act with the rousing chorus and dance, "Stomp Your Foot," Laurie and Martin fall in love and plan to run away together. After Martin goes away without her, Laurie decides to leave alone. The opera closes with an aria by Ma Moss looking to her younger daughter as the continuation of the family.

Copland composed *The Tender Land* in what has been called his "Americana" style. A few folk tunes are incorporated, and the quality of the writing is similar to Copland's earlier *Appalachian Spring.* The harmony is primarily diatonic, with dissonance used only in a few instances for dramatic tension. The orchestration is not complex and the score is devoid of special effects. Copland's intention was to give young American singers material that would be natural to sing and perform.

Copland derived an orchestral suite from *The Tender Land* and prepared arrangements of "The Promise of Living" and "Stomp Your Foot" for chorus and piano four-hands (sometimes used with the orchestral suite). The aria, "Laurie's Song" is arranged for high voice and piano. The opera has been produced only occasionally, sometimes in concert version. In 1987 conductor Murry Sidlin prepared a thirteen-instrument orchestration of *The Tender Land* for a production by the Long Wharf Theater in New Haven, Connecticut. The first complete recording with full orchestra was released in 1990 performed by the soloists, chorus and orchestra of The Plymouth Music Series of Minnesota, music director Philip Brunelle.

—Vivian Perlis

TETRAZZINI, Luisa.

Soprano. Born 29 June 1871, in Florence. Died 28 April 1940, in Milan. Married: 1) Alberto Scalaberni, c. 1890; 2) Pietro Vernati, 1926. Studied at the Istituto Musicale in Florence with Contrucci and Cecherini, and with her sister Eva, herself a soprano and wife of conductor Cleofonte Campanini; debut at the Teatro Pagliano in Florence, as Inez in *L'africaine,* 1890; toured throughout Europe, as well as Russia and Latin America; U.S. debut in San Francisco, 1905; Covent Garden debut as Violetta, 1907, and sang for the summer seasons there from 1908 to 1912; New York debut as Violetta at the Manhattan Opera House, 1908; sang there until 1910; sang for 1911-12 season at the Metropolitan Opera and the 1911-12 and 1912-13 seasons in Chicago; was recorded extensively between 1903 and 1914; toured widely after World War I, singing only concerts; made final appearances in New York in 1931 and London in 1934; in later years was active as a teacher in Milan.

Publications

By TETRAZZINI: books–

The Art of Singing, with Enrico Caruso. New York, 1909.
My Life of Song. London, 1921.
How to Sing. New York, 1923.

About TETRAZZINI: articles–

Richards, J.B. "Luisa Tetrazzini." *Record Collector* 4 (1949): 123.
Shawe-Taylor, D. "A Gallery of Great Singers: Luisa Tetrazzini." *Opera* 14 (1963): 593.
Hiller, C.H. "Der künstlerische Nachlass von Luisa Tetrazzini." *Opernwelt* 31 (December 1990): 63.
Pennino, J. "Tetrazzini at the Tivoli: Success and Scandal in San Francisco." *The Opera Quarterly* 8/2 (1991): 4.

*　　*　　*

Luisa Tetrazzini made her debut in Florence at the Teatro Pagliano (now the Verdi) in 1890 as Inez in Meyerbeer's *L'Africaine*. After singing at the Argentina, Rome, and touring Italian cities, she joined Tomba's opera company at the San Martin, Buenos Aires, in October, 1892, and returned every season until 1895, singing also in Rosario and Mendoza, as well as Uruguay and Brazil. In 1896 she sang in Portugal, Italy, Poland, and Spain. In early 1987 she sang in St Petersburg before returning to Madrid in the spring, where she sang Amina in *La sonnambula*, Lucia, and the *Jollie fille de Perth*'s

Luisa Tetrazzini as Rosina in *Il barbiere di Siviglia*

title role at the Prince Alfonso Theatre. She showed serious signs of vocal decline in *Ugonotti* but fully recovered to win acclaim at the Dal Verme, Milan, the same year, then in 1898 at the Teatro Brunelli, Bologna, and the Teatro de la Opera, Buenos Aires. From the start of 1899 to the spring of 1903 she sang in Warsaw, Moscow, St Petersburg, Berlin, and occasionally in Italy where she triumphed in *Puritani* at the Teatro Adriano, Rome, in April, 1900. From summer 1903 to early 1905 she was mostly in Mexico. Engaged by W.H. Leahy to sing at the Tivoli, San Francisco, for two seasons, she created a furor, as she did at her Covent Garden debut as Violetta in 1907, returning there every season until 1912. She made an equally brilliant debut in the same role in 1908 at the Manhattan, New York, returning every year until 1910. When Hammerstein disbanded his company, she sang for a few performances at the Metropolitan Opera. She reacted against his lawsuit to prevent her singing for other managements by announcing that she would sing in the streets of San Francisco. As a result, she gave her famous Christmas Eve open air concert there in 1910 attended by nearly 250,000 people who heard her clearly without any form of amplification.

After World War I, Tetrazzini ceased appearing in opera and sang instead in popular concerts in Britain and America. In 1925 she starred in the first British Broadcasting Corporation concert heard world-wide.

In 1926, Tetrazzini married Pietro Vernati, twenty-four years younger than she, but they parted after only three years together. She then became involved with charlatans who exploited her obsession with spiritism. Foolishly generous and extravagant, her fortune of five million dollars had vanished by the mid 1930s and she was reduced to giving singing lessons to pupils who boarded with her in Milan, her most successful one being Lina Pagliughi. According to Harry Higgins, who ran Covent Garden for some thirty years, she was the greatest prima donna of his time. He said nothing ever excelled the brilliance of her attack and the abandon of her cadenzas.

John McCormack, who often sang with Tetrazzini at Covent Garden and in New York, was a discerning judge. Above E flat, she was superb, he thought, her chromatic scales upward and downward being marvels of clarity, and her trill unrivalled. "She could get an amazing amount of *larmes dans la voix*, far more than I ever heard from any other coloratura soprano." On the other hand, "the middle of her voice was white and breathy, probably from overwork as a young singer." This criticism refers to what W.J. Henderson of the *New York Sun* described after her Manhattan debut as her worst shortcoming—"the extraordinary emission of her lower medium notes" which were sung with "a pinched glottis and with a color so pallid and a tremolo so pronounced that they were often not a bad imitation of the wailing of a cross infant."

The "tremolo" was probably caused by first night nerves, for this complaint was rarely again made. The distinguished critic, John Pitts Sanborn, observed that when Tetrazzini returned the following season "the crudities had largely disappeared, and her medium register, previously deficient, she had recovered or developed." He thought this improvement due to singing under her brother-in-law Cleofonte Campanini's guidance. Writing in 1912, Sanborn states: "But the apotheosis of Tetrazzini came last spring when, after a year's absence, she returned here to sing in concert. Then the voice was almost perfectly equalised, a glorious organ from top to bottom. Even in the lowest register she was ready with a firm, rich tone. . . . She not only sang great florid arias with perfect command of voice technique and style; she sang Aida's "Ritorna vincitor" as scarcely a dramatic soprano has sung it here. She sang Solvejg' song from *Peer Gynt* like a true Lieder singer, and the page's song from *Figaro* with . . . the most wonderful display of vocal virtuosity since Patti. . . . Her 'Voi che sapete' was the finest piece of Mozart singing I have ever heard, and I have heard both Melba and Sembrich sing the same piece." In his opinion, she was, one of the last exponents of a perfect trill—"two golden hammers beating a faultless interval."

Fortunately, Tetrazzini made many recordings. Her singing of the Carnival of Venice and other examples of her art were included in the "Great Recordings of the Century" LP (Angel COLH 136) issued in 1964. Gerald Fitzgerald in *Opera News* for 12 December that year commented that, like most of her records, "it belies many of the criticisms raised against her, especially the deficiency in the lower region of her voice, which bounds forth jubilantly. . . . More than singing, however, one senses a vibrant personality—generous, uninhibited, warm and joyous that establishes immediate rapport with the listener."

Apart from LPs of Tetrazzini, there is a smoothly transferred Conductart cassette (CV-1002) and compact discs from Pearl (CDS-9220) reproducing most of her records, and from Nimbus (NI-7808) lasting 74′ 35″ and noteworthy for added resonance, while in March, 1991, EMI will be issuing all the Gramophone Company's recordings, transferred by Keith Hardwick. Luisa Tetrazzini's autobiography, *My Life of Song,* published in 1921, which was "ghosted," contains few dates and is extremely unreliable.

—Charles Neilson Gattey

TEYTE, Maggie.

Soprano. Born Margaret Tate, 17 April 1888, in Wolverhampton. Died 26 May 1976, in London. Married: 1) Eugène de Plumon, 1909 (divorced 1915); 2) Sherwin Cottingham, 1921 (divorced 1931). Studied in London, and with Jean de Reszke in Paris, 1904-06; debut in Monte Carlo, singing Tyrcis in *Miriame et Daphné* (an Offenbach pastiche), 1907; that same year appeared as Zerlina at Monte Carlo and in several roles at the Paris Opéra-Comique; in 1908 chosen and coached by Debussy to succeed Mary Garden as Mélisande at Opéra-Comique; with the Beecham Opera Company 1910-11; with Chicago Opera Company, 1911-14, singing among other characters the title role in Massenet's *Cendrillon;* with Boston Opera Company, 1914-17; with British National Opera, 1922-23; during 1920s and 30s appeared in many operettas and musical comedies; recorded highly-acclaimed albums of French songs in 1937 and 1940; New York City Opera debut as Mélisande, 1947; appeared as Belinda in Purcell's *Dido and Aeneas* at the Mermaid Theater in London, 1951; final concert appearance at Festival Hall, 1955; made a Chevalier of the Légion d'honneur in 1957 and D.B.E. in 1958.

Publications

By TEYTE: books—

Star on the Door. London, 1958.

About TEYTE: books—

O'Connor, Garry. *The Pursuit of Perfection: A Life of Maggie Teyte.* London, 1979.

articles—

Tron, D. "Maggie Teyte." *Record Collector* 9 (1954): 129.
Emmons, Shirlee. "Maggie Teyte." *NATS Bulletin* 41/1 (1984): 31.

Although she sang many roles during her long career, Teyte is remembered mostly as one of the first, and for many the finest, interpreters of Mélisande. When she went to be coached by Debussy for her first performance at the Opéra-Comique, she recalled that he exclaimed to himself, "Une autre Ecossaise!"—for Mary Garden, the creator of the part, hailed from Aberdeen.

Teyte's secret of success with Debussy's music lay simply in singing it just as if it had been Mozart. She claimed that he would not allow the repetiteurs at the performance he supervised to interfere with her singing, and as proof of his approval, he accompanied her in recital, just as he had Mary Garden. That these two Scotswomen were the first and for many years just about the only interpreters of this role is rather curious. On all her records of French song, although her diction and phrasing are individual and scrupulous, Teyte sings with an unmistakable British accent.

Although a pupil of Jean de Reszke, and a singer with a natural affinity for French music and particularly for that of Gounod, Debussy, Massenet and Hahn, Teyte had a fierce curiosity which never left her and led her, even at the end of her singing career, which lasted until she was well into her sixties, to expand her repertory to include songs by Stravinsky, Poulenc, Britten, and even to consider Schoenberg (she studied *Pierrot Lunaire,* though she never performed it in public).

Teyte held forthright opinions about the interpretation of opera and the stylistic quirks that generations of singers laid upon various roles. She detested the word "tradition" and until her last years took a keen interest in young performers. She very much admired George Shirley's Pelléas in the 1969 revival at Covent Garden and the adventurous Gustavus of Ragnar Ulfung in *Un ballo in maschera.* She claimed to have heard one of the last castratos sing and lived to hear and discuss the music of Henze and Boulez.

As a woman and as a stage performer she was often accused of being cold, yet her voice on records can have an almost overwhelming intimacy. This has nothing to do with the modern vehemence of singers who have grown up with a knowledge of naturalistic drama, but is always contained within an orthodox technique. In her justly famous recording of "Tu n'es pas beau" from Offenbach's *La Périchole,* the reiteration of "Je t'adore, brigand" or the way in which she attacks the climactic phrases in the finale of act I of Messager's *Monsieur Beaucaire,* an object lesson in vocal technique to hear her withstand the consistently off-pitch singing of her partner, to which she responds with perfectly-placed head notes, all pay tribute to her teacher de Reszke: "When you have done your exercises for staccato, exercises pianissimo, exercises fortissimo, exercises for the diaphragm, exercises for head tone and the raising of the soft palate—all taken or based on operatic motifs—you realise that they are very different from scales."

Although she continued to sing in opera, Teyte was eventually more at home on the concert platform. Her no-nonsense approach to life and art and her outspoken and impatient attitude made her happier where, as she put it, "there was just you and your accompanist—there is no one against you."

—Patrick O'Connor

THAÏS.

Composer: Jules Massenet.

Librettist: Louis Gallet (after Anatole France).

First Performance: Paris, Opéra, 16 March 1894.

Roles: Thaïs (soprano); Athanael (baritone); Nicias (tenor); Crobyle (soprano); Myrtale (mezzo-soprano); Albine (mezzo-soprano); Servant (baritone); Palemon (bass); La Charmeuse (soprano); chorus (SSSATTTBB).

Publications

articles–

Finck, H.T. "Massenet, Thaïs and Farrar." *The Nation* 104 (1917).
Porter, Andrew. Review of *Thaïs. The New Yorker* 6 February (1978).
Opera News 28 January (1978) [*Thaïs* issue].
Avant-scène opéra May (1988) [*Thaïs* issue].
Pines, Roger. Review of *Thaïs. Opera Quarterly* 6/no. 3 (spring 1989): 154.

*   *   *

The once immensely popular *Thaïs* does not figure prominently in today's repertoire; the late 1970s saw a resurgence of interest in the opera, but questions remain as to the overall quality of the drama and the score. Most criticism has centered on the dated subject matter, on Louis Gallet's shallow adaptation of the novel by Anatole France, and, ultimately, on Massenet's inability to delineate the principal characters in musical terms. Roger Pines writes: "Thaïs is a little much for us today. . . . One struggles to care about the fate of Massenet's troubled courtesan and the crazed monk who loves her. The score . . . has not worn as well as either *Manon* or *Werther;* moments of inspiration alternate all too often with tedium." Robert Lawrence, otherwise a defender of Massenet, finds Thaïs to be "a courtesan whose rates and prestige have declined by now."

The opera's insubstantiality may be due in large part to its libretto, which oversimplified Anatole France's novel and was sharply attacked from the start (most notably by France himself). Andrew Porter notes that though France "ranged far beyond the simple moral drama and handled the history in no pious way. . . . There could be no place for this in the opera. Louis Gallet, Massenet's librettist, omitted the irony, the kaleidoscope of daring speculations, and all the jokes. The tone was quite altered."

For Martin Cooper, who wrote the article on Massenet for *The New Grove Dictionary of Music and Musicians,* Massenet's music also lacks a true dramatic quality: "When Massenet attempted the portrait of . . . Thaïs, he was handicapped by his conventionality. Inasmuch as Thaïs is a real person, she is simply a reincarnation of Manon." Furthermore, Cooper notes, though Athanael's "divided personality, and his passion for Thaïs inspired Massenet with some of his rare impassioned music . . . the absence of any comparatively powerful music to express Athanael's asceticism . . . leaves his character and the work unbalanced."

Other critics find the opera still worthy of interest, especially when it is presented well. Despite his negative criticism, Pines also notes that "in the right hands, [the] music still offers some rewards. It is certainly worth enduring a great deal of languid dialogue and quaint salon exoticism in order to savor Thaïs' arias and large chunks of her duets with Athanael. Here Massenet exploits the lyricism and dramatic flair that helped to sustain his immense popularity." And though Porter thought the Met's 1978 revival was marred by poor staging, he found the work to be "a pretty opera, and very skillfully written."

A final assessment seems dependent as well on one's willingness to accept *fin-de-siècle* French culture. As Martin Cooper notes: "the figure of the reformed courtesan . . . was given a devotional tinge very much in line with certain currents in contemporary French Catholicism. . . . The climax of this particular genre was reached with *Thaïs*." Going even further, Gary Lipton feels that Massenet's (and Anatole France's) "special vision of Egyptian antiquity . . . reflects the volatile discussion of equality, social justice and progress in evidence since the literary debates of French Enlightenment figures."

—David Pacun

THÉSÉE [Theseus].

Composer: Jean-Baptiste Lully.

Librettist: Philippe Quinault.

First Performance: Saint-Germain, 12 January 1675.

Roles: Two Pleasures (countertenor, bass); Le Jeu (tenor); Bacchus (countertenor); Vénus (soprano); Cérès (soprano); Mars (bass); Bellone (mute); Eglé (soprano); Cléone (soprano); Arcas (bass); High Priestess of Minerva (soprano); A Fighter (tenor); Egée (baritone); Médée (soprano); Dorine (soprano); Two Old Men from Athens (countertenor, tenor);

Act II of Massenet's *Thaïs*, illustration from first production, Paris Opéra, 1894

Thésée (tenor); A Phantom (mute); Two Shepherdesses (sopranos); Shepherd (countertenor); Minerve (soprano); chorus; ballet; mute figures in the Prologue.

*　　*　　*

Thésée begins with an extended prologue, lamenting King Louis XIV's absence from Versailles and celebrating the recent victories of his army. The drama itself, based on an episode from Ovid's *Metamorphoses*, is set in ancient Athens. The magician princess Médée loves Thésée, the young commander of King Egée's victorious army. Thésée and Egée, however, both love Egée's ward, Princess Eglé, who returns Thésée's love. (A sub-plot involves the confidants of Egée, Eglé, and Médée in a love triangle.) Médée uses her magical powers to torment Eglé, in an effort to make her relinquish Thésée. Unsuccessful, Médée pretends to honor the lovers but persuades Egée to regard Thésée as a threat to the throne and to poison the young hero at a festival in his honor. At the last moment the king recognizes Thésée's sword and realizes what the others already know—that Thésée is his son, who had been raised in a faraway place. Egée gladly gives Thésée Eglé's hand. Still seeking vengeance, Médée orders the forces of hell to destroy the festive palace she has created, but the goddess Minerve replaces it with an indestructible one.

It has been pointed out that Quinault's librettos, though contemporaneous with the tragedies of Racine, bear more resemblance to the tragedies, tragicomedies, machine tragedies, and heroic novels of Corneille's generation: action, adventure, illusion, and tender love take precedence over psychological drama. *Thésée* is no exception. Thanks to Lully's brilliant use of an off-stage chorus and the orchestra, prayers to Minerve at the beginning of the opera are punctuated by distant sounds of battle. Later, Médée transports Eglé to a dreadful desert where "the inhabitants of Hell" torment her, then to an enchanted pastoral island where she must lie to Thésée if she wishes his life to be spared; each location is depicted by appropriate music and action. The heroic initial entrance of Thésée surrounded by his adoring public, the frightening appearance of "phantoms" as Médée destroys the festive palace, the appearance of Minerve in dazzling glory to set things right—all are palpable and convincing.

Yet it was surely Racine who provided the inspiration for female characters like Cybèle and Armide (in *Atys* and *Armide* respectively), not to mention Phèdre in Pellegrin's and Rameau's *Hippolyte et Aricie*—tragic women who are strong and powerful but are devoured by unrequited love, who maintain inappropriate and precarious control over their situations until they are ultimately punished. Médée is the first such woman in French opera. Like the others, she sings powerful monologue airs in ternary or rondeau form, in which she reasons with herself or invokes external powers or internal emotions: "Doux repos," "Dépit mortel," "Sortez, Ombres," "Ah! faut-il me venger." As Volker Kapp has pointed out, *Thésée* symbolically exalts Louis XIV's France by glorifying "la raison d'État": the State, with divine help, surmounts all obstacles. Médée's error is to attempt to impose her will on the king instead of submitting to his laws; Minerve, by stopping Médée, is the symbolic protector of the king of France.

Like several other operas by Lully, *Thésée* was part of the standard repertory of the Paris Opéra through the 1760s; in addition, it was selected to represent Lully when, in 1779, the Opéra programmed an historical survey of French operatic styles.

—Lois Rosow

THESEUS
See THÉSÉE

THILL, Georges.

Tenor. Born 14 December 1897, in Paris. Died 17 October 1984, in Paris. Studied with André Gresse at the Paris Conservatory, and with Fernando De Lucia in Naples; debut as Nicias in *Thaïs,* Paris Opéra, 1924; sang regularly at the Opéra until 1940; appeared at Covent Garden, 1928, 1937; Metropolitan Opera debut as Roméo, 1931; sang with the Metropolitan Opera for two seasons.

Publications

About THILL: books–

Mancini, R. *Georges Thill.* Paris, 1966.
Segond, André. *Georges Thill ou l'age d'or d'opéra.* Lyons, 1980.
———. *Album Georges Thill.* Aix-en-Provence, 1984.

articles–

Celletti, R. "Thill, Georges." In *Le grandi voci,* Rome, 1964.
Avant-scène opéra [Thill issue] September (1984).
Shawe-Taylor, Desmond. "Georges Thill." *Opera* July (1985).

*   *   *

Georges Thill's career was phenomenal. Between his debut at the Paris Opéra in 1924 as Nicias in *Thaïs* and his final performance at a concert in the same city in 1956, he appeared before the public on not far short of 1500 occasions. Until 1940 these were mostly in opera, and he frequently gave more than sixty performances a year. Thereafter he took to the concert stage with up to eighty performances annually. His record year was 1935: with seventy-five performances of opera and twenty-five concerts, he still found time to record.

From the time of his debut Thill rapidly became the leading tenor at the Paris Opéra, while his true métier was as heroic tenor, he sang in an incredible variety of operas, ranging from *Lohengrin,* through *Guillaume Tell* and *Les Huguenots* to *Roméo and Juliet, Werther* and the more standard repertory—*Faust, Carmen, Rigoletto, Aida, Turandot, Tosca.* During the inter-war years Thill was the mainstay of the tenor repertory.

Not until 1928 did Thill sing outside France, appearing at Covent Garden in *Samson and Delilah* with Frozier-Marrot—two equally huge voices! Although he seems to have made only a limited impact in London, this was the beginning of Thill's international career. From 1929 he became a frequent performer at the Teatro Colón in Buenos Aires. In his very first season there he appeared on seventeen occasions in nine different operas and with a variety of distinguished partners. He returned to the Colón in 1930, 1931 and 1938. He also appeared in Montevideo, Rio de Janeiro and the Metropolitan Opera as well as the great European houses—Teatro alla Scala, Vienna and Monte Carlo.

Detailed critical commentary on Thill's performances is not easy to find. His voice is instantly recognizable, but ultimately perhaps not that memorable. He seems to possess enormous vocal resources, but his recorded legacy does not really seem to offer much character differentiation. The somewhat harsh comment that he was the least winning and romantic Roméo and Faust when he appeared at the Metropolitan is understandable when one listens to some of the records, which are occasionally characterized by an unremitting loudness. We are aware of a remarkable heroic tenor which would always be in demand in the opera house, but ultimately there is a shortage of both subtlety and characterization.

On the other hand, the great contemporary critic Hermann Klein commented on the tenderness of an aria from *La bohème* and the charm of one from *Lohengrin,* although he was less impressed with Thill's *La traviata.* There is a remarkable, nearly complete *Werther* sung with Vallin in which Thill gets inside the role. Even better are some extracts from the true repertoire of the French heroic tenor—Massenet's *Cid* and *Hérodiade* and, above all, the 1935 recording of Aeneas's final scene in Berlioz's *Les Troyens.* Here Thill's heroic tones ring out to superb effect: we feel the presence of the legendary hero in this great record.

It may seem slightly surprising that Thill always regarded De Lucia, with whom he spent a considerable period in Naples, as his true teacher, for their vocal styles seem quite dissimilar. However, De Lucia may well have shown his protégé ways in which his voice could be conserved to sustain what must be considered a remarkable career.

—Stanley Henig

THOMAS, (Charles Louis) Ambroise.

Composer. Born 5 August 1811, in Metz. Died, 12 February 1896, in Paris. Studied piano with Zimmermann and harmony and accompaniment with Dourlen at the Paris Conservatory, beginning 1828; studied piano privately with Kalkbrenner, harmony privately with Barbereau, and composition privately with Lesueur; Grand Prix de Rome for his cantata *Hermann et Ketty,* 1832; spent three years in Italy and visited Vienna; returned to Paris and began composing opera; elected to the Académie, 1851; professor of composition at the Paris Conservatory, 1856; director of the Paris Conservatory, 1871.

Operas

La double échelle, F.A.E. de Planard, Paris, Opéra-Comique, Salle des Nouveautés, 23 August 1837.

Le perruquier de la régence, F.A.E. de Planard and P. Dupont, Paris, Opéra-Comique, Salle des Nouveautés, 30 March 1838.

Le panier fleuri, A. de Leuven and L.L. Brunswick, Paris, Opéra-Comique, Salle des Nouveautés, 6 May 1839.

Carline, A. de Leuven and L.L. Brunswick, Paris, Opéra-Comique, Salle des Nouveautés, 24 February 1840.

Le comte de Carmagnola, Eugène Scribe, Paris, Opéra, 19 April 1841.

Le guerillero, T. Anne, Paris, Opéra, 22 June 1842.

Angélique et Médor, T.M.F. Sauvage, Paris, Opéra-Comique, Salle Favart, 10 May 1843.

Mina, ou Le ménage à trois, F.A.E. de Planard, Paris, Opéra-Comique, Salle Favart, 10 October 1843.

Le caïd, T.M.F. Sauvage, Paris, Opéra-Comique, Salle Favart, 3 January 1849.

Le songe d'une nuit d'été, J.B. Rosier and A. de Leuven, Paris, Opéra-Comique, Salle des Nouveautés, 20 April 1850.

Raymond, ou Le secret de la reine, J.B. Rosier and A. de Leuven, Paris, Opéra-Comique, Salle Favart, 5 June 1851.

La Tonelli, T.M.F. Sauvage, Paris, Opéra-Comique, Salle Favart, 30 March 1853.

La cour de Célimène, T.M.F. Sauvage, Paris, Opéra-Comique, Salle Favart, 11 April 1855.

Psyché, J. Barbier and M. Carré, Paris, Opéra-Comique, Salle Favart, 26 January 1857; revised, 21 May 1878.

Le carnaval de Venise, T.M.F. Sauvage, Paris, Opéra-Comique, Salle Favart, 9 December 1857.

Le roman d'Elvire, A. Dumas père and A. de Leuven, Paris, Opéra-Comique, Salle Favart, 4 February 1860.

Mignon, J. Barbier and M. Carré (after Goethe, *Wilhelm Meister*), Paris, Opéra-Comique, Salle Favart, 17 November 1866.

Hamlet, J. Barbier and M. Carré (after Shakespeare), Paris, Opéra, 9 March 1868.

Gille et Gillotin, T.M.F. Sauvage, 1859 (as *Gillotin et son père*), Paris, Opéra-Comique, Salle Favart, 22 April 1874.

Françoise de Rimini, J. Barbier and M. Carré (after Dante), Paris, Opéra, 14 April 1882.

Other works: ballets, sacred and secular vocal works, orchestral works, chamber music, piano and organ pieces.

Publications

About THOMAS: books—

Hanslick, E. *Die moderne Oper.* Vol. 2. Berlin, 1880; 1971; 6th ed., 1911.

Delaborde, H. *Notice sur la vie et les oeuvres de M. Ambroise Thomas.* Paris, 1896.

Hanslick, E. *Die moderne Oper.* Vol. 8. Berlin, 1899; 1971; 3rd ed., 1911.

Cooper, M. *Charles Louis Ambroise Thomas.* London, 1957-58.

articles—

Julien, A. "Ambroise Thomas." *Rivista musicale italiana* 3 (1896): 358.

Simon, J. "Ambroise Thomas." *Revue de Paris* 3/no. 2 (1896): 98.

Berlioz, H. "Le caïd." In *Les musiciens et la musique.* Paris, 1903.

Klein, John W. "A Hundred Years of *Mignon.*" *Opera* November (1966).

Porter, Andrew. "Translating Shakespeare Operas: Thomas's *Hamlet.*" *Opera* July (1980).

*   *   *

Although Ambroise Thomas is a relative unknown today, in the second half of the nineteenth century he was a major force in French music. His twenty operas appeared on all of Paris's leading lyric stages from 1837 onward, and thanks in large measure to the enormous successes of his two masterworks from the 1860s, *Mignon* and *Hamlet,* Thomas served as director of the Paris Conservatory from 1871 until the end of his life. There, for better or for worse, he was in a position to influence the course of French music during the last decades of the century.

Thomas's parents were both music teachers in Metz, and they sent their son to Paris in 1828 to complete his musical education at the Conservatory. He compiled an enviable student record at the august institution, culminating in the Prix de Rome for composition in 1832. During his mandatory three years in the Eternal City, Thomas absorbed well the Italian vocal style, as evidenced by the 1835 collection of six songs *Souvenirs d'Italie,* his first published work and the earliest of nearly forty solo songs he composed throughout his life. Almost immediately upon his return to Paris, Thomas began to write for the lyric stage, at that time the only promising avenue open to a young French composer.

Ambroise Thomas

His first attempt in 1837 was *La double échelle,* a one-act comedy premiered at the Opéra-Comique and generously reviewed by Berlioz in the press. Berlioz especially noted Thomas's skill with orchestration (high praise indeed), an important part of Thomas's musical assets. The next year began a series of seven mostly mediocre works that did little to advance Thomas's career. But in 1849 he succeeded with *Le caïd,* a Rossinian comedy, and in 1850 with *Le songe d'une nuit d'été* which, despite its title, is decidedly non-Shakespearean. Here Falstaff, Elizabeth I and Shakespeare himself appear as characters in the opera, the last-named with a severe drinking problem. Another dry spell followed: six unremarkable operas in nine years. In 1856 Thomas joined the Conservatory faculty as teacher of composition, replacing Adolphe Adam. He turned his creative attention to male choruses, composing about a dozen in the late 1850s and the 1860s. These choruses, sturdy and well crafted, along with the solo songs and operas form the bulk of Thomas's entire output. His other works include three ballets and a quantity of sacred and chamber music.

In 1866 Thomas returned to the boards with *Mignon,* derived from the first part of Goethe's *Wilhelm Meister. Mignon* received immediate acclaim, and enjoyed its 1000th performance at the Opéra-Comique by 1894. Less than two years after *Mignon, Hamlet* was an even greater success at the Opéra, and consolidated Thomas's position as the leading composer of French opera on the eve of the Franco-Prussian War.

After assuming the directorship of the Conservatory, Thomas's new responsibilities left little time for composing large-scale works. His final two operas included one that had been composed before 1870, and his last, *Françoise de Rimini* (1882), was a critical failure said to be the biggest disappointment in Thomas's long life. At the Conservatory, Thomas was a careful and conscientious administrator who raised faculty salaries, improved instructional standards, and expanded the local branch conservatories in the provinces. In 1894, two years before his death, Thomas was awarded the Legion of Honor by the French government.

Mignon and *Hamlet* are still performed today, if infrequently. Thomas's most enduring contribution to musical history has to be considered his pioneering development of a new genre of French opera, opéra-lyrique, midway between opéra-comique and grand opera. Opéra-lyrique was to find full maturity in the works of the next generation of French composers, particularly Bizet, Délibes, Lalo and Thomas's favorite pupil Massenet.

—Morton Achter

THOMSON, Virgil.

Composer. Born 25 November 1896, in Kansas City, Missouri. Died 30 September 1989, in New York City. Served in the United States Army, World War I; studied music with E.B. Hill and A.T. Davison at Harvard University, 1919-23; studied piano with Heinrich Gebhard and organ with Wallace Goodrich in Boston; studied with Nadia Boulanger in Paris, 1921-22; studied composition with Rosario Scalero in New York; organist at King's Chapel in Boston, 1923-24; in Paris, 1925-40; director, Society of Friends and Enemies of Modern Music, 1934-37; music critic of the New York *Herald Tribune* 1940-54; Pulitzer Prize for his score to the film *Louisiana*

Story, directed by R. Flaherty, 1948; sixteen honorary doctorates including Harvard University, 1982; awarded the sixth Annual Kennedy Center Honor for lifetime achievement, 1983.

Operas

Publishers: Boosey and Hawkes, Belwin-Mills, C. Fischer, Peters, Presser, G. Schirmer, Southern.

Four Saints in Three Acts, G. Stein, 1927-28, 1933, Hartford, Connecticut, 8 February 1934.
The Mother of Us All, G. Stein, 1947, New York, 7 May 1947.
Lord Byron, J. Larson, 1966-68, New York, Juilliard School of Music, 20 April 1972.

Other works: ballets, orchestral works, instrumental works, choral works.

Publications

By THOMSON: books–

The State of Music. New York, 1939; 2nd ed., 1962; 1974.
The Musical Scene. New York, 1945; 1968.
The Art of Judging Music. New York, 1948; 1969.
Music Right and Left. New York, 1951; 1969.
Virgil Thomson by Virgil Thomson. New York, 1966; 1977; 1985.
Music Reviewed 1940-1954. New York, 1967.
American Music Since 1910. New York, 1971.
A Virgil Thomson Reader. New York, 1981; 1984.
Page, Tim, and Vanessa Weeks Page, eds. *Virgil Thomson: Selected Letters.* New York, 1987; 1988.
Music with Words. New Haven, 1989.

About THOMSON: books–

Hoover, K., and John Cage. *Virgil Thomson: his Life and Work.* New York, 1959.
Tommasini, Anthony. *The Musical Portraits of Virgil Thomson.* New York, 1985.
Meckna, Michael. *Virgil Thomson: a Bio-bibliography.* Westport, Connecticut, 1986.

articles–

Smith, C. "Gertrude S., Virgil T., and Susan B." *Theatre Arts* 31/no. 7 (1947): 17.
Glanville-Hicks, Peggy. "Virgil Thomson." *Musical Quarterly* 35 (1949): 209.
Smith, C. "Thomson's Four Saints Live again on Broadway." *Musical America* 72/no.7 (1952): 7.
Garvin, H.R. "Sound and Sense in *Four Saints in Three Acts.*" *Bucknell Review* 5/no. 1 (1954): 1.
Helm, E. "Virgil Thomson's *Four Saints in Three Acts.*" *Music Review* 15 (1954): 127.
"Yale Music Library Receives Thomson Papers." *Notes* 36 (1979-80): 78.

unpublished–

Jackson, Richard. "The Operas of Gertrude Stein and Virgil Thomson." M.A. thesis, Tulane University, 1962.
Ward, K.M. "An Analysis of the Relationship between Text and Musical Shape, an Investigation of the Relationship between Text and Surface Rhythmic Details in 'Four

Saints in Three Acts' by Virgil Thomson." Ph.D. dissertation, University of Texas, Austin, 1978.

* * *

Although he studied in Paris with Nadia Boulanger and spent fifteen years composing and writing as an expatriate in stimulating pre-World War II Paris, Virgil Thomson never wholly shed the influences of a boyhood and early youth spent in the very center of the United States. His music with its wit, clever simplicity, and occasional dips into the downright homespun, is American to its heart. An omnivorous reader throughout his life and the author of many books, Thomson was also the deftest of composers for voice, and singers everywhere delight in his wonderfully expressive and apt declamation. His three unconventional operas are testaments to his skill and to his rich and complex American style.

Soon after Thomson met fellow expatriate Gertrude Stein in Paris in 1926, the two began collaborating on the strangely compelling *Four Saints in Three Acts.* Thomson worked at the piano with Stein's stream-of-consciousness text to produce crisply rhythmic, basically diatonic music of enormous vitality. Containing roughly thirty saints in four acts, the setting is the Spain Stein recalled from her travels. Thomson, however, had never been there and leaned heavily on his Southern Baptist upbringing for the religious flavor of the music. Although there are episodes of Anglican chant, his instrumentation and melodies often echo American revivalist meetings, hymn tunes, and even popular dance rhythms. The Hartford, Connecticut premiere on February 8, 1934 featured an all black cast with sets imaginatively designed by Florine Stett-

Virgil Thomson, 1979

heimer of cellophane, crystal, seashells, feathers, and colored lights. The work was an infamous success and the tour of New York and Chicago firmly launched the young composer's career.

Thomson remained in Paris until just before the German occupation in 1940. Arriving in New York with little money and few prospects, he was engaged as music critic for the *New York Herald Tribune* almost immediately and held the post for fourteen years. During this time he also managed to compose a great deal, including the 1946 *The Mother of Us All.* Less abstract than *Four Saints in Three Acts,* the opera's theme is the women's suffrage movement as represented by leader Susan B. Anthony. The nostalgia-tinged music seems familiar since Thomson evokes marches, bugle calls, parlor songs, waltzes, and hymn tunes in the pastiche method which serves him so well. However, with the exception of "London Bridge is Falling Down," all the melodies are original, bearing witness again to Thomson's ever acute ear for musical Americana.

Unable to find an inspiring libretto or librettist, Thomson's third and last opera was not begun until the 1960s. For seven years Thomson worked with poet Jack Larson on the less successful *Lord Byron,* which was premiered in New York at the Juilliard School in 1972. Framed by a choral elegy upon the return of the poet's body to England from Greece and a semi-chorus of welcoming Poets' Corner shades, the opera presents a series of flashback scenes covering Lord Byron's life. Thomson's sensitive and meticulous attention to prosody is evident here too, as well as his playfulness and affinity for deceptively complex simplicity.

Thomson wrote music in all genres with varying degrees of success. He took the musical portrait, a category to which little attention had been paid except for brief essays by Couperin, Schumann, Elgar, and a few others, and made it his own with more than 150 works. However, it was opera that really challenged him and drew upon his musical skills most fully. In general, Thomson's free-wheeling American style may at times lack a deeply personal expressiveness, but there is always an abundance of conviction of some sort, careful craftsmanship, and open-handed wit.

—Michael Meckna

THORBORG, Kerstin.

Contralto. Born 19 May 1896, in Venjan, Sweden. Died 12 April 1970, in Falun, Dalarna. Studied at the Royal Conservatory in Stockholm; debut as Ortrud at the Royal Theater, Stockholm, 1924; remained on roster there until 1930; sang in Prague, Berlin, Salzburg, Vienna, and Covent Garden, 1932-39; Metropolitan Opera debut as Fricka, 1936; remained on the Metropolitan's roster until 1946, then sang there again from 1947-50; taught voice in Stockholm from 1950.

Publications

About THORBORG: articles–

Palatsky, E.H. "Goddess in Retirement." *Opera News* 27 (1963): 32.

Berthelson, B. "Kerstin Thorborg." *Musikrevy* 22 (1967): 345.

*   *   *

The first generation of interwar Wagnerian singers (which included Leider, Olzcewska, Melchior, Janssen, Schorr) was so distinguished that it was hard, at that time, to think they could be replaced. Eventually Flagstad arrived; among the basses there was Ludwig Weber; and there also appeared a contralto, tall of stature, ample of voice, and gifted with outstanding ability as an actress. Kerstin Thorborg had to be seen, not merely heard. She is one of those singers about whom recordings tell less than half; to learn about her full value we have to turn to written records by the critics of the time.

By 1936, the year of her debut at Covent Garden, she was a well-established singer in Germany and Austria as well as in her native Sweden. This was also the year, and indeed the month, of her famous performance in *Das Lied von der Erde* under Bruno Walter in Vienna, from which was made the first recording of Mahler's song-cycle, bringing Thorborg a wider international reputation. She was nevertheless new to England, and she came at a time when memories of the great names of the recent past were still cherished. Ernest Newman still had no doubts about the new arrival: "the finest Fricka I have ever seen or hope to see." Over the next years in London, up to the outbreak of war, she won repeated acclamations of this kind, some of them accompanied by detail that gives substance to the generalities: "All Fricka is expressed, for example, in Madame Thorborg's back as she leaves Wotan after having cowed him in their scene in the second act of the *Valkyrie*." After seeing her as Clytemnestra in *Elektra*, Newman compared her with Chaliapin at his best: "it is difficult to say where singing, acting, costume and make-up severally begin or end, so organically are they fused into one." Later, seeing her "demonic creation" of Ortrud in *Lohengrin*, he saluted her as "the greatest operatic actress of the present day."

Amid all this praise, a warning note appeared from time to time. Of that same performance as Ortrud, Newman remarked that Thorborg's voice seemed a little tired in the highest register, and another English critic, Dynely Hussey, found that when she sang Waltraute in *Götterdämmerung* in 1938 she was "developing an unpleasant shrillness on her upper notes." Recordings from that time onwards also show defects of this sort. She is heard from the stage in several broadcast performances during the 1940s at the Metropolitan; allowing for the poor quality of some of these transcripts, it still appears too frequently for comfort that the notes are imperfectly focussed. One really needs to go back to records made before the time of her international fame to discover just how beautifully she could sing. Not of the most lush, Sigrid Onegin-like quality, her voice was nonetheless rich, pure, and steady. She had fine control over its volume and shading, as is well heard in the arias of Saint-Saëns's Delilah. In Orpheus's lament the famous melody is handled affectionately but without sentimentality. This aspect of Thorborg's art is well captured on these early records; otherwise, the considered admiration of critics such as Newman provides the best testimonial.

—J.B. Steane

THE THREEPENNY OPERA
See DIE DREIGROSCHENOPER

TIBBETT, Lawrence.

Baritone. Born 16 November 1896, in Bakersfield, California. Died 15 July 1960, in New York City. Married: Grace Mackay Smith, 1919 (divorced 1931); two sons. Studied with Frank La Forge and Basil Ruysdael; began career as actor; also sang in church and light operas, and with a travelling quartet; opera debut as Amonasro, Los Angeles, 1923; Metropolitan Opera debut as Lavitsky in *Boris Godunov,* 1923; first major success came there with role of Ford in *Falstaff,* 1925; remained at Metropolitan for twenty-seven seasons, singing in premieres of Taylor's *The King's Henchman* (1927) and *Peter Ibbetson* (1931), Gruenberg's *The Emperor Jones* (1933), Hanson's *Merry Mount* (1934), and Seymour's *In the Pasha's Garden* (1935), and took part in first Metropolitan performances of *Jonny spielt auf* (1929), *Simon Boccanegra* (1932) and *Peter Grimes* (1949); created title role in Goossens's *Don Juan de Mañara* at Covent Garden (1937); sang at San Francisco (1927-49), Chicago (1936-46), and Cincinnati (1943-46); made last Metropolitan appearance in Mussorgsky's *Khovanshchina,* 1950; toured extensively throughout the world and appeared on Broadway and in films; president, American Guild of Musical Artists, 1937-53.

Publications

By TIBBETT: books–

The Glory Road. Brattleboro, 1933. Reprinted (with discography), New York, 1977.

About TIBBETT: books–

Farkas, A., ed. *Lawrence Tibbett: Singing Actor.* Portland, Oregon, 1989.

articles–

Lauri-Volpi, G. *Voci parallele.* Milan, 1955.
Celletti, R. "Lawrence Tibbett." In *Le grandi voci,* Rome, 1964.
Steane, J.B. *The Grand Tradition.* London, 1974.

*   *   *

Lawrence Tibbett is generally recognized as the first American-born, American-trained male opera singer to achieve star status without prior European stage experience.

Tibbett's father, the sheriff of Kern county (California), was killed by an outlaw when Larry was seven years old. His mother then moved with her four children to Los Angeles where Larry grew up. As a youngster he took part in school productions, and after graduation he found various engagements in musicals and plays in the Los Angeles area. For a short while he toured with the Shakespearean company of Tyrone Power, Sr, eventually attracting the attention of the poet Rupert Hughes. Recognizing his talent, Hughes raised a $2,500 loan among his wealthy friends to send Tibbett to

Lawrence Tibbett as Rigoletto

New York to study with Frank La Forge. Soon after Tibbett began his studies in 1922, impresario Charles Wagner hired him to replace Giuseppe de Luca on the Metropolitan Quartet, and he toured with Frances Alda, Giovanni Martinelli, and Carolina Lazzari from 1922 through 1925.

In January 1923, La Forge arranged an audition for Tibbett with the Metropolitan Opera. It was unsuccessful, but in May he tried again and was hired at $60 a week. His inconspicuous debut with the Met followed on 24 November 1923, as Lovitsky in *Boris Godunov* with Chaliapin in the title role. He learned his next role, Valentin in *Faust* (again with Chaliapin), in three days when he had to step in for an ailing Vincente Ballester.

Tibbett sang several small roles in his first season, and his second season started the same way. His big break came when he was asked to take over the role of Ford, again for Ballester, in a new production of *Falstaff* with Antonio Scotti in the title role. Left alone onstage to deliver Ford's monologue, "I let myself go with all I had," he wrote later of that first night on 2 January 1925. "In my aria . . . I tore my heart out." The audience went wild. The ovation lasted for over ten minutes and the performance could not proceed until Tibbett was called back for a solo bow. The incident was written up in all the major newspapers and magazines, and Tibbett became a celebrity overnight.

As Tibbett developed artistically, he was given more challenging assignments. He sang Wolfram, Telramund, Amonasro, Scarpia. In 1926, he took over the role of Neri from Titta Ruffo in *La cena delle beffe* (Giordano), and in 1929, the role of Jonny from Michael Bohnen in Krenek's *Jonny spielt auf.* The first production mounted specifically for him was the Metropolitan premiere of Verdi's *Simon Boccanegra* on 28 January 1932. The performance was a great personal success for Tibbett, and the opera was chosen to open the following season.

Tibbett sang several seasons with the Chicago and San Francisco opera companies, but his artistic home remained the Metropolitan where he performed 442 times in the house, 160 times on tour. During his twenty-seven seasons there he sang forty-nine roles in thirty-seven operas, at times graduating from comprimario to leading roles, from Morales to Escamillo, from Silvio to Tonio, from the Herald to Telramund. He also earned high praise for his portrayals of Rigoletto, Iago, and Falstaff. Equally at home on the concert platform, Tibbett gave solo recitals in many cities throughout the United States. He made his first international tour in 1937, appearing in opera (*Rigoletto, Otello*) and concert in England, France, Hungary, and the Scandinavian countries, to enthusiastic audience reception and critical acclaim. He toured Australia and New Zealand in 1938, Italy in 1946, and London and South Africa in 1947.

In 1940, Tibbett's voice was afflicted by some still undisclosed illness and his gradual vocal decline is traceable to that time. He continued to sing at the Metropolitan until 1950; his last performance in opera was as Ivan Khovansky in *Khovanshchina,* on 24 March 1950. He then appeared in Broadway plays and musicals, and in 1956, he replaced Ezio Pinza in the Broadway production of *Fanny.* He pioneered opera on television and sang the elder Germont in a condensed TV version of *La traviata* in 1950.

His film career began in 1930, with *The Rogue Song,* and in the same year he made his second film, *New Moon,* with soprano Grace Moore. Of his other four films the most interesting from a musical standpoint is *Metropolitan* (1935) with a handful of complete opera arias and songs. Concurrently with his films, Tibbett launched his radio career, and the triple exposure—stage, film, radio—made him a national celebrity.

As contemporary criticism and posterity agree, Lawrence Tibbett's powerful, virile voice ranks with the best of this century. A true bass-baritone with an even scale from a high B natural down to a low F, it was equal to the demands of all the roles in his large repertory. In his best years he could reduce his rich and resonant voice to an exquisite pianissimo or project it over a full orchestra. Although he sang in five languages, Tibbett never learned to speak any of them and had to learn his roles by rote. At the same time his dramatic and expressive phrasing is interpretatively correct, leaving no doubt that he was thoroughly familiar (in translation) with the texts he sang. Giving the right inflection and texture to the words, he was able to weave a magical aura around an aria, a song, a ballad, entering into the psyche of the character. He consistently earned high praise for his acting, and the large number of commercial recordings and airchecks demonstrate that Tibbett was an imaginative performer and an accomplished vocalist who could act with his voice as well. He was a successful interpreter of a wide range of music, equally at home in nineteenth century operas and in new, modern compositions. Some of his recordings, notably his model interpretations of the Toreador Song from *Carmen* and the Te Deum from *Tosca* are arguably in a class by themselves, and his selections from *Porgy and Bess,* sung in dialect and recorded under the supervision of the composer, are interpretative gems.

Tibbett's 78 rpm recording career was exclusively with the Victor Talking Machine Co. and RCA Victor. These recordings captured his voice at its peak, spanning the years 1926 to 1940. The long playing records of songs and arias he made for the Royale and other labels ca. 1955, show the deterioration of his voice and do a great disservice to his memory. Fortunately, an extraordinary number of his radio performances and live Metropolitan Opera broadcasts have survived. Many of these have been privately issued on "The Golden Age of Opera" and UORC labels. These give a fair idea of Tibbett's remarkable talent and great versatility as a singing actor. His exceptionally beautiful and manly speaking voice is preserved on film and in interviews.

Not forgetting his personal and musical origins, Tibbett championed the cause of American artists. He took part in several world premieres: Deems Taylor's *The King's Henchman* (1927) and *Peter Ibbetson* (1931); Louis Gruenberg's *The Emperor Jones* (1933), a great artistic triumph for Tibbett; Howard Hanson's *Merry Mount* (1934); and J.L. Seymour's *In the Pasha's Garden* (1935). In 1937, he created the title role in Eugene Goossens' *Don Juan de Mañara* at Covent Garden. Wanting to protect all performers regardless of status, he organized the American Guild of Musical Artists (AGMA), a national labor union. He became its first president in 1937, and he held the office until 1953.

Because of his language handicap, he could easily identify with the American opera-goer, and he was a lifelong advocate of opera in English. His sunny, open, down-to-earth personality is well captured in his chatty autobiography, *The Glory Road.* But that was in 1933, near the crest of his fame. The downhill slide began seven years later, and his vocal problems and diminished powers reportedly had a destructive effect on his personal life whose details have been kept private by his family. Following an automobile accident, Tibbett was operated on 27 June 1960; he later lapsed into a coma and died on 15 July 1960, in New York City. Fortunately, the many facets of his unique talent have been preserved on recordings and film; they show the quintessential American operatic artist, the first of many who followed in his pioneering footsteps.

—Andrew Farkas

TIEFLAND [The Lowlands].

Composer: Eugen d'Albert.

Librettist: Rudolph Lothar (after the play by Angel Gùimerá, *Terra baixa*).

First Performance: Prague, German Opera, 15 November 1903; revised version, Magdeburg, 16 January 1905.

Roles: Sebastiano (baritone); Marta (mezzo-soprano); Pedro (tenor); Tommaso (bass); Moruccio (baritone); Nuri (soprano); Pepa (soprano); Antonia (soprano); Rosella (contralto); Nando (tenor); Voice (baritone, from chorus); Priest (mute); chorus (SATB).

* * *

Enormously popular in its day, *Tiefland,* Eugen d'Albert's seventh opera, became perhaps his best-known work and held the stage in the Prologue-and-two-act version of 1905 (the 1903 version contained three acts). It is generally regarded as one of the earliest successful German responses to the "verismo" style of the new Italian school and has been compared to works by Leoncavallo, Mascagni, and Puccini. *Tiefland* had its final German heyday in the early years of the Third Reich (receiving over 300 performances in 1934-35), with only occasional revivals thereafter.

Rudolph Lothar's libretto was based upon a strong naturalistic play by the contemporary Catalan writer, Angel Gùimerá (1849-1924); it had been staged in America, England, and France, where it inspired Le Borne's unsuccessful opera *La Catalane* (1907). The action is set in a village in the Catalan lowlands referred to in the opera's title, although the Prologue takes place high above in the Pyrenees: Pedro, a simple shepherd, imagines his dreams realized when his master, the landowner Sebastiano, visits him with a beautiful girl, Marta. She is offered to Pedro as a wife, but he must come down from the mountains to take over the mill her recently deceased "father" had managed. Pedro gladly relinquishes the solitary idyll of his mountain life, only to discover that he has been duped by Sebastiano, who intends to use him as a cover for his own continuing relationship with Marta, whom he has abused for some years after rescuing her from a vagabond life. Only in act II does Pedro come to realize the truth as real love blossoms between him and Marta, whose saviour he becomes. Pedro, the mountain shepherd who once slew a wolf, kills the human wolf Sebastiano and carries Marta away toward the pure air of his mountain pastures as the curtain falls.

Tiefland exemplifies d'Albert's eclectic and inconsistent style, as well as his unfailing craftsmanship and occasionally strong poetic inspiration. The peasant chorus in particular seems to have been revived from an earlier kind of romantic opera, its music borrowed from the world of operetta. Some of Pedro's music is similarly designed, and his second-act duet with Marta contrives to express stereotyped passion.

The orchestral introduction to the opera is typical in its marriage of a salon-style pastoral idiom (although the opening solo clarinet acquires the chromatic inflections of the third-act shepherd's pipe in Wagner's *Tristan und Isolde*) with a more modern lyricism. A Spanish flavor is suggested by a moody A minor dance motif incorporating the major triad on the flattened supertonic. It is in the shadows of this more troubled manner that the complex "verismo" promptings of Marta (who, like some of Puccini's heroines, is both delicate waif and wilful *femme fatale*) and the perverse, persuasive Sebastiano are most at home. The nocturnal conclusion to act I, in which Pedro prepares to sleep on the floor while his unresponsive wife broods upon her fate was admired by otherwise sceptical critics, and it is generally in its darker moments that the opera shines. Of particular note is the fine, slow F-sharp minor processional, again with a pronounced Spanish flavor, that accompanies Marta's grim acceptance of the mantilla in which she is led to her enforced wedding. The theme is developed in authentically Puccinian fashion and, like other motivic material in the opera, recurs later to good effect without being over-worked. At such moments, d'Albert the conventional entertainer becomes a more "modern" musical dramatist—as at the end, where the folk chorus mutters about Sebastiano's death through a mysterious orchestral eddying of whole-tone scales.

—Peter Franklin

TIETJENS [Titiens], Therese Carolina Johanna Alexandra.

Soprano. Born 17 July 1831, in Hamburg. Died 3 October 1877, in London. Studied in Hamburg and Vienna; debut in Auber's *Le maçon,* Hamburg, 1848; major debut as Lucrezia Borgia, Hamburg, 1849; in Frankfurt, 1850-53; created the role of Louise in Lortzing's *Opernprobe,* 1851; at Vienna Hofoper, 1853-59, debut as Mathilde in *Guillaume Tell;* London debut as Valentine in *Les huguenots,* Her Majesty's Theatre, 1858; Covent Garden debut as Lucrezia Borgia, 1868; became British citizen, 1868; toured the United States, 1875.

Publications

About TIETJENS: article–

Foster, Peter. "Titiens—The Earnest Prima Donna." *Opera* 31/March (1980): 224.

* * *

Therese Tietjens was in the great line of sopranos who dominated the London opera stage during the nineteenth century; like Jenny Lind before and Patti and Melba after her, she became a virtual national institution. Little is known of her early life, but she received her musical education in Hamburg and Vienna before making her debut in Auber's *Le maçon* in the former city's St Pauli Theater in August 1848, when she had only just turned seventeen.

In less than a year the young Tietjens was singing Lucrezia Borgia, a role with which she was to be associated throughout her career. After spending some time with the Frankfurt Opera she joined the Vienna Hofoper in 1853; her first two roles were Mathilde in *Guillaume Tell* and Pamina in *Die*

Zauberflöte. During the next six years she sang extensively in Vienna, gradually moving into the more dramatic repertoire, particularly Meyerbeer. She might have stayed in that city had in not been for the astuteness of Benjamin Lumley—the embattled impresario of Her Majesty's Theatre, threatened by the newly rebuilt Covent Garden. On a visit to Vienna he signed her up for his 1858 season. It was to be a decisive move in Tietjens' career.

Luigi Arditi, who conducted her debut performance on 13 April 1858, as Valentine in *Les Huguenots,* gives a graphic description: "Tietjens' fine dramatic presence and imposing voice struck home at once. . . . when that never to be forgotten high C, in the finale of the first act, soared high and brilliantly above the other voices and orchestra, a roar and thunder of applause broke forth. . . . Tietjens established her fame that night once and for all." One critic refers to the "long sustained C alt" in the second act "from which the voice descended in a rapid run." Another praised her execution of the florid passages while pointing out that "like most German singers she pays little regard to embellishment . . . she sang what was set down for her and no more but (it) was accomplished to perfection."

Tietjens was still a member of the Vienna company, but from her return to London in 1859 that city was to be home base for the remaining nineteen years of her life and career. Apart from a long series of highly successful performances in Naples from 1862-4 and appearances in Genoa and Paris, she devoted most of her time outside the London season to extensive tours of the British provinces. She even took British nationality in 1868.

Although Tietjens sang in several London theaters, including Covent Garden, the major focus of her career was the impresario Mapleson, and she was an indispensible element in his extensive and unending operatic campaigns. She gave nearly six hundred performances in London alone in a wide variety of roles. In her first season she followed *Les Huguenots* with *La fille du régiment, La traviata, Il trovatore, Don Giovanni, Le nozze di Figaro* and *Lucrezia Borgia.* The following season she added *Martha, Norma* and *I vespri siciliani* and in 1860 *La favorita, Semiramide* and *Oberon.* Such listing only hints at her incredible versatility for she was later to sing Fidès in *Le prophète* and, incredibly in 1875, Ortrud in *Lohengrin*—"Much to my surprise, I made a success as Ortrud," she said later. She did not add that within a week of her first Ortrud she also sang Norma and Semiramide. It was around this time that Herman Klein first heard Tietjens—"(she) was still vocally in her prime. Her tones had not lost any of their mellowness and power, nor the strong, clear ring that distinguished every note up to the high C." Klein was convinced that the top notes were as reported so long before by Arditi.

Versatility, earnestness and sheer hard work were Tietjens' hallmark. It seems probable that by 1874 she had begun to develop the cancer which was to cause her death, but she still performed many of her favored roles and the critic of *Musical World* opined that "the fine form of Mlle Tietjens throughout the season is a fact specially gratifying in view of seasons to come." In the 1876-77 she embarked on her one and only tour of the USA. In her final season she sang only Norma and Lucrezia Borgia. In her final Lucrezia she was clearly in agony but determined to complete the opera. Klein was not alone in sensing a cry of bodily pain in the last scene when Lucrezia discovers that Gennaro is dead. Indeed she lay unconscious for twenty minutes thereafter.

Tietjens died less than six months after this final performance. The obituary in *Musical World* extended to six columns—"The pure legato style, the perfect phrasing. . . . were unequivocal signs of a great artist . . . We saw . . . her passionate love of the work she was called upon to do, and the manner in which she brought to its discharge all the resources at command. . . . But she was an actress as well as a singer. . . . Hers was the true dramatic instinct. . . . She knew how to identify herself with the character assumed, and to make prominent exactly that phase of it which supplied a key to the whole."

—Stanley Henig

TIPPETT, (Sir) Michael (Kemp).

Composer. Born 2 January 1905, in London. Studied composition with Charles Wood and C.H. Kitson at the Royal College of Music in London, 1923-28; studied piano with Aubin Raymar and conducting with Sir Adrian Boult and Sir Malcolm Sargent; studied counterpoint and fugue with R.O. Morris, 1930-32; directed the South London Orchestra at Morley College, 1933-1940; music director at Morley College, 1940-51; served a three month term in jail for his refusal to serve in the military, 21 June to 21 August 1943; broadcasts for the British Broadcasting Corporation, 1951; director of the Bath Festival, 1969-74; Commander of the Order of the British Empire, 1959; visited the United States, 1965, 1972, 1989, 1991; knighted, 1966.

Operas

Publisher: Schott.

The Village Opera, realization of the ballad opera by C. Johnson (1729) with added music, 1928.
Robin Hood (with D. Ayerst and R. Pennyman), Tippett, D. Ayerst, and R. Pennyman, 1934.
The Midsummer Marriage, Tippett, 1946-52, London, Covent Garden, 27 January 1955.
King Priam, Tippett, 1958-61, Coventry, Belgrade, 29 May 1962.
The Knot Garden, Tippett, 1966-69, London, Convent Garden, 2 December 1970.
The Ice Break, Tippett, 1973-76, London, Covent Garden, 7 July 1977.
New Year, Tippett, 1985-88, Houston, Grand Opera, October 1989.

Other works: choral works, orchestral works (including 4 symphonies), solo vocal works, chamber music, instrumental works, piano pieces.

Publications

By TIPPETT: books–

Moving into Aquarius. London, 1959; 2nd ed., 1974.
E. William Doty Lectures in Fine Arts. Austin, Texas, 1979.
Bowen, M., ed. *Music of the Angels: Essays and Sketchbooks.* London, 1980.

articles–

"A Child of our Time." *The Listener* 38 (1945): 66.
"Purcell and the English Language." In *Eight Concerts of Henry Purcell's Music,* edited by W. Shaw, 46. London, 1951.
"Holst: Figure of our Time." *The Listener* 60 (1958): 800.
"Our Sense of Continuity in English Drama and Music." In *Henry Purcell: Essays on his Music,* edited by I. Holst, 42. London, 1959.
"Conclusion." In *A History of Song* edited by D. Stevens. London, 1960.
"At Work on King Priam." *Score* no. 28 (1961): 58.
"The Gulf in our Music." *The Observer* 14 May (1961): 21.
"Thoughts on Art and Anarchy." *The Listener* 65 (1961): 383.
"Towards the Condition of Music." In *The Humanist Frame,* edited by J. Huxley, 211. London, 1961.
"King Priam: some Questions Answered." *Opera* 13 (1962): 297.
"Music on Television." *The Listener* 71 (1964): 629.
"Music and Poetry." *Recorded Sound* January (1965).
"Schoenberg's Letters." *Composer* no. 15 (1965): 2.
"Schoenberg's Moses and Aron." *The Listener* 74 (1965): 164.
"The BBC's Duty to Society." *The Listener* 74 (1965): 302.
"The Festival and Society." *Musical Times* 110 (1969): 589.
"The Noise in the Pool at Noon." *The Listener* 82 (1969): 804.
Essay on his Concert for Orchestra. In *The Orchestral Composer's Point of View,* edited by R.S. Hines, 203. Norman, Oklahoma, 1970.
"An Englishman Looks at Opera." *Opera News* 29 (1965).
"The Knot Garden." *About the House* 3/no. 7 (1970).
"Tippett on Opera" [with Harold Rosenthal]. *Opera* December (1972)
"The Mask of Time." *Music and Musicians* 35 (1987).

interviews–

"The Composer as Librettist" [interview with P. Carnegy]. *Times Literary Supplement* July (1977): 834.

About TIPPETT: books–

Kemp, Ian. *Michael Tippett: a Symposium on his 60th Birthday.* London, 1965.
Michael Tippett: a Man of Our Time [exhibition catalogue]. London, 1977.
Hurd, Michael. *Tippett.* London, 1978.
White, Eric Walter. *Tippett and his Operas.* London, 1979.
Andrews, P. *Sir Michael Tippett: a Bibliography.* Bedford, 1980.
Matthews, David. *Michael Tippett: an Introductory Study.* London, 1980.
Bowen, Meirion. *Michael Tippett.* New York and London, 1982.
Kemp, Ian. *Tippett: the Composer and his Music.* London, 1984.
Lewis, Geraint, ed. *Michael Tippett, O.M.: a Celebration.* Tunbridge Wells, 1985.
Nicholas, John. *The Operas of Michael Tippett.* New York and London, 1985.
Theil, Gordon. *Michael Tippett: a Bio-bibliography.* New York, 1989.
Scheppach, Margaret A. *Dramatic Parallels in the Operas of Michael Tippett.* Lewiston, New York, 1990.

articles–

Dickinson, A.E.F. "Round about The Midsummer Marriage." *Music and Letters* 37 (1956): 50.
Sutcliffe, T. "Tippett and the Knot Garden." *Music and Musicians* 19/no. 4 (1970): 52.
Warrack, John. "*The Knot Garden.*" *Musical Times* 111 (1970): 1092.
Dickinson, A.E.F. "The Garden Labyrinth." *Music Review* 25 (1971).
Cairns, David. "The Midsummer Marriage." In *Responses.* London, 1973.
Warrack, John. "The Ice Break." *Musical Times* 118 (1977): 553.
Sterfield, Frederick, and David Harvey. "A Musical Magpie: Words and Music in Michael Tippett's Operas." *Parnasus* fall/winter (1982).
Clements, Andrew. "Tippett at 80." *Opera* January (1985).

*   *   *

It is not too much to claim that Michael Tippett's five operas are among his most powerful statements about his belief in humanity, a belief that has consistently informed all his works. To know the operas is to know the composer: his aesthetic creed, the scope of his literary and philosophical influences, the force of his musicianship, and the warmth of his personality.

The operas have appeared at the rate of one in each decade of the sixty years of his career as composer. They reveal significant philosophical and musical thinking and have been influenced by or have influenced works around them in his output.

Tippett's first oratorio, *A Child of Our Time* (1939-1941), focuses on the Jungian idea of human duality, the shadow and light of human nature, and considers the consequences of deeds governed by our darker inclinations. The first opera, *The Midsummer Marriage* (1946-1952), followed soon after and is considered by Tippett as a pendant to the oratorio. It is a lyric, symbolic opera about the reconciliation between our light and dark forces and the ultimate acquisition of wholeness. In its turn, this opera became a powerful source of inspiration for two subsequent orchestral works. The *Piano Concerto* (1952-1955) reflects the opera's "magic" music and the "ascent" music of the heroine as she begins her search for wholeness. The *Second Symphony* (1957) is the orchestral counterpart of the opera, manifesting sound akin to the operatic score and using a Stravinsky-like developmental process that reflects the ritualistic atmosphere of the opera.

The dramatic necessities of Tippett's second opera, *King Priam* (1958-61), an opera about human choice and the relentless consequences thereof, drove Tippett to a drastic change of style. All the works written in the shadow of that opera reflect the change. The *Lullaby for Six Voices* (1960) uses musical ideas that appear in the opera. Its bitonality, for example, foreshadows that of the scene between Paris and Helen in the opera. The *Concerto for Orchestra* (completed in 1963) issued directly out of the opera in that its layered instrumental sounds depict various dramatic ideas, a dramaturgical technique used everywhere in the opera. The form of the *Second Piano Sonata* (1962) is derived from the formal procedures of *King Priam*. The music of the sonata, like that of the opera, proceeds now by flow, now by rest, and the unity comes from constant variation and repetition of new material.

The creative impulse of the third opera, *The Knot Garden* (1966-1969), sheds its light on surrounding works too. Two of the three *Songs for Ariel* that Tippett wrote for a performance of *The Tempest* in 1962 are quoted in the opera. Their use occurs in a scene where, like Prospero in the Shakespeare play, Mangus has the six other characters enact charades in order to help them be reconciled to one another. The first work that stems directly from *The Knot Garden* is *The Songs for Dov* (1970). In the opera, Dov, the white male of a homosexual couple whose black lover has rejected him, is the only one of seven characters whose characterization is incomplete at the opera's end. The *Songs* draw Dov's journey into personal discovery more fully. *Symphony No. 3* (1972) owes the world of its sound to *The Knot Garden*. To give but one example, the Symphony uses the blues both as a stylistic element and, as in the opera, a dramatic means of speaking about human love and understanding.

Tippett's fourth opera, *The Ice Break* (1973-1976), is one of his most realistic and certainly the most violent. If the music of the first three operas is metaphorical for reconciliation and renewal of the human spirit, the realism of the gun shots, police sirens, and foot stomping in *The Ice Break* shows "the extent to which Tippett was prepared to divest his music of metaphor and make his message as clear as possible" (Kemp, 1984, p. 462). The message is for us to abandon faith in the false gods that abound in our time and place it in our own humanity—a constant concept in Tippett's credo. What is unique in *The Ice Break* is the harsh sounds of the chorus as mob-worshipping stereotypical idols constantly breaking into the gentler sounds of the soloists who portray the fear and hope of the individual. Remembrance of the "musique concrète" of the mob scenes almost obviates the gentleness of the ethereal music of hope at the opera's end.

The Ice Break appears to have no direct musical descendants. Having uttered in this opera his strongest statements of distrust of modern society's false gods, Tippett next enters a new world of expression. With *Symphony No. 4* (1976-1977)—already in his mind as *The Ice Break* was being finished—the *Triple Concerto* (1978-1979), the second oratorio *A Mask of Time* (1980-1982), *The Blue Guitar* (1982-1983), *Piano Sonata No. 4* (1983-1984), and the fifth opera *New Year* (1985-1988), Tippett's vision has become both more expansive and more serene, his musical style as challenging as ever, yet more appealing.

Since *The Knot Garden*, jazz and blues-inspired harmony and instrumentation have become a factor in each opera. In *The Ice Break*, use of off-stage electronically projected sounds entered Tippett's "scoring." In *New Year*, Tippett increases his use of electronic sound. He writes taped electronic music that is used to accompany the take-off and landing of a space ship traveling between "today" and "tomorrow." The influence of musical theater is also very significant: there is exciting dance music depicting the energy of street crowds and a character acting as narrator whose singing is pop, not classical.

As with the earlier operas, in *New Year* Tippett once again dramatizes the search for full human potential. Situations, characters, and musical techniques here recall the same in earlier operas; in this fifth opera they appear more gently or more exuberantly handled and in many ways more appealing. The heroine Jo Ann, for example, reminds one of Jenifer in *The Midsummer Marriage*: each must find her true identity by undergoing ritualistic purification. The arias of both heroines bear the stamp of melismatic vocalism typical of Tippett's style for significant characters, but Jo Ann's is a simpler,

more easy-going lyricism, depicting a gentler character than that of Jenifer. Donny, Jo Ann's black adoptive step-brother, is strongly reminiscent of Mel, the black homosexual in *The Knot Garden*. Both represent a kind of primitive who mocks the real world because he does not fit in. Tippett gives to Donny some of the most interesting vocal music and certainly the most physically and musically exciting solo dance music of any that he has written. He thus depicts, in more memorable detail than in *The Knot Garden*, a human being at odds with himself.

Nowhere are the comparisons and contrasts between the operas more significant than in Tippett's messenger figures. Each opera has one. In *The Midsummer Marriage*, the messenger is Sosostris, stunningly assured in her role as visionary. In *King Priam*, the messenger is Hermes, detached but appealing intermediary between the divine and human worlds. Mangus in *The Knot Garden* would untangle the complex web of others' failing relationships but must finally admit that he is no wiser than they. In *The Ice Break*, the androgynous messenger figure, Astron, excels only at self-mockery and tells us to forego the myth of blind hero worship. Pelegrin, the messenger figure in *New Year*, is at the center of the drama, its hero. As space-pilot mediating between "tomorrow" and "today," he seeks out the heroine Jo Ann. Through his disinterested yet deeply loving guidance, she is led from fear of her world to the self-assurance she needs to face its realities.

The messenger figure in his operas is, of course, a metaphor for the composer himself. In 1965, Tippett admitted that Hermes stood for the artist, "for myself—the go-between one world and another . . ." ("Music and Poetry," *Recorded Sound*, January, 1965, 292). He must surely say the same again in 1989 of Pelegrin, the most significantly dramatized messenger figure of his career.

The integrity of Tippett's vision and the unique eclecticism of his musical style point to a man of strong individuality and catholicity of interests. His individuality manifested itself early in his training. While a student of conducting and composition at the Royal College of Music (1923-1928), he taught himself Renaissance counterpoint and the music of the English madrigalists, and arranged to direct a choir to put his study to practical use. In the 1930s he was introduced to left-wing politics, but decided before the decade was out that an active role in politics would stand in the way of his role as musician. So strong was his belief in that role that he endured a three-month prison term in 1943 during the war rather than conform to rules that he considered did not apply to composers who were conscientious objectors.

As Director of Music at Morley College (1940-1951) and Artistic Director of the Bath Festival (1969-1974), Tippett manifested his genius for working well with colleagues, maintaining a cordial atmosphere for music-making and conducting, and developing highly musical and enterprising concert programs.

The inspiration for his varied works springs in part from his catholicity of interests as well as from friends and artistic mentors. The operas alone reflect the breadth of his reading: Shakespeare, Goethe, Frazer, Jung, Fry, Eliot, Pasternak and Solzhenitsyn, to name but a few. T.S. Eliot was the most significant artistic mentor in Tippett's life. Over the years, their considerations of verse and drama finally led Tippett, at Eliot's insistence, to be his own librettist for the oratorios and operas. Since his student days, his voracious appetite for a wide variety of musical styles has influenced his own style. Madrigals, rap, the musical *Fame*, gamelan music, the music of Purcell, Wagner, Stravinsky, Beethoven—he has studied each and assimilated and used them as he saw fit. The continuing vigor of his musical style attests to his enduring capacity to be inspired and—what is more significant—to be inspiring. In 1958 in *Moving into Aquarius,* Tippett stated that his role in this new age is to "... try to transform the everyday by a touch of the everlasting ... to project into our mean world music which is rich and generous." In the last three decades, every major work has fulfilled that pledge.

—Margaret Scheppach

TOSCA.

Composer: Giacomo Puccini.

Librettists: Giuseppe Giacosa and Luigi Illica (after Sardou).

First Performance: Rome, Costanzi, 14 January 1900.

Roles: Floria Tosca (soprano); Mario Cavaradossi (tenor); Scarpia (baritone); Cesare Angelotti (bass); Sacristan (baritone); Spoletta (tenor); Sciarrone (bass); a Jailer (bass); a Shepherd Boy (boy soprano); chorus (SSATTBB).

Publications

books–

Chop, M. *Die Tosca.* Leipzig, 1924.
Winterhoff, H.J. *Analytische Untersuchungen zu Puccinis "Tosca".* Regensburg, 1973.
John, Nicholas, ed. *Giacomo Puccini: "Tosca".* London and New York, 1982.
Courtin, Michèle. *Tosca de Giacomo Puccini.* Paris, 1983.

articles–

Avant-scène opéra September-October (1977) [*Tosca* issue].
Perusse, Lyle F. "*Tosca* and Piranesi." *Musical Times* 121 (1981): 743.
DiGaetani, John Louis. "Puccini's *Tosca* and the Necessity of Antagonism." *Opera Quarterly* 2 (1984): 76.
Döhring, Sieghart. "Musikalischer Realismus in Puccinis *Tosca.*" *Analecta Musicologica* 22 (1984): 249.

Based on a very popular play Victorien Sardou wrote as a vehicle for Sarah Bernhardt, *Tosca* is a thriller with great situations, characters, and philosophical and religious ideas. The libretto by Luigi Illica and Giuseppe Giacosa shortens and tightens the drama of the play. The opera, set in Rome during the revolutionary Napoleonic period, features a famous opera singer in love with the political revolutionary Mario Cavaradossi. Tosca meets her lover in the church of Sant' Andrea della Valle as he paints a scene of Mary Magdalene. But before she arrives, he has helped to hide a political prisoner, Angelotti. Baron Scarpia, the chief of police, enters looking for the political prisoner. By the end of the act, Cavaradossi is implicated and Scarpia decides to question Cavaradossi about the whereabouts of Angelotti.

The second act takes place in the Palazzo Farnese, where Cavaradossi is being tortured to force him to reveal the hiding place of Angelotti. When Tosca enters to negotiate with Scarpia, she hears Mario's screams under torture. Scarpia proposes a deal—if she'll spend the night with him, he will release her lover. In her desperation, she agrees. Scarpia says, however, that he can't release him openly and there will be a sham execution, after which she and Mario will be free to leave Rome. When Scarpia rushes to Tosca for his sexual demands, she stabs him to death instead. In the final act Mario Cavaradossi, imprisoned in Castel Sant' Angelo, is awaiting execution. Tosca rushes in to tell him that she has killed Scarpia, and that the execution will be done with blanks, after which they will be free to leave Rome forever. However, the act ends with Mario's execution and Tosca's suicide.

Thematically, the core of the opera is the conflict between Tosca's belief in God and the Catholic Church and Mario Cavaradossi's agnosticism, perhaps atheism. Between these two ideological poles moves the powerful Baron Scarpia, who outwardly expresses a devout belief in God and the Church but in actuality is a hypocrite who uses his powers as Rome's chief of police to destroy the rebellion against the old regime in any way expedient, and who also uses his political power to force women to go to bed with him.

Tosca's killing of Scarpia in the second act is preceded by her famous aria, "Vissi d'arte," which is at the philosophical core of the opera. She says that she has lived for art and love, and to do good in the world, and she asks God why He is putting her in such a horrible situation. Her prayer includes that most profound question: Why does God allow the suffering of the innocent? Her only response is Scarpia's renewed demands for her favors in exchange for the life of Cavaradossi.

In the last act, Mario sings his final aria, "E lucevan le stelle"—his thoughts before he dies are of the beauty of Tosca's body and the intensity of his love for her. Tosca thinks she has outsmarted Scarpia and that this execution will only be a sham, but she is sadly mistaken. The bullets are real, and Mario is killed; Tosca's final words and suicide in the opera suggest that she does not want to continue living in a world where Mario's philosophy of life prevails.

—John Louis DiGaetani

TOSCANINI, Arturo.

Conductor. Born 25 March 1867, in Parma. Died 16 January 1957, in New York. Studied cello with Carini and composition with Dacci at the Parma Conservatory (won first prize in cello and the Barbacini Prize upon graduation), 1876-1885; cellist with the Italian opera in Rio de Janeiro, 1886, and conductor, from 30 June through the end of the season; conductor at the Teatro Carignano, Turin, November 1886; conducted the Municipal Orchestra, Turin; conducted in many major Italian opera houses, 1887-96, and conducted the premieres of Leoncavallo's *Pagliacci,* 1892, and Puccini's *La bohème,* 1896; conducted symphonic concerts with the orchestra of the Teatro Reggio, Turin, 1896; principal conductor at the Teatro alla Scala, Milan, 1898-1902, 1906-08; conducted opera in Buenos Aires, 1903-04, 1906; principal conductor of the Metropolitan Opera, New York, 1908, where he conducted the premieres of Puccini's *La fanciulla del West,* 1910, and Giordano's *Madame Sans-Gêne,* 1915;

Tosca, **with Julia Migenes-Johnson and Antonio Ordonez, Earl's Court, London, 1991**

in Italy, 1915; toured the United States and Canada with the La Scala Orchestra, 1920-21; artistic director of La Scala, 1921-29; conducted a posthumous premiere of Boito's unfinished opera *Nerone*, which Toscanini completed, 1924; guest conductor of the New York Philharmonic, 1926-29; associate conductor of the New York Philharmonic with Mengelberg, 1929-30, and principal conductor, 1930-36; conducted in Bayreuth, 1930-31; conducted the inaugural concert of the Palestine Symphony Orchestra, Tel Aviv, 26 December 1936; conducted at the Salzburg Festival, 1934-37; conducted in London, 1935, 1937-39; music director of the National Broadcasting Company Symphony Orchestra, 1937; toured South America, 1940, and throughout the United States, 1950, with the NBC Symphony.

Publications

About TOSCANINI: books–

Ciampelli, G. *Arturo Toscanani*. Milan, 1923; revised as *Toscanini*, 1946.

Cozzani, E. *Arturo Toscanini*. Milan, 1927.

Nicotra, T. *Arturo Toscanini*. English translation (from Italian), New York, 1929.

Bonardi, D. *Toscanini*. Milan, 1929.

Stefan, P. *Arturo Toscanini*. Vienna, 1936; English translation, New York, 1936.

Gilman, L. *Toscanini and Great Music*. New York, 1938.

Hoeller, S. *Arturo Toscanini*. New York, 1943.

Della Corte, A. *Toscanini*. Vincenza, 1946.

Nives, D. *Arturo Toscanini*. Milan, 1946.

Sacchi, F. *Toscanini*. Milan, 1951; English translation as *The Magic Baton: Toscanini's Life for Music*, New York, 1957.

Taubman, H. *The Maestro: the Life of Arturo Toscanini*. New York, 1951.

Chotzinoff, S. *Toscanini: an Intimate Portrait*. New York, 1956.

Marsh, R. *Toscanini and the Art of Orchestral Performance*. Philadelphia, 1956; 1962.

Della Corte, A. *Toscanini: Visto da un critico*. Turin, 1958; 1981.

Haggin, B.H. *Conversations with Toscanini*. New York, 1959; 2nd ed., 1979.

Hughes, S. *The Toscanini Legacy*. London, 1959; New York, 1969.

Sacchi, Filippo. *Toscanini. Un secolo di musica*. Milan, 1960.

Antek, S., and R. Hupka. *This Was Toscanini*. New York, 1963.

Frassati, L. *Il maestro Arturo Toscanini e il suo mondo*. Turin, 1967.

Haggin, B.H., ed. *The Toscanini Musicians Knew*. New York, 1967.

Schonberg, H. *The Great Conductors*. New York, 1967.

Fiorda, N. *Arte, beghe, e bizze di Toscanini*. Rome, 1969.

Fedele, A., and R. Paumgartner, eds. *La lezione di Toscanini*. Florence, 1970.

Amara, A., ed. *Toscanini e La Scala*. Milan, 1972.

Barbeau, G., et al. *Toscanini e la Scala*. Milan, 1972.

Mandelli, A. *Toscanini: Appunti per un bilancio critico*. Milan, 1972.

Marek, G. *Toscanini*. New York, 1975.

Wessling, B.W. *Toscanini in Bayreuth*. Munich, 1976.

Sachs, H. *Toscanini*. Philadelphia, 1978.

Matthews, D. *Arturo Toscanini*. Tunbridge Wells and New York, 1982.

Freeman, J. and W. Toscanini. *Toscanini*. New York, 1987.

Horowitz, J. *Understanding Toscanini*. New York, 1987.

Sachs, H. *Arturo Toscanini dal 1915 al 1946: l'arte all'ombra della politica: omaggio al maestro nel 30° anniversario della scomparsa*. Turin, 1987.

articles–

Segre, A. "Toscanini: the First Forty Years." *Musical Quarterly* April (1947).

Taubman, H. "Toscanini in America." *Musical Quarterly* April (1947).

Sartori, C. "The Scala under Toscanini." *Opera* May, June, August, September, October, November, December (1954).

Leinsdorf, E. "Toscanini at Salzburg." *Opera Annual* [New York] 5 (1958).

Klein, J.W. "Toscanini and Alfredo Catalani: a Unique Friendship." *Music and Letters* 48 (1967):213.

Pugliese, G. "Verdi and Toscanini." *Opera* July and August (1967).

Arturo Toscanini enjoyed one of the longest and most influential careers in the history of conducting. The son of a tailor, Toscanini's precocious musicality earned for him a place in the Parma Conservatory when he was just nine years of age. Nine years later, in 1885, he graduated with highest honors, as an accomplished cellist, pianist, student of composition and conductor.

Within a year, Toscanini's meteoric rise to international fame as an opera conductor began. He was on tour in South America with an Italian company and took the podium on very short notice for a production of Verdi's *Aida* in Rio de Janeiro on 30 June 1886. He conducted the entire performance without a score. On this occasion he first demonstrated to a broad public the powerful memory that was to be his stock in trade for the remainder of his career as a conductor.

During the first decade of his career, Toscanini worked in various northern Italian opera theaters, including the Teatro Reggio in Turin and the Teatro alla Scala in Milan, establishing a reputation as a great reformer of conducting methods and techniques. He eschewed the whimsy and arbitrary nuances of conductors in the Wagner tradition, such as Bülow, Mengelberg, Richter, Furtwängler and the Italian Angelo Mariani, who took delight in altering rhythms, agogics, and even the notes themselves in their interpretations. Toscanini rather sought an objective interpretation of the score, basing his interpretation on the actual notation and its markings. At the same time, he required the utmost in concentration and technical precision from his players, from whom he also demanded brilliant playing and precise ensemble. During this period he brought the new repertoire of the Italian *verismo* school into prominence, premiering works such as *Pagliacci* (Milan, 1892) and *La bohème* (Turin, 1896). He also appeared as a champion of Wagner with a masterful Italian premiere performance of *Götterdämmerung* in 1895. (Although Angelo Mariani had performed both *Lohengrin* and *Tannhäuser* some twenty years earlier, he can be represented neither as a champion, nor masterful interpreter).

Toscanini continued to conduct Wagnerian operas, and worked assiduously to develop the operatic repertoire of Giuseppe Verdi during his ensuing years at La Scala. There he also expanded his repertoire to include Debussy, Richard Strauss and Stravinsky, and even lesser known opera composers such as Gluck, Weber and Tchaikovsky. After many years as director at La Scala, during which time he had also taken

Arturo Toscanini conducting at Verdi's burial, 1901

a position at the Metropolitan Opera Company in New York (1907), he walked out. Similarly, after seven seasons at the Met, he again resigned indignantly, just as he had done at Turin in 1895. From that time forward he seemed to prefer activities as a symphonic conductor, conducting the New York Philharmonic until 1936, and in due course he conducted every major orchestra in the world.

Toscanini's operatic activities were sporadic after he left La Scala in 1902. Although he did return in 1921 to rebuild that opera house's activity after World War I, he walked out again in 1936, after being ordered to perform the fascist anthem *Giovinezza*. He remained in Italy long enough to conduct the premiere of Puccini's *Turandot*, then moved back to New York. As World War II approached, he broke off relations with Italy, Germany and Austria, thus shutting off relationships with most of the major opera houses on the continent with which he had worked earlier in his career. By then he had become a legend throughout the musical world, both as operatic and symphonic conductor. His last concert involved opera once again, for the famous lapse of memory which actually caused the NBC to take him off the air took place in the course of a performance of the "Bacchanale" from *Lohengrin*. After that concert, on 4 April 1954, he never conducted again. He died three years later.

—Franklin Zimmerman

DIE TOTE STADT [The Dead City].

Composer: Erich Wolfgang Korngold.

Librettist: Paul Schott [=E.W. and J. Korngold] (after Georges Rodenbach, *Bruges la morte*).

First Performance: Hamburg and Cologne, 4 December 1920.

Roles: Paul (tenor); Marietta (soprano); Frank (baritone); Fritz (tenor); Count Albert (tenor); Brigitta (contralto); Vision of Marie (soprano); Juliette (soprano); Lucienne (mezzo-soprano); Gaston (tenor); Victorin (tenor); chorus (SATB).

*   *   *

Critics call it kitsch, but members of the Erich Wolfgang Korngold Society call *Die tote Stadt* the composer's best opera, possibly even his best work. This opera, his third, premiered when Korngold was only twenty-three years of age; the boy-genius had composed two others while still in his teens. Although *Die tote Stadt* was initially received well, its lush, romantic style grew out of favor, and the work was ignored for years. It was revived in the mid 1970s to mixed reviews, and has maintained a modest place in the operatic repertoire since.

The libretto was based on Georges Rodenbach's novel *Bruges la morte*, a symbolist work about death and decay. In the quiet, almost deserted grey city of Bruges, the hero Hughes has lost his beloved wife, but he cannot accept her death; he begins each day by worshipping at the alter he built to honor her relic—a plait of her hair. One day, he meets a dancer who strongly resembles his dead wife. After spending the night with her, Hughes becomes consumed with guilt, and when she mocks his alter and the sacred tress of hair, he

kills her and collapses, muttering that everything is death in Bruges.

The young Erich Korngold and his father, music critic Julius Korngold, wrote the libretto under the name of Paul Schott: Paul for their hero's name (changed from Hughes to Paul) and Schott for Erich's publishing firm, B. Schott's Söhne in Mainz, to whose senior partner, Ludwig Stecker, the composer dedicated his opera. Korngold took the dark story and lightened it with his youthful perspective. The opera opens in Paul's apartment. Brigitta is showing Frank the alter Paul has made to his dead wife Marie. An excited Paul enters claiming that he has found Marie alive, and tells them how he met Marietta, the dancer, who is the very image of his wife. Frank tries to dissuade him from his fantasy. He leaves, and Paul begins to rhapsodize about his Marie. Marietta appears to pick up the umbrella she left behind. She stays for a while, singing and dancing for Paul. After she leaves, Paul imagines he sees Marie step out from the frame of her portrait. Later, Marietta returns from performing with her troupe. She taunts Paul by dancing with the braided hair of his wife from the alter, and he kills her, and collapses. Then, the door opens, and Marietta appears to ask Paul for her umbrella: he has been dreaming. This time when she asks to stay, he tells her to leave. He has learned from his dream to live in the present, not the past.

Korngold used a rich, expressionistic musical language for his opera. While tonal, the work is filled with rich chromaticisms and dissonances. His orchestration calls upon a large orchestra that includes bass trumpet, two harps, celesta, piano, harmonia, and pipe organ. As a brilliant melodist, he wrote vocal lines of splendid tunes that show off the voices. The work is lush and sonorously luxuriant.

In 1920, *Die tote Stadt* premiered with much fanfare and praise. Two opera companies, one in Hamburg and one in Colgone, gave it its world premiere on the same night, and much was made of the composer's youth. During the following years, it appeared in over eighty opera houses throughout the world, including the Metropolitan Opera in New York in 1921. It received rave reviews. One critic from Hamburg wrote: "The music grows so powerfully out of the text that it determines the significance of the work and turns it into one of the most important operas written in a long time. The intellectual content . . . does not prevent Korngold from writing a thoroughly musicianly work in which genuine melody comes into its own again, without neglecting progressive art and its laws. This combination turns the opera into a musical masterwork and also gives us new hope for the future of German art." But as the serial method of composition rose in favor, Korngold's tonal language became unfashionable, and the opera was dropped. At the outbreak of World War II, Korngold left Europe for Hollywood and put his fine musical drama skills to work for the movies. At the end of the war when he began writing absolute music again, he could not get his works performed. Not only was his music the wrong style, he was further stigmatized as a film composer and was no longer regarded as a "serious composer." It took thirty years—fifteen years after his death—for interest in his music to renew.

In 1972, RCA released a recording of Korngold's film music. Audiences at once recognized the quality of his work and a general revival of his music followed. In 1975, New York City Opera produced *Die tote Stadt;* this production was followed by others throughout Europe. The work is still occasionally performed today. While there has been enough interest to keep it in the repertoire, critics do not all agree as to its quality. Ann Lingg, writing in *Opera News,* called Korngold "a master of surging melody," and praised the opera's "full sonorities, telling leitmotifs, uncanny musical characterization and bold harmonies that never manage to offend the ear." Yet others were less pleased at the revivals. Martin Bernheimer, the Los Angeles critic, called the work "a masterpiece of Junk." He thought the music was "grandiose, overblown, big-band kitsch." The libretto, he wrote, "lent new depths of meaning to such words as mawkish and maudlin." James Helme Sutcliffe, writing in *Opera,* agreed that "with its over-used glockenspiel and ever-present harp and piano glissando's, Korngold's *Die tote Stadt* may not be musically to everyone's taste."

Erich Korngold the child prodigy did not lose his popularity by peaking early and losing his creative edge. Rather, he was a victim of radically changing tastes. Likewise, his opera was dropped from the repertoire not through lack of quality or any intrinsic flaw, but because the lush sound fell out of favor. When the pendulum of fashion swings the other way, the work may become a firm part of the operatic canon.

—Robin Armstrong

TOUREL, Jennie [born Jennie Davidovich].

Mezzo-soprano. Born 22 June 1900, in Vitebsk, Russia. Died 23 November 1973, in New York. Studied with Reynaldo Hahn and Ann El-Tour in Paris; debut in *Prince Igor* at the Opéra Russe, Paris, 1931; American debut in Moret's *Lorenzaccio,* Chicago, 1931; Metropolitan Opera debut as Mignon, 1937; also appeared at Metropolitan Opera 1943-45, 1946-47; became naturalized United States citizen, 1946; created Baba the Turk in *The Rake's Progress,* Venice, 1951; taught at Juilliard and at the Aspen Music Festival.

Publications

About TOUREL: articles–

Offergeld, R. "Some Notes on the Future of Jennie Tourel." *Stereo Review* 35/no. 5 (1975): 78.

*   *   *

Jennie Tourel was born Jennie Davidovich on 22 June 1900 in Vitebsk, Russia. Although Tourel claimed to have been born in Montreal, Canada, in 1910, it appears that this claim was fabricated in order to expedite her entry into the United States. The current opinion is that the 1900 birthdate and the Russia birthplace are correct, and Robert Offergeld in *Stereo Review* (November 1975) points out that her early passports confirm this date and place. She became an American citizen in 1946, and she died in New York City in 1973 of lung cancer.

In the first of a series of moves, which would eventually lead her to the United States, she fled Russia with her family in 1918, settling first in Danzig and then in Paris. Little is known about her musical education in Paris. Although purporting to be self-taught, she admitted to studying briefly in Paris with Anna El-Tour, also a Russian émigré. Martin Bernheimer in his *Grove Dictionary of American Music* article states she also studied in Paris with Raynaldo Hahn. Tourel later acknowledged the influence of the Lieder singer Marya Freund, who championed the early works of Francis Poulenc,

and the Spanish mezzo soprano, Conchita Supervia, who was noted for performing the Rossini heroines in their original keys. Tourel performed the original mezzo version of Rosina in Rossini's *Il barbiere di Siviglia* at the Metropolitan Opera in the mid–1940s. This rekindling of the coloratura mezzo tradition was later associated with the Tourel phenomenon.

Tourel made her operatic debut in 1931 singing Borodin's *Prince Igor* at the Opéra-Russe in Paris. Throughout the ensuing decade Tourel sang primarily in Paris, where her roles included Charlotte in Massenet's *Werther,* Cherubino in Mozart's *Le nozze di Figaro* and the title role of Bizet's *Carmen,* which became her most famous role. Other important performances of this decade included several in the United States. She sang in Ernest Moret's *Lorenzaccio* and Lola in Mascagni's *Cavalleria rusticana* at the Chicago Opera during the 1930-31 season. She also shared the stage with Mary Garden in the world premiere of Hamilton Forrest's *Camille.* In 1937 she made her Metropolitan Opera debut as Mignon in Thomas's opera of the same name.

In 1940, just a few days before the occupation of Paris, she fled to Cuba, where she remained till the end of the year. Having finally obtained an American visa, she arrived in New York City in January 1941. Although this mid-season arrival was untimely in many respects, Tourel almost immediately received offers to perform, including performances of *Carmen* and *Mignon* in Montreal and Tchaikovsky's *Pique Dame* in New York City with the New Opera Company. The year 1944 also marks Tourel's return to the Metropolitan Opera as Mignon. Her roles there included Adalgisa in Bellini's *Norma,* the title role in Bizet's *Carmen* and the original coloratura mezzo-soprano version of Rossini's *Il barbiere di Siviglia.* She also sang her unique interpretation of Bizet's *Carmen* for the inaugural season of the New York City Opera.

Other important milestones for Tourel included a performance of Berlioz's dramatic symphony *Roméo et Juliette* for the gala opening of the New York Philharmonic's 100th anniversary season. She received high praise from *New York Herald Tribune* critic Virgil Thomson (October 1942), who said of her performance, "she is a singer in the great tradition. Her voice is beautiful, her diction clear, her vocalism impeccable and her musicianship tops." She sang with the Boston Symphony Orchestra under Serge Koussevitzky and the National Broadcasting Orchestra under Leopold Stokowski. With Stokowski she gave the American premiere of Prokofiev's cantata *Alexander Nevsky* and in 1943, performed Bach's *Matthäus-Passion* on the Metropolitan Opera stage.

She sang concert versions of two Rossini operas, *Otello* and *Mosè in Egitto* and Offenbach's *La Grande Duchesse de Gérolstein* with the American Opera Society. She appeared in a performance of Tchaikovsky's *Pique Dame* for the National Educational Television in 1971, and in 1972 she performed Pasatieri's *Black Widow* for the Seattle Opera. She created the role of Baba the Turk in the premiere of Stravinsky's *The Rake's Progress* in 1951. Her last operatic appearance was the speaking role of the Duchess of Krakenthorp in Donizetti's *La fille du régiment* with the Chicago Lyric Opera.

This remarkably demanding and diverse musical career was achieved by an instrument which was not of itself extraordinary. Her voice was a rich mezzo soprano capable of coloratura and, although not large in size, capable of great expression. Tourel possessed an enormous aptitude for language. Not only was she fluent in her native languages of French and Russian; during her lifetime she also mastered English, Spanish, Polish, German, Italian, Portuguese and Hebrew. Tourel had a great command for the language of musical expression as well. She was capable of conveying subtle nuances of dynamic expression. She had a breathtaking high pianissimo which sometimes belied her frequent difficulty with sustained high passages. Tourel was also known for the ability to make an entire role her own. Her interpretations of Rosina, Carmen and Charlotte are models even today.

In addition to her considerable career on the operatic stage, Tourel also distinguished herself on the recital stage. Throughout her career she championed a vast repertoire of song literature, particularly the works of Villa-Lobos, Poulenc, Debussy, Ravel, Nin, Obradors, Ginastera, Hindemith, Rorem and Musorgsky.

During the last decade of her life, Tourel taught on the faculty of the Juilliard School of Music, and her public master classes at Carnegie Recital Hall in New York City drew a great following. She was also affiliated with the Rubin Academy of Music in Jerusalem, Israel.

—Patricia Robertson

TOZZI, Giorgio.

Bass. Born 8 January 1923, in Chicago. Studied with Rosa Raisa, Giacomo Rimini, John Daggert Howell, and Giulio Lorandi; debut on Broadway as Tarquinus in Britten's *The Rape of Lucretia,* 1948; Teatro alla Scala debut in Catalani's *La Wally,* 1953; Metropolitan Opera debut in *La Gioconda,* 1955; sang in the premiere of Barber's *Vanessa* at the Met in 1958; has also appeared in films and on television.

Publications

About TOZZI: articles–

Lingg, A.M. "Three American Tsars." *Opera News* 27 (1963): 25.
Ward, H. "Listening in." *Music and Artists* 1/5 (1968): 51.
Katona, P.M. "Das Porträt: Giorgio Tozzi." *Opernwelt* 12 (1969): 46.
Soria, D.J. "Artist life." *High Fidelity/Musical America* 20 (1975): MA4.

* * *

Over his long career Giorgio Tozzi has sung a wide variety of roles in several languages, most of them in nineteenth-century opera. His forays into opera of the eighteenth century (e.g. the title roles of *Don Giovanni* and *Le nozze di Figaro*) and twentieth century (Arkel in Debussy's *Pelléas,* the Doctor in Barber's *Vanessa*) have been relatively rare. But in nineteenth-century opera Tozzi's cosmopolitanism is unsurpassed. He has portrayed Hans Sachs (Wagner's *Die Meistersinger*) and Gurnemanz (*Parsifal*) with great success; he has also sung Farlaf in Glinka's *Ruslan and Lyudmila* and Gremin in Tchaikovsky's *Eugene Onegin;* among his many Italian roles are Don Basilio (Rossini's *Il barbiere di Siviglia*) Fiesco (Verdi's *Simon Boccanegra*) and Scarpia (Puccini's *Tosca*).

Tozzi's is a big voice, not always clear as to pitch in the lower register, but usually warm and lyrical. His skills as an actor often make his performances successful even when he is not in perfect voice. As Hans Sachs at the Metropolitan Opera in 1971 Tozzi was sometimes inaccurate in pitch, but

he still won praise from a critic for his "extroverted, demonstrative Sachs." Portraying Farlaf in *Ruslan and Lyudmila* six years later in Boston, Tozzi was reported to have "projected plenty of personality but not much voice."

Tozzi has recorded several of Verdi's operas. These recordings reveal his strengths, but they also suggest why Tozzi has never risen to the very first rank of Verdi basses. In his portrayal of Count Walter in *Luisa Miller,* recorded in the mid-1960s under Fausto Cleva, we hear a pleasing bass voice, warm in tone but without much sense of character. Walter appears on stage first in act I, scene ii. What kind of person is he? What are his feelings? Tozzi's performance tells us little about such things. When, in his aria "Il mio sangue" he sings of "the punishments of hell," his voice seems to be unengaged with the words. A few moments later, in conversation with his son, the words "lieto annuncio" are not delivered by a singer who *sounds* happy. Act II, scene ii offers listeners a chance to compare Tozzi to another fine bass, Ezio Flagello, as they converse in recitative and duet. Tozzi's enunciation is sufficiently clear; but it rarely sparkles or brings words to life. Flagello colors his words and phrases more vividly than Tozzi, resulting in a character that has more life and vigor than the one portrayed by Tozzi.

The emotional reticence in some of Tozzi's performances may be one reason why operatic producers have tended to cast him as a spiritual leader, a character standing outside the main dramatic conflict of an opera. Among his roles in Verdi's operas are those of Padre Guardiano in *La forza del destino* and of the High Priest Ramfis in *Aida.* As recorded under Solti, Tozzi's Ramfis is an authoritative figure, but does not attract undue attention away from the main characters. His Padre Guardiano (as recorded under Thomas Schippers) is much the same. This is a good performance. It does not give listeners much insight into Padre Guardiano as a man; but perhaps that impersonal quality is one aspect of the role as Verdi conceived it.

—John A. Rice

TRAUBEL, Helen.

Soprano. Born 20 June 1899, in St Louis. Died 28 July 1972, in Santa Monica, California. Studied with Vetta Karst; concert debut with St Louis Symphony Orchestra; Metropolitan Opera debut as Mary Rutledge in Damrosch's *The Man without a Country,* 1937; first major role with the Met was as Sieglinde in 1939; remained there until 1953; also appeared in Chicago and San Francisco.

Publications

By TRAUBEL: books–

St. Louis Woman. New York, 1959; revised edition, 1977.

About TRAUBEL: articles–

Riemens, L. "Traubel, Helen." In *Le grandi voci,* Rome, 1964.

* * *

It seems that Helen Traubel will be remembered as the "other" great Wagnerian soprano of her time, for her career almost directly parallels that of the legendary Kirsten Flagstad. Traubel's Metropolitan Opera debut, in fact, was in *Die Walküre* where she sang Sieglinde to Flagstad's Brünnhilde. And it was the departure of Flagstad for Europe in 1941—amidst a flurry of rumors of Nazi collaboration—which finally opened to Traubel the preeminent position among female Wagnerians at the Metropolitan Opera.

That Traubel's career is somewhat overshadowed by Flagstad should not, however, imply that she was an inferior singer, for in fact Traubel's was a remarkable voice, warm and golden-toned, of great size and solidly placed—a true dramatic soprano. It is only by comparison with Flagstad that she perhaps is found wanting, and then only to a degree. Traubel's top notes, for example, do not satisfy as they should—the powerful and gleaming middle of the voice leaves us anticipating a glorious climax which is not always forthcoming. This flaw became more pronounced as she grew older, but it was noticeable from the start, as off-the-air recordings show her shying away from exposed high passages, and we read that in her Met performances of Isolde she left out the written high Cs.

Like Flagstad, Traubel was not always an involving actress. Her recording of the Narrative and Curse from *Tristan und Isolde,* for example, is among the most impressive pieces of singing on record, but there are many colors and moods to Isolde's character which here are generalized into one. Later, in the love music from the same opera, the shining tone and firmness cannot be faulted, but where passion and involvement are called for, Traubel offers instead an unrelenting, statuesque grandeur.

Perhaps this lack of dramatic spirit explains why she didn't choose to pursue much operatic music outside of the Wagnerian repertoire. Traubel made some records of Italian arias, often not ideally chosen for her (entirely apart from her dramatic gifts, she was never a natural Desdemona or Norma) and again the amplitude and brightness of the voice give much pleasure, but roles like Santuzza and Donna Anna need a passion that just isn't forthcoming.

This said, there are many great records which preserve Traubel at her magnificent best. Her performance of Brünnhilde's Immolation Scene, conducted by Toscanini with all the excitement we would expect, is still among the best ever—here the high notes give her no trouble and at last there is the nobility and excitement which we wanted all along. And there are some lovely souvenirs of Traubel as a recitalist, notably a spacious and superbly secure performance of Richard Strauss' "Zueignung" as well as some Beethoven arrangements of English folksongs where the crisp enunciation and personal warmth are especially pleasing.

What may have limited Traubel's career far more than her few vocal problems was her own overwhelming and rather hearty personality, and in particular her insistence on maintaining a high profile in the popular arts. She appeared frequently on television, and even recorded some comic duets with Jimmy Durante, where her vivid personality fairly jumps off the disc and she reminds us of Sophie Tucker—where is this singer in all of her opera roles? She even developed her own nightclub act, centered around a heavily orchestrated and really quite unappetizing arrangement of "Saint Louis Blues." This secondary career met with substantial disapproval from the Met's general manager, Rudolf Bing, and, after a rather well publicized skirmish between the two, Traubel left the Met in 1953, never to return. This did not end her remarkable career; in 1955 she even appeared in a Broadway musical, *Pipe Dream,* which has the dubious distinction of being the shortest running show in the Rodgers and Hammerstein canon. She had little of the proper manner for this material—some late recordings of American popular song are, like the original cast album of *Pipe Dream,* better left unheard. They are certainly not representative of the soprano who, at her formidable best, may be counted as one of the great Wagner singers of our age.

—David Anthony Fox

LA TRAVIATA [The Strayed Woman].

Composer: Giuseppe Verdi.

Librettist: Francesco Maria Piave (after Dumas *fils, La dame aux camélias*).

First Performance: Venice, La Fenice, 6 March 1853.

Roles: Violetta Valéry (soprano); Alfredo Germont (tenor); Giorgio Germont (baritone); Flora Bervoix (soprano or mezzo-soprano); Baron Douphol (baritone); Gastone (tenor); Marquis D'Obigny (bass); Doctor Grenville (bass); Annina (mezzo-soprano); Joseph (tenor); Commissionaire (bass); Flora's Servant (bass); chorus (SSATTBB).

Publications

book—

Merkling, F., ed. *The Opera News Book of Traviata.* New York, 1967.

articles—

Günther, Ursula. "The Two *Traviatas.*" *Proceedings of the Royal Musical Association* 99 (1972-73).
Avant-scène opéra April (1983) [*La traviata* issue].
Hepokoski, James A. "Genre and Content in Mid-Century Verdi: 'Addio, del passato' (*La traviata,* act III)." *Cambridge Opera Journal* 1 (1989): 249.

After a delicate prelude, which foretells the opera's tragic theme in its simple but expressive, tender pathos, *La traviata* opens with an exuberant celebration in the luxurious apartments of Violetta Valéry. Musically and affectively, the contrast is extraordinary. Verdi employs similar emotive contrasts to underscore various ironies throughout the plot. Violetta is a popular figure in *demi-mondaine* Paris. Beautiful, carefree, and secure in the protection of Baron Douphol, she is devoted to her frivolous existence, and unaware that one of the guests, young Alfredo Germont, has been deeply in love with her for more than a year. But he soon makes known to her the depth of his feeling, first in a magnificent toast before the assembled guests, and then again in an impassioned aria. This aria, *"Di quell' amor ch'e palpito dell' universo"* ("With that love that is the very breath of the universe") becomes the central melody of the opera, symbolic of Alfredo's genuine love for Violetta and, eventually, of hers for him. Verdi plays on the nostalgic quality of this beautiful

La traviata, with Nancy Gustafson as Violetta and Jorge Pita as Alfredo, Scottish Opera, 1989

melody with magnificent psychological effect later, when estrangement and then death separate the lovers.

Reluctant to break off relations with Baron Douphol, and still enamored of her free and easy life, Violetta is at first unwilling to make the total commitment Alfredo seeks. However, his innocence, sincerity, and intensity at last win her over. She accepts both his love and his offer to care for her for the rest of her life. Already, her frequent coughing spells and fits of weakness reveal that she suffers poor health.

Three months later, Violetta and Alfredo are happily living together in a country estate which she has rented. Here, Verdi's music conjures up an idyllic bliss, which also will provide for musical flash-back when tragedy occurs. Upon discovering that Violetta is on the brink of bankruptcy, as a result of the expenses of their new life together, Alfredo hurries away to Paris to draw upon his inheritance and so stave off financial disaster. By mischance, Alfredo's father, Giorgio Germont, arrives during Alfredo's absence. He has come on a special mission, which is to persuade Violetta to end her affair with Alfredo. She resists Germont's arguments, until at last he explains that her past reputation not only is harming Alfredo's prospects, but will inevitably destroy his sister's forthcoming marriage to a young man from a fine family. Faced with this argument, she capitulates, agreeing to leave Alfredo for good at once. This scene is a *tour de force* of impassioned musical declamation, coupled with apt characterization.

Alfredo returns from Paris just as Violetta is finishing her farewell note. (Already she has asked Baron Douphol to take her back.) She conceals its contents from Alfredo until the Baron's carriage has come for her. When she is on her way, a messenger delivers the note, which explains, falsely, that she no longer loves him, and is returning to her former lover. Alfredo's father returns from the garden just then and prevents him from following after Violetta. Alfredo is unwilling to listen to his father's reasoning.

Still nursing his jealous anger, Alfredo attends unbidden a fête at the home of Flora Bevon, Violetta's former friend and confidante. Alfredo gambles recklessly and wins large sums of money, mainly from Baron Douphol, who meanwhile had arrived with Violetta. Alfredo then humiliates Violetta, denouncing her perfidy, and throwing all his winnings at her. His father upbraids him severely for his churlishness, his stern anger bringing Alfredo to his senses. But repentance comes too late to ward off the Baron's challenge to a duel.

Several months later, Violetta, lying on what soon will be her deathbed, receives a letter from Giorgio Germont explaining that the duel has taken place, the Baron has been wounded but recovering, and Alfredo has gone abroad. Alfredo's father has explained her sacrifice, and the two have reconciled. Soon both men visit her, hoping to make amends and start anew. Alfredo renews his vow of love and promises to take Violetta to the country again, where they may live in happiness forever after. But Violetta, sensing the approach of death, gives him a medallion portrait of herself, asking him to show it to the young lady who will one day win his heart. With a brief return of energy, Violetta rises from her bed, only to be overcome by death.

Having startled his public by presenting a plot based on free love, and having broken with convention in choosing a contemporary subject, Verdi composed for *La traviata* one of the deepest and most psychologically revealing scores of his career. The impassioned melody of the aria "Di quell' amore" becomes a veritable *idée fixe,* which at various points in the unfolding story recalls states of former happiness, contrasting these most poignantly with current woes of the main protagonists. Not until he composes *Otello* towards the end of his life will Verdi again find such psychological depth in depicting human tragedy.

—Franklin Zimmerman

TREEMONISHA.

Composer: Scott Joplin.

Librettist: Scott Joplin.

First Performance: New York, 1915.

Roles: Treemonisha (soprano); Monisha (soprano); Lucy (soprano); Remus (tenor); Andy (tenor); Cephus (tenor); Zodzetrick (baritone); Ned (bass); Luddud (bass); Simon (bass); Parson Alltalk (bass); chorus.

*   *   *

Joplin's progress in composition and his disassociation from ragtime is extremely evident in the opera *Treemonisha,* his final extended composition. Although essentially a folk opera, it is conceived in a "grand" manner. An overture precedes the first act and a prelude precedes each of the other two acts. Within the opera there are no spoken parts. Recitatives, arias, and ensembles abound, and in each situation the type of performance sought is indigenous to the story of the opera.

Preparations for *Treemonisha* began early in Joplin's career, perhaps soon after he composed *A Guest of Honor.* Around 1907 Eubie Blake met Joplin in Washington, D.C., and mentioned that Joplin was seeking copyright for the opera. In 1908, Joplin is known to have played portions of the opera for Joseph F. Lamb. However, *Treemonisha* was not published until 1911, and then Joplin had to set up his own publishing company in order to secure publication. It was during this time that Joplin and his publisher John Stark had a serious misunderstanding concerning the awarding of royalties. Between 1911 and 1915, Joplin looked long and in vain for backers, supporters, and producers. An informal performance held in a small Harlem theater in 1915 failed, and the failure apparently broke the back of the "King of Ragtime," for he was soon after committed to a state hospital. Nevertheless, today we have a fine recording and a video of the opera by the Houston Grand Opera company.

As the opera begins the conjurors are intent upon controlling the Negro community, but Treemonisha aims to thwart their purposes. Later Treemonisha is captured by the conjurors, who plan to cast her in the wasps' nest; however, Remus and other men from the community capture the conjurors and rescue Treemonisha, whereupon all proceed back to the plantation. The Negro community wishes to punish the conjurors, but Treemonisha and Remus persuade the people to forgive them. The community hails Treemonisha as their leader, so that they may be free from the plight of conjuring and superstition.

The overture to the first act, the introduction to the second act, and the prelude to the third act of the opera are conceived in a rhapsodic manner, but formal coherence is achieved by the reiteration of themes which express the story and the emotional content of the opera. Several themes from various parts of the opera are heard in the overture, which opens with the theme that Joplin claims is the principal strain in the opera. It appears when Monisha explains why she has named her little girl Treemonisha, and when Treemonisha is rescued from the conjurors. The introduction to the second act and the prelude to the third act of the opera are fairly programmatic in conception, since both signify in their mood the coming events. The somber nature of the introduction to the second act suggests the ensuing conjurors' meeting at the wasps' nest, and the prelude to the third act literally defines the impending joy and utter relief of Treemonisha's mother and father when she is returned to the community. The type of syncopation that occurs in the rags of Joplin may be noticed in the prelude to the third act, but it is softened by a moving bass line rather than the "oompah" bass usually associated with ragtime. Also novel is that each of the instrumental selections that precede an act are closed in structure, rather than open as in a ragtime composition.

The vocal writing in *Treemonisha* makes one overlook what many consider a weak libretto, for it is here that Joplin demonstrates his genius. The vocal writing comprises choruses, recitatives, arias, and ariosos, and in one instance Joplin employs a through-composed aria for one soloist. This is "The Sacred Tree" sung by Monisha when she explains to the community why they must not harm the tree that grew in front of her home. The aria, which is quite lengthy, displays melodic variety and harmonic subtleties of a very high order. Another magnificent aria is "Wrong Is Never Right" sung by Remus after the conjurors have been captured. Though strophic in conception and closing with a choral rendition of the aria, the manner in which Joplin handles the roulades of the aria is particularly astounding.

A particularly striking example of Joplin's genius occurs in the ensemble section entitled "Confusion," which closes the first act of the opera. To express the horror of Treemonisha being captured by the conjurors, Joplin used the device called *Sprechstimme* (speech-song) initiated by Engelbert Humperdinck in 1897 and further developed by Arnold Schoenberg between 1910 and 1913. Joplin gives directions in The Score that women should indicate crying, and that the crying should start on a high pitch and the sound gradually diminish. The men speak in crying tones indicated by headless notes. Joplin also indicates that the crying need not be in strict time, but the accompaniment must be. This is surely an innovative step by Joplin, suggesting his enormous creative ability and giving him a seminal position in music history.

—Addison W. Reed

TREIGLE, Norman.

Bass-baritone. Born 6 March 1927, in New Orleans. Died 16 February 1975. Studied with Elizabeth Wood at Loyola University; debut as Duke of Verona in Gounod's *Roméo et Juliette* with New Orleans Opera Association, 1947; New York City Opera debut as Colline in *La bohème*, 1953, and remained with the company until 1973; appeared at Covent Garden, 1974; also appeared in Hamburg and Milan.

Publications

About TREIGLE: books–

Sokol, M. *Norman Treigle . . . A Man Remembered.* New York, 1975.
Ewen, D. *Musicians since 1900.* New York, 1978.

articles–

"Sermons and Satan." *Time* 94/no. 3 October (1969).
Saal, H. "Double Devil." *Newsweek* 74/no. 6 October (1969).
Obituary. *The New York Times* 18 February (1975).
Eaton, Q. "Norman Treigle." *Opera News* 39/no. 22 (1975).

Norman Treigle (baptized as Adanelle), the youngest of five children of Wilfred and Claudia Treigle, was born in New Orleans, on 6 March 1927. His mother, an accomplished pianist and organist, was responsible for his early interest in music, and he joined the church choir as a boy soprano at the age of nine. Later on, he took part in musical events in high school, where, as an honor student, he graduated at the age of 16. Following a two-year tour of duty in the Navy, he entered Loyola University on a scholarship as a voice major, where he studied with Elizabeth Wood. After winning the New Orleans Opera Auditions of the Air, he made his debut with the New Orleans Opera Association as the Duke of Verona in Gounod's *Roméo et Juliette* on 23 October 1947.

To support himself and to build up some cash reserves, Treigle accepted singing engagements at the First Baptist Church in New Orleans and in nightclubs. He appeared at the Blue Room of New Orlean's Roosevelt Hotel with the bands of Horace Heidt, Jimmy Dorsey, Joe Reichman, and Red Nichols, and toured the American south as a revival singer with Rev. Bob Harrington, the Baptist preacher who later served as a partial model for his role of Olin Blitch. Described as a devout Baptist and "an intensely religious man," Treigle continued to sing in church and recorded three albums of religious music.

After moving to New York City, Treigle was engaged by the New York City Opera where he made his debut as Colline in *La bohème*, on 28 March 1953. During his twenty years with the City Opera, he sang some thirty of the sixty-two major and minor roles in his repertoire, often working with the best directors the company could attract, among them Christopher West, Tito Capobianco, and Frank Corsaro. Although he appeared with many other opera companies in the United States, the City Opera was the scene of his greatest triumphs. His most successful portrayals were Gounod's diabolically fascinating, elegant, and menacing Mephistopheles; Boito's detached, evil, frightening, snake-like Mefistofele; the grotesquely comic King Dodon of *The Golden Cockerel;* the four villains in *Les contes d' Hoffmann;* and the title roles in *Don Giovanni, Giulio Cesare, Boris Godunov, Le nozze di Figaro,* and *Gianni Schicchi.* But he could make an indelible mark even in such brief parts as the toreador in *Carmen.* This reviewer wrote of his Escamillo (*Opera,* 1973) that "he looked and behaved like a toreador; tall, lean, nimble, agile, self-assured, lustful, arrogant—a born winner unafraid of man and beast, at home in the bull-ring and boudoirs, and equally doused in bull's blood and perfume. Vocally Treigle was nothing less than shattering." Arthur Jacobs, reviewing his Mefistofele at the Royal Festival Hall (*Opera,* 1974), wrote of his "marvelously expressive and infinitely malleable voice," calling his performance "spellbinding."

Treigle was equally at home in the modern compositions of Walton, Orff, von Einem, Dallapiccola, Copeland, and Floyd. He created the role of Grandpa Moss in Aaron Copland's *The Tender Land,* and Reverend Hale in Ward's *The Crucible.* He first assumed the role of Olin Blitch in Carlisle Floyd's *Susannah* on 27 September 1956, giving the role a definitive portrayal. He and Phyllis Curtin, creator of the title role, took the performance to the Brussels World's Fair in 1958, to great critical acclaim. In later years, Treigle created three roles composed explicitly for him by Floyd, who called him "an actor-singer with no superiors and few equals . . . an extravagantly gifted man. I am greatly and happily in his debt as a composer."

Opera to Treigle was music drama, with emphasis on the drama. "To me the most important thing is to be an actor who sings," was his artistic credo. *Newsweek* called him "Probably the finest singing actor in opera" (1969), which makes it all the more remarkable that he never appeared at the Metropolitan, only a few hundred yards away from his home theater.

Treigle's voice was a finely grained, well-modulated, and perfectly equalized true bass with an extension that enabled him to sing the most coveted roles of the bass-baritone literature. His timbre, though somewhat reminiscent of the young Pinza, had a color and character of its own, easily recognizable and distinguishable from all others. One of its most remarkable features was its awesome power, wholly unexpected of a 5'11" man weighing only 140 pounds. The best creations in Treigle's repertoire were extraordinary portrayals, unique interpretations that set the singer apart from other exponents of his roles. He was a dynamic, electrifying performer who could fill the stage, dominate a scene, and reduce his less accomplished colleagues to animated props. His conceptions were characterized by a strong sense of theater, and giving proper weight and emphasis to every word he sang, he projected a role physically as well. At times a mere posture or an evocative gesture of his could linger in one's memory as long as the sound of his voice. The recordings that captured his singing—always more impressive in a live performance than in the studio—actually preserved only half of his art.

Treigle recorded for Angel, RCA, ABC, Columbia, Westminster, and some lesser labels. His Mefistofele, Julius Caesar, and Hoffmann villains have been preserved on commercial records. In addition to operatic and religious recital records, there are "private" recordings and tapes of live performances of his Olin Blitch, Mephistopheles, Gianni Schicchi, Cardinal Brogni of a concert performance of *La Juive;* one performance of his King Dodon was issued on records and another is known to exist on videotape.

Treigle believed in the company he served so faithfully for two decades, and when, in his perception, the City Opera was becoming a "glamour house," he resigned to pursue an international career. He partially realized his ambition with an acclaimed concert performance of *Mefistofele* at the Royal Festival Hall (18 March 1974), followed by his Covent Garden debut in *Faust* (22 November 1974), and appearances in Hamburg and Milan. Soon after, on 16 February 1975, he was found dead in his apartment. The New York City Opera honored his memory by establishing in 1975 the Norman Treigle Memorial Fund, with the aim of two permanent scholarships for young American singers. His premature death just two weeks short of his 48th birthday deprived him

and the opera world of a fitting climax to a distinguished career.

—Andrew Farkas

TRIPTYCH.

Einstein on the Beach
Satyagraha
Akhnaten

Composer: Philip Glass.

Librettists: *Einstein on the Beach,* Philip Glass (opera composed with Robert Wilson); *Satyagraha,* C. DeJong (after *Bhagavad Gita*); *Akhnaten,* Philip Glass and others.

First Performances: *Einstein on the Beach,* France, Avignon, 25 July 1976; *Satyagraha,* Rotterdam, 5 September 1980; *Akhnaten,* Stuttgart, 24 March 1984.

Roles: *Einstein on the Beach:* various voices and instruments; *Satyagraha:* M.K. Gandhi (tenor); Miss Schlesen (soprano); Kasturbai (contralto); Mr Kallenbach (baritone); Parsi Rustomji (bass); Mrs Naidos (soprano); Mrs Alexander (contralto); Lord Krishna (bass); Prince Arjunabar; Count Leo Tolstoy, Rabindranath Tagore, Martin Luther King Jr (all non-singing roles); *Akhnaten:* Akhnaten (counter tenor); Nefertiti (contralto); Queen Tye (soprano); Horemhab (baritone); Aye (bass); The High Priest of Amon (tenor); Akhnaten's six daughters (female voices); Funeral Party (eight men's voices); Tourist Guide (voice-over).

Publications

books–

Glass, Philip, with R. Palmer. *Einstein on the Beach* [liner notes for Tomato 4-2901]. 1979.
_____, with C. DeJong. *Satyagraha, M.K. Ghandi in South Africa, 1893-1914: the Historical Material and Libretto Comprising the Opera's Book.* New York, 1980.

articles–

"Creating *Einstein on the Beach:* Philip Glass and Robert Wilson speak to Maxime de la Falaise." *On the Next Wave: the Audience Magazine of BAM's Next Wave Festival* 2/no. 4 (1984): 5.
Jones, R.T. "*Einstein on the Beach:* Return of a Legend." *On the Next Wave: the Audience Magazine of BAM's Next Wave Festival* 2/no. 4 (1984): 1
Taylor, S. "*Einstein* on the Stage." *Brooklyn Academy of Music* (1984): 3.

*   *   *

Although the three operas gathered under the title *Triptych* have on only one occasion been presented in tandem (in Stuttgart in the summer of 1989), Philip Glass has often stated that he did conceive his 1976 *Einstein on the Beach,* his 1980 *Satyagraha* and his 1983 *Akhnaten* as a unit. Each

Akhnaten, **part of Philip Glass's** *Triptych,* **with Christopher Robson as Akhnaten, English National Opera, London, 1985**

of them, he says, is a "portrait" of an individual whose ideas have changed the course of world events, and together, he says, they form a sort of triptych. Their similarities are more philosophical than musical or theatrical.

Satyagraha, which concerns the life of the Indian pacifist Mohandas K. Gandhi, and *Akhnaten,* which deals with the Egyptian pharaoh who supposedly invented the concept of monotheism, indeed seem cut from the same cloth; both feature sumptuously lyric singing set over often soft-textured orchestral accompaniments, and both are cast in the form of vignettes which, although they are presented in something other than chronological order, are comparable in structure to the traditional opera scene. *Einstein on the Beach,* in marked contrast, is a highly abstract work representative of Glass's earlier, more aggressive Minimalist style. The rhythmically insistent score is played for the most part at high volume levels by an ensemble of synthesizers and electronic organs, and the vocal materials are limited to monotone recitations and choral chantings of numbers and solfège syllables. Just as significant, the various segments are not so much scenes as stage pictures, intended as showcases for the virtuosity of designer Robert Wilson. Because of the order in which they are presented, the events portrayed in *Satyagraha* and *Akhnaten* are perhaps hard to follow, but at least they are events clearly based on episodes in the protagonists' lives; in *Einstein on the Beach,* there is very little that in the conventional sense seems narrative.

As different as the first item in the triptych is from its successors, however, all three works are ultimately powerful for the same reason. Even in the more traditionally structured *Satyagraha* and *Akhnaten,* the communication to the audience of text is not an issue; in the one opera the libretto is in Sanskrit, and in the other it is in a variety of archaic languages, and for productions of both the composer has specifically requested that the audience not be provided with translations. The result, as in *Einstein on the Beach,* is a removal of literal meaning from that which is sung; the words have only a cumulative effect, comparable to that of a litany prayed *en masse* in a resonant cathedral. In combination with the aural consistency of Glass's deliberately repetitious, harmonically static scores, the effect—even without vivid stage imagery—can be quite overwhelming.

—James Wierzbicki

TRIPTYCH
See IL TRITTICO

TRISTAN AND ISOLDE
See TRISTAN UND ISOLDE

TRISTAN UND ISOLDE [Tristan and Isolde].

Composer: Richard Wagner.

Librettist: Richard Wagner.

First Performance: Munich, Königliches Hof- und Nationaltheater, 10 June 1865.

Roles: Isolde (soprano); Tristan (tenor); Brangäne (mezzosoprano or soprano); Kurwenal (baritone); King Marke (bass); Melot (tenor); A Shepherd (tenor); A Steersman (baritone); A Sailor's Voice (tenor); chorus (TTBB).

Publications

books–

Kufferath, M. *Guide thématique et analyse de Tristan et Iseult.* Paris, 1894.

Golther, W. *Tristan und Isolde in den Dichtungen des Mittelalters und der neuen Zeit.* Leipzig, 1907.

Lindner, E. *Richard Wagner über Tristan und Isolde: Aussprüche des Meisters über sein Werk.* Leipzig, 1912.

Kurth, E. *Romantische Harmonik und ihre Krise in Wagners 'Tristan'.* Berlin, 1920; 2nd ed., 1923.

Bahr-Mildenburg, A. *Tristan und Isolde: Darstellung der Werke Richard Wagners aus dem Geiste der Dichtung und Musik: vollständige Regiebearbeitung sämtlicher Partien mit Notenbeispielen.* Leipzig, 1936.

Levi, V. *Tristano e Isotta di Riccardo Wagner.* Venice, 1958.

Vogel, M. *Der Tristan-Akkord und die Krise der modernen Harmonie-Lehre.* Düsseldorf, 1962.

Scharschuch, H. *Gesamtanalyse der Harmonik von Richard Wagners Musikdrama 'Tristan und Isolde': unter spezifischer Berücksichtigung der Sequenztechnik des Tristanstiles.* Regensburg, 1963.

Zuckerman, Elliot. *The First Hundred Years of Wagner's Tristan.* New York and London, 1964.

Wagner, W., ed. *100 Jahre Tristan.* Emsdetten, 1965.

Wapnewski, P. *Tristan der Held.* Berlin, 1981.

articles–

Porges, H. "Tristan und Isolde." *Bayreuther Blätter* 25 (1902): 186; 26 (1903): 23, 241; also edited as a separate volume by H. von Wolzogen, Leipzig, 1906.

Golther, W. "Zur Entstehung von Richard Wagners Tristan." *Die Musik* 5 (1905-06): 3.

Prüfer, A. "Novalis Hymnen an die Nacht in ihren Beziehungen zu Wagners Tristan und Isolde." *Richard Wagner-Jahrbuch* 1 (1906): 290.

Grunsky, K. "Das Vorspiel und der erste Akt von 'Tristan und Isolde'." *Richard Wagner-Jahrbuch* 2 (1907): 207.

Anheisser, S. "Das Vorspiel zu 'Tristan und Isolde' und seine Motivik." *Zeitschrift für Musikwissenschaft* 3 (1920-21): 257.

Peyser, H.F. " 'Tristan,' First-hand." *Musical Quarterly* 11 (1925): 418.

Schünemann, G. "Eine neue Tristan-Handschrift." *Archiv für Musikforschung* 3 (1938): 129; 137.

Grunsky, H. " 'Tristan und Isolde': der symphonische Aufbau des dritten Aufzugs." *Zeitschrift für Musikwissenschaft* 113 (1952): 390.

Truscott, H. "Wagner's *Tristan* and the Twentieth Century." *Music Review* 24 (1963): 75.

Mitchell, W.J. "The Tristan Prelude: Techniques and Structure." *Music Forum* 1 (1967): 162.

Voss, E. "Wagners Striche im Tristan." *Neue Zeitschrift für Musik* 132 (1971): 644.

Jackson, R. "*Leitmotive* and Form in the *Tristan* Prelude." *Music Review* 36 (1975): 42.

Dahlhaus, Carl. "*Tristan*—Harmonik und Tonalität." *Melos/Neue Zeitschrift für Musik* 4 (1978): 215.

Raymond, Joely. "The *Leitmotiv* and Musical-Dramatic Structure in Tristan's Third Narration of the Delirium." *Indiana Theory Review* 3 (1980): 3.

Avant-scène opéra July-August (1981) [*Tristan et Isolde* issue].

Burnstein, L. Poundie. "A New View of *Tristan:* Tonal Unity in the Prelude and Conclusion to Act I." *Theory and Practice* 8 (1983): 15.

Frühwald, Wolfgang. "Romantische Sehnsucht und Liebestod in Richard Wagners Oper *Tristan und Isolde.*" *Zeitwende* 54 (1983): 129.

Kinderman, William. "Das 'Geheimnis der Form' in Wagners *Tristan und Isolde.*" *Archiv für Musikwissenschaft* 40 (1983): 174.

Maisel, Arthur. "*Tristan:* a Different Perspective." *Theory and Practice* 8 (1983): 53.

McKinney, Bruce. "The Case Against Tonal Unity in *Tristan.*" *Theory and Practice* 8 (1983): 62.

Knapp, Raymond. "The Tonal Structure of *Tristan und Isolde:* a Sketch." *Music Review* 45 (1984): 11.

Abbate, Carolyn. "Wagner, 'On Modulation' and *Tristan.*" *Cambridge Opera Journal* 1 (1989): 33.

unpublished–

Bailey, R. "The Genesis of *Tristan und Isolde,* and a Study of Wagner's Sketches and Drafts for the First Act." Ph.D. dissertation, Princeton University, 1969.

Stokes, Jeffrey Lewis. "Contour and Motive: a Study of 'Flight' and 'Love' in Wagner's *Ring, Tristan,* and *Meistersinger.*" Ph.D. dissertation, State University of New York, Buffalo, 1984.

* * *

In 1857 Wagner interrupted the composition of *Siegfried* to write *Tristan und Isolde.* He chose a different kind of verse from the alliterative style of *Der Ring,* though his verse was nevertheless criticized as "bombastic" and as "stammering speech, murderous to thought and language" (Hanslick). The opera preserves little of the original legend, using the theme of love to explore the conflict between Will and Circumstance. It thus comes close to the ideals of Schopenhauer, whom Wagner had read in 1854.

In his letters to Liszt, Wagner had talked of developing a kind of drama expressed purely through music, while to Maric Wittgenstein he wrote: "For the moment, music without words: several things I would rather treat in music than in verse." His libretto does indeed call for very little stage action. Where such action is necessary he confines it to the ends of acts: in act I, Tristan and Isolde's embrace; in act II, Tristan's wound; in act III, Tristan's death. The inner drama is portrayed through the orchestra.

The prelude at once projects the listener into a world of mystery and uncertainty. This uncertainty is increased by a feeling of yearning, an element which continues throughout the work until the final bars.

Act I takes place on the ship in which Isolde is being carried to Cornwall to marry the aged King Marke. To her attendant Brangäne, Isolde expresses her rage and humiliation at being taken to an unwelcome marriage by Tristan, the enemy whom she had nursed back to strength even though he had killed her former betrothed. She orders Brangäne to prepare a poisoned potion and offers it to Tristan, as if in atonement. Quickly realizing that it is poisoned, he nevertheless accepts the drink, since he knows his love for Isolde can never be fulfilled. Brangäne, however, has substituted a love potion in place of the poison. The lovers are overcome with longing and embrace each other passionately, oblivious of their arrival in Cornwall.

In act II, Tristan and Isolde meet at night by Marke's castle while the king is away hunting. In a long scene they curse the day that keeps them apart: only at night can their love flourish. Their duet moves to an overwhelming climax, in which the text is reduced to mere pairs of words; its final note, however, is cut short by the arrival of Tristan's squire, Kurwenal. Despite Kurwenal's warning, the lovers are discovered by the king as dawn breaks. Marke gives vent to his grief at Tristan's lack of faith. Melot, a courtier, challenges Tristan with his sword, and during their fight Tristan suddenly lowers his guard and is gravely wounded.

Act III is set on the coast of Brittany, in a deserted ruined castle at Kareol. Tristan survives only in the hope that Isolde might arrive. From delirium, he eventually sinks into unconsciousness. This long monologue is punctuated by a strange, mournful phrase first heard on a shepherd's pipe at the opening of the act. The sound of the pipe changes to joy as Isolde's boat is seen, at which Tristan's outbursts become more and more frenzied. As Isolde enters, he collapses into her arms (a moment emphasized with a musical recollection of their drinking of the love potion) and dies. A second boat arrives bearing King Marke. His agonizing statement of forgiveness is answered only with Isolde's farewell to life, the *Liebestod,* at the end of which she sinks down onto Tristan's body.

Tristan und Isolde was initially conceived to be easily performable by an ordinary opera company, avoiding the difficulties posed by *Der Ring* with its huge orchestra and powerful voices. This ambition was, however, not fulfilled. The first production in Vienna was abandoned after over seventy rehearsals, and it took four years before *Tristan* received its first performance, in Munich. The reasons can easily be explained. While the musical style of the secondary characters follows the established diatonic manner, that for Tristan and Isolde inhabits another world, its highly chromatic idiom so original that even today it can seem unsettling. Moreover, Tristan's delirium in act III is intensified by means of unorthodox rhythmic patterns, including passages of five (5/4) and even seven (4/4 + 3/4) beats, all of which contemporary singers found alien. As Nietzsche commented in *Nietzsche contra Wagner* (1888), these methods produce the effect of music moving in water, without any point of reference.

The use of a smaller orchestra did little to help, since Wagner's approach to the voice remained close to that which he had employed in *Der Ring.* Tristan's role, initially conceived as a "lyric" part, became closer to that of the *Heldentenor* (heroic tenor), and the role is made especially difficult since the singer is on stage for almost the entire work. The relationship between voice and orchestra differed from that of conventional opera: the music is written on a contrapuntal basis where the vocal line is but one of many melodic strands. Nor is the voice necessarily the leading part, for at times it becomes obscured in the overall sound.

Leitmotives are used in *Tristan,* but in a different manner than in *Der Ring.* There are only a small number of them, and they represent not characters or objects but wishes and

Jon Vickers and Helge Dernesch in *Tristan und Isolde,* Salzburg Festival, 1972

emotions. The work's structure is strengthened by such features as the parallel construction of acts I and III and the points of analogy between Tristan's two long monologues in act III. Further coherence comes from the fact that the three acts emphasize in turn the work's three interlocking main themes: love, night, and death.

Such formal organization is all the more necessary in view of the tonal instability of the work's musical language, an instability encapsulated in the famous "Tristan" chord, first heard in the opening phrase of the prelude and unresolved until the final bars. Furthermore, the work avoids closed musical forms, preferring a style that Nietzsche characterized as "infinite melody." Wagner acknowledged this, claiming that his finest art was "the art of transition, for my whole texture consists of such transitions."

—Alan Laing

IL TRITTICO [Triptych].

Il tabarro [The Cloak].
Suor Angelica [Sister Angelica].
Gianni Schicchi.

Composer: Giacomo Puccini.

Librettists: *Il tabarro:* Giuseppe Adami (after Didier Gold, *La houppelande*); *Suor Angelica:* Giovacchino Forzano; *Gianni Schicchi:* Giovacchino Forzano (scenario based on lines from Dante, *Inferno*).

First Performance: New York, Metropolitan Opera, 14 December 1918.

Roles: *Il tabarro:* Giorgetta (soprano); Michele (baritone); Luigi (tenor); Frugola (mezzo-soprano); Tinca (tenor); Talpa (bass); Two Lovers (soprano, tenor); Song Vendor (tenor); chorus (STBB).
Suor Angelica: Sister Angelica (soprano); The Princess (contralto); The Abbess (mezzo-soprano); The Monitor (mezzo-soprano); Mistress of Novices (contralto); Sister Genevieve (soprano); Sister Osmina (mezzo-soprano); Sister Dolcina (mezzo-soprano); Nursing Sister (mezzo-soprano); Two Attending Nuns (mezzo-soprano); Two Novices (mezzo-sopranos); Two Lay-Sisters (soprano, mezzo-soprano); chorus (SSSTB).
Gianni Schicchi: Lauretta (soprano); Rinuccio (tenor); Gianni Schicchi (baritone); Zita (mezzo-soprano); Gherardo (tenor); Nella (soprano); Betto (baritone); Simone (bass); Marco (baritone); La Ciesca (soprano); Master Spinelloccio (bass); Amantio di Nicolso (bass); Gherardino (mezzo-soprano or boy soprano); Pinellino (bass); Guccio (bass).

A scene from the first production of Puccini's *Gianni Schicchi*, from *Il trittico*, Metropolitan Opera, New York, 1918

Publications

book–

Leukel, Jürgen J. *Studien zu Puccinis "Il trittico".* Munich, 1983.

articles–

D'Amico, Fedele. "Una ignorata pagina 'maliperiana' di *Suor Angelica.*" *Rassegna musicale curci* March (1966).
Avant-scène opéra December (1985) [*Gianni Schicchi* issue].

*   *   *

Il trittico consists of three one-act operas bound together by recurrent themes and images. The first of the operas, *Il tabarro,* is based on a play by Didier Gold, with a libretto by Giuseppe Adami. The most *verismo* of Puccini's many operas, it involves adultery, revenge, and murder, all involving poor people. The opera is set on a barge on the river Seine in Paris. Michele, the captain of the barge, is madly in love with his wife Giorgetta, and they have recently suffered the death of their only child. But Giorgetta, much younger than her husband, is having an affair with a young worker, Luigi, on board her husband's barge. Ultimately, and after much suffering, Michele discovers who his wife's lover is and murders him.

The second opera, *Suor Angelica,* has a libretto by Giovacchino Forzano and was based on his own idea. The opera is set in a convent in Italy during the seventeenth century. Convents were places where the Italian nobility stashed away daughters and other females who had caused disgrace to the family. In this case, Suor Angelica has had a child out of wedlock. In the opening of the opera, she and the other nuns sing of their life in the convent, with mixed reactions to their incarceration. Suddenly a relative of Suor Angelica enters, the Zia Principessa, and asks to speak to Angelica alone. She wants her niece to sign some documents involving the family estate, which Angelica obediently does, but she is desperate for news of her son. Her aunt coldly informs her that the child has died, and then hastily leaves. The opera ends with Angelica committing suicide in the hope that God will save her and her son.

Gianni Schicchi, also to a text by Forzano, is based on a few lines from Dante's *Inferno,* concerning the character of Gianni Schicchi, who is placed in hell for falsifying a will. The opera is set in Florence in 1299, and the Donati household is in mourning as their relative, old Buoso Donati, dies. Their grief becomes much more genuine once they find the old man's will and discover that they have all been disinherited— Donati willed his entire estate to a local monastery. In their desperation, the family call upon a lawyer with a dubious reputation, Gianni Schicchi, at the advice of their son Rinuccio, who is in love with Schicchi's daughter, Lauretta. Schicchi then hatches a plot: the family will call in a notary, Schicchi will pretend he is the old and dying Buoso Donati and dictate a new will leaving them everything. This they do, but he outsmarts them by giving them some property while keeping the bulk of the estate for himself. The opera ends with Gianni Schicchi throwing them out of his house, and giving it to the young lovers so they can marry.

All three of the *Trittico* operas involve the themes of death, revenge, and inter-family conflicts. In terms of symbolism, the operas use imagery of water, money, growth, death, and social conflict. Puccini wanted all three operas performed together as a single unit, but very soon after the premiere *Gianni Schicchi* became the audience favorite and is often done without the other two operas. *Gianni Schicchi* has been called the best Italian operatic comedy since Verdi's *Falstaff* and it undoubtedly is, though the other two operas are very fine as well. Recently, some opera companies have staged all three *Trittico* operas together, as Puccini wanted.

—John Louis DiGaetani

TROILUS AND CRESSIDA.

Composer: William Walton.

Librettist: Hassall.

First Performance: London, Covent Garden, 1954; revised, 1975-76.

Roles: Cressida (soprano); Troilus (tenor); Pandarus (tenor); Diomede (baritone); Calkas (bass); Evadne (mezzo-soprano); Antenor (baritone); Horaste (baritone); Woman's Voice (speaking); Two Priests (tenor, baritone); Two Soldiers (tenor, baritone); Three Watchmen (offstage; tenor, two baritones); chorus (SSSSAAAATTTTBBBB).

Publications

articles–

Warrack, John. "Walton's *Troilus and Cressida*." *Opera* December (1954).
Reizenstein, F. "Walton's *Troilus and Cressida*." *Tempo* no. 34 (1954-55): 16.

*   *   *

The story of *Troilus and Cressida* concerns the love of Troilus, Prince of Troy, for Cressida, the daughter of Calkas, High Priest of Pallas, at a time when the Greeks are besieging the city. Act I reveals Calkas, subsequently to be proven a traitor, trying to persuade the Trojans that further resistance is useless. Against this background Troilus meets Cressida and falls in love with her. Pandarus, brother of Calkas, acts as matchmaker. In act II he unites the lovers, but the sudden arrival of Diomede, Prince of Argos, interrupts their new-found happiness. He has come to take Cressida to her father, who has deserted to the Greeks, in exchange for Antenor, Captain of Trojan Spears, whom the Greeks have captured.

Act III shows Cressida in the Greek camp, anxiously awaiting news of Troilus but unaware that her father has arranged for all his messages to be intercepted by Evadne, her servant. Believing herself to be abandoned, she yields completely to Diomede's advances. Then Troilus and Pandarus, admitted through the Greek lines in an hour of truce, come upon Evadne and urge her to fetch Cressida, whose ransom is being arranged. When Troilus reclaims Cressida, Diomede commands her to renounce him, but she refuses. He fights with Diomede, but is mortally wounded in the back by Calkas. Diomede orders Calkas back to Troy, declaring that Cressida must stay behind as a prisoner without privilege. She escapes her fate by taking her own life.

Shortly after finishing the opera, Walton wrote that the theme had commended itself to him because of the human situations which, though set in prehistoric times, were of a universal kind. "If my aim here was a close union of poetic and music drama, it was also my concern to recreate the characters in my own idiom as an example of English *bel canto*, the parts carefully designed to bring out the potentialities of each voice according to its range—in the hope of adding another 'singer's opera' to the repertory."

In fact, Walton had created a masterpiece in which he did indeed establish the principal characters with the sureness of a master's touch. Much of the music is written in his strong romantic lyrical vein (Cressida's arias "Slowly it all comes back to me" and "At the haunted end of the day" are good examples), although some commentators felt that the opera was not full-blooded or romantic enough. Walton's writing for massed voices demonstrates here his ability to create great dramatic effect as he had previously done in such works as *Belshazzars's Feast*. He uses a large orchestra, including triple wind, two harps, celesta and a large percussion section, but the scoring is extremely delicate and colorful. Indeed, he acquired in the composition of this opera new skills and sounds, many of which were to be echoed in subsequent works.

Walton was always dissatisfied with Hassall's libretto, which has been described as too "flowery." Hassall had written libretti for Ivor Novello, and Walton thought that his style had been ruined as a result. Cuts were made in each act for a revival in April 1955, and further incisions in April 1963 accounted for about eight more minutes of music being discarded.

Yet somehow the opera still failed to establish itself as a favorite, even in 1976 when yet further cuts were made and the soprano line lowered to suit Dame Janet Baker's mezzo voice. Nevertheless, many felt that the revisions were ill-considered and that Walton had made a cardinal error in transposing the part. One may therefore look forward to the promised recording of the original version in the complete Chandos series which will use the high soprano of Walton's original conception.

—Stewart R. Craggs

THE TROJANS
See LES TROYENS

THE TROUBADOUR
See IL TROVATORE

TROUBLE IN TAHITI and A QUIET PLACE.

Composer: Leonard Bernstein.

Librettist: *Trouble in Tahiti,* Leonard Bernstein; *A Quiet Place,* Stephen Wadsworth.

First Performance: *Trouble in Tahiti,* Waltham, Massachusetts, Brandeis University, 12 June 1952; *A Quiet Place,* Houston, Houston Grand Opera, 17 June 1983 [revised 1984].

Roles: *Trouble in Tahiti:* Dinah (mezzo-soprano); Sam (bass-baritone); Trio (soprano or mezzo-soprano, tenor, baritone). *A Quiet Place:* Funeral Director (tenor); Bill (baritone); Susie (mezzo-soprano); Analyst (tenor); Doc (bass); Mrs Doc (contralto); Dede (soprano); François (tenor); Junior (baritone); Sam (bass).

Publications

article–

Wadsworth, S. "A Quiet Place: Librettist's Notes." Notes for *A Quiet Place,* Deutsche Grammophon 419 761-2 (1987).

* * *

Although Leonard Bernstein had already ventured into the theatrical medium in the 1940s, *Trouble in Tahiti* (1952) represents his initial effort in the operatic genre. Several years earlier he had made his mark in the musical theater with the scores for the ballet *Fancy Free* (1944) and the Broadway musical *On the Town* (1944, derived from the ballet). It should not seem surprising then that elements from the musical styles of these works emerge in the score for *Trouble in Tahiti,* particularly the jazz-influenced timbres and rhythms, and such popular-song style musical numbers as the opening radio commercial-inspired trio. Bernstein dedicated *Trouble in Tahiti* to Marc Blitzstein, whose caustic influence on the text is felt throughout the work.

Trouble in Tahiti chronicles a single day in the troubled marriage of Sam and Dinah. Sam is self-indulgent and ambitious; Dinah consults an analyst to clarify the desperate circumstances of her life. Caught in the middle is young Junior, who must suffer the neglect of his self-absorbed and uncommunicative parents. Neither Sam nor Dinah can bridge the ever-increasing gap that separates them. In the end both fail in their mutually groping attempts to talk about their estrangement. They escape its consequences by going to a movie together, *Trouble in Tahiti,* where they will not have to confront the bleakness of their shared lives.

Bernstein successfully merges and contrasts elements of the popular musical theater and the conventional opera house in *Trouble in Tahiti.* For example, he employs elements of scat singing in the jazz-inspired Trio—situated either downstage or off-stage—that comments on the action. In contrast, Dinah's aria "There is a Garden," although written in a

popular song form and idiom, reveals Bernstein's close attention to details of larger operatic form and nuance. He interrupts the verses of her aria with brief digressions for Sam and the orchestra. The section then concludes with an elaborate duet for them that paraphrases one of Erik Satie's *Gymnopédies.* This entire section reflects the work's character as an opera perhaps better than any other in the work and represents its musical and dramatic coup.

Less successful however is the merging of styles in *A Quiet Place.* In 1980 Bernstein and Stephen Wadsworth began a collaboration on a sequel to *Trouble in Tahiti* that would eventually become *A Quiet Place.* Along the way to this sequel Bernstein had written *Candide* (1956), *West Side Story* (1957), *Mass* (1971), and even a work entitled *Songfest* (1977), "a study for an American opera." As Wadsworth explains, both men wanted to revitalize and rejuvenate the waning American musical theater and opera, so they worked closely together on the project, revising, rewriting, and trying to recapture the spirit of the earlier work.

A Quiet Place opens with Sam's family in attendance at Dinah's funeral, following her death in an automobile accident. All three acts describe in lurid detail the disintegration of their family over the years, the attempts to bring it together again, and the final, somewhat ambiguously achieved reconciliation.

In its original version *A Quiet Place* consisted of one act with four scenes; it had followed *Trouble in Tahiti* on a double bill. At the urging of conductor John Mauceri, and after poor reviews from the preview in Houston, Bernstein and Wadsworth rewrote *A Quiet Place.* This subsequent version integrates *Trouble in Tahiti* much more thoroughly and ingeniously by incorporating it as two flashbacks (act II) in Sam's mind as he reads through Dinah's diary and later recalls his past.

Much of *A Quiet Place* derives from *Trouble in Tahiti,* both musically and textually, either as a direct quotation, harmonic progression, or musical/textual phrase that clearly alludes to the earlier work. For example, the opening musical passage in the prologue quotes fragments from *Trouble in Tahiti.* By integrating thematic and dramatic elements from *Trouble in Tahiti* into *A Quiet Place,* the collaborators have attempted to magnify and expand on the original idea. One of the most successful examples of this integration occurs in Sam's act I aria "You're Late," which blends textual and motivic elements from *Trouble in Tahiti* with the more contemporary musical idiom of *A Quiet Place.* Ultimately, however, this procedure represents both a strength and weakness of the opera. Whereas it achieves a sense of cohesion between the two temporally and stylistically incongruous works, it also calls attention to the disparity in musical idiom and language. *Trouble in Tahiti,* which works well as a self-sufficient opera in its own right, intrudes upon the textual and compositional style of *A Quiet Place.*

While Bernstein and Wadsworth have endeavored to integrate the two works through the use of common musical motives and textual allusion, they do not realize the dramatic or musical unity and continuity of the earlier opera. Much that fails in *A Quiet Place* should be blamed on the inadequacies of the libretto. Only in isolated instances does the libretto attain the dramatic intensity and concision of the earlier work. By incorporating many of the worst melodramatic elements of ordinary soap opera, it becomes increasingly ineffectual and prosaic on repeated hearings.

Both *Trouble in Tahiti* and *A Quiet Place* contain many autobiographical elements (as Joan Peyser points out in her controversial biography of Bernstein). However, both librettos can and should be interpreted as much wider and serious indictments of contemporary Western/American society, mores, and culture. Although the works are frequently mired in pretentiousness and obscure allusion, their social commentary has not yet received its due recognition. Perhaps the unsavoriness of the material and its peculiar representation have undermined its message.

—William Thornhill

IL TROVATORE [The Troubadour].

Composer: Giuseppe Verdi.

Librettists: Salvadore Cammarano and L.E. Bardare (after García Gutiérrez, *El trovador*).

First Performance: Rome, Apollo, 19 January 1853.

Roles: Manrico (tenor); Count di Luna (baritone); Leonora (soprano); Azucena (contralto or mezzo-soprano); Ferrando (bass); Inez (mezzo-soprano); Ruiz (tenor); chorus (SATB).

Publications

book–

John, Nicholas, ed. *Giuseppe Verdi: Il trovatore.* London, 1983.

articles–

Rosen, David. "*Le trouvère:* Comparing Verdi's French Version with his Original." *Opera News* 41/no. 22 (1977): 16.
Drabkin, William M. "Characters, Key Relations, and Tonal Structure in *Il trovatore.*" *Music Analysis* 1 (1982).
Parker, Roger. "The Dramatic Structure of *Il trovatore.*" *Music Analysis* 1 (1982).
Petrobelli, Pierluigi, et al. "Verdi's *Il trovatore:* a Symposium." *Music Analysis* 1/no. 2 (1982): 125.
Black, John M. "Salvadore Cammarano's Programme for *Il trovatore* and the Problem of the Finale." *Studi verdiani* 2 (1983): 78.
Avant-scène opéra February (1984) [*Le trouvère* issue].
Lawton, David. "*Le trouvère:* Verdi's Revision of *Il trovatore* for Paris." *Studi verdiani* 3 (1985): 79.

*　　*　　*

During the civil wars in fifteenth-century Spain, Ferrando, the captain of the di Luna forces, tells his soldiers how, years before, a gypsy hag was found bending over the cradle of the family's newborn boy, Garzia, and how, when the baby's health began to fail, they hunted the gypsy down and burned her at the stake. Then the gypsy's daughter avenged her mother by stealing the baby from his cradle, and the family, after a frantic search, found only a half-charred infant skeleton on the spot where the old woman had been burned. The lost baby's father died of grief, but not before he had made his other son swear he would never stop searching for his brother.

The son has grown up to be the Count di Luna, enamored of the lady Leonora, who in turn loves a mysterious troubadour. Beneath Leonora's window, the count clashes with the troubadour, who lifts his visor and reveals himself as a political enemy of the di Lunas, Manrico. Later the rivals face each other again in the battle of Pelilla, where Manrico is left for dead.

In the mountains of Biscay, Manrico has been nursed back to health by his mother, the gypsy woman Azucena, who tells him how, long ago, she had stolen the di Luna baby and, with her own infant at her breast, returned to the spot where they had burned her mother, and in crazed confusion cast into the fire there her own infant. The horrified Manrico then wonders about his own identity. He clashes again with the Count di Luna at the convent where Leonora, who has presumed him dead, is about to become a nun. He is finally captured by the count when the di Lunas seize Azucena and he rushes to defend her.

Leontyne Price and Piero Cappucilli in *Il trovatore,* **Salzburg Festival, 1977**

Leonora, in desperation, offers herself to the count in return for Manrico's life. The count assents, then finds that Leonora has secretly taken poison. In fury he orders Manrico's immediate execution, dragging Azucena to the prison window to watch. When the ax falls, Azucena shrieks to the Count what we have feared even to suspect—that he has killed the brother he had sought for all his life. The gypsy woman falls lifeless with the cry, "Mother, you are avenged."

The plot of *Il trovatore,* often unjustly maligned, reflects Verdi's furiously pessimistic view of the world. When he himself was a baby, his mother fled with him in her arms to escape the sabres of a vindictive Russian regiment. He saw his own two children die of illness within the span of a few months, followed in time by their young mother. The year before he wrote *Il trovatore,* his own mother died. His librettist died in the midst of writing it. When the opera appeared, Verdi wrote, "People say that it is too sad, that there are too many deaths in it. But death is all there is to life. What else is there?"

Il trovatore's chaotic text is, on close inspection, full of subtleties, ironies, patterns of imagery. Manrico, for example, is associated in Leonora's first aria with the moon, and the moon emerges from the clouds to reveal his face as he lifts his visor, though no one present knows that his real name is Garzia di Luna (Garzia of the Moon), and eventually he goes to his death never knowing who he was. The four main characters, caught as they are in fixed attitudes, are emotionally charged symbols of life's ironies—Manrico of the inability of any man to know himself, the count of the destructiveness of human passion, Leonora of the futility of self-sacrifice, Azucena of the relentless and confused operation of instinct in a universe that is overwhelmingly cruel to its creatures.

Verdi brought the terrifying story to vivid musical life. Manrico's "Ah sì, ben mio" and Leonore's "D'amor sull' ali rosee," which draw on past *bel canto* traditions, are among the most beautiful arias he ever wrote, while the count's "Il balen" illustrates his new and demanding way of writing for high baritone, and Azucena's music looks forward to the dramatic intensity of his later work. But the source of *Il trovatore*'s strength lies in more than its famous melodies. Francis Toye has said of it, "Something emerges and hits you, as it were, between the eyes, something elemental, furious, wholly true."

—M. Owen Lee

TROYANOS, Tatiana.

Mezzo-soprano. Born 12 September 1938, in New York. Studied with Hans Heinz and at the Juilliard School of Music; debut as Hippolyta in *A Midsummer Night's Dream,* New York City Opera, 1963; member of the Hamburg State Opera, 1965-75; created role of Sister Jeanne in Penderecki's *The Devils of Loudon,* 1969; Covent Garden debut, 1969; engaged by Paris Opéra, 1971; Metropolitan Opera debut as Octavian in *Der Rosenkavalier,* 1976.

Publications

About TROYANOS: articles–

Mayer, Michael. "Tatiana Troyanos." *Opera* March (1985).

*　　*　　*

Tatiana Troyanos is an increasingly rare example of a singer who seems identified in the public's mind with a particular theater—in this case, the Metropolitan Opera. Although she has had a major international career, New York audiences (for whom she has performed regularly since the 1960s) feel a particular sense of pride in her accomplishments. Troyanos has become almost a latter-day Risë Stevens, much beloved by fans who virtually heard her "grow up" at the Met and develop—through nearly three decades and several management regimes—into a mature and special artist, gifted with a burnished mezzo-soprano voice and a vibrant theatrical sense.

These vocal and theatrical attributes have been with Troyanos from the start; over the years her passionate involvement has only increased, while her voice remains remarkably unchanged. At the time of this writing, Troyanos is just over fifty years old but still seems—and sounds—like a young singer. Her voice retains a unique throaty quality which is instantly recognizable, and although the sound has darkened a bit over time, the top is still as bright and assured as that of many sopranos.

It is the glory of her upper register that has made Troyanos such a successful exponent of roles that lie somewhere between soprano and mezzo. Santuzza in *Cavalleria rusticana,* Adalgisa in *Norma,* Giulietta in *Les contes d'Hoffmann,* the Composer in *Ariadne auf Naxos,* Venus in *Tannhäuser* and Kundry in *Parsifal* are just a few examples of these parts: Troyanos, possessed of a perfectly even voice over a wide range, encompasses them all with ease, and brings to each a fervor and ardor which are hers alone. Actually she scored one of her earliest triumphs when she created the soprano role of Sister Jeanne in Penderecki's *Teufel von Loudun,* whose high tessitura and difficult musical intervals say much for Troyanos' vocal skills and musicianship. Her intense portrayal was an acting triumph as well, and it is tempting to find in Troyanos—a New York born singer of Greek descent—links with her heritage, for her flashing brunette goodlooks, the dark glow of her mezzo-soprano and her fiery stage presence remind us of another great singer with a similar background: Maria Callas.

And, like Callas's, there is a distinctive strength and color to Troyanos's lower register as well, and she uses this marvelously shadowy sound to superb dramatic effect. Her physical and vocal gifts make her a natural as Carmen; here as elsewhere the persistent pulse of her vibrato (which, it should be said, is not to every listener's taste) becomes a vital part of the character and one senses a fiercely elemental life force as it rises and ultimately ebbs away. Her Eboli (*Don Carlos*) and Dido (*Les Troyens*) achieve a similar stature and feeling of commitment.

Yet as successful as these assumptions have been, it would do Troyanos a disservice to characterize her as a specialist in the world of fervent and doomed heroines. Her excellent training and technique have given her real skills in florid music. Troyanos has not chosen to sing much Rossini but has given admirably fluent performances of Romeo in Bellini's *I Capuleti ed i Montecchi* and Sesto in Mozart's *La clemenza di Tito.* In recent years, she has also become a noted Handel stylist, and in addition to a distinguished reading of *Ariodante,* Troyanos must be one of very few singers to take on both the roles of Cleopatra and Caesar in *Giulio Cesare.* And she has a marvelous flair for comedy—her Dorabella in *Così fan tutte* is a delight.

Although she has inexplicably never made a recital record, Troyanos has had a long and fruitful recording career. Many of these discs capture her faithfully—or, more properly, as faithfully as is possible without her marvelous physical presence. Her performances as Carmen and the Composer, both with Georg Solti, are worthy souvenirs of these monumental portrayals, and in rather a different vein her recording of Cleopatra under Karl Richter reveals Troyanos' liquid sensuality of tone and ease in coloratura. In fact, she has never made a bad record, and—artist that she is—in every case Troyanos contributes something unique and memorable.

—David Anthony Fox

LES TROYENS [The Trojans].

Composer: Hector Berlioz.

Librettist: Hector Berlioz (after Virgil).

First Performance: Paris, Théâtre-Lyrique, 4 November 1863 (part II); first complete performance in German, as *Die Eroberung Trojas,* Carlsruhe, 5 and 6 December, 1890.

Roles: Part I—*La Prise de Troie*: Cassandra (soprano); Choroebus (baritone); Aeneas (tenor); Helenus (tenor); Ascanius (soprano); Hecuba (mezzo-soprano); Pantheus (bass); Priam (bass); Ghost of Hector (bass); Polyxena (soprano); Andromache (mute); Astyanax (mute); chorus (SSATTBB).

Part II—*Les Troyens à Carthage*: Dido (mezzo-soprano or soprano); Anna (contralto); Aeneas (tenor) Ascanius (soprano); Narbal (baritone); Pantheus (bass); Iopas (tenor); Hylas (tenor); Mercury (baritone); Two Soldiers (baritone, bass); Ghost of Cassandra (soprano); Ghost of Choroebus (baritone); Ghost of Hector (baritone); Ghost of Priam (bass); chorus (SATBB).

Publications

books–

Destranges, E. *Les Troyens de Berlioz: étude analytique.* Paris, 1897.
Kemp, Ian, ed. *Hector Berlioz: Les Troyens.* Cambridge, 1988.

articles–

Jullien, A. "Les Troyens." *Musica* 7 (1908): 43.
Servières, G. "Pièces inédites relatives aux Troyens." *La revue musicale* 5 (1924): 147.
Newman, E. "Les Troyens." In *Opera Nights,* 283. London, 1943.
Klein, J.W. "*Les Troyens.*" *Monthly Musical Record* 87 (1957): 83.
Dickinson, A.E.F. "Berlioz and the Trojans." *Durham University Journal* 20 (1958): 24.
_____. "Music for the Aeneid." In *Greece and Rome,* 2nd series 6 (1959): 129.

Fraenkel, Gottfried. "Berlioz, the Princess, and *Les Troyens.*" *Music and Letters* 44 (1963): 249.
Cairns, David. "Berlioz's Epic Opera." *The Listener* 76 (1966): 364.
_____. "Berlioz and Virgil." *Proceedings of the Royal Musical Association* 45 (1968-69): 97; revised in *Responses,* London, 1973.
Kuhn, H. "Antike Massen: Zu einigen Motiven in *Les Troyens* von Hector Berlioz." In *Opernstudien: Anna Amalie Abert zum 65. Geburtstag,* 141. Tutzing, 1975.
Beye, Charles Rowan. "Sunt lacrimae rerum." *Parnassus* 10 (1982): 75.
Rushton, Julian. "The Overture to Les Troyens." *Music Analysis* 4 (1985): 119.

*   *   *

Part I: *La Prise de Troie.* In the tenth year of the Trojan War, the Greeks appear at last to have sailed away, and the Trojans are jubilant. Only the prophetic princess Cassandra believes that the city is still in danger. She pleads in vain with her lover Choroebus to save himself. Despite her warnings, the Trojans escort into the city a huge wooden horse which the Greeks have left, supposedly as a votive offering, on the shore. That night, as Greek troops pour out of the horse and open the gates of Troy, the Trojan hero Aeneas is warned in a dream by the ghost of the dead prince Hector to escape with what people he can and found a new city in Italy. Cassandra and the Trojan women slay themselves rather than submit to the victorious Greeks.

Part II: *Les Troyens à Carthage.* Aeneas and the survivors of the Trojan War, shipwrecked off the coast of Carthage, are received by Queen Dido. Though she has sworn fidelity to her dead husband Sychaeus, she falls in love with Aeneas when he defends her city against the Numidians and tells her of all the dangers he has passed. They consummate their love in a cave when their royal hunt is interrupted by a storm. But Aeneas, warned by the mysterious cry of the god Mercury and by apparitions of the dead Trojans he has left behind, sets sail again for Italy. Dido, on a terrace by the sea, curses him, falls on his sword, and immolates herself, predicting amid the flames that an avenger (Hannibal) shall rise from her ashes, but seeing too a vision of the imperial Rome that eventually will be the fulfillment of Aeneas' mission.

Virgil was a main source of inspiration for Hector Berlioz, who, named after the noblest Trojan of them all, was moved to tears when, as a boy, he construed the *Aeneid* in Latin with the help of his father. In *Les Troyens,* he limits himself mainly to the first four books of Virgil's twelve-book epic. But the song of the young sailor in the masthead, written by Berlioz with his own sailor son in mind, is derived from the famous Palinurus incident in Book V; Aeneas' touching solo "Others, my son, will teach you to be happy" comes from Book XII; and there are echoes of Virgil's earlier *Eclogues* and *Georgics* in the song of the minstrel Iopas, the figure in the opera who may be thought to represent Virgil himself.

Virgilians will also detect the sound of the dactylic hexameter, "the stateliest measure ever moulded by the lips of man," in such passages as the chorus sung by the Trojans when they first appear, and in the whispering orchestral nocturne that accompanies the love duet of Dido and Aeneas. Another main influence, Shakespeare, enters at that moment, as the lovers trade mythic reminiscences ("In such a night . . .") as Jessica and Lorenzo do in the moonlit night in *The Merchant of*

Venice. On many pages of the score, Berlioz shows his extraordinary sensitivity to the suggestive powers of instruments, while his long-lined melodies remain, after a century, absolutely unique.

Les Troyens was regarded as eccentric and unperformable in Berlioz' day, and he never saw his five-and-a-half-hour epic staged complete. Its rejection was a source of immense sorrow to him, and Gounod remarked that, like his namesake, Hector Berlioz died beneath the walls of Troy. The first publication of the complete score in 1969, the performance that year at Covent Garden, and the subsequent complete recording under Colin Davis, are among the most important musicological events of this century. *Les Troyens* is now rightly thought to be *the* classic of French opera.

—M. Owen Lee

TSAR AND CARPENTER
See ZAR UND ZIMMERMANN

TUCKER, Richard.

Tenor. Born 28 August 1913, in New York. Died 8 January 1975, in Kalamazoo, Michigan. Studied with Paul Althouse; debut as Alfredo in Verdi's *La traviata* with the Salmaggi Opera, New York, 1943; Metropolitan Opera debut as Enzio in *La Gioconda,* 1945; sang at the Met from 1945 until 1975 in 30 leading roles; European debut in *La Gioconda* at the Verona Arena, 1947.

Publications

About TUCKER: articles—

Gualerzi, G. "Tucker, Richard." In *Le grandi voci,* Rome, 1964.
"Richard Tucker," *Opera News* 39 (1975): 7.
Kolodin, I. "The wholly improbable Richard Tucker." *Opera News* 39 (1975): 28.

* * *

Richard Tucker was a leading member of the generation of singers who, during World War II, produced a kind of American golden age of vocalism at the Metropolitan Opera in New York. Even among such artists as his fellow tenor (and brother-in-law) Jan Peerce, baritones Leonard Warren and Robert Merrill, and sopranos Eleanor Steber and Risë Stevens, he was distinguished by the beauty and power of his voice and the fervor and enthusiasm of his style. During his thirty seasons at the Metropolitan Opera he never gave an indifferent performance, skillfully utilizing a *lirico-spinto* tenor voice that could encompass the forcefulness of Canio in *Pagliacci* and the suavity of Ferrando in *Così fan tutte.* He sang some thirty roles and over 400 performances at the Metropolitan, becoming one of its most dependable performers and distinctive personalities. Many regarded him as the finest operatic tenor ever produced by the United States.

Among his warmest admirers was Metropolitan Opera general manager Rudolf Bing, who made Tucker one of the bulwarks of his regime. "Caruso, Caruso, that's all you hear!" Bing said in 1956. "I have an idea that we're going to be proud some day to tell people we heard Richard Tucker."

Tucker was born 28 August 1913 in Brooklyn, New York, the son of poor Jewish immigrants from Bessarabia. His name at birth was Reuben Ticker; he changed it about the time he was beginning his adult singing career, although his family and intimate friends always called him "Ruby." His first job was as a boy alto at the age of six in a Lower East Side Manhattan synagogue, and he later sang at weddings and bar-mitzvahs. After leaving high school (before graduating) he went into the business of making silk linings for fur coats, while pursuing vocal studies with Paul Althouse, the veteran Wagnerian tenor.

Tucker began his professional career as a cantor, conducting services at the Brooklyn Jewish Center, one of the city's largest synagogues. In 1941 he entered the Metropolitan Opera Auditions of the Air, but was not selected as a winner. However, three years later Althouse persuaded Edward Johnson, then the general director of the Metropolitan Opera, to visit the Brooklyn temple to hear him. As Tucker remembered it, Johnson offered him a contract and remarked, "If you can hold an audience of 2,000 in a synagogue, you can hold an audience of 3,600 in an opera house."

Johnson proved to be an accurate prophet, for when Tucker made his Metropolitan Opera debut as Enzo Grimaldo in *La gioconda* on 25 January 1945 he received ovations after "Cielo e mar" and at the conclusion of the opera. Henceforth, he proceeded methodically and with growing artistry through the Italian repertory, and also undertook successfully such French roles as Don José in *Carmen* and Hoffmann in *Les contes d'Hoffmann.* In 1951 Bing asked him to sing Ferrando in an English-language production of *Così fan tutte.* Tucker at first was reluctant to sing Mozart but eventually consented. "I'm glad I did," he said afterward, "it was like honey to my voice." He participated in the Metropolitan Opera recording of *Così,* one of many recordings (including several solo collections) he made.

Possessing a strong and stocky build (he had been an athlete in high school) Tucker was a natural if unpolished actor, who plunged into each new role with unbridled eagerness. He also developed a reputation in the house as a prankster, once inserting a nude picture into the small casket which baritone Robert Merrill was to open during act III of *La forza del destino.* On another occasion he surprised Mr Bing and the audience by bursting into Italian for the aria "M'appari" in an English-language performance of Flotow's *Martha.*

Tucker remained an ordained cantor throughout his life; in 1967 during the Vietnam War he conducted Passover Seder services for Jewish servicemen in Saigon, and his foreign tours took him to Israel as well as to Italy. His religious sensibilities prevented him from wearing a crucifix in operas requiring him to play the roles of priests or prelates. One famous story at the Met tells of the time he was rehearsing the role of Don Alvaro in the final scene of *La forza del destino.* As he lay prostrate in grief and penitence at the feet of Padre Guardino, bass Jerome Hines, playing the monk, unthinkingly began making the sign of the cross over him. Indignantly, Tucker leaped to his feet and shouted: "Not over my dead body, you don't!"

However, Tucker felt honored to be asked to sing César Franck's *Panis Angelicus* at St Patrick's Cathedral at the funeral of Robert Kennedy, and he held honorary degrees from two Roman Catholic universities, Notre Dame and St

John's. He seldom appeared with other American companies, but made an exception to sing at Carnegie Hall in a concert version of Halévy's *La Juive,* an opera he vainly tried to persuade Bing to stage for him at the Metropolitan Opera. "He said it was old-fashioned," complained Tucker. "So what opera isn't?" On the 25th anniversary of his debut, the Metropolitan Opera did him the rare honor of holding a Richard Tucker Gala, during which he appeared opposite Leontyne Price, Joan Sutherland and Renata Tebaldi in one act of three different operas.

Tucker was deeply attached to his wife Sara and inordinately proud of his three sons, a doctor, a lawyer and a stockbroker. At least one, and sometimes all, of the family was in the house whenever he sang. "So far as I am concerned," Tucker once said, "an artist can live on better through a family's love and memories than in annals and archives. That is the real immortality."

Richard Tucker was still in full career when he died of a heart attack on 8 January 1975 as he prepared to give a concert in Kalamazoo, Michigan. His family has established in his honor the Richard Tucker Award which gives an annual stipend of $20,000 to a promising young singer. The annual prize-giving takes place at a Carnegie Hall concert in which many of today's Metropolitan Opera stars participate. It is a memorial very much in the spirit of Richard Tucker.

—Herbert Kupferberg

TURANDOT.

Composer: Ferruccio Busoni.

Librettist: Ferruccio Busoni (after Carlo Gozzi).

First Performance: Zurich, Stadttheater, 11 May 1917.

Roles: Turandot (soprano); Kalaf (tenor); Altoum (bass); Adelma (mezzo-soprano); Barak (baritone); Mother of Black Samarkand Prince (mezzo-soprano); Truffaldino (tenor); Pantalone (baritone); Tartaglia (baritone); Eight Doctors (four tenor, four bass); Singer (soprano); Executioner (mute); chorus (SSATTB).

Publications

articles–

Flinois, Pierre. "Ferruccio Busoni: une autre Turandot." *Avant-scène opéra* May-June (1981).

*   *   *

In 1904 Ferruccio Busoni composed an orchestral suite inspired by the *Turandot* myth, and in 1911 he added two extra items to these seven movements, in order to provide incidental music for Max Reinhardt's Berlin production of Gozzi's play. The idea of turning this music into an opera first entered Busoni's mind when he saw an extravagant production of the play in London in 1913; and so three years later, when he was seeking a companion piece to be staged alongside his own opera *Arlecchino,* he turned to *Turandot.* Busoni described this new work as the result of "the hasty decision to form a two act opera out of the material and substance of *Turandot.* I am rewriting it closer in tone to a pantomime or stage play; the mask-figures, common to both pieces, serve to link them, though they otherwise contrast completely with each other." He provided his own libretto in German, the language in which he believed future performances were most likely, although during the war years he settled in Switzerland and declined professional contact with any of the belligerent nations. The double bill of *Arlecchino* and *Turandot* received its premiere in Zurich in May 1917.

In general terms the plot is that of Puccini's more famous opera of the same name, though there are of course some significant differences. Among these is the role of Barak, servant to Prince Kalaf, who is present in the Busoni version only. The two characters appear together in the first scene of act I, which is set in the central square of Peking. They discuss the story of Princess Turandot and her habit of executing her suitors if they fail to answer three riddles. At that point the Queen Mother of Samarkand passes, cursing Turandot, for her son has just been beheaded. She scornfully throws the Princess's portrait to the ground. Kalaf, on looking at it, falls instantly in love with Turandot and swears to take up the challenge and avenge the Prince of Samarkand.

The chief eunuch Truffaldino prepares the room for the trial, and fanfares announce Emperor Altoum, who shows no appetite for the affair and hopes for a happy resolution. Kalaf kneels before the Emperor, and when Turandot eventually arrives, she is noticeably moved by the Prince's stature. When he has successfully answered the first two riddles—the Human Mind and Tradition—she offers him the opportunity to depart, but Kalaf continues and answers the third riddle correctly: Art. (Busoni's riddles are therefore of a metaphysical nature.) Despite the general rejoicing, Turandot is deeply wounded, and Kalaf offers to free her if she can discover his name and parentage.

In act II the emperor tells Turandot he knows the name but will not reveal it: she should accept her destiny. Her slave Adelma, on the other hand, claims that she too is of royal birth and that the unknown prince once spurned her. As reward for her revelation, Adelma is granted her freedom. In the final scene funeral music is heard for Turandot, but when the dejected Kalaf turns to leave, she calls him back and welcomes him as husband.

Unlike Puccini's Princess, Busoni's Turandot is more than a cruel yet beautiful figure: she has intellectual stature and is driven to savagery in her search for her equal. Likewise, Altoum is here a more sympathetic figure, wise and noble. The masks, Truffaldino and the ministers Pantalone and Tartaglia, are comic creatures, cold-blooded in nature and close to the world of *Arlecchino,* while the chorus is important in representing the people of Peking. Kalaf's idealism, expressed through especially demanding vocal writing, is affirmed at the close.

The opera was written quickly, and musically it draws mainly on existing material. The first scene, for instance, derives from the opening movement of the *Turandot* suite; of all the music in act I, Altoum's dignified and sensitive aria is the most substantial of the new additions. At the beginning of act II, the famous "Greensleeves" tune is heard as slave girls dance. It seems Busoni was unaware of its English heritage, for he had previously used it in a set of piano pieces, under the title *Turandots Frauengemach.*

In the revival for the 1921 Berlin production, Busoni replaced the original spoken dialogue for the moment when Turandot reveals Kalaf's name; and this new music leads straight into the finale, a subtly built apotheosis of all the important themes. The opera ends, as did the suite before it, with lively dance music.

Busoni's *Turandot* is designed primarily as an entertainment rather than as a powerful drama, and though its tendency towards motor rhythms is contrasted against moments of great lyricism, its style can reasonably be identified as neoclassical. Although it will always be overshadowed by Puccini's opera, it should not be underestimated and certainly deserves occasional revival.

—Terry Barfoot

TURANDOT.

Composer: Giacomo Puccini.

Librettists: Giuseppe Adami and Renato Simoni (after Carlo Gozzi).

First Performance: Milan, Teatro alla Scala, 25 April 1926 [unfinished; completed by Franco Alfano].

Roles: Turandot (soprano); Calaf (tenor); Liù (soprano); Timur (bass); Ping (baritone); Pang (tenor); Pong (tenor); Emperor Altoum (tenor); Herald (baritone); chorus (SATTB).

Publications

books–

Marini, R.B. La "Turandot" di Giacomo Puccini. Florence, 1942.

John, Nicholas, ed. Giacomo Puccini: "Turandot". London and New York, 1984.

Ashbrook, William, and Harold Powers. Puccini's "Turandot": The End of the Great Tradition. Princeton, 1991.

articles–

Smith, Gordon. "Alfano and *Turandot*." *Opera* March (1973).

Revers, Peter. "Analytische Betrachtungen zu Puccinis *Turandot*." *Österreichische Musikzeitung* 34 (1979): 342.

Avant-scène opéra May-June (1981) [*Turandot* issue].

Ashbrook, William. "*Turandot* and its Posthumous *prima*." *Opera Quarterly* 2 (1984): 126.

Maehder, Jürgen. "Studien zum Fragmentcharakter von Giacomo Puccinis *Turandot*." *Analecta Musicologica* 22 (1984): 279.

Atlas, Allan W. "Newly Discovered Sketches for Puccini's *Turandot* at the Pierpont Morgan Library." *Cambridge Opera Journal* 3 (1991): 173.

unpublished–

Girardi, Michele. "Turandot: il futuro internotto del melodramma italiana." Ph.D. dissertation, Università degli Studi di Venezia, 1980.

* * *

In March 1920, a meeting between Puccini, Giuseppe Adami (librettist of *La rondine* and *Il tabarro*), and Renato Simoni (a critic at the *Corriere della sera*) brought forth the idea to consider *Turandotte*, a play by the Venetian playwright Carlo Gozzi (1720-1806) for a new opera. *Turandotte* as the model for an opera was by no means a new idea; several composers before Puccini, including Ferruccio Busoni and Antonio Bazzini, one of Puccini's teachers at the Milan conservatory, had already written operas on the subject, with varying degrees of success. Puccini's first introduction to the play was in the form of an Italian translation by Andrea Maffei of Friedrich Schiller's German adaptation of Gozzi's play. He was sufficiently impressed by his reading of the play that he decided to request a libretto from Adami and Simoni. Initial work on the libretto progressed quickly, but many painstaking revisions caused *Turandot* to become Puccini's most fussed over opera since *Manon Lescaut*. In fact, not until September 1924 did Puccini finally receive a version for the final duet that suited him, and this late date is most responsible for Puccini's inability to complete the score before his death.

Adami's and Simoni's libretto, while maintaining essential aspects of Gozzi's play, offers a completely new text which simplifies Gozzi's convoluted plot and adds elements not found in Gozzi. The Princess Turandot, daughter of the Chinese Emperor Altoum, has taken a vow that she will only be the bride of a royal suitor who can solve three riddles which she will pose. The punishment for any suitor who fails to solve all three riddles is death by beheading. Her reason for this vow, as Turandot will explain, is to avenge her ancestress Lo-u-Ling, who was abducted thousands of years ago by the King of the Tartars, who had defeated China in battle. Many suitors have tried to win Turandot, but all have failed, their heads, impaled on stakes, serving as grim reminders of their fate.

At the beginning of the first act, the crowd witnesses the proclamation of a mandarin announcing Turandot's law and the upcoming execution of the Prince of Persia, the latest suitor who has failed to solve all three riddles and is to be executed the same night. Among the crowd are Timur, the old Tartar King, deposed by the Chinese, and his companion, the slave-girl Liù. They soon discover Calaf, Timur's son, whom they had believed was killed in battle with the Chinese. Thus, both Calaf and Timur find themselves fugitives in the country of their enemies.

After the Prince of Persia is led to his execution, Calaf, who at first had cursed Turandot for her cruelty, catches a glimpse of her and falls madly in love. He resolves to conquer her by solving the three riddles. All efforts by Liù (who loves Calaf), by Timur, and by the three courtiers, Ping, Pang, and Pong, to dissuade Calaf, fail, and Calaf strikes the gong as a signal that a new suitor is ready to accept the challenge.

In act II, Calaf is subjected to the three riddles and solves them. The stunned Turandot begs her father not to give her to the unknown stranger, but Altoum explains that the oath is sacred and must be fulfilled. Calaf, who does not want to win Turandot without gaining her love, offers to release her from the oath, if she will solve one riddle he will pose: if by dawn she can discover his name, he will offer her his life.

In the third act, all efforts on Turandot's part to determine the stranger's name fail. When it becomes known that Liù knows his name, she, fearful that she might reveal Calaf's name under torture, takes her own life in order to protect him. Thus, Turandot's last chance to exact the stranger's name has disappeared. In the course of her subsequent encounter with Calaf, he kisses her, and Turandot finally succumbs to her feelings of love for Calaf. Acknowledging defeat, she begs Calaf to leave and to take the mystery of his identity

Turandot, with Gwyneth Jones as Turandot and Plácido Domingo as Calaf, Royal Opera, London, 1984

with him. Calaf, by now certain of her love, reveals his name to her, thus putting himself entirely at her mercy. Turandot, instead of demanding his life for having solved his riddle, proclaims that she has discovered the stranger's name: it is "Love."

Very early in the planning process to the opera, Puccini expressed his intention to find some "authentic" musical source material, just as he did while working on *Madama Butterfly*. In a letter to Adami, apparently from the spring of 1920, Puccini writes: "I shall get some old Chinese music too, and descriptions and drawings of different instruments which we shall put on the stage (not in the orchestra)." As it turns out, Puccini derived some of his "Chinese" material from two sources. One of them was a Chinese music box belonging to Baron Fassini, a friend of Puccini's, who had lived in China for a number of years. It played two tunes, both of which Puccini utilized in the opera. The other source was a book, entitled *Chinese Music*, by J.A. van Aalst. Puccini drew four tunes from this book.

Turandot became the most "exotic" of Puccini's operas, not so much for incorporating a few original tunes as for Puccini's fabrication of *couleur locale* through unorthodox orchestration and freely invented, "exotic" thematic material. Puccini creates *chinoiserie* partly through the use of a greatly expanded percussion section, consisting of fourteen different instruments. Some of these are to be found in Chinese music as well, but the exotic effect does not just emanate from them; rather, it is the size of the percussion section which imitates the large percussive apparatus of Chinese cult and court music. In only a few instances is percussion absent from the score, and combinations of several percussive instruments are frequent.

The basis of the Chinese tonal system is essentially anhemitonic pentatonicism; this characteristic can be observed in the original melodies which Puccini made use of. It is not surprising, therefore, that those "exotic" melodies in *Turandot*, which are freely invented by Puccini, are also by and large pentatonic. Needless to say, large portions of the score are steeped in the expanded tonality of late Romanticism, and it is in these passages that the instrumentation is likewise more conventional—"Puccinian." In such sections, for instance, the strings are usually the main carriers of the melody. This is true in particular for the more melodious passages of the main characters, whose parts are then doubled by the strings, a technique for which Puccini is often, strangely enough, criticized. It is important to note that virtually all pentatonic melodies are supported not by *legato* (as opposed to *pizzicato*) strings, but rather by winds and percussion.

Aside from the pentatonically structured passages and the more conventional, tonally expanded sections, Puccini also uses a more purely dissonant mode of expression, as at the beginning of the opera, where two unrelated triads (D minor and C-sharp major) are superimposed. The function of such dissonant passages, similar to the "exotic" sections, often is to create an "alienation effect," portraying the unusual, shocking, or barbaric aspects of the story.

When Puccini died, he had completed the entire score, including orchestration, up to and including Liù's cortège in act III. For the remainder of the opera, the libretto was completed, and Puccini left thirty-six pages of sketches. With the aid of these, Franco Alfano, commissioned by Toscanini and the Ricordi publishing house, embarked on the task of completing the score. His original completion of the opera, which incorporated much of the sketch material left by Puccini, also contained much original music. Toscanini was not pleased with the result, and insisted on changes and cuts. Thus the reduced version (which is the one published in the

scores and usually performed today) is not only 109 measures shorter, but has also retained ungainly transitions from one passage to another where cuts were performed without smoothing over the edges.

Amazingly, Alfano did not inspect Puccini's orchestration until shortly before he had completed his own score. This certainly accounts for the break in orchestral color, most strongly felt in the complete absence of percussion in the final scene. Much criticism has been directed at Alfano's conclusion, and much of it unfairly. The cut-and-paste job of the second version, having been forced upon Alfano, is a reflection more upon his disillusionment with the project than upon his inability to write a coherent score. There is much of merit in Alfano's completion, even though his failure to absorb Puccini's orchestration is perhaps Alfano's greatest shortcoming.

Ever since its premiere in 1926 at the Teatro alla Scala in Milan, *Turandot* has maintained itself in the repertory. Reactions to the opera have always been mixed, and Turandot as an operatic heroine has caused many reviewers considerable problems. She certainly is not a character who arouses genuine empathy. Unlike other Puccini heroines, such as Mimi, Manon, Butterfly, or Minnie, Turandot appears to be an inhuman character, aloof and cruel. She is not a heroine who sincerely moves us (as Mimi or Butterfly do); that role is left to Liù. To many reviewers, Turandot's coldness and cruelty appear unmotivated, her transformation into a loving woman illogical and unconvincing.

But it is too simple to dismiss Turandot as the frigid queen, whose attributes are grossly exaggerated for mere effect, with no dramatic rationale behind the characterization. Turandot is not an Aristotelian heroine whose suffering arouses pity. Nor is *Turandot,* the opera, music drama in the sense that the actions of the protagonists, be they mythical or verisimilar, are dramatically plausible. There is little that is plausible in *Turandot*. It is false, however, to conclude that for this reason, myth in *Turandot* is emptily employed.

Turandot is arguably Puccini's greatest accomplishment. The work illustrates his complete mastery of orchestration, his unsurpassed melodic inventiveness, and his thorough knowledge of harmonic vocabulary. His unfailing gift to create atmosphere has made *Turandot* a most impressive piece of musical theater; the work may well be considered the apex of Italian opera.

—Jürgen Selk

IL TURCO IN ITALIA [The Turk in Italy].

Composer: Gioachino Rossini.

Librettist: F. Romani (after Caterina Mazzolà).

First Performance: Milan, Teatro alla Scala, 14 August 1814.

Roles: Selim (bass); Fiorilla (soprano); Geronio (bass); Narciso (tenor); Prosdocimo (bass); Zaida (soprano); Albazar (tenor); Isaura (soprano); chorus (SATTB).

Publications

article–

Gavazzeni, G. *"Il turco in Italia." La rassegna musicale* 1 (1959).

*   *   *

The plot of *Il turco in Italia* unfolds within the framework of Prosdocimo the Poet's attempt to write a libretto for an *opera buffa.* Within this conceit, the poet can see every episode as a possible number for his opera, and he is not above manipulating the situation for his own ends. A camp of gypsies provides him with an opening chorus and introduces Zaida, the exiled fiancée of a Turkish prince, and Geronio, husband of the flirtatious Fiorilla. Selim, a Turk (and coincidentally Zaida's former fiancé), happens to be visiting Italy, and the poet plans to arrange a meeting between him and Zaida; however, Fiorilla encounters Selim first and invites him to coffee. In a delightful trio ("Un marito sciumunito": An idiotic husband), the poet presents an opera plot about a foolish husband, a capricious wife, and a lover thrown over for a handsome Turk; Geronio and Narciso (who is in love with Fiorilla) are both insulted and Narciso proposes that the hypothetical poet be beaten. In the lively quartet that follows ("Siete Turchi": You are a Turk), husband, wife, Narciso, and the Turk argue and protest the nature of love and fidelity in the two cultures. Geronio will have none of Fiorilla's willfulness. Selim and Fiorilla have planned an elopement; while he waits for her, he is discovered by Zaida. Narciso, Fiorilla and her friends, and then Geronio arrive: the poet is delighted with the ensuing brawl of a sextet ("Ah! che il cor non m'ingannava": Ah! that my heart was not deceiving) as a first finale.

In the second act the Turk tries to buy Fiorilla from Geronio. The two women want Selim to choose between them, but he is unable to decide. Later at a masked ball Zaida dresses as Fiorilla and Narciso as Selim. The identical couples mistakenly pair with their more appropriate partners, leading to a marvelous *buffo* quintet in which the befuddled Geronio desperately tries to discover and claim his wife. Finally, prompted by the poet, Geronio pretends to divorce Fiorilla and send her home to her parents; she is chastened and reconciled with Geronio. The happy ending sees Selim and Zaida returning together to Turkey and Narciso pardoned.

Despite the suggestion of the title that *Il turco in Italia* was capitalizing on the success of *L'italiana in Algeri* (*The Italian Girl in Algiers*), the plot is not derivative of the earlier work; and despite the fact that the first Milanese audiences felt that Rossini had cheated them by borrowing from himself, almost all of the music is newly composed. It must be noted that an anonymous collaborator wrote not only all the *secco* recitatives of the opera (a typical practice), but also arias for Geronio ("Vado in traccia d'una zingara": I'm looking for a gypsy) and Albazar ("Ah! sarebbe troppo dolce": Ah! it would be too sweet) and the entire second finale. For Rossini the first-act finale is a musical highpoint. His concern centered on the interaction of characters, dramatically and musically, in the unresolved complexities of the mid-point of the opera. The expression of the characters' satisfaction with the resolution of those conflicts at the end of the opera could be entrusted to a collaborator. Indeed, the denouement of some of Rossini's serious operas occurs so swiftly that a tragic ending could be changed to a happy one with minimal disruption to the rest of the opera: he provided both *Tancredi* and *Otello,* for example,

with revised endings which reverse the fortunes of the previous one.

Unfortunately, *Il turco in Italia* was published in the nineteenth century as a Parisian *pastiche:* apparently a one-act reduction Rossini made for the Théâtre-Italien was refleshed with numbers from other operas. The delights of the original version were essentially unknown for a century until its revival with Maria Callas in 1950.

Il turco in Italia is carefully constructed and reveals the strong influence Mozart's comic operas had on the young Rossini. The opera depends largely on its ensembles to develop the dramatic and comic situations as well as to reveal the psychological dimensions of the characters. Their various encounters in sentiment, anger, and confusion inspire Rossini to some of his liveliest music, as in the quintet's canonic passage, "Questo vecchio maledetto": This accursed old fellow), or the trio for Geronio, Narciso, and the poet. There are also lovely moments of reflection, as in the unaccompanied passage of the quintet ("Deh! raffrena, amor pietoso, tanti affetti del cor mio": Ah! gentle love, restrain the abundant feelings of my heart). Fiorilla's aria "Squallida veste, e bruna" (Drab, dark garments), in which she repents her treatment of her husband, reveals an unexpected, deeper level of this apparent coquette's personality.

—Patricia Brauner

THE TURK IN ITALY
See IL TURCO IN ITALIA

THE TURN OF THE SCREW.

Composer: Benjamin Britten.

Librettist: M. Piper (after Henry James).

First Performance: Venice, La Fenice, 14 September 1954.

Roles: Governess (soprano); Mrs Grose (soprano); Miss Jessel (soprano); Peter Quint (tenor); Miles (boy soprano); Flora (soprano).

Publications

books–

Howard, Patricia. *Britten: The Turn of the Screw. Cambridge Opera Guides.* Cambridge, 1985.

articles–

Roseberry, Eric. *"The Turn of the Screw* and its Musical Idiom." *Tempo* no. 34 (1955): 6.
Reininghaus, Frieder. "Wie ein spannender Kriminalfilm. Benjamin Britten's *The Turn of the Screw." Neue Zeitschrift für Musik* 144 (1983): 28.

Hindley, Clifford. "Why Does Miles Die? A Study of Britten's *The Turn of the Screw.*" *Musical Quarterly* (1990).

* * *

The Turn of the Screw adapts one of the world's most celebrated ghost stories for the operatic stage. The compelling events of Henry James's novella are narrated through a series of 16 scenes, interwoven with orchestral interludes—a taut, integrated construction, typical of Britten's chamber operas, and particularly appropriate to this psychological mystery. The central character is an inexperienced and unworldly Governess, who comes to a remote country house to take charge of two young children. She gradually becomes convinced that they are in communication with the previous governess and a manservant—both dead. Her attempts to save the children from these malign influences result in the death of one child, and the fact that there is a second child whose fate is unresolved at the close of the opera gives the chilling drama, in James's words, "another turn of the screw."

Critics still squabble over whether Britten's opera preserves the ambiguities essential to James's story. James leaves open the dual possibilities that either the children are indeed being corrupted by the ghosts, or that their creepy commerce with the dead is only a figment of the Governess's imagination. The continuing controversy suggests that Britten succeeded in reproducing James's puzzle: from the first performance onwards, there have been sufficient champions for both interpretations to prove that the opera tells no less subtle a tale than its source.

In fragmentary sentences and elusive language, close to James's original text, Myfanwy Piper's libretto provides both the everyday exchanges of the schoolroom, and the sweet seduction of ghostly voices, real or imagined. (Giving the ghosts voices, and words to sing, is one of the most criticized aspects of the opera. A producer needs a little ingenuity to preserve the possibility that they are creations of a hysterical brain.) Terse conversations, set-piece songs and the occasional impassioned flare-up of emotion call for a wide range of lyrical and declamatory vocal styles: Britten has them all in his vocabulary, and unifies them with striking consistency, so that the boy Miles is as surely characterized when singing his Latin exercises as when romping with his sister, or flirting timidly with the Governess. The opera does not deal exclusively with horrors: it is also a love story, and delicately hints at the Governess's infatuation with the children's absent guardian, transformed at one moment into a destructive passion for her pupil, at another to a morbid obsession with the dead manservant who also loved the boy.

The opera is a study in tensions. Few operas have matched score and story to such purpose. Each of the two acts runs continuously. The orchestral interludes are no mere "mood music" but comprise a theme and variations for the thirteen instrumentalists that make up the chamber orchestra. The theme is the opera's "screw," using all twelve notes of the chromatic scale, and the variations "turn" it through all the keys, developing in intricacy and menace as the story unfolds. For the listener, the effect is far more than an ingenious technical tour-de-force: the dazzling colors of the score exploit a range of timbres appropriate to a ghost story—rippling celesta arpeggios announce an appearance of the male ghost, Quint, an ominous gong warns of the dead governess, Miss Jessel, a nocturne of birdsong fills the garden at night, and church bells accompany the ironic churchyard scene. *The Turn of the Screw* is among Britten's most important operas,

a worthy analogue of a literary masterpiece, a memorable score, and superb theater.

—Patricia Howard

TURNER, (Dame) Eva.

Soprano. Born 10 March 1892, in Oldham, England. Died 16 June 1990, in London. Studied with Dan Roothan, Giglia Levy, Edgardo Levy, Mary Wilson, and Albert Richards–Broad; debut as a Page in Wagner's *Tannhäuser,* London, 1916; sang with the Carl Rosa Opera Company, 1916-24 in roles that included Santuzza, Tosca, and Brünnhilde; Teatro alla Scala debut as Freia in Wagner's *Das Rheingold,* 1924; sang at Covent Garden, 1928-48; taught at the University of Oklahoma, 1949-59; joined the faculty at the Royal Academy of Music, 1959. Was made a Dame Commander of the Order of the British Empire in 1962.

Publications

About TURNER: articles

English, T. "Eva Turner." *Opera* 1 (1957): 29.
Richards, J.B. "Eva Turner." *Record Collector* 11 (1957): 29.
Cook, I. "This is Eva Turner." *Opera News* (1959):
Owens, R. "Eva Turner, the grand dame of singing." *Missouri Journal of Research in Music Education* 5/2 (1984): 94.
Blythe, A. "Dame Eva Turner: an appreciation." *Gramophone* 68 (1990): 346.
Chricton, R. "Eva Turner." *Opera* 41 (1990): 920.

* * *

Relatively few English-born sopranos of the twentieth century have achieved international fame. Considering the scarcity of truly great dramatic sopranos in this century, it is even more amazing that Eva Turner, born in Oldham, Lancashire, could circumvent so many odds and achieve for herself such a notable place in opera performance. Although her father was a cotton mill engineer and her mother a housewife, her parents considered music essential to Turner's education. In Bristol, her home city during school days, she studied voice with Daniel Rootham, teacher of another renowned English singer, Dame Clara Butt. Hearing a concert version of Wagner's *Die Walküre* and seeing a performance of Verdi's *Il trovatore* kindled young Turner's intense interest in opera.

With five years of study at the Royal Academy of Music with Edgardo Levi and Gigia Levi, she was prepared to audition for the Carl Rosa Opera Company in 1915. Although she began as a chorus member, by asserting herself she was soon able to learn and sing smaller roles. It was during her first year with this company that Turner met and began study with Albert Richards-Broad. Richards-Broad, a member of the Carl Rosa management, was an Australian singing master recognized as an authority on vocal production. With constant work, Turner soon established herself as the prima donna of this provincial English touring ensemble.

In 1924 one of Arturo Toscanini's assistants, having heard Turner in London, urged her to sing for the Maestro at the Teatro alla Scala in Milan. Toscanini engaged her immediately, and from her first performances in Italy her singing

Eva Turner as Turandot

commanded the respect of audiences, colleagues, and conductors. Her singing of operatic roles throughout England, Western Europe, Brazil, Argentina, Venezuela, and the United States during the inter-war years was notable in that she was the only English-born dramatic soprano to achieve this status. She performed such roles as Aida, Santuzza, Sieglinde, Agathe, and Isolde; but persons knowledgeable of her contributions to opera and singing continue to speak and write of her singing of the lead in Puccini's *Turandot*. Her performance of the title role in this work remains the yardstick by which all others are measured.

She first sang the role of Princess Turandot in the Teatro Grande at Brescia, Italy, in 1926, where she gained almost instant recognition. Alfano, who had completed the score of this work following Puccini's untimely death, later stated that Turner was perfect for the role. She first sang it in England in 1928 and eventually retired from the operatic stage after a series of performances of *Turandot* at the Royal Opera House, Covent Garden during the 1947 and 1948 seasons.

Commentators on Turner's career often focus on her huge success in the role of Turandot, ignoring the vast repertoire she presented to audiences throughout her career. Early on, she displayed the musicianship and eagerness to learn contemporary works such as *Le chant fatal* by Georges d'Orlay and *Thais and Thalmae* by Colin Campbell. Her Italian repertoire included, in addition to roles mentioned earlier, such parts as Amelia (*Un ballo in maschera*), Leonora (*Il trovatore*), Musetta (*La bohème*), Donna Anna (*Don Giovanni*), Cio-Cio-San (*Butterfly*), Nedda (*I pagliacci*), Tosca, and Isabeau (from Mascagni's *Isabeau*). Her German repertory was

represented by such roles as Venus and Elisabeth (*Tannhäuser*), Elsa (*Lohengrin*), Brünnhilde (*Siegfried* and *Die Walküre*), Eva (*Die Meistersinger*), and Leonora (*Fidelio*).

Turner's first recordings come during 1926 in Italy, where she, along with other soloists and the chorus from the Teatro alla Scala, put on disc the Triumphant Scene from *Aida* and the ensemble from the end of act III of *La gioconda*. Further recordings preceded her famous 1928 recordings in London. These sessions were unique in that Central Hall, Westminster, was used rather than the traditional studio. Turner said that the space given her voice in this setting provided surroundings similar to those of an opera house. Hearers of these recordings in England, Europe, and the Americas longed to hear this voice in person. Those fortunate enough to do so never ceased talking about the beauty of her full-bodied, trumpet-like tone, which was capable of carrying over chorus and orchestra in stunning fashion. Unable to fault her tone, some critics of Turner, however, cited her failure to deliver the language clearly and her inability to modulate her voice adequately. Those seeing her icy portrayal of Turandot were somewhat reluctant to admit that her acting abilities could encompass the warmth needed for such roles as Aida, Santuzza, and Isolde, but reviews testify that she did achieve a variety of emotions that reflected her sensitivity as an actress.

Another contribution Turner made in the field of opera was in her teaching. In 1949, following her retirement from singing, she was employed by the University of Oklahoma. She remained in this position for ten years before returning to teach at her alma mater, the Royal Academy of Music, and to teach privately in her home. Today Turner's students who serve as singing professors continue teaching the technique she imparted. Several singers she taught or coached have attained success in opera, including Amy Shuard, Pauline Tinsley, Elizabeth Vaughan, Janet Coster, and Linda Esther Gray.

Her highest non-singing honor came in 1962 when Queen Elizabeth II conferred upon her the title of Dame Commander of the British Empire.

Followers of Turner's career were sorely disappointed that she failed to perform Turandot at the Metropolitan Opera. At the height of her successes, both Kirsten Flagstad and Marjorie Lawrence held firm contracts with this house. One cannot help wondering if the situation would have been different if Turner had used someone other than Richards-Broad to serve as her manager. Many of her contracts evolved from what appeared to be casual meetings rather than carefully negotiated and orchestrated business dealings. Although she signed with the agency of Harold Holt, Richards-Broad continued as her manager/teacher until his death in 1940. Shortly after this Turner committed herself to remaining in England for the duration of World War II. By the end of the war, resuming an international career was impossible because of her age.

When she died in June 1990 at the age of ninety-eight, Turner had become almost a legendary figure due to her personality and longevity. Her death left a void in opera. Fortunately, however, her singing has become accessible to audiences by means of compact discs. In 1988 a digitally remastered compact disc containing excerpts from her 1937 performance of *Turandot* was issued with amazing results. Another compact disc containing most of the selections from her older 78s plus two arias from her German repertory was also made available in 1989 in the Great Recordings of the Century series. It would appear that these presentations will continue to allow listeners an opportunity to judge her worth and contributions to opera.

—Rose Mary Owens

TWILIGHT OF THE GODS
See DER RING DES NIBELUNGEN

THE TWO DAYS
See LES DEUX JOURNÉES

THE TWO FOSCARI
See I DUE FOSCARI

THE TWO WIDOWS [Dvě vdovy].

Composer: Bedřich Smetana.

Librettist: E. Züngel (after P.J.F. Mallefille).

First Performance: Prague, Provisional Theater, 27 March 1874; revised, Prague, Provisional Theater, 15 March 1878.

Roles: Karolina (soprano); Aneska (soprano); Ladislav (tenor); Mumlal (bass-baritone); Tonik (tenor); Lidka (soprano); chorus (SATB).

*   *   *

The Two Widows, Bedřich Smetana's sixth opera, is in the nature of a drawing-room comedy. Its humor, witty rather than uproarious, was something of a shock to contemporary audiences, who were expecting another rural comedy like *The Bartered Bride.* The plot concerns two women, cousins, who are both recently widowed. The action takes place at Karolina's wealthy estate; with her is Aneska. Karolina has ultimately accepted her husband's death and is tasting the advantages of independence and power, for she directs the business of her estate and rules over the many people working for her. In stark contrast to her, Aneska is in profound mourning for her husband. In fact, she sees it as her duty to mourn for him for the rest of her life, and do little else.

Soon after the first act begins, Mumlal, Karolina's gamekeeper, enters to complain about a poacher on the grounds whom he can't catch. Mumlal is enraged and also puzzled, for he notes that the intruder never seems to hit any of his targets. This is not much of a surprise to Karolina, as she knows that the poacher is actually trying to attract attention so as to meet Aneska. She knows that he has loved Aneska from a distance even before her husband's death, and she uses the opportunity to bring them together. As she has nothing but contempt for Aneska's perpetual mourning, she is determined to make a match between Ladislav (the poacher) and Aneska. Mumlal, who complains and disapproves of everything and everyone, brings Ladislav to the widows, and Karolina convenes a mock court to try Ladislav, who freely admits his guilt. He is sentenced by Karolina to a half-day's detention in a lovely house on the grounds, and, once there, is met by Aneska, who has been spirited in by Karolina. On declaring his love for Aneska, he is met by her refusal to consider him or anyone else for that matter. The first act ends with the curious workers questioning Mumlal about Ladislav, and Mumlal's angry comments about Karolina's plot to make a cheap woman of his ideal, the self-saddened Aneska.

The second act is given over to further attempts to shake Aneska's attitude. Karolina, seeing that Aneska, despite everything, is attracted to her suitor, hatches several plots to get them to talk to each other. However, none of these plans produces anything as Aneska's answer is always the same. At length, Karolina threatens to pursue Ladislav herself, thinking that this might arouse Aneska's jealousy. Karolina goes to a ball with Ladislav and on returning home is followed by him; Ladislav is determined to apologize for a kiss he gave her at the ball. On hearing this, Aneska, whose determination has been weakening, suddenly changes her attitude. She declares her love for Ladislav, and the opera ends in dancing and general jubilation.

Throughout *The Two Widows,* Smetana reflects a wide range of emotions with exquisite sensitivity. Karolina's music is as energetic as her words and has a rhythmic impetus not shared by any of the other characters. The role needs a dramatic coloratura singer of virtuoso attainments, but it is significant that the technical difficulties are never perceived as an end in themselves. Rather, they are illustrative of an energetic woman whose joy in life (despite her loss) stands diametrically opposed to Aneska's personality. The latter considers herself married to a life of duty and, therefore, noble misery. As such she is the butt of cutting remarks by virtually everyone on stage except Mumlal, who condemns as sinful anything resembling happiness! Smetana treats Aneska's feelings with seriousness, however, and there is no doubt that she has the most beautiful music of the whole opera.

The structure of *The Two Widows* is noteworthy and, to a degree, problematic. Smetana admired Wagner's operas, which he first became acquainted with in the 1860s, and there is little doubt that they had an influence on his operatic work. It was Wagner's contention that the so-called "number opera" was artificial and thus seriously hampered the dramatic validity of the stage action. He therefore advocated the principle of continuous musical and dramatic development unencumbered by the stopping and starting characteristic of earlier operas. To a large extent this is reflected in *The Two Widows,* but it should be noted that Smetana used this principle only partially. Each of the opera's two acts has enough set pieces to make one feel that Smetana is cultivating two very different stylistic principles.

—Harris Crohn

U

ULISSE [Ulysses].

Composer: Luigi Dallapiccola.

Librettist: Luigi Dallapiccola (after Homer, *The Odyssey*).

First Performance: in German as *Odysseus,* Berlin, Deutsche Oper, 29 September 1968; in Italian, Milan, 1969.

Roles: Calypso (soprano); Nausicaa (soprano); Ulysses (baritone); Demodocus (tenor); Circe (mezzo-soprano); Alcinous (bass-baritone); Anticleas (soprano); Tiresias (tenor); Antinous (baritone); Pisandro (baritone); Eurimachus (tenor); Melantho (mezzo-soprano); Eumaeus (tenor); Telemachus (counter-tenor); Penelope (soprano); First Maidservant (contralto); Second Maidservant (soprano); chorus.

Publications

articles–

Drew, D. "Dallapiccola's Odyssey." *The Listener* 80 (1968): 514.
Anon. "I commenti della stampa italiana alla prima in Italia dell' Ulisse di Luigi Dallapiccola." *Nuova rivista musicale italiana* 4 (1970): 205.
Petrobelli, Perluigi. "On Dante and Italian Music: Three Movements." *Cambridge Opera Journal* 2 (1990): 219.

*   *   *

Dallapiccola composed the music for *Ulisse* between 1960 and 1968. The dramatic action is primarily derived from Homer's *The Odyssey* and the libretto, by Dallapiccola himself, was begun prior to the first musical sketch and continued to be fashioned as he composed the score. In Dallapiccola's essay "Birth of a Libretto," from his book *On Opera,* he explains why he wrote his own libretto, details its structure, and lists its many literary sources. He also discusses the psychological nature of his hero, the personalities of the women he encounters, and the divergencies the libretto makes from the conclusion of *The Odyssey.*

Dallapiccola has achieved an incredible distillation of *The Odyssey* in his *Ulisse.* Its two-hour length contains a prologue with three episodes—the second being a symphonic intermezzo—and two acts. Act I has five scenes and act II contains three scenes, a symphonic intermezzo, and an epilogue. The prologue begins with Calypso's lament at Ulysses' departure. Poseidon's storm follows and concludes with Ulysses being washed ashore onto the island of the Phaeacians. Here Ulysses meets the Princess Nausicaa, whom he follows to the court of King Alcinous. Act I opens with the bard Demodocus singing of Ulysses' heroic events to the king. Ulysses agrees to tell the king of his adventures, and in scenes ii, iii, and iv he relates his experiences with the Lotus-eaters, with Circe, and in the Kingdom of the Cimmerians. In this scene Ulysses confronts the shades of Hades, meets his mother's phantom, and finally questions Tiresias, who predicts Ulysses' return to Ithaca where he will encounter violence. Ulysses' departure from the court concludes the act.

The first three scenes of act II are in Ithaca. In the mountains, Antinous plots the assassination of Ulysses' son Telemachus. Ulysses appears dressed as a beggar and goes unrecognized by his servant Eumaeus and by Telemachus. Next Ulysses walks to the palace courtyard, where he becomes enraged at the corrupt and decadent behavior of Melantho and Antinous, and laments that his son did not recognize him. Ulysses vows revenge on his enemies and violently curses Poseidon for his vengeance. The drama's dénouement takes place at a palace banquet. Antinous toasts Poseidon for drowning Telemachus and persuades Melantho to dance with Ulysses' unstrung bow. Melantho performs a lascivious dance and at its climax the bowstring becomes entwined around her neck. Telemachus enters at that moment and all are amazed that he is still alive. While Telemachus recounts how he escaped the ambush, Ulysses removes his disguise, picks up his bow, and says "I too, I have returned!" Ulysses commands Eumaeus to take Melantho away to be hanged, then strings his bow and shoots Antinous. Ulysses' wife Penelope suddenly enters and they reach out to each other as the curtain falls. A symphonic intermezzo follows and leads to the epilogue where Ulysses is alone at sea. Ulysses is tormented over the homicide he has committed—the violence Tiresias had predicted. He despairs, believing that all he has learned is meaningless, and continues to question existence. Then he gazes up at the stars and pleads for the end of his searching for "the Word, the Name and the Truth." Ulysses finally experiences an epiphany of God and no longer feels the aloneness of an individual without faith.

The musical characteristics of *Ulisse* are in a direct line with the great vocal works of the New Viennese School. *Ulisse* incorporates the biblical proportions of Schoenberg's *Moses und Aron,* the predetermined architecture of Berg's *Lulu,* and the crystalline motivic cells and tone-color-melody of Webern's *Das Augenlicht* (The Light of the Eye). Along with these influences, Dallapiccola continued to evolve his personal style which began to manifest itself in his Italian-Neoclassic period and matured in his twelve-tone compositions which use the extended techniques of serial organization and the indeterminate pitch *parlato* (speech) declamation found throughout *Ulisse.*

Dallapiccola is sometimes narrowly viewed as a composer who created only vocal-chamber works; words such as "soft and sweet" and "transparent" are often used to describe them. Indeed, he did create beautiful song-cycles, but his operas and choral pieces are large works of a different order. *Ulisse* is his largest, requiring a cast of fourteen, six dancers, boys choir, mixed chorus and full orchestra with organ. It is also the longest in duration. The libretto is finely written and contains a wealth of strong and varied emotions. The score is rich with color and filled with copious sonic densities often punctuated by abrupt dynamic changes. The symphonic intermezzi are master strokes of invention, linking dramatic action between acts and continuing the psychological development of the protagonist. *Ulisse* is undoubtedly Dallapiccola's great masterpiece written at the peak of his development. It brings together the large questions of existence and projects them in an advanced and challenging musical language.

—Armand Qualliotine

ULYSSES
See ULISSE

UNDINE.

Composer: E.T.A. Hoffmann.

Librettist: E.T.A. Hoffmann (after the novella by de la Motte-Fouqué).

First Performance: Berlin, 3 August 1816.

Roles: Huldbrand (baritone); An Old Fisherman (bass); An Old Fisherwoman (mezzo-soprano); Undine (soprano); Heilmann (bass); Kühleborn (bass); The Duke (tenor); The Duchess (mezzo-soprano); Berthalda (soprano); A Squire (speaking); A Footman (speaking); A Beautiful Child (mute); chorus.

Publications

book–

Schläder, Jürgen. *Undine auf dem Musiktheater. Zur Entwicklungs-geschichte der deutschen Spieloper.* Bonn-Bad Godesberg, 1979.

articles–

Weber, Carl Maria von. Review of *Undine. Allgemeine musikalische Zeitung* 19 (1817):column 201; reprinted in *Sämtliche Schriften von Carl Maria von Weber,* edited by G. Keiser, Berlin and Leipzig, 1908.
Pfitzner, H. "E.T.A. Hoffmanns Undine." *Süddeutsche Monatshefte* 3 (1906): 307; reprinted in *Gesammelte Schriften* vol. 1, p. 55, Munich, 1926.
Thiessen, K. "E.T.A. Hoffmanns Zauberoper Undine und ihre Bedeutung für die Entwicklung der deutschen romantichen Oper." *Neue Musikzeitung* 28 (1907): 491.
Garlington, Aubrey S. Jr. "Notes on Dramatic Motives in Opera: Hoffmann's *Undine.*" *Music Review* 32 (1971): 136.

* * *

In 1811 E.T.A. Hoffmann began work on his major theoretical essay probing the possibilities for German Romantic opera. "Der Dichter und der Komponist" was published serially in the *Allgemeine musikalische Zeitung* in 1813 around the same time Hoffmann completed his last opera, *Undine.* In keeping with the many paradoxes in German Romanticism, there is no apparent connection between the two projects. The polemic in *Der Dichter und der Komponist* presented one possibility for German opera, *Undine* another. Hoffmann had already abandoned his musical career when *Undine* was performed in Berlin in 1816 to limited acclaim. His significance in the history of German Romantic opera, however, remains considerable.

Undine's plot and text was drawn from the celebrated novella of de la Motte Fouqué, but Hoffmann largely wrote his own libretto. The story concerns a water sprite who acquires a human heart permitting her the ability to love. Raised by an elderly fisherman and his wife (taking the place of a daughter they believed drowned), Undine falls in love with a young knight, Huldbrand, and it is by marrying him that she receives a heart.

Throughout the opera Undine is watched over by Kühleborn, a water spirit. She remains perplexed by human behavior, because humans so often take the heart, and love, for granted. Huldbrand soon tires of his wife, and in a boating accident Undine is rescued and taken by Kühleborn to her true home. Huldbrand is attracted to the haughty, apparently well-born Berthalda, actually the long-lost daughter of the old fisherman and his wife. Whereas Undine had loved her foster parents, Berthalda is disgusted with them and ashamed of the truth of her birth.

The story climaxes on Huldbrand's and Berthalda's wedding day when Undine appears from a fountain, kisses her errant lover/husband, and as the crowd looks on in horror draws him beneath the water in a "Liebestod." The final scene of the opera, in the form of a double chorus with one on land and the other in the sea, reveals Huldbrand and Undine together in a fairy-like, watery realm. The human realm had proved too harsh and cruel to tolerate.

The story is an elegantly bitter-sweet Romantic tale, and on occasion the music rises to the challenges presented. Hoffmann makes a sharp distinction between music associated with a sophisticated world and that which reveals the delicate, sensitive nature of Undine. Appropriate recurring motives are heard with Kühleborn's appearances, and although it is a *Singspiel* containing spoken dialogue with sung music, *Undine* owes little to the popular German theater. The most significant music is that heard with Undine's retransformation into a spirit, and returns again as Huldbrand is changed into another entity.

Nevertheless, Hoffmann's musical abilities are inferior to his literary powers. There is little evidence of any technical accomplishment which can match the profound sense of fantasy revealed in the story. While Carl Maria von Weber found much to admire in *Undine,* especially in the use of appropriate associative music to convey meaning, he justly criticized Hoffmann's inadequacy in formal structuring and the overdependence on harmonic clichés. Regardless of the quality of individual moments, *Undine* fails as a stage work but remains a significant and important moment in the on-going quest for German Romantic Opera.

—Aubrey S. Garlington

UNDINE.

Composer: Albert Lortzing.

Librettist: Albert Lortzing (after Friedrich de la Motte-Fouqué).

First Performance: Magdeburg, 21 April 1845.

Roles: Bertalda (soprano); Hugo von Ringstetten (tenor); Kühleborn (baritone); Tobias (bass); Marthe (contralto); Undine (soprano); Father Heilmann (bass); Veit (tenor); Hans (bass); Courtier (speaking); chorus.

Publications

book–

Schlöder, Jürgen. *Undine auf dem Musiktheater. Zur Entwicklungs-geschichte der deutschen Spieloper.* Bonn-Bad Godesberg, 1979.

article–

Bollert, W. "Romantischer Lortzing: Die Schallplatten-Première der Undine." *Fono forum* 12 (1967): 260.

*   *   *

Albert Lortzing's undeniable gifts in the area of comic opera, his facility at portraying the common man, his fluid melodies, and his clear and uncomplicated orchestral textures were precisely those characteristics which worked against him when he attempted his "Romantische Zauberoper," *Undine.* Why he undertook the adaptation of a short novel fairytale by Friedrich de la Motte-Fouqué (1777-1843) is not really known except for the fact that he was in rather serious financial distress, and the offer of a performance in Hamburg under his direction must have encouraged him. The fact that de la Motte-Fouqué had collaborated with E.T.A. Hoffmann on the latter's opera in 1816 did not seem to have influenced either Lortzing's musical concept or his very free adaptation of the original novella.

Act I opens in a poor fisherman's hut. The knight Hugo von Ringstetten and his squire Veit have crossed the magic forest at the request of Bertalda, the beautiful daughter of the duke with whom Hugo is in love. However, an impassable flood of water has trapped them for several months in the poor fisherman's hut belonging to Tobias and Marthe. During their enforced stay, Hugo falls in love with the couple's daughter Undine, and they agree to marry. He knows that Undine was left fifteen years ago on the doorstep on All Soul's Day, the very day Tobias and Marthe's daughter mysteriously disappeared. As the wedding is being prepared, the waters recede. A stranger appears—Kühleborn, the mighty sovereign of the waters. Knowing that Hugo still loves Bertalda, Kühleborn vows to watch over his daughter, Undine.

Act II opens in the great hall of Hugo's castle, where Veit and Hans the cellarmaster discuss the lineage and manner of both ladies. Undine tells her husband that her birth condemns her to be a water spirit without a soul; that only through the true love of a human being can she acquire a soul. Hugo promises her that love. In a fit of jealousy Bertalda reminds Undine of her lowly birth, but Kühleborn appears and tells

Illustration showing the characters in Lortzing's *Undine*, c. 1880

Bertalda that it is she who is the lost child of the poor fisherman and his wife. Bertalda collapses as the water king disappears in the garden pool.

The tragedy of the love triangle unfolds in act III. Hugo expels Undine so that he can marry Bertalda, despite Undine's warning that Kühleborn will never let his infidelity go unpunished. On the wedding night, Undine emerges from the castle well and appears at midnight in the banquet hall where she takes her faithless husband into her arms and sinks into the water's depths.

Although *Undine* was very well received at its premiere (due perhaps to the surface relationships to Romanticism) and for a number of years thereafter, it is at best an historical oddity by a composer whose real talents lay elsewhere. The most successful parts of the opera are, not surprisingly, the buffo scenes and those in which the characters can be natural and immediately appealing. Lortzing's abilities did not lie in the realm of water spirits, the supernatural, and characters without souls.

—Robert H. Cowden

DIE UNGLÜCKSELIGE CLEOPATRA, Königin von Ägypten [The Unhappy Cleopatra, Queen of Egypt].

Composer: Johann Mattheson.

Librettist: Friedrich Christian Feustking.

First Performance: Hamburg, 20 October 1704.

Roles: Cleopatra (soprano); Mark Anthony (tenor); Candace (soprano); Ptolemaeus (contralto); Archibius (baritone); Dercetaeus (tenor); Augustus Caesar (baritone); Mandane (soprano); Juba (tenor); Proculejus (contralto); Nemesis (soprano).

Publications

article–

Buelow, G.J. "Johann Mattheson, the Composer: an Evaluation of his Opera *Cleopatra* (Hamburg, 1704)." In *Studies in Eighteenth Century Music: a Tribute to Karl Geiringer.* London and New York, 1970.

*   *   *

Cleopatra is the only extant score from among Mattheson's seven operas, six of which were composed for performances at Hamburg's famous opera house *am Gänsemarkt* (on the Goose Market). The libretto is derived from Roman history and the account of Mark Anthony as found in Plutarch. The story begins after the disastrous battle at Actium where Anthony, a former Roman general, led the combined naval and army forces of the Egyptians against the Romans and was defeated. Anthony escapes to an island where he swears never again to be lured into the arms of Cleopatra, who had urged him into battle. The latter, however, follows him and quickly persuades her lover to return for yet another attempt to drive the Romans from Egypt. Anthony again engages the Roman forces in a battle outside the gates of Alexandria and

wins. In act II, Augustus develops a new plot to deceive Cleopatra and defeat Anthony's forces. By messenger he proposes that if Anthony lays down his arms and hands over Cleopatra to him, he will restore his former Roman citizenship. The proposal is rejected, but Augustus also communicates to Cleopatra his passionate love for her and his wish to make her Queen of the Roman world if she will abandon Anthony. In act III, Anthony learns of the defeat of the Egyptian fleet by the Romans, and is told (falsely) that Cleopatra has committed suicide. In remorse he kills himself. In Alexandria Augustus enters in triumph, and Cleopatra, her children, and the governor of the city pay homage to him. Augustus again asks for Cleopatra's love, and she promises him her heart and bed. But in the end she realizes Augustus's entreaties are part of a treacherous plan to bring her back to Rome as prisoner. Rather than face disgrace, she commits suicide by the bite of asps hidden in a fruit basket. However, in typical Baroque style, the opera does not end as a tragedy. Rather, a subplot involving the young lovers is climaxed with their marriages being blessed by Augustus, who agrees to be the guardian of the children of Anthony and Cleopatra. The work ends with a ballet for the Egyptian and Roman gentlemen and ladies.

The score to the opera is preserved in a copy made from the manuscript in Hamburg during the early twentieth century and is found in the Library of Congress in Washington, D.C. The original manuscript has been missing since the end of the second world war. The music by Mattheson conforms to the general operatic style prevalent at the Hamburg opera during the late seventeenth and early eighteenth centuries, the only public opera house found in Europe except for those in Venice. The three acts consist entirely of an alternation of recitatives (usually accompanied only by harpsichord and string bass) and arias. Some sixty percent of the solo arias and ensembles are also accompanied only by the basso continuo instruments. The remainder are accompanied by a small string ensemble, sometimes with added oboes or recorders. Mattheson's score relies on an aria style of general tunefulness, frequently cast in strophic, folk-like forms, which avoid all aspects of Italian vocal virtuosity. There are also a number of arias of moving pathos and splendid lyrical beauty, which underscore the composer's oft stated belief that music must be an "oration in tones." There is a strong influence of French music, seen both in the various ballets and other dance forms used for many of the arias. The folk element was an important tradition at the Hamburg opera, and Mattheson employs it especially for the various comic scenes, such as a ballet of chimney sweeps, and also for ribald songs in German dialect (*Plattdeutsch*).

Cleopatra has a particular fame in music history that has overshadowed its merits as one of the composer's major operas. The opera is mostly remembered for an incident that takes place in the biography of George Frideric Handel. The young Handel had come to Hamburg in 1703, where he quickly found a job as violinist in the opera orchestra. He became a good friend of Mattheson, and soon was learning aspects of composing from Mattheson. During one of the performances of *Cleopatra,* in which Mattheson, a fine tenor, sang the role of Anthony, Handel was given the responsibility of harpsichordist-conductor while Mattheson was on stage. However, since Anthony dies early in act III, Mattheson returned to the pit and asked to take over his rightful position at the harpsichord, which Handel refused to yield. In the ensuing altercation, and at the end of the performance, the two high-spirited, gifted young men fought a duel with swords outside the theater. According to Mattheson, Handel's life was saved by a large button on his jacket which Mattheson had struck with his sword.

—George J. Buelow

URBAN, Joseph [Josef].

Designer. Born 26 May 1872, in Vienna. Died 10 July 1933, in New York. Educated at the Art Academy and Polytechnicum, Vienna; worked with Gustav Mahler and Alfred Roller at the Vienna Court Opera; chief scenic designer at the Boston Opera Company, 1912-15; designed over 50 operas for Metropolitan Opera Company, 1917-1933, which remained in use as late as 1951; designed many productions for Broadway, including musicals by Gershwin and Kern, and the Ziegfeld Follies.

Publications

About URBAN: books–

Heylbut, R., and A. Gerber. *Backstage at the Opera.* New York, 1937.
Kolodin, I. *The Story of the Metropolitan Opera.* New York, 1953.
Noble, H. *Life with the Met.* New York, 1954.
Eaton, Q. *The Boston Opera Company.* New York, 1965.
Bordman, G. *American Musical Theatre.* New York, 1978.
Hamilton, D., ed. *The Metropolitan Opera Encyclopedia.* New York, 1987.

*   *   *

Joseph Urban began a wide ranging career as architect, stage designer, director, and illustrator after studying at the Art Academy and the Polytechnicum in his native Vienna, where he also worked with Alfred Roller, chief scenic artist of the Vienna Court Opera. Winner of a prize for his illustrations for Poe's *Masque of the Red Death,* he was soon the recipient of commissions for such enterprises as the redecoration of the Khedive's palace in Egypt and the Esterhazy castle and Town Hall in Vienna, as well as the Tsar's bridge in St Petersburg. In 1910, he was responsible for a dramatic presentation given to celebrate the coronation of King George V of England.

Urban made his first trip to America in 1901 to design the Austrian Pavilion for the 1904 St Louis Fair, and in 1912 Henry Russell engaged him to provide settings for a variety of works at his three-year-old Boston Opera Company. Urban's debut production there, a spectacular *Les contes d'Hoffmann,* overwhelmed audiences and critics with its vivid colors and surprising technical innovations. "For the first time in American theatrical history," wrote one commentator, "every element of the stage—scenery, costumes, properties, and direction—came from a single hand." Given free reign, Urban continued to experiment with "emotion expressed in staging" in such operas as *Tristan, Pelléas, Louise,* and *I gioielli della Madonna,* often without the assistance of the puzzled Boston

technical stage staff or the forebearance of the city's critics. This certainly was not opera as they had ever experienced it before, and they felt confused and frustrated. Even *La bohème* and *Madama Butterfly,* among the repertory pieces, were enlivened by unique touches of lighting and direction that startled placid operagoers.

The collapse of the Boston Opera Company in 1915 released Urban from operatic chores temporarily, and introduced his scenic art to New York through the medium of the Ziegfeld Follies of 1915. This annual extravaganza series, begun in 1907 by Florenz Ziegfeld "to glorify the American girl," consisted of consecutive elaborate production numbers, which Urban designed for the first time "with the flow of the entire production in mind." The 1915 edition, featuring "Urban blue" (his unique trademark), created a sensation, which initiated his collaboration with Ziegfeld's enterprises for the next eighteen years. During this time, Urban's fanciful onstage recreations of the Unter den Linden, a naval battle, the gardens of Versailles, the Grand Canyon, and the Arc de Triomphe in the Follies contrasted with the realistic settings he supplied for the original *Show Boat* and the Mexican-based *Rio Rita.*

Meanwhile, Giulio Gatti-Casazza, general manager of the Metropolitan Opera, who until 1917 had relied principally on painted backcloths and wings for scenery imported from Italy and Germany, discovered in Urban a designer who by now had become a master of many styles, an expert at lighting, and a creator of new and impressive methods of stagecraft. From the impressionistic, as in his *Pelléas* and *Parsifal,* to the realistic, as in *Il barbiere di Siviglia* and *Luisa Miller,* Urban's contribution to set design and staging in America was innovative. While the annual Follies designs were transitory, Urban's Metropolitan Opera sets were conceived to last, and as one observer noted: "Mere painting on canvas was not enough. An Urban church was a real church, and one that could have done duty in many a small town, while an Urban ship stood ready to launch."

Urban settings became as familiar and cherished to several generations of operagoers as many Met singers, and in numerous cases were more lasting. His first designs in 1917 for *Faust,* reported to be "of great beauty, and of such design as to lend themselves to a complete shattering of the conventional stage business," endured in one form or another until 1951. Similarly, a procession of heroines, beginning with Florence Easton in 1923, and including Maria Jeritza and Rosa Ponselle, danced and died in Urban's *Carmen* settings, which were in use until 1951. Between 1917 and his death in 1933, Joseph Urban designed more than fifty productions for the Metropolitan, and as an architect was responsible for the art-deco Ziegfeld Theater (now demolished), the New School for Social Research, and the Central Park Casino in New York City. In 1927, he conceived plans for a cathedral-like Metropolitan Opera House to replace the original one built in 1883, but all ideas for a change were abandoned. His only designs for London were those for the Covent Garden premiere of Montemezzi's *L'amore dei tre re* in 1914. He did not live to see the futuristic buildings he had envisioned for the Century of Progress Exposition which took place in 1933-34 in Chicago.

—Louis Snyder

V

THE VALKYRIE
See DER RING DES NIBELUNGEN

VALLETTI, Cesare.

Tenor. Born 18 December 1922, in Rome. Studied with Tito Schipa; debut as Alfredo in Verdi's *La traviata*, Bari, 1947; Covent Garden debut as Fenton in *Falstaff*, 1950; sang at Teatro alla Scala, 1950-53; sang at the Metropolitan Opera, 1953-60, in roles that included Don Ottavio, Des Grieux, Ferrando in *Così fan tutte*, and Ernesto in *Don Pasquale*; toured and concertized, 1960-68.

Publications

About VALLETTI: articles–

Celletti, R. "Valletti, Cesare." In *Le grandi voci*, Rome, 1964.
Rosenthal, H. "Cesare Valletti." *Great Singers of Today*. London, 1966.
Soria, D.J. "Artist life." *High Fidelity/Musical America* 25 (1975): MA4.

*   *   *

Cesare Valletti, one of the most highly regarded lyric tenors of the 1950s and 1960s, was often described as the successor of Tito Schipa. Like Schipa, he was admired for the refinement of his singing in both opera and recital. Although Valletti's voice was not large and occasionally inclined to thinness above the staff, it was well managed and projected clearly, even in large houses like New York's Metropolitan Opera, where he was a favorite.

Valletti was particularly well known for his interpretations of standard lyric tenor roles by Mozart, Donizetti, and Verdi (principally Alfredo in *La traviata*), but his repertoire also extended to works by Malipiero (*La favola del figlio cambiato*), Mascagni (*L'amico Fritz*), and Wolf-Ferrari (*I quatro rusteghi*). In addition, he was involved in the revival of the bel canto repertoire in the 1950s, appearing in such then-neglected operas as Rossini's *Il Turco in Italia* (in the famous production with Callas in Rome, 1950) and *La donna del lago* (Florence, 1958). He was also heard in earlier operatic music, singing in Cavalli's *Ercole amante* at the Venice Festival of 1952, appearing in Handel's *Acis and Galatea* in New York in 1959, and portraying Nero in Monteverdi's *L'incoronazione di Poppea* at the Caramoor Festival in 1968, a year after his official retirement. His wide-ranging musicality and stylistic versatility were also evident in his recital programs, which embraced French, Spanish, American, and German songs. His Lieder programs at Salzburg in 1960 were particularly well received.

The hallmarks of Valletti's singing are evident in a number of recordings of complete operas made between 1949 and 1962. All reveal an attractive light tenor voice, and—more unusually—all are distinguished by an elegance of musical line combined with dramatic awareness. In *Il barbiere di Siviglia*, for example, he shades and shapes "Se il mio nome" imaginatively, more tentative and lingering in the first verse as he identifies himself as a poor student, and then more confident and ardent in the second after he has heard Rosina's response. He also sings Almaviva's florid music cleanly, including the often-omitted second-act aria, without recourse to aspirates. At the same time, the Count is presented as a fully conceived dramatic character, by turns impetuous and tender. Nor is the comedy slighted. While he is disguised as the drunken soldier, his laughter is genuinely infectious; as the pretended Don Alonzo, he substitutes an amusing accent for the usual nasal tone.

Valletti's sensitivity to differing stylistic demands can be seen by turning to his complete recording of *Madama Butterfly* and the extensive excerpts from *Werther*. In the first, the delicate bel canto line is replaced with a broader approach suitable to verismo, while the latter calls forth a greater variety of shading, including a subtle application of *voix mixte*. Even though Valletti never sang the role of Pinkerton in the theater, the character is as clearly and thoughtfully delineated as that of Werther, a role that formed an important part of his stage repertoire. Both recordings also reveal the command of subtly graded dynamics that Valletti substituted for force, thus allowing him to sing dramatic music convincingly with a light voice.

—Joc K. Law

VALLIN, Ninon.

Soprano. Born 8 September 1886, in Montalieu-Vercieu. Died 22 November 1961, in Lyons. Studied at the Lyons Conservatory; debut in premier of Debussy's *Le martyre de Saint Sébastien*, 1911; sang with the Opéra-Comique, 1912-16; debut at the Teatro Colón in Buenos Aires as Marguerite in Gounod's *Faust*, 1916; sang with the Teatro Colón, 1916-36; Paris Opéra debut as Thaïs, 1920.

Publications

About VALLIN: books–

Fragny, R. de, *Ninon Vallin, princesse du chant*. Lyons, 1963.

articles–

Barnes, H.M. "Vallin, Ninon." *Record Collector* 8 (1953): 53.
Celletti, R. "Vallin, Ninon." In *Le grandi voci*, Rome, 1964.

Alfone, J.M. "Sopranos the Metropolitan missed." *Opera News* 26 (1961): 28.

Pinchard, M. "Hommage à Ninon Vallin." *Musica* 95 (1962): 4.

Albright, W. "Let them sing French: some great Gallic singers and other old friends sing French repertory and more." *Opera Quarterly* 7/3 (1990): 169.

*   *   *

The very epitome of everything that is French in opera singing, Ninon Vallin possessed a voice of great beauty, though not, to judge by her records, of very great power. Although she was admired in Mozart and her roles at the Opéra-Comique included both Micaela and the title role in *Carmen,* she specialized in the music of her own time: Massenet, Charpentier, Hahn, Nin, Falla, Respighi and Fauré were all living composers when she sang their works. She was considered the ideal Manon; her voice was at its richest in the middle and low register, so that Manon does not seem like a soubrette but obtains a depth lacking in more nasal, high soprano interpretations. Vallin could, nevertheless, toss off the coloratura of the *gavotte,* and she recorded arias by Donizetti and Bellini. In the famous recording of Charpentier's *Louise,* supervised by the composer, she partners Georges Thill in a performance that has not been surpassed. In particular the sense of joy and youthfulness that she brings to the final scene obscures the fact that she was already in her fifties when the record was made. Reynaldo Hahn considered her the ideal interpreter of his *mélodies* and accompanied her on a series of recordings; her performance of his song with orchestra "La dernière valse" is the encapsulation of all of Hahn's nostalgia for *la belle époque.* But Vallin's technique was so secure that she seemed able to sing music of each age in its own style. When she was nearing sixty she recorded the third-act aria of the Countess from *Le nozze di Figaro* in French, with no apparent wear on her voice—the trills, runs and long phrases giving her no more trouble than if it had been one of the songs by Bizet or Gounod, which she recorded when she was nearing seventy. Absent from Vallin's singing was that extreme nasal sound which so many French sopranos have developed, partly through necessity in articulating the language, partly through some quirk of national technique. Vallin's prodigious recorded output was a testimony to her popularity, as was her appearance in a rare French "talkie" *La fille de la Madelon.* If her most enduring recorded performances are the complete *Louise, Werther* and the numerous extracts from *Manon* (especially the Saint-Sulpice scene, recorded in 1932 with the Des Grieux of Miguel Villabella) her recordings of songs by Reynaldo Hahn and Joaquin Nin, with the composers at the piano, are the surest examples of her singing at its most confident. In Hahn's setting of Gautier's "Infidélité," at the penultimate line, "L'air est pur, le gazon doux," all sung on one note, her tone has a superb sensual quality which changes effortlessly to a tragic expression for the final "Rien, rien n'a donc changé . . . que vous!" "Ah Ninon!" wrote André Tubeuf, "she could do nothing wrong, nor by halves . . . Vallin was one of the very rare singers in this century who was always not only the epitome of good singing but also of good taste."

—Patrick O'Connor

**THE VAMPIRE
See DER VAMPYR**

DER VAMPYR [The Vampire].

Composer: Heinrich Marschner.

Librettist: Wilhelm August Wohlbrück (after the melodrama by Charles Nodier, François Adrien Carmouche, and Achille de Jouffroy).

First Performance: Leipzig, 29 March 1828.

Roles: Lord Davenaut (bass); Malwina (soprano); Edgar Aubrey (tenor); Lord Ruthven (baritone); Sir Berkley (bass); Janthe (soprano); George Dibdins (tenor); John Perth (speaking part); Emmy (soprano); James Godshill (tenor); Richard Scrop (tenor); Robert Green (bass); Thomas Blunt (bass); Suse (mezzo-soprano); Vampire Master (speaking part); Berkley Servant (bass); chorus.

Publications

articles—

Hanslick, E. "Der Vampyr." In *Musikalisches Skizzenbuch* (*Die moderne Oper,* vol. IV). Berlin, 1896.

Pfitzner, Hans. "Marschners Vampyr." *Neue Musik-Zeitung* 45 (1924): 134.

*   *   *

Marschner's first real operatic success, *Der Vampyr* capitalized on the popularity of Weber's recent *Der Freischütz* (1821), with its mixture of German folk elements and demonic motifs, as well as that of the widespread vampire literature in the wake of Polidori's "The Vampyre: A Tale" of 1819, originally attributed to Byron. From the variety of existing stage versions, the librettist Wohlbrück, Marschner's brother-in-law, drew primarily on Heinrich Ludwig Ritter's *Der Vampyr oder die Todten-Braut,* based in turn on an 1820 French melodrama by Charles Nodier with music by Louis-Alexandre Piccinni (grandson of Niccolò Piccinni).

To prolong his earthly existence by another year, the vampire Lord Ruthven swears to the vampire-master and assembled spirits that he will provide them with three sacrificial brides within twenty-four hours. After an expository recitative and aria describing his bloodthirsty lifestyle, he quickly dispatches his first victim, Janthe, who has rushed out for a nocturnal tryst with him. A posse led by the girl's father discovers the murder and stabs Ruthven. But the vampire is unwittingly rescued by Aubrey, once the beneficiary of Ruthven's aid, who carries his body into a patch of moonlight. Aubrey is forced to swear an oath of secrecy until the new day is past. The scene changes to a hall in the castle of Lord Davenaut. Aubrey greets his beloved Malwina, the Lord's daughter, only to discover that she has been promised to the wealthy Earl of Marsden, in whom he recognizes—to his dismay—the vampire Ruthven.

Act II finds Emmy and George, peasants belonging to the estate of Marsden, preparing to celebrate their wedding.

Emmy's ballad of the "pale man" (*Romanze*, "Sieh, Mutter, dort den bleichen Mann") is ominously interrupted by the appearance of Ruthven. Neither George nor Aubrey (still under oath) is able to prevent the vampire's seduction and murder of Emmy, whom he has enticed away from the festivities. A bullet wound inflicted by George is counteracted by the curative force of the moonlight, once again. In the following scene more wedding festivities are underway in the Davenauts' castle. Aubrey does all he can to dissuade Malwina from this unwanted match and later to hinder the nuptial ceremonies themselves. Both he and Malwina stall for time until finally, as the clock strikes one, Aubrey reveals the horrible identity of Lord Ruthven, who is struck down by a lightning bolt. Thus rescued from an infernal fate, Malwina is given to Aubrey in marriage amidst general rejoicing.

Der Vampyr has often been cited as a link between *Der Freischütz* and Wagner's *Der fliegende Holländer*. Like Weber's opera, it is grounded in the traditions of the *Singspiel* and the recent dramatic *opéra comique*, bringing more fully developed solo and ensemble numbers and extended finales in the manner of recent Italian opera to the older mix of spoken dialogue and simple strophic songs. The vampire story enables Marschner to place the demonic character center stage, unlike Weber's Kaspar, end even to endow him, at least faintly, with qualities of the alienated Byronic anti-hero divided against himself. Ruthven's character stands somewhere between that of two related baritone roles: the amoral seducer Don Giovanni (whose ultimate fate he shares) and Wagner's tragically cursed Dutchman, whose search for salvation also involves repeated sacrifices of innocent young women. His startling appearance at the close of Emmy's F-minor *Romanze* (ballad) has often been cited as a model for the Dutchman's appearance following Senta's ballad, although the sinister narrative romance or ballad type was not itself new (both *Der Freischütz* and Boieldieu's *La dame blanche* had already treated the type with an element of parody.

Numerous melodic and instrumental details of Marschner's score recall Weber, particularly the second theme of the overture (closely resembling that of the *Euryanthe* overture) and the recurring motive of "infernal laughter"—repeated downward leaps in flute, piccolo, or other woodwinds in thirds over a diminished harmony—modeled on a similar gesture associated with Kaspar in *Der Freischütz*. Marschner also makes effective use of melodrama (spoken text to orchestral accompaniment) in act I. The Vampire-Master's brief admonition in the Introduction (over timpani and low string tremolo, resolving to F-sharp minor) is obviously inspired by Samiel in the Wolf's-Glen scene. A more extended piece of melodrama closes the first scene, when Aubrey discovers the wounded Ruthven and carries him to the moonlit hillside. Finally, the various folk-like numbers—the two drinking choruses in act II and the festive music in both finales—recall elements of *Der Freischütz* and *Euryanthe*, respectively.

Marschner's ensembles, however, tend to be more extensive than Weber's, often involving a greater amount of action, as in the chorus of Lord Berkley's nocturnal posse in the first scene ("Wo kann sie sein?"). A desire for increased musical continuity, despite the dialogue format, is manifested in the *attacca* connection of separate numbers, as with the duet (no. 3) following the aforementioned chorus of Berkley's men, or the scene and aria of Malwina (no. 6) and her subsequent duet with Aubrey. Similarly progressive is the extended *grosse Szene* (no. 14) between Aubrey and Ruthven in its discursive treatment of tonality and freely gestural accompaniment; this, again, connects directly with the ensuing aria ("Wie ein schöner Frühlingsmorgen").

Der Vampyr remained current on smaller German stages throughout the nineteenth century, although not reaching the larger theaters of Vienna and Berlin until the end of the century. The score was revised by Hans Pfitzner in the 1920s, who retouched the orchestration and liberally cut what he considered the "weaker passages." Pfitzner also suggested playing the overture *after* the first scene, while the scenery is shifted (an idea he borrowed from Marschner's own procedure in *Hans Heiling*). This revision has served as the basis for a number of modern revivals.

—Thomas S. Grey

VAN DAM, José (Joseph Van Damme).

Bass-baritone. Born 25 August 1940, in Brussels. Studied with Frédéric Anspach at the Brussels Conservatory from 1953 to 1960; debut as Basilio, Liège, 1960; Paris Opéra debut as the Voice of Mercury in *Les Troyens*, 1961; in Paris at Opéra and Opéra-Comique 1961-65; at Geneva Opera 1965-67; sang in premiere of Milhaud's *La mère coupable*, Geneva, 1966; debut at Deutsche Oper, Berlin, 1967; various debuts as Escamillo: Santa Fe, 1967; San Francisco, 1970; Covent Garden, 1973; Metropolitan Opera, 1975; also at Metropolitan Opera sang Golaud, Colline, Wozzeck, Figaro, Jokanaan; sang title role in the world premiere of Messiaen's *St François d'Assise*, Paris Opéra, 1983.

Publications

About VAN DAM: books–

Matheopoulos, Helena. *Bravo*. London, 1986.

articles–

Lipton, G.D. "Wir arme Leute." *Opera News* 44 (8 March 1980): 19.
Wadsworth, S. "Handled with Care." *Opera News* 45/July (1980): 12.
Matheopoulos, Helena. "Flying Belgian José van Dam." *Gramophone* 62/January (1985): 867.
Tubeuf, A. "José van Dam." *Diapason-Harmonie* 317/June (1986): 10.

* * *

José Van Dam possesses one of the most attractive bass-baritone voices of recent decades, coupled with great interpretive intelligence. His range of roles is enormous, encompassing not only the bass-baritone repertoire but some purely baritone and bass roles as well. His greatest roles include Amfortas, Jokanaan, Wagner's Dutchman, Don Alfonso in Mozart's *Così fan tutte*, and Wozzeck. Van Dam tends to play parts for melancholy; his Dutchman is extremely brooding, for which he has been criticized. He does not find, for example, Mozart's Figaro to be a comic role, explaining that "... after five minutes onstage Figaro learns his best friend may be sleeping with Susanna, and I don't think that's funny."

Van Dam considers his ultimate working relationship to have been with Herbert von Karajan, who invited him to the

Salzburg Easter Festival for many productions. Van Dam feels that Karajan's "rapport with his singers amounts to a metaphysical marriage." On recordings Van Dam may be heard in a number of roles under Karajan. He is the Jokanaan on Karajan's *Salome* with Behrens in the title role and manages to invest the prophet with some dramatic interest for once. He sings the part of the monk on Karajan's *Don Carlos* from the Salzburg Easter festival of 1978, sounding at once suitably aged yet steady of tone. On Karajan's *Pelléas et Mélisande* Van Dam sings gloriously as Golaud, managing to elicit sympathy from the listener in a role normally associated with monstrous cruelty. Van Dam's Figaro, an example of great singing and subtle character portrayal by any standards, is featured on the Karajan Decca recording of *Le nozze di Figaro* with a cast that was featured in the Jean-Pierre Ponnelle production at Salzburg. Van Dam is excellent on Karajan's 1984 recording of *Der fliegende Holländer,* displaying gorgeous tone, eloquent phrasing, clear diction, long breath, and a perfect legato in the exquisitely soft singing of "Wie aus der Ferne." For all his admiration of Karajan, Van Dam has turned down a number of roles the maestro proposed to him: Sarastro, Telramund, and Pizarro.

Perhaps Van Dam is an iconoclast in his interpretation of many of the roles he undertakes. Even his Leporello, seen in the Joseph Losey film of *Don Giovanni,* is not a particularly comic character, yet it is a rich interpretation, with many subtleties in the Catalogue aria. The score is conducted by Lorin Maazel, another conductor with whom Van Dam likes to work. Early in his career, Van Dam was invited by Maazel to join the Deutsche Oper, Berlin. There, his first big success was as Paolo in Verdi's *Simon Boccanegra,* a role he recorded on the incomparable DGG set conducted by Claudio Abbado. In Berlin Van Dam also performed, among others, Leporello, Figaro, Attila, Boris, Gianni Schicchi, and Philip in *Don Carlos.* He sang in the 1965 DGG recording of Ravel's *L'heure espagnole* conducted by Maazel. Georg Solti, becoming aware of Van Dam's talents, engaged him as Escamillo at Covent Garden, a role that he subsequently recorded under Solti on Decca and the one in which he made many of his debuts around the world. Van Dam also recorded Berlioz' *La Damnation de Faust* with Solti.

Born in Brussels in 1940, Van Dam sang in a neighborhood church where his voice was discovered by a Jesuit priest. At age 13 he went to Professor Frédéric Anspach at the Brussels Conservatory, where he received a diploma in Lyric Art in 1960. He was then hired by the Paris Opéra, remaining there for four years singing such roles as Marcello, Colline, and Angelotti before leaving for the Geneva Opera for two years and then for Berlin, where his main career may properly be said to have begun. Van Dam is a particularly quick learner but likes to spend a great deal of time preparing a new role, ideally a year between learning and performing. He prefers to read extensively about his characters. In preparing for the role of the devil in Berlioz' *Faust* setting, for example, he discovered the delights of Goethe's *Faust.* Wozzeck, Van Dam feels, is his most arduous role: "It's more of an actor's part than a singer's. . . ." In an *Opera News* interview in 1980 Van Dam revealed that growing up he admired Bjoerling, Warren, Pinza, Siepi, Wunderlich, and, among the ladies, Leontyne Price. "She has a fantastic instrument, a beautiful line." He also looks to instrumentalists for that line, such as Rostropovich, Perlman, Zukerman, and Menuhin. Other notable recordings by Van Dam include Don Alfonso in Muti's 1983 Salzburg *Così fan tutte,* a Massenet *Manon* with

Cotrubas and Kraus under Plasson, and a superb Father in *Louise* with Sills and Gedda.

—Stephen A. Willier

VANESSA.

Composer: Samuel Barber.

Librettist: G.-C. Menotti.

First Performance: New York, Metropolitan Opera, 15 January 1958.

Roles: Vanessa (soprano); Erika (mezzo-soprano); Anatol (tenor); Doctor (baritone or bass-baritone); Baroness (contralto); Nicholas, Majordomo (bass); Footman (bass); Pastor (mute); chorus (SATB).

*   *   *

Samuel Barber's *Vanessa,* completed in 1957 and premiered at the Metropolitan Opera in 1958, was the composer's most ambitious work of the 1950s. Following its premiere, the opera was presented at the Salzburg Festival on 16 August 1958—the first time in history that the Festival presented an American opera and in English. The Metropolitan also staged the work two other seasons, 1958-59 and 1964-65. Thus, *Vanessa* became one among only a few moderately successful American operas to have emerged in the international performance repertoire. However, critics have pointed out that it is an American opera only because the composer was native-born, and not in any nationalistic sense, since neither the libretto nor the score is based on any American "mores or musical lore."

Vanessa, an attractive middle-aged woman who has been grieving over a lost love affair, has withdrawn from the world and lives isolated in a baronial house with her niece Erika "in a northern country." As the opera opens Vanessa awaits the return of her beloved Anatol after twenty years. However, the Anatol who arrives is not her lover but his son, who is an opportunistic adventurer seeking the good life. When Vanessa leaves the scene in disappointment, the young Anatol proceeds to seduce the lonely Erika, who soon realizes he is not serious. In act II, sensing Erika's doubt, Anatol turns his attentions to Vanessa and revives her illusions of youthful love. When the couple's betrothal is announced at the ball in act III, Erika, who is pregnant, attempts suicide. In the final act, Erika is rescued, suffers a miscarriage, and renounces her relationship to Anatol. As Vanessa rides off with Anatol, Erika orders the house be shut up again as she, waiting for love, assumes Vanessa's former role.

Barber had been seeking a libretto for years, discussing opera projects with Dylan Thomas, Thornton Wilder, and Stephen Spender, among others. He was delighted when his friend Gian-Carlo Menotti, who had an excellent working knowledge of the theater as both composer-librettist and stage director, offered to write a text for him. Although Menotti modestly defined a libretto as a "pretext for music," Barber, in his total immersion in any poetry he set, appreciated the economy of Menotti's verbal expression, his pronounced simplicity, and unique theatrical timing—all elements imperative

The first production of Barber's *Vanessa,* with Eleanor Steber in the title role and Regina Resnik as the Baroness, Metropolitan Opera, New York, 1958

for the singing stage. According to Barber, composer and librettist discussed twists and turns of plot and character but Barber changed very few words, and sometimes requested additional text, including an extra aria for the doctor, to be sung by Giorgio Tozzi. Menotti's text, filtered through Barber's musical personality, produced high-style bravura duets, a delightful waltz, as well as pastoral dance tunes, a brilliant coloratura aria for Vanessa, a soliloquy for the doctor, and in the final act, a transporting quintet.

With a Chekhovian quality, *Vanessa* is a subtle character study with recognizable prototypes in the literature of the period. Vanessa's music, through high tessitura and virtuosic demands, reveals her high-strung emotionalism. Erika as a pivotal character has many opportunities—her opening aria, her renunciation of Anatol, and her suicide attempt—for a compelling performance. Anatol, though not so fully developed, reveals a marked weakness. The old Doctor serves as a contrast to the leading participants, and the Baroness— silent and immobile most of the time—must project in her negativity an ominously powerful minor character.

The world premiere under the baton of Dmitri Mitropoulos—the first time in ten years that the Metropolitan Opera had mounted an American opera—was greeted with a standing ovation. Encouraged by this reception, the European premiere in the Festspielhaus at the Salzburg Festival was meticulously planned. Although cordially greeted by an international audience, *Vanessa* was "brutally condemned" by the Austrian and German critics. According to Raymond Ericson's report in *Musical America* (September 1958, vol.

78 no. 10), "Unfortunately, all the best efforts of these distinguished artists could not persuade the critics that Menotti's libretto was not foolishness and that Barber's music was not a pastiche of ideas borrowed from Puccini and Strauss."

However, because of Barber's knowledge and empathy for the human voice, his extraordinary technical skills combined with his inventiveness in infusing formal structures with dramatic content and lyrical expansion, *Vanessa* has survived in the performance repertoire in spite of this evaluation. Further, Winthrop Sargeant in his biographical summary in *The New Grove Dictionary* considers the score "both complex and highly charged with emotional meaning." Indeed, it establishes that an American opera by an American composer "with sufficient knowledge of and feeling for the great international operatic tradition can turn out a near masterpiece in the genre."

—Muriel Hebert Wolf

VARADY, Julia.

Soprano. Born 1 September 1941, in Oradea, Rumania. Married: Dietrich Fischer-Diskau, 1974. Studied with Emilia Popp in Cluj and Arta Florescu in Bucharest; debut as Fiordiligi in Mozart's *Così fan tutte,* Cluj, 1962; sang at the Cluj opera; sang with the Frankfurt Opera, 1970-72; joined the Bavarian State Opera in Munich, 1972; Metropolitan Opera debut as Mozart's Donna Elvira, 1978; created Cordelia in Aribert Reimann's *Lear*, 1978.

Publications

About VARADY: articles–

Mahlke, S. "Saenger-Profile." *Opernwelt Jahrbuch* (1981): 114.
Tubeuf, A. "Julia Varady, le don paisible." *Diapason-Harmonie* 314 (1986): 42.
Geleng, I. "Portraet." *Opernwelt* 31 (1990): 24.

* * *

Few sopranos can match the passion and excitement that Varady brings to her performances of some of opera's greatest heroines; even fewer can match the versatility that she exhibits in performing roles differing widely in musical style and in the type of singing that they demand. Varady can dominate the stage with her performance of Santuzza (*Cavalleria rusticana*). She can perform the title role of *Madama Butterfly* with extraordinary subtlety and emotional effect. Yet she is also recognized as one of our foremost Mozart singers, a specialist in portraying his more distraught heroines. Her Elvira has won applause in Salzburg; her Vitellia in Munich helped bring *La clemenza di Tito* back into the repertory during the 1970s.

Varady's abilities as an interpreter of late eighteenth-century opera were splendidly displayed in a production of *Idomeneo* in Munich in 1975. "Julia Varady triumphed as Electra," wrote Greville Rothon in *Opera*. "She risked the most hazardous technical feats and brought them all off to perfection with the luscious warmth, and powerful and passionate character of her truly outstanding voice. She was a veritable fury."

As Elisetta, the jealous older sister in Cimarosa's *Il matrimonio segreto* (recorded under Barenboim), Varady reveals other aspects of her aptitude for eighteenth-century music. Elisetta is an aggressive snob, but she is also capable of being hurt. When Count Robinson, engaged *in absentia* to Elisetta, arrives and falls for her younger sister Carolina, Varady vividly conveys Elisetta's feelings of pride mixed with vulnerability and humiliation.

Varady's portrayal of Cimarosa's Elisetta is memorable, but there is a weakness in it that one finds in some of Varady's other portrayals as well. Sometimes she sings as if the dramatic situation and the meaning of the words have no importance for her. For example, in the finale of act II, Elisetta overhears voices and believes that Count Robinson and Carolina are engaged in an amorous rendez-vous. But Varady's voice does not convey the excitement and anger that Elisetta must feel. Another illustration of the same lack of emotional involvement is Varady's performance in Johann Christian Bach's *Lucio Silla* (recorded under Günther Kehr). Her portrayal of the heroine Giunia is beautifully sung, but emotionally detached. In the climactic recitative and aria in which Giunia imagines she hears the voice of her lover Cecilio, whom she fears to be dead, Varady does not evoke, with the vividness of which she is capable, Giunia's confused and distraught state of mind.

Varady has sung an astonishingly wide range of nineteenth-century operas. Her interpretations of Wagner heroines have won praise in Berlin (where a critic hailed her Sieglinde "absorbingly acted, thrillingly sung") and Stuttgart (where her first Elsa was described as "a meltingly vulnerable creature with a soaring voice"). She has also been successful in operas by Tchaikovsky and Strauss, and not only in their most familiar works. Typical of Varady's adventurous spirit are her portrayals of leading roles in Tchaikovsky's *Queen of Spades* and Strauss's *Feuersnot*, which she brings to life with the same level of musical and dramatic energy that she brings to more familiar roles.

—John A. Rice

VAUGHAN WILLIAMS, Ralph.

Composer. Born 12 October 1872, in Down Ampney, Gloucestershire. Died 26 August 1958, in London. Married: 1) Adeline Fisher, 1897 (died 1951); 2) the poet Ursula Wood, 7 February 1953. Played violin and viola in the orchestra of the Charterhouse School, London, 1887-90; studied harmony with F.E. Gladstone, theory with Parry, and organ with Parratt at the Royal College of Music, London, 1890-92; studied composition with Charles Wood and organ with Alan Gray at Trinity College, Cambridge, receiving a Mus. B. in 1894 and a B.A. in 1895; studied with Stanford at the Royal College of Music; studied with Max Bruch in Berlin, 1897; Mus. D., Cambridge University, 1901; member of the Folk Song Society, 1904; conductor of the Leith Hill Festival in Dorking, 1905; studied with Ravel in Paris, 1909; served in Salonika and France as a medical orderly and later as an artillery officer in the British Army, 1914-18; professor of composition at the Royal College of Music, 1919-38; conductor of the London Bach Choir, 1920-28; *A Pastoral Symphony* completed 1921; in the United States, 1922; Gold Medal of the Royal Philharmonic Society of London, 1930; lectured at Bryn Mawr College, 1932; Order of Merit from King George V, 1935; composition of his fourth through ninth symphonies, 1931-58; lecture tour of several American universities, 1954.

Operas/Masques

Publishers: Curwen, Oxford University Press, Stainer and Bell.

Hugh the Drover, or Love in the Stocks, H. Child, 1910-14, London, His Majesty's, 14 July 1924; revised, 1956.
The Shepherds of the Delectable Mountains, Vaughan Williams (after Bunyan), 1921, London, Royal College of Music, 11 July 1922 [incorporated into *The Pilgrim's Progress*].
On Christmas Night (masque), A. Bolm and Vaughan Williams (after Dickens), 1926, Chicago, Eighth Street, 26 December 1926.
Sir John in Love, Vaughan Williams (after Shakespeare), 1924-28, London, Royal College of Music, 21 March 1929.
Job (masque), G. Keynes and G. Raverat (after Blake), 1927-30, London, Cambridge Theatre, 5 July 1931.
The Poisoned Kiss (romantic extravaganza), E. Sharp (after R. Garnett), 1927-29, Cambridge, Arts Theatre, 12 May 1936; revised, 1956-57.
Riders to the Sea, Vaughan Williams (after J.M. Synge), 1925-32, London, Royal College of Music, 1 December 1937.

The Bridal Day (masque), U. Wood (after Spenser), 1938-39, British Broadcasting Corporation, 5 June 1953; revised, 1952-53.

The Pilgrim's Progress, Vaughan Williams (after Bunyan, et al.), 1949; London, Covent Garden, 26 April 1951; revised, 1951-52.

Other works: orchestral works (including nine symphonies), ballets, incidental music, sacred and secular vocal works, instrumental and chamber music, many film scores.

Publications

By VAUGHAN WILLIAMS: books–

ed. *The English Hymnal.* 1906.
ed. *Songs of Praise.*
National Music. London, 1934; as *National Music and Other Essays,* London, 1963.
Some Thoughts on Beethoven's Choral Symphony with Writings on other Musical Subjects. London, 1953; reprinted in *National Music and Other Essays,* London, 1963.
The Making of Music. Ithaca, New York, 1955; reprinted in *National Music and Other Essays,* London, 1963.
Vaughan Williams, Ursula, and Imogen Holst, eds. *Heirs and Rebels: Letters Written to Each Other and Occasional Writings on Music,* with Gustav Holst. London, 1959.
Working with Vaughan Williams: the Correspondence of Ralph Vaughan Williams and Roy Douglas. London, 1972; 1988.

articles–

"Conducting" and "Fugue." *Grove's Dictionary of Music and Musicians.* 1900 ed.
"Who Wants the English Composer?" *Royal College of Music Magazine* 9 (1912): 11.

About VAUGHAN WILLIAMS: books–

Dickinson, A.E.F. *An Introduction to the Music of Ralph Vaughan Williams.* London, 1928.
Howes, Frank. *The Dramatic Works of Ralph Vaughan Williams.* London, 1937.
Foss, Hubert. *Ralph Vaughan Williams.* London, 1950.
Pakenham, Simona. *Ralph Vaughan Williams: a Discovery of his Music.* London and New York, 1957.
Day, James. *Vaughan Williams.* London, 1961; 2nd ed., 1975.
Dickinson, A.E.F. *Vaughan Williams.* London, 1963.
Kennedy, Michael. *The Works of Ralph Vaughan Williams.* London, 1964; 1980.
Vaughan Williams, Ursula. *Ralph Vaughan Williams: a Biography* London, 1964.
Ottaway, H. *Vaughan Williams.* London, 1966.
Hurd, M. *Vaughan Williams.* London, 1970.
Lunn, J.E., and Ursula Vaughan Williams. *Ralph Vaughan Williams: a Pictorial Biography.* London, 1971.
Douglas, R. *Working with Ralph Vaughan Williams.* London, 1972.
Mellers, Wilfred. *Vaughan Williams and the Vision of Albion.* London, 1989.
Butterworth, Neil. *Ralph Vaughan Williams: a Guide to Research.* New York, 1990.

articles–

Goddard, S. "The Operas of Vaughan Williams." *The Listener* 20 (1938): 917.
_____. "*The Poisoned Kiss.*" *The Listener* 26 (1941): 737.
Wilson, S. "Hugh the Drover." *Opera* 1 (1950): 29.
Mullinar, M. "The Pilgrim's Progress." *Royal College of Music Magazine* 47 (1951): 46.
Murrill, H. "Vaughan William's Pilgrim." *Music and Letters* 32 (1951): 324.
Smith, C. "The Pilgrim's Progress." *Opera* 2 (1951): 373.
Foss, H.J. "*The Pilgrim's Progress* by Vaughan Williams." In *Music 1952,* edited by A. Robertson, 32. Harmondsworth, 1952.
Ottaway, H. "Riders to the Sea." *Musical Times* 93 (1952): 358.
Warrack, John. "Vaughan Williams and Opera." *Opera* 9(1958): 698.
Vaughan Williams, Ursula. "Vaughan Williams and Opera." *Composer* 41(1971): 25.
Foreman, L. "Vaughan Williams: a Bibliography of Dissertations." *Musical Times* 113 (1972): 962.
Forbes, Anne-Marie H. "Motivic Unity in Ralph Vaughan Williams's *Riders to the Sea.*" *Music Review* 44 (1983): 234.

* * *

Ralph Vaughan Williams, son of an Anglican clergyman, came from a well-to-do middle class background of considerable intellectual distinction, being descended from the Darwins and the Wedgewoods on his mother's side and from a line of professional people on his father's. He showed a talent for music and an interest in the theater from his early childhood; he had a toy theater as a boy at Leith Hill Place in Surrey and composed small pieces to accompany the plays "performed" in it. Titles of some of these have been preserved: *The Ram Opera,* for example, and *The Galoshes (sic!) of Happienes (sic),* found in a musical exercise book dating from the year 1882.

After leaving Charterhouse school in the summer of 1890, the boy went to Munich before entering the Royal College of Music as a student. There, he heard Wagner's *Die Walküre* for the first time; he described the experience as "a feeling of recognition as of meeting an old friend." Two years later, in June 1892, he heard in London a visiting company from the Hamburg opera under Gustav Mahler perform *Tristan und Isolde* and was profoundly affected by the music.

In the autumn of 1895, having graduated in History and having obtained his Bachelor of Music degree at Trinity College, Cambridge, he returned to the Royal College of Music, studying composition with C.V. Stanford. Stanford was not only a fine teacher, scholar and "academic" composer of choral and orchestral music, but also much interested in opera. He had conducted the English premieres of Cornelius's *Barber of Baghdad,* of Schumann's *Genoveva,* and of Delibes's *Le roi l'a dit* earlier in the 1890s. He greatly admired both Verdi and Wagner and composed seven operas himself, including *Shamus O'Brien,* on an Irish theme, first performed in March 1896, which had a successful run of over 100 performances.

Although Vaughan Williams liberated himself from the Brahmsian idiom of his irascible teacher, his operas follow the more traditional kind favored by Stanford himself rather than the Wagnerian music drama. He had discovered the appeal of English folk song, was excited by the freshness of the great Tudor and Stuart composers from Tallis to Purcell, and responded to the beauty and power of Anglo-American literature (Walt Whitman's verse was an early and lifelong enthusiasm). Like many young English musicians of his time, he realized that "second-hand off-scourings of the classics," as he himself put it, were not the way to establish a vital school of English composition. This did not mean, however, that he felt either folk song or a return to the past was the be-all and end-all of any musical renaissance in England. Something more was needed, in his own case, at any rate. He therefore spent three months in Paris in 1908 studying with Maurice Ravel.

In April 1905, music by Vaughan Williams for a masque based on Ben Jonson's *Pan's Anniversary* had been performed at Stratford-on-Avon; another pointer to the future came in 1909, when he composed music for a performance of a dramatized version of Bunyan's *Pilgrim's Progress* at Reigate Priory. Music for a number of Greek plays including *Iphigenia in Tauris, The Bacchae* and *Elektra* followed, but undoubtedly the most successful of these scores was that composed for a production at Cambridge in November 1909 of Aristophanes' *The Wasps*. In 1913, he composed music for other plays, including Maeterlinck's *The Death of Tintagiles* and (for F.R. Benson's Shakespearean season that year at Stratford-on-Avon) *The Merry Wives of Windsor* (to which he was to return for the source of his second full-length opera), *King Richard II, King Henry IV, Part II, King Richard III* and *King Henry V*. Benson also produced Shaw's *The Devil's Disciple,* set in the American colonies in revolt against George III, to which Vaughan Williams contributed the incidental music.

Vaughan Williams was now regarded as the leading English composer of the post-Elgar generation with works such as the *Fantasia on a Theme by Thomas Tallis* (1910), the impressionistic and highly dramatic song cycle *On Wenlock Edge* (1909, poems by A.E. Housman), the *Sea Symphony,* and the *Five Mystical Songs* (1911; poems by George Herbert). By 1910, he felt that he was ready to try his hand at an opera, regardless of whether it might ever reach the stage.

The origin of his first opera, *Hugh the Drover,* was ostensibly the result of a desire to set a prize fight to music, and the boxing match in the first act of *Hugh* is evidence of the fact. Vaughan Williams also wanted to compose a modern equivalent of the ballad operas of the eighteenth century, of which *The Beggar's Opera* had been the first and of which the Savoy operettas of Gilbert and Sullivan were a direct descendant.

The book of *Hugh the Drover* was by Harold Child, a writer on the staff of the London *Times.* "The duty of the words," Vaughan Williams had written in 1902, "is to say just as much as the music has left unsaid and no more." From about August 1910 over a period of years, he gently bullied Child into reshaping his text to do this, and the piece was virtually finished just before the outbreak of war in August 1914.

Despite his age (nearly 42), Vaughan Williams volunteered for military service, first in the Royal Army Medical Corps and then in the Royal Artillery, serving in the Balkans and on the western front. After the armistice, he became Director of Music for the British First Army, and on demobilization in February 1919, he set about revising his *London Symphony* (composed in the years before the war) and *Hugh the Drover.* He also started work on his third (*Pastoral*) symphony, some of the musical ideas for which had occurred to him when in military service. That year, he joined the staff of the Royal College of Music, teaching composition.

Vaughan Williams's music of this period is notable particularly for a ruminatively lyrical strain, evident not only in the *Pastoral Symphony,* but in such works as *The Lark Ascending* (1920) for violin and orchestra (completed before the war but revised after it) and his second opera, *The Shepherds of the Delectable Mountains,* (1922) a one-acter adapted from an episode in Bunyan's *Pilgrim's Progress* and incorporated many years later into the full-length opera he composed on Bunyan's book. In the same year that he composed *The Shepherds,* he also paid his first visit to the United States, to conduct a performance of his *Pastoral Symphony* at the Litchfield County Music Festival, Norfolk, Connecticut. It is amusing to note that he was far more impressed by the bustle of New York than he was by Niagara Falls!

The 1920s saw a broadening and deepening of his idiom. He absorbed something of the neo-classicism of Stravinsky and the brash brightness of "Les Six," but he remained in general true to his own musical past, with works such as the Mass in G minor (1922), the *English Folk Song Suite* for military band (1923) and the Violin Concerto (1926). 1926 also saw the composition of two works in which the power and passion latent in his music reached a new intensity of expression: the oratorio *Sancta Civitas* and the haunting *Flos Campi,* for solo viola, wordless chorus and small orchestra. In the meantime, *Hugh the Drover* reached the professional stage, being produced by the British National Opera Company at His Majesty's Theatre, London, on 14 July 1924.

The success of *Hugh the Drover* stimulated the composer to work on other operatic ventures. The first of these to achieve public performance (on 21 March 1929 at the Royal College of Music) was *Sir John in Love,* a Falstaff opera based on Shakespeare's *The Merry Wives of Windsor,* the text arranged by the composer. The opera marks a distinct advance in stagecraft and musical sophistication over *Hugh,* and the main reason why this delightfully lyrical and strongly characterized piece has not become more popular is probably the sheer number of singers required. It certainly stands up well to the comparison it inevitably courts with Verdi's great masterpiece on the Falstaff story.

There followed what is probably the composer's operatic masterpiece, his setting of J.M. Synge's one-act tragedy *Riders to the Sea.* Work on this began in the 1920s, and although the piece was completed by 1932, it was not performed until 1 December 1937. The taut action and restrained musical idiom of *Riders,* its simplicity and terseness have caused it to become a problem opera; its quality and stageworthiness are indisputable, but because it lasts a mere thirty-five minutes and is difficult to provide with a complementary work of the right scale to fill the rest of the evening, it has been unjustly neglected.

Growing recognition abroad led to a further visit to the United States, this time to lecture at Bryn Mawr University on "National Music." Every new work was now eagerly awaited. The massive "masque for dancing" *Job* (1930, first staged at the Cambridge Theatre, London, 5 July 1931), the powerful Piano Concerto (1931), the violent F minor Symphony (1935) and numerous choral works, including the racy *Five Tudor Portraits* of 1935 and the sombre *Dona Nobis Pacem* (1936) testified to his versatility. Further evidence of this is found in the comic opera *The Poisoned Kiss,* first performed on May 12 1936 at the new Arts Theatre in Cambridge. This work suffers from an irredeemably arch libretto, but it contains some fine music, dramatically apt and lighter in touch than is usually the case with Vaughan Williams. Unlike his other operas and in keeping with its somewhat farcical subject matter, *The Poisoned Kiss* has spoken dialogue.

The Second World War and after saw Vaughan Williams exploiting new fields as well as continuing to cultivate old ones. He composed music to the film *49th Parallel* in 1940-41, the first of many film scores (elements from at least two of which found their way into symphonic compositions), and in 1943, at the age of 70, he produced his luminous and visionary Fifth Symphony, incorporating elements from his unfinished operatic version of *The Pilgrim's Progress.* Many took the Fifth to be his final symphonic testament; few realized that four more symphonies were to follow it, including the pungent and disquieting Sixth (1948) and the *Sinfonia Antartica* (No. 7, 1953), the themes of which were in large measure developed from his music to the film *Scott of the Antarctic.*

Vaughn Williams' final completed opera (he was working on a further operatic project, based on an English folk ballad, when he died) was the *The Pilgrim's Progress,* first performed at the Royal Opera House, Covent Garden, on 26 April 1951. The subject matter and the absence of any conventional operatic love interest and intrigue failed to impress the audience, and a gimmicky production presented the opera in the worst possible light. None the less, the score contains some of his finest music, with a telling theatrical contrast between the sinister mechanical monotone of Apollyon, the Hogarthian ribaldry of the Vanity Fair scene, the laid-back vapidity of the By-Ends episode and the radiant visionary quality of the central figure's apotheosis at the end.

Vaughan Williams is an outstanding figure in the history of twentieth century English music. Basically traditionalist, the individuality, power, depth and intensity of his music at its best have few equals.

—James Day

VENUS AND ADONIS.

Composer: John Blow.

Librettist: unknown.

First Performance: c. 1682.

Roles: Venus (soprano); Adonis (baritone); Cupid (soprano); chorus.

Publications

book–

Lewis, Anthony. Introduction to *J. Blow: Venus and Adonis.* Paris, 1939.

articles–

Lewis, Anthony. "Purcell and Blow's 'Venus and Adonis'." *Music and Letters* 44 (1963): 266.
Luckett, Richard. "A New Source for 'Venus and Adonis'." *Musical Times* 130 (1989): 76.

* * *

Venus and Adonis, a masque consisting of a prologue and three acts by John Blow, librettist unknown, was first given in London in the early 1680s. In *A History of English Opera,*

Eric Walter White gives the probable date of the premiere as "not later than the first three months of 1682," and Curtis Price, in *Henry Purcell and the London Stage,* states that it was "performed about 1682." The heyday of the masque was in the early years of the seventeenth century, when from 1605 to 1631 Ben Jonson, the best-known author of masques, provided them for the court. Blow's *Venus and Adonis* was written during the Restoration for the entertainment of Charles II and is the first example of an English through-composed masque with complete dramatic action. The role of Venus was created for one of the King's mistresses, Mrs Mary ("Moll") Davis; Cupid was undertaken by her daughter, Lady Mary Tudor, only eight or nine years old at the time. There are three principal characters, Venus, Adonis, and Cupid, who comment on love, pleasure and fidelity. In act II the little Cupids receive a spelling lesson on love. Urged by Venus not to forget that "absence kindles new desire," Adonis goes hunting and is fatally wounded and mourned.

The work begins with an overture. Several dances are included in the score, among them a Huntsman's Dance, one for the Cupids, one for the Graces, and a splendid Ground that ends the second act. One especially noteworthy feature of the work is Blow's exemplary setting of the text, capturing the rhythms and nuances of the English language. In the last act, for example, Venus sings passionately of her beloved in the manner of a Monteverdian lament. The opening repetition of her outcries of "Adonis" rise higher each time; sighs are depicted by rising appoggiaturas; chromaticism abounds in the melodic line, which rises by semitones to depict the word "grief"; and there is a diminished fourth on the word "mourn-full." Choral writing is quite prominent and fine; the final four-part dirge, "Mourn for thy servant, mighty God of Love," is a moving ending to the work.

Henry Purcell may have been among those present when *Venus and Adonis* was given at court. In any case the parallels between Blow's work and Purcell's subsequent *Dido and Aeneas* are too many and too obvious to be coincidental. Both works begin in C major and conclude in G minor and have similar dramatic and musical structures. Each is sung throughout and cast in three acts and a French-based prologue; in each a commanding woman loses her beloved; descending chromaticism is used in each to depict grief and ultimate tragedy; both are shaded by moments of comic and pastoral relief; and both end with choruses of mourning and reflection. After the overture, act I of *Venus and Adonis* settles into A minor, a tonality that represents the ill-fated love between the goddess and the young hunter. Hunting music in C major from offstage interrupts the lovers but then the music reverts to A minor. The C major allusion to the hunt does not apply to the hunters themselves, who, as Ellen T. Harris writes, "in Blow's masque remain tonally undifferentiated from the lovers whom they have interrupted." Harris also notes the following alternation of English song types in the first act: symphony (act tune), declamatory air (a 2), symphony (Hunter's Musick), tuneful air, dialogue, and then a final group arranged as chorus and song (cadencing to E minor) and song and chorus (cadencing to A minor). The act ends with a dance that repeats material from the Hunter's Musick.

At the time of the composition of *Venus and Adonis,* Blow was organist of Westminster Abbey and Master of the Children of the Royal Chapel. This was Blow's only work for the stage. None of the score was printed at the time and the retiring Blow did not gain a reputation as a composer for the theater as a result of *Venus and Adonis.*

—Stephen Willier

LES VÊPRES SICILIENNES [The Sicilian Vespers].

Composer: Giuseppe Verdi.

Librettists: Eugène Scribe and Charles Duveyrier.

First Performance: Paris, Opéra, 13 June 1855; revised as *Giovanni di Guzman,* later called *I vespri siciliani,* Milan, Teatro alla Scala, 4 February 1856.

Roles: Montforte (baritone); Henri (tenor); Hélène (soprano); Procida (bass); Bethune (bass); Count Vaudimont (bass); Ninetta (contralto); Daniele (tenor); Tébald (tenor); Robert (bass); Manfred (tenor); chorus (SATTB); chorus (TB).

Publications

articles–

Porter, Andrew. "*Les vêpres siciliennes:* New Letters from Verdi to Scribe." *Nineteenth-Century Music* 2 (1978): 95.
Noske, Frits. "Melodia e struttura in *Les Vêpres siciliennes* di Verdi." *Ricerche musicali* 18/no.4 (1980): 3.
Budden, Julian. "Verdi and Meyerbeer in Relation to *Les Vêpres siciliennes.*" *Studi verdiani* 1 (1982): 11.
Conati, Marcello. "Ballabili nei *Vespri,* con alcune osservazioni su Verdi e la musica popolare." *Studi verdiani* 1 (1982): 21.
Switzer, Richard. "Dawn of *The Vespers.*" *Opera News* 46/no. 14 (1982): 26.
Avant-scène opéra May (1985) [*Les vêpres siciliennes* issue].

* * *

For his first commission from the Paris Opéra, Verdi chose the librettist preferred by Meyerbeer and Halévy, the reigning monarchs of that stage: Eugène Scribe. Though Scribe was supposed to offer an original work, he in fact merely rewrote a libretto Donizetti had attempted to set fifteen years earlier, but failed to complete before succumbing to the venereal disease which eventually killed him. At that time the libretto was called *Le duc d'Albe,* and dealt with Spanish oppression in the Lowlands under the eponymous Duke of Alva. Scribe transferred the oppression to thirteenth-century Sicily, converted the Duke into Guy de Montfort, the cruel governor, changed Amelia, sister of the martyred Count of Egmont, into Hélène, sister of the martyred Regent of Sicily, and Marcel, a revolutionary whom the duke has just discovered to be his illegitimate son, into Henri, Montfort's son under the same circumstances. The major addition to the original libretto is its setting at the moment of a well-known historical event, the uprising of the Sicilians and their massacre of the French as the bells tolled vespers on Easter Sunday, 1282. Verdi also added a character, Procida, who existed in history but seems to have been a diplomat without portfolio rather than the terrorist fanatic the opera makes of him.

Verdi, with his uncanny sense of what would and would not "play," put his finger on a central problem of the libretto. Writing to the Paris Opéra's director, he observed that "M. Scribe offends the French, because Frenchmen are massacred; he offends the Italians by altering the historical character of Procida into the conventional conspirator." Scribe, however, made no alterations, and the opera was given a surprisingly warm reception, the urbane Parisians apparently caring less about seeing their ancestors portrayed as villains than about hearing a good, Meyerbeerian plot realized with Italianate verve. The Italians were denied an opportunity to express themselves on the slandering of Procida, because the Austrians occupying Italy would not permit an opera depicting an Italian nationalist uprising, especially a successful one. For the Italian performance, the action was transferred to the Iberian peninsula, as *Giovanna da Guzman,* with Portuguese patriots and Spanish brutality.

Verdi's criticism of the libretto is cogent, but those of subsequent commentators must be treated with some reservation, since by and large their references are to the eventual Italian translation which, like all Italian translations of the French libretti set by Verdi, Rossini, and Donizetti, reflect a banality of concept and trivialization of motive not found in the originals.

Independent of his reservations about the libretto, Verdi was faced with a difficult task, the writing of "French" music for a Meyerbeerian grand opera. His successful adaptation of *I Lombardi* into the more subtle *Jerusalem* in 1847 had been critically acclaimed in Paris, but there he had adapted an existing score. Now he would have to test himself where both Rossini and Donizetti had succeeded before him, not only in composing music to a libretto in a foreign language (which he, like they, spoke and understood well enough), but also in modifying the essential directness of the Italian operatic idiom into the subtler harmonies, more complex ensembles, and less easily excerptable solo passages preferred by the Parisian public. One hesitates to call this style "French," except geographically: it had its origins in the German Gluck's ideas, while its form had been dictated primarily by the Germanized Italian Spontini and the Italianized German Meyerbeer. Though Verdi would eventually master its requisites perhaps better than anyone else in *Don Carlos* (1867), *Les vêpres siciliennes* can be seen as a laboratory in which Verdi tests his capacity for French expression. Those who know the opera only from its most often played and recorded excerpts, the overture, Procida's act II aria, and Hélène's act V bolero, have heard only the most Italianate parts of the score. Montfort's act III aria and duet with Henri are identifiably Verdian, but more contemplative, less direct than similar pieces from his most recent Italian operas. Henri's aria, proceeding from a complex recitative without the obligatory musical break, is unlike anything Verdi had written up to this time, and can only be compared with the tenor's music in *Stiffelio.* Hélène's act I aria, with its four-movement structure (andante, largo, allegro moderato, allegro giusto) has no model in earlier Verdi, resembling much more closely Fidès' scena in Meyerbeer's *Le prophète.* But it is in the great ensembles concluding the second and fourth acts in which Verdi entirely masters the French style (to the incidental benefit of his later Italian works, especially *Simon Boccanegra* and *La forza del destino*). Again the contrast is between controlled complexity and impetuous simplicity. In the analogous situations a condemned patriot's farewell to his country, in *Il trovatore's* act IV "Miserere" and *Les vêpres'* "Adieu, mon pays," Italian directness is essentially right for the larger-than-life *Trovatore;* the muted antiphony of the *Vêpres* ensemble reflects the more recognizably human reactions of Scribe's characters. *Les vêpres siciliennes* is, finally, not a great opera, but it has great passages, is crucial to Verdi's development, and is fascinating in comparison with both Verdi's later works and the immensely popular works of Meyerbeer and Halévy that the Italian master sought to match in popularity.

—William J. Collins

VERDI, Giuseppe (Fortunino Francesco).

Composer. Born 9 or 10 October 1813, in Le Roncole, near Busseto, Duchy of Parma. Died 27 January 1901, in Milan. Married: 1) Margherite Barezzi, daughter of Verdi's patron, 4 May 1836 (died 18 June 1840); 2) the renowned soprano Giuseppina Strepponi, 29 August 1859 (died 1897). Studied at a very early age with the church organist Pietro Baistrocchi; music lessons with Ferdinando Provesi, director of the municipal music school in Busseto; resident at the home of the merchant Antonio Barezzi, 1831, who paid Verdi's way to Milan for further musical instruction; denied admission to the Milan Conservatory; private study of couterpoint, canon, and fugue with Vincenzo Lavigna; maestro di musica in Busseto, 1834; first opera, *Oberto,* completed 1838, which was accepted and performed at the Teatro alla Scala in Milan, 1839; further opera composition for the Teatro alla Scala, 1839-43; premieres of operas in Venice, Florence, London, St Petersburg, and Paris, 1844-47; elected to and served in the first Italian Parliament, 1861-65; elected to the Académie des Beaux Arts in Paris, 1864; premiere of *Aida* in Cairo, 1871, an international event; nominated a senator of the Italian Parliament, 1875; last operas, *Otello* (1887) and *Falstaff* (1893), composed after years of retirement; the King of Italy named Verdi "Marchese di Busseto," 1893, but Verdi did not accept the title; founded the Casa di Riposo per Musicisti in Milan, 1897.

Operas

Editions: *The Works of Giuseppe Verdi.* Edited by Philip Gosset et al. Chicago and Milan, 1983-.

Oberto, Conte di San Bonifacio, Temistocle Solera? (after A. Piazza, *Rocester, Lord Hamilton*), Milan, Teatro alla Scala, 17 November 1839.

Un giorno di regno, ossia Il finto Stanislao, Felice Romani, revised Temistocle Solera? (after Romani, *Il finto Stanislao* 1812), Milan, Teatro alla Scala, 5 September 1840.

Nabucodonosor (shortened to *Nabucco*), Temistocle Solera (after the ballet by A. Cortesi, 1838), Milan, Teatro alla Scala, 9 March 1842.

I Lombardi alla prima crociata, Temistocle Solera (after Tommaso Grossi), Milan, Teatro alla Scala, 11 February 1843; revised as *Jérusalem,* Gustave Vaëz and Alphonse Royer, Paris, Opéra, 26 November 1847.

Ernani, Francesco Maria Piave (after Hugo, *Hernani*), Venice, La Fenice, 9 March 1844.

I due Foscari, Francesco Maria Piave (after Byron, *The Two Foscari*), Rome, Torre Argentina, 3 November 1844.

Giovanna d'Arco, Temistocle Solera (after Schiller, *Die Jungfrau von Orleans*), Milan, Teatro alla Scala, 15 February 1845.

Alzira, Salvadore Cammarano (after Voltaire), Naples, San Carlo, 12 August 1845.

Attila, Temistocle Solera and Francesco Maria Piave (after Z. Werner), Venice, La Fenice, 17 March 1846.

Macbeth, Francesco Maria Piave and Andrea Maffei (after Shakespeare), Florence, Teatro della Pergola, 14 March 1847; revised, Piave, French translation by Charles Nuitter and A. Beaumont, Paris, Théâtre-Lyrique, 21 April 1865.

I masnadieri, Andrea Maffei (after Schiller, *Die Räuber*), London, Her Majesty's, 22 July 1847.

Il corsaro, Francesco Maria Piave (after Byron, *The Corsair*), Trieste, Grande, 25 October 1848.

La battaglia di Legnano, Salvadore Cammarano (after J. Méry, *La bataille de Toulouse*), Rome, Torre Argentina, 27 January 1849.

Luisa Miller, Salvadore Cammarano (after Schiller, *Kabale und Liebe*), Naples, San Carlo, 8 December 1849.

Stiffelio, Francesco Maria Piave (after E. Souvestre and E. Bourgeois), Trieste, Civico, 16 November 1850; revised as *Aroldo,* Rimini, Nuovo, 16 August 1857.

Rigoletto (originally, *La maledizione*), Francesco Maria Piave (after Hugo, *Le roi s'amuse*), Venice, La Fenice, 11 March 1851.

Il trovatore, Salvadore Cammarano, some changes and additions by L.E. Bardare (after Garcia Gutiérrez, *El trovador*), Rome, Apollo, 19 January 1853.

La traviata, Francesco Maria Piave (after Dumas fils, *La dame aux camélias*), Venice, La Fenice, 6 March 1853.

Les vêpres siciliennes, Eugène Scribe and Charles Duveyrier, Paris, Opéra, 13 June 1855; [revised as *Giovanni di Guzman,* later called *I vespri siciliani,* Milan, Teatro alla Scala, 4 February 1856].

Simon Boccanegra, Francesco Maria Piave and G. Montanelli (after Antonio García Gutiérrez), Venice, La Fenice, 12 March 1857; text revised, Arrigo Boito, music revised by Verdi, Milan, Teatro alla Scala, 24 March 1881.

Un ballo in maschera (originally *Gustavo III*), Antonio Somma (after Eugène Scribe, *Gustave III*), Rome, Apollo, 17 February 1859.

La forza del destino, Francesco Maria Piave (after Angelo Pérez de Saavedra, *Don Alvaro, o La fuerza de sino,* and Schiller, *Wallensteins Lager*), St Petersburg, Imperial Theater, 10 November 1862; text revised, A. Ghislanzoni, music revised by Verdi, Milan, Teatro alla Scala, 27 February 1869.

Don Carlos, François Joseph Méry and Camille Du Locle (after Schiller, W.H. Prescott, *History of Philip II,* and E. Cormon, *Philippe II, roi d'Espagne*), Paris, Opéra, 11 March 1867; translated into Italian by A. de Lauzières and A. Zanardini, with musical revisions by Verdi, for Milan, Teatro alla Scala, 10 January 1884.

Aida, Antonio Ghislanzoni (after a scenario by François Auguste Ferdinand Mariette as sketched in French by Camille Du Locle), Cairo, new Opera House, 24 December 1871.

Otello, Arrigo Boito (after Shakespeare), Milan, Teatro alla Scala, 5 February 1887.

Falstaff, Arrigo Boito (after Shakespeare, *The Merry Wives of Windsor* and *King Henry IV*), Milan, Teatro alla Scala, 9 February 1893.

Other works: choral and other vocal works, piano pieces, a string quartet.

Publications/Writings

By VERDI: books–

Pascolato, Alessandro. *Re Lear e Ballo in maschera: lettere di Giuseppe Verdi ad Antonio Somma.* Città di Castello, 1902.

Cesari, G., and A. Luzio, eds. *Copia lettere.* Milan, 1913; 1973.

Alberti, Annibale. *Verdi intimo: carteggio di Giuseppe Verdi con il conte Opprandino Arrivabene (1861-1886).* Verona, 1931.

Garibaldi, Luigi Agostino. *Giuseppe Verdi nelle lettere di Emanuele Muzio ad Antonio Barezzi.* Milan, 1931.

De Rensis, Raffaello. *Franco Faccio e Verdi: carteggio e documenti inediti.* Milan, 1934.

Luzio, Alessandro. *Carteggi verdiani.* Rome, 1935, 1947.

Bongiovanni, Giannetto. *Dal carteggio inedito Verdi-Vigna.* Rome, 1941.

Osborne, Charles. *Letters of Giuseppe Verdi* [selected and translated from Cesari and Luzio, *Copia lettere,* 1913]. London, 1971.

Busch, Hans. *Verdi's Aida: the History of an Opera in Letters and Documents.* Minneapolis, 1978.

Medici, Mario, and Marcello Conati. *Carteggio Verdi-Boito.* 2 vols. Parma, 1978.

Busch, Hans, trans. and ed. *Giuseppe Verdi Briefe.* Frankfurt am Main, 1979.

Ricordi, Giulio, Franca Cella, and Pierluigi Petrobelli, eds. *Correspondenza e immagini 1881-1890.* Milan, 1982.

Otto, Werner. *Giuseppe Verdi: Briefe.* Kassel, 1983.

Oberdorfer, Aldo, ed. *Verdi: Autobiographie à travers la correspondance.* Paris, 1984.

Busch, Hans, ed. *Verdi's Otello and Simon Boccanegra (Revised Version) in Letters and Documents.* 2 vols. Oxford, 1988.

Petrobelli, Pierluigi, Marisa Di Gregorio Casati, and Carlo Matteo Mossa, eds. *Carteggio Verdi-Ricordi 1880-1881.* Parma, 1988.

About VERDI: books–

Basevi, A. *Studio sulle opere di Giuseppe Verdi.* Florence, 1859.

Hanslick, E. *Die moderne Oper.* Berlin, 1875; 1971.

Soffredini, A. *Le opere di Verdi: studio critico analitico.* Milan, 1901.

Werfel, Franz, and Paul Stefan. *Das Bildnis Giuseppe Verdis.* Vienna, 1926; English translation as *Verdi: the Man in his Letters,* 1942.

Gatti, C. *Verdi.* 2 vols. Verona, 1931; revised edition in 1 vol., 1950.

Mila, Massimo *Il melodramma di Verdi.* Bari, 1933; 1960.

Roncaglia, Gino. *L'ascensione creatrice di Giuseppe Verdi.* Florence, 1940.

Gatti, C. Introduction to *L'abbozzo del Rigoletto di Giuseppe Verdi.* Milan, 1941.

———. *Verdi nelle immagini.* Milan, 1941.

Barblan, Guglielmo. *Un prezioso spartito di Falstaff.* Milan, 1957.

Abbiati, F. *Verdi.* 4 vols. Milan, 1959.

Walker, Frank. *The Man Verdi.* London, 1962; 2nd ed., Chicago, 1982.

Merkling, F., ed. *The Opera News Book of Traviata.* New York, 1967.

Gerhartz, L.K. *Die Auseinandersetzungen des jungen Giuseppe Verdi mit dem literarischen Drama: ein Beitrag zur szenischen Strukturbestimmung der Oper.* Berlin, 1968.

Hughes, Spike. *Famous Verdi Operas.* London, 1968.

Osborne, Charles. *The Complete Operas of Verdi.* London, 1969; 1978.

Baldini, Gabriele. *Abitare la battaglia.* Milan, 1970; English translation as *The Story of Giuseppe Verdi: Oberto to Un ballo in maschera,* edited by Roger Parker. Cambridge, 1980.

Geck, A. *Aida, die Oper: Schriftenreihe über musikalische Bühnenwerke.* Berlin, 1973.

Hopkinson, Cecil. *A Bibliography of the Works of Giuseppe Verdi, 1813-1901.* 2 vols. New York, 1973-78 [vol. 2 treats operatic works].

Budden, Julian. *The Operas of Verdi.* 3 vols. London and New York, 1973-81.

Chusid, Martin. *A Catalogue of Verdi's Operas.* Hackensack, New Jersey, 1974.

Wechsberg, Joseph. *Verdi.* London, 1974.

Baldacci, Luigi, ed. *Tutti i libretti di Verdi.* Milan, 1975.

Godefroy, V. *The Dramatic Genius of Verdi: Studies of Selected Operas.* 2 vols. London, 1975-77.

Weaver, William, ed. *Verdi: a Documentary Study.* London, 1977.

Knaust, Rebecca, *The Complete Guide to "Aida".* New York, 1978.

Moscatelli, C. *Il "Macbeth" di Giuseppe Verdi. L'uomo, il potere, il destino.* Ravenna, 1978.

Osborne, Charles, *Verdi.* London, 1978.

Boito, Arrigo, *Opere.* Milan, 1979.

Marchesi, G. *Verdi, Merli e Cucú.* Busseto, 1979.

Degrada, Francesco. *Il palazzo incantato* [*Macbeth, Don Carlo, Otello*]. Fiesole, 1979.

Lavagetto, Mario. *Quei più modesti romanzi.* Milan, 1979.

———. *Un caso di censura: il "Rigoletto".* Milan, 1979.

Osborne, Charles. *Rigoletto: a Guide to the Opera.* London, 1979.

Wallner-Basté, Franz, comp. and trans. *Verdi aus der Nähe. Ein Lebensbild in Dokumenten.* Zurich, 1979.

Weaver, William, and Martin Chusid, eds. *The Verdi Companion.* New York, 1979; London, 1980.

John, Nicholas, ed. *Giuseppe Verdi: Aida.* London, 1980.

Ross, Peter. *Studien zum Verhältnis von Libretto und Komposition in den Opern Verdis.* Bern, 1980.

Casini, Claudio. *Verdi.* Milan, 1981.

Conati, Marcello, ed. *Interviste e incontre con Verdi.* Milan, 1981; English translation as *Interviews and Encounters with Verdi,* London, 1984.

———. *La bottega della musica, Verdi e la Fenice.* Milan, 1983.

———. *Il "Simon Boccanegra" di Verdi a Reggio Enilia (1857).* Reggio Enilia, 1984.

Csampai, Attila, and Dietmar Holland, eds. *Giuseppe Verdi: Otello: Texte, Materialien, Kommentare.* Reinbek, 1981.

Kimbell, David R.B. *Verdi in the Age of Italian Romanticism.* Cambridge, 1981.

John, Nicholas, ed. *Giuseppe Verdi: Otello,* London, 1981.

———. *Giuseppe Verdi: La traviata.* London, 1981.

Rescigno, E. *"La Forza del destino" di Verdi.* Milan, 1981.

De Angelis, M. *Le carte dell' impresario: melodramma e costume teatrale nell' ottocento.* Florence, 1982.

Gál, Hans. *Giuseppe Verdi und die Oper.* Frankfurt am Main, 1982.

John, Nicholas, ed. *Giuseppe Verdi: Falstaff.* London, 1982.

———. *Giuseppe Verdi: Rigoletto.* London, 1982.

Hepokoski, James A. *Giuseppe Verdi: Falstaff.* Cambridge, 1983.

John, Nicholas, ed. *Giuseppe Verdi: Il trovatore.* London, 1983.

Mila, Massimo. *I costumi della traviata.* Pordenone, 1984.

Rosen, David, and Andrew Porter. *Verdi's "Macbeth": a Sourcebook.* New York and London, 1984.

Budden, Julian. *Verdi.* London, 1985; New York, 1987.

Casati, Marisa Di Gregorio, and Marcello Pavarani, eds. *Ernani ieri e oggi* [symposium] Parma, 1987.

Hepokoski, James A. *Giuseppe Verdi: Otello.* Cambridge, 1987.

Morelli, G., ed. *Tornado a Stiffelio.* Florence, 1987.

Nuove prospettive nella ricerca verdiana. Parma, 1987.

Osborne Charles. *Verdi: a Life in the Theatre.* London, 1987.

Martin, George. *Aspects of Verdi.* New York and London, 1988.

Sopart, Andreas. *Verdis Simon Boccanegra (1857 und 1881): Eine musikalisch-dramaturgische Analyse.* Laaber, 1988.

Abbate, Carolyn, and Roger Parker. *Analyzing Opera: Verdi and Wagner.* Berkeley and Los Angeles, California, 1989.

Jensen, Luke. *Giuseppe Verdi and Giovanni Ricordi. With Notes on Francesco Lucca: From "Oberto" to "La traviata."* New York, 1989.

John, Nicholas, ed. *Giuseppe Verdi: Macbeth.* London, 1990.

Hajtas, Franz. *Studien zur Frühen Verdi-Interpretation. Schalldokumente bis 1926.* Frankfurt-am-main, 1990.

Kaufman, Thomas G. *Verdi and His Major Contemporaries: A Selected Chronology of Performances with Casts.* New York and London, 1990.

articles—

Simone, C. "Lettere al tenore Mario de Candia sulla cabaletta de *I due Foscari.*" *Nuova Antologia* 69 (1934).

Sartori, Claudio. "*Rochester,* la prima opera di Verdi." *Rivista musicale italiana* 43 (1939).

Roncaglia, G. "L'abbozzo del *Rigoletto* di Verdi." *Rivista musicale italiana* 48 (1946); reprinted in *Galleria verdiana.* Milan, 1959.

Cone, E.T. "The Old Man's Toys: Verdi's Last Operas." *Perspectives of New Music* winter (1954): 114.

———. "The Stature of *Falstaff:* Technique and Content in Verdi's Last Opera." *Center* 1 (1954).

Schueller, H. "*Othello* Transformed: Verdi's Interpretation of Shakespeare." In *Studies in Honor of John Wilcox.* Detroit, 1958.

Bollettino dell' Istituto di Studi Verdiani [Parma] 1 (1960) [*Un ballo in maschera* issue].

Hughes, Spike. "An Introduction to Verdi's *Macbeth.*" *Opera* April (1960).

Walker, Frank. "Verdi, Giuseppe Montanelli, and the Libretto of *Simon Boccanegra.*" In *Verdi: bollettino dell' Istituto di Studi Verdiani* 1 (1960).

Roncaglia, Gino. "Annotazioni sul *Falstaff* di Verdi." In *Volti musicali di Falstaff.* Siena, 1961.

Klein, John W. "Some Reflections on Verdi's *Simon Boccanegra.*" *Music and Letters* April (1962).

Quaderni dell' Istituto di Studi Verdiani 1 (1963) [*Il corsaro* issue].

Quaderni dell' Istituto di Studi Verdiani 2 (1963) [*Gerusalemme* issue].

Osthoff, Wolfgang. "Die beiden *Boccanegra*-Fassungen und der Beginn von Verdis Spätwerk." *Analecta Musicologica* 1 (1963).

Klein, John W. "Verdi's *Otello* and Rossini's." *Music and Letters* April (1964).

Bollettino dell' Istituto di Studi Verdiani [Parma] 2 (1961-66) [*La forza del destino* issue].

Pugliese, Giuseppe. "Verdi and Tocanini." *Opera* July and August (1967).

Dean, Winton. "Verdi's *Otello:* A Shakespearean Masterpiece." *Shakespeare Survey* 21 (1968).

Kerman, Joseph. "Verdi's Use of Recurring Themes." In *Studies in Music History: Essays for Oliver Strunk,* 495. Princeton, 1968.

Mila, Massimo "L' unità stilistica nell' opera di Verdi." *Nuova rivista musicale italiana* 2 (1968): 62.

Quaderni dell' Istituto di Studi Verdiani 3 (1968) [*Stiffelio* issue].

1° congresso internazionale di studi verdiani: Venezia 1966. Parma, 1969.

Abert, A.A. "Über Textentwürfe Verdis." In *Beiträge zur Geschichte der Oper,* edited by H. Becker, 131. Regensburg, 1969.

Hauger, George. "*Othello* and *Otello.*" *Music and Letters* January (1969).

Bollettino dell' Istituto di Studi Verdiani [Parma] 3 (1969-73) [*Rigoletto* issue].

Porter, Andrew. "A Sketch for *Don Carlo.*" *Musical Times* 111 (1970).

Barblan, G. "La lunga quarantena de Il Corsaro." Teatro la Fenice program book (1970-71): 291.

2° congresso internazionale di Studi verdiani, Verona, Parma and Busseto, 1969. Parma, 1971.

Quaderni dell' Istituto di Studi Verdiani 4 (1971) [genesis of *Aida* issue].

Kimbell, David R.B. "Poi . . . diventò l'*Oberto.*" *Music and Letters* 52 (1971).

Petrobelli, Pierluigi. "Osservazioni sul processo compositivo in Verdi." *Analecta Musicologica* 43 (1971): 125.

Celletti, R. "*Il Corsaro* e la vocalità di Verdi dall' *Oberto* ai *Vespri.*" Teatro la Fenice program book (1971-72): 321.

Porter, Andrew. "The Making of *Don Carlos.*" *Proceedings of the Royal Musical Association* 98 (1971-72).

Aycock, Roy Edwin. "Shakespeare, Boito, and Verdi." *Musical Quarterly* October (1972).

Budden, Julian. "Varianti nei *Vespri siciliani.*" *Nuova rivista musicale italiana* 6 (1972).

Chusid, Martin. "Rigoletto and Monterone: a Study in Musical Dramaturgy." In *International Musicological Society Congress Report 11. Copenhagen 1972;* reprinted in *Verdi Bollettino* 9 (1982).

Günther, Ursula. "Zur Entstehung der zweiten französischen Fassung von Verdis *Don Carlos.*" In *International Musicological Society Congress Report 11, Copenhagen 1972.*

———. "The Two *Traviatas.*" *Proceedings of the Royal Musical Association* 99 (1972-73).

Osthoff, Wolfgang. "Die beiden Fassungen von Verdi's *Macbeth.*" *Archiv für Musikwissenschaft* 29 (1972).

Porter, Andrew. "A Note on Princess Eboli." *Musical Times* 113 (1972).

Günther, Ursula. "Zur Entstehung von Verdis *Aida.*" *Studi musicali* 2 (1973).

Kerman, Joseph. "Notes on an Early Verdi Opera" [*Ernani*]. *Soundings* 3 (1973): 56.

3° congresso internazionale di studi verdiani, Milan, 1972. Parma, 1974.

Gossett, Philip. "Verdi, Ghislanzoni, and *Aida:* the Uses of Convention." *Critical Inquiry* 1 (1974): 291.

Günther, Ursula. "La genèse de *Don Carlos.*" *Revue de musicologie* 58 (1972): 16; 60 (1974): 87.

Noske, Frits. "Verdi und die Belangerung von Haarlem" [on *La battaglia di Legnano*]. In *Convivium musicorum: Festschrift Wolfgang Boetticher*. Berlin, 1974.

Porter, Andrew. "Prelude to a New *Don Carlos.*" *Opera* 25 (1974): 665.

Sabbeth, Daniel. "Dramatic and Musical Organization in Falstaff." In *3° congresso internazionale di studi verdiani, Milan, 1972*. Parma, 1974.

Günther, Ursula and G. Carrara Verdi. "Der Briefwechsel Verdi-Nuitter-Du Locle zur Revision des *Don Carlo.*" *Analecta Musicologica* 14, 15 (1974, 1975).

Avant-scène opéra May-June (1976) [*Otello* issue].

Avant-scène opéra July-August (1976) [*Aida* issue].

Humbert, J. "A propos de l'égyptomanie dans l'oeuvre de Verdi: attribution à August Mariette d'un scénario anonyme de l'opéra *Aida.*" *Revue de musicologie* 62 (1976): 229.

Noiray, M., and Roger Parker. "La composition d' *Attila*: étude de quelques variantes." *Revue de musicologie* 62 (1976): 104.

Noske, Frits. "Schiller e la genesi del *Macbeth* verdiano." *Nuova rivista musicale italiana* 10 (1976).

Alberti, L. "I progressi attuali [1872] del dramma musicale: note sulla disposizione scenica per l'opera *Aida.*" In *Il melodramma italiano dell'ottocento: studi e richerche per Massimo Mila*, 125. Turin, 1977.

Clémeur, M. "Eine neuentdeckte Quelle für das Libretto von Verdis *Don Carlos.*" *Melos/Neue Zeitschrift für Musik* 3 (1977).

Degrada, Francesco. "Lettura del *Macbeth* di Verdi." *Studi musicali* 6 (1977).

Rosen, David. "*Le trouvère*: Comparing Verdi's French Version with his Original." *Opera News* 41/no. 22 (1977): 16.

———. "Virtue Restored." *Opera News* 42/no. 9 (1977-78): 36; also in *About the House* 6 (1981): 40.

Osthoff, Wolfgang. "Il sonetto nel *Falstaff* di Verdi." In *Il melodramma italiano dell'ottocento: studi e richerche per Massimo Mila*, 157. Turin, 1977.

Lawton, David. "On the 'bacio' Theme in *Otello.*" *Nineteenth-Century Music* 1 (1977-78): 211.

———. "Virtue Restored" [*La traviata*]. *Opera News* 42 (1977-78).

Antokoletz, Elliot. "Verdi's Dramatic Use of Harmony and Tonality in *Macbeth.*" *In Theory Only* 4/no. 6 (1978): 17.

Coe, Doug. "The Original Production Book for *Otello*: an Introduction." *Nineteenth-Century Music* 2 (1978): 148.

Levarie, Siegmund "Key Relationships in Verdi's *Un ballo in maschera.*" *Nineteenth-Century Music* 2 (1978): 143.

Linthicun, David. "Verdi's *Falstaff* and Classical Sonata Form." *Music Review* February (1978).

Porter, Andrew. "*Les vêpres siciliennes*: New Letters from Verdi to Scribe." *Nineteenth-Century Music* 2 (1978): 95.

———. "Observations on *Don Carlos.*" *World of Opera* 1/no. 3 (1978-79): 1.

Avant-scène opéra January-February (1979) [*Simon Boccanegra* issue].

Goldin, Daniela. "Il *Macbeth* verdiano: genesi e linguaggio di un libretto." *Analecta Musicologica* 19 (1979): 336.

Günther, Ursula. "Zur Revision des *Don Carlos*. Postscriptum zu Teil II." *Analecta Musicologica* 19 (1979): 373.

Kimbell, D. "Verdi's First Rifacimento: *I lombardi* and *Jérusalem.*" *Music and Letters* 60 (1979): 1.

Musik-Konzepte 10 (1979) [special Verdi issue].

Noske, Frits. "*Otello*: Drama through Structure." In *Essays on Music for Charles Warren Fox*, edited by Jerald C. Grave, 14. Rochester, New York, 1979.

Palden, Kurt. "Zur Geschichte der *Aida.*" *Österreichische Musikzeitung* 34 (1979): 334.

Hepokoski, James A., "Verdi, Giuseppina Pasqua, and the Composition of *Falstaff.*" *Nineteenth-Century Music* 3 (1980): 239.

Noske, Frits. "Melodia e struttura in *Les Vêpres siciliennes* di Verdi." *Ricerche Musicali* 18/no. 4 (1980): 3.

———. "Verdi's *Macbeth*: Romanticism or Realism?" In *Ars Musica, Musica Scientia. Festschrift Heinrich Hüschen zum fünfundsechzigsten Geburtstag am 2. März 1980*, edited by Detlef Altenburg, 359. Cologne, 1980.

Arc 81 (1981) [special Verdi issue].

Avant-scène opéra March-April (1981) [*Un bal masqué* issue].

Budden, Julian. "Time Stands Still in *Otello.*" *Opera* 32 (1981).

Busch, Hans. "Apropos of a Revision in Verdi's *Falstaff.*" In *Music East and West: Essays in Honor of Walter Kaufmann*, edited by Thomas Noblitt, 339. New York, 1981.

Levarie, Siegmund. "A Pitch Cell in Verdi's *Un ballo in maschera.*" *Journal of Musicological Research* 3 (1981): 399.

Porter, A. "Destination Unknown; or, How Should *Forza* End?" *Opera* November (1981).

Tomlinson, G. "Verdi after Budden." *Nineteenth-Century Music* 5 (1981): 170.

Town, S. "Observations on a Cabaletta from Verdi's *Corsaro.*" *Current Musicology* 32 (1981): 59.

Avant-scène opéra March-April (1982) [*Macbeth* issue].

Budden, Julian. "Verdi and Meyerbeer in Relation to *Les Vêpres siciliennes.*" *Studi verdiani* 1 (1982): 11.

Conati, Marcello. "Ballabili nei *Vespri*, con alcune osservazioni su Verdi e la musica popolare." *Studi verdiani* 1 (1982): 21.

———. "Bibliographia verdiana (1977-1979)." *Studi verdiana* 1 (1982): 107.

Cone, E.T. "On the Road to *Otello*: Tonality and Structure in *Simon Boccanegra.*" *Studi verdiani* 1 (1982): 72.

Della Corte, Andrea, and Marcello Conati. "Saggio di bibliografia delle critiche al *Rigoletto.*" *Verdi* 3 (1982): 1633.

Drabkin, William M. "Characters, Key Relations, and Tonal Structure in *Il trovatore.*" *Music Analysis* 1 (1982).

Kerman, Joseph. "Lyric Form and Flexibility in *Simon Boccanegra.*" *Studi verdiani* 1 (1982): 47.

Lawton, David. "The Corsair Reaches Port." *Opera News* 46 (1982).

———. "Tonal Structure and Dramatic Action in *Rigoletto.*" *Verdi* 3 (1982): 1559.

Marchesi, Gustavo. "L'*Aida* come fiaba." In *Aida al Cairo*, 91. Parma, 1982.

———. "Gli anni del *Rigoletto.*" *Verdi* 3 (1982): 1517.

Parker, Roger. "The Dramatic Structure of *Il trovatore.*" *Music Analysis* 1 (1982).

———. "Levels of Motivic Definition in Verdi's *Ernani.*" *Nineteenth-Century Music* 6 (1982).

Petrobelli, Pierluigi, et al. "Verdi's *Il trovatore*: a Symposium." *Music Analysis* 1/no. 2 (1982): 125.

Rinaldi, M. "Il *Macbeth* di Verdi: un' opera 'più difficile delle altre'." *Studi musicali* 10 (1982).

Rozett, Martha Tuch. "*Othello*, Otello and the Comic Tradition." *Bulletin of Research in the Humanities* 85 (1982): 386.

Sandow, Gregory. "Beyond Convention." *Opera News* 47/no. 7 (1982): 14.

Switzer, Richard. "Dawn of *The Vespers.*" *Opera News* 46/no. 14 (1982): 26.

Várnai, Péter Pál. "Paolo Albiani. Il cammino di un personaggio" [*Simon Boccanegra*]. *Studi verdiani* 1 (1982): 63.

Weiss, P. "Verdi and the Fusion of Genres." *Journal of the American Musicological Society* 35 (1982): 138.

Avant-scène opéra April (1983) [*La traviata* issue].

Biddlecombre, George. "The Revision of 'No, non morrai, che'i perfidi'. Verdi's Compositional Process in *I due Foscari.*" *Studi verdiani* 2 (1983): 59.

Black, John M. "Salvadore Cammarano's Programme for *Il trovatore* and the Problems of the Finale." *Studi verdiani* 2 (1983): 78.

Crutchfield, Will. "Authenticity in Verdi: the Recorded Legacy." *Nineteenth-Century Music* summer (1983).

Della Seta, Fabrizio. "Il tempo della festa. Su due scene della Traviata e su altri luoghi verdiani." *Studi verdiani* 2 (1983): 108.

Giovanelli, Paola Daniela. "La storia e la favola dell' *Oberto.*" *Studi verdiani* 2 (1983): 29.

Marek, George R. "*Falstaff*—Boito's Alchemy." *Opera Quarterly* 1/no. 2 (1983): 69.

Mila, Massimo. "Lettura dell' *Attila* di Verdi." *Nuova rivista musicale italiana* 17 (1983): 247.

Parker, Roger. "Un giorno di regno. From Romani's Libretto to Verdi's Opera." *Studi verdiani* 2 (1983): 38.

Parker, Roger, and Matthew Brown. "Motivic and Tonal Interaction in Verdi's *Un ballo in maschera.*" *Journal of the American Musicological Society* 36 (1983): 243.

Ross, Peter. "Amelias Auftrittsarie im *Maskenball.* Verdis Vertonung in Dramaturgisch-textlichern Zusammenhang." *Archiv für Musikwissenschaft* 40/no. 2 (1983): 126.

Avant-scène opéra February (1984) [*Le trouvère* issue].

Chusid, Martin. "Evil, Guilt, and the Supernatural in Verdi's *Macbeth:* Toward an Understanding of the Tonal Structure and Key Symbolism." In *Verdi's Macbeth: A Sourcebook,* New York and London, 1984.

Sutcliffe, James Helme. "Die sechs 'Fassungen' des *Don Carlos:* Versuch einer Bilanz." *Oper Heute* 7 (1984): 69.

Avant-scène opéra May (1985) [*Les vêpres siciliennes* issue].

Bauman, Thomas. "The Young Lovers in Falstaff." *Nineteenth-Century Music* 9 (1985): 62.

Christen, Norbert. "Auf dem Weg zum szenischen Musikdrama: Verdis *Macbeth* in Vergleich der beiden Fassungen." *Neue Zeitschrift für Musik* 46/nos. 7-8 (1985): 9.

Cohen, H. Robert. "A Survey of French Sources for the Staging of Verdi's Operas: *Livrets de mise en scène,* Annotated scores, and Annotated Libretti in Two Parisian Collections." *Studi verdiani* 3 (1985): 11.

Conati, Marcello. "Aspetti di melodrammaturgia verdiana: a proposito di une sconosciuta versione del finale del duetto Aida-Amneris." *Studi verdiani* 3 (1985): 45.

Conati, Marcello, comp. "Bibliografia verdiana 1983-84: addenda alla bibliografia verdiana 1977-1982." *Studi verdiani* 3 (1985): 141.

Hepokoski, James A. "Under the Eye of the Verdian Bear: Notes on the Rehearsals and Premiere of *Falstaff.*" *Musical Quarterly* 71 (1985): 135.

Lawton, David. "*Le trouvère:* Verdi's Revision of *Il trovatore* for Paris." *Studi verdiani* 3 (1985): 79.

Mauceri, John. "Rigoletto for the 21st Century." *Opera* October (1985).

Parker, Roger, and Matthew Brown. "*Ancora un bacio:* Three Scenes from Verdi's *Otello.*" *Nineteenth-Century Music* 9 (1985): 50.

Puccini, Dario. "Il *Simon Boccanegra* di Antonio García Gutiérrez e l'opera di Giuseppe Verdi." *Studi verdiani* 3 (1985): 120.

Schmidgall, Gary. "Verdi's *King Lear* Project." *Nineteenth Century Music* 9/no. 2 (1985): 83.

Avant-scène opéra April (1986) [*Nabucco* issue].

Avant-scène opéra May-June (1986) [*Falstaff* issue].

Avant-scène opéra September-October (1986) [*Don Carlos* issue].

Chusid, Martin. "Apropos *Aroldo, Stifelio,* and *Le Pasteur,* with a List of 19th-Century Performances of *Aroldo.*" *Verdi Newsletter* 14 (1986).

———. "Editing *Rigoletto.*" *Nuove prospettive nella ricerca verdiana. Vienna, 1983.* Parma, 1987.

———, and Thomas Kaufman. "The First Three Years of *Trovatore.*" *Verdi Newsletter* 15 (1987).

Gualerzi, Giorgio. "Otello: the Legacy of Tamagno." *Opera* February (1987).

Avant-scène opéra September-October (1988) [*Rigoletto* issue].

Hepokoski, James A. "Genre and Content in Mid-Century Verdi: 'Addio, del passatto' (*La traviata,* act III)." *Cambridge Opera Journal* 1 (1989): 249.

Chusid, Martin. "The Tonality of *Rigoletto.*" In *Analyzing Opera,* Berkeley and Los Angeles, 1989.

———. "A Letter by the Composer about *Giovanna d'Arco* and Some Remarks on the Division of Musical Direction in Verdi's Day." *Performance Practice Review* spring (1990); reprinted in *Studi verdiani* 7 (1991-92).

———. "The Inquisitor's Scene in Verdi's *Don Carlos:* Thoughts on the Drama, Libretto, and Music." In *Studies in Musical Sources and Style,* Madison, Wisconsin, 1990.

Taddie, Daniel. "The Devil, You Say: Reflections on Verdi's and Boito's Iago." *Opera Quarterly* spring (1990).

Della Seta, Fabrizio. " 'O cieli azzurri': Exoticism and dramatic discourse in *Aida.*" *Cambridge Opera Journal* 3 (1991): 49.

unpublished—

Lawton, D. "Tonality and Drama in Verdi's Early Operas." Ph. D. dissertation, University of California, Berkeley, 1973.

Moreen, Robert. *Integration of Text Forms and Musical Forms in Verdi's Early Operas.* Ph.D. dissertation, Princeton University, 1975.

Parker, Roger. "Studies in Early Verdi (1832-1844): New Information and Perspectives on the Milanese Musical Milieu and the Operas from *Oberto* to *Ernani.*" Ph. D. dissertation, University of London, 1981.

Detels, Claire Janice. "Giuseppe Verdi's *Simon Boccanegra:* a Comparison of the 1857 and 1881 Versions." Ph.D. dissertation, University of Washington, 1982.

Cordell, Albert O. *The Orchestration of Verdi: A Study of the Growth of Verdi's Orchestral Technique as Reflected in the Two Versions of "Simon Boccanegra."* Ph.D. dissertation, Catholic University, 1991.

* * *

Verdi showed talent and a great love of music early in his life, and was given keyboard lessons as a child. At ten he played the organ in church well enough to replace his teacher, the village organist Pietro Baistrocchi, at the latter's death. By this time Verdi was boarding in Busseto, where he attended school and (in 1825?) began studying music with the composer and organist Ferdinando Provesi, director of the town's church music, the municipal music school and the local philharmonic society.

Giuseppe Verdi, pencil drawing by Giovanni Boldini, 1886

As a teenager, Verdi began assisting his master as organist and in the music school, and he also began writing and arranging for the philharmonic group (marches, overtures, serenades, cantatas, arias, duets, terzets and church music). He also wrote concertos and piano variations to play at the group's concerts. The gifted youth became a protegé of the philharmonic organization's president, the wealthy merchant Antonio Barezzi, and gave music lessons to his daughter Margherita, whom he ultimately married.

Primarily with the financial aid of Barezzi but also with support from the Monte di Pietà of Busseto, Verdi applied for admission to study piano at the Milan Conservatory in 1831. This was denied because of his age (eighteen), the fact that he was not a citizen of Lombardy, and poor positioning of his hands at the keyboard. He was advised to study composition privately and from 1832-1835 did so with Vincenzo Lavigna, composer and *maestro al cembalo* at the Teatro alla Scala for many years. These studies were mainly in counterpoint; but the young Verdi also subscribed to the opera, rented scores and analyzed music with Lavigna. After Provesi's death in 1833, an apparently reluctant Verdi was persuaded to apply for his former teacher's several positions and a protracted struggle ensued between the young musician's supporters, mainly members of the town's philharmonic society, and his detractors, for the most part officials of the church.

After some time had elapsed (Verdi's application had not yet arrived), the clerical faction hired an organist from a neighboring town as director of church music. An attempt to have him made director of the philharmonic society and municipal school of music was foiled by a petition to the Duchess of Parma, Marie Louise. After delaying a year, she ordered a competition for the municipal positions (to take place in February 1836) which Verdi won easily. Before this event Verdi completed his studies with Lavigna and successfully directed, from the keyboard, Haydn's *Creation* (April 1834) and Rossini's *La Cenerentola* (April 1835) at the Teatro Filodrammatico in Milan. In the process he made powerful friends among the Milanese nobles who sponsored these events.

Verdi's new position in Busseto allowed him to marry Margherita, and he attended to his responsibilities well enough. But his primary interest was in opera and he wrote a work entitled *Rocester* which many authorities believe formed the basis for his first performed stage work, *Oberto, Conte di san Bonifacio*. As soon as his first contract expired, Verdi resigned his position in Busseto and took his wife and an infant son to Milan (February 1839). A daughter, the first born, had died some months earlier. Shortly before the relatively successful premiere of *Oberto*, Verdi's son also died (November 1839). Misfortune continued to plague the young composer and he lost his wife while writing his second opera, *Un giorno di regno* (later *Il finto Stanislao*), a farce which proved unsuccessful (September 1840).

Verdi's fortunes turned with *Nabucodonosor* (now universally called *Nabucco*; March 1842), in which his future second wife, Giuseppina Strepponi, sang the role of Abigaille. Strepponi, whose voice declined after a relatively short career as one of Italy's leading dramatic sopranos (1835-1842), was not effective in the difficult role, and the truly phenomenal success of the opera dated from its second season at La Scala, that summer, with an almost entirely new cast of principals. A remarkable string of additional successes followed. The first of these was *I Lombardi alla prima crociata* (February 1843), a sprawling work of little dramatic cogency but with many effective musical numbers. In addition, just as audiences had identified with the Hebrews in their Babylonian captivity in *Nabucco*, they did so no less with the Italian crusaders freeing the Holy land in *I Lombardi*.

Ernani (La Fenice, Venice, March 1844), based on Victor Hugo's play, was the composer's fifth opera and his most successful stage work until *Trovatore*. This was followed the same year by *I due Foscari* (Torre Argentina, Rome November 1844), an intimate, melancholy work based on Byron which had considerable success in the 1840s and 50s, and was still to be heard in the 1860s before disappearing from the repertory.

Verdi returned once more to La Scala with *Giovanna d'Arco* (February 1845), the first of his quartet of operas based on plays by Schiller, and unquestionably the weakest of the four. It was much less successful than its immediate predecessors, although it was heard occasionally in Italy and elsewhere for about twenty years. Verdi believed it to have been poorly staged at La Scala, a complaint he voiced about all his operas performed there in the 1840s and 50s. As a result, he broke off relations with Italy's premier house for almost twenty-five years. Later that year the composer traveled to Naples to direct *Alzira* (August 1845), a work he later considered to be one of his weakest. The following year Verdi returned to Venice to direct *Attila* (March 1846), one of the most successful of the earliest operas, with two lines of text calculated to enflame the patriotic sentiments of Italian audiences, the Roman Ezio's remark to Attila, "You may have the universe, leave Italy to me." Police censors in some Italian cities, in fact, changed these verses.

Verdi's next opera, *Macbeth* (Florence, March 1847), the first of his stage works based on a play by his beloved Shakespeare, is the most original and ambitious of his early operas. Later in life (1875), during a discussion of Wagner, Verdi called Macbeth his own attempt to write music drama. During the late nineteenth century, *Macbeth* had more success in its original version than in Verdi's revision for Paris (April 1865). This may be attributed to a more rapid and effective denouement, the concise manner in which the composer treated the battle music and death of Macbeth in the first version.

Verdi then left Italy, composing first *I masnadieri* for London (July 1847). Although the opera was not particularly successful in England, it did quite well in Italy. In Paris that summer, Verdi began living with Giuseppina Strepponi, his companion and later his wife (1859) for fifty years. He also signed a contract for *Jérusalem* (November 1847), an extensive revision of *I Lombardi* to a French text with the obligatory ballet required by France's premier house. Performed with modest success in cities where French was spoken (e.g. Paris, Brussels and New Orleans) it failed in a retranslation to Italian as *Gerusalemme* (La Scala, December 1850).

Verdi grudgingly fulfilled a contract he had made with the publisher Lucca by writing *Il corsaro* (Trieste, October 1848). Although much of the music is beautiful, this is one of Verdi's less dramatically effective operas. In a departure from his usual habit, the composer refused to direct the premiere. Just days before the proclamation of the short-lived Roman Republic, Verdi joined Giuseppe Mazzini and Giuseppe Garibaldi in Rome where he directed his most blatantly patriotic opera, *La battaglia di Legnano* (January 1848). The story of the defeat of the German emperor Frederick Barbarossa by a league of northern Italian knights, the opera was hampered by censorship in the period after the failure of the revolutions of 1848-49. It had a brief period of success during the early years of the unification of Italy (1859-61) but not thereafter.

With the more intimate *Luisa Miller* (Naples, December 1849), a work for which he had particular affection, Verdi turned away from operas with a political message. The injustices of society, however, especially as they affected individuals, continued to concern him. Here, it is the misuse of unbridled power by a nobleman, Count Walter. In his next opera, *Stiffelio* (Trieste, November 1850), Verdi came to the defense of a minister's wife who commits adultery, but still loves her husband. While there is beautiful music in both works, *Luisa Miller* entered the repertory but *Stiffelio* did not; at least in part it was because of the inherently more logical dramatic development of the former.

With the famous triad of *Rigoletto* (March 1851), *Il trovatore* (Rome, January 1853) and *La traviata* (March 1853), Verdi reached a new level of artistic maturity. He now had full command of the compositional resources of early and mid nineteenth century Italian opera, and he focused these resources on better dramas. Most notably, the characters in these and his later operas are often less stereotypical than in previous operas; they are sometimes grotesque, but they are always intensely human, with well-motivated actions.

Les vêpres siciliennes (June 1855) was Verdi's first completely new opera for Paris. It was followed there a year and a half later by *Le trouvère,* a French translation and revision of *Trovatore* with added ballet. If Verdi's music up to and including *Traviata* may be said to have been mainly influenced by Italian composers such as Rossini, Bellini, Mercadante and especially Donizetti, much of the music he wrote for the stage after *Traviata* may be considered to reflect the influence of French grand opera composers, particularly Meyerbeer. This may be discerned not only in *Les vêpres* and *Don Carlos* (March 1867), both written to French texts specifically as grand operas, but also in such Italian works as *La forza del destino* (St Petersburg, November 1862), *Aida* (Cairo, December 1871) and *Otello* (February 1887). All of these show the massive scale, the greater importance of the drama, the lavish scenery, costumes and staging, the expanded orchestra and richer accompaniments, the rhythmic flexibility (for example, there are far fewer cabalettas with their stereotyped Polonaise or march rhythms) and the approach to structure that stresses the larger, through-composed or tripartite subdivisions that characterize grand opera. The emphasis in these works tends to be less on the soloists, their arias and duets, and more on the ensembles and crowd scenes. Verdi, aware of this changed approach, called his operas of the decade 1862 to 1871 (*Forza, Don Carlos* and *Aida*) his "modern" operas and distinguished them from the earlier operas which he called "cavatina" operas. He specifically included *Traviata* among the "cavatina" operas in which the soloists and their *convenienze* or conventions where stressed. Two of Verdi's operas of the late 1850s, the first version of *Simon Boccanegra* (March 1857) and *Un ballo in maschera* (Rome, February 1859) show elements of both styles. Of the two, *Ballo* is the more brilliant, closer to the older style and was then, and is now, far more successful at the box office (Verdi's measure of an opera's success). Among the reasons for *Ballo*'s success are the fact that the dramatic thread is clearer in *Ballo* than in *Simon Boccanegra,* and the scenes with the secondary characters, Oscar and Ulrica, provide welcome changes of pace, but in addition are crucial for the plot. In Verdi's revision of *Simon Boccanegra* (for La Scala, March 1881), twenty-four years later, the most exciting change occurs with the introduction of a council chamber scene into the finale of act I. Written while the composer was thinking about *Otello,* the music of this scene foreshadows the power and emotional intensity of Verdi's last tragic opera.

Falstaff (February 1893), the composer's final stage work, was written by a mellowing Verdi as he approached eighty, and was undertaken to prove to a doubting musical world that he could successfully set a comedy. Thanks in large part to a brilliant libretto by Arrigo Boito, a composer in his own right who also wrote the librettos for *Otello,* the revision of *Simon Boccanegra* and the *Inno delle nazione, Falstaff* is more tightly constructed than Shakespeare's *Merry Wives of Windsor* on which it is largely based. The opera has magical orchestration, quicksilver melodic ideas and a surprisingly wide range of emotions. It also has a convincing continuity of movement between the individual scenes found consistently only in the final acts of *Aida* and in *Otello.*

As his letters to librettists show, to a certain extent Verdi shared in the construction of his librettos. Sometimes he prepared the *programma,* the summary prose draft of a libretto with which the composer and librettist began their collaboration. This is especially clear in the manuscript materials for the never completed *King Lear* and especially those for *Aida* presently at Verdi's estate, Sant'Agata, where his heirs reside. In two instances the composer literally taught the craft of writing librettos to poets, and the results were successful operas. The works are *Ernani,* Francesco Maria Piave's first libretto, and *Un ballo in maschera,* Antonio Somma's only libretto.

Despite the enormous popularity of most of his operas from *Rigoletto* through *Aida,* it was not until Verdi had written the Manzoni Requiem (1873-74), the finest of his nonoperatic works, and later *Otello* and *Falstaff,* that musicians in Northern Europe and the United States recognized him to be one of the major composers in the history of Western music.

—Martin Chusid

VERRETT, Shirley.

Soprano. Born 31 May 1931, in New Orleans. Studied with Anna Fitziu and Hall Johnson, and with Mme Szekely-Freschl at Juilliard; debut as Lucretia in Britten's *The Rape of Lucretia,* Yellow Springs, Ohio, 1957; New York debut as Irina in Weill's *Lost in the Stars,* 1958; European debut in *Rasputins Tod* by Nabokov, 1959; Teatro alla Scala debut as Carmen, 1966; Metropolitan Opera debut as Carmen, 1968; has sung with the Metropolitan Opera since 1968.

Publications

About VERRETT: articles–

Harris, D. "Shirley Verrett." *Music and Musicians* 21 (1973): 28.
"Shirley Verrett." *Diapason-Harmonie* 348 (1989): 24.
"Artist Profiles." *San Francisco Opera Magazine* 9 (1988): 35.
Dyer, R. "Characteristically Verrett." *Opera News* 54 (1990): 8.

* * *

American diva Shirley Verrett's mid-career transition from mezzo-soprano to soprano has divided critical and popular opinion. Some see the change as an appropriate step for this singer, whose theatrical flair has led her to seek out ever more challenging roles. Others hear the transformation as accompanied by a serious decline in vocal quality and range, and cite her example as a cautionary tale for other mezzos contemplating a similarly reckless path.

Both arguments are valid. Verrett's soprano roles have included at least one portrayal—Verdi's Lady Macbeth—about which critical opinion is almost entirely positive, as well as others (Tosca, even Norma) in which, by and large, she has met the vocal challenges with success, and which have been illuminated by her dramatic presence. At the same time, it is difficult not to hear and regret a separation of vocal registers and substantial wear on the velvety timbre which was such a notable characteristic of one of the most beautiful mezzo-soprano voices of the 1960s and early 70s.

The voice and repertoire of Verrett in her prime were unequivocally those of a mezzo-soprano, although we can hear in the easy upper register the promise of a "higher calling." Verrett's mezzo assayed a large number of roles from coloratura to lyric and dramatic, and to all she brought her instantly recognizable velvety sound as well as a sincerity and nobility of manner which were equally distinctive.

It may be this very diversity that makes Verrett more difficult to characterize than some of her contemporaries. She is not identified as a *bel canto* specialist, for example, unlike her celebrated compatriot Marilyn Horne, though Verrett achieved real distinction in this repertoire, notably in the Metropolitan Opera's production of Rossini's *L'assedio di Corinto* which was also the house debut of Beverly Sills. Neither do we instantly think of Verrett as a Verdi singer, the way we do of Fiorenza Cossotto, though her Azucena, Ulrica and particularly Eboli are among the finest portrayals of those roles in our time.

Perhaps it is in the French repertoire that Verrett has made her most visible and lasting contribution. Her Dalila

is notable for a voluptuous exoticism and superbly sensual vocalism, and she has performed to great acclaim both Didon and Cassandre in *Les Troyens,* where her statuesque grandeur is especially welcome. Audiences who saw Verrett as Carmen (a role she sang in most major international theaters) will never forget her sensuality and fire—though ironically the performance will probably become legend, since Verrett did not record this role (nor many other significant portrayals in her repertoire), and is thus less likely to be remembered by future generations than several other singers in the part.

As Lady Macbeth, a crucial role in her transition to soprano, Verrett came into her own. The voice itself was rather soft-grained for this taxing part, but Verrett's technical security allowed her to negotiate the difficulties with seeming ease; moreover, her powerful physical and vocal acting were precisely right for this flamboyant part. Critics who attended her first performances of the role at the Teatro alla Scala found her the most compelling interpreter of the part since Callas. Fortunately, Verrett's Lady Macbeth was recorded under near ideal circumstances (Claudio Abbado conducting the forces of the Scala revival), and this document goes a long way toward suggesting the impact, both vocal and dramatic, that Verrett can make in the theater. More recent assumptions of soprano roles (including Amelia in *Un ballo in maschera,* and *Aida*) have yielded mixed results, the dramatic thrust and commitment not entirely compensating for increasingly threadbare vocalism—though it should be said that at present Verrett is still a formidable figure on the operatic scene, even if the opulent voice shows unmistakable signs of decline. For a souvenir of that voice at its finest, her Orfeo recorded under the sympathetic baton of Renato Fasano shows Verrett's singing at its richest, the steady tone gleaming with a dark brilliance that few singers have matched.

—David Anthony Fox

Shirley Verrett in *Samson et Dalila*, Royal Opera, London, 1981

**THE VESTAL VIRGIN
See LA VESTALE**

LA VESTALE [The Vestal Virgin].

Composer: Gaspare Spontini.

Librettist: Étienne de Jouy.

First Performance: Paris, Opéra, 15 December 1807.

Roles: Licinio (tenor); Giulia (soprano); Cinna (tenor or baritone); High Priest (bass); High Priestess (soprano or mezzo-soprano); A Consul (bass); A Diviner (bass); chorus (SSATB).

*   *   *

The success of *La vestale,* first performed in Paris in December 1807, established Spontini's position as the leading opera composer of the Napoleonic period. He therefore became another of the Italian emigré composers who, following the

Set design by A. Sanquirico for Spontini's *La vestale*, act I, 1810

example of Lully in the seventeenth century, took on a central role in French musical life, and his style fused French and Italian elements. The opera's libretto, in French, was the work of Étienne de Jouy; it had originally been written for Boieldieu, and later Méhul also declined to set it. The fundamental tension created by the plot is that common operatic tension, the conflict between love and duty, or, more accurately in the case of grand opera, between ceremonial pageantry and individual passion.

Giulia has become a vestal virgin while her lover, the Roman general Licinio, has been away at the wars, for she feared he would never return. When he finally does so, however, his one intention is to win her back, and with this purpose he breaks into the temple by force. Giulia admits that her love for him remains and is stronger than her vows of duty; in their passionate exchanges the lovers do not notice that she has allowed the sacred flame to go out. The High Priest accuses her of neglecting her sacred duties; she accepts the death sentence but refuses to reveal the identity of her lover. Declining to use force, Licinio begs for clemency, and, denouncing the High Priest for his cruelty, declares his own role. Giulia's sentence is that she be buried alive, but as she descends into her tomb, the sky darkens and the flame is restored by a shaft of lightning. The goddess Vesta has forgiven her. Therefore she is released, and the opera ends amid general rejoicing.

The concept of a heroine at odds with her sacred duty has parallels in Gluck's Alceste and Iphigénie, as well as Bellini's Norma. Spontini is able to create a natural intensity because of the plot's natural contrasts between spectacle and intimacy, and for this reason he gave very precise directions for the staging, the more necessary since the sometimes complex groupings of warriors, priests, and priestesses were central to the dramatic thrust. The public ceremonies of temple rituals and triumphal processions, march rhythms often to the fore, still allow for lyricism and character development, although of course the latter focuses only upon Giulia and, to a lesser extent, Licinio.

The conflict of the private and the public leads to sudden turning points in the drama, which are reinforced by the music, often as solo recitatives in the midst of the solemn ceremonial scenes, with emphatic rhythms, wide melodic leaps, and striking harmonic progressions. In fact Spontini developed a highly effective approach to recitative, fusing it with the surrounding numbers, especially relying on *tremolando* strings with heavy arpeggios, contrasted against the intensely felt vocal phrases. In this regard act II has been praised for its ability to convey these powerful tensions; Berlioz, particularly impressed by it, wrote, "The score of *La vestale* is, to my mind, in an entirely different style from that which had been adopted in France by the composers of that period. As regards dramatic expression, character portrayal, accuracy and vehemence of expression, Spontini derived from Gluck. But as regards melodic and harmonic style, scoring and musical colouring, Spontini derives from himself alone. His music has an individual look which it is impossible to mistake."

The best-known scene is that for Giulia in act II, when she prays to Vesta for release from her torment, but then admits that her love for Licinio is all powerful. Scarcely less fine, however, are the passionate love duet and the beautiful aria in which the heroine prays to the gods that her lover's identity will remain a secret. The scale of the spectacle in *La vestale* has tended to overshadow the opera's true value, for it is a work primarily concerned with human passions, expressed through music of vivid dramatic commitment.

—Terry Barfoot

VIARDOT, Pauline [born Pauline Garcia].

Mezzo-soprano. Born 18 July 1821, in Paris. Died 18 May 1910, in Paris. Married author Louis Viardot, 1840. Early vocal training with mother, wife of Manuel García; studied piano with Meysenberg and Liszt, and composition with Reicha; gave vocal concerts in Brussels (1837) and Paris (1838); operatic debut in London as Desdemona in Rossini's *Otello* (1839); after marriage in 1840 the Viardot home became important center for musicians, artists, and literary figures, including Turgenev, Chopin, and George Sand; travelled to Russia in 1843, becoming first foreigner to sing Russian vocal music in the original language; at Covent Garden, 1849-55, with roles including Amina, Rosina, Zerlina, and Azucena; appeared as Fidès in Meyerbeer's *Le prophète,* a role created for her, at the Paris Opéra, 1849; sang in Gluck's *Orphée* in 1859 (from an edition by Berlioz), giving some 150 performances of the work over the next three years; sang female lead in private Paris performance of *Tristan und Isolde* (1860); appeared only rarely after 1863; sang first performance of Brahms' *Alto Rhapsody,* 1870; from 1871 until her death taught and composed in Paris; her compositions include several operettas and many songs.

Publications

By VIARDOT: books–

Ecole classique de chant. Paris, 1861.
Marix-Spire, T., ed. *Lettres inédites de George Sand et de Pauline Viardot 1839-49.* Paris, 1959.

articles–

"La jeunesse de Saint-Saëns." *Musica* 6 (1907): 83.
Baker, T., trans. "Pauline Viardot to Julius Rietz—Letters of a Friendship." *Musical Quarterly* 1 (1915): 350; 2 (1916): 32.

About VIARDOT: books–

La Mara. *Pauline Viardot-Garcia.* Leipzig, 1883.
FitzLyon, A. *The Price of Genius: A Biography of Pauline Viardot.* London, 1964, New York, 1965.
Rozanov, A. *Polina Viardo-Garcia.* Leningrad, 1969; 1982.
Barry, Nicole. *Pauline Viardot.* Paris, 1990.

articles–

Liszt, Franz. "Pauline Viardot-Garcia." *Neue Zeitschrift für Musik* 1 (1859): 49.

Chovelon, Bernadette. "George Sand et Pauline Viardot." In Bancquart, Marie-Claire, et al., *George Sand et la musique.* Echirolles, 1981.
Stegemann, Michael. "Pauline Viardot à Baden-Baden." *Cahiers Ivan Tourguénev, Pauline Viardot, Maria Maliban* 9 (1985): 91.
Dulong, Gustave. "Pauline Viardot tragédienne lyrique." *Cahiers Ivan Tourguénev, Pauline Viardot, Maria Maliban* 10 (1986): 88.

*   *   *

When the seventeen-year-old Pauline Garcia first appeared in Paris (8 October 1839) as Desdemona in Rossini's *Otello,* some people in the audience felt that they were listening to a ghost. It had been one of the greatest parts of her sister, Maria Malibran, who had died three years earlier; comparisons were inevitable. Pauline's voice (c' to f'''), its timbre, and her technique were uncannily similar to those of her dead sister; but discerning critics, such as Alfred de Musset, realised that her temperament and interpretations were very different. Both sisters were outstanding actresses as well as singers. La Malibran had personified the Romantic movement, but by 1839 that movement was already in decline. Pauline's temperament was less frenetic, calmer and more classical, and her debut coincided with a revival of interest in the classical drama, long overshadowed by Romantic excesses.

Although Spanish by birth and Italian by training, Pauline Viardot must be considered a French singer, whereas her sister was an Italian singer. Although Pauline sang the Italian repertory, her greatest successes were not in Italian operas; she never sang in Italy, though appearing frequently in England and in Germany. She was based in Paris for most of her life, and her influence was greatest on French composers, or on "Frenchified" composers such as Meyerbeer. Her high artistic standards and discreet private life did much to improve the status of singers, particularly in France where, at the beginning of her career, the prejudice against stage people was still deeply entrenched.

Although in her youth Pauline sang Rossini and the Romantic repertoire—Bellini, Donizetti—to great acclaim, as she matured she excelled in strong, dramatic parts: Verdi's Lady Macbeth and Azucena; Rachel in Halévy's *La Juive;* Fidès, the elderly mother in *Le prophète*—a part which no other prima donna wanted to tackle, and from which seemingly unpromising material Viardot created an artistic triumph. The summit of her career was reached in Paris in 1859 in the title-role of Gluck's *Orphée* (in Berlioz's edition), in which, according to eye-witnesses, Viardot's tragic intensity was truly sublime.

Pauline Viardot never evoked the mass hysteria which greeted her sister's performances. She appealed to connoisseurs rather than to the wide public—the thinking person's prima donna. Unlike her sister, she was not physically attractive, but she perhaps compensated for this, on and off the stage, by the use of her intelligence and powerful personality. Her voice, too, was not perfect, but she was able to conceal its defects with great skill.

In 1843 Pauline Viardot visited Russia for the first time. She had exceptional success there, and returned for three more seasons. Her relationship with the novelist Ivan Turgenev dates from this first visit, and ended only with his death forty years later in her house. His side of the story is well known and well documented; her attitude to him remains less clear. For the rest of her life, through Turgenev and the many Russian musicians whom she knew personally, Pauline

Viardot was a staunch advocate for Russian music, which was only just beginning to emerge. She learned Russian, and was the first foreigner to sing works by Glinka, Dargomyshsky, Rimsky-Korsakov and Tchaikovsky when they were quite unknown outside Russia. She was an admirer of Borodin, and had the score of Tchaikovsky's *Eugene Onegin* in Paris even before it was performed in Moscow. She composed songs to Russian texts, and had many Russian pupils. She was one of the most important links between Russian composers and the West.

Pauline Viardot's vocal and dramatic gifts inspired many very different composers: Meyerbeer, who wrote *Le prophète* for her; Berlioz, who for a time envisaged her as both Cassandra and Dido in *Les Troyens;* Saint-Saëns, who hoped that she would be his Dalila. She gave private performances of parts of *Les Troyens* and of *Samson et Dalila,* but by the time these works were publicly performed she was too old to take part. In Paris in 1860 she gave a private performance of *Tristan und Isolde,* singing Isolde to Wagner's Tristan.

Pauline Viardot and her husband Louis, a writer, were the centre of a distinguished international circle of musicians, artists and writers, which included George Sand, Chopin, Liszt, Delacroix, Dickens and the Rubinstein brothers. With her immense prestige as an artist and her many friends, Viardot had considerable influence, which she was always ready to use to help younger musicians. By appearing in their early works she launched Gounod (*Sapho*) and Massenet (*Marie-Magdeleine*).

Although she was a fine Donna Anna and, when young, an enchanting Zerlina, and was much admired as Valentine in *Les Huguenots,* Pauline Viardot was supreme only in certain parts: Fidès, Rachel, Orphée, Alceste; in these she had no rivals. She may not have been the greatest prima donna of the nineteenth century—although Berlioz considered her to be ". . . one of the greatest artists . . . in the past and present history of music"—but she was certainly the most intelligent prima donna of her epoch, and had more influence on a wide range of composers and writers than any other singer.

—April FitzLyon

VICKERS, Jon.

Tenor. Born 29 October 1926, in Prince Albert, Saskatchewan. Married: Henrietta Outerbridge, 1953; three sons, two daughters. Studied with George Lambert at the Royal Conservatory of Music in Toronto; debut as Duke in *Rigoletto,* Toronto, 1952; sang regularly for Canadian radio; Covent Garden debut as Riccardo in *Un ballo in maschera,* 1957; at Covent Garden until 1969; sang Siegmund at both Bayreuth and London, 1958; sang Siegmund, Don José, Radames, and Canio at Vienna Staatsoper, 1959; Metropolitan Opera debut as Canio, 1960; remained there for twenty seasons; sang Peter Grimes at Metropolitan in 1967, and repeated role in London in 1969, 1971, and 1975; sang in U.S. premiere of Handel's *Samson,* Dallas, 1976; retired in 1988; was made Companion of Honor of the Order of Canada, 1969.

Publications

About VICKERS: books–

Cairns, D. *Responses.* London, 1973.

articles–

Goodwin, Noël. "Jon Vickers." *Opera* 4 (1962): 233.
Ardoin, John. "Jon Vickers." In H.H. Breslin, ed., *The Tenors,* 43. New York, 1974.
Ludwig, H. "Jon Vickers Interview." *Opernwelt* (October 18, 1975).
"Jon Vickers in Conversation with Michael Oliver." *Opera* 33/4 (1982): 362.
"Jon Vickers on Peter Grimes" (conversation with Max Loppert). *Opera* 35/8 (1984): 835.
Williams, J. "A Sense of Awe: The Career of Jon Vickers as Seen in Reviews." *Opera Quarterly* 7/3 (1990): 36.

From the beginning of his career in the mid-1950s until 1988, Jon Vickers was without peer as a dramatic tenor. The character of his voice was atypical and strikingly individual—rugged, sinewy, tough, but capable of great warmth and lyrical beauty—and the range of vocal colors that he commanded allowed him to be equally persuasive in the English, Italian, French, and German repertoires.

During his early years of study in Toronto, the brilliant ring of his voice was evident, but his teacher, George Lambert, laid a vocal foundation for Vickers with the music of Bach, Handel and Purcell. While far from the dramatic repertoire in which Vicker's became famous, this music provided a source to which he returned throughout his career. As he once put it in an interview, "Last season, after singing Siegmund, I felt my voice crying out for an antidote of Handel and Bach." In the 1950s in Canada he had the opportunity to sing such diverse roles as the Duke in *Rigoletto,* Alfredo in *La traviata,* Ferrando in *Così fan tutte,* Troilus in *Troilus and Cressida,* the Male Chorus in *The Rape of Lucretia,* as well as radio performances of Act I of *Die Walküre* and the final scene of *Parsifal,* and oratorios of Handel and Haydn. By the time he reached Covent Garden and the international stage in 1957, he was vocally accustomed to a variety of musical demands, and he had the experience and the interest to maintain that variety.

Throughout his long career Vickers sang with virtually every major conductor, singer, and director of the time, among whom he developed a particularly fruitful relationship with Herbert Von Karajan. Although he appeared in all the great opera houses of Europe and America, he nevertheless severely restricted the number of his performances in any one season, and he chose carefully when he would add a role to his repertoire and when he would leave it. His resources were maintained and nourished, and when he closed his career with the second act of *Parsifal* at Kitchener, Ontario, in 1988, he did so with the compelling, full-throated affirmation that had distinguished his performances for thirty-five years.

Vickers did not record or publicly perform single arias to show off his voice and beguile the public, because for him the voice was to be at the service of the music, not the reverse. For Vickers, an aria would make sense only in the context of the drama to which it belonged, and almost all his operatic recording is of complete works. His recorded legacy is, in fact, relatively small considering his prominence and stature.

Recordings in any case convey only inadequately a Vickers performance. Vocal effects such as his use of half-voice or head-tone, or a tendency to portamento, can stand out on a recording as vocal mannerisms, but they could have tremendous effect in the theater because they were so dramatically motivated. Moreover, Vickers is a powerfully built man whose physical presence in itself carries great force, and on the stage he understood fully how to express in external gesture and movement his understanding of the inner feelings and motivations of the characters he portrayed.

Vickers could produce a heroic sound, but he could also sing quietly with sensual beauty and intimacy, and he could accomplish this dynamic range without a break in timbral continuity. He used this range to extraordinary effect, and this is something that can be grasped from his recordings. The final act of *Tristan und Isolde* he sang like chamber music, as if offering to the listener the chance of merely overhearing the interior musings of the delirious Tristan, but the arrival of Isolde would bring forth a torrent of sound, only to die literally in his mouth as Tristan himself dies. Similarly in *Peter Grimes,* Vickers makes Peter's final monologue a *tour de force* of expressive singing as Peter's emotions and reminiscences thrash about, from the rage of "Now is gossip put on trial" to the distant and heart-breaking quietness of the phrase "Turn the skies back and begin again."

The song recital played a relatively small part in Vickers's career, but his ability to adjust the vocal scale of his performance was especially evident there. A recording of songs that he made for the Canadian Broadcasting Corporation in 1969 is sung with compelling simplicity and a directness of communication from singer to listener. His performances of Schubert's *Die Winterreise* were a highly personal interpretation of those often bleak songs, with an intimacy that demanded the utmost concentration of the listener.

Vickers included among his greatest roles the monumental figures of Otello, Tristan, Parsifal, Siegmund, Aeneas and Peter Grimes, but he was as convincing in lesser masterpieces such as *Samson et Dalila, I pagliacci, The Bartered Bride,* or *Carmen* because of the complete conviction and understanding that he carried to a performance. Since opera was not for him merely entertainment, he had to find in a role some moral force, whether it be Tristan's struggle to overcome desire or the consequences of Samson's broken vows. It was this conviction, the absolute certainty of his own understanding, and uncompromising standards that he brought to his performances and which made them so thrilling.

—Carl Morey

LA VIDA BREVE [The Short Life].

Composer: Manuel de Falla.

Librettist: Carlos Fernández Shaw.

First Performance: Nice, Casino Municipal, 1 April 1913.

Roles: Salud (soprano); Her Grandmother (mezzo-soprano or contralto); Paco (tenor); Uncle Sarvaor (bass or baritone);

Carmela (mezzo-soprano); Manuel (baritone); Singer (baritone); Four Peddlers (sopranos, mezzo-soprano); Voices (tenors); chorus (SSAATTBB).

* * *

La vida breve is a two-act opera composed by Manuel de Falla in 1904 and 1905. It is based upon a poem entitled *El chavalillo* by Carlos Fernández Shaw, a poet who frequently collaborated in the production of *zarzuelas,* and who expanded the work into the libretto Falla used. The opera was awarded a prize for the best lyrical drama by a Spanish composer by the Real Academia de Bellas Artes of Madrid. Since the award did not entail a production of the opera, the premiere had to be postponed for a number of years. The first performance of *La vida breve* did not take place until 1 April 1913, when it was produced at the Nice Casino Municipal under the direction of J. Miranne, with the soprano Lillian Grenville and the tenor David Devriès in the roles of Salud and Paco. Subsequent performances took place at the Opéra-Comique of Paris, 7 January 1914, under the direction of Franz Ruhlmann; Teatro de la Zarzuela of Madrid, 14 November 1914; and, the New York Metropolitan Opera, 7 March 1926.

The plot revolves around Salud, a simple girl from Granada, who lives with her grandmother and her uncle. She has fallen in love with Paco, a dashing young man of ostentatious vanity, to whom she swears eternal love. But Paco deserts Salud for the rich *novia,* Carmela, whom he plans to marry. Salud watches the wedding banquet through an iron railing and, overcome with anger, she bursts into the festivities and falls dead at Paco's feet. (We are never really sure what is the cause of the heroine's death.) Pandemonium follows and the curtain falls.

Manuel de Falla continued to compose a considerable amount of music for some fifteen years after he had completed *La vida breve.* The music of his later years became a synthesis of the Spanish spirit with the style of the early Spanish Renaissance polyphonists. Therefore, while later works such as *Master Peter's Puppet Show* and the Concerto for harpsichord do have a stylized Spanish quality, the earlier *La vida breve* has a more immediate Spanish identity for most listeners. Within this work the melodies employ characteristics of the *cante hondo* style found among Falla's countrymen, including a restricted tessitura and a modal basis colored with oriental inflections. Many of the rhythms throughout the opera are dotted, displaying syncopated patterns typical of popular Andalusian dances.

The opera as a drama is problematic. It contains a plot with very little action or development. Fernández Shaw hastily wrote the lyrics for *La vida breve* in the manner in which he was accustomed to writing librettos for the popular *zarzuelas.* Nevertheless, because of Falla's devoted study and keen understanding of true Spanish music, *La vida breve* is one of the most Spanish of all operas. Not only does the music capture the sounds of the country, it also expresses the sense of strong emotion found in the daily lives of Spaniards throughout much of their turbulent history.

—Roger F. Foltz

VILLA-LOBOS, Heitor.

Composer. Born 5 March 1887, in Rio de Janeiro. Died 17 November 1959, in Rio de Janeiro. Studied music with his father; collected folk songs in northern Brazil, 1905-07; studied with Frederico Nascimento, Angelo França, and Francisco Braga at the National Institute of Music in Rio de Janeiro, 1907-1912; gathered Indian songs in the interior of Brazil, 1912; presented a very successful concert of his compositions in Rio de Janeiro, 13 November 1915; met pianist Artur Rubenstein, and composed *Rudèpoêma* for him (1921-26); in Paris on a Brazilian government grant, 1923; returned to Brazil, 1930; appointed director of music education, Rio de Janeiro, 1930; developed his own method of solfeggio for children; concert tour of the United States, 1944-45; established the Brazilian Academy of Music in Rio de Janeiro, 1945; from 1947, Villa-Lobos lived part of each year in the United States, Brazil, and Europe until his death.

Operas

Publishers: Associated, Consolidated, Eschig, Napoleão, Peters, Ricordi, Robbins, Southern, Tonos, Vitale.

Izaht, Azevedo, Júnior, and Villa-Lobos, 1912-14, Rio de Janeiro, Municipal, 13 December 1958.
Magdalena ("musical adventure"), R. Wright and G. Forrest, 1948, Los Angeles, 26 July 1948.
Yerma, after Lorca, 1955-56, Sante Fe, 12 August 1971.
A menina des nuvens ("musical adventure"), L. Benedetti, 1957-58, Rio de Janeiro, Municipal, 29 November 1960.

Other works: ballets, film scores, vocal works, orchestral works, chamber music, piano pieces.

Publications

By VILLA-LOBOS: books–

O ensino popular da música no Brasil. Rio de Janeiro, 1937.
A música nacionalista do Governo Getúlio Vargas. Rio de Janeiro, 1937.

articles–

"A música: fator de comunhão entre os povos." *Anuário brasileiro* 3 (1939): 32.

About VILLA-LOBOS: books–

Muricy, Andrade. *Villa-Lobos: uma interpretação.* Rio de Janeiro, 1961.
Peppercorn, Lisa M. *Heitor Villa-Lobos: Leben und Werk des brasilianischen Komponisten.* Zurich, 1972.
Mariz, W. Vasco. *Heitor Villa-Lobos: Life and Work of the Brazilian Composer.* Washington, D.C., 1970; 5th ed., 1977.
Schoenbach, Peter J. *Classical Music of Brazil.* Albuquerque, New Mexico, 1985.
Appleby, David, P. *Heitor Villa-Lobos: a Bio-bibliography.* Westport, Connecticut, 1988.
Peppercorn, Lisa M. *Villa-Lobos: the Music (an Analysis of his Style). London, 1991.*

articles–

Peppercorn, Lisa M. "A Villa-Lobos Opera." *New York Times* 28 April (1940).
_____."Uma Opera de Villa-Lobos." *Musica Viva* [Rio de Janeiro] 1/no. 3 (1940).
_____. "Some Aspects of Villa-Lobos' Principles of Composition." *Music Review* 6 (1943): 28.
_____. "Villa-Lobos's Stage Works." *Revue belge de musicologie* 36-38 (1982-84): 175.
_____. "Villa-Lobos's Commissioned Compositions." *Tempo* no. 151 (1984).
Rickards, Guy S. "Yerma." *Tempo* no. 170 (1989).

* * *

Villa-Lobos was not a prolific opera composer. The research of Lisa Peppercorn has shown that only two operas, *Izaht* and *Yerma,* can be claimed with any certainty to have ever been written, plus two musicals or operettas, *Magdalena* and *A menina des nuvens.* Other works may have been begun, but precious little has survived if so. Villa-Lobos's career, like Sibelius's, is littered with unrealized projects and might-have-beens, but unlike Sibelius, Villa-Lobos claimed at various times to have composed several operas which had even been performed, when in fact not a note had been set down. To be sure, he claimed as much for other forms of music as well; the Second Symphony, for example, was almost certainly not written until the 1940s, post-dating the Third, Fourth and Fifth Symphonies at least, works which had been performed shortly after the end of the Great War.

Villa-Lobos was never really comfortable writing for the stage, whether ballet or opera. If more at ease with dance, he nonetheless realized the cardinal importance of opera as a form to his hopes of becoming an established major composer. The first recorded references to any kind of stage works appear on a generally fictional list of compositions drawn up in about 1908 on the back of a piano piece from a few years earlier. To be fair, this list may be little more than a list of what he intended to write, but not much survives, and probably little more was ever written. However, one piece, an untitled operetta with thirty-six numbers was at least begun, an intermezzo from act four revealing that a title of *Dulcinda* had been selected. Omitted from the list, however, is another work entitled *Comedia lirica,* of which a piano score of some dozen numbers from the first two acts survives, the first substantial theater music he ever penned. It is possible that one of these two pieces is what persisted later on as the opera *Femina,* allegedly fully rehearsed by a company that went bust on the day of the premiere.

In 1915 a further operatic project was conceived: *Izaht.* This eventually turned out to be the first completed opera by Villa-Lobos, but it took some twenty-five years to become so. The overture was written to satisfy the requirements of a concert in 1917, and the following year Villa-Lobos conducted the fourth (and last) act, presumably in the hope of stimulating a complete performance for which he would then no doubt have composed the rest of the work. The reactions to these extracts were not encouraging, however: the overture was damned for being unduly dissonant, while the final act, bereft of context and without staging, so completely baffled the audience that no one knew what to make of it. Despite tirelessly organizing concerts both in France and Brasil over the next decade, it would seem not a note of *Izaht* was heard, and yet in 1928, Villa-Lobos declared that the complete opera had been performed four times but that he had stopped all further performances in order to concentrate on new compositions. Further claims that *Izaht* had been written in four months and had made his reputation in Brasil were pure fantasy.

Izaht was finally completed for a performance in Brasil in 1940, a fate not shared by such other projects as *Femina, Aglaia, Elisa, Jesus* (a Biblical epic), *Zoe* (an opera supposedly about a dancer and her role within contemporary society) and *Malazarte,* which last (according to its composer based wholly on folk elements and nearly impossible to stage) seems never to have been written down, though to what extent it really had formed in Villa-Lobos's head must remain a matter of scepticism.

Once the all-important breakthrough had been made in the United States in the mid-1940s, Villa-Lobos began to receive commissions for all manner of different works. One of the first of these was for a two-act "musical adventure," *Magdalena* (the title refers to a Colombian river), for the Los Angeles Light Opera Association. The original idea had been for two Broadway producers to construct a musical from existing music in a manner similar to *The Song of Norway,* but Villa-Lobos offered a new work instead. Despite well over a hundred performances in Los Angeles, San Francisco and New York, it failed to make a lasting impression, and in between the West and East Coast performances, extensive alterations to the plot and music irked the composer so much that he threatened (but did not carry out) a public denial of the music as his. In reality an operetta or musical rather than an opera, it has now been recorded by CBS.

A second "musical adventure," *A menina des nuvens* (*The Daughter of the Clouds*) followed in 1958. Styled an opera for children in three acts to a libretto by L. Benedetti, it stands in relation to Villa-Lobos's works much as *Let's Make An Opera!* does to Benjamin Britten's.

Fortunately, the failure of *Magdalena* did not deter the would-be commissioners of Villa-Lobos's second (and last completed) proper opera, *Yerma,* based on the play (of the same name) in Federico Garcia Lorca's folktrilogy. It is solely on *Yerma* that Villa-Lobos's reputation as an opera composer rests. Its Puccinian flavor has been much commented on, but too much can be made of this, since Villa-Lobos grew up with Puccini's music (his father having been a keen fan), so that a Puccinian model for his own opera was only natural, as Beethoven was for the symphonies. Ironically, Villa-Lobos was never to hear a note in performance of his only commissioned opera, which had to wait until 1971 for Santa Fe Opera's premiere production. If Villa-Lobos had ever any intention of setting the other Lorca plays, no trace has survived.

—Guy Rickards

A VILLAGE ROMEO AND JULIET.

Composer: Frederick Delius.

Librettist: Frederick Delius (after Gottfried Keller, *Romeo und Julia auf dem Dorfe*).

First Performance: Berlin, Komische Oper, 21 February 1907.

Roles: Manz (baritone); Marti (baritone); Sali (tenor); Vreli (soprano); Dark Fiddler (baritone); Two Peasants (baritones); Three Women (contralto, two sopranos); Ginger-Bread Woman (soprano); Wheel-of-Fortune Woman (soprano); Cheap Jewelry Woman (contralto); Showman (tenor); Merry-Go-Round Man (baritone); Shooting-Gallery Man (bass); Slim Girl (soprano); Wild Girl (contralto); Poor Horn Player (tenor); Hunchback Bass Fiddler (bass); Three Bargemen (two baritones, tenor); chorus (SATBB).

The original story from which Delius fashioned the consistently beautiful score for *A Village Romeo and Juliet* was drawn from a real life occurrence. On 3 September 1847, a Zurich newspaper had reported the deaths of two youths whose bodies had been found in a field. Children of poor background from a village near Leipzig, they had not been allowed to marry because of enmity between their families. After dancing one night at a nearby inn, they had shot themselves. The story caught the attention of the Swiss author Gottfried Keller, who jotted down in his diary shortly afterwards a possible motive for the feud: a dispute over a strip of land between the farms of the respective families. In 1885 this peasants' dispute and the Romeo and Juliet theme were interwoven by Keller to become the subject of his most famous novella, *Romeo und Julia auf dem Dorfe,* published the following year in the first of the two volumes which comprised the collection of stories entitled *Die Leute von Seldwyla.*

When Delius first encountered Keller's tale is not known, but a friend noted in September 1897 that the composer "had long had it in mind to use it as an opera." Earlier, in 1894, Delius had written: "I have a vague idea of writing 3 works: one on the Indians *[The Magic Fountain],* one on the Gypsies and one on the Negroes and quadroons *[Koanga]*." It may well be that the loose group of wanderers and social outcasts who appear towards the end of Keller's novella represent in Delius's opera the vestigial gypsies of that projection.

The principal characters of *A Village Romeo and Juliet* are Salomon (Sali) Manz and Vrenchen (Vreli) Marti. Delius presents the two as young children in just the first scene of his "lyric drama in six scenes." Scene ii takes place six years later, and the remaining action probably just some months after that. The dispute between the farmers Manz and Marti, which results in ruinous litigation between them, is contained within the first two scenes of the opera, whereas the quarrel and its aftermath play a major role continuing well into the second half of Keller's original. Delius, however, wished his Romeo and Juliet to take center stage as early as possible, with the result that for the purposes of the opera the farmers' wives and other subsidiary characters in Keller are excised completely from the score. On the other hand, the role of the Dark Fiddler—the true but dispossessed inheritor of the strip of "wildland" that is at the root of the whole tragedy—is much expanded in Delius's hands. The grandson of the original owner of the now-disputed land, he has never been able to prove title to it (Delius adopts the device of illegitimacy to explain why), and he appears in the first scene of the opera, while the children are playing on the wildland that is gradually being ploughed into by each father, to warn them that time may well avenge him. Following his departure, farmers Manz and Marti quarrel and separate the children, who must no longer play together.

Six years later, their fathers now impoverished, Sali finally seeks out Vreli again. Love dawns. They agree to meet secretly on the wildland where, however, the Dark Fiddler disturbs them once again. He bears them no ill will, though he finds a grim satisfaction in their fathers' downfall and suggests that as they too have become reduced to such beggarly circumstances, they should join him in his wanderings. Even if they choose not to do so, "We'll meet again, no doubt, further down the hill." Left alone, the lovers take their first kiss, but are seen by Marti, looking for his daughter. While trying to drag her away he is knocked unconscious by Sali. The blow has terrible consequences: Marti is from then on confined in an asylum in the nearby town of Seldwyla. Vreli is left alone.

Time passes, and Vreli is spending her last night in the family home, now sold to pay her father's debts. As the twilight deepens, Sali returns and vows never to leave her again. They talk until darkness and then fall asleep in each other's arms. Each dreams of their wedding. Early next morning they take their leave of the house and make their way to the annual September fair at the village of Berghald. Wandering around the booths and stalls, they find their happiness cut short when they are recognized by other fairgoers from Seldwyla. Miserably self-conscious in their poor clothing, they decide to move on and at twilight reach an old riverside inn, the *Paradiesgärtlein*. Although here, at least, they do not expect to be recognized, they soon find that the inn is frequented by the Dark Fiddler and the vagabonds who are his friends. Welcomed by the group, Sali and Vreli again have temptation put in their way. Should they not after all join the fiddler and his companions in their nomadic life, free of all bourgeois moral restraints? Vreli has, after all, sung earlier of wandering "like gypsies on the great road." The youngsters' innate innocence and integrity will not, however, permit them to do so. They rather choose to consummate their love and die. Sali sees a hay-barge moored nearby, lifts Vreli into it and casts off. He will sink the boat and the lovers will drown in each other's arms.

Like all of Delius's operas, with the exception of the fairy tale *Irmelin,* the emphasis of *A Village Romeo and Juliet* is on alienation—between individuals, classes, or races. One or another set of circumstances decrees that the principal actors on Delius's stage will be outcasts, with death usually the outcome. The wellspring of tragedy in *The Magic Fountain* is racial conflict, as it is again in *Koanga.* In the one case it is the North American Indian, in the other the Afro-American whose downfall is brought about, willingly or unwillingly, by the white man. The outcasts of *Margot la Rouge* are the apache underclass of Parisian society. *Fennimore and Gerda* too is in major part the story of the alienation (for the first and only time on a bourgeois level in Delius's operas) between the three people at the heart of the main "Fennimore" episode. In *A Village Romeo* the alienation of each of the principal characters is virtually complete. Society rejects them all. Through their greed for land, Manz and Marti become impoverished and are then the direct cause of the years of separation between their children. The Dark Fiddler has long been a social outcast: interestingly, he remains so throughout, the only character who has adjusted to his life and achieved some kind of happiness. Sali and Vreli are innocent outcasts who end by being completely unable to relate to the world around them. They elect to die because they can envision this quite clearly, and not because they take a nihilistic or fatalistic view of the world. Triumphantly, the process of alienation is brought to an end by the unity of their love and death.

In 1897 and 1898 Delius had two writer friends make separate attempts to produce a libretto from Keller's story.

The first was C.F. Keary, *Koanga's* librettist, the second Karl-August Gerhardi, who started to fashion a suitable German text. Neither satisfied Delius, who, beginning to see the shape of his opera, decided in the autumn of 1899 to write his own libretto, which he swiftly completed. By November he was hard at work on the music, several successive months going into composition. After various interruptions, the opera was completed in 1901. Thomas Beecham, who gave it in London in 1910 and again in 1920, made with Delius's agreement certain revisions to the text, and this is the work's authentic libretto. The fresh English libretto (or "new translation") commissioned for the opera's revival in 1962 derived from the mistaken belief that Jelka Delius's excellent German translation of Delius's text was in fact the original libretto. It was finally—and one hopes irrevocably—abandoned when the 1989 film of the opera largely reverted to the Delius/Beecham version.

Peter Weigl's film has in fact confirmed what Frank Corsaro's 1970s production of *A Village Romeo,* with its cinematographic commitment to the scenic qualities as well as the moods evoked by the music, had already suggested: that Delius wrote, as it were, a film scenario and then composed an almost seamless stream of ravishingly beautiful music to mirror and amplify it. Claus Helmut Drese, at the time of his Zurich production in 1980, spoke of the challenge presented by the fact that some forty minutes of the score were purely orchestral. There is for most of this time comparatively little stage action. It is this kind of almost wilful disregard for the expectations of conventional operagoers that has received wry acknowledgement by successive (and largely sympathetic) commentators on *A Village Romeo and Juliet.* In 1923 Heseltine first hinted at the possibilities the gramophone may open up for the work; in 1948 Hutchings saw radio broadcasting as providing its most effective future; in 1970 Jefferson wrote of the possibility of its "triumphing" as a film. It is perhaps not surprising that earlier critics were disappointed at this lack of action. After all, in spite of requiring a large orchestra, the piece has at its core little more than the intimate interaction of the two young lovers who hold the center of the stage throughout. This rather static quality—shared in many respects with Debussy's *Pelléas et Mélisande*—is likely to demand more from an audience than, say, most of its verismo contemporaries, and the finest productions have been those in which the quality of the acting, as well as the singing, of the Sali and Vreli characters has served to draw the audience deeply into the taut intimacy of the drama, a drama impelled to its tragic conclusion by Delius's extraordinarily cogent and sinuous score. The composer, incidentally, always insisted on his singers' acting "from the music and not from the stage."

A Village Romeo and Juliet is to all intents and purposes the fruit of the happy circumstance of compositional maturity reached at the same time as the discovery of a virtually perfect vehicle for the composer's genius. The descriptive power of Delius's music, particularly in relation to the kind of pantheism that so attracted him, was already evident in his earliest orchestral works dating from the later 1880s and was fully assured by the time of the composition of the symphonic poem *Paris,* immediate predecessor of *A Village Romeo.* All of Delius's rich harmonies are there, as indeed are longer melodic lines than his previous operas have tended to give us, together with a characteristic translucence in the scoring. The score is in fact remarkably faithful to its source, and those very qualities of restraint, indeed reticence, that characterize Keller's economically-expressed story are also present in the music. Apart from the opportunity offered by the village fair music, with its striking pre-echoes of Stravinsky's *Petrushka,* there are remarkably few "theatrical" effects, and indeed some productions have given emphasis scenically to a perceived dream-like character inherent in the work—a character that may obviously be epitomized as the very antithesis of verismo. We are indeed far from Verona with this almost Nordic Romeo and Juliet, and there is no doubt that Delius saw his work to some extent as a psychological drama pointing the way to the J.P. Jacobsen-inspired *Fennimore and Gerda* a few years later. But whereas in the main "Fennimore" episode there is a darker, more troubled and even claustrophobic aspect to this later score, it is the quality of freshness and light which predominates in *A Village Romeo.* From the opening orchestral outburst (already giving us one of the opera's main leitmotifs) in all its sun-drenched vigor, evoking the dazzling beauty and the vibrant late-summer air of the countryside, to the final passionate duet, lit by moonlight, the elemental forces of nature and, with them, the oneness of human life are evoked, giving us some of Delius's finest music. Each of the opera's six scenes has its prelude, the first five being purely orchestral, the last taking the form of a distant mixed chorus set against the lower strings and followed by echoing horn-calls, and among them are ravishing examples of Delius's evocative use of woodwind, horns and strings (see particularly the transition between scenes ii and iii leading to Sali and Vreli's meeting on the wildland). Otherwise the best-known of the orchestral interludes is "The Walk to the Paradise Garden," only composed in 1907 when the scene-changing exigencies of Hans Gregor's production at Berlin's newly-founded Komische Oper demanded its interpolation.

The number of European productions in the 1980s has given scope for a full reassessment of *A Village Romeo and Juliet,* and Weigl's film of the opera has at last provided us with a view of the work as nearly as possible as Delius would have wished to see it. Those earlier critical views of Delius' characters as little more than prototypes or symbols, moving in dreamlike sequence to their predestined end, are seen to be very wide of the mark: the lovers are flesh and blood, and their passion, so long held in check and finally fully released, is committed, believable and deeply moving. Heseltine was right from the start: "There is never any disparity between the music and the action. . . . If opera be defined as perfect co-relation between music and action, then *A Village Romeo and Juliet* is one of the most flawless masterpieces that have ever been given to the world."

—Lionel Carley

THE VILLAGE SOOTHSAYER
See LE DEVIN DU VILLAGE

LE VILLI [The Willis].

Composer: Giacomo Puccini.

Librettist: Ferdinando Fontana.

First Performance: Milan, Teatro dal Verme, 31 May 1884; revised Turin, Regio, 26 December 1884.

Roles: Guglielmo Wulf (baritone); Anna (soprano); Roberto (tenor); chorus (SATTB).

Publications

article—

Budden, Julian. "The genesis and literary source of Giacomo Puccini's first opera." *Cambridge Opera Journal* 1 (1989): 79.

When Puccini entered the conservatory in Milan as a student in 1880, he found himself in a much more stimulating environment than his native Lucca had been. While he was instructed at the conservatory by Amilcare Ponchielli and Antonio Bazzini, he also benefited greatly from his exposure to a wide spectrum of operatic repertoire being performed in the city. Milan had to be counted as one of the most significant opera centers in Italy. Despite being chronically short on cash, Puccini managed to attend a good many performances. Milan was not only a Verdi stronghold; French opera was all the rage as well, the most popular composers being Massenet, Gounod, Halévy, Meyerbeer, and Bizet.

Puccini set out to compose his first opera, *Le villi,* in 1883. In July of that year, he had first met his librettist, Ferdinando Fontana, who had suggested the subject to him. The plot is drawn from Heine, who had related the legend in his *Elementargeister und Dämonen.* The *Willis* (as they are called in the legend) are ghostly maiden dancers, brides who died before their wedding. Within their dead hearts, there remains the unfulfilled yearning to dance, and at midnight, the *Willis* ascend from their graves and gather on the highways. Any young man who happens upon them is doomed; he must dance with them, and the *Willis,* holding him in their embrace, dance with him relentlessly until he falls dead.

Upon the background of this legend, Fontana constructed a simple plot. The action is set in two scenes (or acts in the later expanded two-act version). Guglielmo Wulf's daughter Anna is celebrating her engagement to Roberto, who is about to leave for Mainz, where he intends to collect a major inheritance he has just received. Before he departs, he and Anna pledge each other eternal loyalty. In Mainz, however, Roberto is led astray by a "siren" who lures him to an "obscene orgy," and he forgets all about his love for Anna. Meanwhile, Anna waits in vain for Roberto's return. By winter, she dies of a broken heart.

When the "siren" abandons Roberto, he decides to return to Anna, not knowing that she has died. When he returns home, the *villi,* among them Anna, are lying in wait for him. When he first hears Anna's voice, he believes her to be alive, but when she appears, she tells him that she is no longer "love," but "revenge." Roberto, full of remorse, realizes that she is dead. When he runs towards her, Anna embraces him while the *villi* gather around them. They announce to him that a man who in life was deaf to love will find no forgiveness in death. The terrified Roberto tries to escape, but the *villi* mercilessly surround him. His fate is sealed as he is forced to dance himself to death with Anna.

In Fontana's elaboration of the plot, the *villi* become the ghosts of betrothed maidens whose deaths are caused specifically by having been abandoned by their lovers. While the story is typical of the general interest in the demonic aspects of German Romanticism in Italy around 1870-1880 (cf. Boito's *Mefistofele* or Catalani's *Elda*), it cannot be seen to indicate a particular preference for the subject on Puccini's part. Puccini was primarily interested in entering an opera in the competition sponsored by the publisher Sonzogno. For this he needed a libretto and, lacking adequate funds, he was hardly in a position to be choosy. He was also working against a deadline, so that he must have been eager to get his hands on any libretto at all.

Even though *Le villi* failed to win the Sonzogno competition, it gained the recognition of several influential men, among them Ponchielli, Arrigo Boito, and Giulio Ricordi, who saw the merits in this first opera by a young composer and undertook to have the work staged. It was first performed in 1884, and its reception was positive among critics and the public alike. While there were some novel aspects to the score (as for instance the two intermezzi, before each of which the audience was provided with essential dramatic information), *Le villi* was still a number opera in the old tradition. At the same time, melody was already establishing itself as the foremost characteristic of Puccini's style, even though this opera has little affinity with the kind of melodic writing Puccini would develop later on in his career. Few melodies display the same kind of broadly painted contour that later became the trademark of Puccini's style.

While the influence of Ponchielli is noticeable throughout the score, so is the influence of the French composers whose music Puccini was exposed to in Milan; especially, it would appear, Massenet and Bizet. But in the orchestral preludes, there is also a trace of Wagner, whose music had first been performed in Italy in 1871. But overall, *Le villi* is characterized by a quite conventional harmonic vocabulary, devoid of copious chromaticism. The orchestration as well shows Puccini under the influence of the French masters. Generally, the orchestral texture is light, often emphasizing the winds, making for a bright sound. The very beginning of the opera, dominated by the winds, illustrates this aspect of Puccini's orchestration. Even though the orchestration is at times rather awkward, Puccini often displays some quite imaginative scoring.

For all its merits as the first opera of one of the most influential composers from the turn of the century, *Le villi* cannot claim a stake in the repertory. The score is the promising work of a fledgling composer, but not an early masterpiece. The greatest shortcoming, however, must be seen in the libretto. While the language is mostly unimaginatively conventional, if not pretentious, the almost complete absence of action makes it all but impossible to sustain interest in the story, all the more so because none of the characters is developed enough to allow the audience to feel any empathy for them. As a dramatic piece, *Le villi* is a failure, but it does contain a fair amount of charming music.

—Jürgen Selk

VINAY, Ramón.

Tenor and baritone. Born 31 August 1912, in Chillán, Chile. Studied engineering in France, voice in Mexico City with José Pierson; baritone debut as Count di Luna in *Il trovatore,* Mexico City, 1938; tenor debut as Don José in *Carmen,* Mexico City, 1943; New York City Opera debut as Don José, 1945; Metropolitan Opera debut as Don José, 1946; at Metropolitan Opera, 1946-62 and 1965-66; Teatro alla Scala debut as Otello, 1947; Salzburg debut, 1951; at Bayreuth,

1952-57; Covent Garden debut, 1955; Paris debut, 1958; artistic director of The Santiago Opera, 1969-71.

Publications

About VINAY: articles–

Rosenthal, Harold. "Ramón Vinay." *Opera* 6/June (1958): 355.
Celletti, Rodolfo. "Vinay, Ramón." *Le grandi voci.* Rome, 1964.
Rosenthal, Harold. "Ramón Vinay." *Great Singers of Today.* London, 1966.

Fairly early in his career, Ramón Vinay staked out his operatic territory and took psychological siege. There was heroic agony in his sound, but sorrow and tenderness, too. He could suggest the noble pain of a tenor like Giovanni Martinelli, but with an intellectual frenzy all his own. Vinay's was a dark voice of medium size, called rich on good nights and thick on problematic ones, shadowed and occasionally unsteady but at its peak possessing great warmth, like sunlight in a thicket. In the theater it lacked a cutting edge, the *squillo* of Mario del Monaco or Franco Corelli, but it had a complexity of color that gave his Otello vulnerability, his Don José tragic stature, and his Wagnerian roles spiritual profundity. The lower range connoted authority and the upper an implacable yearning.

Like Renato Zanelli, Lauritz Melchior, and Set Svanholm, Vinay began as a baritone. His international career, though, started in 1944 with a Mexican performance of Verdi's *Otello.* In two years his "Rembrandtian tone quality" (as Arthur Bloomfield put it) led him to the Metropolitan Opera in this and other tenor roles, and then to Bayreuth for half a dozen seasons in Wagner, and meanwhile to Salzburg, San Francisco, Holland, London, and Italy, singing his famous Moor and Don José, Samson, Canio, Radames, Tannhäuser, Siegmund, Tristan, Parsifal, and Herod. In the 1960s he returned to lower roles: Falstaff, Telramund, Iago, Scarpia, Dr Schoen, and even Bartolo (*Il barbiere di Siviglia*), Varlaam (Lord Harewood reportedly thought it the best characterized he had ever seen), and the Grand Inquisitor in *Don Carlo.* He closed his singing career in Chile singing tenor one more time, in the final act of *Otello.*

As can be seen, Vinay had his triumphs in roles of the greatest motivational complexity. The voice was best heard in a house the capacity of Bayreuth—about 2000; faced with Wagner at the Metropolitan Opera (nearly twice that size), he might push. His expressive qualities were already finely developed in his first studio recording, some highlights from *Carmen* done with Gladys Swarthout in 1946. Pride and intimate yearning shape his performance. His Flower Song is deeply committed rather than declamatory, his reading of "Carmen, je t'aime" at its conclusion an exposed private moment. Vinay's characterization in the final duet is equally adult: forgiving and demanding, desperate, restrained, and impossible all at once, without either vulgarity or pretension, but suggesting more fully than any later singer but Jon Vickers the nobility of Don José's sexual passion.

These qualities dominated Vinay's other roles, too. His Otello under Toscanini (1947) may lack some of the suffocating tenderness of Martinelli's, but it too is profoundly indicative of both public valor and private frailty. Under Fritz

Busch's direction at the Metropolitan Opera (1948) he deepens the frenzy, and with Furtwängler in Salzburg (1951) the element of reverie.

By that time Vinay had begun his forays into Wagner with an initial Tristan in San Francisco with Kirsten Flagstad (1950), and his Bayreuth career in tenor leads was about to begin. Some of those performances may be even more satisfying on records than they were in the opera house, where the visceral impact of the voice was less and the details could be lost in a single hearing. One would expect him to enact the frenzies of Tristan's third act movingly, but the erotic passion of act II is more difficult for a voice blunt in tone, a little tight at the climaxes, and not always free. Nevertheless, in a Bayreuth performance of July 1952 a despairing idealism always illuminates the mature sound, and towards the end of the love duet Vinay's spiritual quietude highlights amazingly the ensuing ecstasy of the climax. By contrast, the Melchior performance of 1936 (Covent Garden)—a touchstone—is incomparably beautiful in timbre: a tender seduction unequaled in my experience of this opera, but without the rapturous pain that makes the Vinay version an endless stimulation. Likewise, Melchior's subsequent appeal to Isolde to follow him into death is infinitely comforting, but Vinay's remains filled, uniquely, with exhausted longing. These traits are also found in his 1954 Bayreuth Tannhäuser. As one might expect, he sounds more industrious than joyful in the Venusberg salute, but the Rome Narration, chronicling the hero's damnation, has all the rage and sorrow implicit in the music and demonstrates most strikingly Vinay's special gifts. His revelation is one of increasing anguish. In this performance, the words of the Pope are indeed the words of anathema and the call to Venus a final cry of spiritual exhaustion. In his 1957 Parsifal, the voice is even older, but his response to seduction by Kundry is movingly agonized and the final redemption suffuses his tone with joy.

Vinay's baritone period is not so fully documented, though his Telramund and Iago (both 1962) show strong musical profile if not much vocal glamour. In the Verdi, he uses rhythm as a dramatic weapon and brings immense energy and craft to his work. "Era la notte" is strikingly intimate *and* obscene, and the duets with the Otello of Del Monaco are interesting for their differently projected voices: Del Monaco's is a sword and Vinay's a truncheon.

A commanding man onstage, Vinay was a singing actor of profound feeling in his French and Italian roles, and the subtlest and most heroic in spirit of the tenors of the Bayreuth renaissance in the early 1950s. His characterizations remain unique, but some of his work reminds one fondly of Jon Vickers, who has expressed deep admiration for Vinay's accomplishments.

—London Green

VISCONTI, Luchino.

Producer and designer. Born Count Don Luchino Visconti di Modrone, 2 November 1906, in Milan. Died 17 March 1976, in Rome. Collaborated with Jean Renoir on an opera film, *La Tosca,* 1939; later a director of films and theater in Italy; first film as director, *Ossessione,* 1942; operatic debut, *La vestale,* Teatro alla Scala, 1954; in collaboration wrote the libretto for Mannino's opera *Il diavolo in giardino,* Palermo, 1963.

Opera Productions (selected)

La vestale, Teatro alla Scala, 1954.
La sonnambula, Teatro alla Scala, 1955.
La traviata, Teatro alla Scala, 1955.
Anna Bolena, Teatro alla Scala, 1957.
Iphigénie en Tauride, Teatro alla Scala, 1957.
Macbeth, Spoleto Festival, 1958.
Don Carlos, Covent Garden, 1958.
Duca d'Alba, Spoleto Festival, 1959.
Salome, Spoleto Festival, 1961.
La traviata, Spoleto Festival, 1963.
Il diavolo in giardino, Palermo, 1963.
Il trovatore, Covent Garden, 1964.
Der Rosenkavalier, Covent Garden, 1966.
Falstaff, Vienna, 1966.
La traviata, Covent Garden, 1967.
Manon Lescaut, Spoleto Festival, 1972.

Publications

By VISCONTI: books–

Three Screenplays: White Nights, Rocco and His Brothers, The Job. Translated by Judith Green. New York, 1970.

articles–

"Maria Callas." *Opera* 21 (1970): 806 and 911.

About VISCONTI: books–

Estève, M., ed. *"Luchino Visconti: l'histoire et l'esthétique.* Paris, 1963.
Guillaume, Y. *Luchino Visconti.* Paris 1966.
Nowell-Smith, Geoffrey. *Luchino Visconti.* London, 1967.
Baldelli, P. *Luchino Visconti.* Milan, 1973.
Stirling, Monica. *A Screen of Time: A Study of Luchino Visconti.* New York, 1979.
Servadio, Gaia. *Luchino Visconti, a Biography.* New York, 1983.
Schifano, L. *Luchino Visconti: Fuerst des Films.* Gernsbach, 1989.

articles–

Alberti, L. "Luchino Visconti regista d'opera." *La Rassegna Musicale* 26 (April 1956): 130-33.
Weaver, W. "Luchino Visconti." *Opera* 9 (May 1958): 289-92.
"Covent Garden Opera." *Musical Opinion* 81 (June 1958): 569.
Ardoin, J. "Luchino Visconti, Master Magician." *Musical America* 81 (November 1961): 14-15.
Hanson, W. "*The Leopard;* Luchino Visconti Commands Both Opera and Film." *Opera News* 28 (28 September 1963): 16-18.
Weaver, W. "Palermo: Visconti as Librettist." *Opera* 14 (May 1963): 330-31.
Ardoin, J. "Opera Abroad, A Busman's Holiday." *Musical America* 84 (September 1964): 15.
Smith, P.J. "Gli Italiani in New York." *Opera* 19 (September 1968): 714-16.
Wechsberg, J. "Visconti's Monumental Joke." *Opera* 20 (June 1969): 491-93.
"Viskonti i operniyat teatur." *Bulgarska Muzika* 20, no. 8 (1969): 89.

Schmidt-Garre, H. "Italienische Oper—englisch zubereitet." *Neue Zeitschrift für Musik* 131 (June 1970): 278.

d'Amico, F., and others. "The Callas Debate." *Opera* 21 (September 1970): 806-19; (October 1970): 911-21.

"Albums: Visconti's Inventory." *Melody Maker* 53 (14 January 1978): 20.

Mannino, F. "Musica e spettacolo: esperienze con Luchino Visconti." *Rassegna Musicale Curci* 41, no. 3 (1988): 39-49.

*   *   *

When asked the date of his birth, Visconti sometimes replied, "Soon after the curtain went up at La Scala." According to his biographer, Monica Stirling, his first experience of an opera was *La traviata*. Coming from an upper-class, wealthy background, the theater was hardly thought of as an appropriate career for a young man. Visconti's radical ideas, which found their outlet in films like *Ossessione, La terra trema* and *Rocco,* were hardly compatible with the opera, as a symbol of *ancien-régime* conventions. However, what eventually became Visconti's best-known contribution to opera and cinema was the evocation of 19th-century works in modern terms: operas by Donizetti, Bellini, and Verdi, and films like *Senso, Il gattopardo* and *L'innocente.*

Visconti first worked in the cinema as an assistant to Jean Renoir; one of their (unfinished) projects was a film of *Tosca,* using Puccini's score as background music. Before he had begun to direct opera regularly, Visconti included, at the start of *Senso,* a stunning recreation of a performance of *Il trovatore* at La Fenice. The greatest successes of Visconti's opera career were with Maria Callas—productions at Teatro alla Scala of Spontini's *La vestale,* Bellini's *La sonnambula,* Verdi's *La traviata,* Donizetti's *Anna Bolena,* and Gluck's *Iphigénie en Tauride.* In Callas, Visconti found a singer-actress who brought to the bel canto repertory an instinct for stage action which had both traditional operatic grandeur and a more contemporary psychological awareness. During an interview in 1970 he said: "In opera, the stage characterization is the natural outcome of the musical one . . . she is one of those artists who, having worked out and perfected a detail, don't keep changing it." This perfectly suited Visconti's approach, which grew out of his work in the cinema and demanded a detailed choreography rather than the more robust theatricality of the old Italian opera. Although nearly all of his opera productions relied on traditional settings, the notion behind them often had a precise, more intellectual idea. The *La sonnambula* was like a Victorian lithograph of ballerinas—the Romantic age glimpsed from afar; *Iphigénie en Tauride,* an attempt to match Gluck's music with a Tiepolo *fresco.* Visconti seldom restaged a work, but *La traviata* held a fascination for him and he returned to it after the 1955 La Scala production, first at Spoleto in 1963, then at Covent Garden in 1967. The Callas-La Scala version had settings moved forward to the 1880s, the Spoleto one returned to the 1840s of the original. In his final view of *La traviata,* a black-and-white decor, inspired by the drawings of Aubrey Beardsley, was considered too provocative even for London in the swinging 1960s.

Visconti's most enduring productions were those of Verdi's *Don Carlos,* first presented at Covent Garden in 1958, which continued to be revived for 30 years, and *Le nozze di Figaro,* first presented in Rome in 1964. *Don Carlos* was hailed as a production that had "completely vindicated Italian grand opera." In this, and in a less well-received *Il trovatore* in 1963,

Visconti worked within obviously painted sets and exaggerated false perspectives but produced acting which, while seeming traditional, achieved a modern impact. The art-nouveau *Der Rosenkavalier* in London (1966) and a symbolistic, semiabstract *Simon Boccanegra* in Vienna (1969) were both deemed unsuccessful. His final opera production, Puccini's *Manon Lescaut* at Spoleto in 1973, was a return to form. Although Visconti did not direct an opera by Wagner, his bio-pic of Ludwig of Bavaria (*Ludwig,* 1972) is suffused with Wagner's music and images derived from his operas. Similarly, the final moments of Visconti's last film, *L'innocente,* seem like an homage to the finale of act II of *Tosca.*

Valentine Lawford, summing up Visconti's work, wrote that "a certain dualism perceptible in Visconti's own personality—outwardly impressive, authoritive, dictatorial, but gentle, humble, vulnerable at heart—is reflected, magnified in his work." While Visconti may have had "a feeling for luxury and a fascination with decadence," it was ultimately his good taste that showed in all the best of his productions. Commenting on the famous Teatro alla Scala *Anna Bolena* in 1957, Desmond Shawe-Taylor wrote, "It is one of the great merits of Luchino Visconti's production that he is never afraid of simple effects when they are truly called for."

—Patrick O'Connor

VISHNEVSKAYA, Galina.

Soprano. Born 25 October 1926, in Leningrad. Married: cellist/conductor Mstislav Rostropovich, 1955; two daughters. Studied in Leningrad with Vera Garina; debut in operetta, 1944; toured with Leningrad Light Opera Company, 1944-48; soloist with the Leningrad Philharmonic, 1948-52; joined Bol'shoy Theater in Moscow, 1952 (debut as Tatyana in *Eugene Onegin*); Metropolitan Opera debut as Aida, 1961; Covent Garden debut in same role, 1962; Teatro alla Scala debut as Liù in *Turandot,* 1964; appeared in film of Shostakovich's *Katerina Izmaylova* (1966) and sang in first performance of his Symphony No. 14 (1969); left USSR with husband in 1974; Soviet citizenship stripped in 1978 but restored in 1990.

Publications

By VISHNEVSKAYA: books–

Galina: A Russian Story. San Diego, 1984.

About VISHNEVSKAYA: books–

Samuel, Claude. *Entretiens avec Mstislav Rostropovich et Galina Vishnevskaya sur la Russie, la musique, la liberté.* Paris, 1983.

articles–

Timokhin, V. "Galina Vishnevskaya." *Muzikal'naya zhizn'* no. 12 (1964): 9.

*   *   *

Since first becoming a soloist with the Bol'shoy Theatre in 1952, Galina Vishnevskaya's name has become increasingly well known throughout the musical world. Following an international tour in 1955 embracing Eastern Europe, Yugoslavia, Italy, Austria, France, England, the United States, Australia, New Zealand, and Japan, her performances of such roles as Tatyana and Lisa in Tchaikovsky's *Eugene Onegin* and *The Queen of Spades,* Kupava and Marfa in Rimsky-Korsakov's *The Snow Maiden* and *The Tsar's Bride,* Aida and Violetta in Verdi's *Aida* and *La Traviata,* Madama Butterfly and Tosca in Puccini's operas of the same titles, Leonora in Beethoven's *Fidelio,* Cherubino in Mozart's *Le nozze di Figaro* and the solo part in Poulenc's *La voix humaine*—all have been highly commended. She was the first performer of the role of Katarina in Shebalin's *The Taming of the Shrew* at the Bol'shoy in 1957, of Natasha Rostova in Prokofiev's *War and Peace* in 1959, of Marina in Muradeli's *October* in 1964, and of Sofiya Tkachenko in Prokofiev's *Semen Kotko* in 1970. In 1966 she sang the title role in the screen adaptation of Shostakovich's opera *Katerina Izmaylova* (a modified version of the earlier opera *The Lady Macbeth of the Mtsensk District*).

Vishnevskaya's superb artistry has often been a source of inspiration to composers. Benjamin Britten dedicated to her and her husband, Mstislav Rostropovich, his song cycle to words of Pushkin, *The Poet's Echo.* For her also was intended the soprano part in Britten's *War Requiem.* Shostakovich dedicated to her his Seven Romances, op. 127, likewise including a part for cello, and she was also a performer in the premiere of his Symphony No. 14 (1969).

Since 1974, following the emigration of Vishnevskaya and her husband to the West, both artists have been tremendously active often in joint projects (Rostropovich acting either as conductor or piano accompanist). In Britain alone both have appeared regularly at the Edinburgh Festival, the Aldeburgh Festival, Covent Garden, the Royal Festival Hall, and at the more recent Rostropovich Festival in Snape. Galina Vishnevskaya is a master in the art of creating mood, and it has been frequently stated that, even if the listener lacks an understanding of Russian, in her performance the underlying meaning of a song or aria could still be felt.

While Vishnevskaya's acting (influenced, like her singing, by Russian traditions) has on occasion been criticized as being a little "old-fashioned" (some critics consider her interpretation of Tatyana in Tchaikovsky's *Eugene Onegin* to be somewhat stylized), critics are unanimous in acknowledging the superb quality of her voice and the beauty of her tone. Equally at home in Russian, English, French, and Italian, she captures the essential features of each composer, be it Shostakovich, Britten, Poulenc or Verdi. Her performance as the passionate Katerina in Shostakovich's *Katerina Izmaylova* in the HMV recording of the work must certainly be regarded as one of her masterpieces; the *Gramophone* reviewer writes of "the moments of tenderness beautifully controlled, the voice coloured in great effect to convey a whole range of moods.... With Vishneskaya the character achieves a truly tragic stature." Impressive, too, is her portrayal of Pushkin's naive and guileless Tatyana in Tchaikovsky's *Eugene Onegin,* in which her interpretation is equally telling in its psychological insight. Though Vishnevskaya has occasionally been criticized for unevenness of performance, her voice is one that commands our attention and thus our emotions: in the final analysis, her supreme artistry prevails.

—Gerald Seaman

VIVALDI, Antonio.

Composer. Born 4 March 1678, in Venice. Died (buried) 28 July 1741, in Vienna. Studied violin probably with his father, Giovanni Battista Vivaldi, violinist at San Marco; commenced training for the priesthood 1693, ordained 1703; violin teacher at the Ospedale della Pietà in Venice 1703-9, 1711-17, 1735-8; music director at the court in Mantua of Prince Philip of Hesse-Darmstadt 1718-20; invited to Vienna by Charles VI, to whom he dedicated his twelve violin concertos entitled *La cetra,* 1727; composed many operas for Venice and other cities both inside and outside Italy.

Operas

Ottone in villa, D. Lalli, Vicenza, Teatro delle Garzerie, May 1713.

Orlando finto pazzo, G. Braccioli, Venice, Sant' Angelo, fall 1714.

Nerone fatto Cesare, M. Noris, Venice, Sant' Angelo, carnival 1715 [lost].

La costanza trionfante degl' amori e de gl'odi, A. Marchi, Venice, San Moisè, carnival 1716 [lost]; revised as *L'Artabano, re de' Parti,* Venice, San Moisè, carnival 1718; revised as *L'Artabano,* Mantua, carnival 1725; revised? as *Doriclea,* Prague, Sporck, carnival 1732.

Arsilda, regina di Ponto, D. Lalli, Venice, Sant' Angelo, 27/28 October 1716.

L'incoronazione di Dario, A. Morselli, Venice, Sant' Angelo, 23 January 1717.

Tieteberga, A.M. Lucchini, Venice, San Moisè, 16 October 1717 [lost].

Scanderbeg, A. Salvi, Florence, Teatro della Pergola, 22 June 1718 [lost].

Armida al campo d'Egitto, G. Palazzi, Venice, San Moisè, carnival 1718 [act 2 lost]; revised, Mantua, Arciducale, 1718; revised?, Lodi, 1719; revised as *Gl'inganni per vendetta,* Vicenza, Teatro delle Grazie [lost].

Teuzzone, Zeno, Mantua, Arciducale, carnival 1719.

Tito Manlio, M. Noris, Mantua, Arciducale, carnival 1719.

Tito Manlio (pasticcio) (with G. Boni and G. Giorgio), Rome, Teatro della Pace, carnival 1720 [lost].

La Candace o siano Li veri amici, F. Silvani and D. Lalli, Mantua, Arciducale, carnival 1720 [lost].

La verità in cimento, G. Palazzi and D. Lalli, Venice, Sant'-Angelo, 26 October 1720.

Filippo, re di Macedonia (with G. Boniventi), D. Lalli, Venice, Sant' Angelo, 27 December 1720 [lost].

La Silvia, E. Bissari?, Milan, Ducale, 28 August 1721 [lost].

Ercole su'l Termodonte, G.F. Bussani, Rome, Capranica, 23 January 1723 [lost].

Giustino, N. Berengani, Rome, Capranica, carnival 1724.

La virtù trionfante dell'amore e dell'odio overo Il Tigrane (with B. Micheli and N. Romaldi), F. Silvani, Rome, Capranica, Carnival 1724.

L'inganno trionfante in amore, M. Noris and G.M. Ruggieri, Venice, Sant' Angelo, fall 1725 [lost].

Cunegonda, A. Piovene, Venice, Sant' Angelo, 29 January 1726 [lost].

La fede tradita e vendicata, F. Silvani, Venice, Sant' Angelo, 16 February 1726 [lost]; revised as *Ernelinda* (pasticcio) (music mostly by F. Gasparini, B. Galuppi and Vivaldi), F. Silvani, Venice, San Cassiano, carnival 1750 [lost].

Dorilla in Tempe, A.M. Lucchini, Venice, Sant' Angelo, 9 November 1726; revised?, Prague, Sporck, 1732; revised, Venice, Sant' Angelo, 1734.

Ipermestra, A. Salvi, Florence, Teatro della Pergola, carnival 1727 [lost].

Siroe, re di Persia, Metastasio, Reggio Emilia, Pubblico, May 1727 [lost]; revised, Ancona, Fenice, 1738; revised, Ferrara, Bonacossi, 1739.

Farnace, A.M. Lucchini, Venice, Sant' Angelo, 10 February 1727; revised, Venice, Sant' Angelo, 1727; revised?, Prague, Sporck; 1730; revised, Pavia, Omodeo, 1731.

Orlando, G. Braccioli, Venice, Sant' Angelo, fall 1727; revised?, Este, Grillo, 1740.

Rosilena ed Oronta, G. Palazzi, Venice, Sant' Angelo, carnival 1728 [lost].

L'Atenaide o sia Gli affetti generosi, Zeno, Florence, Teatro della Pergola, 29 December 1728.

Argippo, D. Lalli, Prague, Sporck, fall 1730 [lost].

Alvilda, regina de' Goti, Prague, Sporck, spring 1731 [lost].

La fida ninfa, S. Maffei, Verona, Filarmonico, 6 January 1732.

Semiramide, Zeno, Mantua, Arciducale, carnival 1732 [lost].

Motezuma, G. Giusti, Venice, Sant' Angelo, 14 November 1733 [lost].

L'Olimpiade, Metastasio, Venice, Sant' Angelo, 17 February 1734.

L'Adelaide, A. Salvi, Verona, Filarmonico, carnival 1735 [lost]; revised?, Graz, Tummelplatz, 1735.

Griselda, Zeno (additions by C. Goldoni), Venice, San Samuele, 18 May 1735.

Tamerlano (Bajazet) (pasticcio), A. Piovene, Verona, Filarmonico, carnival 1735; revised? as *Bajazette,* Vicenza, Teatro delle Garzerie, 1738.

Ginevra, principessa di Scozia, A. Salvi, Florence, Teatro della Pergola, January 1736 [lost].

Catone in Utica, Metastasio, Verona, Filarmonico, May 1737 [act 1 lost]; revised?, Graz, Tummelplatz, 1740.

L'oracolo in Messenia, Zeno, Venice, Sant' Angelo, 30 December 1737 [lost]; revised, Vienna, Kärntnertor, 1742.

Rosmira (pasticcio), S. Stampiglia, Venice, Sant' Angelo, 27 January 1738; revised?, Graz, Tummelplatz, 1739.

Feraspe, F. Silvani, Venice, Sant' Angelo, 7 November 1739 [lost].

Other works: serenatas, cantatas, oratorios, sacred vocal works, solo sonatas, trio sonatas, concertos.

Publications/Writings

About VIVALDI: books–

Goldoni, Carlo. *Mémoires de M. Goldoni pour servir à l'histoire de sa vie et à celle de son théâtre,* vol. 1, 286. Paris, 1787.

Stefani, Federigo. *Sei lettere di Antonio Vivaldi veneziano.* Venice, 1871.

Chigiana 1 (1939) ["Antonio Vivaldi: note e documenti sulla vita e sulle opere"].

Pincherle, Marc. *Vivaldi.* Paris, 1955; English translation as *Vivaldi: Genius of the Baroque,* London, 1958.

Kolneder, Walter. *Vivaldi. Leben und Werk.* Wiesbaden, 1965; English translation as *Antonio Vivaldi: his Life and Work,* London, 1970.

Giazotto, Remo. *Antonio Vivaldi.* Turin, 1973.

Strohm, Reinhard. *Italienische Opernarien des frühen Settecento (1720-30).* 2 vols. Cologne, 1976.

Ryom, Peter. *Les manuscrits de Vivaldi.* Copenhagen, 1977.

Degrada, Francesco, and Maria Teresa Muraro, eds. *Antonio Vivaldi da Venezia all' Europa.* Milan, 1978.

Degrada, Francesco, ed. *Vivaldi veneziano europeo.* Venice, 1980.

Rinaldi, Mario. *Il teatro musicale di Antonio Vivaldi.* Florence, 1978.

Vivaldi-Studien. Dresden, 1978.

Talbot, Michael. *Vivaldi.* London, 1978; 1984.

Strohm, Reinhard. *Die italienische Oper im 18. Jahrhundert.* Wilhelmshaven, 1979.

Cross, Eric. *The Late Operas of Antonio Vivaldi, 1723-38.* 2 vols. Ann Arbor, Michigan, 1981.

Bellina, Anna Laura, Bruno Brizi, and Maria Grazia Pensa. *I libretti vivaldiani: recenzione e collazione dei testimoni a stampa.* Florence, 1982.

Bianconi, Lorenzo, and Giovanni Morelli, eds. *Antonio Vivaldi: teatro musicale, cultura e società.* 2 vols. Florence, 1982.

Kolneder, Walter. *Antonio Vivaldi: Dokumente seines Lebens und Schaffens.* Wilhelmshaven, 1979; English translation as *Antonio Vivaldi: Documents of his Life and Works.* New York, 1982.

Collins, Michael, and Elise K. Kirk, eds. *Opera and Vivaldi.* Austin, Texas, 1984.

Strohm, Reinhard. *Essays on Handel and Italian Opera.* Cambridge, 1985.

Stipcevic, Ennio. *Sull' opera Scanderbeg di Antonio Vivaldi.* Bologna, 1985-6.

Fanna, Antonio, and Giovanni Morelli, eds. *Nuovi studi vivaldiani: edizione e cronologia critica delle opere.* Florence, 1988.

Talbot, Michael. *Antonio Vivaldi: a Guide to Research.* New York, 1988.

Chigiana 41 (1989) ["Atti del convegno internazionale di studi *La prima 'Settimana Musicale Senese' e la Vivaldi Renaissance (1939-1989)'"*].

Heller, Karl. *Vivaldi: cronologia della vita e dell' opera.* Florence, 1991.

articles–

Wolff, Hellmuth Christian. "Vivaldi und der Stil der italienischen Oper." *Acta musicologica* 40 (1968): 179.

"Facsimilé et traductions de cinq lettres de Vivaldi à Bentivoglio." *Vivaldiana* 1 (1969): 117.

Cross, Eric. "Vivaldi as Opera Composer: *Griselda.*" *Musical Times* 119 (1978): 411.

_____. "Vivaldi's Operatic Borrowings." *Music and Letters* 49 (1978): 429.

Hill, John Walter. "Vivaldi's Griselda." *Journal of the American Musicological Society* 31 (1978): 53.

Mangini, Nicola. "Sui rapporti del Vivaldi col Teatro Sant'-Angelo." In *Venezia e il melodramma nel Settecento,* edited by Maria Teresa Muraro, 263. Florence, 1978.

Ryom, Peter. "Antonio Vivaldi: les relations entre les opéras et la musique instrumentale." In *Venezia e il melodramma nel Settecento,* edited by Maria Teresa Muraro, 249. Florence, 1978.

Strohm, Reinhard. "Zu Vivaldis Opernschaffen." In *Venezia e il melodramma nel Settecento,* edited by Maria Teresa Muraro, 237. Florence, 1978.

Rinaldi, Mario. "Dati certi su Vivaldi operista." *Nuova rivista musicale italiana* 13 (1979): 150.

Ryom, Peter. "Les catalogues de Bonlini et de Groppo." *Informazioni e studi vivaldiani* 2 (1981): 3.

Tàmmaro, Ferruccio. "Contaminazioni e polivalenze nell'*Orlando finto pazzo.*" *Rivista italiana di musicologia* 17 (1982): 71.

Hill, John Walter. "Vivaldi's 'Ottone in villa' (Vicenza, 1713): a Study in Musical Drama." Introductory essay to Domenico Lalli and Antonio Vivaldi, *Ottone in villa,* ix-xxxvii. Milan, 1983.

Hortschansky, Klaus. "Arientexte Metastasios in Vivaldis Opern." *Informazioni e studi vivaldiani* 4 (1983): 61.

Pensa, Maria Grazia. "La felicità delle lettere, ossia l'edizione veneziana della *Drammaturgia* di Leone Allacci." *Informazioni e studi vivaldiani* 4 (1983): 20.

Selfridge-Field, Eleanor. "Dating Vivaldi's Operas." *Informazioni e studi vivaldiani* 5 (1984): 53.

Weiss, Piero. "Venetian Commedia Dell'Arte 'Operas' in the Age of Vivaldi." *Musical Quarterly* 70 (1984): 195.

Tàmmaro, Ferruccio. "Il 'Farnace' di Vivaldi: problemi di ricostruzioni." *Studi musicali* 15 (1986): 213.

Cataldi, Luigi. "La rappresentazione mantovana del 'Tito Manlio' di Antonio Vivaldi." *Informazioni e studi vivaldiani* 8 (1987): 52.

Strohm, Reinhard. "Vivaldi's and Handel's Settings of 'Giustino'." In *Music and Theatre: Essays in Honour of Winton Dean,* edited by Nigel Fortune, 131. Cambridge, 1987.

Hill, John Walter. "A Computer-Based Analytical Concordance of Vivaldi's Aria Texts: First Findings and Puzzling New Questions about Self-Borrowing." *Studi musicali* 17 (1988): 511.

Vitali, Carlo. "Vivaldi e il conte bolognese Sicinio Pepoli. Nuovi documenti sulle stagioni vivaldiane al Filarmonico di Verona." *Informazioni e studi vivaldiani* 10 (1989): 25.

Talbot, Michael. "Vivaldi in the Sale Room: a New Version of 'Leon feroce'." *Informazioni e studi vivaldiani* 12 (1991): 5.

Vitali, Carlo. "I fratelli Pepoli contro Vivaldi e Anna Girò. Le ragioni di un' assenza." *Informazioni e studi vivaldiani* 12 (1991): 19.

unpublished—

Caffi, Francesco. *Storia della musica teatrale in Venezia.* Manuscript, c. 1850.

Rowell, Lewis E. "Four Operas of Antonio Vivaldi." Ph.D. dissertation, University of Rochester, 1958.

Maurer, Helen. "The Independent Arias of Antonio Vivaldi in Foà 28." Mus.D. dissertation, Indiana University, 1974.

Wilson, Kenneth. *"L'Olimpiade:* Selected Eighteenth-Century Settings of Metastasio's Libretto." Ph.D. dissertation, Harvard University, 1982.

Roseman, Ulysses. "Antonio Vivaldi's *Orlando finto pazzo:* An Analysis and Critical Edition." M.A. dissertation, University of California at Los Angeles, 1989.

Antonio Vivaldi, caricature by Pier Leone Ghezzi

*　　*　　*

Were one to take the date of Vivaldi's first opera, *Ottone in villa* (Vicenza, 1713), as the deciding factor, one would conclude that he came late to the genre, at the age of thirty-five. This impression is misleading, however, since both he and his violinist father were actively involved with opera as performers and in management long before then; in fact, already in 1708 Vivaldi had composed a dramatic cantata for five voices, *Le gare del dovere,* that deploys the full range of musical resources found in opera.

Having made his debut outside his native Venice, Vivaldi concentrated his operatic efforts during the years up to 1718 on his native city. Much of the time he acted not only as composer but also as arranger (of other men's operas), musical director and impresario. From 1713 to 1717 he worked at the little Sant' Angelo theater, in 1717-18 at the hardly more pretentious San Moisè house. Although Vivaldi did not enjoy the prestige and patronage that came from activity in Venice's premier theaters (the Venetian nobles who controlled them tended to despise him as a parvenu), his wearing of so many "hats" at once—impossible in the larger houses—enabled him to develop an integrated view of opera that, while in no sense revolutionary, allowed his musical language to develop in fruitful ways.

The function of music in Italian opera of the early eighteenth century was more modest than that to which we have grown accustomed from Gluck onwards. Whereas in a modern opera music is a full partner in the drama and is expected to make a contribution to it independent of (and even sometimes in opposition to) the words and stage action, in late baroque "heroic" opera (*opera seria*) music is expected—like scenery, stage machinery, and costume—to provide appropriate "clothing" for a pre-existing drama that essentially inheres in the poet's libretto alone. The task of the composer is to set the words efficiently, with respect for accent and poetic meter (this especially in recitatives), to reflect in music the imagery and feelings of the text by drawing on traditional figures and devices, to satisfy the singers' need for vocal display (paying careful attention to the special qualities of each singer and the relative status of each), and to control the pace of the action so that the stage effects succeed.

Vivaldi fulfilled this basic set of requirements with great skill, but he also brought to opera the experience of a composer who had already distinguished himself in orchestral music. His first set of violin concertos (*L'estro armonico* Op. 3, 1711) had created a sensation all over Europe and was the object of much admiration and imitation. As one might expect, Vivaldi introduced the same degree of liveliness, complexity and feeling for sonority into the accompaniments of his operatic arias. The backbone of his orchestra was the string section, but every opera contains one or two arias featuring one or more "novelty" instruments such as recorder, bassoon, viola d'amore or a pair of horns. In these Vivaldi demonstrates his keen sense of tone color and idiomatic instrumental writing. On occasion, the orchestral writing in his arias is so elaborate and prominent that one almost has the sensation of a Wagnerian texture in which the instruments supply the foreground and the voice—weaving a free counterpoint against them—the background. Not that Vivaldi's vocal writing is undistinguished; particularly in arias of a more "popular" type he evinces real flair and produces melodies of true memorability. It is, however, true that his attentiveness to accuracy of word-setting and sensitivity of word-painting is sometimes found wanting. This is often the result of a concern to develop motives to the full, which may lead him to persist in using the opening musical ideas of an aria even when they are no longer metrically or dramatically apposite.

As in all Italian opera of his time, two well-defined types of musical setting predominate: recitative and aria (ensembles and choruses are rare, and the latter are often very perfunctory). Recitative is the core of the drama, carrying the action forward in a musical language that, although neutral and conventional in its basic form, is able through harmony, modulation and vocal inflection subtly to reflect the dramatic situation. Arias are conceived as static "moments" illustrating a character's feelings at a given point. They are like stills in a moving picture. In consequence, their structure is nondynamic and nearly always has recourse to the "da capo" plan in which following a middle section the opening section returns in unvaried form, except for the addition of improvised vocal embellishment. Vivaldi is always content to accept the traditional division of labor between recitative and aria, although on occasion he will employ special varieties of recitative (such as instrumentally accompanied recitative and arioso) for emotionally charged scenes.

Vivaldi continued along the same path during the three-year period (1718-20) he spent at the court of Mantua as director of secular music. Soon after his return to Venice, Benedetto Marcello's pamphlet *Il teatro alla moda* (*The Fashionable Theater*) appeared, a mordant satire on contemporary Italian opera. It has been thought that Vivaldi was a particular target of Marcello, but today the general opinion among scholars is that the satirist included Vivaldi merely as the most prominent representative of the general operatic practice of his time. Marcello criticizes, for example, the frequent use of unison writing in the orchestra, a device that Vivaldi certainly liked and which several other composers had taken up under his influence. The pamphlet did nothing to impede his career as a composer of opera during the 1720s, which saw him at the height of his productivity and reputation. During this decade he received several commissions from houses in other cities such as Rome and Florence, and several of his works were revived inside and outside Italy, often without his active participation. He also began to act as a roving impresario, taking opera (his own works included) to provincial centers.

Musically, however, the 1720s were a decade of crisis for Vivaldi. In the middle years composers of Neapolitan origin including Vinci, Porpora and Leo became dominant on the Venetian stage. Their musical language reasserted the primacy of the singer, whose part became ever more ornate and finely nuanced, and pushed the orchestral accompaniment into the background. To some extent Vivaldi accommodated this new fashion, though he never repudiated totally the personal style that he had already forged. It is notable how rarely he set libretti by Metastasio, the poet *par excellence* of the Neapolitan school; the latter's bias towards reflection rather than action was perhaps at odds with Vivaldi's preference for a more vigorous approach. His later operas show a greater variety of treatment than his earlier ones, but at some cost to stylistic integrity. Several of them include ensembles of great distinction (the quartet in *Farnace* differentiates the characters as finely as Mozart would have done), while one (*Giustino*) has a powerful final chorus styled as a full-length chaconne.

Following his return from a visit to central Europe in 1729-30, Vivaldi, now ageing, found it impossible to maintain his pre-eminent position in Venetian opera. Increasingly, his opportunity to compose operas became dependent on his parallel activity as a freelance impresario, since commissions had become less frequent. The focus of his activity gravitated away from Venice, now firmly in the grip of the Neapolitans, towards the minor operatic centers of the Italian mainland. His operatic projects met by turns with spectacular success and miserable failure, and their financial returns fluctuated correspondingly. He was particularly unlucky in Ferrara, where three consecutive seasons (1737-39) ended in frustration for him (on one occasion because, as a priest, he was forbidden by the papal legate to direct the performances). Nevertheless, a late opera such as *Catone in Utica* (*Cato in Utica,* Verona, 1737) shows few signs of waning inspiration. It is symptomatic of the precarious nature of Vivaldi's operatic activity at the end of his life that he journeyed from Venice to Vienna, leaving behind a legal tussle arising from one opera (*Feraspe*), only to find that the work he had planned for Vienna could not be staged because of a compulsory period of public mourning following the unexpected death of Emperor Charles VI. Cast adrift in the imperial capital, he died in great poverty.

Always given to exaggeration, Vivaldi claimed in 1739 to have composed ninety-four operas. Fewer than fifty have been identified, and of these only sixteen survive in a complete enough form to make their revival possible today. In fact, the "survival rate" evidenced by those figures is remarkably high for its time. It arises, first, from the fact that in his role as impresario Vivaldi was able to retain the scores that he had supplied to himself as composer (rather than give them up to the commissioning opera house) and, second, from the near-miraculous survival of his collection of his own manuscripts, today preserved in the Foà and Giordano bequests in the Biblioteca Nazionale, Turin.

The old view that Vivaldi's operas were "concertos in vocal dress" is discredited, and the musical value of his operas, as of all his vocal music, is nowadays generally recognized. That said, they do not depart in the least from the norms of Italian *opera seria* as practiced in the age of Zeno and Metastasio, and their appreciation on the stage depends greatly on the modern audience's acceptance of the underlying conventions, in particular those pertaining to the poetry and dramaturgy of the literary text. It is a mistake, for example, to imagine that a da capo aria can successfully be turned into a forward-moving event by means of the anachronism of cleverly devised accompanying action; it is far better to accept, and capitalize on, its intentionally static character. Given the importance to the drama of the recitative, it is desirable to cut it as little as possible and deliver it in a swift, unexaggerated and continuous manner.

Of the pre-1720 operas *L'incoronazione di Dario, La verità in cimento* and *Tito Manlio* have all been presented successfully in modern times; of the later operas *Giustino, Farnace, Orlando (furioso), La fida ninfa, Griselda* and *L'Olimpiade* have all been revived. The early *Ottone in villa* and *Orlando finto pazzo* have not yet been given modern performances but deserve them. Although Vivaldi cannot claim the artistic and historical importance of Handel or even Alessandro Scarlatti in the domain of opera, he is a figure with a distinct and attractive voice.

—Michael Talbot

LA VOIX HUMAINE [The Human Voice].

Composer: Francis Poulenc.

Librettist: Francis Poulenc (after Jean Cocteau).

First Performance: Paris, Opéra-Comique, 6 February 1959.

Roles: The Woman (soprano).

Publications

articles—

Lockspeiser, E. "An Introduction to Poulenc's *La voix humaine.*" *Opera* August (1960).
Avant-scène opéra 52 (1983) [*Dialogues des carmélites* and *La voix humaine* issue].

* * *

Barely a year after the January 1957 premiere of *Dialogues des Carmélites,* Francis Poulenc's second opera, he was approached by the Paris director of Ricordi, the company that had commissioned and published *Dialogues,* with a suggestion for a new project. Would Poulenc, who was now a recognized musical dramatist, be interested in setting Jean Cocteau's monodrama, *La voix humaine*? Poulenc agreed quickly and enthusiastically, but rejected an additional suggestion that the single role in the opera (a character known simply as "Elle" ["She"]) be created for Maria Callas; instead, Poulenc had in mind his now-favorite leading lady, Denise Duval. The forty minute, one-act "tragédie-lyrique" was composed quickly, between February and June 1958, and Cocteau himself worked closely with Poulenc on the libretto, as well as handling design and production for the premiere.

For the second time in five years, Poulenc was obsessed by a composition, as he had been with *Dialogues,* writing to a friend that he composed *La voix* "in a trance." It was the intense mood of grief and solitude pervading *La voix* that caused Poulenc's state of agitation: "I think that I needed the experience of spiritual and metaphysical anguish in *Dialogues* so as not to betray the terribly human anguish of Jean Cocteau's superb text."

Cocteau's 1930 monodrama reveals to us a young, attractive woman who has been jilted by her lover. As the only character on stage, she prowls around her bedroom like a caged animal, pouring out her mixed emotions in a telephone conversation with this lover, whom we neither see nor hear.

A disturbing intrusion upon this already pathetic monologue are the notorious hazards of the French telephone system at that time: the conversation is actually cut off twice and interrupted once. Because of this and because it represents her sole link to her lover, the telephone receiver almost becomes a second on-stage character. These problems only intensify the woman's anxiety. She is barely coherent at times; she is mad with jealousy and suspicion; she has attempted suicide; she soars to ecstasy and descends to despondency; and her voice rises to a cry of anguish as the opera ends and she realizes she will never speak to her lover again.

Since this is an opera for a single character, we can focus our attention on the style and contour of the vocal line. The following characteristics are observed: repeated notes abound; intervals greater than a fifth are rare, while stepwise motion and thirds predominate; rhythm and accents are designed to reflect actual speech patterns, particularly the pauses and hesitations of a telephone conversation. Thus, much of the vocal writing suggests plainchant, and the restrained style is appropriate since the main character is trying to contain her emotions throughout most of the conversation. She gives her feelings free rein only three times: during a particularly dramatic passage in which she laments losing the intimacy they shared with each other; and two lyric passages, when she speaks fondly of a happy occasion the two of them had shared, and when she speaks of her suicide attempt and her pathetic dream. This latter passage must be considered the most emotional part of the opera, and in it the vocal line finally becomes lyrically shaped and tonally stable.

Indeed, *La voix humaine* is one of Poulenc's most tonally unstable, ambiguous works, for it is filled with nonfunctional progressions, unresolved dissonances, particularly sevenths and ninths, diminished sevenths which do not resolve in a conventional manner, and progressions of chords related chromatically. Tonality is established definitively only in the most lyric passages, or by short orchestral motives based on functional harmonies.

This is but one way in which the orchestra serves to hold this fragmentary, declamatory opera together. A series of orchestral motives—not leading motives since they have no single dramatic reference—serves to unify the work. Many of these motives, nine of which are readily identifiable, can be traced back to similar or identical passages in *Dialogues des Carmélites,* the seminal work of Poulenc's mature style. In addition, the orchestra portrays the ringing of the telephone with repeated notes on the xylophone; it expresses the singer's agitation and confusion while trying to reach her former lover; it even suggests the jazz which she hears in the background over the phone. Most importantly, however, the orchestra fills in the voids created by the inherently dry, disjointed vocal line. If *La voix humaine* succeeds as a piece of music, it is because of the orchestral framework. Poulenc himself, in a preface to the opera, says: "The entire work should be bathed in the deepest orchestral sensuality."

Ultimately, then, Poulenc saw *La voix humaine* as an expressive, romantic work. It is certainly a fine, challenging vehicle for a singing actress and, though major opera companies seldom perform this, or any other, solo opera, there seems to be a place for Poulenc's last opera in the hands of a serious dramatic soprano.

—Keith W. Daniel

VON HEUTE AUF MORGEN [From Today till Tomorrow].

Composer: Arnold Schoenberg.

Librettist: M. Blonda [=G. Schoenberg].

First Performance: Frankfurt, Opernhaus, 1 February 1930.

Roles: Man (baritone); Woman (soprano); Girlfriend (soprano); Singer (tenor); Child (speaking).

Publications

article–

Kirsch, Winfried. "Die 'Opera domestica'. Zur Dramaturgie des bürgerlichen Alltags im aktuellen Musiktheater der 20er Jahre." *Hindemith-Jahrbuch* 9 (1980): 179.

*　　*　　*

In November of 1928, Schoenberg wrote to his publisher of his interest in writing a one-act comic work. By early 1929 he was eliciting comments from his students about the libretto for *Von Heute auf Morgen,* written by his second wife, Gertrude Kolisch, under the pseudonym Max Blonda. As a comic work, the opera stands in marked contrast to *Erwartung* and *Die glückliche Hand,* which preceded it by over a decade, as well as to *Moses und Aron,* on which Schoenberg was concurrently working.

Von Heute auf Morgen is a satiric, contemporary domestic drama not unlike Hindemith's *Neues vom Tage* (1929) or even Richard Strauss' *Intermezzo* (1924). The couple, referred to simply as *Frau* and *Mann* in the manner of expressionist drama and reminiscent of Schoenberg's own earlier works, experience the perennial problem of marital boredom. The husband becomes infatuated with his wife's single girlfriend, an emancipated "new woman" of the world, whom he finds more desirable than his dependable *Hausfrau* wife. In retaliation, the wife pretends to fall in love with a tenor. (The singer and girlfriend are also referred to in an objective manner as simply *der Sänger* and *die Freundin.*) This modern pair are revealed as shallow, wishing only wine, dance and music, and the husband realizes the foolishness of his attraction. The work ends with the couple's son, a speaking role, asking "Mama, what are they, modern people?" thus providing a moral of sorts about superficial modernity that changes overnight, or "von heute auf morgen."

Schoenberg had used this same expression earlier in the foreword to his *Drei Satiren* (1926), in which he likewise condemned as faddish certain postwar musical experiments, singling out in particular the neo-classicism of Stravinsky and the everyday aesthetic of Krenek most clearly articulated in his successful opera *Jonny spielt auf* (1927). As Krenek had judged against the supposed elitism and isolationist position of Schoenberg in his opera, so Schoenberg here repudiates, through the husband's foolish obsession with the modern woman, Krenek's *Zeitoper* and its concern for art that reflected its time.

Schoenberg claimed that his twelve-tone score was light and cheerful. His large and colorful orchestration included saxophones, piano, mandolin, and guitar or banjo, instruments popular with composers of *Zeitopern* for their recognizable jazz timbres. Although Schoenberg specified the up-to-date stage properties also beloved of Krenek, he did not use popular dance idioms in his score as Krenek and others had done. At one point the wife does hum nine measures of a modern dance, so called in the score, as she attempts to dance with her husband while the alto saxophone doubles her melody line. With this exception, Schoenberg chose to use the instrument identified with jazz in an absolute manner, as if to deny any other cultural or popular connotations. Formally Schoenberg set off numbers with clearly marked recitatives and relied on extensive fugal procedures, which work particularly well for the feuding couple. The final section, wherein the couple reconciles, thus providing the aesthetic moral, is set off in *Sprechstimme.*

Although Schoenberg expressed dissatisfaction with the production, the work was popular with the opening night audience in Frankfurt am Main where it was paired with Pergolesi's *Il maestro di musica,* now deemed spurious. It gained critical acclaim but received only three other performances and ultimately fell from the repertory.

—Susan C. Cook

VON STADE, Frederica.

Mezzo-soprano. Born 1 June 1945, in Somerville, New Jersey. Married: singer Peter Elkus (divorced). Studied with Sebastian Engelberg, Paul Berl, and Otto Guth at Mannes College, New York; debut as the Third Boy in *Die Zauberflöte,* Metropolitan Opera, 1970; Paris debut as Cherubino in *Le nozze di Figaro,* 1973; Glyndebourne debut as Cherubino, 1973; sang Penelope in the American premiere of *Il ritorno d'Ulisse in patria,* Washington, 1974; Covent Garden debut as Rosina in *Il barbiere di Siviglia,* 1975; created the role of Maria in Villa-Lobos's *Yerma,* Santa Fe.

Publications

About VON STADE: articles–

Movshon, George. "Frederica von Stade." *Opera* 31/January (1980): 31.

Mai, C. "Das Interview." *Opernwelt* 22/8-9 (1981): 19.

Greenfield, E. "Here and There: Frederica von Stade." *Gramophone* 60/June (1982): 18.

Tassel, J. "A Real Thoroughbred." *Opera News* 47/9 (April 1983): 16.

Soria, D.J. "Frederica von Stade." *Hi Fidelity/Musical America* 33/12 (1983): MA6.

Profile. *San Francisco Opera Magazine* 3/Fall (1984): 41; 69/3 (1991): 34.

Doherty, M. Stephen. "Alexandra Grinnell Clark Portrays the Grandeur of the Opera and One of its Greatest Artists." *American Artist* 50/June (1986): 64.

Paolucci, Bridget. "A Time for Soul-Searching." *Opera News* 52 (9 April 1988): 28.

"On lednuti za Praz skym jarem (interview)." *Hudebni Rozhledy* 41/9 (1988): 396.

Shirakawa, S.H. "Frederica von Stade: After Nearly 20 Years in the Opera House, Broadway Musicals Beckon." *Ovation* 9/November (1988): 20.

*　　*　　*

In an age when most leading opera singers specialize in some relatively restricted repertory, Frederica von Stade's repertory covers two centuries and extends into two more; she has brought to her portrayal of Monteverdi's Penelope (*Il ritorno d'Ulisse in patria*) as much dramatic intensity and musicality as she displayed in her performances, at the Metropolitan Opera and several of the world's other leading houses, of Debussy's Mélisande.

Von Stade has brought comic and tragic roles to life with equal vividness. One can hear and see this clearly in her portrayals of Rossini heroines, both comic and serious. In the performances of Rossini's *Il barbiere di Siviglia* with which she made her Covent Garden debut in 1975, she sang Rosina with liveliness, sweetness, and a command of Rossinian coloratura; in a recording of Rossini's rarely performed opera seria *Otello,* she sang the role of Desdemona with a touching sense of tenderness and vulnerability. Von Stade displayed a stunningly beautiful legato in Rossini's Willow Song and the recitative that precedes it, spinning out Rossini's lines with perfect artistry.

Von Stade has won much applause for her performances of nineteenth-century French opera. Charlotte (*Werther*) is among several Massenet roles that she has performed with particular beauty and dramatic effect; she contributed much to a recording (under Rudel) of Massenet's *Cendrillon.* She has also sung the role of Béatrice in Berlioz's *Béatrice et Bénédict* with great success.

Von Stade is clearly an adventurous and ambitious singer, constantly expanding her repertory and seeking new roles. At the same time she has remained faithful to certain roles and types of roles with which she has been successful through most of her career. Von Stade is comfortable wearing trousers. Her slim figure, handsome face and bright, silvery high mezzo-soprano voice have helped her become the busiest female portrayer of boys and young men in all opera. Idamante (Mozart's *Idomeneo*), Stephano (Gounod's *Roméo et Juliette*), Fréderic (Thomas's *Mignon*), Octavian (Strauss's *Rosenkavalier*) and Hänsel (Humperdink's *Hänsel und Gretel*) are among her roles; but it is especially as Cherubino (in Mozart's *Le nozze di Figaro*) that von Stade has won applause throughout her career, bringing to that role just the right combination of sensuality and innocence, of mischief and charm. Her Cherubino was praised by one critic near the beginning of her career (San Francisco, 1972) as "nimble, milky-toned, vocally aristocratic." Fifteen years later she was still singing the role to universal applause, welcomed at the Metropolitan in 1987 as a "wonderous Cherubino." She has also sung the role at Glyndebourne, the Paris Opéra, and many other theaters.

One can hear much of what makes von Stade so successful in one of her lesser-known trouser roles, that of Annio in Mozart's *La clemenza di Tito* (as recorded under Colin Davis). Annio is not one of the opera's leading roles; yet von Stade is an exciting, interesting Annio; she brings all her musical and dramatic energy to the part, coloring words and phrases vividly. Listen, for example, to the way in which she gives a tragic quality to the words "il nostro dolore" in the aria "Tu fosti tradito." Only a quivering, almost constant vibrato detracts from an otherwise perfect performance.

—John A. Rice

W–X

WÄCHTER, Eberhard.

Baritone. Born 9 July 1929, in Vienna. Studied with Elisabeth Rado in Vienna; debut as Silvio in *I pagliacci,* Vienna Volksoper, 1953; joined Vienna State Opera, 1955; Covent Garden debut as Count Almaviva in *Le nozze di Figaro,* 1956; Salzburg debut as Arbaces in *Idomeneo,* 1956; Covent Garden debut as Count Almaviva, 1956; Bayreuth debut as Amfortas in *Parsifal,* 1958; Paris debut as Wolfram in *Tannhäuser,* 1959; Teatro alla Scala debut as Count Almaviva, 1960; Metropolitan Opera debut as Wolfram, 1961; sang in first performances of Martin's *Der Sturm* (1956), Einem's *Der Besuch der alten Dame* (1971), in Vienna; director of Vienna Volksoper and the Vienna State Opera, 1991-; son Franz also a baritone.

Publications

About WÄCHTER: articles–

"Bundestheater: ein neuer Abschnitt." *Bühne* 307/April (1984): 11.
Loebl, H. "Der Kreis hat sich geschlossen." *Bühne* 348/September (1987): 6.
Fabian, Imre. "Interview." *Opernwelt* 28/9 (1987): 13.
Rohde, G. "Das Phantom in der Oper ist jetzt ein Agent." *Neue Musikzeitung* 37/August-September (1988): 1.
Fabian, Imre. "Eine Farce? Wie man in Wien den Staatsoperdirektor behandelt und seinen Nachfolger ernennt." *Opernwelt* 29/November (1988): 11.

*   *   *

Eberhard Wächter, the Austrian dramatic baritone, was born in Vienna on 9 July 1929. After completing his Abitur in 1947, he studied piano and music theory at the Vienna Hochschule für Musik and in 1950 began his voice studies with Elisabeth Rado. Wächter made his operatic debut in 1953 at the Vienna Volksoper as Silvio in *I pagliacci.* In 1955 he became a member of the Vienna State Opera. From then on his career became a series of important international successes with guest performances in Italy, at Milan's Teatro alla Scala and in Rome, at Covent Garden (the Count in *Le nozze di Figaro* in 1956 and Amfortas and Renato in *Un ballo in maschera* in 1959), as well as in Munich, Stuttgart, Wiesbaden, Berlin, and Brussels. Beginning in 1956, Wächter was a regular guest at the Salzburg Festival where his outstanding portrayals in Mozart's baritone repertoire included Arbaces in *Idomeneo* in 1956 and 1961, the Count in 1958, Don Giovanni in 1960 and 1961, and the role of Orest in Richard Strauss' *Elektra* in 1964.

Eberhard Wächter was also engaged for the Edinburgh and Glyndebourne Festivals, and in 1960 he performed in both Dallas and San Francisco. His debut at New York's Metropolitan Opera took place in 1961. The Bayreuth Festival during the years 1957-59, 1962-63, and 1966 saw his outstanding portrayals of Amfortas in *Parsifal* and as Wolfram in *Tannhäuser.*

Wächter took part in the first performances of Frank Martin's *Der Sturm* on 17 June 1956 and Gottfried von Einem's *Der Besuch der alten Dame* on 23 May 1971 at the Vienna State Theater. Other roles included Rodrigo in *Don Carlos,* Simon Boccanegra, the Count di Luna in *Il trovatore,* and the name role in *Dantons Tod.* Besides his great successes as an opera singer, Eberhard Wächter's expressive singing led him to have an almost equally rewarding career in concert and recitals.

Among Wächter's many recordings are complete versions of *Tristan und Isolde* and *Der Freischütz* on the DGG label; *Salome, Arabella, Das Rheingold, Die Fledermaus, Wozzeck,* and *Lulu* on Decca; *Le nozze di Figaro, Don Giovanni, Die Fledermaus, Der Rosenkavalier,* and *Capriccio* on Columbia; *Don Giovanni, Tannhäuser,* and *Tiefland* on Philips; *Cavalleria rusticana* on Ariola-Eurodisc; Dallapiccola's *Il prigioniero* on Italia; and a third *Die Fledermaus* for RCA. His performances in opera highlights are to be found on Replica (the Heerrufer in *Lohengrin* from the 1958 Bayreuth recording), on Melodia (*Parsifal* and *Lohengrin,* Bayreuth 1958 and 1960), on Movimento Musica (*Fidelio, Die Zauberflöte,* and from the Salzburg Festivals of 1960 and 1961, *Don Giovanni* and *Idomeneo*).

Wächter's son Franz is also a baritone. In 1991-92 Eberhard Wächter was named Intendant of both the Vienna Volksoper and the State Opera.

—Suzanne Summerville

WAGNER, (Wilhelm) Richard.

Composer. Born 22 May 1813, in Leipzig. Died 13 February 1883, in Venice. Married: 1) Christine Wilhelmine ("Minna") Planer, actress, 24 November 1836; 2) Cosima Liszt, daughter of the composer and piano virtuoso Franz Liszt and former wife of the famous conductor Hans von Bülow, 25 August 1870 (one daughter, one son). Student at the Dresden Kreuzschule, 1822-27; studied piano with Humann and violin with Robert Sipp, 1825; studied classics with his uncle Adolf Wagner; entered the Nikolaischule in Leipzig, 1828; studied harmony with Christian Gottlieb Müller; entered the Thomasschule, 1830; his *Overtüre* in B-flat performed at the Leipzig Theater, conducted by Heinrich Dorn, 24 December 1830; studied composition and counterpoint with Theodor Weinlig, cantor of the Thomaskirche; music director of Heinrich Bethmann's theater company, Magdeburg, 1834; director of the Königsberg town theater, 1 April 1837; music director of the theater in Riga, 1837-39; met Meyerbeer in Boulogne; arranged piano scores for operas and wrote for the *Gazette musicale* in Paris, 1839-42; in debtor's prison, 28 October-17 November 1840; *Rienzi* accepted for production in Dresden,

1842; named second Hofkapellmeister in Dresden, 1843; an order for Wagner's arrest was issued for his participation in the Dresden uprising, 1849; met Liszt in Weimar; in Zurich by July, 1849; received loans for the production of his operas from the merchant Otto Wesendonck, 1854; conducted concerts of his own music in London, 1855, where he met Queen Victoria; moved to Venice, 1858; in Lucerne, still escaping the Dresden government, 1859, and then in Paris; Napoleon III ordered the director of the Paris Opéra to produce Wagner's *Tannhäuser,* 1860; partial amnesty by Dresden authorities, 1860 (total amnesty given 1862); moved to Biebrich, 1862; offered unlimited patronage by King Ludwig II of Bavaria, 1864; cornerstone of the Bayreuth Festspielhaus laid, 22 May 1872; premiere of the *Ring* cycle conducted by Hans Richter and attended by Kaiser Wilhelm I, among others, 1876; Wagner's grave is at his family home, the villa *Wahnfried* at Bayreuth.

Operas

Editions:

Richard Wagners Werke. Edited by M. Balling. Leipzig, 1912-29; 1971.
R. Wagner: Sämtliche Werke. Edited by Carl Dahlhaus. Mainz, 1970-.

Die Hochzeit, Wagner, after J.G. Büsching: Ritterzeit und Ritterwesen, 1832-33, Leipzig, Neues Theater, 13 February 1938 [partially lost].
Die Feen, Wagner (after C. Gozzi, *La donna serpente*), 1833-34, Munich, Königliches Hof- und Nationaltheater, 29 June 1888.
Das Liebesverbot, oder Die Novize von Palermo, Wagner (after Shakespeare, *Measure for Measure*), 1834-36, Magdeburg, 29 March 1836.
Rienzi, der Letzte der Tribunen, Wagner (after E. Bulwer Lytton and M.R. Mitford), 1837-1840, Dresden, Königliches Hoftheater, 20 October 1842; revised, 1843.
Der fliegende Holländer, Wagner (after Heine, *Aus den Memoiren des Herrn von Schnabelewopski*), 1841, Dresden, Königliches Hoftheater, 2 January 1843; revised, 1846; revised, 1852.
Tannhäuser und der Sängerkrieg auf Wartburg (originally *Der Venusberg*), Wagner, 1843-45, Dresden, Königliches Hoftheater, 19 October 1845; revised, text alterations with C. Nuitter, 1860-61, Paris, Opéra, 13 March 1861; revised, 1865, Munich, Königliches Hof- und Nationaltheater, 5 March 1865; slightly revised, 1875, Vienna, Hofoper, 22 November 1875.
Lohengrin, Wagner, 1845-47, Weimar, Hoftheater, 28 August 1850.
Der Ring des Nibelungen, Wagner, first text draft 1848; 1) *Das Rheingold,* 1851-54, Munich, Königliches Hof- und Nationaltheater, 22 September 1869; 2) *Die Walküre,* 1851-56, Munich, Königliches Hof- und Nationaltheater, 26 June 1870; 3) *Siegfried* (originally *Der junge Siegfried*), 1851-71, Bayreuth Festspielhaus, 16 August 1876; 4) *Götterdämmerung,* 1850-74, Bayreuth Festspielhaus, 17 August 1876; performance of the entire cycle, Bayreuth Festspielhaus, 13, 14, 16, 17 August 1876.
Tristan und Isolde, Wagner, 1856-59, Munich, Königliches Hof- und Nationaltheater, 10 June 1865.
Die Meistersinger von Nürnberg, 1845, 1865-67, Munich, Königliches Hof- und Nationaltheater, 21 June 1868.
Parsifal (originally *Parzival*), Wagner, 1857, 1865, 1876-82, Bayreuth Festspielhaus, 26 July 1882.

Other works: orchestral works, incidental music, choral and other vocal works, chamber music, piano pieces.

Publications/Writings

By WAGNER: books–

Correspondence of Wagner and Liszt. 2 vols. London, 1888.
R. Wagner: Gesammelte Schriften und Dichtungen. 9 vols. Leipzig, 1871-73, 1883; 1887; 1976; English translation and edition by W.A. Ellis as *Wagner: Complete Prose Works.* 8 vols. London, 1892-99; 5th ed. edited by H. von Wolzogen and R. Sternfeld, *Sämtliche Schriften und Dichtungen,* 16 vols. Leipzig, 1911-16.
Mein Leben. 2 vols. 1864; edited by Martin Gregor-Dellin, 3 vols., Munich, 1963; 1976; English translation, London, 1911; revised edition, New York, 1924; edited by Mary Whittall, Cambridge, 1983; French translation, Paris, 1978.
Letters to August Röckel. Bristol, 1897.
Letters to Mathilde Wesendonck. London, 1904.
Burk, John, ed. *Letters.* New York, 1950.
Goldman, A., and E. Sprinchorn, eds. *Wagner on Music and Drama: a Compendium of Richard Wagner's Prose.* New York, 1964.
Strobel, G., and W. Wolf. *Richard Wagner: Sämtliche Briefe.* Leipzig, 1967-.
Bergfeld, Joachim, ed. *Das braune Buch: Tagebuchaufzeichnungen 1865 bis 1882.* Zurich, 1975; English translation as *The Brown Book,* London, 1980.
Kesting, Hanjo, ed. *Briefe* [selection]. Munich, 1983.
Spencer, Stewart, and Barry Millington, eds. *Selected Letters.* London, 1987.

About WAGNER: books–

Kufferath, M. *Parsifal de Richard Wagner: légende, drame, partition.* Paris, 1890; English translation, 1904.
Kufferath, M. *Guide thématique et analyse de Tristan et Iseult.* Paris, 1894.
Peladan, Joséphine. *Le théâtre complet de Wagner. Les XI opéras scène par scène.* Chamuel, 1894; Paris and Geneva, 1981.
Bowen, A.M. *The Sources and Text of Wagner's 'Die Meistersinger von Nürnberg'.* Munich, 1897.
Shaw, George Bernard. *The Perfect Wagnerite: a Commentary on the Niblung's Ring.* London, 1898; 4th ed., 1923; 1972.
Wechsler, E. *Die Sage vom heiligen Gral in ihrer Entwicklung bis auf Richard Wagners "Parsifal".* Halle, 1898.
Smolian, A. *The Themes of 'Tannhäuser'.* London, 1891.
Tiersot, J. *Etude sur les Maîtres-chanteurs de Nuremberg de Richard Wagner.* Paris, 1899.
Smolian, A. *Richard Wagners Bühnenfestspiel Der Ring des Nibelungen: ein Vademecum.* Berlin, 1901.
Golther, W. *Die sagengeschichtlichen Grundlagen der Ringdichtung Richard Wagners.* Berlin, 1902.
———. *Tristan und Isolde in den Dichtungen des Mittelalters und der neuen Zeit.* Leipzig, 1907.
Kloss, E. *Richard Wagner über die 'Meistersinger von Nürnberg': Aussprüche des Meisters über sein Werk.* Leipzig, 1910.
Krienitz, W. *Richard Wagners 'Feen'.* Munich, 1910.
Golther, W. *Parsifal und der Gral in deutscher Sage des Mittelalters und der Neuzeit.* Leipzig, c. 1911.
Lindner, E. *Richard Wagner über Tristan und Isolde: Aussprüche des Meisters über sein Werk.* Leipzig, 1912.

Kloss, E., and H. Weber. *Richard Wagner über den Ring des Nibelungen: Aussprüche des Meisters über sein Werk in Schriften und Briefen.* Leipzig, 1913.

Lindner, E. *Richard Wagner über 'Tannhäuser': Aussprüche des Meisters über sein Werk.* Leipzig, 1914.

Wolzogen, H. von. *Richard Wagner über den 'Fliegenden Holländer': die Entstehung, Gestaltung und Darstellung des Werkes aus den Schriften und Briefen des Meisters zusammengestellt.* Leipzig, 1914.

Kurth, E. *Romantische Harmonik und ihre Krise in Wagners 'Tristan'.* Berlin, 1920; 2nd ed., 1923.

Debussy, C. *Monsieur Croche antidilettante.* Paris, 1921; 2nd ed., 1926; English translation, 1962.

Zademack, F. *Die Meistersinger von Nürnberg: Richard Wagners Dichtung und ihre Quellen.* Berlin, 1921.

Lorenz, A. *Das Geheimnis der Form bei Richard Wagner.* 4 vols. Berlin, 1924-33.

Wiessner, H. *Der Stabreimvers in Richard Wagners "Ring des Nibelungen."* Berlin, 1924; 1967.

Leroy, L.A. *Wagner's Music Drama of the Ring.* London, 1925.

Hapke, W. *Die musikalische Darstellung der Gebärde in Richard Wagners Ring des Nibelungen.* Leipzig, 1927.

Thompson, H. *Wagner and Wagenseil: a Source of Wagner's Opera "Die Meistersinger".* London, 1927.

Strobel, O. *Richard Wagner: Skizzen und Entwürfe zur Ring-Dichtung, mit der Dichtung 'Der junge Siegfried'.* Munich, 1930.

Buesst, A. *Richard Wagner: The Nibelung's Ring.* London, 1932; 2nd ed., 1952.

Newman, Ernest. *Life of Richard Wagner.* 4 vols. London, 1933-37.

Grisson, R. *Beiträge sur Auslegung von Richard Wagners "Ring des Nibelungen."* Leipzig, 1934.

Bahr-Mildenburg, A. *Tristan und Isolde: Darstellung der Werke Richard Wagners aus dem Geiste der Dichtung und Musik: vollständige Regiebearbeitung sämtlicher Partien mit Notenbeispielen.* Leipzig, 1936.

d'Indy, V. *Introduction à l'ètude de Parsifal.* Paris, 1937.

Gilman, Lawrence. *Wagner's Operas.* St Clair Shores, Michigan, 1937; 1979.

Hutcheson, E. *A Musical Guide to the Richard Wagner Ring of the Nibelung.* New York, 1940; 1972.

Rayner, Robert M. *Wagner and "Die Meistersinger".* London, 1940.

Newman, Ernest. *Wagner Nights.* London, 1949; 8th ed., New York, 1981.

Barth, H., ed. *International Wagner-bibliographie 1945-55.* Bayreuth, 1956; supplements, 1961, 1963.

Kerman, J. *Opera as Drama.* New York, 1956; 2nd ed., Berkeley, 1988.

Levi, V. *Tristano e Isotta di Riccardo Wagner.* Venice, 1958.

Vogel, M. *Der Tristan-Akkord und die Krise der modernen Harmonie-Lehre.* Düsseldorf, 1962.

Williamson, Audrey. *Wagner Opera.* London, 1962; 2nd ed., 1982.

Donington, Robert. *Wagner's "Ring" and its Symbols: the Music and the Myth.* London, 1963; 3rd ed., 1974.

Engel, H. "Über Richard Wagners Oper *Das Liebesverbot.*" In *Festschrift Friedrich Blume.* Kassel, 1963.

Scharschuch, H. *Gesamtanalyse der Harmonik von Richard Wagners Musikdrama 'Tristan und Isolde': unter spezifischer Berücksichtigung der Sequenztechnik des Tristanstiles.* Regensburg, 1963.

Steinbeck, D. *Interszenierungsformen des Tannhäuser (1845-1904): Untersuchungen zu Systematick der Opernregie.* Regensburg, 1964.

Zuckerman, Elliot. *The First Hundred Years of Wagner's Tristan.* New York and London, 1964.

Stoffels, Hermann. *Die Meistersinger von Nürnberg von Richard Wagner.* Berlin, 1965.

Wagner, W., ed. *100 Jahre Tristan.* Emsdetten, 1965.

Gutman, R.W. *The Man, his Mind, and his Music.* New York and London, 1968.

Steinbeck, D., ed. *Richard Wagners Tannhäuser-Szenarium: das Vorbild der Erstaufführung mit der Kostümbeschreibung und den Dekorations-plänen.* Berlin, 1968.

Westernhagen, Curt von. *Wagner.* Zurich, 1968; English translation, 1979.

Magee, Bryan. *Aspects of Wagner.* Oxford, 1968; 1972; 1988.

Dahlhaus, Carl. *Die Bedeutung des Gestischen in Wagners Musikdramen.* Munich, 1970.

Dahlhaus, Carl, ed. *Das Drama Richard Wagners als musikalisches Kunstwerk.* Regensburg, 1970.

Geck, M., and E. Voss, eds. *Dokumente zur Entstehung und ersten Aufführung des Bühnenweihfestspiels Parsifal. R. Wagner: Sämtliche Werke* 30. Mainz, 1970.

Dahlhaus, Carl. *Die Musikdramen Richard Wagners.* Velber, 1971; English translation, 1979.

———. *Wagners Konzeption des musikalischen Dramas.* Regensburg, 1971.

Hopkinson, C. *Tannhäuser: an Examination of 36 Editions.* Tutzing, 1973.

Westernhagen, Curt von. *Die Entstehung des 'Ring', dartestellt an den Kompositionsskizzen Richard Wagners.* Zurich, 1973; English translation, 1976.

Greig, W., and H. Faldt, eds. *Dokumente zur Entstehungsgeschichte des Bühnenfestspiels Der Ring des Nibelungen. R. Wagner, Sämtliche Werke* 29/1. Mainz, 1976.

Culshaw, John. *Reflections on Wagner's Ring.* New York, 1976.

Westernhagen, Curt von. *Die Entstehung des "Ring".* Zurich, 1973; English translation as *The Forging of the "Ring".* Cambridge, 1976.

Bauer, H.-J. *Wagners Parsifal: Kriterien der Kompositionstechnik.* Munich, 1977.

Deathridge, John. *Wagner's Rienzi: a Reappraisal based on a Study of the Sketches and Drafts.* Oxford, 1977.

DiGaetani, John Louis, ed. *Penetrating Wagner's Ring: an Anthology.* Rutherford, New Jersey, 1978; New York, 1983.

Chancellor, John. *Wagner.* London, 1978.

Kunze, Stefan, ed. *Richard Wagner: von der Oper zum Musikdrama.* Bern, 1978.

Mayer, Hans. *Richard Wagner. Mitwelt und Nachwelt.* Stuttgart and Zurich, 1978.

Wapnewski, P. *Der traurige Gott: Richard Wagner in seinen Helden.* Munich, 1978.

Burbridge, P., and R. Sutton, eds. *The Wagner Companion.* New York, 1979.

Chailley, Jacques. *"Parsifal" de Richard Wagner, opéra initiatique.* Paris, 1979.

Cooke, Deryck. *I Saw the World End: a Study of Wagner's Ring.* London, 1979.

Mack, Dietrich, ed. *Richard Wagner, "Tannhäuser".* Frankfurt am Main, 1979.

Reinhardt, Heinrich. *Parsifal. Studien zur Erfassung des Problemhorizonts von Richard Wagners letztem Drama.* Straubing, 1979.

Barth, Herbert, ed. *Bayreuther Dramaturgie. "Der Ring des Nibelungen."* Stuttgart and Zurich, 1980.

Blyth, Alan. *Wagner's "Ring": an Introduction.* London, 1980.

Gregor-Dellin, Martin. *Richard Wagner: Sein Leben, sein Werk, sein Jahrhundert.* Munich, 1980; English translation, London and San Diego, 1983.

Beckett, Lucy. *Richard Wagner: Parsifal.* Cambridge, 1981.

Wapnewski, P. *Tristan der Held.* Berlin, 1981.

Bauer, O. *Richard Wagner: die Bühnenwerke von der Uraufführung bis heute.* Berlin, 1982.

Borchmeyer, D. *Das Theater Richard Wagners.* Munich, 1982; English translation as *Richard Wagner: Theory and Theater,* Oxford, 1991.

Deathridge, John. *An Introduction to "The Flying Dutchman".* London, 1982.

Ewans, Michael. *Wagner and Aeschylus: the "Ring" and the "Oresteia".* London, 1982.

Ingenschay-Goch, Dagmar. *Richard Wagners neu erfundener Mythos. Zur Rezeption und Reproduktion des germanischen Mythos in seinen Opern texten.* Bonn, 1982.

John, Nicholas, ed. *Richard Wagner: "Der fliegende Holländer".* London, 1982.

McCreless, Patrick. *Wagner's "Siegfried": its Drama, History, and Music.* Ann Arbor, 1982.

Osborne, Charles. *The World Theatre of Wagner.* Oxford, 1982.

Benvenga, Nancy. *Kingdom on the Rhine: History, Myth and Legend in Wagner's "Ring".* Harwick, Essex, 1983.

Cord, William O. *An Introduction to Richard Wagner's Der Ring des Nibelungen: a Handbook.* Athens, Ohio, 1983.

John, Nicholas, ed. *Richard Wagner: "Die Walküre".* London, 1983.

————. *Richard Wagner: "Die Meistersinger von Nürnberg".* London, 1983.

Csampai, Attila, and Dietmar Holland. *Richard Wagner, "Parsifal": Texte, Materialien, Kommentare.* Reinbek bei Hamburg, 1984.

Dahlhaus, Carl, and John Deathridge. *The New Grove Wagner.* London, 1984.

Fay, Stephen. *The Ring: Anatomy of an Opera.* London, 1984.

John, Nicholas, ed. *Richard Wagner: "Siegfried".* London, 1984.

Loos, Helmut, and Günther Massenkeil, eds. *Zu Richard Wagner: Acht Bonner Beiträge im Jubiläumsjahr 1833.* Bonn 1984.

Millington, Barry. *Wagner.* London, 1984.

Bailey, Robert, ed. *Prelude and Transfiguration from "Tristan und Isolde".* New York, 1985.

Dahlhaus, C., and E. Voss, eds. *Wagnerliteratur—Wagnerforschung: Bericht über das Wagner-Symposion München 1983.* Mainz, 1985.

Deathridge, J., M. Geck, and E. Voss, eds. *Verzeichnis der musikalischen Werke Richard Wagners und ihrer Quellen.* Mainz, 1986.

Müller, Ulrich, and Peter Wapnewski, eds. *Wagner Handbuch.* Stuttgart, 1986.

Pahlen, Kurt, ed. *Richard Wagner: Die Meistersinger von Nürnberg.* Munich, 1986.

Fitzgerald, Gerald, and Patrick O'Connor, eds. *The Ring: Metropolitan Opera.* New York, 1988.

John, Nicholas, ed. *Wagner: Tannhäuser.* London, 1988.

White, David A. *The Turning Wheel: a Study of Contracts and Oaths in Wagner's Ring.* Selinsgrove, Pennsylvania, 1988.

Abbate, C., and R. Parker, eds. *Analyzing Opera: Verdi and Wagner.* Berkeley and Los Angeles, 1989.

Gray, Howard. *Wagner.* London, 1990.

Osborne, Charles. *The Operas of Wagner.* London, 1990.

Magee, Elizabeth. *Richard Wagner and The Nibelungs.* Oxford, 1991.

articles—

Draeseke, Felix. "Die sogenannte Zukunftsmusik und ihre Gegner." *Neue Zeitschrift für Musik* 55 (1861), vols. 9 and 10; reprinted in *Felix Draeseke. Schriften 1855-61,* ed. by Martella Gutiérrez-Denhoff and Helmut Loos, Bad Honnef, 1987.

Die Musik 1 (1901-02).

Porges, H. "Tristan und Isolde." *Bayreuther Blätter* 25 (1902): 186; 26 (1903): 23, 241; also edited as a separate volume by H. von Wolzogen, Leipzig, 1906.

Altmann, W. "Richard Wagner und die Berliner General-Intendantur: Verhandlungen über den 'Fliegenden Holländer' und Tannhäuser'." *Die Musik* 2/no. 11 (1902-03): 331; no. 14 (1902-03): 92; no. 16 (1902-03): 304.

Golther, W. "Die französische und die deutsche Tannhäuser-Dichtung." *Die Musik* 2 (1902-03): 271.

Ellis, W.A. "Die verschiedenen Fassungen von "Siegfrieds Tod." *Die Musik* 3 (1903-04): 239, 315.

Abert, H. "Gedanken zu Richard Wagners 'Die Meistersinger von Nürnberg'." *Die Musik* 4 (1904-05): 254.

Golther, W. "Zur Entstehung von Richard Wagners Tristan." *Die Musik* 5 (1905-06): 3.

Drews, A. "Mozarts 'Zauberflöte' und Wagners 'Parsifal': eine Parallele." *Richard Wagner-Jahrbuch* 1 (1906): 326.

Sakolowski, P. "Wagners erste Parsifal-Entwürfe." *Richard Wagner-Jahrbuch* 1 (1906): 317.

Prüfer, A. "Novalis Hymnen an die Nacht in ihren Beziehungen zu Wagners Tristan und Isolde." *Richard Wagner-Jahrbuch* 1 (1906): 290.

Grunsky, K. "Das Vorspiel und der erste Akt von 'Tristan und Isolde'." *Richard Wagner-Jahrbuch* 2 (1907): 207.

Petsch, R. "Der 'Ring des Nibelungen' in seinen Beziehungen zur griechischen Tragödie und zur zeitgenössischen Philosophie." *Richard Wagner-Jahrbuch* 2 (1907): 284.

Panzer, F. "Richard Wagners Tannhäuser: sein Aufbau und seine Quellen." *Die Musik* 7 (1907-08): 11.

Dinger, H. "Zu Richard Wagners 'Rienzi'." *Richard Wagner-Jahrbuch* 3 (1908): 88.

Grunsky, K. "Die Rhythmik im Parsifal." *Richard Wagner-Jahrbuch* 3 (1908): 276.

Istel, E. "Richard Wagners Oper 'Das Liebesverbot' auf Grund der handschriftlichen Originalpartitur dargestellt." *Die Musik* 8 (1908-09): 3.

Kloss, E. "Richard Wagner über 'Lohengrin': Aussprüche des Meisters über sein Werk." *Richard Wagner-Jahrbuch* 3 (1908): 132.

Porges, H. "Ueber Richard Wagners 'Lohengrin'. *Bayreuther Blätter* 32 (1909): 173.

Ostel, E. "Wagners erste Oper 'Die Hochzeit' auf Grund der autographen Partitur dargestellt." *Die Musik* 9 (1909-10): 331.

Heuss, A. "Zum Thema, Musik und Szene bei Wagner: im Anschlass an Wagners Augsatz, Bemerkungen zur Aufführung der Oper 'Der fliegende Holländer'." *Die Musik* 10 (1910-11): 3, 81.

Istel, E. "Wie Wagner am 'Ring' arbeitete: Mitteilungen über die Instrumentationsskizze des 'Rheingold' und andere Manuskripte." *Die Musik* 10 (1910-11): 67; abridged English translation in *Musical Quarterly* 19 (1933): 33.

Altmann, W. "Zur Geschichte der Entstehung und Veröffentlichung von Wagners 'Der Ring des Nibelungen'." *Allgemeine Musik-Zeitung* 38 (1911): 69, 101, 129, 157, 185, 217, 245.

Kapp, J. "Die Urschrift von Richard Wagners 'Lohengrin'-Dichtung." *Die Musik* 11 (1911-12): 88.

Altmann, W. "Zur Entstehungsgeschichte des 'Parsifal'." *Richard Wagner-Jahrbuch* 4 (1912): 162.

Koch, M. "Die Quellen der 'Hochzeit'." *Richard Wagner-Jahrbuch* 4 (1912): 105.

Petsch, R. "Zur Quellenkunde des 'Parsifal'." *Richard Wagner-Jahrbuch* 4 (1912): 138.

Wolzogen, H. von. "Parsifal-Varianten: eine Übersicht." *Richard Wagner-Jahrbuch* 4 (1912): 168.

Heuss, A. "Die Grundlagen der Parsifal-Dichtung." *Die Musik* 12 (1912-13): 206, 323.

Istel, E. "Autographe Regiebemerkungen Wagners zum 'Fliegende Holländer'." *Die Musik* 12 (1912-13): 214.

Mehler, E. "Beiträge zur Wagner-Forschung: unveröffentliche Stücke aus 'Rienzi,' 'Holländer' und 'Tannhäuser'." *Die Musik* 12 (1912-13): 195.

Altmann, W. "Zur Geschichte der Entstehung und Veröffentlichung von Richard Wagners 'Die Meistersinger von Nürnberg'." *Richard Wagner-Jahrbuch* 5 (1913): 87.

Grunsky, K. "Reim und musikalische Form in den Meistersingern." *Richard Wagner-Jahrbuch* 5 (1913): 138.

Mehler, E. "Die Textvarianten der Meistersinger-Dichtung: Beiträge zur Textkritik des Werkes." *Richard Wagner-Jahrbuch* 5 (1913): 187.

Roethe, G. "Zum dramatischen Aufbau der Wagnerschen Meistersinger." *Sitzungberichte der Preussischen Akademie* no. 37 (1919).

Anheisser, S. "Das Vorspiel zu 'Tristan und Isolde' und seine Motivik." *Zeitschrift für Musikwissenschaft* 3 (1920-21): 257.

Robertson, J.G. "The Genesis of Wagner's Drama 'Tannhäuser'." *Modern Language Review* 18 (1923): 458.

Peyser, H.F. " 'Tristan,' First-hand." *Musical Quarterly* 11 (1925): 418.

Strobel, O. " 'Winterstürme wichen dem Wonnemond': zur Genesis von Siegmunds Lenzgesang." *Bayreuther Blätter* 53 (1930): 123.

Unger, M. "The Cradle of the Parsifal Legend." *Musical Quarterly* 18 (1932): 428.

Strobel, O. "Zur Entstehungsgeschichte der *Götterdämmerung*: unbekannte Dokumente." *Die Musik* 25 (1932-33): 336.

———. "Wagners Prosaentwurf zum 'Fliegende Holländer'." *Bayreuther Blätter* 56 (1933): 157.

Schünemann, G. "Eine neue Tristan-Handschrift." *Archiv für Musikforschung* 3 (1938): 129, 137.

Abraham, G. " 'The Flying Dutchman': Original Version." *Music and Letters* 20 (1939): 412.

Grunsky, H. " 'Tristan und Isolde': der symphonische Aufbau des dritten Aufzugs." *Zeitschrift für Musikwissenschaft* 113 (1952): 390.

Hess, W. " 'Die Meistersinger von Nürnberg': ihre dichterische musikalische Gesamtform." *Zeitschrift für Musik* 113 (1952): 394.

Engel, H. "Versuch einer Sinndeutung vom Richard Wagners *Ring des Nibelungen*." *Die Musikforschung* 10 (1957): 225.

Serauky, W. "Die Todesverkündigungsszene in Richard Wagners *Walküre* als musikalisch-geistige Achse des Werkes." *Die Musikforschung* 12 (1959): 143.

Engel, H. "Über Richard Wagners Oper *Das Liebesverbot*." In *Festshrift Friedrich Blume*. Kassel, (1963): 80.

Truscott, H. "Wagner's *Tristan* and the Twentieth Century." *Music Review* 24 (1963): 75.

Adorno, T.W. "Zur Partitur des 'Parsifal'." In *Moments musicaux*, 52. Frankfurt am Main, 1964.

Westernhagen, Curt von. "Die Kompositions Skizze zu 'Siegfrieds Tod' aus dem Jahre 1850." *Neue Zeitschrift für Musik* 124 (1968): 178.

Steinbeck, D. "Zur Textkritik der Venus-Szenen im 'Tannhäuser'." *Die Musikforschung* 19 (1966): 412.

Mitchell, W.J. "The Tristan Prelude: Techniques and Structure." *Music Forum* 1 (1967): 162.

Bailey, Robert. "Wagner's Musical Sketches for *Siegfrieds Tod*." In *Studies in Music History: Essays for Oliver Strunk*, edited by Harold Powers, 459. Princeton, 1968.

Dahlhaus, Carl. "Formprinzipien in Wagners 'Ring des Nibelungen'." In *Beiträge zur Geschichte der Oper*, edited by H. Becker, 95. Regensburg, 1969.

Geck, M. "Rienzi-Philologie." In *Das Drama Richard Wagners als musikalisches Kunstwerk*, edited by Carl Dahlhaus, 183. Regensburg, 1970.

Kunze, Stefan. "Naturszenen in Wagners Musikdrama." *Gesellschaft für Musikforschung Kongressbericht* (1970): 199.

Voss, E. "Wagners Striche im Tristan." *Neue Zeitschrift für Musik* 132 (1971): 644.

Bailey, Robert. "The Evolution of Wagner's Compositional Procedure after Lohengrin." In *International Musicological Society Congress Report 11, Copenhagen 1972*.

Brinkmann, R. " 'Drei der Fragen stell'ich mir frei': zur Wanderer-Szene im I. Akt von Wagners 'Siegfried'." *Jahrbuch des Staatlichen Institut für Musikforschung Preussicher Kulturbesitz 1972*: 120.

Steinbeck, D. "Richard Wagners *Lohengrin*-Szenarium." In *Klein Schriften der Gesellschaft für Theatergeschichte*, 25. Berlin, 1972.

Dahlhaus, Carl. "Wagner and Program Music." *Studies in Romanticism* 9 (1970): 3; German original in *Jahrbuch des Staatlichen Institut für Musikforschung Preussischer Kulturbesitz 1973*.

———. "Zur Geschichte des Leitmotivtechnik bei Wagner." In *Richard Wagner: Werk und Wirkung*, 17. Regensburg, 1971.

Machlin, Paul S. "Wagner, Durand, and *The Flying Dutchman*: the 1852 Revisions of the Overture." *Music and Letters* 55 (1974).

Jackson, R. "*Leitmotive* and Form in the *Tristan* Prelude." *Music Review* 36 (1975): 42.

Nitsche, P. "Klangfarbe und Form: das Walhallthema in Rheingold und Walküre." *Melos/Neue Zeitschrift für Musik* 1 (1975): 83.

Avant-scène opéra November-December (1976) [*L'or du Rhine* issue].

Strohm, Reinhard. "*Rienzi* and Authenticity." *Musical Times* (1976).

Avant-scène opéra January-February (1977) [*La Walkyrie* issue].

Avant-scène opéra November-December (1977) [*Siegfried* issue].

Deathridge, John. "Wagner's Sketches for the *Ring*." *Musical Times* 118 (1977).

Bailey, Robert. "The Structure of the *Ring* and its Evolution." *Nineteenth-Century Music* 1 (1977-78).

Strohm, Reinhard. "Dramatic Time and Operatic Form in Wagner's *Tannhäuser*." *Proceedings of the Royal Musical Association* 104 (1977-78).

Avant-scène opéra nos. 13-14 (1978) [*Le crépuscle des Dieux* issue].

Dahlhaus, Carl. "*Tristan*—Harmonik und Tonalität." *Melos/Neue Zeitschrift für Musik* 4 (1978): 215.

McDonald, William E. "Words, Music, and Dramatic Development in *Die Meistersinger*." *Nineteenth-Century Music* 1 (1978): 246.

Várnai, Péter Pál. "Survival of Italian Operatic Traditions in Wagner's Music Drama." *Ricerche musicali* 2/no. 2 (1978): 71.

Vetter, I. "Holländer-Metamorphosen." *Melos/Neue Zeitschrift für Musik* 4 (1978).

Blissett, William. "The Liturgy of *Parsifal*." *University of Toronto Quarterly* 49 (1979): 117.

Avant-scène opéra November-December (1980) [*Le vaisseau fantôme* issue].

Breig, Werner. "Der 'Rheintöchtergesang' in Wagners *Rheingold*." *Archiv für Musikwissenschaft* 38 (1980): 241.

Coren, David. "Inspiration and Calculation in the Genesis of Wagner's *Siegfried*." In *Studies in Musicology in Honor of Otto E. Albrecht*, edited by John Walter Hill, 266. Kassel, 1980.

Kinderman, W. "Dramatic Recapitulation in Wagner's *Götterdämmerung*." *Nineteenth-Century Music* 4 (1980): 101.

Raymond, Joely. "The *Leitmotiv* and Musical-Dramatic Structure in Tristan's Third Narration of the Delirium." *Indiana Theory Review* 3 (1980): 3.

Avant-scène opéra July-August (1981) [*Tristan et Isolde* issue].

Avant-scène opéra January-February (1982) [*Parsifal* issue].

Berkemeier, Georg. " 'Hin Ritter, wisst: Sixtus Beckmesser Merker ist!': 'Was nutzt mir meine Meisterpracht?' Noch eine anmerkung zum Merker in Wagners *Die Meistersinger von Nürnberg*." In *Sequenzen. Maria Elizabeth Brockhoff zum 2.4.1982 gewidmet von Schülern, Freunden und Kollegen*, edited by Georg Berkemeier and Isolde Maria Weineck. Hagen, 1982.

Brinkmann, Reinhold. " '. . . einen Schluss Machen!' Über externe Schlüsse by Wagner." *Beiträge für Musikwissenschaft* 24 (1982): 119.

———. "Richard Wagner der Erzähler." *Österreichische Musikzeitung* 37 (1982): 297.

Der Lek, Robbert van. "Zum Begriff Übergang und zu seiner Anvendung durch Alfred Lorenz auf die Musik von Wagners *Ring*." *Die Musikforschung* 35 (1982): 129.

Hamilton, David. "At the Start" [*Die Feen*]. *Opera News* 46/no. 13 (1982): 14.

Musik-Konzepte 25 (1982) [special *Parsifal* issue].

Rienäcker, Gerd. "Zur Dramaturgie der Bühnfestspiele Richard Wagners. Beobachtungen, Fragen, Hypothesen." *Beiträge für Musikwissenschaft* 24 (1982): 159.

Schäfer, Wolf Dieter. "Syntaktische und semantische Bedingungen der Motivinstrumentation in Wagners *Ring*." In *Festschrift Heinz Becker zum 60. Geburtstag am 26. Juni 1982*, edited by Jürgen Schläder and Reinhold Quandt, 191. Laaber, 1982.

Seelig, Wolfgang. "Ambivalenz und Glauben." *Österreichische Musikzeitung* 37 (1982): 307.

Sutcliffe, James Helme. "*Parsifal*: Summation of a Musical Lifetime." *Opera* July-August (1982).

Weiner, Marc A. "Richard Wagner's Use of E.T.A. Hoffmann's *The Mines of Falcun*." *Nineteenth-Century Music* 5 (1982): 201.

Wildgruber, Jens. "Das Geheimnis der 'Barform' in R. Wagners *Die Meistersinger von Nürnberg*. Plädoyer für eine neue Art des Formbetrachtung." In *Festschrift Heinz Becker zum 60. Geburtstag am 26. Juni 1982*, edited by Jürgen Schläder and Reinhold Quandt, 205. Laaber, 1982.

Coren, D. "The Texts of Wagner's *Der junge Siegfried* and *Siegfried*." *Nineteenth-Century Music* 6 (1982-83).

Abbate, C. "The Parisian 'Venus' and the 'Paris' Tannhäuser." *Journal of the American Musicological Society* 36 (1983).

Burnstein, L. Poundie. "A New View of *Tristan*: Tonal Unity in the Prelude and Conclusion to Act I." *Theory and Practice* 8 (1983): 15.

Cumbow, Robert C. "The Ring is a Fraud: Self, Totem, and Myth in *Der Ring des Nibelungen*." *Opera Quarterly* 1 (1983): 107.

Dahlhaus, Carl. "Tonalität und Form in Wagners *Ring des Nibelungen*." *Archiv für Musikwissenschaft* 40 (1983): 165.

Deathridge, John. "*Rienzi* . . . a Few of the Facts." *Musical Times* 124 (1983): 546.

Floros, Constantin. "Der 'Beziehungszauber' der Musik im *Ring des Nibelungen* von Richard Wagner." *Neue Zeitschrift für Musik* 144 (1983): 8.

Frühwald, Wolfgang. "Romantische Sehnsucht und Liebestod in Richard Wagners Oper *Tristan und Isolde*." *Zeitwende* 54 (1983): 129.

Gloede, Wilhelm. "Dichterisch-musikzlische Periode und Form in Brünnhildes Schlussgesang." *Österreichisches Musikzeitung* 38 (1983): 84.

Hirsbrunner, Theo. "Wagners *Götterdämmerung*. Motivgeschichte in Tradition und Gegenwart." *Universitas* 38 (1983): 43.

Kestner, Joseph. "Romantic Rebel: Wagner's Hero Tannhäuser, Forged from a Wealth of Literary Sources, Straddles Worlds Sacred and Profane—Much Like its Creator." *Opera News* 47 (1983): 16.

Kinderman, William. "Das 'Geheimnis der Form' in Wagners *Tristan und Isolde*." *Archiv für Musikwissenschaft* 40 (1983): 174.

Lee, M. Owen. "Wagner's *Ring*: Turning the Sky Round." *Opera Quarterly* 1 (1983): 28.

Maisel, Arthur. "*Tristan*: a Different Perspective." *Theory and Practice* 8 (1983): 53.

McKinney, Bruce. "The Case Against Tonal Unity in *Tristan*." *Theory and Practice* 8 (1983): 62.

Newcomb, Anthony. "Those Images that Yet Fresh Images Beget." *Journal of Musicology* 2 (1983): 227.

Nitsche, Peter. "Operntraditionen im Musikdrama Richard Wagners. Zu Formkonzeption des ersten Aufzugs der *Walküre*." *Musica* 37 (1983): 29.

Potter, John. "Brünnhilde's Choice." *Opera News* 47 (1983): 8.

Schubert, Bernhard. "Wagners 'Sachs' und die Tradition des romantischen Künstlerselbstverständnisses." *Archiv für Musikwissenschaft* 40 (1983): 212.

White, David A. "Who is Parsifal's 'pure fool'? Nietzsche on Wagner." *Music Review* 44 (1983): 203.

Avant-scène opéra April-May (1984) [*Tannhäuser* issue].

Dahlhaus, Carl. "Entfremdung und Erinnerung: zu Wagners *Götterdämmerung*." In *Bericht über den Internationalen Musikwissenschaftlichen Kongress Bayreuth, 1981*, edited by Christoph Hellmut Mahling and Sigrid Wiesmann, 416. Kassel, 1984.

Daverio, John. "Narration as Drama: Wagner's Early Revisions of *Tannhäuser* and their Relation to the Rome Narrative." *College Music Symposium* 24 (1984): 55.

Gloede, Wilhelm. "Zur Verhältnis zwischen den Anfangs und den Endtonarten in Wagners Musikdramen." *Musica* 38 (1984): 429.

Hirsbrunner, Theo. "Musik über Musik: zu Wagners *Götterdämmerung*." In *Analysen: Beiträge zu einer Problemgeschichte des Komponierens. Festschrift für Hans Heinrich Eggebrecht zum 65. Geburtstag*, edited by Werner Breig et al., 292. Wiesbaden, 1984.

Kinderman, William. "Bayreuth 1983." *Nineteenth-Century Music* 8 (1984): 60.

Knapp, Raymond. "The Tonal Structure of *Tristan und Isolde:* a Sketch." *Music Review* 45 (1984): 11.

Lewin, David. "Amfortas's Prayer to Titurel and the Role of D in *Parsifal:* the Tonal Spaces of the Drama and the Enharmonic C-flat/B." In *Essays for Joseph Kerman,* edited by D. Kern Holoman. *Nineteenth-Century Music* 7 (1984).

Vetter, Isolde. "Die Entstehung des *Fliegenden Holländers* von Richard Wagner." In *Bericht über den Internationalen Musikwissenschaftlichen Kongress Bayreuth, 1981,* edited by Christoph Hellmut Mahling and Sigrid Wiesmann, 436. Kassel, 1984.

Wolf, Hugo, et al. "*Tannhäuser und der Sängerkrieg auf Wartburg* von Richard Wagner." *About the House* 6/no. 12 (1984): 33.

Kinderman, William. "Wagner's *Parsifal:* Musical Form and the Drama of Redemption." *Journal of Musicology* 4 (1986): 431; 5 (1987): 315.

Dyson, J. Peter. "Ironic Dualities in *Das Rheingold.*" *Current Musicology* 43 (1987).

Darcy, Warren. " 'Everything that is, ends!': the Genesis and Meaning of the Erda Episode in *Das Rheingold.* " *Musical Times* September (1988).

Avant-scène opéra January-February (1989) [*Les maîtres chanteurs de Nuremburg* issue].

Abbate, Carolyn. "Wagner, 'On Modulation,' and *Tristan.*" *Cambridge Opera Journal* 1 (1989): 33.

Chytry, Josef. *The Aesthetic State* [Wagner chapter]. Berkeley and Los Angeles, 1989.

Darcy, Warren. "*Creatio ex nihilo:* The Genesis, Structure, and Meaning of the *Rheingold* Prelude." *Nineteenth-Century Music* 13 (1989): 79.

McCreless, Patrick. "Motive and Magic: A Referential Dyad in *Parsifal.*" *Music Analysis* 9 (1990): 227.

Borchmeyer, Dieter. "Wagner Literature: A German Embarrassment." *Wagner* 12 (1991): 51.

unpublished–

Lorenz, Alfred. "Gedanken und Studien zur Musikalische Formgebung in R. Wagners Ring des Nibelungen." Ph.D. dissertation, Frankfurt-am-Main, 1922.

Bailey, R. "The Genesis of *Tristan und Isolde,* and a Study of Wagner's Sketches and Drafts for the First Act." Ph.D. dissertation, Princeton University, 1969.

Coren, D. "A Study of Richard Wagner's 'Siegfried'." Ph.D. dissertation, University of California, Berkeley, 1971.

Breig, W. "Studien zur Entstehungsgeschichte von Wagners 'Ring des Nibelungen'." Ph.D. dissertation, University of Freiburg, 1973.

Machlin, P.S. "The Flying Dutchman: Sketches, Revisions and Analysis." Ph.D. dissertation, University of California, Berkeley, 1976.

Heidgen, Norbert. "Textvarianten in Richard Wagners *Rheingold* und *Walküre.*" Ph.D. dissertation, Technische Universität, Berlin, 1981.

Stokes, Jeffrey Lewis. "Contour and Motive: a Study of 'Flight' and 'Love' in Wagner's *Ring, Tristan,* and *Meistersinger.*" Ph.D. dissertation, State University of New York, Buffalo, 1984.

Abbate, Carolyn. "The 'Parisian' *Tannhäuser.*" Ph.D. dissertation, Princeton University, 1984.

*   *   *

In the works of Wilhelm Richard Wagner elements of the tradition of German romantic opera stemming from Mozart's *Zauberflöte* and Weber's *Der Freischütz* were incorporated into a highly original artistic synthesis often described as *Musikdrama,* although that term was disowned by Wagner himself. The influence of Wagner has been immense and many-faceted, extending beyond opera and drama into aesthetic theory, literature, politics, and performance practice. A prolific writer, Wagner composed the texts as well as the music of his works, adapting material from medieval epics such as the *Nibelungenlied,* the *Edda,* Gottfried von Strassburg's *Tristan,* and Wolfram von Eschenbach's *Parzifal.* Wagner's music shows major innovations in its form, orchestration, and harmonic language. In the works of his most advanced style, beginning with *Tristan und Isolde,* an expanded tonal practice based on the twelve chromatic modes, a richly allusive, polyphonic motivic texture, and a formal control over vast temporal spans all contribute to an artistic synthesis in which the music assumes a central if not dominant role. In order to realize his ideals, Wagner founded a center for performance of his works at Bayreuth, Germany, where a theater was constructed according to the composer's specifications, and festivals have continued since 1876.

Wagner's earliest operas reveal comparatively little of his originality. The most important of these, *Rienzi,* owes much to the grand opera of Spontini and Meyerbeer. Wagner later polemicized vigorously against "opera," but some features of grand opera style nevertheless reemerge in certain of his ripest works, such as *Die Meistersinger* and *Götterdämmerung.* It was in the first of his German romantic operas, *Der fliegende Holländer* of 1841, that Wagner successfully developed material from legend centered on his favorite theme of redemption, involving here an accursed sea captain seeking release through the unconditional love of a woman, Senta.

Der fliegende Holländer and Wagner's succeeding works from the 1840s also show some important musical innovations. Wagner goes beyond the strict sectional divisions and stereotyped conventions of opera in his treatment of Senta's ballade, with its startling interruption of the spinning song and its powerful evocation of the chromatic music in the minor associated with the Dutchman, with whom she is obsessed. That music, in turn, is first heard at the beginning of the overture, where its open fifths in D minor, projected in the string tremoli and ghostly horn call, recall the opening of Beethoven's Ninth Symphony. In the two following operas written while he was Kapellmeister at Dresden, *Tannhäuser* and especially *Lohengrin,* Wagner tended to blur or eliminate divisions between successive set-numbers, and merge the functions of recitative and aria into an arioso-like *Sprechgesang,* or "speech song," while imposing a unity of tone on the whole, in part through the resourceful use of recurring motives in the orchestra. In *Lohengrin* not only themes and motives but also keys assume consistent dramatic associations: the A major of the prelude, for instance, is linked with Lohengrin and the Grail, and F# minor with Ortrud.

During the 1840s Wagner also identified the dramatic material for all of his later works except *Tristan,* thereby setting out the major goals of his career long in advance. *Die Meistersinger von Nürnberg* was originally conceived as a comic pendant to *Tannhäuser,* whereas the mythological material for *Lohengrin* is closely associated with *Parsifal.* (In the medieval sources, Parzifal is Lohengrin's father.) Wagner was keenly aware of such interconnections between his works, and sometimes deliberated for years over the necessary adaption and compression of his source material, making prose sketches well in advance of the writing of the dramatic poems. It was

Richard Wagner, photographed in 1871

during the 1840s as well that Wagner assimilated some of the vocabulary and conceptual apparatus of Hegelian dialectics, with its questionable indulgence in sweeping generalization based on evolutionary historicism. This ideological approach surfaces in many of Wagner's prose writings, from his famous polemic about the end of the symphony after Beethoven's Ninth to his infamous pronouncements about the Jews in *Judaism in Music* of 1850, a treatise Wagner reissued in 1869. Wagner's antisemitism needs to be understood in an historical context, but the issue has done much damage to his reputation, and points of connection do exist between his legacy of Bayreuth and the murderous regime of Hitler.

Wagner's involvement with the unsuccessful revolutionary uprisings at Dresden in 1849 led to a call for his arrest, and with Liszt's help, he fled to Switzerland, where he spent several years occupied not with musical composition but with prose writings and the poem of his gigantic cycle *Der Ring des Nibelungen*. The most central of his theoretical writings is *Oper und Drama* of 1851, the doctrines of which correspond closely to the earlier parts—but not the last third—of the *Ring*. The *Ring* cycle consists of the prologue *Das Rheingold* and three main dramas, *Die Walküre*, *Siegfried*, and *Götterdämmerung*. The works were initially conceived in reverse order, the oldest being *Siegfried's Tod*, the original title of *Götterdämmerung*, but Wagner soon resolved to expand the project to unprecedented dimensions. The subject of this cycle of epic dramas thus begins not with the tale of Siegfried but with the theft of the Rhine gold—or rape of nature—committed by the Nibelung Alberich, who foreswears love to gain power. Wotan, leader of the gods, seizes Alberich's ring and hoard in order to discharge his financial obligations for the building of the palace of Walhalla, but increasingly loses his ability to control events, and ultimately Walhalla—symbol of the established order—is consumed in flame at the dawn of a new era, as the ring is returned to the Rhinemaidens. The story is rich in political overtones, and parts of it have been interpreted as a socialist allegory.

For the music of this vast cycle, Wagner devised a large number of motives and themes that have often been labeled as *leitmotives* or "leading motives." The term *leitmotive* does not stem from Wagner, however, and the familiar labels have little meaning in themselves and can easily mislead, by giving the false impression of a fixed and constant symbolic association. Actually, Wagner's motives tend to evolve in their dramatic associations as well as in their intervallic configuration, so their significance is usually dependent on the larger context.

The central innovation of Wagner's *Ring* and later works is his abolishment of set-numbers as such, and his equation of the development of music with the development of the entire drama. The slow pacing and enormous time-scale of Wagner's music makes possible this identification, whereby, in Wagner's words from one of his later treatises, "the music spreads itself over the entire drama, and not just over small, isolated, arbitrarily separated parts of the whole." One is reminded of Beethoven's imposition of a tighter musical and dramatic interconnection between the successive movements of pieces like the Fifth and Ninth Symphonies; Wagner could claim with some justification to be Beethoven's heir in this respect.

The constant recall of short motives and more extended themes—however important—would not always suffice to articulate the major events of the drama on such a massive time-scale, and Wagner also relies not infrequently on extended, varied musical recapitulation. In the *Ring*, these recapitulatory elements are especially prominent in *Götterdämmerung*, which begins and ends with references to the

beginning of the cycle, and culminates in a great recapitulation from the preceding drama leading to a new outcome. The opening of its prelude, for example, recalls not only the chords from Brünnhilde's awakening in *Siegfried* but also the rising motivic arpeggiations from the outset of *Das Rheingold*. The very first vocal theme of the cycle, the Rhinemaidens' "Weia! Waga! Woge, du Welle, walle zur Wiege!" (an extreme example of the alliteration which replaces end-rhyme in the *Ring* poem) recurs for the last time near the close of *Götterdämmerung*, where Flosshilde's music at the recovery of the ring corresponds closely, even in its pitch level, to the initial appearance of this theme from the prologue; the theme is then transposed, and combined and juxtaposed with other motives as the Rhinemaidens swim into the depths with their prize. The setting of Siegfried's final narrative, death and funeral procession earlier in the last act of *Götterdämmerung*, on the other hand, involves a massive varied recapitulation of material drawn from both acts II and III of the preceding drama, *Siegfried*, which is even grouped into a modulatory structure passing from E to C that recalls and transforms the tonal progression from Brünnhilde's awakening in *Siegfried*. Such modulatory structures often assume an important dramatic and architectural role in the later works, but as Robert Bailey has shown, Wagner had determined an overall framework of tonalities with dramatic associations already at a formative stage in the composition of the *Ring*.

Other innovations of the *Ring* include the use of the so-called Wagner tubas—instruments specifically designed for this work and later employed by Bruckner and Richard Strauss—and the curtailment of duet and ensemble singing in those portions of the cycle composed up to 1857, namely *Das Rheingold*, *Die Walküre*, and the first two acts of *Siegfried*. The music of the later portions of the *Ring* was composed only in 1869-74, following a twelve-year hiatus during which Wagner wrote *Tristan und Isolde* and *Die Meistersinger von Nürnberg*. There is consequently a noticeable stylistic shift within the *Ring* to a more advanced and polyphonic musical style in the last act of *Siegfried* and in *Götterdämmerung*, whose text is nevertheless the oldest and the most conventionally operatic. A somewhat analogous stylistic discontinuity was introduced into the final version of *Tannhäuser* written for Paris in 1861, when Wagner added chromatic music in a Tristanesque style to the Venusberg scene, in striking contrast to the rest of the score.

As a culminating monument to romanticism and a starting-point of modern music, *Tristan und Isolde* assumes a pivotal position in music history. The initially unexpressed love of Tristan and Isolde grows after the drinking of the potion into a passion and longing for night, and ultimately into a metaphysical separation from outward existence as symbolized in Isolde's concluding transfiguration and apparent death. Such a symbolic treatment of "Night" as an alternative realm builds upon literary models such as Novalis's *Hymnen an die Nacht*, and celebrates the triumph of the suprarational through the articulating power of music. The famous chromatic music of the prelude embodies the unfulfilled yearning of the lovers not only through its use of the harmonically ambiguous "Tristan" chord (a minor triad with added sixth), rising semitone motion, and the melodic intensity and rich contrapuntal texture of its "infinite" melody—to use Wagner's term—but also through its tonal context: a tonal center of A minor is implied, but its actual triad is withheld. In the structural unit comprising the first seventeen bars, the music outlines a chromatic ascent through the octave from G# to G# an octave higher—leading tones of the implied tonic—while the chords at the phrase endings sound the dominant-seventh chords of the triad degrees of A minor. Here, as elsewhere, the cadence at the end of the progression is deceptive, since a resolution to the implied tonic would break the tension and disrupt the musical continuity, and furthermore would be dramatically unmotivated. This example shows how Wagner's dramatic effects can be embedded in the larger musical structure, and not only reflected in referential motives. Wagner's later music, in becoming more autonomous and less dependent on the text in specific details, often becomes thereby an ever greater and more generalized function of the drama.

Wagner restates this entire progression at several important junctures of the drama (at the drinking of the love potion in act I, at Tristan's confrontation with King Marke in act II, and at Tristan's death in the final act). Most consequential for the drama as a whole, however, is Wagner's transformation of the structural basis for the passage at the climax of the love-duet in act II, and again in the closing moments of Isolde's transfiguration in act III (this conclusion of *Tristan* is often described as her *Liebestod* or "Love-Death," but Wagner used that word only in reference to the first act prelude, and his description of the conclusion as a *Verklärung* or transfiguration is more fitting). In these passages, the idea of the chromatic ascent through the octave from G♯ is retained in a new texture of more ecstatic character, and the harmonic support to the G♯ is altered through the substitution of one pitch—F♯ for F♭—purging thereby the mysterious ambiguity of the "Tristan" chord. The resulting appoggiatura chord then becomes the stable tonic of B major, but only at the conclusion of Isolde's transfiguration is the cadence, with its accompanying large-scale rhythmic resolution, supplied. Isolde's text in this section is allied solely with the inward, metaphysical action, since she finds Tristan "awake" and describes the "ringing sound"—that is, the music—that envelopes her. The great cadence, treated as the culmination of a large-scale recapitulatory gesture, is Wagner's means of symbolizing Isolde's ascent into Night, and the all-encompassing nature of the resolution is underlined by his recall of the "Tristan" chord in the final moments. The revolutionary chromaticism of *Tristan* still depends crucially on the diatonic background of this resolution, which signals the dramatic breakthrough as the lovers disappear, as it were, from the level of the visible action.

Wagner completed *Tristan* in 1859, while still in exile, and the years that followed were some of the most difficult of his life. The breaking-off of Wagner's relationship with Mathilde Wesendonck (who acted as an inspiration behind the composition of *Tristan*), his inability to mount performances of the work, his usual problems with debts, and the *Tannhäuser* scandal at Paris in 1861 all tended to undermine his tenacity. Wagner did much conducting of his own works in various cities during this period (his contributions to the art of conducting were substantial, and include the important treatise *On Conducting* published in 1869). Then, on 3 May 1864, in an astonishing turn of events, he was summoned by the eighteen-year-old Ludwig II, the new King of Bavaria, who supported Wagner financially and placed the musical resources of Munich at his disposal, opening up the last and most successful phase of Wagner's career. Yet in spite of Ludwig's support, less than two years later Wagner was forced to leave Munich. One of the main reasons was his relationship with the wife of his conductor Hans von Bülow, Liszt's daughter Cosima, whom Wagner married in 1870. Wagner left Munich for Tribschen, Switzerland (near Lucerne), where he finished *Die Meistersinger* in October of 1867. *Tristan* had already been given its successful premiere at Munich in 1865 and *Die Meistersinger* followed in 1868. By that time, however,

Wagner's plans for a festival theater for the performance of the *Ring* in Munich were doomed to failure, and his attention was soon to turn to Bayreuth.

Die Meistersinger, Wagner's major work of the 1860s and the only comic opera of his maturity, centers on the relation between art and society. The singing contest between Walther von Stolzing—a "natural" genius—and Beckmesser—sterile pedant and caricature of Viennese critic Eduard Hanslick—reflects just one aspect of the theme. The only one of the masters who fully understands art is Walther's instructor, the widower Hans Sachs, who is sorely tempted to join the contest for Eva Pogner's hand, but does not do so out of a gesture of "bitter resignation" and commitment to the "angel" who holds him in an artistic "paradise" counterpoised to the *Wahn* or "delusion" of earthly existence. Carl Dahlhaus has observed how the predominant diatonicism of *Die Meistersinger*—with social roots in its chorales, marches, and dances—is rendered fragile through a juxtaposition with chromaticism, and this is nowhere more evident than in the scenes for Eva and Sachs in act III, culminating in an explicit quotation from *Tristan.* The influence of Schopenhauer is felt here no less than in *Tristan,* both in the idea of denial of the will to life and in the elevation of musical art, which for Schopenhauer represented no less than "the inner nature, the in-itself of all phenomena," a cosmic force unifying the spiritual and material poles of existence. The final choral scene of *Die Meistersinger* has been misused for chauvinistic purposes, but it actually glorifies not the state, but art ("should the Holy Roman Empire dissolve in mist, there would remain the holy German Art!"), and was criticized for precisely this reason in Germany during the Second World War.

After the completion of the *Ring* and its first performance at Bayreuth in 1876, Wagner succeeded in finishing one remaining work, the *Bühnenweihfestspiel* ("stage consecration festival play") *Parsifal.* (Another projected work based on Buddhist sources, *Die Sieger* was left unrealized.) *Parsifal* is the only one of Wagner's major works composed at Bayreuth, and its orchestral subtleties take full advantage of the sunken orchestra pit and superb acoustics of the Bayreuth Festival Theater. Performances of *Parsifal* reopened the Bayreuth Festival in 1882, after several years when the future of the project was in financial jeopardy.

Parsifal is perhaps the most advanced and controversial of all Wagner's works. The theme of redemption takes on a more radical, collective character in *Parsifal,* as aspects of Christianity are assimilated into Wagner's temple of art. Thus the "transfiguration" of the central protagonist(s) occurs not as an end point to the action, as in *Der fliegende Holländer* or *Tristan,* but begins already in act II, as Parsifal recoils from Kundry's seduction attempt, with its musical embodiment in the contaminating chromaticism of her music. Parsifal's denial of the temptation of the senses is connected to his capacity for compassion; Agapē overcomes Eros. Musically, there can be no resolution of chromaticism into diatonicism here, as in *Tristan,* but rather a purification *from* chromaticism of the diatonic themes and motives of the Grail, which are integrated and combined for the first time in the closing recapitulatory synthesis at the end of act III, after Parsifal appears as redeemer and reveals the Grail. At the same time, the wound of the Grail King Amfortas—outward symbol of his sinful condition—is healed by Parsifal, and Kundry, whom he has baptized, is released from her curse through death. The symbolism of *Parsifal* is especially complex, and resists unambiguous interpretation, but the indispensable essence of the drama is conveyed in the music. *Parsifal* is a major monument to the aesthetic of the sublime and to Wagner's conviction, expressed in *Religion and Art* of 1880, that art could "salvage the kernel of religion" through its "ideal representation" of mythical religious images. Wagner's attempts to express the inexpressible, or at least the extraordinary, were carried to their limits in *Parsifal*, and not surprisingly, it proved difficult if not impossible for subsequent composers of opera to build further on this line of approach. In recognition of its exhaustive character, Debussy once described Wagner's legacy as "a beautiful sunset that was mistaken for a dawn."

—William Kinderman

WAGNER, Wieland Adolf Gottfried.

Director. Born 5 January 1917, in Bayreuth; died 17 October 1966, in Munich. Grandson of Richard, son of Siegfried, elder brother of Wolfgang. Trained at Bayreuth, observed productions of Emil Preetorius, Alfred Roller; first professional work at Altenburg; designed *Parsifal*, 1937, and *Die Meistersinger von Nürnberg*, 1943, for Bayreuth; co-director Bayreuth Festival 1951-66. Produced all of Wagner's operas at Bayreuth from *Rienzi* to *Parsifal*.

Opera Productions (selected)

Parsifal, Bayreuth, 1951.
Der Ring des Nibelungen, Bayreuth, 1951.
Tristan und Isolde, Bayreuth, 1952.
Orfeo ed Euridice, Stuttgart Staatsoper, 1953.
Fidelio, Stuttgart Staatsoper, 1954.
Tannhäuser, Bayreuth, 1954.
Die Meistersinger von Nürnberg, Bayreuth, 1956.
Antigonae, Stuttgart Staatsoper, 1956.
Lohengrin, Bayreuth, 1958.
Der fliegende Holländer, Bayreuth, 1959.
Carmen, Hamburg Staatsoper, 1959.
Tannhäuser, Bayreuth, 1961.
Salome, Stuttgart Staatsoper, 1962.
Tristan und Isolde, Bayreuth, 1962.
Die Meistersinger von Nürnberg, Bayreuth, 1963.
Der Ring des Nibelungen, Bayreuth, 1965.
Wozzeck, Frankfurt am Main, 1966.

Publications

By WAGNER: books—

Editor. *Richard Wagner und das neue Bayreuth*. Munich, 1962.
Editor. *Hundert Jahre Tristan: Neunzehn Essays*. Emsdetten, 1965.

articles—

"Tradition and Innovation." *Opera News* 16 (31 December 1951): 4.
"Denkmalschutz für Wagner." *Österreichische Musikzeitschrift* 13/September (1958): 357.
Foreword to Skelton, Geoffrey, *Wagner at Bayreuth: Experiment and Tradition*. London, 1965; second edition, revised and enlarged, 1976.

Afterword to Gollancz, Victor, *The Ring at Bayreuth and Some Thoughts on Operatic Production*. London, 1966.

About WAGNER: books—

Ruppel, K.H., editor. *Wieland Wagner inszeniert Richard Wagner: ein Bildwerk*. Konstanz, 1960.
Panofsky, W. *Wieland Wagner*. Bremen, 1964.
Skelton, Geoffrey. *Wagner at Bayreuth: Experiment and Tradition*. London, 1965; second edition, revised and enlarged, 1976.
Gollancz, Victor. *The Ring at Bayreuth and Some Thoughts on Operatic Production*. London, 1966.
Goléa, Antoine. *Entretiens avec Wieland Wagner*. Paris, 1967.
Barth, H. *Internationale Wagner-Bibliographie 1961 bis 1966 und Wieland Wagner Bibliographie*. Bayreuth, 1968.
Lust, C. *Wieland Wagner et la survie du théâtre lyrique*. Lausanne, 1969.
Schäfer, W.E. *Wieland Wagner: Persönlichkeit und Leistung*. Tübingen, 1970.
Skelton, Geoffrey. *Wieland Wagner: The Positive Skeptic*. London, 1971.
Wagner, W.S. *The Wagner Family Albums*. London, 1976.
Musique en jeu nos. 22-23 (1976) [special issues].
Bauer, Owald George. *Richard Wagner: The Stage Designs and Productions from the Premiers to the Present*. New York, 1983.

articles—

Moor, P. "Wagner's Grandson, Wieland, Breaks the Traditions." *Theatre Arts* 35/November (1952): 68.
Toëg, G. "Wieland Wagner, musicien de Bayreuth." *La vie musicale* 2/November (1952): 9.
Fuchs, P.P. "Opera in West Germany; Post-War Conditions Have Produced New Visual Approaches and Techniques." *Musical American* 76 (15 February 1956): 16.
"Wieland Wagner Talking." *Opera* 9/August (1958): 487.
Eckstein, P. "Wieland Wagner o problemache soudobe opera." *Hudebni Rozhledy* 14/18 (1961): 774.
Joachim, H. "Günther Rennert, Oskar Fritz Schuh, Wieland Wagner—Three Eminent Opera Producers." *Canon* 16/December-January (1962-63): 16.
Garbutt, J. and J. Derry. "Reflections on the New Bayreuth." *The Music Review* 25/1 (1965): 34.
Loney, Glenn. "Cult and Myth on the Green Hill." *Hi Fidelity/Musical American* 14/October (1965): 160.
von Lewinsky, W.E. "Wieland Wagner's *Wozzeck* unter Pierre Boulez." *Melos* 33/June (1966): 186.
Goléa, Antoine. "Wieland Wagner et Wozzeck face à face." *Musica* 148-149/July-August (1966): 8.
"Wieland Wagner 1917-1966." *Orchester* 14/November (1966) 427.
McMullen, R. "The Phantom of the Festspielhaus; An Only Partly Imaginary Conversation between Richard and Wieland Wagner." *Hi Fidelity/Musical American* 16/November (1966): 60.
Boulez, Pierre. "Der Raum wird hier zur Zeit." *Melos* 33/December (1966): 400.
Porter, Andrew, et al. "Wieland Wagner (list of productions)." *Opera* December 1966: 931.
Salzman, Eric. "The World of Wieland Wagner." *Opera News* 31 (21 January 1967): 8.
London, G. "The World of Wieland Wagner." *The Saturday Review* 50 (28 January 1967): 59.
"The Late Wieland Wagner." *Music (SMA)* 1/2 (1967): 46.

Wieland Wagner's production of *Parsifal* (act I), Bayreuth Festival, 1953

Spingel, H.O., et al. "Dienst am Werk oder Interpreten-Willkür?" *Opernwelt* August 1967: 27.

Moushon, G. "Bayreuth: The Wagner Legacy Imperiled." *Hi Fidelity/Musical American* 18/October (1968): MA25.

Guiomar, M. "Problèmes permanents d'esthétique wagnérienne des quelques publications récentes." *Revue d'esthetique,* 1969.

Wodnansky, W. "The Opera and Wieland Wagner." *Music Journal* 28/February (1970): 34.

Everding, A. "Was bleibt Wieland Wagner?" *Opernwelt* 3/March (1972): 26.

Jungheinrich, H.K. "Vom Neo-Mythos zum politischen Aufklärungstheater: zur Wagnerbühne nach Wieland Wagner." *Opernwelt* 3/March (1972): 27.

Porter, Andrew. "Approaches to *Tannhäuser.*" *About the House* 4/3 (1973): 12.

Kolodin, Irving. "The Wagners of Bayreuth 1876-1976." *The Saturday Review* 3 (24 July 1976): 30.

Flinois, Pierre. "*Les Maîtres* de Wieland Wagner." *Avant-scène opéra.* January-February 1978.

Asche, G. "Leonie Rysanek: Wieland hatte Mühe, mich zu zähmen." *Opernwelt* Yearbook 1981: 23.

Liebermann, R. "In Support of 'Music theatre'." *Opera* 34/February (1983): 135.

Von Buchau, S. "All About Anja (interview with Anja Silva)." *San Francisco Opera Magazine* 3/Fall (1983): 45.

Lehmann, H.P. "Begegnungen mit Wieland Wagner." *Opernwelt* 27 (Yearbook 1986): 61.

Littlejohn, D. "Whither Breastplates? Stagings of Wagner's Ring since 1876." *San Francisco Opera Magazine* 68/2 (1990): 28.

Wagner, G.H. "Als ein Wagner in Israel." *Dissonance* 25/August (1990): 4.

*   *   *

Wieland Wagner's "new Bayreuth style," introduced when he and his brother Wolfgang reopened Wagner's Festspielhaus in 1951 following its wartime closure, was based on the conviction that the realistic way in which Wagner's music dramas had traditionally been staged prevented them from making their full impact. He set himself to evolve a production style, based on a close study of the words and music of the works themselves rather than slavishly following Wagner's stage directions. The rich expressiveness of Wagner's music, he realized, conveyed much more to the ear than stage action and settings did to the eye, and he deliberately aimed at reducing the spectacular element in order to allow words and music (the essence of the drama) to make their full impact.

Lighting became the main scenic ingredient, and in particular the spotlight. Wieland Wagner's first stagings at Bayreuth of *Parsifal* (1951), *Der Ring des Nibelungen* (1951) and *Tristan und Isolde* (1952) were notable for the bareness of their stage settings, many of the scenes being played in darkness or semi-darkness with copious use of the spotlight to create a scene within a scene. Whenever the stage was put to full use, however, (as in the scene between Brünnhilde and Wotan at the end of *Die Walküre* and the final scene of *Siegfried*), the effect was breathtaking, for Wieland Wagner was by inclination and training a painter, and in his stage work he handled lighting like paint, using it not just to illuminate external objects but to act on the emotions. When in subsequent years he came to produce Wagner's earlier works (*Der fliegende Holländer, Tannhäuser, Lohengrin*) he allowed more in the way of stage settings in keeping with the composer's historical treatment of the action, though he continued to regard Wagner's stage directions as "inner visions," not practical demands. The lighting also became brighter, the costumes (all of which, like the stage settings, Wieland Wagner designed himself) more colorful.

Movement played a very important part in Wieland Wagner's presentation of the dramas, particularly in scenes involving a large number of singers. The knights of the Grail in *Parsifal,* the pilgrims, the knights and their ladies in *Tannhäuser,* and the people of Brabant in *Lohengrin* were dressed in identical costumes and they moved in formal patterns. By lighting and by subtle variations to their symmetry these groups served an additional function as a fluid part of the scenery.

Wieland Wagner demanded a high caliber of acting from his singers, and his intensive rehearsals with them, singly and in ensemble, were aimed at ensuring that they had a clear idea of what they were doing and saying. He considered that in opera, as in the spoken drama, the basic theme (what he called "the dramatic idea") was all-important, and his main efforts were directed towards bringing Wagner's psychological insights well to the fore.

Wieland Wagner had a horror of preconceived ideas, his own as well as those of others, and throughout his career he was constantly making changes in his productions or redoing them entirely. His restlessness was not the result of uncertainty but of an inventive imagination that was always striving towards something that, being different, might turn out to be better. There were radical differences between his productions of those works he staged more than once in Bayreuth (the *Ring, Tristan, Die Meistersinger, Tannhäuser*), the bareness of the stage in the early years giving way to pieces of scenery more symbolic than realistic (e.g., the vaguely Celtic structures in *Tristan* that suggested successively the prow of a ship, a watchtower and a sail, at the same time reflecting the emotional conflicts with which each act deals).

Though he claimed to be largely self-taught, Wieland Wagner's production style evolved from his intensive reading of his grandfather's prose works as well as the text and music of the works themselves, and also from his study of the ideas of Adolphe Appia and Edward Gordon Craig. He saw Wagner's music dramas as mystery plays requiring a timeless, non-realistic approach, but he never made use of modern dress. The style he evolved was well-suited to all of Wagner's works except *Die Meistersinger,* as he himself acknowledged. His two stagings of Wagner's comedy at Bayreuth, the first impressionistic, the second Shakespearean in style, had their revelatory moments, but on the whole were his least successful.

Though at the time much attacked by traditionalists, the "new Bayreuth style" was widely copied throughout the world. Its main drawback was that, in the hands of a producer less thorough, less imaginative and less sensitive than Wieland Wagner, it ran the risk of looking too plain and consequently rather boring.

His work in the Festspielhaus left Wieland Wagner little time to apply his ideas to the works of other composers, but occasional stagings outside Bayreuth (mainly in Stuttgart) did produce some interesting, if inconclusive results. His influence on the succeeding generation of producers can be seen less in the detail of his method than in the general prevalence of non-realistic operatic stagings based, like his own, on a "dramatic idea."

—Geoffrey Skelton

WAGNER, Wolfgang.

Director. Born 30 August 1919, in Bayreuth. Grandson of Richard, son of Siegfried, and brother of Wieland. Studied music privately in Bayreuth; theatrical training with Emil Preetorius; co-director Bayreuth Festival 1951-66; director Bayreuth Festival 1966-.

Opera Productions (selected)

Lohengrin, Bayreuth, 1953.
Der fliegende Holländer, Bayreuth, 1955.
Tristan und Isolde, Bayreuth, 1957.
Der Ring des Nibelungen, Bayreuth, 1960.
Lohengrin, Bayreuth, 1967.
Die Meistersinger von Nürnberg, Bayreuth, 1968.
Der Ring des Nibelungen, Bayreuth, 1970.
Die Meistersinger von Nürnberg, Bayreuth, 1973.
Parsifal, Bayreuth, 1975.
Tristan und Isolde, Milan, Teatro alla Scala, 1978.
Die Meistersinger von Nürnberg, Bayreuth, 1981.
Tannhäuser, Bayreuth, 1985.
Parsifal, Bayreuth, 1989.

Publications

By WAGNER: articles–

Foreword to Bauer, Owald George, *Richard Wagner: die Bühnenwerke von der Uraufführung bis heute.* Frankfurt am Main, 1982.
"Grusswort: hommage à Birgit Nilsson." *Opernwelt* Yearbook 1987: 9.

About WAGNER: books–

Gollancz, Victor. *The Ring at Bayreuth and Some Thoughts on Operatic Production.* London, 1966.
Skelton, Geoffrey. *Wagner at Bayreuth: Experiment and Tradition.* London, 1965; second edition, revised and enlarged, 1976.
Barth, Herbert, editor. *Wolfgang Wagner zum 50. Geburtstag.* Bayreuth, 1969.
Wagner, W.S. *The Wagner Family Albums.* London, 1976.
Musique en jeu nos. 22-23 (1976) [special issues].
Bauer, Owald George. *Richard Wagner: die Bühnenwerke von der Uraufführung bis heute.* Frankfurt am Main, 1982.
Sabor, R. *Die wahre Wagner; Dokumente beantworten die Frage: Wer war Wagner wirklich?* 1987.

articles–

"The Younger Wagner." *Opera News* 25/October (1960): 24.
Dew, J. "The Bayreuth Style." *Opera* 17/October (1966): 783.
Gregor-Dellin, Martin. "Guardian of Bayreuth." *Music and Musicians* 16/November (1967): 27.
Guiomar, M. "Problèmes permanents d'esthétique wagnérienne des quelques publications récentes." *Revue d'esthétique,* 1969.
Ludwig, H. "Reizfaktor: die menschlichen Probleme." *Opernwelt* 9/September (1972): 19.
Seifert, W. " 'Der Mietvertrag sichert dem Unternehmer die künstlerische Freiheit'; oder, Neubayreuth in neuer Form—ein Gespräch mit Wolfgang Wagner über die Richard-Wagner-Stiftung Bayreuth." *Neue Zeitschrift für Musik* 135/8 (1974): 485.

Hauser, V.T. "In the Spirit of Richard Wagner—Wolfgang Wagner and the Bayreuth Tradition." *Opera Canada* 16/5 (1975): 12.
Kolodin, Irving. "The Wagners of Bayreuth 1876-1976." *The Saturday Review* 3 (24 July 1976): 30.
Sutcliffe, J.H. "Wolfgang Wagner: An Interview." *Opera News* 41/August (1976): 26.
Woznica, H. "O problemach festiwali w Bayreuth mowi Wolfgang Wagner." *Ruch Muzyczny* 22/9 (1978): 17.
"Kontinuität des Aufbruchs—Wolfgang Wagner zum 60. Geburtstag." *Neue Zeitschrift für Musik* 28/5 (1979): 2.
Kanski, J. "Mowi Wolfgang Wagner." *Ruch Muzyczny* 24/20 (1980): 13.
Asche, G. "Wolfgang Wagner: Die Aussage des Werkes neu überprüfen." *Opernwelt* Yearbook 1981: 7.
Dannenberg, P. "Verbündet mit den Jungen; ein Porträt des Festspielleiters Wolfgang Wagner." *Opernwelt* 25/10 (1984): 12.
Plagemann, B. "Bayreuther Festspiele—Bilanz und ein Interview mit dem Chef des Hauses zu seinem 65. Geburtstag." *Orchester* 32/November (1984): 989.
Koltai, Tamas. "Fesztival kultusz nelkuel Beszelgetes Wolfgang Wagnerrel." *Muzsika* 28/November (1985): 26.
Mayo, A.F. "Bayreuth: la gestion de Wolfgang Wagner." *Monsalvat* 140/July-August (1986): 8.
Kanski, J. "Z Wolfgangiem Wagnerem o *Parsifalu* oraz *Spiewakach norymberskich*—i nie tylko." *Ruch Muzyczny* 31/2 (1987): 16.
Kanski, J. "Przyblizye trudne dzielu widzom." *Ruch Muzyczny* 33/22 (1989): 20.

Wolfgang Wagner, younger son of Siegfried Wagner, studied in Berlin with Emil Preetorius. From 1942 until 1944, when all German theaters and opera houses were closed, he worked as an assistant to Heinz Tietjen, chief producer at the Bayreuth Festspielhaus, where Siegfried Wagner's widow Winifred was director. When Bayreuth re-opened after the second world war in 1951, the Festival was jointly directed by the brothers, Wieland and Wolfgang Wagner. At first most productions were staged by Wieland, while Wolfgang was chiefly occupied with administrative duties, but in 1953 Wolfgang produced and also designed *Lohengrin.* His production, though less individual and more traditional than those of Wieland, was in the same austere style—a style that was congenial to the brothers (especially to Wieland) and made necessary by financial stringency.

In 1955 Wolfgang Wagner staged *Der fliegende Holländer* and in 1957 a successful production of *Tristan und Isolde.* In 1960 he tackled *Der Ring des Nibelungen* for the first time. His set, a large segmented disc that began and ended the cycle perfectly round and flat, with many variations of shape in between, was more admired than his handling of the characters, which lacked both the subtlety and authority of Wieland. This *Ring* cycle lasted until 1964. When Wieland Wagner died in 1966, Wolfgang became sole artistic director. His next production, another *Lohengrin* in art nouveau style (1967), was a great success, while *Die Meistersinger* (1968), a popular triumph, underlined the basic differences between the brothers: if Wieland was the dramatic visionary, Wolfgang was the practical man of the theater.

After Wieland's death, Wolfgang broke with tradition and started to invite other producers and designers to Bayreuth: August Everding was the first choice, to be followed by the more controversial Götz Friedrich. Meanwhile, in 1970,

Wolfgang staged a second *Ring* cycle, which was revived until 1975, when he produced a new *Parsifal* (his first) to replace the old, much loved and cherished staging by Wieland. In 1976, which marked the centenary of the first complete *Ring* cycle, Patrice Chéreau caused a scandal with a production that, after a few seasons, was widely accepted as interesting as well as innovative.

On an infrequent excursion outside Bayreuth Wolfgang staged a successful *Tristan und Isolde* at the Teatro alla Scala, Milan in 1978; at Bayreuth he re-staged *Die Meistersinger* in 1981; this time the production, which saw all the characters as unusually youthful, was rather less popular than before. A *Tannhäuser* in 1985 was found too conventional, harking back to the style of the 1950s, while the *Parsifal* of 1989 was subjected to similar criticism. Ironically, Wolfgang Wagner as producer/designer was suffering from the necessary and beneficial changes at Bayreuth inaugurated by himself, in his capacity as artistic director and administrator. His introduction of producers such as Friedrich, Chéreau and Harry Kupfer made his own work appear old-fashioned by comparison.

—Elizabeth Forbes

DIE WALKÜRE (THE VALKYRIE)
See DER RING DES NIBELUNGEN

WALLACE, (William) Vincent.

Composer. Born 11 March 1812, in Waterford, Ireland. Died 12 October 1865, in Château de Bagen (Haute-Garonne), France. Married: 1) Isabella Kelly, 1831; 2) Helen Stoepel, American pianist, 1850. Played violin in theaters and organ in churches in Dublin beginning 1827; tours of Australia, South America, Mexico, the United States, and Germany; successfully produced his opera *Maritana* in London, 1845.

Operas

Maritana, E. Fitzball, London, Drury Lane, 15 November 1845.
Matilda of Hungary, A. Bunn, London, Drury Lane, 22 February 1847.
Lurline, E. Fitzball, 1847, London, Covent Garden, 23 February 1860.
The Amber Witch, H.F. Chorley, London, Her Majesty's, 28 February 1861.
Love's Triumph, J.R. Planché, London, Covent Garden, 3 November 1862.
The Desert Flower, A. Harris and T.J. Williams, London, Covent Garden, 12 October 1863.
The Maid of Zurich [unperformed].
The King's Page, J.E. Carpenter [unperformed].
Estrella, H.B. Farnie [unfinished].
Gulnare (Italian operetta) [unperformed].
Olga (Italian operetta) [unperformed].

Other works: vocal works, piano music.

Publications

About WALLACE: books–

Berlioz, H. *Les soirées de l'orchestra*. Paris, 1852.
Pougin, A. *William Vincent Wallace: étude biographique et critique*. Paris, 1866.
Shaw, G.B. *London Music in 1888-89 as heard by Corno di Bassetto* [351]. London, 1937.
White, E.W. *The Rise of English Opera*. London, 1951.

articles–

Guernsey, W. "William Vincent Wallace." *Musical World* 43 (1865): 656.
Klein, J.W. "Vincent Wallace (1812-65): a Reassessment." *Opera* 16 (1965): 709.
Temperley, Nicholas. "The English Romantic Opera." *Victorian Studies* 9 (1966): 293.

Though William Wallace is remembered today for only one work, he composed some nine operas and two operettas, all of which attest to his good knowledge of vocal writing, orchestral instruments and their musical capabilities. The great success of his *Maritana*, written and performed in 1845 in London, following his years of peripatetic existence in Australia and the New World, was never repeated, though, as will be seen, some good numbers are to be found in the pages of some of his subsequent work.

The failure of his *Matilda of Hungary* (largely due to a poor libretto), composed and performed in 1847, seems to have temporarily dulled his enthusiasm for opera, and though his *Lurline* (1847) was commissioned for the Paris Opéra for performance in 1848, it was not performed. In its revised version, however, *Lurline* was given at Covent Garden in 1860 and achieved moderate success. Using a variant of the Lorelei legend and having as its theme the power of music, it is essentially a romantic opera, using such elements as an antique castle on the banks of the Rhine, the river itself with Lurline and her enchanted harp and song, the coral caves beneath the waters, choruses of naiads, huntsmen and the like. Chorus numbers are often quite extensive and the music is continuous, while some numbers such as "Lurline's Romance," entitled in the score "The Spell," (utilizing an ensemble of naiads and harp), and number 17, the "Drinking Song" sung by the gnome, are particularly effective. Number 21 takes the form of an "Ave Maria" (the religious element occurs frequently in Wallace's works), while number 30 is a chorus and ballet. The overture is of substantial proportions and some use is made of theme repetition.

Large-scale structure is again seen in *The Amber Witch*, a four-act opera written to a libretto by the critic H.F. Chorley. In this, number 21 is a "Latin Hymn with chorus," in which the falsely accused Mary sings a Latin hymn to interpolations from the crowd, before being saved from the stake at the very last gasp, the whole thing being reminiscent of Meyerbeer. The Introduction includes a chorale for wind instruments, which recurs later in the action, number 4 is a trio with chorus and with bell accompaniment, number 5 is a postman's song with posthorn, while number 9, a rondo sung by Mary, has some real coloratura writing. Number 11 is a big quintet with chorus.

A scene from Vincent Wallace's opera *Lurline,* **Royal Italian Opera, London, 1860**

Some charming elements are to be found in *Love's Triumph,* a three-act opera with libretto by J.R. Planché, particularly in the trio (number 6) entitled "A Simple Cymon, a romantic swain," in which the staccato accompaniment in the *Allegretto moderato* section is both novel and effective. Like most of Wallace's operas, though, the work is more a succession of songs, ballads and romances (plus the occasional concerted number) than opera proper, and it is significant that many of the numbers (as notes in the scores tell us) were available for individual sale in other keys. By and large, though, the libretto of *Love's Triumph* is weak and the words little more than doggerel.

The remaining opera, *The Desert Flower,* a three-act romantic opera written by A. Harris and T.J. Williams, was given at Covent Garden in 1863. Though the work has been described as "a weak perversion of the narrative of Captain Smith and the faithful Pocohontas," the work nevertheless contains some interesting elements. The overture introduces themes heard later in the action, the strong rhythmic elements associated with the Indians being of importance. Oanita, the Indian queen, has some coloratura elements in aria number 3; number 5 (finale to act I) contains interesting rhythmic clashes; act II, number 11 takes the form of a march and war song, followed by an Indian chorus and ballet. The start of act II reintroduces the motto theme heard in the overture and this is taken up by a chorus behind the scenes, while act III, number 18 has some attempt at Indian coloring, with open fifths and a repeated chant which is theatrically effective. Seen as a whole, therefore, it must be admitted that

Wallace was never lacking in good ideas, and had the ability to think in grandiose terms. His principal weaknesses were an inability to reveal individual character and a tendency towards a motleyness of styles. On occasion, however, as in his masterpiece, *Maritana,* his music rose above that of mediocrity and no doubt served as a model for later English composers, especially Sullivan, anticipations of whom may be found on more than one occasion.

—Gerald Seaman

WALLERSTEIN, Lothar.

Producer. Born 6 November 1882, in Prague. Died 13 November 1949, in New Orleans, Louisiana. Studied art and music in Prague and Munich and attended the Geneva Conservatory; initially a physician; in 1908 began teaching piano at the Geneva Conservatory; répétiteur, Dresden Court Opera, 1909; conductor, Poznán, 1910-14; stage director, Breslau, 1918-22; Duisburg, 1922-24; Frankfurt, 1924-27; producer, Vienna Staatsoper, 1927-38; Salzburg Festival, 1926-37; conducted at Teatro alla Scala, Milan, 1929; fled Austria, 1938 (later became U.S. citizen); established opera school at The Hague, 1939; stage director, Metropolitan Opera, 1941-46; first resident stage director, New Orleans Opera.

Opera Productions (selected)

The Island God, Metropolitan Opera, 1942.
Lucia di Lammermoor, Metropolitan Opera, 1942.
La serva padrona, Metropolitan Opera, 1942.
Ilo e Zeus, Metropolitan Opera, 1942.
Tristan und Isolde, Metropolitan Opera, 1942.
Tosca, Metropolitan Opera, 1942.
Boris Godunov, Metropolitan Opera, 1942.
Der Rosenkavalier, Metropolitan Opera, 1943.
Norma, Metropolitan Opera, 1943.
Aida, New Orleans Opera.
Pelléas et Mélisande, Holland Festival, Amsterdam, 1948.

Publications

About WALLERSTEIN: books–

Berger, A. *Über die Spielleitung der Oper. Betrachtungen zur musikalischen Dramaturgie Dr. Lothar Wallersteins.* Graz, 1928.

*   *   *

Czechoslovakian producer Lothar Wallerstein was one of the most distinguished opera producers of his generation. His collaboration with conductor Clemens Krauss and designer Ludwig Sievert in Frankfurt from 1924 to 1927 has been called the golden age of the Frankfurt Opera. Their subsequent collaboration in Vienna saw a needed period of stability and a carefully rehearsed ensemble in that often volatile opera house. Richard Strauss called on Wallerstein's keen sense of theater to help with the composition of several of his last operas and the revision of other works.

Wallerstein was a man of many talents. Before moving to production, he had trained and worked as a conductor and as a medical doctor. Wallerstein took a traditional, realistic approach to opera production. While not an innovator like Max Reinhardt or given to fastidious matching of movement to music like Carl Ebert, he nevertheless gave imaginative and creative productions, especially in his collaborations with Krauss and Sievert. When called to Vienna by Franz Schalk, he teamed up with the old master designer, Alfred Roller, whose constant search for striking stagings stimulated his new colleague. Wallerstein was at his best in handling crowds, although he did not leave his principals to their own stand-and-gesture devices. At the Metropolitan Opera after he left Austria, Wallerstein established acting classes for young singers in which he coached them extensively in their roles.

Like his colleague Krauss, Wallerstein was liable to tinker with the structure of operas in an attempt to improve what he saw as failings in their dramatic construction. Their Verdi cycle in Vienna saw productions of Franz Werfel's rewriting of *La forza del destino, Don Carlos,* and *Simon Boccanegra.* Richard Strauss, who as a young man had revised Gluck's *Iphigénie en Tauride* in an attempt to eliminate what he saw as its deficiencies, turned his attention to Mozart's *Idomeneo* in 1930 and asked Wallerstein to rewrite the libretto in German. Besides transforming the character of Elektra into a priestess named Ismene, Wallerstein completely rearranged the last two acts. Act II was changed to begin with Idomeneo's "Fuor del mar;" Ilia's aria that originally preceded it now came later, and her "Zeffiretti lusinghieri" was moved

from the third act. Strauss recomposed the opera as an almost Wagnerian through-composed, leitmotivic score.

Wallerstein also turned his hand to one of Strauss's own operas, *Die ägyptische Helena,* at the composer's request. After Hofmannsthal's death, Strauss decided to rework two aspects of the second act: the structure, in which the mixing scene, hunt, and Altair's aria are each divided into two parts and separated by other material; and some overly philosophical or overly subtle passages that obscure information necessary for the plot. Whether the dramatic structure needed improvement is open to question, but Wallerstein did a competent job of uniting the halves of the various scenes. The best of his revisions clarifying the plot is a new prayer (which evolves into a new trio) for Aithra in which she calls upon Poseidon's aid. This is a beautiful and dramatically effective text. Wallerstein also played a role in the creation of the last of Strauss's operas, when the composer consulted him in his collaborations with Joseph Gregor.

Wallerstein's wide range of expertise can be seen in his early work in Frankfurt. Before moving there he guest-produced Hermann Goetz's version of *The Taming of the Shrew, Der widerspenstigen Zähmung,* as well as Gluck's *Orfeo ed Euridice.* Wallerstein's and Krauss's first production in Frankfurt was *Pique Dame,* and they began a new *Der Ring des Nibelungen* in their first season. After Wallerstein fled Austria he founded an opera school at The Hague, then spent the last years of his life in the United States, where he staged productions at the Metropolitan Opera. One anecdote of Wallerstein's term there sums up his professionalism: he demanded that his name be removed from a production of *Die Walküre* because he believed he had not had enough time and resources to do it well.

—David Anderson

WALLMANN, Margherita.

Director, choreographer. Born 22 June 1904, in Vienna. Dancer, then choreographer for the Salzburg Festival, 1933-39; ballet director in Vienna, 1934-39; at Teatro Colón, Buenos Aires, 1937-48; produced a number of operas at Teatro alla Scala in the 1950s; director of productions, Monte-Carlo, beginning 1972. Directed world premieres of Milhaud's *David,* 1955; Poulenc's *Les dialogues des Carmélites,* 1957, Pizzetti's *Assassinio nella cattedrale,* 1958, and *Clitennestra,* 1965; Martin's *Mystère de la nativité,* 1960; Castelnuovo-Tedesco's *Mercante de Venezia,* 1961; Becaud's *Opéra d'Aran,* 1962; Rossellini's *Leggende del ritorno,* 1966, and *La reine morte,* 1973; Lesur's *Andrea del Sarto,* 1969; Bondeville's *Antoine et Cléopatre,* 1974; Bentoiu's *Hamlet,* 1974. Awards: First prize for opera staging, Salzburg Festival; Toscanini Medal; Puccini Prize; Max Reinhardt Medal.

Opera Productions (selected)

Orfeo ed Euridice, choreographer, Salzburg, 1933.
Oberon, choreographer, Salzburg, 1934.
Falstaff, choreographer, Salzburg, 1935.
Don Giovanni, choreographer, Salzburg, 1935.
Alceste, Milan, Teatro alla Scala, 1954.
Medea, Milan, Teatro alla Scala, 1954.
Norma, Milan, Teatro alla Scala, 1955.
David, Milan, Teatro alla Scala, 1955.

Un ballo in maschera, Milan, Teatro alla Scala, 1957.
Les dialogues des Carmélites, Milan, Teatro alla Scala, 1957.
Assassinio nella cattedrale, Milan, Teatro alla Scala, 1958.
Mystère de la nativité, Salzburg Festival, 1960.
Mercante de Venezia, Florence Festival, 1961.
Opéra d'Aran, Paris, 1962.
Lucia di Lammermoor, New York, Metropolitan Opera, 1964.
Clitennestra, Milan, Teatro alla Scala, 1965.
La gioconda, New York, Metropolitan Opera, 1966.
Leggende del ritorno, Milan, Teatro alla Scala, 1966.
Robert le diable, Florence Festival, 1968.
Andrea del Sarto, Marseilles, 1969.
La reine morte, Opéra Monte-Carlo, 1973.
Antoine et Cléopatre, Rouen, 1974.
Hamlet, Marseilles, 1974.
Francesca da Rimini, Rome, 1976.
Turandot, Buenos Aires, Teatro Colón, 1977.
La forza del destino, Los Angeles, 1982.

Publications

By WALLMANN: book–

Les Balcons du ciel. Paris, 1976.

About WALLMANN: articles–

de Weerth, E. "Superwoman." *Opera News* 23 (6 April 1959): 26.
"Le retour de Marguerite Wallmann." *Musica* 94/January (1962): 12.
Downes, E. "A Chic, Blond Dynamo." *The New York Times* 114 (11 October 1964): 11, section 2.
"Determined Lady." *Opera News* 29 (17 October 1964): 14.
Legge, W. "Opera on Three Fronts." *Hi Fidelity/Musical American* 16/March (1966): 138.
Kessler, G. "Ein Zeitgenosse Verdis." *Opernwelt* 6/June (1967): 23.
———. "Ehrung für Toscanini." *Opernwelt* 7/July (1967): 21.
———. "Unverwelkter Charme und pikante Komik." *Opernwelt* 5/May (1968): 30.
———. "Primadonnenglanz in der Scala." *Opernwelt* 7/ July (1968): 24.
Weaver, W. "Maggio Musicale—A Dying Institution?" *Hi Fidelity/Musical American* 18/August (1968): MA28.
Wutschek, P. "Man muss als Regisseur Respekt vor dem Komponist haben—Gespräch mit der italienischen Regisseurin Margherita Wallmann." *Opernwelt.* 3/March (1976): 31.
Fabian, Imre. "Es ist das beste Theater der Welt." *Opernwelt* 20/5 (1979): 43.

*   *   *

In the period following the Second World War, before the emergence of the producer as a dominant force in the opera-house, Margherita Wallmann was well known for her productions of large-scale works in which the chorus plays an important part. A firsthand knowledge of choreography and mime enabled Wallmann to create stagings which were effective in the world's biggest opera-houses, where intimate gestures tend to get lost and the overall stage picture is what counts.

Born in 1904 into a cultured milieu in Vienna, Wallmann renounced a religious vocation and became a dancer. She went to Berlin where she benefited from the instruction of Mary Wigman, one of the early "high priestesses" of modern dance. Wallmann showed considerable promise both as a dancer and as a choreographer. After dancing in her own balletic version of Gluck's *Orfeo* (with Ted Shawn in the title role) at the Munich International Dance Festival, she was engaged by Bruno Walter to choreograph the dances in the operatic *Orfeo* at the 1933 Salzburg Festival, where she had already appeared with her own dance group. This was followed by choreography for *Oberon* (1934), *Falstaff* and *Don Giovanni* (both in 1935).

While rehearsing a revival of *Orfeo* in Vienna on a split-level set (which later became one of her trademarks), Wallmann fell and was badly injured. Unable to continue as a performer, she devoted the remainder of her career to choreography and, in particular, to producing opera. The clarity of her stagings meant that Wallmann was much in demand by the opera-houses with the most stage space to fill—Vienna, Paris, Buenos Aires, Chicago, and particularly the Teatro alla Scala. She worked with designers who understood the need for massive, painted sets (Benois, Wakhévitch, Fiume) to provide the spectacle that audiences wanted, especially in Verdi and other nineteenth–century operas. She also made incursions into an earlier repertory which also called for tightly controlled production, such as *Alceste* and *Medea,* both with Callas at the Teatro alla Scala in 1953 and 1954.

Wallmann also choreographed many new ballets and staged the first performances of many new operas, often with a religious theme (e.g. Pizzetti's *Assassinio nella cattedrale*), and she was able to combine this with her talent for memorable crowd scenes in what was, perhaps, her most famous production—the world premiere of Poulenc's *Les dialogues des Carmélites* at the Teatro alla Scala in 1957, a staging which was reproduced in several other leading opera houses.

As styles of opera production evolved, Wallmann's approach began to fall out of favor. An attempt at collaborating with the more avant-garde designer Svoboda on *Robert le diable* for the 1968 Florence Festival was not well received; the starkness of the sets was not what was expected of a Wallmann staging. Smaller theaters continued to use Wallmann's services, though generally on operas which were smaller in scale than those with which she made her name (e.g. *Katya Kabanová* in Trieste). Her career ended in Monte Carlo where she had been appointed director of productions in 1972.

—Oliver Smith

LA WALLY.

Composer: Alfredo Catalani.

Librettist: Luigi Illica (after the novella by Wilhelmine von Hillern *Die Geyer-Wally*).

First Performance: Milan, Teatro alla Scala, 20 January 1892.

Roles: Wally (soprano); Stromminger (bass); Walter (soprano); Giuseppe Hagenbach of Sölden (tenor); Vincenzo Gellner of Hochstoff (baritone); Afra (mezzo-soprano); Wanderer (bass); chorus (SSATTBB).

*   *   *

In 1878, the Lombard artist Tranquillo Cremona provoked something of a scandal with a painting of the twenty-four-year-old Alfredo Catalani. Cremona and his subject were fellow *scapigliati* (roughly "bohemians"), disaffected adherents of a Milanese artistic movement. The disturbing portrait, a canvas entitled *L'edera* ("Ivy"), depicted the pale and sickly Catalani—he would die of tuberculosis—desperately clinging to a robust but aloof Milanese beauty, Elisa Cagnoli. Glacial indifference is only one aspect of the *femme fatale,* a figure that resonated in the arts throughout the period of the "decadence." The *femme fatale* was equally apt to figure as the predatory female, whether in the paintings of Gustave Moreau, the poetry of Stéphane Mallarmé, or the operas of Catalani. If the *femme fatale* tended to take on the aspect of Salomé or the Sphinx in France, Catalani's deep involvement with German Romanticism led him to discover her image in German folklore. In Catalani's penultimate opera, *Loreley* (1890), the hero struggles with the conflicting passions he experiences for his beloved, a mortal girl, and the water nymph Loreley. For his last opera, Catalani turned to a novella by Wilhelmine von Hillern, *Die Geyer-Wally* or *The Vulture Wally,* which was serialized in a Milanese newspaper.

In the libretto that Luigi Illica prepared for Catalani— Illica was later the co-librettist for a number of Puccini's operas—the vulturine aspects of Catalani's eponymous heroine are notably downplayed. Unlike the novella, the opera ends with the destruction of ill-fated lovers at Nature's hands, as Boito had suggested it should. Like the novella's heroine, however, the opera's heroine is closely identified with nature. *La Wally* is set in the village of Hochstoff in the Tyrol, where the wealthy landowner Stromminger's seventieth birthday is

Catalani's *La Wally,* cover of first edition of score, with illustration by Adolfo Hohenstein, 1892

being celebrated. When Hagenbach and other huntsmen from neighboring Sölden turn up to boast of their exploits, Stromminger and Hagenbach come to blows. Stromminger's untamed daughter Wally intervenes, but Hagenbach and Wally are immediately smitten with one another, to Stromminger's chagrin. Stromminger promises Wally's hand to his bailiff, Gellner, but Wally spurns Gellner's advances and is exiled from her father's estate. At the feast of Corpus Christi a year later, Gellner taunts Wally, who has inherited her father's estate, with the information that Hagenbach is engaged to marry Afra. When Wally insults Afra, Hagenbach is urged to avenge Afra by stealing a kiss from Wally during the torrid kissing dance, the *Walzer del bacio.* Dancing with Wally rekindles Hagenbach's passion for her, however, and, oblivious of the crowd, he wrests a passionate kiss from her. The crowd cheers, publicly humiliating Wally, and Hagenbach is dragged away by his companions before he can assure Wally of his true feelings. Wally promises Gellner her hand if he will kill Hagenbach. That night Gellner pushes Hagenbach into a deep ravine and leaves him for dead. Regretting the events she has set in motion, Wally manages the dangerous feat of climbing down into the ravine and rescuing the unconscious Hagenbach. Wally retires to the seclusion of the mountains where Hagenbach ultimately pursues her. Hagenbach defends his kiss as a token of his true feelings for Wally, who confesses her role in Hagenbach's near-fatal accident. A violent snowstorm has developed and Hagenbach is killed in an avalanche. Wally leaps from a precipice, joining Hagenbach in death.

Although Illica's characters remain paste-board, his libretto afforded Catalani abundant opportunity for rendering nature and for bringing the atmosphere of a Swiss mountain village vividly to life. Catalani certainly possessed the evocative power necessary for such atmospheric effects. Throughout the opera, Wally and her relationship to nature are simply yet effectively suggested with horn fifths and tremolo strings. With its Alpine setting, the fourth act in particular provided Catalani with opportunities for evoking nature. The act opens with an atmospheric prelude suggesting the endless desolation of the Alps and Wally's own isolation within them. Essentially a ternary form, the prelude is spun out of a somber and modally inflected motive. Catalani drew upon a number of sources within his immediate Italian tradition for a vivid depiction of the brewing snow storm later in the act. From the last act of Verdi's *Rigoletto,* Catalani borrowed the device of an offstage chorus humming in imitation of the sound of the wind. With the duet of the reunited Wally and Hagenbach ("Vieni, vieni; una placida vita"), Catalani managed a synthesis of the "Lontano, lontano" duet from Boito's *Mefistofele* and the duet for Helen of Troy and Faust from the same opera.

Catalani's real allegiance was to German Romantic opera of the pre-Wagnerian variety, and he was sometimes hampered by the framework of the conventions that he inherited from the Italian tradition in which he labored, yet the operas of Carl Maria von Weber that he so much admired no more provided a model for Catalani's symphonic continuities than did the operas of Catalani's Italian predecessors. Catalani was a master of transitions and atmospheric effects, but he was less successful in spinning out the sort of formal melodies necessary for creating fully convincing set pieces. Consequently, *La Wally*'s set pieces can seem inert within the context of so flexible a continuum. In *La Wally* Catalani made supple and effective use of all of those forms of musical declamation intermediate between aria and recitative, of various effects of *arioso* and *parlando.* There is a measure of true motivic development in the opera, too, as in the opening tableau with its villagers and hunters, where horn calls and fragments of folk melody are woven into a developing contrapuntal fabric. In addition to other forms of melodic reminiscence and recall, Catalani even used what can only be considered a Wagnerian leitmotiv for the music expressing the love at first sight of Wally and Hagenbach, which is transformed on its successive reappearances. Such developmental and motivic processes required the freedom to be found in the varied patches between the opera's set pieces, and the quasi-symphonic continuity throughout much of *La Wally* is remarkable not only for its originality, but for its independence from the alternative models provided by Wagnerian music drama and Verdi's *Otello*. At the same time, *La Wally* is not without full-blown lyrical melody, as its most famous excerpt, "Ebben? Ne andrò lontana," serves to confirm, although Catalani adapted this aria from a *Chanson groënlandaise* he had composed in 1876. This aria has found a wide public in recent years through Jean-Jacques Beineix's 1981 film, *Diva*.

—David Gable

WALTER [Schlesinger], Bruno.

Conductor. Born 15 September 1876, in Berlin. Died 17 February 1962, in Beverly Hills, California. Studied with H. Ehrlich, L. Bussler, and R. Radecke at the Sterns Conservatory in Berlin, beginning 1884; public performance as a pianist, 1885; vocal coach and conductor at the Cologne Opera, 1893; assistant conductor under Gustav Mahler at the Hamburg Stadttheater, 1894; second conductor at the Stadttheater in Breslau, 1896-97; principal conductor in Pressburg, 1897; principal conductor in Riga, 1898-1900; conductor at the Berlin Royal Opera, 1900-01; assistant to Mahler at the Vienna Court Opera, 1901; guest conducted the Royal Philharmonic Society, London, 1909; conducted the posthumous premiere of Mahler's *Das Lied von der Erde,* 1911, and his Symphony No. 9, 1912; Royal Bavarian Generalmusikdirektor in Munich, 1913; conducted the "Bruno Walter Concerts" with the Berlin Philharmonic, 1921-33; conducted at the Salzburg Festival, 1925; guest conducted the New York Symphonic Society, 1923, 1924, 1925; conductor of the Städtische Oper in Berlin-Charlottenburg, 1925-29; succeeded Furtwängler as conductor of the Gewandhaus Orchestra, Leipzig, 1929; associate conductor of the New York Philharmonic with Toscanini, 1932-35; his various concerts in Berlin were cancelled with the rise of the Nazis, 1933; music director of the Vienna State Opera, 1936, but lost this post as a result of the annexation of Austria, 1938; in France, where he obtained citizenship, and then in America, where he became a naturalized citizen; guest conductor of the National Broadcasting Company Symphony Orchestra, 1939; conducted at the Metropolitan Opera, New York, beginning 1941; conductor and musical adviser of the New York Philharmonic, 1947-49; regular guest conductor of the New York Philharmonic until 1960; numerous conducting engagements in Europe, 1949-60. Walter was also a composer, whose works include two symphonies.

Publications

By WALTER: books–

Von den moralischen Kräften der Musik. Vienna, 1935.
Gustav Mahler. Vienna, 1936; 2nd ed., 1957; English translation, 1937.
Theme and Variations: an Autobiography. New York, 1946.
Von der Musik und vom Musizieren. Frankfurt am Main, 1957; English translation, 1961.
Walter-Lindt, L., ed. *Briefe 1894-1962.* Frankfurt am Main, 1970.

interviews–

"Bruno Walter in Conversation with Albert Goldberg." In *Conversations with Conductors,* edited by Robert Chesterman. London, 1976.

About WALTER: books–

Komorn-Rebhan, M. *Was wir von Bruno Walter lernten.* Vienna, 1913.
Stefan, P. *Bruno Walter.* Vienna, 1936.
Gavoty, B. *Bruno Walter.* Geneva, 1956.
Schonberg, H. *The Great Conductors.* New York, 1967.

articles–

Mann, T. "To Bruno Walter on his 70th Birthday." *Musical Quarterly* October (1946).

*   *   *

In 1889 Bruno Walter saw Hans von Bülow conduct, which persuaded him to pursue conducting as a career for himself. His first operatic performance was in Cologne, where he conducted Lortzing's *Der Waffenschmied,* but it was his move to a similar post as assistant conductor in Hamburg under Mahler which was to exert a significant musical influence upon him for the rest of his life.

By the turn of the century, Walter was a colleague of Strauss and Karl Muck in Berlin, where he conducted his first *Ring* and Gilbert and Sullivan's *The Mikado* to critical acclaim. He also conducted Siegfried Wagner's *Der Bärenhäuter* in the approving presence of the composer's mother Cosima, and gave the first performance of Pfitzner's opera *Der arme Heinrich* in Berlin. Problems with opera house politics and Prussian officialdom, however, which Walter was totally unsuited to deal with, led him to accept Hans Richter's vacated post in Vienna as a Kapellmeister under his mentor Mahler in 1901.

As Mottl's successor in Munich, Walter supported many contemporary composers and over a decade gave the first performances of such operas as Pfitzner's *Palestrina* and Korngold's *Violanta* and the *Ring des Polykrates.* It was as an interpreter of Mozart's operas ("the Shakespeare of opera" as Walter described him), however, that Walter's reputation has endured. He was renowned for meticulous preparation, particularly in the ensemble operas of Mozart, but his pre-war work in London was also famous for brilliant interpretations of Wagner's *Ring* and Strauss' *Der Rosenkavalier* with Lotte Lehmann, Elisabeth Schumann and Richard Mayr. The advent of Hitler's Third Reich forced him to flee to America

Bruno Walter, Berlin, 1929

and his first operatic engagements at the New York Metropolitan Opera were his famous performances of *Fidelio, Don Giovanni* and Smetana's *The Bartered Bride.*

In his conducting Walter was not obsessed by technique, saying that "by concentrating on precision one arrives at technique, but by concentrating on technique one does not arrive at precision." His highly refined and cultured personality was dominated by an excessive humility toward the work and its composer, and this often resulted in deferential performances full of warmth and lyricism yet lacking the rhythmic stamp of a strong interpretation. Sir Adrian Boult said of Walter that "he was so immersed in the music he was doing that he managed somehow to convey it just as telepathically I think as by putting it into the stick." Where this might have been seen as a weakness on the concert platform, it became a strength in the opera house where his flexibility in rhythm enabled him to provide a fluid, rhapsodical and adaptable accompaniment for his singers. Lotte Lehmann said that "when he accompanies me I have the feeling of the utmost well-being and security. The end of his baton is like a cradle in which he rocks me."

The essence of Walter's conducting lay in a nobility and compassion which exuded romanticism in his smoothly flowing tempi; these were never hurried and succeeded in conveying to his listeners a deep love for the work in hand. His tactful and highly moral outlook, coupled with a totally non-dictatorial approach to his players encouraged a chamber music-like input from them which surprised and disarmed them. He placed much emphasis on tone production and color, but in his own words "my concern was for a higher clarity than that of sound: to wit, the clarity of musical meaning."

—Christopher Fifield

WALTON, (Sir) William (Turner).

Composer. Born 29 March 1902, in Oldham, Lancashire. Died 8 March 1983, in Ischia, Italy. Married: Susana Gil Passo. Enrolled in the Cathedral Choir School at Christ Church, Oxford; entered Christ Church, but never graduated; string quartet performed at the International Society for Contemporary Music, 1923; composed *Crown Imperial March* for the coronation of King George VI, 1937; honorary doctorate from Oxford University, 1942; knighted in 1951; composed *Orb and Sceptre* for the coronation of Queen Elizabeth II, 1953.

Operas

Troilus and Cressida, Hassall, 1947-54, London, Covent Garden, 1954; revised, 1975-76.
The Bear (extravaganza), P. Dehn (after Chekhov), 1965-67, Aldeburgh, 1967.

Other works: orchestral works, film scores, choral and solo vocal works, chamber and instrumental music, incidental music.

Publications

By WALTON: interviews–

Warrack, J. "Sir William Walton talks to John Warrack." *The Listener* 80 (1968): 176.

About WALTON: books–

Howes, F. *The Music of William Walton.* 2 vols. London, 1942-43.
Howes, F. *The Music of William Walton.* London, 1965; 2nd ed., 1974.
Ottaway, Hugh. *William Walton.* Sevenoaks, 1972.
Tierney, Neil. William Walton. London, 1985.
Smith, Carolyn J. *William Walton: a Bio-bibliography.* Westport, Connecticut, 1988.
Walton, Susana. *William Walton: Behind the Facade.* Oxford, 1988.
Kennedy, Michael. *Portrait of Walton.* Oxford, 1989.
Craggs, Stewart R. *William Walton: a Catalogue.* Oxford, 1990.
———. *A Walton Source Book.* Aldershot, 1992.

articles–

Zoete, B. de. "William Walton." *Monthly Musical Record* 59 (1929): 321, 356.
Frank, A. "The Music of William Walton." *The Chesterian* 20 (1939): 153.
Foss, H.J. "William Walton." *Musical Quarterly* 26 (1940): 456.
Evans, E. "William Walton." *Musical Times* 85 (1944): 329, 364.
Avery, K. "William Walton." *Music and Letters* 28 (1947): 1.
Mitchell, D. "Some Observations on William Walton." *The Chesterian* 26 (1952): 35, 67.
Warrack, John. "Walton's *Troilus and Cressida.*" *Opera* December (1954).
Reizenstein, F. "Walton's *Troilus and Cressida.*" *Tempo* no. 34 (1954-55): 16.
Craggs, Stewart R. "*Façade* and the Music of Sir William Walton." *Library Chronicle of the University of Texas at Austin* nos. 25-26 (1984): 101.

*　　*　　*

Walton, in his long career, wrote only one full-length opera, *Troilus and Cressida* (1947-1954), and one comic opera, *The Bear* (1964-1967). In addition, however, he had begun a correspondence with Cecil Grey in May 1941 about the possibility of collaborating on an opera. The composer Carlo Gesualdo, Prince of Venosa, who in 1590 had murdered his wife and lover, was their chosen subject. This collaboration lasted until the end of 1942 when Walton's interest began to fade.

Three events may have helped to re-kindle his interest in opera after World War II. The first was the production of Britten's *Peter Grimes* at Sadler's Wells in June 1945; the second was the acceptance of a commission from the British Broadcasting Corporation in February 1947 for an opera for broadcasting; and the last was the encouragement of Alice Wimbourne, who brought Walton in contact with his librettist, Christopher Hassall.

Lady Wimbourne died the following year, and Walton later traveled to Buenos Aires for a Performing Right Society conference. Here he met Susana Gil, and, despite parental opposition, married her. They returned to England and decided to settle on the island of Ischia in the Bay of Naples. Here Walton returned to the writing of *Troilus and Cressida* with renewed vigor.

The Mediterranean atmosphere consequently had a bearing on *Troilus and Cressida* which relates to the operatic tradition of Verdi and Puccini more than to any other. The treatment of the opera's subject is derived from Chaucer (Shakespeare's play was the least helpful version of the legend) and resulted in the romantic theme of a lonely, frightened individual seeking shelter from an alien world.

The opera contains some of Walton's best music and may be regarded as the culmination of his composing career. Many features of his previous music re-appear: the vocal and dramatic intensity of *Belshazzar's Feast* (Walton brought a superb sense of theater to the opera); the tension and the ferocity of the First Symphony; the sensuousness, beauty and brilliance of both the Viola Concerto and the Violin Concerto. The music of Pandarus also includes elements from *Façade*, besides being influenced by Britten.

Walton was always anxious to write another opera, and indeed announced, in May 1963, that he was beginning work on a new opera, again with Christopher Hassall as librettist. Alas, this was not to be because of Hassall's untimely death.

In October 1958, however, Walton had been offered (and accepted) a commission by the Koussevitsky Music Foundation in the Library of Congress for an opera which finally resulted in his one-act extravaganza, *The Bear.* The idea of turning Chekhov's play into an opera originated with Peter Pears, who had suggested to Walton that he should read Chekhov's three vaudevilles or jests. From these, he chose *The Bear.*

Walton started to compile his own libretto, but then decided that he required the services of a professional, and Paul Dehn, one of the most versatile writers of his generation, was brought in. Work on the opera was brought temporarily to a halt in January and February 1965 because of Walton's grave ill-health, and it was not until the summer that he was really fit to work again.

Composition continued until April 1967 when it was decided that the first performance should be given at the Aldeburgh Festival the following June. The opera contains much satirical wit and parody; indeed, among the composers parodied are Offenbach, Tchaikovsky, Poulenc, Verdi, Britten (*A Midsummer Night's Dream*), and Walton himself (*Troilus and Cressida* and *Façade*).

Walton always wanted to write a companion piece for *The Bear* and eventually found a suitable librettist, the writer Alan Bennett, in 1980. It was originally hoped that the English Music Theatre Company might perform the proposed opera at Aldeburgh, in celebration of the composer's 80th birthday in March 1982. Unfortunately, this plan had to be abandoned.

—Stewart R. Craggs

WAR AND PEACE [Voyna i mir].

Composer: Sergei Prokofiev.

Librettist: Sergei Prokofiev (after Tolstoy).

First Performance: concert performance, Moscow, 16 October 1944; complete performance, Moscow, Stanislavsky, 8 November 1957; revised, 1946-52.

Roles: Prince Andrei Bolkonsky (baritone); Count Rostov, Ilya (bass); Natasha (soprano); Pierre (tenor); Hélène (contralto or mezzo-soprano); Anatole (tenor); Dolokhov (bass); Prince Kutuzov, Michael (bass); Denisov (baritone); Prince Bolkonsky, Nicolai (bass); Princess Marie (mezzo-soprano); Sonya (mezzo-soprano); Princess Mariya Akhrosimova (soprano); Karataev (tenor); more than fifty additional lesser roles, many of which may be doubled; chorus (SSATTBB).

Publications

articles—

Sabinina, M. " 'Voyna i mir'." *Sovetskaya muzika* no. 12 (1953).

Keldïsh, Ya. "Eshcho ob opere 'Voyna i mir'." *Sovetskaya muzika* no. 7 (1955).

McAllister, R. "Prokofiev's Tolstoy Epic." *Musical Times* 113 (1972): 851.

Brown, M.H. "Prokofiev's *War and Peace:* A Chronicle." *Musical Quarterly* 63 (1977): 297.

Prokofiev's *War and Peace* occupied his attention from 1941 until his death in 1953, during which time it underwent several transformations, including placing greater emphasis on melody and on the part played by Kutuzov and the Russian army of 1812. Lasting over four hours if given in its entirety, *War and Peace,* like its literary counterpart, is one of the great Russian epics.

The opera opens with an overture, though this is often replaced by a choral epigraph, using Tolstoy's and Denis Davydov's original words extolling the strength of the Russian people in the face of aggression. Scene i opens in the house and garden of Count Rostov at Odradnoe in May 1809. Prince Andrei Bolkonsky, recently widowed, reads by the window, but is roused from his melancholy by the sound of young girls' voices. The lyrical duet of Natasha and Sonya, as they comment on the beauty of the spring night, fills Andrei with fresh hope. Scene ii takes the form of a ball given by a grandee of Catherine's day in St Petersburg, 1810. As a chorus is sung, Count Rostov appears with Natasha and Sonya, followed by Count and Countess Bezukhov (Pierre and Hélène). Pierre Bezukhov approaches his old friend Prince Andrei and suggests that he invite Natasha to dance with him. Natasha has already attracted the attention of the dissolute Prince Anatole Kuragin (Hélène Bezukhov's brother).

The next scene takes place a year later, in February 1812. Natasha is engaged to Prince Andrei, who has been obliged by his father, who is opposed to the marriage, to spend a year abroad. In a soliloquy Natasha expresses her love for Andrei. In scene iv, Anatole gives Natasha a letter in which he suggests that they elope.

In scene vi, which takes place in the house of Mariya Akhrosimova where Natasha and Sonya are staying in the count's absence, Dunyasha the chambermaid warns Natasha that Sonya has told Mariya about the intended elopement. When Anatole appears, his way is barred by the butler; after a struggle, Anatole and Dolokhov make their escape. Akhrosimova remonstrates with Natasha, who runs off in tears. Pierre Bezukhov enters and on Mariya's instigation tries to talk to Natasha, telling her that Anatole is already married. Natasha, overwhelmed with remorse and shame at her stupidity, tries to commit suicide but is saved by Sonya. Scene vii takes place in Pierre's study the same night. When alone with Anatole, Pierre demands that Natasha's love letter agreeing to the elopement be handed over to him, which is done. In a soliloquy Pierre muses on the uselessness of his life and confesses that he himself loves Natasha. News is brought in that Napoleon is at the Russian frontier.

Part II: War opens on the Field of Borodino, preceding the battle on 25 August 1812. Against a background of patriotic soldiers' songs, Prince Andrei and Lieutenant-Colonel Denisov discuss the possibility of cutting Napoleon's lines of communication with a partisan detachment. Andrei's thoughts go back to Natasha and the unhappiness she has brought him. While two German generals discuss military strategy, Andrei tells Pierre that the Russians will win since they are defending their homeland. They embrace. Field Marshall Kutuzov appears and is acclaimed by his men, whom he inspires. The battle commences.

Scene ix takes place later the same day in the French camp, where Napoleon's confidence is shaken as reports indicate that the battle is not going as expected. Scene x occurs two days later in a peasant hut at Fili, where Kutuzov is discussing tactics with his generals. Is it better to try to defend Moscow and possibly risk total defeat, or to abandon Moscow and keep the army intact? Kutuzov decides to sacrifice the old capital. Left alone he expresses his patriotism in a moving aria.

Scene xi takes place in September-October. Moscow, captured by the French, has been set on fire. The soldiers are looting. Pierre learns that the Rostovs have left the city with some of the wounded, among whom (though unknown to Natasha) is Andrei. Pierre himself is arrested and sentenced to death as an arsonist; though reprieved, he remains a prisoner. Napoleon walks through the city, saddened by the outcome, though marveling at the Russian people's resilience and courage.

In scene xii Prince Andrei is lying in a hut outside Moscow, mortally wounded. In his delirium he dreams of Natasha, Moscow, his country. Natasha enters, dressed in white, and begs for forgiveness. They reaffirm their love and, in a poignant scene, he dies.

The final scene takes place in November 1812 on the road to Smolensk. A blizzard is raging, and at the end of Napoleon's retreating army is a column of Russian prisoners, among whom are Pierre and Karataev. Karataev falls to the ground exhausted and is shot. However, partisans appear who attack the French and free Pierre, followed by a group of women partisans. In the final moments Kutuzov and soldiers enter. "The enemy is beaten" cries the Field Marshall, "Russia is saved." All join in a final patriotic chorus.

It is a tribute to Prokofiev's skill that he was able to condense Tolstoy's enormous work into a coherent whole and produce an opera that nearly always holds one's attention. To achieve this, the action is interspersed with a variety of numbers—orchestral interludes, dances, arias, duets, and choral items, including some of the composer's most lyrical numbers. The splendid duet in scene i, Natasha's soliloquy in scene iii, Pierre's monologue in scene vii, Kutuzov's aria in scene x are only some of the impressive numbers, while mention must be made of the numerous choruses in a distinctive national idiom which give the opera a unique flavor. Running through the opera is a series of motto themes, knowledge of which enhances one's understanding of what is taking place, since the motives are sometimes used in the manner of the Wagner *Leitmotiv* to refer to characters not present on the stage or to convey general concepts, such as the idea of patriotism and victory. Though *War and Peace* is inferior to Prokofiev's earlier works such as *The Love for*

Three Oranges and *The Fiery Angel*, it is not only an outstanding example of the Soviet ideological thinking of the time but manages to transcend national boundaries. Prokofiev himself, rightly or wrongly, regarded it as his finest work.

—Gerald Seaman

WARD, Robert (Eugene).

Composer. Born 13 September 1917, in Cleveland. Studied with Howard Hanson and Bernard Rogers at the Eastman School of Music; B. Mus. from Eastman, 1939; studied composition with Frederick Jacobi and conducting with Albert Stoessel at the Juilliard School of Music; M. A. from Juilliard, 1946; taught at the Juilliard School, 1946-56; Vice President and Managing Editor of Galaxy Music Corporation, 1956-66; Pulitzer Prize for *The Crucible,* 1962; chancellor of the North Carolina School of the Arts, 1967-72; elected to the National Institute of Arts and Letters, 1967; Mary Duke Biddle Professor of Music at Duke University, 1979.

Operas

Publishers: Associated, Galaxy, Highgate.

Pantaloon [later, *He Who Gets Slapped*], B. Stambler (after Andreyev), 1955, New York, City Center Opera Company, 1959; revised, 1973.
The Crucible, B. Stambler (after A. Miller), New York, 1961.
The Lady from Colorado, B. Stambler (after H. Croy), Colorado, Central City Opera, summer 1964.
Claudia Legare, B. Stambler (after Ibsen, *Hedda Gabler*), 1973, Minneapolis, Minnesota Opera Company, 14 April 1978; revised, 1978.
Abelard and Heloise. J. Hartman, Charlotte, North Carolina, Charlotte Opera Association, 1981.
Minutes till Midnight, Ward and D. Lang, 1978-82, Miami, New World Festival of the Arts, June 1982.

Other works: orchestral works, vocal works, instrumental music.

Publications

About WARD: articles–

Stambler, B. "Robert Ward." *American Composers Alliance Bulletin* 4/no. 4 (1955): 3.
Fleming, S. "Robert Ward." *HiFi/Musical America* 32/no. 5 (1982): 4.

*   *   *

Robert Ward's emergence as an opera composer did not occur until 1956 when the opera *Pantaloon* was given in New York by the Juilliard School where Ward was an instructor. The opera was based on the play *He Who Gets Slapped* by Leonid Andreyev. A colleague at Juilliard, Bernard Stambler, collaborated with Ward in adapting the play for an opera. The work was later published under the original play title and also performed by the New York City Center Opera Company in 1959. For many of Ward's admirers this opera remains one of his finest operatic works, and Ward stated much later that it was "still as good an opera an any I've written."

The success which Ward and Stambler had with *He Who Gets Slapped* led them to collaborate on three more works: *The Crucible* (1961), *The Lady from Colorado* (1964), and *Claudia Legare* (1978). Most important was *The Crucible,* which was premiered in 1961. This opera was based on Arthur Miller's play of the same name and recreates the atmosphere of the New England witch trials of colonial America. The work has become Ward's most successful and important opera and received the 1962 Pulitzer Prize and the New York Music Critics' Circle Award. *The Lady from Colorado* was based on a book by Homer Croy. Commissioned by the Central City (Colorado) Opera House, the opera was performed fifteen times during the 1964 summer season. The work was an attempt to blend serious opera with light, musical comedy and the result received mixed reviews. Ross Parmenter wrote in the *New York Times,* "The "Lady" is nearly all corn. Its chief characters are stereotyped and the music, far from having naivete of genuine innocence, has the professionalism of opera companies turning their hands to a "paint your wagon" type of Broadway show." In contrast, Allen Young's review in *Musical America* states "the melodies are expansive and goodnatured, its rhythms supple and varied achieving a consistently mobile and buoyant texture."

It is perhaps the disappointment in the reception of *The Lady From Colorado* that Ward turned his attention away from opera for several years. However, in the 1970s, he resumed his operatic compositions and completed *Claudia Legare,* a commission from the New York Center Opera Company, in 1977. The work was based on the play *Hedda Gabler* by Henrik Ibsen. The opera was first given 14 April 1978 in Minneapolis by the Minnesota Opera Company. A large work of four acts, the opera was revised into a chamber version in 1978 to be more accessible for performance. Ward maintains his conservative, tonal style in this work.

Ward's next opera was *Abelard and Heloise,* which was a commission from the Charlotte (North Carolina) Opera Association. The premiere was given in 1982 by the Charlotte Opera Association. The librettist was Jan Hartman and the story deals with the famous love affair in the Middle Ages between Abelard and his beloved Heloise. Ward's musical style is well-suited for this story and the result is a romantic and dramatic opera which may be compared to *The Crucible* for its favorable critical reviews. Claire McPhail of the Charlotte Post wrote, "It is romantic, dramatic, poignant and completely theatrical. Visually, dramatically and aurally the opera reaches a majestic height in the Cathedral of Sens."

Ward's most recent opera is *Minutes till Midnight.* A large work of nine scenes in three acts, the opera was commissioned by the Southeast Bank of Florida and was given its premiere at the New World Festival of the Arts in Miami, June 1982. The librettist was Daniel Lang. For the first time Ward was challenged by a story which deals with a current topic. The main character is Emil Roszak, a physicist, who worked on the atomic bomb and is on the threshold of completing a formula for the use of cosmic energy. His assistant, Chris, envisions this new energy source as the panacea for the world's ills. Unfortunately Roszak is summoned to the White House to develop his cosmic energy into a cosmic bomb as the enemy is also working on one. Roszak is tormented by the idea that the world will be destroyed, and he boldly publishes his formula in an international journal. The message of the opera appears to be that all information, especially that which can endanger mankind, should be made available to all. The opera received considerable criticism in that "the

music is too lyrical and sweet to underscore such mind-boggling consequences as global destruction and the annihilation of mankind." It is hoped a revival of the opera will enable further consideration of the work and its importance as an American opera.

Robert Ward has made considerable contributions to the American operatic repertoire. He has shown his ability to project a definite nationalistic character into his operas and deserves consideration as one of the outstanding composers of American opera. Although his musical style is conservative, his eclecticism enables him to utilize not only American jazz, cowboy songs, and non-western melodies but also moments which can only be attributed to the influence of Arnold Schoenberg and his followers. The resultant operatic works have been accessible to most audiences and his style offers a link with the past. It is difficult to make a critical judgment on the totality of Ward's operas at this point in time, but there is general agreement that his Pulitzer Prize winning opera *The Crucible* is an important contribution to the American repertoire of the twentieth century.

—Robert F. Nisbett

WARREN [Varenov], Leonard.

Baritone. Born 21 April 1911, in New York City. Died 4 March 1960, on the stage of the Metropolitan Opera House, New York City, during a performance of *La forza del destino.* Studied with Sidney Dietsch, Giuseppe De Luca, Giuseppe Pais, and Riquardo Picozzi. Sang in Radio City Music Hall chorus; Metropolitan Opera debut as Paolo in *Simon Boccanegra,* 1939; for twenty-two seasons, the company's leading "Italian" baritone; twenty-six roles included Rigoletto, Iago, Germont, Escamillo, Falstaff, Macbeth, Simon Boccanegra, Scarpia; created the role of Ilo in Menotti's *Island God,* 1942; at San Francisco, 1943-56; Chicago, 1944-46; Teatro alla Scala debut, 1953; Soviet tour 1958.

Publications

About WARREN: articles–

Miller, Philip L. "Leonard Warren 1911-1960." *Opera* 6/ June (1960): 396.
Riemens, L. "Warren, Leonard." In *Le grandi voci* ed. by R. Celletti, Rome, 1964.
Webster, M. "Everyone Suddenly Burst Out Singing . . ." *Opera Quarterly* 7/2 (1990): 37.

*   *   *

Before American baritone Leonard Warren made his Metropolitan Opera debut (as Paolo in Verdi's *Simon Boccanegra* in 1939), he had virtually no operatic experience. His only previous appearance on the operatic stage was in excerpts from Verdi's *La traviata* and Leoncavallo's *I pagliacci* the previous year. After Paolo, his roles at the Metropolitan Opera, in the order in which he assumed them, were Rangoni and Shchelkalov in Musorgsky's *Boris Godunov* (1939), Valentin in Gounod's *Faust* (1939), the Herald in Wagner's *Lohengrin* (1940), Amonasro in Verdi's *Aida* (1940), Barnaba in Ponchielli's *La gioconda* (1940), Escamillo in Bizet's *Carmen* (1940), Alfio in Mascagni's *Cavalleria rusticana* (1941), the High Priest in Gluck's *Alceste* (1941), the High Priest in Saint-Saëns's *Samson et Dalila* (1941), Giorgio Germont in Verdi's *La traviata* (1942), Ilo in Menotti's *The Island God* (1942), Enrico in Donizetti's *Lucia di Lammermoor* (1942), Count di Luna in Verdi's *Il trovatore* (1943), Carlo in Verdi's *La forza del destino* (1943), Renato in Verdi's *Un ballo in maschera* (1943), Tonio in Leoncavallo's *I pagliacci* (1943), Verdi's *Rigoletto* (1943), Verdi's *Falstaff* (1944), Iago in Verdi's *Otello* (1946), Verdi's *Simon Boccanegra* (1949), Gérard in Giordano's *Andrea Chénier* (1954), Scarpia in Puccini's *Tosca* (1955), Don Carlo in Verdi's *Ernani* (1956), and Verdi's *Macbeth* (1959). In 1944 he participated in the legendary Red Cross benefit performance at Madison Square Garden of the final act of *Rigoletto,* conducted by Arturo Toscanini. By the end of his career, which was cut short by his death on the stage of the Metropolitan Opera House in 1960 during a performance of Verdi's *La forza del destino,* Warren had become the company's leading Verdi baritone. Although his career took him to a number of other opera houses, notably in Rio de Janiero, in Mexico City, and at the Teatro alla Scala, as well as on a tour of Russia in 1958, the overwhelming majority of Warren's performances were at the Metropolitan Opera.

Warren was one of a long line of American baritones; many saw him as the successor to Lawrence Tibbett, and such latter-day American baritones as Sherrill Milnes have acknowledged Warren's influence on their careers.

With a voice marked by a beautiful, rich tone, a firm line, power, and an easy upward extension beyond high A, Warren was a nearly ideal singer for the Verdi baritone roles, most of which lie relatively high, and it was largely in these parts, notably Iago, Rigoletto, Simon Boccanegra, and Macbeth, that his fame lies. His greatness lay in the sheer sound of his voice. His virtues were more vocal than dramatic, although his voice had a basically dramatic sound; he worked hard—with success—to improve his acting ability as his career progressed. The sound of his voice has been described as mellifluous, generous, imposing, and sympathetic. The voice was employed with a mastery of phrasing founded on a solid, confident technique. He was adept at producing soft notes that retained their body, as well as powerful, ringing high notes. Toward the end of his career, his voice became somewhat dryer, with a more pronounced vibrato, but the overall sound was retained. The beauty and smoothness of Warren's voice reaped benefits outside the Verdi canon as well, not least in the verismo roles he sang, as seen, for example, in the chilling elegance he brought to Puccini's Scarpia.

Warren made relatively few recordings of complete operas, The roles he did record include Rigoletto (1950, under Cellini), Count di Luna (1952, under Cellini, and 1959, under Basile), Renato (abridged, 1955, under Mitropoulos), Amonasro (1955, under Perlea), Macbeth (1959, under Leinsdorf), Giorgio Germont (1956, under Monteux), Scarpia (1957, under Leinsdorf), Barnaba (1957, under Previtali), and the Don Carlo in *La forza del destino* (1958, under Previtali).

—Michael Sims

WEBER, Carl Maria (Friedrich Ernst), Freiherr von.

Composer. Born 18 November 1786, in Eutin, Oldenburg. Died 5 June 1826, in London. Married the singer Caroline

Brandt. His first teacher was his stepbrother Fritz, a student of Haydn; studied piano with J.P. Heuschkel in Hildburghausen, 1796; studied counterpoint with Michael Haydn in Salzburg, 1797; studied singing with Valesi (J.B. Wallishauser) and composition with J.N. Kalcher in Munich, 1798-1800; further study with Michael Haydn in Salzburg, 1801; studied the works of previous masters under the tutelage of the Abbé Vogler in Vienna, 1803; conductor of the Breslau City Theater, 1804; Musik-Intendant to Duke Eugen of Württemberg at Schloss Carlsruhe, 1806; private secretary to Duke Ludwig in Stuttgart, and music teacher to his children, 1807; his opera *Silvana,* Frankfurt 1810, successful; piano concert tours of Frankfurt, Würzburg, Nuremberg, Bamberg, Weimar, Gotha and other German cities; conductor of the German opera in Prague, 1813; asked by the King of Saxony to take over the German Opera Theater in Dresden, 1817; treated for tuberculosis in Marienbad, 1824; led the enormously successful performances of his *Oberon* in London.

Operas

Edition: *C.M. von Weber: Musikalische Werke: erste kritische Gesamtausgabe.* Edited by H.J. Moser et al. Augsburg and Brunswick, 1926-.

Die Macht der Liebe und des Weins (Singspiel), 1798 [lost].
Das Waldmädchen, C. von Steinsberg, Freiburg, 24 November 1800 [fragments].
Peter Schmoll und seine Nachbarn, J. Türk (after C.G. Cramer), 1801-02, Augsburg, March? 1803.
Rübezahl, J.G. Rhode, 1804-05 [fragments].
Silvana, F.C. Hiemer (after *Das Waldmädchen*), 1808-10, Frankfurt am Main, 16 September 1810.
Abu Hassan (Singspiel), F.C. Hiemer (after *The 1001 Nights*), 1810-11, Munich, Residenz, 4 June 1811.
Der Freischütz, F. Kind (after J.A. Apel and F. Laun, *Gespensterbuch*), 1817-21, Berlin, Schauspielhaus, 18 June 1821.
Die drei Pintos, T. Hell (after C. Seidel), 1820-21, Leipzig, Neues Stadt-Theater, 20 January 1888 [unfinished; finished by G. Mahler].
Euryanthe, H. von Chezy, 1822-23, Vienna, Kärntnertor, 25 October 1823.
Oberon, J.R. Planché (after C.M. Wieland), 1825-26, London, Covent Garden, 12 April 1826.

Other works: incidental music, sacred and secular vocal works, chamber music, piano pieces.

Publications/Writings

By WEBER: books—

Hell, T., ed. *Hinterlassene Schriften von Carl Maria von Weber.* Dresden, 1828; 2nd ed., 1850.
Weber, M.M. von, ed. *Carl Maria von Weber: ein Lebensbild.* Leipzig, 1866.
Weber, Caroline von, ed. *Reise-Briefe an seine Gattin Caroline.* Leipzig, 1886.
Rudorff, E., ed. *Briefe von Carl Maria von Weber an Hinrich Lichtenstein.* Brunswick, 1900.
Kaiser, G., ed. *Sämtliche Schriften von Carl Maria von Weber: Kritische Ausgabe.* Berlin, 1908.
Kaiser, G., ed. *Weber's Briefe an den Grafen Karl von Brühl.* Leipzig, 1911.

Hellinghaus, O., ed. *Karl Maria von Weber: seine Persönlichkeit in seinen Briefen und Tagebüchern und in Aufzeichnungen seiner Zeitgenossen.* Freiburg, 1924.

Hirschberg, L., ed. *Siebenundsiebzig bisher ungedruckte Briefe Carl Maria von Webers.* Hildburghausen, 1926.

Laux, K., ed. *Carl Maria von Weber: Kunstansichten.* Leipzig, 1969; 2nd ed., 1975.

Reynolds, David. *Weber in London, 1826. Selections from Weber's Letters to his Wife.* London, 1976.

Kunstansichten. Ausgewählte Schriften. Wilhelmshaven, 1978.

Warrack, John, ed. *Writings on Music.* Translated by M. Cooper. Cambridge, 1981.

Worbs, Hans Christoph. *Carl Maria von Weber: Briefe.* Frankfurt am Main, 1982.

articles–

"Letters for G. Weber." *Caecilla* 4 (1826): 302; 7 (1828): 20; 15 (1833): 30.

"14 letters to F. von Mostel, 1 to Dr Jungh." *Wiener allgemeine Zeitung* 6 (1846): 473.

Kapp, J. "Webers Aufenthalt in Berlin im August 1814 nach unveröffentlichten Briefen an seinen Braut." *Die Musik* 18 (1925-26): 641.

Kinsky, G. "Ungedruckte Briefe Carl Maria v. Webers." *Zeitschrift für Musik* 93 (1926): 335, 408, 482.

Haus, John. "Carl Maria von Weber: Unveröffentlichte Briefe." *Beiträge zur Musikwissenschaft* 20 (1978): 186.

About WEBER: books–

Brühl, C. *Neueste Kostüme auf beiden königlichen Theatern in Berlin.* Berlin, 1822.

Kind, Friedrich. *Freischütz-Buch.* Leipzig, 1843.

Schumann, R. *Gesammelte Schriften über Musik und Musiker.* Leipzig, 1854; 4th ed., 1914.

Benedict, J. *Weber.* London, 1881; 5th ed., 1899.

Servières, G. *Freischütz.* Paris, 1913.

Hasselberg, E., ed. *Der Freischütz: Friedrich Kind Operndichtung und ihre Quellen.* Berlin, 1921.

Goslich, S. *Beiträge zur Geschichte der deutschen romantischen Oper.* Leipzig, 1937.

Cornelissen, T. *Carl Maria von Webers Freischütz als Beispiel einer Opernbehandlung.* Berlin, 1940.

Schnoor, H. *Weber auf dem Welttheater: ein Freischützbuch.* Dresden, 1942; 4th ed., 1963.

Dünnebeil, H. *Carl Maria von Weber.* Berlin, 1953.

Schnoor, H. *Weber: Gestalt und Schöpfung.* Dresden, 1953.

Kron, W. *Die angeblichen Freischütz-Kritiken E.T.A. Hoffmanns.* Munich, 1957.

Mayerhofer, G. *Abermals voms Freischützen: Der Münchener Freischütze von 1812.* Regensburg, 1959.

Becker, W. *Die deutsche Oper in Dresden unter der Leitung von Carl Maria von Weber 1817-26.* Berlin, 1962.

Laux, K. *Carl Maria von Weber.* Leipzig, 1966.

Warrack, J. *Carl Maria von Weber.* London, 1968; 2nd ed., 1976.

Goslich, S. *Die deutsche romantische Oper.* Tutzing, 1975.

Csampai, Attila, and Dietmar Holland, eds. *Carl Marìa von Weber. Der Freischütz: Texte, Materialien, Kommentare.* Reinbek bei Hamburg, 1987.

Henderson, Donald, and Alice Henderson. *Carl Maria von Weber: a Guide to Research.* New York, 1990.

articles–

"Oberon, or The Elf King's Oath." *Quarterly Musical Magazine and Review* 8 (1826): 84.

Chezy, H. von. "Carl Maria von Webers Euryanthe: ein Beitrag zur Geschichte der deutsche Oper." *Neue Zeitschrift für Musik* 13 (1840): 1, 9.

Berlioz, H. "Le Freyschütz de Weber." *Voyage musicale en Allemagne et en Italie,* vol. 1, 369. Paris, 1844.

Wagner, R. "Der Freischütz in Paris." In *Gesammelte Schriften und Dichtungen,* vol. 1. Leipzig, 1871; English translation as *Richard Wagner's Prose Works,* edited and translated by W.A. Ellis, volume 7, London, 1898.

Kapp, J. "Die Uraufführung des Freischütz." *Blätter der Staatsoper* [Berlin] 1/no. 8 (1921): 9.

Abert, H. "Carl Maria von Weber und sein Freischütz." *Jahrbuch der Musikbibliothek Peters* (1926): 9; reprinted in *Gesammelte Schriften und Vorträge,* edited H. Blume, Halle, 1929; 2nd ed., 1968.

Engländer, R. "The Struggle between German and Italian Opera at the Time of Weber." *Musical Quarterly* 31 (1945): 479.

Kirby, P. "Weber's Operas in London, 1824-26." *Musical Quarterly* 32 (1946): 333.

Virneisel, W. "Aus dem Berliner Freundeskreise Webers" [includes 31 letters to F. Koch]. In *Carl Maria von Weber: eine Gedenkschrift,* edited by G. Hausswald. Dresden, 1951.

Dent, Edward J. "Der Freischütz." *Opera* March (1954).

Abert, A.A. "Webers Euryanthe und Spohrs Jessonda als grosse Opern." In *Festschrift für Walter Wiora,* 435. Kassel, 1967.

Laux, K. "In Erinnerung gebraucht" [on *Die drei Pintos*]. In *Musikbühne 76,* edited by H. Seeger. Berlin, 1976.

Jones, G. "Weber's 'Secondary Worlds': the Later Operas of Carl Maria von Weber." *International Review of the Aesthetics and Sociology of Music* 7 (1976): 219.

Warrack, John. "Oberon und der englische Geschmack." In *Musikbühne 76,* edited by H. Seeger. Berlin, 1976.

Maehder, Jürgen. "Die Poetisierung der Klangfarben in Dichtung und Musik der deutschen Romantik" [Der Freischütz]. *Aurora* 38 (1978): 9.

Stephan, Rudolf. "Bemerkungen zur Freischütz-Musik." In *Studien zur Musikgeschichte Berlins in frühen 19. Jahrhundert,* edited by Carl Dahlhaus, 491. Regensburg, 1980.

Dahlhaus, Carl. "Webers Freischütz und die Idee der romantischen Oper." *Österreichische Musikzeitschrift* 38 (1983): 381.

Finscher, Ludwig. "Weber's *Freischütz:* Conceptions and Misconceptions." *Proceedings of the Royal Musical Association* 110 (1983-84): 79.

Tusa, Michael C. "Weber's *Grosse Oper:* a Note on the Origins of *Euryanthe.*" *Nineteenth-Century Music* 8 (1984): 119.

Avant-scène opéra April (1985) [*Oberon* issue].

Avant-scène opéra January-February (1988) [*Freischütz* issue].

unpublished–

Jones, G. "Backgrounds and Themes of the Operas of Carl Maria von Weber." Ph.D. dissertation, Cornell University, 1972.

*　　*　　*

As the son of a theater director and a singer, Weber grew up with the theater in his blood, and composed his first *Singspiel* (in other words, a German play mostly set to music) when he was eleven, while as a precocious seventeen-year-old he took charge of a Breslau theater and trod on a number of toes by initiating what he saw as necessary reforms, from repertory to his orchestra's seating arrangements. After he was laid low for some weeks by his strange accident of poisoning himself with engraving acid, he found that his many enemies had reversed most of his innovations and he resigned. Already by the age of twenty he was an experienced man of the theater, although he was inclined to be disillusioned about human nature, and he went on to hold a number of important positions in major opera houses, conducting standard repertory and introducing new pieces in a way that gave him an unrivaled knowledge of opera as it existed at the time in northern Europe.

The vigor of Weber's activities as a conductor and composer was sustained throughout his comparatively short life, and it undoubtedly contributed to the brevity of his life. Indeed, it belied his uncertain health and the fact that he walked with a slight limp (and perhaps some pain also) owing to a damaged hip, and the personality expressed in his music is a genial and attractive one as well as abounding in energy and imaginative force. He was still in his twenties when he first came across the story of his most famous work, *Der Freischütz,* and when the opera was produced in 1821 it was clear that he offered a new genre of "romantic opera" (as it was designated). In *Der Freischütz,* ordinary people plausibly confront mysterious powers of good and evil in a story of love and ambition set in a Bohemian village. The music has a folk-like idiom in some numbers such as the choruses of huntsmen and bridesmaids, but in the celebrated Wolf's Glen scene in which the magic bullets are cast, the composer's orchestral mastery is to the fore (for example, in his use of horns and drums) along with his capacity for tellingly sinister harmonies. Such Gothic horrors were much to the taste of a new German middle-class audience, particularly when they were fairly sure that all would be resolved in a happy ending.

To understand what Weber aimed at, we need to have some idea of what he meant by "romantic opera," a term he applied also to his *Euryanthe* and *Oberon.* The concept of romanticism itself is vast, but one definition that this composer might have agreed with was "the addition of mystery to beauty," and folk-lore, ballads and fairy tales of all kinds provided him with supernatural and exotic elements in plenty. He called *Euryanthe* a "grand heroic-romantic opera," and it is a complex tale of love and intrigue set in twelfth century France. Its music is continuous, unlike that of *Der Freischütz* with its occasional spoken dialogue, and in it he also went further with the technique of relating persons or dramatic concepts to musical "motives" (small but recognizable melodic and rhythmic fragments) or tone colors in a way that was to flower fully half a century later with Wagner, who indeed acknowledged German music's debt to Weber. *Oberon* is really something of a pantomime, a thirteenth-century story, telling of chivalry, magic, fairies, pirates and mermaids and set in locations as far afield as Baghdad and Tunis. Weber was no stranger to such armchair travel, and even his early one-act *Singspiel* called *Abu Hassan* takes its story from the Arabian collection called *The Thousand and One Nights.*

Such adventurousness has dangers as well as advantages. We may well feel that Weber's penchant for the exotic prevented him from creating the really believable human characters we look for in opera, except perhaps for the lovers Max and Agathe in *Der Freischütz.* The craggy heroes of Wagner's operas are not for him, nor the heroines such as we find at the center of Puccini's or Massenet's, nor, for that matter, Mozart's social comment or the political and psychological insights of Verdi. But with his pioneering imaginative writing for voices and his mastery of the orchestra he is a central figure in the development of German opera, and one above all who paved the way for Wagner, not least in his use of folk-lore, and the way in which he told of the supernatural and its interaction with human beings.

—Christopher Headington

Carl Maria von Weber

WEBER, Ludwig.

Bass. Born 29 July 1899, in Vienna. Died 9 December 1974, in Vienna. Studied with Alfred Boruttau in Vienna; debut at Vienna Volksoper, 1920; at Bavarian State Opera, Munich, 1933-45; Covent Garden debut, 1936; created the Holsteiner in *Friedenstag,* 1938; at Salzburg, 1939-47; sang in first performance of von Einem's *Dantons Tod,* Salzburg, 1947; with Vienna State Opera, 1945-60; at Bayreuth, 1951-63, debuting as Gurnemanz in *Parsifal.* Specialized in Wagner and Mozart.

Publications

About WEBER: articles—

Brass, Dennis. "Ludwig Weber." *Opera* 2/June (1951): 352.

*   *   *

Although Ludwig Weber was considered one of the finest Wagnerian basses of the century, he was also famous for his portrayals of the Mozart bass roles and was a memorable Baron Ochs in Strauss's *Der Rosenkavalier.* He made his debut at the Vienna Volksoper in 1920. In 1923 he sang at the Bremen Stadttheater as Fiorello in Rossini's *Il barbiere di Siviglia.* He later appeared in the opera houses of Düsseldorf (1930), Cologne (1932), Munich (1933-45, as part of Clemens Krauss's ensemble), Vienna (from 1945), and the Bayreuth Festival (from 1951). During his long career he appeared at Covent Garden, the Salzburg Festival, the Maggio Musicale Fiorentino, La Scala, the Colón in Buenos Aires, Brussels, the Hague, Paris, and Budapest.

Weber was closely associated with the Wagnerian bass roles: Gurnemanz in *Parsifal;* Daland in *Der fliegende Holländer;* Fafner, Fasolt, Hagen, and Hunding in *Der Ring des Nibelungen;* King Mark in *Tristan und Isolde;* and Pogner and Kothner in *Die Meistersinger von Nürnberg.* Non-Wagnerian parts included the Mozart roles of Sarastro in *Die Zauberflöte,* Osmin in *Die Entführung aus dem Serail,* and the Commendatore in *Don Giovanni;* he also sang Rocco in Beethoven's *Fidelio,* Caspar in Weber's *Der Freischütz,* and Mussorgsky's Boris Godunov.

Weber created the role of the Holsteiner in the world premiere of Richard Strauss's *Friedenstag* in 1938 and appeared in the first performance of von Einem's *Dantons Tod* at Salzburg in 1947. He was also involved in two notable performances of *Die Entführung aus dem Serail:* the 1938 revival at Covent Garden under Sir Thomas Beecham, and a new production in Vienna in 1946 that starred Elisabeth Schwarzkopf as Constanze. He sang Gurnemanz in the performance of *Parsifal* given in the season that marked the reopening of Bayreuth after the Second World War in 1951. This performance highlighted the warmth and generosity of the character and moved recording producer John Culshaw to call Weber "without any doubt . . . the great Gurnemanz of his generation."

By the 1952 Bayreuth Festival, however, Weber's age had become more apparent, and his vocal problems had begun to undermine his interpretive abilities, his singing exhibiting a roughness that had not previously been apparent. By this time he benefited from a strong conductor who could keep him in check, lest his tendency toward bathos—no doubt a compensation for his declining vocal resources—would take over. He continued to sing through the 1950s, and was still singing at the Bayreuth Festival as late as 1963 (as Titurel in *Parsifal*).

Weber is remembered as an imaginative singer. His versatility is seen in an ability to encompass both the evil, dangerous characters of Wagner and the comic roles of Baron Ochs and Osmin. His portrayal of Daland, which he sang, among other times, at Covent Garden in 1937, managed to convey both the greed of the character and his genial side, a subtle, affectionate performance. He portrayed an evil Hagen—but the blackness was in the coloring of the words, not in the inherent quality of the voice—with a rich, ripe tone, a relishing of the words, and the ability to darken his sound to match the character's sinister thoughts. At the same time, he could create a sympathetic character through coloring his tone, as with his Fasolt in the 1950 Teatro alla Scala *Der Ring des Nibelungen* conducted by Furtwängler. His Osmin maintained a balance between the odious and the clownish, creating a lively, human portrait. He was less successful in the Italian repertoire, never having perfected the legato that such music requires.

Weber's recording career began with some performances as Wotan in extracts from Wagner's *Der Ring des Nibelungen* made in the early 1930s, and he recorded excerpts from *Der Rosenkavalier* as Baron Ochs under Ackermann in 1949. His participation in complete operatic recordings, other than those derived from staged performances, includes Sarastro under Karajan (1950), the First Nazarene in *Salome* under Krauss (1954), and Baron Ochs under Erich Kleiber (1954); he recorded his imposing Commendatore, still able to convey the voice of doom, under Moralt in 1955.

—Michael Sims

WEIKL, Bernd.

Baritone. Born 29 July 1942, in Vienna. Studied economics at the University of Mainz and started vocal studies in 1965. Graduated from Hanover Hochschule für Musik, 1970; debut as Tsar Peter in Lortzing's *Zar und Zimmermann,* Düsseldorf, 1970; appeared as Melot in Karajan's *Tristan* production, Salzburg Easter Festival, 1972; appeared at Bayreuth 1972-92; Vienna Volksoper debut as Billy Bigelow in *Carousel;* Covent Garden debut as Figaro in *Il barbiere di Siviglia,* 1975; Metropolitan Opera debut as Wolfram, 1977; appeared in Tokyo in 1980 and Paris in 1982; Teatro alla Scala debut as Iago, 1990; has also appeared on film and television.

*   *   *

From his first appearance in Bayreuth as Wolfram in Götz Friedrich's 1972 production of *Tannhäuser,* Bernd Weikl appeared upon the operatic firmament as a special presence, and this only two years after graduating from the Hanover School of Music. His development from lyric baritone (Lortzing, Donizetti) to roles requiring more spinto heft (Onegin, Rossini's Figaro, Hans Heiling) to Wagner's most lyrical baritone role took place so rapidly that some may have anticipated an early demise of his bright voice, even timbred through an extraordinary range, perhaps because of the rapid, expressive vibrato which gives it its special appeal and can be shaded or colored for any dramatic situation. They would not have been reckoning with the absolute control which he has exercised over every stage of his career, feeling that a voice must develop in its own way and within its own time span, never being artificially darkened or pushed for more volume. For this reason, he allowed himself much time before singing dramatic baritone roles, partly because he at first had difficulty finding the kernel or vocal center of gravity, as he describes it. In search of this personal ideal he has sought out the most distinguished teachers in several centers, forces himself to test his own development by the most rigorous standards and regularly returns to a famous vocal coach to have the state of his art analysed. Waiting until he was vocally and spiritually ready for a role has been a first principle. His first Hans Sachs was at thirty-nine. Though Wagner's was thirty-three, Weikl was determined not to open himself to the charge of being too young for the role, although Sachs has to be young enough to make Eva's attraction to him believable. His first Holländer was at forty-eight. By then he had left some roles behind—Rossini's Figaro, Eisenstein and Falke—and added some: Boccanegra and Iago. Nabucco may lie in the future, perhaps even Scarpia. Wotan never, although conductors constantly beleager him. He has twice been under contract to sing Falstaff, which he feels to be the great Italian counterpart of Sachs, but in each case he has cancelled because he felt his voice was too young, and he was searching for a great conductor to work on the characterization of the role with him.

Weikl is the averred enemy of jet-set opera, approving of stagione and festivals because they allow a singer to develop a role over a series of performances. He feels the best performance is often the fifth or seventh, and refuses to alternate roles in repertory that requires different vocal color.

He has made passionate appeals in print for designers to create sets which help a singer project the voice, and condemnations of directors who know nothing about vocal technique and therefore require action which hampers breath control or positions which make support of the vocal tone impossible. He wishes more conductors would discuss their roles with the singers, learn to phrase vocally, breathe with the singers and adjust orchestral volume to the characteristics of each voice. Opera, he feels, must be approached (by the artist) with love, not egomania or calculating commercialism.

—James Helme Sutcliffe

WEILL, Kurt.

Composer. Born 2 March 1900, in Dessau. Died 3 April 1950, in New York. Married: singer/actress Lotte Lenya. Studied privately with Albert Bing in Dessau, 1914-18; studied with Humperdinck and Krasselt at the Berlin Hochschule für Musik, 1918; opera coach in Dessau; conductor at the theater in Lüdenscheid; studied privately with Busoni in Berlin, 1921; completed his *Berliner Symphonie*, 1921; collaboration with Brecht on *Die Dreigroschenoper*, Berlin 1928 (200 years after the premiere of Gay and Pepusch's *The Beggar's Opera*); in Paris, London, and then the United States, 1935; United States citizen, 1943.

Operas and Musicals

Der Protagonist, G. Kaiser, 1924-25, Dresden, 27 March 1926.
Royal Palace (ballet-opera), Goll, 1925-26, Berlin, Staatsoper, 2 March 1927.
Na und?, F. Joachimson, 1926-27 [not performed; lost].
Der Zar lässt sich photographieren, Kaiser, 1927, Leipzig, 18 February 1928.
Mahagonny (Songspiel), B. Brecht, 1927, Baden-Baden, 17 July 1927; revised as *Aufstieg und Fall der Stadt Mahagonny,* 1927-29, Leipzig, Neues Theater, 9 March 1930.
Die Dreigroschenoper (play with music), B. Brecht and E. Hauptmann (after John Gay, *The Beggar's Opera*), 1928, Berlin, Theater am Schiffbauerdamm, 31 August 1928.

Happy End (play with music), E. Hauptmann and B. Brecht, 1929, Berlin, Theater am Schiffbauerdamm, 2 September 1929.
Der Jasager (school opera), B. Brecht, 1930, Berlin Radio, 23 June 1930.
Die Bürgschaft, C. Neher, 1930-31, Berlin, Städtische Oper, 10 March 1932.
Der Silbersee, G. Kaiser, 1932-33, Leipzig, Altes Theater, 23 February 1933.
Der Kuhhandel (operetta), R. Vambery, 1934 [not performed]: revised as *A Kingdom for a Cow* (musical comedy), R. Arkell and D. Carter, London, Savoy, 28 June 1935.
Der Weg der Verheissung (biblical drama), Werfel, 1934-35 [not performed]; revised as *The Eternal Road,* L. Lewisohn, 1935-36, New York, Manhattan Opera House, 7 January 1937.
Johnny Johnson (fable), P. Green, 1936, New York, 44th Street, 19 November 1936.
Knickerbocker Holiday (operetta), M. Anderson, 1938, New York, Ethel Barrymore, 19 October 1938.
Ulysses Africanus (play with music), M. Anderson, 1939 [incomplete].
The Firebrand of Florence (operetta), E.J. Mayer and I. Gershwin, 1944, New York, Alvin, 22 March 1945.
Street Scene (Broadway opera), E. Rice and L. Hughes, 1946, New York, Adelphi, 9 January 1947.
Down in the Valley (college opera), A. Sundgaard, 1945-48, Bloomington, Indiana, School of Music, 15 July 1948.

Other works: film scores, incidental music, ballets, orchestral works, vocal works, chamber and instrumental music.

Publications

By WEILL: articles–

contribution to Kenedi, János, ed. *Film + zene = filmzene? Irások a filmzenérol.* Budapest, 1978.

About WEILL: books–

Wagner, G. *Weill und Brecht: das musikalische Zeittheater.* Munich, 1977.
Die Komische Oper Berlin in drei Jahrzehnten: Fotos, Entwürfe, Notate, Dokumente. Berlin, 1979.
Kowalke, Kim H. *Kurt Weill in Europe.* Ann Arbor, Michigan, 1979.
Sanders, Ronald. *The Days Grow Shorter: the Life and Music of Kurt Weill.* London, 1980.
Jarman, Douglas. *Kurt Weill: an Illustrated Biography.* Bloomington, Indiana, 1982.
Brecht und die Musik. Edited under the auspices of the Verband der Theaterschaffenden der DDR. Berlin, 1984.
Engelhardt, Jürgen. *Gestus und Verfremdung: Studien zum Musiktheater bei Strawinsky und Brecht/Weill.* Munich and Salzburg, 1984.
Schebera, Jürgen. *Kurt Weill: Leben und Werk mit Texten und Materialien von und über Kurt Weill.* Königstein, 1984.
Kowalke, Kim H., ed. *A New Orpheus: Essays on Kurt Weill.* New Haven, 1986.
Drew, David. *Kurt Weill: a Handbook.* Berkeley, 1987.
Cook, Susan C. *Opera for a New Republic: the "Zeitopern" of Krenek, Weill, and Hindemith.* Ann Arbor, 1988.
Mercado, Mario R. *Kurt Weill: a Guide to his Works.* New York, 1989.

Spoto, Donald. *Lenya: a Life*. New York and London, 1989.

Hilton, Stephen. *Kurt Weill: The Threepenny Opera*. Cambridge, 1990.

articles–

Horenstein, J. "Kurt Weill: 'Der Protagonist'." *Musikblätter des Anbruch* 8 (1926): 225.

Schrenk, W. "Der Protagonist." *Blätter der Staatsoper* [Berlin] no. 7 (1928): 8.

Pringsheim, K. "Kurt Weill." *Blätter der Staatsoper* [Berlin] no. 9 (1928): 1.

Machabey, A. "Kurt Weill et le théâtre musical allemand contemporain." *Revue d'Allemagne* 3 (1931): 317.

Bekker, P. "Von der 'Rose' bis zur 'Bürgschaft'." *Die Musik* 25 (1932): 7.

Courcy, G. de. "New Opera by Kurt Weill." *Musical America* 52 (1932): 5, 41.

Machabey, A. "Kurt Weill et le drame lyrique allemand." *Revue d'Allemagne* 7 (1933): 632.

Thomson, Virgil. "Most Melodious Tears." *Modern Music* 11 (1933): 13.

Einstein, A. "A German Version of 'The Beggar's Opera'." *Radio Times* 1 February (1935): 13.

Blitzstein, M. "Weill Scores for 'Johnny Johnson'." *Modern Music* 14 (1936): 44.

Mitchell, D. "Kurt Weill's 'Dreigroschenoper' and the German Cabaret-opera in the 1920s." *The Chesterian* 25 (1950): 1.

Blitzstein, M. "On Mahagonny." *Score* no. 23 (1958): 11.

Drew, D. "Brecht versus Opera: some Comments." *Score* no. 23 (1958): 7.

Skulsky, A. "Rise and Fall of the City of Mahagonny." *American Record Guide* October (1958): 113.

Hartung, G. "Zur epischen Oper Brechts und Weills." *Wissenschaftliche Zeitschrift der Martin-Luther-Universität* 8 (1959): 659.

Drew, D. "The History of Mahagonny." *Musical Times* 104 (1963): 18.

———. "Weill's School Opera." In *Opera 66*, edited by C. Osborne, 169. London, 1966.

Brock, Hella. "Brechts Bedeutung für die Musikerziehung" [*Der Jasager*]. *Musik und Gesellschaft* 28 (1978): 72.

Ringer, Alexander L. "Weill, Schönberg und die 'Zeitoper'." *Die Musikforschung* 33 (1980): 465.

Rienäcker, Gerd. "Thesen zur Opernästhetik Kurt Weills." *Jahrbuch der Musikbibliothek Peters 1980* 3 (1981): 126.

Kahnt, Hartmut. "Die Opernversuche Weills und Brechts mit Mahagonny." In *Musiktheater heute*, edited by Hellmut Kühn, 63. Mainz, 1981.

Collisani, Amalia. "*Der Jasager*: musica e 'distacco'." *Rivista italiana di musicologia* 18 (1982): 310.

Rorem, Ned. "Notes on Weill." *Opera News* 48 (1984): 12.

Ruf, Wolfgang. "Gebrauchsmusik in der Oper: Der 'Alabama-Song' von Brecht und Weill." In *Analysen: Beiträge zu einer Problemgeschichte des Komponierens. Festschrift für Hans Heinrich Eggebrecht zum 65. Geburtstag*, edited by Werner Breig et al., 411. Wiesbaden, 1984.

Kowalke, Kim H. "Accounting for Success: Misunderstanding *Die Dreigroschenoper*." *Opera Quarterly* spring (1989).

* * *

Kurt Weill's music occupies a unique position in the history of musical theater and opera, and he represents to scholars of theatrical music one of the most enigmatic figures in twentieth century music. While in the midst of a highly successful career in the European theater, where he was regarded as one of the bright lights of contemporary German composition, Weill fled his native continent, came to America in 1935, and radically altered his compositional style to accommodate the musical idiom of the Broadway stage. As a result of his attempt to integrate his personal style effectively into the popular American musical theater and to compose "the American opera," we possess a series of works that often transcend the usual boundaries of plot/theme and musical sophistication found on the Broadway stage. Because of this extraordinary adjustment in idiom and technique, Weill presents to the music critic one of the most difficult of all careers to assess.

Weill's earliest works, including the opera *Der Protagonist* (1925) with which he established his reputation, utilize a complex contrapuntal and harmonic vocabulary influenced by the Germanic/Austrian musical language inherited and developed by Arnold Schoenberg and his followers. However, with his next work, *Der neue Orpheus* (1925, cantata for soprano, solo violin and orchestra), he embarked on a "new type of expression" that embraced sociological goals and a simpler musical idiom incorporating popular elements. His next opera, *Royal Palace* (1927), incorporated these new materials into a theatrical work for the first time. For the remainder of the 1920s and the early 1930s he made a conscious effort to write his works in a more accessible vein for a wider audience. Each of these introduces popular musical styles and forms, and shows, to a small extent, the influence of jazz. Eventually this shift in emphasis proved to be the turning point in his theatrical career, and helped bind together many of the seemingly disparate elements that appear in his work.

Two of Weill's most widely known operas date from this time: *Die Dreigroschenoper* (1928) and *Aufstieg und Fall der Stadt Mahagonny* (1929), both with librettos by Bertolt Brecht. Also during this time Weill wrote the first of his school operas, *Der Jasager* (1930, also with Brecht), a work that has affinities with the "Gebrauchsmusik" idiom of Paul Hindemith and the didactic operas of Hanns Eisler. Together with Brecht, he helped develop a kind of socially relevant musical theater, *Zeitoper*, and laid the groundwork for the "epic theater." His later American works would further explore and exploit the popular styles introduced here, but within the context of the Broadway theater.

With the world premiere of the three-act opera *Die Bürgschaft* in 1932, Weill believed he had again created the foundation for a new opera form, the promise of which was unfortunately thwarted by the political situation that eventually sent Weill on to America.

In September, 1935, Weill and his wife Lotte Lenya arrived in New York City for the production of his Biblical drama *The Eternal Road*. Undoubtedly one of the most significant sights he saw in those first few months in America was a rehearsal of George Gershwin's *Porgy and Bess* (1935). When he had completely absorbed the production before him, he recognized immediately that his vision of writing an American opera presented a real possibility.

Certain aspects of Weill's European thought became integral to his theoretical approach in America. Similarly, many of his goals for the theater remained constant, such as trying to write music accessible to a wide variety of listeners. It should come as no surprise then that when Weill arrived in America he chose to work primarily in the Broadway theater. He realized wisely that if he wanted to write relevant works

Kurt Weill with his wife, singer/actress Lotte Lenya, at the time of the 1928 premiere of *Die Dreigroschenoper* (*The Threepenny Opera*)

for the dramatic stage comparable to those he had already done in Europe, his outlet for performances would be restricted to that on Broadway. No other medium in this country could compare favorably with the subsidized theater in which he had worked in Europe. The Metropolitan Opera at that time was not in the habit of staging or commissioning commercial fare of the type he wanted to write. Rather than accept Broadway as a limiting medium, he utilized it to attempt his own new brand of musical theater that could offer new possibilities and forms for integrating text and music. Clearly, his thought processes and musical instincts for the theater remained steadfast despite the obvious change in perspective.

One of Weill's primary goals in the United States was to write a definitive American opera, using indigenous American materials and sources. He believed that this could be achieved only in the "living American theater," that is, on the Broadway stage. As Weill modified his musical language for the Broadway stage, he nevertheless maintained a concern for socially relevant themes, and wrote works that, for the most part, belie the mainstream of the traditional Broadway musical theater. Weill's search for the right combination of elements and circumstances for an opera production became quite determined, almost obsessive at times. His folk opera *Down in the Valley* (composed 1945-48, and originally conceived as a radio opera) certainly contained the indigenous raw material for an American opera, utilizing as it did five representative folk songs, but it failed to satisfy his desire for

a professional opera on Broadway. Ultimately he believed that *Street Scene* (1947) fulfilled this role.

Perhaps the most important and influential decision Weill made early in his European career was to work primarily with playwrights, so that he could take advantage of the modern theatrical techniques they offered. Similarly, in America, Weill generally eschewed the traditional Broadway approach toward collaboration which brought together established lyricists and book writers. He had already worked with several of Europe's most outstanding playwrights, such as Bertolt Brecht (*Die Dreigroschenoper*), Georg Kaiser (*Der Protagonist*), and Caspar Neher (*Die Bürgschaft*) (to name a few), and was to collaborate with some of the finest American playwrights of the 1930s and 1940s, such as Paul Green (*Johnny Johnson*), Maxwell Anderson (*Lost in the Stars*), and Elmer Rice (*Street Scene*), among others. This decision unquestionably influenced his choice of librettos and helped develop in him a theatrical experience and acumen deliberately calculated for operatic diversity.

While most critics tend to divide Weill's career into two radically independent stages, it now seems much more evident that the American career evolved almost inevitably from his European one. Weill confirmed this view near the end of his life when he succinctly summarized his personal objectives as a composer. In his notes to the recording of his Broadway opera *Street Scene* he stated: "Ever since I made up my mind, at the age of 19, that my special field of activity would be the theatre, I have tried continuously to solve, in my own way, the form problems of the musical theatre, and through the years I have approached these problems from all different angles." This remark represents one of the most important and fundamental considerations for understanding Weill's entire career. If his relationship to opera and musical theater in general is viewed as a constant effort to develop new directions and paths, then this statement throws into relief the wide variety of works he composed for the theater.

Weill was never satisfied with the musical theater as he had inherited it, and he was never satisfied completely with his own efforts on its behalf. When he stated in the same notes cited above that all of his works prior to *Street Scene* represent "stepping stones" toward that work's composition, he implied that all of his works are integrated in some manner. Each individual work along the way reveals through its form a link in his continued search for an adequate means to express his artistic vision. It also explains why, in an attempt to convey the underlying meaning of that form, his works display such a wide variety of descriptive titles and genres.

Nearly all of Weill's theatrical works skirt or straddle the lines between the usually accepted genres. To consider any of his European works as operas in the traditional sense of the word would alter its meaning almost beyond comprehension. Likewise none of his Broadway works falls into any traditional type; rather they tend to create their own autonomous categories. In fact, he usually designated his operas by various distinctive titles to suggest their general form and means of expression: *Die Dreigroschenoper* was called a "Play with music"; *Der Jasager* a "School opera"; *Down in the Valley* a "Folk-opera"; and *Street Scene* "An American Opera." The generic description functions as a reminder that the works stand outside the usual boundaries prescribed by opera.

Weill scholar Kim Kowalke has demonstrated in his book *Kurt Weill in Europe* that Weill's application of certain compositional elements and techniques unite the European works. It should not seem surprising that some of these same elements appear, albeit somewhat altered, in the American works, thus transcending their original purpose. In addition, Weill's highly sophisticated musical vocabulary provided him with a means of organization and musical variety not always available to the popular songwriter. As a result, the musical continuity of his American works—*Street Scene* in particular—suggests a direct influence from his earlier theatrical career in Europe. In fact, the mixture of popular elements, jazz-derived idioms, and cliché, and the attempt at tight musical organization, represents in some ways a remarkable continuation of his late European technique.

Superficially, the popular musical techniques remain his most faithful and consistent strain between the two musical worlds of the European and America theater. However, some of the compositional procedures in *Street Scene* vividly recall the more complex European techniques discussed in detail by Kowalke. Also, because both the European and American careers embrace many of the same ideological goals, the connection between them is less tenuous than often perceived, despite the disguise of a different musical language and medium. It is these connections, rather than the disparities, that make of Weill's music and career one of the most influential, innovatory, adventurous, and original contributions to twentieth century opera and musical theater.

From 1925 until his death in 1950, Weill wrote a series of works which run the gamut of theatrical subject matter and musical style, ranging from the expansive *Aufstieg und Fall der Stadt Mahagonny* and *Die Bürgschaft,* to his school operas *Der Jasager* and *Down in the Valley,* and finally to the combination of Broadway and traditional operatic elements in *Street Scene.* The result was a dramatic legacy distinguished by its diversity, innovative intentions, and ultimately by its overall musical content.

—William Thornhill

WEINBERGER, Jaromir.

Composer. Born 8 January 1896, in Prague. Died 8 August 1967, in St Petersburg, Florida. Married: Hansi Lemberger. Studied with Křička and Hofmeister at the Prague Conservatory; studied with Max Reger in Leipzig; taught at the Ithaca Conservatory, New York, 1922; returned to Europe, and taught in Bratislava, Prague, and Vienna; moved to the United States, where he settled in St Petersburg, Florida, 1939.

Operas

Publishers: Associated, Boosey and Hawkes, H.W. Gray, Universal.

Kocourkov, c. 1927 [not performed].
Shvanda the bagpiper [Švanda Dudák]. M. Brod and M. Kareš, Prague, 27 April 1927.
Die geliebte Stimme [Milovany Hlas]. Weinberger, Munich, 28 February 1931.
The outcasts of Poker Flat [Lidé z Pokerflatu]. M. Kareš (after B. Harte), Brno, 19 November 1932.
Frühlingssturm, Berlin, 1933.
Apropo co dela Andula.
A Bed of Roses [Na ruzich ustlano] (operetta), Prague, 1934 [lost].
Wallenstein [Valdštejn]. M. Kareš (after Schiller), Vienna, 18 November 1937.
Cisar pan na tresnich [lost].

Other works: orchestral works, vocal works, chamber and instrumental music, piano pieces.

Publications

By WEINBERGER: articles–

"Zur Kompositionen von Volksliedtexten." *Österreichische Musikzeitschrift* 17 (1962): 231.

About WEINBERGER: articles–

Erhardt, O. "Schwanda and the Czech Folk Opera." *Sackbut* 11 (1930): 23.
Balatka, A. "J. Weinberger, M. Brod, i M. Kares." *Divadelni list* 8 (1932): 142, 169; 9 (1933): 2, 10, 37.
Lee, A. "Jaromir Weinberger." In *A Critic's Notebook,* 72. Boston, 1943.
Lindlar, H. ed. "Jaromir Weinberger." In *Tschechische Komponisten,* vol. 8, *Musik der Zeit,* 37. Bonn, 1954.
Kushner, David Z. "Jaromir Weinberger (1896-1967): from Bohemia to America." *American Music* 6 (1988): 293.

*   *   *

Jaromir Weinberger, composer of one of this century's greatest box office successes, the folk opera *Švanda Dudák* (1927), is, surprisingly, given scant attention in dictionary and encyclopedia articles dealing with Czechoslovakian music despite the national flavor of *Shvanda* and other important compositions.

A *wunderkind,* Weinberger began to compose as a child. His earliest teachers included Jaroslav Křička, Václav Talich, and Rudolf Karel. Later, at the Prague Conservatory, he produced his *Lustspiel Overture* (1913) under the supervision of Vitěslav Novák. After further study with Karel Hofmeister in Prague and Max Reger in Leipzig, he discarded an early affinity for French impressionism and began to develop the style which characterizes much of his work, a style rooted in the Bohemian national tradition of Dvořák and Smetana. From his studies with Reger and Novák, Weinberger developed a solid contrapuntal technique, an adroit blending of polyphonic textures with a coloristic use of the large Romantic orchestra, and a post-Romantic sense of harmonic structure.

Following a brief flirtation with American academic life (director of the theory and composition department at the conservatory in Ithaca, New York, fall term, 1922), Weinberger returned to Europe, where he had already established a sizable following among the critics and the public. The early piano setting of *Hatikvah* (1918), written for the Herzel Zionist group in Prague, reflects his Jewish heritage, a factor in his ultimate fate as a creative artist. Weinberger also developed in this period an affinity for the works of such American literary personalities as Walt Whitman, Mark Twain, Henry Wadsworth Longfellow, and Bret Harte. Disillusioned with the emphasis on industrialization in America, Weinberger nevertheless praised Americans for their ability to absorb complicated rhythms and melodic intervals. At that time, however, a musician needed to be established in Europe before attempting to succeed in the United States, and, indeed, that is precisely what he set about to do.

Shvanda established Weinberger as an international celebrity; the work was performed some 2000 times between 1927 and 1931, and translated into many languages. *Christmas,* inspired by old Czech Christmas carols, was another nationalistic work performed throughout Europe; in Prague, it was rendered every Christmas Eve until the German occupation brought the practice to a stop. Other compositions of the 30s include the operas *Die geliebte Stimme, The outcasts of Poker Flat* (based on a Bret Harte story), and *Wallenstein* (modeled after Schiller's tragedy). The latter introduces realistic spoken dialogue and leit-motifs.

After the rise of Nazism, Weinberger spent time in France and England before arriving in New York in January 1939. The royalties for his pre-1933 works ceased in Germany and Austria, and *Wallenstein,* which was produced in Vienna in November 1937, was placed on Hitler's index. Chancellor von Schuschnigg, the dedicatee of the opera, was sent to prison. In the United States, Weinberger achieved success with a number of orchestral, chamber, and vocal works.

Weinberger and his wife Hansi Lemberger settled in St Petersburg, Florida in January 1949. He spent virtually all his remaining years in near seclusion and sinking gradually into a deep state of melancholia. His last days were spent playing the piano almost ceaselessly. On August 8, 1967 he took an overdose of sedative drugs and expired.

An anachronism in his own time and by his own admission, Weinberger lived in the past as a composer. He saw no future in the twelve-tone method or in other avant-garde approaches to the craft of musical composition. He was at his best in the nationalistic works whose style he inherited and expanded

upon, masterly in their technique and orchestration, tuneful and colorful. *Shvanda* perhaps best exemplifies Weinberger's creative gifts.

—David Z. Kushner

WEINGARTNER, (Paul) Felix.

Conductor. Born 2 June 1863, in Zara, Dalmatia. Died 7 May 1942, in Winterthur. Married: 1) Marie Juillerat, 1891 (divorced); 2) Baroness Feodora von Dreifus, 1903 (divorced); 3) Lucille Marcel, mezzo-soprano. Studied music with W.A. Rémy in Graz, 1868; recommendation from Brahms for a stipend that allowed Weingartner to study at the Leipzig Conservatory with Reinecke, Jadassohn, and Paul, 1881-83; Mozart Prize from the Leipzig Conservatory, 1883; met Liszt, who recommended producing Weingartner's opera *Sakuntala,* Weimar, 1884; conducted in Königsberg, 1884-85, Danzig, 1885-87, Hamburg, 1887-89, and Mannheim, 1889-91; conducted the Hofoper in Berlin, 1891-98; conducted the Kaim Orchestra in Munich, 1898-1905; succeeded Mahler as music director of the Vienna Court Opera, 1908-11; conductor at the Municipal Opera in Hamburg, 1912-14; directed the Darmstadt Orchestra, 1914-18; music director of the Vienna Volksoper, 1919-24; conducted the Vienna Philharmonic, 1908-27; director of the Basel Conservatory, 1927; guest conductor, 1934-35, and director, 1935-36, of the Vienna State Opera; conducted many major European and American orchestras and opera companies; conducted *Tristan und Isolde* with the Boston Opera Company, 1912; conducted *Parsifal* at Covent Garden, 1939. Weingartner was also a composer, whose works include numerous operas and symphonies.

Publications

By WEINGARTNER: books–

Die Lehre von der Wiedergeburt und das musikalische Drama. Leipzig, 1895.
Über das Dirigieren. Berlin, 1896; 5th ed., Leipzig, 1913.
Bayreuth 1876-1896. 1897; 2nd ed., Berlin, 1904.
Die Symphonie nach Beethoven. Berlin, 1897; 4th ed., 1901; English translation, London, 1904; new English translation as *The Symphony since Beethoven,* London, 1926.
Ratschläge für Aufführungen der Sinfonien Beethovens. Leipzig, 1906; 3rd ed., 1928; English translation, London, 1907.
Akkorde: gesammelte Aufsätze von Felix Weingartner. Leipzig, 1912.
Erlebnisse eines "Königlichen Kapellmeisters" in Berlin. Berlin, 1912.
Ratschläge für Aufführung der Sinfonien Schuberts und Schumanns. Leipzig, 1918.
Eine Künstlerfahrt nach Südamerika: Tagebuch Juni-November 1920. Vienna, 1921.
Ratschläge für Aufführungen der Sinfonien Mozarts. Leipzig, 1923.
Lebenserinnerungen. 2 vols. Zurich, 1923-29; English translation as *Buffets and Rewards: a Musicians Reminiscences,* London, 1937.
Unwirkliches und Wirkliches: Märchen, Essays, Vorträge. Vienna, 1936.

Weingartner on Music and Conducting. New York, 1969.

About WEINGARTNER: books–

Krause, E. *Felix Weingartner als schaffender Künstler.* Berlin, 1904.
Hutschenruyter, W. *Levensschets en portret van Felix Weingartner.* Haarlem, 1906.
Riesenfeld, P. *Felix Weingartner. Ein kritischer Versuch.* Breslau, 1906.
Lustig, J. *Felix Weingartner. Persönlichkeiten.* Berlin, 1908.
Festschrift für Dr. Felix Weingartner zu seinem siebzigsten Geburtstag. Basel, 1933.
Jacob, W. *Felix Weingartner.* Wiesbaden, 1933.
Schonberg, H. *The Great Conductors.* New York, 1967.
Dyment, C. *Felix Weingartner: Recollections and Recordings.* Rickmansworth, 1975.

articles–

Raabe, P. "Felix Weingartner." *Die Musik* January (1908).

Felix Weingartner's career often led him into confrontation and controversy, largely due to his remote and egocentric personality dominated by his aristocratic, man-of-the-world bearing. Born at the heart of the Romantic era he nevertheless became an implacable foe of the flexible style of conducting adopted by Bülow and perpetuated by Nikisch. The *tempo rubato,* as he called it in his own memoirs, in which its

Felix Weingartner, caricature by H. Lindloff

exponents "sought to make the clearest passages obscure by hunting out insignificant details . . . these little tricks were helped out by continual alterations and dislocations of tempo; where a gradual animation or a gentle and delicate slowing-up is required, a violent spasmodic *accelerando* or *ritenuto* was made," was anathema to him. The style he most admired was that adopted by Richter, Levi and Muck, all of whom made loyalty to the printed score the prime motivation behind their musical interpretations. Indeed the *Musical Times* described Weingartner, after his London debut in May 1898, as a "thoroughly sound and sane musician, bent on reproducing the great masters *ipsissima verba,* inflicting no far-fetched new readings," and whose sense of rhythm was "enchanting; wonderful elasticity combined with absolute clearness and perfection of detail."

The other area in which Weingartner aroused a storm of argument was on the question of cuts. When he followed Mahler in Vienna as music director, Weingartner immediately reversed his predecessor's policy of performing works uncut, stating that he had "reached the conclusion that many passages of the *Ring, Tannhäuser* and even the short *Fliegende Holländer* are too long, not only in actual time but also in organic structure, dramatic necessities and (in the two first-named works) unity of style. I consider judicious cutting an artistic duty that greatly enhances the aesthetic pleasure to be obtained."

Weingartner's temperament caused particular problems in his dealings with opera houses, their managements (he ran into difficulties with Hülsen, intendant in Berlin, for example), singers, the critics (in particular Julius Korngold, who followed Hanslick on Vienna's *Neue freie Presse*), and some of the public. As Mahler's successor in the Austrian capital, Weingartner managed to antagonize everyone very soon, throwing out Roller's *Fidelio* designs, complaining about such singers as Bahr-Mildenburg, Gutheil-Schoder and Weidemann, all of whom had been virtually "sung-out" by the demanding Mahler, and having contractual difficulties with Leo Slezak and Selma Kurz.

A prolific composer himself, Weingartner harbored a jealousy of Richard Strauss (whose *Elektra* overshadowed Weingartner's own opera *Orestes*), but with other contemporary composers he showed a more positive approach. In Vienna he performed Debussy's *Pelléas et Mélisande,* Puccini's *Tosca,* Goldmark's *Wintermärchen* and d'Albert's *Tiefland.* He also took a backward glance into the nineteenth century and staged Méhul's *Joseph,* Adam's *Le postillon von Lonjumeau,* Auber's *Fra diavolo, Djamileh* and *Le domino noir,* Flotow's *Stradella,* Lortzing's *Waffenschmied, Wildschütz* and *Zar und Zimmermann* and Cornelius's *Barbier von Baghdad.*

Weingartner's first Viennese period (1908-11) ended with Berlioz's *Benvenuto Cellini,* by which time, as is invariably the case with the fickle–minded public and critics, he was favored by many who had initially opposed him. In 1934 he was recalled, a more mellowed man of seventy, and during this second tenure of only eighteen months Weingartner celebrated his golden jubilee as a conductor with *Götterdämmerung.*

Weingartner's command of stick technique was infallible, clear and precise in combining expressiveness with constant rhythm. His movement on the podium was restrained, precise yet elegant as befitting his aristocratic background, the smallest flick of the wrist or the tiniest gesture of the left hand, which characteristically had the two pairs of fingers separated by a gap. It is clear from his recorded legacy (dominated by orchestral rather than operatic music) that among his many attributes was a gift of timing which allowed the music to breathe expressively and yet maintain a regular and strict inner pulse. He had an acute awareness of dynamic gradation coupled with detailed instrumental balance, and a masterly sense of rhythm and tempo. The result might have produced a cold and calculated method of music-making, but this was far from the truth. He was capable of warm and poetic feeling despite his powers of analysis, for he had the subtlest of judgment and could produce the most delicate details when proportioning his readings.

—Christopher Fifield

WELITSCH, Ljuba.

Soprano. Born Ljuba Veličkova, 10 July 1913, in Borissovo, Bulgaria. Studied with Gyorgy Zlatov in Sofia, and in Vienna with Lierhammer; debut at Sofia Opera, in small part in *Louise*, 1934; sang at Graz, 1937-40; at Hamburg, 1941-43; at Vienna Volksoper, 1940-44; at Munich, 1943-46; sang in special Vienna performance of Strauss's *Salome*, with the composer conducting, 1944; joined Vienna Staatsoper, 1946, and made debut at Covent Garden (as Salome) during a visit by the company in 1947; sang Donna Anna in *Don Giovanni* (1948) and Amelia in *Un ballo in maschera* (1949) in Edinburgh with Glyndebourne Opera; Metropolitan Opera debut as Salome, 1949, and appeared there for four seasons; sang *Queen of Spades* at Covent Garden, 1953; final operatic role was in Egk's *Der Revisor*, Vienna, 1959; took the speaking part of the Duchess of Crakentorp in Met production of *La fille du régiment* (1972).

Publications

About WELITSCH: books–

Bonchev, Martin. *Slaveiat s ime Liubov: Liuba Velichkova.* Sofia, 1979.
Dusek, Peter, and Volkmar Parschalk, eds. *Nicht nur Tenöre: Das beste aus der Opernwerkstatt.* Vol. 2. Vienna, 1986.

articles–

Earl of Harewood, and Harold Rosenthal. "Ljuba Welitsch." *Opera* 4 (1953): 72.
"Another View." *Opera News* 55 (1990): 45.

* * *

Welitsch's name is associated above all with the role of Salome, one that she studied with the composer and sang under his direction. In London she was also particularly remembered for her performance of this opera in a once notorious production by Peter Brook, with decor by Salvador Dali. Although in retrospect this seems a fairly mild-mannered interpretation of the opera, at the time it was received by a conservative public and press, unused to any form of experimental reinterpretation, as if it were scandalous.

In her years as a member of the ensemble at Graz, and later in Munich and Vienna, Welitsch sang a large number of parts encompassing much of the soprano repertory from Cherubino in *Le nozze di Figaro* to Aida, Tosca, Senta and

Salome. Because her career reached its peak during the Second World War and its immediate aftermath, Welitsch's international renown was consequently shortlived. Her debut at the Metropolitan Opera was in 1949; by 1955 she had virtually retreated from large roles, although she continued to perform in Vienna both as an actress in drama and in character roles at the Volksoper. It is tempting to ascribe this cessation of her singing career, like that of Callas in her forties, to misuse of the natural range of her voice, stretching it from lyric to dramatic roles.

Those who heard Welitsch in her prime describe a voice of apparently limitless resources, a musicality that was of instrumental purity, wedded to a stage presence of enormous charm, warmth and fascination. Lord Harewood wrote in *Opera* (Feb 1953): "A more full-blooded and generous performer probably does not exist today" and of her Aida, "the way she dominated the great ensemble of the Triumph scene seemed to me nothing short of uncanny, and older operagoers have confirmed that they had perhaps never heard that part of the role so well realised."

On records Welitsch's generosity of breath, phrasing, for instance, "Vissi d'arte" with wonderful swelling and diminishing of tone, and seeming to employ her intake of breath for purely dramatic purposes, and her victorious attack on the repeated high notes and runs in the Csardas from *Die Fledermaus*, confirm the contemporary reports. Her top notes were compared by the conductor Boyd Neel to "a saw-mill," a characteristically unromantic description of something of the relentless security she seemed to be able to muster. The critic Philip Hope-Wallace chose her as "The most beautiful woman I know" and described her "princely/ feline stride, red-gold hair, that *strahlende sopran* . . . Welitsch sang on her nerves—clear stream of tone like Rethberg, a diamond top C like the evening star."

Of the few complete recordings of operas with Welitsch that survive, her Chrysothemis in a Beecham-conducted *Elektra*, Donna Anna in a Furtwängler *Don Giovanni* with Gobbi in the title role, and a *Salome* from the Metropolitan Opera, all confirm that hers was a supremely theatrical voice and presence. Her Mozart performances were received in their time as models of style, though today they would be considered somewhat sketchy; that she could refine her art and produce an intimate, less flamboyant mood can be heard on some records of lieder, notably an impassioned *Im Walde* by Schubert, recorded in 1947, and nearly fifteen years later, her last record, as a guest in the party scene of Karajan's direction of *Die Fledermaus*, when she sings a beautifully phrased though insecure, "Wien, Wien nur du allein." Welitsch inspired the sort of adoration in public and critics that is accorded to few, when in 1953 she returned to Covent Garden as Lisa in *The Queen of Spades*. While already her voice was beginning to present her with problems, William Mann wrote, "The flexibility, the melting purity of tone and the artistry are perhaps even more mature than before. Even if the voice proves to have lost its carrying power, I would rather hear and see Welitsch in her own repertory than any other living singer."

—Patrick O'Connor

WERTHER.

Composer: Jules Massenet.

Librettist: Édouard Blau, Paul Milliet, and Georges Hartmann (after Goethe) [libretto translated into German by Max
Kalbeck].

First Performance: Vienna, Court Opera, 16 February 1892.

Roles: Charlotte (mezzo-soprano); Sophie (soprano);
Werther (tenor); Albert (baritone); Le Bailli (baritone or
bass); Schmidt (tenor); Johann (baritone or bass); chorus
(SSAA).

Publications

book–

Hanslick, E. *Fünf Jahre Musik,* pp. 23 ff. Berlin, 1896.

articles–

Debussy, Claude. "Reprise de *Werther* à l'Opéra-Comique."
Gil Blas 27 April (1903); reprinted in *Monsieur Croche et
autres écrits,* edited by François Lesure, 154, Paris, 1980;
English translation, London and Cambridge, Massachusetts, 1987.
Béraud, H. "Werther au phonographe." *Le menéstrel* 99
(1932): 9.
Earl of Harwood. "Massenet's Opera *Werther.*" *Opera* 3
(1952): 69.
Commons, J. "Genesis of *Werther.*" In *Music and Musicians*
14/no. 10 (1966): 18.
Harding, J. "Massenet's *Werther.*" *The Listener* 75
(1966): 958.
Becker, Heinz. "Massenets *Werther:* Oper oder vertonter Roman?" In *Ars musica, musica scientia. Festschrift Heinrich
Hüschen zum fünfundsechzigsten Geburtstag am 2. März
1980,* edited by Detlef Altenburg, 30. Cologne, 1980.
Avant-scène opéra March (1984) [*Werther* issue].

unpublished–

Stocker, L.L. "The Treatment of the Romantic Literary Hero
in Verdi's 'Ernani' and in Massenet's 'Werther'." Ph.D.
dissertation, Florida State University, 1969.

*   *   *

When a Viennese operatic commission came Massenet's way,
he had a subject ready in Goethe's novel *Die Leiden des
jungen Werthers,* a profoundly influential work of the Romantic movement, which he had read while traveling in Germany.
It tells of a young intellectual who suffers and dies for love,
whose repudiation of common sense and convention stirred
many thinking people in a period when much of the social
and moral order was being questioned and found wanting.

Like Puccini, Massenet usually liked to have a woman as
his central character in an opera, and his Hérodiade, Manon,
and Thaïs are all memorable characters in the works which
bear their names. Here, the protagonist is a man, a young
German poet aged twenty-three, but he is no ordinary strong
hero in the Wagnerian sense, and in that, perhaps, he resembles Tchaikovsky's Eugene Onegin; certainly he shares with
that character a difficulty in knowing his own mind. The

prelude to the opera, in D minor and then D major, perhaps
describes him in being contemplative and passionate by turns.
Then at the start of the opera, set around 1780 in Frankfurt,
we find that he is in love with Charlotte, but that she, while
returning something of his affection, is to be married to his
friend Albert, who is a year or two older than he and seen by
her respectable bourgeois family as a practical man and not
the dreamer that Werther is. It becomes clear that the decision as to Charlotte's future is a firm one and that Werther
must accept it, though he cries in despair, "she'll be another
man's wife!"

Werther has moved out of Charlotte's life, but having done
so he finds himself unable to forget her, and in act II he
returns to find her and Albert happy after three months of
marriage. Albert sees him sitting disconsolately and generously greets him and welcomes him. Again Werther realizes
that he should stay away, and resolves to respect his friend's
marriage, but as soon as he is alone with Charlotte he renews
his declaration of love and she begs him to go, at least until
Christmas. When he rather dramatically tells her younger
sister Sophie that he is departing "never to return," Sophie
tells Charlotte and Albert, who now realizes with certainty
and distress that Werther is still in love with his wife.

By the beginning of act III, set at Christmas time, Werther
is writing love letters to Charlotte, who responds in spite of
herself and is deeply disturbed and tearful although she does
her best to hide her feelings from those around her, praying
for strength to bear her difficult situation. Finally, Werther
appears, saying that he could no longer stay away; the two
of them reminisce about happy times past, he sings the despairing aria with harp obbligato, "Pourquoi me réveiller?"
and finally they embrace. But now Charlotte is overwhelmed
by her feelings and rushes off to a locked room. Albert returns, having heard of Werther's return and at once fearing
the outcome. A servant enters with a message from Werther,
asking for the loan of his pistols, and Albert coldly tells
Charlotte to hand them over, which she does as if in a dream.
Act IV which is relatively short, serves as an epilogue.
Werther, who lies dying, is contented when Charlotte tells
him, in some of the most passionate music of the opera, that
he has always had her love. The voices of children celebrating
Christmas in a joyful carol in G major are heard as the opera
ends.

The story of *Werther,* though deeply touching, is somewhat
thin in itself to be spread over a whole opera, and there are
of course skilful dramatic tributaries. The family atmosphere
of Charlotte's parental home is well drawn, and Werther
himself sings of it in his A flat major aria "O spectacle idéal
d'amour et d'innocence." Albert has a quiet domestic exchange with his wife in act II, and he is most effective when
he hands the pistols to Charlotte to be given to Werther and
leaves the room with an angry gesture. However, inevitably
his is not a very sympathetic or fully drawn role compared
to that of his less stable but dramatically more interesting
rival. One feature of the opera that even a seasoned operagoer
may find hard to swallow is that the last exchange between
Charlotte and Werther occupies no less than twenty pages of
the opera's vocal score.

One could argue that Massenet, with his occasional sentimentality, was not the ideal composer for this powerful and
passionate German story, and that Verdi or Richard Strauss
might have handled it more strongly—just as it might be
suggested of the famous treatment of Goethe's *Faust* by another French composer, Gounod. But whatever the case,
Massenet's music is invariably elegant and often moving, and
its moments of tenderness are not confined to the lovers.
Indeed, the family scenes and the final children's carol are

José Carreras and Frederica Von Stade in Massenet's *Werther*, Royal Opera, London, 1980

among the most evocative and touching in the opera, while the writing for the solo voices is always fluent, skilful, and sweet, Werther's role being especially demanding.

—Christopher Headington

THE WHITE LADY
See LA DAME BLANCHE

THE WIFE OF BERNAUER
See DIE BERNAUERIN

DER WILDSCHÜTZ, oder Die Stimme der Natur [The Poacher, or The Voice of Nature].

Composer: Albert Lortzing.

Librettist: Albert Lortzing (after Kotzebue, *Der Rehbock*).

First Performance: Leipzig, Municipal Theater, 31 December 1842.

Roles: Baculus (bass); Count Eberbach (baritone); Baron Kronthal (tenor); Gretchen (soprano); Countess Eberbach (contralto or mezzo-soprano); Baroness Freimann (soprano); Nannette (mezzo-soprano); Pankratius (bass); A Guest (bass).

* * *

The fusion of text and music, both of them of the highest quality, in *Der Wildschütz* mark it as Albert Lortzing's finest opera. There is a fluidity, clarity, and engaging character to this work which guarantee it, at least in German-speaking lands, a permanent place in the repertoire. The opera opens with the engagement celebration of Gretchen and Baculus, which is interrupted by the arrival of a letter containing Baculus' dismissal from the count's service because of his alleged poaching, in this case a deer to be roasted for the wedding feast. Baculus becomes jealous at the thought of

Gretchen pleading his case with the count. Baroness Freimann, sister of the count, and her maid appear disguised as students, and the baroness offers to go to the count disguised as Gretchen, in an effort to look over her brother's choice of a new husband for her and to plead for Baculus. The count's hunting party arrives, including among others Baron Kronthal, brother of the countess, who, unrecognized, has taken a position as estate manager. As an excuse for pursuing the two women, the count invites everyone to his birthday party the following day.

Act II takes place in the billiard room at the castle, where the countess is eloquently reading Sophocles to her uncomprehending servants. Baculus, pleading his case with frequent classical quotations, is interrupted by the count. Before Baculus can be thrown out, the baroness, disguised as Gretchen, arrives. The baron and the count are charmed and, when the countess intercedes for Baculus, the count decides to reconsider. A storm conveniently develops so both the baroness and Baculus have to remain at the castle overnight. The baron and the count parry for the attentions of the baroness. As the competition increases during the famous billiard quintet, the countess arrives to rescue the baroness. In frustration the baron offers Baculus five thousand gold pieces to break his engagement, and Baculus accepts.

The count's promised party opens the final act in the garden, where the villagers are celebrating their patron's generosity. Baculus offers the real Gretchen to the baron, who refuses. Upon learning that the other Gretchen (the baroness) is a student in disguise, the baron discovers her identity and declares his love. Mutual recognition follows, and each character explains away his guilt by referring to the subtitle of the opera—each was following the Voice of Nature. And the schoolmaster is forgiven, for in the twilight he had shot his own donkey instead of one of the count's beloved deer.

Following his established pattern, Lortzing selected a contemporary play by August von Kotzebue which caused a sensation when it was first printed in 1815. The composer acted in the work while engaged in Detmold, and he adhered to its major outlines while recasting a disagreeable farmer into the likable schoolteacher Baculus, and injecting a gushing enthusiasm for Greek tragedy into the character of the countess. This latter touch was intended to capitalize on the tremendous public reception accorded Sophocles' *Antigone* when it was premiered in Leipzig on March 5, 1842 with incidental music by Felix Mendelssohn. The affected public mania for Greek expression was too good an opportunity to pass up, so he revised his libretto to give the text an immediacy by satirizing the prevailing mood in the figure of the countess. The other minor changes such as ages and names serve to bring the opera closer to the spirit of Beaumarchais and Mozart, and the end result is certainly the finest libretto Lortzing created.

The title, *Der Wildschütz* (*The Poacher*), is extremely well chosen in that it has a direct relationship to all the major characters. Baculus' act of poaching on the count's estate is the main event, but in much more subtle terms each major character is guilty of poaching other people's property. The baron and the count try to win a girl whom they believe to be another's fiancée. The baroness and the countess are infatuated with the estate manager whose social position should make a serious relationship impossible. Baculus and Gretchen are lured by the charms of forbidden fruit; the former by money and the latter by her feminine instinct to flirt. The subtitle, *Die Stimme der Natur* (*The Voice of Nature*), points to the fact that each major character was misled and later excused by his intuitive feelings or the voice of nature. *Der Wildschütz* is a comedy of love showing the humor of love's jealousy (Baculus), the naive and practical aspects of love (Gretchen), love's melancholy and abandon (baron), love's insatiable sexual force (count), love's disappointments and hopes (countess), and the flirtations and curiosity of love (baroness). The humorous aspects of love can be seen in the infatuation of the unsuspecting countess for the baron, in the competition between the baron and count for the latter's sister, and in the flirtation of Baculus with the mirage of fame and fortune, and, of course, in exaggerated readings of Sophocles.

On the surface at least *Der Wildschütz* is a typical comedy of manners in which there is a great deal of play acting and role playing with lots of disguise, cynicism, parody, and illusion. Certainly real love is not much in evidence, but this is no critique of the social structure of Lortzing's time, and that is clearly evident in the musical score. Lortzing, the man who had been on or near a stage every day for twenty years, knew what affected audiences. With no desire to write for posterity, he catered to a middle class which sought entertainment and distraction. As a master of small forms, he could string together theatrically effective scenes skillfully segued by tuneful and attractive music. The score is delightfully Mozartian, and it conforms to the master's use of instruments beginning with *Die Entführung aus dem Serail* some sixty years earlier. And the music does cause us to smile. It engages our attention but does not force our aesthetic commitment, and it is flexible to the needs of the drama without creating a form of its own.

—Robert H. Cowden

WILLIAM TELL
See GUILLAUME TELL

THE WILLIS
See LE VILLI

WILSON, Robert.

Director and designer. Born 4 October 1941, in Waco, Texas. Educated at the University of Texas, Austin, 1959-62, and Pratt Institute, 1962-65, where he earned a BFA in architecture; studied painting with George MacNeil, 1964; apprenticed to Paolo Soleri, Arcosanti Community, Arizona, 1966; artistic director of the Byrd Hoffmann Foundation, New York, from 1969, which has produced most of his works; design debut, *America Hurrah*, 1965; opera debut, *Einstein on the Beach*, 1976. Specialist in performance art; has taught and lectured in the United States and Europe; has exhibited as a sculptor and artist in New York, Bonn, Milan, and elsewhere; winner of numerous awards in the United State and Europe.

Opera Productions (selected)

Einstein on the Beach, Festival d'Avignon, France, 1976.
Médée, Opera de Lyon, France, 1984.
Einstein on the Beach, Brooklyn Academy of Music, New York, 1984.
the CIVIL warS, 1983-85.
Alceste, Wurtemburg Staatsoper, Stuttgart, 1986.
Salome, Teatro alla Scala, 1987.
Le martyre de Saint Sébastien, Maison de la Culture de la Seine-St. Denis, Bobigny, 1988.
Doktor Faustus, Teatro alla Scala, 1989.
De Materie, Netherlands Opera, Muziektheater, Amsterdam, 1989.
Alceste, Lyric Opera of Chicago, 1990.
Die Zauberflöte, Bastille Opera, Paris, 1991.
Parsifal, Hamburg Staatsoper, 1991.

Original Performance Pieces (selected)

Alley Cats, New York, 1968.
The King of Spain, Anderson Theatre, New York, 1969.
The Life and Times of Sigmund Freud, Brooklyn Academy of Music, 1969.
Deafman Glance, University of Iowa, Iowa City, 1970.
Program Pologue Now, Overture for A Deafman, Paris, 1971.
KA MOUNTAIN AND GUARdenia TERRACE, A Story about A Family and Some People Changing, Shiraz Festival of Arts, Iran, 1972.
The Life and Times of Joseph Stalin, Copenhagen and Brooklyn Academy of Music, 1973.
A Letter for Queen Victoria, Spoleto Festival, 1974.
A Mad Man A Mad Giant A Mad Dog A Mad Urge A Mad Face, 1974.
The Life and Times of Dave Clark, 1974.
The $ Value Man, 1974.
Death, Destruction and Detroit, 1979.
Medea, 1984.
Hamletmachine, 1986.
The Black Rider, Paris, 1990.

Publications

By WILSON: books–

Death Destruction and Detroit. Berlin, 1979.
The Golden Windows. Munich, 1982.
the CIVIL warS (Dutch section). Paris, 1983.
the CIVIL warS (German section). Frankfurt, 1984.
the CIVIL warS (Italian section). Rome, 1984.
Robert Wilson's Vision: An Exhibition of Works by Robert Wilson, with a Sound Environment by Hans Peter Kuhn. New York, 1991.

articles–

"I Was Sitting on My . . ." *The Drama Review* 21 (December 1977).
"Tale of Two Cities (D D & D)," *Performance Art* 1 (1979).

About WILSON: books–

Croyden, Margaret. *Lunatics, Lovers and Poets.* New York, 1974.
Marranca, Bonnie, ed. *The Theatre of Images.* New York, 1977.

Brecht, Stefan. *The Theatre of Visions: Robert Wilson.* Frankfurt, 1978.
Wirth, Andrezj. *Robert Wilson: The Theater of Images.* New York, 1984.
Stearns, R., ed. *Robert Wilson: The Theater of Images.* New York, 1984.
Donker, Janny. *The President of Paradise: A Traveller's Account of the CIVIL warS.* Amsterdam, 1986.
Shyer, Lawrence. *Robert Wilson and His Collaborators.* New York, 1989.

articles–

Sabbe, H. "Wilson-Glass: een mijilpaal in de operageschiedenis?" *Mes en melodie* (January 1977): 12-14.
na Gopaleen, T. "Robert Wilson: Multinationalizing the Avant-Garde." *Village Voice* 28 (6 December 1983): 95.
Rich, A. "Robert Wilson and the Olympic Scandal." *Vanity Fair* 47 (June 1984): 94-97.
Dalton, J. "Robert Wilson: Seeing the Forest for the Trees." *Ear, Magazine of New Music* 13, no. 8 (1988): 18-21.
Baier, C. "Die neue Romantik: Robert Wilson, William S. Burroughs, Tom Waits und *The Black Rider.*" *Österreichische Musikzeitschrift* 45 (May 1990): 260-61.
Rockwell, John. "The West German Season of Robert Wilson." *The New York Times* 139 (20 June 1990): B1 or C11.
Wilson, P.N. "Fantasie ueber ein deutsches Thema: *The Black Rider—ein Freischuetz-Musical* von Robert Wilson, Tom Waits und William Burroughs." *Neue Zeitschrift für Musik* 151 (July-August 1990): 61.
Marx, R. "Image Maker (Visionary Theater Artist)." *Opera News* 55 (September 1990): 24.
"*The Black Rider.*" *Diapason-Harmonie* no. 365 (November 1990): 32.
Rieff, David. "The Exile Returns. Is the Director-Artist Robert Wilson, a Popular Success in Europe, Too Visionary for American Audiences?" *Connoisseur* 221 (June 1991): 28.
Tubeuf, A. "Bob Wilson, le maître du temps." *Diapason-Harmonie* no. 372 (June 1991): 22.
Kupfer, H., and others. " 'Noch nicht am Ende, aber . . .'" *Die Buehne* (Summer 1991): 30.

* * *

Director and designer Robert Wilson has collaborated with contemporary composers in the creation of musical theater pieces. His first operatic work with Philip Glass, *Einstein on the Beach,* has been seen throughout Europe and was presented on the stage of the Metropolitan Opera House in 1976 (in 1984 it was presented at the Brooklyn Academy of Music). He has also created and staged his own dramatic works and has mounted productions of nonoperatic works from the classic repertoire. Wilson's *the CIVIL warS* was planned for the Los Angeles Olympic Arts Festival in 1984, but was canceled for financial reasons. This unfinished epic was a collaborative effort involving, among others, composers David Byrne and Philip Glass. Its various parts were developed in workshops around the world and have been performed by numerous companies. The music of connecting sections, composed by Byrne and called as a group *the Knee Plays,* was seen first at Minneapolis's Walker Arts Center and then, in 1987, at New York's Alice Tully Hall; act V was staged at the Brooklyn Academy of Music in the same year. Other mountings of various parts have taken place in Cambridge, Massachusetts, and in Cologne. In 1989 Wilson staged Louis Andriessen's

Die Materie in Amsterdam and Giacomo Manzoni's *Doktor Faustus* at La Scala.

Wilson's approach to repertory operas is decidedly interventionist, with the imposition of stylized movements allied to bold geometric designs. Some critics have found Wilson's work mannered, static, and self-indulgent, while others have been impressed by his control of design and movement and the precision with which these movements are executed, finding in his stagings a cumulative dramatic impact.

Wilson's first staging of a standard opera was Charpentier's *Médée* at Lyons in 1984, presented in conjunction with a production of Gavin Bryar's opera of the same name that was later seen at the Théâtre des Champs Elysées in Paris. Both *Medeas* were presented on the same Wilson-designed blue cyclorama. Two years later he created in tandem productions Euripides's play *Alcestis* and Gluck's opera *Alceste*. Wilson's staging of *Alceste,* first seen in Stuttgart in 1986 and later as the opening opera in the 1990-91 season of the Chicago Lyric Opera, is illustrative of his approach to stagings of traditional operas. The singers employ stylized gestures, usually in slow motion, and occasionally freeze into contorted poses, adding an element of unreality to the work that—in the case of Gluck's opera—contradicts the stated aims of the composer. Apparently a reaction against what he feels are old-fashioned sentiments—simplicity and naturalness—Wilson applies layers of the esoteric and unnatural, calling upon the traditions of mime and the theater of the Far East. In its Chicago incarnation, the chorus was placed in the orchestra pit, reducing its role from an important dramatic protagonist to an accompanist for the soprano, whose role is thereby turned into a concert solo, although she shared the stage with dancers in act II. The set designs featured, in addition to Wilson's characteristically bold geometric shapes, a continuously rotating cube suspended over the playing area.

Plans for Wagner's *Parsifal* at Bayreuth did not materialize, and a staging of the same work in Cassel scheduled for 1981 was canceled—reportedly because the sets did not arrive on time. Wilson's production of *Parsifal,* finally seen in Hamburg in 1991, was a static staging of a work in which stasis is raised to a spiritual level. The staging was criticized as being inappropriate for a work about complex characters, reducing them to "statues in Kabuki costumes" (*Opera,* July 1991). A new production was seen in Chicago in 1992, and was notable for its employment of one of Wilson's most characteristic features: the relegation of most of the cast—aside from the title character—to the wings or the orchestra pit, to be replaced on stage by mimes or to remain disembodied voices.

Richard Strauss's *Salome* was staged at Teatro alla Scala in 1987 with Montserrat Caballé in the title role. The production featured Kabuki-inspired movements, with actions, gestures, and sounds treated as if they occupied separate universes. It involved a mixture of images derived from sources as diverse as punk culture and Lewis Carroll.

In 1988 Wilson staged and designed the gala opening concert of the Opéra Bastille de Paris. Mozart's *Die Zauberflöte* received a staging by Wilson in the same theater in 1991, one that deemphasized the comic elements of the work. Wilson dressed his singers in Noh-style costumes to resemble warriors. He placed the action on spare, angular sets that revealed the influence of Calder and Arp, and punctuated them with laser beams. Wilson further imposed his conception on the work by reordering the arias and using electronic sounds at the start of each scene to create an atmosphere. One striking image in this production was an enormously tall Queen of the Night on stilts.

The premiere of a Glass-Wilson opera has been planned for 1992 in Lisbon, and the production is scheduled to travel to the World's Fair in Seville.

—Michael Sims

WINDGASSEN, Wolfgang.

Tenor. Born 26 June 1914, in Annemasse, Haute Savoie. Died 8 September 1974, in Stuttgart. Married: singer Lore Wissman. Studied with his father, tenor Fritz Windgassen; with Maria Ranzow and Alfons Fischer, Stuttgart Conservatory; debut as Alvaro in *La forza del destino,* Pforzheim, 1941; Stuttgart, 1945-72; at Bayreuth, 1951-70, debuting as Parsifal; Teatro alla Scala debut as Florestan in *Fidelio,* 1952; Paris Opéra debut, 1954; Covent Garden debut as Tristan, 1954; regularly sang Siegfried in *Ring* cycles at Covent Garden; Metropolitan Opera debut as Siegmund, 1957; director of Stuttgart Opera, 1972-74.

Publications

About WINDGASSEN: books–

Wessling, Berndt W. *Wolfgang Windgassen.* Bremen, 1961.
Honolka, Kurt. *Wolfgang Windgassen.* Stuttgart, 1962.

articles–

Honolka, Kurt. "Wolfgang Windgassen." *Opera* September (1962).
Ashbrook, W. "Perspectives on an aria: *In des Lebens Frühlingstagen.*" *Opera News* 46 (3 April 1982): 38.
Verdino-Suellwold, C.M. "The Heldentenor in the Twentieth Century: Refining a Rare Breed." *Opera Journal* 20/3 (1987): 24.
Norquet, M. "Bayreuth-Protagonisten von einst: Aufnahmen mit Astrid Varnay und Wolfgang Windgassen." *Opernwelt* 30/September (1989): 64.

*   *   *

For most of the 1950s and 1960s, Wolfgang Windgassen was the greatest living Heldentenor. As John Steane notes in *The Grand Tradition,* Windgassen "came on the scene just as the hunger for a listenable Heldentenor was reaching starvation point." After studying with his father Fritz Windgassen, a leading tenor, Wolfgang completed studies at the Stuttgart Conservatory with Maria Ranzow and Alfons Fischer and made his debut as Alvaro in Verdi's *La forza del destino* in 1941. Wolfgang's mother was likewise a singer, the coloratura soprano Vally van Osten (1882-1923). Windgassen was a regular member of the Stuttgart Opera from 1945 until 1972; from 1972 until his death in 1974 he served as director of that company. Initially specializing in relatively lighter roles such as Hoffmann, Tamino, Don José, Max in Weber's *Der Freischütz,* and in works by Lortzing, Windgassen soon moved into the Wagnerian roles that comprised his main career. He gained international attention in the role of Parsifal at Bayreuth at its reopening in 1951 and returned there nearly every summer until 1970. At Bayreuth he performed nearly all the major tenor roles, including Siegmund, Siegfried, Tristan, Loge, Lohengrin, Walther von Stolzing, Erik in *Der fliegende Holländer,* and Tannhäuser. For much of his career he specialized in Siegfried and Tristan. He had also a repertoire of Italian operas that he performed in German, Verdi's *Otello,* for example. His best roles outside of Wagner were, in addition to Otello, Adolar in Weber's *Euryanthe,* the Emperor in Strauss's *Die Frau ohne Schatten,* and Florestan in *Fidelio.* Windgassen sang only six performances at the Metropolitan Opera in New York but was a regular singer at the Teatro alla Scala from 1952, the Paris Opéra from 1954, and at Covent Garden from 1954. He was also a regular guest at the Staatsoper in Vienna.

Windgassen's abilities are well documented on a fairly large number of recordings both live and commercial. He is perhaps at his lyrical best in the 1953 *Lohengrin* from Bayreuth with Eleanor Steber as a radiant Elsa, conducted by Keilberth. At times Windgassen is somewhat unsteady, but in the Narrative and in other passages calling for bel canto singing, the voice is firm and beautiful. In Solti's *Ring* cycle on Decca his Siegfried is sufficiently heroic but also human, intelligent, and affecting. It remains one of the very best examples of this thoughtful singer's work. Windgassen also recorded Siegfried for Philips's *Ring* cycle under Karl Böhm. Windgassen's Parsifal is preserved in his 1951 debut performance from Bayreuth, conducted by Hans Knappertsbusch. This is widely considered to be one of the greatest of all opera recordings, both for the level of singing and because of Knappertsbusch's sense of musical architecture.

During his Bayreuth years Windgassen became a believable actor under the guidance of Wieland Wagner. For Windgassen Wagner directed a production of his grandfather's seldom-performed *Rienzi* in Stuttgart. The 1966 Bayreuth *Tristan und Isolde* production with Birgit Nilsson and Windgassen, under the direction of Wieland Wagner with Karl Böhm conducting, was recorded by DGG. Windgassen's third act is especially compelling, the tenor making up for vocal deterioration by interpretive greatness. In the first two acts he seems not to have yet fully assumed the role. From 1961 there are highlights of the famous Bayreuth *Tannhäuser* with De Los Angeles as Elisabeth and Grace Bumbry as Venus. Here Windgassen is not in his best vocal estate; his singing is at times rough and he resorts too often to aspirates. For DGG Windgassen made complete recordings of Walther in *Die Meistersinger von Nürnberg* and Erik in *Der fliegende Holländer.* In the latter, recorded in 1955 under Fricsay, Windgassen gives an eloquent performance. His reliability in this role may also be judged in live Bayreuth recordings. A 1953 recording of *Fidelio* for HMV under Furtwängler finds Windgassen's Florestan well sung but lacking conviction and heroic stature. In highlights from Verdi's *Otello* sung in German, Alan Blyth finds the tenor "a taxed but moving Moor."

By the standards of Windgassen's predecessor, the incomparable Lauritz Melchior, Windgassen's voice lacked the ultimate force and volume needed for these Wagnerian roles, yet, in the words of Steane, he "has been as scrupulous a lyricist as any Wagnerian singer of the earlier generation," and he was "the most human and humane of Siegfrieds." In hundreds of performances of these roles throughout his career, Windgassen proved to be steady and reliable. Because of the vocal demands of Wagner he sometimes tended to save himself for the big moments and if there is a lack of thrust and bite needed for passages such as Siegfried's Forging Scene, his 1974 obituary in *Opera* noted that "Few Tristans or Siegfrieds were able to sing the lyrical portions of their music with as much beauty of tone and at the same time rise to the more dramatic moments of the score."

—Stephen A. Willier

WOLF, Hugo.

Composer. Born 13 March 1860, in Windischgraz. Died 22 February 1903, in Vienna. Studied with his father and with the schoolmaster Sebastian Weixler; enrolled for one semester in the secondary school in Graz, 1870; enrolled in the seminary of the Benedictine monastery of St Paul in Carinthia, 1871; attended the Gymnasium in Marburg, 1873; studied piano with Wilhelm Schenner and harmony with Robert Fuchs at the Vienna Conservatory, 1875; met Wagner in 1875; expelled from the Vienna Conservatory, 1877; met Brahms in 1879; chorus master in Salzburg, 1881; music critic of the *Wiener Salonblatt,* 1883-87; his symphonic poem *Penthesilea,* performed by the Vienna Philharmonic under Richter in 1885, was a failure; publication of a number of his songs in 1889; numerous performances of his works in Germany; establishment of the Hugo Wolf-Verein in Vienna by Michael Haberlandt, 1897; nervous breakdown, 1897; travel in Italy and Austria, 1898; died in a state asylum in Vienna.

Operas

Edition: *H. Wolf: Sämtliche Werke.* Internationalen Hugo Wolf-Gesellschaft. Vienna, 1960-.

König Alboin, P. Peitl, 1876-77 [fragmentary (21 measures)].
Der Corregidor, R. Mayreder (after Alarcón, *El sombrero de tres picos*), 1895, Mannheim, 7 June 1896; revised, 1896, 1897, 1898.
Manuel Venegas, M. Hoernes (after Alarcón, *El niño de la bola*), 1897, Mannheim, 1 March 1903 [unfinished].

Other works: incidental music, sacred and secular vocal music (including over 300 songs), orchestral works (including 3 symphonies), chamber music, piano pieces.

Publications/Writings

By WOLF: books–

Batka, R., and H. Werner, eds. *H. Wolf: Musikalische Kritiken.* Leipzig, 1911; 1976.
Pleasants, Henry, ed. *The Music Criticism of Hugo Wolf.* New York, 1978.

letters–

Werner, H. *Hugo Wolf: Briefe an Rosa Mayreder, mit einem Nachwort der Dichterin des "Corregidors".* Vienna, 1921.
Hilmar, Ernst, and Walter Obermaier. *Hugo Wolf: Briefe an Frieda Zerny.* Vienna, 1978.

Note: for additional published letters, see the *New Grove Dictionary of Music and Musicians,* 1980 ed.

About WOLF: books–

Newman, E. *Hugo Wolf.* London, 1907; 1966.
Walker, F. *Hugo Wolf: A Biography.* London, 1951; 2nd ed., 1968.
Lindner, D. *Hugo Wolf.* Vienna, 1960.
Werba, E. *Hugo Wolf oder der zornige Romantiker.* Vienna, 1971.
Cook, P. *Hugo Wolf's Corregidor.* London, 1976.
Rostand, Claude. *Hugo Wolf. L'homme et son oeuvre.* Paris and Geneva, 1982.
Saary, Margarete. *Persönlichkeit und musikdramatische Kreativität Hugo Wolfs.* Tutzing, 1984.

articles–

Fellinger, I. "Die Oper im kompositorischen Schaffen von Hugo Wolf." *Jahrbuch des Staatlichen Instituts für Musikforschung Preussischer Kulturbesitz* 5 (1972): 87.
Spitzer, L. "Rosa Mayreders Textbuch zu Hugo Wolfs 'Manuel Venegas'." *Österreichische Musikzeitschrift* 28 (1973): 443.
————. "Hugo Wolfs 'Manuel Venegas'. Ein Beitrag zur Genese." *Österreichische Musikzeitschrift* 32 (1977): 68.
Youens, Susan. "Hugo Wolf and the Operatic Grail: the Search for a Libretto." *Cambridge Opera Journal* 1 (1989): 277.

* * *

Although Hugo Wolf's reputation rests almost entirely on his songs, his life-long goal was to compose an opera, and there is reason to believe that, had he lived longer, he would have turned his attention increasingly towards this genre.

From the time he saw his first opera (Donizetti's *Belisario*) at age eight, through his student years, and into maturity, opera held a special fascination for Wolf. Beginning in September 1875, when he enrolled at the Vienna Conservatory, Wolf attended operas quite frequently. He heard works by Mozart, Beethoven, Weber, Meyerbeer (he was especially fond of *Les Huguenots*), and others. He was deeply impressed by Wagner's *Tannhäuser* and *Lohengrin,* and during one of his visits to Vienna (December 1875) Wagner encouraged Wolf in his compositional pursuits.

As early as 1876 Wolf was searching for a suitable operatic subject. He briefly considered Theodor Körner's libretto on Alfred the Great. In a letter of 31 August to his cousin, Anna Vinzenzberg, Wolf mentions a four-act romantic opera entitled *König Alboin,* on a libretto by a friend, the Viennese writer Paul Peitl. All that survives is a twenty-one-measure fragment of instrumental music (dated 9 April 1877) accompanying a duel between King Alboin and his enemy Lintram in act III.

A letter from Dr Friedrich von Hausegger, a professor at the University of Graz, reveals that in 1878 Wolf was again thinking of composing an opera, if only he could find a suitable libretto. This idea was apparently on his mind in the early 1880s, too. In Maierling during the summer of 1882 Wolf investigated the possibility of writing an opera, with his own libretto, on the legend of the fairy princess, Ilse, but he soon lost interest in this project. The following winter he drafted the libretto of a comic opera set in Seville at carnival time. Though the sketches break off in act II, these fragmentary drafts illustrate Wolf's early interest in southern themes. This was to assume greater importance later in his career in works such as the *Spanisches Liederbuch* (1889-90) and the *Italienisches Liederbuch* (1890-91, 1896), and in the operas *Der Corregidor* and *Manuel Venegas,* after stories by the Spanish novelist Pedro de Alarcón.

Towards the end of the decade Wolf became increasingly preoccupied with the idea of writing an opera and devoted much time and effort to the search for a libretto. In a letter to his mother in late 1888, he spoke of his plans to compose an opera in the coming year. The subject of Wolf's projected work was Alarcón's *El sombrero de tres picos,* which recently had been published in a German translation. In a letter to his brother-in-law, Josef Strasser, from around this time (10 September 1888), Wolf mentions that he planned to treat this subject in operatic form and to write his own libretto. During a stay at the home of his friends the Werners in Perchtoldsdorf the next May, however, Wolf took up a different project, an opera based on Schlegel's translation of *A Midsummer Night's Dream.* The *Elfenlied* for soprano solo, women's chorus, and orchestra, and the *Lied des transferierten Zettel,* both of which were composed at this time, are apparently fragments of the music intended for this opera; a sketch of the planned libretto is preserved in the City Library in Vienna.

Long before he was ready to write it, Wolf seems to have had a clear idea of the kind of opera he wished one day to create. As early as 28 June 1890, in a letter to his friend Oskar Grohe, Wolf mentioned that it would contain "strumming guitars, sighs of love, moonlit nights, champagne carousals." By then he had already given up his own attempt to draft a libretto based on *El sombrero de tres picos,* and earlier that year he had furiously rejected a version prepared by the feminist writer Rosa Mayreder. Thereafter, over a period of nearly five years, Wolf considered, and rejected, many different suggestions for possible subjects by authors from Shakespeare to Ibsen, including *The Tempest,* the story of Pocohontas, the life of Buddha, and the story of Cupid and Psyche from *The Golden Ass* of Apuleius.

In March 1892, at the first Wolf recital in Berlin, the composer met a librettist, Richard Genée, who recommended that he consider Alarcón's *El niño de la bola,* which had been published in German as *Manuel Venegas.* Later that year several individuals—including his friends Gustav Schur, Adalbert von Goldschmidt, and Hermann Wette—all tried their hand at providing a libretto on *Manuel Venegas.* Wolf rejected every version.

With the success of Humperdinck's *Hänsel und Gretel* in December 1894, Wolf desired more intensely than ever to compose an opera of his own. Shortly thereafter, he read a new version of *El sombrero de tres picos* by Franz Schaumann, chairman of the Wagner-Verein. Although he rejected it, too, Schaumann's libretto reminded Wolf of the earlier one by Mayreder. He reread it and decided that—after all—her version was the text which had eluded him for so long. In April 1895 he began work on *Der Corregidor;* by early July all four acts were completed in piano score, and it was orchestrated by the end of the year. The first performance, on 7 June 1896 in Mannheim, was quite successful, although enthusiasm waned at the next performance. The score and parts were revised extensively in 1896 and early 1897.

Wolf soon became anxious to write a second opera. He rejected *Eldas Untergang,* an original libretto by Rosa Mayreder, but urged her to write a new version of *Manuel Venegas.* While waiting for her libretto, Wolf briefly considered setting Kleist's *Amphitrion.* In May 1897, Wolf rejected Mayreder's *Manuel Venegas,* but accepted a version by Moritz Hoernes, a professor at the University of Vienna. In September he began intensive work on the new opera. After composing about sixty pages of piano score (five scenes) in three weeks,

Wolf's mind gave way, the result of an advanced case of syphilis coupled with a distressing personal setback. Wolf had attempted to interest the new director of the Vienna Opera, his former classmate Gustav Mahler, in producing *Der Corregidor* during the 1897-98 season. Although initially the prospects seemed encouraging, in the late summer of 1897 Mahler and Wolf had a falling out, and Mahler decided not to perform the work. Soon Wolf began to claim that he had been appointed Mahler's successor as director of the Vienna Opera, and announced that from then on only his works (most of which were unfinished or unwritten) would be performed. He was removed under restraint to the asylum of Dr Wilhelm Svetlin. His letters describe grandiose plans for world tours of his operas with the support of the Weimar theater.

The surviving fragment of *Manuel Venegas* betrays no hint of Wolf's mental deterioration. Indeed, the "Spring Chorus" which opens the work is one of the loveliest pieces in his entire *oeuvre*. Although its unfinished state obviously precludes its acceptance into the operatic canon, the feasibility of concert performances of *Manuel Venegas*, along the lines of those by the Hugo Wolf-Gesellschaft in the late 1970s, should not be overlooked.

—Stephen A. Crist

WOLFF, Albert (Louis).

Conductor/Composer. Born 19 January 1884, in Paris. Died 20 February 1970, in Paris. Studied with Leroux, Gédalge, and Vidal at the Paris Conservatory; pianist in cabarets; organist at St Thomas Aquinas, 1906-10; on the staff of the Opéra-Comique, Paris, 1908; chorus master, and then conductor at the Opéra-Comique, 1911; conductor of the French repertoire, Metropolitan Opera, New York, 1919-21; conducted the premiere of his own opera, *L'oiseau bleu,* at the Metropolitan, 27 December 1919; succeeded Messager as music director of the Opéra-Comique, 1921-24; conducted the premiere of Ravel's *L'enfant et les sortilèges,* 1925; second conductor, 1925, and principal conductor, 1934-40, of the Concerts Pasdeloup; conductor of the Concerts Lamoureux, 1928-34; toured South America, 1940-45; general director of the Opéra-Comique, 1945-46; conducted the premiere of Poulenc's *Les mamelles de Tirésias,* 1947.

Publications

About WOLFF: articles–

Wolff, S. "Albert Wolff, doyen de l'Opéra-Comique." *Guide du Concert et du Disque* 3 October (1958).

* * *

Conductor Albert Wolff enjoyed an association with the Paris Opéra-Comique from 1908 until well into the 1960s. This was not, however, the whole of his many and varied accomplishments. During the seasons of 1919-20 and 1920-21, Wolff was a busy conductor at the Metropolitan Opera in New York, where he made his debut leading *Faust* with Farrar, Martinelli, and Rothier. Also that season he conducted *Carmen* with those same principals, *Samson* with Caruso, *Manon*

(Farrar), Rabaud's *Marouf,* and the world premiere of his own opera, *L'oiseau bleu.* The following season he led all of those except *Marouf,* plus the Metropolitan premiere of *Louise,* also with Farrar.

Appointed music director of the Opéra-Comique to succeed André Messager, he left the Metropolitan, but in 1924 he was with the Concerts Pasdeloup, founder of the Concertes Moderne specializing in contemporary music. He was also music director of the Champs Elysées theater; in 1937, he led *Pelléas et Mélisande* at Covent Garden, and he was also conductor of the Concerts Lamoureux.

Wolff spent the years of the Second World War conducting in South America, where he had conducted previously at the Colón. He returned to France in 1945 to become Director General of the Opéra-Comique. Leaving that post, he continued to conduct there, at the Paris Opéra, and for symphonic concerts in France and abroad.

Wolff led a performance of *Manon* for Denmark Radio which was rebroadcast by that organization year after year. As late as the 1960s, Wolff's performances of *Werther* and *Les pêcheurs de perles* at the Opéra-Comique, with the ragtag orchestra that existed there at that time, were absolutely superb.

Albert Wolff was a great French conductor, master of that ineffable subtle but lush mystery which makes for authentic musical "Frenchness." He also led several important first performances of works by, among others, Ravel (*L'enfant*), Debussy, Roussel, and Poulenc. He died in 1970, and his memory is still revered by many musicians and audience members alike.

Wolff recorded prolifically in all repertoires throughout his career. Few of these performances are available today. Best known are the complete recordings of *Carmen* and *Manon,* although there are, somewhere, excerpts from *Madama Butterfly* and *Les contes d'Hoffmann.*

—Bert Wechsler

WOLF-FERRARI, Ermanno.

Composer. Born 12 January 1876, in Venice. Died 21 January 1948, in Venice. Studied with Rheinberger in Munich, 1893-95; his oratorio *La Sulamite* successfully performed in Venice, 1899; director of the Liceo Benedetto Marcello in Venice, 1902-07; taught at the Salzburg Mozarteum; lived for many years in Neu-Biberg, near Munich.

Operas

Publishers: Fantuzzi, Leuckart, Rahter, Ricordi, Schott, Sonzogno, Weinberger.

Irene, Wolf-Ferrari, 1895-96 [not performed].
La Camargo, M. Pezzè-Pascolato (after de Musset), c. 1897 [unfinished].
Cenerentola, M. Pezzè-Pascolato (after Perrault), Venice, La Fenice, 22 February 1900; revised Bremen, 31 January 1902.
Le donne curiose, L. Sugana (after C. Goldoni), 1902-03, Munich, Residenz, 27 November 1903.
I quattro rusteghi, L. Sugana and G. Pizzolato (after C. Goldoni), Munich, Hoftheater, 19 March 1906.

Il segreto di Susanna (intermezzo), E. Golisciani, Munich, Hoftheater, 4 December 1909.

I gioielli della Madonna, E. Golisciani and C. Zangarini, Berlin, Kurfürstenoper, 23 December 1911.

L'amore medico, E. Golisciani (after Molière), Dresden, Hoftheater, 4 December 1913.

Gli amanti sposi, L. Sugana, G. Pizzolato, E. Golisciani, and G. Forzano (after C. Goldoni), libretto 1904, music c. 1916, Venice, La Fenice, 19 February 1925.

Das Himmelskleid (La veste di cielo), Wolf-Ferrari (after Perrault), c. 1917-25, Munich, National, 21 April 1927.

Sly, ovvero La leggenda del dormiente risvegliato, Forzano (after Shakespeare), Milan, Teatro alla Scala, 29 December 1927.

La vedova scaltra, M. Ghisalberti (after C. Goldoni), Rome, Opera, 5 March 1931.

Il campiello, M. Ghisalberti (after C. Goldoni), Milan, Teatro alla Scala, 11 or 12? February 1936.

La dama boba, M. Ghisalberti (after Lope de Vega), Milan, Teatro alla Scala, 1 February 1939.

Gli dei a Tebe, L. Andersen [=L. Strecker] and M. Ghisalberti, Hanover, Oper, 4 June 1943.

Other works: vocal works, orchestral and instrumental music, piano pieces.

Publications/Writings

By WOLF-FERRARI: books–

Considerazioni attuali sulla musica. Siena, 1943.

Lothar, Mark, ed. *Wolf-Ferrari: Briefe aus einem halben Jahrhundert.* Munich and Vienna, 1982.

Note: for additional writings by WOLF-FERRARI, see *Die Musik in Geschichte und Gegenwart,* edited by Friedrich Blume, Kassel, 1949-68; supplements, 1968-.

interviews–

Würz, A. "Begegnung mit Ermanno Wolf-Ferrari." *Zeitschrift für Musikwissenschaft* 103 (1936): 221.

About WOLF-FERRARI: books–

Rensis, Raffaello de. *Ermanno Wolf-Ferrari: la sua vita d'artista.* Milan, 1937.

Grisson, Alexandra Carola. *Ermanno Wolf-Ferrari.* Regensburg, 1941. Zurich, 1958.

Rebois, H. *Des rustres de Goldoni aux quatre rustres de Wolf-Ferrari.* Nice, 1960.

articles–

Mauke, W. "Le donne curiose." *Rivista musicale italiana* 11 (1904): 366.

———. "I quattro rusteghi." *Rivista musicale italiana* 13 (1906): 315.

Schmidt, L. "Die neugierigen Frauen," "Die vier Grobiane." In *Aus dem Musikleben der Gegenwart,* 140, 143. Berlin, 1909.

Bontempelli, E. "Il segreto di Susanna." *Rivista musicale italiana* 18 (1911): 839.

Candida, F. "Without Benefit of Formula" [interview summary] *Musical Digest* 6/no. 12 (1924): 40.

Gatti, G.M. " 'Sly' von Wolf Ferrari, und einige allgemeine Bemerkungen." *Melos* 7 (1928): 537.

Lualdi, A. "*Sly,* opera in tre atti di E. Wolf-Ferrari." *Musica d'oggi* [Milan] 10 [series 1] (1928): 8.

Rensis, Raffaello de. "In occasione della *Vedova scaltra,* un aspetto sconosciuto di Wolf-Ferrari." *Nuova Italia musicale* [Rome] 4/no. 3 (1931): 5.

Gasco, A. "*I quattro rusteghi* al Costanzi (1923)," "*La vedova scaltra* e un musicista più scaltra di lei (1931)." In *Da Cimarosa a Strawinsky,* 385, 392, 398. Rome, 1939.

Gavazzeni, G. "Lettera da Milano: *La dama boba* di Wolf-Ferrari alla Scala." *La rassegna musicale* 12 (1939): 78.

Zentner, W. "Zum Opernschaffen Ermanno Wolf-Ferraris." *Zeitschrift für Musikwissenschaft* 108 (1941): 13.

Hübsch-Pfleger, L. "Unveröffentlichte Briefe Ermanno Wolf-Ferraris." *Zeitschrift für Musikwissenschaft* 117 (1951): 24.

Smith, C. "City Opera Presents *I quattro rusteghi.*" *Musical America* 71/no. 4 (1951): 5, 23.

Vigolo, G. "Pudori perduti" [*I gioielli della Madonna*]. In *Mille e una sera all' opera e al concerto,* 255. Florence, 1971.

Keller, Hans. "Ermanno Wolf-Ferrari: the Problem of Our Time." *Opera* January (1976).

unpublished–

Pfannkuch, W. "Das Opernschaffen Ermanno Wolf-Ferraris." Ph.D. dissertation, University of Kiel, 1952.

* * *

Ermanno Wolf-Ferrari was Venetian by birth, although his painter father came from Bavaria. By adding his mother's maiden name to the plain German surname Wolf, he seems to have wished to emphasize his Italian nationality, though he did not drop his Christian name, one which is uncommon in Italy and corresponds to the very Germanic-sounding Hermann. His studies in Rome and Munich seem also to symbolize his dual national allegiance, but the Italian publisher Ricordi would not take him on as a composer, and from his mid-twenties he seems to have accepted the fact that his operas had more success north of the Alps than in Italy. Along with that success, however, his work as a teacher in his native Venice meant that his life was largely divided between that city and Munich. The War seems to have deeply shocked him, and for some time he took refuge in Zurich and composed little or nothing.

Wolf-Ferrari composed no less than fifteen operas (the first of them, *Irene* at the age of twenty to his own text), and it seems more than likely that until we know more than just the two or three which are popular it will remain difficult to make an assessment of his contribution to the genre. An examination of the scores, or even listening to a recording or broadcast, is not the same as knowing if these works could appeal lastingly to that wide public which is, after all, arguably the ultimate judge of an opera's viability and quality in the theater. In the meantime it looks as if there is more to Wolf-Ferrari than has met the eye; for example, although he could and usually did write conventionally, although elegantly and delightfully, in melody and harmony, he can also be boldly dissonant (as in the opening bars of his Cinderella opera *Cenerentola* and the quarrel in act III of *Il campiello*) or emotionally complex (as in parts of *Gli amanti sposi* and the almost unknown *Sly, ovvero La leggenda del dormiente risvegliato.* It is strange, too, to realize that his last opera, *Gli dei a Tebe* dates from as late as 1943 and had its first production in Hanover during World War II. However, the major upheavals that had by now taken place in European music had not affected his style fundamentally, and his dual Italian-German cultural nature seems to have remained to the last.

The influences of other styles on Wolf-Ferrari had come earlier. One was Wagner's *Tristan und Isolde* which dealt with human emotion more than gods and legends. Another was that of Italian *verismo* or "realism" *à la* Mascagni and Leoncavallo, which first made itself felt in *I gioielli della Madonna,* doubtless partly because of the Neapolitan setting and the references to the Catholic faith, but also perhaps because Wolf-Ferrari felt he needed to win over the branch of Italian opinion which favored such an approach to opera (though this particular work had its premiere not in Italy but Berlin). It has been argued, and perhaps rightly, that his essentially sensitive nature was not in sympathy with the cruder kinds of musical and dramatic effects, although he must have known that the ability to be direct and even raw in utterance is among the strengths of several major operatic composers including Verdi, Wagner and Puccini. He seems to have been happiest and most successful in comedy and in portraying the gentler emotions.

Of Wolf-Ferrari's operas, only the one-act *intermezzo Il segreto di Susanna* is really familiar to audiences everywhere for its amusingly topical story (the secret is her smoking), elegant humor and lively melody. *I quattro rusteghi,* inspired by Goldoni's Venetian comedy, has a brisk and attractive *buffo* quality as well as some romantic moments that may be indebted to Verdi's *Falstaff.* The earlier opera *Le donne curiose* is also taken from the same lively eighteenth century writer, as are the late pieces *La vedova scaltra* and *Il campiello,* and this fellow Venetian clearly had a lasting appeal to this perhaps self-doubting composer.

—Christopher Headington

THE WOMAN WITHOUT A SHADOW
See DIE FRAU OHNE SCHATTEN

THE WORLD OF THE MOON
See IL MONDO DELLA LUNA

WOZZECK.

Composer: Alban Berg.

Librettist: Alban Berg (after Georg Büchner).

First Performance: Berlin, Staatsoper, 14 December 1925.

Roles: Marie (soprano); Captain (tenor); Drum Major (tenor); Wozzeck (baritone); Doctor (bass); Margaret (mezzo-soprano or contralto); Andres (tenor); Child (child soprano); Two Apprentices (bass and baritone); Fool (tenor); Soldier (tenor); Townsman (tenor); chorus (SATTBBBB).

Publications

books–

Musikblätter des Anbruch: Alban Bergs "Wozzeck" und die Musikkritik. Vienna, 1926.

Mahler, Fritz. *Zu Alban Berg's Oper "Wozzeck".* Vienna, 1957.

Ploebsch, G. *Alban Bergs "Wozzeck".* Strasbourg, 1968.

Hilmar, E. *Wozzeck von Alban Berg: Entstehung—erste Erfolge—Repressionen (1914-1935).* Vienna, 1975.

Vogelsand, L. *Dokumentation zur Oper "Wozzeck" von Alban Berg: die Jahre des Durchbruchs 1925-32.* Laaber, 1977.

Kolleritsch, O. ed. *50 Jahre Wozzeck von Alban Berg: Vorgeschichte und Auswirkungen in der Opernästhetik.* Gratz, 1978.

Perle, George. *The Operas of Alban Berg, I: Wozzeck.* Berkeley, 1980.

Schmalfeldt, Janet. *Berg's "Wozzeck": Harmonic Language and Dramatic Design.* New Haven, 1983.

Jarman, Douglas. *Alban Berg: Wozzeck.* Cambridge, 1989.

articles–

Viebig, E. "Alban Bergs 'Wozzeck': ein Beitrag zum Opernproblem." *Die Musik* 15 (1923): 506.

Berio, Luciano. "Invito a Wozzeck." *Il diapasion* 3 (1952): 14.

Blaukopf, K. *Autobiographische Elemente in Alban Bergs 'Wozzeck'.* Österreichische Musikzeitschrift 9 (1954): 155.

Treitler, Leo. " 'Wozzeck' et l'Apocalypse." *Schweizerische Musikzeitung/Revue musicale suisse* 106 (1976): 249; English version in *Critical Inquiry* winter (1976).

Schmidt, Henry J. "Alban Berg's Wozzeck." In *Georg Büchner. The Complete Collected Works,* translated and edited by Henry J. Schmidt, 388-92. New York, 1977.

Peterson, Peter. "Wozzecks persönliche Leitmotive." *Hamburger Jahrbuch für Musikwissenschaft* 4 (1980): 33.

Radice, Mark A. "The anatomy of a libretto: the music inherent in Büchner's *Wozzeck.*" *Music Review* 41 (1980): 233.

Avant-scène opéra 36 (1981) [*Wozzeck* issue].

Rosenfeld, Gerhard, Siegfried Matthus, and Pavel Eckstein. "Der epochale *Wozzeck* zum 100. Geburtstag von Alban Berg." *Oper Heute* 7 (1984): 110.

Ardoin, John. "Apropos *Wozzeck.*" *Opera Quarterly* 3 (1985): 68.

Greene, Susan. "Wozzeck, and Marie: Outcast in Search of an Honest Morality." *Opera Quarterly* 3 (1985): 112.

* * *

Wozzeck, a soldier of the lowest rank, is ridiculed by his Captain, his fellow soldier Andres, and the Doctor, for whose bizarre dictary experiments Wozzeck acts as a subject in order to supplement his meagre income. All these are his intellectual and spiritual inferiors, and none has his acute appreciation of social injustice. Marie, the mother of Wozzeck's child, is unable to resist the charms of the shallow Drum Major and is seduced by him. His attention having been drawn to Marie's infidelity, Wozzeck challenges her to admit it, but she refuses. Her spiteful reaction ("Rather a knife in my body than a hand laid on me") and the sight of her dancing openly with the Drum Major arouse Wozzeck's imagination. He kills Marie before she has an opportunity to convey her repentance to him. Guilt and terror lead Wozzeck back to the scene of the crime, where he drowns himself.

GEORG BÜCHNERS

WOZZECK

OPER
IN 3 AKTEN (15 SZENEN)

VON

ALBAN BERG

Op. 7

PARTITUR

UNIVERSAL-EDITION A. G.
WIEN U. E. Nr. 7379 LEIPZIG

Wozzeck, title page of first edition of score, 1926

Their child, on hearing of his mother's death, is drawn by innocent curiosity to look at the body.

Berg's first essay in operatic composition was not only a resounding commercial success on its appearance in 1925 but has maintained its place in the repertoire throughout the postwar period. Regarded by some as atonal, its musical language is perhaps best thought of as an eclectic blend which draws on the resources heard in Schoenberg's *Erwartung* while maintaining strong links with the expanded tonality characteristic of Strauss's *Elektra*. Its musico-dramatic orientation also embodies compromise, coming close to Expressionism at some points—notably Marie's murder—but essentially naturalistic in the manner of Berg's Austrian contemporaries. His literary source, Büchner's *Woyzeck*, was the product of a revolutionary sensibility which stressed the plight of the working class and held bourgeois values up to ridicule, and thus through a fortunate accident of history needed no major reinterpretation in order to mesh with the aesthetics of Krausian Vienna.

Only judicious cuts were needed for Berg to adapt the text of his libretto from Franzos's masterly realization of Büchner's hastily written drafts. In devising the format of the opera, however, he showed a sense of musico-dramatic vision which compares with Boito's. The fifteen short scenes are organized, according to Berg's own description, through abstract musical forms: baroque suite, rhapsody, military march, lullaby, passacaglia and rondo (act I); a five-movement symphony (act II); inventions on a theme, a note, a rhythm, a chord, a key and a *moto perpetuo* (act III). That this well known account of the work is slightly forced merely underlines its quality of deliberation and artifice, which complements the music's wide-ranging harmonic and motivic language. But closer study also reveals a careful web of cross-references within the musical substance, including literalistic leitmotives of the Straussian kind as well as a more abstract system of organization which arguably supports the consistency of forceful expression that is the opera's hallmark.

Despite the organization of the opera into discrete formal units, an impression of through-composed music-drama is generated by the orchestral interludes which link the scenes of each act. These tend either to summarize the music of the preceding scene through abbreviated and concentrated recapitulation, producing an effect of heightened reflection, or to introduce a complex musical texture—as with the off-stage military music (act I, scene 3) or the dance music of the large tavern scene (act II, scene 4)—so as to establish a rich context for the vocal exchanges of the following scene. After the scene of Wozzeck's death, the final orchestral interlude— which begins in a clear D minor—carries the entire burden of his tragedy, and the children's scene which follows is also sustained by the orchestra's glinting *moto perpetuo*. The post-Wagnerian credentials of Berg's approach to operatic composition are also confirmed by the absence of arias and other set pieces, despite the apparent reliance on conventional forms. This is true even of Marie's famous lullaby (act I, scene 3) and her other intimate exchanges with the child (act II, scene 1; act III, scene 1), and of the stylized folk songs sung by Andres (act I, scene 2; act II, scene 4), all of which are conceived as indicators of social status and projected as stage music by a recognizable simplification of musical language.

Berg reserves the effect of alienation, which one may easily read into Büchner's drama throughout, for the final scene of the opera, in which the children greet the news of Marie's death much as they might the arrival of a traveling showman. Elsewhere, the narrative focus and the play of motivic musical materials project a sympathy for Wozzeck—famously enhanced by Fischer-Dieskau in his recorded performance (1965)—which is thought by some to distort the play. The other roles are less troublesome, and all are well characterized; those of Wozzeck and Marie are notable in their own right. The opera makes sensitive use of *Sprechstimme*, together with sung delivery of all kinds including *bel canto*. *Lulu*—a very different opera—is now regarded as the composer's masterpiece, but *Wozzeck's* historical position is no less assured.

—Anthony Pople

THE WRECKERS.

Composer: Ethel Smyth.

Librettist: Ethel Smyth (with Henry Bennet Brewster).

First Performance: Leipzig, 1906.

Publications

article–

Abromeit, Kathleen A. "Ethel Smyth, *The Wreckers*, and Sir Thomas Beecham." *Musical Quarterly* 73 (1989).

*   *   *

In the early 1900s, when Ethel Smyth was searching for a suitable theme for her next opera, she recalled a visit she had paid to the Piper's Hole in the Isles of Scilly. This cave near the sea made a deep impression on her at the time. She later asked her philosopher-friend, Henry Bennet Brewster, to write a libretto based on the images of that visit, combined with stories of the old Cornish wreckers.

The resulting libretto depicts the inhabitants of a Cornish village who depend on the plunder of shipwrecks for their livelihood. The shipwrecks are arranged by the planting of false beacons or the removal of real ones. Smyth summarizes the plot as follows: "Two lovers who, by kindling secret beacons, endeavoured to counteract the savage policy of the community—how they were caught in the act by the Wreckers' Committee, a sort of secret court which was the sole authority they recognized—and condemned to die in one of those sea-invaded caves."

The libretto was originally in French and titled *Les Naufrageurs* (The Wreckers). Rumor had it that French conductor Andre Messager would be the new artistic director of the English opera company, Covent Garden. Because of this, Smyth and Brewster felt that a French libretto would give *The Wreckers* its best chance for a performance in England. However, for unknown reasons, the work was never performed in its original French version. Usually, the work is performed in English, although there is a German version as well (*Strandrecht*).

Smyth encountered difficulties in obtaining performances of *The Wreckers* despite the fact that she worked very hard to "sell" the work. According to Charles Reid in *Thomas Beecham: An Independent Biography*, "For five years Ethel Smyth, wearing mannish tweeds and an assertively cocked felt hat, had been striding about Europe, cigar in mouth, trying to sell her opera *The Wreckers* to timorous or stubborn impresarios." Whenever she could induce a conductor or musical director to consider the work, and let her play it, it was received with such enthusiasm that she thought an offer to produce it was bound to follow. Frequently the score was returned with a letter giving all sorts of reasons for the impossibility of producing this "noble and original" work in the near future.

One of the most successful productions of *The Wreckers* was under the baton of Sir Thomas Beecham. Beecham was very excited to conduct the six afternoon performances and have the opportunity to introduce himself to London as an opera conductor. Unfortunately, the preparation for *The Wreckers* was far from adequate. Beecham crammed all the rehearsals into ten days and nights. Smyth was very disappointed in Beecham's approach to the opera, and she openly expressed her opinions to him. Despite the problems in the preparation, it was a success in the eyes of the public as well as a professional success for Smyth and Beecham.

Smyth uses a large orchestra throughout *The Wreckers*. In addition, she employs leitmotifs that serve as a means of both symphonic development and dramatic allusion. Smyth also relies heavily on dense contrapuntal writing. All these techniques demonstrate a Wagnerian influence. *The Wreckers* is considered by many scholars to be the most powerful English opera of its period.

—Kathleen A. Abromeit

WUNDERLICH, Fritz.

Tenor. Born 26 September 1930, in Kusel, Germany. Died 17 September 1966, in Heidelberg. Studied with Margarethe von Winterfeldt at the Freiburg Hochschule für Musik; debut as Tamino in *Die Zauberflöte,* Freiburg, 1954; sang in Stuttgart, 1955-58, Frankfurt, 1958-60, and in Munich from 1960; also sang in Vienna from 1962; Covent Garden debut as Don Ottavio, 1965.

Publications

About WUNDERLICH: articles–

Steane, J.B. *The Grand Tradition.* London, 1974.
Canning, Hugh. "Fritz Wunderlich: Unforgettable, Unforgotten." *Opera* September (1990).

*   *   *

The outstanding German lyric tenor of his generation, Fritz Wunderlich was first and foremost a melodist. Although he played many operatic roles in his brief career (which ended in a tragic accident) they were those in which qualities of sweetness were more important than those of strength. In some ways the role of Mozart's Prince Tamino, the hero of *Die Zauberflöte,* seemed tailor-made for him, and it is appropriate that he began and ended his work in the opera house with it. Tamino is an innocent figure who nevertheless has the character and courage to face the unknown in a series of trials that lead him to love and a more mature understanding of himself, and while Schikaneder's story and libretto in themselves can seem a little silly, it can convince us fully when allied to Mozart's music sung by an artist such as Wunderlich.

It was in Mozart, and as Tamino above all, that Wunderlich was seen at his finest, and also as an actor who characterized his role with his voice as much as with his physical presence. Although he could elicit sympathy as Don Ottavio, the lover of Donna Anna in *Don Giovanni,* inevitably the baritone who played Giovanni dominated the stage proceedings. In fact, many of the roles that Wunderlich played, and played well, did not allow his qualities of firmness and essential goodness to shine fully: another example is his portrayal of Onegin's friend Lensky in Tchaikovsky's *Eugene Onegin.* Still, both Don Ottavio and Lensky take up moral attitudes against an unscrupulous man, and in this respect the roles suited him. As Alfredo in Verdi's *La traviata* he could also show a devoted earnestness and fidelity of character. In Pfitzner's *Palestrina,* he played the Italian Renaissance composer himself, a leading role though not a romantic one. Palestrina is shown here as undergoing various uncertainties

Fritz Wunderlich as Don Ottavio in *Don Giovanni*

of mind and feeling external pressures but ultimately saving the art of liturgical music for the Catholic Church. The opera is set in 1563, when the real Palestrina was approaching forty; Wunderlich himself was in his mid-thirties and identified well with the role of an artist seeking to serve his God in an imperfect world, while the spirituality of his voice made a deep impression on those who heard these Vienna performances in 1965.

With his sweet, firm, yet sensitive tone and an easy stage presence, Wunderlich was also effective in the comedy role of the young actor Henry in Strauss's *Die Schweigsame Frau* and the Greek shepherd boy Leukippos in the same composer's *Daphne.* He also sang successfully in operetta. At the time of his death, he was considering singing some of the major Wagnerian roles, and the idea of him as Parsifal in Wagner's opera is perhaps one of the major might-have-beens in the history of 20th-century opera; here his performance might have been a revelation. Nor do we have memories or recordings of Wunderlich as the apprentice David in *Die Meistersinger,* although tantalizingly, the richness of his expressive characterization in the deeper kind of German music

is to be heard outside opera in his recorded performance with Klemperer of Mahler's *Das Lied von der Erde.*

Fritz Wunderlich made a number of recordings, including Tamino in *Die Zauberflöte,* Wozzeck's soldier friend Andres opposite Dietrich Fischer-Dieskau in Berg's gloomy and powerful opera *Wozzeck,* and Jenik in Smetana's *The Bartered Bride.* There are too few recordings of entire operas with Wunderlich, however, and they do not always feature him in important roles. He may have been happier in his recorded recitals of individual numbers from opera and operetta which feature such composers as Handel, Mozart, Donizetti, Verdi, Puccini, Lortzing, Johann Strauss, Lehár and Kálmán.

—Christopher Headington

XERXES
See SERSE

Y

YERMA.

Composer: Heitor Villa-Lobos.

Librettist: Heitor Villa-Lobos (after Lorca).

First Performance: Santa Fe, August 1971.

Roles: Yerma (soprano); Juan (tenor); Victor (baritone); Maria (mezzo-soprano); Dolores (mezzo-soprano); Old Woman (mezzo-soprano); Six Laundresses (three sopranos, three mezzo-sopranos); Masked Man (tenor); Masked Woman (soprano); chorus (SSSAATTBBB).

*   *   *

There are minimal differences between Federico Garcia Lorca's original play, *Yerma,* and the libretto Villa-Lobos set. The play itself, usually regarded as the centerpiece of a folk-triptych also comprising *Blood Wedding* and *The House Of Bernarda Alba,* is entirely self-contained, and the essentially static nature of its scenes and the world they depict make *Yerma* a fine vehicle for operatic treatment. When commissioned, the original objective had been to set the text in English for the American and British markets, and a translator was even engaged. Villa-Lobos, however, decided that only the Spanish text would do and independently started composing. The use of the original language has unjustly kept *Yerma* off the stage; opera houses would not countenance performances in Spanish and consequently the work languished for sixteen years until the Santa Fe premiere in 1971, twelve years after Villa-Lobos had died. The opera waited another eighteen years to cross the Atlantic for its British premiere, and then only in a concert performance in the Queen Elizabeth Hall.

Although the music is unmistakably Villa-Lobos', stylistically the composer relied on Puccini (a favorite composer of Villa-Lobos' father) as a model. One will look as much in vain, though, for any outright reminder of the composer of "Nessun dorma" as one would for the familiar style of the *Bachianas Brasileiras.* Structurally, the first act is the least successful (it is also the longest) and the at times workaday recitative in the first scene indicates clearly that its composer took a little time to warm thoroughly to the task (it should be remembered that Villa-Lobos was by no means an experienced or prolific writer of operas: *Yerma* was his second, whatever he may have claimed at various times). The prelude, though, is of greater moment: brooding and heavy with a suppressed sensuality that, while it is gradually dispelled during act I, is never entirely absent, and returns to erupt violently in the final scene of the work with tragic results.

Into this repressive atmosphere so expressive of the chauvinistic culture of Southern Spain, Yerma herself is cast. The very name, an invention of Lorca's meaning "She who is barren," encapsulates her situation: she is childless, but it is clear that it might be her husband, Juan, who is unwilling or infertile. Yerma is a proud and turbulent woman whose intense and active nature contrasts starkly with her surroundings. Some productions of the play have concentrated Yerma's dilemma solely into conflict with her husband, but this is a mistake that Villa-Lobos did not make. Whatever Juan's motives, both he and Yerma are prisoners of their situation, and if he copes less than tactfully with his wife, it is not so much a personal failing as a cultural one. The odds are stacked in his favor, but the viewpoint of the opera is most definitely Yerma's; she is onstage nearly throughout, and when absent she is the sole topic of conversation. The roles of Victor (Yerma's childhood sweetheart) and the pregnant (later maternal) Maria (originally created by Frederica von Stade in 1971) are in reality just part of the scenery: they are personifications of Yerma's imprisonment and isolation just as surely as any gaoler would be.

There are some striking moments in the score, perhaps the best being the magnificent depiction of a mountain shrine at the start of the very last scene, and the opening of act II, which begins with six raucous village-women, washing their clothes and gossiping vociferously about Yerma. This short five-minute scene acts like a scherzo preceding the profound inner heart of the whole work which follows in the next. This, at over half-an-hour, is the longest scene in the work, longer even than the entire final act. It contains the deepest and most intense music as the seeds of the eventual tragedy are sown. Chamber musical textures are frequently employed, and there is an overpowering intimacy that Villa-Lobos' Italian master would have been proud of. The tolling timpani chords embody in sound the very hopelessness of Yerma's life, being both percussively active and utterly immovable. The second act closes with low wind instruments, shepherds' bells, and the wailing of Juan's sisters in a spectral music of almost supernatural power.

The supernatural is of no help to Yerma, though. She tries magic and ritual, ultimately religion, all in vain. Her desperation is never so complete that she will contemplate infidelity to Juan to fulfill her white-hot desire for a child, and she rejects just such a proposition from a young man's mother as an unacceptable compromising of family honor. In both short scenes of the third act, Yerma is confronted by her husband who becomes increasingly hostile. Juan's motives are certainly open to interpretation as to whether he wishes to keep his wife's affection uncluttered by children for himself or merely esteems her as a sex object, but Yerma's frustration as his unfulfilled ornament boils over and, driven by his unthinking and unfeeling indifference to her needs, she strangles him. Her final solo is the most moving point in the score: as soon as Juan collapses, she realizes that her only chance for a child has died with him. The final ironies are most telling, for in killing Juan to free herself she has merely bolted the door of her childlessness the more, and she laments not for her once-living husband but the unconceived child of her fantasies that she can now never bear.

—Guy Rickards

THE YOUNG LORD
See DER JUNGE LORD

Z

ZAMPA, ou La fiancée de marbre.

Composer: Ferdinand Hérold.

Librettist: Anne Honoré Joseph Duveyrier.

First Performance: Paris, Opéra-Comique, 3 May 1831.

Publications

article–

Berlioz, Hector. "De la partition de *Zampa.*" *Journal des débats* 27 September (1835).

*　　*　　*

Ferdinand Hérold was a talented composer who spent what seems an inordinate amount of time attempting to crack the institutions of French opera. After his return to France in 1815 following a sojourn in Italy under the auspices of the *Prix de Rome* where he apparently spent more time working in Neapolitan theaters than elsewhere, he became a *maestro al cembalo* at the Théâtre Italiènne in Paris. From 1815 to 1830 he also worked in various capacities at both the Opéra Comique and the Opéra. Only with *Zampa,* an *opéra comique* in three acts with a text by Anne Duveyrier which premiered 3 May 1831, did the composer find the success long overdue him. *La pré aux clerc,* which followed in 1832, was even more successful, if not as competent as *Zampa,* but Hérold was unable to build upon these successes due to illness. He died of tuberculosis the following year.

Zampa is particularly interesting since it is the only French opera which attempts to recreate some aspect of the Don Juan legend. Zampa is a libertine nobleman and pirate, who is willing to kill Alphonse in order to seduce, then marry, Alphonse's fiancee, Camille, whose father is held hostage to Zampa's outrageous demands. During a drinking party, Zampa places a ring on the finger of a stone statue of his former bride, Albena, whom he had abandoned. The statue's fingers grasp the ring, and while the company is horrified, Zampa dismisses the apparition with a swagger and a ribald, giddy tune. When Camille pleads for mercy, Zampa reveals himself to be a nobleman as well as Alphonse's brother. As a result Alphonse will not fight Zampa, but Zampa orders him to prison and demands that Albena's statue be tossed into the sea. As he fights with Camille, the statue's stony fingers grasp Zampa and will not release him. Albena takes Zampa into the sea; Camille is reunited with Alphonse, and her father is released from prison. At the end the statue rises from the sea to bless the happy couple.

The solemnity of the situations is interspersed with frivolous music. Hérold reveals himself a master at the juxtaposition of disparate elements, a feature of French Romantic thought which had risen to the fore in Hugo's *Préface* to *Cromwell* in 1826. Elegantly satirical melodies and scenes intensify the horror of Zampa's treatment of Camille and Albena. In terms of Romantic theater, however, the most telling stroke is the presence of a notable anti-hero whose misdeeds are punished not by divine retribution but by supernatural intervention by a former lover. The theme of the wronged wife who takes an errant lover/husband to an eternal reward is a common enough theme in Romantic myth as well as opera.

—Aubrey S. Garlington

———————

ZANDONAI, Riccardo.

Composer. Born 30 May 1883, in Sacco Trentino. Died 5 June 1944, in Pesaro. Married: soprano Tarquinia Tarquini, 1917. Studied with Gianferrari at Rovereto, 1893-98; studied with Mascagni at the Liceo Rossini in Pesaro, 1898-1902; international success with *Conchita,* 1911; involved in a political movement for the return of former Italian provinces during World War I; director of the Liceo Rossini in Pesaro, 1939.

Operas

Publisher: Ricordi.

La coppa del re, G. Chiesa (after Schiller), c. 1906 [unperformed].

L'uccellino d'oro (children's opera), G. Chelodi (after Grimm), Sacco di Rovereto, 1907.

Il grillo del focolare, C. Hanau (after Dickens), Turin, 1908.

Conchita, M. Vaucaire and C. Zangarini (after P. Louÿs), Milan, 1911.

Melenis, M. Spiritini and C. Zangarini (after L. Bouillet), Milan, 1912.

Francesca da Rimini, d'Annunzio (abridged by T. Ricordi), Turin, 1914.

La via della finestra, G. Adami (after Scribe), Pesaro, 1919; revised, Trieste, 1923.

Giulietta e Romeo, A. Rossato (after da Porto and Shakespeare), Rome, 1922.

I cavalieri di Ekebù, A. Rossato (after S. Lagerlöf), Milan, 1925.

Giuliano, A. Rossato (after J. da Varagine), Naples, 1928.

Una partita, A. Rossato (after Dumas père), Milan, 1933.

La farsa amorosa, A. Rossato (after Alarcón), Rome, 1933.

Il bacio, A. Rossato and E. Mucci (after G. Keller), 1940-44 [unfinished].

Other works: incidental music, orchestral works, vocal works, chamber music.

Publications

About ZANDONAI: books–

Ziliotto, B. *Francesca da Rimini: guida attraverso il poema e la musica*. Milan, 1923.

Barblan, G., R. Mariani et al. *A Riccardo Zandonai*. Trent, 1952.

Tarquini, T. Zandonai. *Da "Vie del paradiso" al n. 1 (ricordi vicini e lontani)*. Rovereto, 1955.

Cagnoli, B. *Riccardo Zandonai*. Trent, 1978.

Bassi, Adriano. *Riccardo Zandonai, tracce di vita*. Poggibonsi, 1982.

Chiesa, Renato, ed. *Riccardo Zandonai*. Milan, 1983.

articles–

Barini, G. "*Conchita* di Riccardo Zandonai." *Nuova antologia* 242 (1912): 714.

Angeli, A. d'. "*Francesca da Rimini* di R. Zandonai." *Cronaca musicale* [Pesaro] 18 (1914): 136.

Mondaldi, G. "La *Francesca da Rimini* di Riccardo Zandonai." *Nuova antologia* 254 (1914): 322.

Cesari, G. "*Giulietta e Romeo* di Arturo Rossato e Riccardo Zandonai." *Rivista musicale italiana* 29 (1922): 113.

Pratella, F.B. "*Giulietta e Romeo* di Riccardo Zandonai." *Pensiero musicale* [Bologna] 2 (1922): 64.

Lualdi, A. "*I cavalieri di Ekebù* di R. Zandonai alla Scala." *Serate musicali* [Milan] (1928): 171.

Napolitano, F.N. "Lettera da Napoli" *[Giuliano]*. *La rassegna musicale* 1 (1928): 192.

Pannain, G. "Le prime esecuzioni: Zandonai: *Giuliano*." *Rivista musicale italiana* 35 (1928): 161.

Rossi-Doria, G. "Lettera da Roma" *[La farsa amorosa]*. *La rassegna musicale* 6 (1933): 117.

Gasco, A. "Zandonai e *Giulietta e Roma*," "I sorrisi della *Farsa amorosa*." In *Da Cimarosa a Strawinsky*, 258, 268. Rome, 1939.

Tomelleri, L. "Francesca da Rimini: d'Annunzio e Zandonai." In *Gabriele d'Annunzio e la musica*, 28. Milan, 1939; reprinted in *Rivista musicale italiana* 43 (1939): 188.

Barblan, G. "Riccardo Zandonai e la fede nel melodramma." *Ricordiana* [Milan] 2/new series (1962): 422; English translation, *Ricordiana* [London]7/no. 1 (1962): 8, 13.

Chiesa, R. "La *Francesca da Rimini* di d'Annunzio nella musica di Riccardo Zandonai." *Quaderni dannunziani* [Brescia] nos. 32-33 (1965): 320.

Vigolo, G. "Zandonai con d'Annunzio." In *Mille e una sera all' opera e al concerto*, 484. Florence, 1971.

Conrad, Peter. "A Woman in Flames." *Opera News* 48/no. 14 (1984): 14.

Kestner, Joseph. "Legend of Lovers: from Dante to Zandonai, the Tale of Ill-Fated Paolo and Francesca has Fired the Imagination of Many an Artist." *Opera News* 48/no. 14 (1984): 8.

Zondergeld, Rein A. "Riccardo Zandonai: the Master of Fake Emotion." *Opera* November (1984).

*   *   *

Riccardo Zandonai belonged to what was later to be called the "eighties generation" *(generazione dell'ottanta)* by the musicologist Massimo Mila. These composers were linked by little more than their dates of birth; in fact they display all the diversity of Italian music in the first half of the twentieth century. While most reflected the contemporary desire in Italy to change the balance of music from opera to instrumental music (chiefly on Austro-German models), others were content to expand on the elements of Austro-German music which had already been adopted in Italian opera.

Just as in 1890, when the tradition of opera composition in Italy seemed to receive new impetus with the work of Mascagni and the other members of the "young school" *(giovane scuola)*, so in 1914 a new start seemed likely with Zandonai's *Francesca da Rimini*. On the eve of the First World War, operatic life in Italy was about to change from a repertoire based on contemporary works to the situation which has held for the rest of the century—a repertoire based on classic works from the past. Zandonai was the choice of the most powerful music publisher, Ricordi, to continue their prestigious line of composers and be "Puccini's successor."

Arrigo Boito personally recommended Zandonai to Giulio Ricordi in 1907 and the composer was immediately contracted to write an opera with a ready-made libretto on Dickens's *The Cricket on the Hearth*. Next he was offered Pierre Louÿs's *La femme et le pantin*, a subject with a Spanish setting which Puccini had already turned down. Zandonai was not daunted by a piece which so strongly echoed *Carmen*, and Ricordi sent him to Spain to capture the atmosphere for his work.

A letter from Seville to Ricordi in 1909 records Zandonai's strong impression of Spanish folk music and the declaration that "even Bizet neglected the most interesting types of Spanish song." Zandonai was determined that his *Conchita* (as the opera was eventually called) should be "really Spanish-speaking." Other comments in this letter give hints about Zandonai's approach to composition and show how a composer who feels himself to be part of a living tradition can confidently find musical material from extra-musical stimuli. He writes about the great buildings of Seville as "grandiose tone-poems" and the little alleys with their "incredibly white building and little balconies" being "little snatches of music which an artist can capture and reproduce."

Following the successful production of *Conchita* and the far less popular *Melenis*, Zandonai's moment of glory came with *Francesca da Rimini*. Here he catches perfectly the precious medievalism of D'Annunzio's text, and creates a magically colored score of passion and refinement. It was his only significant international success, and is still occasionally revived in Italy and elsewhere. Thereafter the story of Zandonai's career is one of decline. A single collaboration with Giuseppe Adami brought into existence the comic opera *La via della finestra*, and later the composer found a long-term collaborator in the journalist Arturo Rossato. Their first work together (and Rossato's first libretto) was *Giulietta e Romeo*, effectively a return to the terrain and manner of *Francesca*. Zandonai felt that he had reached his compositional maturity with their later opera *I cavalieri di Ekebù*, with its Nordic setting. The composer's last years were spent in Pesaro, where he succeeded his teacher Mascagni as the Director of the Conservatory. After the fall of Mussolini and the German occupation, he and his wife took refuge in a monastery above Pesaro, where he worked on an opera, *Il bacio*, incomplete at his death.

Zandonai was effectively trapped by the passing of the Romantic period in music. His inheritance was the symphonically structured operatic idiom that held sway in Italy after Verdi's *Falstaff* (1893). His scores are shaped by the orchestral web, into which the vocal lines are woven. His orchestral sound is profoundly colored by the work of Strauss and Debussy, while the vocal delivery is essentially that of the *verismo* opera, robust declamation and lyrical passages alike being supported by a weighty orchestral sound.

Zandonai's harmony is still tonal, but harmonic movement is by way of parallels, altered dominants and subdominants. Modal and whole-tone passages sit side by side, while passages in a specific key may be qualified by a "foreign" chord: D flat major—G flat major—A flat major—G7—D flat major. Textures are created out of a selection of motifs attached to characters and ideas in the general Italian post-Wagner manner ("Wagner explained to the masses," in the words of Rubens Tedeschi). The motifs themselves are generally well-characterized, and steer clear of the obvious immediacy and occasional vulgarity of some of the *verismo* composers.

Zandonai's vocal writing accepts the norms of *verismo:* the tenor lover, soprano heroine and evil baritone. In each case the writing makes extreme demands on the singer in terms of tessitura and sheer power and weight. A feature of some of Zandonai's operatic scores is the extended descriptive orchestral passage, like the third-act prelude in *Conchita* (an impression of the Sevillian night) and the "Cavalcata" in *Giulietta e Romeo*, which describes Romeo's frantic ride back to Verona. Zandonai also wrote a number of orchestral pieces in their own right, often with a descriptive intention, such as *Primavera in Val di Sole* (Spring in the Val di Sole), and *Concerto andaluso* (Andalusian concerto).

With the passing of this late-Romantic style and the establishment of the Fascist state after 1922, Zandonai's aesthetic was well in tune with the provincial and backward-looking nature of much music during the period. In 1932 he was one of the co-signatories of Alceo Toni's Manifesto of Italian Musicians for the Tradition of Nineteenth-Century Romantic Art. This unequivocally expressed the desire to turn away from the experimentation current in Western music elsewhere in favor of the standards of the turn of the century. While a totalitarian, repressive state is not a necessary condition of provincialism and regression in music, the opportunism of the period created the backdrop against which Zandonai's later works were composed.

—Kenneth Chalmers

ZAR UND ZIMMERMANN, oder Die Zwei Peter [Tsar and Carpenter, or the Two Peters].

Composer: Albert Lortzing.

Librettist: Albert Lortzing (after C.C. Römers).

First Performance: Leipzig, Municipal Theater, 22 December 1837.

Roles: Peter I, alias Peter Mikailov (baritone); Peter Ivanov (tenor); Van Bett (bass); Marie (soprano); Marquis de Châteauneuf (tenor); Admiral Lefort (bass); Lord Syndham (bass); Widow Browe (contralto); chorus (SSAATTBB).

Publications

article–

Sanders, E. "*Oberon* and *Zar und Zimmermann*." *Musical Quarterly* 40 (1954): 521.

* * *

Lortzing achieved his first great success with *Zar und Zimmermann, oder Die zwei Peter* which was based on a German translation of the three-act French comédie héroique, *Le Bourgomestre de Sardam ou les deux Pierres* by Mélesville, Boirie, and Merle. He had often acted the role of Châteauneuf in the German translation of the play and knew the material well. As his first mature work, it is one of the cornerstones of German comic opera. For the very first time a composer created a world in which the thoughts and feelings of the German common man were portrayed with insight and charm. At the premiere in Leipzig on 22 December 1837, Lortzing sang the role of Peter Ivanov and his mother played the widow Browe.

The plot revolves around two Russians, tsar Peter who, under the name of Peter Mikailov, is working as a carpenter in the shipyard of the widow Browe in Saardam, and a young deserter, Peter Ivanov. The latter is in love with the mayor's niece, Marie. The mayor, van Bett, has an offer of £2,000 from the English ambassador to check up on a carpenter named Peter, but which Peter? To further complicate matters, the French ambassador is making a play for Marie and, in addition, penetrates the tsar's disguise. The seeds of intrigue, jealousy, and political maneuvers are in place.

Act II begins in the garden, where the wedding feast is under way. Soldiers arrive to check the identity of the foreigners present, and the mayor interrogates several of them. When he tries to have both Mikailov and Ivanov arrested, the English ambassador proclaims the former as the French ambassador and the latter as the Russian tsar. Naturally, confusion reigns at this point.

The final act takes place in the Town Hall where van Bett is rehearsing the formal welcome for the tsar. Mikailov assures Marie that all is well, and after taking Ivanov's identification in return for a sealed letter, he exits. Tsar Peter I sails away triumphantly at the head of his fleet having appointed Ivanov in the letter to an official post in Moscow.

Zar und Zimmermann contains all of the elements that have made Lortzing such an enduring presence in the opera houses of German-speaking countries. The humor is down to earth and infectious; the tunes are attractive and lively; and the plot moves forward briskly, helped in large part by the use of spoken dialogue. From the overture, which is a medley of the best numbers, to van Bett's brilliant opening buffo aria, "O sancta justitia!," to the famous second act sextet, to Marie and Ivanov's final duet, *Zar und Zimmermann* bubbles along with zest and a realistic insight into the human condition.

What makes this particular piece so impressive is that at one stroke Lortzing managed to encapsulate all of the necessary elements of the German comic opera. With few examples to follow, he deftly projected the German character, or at least that side of it which the average public understood. This work did for Germany what Gilbert and Sullivan's *H.M.S. Pinafore* was to do for England some forty years later—it captured the spirit of a time and of a nation.

—Robert H. Cowden

DIE ZAUBERFLÖTE [The Magic Flute].

Composer: Wolfgang Amadeus Mozart.

Librettist: Emanuel Schikaneder.

First Performance: Vienna, Theater auf der Wieden, 30 September 1791.

Roles: Queen of the Night (soprano); Pamina (soprano); Tamino (tenor); Papageno (baritone); Sarastro (bass); Papagena (soprano); Monostatos (tenor); Three Ladies (sopranos, mezzo-soprano); Three Genii (soprano, mezzo-soprano, contralto); Speaker of the Temple (bass); Two Priests (tenor, bass); Two Men in Armor (tenor, bass); chorus (SATTBB).

Publications

books–

Brukner, F. *Die Zauberflöte: unbekannte Handschriften und seltene Drucke aus der Frühzeit der Oper.* Vienna, 1934.

Stefan, P. *Die Zauberflöte: Herkunft, Bedeutung, Geheimnis.* Vienna, 1937.

Friedrich, Götz. *Die humanistische Idee der "Zauberflöte": Ein Beitrag zur Dramaturgie der Oper.* Dresden, 1954.

Brophy, Brigid. *Mozart the Dramatist.* London, 1964; 1988.

Rosenberg, A. *Die Zauberflöte: Geschichte und Deutung.* Munich, 1964.

Moberley, Robert B. *Three Mozart Operas: Figaro, Don Giovanni, The Magic Flute.* London, 1967.

Chailley, J. *La flûte enchantée: opéra maçonnique: essai d'explication du livret et de la musique.* Paris, 1968; English translation by Herbert Weinstock as *"The Magic Flute": Masonic Opera,* New York, 1972.

Batley, E.M. *A Preface to The Magic Flute.* London, 1969.

Ascher, Gloria. *"Die Zauberflöte" und "Die Frau ohne Schatten": Ein Vergleich zwischen zwei Operndichtungen der Humanität.* Berne, 1972.

Pahlen, Kurt. *Wolfgang Amadeus Mozart—"Die Zauberflöte." Ein Opernführer.* Munich, 1978.

Gammond, Peter. *The Magic Flute: A Guide to the Opera.* London, 1979.

Hocquard, Jean-Victor. *La flûte enchantée.* Paris, 1979.

Csampi, Attila, and Dietmar Holland, eds. *Wolfgang Amadeus Mozart: "Die Zauberflöte". Texte, Materialien, Kommentare.* Reinbek bei Hamburg, 1982.

Peter, Christoph. *Die Sprache der Musik in Mozarts Zauberflöte.* Stuttgart, 1983.

Dieckmann, Friedrich, ed. *"Die Zauberflöte": Max Slevogts Randzeichnungen zu Mozarts Handschrift, mit dem Text von Emanuel Schikaneder.* Berlin, 1984.

articles–

Blümml, Emil Karl. "Ausdeutungen der 'Zauberflöte'." *Mozart-Jahrbuch* 1 (1923): 109.

Komorzynski, E. "Die Zauberflöte: Entstehung und Bedeutung des Kunstwerks." *Neues Mozart-Jahrbuch* 1 (1941): 147.

King, A.H. "The Melodic Sources and Affinities of *Die Zauberflöte*." *Musical Quarterly* 36 (1950): 241.

Branscombe, P. " 'Die Zauberflöte': Some Textual and Interpretative Problems." *Proceedings of the Royal Musical Association* 92 (1965-66): 45.

Gruber, G. "Das Autograph der 'Zauberflöte'." *Mozart-Jahrbuch* (1967): 127; (1968-70): 99.

———. "Bedeutung und Spontaneität in Mozarts 'Zauberflöte'." In *Festschrift Walter Senn,* 118. Munich and Salzburg, 1975.

Koenigsberger, D. "A New Metaphor for Mozart's *Magic Flute*." *European Studies Review* 5 (1975): 229.

Starobinsky, Jean. "Pouvoir et lumières dans la *Flûte enchantée*." *XVIIIe siècle* 10 (1978): 435.

Godwin, Jocelyn. "Layers of Meaning in *The Magic Flute*." *Musical Quarterly* 65 (1979): 471.

Wangermée, Robert. "Quelques mystères de *La flûte enchantée*." *Revue belge de musicologie* 34-35 (1980-81): 147.

Köhler, Karl-Heinz. "Zu den Methoden und einigen Ergebnissen der philologischen Analyse am Autograph der *Zauberflöte*." *Mozart-Jahrbuch* (1980-83): 282.

Gurewitsch, Matthew. "In the Mazes of Light and Shadow: A Thematic Comparison of *The Magic Flute* and *Die Frau ohne Schatten*." *Opera Quarterly* 1 no. 2 (1983): 11.

Cole, Malcolm S. "*The Magic Flute* and the Quatrain." *Journal of Musicology* 3 (1984): 157.

Wolff, Christoph. " 'O ew'ge Nacht! Wann wirst du schwinden?' Zum Verständnis der Sprecherszene im ersten Finale von Mozarts *Zauberflöte*." In *Analysen: . . . Festschrift für Hans Heinrich Eggebrecht zum 65. Geburtstag,* edited by Werner Breig et al., 234. Stuttgart, 1984.

Freyhan, Michael. "Toward the Original Text of Mozart's *Die Zauberflöte*." *Journal of the American Musicological Society* 39 (1986): 355.

* * *

Labeled simply a *Grosse Oper* (Grand Opera), *Die Zauberflöte* is Mozart's last opera. Made in collaboration with an old friend, Emanuel Schikaneder (1751-1812), director of the Theater auf der Wieden (Freihaus Theater) since 1789, it is a *Singspiel* consisting of musical numbers and spoken dialogue.

Set in Egypt, colored by Enlightenment ideals and Masonic precepts, and seasoned with comic episodes, magic, and stage machinery, the plot hinges upon a theme of trial and purification, a quest for wisdom guided by friendship and supported by love. Pursued by a frightful serpent, the foreign prince Tamino rushes on stage and faints, most unheroically. Three ladies rescue him. Their mistress, the Queen of the Night, implores Tamino to rescue her beautiful daughter Pamina from the wicked sorcerer Sarastro. Inspired by love, armed with magic bells and a magic flute, and accompanied by the comic bird-catcher Papageno, Tamino embarks upon his journey. Having reached Sarastro's realm, Tamino discovers not a sorcerer but an enlightened ruler. With the truth revealed, Tamino readily agrees to undergo the trials which will make him an initiate of the Sun Temple. United after much tribulation, Tamino and Pamina successfully pass the tests of fire and water. Papageno finds his Papagena, the Queen and her minions are vanquished, and the community rejoices, praising the victory of strength, beauty, and wisdom.

No other Mozart dramatic work has such a complicated early history. Frustratingly little is known about the circumstances that led to the opera's creation. No contract survives. No correspondence chronicles Mozart's creative process. Never before had a libretto been compiled from such a remarkable range of sources: books, contemporary stage works, Masonic ritual and numerology (especially the number three), Schikaneder's earlier works and his Shakespearean experience, and prior compositions of Mozart (e.g., *Zaide, Thamos, König von Ägypten,* and *Die Entführung aus dem Serail*). Selecting ideas, scenes, characters, and plot details, the collaborators assembled from these disparate elements an action-packed entertainment, filled with suspense, spectacle, low comedy, and lofty idealism.

Generally discredited now is the theory that Schikaneder and Mozart reversed the plot in midstream, changing Sarastro from a sorcerer to an enlightened ruler and the Queen of the Night from a sorrowing mother to a destructive force. Generally accepted, on the other hand, is the view that while others such as Karl Ludwig Giesecke or Pater Cantes may

Die Zauberflöte, frontispiece to original libretto, engraving by Ignaz Albert, 1791

have contributed details, Schikaneder was the guiding force who wrote the bulk of the text. A more intriguing question cannot be answered: what was Mozart's share in the fashioning of the libretto? The text—simple in diction, pictorial, intelligible, and often inspiring—stands well above the average German opera libretto of its time. Surface inconsistencies notwithstanding, it fired Mozart's musical imagination. Within its frame, his music could unfold fully.

Aligned on the sides of darkness and light, the seven principal characters form a hierarchy. At the bottom, Monostatos (Italian *opera buffa* style) opposes Papageno and Papagena (folklike German songs). At the top, the Queen of the Night (Italian *opera seria* style) opposes the wise Sarastro (simple, exalted hymn style). In the middle, with no counterparts on the side of darkness, stand the central characters, the noble lovers Tamino and Pamina, whose expressive arioso style unites Italian lyricism with German intensity. Not only are these characters memorable individuals; they are also symbols. *Die Zauberflöte* is an allegory depicting the triumph of light over darkness and of good over evil, the victory of virtue and brotherhood, and extolls universal love and friendship. Although Schikaneder and Mozart left no hints, commentators soon believed that the characters embodied other meanings or represented real people in politics, Freemasonry, or music.

For the opera's production, Schikaneder fully exploited the resources of his theater, transforming the often poetic stage directions into the spectacle that he and his public relished. Beyond an engraving of Schikaneder in his Papageno costume, little if anything survives to show how the production might have looked.

A new serenity, a heightened sense of control, and a ceremonial/religious tone characterize Mozart's music for *Die Zauberflöte*. Propelled by march and dance rhythms, his melodies animate the characters and illuminate the dramatic situations. Enriching Mozart's basic harmonic vocabulary at crucial spots is an expressive chromaticism that heightens intensity or adds poignance, as appropriate. The inclusion of counterpoint in the Bach tradition evokes a time and place foreign to the Vienna of 1791. Not only does the fugal section of the overture foreshadow the trials to be endured by the lovers; almost paradoxically, the rapid repeated notes and bright orchestral colors of its theme presage the comic side of the proceedings. For the Two Men in Armor, who intone a paraphrase of a biblical text, Mozart exhumes the venerable Lutheran chorale-prelude, in which a hymn tune unfolds in slow note values above a more rapidly moving contrapuntal accompaniment.

Mozart knew his singers and understood their voices. A kaleidoscope of vocal color, *The Magic Flute* offers solos, ensembles ranging from duets to quintets, and choruses. Supplementing the adult male and female voices is the cool, serene sound of the Three Boys. Similarly, Mozart had at his disposal a capable orchestra of thirty-five players. In addition to the special effects of Glockenspiel and panpipes, he also includes solemn trombones and the basset horns associated with his Masonic music. The opera exhibits a dazzling variety of musical types. Distributed among its twenty-one numbers are folklike strophic songs, elaborate coloratura arias, expressive ariettes, a hymn, an instrumental march, numerous ensembles, choruses, an *introduzione,* and two enormous ensemble finales, each a *tour de force* of the dramatic composer's art.

The sharp contrasts of musical material are self-evident. More difficult to assess are the factors that forge this opera into such a powerful unity. Schikaneder's drama supplies the poetic kernal. Mozart furnishes the rest. Certain recurring musical figures, rhythmic patterns, and harmonic progressions are readily audible. Operative too is Mozart's singular ability to reconcile musical and dramatic demands. His key scheme, for example, makes sense musically and, at the same time, relates closely to the course of the drama and to the contents of the individual numbers. E-flat major (three flats) is the Masonic key, C minor (also three flats) represents the dark side, while C major, to the Age of the Enlightenment, is the key of light. He creates a unity of sound, bathing his characters in a radiant glow. Perhaps the greatest binding force is a unity of musical conception that mediates and ultimately resolves the conflicting opposites: dark-light, evil-good, masculine-feminine, sublime-ridiculous.

The Magic Flute quickly became Mozart's greatest success, a triumph he could relish for only two months. It proved to be Schikaneder's greatest success as well, the springboard to the fulfillment of his ultimate dream, the Theater an der Wien. Two centuries later, this enigmatic, sublimely beautiful opera remains a repertory staple.

—Malcolm S. Cole

ZAZÀ.

Composer: Ruggero Leoncavallo.

Librettist: Ruggero Leoncavallo (after P. Berton and C. Simon).

First Performance: Milan, Lirico, 10 November 1900.

Roles: Zazà (soprano); Anaida (mezzo-soprano); Milo Dufresne (tenor); Madame Dufresne (soprano); Toto (speaking); Cascart (baritone); Malardot (tenor); Floriana (soprano); Bussy (baritone); Natalia (soprano); Lartigon (bass); Duclou (baritone); Michelin (tenor); Marco (tenor); Courtois (bass); Augusto (tenor); chorus.

Publications

article–

Korngold, J. "Ruggiero Leoncavallo: *Zazà* (1909)." In *Die romantische Oper der Gegenwart*, 103. Vienna, 1922.

*   *   *

Zazà is an opera in four acts by Ruggiero Leoncavallo, composed in 1900. The libretto was written by Leoncavallo, as were the librettos for all his operas, and was based on the play by Pierre Berton and Charles Simon. Considered a sentimental comedy, *Zazà* was influenced by Massenet.

The plot revolves around a woman named Zazà, a café singer, and takes place in France towards the end of the nineteenth century. Zazà, who has many admirers, favors Milio Dufresne, who is indifferent to her interests. Zazà places a bet with Bussy, a journalist, that she can seduce Dufresne and win his affections. Dufresne does not respond initially but finally yields.

Dufresne announces to Zazà that he must go to Paris to attend to urgent business. Zazà protests, but finally professes her love to him and bids him farewell. In an effort to break up the love affair, Zazà's mother and partner tell her that Dufresne was seen in Paris with another woman. Zazà departs immediately for Paris to find out if there is any truth to this statement. During her brief stay in Paris, Zazà not only discovers that Dufresne is married, but she also meets his daughter, Toto.

Heartbroken, Zazà returns home. Hoping that Dufresne does love her, she agrees to see him again. When he maintains the old deception, Zazà confronts him, and Dufresne becomes furious. Zazà realizes that he does love his wife. She assures Dufresne that his wife knows nothing of their affair and sends him home to his family. Left alone, she wails in grief and despair.

Zazà was written ten years after *I pagliacci* ("The Clowns"), which was clearly Leoncavallo's most successful opera. While *Zazà* became fairly widely known, the composer was never able to duplicate the success of *I pagliacci*. *Zazà* had a successful opening with performances in French, Italian, Russian, German, Polish, Czech, and Hungarian. Its popularity died out in the 1920s, and it is only occasionally revived in Italy, primarily for its strong writing for the principals.

This work is usually referred to as a vivid example of "verismo," a term used to classify Italian opera of a sensational, supposedly "realistic" kind. Verismo operas deal with everyday situations as opposed to costume plays and legends. Musically, these realistic librettos are set with a great deal of dissonance, large orchestral sound, and the other musical devices which were used to stimulate jaded sensibilities. Verismo was short-lived and not widely known in its time, though it had some repercussions in France and Germany.

—Kathleen A. Abromeit

ZEFFIRELLI, Franco [born Gian Franco Corsi].

Producer and designer. Born 12 February 1923, in Florence. Attended Licèo Artistico, Florence and the University of Florence School of Architecture, 1941-46; studied voice; first operatic experience as director and designer of amateur productions in Siena; began a theatrical career as a radio actor, 1945; joined Visconti's Morelli-Stoppa Company as actor and stage manager, 1946; designed sets for *Livietta e Tracollo*, 1946, and *Serenata e tre*, 1947; designer and assistant to Visconti for plays and films, 1948-52; designed operas and plays throughout Italy in the late 1940s; first major operatic work as designer of *L'Italiana in Algeri*, Teatro alla Scala, 1952/53; producer and designer of *La cenerentola*, Teatro alla Scala, 1953, which was followed by many productions there; during the early 1960s, led the neoromantic revival in opera staging and design with Visconti; first Broadway assignment, designer and director of *The Lady of the Camellias*, Winter Garden, 1963; since 1964 has devoted himself primarily to theater and films, where he is well-established in historic drama. Recipient, Liberty award, 1986.

Opera Productions and Designs (selected)

L'Italiana in Algeri, Teatro alla Scala, 1952/53.
La cenerentola, Teatro alla Scala, 1953.
L'elisir d'amore, Teatro alla Scala, 1955.
Il Turco in Italia, Teatro alla Scala, 1955.
Falstaff, Holland Festival, Amsterdam, 1956.
La traviata, Dallas Opera, 1958.
Mignon, Teatro alla Scala, 1958.
Lucia di Lammermoor, Covent Garden, 1959.
Cavalleria rusticana, Covent Garden, 1959.
Pagliacci, Covent Garden, 1959.
Vivì, San Carlo, Naples, 1959.
Alcina, Dallas Opera, 1960; Covent Garden, 1962.
Falstaff, Covent Garden, 1961.
L'elisir d'amore, Glyndebourne, 1961.
Aida, Teatro alla Scala, 1963.
La bohème, Teatro alla Scala, 1963.
Tosca, Covent Garden, 1964.
Rigoletto, Covent Garden, 1964.
Falstaff, Metropolitan Opera, 1964.
Antony and Cleopatra, Metropolitan Opera, 1966.
Cavalleria rusticana, Metropolitan Opera, 1970.

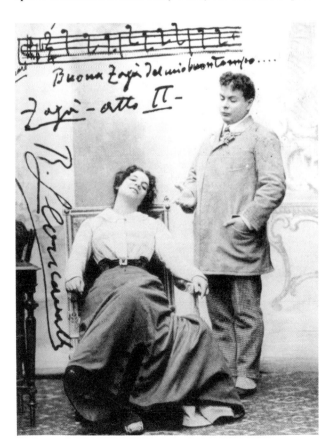

Rosina Storchio and Mario Sammarco in Leoncavallo's *Zazà*, 1903

Pagliacci, Metropolitan Opera, 1970.
Otello, Metropolitan Opera, 1972.
Don Giovanni, Staatsoper, Vienna, 1972.
Un ballo in maschera, Teatro alla Scala, 1972.
Otello, Teatro alla Scala, 1976.
Carmen, Staatsoper, Vienna, 1978.
La bohème, Metropolitan Opera, 1981.
Turandot, Metropolitan Opera, 1987.

Opera Films and Television productions

Fidelio, 1970.
Pagliacci, 1981.
La traviata, 1983.
Cavalleria rusticana, 1986.
Otello, 1986.

Publications

By ZEFFIRELLI: books–

Franco Zeffirelli's Jesus: A Spiritual Diary. Translated by
    Willis J. Egan. San Francisco, 1984.
Zeffirelli: The Autobiography of Franco Zeffirelli. New York,
    1986.

articles–

————, and Rosenthal, H. "On Producing Italian Come-
    dies." *Opera* 12 (June 1961): 365-68.
"Thoughts on Producing *Alcina.*" *The Musical Times* 103
    (March 1962): 166-67.

About ZEFFIRELLI: articles–

Bonynge, Richard. "Franco Zeffirelli." *Opera* 10 (December
    1959): 771-77.
Rosenthal, H., and N. Goodwin. "Does Opera Need Zeffire-
    lli?" *Music and Musicians* 12 (April 1964): 12-14.
"Talking to Zeffirelli." *About the House* 1, no. 6 (1964): 40-
    42.
Rasponi, L. "Franco Zeffirelli: The Romantic Realist." *Opera
    News* 46 (16 January 1982): 8-12.
Boehm, G. "Franco Zeffirelli." *Die Buehne* no. 305 (February
    1984): 8-9.
Solomon, R.E. "A Critical Study of Franco Zeffirelli's *La
    traviata.*" *Dissertation Abstracts* 48 (August 1987): 329A.

*   *   *

Like Luchino Visconti whom he assisted and with whom he
has often been compared, Zeffirelli has both designed and
produced plays, operas, and films. As a young man Zeffirelli
studied architecture and singing, both of which he abandoned
to join Visconti's company as an actor, designer, and production assistant. While never completely giving up the
"straight" theater, Zeffirelli was best known as a producer of
opera before achieving more general fame as a director of
films.

Zeffirelli's first opera designs were for the small-scale Siena
Settimana Musicale, and his first important operatic commission came in 1952 when he was asked to design *L'Italiana in
Algieri* for the Teatro alla Scala. The first opera which he
both designed and produced was *La cenerentola* (Teatro alla
Scala 1953/54), but it was with *Il Turco in Italia*—(Teatro
alla Scala 1955)—his first production with Maria Callas—
that his mature style began to emerge. Zeffirelli's early designs
had been lighthearted and airy, using traditional backcloths
and flats, but the Teatro alla Scala *Il Turco in Italia* marked
his first steps towards "*riesumazione*": recreating the look
and feel of the period in which the opera is set, while filtering
it through the aesthetic of the period of its composition.

Shakespeare, both as playwright and as a source of libretti,
inspired some of Zeffirelli's best work. Zeffirelli first staged
Falstaff (conducted by Giulini) at the 1956 Holland Festival,
a production which was to set a pattern followed for much
of his career—the remounting of successful stagings for other
theaters with small variations in scale. Zeffirelli's staging of
La traviata, which was first seen in Dallas in 1959, followed
this pattern.

For the Covent Garden production of *Lucia di Lammermoor* in 1959, which made Joan Sutherland a *prima donna
assoluta,* Zeffirelli produced a lighting which gave the illusion
that the engravings from which his sets were derived had
been brought to life. The production was widely acclaimed
and described as being quintessential Zeffirelli. As a result,
Zeffirelli staged other operas at Covent Garden, several of
which (*Cavalleria rusticana, Pagliacci, Rigoletto,* and *Falstaff*) have remained in use over a long period of time. Other
opera houses gave Zeffirelli the chance to produce a wide
range of works, and his style became increasingly lavish until
it seemed that the singers were swamped by the scenery. It
now appeared inevitable that Zeffirelli's ideas could only be
fully realized in the film studio. The culmination of Zeffirelli's
operatic work came in 1964 with the two productions he
staged for Maria Callas, then approaching the end of her
stage career—*Tosca* at Covent Garden and *Norma* in Paris.

From then on, Zeffirelli staged only a handful of operas
(*Turandot, La bohème, Otello,* and *Don Giovanni*) in the few
opera houses big enough to both accommodate and afford
his highly realistic productions. The exception was Samuel
Barber's *Antony and Cleopatra,* presented at the opening of
the new Metropolitan in 1966. (Zeffirelli also assisted in writing the libretto.)

Zeffirelli's films of *La traviata* and *Otello* certainly made
his operatic work known to a wider public: the former was a
fairly successful adaptation of the flashback techniques staged
in Dallas while the latter took far more liberties with Verdi's
opera and was neither a critical nor a public success. In these
times of "produceritis," many an older opera-goer may long
for a return to the Zeffirelli style, but few are the opera houses
which can afford such self-indulgent (in his detractors' eyes)
opulence.

—Oliver Smith

Franco Zeffirelli's production of *Lucia di Lammermoor* with Joan Sutherland in the title role, Lyric Opera of Chicago, 1961

ZÉMIRE ET AZOR.

Composer: André Grétry.

Librettist: Jean-François Marmontel (after Beaumont, *La belle et la bête*).

First Performance: Fontainebleau, 9 November 1771.

Roles: Azor (tenor); Sander (bass); Ali (tenor); Zémire (soprano); Fatmé (soprano); Lisbé (soprano or mezzo-soprano); Fairy (mute); chorus.

Publications

article–

Charlton, David. "The Appeal of the Beast: a Note on Grétry and *Zémire et Azor.*" *Musical Times* 121 (1980): 169.

*   *   *

Grétry's four-act comedy-ballet is set to the verse of Jean-François Marmontel, based on Mme de Beaumont's setting of the fairy tale *Beauty and the Beast*, Charles Favart's *La fée Urgèle* [The Fairy Urgèle], and la Chaussée's play *Amour pour amour* [Love for Love, 1742]. Marmontel blends comedy and sentiment while teaching virtues and morals by means of contrast. The metaphors are significant of deeper human truths as conceived by the eighteenth-century Enlightenment.

Shipwrecked in a storm, Sander and his servant Ali have lost all possessions and seek shelter in an enchanted palace. Magically, a table of provisions appears. Sander eyes a rose bush which reminds him of his daughter's gift wishes: Fatmé and Lisbé had requested ribbons and lace, but Zémire wanted a rose. No sooner has Sander plucked the rose than the repulsive, threatening figure of Azor appears and demands as payment a human life. Sander promises one of his daughters. After a stern warning not to deceive him, Azor provides transportation home via a magic cloud.

Act II takes us to Sander's simple dwelling on the Gulf of Ormus. The three daughters express concern about their father's prolonged absence. Sander and Ali arrive home, but Sander conceals his promise to Azor and prepares to return alone to him. He writes a brief note to his daughters, adding that the journey may be much longer this time. Ali tells the whole story to Zémire, who then coaxes Ali into accompanying her to the fairy palace.

In act III, Azor, alone in his palace, vents his suffering and laments his ugly frame. Zémire and Ali enter the palace; she takes stock of her new abode with wonder, noting the harpsichord, the many books, and a door engraved with her name. Suddenly Azor materializes. After the initial shock Zémire responds to his warmth and sensitivity; Azor pronounces her queen of the palace. In response to Zémire's nostalgia for her family, Azor conjures up a magic picture in which Sander and Zémire's sisters appear visibly upset. Zémire desires to return, so Azor provides a ring, which if worn will give her freedom from him, but if thrown away will return her to him.

In act IV, Zémire arrives back home in a chariot drawn by two winged dragons. She reassures her family that all is indeed well, but that she must return before sundown or Azor will die. They argue heatedly and Zémire tosses the ring away; she is instantly whisked away. Back at the grotto of the fairy castle garden; where the sun has set and Azor is near death, Zémire enters the palace calling for Azor. She professes her love for him, and the scene changes immediately to a throne room in the fairy palace: Azor, redeemed through Zémire's love, is enthroned in splendor. Zémire's family is transported to the palace to join in the wedding festivities.

The orchestra consists of two oboes, two flutes, two clarinets, two bassoons, two horns, strings, and basso continuo. The clarinets play with particular effect in act III, scene vi, the *pièce de résistance* of the opera, as part of a wind sextet, which is placed backstage. This lends an eerie quality to the vision of Zémire's home. After the instrumental introduction, during which Sander, Fatmé and Lisbé can be seen, but not heard, Grétry inserts spoken dialogue allowing Zémire to ask Azor why she cannot hear their discussion. He reluctantly adds the voices to the weird strains.

Good examples of tonal painting include the thunder storm which connects the overture with the first air and the dripping of water in the grotto. Grétry's orchestra reflects stage action in the air "Ne va me tromper" ("Don't deceive me," act I, scene ii), where he writes three rising scalar fragments in the introduction to which the beast pulls himself up to his full height to warn Sander. The orchestra imitates a plucked guitar with pizzicato strings in a popular romance (act I, scene ii), where Sander's pleas for leniency make their effect in a pathetic F-minor key. The orchestra is able to contradict Ali's claims that the storm is lifting (act I, scene i) by indicating strong gusts of wind and torrents of rain. Sander decides to depart to pulsating bursts of adrenaline and syncopated rhythms. But Ali is ready for a snooze; yawning bassoons and celli arch in thirds downward accompanying Ali's lethargical whole notes which descend a full ninth. Sander declaims rhythmically, punctuated by orchestral staccati and restless forte/piano alternations. Echo devices balance Zémire's clear soprano voice with flutes in act III, scene v. In her final air (act IV, scene iv), Grétry places two solo horns and two flutes high above the stage to lend a sense of distance inside the hollow grotto.

National styles blend in Azor's air "Ah! quel tourment" ("Ah what torment," act III, scene iii): the French lyric tragedy monologue in the long introduction; the Italian cantilena of the slow E-flat major [A] section; the German *Storm and Stress* in the B-flat minor [B] section with its agitated tremoli, wildly contrasting dynamics [Sf-p], and passionate vocal declamation.

Two accompanied recitatives are reserved for impassioned cries: while Sander scribbles his note in act II, scene vii, a ripple of script is heard in the muted strings. A motive of four descending half-notes in the celli indicates danger. When he reads his note aloud, he is virtually unaccompanied. Azor, near death, sings an accompanied recitative to a dripping water figure in a 6/8 siciliano meter. A second motive etches the shape of the setting sun.

The redemption through love theme was appealing to the bourgeoisie, as were the lessons in virtue and morals; all the wide range of emotions, variety of contrasts and true-to-life musical characterizations influenced the next five decades of operatic composition, among them Mozart's *Die Zauberflöte*

(1791), Spohr's *Zemire und Azor* (1819), and Marschner's *Hans Heiling* (1833).

—Linda M. Stones

ZEMLINSKY, Alexander von.

Composer. Born 14 October 1871, in Vienna. Died 15 March 1942, in Larchmont, New York. Studied piano with Door and composition with Krenn, R. Fuchs and J.N. Fuchs at the Vienna Conservatory, 1887-92; joined the Tonkünstlerverein, 1893; involved with the orchestral society Polyhymnia, 1895, and became associated with Arnold Schoenberg; opera *Es war einmal* conducted by Mahler at the Vienna court opera, 1900; conductor of the Karlstheater in Vienna, 1900-06; conducted at the Theater an der Wien, 1903; principal conductor of the Volksoper, and organized with Schoenberg the Union of Creative Musicians, 1904; conductor of the German Opera in Prague and taught at the Prague College of Music, 1911; assistant conductor to Otto Klemperer at the Kroll Opera in Berlin, 1927; emigrated to the United States, 1938.

Operas

Sarema, Adolph von Zemlinsky (after R. von Gottschall, *Die Rose vom Kaukasus*), c. 1895, Munich, Hofoper, 10 October 1897.
Es war einmal, Drachmann, 1897-99, Vienna, Hofoper, 22 January 1900.
Der Traumgörge, L. Feld, 1904-06.
Kleider machen Leute, L. Feld (after G. Keller), c. 1908, Vienna, Volksoper, 2 October 1910; revised, 1922.
Eine florentinische Tragödie, Wilde (translated by M. Meyerfeld), 1915-16, Stuttgart, 30 January 1917.
Der Zwerg, G.C. Klaren (after Wilde, *The Birthday of the Infanta*), 1920-21, Cologne, 28 May 1922.
Der Kreidekreis, after Klabund, 1932, Zurich, 14 October 1933.
Der König Kandaules, Gide (translated by F. Blei), c. 1935 [unfinished].

Other works: orchestral works, choral works, chamber and instrumental music, songs.

Publications/Writings

By ZEMLINSKY: articles–

"Jugenderinnerungen." In *Arnold Schönberg zum 60. Geburtstag*, 33. Vienna, 1934.

About ZEMLINSKY: books–

Kolleritsch, O. ed. *Alexander Zemlinsky: Tradition im Umkreis der Wiener Schule, Studien zur Wertungsforschung*, 7. Graz, 1976.
Weber, H. *Österreichische Komponisten des 20. Jahrhunderts* Vienna, 1977.
Stephan, R. *Alexander Zemlinsky: ein unbekannter Meister der Wiener Schule*. Kiel and Vienna, 1978.

articles–

Hoffmann, R.S. "Alexander von Zemlinsky." *Der Merkur* 2 (1911): 193.

Der Auftakt 1 (1921) [Zemlinsky issue].

Adorno, T.W. "Zemlinsky." In *Quasi una fantasia: musikalische Schriften,* vol. 2, p. 155. Frankfurt, 1963.

Mahler, A. "Alexander Zemlinsky." *Die Musikforschung* 24 (1971): 250.

Weber, H. "Zemlinsky in Wien 1871-1911." *Archiv für Musikwissenschaft* 28 (1971): 77.

Mahler, A. "Alexander Zemlinskys Prager Jahre." *Hudebni veda* 9 (1972): 237.

Weber, H. "Jugendstil und Musik in der Oper der Jahrhundertwende." *Die Musikforschung* 27 (1974): 171.

Schöny, Heinz. "Alexander von Zemlinsky." *Genealogie* 27 (1978): 97.

Weber, H. "Krise der Identität. Zu sozialen und psychischen Konflikten Alexander Zemlinskys." *Musica* 34 (1980): 3.

Wildner-Partsch, Angelika. "Die Opern Alexander Zemlinskys. Betrachtungen anhand zweier repräsentativer Werke." *Studien zur Musikwissenschaft* 33 (1982): 55.

unpublished–

Partsch, Angelika. "Das Opernschaffen Alexander Zemlinskys." Ph.D. dissertation. University of Vienna, 1979.

*　　*　　*

Influential in turn-of-the-century Vienna as a modernistically-inclined composition teacher, Zemlinsky in fact devoted the major part of his creative energy to opera, both

Alexander von Zemlinsky

as an innovative conductor and as a composer. His seven completed works in the genre appeared at strategic points throughout his career (an eighth, *Der König Kandaules,* after Gide, was left uncompleted). They negotiate an interesting path between the demands of popular musical theater and an idealistic refinement of taste and purpose.

Zemlinsky was by nature inclined to the fairy-tale romanticism of Humperdinck as much as the more severe, expressionistic modernism of his close friend Arnold Schoenberg, whose experimental harmonic language was at times eclipsed by Zemlinsky's before the First World War. Strong though his sympathetic association with the Second Viennese School was, Zemlinsky came to admire the works of Gustav Mahler above those of his younger contemporaries. The senior composer was to play an important role in the development of Zemlinsky's career when he accepted his second opera, *Es war einmal,* for performance at Vienna's Hofoper in 1900.

Mahler had initially considered Zemlinsky's prize-winning first opera, *Sarema* (first performed in Munich, 1897) for performance in Vienna. This work was of the heroic post-Wagnerian type, was set in the eighteenth century on the Russian-Caucasian border and concerned the relationship between a Russian officer and a Caucasian girl, Sarema, who kills herself after struggling between love and loyalty to her oppressed people. In the event Mahler seems to have realized that Zemlinsky was more at home in the subtler world of *Es war einmal,* the preparation of whose final version Mahler supervised (making changes to the libretto and orchestration, lengthening the interlude following the prologue and recomposing the conclusion of act I). This work incidentally established a first, indirect connection between Mahler and his future wife, Alma Schindler, a pupil and near-fiancée of Zemlinsky's. It is not impossible that she played a part in Zemlinsky's attraction to Holger Drachmann's fairy-tale comedy in which a haughty princess is compromised into banishment by a "gypsy" who reveals himself as the Prince of Northland only after having tamed her shrewish ways and having inspired her passively submissive love.

The first act of *Es war einmal* is an impressive, state-of-the-art essay in post-Wagnerian style influenced not only by Humperdinck, but also Tchaikovsky and Rimsky-Korsakov (Dukas and Debussy subsequently attracted Zemlinsky; later still, Stravinsky and Weill). Statuesque Wagnerian rhetoric is replaced by a more naturalistic vocal declamation, borne upon a symphonically evolving and kaleidoscopically colored orchestral discourse. This is nevertheless always ready to retreat before the closed-form songs and dances that Zemlinsky incorporates (often of a characteristic or specifically "gypsy" nature).

Rehearsals for *Der Traumgörge* were shelved after Mahler's departure from Vienna in 1907 and this remarkable experiment in through-composed "magic realism" remained unperformed in Zemlinsky's lifetime. He seems to have sensed, however, that the virtuosity of its advanced orchestral and harmonic language, rarely permitting the crystallization of extended periodic melody, would not have attracted a wider audience. *Kleider machen Leute* (1910) seems deliberately to reintroduce clearer recurring melodic material and occasional closed forms. This gently comic opera, revised in 1922, was derived from the Seldwyla stories of Gottfried Keller (amongst which Delius discovered his *A Village Romeo and Juliet*). Wenzel Strapinski, a ne'er-do-well tailor, encourages the social confusion caused by his fine clothes when he arrives in an unfamiliar village; he is taken for a Polish count before finding a little post-Wagnerian redemption in the arms of a girl who will love him even when his true identity is revealed. Although Leo Feld's libretto shares some of the faults of that for *Der Traumgörge* and detracted from the opera's complete success in its first, three-act version, Strapinski's melodically folksy (if harmonically sophisticated) little song provides a source of effective devices for focusing Straussian lushness in this satire upon petty-bourgeois self-deception.

Criticism of the opera's lack of strong effects nevertheless dogged *Kleider machen Leute* and may have led Zemlinsky to change direction somewhat in the two one-act operas he composed during his time in Prague. *Eine florentinische Tragödie* (1917) and *Der Zwerg* (1922—posthumously revived as *Der Geburtstag der Infantin*) explore more extreme areas of decadent emotionalism and were both based on Oscar Wilde (like Strauss's *Salome*). *Der Zwerg* is striking not least for its harrowing central role for the tenor: a grotesque dwarf whose natural innocence is shattered into expressionistic nightmare by the wilful, musically somewhat neoclassical Infanta (she would prefer a toy that does not have a heart). This powerful work successfully unites deliberately contrasted musical styles in a way that was still more elaborately explored in *Der Kreidekreis,* which drew on the same, originally Chinese, source as Brecht's *The Caucasian Chalk Circle*. Composed during Zemlinsky's Kroll Opera period in Berlin, it alluded to jazz (for the less savory characters) as well as something of the Brecht-Weill manner of closed-form "numbers" with spoken dialogue in its fusion of romantic idealism and sharp social criticism. It was successfully premiered in Zurich in 1933, although the events of history gave it no better chance of achieving the conclusive public success that had eluded Zemlinsky's earlier operas.

—Peter Franklin

ZENATELLO, Giovanni.

Baritone/tenor. Born 22 February 1876, in Verona. Died 11 February 1949, in New York City. Married: mezzo-soprano Maria Gay, 1913; two sons, one daughter. Studied as baritone with Zannoni and Moretti in Verona; debut as Silvio in *Pagliacci,* Belluno, 1898; took role of Canio in *Pagliacci* at the Teatro del Fondo, Naples, 1899, and thereafter sang tenor; appeared at Lisbon, 1902; at Teatro alla Scala 1902-07, with debut in *La damnation de Faust;* created the principal tenor roles in first performances of Giordano's *Siberia,* 1903 and *Madama Butterfly,* 1904; appeared frequently at Buenos Aires, 1903-10; Covent Garden debut as Riccardo, 1905; New York debut at Manhattan Opera House as Enzo in *La gioconda,* 1907; debut with Metropolitan Opera on tour in 1909, replacing Caruso, but never sang with the company in New York; sang in Boston, 1910-17, and Chicago, 1912-13; sang Radames at opening of Verona Arena, 1913; sang Otello at Covent Garden, 1926; retired in 1928; directed singing school with wife, and managed the Verona Arena for several seasons.

Publications

About ZENATELLO: books–

Lauri-Volpi, G. *Voci parallele*. Milan, 1955.
Consolaro, Nina Zenatello. *Giovanni Zenatello, tenore: Ideatore degli spettacoli lirici dell'Arena di Verona (1913)*. Verona, 1976.

articles–

Hutchinson, T., and C.W. Williams. "Giovanni Zenatello." *Record Collector* 14 (1961): 101.

When Francesco Tamagno, the tenor for whom Verdi wrote *Otello,* died in 1905, there were several worthy successors to the role, but none became more associated with it than Giovanni Zenatello. Indeed, his fame in that part eventually rivaled that of Tamagno himself, even though their voices were quite different. The older tenor, whose clarion tones were said to "shake the chandelier at Covent Garden," possessed an enormous voice of a trumpet-like, rather open quality but one truly tenorial in timbre. Zenatello, who began as a baritone and never lost a baritonal darkness and weight of timbre, possessed a vocal quality more akin to what we now think of as an "Otello voice."

But even this is not the full story. To compare Zenatello with two later, famous exponents of Otello, Renato Zanelli and Ramon Vinay, both of whom also began as baritones, would be inappropriate. Neither Zanelli nor Vinay managed to integrate into his vocal method a ringing high register as Zenatello did; the latter's voice, though of dark timbre, avoided the baritonal constriction of the upper register that plagued Vinay and Zanelli throughout their careers. Zenatello happily developed an ability to sing both lyric and dramatic parts throughout his long career. He was a famous Rodolfo (*La bohème*), Riccardo (*Un ballo in maschera*), Faust, and Don José (*Carmen*) as well as the more immediately obvious dramatic roles such as Canio (*Pagliacci*) and Radames (*Aida*). The impression Zenatello made on his audience is eloquently conveyed by the critic of the *Times,* writing after the tenor's Covent Garden debut as Riccardo: "It is not often that a singer having a great reputation in his own country shows at once the grounds for that reputation on his first appearance at Covent Garden; and although in the early part of the opera Signor Zenatello's voice seemed a little small, its beautiful quality was immediately apparent, while once having felt his way and accustomed himself to the new surroundings, he sang superbly. . . . . His tenor voice is a happy combination of the lyric and the heroic, robust yet delicate when delicacy is required and full of colour and he is singularly free from the excessive exuberance of many of his race. As he acts with fine liveliness, he is certain to earn the greatest credit here."

It is a testimony to Zenatello's histrionic ability and fine technique that, as Otello, he achieved world fame, and was said to have sung the role over 500 times throughout the course of his long career. Few tenors in operatic history have equalled this achievement, and we are fortunate to have actual documentary evidence in a live recording of Zenatello in this role from 1926, commercially recorded by HMV during a performance at Covent Garden. The voice is still in excellent condition after a career of nearly three decades, and his interpretation and personality practically leap from the grooves at the listener.

Zenatello was fortunate in having recorded prolifically. His first recordings for Black G&T were made in 1903 and, though technically somewhat crude, the young voice is well captured, robust and ringing.

Much of his best work was for the excellent Fonotipia Company, reflecting the wide-ranging repertoire that he sang on stage. They are historically important too, for they preserve his interpretation of several of the roles he created, most notably his Pinkerton (*Madama Butterfly*), which is represented by his participation in the love duet of act I.

Zenatello also recorded for Columbia (rather dim and backward technically) and with more success for Edison. But perhaps the best idea of Zenatello's singing can be gained from the Victors, recorded between 1928 and 1930. Though by now the voice had largely lost the lyricism of earlier years, this is compensated for by a dramatic intensity, a wide palette of vocal color, and a trumpet-like tone that is thrilling in its ardour. Yet, the technique is unimpaired and he is still able to sing softly when demanded by the score. Most remarkable of all is a snatch of his singing of Otello's death during a radio interview from 1948 when Zenatello was over seventy, the voice still amazingly steady. All in all, it is a worthy souvenir of a great artist and one of the most important tenors of this century.

—Larry Lustig

ZENO, Apostolo.

Librettist/Poet/Scholar. Born 11 December 1668, in Venice. Died 11 November 1750, in Venice. Studied in the seminary of the Somaschi fathers; one of the founders of the Accademia degli Animosi, 1691 (became the Venetian branch of the Roman Arcadian Academy, 1698); success as a librettist with *Lucio Vero,* 1700; with Scipione Maffei, Antonio Vallisnieri, and his brother Pier Caterino Zeno, founded the *Giornale dei letterati d'Italia,* 1710; invited to the Hapsburg Court in Vienna to become Poeta e istorico di S.M. Cesarea, 1718; retired in Venice, 1729.

Librettos

Gl' inganni felici, C.F. Pollarolo, 1695.
Il Tirsi, 1696.
Il Narcisso, F.A. Pistocchi, 1697.
I rivali generosi, M.A. Ziani, 1697.
Eumene, M.A. Ziani, 1697.
Odoardo, M.A. Ziani, 1698.
Faramondo, C.F. Pollarolo, 1699.
Lucio Vero, C.F. Pollarolo, 1700.
Temistocle, M.A. Ziani, 1700.
Griselda, A. Pollarolo, 1701.
Il Venceslao, C.F. Pollarolo, 1702.
Aminta, T. Albinoni, 1703.
Pirro, G.A.V. Aldrovandini, 1704.
Antioco (with P. Pariati), F. Gasparini, 1705.
Artaserse (with P. Pariati), A. Zanettini, 1705.
Ambleto (with P. Pariati), F. Gasparini, 1705.
Statira, (with P. Pariati), F. Gasparini, 1705.
Il Teuzzone, P. Magni and C. Monari, 1706.
L'amor generoso, F. Gasparini, 1707.
La Svanvita (with P. Pariati), A. Fiorè, 1707.
Anfitrione (with P. Pariati), F. Gasparini, 1707.
Flavio Anicio Olibrio (with P. Pariati), F. Gasparini, 1707.
Engelberta (with P. Pariati), F. Gasparini, 1708.
Astarto (with P. Pariati), Albinoni, 1708.
Il falso Tiberino (with P. Pariati), C.F. Pollarolo, 1708.
Atenaide, A. Fiorè, A. Caldara, and F. Gasparini, 1709.
Sesostri (with P. Pariati), F. Gasparini, 1709.
Scipione nelle Spagne, c. 1710.
Merope, F. Gasparini, 1711.

Alessandro Severo, A. Lotti, 1716.
Ifigenia in Aulide, A. Caldara, 1718.
Sirita, A. Caldara, 1719.
Lucio Papirio dittatore, A. Caldara, 1719.
Don Chisciotte in Sierra Morena (with P. Pariati), F.B. Conti, 1719.
Meride e Selinunte, G. Porsile, 1721.
Ormisda, A. Caldara, 1721.
Alessandro in Sidone (with P. Pariati), F.B. Conti, 1721.
Nitocri, A. Caldara, 1722.
Euristeo, A. Caldara, 1724.
Andromaca, A. Caldara, 1724.
Gianguir, A. Caldara, 1724.
Semiramide in Ascalona, A. Caldara, 1725.
I due dittatori, A. Caldara, 1726.
Imeneo, A. Caldara, 1727.
Ornospade, A. Caldara, 1727.
Mitridate, A. Caldara, 1728.
Cajo Fabbrizio, A. Caldara, 1729.
Enone, A. Caldara, 1734.

Publications

About ZENO: books–

Negri, F. *La vita di A. Zeno.* Venice, 1816.
Pistorelli, L. *I melodrammi di A. Zeno.* Padua, 1894.
Menghi, A. O. *Zeno e la critica letteraria.* Camerino, 1901.
Wotquenne, A. *Zeno, Metastasio et Goldoni. Table alphabétique des morceaux mesurés contenus dans leurs oeuvres dramatiques.* Leipzig, 1905.
Pietzsch, A. *A. Zeno in seiner Abhängigkeit von der französischen Tragödie.* Leipzig, 1907.
Fehr, M. *A. Zeno und seine Reform des Operntextes.* Zurich, 1912.
Giazotto, R. *Poesia melodrammatica e pensiero critico nel settecento.* Milan, 1952.
Freeman, Robert. *Opera Without Drama.* Ann Arbor, 1981.
Gallarati, P. *Musica e maschera. Il libretto italiano del settecento.* Turin, 1984.

articles–

Pistorelli, L. "Due melodramme inediti di A. Zeno." *Rivista musicale italiana* 3 (1896): 261.
Giazotto, R. "A. Zeno, P. Metastasio e la critica del settecento." *Rivista musicale italiana* 48 (1946): 324; 49 (1947): 46; 50 (1948): 39, 248; 51 (1949): 43, 130.
Freeman, R. "Apostolo Zeno's Reform of the Libretto." *Journal of the American Musicological Society* 21 (1968): 321.
Grout, D.J. "La 'Griselda' di Zeno e il libretto dell' opera di Scarlatti." *Nuova rivista musicale italiana* 2 (1968): 207.
Burrows, D. "Stile nella cultura: Vivaldi, Zeno, Ricce." In *Mitologie. Convivenze di musica e mitologia,* edited by G. Morelli. Venice, 1979.

*   *   *

The reforms of the libretto which led to the operatic style of the "Neapolitan" group of composers, nowadays called *opera seria* and typified by J.A. Hasse, have traditionally been attributed to two dramatists, Apostolo Zeno and Pietro Metastasio. The latter's importance is assured, but Zeno's position is more questionable. It is true that most of the new features— the ubiquitous *ingresso* or exit-aria, the banishment of comic characters and mythology, the reduction in the number of scenes, the regularization of the aria form—are already evident in Zeno's texts, but they are equally so in those of contemporaries like Stampiglia and Bernardoni. Nevertheless, certain details of Zeno's talents and taste may have set the direction for many of these changes, both for good and ill.

Zeno was a man of profound learning, a historian and literary scholar, author of an unfinished Latin history of Italy and a series of biographies, including one of Giambiattista Guarini, a poetic dramatist whose work Zeno did not hesitate to plunder. As a poet he was committed to the Arcadian tradition (he was co-founder of an Arcadian academy in Venice), which called for the refinement and standardization of the Italian language, for rational good sense, clarity, vivacity in the composition of verse, and for a return to the moral grandeur of classical times. Partly as a result of this, writers turned on one hand to small pastoral lyrics, suitable for musical setting as cantatas and serenatas, on the other hand to heavy classical dramas, theatrically stillborn.

It was the pastoral element in this movement which was to form Metastasio's style. Zeno, however, was a clumsy poet with a poor ear for verbal harmony; only in the occasional pastoral aria does he achieve the facility which was natural to Metastasio. He knew nothing of music, which he regarded as an unfortunate necessity in opera, along with elaborate stage effects. When a complete edition of his dramas was undertaken, their origin as musical texts was concealed. Thus, the clear separation of recitative and aria, the recitative restricted to the declamatory meters of *endecasillabo* and *settenario*, was natural for Zeno, as was the long aria-free sequence in the last act, where the denouement, the dramatist's most important moment, had to be protected from interference by the composer.

Zeno was conscious of his inability as a comic writer. When he took up his appointment as Imperial Poet at the Viennese court (Metastasio was to be his successor) he specified that he was never to be asked to write comedy. The comic scenes in works like *Flavio Anicio Olibrio* (1707-1708) and *Don Chisciotte in Sierra Morena* (1719) were probably the work of his collaborator, Pietro Pariati.

Zeno's knowledge of history, however, enabled him to give verisimilitude to his dramas and perhaps promoted the separation of history from mythology. Mythical characters and plots survived only in occasional genres like the serenata and *dramma pastorale* and, in Vienna, the *festa teatrale*. The printed texts of Zeno's serious dramas are preceded by *argomenti*, summaries of the plot and its background, which quote over eighty classical and contemporary sources.

Perhaps the reputation of Zeno as the "architect" of the new kind of opera (De Sanctis) rests on the continued setting of his texts throughout the eighteenth century and into the nineteenth. They were nearly always altered and shortened (for example, Rolli adapted *Scipione nelle Spagne* in 1726 for Handel) and the arias were often rewritten. It has to be admitted that these adaptations were often improvements. Furthermore, Zeno's plots were often reused and individual scenes were copied by later dramatists; Metastasio's *Siroe* is a rehash of Zeno's *Ormisda*, his *Il re pastore* of Zeno's *Alessandro in Sidone*. When act I, scene iv of Zeno's *Temistocle* reappears as act II, scene viii of Metastasio's drama of the same name, the liveliness of the dialogue, the warmth of the feelings reveal the superiority of the later writer.

Contemporaries spoke of Zeno's pomp and gravity; Calzabigi wrote to Alfieri in 1783 that Zeno was "more theatrical, more serious, more thoughtful, more varied than Metastasio." Unfortunately, it was the *melodramma*'s pretensions to tragedy which produced stiff characters and mechanical plots, infected with a kind of abstract heroism which was ridiculed by later writers. This, and the Procrustean bed of recitative and aria, were the very features which the next "reform," that of Calzabigi and Gluck, set about changing. Zeno's literary personality may have encouraged tendencies in *opera seria* which marked the style, but they eventually brought about its downfall. His position as its originator, however, is no longer accepted.

—Raymond Monelle

ZIMMERMANN, Bernd Alois.

Composer. Born 20 March 1918, in Bliesheim, near Cologne. Died 10 August 1970, in Königsdorf. Studied philology at the universities of Bonn, Cologne, and Berlin; studied composition with Philipp Jarnach in Cologne; attended lectures by Wolfgang Fortner and René Leibowitz at Darmstadt; lecturer in composition at the Hochschule für Musik in Cologne, 1958.

Operas

Die Soldaten, Zimmermann (after Lenz), 1958-60; revised 1963-64.
Medea, H.H. Jahnn, [unfinished].

Other works: orchestral works, vocal works, chamber and instrumental music, music for tape, incidental music.

Publications

By ZIMMERMANN: books—

Intervall und Zeit: Aufsätze und Schriften zum Werke. Mainz, 1974.
Die Soldaten [libretto, correspondence, texts, studies]. Strasbourg, 1988.

articles—

"Jenseits des Impressionismus: von Debussy bis zur Jeune France." *Musica* 3 (1949): 339.
"Material und Geist." *Melos* 18 (1951): 5.
"Unzeitgemässe Betrachtungen zur Musik und der jungen Generation." *Melos* 19 (1952): 305.
" 'Zeitgenössische' oder 'neue Musik'." In *Köln: eine Vierteljahresschrift für die Freunde der Stadt.* Cologne, 1960.
"Ludwig Strecker 80 Jahre alt." *Melos* 30 (1963): 1.

interview—

Danler, K-R. "Gespräch mit Bernd Alois Zimmermann." *Musica* 21 (1967): 180.

About ZIMMERMANN: books—

Konold, Wulf. *Bernd Alois Zimmermann: der Komponist und sein Werk.* Cologne, 1986.
Niemöller, Klaus, and Wulf Konold, eds. *Zwischen den Generationen: Bericht über das Bernd-Alois-Zimmermann-Symposion, Köln 1987.* Regensburg, 1989.

articles–

Baruch, G.W. "Zeitgenössische Komponisten: Bernd Alois Zimmermann." *Melos* 20 (1953): 319.

Schubert, R. "Bericht über die Perspektiven." *Die Reihe* 4 (1958): 103; English translation in *Die Reihe* 4 (1960): 103.

Rothärmel, M. "Der pluralistische Zimmermann." *Melos* 30 (1968): 97.

Bienek, H. "Kommen wird der Tod." *Melos* 37 (1970): 427.

Krellmann, H. "Bernd Alois Zimmermann." *Musica* 24 (1970): 485.

Stuckenschmidt, H.H. "Ein starker, ein freier Geist." *Melos* 37 (1970): 349.

Seipt, A. "Die Soldaten." In *Neue Musik seit 1945,* 360. Stuttgart, 1972.

Halbreich, H. "Berndt Alois Zimmermann." In *Festschrift für einen Verleger: Ludwig Strecker,* 242. Mainz, 1973.

Häusler, J. "Bernd Alois Zimmermann und sein Werk für zeitgenössische Musik." *Universitas* 28 (1973): 1117.

Kirchberg, K. "Omnia tempus habent: ein Rückblick auf Leben und Werk Bernd Alois Zimmermanns." In *Neue Musik in der Bundesrepublik,* 35. Cologne, 1974.

Karbaum, M. "Zur Verfahrensweise im Werk Bernd Alois Zimmermanns." In *De ratione in musica: Festschrift Erich Schenk,* 275. Kassel, 1975.

Musik und Bildung 10 (1978) [special Zimmermann issue].

Becker, Peter. "Aspekte der Lenz-Rezeption in Bernd Alois Zimmermanns Opera *Die Soldaten.*" In *Musiktheater heute,* edited by Hellmut Kühn, 94. Mainz, 1981.

Fischer, Erik. "Bernd Alois Zimmermanns Oper *Die Soldaten.* Zum Deutung der musikalisch-dramatischen Struktur." In *Festschrift Heinz Becker zum 60. Geburtstag am 26. Juni 1982,* edited by Jürgen Schläder and Reinhold Quandt, 268. Laaber, 1982.

Konold, Wulf. "B.A. Zimmermanns zweites Opernprojekt." In *Für und Wider die Literaturoper. Zur Situation nach 1945,* ed. Sigrid Wiesmann, 113. Laaber, 1982.

Wiesmann, Sigrid. "Bedingungen der Komponierbarkeit. Berndt Alois Zimmermanns *Die Soldaten,* György Ligetis *Le grand macabre.*" In *Für und Wider die Literaturoper. Zur Situation nach 1945,* ed. Sigrid Wiesmann, 27. Laaber, 1982.

Gruhn, Wilfried. "Integrale Komposition. Zu Bernd Alois Zimmermanns Pluralismus-Begriff." *Archiv für Musikwissenschaft* 40 (1983): 287.

* * *

Bernd Alois Zimmermann's single opera, *Die Soldaten* 1958-60; revised 1963-64, has been widely recognized as one of the most significant contributions to the genre by a composer of Germanic origin since Alban Berg's *Wozzeck* (1921). Its historical importance derives from three factors: 1) it is the first opera composed by a person closely associated with the post-war avant garde; 2) it is the first opera in which techniques of integral serialism are utilized as an organizational basis; 3) quotation and collage are introduced as significant aspects of the dramatic and musical design.

This last aspect, the use of musical material borrowed from other sources in a manner similar to the technique of collage in the visual arts, is perhaps the single most innovative feature of the opera. Not only does Zimmermann quote composers of the past (primarily Bach) and allude stylistically to jazz and other "vernacular" idioms, he is able to integrate these materials into the musical and dramaturgical fabric. The barriers between past, present, and future are broken down through musical and dramatic juxtapositions; all of history is presented as completely present in a pluralistic and contemporary world view. One way this is achieved is through the simultaneous presentation of separate "scenes" on different levels of the stage; in this way, the dramatic stage presentation parallels the equally pluralistic attitude shown in the use of stylistic and material borrowings superimposed upon the composer's "own music."

Despite his limited operatic output, Zimmermann's primary musical orientation was toward the dramatic. Throughout his career, he displayed a keen interest in musical forms which are inherently dramatic: the solo sonata, the symphony, the ballet, and especially the concerto. He was also active as a composer of music for dramatic productions in radio and film. It would seem that this dramatic orientation was pivotal in his espousal of pluralistic techniques of collage and quotation for most of his works following *Die Soldaten.*

Zimmermann's first mature works were in the particular vein of neo-classicism which dominated Germany's musical life during the inter-war years. His earliest published composition, the five Extemporale für Klavier (1938-46), shows the influence of Hindemith in the use of unusual yet still diatonically derived harmonies. *Enchiridion: Kleine Stücke für Klavier* (1949-51) is similar, but incorporates the diatonic harmonies within a quickly moving chromatic linear design. This work is one of the first in which Zimmermann incorporated the twelve-tone techniques of Arnold Schoenberg which had recently begun to resurface following the suppression of Schoenberg's music by the Nazis.

Building on the models of his teachers Wilhelm Fortner and René Leibowitz, Zimmermann composed several works in which he attempted to reconcile Schoenberg's twelve-tone techniques with the dominant formal tradition of Central European music as exemplified by such composers as Igor Stravinsky, Béla Bartók, and Paul Hindemith. Typical of this period are his Violin Concerto (1949/50), and Oboe Concerto (1952), each of which adheres stylistically to neo-classicism, while incorporating thematic material derived from twelve-tone series. The renewed interest in Schoenberg's twelve-tone technique following the Second World War was reflected in the organization in 1946 of the "Darmstädter Ferienkurse für Neue Musik." These seminars were attended by many of the most talented young composers of the time, including Zimmermann in 1948 and 1950, and were pivotal in reacquainting composers and the public with the music of Schoenberg, Berg, and Webern. It was in Darmstadt that Zimmermann studied with Fortner, Leibowitz and Hindemith, who were among the first to be engaged as leaders of the composition seminars. It was also here that Zimmermann became associated with the somewhat younger composers of the post-war avant-garde who were just beginning to radically alter the course of European music.

By the mid-fifties, the attitudes of many composers in Europe had changed dramatically: twelve-tone serialism was no longer seen as simply the basis for the creation of themes within a neoclassical style, but as a systematic mode of organization to be applied to the entire musical fabric. This more thorough-going integration of serialism is evident in Zimmermann's works of the period, such as Perspektiven (1955/56), Canto di speranza (1953/57), and the Cello Sonata (1959/60). This last work also exemplifies Zimmermann's continuing occupation with music of a dramatic thrust. The structural rigor of serialism did not hinder Zimmermann's ability to create dramatic intensity. Like his earlier neo-classical concertos, the Cello Sonata is music requiring extreme virtuosity and dramatic flair from the performer.

Although Zimmermann's serial orientation would remain basically unaltered for the remainder of his career, he began increasingly to use stylistic and material quotation within serially structured works. He had already shown an openness to pre-existing materials in his work during the years when he was first exploring integral serialism. His Trumpet Concerto entitled *Nobody knows de trouble I see* (1954) uses, as the title suggests, the African-American spiritual of the same title as what Zimmermann terms its "geometrical center" (letter to Karl Amadeus Hartmann, 30 October 1956; quoted in Konold, 1986, p. 95). Even before this, in *Kontraste* (1953), the composer had called up the ghosts of such eminent forebears as Claude Debussy, Maurice Ravel and Johann Strauss to preside over this first in his series of "Imaginary Ballets."

Zimmermann would, however, go beyond the use of stylistic allusion—already evident, at any rate, in his earlier neo-classicism—in works such as *Die Soldaten* (1958/64), and *Dialoge* (1960/65). In these works, actual quotation of pre-existing material is used. In each case, the overall conception is serial and the quotations appear superimposed over one another along with Zimmermann's "own music." In one section alone of *Dialoge* the composer quotes Debussy's *Jeux,*

Mozart's Piano Concerto in C Major, K.467, and the hymn *Veni creator spiritus.* In both *Die Soldaten* and *Dialoge,* quotation is confined to relatively small portions of each work. But in Zimmermann's most extreme use of quotation, his *Musique pour les soupers du roi Ubu* (1966), the composer pieces together a work consisting entirely of pre-existing music by himself and others. Zimmermann's quotations sometimes emerge as part of a continuous musical fabric, alluding to the past as simply another element available for a composer's use. At other times, they appear as interruptions, startling the music, as it were, as abrupt and foreign-sounding elements.

The pluralistic attitude which Zimmermann and others began to display in the 1960s toward the music of the past has been seen by some as a transformation of serial procedures. Robert P. Morgan has compared Zimmermann's careful manipulation of pre-existing material through "combinational and permutational methods" in *Musique pour les soupers du roi Ubu* to the use of serial procedures with more usual "pre-formed" materials such as pitch or rhythm (*Twentieth-Century Music,* New York 1991, 412).

—Richard R. Blocker

TITLE INDEX

The *International Dictionary of Opera* Title Index includes all titles found in the "Operas" lists in the book's nearly 200 composer entries. The names in parentheses after the title refer to the composer entry where full composition information may be found; the page number on which this data is located follows for quick access. Boldface page numbers refer to the location of the full entry on that opera.

A **Boldface** page number refers to the full entry for the title.

A **Boldface** page number refers to the full entry for the title.

C

A **Boldface** page number refers to the full entry for the title.

A **Boldface** page number refers to the full entry for the title.

E

Éclair (Halévy): 566
Écossais de Chatou (Delibes): 319
Ecuba (Malipiero): 795
Edelmüthige Porsenna (Mattheson): 828
Edgar (Puccini): **378,** 1060
Edipo re (Leoncavallo): 735
Edmea (Catalani): 225
Eduardo e Cristina (Rossini): 1145
Éducation manquée (Chabrier): 237
Egeria (Hasse): 586
Egg (Menotti): 856
Egisto (Cavalli): 229
Einstein on the Beach (Glass): 514
    See Triptych
Elda (Catalani): 225
Electre (Grétry): 554
Elegy for Young Lovers (Henze): **382,** 596
Elektra (Strauss): **382,** 1287
Elen e Fuldano (Malipiero): 795
Elena (Cavalli): 229
Elena (Elena e Costantino) (Mayr): 835
Elena da Feltre (Mercadante): 859
Elfrida (Arne): 57
Elfrida (Balfe): 77
Elfrida (Paisiello): 980
Eliogabalo (Cavalli): 229
Elisa e Claudio, ossia L'amore protetto dall' amicizia (Mercadante): 859
Elisa, ossia Il monte San Bernardo (Mayr): 835
Elisa, regina di Tiro (Galuppi): 483
Elisabetta, regina d'Inghilterra (Rossini): 1145
Élisca, ou l'amour maternel (Grétry): 555
Elisi delusi (Spontini): 1270
Elisir d'amore [The Elixir of Love] (Donizetti): 356, **385**
Elixir of Love
    See Elisir d'amore
Eliza (Arne): 56
Eliza, ou Le voyage aux glaciers du Mont St-Bernard (Cherubini): 247
Elizabeth, o Il castello di Kenilworth (Donizetti): 356
Elodie, ou Le forfait nocturne (Offenbach): 954
Elvezi, ovvero Corrado di Tochemburgo (Pacini): 973
Elvida (Donizetti): 354
Elvira (Paisiello): 980
Embarras des richesses (Grétry): 554
Emilia di Liverpool (Donizetti): 354
Emilie, ou La belle esclave (Grétry): 554
Emireno o vero Il consiglio (Scarlatti): 1185
Emma d' Antiocchia (Mercadante): 859
Emma di Resburgo (Meyerbeer): 867
Emma, ou La prisonnière (Boieldieu): 158
Emma, ou La promesse imprudente (Auber): 66
Emmeline (Hérold): 600
Emperor Jones (Gruenberg): **386,** 560
Emperor's New Clothes (Moore): 898
Enchantress (Balfe): 77
Ende einer Welt (Henze): 596
Endimion (Charpentier): 242
Endimione (Hasse): 586
Endimione, ovvero Il trionfo d'amore (Jommelli): 654
Enea e Lavinia (Sacchini): 1163
Enea in Cuma (Piccinni): 1017
Enea nel Lazio (Jommelli): 654, 655
Enea nel Lazio (Porpora): 1038
Enfant et les sortilèges [The Bewitched Child] (Ravel): **386,** 1086
Enfant prodigue (Auber): 67

Enfant roi (Bruneau): 187
English Cat (Henze): 596
Enlèvement des Sabines (Piccinni): 1018
Enrico (Galuppi): 484
Enrico di Borgogna (Donizetti): 354
Enrico II (Rosmonda d'Inghilterra) (Nicolai): 931
Enrico IV al passo della Marna (Balfe): 77
Entdeckte Verstellund oder Die geheime Liebe der Diana (Keiser): 676
Entente cordiale (Smyth): 1258
Entführung aus dem Serail [The Abduction from the Seraglio] (Mozart): **387,** 906
Entrez, messieurs, mesdames (Offenbach): 953
Eolf (Boughton): 176
Epicure (Cherubini): 247
Epicure (Méhul): 846
Epilogue for Mayr's Elise (Paisiello): 981
Equivoci in amore o vero La Rosaura (Scarlatti): 1185
Equivoci nel sembiante (Scarlatti): 1184
Equivoco (Piccinni): 1017
Equivoco stravagante (Rossini): 1145
Equivoco, ovvero Le Bizzarie dell' amore (Mayr): 835
Eraclea (Scarlatti): 1185
Eraclito e Democrito (Salieri): 1170
Eraldo ed Emma (Mayr): 835
Ercole al Termedonte (Piccinni): 1018
Ercole amante (Cavalli): 229
Ercole in Lidia (Mayr): 835
Ercole su'l Termodonte (Vivaldi): 1413
Ergilda (Galuppi): 483
Erifile (Sacchini): 1163
Erismena (Cavalli): 229
Eritrea (Cavalli): 229
Ermenegildo (Porpora): 1038
Ermione (Rossini): 1145
Ernani (Bellini): 106
Ernani (Verdi): **391,** 1393
Ero e Leander (Boito): 161
Ero e Leandro (Paer): 976
Erode, ossia Marianna (Mercadante): 859
Eroe cinese (Cimarosa): 261
Eroe cinese (Galuppi): 484
Eroe cinese (Hasse): 586
Eroe cinese (Sacchini): 1163
Eroi di Bonaventura (Malipiero): 795
Eroismo in amore (Paer): 976
Eroismo ridicolo (Spontini): 1270
Erostrate (Halévy): 566
Erreur d'un moment (Auber): 66
Errore amoroso (Jommelli): 653
Erschöpfung der Welt (Kagel): 669
Erwartung [Expectation] (Schoenberg): **393,** 1199
Erzsébet (Erkel): 390
Es war einmal (Zemlinsky): 1480
Escavazione del tesoro (Pacini): 973
Esclarmonde (Massenet): **394,** 821
Esclave de Camoëns (Flotow): 453
Esmeralda (Dargomïzhsky): 311
Esmeralda (Massenet): 821
Estelle et Némorin (Berlioz): 127
Ester d'Engaddi (Pacini): 974
Esther de Carpentras (Milhaud): 875
Estrella (Wallace): 1434
Esule di Granata (Meyerbeer): 867
Esule di Roma, ossia Il proscritto (Donizetti): 356
Etienne Marcel (Saint-Saëns): 1169
Étoile (Chabrier): 237

A **Boldface** page number refers to the full entry for the title.

F

A **Boldface** page number refers to the full entry for the title.

H

A **Boldface** page number refers to the full entry for the title.

J

K

A **Boldface** page number refers to the full entry for the title.

M

A **Boldface** page number refers to the full entry for the title.

N

A **Boldface** page number refers to the full entry for the title.

P

A **Boldface** page number refers to the full entry for the title.

Q

R

A **Boldface** page number refers to the full entry for the title.

S

A **Boldface** page number refers to the full entry for the title.

A **Boldface** page number refers to the full entry for the title.

U

V

W

A **Boldface** page number refers to the full entry for the title.

NATIONALITY INDEX

AMERICAN

Adams, John
Albanese, Licia
Amato, Pasquale
Anderson, June
Anderson, Marian
Argento, Dominick
Arroyo, Martina
Auden, W. H.
Bampton, Rose
Barber, Samuel
Battle, Kathleen
Beeson, Jack
Bernstein, Leonard
Blitzstein, Marc
Bloch, Ernest
Bumbry, Grace
Caldwell, Sarah
Callas, Maria
Copland, Aaron
Corsaro, Frank
Curtin, Phyllis
Eames, Emma
Eaton, John
Elias, Rosalind
Ewing, Maria
Farrar, Geraldine
Farrell, Eileen
Floyd, Carlisle
Foss, Lukas
Fremstad, Olive
Gershwin, George
Giannini, Dusolina
Glass, Philip
Glossop, Peter
Graf, Herbert
Grist, Reri
Gruenberg, Louis
Hindemith, Paul
Hines, Jerome
Homer, Louise
Horne, Marilyn
Janssen, Herbert
Joplin, Scott
King, James
Kipnis, Alexander
Korngold, Erich Wolfgang

Krenek, Ernst
Kurka, Robert
Lear, Evelyn
Lehmann, Lilli
Leinsdorf, Erich
Levine, James
London, George
Maazel, Lorin
MacNeil, Cornell
McCormack, John
Menotti, Gian Carlo
Merrill, Robert
Merriman, Nan
Milnes, Sherrill
Moffo, Anna
Monteux, Pierre
Moore, Douglas
Moore, Grace
Morris, James
Nordica, Lillian
Norman, Jessye
Pagliughi, Lina
Peerce, Jan
Peters, Roberta
Pons, Lily
Ponselle, Rosa
Price, Leontyne
Prince, Harold
Ramey, Samuel
Raskin, Judith
Resnik, Regina
Rethberg, Elisabeth
Rudel, Julius
Sanderson, Sybil
Schippers, Thomas
Schumann-Heink, Ernestine
Schwarzkopf, Elisabeth
Sellars, Peter
Sendak, Maurice
Sessions, Roger
Shirley, George
Sills, Beverly
Steber, Eleanor
Stevens, Risë
Stich-Randall, Teresa
Szell, George
Thomson, Virgil
Tibbett, Lawrence

Tourel, Jennie
Tozzi, Giorgio
Traubel, Helen
Treigle, Norman
Troyanos, Tatiana
Tucker, Richard
Verrett, Shirley
Von Stade, Frederica
Wallerstein, Lothar
Ward, Robert
Warren, Leonard
Wilson, Robert

ARGENTINIAN
Ginastera, Alberto
Kagel, Mauricio

AUSTRALIAN
Lawrence, Marjorie
Mackerras, Charles
Melba, Nellie
Minton, Yvonne
Moshinsky, Elijah
Sutherland, Joan

AUSTRIAN
Bahr-Mildenburg, Anna
Berg, Alban
Berry, Walter
Bodanzky, Artur
Böhm, Karl
Cavalieri, Catarina
Cebotari, Maria
Dernesch, Helga
Einem, Gottfried von
Felsenstein, Walter
Graf, Herbert
Gregor, Joseph
Gueden, Hilde
Haydn, Franz Joseph
Hofmannsthal, Hugo von
Karajan, Herbert von
Kleiber, Carlos
Kleiber, Erich
Konetzni, Anny
Konetzni, Hilde
Krauss, Clemens
Krenek, Ernst
Krips, Josef
Kunz, Erich
Kurz, Selma
Leinsdorf, Erich
Ligeti, György
Lipp, Wilma
Mahler, Gustav
Mottl, Felix
Mozart, Wolfgang Amadeus
Patzak, Julius
Popp, Lucia
Reinhardt, Max
Richter, Hans
Roller, Alfred
Rosbaud, Hans
Rudel, Julius
Rysanek, Leonie
Schalk, Franz
Schenk, Otto

Schmidt, Franz
Schoenberg, Arnold
Schreker, Franz
Schubert, Franz
Schuch, Ernst von
Schumann-Heink, Ernestine
Slezak, Leo
Tauber, Richard
Urban, Joseph
Wächter, Eberhard
Wallmann, Margherita
Weber, Ludwig
Weikl, Bernd
Weingartner, Felix
Wolf, Hugo
Zemlinsky, Alexander von

BELGIAN
Cluytens, André
Danco, Suzanne
Gorr, Rita
Grétry, André-Ernest-Modeste
Heldy, Fanny
Pousseur, Henri
Van Dam, José

BRAZILIAN
Gomes, Antonio Carlos
Sayão, Bidú
Villa-Lobos, Heitor

BULGARIAN
Christoff, Boris
Ghiaurov, Nicolai
Welitsch, Ljuba

CANADIAN
Albani, Emma
Johnson, Edward
London, George
Simoneau, Léopold
Stratas, Teresa
Vickers, Jon
Vinay, Ramón

CZECHOSLOVAKIAN
Blachut, Beno
Burian, Karel
Destinn, Emmy
Dvořák, Antonín
Janáček, Leoš
Jeritza, Maria
Korngold, Erich Wolfgang
Kubelík, Rafael
Martinů, Bohuslav
Novotná, Jarmila
Popp, Lucia
Slezak, Leo
Smetana, Bedřich
Stolz, Teresa
Svoboda, Josef
Wallerstein, Lothar
Weinberger, Jaromir

DANISH
Melchior, Lauritz
Nielsen, Carl
Roswaenge, Helge

Corena, Fernando
Cuénod, Hugues
Della Casa, Lisa
Einem, Gottfried von
Honegger, Arthur
Mathis, Edith
Rousseau, Jean-Jacques

UKRAINIAN
Kipnis, Alexander

WELSH
Burrows, Stuart
Evans, Geraint
Jones, Gwyneth
Price, Margaret

YUGOSLAVIAN
Dermota, Anton
Jurinac, Sena
Milanov, Zinka

NOTES ON ADVISERS AND CONTRIBUTORS

ABROMEIT, Kathleen A. Public services librarian, Conservatory Library, Oberlin College. Author of articles on Ethel Smyth, *The Wreckers*, and Anna Bon. Author of CD-ROM reviews for *Mad River Review* and reviews for *Choice*. **Essays:** *Bohème* [Leoncavallo]; Caldwell; *Debussy; Pelléas et Mélisande;* Smyth; *Wreckers; Zazà.*

ACHTER, Morton. Professor of music and chairman of department of music, Otterbein College, Westerville, Ohio. Former chairman of Fine Arts at Bloomfield College; faculty appointments also at the University of Michigan and Boston University. **Essays:** *Hamlet; Mignon;* Thomas.

ADAMS, Byron. Composer, conductor, and assistant professor of music, University of California, Riverside. Author of articles for *MLA Notes, Music and Letters,* and *Musical Quarterly.* **Essays:** *Pilgrim's Progress;* Adams.

ANDERSON, David E. Doctoral candidate at the University of Chicago. Author of articles for *Music Review, The Opera Quarterly,* and *Notes.* **Essays:** *Ägyptische Helena;* Blitzstein; Busch; *Dantons Tod;* Ebert; Einem; *Elegy for Young Lovers;* Gregor; Hartmann; Henze; *Regina;* Roller; Schmidt; Wallerstein.

ANTOKOLETZ, Elliott. Head of musicology division and professor of musicology, University of Texas, Austin. Editor of the *International Journal of Musicology.* Author of *The Music of Béla Bartók,* 1984, *A Guide to Béla Bartók Research,* 1988, and *Twentieth Century Music,* 1992. **Essay:** *Duke Bluebeard's Castle.*

ARMSTRONG, Robin. Free-lance writer. Contributor of articles to *Contemporary Musicians, Contemporary Black Biography,* and *African-American Almanac.* **Essays:** *Adriana Lecouvreur;* Bohnen; *Cendrillon;* Gadski; Neidlinger; Schlusnus; Schorr; *Tote Stadt.*

ASHBROOK, William. Professor Emeritus of music, Indiana State University. Author of *Donizetti,* 1965, *The Operas of Puccini,* 1968, *Donizetti and His Operas,* 1982, and *Puccini's Turandot: The End of the Great Tradition,* with Harold Powers, 1991. Contributing editor for *The Opera Quarterly* and member of editorial board of *Cambridge Opera Journal.* **Essays:** Donizetti; Puccini.

BACKUS, Joan. Visiting assistant professor, University of Victoria, British Columbia, Canada. Author of articles on Liszt for *19th Century Music* and *Journal of the American Liszt Society.* **Essays:** Albani; Johnson.

BARFOOT, Terry. Senior lecturer in history of music, The South Downs College, England. Coauthor of *Opera: A History,* 1987. Editor of *The Classical Music Repertoire Guide* and *Quarternote.* Feature writer for *Classical Music Magazine,* music critic for *The News* (Portsmouth), and author of program notes for various concert series and opera companies throughout England. **Essays:** Bailey; Baker; Cimarosa; *Comedy on the Bridge; Dalibor;* Glossop; *Libuše;* Martinů; *Matrimonio segreto;* Smetana; Spontini; *Turandot* [Busoni]; *Vestale.*

BARWICK, Steven. Professor Emeritus of music, Southern Illinois University. Author of *The Franco Codex of the Cathedral of Mexico,* 1965, and *Two Mexico City Choirbooks of 1717,* 1982. **Adviser.**

BEACHAM, Richard C. Reader in theatre studies, Joint School of Theatre, University of Warwick, England. Author of *The Roman Theatre and Its Audience,* 1991. Editor and translator of *Adolphe Appia: Texts on Theatre,* 1992. Author of articles on Appia for *Maske und Kothurn, The Opera Quarterly,* and *New Theatre Quarterly.* **Essay:** Appia.

BERRETT, Joshua. Professor of music, Mercy College, Dobbs Ferry, New York. Editor of *Symphonies of Louis Spohr, Series C, Vol. IX, The Symphony 1720-1840,* 1980, and *Symphonies of Andreas Romberg and Bernhard Romberg, Series C, Vol. XIV, The Symphony 1720-1840,* 1985. Author of articles for *Journal of Jazz Studies, The Black Perspective in Music,* and *Musical Quarterly.* **Essays:** *Jessonda;* Mahler; Spohr.

BIRKIN, Kenneth. Free-lance writer and reviewer; musician. Author of *Richard Strauss's "Arabella,"* 1989,

"Friedenstag and Daphne": An Interpretative Study of the Literary and Dramatic Sources of the Richard Strauss Operas, 1989, and editor of *Stefan Zweig/Joseph Gregor: Briefwechsel, 1921-1938,* 1991. Author of record sleeves as well as reviews and articles for *International Richard Strauss Gesellschaft-Wein, Music and Letters, Musical Times, Opera,* and *Tempo.* **Essays:** *Arabella;* *Daphne;* Hofmannsthal; Krauss; Strauss.

BLOCKER, Richard R. Lecturer in music, DePaul University. Former lecturer in music, The University of Chicago. **Essays:** *Soldaten;* Zimmermann.

BLYTH, Alan. Music critic and editor. Author of *The Enjoyment of Opera,* 1969, and several biographies. Editor of *Opera on Record,* volume 1, 1979, volume 2, 1983, and volume 3, 1984; *Song on Record,* 1986; and *Choral Music on Record,* 1992. Music critic for the London *Times,* and the *Daily Telegraph.* Author of articles for *Gramophone* and *Opera.* **Adviser.**

BRAUNER, Charles S. Professor of music history and literature, and chairman, department of theory, history, and composition, Chicago Musical College, Roosevelt University. Author of articles for *Journal of the American Musicological Society* and *Musical Quarterly.* Contributor of articles to *Studies in the History of Music, Volume 2,* 1988, and *Musical Humanism and Its Legacy,* 1992. **Essay:** *Capuleti ed i Montecchi.*

BRAUNER, Patricia B. Coordinator of the Center for Italian Opera Studies, University of Chicago; and musicological consultant and research associate, Fondazione Rossini. Author of articles on Gioacchino Rossini. **Essays:** *Cenerentola; Mosè in Egitto; Siège de Corinthe; Turco in Italia.*

BUDDEN, Julian. Member of British Broadcasting Corporation music staff, 1951-1983. Author of *The Operas of Verdi* (volume 1, 1973; volume 2, 1978; volume 3, 1981), and *Verdi,* 1985. Author of numerous articles on Italian opera for many music periodicals. **Adviser.**

BUELOW, George J. Professor of musicology, Indiana University. Author of *The "Ariadne auf Naxos" by Hugo von Hofmannsthal and Richard Strauss,* with D. Daviau, 1975, and *Thorough-Bass Accompaniment According to Johann David Heinichen,* 1986. Author of articles and reviews for *Acta Musicologica, Bach, Journal of Music Theory, Journal of the American Musicological Society,* and other journals. Contributor to *The New Grove Dictionary of Music and Musicians,* 1980, and *The New Grove Dictionary of Opera,* 1992. **Essays:** Mattheson; *Unglückselige Cleopatra.*

BURIAN, Jarka M. Professor of theatre, State University of New York at Albany. Author of *The Scenography of Josef Svoboda,* 1971, and *Svoboda: Wagner,* 1983. **Essays:** Koltai; Svoboda.

BURROUGHS, Bruce. Editor-in-chief, *The Opera Quarterly,* Van Nuys, California. Author of articles for *The Houston*

Post, Musical Journal, Los Angeles Times, and *Opera News.* **Essays:** Albanese; Bori; Milanov; Onegin; Pons; Ponselle; Scotti; Singher. **Adviser.**

BUSHNELL, Howard. Author of *Maria Malibran: A Biography of the Singer,* 1979. **Essays:** Garcia; Malibran.

CARLEY, Lionel. Honorary archivist and adviser to Delius Trust, England. Author of *Delius: The Paris Years,* 1975, *Delius: A Life in Pictures,* 1977, *Delius: A Life in Letters,* with Robert Threlfall, 1988, and *Grieg and Delius: Marion Boyars—A Correspondence,* in press. **Essays:** *Koanga; Village Romeo and Juliet.*

CARR, Maureen A. Professor of music theory, Pennsylvania State University. Author of *Sightsinging Complete,* 5th ed., with Bruce Benward, 1991, and *Introduction to Sightsinging and Ear Training,* 2nd ed., with Bruce Benward and J. Timothy Kolosick, 1992. **Essays:** *Boris Godunov;* Crosse; *Opera; Purgatory; Rossignol; Sadko.*

CARTER, Tim. Reader in music, Royal Holloway and Bedford New College, University of London, England. Author of *W.A. Mozart: "Le nozze di Figaro,"* 1987, *Jacopo Peri (1561-1633): His Life and Works,* 1989, and *Music in Late Renaissance and Early Baroque Italy,* 1992. Contributor to *The New Grove Dictionary of Opera* and *The Penguin Opera Guide.* Author of articles on late Renaissance music for many scholarly journals. **Essays:** Busenello; *Così fan tutte; Nozze di Figaro.*

CHALMERS, Kenneth. Composer. Regular translator for *Opera* magazine. **Essays:** *Francesca da Rimini;* Zandonai.

CHEER, Clarissa Lablache. President of the Luigi Lablache Society, Harbor City, California. Currently writing a biography on Luigi Lablache. **Essay:** Lablache.

CHERNISS, Michael. Essayist. **Essay:** Cigna.

CHUSID, Martin. Professor of music and director of American Institute for Verdi Studies, New York University. Author of *A Catalog of Verdi Operas,* 1974, and *The Verdi Companion,* 1979. Author of articles for *Acta Musicologica, Mozart-Jahrbuch, Opera News, The Opera Quarterly,* and other journals. Editor of the *Verdi Newsletter* since 1984. **Essays:** Cammarano; *Rigoletto;* Verdi.

CLARK, Caryl. Post-doctoral fellow in music, University of Toronto, Ontario, Canada. Author of reviews for *The Journal of Musicology, Journal of Musicological Research,* and articles for *Current Musicology.* Contributor to *The New Grove Dictionary of Opera,* 1992. **Essays:** *Fedeltà premiata; Mondo della luna.*

CLINKSCALE, Martha Novak. Lecturer, University of California, Riverside. Author of *Makers of the Piano 1700-1820,* in press. Editor of *Journal of the American Musical Instru-*

ment Society. Contributor to *The New Grove Dictionary of Opera*, 1992, and *Encyclopedia of Keyboard Instruments*, in press. **Essays:** *Calisto;* Cavalli; *Ormindo.*

COLE, Malcolm S. Professor of musicology, University of California, Los Angeles. Author of *Armseelchen: The Life and Music of Eric Zeisl*, with Barbara Barclay, 1984, and *Guided Listening*, with Eleanor Hammer, 1992. Author of articles and reviews for *Journal of the American Musicological Society, Journal of Musicology*, and *Performance Practice Review*. Contributor to *The New Grove Dictionary of Music and Musicians*, 1980. **Essays:** *Freischütz;* Schikaneder; *Zauberflöte.*

COLLINS, William J. Member of English department faculty, Kutztown University, Pennsylvania. Coauthor of *Black Bart: The True Story of the West's Most Famous Stagecoach Robber*, 1992, and *EJS: A Discography of the Private-Label Recordings of Edward J. Smith*, in press. Author of articles on opera for *The Record Collector*. **Essays:** *Africaine;* Balfe; *Bohemian Girl;* Campanini, Italo; De Reszke, Jean; De Sabata; Flotow; Gomes; *Martha;* Meyerbeer; *Nerone;* Ponnelle; *Robert le Diable;* Tebaldi; *Vêpres siciliennes.*

COOK, Susan C. Associate professor of music and women's studies, University of Wisconsin—Madison. Author of *Opera for a New Republic*, 1988, and articles for *American Music* and *The Journal of Musicology*. **Essays:** *Jonny spielt auf;* Krenek; *Neues vom Tage; Von Heute auf Morgen.*

COOPER, David. Lecturer in music, University of Leeds, England. Composer and director of electroacoustic studio works, including a one-act opera, *Belisa*, 1982. **Essays:** *Arden Must Die;* Goehr; Maw; *Rising of the Moon.*

CORSE, Sandra. Associate professor of English, Georgia Institute of Technology. Author of *Opera and the Uses of Language*, 1987, and *Wagner and the New Consciousness*, 1989. **Essays:** *Death in Venice; Dreigroschenoper.*

COWDEN, Robert H. Professor of music, San José State University. Author of the bibliographic works *Concert and Opera Singers*, 1985, *Concert and Opera Conductors*, 1987, and *Instrumental Virtuosi*, 1989; and editor-in-chief of *Opera Companies of the World: Selected Profiles*, 1992. **Essays:** Lortzing; *Undine* [Lortzing]; *Wildschütz; Zar und Zimmermann.*

CRAGGS, Stewart R. Development services librarian, University of Sunderland Library, England. Author of catalogues for the works of William Walton and biobibliographic works on Arthur Bliss, Richard Rodney Bennett, and John McCabe. Author of articles for *Musical Times* and *Perspective in Music*. **Essays:** *Troilus and Cressida;* Walton.

CRIST, Stephen A. Assistant professor of music, Emory University. Author of articles for *Bach Perspectives, Bach Studies*, and *Early Music*. **Essays:** *Corregidor;* Wolf.

CROHN, Harris N. Associate professor of music, piano faculty, Southern Methodist University. Active recitalist, chamber

music performer, accompanist, and conductor. **Essays:** Blachut; Cornelius; *Cunning Little Vixen; Devil and Kate;* Dvořák; Janáček; *Makropoulos Case; Two Widows.*

CYR, Mary. Chair, department of music, University of Guelph, Quebec, Canada. Author of *Performing Baroque Music*, 1992. Editor of *Canadian University Music Review* and contributor to *The New Grove Dictionary of Opera*, 1992. Author of articles on Jean-Phillipe Rameau and eighteenth-century opera for *Early Music, Music and Letters*, and *Musical Times*. **Essays:** *Castor et Pollux;* Rameau.

D'ANGELO, James. Member of the faculties of Goldsmiths College, University of London, Webster University, and The Westminister Institute, England. Author of *Tonality Symbolism in Paul Hindemith's Opera "Die Harmonie der Welt,"* 1985, and *The Tuning of the Universe*, 1991. **Essays:** *Harmonie der Welt;* Hindemith.

DANES, Robert H. Associate professor of music and associate dean of College of Arts and Sciences, Washburn University, Topeka, Kansas. Author of articles for *Diapason* and *Washington Opera Magazine*. **Essays:** *Erwartung; Rake's Progress.*

DANIEL, Keith W. Music teacher, Concord Academy, Concord, Massachusetts. Author of *Francis Poulenc: His Artistic Development and Musical Style*, 1982. Author of articles for *In Theory Only, American Choral Review*, and *Stagebill*. **Essays:** *Dialogues des Carmélites;* Poulenc; *Voix Humaine.*

DARCY, Warren. Professor of music theory, Oberlin College Conservatory of Music. Contributor to *The Opera Quarterly* and *19th Century Music*. **Essay:** *Fliegende Holländer.*

DAVIDIAN, Teresa. Visiting assistant professor, Bowdoin College. Author of articles for *Journal of Musicological Research* and *Theory and Practice*. **Essays:** *Fervaal; Heure espagnole;* Ravel.

DAY, James. Free-lance writer and lecturer and former principal, Cambridge Eurocentre, England. Author of *Vaughan Williams*, 1961, *The Literary Background to Bach's Cantatas*, 1961, and *Music and Aesthetics in the 18th and 19th Century*, with Peter le Huray, 1981. **Essays:** Davis; Holst; *Hugh the Drover;* Leppard; *Savitri;* Vaughan Williams.

DEL MAR, NORMAN. Conductor. Author of the three-volume *Richard Strauss*, 1962-72, *Mahler's Sixth Symphony: A Study*, 1980, *Orchestral Variations*, 1981, *Anatomy of the Orchestra*, 1981, *Companion to the Orchestra*, 1987, and *Conducting Beethoven*, 1992. **Adviser.**

DENNIS, Lawrence J. Professor of philosophy of education, Southern Illinois University. Reviewer for *Opera Canada*. Previously a pianist and teacher at McGill University, Canada, and reviewer for *Music and Musicians*. **Essays:** Graham; *Lucio Silla; Mitridate, Rè di Ponto; Orfeo ed Euridice.*

DETELS, Claire. Associate professor of music, University of Arkansas. Author of articles for *Opera Journal* and *Yearbook of Interdisciplinary Studies in the Fine Arts.* **Essays:** *Falstaff;* Macbeth [Verdi]; *Madama Butterfly; Manon Lescaut; Otello* [Verdi]; *Simon Boccanegra.*

DIGAETANI, John Louis. Associate professor of English, Hofstra University. Author of *Richard Wagner and the Modern British Novel,* 1978, *Puccini the Thinker,* 1987, *An Invitation to the Opera,* 1990, and *Penetrating Wagner's Ring: An Anthology,* 1990. Author of articles for *Opera Canada, Opera Digest, Opera News,* and *The Opera Quarterly.* **Essays:** *Fanciulla del West;* Nilsson, Birgit; *Ring des Nibelungen; Tosca; Trittico.*

DOMMETT, Kenneth. Free-lance writer for *High-Fi News.* Former lecturer at Birmingham University and music critic for the *Birmingham Post.* **Essays:** *Bánk Bán;* Erkel; *Greek Passion; Háry János; Julietta;* Kodály; *Maskarade;* Nielsen; *Red Line;* Sallinen; *Saul og David.*

DRAKE, James A. Executive director, Greenville University Center, Clemson University. Author of *Ponselle: A Singer's Life,* 1982, *Richard Tucker: A Biography,* 1984, and *Rosa Ponselle: A Profile in Perspective,* in press. Author of articles for *High/Fidelity, Musical America, The Opera Quarterly,* and other periodicals. **Essays:** Morris; Tamagno.

DRUMMOND, Andrew. Professor of theatre arts, Kingsburough Community College of the City University of New York. Author of *American Opera Librettos,* 1973. **Essays:** *Good Soldier Schweik; Lizzie Borden; Susannah.*

DYSON, Peter. Associate professor of English, University of Toronto, Ontario, Canada. Reviewer and feature writer for *Opera Canada* and *Opera.* Author of articles on opera for *Current Musicology* and *Henry James Review.* **Essays:** *Andrea Chénier;* Crespin; *Due Foscari;* Janowitz; London; *Nabucco;* Sills; *Stiffelio.*

ELLIOTT, Jonathan. Composer and member of music faculty, Saint Ann's School, Brooklyn, New York. Contributing editor for MCR Productions, The Netherlands. **Essays:** *Antony and Cleopatra;* Beeson; Ginastera.

EWANS, Michael. Associate professor of drama and warden of the Central Coast Campus of the University of Newcastle, New South Wales, Australia. Author of *Janáček's Tragic Operas,* 1977, *Wagner and Aeschylus: The "Ring" and the "Orestei,"* 1982, *Georg Büchner's Woyzeck: Translation and Theatrical Commentary,* 1989, and numerous articles and essays on Greek tragedy and opera. **Essays:** Bartók; *From the House of the Dead; Jenůfa; King Priam; Lulu; Midsummer Marriage.*

FANNING, David. Lecturer in music, Manchester University, England. Author of articles for *Royal Musical Association.* **Essays:** *Lady Macbeth of Mtsensk District;* Shostakovich.

FARISH, Stephen T., Jr. Professor of music and associate

dean for academic affairs, College of Music, University of North Texas. Author of *Lessons in French Diction for Singers,* 1969, with a new and expanded edition in progress. Contributor to *The 371 Chorales of Johann Sebastian Bach,* 1966. Author of articles for *Journal of Research in Singing.* **Essays:** Arne; *Artaxerxes.*

FARKAS, Andrew. Director of libraries and professor of library science, University of North Florida. Editor, contributor, and translator of *Tita Ruffo: An Anthology,* 1984; author of *Opera and Concert Singers: An Annotated International Bibliography,* 1985; editor of *Lawrence Tibbett: Singing Actor,* 1989; and coauthor of *Enrico Caruso: My Father and My Family,* with Enrico Caruso, Jr. Author of articles for numerous publications, including *Opera, Opera News, The Opera Quarterly,* and *Record Collector.* **Essays:** Caruso; Dal Monte; Ruffo; Tibbett; Treigle. **Adviser.**

FELDMAN, James Allen. Professor of music theory, Baldwin-Wallace College Conservatory, Berea, Ohio. **Essays:** *Albert Herring; Manon; Medium; Midsummer Night's Dream; Norma; Riders to the Sea; Rienzi.*

FEND, Michael. Fellow of German Academic Exchange Service (DAAD), England. Author of *Europäische Hochschulschriften,* 1989. **Essay:** *Deux Journées.*

FIFIELD, Christopher. Free-lance conductor, writer, and broadcaster. Director of music, University College, London, England, 1980-1990. Author of *Max Bruch,* 1988, *Wagner in Performance,* 1992, and *True Artist and True Friend: A Biography of Hans Richter,* in press. **Essays:** Blech; Bülow; Coates; Klemperer; Knappertsbusch; Levi; Muck; Nikisch; Richter; Schalk; Schuch; Walter; Weingartner.

FITZLYON, April. Free-lance writer and translator. Author of *Lorenzo da Ponte,* 1956, *The Price of Genius,* 1964, and *Turgenev and the Theatre,* 1983. Contributor to *The New Grove Dictionary of Music and Musicians,* 1980. Author of articles for many periodicals. **Essay:** Viardot.

FOLTZ, Roger E. Professor of music, University of Nebraska. Author of *Sight Singing and Related Singing,* 1973, 1978, and *Sight Singing: Melodic Structures in Functional Tonality,* 1978, both with Anne Marie de Zeeuw. Author of articles for *Clavier Magazine, Indiana Theory Review, Journal of Music Theory Pedagogy,* and other journals. **Essays:** Argento; Falla; *Postcard from Morocco; Vida breve.*

FORBES, Elizabeth. Free-lance music journalist. Author of *Opera From A to Z,* 1978, *The Observer's Book of Opera,* 1982, and *Mario and Grisi,* 1985. Consulting editor and contributor to *The New Grove Dictionary of Opera,* 1992. **Essays:** Berghaus; Dexter; Friedrich; Herz; Kupfer; Miller; Shaw; Wagner, Wolfgang.

FOX, David Anthony. Associate director, College of General Studies, University of Pennsylvania. Formerly director of special programs at University of California, Los Angeles. Author of reviews for *The Opera Quarterly, Pulse,* and other musical journals. **Essays:** *Ariadne auf Naxos;* Borkh; Brouwenstijn; Danco; Della Casa; Fassbaender; *Frau ohne Schatten;* Gluck; Gorr; Gueden; Jurinac; Kunz; Ludwig; Merriman; Popp; Resnik; Schwarzkopf; Stich-Randall; Traubel; Troyanos; Verrett.

FRANKLIN, Peter. Lecturer in music, University of Leeds, England. Author of *The Idea of Music: Schoenberg and Others,* 1985, and *Mahler's Third Symphony,* 1991. **Essays:** d'Albert; Delius; *Ferne Klang; Florentinische Tragödie; Palestrina;* Pfitzner; Schreker; *Tiefland;* Zemlinsky.

FREEMAN, John W. Associate editor for *Opera News,* New York. Author of *The Metropolitan Opera Stories of the Great Operas,* 1984, and *Toscanini: A Pictorial Biography,* with Walfredo Toscanini, 1987. **Essays:** Bampton; Novotná.

FURMAN, Nelly. Professor of French and past director of women's studies program, Cornell University. Author of *La Revue des Deux Mondes et le Romantisme (1831-1848),* 1975, and coeditor of *Women and Language in Literature and Society,* 1980. **Essay:** *Carmen.*

GABLE, David. Doctoral candidate, Harper Fellow, The University of Chicago. Coeditor of *A Life for New Music: Selected Papers of Paul Fromm,* 1988, and *Alban Berg: Historical and Analytical Perspectives,* 1991. Author of articles for *Journal of Musicology* and *Journal of the American Musicological Society.* **Essays:** *Barbier von Bagdad;* Catalani; *Joseph;* Kagel; Méhul; *Wally.*

GALANTE, Jane Hohfeld. Chamber music pianist, and trustee, Morrison Chamber Music Foundation. Former music editor for *A Journal of Modern Culture* and instructor, history of opera at Mills College and the University of California, Berkeley. **Essays:** *Christophe Colomb;* Milhaud.

GARLINGTON, Aubrey S. Professor of music, University of North Carolina. Author of *Confraternity and "Carnivale" at San Giovanni Evangelista, Florence, 1820-1920,* 1991. Author of articles for *Journal of the American Musicological Society, Musical Quarterly,* and *Yearbook of Interdisciplinary Studies in the Fine Arts.* **Essays:** *Armide* [Gluck]; Cavalieri, Catarina; Delibes; Hérold; Hoffmann; Lalo; Malipiero; Mayr; *Roi d'Ys;* Salieri; Sanquirico; *Tarare; Undine* [Hoffmann]; *Zampa.*

GATTEY, Charles Neilson. Biographer, playwright, lecturer, and author. Author of *Queens of Song,* 1979, *The Elephant That Swallowed a Nightingale and Other Operatic Wonders,* 1981, *Peacocks on the Podium,* 1982, and *Foie Gras and Trumpets,* 1984. Regular contributor to *About the House.* **Essays:** Hempel; Lind; Pagliughi; Patti; Tetrazzini.

GRAY, Timothy O. Legal proofreader, free-lance editor, and doctoral candidate, Loyola University of Chicago. **Essays:** Böhm; Corelli; Muzio; Sass.

GREEN, London. Professor of drama and stage director, Bishop's University, Quebec, Canada; writer, radio commen-

tator, and stage director. Author of *Metropolitan Opera Guide to Recorded Opera,* in press. Author of articles for *Opera Canada, Opera News, The Opera Quarterly, Theatre Research International,* and *Theatre Journal.* **Essays:** Caniglia; Gobbi; Lehmann, Lilli; Olivero; Peerce; Rossi-Lemeni; Scotto; Stignani; Vinay.

GREENSPAN, Charlotte. Free-lance writer. Translator of *Haydn Keyboard Sonnets,* 1982. Contributor to *The New Harvard Dictionary of Music,* 1986. Editor of *Maria Malibran, Album Lyrique, and Dernières Pensées,* 1984. **Essays:** *Beatrice di Tenda;* Bellini; *Puritani;* Romani; *Sonnambula; Straniera.*

GREY, Thomas S. Assistant professor of music, Stanford University. Contributor to *Analyzing Opera,* 1989, *Wagner Compendium,* 1992, and *Music and Text: Critical Inquiries,* 1992. Author of articles for *19th Century Music.* **Essays:** Auber; Boieldieu; *Dame blanche; Don Pasquale; Fra Diavolo;* Goldmark; Halévy; *Juive; Königin von Saba; Lituani; Lustigen Weiber von Windsor;* Marschner; Nicolai; *Prophète; Vampyr.*

GRIFFITHS, Paul. Staff member of *The New Yorker.* Author of *A Concise History of Modern Music,* 1978, *Modern Music: The Avant-Garde Since 1945,* 1981, *The String Quartet,* 1983, *New Sounds, New Personalities: British Composers of the 1980s,* 1985, and *An Encyclopedia of 20th Century Music,* 1986. Contributor to *The New Grove Concise Dictionary of Music and Musicians,* 1988. Former member of editorial team for The New Grove Dictionaries. Former music critic for the London *Times.* **Adviser.**

GRIM, William E. Assistant professor of music, Worcester State College, Massachusetts. Author of *The Faust Legend in Music and Literature,* vol. 1, 1988, vol. 2, 1992, *Max Reger: A Bio-Bibliography,* 1988, and *Haydn's Sturm und Drang Symphonies: Form and Meaning,* 1990. Editor of *Yearbook of Interdisciplinary Studies in Fine Arts.* **Essays:** Boito; d'Indy; *Doktor Faust; Faust; Mefistofele;* Schippers; Steber.

GROOS, Arthur. Professor of German studies, Cornell University. Coauthor of *Giacomo Puccini: La Bòheme,* 1986, and author of *Reading Opera,* 1988. Coeditor of *Cambridge Opera Journal.* Author of numerous articles on opera, especially on Wagner and Puccini. **Adviser.**

GROVER, Ralph Scott. Associate professor Emeritus of music, Lafayette College, Easton, Pennsylvania. Author of *Ernest Chausson: The Man and His Music,* 1980, and *The Music of Edmund Rubbra,* in press. **Essays:** Chausson; *Roi Arthus.*

GUENTHER, Roy J. Professor of music and chairman of department of music, George Washington University, Washington, D.C. Music critic for the *Washington Post.* Author of *Musorgsky's Days and Works: A Biography in Documents,* 1983, and contributor to *Russian Theoretical Thought in Music,* 1983. **Essays:** *Khovanshchina;* Musorgsky.

GUTMAN, David. Senior Discographer (classical), National Discography, MCPS, England. Author of *Prokofiev,* 1988.

Editor of *The Lennon Companion,* 1987, and *The Dylan Companion,* 1990, both with Elizabeth Thomson. **Essays:** *Gambler; Love for Three Oranges.*

HALL, Michael. Free-lance broadcaster, conductor, and writer. Founder of the Northern Sinphonia Orchestra. Author of *Harrison Birtwistle,* 1984. **Essays:** Birtwistle; *Mask of Orpheus; Punch and Judy.*

HARDING, James. Lecturer, broadcaster, and writer. Author of *Saint-Saëns and His Circle,* 1965, *Massenet,* 1970, *Rossini,* 1971, *Gounod,* 1973, *Folies de Paris: The Rise and Fall of French Operetta,* 1979, *Jacques Offenbach,* 1980, *Maurice Chevalier: His Life,* 1982, *Ivor Novello,* 1987, *Gerald du Maurier: The Last Actor Manager,* 1989, and *George Robey and the Music Hall,* 1991. **Essays:** Charpentier; *Cid; Don Quichotte;* Gallet; Gounod; *Jongleur de Notre Dame; Louise;* Massenet; Meilhac; *Roméo et Juliette;* Saint-Saëns; *Samson et Dalila;* Scribe.

HARRIS, Ellen T. Professor of music and associate provost for the Arts, Massachusetts Institute of Technology. Author of *Handel and the Pastoral Tradition,* 1980, and *Henry Purcell's "Dido and Aeneas,"* 1987. Editor of *Henry Purcell: "Dido and Aeneas,"* 1989, and *The Librettos of Handel's Operas,* 1989. Author of articles for *Händel-Jahrbuch* and *The Journal of Musicology.* **Essays:** *Alcina; Dido and Aeneas;* Handel; Haym; *Orlando* [Handel]; *Radamisto; Rinaldo;* Rolli; *Serse.*

HARTWELL, Robin. Lecturer in music, Liverpool Institute of Higher Education. Former member of faculties of University of Sussex, University of Keele, and University of Liverpool. **Essays:** *Devin du village; Grand Macabre;* Ligeti; *Lighthouse;* Rousseau.

HATCH, Christopher. Previously a lecturer in music, Columbia University. Editor of *Music and Civilization: Essays in Honor Paul Henry Lang,* with Edmond Strainchamps and Maria Rika Maniates, 1984, and editor of *Music Theory and the Exploration of the Past,* with David W. Burnstein, 1992. Author of articles for *Musical Quarterly* and *The Opera Quarterly.* **Essays:** *Ballad of Baby Doe;* Moore, Douglas.

HEADINGTON, Christopher. Composer, pianist, author, and teacher. Author of *The Bodley Head History of Western Music,* 1974, *Illustrated Dictionary of Musical Terms,* 1980, *The Performing World of the Musician,* 1981, *Britten,* 1981, and *Listener's Guide to Chamber Music,* 1982. Coauthor of *Opera: A History,* 1987, and *Sweet Sleep,* 1992. **Essays:** Allen; *Bartered Bride;* de Los Angeles; *Entführung aus dem Serail; Euryanthe;* Evans; Ferrier; Flagstad; Goodall; Guthrie; Hammond; *Hänsel und Gretel;* Humperdinck; *Königskinder;* Lewis; Magnard; Monteux; *Oberon;* Pritchard; Shirley-Quirk; Solti; Weber, Carl Maria von; *Werther;* Wolf-Ferrari; Wunderlich. **Adviser.**

HELLER, Wendy. Doctoral candidate, Brandeis University, Waltham, Massachusetts. Contributor to *The New Book of Knowledge,* in progress. **Essays:** Aureli; Cicognini; Gay; Monteverdi; Rinuccini; Rospigliosi; Striggio.

HENIG, Stanley. Head of Centre for European Studies, University of Central Lancashire, England. Former chairman, Court of Royal Northern College of Music and Secretary, Historic Masters Ltd. and Historic Singers Trust. Contributor to *Opera.* **Essays:** Alboni; Bahr-Mildenburg; Battistini; Bonci; Destinn; *Forza del Destino; Hérodiade;* Horne; Jadlowker; Kurz; Maurel; Nilsson, Christine; Pasta; Ricciarelli; Sanderson; Storchio; Thill; Tietjens.

HEYER, John Hajdu. Dean, College of Fine Arts, Indiana University of Pennsylvania. Editor of *Gilles "Messe de morts,"* 1984, and *Lully and the Music of the French Baroque,* 1989. Contributor to *The New Grove Dictionary of Music and Musicians,* 1980. **Essays:** *Atys;* Lully.

HIGGINS, John. Obituary editor, the London *Times,* England. Author of *The Making of an Opera,* 1977, and editor of *Glyndebourne: A Celebration,* 1984. Formerly arts editor for *Financial Times* and the London *Times.* **Adviser.**

HINDLEY, Clifford. Independent scholar. Author of articles on Benjamin Britten and *Billy Budd* for *Music and Letters* and *Musical Quarterly.* **Essays:** *Billy Budd; Peter Grimes.*

HODGES, Shelia. Writer. Author of *Gollancz: The Story of a Publishing House,* 1978, *God's Gift: A Living History of Dulwick College,* 1981, and *Lorenzo Da Ponte,* 1985. Author of articles for various international music magazines. **Essays:** Bene; Da Ponte; Storace.

HOLM, Barbara A. K. Essayist. **Essay:** Bergman.

HOWARD, Patricia. Tutor and lecturer in music, The Open University, England. Author of *Gluck and the Birth of Modern Opera,* 1963, *The Operas of Benjamin Britten: An Introduction,* 1969, *Haydn in England,* 1980, *Mozart's "Marriage of Figaro,"* 1980, *C.W. Gluck: "Orfeo,"* 1981, *Benjamin Britten: "The Turn of the Screw,"* 1985, *Christoph Willibald Gluck: A Guide to Research,* 1987, *Music in Vienna 1790-1800,* 1988, and *Beethoven's "Fidelio,"* 1988. **Essays:** Gluck, Christoph Willibald von; Guadagni; *Iphigénie en Aulide;* Quinault; *Rape of Lucretia; Turn of the Screw.*

HUNTER, Mary. Associate professor of music, Bates College, Lewiston, Maine. Contributor to *The New Grove Dictionary of Opera,* 1992, and to *Cambridge Opera Journal* and *Journal of Musicology.* **Essay:** Haydn.

HURLEY, David Ross. Musicologist, Center for Italian Opera Studies, University of Chicago. **Essay:** Keiser.

JEFFERSON, Alan. Writer. Author of *Delius,* 1972, *Inside the Orchestra,* 1974, *The Glory of Opera,* 1976, *Sir Thomas Beecham,* 1979, *The Complete Gilbert & Sullivan Opera Guide,* 1984, *Der Rosenkavalier,* 1986, *Lotte Lehmann,* 1990, and several works on Richard Strauss. Past editor of *The Monthly Guide to Recorded Music.* **Essays:** Beecham; Callas; Dermota; Galli-Marié; Jeritza; Konetzni, Hilde; Lehmann, Lotte; Lemnitz; Patzak; Pinza; Schumann; Seefried; Siems; Stabile; Supervia.

JONES, J. Barrie. Lecturer in music, The Open University, England. Author of *Gabriel Fauré: A Life in Letters,* 1989. Contributor to *Makers of Nineteenth-Century Culture,* 1982. Author of articles and reviews on Fauré, Liszt, Granados, and others for *Liszt Society, The Musical Review,* and *Tempo.* **Essays:** Chabrier; *Gwendoline; Roi malgré lui.*

KAUFMAN, Thomas G. Author of *Annals of Italian Opera, Volume I: Verdi and His Major Contemporaries,* 1990. Contributor of chronologies to several publications and to *Verdi's "Macbeth"—A Source Book,* 1984. Author of articles and reviews for *The Opera Quarterly* and *Journal of the Donizetti Society.* **Essays:** Grisi, Giuditta; Grisi, Giulia; Mario; Mercadante; Pacini; *Saffo;* Tamberlick. **Adviser.**

KELLY, Barbara L. Doctoral candidate, University of Liverpool, England. **Essay:** *Pauvre matelot.*

KERMAN, Joseph. Professor of music, University of California, Berkeley. Author of *Opera as Drama,* 1956, *The Elizabethan Madrigal,* 1962, *The Beethoven Quartets,* 1967, *Listen,* 1972, *Beethoven's "Kafka Sketchbook,"* 1970, *The Masses and Motets of William Byrd,* 1981, and *Contemplating Music,* 1985. Author of articles and reviews for publications, including *Critical Inquiry, Hudson Review,* and *New York Review of Books.* Editor of *19th Century Music* and *California Studies in 19th Century Music.* **Adviser.**

KINDERMAN, William. Professor of music, University of Victoria, British Columbia, Canada. Author of *Beethoven's Diabelli Variations,* 1989. Editor of *Beethoven's Compositional Process,* 1991. Author of articles on Wagner for *Archiv für Musikwissenschaft, Journal of Musicology,* and *19th Century Music.* **Essays:** *Parsifal;* Wagner, Richard.

KOTZE, Michael. Professional singer. **Essay:** Hotter.

KUPFERBERG, Herbert. Senior editor, *Parade* magazine, New York. Author of *The Mendelssohns: Three Generations of Genius,* 1972, *Opera,* 1975, *Basically Bach,* 1985, *Amadeus: A Mozart Mosaic,* 1987, and *The Book of Classical Music Lists,* 1988. Past music critic for *Atlantic Monthly* and *National Observer;* contributor to many magazines. **Essays:** *Barbiere di Siviglia* [Rossini]; *Elisir d'amore; Rosenkavalier;* Rudel; Tucker.

KUSHNER, David Z. Professor of music and coordinator of musicological studies, University of Florida. Contributor to *The New Grove Dictionary of Music and Musicians,* 1980, *The New Grove Dictionary of American Music,* 1984, and *Great Lives from History: Renaissance to 1900,* 1989. Music book reviewer for *American Music Teacher.* **Essays:** Bloch; *Cradle Will Rock;* Dargomïzhsky; *Macbeth* [Bloch]; Nono; *Stone Guest;* Weinberger.

LAING, Alan. Lecturer, University of Hull, England, and composer. Author of articles for *Association of Teachers of Italian Journal;* composer. **Essays:** *Edgar; Hans Heiling; Meistersinger von Nürnberg; Tristan und Isolde.*

LARRAD, Mark. Musicologist, University of Liverpool, England. Author of articles on Spanish music of the nineteenth and twentieth centuries for *Revista de musicología* and *Revista musical catalana.* **Essays:** *Goyescas;* Granados.

LAW, Joe K. Writing instructor, Texas Christian University. Author of articles on opera or opera and literature for *Opera Journal, The Opera Quarterly, Review of English Studies,* and *Twentieth Century Literature.* **Essays:** Auden; Duprez; Pears; Sontag; Valletti.

LEE, M. Owen. Professor of classics, St. Michael's College, University of Toronto, Ontario, Canada. Author of *Word, Sound, and Image in the Odes of Horace,* 1969, *Fathers and Sons in Virgil's "Aeneid,"* 1979, *Death and Rebirth in Virgil's Arcadia,* 1989, and *Wagner's Ring: Turning the Sky Round,* 1990. Author of many articles on classics and music for journals, including *Opera News* and *The Opera Quarterly.* **Essays:** *Aida; Lohengrin;* Simoneau; *Tannhäuser; Trovatore; Troyens.*

LESSEM, Alan. Deceased, February 1992. Former associate professor of music, York University, Ontario, Canada, and editor of *Canadian University Music Review.* Author of articles for *Journal of the Arnold Schoenberg Institute* and *Musical Quarterly.* **Essays:** *Glückliche Hand; Mahagonny.*

LINDENBERGER, Herbert. Professor of comparative literature, Stanford University. Author of *On Wordsworth's "Prelude,"* 1966, *George Büchner,* 1964, *George Trakl,* 1971, *Historical Drama: The Relation of Literature and Reality,* 1975, *Saul's Fall: A Critical Fiction,* 1979, *Opera: The Extravagant Art,* 1986, and *The History in Literature: On Value, Genre, Institutions,* 1990. Author of articles for numerous scholarly journals. **Adviser.**

LITTLEJOHN, David. Professor of journalism, University of California, Berkeley, and music critic for *The Wall Street Journal.* Author of *The Life and Work of Charles W. Moore,* 1984, and *The Ultimate Art: Essays Around and About Opera,* 1992. Formerly music and arts critic for PBS Television, and the London *Times.* **Essay:** Sellars.

LUSTIG, Larry. Editor, *The Record Collector,* Broomfield, England. **Essays:** Barrientos; Bellincioni; Bergonzi; Burian; Cossutta; De Reszke, Edouard; Faure, Jean-Baptiste; Fleta; Lauri-Volpi; Pertile; Smirnov; Tagliavini; Zenatello.

LUSTIG, Roger L. Writer. Author of articles and reviews for *Chorus!, Händel-Jahrbuch, Notes,* and *Proceedings of the RMA Mozart Conference.* **Essays:** *Fierabras; Genoveva;* Schubert; Schumann.

MACDONALD, Malcolm. Editor, *Tempo* magazine. Author of *Schoenberg,* 1976; *The Symphonies of Havergal Brian,* volume 1, 1974, volume 2, 1978, volume 3, 1983; *John Foulds: His Life in Music,* 1975; *Ronald Stevenson,* 1989; and *Brahms,* 1990. Compiler of *The Gramophone Classical Catalogue,* 1974-1978. **Essays:** *Arlecchino;* Busoni; Fauré, Gabriel; *Moses und Aron; Pénélope;* Schoenberg.

MACONIE, Robin. Composer and writer on music, and quotations manager, Dawson UK, Book Division, England. Author of *The Works of Karlheinz Stockhausen*, 1976, and *The Concept of Music*, 1990. Compiler and editor of *Stockhausen on Music*, 1989. Contributing music editor to Helicon (formerly Hutchinson Encyclopedias). **Essays:** *Licht: die sieben Tage der Woche;* Stockhausen.

MARTIN, George. Writer. Author of *The Opera Companion*, 1961, *Verdi: His Music, Life and Times*, 1963, *The Companion to Twentieth-Century Opera*, 1979, *The Damrosch Dynasty*, 1983, *Aspects of Verdi*, 1988, and *Verdi at the Golden Gate*, in press. Featured book critic for *The Opera Quarterly*. **Adviser.**

MECKNA, Michael. Associate professor of music, Texas Christian University. Author of *Virgil Thomson: A Bio-Bibliography*, 1986, and of articles for *American Music, Music Journal, Musical Quarterly,* and *Musical Times.* Contributor to *The New Grove Dictionary of American Music*, 1984, and *The New Grove Dictionary of Opera*, 1992. **Essays:** *Four Saints in Three Acts; Mother of Us All;* Thomson.

MINTZER, Charles B. Essayist. **Essays:** Amato; Cavalieri, Lina; Kipnis; Matzenauer; Raisa.

MITCHELL, Jerome. Professor of English, University of Georgia. Author of *Thomas Hoccleve: A Study in Early Fifteenth-Century English Poetic*, 1968, *The Walter Scott Operas*, 1977, and *Scott, Chaucer, and Medieval Romance*, 1987. **Essay:** Gigli.

MONELLE, Raymond. Senior lecturer in music, University of Edinburgh, Scotland. Author of *Linguistics and Semiotics in Music*, 1992. Music critic for *The Independent* and *Opera*. **Essays:** Calzabigi; Giacosa; Hasse; Illica; Piave; Zeno.

MONSON, Dale E. Associate professor of music, Pennsylvania State University. Former editor of *Current Musicology*. Contributor to *The New Grove Dictionary of Opera*, 1992. Author of articles for *International Review of the Aesthetics and Sociology of Music,* and *Pergolesi Studies.* **Essays:** *Adriano in Siria;* Bernacchi; *Buona figliuola; Clemenza di Tito; Filosofo di campagna;* Galuppi; Goldoni; Jommelli; Metastasio; Pergolesi; Piccinni; Porpora; *Rè pastore;* Senesino; *Serva Padrona.*

MORAN, William R. Founder and honorary curator of the Stanford Archive of Recorded Sound, California. Author of *Melba: A Contemporary Review*, 1985, and *The Recordings of Lillian Nordica.* Contributor to *Opera and Concert Singers*, 1985. Author of articles, reviews and discographies for *High Fidelity, The Opera Quarterly, Record Collector, Record News, Recorded Sound,* and other journals. **Essays:** Giannini; Melba; Nordica; Sayão; Schumann-Heink. **Adviser.**

MOREY, Carl. Jean A. Chalmers Professor of Music, University of Toronto, and director of Institute for Canadian Music, Ontario, Canada. Author of articles for *Opera Canada.* Contributor of articles to *The Concise Oxford Dictionary of*

Opera, 1979, Encyclopedia of Music in Canada, 1981, The Encyclopedia of Opera, 1976, and *The New Grove Dictionary of Opera,* 1992. **Essays:** Stratas; Vickers.

MOSHELL, Gerald. Associate professor of music, Trinity College, Hartford, Connecticut. Stage director and conductor of numerous productions of twentieth-century opera and musical theatre. Theatre critic and music critic for *The Hartford Courant.* **Essays:** *Capriccio; Enfant et les sortilèges; Oedipus Rex; Retablo de Maese Pedro.*

NASH, Elizabeth H. Professor of theatre arts, University of Minnesota. Author of *Always First Class: The Career of Geraldine Farrar*, 1981, and *The Luminus Ones: A History of the Great Actresses*, 1991. **Essay:** Farrar.

NEILL, Edward. Music critic. Author of *Musica, tecnica ed estetica del canto degli uccelli*, 1978, *Niccolo Paganini: Epistolario*, 1982, *Niccolo Paganini: Il cavaliere filarmonico*, 1990, and *Niccolo Paganini: Il registro di lettere*, 1991. Cofounder of Institute for Paganini Studies, founder of The Italian Bruckner Society, and founder and head of Istituto Demologico Ligure. **Essay:** *Segreto di Susanna.*

NEUMEYER, David. Professor of music, Indiana University. Author of *The Music of Paul Hindemith*, 1986. Author of articles on Hindemith for *Hindemith-Jahrbuch, Journal of the Arnold Schoenberg Institute, Music Theory Spectrum,* and *Musik Theorie.* **Essay:** *Mathis der Maler.*

NEWCOMB, Anthony. Professor of music, University of California, Berkeley. Author of *The Madrigal in Ferrara 1579-1597*, 2 volumes, 1981, and editor of *Complete Works of Luzzasco Luzzaschi.* Past editor of *Journal of the American Musicological Society.* Author of articles for *Annuales musicologiques, Early Music, Journal of the American Musicological Society, 19th Century Music, Rivista italiana di musicologia,* and *Studi musicali.* **Adviser.**

NIEZEN, Richard. Essayist. **Essay:** Furtwängler.

NISBETT, Robert F. Chair and associate professor, department of music, theatre, and dance, Colorado State University. Contributor to *The New Grove Dictionary of Opera*, 1992. Author of articles for *American Music, Current Musicology,* and *Sonneck Society Bulletin.* **Essays:** *Crucible; Emperor Jones;* Gruenberg; Ward.

NOBUSAWA, Kiko. Free-lance writer. Author of concert reviews and editorials for *The Vermont Times.* **Essays:** Anderson, Marian; Ciceri; Soyer.

O'CONNOR, Patrick. Free-lance writer. Editor-in-chief, *Opera News,* and deputy editor, *Harpers & Queen.* Author of *Josephine Baker*, 1988, *Toulouse-Lautrec: The Nightlife of Paris*, 1991, and *The Amazing Blonde Woman*, 1991. Regular contributor to *Daily Telegraph, Literary Review,* and *Times Literary Supplement.* **Essays:** Bacquier; Brecht; Hockney; Honegger; *Mamelles de Tirésias;* Marcoux; Mödl; Silja; Söderström; Sutherland; *Teyte;* Vallin; Visconti; Welitsch.

OGLESBY, Donald. Associate professor of music, University of Miami, and artistic director and conductor, Miami Bach Society, Florida. Author of *A Conductor's Study of Marc-Antoine Charpentier's "Judicium,"* 1979, and *Score Preparation: A Study Guide for Conducting Students,* 1981. **Essays:** Charpentier; *Médée* [Charpentier].

OLMSTEAD, Andrea. Chair, department of music history, The Boston Conservatory. Author of *Roger Sessions and His Music,* 1985, *Conversations with Roger Sessions,* 1987, and *The Correspondence of Roger Sessions,* 1992. Formerly a music history teacher at The Juilliard School and Aspen Music School. **Essays:** *Montezuma* [Sessions]; Serban; Sessions.

OSBORNE, Richard. Writer and broadcaster/presenter for BBC Radio 3's *Saturday Review.* Author of *Rossini,* 1986, and *Conversations with Karajan,* 1989. Contributor to *Opera on Record.* Contributor to *Gramophone.* **Essay:** Karajan.

OWENS, Rose Mary. Professor of music, Southwest Missouri State University. Author of *Eva Turner: The Grand Dame of Singing: A Study of her Life as a Singer and as a Teacher,* 1983, and *Study Guide to Accompany Stanley Sadie's Brief Guide to Music,* 1987. Regular reviewer for *The Choral Journal.* **Essays:** Bumbry; Curtin; Farrell; Hines; Peters; Price, Leontyne; Raskin; Turner.

PACUN, David E. Lecturer in music, University of Vermont; doctoral candidate, University of Chicago. **Essays:** Boito; Floyd; Forzano; Ghislanzoni; Korngold; Kurka; Raaff; *Thaïs.*

PARKER, C.P. Gerald. Music librarian, Bibliothéciare de Musique, University of Quebec, Montreal, Canada. Author of articles for *ARSC Journal, Fanfare, The Opera Quarterly, Spectrum,* and other journals. **Essay:** Cilèa.

PARSONS, James. Visiting assistant professor, department of music, University of Missouri. Contributor of essays to *Four Centuries of Opera: Manuscripts and Printed Editions in The Pierpont Morgan Library,* 1983. Author of articles and reviews for *Early Music, Journal of Musicology, Notes, Opera, Opera Canada, Opera News, Opera Journal, Opus,* and *Stagebill.* **Essays:** Beethoven; *Dardanus; Ernani; Euridice* [Peri]; *Fidelio; Indes galantes; Orlando* [Vivaldi]; Peri; *Roland; Rusalka.*

PATTON, Elizabeth W. Free-lance writer. Music critic for the *Ann Arbor News.* **Essays:** *Contes d'Hoffmann; Demon; Eugene Onegin; Life for the Tsar; Maid of Orleans; Mavra; May Night;* Offenbach; *Ruslan and Lyudmila; Salome; Snow Maiden.*

PENNINO, John. Assistant archivist, Metropolitan Opera, New York. Author of articles for *The Opera Quarterly.* **Essays:** Campanini, Cleofonte; Garden; Levine; Moore, Grace; Siepi; Stevens.

PERLIS, Vivian. Director, Oral History, American Music, School of Music, Yale University. Author of *Charles Ives Remembered: An Oral History,* 1974, *An Ives Celebration,* 1977, *Copland: 1900 Through 1942,* 1984, and *Copland: Since 1943,* 1989. **Essays:** Copland; Foss; Knussen; *Tender Land.*

POPLE, Anthony. Lecturer in music, Lancaster University, England. Editor of the journal *Musicus: Computer Applications in Music Education.* Author of *Skryabin and Stravinsky: Studies in Theory and Analysis,* 1988, and *Berg: Violin Concerto,* 1991. Author of articles for *Music Analysis, Music and Letters,* and *The Musical Times.* **Essays:** Berg; *Wozzeck.*

POULOS, Helen. Associate professor of music and coordinator of graduate studies in music, Southern Illinois University. Author of articles for *American String Teacher's Association Journal.* **Essay:** Lawrence.

POULTNEY, David. Professor of music, Illinois State University. Author of *Studying Music History,* 1983, and *Dictionary of Church Music,* 1991. Author of articles for *Musical Quarterly.* **Essays:** *Barbiere di Siviglia* [Paisiello]; De Lucia; *Mitridate Eupatore;* Nourrit; Paisiello; Scarlatti.

PRATT, Stephen. Head of Music, Liverpool Institute of Higher Education, England. Composer. **Essay:** *Staatstheater.*

PRICE, Walter. Essayist. **Essay:** Warren.

PURKIS, Charlotte. Lecturer in Music and Performing Arts, University of Southampton, England. **Essay:** Boughton.

QUALLIOTINE, Armand. Guitar instructor at Boston and Brandeis Universities, and private teacher of composition, theory, and guitar. Author of *Extended Set Procedures in Two Compositions of Luigi Dallapiccola,* 1986. **Essay:** *Ulisse.*

REED, Addison W. Deceased, 1991. Former chair, department of music, Northern Kentucky University. Contributor to *The New Grove Dictionary of Music and Musicians,* 1980, *Black Journals of the United States,* 1982, and *Ragtime, Its History, Composers, and Music,* 1985. Author of articles for *The Black Perspective in Music* and *Piano Quarterly.* **Essays:** Joplin; *Treemonisha.*

RICE, John A. Assistant professor of music, University of Houston. Author of *W.A. Mozart: "La Clemenza di Tito,"* 1991. Author of articles and reviews for *Early Music, Haydn Yearbook, Music and Letters, Notes, Studi musicali,* and other periodicals. **Essays:** Alva; *Arbore di Diana;* Baccaloni; Benucci; Berganza; Berry; Bruscantini; Burrows; *Comte Ory; Cosa Rara;* Cotrubas; Freni; Ghiaurov; Grist; Gruberova; *Italiana in Algeri;* Jerusalem; Lorengar; Martín y Soler; Mathis; Minton; *Otello* [Rossini]; Price, Margaret; Rossini; Sacchini; Schreier; Shirley; Streich; *Tancredi;* Tozzi; Varady; Von Stade.

RICKARDS, Guy. Essayist. Contributor to *Contemporary Composers,* 1992, and author of articles for *Gramophone, Havegal Brian Society Newsletter, Journal of the British Music Society,* and *Tempo.* **Essays:** *Aniara;* Blomdahl; Dallapiccola; Egk; *Peer Gynt; Prigioniero;* Villa-Lobos; *Yerma.*

ROBERTSON, Patricia Connors. Instructor of music, Ball State and Taylor universities, Indiana. **Essays:** Adams; Anderson, June; *Consul;* Galli-Curci; MacNeil; Moffo; *Nixon in China;* Tourel.

ROBINSON, Harlow. Associate professor, Department of Slavic Languages and Literatures, State University of New York at Albany. Author of *Sergei Prokofiev: A Biography,* 1987. Regular contributor to *Musical America, New York Times, Opera News, The Opera Quarterly,* and *Stagebill.* **Essays:** *Betrothal in a Monastery;* Borodin; *Katia Kabanová; Prince Igor;* Prokofiev.

ROSE, Bob. Opera review critic, Davis Enterprise, Davis, California. Author of record sleeve notes, 1978-1991, for recordings of complete opera and operatic recitals for *Voce Records.* **Essays:** Anders; Borgioli; Roswaenge; Schipa; Tauber.

ROSEBERRY, Eric. Free-lance musician and writer. Author of *The Life and Times of Dmitri Shostakovich,* 1986, *Cambridge Opera Handbook: "Death in Venice,"* 1987, and *Ideology, Style, Content and Thematic Process in the Music of Shostakovich,* 1989. Contributor of essays to *Britten Companion,* 1984. Author of articles and reviews for *CD Review, Music and Letters, Musical Quarterly, Musical Times, Tempo,* and other musical journals. **Essays:** *Church Parables; Nose; Owen Wingrave.*

ROSOW, Lois. Associate professor of music, Ohio State University. Contributor of articles to *Jean-Baptiste Lully and the Music of the French Baroque: Essays in Honor of James R. Anthony,* 1989, *Lully: Actes du Colloque/Kongressbericht: Saint-Germain-en-Laye--Heidelberg,* 1990, and *The New Grove Dictionary of Opera,* 1992. Author of articles for *Early Music,* and *Journal of the American Musicological Society.* **Essays:** *Alceste* [Lully]; *Armide* [Lully]; *Thésée;.*

ROUTH, Francis. Composer. Author of *Contemporary Music,* 1968, *Contemporary British Music,* 1970, *Early English Organ Music,* 1973, and *Stravinsky,* 1975. Former editor of *Composer.* Author of articles for *The Annual Register.* **Essay:** Stravinsky.

RUNYAN, William E. Assistant dean of the College of Arts and Liberal Arts, Colorado State University. Author of articles for *Brass Bulletin, Journal of the Conductor's Guild, Notes,* and *The Opera Journal.* **Essays:** Björling; *Guillaume Tell; Huguenots; Muette de Portici.*

RUSHTON, Julian. Professor of music, University of Leeds, England; past general editor of Cambridge Music Handbooks. Author of *W.A. Mozart: "Don Giovanni,"* 1981, *The Musical Language of Berlioz,* 1983, *Classical Music: A Concise History,* 1986, and *W.A. Mozart: "Idomeneo,"* in press. Editor of *New Berlioz Edition,* 4 vols., 1970-1991. Author of numerous articles, conference papers, and reviews. **Essays:** *Béatrice et Bénédict; Benvenuto Cellini;* Berlioz. **Adviser.**

RUTSCHMAN, Edward. Associate professor of music,

Western Washington University. Contributor to *L'Opera italiana a Vienna prima di Metastasio,* 1990. Author of articles for *Current Musicology.* **Essays:** Caccini; Cesti; *Dafne; Euridice* [Caccini]; Gagliano; *Pomo d'oro.*

SALMON, Gregory. Deceased, October 1991. Doctoral candidate, University of California, Berkeley. **Essays:** Glinka; Rimsky-Korsakov; Rubinstein; Tchaikovsky.

SALOMAN, Ora Frishberg. Professor of music, Baruch College of the City University of New York. Contributor of articles to *Music and Civilization: Essays in Honor of Paul Henry Lang,* 1984, and *The New Grove Dictionary of Opera,* 1992. Author of articles for journals, including *Acta Musicologica, American Music,* and *Journal of Musicology.* **Essay:** *Iphigénie en Tauride.*

SAMSON, Jim. Professor of musicology, University of Exeter, England. Author of *Music in Transition: A Study in Tonal Expansion and Early Atonality 1900-1920,* 1977, *The Music of Szymanowski,* 1980, *The Music of Chopin,* 1985, and *Chopin: The Four Ballads,* 1992. Editor of *The Cambridge Companion to Chopin,* 1982, *Chopin Studies,* 1988, and *The Late-Romantic Era: Man and Music, Volume 7,* 1991. **Essays:** *Halka; Król Roger;* Moniuszko; Szymanowski.

SANSONE, Matteo. Lecturer in English, Conservatorio di Musica Luigi Cherubini, Florence, Italy. Author of *Italian and Maltese Music (1573-1809) in the Cathedral Museum of Malta,* with John Azzopardi, 1992. Author of articles for *Bulletin for the Society for Italian Studies, Italian Studies,* and *Music and Letters.* **Essays:** *Cavalleria rusticana; Fedora; Gioielli della Madonna;* Giordano; Leoncavallo; Mascagni; *Pagliacci.*

SCHEPPACH, Margaret. Professor of music, College of Saint Rose, Albany, New York. Author of *Dramatic Parallels in the Operas of Michael Tippett,* 1990. **Essays:** *Ice Break; Knot Garden; New Year;* Tippett.

SCHULKEN, Samuel B., Jr. Professor of music, Southwest Virginia Community College. Author of *Introduction to Music History-Appreciation Correspondence Study,* 1967. **Essays:** *Elektra; Schweigsame Frau.*

SEAMAN, Gerald R. Associate professor of musicology, University of Auckland, New Zealand. Author of *History of Russian Music,* 1967, and *Rimsky Korsakov: A Bibliographical Research Guide,* 1988. General Editor of *Encyclopaedic Dictionary of Russian and Soviet Music,* in press. **Essays:** Benedict; Chaliapin; *Colas Breugnon; Fiery Angel; Golden Cockerel; Iolanta;* Kabalevsky; *Legend of the Invisible City of Kitezh and the Maiden Fevroniya; Maritana;* Meyerhold; Nemirovich-Danchenko; *Queen of Spades;* Stanislavsky; Vishnevskaya; Wallace; *War and Peace.*

SELK, Jürgen. Doctoral candidate and research assistant, Center for Italian Opera Studies, University of Chicago. **Essays:** *Bohème* [Puccini]; *Rondine; Turandot* [Puccini]; *Villi.*

SELLS, Michael. Opera singer; professor of music and dean, Jordan College of Fine Arts, Butler University, Indianapolis, Indiana. **Essays:** Britten; *Paul Bunyan.*

SESHADRI, Anne Lineback. Lecturer in musicology and ethnomusicology, University of Maryland. **Essays:** Graun; *Montezuma* [Graun].

SHAMAN, William. Librarian and assistant professor of librarianship, Bemidji State University, Bemidji, Minnesota. Author of *Discography of the Edward J. Smith Recordings,* 1992, and *Guiseppe De Luca: A Discography,* 1992. Contributor to *The New Grove Dictionary of Opera,* 1992. Author of many reviews for *American Music, The Journal of the Association for Recorded Sound Collections, Notes,* and *Record Collector.* **Essays:** Boninsegna; Calvé; De Luca; Eames; Figner; Fremstad; Mei-Figner; Rethberg; Slezak; Stracciari; Svanholm.

SHAY, Robert. Assistant professor of music, Arkansas College. **Essay:** Blow.

SHERLAW-JOHNSON, Robert. Fellow, Worcester College, Oxford University, England. Author of *Messiaen,* 1976. **Essays:** Messiaen; *St François d'Assise.*

SIMPSON, Adrienne. Research fellow, National Library of New Zealand. Author of *Opera in New Zealand: Aspects of History and Performance,* 1990, and *Southern Voices: International Opera Singers of New Zealand,* with Peter Downes, 1992. Contributor to *The New Grove Dictionary of Music and Musicians,* 1980, and *The New Grove Dictionary of Opera,* 1992. Author of numerous scholarly articles for journals in Europe and Australasia. **Essays:** Alda; McIntyre.

SIMS, Michael. Managing editor, The MIT Press, Cambridge, Massachusetts. **Essays:** Arnoldson; Arundell; Battle; Behrens; Bockelmann; Borgatti; Brook; Cappuccilli; Chailly; Christoff; Cluytens; Copley; Cox; Del Monaco; Everding; Freeman; Gedda; Gentele; Hall; Keilberth; Kempe; King; Kleiber, Carlos; Kubelík; Lipp; Maazel; Mariani; Melchior; Moll; Moshinsky; Mottl; Mugnone; Nesterenko; Pountney; Prince; Ramey; Rennert; Rosbaud; Rothenberger; Sanzogno; Sawallisch; Schenk; Schneider-Siemssen; Seidl; Sendak; Stolz; Te Kanawa; Weber, Ludwig; Wilson.

SKELTON, Geoffrey. Writer and translator. Author of *Wagner at Bayreuth: Experiment and Tradition,* 1965, *Wieland Wagner: The Positive Sceptic,* 1971, *Paul Hindemith: The Man Behind the Music,* 1975, *Richard and Cosima Wagner: Biography of a Marriage,* 1982, and *Wagner in Thought and Practice,* 1991. Translator of *Cosima Wagner's Diaries,* 2 volumes, 1978, 1980. **Essays:** Wagner, Weiland.

SLOOP, Jean C. Professor of music, Kansas State University. **Essays:** *Amahl and the Night Visitors; Amelia al ballo; Bernauerin; Kluge;* Menotti; *Mond;* Orff; *Saint of Bleecker Street.*

SMITH, Carolyn J. Humanities bibliographer/associate professor, Kansas State University Library. Author of *William*

Walton: A Bio-Bibliography, 1988. **Essays:** *Bear;* Davies, Peter Maxwell; *Taverner.*

SMITH, Oliver. Chargé de cours, EAP, Paris. Author of *Guide du voyageur,* 1990. Translator of opera travel and advertising. **Essays:** Benois, Alexandre; Benois, Nicola; Chéreau; Pizzi; Strehler; Wallmann; Zeffirelli.

SNOWMAN, Daniel. Writer and broadcaster, British Broadcasting Corporation, England. Author of *The Amadeus Quartet: The Men and the Music,* 1981, and *The World of Placido Domingo,* 1985. Former Chairman, London Philharmonic Choir. Author of articles and reviews for *Gramophone, The Musical Times, The Washington Opera Magazine,* and other newspapers and journals. **Essay:** Domingo.

SNYDER, Louis. Free-lance journalist. Author of *Community of Sound: Boston Symphony and Its World of Players,* 1979. Author of articles for *Musical America, Opera News,* and *Variety.* **Essays:** Graf; Homer; *Mireille;* Sembrich; Urban.

SOLOMON, Jon. Associate professor of classics, University of Arizona. Associate editor of the *Greek and Latin Music Theory Series,* University of Nebraska Press. Author of articles for *American Journal of Philology, Classics and Cinema, Journal of Musicology,* and *Music and Letters.* **Essays:** *Anima del Filosofo; Antigonae; Bassariden; Idomeneo; Oedipe à Colone; Semiramide.*

STEANE, John B. Free-lance writer and broadcaster. Author of *The Grand Tradition: 70 Years of Singing on Record,* 1974, and *Voices: Singers and Critics,* 1992. Regular reviewer of vocal records for *Gramophone.* Frequent broadcasts for BBC Radio 3 and World Service. Author of articles for *The Musical Times, Opera, Opera News,* and *Opera Now* (monthly). Contributor to *The New Grove Dictionary of Opera,* 1992. **Essays:** Heldy; Janssen; Journet; Pasero; Sammarco; Thorborg. **Adviser.**

STEARNS, David Patrick. Music critic for *USA Today;* correspondent for *The Independent* in London; music commentator for National Public Radio; contributing editor of *Stereo Review.* **Essays:** Dernesch; Giulini; *Junge Lord;* Sinopoli.

STEIN, Louise. Writer on opera, ballet, and films. **Essays:** *Amico Fritz;* Felsenstein; Reinhardt.

STEVENS, Denis. President, Accademia Monteverdiana. Author of *The Mulliner Book,* 1952, *Thomas Tomkins,* 1957, *Tudor Church Music,* 1966, *Musicology: A Practical Guide,* 1980, *The Letters of Claudio Monteverdi,* 1980, *Musicology in Practice,* 1987, and *The Joy of Ornamentation,* 1989. Editor of *Grove's Dictionary of Music,* 5th ed. and *A History of Song,* 1960. **Essays:** Bordoni; Caffarelli; Cuénod; *Fairy Queen;* Farinelli; *Favola d'Orfeo; Incoronazione di Poppea;* Rubini; Schröder-Devrient. **Adviser.**

STILWELL, Robynn J. Doctoral candidate, University of Michigan. **Essay:** Corsaro.

STONES, Linda M. Professor of music, California State University, Northridge. **Essays:** Grétry; *Richard Coeur-de-Lion; Zémire et Azor.*

STUDWELL, William E. Principal cataloger and professor, University Libraries, Northern Illinois University. Editor of *Music Reference Services Quarterly.* Author of *Adolphe Adam and Leo Delibes: A Guide to Research,* 1987. Author of many articles on library science and music for journals and other publications. **Essays:** Adam; *Attaque du moulin;* Bruneau; *Lakmé; Lily of Killarney; Mazeppa; Postillon de Longjumeau.*

SUMMERVILLE, Suzanne. Professor of music, University of Alaska. Music director, Fairbanks Choral Society. Author of articles for *National Association of Teachers of Singing Bulletin, The Opera Quarterly,* and *Unitas Fratrum.* **Essays:** Berger; Kollo; Konetzni, Anny; Köth; Leider; Wächter.

SUTCLIFFE, James Helme. Free-lance opera critic and composer. Regular contributor to *Musica, Musical America, Opera, Opera Canada, Opera News,* and *Opernwelt Zürich,* **Essays:** *Lear;* Lear, Evelyn; Reimann; Weikl.

TALBOT, Michael. Professor of music, University of Liverpool, England. Author of *Vivaldi,* 1978, *Antonio Vivaldi: A Guide to Research,* 1988, and *Tommaso Albinoni: The Venetian Composer and His World,* 1990. Author of articles on late Baroque Italian music for *Music and Letters, Music Review, Rivista italiana de musicologia, Soundings,* and other journals. **Essays:** *Fida ninfa; Pimpinone;* Telemann; Vivaldi. **Adviser.**

TÉREY-SMITH, Mary. Professor of musicology and director of the Collegium Musicum, Western Washington University. Author of articles for *Arts Inquiry, Canadian Association of University Schools of Music, Revue de musique des universités canadiennes,* and *Studia musicologica.* **Essay:** Abaris.

THORNHILL, William. Professor of music history, Ohio State University. **Essays:** Abbado; Bernstein; Damrosch; *Street Scene; Trouble in Tahiti* [and] *A Quiet Place;* Weill.

TYLER, Linda. Adjunct associate professor, Drew University. Author of *Edward Burlingame Hill,* 1990, and contributor to scholarly periodicals, including *Cambridge Opera Journal, Mozart Jahrbuch, Music and Letters,* and *Opera Journal.* **Essays:** *Bastien und Bastienne;* Mozart; *Schauspieldirektor.*

TYSON, Alan. Senior research fellow, All Souls College, Oxford University, England. Author of *Mozart: Studies of the Autograph Scores,* 1987, and *W.A. Mozart: "Le Nozze di Figaro," Eight Variant Versions,* 1989. Contributor of many articles to music journals. **Adviser.**

WAKELING, Dennis W. Deceased, May 1992. Former director of opera, College of Music, University of North Texas. Regular reviewer of books and records for *The Opera Quarterly.* **Essays:** *Ariane et Barbe-Bleue; Aspern Papers; Attila; Battaglia di Legnano;* Dukas; *Feuersnot; Gloriana; Intermezzo; Leonora; Luisa Miller; Masnadieri;* Paer.

WALTON, J. Michael. Head of department of drama and reader in theatre history, University of Hull, England. Author of *The Greek Sense of Theatre: Tragedy Reviewed,* 1984, *Living Greek Theatre: A Handbook of Classical Performance and Modern Production,* 1987, and *Greek Theatre Practice.* **Essay:** Craig.

WEATHERSON, Alexander. Principal lecturer in visual and performing arts, The Leeds Polytechnic, and chairman of the Donizetti Society. Editor of *The Journal of the Donizetti Society.* Author of *"Ugo, conte di Parigi": Its Source, and the "Convenienze Teatrali" Which Led to Its Short Life on the Stage,* 1985, and *"I fratelli Ricci": due compositori divisi dalla stessa opera,* 1989. **Essays:** *Anna Bolena; Favorite; Lucia di Lammermoor; Lucrezia Borgia; Roberto Devereux.*

WECHSLER, Bert. Free-lance writer. Author of articles for *Dance Magazine, High Fidelity, New York Times, Opera News, Video Review,* and other newspapers and periodicals. **Essays:** Barbieri; Berglund; Bodanzky; Cebotari; Elias; Ewing; Frick; Kiepura; Lorenz; Pilarczyk; Tajo; Talvela; Wolff.

WHITTALL, Arnold. Professor of music theory and analysis, King's College, University of London, England. Author of articles on nineteenth- and twentieth-century music, with special emphasis on the operas of Wagner, Strauss, Britten, and Tippet. **Adviser.**

WHITTON, Kenneth S. Professor Emeritus of European cultural studies and German, University of Bradford, England. Author of *The Theatre of Friedrich Dürrenmatt,* 1980, *Dietrich Fischer-Dieskau: Mastersinger,* 1981, *Lieder: An Introduction to German Song,* 1984, and *Dürrematt: Reinterpretation in Retrospect,* 1990. **Essay:** Fischer-Dieskau.

WHYTE, Sally. Free-lance international arts writer, reviewer, and correspondent. Regular correspondent on music and the arts for *Ha'Aretz (The Nation)* and *Arts Review,* London. **Essay:** Rè in Ascolto.

WIERZBICKI, James. Music editor, *St. Louis Post-Dispatch.* **Essays:** Barber; Gershwin; Glass; Penderecki; *Porgy and Bess; Triptych.*

WILLIER, Stephen. Professor of music history, Temple University. Lecturer and program annotator for the Opera Company of Philadelphia and the Pennsylvania Opera Theater. Author of articles and reviews for *Fontes artis musicae, Journal of the American Musicological Society, Opera News,* and *The Opera Quarterly.* Contributor to *The New Grove Dictionary of Opera,* 1992. **Essays:** *Alceste* [Gluck]; *Amore dei tre re;* Arroyo; Caballé; Carreras; Di Stefano; *Don Carlos; Donna del lago; Esclarmonde;* Faccio; Falcon; *Fille du régiment; Finta giardiniera; Gioconda;* Hidalgo; *Iris;* Ivogün; Jones; Kleiber, Erich; Kraus; Krips; *Lombardi alla Prima Crociata;* Lubin; Mackerras; *Maria Stuarda;* Martón; McCormack; Montemezzi; Muti; *Nina;* Norman; Pavarotti; *Pirata;* Pizzetti; Ponchielli; Prêtre; Prey; Reiner; *Rodelinda; Roi de Lahore;* Rysanek; Serafin; Simionato; Solera; Strepponi; Szell; Van Dam; *Venus and Adonis;* Windgassen.

WILLIS, Stephen C. Head of archives, music division, National Library of Canada. **Essays:** Cherubini; *Médée* [Cherubini].

WOLF, Muriel Hebert. Professor of music, State University of New York at Buffalo. Author of articles for *Overture, The Opera Journal,* and *The Opera Quarterly.* **Essays:** *Cardillac; Devils of Loudon;* Pousseur; *Vanessa.*

WRIGHT, H. Stephen. Music librarian, Northern Illinois University. Contributor to *Film Music 1,* 1989. Author of book reviews for *Fontes artis musicae.* **Essays:** *Cry of Clytaemnestra;* Eaton.

WRIGHT, Lesley A. Associate professor of musicology, University of Hawaii. Author of *Georges Bizet: Letters in the Nydahl Collection,* 1988. Contributor to *The New Grove Dictionary of Opera,* 1992. Author of articles for *English National Opera Guide, 19th Century Music,* and *Studies in Music.* **Essays:** Bizet; *Jolie fille de Perth; Pêcheurs de perles.*

WYNNE, Meredith. Essayist. **Essays:** *Beggar's Opera;* Pepusch.

ZIMMERMAN, Franklin B. Professor of music, University of Pennsylvania, and director, Pennsylvania Promusica. Author of *Henry Purcell: An Analytical Catalog of His Complete Works,* 1963, *Henry Purcell: His Life and Times,* 1967, *Henry Purcell: An Index to His Complete Works,* 1971, *The Symphonies of C.F. Abel,* 1982, and *Henry Purcell: A Guide to Research,* 1988. Coauthor of other works on Purcell. **Essays:** *Ballo in maschera;* Boulez; *Don Giovanni; Giulio Cesare in Egitto;* Kelly; *King Arthur;* Leinsdorf; Purcell; *Ritorno d'Ulisse in Patria;* Toscanini; *Traviata.*

ZUCKER, Stefan. Editor, *Opera Fanatic,* and host of the radio show of that name. Author of articles for *American Record Guide, La Follia, New World, New York Tribune, Opera News, The Opera Quarterly, Professione Musica,* and other publications. **Essays:** Araiza; Corena; Merrill; Milnes.

PICTURE ACKNOWLEDGMENTS

Photos and illustrations for entries in the *International Dictionary of Opera* have been used by permission of the following organizations and individuals:

Archiv für Kunst und Geschichte, Berlin: Adam, *Arlecchino*, *Armide* [Gluck], Auber, *The Bartered Bride*, Bartók, *The Beggar's Opera*, *Benvenuto Cellini*, Bizet, *La bohème* [Puccini], Böhm, Bordoni, Brecht, Britten, Bülow, Busoni, Caccini, *Cardillac*, Cavalli, Cherubini, Cimarosa, *La clemenza di Tito*, *Les contes d'Hoffmann*, Copland, *La Dafne*, Da Ponte, Debussy, Destinn, *Don Giovanni*, Donizetti, Dvořák, Egk, *Elektra*, *Die Entführung aus dem Serail*, Erkel, *La favola d'Orfeo*, Farinelli, Farrar, Fischer-Dieskau, *Der fliegende Holländer*, Flotow, *Fra Diavolo*, *Die Frau ohne Schatten*, *Der Freischütz*, Furtwängler, Garcia, Gershwin, *Giulio Cesare*, Glinka, Christoph Willibald von Gluck, *The Golden Cockerel*, Goldoni, Grisi, Haydn, Henze, Hoffmann, Hofmannstahl, Holst, Hotter, Humperdinck, *Idomeneo*, *Iphigénie en Aulide*, Ivogün, Janáček, Jommelli, *Jonny spielt auf*, Klemperer, *Die Kluge*, Kodály, *Die Königskinder*, Korngold, Krauss, Krenek, *Libuše*, *A Life for the Tsar*, Ligeti, London, *Lulu*, Mahler, *Martha*, Martín y Soler, Mascagni, Massenet, Melchior, Metastasio, Meyerbeer, Milhaud, Mödl, Monteverdi, Musorgsky, *Le nozze di Figaro*, *Oberon*, *Otello* [Rossini], Paisiello, *Parsifal*, Penderecki, Pepusch, Pergolesi, Piave, Ponelle, *Porgy and Bess*, *Prince Igor*, Prokofiev, Puccini, Rameau, Ravel, Richter, *Der Ring des Nibelungen: Das Rheingold, Die Walküre, Götterdämmerung*, Rubinstein, Salieri, *Salome*, Sanderson, Scarlatti, Schalk, *Der Schauspieldirektor*, Schikaneder, Schoenberg, Schreker, Schröder-Devrient, Scribe, Shostakovich, Smetana, Steber, Storace, Strauss, *Tannhäuser*, Tchaikovsky, Telemann, *Thaïs*, *Undine* [Lortzing], Richard Wagner, Wieland Wagner, Walter, Carl Maria von Weber, Weill, Weingartner, *Wozzeck*, *Die Zauberflöte*, Zemlinsky

Bibliotheca Cantonale Locarno, Fondo Ruggero Leoncavallo: Leoncavallo

Bibliothèque Nationale, Paris: *L'Africaine*, *Armide* [Lully], Alexandre Benois, Berlioz, *Don Carlos*, *Mavra*, Offenbach, *Orfeo ed Euridice*, *Les pêcheurs de perles*, *Pénélope*, Rimsky-Korsakov

Bibliothèque royale Albert Ier, Brussels (Cabinet des Estampes): *La muette de Portici*

British Library: *Un ballo in maschera*, Blow, *Rinaldo*, *Tamerlano*

British Museum, London: Cuzzoni

Deutsches Theatermuseum, Munich: Raaff

Donald Cooper/Photostage, London: *Albert Herring*, *Anna Bolena*, *Ariadne auf Naxos*, *Attila*, Baker, *Il barbiere di Siviglia* [Rossini], *Billy Budd*, *Boris Godunov*, *Capriccio*, Copley, *Così fan tutte*, *The Cunning Little Vixen*, Domingo, *Dreigroschenoper*, Ewing, Falstaff, Fassbaender, Fidelio, Freeman, Freni, Glass, *Hänsel und Gretel*, Herz, Hockney, Horne, *Jenůfa*, *Kat'a Kabanová*, Kraus, Kupfer, *Lady Macbeth of the Mtsensk District*, *Lear*, *Licht*, *The Love for Three Oranges*, *Lucrezia Borgia*, *Macbeth*, *Madama Butterfly*, Martón, *The Mask of Orpheus*, Miller, Moshinsky, *New Year*, *Oedipus Rex*, Pavarotti, Pears, Pountney, *The Rake's Progress*, Ricciarelli, *Rigoletto*, *Il ritorno d'Ulisse in patria*, Scotto, Sellars, Serban, *Serse*, *Simon Boccanegra*, *Street Scene*, Te Kanawa, *Tosca*, *La traviata*, *Triptych: Akhnaten*, *Turandot*, Verrett, *Werther* (All illustrations copyright © Donald Cooper/Photostage)

Giancarlo Costa, Milan: *Andrea Chénier*, Bellini, Boito, *Don Quichotte*, *L'elisir d'amore*, Faccio, *The Fiery Angel*, *Il filosofo di campagna*, Forzano, *Francesca da Rimini*, Ghislanzoni, Giacosa, *La Gioconda*, Halévy, *Iláry János*, Illica, *The Legend of Kitezh*, Louise, *Luisa Miller*, Manon, *Manon Lescaut*, *Il matrimonio segreto*, Maurel, *Médée* [Cherubini], *Mefistofele*, *Nabucco*, *Norma*, Ponchielli, Rinuccini, Romani, Rossini, Rubini,

Sadko, The Saint of Bleecker Street, Semiramide, La sonnambula, Toscanini, Verdi, *La vestale,* Vivaldi, *La Wally* (All illustrations copyright © Giancarlo Costa)

Hamburg Oper: Dexter

Internationale Louis Spohr Gesellschaft e.V., Louis Spohr-Gedenk-und Forschungsstatte, Kassel: Spohr

Siegfried Lauterwasser, Überlingen am Bodensee: Abbado, Behrens, Boulez, Chéreau, Everding, Friedrich, Giulini, Hall, Jones, Karajan, Levine, *Lohengrin, The Makropoulos Case, Die Meistersinger von Nürnberg,* Muti, Birgit Nilsson, Leontyne Price, Rennert, *Der Ring des Nibelungen: Siegfried, Der Rosenkavalier,* Solti, *Tristan und Isolde, Il trovatore* (All illustrations copyright © Siegfried Lauterwasser)

Lyric Opera of Chicago: Argento (photo by Dan Rest); *The Gambler* (photo by Tony Romano); Zeffirelli (photo by Nancy Sorenson)

Mary Evans Picture Library, London: *Die Ägyptische Helena, Aida, La donna del lago,* Duprez, Lind, *I Lombardi, Rienzi, Roméo et Juliette, Samson et Dalila*

Metropolitan Opera Archives, New York: Marian Anderson, *La fanciulla del West, Goyescas, Lakmé,* Tibbett, *Il trittico, Vanessa*

Charles B. Mintzer, New York: Amato, Lina Cavalieri, Kipnis, Matzenauer, Raisa

Mozart-Archiv, Internationale Stiftung Mozarteum, Salzburg: Mozart (Copyright © Mozart-Archiv, Internationale Stiftung Mozarteum)

Musée des Beaux-Arts, Rouen: Boieldieu

Muzeum Antonína Dvoráka, Prague: *Rusalka*

National Portrait Gallery, London: Arne, Handel, Purcell (All illustrations copyright © National Portrait Gallery)

Österreichisches TheaterMuseum, Vienna: *Jessonda*

Pierpont Morgan Library, New York: Berg, *Le devin du village* (PML 17476)

Pierpont Morgan Library, New York (Mary Flagler Cary Music Collection): *L'Euridice, Iphigénie en Tauride* (Cary 70), *Roland*

Royal College of Music, London: *Dido and Aeneas*

Royal Opera House Archives, Covent Garden, London: *Arabella, Don Pasquale,* Gigli

Royal Opera, Stockholm: *The Consul,* Gentele

Staatliche Kunstsammlungen Dresden, Kupferstichkabinett (photo Sächsische Landesbibliothek): *I Capuleti ed i Montecchi*

Statens konstmuseer, Stockholm (National museum): *Atys*

The Stuart-Liff Collection, Port Erin, Isle of Man: Albani, Alda, *L'amore dei tre re,* Bahr-Mildenburg, Battistini, Bellincioni, Bonci, Boninsegna, Borgioli, Bori, Borkh, Burian, Callas, Calvé, Caruso, *Cavalleria rusticana,* Chaliapin, Christoff, Corelli, Dal Monte, Della Casa, De Los Angeles, De Luca, De Lucia, De Reske,